THE LAW OF OBLIGATIONS
ROMAN FOUNDATIONS OF THE
CIVILIAN TRADITION

AF691275

The Law of Obligations
Roman Foundations of the Civilian Tradition

REINHARD ZIMMERMANN

Dr. iur (Hamburg)
Professor für Privatrecht, Römisches Recht und Historische Rechtsvergleichung, Universität Regensburg; formerly W.P. Schreiner Professor of Roman and Comparative Law, University of Cape Town

CLARENDON PRESS · OXFORD

Oxford University Press, Walton Street, Oxford OX2 6DP
Oxford New York
Athens Auckland Bangkok Bogota Bombay
Buenos Aires Calcutta Cape Town Dar es Salaam
Delhi Florence Hong Kong Istanbul Karachi
Kuala Lumpur Madras Madrid Melbourne
Mexico City Nairobi Paris Singapore
Taipei Tokyo Toronto

and associated companies in
Berlin Ibadan

Oxford is a trade mark of Oxford University Press

Published in the United States
by Oxford University Press Inc., New York

© Juta & Co, Ltd, South Africa 1990 and 1996

First published in hardback by Juta and Co, South Africa, 1990
Reprinted 1992
First issued in paperback by Oxford University Press 1996

All rights reserved. No part of this publication may be reproduced, stored in a retrieval system, or transmitted, in any form or by any means, without the prior permission in writing of Oxford University Press. Within the UK, exceptions are allowed in respect of any fair dealing for the purpose of research or private study, or criticism or review, as permitted under the Copyright, Designs and Patents Act, 1988, or in the case of reprographic reproduction in accordance with the terms of the licences issued by the Copyright Licensing Agency. Enquiries concerning reproduction outside these terms and in other countries should be sent to the Rights Department, Oxford University Press, at the address above

This book is sold subject to the condition that it shall not, by way of trade or otherwise, be lent, re-sold, hired out or otherwise circulated without the publisher's prior consent in any form of binding or cover other than that in which it is published and without a similar condition including this condition being imposed on the subsequent purchaser

British Library Cataloguing in Publication Data
Data available

Library of Congress Cataloging in Publication Data
ISBN 0 7021 2347 1 (HB)
ISBN 0–19–876426–X (PB)

Printed in Great Britain by
Biddles Ltd., Guildford and King's Lynn

[N]ihil es[t] homine nobili dignius quam cognitio[. . .] juris. Primum quidem ejus quod omnes homines hominibus, et gentes gentibus sociat; deinde vero patri[i], cujus partem non exiguam facit jus Romanum a plerisque populis adoptatum, per se quoque supra omnia Civitatum jura dignissimum nosci, ut quod perfectum excultumque sit experimentis tam magni tamque diuturni Imperii. . . . Tam evidens . . . est ejus Juris in plerisque partibus, iis maxime, quae ad contractus aut damnum injuria datum pertinent, aequitas, ut, ad quos populos Romana arma pertingere nunquam potuerunt, . . . eo leges Romanae sine vi ulla, justitiae suae vi triumphantes, pervenerint.

Hugo Grotius, *Epistolae ad Gallos*, CLVI
(Hamburgi, XVI. Novemb. 1633)

(There is nothing more worthy of a gentleman than the study of Law: in the first place the study of that law which links man to man and nation to nation; then the study of the law of our fatherland. No small part of this consists in the Roman law, adopted by most peoples, but in itself also the most worthy of study, above all national laws, for having been developed and perfected by the experiences of so great and longlived an empire. So apparent is the equity of that law in its several parts, but especially in those which pertain to contract and unlawful damage, that it prevails even among those peoples whom the Romans could never conquer by arms, and it does so without any force, triumphing merely by virtue of its innate justice.)

Foreword

For a book which is merely new no introduction is really called for, but a minor fanfare may perhaps be in order for a work of an altogether novel kind. This is such a work: no previous book is at all like it.

'I have tried to write the type of book that I would have liked my students to have' says the author, and so successful is he in this enterprise that every other teacher of Roman Law (may their tribe increase!) should *insist* on his students' having this book to hand, all the more so now that Oxford, in its *Liber Pauperum* tradition, has made it readily available. They should be told that only in its size is it at all daunting. A glance inside will show how user-friendly it is, for all the great learning it contains; a little Latin will help (as it helped Shakespeare), but the learning is lightly worn, lucid exposition and contextual explanation go trippingly hand in hand, and the whole is couched in a relaxed and confident style which it is a joy to read.

The work is especially well-suited to English students because, *more romano et anglico*, it emphasises actual cases as illustrations of rules and examples of approaches in a coverage which the Table of Cases shows to be much wider than the title might suggest.

It is not only Romanists and their confrères in comparative law and legal history who will find this book an inexhaustible source of personal pleasure and professional profit: it will be illuminating to anyone with any interest in private law as a vital strand in our European civilisation—'vital' as in both 'essential' and 'living'. Here are the Italian Glossators and Commentators, the Spanish late scholastics, humanists from France and Holland, and the great German scholars of the nineteenth century, quoted in such a way as to let us feel the tone as well as appraise the substance of their contributions to our common heritage. To that tradition this work is a monument and an important addition.

Nor are those heroes irrelevant today: after all, had Germany not embraced the Roman Law they nurtured and embellished, it is very doubtful that a European Union could even be being proposed today, for law is its cement and faith in law its spiritual foundation.

Tony Weir
Trinity College, Cambridge

2 November 1995

Preface

I.

The story is told of a professor who was asked, at short notice, to deliver a lecture. How much time would he need for preparation? That depended entirely on how long he was supposed to talk, the professor answered. A two-hour lecture he could give off the cuff, but for a presentation of 10 or 20 minutes he would need much longer.

In the light of this anecdote, I should like to assure the reader that, despite appearances, this book is rather short. Considering the time-span and the subject-matter which it sets out to cover within a mere 1241 pages, the treatment may even be considered to be alarmingly short. On much more specific topics such as, for example, contractual liability in Roman law, there are a whole variety of modern monographs running into several hundred pages each; for many specific contracts there is a specialized literature that is abundantly rich; and even to individual facets of a contract, such as liability for latent defects in the Roman law of sale, not only comprehensive articles but entire books have been devoted. Apart from that, there is the literature written by countless generations of lawyers since the days of the glossators, who have, again and again, worked their way through the Roman texts; and, finally, there are all those who have written not so much on the rules of Roman law as such as on the history of their reception, further refinement and generalization, on how they have been reinterpreted, misunderstood or used to promote entirely new policies. Innumerable individual topics (the concepts of interesse—or damages, of error in substantia, or of dolus, the error requirement in the condictio indebiti, the notion of iniuria in terms of the actio iniuriarum or of the lex Aquilia, the doctrine of causa—or of its English equivalent: consideration—or the medieval theories surrounding the notion of usury, to mention just a few) constitute what the medieval lawyers were wont to describe as a shoreless ocean onto which no one was able to venture without running a grave risk of drowning. The present book is therefore based, chapter for chapter, on a process of selection, on an attempt to sift, to compress and to put into shape an abundant body of material. Which criteria have governed this process of selection?

Here I must say a few words about the aims that I have pursued in writing this book. Essentially, it is, of course, a book on Roman law and the question thus arises why it should be important to deal with a subject that appears to be so far removed from our time. Many different answers may be given to this question, and one can approach a discussion of the "relevance" of Roman law, quite legitimately, from a variety of entirely different perspectives. To me, two points have always been of particular importance—two points with regard to which Roman law differs significantly from any other historical legal system. On the one hand, it constitutes, in its ensemble, such a high level of cultural achievement that it will always retain its character as a model for the rational solution of legal conflicts. The problems raised, the arguments advanced and the solutions found by the Roman lawyers have in many instances, over the centuries, maintained both their topicality and their educational value. In other words: by analysing a crisp opinion given by Celsus or Ulpian, one can frequently learn more about legal ingenuity than by wading through the elaborate treatises of many modern law professors.

On the other hand, however, and more importantly, our way of thinking about law (in the present context, more specifically about the law of obligations) has been decisively moulded by the Roman lawyers. The contract–delict dichotomy; unjustified enrichment as an independent source of liability; the concept of a consensual contract; or even the basic notion of an obligation: these are only some of the fundamental ingredients which have shaped the civilian tradition. Many individual legal institutions have been preserved, either entirely unchanged or in a modernized form; and many rules of Roman law, in some or other codified version, still determine, for better or worse, the outcome of legal disputes at the end of the 20th century. Even where a new regime prevails, it has usually been introduced consciously or unconsciously in opposition to a rule of Roman law; and even in those cases, it is often only on the basis of a proper understanding of the Roman rule in question that one is able to appreciate, evaluate and understand the development. Even in defeat, Roman law therefore retains a key function for any more than superficial comprehension of the modern law. And apart from that, such defeats have occasionally not been of a lasting character. The idea that a codification should be able to sever all ties with the past, and thus entirely cut off the continuity of historical development, has proved to be a rather simplistic illusion. Even in a codified legal system the reappearance of ideas and solutions from the treasure house of the ius commune is by no means a rare—though usually an unacknowledged—phenomenon. The contents of that treasure house, however, are largely of Roman provenance.

Underlying both the form and content of the present book is therefore the belief that for a proper understanding of modern law one needs to know about the origin of its rules and institutions: why and how they have been developed, in which form they have been received, why and how they have been retained, changed, adapted or rejected. I have therefore always regretted the prevailing division of legal literature into books devoted to Roman law "proper" and to the modern history of private law. The study of legal history tends to become a rather sapless, purely "academic" affair, and is in danger of losing much of its legitimacy as an essential part of an educated lawyer's intellectual equipment if one omits to ask what a particular idea has contributed to the development of modern institutions. Roman law has made a particularly significant contribution, and the modern lawyer may thus legitimately expect a professor of Roman law to describe and analyse the details of this impact. Or, to put the matter slightly more pointedly: suretyship transactions in Babylonian law are a matter for the specialist; "alterum non laedere", "ex nudo consensu oritur actio" or "neminem ex alterius detrimento locupletiorem facere", on the other hand, do not concern only the professional legal historian, but every modern lawyer.

II.

One further point must immediately be added. Roman law does not only form the historical basis of only one particular, national legal system; it provides the most essential foundations of the "civilian" tradition. The term "civilian", in the terminology of English comparatists, refers to the legal systems on the European continent. It is used in contrast to the (English) common law. This distinction is very valuable in one respect; however, one has to beware of two different kinds of misconception.

On the one hand, it emphasizes correctly the basic unity of the European legal tradition; for the modern division of the science of law into national legal disciplines is of comparatively recent origin. From the late Middle Ages until the time of the French Revolution, the countries of Western and Central Europe had a common law and a common legal science. The creation of this ius commune was part of a most dramatic and far-reaching civilizatory phenomenon: the so-called Renaissance of the 12th century. Both the Roman Church and the Roman Empire (of the German nation) claimed to be supreme and universal authorities, and they needed rational legal systems as a source of legitimacy and as a means of control and organization. Thus, the new scholastic method of analysing and synthesizing was applied to the authoritative texts: the canones, on the one hand, and the recently rediscovered Justinianic law as compiled in what came to be known as the Corpus Juris Civilis, on the other. Roman law thus became one of the two principal ingredients of the medieval ius utrumque; but its counterpart, the canon law, was heavily influenced by it as well ("Ecclesia vivit lege Romana"). It was this ius utrumque which was taught at the universities and which the graduates, first of Bologna, then of all the other law schools that spread over Europe, tended to apply when they moved into key positions in the administration of their various kingdoms, principalities and cities. Large parts of Roman law therefore came to be "usu receptum" and constituted the basis of a European Roman-canon "common" law. This development tied in well, if not with a political concept of a Roman continuity (the doctrine of a translatio imperii from the Roman principes to Charlemagne and his successors), then with the general cultural Rome-ideal of the Middle Ages. Eventually Roman law came to be regarded as the embodiment of both ratio and aequitas. Local laws and older territorial customs were to some extent inserted into, absorbed by and amalgamated with the ius commune.

It is particularly important to emphasize the European character of these developments. True, Roman law was not received at the same time in all places. The movement started in Italy in the 12th century, it reached the northern part of France and Holland in the 13th and 14th centuries and in Germany it was only in the 16th century that Roman law succeeded in establishing itself as the ius commune. Also, in the course of time different countries took the lead as far as further refinement of academic study or practical application of Roman law was concerned. But the general pattern of the development was essentially the same everywhere. In the Middle Ages, the whole of educated Europe formed a single and undifferentiated cultural unit; and the Roman-canon "common" law was part and parcel of this European culture. Law professors moved freely from a chair in one country to one in another; the same textbooks were used at Pavia or Bologna as much as at Halle, Alcalà or Oxford; and it was on a European level, too, that all the major transformations of that common law took place. Moving with the same cultural tides and moored to a common language, European legal science remained an essentially homogeneous intellectual world. It was the international communis opinio doctorum that became authoritative for the application and development of the law. Thus, what we usually refer to as usus modernus pandectarum existed not only in Germany, but in the whole of Central and Western Europe.

It is this tradition to which the word "civilian" is usually applied and to which Roman law has made a major contribution; and it is one of the concerns of the present book to revive the interest of the modern lawyer in that contribution, to bring to his mind the extent of our indebtedness to Roman legal science, and thus to enhance his appreciation of its achievements. This is not only an exercise in antiquarianism. For the civilian tradition lives on, albeit often unrecognized, in the modern national legal systems. All the major European codes find their roots at one stage or another in the development of the ius commune which they were designed to supplant; and the ius commune therefore usually presents the most appropriate starting point for comparative research in the traditional core areas of continental private law. Apart from that, however, it provides the intellectual and doctrinal framework within which a new European legal unity may one day emerge. Anyone attempting to bolster the move towards greater political and economic unity by a harmonization of the legal rules applying in the various European countries would neglect their common historical basis at his peril. The ius commune even today constitutes a unifying force of great potential.

On the other hand (and here we come to the two more problematic features of the terminological distinction referred to above), the "European" ius commune and the "English" common law were (and are) not really so radically distinct as is often suggested. This applies to the methodological approach and framework within which the law developed as much as to the substantive legal rules. Thus, firstly, the continental ius commune of the 16th, 17th and 18th centuries displayed many features that we like to regard today as typically English. For it was not a professorial law characterized by impractical abstractions, deductive reasoning and conceptual jurisprudence; to a large extent, it was judicial law, jurisprudentia forensis, developing through lawyers' interpretations and judicial opinions, creating a continuous literary legal tradition and leading towards an authoritative communis opinio. It was thus, incidentally, not very different in spirit from classical Roman law. And secondly: England in reality was never completely cut off from continental legal culture. Indeed, in its very inception, the common law, which became a hallmark of English life, was not English at all. It was "a species of continental feudal law developed into an English legal system by kings and justices of continental extraction" (Maitland). Throughout the centuries, Roman (civil) law never ceased, through various channels, to exercise a considerable influence on English law and jurisprudence. This does not mean that the common law can be described merely as an offshoot of either Roman law or canon law. Of course, a whole variety of indigenous threads were woven into its tapestry; and even where there was some civilian influence, English courts and writers have often proceeded to develop the law along different lines than their continental counterparts. But it would appear to be a fruitful exercise to try to explore a common basis for comparative legal studies, to trace explicit as well as cryptic reception processes, to concentrate one's attention, for once, not so much on the distance and the differences between common law and civil law as on their proximity and similarities; and to attempt a comparison of legal solutions against the background of a common "Western" civilization. It is for this reason that I have included, wherever appropriate, references to the English common law.

III.

The present book is based on seven years' experience of teaching Roman law at the University of Cape Town. I have tried to write the type of book that I would have liked my students to have; or, which is essentially the same, the type of book that I would have enjoyed to read when I studied for my law degree at the University of Hamburg. I do not think that Roman law can adequately be presented in terms of abstract propositions. It has been developed, largely, in a casuistic fashion, and as soon as one neglects this vital feature, the study of Roman law tends to become a rather flat and uninteresting affair. In contradistinction to many other books on Roman law, I have therefore always attempted to start with the concrete and specific and to proceed from there to topics and propositions of a more general nature. (Chapters 1 and 27, however, constitute certain unavoidable exceptions to this manner of presentation.) Also, the emphasis throughout my book falls squarely on the individual cases discussed by the Roman jurists. Of course, I have tried to select those which have played a key role in the development of a specific legal rule or institution within the history of Roman law or of the later ius commune, or which are characteristic of the way in which the Roman jurists thought or argued. I have also tried to add colour to the discussion by providing the kind of background information which I believe one needs in order to evaluate the sources in their historical setting.

It is obvious that one cannot, under these circumstances, aim at encyclopedic completeness. The present book is therefore not in the nature of a comprehensive reference work which would meticulously list and soberly, if somewhat tediously, describe all conceivable particulars of the Roman law of obligations. I have rather chosen what I consider to be its most characteristic and important facets and tried to deal with them more thoroughly than would otherwise have been possible. The selection, again, has largely been determinded by the contribution which a specific legal institution has made to the modern law of obligations. Thus, to mention one example, discussion of the contract litteris has been reduced to a mere footnote. But not only topics which are of purely historical interest have been largely neglected; the ancient history of the Roman law of obligations, too, features only as far as this is absolutely necessary in order to appreciate the position in classical Roman law. And the problems connected with determining whether or not a particular text is interpolated have been highlighted only once by way of example. Essentially, then, I have attempted to tell the story of the characteristic concepts and institutions of the Roman law of obligations, commencing with what we usually refer to as classical Roman law but carrying it, beyond Justinian, into the modern law.

As far as this extension of the story into the ius commune is concerned, I had to confine myself even more drastically. Generally speaking, I have only been able to emphazise certain episodes within the history of the ius commune which have been of particular importance for the process of adaptation, transformation and modernization of the Roman law. The contributions of the canon lawyers, of the Roman-Dutch jurists and of the usus modernus pandectarum feature particularly prominently in this respect. Among the modern legal systems into which the story could have been carried, I have selected

German, South African and English law. The references to modern French law are too haphazard to deserve to be mentioned in this context. Why just the legal systems of these three countries? The cynic may be inclined to say that they happen to be the ones with which the author is most familiar. And in a way, of course, the cynic is right. Nevertheless, I do not think that the choice is unjustifiable from a more objective point of view. The German BGB is one of the major European codifications, and it is based, for better or for worse, more purely on Roman legal learning than any of the others. Unlike, especially, the French and Austrian codifications, it has absorbed the results of pandectist legal science, that last, scintillating blossom on the tree of the ius commune. The choice of English law has already been explained. South African private law, in turn, constitutes one of the last preserves in the modern world where the tradition of the ius commune still lives on, untrammelled, largely, by the intervention of the legislator. Courts and legal writers still derive their inspiration directly from the sources of (classical) Roman-Dutch law, and through them, from Justinian's Corpus Juris Civilis. Moreover, South African law is also of particular interest to the modern comparative lawyer since it is one of only a handful of "mixed jurisdictions"—of legal systems, that is, which are not only based on traditional civilian learning, but which have also absorbed much English law. This reception of English legal ideas occurred in the course of the 19th century and by a process that reveals certain intriguing similarities to the spread of Roman law over Europe. Thus, the two main emanations of the "Western", or European (in the broader sense), tradition have here been blended together, and the processes of a mutual assimilation that have occurred over the years offer stimulating insights as well as valuable experiences for anyone interested in the prospect of a future European common law.

I should perhaps stress that the present book deals specifically with the *Roman* roots of the civilian tradition. Thus, it confines itself to the traditional core areas of the law of obligations; it does not discuss the emergence of those of its more modern branches, which derive their origin from other sources. The book is therefore not a textbook of the ius commune. Also, its subject matter is purely the substantive private law. More specifically, therefore, the law of procedure has not been dealt with, at least not as far as the ius commune or modern legal systems are concerned. Classical Roman law, on the other hand, cannot be understood except from a procedural perspective, and this procedural perspective thus often influences the discussion. But here, again, the Roman law of civil procedure is not explained as such; a basic knowledge of its characteristic features is taken for granted.

Thirty out of the 32 chapters were written during the seven years I spent at the University of Cape Town. I have thus been able to draw on certain sources (South African monographs, dissertations and, in particular, court decisions) which are not readily available in European libraries. On the other hand, however, it was often exceedingly difficult to obtain more specialized European works, particularly modern Italian monographs and law reviews. I have, intermittently, been able to spend some time in Hamburg working in the library of the seminar for Roman law and comparative legal history; in a few urgent cases German colleagues have also helped by sending me photocopies. Although this considerably facilitated my task, there remain certain works which I have, unfortunately, not been able to consult, since even the inter-library loan services failed to locate them. I have sifted through and, where appropriate, included in the footnotes all the literature that was available to me by the end of 1988; in some instances it was also still possible to incorporate relevant contributions which appeared in 1989. This does not, regrettably, apply to vol. II of Helmut Coing's magisterial treatise *Europäisches Privatrecht*, nor to the third edition of *Farlam and Hathaway, Contract, Cases, Materials, Commentary* (by G. Lubbe and Chr. Murray). Generally, references in the footnotes to older literature on Roman law have been confined to works which I regard as specifically significant. From them, the reader will always be able to trace further secondary sources. Apart from that he can, of course, as far as the literature up to 1975 is concerned, always consult the two volumes of Max Kaser's *Römisches Privatrecht*. I have not deemed it necessary to try to emulate the bibliographic comprehensiveness of these standard works which must, surely, be available to whoever wishes to embark on specialized research in Roman law. Only the more recent literature, which would otherwise be difficult to trace, has been referred to more comprehensively. Furthermore, since one common denominator of all future readers of this book will be their command of English, I have also endeavoured to draw their attention to all the secondary literature in that language that was available to me and that was not too outdated.

IV.

A foreword not only confronts an author with the slightly awkward task of explaining why he has set out to write his book, of justifying the approach he has adopted, and of preparing the reader, as gently as possible, for the arduous task that lies ahead. It also provides the welcome opportunity of thanking all those persons who and institutions which have made a special contribution towards its existence.

First of all, it must be obvious to every reader how much the present book owes, where it deals with classical Roman law, to the work of Max Kaser. His three great handbooks, in particular, have shaped my way of thinking on Roman law, and they have invariably provided the starting point for my own research. I am very grateful to have had the chance to become, so to speak, a Kaser pupil of the second generation and to have been a student, later a junior colleague, of Professor Dr. Hans Hermann Seiler (Hamburg) and Professor Dr. Jens-Peter Meincke (Cologne) in their respective departments. Apart from that, I must confess that as a student Fritz Schulz' two books on *Classical Roman Law* and on the *Principles of Roman Law* made a particularly deep impression on me; they were written in a style which continues to attract me more than the balanced, detached and impersonal tone in which German scholarship usually presents itself. But then, I must also immediately say that my interest in Roman law has never been a purely antiquarian one; and the call to Cape Town provided me with an ideal opportunity of studying the history of the ius commune and the impact of Roman law on modern legal systems. In that regard, I have drawn much inspiration from the work of Professors Feenstra and Coing.

In the second place, I should like to mention my colleagues and friends in Cape Town. Their hospitality and kindness have been a major source of strength and have largely contributed to these seven years spent on the slopes of the Magic Mountain being so immensely rich and rewarding. I do not want to suggest for a minute that those years have always been easy. On the contrary: life as a law professor in a deeply polarized society, in which basic human rights and fundamental precepts of justice are infringed daily and almost as a matter of routine, is riddled with moral dilemmas. The teaching of law is demeaned if the idea of justice is flouted in practice; and not even a subject such as Roman law remains unaffected at a time when the traditional values upon which a university training is founded become caught up in a maelstrom of partisanship and intolerance, of repression and opportunism, of violence and counterviolence. And yet, Cape Town still remains for me a very special place: "ille terrarum mihi praeter omnes Angulus ridet." It is a smile that is both bewitchingly charming and distressingly sad.

Among the people I met in the Cape I have to mention one by name: Professor C.G. van der Merwe, my oldest South African friend and colleague at the University of Stellenbosch. From the time we first met, he and his family displayed a kind and generous hospitality towards me that one rarely, if ever, meets in Europe. It was he who encouraged me to accept the call to Cape Town in 1980 and who, some years later, also persuaded me to write the present book.

I should like to thank, furthermore, the University of Cape Town for providing me with a research grant and my colleagues at the University of Regensburg (as well as the Bavarian minister for science and culture) for granting me six months' sabbatical leave—only one semester after I had taken up my new duties at Regensburg—in order to complete this book. I gratefully acknowledge the help of Mrs Lisa Duminy who read the whole manuscript and suggested stylistic improvements and who also very kindly helped with the reading of the first set of proofs. The task of typing the manuscript—not always an easy one—was largely carried out by my former secretary at UCT, Mrs Margaret Schubert. Five of my former Roman law students at UCT came to Regensburg for some months as research assistants and contributed in various ways to the completion of the book. Diane Davis, inter alia, double-checked all quotations from the various parts of the Corpus Juris Civilis and from the *Institutes* of Gaius, as well as all references to extra-legal sources and to the medieval jurists. Bruce Cleaver and Anton Fagan checked the references to Anglo-American and South African cases and helped with the list of abbreviations. Above all, however, they rendered me an invaluable assistance by feeding all corrections and amendments to the original text into a computer which, at times, displayed a rather inordinate appetite for all kinds of textual delicacies: it irretrievably devoured them. John Butler and Deon de Klerk spotted further mistakes when they checked the various indexes; they also helped with the reading of the proofs, particularly those of the preliminary and end matter. Back in Cape Town, John Linnegar most meticulously edited the final version of my manuscript before it went into print, liaised with the printers and cleared up all loose ends on the proofs. For his assistance, too, I am very grateful.

Last, but not least, I should like to thank Richard Cooke, Simon Sephton and Madeline Lass of Juta & Co. most sincerely for their wholehearted co-operation and unfailing support throughout the various stages of the production of this book.

REINHARD ZIMMERMANN

Newlands, 10 October 1989

The favourable reception of this book has necessitated a second impression. I have taken the opportunity to eliminate a handful of printing mistakes. But the substance remains unchanged.

The book will now be published jointly by Juta & Co., C. H. Beck and Kluwer. I am most grateful to Richard Cooke in Cape Town and Dr. Wilhelm Warth in Munich for their ready co-operation.

REINHARD ZIMMERMANN

Regensburg, September 1992

Summary of Contents

Table of Contents

Chapter 12 — LOCATIO CONDUCTIO II

Chapter 13 — MANDATUM

Page

Chapter 14 — NEGOTIORUM GESTIO

Chapter 15 — SOCIETAS

Page

Chapter 17 — PACTA AND INNOMINATE REAL CONTRACTS

Page

Chapter 18 — FORMATION OF CONTRACT

Page

Chapter 19 — ERROR

Chapter 20 — INTERPRETATION OF CONTRACTS

CHAPTER 22 — INVALIDITY AND REASONS FOR INVALIDITY

CHAPTER 26 — UNJUSTIFIED ENRICHMENT

Page

Chapter 27 — DELICT IN GENERAL

Chapter 28 — FURTUM

List of abbreviations

Abbreviation	*Full citation, name or spelling*	*Place or origin*
A	Appellate Division	SA
A.D.	anno Domini	
ABGB	Allgemeines Bürgerliches Gesetzbuch	Ö
AC	Law Reports, Appeal cases	Eng
AD	Appellate Division Reports	SA
Ad & El	Adolphus & Ellis's Reports, King's Bench and Queen's Bench	Eng
ADHO-RIDA	Archives d'histoire du droit oriental (1952–53 combined with RIDA)	B
Afr.	Africanus	
AG	Amtsgericht	Ger
AGBG	Gesetz zur Regelung des Rechts der Allgemeinen Geschäftsbedingungen	Ger
AHDE	*Anuario de historia del derecho espanol*	E
AJ	Acting Judge	
AJA	Acting Judge of Appeal	
Alex. Sev.	Alexander Severus	
Aleyn	Aleyn's Reports, King's Bench	Eng
Alf.	Alfenus	
All ER	All England Law Reports	Eng
Annali Bari	*Annali della Facoltà di Giurisprudenza dell' Università di Bari*	I
Annali Catania	*Annali del Seminario Guiridico dell' Università di Catania*	I
Annali Palermo	*Annali del Seminario Giuridico dell' Università di Palermo*	I
anon.	anonymous	
ANRW	*Aufstieg und Niedergang der römischen Welt, Geschichte und Kultur Roms im Spiegel der neueren Forschung* (ed. H. Temporini, W. Haase, pp. 1972 sqq.)	Ger
Ant.	Antoninus	
App DC	Appeal Cases, District of Columbia	USA
Arcad.	Arcadius	
arg.	argument	
art., Art.	article	
artt., Artt.	articles	
A^sA^s	Aulus Agerius	
Aug.	Augustus	
Aus	Australia	
Australian LJ	*Australian Law Journal*	Aus
B	Belgium	
B & Ald	Barnewall and Alderson's Reports, King's Bench	Eng
B & S	Best & Smith's Reports, Queen's Bench	Eng
B.C.	before Christ	
BAGE	Entscheidungen des Bundesarbeitsgerichts	Ger
BGB	Bürgerliches Gesetzbuch	Ger
BGBl	Bundesgesetzblatt	Ger

Abbreviation	*Full citation, name or spelling*	*Place or origin*
BGH	Bundesgerichtshof	Ger
BGHZ	Entscheidungen des Bundesgerichtshofs in Zivilsachen	Ger
BIDR	*Bulletino dell'Istituto di diritto romano*	I
Bing	Bingham's Reports, Common Pleas	Eng
Bing (NC)	Bingham's New Cases, Common Pleas	Eng
Black W	William Blackstone's Reports, King's Bench and Common Pleas	Eng
Boston University LR	*Boston University Law Review*	USA
Bpk.	Beperk (= Limited)	
Buch	Buchanan's Reports	SA
Buch AC	Buchanan's Appeal Cases, Cape Appeal Court	SA
Burr	Burrow's Reports, King's Bench	Eng
Butterworth's South African LR	*Butterworth's South African Law Review*	SA
BVerfG	Bundesverfassungsgericht	Ger
BVerfGE	Entscheidungen des Bundesverfassungsgerichts	Ger
BW	Burgerlijk Wetboek	
C	Cape Provincial Division	SA
C.	Codex Iustinianus	
c.	canon (Corpus Juris Canonici)	
CA	Court of Appeal	Eng
California LR	*California Law Review*	USA
Call.	Callistratus	
Cambridge LJ	*Cambridge Law Journal*	Eng
Camp	Campbells's Reports Nisi prius	Eng
Can	Canada	
Can.	Canon (Codex Juris Cononici)	
Cap., cap.	Caput	
Carac.	Caracalla	
Cases T. Talbot	Cases in Equity temp. Talbot	Eng
Cass.	Cassius	
CB	Chief Baron; Common Bench Reports	Eng
CB (NS)	Common Bench Reports (New Series)	Eng
c.c.	code civil	Fr
CCC	Constitutio Criminalis Carolina	
Cels.	Celsus	
cf.	confer	
Ch	Law Reports, Chancery Division	Eng
CH	Switzerland	
Ch. réun.	Cour de Cassation, Chambres réunies	Fr
chap.	chapter	
ChD	Chancery Division; Law Reports Chancery Division	Eng
Cilsa	*The Comparative and International Law Journal of Southern Africa*	SA
CJ	Chief Justice	
CLR	Commonwealth Law Reports	Aus
Cmnd.	Command Papers, 5th series	Eng
Co Rep	Coke's Reports	Eng
Co.	Company	
Cod.	Codex	

Abbreviation	*Full citation, name or spelling*	*Place or origin*
col.	column	
Coll.	Mosaicarum et Romanarum legum collatio	
Columbia LR	*Columbia Law Review*	USA
Concl.	Conclusio	
Cons.	Consilium	
Const.	Constantinus; Constitutio	
Cowp	Cowper's Reports, King's Bench	Eng
Cox	Cox's Equity Cases	Eng
CP	Law Reports, Common Pleas	Eng
CPD	Reports of the Cape Provincial Division	SA
Cro Jac	Croke's Reports temp. James I., King's Bench and Common Pleas	Eng
CT	Codex Theodosianus	
D	Dunlop, Court of Session Cases (Scotland); Durban and Coastal Local Division (South Africa)	
D & R	Dowling & Rylands's Reports, King's Bench	Eng
D.	Digesta	
DC Cir	District of Columbia Court of Appeal Cases	USA
Dec., Decis.	Decisio	
Diocl.	Diocletianus	
Disp.	Disputatio	
Dist.	Distinctio	
Dougl	Douglas' Reports, King's Bench	Eng
Dr & Sm	Drewry and Smale's Reports, Chancery	Eng
E	Spain	
E I	First draft of the German Civil Code (BGB)	Ger
e.g.	for example	
East	East's Reports, King's Bench	Eng
ED	*Enciclopedia del diritto*	I
ed., eds.	edition, editor; editions, editors	
EDC	Reports of the Eastern Districts Court of the Cape of Good Hope	SA
EDL	Reports of the Eastern Districts Local Division	SA
Edms.	Eiendoms (= Proprietary)	
Edw	Edward	Eng
EheG.	Ehegesetz	Ger
Eins.	Eiendoms (= Proprietary)	
El & Bl	Ellis and Blackburn's Reports, Queen's Bench	Eng
Eng	England	
Eq	Equity Reports; Equity Cases	Eng
esp.	especially	
Ex D	Law Reports, Exchequer Division	Eng
Exch	Exchequer; Law Reports Exchequer	Eng
Exerc.	Exercitatio	
F	Federal Reporter	USA
F 2d	Federal Reporter, 2nd Series	USA
FC	Federal Supreme Court of Southern Rhodesia	ZB
FIRA, vol. III	*Fontes Iuris Romani Antejustiniani*, Pars tertia, Negotia (ed. V. Arangio-Ruiz), 2nd ed., 1972	

	Full citation, name or spelling	*Place or origin*
Flor.	Florentinus	
Foord	Foord's Reports, Cape Supreme Court	SA
Fr	France	
Fr. vat.	Fragmenta vaticana	
Gai.	Gaius	
Gall.	Gallienus	
Ger	Germany	
GG	Grundgesetz	Ger
gl.	glossa	
Gord.	Gordianus	
GrünhZ	*Zeitschrift für das Privat- und Öffentliche Recht der Gegenwart*	Ger
H	Greece	
H & C	Hurlstone & Coltman's Reports, Exchequer	Eng
H Bl	Henry Blackstone's Reports, Common Pleas	Eng
Harvard LR	*Harvard Law Review*	USA
Hastings International and Comparative LR	*Hastings International and Comparative Law Review*	USA
HCG	Reports of the High Court of Griqualand	SA
Hermog.	Hermogenianus	
HL	House of Lords	UK
HLC	Clark's Reports, House of Lords	Eng
HRG	Handwörterbuch zur deutschen Rechtsgeschichte (see bibliography)	
I	Italy	
I Itp.	Index Interpolationum	
i.e.	id est	
i.f.	in fine	
Iav.	Iavolenus	
ibid.	ibidem	
Imp.	Imperator	
Impp.	Imperatores	
Index	Index, Quaderni camerti di studi romanistici	I
Inst.	*Institutiones Justiniani*	
itp.	interpolated	
Iul.	Iulianus	
Iura	*Rivista internazionale di diritto romano e antico*	I
J	Judge	
JA	Judge of Appeal	
JhJb	*Jherings Jahrbücher für die Dogmatik des bürgerlichen Rechts*	Ger
JJP	*The Journal of Juristic Papyrology*	P
JP	Judge President	
JRS	*Journal of Roman Studies*	Eng
Juridical Review	*The Juridical Review*	Sc
Just.	Justinian	
KB	King's Bench; Law Reports King's Bench Division	Eng
KG	Kammergericht	Ger

Abbreviation	*Full citation, name or spelling*	*Place or origin*
Klio	Klio, Beiträge zur alten Geschichte	Ger
Lab.	Labeo	
Labeo	*Labeo, Rassegna di diritto romano*	I
LC	Lord Chancellor	Eng
Ld Raym	Lord Raymond's Reports, King's Bench and Common Pleas	Eng
LG	Landgericht	Ger
Lib.	Liber	
Lic. Ruf.	Licinnius Rufus	
LJ	Lord Justice	Eng
loc. cit.	loco citato	
LQR	*Law Quarterly Review*	Eng
LR; *LR*	Law Reports; *Law Review*	Eng
LT	Law Times Reports	Eng
Ltd.	Limited	
M & W	Meeson & Welsby's Reports, Exchequer	Eng
Maec.	Maecianus	
Marc.	Marcellus	
Marci.	Marcianus	
Max.	Maximinianus	
McGill LJ	*McGill Law Journal*	Can
Menz	Menzies' Reports	SA
Michigan LR	*Michigan Law Review*	USA
Mod Rep	Modern Reports	Eng
Mod.	Modestinus	
Modern LR	*Modern Law Review*	Eng
MR	Master of the Rolls	
N	Natal Provincial Division	SA
n., nn.	note, notes	
n.d.	no date	
NE	North Eastern Reporter	USA
Nelson	Nelsons's Chancery Reports	Eng
Ner.	Neratius	
NL	The Netherlands	
NLR	Natal Law Reports	SA
Nov.	Novellae Iustiniani	
NPD	Reports of the Natal Provincial Division	SA
NRH	*Nouvelle revue historique de droit francais et étranger*	Fr
N^sN^s	Numerius Negidius	
NY	New York Reports	USA
O	Orange Free State Provincial Division	SA
Ö	Austria	
OLG	Oberlandesgericht	Ger
op. cit.	opere citato	
OPD	Reports of the Orange Free State Provincial Division	SA
OR	Official Reports of the High Court of the South African Republic (South Africa); Schweizerisches Obligationenrecht (CH)	
P	Poland	

Abbreviation	*Full citation, name or spelling*	*Place or origin*
p., pp.	pagina (page), paginae (pages)	
Pap.	Papinianus	
Paul.	Paulus	
Paul. Sent.	Pauli Sententiae	
PC	Judicial Committee of the Privy Council	
PH	Prentice Hall, Weekly Legal Service	SA
Pomp.	Pomponius	
pr.	principium	
PrALR	Preussisches Allgemeines Landrecht	Ger
Proc.	Proculus	
Prot.	Protokolle	
Pty.	Proprietary	
Pvt.	Private (Company)	
QB	Queens Bench; Law Reports Queen's Bench Division	Eng
Qd	Queensland Reports	Aus
Quaest.	Quaestio	
Quint. Muc.	Quintus Mucius	
R	Rettie, Court of Session Cases (Scotland); Rhodesia	
R	Rhodesia	
R & N	Rhodesia and Nyasaland Law Reports	ZB
RabelsZ	*Zeitschrift für ausländisches und internationales Privatrecht*	Ger
RAD	Rhodesian Apellate Division	ZB
RE	*Paulys Realencyclopädie der classischen Altertumswissenschaft* (G. Wissowa, W. Kroll, K. Mittelhaus, K. Ziegler, 1893 sqq.)	
RGZ	Entscheidungen des Rechtsgerichts in Zivilsachen	Ger
RH	*Revue historique de droit francais et étranger*	Fr
RHDI	*Revue hellénique de droit international*	H
RheinZ	*Rheinische Zeitschrift für Zivil- und Prozessrecht*	Ger
RIDA	*Revue internationale des droit de l'antiquité*	B
RISG	*Rivista italiana per le scienze giuridiche*	I
RJ	*Rechtshistorisches Journal*	Ger
Roscoe	Roscoe's Reports, Cape Supreme Court	SA
Russ & Ry	Russel & Ryan's Crown Cases Reserved	Eng
s., ss.	section, sections	
s.v.	sub voce	
SA	South Africa; South African Law Reports	SA
Sab.	Sabinus	
SALJ	*South African Law Journal*	SA
Salkeld	Salkeld's Reports, King's Bench	Eng
SAR	Reports of the High Court of the South African Republic	SA
Sc	Scotland	
SC	senatus consultum; Session cases (Scotland); Cape Supreme Court (South Africa)	
Scaev.	Scaevola	
SDHI	*Studia et documenta historiae et iuris*	I
Sept. Sev.	Septimius Severus	
Serv. Sulp.	Servius Sulpicius Rufus	

Abbreviation	*Full citation, name or spelling*	*Place or origin*
SeuffA.	Seufferts Archiv für Entscheidungen der obersten deutschen Staaten	Ger
sq., sqq.	et sequens, et sequentes	
SR	Reports of the High Court of Southern Rhodesia	ZB
Stanford LR	*Stanford Law Review*	USA
StGB	Strafgesetzbuch	Ger
Suppl.	Supplementum	
SWA	South-West Africa Provincial Division; Reports of the High Court of South West Africa	SA
T	Transvaal Provincial Division	SA
Tab. Herc.	Tabulae Herculanenses	
Tennessee LR	*Tennessee Law Review*	USA
Ter. Cl.	Terentius Clemens	
TH	Reports of the Witwatersrand High Court	SA
Theod.	Theodosius	
THRHR	*Tydskrif vir Hedendaagse Romeins-Hollandse Reg*	SA
Tit.	Titulus	
TLR	Times Law Reports	Eng
Tothill	Tothill's Transactions in Chancery	Eng
TPD	Reports of the Transvaal Provincial Division	SA
TR	*Tijdschrift voor rechtsgeschiedenis*	NL
Tract.	Tractatus	
trans.	translated	
Tryph.	Tryphoninus	
TS	Reports of the Transvaal Supreme Court	SA
TSAR	*Tydskrif vir die Suid-Afrikaanse Reg*	SA
Tulane LR	*Tulane Law Review*	USA
UE	Tituli ex corpore Ulpiani (Ulpiani epitome)	
UK	United Kingdom	
Ulp.	Ulpianus	
University of British Columbia LR	*University of British Columbia Law Review*	Can
University of California at Los Angeles LR	*University of California at Los Angeles Law Review*	USA
University of Chicago LR	*University of Chicago Law Review*	USA
University of Toronto LR	*University of Toronto Law Review*	Can
US	Reports of Cases in the Supreme Court in the United States of America	USA
USA	United States of America	
Val.	Valentinianus	
Val. Max.	Valerius Maximus	
vat.	see Fr. vat.	
VC	Vice Chancellor	Eng
vd.	vide	
Ven.	Venuleius	
Viv.	Vivianus	
viz.	videlicet	
vol., vols.	volume, volumes	

Abbreviation	*Full citation, name or spelling*	*Place or origin*
W	Witwatersrand Local Division	SA
Wheat	Wheaton's Supreme Court Reports	USA
Wils	G. Wilson's Reports, King's Bench and Common Pleas	Eng
WLD	Reports of the Witwatersrand Local Division	SA
WLR	Weekly Law Reports	Eng
WLR (Canada)	Western Law Reporter	Can
Yale LJ	*Yale Law Journal*	USA
YB	Year Books	Eng
Z	Zimbabwe, Supreme Court	ZB
ZB	Rhodesia, Zimbabwe	
ZHR	*Zeitschrift für das gesamte Handelsrecht und Wirtschaftsrecht*	Ger
Zimbabwe LJ	*Zimbabwe Law Journal*	ZB
ZNR	*Zeitschrift für neuere Rechtsgeschichte*	Ger
ZPO	Zivilprozessordnung	Ger
ZSS	*Zeitschrift der Savigny-Stiftung für Rechtsgeschichte* (romanistische Abteilung)	Ger
ZSS (GA)	*Zeitschrift der Savigny-Stiftung für Rechtsgeschichte* (germanistische Abteilung)	Ger
ZSS (KA)	*Zeitschrift der Savigny-Stiftung für Rechtsgeschichte* (kanonistische Abteilung)	Ger
ZStrW	*Zeitschrift für die gesamte Strafrechtswissenschaft*	Ger
ZStW	*Zeitschrift für die gesamte Staatswissenschaft*	Ger

Principal Works Cited

This bibliography contains only those works that have been referred to in abbreviated form in more than one chapter.

Accursius, *Corpus Iuris Civilis Iustinianei cum commentariis Accursii* (Lugduni, 1627)
Albanese, Bernardo, *Gli atti negoziali nel diritto privato romano* (1982)
Apathy, Peter, *Animus novandi, Das Willensmoment beim römischen Schulderneuerungsvertrag* (1975)
Arangio-Ruiz, Vincenzo, *Instituzioni di diritti romano* (14th ed., 1968)
Arangio-Ruiz, Vincenzo, *La compravendita in diritto romano,* vol. I (1961); vol. II (1954)
Arangio-Ruiz, Vincenzo, *Responsabilità contrattuale in diritto romano* (2nd ed., 1958)
Arndts, Ludwig, *Lehrbuch der Pandekten* (6th ed., 1868)
Arp, Torsten, *Anfängliche Unmöglichkeit, Zum Verständnis von 306 BGB* (1988)
Atiyah, Patrick S., *Pragmatism and Theory in English Law* (1987)
Atiyah, Patrick S., *Essays on Contract* (1986)
Atiyah, Patrick S., *The Rise and Fall of Freedom of Contract* (1979)
Azo, *Summa Codicis* (Lugduni, 1552)

Baldus de Ubaldis, *In Quartum et Quintum Codicis Libros Commentaria* (Augustae Taurinorum, 1576)
Baldus de Ubaldis, *Commentaria in Decretales* (Venetiis, 1595)
Baldus de Ubaldis, *Consilia, sive responsa* (Venetiis, 1575)
Baron, J., *Pandekten* (4th ed., 1882)
Bartolus de Saxoferratis, *Commentaria* (Lugduni, 1552)
Bechmann, August, *Der Kauf nach gemeinem Recht,* vol. I (1876); vol. II (1884); vol. III (1905/08)
Behrends, Okko, *Die fraus legis, Zum Gegensatz von Wortlaut- und Sinngeltung in der römischen Gesetzesinterpretation* (1982)
Benöhr, Hans-Peter, *Das sogenannte Synallagma in den Konsensualkontrakten des klassischen römischen Rechts* (1965)
Berger, Adolf, *Encyclopedic Dictionary of Roman Law* (1953) (Berger, ED)
Berman, Harold J., *Law and Revolution, The Formation of the Western Legal Tradition* (1983)
Betti, Emilio, *Diritto romano,* vol. I (1935)
Betti, Emilio, *Istituzioni di diritto romano,* vol. II, 1 (1960)
Biondi, Biondo, *Contratto e stipulatio* (1953)
Biondi, Biondo, *Il diritto romano christiano* (1952 sqq.)
Birks, Peter, *An Introduction to the Law of Restitution* (1985)
Blackstone, Sir William, *Commentaries on the Laws of England* (London, 1791)
Boberg, P.Q.R., *The Law of Delict* vol. I (1984)
Boehmer, Justus Henning, *Ius ecclesiasticum protestantium,* vols. I–III (5th ed., 1756, 1762, 1774); vol. IV (4th ed, 1754); vol. V (3rd ed., 1763), all Halae Magdeburgicae
Brinz, Alois, *Lehrbuch der Pandekten* (1857 sqq.)
Brunnemann, Johannes, *Commentarius in Codicem* (Lipsiae, 1699)
Brunnemann, Johannes, *Commentarius in Pandectas* (4th ed., Francofurti ad Moenum, 1692)
Buckland, W.W.; McNair, A.D., *Roman Law and Common Law, A Comparison in Outline* (2nd ed., 1952)
Buckland, W.W.; Stein, Peter, *A Text-Book of Roman Law from Augustus to Justinian* (3rd ed., 1963)
Burge, William, *Commentaries on the Law of Suretyship* (1849)

Cannata, Carlo Augusto, *Ricerche sulla responsabilità contrattuale nel diritto romano* (1966)
Cannata, Carlo Augusto, *Per lo studio della resonsabilità per colpa nel diritto romano classico* (1967–68)
Carcopino, Jérôme, *Daily Life in Ancient Rome* (Pelican, 1956)
Carpzov, Benedict, *Jurisprudentia forensis Romano-Saxonica* (Francofurti ad Moenum, 1650)
Chitty on Contracts (25th ed., 1983)
Chorus, Jeroen M.J., *Handelen in strijd met de wet* (1976)
Christie, R.H., *The Law of Contract in South Africa* (1981)

Claus, Axel, *Gewillkürte Stellvertretung im Römischen Privatrecht* (1973)
Cocceji, Samuel de, *Jus civile controversum* (2nd ed., Francofurti et Lipsiae, 1729)
Coing, Helmut, *Europäisches Privatrecht,* vol. I (1985)
Covarruvias a Leyva, Didacus de, *Opera omnia,* vol. I (Venetiis, 1604); vol. II (Lugduni, 1668)
Cuiacius, Iacobus, *Opera* (Venetiis, 1758)
Darjes, Joachim Georg, *Institutiones iurisprudentiae universalis* (Ienae, 1740)
Daube, David, *Roman Law, Linguistic, Social and Philosophical Aspects* (1969)
De Martino, Francesco, *Wirtschaftsgeschichte des alten Rom* (1985)
De Neeve, P.W., *Colonus, Private Farm-Tenancy in Roman Italy During the Republic and the Early Principate* (1984)
De Robertis, Francesco M., *La disciplina della responsabilità contrattuale,* vol. I (1962); vol. II (1964); vol. III (1972)
De Vos, Wouter, *Verrykingsaanspreeklikheid in die Suid-Afrikaanse Reg* (3rd ed., 1987)
De Wet, J.C.; van Wyk, A.H., *Kontraktereg en Handelsreg* (4th ed., 1978) (De Wet en Yeats)
De Zulueta, Francis, *The Roman Law of Sale* (1945)
De Zulueta, Francis, *The Institutes of Gaius,* vol. II (1953)
Dernburg, Heinrich, *Pandekten* (6th ed., 1900)
Diesselhorst, Malte, *Die Lehre des Hugo Grotius vom Versprechen* (1959)
Dilcher, Hermann, *Die Theorie der Leistungsstörungen bei Glossatoren, Kommentatoren und Kanonisten* (1960)
Diosdi, György, *Contract in Roman Law, From the Twelve Tables to the Glosssators* (1981)
Domat, Jean, *Les loix civiles dans leur ordre naturel* (Paris, 1689 sqq.)
Donellus, Hugo, *Opera omnia* (Florentiae, 1840 sqq.)
Duncan-Jones, Richard, *The Economy of the Roman Empire, Quantitative Studies* (1974)
Durantis, Wilhelm, *Speculum iudiciale* (Basileae, 1574)

Endemann, Wilhelm, *Studien in der romanisch-kanonistischen Wirtschafts- und Rechtslehre bis gegen Ende des 17. Jahrhunderts,* vol. I (1874); vol. II (1883)
Étienne, Robert, *Pompeji* (2nd ed., 1976)
Fachinaeus, Andreas, *Controversiae iuris, Coloniae Agrippinae* (1649)
Feenstra, Robert, *Vergelding en vergoeding* (1982)
Feenstra, Robert; Ahsmann, Margreet, *Contract, Aspecten van de begrippen contract en contractsvrijheid in historisch perspectief* (1980)
Fleming, John G., *The Law of Torts* (7th ed., 1987)
Flume, Werner, *Allgemeiner Teil des Bürgerlichen Rechts, Zweiter Band, Das Rechtsgeschäft* (3rd ed., 1979) (Flume, AT)
La formazione storica del diritto moderno in Europa, Atti del terzo congresso internazionale della società italiana di storia del diritto (1977)
Frezza, Paolo, *Le garanzie delle obbligazioni,* vol. I (1962); vol. II (1963)
Frier, Bruce W., *Landlords and Tenants in Imperial Rome* (1980)
Frier, Bruce W., *The Rise of the Roman Jurists* (1985)

Glanvill, *The treatise on the laws and customs of the realm of England commonly called Glanvill* (ed. G.D.G. Hall, 1965)
Glück, Christian Friedrich, *Ausführliche Erläuterung der Pandekten,* vols. 1–34 (Erlangen, 1797 sqq.); vols. 35-43 continued by Christian Friedrich Mühlenbruch (Erlangen, 1832 sqq.)
Goff, Sir Robert; Jones, Gareth, *The Law of Restitution* (2nd ed., 1978)
Goris, Lambertus, *Adversariorum iuris subcisivorum ad lucem consuetudinis Ducatus Gelriae et Comitatus Zutphaniae ac vicinarum Belgii provinciarum,* Tractatus quatuor (3rd ed., Arnhemii, 1651)
Groenewegen van der Made, Simon à, *Tractatus de legibus abrogatis et inusitatis in Hollandia vicinisque regionibus* (Amstelaedami, 1669)
Grosso, Guiseppe, *Il sistema romano dei contratti* (3rd ed., 1963)
Grotius, Hugo, *De jure belli ac pacis* libri tres (Amsterdami, 1631)
Grotius, Hugo, *Inleiding tot de Hollandsche Rechtsgeleertheyd* ed. by Robert Warden Lee (2nd ed., 1953)
Gudelinus, Petrus, *Commentarii de iure novissimo* (Florentiae, 1839)

Hammen, Horst, *Die Bedeutung Friedrich Carl von Savignys für die allgemeinen dogmatischen Grundlagen des Deutschen Bürgerlichen Gesetzbuches* (1983)
Handwörterbuch zur deutschen Rechtsgeschichte, eds.: Adalbert Erler, Ekkehard Kaufmann (1971 sqq.) (HRG)

Hasse, Johann Christian, *Die Culpa des Römischen Rechts* (2nd ed., 1838)
Hausmaninger, Herbert, *Schadenersatzrecht der lex Aquilia* (3rd ed. 1987)
Hausmaninger, Herbert; Selb, Walter, *Römisches Privatrecht* (4th ed., 1987)
Heimbach, G.E. (et al.), ed(s)., *Basilicorum* libri LX (1833 sqq.)
Heineccius, Io. Gottlieb, *Elementa iuris civilis* (4th ed., Amstelaedami, 1740)
Heumann, H.; Seckel, E., *Handlexikon zu den Quellen des römischen Rechts* (10th ed., 1958)
Hochstein, Reiner, *Obligationes quasi ex delicto. Untersuchungen zur dogmengeschichtlichen Entwicklung verschuldensunabhängiger Deliktshaftung unter besonderer Berücksichtigung des 16. bis 18. Jahrhunderts* (1971)
Hoffmann, Hans-Joachim, *Die Abstufung der Fahrlässigkeit in der Rechtsgeschichte* (1968)
Holdsworth, Sir William, *A History of English Law* 17 vols. (reprint 1966)
Holmes, Oliver Wendell, *The Common Law* (1881)
Honsell, Heinrich, *Die Rückabwicklung sittenwidriger oder verbotener Geschäfte* (1974)
Honsell, Heinrich, *Quod interest im bonae-fidei-iudicium, Studien zum römischen Schadensersatzrecht* (1969)
Honsell, Heinrich; Mayer-Maly, Theo; Selb, Walter, *Römisches Recht* (= Paul Jörs, Wolfgang Kunkel, Leopold Wenger, *Römisches Recht* 4th ed., 1987)
Horak, Franz, *Rationes decidendi, Entscheidungsbegründungen bei den älteren römischen Juristen bis Labeo* (1969)
Huber, Ulrich, *Heedendaegse Rechtsgeleertheyt* (Amsterdam, 1768)
Huber, Ulrich, *Praelectiones juris civilis* (4th ed., Francofurti et Lipsiae, 1749)
Jhering, Rudolf von, *Geist des römischen Rechts auf den verschiedenen Stufen seiner Entwicklung* (6th–8th eds., 1923 sqq.)
Jolowicz, H.F., *Roman Foundations of Modern Law* (1957)
Jolowicz, H.F.; Nicholas, Barry, *Historical Introduction to the Study of Roman Law* (3rd ed., 1972)
Jones, Sir William, *An Essay on the Law of Bailments* (9th ed., Philadelphia, 1836)
Joubert, D.J., *General Principles of the Law of Contract* (1987)
Jörs, Paul; Kunkel, Wolfgang; Wenger, Leopold, *Römisches Privatrecht* (3rd ed., 1949)
Kaser, Max, *Das altrömische ius* (1949)
Kaser, Max, *Das römische Privatrecht,* Erster Abschnitt (2nd ed., 1971) (Kaser, *RPr* I)
Kaser, Max, *Das römische Privatrecht,* Zweiter Abschnitt (2nd ed., 1975) (Kaser, *RPr* II)
Kaser, Max, *Das römische Zivilprozessrecht* (1966) (Kaser, *RZ*)
Kaser, Max, *Über Verbotsgesetze und verbotswidrige Geschäfte im römischen Recht* (1977)
Kaufmann, Horst, *Die altrömische Miete* (1964)
Kaufmann, Horst, *Rezeption und usus modernus der actio legis Aquiliae* (1958)
Kelly, John Maurice, *Roman Litigation* (1966)
Kerr, A.J., *The Law of Sale and Lease* (1984)
Kerr, A.J., *The Principles of the Law of Contract* (3rd ed., 1980)
Knütel, Rolf, *Contrarius consensus, Studien zur Vertragsaufhebung im römischen Recht* (1968)
Knütel, Rolf, *Stipulatio ponae, Studien zur römischen Vertragsstrafe* (1976)
König, Detlef, *Ungerechtfertigte Bereicherung, Tatbestände und Ordnungsprobleme in rechtsvergleichender Sicht* (1985)
Kupisch, Berthold, *Die Versionsklage, Ihre Entwicklung von der gemeinrechtlichen Theorie des 17. Jahrhunderts bis zum Österreichischen Allgemeinen Bürgerlichen Gesetzbuch* (1965)
Lange, Hermann, *Schadensersatz und Privatstrafe in der mittelalterlichen Rechtstheorie* (1955)
Lange, Hermann, *Schadensersatz* (1979)
Lauterbach, Wolfgang Adam, *Collegium theoretico-practicum* (Tubingae, 1723 sqq.)
Lawson, F.H.; Markesinis, B.S., *Tortious Liability for Unintentional Harm in the Common Law and the Civil Law,* vol. I (1982)
Lee, Robert Warden, *Introduction to Roman-Dutch Law* (5th ed., 1953)
Lenel, Otto, *Das Edictum perpetuum* (3rd ed., 1927) (Lenel, *EP*)
Leser, Hans C., *Der Rücktritt vom Vertrag, Abwicklungsverhältnis und Gestaltungsbefugnisse bei Leistungsstörungen* (1975)
Levy, Ernst, *Die Konkurrenz der Aktionen und Personen im klassischen römischen Recht,* vol. I (1918); vol. II, 1 (1922)
Levy, Ernst, *West Roman Vulgar Law, The Law of Property* (1951)
Levy, Ernst, *Weströmisches Vulgarrecht, Das Obligationenrecht* (1956)
Levy, Ernst, *Sponsio, fidepromissio, fideiussio* (1907)
Leyser, Augustin, *Meditationes ad Pandectas* (Franckenthalii, 1778 sqq.)

Liebs, Detlef, *Die Klagenkonkurrenz im römischen Recht, Zur Geschichte der Scheidung von Schadensersatz und Privatstrafe* (1972)
Liebs, Detlef, *Römisches Recht* (3rd ed., 1987) (Liebs, *RR*)
Lübtow, Ulrich von, *Beiträge zur Lehre von der condictio nach römischem und geltendem Recht* (1952)
Lübtow, Ulrich von, *Die Entwicklung des Darlehensbegriffs im römischen und im geltenden Recht mit Beiträgen zur Delegation und Novation* (1965)
Lübtow, Ulrich von, *Untersuchungen zur lex Aquilia de damno iniuria dato* (1971)

Mackeldey, Ferdinand, *Systema iuris Romani hodie usitati* (1847)
Magdelain, André, *Le consensualisme dans l'édit du préteur* (1958)
Maine, Sir Henry, *Ancient Law* (Everyman's Library edition, 1917)
Maschi, Carlo Alberto, *La categoria dei contratti reali* (1973)
Masi, Antonio, *Studi sulla condizione nel diritto romano* (1966)
Mayer-Maly, Theo, *Locatio conductio* (1956)
Mayno, Yason de, *Commentaria in Digestas* (Venetiis, 1590)
Medicus, Dieter, *Id quod interest, Studien zum römischen Recht des Schadenersatzes* (1962)
Mevius, David, *Decisiones super causis praecipuis ad summum tribunal regium Vismariense delatis* (Francofurti ad Moenum, 1712)
Michel, Jacques, *Gratuité en droit romain* (1962)
Misera, Karlheinz, *Der Bereicherungsgedanke bei der Schenkung unter Ehegatten* (1974)
Molina, Lodovicus, *De iustitia et iure* (Moguntiae, 1602 sq.)
Molinaeus, Carolus, *Omnia quae extant opera* (Parisiis, 1681)
Mommsen, Friedrich, *Die Unmöglichkeit der Leistung in ihrem Einfluß auf obligatorische Verhältnisse* (1853)
Mommsen, Theodor, *Römisches Staatsrecht* (3rd ed., 1887/88; 4th ed., 1895)
Mommsen, Theodor, *Römisches Strafrecht* (1899)
Mugdan, Benno, *Die gesammten Materialien zum Bürgerlichen Gesetzbuch für das Deutsche Reich*, ed. Benno Mugdan (1899 sq.)
Mühlenbruch, Christian Friedrich, *Doctrina pandectarum* (4th ed., 1838 sqq.)

Nanz, Klaus-Peter, *Die Entstehung des allgemeinen Vertragsbegriffs im 16. bis 18. Jahrhundert* (1983)
Nicholas, Barry, *An Introduction to Roman Law* (1962)
Nicholas, Barry, *French Law of Contract* (1982) (Nicholas, *FLC*)
Nörr, Dieter, *Causa mortis* (1986)
Nörr, Dieter, *Rechtskritik in der römischen Antike* (1974)

Ogorek, Regina, *Untersuchungen zur Entwicklung der Gefährdungshaftung im 19. Jahrhundert* (1975)

Parladorius, Joannes Yanes, *Rerum quotidianarum libri duo, Trajecti ad Rhenum* (1680)
Pauly, (Der Kleine Pauly), *Lexikon der Antike* (1979)
Pauw, Pieter, *Persoonlikheidskrenking en skuld in die Suid-Afrikaanse privaatreg—'n regshistoriese en regsvergelykende ondersoek* (unpublished Dr. iur. thesis, Leiden, 1976)
Perezius, Antonius, *Praelectiones in duodecim libros codicis* (Amstelodami, 1671)
Pernice, Alfred, *Labeo, Römisches Privatrecht im ersten Jahrhundert der Kaiserzeit* (1873 sqq.)
Pernice, Alfred, *Zur Lehre von den Sachbeschädigungen nach römischem Rechte* (1867)
Peters, Frank, *Die Rücktrittsvorbehalte des römischen Kaufrechts* (1973)
Peters, Frank; Zimmermann, Reinhard, 'Verjährungsfristen—Der Einfluß von Fristen auf Schuldverhältnisse; Möglichkeiten der Vereinheitlichung von Verjährungsfristen', in: *Gutachten und Vorschläge zur Überarbeitung des Schuldrechts*, vol. I (1981)
Pistoris, Modestinus, *Consilia sive responsa* (Lipsiae, vol. I (1586); vol. II (1588))
Plucknett, Theodor F.T., *A Concise History of the Common Law* (5th ed., 1956)
Pollock, Sir Frederick; Maitland, Frederic William, *The History of English Law Before the Time of Edward I* (2nd ed., 1898)
Pothier, Robert Joseph, *Oeuvres* (Paris, 1835) (Pothier, *Traité de …*)
Pothier, Robert Joseph, *Pandectae Justinianae in novum ordinem digestae* (Parisiis, 1818 sqq.)
Pringsheim, Fritz, *The Greek Law of Sale* (1950)
Puchta, G.F., *Pandekten* (11th ed., 1872)
Pufendorf, Samuel, *De jure naturae et gentium libri octo* (Francofurti ad Moenum, 1694)

Rabel, Ernst, *Das Recht des Warenkaufs, Eine rechtsvergleichende Darstellung* (reprint 1964)
Rabel, Ernst, *Grundzüge des römischen Privatrechts* (2nd ed., 1955)

Raber, Fritz, *Grundlagen klassischer Injurienansprüche* (1969)
Regelsberger, Ferdinand, *Pandekten*, vol. I (1893)
Rheinstein, Max, *Die Struktur des vertraglichen Schuldverhältnisses im anglo-amerikanischen Recht* (1932)
Riccobono, Salvatore; Kerr Wylie, J.; Beinart, Ben, *Stipulation and the Theory of Contract* (1957)

Sande, Joannis à (van de), *Opera omnia juridica* (Bruxellis, 1721)
Savigny, Friedrich Carl von, *Das Obligationsrecht*, vol. I (1851); vol. II (1853)
Savigny, Friedrich Carl von, *System des heutigen römischen Rechts* (1840 sqq.)
Scherner, Karl Otto, *Rücktrittsrecht wegen Nichterfüllung, Untersuchungen zur deutschen Privatrechtslehre der Neuzeit* (1965)
Schilter, Johann, *Praxis juris Romani in foro Germanico* (3rd ed., Francofurti et Lipsiae, 1713)
Schindler, Karl-Heinz, *Justinians Haltung zur Klassik* (1966)
Schipani, Sandro, *Responsabilità "ex lege Aquilia", Criteri di imputazione e problema della "culpa"* (1969)
Schmidlin, Bruno, *Die römischen Rechtsregeln, Versuch einer Typologie* (1970)
Schubert, Werner (ed.), *Die Vorlagen der Redaktoren für die erste Kommission zur Ausarbeitung des Entwurfs eines Bürgerlichen Gesetzbuches* (1980 sqq.)
Schulz, Fritz, *Classical Roman Law* (1951) (Schulz, *CRL*)
Schulz, Fritz, *Einführung in das Studium der Digesten* (1916)
Schulz, Fritz, *History of Roman Legal Science* (1946) (Schulz, RLS)
Schulz, Fritz, *Principles of Roman Law* (1936)
Schwarz, Fritz, *Die Grundlage der condictio im klassischen römischen Recht* (1952)
Seiler, Hans Hermann, *Der Tatbestand der negotiorum gestio im römischen Recht* (1968)
Siber, Heinrich, *Römisches Recht in Grundzügen für die Vorlesung*, vol. II: Römisches Privatrecht (1928)
Simpson, A.W.B., *A History of the Common Law of Contract* (1975)
Staudinger, J. von, *Kommentar zum Bürgerlichen Gesetzbuch* (12th ed., 1978 sqq.)
Stein, Peter, *Fault in the Formation of Contract in Roman Law and Scots Law* (1958)
Story, Joseph, *Commentaries on the Law of Bailments* (9th ed., Boston, 1878)
Struve, Georg Adam, *Syntagma jurisprudentiae secundum ordinem Pandectarum concinnatum* (Jenae, 1702)
Stryk, Samuel, "Specimen usus moderni pandectarum", in: *Opera omnia* (Florentiae, 1837 sqq.)
Sturm, Fritz, *Stipulatio Aquiliana* (1972)

Tafaro, Sebastiano, *Regula e ius antiquum in D. 50, 17, 23* (1984)
Thibaut, Anton Friedrich Justus, *System des Pandekten-Rechts* (8th ed., 1834)
Thielmann, Georg, *Die römische Privatauktion, Zugleich ein Beitrag zum römischen Bankierrecht* (1961)
S. Thomae Aquinatis, *Summa Theologiae* ed. by Petrus Cramello (1952 sqq.)
Thomas, J.A.C., *Textbook of Roman Law* (1976) (Thomas, *TRL*)
Thomas, J.A.C., *The Institutes of Justinian* (1975)
Treitel, G.H., *The Law of Contract* (7th ed., 1987)

Van Bynkershoek, Cornelis, *Observationes tumultuariae* (Harlemi, 1926 sqq.)
Van den Heever, F.P., *Aquilian Damages in South African Law* (1945)
Van der Keessel, D.G., *Praelectiones iuris hodierni ad Hugonis Grotii introductionem ad iurisprudentiam Hollandicam* (Amstelodami, Promunturii Bonae Spei in Urbe, 1961 sqq.)
Van der Walt, J.C., *Delict* (1979)
Van Damhouder, Joost, *Praxis rerum criminalium* (Antverpiae, 1562)
Van Leeuwen, Simon, *Censura forensis theoretico-practica* (4th ed., Lugduni in Batavis, 1741)
Van Leeuwen, Simon, *Het Rooms-Hollands-Regt* (Amsteldam, 1678)
Van Zyl, D.H., *Negotiorum gestio in South African Law* (1985)
Vangerow, Karl Adolph von, *Lehrbuch der Pandekten* (7th ed., 1876)
Vinnius, Arnoldus, *In Quatuor Libros Institutionum Imperalium Commentarius* (Lugduni, 1761)
Visky, Karoly, *Spuren der Wirtschaftskrise der Kaiserzeit in den römischen Rechtsquellen* (1983)
Voci, Pasquale, *Diritto ereditario romano* (2nd ed., vol. I (1967); vol. II (1963) (Voci, *DER*)
Voci, Pasquale, *L'errore nel diritto romano* (1937)
Voci, Pasquale, *Le obbligazioni romane*, vol. I, 1, Il contenuto dell'obbligatio (1969)
Voet, Johannes, *Commentarius ad Pandectas* (Parisiis, 1827, 1829)

Wächter, Carl Georg, *Pandekten* (1880 sq.)
Watson, Alan, *Contract of Mandate in Roman Law* (1961)
Watson, Alan, *Failures of the Legal Imagination* (1988)
Watson, Alan, *Legal Transplants* (1974)
Watson, Alan, *The Evolution of Law* (1985)
Watson, Alan, *The Law of Obligations in the Later Roman Republic* (1965)
Wesenbecius, Matthaeus, *In pandectas iuris civilis comentarii* (Basileae, 1589)
Wesenberg, Gerhard, *Verträge zugunsten Dritter* (1949)
Wesenberg, Gerhard; Wesener, Gunter, *Neuere deutsche Privatrechtsgeschichte* (4th ed., 1985)
Wessels, Sir J.W., *The Law of Contract in South Africa* (2nd ed., 1951)
Wieacker, Franz, *Privatrechtsgeschichte der Neuzeit* (2nd ed., 1967)
Wieacker, Franz, *Römische Rechtsgeschichte,* Erster Abschnitt (1988) (Wieacker, *RR*)
Wieacker, Franz, *Societas, Hausgemeinschaft und Erwebsgesellschaft* (1936)
Wieacker, Franz, *Vom römischen Recht,* Zehn Versuche (2nd ed., 1961)
Wieling, Hans Josef, *Interesse und Privatstrafe vom Mittelalter bis zum Bürgerlichen Gesetzbuch* (1970)
Windscheid, Bernhard; Kipp, Theodor, *Lehrbuch des Pandektenrechts* (9th ed., 1906)
Winfield, Sir Percy Henry, *The Province of the Law of Tort* (1931)
Winfield and Jolowicz on Tort (12th ed. by W.V.H. Rogers, 1984)
Wissenbach, J.J., *Exercitationes ad Quinquaginta Libros Pandectarum* (4th ed., Lipsiae, 1673)
Wittmann, Roland, *Die Körperverletzung an Freien im klassischen römischen Recht* (1972)
Wolf, Joseph Georg, *Causa stipulationis* (1970)
Wolf, Joseph Georg, *Error im römischen Vertragsrecht* (1961)
Wolff, Christian, *Institutiones iuris naturae et gentium* (Halae Magdeburgicae, 1750)
Wolff, Christian, *Jus naturae* (Francofurti et Lipsiae, 1740)
Wollschläger, Christian, *Die Entstehung der Unmöglichkeitslehre, Zur Dogmengeschichte des Rechts der Leistungsstörungen* (1970)
Wolter, Udo, *Ius canonicum in iure civili* (1975)
Wunner, Sven E., *Contractus, Sein Wortgebrauch und Willensgehalt im klassischen römischen Recht* (1964)

Zasius, Udalricus, *Opera omnia* (Lugduni, 1550)
Ziegler, Karl-Heinz, *Das private Schiedsgericht im antiken römischen Recht* (1971)
Zimmermann, Reinhard, *Das römisch-holländische Recht in Südafrika* (1983) (Zimmermann *RHR*)
Zimmermann, Reinhard, *Richterliches Moderationsrecht oder Totalnichtigkeit?, Die rechtliche Behandlung anstössig-übermässiger Verträge* (1979)
Zweigert, Konrad; Kötz, Hein, *Einführung in die Rechtsvergleichung auf dem Gebiete des Privatrechts,* vol. I (2nd ed., 1984) (Zweigert/Kötz, vol. I)
Zweigert, Konrad; Kötz, Hein, *Einführung in die Rechtsvergleichung auf dem Gebiete des Privatrechts,* vol. II, 2nd ed., 1984) (Zweigert/Kötz)
Zweigert, Konrad; Kötz, Hein; Weir, Tony, *An Introduction to Comparative Law,* vol. II (1977) (Zweigert/Kötz/Weir)

CHAPTER 1

Obligatio

I. THE CONCEPT AND ITS HISTORICAL DEVELOPMENT

1. Obligare—obligatio—obligation

"Nam fundi et aedes obligatae sunt ob Amoris praedium" said Astaphium ancilla in Plautus' play *Truculentus* (at 214), thus providing us with the oldest source in which the word "obligare" is used. The substantive "obligatio" can be traced back to Cicero.[1] As to the literal meaning of the term, its root "lig-" indicates that something or somebody is bound;[2] just as we are all "bound back" (to God) by virtue of our "re-ligio". This idea is still clearly reflected in the famous definition which Justinian advanced in his *Institutes*, where he introduced the subject of the law of obligations: "obligatio est iuris vinculum, quo necessitate adstringimur alicuius solvendae rei secundum nostrae civitatis iura."[3] Today the technical term "obligation" is widely used to refer to a two-ended relationship which appears from the one end as a personal right to claim and from the other as a duty to render performance. The party "bound" to make performance is called the debtor (debitor, from debere), whilst at the other end of the obligation we find the "creditor", who has put his confidence in this specific debtor and relies (credere) on the debtor's will and capacity to perform. As far as the Roman terminology is concerned, "obligatio" could denote the vinculum iuris looked at from either end; it could refer to the creditor's right as well as to the debtor's duty. This obviously makes it somewhat difficult to render the Roman idea in English, for the English term "obligation" is merely oriented towards the person bound, not towards the person entitled. With the words "my obligations" I can refer only to my duties, not to my rights.[4]

2. Delictual liability: from revenge to compensation

The carving out of the concept of an "obligatio" and the development of a law of obligations was one of the great contributions of classical Roman jurisprudence to the science of law. Fritz Schulz refers to it as

[1] *Epistulae ad M. Brutum* 1, 18, 3: see Schulz, *CRL*, pp. 455 sqq.

[2] The same connotation is inherent in the Dutch (and Afrikaans) word for obligation: "ver*bint*enis".

[3] Inst. III, 13 pr. On the origin of this definition cf., most recently, Bernardo Albanese, "Papiniano e la definizione di 'obligatio' in J. 3, 13, pr.", (1984) 50 *SDHI* 166 sqq. According to him, it is attributable to Papinian.

[4] See, for example, Peter Birks, "Obligations: One Tier or Two?", in: *Studies in Justinian's Institutes in memory of J.A.C. Thomas* (1983), pp. 19 sq.

"[a] unique achievement in the history of human civilisation".[5] Indeed, the concept of "obligatio" is a very advanced and refined one which was not part of the primitive thinking patterns of archaic Roman law (let alone any other legal system), but which stood at the end of a long evolution.[6] Like Greek or Germanic law, Roman law in its early stages can be conceived of, by and large, as the law of the family units[7] which constituted the ancient rural community. Family relationships, succession and property: these were the main areas with which the law had to concern itself—all of them as part and parcel of a broadly conceived family law and under the umbrella of the extensive powers of that almost absolute monarch of each familia, the paterfamilias. However, already at an early stage it was recognized that certain situations did not fit into the internal power structure of the familia: situations where, for instance, a person in one familia was allowed to exercise a legal power over a paterfamilias of another familia. The purpose of exercising this power was not to incorporate this other person into the family unit but to expiate a wrong which might have been inflicted and for which the other party was "liable". Thus, the early roots of liability in private law lie in what we today call delict. At a time when State authority was still too weak to enforce law and order, and either to administer criminal sanctions or to develop a system according to which a wronged party could be compensated, the individual had to take the law into his own hands. Whoever had committed a wrongful act against the body or property of another person was exposed to the vengeance of the victim of this wrong. The wronged party gained a right of seizure over the body of the wrongdoer, in order to execute his vengeance.

Initially this execution took the harshest possible form, namely the infliction of death. It is obvious that for the community at large such a state of affairs in which its members were allowed to kill each other was hardly satisfactory. Soon, therefore, we find the State interfering. On the one hand, seizure of the wrongdoer was tied to formal proceedings under State supervision (manus iniectio); on the other, the powers of the victim were reduced. In the case of membrum ruptum, the lex talionis[8] took the place of killing: if the wrongdoer had broken the

---

[5] *CRL*, p. 463; cf. also Kaser, *RPr* I, pp. 478 sq. (law of obligations is the area of the law where pre-classical and classical jurisprudence have accomplished their most valuable and lasting creative achievements).

[6] See, especially, Kaser, *Altrömisches ius*, pp. 179 sqq.; idem, *RPr* I, pp. 146 sqq.; Emilio Betti, *La struttura dell' obbligazione romana e il problema della sua genesi* (1955); Okko Behrends, *Der Zwölftafelprozess—Zur Geschichte des römischen Obligationenrechts* (1974), pp. 33 sqq. and passim; Mario Talamanca, "Obbligazioni", in: *ED*, vol. 29 (1979), pp. 1 sqq.; Wieacker, *RR*, pp. 256 sqq. Due to a lack of definite historical sources, many details of the development (as, for example, the question of the historical priority of delict or contract) are disputed.

[7] As to the term "familia", see Ulp. D. 50, 16, 195, 1–5.

[8] With regard to the lex talionis certain texts from the Old Testament spring to mind, especially Exodus 21, 23–25: ". . .if any harm follows, you shall give life for life, eye for eye, tooth for tooth, hand for hand, foot for foot, burn for burn, wound for wound, stripe for stripe. . . ." For comment, see, most recently, Mervyn Tower, "Popular misconceptions: A

victim's limb, the victim was allowed only to break the wrongdoer's limb in return—to let him inflict a graver injury than he had received himself now seemed to be excessive satisfaction. However, taliation (even though historically introduced as a means of mitigation) was still a relatively crude way of dealing with the consequences of wrongful acts. Therefore, already at a time before the XII Tables were drafted, the victim's right to vengeance was made redeemable: at first he was allowed, later expected, and finally indirectly forced, to accept a composition consisting of a sum of money (earlier on, probably cattle)[9] which either the wrongdoer himself or somebody else—usually a relative—might offer[10] in order to make the victim abstain from taking vengeance.[11] This was a development which the State tried to support by standardizing the amount of the composition for various delicts. At that stage, liability for delict began to be seen increasingly in financial rather than retaliatory terms.[12] Still, however, the law focused on the aspect of liability: the wrongdoer had the option of "buying-off" the right of vengeance, but if he was not able to do that and if nobody else was willing to redeem him either, manus iniectio was granted, i.e. the victim was now allowed to exercise his power of seizure. If the worst came to the worst, the wrongdoer was liable to be sold into slavery (trans Tiberim) or even to be cut into pieces.[13]

Note on the Lex Talionis", (1984) 80/81 *Law and Justice* 25 sqq. Exodus 21, too, represents a comparatively refined stage of the legal development. Cf. still the song of Lamech (son of Methusalem and father of Noah) in Genesis 4, 23 and 24: "Hear my voice, ye wives of Lamech, hearken unto my speech: for I have slain a man to my wounding, and a young man to my hurt. If Cain shall be avenged sevenfold, truly Lamech seventy and sevenfold."

[9] The word "pecunia" is derived from pecus. For further discussion of the origin of money in Rome and of the etymology of pecunia and pecus, see Wieacker, *RR*, pp. 238 sqq. (239).

[10] Provisions such as § 267 I BGB ("If a debtor does not have to perform in person, a third party may also make performance. The approval of the debtor is not necessary") go back to this privilege that a debtor, liable for execution on his person, could be redeemed by third parties.

[11] This account largely represents the prevailing opinion: the development of delictual liability is seen as an evolution from revenge (but cf. also Herman van den Brink, *The Charme of Legal History*, 1974, pp. 51 sqq.; Wieacker, *RR*, pp. 286 sq.) to compensation. Cf. already Jhering, *Geist* I, pp. 118 sqq.; today: Kaser, op. cit. For a different view based mainly on comparative evidence derived from primitive societies, see Geoffrey MacCormack, "Revenge and Compensation in Early Law", (1973) 21 *The American Journal of Comparative Law* 69 sqq.

[12] That liability, at that stage, had become redeemable by payment of a sum of money, seems to have been the historical reason for a basic feature of the Roman law of civil procedure: omnis condemnatio pecuniaria. See Paul Koschaker, (1916) 37 *ZSS* 355 sqq.; Kaser, *RZ*, p. 287.

[13] For details, see the XII Tables; especially Tables 3, 1: "Post deinde manus iniectio esto. In ius ducito", 3, 2: "Ni iudicatum facit aut quis endo eo in iure vindicit, secum ducito. Vincito aut nervo aut compedibus XV pondo ne maiore aut si volet minore vindicito" and 3, 6: "Tertiis nundinis partis secanto. Si plus minusve secuerunt, se fraude esto." These and other provisions seem fairly harsh to us, but it was the aim of the XII Tables to protect the debtor against arbitrary cruelty on the part of the creditor. Thus the weight of the chains, with which the debtor was kept imprisoned in the house of the creditor, was not to exceed 15 pounds. There are provisions as to how the debtor was to be fed. He had to remain imprisoned for 60 days, then the creditor had to bring him to three successive market-days

3. The origin of contractual liability

The Romans soon discovered that such a redeemable, pledge-like power of seizure was a convenient means of exerting pressure on the other person. They saw no reason why this pressure should be applied only to enforce payment of a monetary composition in the case of delict and not to enforce other performances as well. Thus, if one party wanted to obligate another to make a specific performance, he would ask the latter to subject himself to this power of seizure in case he failed to perform. This he did by entering into a transaction with the other party; the object of this transaction was to create the same type of liability by artificial means (i.e. by asking the other party to subject himself to it voluntarily) which arose "ex lege" in case of delict. One of the oldest of these transactions was the highly controversial nexum:[14] by way of an act per aes et libram the debtor would settle his condition as nexus ("entangled"), that is, he was liable to the creditor if he did not redeem himself by timeously paying back a specific sum he had received.[15] The primary economic purpose of nexum was to ensure repayment of a loan.[16] By the time of classical law it had already

(all this in order still to make redemption possible). It never seems to have happened in practice that a debtor was ultimately killed (thrown down from the Tarpeian rock) or (in the case of several co-creditors) cut into pieces (this probably referred only to his corpse); cf., for example, Cassius Dio, *Historia Romana* IV, 17, 8). Nevertheless, the old story of the creditor demanding his pound of flesh from the debtor's body (immortalized by Shakespeare in his *Merchant of Venice*) appears to have its origin in the "partes secanto" of the XII Tables. Usually, the unredeemed debtor had to work off his debt in the service of the creditor. On all this, see Behrends, op. cit., note 6, pp. 113 sqq. (he argues, however, contrary to established doctrine, that the creditor acquired the same kind of power over his debtor that a paterfamilias had over his dependants; but see Franz Horak, "Kreditvertrag und Kreditprozess in den Zwölftafeln", (1976) 93 *ZSS* 261 sqq., 278 sqq.); cf. also Carlo Augusto Cannata, "Tertiis nundinis partis secanto", in: *Studi in onore di Arnaldo Biscardi*, vol. IV (1983), pp. 59 sqq. For a comparative analysis of concept and development of (delictual) liability in ancient societies cf. Josef Kohler, *Shakespeare vor dem Forum der Jurisprudenz* (2nd ed., 1919), pp. 50 sqq.

[14] Buckland/Stein, pp. 429 sqq.; Francis de Zulueta, "The Recent Controversy about Nexum", (1913) 29 *LQR* 137 sqq.; Jolowicz/Nicholas, pp. 164 sqq.; Kaser, *Altrömisches ius*, pp. 119 sqq., 138 sqq., 233 sqq.; idem, *RPr* I, pp. 166 sq.; Liebs, *RR*, pp. 229 sqq.; Ulrich von Lübtow, "Zum Nexumproblem", (1950) 67 *ZSS* 112 sqq.; Maine, pp. 185 sqq.; Talamanca, *ED*, vol. 29, pp. 4 sqq.; Herman van den Brink, *Ius fasque* (1968), pp. 158 sqq.; Wieacker, *RR*, pp. 336, 582. Recently, the existence of a specific nexum transaction has been denied by Okko Behrends, "Das nexum im Manzipationsrecht oder die Ungeschichtlichkeit des Libraldarlehens", (1974) 21 *RIDA* 137 sqq. That the Germanic tribes knew institutions similar to nexum is testified by Tacitus, *Germania* XXIV, 2. As to the history of the penal bond in the English common law ("a sophisticated form of self-pledge"), see Simpson, *History*, pp. 88 sqq., 123 sqq.

[15] Even if he paid what he owed, a formal counteract per aes et libram was necessary to discharge him. Otherwise the debtor would have remained obligatus. This solutio per aes et libram survived in classical law as a means of releasing the debtor from his debt; cf. infra p. 756.

[16] For a comparative analysis of loan transactions in primitive legal systems, see Obrad Stanojevic, "Observations sur le prêt dans les droits primitifs", in: *Studi in onore di Edoardo Volterra*, vol. III (1971), pp. 429 sqq.

disappeared[17] and its function had been taken over by the informal contract of mutuum.

It is obvious that nexum and certain similar formal transactions of the ancient Roman law are the historical roots of what were later to be classified as contractual obligations. Yet at this early stage we can hardly speak of a law of obligations because the most important constituent element of the concept of an obligation was still missing: the wrongdoer/promisor did not "owe" the payment of a composition or whatever he had promised; such payment/performance was just a means of warding off the impending execution on his person. The law initially concerned itself only with the question of liability.[18] Quite soon, however, this stage of the development was left behind. It gradually came to be recognized that the debtor was under a duty to make performance and that the other party had a corresponding right to claim such performance. Thus, obligatio in classical Roman law implied both "duty" and "liability": a relation existed in terms of which the debtor ought to (i.e. was "bound" to) perform whatever he had promised to perform (or, in the case of delict, to compensate the victim); only if he failed to comply with this duty did he become liable in the sense that his body and/or property were exposed to execution.

Yet, even at a mature stage, the Roman concept of obligatio always retained certain archaic features.[19] The very word "obligatio" always reminded the Roman lawyer of the fact that, in former times, the person who was to be liable, that is, over whose body the creditor acquired the pledge-like power of seizure, was physically laid in bonds; and, even though this piece of symbolism was soon abandoned and the idea came to prevail that the debtor could be legally bound even if his body was not physically put into chains, the concept of an obligation, in the minds of laymen as well as lawyers, seems to have retained the connotation of some sort of invisible rope around the neck of the debtor, tying a specific debtor to a particular creditor. The obligation thus gave rise to an intensely personal relationship: when one considers that the law was originally concerned, not with the duty aspect of obligation, but with personal liability of the strictest kind,[20] there is, at

---

[17] Plebeian nexi had to suffer considerable hardship from their patrician creditors (cf. e.g. Livius, *Ab urbe condita*, Liber II, XXIII, 1 and 6); thus, nexum was probably prohibited in the course of the 4th century as a result of the class struggles.

[18] As to the famous conceptual difference between "*Schuld*" and "*Haftung*" (duty and liability), see Alois Brinz, "Der Begriff der obligatio", (1874) 1 *GrünhZ* 11 sqq.; De Zulueta, *Gaius* II, pp. 144 sq.; Jolowicz/Nicholas, pp. 160 sqq.; Rabel, *Grundzüge*, pp. 89 sq.; Talamanca, *ED*, vol. 29, pp. 20 sqq.; as far as Germanic legal history is concerned, cf. e.g. Otto von Gierke, *Deutsches Privatrecht*, vol. III (1917), pp. 8 sqq. For a general evaluation, see Bernhard Diestelkamp, "Die Lehre von Schuld und Haftung", in: Helmut Coing, Walter Wilhelm (eds.), *Wissenschaft und Kodifikation im 19. Jahrhundert*, vol. VI (1982), pp. 21 sqq.

[19] "The image of a vinculum iuris colours and pervades every part of the Roman law of Contract and Delict": Maine, p. 190.

[20] At this early stage of the development, both delictual and contractual obligations died with the person liable; he had been the hostage, and when he died, there was nothing that

least historically, nothing strange in this idea of "privity" of obligation. The practical consequences that were to flow from this will be discussed in Chapter 2 of this work. Further terminological evidence for the development sketched above is provided by the word used in classical law to indicate fulfilment of an obligation: the term "solvere" (= to loosen) refers back to the stage where payment was a means of securing release from power of seizure, that is, of loosening the (not merely metaphorical) bond around the debtor's body.[21]

4. Dare facere praestare oportere

The essential element of an obligation in developed Roman law, therefore, was the fact that the debtor was directly bound to make performance. The performance which was owed could take the form of dare facere praestare—"[o]bligationum substantia non in eo consistit, ut aliquod corpus nostrum aut servitutem nostram faciat, sed ut alium nobis obstringat ad dandum aliquid vel faciendum vel praestandum":[22] dare referring mainly to the transfer of quiritary ownership,[23] facere comprising all kinds of acts (including a dare) as well as omissions, and praestare vaguely implying a guarantee for a certain result.[24] As one can see, these terms overlap; they date back to a time when one was not too particular about clear-cut conceptual analysis. They had been taken over from the procedural formulae as terms of substantive law to describe the possible content of an obligation;[25] since Roman law was an actional law, it mattered little whether an agreement was to be regarded as binding if no suitable procedural formula was available to enforce it: only where there was a remedy was there a right ("ubi remedium, ibi ius"). This remedy, in the case of obligations, was always an actio in personam: the plaintiff was not asserting a relationship between a person and a thing (in the sense that he could bring his remedy against whoever was, by some act, denying the

could devolve on the heirs. Delictual obligations in Roman law always remained passively intransmissible: the request for expiation could be directed only against the person who had committed the wrong. The liability of heirs under transactions entered into by the deceased, on the other hand, was already recognized by the XII Tables. See Max Kaser, "Die altrömische Erbenhaftung", (1952) 1 *AHDO-RIDA* 507 sqq.; Voci, *DER*, vol. I, pp. 45 sqq. For medieval English law and its rule of "actio personalis moritur cum persona", see Simpson, *History*, pp. 41 sq., 558 sqq. The situation changed only with the rise of assumpsit.

[21] See, for example, Liebs, *RR*, pp. 231 sq. On solutio, see generally D. 46, 3 and Buckland/Stein, pp. 564 sq.; Kaser, *RPr* I, pp. 635 sqq. The old and original meaning of solutio is still reflected in what Gaius tells us about the form of release per aes et libram. "Me eo nomine a te solvo libroque" were the words, which had to be used by the person to be released: Gai. III, 174.

[22] This is Paulus' famous definition of an obligation, contained in D. 44, 7, 3 pr.; on which, see, for example, Talamanca, *ED*, vol. 29, pp. 28 sqq.

[23] Gai. IV, 4.

[24] Sturm, *Stipulatio Aquiliana*, pp. 111 sqq. The term derives from "praesstare" (to stand in as a hostage) and had been carried over from the days when the person liable was bound as a hostage.

[25] See Gai. IV, 2.

plaintiff's alleged right to the object in question—that was the crucial point in an actio in rem), but rather a relationship between two persons; the plaintiff set out to sue the particular defendant because he, personally, was under a duty towards him, and not because (for instance) he happened to be in possession of some of the plaintiff's property. If one translates this into the language of substantive law, one can say that the law of obligations is concerned with rights in personam, whilst rights in rem are the subject matter of the law of property.[26] This is what Paulus emphasized in the fragment quoted at the beginning of this paragraph.

5. Unenforceable obligations ("obligationes naturales")

It has just been pointed out that obligations were enforceable by means of actiones civiles (or honorariae). There were some situations, however, where the creditor had no way of compelling his debtor to comply with what he had undertaken to do. I am referring here to what has been known as "obligationes naturales"[27] since the time of classical law: obligations contracted by slaves, children and women in power and debts owed to such persons, to mention the original examples. Sensu stricto, they are not obligations because they lack enforceability: persons in power could normally not be parties to a lawsuit; and where they could (sons in power in the position of a defendant), the other party could not proceed to execution under the judgment. On the other hand, we are not dealing with a case of invalidity: obligationes naturales were not legally irrelevant, but had certain secondary effects of an obligation. For instance, there was no reason why anything which had been performed in fulfilment of such a debt should be allowed to be claimed back:[28] the receiver had not been enriched without legal ground because what was owed was, after all, a debitum (even though the claim was not enforceable). Furthermore, a naturalis obligatio could be the object of a novation,[29] it could be used for a set-off against a claim of the debtor[30] and, to

[26] For a clear analysis of this fundamental distinction, see Nicholas, *Introduction*, pp. 99 sqq.

[27] Cf. Buckland/Stein, pp. 552 sq.; Pierre Cornioley, *Naturalis obligatio* (1964); Kaser, *RPr* I, pp. 480 sqq.; Enrico Moscati, "Obbligazioni naturali", in: *ED*, vol. 29 (1979), pp. 353 sqq.; Gaetano Scherillo, "Le obbligazioni naturali", (1968) 175 *Archivo giuridico* 516 sqq.; J.A.C. Thomas, "Naturalis obligatio pupilli", in: *Sein und Werden im Recht, Festgabe für Ulrich von Lübtow* (1970), pp. 457 sqq.; Paul van Warmelo, "Naturalis obligatio", in: *Huldigingsbundel Pont* (1970), pp. 410 sqq.; Windscheid/Kipp, § 287 sqq. "Naturalis" obligatio in this context, therefore, means as much as "non-genuine" obligation. Cf. Iul. D. 46, 1, 16, 4 "per abusionem".

[28] Cf. Iul. D. 46, 1, 16, 4; Ulp. D. 44, 7, 10.

[29] Ulp. D. 46, 2, 1 pr., 1.

[30] Ulp. D. 16, 2, 6 (but see Buckland/Stein, p. 552); *Fensham v. Jacobson* 1951 (2) SA 136 (T) at 137H–138F.

secure its fulfilment, a pledge could be given or a surety provided.[31]

In modern legal systems, too, the situation occurs that the law recognizes some effects of certain transactions, without, however, being disposed to assist the "creditor" in enforcing his right.[32] In South African law, the term "naturalis obligatio" is still used in these instances,[33] but the concept is known in substance even where, as in the German Civil Code, it has been abolished in name. Yet, the type of transaction falling into this category has changed drastically. In the place of relationships affected by the paternal power over one of the parties we now find, to take the main examples in German law, the promise of a fee to a marriage broker[34] and gaming and betting.[35] These are transactions which the legislator has disapproved of—for reasons which, incidentally, seem to be a little outdated in the one case[36] and somewhat paternalistic in the other.[37] A situation similar in its practical result, but different as far as the legal construction is concerned, occurs where the period of prescription for a claim has expired. Here the creditor is entitled to claim (i.e. his right remains enforceable), but the debtor may refuse performance. Yet, once performance has been rendered, it may not be reclaimed.[38] German commentators generally do not fail to observe that this case cannot be brought under the concept

---

[31] Cf. e.g. Gai. III, 119 a; William Burge, *Commentaries on the Law of Suretyship* (1849), p. 7.

[32] See Mario Rotondi, "Alcune considerazioni sul concetto di obbligazione naturale e sulla sua evoluzione", (1977) 75 *Rivista del diritto commerciale* 213 sqq.

[33] Cf. especially the comprehensive analysis by Wessels, *Contract*, vol. I, pp. 386 sqq.

[34] § 656 BGB.

[35] §§ 762 sqq. BGB. For South African law, cf. *Fensham v. Jacobson* 1951 (2) SA 136 (T) and *Gibson v. Van der Walt* 1952 (1) SA 262 (A). Cf. also Pothier, *Traité du jeu*, n. 58; § 1271 ABGB, art. 514 II OR. On gaming in Rome and on the reaction of the Roman authorities, cf. Marek Kurylowicz, "Die Glücksspiele und das römische Recht", in: *Studi in onore di Cesare Sanfilippo*, vol. IV (1983), pp. 267 sqq.

[36] 656 BGB has been severely criticized as being discriminatory and infringing the basic rights of the German "*Grundgesetz*"; it has been said to be pushing a trade with a legitimate social function into the twilight of doubtful seriosity and thus impeding, rather than facilitating, judicial control of real abuses. The courts are now increasingly faced with difficult problems arising from situations where the fee paid to a marriage broker has been pre-financed by the broker's bank. Also, a flourishing business of escort agencies has sprung up in recent years to accommodate the increasing number of "singles". Into which contractual category do the various partnership service transactions fall? And is § 656 BGB applicable in all these cases? On these questions, see Peter Gilles, "Partnerschaftsservice statt Ehemakelei", 1983 *Neue Juristische Wochenschrift* 362 sqq.

[37] Is it really acceptable to maintain that the law has to prevent people from ruining themselves by indulging in gaming and betting? A more pragmatic approach as to why gaming and betting contracts should be unenforceable is advanced in judicial pronouncements such as *Graham v. Pollok* (1848) 10 D 646 at 648 ("However laudable the sport may be, we have far more serious matters to attend to") or *Christison v. McBride* (1881) 9 R 34 ("The Queen's Court does not exist for settling disputes as to who drew the winning number in a lottery") (both Scottish cases).

[38] § 222 BGB; cf. also *Pentecost & Co. v. Cape Meat Supply Co.* 1933 CPD 472 and now ss 10, 17 of the South African Prescription Act 68/1969. For further discussion and comparative material, see Karl Spiro, *Die Begrenzung privater Rechte durch Verjährungs-, Verwirkungs- und Fatalfristen*, vol. I (1975), § 244.

of an obligatio naturalis.[39] The Romans, on the other hand, had no objection to extending the term to cases (as, for example, that of the senatus consultum Macedonianum) where an exceptio could be raised to bar the claim.[40] That goes to show that historically here, as in many other areas, we are not dealing with a clearly definable terminus technicus: the classical Roman lawyers did not think in terms of neat and logical conceptual categories.[41] Apart from that, the Corpus Juris Civilis also contains texts of post-classical origin which are based on another understanding of the notion of an obligatio naturalis. They refer to merely moral or ethical and, in this sense, "natural" duties:[42] where, for instance, a freedman has rendered certain services to his patronus which were not, in fact, legally owed ("condicere eum non posse, quamvis putans se obligatum solvit . . .: natura enim operas patrono libertus debet"),[43] or where someone has returned somebody else's present.[44] Furthermore, to add to the confusion, Paulus sometimes spoke of naturales obligationes in a totally different sense; he used the term to refer to those (enforceable!) obligations which were not peculiar to the Roman ius civile (like the formal stipulatio) but based on the naturalis ratio and which were part, as such, of the ius

---

[39] See e.g. Staudinger/H. Dilcher (1979), § 222, n. 3.

[40] Paul. D. 14, 6, 10. Another interesting case, where Roman lawyers used the term "naturalis obligatio", concerned the actio de peculio. If the paterfamilias granted a peculium to his son in power or slave, he was liable for all commercial debts incurred by that person in power. This liability was "dumtaxat de peculio", limited by the amount of the peculium at the moment of condemnation. As far as the computation of the value of the peculium was concerned, whatever the paterfamilias "owed" to the peculium was added, whatever "claims" he had against the peculium were deducted from it. Of course, any transactions between two members of the same familia could never give rise to an "obligation". Yet they were not a legal non-entity, because in the context of the calculation of the peculium they were taken into consideration. In the course of time, quite a few other cases of "naturales obligationes" were added: obligations incurred by a ward without auctoritas tutoris (Paul. D. 12, 6, 13, 1), obligations extinguished due to capitis deminutio (Ulp. D. 4, 5, 2, 2) or litis contestatio (Ulp. D. 46, 1, 8, 3) etc.

[41] "It would be wholly incorrect to say that there were no general concepts in the Roman law of the time of Justinian and before; on the contrary, Roman jurists eagerly discussed situations in which a contract would be void because of 'mistake', situations in which the enforcement of an informal obligation was required by 'good faith', and various other types of situations in which legal results involved a reference to concepts. . . . However, these concepts were not treated as ideas which pervaded the rules and determined their applicability. They were not considered philosophically. The concepts of Roman law, like its numerous legal rules, were tied to specific types of situations. Roman law consisted of an intrinsic network of rules; yet these were not presented as an intellectual system but rather as an elaborate mosaic of practical solutions to specific legal questions. Thus one may say that, although there were concepts in Roman law, there was no concept of a concept" (Berman, *Law and Revolution*, pp. 149 sq.).

[42] Cf. e.g. Cornioley, op. cit., note 27, pp. 256 sqq.; Van Warmelo, *Huldigingsbundel Pont*, pp. 419 sqq.

[43] D. 12, 6, 26, 12. For all details, see Wolfgang Waldstein, *Operae libertorum* (1986) (on Ulp. D. 12, 6, 26, 12 cf. pp. 363 sqq.).

[44] D. 5, 3, 25, 11.

gentium common to all peoples (as, for instance, the consensual contracts).[45]

Under these circumstances one can well understand that lawyers of later centuries, who were trying to analyse the concept of natural obligations on the basis of the Roman sources, sometimes tended to despair: "Sunt hac in re multae leges quae pugnant invicem, et est summus labor in eis adducendis in concordiam; fuit mihi olim maximus et diu in desperatione fui", as the humanist Cuiacius confessed.[46] By his time, however, the discussion had become largely theoretical. Many of the classical Roman examples had become obsolete. Where an attempt was made to define a naturalis obligatio in the spirit of the Corpus Juris Civilis, if somewhat vaguely, as "quae solo nititur aequitatis naturalis vinculo,"[47] the question immediately arose under which circumstances such an equitable or moral obligation was to be recognized. But since this was dependent on each individual's sense of tact, morality and piety, general rules could hardly be established.[48] If, furthermore, on the evidence of some centuries of discussion,[49] one accepts that great caution is necessary not to generalize consequences and effects of natural obligations as far as accessory rights, compensation, etc. are concerned, the question may well be asked whether modern legislators have not been wise to abandon a makeshift term[50] with such a notorious potential for confusion.[51]

II. DIVISIO OBLIGATIONUM

1. The contract—delict dichotomy

In the course of our discussion of the origins of liability we have been referring to contractual and delictual obligations. This is the summa divisio obligationum, which Gaius—probably putting the old Aristotelian distinction between voluntary and involuntary transactions to

---

[45] Cf. e.g. Paul. D. 50, 17, 84, 1; 45, 1, 126, 2.

[46] Cf. Van Warmelo, *Huldigingsbundel Pont*, p. 433, n. 1.

[47] Cf. e.g. Voet, *Commentarius ad Pandectas*, Lib. XLIV, Tit. VI, III.

[48] Cf. therefore Wessels, *Contract*, vol. I, p. 394: "Our law does not favour the extension of the scope of the natural obligation, and therefore mere debts of honour and promises pietatis causa are not to be regarded as giving rise to natural obligations." Would gaming, betting or marriage broking fall into this class of cases?

[49] For an outline of the historical development, see J.E. Scholtens, *De Geschiedenis der natuurlijke Verbintenis sinds het Romeinsche Recht* (1931); Van Warmelo, *Huldigingsbundel Pont*, pp. 421 sqq., Rotondi, (1977) 75 *Rivista del diritto commerciale* 213 sqq.; cf. also Savigny, *Obligationenrecht*, vol. I, §§ 5 sqq.; Windscheid/Kipp, § 287 sqq.

[50] Hausmaninger/Selb, p. 250.

[51] On a similar note, Van Warmelo, *Huldigingsbundel Pont* (for modern South African law), concludes by saying: "Hierdie reëlings sal en moet gehandhaaf word, maar om hulle (nou en dan) as natuurlike verbintenisse te noem lei tot niks en skep eerder onduidelikheid en onsekerheid."

systematical use[52]—introduced in his *Institutes.*[53] It has remained fundamental ever since and is a reflection of the fact that different rules are needed to govern the voluntary transfer of resources between two members of the legal community on the one hand, and possible collisions between their private spheres on the other:[54] the one body of rules being concerned with the fulfilment of expectations engendered by a binding promise, the other with the protection of the status quo against wrongful harm.[55] However, the borderline between contract and delict is by no means as clear as might be imagined. That it has been considerably blurred becomes apparent when one compares how different modern legal systems have tried to cope with the demands for extension of liability, arising as a result of the complexities of the technological age.[56] The protection of the consumer against defective products by means of a claim against the manufacturer is a matter for the law of torts in English law,[57] whilst the French courts have been prepared to grant him a direct contractual claim.[58] In the case of negligent statements, the German courts operate with contractual liability (even though in some cases the fictitious nature of the contractual construction can hardly be concealed: the defendant is liable, not because he wants to be bound, but because he is—under certain circumstances—*supposed* to be liable);[59] the House of Lords, by contrast, in the celebrated case of *Hedley Byrne and Co. Ltd. v. Heller and Partners Ltd.*,[60] based the action on tort. In addition, Rudolf von Jhering's famous "discovery"[61] of culpa in

[52] See A.M. Honoré, *Gaius* (1962), pp. 97 sqq. (100); Witold Wolodkiewicz, "Le fonti delle obbligazioni nelle istituzioni di Gaio e nelle res cottidianae", (1970) 24 *Rivista italiana per le scienze giuridiche* 138 sqq.

[53] Gai. III, 88: "Nunc transeamus ad obligationes. quarum summa divisio in duas species diducitur: omnis enim obligatio vel ex contractu nascitur vel ex delicto."

[54] See, for example, Arthur van Mehren, "A General View of Contract", in: *International Encyclopedia of Comparative Law*, VII, 1, nn. 1 sqq.; Charles Fried, *Contract as Promise* (1981), p. 4 and passim.

[55] A.S. Burrows, "Contract, Tort and Restitution. A Satisfactory Division or Not?", (1983) 99 *LQR* 217 sqq.; cf. also Fried, op. cit., note 54, pp. 2 sq.: "The law of property defines the boundaries of our rightful possessions, while the law of torts seeks to make us whole against violations of those boundaries, as well as against violations of the natural boundaries of our physical person. Contract law ratifies and enforces our joint ventures beyond those boundaries."

[56] B.S. Markesinis, "The Not So Dissimilar Tort and Delict", (1977) 93 *LQR* 78 sqq.

[57] See especially the two famous cases of *MacPherson v. Buick Motor Co.* (1916) 217 NY 382, 111 NE 1050 and *Donoghue v. Stevenson* [1932] AC 562 (HL); Friedrich Kessler, "Products Liability", (1966/67) 76 *Yale LJ* 887 sqq.; R.W.M. Dias/B.S. Markesinis, *The English Law of Torts: A Comparative Introduction* (1976), pp. 61 sqq.

[58] See, for example, H. Mazeaud, "La responsabilité civile du vendeur fabricant", (1955) 53 *Revue trimestrielle de droit civil* 611 sqq.

[59] See Werner Lorenz, "Das Problem der Haftung für primäre Vermögensschäden bei der Erteilung einer unrichtigen Auskunft", in: *Festschrift für Larenz* (1973), pp. 575 sqq.

[60] [1964] AC 465 (HL). For the broader context of this discussion, see Atiyah, *Rise and Fall*, pp. 771 sqq.

[61] Hans Dölle, *Juristische Entdeckungen, Verhandlungen des 42. Deutschen Juristentages*, vol. II (1959), pp. B 1 sqq.

contrahendo,[62] applied by him to a fairly restricted number of situations,[63] has been used (or abused?) by the German courts to make large inroads into the law of delict;[64] thus, they have granted a contractual action for damages where a prospective purchaser, while inspecting some carpets in a store, was hit by a linoleum carpet which had been negligently handled by an employee of that store,[65] or even where the daughter of a prospective customer slipped on a lettuce leaf while entering the store with her mother.[66] As a result, it has been said that "the distinction between contract and tort is rapidly breaking down",[67] and in England as well as America the "death of contract" has been proclaimed.[68]

---

[62] Rudolf von Jhering, "Culpa in contrahendo, oder Schadensersatz bei nichtigen oder nicht zur Perfektion gelangten Verträgen", (1861) 4 *JhJb* 1 sqq.

[63] Erich Schanze, "Culpa in contrahendo bei Jhering", (1978) 7 *Ius Commune* 326 sqq.

[64] For an overview of the development in German law, see Peter Gottwald, "Die Haftung für culpa in contrahendo", 1982 *Juristische Schulung* 877 sqq.; Dieter Medicus, *Verschulden bei Vertragsverhandlungen, Gutachten und Vorschläge zur Überarbeitung des Schuldrechts*, vol. I (1981), pp. 479 sqq. For a comparative analysis, see Friedrich Kessler/Edith Fine, "Culpa in Contrahendo, Bargaining in Good Faith, and Freedom of Contract: A Comparative Study", (1964) 77 *Harvard LR* 401 sqq.

[65] The famous linoleum carpet case: RGZ 78, 239 sqq.

[66] The vegetable leaf case: BGHZ 66, 51 sqq., in which culpa in contrahendo and the contract with protective function in favour of a third party were combined.

[67] Markesinis, (1977) 93 *LQR* 122; cf. also J.C. Smith, "Economic Loss and the Common Law Marriage of Contracts and Torts", (1984) 18 *University of British Columbia LR* 95 sqq.

[68] See Grant Gilmore's elegant series of lectures "The Death of Contract" (1974). The modern English law of contract grew up around the action of assumpsit. Historically, this action was an offspring of the action of trespass on the case (that is, of the law of torts): see Simpson, *History*, pp. 199 sqq. According to Gilmore, contract is today being reabsorbed into the mainstream of tort, the residual category of civil liability (pp. 87 sqq.). For the rise (especially during the age of individualism since the latter half of the 18th century) and the modern decline of contract (since about 1870) in England, see the fascinating analysis by Atiyah, *Rise and Fall*, esp. pp. 345 sqq., 388 sqq., 398 sqq., 681 sqq., 716 sqq. Atiyah argues that in the English common law benefit and reliance (as opposed, especially, to mere promise) were the traditional key concepts of liability. Accordingly, there was no inherent difference between contractual and delictual obligations. It was only with "the settling of classical contract theory" (developed during the age of freedom of contract, stimulated by and intimately linked to the rise of individualism, *laissez faire* and the free market ideology, legal formalism, positivism and principle orientation), that a firmer line between contractual and non-contractual duties came to be established: due, mainly, to the creation (or formulation) of general rules governing contractual relationships, with clearly defined abstract concepts and based on the will theory, by doctrinal writers (starting with the treatises by Pollock and Anson) since the 1870s. These writers drew heavily on Roman law and on modern continental lawyers such as Pothier or Savigny. Their works "continued to exercise a dominating influence on English contractual thought through the next hundred years, and indeed, may be said to still rule us from their graves" (p. 682; cf. also F.H. Lawson, "Doctrinal Writing: A Foreign Element in English Law?", in: *Ius Privatum Gentium, Festschrift für Max Rheinstein*, vol. I (1969), pp. 191 sqq. and A.W.B. Simpson, "The Rise and Fall of the Legal Treatise: Legal Principles and the Forms of Legal Literature", (1981) 48 *University of Chicago* LR 632 sqq.). In Atiyah's view, this later idea "that tort liabilities are wholly different from contractual liabilities because the latter arise from consensual obligations is not soundly based, either in logic or in history" (p. 505). He argues that with the decline of contract a resurgence of benefit-based and reliance-based liabilities is taking place today. Thus, in his opinion, the time "is plainly ripe for a new theoretical structure for

Yet one must not overlook the fact that these developments, in so far as they appear to be illegitimate extensions of either of these regimes, have their origin in certain doctrinal idiosyncrasies that have prevented a (systematically) more adequate approach. Certain deficiencies in the law of delict (particularly the absence of strict vicarious liability)[69] which the courts were not able and Parliament was too weak to overcome have led to the German courts achieving by means of the law of contract what other jurisdictions have managed to resolve in the area of torts. If, on the other hand, English judges have tended to expand the common law of torts,[70] they were forced to do so because of the limitations of their law of contract, especially the one imposed by the doctrine of consideration. "If it were possible in English law," as Lord Devlin has put it in the *Hedley Byrne* case,[71] "to construct a contract without consideration, . . . the question would be, not whether on the facts of the case there was a special relationship [sc: giving rise to a duty of care], but whether on the facts of the case there was a contract." Of course, there are borderline cases which present genuine delictual as well as contractual aspects. The contract/delict dichotomy can, therefore, hardly be carried through with dogmatic rigidity. That does not detract from the fact that contract is still alive and well today and that, in all likelihood, contract and delict will, and should, remain distinct bodies of law.[72] As Arthur van Mehren has pointed out, the rise of insurance has probably even sharpened the differences between the two regimes.[73]

---

contract . . . (and for the) redrawing of conceptual categories of the law" (pp. 778, 779). Cf. also Gerhard Kegel, "Verwirkung, Vertrag und Vertrauen", in: *Festschrift für Klemens Pleyer* (1986), pp. 528 sqq. and, for German law, Eduard Picker, "Vertragliche und deliktische Schadenshaftung", 1987 *Juristenzeitung* 1041 sqq. (also advocating abolition of the dichotomy of contractual and delictual liability for damages; according to Picker, liability for damages always arises ex lege and it is only the duty to render performance that is based on private autonomy, i.e. contract).

[69] § 831 BGB allows the "person who employs another to do any work" to escape liability for damage done by his employee, by proving that he has exercised the necessary care in the selection of the employee and that, where he had to supply equipment or to supervise the work, he has also exercised ordinary care as regards such supply or supervision. For a comparative analysis of this rather unfortunate rule, see Zweigert/Kötz/Weir, pp. 294 sqq.; cf. also infra pp. 1125 sq.

[70] Cf. recently A.J.E. Jaffey, "Contract in tort's clothing", (1985) 5 *Legal Studies* 77 sqq., who concludes his analysis of the case law with the comment: "By all means let the relevant rules of contract be reformed. But to use tort at random to evade them leads to confusion, uncertainty and inconsistency in the law" (p. 103).

[71] [1964] AC 465 (HL) at 525–6.

[72] In this vein, against the "Death of Contract" school see, for example, A.S. Burrows, (1983) 99 *LQR* 217 sqq., 255 sqq., 263 sqq.; Fried, op. cit., note 54, pp. 1 sqq.; Smith, (1984) 18 *University of British Columbia LR* 108 sqq., 125.

[73] Op. cit., note 54, n. 2. Owing to the availability of insurance, the tortfeasor who is liable in delict today typically does not ultimately have to bear the loss. Delictual rules, therefore, have to take into account the fact that in all likelihood losses will not be borne by individuals but will be shifted to groups. Contractual relations involve different kinds of risk; here, typically, the individual parties will bear the loss assigned to them.

2. From twofold to fourfold subdivision

The distinction between contractual and delictual obligations does, of course, not represent an exhaustive basis for the systematic analysis (a divisio in the technical sense) of the law of obligations. That would not have been disputed even by Gaius. In actual fact, the "summa divisio" in III, 88 of his *Institutes* seems to have been established mainly for didactical purposes, in order to provide the law student with a broad outline of the material covered; systematic completeness does not appear to have been intended.[74] Only a few lines later Gaius discusses a case of unjustified enrichment and makes it quite plain that the obligation to render restitution cannot be regarded as a contractual one.[75] Of course, it is not of a delictual nature either. In his amended and revised version of the *Institutes*, probably published posthumously under the somewhat peculiar title of *Res cottidianae sive aurea*, Gaius added a third category in order to accommodate these and other cases: "Obligationes aut ex contractu nascuntur aut ex maleficio aut proprio quodam iure ex variis causarum figuris."[76] But this lumping together of everything which did not really fit under either delict or contract into a hotchpotch of "various causes" could not, of course, appeal to the more systematically oriented minds of the East-Roman school jurists. Thus, by the time the official Justinianic textbook was compiled, this residual category had been subdivided on the model of the contract/delict dichotomy, and as a result a fourfold scheme had been arrived at: ". . .divisio [obligationum] in quattuor species diducitur: aut enim ex contractu sunt aut quasi ex contractu aut ex maleficio aut quasi ex maleficio."[77]

As far as systematic exposition and classification of topics are concerned, Justinian took great delight in the number four: not only does he present four sources of obligations, he also gives a fourfold subdivision of contractual obligations; then, there are four kinds of contracts re, four cases of contracts verbis and four instances of contracts consensu; furthermore, four delicts and four quasi-delicts are

[74] Max Kaser, "Divisio obligationum", in: *Studies Thomas*, p. 85; contra: Arnaldo Biscardi, "Some Critical Remarks on the Roman Law of Obligations", (1977) 12 *The Irish Jurist* 372 sqq., according to whom Gaius saw the delict/contract dichotomy as exhaustive. Cf. also Thomas, *TRL*, p. 2.

[75] Gai. III, 91.

[76] Gai. D. 44, 7, 1 pr.; cf. Wolodkiewicz, (1970) 24 *Rivista italiana per le scienze giuridiche* 78 sqq.

[77] Inst. III, 13, 2. For details of the development of the divisio obligationum from Gaius' two- and threefold down to Justinian's fourfold division, see Kaser, *Studies Thomas*, pp. 73 sqq.; Theo Mayer-Maly, "Divisio obligationum", (1967) 2 *The Irish Jurist* 375 sqq. (in English); Giuseppe Grosso, *Il sistema romano dei contratti* (3rd ed., 1963), passim; Talamanca, *ED*, vol. 29, pp. 38 sqq. Cf. also Diosdy, pp. 112 sqq., who has recently advanced the supposition that the trichotomy of the sources of obligations, as laid down in D. 44, 7, 1 pr., never existed in Roman law.

mentioned.[78] This method of arranging and systematizing the law was neither accidental[79] nor merely adopted for the sake of (a somewhat artificial) symmetry of exposition: like most people in the ancient world, he was influenced by the symbolism of numbers. The number four has always had a special significance, usually relating—in contrast to the sacred number three[80]—to the more external or secular structure of the world.[81] (Of course, the addition of four and three equals the mystical number seven,[82] multiplication of them the holy number twelve.)[83]

3. Quasi-contractual and quasi-delictual obligations

But what did the two residual categories consist of? Under the heading of "obligationes quasi ex contractu" we find, most importantly, indebitum solutum; furthermore, negotium gestum, tutela, communio and legatum per damnationem[84] (i.e. obligations arising from unjustified enrichment, from (unauthorized) management of (another's)

---

[78] Cf. the (too severely) critical analysis by H. Goudy, "Artificiality in Roman Juristic Classifications", in: *Studi giuridici in onore di Carlo Fadda*, vol. V (1906), pp. 209 ff. (214 sqq.).

[79] That Justinian was very conscious of the role of symbolic numbers in the arrangement of the Corpus Juris Civilis appears from § 1 of his Constitutio Tanta.

[80] Some examples from the Bible: Three is the number of the Holy Trinity, three angels visited Abraham, for three days Christ was buried, three times Christ asked his Father that the cup might pass, three times Peter renounced Christ, three times Christ showed himself to his disciples after his resurrection. In our modern, heathen, usage, man no longer piously accepts the harmonic structure of the world (as expressed in perfect numbers), but still clings to the somewhat superstitious aura attaching to the "lucky three". For the symbolic influence of the number three in Roman law, see H. Goudy, *Trichotomy in Roman Law* (1910).

[81] For example the four cardinal points of the compass, the four seasons, the four elements, the four temperaments, the four ground colours of the rainbow, the four years between two intercalary days, the sequence of the four empires according to St. Hieronymus, underlying the doctrine of translatio imperii. For further discussion, see Desmond Varley, *Seven, The Number of Creation* (1976), pp. 43 sqq.

[82] As to the importance for the Greeks of the number seven, cf., for example, Wilhelm H. Roscher, *Die Hebdomadenlehren der griechischen Philosophen und Ärzte* (1906); *RE*, vol. XIV, col. 2579; Joachim Ritter, *Historisches Wörterbuch der Philosophie*, vol. III (1974), pp. 1022 sq.; for the Romans, cf., for example, Aulus Gellius, *Noctes Atticae*, Lib. III, 10; cf. also the comparative material in the annotations by Fritz Weiss, in: Aulus Gellius, *Die Attischen Nächte*, vol. I (1875), pp. 193 sqq.; Varley, op. cit., note 81, pp. 19 sqq. and passim. The book of Revelation contains no fewer than 54 instances of Sevens.

[83] Goudy, *Trichotomy*, p. 5, asks rhetorically: "What literary . . . author nowadays, in dividing his treatise into parts, books, etc., or dividing his subject-matter into heads and categories or genera and species, would attach any special importance to what the number of these might be?" However, one can point to Thomas Mann, whose entire work (esp. the *Magic Mountain*, *Joseph and his Brothers* and *Doctor Faustus*) is profoundly influenced by the symbolism of numbers. Cf., for example, the brilliant essay by the American Germanist, Oskar Seidlin, "Das hohe Spiel der Zahlen", in: O. Seidlin, *Klassische und moderne Klassiker* (1972), pp. 103 sqq.; for the English version, see (1971) 86 *Publications of the Modern Language Association* 924 sqq.

[84] A legatum per damnationem gave rise to a personal claim of the legatee against the heir. We are not concerned here with the other important type of legacy, the legatum per vindicationem. Here the legatee acquired ownership of the object left to him immediately at the death of the de cuius, and as a result he could avail himself of the rei vindicatio. A third type of legacy, the legatum sinendi modo, was of little practical relevance in classical times.

affairs, from the tutor's conduct of his ward's affairs, from the relationship between co-owners and from specific instructions contained in a will).[85] The four cases of quasi-delictual liability, on the other hand,[86] referred to the judge who, through breach of his official duties, caused damage to another person (iudex qui litem suam fecit; literally "the judge who makes the trial his"),[87] to anybody from whose dwelling something was thrown down or poured onto the street so as to injure another person (deiectum vel effusum),[88] or from whose building objects placed, or suspended, on an eave or projecting roof fell down and endangered the traffic (positum vel suspensum),[89] and to sea carriers, innkeepers and stablekeepers, whose employees had stolen or damaged the property of one of their customers (furtum vel damnum in navi aut caupone aut stabulo).[90] To find a common denominator for what has been lumped together here, is not at all easy. In the case of quasi-contractual obligations it was probably the fact that—just as in contractual situations—some kind of negotium had taken place. Thus, the actions granted to enforce quasi-contractual obligations were all very closely modelled on specific contractual actions.[91]

As far as the "obligationes quasi ex delicto" are concerned, Buckland has ventured the proposition[92] that they were based on the idea of vicarious liability. But that does not explain the iudex qui litem suam

---

[85] Inst. III, 27.

[86] Inst. IV, 5.

[87] That can mean either that the judge now has to step into the role of the defendant and, in that sense, brings a suit on himself, or that the judge has become (emotionally) so entangled in the case that he lacks the necessary impartiality (he treats the case as if it were his own). On this topic, see Kelly, *Roman Litigation*, pp. 102 sqq.; further David Pugsley, "Litem suam facere", (1969) 4 *The Irish Jurist* 351 sqq. (with parallels in English law); D.N. MacCormick, "Iudex Qui Litem Suam Fecit", 1977 *Acta Juridica* 149 sqq.; Geoffrey MacCormack, "The Liability of the Judge in the Republic and Principate", in: *ANRW*, vol. II, 14 (1982), pp. 5, 9 sq., 16 sqq.; Alvaro D'Ors, "'Litem suam facere'", (1982) 48 *SDHI* 368 sqq.; P.B.H. Birks, "A New Argument for a Narrow View of litem suam facere", (1984) 52 *TR* 373 sqq.

[88] Cf. D. 9, 3; Inst. IV, 5, 1; Gai. D. 44, 7, 5, 5; further, for example, Wittmann, *Körperverletzung*, pp. 62 sqq.; Giannetto Longo, "I quasi-delicta—actio de effusis et deiectis—actio de positis ac suspensis" in: *Studi in onore di Cesare Sanfilippo*, vol. IV (1983), pp. 428 sqq.; Enrique Lozano y Corbi, "Popularidad y regimen de legitimacion en la 'actio de effusis et deiectis'", in: *Studi in onore di Arnaldo Biscardi*, vol. V (1984), pp. 311 sqq.

[89] Cf., for example, Alan Watson, "Liability in the Actio de Positis ac Suspensis", in: *Mélanges Philippe Meylan*, vol. I (1963), pp. 379 sqq.; William M. Gordon, "The Actio de Posito Reconsidered", in: *Studies Thomas* (1983), pp. 45 sqq.; Longo, *Studi Sanfilippo*, vol. IV, pp. 428 sqq.

[90] Cf., for example, Wolodkiewicz, (1970) 24 *Rivista italiana per le scienze giuridiche* 210 sqq.

[91] The connection between negotiorum gestio and tutela, on the one hand, and mandatum (mandate) on the other, is obvious. In the case of indebitum solutum, the condictio (i.e. the action applicable for the recovery of a loan-mutuum) was granted. On the historical relationship between the claims for unjustified enrichment (the law of condictiones) and the old procedural remedy of condictio, see infra, pp. 835 sqq. Communio resembled societas (partnership), and in the case of legatum per damnationem the actio ex testamento was granted, which was closely related to the actio ex stipulatu.

[92] Buckland/McNair, pp. 395 sqq.

fecit. A striking feature of at least the three last-mentioned quasi-delicts is, however, that liability was imposed regardless of fault: where the contents of a chamber-pot were emptied on the head of whoever just happened to pass by,[93] where a flower-box embellishing the eaves was blown down onto the street, or where the trusting traveller was stripped of his belongings by the chambermaid, the person in charge of the place where the disaster had occurred was liable irrespective of whether he had been negligent or not.[94] True: Justinian, who generally liked to stress and strengthen subjective elements in the law and who, more particularly, carved out "culpa" as the cornerstone for delictual liability, tried to rationalize the cases of quasi-delict on this basis and therefore implanted culpa elements in this (as in other) area(s): nautae, stabularii and caupones were held liable, because they were presumed to have been negligent in the choice and supervision of their employees (culpa in eligendo),[95] and in the case of deiectum vel effusum, too, negligence on the part of the person in charge was presumed ("culpa enim penes eum est").[96] Classical lawyers, on the other hand, generally emphasizing more objective criteria of liability, did not have any difficulty in taking these situations for what they were: namely, cases of strict liability. Inhabitatores, stabularii, etc. were held to be responsible because they were in charge of the place where or from where the injurious act occurred. In other words, they were in control of a potential source of danger to other people's lives, health and property. If this aspect was originally the connecting link between three out of the four quasi-delicts, it may possibly also have applied to the fourth one: for the liability of the judge in classical law was not

---

[93] As there was no refuse collection in Rome, it seems that one usually got rid of one's garbage by throwing it out of the window. Furthermore, many people apparently found it amusing to throw things down on passers-by. As the Roman streets were narrow and the houses fairly tall (five to six storeys were by no means uncommon), one can understand Juvenal's caustic warning that it would be frivolous to walk to a supper invitation without having made one's last will first. On all this cf. Juvenal, *Satura* III, 268 sqq.; Carcopino, pp. 57 sqq.; cf. also the eloquent and comprehensive note by Johannes van der Linden, printed in translation by Percival Gane, *The Selective Voet*, vol. II (1955), pp. 596 sqq.

[94] Whether there was strict liability in the case of positum aut suspensum, is, however, questionable. It depends on the interpretation of Ulp. D. 9, 3, 5, 10. Perhaps this case was classified as a quasi-delict because it was so closely related to the actio de deiectis vel effusis and because there did not have to be an injury for liability to arise. The habitator was therefore liable for the danger he had created. Strict liability is also disputed as far as the iudex qui litem suam fecit is concerned: see Peter Birks, "The Problem of Quasi-Delict", (1969) 22 *Current Legal Problems* 172 sqq.; idem, (1984) 52 *TR* 373 sqq. Birks himself argues that the key to quasi-delict "may lie in [the] possibility of liability without misfeasance from which flows the need for the assumption of a special position" ((1969) 22 *Current Legal Problems* 174). One of the decisive questions is how to interpret texts such as Gai. IV, 52, where no reference to the judge's state of mind is made. Did a presumption of dolus operate in these cases? Contra, inter alios, A.M. Honoré, *Gaius* (1962), p. 102.

[95] Cf. Inst. IV, 5, 3. As to the concept of culpa in eligendo, cf. Geoffrey MacCormack, "Culpa in eligendo", (1971) 18 *RIDA* 525 sqq. (here specifically pp. 547 sqq.).

[96] Ulp. D. 9, 3, 1, 4; for the liability of the iudex ("licet per imprudentiam"), Gai. D. 44, 7, 5, 4.

dependent either on whether he had negligently (or possibly even intentionally) given the wrong judgment. Thus, one can argue that here, as well, the person held liable was the one who was in control of, or supposed to be in control of, the vagaries and risks connected with a lawsuit.[97]

4. The reception of Justinian's scheme

(a) General observations

Justinian's fourfold scheme was received in Europe together with the substantive Roman law; it has provided, historically, the most influential model for structuring the law of obligations.[98] Throughout the centuries systematic treatises have been based on it: from Donellus' *Commentarii de Jure Civili* and Georg Adam Struve's *Jurisprudentia Romano-Germanica Forensis* to Thibaut's *System des Pandektenrechts*, to mention three important works from the times of humanism, usus modernus pandectarum and pandectism.[99] It has also been given legislative endorsement, for instance in the French Civil Code, which states in art. 1370 IV, at the outset of its fourth title ("*Des engagements qui se forment sans convention*") and after having dealt with contractual obligations in the previous title, "*les engagements qui naissent d'un fait personnel à celui qui se trouve obligé, résultent ou des quasi-contrats, ou des délits ou quasi-délits*". In the course of time, however, and especially since Roman law was no longer unquestioningly accepted as ratio scripta, criticism was levelled against this system. The most radical attempt to move away from it was undertaken by the natural lawyers. They attempted to develop a functional scheme, classifying the obligations according to content and effect[100] rather than emphasizing the various ways in which obligations originate. This way of looking at the law of obligations has become widely accepted as far as

[97] Cf. Hochstein, *Obligationes*, pp. 26 sqq.; Peter Stein, "The Nature of Quasi-Delictual Obligations in Roman Law", (1958) 5 *RIDA* 563 sqq. Cf. also Thomas, *TRL*, p. 377 ("a kind of insurance for the victim of harm, dictated by public policy"); D'Ors, (1982) 48 *SDHI* 368 sqq. (objective liability); MacCormick, 1977 *Acta Juridica* 149 sqq. But see Witold Wolodkiewicz, "Sulla cosidetta responsabilità dei 'quasi delitti' nel diritto romano ed il suo influsso sulla responsibilità civile moderna", in: *La formazione storica*, vol. III, pp. 1277 sqq. (no common denominator for the quasi-delicts); Longo, *Studi Sanfilippo*, vol. IV, pp. 401 sqq.

[98] For details, see Hans Hermann Seiler, *Die Systematik der einzelnen Schuldverhältnisse in der neueren Privatrechtsgeschichte* (Diss. Münster, 1957), pp. 15 sqq.; as far as 19th-century codifications are concerned, cf. also Carlo Augusto Cannata, "Sulla classificazione delle fonti delle obbligazioni dal 1804 ai nostri giorni", in: *La formazione storica*, vol. III, pp. 1177 sqq.

[99] Cf. also Windscheid/Kipp, § 362, n. 1, albeit in very cautious terms: ". . . *in letzter Linie Sache des Taktes*" (in the last resort a matter of tact).

[100] See Pufendorf, *De jure naturae et gentium*, esp. Lib. V, but also already Hugo Grotius, *De jure belli ac pacis*, esp. Lib. II, Cap. XII, 1 sq. Cf. also the system of the *Preussisches Allgemeines Landrecht* (Prussian General Land Law), which does not have a title on obligations or even on contracts, but deals with the individual obligations in the context and from the point of view of their function for acquisition, loss and transfer of ownership.

arrangement and classification of the specific contracts is concerned,[101] but has otherwise remained a short-lived episode. Most expositors contented themselves with rather adapting and adjusting the Justinianic system. Some of them advocated a return to Gaius' threefold scheme.[102] Others even moved back to the original subdivision between contract and delict.[103] Some added a fifth (or a third) category ("obligationes ex lege")[104] in order to accommodate, for instance, the actio ad exhibendum (available to force the defendant to produce in court a thing which he had in his possession or detention), which had always fallen between the four stools of Justinian's scheme. Yet others used this category of obligationes ex lege[105] to throw together whatever could not be accommodated in either the contractual or delictual niche.[106]

(b) The distinction between delict and quasi-delict

Generally speaking, it appears that the two quasi-categories were regarded as the major source of uneasiness and dissatisfaction. As far as the distinction between delict and quasi-delict is concerned, Justinian himself had already largely removed its raison d'être by tampering with the quasi-delicts under the auspices of a generalized fault requirement. If liability for delict, as well as for quasi-delict, is based on fault, one can, of course, try to distinguish between different types of fault. Thus we find the theory that delict is characterized by the fault of the tortfeasor himself, quasi-delict by culpa imputativa.[107] Others confined liability for delict to the infliction of intentional harm and regarded negligence, culpa propria, as the distinctive characteristic of quasi-delicts (". . .delictum est vel verum, vel quasi delictum. Illud ex dolo, hoc ex culpa committitur").[108] But these propositions are unsatisfac-

---

[101] Cf., for example, Mühlenbruch, *Doctrina Pandectarum*, Lib. III, II (Singulae obligationum species); Windscheid/Kipp, IV. Buch, Zweites Kapitel.

[102] E.g. Antonius Merenda, *Controversiarum iuris libri* XXIV, Tom. III (Bruxellis, 1746), nn. 2, 11 sqq. ("distingui non possunt obligationes quasi ex contractu orientes ab iis, quae nascuntur quasi ex maleficio").

[103] Cf. Brinz, *Pandekten*, § 94 (*Geschäftsforderungen und Strafforderungen*); further Seiler, op. cit., note 98, pp. 94 sqq.

[104] Windscheid/Kipp, IV. Buch, Zweites Kapitel III; Vangerow, *Pandekten*, 5. Buch, 4.–6. Kapitel; cf. also art. 1370 II c.c.

[105] Dating back to Mod. D. 44, 7, 52 pr., 5. On this text and on the concept of obligationes ex lege generally, see Theo Mayer-Maly, "Das Gesetz als Entstehungsgrund von Obligationen", (1965) 12 *RIDA* 437 sqq.; idem, (1967) 2 *The Irish Jurist* 380.

[106] Mayer-Maly, (1965) 12 *RIDA* 449; cf. also art. 1173 codice civile.

[107] Struve, *Syntagma*, Exerc. VIII, Lib. IV, Tit. IX, CXIII ("[Q]uasi delict[um] . . . consistit in aliqua culpa, ut ita loquar, imputativa, hoc est quae alicui ex alieno facto eorum, quos quis adhibet, imputatur."); Samuel Stryk, *Tractatus de actionibus forensibus* (Wittembergae, 1708), Sectio I, X, § LV.

[108] Johann Gottlieb Heineccius, *Recitationes in elementa iuris civilis secundum ordinem Institutionum* (Vratislawiae, 1773), Lib. IV, Tit. V, § MXXXII. Further e.g. Pothier, *Traité des obligations*, n. 116: "*On appelle délit le fait par lequel une personne, par dol ou malignité, cause du dommage ou quelque tort une autre. Le quasi-délit est le fait par lequel une personne, sans malignité, mais par une imprudence qui n'est pas excusable, cause quelque tort une autre.*"

tory. The former cannot accommodate the iudex qui litem suam fecit, the latter, especially if it is carried through even in cases of liability under the lex Aquilia, leads to a restructuring that looks, at first glance, as dramatic as it is irrelevant in its practical effect; for wherever negligent and intentional causation of harm are put on an equal footing—as, typically, in artt. 1382, 1383 of the code civil—a classification of delicts based on the culpa/dolus dichotomy does not serve a structurally useful purpose. It is not surprising, therefore, that the distinction between *délit* and *quasi-délit* is without practical relevance in French law,[109] and that, generally, in the course of the 19th century, both categories were merged into one.[110] The unfortunate consequence of this age-old misinterpretation of the true basis of the law of quasi-delict, and of its final amalgamation with the law of delict, was the fact that strict liability did not fit into the system any longer. Both the traditional instances of no-fault liability and the ones that gradually emerged during the age of industrialization were therefore regarded as corpus alienum—as some sort of doctrinal waif without a legitimate place in the system of private law.[111]

(c) The distinction between contract and quasi-contract

The quasi-contracts did not have a much smoother passage through the history of private law. Neither the haphazard composition of this category nor the perceived lack of a positive common criterion distinguishing it from contract, delict and quasi-delict could appeal to systematically minded jurists. Attempts were therefore made, particularly during the 19th century, to tag the various quasi-contracts to those (proper) contracts with which they appeared to be most closely related, and in this way to amalgamate the two categories.[112] This approach, however, was bound to lead to insurmountable difficulties in the case of unjustified enrichment; for whilst the contract of loan for consumption and the claims for unjustified enrichment grew historically from the same root, the two institutions no longer had much in common once the condictio as the procedural remedy applicable to

---

[109] The cases of strict liability laid down in artt. 1384–1386 do not fall under "*quasi-délit*" but are generally referred to by the term "*responsabilité*". On the origin of these provisions, see, most recently, Watson, *Failures*, pp. 1 sqq.

[110] On the history of quasi-delicts generally, see Hochstein, *Obligationes*, pp. 34 sqq.; cf. also Wolodkiewicz, in: *La formazione storica*, vol. III, pp. 1288 sqq.

[111] Cf. in this context the observation already made by Lorenz von Stein, *Zur Eisenbahnrechts-Bildung* (1872), p. 15: "*Deutschland ist geradezu unerschöpflich in Abhandlungen über Ulpian und Papinian, aber vom Eisenbahnrecht weiss es so gut als nichts*" (Germany is just about inexhaustible in treatises on Ulpian and Papinian, but of railway law it knows little more than nothing). On the treatment of non-contractual liability for damages without fault by the natural lawyers and in the codifications influenced by them, see Hans-Peter Benöhr, "Ausservertragliche Schadensersatzpflicht ohne Verschulden? Die Argumente der Naturrechtslehren und -kodifikationen", (1976) 93 *ZSS* 208 sqq.

[112] Cf., for example, Arndts, *Pandekten*, § 242 and passim; Puchta, *Pandekten*, 6. Buch, 2. Kapitel; Vangerow, *Pandekten*, 5. Buch, 4. Kapitel.

both of them had been abandoned.[113] As a result, the Swiss codification[114] confined the third category (besides contract and delict) to unjustified enrichment as the "most relevant"[115] quasi-contract. However, it is hardly justifiable to attach so much more weight and significance to the law of unjustified enrichment than to negotiorum gestio.[116]

5. The attitude adopted by the BGB

At the time of codification in Germany, the category of quasi-contracts had become more or less decomposed and was as discredited as the quasi-delicts. The fathers of the BGB in the end abandoned any attempt to systematize the law of obligations and simply placed 25 different types of obligations side by side: ranging from sale and exchange (title 1) to production of things (the old actio ad exhibendum, title 23), unjustified enrichment (title 24) and delict (title 25).[117] Such an attitude (one can only call it a capitulation) does not sufficiently appreciate the fact that the endeavours to find a satisfactory divisio obligationum are not an idle glass-bead game, but serve to find a rational justification and basis for imposing and recognizing obligations.[118] Like any system, it should be designed to demonstrate "veritat[es] inter se connexa[e]".[119] Interestingly, though, a revival of the dogmatic categories of quasi-contract and quasi-delict has recently been suggested.[120] This specific suggestion forms part of a strong move to overcome, once again, the crude bipartite division into contract/quasi-contract and delict/quasi-delict to which Justinian's scheme was reduced in the

[113] But see, for example, Vangerow, *Pandekten*, §§ 623 sqq.; Puchta, *Pandekten*, §§ 304 sqq., who still puts loan and unjustified enrichment on a par.

[114] *Schweizerisches Obligationenrecht* (1911), artt. 62 sqq.

[115] Andreas von Tuhr, *Allgemeiner Teil des schweizerischen Obligationenrechts, 1. Halbband* (1924), p. 39.

[116] The Italian codice civile (1942) subdivides the law of obligations into specific contracts, unilateral promises, negotiable instruments, negotiorum gestio, unjustified enrichment and delicts. South African law, incidentally, treats quasi-contracts without much kindness. They are dealt with neither in textbooks on contract nor in those on delict. Even in a textbook on the law of obligations (Lee and Honoré (2nd ed, 1978, by Newman and McQuoid-Mason)), the quasi-contracts are not mentioned. In other works (such as Hosten/Edwards/Nathan/Bosman, *Introduction to South African Law and Legal Theory* (1980), pp. 506 sqq.), enrichment appears as a brief appendix to the law of delict, negotiorum gestio, in turn, as an appendix to enrichment. There is only one major monograph each on enrichment and negotiorum gestio. On "quasi-contract" in the French Civil Code, cf., for example, Carlo Augusto Cannata, "Das faktische Vertragsverhältnis oder die ewige Wiederkunft des Gleichen", (1987) 53 *SDHI* 310 sqq.

[117] On the history of the BGB in this respect, see Seiler, op. cit., note 98, pp. 72 sqq.

[118] Theo Mayer-Maly, "Vertrag und Einigung", in: *Festschrift für H.C. Nipperdey*, vol. I (1965), p. 522. Cf. also Seiler, op. cit., note 98, pp. 112 sqq.; Helmut Coing, "Bemerkungen zum überkommenen Zivilrechtssystem", in: *Vom deutschen zum europäischen Recht, Festschrift für Hans Dölle*, vol. I (1963), p. 25.

[119] Christian Wolff, *Institutiones juris naturae et gentium*, § 62.

[120] Hochstein, *Obligationes*, pp. 11 sqq., 150 sq.; Heinz Hübner, "Zurechnung statt Fiktion einer Willenserklärung", in: *Festschrift für H.C. Nipperdey*, vol. I (1965), pp. 397 sqq.; Mayer-Maly, (1965) 12 *RIDA* 450 sq.

course of the 19th century.[121] For, on the one hand, strict liability can no longer be regarded as an anomaly only to be dealt with in special, somewhat haphazard, statutes; it has to be accepted as an integral part of a modern law of loss allocation, and that is, as a second track of liability besides delict.[122] On the other hand, the need for a quasi-contractual liability based on justifiable reliance has become increasingly apparent: a new and independent line of liability that can be regarded neither as contractual (because it presupposes no valid contract but merely a special relationship based on business contact) nor as delictual (because of the increased intensity of duties owed to the other party, going beyond what is owed to everybody in the course of daily life).[123]

6. "De facto" contracts and implied promises

Establishing either an unstructured numerus clausus of obligations or sticking to an exclusive contract/delict dichotomy entails a specific danger: the temptation to pervert the law of contract in order to accommodate cases that do not happily fit into the established categories. Thus, for instance, German courts and writers have construed "de facto" contracts where there is no legally relevant contractual agreement between the parties: in cases where, for instance, a person uses a parking bay whilst not being prepared (as he specifically declares) to pay the appropriate parking fee.[124] This danger is much more obvious, however, if one looks at the history, in English law, of what we would call enrichment liability. "[B]roadly speaking", as Viscount Haldane LC put it in his speech in *Sinclair v. Brougham*,[125] "so far as proceedings in personam are concerned, the common law of England really recognizes (unlike Roman law) only actions of two classes, those founded on contract and those founded on tort." Thus, in the old common law, governed by specific forms of actions, the remedy of indebitatus assumpsit had to be used—on the basis of an implied promise—where it was felt that an obligation should be imposed.

---

[121] Seiler, op. cit., note 98, pp. 95 sq. and passim.

[122] Josef Esser, "Die Zweispurigkeit unseres Haftpflichtrechts", 1953 *Juristenzeitung* 129 sqq.; Hein Kötz, "Gefährdungshaftung", in: *Gutachten und Vorschläge zur Überarbeitung des Schuldrechts*, vol. II (1981), pp. 1779 sqq.; in English, for example, Lawson/Markesinis, pp. 142 sqq., and Zweigert/Kötz/Weir, pp. 309 sqq. with many references.

[123] Cf. esp. Claus-Wilhelm Canaris, "Schutzgesetze—Verkehrspflichten—Schutzpflichten", in: *II. Festschrift für Karl Larenz* (1983), pp. 27 sqq. (pp. 85 sqq.: "*Die Haftung für 'Schutzpflichtverletzungen' als 'dritte Spur' zwischen Delikts- und Vertragshaftung*") with many other references.

[124] Cf. BGHZ 21, 319 sqq.; Günter Haupt, *Über faktische Vertragsverhältnisse* (1941); Karl Larenz, *Allgemeiner Teil des Bürgerlichen Rechts* (6th ed., 1983), pp. 525 sqq., criticized, in the present context, by Mayer-Maly, *Festschrift Nipperdey*, vol. I, pp. 514 sqq.; idem, (1967) 2 *The Irish Jurist* 376 sqq.; cf. also Eugen Dietrich Graue, "Vertragsschluss durch Konsens?" in: *Rechtsgeltung und Konsens* (1976), pp. 105 sqq., 112 sqq. For a rather unconventional historical evaluation of this trend, cf. Cannata, (1987) 53 *SDHI* 297 sqq.

[125] [1914] AC 398 (HL) at 415.

> "The basic reason for the development of implied assumpsit was the desire to use a convenient form of action to remedy certain duties or obligations recognized either directly by law or by common sense or justice. For example, the law said that debts should be paid, but if the action of assumpsit was to be used to ensure that this was done there had to be a promise; if in fact there had been no promise in reality then the solution (if one wanted to permit assumpsit) was to engage in some deeming."[126]

Liability was imposed where it was felt that payment ought to be made: not only where the implication of a promise was a genuine inference from the acts or words of the parties, but also where the implication was purely fictional.[127] This somewhat artificial judicial construction was bound to lead to conceptual confusion; the problem of how and under which circumstances unjust benefits have to be skimmed off and (re-)transferred became contaminated by contractual doctrine.[128] In the course of the second half of the 18th century and during the 19th, the civilian notion of quasi-contract was imported into English jurisprudence,[129] and the distinction between contract and quasi-contract gradually replaced the old English categories of express and

[126] Simpson, *History*, pp. 489 sq.; cf. also Goff and Jones, *Restitution*, pp. 5 sqq.

[127] Continental writers, too, have sometimes argued that the obligations quasi ex contractu are based on a consensus fictivus or praesumptus: see, for example, Van Leeuwen, *Censura Forensis*, Pars I, Lib. IV, Cap. XXV; Voet, *Commentarius ad Pandectas*, Lib. XLIV, Tit. VII, v. ("Quasi contractus sunt praesumtae conventiones, ex quibus mediante facto valida nascitur obligatio"). But see the critical analyses by Vinnius, *Institutiones*, Lib. III, Tit. XXVIII pr., n. 3 sq. and Pothier, *Traité des obligations*, nn. 113, 117; they derive the quasi-contracts from aequitas (utilitas). On Vinnius' view and the response it drew (on the Continent as well as in England), see Peter Birks, "English and Roman Learning in *Moses v. Macferlan*", (1984) 37 *Current Legal Problems* 11 sqq. Cf. further Cannata, (1987) 53 *SDHI* 306 sqq. For a more detailed analysis of civilian opinion on the dogmatic foundation of quasi-contractual liability, see now Peter Birks/Grant McLeod, "The Implied Contract Theory of Quasi-Contract: Civilian Opinion Current in the Century Before Blackstone", (1986) 6 *Oxford Journal of Legal Studies* 46 sqq., 55 sqq.

[128] Cf. Birks, (1969) 22 *Current Legal Problems* 165. A very different perspective on these developments is adopted by Atiyah, *Rise and Fall*, pp. 181 sqq., 480 sqq. According to him, the close affinity between contract and quasi-contract is confusing only to the modern lawyer, and on the basis of the will theory of contract. Eighteenth-century lawyers, on the other hand, were concerned primarily about the recompense of benefits; whether a man promised to make a recompense or failed to promise when he plainly ought to make a recompense was a secondary matter.

[129] Cf., for example, John Austin, *Lectures on Jurisprudence* (5th ed., 1911), pp. 911 sqq., 984 sq.; Maine, pp. 201 sq.; Birks, (1984) 37 *Current Legal Problems* 9 sqq. According to Birks, it was Lord Mansfield (*Moses v. Macferlan* (1760) 2 Burr 1005) who introduced the notion of quasi-contract into the English common law. "It is as certain as anything can be", writes Birks, "that no Roman lawyer ever intended quasi ex contractu to suggest the shadow of a contract . . . [But] it is likely that [Lord Mansfield] . . . under[stood] it as 'sort-of-contract' because that interpretation was already current among contemporary civilians" (p. 10). This is the "dark side" of the famous decision in *Moses v. Macferlan* (on its "bright side", see infra p. 894). Whatever Lord Mansfield's reasons for appealing to Roman law in order to explain the non-contractual range of indebitus assumpsit (on which cf. infra pp. 892 sq.) may have been, it was the kind of appeal which "beckons to disaster" (p. 5). With *Moses v. Macferlan* contractual doctrine started to overshadow and to deform the English law of restitution. Via Blackstone's *Commentaries on the Law of England* (Book III, Chapter 9) the "anti-rational" (p. 23) fiction became firmly ingrained in the English common law. Cf. further Birks/ McLeod, (1986) 6 *Oxford Journal of Legal Studies* 46 sqq., 77 sqq.

implied contracts.[130] To quote the words of Lord Wright in the famous *Fibrosa* case:[131] "The obligation is a creation of the law, just as much as an obligation in tort. The obligation belongs to a third class, distinct from either contract or tort, though it resembles contract rather than tort." The concept of implied contract, "[t]hese fantastic resemblances of contracts invented in order to meet requirements of the law as to forms of action which have now disappeared",[132] has been abandoned as a misleading anachronism, and "restitution" is rapidly establishing itself as an independent, "quasi-contractual" branch of the law of obligations.[133]

III. THE PLACE OF OBLIGATIONS WITHIN THE SYSTEM OF PRIVATE LAW

Practical lawyers are not usually overconcerned with bringing the law into a neat systematical order so that it appears as a logically consistent whole of legal rules and institutions. For the writer of a textbook, especially if it is an elementary one, this is, however, essential; after all, he has to prevent his student readers from getting lost in a totally indigestible mass of casuistry. Thus, significantly, it was Gaius who started subdividing the law of obligations in a rational manner. Other classical jurists, if they made any attempt at all,[134] merely enumerated various ways in which obligations could arise. A similar attitude was displayed by them towards the whole of Roman private law: it was also not perceived to constitute an organized system.[135] Abstract conceptualization was not taken beyond the various legal institutions which made up Roman private law, and in Quintus Mucius' and Sabinus' compilations—the latter was based on the former and provided, in turn, the cornerstone for the restatement of the interpretation of civil law in the great commentaries by Paulus and Ulpianus and Pomponius—these institutions were arranged in a "convenient leisurely fashion",[136] dictated by associative thinking rather than methodical reflection. Quintus Mucius' *Ius Civile* has been said to have laid "the foundation not merely of Roman but European

[130] For a comparison between quasi-contract in Roman and English law, see Buckland/McNair, pp. 329 sqq.

[131] *Fibrosa Spolka Akcyjna v. Fairbairn Lawson Combe Barbour Ltd.* [1943] AC 32 (HL) at 62.

[132] Per Lord Atkin, *United Australia Ltd. v. Barclay's Bank Ltd.* [1941] AC 1 (HL) at 29.

[133] Cf., for example, A.S. Burrows, "Contract, Tort and Restitution. A Satisfactory Division Or Not?", (1983) 99 *LQR* 217 sqq.; for further discussion, see infra pp. 893 sqq.

[134] Cf. Mod. D. 44, 7, 52 pr.: "Obligamur aut re aut verbis aut simul utroque aut consensu aut lege aut iure honorario aut necessitate aut ex peccato." On obligari lege, cf. Theo Mayer-Maly, (1965) 12 *RIDA* 437 sqq.; on obligari necessitate, cf. Theo Mayer-Maly, (1966) 83 *ZSS* 47 sqq.

[135] Just as in modern English law, where private law is not seen as a system either.

[136] Cf. Schulz, *Principles*, p. 57; on the approach of the Roman lawyers towards abstraction (and systematization) generally, cf. already pp. 40 sqq. and idem, *RLS*, p. 257.

jurisprudence"[137] and his main achievement, in the words of Pomponius, was: "ius civile primus constituit generatim in libros decem et octo redigendo."[138] But, however progressive his scheme was by comparative standards, it displays no interest in a logical structuring of the legal material.[139]

1. Gaius: personae, res, actiones

Again, the first attempt in that direction came from Gaius, the outsider. Looking at the civil law as a whole and trying to identify the constituent elements of which it was formed, he superimposed upon the traditional contents of the civil law (that is, on the material dealt with by Mucius and Sabinus, which in turn was mainly that covered by the XII Tables) a subdivision into persons and things; and as he added a book dealing with actions, he arrived at a tripartite subdivision: "Omne autem ius quo utimur vel ad personas pertinet vel ad res vel ad actiones."[140] This is the famous institutional system, the fons et origo of all attempts in later times to structure the subject matter of private law. We cannot here examine critically all its details and implications: ius personarum, for instance, was neither—as one might think—the law of rights and duties of persons in specific, exceptional positions (as, for example, children or slaves) nor family law, but dealt substantially with questions of status.[141] In the present context we have to confine our attention to one specific, rather interesting feature: unlike in modern legal systems, the law of obligations does not appear as a distinct entity. This is due to the fact that "res", the law of things, was not only concerned with real rights but was conceived of as the law of the patrimony in a broad sense.[142] Thus, the second part of Gaius' *Institutes* deals with the law of things in a narrower sense, with succession and with obligations.[143]

This arrangement, leading to a second tripartite subdivision, is somewhat strange in that Gaius seems to have mixed two different

---

[137] Schulz, *RLS*, p. 94. Cf. also, for example, Frier, *Roman Jurists*, p. 171: "Quintus Mucius is the father of Roman legal science and of the Western legal tradition. He is the inventor of the legal profession"; generally on Quintus Mucius, see Richard A. Bauman, *Lawyers in Roman Republican Politics* (1983), pp. 340 sqq.; Wieacker, *RR*, pp. 549 sqq., 595 sqq. 630 sq.

[138] D. 1, 2, 2, 41. For details, see Alan Watson, *Law Making in the Later Roman Republic* (1974), pp. 143 sqq., 179 sqq.

[139] Cf. Peter Stein, "The Development of the Institutional System", in: *Studies Thomas*, pp. 151 sqq.; cf. further Frier, *Roman Jurists*, pp. 155 sqq.; Wieacker, *RR*, pp. 597 sqq.

[140] Gai. I, 8; cf. especially Stein, *Studies Thomas*, pp. 154 sqq.; Jolowicz, *Roman Foundations*, pp. 61 sqq.; Buckland/Stein, pp. 56 sqq. Thus, Gaius was moving from "divisio" (i.e. dividing the material merely into categories) to "partitio" (breaking it down into its constituent elements). Cf. generally Dieter Nörr, *Divisio und Partitio* (1972).

[141] Cf., for example, De Zulueta, *Gaius* II, pp. 23 sq.; Jolowicz, *Roman Foundations*, pp. 63 sqq.

[142] Cf. Hans Kreller, "Res als Zentralbegriff des Institutionensystems", (1948) 66 *ZSS* 572 sqq.

[143] "A decidedly heterogeneous assemblage": Schulz, *RLS*, p. 160.

criteria as the basis for his scheme. On the one hand, he adopts a distinction between corporeal and incorporeal things, incorporeal being "[res] quae tangi non possunt, qualia sunt ea quae iure consistunt, sicut hereditas, . . . obligationes quoquo modo contractae".[144] But he does not really carry it through, for in the first subdivision—which, incidentally, does not bear a Latin name—Gaius not only deals with corporeal objects but also with usufructs and praedial servitudes. It is, therefore, not only in the second and third subdivision that he discusses incorporeal objects. On the other hand, Gaius distinguishes between acquisition of single objects and acquisition per universitatem; indeed, he introduces the discussion of his second subdivision with the words: "Hactenus tantisper admonuisse sufficit quemadmodum singulae res nobis adquirantur. . . . videamus itaque nunc quibus modis per universitatum res nobis adquirantur."[145] This criterion, however, is not without problems either; for whilst the second subsection does, in fact, deal with certain forms of universal succession other than by way of inheritance,[146] an exposition of the law of succession is quite clearly its main concern—so much so, that a discussion of the law of legacies is included even though, as Gaius himself acknowledges, "quo et ipso singulas res adquirimus".[147] Moreover, the arrangement of subject matter according to whether individual objects are acquired or whether universal succession takes place cannot account for the fact that the law of obligations is introduced into the scheme as a third category, i.e. after universal succession—which, after all, affects the rights and duties created by an obligation in the same way as real rights—has already been dealt with. Gaius himself, incidentally, does not even attempt to demonstrate the logic of his system; he simply presses on with the words: "Nunc transeamus ad obligationes."[148] (As Fritz Schulz has remarked with mild irony: "*il y a beaucoup de 'puis' dans cette histoire.*")[149]

2. Justinian's *Institutiones* and the relation between actions and obligations

All in all, despite the fact that the institutional system involved considerable conceptual progress (especially in distinguishing corporeal and incorporeal objects, classifying obligations as incorporeal objects and bringing together the various hitherto scattered contracts and delicts and linking them as sources of obligations),[150] it is no

---

144 Gai. II, 14. One would expect ownership, like any other right, to be a res incorporalis. By a strange sort of logical leap, however, dominium was treated as a res corporalis and thus identified with its object. On the res corporalis/incorporalis distinction in modern law, see Kreller, (1948) 66 *ZSS* 592 sqq.

145 Gai. II, 97.

146 Gai. III, 82 sqq.

147 Gai. II, 97.

148 Gai. III, 88.

149 *Principles*, p. 56.

150 Stein, *Studies Thomas*, p. 154.

exaggeration to say that the tripartite division into personae, res, actiones, "which has probably left its mark on every existing code and every general legal textbook,[151] has never been quite easy to understand".[152] That was already true of the compilers of the Corpus Juris Civilis. Whilst both Digest and Code, in their sections dealing with private law, generally follow the sequence of the praetorian Edict—which in turn had been built up from a procedural point of view and did not pretend to structure the substantive law according to rational principles—in Justinian's introductory textbook the scheme developed by Gaius was taken over. Like Gaius, the authors of the *Institutes* dealt with personae, res, actiones in four books—and thus arrived not only at a seemingly more balanced structure but also at a numerically desirable combination of three in four; unlike Gaius, however, they no longer saw the basic trichotomy as a simple framework within which the established legal institutions could be conveniently discussed, but rather understood it as providing a structure for the who (persons), the what (objects) and the how (actions) in the law.[153]

Yet the third of these subdivisions had become somewhat messy. For neither did Justinian's compilers wish to indulge in legal history and give an account of the actions of classical law (or perhaps even, as Gaius had still done, of the ancient legis actiones); after all, the formulary system had by then been superseded by the procedure per libellum. Nor did they regard the *Institutes* as the appropriate place to discuss the law of procedure as such. In classical law, when the question whether a person had an action determined whether he had a right in substantive law, the institutional treatment of actions had been absolutely essential, for substantive law could hardly be understood without it. Now, a uniform procedure had been developed which served to enforce all kinds of claims and[154] its technical details no longer constrained and determined the development of substantive law. Thus, the Byzantine lawyers were moving towards the separation of substantive private law

---

[151] Not only, incidentally, on the Continent, but also in Scotland, namely on Lord Stair's influential *Institutions of the Law of Scotland* (1681) (see D.M. Walker, "The Structure and Arrangement of the Institutions", in: Stair, *Tercentenary Studies* (1981), pp. 100 sqq.); and even in England. Sir Matthew Hale, who for the first time attempted to tidy up and systematize the whole of the English common law (until then a casuistic jumble, as is well reflected in Sir Edward Coke's writings) based his scheme on Justinian's Institutes. Hale's *Analysis of the Laws of England* (1713), was then in turn adopted by Blackstone (himself essentially a civilian and an academic) in his famous *Commentaries on the Laws of England* (1765–69). See Simpson, (1981) 48 *University of Chicago LR* 632 sqq.; Peter Stein, *Roman Law and English Jurisprudence Yesterday and Today* (Inaugural Lecture, Cambridge, 1969), pp. 7 sqq.; F.H. Lawson, "Institutes", in: *Festschrift für Imre Zajtay* (1982), pp. 339 sqq. More specifically on the role of Sir Matthew Hale in the development of English jurisprudence, and on the influence of civilian methodology on his thinking, see Daniel R. Coquillette, *The Civilian Writers of Doctors' Commons* (London, 1988), pp. 264 sqq.

[152] Jolowicz, *Roman Foundations*, p. 62.

[153] Cf. Stein, *Studies Thomas*, pp. 159 sqq.

[154] For details, see especially Kaser, *RZ*, pp. 410 sqq.

and the law of civil procedure, which has, over the centuries, become a well-established feature of the civilian systems. Under the heading of "actiones" in Book Four they did not give an account of how legal proceedings had to be instituted or continued but only discussed different types of actions (such as actiones in rem, in personam, noxales, perpetuae and temporales), transmissibility of actions, and similar matters. Significantly, however, they included the discussion of parts of the law of obligations in this same Book Four, and they did this not just in order to accommodate an overspill from Book Three, and to arrive at a more balanced arrangement of the material over the four books, but because of the inner relationship which the East-Roman school had come to see between the two topics.[155] Thus, for them, it seemed to be at least as apposite to take obligations, in their traditional place, to constitute an introduction to actions, as it had been for Gaius to deal with the law of obligations at the end of his subsection on things. For, with the demise of the formulary system, the classical actiones had not completely disappeared. Justinian, always eager to hark back to the achievements of classical jurisprudence—or at least to pretend to do so—had retained the names of the old actions and even introduced some new ones. However, an action was now something entirely different to what it had been in classical law.[156] Since it was no longer tied to the procedural formula, "actio" had by now become a term of substantive law, indicating the right to demand some performance from another party. But that was basically what obligations were all about. The various kinds of obligations could, therefore, be regarded as causae actionum or, as one of the compilers of the Institutes, the Constantinopolean professor Theophilus put it, as the "mothers" of actions.[157] If there was a contract of sale, such a contract gave rise to certain duties. In the case of breach of one of these duties, the other party could sue; however, the action would not, strictly speaking, be an action for breach of contract,[158] but the action on sale, i.e. the actio empti or venditi. The essential content of an obligation was thus that it entitled the creditor to bring an action.[159]

---

[155] See the analysis by Stein, *Studies Thomas*, pp. 160 sqq. On obligatio and actio in classical law, cf. Emilio Betti, *La struttura dell' obbligazione romana* (2nd ed., 1955); Honsell/Mayer-Maly/Selb, pp. 218 sqq.

[156] On actions in post-classical law, Kaser, *RPr* II, pp. 65 sqq.; *RZ*, pp. 467 sqq.; cf. also Jolowicz, *Roman Foundations*, pp. 75 sqq.

[157] Theophilus, *Paraphrasis institutionum*, Lib. III, Tit. XIII: " μήτερες γὰρ τῶν ἀγωγῶν αἱ ἐνοχαί."

[158] This is the difference to English law; cf. Buckland, "Cause of action: English and Roman", (1943) 1 *Seminar* 4 sqq.

[159] If the action had been brought, that is, if litis contestatio had taken place, no other action could be brought under the same contract: the barring effect of litis contestatio.

3. From Justinian's scheme to the "*Pandektensystem*"

The opinion that actions and obligations really belong together was widely accepted in the Middle Ages;[160] further support for it was found in two titles of the Corpus Iuris, D. 44, 7 and C. 4, 10, which are both headed "De obligationibus et actionibus". Savigny still discussed it fairly extensively,[161] even though in the wake of humanistic jurisprudence its weakness had already been exposed:

> "Hoc autem falsam esse, vel ex uno hoc apparet, quod ista consideratione non magis obligatio ad actiones pertinet, quam dominium, quam ceterum in rem jura, quam ipsum jus personae: quippe quae et ipsa singula suas actiones habent, et pariunt."[162]

Of course, it was not only the appropriate position of the law of obligations which was a matter for dispute. In the 16th century both the lawyers of the humanist persuasion and, quite independently of them, the Spanish scholastics of the school of Salamanca had begun to move away in their expositions of the law from the so-called "legal order" (or rather, disorder), i.e. the sequence of topics as dictated by the Digest.[163] Until the 19th century, private lawyers were to battle continuously with the difficulties of systematization,[164] generally on the basis of Justinian's *Institutes* which had received increased attention.[165] If, for instance, one looks at the great codifications produced around the turn of the 18th century, one still finds a tripartite division in both the code civil and the ABGB. But whilst the ABGB followed the system of Gaius fairly closely, turning the third book into some sort of general part dealing with provisions common to the law of persons (Book One) and things (Book Two), the code civil devoted its third book to "*des differentes manières dont on acquiert la propriété*", (including, inter alia, succession, obligations and matrimo-

---

[160] Cf. Jolowicz, *Roman Foundations*, pp. 62 sqq.; for the usus modernus, Coing, p. 393; questions of the law of obligations were still occasionally treated as part of the law of actions.

[161] *System*, vol. I, pp. 401 sqq.

[162] Vinnius, *Institutiones*, Lib. III, Tit. XIV, 2.

[163] It was only in the 18th century that the French lawyer Pothier set himself the task of putting the texts of the Digest into a systematic order; see his *Pandecta Iustinianae in novum ordinem Digestae*.

[164] Cf. the accounts given by Jolowicz, *Roman Foundations*, pp. 61 sqq.; Peter Stein, "The Fate of the Institutional System", in: *Huldigingsbundel Paul van Warmelo* (1984), pp. 218 sqq.; Andreas B. Schwarz, "Zur Entstehung des modernen Pandektensystems", (1928) 42 *ZSS* 578 sqq. and Lars Björne, *Deutsche Rechtssysteme im 18. und 19. Jahrhundert* (1984), pp. 131 sqq. More specifically on the system developed by the Spanish scholastics (which was based on their restitution doctrine), see Günther Nufer, *Über die Restitutionslehre der spanischen Spätscholastiker und ihre Ausstrahlung auf die Folgezeit* (unpublished Dr. iur. thesis, Freiburg, 1969), pp. 16 sqq., 59 sqq.; Coing, pp. 190 sq.

[165] The system of Justinian's *Institutes* was also essential in the shaping of the national legal systems in the 17th and 18th centuries; on these "Institutes of National Law", see Klaus Luig, 1972 *Juridical Review* 193 sqq. Luig has coined the term "Institutionalists" on the model of the "Institutional writers" of Scottish law, i.e. the authors of systematic expositions of private law. As far as Institutional writing in Scotland, England and America is concerned, see Lawson, *Festschrift Zajtay*, pp. 339 sqq.

nial property law!).[166] Only with the acceptance of Georg Arnold Heise's celebrated five-membered scheme[167] did the discussion finally die down; it came to be known as "*Pandektensystem*" and forms the systematic basis of the BGB: general part, obligations, things, family law and succession. The differentiation between the law of obligations and things is, of course, of Roman origin, in so far as it represents the transformation into substantive law of the dichotomy between actiones in rem and in personam. It had been emphasized, for instance, by Grotius, who devoted the second book of his *Inleiding* to "Beheering" (defined as " 't recht van toe-behooren bestaende tusschen den mensch ende de zaecke zonder noodigh opzicht op een ander mensch"),[168] the third to "Inschuld" (" 't recht van toe-behooren dat den eenen mensch heeft op den anderen om van hem eenige zahe ofte daed to genieten").[169,170] Family law owes its recognition as a separate systematic entity to the natural lawyers who based their systems on the double nature of man—as an individual and, at the same time, as a part of larger groups in society. They thus dealt first with rules relating to the individual as such (including, especially, the law of property) before then proceeding in widening circles to matters such as family law (which they separated from the law of persons), the law of companies and other associations, societas, public law and public international law.[171] The position of the law of succession varied greatly. Quintus Mucius and Sabinus had placed it right at the beginning of their "ius civile". Then it was merged for a long time with the law of things as being one of the ways of acquiring ownership. If we today usually conclude our system with the law of succession, this tradition also dates back to the natural lawyers: with the separation of family law from the law of persons, the former began to exert a considerable attraction on succession, especially intestate succession.[172] Persons, or rather what was left of it, remained right at the beginning of the system—not, however, as a separate entity but as part and parcel of the general part.

---

[166] The composition of Book Three is based on the system adopted by Donellus, *Commentarii de Jure Civili*. As to the Prussian Code, which was based on a totally different system, cf. supra, note 100.

[167] Cf. his *Grundriss eines Systems des gemeinen Civilrechts zum Behuf von Pandekten-Vorlesungen* (1807).

[168] II, I, 58.

[169] II, I, 59. The first book is entitled "Van de beginselen der rechten ende van der menschen rechteliche gestaltenisse".

[170] Others had rather blurred this distinction. The extent to which the question of systematization had been controversial is demonstrated by the fact that, while traditionally obligations had been dealt with as part and parcel of "res", attempts were not wanting to accommodate, the other way round, the law of things within the framework of the law of obligations. Cf. e.g. Jean Domat, *Les loix civiles dans leur ordre naturel*, who subdivided the law into engagements and successions.

[171] This systematic approach goes back to Samuel Pufendorf, *De jure naturae et gentium* (1672). It found legislative realization in the Prussian Code.

[172] Cf., for example, the structure of Christian Wolff's *Institutiones iuris naturae et gentium* and of part II, 2 PrALR.

This "general part" is the truly distinctive feature of the "*Pandektensystem*"; it has left its mark not only on the BGB, but on the whole science of law in Germany (and all the systems influenced by German law). To abstract and bring forth a body of general rules has great systematic advantages as well as severe inherent dangers.[173] It has a rationalizing effect and contributes to the scientific precision of legal analysis. On the other hand, comprehension of the law is rendered extremely difficult for someone not specifically trained in legal thinking. Thus, for example, the possibility of placing a person under guardianship is envisaged in § 6, but the details of the procedure are set out only in §§ 1896 sqq. Many of the general rules about the law of obligations are not, in fact, to be found in Book Two, but in the general part: how contracts are to be concluded, the effect of error or metus on the validity of contracts, etc. And if, for instance, one is dealing with the sale of some hinnies or pigs, one has to consult—the order being determined by the rule of lex specialis derogat legi generali—the special rules about the purchase of livestock, the more general (but still fairly special) rules given for the contract of sale, the general part of the law of obligations and, finally, the general part of the BGB. The general part is a child of legal formalism; legal philosophies based on social ethics are bound to reject this abstract,[174] technical and unconcrete way of structuring law and legal analysis. As far as, in particular, the BGB is concerned, additional criticism can be levelled at the content of its general part: for it does not contain rules about the basic principles of legal behaviour, about the exercise of rights in society,[175] principles of statute interpretation, the sources of law or the powers of a judge; instead, a variety of topics are included, which one should hardly expect there, such as the law of associations, foundations, extinctive prescription or the giving of security.

Yet, all in all, and even though it is not based on uniform principles of classification—whilst the law of things and the law of obligations are subdivided because the one deals with absolute and the other with relative rights, family law and succession are characterized as systematic entities by nothing but the simple fact that all rules relating to two areas of social reality have been put together[176]—the "*Pandektensystem*" has become firmly engrained in German private law. As a result, the law of obligations is today allocated an undisputed compartment of its own.

[173] On the history, content and value of the general part, see Schwarz, (1921) 42 *ZSS* 587 sqq.; Wieacker, *Privatrechtsgeschichte*, pp. 486 sqq.; Ernst Zitelmann, "Der Wert eines 'allgemeinen Teils' des bürgerlichen Rechts", (1906) 33 *GrünhZ* 1 sqq.; Philipp Heck, "Der allgemeine Teil des Privatrechts", (1939) 146 *Archiv für die civilistische Praxis* 1 sqq.; Gustav Boehmer, *Einführung in das bürgerliche Recht* (2nd ed., 1965), pp. 73 sqq.; Björne, op. cit., note 164, pp. 250 sqq.

[174] On the "German Abstract Approach to Law" and for comments on the system of the BGB, see Folke Schmidt, (1965) 9 *Scandinavian Studies in Law* 131 sqq.

[175] See, for example, art. 2 ZGB (Switzerland): Everyone must act in good faith in exercising his rights and performing his duties.

[176] Cf., for example, Boehmer, op. cit., note 173, pp. 71 sq.

IV. PLAN OF TREATMENT

In the chapters that follow, first the law of contract, then unjustified enrichment, and finally the law of delict will be dealt with. The discussion of contract commences with the special contracts before it focuses on general doctrines. This progression from the concrete to the more abstract and general would appear to accord best with the way the Roman lawyers developed their law of contractual obligations. As far as the special contracts are concerned, contracts verbis, litteris, re and consensu are distinguished. This fourfold (!) scheme of contractual obligations is based on the manner in which the contract was concluded; as with the two other important systems discussed in this chapter, it dates back to Gaius.[177]

Fundamental, however, to the subject matter of this book is the Roman concept of an obligation and it appears to be apposite, therefore, first to consider three of its most important implications (Chapter 2). We shall then proceed to discuss the stipulation, prototype of a contract verbis and cornerstone of the Roman contractual system. Two particularly important types of transaction (conventional penalties and suretyship) which had to be concluded by way of a stipulation will be examined next (Chapters 4 and 5). The following two chapters are devoted to the four real contracts (mutuum, commodatum, depositum, pignus), the next eight to the four consensual contracts (emptio venditio, locatio conductio, mandatum and societas).[178] Though not a

---

[177] Gai. III, 89 (also 119 a); cf. also Gai. D. 44, 7, 1, 1; *Inst.* III, 13, 2. This scheme is discussed by Ulrich von Lübtow, *Betrachtungen zum gaianischen Obligationenschema, Atti Verona*, vol. III (1951), pp. 241 sqq.; Max Kaser, "Gaius und die Klassiker", (1953) 70 *ZSS* (RA) 157 sqq.; Grosso, *Sistema*, pp. 73 sqq.; Carlo Augusto Cannata, "La 'distinctio' re-verbis-litteris-consensu et les problèmes de la pratique", in: *Sein und Werden im Recht, Festgabe für Ulrich von Lübtow* (1970), pp. 431 sqq.; cf. also idem, "Sulla 'divisio obligationum' nel diritto romano repubblicano e classico", (1970) 21 *Iura* 52 sqq. On the further history and reception of this classification, see Seiler, op. cit., note 98, passim.

[178] The rather mysterious (Vincenzo Arangio-Ruiz, *Istituzioni di diritto romano* (14th ed., 1968), p. 328) obligatio litteris mentioned (only!) in the *Institutes* of Gaius (III, 128 sqq.) will be passed over since it did not form part of the legacy of classical Roman law to the European ius commune. It may have originated as a consequence of the expansion of trade and commerce during the time after the second Punic war, when it became increasingly inconvenient to use the form of a stipulation (requiring the presence of both parties in one and the same place) in order to oblige somebody to pay a sum of money. The obligatio litteris (giving rise to an obligatio stricti iuris) arose as a result of the entry ("expensum ferre": cf. Gai. III, 129; Cicero, *Pro Q. Roscio comoedo*, I, 2) by the creditor into his codex accepti et expensi. This codex (mentioned by Cicero, op. cit., II, 5 sqq.) appears to have been a kind of inventory which was drawn up by a Roman paterfamilias (usually monthly) in order to record (in chronological sequence) all receipts, expenses, claims and debts. It thus reflected the development of a family's financial position and was the basis of the accounting system of a Republican household; as such it enjoyed a specific vis, diligentia and auctoritas (cf. Cicero, op. cit., II, 5 sqq., when he also refers to the codices as "aeterna, servantur sancte, perpetuae existimationis fidem et religionem amplectuntur"). The entry that gave rise to the obligatio litteris appears to have been made by the creditor at the request of his debtor (usually in the form of a—written—iussum); it was based on a fictitious loan (a pecuniam credere with regard to which neither a datio (cf. infra, p. 153) nor a stipulation had been effected) and had a novatory effect: it replaced another obligation, for instance one

contract, negotiorum gestio will be dealt with, for the sake of convenience, as an appendage to mandatum. Donation will be discussed last (Chapter 16); it was not a contract in classical Roman law, but became one in post-classical times. The chapter on pacta and innominate real contracts will take us into the general part of our study of the law of contract, for it is here that we find the doctrinal bridge towards the modern general law of contract. In the subsequent chapters consideration will therefore be given to the most important problem areas affecting every type of contract: how does it come into existence and what is it based upon; what are the effects of error, of metus and of dolus on the contractual relationship between the parties; what are the principles governing the interpretation of contracts; under which circumstances are contracts invalid and how can the obligations arising therefrom be terminated; which provisions may the parties include in their contract (conditions and time clauses will be dealt with as an example of two particularly important examples); and what are the consequences of a breach of contract. The law of unjustified enrichment forms the subject of Chapter 26; together with negotiorum gestio (Chapter 14), it is the only "quasi-contract" considered in some detail. With Chapter 27 we embark on our discussion of the law of delict; some general comments will be followed by a consideration of the most important specific delicts: furtum, damnum iniuria datum and iniuria. Finally, we shall turn our attention to certain instances of strict liability.

---

arising from a contract of sale. For a thorough analysis along these lines, cf. Ralf Michael Thilo, *Der Codex accepti et expensi im Römischen Recht* (1980), pp. 42 sqq., 79 sqq. (on the Roman bookkeeping and accounting system), pp. 162 sqq. (on the codex accepti et expensi), pp. 276 sqq. (on the contract litteris); cf. further, for example, Savigny, *Vermischte Schriften*, vol. I (1850), pp. 205 sqq.; De Zulueta, *Gaius* II, pp. 163 sqq.; Thielmann, *Privatauktion*, pp. 110 sqq.; 196 sqq.; Watson, *Obligations*, pp. 18 sqq.; Pierre Jouanique, "Le codex accepti et expensi chez Cicéron", (1968) 46 *RH* 5 sqq.; M.W.E. Glautier, "A Study in the development of Accounting in Roman Times", (1972) 19 *RIDA* 310 sqq.; Honsell/Mayer-Maly/Selb, pp. 251 sqq.

CHAPTER 2

Stipulatio alteri, Agency and Cession

I. STIPULATIO ALTERI

The concept, sketched in the preceding chapter, of the obligatio as being a strictly personal bond between the two parties who had concluded the contract found highly characteristic expression in the fact that Roman law did not recognize contracts in favour of third parties, (direct) agency and the cession of rights.

1. Alteri stipulari nemo potest

(a) The rule

"A contract may stipulate performance for the benefit of a third party, so that the third party acquires the right directly to demand performance." This is how the BGB (§ 328 I) introduces its title on contracts in favour of third parties. For a Roman lawyer such a statement would have been inconceivable. ". . . vulgo dicitur", said Gaius (II 95),[1] "per extraneam personam nobis adquiri non posse": Roman law generally refused to acknowledge the validity of agreements in terms of which third parties were intended to acquire rights. It is safe to assume that in early Roman law "privity of contract", in this sense, was so much a matter of course that it hardly needed to be emphasized: legal acts and their effects were seen as a unity. Legal effects were not abstracted from the persons performing the formalities and could therefore not be made to originate in the person of an independent outsider.[2] "Decem milia Titio dari spondes?": under a stipulation of this type it was, as a result, impossible for the two contracting parties to confer the right on Titius to claim the ten thousand from the promisor. But did that mean that stipulations of this kind were invariably invalid? Was it not conceivable to regard the promisor as bound to the *stipulator*, i.e. his contractual partner, who could then force him to make performance to Titius? In such a "non-genuine" contract in favour of a third party, legal effects would arise and exist only between the acting parties. The answer of the Roman lawyers was succinctly summed up by Ulpianus (D. 45, 1, 38,

[1] Cf. also *Inst.* II, 9, 5. On this maxim, see, most recently Renato Quadrato, "Rappresentanza", in: *ED*, vol. 38, 1987, pp. 426 sqq. (proposing a new and very narrow construction of the crucial term "extraneus"; it did not, for instance, cover liberti and amici).

[2] Schmidlin, *Rechtsregeln*, pp. 70 sqq.

17): "Alteri stipulari nemo potest, praeterquam si servus domino, filius patri stipuletur." The origin of this famous rule, which had such a lasting effect in the history of private law, has to be seen according to traditional opinion in the formalities required for a stipulation.[3] A conceptio verborum of the above-mentioned type did not comply with the set form of question and answer, because, at least in the beginning, a stipulation had to contain the word "mihi", and it thus had to secure performance to the stipulator, not to Titius.[4] However, the rule was not abandoned even at a time when the formalities were seen in a more liberal light by the jurists; on the contrary, it was probably only then that its implications for the freedom of the parties to adapt and vary their formal declarations were fully realized and that the rule was framed and formulated.[5] Also, its application was not confined to stipulations but extended to all obligations: "Nec paciscendo nec legem dicendo nec stipulando quisquam alteri cavere potest."[6]

(b) The interest requirement

Roman lawyers tried to rationalize the rule and they explained it on the basis that the stipulator did not have any actionable interest in the conclusion of a stipulatio alteri: ". . . inventae sunt enim huiusmodi obligationes ad hoc, ut unusquisque sibi adquirat quod sua interest: ceterum ut alii detur, nihil interest mea" (Ulp. D. 45, 1, 38, 17).[7] These considerations may not be altogether convincing for a modern lawyer[8]—some sort of interest must, typically, also exist in a stipulatio alteri, otherwise a sensible man would hardly enter into such an agreement. This in itself is no reason to reject the text as spurious. The same argument is documented in other texts;[9] it relates to the procedural rule of omnis condemnatio pecuniaria.[10] If every judgment had to be for a definite sum of money, then performance had to be

[3] Wesenberg, *Verträge zugunsten Dritter*, pp. 11 sq., but see infra, pp. 72 sqq.

[4] Kaser, *RPr* I, pp. 539 sq., 543, n. 49.

[5] Schmidlin, *Rechtsregeln*, pp. 71 sq.; cf. also Okko Behrends, "Überlegungen zum Vertrag zugunsten Dritter im römischen Privatrecht", in: *Studi in onore di Cesare Sanfilippo*, vol. V (1984), pp. 1 sqq.

[6] Q.M. Scaevola D. 50, 17, 73, 4. The reference to pacta and leges dictae has often been regarded as interpolated. However, in this fragment Scaevola succinctly refers to the three possibilities which might conceivably create effects in favour of third parties, and there is no reason why such enumeration should not be classical. Contracts are probably not mentioned because the naming of a third party was regarded by the jurist as such a deviation from the typical pattern that it was treated as an incidental provision (lex dicta); cf. Wesenberg, *Verträge zugunsten Dritter*, pp. 9 sq. Further on D. 50, 17, 73, 4, see Wieacker, *RR*, p. 578. On pacta in favorem tertii, see Peter Apathy, "Zur exceptio pacti auf Grund eines pactum in favorem tertii", (1976) 93 *ZSS* 97 sqq.

[7] On this text and its implications, cf., most recently, Behrends, *Studi Sanfilippo*, vol. V, pp. 5 sqq.

[8] Cf. the criticism by Schulz, *CRL*, n. 822.

[9] Cels. D. 42, 1, 13 pr.; 45, 1, 97, 1; Pomp. D. 45, 1, 112, 1; Pap. D. 45, 1, 118, 2; cf. Medicus, *Id quod interest*, pp. 217 sqq.

[10] Kaser, *RZ*, pp. 286 sqq.

capable of being evaluated in monetary terms.[11] That was possible only if every obligation involved an interest, the pecuniary value of which could be estimated. If the plaintiff sued for a certum,[12] the objective value of the objects due to be delivered had to be ascertained.[13] If an incertum was being sued for,[14] the judge had to assess the loss suffered by the creditor as a result of non- or malperformance. But how could an estimation of quod interest[15] be made if the stipulator breached his duty to perform towards a third party? That need not normally have bothered the stipulator. Yet there are cases in which the stipulator has an obvious interest in the promisor carrying out his duties towards the third party, and it is quite in keeping with the argument advanced in D. 45, 1, 38, 17 that here the lawyers were prepared to grant an action, i.e. to treat a stipulatio alteri as valid.[16] Such an interest could arise out of the fact that the stipulator was liable to the third party for the performance of the promisor. An example of such a situation is provided by Ulp. D. 45, 1, 38, 20:

> "Is, qui pupilli tutelam administrare coeperat, cessit administratione contutori suo et stipulatus est rem pupilli salvam fore. ait Marcellus posse defendi stipulationem valere: interest enim stipulatoris fieri quod stipulatus est, cum obligatus futurus esset pupillo, si aliter res cesserit."

Here a tutor wanted to leave the entire administration of the ward's property to his co-tutor and asked him for a cautio rem pupilli salvam fore, that is, for a guarantee (in the form of a stipulation) that he would properly administer this property. As this stipulation had been concluded between the two tutors and provided the tutor cessans with an actio ex stipulatu against the tutor gerens, but imposed a duty on the latter to see to it that his administration of the ward's property would not prove to be detrimental, it was a contract in favour of a third party.[17] However, both Marcellus and Ulpianus regarded the stipulation as valid. The first tutor, although he had ceased to act as a tutor,

---

[11] Cf. Ulp. D. 40, 7, 9, 2; Voci, *Le obbligazioni romane*, vol. I, 1 (1969), pp. 229 sqq.

[12] Cf. e.g. the condictio certae rei: "Si paret Num Num Ao Ao tritici Africi optimi modios centum dare oportere, quanti ea res est, tantam pecuniam iudex Num Num Ao Ao condemnato, si non paret, absolvito."

[13] In the case of certa pecunia (cf. the condictio certae pecuniae) condemnation was for that specific sum of money.

[14] Cf. e.g. the actio empti: "Quod As As de No No hominem Stichum emit, quidquid ob eam rem Num Num Ao Ao dare facere oportet ex fide bona, eius iudex Num Num Ao Ao condemnato, si non paret, absolvito."

[15] Cf. generally Medicus, *Id quod interest*; H. Honsell, *Quod interest*; and infra pp. 826 sq.

[16] Cf. the general statement in *Inst.* III, 19, 20; C. 8, 38, 3 pr. (Diocl. et Max.) (see the interpretation by Max Kaser, "Zur Interessenbestimmung bei den sog. unechten Verträgen zugunsten Dritter", in: *Festschrift für Erwin Seidl* (1975), pp. 82 sqq.).

[17] Towards the ward the second tutor is in any event liable for maladministration under the actio tutelae. Normally the cautio would have been concluded between tutor and ward. It mainly served the function of providing a basis for suretyship stipulations.

was still liable if the ward's affairs were badly administered.[18] He had left the administration to his co-tutor suo periculo and thus had an interest in reducing this periculum by providing for himself a means of forcing the tutor gerens to carry out his obligations.[19] Another example is discussed in Ulp. D. 45, 1, 38, 21 where the promisor of an insula facienda had asked a substitute to promise that he would carry out the building operations for the original stipulator. The (second) stipulation was valid because the stipulator was himself liable as promisor in the first stipulation.

(c) Origin of the rule

More examples could be cited.[20] In analysing them, one is driven to the conclusion that the "interest requirement" only states something obvious: the plaintiff can sue if he has a (financial) interest capable of being assessed by the judge. One would hardly need a rule such as "alteri stipulari nemo potest" to exclude actionability in cases where there is no such interest. On the other hand, one has to take into consideration that it was impossible for the judge to grant an action to the stipulator/plaintiff where the content of the stipulation was (alteri) certum dare. For, according to the wording of the applicable actions,[21] the judge could condemn the defendant only in the sum of money or the objective value of the objects due; he did not have the discretion (by virtue of a "quidquid . . . oportet" clause) to assess any other interest. In the case of a stipulatio alteri, however, the sum of money or the objects concerned are not due to the stipulator/plaintiff and so there was no possibility for him to sue. Thus it seems more convincing to see the origin of the "alteri stipulari nemo potest" (or, preferably, the "alteri dari stipulari nemo potest") rule as lying in the peculiarities of the Roman law of procedure[22] rather than in the formalities of the stipulation: where a promise of (alteri) certum dari had been made, no action was available;[23] in all other cases[24] the promisee could sue,

[18] Even though only in subsidio. On the liabilities of co-tutors, especially the relationship of tutor gerens and cessans, see Ernst Levy, "Die Haftung mehrerer Tutoren", (1916) 37 *ZSS* 14 sqq., 59 sqq.

[19] A different interpretation is given by Wesenberg, pp. 12 sqq. But see Max Kaser, "Die römische Eviktionshaftung nach Weiterverkauf", in: *Sein und Werden im Recht, Festgabe für Ulrich von Lübtow* (1970), p. 491; Alejandro Guzman, *Caucion tutelar en derecho romano* (1974), pp. 272 sqq.

[20] Cf. Kaser, *Festschrift Seidl*, pp. 75 sqq.; Apathy, (1976) 93 *ZSS* 102 sqq.

[21] Cf. e.g. supra, notes 12 and 13.

[22] Hans Ankum, "Une nouvelle hypothèse sur l'origine de la règle Alteri dari stipulari nemo potest", in: *Études offertes à Jean Macqueron* (1970), pp. 21 sqq.

[23] Cf. Gai. III, 103; also Paul. D. 45, 1, 126, 2. See Ankum, *Études Macqueron*, pp. 25 sq.

[24] That is, with regard to contracts for incertum dare or facere. But see Pap. D. 45, 1, 118, 2, where the alteri certum dari is regarded from the point of view of the stipulator as facere, i.e. an incertum.

provided he had an actionable interest.[25] With the decline of the formulary procedure these distinctions were bound to become meaningless. Instead, however, of abolishing "alteri (dari) stipulari nemo potest", Justinian emphasized it as a general rule and finally eliminated the "dari".[26] Yet, at the same time, by also generalizing the idea that the promisee had to be able to sue wherever there was an actionable interest, he emasculated it for all practical purposes.

2. Strategies to evade the restriction

Furthermore, the awkward problem of the lack of interest could easily be avoided by the parties; they simply had to add a stipulatio poenae and to make forfeiture of the penalty dependent on non-performance by the promisor towards the third party: "ergo si quis stipuletur Titio dari, nihil agit, sed si addiderit de poena 'nisi dederis, tot aureos dare spondes?' tunc committitur stipulatio" (*Inst.* III, 19, 19). It was one of the functions of stipulationes poenae to render unnecessary the assessment of what was owed as a consequence of a breach of the promise.[27] Irrespective of whether there was an interest or not, if what had been promised had not been given, the lump sum of "tot aureos" was forfeited:

> "[P]lane si velim hoc facere, poenam stipulari conveniet, ut, si ita factum non sit, ut comprehensum est, committetur stipulatio etiam ei, cuius nihil interest: poenam enim cum stipulatur quis, non illud inspicitur, quid intersit, sed quae sit quantitas quaeque condicio stipulationis" (Ulp. D. 45, 1, 38, 17).

In this way, a (non-genuine) contract in favour of a third party could be made indirectly enforceable. The penalty clause put the promisor under some pressure to honour his promise and, thus, the practical effects of the "alteri stipulari nemo potest" rule were less dramatic than would appear at first glance.[28] Also, the parties could avail themselves of the institution of a solutionis causa adiectus.[29] While a promise could not be

---

[25] Interestingly, an "interest-theory" of a very similar kind ("He that hath interest in the promise shall have the action") played a crucial role in the shaping of the English "privity of contract" doctrine (on which see infra, p. 45). For a modern analysis, see Vernon V. Palmer, "The History of Privity—The Formative Period (1500–1680)", (1989) 33 *American Journal of Legal History* 7 sqq.

[26] Cf. Ulp. D. 45, 1, 38, 17, which, from this point of view, has to be regarded as partially interpolated. See Kaser, *Festschrift Seidl*, p. 87. Paul. D. 45, 1, 126, 2 seems to have escaped the attention of the compilers.

[27] Cf. infra, pp. 95 sq.

[28] Cf. in this context the interesting considerations of Wesenberg, *Verträge zugunsten Dritter*, p. 20; he argues that the main function of the modern contract in favour of a third person (as, for example, regulated in the BGB) is to make provision for relatives. The father of a family wants to protect wife and children against the possibility that the estate might not suffice for their maintenance after his death. In Roman times the subsistence minimum of the civis Romanus and his relatives was provided for by other means (cf., for example, the cura annonae).

[29] This institution has been analysed in great detail by the Roman lawyers. Cf. the casuistry in Pothier, *Pandectae Justinianae IV* (1819), pp. 266 sqq.; Wesenberg, *Verträge zugunsten Dritter*, pp. 20 sqq.

made in favour of Titius, it could be made in favour of either me or Titius. A stipulation of the type "mihi aut Titio dari spondesne?" was valid; although, of course, no right to claim payment was being conferred on Titius, he was entitled to receive payment: "Titius nec petere nec novare nec acceptum facere potest, tantumque ei solvi potest" (Paul. D. 46, 3, 10). Thus, the situation here is similar to the one arising under a (non-genuine) penalty clause:[30] performance only to me is "in stipulatione", performance to Titius is a datio merely "in exsolutione". If, on the other hand, the addition of Titius could not only be regarded as solutionis causa, but if (part-)performance to him was the object of the stipulation ("mihi *et* Titio decem dari spondesne?"), the stipulation, at least as far as this addition was concerned, could not be regarded as valid.[31] The Sabinians, following a very formal "blue-pencil approach",[32] simply struck out what was invalid—i.e. the word "et Titio". The result was that, contrary to the obvious intention of the parties, the ten were owed to the stipulator. The Proculians, however, went beyond the strictly literal interpretation of the formal declaration and regarded "et Titio" not merely as an invalid part of the formula but as an invalid negotium. It would be strange, they argued, if the invalidity of the stipulation in favour of Titius were to have the effect of automatically increasing the amount owed to the stipulator. Thus they advocated upholding the stipulation in the stipulator's favour for five.[33] Furthermore, delegatio solvendi[34] and adstipulatio[35] served to compensate for the lack of, and to satisfy the need for, a contract in favour of third parties.

3. Changes in post-classical law

Still, however, the principle that the third party could not acquire a right was maintained. This began to change only in late classical imperial law. Here we find texts such as C. 8, 54, 3 (Diocl. et Max.):

> "Quotiens donatio ita conficitur, ut post tempus id quod donatum est alii restituatur . . . benigna iuris interpretatione divi principes ei [in quem liberalitatis compendium conferebatur] utilem actionem iuxta donatoris voluntatem competere [admiserunt]."

A donatio sub modo had been concluded; the donee had to pass on the donation to a third party after a specified period. According to ius vetus, neither the donor (a donee charged with a modus could, as a rule, be sued for performance only if the modus had been strengthened by

[30] Cf. Paul. D. 44, 7, 44, 5; infra, pp. 98 sq.
[31] Gai. III, 103 and Schmidlin, *Rechtsregeln*, pp. 72 sqq.
[32] On which, see infra, p. 78.
[33] This is the line taken by Justinian: *Inst.* III, 19, 4. Cf. also Iav. D. 45, 1, 110 pr.
[34] The creditor authorizes the debtor to make performance to a third person; cf. e.g. Afr. D. 46, 3, 38, 1.
[35] An accessory creditor, who was entitled both to receive performance and to sue; his right, however, depended on that of the main creditor. Cf. Gai. III, 110 sqq.; Schulz, *CRL*, pp. 491 sqq.

stipulation) nor the third party had an action to enforce the agreement. Under these circumstances, the emperors granted an equitable action to the third party.[36] This recognition of a genuine agreement in favour of a third party constituted the first direct inroad into the "per extraneam personam nobis adquiri non posse" principle. The authenticity of this text is borne out by the Fragmenta vaticana.[37] We find a series of other cases in the Codex and even in the Digest,[38] as, for example, Ulp. D. 13, 7, 13 pr.,[39] where an actio in factum is granted to a pledgor after the pledgee, in the course of selling the pledged object, had agreed with the purchaser that the debtor should be able to redeem his object from the purchaser; there is also C. 3, 42, 8,[40] where the two parties to a depositum had arranged that the depositee should return the property, not to the depositor, but to a third party, and where this third party is given an actio depositi utilis.[41] But these texts are all very probably interpolated. They show, however, that by the time of Justinian the range of exceptions to the classical principle had been considerably increased. Thus, the compilers had brought a certain amount of inconsistency and confusion into the sources.[42] While still retaining and even emphasizing the principles of "alteri stipulari nemo potest" and "per extraneam personam nobis adquiri non potest", they had taken over, extended or introduced a number of situations in which these principles did not apply. Reconciliation and harmonization of the sources in later times therefore became a difficult and cumbrous undertaking. Also, some of those exceptions lent themselves to an unhinging of the principles. Thus, the history of the contract in favour of a third person is rather varied and eventful.[43]

---

[36] Cf. Wesenberg, *Verträge zugunsten Dritter*, pp. 29 sqq.; Ankum, *Études Macqueron*, p. 23.

[37] Vat. 286.

[38] They are specified and discussed by Wesenberg, *Verträge zugunsten Dritter*, pp. 23 sqq. Cf. also Windscheid/Kipp, § 316, 2; Hans Ankum, *De voorouders van een tweehoofdig twistziek monster* (1967), pp. 15 sqq.; Behrends, *Studi Sanfilippo*, vol. V, pp. 48 sqq.

[39] "Si, cum venderet creditor pignus, convenerit inter ipsum et emptorem, ut, si solverit debitor pecuniam pretii emptori, liceret ei recipere rem suam, scripsit Iulianus et est rescriptum ob hanc conventionem pigneraticiis actionibus teneri creditorem, ut debitori mandet ex vendito actionem adversus emptorem. sed et ipse debitor aut vindicare rem poterit aut in factum actione adversus emptorem agere."

[40] "Si res tuas commodavit aut deposuit is, cuius precibus meministi, adversus tenentem ad exhibendum vel vindicatione uti potes. Quod si pactus sit, ut tibi restituantur, si quidem ei qui deposuit successisti, iure hereditario depositi actione uti non prohiberis: si vero nec civili nec honorario iure ad te hereditas eius pertinet, intellegis nullam te ex eius pacto contra quem supplicas actionem stricto iure habere: utilis autem tibi propter aequitatis rationem dabitur depositi actio" (Diocl. et Max.).

[41] The common denominator of all these exceptions seems to be that an action was granted "to the third person . . . against one who took a thing with notice of [the third person's] right": Thomas, *TRL*, p. 247.

[42] Kaser, *RPr* II, pp. 339 sq.; Emilio Albertario, "I contratti a favore di terzi", in: *Festschrift für Paul Koschaker*, vol. II (1939), pp. 26 sqq.

[43] See Ankum, *De voorouders*, op. cit., note 38, pp. 17 sqq.; Coing, pp. 423 sqq.; Ulrich Müller, *Die Entwicklung der direkten Stellvertretung und des Vertrages zugunsten Dritter* (1969),

4. The evolution of the modern contract in favour of a third party

(a) *Alteri stipulari nemo potest: rule and exceptions*

It took a long time before the "alteri stipulari nemo potest" principle was finally overcome; this principle, incidentally, was taken to prohibit what we today call genuine contracts in favour of a third party, non-genuine contracts in favour of a third party and (direct) representation—i.e. every contract which would either aim at creating rights, or rights and obligations, in the person of a third party, or bind one of the contracting parties to perform in favour of the third. Some authors extended the application of C. 8, 54, 3 and used this constitution as a crystallization point for rules about stipulationes alteri.[44] Others availed themselves of the transformative potential inherent in the "interest" concept.[45] By accepting more and more liberally an interest of the creditor in the conclusion of such a contract, the rule against (non-genuine) contracts in favour of third parties could be totally eroded. Thus we find Gothofredus categorically stating "[H]ominem beneficio adfici nostra interest".[46] Other writers, again, argued that all the exceptions already recognized in Roman law negated the rule.[47] Savigny saw the solution to the problem largely in an extensive application of unauthorized agency.[48] The glossator Martinus Gosia, one of the famous quattuor doctores, maintained that "alteri stipulari nemo potest" referred only to the actio directa and did not prevent the third party from acquiring an actio utilis.[49] According to the commentators, the principle did not apply to "personae publicae" such as notarii or iudices.[50] The canonists recognized an interesting exception in cases where the promise in favour of a third party had been affirmed by oath: if the promise had to be regarded as invalid, perjury

---

pp. 29 sqq.; Wesenberg, *Verträge zugunsten Dritter*, pp. 101 sqq.; Johannes Christiaan de Wet, *Die ontwikkeling van die ooreenkoms ten behoewe van 'n derde* (1940), pp. 28 sqq.

[44] De Wet, op. cit., note 43, e.g. pp. 63 sqq., 68 sqq., 140.

[45] Cf. for the humanists, for example, Franciscus Duarenus, *In Tit. de Pactis*, cap. III, 7 sq.; for the usus modernus e.g. Benediktus Carpzovius, *Definitiones Forenses ad Constitutiones Electorales Saxonicas, Lipsiae et Francofurti* (1694), Pars II, Constitutio XXIX, Def. XX, nn. 1 sqq.; Constitutio XXXIII, Def. XXVII.

[46] Dionysius Gothofredus, *Corpus Juris Civilis Romani*, Lib. XLV, Tit. I, 38, § 17, t; cf. also e.g. Vinnius, *Institutiones*, Lib. III, Tit. XX, 4, n. 3, but see also 19.

[47] Cf. Stryk, *Usus modernus pandectarum*, Lib. II, Tit. XIV, § 12: ". . . et sic non negatur aptitudo, per alium quaerendi obligationem, sed negatur regalia [sic; regula?]."

[48] Savigny, *Obligationenrecht*, vol. II, pp. 81 sqq.

[49] Cf. the analysis by Müller, op. cit., note 43, pp. 44 sqq.; Wesenberg, *Verträge zugunsten Dritter*, pp. 102 sqq.; as to the discussion amongst the medieval legists and canonists generally, cf. also Hans Ankum, "Die Verträge zugunsten Dritter in den Schriften einiger mittelalterlicher Romanisten und Kanonisten", in: *Sein und Werden im Recht, Festgabe für Ulrich von Lübtow* (1970), pp. 559 sqq.; idem, *De voorouders*, op. cit., note 38, pp. 17 sqq.

[50] Cf. already Accursius, gl. Nihil agit ad I. 3, 20, 4. This exception was based mainly on Ulp. D. 46, 6, 2–4, which deals with a servus publicus. Cf. esp. Hermann Lange, " 'Alteri stipulari nemo potest' bei Legisten und Kanonisten", (1956) 73 *ZSS* 279 sqq.; Coing, p. 425.

(which meant sin) would have been sanctioned.[51] And some influential Spanish writers (such as Antonio Gomez and Covarruvias)[52] argued that alteri stipulari nemo potest had been rendered practically obsolete as a result of the widespread recognition of "ex nudo pacto oritur actio":[53] for even if a stipulation in favour of a third party might have to be regarded as invalid,[54] an informal pactum to the same effect did not incur objections.[55] Generally, however, until the 17th century and partially even until the end of the 19th century, the "alteri stipulari nemo potest" rule was reaffirmed and applied—be it out of reverence for the sources of Roman law,[56] be it because a stipulatio alteri was regarded as a logical impossibility[57] or as irreconcilable with the nature of stipulations,[58] or be it that no specific need for agreements in favour of third parties was recognized: under these circumstances, and in view of the fact that obligations constituted limitations on the natural freedom, it was not regarded as justifiable to grant recognition to this kind of transaction.[59] At the height of pandectism, Alois Brinz, in his famous textbook, still tried to reconcile the Justinianic exceptions with the "alteri stipulari nemo potest" principle in order to prove both its logical stringency and its historical significance.[60]

(b) The abandonment of the rule

But these attempts were hardly more than the last thunderings of a lost battle. In the 17th century the great breakthrough towards the recognition of the contract in favour of a third party had taken place and the prevailing new attitude had already influenced many of the codes of that time. In contrast to the contemporary lawyers in Italy, France and Germany, the "elegant" jurisprudence in the Netherlands had turned away from the Roman principle of "alteri stipulari nemo potest".[61]

---

[51] Cf. Lange, (1956) 73 *ZSS* 297 sqq. Note in this context the promise required of schismatic bishops who returned to the church: ". . . promitto tibi N. et per te sancto Petro apostolorum principi, atque eius Vicario N. beatissimo Gregorio, vel successoribus ipsius."

[52] Cf. Coing, p. 425.

[53] Cf. infra, pp. 537 sqq.

[54] On the essence and significance of stipulations under the ius commune cf., however, infra, pp. 546 sqq.

[55] This line of argument (despite not being supported by the Roman sources) also commended itself to some writers of the German usus modernus (cf. Stryk, *Usus modernus pandectarum*, Lib. II, Tit. XIV, § 12) and of Roman-Dutch law (Van Leeuwen, *Censura Forensis*, Pars I, Lib. IV, Tit. XVI, n. 8); cf. also Grotius, *De jure belli ac pacis*, Lib. II, Cap. XI, § 10.

[56] Especially by the humanists; cf. Müller, op. cit., note 43, pp. 73 sqq.

[57] Cf. Brinz, *Pandekten*, § 374 (p. 1627). Cf. also Savigny, *Obligationenrecht*, vol. II, p. 84 (stating that, from the point of view of "good and accurate theory" the doctrine has to be rejected "out of hand").

[58] Brunnemann, *Commentarius in Pandectas*, Lib. XLIV, Tit. VIII, Ad. L. 11, n. 1.

[59] Donellus, *Commentarii de Jure Civili*, Lib. XII, Cap. XVI, 9 sq.; Savigny, *Obligationenrecht*, vol. II, p. 76.

[60] § 375.

[61] See especially Ankum, *De voorouders*, op. cit., note 38, pp. 27 sqq.; De Wet, op. cit., note 43, pp. 104 sqq.; Müller, op. cit., note 43, pp. 98 sqq.

This move was possibly indirectly influenced by a law of King Alfons XI of Spain from 1348,[62] but it was mainly based on the needs and usages of the rapidly expanding Dutch economy. One of the first to take the "consuetudo" into account was Johannes Jacob Wissenbach, who stated the Roman rule and then continued:

> "Et moribus hodiernis vel paciscendo, vel legem dicendo, vel stipulando alter alteri cavere potest . . . Neque id mirum videri debet. Nam roganti, quare Jure Civili alteri stipulari nemo possit, vix aliam dederis rationem, in quo acquiescat, quam hanc, quia ita legislatori placuit . . . Mores ergo id Romanorum placitum, facile subigere poterant."[63]

A couple of years later, Simon van Leeuwen had this to say in his *Censura Forensis* about bills of exchange: "Nostris autem vicinisque regionibus, praesertim inter mercatores nihil frequentius quam quod in litterarum obligationibus, non modo sibi aut alteri, sed in genere cuicunque literatum latori valide stipuletur."[64]

However, the frontal attack on "alteri stipulari nemo potest" was launched by the natural lawyers, led by Hugo Grotius. Significantly,[65] in his *Inleiding tot de Hollandsche Rechtsgeleertheyd*, Grotius had still stated that "niemand door een ander inschuld bekomen [kan] zonder opdracht".[66] It was only in his *De Jure Belli ac Pacis* that he asserted the incompatibility of "alteri stipulari nemo potest" with natural law:

> "Si mihi facta est promissio, omissa inspectione an mea privatim intersit, quam introduxit ius Romanuma, naturaliter videtur mihi acceptandi ius dari efficendi ut ad alterum ius perveniat, si et is acceptet. . . . Nam is sensus iuri naturae non repugnat."[67]

The recognition of the contract in favour of a third party thus came as a consequence of the emphasis which Grotius put on will and consensus as essential elements of the contract.[68] Another consequence, however, is the specific limitation of this construction which lies in the fact that the third party does not (directly) acquire a right under the contract between the other two, but that a declaration is required to accept the benefit. Strictly speaking, therefore, the right of the third party arises from a vinculum iuris between himself and the promisor. The situation

---

[62] Cf. Didacus de Covarruvias a Leyva, "Variae Resolutiones Juridicae", in: *Opera Omnia* (Francofurti, 1573), Lib. I, Cap. XIV, 11. Both Müller, op. cit., note 43, and Coing, p. 430, emphasize that the break with the "alteri stipulari nemo potest" rule ultimately originated in Spanish legal science; cf., for example, the discussion in Perezius, *Praelectiones*, Lib. VIII, Tit. LV, n. 9.

[63] *Exercitationes,* Ad Regulas Juris, Disput. XI, l. 73, 5 (should read: 16).

[64] Pars I, Lib. IV, Cap. XVI, 8. The discussion among the Dutch jurists has been summed up by Voet, *Commentarius ad Pandectas*, Lib. XLV, Tit. I, III; cf. also Groenewegen, De legibus abrogatis, Inst. Lib. III, Tit. XX, § 19 alteri.

[65] Cf. Reinhard Zimmermann/David Carey-Miller, "Hugo Grotius—Generis humani iuris consultus", 1984 *Jura* 1 sqq.

[66] III, I, 36; but see also III, III, 38.

[67] Lib. II, Cap. XI, § 18. As so often (cf. Otto Wilhelm Krause, *Naturrechtler des sechzehnten Jahrhunderts* (1982), pp. 150 sqq.), Grotius built on the foundations laid by the late scholastic Spanish legal science (cf. supra, note 62.).

[68] Wieacker, *Privatrechtsgeschichte*, pp. 293 sq. and especially, Diesselhorst, *Hugo Grotius*, passim: cf. infra, p. 544.

is thus not dissimilar from what we are accustomed to call unauthorized agency.[69] It was in this form that the contract in favour of a third party made its way into the Prussian,[70] Bavarian,[71] and Saxonian[72] codifications. The Austrian code was more conservative in this respect and retained the "alteri stipulari nemo potest" principle.[73] So did, under the influence of Robert-Joseph Pothier,[74] the French code civil.[75] It made provision for only two narrowly defined exceptions in art. 1121: a "*stipulation au profit d'un tiers*" is valid, "*lorsque telle est la condition d'une stipulation que l'on fait pour soi-meme ou d'une donation que l'on fait a un autre.*"[76] The Roman idea of the actionable interest necessary for a valid stipulation (Ulp. D. 45, 1, 38, 17), as well as the donatio sub modo in C. 8, 54, 3 are clearly evident in this provision. The French courts have, however, regarded the first alternative (namely that the contract must not only be for the benefit of the third party but that there must be a simultaneous promise for the benefit of the promisee) as being satisfied if the promisee derives any "profit moral" from the transaction.[77] Thus, they have unhinged the principle of art. 1165 and introduced into French law—contra legem, as it were—the modern contract in favour of third parties. According to the "*théorie de la création directe de l'action*" the third party acquires the right directly at the time when promisor and promisee conclude their contract; his own declaration does not have a constitutive effect. This has brought French law into line with modern German law; the "mature"[78] solutions found in 328 sqq., providing, inter alia, for life insurance contracts and farm surrender agreements, are due to the conceptual clarity achieved by the pandectists.[79] Grotius' construction, on the other hand, lives on to this

[69] It is hardly surprising that both sometimes get mixed up in South African law; cf. e.g. Leslie Rubin, "The Legal Consequences of Contracts Concluded by a negotiorum gestor", 1954 *Butterworth's South African LR* 131 sq.; Lee, *Introduction* p. 439.

[70] § 75 I 5 PrALR.

[71] Theil 4, Cap. 1, § 13 Codex Maximilianeus.

[72] § 854 Sächsisches Gesetzbuch.

[73] § 881 ABGB; reformed, however, by the third Theilnovelle in 1916.

[74] *Traité des obligations*, nn. 54 sqq.

[75] Art. 1165 code civil; on the origin of the provisions regarding contracts in favour of a third party in the French and Dutch codifications, see Ankum, *De voorouders*, op. cit., note 38, pp. 30 sqq.; as far as French law is concerned, cf. also Edouard Lambert, *Du contrat en faveur des tiers* (1893), passim.

[76] This provision has been received in Louisiana (but has been changed subsequently). On the history of "stipulations pour autrui" in Louisiana, see J. Denson Smith, (1936) 11 *Tulane LR* 18 sqq.

[77] The most important parts of the "vast edifice which the French courts have constructed on the frail foundation of art. 1121", especially Despretz c. Wannebroucq, Cass. civ. 16.1.1888, are easily accessible in Kahn-Freund/Lévy/Rudden, *A Source-book on French Law* (2nd ed., 1979), pp. 454 sqq.; cf. also Nicholas, *FLC*, pp. 177 sqq.

[78] Zweigert/Kötz/Weir, pp. 126 sqq., 138.

[79] Cf. especially Windscheid/Kipp, § 316. In § 316 a, a variety of theories and constructions (mostly based on fictions) is discussed which were proposed in the course of the 19th century in order to get around the effects of the "alteri stipulari nemo potest" rule.

day in the modern Roman-Dutch law of South Africa.[80]

(c) Privity of contract

All in all, the civil-law systems seem more or less to have thrown off the fetters of the Roman "alteri stipulari nemo potest" principle.[81] If, therefore, one wants to name a legal system that to this day quite obstinately conceives of contractual obligations as necessarily bilateral "vincula iuris", in a way which is very unabstract and similar to the Roman view, one has to look at the English common law.[82] There, in the words of Viscount Haldane LC, "certain principles are fundamental. One is that only a person who is a party to a contract can sue on it. Our law knows nothing of a ius quaesitum tertio arising by way of contract".[83] This rule is usually justified by reference to the doctrines of "privity of contract" and "consideration" (consideration must move from the promisee). However, again not unlike their Roman counterparts, English lawyers have not been able altogether to ignore the practical need for allowing third parties to sue and have, therefore, in some cases found other means of achieving this end. More particularly, trust constructions (usually of a more or less fictitious nature) have been employed in this context.[84]

II. AGENCY

1. Direct representation: introduction

Not only the contract in favour of a third party but also the modern law of agency have been developed, in the civil-law systems, largely in opposition to the situation in Roman law. Again, it was the "alteri stipulari nemo potest" principle which stood in the way; again, however, matters were complicated by the fact that the Corpus Juris Civilis did not really present a very clear and consistent picture. Again, it was Hugo Grotius who had a major impact on the development; in particular, he advanced the legal analysis by distinguishing for the first time between contracts in favour of a third party and agency: "Solent

Cf. in this context the polemic though instructive remarks by von Kirchmann, *Die Werthlosigkeit der Jurisprudenz als Wissenschaft* (1848), as quoted by Zweigert/Kötz/Weir, p. 126.

[80] Cf. e.g. *Mutual Life Insurance Co. of New York v. Hotz* 1911 AD 556 sqq.; *McCullogh v. Fernwood Estate Ltd.* 1920 AD 204 sqq. and the criticism by De Wet, op. cit., note 43, pp. 146 sqq.; De Wet en Yeats, pp. 94 sqq. For a different view, see J. Kerr Wylie, "Contracts in favour of third parties", (1943) 7 *THRHR* 94 sqq.

[81] Cf. the comparative analysis by Zweigert/Kötz/Weir, pp. 124 sqq.

[82] Cf. the comparative analysis by Zweigert/Kötz/Weir, pp. 133 sqq.; and the historical analysis by Palmer, (1989) 33 *American Journal of Legal History* 3 sqq.

[83] *Dunlop Pneumatic Tyre Co. Ltd. v. Selfridge and Co. Ltd.* [1915] AC 847 (HL) at 853; cf. also *Beswick v. Beswick* [1967] 2 All ER 1197 (HL); Treitel, *Contract*, pp. 458 sqq.

[84] Cf. Buckland/McNair, pp. 214 sqq.; Arthur L. Corbin, *Contracts for the Benefit of Third Persons*, (1930) 46 *LQR* 12 sqq.; Louise Wilson, "Contract and Benefits for Third Parties", (1987) 11 *Sydney LR* 230 sqq.

et controversiae incidere de acceptatione pro altero facta: in quibus distinguendum est inter promissionem mihi factam de re danda alteri, et inter promissionem in ipsius nomen collatam cui res danda est."[85] This distinction is based on Grotius' general emphasis on the will of the contracting parties, and it has remained fundamental ever since.[86] It was developed as a consequence of the rejection of the "alteri stipulari nemo potest" principle. As long as this principle was applied, it was seen to refer to all situations in which an independent third party acquired a right under a contract which had been concluded between two other parties. This is exactly what (genuine) contracts in favour of third parties and agency have in common, and therefore it had hardly been necessary thus far to differentiate cases which were prohibited anyway. Agency, as we see it today, refers to a situation where one person (the agent), authorized by a third party (the principal), concludes a transaction on behalf of the latter with another person, with the result that such transaction will take effect between the *principal* and this other person.[87] Thus, the main difference from what we call a contract in favour of a third party lies in the fact that in the one case the principal in every respect becomes party to the contract that has been concluded by the agent; the agent is merely acting as a conduit pipe and has no concern with the effects of the transaction. In the other case, the third party acquires only the right to claim performance. He does not become a party to the contract which is concluded, and becomes effective, between promisor and promisee. Thus, the imposition of a *duty* to perform is conceivable only in the case of agency; a contract not only for the benefit of, but casting a burden on a third party is not, and has never been, admissible.[88] If one looks at the will of the parties concerned, one can say that the agent wants to accept the promise in the name of the principal, whereas the promisee under a contract in favour of a third party wants to act in his own name for the benefit of the third party. For agency, the continental legal systems specify a further requirement: the agent has to act in the name of the principal,[89] and

[85] *De jure belli ac pacis*, Lib. II, Cap. XI, 18.

[86] The distinction is sometimes blurred; cf., for example, supra, notes 48, 69.

[87] Thus, one person acts, but the effects of that act arise in a third party. Rabel, "Die Stellvertretung in den hellenistischen Rechten und in Rom", in: *Atti del congresso internazionale di diritto romano*, vol. I (1934), p. 238, has called this a legal miracle ("*Ursprünglich gibt es nirgends eine direkte Stellvertretung. Sie ist ein juristisches Wunder*").

[88] Cf. Paul. D. 45, 1, 83 pr.; Windscheid/Kipp, § 317; Klaus-Peter Martens, "Rechtsgeschäft und Drittinteressen", (1977) 177 *Archiv für die civilistische Praxis* 139 sqq. The validity of such a transaction is (in modern times) incompatible with the autonomy of each individual to enter into legal transactions (*Privatautonomie*). In the case of agency, this problem does not arise, as the principal has conferred the power of agency on the agent.

[89] Cf., for example, Windscheid/Kipp, § 73, n. 15; Wolfram Müller-Freienfels, *Die Vertretung beim Rechtsgeschäft* (1955), pp. 15 sqq.; Karsten Schmidt, "Offene Stellvertretung" 1987 *Juristische Schulung* 425 sqq.; cf. also art. 1984 code civil; art. 1388 codice civile. For a comparative evaluation, see Philippos Doris, "Die unmittelbare Stellvertretung des BGB im

must therefore make it clear to the other party that he is not acting in his own name.[90] This is the publicity principle[91] which, incidentally, had also already been enunciated by Grotius and the other natural lawyers.[92] In contradistinction, English law recognizes the "undisclosed principal":[93] as long as the agent has authority to act at the time when the contract is made, the principal acquires rights and duties under this contract even if the agent did not reveal the fact that he was acting on behalf of another. Although this has often been regarded as a strange anomaly of English law,[94] the undisclosed principal has managed to creep into one civil-law system, namely the usus hodiernus of Roman-Dutch law.[95] According to the South African Appellate Division, the opportunity to expel the uncouth intruder has unfortunately been lost.[96]

2. No general concept of agency in Roman law

Roman law did not know a general concept of agency. Certain situations were recognized in which persons could act through middlemen, but a comprehensive legal institution of agency was never developed.[97] This, as far as the acquisition of rights through an agent is concerned, was another consequence of "per extraneam personam nihil nobis acquiri potest".[98] That, in turn, one could not incur obligations

---

Lichte funktions- und strukturähnlicher Rechtsgebilde in anderen Rechtsordnungen", in: *II. Festschrift für Karl Larenz* (1983), pp. 161 sqq.

[90] Cf. § 164 II BGB, which formulates with unsurpassed elegance: "In the case, that the will to act in another person's name, is not apparent, the absence of the will to act in one's own name is not to be taken into consideration."

[91] It aims at protecting both the party with whom the "agent" contracts and third parties (who have an interest in the certainty and clarity of legal relations).

[92] Cf. e.g. Christian Wolff, *Institutiones juris naturae et gentium*, § 551.

[93] Cf. Wolfram Müller-Freienfels, "The Undisclosed Principal", (1953) 16 *Modern LR* 299 sqq.; idem, "Comparative Aspects of Undisclosed Agency", (1955) 18 *Modern LR* 33 sqq.; S.J. Stoljar, *The Law of Agency* (1961), pp. 203 sqq.

[94] Cf. e.g. G.H.L. Fridman, *The Law of Agency* (4th ed., 1976), pp. 191 sqq.

[95] *Lippert & Co. v. Desbats* 1869 Buch 189; *O'Leary v. Harbord* (1888) 5 HCG 1; cf. J.C. van der Horst, *Die Leerstuk van die "Undisclosed Principal"* (1971).

[96] *Cullinan v. Noordkaaplandse Aartappelkernmoerkwekers Koöperasie Bpk.* 1972 (1) SA 761 (A) at 767F–G: "Ofskoon . . . die leerstuk . . . inderdaad indruis teen die grondbeginsels van ons reg, is die onderhawige myns insiens nie 'n geval waar ingegryp en die leerstuk oorboord gegooi kan word nie. . . ."

[97] Cf. Axel Claus, *Gewillkürte Stellvertretung im Römischen Privatrecht* (1973); G. Hamza, "Aspetti della rappresentanza negoziale in diritto romano", (1980) 9 *Index* 193 sqq.; idem, "Fragen der gewillkürten Stellvertretung im römischen Recht", (1983) 25 *Acta Juridica Academiae Scientiarum Hungaricae* 89 sqq.; Kaser, *RPr* I, pp. 260 sqq.; idem, "Zum Wesen der römischen Stellvertretung", (1970) 9 *Romanitas* 333 sqq.; idem, "Stellvertretung und 'notwendige Entgeltlichkeit'", (1974) 91 *ZSS* 146 sqq.; Ludwig Mitteis, *Die Lehre von der Stellvertretung* (1885); Müller, op. cit., note 43, pp. 14 sqq.; Joseph Plescia, "The Development of Agency in Roman Law", (1984) 30 *Labeo* 171 sqq.; Raphael Powell, "Contractual Agency in Roman Law and English Law", 1956 *Butterworth's South African LR* 41 sqq.; Quadrato, *ED*, vol. 38, pp. 417 sqq.; Rabel, *Atti*, op. cit., note 87, pp. 235 sqq.; idem, *Grundzüge*, §§ 118 sqq.

[98] But cf. Alessandro Corbino, "Forma librale ed intermediazione negoziale", in: *Sodalitas, Scritti in onore di Antonio Guarino*, vol. V (1984), pp. 2257 sqq.

through an independent third person seems to have been so obvious that a similar rule did not even have to be formulated. For an explanation one has to look back to the formalism of the old law with its magical roots: the ceremonies connected with transactions such as mancipatio and nexum and the sacral elements of the old stipulatio seem to have necessitated performance of the formal acts in personam.[99] That Roman lawyers clung to this principle during the more advanced stages of legal development and even applied it to the informal contracts, some of which came to be the main transactions of daily life and of commercial intercourse, provides striking evidence of their characteristic traditionalism.[100] To us, today, agency appears to be an essential device in any developed and sophisticated economy which avails itself of the advantages of a division of labour for the production and distribution processes.[101] How could the Romans do without it? They were, after all, a nation whose economic and social structure,[102] from about the time of the Punic wars, was no longer determined so much by agriculture as by commerce, finance and city life.[103] The answer lies partly in the structure of the Roman economic system, more particularly in the organization and functioning of the family unit; besides, the Romans used other devices which allowed them to approximate the practical effects of agency. Also, the rule regarding the exclusion of agency was not as rigidly applied as is sometimes suggested; if their traditionalism led the Roman lawyers to retain the

---

[99] Cf. Mitteis, op. cit., note 97, pp. 13 sqq.; Kaser, *RPr* I, p. 260. A totally different hypothesis has recently been advanced by Claus, *Stellvertretung*, pp. 14 sqq. According to him, (ancient) Roman law did not object to agency in the sense that a free person could acquire rights and incur obligations on behalf of somebody else. Taking as his point of departure what Erwin Seidl (for example in: *Ägyptische Rechtsgeschichte der Saiten- und Perserzeit* (2nd ed., 1968), pp. 45 sqq.) has called "the principle of necessary remunerativeness"—which, according to Seidl, originally applied in Roman law just as in all other (early) legal systems (cf. for England the doctrine of consideration)—he argues that if the remuneration had come from the property of a third party or if what had been acquired had benefited the property of the third party, that third party, and not the person concluding the contract, would be liable and entitled under the transaction. Only later on, when the will of the parties began to be emphasized and ultimately replaced the principle of necessary remunerativeness as the basis of the contractual transactions (that is, since the end of the third century B.C.) did the jurists introduce the prohibition of agency. For a refutation of this theory, see Kaser, (1974) 91 *ZSS* 146 sqq.

[100] On this topic generally, see Schulz, *Principles*, pp. 83 sqq.; Dieter Nörr, "Zum Traditionalismus der römischen Juristen", in: *Festschrift für Werner Flume*, vol. I (1978), pp. 153 sqq.

[101] Müller-Freienfels, *Vertretung*, op. cit., note 89, p. 53.

[102] Cf. M.I. Finley, *The Ancient Economy* (1973); Tenney Frank (ed.), *An Economic Survey of Ancient Rome*, vol. I, v (1959); M. Rostovtzeff, *The Social and Economic History of the Roman Empire* (1926); and the essays collected in M.I. Finley (ed.), *Studies in Ancient Society* (1974) and Helmuth Schneider (ed.), *Zur Sozial- und Wirtschaftsgeschichte der späten römischen Republik* (1976); Wieacker, *RR*, pp. 347 sqq.

[103] As to what follows cf. especially the clear and instructive analysis by Kaser, (1970) 9 *Romanitas* 333 sqq.; also Rabel, *Grundzüge*, §§ 118 sqq. On the reasons for an increasing need for agency (and thus: for the intervention of the praetor), see Powell, 1956 *Butterworth's South African LR* 42 sqq.

principle,[104] their pragmatism allowed for exceptions where necessary. Roman law was never conceived of and developed as a system of rigid rules, but rather from a casuistic point of view.[105]

3. Acting for (and through) others in Roman law

(a) Indirect representation and other substitute devices

Firstly, the Romans knew, of course, what we would call indirect representation:[106] the "agent" could conclude the contract (e.g. of sale) in his own name and demand transfer of ownership to himself; he was then obliged under whatever his relationship with the "principal" might be (often a mandatum) to hand over to the "principal" whatever he received. Indirect representation is based on a iussum (or ratihabitio),[107] the (informal) declaration of the "principal" to the "agent" acknowledging the results of the "agent's" acts. This "iussum" is different from the modern "authority" in that it had no "external effect": it did not give rise to a contractual relationship between the "principal" and the party with whom the "agent" contracted. Legal relationships existed only between the "principal" and "agent" on the one hand, and the "agent" and his contractual partner on the other. Thus, indirect representation is cumbersome in that it requires two legal transactions instead of only one. The "principal" is in a comparatively weak position: it is only the "agent" who can sue under the contract concluded by him; once ownership has been transferred to

---

[104] But cf. W.M. Gordon, "Agency and Roman Law", in: *Studi in onore di Cesare Sanfilippo*, vol. III (1983), pp. 341 sqq., who argues that "Roman law gradually reached a position where the advantage of going further was more theoretical than practical and Roman law reached this situation in a way which gave practical results which were in certain respects preferable to those which would follow from the adoption of direct agency" (p. 343). For a critical evaluation of the traditional opinion, see also Quadrato, *ED*, vol. 38, pp. 417 sqq.

[105] Cf. esp. Max Kaser, "Zur Methode der römischen Rechtsfindung", in: *Ausgewählte Schriften*, vol. I (1976), pp. 3 sqq.

[106] The institutions of buying commission and commission for sale are modern examples of indirect agency. They are based on the desire to make use of independent entrepreneurs at foreign trading centres and on the preference of the buyers or sellers at these foreign trading centres to contract with the representative on the spot rather than with some unfamiliar and far-off principal. Transactions through commission agents were very popular in the 19th century; owing to the modern means of transport and communication their importance has decreased considerably, cf. Karsten Schmidt, *Handelsrecht* (3rd ed., 1987), pp. 762 sqq. Agency, for the fathers of the BGB, meant "direct agency" (cf. supra, p. 46); they regarded (rules about) indirect agency as obsolete and dispensable. Time has shown that this attitude was too rigid; the need for indirect agency in certain circumstances has had to be accommodated by the courts (cf., for example, the *Geschäft für den, den es angeht* (transaction for whom it concerns), on which, see Karl August Bettermann, *Vom stellvertretenden Handeln* (1937), pp. 90 sqq.; Klaus Müller, "Das Geschäft für den, den es angeht", 1982 *Juristenzeitung* 777 sqq.). As far as Roman law is concerned, the importance of indirect agency as a satisfactory alternative to direct agency is stressed by Gordon, *Studi Sanfilippo*, vol. III, pp. 344 sqq.

[107] Ratihabitio is subsequent assent; cf., for instance, Ulp. D. 46, 8, 12, 1; 3, 5, 5, 11. On the theory and history of ratification in the law of agency, see Gualtiero Procaccia, (1978–79) 4 *Tel Aviv University Studies in Law* 9 sqq.

the "agent", the "principal" can avail himself of an actio in personam only to enforce the passing on of ownership to himself. As a result, he is, for instance, exposed to the risk of his "agent's" insolvency.

Secondly, there was the possibility of concluding a contract by means of a nuntius.[108] While in the case of agency it is the agent who makes the declaration leading to the contract—in his own name (indirect representation) or in the name of the principal (direct representation), but in any event as his own declaration—the messenger merely transmits somebody else's declaration.[109] He is not involved in the formation of the contract but in a purely mechanical way; what he transmits is not regarded as his own, but as his "principal's" declaration. The situation is thus similar to the conclusion of a contract by way of letter.[110]

In the third place, Roman law provided for certain situations where one party acted for another not as an agent but in his own right. This was the concept of trusteeship: the trustee held a right in somebody else's interest; on account of the fiduciary relationship he was bound, however, to safeguard these interests of the beneficiary. Fiducia fits into this category (be it cum creditore or cum amico contracta).[111] Also, the procurator ad litem may be mentioned here: he did not act as a representative in the way that the dominus litis would have become party to the litigation; he litigated over somebody else's claim, or obligation, in his own right.[112] Another example is tutela. Even though the law made the greatest efforts to enable persons under tutela to undertake the required legal acts themselves (subject to auctoritas tutoris), there remained situations where the tutor had to act *for* them.[113] This he did domini loco,[114] i.e. he was apparently regarded as having some sort of (functionally limited) title over the person and property of the ward.[115] Interestingly enough, however, this view seems to have undergone some change. Already according to classical law the tutor could acquire possession and (as far as this was possible through the acquisition of possession, as, for instance, in the case of

[108] This applies to the informal transactions only. Where, for example, formal oral declarations by the stipulator and promisor are required (stipulatio), the parties could not make use of nuntii.

[109] As to the concept of a nuntius, cf. Flume, *AT*, § 43, 4; Götz Hueck, "Bote—Stellvertreter im Willen—Stellvertreter in der Erklärung", (1952–53) 152 *Archiv für die civilistische Praxis* 432 sqq.; Mitteis, op. cit., note 97, pp. 128 sqq.

[110] Paul. D. 18, 1, 1, 2: "Est autem emptio iuris gentium, et ideo consensu peragitur et inter absentes contrahi potest et per nuntium et per litteras."

[111] Gai. II, 60.

[112] Kaser, *RZ*, pp. 152 sqq.; Claus, *Stellvertretung*, pp. 52 sqq.

[113] As, for example, where the impubes was still an infans or where he was absens.

[114] Paul. D. 26, 7, 27: "Tutor, qui tutelam gerit, quantum ad providentiam pupillarem domini loco haberi debet."

[115] Cf. especially Max Kaser, "Ruhende und verdrängende Hausgewalt im älteren römischen Recht", (1939) 59 *ZSS* 31 sqq. (35 sqq.).

traditio or usucapio) ownership for the ward.[116] The inadmissibility of agency was apparently limited by the Roman lawyers to the strictly legal sphere, and possession was not regarded as a right but as a mere factum. Gradually, however, the praetor also started, after the termination of the tutela, to grant actiones utiles for and against the former ward where the tutor had acquired contractual rights[117] and incurred obligations[118] on behalf of the ward.[119] Here the basic principle against agency was certainly disregarded.

Fourthly, third parties could, under certain circumstances, *dispose* over the rights of others and in this way act for those other persons. The non-owner could transfer property or encumber it with a right of pledge, the non-creditor could release the debtor from his debt by means of a pactum de non petendo, etc., provided only that the transaction required no formalities and that the true owner, creditor, etc., had either approved of the transaction or ratified it.[120] The Romans did not regard the third party as an agent in these cases; he was not acting on behalf of the party entitled to the right, but was entering into a transaction of his own.

(b) The paterfamilias acting through his dependants

All these devices would still not have obviated the need for agency in Roman law. Fifthly, therefore, and most importantly, the fact has to be taken into account that a paterfamilias could act through his children in power and his slaves. These persons were not able to have proprietary rights; thus, whatever they acquired fell to the paterfamilias.[121] Whether they had acted in their own name or not was irrelevant; neither did it (usually) matter whether the paterfamilias knew of or had willed their acts.[122] Max Kaser[123] has explained this phenomenon in terms of the concept of "*Organschaft*": in the same way as a human being uses his limbs or as (today) a juristic person uses his organs to act, the Roman paterfamilias was able to act through his dependants. For the purposes of acquisition, they served the function of animated

---

[116] Ner. D. 41, 1, 13, 1; Paul. D. 41, 2, 1, 20.

[117] Cf. Ulp. D. 26, 7, 9 pr.; Ulp. D. 13, 5, 5, 9.

[118] Cf. Scaev. D. 36, 3, 18, 2.

[119] Actiones utiles were also granted for and against municipia on account of the acts of their actor (representative in court): Paul. D. 3, 4, 10; Ulp. D. 13, 5, 5, 7 sqq.; cf. further Ulp. D. 12, 1, 27.

[120] Cf. Gai. D. 41, 1, 9, 4; Ulp. D. 6, 1, 41, 1; Paul. D. 13, 7, 20 pr.

[121] Cf. recently Wolfgang Krüger, *Erwerbszurechnung kraft Status* (1979), pp. 21 sqq.; as far as the acquisition of *possession* through persons in power is concerned, see Hans-Peter Benöhr, *Der Besitzerwerb durch Gewaltabhängige im klassischen römischen Recht* (1972). On the problems arising in situations where a slave has several domini, see Geoffrey MacCormack, "Nomination: Slaves and Procurators", (1976) 23 *RIDA* 191 sqq.

[122] Cf. Gai. II, 86 sqq.

[123] (1970) 9 *Romanitas* 343 sqq.

instruments.[124] Thus, the acquisitive acts were not, as would also have been conceivable, regarded as totally ineffective or irrelevant. Where, on the other hand, the filiusfamilias or slave had incurred an obligation, the paterfamilias was not normally bound.[125] In fact, the position of the creditor was very weak: slaves could not be parties to a lawsuit, and execution against children in power, as long as they did not have proprietary capacity, was excluded. In classical law these obligations against persons in power were regarded as obligationes naturales.[126] As a result, it must have appeared unattractive and risky to contract with a filiusfamilias or a slave. Thus, in order not to stifle legal relations and business life, the praetor intervened and was prepared, under certain circumstances, to grant actiones "adiecticiae qualitatis"[127] against the paterfamilias. The common denominator of most of these actions was a (tacit or express, general or specific) authority given to the person in power to act on behalf of the paterfamilias. This is particularly obvious in the case of the actio quod iussu,[128] where an express (formless) authority even had to have been communicated to the party with whom the person in power was about to contract, but it also applied to the actio de peculio,[129] where the son in power or the slave had been given a peculium (the paterfamilias was then liable for all commercial debts incurred up to the value of the peculium at the time of condemnation); to the actio exercitoria,[130] which lay against the exercitor navis for commercial debts incurred (within the terms of the so-called "praepositio")[131] by his magister navis, and to the actio institoria,[132] which was available against an employer for commercial debts incurred (again: within the terms of the praepositio) by an employee who had been put in charge of a taberna or some other negotiatio.[133] Besides these, an actio de in rem verso[134] was available if the person in power had used what he had acquired under the contract

---

[124] We find the same idea in public law: populus Romanus and municipia act through their magistratus. Cf. also the post-classical concept of the delegatus principis (C. 1, 50 and 51).

[125] Cf., for example, Gai. D. 50, 17, 133: "Melior condicio nostra per servos fieri potest, deterior fieri non potest." Could slaves alienate property for their masters? For details, see Hans Ankum, "Mancipatio by Slaves in Classical Roman Law?", 1976 *Acta Juridica* 1 sqq.; idem, "Mancipatio by Slaves in Classical Roman Law", in: *Huldigingsbundel Paul van Warmelo* (1984), pp. 6 sqq.

[126] Cf., for example, Ulp. D. 44, 7, 14.

[127] Cf. generally e.g. Claus, *Stellvertretung*, pp. 64 sqq. and passim. The term has its origin in Paul. D. 14, 1, 5, 2: "[H]oc enim edicto non transfertur actio, sed adicitur."

[128] D. 15, 4; C. 4, 26.

[129] Gai. IV, 72a–74a; *Inst.* IV, 7, 4–4c; D. 15, 1; C. 4, 26.

[130] D. 14, 1; C. 4, 25.

[131] "Non tamen omne, quod cum institore [sc.: vel exercitore] geritur, obligat eum qui praeposuit, sed ita, si eius rei gratia cui praepositus fuerit, contractum est, id est dumtaxat ad id quod eum praeposuit" (Ulp. D. 14, 3, 5, 11).

[132] D. 14, 3; C. 4, 25.

[133] On the interpretation of the term "institor", cf. the analysis by Nikolaus Benke, "Zu Papinians actio ad exemplum institoriae actionis", (1988) 105 *ZSS* 597 sqq.

[134] D. 15, 3.

to enrich the property of his paterfamilias. The most interesting of these remedies in the present context were the actiones exercitoria and institoria because they were granted irrespective of whether or not the exercitor navis or institor was a person in power.[135] Thus, we are dealing here with instances where a freeman was able to obligate a third party who had authorized him to do business on his behalf. This approximated agency. However, magister navis and institor were and remained the parties to the contract which had been concluded; the liability was extended only to the exercitor navis/employer, who could now be sued in solidum.[136] Also, these "principals" were sometimes granted the contractual actions of their "agents" against the other party as actiones utiles.[137]

(c) *Procuratio*

Sixthly, attention has to be drawn to the institution of procuratio.[138] Wealthy people used to have a procurator omnium bonorum to look after and administer their property. In pre-classical times they would appoint to this position one of their own freedmen who had been specifically trained for the job and who, on account of the patronal power, was still very much dependent upon his (former) master even after manumissio had taken place. Later on, this power gradually dwindled and the freedman was increasingly regarded as a legally independent person (with the effect that reciprocal claims between procurator and principal became possible); also, freeborn persons were now employed as procuratores. As with tutors, procurators could acquire possession and (through the acquisition of possession) ownership for the principal.[139] As in the case of the institor and the magister navis, contractual rights acquired by the procurator were also granted to the principal as actiones utiles.[140] Eventually, Papinian also made the principal liable for the debts incurred by the procurator in connection with the range of activities for which he was appointed: he

---

[135] Gai. IV, 71; Ulp. D. 14, 1, 1, 4; Ulp. D. 14, 3, 7, 1.

[136] Liability in solidum = several persons owe one performance in such a manner that each of them is bound to effect the whole performance, but the creditor is entitled to demand the performance only once. Cf. today, for example, § 421 BGB.

[137] Cf. Marcell./Ulp. D. 14, 3, 1; Paul. D. 46, 5, 5.

[138] Piero Angelini, *Il procurator* (1971); Okko Behrends, "Die Prokuratur", (1971) 88 *ZSS* 215 sqq.; Hamza, (1983) 25 *Acta Juridica Academiae Scientiarum Hungaricae* 97 sqq.; J.-H. Michel, "Quelques observations sur l'évolution du procurator en droit romain", in: *Études offertes à Jean Macqueron* (1970), pp. 515 sqq.; Kaser, *RPr* II, pp. 100 sq.; idem, (1974) 91 *ZSS* 186 sqq.; Renato Quadrato, "D. 3, 3, 1 pr. e la definizione di 'procurator'" (1974) 20 Labeo 210 sqq.; idem, *ED*, vol. 38, pp. 422 sqq.; Watson, *Obligations*, pp. 193 sqq.

[139] Cf., for example, Gai. II, 95; (on which, see Claus, *Stellvertretung*, pp. 174 sqq., but also Quadrato, *ED*, vol. 38, pp 426 sqq.); *Inst.* II, 9, 5. Nomination by the procurator determined whether he or his principal acquired: see MacCormack, (1976) 23 *RIDA* 191 sqq.

[140] Pap./Ulp. D. 19, 1, 13, 25.

advocated an analogous application of the actio institoria to the free procurator as actio ad exemplum institoriae actionis.[141]

Finally, exceptions to the rule against agency were admitted with regard to certain honorarian obligations (precarium, receptum nautarum, etc.).[142] Another rule is probably attributable to Greek influence: if somebody gave a loan on behalf of another person, the action against the borrower to reclaim what had been handed over (the "condictio") was granted to that other person.[143] Very liberal rules were applied in the cognitio extra ordinem procedure.[144]

4. The erosion of the rule against agency

Thus far we have been looking at classical law. West-Roman vulgar law[145] brought about considerable changes and some (dogmatically and conceptually crude) advancement towards the recognition of agency. That was due partly to certain transformations in the legal position of those persons who were used to act on behalf of others, partly to a lack of comprehension and appreciation of the formalistic inhibitions that had prevented the lawyers in earlier times from allowing extranei to act for each other. East-Roman classicism, however, frowned upon these developments and went back to the classical rules. Only in some minor respects did Justinian advance and consolidate the position.[146] Merely on the basis of the Corpus Juris Civilis, it was therefore hardly possible in later ages to argue for the general recognition of agency. "Generale est, ex alterius stipulatione alteri accionem non queri",[147] had to be the general principle at times when Roman law enjoyed supreme

---

[141] Pap. 14, 3, 19 pr.; Pap./Ulp. D. 19, 1, 13, 25; Pap./Ulp. D. 17, 1, 10, 5; Ernst Rabel, "Ein Ruhmesblatt Papinians", in: *Festschrift für Ernst Zitelmann* (1913); Claus, *Stellvertretung*, pp. 259 sqq.; Quadrato, *ED*, vol. 38, pp. 431 sqq.; Benke, (1988) 105 *ZSS* 607 sqq.

[142] Cf., for example, Ulp. D. 43, 26, 6, 1; Ulp. D. 4, 9, 1, 3.

[143] Cf. e.g. Afr./Ulp. D. 12, 1, 9, 8; Scaev. D. 39, 5, 35, 2; Paul. D. 45, 1, 126, 2; Kaser, (1974) 91 *ZSS* 177 sqq.; Ulrich von Lübtow, "Die Darlehensgewährung durch den Prokurator", in: *Studi in onore di Edoardo Volterra*, vol. I (1971), pp. 149 sqq.; Fritz Pringsheim, *Der Kauf mit fremdem Geld* (1916), p. 109.

[144] Ulp. D. 14, 1, 1, 18; Paul. D. 14, 5, 8. On the cognitio extra ordinem, the latest form of civil proceedings in Roman law, which was first concurrent with, but later replaced the formulary procedure, cf. Kaser, *RZ*, pp. 339 sqq., pp. 410 sqq.; Honsell/Mayer-Maly/Selb, pp. 557 sqq.

[145] Levy, *Obligationenrecht*, pp. 60 sqq. On the post-classical developments, see also Sandro Angelo Fusco, "*Pecuniam commodare*" (1980), pp. 44 sqq.

[146] Cf. the details in Kaser, *RPr* II, pp. 99 sqq.; Claus, *Stellvertretung*, pp. 337 sqq. Probably the most important change related to the acquisition of possession (and through possession, ownership) through extranei which was now no longer restricted to tutores and procuratores, but generally admitted: *Inst.* II, 9, 5; C. 7, 32, 1. This generalization, however, possibly dates back already to late classical times: cf. Alan Watson, "Acquisition of Ownership by 'traditio' to an 'extraneus' " (1967) 33 *SDHI* 189 sqq.; Kaser, (1974) 91 *ZSS* 194 sq.

[147] Irnerius, "gl. danda ad D. 3, 3, 27, 1", in: Enrico Besta, *L'opera d'Irnerio*, vol. II (1896), p. 42.

authority.[148] Even canon law, in accordance with "ecclesia vivit lege Romana",[149] did not abandon the principle of "alteri stipulari nemo potest",[150] although the Church clearly favoured representation as an essential element of Christian life and belief.[151] Down to the 19th century there were legal writers who regarded it as irreconcilable with the nature of an obligation for a contractual right to arise directly in the person of a third party. The "principal" (mandator) could acquire that right only through a cession by the "agent" (mandatary).[152]

On the other hand, of course, the scene was set for a gradual erosion of the rule against agency. Already the commentators formed stratagems to bypass it under certain circumstances: they argued, for instance, that an actio utilis should be granted to the principal in all the cases where the actio directa could not be ceded.[153] Also, one finds attempts to water down the relevance of the procurator's, magister navis's and institutor's obligation: with the termination of their office it would fall away.[154] According to Martinus Gosia[155] (whose opinion, however, did not gain acceptance)[156] the prohibition of Roman law

---

[148] Especially at the time of the glossators and the humanists. For a general discussion, see Coing, pp. 423 sqq.; J.C. de Wet, " 'n Bydrae tot die geskiedenis van die ontwikkeling van direkte verteenwoordiging by die sluiting van ooreenkomste", (1942) 6 *THRHR* 99 sqq., 210 sqq.; Müller, op. cit., note 43, pp. 29 sqq.; Paolo Cappellini, "Rappresentanza", in: *ED*, vol. 38 (1987), pp. 435 sqq.; Hasso Hofmann, *Repräsentation* (1974), pp. 152 sqq.; for the more modern history, see Wolfram Müller-Freienfels, "Die Abstraktion der Vollmachterteilung im 19. Jahrhundert", in: Helmut Coing, Walter Wilhelm (eds.), *Wissenschaft und Kodifikation des Privatrechts im 19. Jahrhundert*, vol. II (1977), pp. 144 sqq. For a discussion of the (comparative) history of agency, see also Gualtiero Procaccia, "On the History of Agency", (1976) 2 *Tel Aviv University Studies in Law* 56 sqq.

[149] See, for example, Adalbert Erler, in *HRG*, vol. I (1971), cols. 798 sq.

[150] The oft-quoted brocard (esp. in English law) "qui facit per alium, facit per se" goes back to two regulae contained in the Liber Sextus, Lib. V, Tit. XII, De regulis iuris LXVIII and LXXII (Bonifacius VIII). It was, however, hardly more than a guideline and did not establish a legal rule about agency (in private law) which would have abrogated the Roman principle. Cf. Hermann Lange, (1956) 73 *ZSS* 286 sqq.; Müller, op. cit., note 43, pp. 62 sqq., but see also Procaccia, (1976) 2 *Tel Aviv University Studies in Law* 70 sqq.

[151] One may think, for instance, of Christ's death as satisfactio vicaria for Adam's fall (likewise a peccatum vicarium) or of the Pope as vicarius Christi. Also the hierarchical structure of the Church has always necessitated acting for others. For details cf., for example, J. Ratzinger, "Stellvertretung", in: H. Fries (ed.), *Handbuch theologischer Grundbegriffe* (1963), vol. II, pp. 566 sqq.; Hofmann, op. cit., note 148, pp. 47 sqq., 116 sqq. and passim; Settimio Carmignani Caridi, *Rappresentanza*, in: *ED*, vol. 38 (1987), pp. 485 sqq. On the development of agency in the early canon law, cf. Anton Kradepohl, *Stellvertretung und katholisches Eherecht* (1964), pp. 28 sqq. On agency in the conclusion of a marriage according to canon law, see Kradepohl, pp. 64 sqq.

[152] Cf. Vangerow, *Pandekten*, § 608 (vol. III, pp. 293 sqq.); Mühlenbruch, *Doctrina Pandectarum*, § 131.

[153] ". . . in his quae adeo sunt personalia, quod ex persona procuratoris non possunt transire in dominum procurator repraesentat persona domini directo sicut nuncius": Bartolus, *Commentaria*, D. 39, 2, 13, § Si alieno, 3. This thought was based on texts such as Ulp. D. 14, 3, 1; Paul. D. 46, 5, 5; vide supra, note 137.

[154] Cf. e.g. Bartolus, *Commentaria*, D. 3, 3, 67, § Procurator qui pro evictione.

[155] Cf. supra, p. 41 (note 49).

[156] But it was approved and taken over in the 16th century by Franciscus Hotomanus; cf. the analysis by Müller, op. cit., note 43, pp. 96 sq.

related only to the acquisition of the actio directa by the third party and not to the acquisition of an actio utilis. Throughout the centuries lawyers attempted to find ways and means of extending whatever approximated agency in the Digest. Friedrich-Carl von Savigny, for instance, used the institution of nuntius to try to show that the Romans had recognized agency;[157] furthermore, he alleged that the "alteri stipulari nemo potest" rule had been applied only to stipulations: since stipulations no longer existed, the rule had, for all practical purposes, been abrogated and therefore did not stand in the way of agency.[158, 159]

5. The evolution of the modern concept of agency

By this time, however, despite all the theoretical disputes, the institution of agency was firmly entrenched in practice. The needs of the expanding commerce had, since the Middle Ages, been the most important impetus for the recognition of this device; also, the changes in economic, political and social structures[160] somehow had to be accommodated. It is therefore hardly surprising to find the "alteri stipulari nemo potest" principle already abandoned in the statutes of the upper Italian city states, those early centres of flourishing trade and commerce,[161] and then in 17th century Roman-Dutch jurisprudence.[162] Even though the Dutch authors did not yet distinguish between agency and stipulatio alteri, they carved out and emphasized some aspects which to us are of fundamental importance for the law of agency today: the agent's acts *directly* bind the principal (Ulrich Huber:[163] "Moribus hodiernis ut obligatio immediate per alium cui mandatum dedimus in nos transit, ita nec dubium est"); the agent must have acted in the name of the principal (Johannes Voet:[164] ". . . quas [actiones] tamen nostris moribus cedi haud opus, quoties mandatarium non suo, sed mandantis nomine contraxisse expressum est; . . . si suo nomine procurator contraxerit, cessionem actiones fieri necesse est");[165] and the principal is

---

157 *Obligationenrecht*, vol. II, § 57.

158 *Obligationenrecht*, vol. II, § 56.

159 On the relationship and mutual impact of the actio de in rem verso and agency, see Kupisch, *Versionsklage*, pp. 30 sqq.

160 It is rather surprising to see how, for instance, some of the humanists condemned slavery as not being reconcilable with the Christian teaching, but nevertheless extensively discussed and regarded as binding the sources of Roman law relating to the legal position of slaves (for instance, in the present context, as one of the exceptions to "alteri stipulari nemo potest"). But see, on the other hand, Simon van Leeuwen (*Censura Forensis*, Pars I, Lib. II, Cap. XII, n. 2), who argued that since slavery had been abolished, the Roman rules relating to acquisition through slaves had to be applied to those free persons ("famulos, et ministros liberos homines, qui nobis operis suis inserviunt") who had taken their place.

161 Cf. analysis and references in Müller, op. cit., note 43, pp. 55 sqq.

162 Cf. De Wet, (1942) 6 *THRHR* 210 sqq.; D.J. Joubert, *Die Suid-Afrikaanse Verteenwoordigingsreg* (1979), pp. 13 sqq.

163 *Disputationes Iuris Fundamentales* (Franequerae, 1688), Disp. LI, n. 9.

164 *Commentarius ad Pandectas*, Lib. XVII, Tit. I, IX.

165 In the same passage, Voet, incidentally, compares procuratores and nuntii: ". . . quia procuratores hodie in negotiis contrahendis considerantur magis ut nuncii." This has been

not only an additional debtor but he is liable *in the place of* the agent (Simon van Leeuwen: "A quibus tamen moribus nostris in tantum receditur, ut non in institores aut praepositos directa detur actio, sed adversus ipsos Dominos praeponentes agi debeat, qui institorum nomine tenentur, nisi cum iis sit actum quos institores aut praepositos suos negant").[166]

Whilst the writers of the Dutch jurisprudence, and later on also of the German usus modernus pandectarum, argued from the point of view of commercial practice and the mores hodierni, it was left to the natural lawyers (who subjected Roman law to criticism from the point of view of natural justice) to break away decisively from the principle of "alteri stipulari nemo potest" and to lay the conceptual cornerstones for the future.[167] This state of affairs is reflected in the first wave of codifications inspired by natural law and enlightenment.[168] In the course of the 19th century, the conceptual framework was further refined. Brinz[169] and Windscheid[170] firmly established the so-called representation theory: it is the agent's will (not the principal's as expressed through the agent) that is necessary for the conclusion of the contract. Thus, the agent is not to be regarded as some sort of juristic organ through which the principal acts.[171] As a consequence of this perspective, the requirements for the validity of the contract concluded through the agent (as, for instance, whether there was fraud, duress or error) have to be judged with a view to the person of the agent, not the principal.[172] Paul Laband[173] eventually introduced the conceptual distinction between the grant of authority and the legal relationship giving rise to it (mandate). This became known as the doctrine of

translated by Percival Gane (*The Selective Voet*, vol. III (1956) in the following way: ". . . because agents are rather regarded today in making business contracts as messengers." On that basis, Voet's opinion has been criticized in (1910) 27 *SALJ* 385. According to Müller, op. cit., note 43, p. 109, Voet is saying that the agent is more than a nuntius.

[166] *Censura Forensis*, Pars I, Lib. IV, Cap. III, n. 10.

[167] Cf. supra, pp. 43, 45 sq., and Müller, op. cit., note 43, pp. 123 sqq. This was then also taken over in the usus modernus, cf. e.g. Leyser, *Meditationes ad Pandectas*, Spec. DXIX; for France, see Pothier, *Traité des obligations*, nn. 74 sqq. For details of the development, see, in particular, Coing, pp. 426 sqq., 429 sq.; Cappellini, *ED*, vol. 38, pp. 447 sqq.

[168] Cf. § 85 I 13 PrALR; §§ 1002 sqq. ABGB; Theil 4, Cap. 9, § 7 Codex Maximilianeus; § 788 Sächsisches Gesetzbuch; artt. 1984, 1998 code civil.

[169] Brinz, *Pandekten*, § 371.

[170] Windscheid/Kipp, § 73 (pp. 350 sqq.).

[171] This had been Savigny's opinion (*Obligationenrecht*, vol. II, §§ 54 sqq., 57, 59) ("*Geschäftsherrntheorie*"; organ theory); for an analysis, see Heinz Mohnhaupt, "Savignys Lehre von der Stellvertretung", (1979) 8 *Ius Commune* 60 sqq.; cf. for England also Stoljar, op. cit., note 93, pp. 14 sq.

[172] Cf., for example, § 166 BGB; Flume, *AT*, § 43, 3. This is also the situation pertaining in modern Roman-Dutch law; see, for example, De Wet en Yeats, p. 87 sq.; Joubert, op. cit., note 162, pp. 24 sqq.

[173] "Die Stellvertretung bei dem Abschluss von Rechtsgeschäften nach dem Allgemeinen Deutschen Handelsgesetzbuch", (1866) 10 *ZHR* 183 sqq.

abstraction in agency,[174] on which the BGB and most subsequent codifications of private law around the world are based.[175] Whilst the mandate relates to the (internal) relationship between principal and agent, the grant of authority determines the (external) relationship between the principal and the other party with whom the agent concludes the contract. Both acts are independent of each other: there can be a mandate without grant of authority, just as it is possible to have a grant of authority without mandate. Not much differently, English law distinguishes between agency as a contract engendering rights and duties and as a transfer of authority;[176] it does not, however, put this insight to any systematic use.[177] In modern Roman-Dutch law, the concept of authorization as an abstract (unilateral) juristic act[178] is still vying with the traditional view of agency as one of the specific contracts ("mandat"), namely "*un acte par lequel une personne donne une autre le pouvoir de faire quelque chose pour le mandant et en son nom*".[179]

III. CESSION

1. Nomina ossibus inhaerent

Finally, assignment (cession)![180] "Nomina ossibus inhaerent" said the medieval lawyers in their metaphorical way:[181] the action arising from the obligation hinges on the bones and entrails of the creditor and can no more be separated from his person than the soul from the body. If the obligation is something highly personal, a vinculum iuris that attains its individuality by virtue of having been created between two specific parties, it is clear that it could not be regarded as transferable in

[174] Cf. especially Müller-Freienfels, in: *Wissenschaft und Kodifikation*, op. cit., note 148, pp. 144 sqq.; for a comparative view, see also Procaccia, (1976) 2 *Tel Aviv University Studies in Law* 81 sqq.; Gerd Justus Albrecht, *Vollmacht und Auftrag* (unpublished Dr. iur. thesis, Kiel, 1970), passim.

[175] Cf. e.g. §§ 164 sqq. BGB; artt. 1387 sqq. codice civile; §§ 211 sqq. Civil Code (Greece). For a comparative analysis of agency in modern civil-law systems, see Wolfram Müller-Freienfels, "The Law of Agency", in: A.N. Yiannopoulos (ed.), *Civil Law in the Modern World* (1965), pp. 77 sqq.

[176] Cf., for example, Fridman, op. cit., note 94, pp. 8 sqq.

[177] Zweigert/Kötz/Weir, p. 101. On the history of agency (and its relationship with the privity requirements of modern contractual doctrine), see, most recently, Palmer, (1989) 33 *American Journal of Legal History* 28 sqq.

[178] J.C. De Wet, "Agency and Representation", in: Joubert (ed.), *The Law of South Africa*, vol. I (1976), n. 115.

[179] These are the words of art. 1984 code civil. They are based on Pothier, *Traité des obligations*, nn. 74 sqq. In South African law this view is maintained by A.J. Kerr, *The Law of Agency* (1979), pp. 1 sqq., 15 sqq., whose whole treatise is, in turn, greatly influenced by Pothier. (The *Traité du contrat de mandat* has, incidentally, been translated into English: B.G. Rogers, *Pothier's Treatise on the Contract of Mandate* (1979).)

[180] The word "assignment" is derived from assignare (assignatio), cession from cedere (cessio). Only the latter expression occurs in the Roman sources (C. 4, 35, 22 sq.).

[181] Cf., for example, Azo, *Summa Codicis*, ad C. 4, 10 (p. 118, left col.); cf. Erich Genzmer, "Nomina ossibus inhaerent", in: *Mélanges Philippe Meylan*, vol. I (1963), pp. 159 sqq.

early and classical Roman law: the claims were taken as being inseparably related to the one individual creditor–debtor relationship.[182] However, each society in which commerce plays a role sooner or later has to face a strong demand to increase the circulation of credit; to us today it is a matter of course that the right to claim, i.e. the expectation to receive what is owed, constitutes an asset within the estate of the creditor,[183] which he should be able to sell, to exchange, or to donate and which, therefore, has to be easily transferable. All modern legal systems do indeed provide some way in which such a transfer can be effected.[184] Thus, the BGB boldly provides that "a claim may, by contract with another person, be assigned by the creditor to him (assignment). On the conclusion of the contract the assignee takes the place of the assignor."[185] Other systems have not gone quite so far: the code civil, for instance, attributes only a relative effect to the assignment—the agreement to assign the claim is valid between assignor and assignee; as far as third parties are concerned, the assignee is regarded as having acquired the claim only once the debitor cessus has been formally (i.e. through the agency of a bailiff) notified of the assignment, or if he has "accepted" the assignment by judicial or notarial document.[186] But how did Roman law manage to do without cession? In order to accommodate the needs of commercial life the lawyers availed themselves of two other legal institutions to achieve

[182] Cf. Schulz, *CRL*, p. 628: "It could not be otherwise. A law in which execution on the person of the debtor is a living institution cannot allow a creditor to transfer his right to another without the consent of the debtor, thereby perhaps substituting a harsh creditor for a mild one." For the same consideration in Jewish law, see S.J. Bailey, "Assignment of Debts in England from the Twelfth to the Twentieth Century", (1931) 47 *LQR* 535.

[183] Cf. already Hugo Donellus, *Commentarii de Jure Civili*, Lib. XV, Cap. XLIV, VIII ("Nam et hae sunt in bonis nostris").

[184] Cf. the analysis in Zweigert/Kötz/Weir, pp. 108 sqq.

[185] § 398 BGB. As to the history of this section cf. Klaus Luig, *Zur Geschichte der Zessionslehre* (1966), pp. 100 sqq., 130 sqq. In the civil-law systems we speak of singular succession to obligations (as opposed to the universal succession of the heir). The assignment is usually based on a sale of the right: the contract of sale provides the obligationary agreement to cede or, put differently, the assignment is the real agreement executing the obligation incurred by virtue of the sale of the right. (The situation is thus similar to the sale of corporeal objects, where both traditio and a "real" agreement are necessary to transfer ownership; cf. infra, p. 239). This applies to legal systems (such as the German and the South African) which require an act separate from the obligationary contract (e.g. of sale) to transfer the right. The matter is different in French law, where ownership of corporeal objects passes on account of the contract of sale. Consequently, the French Code also deals with *cession de créance* in the context of the law of contract.

[186] Artt. 1689 sq. code civil. These provisions are based on the writings of Domat and Pothier and, through them, ultimately on the *Coutume de Paris* (with the famous rule: *un simple transport ne saisit point*—a mere cession does not place the "assignee" in "possession" of the claim); cf. Frans Heinrich Grosskopf, *Die geskiedenis van die sessie van vorderingsregte* (1960), pp. 78 sqq. Even though they have been not inconsiderably modified by the courts, they have proved to be too cumbersome for commercial practice. Both legislator and courts have found ways to get around them, as, for instance, by using the institution of *"subrogation personnelle"* (artt. 1249 sqq.). Cf. Ghestin, "La transmission des obligations en droit français positif", in: *La transmission des obligations* (IXes Journées d'étude juridique Jean Dabin, 1980), pp. 3 sqq., 36 sqq.

results similar to an assignment: novation and procedural representation.[187]

2. The use of novation and procuratio in rem suam

"[N]am quod mihi ab aliquo debetur, id si velim tibi deberi . . . opus est ut iubente me tu ab eo stipuleris; quae res efficit ut a me liberetur et incipiat tibi teneri; quae dicitur novatio obligationis";[188] the old creditor would authorize the debtor to assume a new obligation towards a third party. This was called a delegatio obligandi[189] and had a novatory effect in so far as the new obligation replaced the old one. "Quod Titio (Titius being the old creditor) debes, mihi dari spondesne?" would be the question of the new creditor, and with the debtor's answer, "spondeo", the transaction was concluded. The new obligation had exactly the same content as the old one (idem debitum), but contained one new element (novum),[190] namely the change of creditors. Compared to a straightforward assignment of a right, this way of proceeding had three obvious disadvantages: as we are dealing with a novation, the new obligation had to be couched in the form of a stipulatio, which might not always be convenient; as the debtor had to be party to the new stipulation, the success of the whole transaction depended on his co-operation; and as the old obligation was not transferred but extinguished, all accessory security rights which might have been created automatically lapsed and had to be constituted anew.

These disadvantages could be avoided if the (old) creditor appointed the person to whom he wanted to transfer the claim as his cognitor or procurator in rem suam,[191] i.e. he authorized the "assignee" to sue the

---

[187] Cf. esp. Biondo Biondi, "Cessione di crediti e di altri diritti", in: *Novissimo Digesto Italiano*, vol. III (1959), pp. 152 sqq.; Luig, op. cit., note 185, pp. 2 sqq.; Georg H. Maier, "Zur Geschichte der Zession", in: *Festschrift für Ernst Rabel*, vol. II (1954), pp. 205 sqq.; Wladyslaw Rozwadowski, "Studi sul trasferimento dei crediti in diritto romano", (1973) 76 *BIDR* 11 sqq. On the possibility of achieving a change of creditors by way of an oath (iusiurandum), see Fritz Sturm, "Der Eid im Dienste von Abtretung und Schuldübernahme", in: *Studi in onore di Gaetano Scherillo*, vol. II (1972), pp. 514 sqq.

[188] Gai. II, 38.

[189] Paolo Cosentino, "Osservazioni in tema di mandatum e di delegatio", (1966) 69 *BIDR* 299 sqq.; Wolfgang Endemann, *Der Begriff der Delegatio im klassischen Römischen Recht* (1958).

[190] Ulp. D. 46, 2, 1 pr.: "Novatio est prioris debiti in aliam obligationem vel civilem vel naturalem transfusio atque translatio, hoc est cum ex praecedenti causa ita nova constituatur, ut prior peremätur novatio enim a novo nomen accepit et a nova obligatione." Cf. also Gai. III, 176 and Kaser, *RPr* I, pp. 647 sqq.

[191] The power to act as cognitor was conferred by formal declaration upon the procedural opponent (cf. e.g. Gai. IV, 83). The appointment of a procurator in rem suam required neither a formal act nor a declaration to the procedural opponent; an internal arrangement between dominus litis and procurator was sufficient. Cf. Kaser, *RZ*, pp. 152 sqq. On the role of "paraprofessional" cognitores within the Roman judicial system, see Frier, *Roman Jurists*, pp. 65 sqq.

debtor in his own name[192] and to keep whatever he received. Thus the "assignee" acted "in rem suam" for his own benefit. This authorization is often referred to as a mandatum ad agendum. The term "mandate", however, should be used with circumspection, as in the present context it does not refer to the consensual contract of mandatum,[193] but is an untechnical equivalent of the terminus technicus "iussum".[194] While procedural representation of this type could largely achieve the economic results of an assignment, without being dependent on the co-operation of the debtor, it had certain other drawbacks: the "assignor", after all, remained creditor and could, by instituting a claim himself, by accepting the debtor's performance, by releasing the debtor from his obligation, etc., still frustrate the purpose of the whole transaction. This situation changed only once litis contestatio had taken place: due to what has sometimes been called the "novatio necessaria" connected with the founding of the trial,[195] the new creditor now replaced the old one.[196] Up to the time of litis contestatio the "assignor" could also freely revoke the "assignee's" authority to sue.[197] Furthermore, the iussum ad agendum in rem suam possibly came to an end with the death of either of the two parties.[198] This somewhat precarious situation of the "assignee" was to a certain extent ameliorated by means of a cautio: the old creditor had to promise by way of stipulation (to which a penalty could be attached)[199] not to

---

[192] "Sine vero hac novatione non poteris tuo nomine agere, sed debes ex persona mea quasi cognitor aut procurator meus experiri": Gai. II, 39. Cf. Wulf-Dieter Gehrich, *Kognitur und Prokuratur in rem suam als Zessionsformen des klassischen römischen Rechts* (1963); Rozwadowski, (1973) 76 *BIDR* 39 sqq.

[193] The contract of mandatum would be invalid, because the whole transaction is "tua tantum gratia", cf. infra, p. 422.

[194] Cf. Kaser, *RPr* I, pp. 265 sq., 653. Thus, a distinction has to be drawn between the authority as such (iussum) and the causal transaction giving rise to the granting of such authority, e.g. the purchase of the claim (or, in the case of procuratio in rem alienam a mandatum stricto sensu).

[195] In the case of iudicia legitima and as far as actiones in personam were concerned, litis contestatio had the effect of extinguishing the cause of action (dare facere oportere) and replacing it by a condemnari oportere, the defendant's subjection to the possible condemnation (actio consumitur): Gai. III, 180. The similarity to novation is obvious. One of the differences, however, lies in the fact that accessory rights did not fall away with the extinction of the old obligation: cf., for example, Marci. D. 20, 1, 13, 4 for hypotheka.

[196] Whether litis contestatio had this effect only in regard to a cognitor or also to a procurator in rem suam is disputed: cf. Gehrich, op. cit., pp. 74 sqq.; Rozwadowski, (1973) 76 *BIDR* 97 sqq.

[197] Cf. Paul. D. 3, 3, 16, 7; Paul. D. 3, 3, 42, 2.

[198] That does not already follow from the intransmissibility of the contract of mandatum, for we are concerned here with a iussum. As to the death of the dominus litis, see Ulp. D. 3, 3, 15 pr., a text which has since the times of the French humanist, Antonius Faber, often been regarded as spurious—the question is very controversial: Gehrich, op. cit., note 192, pp. 28 sqq.; Grosskopf, op. cit., note 186, pp. 9 sqq.; Maier, op. cit., note 187, pp. 207 sqq.; Rozwadowski, (1973) 76 *BIDR* 70 sqq. For the death of the "assignee", see C. 8, 53, 33 pr.

[199] See Rabel, *Grundzüge*, p. 130.

interfere with the "assignee's" right.[200] However, such a cautio did not, of course, transfer the claim to the "assignee"; legally, the (old) creditor was still able to proceed and thus to upset the position of the "assignee", who in turn could claim only what the "assignor" had recovered from the debt (or the penalty).

3. Post-classical developments, Corpus Juris and ius commune

All in all, while meeting the commercial demand for circulation of claims to a not inconsiderable degree, neither novation nor procedural representation could be regarded as really satisfactory substitutes for assignment. It is, therefore, hardly surprising to find under the imperial law from the time of Antoninus Pius onwards a growing tendency to improve the position of the assignee by making it more independent of the assignor. This was done by the granting of an actio utilis in cases where the mandate to act as cognitor or procurator in rem suam had been terminated due to the death of either of the parties,[201] but (more importantly) also totally independently of any kind of procedural representation: first in a case of purchase of an inheritance,[202] but soon also when an individual claim had been sold,[203] given as a dos,[204] etc. By the time of Justinian,[205] the actio utilis was granted whenever the parties had intended to transfer a claim, no matter what transaction was involved.[206] The assignee was thus no longer claiming as a mere cognitor or procurator, that is, on account of an actio mandata, but in his own right[207]—a right which could no longer be affected by revocation or death. However, the actio utilis did not really transfer the claim either, because the old creditor's actio (directa) continued to exist: if, for instance, the debtor performed towards the creditor, the "assignee's" action was thwarted. On the other hand, the debtor could possibly raise an exceptio doli against the actio directa, which considerably weakened the "assignor's" position.[208] But that was possible only if the debtor knew of the assignment. Such knowledge obviously being in the "assignee's" interest, we find that in

---

[200] Cf. Gai. II, 252; Maier, op. cit., note 187, pp. 218 sqq.; Rozwadowski, (1973) 76 *BIDR* 73 sqq.

[201] C. 4, 10, 1 (Gord.).

[202] Ulp. D. 2, 14, 16 pr.: "Si cum emptore hereditatis pactum sit factum et venditor hereditatis petat, doli exceptio nocet. nam ex quo rescriptum est a divo Pio utiles actiones emptori hereditatis dandas, merito adversus venditorem hereditatis exceptione doli debitor hereditarius uti potest."

[203] Diocl. et Max., C. 4, 39, 8.

[204] Val. et Gall., C. 4, 10, 2.

[205] He closed the last gap by deciding the case that a claim had been donated: C. 8, 53, 33.

[206] Cf. generally Fridolin Eisele, *Die actio utilis des Zessionars* (1887); Max Kaser, "Zum 'pignus nominis' ", (1969) 20 *Iura* 177 sqq.; Rozwadowski, (1973) 76 *BIDR* 124 sqq.

[207] His name would thus appear in the intentio of the formula; in the case of procedural representation, the intentio gives the name of the "assignor", while only the condemnatio is framed in favour of the representative.

[208] Luig, op. cit., note 185, pp. 6 sq.

post-classical East-Roman law the practice of denuntiatio, i.e. a notification of the debtor by the "assignee", gradually became entrenched. Soon the situation was further improved in that the debtor, as a consequence of denuntiatio, could now no longer discharge his obligation by rendering performance towards the old creditor.[209] Details concerning the denuntiatio (did this practice originate in late classical law?; did it have the effect of extinguishing the "assignor's" actio directa?; did the same consequences arise if the debtor obtained notice of the assignment otherwise than by denuntiatio?) are controversial.[210] But if one takes into consideration the breakdown of the classical concept of an "actional law" in post-classical times and the change in meaning, nay pointlessness,[211] of the concept of actiones utiles that went with it, one can say that for all practical purposes assignment as a transfer of the substantive right from the old to the new debtor (i.e. a singular succession to obligations) had become recognized by the time of Justinian.[212]

However, Justinian incorporated into his Corpus Juris Civilis classical sources dealing with procuratores in rem suam, actiones mandatae and utiles and thus juxtaposed as existing law the various stages through which the development of assignment had passed. It is small wonder that this sort of arrangement caused great confusion after the Digest had been rediscovered and Roman law was to be applied again.[213] The glossators,[214] in their attempt to explain and harmonize the conflicting sources by logical means, reverted to the old dogma of the untransferability of rights. How, they argued, could claims be regarded as transferable if one of the most common ways of "ceding" a claim had obviously been the appointment of a procurator in rem suam? The use of this institution would otherwise have been impossible. Also, if up to the time of denuntiatio or litis contestatio payment to the old creditor released the debtor from his obligation, how could that be explained rationally other than by assuming that the "assignor's" claim still existed? As far as the meaning and effect of the

---

[209] Cf. Alex., C. 8, 16, 4; Gord., C. 8, 41, 3 (probably interpolated).

[210] Discussion and references in Rozwadowski, (1973) 76 *BIDR* 91 sqq., 155 sqq.; Luig, op. cit., note 185, pp. 6 sqq. On the significance of the denuntiatio in the ius commune (does "denuntiatio simplex" suffice or is the drawing up—and handing over—of a formal instrument required?; what is the effect of denuntiatio or—in France—insinuatio?), cf. Coing, pp. 447 sq.

[211] As Groenewegen, *Tractatus de legibus abrogatis*, Cod. Lib. VIII, Tit. XLII, l. 3, n. 3, aptly put it: "Sed quemadmodum hodie sublatis actionum formulis, . . . extra ordinem, . . . et suppresso actionum nomine . . . jus dicitur, ideoque directae et utilis actionis distinctio penitus sublata est."

[212] Cf. Levy, *Obligationenrecht*, pp. 155 sqq. In the Codex we find terms such as "actiones transmittere" (C. 8, 53, 33) and "actiones per cessionem transferre" (C. 5, 12, 31 pr.).

[213] For the history of assignment in the European ius commune, see the works by Grosskopf and Luig, also the overview by Coing, pp. 445 sqq.; Bruno Huwiler, *Der Begriff der Zession in der Gesetzgebung seit dem Vernunftrecht* (1975), pp. 1 sqq.; Susanna Johanna Scott, *Sessie in die Suid-Afrikaanse reg* (1977), pp. 4 sqq.

[214] Cf. the analysis by Grosskopf, op. cit., note 186, pp. 43 sqq.

actio utilis and its connection or interrelationship with the actio mandata were concerned, a whole host of theories, hypotheses and speculations were developed.[215] These disputes carried on throughout the centuries; in Germany it was maintained until well into the 19th century that rights, by nature of the concept of an obligatio, could not be regarded as transferable.[216] Christian Friedrich Mühlenbruch tried to show that the introduction of the actio utilis had not, in fact, changed the principle of the "assignee" merely acting as procurator of the "assignor". According to him, the actio utilis had been based on the fiction of a mandate: it was *as if* the "assignee" had been authorized to act as procedural representative.[217] What was transferred was *in any event* never the claim but merely the exercitium actionis. So influential was Mühlenbruch's theory that during the first half of the 19th century it totally dominated the scene.[218] That might seem surprising to us, because he did not make any reference to the sources of Roman law for the fiction which he introduced. But at that time the construction of logically consistent systems was what one aimed for, and axiomatic arguments, based on the nature or essence of a certain concept, and the use of fictions were well-recognized and oft-used tools for that purpose.[219]

4. The turning of the tide

From about 1855, however, the tide was turning. Bernhard Windscheid[220] refuted Mühlenbruch's theory as being conceptually and historically wrong; he showed that the granting of the actio utilis had finally been recognized as a full transfer of the claim. In his view, the assignor ceased to be creditor once the assignee had "taken possession" of this action; i.e. especially if either denuntiatio or litis contestatio had taken place. Otto Bähr[221] went further and argued that denuntiatio was not required for a transfer of the claim; by mere agreement with the

---

[215] Cf. the desperate exclamation by Cacheranus, as quoted by Grosskopf, op. cit., note 186, p. 75: "Videtis igitur, doctissimi Lectores, varias Doctorum opiniones, et doctrinas, a quibus facile se extricare non est, nisi elevemus oculos ad Christum Iesum, Dei veritatem et sapientiam."

[216] Cf., for example, Christian Friedrich Mühlenbruch, *Die Lehre von der Cession der Forderungsrechte* (3rd ed., 1836), p. 22; Mackeldey, *Systema iuris Romani*, § 333; Vangerow, *Pandekten*, § 574, n. 1.

[217] Mühlenbruch, op. cit., note 216, pp. 147 sqq.

[218] As far as the pandectist literature is concerned, cf. Luig, op. cit., note 185, pp. 47 sqq.

[219] Generally on the use of fictions, see Maine, pp. 13 sqq.; Gustav Demelius, *Die Rechtsfiktion in ihrer geschichtlichen und dogmatischen Bedeutung* (1858); Josef Esser, *Wert und Bedeutung der Rechtsfiktionen* (2nd ed., 1969); Lon L. Fuller, *Legal Fictions* (1967); Karl Larenz, *Methodenlehre der Rechtswissenschaft* (5th ed., 1983), pp. 251 sqq.; Peter Birks, "Fictions Ancient and Modern", in: *The Legal Mind, Essays for Tony Honoré* (1986), pp. 83 sqq.; Wieacker, *RR*, pp. 324 sqq.; Tomasz Giaro, "Über methodologische Werkmittel der Romanistik", (1988) 105 *ZSS* 223 sqq.

[220] *Die Actio des römischen Civilrechts vom Standpunkte des heutigen Rechts* (1856), pp. 148 sqq.; also in Windscheid/Kipp, §§ 329 sqq.

[221] "Zur Zessionslehre", (1857) 1 *JhJb* 351 sqq.

assignor the assignee could attain the position of—exclusive—creditor. This agreement, like traditio in the case of corporeal objects, is independent of the obligatory transaction (the causa) on account of which the transfer is effected. This is what was finally incorporated into the BGB.[222]

Even before the time of Mühlenbruch, incidentally, there had for a long time been tendencies to contest the traditional dogma that had been handed down from the glossators to the commentators and from them to the humanists. "Inspecta porro consuetudine existimarim cedentem facta semel cessione nullam penitus retinere actionem, et quicquid juris habuerit in cessionarium transferri": this statement by Lambertus Goris[223] is representative of the practically oriented jurisprudence in the Northern Netherlands during the 17th and 18th centuries;[224] acknowledgment of the needs of commercial practice led to the abrogation, as a matter of customary law, of the Roman doctrines about cession. This view both influenced the usus modernus in Germany[225] and provided the basis for modern South African law.[226] The natural lawyers, too, in opposition to the doctrines espoused by the humanists, recognized assignment as a full transfer of the right. They construed assignment of rights as the transfer of ownership of res incorporales and systematically juxtaposed it with the transfer of ownership of res corporales (which, in their view, also required consensus ad idem between alienor and alienee).[227, 228] This functional parallel between transfer of ownership and assignment, and the idea of a conceptually independent contract effecting the transfer of the right, has also had a lasting effect on the modern civil-law systems.[229] It was

[222] Cf. also already §§ 376 sqq. I 11 PrALR.

[223] *Adversariorum iuris tractatus*, Tract. III, Pars I, Cap. I, 5.

[224] Cf. the analysis by Grosskopf, op. cit., note 186, pp. 103 sqq., 116 sqq.

[225] Vide Johann Schilter, *Praxis iuris Romani in foro Germanico, Francofurti et Lipsiae* (1713), *Exercitatio ad Pand. XXX*, §§ LXII sqq.

[226] Cf. De Wet en Yeats, pp. 225 sqq.; P.M. Nienaber, in: Joubert (ed.), *The Law of South Africa*, vol. II (1977), nn. 324 sqq.; Susanna Johanna Scott, *The Law of Cession* (1980). Very influential in South African practice has been Johann van de Sande's book *De Actionum Cessione*. Being, however, a Frisian author, he can be regarded as authority for Roman-Dutch law strictu senso only with circumspection. The reception of Roman law in Friesland has been more far-reaching than in Holland. The problem of cession provides a good example, for in accordance with what they understood the Roman law to be, both Van de Sande and Ulrich Huber did *not* regard claims as transferable (cf. e.g. Van de Sande, Cap. VIII, 19: "[actio] intra viscera ejus, cui debetur, haere[a]t").

[227] Cf. e.g. Christian Wolff, *Institutiones juris naturae et gentium*, §§ 313 sqq.; Darjes, *Institutiones iurisprudentiae universalis*, §§ 489 sqq. For a detailed analysis, see Huwiler, op. cit., note 213, pp. 45 sqq.

[228] On the concept of cession in the codifications influenced by natural law (Codex Maximilianeus Bavaricus, PrALR and ABGB), see Huwiler, op. cit., note 213, pp. 103 sqq.

[229] Even though we would not today regard the holder of a right as its "owner", assignment (as with transfer of ownership) both in German and South African law is an abstract legal act (abstract, that is, from the obligational agreement; a different view based on the tradition of "cessio sine causa facta non valet" was still adopted, for instance, by Van de Sande, *De Actionum Cessione*, Cap. II, 3). As to the development of the concept of cession

thus only at the end of a long historical development that first the Roman law, and then again the European ius commune, recognized claims as fully transferable items of property.

Two final remarks may be apposite. Once the interests of trade and commerce have been thus accommodated (in that the right of the assignee has been strengthened to the extent that he—and only he—is entitled to claim on account of his agreement with the assignor), the protection of the debtor must become the main concern of the law.[230] After all, he is facing a new creditor without his having had any say in the matter. His interests demand a restriction of the assignee's position in at least two ways: the debtor must not be worse off after the claim has been assigned than he was before, i.e. the assignment must not curtail any defences he might have been able to raise against the assignor;[231] and payment made to the assignor must discharge the obligation, provided the debtor did not know of the assignment.[232] Post-classical Roman law further provided a special protection against professional purchasers of claims who wanted to benefit from the bad economic climate: if they had paid less than the actual amount of the debt when purchasing the claim, they could not recover more from the debtor than they had paid themselves.[233] Like Anastasius, later legislators and courts have from time to time viewed assignment with a somewhat suspicious eye.

The second point is that the same type of development can also be observed in other legal systems. Like Roman law, the old English common law regarded the contractual vinculum iuris as something so personal that the claims arising therefrom could not be transferred to a

---

as an abstact legal act, see Klaus Luig, "Zession und Abstraktionsprinzip", in: Coing/Wilhelm (ed.), *Wissenschaft und Kodifikation des Privatrechts im 19. Jahrhundert*, vol. II (1977), pp. 112 sqq.

230 Cf. especially Luig, in: *Wissenschaft und Kodifikation*, op. cit., note 229, pp. 112 sqq.

231 Cf. Paul. D. 18, 4, 5; § 404 BGB; *Van Zyl v. Credit Corporation of SA Ltd.* 1960 (4) SA 582 (A) at 588F–H. The general principle in South African law, as in German law, seems to be that the position of the debtor must not be adversely affected as a result of the cession: cf. Voet, *Commentarius ad Pandectas*, Lib. XVIII, Tit. IV, XIII; De Wet en Yeats, pp. 231 sq. As to the position of the debtor where assignor and assignee have tried, by means of the assignment, to deprive him of his counterclaims, see the fascinating decision *L.T.A. Engineering Co. Ltd. v. Seacat Investments Ltd.* 1974 (1) SA 747 (A) with a full discussion by Jansen JA of Ulp. D. 3, 3, 33, 5 and Gai. D. 3, 3, 34. Cf. Paul van Warmelo, (1974) 91 *SALJ* 298 sqq.; Zimmermann, *RHR*, pp. 66 sq.

232 Cf. C. 8, 16, 4 (Alex.); § 407 BGB; *Lovell v. Paxinos and Plotkin: in re Union Shopfitters v. Hansen* 1937 WLD 84 at 86. In French practice (since about the 16th century) the debtor has been protected in a different manner: by formalizing the act of cession and requiring "signification" of the debtor. Only such signification (denuntiatio) was seen to transfer the claim; cf. e.g. supra, pp. 59, 63.

233 The lex Anastasiana: C. 4, 35, 22. Cf. still Windscheid/Kipp, § 333; Van de Sande, *De Actionum Cessione*, Cap. XI, and also artt. 1699 sqq. code civil. The rule has not been adopted in the BGB; in South Africa it is regarded as having been abrogated by disuse: cf. *Seaville v. Colley* (1892) 9 SC 39.

third person.[234] However, the old creditor could authorize the "assignee" to sue on his behalf and then to keep the proceeds.[235] This institution of a "power of attorney" served a rather similar function to the Roman procuratio in rem suam. A sophisticated system of transfer of claims had already been developed in the first two hundred years after the Battle of Hastings under the influence of Jewish law—the Jews had soon begun to monopolize the financial business—but had disappeared with the banishment of the Jews at the end of the 13th century.[236] Thus it was left to equity to improve the situation of the "assignee": where a claim enforceable in equity had been assigned, the equity judges allowed him to claim directly in his own name. Where, however, a "legal chose in action"[237] was involved (that is, a right which had to be sued for "at law" before the King's judges), two trials were necessary: the assignee had to obtain a judgment in equity requiring the assignor to tolerate the claim in his name, as well as one "at law" against the debtor. It was only the Judicature Act in 1873 that brought about a long-overdue procedural simplification.[238]

[234] Cf., for example, Holdsworth, *HEL*, vol. VII (2nd ed., 1937), p. 520: ". . . the assignment of such a right of action by the act of two parties was unthinkable."

[235] Pollock and Maitland, vol. II, pp. 224 sq.

[236] On this interesting episode and on the traces that it left in English law (as, for example—possibly—the common-law exceptions in favour of such assignments as concerned the King; the Jews, as the King's villains, were considered to be dealing in his property and on his behalf), see Bailey, (1931) 47 *LQR* 516 sqq. As the reasons for the rejection of the customs of the Jewry (which would have made debts freely assignable) Bailey refers to the unpopularity of their originators, the reaction of a people released from hated oppression, and the obstinate inertia of the common law.

[237] As to this term (which is still in use today), see Holdsworth, *HEL*, vol. VII, pp. 515 sqq.

[238] On the historical development in England, see Percy H. Winfield, "Assignment of Choses in Action in Relation to Maintenance and Champerty", (1919) 35 *LQR* 143 sqq.; Bailey, (1932) 48 *LQR* 248 sqq., 547 sqq. Bailey sums up his analysis in the following words (p. 579): "The history of this subject shows clearly that the common law Courts obstructed the development of a sound and uniform doctrine of assignment. . . . This was due to their inability to harmonize any such doctrine with the general principles which they evolved."

PART II

CHAPTER 3
Stipulatio

1. The classical stipulation

By far the most important of the verbal contracts was the stipulatio.[1] "Verbis obligatio fit ex interrogatione et responsione, veluti: 'dari spondes?' 'spondeo', 'dabis?' 'dabo', 'promittis?' 'promitto', 'fidepromittis?' 'fidepromitto', 'fideiubes?' 'fideiubeo', 'facies?' 'faciam'."[2] Thus a stipulation required question and answer: the future debtor (promisor) would make a certain promise after having been requested by the future creditor (stipulator) to do so. Question and answer had to correspond (so that when the question was "fidepromittis?", the answer could not be "fideiubeo") and had to follow each other immediately (the requirement of "unitas actus"). Of course, the question had to precede the answer. With these essential characteristics, the stipulation was one of the most important and original creations of Roman law.[3] It was based on the "fides Romana" and shows, in the words of Fritz Schulz, "the true Roman predilection for accuracy, brevity and simplicity".[4] It corresponds with the rules—well worth heeding!—stated by Aulus Gellius for dialectics:

> "Legem esse aiunt disciplinae dialecticae, si de quapiam re quaeratur disputeturque atque ibi quid rogere ut respondeas, tum ne amplius quid dicas quam id solum quod es rogatus aut aias aut neges; eamque legem qui non servent, . . . existumantur indoctique esse disputandique morem atque rationem non tenere . . . Indefinitus namque inexplicabilisque sermo fiat, nisi interrogationibus responsionibusque simplicibus fuerit determinatus."[5]

Verbosity begets obscurity, and obscurity gives rise to disputes. If the stipulator is forced to sum up his proposed transaction in a question, its content becomes clear and indisputable. In addition, as the promisor is made to listen to this question and to give an explicit, corresponding answer, there is little room for misunderstanding: much less than where contracts can be concluded inter absentes and/or by signing lengthy documents that have often not been read (let alone understood), such as

---

[1] Others were the dotis dictio and the promissio operarum of a libertus: Gai. III, 95 a, 96; for an overview cf. Albanese, *Atti negoziali*, pp. 68 sqq.; specifically on the promissio operarum libertorum cf. Wolfgang Waldstein, *Operae libertorum* (1986), pp. 239 sqq.

[2] Gai. III, 92; cf. also *Inst.* III, 15 pr. and 1.

[3] Kaser, *RPr* I, p. 538.

[4] *CLR*, p. 474.

[5] *Noctes Atticae*, Lib. XVI, II. ("They say that it is a rule of the dialectic art that if there is inquiry and discussion of any subject and you are called upon to answer a question which is asked, you should answer the question by a simple 'yes' or 'no'. And those who do not observe that rule . . . are thought to be both uneducated and unobservant of the customs and laws of debate . . . For a discussion will become endless and hopelessly involved, unless it is confined to simple questions and answers"; trans. John C. Rolfe, *The Attic Nights of Aulus Gellius*, vol. III (1928), p. 133.)

(for example) modern standard contract forms.[6] This is especially true where the promisor repeats everything spelt out in the question: if the stipulator asks "decem mihi dari spondes?" and the answer is "viginti tibi dari spondeo", it is immediately obvious that no consensus has been reached. Already in Cicero's time[7] it was, however, recognized that the answer could consist of one word. But even then it had to be the right word, namely the exact verb the stipulator had used in his question ("centum mihi dari spondes?"—"spondeo"). The promisor could not, for instance, shrug off the question and thus try to avoid a reflection of its content by simply answering "yes";[8] the Latin language does not provide any equivalent for this abstract affirmation. It made allowance only for the concrete way of affirmatively responding to what had been asked in each particular instance by forming a small sentence consisting at least of subject and verb: an interesting example of how language reflects (or moulds?) a people's mind.[9]

2. Evaluation of the oral formality

The insistence on question and answer with the characteristic repetition of at least a key word (the verb) also made it abundantly clear when a contract had in actual fact been concluded. In modern law it is often difficult to determine whether certain declarations still form part of the preliminary negotiations or are already intended as a binding offer or acceptance. In Rome a question in which "spondes?" (or a similar verb) was used immediately set an imaginary little warning light flickering, because everybody knew then that, by giving the appropriate answer, he would become contractually bound.[10] Furthermore, it is probably fair to say[11] that from a psychological point of view the binding force of a formal oral promise given to the other party in his presence was greater than that of a signature underneath a lengthy and involved document, drafted by the other party: for whilst many people today seem to have an exaggerated reverence for what has been written down, the Roman ideas of fides (supposed to derive from "fit quod *dicitur*") and constantia demanded that a man keep his word, whether it was embodied in a document or not.[12] Quite characteristically, Cicero

---

[6] It is one of the main aims of legislative consumer protection against the "small print" to ensure that special attention is drawn to the standard clauses and that the consumer is provided with a reasonable opportunity to take note of their contents; cf. e.g. § 2 AGBG.

[7] Cf. *Oratio pro A. Caecina* III—7.

[8] The point is made by Rudolf von Jhering, *Geist* II, pp. 556 sqq., quoting J. Christiansen, *Institutionen des römischen Rechts*.

[9] On the attitude of Roman lawyers towards abstraction (reserve and disinclination), see Schulz, *Principles*, pp. 40 sqq.

[10] Cf. also Maine, pp. 193 sq.

[11] See Schulz, *CRL*, p. 474.

[12] Schulz, *Principles*, pp. 223 sqq.; Luigi Lombardi, *Dalla "fides" alla "bona fides"* (1961), pp. 1 sqq.; Harald Fuchs and Ernst Meyer, in: Hans Oppermann (ed.), *Römische Wertbegriffe* (1983), pp. 23 sqq., 529 sqq.; Wieacker, *RR*, pp. 506, 643 sq.

writes: "Fundamentum autem est iustitiae fides, id est dictorum conventorumque constantia et veritas."[13]

To us, today, the disadvantages of the Roman form of stipulation are obvious. To start with, this type of transaction was not accessible to everybody; by virtue of the oral formality, deaf or mute people were excluded.[14] Furthermore, the conclusion of a stipulation required both parties to be present at the same time at the same place.[15] This presented no problem at a time when Rome was still essentially a medium-sized country town and when the range of commercial activities of its inhabitants was fairly limited. But it became increasingly cumbersome with the expansion of the Empire after the second Punic war: even if one takes into consideration that a stipulator could, of course, always send his slaves or sons in power to "represent" him. Thirdly, insistence on the oral form can, in individual cases, lead to harsh results. To deny that a stipulation is valid only because one of the parties had used a wrong word or had sneezed before being able to give his answer might seem inequitable. In fact, we find Justinian pouring scorn upon the subtilitas, scrupulositas and difficultas of the oral solemnities with their rigorous consequences: "multas . . . ambages scrupulososque circuitus correximus", he said, referring proudly to "nuper leg[es] a nobis script[ae]".[16] The formalities which enveloped the classical law were not to his liking.

Finally, what strikes us as odd is that even though the stipulation was a formal act, the parties were not required to put its content in writing; where we refer to formal acts today, we usually have the requirements of writing, notarial authentication or official certification in mind. The reason is that such documents enormously facilitate proof of the conclusion and content of the transaction; to us this is, in fact, one of the main functions of formalities. The Romans, on the other hand, as far as the development of their rules of substantive law was concerned, were surprisingly unconcerned about problems of evidence. Whether certain allegations could be taken as proven in court and how this was to be done was a matter of concern for the iudex, who was appointed by the magistrate, not for the lawyers, who administered the ius civile. In the case of stipulations, Roman fides seems to have afforded sufficient security for the purely oral promise to become a viable and practical institution of Roman law.[17] In this context, one must also take

---

[13] *De officiis*, 1, VII—23.

[14] Gai. III, 105.

[15] Gai. III, 136 (in fine); Paul. *Sent.* V, VII, 2 ("Verborum obligatio inter praesentes non etiam inter absentes contrahitur.").

[16] C. 2, 55, 4, 7; generally on the contemptuous attitude of the Byzantines towards the oral forms of Roman law, see Riccobono/Kerr Wylie/Beinart, pp. 86 sqq.

[17] The necessity for formalities designed to provide evidence may not have been felt so strongly in former times because, until fairly recently, the memory of most people was much more reliable than it is today.

into consideration that sponsio (etymologically descending from σπένδω, to present a drink-offering) had a sacral origin with the promisor being forfeited in case of non-compliance with his promise to the god or goddess who had been invoked.[18] Thus, one can well imagine that many Romans still sensed certain oath-like connotations when using the word "spondeo" at a time when all sacral effects and sanctions had long fallen away. However, during the later Republic a moral decline set in and people were less and less prepared to adjust their lives in accordance with the traditional behaviour patterns based on the old Roman virtues; also, as we have seen in the Gaius fragment quoted above, words other than spondere came to be used—a development largely due to the influence of the increasing number of legal relations with peregrini. Thus, if we look at the development of the practice of stipulations, we find a gradual rise in the use of written documents.[19] Hand in hand with this went a tendency to relax the rigidity of the old law.[20] These two developments will now have to be examined more closely. Whilst their general trend cannot be disputed, it has to be emphasized that many details as to the time when specific decisions were taken and when the classical stipulation started to undergo major transformations are in dispute. Many of the texts in point have been or are still regarded as spurious. It must be borne in mind that Justinian's reform of the law of stipulation is "one of the most imposing that we find in the Corpus Juris".[21] On the one hand, Justinian tried to save the richness of thought and argument that had been tied up with the classical stipulation; thus, he took over many of the old texts dealing with stipulations.[22] On the other hand, of course, he had to take account of the large-scale development of the law that had taken place since then, and in his Corpus Juris he had to accommodate the law and custom of his time. In order to achieve this,

---

[18] On the origin and early history of stipulatio and sponsio, see Okko Behrends, *Der Zwölftafelprozess* (1974), pp. 34 sqq.; David Daube, "Sponsor and the History of Contract", (1946) 62 *LQR* 266 sqq.; Rudolf Düll, "Zur römischen Stipulatio", (1951) 68 *ZSS* 191 sqq.; Jolowicz/Nicholas, pp. 280 sqq.; Kaser, *Altrömisches ius* (1949), pp. 256 sqq.; idem, *RPr* I, pp. 168 sqq.; but cf. also Pierre Cornioley, "De la 'sponsio' à la stipulation: procedure et 'contrat'", in: *Sodalitas, Scritti in onore di Antonio Guarino*, vol. VI (1984), pp. 2891 sqq.

[19] Generally on the increased use of writing in Roman law, see Jolowicz/Nicholas, pp. 414 sqq.; Kaser, *RPr* I, pp. 230 sqq.

[20] "The degeneration of the purely oral stipulation is twofold. On the one hand . . . the strictness of the formal oral requirements is relaxed. . . . On the other hand . . . the oral stipulation eventually disappears from practical use and gives place entirely to the written. This is, indeed, not degeneration at all, but atrophy. It is, moreover, impossible, and is likely to remain so, to determine how far advanced this atrophy was at any particular period": Barry Nicholas, "The Form of the Stipulation in Roman Law", (1953) 69 *LQR* 241.

[21] Riccobono/Kerr Wylie/Beinart, p. 84.

[22] Cf. Levy, *Obligationenrecht*, p. 53: "*Fasziniert von der Mission, als Restaurator der goldenen Zeit des römischen Rechtes in die Geschichte einzugehen, und tief beeindruckt von der lichtvollen Durcharbeitung, die einst der Verbalvertrag empfangen hatte, versucht er durch weite Strecken, die klassische Analyse zu retten.*" (Fascinated by the mission to go down in history as the restorer of the golden age of Roman law and deeply impressed by the inspired manner in which the verbal contract had been shaped, he sought to a large extent to save the classical analysis.)

he used fictions and interpolations. How far he went in the use of the latter method, however, is very difficult to determine.

3. Relaxation of the word formalism

(a) The words to be used

We have already seen that one of the forms of stipulation (namely the one characterized by the use of the word "spondere") was of sacral origin. There may have been a second, non-sacral root to stipulation.[23] But it is also possible that "stipulari", in ancient Roman law, was always connected with an oath (i.e. the act of sponsio).[24] Originally, there were probably further formalities, as can still be seen in the word "promise" (derived from "promittere", literally: "to stretch forward" (sc.: one's hand)). The word "stipulari" itself goes back to "stips", so that some staff ritual was probably involved as well.[25] In the later Roman Republic, however, there was no longer any sign of that. What remained was the simple and convenient oral formality. The sponsio stipulatio was not treated any differently from the other forms, except that its use was restricted to Roman citizens.[26]

Peregrines could use the other verbs mentioned in Gai. III, 92; these then became available to Roman citizens too. There is some dispute as to how far this relaxation of the word formalism went. According to Nicholas,[27] the list given by Gaius represents a numerus clausus: only those verbs could be used to conclude a valid stipulation. One would then have to take "veluti" to mean "as follows" and not translate it as "for example". That is not impossible, but it is unlikely. The prevailing opinion[28] therefore maintains that Gaius, as a good teacher would, merely gave a couple of examples, but that any other verbs could also be used. Indeed, it is difficult to see why "facias?" "facio"—should have been allowed, but not a more specific term describing what type of work had been promised in the individual case. Moreover, even the use of Greek (and possibly also the Punic and Syriac languages) was permissible, provided each of the parties understood the language

---

[23] Cf. e.g. Kaser, *RPr* I, p. 169.

[24] Cf. e.g. Behrends, op. cit., note 24, p. 35.

[25] Or a symbolic binding with a haulm (stipula)? For these and other hypotheses cf., for example, Düll, (1951) 68 *ZSS* 191 sqq.; Detlef Liebs, "Contrarius actus. Zur Entstehung des römischen Erlassvertrags", in: *Sympotica Franz Wieacker* (1970), pp. 134 sq.; Geoffrey MacCormack, "Formalism, Symbolism and Magic in Early Roman Law", (1969) 37 *TR* 453 sqq. Cf. also already *Inst.* III, 15 pr.: "Quae hoc nomine inde utitur, quia stipulum apud veteres firmum appellabatur, forte a stipite descendens."

[26] Gai. III, 93, 94. On the relationship between sponsio and stipulatio, see, most recently, Cornioley, *Scritti Guarino*, vol. VI, pp. 2891 sqq.; Malte Dobbertin, *Zur Auslegung der Stipulation im klassichen römischen Recht* (1987), pp. 45 sqq.

[27] "The Form of the Stipulation in Roman Law", (1953) 69 *LQR* 63 sqq.

[28] Cf. e.g. Annemarie Winkler, "Gaius III, 92", (1958) 5 *RIDA* 603 sqq.; De Zulueta, *Gaius* II, pp. 153 sqq.

used.[29] Of course, question and answer had to correspond, but it seems not even to have been imperative that they had to be in the same language. Thus, for example, the question might have been "ὁμολογεῖς?", the answer the Punic equivalent to "promitto".

(b) *Unitas actus*

Apart from the verb as the key word, unitas actus and correspondence of question and answer were essential elements of the Roman stipulation. Both gave rise to discussions too. As to the first, the rule is stated by Venuleius: "Continuus actus stipulantis et promittentis esse debet . . . et comminus responderi stipulanti oportet. ceterum si post interrogationem aliud acceperit, nihil proderit, quamvis eadem die spopondisset."[30] The compilers, after "debet", added a little gloss: "ut tamen aliquod momentum naturae intervenire possit." One is left to speculate what "a short interval dictated by nature" may have implied: was the promisor allowed to spend a penny before he gave the answer? Or did it refer, for instance, to a sneeze or a bout of coughing? Of course, formalism would have been carried to ridiculous extremes had provision not been made for the latter type of incident. So the promisor was granted a moment of reflection; even a witticism or an elegant quotation was allowed to intervene, so that, for instance, a bit of Vergil that had been recited between question and answer[31] was passed over indulgently as "supervacuus". According to D. 45, 1, 1, 1, Ulpian seems to have gone so far as to accept an intervening absence of the stipulator, provided he had been away only for an "intervallum medium" before returning to hear the answer. But when is an intervallum "medium"? Did it matter whether any other affairs were attended to in the meantime? According to Venuleius, that did invalidate the stipulation; otherwise, that is, where no other business was conducted, he seems to imply that the intervallum might extend to a full day.[32] But this limit is as arbitrary as any other would have been. It is very likely that both Ulpian's medium intervallum and Venuleius' one-day period were interpolated.[33] Classical law probably still required continuous presence of the parties; possibly the question was beginning to be disputed.

(c) *Correspondence between question and answer*

As far as the correspondence between question and answer is concerned, it has been mentioned that the reply could have been in one

---

[29] Ulp. D. 45, 1, 1, 6; Gai. III, 93; *Inst.* III, 15, 1. Thus, in developed law there was no magic in the use of particular words. As to the use of "Poenum . . . vel Assyrium . . . lingua" cf. Riccobono/Kerr Wylie/Beinart, pp. 39 sq.

[30] Ven. D. 45, 1, 137 pr.

[31] "Arma virumque cano" (*Aeneis*, Lib. I, 1); cf. Flor. D. 45, 1, 65 pr.

[32] D. 45, 1, 137 pr.: ". . . ceterum si post interrogationem aliud acceperit, nihil proderit, quamvis eadem die spopondisset."

[33] Riccobono/Kerr Wylie/Beinart, pp. 35 sq.

word. By the time of the later Republic, the promisor did not have to repeat everything said in the question. Throughout the classical period, however, he had to use the same verb as the stipulator. Simply to give a nod of assent was not sufficient; and that Ulpian should have allowed the answer "quid ni" is not credible at all.[34] It was only later that the formal correspondence came to be watered down to that extent. Also, of course, the promisor was not allowed to change the terms of the contract, even though he might have used the correct verb; therefore, if the question had been "intra calendas quintas dabis?", the answer "dabo idibus"[35] was no good. Similarly, the promisor could not introduce a condition ("si illud factum erit, dabo") which had not been part of the question ("dabis?"). But what if the stipulator had asked for the delivery of Pamphilus and had received the answer "Pamphilum et Stichum dabo"? Strictly speaking, question and answer did not correspond. Yet, to regard the whole transaction as invalid seemed to be unduly strict, even to the classical lawyers. After all, as far as Pamphilus was concerned, there had been both question and answer. Thus, by way of fiction, the one stipulation was seen as two separate stipulations, the one referring to Pamphilus and the other to Stichus. This way of looking at things was summed up in the rule "tot stipulationes quot res"[36]—in the law of stipulations, it is to be assumed that as many stipulations have been concluded as there are objects involved. Therefore, whilst the transaction regarding Stichus failed owing to the lack of a question, there was a valid stipulation with regard to Pamphilus.[37] It is tempting to apply a similar type of reasoning where the discrepancy between question and answer related not to the number of objects involved but to a sum of money:

> "Si stipulanti mihi 'decem' tu 'viginti' respondeas, non esse contractam obligationem nisi in decem constat. ex contrario quoque si me 'viginti' interrogante tu 'decem' respondeas, obligatio nisi in decem non erit contracta: licet enim oportet congruere summam, attamen manifestissimum est viginti et decem inesse."[38]

The argument is here not "tot stipulationes quot res", but "in maiore minus inest", a rather plausible maxim which we come across repeatedly in the Digest.[39] Whether it was applied in classical law in a

---

[34] D. 45, 1, 1, 2: "Si quis ita interroget 'dabis?' responderit 'quid ni?' et is utique in ea causa est, ut obligetur: contra si sine verbis adnuisset."

[35] Cf. the example given in Ulp. D. 45, 1, 1, 3.

[36] Ulp. D. 45, 1, 29 pr.; D. 45, 1, 86; Paul. D. 45, 1, 140 pr.; cf. Schmidlin, *Rechtsregeln*, pp. 73 sq.

[37] Ulp. D. 45, 1, 1, 5: ". . . Stichi adiectionem pro supervacuo habendam puto: . . . duae sunt quodammodo stipulationes, uni utilis, alia inutilis, neque vitiatur utilis per hanc inutilem."

[38] Ulp. D. 45, 1, 1, 4.

[39] Cf., for example, Wunner, *Contractus*, pp. 204 sq.; Hans Josef Wieling, *Testamentsauslegung im römischen Recht* (1972), pp. 92 sq., 125 sq., 266. For details of the application and significance of this maxim cf., in particular, Ralph Backhaus, "In maiore minus inest", (1983) 100 *ZSS* 136 sqq.

case such as this is, however, extremely doubtful; for, in contrast to the previous example, where Pamphilus was mentioned in both question and answer, there is no longer any *formal* correspondence where the question is for ten and the reply for twenty, or vice versa; on the other hand, there is, however, *substantive* correspondence concerning part of the performance. "Nisi in decem" and the whole passage from "licet" to "inesse" may well have been interpolated;[40] however, one cannot exclude the possibility that our text represents a view already held in late classical jurisprudence.[41]

4. Excursus: utile per inutile non vitiatur

(a) Partial invalidity in Roman law

It is convenient, at this point, to pause for a little while and to consider the concluding phrase of Ulp. D. 45, 1, 1, 5: "neque vitiatur utilis per hanc inutilem." Innocuous and insignificant as it might look, this little sentence certainly made history. It addresses the question whether the one stipulation ("Pamphilum dari spondes?"—"Spondeo"), in itself valid, might not have to be regarded as invalid because the other one (to which there is only the answer: "Stichum dari spondeo") is invalid. Both stipulations, as will be remembered, were not only part and parcel of a single transaction, but had in actual fact been drawn together in one single act. Thus, one could have argued that invalidity of part of the act leads to invalidity of the whole transaction. This, however, is not the answer given by Ulpianus. The valid stipulation, in his view, remains unaffected by the invalidity of part of the transaction. One must be cautious not to take this (as was indeed done in later ages) as the basis for a hard-and-fast rule governing the question of partial invalidity of a legal transaction: Ulpian's comment relates to this one specific case only ("hanc inutilem"). While, therefore, it would not be true to say that the whole idea of partial invalidity is of post-classical origin,[42] it would be equally incorrect to assume that the classical lawyers had pinpointed the problem of partial invalidity as such and subjected the various cases to a general rule. Rather, they tackled the cases as they arose, adapting the result and reasoning to the individual circumstances.[43] No abstraction was attempted. We do, however, find a tendency to uphold the transaction without its invalid part, wherever possible. The Digest preserves a variety of examples: a piece of land has been sold, but it transpires that the parties failed to reach agreement with regard to a slave who was to be transferred as part of the

---

[40] Cf. e.g. Gai. III, 102; Giovanni Criscuoli, *La nullità parziale del negozio giuridico* (1959), pp. 27 sq.

[41] Cf. e.g. Paul Kretschmar, "Kritik der Interpolationenkritik", (1939) 59 *ZSS* 186 sq.

[42] This is the view, for instance, of Betti, *Diritto Romano*, pp. 333 sq.

[43] Cf. Hans Hermann Seiler, "Utile per inutile non vitiatur", in: *Festschrift für Max Kaser* (1976), pp. 127 sqq.

accessories;[44] a clause has been added in a contract of loan for use exempting the borrower from liability for dolus;[45] the name of one of the heirs in a will has been struck out;[46] a promise has been given, by way of stipulatio, to pay a certain sum to the stipulator and to a third party.[47] In all these cases, the invalidity of part of the transaction, either explicitly or implicitly, was held not to affect the whole transaction.[48] Where, on the other hand, partial invalidity would clash with overriding policy considerations (as, for instance, that the parties strike their bargain themselves and that arbitrary—judicial—intervention into the terms of the transaction be avoided), the jurists did not hesitate to opt for total invalidity.[49]

(b) Generalization of Ulp. D. 45, 1, 1, 5

From the Middle Ages onwards, however, lawyers latched on to D. 45, 1, 1, 5 and generalized Ulpian's phrase at the end of that fragment. The rule of "utile per inutile non vitiatur" became part of the ius commune and dominated the discussion of partial invalidity[50] from the time of the gloss[51] down to the pandectists.[52] Taken as a general rule, however, and not only as a guideline or presumption, it is apparent that "utile per inutile non vitiatur" inevitably leads to many unsatisfactory results, for instance in cases where the invalid part constitutes a major component of the transaction.

Attempts were not wanting to water down the rule in order to achieve greater flexibility. Thus, on the basis of Paul. D. 50, 17, 129, 1 ("Cum principalis causa non consistit, ne ea quidem quae sequuntur locum habent") and Paul. D. 50, 17, 178 ("Cum principalis causa non consistat, plerumque ne ea quidem quae sequuntur locum habent") attempts were made to establish some sort of counter-rule.[53] In particular, however, the intention of the parties to the transaction came

---

[44] Paul. D. 18, 1, 34 pr.: "Si in emptione fundi dictum sit accedere Stichum servum neque intellegatur, quis ex pluribus accesserit, cum de alio emptor, de alio venditor senserit, nihilo minus fundi venditionem valere constat."

[45] Paul. D. 13, 6, 17 pr.: "In commodato haec pactio, ne dolus praestetur, rata non est."

[46] Ulp. D. 28, 4, 2: "Cancellaverat quis testamentum vel induxerat et si propter unum heredem facere dixerat: id postea testamentum signatum est. quaerebatur de viribus testamenti deque portione eius, propter quem se cancellasse dixerat. dicebam, si quidem unius ex heredibus nomen induxerit, sine dubio ceteram partem testamenti valere et ipsi soli denegari actiones. . . ."

[47] Gai. III, 103; the second part of this stipulation infringes the rule "alteri stipulari nemo potest." Cf. supra, pp. 34 sqq. In the present context it is of interest to note that neither the Proculiani nor the Sabiniani advocated invalidity of the whole promise.

[48] For further discussion, see Seiler, *Festschrift Kaser*, pp. 128 sqq.

[49] Cf., for example, Marci. D. 18, 1, 44, as discussed by Seiler, *Festschrift Kaser*, pp. 130 sq.

[50] Criscuoli, op. cit., note 40, pp. 49 sqq., Theo Mayer-Maly, "Über die Teilnichtigkeit", in: *Privatrechtliche Beiträge, Gedenkschrift Franz Gschnitzer* (1969), pp. 281 sq.

[51] Accursius, gl. Per hanc inutilem, ad. D. 45, 1, 1, 5.

[52] Cf. e.g. Dernburg, *Pandekten*, vol. I, § 124, 3.

[53] Cf. Puchta, *Pandekten*, § 67.

to be emphasized;[54] and it is this recourse to the fundamental freedom of the individuals to regulate their own affairs that influenced the modern codifications.[55] Utile per inutile non vitiatur was therefore reduced to a presumption operating only where it cannot be ascertained what the parties had envisaged, in the event of part of their transaction turning out to be invalid.[56] Some codifications, amongst them the BGB, moved even further away from Roman law and reversed the presumption:[57] utile per inutile vitiatur, unless it may be assumed, in the words of the BGB, "that [the transaction] would have been entered into even if the void part had been omitted".[58] But in most cases it is very difficult, if not impossible, to determine what the parties would have done had they known that part of their transaction was invalid: parties normally do not consider this eventuality at the time of entering into the contract. Thus, the real will of the parties is usually replaced by an enquiry into their "hypothetical will",[59] i.e. by an evaluation of interests according to the standard of the reasonable man. But that, in the final analysis, makes the subsidiary presumption (be it utile per inutile non vitiatur or utile per inutile vitiatur) rather superfluous. Under the guise of the hypothetical will, the courts have thus acquired, once again, the far-reaching discretion of the Roman jurists to find suitable solutions to each individual case in which the question of partial invalidity arises.[60] As a result, the above-mentioned rules of the European codifications have been characterized as relics from past epochs, which attempted, on the basis of a misconceived Roman tradition, to lay down and settle the consequences of partial invalidity in a general legal rule.[61]

(c) Severability

Surprisingly, in South African law, neither utile per inutile non vitiatur nor the Roman sources seem to have influenced the discussion. Instead, the courts have received English law in this regard.[62] There the question has always been whether the unobjectionable parts of a contract may be enforced and the objectionable disregarded as "severed". As far as such severance is concerned, the courts seem to

---

[54] Cf. Windscheid/Kipp, § 82, n. 12.

[55] For a comparative analysis, see Alexander Ligeropoulos, "Teilnichtigkeit des Rechtsgeschäfts unter Ausschluss der Gesamtnichtigkeit", (1971) 24 *RHDI* 1 sqq.

[56] Cf. e.g. art. 20 II OR; art. 1419 II codice civile (on which, see Criscuoli, op. cit., note 40, pp. 59 sqq.).

[57] Cf. art. 1172 code civil; Art. 181 Greek Civil Code.

[58] § 139 BGB. But see, more recently, § 6 I ABGB, dealing with partially invalid standard contract terms. Here the German legislator has returned to utile per inutile *non* vitiatur.

[59] Mayer-Maly, in: *Münchener Kommentar*, vol. I (2nd ed., 1984), § 139, nn. 24 sqq.

[60] The German courts use this discretion to avoid invalidity of the whole transaction to a far greater extent than envisaged by the legislator. Thus, one might ask whether the presumption of utile per inutile vitiatur still reflects the practice of the courts.

[61] Seiler, *Festschrift Kaser*, p. 147; cf. also Honsell/Mayer-Maly/Selb, p. 116.

[62] Cf. Christie, *Contract*, pp. 360 sqq., 379 sqq.; Wessels, *Contract*, vol. I, nn. 605 sqq.

have been guided by two basic principles,[63] namely that the courts must not make a new contract for the parties and that they will sever the unenforceable parts of a contract only if it is in accordance with public policy to do so.[64] As far as the first of these principles is concerned, English courts have employed the "blue-pencil test": severance will only be effected if the illegal part can be crossed out by running a "blue pencil" through it (that is, where the courts do not have to rewrite the existing contract).[65] Such a guideline would also be of use in German law where the courts display an increasing tendency to reduce exorbitant terms of a contract to an acceptable level instead of declaring the contract null and void.[66] One of the policy considerations militating against such a tendency has been spelt out—with regard to the practically very important employer and employee covenants in restraint of trade—in the following terms:

> "It would in my opinion be pessimi exempli if, when an employer had exacted a covenant deliberately framed in unreasonably wide terms, the courts were to come to his assistance and, by applying their ingenuity and knowledge of the law, carve out of this void covenant the maximum of what he might validly have required. It must be remembered that the real sanction at the back of these covenants is the terror and expense of litigation, in which the servant is usually at a great disadvantage, in view of the longer purse of his master."[67]

5. The atrophy of the classical stipulation

(a) The use of documents (with evidentiary function)

Back to the stipulations! For as long as Rome and Roman tradition were dominant in the application and development of the law, the basic structure of the stipulation remained unchanged, even though, as we have seen, various concessions were made to facilitate its use in commercial practice. The degeneration (or atrophy) of the classical

---

[63] Cf. *Chitty on Contracts*, vol. I, nn. 1181 sqq. As is pointed out in n. 1183, many authorities cannot easily be reconciled with these principles. The confusion in the law of severance (which does not really commend itself for reception purposes) seems to be attributable on the one hand to the fact that the courts have traditionally distinguished between promises rendered illegal by statute and promises illegal at common law ("The statute is like a tyrant; when he comes he makes all void; but the common law is like a nursing father, makes void only that part where the fault is and preserves the rest": see Twisden J, in *Maleverer v. Redshaw* (1669) 1 Mod. Rep. 35 sq.); on the other hand, it is attributable to the tendency of certain tests "to crystallize into a firm rule of law, divorced from the underlying considerations of public policy which originally inspired [them]"—cf. esp. the rule that a consideration which is partly illegal can never be severed: Norman S. Marsh, "The Severance of Illegality in Contract", (1948) 64 *LQR* 230 sqq. (231), 347 sqq.

[64] Thus, English law places less emphasis on the (presumed or real) intention of the parties: cf. Marsh, (1948) 64 *LQR* 230 sqq.

[65] Cf. e.g. *Attwood v. Lamont* [1920] 3 KB 571 (CA) at 577–8.

[66] The problem of quantitative severability of contracts: cf. Zimmermann, *Moderationsrecht*, pp. 19 sqq. and passim; contra: Johannes Hager, *Gesetzes- und sittenkonforme Auslegung und Aufrechterhaltung von Rechtsgeschäften* (1983); Alfons Bürge, *Rechtsdogmatik und Wirtschaft—Das richterliche Moderationsrecht beim sittenwidrigen Rechtsgeschäft im Rechtsvergleich—Bundesrepublik Deutschland—Schweiz—Österreich—Frankreich* (1987).

[67] Lord Moulton, in *Mason v. Provident Clothing and Supply Co. Ltd.* [1913] AC 724 (HL) at 745.

stipulation,[68] in the course of which the oral formality gradually lost all significance, came about under the influence of commercial practice in the Hellenistic provinces. Even in classical Roman law already a document embodying the content of the stipulation was usually drawn up.[69] Such a document had a purely evidentiary function and was neither required for the validity of the transaction nor could it replace the oral exchange of question and answer.[70]

Lay people tend to attach greater significance to written documents than these deserve from a legal point of view: that was probably as true in imperial Rome as it is today. Hence the belief started to gain ground that the recording of the transaction was essential for its validity.[71] This belief was influenced by the obligatory effect of writing in the Hellenistic East and especially by the Greek practice of drawing up instruments of indebtedness[72]—instruments which could be enforced in Roman courts too.[73] It was further supported by the practice of draftsmen and notaries to attach a stereotype "stipulatory clause" to their documents.[74] If, for instance, we look through the Egyptian papyri, we find that after the enactment of the constitutio Antoniniana[75] this clause (καὶ ἐπερωτηθε ὶς ὡμολόγησα—interrogatus spopondit) became an essential element of the documentation of legal transactions,[76] its purpose obviously being to render the obligation enforceable according to Roman law.[77]

---

[68] The literature on this topic is abundant. The details of the development are controversial; see esp. (of the more recent literature) Kaser, *RPr* II, pp. 373 sqq.: Levy, *Obligationenrecht*, pp. 34 sqq.; Geoffrey MacCormack, "The Oral and Written Stipulation in the Institutes", in: *Studies in Justinian's Institutes in memory of J.A.C. Thomas* (1983), pp. 96 sqq.; Nicholas, (1953) 69 *LQR* 77 sqq., 233 sqq.; J.C. van Oven, "La stipulation a-t-elle dégénéré?", (1958) 26 *TR* 409 sqq.; Fritz Pringsheim, in: *Gesammelte Abhandlungen*, vol. II (1961), pp. 194 sqq.; Riccobono/Kerr Wylie/Beinart, pp. 48 sqq., 55 sqq., 91 sqq.; Dieter Simon, *Studien zur Praxis der Stipulationsklausel* (1964), pp. 26 sqq.; Dietrich V. Simon, *Konstantinisches Kaiserrecht* (1977), pp. 93 sqq.

[69] Such cautio stipulatoria could contain all the elaborate details of the transaction which it would have been difficult to include in the oral question-and-answer form. To this document the parties could then simply refer in their stipulation ("Ea omnia, quae supra scripta sunt, dari?": Paul. D. 45, 1, 140 pr.; cf. also Paul. D. 17, 2, 71 pr.) and record the oral act in a stereotype clause appended to the cautio; cf. Ulp. D. 2, 14, 7, 12 (". . . novissima parte pactorum ita solet inseri 'rogavit Titius, spopondit Maevius' . . .").

[70] Contra: Diósdi, pp. 51 sqq. [71] Cf. e.g. Gai. III, 134; Diósdi, pp. 62 sq.

[72] Cf. Cicero (*Topica*, XXVI—96), who took stipulations to be res quae ex scripto aguntur.

[73] Kaser, *RPr* II, pp. 374 sq.

[74] Cf. supra, note 69, and especially Pringsheim, op. cit., note 68, pp. 194 sqq.; Dieter Simon, op. cit., note 68, pp. 1 sqq.

[75] The importance of the constitutio Antoniniana for the degeneration of the stipulation is emphasized by Schulz (*CRL*, p. 476) in the following words: "With [this enactment] the stipulation was doomed. It was too closely connected with Roman customs and the peculiar Roman temperament and too alien to Eastern legal thought to be fully understood and properly applied by the vast mass of new Roman citizens."

[76] It was appended in a curiously overcautious and tremulous way, not uncommon for notaries, to all sorts of contracts and even to wills or documents relating to a release from slavery.

[77] However, during the time up to Justinian, there seems to have been a shift from *"promissorische Sanktionsklausel"* to *"konfirmatorische Sanktionsklausel"*; see the detailed analysis of the sources by Dieter Simon, op. cit., note 68, pp. 41 sqq.

(b) Gradual conversion of the stipulation into a written contract

Nevertheless, the late classical lawyers still maintained the oral nature of the stipulation, even if increasingly as a matter of theory. If, at the end of the document, it had been indicated that question and answer had been properly put,[78] there was no reason for the courts not to accept this as true, unless the contrary was positively proven. The document thus provided the basis for a (factual) presumption that the oral formality had been complied with. Papinian (himself probably born in the East) went even further: "Licet epistulae, quam libello inseruisti, additum non sit stipulatum esse eum cui cavebatur, tamen, si res inter praesentes gesta est, credendum est praecedente stipulatione vocem spondentis secutam."[79] Here the letter did not even mention that oral question and answer had been given. Yet, as long as the transaction had taken place inter praesentes, on the basis of the promise being put down in writing, it was accepted that a stipulation had been concluded! Thus, in actual practice, the oral formality was increasingly neglected and the stipulation was largely converted into a promise in writing.[80] Of course, it was still open to the debtor to prove that the formal oral act had not in fact taken place; but apart from showing that it *could* not have taken place (e.g. because one of the parties was not present at the alleged time and place), such proof of the negative is notoriously difficult.

This fundamental structural change in the nature of the stipulation was formally recognized in the fifth century. Even though his words leave some room for interpretation, it is today widely accepted that Emperor Leo dispensed with the old Roman question-and-answer ritual which by that time must have seemed somewhat atavistic: "Omnes stipulationes, etiamsi non sollemnibus vel directis, sed quibuscumque verbis pro consensu contrahentium compositae sint, legibus cognitae suam habeant firmitatem."[81] The words no longer

[78] Cf. e.g. Ulp. D. 2, 14, 7, 12.

[79] C. 8, 37, 1 (Sev. et Ant.). This rescript is dated April 200. At this time, as Tony Honoré has argued, Papinian was secretary a libellis: cf. *Emperors and Lawyers* (1981), pp. 56 sqq.

[80] Cf. further, for example, Paul. D. 24, 1, 57; 45, 1, 134, 2.

[81] C. 8, 37, 10 (a. 472). Interpretation and evaluation of this Constitution provide a good example of the disputes surrounding the later history of the Roman stipulation. On the one hand, it is held that late classical law had already gone the whole way from verba to scriptura, so that Leo's Constitution merely (re-)states what was already recognized (cf. e.g. Jörs/Kunkel/Wenger, p. 98). On the other hand, it is suggested that, up to the time of Leo, the formality of oral question and answer reigned supreme. Leo dispensed with the necessity of formal question and answer, but did not change the nature of the stipulation as an oral act. Only Justinian replaced the oral act by the written document (cf. e.g. Riccobono/Kerr Wylie/Beinart, pp. 51 sqq.). Others, again, see this transformation as having taken place with Leo's Constitution; according to them, each written contract was to be taken as a stipulation (e.g. Levy, *Obligationenrecht*, p. 39). Nicholas, (1953) 69 *LQR* 63 sqq., 233 sqq. argues that even Leo still retained the form of (oral) question and answer; the purpose of C. 8, 37, 10 was only to do away with what he believes to have been the numerus clausus of the formal words (cf. Gai. III, 92 and supra. p. 72) and to allow the use of other than these

mattered; of importance was only that the parties had reached consensus at the same time and the same place. The sole remaining ground on which this "stipulation" could still be invalidated was that either of the parties (or both of them) had not been present. In the course of the next fifty years this obviously proved to be a loophole through which, in the words of Justinian,[82] litigious men would try to escape liability, maintaining—after a while—that either they or their opponents had been absent when the contract was concluded. Justinian tried to curb undesirable lawsuits of that nature and therefore provided for a strong presumption: ". . . tales scripturas, quae praesto esse partes indicant, omnimodo esse credendas."[83] This could be refuted only if it was shown ". . . manifestissimis probationibus et melius quidem, si per scripturam . . . ostenderit"[84] that the parties had not been in the same town on the day the instrument was executed.[85] Thus he substituted "the mere possibility that the parties may have been present . . . for the material fact of their presence".[86] In a way, therefore, one can say that Justinian's legislation falls in line with previous developments: for all practical purposes the stipulation had now been converted into a written contract. In the practice of his time the formal oral stipulation no longer existed.[87] And yet, as has been pointed out already, in order to preserve the wealth of ideas from the classical law of contract, Justinian had to take over into his Digest—as if they still represented the law of his time—many texts based on the oral formalities. He bridged that gap by way of a fiction: if the parties had put their transaction down in writing and had indicated in this document that both parties had been present, then, unless it could be proved that one of the parties had in fact been absent from the town for the whole day, the promise was taken to have been given orally. With regard to his theoretical conception of a stipulation, Justinian therefore

---

"sollemnia verba". According to van Oven, (1958) 26 *TR* 415 sqq., too, Leo's Constitution did not change very much. He sees the sollemnitas that was abolished in the correspondence of the verb used in question and answer. Also according to MacCormack, *Studies Thomas*, pp. 99 sq., the stipulation remained an oral act. He, however, takes the constitution to have been of a purely declaratory nature (". . . [it] cannot have abolished any particular requirement") and argues that the correspondence requirement had already been watered down in classical law. For older literature, see Windscheid/Kipp, § 312, n. 2.

[82] Inst. III, 19, 12; C. 8, 37, 14, 2.

[83] Inst. III, 19, 12.

[84] C. 8, 37, 14, 2.

[85] To show his displeasure at these kinds of stories, Justinian used strong language ("improbis allegationibus").

[86] Riccobono/Kerr Wylie/Beinart, p. 57.

[87] Differently, MacCormack, *Studies Thomas*, pp. 96 sqq.; to some extent also Diósdi, pp. 61 sq.

fell behind what had been accepted by Leo. By somehow trying to reconcile the irreconcilable (i.e. classical theory and modern practice)[88] and by admitting texts and enactments from different stages of the development into his Corpus Juris Civilis, he left the law of stipulation on a rather discordant note in this enactment.[89]

6. The importance of form and formality

(a) Form as the oldest norm

The history of stipulation provides a good example of the importance of form and formalism in Roman law.[90] Legal effects in ancient Roman law, as in other early legal systems, could be achieved only by way of formal acts. When we think of formal transactions today, we see the form as *accompanying* the legal act; it has usually been introduced by the legislator, for specific policy considerations, as an *additional* requirement for the validity of that act.[91] But this, in the development of a legal system, is a relatively modern thinking pattern. Originally, form itself created the legal effect; it was, as Gerhard Dulckeit[92] has put it, *"Wirkform"* (effective form) rather than *"Schutzform"* (protective form). Compliance with the form was the actual *reason* (not only a necessary requirement) for the existence and recognition of a legal effect. Historically, this concept of form is based on a primitive belief in its magical nature.[93] If we take, for example, the law of obligations, we have seen that, originally, the hostage given to the creditor as a pledge was probably physically bound: "obligatus" in the literal sense. When this real bond was in the course of time superseded by an ideal, imaginary bond, the binding nature of the latter had to be secured somehow. Therefore, the creditor's real power over the body of the

---

[88] As to the "two souls in Justinian's bosom" in this context, see, Levy, *Obligationenrecht*, p. 59.

[89] For the later history of stipulation cf. infra, pp. 546 sqq.

[90] One of the best accounts is still that by R. von Jhering, *Geist* II, pp. 470 sqq.; cf. also Ludwig Mitteis, *Römisches Privatrecht bis auf die Zeit Diokletians*, I (1908), pp. 225 sqq.

[91] Differently, for example, art. 1341 code civil, which prescribes that all transactions of more than 5 000 ffrs must take the form of private writing or of a notarial document. But non-observance of the form does not entail invalidity of the transaction. Only the testimony of witnesses is excluded; in other words, the informal transaction cannot be proved in court. Also, according to the Statute of Frauds (1677, England), transactions which do not observe the prescribed forms ("a note or memorandum of the agreement in writing and signed by the party to be charged therewith") are not void, but rather unenforceable; on the Statute of Frauds, Simpson, *History*, pp. 599 sqq. For alternative consequences of a lack of form in German law, cf. Rudolf Westerhoff, "Wie begründen wir Formnichtigkeit?", (1984) 184 *Archiv für die civilistische Praxis* 376 sq.

[92] "Zur Lehre vom Rechtsgeschäft im klassischen römischen Recht", in: *Festschrift für Fritz Schulz*, vol. I (1951), pp. 160 sqq. Cf. also Jörs/Kunkel/Wenger, p. 90; Kaser, *RPr* I, pp. 39 sq.

[93] Cf. Kaser, *Altrömisches ius*, pp. 301 sqq.; idem, *RPr* I, p. 28; Dulckeit, *Festschrift Schulz*, vol. I, pp. 162 sq.; contra: Geoffrey MacCormack, "Formalism, Symbolism and Magic in Early Roman Law", (1969) 37 *TR* 439 sqq., 447 sqq.; idem, "Haegerstroem's Magical Interpretation of Roman Law", (1969) 4 *The Irish Jurist* 153 sqq.

person who was liable came to be replaced by a magical power over him and it was for this purpose that a formal ritual had to be performed. These rituals were devised by the state priests who, at that time, were not only in charge of sacral affairs, but were also responsible for the application and development of the law.[94] They all entailed the uttering of precisely set, formal words, often reinforced by the performance of symbolic acts, as, for example, laying one's hands or a staff on the object of the transaction. It was only by means of these rituals that legal transactions could be effected: compliance with the ritual formalities brought about a real (but invisible and in so far magical) change in the relationships between the parties concerned. The slightest mistake would wreck the whole transaction: every reader of fairy tales knows that magical effects can be engendered only by a most punctilious recital of a set formula. Procedure has always been a prominent arena for this kind of formalism and thus we cannot be surprised to read what Gaius reports about "nimia subtilitas veterum" relating to the legis actio procedure:

> "unde eum qui de vitibus succisis ita egisset, ut in actione vites nominaret, responsum est rem perdidisse, quia debuisset arbores nominare, eo quod lex XII tabularum, ex qua de vitibus succisis actio competeret, generaliter de arboribus succisis loqueretur."[95]

A very similar formalism is known to have governed the old Germanic procedure:[96] qui cadit a syllaba, cadit a causa. But whilst the old legis actiones were by the time of classical law no longer in use, many of the formal transactions of private law were; and the stipulatio (besides mancipatio and in iure cessio) was one of the most important of them. Even though there was now, of course, no longer any magic in an exchange of oral question and answer in free, if corresponding, words, its basic structure had, as we have seen, been reverently preserved. As a consequence, the liability of whoever had made a promise could not extend beyond what was covered by the words used; but, on the other hand, he would also be held relentlessly bound by those words. As long as the formalities had been correctly executed, the act was fully

---

[94] As to the pontifical nature of the ancient Roman jurisprudence, cf. Jhering, *Geist* II, pp. 390 sqq.; Kaser, *Altrömisches ius*, pp. 345 sqq.; Schulz, *RLS*, pp. 6 sqq., 15 sqq.; Wieacker, *RR*, pp. 310 sqq. and passim.

[95] Gai. IV, 11; cf. also IV, 30.

[96] Cf. E. Kaufmann, in: *HRG*, vol. I, col. 1163 sqq.; for grotesque extremes in the 13th/14th centuries cf., for example, 68, 7 of the *Lehenrecht of the Sachsenspiegel*, where Eike von Repgow found it necessary to state: *"Wenn der Mann im Lehengericht sich die Nase putzt oder sich schneuzt oder spuckt oder gähnt oder wenn er hustet oder niest oder auf der anderen Seite seines Vorsprechers steht, als er zunächst stand, oder wenn er sich schicklich umschaut oder Fliegen, Mücken oder Bremsen schicklich von sich scheucht, so hat er deswegen kein Strafgeld verwirkt, obwohl dies einige Leute glauben"* (cf. the edition by C. Schott, 1984) (If, in the feudal court, the man blows his nose or spits or yawns or when he coughs or sneezes or stands on the other side of his prompt than he first stood, or if he turns around in gentlemanly fashion or brisks away in gentlemanly fashion flies, mosquitoes or horseflies, he does not on that account incur a penalty, although some people think so).

effective, no matter whether those effects had in actual fact been willed or not. It is obvious that under those circumstances a gap could develop between what was wanted and what was formally declared and, if one took only the latter into consideration, hard and inequitable results were likely to ensue. But it is quite ahistorical to envisage the problem in this way with regard to an ancient legal system. Right until the Republic it would not have occurred to the Roman lawyers that a discrepancy between will and word could exist.[97] The actual reason for the desired legal result was not the consent between the parties but the formal exchange of the words. The true will of the parties could be discovered only from the words.[98]

One may, incidentally, well raise the question whether strict adherence to this principle was really as harsh as it seems to us today. When we are inclined to take offence at the fact that a deviation from the required form would invalidate the whole transaction, even though there might have been substantive agreement between the parties, we proceed from the supposition that the parties really wanted to be bound under those circumstances and merely somewhat carelessly neglected to observe the form. But it is equally possible that non-compliance with the form signified the intention of the parties not to be bound! Considering the simple and uncomplicated nature of the stipulation, so familiar to every Roman citizen, the second possibility is arguably the rule rather than the exception.[99] Furthermore, in predominantly agrarian early societies legal transactions were not as commonplace as they are today and were therefore approached with gravity and concentration. Considering the importance of the act, one therefore did not mind the demands made upon the parties' precision and attention. Thus what we regard as formalism today was not perceived as such in early Roman law. Form, then, in this sense, can be said to be the oldest norm.[100]

(b) From "effective" form to "protective" form

In the course of time, however, this attitude changed. In the wake of the rise of the informal contracts, the meeting of the minds, the agreement of the parties concerned, came to be accepted increasingly as the cornerstone of and actual effective reason for all contractual

---

[97] The same applies to other early legal systems. Two examples from the Bible spring to mind: Jacob's marriage to Leah and Isaac's blessing given to Jacob instead of to Esau were both unquestionably valid despite Jacob's and Laban's deceit.

[98] Along the same line Celia Wasserstein Fassberg, "Form and Formalism: A Case Study", (1983) 31 *American Journal of Comparative Law*, 630: "Nothing had happened if the form was absent because only by means of form were the public, religious requirements of certainty and society fulfilled. For the same reason, just as nothing had happened in law, nothing had happened in fact.".

[99] Jhering, *Geist* II, p. 492.

[100] Wilhelm Ebel, *Recht und Form* (1975), pp. 13 sq.; Wieacker, *Vom römischen Recht*, p. 76; idem, *RR*, pp. 320 sqq.

obligations. This agreement, as far as all the more important transactions were concerned, would as a matter of course be recorded, but such a document served an evidentiary purpose only. Thus, with the increase in the use of writing[101] we find a shift from "effective form" to "protective form".[102] The documentation merely accompanied the transaction and did no longer in itself represent and embody it; where it was made mandatory, it served to promote specific policy considerations: certainty of the law, facilitation of tax enforcement, etc. As far as the stipulation was concerned, however, the effective and protective functions in post-classical law became somewhat confused. As we have seen, the oral formality was gradually superseded by the drafting of an instrument. When this happened, under the influence of Hellenistic practice and tradition,[103] one of the characteristics of the question-and-answer ritual, namely its obligatory effect, passed to the instrument. This is where the roots of the modern law of negotiable instruments are to be found.[104] But as, on the other hand, no sharp distinction was drawn between constitutive and simply evidentiary documents, the original idea of the written document merely providing evidence for the (oral) conclusion of a stipulation was never entirely lost.

(c) Formal requirements in modern contract law

Modern legal systems still know the written record (in its many variants ranging from simple writing to a document attested by an independent public official)[105] as a formal requirement, though only for specific transactions and as an exception to the general rule that all formless agreements are enforceable.[106] Often, certain formalities have to be observed with regard to the contract of sale of land,[107] (usually justified by the consideration that landed property, as a rule, is the most important of the seller's assets).[108] Contracts of guarantee are another typical example,[109] it being assumed that the dangers inherent

[101] Cf. e.g. Jolowicz/Nicholas, pp. 414 sqq.
[102] Kaser, *RPr* II, pp. 73 sqq.
[103] Kaser, *RPr* II, pp. 76 sq., 376 sq.
[104] Cf. Heinrich Brunner, *Zur Rechtsgeschichte der römischen und germanischen Urkunde* (1880), pp. 44 sqq., 86 sqq.; H.-A. Schultze von Lasaulx, *Beiträge zur Geschichte des Wertpapierrechts* (1931), pp. 25 sqq.
[105] The notary in Germany is entrusted with the recording of legal transactions; there is no comparable official in English law.
[106] Cf. the comparative analysis by Zweigert/Kötz/Weir, pp. 53 sqq.
[107] Cf. § 313 BGB; s. 40 Law of Property Act (1925, England); Alienation of Land Act, 68/1981 (South Africa); for a thorough comparative discussion, see Bernd von Hoffmann, *Das Recht des Grundstückskaufs* (1982), pp. 111 sqq.
[108] Questioned by Zweigert/Kötz/Weir, p. 51 (". . . [this consideration] gives immovable property a special status not justified by modern conditions, but it is in any case unavoidable to require some degree of formality for transactions in land since otherwise there would be no clear basis for making entries in the Land Register"). Cf. also von Hoffmann, op. cit., note 107, pp. 4 sqq.
[109] § 766 BGB; Statute of Frauds.

in standing surety are not realized by many; promises of gift can be mentioned as a third[110]—here it would otherwise often be difficult to determine whether a specific declaration was meant to be taken seriously. Sometimes the legislator subjects new types of legal transactions to a statutory form: one may think of § 2 AGBG[111] and § 1a AbzG[112] which have been introduced in the interest of consumer protection. Still, the general trend is towards informality, at least as far as the traditional core areas of private law are concerned. "Ius vigilantibus scriptum" was the call of 19th-century liberalism, in the spirit of which the excessive formal requirements enacted under the patronizing and paternalistic aegis of enlightened absolutism[113] were shaken off: people should normally be able to look after their interests themselves and should not have to be tied to the apron strings of statutory formalities. But even where specific forms are still required, a tendency is often observable in the practice of the courts to water down such rules.[114] They have all been introduced in order to achieve certain legislative purposes: to facilitate proof of the transaction,[115] to give an opportunity for thoughtful consideration and thus to prevent rash and precipitate declarations, or—in the case of notarial authentication—to provide for legal consultation.[116] It is, of course, perfectly possible that, in an individual case, these aims could have been realized in other ways, even though the formal requirements were not met by the parties: anxious consideration of all the risks involved may well have preceded the oral promise to stand surety; the oral promise to sell a piece of land may have been given by a professor of property law (who, one would assume, hardly needed legal advice); the

---

[110] § 518 BGB, art. 931 code civil.

[111] Cf. supra, note 6.

[112] Writing required in the case of instalment sales (so that the purchaser's attention is drawn to the financing charges).

[113] Cf., for example, as to the provisions of the PrALR, the comment by Jhering, *Geist* II, pp. 483 sq.

[114] "English Judges have done their best to restrict the area of application of the Statute of Frauds, helped in their tortuous construction by the remarkable opacity of the statutory text": Zweigert/Kötz/Weir, p. 46. In France the courts have watered down art. 1341 code civil by means of a widely construed doctrine of "commencement de preuve par écrit": testimony of witnesses is admitted, whenever the leading of evidence can at least be started off with a written document. For the attitude of the German courts, see n. 119.

[115] This was the reason for the enactment of the Statute of Frauds: "For the prevention of many fraudulent Practices which are commonly endeavoured to be upheld by Perjury and Subornation of Perjury", i.e. fraudulent plaintiffs bringing claims on non-existent contracts; the background is sketched by Simpson, *History*, pp. 599 sq.; cf. further esp. Ernst Rabel, "The Statute of Frauds and Comparative Legal History", (1947) 63 *LQR* 174 sqq. An amusing example of the evidentiary function of form is related by Paul Vinogradoff, *Outlines of Historical Jurisprudence*, vol. I (1920), p. 364: in early Bavaria and Alemannia transfers of land had to be performed in the presence of a certain number of small boys who, after attending the ceremony, were treated to a box on the ear in order that they might keep a vivid remembrance of what had happened. Without such a box, the transfer was void.

[116] Cf. e.g. Karl Heldrich, "Die Form des Vertrages", (1941) 147 *Archiv für die civilistische Praxis* 91 sqq.; Lon L. Fuller, "Consideration and Form", (1941) 41 *Columbia LR* 799 sqq. (who adds what he refers to as the "channeling function").

testator might have made his intention to institute his niece as heir absolutely clear.[117] The sanction of invalidity therefore seems to overshoot the mark: it is not demanded by the policy underlying the rules requiring formality of the act. Strict and uncompromising application of the law under these circumstances is often denounced as "formalistic".[118] Equitable inroads have therefore from time to time been made into the domain of statutory forms. One of the most notable instances has been the willingness of the German Federal Supreme Court to enforce contracts for the sale of land, which lack the form prescribed in § 313 BGB, if the basic principle of good faith so demands: this, in the view of the court, is the case if the result would otherwise be "plainly intolerable" (sc.: and not only "hard") for the party relying on the validity of the transaction.[119] Such tendencies, however, are of a questionable nature. Ours is an age of formlessness. We like to focus our attention on the individual case and therefore tend to overemphasize the disadvantages of form. Indeed, it is indisputable that form not only entails a certain amount of inconvenience; it is also dangerous, in that a small flaw can have grave, harsh and unexpected consequences.

(d) Formalism or flexibility?

The advantages of form, on the other hand, are less noticeable, because they are of a negative nature.[120] Whenever a transaction is held invalid due to a formal lapsus, one's sense of equity is incensed;[121] it is hardly ever emphasized, however, how many rash, ill-conceived and

---

[117] The law of (testate) succession is, of course, one of the main battlefields with regard to this problem. See, for instance, for Germany, the classic monograph by Fritz von Hippel, *Formalismus und Rechtsdogmatik* (1935); for a recent comparative survey Fassberg, (1983) 31 *American Journal of Comparative Law* 627 sqq.; and for South Africa, see Ellison Kahn, "The Will that Won't", in: *Huldigingsbundel Paul van Warmelo* (1984), pp. 128 sqq.

[118] On formal and formalistic reasoning in contract law, see P.S. Atiyah, "Form and Substance in Legal Reasoning: the Case of Contract", in: *The Legal Mind, Essays for Tony Honoré* (1986), pp. 19 sqq.

[119] The line of the Federal Supreme Court has varied; cf. the analysis by Joachim Gernhuber, "Formnichtigkeit und Treu und Glauben", in: *Festschrift für Walter Schmidt-Rimpler* (1957), pp. 151 sqq.; Ludwig Häsemeyer, *Die gesetzliche Form der Rechtsgeschäfte* (1971), pp. 36 sqq.

[120] On the advantages and disadvantages of form, see Jhering, *Geist* II, pp. 470 sqq.; on form and substance in legal reasoning cf. Atiyah, *Essays Honoré*, pp. 19 sqq., 33 sqq.

[121] A frontal attack on the formal requirements for wills has been launched by Gerhard Kegel, "Die lachenden Doppelerben", in: *Festschrift für Werner Flume* (1978), vol. I, pp. 545 sqq. In case of a failure of a will as a result of the testator's lawyer's negligence, the intended beneficiary, according to Kegel, may take directly under the will (and thus dethrone the intestate heir). The Federal Supreme Court, on the other hand, has adopted the view that the intended beneficiary may claim damages from the negligent lawyer (as a result of which we would have, in actual fact, one person taking under the will, the other by way of claiming damages). Against both solutions cf. Reinhard Zimmermann, "Lachende Doppelerben?—Erbfolge und Schadensersatz bei Anwaltsverschulden", 1980 *Zeitschrift für das gesamte Familienrecht* 99 sqq. Cf. also John G. Fleming, "Comparative Law of Torts", 4 *Oxford Journal of Legal Studies* 239 sq.; Owen Rogers, "The Action of the Disappointed Beneficiary", (1986) 103 *SALJ* 583 sqq.

inequitable transactions have been *prevented* due to compliance with a statutory form. It is in the interest of these many cases that hardship in an individual situation has to be accepted. The broader legislative purpose behind provisions which lay down formal requirements can be achieved only if they are strictly applied. The extent to which that is possible naturally depends largely on the general appropriateness of such provisions in pursuing the legislative policy,[122] and on whether there has been reasonable reliance which needs to be protected.[123] But it should be clearly recognized that an individualizing approach misses the essence of statutory form in its typifying purport. Insurmountable difficulties in defining and demarcating exceptional cases (what is only "hard" as opposed to "plainly intolerable"?) are the consequence.

The attitude of a legal culture towards form reflects its self-image and maturity. At the same time, the form in which the law appears and finds expression is an image of the general spirit of the age. Strict formalism and rigidity are characteristic of the archaic agrarian society, governed by strict discipline and living in accordance with typified behaviour patterns. The other extreme is absolute freedom, unlimited individualism and arbitrariness. Its legal expression is formlessness and the boundless sway of equity; its general intellectual background is one of superabundance and profusion of material, spinelessness and mental exhaustion.[124] Formalism and flexibility are intrinsically opposed to each other. The one makes for certainty of the law, the other for equity—the two principles on which justice is based. These principles are antagonistic. Yet the legal system must try to realize both simultaneously. That makes ideal justice a Utopian idea, for the one principle must always be precariously balanced against the other. To carry through the one without any regard to the other would lead to extreme injustice: summum ius summa iniuria.[125] The legal system thus has to strive for a *coincidentia oppositorum* on the highest attainable level. It is submitted that Roman jurisprudence under the Principate

---

[122] As a negative example, cf. the formalities required for the holograph will before the *Testamentsgesetz* of 1938; a will was void, even if only the place where it had been drawn up had not been written by hand, because it was printed on the letter paper of a hotel.

[123] Cf. the English doctrine of part performance: on its evolution by the Court of Chancery, see Simpson, *History*, pp. 613 sqq.; cf. also the (American) Restatement Contracts 2d (1982), § 129.

[124] Zimmermann, *Moderationsrecht*, pp. 189 sq. This development from self-assured primitivity to artistic perfection coupled with formal disintegration and depletion of meaning is usually well illustrated by the development of art; a comparison between the early Greek *kouroi* with their strictly mathematical and rectilinear frame of reference with the Hellenistic sculptures is particularly instructive.

[125] Cf. Cicero, *De officiis* 1, X—33, probably of Greek origin; cf. Georg Eisser, "Zur Deutung von 'summum ius summa iniuria' im römischen Recht", in: *Summum ius summa iniuria* (1963), pp. 1 sqq. Thus, Rudolf von Jhering could state, in a seemingly paradoxical way: "*Die Form ist die geschworene Feindin der Willkür, die Zwillingsschwester der Freiheit*" (Form is the archfoe of arbitrariness, the twin sister of freedom): *Geist* II, p. 471.

came as close as is humanly possible to achieving such harmonization and therefore truly deserves the epithet "classical".[126]

7. The flexibility of the Roman stipulation: range of application

Contrary to Germanic law, Roman law displays a remarkable inclination towards clarity and simplicity.[127] This is quite obvious if one looks at the formal transactions of classical Roman law. There was a notable restraint in developing new forms. In general, existing forms were used and, if necessary, adapted, extended or made—with or without modification—to serve new purposes. Thus Ernst Rabel has coined the term *"nachgeformte Rechtsgeschäfte"*[128] (transactions shaped in the old mould), and one has only to think of in iure cessio and mancipatio for a whole variety of examples: in iure cessio constituted a ritual imitating legal proceedings in the course of which the defendant acknowledged the plaintiff's allegations, and it could thus be used to effect a transfer of certain rights between two parties; mancipatio nummo uno, essentially an imaginary cash sale, could conveniently be employed to become, for example, the main form of making a will. In the case of stipulatio, its usefulness and flexibility made it the cornerstone of the Roman contractual system, a cornerstone which, incidentally, has no parallels in other historical legal systems.[129] As it was their form and not their content upon which the legal effects of stipulations were based and as this form was simple, clear and unspecific (i.e. not stamped by the peculiarities of specific types of transactions which they might have been designed to accommodate), stipulations were apt to be employed for very different purposes; in fact, they could be made to accommodate everything that could conceivably be the object of a contractual obligation: dare, facere, praestare (as long, of course, as such content was not illegal or immoral).[130] In the beginning there was possibly only the stipulation for a certum, which was enforceable by means of a condictio (or: actio certae creditae pecuniae) as long as certa pecunia was involved, and by

---

[126] As to the "classicity" of classical Roman law, cf. also Schulz, *RLS*, pp. 99 sqq. As far as the concept "classical" is concerned, see generally, in the sense indicated in the text above, Fritz Schachermeyr, *Forschungen und Betrachtungen zur griechischen und römischen Geschichte* (1974), pp. 145 sqq.

[127] Cf. generally Schulz, *Principles*, pp. 66 sqq.; also Jhering, *Geist* III, pp. 139 sqq., 178 sqq.

[128] Ernst Rabel, "Nachgeformte Rechtsgeschäfte", (1906) 27 *ZSS* 290 sqq.; (1907) 18 *ZSS* 311 sqq.; cf. also Liebs, *Sympotica Wieacker*, pp. 111 sqq.

[129] But see F.H. Lawson, "Analogues of the Stipulatio in English Law", in: *XXth century Comparative and Conflicts Law, Legal Essays in Honor of Hessel E. Yntema* (1961), pp. 117 sqq. However, Lawson does not deal so much with the form of the stipulation but highlights two other aspects: the fact that the promisee, if he is to be able to sue on the promise, must extract it from the promisor, and that he must draft the terms that he wants, i.e. that the promisee must take the initiative.

[130] Cf. e.g. Riccobono/Kerr Wylie/Beinart, pp. 26 sq.; Siber, *Römisches Privatrecht*, pp. 178 sq.

means of a condictio certae rei as far as specific objects or a certain quantity of fungible things was concerned. The formula of the condictio was simply: "Si paret N^m N^m A^o A^o decem milia dare oportere, iudex N^m N^m A^o A^o decem milia condemnato, s.n.p.a." In the case of the condictio certae rei the intentio did not contain a sum of money but, for example, "tritici Africi optimi modios". Thus, because of "omnis condemnatio pecuniaria", the iudex had to be directed in the condemnatio to estimate the pecuniary value of the claim (". . . quanti ea res est, tantam pecuniam . . ."). But once this discretion of the judge was recognized, there was nothing in principle opposed to admitting stipulations for an incertum: stipulations where even the object of the claim was not at all fixed, but was left for judicial determination. On the basis of such an actio ex stipulatu, the judge had to condemn the defendant in "quidquid ob eam rem N^m N^m A^o A^o dare facere oportet".[131] An example is discussed in Ulp. D. 45, 1, 75, 4: "Illud dubitationem recipit, si quis id, quod ex Arethusa ancilla natum erit, aut fructus, qui in fundo Tusculano nati erunt, dari sibi stipulatus sit, an certum stipulatus videatur. sed ipsa natura manifestissima est incerti esse hanc stipulationem." Here the stipulation was "Id quod ex Arethusa ancilla natum erit (fructus qui in fundo Tusculano nati erunt), dari spondes?" "Spondeo". Not only the estimation of the pecuniary value of the object but the object itself had to be determined before judgment would be given.

Thus the scope of the contract of stipulation was immense indeed.[132] As Roman law never recognized the general principle of "ex nudo pacto oritur actio",[133] the stipulation was the means to achieve what could not be achieved by formless consent. But even where informal contracts would have been at hand the Romans often availed themselves of the stipulation in order to create an obligation. Thus, stipulations were regularly used to strengthen a loan (and to add certain ancillary clauses that could accompany a loan), to replace an already existing obligation with a new one (novation), to make a donation or to promise a dowry, to buy a specific quantity of unascertained goods (this was of particular importance since a consensual sale by description was not enforceable),[134] or to give specific guarantees (these are the manifold "cautiones" that we find both in private law and in the law of procedure:[135] the cautio usufructuaria, the cautiones rei uxoriae or rem pupilli salvam fore, the stipulatio duplae, the cautio damni infecti or the cautio iudicatum solvi to mention a few). By way of example, two areas of application (conventional penalties and suretyship contracts) will be examined more closely in the following chapters.

[131] Gai. IV, 136.
[132] Schulz, *CRL*, p. 478.
[133] Cf. infra, pp. 509 sqq.
[134] Cf. infra, pp. 236 sqq.
[135] Kaser, *RZ*, pp. 335 sq.

As with the other strictly formal acts of the old ius civile, the stipulation gave rise to only one obligation, not to mutual ones.[136] One party (the debtor) would be bound to perform towards the other (the creditor), but could not, under the same stipulation, acquire a counterclaim. Or, the other way round: the stipulation granted the creditor a right, without, at the same time, imposing a duty on him. The stipulation was a unilaterally binding contract. If, therefore, the parties wished to cast a bilateral agreement (as, for example, a contract of sale) in the form of a contract verbis, they had to make two stipulations: the one relating to the purchase price, the other obliging the seller to make delivery. If the promisor wanted to make sure that the stipulator did not take advantage of the unilateral nature of the transaction by trying to enforce his right without having rendered performance, he would link the two promises to each other by means of a condition: "Centum mihi dari spondes, si Pamphilum tibi dederim?" "Spondeo"; similarly, the second stipulation would then normally be: "Pamphilum mihi dari spondes, si centum tibi dederim?" "Spondeo".[137]

8. The framing of the stipulation

(a) Abstract or causal?

As far as the framing of the stipulation was concerned, we have already seen that there had to be formal correspondence between question and answer. But, apart from that, the use of specific words was not prescribed. That was what made the form of stipulation such a flexible tool. It could be used to promise whatever dare, facere or praestare the parties had in mind. If that was payment of one hundred, they could, for instance, merely say: "Centum mihi dari spondes?" "Spondeo." But, of course, nobody is likely to promise centum just like that. People usually have a reason for making such a promise. In our example the hundred might have been promised as a dowry or because the parties wanted to reaffirm an obligation based on a contract of sale; or perhaps the hundred was simply meant as a gift. This underlying purpose of the promise did not have to be mentioned in the stipulation; the stipulation—as in our example above—was then framed abstractly. Why the hundred had been promised, was anybody's guess; it certainly

[136] The unilateral nature of legal relationships in the old Roman law is stressed by Jhering, *Geist* III, pp. 199 sqq. and ties in with the principle of simplicity. *"Der Gedanke der Gegenseitigkeit ist kein ursprünglicher Gedanke des römischen Zivilrechts, das spezifisch Römische ist die Einseitigkeit. . . . Die einseitige Obligation ist nicht bloss die einfachste Obligationsform im analytischen Sinne, sondern auch im praktischen Sinn, d.h. die am leichtesten zu handhabende"* (The notion of reciprocity is not an original idea of Roman private law; unilaterality is the specifically Roman notion . . . The unilateral obligation is not only the simplest type of obligation from an analytical perspective, but also from a practical point of view, i.e. it is the one that can most easily be handled). Cf. also Wieacker, *RR*, pp. 327 sq.

[137] As will be seen, the two reciprocal stipulations could also be connected by means of an exceptio (in this instance the exceptio mercis non traditae would have been applicable).

could not be ascertained from the stipulation itself. The promise was therefore valid according to the ius civile, irrespective of whether anything had gone wrong as far as this underlying causa was concerned. On the other hand, the parties could also expressly include the causa stipulationis in the wording of question (and answer) and thus draft the stipulation causally: "Centum mihi dotis causa spondes?" "Spondeo" (or: "Centum tibi dotis causa spondeo"); or: "Quod mihi ex empto debes, dari spondes?" "Spondeo"; or: "Centum mihi donationis causa spondes?" "Spondeo". Here the obligatory effect of the promise was tied to the validity of dos, sale or donation. A clear comprehension of these two ways of drafting a stipulation is also relevant as far as the interpretation of stipulations is concerned. A good example is Iav. D. 24, 3, 66, 4: "Mulier, quae centum dotis apud virum habebat, divortio facto ducenta a viro errante stipulata erat. Labeo putat, quanta dos fuisset, tantam deberi, sive prudens mulier plus esset stipulata sive imprudens: Labeonis sententiam probo." Here, the value of the dos was 100, but the ex-husband mistakenly promised to pay back 200. Both Labeo and Iavolenus think that only 100 are owed. This decision must seem either very strange or astonishingly "progressive" to anybody who would assume this stipulation to have been something like "Ducenta mihi dari spondes?" "Spondeo". For how could a clear and unambiguous promise of ducenta be held to mean centum by any classical lawyer, let alone by an early classical writer such as M. Antistius Labeo? Stipulations, after all, were strictly construed, and circumstances not embodied in their wording were normally not taken into consideration.[138] Things look quite different if one takes the possibility into account that the stipulation had been framed causally—and would thus have mentioned that the promise was given for the purpose of repayment of the dos. Looking at the stipulation now, one is faced with a glaring inconsistency: the parties spelt out the sum of two hundred, but they actually envisaged (as is apparent from the text of the stipulation, too) the sum of one hundred. The promise therefore seems to be for one hundred and for two hundred at the same time. The fact that Labeo, under these circumstances, chose to interpret the stipulation in the way he did (because one hundred was what the parties really had in mind) would then have attested to his skill in finding the most sensible solution to the problem. It is more than likely that, indeed, the problem presented itself in terms of the second alternative. For it has to be taken into consideration that "mulier" would, in any event, after termination of her marriage have had a claim for restoration

---

[138] Therefore the text has been regarded as spurious (Riccobono/Kerr Wylie/Beinart, pp. 105 sqq.). Wunner, *Contractus*, pp. 206 sqq., on the other hand, accepts the text as evidence for both the prevalence of voluntas over quod dictum est in the law of stipulation and for quantitative severability of contracts. Contra Zimmermann, *Moderationsrecht*, pp. 132 sq. On the principles governing interpretation cf. infra, pp. 621 sqq.

of the dos and would thus have been able to avail herself of the actio rei uxoriae. The stipulation therefore appears to have had a novatory function; we know, however, that stipulations of a novatory character always stated as their content that which was owed under the previous obligation; in other words, that they were framed causally.[139]

(b) The exceptio non numeratae pecuniae

On the other hand, the practical difference between the abstract and causal way of drafting the stipulation should not be overrated. Abstraction did not entirely exclude recourse to the causa—it only made it more difficult. Where the creditor tried to enforce an abstractly framed stipulation, the debtor could still defend himself by pointing out that the hundred were meant to be a dos and that the marriage had not taken place, or that the promise was based on a contract of sale which had been invalid, etc. But it was only by way of an exceptio, usually the exceptio doli (which the defendant had to get inserted into the formula), that all this could be taken into account: the argument being that a creditor enforcing a stipulation sine causa was acting in breach of good faith.[140] For certain situations special exceptiones were available: the exceptio mercis non traditae where a purchase price had been—abstractly—stipulated and where this stipulation was now enforced without the goods having been delivered;[141] the exceptio non numeratae pecuniae where the defendant objected that he had in actual fact not received the loan for the return of which he was now being sued. This latter exceptio was introduced in late classical law in order to meet the situation where the debtor had acknowledged receipt of, and promised to repay, the sum agreed upon before it had actually been handed over to him.[142] That prospective creditors should have asked for such an anticipatory promise does not seem to have been uncommon at all;[143] the borrowers, in order to receive the capital, would have complied with this request by way of stipulation; and evidence of this stipulation would, by that time, generally have been a written document (which in the course of the further development was to acquire an increasingly dispositive function after the model of the Greek συγγραφή). Of course, under these circumstances it was bound to happen that what had in actual fact already been acknowledged did not take place and that the loan was not handed over after all. If the creditor then presented the instrument and sued for repayment, he

[139] Cf., for example, Ulp. D. 45, 1, 75, 6.

[140] Cf. Wolf, *Causa stipulationis*, pp. 1 sqq., 76 sqq.; Andreas Wacke, "Zur causa der Stipulation", (1972) 40 *TR* 237 sqq.; Dobbertin, op. cit., note 26, pp. 60 sqq.

[141] Gai. IV, 126 a; Iul. D. 19, 1, 25; cf. Thielmann, *Privatauktion*, pp. 141 sqq.

[142] See esp. Ernst Levy, "Die querela non numeratae pecuniae", (1953) 70 *ZSS* 214 sqq.; Buckland/Stein, pp. 442 sq.; Kaser, *RPr* I, p. 542; idem, *RPr* II, pp. 379 sq.; Thomas, *TRL*, pp. 268 sq.; and, most recently, Maria Rosa Cimma, *De non numerata pecunia* (1984); Hervé Trofimoff, "La cause dans l'exception non numeratae pecuniae", (1986) 33 *RIDA* 215 sqq.

[143] Cf. e.g. Gai. IV, 116 a, 119; Ulp. D. 44, 4, 2, 3.

could normally be met with the exceptio doli.[101] But sometimes this avenue was not open to the debtor: "Adversus parentes patronosque neque doli exceptio neque alia quidem, quae patroni parentisve opinionem . . . suggillet, competere potest."[102] Therefore, an exceptio in factum had to be introduced and this was the exceptio non numeratae pecuniae. It could also be used where the creditor had not behaved fraudulently, perhaps because, as a "cessionary", or as the heir of the creditor, he did not know that the loan had actually never been paid out. But its impact went far beyond these cases. Normally the defendant (borrower) would, in order to substantiate his exceptio doli, have had to prove a negative fact, namely that he had *not* received the loan.[103] That was, of course, very difficult. The main effect of the exceptio non numeratae pecuniae therefore consisted in the fact that the burden of proof, as far as the advancement of the loan was concerned, was shifted (back, as it were) upon the plaintiff. But even independently of any action on the part of the plaintiff, the defendant could contest his obligation by means of a querela non numeratae pecuniae.[104] Both the exceptio and the querela at first prescribed after one year, later after five years, and finally, since the time of Justinian, after two years.[105] If the remedies were raised in time, neither a stipulation nor any document was of much assistance to the creditor any longer. Otherwise, that is, when the time set for bringing these remedies had expired, the written acknowledgement of the debt was to become, in post-classical times, irrebuttable proof that the loan had in fact been paid out.[106]

---

[101] Gai. IV, 116 a.

[102] Ulp. D. 44, 4, 4, 16 (on which cf. e.g. Cimma, op. cit., note 142, pp. 38 sqq.).

[103] Cf., however, Levy, (1953) 70 *ZSS* 219 sqq.

[104] Cf. e.g. C. 4, 30, 4 (Ant.); for a recent discussion, see Jean Philippe Lévy, "A quels faits la 'querela non numeratae pecuniae' tendait-elle à remédier?", in: *Studi in onore di Cesare Sanfilippo*, vol. IV (1983), pp. 339 sqq.; Cimma, op. cit., note 142, pp. 60 sqq., 166 sqq.; Trofimoff, (1986) 33 *RIDA* 236 sqq.

[105] C. 4, 30, 14 pr.; *Inst.* III, 21; generally, for Justinian's law on the topic, cf. C. 4, 30, 14–16 and Cimma, op. cit., note 142, pp. 171 sqq.

[106] On the usus modernus of the exceptio non numeratae pecuniae, see Coing, pp. 470 sq.; for the 19th century, see Windscheid/Kipp, § 372 (concluding, de lege ferenda, on a very critical note). The exceptio has not been incorporated into the modern codifications. It is still in use in South African law (though usually renounced by the parties to the loan); cf. D.J. Joubert, in: Joubert (ed.), *The Law of South Africa*, vol. 15 (1981), n. 293.

CHAPTER 4

Stipulatio poenae

1. The functions of penalty clauses

The imposition of penalties is generally seen today as a concern of the State authorities. Penal elements in private law are very much the exception. Yet all civil-law jurisdictions recognize the possibility of voluntary subjection to a private penalty: a person may promise payment of a sum of money in the event of his doing, or refraining from doing, some act, especially in the event of his not performing an obligation which he has undertaken, or not performing it in the proper manner. Such conventional penalty clauses are useful for two reasons.[1] On the one hand they serve as a means of exerting pressure on the other party to behave or not to behave in a specific way; on the other hand, they relieve the creditor of the necessity of assessing and proving his claim for damages in case of non-compliance.

(a) Assessment of damages

Roman lawyers were familiar with both these functions.[2] Their conventional penalty was normally cast in the form of a stipulation.[3] The use of such stipulationes poenae was highly recommended by Justinian:

> "Non solum res in stipulatum deduci possunt, sed etiam facta: ut si stipulemur fieri aliquid vel non fieri. et in huiusmodi stipulationibus optimum erit poenam subicere, ne quantitas stipulationis in incerto sit ac necesse sit actori probare, quid eius intersit."[4]

In the same vein, we find Venuleius arguing:

> "In eiusmodi stipulationibus, quae 'quanti ea res est' promissionem habent, commodius est certam summam comprehendere, quoniam plerumque difficilis probatio est, quanti cuiusque intersit, et ad exiguam summam deducitur."[5]

It is often difficult and cumbersome to establish "quanti ea res est", that is, the amount in which the judge was instructed to condemn, where

---

[1] Cf. "Motive", in: *Mugdan*, vol. II, p. 275; Alfred Söllner, in: *Münchener Kommentar*, vol. II (2nd ed., 1985), Vor § 339, n. 3; Detlev Fischer, *Vertragsstrafe und vertragliche Schadensersatzpauschalierung* (1981), passim.

[2] Knütel, *Stipulatio poenae*, pp. 45 sqq. Early Roman law (like all early legal systems) had focused on the "in terrorem" function; the penalty was used as a sanction for a private wrong. In the course of time the compensatory function came to the fore; it was, in turn, to dominate the scene during the development of the ius commune. Classical Roman law presents the model of a well-balanced bifunctional approach.

[3] A penalty could, however, also be added to one of the consensual contracts by way of a pactum adiectum. The penalty could then be claimed with the bonae fidei action arising from that contract.

[4] *Inst.* III, 15, 7.

[5] D. 46, 5, 11.

we are dealing with a condictio certae rei. Even more so in cases of a facere stipulation,[6] where the judge had to assess "quidquid ob eam rem N^{um} N^{um} A^{o} A^{o} dare facere oportet": one always has to remember that, due to "omnis condemnatio pecuniaria", specific performance could never be enforced and that the problem of fixing monetary compensation or damages thus arose on a much broader scale than it does today. Correspondingly more important were penalty clauses obviating the need to adduce evidence, dispensing with the vagaries of judicial discretion and allowing parties to recover more safely, more speedily and more completely.[7] The fact that the English common law traditionally also does not render judgments obliging the debtor to perform his promise and, instead, confines the creditor to a claim for breach of contract,[8] seems to be one of the reasons why penal bonds in medieval English law were as popular as stipulationes poenae were in Roman law.

(b) "In terrorem" function

As far as the first of the above-mentioned functions of stipulationes poenae is concerned, C. 2, 55, 1 may be referred to:

> "Ex sententia arbitri ex compromisso iure perfecto aditi appellari non posse saepe rescriptum est, quia nec iudicati actio inde praestari potest et ob hoc invicem poena promittitur, ut metu eius a placitis non recedatur. . . ."

An appeal against an arbiter's award cannot be entertained; one of the reasons given by Emperor Caracalla relates to the stipulationes poenae entered into by the parties when they made their "compromissum": it was their purpose to deter the parties from not abiding by the arbiter's decision, and this purpose would be frustrated were one to allow an appeal. The "in terrorem" function of penalty clauses is also highlighted in Pap. D. 35, 1, 71, 1:

> "Titio centum relicta sunt ita, ut Maeviam uxorem quae vidua est ducat: condicio non remittetur et ideo nec cautio remittenda est. huic sententiae non refragatur, quod, si quis pecuniam promittat, si Maeviam uxorem non ducat, praetor actionem denegat: aliud est enim eligendi matrimonii poenae metu libertatem auferri, aliud ad testamentum certa lege invitari."

Where somebody promises to pay a penalty if he does not marry Maevia, such promise will be disapproved of. The case is different where some money has been left to Titius provided he marries Maevia. This condition is not objectionable, because it constitutes an "invitation", an inducement to marry. Titius will get a special reward for marrying Maevia, but won't lose anything if he decides otherwise. In the first case, however, he is put under pressure to marry Maevia, and

[6] Vide supra, pp. 37 (note 24), 90.
[7] Knütel, *Stipulatio poenae*, p. 53.
[8] Cf. infra, pp. 776 sqq.

that would be in conflict with the rule of "libera sunt matrimonia".[9] It is obvious that this side of a stipulatio poenae is—or can be—problematical. Few legal systems have, however, gone as far as the English common law, which disallows penalty clauses altogether.[10]

(c) Indirect enforcement of unenforceable acts

Stipulationes poenae served a further, very important, function in Roman law: they could be used to enforce performance of, or forbearance from, an act which was not already owed; that is, to make (indirectly) enforceable what had not been made directly enforceable by the parties. One might be tempted to ask why the creditor would contemplate this roundabout way of going about things, instead of making what he wanted the other party to do or not to do the object of an obligation itself. The answer is that in quite a few cases he was not able to do so. Again, we are here touching upon certain consequences of the "omnis condemnatio pecuniaria" rule: where the performance had no pecuniary value for the recipient, a condemnation could not be pronounced. Thus, a stipulatio poenae was the only way of securing immaterial (non-pecuniary) interest. The same applies, as has already been discussed, to contracts in favour of a third party.[11] A stipulatio alteri was not enforceable, a stipulatio poenae was. If forfeiture of the penalty was made dependent upon non-performance to the third party, this was a convenient device to exert pressure on the promisor to perform rather than to pay the penalty. Another example is given by Ulpianus in D. 45, 1, 38, 2: ". . . si quis velit factum alienum promittere, poenam . . . potest promittere". If a vendor had guaranteed that the purchaser would not be disturbed in his position ("habere licere"), the question arose whether such a promise covered interferences by third parties too.[12] An interpretation along those lines would have clashed with the rule that one cannot promise what somebody else will or will not do. Ulpianus shows the way out: a penalty, forfeiture of which is dependent upon third-party interference with the purchaser's habere.

---

[9] C. 8, 38, 2 and today § 1297 II BGB. Differently § 113 II 1 PrALR.

[10] Vide infra, pp. 107 sq. In the Middle Ages penal bonds were very popular, but in theory their function was apparently compensatory. Even where—as was commonly done—the penalty was fixed at twice the sum owed, it served to compensate the creditor for his loss of interesse. The practice of relieving defaulting debtors from forfeiture of the penalty "in equity" (that is, by the Court of Chancery) led to the decline of the penal bond and finally to the rejection of penalties by the common law. On the history of penal bonds, on their decline and on the establishment of the compensatory principle, see Simpson, *History*, pp. 90 sqq., 118 sqq., 123 sqq. Not dissimilar is the development that took place under the influence of canon law in the early ius commune. Cf. André Fliniaux, "L'évolution du concept de clause pénale chez les canonistes du Moyen-Age", in: *Mélanges Paul Fournier* (1929), pp. 233 sqq.

[11] Vide supra, p. 38.

[12] Ulp. D. 45, 1, 38 pr.

2. Non-genuine conventional penalty clauses

All these stipulationes poenae which are not attached to an already existing obligation (that is, those that perform the third of the above-mentioned functions) are usually referred to as independent or non-genuine conventional penalties. Their legal nature is described by Paulus in the following words: "Si ita stipulatus sim: 'si fundum non dederis, centum dare spondes?' sola centum in stipulatione sunt, in exsolutione fundus."[13] Only "centum" are owed; the promisor is under no obligation to transfer the tract of land. Such a transfer, however, is one way of discharging his obligation. We still find the non-genuine penalty in modern German law,[14] but it is living the sad life of a pitiful little wallflower. Its loss of significance is due largely to the fact that modern law has moved away from the principle of necessary condemnatio pecuniaria and has also broadened the scope of contractual freedom of the parties. Yet, analytically, even today it is the most basic form of conventional penalty, of which the genuine conventional penalty merely represents a specialized modification.[15] In Rome the non-genuine form was of great practical importance and was regularly employed, even in cases where that which was contained in the conditional part of the penalty stipulation could well have been the object of an obligation in itself. The agreement to submit a dispute to arbitration has been mentioned above. A mere pactum on those lines was not enforceable. Indeed, the technical term "compromissum" indicates that formal promises by both parties had to be given to abide by the award of the arbiter. Of course, the parties could execute two straightforward stipulations to that effect,[16] but the resulting protection was so unsatisfactory that it was general practice to enter into a penalty stipulation without any further ado: ". . . quod . . . arbiter ex compromisso . . . sententiam prove sententia dicat dicive iubeat . . .: si quid adversus ea factum erit sive quid factum non erit HS M probos recte dari."[17] This is a non-genuine penalty. The parties seem not to have bothered to promise, first of all, to abide by "sententia arbitri". The reason why the penalty was so much more important is obvious:

---

[13] D. 44, 7, 44, 5.

[14] Mentioned, but rather in passing and by no means fully regulated, in § 343 II BGB. South African law, like most other modern legal systems, does not recognize an undertaking of this kind as a penalty: cf. De Wet en Yeats, p. 218 and Guenther H. Treitel, "Remedies for Breach of Contract", in: *International Encyclopedia of Comparative Law*, vol. VII, 16 (1976), p. 91, discussing the English case of *Alder v. Moore* [1961] 2 QB 57 (CA), where a professional football player who received a sum of money from an insurance company on account of a personal injury undertook to repay that money in the event of his playing professional soccer again.

[15] The practical and dogmatic importance of the independent conventional penalty has been emphasized by Eduard Bötticher, "Wesen und Arten der Vertragsstrafe sowie deren Kontrolle" 1970 *Zeitschrift für Arbeitsrecht* 3 sqq.

[16] Cf. Ulp. D. 4, 8, 27, 7.

[17] Cf. Tab. Herc. 76. On this fragment and on the structure and content of the compromissum, see Ziegler, *Privates Schiedsgericht*, pp. 47 sqq. (64, 93).

"Cum poena ex compromisso petitur, is qui commisit damnandus est, nec interest, an adversarii eius interfuit arbitri sententia stari nec ne."[18]

Historically, furthermore, the non-genuine conventional penalties were the earliest form of stipulationes poenae and had a considerable influence on the development of the law of obligations.[19] At some early stage, a binding promise, enforceable by means of the legis actio per iudicis arbitrive postulationem,[20] could have only certa pecunia as its content. Commitment, for instance, to a facere could be achieved only indirectly: by making the other party promise certa pecunia if the desired act was not forthcoming.[21] It is from this starting point that certa res and, finally, incertum gradually gained recognition as things that could be owed directly, that is, become acceptable objects of a stipulation in their own right.[22] Thus (non-genuine) conventional penalties can well be said to have paved the way for the comprehensive range of classical stipulatio. A similar development (namely an advance from the use of—independent—penalties made conditional upon the occurrence or non-occurrence of a specific act to the recognition of the binding character of this act itself) is observable in the medieval English common law. Like the Roman jurists, the common lawyers started off, not with a general principle of actionability, but with a list of transactions which were actionable through the procedural forms. This formulary system, as in Roman law, determined the content and structure of the common law to a very considerable extent. The most commonly used of the medieval contractual actions was the writ of debt.[23] It was available, wherever a "sum certain" was due in law by debtor to creditor. This would usually be the case on the basis of a bond, a sealed instrument, whereby the one party had acknowledged to be the debtor of the other. Where such a bond was made subject to a condition, it became a most flexible institution which could be used to accommodate any lawful agreement.[24] These conditional penal bonds "function[ed] in what appears to us to be a peculiarly topsy-turvy way. Performance of what may be called the underlying agreement is not imposed as a duty; instead performance is only relevant as providing a defence to an action of debt for the penalty."[25] They are what we would call in civil-law terms non-genuine penalties.

---

[18] Mod. D. 4, 8, 38.

[19] Knütel, *Stipulatio poenae*, pp. 62, 65 sqq.

[20] Gai. IV, 17 a.

[21] The conditional promise was probably preceded, historically, by an alternative one ("Stichum aut decem dari spondes?"): cf. Kaser, *RPr* I, pp. 170, 519.

[22] The process was reversed in the interesting fragment Paul. D. 38, 1, 39 pr.: an invalid independent (!) penalty is reinterpreted (converted) into a valid promise of what had been in condicione. Cf. Knütel, *Stipulatio poenae*, pp. 76 sqq.

[23] Simpson, *History*, p. 53.

[24] Idem, *History*, pp. 90, 112 sqq.

[25] Idem, *History*, p. 112.

3. Genuine conventional penalty clauses

It will not come as a surprise that it is the genuine (or accessory) penalty clause[26] that the non-genuine conventional penalty is distinguished from. As § 339 BGB puts it: "If the debtor promises the creditor the payment of a sum of money as a penalty in case he does not perform his obligation or does not perform it in the proper manner. . . ." Here, the penalty secures (proper) performance of what is already owed. Hence, as far as genuine penalty clauses are concerned, we are always dealing with a two-membered transaction. Often the obligation, to which a stipulatio poenae was added, had also been cast in the form of a stipulation. Then we have a double stipulation of the type: "Pamphilum dari spondes?" "Spondeo." "Si Pamphilum non dederis, decem dari spondes?" "Spondeo." This would have been the most correct form, but if the promisor's answer was given only once ("Pamphilum dari spondes? Si non dederis, decem dari spondes?" "Spondeo."), that was acceptable too.[27] A stipulatio poenae could, however, also be attached to other obligations, for instance to a contract of sale.[28]

One problem, in particular, is raised by the specific structure of this type of stipulatio poenae: what is the relationship between the obligation to give Pamphilus and the obligation to pay one hundred, once the penalty of centum has become exactable?[29] Three different solutions are possible:[30] the two obligations can be cumulatively, alternatively or successively linked, i.e. the plaintiff can be allowed to claim both Pamphilus and centum, or he can have the option of choosing either the one or the other, or he can be confined to claiming only centum. As far as the double stipulations are concerned, the following fragment is of particular interest:

> "Sed si navem fieri stipulatus sum et, si non feceris, centum, videndum, utrum duae stipulationes sint, pura et condicionalis, et existens sequentis condicio non tollat

---

[26] In many modern systems the concept of a "penalty clause" is confined to these cases. Cf., for example, Treitel, op. cit., note 14, p. 94: ". . . the general principle that a penalty clause contains a merely accessory obligation". Treitel also quotes art. 2117 of the Louisiana Civil Code, where the accessory nature of the penalty clause is expressed very clearly: "A penal clause is a secondary obligation entered into for the purpose of enforcing performance of a primary obligation." As to the consequences of the accessoriness (if principal obligation is invalid, penalty is invalid, as well; assignment of principal obligation involves assignment of the penalty, etc.), cf. § 344 BGB; Söllner, op. cit., note 1, § 339, nn. 6 sqq.; De Wet en Yeats, pp. 219 sq.

[27] Cf. Pap. D. 45, 1, 115, 2; Paul. D. 17, 2, 71 pr.

[28] Cf., for example, Iul. D. 19, 1, 28. Also settlements and other pacta on the basis of which the praetor would grant an exceptio pacti could be secured by penalties: cf. e.g. Scaev. D. 45, 1, 122, 3; Paul. D. 23, 4, 12, 2.

[29] "On the problem of a penal stipulation combined with another, the sources are in a sad state of confusion": David Daube, "Slightly Different", (1961) 12 *Iura* 91. But see Levy, *Konkurrenz*, vol. II, 1, pp. 117 sqq. and, more recently, the detailed discussion by Knütel, *Stipulatio poenae*, pp. 262 sqq. (double stipulations), pp. 291 sqq. (pacta), pp. 320 sqq. (bonae fidei contracts).

[30] Windscheid/Kipp, § 285, 4.

priorem? an vero transferat in se et quasi novatio prioris fiat? quod magis verum est."[31]

The problem seems to have been controversial. While an older opinion has probably advocated elective concurrence (that is, the regime of alternativity),[32] Paulus favoured successivity. Up to the time when centum was exactable, the plaintiff could sue only on the first obligation (here: a facere obligation, namely to build a ship); afterwards, only on the second. When the penalty had fallen due, the binding force of the first obligation ceased to exist: the second obligation absorbed the first one in a way which was not dissimilar to a novatio.[33] With this decision, Paulus emphasized the compensatory function of the penalty clause:[34] the underlying policy consideration seems to be that the creditor must be held bound by whatever pre-estimate of his potential damages he made in fixing the quantum of the penalty. If the penalty then turned out not to cover his interest, he should not be able to revert to a claim for damages on the first stipulation.[35] The modern Swiss and German codes have decided differently:[36] by introducing a penalty clause into the contract, the creditor certainly wanted only to strengthen his position; therefore, he should still be allowed to fall back on his primary action for damages where the penalty has failed to provide sufficient protection. The forfeited penalty thus represents the minimum amount of the damage; but then could the creditor not have stipulated a higher penalty in the first place? Also, he could have excluded this regime of successivity of actions by specifically asking for cumulative or elective concurrence of remedies.[37]

However, § 340 II BGB and art. 161 II OR, in turn, also go back to Roman law; they are based on Iul. D. 19, 1, 28, the key fragment dealing with the concurrence of actions arising from bonae fidei contracts and penal stipulations that had been attached to them.

"Praedia mihi vendidisti et convenit, ut aliquid facerem: quod si non fecissem, poenam promisi. respondit: venditor antequam poenam ex stipulatu petat, ex vendito agere potest: si consecutus fuerit, quantum poenae nomine stipulatus esset, agentem ex stipulatu doli mali exceptio summovebit: si ex stipulatu poenam

[31] Paul. D. 44, 7, 44, 6.

[32] Even though, after forfeiture of the penalty, there were, strictly speaking, two obligations, both valid and enforceable, cumulation was generally regarded as inequitable by the Roman lawyers (Lab./Ulp. D. 44, 4, 4, 7; Sab./Ulp. D. 2, 14, 10, 1; Mela/Paul. D. 23, 4, 12, 2) and has been accepted only under exceptional circumstances.

[33] "Quasi novatio". Stricto sensu we cannot speak of a novatio, because "navem facere" and "centum" are not "idem debitum". Cf. supra, p. 60 and infra, pp. 634 sq.

[34] Knütel, *Stipulatio poenae*, p. 269.

[35] See also art. 1229 code civil; § 1336 I ABGB and, for South African law, De Wet en Yeats, pp. 220 sq.

[36] § 340 II BGB, art. 161 II OR.

[37] On such agreements between the parties as to the concurrence of actions, see Knütel, *Stipulatio poenae*, pp. 281 sqq.

consecutus fueris, ipso iure ex vendito agere non poteris nisi in id, quod pluris eius interfuerit id fieri."[38]

Some tracts of land have been sold; as part of the agreement the purchaser has undertaken not only to pay the purchase price, but also "to do something", for example to repair the vendor's house.[39] A stipulatio poenae provides for the possibility of his failure to do this job. Which actions does the vendor have, once the penalty is exactable? According to Iulianus, he is not confined to one based upon the stipulatio poenae, but can still avail himself of the actio venditi. In other words, he may choose which action he wants to use, but he cannot cumulate the two. If the vendor proceeds under the actio venditi, he cannot afterwards sue for the penalty; that second claim can then be countered with an exceptio doli. Where, on the other hand, he claims the penalty, he cannot sue for the same sum with the actio venditi. To prevent him from doing so (that is, to bar the actio venditi), the purchaser does not even have to plead an exceptio; the exceptio doli is inherent in all bonae fidei iudicia.[40] What Iulianus advocates, in this instance, is basically the principle of alternativity of remedies. But it is qualified in that the second claim is barred only up to the amount which the creditor (in our case, the vendor) has been able to recover in whichever action he brought first. The actual damages might exceed the sum fixed as a penalty. Then the actio venditi was still available to recover this additional amount. On the other hand, the penalty might have been beyond whatever damages had been suffered. If in this instance the vendor chose to use the actio venditi first, he was still able to bring a supplementary claim on the basis of the stipulatio poenae. The condictio was barred only up to the amount that had already been recovered, as can be deduced from the words "quantum poenae nomine stipulatus esset". Hence Roman lawyers do not seem to have stressed the purely compensatory side of penalty clauses to the same extent as in the case of double stipulations. Contracts bonae fidei gave rise to a whole range of duties, and the argument that the penalty could be treated as a genuine and binding pre-estimate of whatever damage might arise as a result of failure on the part of the debtor to comply with them did not really commend itself under these circumstances. Similarly, any parallel to novatio would have been rather far-fetched, especially in cases such as the one discussed by Iulianus, where the penalty served to secure only part of the contract of sale.[41]

---

[38] Interpolated, according to, for example, Levy, *Konkurrenz*, vol. II, 1, pp. 126 sqq.; but see Knütel, *Stipulatio poenae*, pp. 320 sqq.; Liebs, *Klagenkonkurrenz*, p. 208.

[39] Cf. e.g. Pomp. D. 19, 1, 6, 1.

[40] Vide infra, pp. 509, 667, 674.

[41] Knütel, *Stipulatio poenae*, p. 363.

4. Range of application

Stipulationes poenae were employed in Roman law in conjunction with all sorts of transactions.[42] They were used to secure the observance of obligations arising from sale, hire or partnership agreements,[43] the enforcement of settlements or the repayment of a loan; their field of application extended to the law of property, to family law[44] and to succession.[45] In three types of transactions, however, penalty stipulations found a particularly prominent expression: compromissa, stipulationes duplae and cautiones vadimonium sisti. The first two have been or will be discussed at other places,[46] the cautio relates to the law of procedure: "Cum autem in ius vocatus fuerit adversarius, neque eo die finiri potuerit negotium, vadimonium ei faciendum est, id est, ut promittat se certo die sisti."[47] Where the proceedings in iure could not be concluded within one day, the praetor permitted the plaintiff to fix the time when the defendant had to reappear in court.[48] The defendant then had to make a promise in something like the following terms: "[T]e sisti in certo loco: si non steteris, quinquaginta aureas dari spondes?"[49] The penalty would usually be fixed at half the amount in dispute.[50] Whether we are dealing here with an independent or accessory conventional penalty is not entirely clear.[51] It is in keeping with the practical relevance of stipulationes poenae that the Roman lawyers went to great pains to find the most suitable and expedient form of drafting them. Thus Labeo recommends the following versions, according to whether a duty to do or to refrain from doing something is involved:

> "Si ut aliquid fiat stipulemur, et usitatius et elegantius esse Labeo ait sic subici poenam: 'si ita factum non erit': at cum quid ne fiat stipulemur, tunc hoc modo: 'si adversus ea factum erit': et cum alia fieri, alia non fieri coniuncte stipulemur, sic comprehendum: 'si non feceris, si quid adversus ea feceris'."[52]

Forfeiture of the penalty would then be decided accordingly: where the stipulatio poenae aimed at securing forbearance ("Si in Capitolium

---

[42] Cf., for example, Adolf Berger, *Die Strafklauseln in den Papyrusurkunden* (1911), pp. 102 sqq.

[43] See e.g. Alf./Paul. D. 17, 2, 71 pr. On this fragment, see Daube, (1961) 12 *Iura* 88 sqq.

[44] Cf. the "stipulatio ex bonis moribus concepta" in Pap. D. 45, 1, 121, 1, which had been promised by a husband in case he would fall back into "consuetudo concubinae". Otherwise penalty stipulations in the field of family law were often disapproved of for moral reasons; cf., for example, supra, pp. 96 sq.

[45] Restrictions of the freedom of testation by means of stipulationes poenae ("si heredem me non feceris, tantum dare spondes?") were regarded as invalid: Iul. D. 45, 1, 61. The question was disputed in the later ius commune (cf. Windscheid/Kipp, § 529, n. 4); the BGB (§§ 2302, 344) has returned to the Roman solution.

[46] Vide supra, pp. 98 sq., and infra, pp. 295 sq. and 526 sqq.

[47] Gai. IV, 184.

[48] Cf. Kaser, *RZ*, pp. 167 sq.

[49] Cf. Pap. D. 45, 1, 115 pr.

[50] Cf. Gai. IV, 186.

[51] Cf. the discussion by Knütel, *Stipulatio poenae*, pp. 71 sqq.

[52] Lab./Ven. D. 45, 1, 137, 7; cf. also Ulp. D. 45, 1, 71.

ascenderis, centum mihi dari spondes?"), the penalty became exactable in case of contravention; where the penalty was used to exert pressure to act ("Si intra biennium Capitolium non ascenderis, centum mihi dari spondes?"), forfeiture occurred in case of failure to do the act.

5. Forfeiture of the penalty

(a) *If no time has been set for performance*

That sounds simple enough, but the latter situation especially gave rise to intricate problems of interpretation. What if no time had been set within which the act was to take place?[53] One can think essentially of two solutions, and both were advocated in Roman law.

According to Sabinus, the penalty became exactable if what had been promised was not done immediately ("statim").[54] Pegasus preferred an interpretation more favourable to the debtor: in his opinion, the debtor had to pay the penalty only if and when it had become impossible to carry out the act.[55] Papinian, who relates this dispute,[56] distinguishes between the two solutions. With regard to genuine conventional penalties, he follows Sabinus. The main obligation ("In Capitolium ascendere spondes?" "Pamphilum dari spondes?") is due immediately: quotiens dies non ponitur, praesenti die debetur.[57] It would, therefore, frustrate the purpose of the penalty clause to quite a considerable extent if the penalty became due only at a much later date and not as soon as the debtor had not availed himself of the first opportunity to act. This reasoning is based on the accessory nature of the genuine penalty clause and does not apply to non-genuine conventional penalties. Here Papinian comes to share Pegasus' view and, in doing so, adopts a very literal interpretation of the conditional clause. For, strictly speaking, the condition "si in Capitolium non ascenderis" can be said to have been fulfilled with any degree of certainty only when it has become impossible for the promisor to climb the Capitol. This approach is in accordance with the general principle of interpretatio contra stipulatorem:[58] had the stipulator wished the penalty to be due immediately, he could (and should) have said so expressly.[59]

However, even where a time had been set within which the act had to be performed, problems could arise. Did the stipulator have to wait

[53] Otherwise, expiry of the time set for performance would mark the forfeiture of the penalty: Pomp. D. 45, 1, 27, 1.
[54] Sab./Pap. D. 45, 1, 115, 2: "Item si quis ita stipuletur: 'si Pamphilum non dederis, centum dari spondes?' . . . Sabinus . . . existimabat ex sententia contrahentium, postquam homo potuit dari, confestim agendum. . . ."
[55] Peg./Pap. D. 45, 1, 115, 2: "Pegasus respondit non ante committi stipulationem, quam desisset posse Pamphilus dari."
[56] Pap. D. 45, 1, 115, 2.
[57] For this principle, see Ulp. D. 45, 1, 41, 1; Pomp. D. 50, 17, 14; cf. also *Inst.* III, 15, 2.
[58] Vide infra, pp. 639 sq.
[59] See, too, Knütel, *Stipulatio poenae*, pp. 131 sq.

until the time had lapsed (that is, for two years in our example above), even if it had already become clear that the act had become impossible?

> " 'Insulam intra biennium illo loco aedificari spondes?' ante finem biennii stipulatio non committitur, quamvis reus promittendi non aedificaverit et tantum residui temporis sit, quo aedificium extrui non possit: neque enim stipulationis status, cuius dies certus in exordio fuit, ex post facto mutatur."[60]

Here it had become impossible to erect the building within whatever time remained of the two years the promisor had originally been given. Nevertheless, the penalty was due only after the full period had lapsed. According to Papinian, the status of the stipulation cannot be changed by subsequent events. Paulus decided likewise, but gave a different reason: ". . . tota enim obligatio sub condicione et in diem collata est."[61] Forfeiture of the penalty was subject not only to a condition but also to a time clause ("dies"); the fact that the condition had been satisfied did not entail that the time, too, had lapsed.

(b) "Si per debitorem stetit . . ."

The most intricate question, however, as far as forfeiture of the penalty was concerned, related to a more general question: did the penalty become due when the condition was (objectively) fulfilled or did forfeiture also depend upon a subjective requirement, so that it would have occurred only where the promisor was in some way responsible for the non-fulfilment?

Our sources do not provide us with a clear and distinct picture; consequently, a number of theories have been developed by modern writers as to the position in classical Roman law.[62] But here, as in many other cases, one would be missing the casuistic nature of Roman law were one to try to extract a uniform, general rule from the available texts. Generally speaking, there seems to have been a development from a very strict and formalistic to a more subjective and equitable (that is, debtor-oriented) approach, stimulated by Sabinus (who is quoted in the following terms: ". . . et tamdiu ex stipulatione non posse agi, quamdiu per promissorem non stetit, quo minus hominem daret")[63] and promoted by his school.[64] The Proculians at first carried on to proceed from the principle of objective liability,[65] but after Celsus

---

[60] Pap. D. 45, 1, 124.

[61] Paul. D. 45, 1, 8.

[62] Frezza, *Garanzie*, vol. I, pp. 347 sqq.; Jörs/Kunkel/Wenger, p. 181; Kaser, *RPr* I, pp. 520 sq.; Pasquale Voci, "La responsabilità del debitore da stipulatio poenae", in: *Studi in onore di Edoardo Volterra*, vol. III (1971), pp. 319 sqq.; Windscheid/Kipp, § 285, 3. The question has now been comprehensively investigated by Knütel, *Stipulatio poenae*, pp. 195 sqq.

[63] Pap. D. 45, 1, 115, 2, relating to "si Pamphilum non dederis, centum dari spondes?".

[64] Cf., for example, Iul./Afr. D. 44, 7, 23 (for poena traiecticiae pecuniae); on which cf. infra, p. 185.

[65] Lab. D. 22, 2, 9.

abandoned it in favour of the Sabinian view[66] it seems to have become the prevailing opinion that the penalty was exactable only if the debtor was responsible for the performance or non-performance of what had primarily been envisaged by the parties. This responsibility was usually expressed in the words "Si per debitorem stetit quo minus (daret, non daret, veniat etc.)": a flexible concept that varied according to the standard of liability applicable in the particular context and therefore did not necessarily entail fault in the modern sense.[67] In similarly broad terms ("si per creditorem stetit, . . .") even the Proculians had already excluded liability for the penal sum, where forfeiture had its origin in the creditor's sphere.[68] However, some exceptional cases of "strict" liability continued to exist, and, especially with regard to the oldest type of penal promises, the cautio vadimonium sisti, the new approach never seems to have been adopted, probably because protection of the debtor had already been ensured by praetorian intervention.[69] A variety of exceptiones was available to him, on the basis of which he could allege, for instance, that he had been prevented from reappearing in court owing to dolus malus of the plaintiff or "valetudine vel tempestate vel vi fluminis";[70] where he had failed to do so "si ab alio sit impeditus",[71] the penalty was payable, but he was granted an action for damages against that third party. Today the penalty can generally be exacted only if the debtor has been at fault in not fulfilling his contractual obligations;[72] the parties can, however, provide differently.

6. The problem of excessive penalty clauses

(a) *The dangers of conventional penalties*

Conventional penalties, as may have become apparent already, are dangerous. Where there is unequal bargaining power, the creditor tends to put the economically less potent debtor under considerable pressure by stipulating penalties that, on occasion, may well exceed every reasonable or legitimate interest. The debtor, on the other hand, often has the freedom to "take it (upon the conditions offered) or leave it" only, and therefore cannot effectively negotiate the amount of the penalty. Furthermore, as the clause does not put him under any immediate obligation but only under a conditional one, the natural confidence in his own ability to render due performance will lead the

---

66 Cels./Ulp. D. 4, 8, 23, 3.
67 Cf. infra, pp. 385, 730, 785 sqq., 820, 822.
68 Serv./Ulp. D. 22, 2, 8; Pomp. D. 4, 8, 40.
69 Knütel, *Stipulatio poenae*, pp. 198 sqq.
70 Ulp. D. 2, 11, 2, 3–8.
71 Ulp. D. 2, 10, 1, 3.
72 Cf. § 339 BGB (". . . the penalty is forfeit if he is in default"; mora debitoris (default) entails fault: § 285 BGB); implicitly also De Wet en Yeats, pp. 217 sqq. (breach of contract); cf. also Treitel, op. cit., note 14, p. 94 ("Thus if 'fault' on the part of a debtor is an essential ingredient of contractual liability, it must exist before the penalty can be exacted").

debtor to underrate its gravely detrimental nature. Thus he may find himself to be exposed, rather surprisingly, to considerable claims, going far beyond the value his performance may conceivably have had for the creditor. Such considerations raise the question whether a legal system should lend its hand to the enforcement of excessive penalty clauses.[73] Roman lawyers, loath to interfere with what the parties had agreed upon, seem to have had no qualms about such clauses. They did not object to stipulationes poenae simply because the stipulated sum was too high. Until fairly recently, the French code civil followed the same principle of giving liberal effect to penalty clauses, even where the amount in question was excessive or derisory.[74] This attitude is based on individualism and freedom of contract; Johannes Voet[75] summed up the underlying policy consideration in the following words: ". . . ac merito regeri promissori poenae conventionalis, illum imputare sibi debere, quod sponte sua sibi talis imposuerit tantaeque poenae necessitatem"; the debtor has but himself to blame—had he not agreed to the clause, he would not have found himself in such a predicament. After all, we are dealing with a *conventional* penalty. Such an attitude, however, for the reasons mentioned above, is not acceptable under modern economic circumstances.

(b) The approach of modern European legal systems

An entirely different approach has been followed by English law, where penalty clauses "stipulated as in terrorem of the offending party"[76] are rejected as wholly invalid. Only where the clause is a genuine attempt to estimate the damages likely to ensue as a consequence of the breach of promise will the claim be entertained by the courts.[77] Thus, while saving the debtor from a situation where he would have had to pay what appears to be an extravagant and unconscionable amount compared with the greatest loss "that could conceivably be proved to have followed from the breach",[78] the English courts have introduced a distinction between penalties in a narrow sense and liquidated damages clauses, a distinction that has proved to be cumbersome and unsatisfactory. In each case the purpose of the clause has to be determined, and certain rules and presumptions

[73] For a comparative analysis, see Treitel, op. cit., note 14, pp. 90 sqq., 97 sqq.; James J. Cox, "Penal Clauses and Liquidated Damages", (1958) 33 *Tulane LR* 180 sqq.; J.C. de Wet, *Opuscula Miscellanea* (1979), pp. 209 sqq.

[74] Cf. artt. 1152 and 1231 code civil, amended, however, and brought into line with the other Continental systems in 1975. Cf. e.g. Fischer, op. cit., note 1, pp. 132 sqq.; Nicholas, *FLC*, pp. 229 sqq.

[75] *Commentarius ad Pandectas*, Lib. XLV, Tit. I, XII.

[76] *Dunlop Pneumatic Tyre Co. Ltd. v. New Garage and Motor Co. Ltd.* [1915] AC 79 (HL) at 86.

[77] Cf., for example, Treitel, *Contract*, pp. 769 sqq.

[78] *Dunlop Pneumatic Tyre Co. Ltd. v. New Garage and Motor Co. Ltd.* [1915] AC 79 (HL) at 87.

have been laid down to aid the courts in their task. But they achieve neither certainty of the law nor equitable solutions in each individual case, and therefore have been said to "manage to get the worst of both worlds".[79] Continental codifications generally recognize the validity of conventional penalties, subject, however, to judicial discretion to reduce the amount. By way of example, we may refer to the BGB: if a penalty which is due is disproportionately high, it may be reduced to a reasonable amount by a court's decision, upon application by the debtor. As far as the determination of reasonableness is concerned, the code provides that every legitimate interest (and not only pecuniary interests) shall be taken into consideration.[80] This judicial power to modify a contractual term was clearly recognized as highly exceptional[81] and was accepted only after much toing and froing in the final draft of the BGB.[82] It was also in conflict with pandectist doctrine, which faithfully supported the liberal Roman principle of literal enforcement of penalty clauses.

(c) Ius commune and South African law

Nevertheless, this attitude did not always reign supreme in the course of the development of the ius commune. There was a long, drawn-out dispute as to whether the rule in C. 7, 47 limiting the amount of damages claimable to double the value of what had been promised[83] was applicable to conventional penalties. "Haec quaestio antiquis, et neotericis multum ambagiosa est, et male discussa", as Molinaeus[84] bluntly remarks, answering this question himself in the affirmative. If the penalty is, with regard to its nature and function, a substitute for the recovery of whatever damages have arisen,[85] then its amount should

---

[79] Treitel, op. cit., note 14, p. 103. Strangely enough, the German courts have more recently cumbered themselves with very much the same problem. They have started distinguishing between penalty clauses (which, however, contrary to English law, are not invalid, but subject to the rules laid down in § 339 sqq.) and liquidated damages (which are not subject to these provisions of the code). In the literature, too, attempts have not been wanting to confine application of the § 339 sqq. to "in terrorem" clauses. Cf. the critical discussion by Fischer, op. cit., note 1, pp. 42 sqq.

[80] § 343 BGB; cf. also § 1336 ABGB, art. 163 III OR, art. 1384 codice civile.

[81] Cf. Heinrich Siber, in: Planck, *Kommentar zum Bürgerlichen Gesetzbuch* (4th ed.), vol. II, 1 (1914), § 343, 1: *"anomales Recht"* and Zimmermann, *Moderationsrecht*, pp. 89 sq.

[82] Cf. "Protokolle", in: *Mugdan*, vol. II, pp. 722 sqq.; cf. also *Verhandlungen des 20. Deutschen Juristentages*, vol. II (1889), pp. 23 sqq., 43 sqq.

[83] A notorious constitution, the wording of which (according to J.C. de Wet, *Opuscula Miscellanea* (1979), p. 205) is "so confused and obscure that it defies interpretation and even translation". Yet it became part and parcel of the ius commune. On C. 7, 47 in Roman law, see Medicus, *Id quod interest*, pp. 288 sqq.; H.J. Erasmus, " 'n Regshistoriese Beskouing van Codex 7, 47", (1968) 31 *THRHR* 213 sqq.; on the ius commune, see Coing, pp. 438 sqq. and H.J. Erasmus, "Aspects of the History of the South African Law of Damages", (1975) 38 *THRHR* 115 sqq.; for modern South African law, see Erasmus, (1968) 31 *THRHR* 237 sqq. For further details cf. also infra pp. 828 sqq.

[84] Carolus Molinaeus, *Tractatus de eo quod interest* (Venetiis, 1574), n. 159.

[85] As can be seen from this argument, the focus was very much on the purely compensatory function of penalty clauses. This attitude dates back to canon law empha-

also be limited in the same way as damages are: this was an oft-repeated argument of those who wanted to impose the limit of duplum upon penalty clauses.[86] Their view found legislative sanction, for instance in the Prussian Code.[87] But in the long run the contrary view prevailed.[88] In some places, however, and especially in the law of the Netherlands, a custom had come to be recognized that if the penalty was much larger than the actual loss suffered, it was within the competence of the court to reduce it "ad bonum et aequum"[89] so that Voet, while rejecting the applicability of C. 7, 47,[90] could state:

> "Denique moribus hodiernis volunt, ingente poena conventioni apposita, non totam poenam adjudicandam esse, sed magis arbitrio judicis eam ita oportere mitigari, ut ad id prope reducatur ac restringatur, quanti probabiliter actoris interesse potest."[91]

This was also, of course, what was transplanted to the Cape of the Good Hope, and the same principle, incidentally, is today recognized in South Africa, albeit on a statutory basis. The development leading to the enactment of the South African Conventional Penalties Act[92] is colourful, interesting and not atypical of the more recent South African legal history. While at first both the Cape Supreme Court and, especially, the Transvaal Supreme Court strove to follow the Roman-Dutch principle,[93] under the influence of Lord De Villiers and the Privy Council the English law relating to penalty clauses came to be received.[94] Thus, instead of enforcing penalties subject to a moderating jurisdiction of the court, the courts started drawing a distinction between (unenforceable) penalties and genuine estimates of damages. A half-hearted attempt by the Appellate Division to reverse the development[95] was rejected by the Privy Council,[96] until 1950 the highest court for the Union of South Africa. Naturally, the Privy Council, which was not staffed with Roman-Dutch lawyers, did not find the South African development unacceptable at all. With the rise of

---

(emphasizing, for moral reasons, the protection of the debtor and arguing that whatever was beyond a reasonable pre-estimate of damages constituted an unjustified gain for the creditor) and prevailed down to the time of the natural-law codifications. Only the 19th century saw a renascence of the "in terrorem" function of penalty clauses; their character, as private sanctions for the wrong of breach of contract, was (re-)accentuated—conventional penalties as *"eine durch Privatwillkür begründete Criminalanstalt im Kleinen"* (Savigny).

[86] Cf., for example, Pothier, *Traité des obligations*, n. 345.

[87] § 301 I 5 PrALR.

[88] Cf., for example, Fachinaeus, *Controversiae iuris*, vol. I, p. 50; Glück, vol. IV, p. 532, n. 3.

[89] Van Leeuwen, *Censura Forensis*, Pars I, Lib. IV, Cap. XV, 2.

[90] *Commentarius ad Pandectas*, Lib. XLV, Tit. I, XII.

[91] *Commentarius ad Pandectas*, Lib. XLV, Tit. I, XIII; cf. also Groenewegen, *De legibus abrogatis*, Cod. Lib. VII, Tit. XLVII, n. 10.

[92] Act 15/1962. Cf. De Wet en Yeats, pp. 211 sqq.; J.C. de Wet, *Opuscula Miscellanea* (1979), pp. 206 sqq.

[93] Cf. *Steytler v. Smuts* (1833) 1 Menz 40; *Mann and Harris v. Cohen* 1902 TH 261.

[94] *Otto v. Lategan* (1892) 9 SC 250; *Commissioner of Public Works v. Hills* [1906] AC 368 (PC).

[95] *Pearl Assurance Co. Ltd. v. Union Government* 1933 AD 277.

[96] *Pearl Assurance Co. v. Union Government* 1934 AD 560 (PC).

the purist approach to South African law, however, the decision in *Pearl Assurance Co. v. Union Government* was bound to receive harsh criticism; Van den Heever JA branded it as a "blemish on our legal system which militates against good faith, trust and business morality".[97] Yet little could be done by the courts against a precedent of that calibre, and thus only the legislature was able to remedy the situation. It acted in 1962.[98]

7. Semel commissa poena non evanescit

(a) *The Celsinian interpretation*

Roman law, as we have seen, did not provide for the reduction of excessive conventional penalties. This did not mean, however, that the Roman lawyers were totally unsympathetic towards the debtor and did not develop ways and means to assist him against creditors claiming the penalty. Reduction clauses are not the only means of diffusing the dangers inherent in penalty clauses. The same end can, to a certain extent, be achieved by careful analysis of the requirements for forfeiture.[99] In particular, however, a legal system can condone subsequent rendering of whatever performance had been due and thus allow the debtor unilaterally to purge forfeiture of the penalty. Such purgatio is, historically, the older device to protect the debtor, and the Roman lawyers, in fact, went out of their way to use it. It is largely forgotten today,[100] quite wrongly so, as Rolf Knütel has demonstrated.[101]

Semel commissa poena non evanescit:[102] a penalty, once payable, will not subsequently fall away. This sounds like a very general statement, but it would be wrong to take it as a hard-and-fast rule of Roman law. It was restricted owing to a very bold and flexible interpretation of penalty clauses, which goes back to Celsus[103] (who is generally

---

[97] *Tobacco Manufacturers Committee v. Jacob Green and Sons* 1953 (3) SA 480 (A) at 493F.

[98] Conventional Penalties Act 15/1962. Sec. 3 of this Act provides: "If upon the hearing of a claim for a penalty, it appears to the court that such penalty is out of proportion to the prejudice suffered by the creditor by reason of the act or omission in respect of which the penalty was stipulated, the court may reduce the penalty to such extent as it may consider equitable in the circumstances. . . ."

[99] Cf. supra, pp. 104 sqq.

[100] It was specifically excluded by § 306 I 5 PrALR. As to modern German law, cf. Söllner, op. cit., note 1, § 339, nn. 17 sqq.

[101] Rolf Knütel, "Verfallsbereinigung, nachträglicher Verfall und Unmöglichkeit bei der Vertragsstrafe", (1975) 175 *Archiv für die civilistische Praxis* 44 sqq.

[102] Cels./Ulp. D. 4, 8, 23 pr.; cf. also Gai. D. 21, 2, 57, 1 and Voci, *Studi Volterra*, vol. III, pp. 335 sqq.

[103] Cels./Ulp. D. 4, 8, 21, 12, Paul. D. 4, 8, 22, Cels./Ulp. D. 4, 8, 23 pr.: "Intra quantum autem temporis, nisi detur quod arbiter iusserit, committatur stipulatio, videndum est. et si quidem dies adiectus non sit, Celsus scribit libro secundo digestorum inesse quoddam modicum tempus: quod ubi praeterierit, poena statum peti potest: et tamen, inquit, et si dederit ante acceptum iudicium, agi ex stipulatu non poterit: utique nisi eius interfuerit tunc solvi. Celsus ait, si arbiter intra kalendas Septembres dari iusserit nec datum

regarded as one of the most original thinkers among the Roman lawyers). He drew a distinction according to whether the penalty clauses in question contained a reference to a specific date up to which performance had to have been made or not. To take a compromissum between Gaius and Seius as an example, the promise might have been something like: "Si quid adversus sententiam arbitri factum erit sive quid ita factum non erit, centum dari spondes?". "Spondeo." The arbiter might then have decided that the slave, Pamphilus, had to be given to Seius; just as well he might have requested Gaius more specifically to hand the slave over before the tenth of October. In the first case it had to be decided when the penalty was exactable. In Celsus' view, performance had to be rendered within "modicum tempus"; accordingly, forfeiture occurred after the lapse of whatever time was deemed to be "modicum" under the circumstances. However, even when Pamphilus had been given later on (that is, after the lapse of "modicum tempus" and after forfeiture of the penalty), that was still in accordance with a literal interpretation of the compromissum: Gaius had promised to act according to the award of the arbiter; this sententia had been to hand over Pamphilus, and that, finally, was what Gaius had done. Hence the paradox that forfeiture, which had actually taken place, was taken not to have occurred after all. The practical result was that payment of the penalty could still be avoided, until the creditor had brought an action—that is, until litis contestatio had taken place. At the time of litis contestatio, of course, the programme of litigation was fixed conclusively[104] and later developments could no longer be taken into consideration.

One might ask whether such an interpretation did not both unduly prejudice the interests of the creditor[105] and disregard the "in terrorem" function of the penalty. But the creditor was allowed to reject any performance tendered after the lapse of modicum tempus, if his interest in receiving it had fallen away in the meantime.[106] Also, it was in his hands to force the debtor either to make performance or to pay the penalty; once modicum tempus had passed, he could resort to litigation and thus preclude the debtor from unilaterally purging forfeiture. As far as the penalty itself is concerned, it seems to have fulfilled its "in terrorem" function if the debtor had rendered performance; if he had

erit, licet postea offeratur, attamen semel commissam poenam compromissi non evanescere, quoniam semper verum est intra kalendas datum non esse: sin autem oblatum accepit, poenam petere non potest doli exceptione removendus." Cf. also Marci. D. 4, 8, 52; Scaev. D. 45, 1, 122, 2. For a full discussion, see Knütel, *Stipulatio poenae*, pp. 147 sqq.

[104] Kaser, *RZ*, pp. 225 sq.

[105] Because, as a consequence of this interpretation, he had to accept the belated performance. If he did not do so (that is, if the fulfilment of the condition was brought about by the party to whose advantage it operated), the condition was deemed not to have been fulfilled. Vide infra, p. 729.

[106] Paul. D. 4, 8, 22.

finally done what was expected of him, the enforcement of what was designed to put pressure on him surely must be out of place.[107]

(b) Praetorian intervention

In the second of the above-mentioned cases, however, there was no room for such a flexible approach. Where a specific date had been set and the penalty become payable at that time, subsequent performance could no longer change this situation. Thus it is only in these instances that "semel commissa poena non evanescit" becomes relevant. But even here it was not applied as a general rule of a binding character, for now and then we find the praetor coming to the rescue of the debtor, even where, according to the unequivocal wording of the stipulatio, the penalty had become payable. He was prepared to grant an exceptio doli where it seemed unreasonable of the creditor to enforce the penalty, even though his position had not really been adversely affected by the delay in performance.[108] Another very interesting instance of praetorian intervention is Ulp. D. 2, 11, 9, 1:

> "Si plurium servorum nomine iudicio sistendi causa una stipulatione promittatur, poenam quidem integram committi, licet unus status non sit, Labeo ait, quia verum sit omnes statos non esse: verum si pro rata unius offeratur poena, exceptione doli usurum eum, qui ex hac stipulatione convenitur."

Here obviously an actio noxalis[109] had been brought; the defendant had promised, by way of a cautio, vadimonium sisti, (re)appearance in court of the several slaves in question. Even if only one of the slaves was missing, according to a strict reading of the cautio, the penalty, in its entirety, became exactable. Where, however, the debtor offered a pro rata share of the penalty he was granted an exceptio doli against the claim for the whole sum. Thus, for considerations of equity, we find Labeo/Ulpianus here allowing what amounts to a reduction of the

---

[107] In a similar vein, see Knütel, (1975) 175 *Archiv für die civilistische Praxis* 56 sq.

[108] Paul. D. 21, 2, 35: "Evictus autem a creditore tunc videtur, cum fere spes habendi abscisa est: itaque si Serviana actione evictus sit, committitur quidem stipulatio: sed quoniam soluta a debitore pecunia potest servum habere, si soluto pignore venditor conveniatur, poterit uti doli exceptione." For a very interesting parallel in the old English common law (to which Professor R. Knütel, Bonn, has drawn my attention), see the decision by Bereford CJ in *Umfraville v. Lonstede* YB 2 and 3 Edw II (Selden Society) 58 and the comment by F.W. Maitland in his Introduction (p. xiii) to this volume: "A man has bound himself to pay a certain sum if he does not hand over a certain document on a certain day. Being sued upon his bond, he is unable to deny that he did not tender the document on the day fixed for the transfer; but he tenders it now, excuses himself by saying that he was beyond the sea, having left the document with his wife for delivery, and urges that the plaintiff has suffered no damage. . . . To our surprise, Bereford CJ . . . exclaims: 'What equity would it be to award you the debt when the document is tendered and you cannot show that you have been damaged by the detention?' (*Quel equité serra de agarder à vous le dette de pus que l'escrit est prest, si vous ne porriez monstrer que vous fustes endamagé par la detenue?*) In the end the plaintiff is told that he will have to wait seven years for his judgement. Here certainly we seem to see 'relief against penalties' and relief that is granted in the name of 'equity', though it takes the clumsy form of an indefinite postponement of that judgement, which is dictated by the rigours of the law."

[109] On which see infra pp. 916 sq., 1099 sq., 1118 sq.

penalty in case of part performance; this idea was, later on, adopted by the French legislator and provided the historical basis for the ius moderandi, *"lorsque l'engagement a été exécuté en partie"*, contained in art. 1231 of the code civil.[110]

[110] Already in its original form, i.e. before the alteration in 1975. Cf. also art. 1384 codice civile.

CHAPTER 5

Suretyship

I. INTRODUCTION

1. The contract of suretyship

Where someone incurs a contractual obligation towards another, he will often be asked by his new creditor to promise a penalty in case of non-fulfilment. Stipulationes poenae can therefore be seen as one way of ensuring that promises are honoured. However, they give the creditor only another actio in personam against the debtor. Thus they do not protect him against the risk that the debtor may, once the debt has fallen due, have become insolvent or have disappeared. The creditor will therefore normally try to minimize the risk of losing out in one of two ways: he will either ask to be allocated a specific item belonging to the debtor (or to a third party) from which he will, in case of default or non-performance, be able to obtain satisfaction; or he may ask some other party (or parties) to guarantee fulfilment of the principal obligation. In other words, he will try to secure his position either by way of a real right (ownership, right of pledge, mortgage) or by actions in personam against one or more additional debtors (personal security).

Traditionally, the most important type of personal security is the contract of suretyship, where, in the words of the BGB, the surety binds himself to the creditor of a third party to be responsible for the fulfilment of the obligation of that third party.[1] Suretyship is well known in all modern (and ancient) legal systems.[2] Roman law displayed a striking predilection for this type of security transaction (adpromissio). Like conventional penalties, adpromissiones had to be cast in the form of a stipulation. Three different types were known in classical Roman law: sponsio, fidepromissio and fideiussio. Their refined and elaborate structure made them a model for all times; thus, the rules governing suretyship today are still essentially Roman.

---

[1] § 765 I BGB.

[2] Cf. especially the contributions published under the title "Les sûretés personnelles" as vols. 28 (1974), 29 (1971) and 30 (1969) of the *Recueils de la société Jean Bodin pour l'histoire comparative des institutions*. For more than 1 800 pages, the law of suretyship is discussed in a wide variety of historical and contemporary legal systems. The contributions range from Sumerian-Akkadian to (for example) Cambodian law. Neither Hungarian law from the 13th to the 18th century nor medieval Lotharingian law is neglected (although Roman-Dutch and Scottish law are). Very useful, too, for the modern comparative history of suretyship is William Burge, *Commentaries on the Law of Suretyship* (1849); cf. further Ralph Slovenko, "Suretyship" (1964–65) 39 *Tulane LR* 427 sqq.; Philip K. Jones, "Roman Law Bases of Suretyship in Some Modern Civil Codes", (1977–78) 52 *Tulane LR* 129 sqq.

2. Real security and personal security

As is evident both from the standard of jurisprudential analysis and the amount of legislative activity, personal security was much more important in Roman law than it is today. Today creditors usually prefer real security.[3] It provides them with assets of a rather stable value which can be converted into cash even in the event of insolvency and it excludes the risk of a (second) lawsuit against the surety (who may be unwilling to pay), or of being faced with *his* financial collapse too. "Plus cautionis in re est quam in persona"[4]—this statement by Pomponius would be a fair reflection of the modern trend in commercial life. As far as Roman law is concerned, however, the reverse was true. Two (possibly three) reasons can be given for the emphasis in Roman law on personal security.[5]

The first and most important reason relates to the value system that permeated Roman law and society. Friendship played a far greater social role than it does today; amicitia was a permanent relationship based on fidelity which gave rise to numerous and strict (extralegal) duties.[6] "Omnia . . . alter pro altero suscipiet":[7] this is a characteristic expression of such an attitude; and one of the things friends undertook as a matter of course was to stand surety for each other.[8] It was part of the "officium" to help one's friend in every situation and no matter what the sacrifice—so much so that Cicero could state with only a mild degree of rhetorical exaggeration: ". . . sine amicitia vitam esse nullam, si modo velint aliqua ex parte liberaliter vivere."[9] While, therefore, amicitia made personal security a much more viable and popular institution in Roman society, Roman fides, to quite a considerable extent, alleviated the risks involved in it for the creditor: if it was in any event of prime concern for the Roman citizen to keep his word, he would certainly do everything in his power to honour a promise given for a friend.

Secondly, personal security had a much more potent effect than security by pledge; the harshness of personal execution made whoever was personally liable try to discharge his obligation almost at all cost. And, finally, one should also mention in this context the relatively unsatisfactory nature of the Roman law of real security, even though that was probably to a large extent a consequence of, rather

---

[3] On the relative importance of personal and real security generally, see John Gilissen, "Esquisse d'une histoire comparée des sûretés personnelles", in: *Les sûretés personnelles*, vol. 28, pp. 87 sqq.

[4] Pomp. D. 50, 17, 25.

[5] Cf. especially Schulz, *CRL*, pp. 400 sqq. and also Kaser, *RPr* I, pp. 660 sq.; Nicholas, *Introduction*, pp. 149 sqq.

[6] Schulz, *Principles*, pp. 233 sqq.; Karl Meister, "Die Freundschaft bei den Griechen und Römern", (1950) 57 *Gymnasium* 5 sqq.

[7] Cicero, *Laelius de amicitia*, XXII, 82.

[8] Schulz, *Principles*, p. 237.

[9] *Laelius de amicitia*, XXIII 86.

than a reason for, the attractiveness of personal security. Usefulness and reliability of real security were seriously impaired by the lack of publicity: already by the time of the Republic, a right of pledge could be granted without transfer of the object to the creditor; later on, statutory liens with automatic priority in rank were introduced and in addition (non-possessory) general hypothecs over a whole property or parts of it gained considerable importance. Particularly during the 19th century, the deficiencies of the Roman law of real security were overemphasized (*"eine wahre Pest"*, *"etwas Fürchterliches"*).[10] The absence of a secure mortgage of land may well have contributed towards the rise of latifundia in Italy: whoever wanted to invest in land had to buy; the small farmers, in turn, because of the unavailability of real credit, were often forced to sell.[11] On the other hand, a desirable result was achieved in that at least free (i.e. largely unencumbered) ownership of land had been preserved.[12] Now, in the wake of 19th-century liberal expansionism, the "freedom" was proclaimed to incur debts by way of mortgage loans. A refined and consolidated land register provided the basis for what was called "mobilization of land value".[13] The consequence was that landed property soon became overcharged with debts. Before the First World War in Germany a total of 60 billion Marks was invested in mortgages, the sum total of the national wealth being less than 350 billion Marks.[14] Also, as far as the right of pledge on moveable things was concerned, the 19th century saw a move away from Roman law: delivery of the pledge to the creditor was made a mandatory requirement in terms of § 1205 BGB.[15] It did not take long, however, before what is effectively a non-possessory pledge slipped in again through the back door: the constitutum possessorium of § 930 BGB provided a convenient starting point for the "modern" lease back transactions (*"Sicherungsübereignung"*). They have dramatically reduced the practical significance of all the elaborate provisions contained in §§ 1204 sqq. BGB, and constitute a remarkable reversion back to the Roman fiducia.[16] While real security has therefore become more attractive today, it has remained a double-edged sword, beset with both new and old flaws and dangers. Personal security continues to play a significant role in those areas

[10] Cf. Justus Wilhelm Hedemann, *Die Fortschritte des Zivilrechts im XIX. Jahrhundert*, II, 2 (1935), pp. 6 sq. (the quotations (a real plague; something dreadful) are taken from Thibaut and Hugo).

[11] Schulz, *CRL*, p. 404.

[12] Schulz, *CRL*, p. 404.

[13] Justus Wilhelm Hedemann, *Die Fortschritte des Zivilrechts im XIX. Jahrhundert*, II, 1 (1930), pp. 42 sqq., 94 sqq.

[14] Cf. Hedemann, *Fortschritte*, II, 1, p. 98.

[15] Cf. Wolfgang Hromadka, *Die Entwicklung des Faustpfandprinzips im 18. und 19. Jahrhundert* (1971), pp. 41 sqq.

[16] Cf. e.g. Andreas Wacke, *Das Besitzkonstitut als Übergabesurrogat in Rechsgeschichte und Rechtsdogmatik* (1974), pp. 59 sqq.

where, ironically, it is not a natural person who stands surety but either a State institution or a bank.[17] Here, especially, the risk of insolvency appears to be considerably reduced.

II. SPONSIO, FIDEPROMISSIO AND FIDEIUSSIO

1. Sponsio

Of the three above-mentioned adpromissiones, sponsio was the oldest. It was characterized by the use of the word "spondere": "idem dari spondes?" "spondeo".[18] This "idem" that the surety promised would have been spelt out in the promise of the main debtor, which had been concluded beforehand. We have already come across the institution of sponsio in a broader sense, signifying any stipulation (that is, not only a suretyship stipulation) in which the verb "spondere" was used.[19] Because of a lack of sources, the early history of sponsio stipulatio is somewhat obscure. It is an open question whether the law of contract evolved from suretyship (in that sponsio was at first used exclusively to accept liability for others, then made available for the debtor to stand surety for himself, and only in the end turned into a method of creating debt and liability in one and the same person, that is, of making ordinary promises;[20] sponsio in this broad sense would then possibly have emerged only after the time of the enactment of the XII Tables)[21]—or whether, alternatively, sponsio was applicable, right from the beginning, for purposes other than suretyship.[22] Any answer must take into consideration certain terminological factors (namely, that "spondere" means "to promise"—in the broad sense; the word "sponsor",[23] on the other hand, always seems to have been used for a person who promised for somebody else)[24] and it is further complicated

---

[17] Details of the economically most important areas in Walther Hadding, Franz Häuser, Reinhard Welter, "Bürgschaft und Garantie", in: *Gutachten und Vorschläge zur Überarbeitung des Schuldrechts*, vol. III (1983), pp. 584 sqq.

[18] Gai. III, 116.

[19] Cf. supra, pp. 71, 72.

[20] Cf. especially Ludwig Mitteis, "Über die Herkunft der Stipulation. Eine Hypothese", in: *Aus römischem und bürgerlichem Recht, Festschrift für Ernst Immanuel Bekker* (1907), pp. 107 sqq.; also, for example, De Zulueta, *Gaius* II, pp. 145 sq., 152.

[21] Cf. e.g. Robert Feenstra, "Die Bürgschaft im römischen Recht und ihr Einfluss auf die mittelalterliche und spätere Rechtslehre", (1974) 28 *Recueils* (op. cit., note 2) 307 sqq.

[22] Cf. esp. Ernst Levy, *Sponsio, fidepromissio, fideiussio* (1907), pp. 1 sqq.

[23] Cf. Jean Triantaphyllopoulos, "Sponsor", (1961) 8 *RIDA* 373 sqq.

[24] Boggling at this discrepancy in meaning between verb and agent noun, many writers have attempted to harmonize the two. While some authors have imputed the wide range of "spondere" to "sponsio" (cf., for example, Levy, loc. cit.), others have argued that the verb was originally used in the same narrow sense as the noun (cf., for example, Mitteis, loc. cit.). Both views have been criticized by David Daube (*Roman Law, Linguistic, Social and Philosophical Aspects* (1969), pp. 4 sqq.), who finds any argument based on the assumption of absolute agreement between a verb and its agent noun "utterly unconvincing". Daube shows that the agent noun "tends to be confined to the striking" (p. 2) and gives the following illustration: "Merere or mereri means to earn, meretrix, literally, the earneress.

by the uncertainty about whether sponsio stipulatio had always been one single transaction, or whether it constituted an amalgamation of what were once two different roots.[25] Be that as it may, for our purposes it is important to note that the sponsor was always liable for somebody else's debt; this is the characteristic difference from other sureties in the ancient law who, like vades and praedes, guaranteed the presence of the person of the wrongdoer/debtor or of the object in dispute in court (*"Gestellungsbürgen"*).[26] Sponsio continued to be used for suretyship purposes; by the time of the later Roman Republic it had become, together with the closely related fidepromissio, the only form in which a promise to stand surety could be cast.[27]

2. The limitations of sponsio

Sponsio could, however, guarantee no debts except those which had themselves been created by way of a stipulation.[28] If another obligation (as, for example, one arising from a consensual contract of sale) was to be secured, a novatio had to take place first, in order to recast it in the form of a stipulation. Only then could the sponsio follow.

Originally, both the stipulation that was to be secured and the sponsio itself had to be concluded in one uninterrupted act. This requirement of "unitas actus" did not, however, imply that both stipulations were drawn together into one act, where the creditor first asked the debtor and then the surety ("Sei, decem mihi dari spondes? Maevi, idem dari spondes?") before both gave their answer, "spondeo".[29] Rather, both stipulations were kept separate (so that the main debt—"Sei, decem mihi dari spondes?" "Spondeo"—was created before the promise to stand surety was made); only, the one had to follow the other immediately. But this requirement was abandoned by the Proculians; they allowed sponsiones that had been concluded

---

Was the noun at one time wide, including a schoolmistress? Or was the verb narrow and there is no profit and no merit but goes back to the example set by the call-girl? In reality the noun is from the outset confined to a sector of the verb. The lady is called earneress because she makes a profession of earning, because she sets about earning in a rather special fashion, and indeed because the very fact that a woman earns is striking—there were not at the time many other ways, this kind of woman is *the* earneress" (p. 10). In the same way, according to Daube, the agent noun sponsor describes him "whose promise stands out" (p. 5).

[25] Cf. supra, p. 72, furthermore, especially, Vincenzo Arangio-Ruiz, "'Sponsio' e 'stipulatio' nella terminologia romana", (1962) 65 *BIDR* 193 sqq., who shows that the terms "stipulatio" and "sponsio", at least as far as we can trace them back, have always indicated the two sides of one and the same transaction. For a brief summary of the discussion relating to the origins of stipulatio, cf. also Jolowicz/Nicholas, pp. 280 sq.

[26] Cf. Kaser, *Altrömisches ius*, pp. 270 sqq.; Wesener, *RE*, Suppl. vol. XIV, pp. 447 sqq.; Teresa Gimenez-Candela, "Notas en torno al 'vadimonium'", (1982) 48 *SDHI* 126 sqq.

[27] *"Gestellungsbürgschaft"* by means of vades or praedes had been turned into the promise of vadimonium or cautio pro praede (both in the form of stipulations). The old praedes survived only in exceptional cases; cf. e.g. Jolowicz/Nicholas, p. 299.

[28] Gai. III, 119.

[29] This would be the case of joint debtors (plures rei promittendi): see *Inst.* III, 16 pr.

subsequently and in the absence of the main debtor.[30] This view, of course, entailed a change in the standard formula used for the purpose of sponsio. "Idem dari spondes?" was hardly the appropriate question where what was being referred to had taken place some months before. The stipulator had to be more precise as to what he wanted the surety to guarantee: "Quod Seius mihi dare spopondit dari spondes?" or, for instance: "Decem, quae Seius mihi debet, dari spondes?" These, however, were exactly the forms which the parties would also have had to use for the purposes of a novatio. Thus intricate problems of interpretation could arise.[31]

A surety binds himself to be responsible for the fulfilment of somebody else's obligation. He often acts altruistically, especially where—as in Rome—the debtor did not have to draw so much on commercial banks, but could rely on his friends, who readily lent him their help as part of the officium amicitiae. Yet, as sureties, these friends were liable in the same way as the debtor, that is, they faced the dire consequences of personal execution if they could not or did not want to pay, once they were called upon to do so. Thus, there was a strong tendency to relieve the lot of sureties which resulted in quite an unusual degree of legislative activity.[32] As a creditor normally had several sureties guaranteeing one debt, the first concern of the legislator was to spread the load evenly between them. A lex Appuleia gave an action to any surety who had paid more than his share against the others for the excess: ". . . inter sponsores . . . lex Appuleia quandam societatem introduxit", as Gaius put it.[33] Then came the lex Furia that made the creditor divide his debt among the co-sureties who were alive at the time when the debt fell due.[34] Thus he was no longer able to sue each of them for the whole; instead, he was faced with the prospect of having to bring an action against all co-sureties for their aliquot part—that is, of having to conduct a multiplicity of lawsuits. An important implication of the lex Furia was that the shares were fixed, regardless of whether all the co-sureties were solvent when the debt fell due. In other words: it was the creditor rather than the other co-sureties who carried the risk of insolvency of one (or several) of the sureties! If, for example, A, B, C and D were sureties for a debt of 120 and A had died before the debt fell due, B and C were liable for only 40 each, irrespective of whether the creditor could exact the third share of 40 from D or not. With the introduction of the lex Furia, incidentally, it became doubtful whether the beneficium legis Appuleiae still survived.

[30] Frezza, *Garanzie*, vol. I, pp. 23 sqq.

[31] Cf. Peter Apathy, "Zur Abgrenzung von Novation und Bürgschaft", (1971) 18 *RIDA* 381 sqq., 399 sqq., 409 sqq., 427 sqq.

[32] For a general outline, see Jean Triantaphyllopoulos, "La législation romaine sur le cautionnement", (1961) 39 *RH* 501 sqq.; Frezza, *Garanzie*, vol. I, pp. 14 sqq.

[33] Gai. III, 122.

[34] Gai. III, 121.

Seeing that a creditor who had exacted more than his rateable part from a sponsor became liable to manus iniectio himself,[35] there no longer seems to have been any need for it. The situation was different in the provinces, because the lex Furia (in contrast to the lex Appuleia) applied in Italy only.[36]

But how could the sureties know what their share was? It was often only the creditor (and probably also the debtor) who knew the number of sureties securing a particular debt. A lex Cicereia therefore required the creditor to announce publicly and in advance for which obligation he was about to secure himself and how many sureties he was going to take.[37] If he failed to give this notice, the sureties could within 30 days ask for a declaratory judgment (praeiudicium) to determine this point. If it was found that no proper notice had indeed been given, they were discharged.

One can well imagine that all these provisions made the sponsio increasingly cumbersome and unattractive to the creditor. A further point was that the liability of a sponsor did not descend to his heirs;[38] all the primitive obligations had been (passively) intransmissible, and in the case of sponsio this might have remained so as a result of its (originally) sacral nature.[39] "As if this were not enough",[40] the lex Furia also limited the liability of the sponsor himself to two years. After the lapse of this time, he automatically became free.

3. Fidepromissio and the transition to fideiussio

Fidepromissio did not offer the creditor a more viable alternative, because it was subject to the same defects and limitations as sponsio.[41] All the rules mentioned so far applied also to fidepromissio. The main difference between these two types of suretyship was merely that sponsio was confined to Roman citizens whereas fidepromissio stipulations were available to non-Romans too.

By the end of the Republic, therefore, while sureties were well protected, creditors started to look for better security. Thus a third type of suretyship stipulation emerged which was subject to none of the above-mentioned limitations.[42] It soon began to supersede sponsio and

---

35 Gai. IV, 22.

36 Gai. III, 121 a.

37 Gai. III, 123.

38 Gai. III, 120.

39 Cf. supra, p. 72 and Kaser, *RPr* I, pp. 168 sq., cf. further Levy, *Sponsio*, pp. 45 sqq.

40 De Zulueta, *Gaius* II, p. 161.

41 As to fidepromissio, see Jean Triantaphyllopoulos, "Peregrinus fidepromissor (Gai. inst. 3, 120)", in: *Mélanges d'histoire ancienne offerts à William Seston* (1974), pp. 473 sqq. and also Franz Wieacker, "Zum Ursprung der bonae fidei iudicia", (1963) 80 *ZSS* 13 sq.

42 That fideiussio was developed mainly in order to evade the suretyship legislation is the prevailing opinion; see e.g. De Zulueta, *Gaius* II, p. 161; Feenstra, op. cit., note 21, p. 315; Jolowicz/Nicholas, p. 300. Contra: Levy, *Sponsio*, pp. 124 sqq.; Werner Flume, *Studien zur Akzessorität der römischen Bürgschaftsstipulationen* (1932), pp. 36 sqq.

fidepromissio in practice and has become the prototype of the modern contract of suretyship. This development provides a good example of how well-intentioned legislation, designed to achieve better protection of the debtor, can in the end defeat this very purpose. The new type of suretyship was called fideiussio and the question and answer required for its conclusion were as follows: "Quod Maevius mihi debet, id fide tua esse iubes?" "Fideiubeo."[43] Fideiussio was not subject to the provisions of the lex Appuleia, the lex Furia or the lex Cicereia.[44] Otherwise than in the case of sponsio or fidepromissio, the obligation was transmissible on death, i.e. the creditor could sue the heirs of a deceased fideiussor.[45] Furthermore, fideiussio was not restricted to securing stipulations; it could be used to guarantee any debt, however created.[46] It has been suggested that there was a further, more fundamental and structural difference between the new and the two older forms of suretyship and that this is what Gaius really had in mind when he emphasized: "Sponsoris vero et fidepromissoris similis condicio est, fideiussoris valde dissimilis":[47] fideiussio, it is said, was "accessory", while sponsio and fidepromissio were not.[48]

III. THE ACCESSORINESS OF SURETYSHIP IN ROMAN LAW

1. Limited accessoriness of fideiussio

(a) ". . . nec plus in accessione [est]"

Any discussion of the accessory nature of the Roman suretyship stipulations immediately involves the danger of superimposing modern concepts and thinking patterns upon historical legal system. Suretyship, in modern law, is an "accessory" contract,[49] accessoriness indicating, in the present context, dependence, to a greater or lesser extent, of the surety's obligation upon that of the principal debtor. Both the term and the idea do, indeed, go back to Roman law, but it would, of course, be ahistorical to expect the Roman sources to conform to, for instance, the rigid conceptualization of the BGB: "The

[43] On the notion of "fides" as part of the declarations required for "fide-iussio", see Flume, op. cit., note 42, pp. 52 sqq.

[44] A lex Cornelia (81 B.C.), limiting the sum for which one person could stand surety for the same debtor to the same creditor in any one year to 20 000 sesterces, did, however, apply to all three types of suretyship promises: Gai. III, 124.

[45] Gai. III, 120.

[46] Gai. III, 119 a.

[47] Gai. III, 118.

[48] Wilhelm Girtanner, *Die Bürgschaft nach gemeinem Civilrecht* (1850–51), pp. 20 sqq.; Flume, op. cit., note 42, pp. 64 sqq.; Schulz, *CRL*, pp. 495 sqq.

[49] Cf. e.g. John Gilissen, "Esquisse d'une histoire comparée des sûretés personnelles", (1974) 28 *Recueils* (op. cit., note 2) 100 sqq.; Albert Kiralfy, "History of the Law of Personal Guarantee in England since 1500", (1971) 29 *Recueils* (op. cit., note 2) 411 sqq., 421 sqq.; L.R. Caney, C.F. Forsyth, *The Law of Suretyship in South Africa* (1982), p. 28; Burge, *Suretyship*, p. 3.

extent of the principal obligation at any time determines the obligation of the surety."[50] Whilst, in fact, many of their decisions would fit in well with this definition, the Roman lawyers took a much more flexible line and never allowed themselves to be hemmed in by rigid dogmatic categories such as "accessoriness".[51] Nor did they actually use that term in the modern technical sense. When Gaius says, "[n]am [sponsores et fidepromissores] quidem nullis obligationibus accedere possunt nisi verborum"[52] or ". . . et horum [referring to sponsores, fidepromissores *and* fideiussores] obligatio accessio est principalis obligationis",[53] he merely describes the obligation of the surety as one which is added to that of the principal debtor. The adjective "accessorius", incidentally, was created by the glossators ("in accessione . . . id est in accessoria obligatione"). How far, then, was this "added" obligation of the fideiussor dependent upon the obligation it was designed to secure? The answer of the Roman lawyers was, in a nutshell: in so far as the structure, function and purpose of the surety's promise required. Thus, for example, the obligation of the fideiussor could not exceed the principal obligation: ". . . nec plus in accessione esse potest quam in principali re."[54] If, in the framing of the fideiussio, reference had to be made to the main obligation, it is hardly imaginable how the surety could be made to promise "eadem quindecim quae Maevius debet", where Maevius in fact only owed decem. On the other hand, the surety could be liable for less than the main debtor, for if the latter owed ten, he would in any event and by implication also owe the five which the surety might have made himself liable for: minus in maiore inest.[55] Generally speaking, one can say that the surety was not to be liable more strictly than the main debtor. Suretyship is a way of ensuring that the creditor gets what the debtor owes him; where the debtor does not owe anything, the third party cannot really be said to stand surety. This type of reasoning can also be applied, for instance, to conditional promises:[56] where the main obligation was conditional, the fideiussor could not be made to promise unconditionally. Yet it was perfectly possible to secure a promise that was not itself subject to a condition, by means of a conditional fideiussio.[57]

---

[50] § 767; cf. already the pandectist writers, e.g. Girtanner, op. cit., note 48, pp. 402 sqq.
[51] Cf. e.g. Ernst Levy, "Principal and Surety in Classical Roman Law", (1951) 14/15 *BIDR* 217: "No doubt, the liability of the fideiussor was accessory, i.e. dependent in some way upon the principal's obligation. How far, however, this dependence made itself felt, is another matter."
[52] Gai. III, 119.
[53] Gai. III, 126.
[54] Gai. III, 126.
[55] Cf. supra, p. 74 (note 39).
[56] As Justinian put it: "Non solum enim in quantitate, sed etiam in tempore minus et plus intellegitur" (*Inst.* III, 20, 5).
[57] Cf. *Inst.* III, 20, 5.

(b) The availability of the debtor's exceptions

Similar considerations seem to have been relevant in determining whether the fideiussor could avail himself of the exceptiones which the debtor was entitled to raise. This problem crops up in a variety of texts. Celsus D. 12, 6, 47 provides an example:

> "Indebitam pecuniam per errorem promisisti: eam qui pro te fideiusserat solvit. . . . si[n autem] fideiussor suo nomine solverit quod non debebat, ipsum a stipulatore repetere posse, ..."[58]

Maevius (the main debtor) promised, by mistake, to pay what he did not in actual fact owe. Seius stood surety for this promise. In order to discharge his suretyship obligation, Seius then paid the money to Titius (the creditor). As a consequence of the mistake, Titius is unjustifiedly enriched. The question is, however, whether Seius or Maevius can institute the condictio indebiti.[59] On the one hand, one may argue that Seius has paid a debitum; thus, he can sue Maevius only for reimbursement, and it is up to the latter to claim the unjustified enrichment back from Titius. Celsus opines otherwise: Maevius could have raised an exceptio doli should Titius have tried to sue him. The same exceptio was available to Seius, who, in honouring his obligation arising from the fideiussio, has paid something he did not have to pay—an indebitum which he will now be able to claim back himself. A similar view is expressed in many other sources.[60] But it would be rash to accept the generalizing statement by Marcianus (D. 44, 1, 19): "Omnes exceptiones, quae reo competunt, fideiussori quoque etiam invito reo competunt" at face value. If a debtor became insolvent owing to misfortune, he was able to avoid the harshness of personal execution by way of cessio bonorum, i.e. by ceding his property to the creditors.[61] Once he had done that, he could bar further claims with the exceptio nisi bonis cesserit. Defences of this kind, which were based on certain snags pertaining to the person of the main debtor, rather than the principal obligation, could not be raised by the fideiussor: ". . . ideo quia, qui alios pro debitore obligat, hoc maxime prospicit, ut, cum facultatibus lapsus fuerit debitor, possit ab his quos pro eo obligavit suum consequi."[62] But if the fideiussio was designed to protect the creditor against exactly this type of eventuality, it was certainly not intended to provide him with a sum of money which the principal debtor had promised only by mistake and which he was therefore

---

[58] This text is discussed by Fritz Schulz, "'Condictio indebiti' und die Accessorietät der 'sponsio' und 'fideiussio' (D. 12. 6. 47.)", (1952) 3 *Iura* 15 sqq. and Max Kaser, "Celsus D. 12. 6. 47 und die Akzessorietät der Bürgschaft", in: *Festgabe für Arnold Herdlitczka* (1972), pp. 143 sqq.

[59] The most important of the unjustified enrichment claims. For details, see infra pp. 848 sqq.

[60] Cf. e.g. Ulp. D. 17, 1, 29 pr.; Pap. D. 46, 1, 49 pr.; Iul. D. 46, 1, 15 pr.; Ulp. D. 36, 4, 1 pr.

[61] Kaser, *RZ*, pp. 316 sq.

[62] *Inst.* IV, 14, 4.

entitled neither to receive nor to retain. This is the underlying policy reason for Celsus' decision discussed above;[63] to sue the surety while the main debtor can raise the exceptio doli is in itself a breach of good faith which may, in turn, be met with an exceptio doli.

(c) Invalidity of the principal obligation

If the principal obligation was invalid (perhaps because it was illegal or immoral), a contract of suretyship could not be validly created either, for there was nothing to secure. The position was different in the case of a naturalis obligatio: where a ward or woman had incurred an obligation sine auctoritas tutoris, a fideiussio undertaken to secure his or her (natural) obligation was valid and enforceable.[64] Again, the "snag" about the principal obligation related to the person of the main debtor, and it did not run counter to the function of suretyship to afford coverage for the creditor in these cases: the surety is supposed to secure the creditor against any inability on the part of the debtor to pay his debt, whatever the reason. The same principle applied where somebody had stood surety, for instance, for the obligation of a slave.[65] By the same token, the surety's obligation normally[66] expired when the principal obligation came to an end. Thus, where the debtor had paid what he owed, or where he had been released by acceptilatio, where his obligation was discharged by novatio or where, for example, the creditor became his universal successor (confusio), the fideiussor automatically became free too.[67] Problems could arise where fulfilment of the principal obligation had become impossible through no fault of the principal debtor: both principal debtor and fideiussor were free. This was the situation even if the fideiussor had been responsible for the fact that the debtor had become unable to render performance. If, for instance, Seius (the surety) killed the slave that Maevius (the principal debtor) had promised to deliver to Titius, Maevius' obligation was discharged and, as a consequence, Seius' obligation fell away as well. This result was, of course, intolerable and thus we find the praetor granting either an actio utilis or an actio de dolo against the fideiussor.[68]

---

[63] Kaser, *Festgabe Herdlitczka*, pp. 154 sqq.

[64] Gai. III, 119 a. As far as the example of the woman or ward is concerned, Gaius confines his statement (III, 119) to sponsio and fidepromissio; it is very unlikely, however, that stipulations of these persons, incurred without auctoritas tutoris, should have provided a sufficient basis for sponsio and fidepromissio, but not for fideiussio; here it did not even matter whether the woman or ward had engaged (sine auctoritas tutoris) in a stipulation (cf. esp. Francesco de Martino, *Le garanzie personali dell'obbligazione I* (1940), pp. 86 sqq.; Frezza, *Garanzie*, vol. I, pp. 43 sqq.). In late classical law they were regarded as naturales obligationes: Pap. D. 46, 3, 95, 4; Ulp. D. 46, 2, 1, 1.

[65] Gai. III, 119 a.

[66] For exceptions (based, again, on the creditor's security interest), see Kaser, *RPr* I, p. 664, n. 44; Buckland/Stein, p. 446, n. 1.

[67] Schulz, *CRL*, pp. 500 sq.

[68] Ner./Iul./Pap. D. 4, 3, 19; Paul. D. 45, 1, 49 pr.; Flume, op. cit., note 42, pp. 105 sqq.; Frezza, *Garanzie*, vol. I, pp. 87 sqq.

All in all, therefore, one can conclude that the obligation of the fideiussor *was* dependent upon that of the main debtor, but only in a limited way.[69] Thus, to characterize fideiussio as "accessory" is safe only as long as it is kept in mind that one does not thereby describe the precise nature and scope of all legal effects involved.[70]

2. Sponsio and fidepromissio

If, then, the first part of the above-mentioned proposition (fideiussio was accessory) can be maintained only cum grano salis, the other half is open to far more serious criticism. The opinion that sponsio and fidepromissio were not "accessory" to a principal obligation, but independent, is based on far-reaching interpolation hypotheses, supported, in some instances, by large-scale rewriting rather than careful reconstruction of the available sources.[71] The main problem is that very little direct evidence is available, for sponsio and fidepromissio had already disappeared as living institutions soon after the end of the classical period.[72] By the 6th century they had become totally obscure. Justinian, therefore, systematically removed sponsores and fidepromissores from the classical sources and substituted the fideiussor in their place. Thus, while we certainly have to expect a certain degree of corruption in our texts dealing with suretyship, it is hardly justified to relate whatever does not seem to tie in with the idea of accessoriness in our sources to the older sponsio/fidepromissio layer of the law. Both sponsio and fidepromissio were certainly not accessory in any strict or dogmatic sense of the word,[73] but they were also, in all likelihood, no more independent of the main obligation than fideiussio was.[74]

IV. IDEM DEBITUM

1. The classical principle of "*Konsumptionskonkurrenz*"

One further very important aspect was common to sponsio, fidepromissio and fideiussio (even though that has also been disputed). The surety promised "idem" or "id quod Maevius mihi debet". As a result, he and the main debtor owed the same; their obligations were

[69] Kaser, *RPr* I, pp. 661, 663.
[70] Levy, (1951) 14/15 *BIDR* 217.
[71] An example of this method is the restoration of the Celsus text (D. 12, 6, 47, discussed supra, p. 123) by Schulz, (1952) 3 *Iura* 18. Contra: Kaser, *Festgabe Herdlitczka*, pp. 143 sqq., 146 sqq.
[72] Levy, *Obligationenrecht*, pp. 196 sqq.
[73] Cf. Gai. III, 119: ". . . interdum ipse qui promiserit non fuerit obligatus, velut si mulier aut pupillus sine tutoris auctoritate, aut quilibet post mortem suam, dari promiserit. at illud quaeritur, si servus aut peregrinus spoponderit, an pro eo sponsor aut fidepromissor obligetur."
[74] Robert Feenstra, "Le caractère accessoire des différents types de cautionnement 'verbis' en droit romain classique", in: *Études offertes à Jean Macqueron* (1970), pp. 301 sqq.; Kaser, *Festgabe Herdlitczka*, pp. 154 sqq.

considered eadem res.[75] From the point of view of the creditor, this entailed a certain risk relating to the enforcement of his claim. For reasons of procedural economy and respect for the judicial function, nobody was allowed to come to court more than once in the same matter: bis de eadem re agere non liceat[76] had been the hallowed rule since the days of the legis actiones. The key moment was litis contestatio; once this joinder of issue had taken place, the action was consumed[77] and any attempt to institute a second trial would (as far as iudicia legitima in personam with a formula in ius concepta were concerned)[78] have been met by denegatio actionis.[79] If, therefore, the actions against main debtor and surety were identical with respect to both their causa and their objective, any action brought against the one automatically made the other's obligation fall away too: not only did litis contestatio with the main debtor destroy the obligation of the surety (that could possibly still have been explained on the basis of the "accessoriness" of the latter)[80] but litis contestatio with the surety also extinguished the obligation of the main debtor.[81]

Thus, the creditor had to be careful about whom he chose to sue. Once, for instance, he had brought his action against the main debtor without being able to obtain full satisfaction, he was barred from suing the surety. The concurrence of actions, as Levy[82] has put it, was determined in the sense of reciprocal process consumption (*"Konsumptionskonkurrenz"*).

2. From *"Konsumptionskonkurrenz"* to *"Solutionskonkurrenz"*

To any modern lawyer this must seem rather strange.[83] The Romans, however, can hardly have considered these effects of litis consumptio as

---

[75] Cf. e.g. Levy, *Konkurrenz*, vol. I, pp. 190 sqq.; Liebs, *Klagenkonkurrenz*, p. 250.

[76] Quintilianus, *Declamationes*, 226; cf. Levy, *Sponsio*, pp. 48 sqq.; Kaser, *Altrömisches ius*, pp. 115 sqq.

[77] Hence the old saying (Gai. III, 180): "Ante litem contestatam dare debitor oportet, post litem contestatam condemnari oportet, post condemnationem iudicatum facere oportet." For a discussion, see Detlef Liebs, "Die Klagenkonsumption des römischen Rechts", (1969) 86 *ZSS* 169 sqq.

[78] Gai. III, 180 sq., IV, 106 sq.; in the case of all other actions, consumption was effected by granting to the defendant the exceptio rei iudicatae vel in iudicium deductae.

[79] As to the barring effect of litis contestatio, cf. Kaser, *RZ*, pp. 229 sqq.; Buckland/Stein, pp. 695 sqq.; cf. also supra p. 61, note 195.

[80] This is the line of argument adopted by William Warwick Buckland, "Principal and Fideiussor. Consumptio litis", (1941) 53 *Juridical Review* 281 sqq.

[81] But see Buckland, (1941) 53 *Juridical Review* 281 sqq., who disputes eadem res as far as fideiussio was concerned. His view, shared e.g. by Schulz, *CRL*, p. 501, has been refuted by Ernst Levy, "Principal and Surety in Classical Roman Law", (1951) 14/15 *BIDR* 207 sqq.; cf. also Frezza, *Garanzie*, vol. I, pp. 129 sqq. Schulz, incidentally, comes to the same conclusion for sponsio and fidepromissio (p. 497); if the creditor sued the principal debtor, so he argues, the obligation of the sponsor/fidepromissor remained intact. This is a consequence of his view that sponsio was not accessory.

[82] *Konkurrenz*, passim.

[83] According to Liebs, *Klagenkonkurrenz*, pp. 183 sq., 251, 252 sq., the reciprocal process

unbearable in practice.[84] There were ways and means for creditors to avoid them: in place of fideiussio they could have used the mandatum credendae pecuniae (or: qualificatum) in order to obtain a surety;[85] and the promissio indemnitatis,[86] as Levy[87] has pointed out, was invented for the very purpose of thwarting litis consumptio. Yet, fideiussio remained the central suretyship institution. Even in post-classical vulgar law the principle of reciprocal process consumption was faithfully retained,[88] although by now the bipartite formulary procedure had fallen into disuse and litis contestatio had consequently lost its technical significance. With these changes, as far as the procedural background was concerned, the time was now ripe to adopt a more rational approach. The decisive step was eventually taken by Justinian:

> "Generaliter sancimus, quemadmodum in mandatoribus statutum est, ut contestatione contra unum ex his facta alter non liberetur, ita et in fideiussioribus observari. Invenimus enim et in fideiussorum cautionibus plerumque ex pacto huiusmodi causae esse prospectum, et ideo generali lege sancimus nullo modo electione unius ex fideiussoribus vel ipsius rei alterum liberari, vel ipsum reum fideiussoribus vel uno ex his electo liberationem mereri, nisi satisfiat creditori, sed manere ius integrum, donec in solidum ei pecuniae presolvantur vel alio modo satis ei fiat."[89]

Here, the barring effect of litis contestatio was relinquished between surety and principal debtor as well as between several co-sureties: both principal and sureties were now to be liable until payment was rendered or until the creditor had otherwise obtained full satisfaction. Thus, process consumption had been replaced by what one could call a principle of concurrence of solutiones (satisfaction consumption, "*Solutionskonkurrenz*"): the actions concur in the sense that it is no longer litis contestatio with regard to the one, but rather solutio, that makes the creditor lose the other. The same reform, incidentally, was

---

consumption in classical Roman law was a relic from the days when personal execution held sway. Where personal liability was the ultimate and only consequence, it did not matter that all other (security) rights fell away once proceedings had been instituted: execution was always possible and could never turn out to be unsuccessful (because of insolvency).

[84] Cf. Buckland, (1941) 53 *Juridical Review* 285.

[85] Cf. infra, pp. 139 sqq.

[86] "Quanto minus a Titio debitore exegissem, tantum dari spondes?" (cf. Ulp. D. 46, 2, 6 pr.); see Levy, *Sponsio*, pp. 149 sqq.; Frezza, *Garanzie*, vol. I, pp. 136 sqq.; Rolf Knütel, "Zur Frage der sog. Diligenzpflichten des Gläubigers gegenüber dem Bürgen", in: *Festschrift für Werner Flume* (1978), vol. I, pp. 568 sqq.

[87] (1951) 14/15 *BIDR* 216.

[88] Cf. e.g. Gai. Epitome II, 9, 2: "Creditor autem, qui pecuniam dedit, in potestate habet ad reddendam pecuniam, quem velit tenere, utrum ipsum debitorem an fideiussorem. Sed si debitorem tenere elegerit, fideiussorem absolvet: si vero fideiussorem tenuerit, debitorem absolvet; quia uno electo, quem idoneum creditor iudicavit, alterum liberat"; Levy, *Obligationenrecht*, pp. 199 sqq.

[89] C. 8, 40, 28 pr. and 1. This reform, according to Justinian, had been prompted by an increasingly popular practice of the parties to set aside the effects of litis consumptio by special agreement: "Si enim pactis conventis hoc fieri conceditur et in usu quotidiano semper hoc versari adspicimus, quare non ipsa legis auctoritate hoc permittatur, ut nec simplicitas suscipientium contractus ex quacumque parte possit ius creditoris mutilare?" (C. 8, 40, 28, 3). Cf. Levy, *Obligationenrecht*, pp. 204 sq.

carried out with regard to plures rei promittendi,[90] the closely related prototype of a situation where two or more persons were liable for eadem res.[91] Over and above this, all the other instances in which a plurality of debtors lead to joint obligations[92] had to be brought in line with this new approach. Hence, Justinian faced the formidable task of eliminating litis consumptio, across the board, from all the texts he intended to incorporate into the Digest as well as the Codex.[93] Inadvertently, however, he left a number of the classical texts unchanged.[94] And as in some instances—especially as far as bonae fidei iudicia were concerned—the classical jurists had already abandoned process consumption in favour of concurrence of solutiones,[95] the most dramatic confusion was bound to arise as soon as legal writers set themselves the task of constructing a logically consistent doctrinal building on the basis of the Roman sources—on the basis, that is, of a veritable heap of ruins.[96]

3. Correality and solidarity

This is exactly what happened, however, in the course of the 19th century. A distinction was drawn between (simple) solidarity[97] and correality:[98] the term "solidarity" was used to indicate two (or more) obligations directed to one and the same juristic end, but not identified, and thus extinguished only by solutio; correality, on the other hand, was taken to refer to the concurrence of two (or more) obligations which were objectively identified so as constructively to form one, the liability of correi falling away as soon as litis contestatio with one of them had taken place. Fideiussor and main debtor, for example, in these terms were related to each other in the form of correal liability (as were plures rei promittendi). As far as the basis for this distinction was

[90] C. 8, 40, 28, 2. As to the structure of the whole enactment contained in C. 8, 40, 28 (pieced together in various stages), cf. Fritz Schulz, "Interpolationen in den Justinianischen Reformgesetzen des Codex Justinianus vom Jahre 534", in: *Studi in onore di Pietro Bonfante*, vol. I, pp. 357 sqq.; Liebs, *Klagenkonkurrenz*, pp. 38 sqq.; cf. further Giuseppina Sacconi, *Studi sulle obbligazioni solidali da contratto in diritto romano* (1973), pp. 4 sqq.

[91] Cf. supra, p. 118.

[92] Overview in Kaser, *RPr* I, p. 657; Sacconi, op. cit., note 90, pp. 51 sqq.

[93] Cf. e.g. the interpolations discussed by Liebs, *Klagenkonkurrenz*, pp. 60 sqq.

[94] Cf. e.g. Paul. D. 11, 1, 8 (Liebs, *Klagenkonkurrenz*, pp. 71 sq.) and the references in Kaser, *RPr* I, p. 658.

[95] Pap. D. 46, 1, 52, 3; Iul. D. 26, 7, 18, 1; Ulp. D. 16, 3, 1, 43; Ulp. D. 13, 6, 5, 15; Liebs, *Klagenkonkurrenz*, pp. 184 sqq.; Sacconi, op. cit., note 90, pp. 51 sqq.

[96] Jörs/Kunkel/Wenger, p. 210 (*"Für das klassische Recht haben wir ein Trümmerfeld vor uns. Die justinianischen Kompilatoren haben tiefgreifende Interpolationen vorgenommen und durch Spezialgesetze neue Grundsätze eingeführt, aber einen einheitlichen, in sich gefestigten Neubau nicht zu schaffen vermocht"*).

[97] Each of the several debtors is liable for the whole ("in solidum"); hence the term "solidarity".

[98] This term has been derived from "correus" (conreus), which, however, appears only once in our sources (Ulp. D. 34, 3, 3, 3).

concerned, the sheer quantity of literature[99] that came to be produced was equalled only by its absolute barrenness. Rudolf von Jhering referred to the correal obligations as a legal figure "possessed with a truly demoniacal obstinacy",[100] and the refined and esoteric levels of analysis to which they were elevated is probably the most striking example of what he described in the following terms:

> "Then there arise opinions and theories which can maintain their life only in the place where they received the same, to wit, in the lecturer's chair, but which, if they venture into the outside world, at once prove that they cannot bear the raw air of reality; opinions . . . in the highest degree learned, but also in the highest degree perverted—hot-house plants without sap and energy, bastards of logic and erudition with law, unsound lecture-room jurisprudence."[101]

It was pandectism at its worst.[102] Today, such theorizing in terms of "solidarity" and "correality" should be avoided, not only for the reasons given by Jhering but also because it would be an entirely ahistorical enterprise. The Roman lawyers neither knew this terminology nor were they concerned with abstract analyses concerning the conceptual nature of the various cases of plurality of debtors.

V. THE TRIPLET OF PRIVILEGES AVAILABLE TO THE FIDEIUSSOR

1. Beneficium excussionis vel ordinis

C. 8, 40, 28 paved the way for another reform regarding fideiussio. In Novellae 4, 1 we read:

> "Si quis igitur crediderit et fideiussorem . . . acceperit: is non primum adversus . . . fideiussorem . . . accedat, . . . sed veniat primum ad eum qui . . . debitum . . . contraxit. Et si quidem inde receperit, ab aliis abstineat."

With this enactment[103] the liability of the surety became subsidiary: the fideiussor could avail himself of a defence (later on called beneficium

---

[99] Starting with F.L. Keller, *Ueber Litis Contestation und Urtheil nach classischem Römischem Recht* (1827), and Georg Julius Ribbentrop, *Zur Lehre von den Correal-Obligationen* (1831); cf. further Windscheid/Kipp, § 292, pp. 197 sq. They quote a statement from 1829 ("Es ist . . . nicht leicht über irgend einen anderen Hauptpunkt des römischen Rechts die Literatur so dürftig, wie über diesen") and comment, somewhat sarcastically: "Mancher möchte wohl diesen Zustand zurückwünschen" (Not easily will one find another main problem in Roman law about which the literature is equally scarce; many a one would probably desire the return of this state of affairs).

[100] *Scherz und Ernst in der Jurisprudenz* (13th ed., 1924), p. 8.

[101] Jhering, *Geist*, vol. II 2, p. 324 (as translated by J. Kerr Wylie, *Solidarity and Correality* (1923), pp. 5 sq.). Cf. also, again, Rudolf von Jhering, *Scherz und Ernst*, op. cit., note 100, p. 9: "A juristic writing which fundamentally ignores the practical application of its subject! a cunningly constructed watch which is not intended to go!"

[102] For a new version of pandectism, namely exclusive emphasis on doctrinal consistency (even at the expense of extensive reconstruction of the sources), see J. Kerr Wylie, *Solidarity and Correality* (1923).

[103] On its history cf. Schindler, *Justinians Haltung zur Klassik*, pp. 36 sqq.

excussionis vel ordinis)[104] which lasted until the creditor had brought action against the principal and execution under the resulting judgment had proved to be abortive; if the debtor was absent, the fideiussor could ask the praetor to be granted some time within which to produce him.

It is obvious that a regulation such as this had not been conceivable at a time when litis contestatio still had its barring effect: it would have made suretyship practically worthless. Thus, indeed, throughout the classical period and up to the time of Justinian, the debtor and his surety were liable on an equal footing and not the one only if satisfaction could not be obtained from the other:[105] in other words, the creditor was free to choose whom of the two he wanted to sue first. And yet, this statement has to be qualified to a certain extent: it is correct, as far as the strictly legal side of things was concerned; in actual practice, however, the surety was what he was (arguably) only intended to be, namely a subsidiary debtor. Public policy and well-established business morals required the creditor to approach the debtor first (out of court, obviously) and turn against the surety only as a last resort: "Non enim aliter salvo pudore ad sponsorem venit creditor quam si recipere a debitore non possit."[106] To sue the surety when the debt was fairly easily obtainable from the "principal" debtor was regarded as offensive and whoever did this could become liable under the actio iniuriarum: not for having behaved improperly towards the surety but for having insulted the "principal" debtor; "[s]i creditor meus, cui paratus sum solvere, in iniuriam meam fideiussores meos interpellaverit, iniuriarum tenetur."[107] The Romans were somewhat touchy in pecuniary matters, especially as far as their creditworthiness was concerned;[108] and even though gossip may no longer have been as important in the Augustan metropolis as in the country town of the times before the Punic wars,[109] the mere fact that the creditor had, by implication, not considered the debtor to be able to honour his debt was enough seriously to jeopardize the reputation and social status of the latter. Whether animus iniuriandi (i.e. the intention to embarrass the debtor by proceeding in the way he

---

[104] "Excussionis" from "excutere", in the sense of bringing action and attempting execution against one debtor before another debtor could be sued; "ordinis" because an order was established in which the creditor had to pursue his remedies. Cf. e.g. Burge, *Suretyship*, pp. 332 sq. Sometimes, too, the term "beneficium discussionis" is used.

[105] Unless the suretyship stipulation had been drafted accordingly; cf. e.g. Iul. D. 46, 1, 16, 6 (fideiussio indemnitatis).

[106] Quintilianus, *Declamationes*, 273. Cf. also Cicero, *Epistulae ad Atticum*, 16, 15, § 2, and, generally, Levy, *Sponsio*, pp. 41 sqq. The Cicero text, incidentally, has recently been subjected to a detailed analysis by Berthold Kupisch, "Cicero ad Atticum 16, 15, 2", (1979) 96 *ZSS* 43 sqq.; it provides the basis for his argument that litis contestatio was not an essential element of classical formulary procedure. The traditional doctrine has, however, in the meantime, been reasserted by Max Kaser, "Cicero 'ad Atticum' 16. 15. 2. Formularprozess ohne 'litis contestatio'?", in: *Sodalitas, Scritti in onore di Antonio Guarino*, vol. VII (1984), pp. 3151 sqq.

[107] Gai. D. 47, 10, 19. Cf. further Ulp. D. 47, 10, 15, 32 sq.; Mod. D. 47, 10, 20.

[108] Cf. e.g. Kelly, *Roman Litigation*, p. 21.

[109] Cf. Schulz, *CRL*, p. 496.

did) was required on the part of the creditor to make him liable is not entirely clear;[110] in any event, he had to be careful because condemnation involved infamia[111] and this, in turn, severely affected his own standing within the community. But even apart from this, a necessity to create *legal* rules about the order in which "principal" debtor and surety had to be approached seems not to have really arisen in classical law, because suretyship was not primarily regarded as an alternative avenue to obtain satisfaction, but rather as a means to exercise pressure.[112] If amicitia demanded that one stood surety for one's friend, then, by the same token, it was the debtor's officium to do everything in his power not to let his friend's liability materialize. Similar considerations applied where the wealthy patronus succoured his clients: their social status being ultimately dependent on his patronage, they must have considered it imperative to avoid any inconvenience to their benefactor. Thus, again, they would have tried their best, without further ado, to bring his liability to an end. Therefore, even where it had become necessary for the creditor to remind either "principal" debtor or surety that the debt had fallen due, the ensuing negotiations between creditor and debtor or between surety and debtor usually resulted in the debtor settling his debt (as long, of course, as the claim against him was well founded and he was able to pay) rather than having to face the consequences of the creditor's taking action against the surety.

2. Beneficium divisionis

In another very important respect, the lot of sureties had already been relieved in classical law by a rescript of the Emperor Hadrian.

> "[F]ideiussores . . . perpetuo tenentur, et quotquot erunt numero, singuli in solidum obligantur. itaque liberum est creditori a quo velit solidum petere. sed nunc ex epistula divi Hadriani compellitur creditor a singulis, qui modo solvendo sint, partes petere."[113]

This sounds like the lex Furia rediviva: the debt was to be divided per capita between the various co-sureties. But there were important differences between that earlier piece of legislation and the epistula Hadriani. The latter granted only a beneficium divisionis of which each surety, when sued, could, but need not, avail himself. In law, fideiussores remained liable in full. Thus if one of them had paid the whole amount, only to find out that the "principal" debtor had fallen insolvent, the loss was entirely his. Neither was the creditor unjustifiedly enriched (the surety had not paid indebitum), nor was there, failing special legislation after the model of the lex Appuleia, a

---

[110] Raber, *Injurienansprüche*, pp. 150 sqq.
[111] Gai. IV, 182. On infamia cf. infra, p. 207.
[112] J. Macqueron, "Le cautionnement moyen de pression", (1957) 50 *Annales de la Faculté de droit d'Aix-en-Provence* 97 sqq.
[113] Gai. III, 121. For the background cf. Liebs, *Klagenkonkurrenz*, pp. 186 sqq.

general right of recourse against the other fideiussores. ". . . et sibi imputare debet, cum potuerit . . . desiderare ut pro parte in se detur actio":[114] he has only himself to blame, since he could have availed himself of the beneficium. The fact that the obligation was not divided ipso iure as between the various co-sureties,[115] but that this concession had to be applied for, before the magistrate, at the time when action was brought, had another important consequence: no longer was each co-surety liable for his proportionate share, regardless of whether one or more of the others had in the meantime become insolvent;[116] for the calculation of the shares it mattered only how many co-sureties were solvent "litis contestatae tempore".[117] If, for example, A, B and C had been fideiussores for a debt of 120, the creditor could claim 40 from each of them, if all were solvent at the time of litis contestatio and had availed themselves of the beneficium divisionis. If, however, C was insolvent at the time when A and B were sued, the liability of each of them increased to 60. Thus, in contrast to the rather inflexible regime of the lex Furia, the co-sureties now had to carry the risk of insolvency of one or more of their number,[118] and this, undoubtedly, represents the more appropriate solution to the problem.

3. Beneficium cedendarum actionum

The triplet of privileges available to the surety was completed by the so-called beneficium cedendarum actionum. It had classical roots, but was first shaped into a general right by Justinian. It aimed at providing the surety who had discharged the obligation, with a right of recourse against the principal debtor and/or his co-sureties.

(a) The problem of the surety's right of recourse against the main debtor

Such a right of recourse against the principal debtor had always existed with regard to sponsio: according to a lex Publilia (dating from about the 4th/3rd century B.C.), the sponsor could avail himself of an actio depensi if he had not been reimbursed within six months.[119] This liability of the debtor towards the sponsor, incidentally, had not been introduced by the lex Publilia.[120] Sponsio was one of the early "liability transactions" by means of which the pledge-like power of seizure, which arose as a consequence of wrongful acts, could be created by the parties.[121] Where a third party had released the debtor from the

---

[114] *Inst.* III, 20, 4.
[115] Gai. D. 46, 1, 26.
[116] Cf. supra, p. 119.
[117] *Inst.* III, 20, 4.
[118] Gai. III, 121.
[119] Gai. III, 127; IV, 22. For a recent discussion, see Max Kaser, "'Unmittelbare Vollstreckbarkeit' und Bürgenregress", (1983) 100 *ZSS* 106 sqq.
[120] For the following, see Kaser, *RPr* I, p. 153; idem, *Altrömisches ius*, p. 131 sq.; idem, (1983) 100 *ZSS* 100 sqq.
[121] Cf. supra, pp. 4 sqq.

creditor's power, the formal solutio per aes et libram originally[122] effected a transfer of the creditor's power over the debtor to the third party, in return for payment (depensum—from "dependere", "to weigh out") of the ransom. This liability under the third party's recourse, arising from the transfer of power, was at first immediately executable; later on, an action was introduced which had to be brought first, so as to allow a court to go into the matter and examine possible defences of the debtor before manus iniectio could take place.[123] This was the actio depensi.[124] The purpose of the lex Publilia, in the days when recourse could be had by the sponsor without prior lawsuit and judgment, had been to alleviate his position by granting a period of six months within which to satisfy the claim of his new creditor.[125]

In the case of fideiussio,[126] the actio depensi did not apply. That did not mean that the fideiussor never had any right of recourse against the principal debtor; whether or not he had depended entirely on his internal relationship with the latter. In most cases, the fideiussor would have stood surety at the request of the principal debtor, with the result that a contract of mandatum would have come into existence.[127] Thus, the surety had the actio mandati contraria to claim reimbursement for his expenses incurred, that is, in this instance, the sum he had to pay the creditor.[128] Where, on the other hand, the surety had not acted under an express or tacit mandate, but had, for example, wanted to assist his absent friend by standing surety for him, the actio negotiorum gestorum contraria was available to him.[129] So it was normally only where the suretyship obligation had been incurred against the wishes of

---

[122] See Kaser, *RPr* I, p. 172; idem, *Altrömisches ius*, pp. 240 sqq.; Rolf Knütel, "Zum Prinzip der formalen Korrespondenz im römischen Recht", (1971) 88 *ZSS* 75.

[123] However, litiscrescence (infitiando lis crescit in duplum) remained a characteristic of this action: see Gai. IV, 9; 171 and Kaser, *Altrömisches ius*, pp. 118 sqq.

[124] "Depensi", because the action arose where payment had been effected by the third party by means of an act per aes et libram, in the course of which the sum had originally been weighed out. In classical law, solutio per aes et libram was used only for the purpose of release and took place nummo uno: see Gai. III, 173–5, and infra, p. 756.

[125] Paul Koschacker, (1916) 37 *ZSS* 361 sqq.; differently e.g. Francesco de Martino, *Studi sulle garanzie personali* II (1938), pp. 42 sqq.

[126] And also of fidepromissio. The applicability of the actio depensi and lex Publilia were the only questions in regard to which there was a significant difference between the rules relating to sponsio and fidepromissio. As far as the redress of the fidepromissor against the principal debtor was concerned, see Watson, *Obligations*, pp. 7 sq.

[127] Gai. III, 127; Ulp. D. 50, 17, 60; Frezza, *Garanzie*, vol. I, pp. 162 sqq.; Gunter Wesener, "Die Durchsetzung von Regressansprüchen im römischen Recht", (1965) 11 *Labeo* 343 sqq.; cf. also Roger Vigneron, "Fideiussor, qui pecuniam deposuit, confestim agere mandati potest", (1974) 77 *BIDR* 443 sqq.; Kaser, (1983) 100 *ZSS* 124 sqq.

[128] The surety, however, must not have failed to set up exceptiones which were available against the debtor and of which he was aware, and he generally had to have been diligent in conducting the case: cf. Ulp. D. 17, 1, 29 pr., 2–4.

[129] Paul. D. 17, 1, 20, 1; Seiler, *Negotiorum gestio*, pp. 120 sqq.

the principal debtor that an avenue for recourse did not exist.[130] Nevertheless, the classical lawyers conceived of another possibility enabling the fideiussor to secure his position as far as his right of recourse was concerned: he had to pay only once the creditor had transferred to him, by way of procuratio in rem suam, his own claim against the debtor.[131] The surety could then use the creditor's old claim for reimbursement purposes.

One might ask what advantage there was for the surety in acquiring this additional action. Indeed, under the actiones mandati contraria and negotiorum gestorum contraria, he could claim not only the amount of the debt he had paid but also any other loss or expense incurred by him as a result of the debtor not having met his obligation—and this was not possible if he used the creditor's claim that had been ceded to him. But then this latter claim was independent of whatever internal relationship might have existed between the principal debtor and the surety and it was available even where the requirements of the actions arising from mandate or negotiorum gestio did not exist, or (especially) where they could not be proved (or were difficult to prove). Furthermore, these latter remedies were often practically useless, for, where the surety had been called upon to pay, it was not unlikely that the debtor was insolvent. The creditor's right, on the other hand, might well have been superior: either by virtue of being privileged in rank or of being strengthened by real security.[132]

(b) The construction of the beneficium cedendarum actionum

There was, however, one particular difficulty as far as this "cession" of the creditor's right was concerned. Once the surety had paid, not only his own but also the principal debtor's obligation was discharged. Consequently, the creditor, having obtained full satisfaction, no longer had any right to cede; to effect this cession before payment was made did not obviate the problem, for payment still extinguished the obligation. How, therefore, could the surety assert the creditor's right when this had ceased to exist?[133] The answer of the Roman jurists can be found in texts such as Paul. D. 46, 1, 36:

> "Cum is qui et reum et fideiussores habens ab uno ex fideiussoribus accepta pecunia praestat actiones, poterit quidem dici nullas iam esse, cum suum perceperit et

---

[130] Cf. Paul. D. 17, 1, 40. This is in accordance with the prevailing opinion (C. 2, 18, 24) that there was no claim for reimbursement of outlays for the gestor who had acted against the will of the principal; cf. Seiler, *Negotiorum gestio*, pp. 86 sqq.; also Wessels, *Contract*, §§ 4155 sq.

[131] Frezza, *Garanzie*, vol. I, pp. 180 sqq.; Wesener, (1965) 11 *Labeo* 346 sqq.; Giuseppe Provera, "Riflessioni sul beneficium cedendarum actionum", in: *Studi in onore di Cesare Sanfilippo*, vol. IV (1983), pp. 609 sqq.

[132] Cf. e.g. the case on which the decision C. 8, 40, 2 is based.

[133] A further problem could arise where the creditor had sued the surety: litis contestatio would then (even before solutio) have destroyed not only the surety's but also the main debtor's obligation (both were for eadem res). Here, the Roman lawyers seem to have helped by means of in integrum restitutio: cf. Levy, *Konkurrenz*, vol. I, pp. 225 sqq.

perceptione omnes liberati sunt. sed non ita est: non enim in solutum accipit, sed quodammodo nomen debitoris vendidit."

The whole device is treated as a contract of sale, where the surety purchases the creditor's action rather than discharges his obligation. By how far that misses the psychological realities of the situation hardly needs to be stressed; the fiction has, accordingly, been severely criticized.[134] Yet, to object to the unrealistic nature of the argument does not seem entirely fair; for the characteristic feature of a fiction is that it deals with a particular set of facts as if a different set of facts were at issue.[135] Also, the Roman lawyers always seem to have been aware of the fictitious nature of this purchase contract[136] and were not led to inappropriate consequences and distortions.[137] As far as the development of recourse devices is concerned, the argument certainly played a very useful role.[138] In fact, it seems to have been extended in the course of time.[139] At first, a specific agreement concerning the cession between surety and creditor was probably necessary (only the interpretation of this agreement as a contract of sale was fictitious), and this agreement, of course,[140] had to be made before solutio had taken place.[141] We find other texts, however, where no such time limit was acknowledged; Paul. D. 46, 1, 36 provides an example: the ablativus absolutus "accepta pecunia" indicates that the surety had already paid before the action was ceded to him. In cases such as this, some Roman lawyers apparently did not want to let the principal debtor benefit from a lack of circumspection on the part of the surety. Thus, they did not even require a real conventio between the two parties (which had to have taken place before solutio) any more, but boldly read this whole agreement into the transaction by way of fiction. The Imperial chancellery, however, does not seem to have adopted this broader view,[142] but rather started to *require* the creditor to effect this transfer of

---

[134] Cf. e.g. Fritz Schulz, *Rückgriff und Weitergriff* (1907), p. 27.

[135] Cf. esp. Dieter Medicus, "Der fingierte Klagenkauf als Denkhilfe für die Entwicklung des Zessionsregresses", in: *Festschrift für Max Kaser* (1976), pp. 391 sqq.; 396 sqq. On the use of fictions generally, cf. the references quoted supra, p. 64, note 219.

[136] Cf. Paul. D. 46, 1, 36: "quodammodo"; Mod. D. 46, 3, 76: "magis . . . videatur".

[137] This is one of the great dangers of developing the law by means of fictions.

[138] It was still used by the German legislator to justify the cessio legis of § 774 BGB: cf. "Motive", in: *Mugdan*, vol. II, p. 376.

[139] Medicus, *Festschrift Kaser*, pp. 402 sqq.

[140] Payment was supposed to discharge the actio venditi and thus to leave the claim for which the surety had made himself liable intact. If no contract of "sale" had been made at the time of solutio, solutio could be taken only to have discharged the main debtor's (and the surety's) obligation.

[141] Cf. Mod. D. 46, 3, 76: "Modestinus respondit, si post solutum sine ullo pacto omne, quod ex causa tutelae debeatur, actiones post aliquod intervallum cessae sint, nihil ea cessione actum, cum nulla actio superfuerit: quod si ante solutionem hoc factum est vel, cum convenisset, ut mandarentur actiones, tunc solutio facta esset mandatum subsecutum est, salvas esse mandatas actiones, cum novissimo quoque casu pretium magis mandatarum actionum solutum quam actio quae fuit perempta videatur."

[142] C. 5, 58, 1 (Sev. et. Ant.); 8, 40, 11 (Alex).

his rights against the principal debtor:

> "Creditori, qui pro eodem debito et pignora et fideiussorem accepit, licet, si malit, fideiussorem convenire in eam pecuniam, in qua se obligaverit. quod cum facit, *debet* ius pignorum in eum transferre."[143]

It is along these lines that Justinian introduced the beneficium cedendarum actionum as a general right of the surety to demand cession before discharging his suretyship obligation.[144]

(c) The recourse of the surety against his co-sureties

Regarding the recourse of the surety who had paid the whole amount against possible co-sureties, the matter had been regulated by the lex Appuleia for sponsio and fidepromissio transactions. Whether the provisions of this law had survived the introduction of the lex Furia is, as we have seen,[145] very doubtful. Seeing that the surety was now liable for his aliquot part only, he hardly needed any action against his co-sureties any longer. Again, however, this regime did not apply to fideiussio. In contrast to the situation governing his recourse against the principal debtor, the surety did not normally have any actions arising from an internal relationship with the co-sureties either: unless, for instance, they had contracted inter se to bear their share of the debt, a contractual or quasi-contractual nexus between them usually did not exist; and failing specific legislation to this effect, one could not simply somehow throw them together into some sort of partnership ("quandam societatem").[146] In this predicament, the Roman lawyers once again helped with a beneficium cedendarum actionum, again dressed up, initially as a contract of sale. From D. 46, 1, 17[147] we know that, already by the time of Iulianus, the praetor was prepared to force the creditor to cede his action against the debtor to the surety. However, the introduction of the beneficium divisionis under Hadrian had a similar effect on the praetor's willingness to intervene in this way as the lex Furia had had on the provisions of the lex Appuleia: where a surety could avail himself in the first place of this more favourable beneficium, which enabled him to reduce his liability to his aliquot share, there was no longer any necessity for the praetor to rush to his aid. Of course, the creditor was perfectly free to cede his actions against the co-sureties voluntarily. But otherwise we find the praetor intervening on behalf of the surety only in situations where the

---

143 C. 8, 40, 2 pr. (Sev. et. Ant.).

144 Nov. 4, 1 in fine (". . . a creditore actionibus sibi cessis").

145 Supra, pp. 119 sq.

146 Gai. III, 122, referring to the lex Appuleia.

147 "Fideiussoribus succurri solet, ut stipulator compellatur ei, qui solidum solvere paratus est, vendere ceterorum nomina." On this text, see Medicus, *Festschrift Kaser*, pp. 394 sqq.; Provera, *Studi Sanfilippo*, vol. IV, pp. 636 sqq.

beneficium divisionis had not been available to him.[148] This is the background of Pap. D. 46, 6, 12: "Si plures fideiussores a tutore pupillo dati sunt, non esse eum distringendum, sed in unum dandam actionem ita, ut ei, qui conveniretur, actiones praestarentur." Where a tutor had provided for several co-sureties on behalf of his ward, the ward was allowed to sue each of them for the whole; in the interests of the ward, the beneficium divisionis was not granted under these circumstances. On the other hand, it was then only just and reasonable to require the ward to cede his actions against the co-sureties. In the end, therefore, it was not the ward but one of the sureties who had to face the problem of getting his money back from all the others. Again, however, it was Justinian who generalized this idea by granting a beneficium cedendarum actionum to any surety[149] (and, indeed, to all joint debtors)[150] who had paid solidum.

VI. SPECIAL TYPES OF SURETYSHIP TRANSACTIONS

1. Promissio indemnitatis and fideiussio fideiussoris

We have so far largely been dealing with the standard form of fideiussio. Suretyship, however, gave the Roman lawyers ample opportunity to display their ingenuity in devising special types of transactions to meet special circumstances or to get around some of the more cumbersome edges of fideiussio. Promissio indemnitatis has been mentioned already.[151] This way of drafting the suretyship stipulation seems to have become fairly popular in classical law, because it had advantages for both the creditor and the surety: for the creditor it provided a convenient way of avoiding the consequences of litis consumptio; for the surety it was favourable in that it made his liability a subsidiary one. The fideiussor fideiussoris (achterborg, *Nachbürge*, rear-surety) is another example.[152] He undertook a suretyship for a surety, thus guaranteeing not the obligation of the principal debtor but that of the first surety. By using this form of rear-suretyship, the creditor had the benefit of the additional security afforded by a plurality of sureties, while on the other hand evading the inconvenience of having to sue all of them individually for their proportionate share (in case they chose to avail themselves of the beneficium divisionis).

---

148 Cf. Levy, *Sponsio*, pp. 164 sqq.; Frezza, *Garanzie*, vol. I, pp. 186 sqq.; but see Provera, *Studi Sanfilippo*, vol. IV, pp. 636 sqq.

149 Cf. e.g. Windscheid/Kipp, § 481, 3.

150 As far as the right of recourse between joint debtors is concerned, cf. Wesener, (1965) 11 *Labeo* 350 sqq.; Kaser, *RPr* II, pp. 456 sq. For an evaluation of the historical development of the right of recourse in Roman law generally, see Wesener, pp. 360 sq.

151 Cf. supra, note 86.

152 Cf. e.g. Ulp. D. 46, 1, 8, 12 and Caney/Forsyth, op. cit., note 49, p. 48.

2. The use of emptio venditio for the purpose of suretyship

Even more interesting are the cases where the Roman lawyers used consensual contracts for the purpose of suretyship. Thus, for instance, the late Republican jurists already seem to have devised a transaction, by means of which a result very similar to fideiussio could be achieved, but which avoided certain of its disadvantages, especially litis consumptio, and also all the inconveniences relating to the oral formality of stipulation. The creditor would ask his debtor to mandate a third party (Seius) to buy his claim. Normally, the purchase price which Seius had to pay was less than the amount of the debt which was the object of the transaction. Thus, the creditor could claim the purchase price from Seius (not the full amount of his claim against the debtor; that was the disadvantage of this construction) in case the debtor fell insolvent or was not able to pay for any other reason. Once Seius had paid the purchase price, he (Seius) could try to recover his expenses from the debtor (on the basis of his actio mandati contraria). A transaction of this type had been concluded in the much-disputed fragment Ofilius/Ulp. D. 44, 4, 4, 6:

> "Quod si is, cui pecunia debeatur, cum debitore decidit et nomen eius vendidit Seio, cui debitor mandaverat, ut nomen emeret, deque ea re emptor stipulatus est, deinde creditor eam pecuniam retinet, quam per iudicem abstulit, an emptor ex stipulatu possit experiri? et Ofilius putat, si venditor nominus paratus non sit reddere, quantum ab emptore acceperit, non nocituram exceptionem doli mali: et puto sententiam Ofilii veram."[153]

Here, the debtor had agreed to mandate Seius to buy the creditor's claim as part of a settlement ("decidit") with his creditor (who, in turn, might have granted indulgence; the text does not inform us about the creditor's concession). The purchase of the claim had been accompanied by a stipulation, according to which (i.a.) the creditor had promised to hand over to Seius whatever he might receive under his claim from the debtor. The creditor thus had a choice: he could either sue his debtor and then, if unsuccessful, proceed against Seius, or he could claim the purchase price from Seius immediately. This is what he seems to have done in the present instance. However, later on, and against all expectations, he received the full debt from the debtor. It is obvious that under these circumstances he could not be allowed to keep both sums. The question is whether he now had to hand over to Seius the full amount he had received from his debtor or whether he could keep the amount by which the debt exceeded the purchase price. According to Ofilius, the creditor could meet Seius' action arising from the stipulation with an exceptio doli, if he was prepared to pay back as

---

[153] As to the interpretation of this text, I follow Andreas Wacke, "Ofilius D. 44, 4, 4, 6. Ein Forderungskauf zu Bürgschaftszwecken", (1970) 17 *RIDA* 345 sqq.; cf. also Dieter Nörr, "Bemerkungen zur spätrepublikanischen Kautelarpraxis", in: *Eranion in honorem G.S. Maridakis* (1963), vol. I, pp. 204 sqq.; Geoffrey MacCormack, "'Dolus' in Republican Law", (1985) 88 *BIDR* 35 sq. and (differently) Watson, *Obligations*, pp. 261 sqq.

much as he had received from him (Seius). In other words: Seius was not meant to benefit from the transaction; it would not have been in accordance with what the parties had intended (namely a form of suretyship) if Seius had been able to claim the full sum of the debt which the creditor had been able to recover. Should he have tried to do that, his behaviour would have been classified as fraudulent, i.e. the creditor could have raised the exceptio doli.

3. The use of mandatum, especially the mandatum qualificatum

More often than emptio venditio, however, the Romans employed the contract of mandatum in the present context. That could happen even where a fideiussio had already been concluded. Thus, the creditor could arrange with the fideiussor to be mandated by him to sue the debtor.[154] In this way, the vexed problem of litis consumptio could be obviated; for whilst the creditor's action arising from the fideiussio was still consumed, an actio mandati contraria remained available to him against the fideiussor even after his unsuccessful attempt to obtain his satisfaction from the debtor. At the same time, this construction ensured that the creditor instituted legal proceedings against the principal debtor first, before turning to the fideiussor. More importantly, however, the contract of mandate could often be used in the place of fideiussio, i.e. as an alternative form of suretyship.[155] If Maevius requested Titius to lend money to Seius, he had in actual fact become surety for Seius: for if the latter failed to repay, Titius could sue Maevius with the actio mandati contraria for reimbursement on the ground of his having suffered loss in carrying out the request.[156] The validity of this type of transaction (which came to be called "mandatum qualificatum" since the days of the commentators) was disputed at first, because, according to Servius Sulpicius, the mandator/surety himself (Maevius) had no actionable interest in the fulfilment of the mandate; however, Sabinus' opposite opinion seems to have prevailed,[157] and in classical law this device was apparently fairly popular.[158] It differed from fideiussio in that litis contestatio with the debtor did not consume the action against the mandator/surety.[159] Thus, the creditor could

[154] Paul. D. 17, 1, 22, 2; cf. also Inst. III, 26, 2.

[155] Cf. G. Bortolucci, "Il mandato di credito", (1915) 27 *BIDR* 129 sqq., (1916) 28 *BIDR* 191 sqq.; Frezza, *Garanzie*, vol. I, pp. 199 sqq.; Antonio Guarino, *Mandatum credendi* (1982); Buckland/Stein, pp. 519 sqq.; Kaser, *RPr* I, p. 666; II, pp. 460 sq.; Schulz, *CRL*, p. 558; Girtanner, pp. 60 sqq.; Windscheid/Kipp, § 412, 2; 476, n. 3.

[156] A practical disadvantage of the mandate was that it had to be undertaken before the principal obligation (cf. Ulp. D. 17, 1, 12, 14: "Si post creditam pecuniam mandavero creditori credendam, nullum esse mandatum rectissime Papinianus ait"), whereas the fideiussor could accede beforehand or (as is the usual case) afterwards. As to the question of ratihabitio, see Frezza, *Garanzie*, vol. I, pp. 212 sqq.

[157] Gai. III, 156.

[158] Jolowicz/Nicholas, p. 301 even say "extremely common"; cf. also Watson, *Mandate*, p. 84.

[159] Pap. D. 46, 1, 52, 3; Just. C. 8, 40, 28 pr. (by implication).

choose whom to sue first;[160] in case he did not obtain satisfaction from the one, he was not barred from proceeding against the other. Furthermore, due to the informal, consensual nature of mandatum, this type of suretyship could be concluded inter absentes, which was, of course, not possible in the case of fideiussio. Also, the mandatum qualificatum, like all consensual contracts, gave rise to iudicia bonae fidei: the judge, according to the procedural formula, was requested to condemn the defendant into "quidquid . . . dare facere oportet ex fide bona" and therefore had a wide discretion to assess the obligations of the parties in accordance with the equities of the individual case. The action arising from fideiussio, on the other hand, was stricti iuris. Thus, for instance, the creditor lost his right of recourse against the surety/mandator where a mandatum qualificatum had been concluded, if his action against the debtor failed due to his own negligence: "Si creditor a debitore culpa sua causa ceciderit, proper est, ut actione mandati nihil a mandatore consequi debeat, cum ipsius vitio acciderit, ne mandatori possit actionibus cedere." The creditor was therefore taken to owe a duty of care towards the surety. There was no room for duties of this kind in the case of fideiussio. The stipulation by means of which it was concluded was a unilaterally binding contract which only placed the surety under an obligation to perform. As the action was stricti iuris, the judge did not have any discretion to derive reciprocal duties from or ascribe them to this contract.[161]

The Roman lawyers, of course, realized the true function of this type of mandatum. Thus a tendency is noticeable to treat it as a kind of suretyship and to apply, for instance, the beneficium divisionis where there was a plurality of mandators,[162] or to allow the mandator to raise not only his own but also the debtor's exceptiones when he was sued by the creditor.[163] On the other hand, due to the bonae fidei nature of its actions, mandatum qualificatum sometimes served as a model for the

---

[160] Schindler, *Justinians Haltung zur Klassik*, pp. 38 sqq.

[161] Cf. Scaev. D. 46, 1, 62: "Si fideiussor creditori denuntiaverit, ut debitorem ad solvendam pecuniam compelleret vel pignus distraheret, isque cessaverit, an possit eum fideiussor doli mali exceptione summovere? respondit non posse." There was, however, one instance of fideiussio in which the creditor did have such a duty: promissio indemnitatis. Mod. D. 46, 1, 41 pr.: "Respondit, si fideiussores in id accepti sunt, quod a curatore servari non possit, et post impletam legitimam aetatem tam ab ipso curatore quam ab heredibus eius solidum servari potuit et cessante eo, qui pupillus fuit, solvendo esse desierit: non temere utilem in fideiussores actionem competere." The reason for this decision is not given by Modestinus; it seems to lie in the nature of a fideiussio indemnitatis as a conditional promise (Paul./Pap. D. 45, 1, 116), to which the rule applied that the condition is deemed not to have been fulfilled, if the party to whose advantage it would have operated was responsible for its fulfilment. Cf. Rolf Knütel, "Zur Frage der sog. Diligenzpflichten des Gläubigers gegenüber dem Bürgen", in: *Festschrift für Werner Flume*, vol. I (1978), pp. 568 sqq. and infra, p. 729.

[162] Cf. Pap. 27, 7, 7 in fine (interpolated?) and Just. C. 4, 18, 3; Karl-Heinz Schindler, "Zum Problem byzantinischer Bearbeitungen des ersten Codex", in: *Studi in onore di Edoardo Volterra*, vol. II (1971), pp. 371 sqq., but Liebs, *Klagenkonkurrenz*, pp. 187 sq.

[163] Ulp. D. 46, 1, 32; Diocl. C. 4, 30, 12. Both texts have often been regarded as spurious; but see Kaser, *RPr* II, pp. 460 sq. (n. 28).

development of the more inflexible fideiussio. Thus it was already recognized in classical law that the creditor could demand payment from the mandator/surety only if he was willing to cede to him his repayment claim against the debtor.[164] This idea, in the course of time, came to be applied to fideiussio as beneficium cedendarum actionum. Justinian rounded these developments off by equating mandatores and fideiussiores for all practical purposes.[165] It was not difficult, therefore, for later writers such as the Roman-Dutch jurists to weave these two strands into one and to fuse the equitable approach underlying mandatum with the fideiussio.[166] Even in countries such as Germany, where mandatum qualificatum did not entirely disappear but continues to occupy a little niche of its own,[167] it has come to be generally recognized that the obligations arising from fideiussio/suretyship are to be judged "ex bona fide" too.[168]

[164] Iul. D. 46, 1, 13; Gai. D. 17, 1, 27, 5; Mod. D. 46, 1, 41, 1; Wesener, (1965) 11 *Labeo* 347. Of course, the difficulties encountered with regard to fideiussio (that solutio or litis contestatio consumed both actions) did not arise in this case.

[165] Bortolucci, (1915) 28 *BIDR* 239 sqq.; cf. also Liebs, *Klagenkonkurrenz*, pp. 41 sq.; Guarino, op. cit., note 155, pp. 21 sqq.

[166] There was a third strand in the form of constitutum debiti alieni, a praetorian pact which served the function of suretyship; Justinian was the first to subject it to the rules pertaining to suretyship (by extending the beneficia divisionis, excussionis and cedendarum actionum). In contrast to fideiussio, constitutum could be made "in durior causa". Cf. Caney/Forsyth, op. cit., note 49, pp. 18 sqq.; Frezza, *Garanzie*, vol. I, pp. 229 sqq., 282 sqq.; Girtanner, op. cit., note 48, pp. 47 sqq.; Jolowicz/Nicholas, p. 301; Kaser, *RPr* II, p. 461.

[167] Cf. Windscheid/Kipp, §§ 412, 2; 476, n. 3; Franz Philipp von Kübel, "Recht der Schuldverhältnisse, Teil 3", in: Werner Schubert (ed.), *Vorentwürfe*, pp. 89 sqq. § 778 BGB reads: "A person who gives a mandate to another to give credit to a third party in the person's own name and for his own account is liable to the mandatary *as a surety* for the obligation of the third party arising from the giving of credit." Constitutum debiti alieni, on the other hand, has disappeared as a separate institution on its own; cf. e.g. Girtanner, op. cit., note 48, pp. 373 sqq. On constitutum debiti in general, cf. also infra, pp. 511 sqq.

[168] This has practical consequences, for instance, regarding the question whether the creditor owes a duty of care towards the surety (cf. supra, p. 140). Such a duty was widely recognized in 19th-century legislation and literature. In the BGB, however, we find a strange relapse into the old Roman law of fideiussio; its §§ 765 sqq. are based on the assumption that, in accordance with its nature as a unilaterally binding contract, suretyship can give rise only to rights and not to duties in the person of the creditor. Thus the creditor is perfectly free to watch his debtor become insolvent without being barred, later on, from claiming from the surety that which can then no longer be claimed from the debtor. The courts have tried to remedy this situation to the best of their ability and have reintroduced, through the back door, and in a very limited way, the more equitable principle of the ius commune. Cf. the analysis by Knütel, *Festschrift Flume*, pp. 559 sqq. This, incidentally, is a development that can be observed in many cases where a legislator has rather tried to break with tradition. The approach of the BGB, in this particular instance, may have to be seen in the context of the economic crisis of the 1870s and the increasing importance, for the banks, of transactions on credit; hence the desire to make suretyship more attractive/viable from the point of view of the creditor: cf. Knütel, pp. 564 sq.

VII. THE IMPACT OF FIDEIUSSIO ON MODERN LEGAL SYSTEMS

1. Roman-Dutch law

The Roman law of suretyship has had a profound influence on modern legal systems. The suretyship contract in all countries that have received Roman law derives directly from Justinian's fideiussio.[169, 170] This is most obvious in the usus hodiernus of Roman-Dutch law.[171] Suretyship is an accessory contract and the position of the surety is still governed by the venerable triplet of privileges: he can avail himself of the beneficium excussionis, the beneficium divisionis (where there is a plurality of sureties) and the beneficium cedendarum actionum. With regard to the latter, an interesting development has taken place. Some of the classical Roman-Dutch writers found it repugnant that the surety who paid should remain burdened with the whole debt if he forgot to ask for cession in good time. Thus, in order not to let the co-sureties benefit from his carelessness, they allowed cession to take place at any time, even long after payment had been rendered.[172] But once that was accepted, the question was bound to arise sooner or later whether the whole act of cession had not under those circumstances become a meaningless formality which the law could just as well dispense with. This, indeed, was the view taken by Wessels J, in *Kroon v. Enschede*,[173] who thereby brought South African law in line with the English

---

[169] Cf. the contributions in *Les sûretés personnelles*, op. cit., note 2, for example, Jean Gilissen, vol. 28, pp. 94 sqq.; Burge, *Suretyship*, passim; Jones, (1977–78) 52 *Tulane LR* 136 sqq. (describing, for instance, the French Code Civil as "almost a restatement of the Roman law as clarified and modified by such jurists as Pothier and Domat"). In many modern systems, writing is prescribed for suretyship contracts (cf. e.g. § 766 BGB (but see § 350 HGB, if the surety is a merchant), s. 6 Act 50/1956 (South Africa), and, generally, Ernst J. Cohn, "The Form of Contracts of Guarantee in Comparative Law", (1938) 54 *LQR* 220 sqq.). In the European usus modernus of Roman law, fideiussio was an informal contract: the oral formality of the Roman stipulatio had become obsolete, and the symbolic forms of Germanic law which existed for the contract of suretyship had been suppressed by the reception of Roman law. Thus, the (re-)introduction of the formal requirements had to take place by deliberate acts of legislation.

[170] The promissio (or fideiussio) indemnitatis (cf. supra, note 86), incidentally, lives on in the modern contract of indemnity ("a promise to save another harmless from the result of a transaction into which he enters at the instance of the promisor": Anson/Guest, *Law of Contract* (24th ed., 1975), p. 76; in German: *"Garantievertrag"*); cf. esp. Rudolf Stammler, "Der Garantievertrag", (1886) 69 *Archiv für die civilistische Praxis* 1 sqq. and, more recently, Jörg Käser, "Garantieversprechen als Sicherheit im Handelsverkehr", (1971) 35 *RabelsZ* 593 sqq.; Hadding/Häuser/Welter, op. cit., note 17, pp. 682 sqq.

[171] Cf. De Wet en Yeats, pp. 344 sqq.; Wessels, *Contract*, §§ 3771 sqq. and Caney/Forsyth, loc. cit.

[172] Groenewegen, *De legibus abrogatis*, Cod. Lib. VIII, Tit. XLI, l. 11 cum alter; Voet, *Commentarius ad Pandectas*, Lib. XLVI, Tit. I, XXX; cf. later on, also Girtanner, op. cit., note 48, pp. 533 sqq.; contra, e.g., Grotius, *Inleiding*, III, III, XXXI.

[173] 1909 TS 374; but cf. also Voet, *Commentarius ad Pandectas*, Lib. XLVI, Tit. I, XXX; Pothier, *Traité des obligations*, n. 445; Burge, *Suretyship*, pp. 381 sqq.

doctrine of contribution:[174] without any assignment, the surety who has paid the debt, is entitled to recover from his co-sureties. Thus, he does not pursue the creditor's right, but his own right based not on contract but on general equity. Besides this "automatic" right to contribution against his co-sureties and his right of recourse against the principal debtor arising from their internal relationship (mandate or negotiorum gestio),[175] the beneficium cedendarum actionum has not sunk into oblivion; it is still vitally important where the creditor's claim enjoyed a privileged position or where it was secured by accessory real rights.

Kroon v. Enschede, by the way, is but one example of quite a number of decisions of South African courts in this field which fascinate the reader on account of their extensive investigation into the sources of Roman-Dutch law. Sometimes the very question of what these sources are has been the bone of contention. The *cause célèbre* is *Wolson v. Gerber*.[176] Seven persons had stood surety for repayment of a loan "jointly and severally and as sureties and co-principal debtors . . . renouncing the legal exceptions . . . ordinis seu excussionis et divisionis", as the parties had specified. After one of them, a certain Wolson, had paid the creditor the whole amount, the question arose as to how much he would be able to claim, by way of recourse, from Gerber, another of the co-sureties. According to Voet,[177] Sande[178] and Perezius,[179] he could sue any of the remaining co-debtors for the whole of the original debt minus only his own pro rata share (that is, in this instance, for six-sevenths). Pothier,[180] on the other hand, had advocated a restriction of his right of recourse against each of the co-debtors; as a result, he would have been able to recover only one-seventh of what he had paid to the creditor from the defendant.[181] Faced with this conflict of opinion, the court came to the conclusion that the more modern opinion of Pothier could not be followed:

> "Pothier is of course a great authority on the Civil law . . . [and] as an interpreter of the Roman law, our law in subsidio, on questions on which the Dutch jurists are

---

[174] Cf. e.g. *Fleetwood v. Charnock* (1629) Nelson 10; *Dering v. Earl of Winchelsea* (1787) 1 Cox 318 at 320.

[175] As far as the right of recourse against the principal debtor is concerned, an (automatic) "subrogation" is unknown in South African law; cf. e.g. J.E. Scholtens, (1959) 76 *SALJ* 266 sqq.

[176] 1954 (3) SA 94 (T); the decision of the Appellate Division of the South African Supreme Court is to be found sub nom. *Gerber v. Wolson* in 1955 (1) SA 158 (A).

[177] *Commentarius ad Pandectas*, Lib. XLVI, Tit. I, XXIX.

[178] *De Actionum Cessione*, Cap. VI, 33.

[179] Perezius, *Praelectiones*, Lib. VIII, Tit. LIX, 41 (p. 498).

[180] *Traité des obligations*, n. 281; cf. also the references in Berlichius, *Conclusiones practicales secundum ordinem Constitutionum Divi Augusti, Electoris Saxoniae* (4 ed., Leipzig, 1670), Pars II, Concl. XXII, nn. 88 f.

[181] This solution was adopted by Burge, *Suretyship*, p. 417 and in the code civil (artt. 1214, 2033).

> silent, his opinions naturally carry much weight . . . But [his authority] cannot prevail against the opinions of the accepted Dutch authorities."[182]

It is not without irony, however, to see that, notwithstanding these general pronouncements about his relevance for South African courts, Pothier at least scored an indirect victory; the majority of the court did, in the end, limit the right of recourse to one-seventh but based their decision on a somewhat unsatisfactory fiction, namely on an implied agreement between the seven co-sureties limiting their reciprocal rights of recourse to the pro rata share.[183]

2. German law and the English common law

In modern German law, too, suretyship is characterized by its accessoriness.[184] According to § 771 BGB, the surety may refuse to satisfy the creditor as long as the latter has not attempted compulsory execution against the principal debtor without success: a statutory version of the beneficium excussionis. Hadrian's beneficium divisionis, however, has not been adopted: co-sureties are liable as joint debtors for the whole debt (unless, of course, something else was agreed upon by the parties). The beneficium cedendarum actionum has been developed into a cessio legis: where the surety satisfies the creditor, the latter's claim against the principal debtor is (automatically) transferred to him.[185] As a consequence of this, all ancillary rights pass to the assignee, too.[186] Hence, the surety who has paid also acquires the claims of the creditor against the other (co-)sureties, but only to the extent of their pro rata share.[187] Even the English law of suretyship "has been much influenced by Roman law, partly directly, partly through medieval mercantile law which had been in contact with Roman law, partly through the system of 'Equity' administered by the English chancellors, which was itself influenced by canon law and late Roman law".[188] The rules relating to fideiussio have shaped the accessory nature of the surety's liability.[189] The beneficium cedendarum actionum lives on in the form of a duty of contribution between co-sureties and of the doctrine of subrogation.[190] Sureties do not, however, have the

---

[182] Van den Heever JA, in *Gerber v. Wolson* 1955 (1) SA 158 (A) at 170H–171A. Similarly, Steyn J in *Wolson v. Gerber* 1954 (3) SA 94 (T) at 99 sq. Differently Fagan JA, in *Gerber v. Wolson* 1955 (1) SA 158 (A) at 183. On the influence of Pothier on South African law, in theory and in actual practice, see generally Reinhard Zimmermann, "Der Einfluss Pothiers auf das römisch-holländische Recht in Südafrika", (1985) 102 *ZSS* (GA) 176 sqq.

[183] Cf. Zimmermann, (1985) 102 *ZSS* (GA) 200 sqq.

[184] Cf. §§ 767, 768, 770 BGB and "Motive", in: *Mugdan*, vol. II, pp. 369 sqq.

[185] § 774 I BGB.

[186] §§ 412, 401 BGB.

[187] §§ 774 II, 426 I BGB.

[188] Albert Kiralfy, "History of the Law of Personal Guarantee (Suretyship) in England since 1500", in: (1971) 29 *Recueils* (op. cit., note 2) 400.

[189] Cf. Kiralfy, op. cit., pp. 410 sqq.; for details of the English law in this regard, see Johan Steyn, "Guarantees: The Co-extensiveness Principle", (1974) 90 *LQR* 246 sqq.

[190] Burge, *Suretyship*, pp. 352 sqq., 384 sqq.

right to compel the creditor to proceed against their co-sureties (beneficium divisionis). Nor, in fact, is the creditor required to sue the principal debtor first; the beneficium excussionis, recognized in medieval English law,[191] has not managed to establish itself in the modern common law.[192]

It is not accidental that neither the beneficium divisionis nor the beneficium excussionis became part of the English law. Even in those legal systems where they have been received, their operation is usually excluded by the parties.[193] Thus, if one looks, not at the common law or statute book, but into how suretyship is actually practised today, one will generally find the sureties to be in the position of joint and several debtors: liable for the whole debt and as a principal debtor. In so far as certain Germanic forms of suretyship still live on in this practice, the history of suretyship could indeed be written as a struggle of indigenous custom against the received rules of Roman law.[194]

VIII. WOMEN AS SURETIES

1. The senatus consultum Vellaeanum

Before concluding this chapter, a small arabesque should be added. At some time between A.D. 41 and 65[195] the Roman Senate enacted the following law:

> "Quod Marcus Silanus et Velleus Tutor consules verba fecerunt de obligationibus feminarum, quae pro aliis reae fierent, quid de ea re fieri oportet, de ea re ita censuere: quod ad fideiussiones et mutui dationes pro aliis, quibus intercesserint feminae, pertinet, tametsi ante videtur ita ius dictum esse, ne eo nomine ab his petitio neve in eas actio detur, cum eas virilibus officiis fungi et eius generis obligationibus obstringi non sit aequum, arbitrari senatum recte atque ordine facturos ad quos de ea re in iure aditum erit, si dederint operam, ut in ea re senatus voluntas servetur."[196]

These are the words of the famous (or notorious) senatus consultum Vellaeanum by which women were prohibited from "interceding", that is, from incurring liability for the benefit of others (pro aliis reas fieri), as, for instance, in the case of suretyship contracts.

---

[191] Cf. already Glanvill, X, 3, in fine: ". . . si principalis debitor ita inde defecerit quod non habeat unde solvere possit, tunc demum recuperandum erit ad plegios" and then the Statute of Merchants 1285 (13 Edward I) (on which, see Theodore Plucknett, *Legislation of Edward I* (1962), pp. 138 sqq.).

[192] Burge, *Suretyship*, pp. 341 sq.

[193] As has been the case, for instance, in *Wolson v. Gerber*, supra, note 176.

[194] Cf. Feenstra, op. cit., note 21, pp. 296 sqq., 322 sqq.; Werner Ogris, "Die persönlichen Sicherheiten in den westeuropäischen Rechten des Mittelalters", (1971) 29 *Recueils* (op. cit., note 2) 21 sqq. For the "Dogmengeschichte" of the suretyship contract generally, see Girtanner, op. cit., note 48, pp. 151 sqq.; for its Germanic roots, see Franz Beyerle, "Die Ursprung der Bürgschaft", (1927) 47 *ZSS* (GA) 567 sqq.

[195] Cf. the arguments advanced by Hans Kreller, *Das Verbot der Fraueninterzession von Augustus bis Justinian, Anzeiger der phil.-hist. Klasse der Österreichischen Akademie der Wissenschaften* (Wien), pp. 6 sq.

[196] Ulp. D. 16, 1, 2, 1.

Reading this enactment, one is not struck by its precision and lucidity. But that in itself is no reason to regard the text, as it has been handed down to us, as largely interpolated.[197] Modern legislators have not always done much better as far as the clarity of expression and stylistic elegance of their enactments are concerned; the science (or art) of how to legislate has, until very recently, received hardly any attention in academic legal circles.[198] Besides, the Roman Senate was not composed of private lawyers; the wording of its consulta was often based, quite probably, on the motions brought before it, and these motions, frequently containing not only a specific rule but also the motivation for it, were not necessarily skilfully drafted.[199] It is, however, precisely its somewhat clumsy wording that makes this senatus consultum such an instructive example of how classical lawyers interpreted statutory provisions in order to make them workable tools for the implementation of the legislative policy.

2. The policy of the senatus consultum

But what was this policy underlying the senatus consultum Vellaeanum? According to Fritz Schulz, it was "an outspokenly reactionary enactment in conformity with the general attitude of the Senate which at that period was the centre of reaction".[200] Since the time of the Punic wars the increasing emancipation of women[201] had led to a deplorable decay of the good old mores maiorum, and the Senate now tried to reverse this development by preventing women from indulging in business transactions and by bringing them back to their proper place, which, according to traditional opinion, is, of course, at home.[202] But

---

[197] Heinrich Vogt, *Studien zum Senatus Consultum Velleianum* (1952), pp. 2 sqq.

[198] Cf., however, Peter Noll, *Gesetzgebungslehre* (1973) (by now a classic); now also Jürgen Rödig, *Studien zu einer Theorie der Gesetzgebung* (1976); Hans Schneider, *Gesetzgebung* (1982).

[199] Cf. Dieter Medicus, *Zur Geschichte des Senatus Consultum Velleianum* (1957), p. 19. As to the style and structure of senatus consulta in general, cf. David Daube, *Forms of Roman Legislation* (1956), pp. 78 sqq. (". . . as a senatusconsult is addressed not to the people at large but to a magistrate . . ., its language is much freer and more general than that of statutes or edicts. It is not intended as a precise guide for the ordinary man, but as advice for an official, who will be quite capable of judging exactly how far and in what way to follow it out. A great deal, that is, must be left to the discretion of the recipient").

[200] *CRL*, p. 569.

[201] Cf. e.g. Schulz, *CRL*, pp. 180 sqq.; Johannes Georg Fuchs, *Die rechtliche Stellung der Frau im alten Rom* (1960), pp. 9 sqq.; cf. also, more recently, the studies by Suzanne Dixon, "Infirmitas sextus: Womanly Weakness in Roman Law", (1984) 52 *TR* 343 sqq; Leo Peppe, *Posizione giuridica e ruolo sociale della donna romana in età repubblicana* (1984); Jane F. Gardner, *Women in Roman Law and Society* (1986), and O.F. Robinson, "The Status of Women in Roman Private Law", 1987 *Juridical Review* 143 sqq.

[202] That the senatus consultum was a measure directed *against* the women has been asserted, especially, by Vogt, op. cit., note 197, pp. 6 sqq.; cf. also J.E. Spruit, "Het Raets-besluit van Burgemeester Velleius", in: *Huldigingsbundel Paul van Warmelo* (1984), pp. 197 sq. and 194 sq. with quotations from Philips van Leyden (14th century): "mulieres vagari non convenit nec se virorum coetibus immiscere", "mulieres commodius domesticorum curam gerunt." During the Middle Ages, women were denounced not only for being too earthbound to give due thought to matters of business but also for being unable

even though some of the senators may indeed have thought so, the predominant intention of the enactment was a less sinister one: if the senate took "intercedere" to be a matter for men only ("virile officium"), this seems to have been primarily an assessment (possibly a paternalistic one) of what was in the women's best interest. In other words, the senatus consultum was designed to be an instrument of protection, and in that sense a privilege—or, in the words of Hugo Grotius: a "voordeel" for "vrou-menschen".[203] This appears from the enactment itself[204] and is also, for instance, borne out by the way in which the condictio was handled: where a woman had actually performed what she had promised in violation of the senatus consultum, and had done so in full knowledge of the legal position, she was not able to claim her performance back.[205] Obviously, under these circumstances, she did not need to be protected by the law. Thus, there was no necessity for the lawyers to deviate from the normal rule that no enrichment claim can be brought where the person performing knew that he or she was not bound to effect the performance.[206]

However, this way of looking at the enactment raises two questions: why did the enactment relate to women only, and why did it prevent women from "intercedere" rather than, for instance, from incurring obligations in their own interest too? The answer is to be found in what the Roman lawyers described as sexus imbecillitas,[207] infirmitas[208] or fragilitas feminarum.[209] Even though the realities of Roman life had, to a certain extent, left behind the stage at which women were "content to sit at the distaff or the weaving loom",[210] and even though a lawyer such as Gaius—albeit a good hundred years later!—regarded the common idea of levitas animi feminarum as more specious than true,[211] these arguments should not simply be discounted as rhetorical phraseology or the professorial wisdom of reactionary philistines.[212] As

---

to devote themselves to divine things. Woman was, in the words of Vincent de Beauvais, "the confusion of man, an insatiable beast, a continuous anxiety, an incessant warfare, a daily ruin, a house of tempest, a hinderance to devotion" (cf. Gerald R. Owst, *Literature and Pulpit in Medieval England* (2nd ed., 1961, p. 378)).

[203] *Inleiding*, III, III, XV; cf. also Girtanner, op. cit., note 48, pp. 135 sq., 335 sq.; Medicus, op. cit., note 199, pp. 18 sqq. and passim; Dixon, (1984) 52 *TR* 356 sqq., 363 sqq.; as to the older literature, see Glück, vol. 14, pp. 447 sqq.; Spruit, *Huldigingsbundel van Warmelo*, pp. 200 sqq. By implication, then, the necessity of enacting the senatus consultum Vellaeanum shows the decay, at that time already, of the other protective devices, especially the tutela mulierum.

[204] "Et eius generis obligationibus obstringi non sit aequum": it is not the activity of the woman but the fact that she is bound that is considered inequitable.

[205] C. 4, 29, 9 (Gord.); Medicus, op. cit., note 199, pp. 30 sqq.

[206] Cf. Schwarz, *Condictio*, pp. 65 sqq.

[207] Ulp. D. 16, 1, 2, 2.

[208] Ulp. D. 16, 1, 2, 3.

[209] C. 4, 29, 22 (Just.). On these topoi cf. Dixon, (1984) 52 *TR* 343 sqq.

[210] Schulz, *CRL*, p. 183.

[211] Gai. I, 190.

[212] Schulz, *CRL*, p. 184.

a rule, it was the paterfamilias who administered the property of the family, and as a result of this and of tutela mulierum, the average Roman woman did in fact lack business experience. That made it particularly difficult for her coolly to assess the risks involved in those transactions which did not immediately affect her own affairs. The senatus consultum Vellaeanum dealt with situations where the woman acted in the interest of somebody else; this third party was the "true" debtor, who was to be ultimately responsible for the debt incurred. Thus, the woman could easily be tempted to think of her own obligation as a mere formality which she would never be required to fulfil. Emotionally inclined to rush to somebody else's help when required to do so, acting with undue confidence in this other person's ability and readiness to honour his promise, unable, especially, to withstand the importunacy of their husbands or friends, and generally prone to be influenced by unscrupulous or well-meant but unsound advice—so one probably thought—women tend to be somewhat frivolous, over-optimistic and reckless of their own interests. The danger therefore existed that they would all too readily bind themselves for others (pro aliis reas fieri), and it was this specific danger that the Senate set out to combat.[213]

3. The interpretation of the senatus consultum by the Roman lawyers

(a) Protection of the woman

The senatus consultum Vellaeanum was interpreted and applied with this purpose in mind; in modern parlance, one might say that the Roman lawyers followed a purposive or teleological[214] approach. Thus, they were ready to apply the enactment to all situations that were dangerous in the above-mentioned sense: where a woman stood surety,

---

[213] For a slightly different analysis, see Dixon, (1984) 52 *TR* 356 sqq., 363 sqq. She argues that the senatus consultum was in line with the Augustan legislation preventing the husband from selling dotal land in Italy without the permission of his wife (cf. Gai. II, 63; *Inst.* II, 8 pr.) and that it was thus intended to protect her fortune from inroads by the husband. The wording of the enactment as it has come down to us "is concerned with the proper sphere of women rather than their intrinsic character" (p. 369). Dixon admits, however, that the notion of female weakness soon began to play its part in the application of the senatus consultum.

[214] "[The European countries] adopt a method which they call in English by strange words—at any rate they were strange to me—the 'schematic and teleological' method of interpretation. It is not really so alarming as it sounds. All it means is that the judges do not go by the literal meaning of the words or by the grammatical structure of the sentence. They go by the design or purpose which lies behind it. When they come upon a situation which is to their minds within the spirit—but not the letter—of the legislation, they solve the problem by looking at the design and purpose of the legislature—at the effect which it was sought to achieve. They then interpret the legislation so as to produce the desired effect. This means that they fill in gaps, quite unashamedly, without hesitation. They ask simply: what is the sensible way of dealing with this situation so as to give effect to the presumed purpose of the legislation? They lay down the law accordingly": Lord Denning MR in *James Buchanan & Co. Ltd. v. Babco Forwarding & Shipping (UK) Ltd.* [1977] QB 208 (CA) at 213F–H.

incurred joint obligations,[215] gave security for another by way of pledge,[216] released the debtor by means of novatio,[217] or took out a loan on somebody else's behalf and thus saved him from incurring any liability himself.[218] Furthermore, even contracts of sale[219] or hire[220] could be hit by the senatus consultum and it was also taken to cover cases where a woman had not interceded herself on behalf of the third party but had mandated a fourth party to do so for her.[221]

From another angle, however, we find the lawyers displaying a very restrictive tendency, willing to recognize exceptions where the requirements of the senatus consultum had, in a very literal sense, in actual fact been met.[222] The common denominator of these situations appears to lie in the absence of a necessity to protect the interceding woman. Hence, for example, decisions such as Paul. D. 16, 1, 24 pr.: "Debitrix mulier a creditore delegata pro eo cui delegata est promisit: non utetur exceptione." Here the woman had incurred an obligation on behalf of, i.e. interceded for, a third party. However, she had been authorized to do so by her creditor by way of delegatio obligandi, which meant a change of creditor and involved a novation. Thus, by assuming the new obligation, the woman got rid of her old one, and this meant that her intercession did not entail a specific risk or danger. It was "neutral", in so far as in being released from the old obligation she received a compensation for facing the prospect of liability to the new creditor. Therefore, the transaction was not treated as invalid. The same could apply where the woman had interceded donandi animo, i.e. in order to donate the sum, for which she had made herself liable, to the debtor: "Item si [mulier] quid liberaliter fecerit, veluti ne iudicatus pater eius propter solutionem vexetur, non erit tuta senatus consulto."[223] There was no misconception, in a case such as this, about the financial risk involved. Nor was the senatus consultum Vellaeanum applied where the woman had pursued her own interest:

---

[215] Afr. D. 16, 1, 17, 2.

[216] Ulp. D. 16, 1, 8 pr.; Pomp. D. 16, 1, 32, 1.

[217] C. 4, 29, 1 (Ant.); 4, 29, 4 pr. (Alex.).

[218] This case is mentioned in the text of the senatus consultum, but nevertheless disputed by Vogt, op. cit., note 197, pp. 43 sqq. Contra: Medicus, op. cit., note 199, pp. 101 sqq.

[219] Pomp. D. 16, 1, 32, 2.

[220] C. 4, 29, 10 (Phil.).

[221] Pomp. D. 16, 1, 32, 3. If the fourth party had incurred expenses as a result of having interceded (because he was called upon to pay), he could claim reimbursement from the woman by way of the actio mandati contraria. Thus, from the point of view of the rationale of the senatus consultum, the woman was in very much the same position as when she had interceded herself.

[222] For a detailed analysis, see Medicus, op. cit., note 199, pp. 34 sqq.; cf. also e.g. Voet, *Commentarius ad Pandectas*, Lib. XVI, Tit I, XI.

[223] Call. D. 16, 1, 21, 1; cf. also Ulp. D. 16, 1, 4 pr.

> "Aliquando, licet alienam obligationem suscipiat mulier, non adiuvatur hoc senatus consulto: quod tum accidit, cum prima facie quidem alienam, re vera autem suam obligationem suscipiat. ut ecce si . . . pro fideiussore suo intercedat."[224]

Here, the woman had interceded on behalf of a third party and therefore, prima facie, acted for the benefit of somebody else. But since this third party was her own surety, she had "re vera" incurred the obligation in her own interest. It was characteristic of their general approach to this enactment that the Roman lawyers looked at the real interest situation rather than contenting themselves with a formal classification of the transaction.[225]

(b) Protection of the creditor

The lawyers, however, had to be concerned with the protection of the creditor too. To strengthen his position was not problematic as long as that did not affect the woman. According to the senatus consultum, any action against a woman who had interceded was barred by an exceptio.[226] That left the creditor in a very unsatisfactory position where this intercession had had the effect of releasing the debtor, or of saving the third party in whose interest the woman had incurred her obligation, from assuming any liability himself. Thus two new (praetorian) remedies had to be developed: an actio restitutoria,[227] for the first of these two situations, in order to reinstate the creditor into his former claim against the debtor, and an actio institutoria,[228] which enabled the creditor to proceed against the third party, just as if the contract had been concluded with him instead of with the woman.

(c) Policy conflict

But the policies of protecting the woman and of avoiding unreasonable consequences for the creditor could clash. That was the case especially where a third party had interceded on behalf of the woman or where the woman had concluded a transaction that was not immediately recognizable as an intercession. This conflict of interests was resolved in favour of the creditor: the exceptio senatus consulti Vellaeani was to be employed only where the creditor had known of the intercessory nature of the woman's transaction (as, for instance, always in the case of

---

[224] Gai. D. 16, 1, 13 pr.; cf. also Pomp. D. 16, 1, 32 pr., Mod. D. 16, 1, 25 pr., Pap. D. 16, 1, 27, 2.

[225] Cf. also e.g. supra, pp. 148 sq.

[226] That exceptio was (probably) inserted by the praetor ex officio (i.e. even invita muliere): cf. Medicus, op. cit., note 199, pp. 30, 48.

[227] Ulp. D. 16, 1, 8, 7 sqq.; cf. further Arthur Hartkamp, "Die Drittwirkung der 'in integrum restitutio'", in: Daube Noster, *Essays in Legal History for David Daube* (1974), pp. 150 sqq.

[228] Ulp. D. 16, 1, 8, 14; cf. further Giovanni Bortolucci, *Actio quae instituit obligationem* (1915), pp. 9 sqq.

suretyship).[229] This, of course, limited the applicability of the senatus consultum quite drastically. Yet it was the only means not only of protecting the creditor but also of generally maintaining the creditworthiness of women: "Si mulier tamquam in usus suos pecuniam acceperit alii creditura, non est locus senatus consulto: alioquin nemo cum feminis contrahet, quia ignorari potest, quid acturae sint."[230] The prospect of being faced with the exceptio even where the creditor had assumed that the woman had acted on her own behalf was not at all unlikely to curtail the willingness of cautious businessmen to grant credit to women, even if the latter did in actual fact act in their own interest.

4. Justinian's contribution

Justinian modified the prohibition on intercessiones by women not inconsiderably; he generally followed the policy of (further) reducing the protection afforded to women by the senatus consultum Vellaeanum and of thus recognizing their increasing emancipation and business experience.[231] Most importantly, he created for women the possibility of validating their acts of intercession by confirming them after a lapse of two years,[232] or by acknowledging the receipt of compensation in a formal document, drawn up by a tabellio and signed by three witnesses.[233] The use of such documents containing, where necessary, a merely fictitious compensation, made intercessiones fairly freely available to women; only the formality of the act was left to prevent a woman from foolishly rushing into these types of transactions.

In one particular case, however, Justinian tightened the screws: he imposed an absolute prohibition on women to intercede on behalf of their husbands, unless (and that was the only exception) the money received as a result of their intercessions was spent for the benefit of the women themselves.[234] This enactment, later known as the Authentica si qua mulier,[235] effectively re-enforced the policy of the senatus consultum Vellaeanum for that situation in which women had always been particularly susceptible of acting in an unduly altruistic and

---

[229] Cf. e.g. Pap. D. 16, 1, 27 pr., Scaev. D. 16, 1, 28, 1; Medicus, op. cit., note 199, pp. 54 sqq.

[230] Paul. D. 16, 1, 11.

[231] For the details, see Medicus, op. cit., note 199, pp. 66 sqq., 77 sqq.; Kreller, op. cit., note 195, pp. 9 sq.; Kaser, *RPr* II, p. 462; Antonio Díaz Bautista, "L' intercession des femmes dans la législation de Justinien", (1983) 30 *RIDA* 81 sqq.

[232] C. 4, 29, 22 pr.

[233] C. 4, 29, 23, 1 ("Sed si quidem in ipso instrumento intercessionis dixerit sese aliquid accepisse et sic ad intercessionem venisse et hoc instrumentum publice confectum inveniatur et a tribus testibus consignatum, omnimodo esse credendum eam pecuniam vel res accepisse, et non esse ei ad senatus consulti Velleiani auxilium regressum. . . .").

[234] Nov. 134, 8.

[235] Cf. e.g. Spruit, *Huldigingsbundel van Warmelo*, pp. 200 sqq.

unbusinesslike manner, and from which, historically, the idea of preventing women from interceding had actually originated.[236]

5. The position in modern law

Both senatus consultum Vellaeanum and Authentica si qua mulier appear to be somewhat out of tune with modern notions about equality of the sexes. As Van den Heever J once put it when faced with the necessity of applying these legal fossils in the 20th century:

> "One of the incongruities of this inconsequent age is the fact that women while enjoying full rights of citizenship, including that of making or marring policies of the State as effectively as any male, are able in their private affairs to invoke a defence based on their innate fecklessness and incapacity and so avoid liability in respect of obligations which they have deliberately assumed."[237]

Yet it took almost another 30 years before this part of the Roman-Dutch common law was repealed in South Africa (by legislation),[238] as it had already been in the other countries of the ius commune tradition (in France as early as 1606, in some parts of Germany only with the coming into operation of the BGB).[239] Thus, today, the disputes enveloping the senatus consultum Vellaeanum have lost their practical relevance.[240] Yet the enactment is still worth studying from a historical perspective, as it provides an important mosaic stone for the evaluation of the role of women in Roman society and of the way in which the Roman jurists applied and developed the law.

---

[236] Ulp. D. 16, 1, 2 pr.

[237] *Van Rensburg v. Minnie* 1942 OPD 257 at 259.

[238] Suretyship Amendment Act 57 of 1971. On its history, see Ellison Kahn, "Farewell Senatus consultum Velleianum and Authentica Si Qua Mulier", (1971) 88 *SALJ* 364 sqq. As late as 1965 the Law Revision Committee had urged not only that the benefits should be retained but, preferably, that they should be made more effective.

[239] On the history and the application of the senatus consultum Vellaeanum since the Middle Ages, see Girtanner, op. cit., note 48, pp. 258 sqq., 335 sqq.; Glück, vol. 14, pp. 433 sqq., vol. 15, pp. 1 sqq.; Spruit, *Huldigingsbundel van Warmelo*, pp. 210 sqq. For Roman-Dutch law, see Voet, *Commentarius ad Pandectas*, Lib. XVI, Tit. I; Caney, *The Law of Suretyship in South Africa* (2nd ed., 1970), pp. 163 sqq.; Spruit, *Huldigingsbundel van Warmelo*, pp. 204 sqq.; Oskar Lehner, "Senatus Consultum Velleianum—Die Wiederkehr einer antiken Rechtsfigur im frühnenzeitlichen österreichischen Recht", (1988) 105 *ZSS* (GA) 270 sqq.; Wessels, *Contract*, §§ 3815 sqq.; for the pandectists, see Windscheid/Kipp, §§ 485 sqq. As in the case of suretyship, the widespread use of renunciation clauses since the Middle Ages (". . . renuncians . . . et specialiter beneficio Velleiani"—on these Spruit, *Huldigingsbundel van Warmelo*, pp. 201 sqq.) reveals a certain reaction of indigenous practice against the received rule of Roman law. The renunciation of the exceptio senatus consulti Vellaeani was generally regarded as admissible, because of the nature of this remedy as being "in favorem mulieris".

[240] So, incidentally, has the "artificial" (Schulz, *CRL*, p. 570) conception of "intercedere", "intercessio" as a terminus technicus.

PART III

CHAPTER 6

Mutuum

I. THE ROMAN CONTRACT OF MUTUUM

1. The nature of mutuum

We turn now to the real contracts, the prototype of which was mutuum, the loan for consumption. It is, in fact, the only real contract Gaius specifically deals with in his *Institutes*. He describes it in the following terms:

> "[M]utui autem datio proprie in his fere rebus contingit quae pondere numero mensura constant, qualis est pecunia numerata, vinum, oleum, frumentum, aes, argentum, aurum. quas res aut numerando aut metiendo aut pendendo in hoc damus, ut accipientium fiant et quandoque nobis non eadem, sed aliae eiusdem naturae reddantur";[1]

and he adds a speculation as to why this type of contract was called mutuum: "[U]nde etiam mutuum appellatum est, quia quod ita tibi a me datum est, ex meo tuum fit."[2] This is a pseudo-etymology.[3] Mutuum is probably derived from "mutare", which means "to change", "to swop".[4] Yet, ex meo tuum facere was an essential feature of the contract of mutuum. A datio had to take place[5] on account of which ownership of the object(s) lent passed to the borrower. Once this datio had been effected, the borrower became obligated to the lender not to return the very things that he had received, but (in the case of money) an equal sum or (as far as other fungibles were concerned) objects of the same kind, quantity and quality.[6] To enforce this obligation, the lender could avail himself of the condictio (actio certae creditae pecuniae).[7] Owing to the fact that its intentio was abstractly framed (that is, it did not refer to the obligatory basis of the claim), this action was very flexible and apt to cater for all situations where certum dare was owed. That is why we have already come across the condictio in the cases of stipulationes certi and contracts litteris.[8]

---

[1] Gai. III, 90.

[2] Cf. also Paul. D. 12, 1, 2, 2.

[3] On its origin, see von Lübtow, *Darlehensbegriff*, pp. 1 sqq., 19 sq.

[4] A. Walde, J.B. Hofmann, *Lateinisches etymologisches Wörterbuch* (3rd ed.), vol. II (1954), pp. 137 sq.; cf. also J.M. Kelly, "A Hypothesis on the Origin of Mutuum", (1970) 5 *The Irish Jurist* 155 sqq. with further speculation.

[5] For this central requirement of mutui datio cf. V. Stanojevic, "La 'mutui datio' du droit romain", (1969) 15 *Labeo* 311 sqq.

[6] Cf., for example, Pomp. D. 12, 1, 3.

[7] *Inst.* III, 14 pr.

[8] Cf. supra, pp. 32 sq., 89 sq.

Three obvious inferences can be drawn from what has been said so far. Whereas not every loan of fungibles[9] can be classified as a mutuum (in the case of fungible objects which are ordinarily used without being consumed, the lender will often want to get back the thing itself and not only its equivalent in kind; already, therefore, a transfer of ownership to the borrower is not envisaged by the parties), non-fungible objects cannot be the object of a mutuum: the borrower's obligation presupposes the existence of an equivalent in kind.[10] Secondly, as both ownership and possession pass to the borrower and as a contractual obligation does not come into existence without this transfer having taken place, risk problems cannot arise. If the borrower loses the money or the goods received, this is entirely his own affair and does not have any effect on his obligatio arising from the mutuum: "et is quidem qui mutuum accepit, si quolibet fortuito casu quod accepit amiserit, veluti incendio, ruina, naufragio aut latronum hostiumve incursu, nihilo minus obligatus permanet."[11] This is entirely in accordance with the natural principle of casum sentit dominus (or res perit suo domino):[12] it is the owner who has to bear the risk of accidental loss or destruction and, except by way of insurance, he cannot shift the risk onto somebody else's shoulders. Thirdly, prior to the datio (that is, the vesting of ownership in the borrower), no obligation could come into existence. A pactum de mutuo dando, i.e. the promise to grant a loan in future, was unenforceable—unless, of course, it was couched in the form of a stipulation.

2. Mutuum and stipulatio

A further, very important characteristic of mutuum is the fact that the contract gave rise to only one action (the condictio of the lender against the recipient of the loan) and consequently only to one obligation (namely that of the borrower to return res aliae eiusdam naturae). Thus, especially, a claim for interest could not be enforced. The condictio was, after all, an actio stricti iuris. The judge therefore did not have any discretion to give effect to informal, ancillary agreements between the parties, or to equitable considerations; he could only condemn the borrower in as much as the latter had received from the lender. Strictly speaking, mutuum was thus a unilaterally binding, gratuitous contract.

---

[9] As to the term "fungibles" (derived from the Latin "fungibiles"), see Pothier, *Traité du contrat du prêt de consomption*, n. 25: "Earum natura est, ut aliae aliarum ejusdem generis rerum vice fungantur."

[10] Cf. e.g. Nicholas, *Introduction*, p.167.

[11] *Inst.* III, 14, 2.

[12] Cf. C. 4, 24, 9; also Ulp. D. 50, 17, 23 in fine. This remains true as long as there is no specific reason to shift the loss. Such shift is justified normally on the basis of culpa or dolus (delictual liability), but there are certain instances where even accidental loss does not lie with the owner. On the precise ambit of casum sentit dominus, see Andreas Wacke, "Gefahrerhöhung als Besitzerverschulden", in: *Festschrift für Heinz Hübner* (1984), pp. 670 sqq.

In commercial practice, however, few people were (and still are) prepared to make loans on an entirely altruistic basis.[13] Yet, if the lender wished to receive interest on the capital loaned, he had to extract from the borrower a promise in the form of a stipulation,[14] i.e. the parties had to enter into a separate, additional contract. This is in fact what usually happened; and since a stipulation had to be made anyway, if the loan was to be given for interest, the parties usually took the opportunity to incorporate the principal debt as well, so that the borrower's obligation to return the capital was very often reaffirmed by way of stipulation.[15] At the same time, this was a convenient way to make certain incidental provisions binding—for instance, those relating to the time of repayment or the place of performance. Under these circumstances the transaction was re et verbis[16] rather than merely re: datio and stipulatio were two acts, both giving rise to the obligation to restore the capital, and both, incidentally, enforceable by means of the condictio. Naturally, however, performance had to be made only once, and in case of failure of performance the creditor could also bring the condictio only once. This he probably did on the basis of the stipulatio, for the Roman lawyers seem to have been of the opinion that the obligatio re was absorbed by the obligatio verbis:

> "Cum enim pecunia mutua data stipulamur, non puto obligationem numeratione nasci et deinde eam stipulatione novari, quia id agitur, ut sola stipulatio teneat, et magis implendae stipulationis gratia numeratio intellegenda est fieri."[17]

---

[13] Even a loan without interest is, however, not always (perhaps even: not usually) made for purely altruistic reasons. Roman society was characterized by a network of (informal) relationships which could either be created by, or which engendered a (moral) duty to grant, a (seemingly) gratuitous loan. Thus, for instance, loans could be given not in order to receive interest but to gain political influence, to generate loyalty or to create a situation of dependence. Furthermore, the usual duties arising from the Roman concept of "amicitia" (on which cf. e.g. supra, p. 115) must be taken into consideration. Both the granting of a (usually short-term) loan in order to allow the borrower to cope with a momentary problem of liquidity and the (informal) "remuneration" of such friendly service with other services or favours were natural implications of the officium amici. The average Roman paterfamilias did not go to a professional moneylender (fenerator) but turned to his amici when he was in need of capital. For all details, particularly the social and economic background as it can be reconstructed on the basis of Roman literary sources, cf. Alfons Bürge, "Vertrag und personale Abhängigkeiten im Rom der spätem Republik und der frühen Kaiserzeit", (1980) 97 *ZSS* 114 sqq. On the (low) social position of the feneratores (and on banking business in general) cf. idem, "Fiktion und Wirklichheit: Soziale und rechtliche Strukturen des römischen Bankwesens", (1987) 104 *ZSS* 488 sqq., 495 sqq. The fact that credit was readily available through private connections substituted for (and in turn contributed to) the lack of a large-scale banking system in Rome. Cf. also infra, pp. 217 sq.

[14] Afr. D. 19, 5, 24.

[15] Cf. e.g. Paul. D. 12, 1, 40; Scaev. D. 45, 1, 122, 1; Paul. D. 45, 1, 126, 2; Ulp. D. 46, 2, 6, 1.

[16] Ulp. D. 12, 1, 9, 3; Mod. D. 44, 7, 52 pr. These texts have often been regarded as spurious; cf., for example, Alfred Pernice, "Der sogenannte Realverbalkontrakt", (1892) 13 *ZSS* 246 sqq.; Schulz, *CRL*, p. 507; but see Max Kaser, "'Mutuum' und 'stipulatio'", in: *Eranion G.S. Maridakis*, vol. I (1963), pp. 155 sqq.

[17] Pomp. D. 46, 2, 7; cf. Fritz Pringsheim, "Id quod actum est", (1961) 78 *ZSS* 79 sqq.; Kaser, *Eranion Maridakis*, pp. 157 sqq.

Of the above-mentioned incidental provisions, the fixing of a date for repayment of the capital is obviously of particular interest to a borrower. A loan transaction can hardly achieve its purpose if the capital has to be repaid immediately after it has been handed over by the lender to the borrower. Yet this was, strictly speaking, the case where the mutuum was not accompanied or reaffirmed by a stipulation. For it was the datio that gave rise to the obligation to repay the capital, and this obligation came into effect immediately. The due date for repayment could, at least originally, not be deferred by the parties because whatever they might have agreed upon informally could not be considered in iure civili. This result was less inconvenient than it sounds, because mutuum was used, at first, between friends or neighbours for the purposes of short-term loans without interest.[18] Here, social ties arising from amicitia and humanitas were strong enough to prevent the creditor from (ab-)using his formal position and bringing the condictio immediately. For commercial loan transactions the formal, but very dangerous, nexum was available.[19] When it disappeared during the period of the Republic, mutuum took over this function too and became the universal loan transaction. But in the commercial context it was, in actual practice, always accompanied by a stipulation containing all the special arrangements of the parties.

3. The consensual element of mutuum

(a) Consensus and rei interventio

Furthermore, even with regard to mutuum proper the consensual element came to be increasingly emphasized in the course of time. It is obvious that not every datio could give rise to a condictio. Perhaps the property had been transferred in order to enrich the recipient permanently (as in the case of a donation), to discharge an obligation or, for instance, to give a dowry. Thus, to classify a transaction as mutuum, we need not only the transfer of fungible things but also some sort of understanding between the parties that this specific transfer takes place in order to effect a loan, i.e. that the recipient has to restore the value of what is being transferred to him. Thus we find Paulus stating:

> "Non satis autem est dantis esse nummos et fieri accipientis, ut obligatio nascatur, sed etiam hoc animo dari et accipi, ut obligatio constituatur. itaque si quis pecuniam

---

[18] Kaser, *RPr* I, p. 170; Watson, *Evolution*, pp. 9 sqq. Cf. also Kelly, (1970) 5 *The Irish Jurist* 156 sqq. (according to whom mutuum originated as barter) and Geoffrey MacCormack, "Gift, Debt, Obligation and the Real Contracts", (1985) 31 *Labeo* 139 sqq., who specifically links mutuum with gift.

[19] Cf. supra, pp. 4 sq. Nexum may have been immediately enforceable by execution, without prior lawsuit and judgment: cf. Kaser, *Altrömisches ius*, pp. 119 sqq.; but see Ludwig Mitteis, "Über das Nexum", (1901) 22 *ZSS* 96 sqq.; Max Kaser, "'Unmittelbare Vollstreckbarkeit' und Bürgenregress", (1983) 100 *ZSS* 111.

suam donandi causa dederit mihi, quamquam et donantis fuerit et mea fiat, tamen non obligabor ei, quia non hoc inter nos actum est."[20]

This mental element, the animus, ut obligatio constituatur,[21] for a long time merely qualified the purpose for which the datio had been made; it was not a proper contractual agreement and left no room for the regulation of details concerning the loan. However, it is apparent from the sources that a development took place in this regard.[22] First of all, the ius honorarium offered opportunities to take into consideration informal arrangements between the parties concerning the time of repayment. On the basis of such pacta de non petendo intra certum tempus the praetor was prepared to grant an exceptio pacti; alternatively, he could also help with an exceptio doli.[23] But in the course of time mutuum became transformed into a true obligatory contract based, like all contracts, on consensus,[24] but it was dependent, in addition, on rei interventio. There is some evidence that the consensual leg of mutuum was already far enough developed in classical law that arrangements relating to the time of repayment could be accommodated; this would have meant that the bringing of the condictio according to the ius civile was regarded as deferred until that time had expired.[25] This development, of course, continued in post-classical times with the general disintegration of the system of contracts of classical law. The emphasis was squarely on the consensus between the parties; the datio (distinguishing mutuum from other contracts and making it a contractus re) remained as a mere additional requirement.[26] Vinnius put it very clearly when he wrote, some hundred years later: "Constituitur mutuum non solo ac nudo consensu, sed rem intervenire ac tradi oportet."[27]

A good example of how the classical Roman lawyers tried to give effect to what the parties had actually agreed upon—without, however, unduly prejudicing the "real" nature of mutuum—is provided by Ulp. D. 12, 1, 11, 1:

"Si tibi dedero decem sic, ut novem debeas, Proculus ait, et recte, non amplius te ipso iure debere quam novem. sed si dedero, ut undecim debeas, putat Proculus amplius quam decem condici non posse."

---

[20] Paul. D. 44, 7, 3, 1. On this text, see Fritz Raber, "Hoc animo dare", (1965) 33 *TR* 58 sqq.

[21] Pringsheim, (1961) 78 *ZSS* 79 sqq.; O. Stanojevic, (1969) 15 *Labeo* 311 sqq., 317.

[22] For a detailed analysis, see Kaser, *Eranion Maridakis*, pp. 171 sqq.; also Raber, (1965) 33 *TR* 58 sqq. and Giuseppina Sacconi, "'Conventio' e 'mutuum'", (1987) 15 *Index* 423 sqq.

[23] Flor. D. 2, 14, 57 pr.; Ulp. D. 44, 4, 2, 6. Cf. von Lübtow, *Condictio*, p. 135.

[24] Cf. Ulp. D. 2, 14, 1, 3: ". . . ut eleganter dicat Pedius nullum esse contractum, nullam obligationem, quae non habeat in se conventionem, sive re sive verbis fiat."

[25] Iul. D. 12, 1, 22; Gai. D. 13, 3, 4; Kaser, *Eranion Maridakis*, p. 162; but see also Stanojevic, (1969) 15 *Labeo* 318: ". . . *le consensus, la volonté des parties, est resté jusqu'à la fin dans l'ombre projeté par l'acte matériel—la datio*."

[26] As to the law of Justinian, see Kaser, *RPr* II, pp. 369 sqq.

[27] *Institutiones*, Lib. 3, Tit. XV, pr., 1.

Two cases are discussed in this fragment and in both there is a discrepancy between the real and the consensual aspect of the transaction. In the first case ten were given on the understanding that only nine had to be returned; in the second, the borrower agreed to return eleven, even though, again, he had received only ten.[28] If, in the first case, Proculus/Ulpianus granted a condictio for nine only, this was a relaxation of the rule that the exact equivalent of what had been received had to be returned. However, the jurists did not hesitate to give effect to what the parties actually agreed upon; for as far as this lesser sum was concerned, the requirement of rei interventio had been complied with, too: minus in maiore inest.[29] If the lender receives nine, he does not get anything back for which he has not previously handed over an equivalent to the borrower. This is different in the second case. As far as the eleventh coin is concerned, the "real" aspect of the contract of mutuum has not been satisfied. If ten were given, there was no rei interventio, as far as number eleven is concerned. Thus the condictio cannot lie for more than ten.[30]

(b) Ex meo tuum facere

According to the pseudo-etymological basis of mutuum ("ex meo tuum"), there had to be a direct transfer of ownership from the creditor to the recipient of the loan. As Paulus put it figuratively, "item mutuum non potest esse, nisi proficiscitur pecunia";[31] there can be no contract of mutuum, unless the coins "wander" (sc.: from the hands of the creditor into those of the debtor). It is obvious that such a conceptually restricted view was bound to lead to cumbersome and very formalistic results. What, for instance, if the debtor was already in possession of the sum of money he wished to borrow because it had been deposited with him by the creditor at an earlier stage? Should one require the depositee under these circumstances to hand the money back to the depositor (thus discharging his obligation under the contract of depositum) only in order to have the very same sum returned to him immediately afterwards, now sub specie mutui? This would have been an inconvenient complication, to say the least. Thus we find already Iulianus taking the more practical view that ". . . si pecuniam apud te depositam convenerit ut creditam habeas, credita fiat, quia tunc nummi, qui mei erant, tui fiant".[32] This decision was facilitated by the fact that the money had actually once "wandered"

[28] Cf. also Paul. D. 2, 14, 17 pr.
[29] Cf. supra, p. 74.
[30] The fact that, as to the eleventh coin, no datio had taken place, and that no valid mutuum had therefore come into existence with regard thereto, does not have the consequence that the whole transaction is invalid: utile per inutile non vitiatur (cf. supra, pp. 75 sqq.). As far as the ten coins are concerned, the condictio can be granted.
[31] Paul. D. 12, 1, 2, 3.
[32] Iul./Afr. D. 17, 1, 34 pr.; also Ulp. D. 12, 1, 9, 9.

from the creditor to the debtor; a direct transfer of the coins had taken place (even though, at that stage, no transfer of ownership had been envisaged). In a very wide sense, therefore, one could still reconcile this situation with the "ex meo tuum" requirement. Yet it was the first step towards the recognition of a mere loan by agreement. A subsequent step had to be taken in response to the rise of a commercial banking system. Financial transactions were effected by credit transfers, payments made by what we would call an order of remittance or by a simple change of entry in the books of the argentarius.[33] Under these circumstances it was no longer feasible to insist on a direct transfer of individual coins in the case of mutuum: this would have meant the death of mutuum as the central loan transaction. Thus it was recognized, by way of a ius singulare,[34] that transfer of the sum to be advanced could be effected by delegatio solvendi:

> "Singularia quaedam recepta sunt circa pecuniam creditam. nam si tibi debitorem meum iussero dare pecuniam, obligaris mihi, quamvis meos nummos non acceperis."[35]

The creditor ("ego") has ordered his debtor to pay the money to a third party ("tu") to whom he wished to lend it. A contract of mutuum is thereby created between the creditor and the third party, even though the latter has not received his money from the creditor/lender. The same conclusion had already been reached by Iulianus: ". . . quod, si a debitore meo iussero te accipere pecuniam, credita fiat, id enim benigne receptum est."[36] If we compare this with his opinion regarding the previous case (depositum), we see that his reasoning no longer rests on the "ex meo tuum" basis. "Benigne (or possibly: utilitatis causa) receptum" is a clear recognition of what Ulpianus refers to as singularium (receptum), namely, the exceptional nature of this decision, for the sake of practical convenience. Dogmatically, this exception is probably based on a (double) fiction: the transfer from debtor to borrower merely serves as a short cut in order to avoid a cumbersome double transaction. The device is acceptable, because it can be deemed that the money has travelled from debtor to creditor and then from creditor to borrower. This ties in well with the Celsinian construction of delegatio solvendi,[37] based on the understanding (still fundamentally important for the modern law of unjustified

---

[33] Von Lübtow, *Darlehensbegriff*, pp. 25 sq. On argentarii, see infra, pp. 514, 764 sq.

[34] Paul D. 1, 3, 16: "Ius singulare est, quod contra tenorem rationis propter aliquam utilitatem auctoritate constituentium introductum est."

[35] Ulp. D. 12, 1, 15.

[36] Iul./Afr. D. 17, 1, 34 pr.

[37] Cf. Ulp. D. 24, 1, 3, 9–13; von Lübtow, *Darlehensbegriff*, pp. 30 sqq.; Max Kaser, "Zur Frage einer condictio aus gutgläubigem Erwerb oder gutgläubiger Leistung im römischen Recht", in: *Festschrift für Wilhelm Felgentraeger* (1969), pp. 277 sqq., 289 sqq.; Hans Julius Wolff, "Julian und die celsinische 'Durchgangstheorie'", in: *Mélanges Philippe Meylan*, vol. I (1963), pp. 409 sqq.

enrichment[38]) that payment by the debtor (drawee) to the borrower (payee) has two legal effects: it is to be regarded as performance by the drawee towards the creditor/drawer (thus effecting a discharge of this debt) and, at the same time, as a performance by the creditor towards the borrower (thus giving rise to the obligation of the latter).

Both Iulianus and Africanus were not prepared, however, to extend this exception to other cases. For their restrictive tendency they advanced an argumentum ad absurdum, ". . . alioquin dicendum ex omni contractu nuda pactione pecuniam creditam fieri posse", thereby dismissing the suggestion that a contract of mutuum might have come into existence in the following case:

> "Qui negotia Lucii Titii procurabat, is, cum a debitoribus eius pecuniam exegisset, epistulam ad eum emisit, qua significaret certam summam ex administratione apud se esse eamque creditam sibi se debiturum cum usuribus semissibus."[39]

Lucius Titius' procurator had collected some money from his debtors. He then wrote to his principal asking him whether he could keep part of this sum as a loan. Even if the principal acceded to this request, a mutuum did not come into existence; otherwise the real element, essential for this type of contract, would, for all practical purposes, have been abolished and mutuum would have become a purely consensual contract.

(c) Towards a loan by agreement

But was it not possible to apply the concept of the double fiction to this type of case, as well?

> "[Q]uod igitur in duabus personis recipitur, hoc et in eadem persona recipiendum est, ut, cum ex causa mandati pecuniam mihi debeas et convenerit, ut crediti nomine eam retineas, videatur mihi data pecunia et a me ad te profecta"

opined Ulpianus[40]—and any attempt to reconcile this statement with that of Iulianus/Africanus[41] would be an absolutely futile piece of *Pandektenharmonismus* ("pandect harmonism"). The texts, relating as they do to exactly the same situation, are in direct conflict. However, Ulpianus wrote about two generations later than Africanus, and by his time the old "ex meo tuum" requirement had been further relaxed, if not disbanded. Iulianus/Africanus had still emphasized the element of datio, even though the sum did not have to be advanced (directly) by the creditor but could be handed over by a third party, acting under his direction or in his name. Now, all that was left was an agreement between debtor and creditor that what was owed, was owed as a loan. And, indeed, if the direct payment from the debtor to the borrower in

---

[38] Cf., for example, Lieb, in: *Münchener Kommentar*, vol. III 2, (2nd ed., 1986), § 812, nn. 30 sqq.; Reinhard Zimmermann, "A road through the enrichment-forest?", 1985 *Cilsa* 14 sqq.

[39] Iul./Afr. D. 17, 1, 34 pr.

[40] Ulp. D. 12, 1, 15.

[41] Cf. e.g. Ph. E. Huschke, *Die Lehre des Römischen Rechts vom Darlehn* (1882), pp. 57 sqq.

a three-cornered relationship can be looked upon as if two dationes had in actual fact taken place, then the same argument must surely be applicable where debtor and borrower are one and the same person. Instead of requiring the debtor (that is, the procurator in Africanus' case) to hand the money over to the creditor (on account of the actio mandati directa) and then to receive it back subsequently as a loan, the procedure can be considerably simplified by allowing the debtor/borrower to keep the money and to regard the two dationes as having been performed. Ulp. D. 12, 1, 15 has become the basis for § 607 II BGB ("A person who owes money or other fungibles for any other reason may agree with the creditor that the money or the things shall be owed as a loan"), and it has been argued that the structure of this provision can still only be properly understood on the basis of Ulpian's double fiction.[42] On the same basis other cases, too, could now be fitted into the framework of mutuum. Of particular interest is Ulp. D. 12, 1, 11 pr.:

> "Rogasti me, ut tibi pecuniam crederem: ego cum non haberem, lancem tibi dedi vel massam auri, ut eam venderes et nummis utereris. si vendideris, puto mutuam pecuniam factam."

Here, "ego" was quite willing to lend some money to "tu", but did not have any cash available himself. He therefore gave "tu" a dish or a lump of gold so that he could sell the same and then keep the proceeds as a loan. The cautious "puto" betrays a conflict of opinion and, not surprisingly, we find Africanus still rejecting the idea that a contract of mutuum could be created in this manner.[43] But it is not surprising, either, to see Ulpianus taking a more liberal view. The same arguments as in Ulp. D. 12, 1, 15 could be advanced: "tu", for the sake of avoiding cumbersome and unnecessary formalities, should be placed in the position in which he would have been had he first surrendered the proceeds from the sale to "ego" and then received the same from him as a loan.

(d) Contractus mohatrae

Still, however, for the mutuum to come into existence between "ego" and "tu", it was required that the latter did in actual fact sell the object and receive the purchase price.[44] It was only at the time of Diocletian that one further step towards the recognition of a loan by agreement was taken: if the borrower received certain objects from the lender and both parties were agreed as to the value of these objects, then this estimated value was to be taken as the sum which the borrower was under an obligation to return. Whether he used what had been given to

---

[42] Cf. von Lübtow, *Darlehensbegriff*, pp. 81 sqq., 156 sqq.; idem, "Ulpians Konstruktion des sogenannten Vereinbarungsdarlehens", in: *Synteleia Vincenzo Arangio-Ruiz*, vol. II (1964), pp. 1212 sqq.

[43] Iul./Afr. D. 17, 1, 34 pr.

[44] Cf. also Ulp. D. 19, 5, 19 pr.

him by the lender in order to obtain the money he needed or in any other way, was left entirely to him and was no longer of any concern to the lender. He could sue the borrower with the actio certae creditae pecuniae for the return of a loan on the basis of having given him the objects in the place of money.[45] This conceptual advance was bound to have consequences for the question of who had to carry the risk of these objects getting lost or being destroyed before the sale had been effected by the borrower. It is clear that in post-classical law that risk lay with the borrower—a corollary of the fact that it was now left to him to decide how best to make use of the objects given to him, and that the contract of mutuum came into existence no matter whether he had sold them or not. In late classical law, on the other hand, one might expect the risk to have remained with the lender, until the objects had been sold and that sale had been fully carried out. Only then did the lender lose ownership; only then, too, did the contract of mutuum come into existence. This solution would have been in accordance with the general rule of "casum sentit dominus": the risk of any accidental loss, deterioration or destruction of a thing normally falls on its owner. But the results would not always have been in accordance either with equity or with the interests and presumed intentions of the parties. Where the lender gave a golden vase, which he would never have sold himself, to a friend of his who was in need of money, charging him to sell the vase and to keep the purchase price as a loan, it was hardly equitable to burden the lender with the risk; he had, after all, gone out of his way in order to accommodate the would-be borrower. The latter was now not only in control of the vase, but the whole transaction had also been undertaken in his interest. This is why we find Nerva drawing the following distinction (Ulpianus concurring):

> ". . . multum interesse, venalem habui hanc lancem vel massam nec ne, ut, si venalem habui, mihi perierit, quemadmodum si alii dedissem vendendam: quod si non fui proposito hoc ut venderem, sed haec causa fuit vendendi, ut tu intereris, tibi eam perisse, et maxime si sine usuris credidi."[46]

The allocation of risk is therefore based on the consideration whether the sale was solely in the interest of the prospective borrower, or whether it was also in the lender's interest, because he wanted to sell those particular objects anyway.

The problem discussed in Ulp. D. 12, 1, 11 pr. was interesting, not only from a dogmatical point of view, but also because it showed how a contract of sale could be used to effect a loan. In the Middle Ages the lawyers began to avail themselves of this possibility in a very ingenious

---

[45] C. 4, 2, 8. What the borrower owed was the value of the objects as estimated by the parties. If, in actual fact, he could only sell them for less, that was his risk; it did not affect his obligation. In the case of Ulp. D. 12, 1, 11 pr., on the other hand, the borrower would have been liable only for the sum that he had in actual fact received from the sale.

[46] Ulp. D. 12, 1, 11 pr. See Max Kaser, "Die Verteilung der Gefahr beim sogenannten 'contractus mohatrae'", in: *Synteleia Arangio-Ruiz*, vol. I (1964), pp. 74 sqq.

way. If A sells his golden vase (value 100) to B for 120, allowing him to pay the purchase price after the lapse of a certain time, and if B then sells the vase to C for 100, B is in actual fact in the position of a person who, having borrowed 100 from A, has to repay this loan with 20 % interest. The procedure can be greatly simplified by leaving the third party out of the picture and thus confining the transaction to A and B:

> ". . . quis egens pecunia emit summo pretio in diem solvendo a mercatore merces, et statim eidem pecunia numerata pretio infimo revendit."[47]

If, for example, A sold his vase to B for 120 and B immediately resold it to A for 100, the second "purchase price" being due immediately, the first one only after the lapse of a certain time (such interval, of course, in reality constituting the period of the loan), the same result was achieved and it did not even matter whether the vase was in actual fact transferred and re-transferred or not. A fictitious double sale could thus be used as a substitute for mutuum and interest stipulation. Naturally, the question will be asked why the lawyers, down to the 17th century, went about what appears to be a fairly straightforward business deal in such a roundabout way. The answer is that, under the influence of medieval canon law, the European ius commune recognized a general prohibition on the charging of interest rates.[48] The contractus mohatrae, as this type of loan, disguised in the form of two contracts of sale, came to be called (in the Latinized version of an Arabian term),[49] was thus a device—one of many!—to sidestep this idealistic but impractical canonical restraint on contractual freedom and on business life in general.[50]

4. On the "reality" of real contracts

Roman law never merged mutuum, pactum de mutuo dando and interest stipulation into a single consensual contract to be transformed into a bonae fidei iudicium. A mere pactum de mutuo dando remained unenforceable and interest had to be stipulated for separately; mutuum had become a true contract, but remained a "real" one. There seems to have been a certain reluctance to improve and streamline this area of the law, and thus to promote the danger of usurious dealings.[51] Both the insistence on formality (as far as interest was concerned)[52] and on the principle that the (future) granting of a loan could not be validly promised, served a very useful warning function, preventing lender as well as borrower from entering rashly into dangerous credit transac-

---

[47] Pufendorf, *De jure naturae et gentium*, Lib. V, Cap. VII, § 12.
[48] Cf. infra, pp. 170 sqq.
[49] Windscheid/Kipp, § 261, n. 5.
[50] On the contractus mohatrae, see, for example, Stryk, *Usus modernus pandectarum*, Lib. XXII, Tit. I, § 21; Gustav Klemens Schmelzeisen, *Quellen zur Neueren Privatrechtsgeschichte Deutschlands*, vol. II, 1 (1968), p. 85.
[51] Von Lübtow, *Condictio*, pp. 139 sqq.; idem, *Darlehensbegriff*, pp. 95 sq.
[52] But cf. infra, p. 218, note 226 and p. 538, note 189.

tions. The Roman idea of mutuum as a real contract, giving rise to only one obligation (namely that of the borrower to repay the loan) was bound to become very problematic when, as a result of the general recognition of "pacta sunt servanda",[53] pacta de mutuo dando and informal arrangements about interest could be and were in actual fact regarded as valid and binding.[54] Instead, however, of advancing the process of amalgamation and "consensualization", the authors of the ius commune, particularly in the 19th century, entrenched the idea of the Roman real contracts as something logically necessary and conceptually cogent.

> "The . . . real contracts," we read, "are 'real' in the fullest sense of the term: by the very nature of the case they are, and always will be, real contracts, because they all involve an entrusting of property by one person to another [with a duty in that other to restore it], so that the 'res', in this instance, determines both the ground and the nature of the obligation. Accordingly the nominate real contracts are real contracts to this very day: a claim for a return of property can only be supported on the ground of the previous delivery."[55]

By the same token, however, the contract of lease would have to be regarded as a real contract, because there, too, the duty to restore the property comes into existence only once delivery has taken place.[56] What the pandectists tended to overlook, was, firstly, the fact that in modern law (otherwise than in Roman law) every performance—as long as it is not illegal or immoral—can be the object of a binding contractual agreement. Secondly, they overemphasized the obligation of the borrower to restore what he had received, without duly taking into consideration that the creation of such an obligation in the person of the borrower can hardly be the content and main purpose of the whole transaction;[57] otherwise the lender might as well have kept his property in the first place. A loan, in other words, is not made in order to get back the money; it is made in order to let the other party have the use of the capital[58] for a certain period of time and (perhaps) to earn some interest for the temporary transfer of such value.[59] It took a long time to overcome such conceptual thinking still based, essentially, on the Roman actional system. According to § 607 BGB, the essence of a loan consists in a person who has received money or other fungibles as a loan, being bound to return to the lender what he has received, in things of the same kind, quality and quantity. No mention is made of

[53] Cf. infra, pp. 542 sqq., 576.

[54] Cf. e.g. Stryk, *Usus modernus pandectarum*, Lib. XII, Tit. I, §§ 3, 5, 9; Van der Keessel, *Praelectiones ad Gr.* III, X, 4 and 8; Windscheid/Kipp, § 370, 2 (n. 18), § 371, n. 6.

[55] Rudolph Sohm, *The Institutes* (trans. by James Crawford Ledlie, 3rd ed., 1907), p. 380.

[56] Philipp Heck, *Schuldrecht*, (1929), pp. 248, 327.

[57] But see Andreas von Tuhr, *Der Allgemeine Teil des Deutschen Bürgerlichen Rechts*, vol. II 2 (1918), p. 70.

[58] Cf. e.g. Plautus, *Persa*, Act I, l. 118, "nummos . . . mutuos utendos".

[59] Cf., for example, RGZ 161, 52 (53 sqq.), dealing with the tricky problem of the application of the "in pari turpitudine" rule in cases of usurious loans.

any duties on the part of the lender. It is not surprising, on this basis, that the "Realvertragstheorie" has still found staunch supporters in this century:[60] the agreement to give a loan,[61] in their view, is only a pactum de contrahendo, the loan itself a contract re.[62] Today, however, the unsuitability of this view, both on a conceptual level and as far as the practical consequences are concerned, has been widely recognized.[63] Loan, therefore, is usually regarded as a consensual contract in modern law;[64] the handing over of the capital to the borrower takes place solvendi, and not obligandi causa. A loan at interest, then, is a reciprocal contract, and even where no interest has been agreed upon, duties do not only arise in the person of the borrower (that is, the contract is not any longer merely unilaterally binding). Thus, the lender is obliged to transfer the capital to the borrower and to let him have the use of the value for the time agreed upon; he can be liable on account of defects in title or defects in quality, etc.[65, 66]

---

[60] Enneccerus/Lehmann, *Recht der Schuldverhältnisse* (15th ed., 1958), § 142 I.

[61] Cf. § 610 BGB.

[62] This view still prevails in France (on the basis of art. 1892 code civil) and in Italy (art. 1813 codice civile): cf. the comparative survey by Dieter Henrich, *Vorvertrag, Optionsvertrag, Vorrechtsvertrag* (1965), pp. 78 sq.

[63] See especially Gustav Boehmer, "Realverträge im heutigen Recht", (1913) 38 *Archiv für bürgerliches Recht* 314 sqq.; but see Carlo Alberto Maschi, *La categoria dei contratti reali* (1973), pp. 1 sqq.

[64] Von Lübtow, *Darlehensbegriff*, pp. 89 sqq.; Karl Larenz, *Lehrbuch des Schuldrechts*, vol. II (12th ed., 1981), § 51.

[65] As to the possibility of a contrarium iudicium, i.e. a claim by the borrower against the lender in case the latter had given the money in foreign currency, so that the borrower had to exchange it at a loss, cf. already Savigny, *System*, vol. V, p. 509. A similar problem can arise, for instance, in the case of a loan of seed corn, if the seed corn is of a bad quality and causes damage (cf. Windscheid/Kipp, § 371, n. 2). In modern German law, § 493 BGB is taken to cover this situation, provided the loan was at interest ("The provisions relating to the obligation of the seller in respect of warranty against defects of quality apply mutatis mutandis to other contracts which are for alienating . . ., for value").

[66] In South African law, according to D.J. Joubert in: Joubert (ed.), *The Law of South Africa*, vol. 15 (1981), sub titulo "Loan", loan is a consensual contract. In view of the fact that the authors of the ius commune used to emphasize the rei interventio as a requirement for the contract of mutuum, this statement seems to rest on a somewhat shaky basis, namely a statement by De Villiers AJA in *Conradie v. Rossouw* 1919 AD 279 at 310 sq. ("the promise of a loan which formerly could only be effected by means of the stipulatio de mutuo dando . . . could now [sc.: in classical Roman-Dutch law] be validly made by means of a simple promise"). Lee, *Introduction*, p. 312 simply remarks: "Loan for Consumption—Loan for Use. All this is Roman law." See further the detailed treatment by Voet, *Commentarius ad Pandectas*, Lib. XII, Tit. I, on which Sir Percival Gane in his translation (*The Selective Voet*, vol. II (1955), p. 750) remarks: "Even at the present day this title may serve almost in detail as an accurate and exhaustive treatment of the law of the loan of fungibles, since no dissent has as yet been expressed from its principles in any of the more than thirty decided South African cases in which it has figured."

II. THE HISTORY OF THE INTEREST RATES AND USURY

1. Policies of the Roman Republic

Moneylending transactions, in so far as they go beyond loans between friends or neighbours, have at all times posed a challenge to the legislator.[67] The borrower is usually in a weak position economically (otherwise he would not be in need of money), and thus a strong possibility exists that the lender may be tempted to exploit his predicament. In order to prevent usurious[68] abuses, the State is therefore called upon to interfere and to afford some protection to the disadvantaged party. The Roman legislator responded to this challenge in a twofold way. He tried to combat usurious interest rates and he addressed himself specifically to the situation where sons in power had taken up a loan.

Roman law is marked by its emphasis on the autonomy of the contracting partners to regulate their own affairs, based on the principle of liberty and corresponding to the authoritative position of the paterfamilias in Roman society.[69] Thus, for instance, Roman law never provided for judicial reconsideration of contracts of sale or lease in cases of gross imbalance between performance and counterperformance. Yet, there is one area in which the law intervened at an early stage: usurious interest rates. In contracts of loan, the freedom of the parties to negotiate usually amounts to the freedom of the creditor to dictate the terms of the contract. The XII Tables already contained a rule "ne quis unciario faenore amplius exerceret".[70] The term "unciarium fenus" (interest of $\frac{1}{12}$ of the capital) is somewhat enigmatical and has led modern scholars to argue about whether it constituted a ceiling rate of $8\frac{1}{3}$ %, 10 %, $83\frac{1}{3}$ % or 100 %.[71] This dispute arises because it is uncertain whether the interest, according to the XII Tables, had to be calculated per year or per month, and whether the calculation was based on a year

---

[67] Cf., for instance, the comparative analysis by Eike von Hippel, *Verbraucherschutz* (3rd ed., 1986), pp. 214 sqq.

[68] The terms "usury" and "usurious" are used here to refer to situations where the interest rate is unreasonable/illegal; etymologically, they are derived from "usura", which means "interest" generally. In the Middle Ages, when the taking of interest was prohibited, both meanings actually amounted to the same thing.

[69] Cf. esp. Schulz, *Principles*, pp. 140 sqq.

[70] Tacitus, *Annales*, Lib. VI, 16; Cato, *De agri cultura, praefatio*.

[71] Cf. Gustav Billeter, *Geschichte des Zinsfusses im griechisch-römischen Altertum bis auf Justinian* (1898), pp. 157 sqq.; Fritz Klingmüller, "Streitfragen um die römische Zinsgesetzgebung", (1902) 23 *ZSS* 68 sqq.; C. Appleton, "Le taux du 'fenus unciarium'", (1919) 43 *NRH* 467 sqq.; Francesco De Martino, "Reforme del IV Secolo A.C.", (1975) 78 *BIDR* 62 sqq. The latter two figures seem to be surprisingly high; however, they are not atypical for archaic legal systems dominated by a primitive barter economy; also, one has to take into account the general distrust prevailing in an agrarian society not well versed in economic affairs.

containing ten or twelve months.[72] It is clear, however, that in case of contravention the usurer incurred a criminal sanction: he had to pay the poena quadrupli. In the course of the following centuries, this limit for the charging of interest rates varied; in 347 B.C., for instance, it was cut down by half (fenus semiunciarium).[73] In practice, however,[74] higher interest rates often seem to have been charged and the borrowers were far from being well protected. Therefore, only five years later, a lex Genucia forbade the charging of interest altogether.[75] But even that did not stop usurious practices. From Appian[76] we hear about a dramatic uprising in 89 B.C.:

> "About the same time dissensions arose in the city between debtors and creditors, since the latter exacted the money due to them with interest, although an old law distinctly forbade lending on interest and imposed a penalty upon any one doing so. . . . But, since time had sanctioned the practice of taking interest, the creditors

[72] The old Roman year is said to have contained only 10 months. It started with the month of March, i.e. the time of thaw, when nature awoke and flora and fauna regained their vitality; the flowing of the life-sap was seen, apparently, as something essentially male, for the term "Martius" derives from mas, -aris. It is not clear whether this year ran from spring to spring (an interest rate of fenus unciarium based on a yearly calculation would then amount to $8\frac{1}{3}$ %) or whether it comprised only the period of agrarian productivity, so that the time of nature's hibernation was not counted (under these circumstances, $\frac{1}{12}$ for ten months would amount to $\frac{1}{10}$ for twelve months = 10 %). King Numa is said to have added two further months (namely Januarius and Februarius, as nos. 11 and 12) and he thus introduced a year based on twelve months and containing 355 days. Because the year was running ahead of the solar year by $10\frac{1}{4}$ days, intercalations were necessary. Normally, therefore, every second year in the middle of February a whole mensis intercalaris of either 22 or 23 days was inserted. On that basis, however, the calendar overshot the solar year by one day. The question of intercalations seems to have been handled very arbitrarily and was sometimes dependent upon considerations of political expediency. In 190 B.C., for instance, the calendar was 190 days out of step with the solar year. Julius Caesar was the first to introduce a rational system of intercalations. After having intercalated 90 days in the year 46, he started the new (Julian) calendar on 1 January 45. The year consisted of 12 months (January now being the first month) or 365 days; every fourth year, one day in February (the 24th or 25th) was counted twice, thus bringing it up to 366 days. In the Middle Ages it became apparent that the calendar had, again, run out of tune with the tropical year. Thus, in his bull "Inter Gravissimas" Pope Gregory XIII (one of many lawyers on the Holy See), decreed that 10 days, the 5th to the 14th October 1582, had to be leaped over and that henceforth every centenary year (except every fourth one, starting from 1600) should cease to have the intercalary day. During the Middle Ages, incidentally, the year was considered to begin at Easter, which might be at any time between 22 March and 22 April. Usually, however, a fixed date was set (25 March). All the names of our months (with two exceptions) go back to the old Roman calendar prior to the Julian reform. The names September to December, based on the numerals from seven to ten, still bear witness to the fact that, at that time, the year commenced on 1 March. The Quintilis was changed to July in honour of Julius Caesar (his birthday was on 13 July), Sextilis to Augustus in honour of the first princeps (who had conquered Alexandria, and thus finally triumphed over his rival Antonius during the first days of August in 30 B.C.). For further details, see A. Michels, *The Calendar of the Roman Republic* (1967); Hans Kaletsch, *Tag und Jahr* (1970); Alan E. Samuel, *Greek and Roman Chronology* (1972), pp. 153 sqq.

[73] Tacitus, *Annales*, Lib. VI, 16; Livius, *Ab urbe condita*, Lib. VII, XXVII, 3.

[74] On what was ordinarily charged in practice, see Billeter, op. cit., note 71, pp. 163 sqq., 228 sqq.

[75] Cf. Max Kaser, *Verbotsgesetze*, p. 36; Giuseppe Tilli, ". . . postremo vetita versura", (1984) 86/87 *BIDR* 147 sqq. See, in this context, too, the lex Marcia, mentioned in Gai. IV, 23.

[76] *Bella civilia*, Lib. I, 54.

> demanded it according to custom. The debtors, on the other hand, put off their payments on the plea of war and civil commotion. Some indeed threatened to exact the legal penalty from the interest-takers. The praetor Asellio, who had charge of these matters, as he was not able to compose their differences by persuasion, allowed them to proceed against each other in the courts, thus bringing the deadlock due to the conflict of law and custom before the judges. The lenders, exasperated that the now obsolete law was being revived, killed the praetor."

Asellio was slain in the centre of the forum Romanum. The Senate offered a reward to anybody who would give testimony leading to the conviction of the murderers of Asellio, but to no avail. The moneylenders covered up everything.

2. Maximum rates from the end of the Republic until Justinian

It is clear from this vivid description that very drastic provisions do not always lead to a satisfactory state of affairs. In fact, they can sometimes be counterproductive. Sulla, therefore, in 88 B.C. seems to have introduced the old fenus unciarium. Towards the end of the Republic, however, the so-called centesimae usurae came into use ($\frac{1}{100}$ per month, i.e. 12 % per year).[77, 78] They were maintained, essentially unchanged,[79] as maximum rates during the imperial times right down to the 6th century.[80] Alexander Severus enjoined senators not to charge interest, but soon thereafter a special limit, the usurae dimidiae centesimae (6 %), was fixed for them.[81] Justinian, under the influence of Christianity, was not favourably disposed towards the charging of interest. He tightened the usury laws and reduced the ordinary maximum rate to 6 % and to 4 % for senators.[82] A special concession was made to those "qui ergasteriis praesunt vel aliquam licitam

[77] As to the terminology which was used for the various interest rates (sextans, i.e. the sixth part of 12 % = 2 %, quadrans = 3 %, etc.), cf. *Inst.* II, 14, 5. In the Middle Ages the words "centesimae usurae" were taken to mean 100 % per year: cf. Wieling, *Interesse und Privatstrafe*, p. 199.

[78] In 56 B.C., however, it was still possible for two Roman moneylenders (M. Scaptius and P. Matinius) to charge an interest rate of 48 % for a loan to the town of Salamis in Cyprus. The island of Cyprus had been conquered by the Romans (and added to the province of Cilicia) two years before. The Salaminians needed the money in order to bribe the Roman governor, P. Cornelius Lentulus Spinther, and thus to induce him not to billet his soldiers on them during the winter. A long drawn-out dispute arose as to when the loan had to be paid back. During the course of it, Scaptius once prevented the senators of Salamis from leaving their town hall, until five of them had died of starvation. Cicero, when he was governor of Cilicia in 51–50 B.C., tried to settle the dispute. He proposed to reduce the interest rate to 12 % but to allow inclusion of the accrued interest in the capital sum (anatocism) ("Confeceram, ut solverent (sc.: Salaminii) centesimis sexenni ductis cum renovatione singulorum annorum": *Epistulae ad Atticum*, 6, 1, § 5). This proposal was rejected by Scaptius. For further details, see Klaus Wille, *Die Versur* (1983), pp. 13–56.

[79] But see Levy, *Obligationenrecht*, pp. 160 sqq.

[80] Billeter, op. cit., note 71, pp. 267 sqq.

[81] *Codex Theodosianus*, 2, 33, 4.

[82] C. 4, 32, 26, 2. Cf. Billeter, op. cit., note 71, pp. 306 sqq.; Mariagrazia Bianchini, "La disciplina degli interessi convenzionali nella legislazione giustinianea", in: *Studi in onore di Arnaldo Biscardi*, vol. II (1982), pp. 391 sqq.

negotiationem gerunt": they could charge up to 8%.[83] Regarding policy, it is interesting to see that the problem of usury was tackled in Roman law by way of penal sanctions.[84] Like all statutory prohibitions in early law,[85] the usury laws were not "perfect",[86] that is, as long as the correct form had been observed, the illegal act was not invalid. However, according to classical law, the debtor did not have to pay the usurious rate of interest:

> "Placuit, sive supra statutum modum quis usuras stipulatus fuerit sive usurarum usuras,[87] quod illicite adiectum est pro non adiecto haberi et licitas peti posse."[88]

The contract was still valid, but the borrower had to pay only the legal maximum rate. Marcianus arrived at this result by introducing a legal fiction: he treated the stipulation as if the parties had made a core stipulation, involving this legal maximum, to which the illegal part exceeding it had then been added. Thus, one only had to subtract this illegal addition ("pro non adiecto haberi"). This operation did not constitute a major interference with the contractual agreements of the parties: particularly the right of the creditor to claim back his capital remained, of course, entirely unaffected;[89] mutuum and interest-stipulation were two separate contracts. If the excessive interest had

---

[83] Cf. also Nov. 136, 4, as far as bankers are concerned. For further special rates cf., for example, C. 5, 12, 31, 5; C. 5, 13, 1, 7 b and C. 7, 54, 2 sq.

[84] In the same way Roman law dealt with unconscionable bargains relating to the sale of corn and with syndicates formed in order to push up the corn price (societatem coire quo annona carior fiat). However, the State had started, at an early stage, to take over responsibility for providing the Roman people with grain; towards the end of the Republic, this culminated in a free corn supply for everybody; later on for the underprivileged classes only. At the time of Augustus, the number of recipients was 320 000. For all this, see e.g. Stephan Brassloff, *Sozialpolitische Motive in der römischen Rechtsentwicklung* (1933), p. 16 sqq., 50 sqq. Some 150 000 tons of corn travelled annually from Alexandria to Rome during the first three centuries A.D., involving "probably the most ambitious maritime enterprise of the ancient world" (Lionel Casson, "The Alexandria–Rome Sailing Schedule", in: *Ships and Seamanship in the Ancient World* (1971), pp. 297 sqq.).

[85] Kaser, *Verbotsgesetze*, pp. 13 sqq., 18 sq.

[86] Cf. infra, pp. 697 sq., 700 sq.

[87] Interest on interest (usurae usurarum) could not be charged; see Ulp. D. 12, 6, 26, 1; Mod. D. 42, 1, 27; C. 4, 32, 28. An easy way of evading this restriction consists in capitalizing the accrued interest, i.e. including it in the capital sum, on which in turn an increased amount of interest has to be paid (anatocism, anatocismus coniunctus). This could be achieved by way of a transaction called versura, an act either litteris or verbis (usually a συγγραφή was drawn up) which had the effect of a novation. For details, see Wille, op. cit., note 78, pp. 46 sqq. Only Justinian prohibited anatocism: C. 4, 32, 28; 7, 54, 3 pr. Cf. also Glück, vol. 21, pp. 115 sqq., Windscheid/Kipp, § 261, and § 248 I BGB: "An agreement *made in advance* to the effect that arrears of interest shall again bear interest is void." (For details, see Karsten Schmidt, "Das 'Zinseszinsverbot'", 1982 *Juristenzeitung* 829 sqq.) Neither, incidentally, could arrears of interest be charged to the extent that they exceeded the amount of the capital that had been borrowed: Ulp. D. 12, 6, 26, 1 ("supra duplum autem usurae"); C. 4, 32, 10 (Ant.); Laura Solidoro, "Ultra sortis summam usurae non exiguntur", (1982) 28 *Labeo* 164 sqq.; Bianchini, *Studi Biscardi*, vol. II, pp. 399 sqq. In post-classical times the accrual of interest also ceased, rather strangely, when the amount of interest *paid* had reached the amount of the capital sum: Nov. 121, 2; 138; 160 pr. Cf. Kaser, *RPr* II, p. 342.

[88] Marci. D. 22, 1, 29.

[89] Paul. D. 22, 1, 20; C. 4, 2, 8.

already been paid by the borrower, the excess was credited against the capital; if it exceeded the capital or if it had been paid per errorem, it could be reclaimed:

> "Usurae supra centesimum solutae sortem minuunt, consumpta sorte repeti possunt. usurae, quae centesimam excedunt, per errorem solutae repeti possunt."[90]

3. The canonical prohibition on usury in the Middle Ages

The history of the law relating to usury is a very interesting and varied one. The development in the Middle Ages was dominated by a rule of canon law which prohibited the charging of interest.[91] It was based on a number of scriptural texts, as, particularly St. Luke's exhortation "mutuum date nihil inde sperantes",[92] but it also tied in with economic and dogmatic considerations: the charging of interest entails the exploitation of need and leads to the further pauperization of the debtor; furthermore, it was argued that money, in the nature of things, cannot yield fruits:[93] pecunia pecuniam parere non potest.[94] The Church, traditionally, regarded commercial profits as a danger to salvation. ". . .homo mercator vix aut nunquam potest Deo placere. Et ideo nullus Christianus debet esse mercator, aut, si voluerit esse, proiiciatur de ecclesia Dei." This was the view of St. John Chrysostomus about merchants,[95] and it applied, of course, a fortiori to a usurer. If the Church tried to imprint its economic ethics on the secular law,[96] it was, generally speaking, only partially successful; the canonical prohibition on interest did, however, come to be received, in principle, in iure civili.[97] The

[90] Paul. Sent. II, XIV, 2 and 4; cf. further Ulp. D. 12, 6, 26 pr.

[91] Cf. the *Decretales Gregorii* IX., Lib. V, Tit. XIX, especially the decree of the third Lateran Council in Lib. V, Tit. XIX, Cap. III.

[92] St. Luke 6, 35 (but see also St. Luke 19, 11 sqq. = St. Matthew 25, 14 sqq., the parable of the talents!); from the Old Testament cf. Exodus 22, 25; Deuteronomy 23, 19; Leviticus 25, 35 sqq.; Nehemiah 5, 6–11; Ezekiel 18, 17 (usury forbidden against "poor" and "brother"; cf. also Psalm 15, 5 (innocent)); it was, however, allowed against strangers (Deuteronomy 23, 20: ". . . unto a stranger thou mayest lend upon usury; but unto thy brother thou shalt not lend upon usury"). "Stranger" is the translation of "Kanaanite", the word that was used in the old Hebrew language for "businessman", "banker", "trader".

[93] The doctrine that money is "sterile" goes back to Aristotle's *Politika*, Book I, III, 16 (1257 b) and has been built upon by St. Augustin and St. Thomas Aquinas.

[94] On the "scholastic analysis of usury", see the comprehensive work, thus entitled, by John T. Noonan, (1957), furthermore especially the classic work by Wilhelm Endemann, *Studien in der romanisch-kanonistischen Wirtschafts- und Rechtslehre bis gegen Ende des 17. Jahrhunderts*, 2 vols. (1874 and 1883); also Raymond de Roover, *La pensée économique des Scolastiques. Doctrines et méthodes* (1971); Winfried Trusen, *Spätmittelalterliche Jurisprudenz und Wirtschaftsethik, dargestellt an Wiener Gutachten des 13. Jahrhunderts* (1961).

[95] Cf. Decretum Gratiani, Prima Pars, Dist. LXXXVIII, c. 11. Cf., too, Henri Pirenne, *A History of Europe*, vol. II (1958), p. 229: men "could hardly imagine the merchant's strongbox without picturing the devil squatting on the lid".

[96] Cf., for example, *Constitutiones Clementis V.*, Lib. V, Tit. V, § 1, threatening those who enact statutes providing for the possibility of charging interest with excommunication.

[97] Cf. e.g. Windscheid/Kipp, § 260, n. 3; cf. also Wolfgang Kunkel, *Quellen zur neueren Privatrechtsgeschichte Deutschlands*, vol. I, 2 (1938), p. 409 sub "Wucher", for the local laws during the time of the reception of Roman law. Generally on the history of usury in the Holy Roman Empire of the German nation, see Max Neumann, *Geschichte des Wuchers in*

sanctions against usury were strict. The usurious transaction was invalid and whatever the usurer had taken in excess of the loan was treated as stolen goods. The usurer was also liable for punishment.[98]

But this is only one side of the story. The economic realities were stronger than the monastic ideals of the early Christian Church. With a general prohibition of interest, not even the need to borrow merely for consumption, which arises in a predominantly agrarian society, could be adequately tackled. But in the late 11th and early 12th centuries, the whole economic situation began to change. The rise of commercial capitalism, in its vigour and in the relative rapidity of its development, has been compared with the industrial revolution of the 19th century.[99] Money came to be lent for production or investment; large sums were needed for financing venturesome economic and military enterprises. The crusades, launched by the Church itself, are one obvious example. Thus, "legitimate trade based on good faith was distinguished from illegitimate trade based on avarice";[100] lawful credit devices were distinguished from the sin of usury. The history of the prohibition of usury from the Middle Ages onwards could well, therefore, be written as the history of its gradual erosion. A variety of transactions were developed and used simply for the purpose of circumventing the prohibition;[101] the contractus mohatrae, where two contracts of sale disguised a loan on interest, has already been mentioned as an example. They necessitated the extensions of the usury rule to contracts of sale and other transactions. This in turn gave rise to a voluminous body of casuistry.[102] Very fine lines, too, had to be drawn to distinguish between illicitae usurae lucratoriae and usurae

---

Deutschland bis zur Begründung der heutigen Zinsgesetze (1654) (1865); cf. also Wieling, *Interesse und Privatstrafe*, pp. 197 sqq. Endemann, *Studien*, vol. I, p. 2 sums up the influence of the canonical usury doctrine in the following words: "*Die Darstellung der Wucherlehre ergibt, dass sich die Konsequenzen jenes Dogma's allmählich über das gesammte Wirthschaftsleben, und über Handel und Verkehr erstreckten. . . . Die Rechtshistorie des Verkehrsrechts jener Zeiten kann nichts Anderes sein, als die Geschichte der Herrschaft der Wucherlehre in der Rechtslehre*" (The analysis of the usury doctrine shows that its consequences gradually extended over the entire economic sphere, over trade and commerce in general. . . . The history of the law relating to commercial transactions of those times cannot be but the history of the ascendancy of the usury doctrine in contemporary jurisprudence).

[98] Molina, *De iustitia et iure*, Tract. II, Disp. 334.

[99] Henry Pirenne, *Sozial- und Wirtschaftsgeschichte Europas im Mittelalter* (2nd ed., 1971), pp. 156 sqq., 199 sqq.

[100] Berman, *Law and Revolution*, p. 338.

[101] "Sed ita mores avarorum et pessimorum hominum sunt comparati, ut semper novas vias, et artes avaritiam exercendi inveniant": Stryk, *Usus modernus pandectarum*, Lib. XXII, Tit. I, § 1.

[102] For details about transactions for the purpose of evading the prohibition of interest cf. e.g. Stryk, *Usus modernus pandectarum*, Lib. XXII, Tit. I, §§ 19 sqq.; Molina, *De iustitia et iure*, Tract. II, Disp. 303 sqq.; §§ 1–7 of the XVII. title of the *Reichspolizeiordnung* (1577); Neumann, op. cit., note 97, pp. 440 sqq.; Trusen, op. cit., note 94, pp. 60 sqq. As to the casuistic approach adopted in the usury legislation of the time, cf. Helmut Schmidt, *Die Lehre von der Sittenwidrigkeit der Rechtsgeschäfte in historischer Sicht* (1973), pp. 33 sqq. On the practice of medieval English Church courts, cf. R.H. Helmholz, *Canon Law and the Law of England* (1987), pp. 323 sqq.

compensatoriae;[103] availing themselves of the Roman concept of quod interest (interesse),[104] the medieval lawyers allowed the creditor to claim a surcharge in the form of (lawful) interest as a compensation for lucrum cessans, damnum emergens and periculum sortis, or to charge interest in case of delay of performance. Another intricate distinction was that between usury and emptio annuorum redituum (purchase of an annuity, *Rentenkauf*).[105] The latter, defined as "contractus institutus a consuetudine, ex quo unus vendit, et alter emit ius certi reditus, singulis annis solvendi in pecunia",[106] had always been regarded as valid, even though the obligation to pay an annual return (census or reditus) usually went ultra sortem and might well have been regarded as a contravention of the prohibition of interest. Especially in Germany, this transaction has been of enormous practical importance as an opportunity to raise and invest capital and thus to create credit.

4. A clash between theory and practice?

It would be going much too far even to mention all the real and quasi-exceptions to the general usury prohibition which were recognized in the Middle Ages[107] and which permitted trade and commerce to flourish. The disputes and discussions clustering around the principle challenged the ingenuity of merchants and lawyers alike. Besides, the Church tolerated usury by Jews: excluded from agriculture, not allowed to own landed property, unable to join the guilds and thus become artisans or ordinary merchants, they were forced to take up the shadier business of moneylending/pawnbroking.[108] Rejecting Christ as Saviour and doggedly refusing to accept the new law of the Gospel, often charged with well-poisoning and other wicked acts, they were taken to be damned anyway. But special privileges were also granted to

[103] For the difference cf., for example, Pothier, *Traité du contrat du prêt de consomption*, n. 53.

[104] Cf. Lange, *Schadensersatz und Privatstrafe*, pp. 10 sqq.

[105] W. Ogris, *Der mittelalterliche Leibrentenvertrag* (1961), pp. 104 sqq.; Coing, pp. 378 sq.; Winfried Trusen, "Zum Rentenkauf im Spätmittelalter", in: *Festschrift für Hermann Heimpel*, vol. II (1972), pp. 140 sqq.

[106] Feliciano de Solis, *Commentarii de censibus quatuor libris* (Francofurti, 1605), Lib. I, Cap. IV, 8.

[107] Cf. the details in John Gilchrist, *The Church and Economic Activity in the Middle Ages* (1969), pp. 62 sqq.; Noonan, op. cit., note 94, pp. 100 sqq.; Endemann, *Studien*, vol. II, pp. 366 sqq.; Neumann, op. cit., note 97, pp. 109 sqq.

[108] As to the social, economic and legal position of Jews, cf. Justus Henning Boehmer, *Ius ecclesiasticum protestantium*, Lib. V, Tit. 6; Guido Kisch, *The Jews in Medieval Germany* (1949); idem, *Jewry-Law in Medieval Germany* (1959); idem, *Fragen zur Rechts- und Sozialgeschichte der Juden in Deutschland während des Mittelalters* (1955); cf. also the eminently readable account by Paul Johnson, *A History of the Jews* (1987), pp. 169 sqq. (passim). According to Talmudical theology, usury is a sin (cf. the texts from the Old Testament, referred to in note 92 supra), but only if it is committed against another Jew ("Kanaanite" was now (mis-)understood in the sense of "stranger", "non-Jew"; hence the rule that no interest is to be extracted from Jews, even if they are businessmen. On the other hand, the taking of interest from Gentiles is allowed even if they are not businessmen or if they are poor). Cf. e.g. Eberhard Klingenberg, *Das israelitische Zinsverbot in Torah, Misnah und Talmud* (1977).

the montes,[109] financial institutions designed at first by the Italian city states to boost their rather run-down public finances by way of forced government loans, yet, in the course of time also engaging in other financial and credit transactions—especially deposit banking.[110] In these montes the great public banking corporations originated, of which the Casa di San Giorgio in Genoa eventually became the most important. Since the second half of the 15th century, even the Church started to establish and to run banks, though, of course, these institutions were not called banks but montes pietates (mountains of piety).[111]

In view of all this, one may be inclined to wonder at the hypocrisy of Church and canon lawyers, or at least to deplore the deep rift that seems to have existed between the ascetic theory behind the usury prohibition and the very mundane commercial activities which the canonists condoned.[112] But, in fact, they not only condoned them—by analysing and systematizing the law of usury for the first time, they actually provided a rational foundation for the dramatic growth of commercial and financial life during the Middle Ages;[113] and it is very likely that this was fully in accordance with contemporary Christian social theory. For the Western Church in the 12th century was no longer fundamentally otherworldly;

> "it believed in the possibility of reconciling commercial activity with a Christian life. . . . The secular activities of those engaged in commercial enterprise were to be organized in ways that would redeem them from the sin of avarice. The merchants were to form guilds that would have religious functions and would maintain

---

[109] Cf. Endemann, *Studien*, vol. I, pp. 431 sqq.; Raymond de Roover, *Money, Banking and Credit in Medieval Bruges* (1948); Winfried Trusen, "Die Anfänge öffentlicher Banken und das Zinsproblem, Kontroversen im Spätmittelalter", in: *Recht und Wirtschaft in Geschichte und Gegenwart, Festschrift für Johannes Bärmann* (1975), pp. 113 sqq.

[110] Based on the Roman depositum irregulare (cf. e.g. Johann Marquard, *Tractatus politico-juridicus de jure mercatorum et commerciorum singulari* (Francofurti, 1662), Lib. II, Cap. IX, nn. 21 sqq.), which could thus be used as yet another avenue to sidestep the canonical usury rule; the transaction, in effect, was a loan of money for investment purposes on interest. Transactions involving bills of exchange were another means of creating credit, which came to be handled by the montes and which entailed, de facto, an infringement of the prohibition of interest. On the history of bills of exchange, see Endemann, *Studien*, vol. I, pp. 75 sqq.; Raymond de Roover, *L'évolution de la Lettre de Change, XIV–XVIII siècles* (1953); Coing, pp. 537 sqq.

[111] The first montes pietatis were constituted in 1461 and 1462 in Perugia and Orvieto. They were public pawnshops, normally financed by charitable donations and run not for profit but for the service of the poor. They charged a small fee for their care of the pawns and for the expenses of administration (usually 6 %). At the end of the 18th century, there were 80 montes pietatis in Italy. But gifts alone did not provide sufficient funds. Thus, the montes were soon permitted to raise money by paying interest. Several 16th-century pontiffs authorized the montes to accept deposits and pay interest upon them. On the montes pietatis, see Endemann, *Studien*, vol. I, pp. 460 sqq. The Popes also actively supported the Medici Bank in Florence: cf. Raymond de Roover, *The Rise and Decline of the Medici Bank 1397–1494* (1963), pp. 194 sqq.

[112] Max Weber, "Die protestantische Ethik und der Geist des Kapitalismus", in: *Gesammelte Aufsätze zur Religionssoziologie* (5th ed., 1963), pp. 56 sqq.

[113] Gilchrist, op. cit., note 107, p. 107.

> standards of morality in commercial transactions. . . . Thus the social and economic activity of merchants was not left outside the reach of moral issues. A social and economic morality was developed which purported to guide the souls of merchants toward salvation. And that morality was embodied in law. Law was a bridge between mercantile activity and the salvation of the soul."[114]

This, incidentally, ties in with what C.S. Lewis has called "the undying paradox, the blessedly two-edged character of Christianity".[115] Christianity is world-denying and world-affirming at the same time, and it is the latter by virtue of being the former: "Because we love something else more than this world, we love even this world better than those who know no other."[116]

5. Usura non est lucrum, sed merces

But be this as it may, in the course of the 16th century it became apparent that the canonical prohibition on usury was no longer tenable in iure civili. The main attack came in the wake of the Reformation:[117] from Calvin in regard to its theological justification, from Carolus Molinaeus[118] and Claudius Salmasius[119] as far as its legal and economic basis was concerned. The words of the Lord in Luke 6, 35 had been misunderstood according to Molinaeus; they did not refer to contracts of loan, but merely to alms. Thus, money that had been given with a charitable intention must never be reclaimed with interest. A loan given per modum negociationis, on the other hand, was valid, as long as only a moderate amount of interest and not turpes usurae had been promised. The Roman rules relating to usury, not being in conflict with Divine law, could therefore still be applied. Salmasius, on the other hand, set about attacking the "sterility of money" doctrine. He regarded the granting of a loan as the hire of the money involved, the interest consequently as the rent to be paid for its use: "Locatur pecunia, quae foenori[120] datur, non alio modo, quam aedes aut ager aut opera, pro quibus merces exigitur ab his, qui ea conduxerunt."[121] Consequence:

> ". . . usura non est proprie lucrum, sed merces. Nec propter officium mutuationis accipitur, sed propter usum pecuniae. Aliud autem est merces, aliud lucrum. Hoc adventicium est, et extra rem. Illa profecticia ex ipsa re."

By the time the imperial legislation, in 1654,[122] for the first time

---

[114] Berman, *Law and Revolution*, pp. 378 sq.

[115] "Some Thoughts", in: *First and Second Things* (1985), p. 91.

[116] Op. cit., note 115, p. 95.

[117] Endemann, *Studien*, vol. I, pp. 62 sqq.; Noonan, op. cit., note 94, pp. 365 sqq.

[118] *Tractatus commerciorum et usurarum redituumque pecuniae et monetarum* (Parisiis, 1546).

[119] *De usuris* (Lugduni Batavorum, 1638).

[120] Like Calvin and Molinaeus, Salmasius drew a distinction between (illegal) mutuum and (lawful) foenus.

[121] Op. cit., note 119, Cap. 5.

[122] *Jüngster Reichsabschied*, § 174 (*NS = Neue und vollständige Sammlung der Reichs-Abschiede* (1747), vol. III, 673).

acknowledged the possibility of charging usurae in principle, loans at interest had already become very common in practice.[123] The canonical prohibition came to be regarded as abrogated by general custom.[124] At the same time there was a general move back to the Roman rules relating to interest, modified in many places only in that the maximum rate for ordinary loans was reduced from 6 % to 5 %, either by way of legislation or by customary recognition.[125] In the Catholic countries (Spain, France and Italy), on the other hand, the canonical prohibition continued to be maintained in principle. In 18th-century French literature it still found support in the influential writings of Domat[126] and Pothier.[127, 128]

6. The flexible rule of the BGB

As far as Germany is concerned, this chapter in the history of the laws against usury drew to a close in 1867. In this year, under the influence of economic liberalism, all limitations on interest rates were abolished.[129] In practice the usury laws were very often circumvented[130] and were regarded as arbitrary and unjustifiable restrictions on the freedom of contract. However, in the years that followed, complaints about usurious exploitation increased. The liberalistic hopes and theories turned out to be castles in the air: with the abolition of criminal sanctions the criminal behaviour itself does not normally disappear. Thus, some control had to be reintroduced. But there was no return to the old policy of fixing maximum rates.[131] Any limit would have been entirely arbitrary. On what basis could 5 % (or

---

[123] Neumann, op. cit., note 97, pp. 506 sq., 511 sqq., 537 sq.; Wieling, *Interesse und Privatstrafe*, pp. 207 sqq.

[124] David Mevius, *Vollständiger Commentarius von wucherlichen Contracten* (Franckfurt/ Leipzig, 1710), I, Cap. VI, § 7; Glück, vol. 21, pp. 100 sq.

[125] Cf. the survey in Boehmer, *Ius ecclesiasticum protestantium*, Lib. V, Tit. 19, §§ III sqq.; Neumann, op. cit., note 97, pp. 545 sqq. Attempts were also made either to subject Jews to these maximum rates or to exclude them from the moneylending business; cf. e.g. *Reichspolizeiordnung* (1577) Tit. XX, 6; Gustav Klemens Schmelzeisen, *Polizeiordnungen und Privatrecht* (1955), p. 475 sqq.

[126] Domat, *Les loix civiles*, Lib. I, Tit. VI, Introduction.

[127] Pothier, *Traité du contrat du prêt de consomption*, nn. 53 sqq. Cf. also Franciscus Hotomanus, *Quaestiones illustres* (Hanoviae, 1601), n. 40.

[128] In the new Codex Juris Canonici the prohibition on usury is no longer mentioned. But cf. still canon 1534 of its predecessor, the Codex Juris Canonici of 1917.

[129] BGBl (*Norddeutscher Bund*) 1867, 159; applicable at first only to the Confederation of Northern Germany, but soon to the Reich, too (exception: Bavaria). On the history of these enactments, see Peter Landau, "Die Gesetzgebungsgeschichte des § 247 BGB. Zugleich ein Beitrag zur Geschichte der Einführung der Zinsfreiheit in Deutschland" in: *Beiträge zur Rechtsgeschichte, Gedächtnisschrift für Hermann Conrad* (1979), pp. 388 sqq.

[130] Cf. Goldschmidt, "Gesetzgebungsfrage, betr. die Aufhebung der Wuchergesetze", in: *Verhandlungen des Sechsten Deutschen Juristentages*, vol. I (1865), pp. 232 sqq. He referred to the usury laws as "conventional lies".

[131] This policy is still pursued in South Africa. Interest rates (in modern parlance: finance charges) are limited by the Limitation and Disclosure of Finance Charges Act 73/1968, amended by Act 90/1980. On this Act and its predecessors, see D.J. Joubert, op. cit., note 66, n. 295.

any other amount) be regarded as legal and 5,5 % as illegal and punishable? Therefore, a flexible rule was introduced in 1880, first in the field of criminal law. This provision was extended in 1892 to cover contracts other than loan; in 1896 it was incorporated into the new codification of private law.[132] There it is considered as a special case of a legal transaction contra bonos mores:

> "A legal transaction is also[133] void whereby a person exploiting the distressed situation, inexperience, lack of judgmental ability or grave weakness of will of another, causes to be promised or granted to himself or to a third party in exchange for a performance, pecuniary advantages, which exceed the value of the performance to such an extent that, under the circumstances, the pecuniary advantages are in obvious disproportion to the performance."[134]

If one compares this to the policy adopted in Roman law, one will find at least four differences: there is no fixed limit, but a flexible one that has to be decided on in each individual case before the courts;[135] the rule is applicable not only to contracts of loan but also to contracts of sale, lease, contract for work, etc.; certain subjective criteria have been introduced that have to be satisfied if a contract is challenged on the basis of being usurious, i.e. an obvious disproportion between performance and counterperformance per se is not sufficient; and we are dealing with a lex perfecta, that is, any contract in violation of § 138 II BGB is void. This latter point, incidentally, leads to problems concerning the law of restitution. If the capital has been handed over to the borrower and it later transpires that the contract of loan is usurious and therefore void, the lender will usually try to get back his capital by means of an unjustified enrichment claim (condictio indebiti). This action, however, seems to be barred by virtue of the fact that the "in pari turpitudine" rule[136] has to be applied analogously in cases of turpitudo solius dantis.[137] But does this mean that the party who was

---

[132] On the history of usury legislation in the 19th century, see Klaus Luig, "Vertragsfreiheit und Äquivalenzprinzip im gemeinen Recht und im BGB", in: *Aspekte europäischer Rechtsgeschichte, Festgabe für Helmut Coing* (1982), pp. 171 sqq.; Zimmermann, *Moderationsrecht*, pp. 145 sqq. Cf. also John P. Dawson, "Economic Duress and the Fair Exchange in French and German Law", (1937) 12 *Tulane LR* 42 sqq.

[133] The "also" refers to § 138 I BGB which reads: "A legal transaction which is contra bonos mores is void."

[134] § 138 II BGB.

[135] For details, see Mayer-Maly in: *Münchener Kommentar*, vol. I, (2nd ed., 1984), § 138, nn. 117 sqq.

[136] Cf. infra, pp. 846 sq., 863 sqq.

[137] The in pari turpitudine rule is laid down in § 817, 2 BGB: "The claim for return is barred if the person performing has committed a similar infringement. . . ." This refers to the condictio ob turpem vel iniustam causam (§ 817, 1 BGB) which lies in cases where the acceptance of the performance by the recipient constitutes an infringement of a statutory prohibition or is contrary to public policy. Literally, therefore, § 817, 2 BGB is applicable only if both parties acted immorally or illegally. The practical effect of that rule is that a person who received something under an illegal or immoral contract may keep it. It would be absurd, however, if only a recipient who had acted immorally himself were allowed to keep the object of the performance, whereas the condictio would not be barred against a

exploited in the first place is now allowed to make a comfortable profit by being able to keep the money (for ever[138] or at least for the time that the parties had—in their invalid contract—agreed upon) without paying interest at all? This, indeed, is the prevailing opinion today.[139] I think, however, that a case can be made out for granting to the usurer an action against the borrower, based on unjustified enrichment, for the value of the use of the money.[140]

III. SPECIAL TYPES OF LOAN

1. Loans to sons in power

(a) The senatus consultum Macedonianum and its policy

The other piece of legislation dealing with specific dangers resulting from moneylending transactions was passed at the time of either Claudius[141] or Vespasian.[142] It was the senatus consultum Macedonianum, named, for once, not after the proposer, but after the person whose scandalous behaviour occasioned it. We find its words recorded by Ulpian in the following way:

> ". . . placere, ne cui, qui filio familias mutuam pecuniam dedisset, etiam post mortem parentis eius cuius in potestate fuisset, actio petitioque daretur, ut scirent, qui pessimo exemplo faenerarent nullius posse filii familias bonum nomen expectata patris morte fieri."[143]

The enactment provided that the lender who has given money to a son in power should have no action to reclaim his money, even after the death of the latter's father.[144] It was the legislatorial reaction to an incident which has been described by Theophilus:

> "There lived at Rome a person called Macedo. When still under patria potestas, he borrowed money from somebody, hoping that after his father's death he would be able to repay the debt. As time dragged on, the creditor pressed him hard, demanding his debt. Macedo had nothing wherewith to pay (how could he, being

---

blameless receiver. Thus, 817, 2 BGB must also be applied in cases of turpitudo solius dantis. For a more detailed discussion, see Zimmermann, *Moderationsrecht*, pp. 156 sqq.

[138] This, amazingly, was the solution arrived at in RGZ 151, 70 (72 sqq.). It has been abandoned since RGZ 161, 52 (53 sqq.).

[139] RGZ 161, 52 (53 sqq.); Gustav Boehmer, *Grundlagen der bürgerlichen Rechtsordnung*, vol. I (1950), pp. 55 sq.

[140] Cf. Dieter Medicus, "Vergütungspflicht des Bewucherten", in: *Gedächtnisschrift für Rolf Dietz* (1973), pp. 61 sqq. There is a tendency to avoid these difficulties by interfering with the contract and reducing the usurious interest rate to an acceptable level, rather than to regard the contract as totally void: cf. e.g. Mayer-Maly, op. cit., note 135, § 138, nn. 132 sqq. and Lieb, in: *Münchener Kommentar*, vol. III, 2 (2nd ed., 1986), § 817, nn. 16 sqq. Contra: Zimmermann, *Moderationsrecht*, pp. 177 sqq. and passim.

[141] Cf. Tacitus, *Annales*, Lib. XI, 13, 2.

[142] Suetonius, *De vita Caesarum, Divus Vespasianus*, XI; Kaser, *RPr* I, p. 532. For a possible reconciliation, see Glück, vol. 14, p. 308.

[143] Ulp. D. 14, 6, 1 pr.

[144] The praetor either refused an action (denegatio actionis) or he (more often) granted the exceptio senatus consulti Macedoniani (to enable the iudex to examine the facts alleged). See Schulz, *CRL*, p. 511.

> alieni iuris?); so he killed his father. The matter was brought before the senate: Macedo suffered the penalty for patricide, and the senatus consultum called Macedonianum was made."[145]

This story has been challenged more than once: Gerhard von Beseler, the chief interpolation-hunter, has denounced it as a silly Byzantine legend.[146] Theophilus' account has, however, been vindicated most elegantly and convincingly by David Daube,[147] who answered the question "Did Macedo murder his father?" in the affirmative: "It is to be feared that he did." In fact, Theophilus' paraphrase provides us with the background against which we can appreciate the true intention of the senatus consultum. The most important point is that it barred the lender's claim after the father's death.[148] During his lifetime, of course, no judgment rendered against the son on account of the obligation he had incurred, was enforceable; any attempt to carry out the execution would have interfered with the patria potestas. If, therefore, before the senatus consultum had been enacted, a capitalist had lent money to a son in power, it was inevitable that the parties to such a loan

> "should often look forward to the father's death as a welcome event: it was the father who stood between the filiusfamilias and his inheritance and freedom, and between the moneylender and an unhampered prosecution of his claim".[149]

This is exactly the situation in which Macedo found himself. Unfortunately, his father proved long-lived. Having already committed a number of more minor illegalities[150] (such as possibly embezzling the family's jewels), and thus being conspicuously susceptible to blackmail, Macedo did not seem to have seen any other way of coping with the demands of his troublesome creditor than to bring his father's life to a premature end. The aim of the senatus consultum, under these circumstances, was to make loans to sons in power as unattractive as possible: which moneylender would still be prepared to make a loan which the law could never assist him to recover? Secondly, even if a moneylender still took the risk, the provisions of the senatus consultum removed any interest the moneylender might have had in the murder of his debtor's father. This crime would no longer improve his position ; neither before nor after the father's death did he have an enforceable claim.[151] The intention of the senatus consultum was therefore not to protect improvident and thoughtless young men from the dangers of leading a sumptuous life on credit: it applied to grey-haired senators

---

145 *Paraphrasis institutionum*, Lib. IV, Tit. VII, 7.

146 *Beiträge zur Kritik der römischen Rechtsquellen*, vol. IV (1920), pp. 130 sq.; cf. also Schulz, *CRL*, p. 512 ("obviously, this story cannot be true").

147 "Did Macedo murder his father?", (1947) 65 *ZSS* 261 sqq.

148 Also, if the son had been granted a peculium, the actio de peculio against the paterfamilias: C. 4, 28, 6 pr.

149 Daube, (1947) 65 *ZSS* 268.

150 Cf. Ulp. D. 14, 6, 1 pr.: ". . . et saepe materiam peccandi malis moribus praestaret. . . ."

151 Daube, (1947) 65 *ZSS* 269.

and consuls, as long as they were alieni iuris,[152] but it did not apply to effervescent teenagers, as long as they were sui iuris. Its application was confined to filiifamilias, that is, to cases where the temptation to eliminate the father could have existed.[153] In enacting the senatus consultum Macedonianum, the Roman Senate seems therefore to have had in mind the protection of the paterfamilias against the attacks of desperate sons following Macedo's fearful example. The legislation was intended to avert patricide, which is most likely where a depraved filiusfamilias acts under the guidance of a moneylender.[154] The latter was seen to be the principal culprit behind all these sinister machinations,[155] and the main thrust of the senatus consultum was therefore directed at eradicating the villainous character of an usurer inciting his debtor to take these desperate steps.

(b) The application of the senatus consultum by the Roman jurists

It was with this intention in mind that the senatus consultum Macedonianum was applied. As in the case of the senatus consultum Vellaeanum, we find the Roman lawyers adopting a purposive or teleological approach in establishing the scope and rational limitations of the enactment.[156] Thus, for instance, we read:

> ". . . si quidem eius causa exceptio datur cum quo agitur, solutum repetere potest, ut accidit in senatus consulto de intercessionibus: ubi vero in odium eius cui debetur exceptio datur, perperam solutum non repetitur, veluti si filiusfamilias contra Macedonianum mutuam pecuniam acceperit et paterfamilias factus solverit, non repetit."[157]

Unlike the exceptio senatus consulti Vellaeani, the defence under the senatus consultum Macedonianum was not granted in the interest of the person who had incurred the obligation (the defendant, i.e. the woman and the son in power respectively); its function was to thwart the creditor.[158] Thus, a son in power who accidentally paid back the loan after having become sui iuris was not allowed to recover the money.[159] Normally a person to whom a perpetual (as opposed to a merely

[152] Cf. Ulp. D. 14, 6, 1, 3: "In filio familias nihil dignitas facit quominus senatus consultum Macedonianum locum habeat: nam etiamsi consul sit vel cuiusvis dignitatis, senatus consulto locus est."

[153] Cf. e.g. Ulp. D. 14, 6, 3, 3: ". . . nam pecuniae datio perniciosa parentibus eorum visa est."

[154] Daube, (1947) 65 *ZSS* 308. Cf. also, in a broader context, Daube, *Roman Law*, pp. 87 sqq.

[155] Cf., too, Kaser, *RPr* I, p. 532.

[156] Cf. the compilation in Buckland/Stein, pp. 465 sq.; cf. also Windscheid/Kipp pp. 583 sqq.

[157] Marci. D. 12, 6, 40 pr.

[158] Cf. also Pomp. D. 12, 6, 19 pr.: "Si *poenae causa* ius cui debetur debitor liberatus est, naturalis obligatio manet. . . ." The senatus consultum, incidentally, did not apply if the moneylender had had no reason to think that his prospective debtor might be alieni iuris: cf. Ulp. D. 14, 6, 3 pr.–2.

[159] He is, as Paulus puts it, under a naturalis obligatio; cf. also Pomp. D. 12, 6, 19 pr. and Pierre Cornioley, *Naturalis obligatio* (1964), pp. 243 sqq.

temporary, dilatory) exceptio is available may reclaim what has been paid in error.[160]

Of course, a fortiori, deliberate ratification of the debt, once the son had ceased to be alieni iuris, was permissible too. Thus, the former son in power, now paterfamilias in his own right, could no longer plead the exceptio senatus consulti Macedoniani once he had actually started to pay back the loan[161]—the transaction had now become fully effective. Furthermore, the paterfamilias did not deserve any protection where the son had incurred the obligation from the mutuum with his consent, or where he (the paterfamilias) had subsequently ratified the transaction.[162] Repayment of part of the loan by the paterfamilias, again, was taken to imply such ratification; the paterfamilias was therefore barred from relying on the protection afforded by the senatus consultum Macedonianum under these circumstances.[163] There were other cases in which it could be presumed that the son in power, in taking up the loan, did not do so in order to embark on a life of reckless intemperance, but acted in accordance with the wishes and intentions of his father: for instance, if the money was needed for study purposes by a student who had to maintain himself at an overseas university; or if it was used to cover reasonable expenses which the father ordinarily paid.[164] The same applied if the money was used for the benefit of his father's property.[165] Entirely logical, too, was the solution adopted where the status of the borrower had changed after he had promised repayment of the money, but before it had actually been paid out to him. If the final, decisive act of lending was made to a paterfamilias, the senatus consultum did not apply, even though the receiver had previously been alieni iuris.[166] Conversely, if a person sui iuris had made the promise, but had received the money at a time when he had, by way of adrogatio, become alieni iuris, the exceptio was applicable.[167] This differentiation is explicable on the basis that the senatus consultum was intended to prevent crimes such as the one

---

[160] Marc. D. 12, 6, 40 pr.: "Qui exceptionem perpetuam habet, solutum per errorem repetere potest." Cf. § 813 I BGB: "What was done with the object of fulfilling an obligation may be demanded back even if there was a defense to the claim whereby the enforcement of the claim was permanently barred."

[161] Ulp. D. 14, 6, 7, 16: "Si paterfamilias factus solverit partem debiti, cessabit senatus consultum nec solutum repetere potest."

[162] C. 4, 28, 7 (Iust.). What if the father had agreed to the transaction, but the grandfather was still alive? This was the problem in Iul. D. 14, 6, 14: "Filium habeo et ex eo nepotem: nepoti meo creditum est iussu patris eius: quaesitum est, an contra senatus consultum fieret. dixi, etiamsi verbis senatus consulti filii continerentur, tamen et in persona nepotis idem servari debere: iussum autem huius patris non efficere, quo minus contra senatus consultum creditum existimaretur, cum ipse in ea causa esset, ut pecuniam mutuam invito patre suo accipere non possit."

[163] Ulp. D. 14, 6, 7, 15.

[164] Ulp. D. 14, 6, 7, 13.

[165] Ulp. D. 14, 6, 7, 12.

[166] Ulp. D. 14, 6, 3, 4.

[167] Scaev. D. 14, 6, 6.

committed by Macedo, not on the assumption that it was primarily aimed at the protection of irresponsible youth.

Was the senatus consultum Macedonianum, in accordance with its wording, applied only to loans of money or was it extended, by way of interpretation, to other transactions? Did it cover the filiusfamilias breakfasting every morning on nightingales bought on credit?[168] "Is autem solus senatus consultum offendit, qui mutuam pecuniam filio familias dedit, non qui alias contraxit, puta vendidit locavit."[169] The rationale is set out by Daube:[170]

> "A filius familias was free to squander all his prospective wealth, and more—provided he obtained the credit from ordinary business men, in an honest manner. He might even stand surety for a prodigal friend:[171] that was not a dirty, underhand arrangement. . . . What the senate was out to prevent or at any rate render harmless was the pure money loan from an usurer. It was this transaction which so easily led to crime."[172]

On the other hand, of course, the parties could not be allowed to sidestep the provisions of the senatus consultum by simply disguising the loan. If a contract of sale had been entered into between the moneylender and the son in power, though the purpose of the transaction really was to effect a loan, the senatus consultum was held to apply.[173]

Even though the senatus consultum Macedonianum was closely linked to the entire system of patria potestas, it survived in Germany until the end of the 19th century.[174] In Roman-Dutch law, on the other hand, its application was restricted to persons under the age of 25.[175]

2. Loans to merchants involved in overseas trade

(a) Pecunia traiecticia as a form of marine insurance

It has been said above that the borrower remains liable even though he might have lost what he had received by fire, earthquake or shipwreck. The risk, as a matter of course, was on the borrower/owner. Yet, there was one situation in which the capital was supposed to be at the risk of the lender: pecunia traiecticia[176] or, to use the more accurate

---

[168] Daube, (1947) 65 *ZSS* 280.

[169] Ulp. D. 14, 6, 3, 3. Cf., too, C. 4, 28, 3: "Si filius familias aliquid mercatus pretium stipulanti venditori cum usurarum accessione spondeat, non esse locum senatus consulto, quo fenerare filiis familias prohibitum est, nemini dubium est: origo enim potius obligationis quam titulus actionis considerandus est."

[170] (1947) 65 *ZSS* 293 sq.

[171] For this example, see Ulp. D. 14, 6, 7 pr.

[172] Cf. Ulp. D. 14, 6, 3, 3, as quoted supra, note 153.

[173] Ulp. D. 14, 6, 3, 3: "quod ita demum erit dicendum, si non fraus senatus consulto sit cogitata, ut qui credere non potuit magis ei venderet, ut ille rei pretium haberet in mutui vicem."

[174] Cf. e.g. the detailed treatment by Windscheid/Kipp, § 373.

[175] Groenewegen, *De legibus abrogatis,* Cod. Lib. IV, Tit. XXVIII; cf. also Voet *Commentarius ad Pandectas,* Lib. XIV, Tit. VI, II. But see Huber, *Hedendaegse Rechtsgeleertheyt,* III. Boek, XVI. Kap., 23 sqq.

[176] D. 22, 2.

post-classical term, fenus nauticum.[177] This was a loan of money given to a merchant involved in overseas trade, who lacked the capital to buy the merchandise and to ship it at his own risk. Sea voyages on the Mediterranean were dangerous in Greek and Roman times because of storms and pirates[178] and the average merchant therefore looked for some kind of marine insurance. This was the function served by fenus nauticum: the money had to be repaid only if the ship arrived safely in port with the cargo on board (si navis intra certum tempus pervenerit in portum). Usually, the loan was given for both the voyage out and the return journey: the merchant would use the money to buy articles suitable for exporting at the port of departure, in order to sell them overseas. He would then avail himself of the proceeds to import other articles on the homebound journey. Because of the risk which the lender assumed, the rate of interest, up to the time of Justinian, was not limited;[179] to charge high interest rates was not regarded as objectionable and usurious as it was not merely a compensation for the use of the capital but a premium periculi,[180] an equivalent for the assumption of the risk of the various maritime vagaries.[181] We do not know what rates were in accordance with ordinary trade usage in Rome; Greek moneylenders during the 4th century B.C. charged between $22\frac{1}{2}$ and

---

[177] C. 4, 33. As to the Roman terminology, cf. Wieslaw Litewski, "Römisches Seedarlehen", (1973) 24 *Iura* 113 sqq.; Hans Ankum, "Tabula Pompeiana 13: ein Seefrachtvertrag oder ein Seedarlehen?", (1978) 29 *Iura* 170 sq.

[178] During the time of the Roman Republic, piracy posed a grave danger for all sea voyages. Cf., for example, Plutarch, *Vitae*, Pompeius 25–28; Theodor Mommsen, *Römische Geschichte*, vol. II (14th ed., 1933), p. 64: ". . . *die Piratenflotte [war] die einzige ansehnliche Seemacht im Mittelmeere, der Menschenfang das einzige daselbst blühende Gewerbe. Die römische Regierung sah den Dingen zu, die römischen Kaufleute aber standen als die besten Kunden auf dem Sklavenmarkt mit den Piratenkapitänen als den bedeutendsten Grosshändlern in diesem Artikel auf Delos und sonst in regem und freundlichem Geschäftsverkehr.*" Pompeius, in his war against the pirates (67 B.C.), largely eradicated piracy in the Mediterranean Sea. For details, see Henry A. Ormerod, *Piracy in the Ancient World* (1924); Friedrich Berber, "Von der Piraterie in der Antike", in: *Recht über See, Festschrift für Rolf Stödter* (1979), pp. 147 sqq. and Karl Heinz Ziegler, "Pirata communis hostis omnium", in: *De iustitia et iure, Festgabe für Ulrich von Lübtow* (1980), pp. 93 sqq.

[179] C. 4, 33, 2 (Diocl.); C. 4, 32, 26, 2 (Just.); Paul. Sent. II, XIV, 3 ("Traiecticia pecunia propter periculum creditoris, quamdiu navigat navis, infinitas usuras recipere potest"). Justinian fixed the maximum rate of interest at 12 % (cf. e.g. Arnaldo Biscardi, *Actio pecuniae traiecticiae* (2nd ed., 1974), pp. 54 sqq.; Bianchini, *Studi Biscardi*, vol. II, pp. 418 sqq.). Already in (late) classical law, interest no longer had to be specifically stipulated for. A mere pactum was sufficient. Cf. Paul. D. 22, 2, 7 and Kaser, *RPr* I, p. 409, n. 37; Litewski, (1973) 24 *Iura* 165 sqq.; contra: Arnaldo Biscardi, "'Pecunia traiecticia' e 'stipulatio poenae'", (1978) 24 *Labeo* 282 sqq.

[180] Cf. Scaev. D. 22, 2, 5 pr.; cf. also Paul. Sent. II, XIV, 3.

[181] Consequently, the high interest rate had to be paid only for the days the ship was at sea, not when it was in port (cf. e.g. Mod. D. 22, 2, 1; Mod. D. 22, 2, 3; Paul. Sent. II, XIV, 3). On the other hand, the debtor was released from the duty to repay the loan only if the merchandise was lost due to a typical risk of the sea (marina tempestas: C. 4, 33, 4; naufragium: C. 4, 33, 5; also piratarum insidiae: cf. Gai. D. 13, 6, 18 pr.), not in case of other accidents or carelessness on the part of the debtor. For details of the periculum creditoris, see Litewski, (1973) 24 *Iura* 125 sqq.; idem, "Bemerkungen zum römischen Seedarlehen", in: *Studi in onore di Cesare Sanfilippo*, vol. IV (1983), pp. 384 sqq.

$33\frac{1}{3}$ per cent depending on the distance to be covered by the ship.[182] The merchants, of course, were sometimes tempted to avoid having to pay such large parts of their profit margin to the lender; thus we read of feigned shipwrecks and intentional sinkings of the ships concerned.[183] To avoid manipulations of this kind, the lender usually sent one of his slaves to take part in the whole voyage.

(b) Greek custom and Roman practice

This form of marine insurance by way of fenus nauticum, like most Roman rules of maritime law, came from the Hellenistic East. The Greek bottomry loan was essentially based on the idea of surrogation.[184] Otherwise than in Roman law, the lender still seems to have been entitled to the capital, even after it had been handed over. Likewise, he was entitled to whatever was bought with this money. Thus the merchandise was regarded as pledged to him. If the goods got lost during the sea journey, the creditor had lost the object to which the liability of the borrower attached and, as a consequence, his claim for repayment fell away too. The Roman lawyers seem to have had certain difficulties in accommodating this foreign custom and translating it into the terms and concepts of their law.[185] That is apparent, for instance, from the term "pecunia traiecticia" and from the definition given by Modestinus: "Traiecticia ea pecunia est quae trans mare vehitur."[186] This statement does not reflect the main characteristic of the transaction, namely the assumption of risk on the part of the lender. But even on a descriptive level it is inaccurate,[187] for it was normally not the money that travelled overseas (that would not have been a very meaningful form of a fenus nauticum because it would have exposed the money to the perils of the sea without using it to yield a profit); it was the merchandise bought with the borrowed money that was in danger of perishing in one of the many possible maritime disasters. Nevertheless, Roman practice followed the Greek custom (in classical times some sort of ius gentium of all seafaring nations) very closely.[188] An instructive example is the detailed account by Quintus Cervidius Scaevola of a transaction concerning a merchant by the name of

---

[182] Billeter, op. cit., note 71, pp. 303 sqq.

[183] Livius, *Ab urbe condita*, Lib. XXVI, III, 10.

[184] Fritz Pringsheim, *Der Kauf mit fremdem Geld* (1916), pp. 4 sqq.

[185] Until the time of Justinian their aim was never to introduce new rules, or to change the Greek custom, but merely to understand and incorporate it into their legal system. Cf. e.g. Nov. 106 and Pringsheim, op. cit., note 184, p. 146.

[186] Mod. D. 22, 2, 1.

[187] But see Litewski, (1973) 24 *Iura* 120 sqq. He contends that it was, in fact, originally the money that was transported overseas, in order to buy and then import the merchandise; only later was the fenus nauticum used for both import and export purposes.

[188] Pringsheim, op. cit., note 184, pp. 143 sqq. On the relationship between maritime loans in Greek and Roman practice see, most recently, Gianfranco Purpura, "Ricerche in tema di prestito marittimo", (1987) 39 *Annali Palermo* 202 sqq.

Callimachus.[189] Stichus, a slave of a (Roman) moneylender, had handed over a certain sum of money as a loan to Callimachus in Berytus. The latter was supposed to buy merchandise and to ship it to Brentesium (Brindisi); there he had to sell the goods, use the proceeds to buy import articles and ship them back to the home port, Berytus. Both the merchandise bought in Berytus and that acquired in Brentesium served as a pledge for the lender's claim and travelled at his risk.[190] Callimachus, furthermore, was liable for the maintenance of the lender's slaves accompanying the transport (in the end, however, only the slave Eros took part in the voyage). Finally, the loan had been given to Callimachus for a maximum period of 200 days, within which both the outward journey and return trip had to be completed. However, it was also agreed that he had to leave Brentesium intra idus Septembres, i.e. on or before 13 September, and to head back directly to Syria.[191] The whole of the contract was affirmed by way of stipulation;[192] observance of the right time of departure from Brentesium was secured by stipulatio poenae: if Callimachus should still be in Brentesium on

[189] Scaev. D. 45, 1, 122, 1. On the fragment, see Ulrich von Lübtow, "Das Seedarlehen des Callimachus", in: *Festschrift für Max Kaser* (1976), pp. 329 sqq.; Purpura, (1987) 39 *Annali Palermo* 212 sqq., 301 sqq.

[190] Generally on pledges in connection with fenus nauticum, Litewski, (1973) 24 *Iura* 169 sqq. An interesting case (Paul. D. 22, 2, 6) is discussed by Robert Röhle, "Zum Beispiel D. 22, 2, 6", (1979) 45 *SDHI* 549 sqq. He vindicates the exegesis given by Cuiacius (*Commentarii in Lib. XXV Quaest. Pauli*, col. 1216 sqq.) against modern interpretations. The key to the solution is the accessoriness of pignus. Cf. also Purpura, (1987) 39 *Annali Palermo* 273 sqq.

[191] This date of departure from Brindisi had to be specifically agreed upon in view of the fact that the period of 200 days might otherwise have run into the winter season, during which the seas were "closed" (Vegetius, *Epitoma rei militaris*, Lib. IV, XXXIX: "a die VI. kal. Junios usque in Arcturi ortum, id est in diem VIII decimum kal. Octobres, secura navigatio creditur, . . . post hoc tempus usque in tertium idus Novembres incerta navigatio est. . . . Ex die . . . tertio idus Novembris usque in diem sextum idus Martias maria clauduntur"; that is: from 8 June to 14 September navigation was safe; between 11 March and 8 June and from 14 September to 10 November navigation was uncertain; between 11 November and 10 March seas were closed). Winter sailing was particularly dangerous, not so much on account of the storms (the summer storms, in the Mediterranean, especially the Mistral and the Etesianus are notorious too), but because of the reduced visibility, severely hampering orientation in an age that did not yet know the mariner's compass: "lux minima noxque prolixa, nubium densitas, aeris obscuritas, ventorum imbri vel nivibus geminata saevitia" (Vegetius, loc. cit., on the dangers of winter sailing). Thus, St. Paul's shipwreck (Acts 27, 9) happened because the shipper risked sailing from Crete after the season had closed. On all this cf. Jean Rougé, *Recherches sur l'organisation du commerce maritime en Mediterranée sous l'Empire Romain* (1966), pp. 31 sqq.; Lionel Casson, *Ships and Seamanship in the Ancient World* (1971), pp. 270 sqq. Even if Callimachus had set out from Berytus immediately after the opening of the sailing season (i.e. on 11 March), he would have had until 26 September before he had to be back. The distance between Brindisi and Berytus was easily manageable between 13 and 26 September. With a wind from the right direction, ancient sailing ships could travel a speed of between $4\frac{1}{2}$ and 6 knots. We know, for instance, that under favourable wind conditions the distance from Carthage to Gibraltar (820 nautical miles) could be covered within 7 days. For details, see Casson, pp. 281 sqq.

[192] Generally on the form in which a fenus nauticum was concluded, Litewski, (1973) 24 *Iura* 137 sqq.; Ankum, (1978) 29 *Iura* 171 sq.

14 September, the whole of the capital plus interest would become exactable "quasi perfecto navigio".[193]

This transaction contains all the typical elements of a fenus nauticum;[194] of course, many variations were possible. Thus, we find an ingenious combination of fenus nauticum and commercial partnership in Cato's moneylending transactions.[195] He gave the capital to one of his liberti (a certain Quinctius) who had to get together 50 shipowners and merchants for the purpose of overseas trading. Thus, the partners could share the risk involved; if one of the 50 ships sank, the proportional share of the loss for each of them was only $\frac{1}{50}$. Cato, who incidentally was not very keen on voyages by ship himself,[196] has been criticized by his biographer, Plutarch, for indulging in this "most condemnable of loan transactions" (namely fenus nauticum). Such an evaluation, however, does not do justice to a man whom Livius refers to as "vir sanctus et innocens"[197] and who has gone down in history as the epitome of Roman austerity and uprightness; it is based on an un-Roman perception of business activities involving the loan of money on a commercial basis as something dishonest and discreditable.[198]

Writers in later centuries struggled to comprehend dogmatically and fit in the fenus nauticum;[199] nevertheless, it continued to be practised.

---

[193] In the end, of course, Callimachus did not start his return journey in time; he left Brentesium only after 13 September, even though he had already loaded the freight before that date. Eros, however, had agreed to this belated departure. On this case and the problems raised by it, see von Lübtow, *Festschrift Kaser*, pp. 329 sqq.; Purpura, (1987) 39 *Annali Palermo* 212 sqq., 301 sqq.

[194] As to the stipulationes poenae that were usually attached to fenora nautica, see Károly Visky, "Das Seedarlehn und die damit verbundene Konventionalstrafe im römischen Recht", (1969) 16 *RIDA* 389 sqq.; Litewski, (1973) 24 *Iura* 173 sqq.; Arnaldo Biscardi, *Actio pecuniae traiecticiae* (2nd ed., 1974), passim; Knütel, *Stipulatio poenae*, pp. 39 sq.; Biscardi, (1978) 24 *Labeo* 276 sqq.; Litewski, *Studi Sanfilippo*, vol. IV, pp. 390 sqq.; Visky, *Spuren*, pp. 85 sqq.

[195] Cf. Plutarch, *Vitae*, Cato Maior 21, 5–7. See Ulrich von Lübtow, "Catos Seedarlehen", in: *Festschrift für Erwin Seidl* (1975), pp. 103 sqq.; Purpura, (1987) 39 *Annali Palermo* 235 sqq.

[196] He is reported to have said that he made three mistakes in his life: he told a secret to his wife, he took a boat when he could have walked, and he spent an entire day without a will: Plutarch, *Vitae*, Cato maior, 9, 9.

[197] *Ab urbe condita*, Lib. XXXII, XXVII, 2–4.

[198] Cf., concerning Cato, the analysis by Von Lübtow, *Festschrift Seidl*, pp. 108 sqq. Cato must have been a very wealthy man (D. Kienast, *Cato, Der Zensor* (1954), pp. 33 sqq.). He used to say that as a young man he had had only two sources of income: agriculture and frugality. Later on, he increased his property by investing his money in various commercial enterprises. He regarded his wealth as the material basis for his independence; it enabled him to devote his time to the Roman political life. On Cato as jurist and politician cf., most recently, Richard A. Bauman, *Lawyers in Roman Republic Politics* (1983), pp. 148 sqq.; Wieacker, *RR*, pp. 538 sq.

[199] Cf., for example, the rather tortuous analysis by Huschke, op. cit., note 41, p. 223.

During the time of the usus modernus, it came to be amalgamated with the medieval bottomry loan.[200]

3. Loans to professional sportsmen

In the case of fenus nauticum, repayment of the loan was dependent upon whether the ship arrived safely at its destination, with its cargo on board. Whether or not this condition was satisfied depended on the occurrence or non-occurrence of events entirely outside the control of the parties (shipwreck due to storm, piracy, etc.). There were other cases, however, where whether or not the loan had to be paid back was determined, to a certain extent, by the borrower himself. As long as such transactions did not take on the character of gambling ("si modo in aleae speciem non cada[n]t"),[201] they were entirely valid. Quintus Cervidius Scaevola mentions two examples:

> ". . . nec dubitabis, si piscatori erogaturo in apparatum plurimum pecuniae dederim, ut, si cepisset, redderet, et athletae, unde se exhiberet exerceretque, ut, si vicisset, redderet."[202]

The more interesting of these is the case of the professional athlete who received a loan in order to be able to maintain himself and to cover all expenses incurred in connection with his exercise programme, equipment, etc.[203] The money had to be repaid only once the borrower had gained a victory.[204] Success in sport offered the opportunity of

[200] Coing, pp. 552 sq.; as far as medieval law is concerned, cf. also Berman, *Law and Revolution*, pp. 349, 621. He points out that the sea loan was criticized as usurious and condemned by Pope Gregory IX in 1236. For a detailed analysis, see Pothier, *Traité du prêt à la grosse aventure*. "Bottomry", incidentally, seems to be a Flemish term derived from the figurative use, pars pro toto, of the bottom or keel to designate the whole ship. The bottomry loan was received into the English law via the Law Merchant and through the court of Admiralty, one of the strongholds of the "Civilians" (on which see, most recently, the comprehensive account by Daniel R. Coquilette, *The Civilian Writers of Doctors' Commons* (London, 1988)). It first occurs in the records in 1593. Cf. Holdsworth, *HEL*, vol. VIII, p. 261.

[201] Scaev. D. 22, 2, 5 pr.

[202] D. 22, 2, 5 pr. On this text (and the question of its classicity), see Glück, vol. 21, pp. 153 sqq., 164 sqq.; Litewski, (1973) 24 *Iura* 160 sqq.

[203] For all details cf. especially Andreas Wacke, "Athleten als Darlehensnehmer nach römischem Recht", (1978) 44 *SDHI* 439 sqq.

[204] Such conditions, where the existence of an obligation was made dependent upon a certain achievement on the part of the (potential) debtor, were not entirely unusual. Cf., for instance, the logical paradox related in Aulus Gellius, *Noctes Atticae*, Lib. V, X. Protagoras ("sophistarum acerrimu[s]") had been promised by his pupil Euathlos "mercedem grandem pecuniam", payable at the time the latter won his first lawsuit ("quo primum die causam apud iudices orasset et vicisset"). For a long time Euathlos remained Protagoras' pupil without, however, undertaking any trial work. Protagoras therefore ultimately decided to sue him for his fee, arguing as follows: ". . . si contra te [sc.: Euathle] lis data erit, merces mihi et sententia debebitur, quia ego vicero; sin vero secundum te iudicatum erit merces mihi ex pacto debebitur, quia tu viceres." Euathlos, however, replied: ". . . si iudices pro causa mea senserint, nihil tibi ex sententia debebitur, quia ego vicero; sin contra me pronuntiaverint, nihil tibi ex pacto debebo, quia non vicero." The judges were unable to give a decision and postponed the matter indefinitely: "Tum iudices, dubiosum hoc

considerable prestige and social and economic advancement,[205] but it entailed devotion and training for years and on a full-time basis.[206] Thus it was essential for a young and talented sportsman to find a sponsor who would be prepared to bear the risk that all these efforts might in the end turn out to be in vain. Obviously, this risk was a considerable one, for it must be borne in mind, inter alia, that Baron de Coubertin's comforting emphasis on participation rather than victory would have been entirely out of place in the ancient world.[207] One was either the winner or a loser; there were no prizes for those placed second or third.[208] Thus, as a praemium periculi, the moneylender was entitled to charge higher interest rates than usual;[209] as in the case of fenus nauticum, the interest did not have to be specifically stipulated for.[210]

One may ask whether, under these circumstances, the athlete might not have been tempted to abandon striving for victory rather than having to repay loan plus interest. There was the danger, too, that he might accept a bribe from one of his competitors in order to let him win.[211] But on the one hand, the financial incentives and the material and immaterial advantages of victory normally seem to have outweighed such considerations. Successful athletes went from one competition to the other year after year and had a good chance of becoming wealthy men.[212] On the other hand, according to general principles, the condition on which repayment of the loan depended was deemed to be fulfilled if actual fulfilment was prevented, mala fide, by the party which had an interest in its non-fulfilment (i.e. the—potential—debtor).[213]

---

inexplicabileque esse quod utrimque dicebatur rati, ne sententia sua, utracumque in partem dicta esset, ipsa sese rescinderet, rem iniudicatam relinquerunt causamque in diem longissimam distulerunt."

[205] Cf. Mario Amelotti, "La posizione degli atleti di fronte al diritto romano", (1955) 21 *SDHI* 123 sqq.; Henri W. Pleket, "Zur Soziologie des antiken Sports", in: (1974) 36 *Mededelingen van het Nederlands Instituut te Rome* 57 sqq., 74 sqq.

[206] The Greek word ἀθλητής usually referred to professional athletes, as opposed to an ἰδιώτης (amateur; literally: idiot).

[207] On sport in Greek and Roman antiquity generally, see e.g. Julius Jüthner, *Die athletischen Leibesübungen der Griechen*, 2 vols (1965–68); Harold Arthur Harris, *Sport in Greece and Rome* (1972); Edward Norman Gardiner, *Athletics of the Ancient World* (1967); Ingomar Weiler, *Der Sport bei den Völkern der Alten Welt* (2nd ed., 1988).

[208] Henri W. Pleket, "Games, Prizes, Athletes and Ideology", (1975) 1 *Stadion* 49 sqq. (74 sqq.).

[209] In this specific instance the parties had agreed that the creditor should get "insuper aliquid praeter pecuniam", i.e. a lump sum by which the repayable capital was increased ("ad augendam obligationem"). The state of dependence upon his sponsor which an athlete could get into, under these circumstances, is illustrated by the case in Ulp. D. 4, 2, 32, 2.

[210] Cf. Scaev. D. 22, 2, 5, 1.

[211] On bribery scandals in ancient sport cf. Clarence A. Forbes, "Crime and Punishment in Greek Athletics", (1952) 47 *Classical Journal* 169 sqq., 202 sqq. Revealing, too, C. 10, 54, 1 (Diocl.) ("non aemulis corruptis ac redemptis").

[212] Wacke, (1978) 44 *SDHI* 446 sq.

[213] Cf. infra, pp. 730 sq.

CHAPTER 7

Commodatum, Depositum, Pignus

I. COMMODATUM

1. Commodatum and mutuum

Mutuum was available only where a party wanted to borrow money or fungibles; an equivalent in kind had to be returned. Where the lender, on the other hand, expected the very same thing that he had handed over to the borrower to be returned, the contract was not mutuum but commodatum. Commodatum was the gratuitous loan of a thing for use.[1] Like mutuum, it was a real contract, that is, it could not be created by a formless pact; nor could the lender bind himself by way of letter or any other means (except, of course, by way of stipulation) to grant a loan.[2] The contract of commodatum, and with it the obligation to restore, came into existence only once the object had been handed over.[3] This object was normally a non-fungible thing. However, a commodatum could come into existence in respect of fungibles too. The famous textbook examples are the food to be used as a show-dish or the cash to be spread out on a moneylender's table: "Non potest commodari id quod usu consumitur, nisi forte ad pompam vel ostentationem"[4]—consumable goods were normally lent by way of mutuum; if, however, they were not intended to be consumed, but merely to be displayed for the purpose of "pomp or ostentation" and then to be handed back again, a commodatum came into existence.

Thus we find two different forms of loan in Roman (and in modern) law: the one where the individual thing is lent (and has to be restored), the other where it is not the money or fungible object itself, but rather its value that is lent. Whereas, however, the terminological distinction drawn by the Roman lawyers "very happily expresses the fundamental difference" between these two forms of loan, "our poverty (sc.: the English language) is reduced to confound (them) under the vague and common appellation of a loan".[5] Or, to quote Pollock and Maitland:

[1] "Commodare" has been defined by Donellus in the following terms: ". . . rem quae usu non consumitur, seu mobilem seu immobilem utendam gratis dare certo praescripto utendi fine aut modo": *Commentarii de Jure Civili,* Lib. XIV, Cap. II, II).

[2] Cf., for example, the case in Scaev. D. 39, 5, 32.

[3] Cf., for example, Inst. III, 14, 2.

[4] Ulp. D. 13, 6, 3, 6.

[5] Edward Gibbon, *Decline and Fall of the Roman Empire,* 1962 sqq., vol. IV, chap. 44, pp. 427 sqq.

> "To this day Englishmen are without words which neatly mark this distinction. We lend books and halfcrowns to borrowers; we hope to see the same books again, but not the same halfcrowns; still in either case there is a loan."[6]

On the model of the French *prêt à usage*[7] the term "loan for use" has been introduced by Sir William Jones in his *Essay on the Law of Bailments*[8]—the first English monograph, incidentally, which can properly be called a legal treatise.[9] The German Code distinguishes between *Leihe*[10] (commodatum) and *Darlehen*[11] (mutuum); the somewhat artificial term of *Darlehen*, alien to Germanic law,[12] has never managed to establish itself in common parlance.[13]

2. History and gratuitous nature of commodatum

Commodatum, being necessarily gratuitous, is not one of the cornerstones of commercial life. It usually occurs between friends, relatives or neighbours,[14] and litigation involving problems arising from loan is rare.[15] It is therefore not surprising that commodatum as a legally recognized and enforceable contract appeared comparatively late in Roman legal history, namely only towards the end of the Republic.[16] Before that time, a loan was regarded as a matter of amicitia, falling, as it were, outside the sphere of law. Thus, only the general delictual remedies might have been available where the "borrower" exceeded what had been granted to him as a favour.[17] A contractual action enabling the lender to sue the borrower for the return of his object was first recognized by the praetor.[18] This was the actio commodati, and it was based on a formula in factum concepta:

> "Si paret A^m A^m N^o N^o rem qua de agitur commodasse eamque A^o A^o redditam non esse, quanti ea res erit, tantam pecuniam iudex N^m N^m A^o A^o condemnato, si non paret, absolvito."[19]

---

[6] *History*, vol. II, 170.

[7] Art. 1874 code civil; cf. also Pothier, *Traité du prêt à usage et du précaire*.

[8] N. 64.

[9] Cf. A.W.B. Simpson, "The Rise and Fall of the Legal Treatise: Legal Principles and the Forms of Legal Literature", (1981) 48 *The University of Chicago LR* 658 sqq.

[10] § 598 BGB.

[11] § 607 BGB.

[12] W. Ogris, "Darlehen", in: *HRG*, vol. I (1971), col. 662 sqq.

[13] Cf. further Schulz, *CRL*, pp. 508 sq.

[14] Pierluigi Zannini, *Spunti critici per una storia del commodatum* (1983), pp. 115 sqq.; Michel, *Gratuité*, n. 140.

[15] As Story, *Bailments*, § 285, puts it: "[Gratuitous loans have] furnished very little occasion for the interposition of judicial tribunals, for reasons equally honorable to the parties, and to the liberal spirit of polished society."

[16] Cf., for example, Carlo-Maria Tardivo, "Studi sul 'commodatum'", (1984) 204 *Archivio Giuridico* 225 sqq.; but see Zannini, op. cit., note 14, pp. 67 sqq., 138 sqq. and passim (according to whom the legis actio per condictionem was available).

[17] Kaser, *RPr* I, p. 533; cf. also Zannini, op. cit., note 14, pp. 127 sqq.

[18] Cf. Ulp. D. 13, 6, 1 pr.

[19] Lenel, *EP*, p. 252; for a detailed discussion, see Maschi, *Contratti reali*, pp. 150 sqq.; Tardivo, (1984) 204 *Archivio Giuridico* 234 sqq.

By the time the praetorian edict was codified, the lender could, instead, choose to proceed under a formula in ius concepta.[20] Whether the latter was a iudicium bonae fidei or not[21] cannot be established with certainty and remains a matter of speculation.[22] With its intentio incerta (". . . quidquid ob eam rem N^m N^m A^o A^o dare facere oportet")[23] it gave the judge a greater discretion in the process of adjudication, anyway. Under the formula in factum concepta, the defendant could only be condemned into "quanti ea res erit", that is, the objective value of the object and what had been obtained from it.[24]

Commodatum as the gratuitous transfer of a thing for use was different from fiducia cum amico contracta in that it did not involve the transfer of ownership; nor was it confined to res mancipi. In this respect it was similar to precarium.[25] In contrast to precarium, however, commodatum gave the borrower only detention of the thing and not interdictal possession. On the other hand, precarium did not give rise to a legal relationship; it was a mere factum, revocable at any time.[26] In commodatum the lender was bound to leave the thing with the borrower for whatever time the parties had agreed upon, otherwise until the object had been or could have been used in the way envisaged in the contract.[27] If the lender claimed his thing back prematurely, the borrower could defend the action successfully.[28] The precario tenens at first did not enjoy any protection against the owner; in late classical law, however, we find a tendency to institutionalize precarium as a kind of loan transaction "ad tempus".[29]

Commodatum was distinguished from hire (locatio conductio rei) by the fact that it was gratuitous.[30]

---

[20] Gai. IV, 47.

[21] This is essential for a variety of questions: whether pacta adiecta or a dolus in contrahendo could be taken into consideration, whether the exceptiones doli or pacti had to be raised or were inherent in the iudicium, etc.

[22] Cf. on the one hand Ernst Levy, "Zur Lehre von den sog. actiones arbitrariae", (1915) 36 *ZSS* 1 sqq. (formula did not contain ex bona fide clause), on the other hand, for example, Schulz, *CRL*, pp. 513 sq. The various arguments are discussed by Max Kaser, "Oportere und ius civile", (1966) 83 *ZSS* 30 sqq. But see, more recently, Maschi, *Contratti reali*, pp. 218 sqq., 231, offering a reconstruction of the formula in ius concepta with the ex bona fide clause; cf. also Tardivo, (1984) 204 *Archivio Giuridico* 240 sqq.

[23] Lenel, *EP*, p. 252.

[24] These strict and objective principles of estimation could sometimes be of advantage to the plaintiff; cf. Max Kaser, *Quanti ea res est* (1935), pp. 65 sqq.

[25] Cf. Ulp. D. 43, 26, 1 pr. and 3.

[26] Cf. e.g. Max Kaser, "Zur Geschichte des precarium", (1972) 89 *ZSS* 94 sqq.

[27] Even if it suddenly turned out that the lender needed the object himself? On this problem, see Glück, vol. 13, pp. 446 sq.

[28] Either by raising an exceptio doli (in the case of the formula in factum concepta and also under the formula in ius concepta, provided it did not contain the ex bona fide clause) or on account of the bona fide clause.

[29] For details and references cf. Kaser, (1972) 89 *ZSS* 100 sqq., 113 sqq.; contra: Pierpaolo Zamorani, *Precario habere* (1969).

[30] Cf. Ulp. D. 13, 6, 5, 12.

3. Gratis habitare

A difficult problem of delimitation cropped up where free habitation was granted.[31] Was this still commodatum or did it not rather have to be considered as a case of donation? According to Labeo and the Proculians, land could not be the object of commodatum.[32] This opinion, however, did not prevail: "sed ut apparet, proprie commodata res dicitur et quae soli est, idque et Cassius existimat."[33] On that basis Vivianus was able to answer the question "Si gratuitam tibi habitationem dedero, an commodati agere possim?", in the affirmative.[34] It is, however, not entirely clear whether gratis habitare was generally considered to fall under commodatum. Pomponius, for instance, applied the law of donation:

> "In aedibus alienis habitare gratis donatio videtur. id enim ipsum capere videtur qui habitat, quod mercedem pro habitatione non solvit. potest enim et citra corporis donationem valere donatio, velut si donationis causa cum debitore meo paciscar, ne ante certum tempus ab eo petam."[35]

This fragment refers to the lex Cincia de donis et muneribus, which limited gifts to a certain maximum amount.[36] It can be read to imply a straightforward classification of gratis habitare as donation.[37] It has been argued,[38] however, that Pomponius, while not disputing the classification of this transaction as commodatum, nevertheless applied certain rules relating to the law of donation by analogy—the analogy being based on a fictitious splitting-up of the transaction into a contract of hire and a remissio mercedis, a remission of the rent. The latter, obviously, implies a gift of money. The problem, incidentally, is still exercising lawyers' minds today. The German Federal Supreme Court has in recent times managed to perform a surprising double-volte. Contrary to previous decisions, it has described in two pronouncements of 1970 the granting of free habitation as a donation of possession and use.[39] In 1981 the court again changed its opinion; the transaction is now once more considered to constitute a loan for use.[40]

---

[31] For a detailed analysis, see Klaus Slapnicar, *Gratis habitare, Unentgeltliches Wohnen nach römischem und geltendem Recht* (1981), pp. 41 sqq.; cf. also Glück, vol. 13, pp. 450 sqq.

[32] Ulp. D. 13, 6, 1, 1.

[33] Ulp. D. 13, 6, 1, 1.

[34] Ulp. D. 19, 5, 17 pr. (". . . et Vivianus ait posse"). Cf. also Ulp. D. 13, 6, 1, 1 in fine: "Vivianus amplius etiam habitationem commodari posse ait."

[35] Pomp. D. 39, 5, 9 pr.

[36] Cf. infra pp. 482 sqq.

[37] Cf. also Pomp. D. 24, 1, 18, dealing with the prohibition of donation between spouses ("valet donatio").

[38] Slapnicar, op. cit., note 31, pp. 82 sqq., 185 sqq.

[39] BGH, 1970 *Neue Juristische Wochenschrift* 941; BGH 1970 Wertpapier-Mitteilungen 1247.

[40] BGHZ 82, 354 sqq.; for an evaluation of this decision from a historical point of view, see Klaus Slapnicar, "Unentgeltliches Wohnen nach geltendem Recht ist Leihe, nicht Schenkung—Dogmengeschichtliches zu BGHZ 82, 354", 1983 *Juristenzeitung* 325 sqq.

4. The liability of the borrower

(a) The diligentissimus paterfamilias

"Rei commodatae et possessionem et proprietatem retinemus: nemo enim commodando rem facit eius cui commodat."[41] The position of the borrower was weak. Ownership of the borrowed object did not pass to the borrower; nor did he become possessor. He was a mere detentor. Apart from that, he was subject to a very strict type of liability. As to the range of this liability, the Digest has this to say:

> "In rebus commodatis talis diligentia praestanda est, qualem quisque diligentissimus pater familias suis rebus adhibet, ita ut tantum eos casus non praestet, quibus resisti non possit, veluti mortes servorum quae sine dolo et culpa eius accidunt, latronum hostiumve incursus, piratarum insidias, naufragium, incendium, fugas servorum qui custodiri non solent."[42]

And then, again, following on from the discussion of mutuum:

> ". . . is vero qui utendum accepit, si maiore casu, cui humana infirmitas resistere non potest, veluti incendio ruina naufragio, rem quam accepit amiserit, securus est. alias tamen exactissimam diligentiam custodiendae rei praestare compellitur."[43]

Both texts, interestingly, enumerate a couple of catastrophes for which the borrower could *not* be held liable. However, they also try to define, positively, what is expected of the borrower. But the superlatives used in this context (diligentissimus paterfamilias, exactissima diligentia) are not easy to understand. For normal negligence, we would expect to find a reference to the diligens paterfamilias.[44] Can one be more diligent than diligent? The medieval lawyers evidently thought so and consequently came to distinguish various grades of negligence. As a counterpart to exactissima diligentia, the standard of culpa levissima was developed[45] and dominated the discussion about the liability in commodatum (and certain other contracts) down to the 19th century.[46] Or is the diligentissimus paterfamilias not a rather Utopian ideal, a paragon of circumspection endowed with the prophetic vision of the clairvoyant[47] and thus able to prevent incidents for which one cannot blame a normal human being? But why then introduce this awesome creature in an attempt to define in subjective terms what obviously seems to have been liability attributed according to objective criteria, that is, independent of a blameworthy state of mind of the borrower? The answer to this question lies in Justinian's tendency, originating in Greek philosophy and reinforced by the Christian religion, to make

[41] Pomp. D. 13, 6, 8 and Ulp. D. 13, 6, 9.

[42] Gai. D. 13, 6, 18 pr.

[43] Gai. D. 44, 7, 1, 4. On exactissima diligentia, see De Robertis, *Responsabilità contrattuale*, pp. 323 sqq.; Tardivo, (1984) 204 *Archivio Giuridico* 296 sqq.

[44] Cf. e.g. Paul. D. 10, 2, 25, 16; Paul. D. 19, 1, 54 pr.

[45] Cf. Accursius, gl. Diligentissimus ad D. 19, 2, 25, 7; Bartolus, D. 13, 6, 18 pr., § In rebus; cf. also e.g. Pothier, *Traité du prêt à usage et du precaire*, nn. 48 sqq.

[46] For details of the development, cf. Hoffmann, *Fahrlässigkeit*, passim.

[47] Cf. *Hawkins v. Coulsdon and Purley Urban District Council* [1954] 1 QB 319 at 341.

fault the central element of the law relating to liability.[48] As usual, he somehow tried to reconcile the old and the new, and thus he superimposed a subjectivizing terminology on the decisions of the classical lawyers.[49] They, in turn, had held the borrower liable not only where he had been at fault but also for certain typical accidents. This is known as custodia liability.[50] It was demarcated in a concrete and casuistical way and cannot therefore adequately be cast into an abstract formula.

(b) *The nature of custodia liability*

The essence of custodia liability has been succinctly summed up by Fritz Schulz:[51]

> "[The borrower] was absolutely liable for certain typical accidents which were regarded as avoidable by properly watching and guarding the borrowed thing, and on the other hand he was not liable for other typical accidents which were invariably regarded as not avoidable by the exercise of care."

If a borrowed horse was stolen by a third person or if it was killed or injured by one of the borrower's friends, the borrower was responsible to the lender irrespective of whether he had in actual fact looked after the horse as well as possible, i.e. whether he could have prevented the incident in this individual case or not. If, on the other hand, the horse was taken away, injured or slaughtered by invading enemies or a gang of robbers, the borrower was not liable. Accidents of the latter type (of which Gaius gives a list of examples in both D. 13, 6, 18 pr. and D. 44, 7, 1, 4)[52] are normally referred to as vis maior[53] (or, to use the English terminology, as acts of God).[54] Thus one can say that "liability for custodia implied a liability for lesser accidents (casus minor), i.e. . . . a liability for any loss not to be attributed to vis maior".[55] This has come to be the prevailing view amongst Romanists in the 20th century,[56] but

[48] On the (Justinianic) concept of diligentia and the yardstick of the diligens paterfamilias, see Wolfgang Kunkel, "Diligentia", (1925) 45 *ZSS* 266 sqq., 301 sqq.; Arangio-Ruiz, *Responsabilità contrattuale*, passim; De Robertis, *Responsabilità contrattuale*, passim, e.g. pp. 171 sqq.; Tafaro, *Regula*, pp. 218 sqq. Cf., in our context, *Inst.* III, 14, 2 ("exacta diligentia custodiendae rei").

[49] Both Gai. D. 13, 6, 18 pr. and Gai. D. 44, 7, 1, 4 are, in so far, interpolated. Cf. e.g. Kunkel, (1925) 45 *ZSS* 271 sq.; Arangio-Ruiz, *Responsabilità contrattuale*, pp. 66 sqq.

[50] Gai. III, 206; Ulp. D. 13, 6, 5, 5.

[51] *CRL*, p. 515.

[52] Cf. also *Inst.* III, 14, 2 and Ulp. D. 50, 17, 23.

[53] Theo Mayer-Maly, "Höhere Gewalt: Falltypen und Begriffsbildung", in: *Festschrift für Artur Steinwenter* (1958), pp. 58 sqq.; Giuseppe Ignazio Luzzatto, *Caso fuortuito e forza maggiore come limite alla responsabilità contrattuale*, vol. I (1938); Imre Molnár, "Die Ausgestaltung des Begriffes der vis maior im römischen Recht", (1981) 32 *Iura* 73 sqq.

[54] Or, to quote Heineccius, *Elementa Iuris Civilis*, Lib. III, Tit. XIV, § 784: "Casus est eventus a divina providentia profectus, cui resisti non potest."

[55] Schulz, *CRL*, p. 515.

[56] First put forward by J. Baron, "Die Haftung bis zur höheren Gewalt", (1892) 78 *Archiv für die civilistische Praxis* 203 sqq. and Emil Seckel, in: Heumann/Seckel, pp. 116 sqq. Cf. today e.g. Antonino Metro, *L'obbligazione di custodire nel diritto romano*, passim; Cannata, *Responsabilità contrattuale*; Kaser, *RPr* I, pp. 506 sqq.; Honsell/Mayer-Maly/Selb, pp. 233 sqq.

it has not remained unchallenged.[57] Custodia, in the sources, is not used as an unequivocal technical term of law. Thus, it has been argued that it expresses not a general category of liability but the content of an obligation. And, indeed,[58] "custodiam praestare" originally and primarily meant to furnish (and not to be liable for) custodia; it referred to the actual behaviour required of the person under the obligation, namely to keep the object safe. What he owed was in the first place the prevention of theft; in classical law, the content of his obligation was extended to cover certain cases of damage done to the object by third persons.[59] As a corollary, or spin-off, of this obligation, however, custodia came to be used also as a standard of liability: in case of breach of custodia (i.e. when a theft or some damaging event had occurred) the lender could bring the actio commodati, just as, for instance, the depositor could bring the actio depositi if the depository had acted fraudulently. Custodia therefore contained a guarantee to provide a certain result—namely to keep the object safe—which was tacitly implied in certain types of obligations (as, for instance, commodatum), but could also be expressly undertaken in others.[60] Yet, this guarantee (and consequently: liability for custodiam praestare) was not considered to be an absolute one; it was not taken beyond the limits of what could still be regarded, from an objective point of view, as humanly possible. Impossibilium nulla obligatio est:[61] nobody can promise what is impossible, namely to furnish a degree of custodia that will exclude damage by, say, an earthquake. These limitations of custodia, as has already been pointed out, came to be characterized as cases of vis maior,

The literature is virtually boundless ("[The subject is] snowed under with books and articles, with theories, comments, opinions and prejudices to such a degree, that hardly anybody ventures to undertake (a) reappraisal": Van den Bergh, infra, note 57, p. 59). There are three main problems that have triggered off this prolific production of legal literature on custodia: a terminological one (the ambiguous nature of the term custodia in classical law), a historical one (the difference between classical and Justinianic law) and a policy-oriented one (custodia, esp. in the 19th century, as one of the battle grounds for the basis of the law concerning liability: necessarily subjective, i.e. based on fault, or not?). For the traditional (pre-Baron and -Seckel) approach (custodia as a mere species diligentiae), see e.g. Hasse, *Culpa*, pp. 281 sqq. It is on this basis, incidentally, that custodia liability has not been incorporated into the BGB (with the exception of § 701 I 2; see infra, p. 521): "Motive", in: *Mugdan*, vol. II, p. 15.

[57] Cf. particularly Geoffrey MacCormack, "Custodia and Culpa", (1972) 89 *ZSS* 149 sqq. (e.g. p. 155: "A person required to show custodia is not normally liable for loss through theft or otherwise unless there has been fault on his part") and G.C.J.J. van den Bergh, "Custodiam praestare: custodia-Liability or Liability for failing custodia", (1975) 43 *TR* 59 sqq. (e.g. p. 71: "Custodia was . . . a liability for failure to guard properly over things one has in his keeping for reasons of profit"); idem, "Custodia and furtum pignoris", in: *Studi in onore di Cesare Sanfilippo*, vol. I (1982), pp. 601 sqq.; most recently, cf. René Robaye, *L'obligation de garde. Essai sur la responsabilité contractuelle en droit romain* (1988).

[58] As to the following, cf. especially Cannata, *Responsabilità contrattuale*, passim.

[59] Iul./Marcell. D. 19, 2, 41 as opposed to Iul. D. 13, 6, 19. On these texts, Cannata, *Responsabilità contrattuale*, pp. 61 sqq., 85 sqq.

[60] Cannata, *Responsabilità contrattuale*, pp. 102 sqq.; Kaser, *RPr* I, p. 507.

[61] Cels. D. 50, 17, 185. On philosophical implications of this maxim ("ought implies can"), see Joachim Hruschka, "Zwei Axiome des Rechtsdenkens", in: *Aus dem Hamburger Rechtsleben, Festschrift für Walter Reimers* (1979), pp. 459 sqq.

but were always conceived in a casuistic manner: they constituted a certain class of situations in which liability was excluded, because the fact that the guarantee had not been kept could typically not be attributed to the debtor. Custodia liability, therefore, did not presuppose fault.

This specific feature of classical Roman law should, I think, not be regarded as archaic or primitive.[62] Over the last hundred years we can observe a growing dissatisfaction with fault. Culpa as the essential cornerstone of our system of liabilities has come under attack, and the idea of allocating and demarcating spheres of risk according to objective criteria rather than necessarily basing liability on individual responsibility is a thoroughly modern one.[63] The "*Sphärentheorie*" in modern German labour law, established by the Supreme Court of the German Reich and further refined, after the Second World War, by the Federal Labour Court, is but one example.[64]

(c) The range of liability; instances of liability for vis maior

Of course, whoever was responsible for custodia was a fortiori liable for dolus and culpa too.[65] The borrower was not liable for any deterioration of the object arising from wear and tear through normal use; he was liable, however, for careless handling:

> "Eum, qui rem commodatam accepit, si in eam rem usus est in quam accepit, nihil praestare, si eam in nulla parte culpa sua deteriorem fecit, verum est: nam si culpa eius fecit deteriorem, tenebitur."[66]

Where the borrower, through his negligence, enabled a third party to steal or damage the object, he was obviously liable. His fault normally did not even matter (and thus did not have to be proved), as he was liable for custodia anyway. It did, however, become relevant where the borrower had used the thing contrary to the terms of the contract. The

[62] See, however, Schulz, *CRL*, p. 515.

[63] Cf. e.g. Walter Wilburg, *Die Elemente des Schadensrechtes* (1941), pp. 112 sqq., 124 sqq.

[64] RGZ 106, 272 sqq.; BAGE 3, 346 sqq. If an employee is unable to perform his services, the decision whether or not he can demand remuneration depends on whether this inability has its origin in the sphere of the employer (breakdown of electricity supply, unavailability of raw materials, fire, defects in the machinery, etc.) or of the employee (strike in his own or in other factories). Cf. for details Schaub, in: *Münchener Kommentar*, vol. III 1 (2nd ed., 1988), § 615, nn. 93 sqq.; for a most interesting historical analysis, see Eduard Picker, "Richterrecht oder Rechtsdogmatik—Alternativen der Rechtsgewinnung?—Teil 2", 1988 *Juristenzeitung* 62 sqq.

[65] Cf. e.g. Kaser, *RPr* I, p. 511; Joachim Rosenthal, "Custodia und Aktivlegitimation zur Actio furti", (1951) 68 *ZSS* 258 sqq.

[66] Ulp. D. 13, 6, 10 pr.; cf. also § 602 I BGB. What if during a fire the borrower saved his own property in preference to what he had borrowed? ". . . si incendio vel ruina aliquid contigit vel aliquid amnum fatale, non tenebitur, nisi forte, cum possit res commodatas salvas facere, suas praetulit" (Ulp. D. 13, 6, 5, 4). This case, "which is somewhat nice and curious" (Story, *Bailments*, § 245), has been interpreted in various ways, usually as indicating that to prefer one's own property in a dangerous situation amounts to negligence; cf. e.g. Voet, *Commentarius ad Pandectas*, Lib. XIII, Tit. VI, IV; Pothier, *Traité du prêt à usage et du précaire*, n. 56; Glück, vol. 13, pp. 438 sqq.; Story, *Bailments*, §§ 245 sqq.

contract of commodatum gave the borrower the right to use what was handed over to him for a specific purpose.[67] If he used it for purposes other than the one agreed upon, or if he went beyond what the parties had in actual fact envisaged, he did not only commit (in modern terminology) a breach of contract; the borrower, in these instances, unlawfully appropriated to himself a specific use of the object lent to him, and in Roman law such "stealing" of the use ("furtum usus") satisfied the requirements for the delict of theft.[68] Thus, for instance, a horse borrowed for the purpose of joy-riding must neither be taken further than the distance agreed upon nor be used as a battle horse.[69] If somebody has been given silver cutlery to be used for a dinner party, he must not take it on a sea voyage overseas.[70] If a slave has been lent to work as a fresco painter on the ground, the borrower must not put him on a scaffold and ask him to decorate the third storey of his house.[71] In all these instances, the unauthorized conversion of use had the consequence of increasing the borrower's liability, beyond custodia, so as to cover incidents of vis maior too.[72] If the horse was killed by the enemies, if the cutlery was taken by Silician corsairs, if the fresco painter on his scaffold was struck by lightning: in all these cases the borrower was now liable under the actio commodati, even though the incidents normally fell outside his responsibility for custodia. The borrower, in other words, had to carry the full periculum rei: whatever happened to the thing, subsequent to the furtum usus, was attributed to him. It is not entirely clear from the sources whether there had to be a specific (causal) connection between the wrongful act of the borrower and the occurrence of the vis maior; so that, for instance, the borrower would not have been liable if the horse that he took (but was not supposed to take) on a ride to Rome was injured by an earthquake, which would also have struck it had it been quietly grazing on the borrower's pasture.[73] Depending on the answer to this question, the

---

[67] Glück, vol. 13, pp. 430 sqq. Cf. also e.g. supra, note 1.

[68] Gai. III, 196. If the borrower believed that the lender would have approved of this deviation from the contract, he was not liable: "Qui re sibi commodata . . . usus est aliter atque accepit, si existimavit se non invito domino id facere, furti non tenetur" (Pomp. D. 47, 2, 77 pr.). Further on furtum and furtum usus, cf. infra, pp. 922 sqq.

[69] Cf. Pomp. D. 13, 6, 23; Ulp. D. 13, 6, 5, 7.

[70] Cf. Gai. D. 13, 6, 18 pr.; Gai. D. 44, 7, 1, 4.

[71] Cf. Ulp. D. 13, 6, 5, 7.

[72] Cf. e.g. Gai. D. 44, 7, 1, 4: "sed et in maioribus casibus, si culpa eius interveniat, tenetur"; Ulp. D. 13, 6, 5, 4: ". . . nisi aliqua culpa interveniat." Cf. also Lord Holt in *Coggs v. Bernard* (1703) 2 Ld Raym 909 at 915 (". . . as if a man should lend another a horse, to go westward . . .; if the bailee go northward . . ., if any accident happen to the horse in the northern journey, . . . the bailee will be chargeable; because he has made use of the horse contrary to the trust he was lent to him under, and it may be if the horse had been used no otherwise than he was lent, that accident would not have befallen him", quoting Bracton for this proposition); *Lilley v. Doubleday* [1881] 7 QB 510 at 511 (per Grove J); Jones, *Bailments*, pp. 67 sq.; Story, *Bailments*, §§ 232 sq., 241 sq.

[73] Cf. e.g. Windscheid/Kipp, § 375, n. 10 a, on the one hand, Van Leeuwen, *Censura Forensis*, Pars I, Lib. IV, Cap. V, 4 ("De casu fortuito commodatarius numquam tenetur.

borrower's liability was either based on culpa in these cases,[74] or on the idea that a wrong, once committed, taints all the consequences flowing therefrom: versanti in re illicita, omnia imputantur quae ex delicto sequuntur, to quote the famous adage of the medieval canon lawyers,[75] the origin of the notorious versari doctrine of modern criminal law.[76]

Except for these cases, where culpa aliqua interveniat, the borrower could be liable for vis maior on account of a special agreement to this effect. The parties to a contract were free to vary the standard of liability (". . . sed haec ita, nisi si quid nominatim convenit (vel plus vel minus) in singulis contractibus")[77] and thus the custodia liability of the borrower was by no means mandatory.[78] Just as, therefore, the borrower could undertake to be liable only for dolus, or for dolus and culpa,[79] so he could assume the full periculum rei ("*Versicherungshaftung*").[80] When and how far he had in actual fact done so, was often a matter of interpretation; one of the most interesting cases in this context (which has left its traces in some modern codes),[81] is the valued loan. Where goods have been estimated at a certain price, the borrower, according to Ulpian, must be considered as bound to restore either the objects lent or their value, no matter what has happened: ". . . omne periculum praestandum ab eo, qui aestimationem se praestaturum recepit."[82]

Nisi expresse ita convenerit, aut si culpa casui occasionem aut causam dederit") on the other. One could also think of restricting the liability of the borrower to cases where his wrongful act has increased the risk of this specific vis maior, e.g. if the silver plates, which the borrower was supposed to have used at home, had been lost in a shipwreck; not so if they had been struck by lightning (which could just as well have happened at home). For further examples, see Story, *Bailments*, §§ 241 sqq.

[74] Cf. Van Leeuwen, loc. cit.: "Sed hoc casu, non tamen propter casum, quam propter culpam tenetur."

[75] For details, see Horst Kollmann, "Die Lehre vom versari in re illicita im Rahmen des Corpus juris canonici", (1914) 35 *ZStW* 46 sqq.; H.L. Swanepoel, *Die leer van "versari in re illicita" in die strafreg* (1944). For a legislative realization of this doctrine, see art. 146 CCC.

[76] As far as modern private law is concerned, liability for accidental loss continues to be imposed on the borrower who exceeds his right of use, by art. 1881 code civil, art. 1805 II codice civile and many other modern codifications. The German BGB is silent on the point; hence the dispute in modern literature (cf. e.g. Kollhosser, in: *Münchener Kommentar*, vol. III 1 (2nd ed., 1988), §§ 602, 603, n. 3). For a discussion of the problem in modern law and its historical ramifications, see Andreas Wacke, "Gefahrerhöhung als Besitzverschulden", in: *Festschrift für Heinz Hübner* (1984), pp. 689 sqq.

[77] Ulp. D. 50, 17, 23.

[78] Cf. e.g. C. 4, 23, 1.

[79] Cf. Ulp. D. 13, 6, 5, 10.

[80] That is, he could insure the lender against accidental loss, even where it originated in an incident of vis maior. Cf. Paul Krückmann, "Versicherungshaftung im römischen Recht", (1943) 63 *ZSS* 1 sqq. Cf. also Story, *Bailments*, § 252.

[81] Cf. art. 1883 code civil and art. 2901 Louisiana Civil Code, discussed by Alan D. Ezkovitch, (1983–84) 58 *Tulane LR* 359 sqq.

[82] Ulp. D. 13, 6, 5, 3; cf. also Ulp. D. 19, 3, 1, 1 and Pothier, *Traité du prêt à usage et du précaire*, nn. 62 sqq.; Jones, *Bailments*, pp. 71 sq.; Glück, vol. 13, pp. 434 sqq.

(d) The principle of utility

If we attempt to determine why the borrower was (normally) liable to the strictest possible degree, we must look at who benefited from and therefore had a specific interest in the contract. The Roman lawyers, in determining the degree of diligence that the contractual partners could reasonably expect from each other, were guided by the principle of utility ("*Utilitätsgedanke*").[83] He who asks a favour has no right to expect very favourable treatment when it comes to determining the question of liability for loss or destruction; he, on the other hand, who accepts a burden, may reasonably presume that he will not be required to exercise the same amount of diligence as if he had received a benefit.[84] Fraudulent behaviour, however, can under no circumstances be condoned. Dolus, therefore, must be the minimum for which contractual partners are liable to each other in any event. In the case of commodatum, things are lent "oftenest to the borrower's use alone".[85] Hence his custodia liability:

> "Quae de fullone aut sarcinatore diximus, eadem transferemus et ad eum cui rem commodavimus. nam ut illi mercedem capiendo custodiam praestant, ita hic quoque utendi commodum percipiendo similiter necesse habet custodiam praestare."[86]

It follows from this that where, for once, the loan was made in the interest of the lender (as, for instance, where "a passionate lover of music were to lend his own instrument to a player in concert, merely to augment his pleasure")[87] the borrower's liability cannot be for custodia, but "[he] is holden only for the grossest faults":[88] for dolus, according to Roman law.[89] Ulpianus provides some further examples of lenders keen to boast with the wealth of their (future) wives or with the splendour of games which they were about to organize:

> "Interdum plane dolum solum in re commodata qui rogavit praestabit, ut puta si quis ita convenit: vel si sua dumtaxat causa commodavit, sponsae forte suae vel uxori, quo honestius culta ad se deduceretur, vel si quis ludos edens praetor scaenicis commodavit, vel ipsi praetori quis ultro commodavit."[90]

---

[83] Cf. esp. Bernhard Kübler, "Das Utilitätsprinzip als Grund der Abstufung bei der Vertragshaftung im klassischen römischen Recht", in: *Festgabe der Berliner juristischen Fakultät für Otto v. Giercke* (1910), vol. II, pp. 235 sqq.; Dietrich Nörr, "Die Entwicklung des Utilitätsgedankens im römischen Haftungsrecht", (1956) 73 *ZSS* 68 sqq.; Michel, *Gratuité*, pp. 325 sqq.; Hoffmann, *Fahrlässigkeit*, pp. 16 sqq.; Tafaro, *Regula*, pp. 123 sqq., 207 sqq.; for Justinian's time, see Afr. D. 30, 108, 12; Ulp. D. 50, 17, 23 (both spurious) and De Robertis, *Responsibilità contrattuale*, pp. 13 sqq. Cf. also *Coggs v. Bernard* (1703) 2 Ld Raym 909 at 915.

[84] Story, *Bailments*, § 17.

[85] Stair, *The Institutions of the Law of Scotland* (Edinburgh, 1832), I, 11, 9.

[86] Gai. III, 206.

[87] Jones, *Bailments*, p. 72.

[88] Stair, loc. cit.

[89] In later times usually for gross negligence also; cf. e.g. Voet, *Commentarius ad Pandectas*, Lib. XIII, Tit. VI, IV; "Motive", in: *Mugdan*, vol. II, p. 250 and D.J. Joubert, in: Joubert (ed.), *The Law of South Africa*, vol. 15 (1981), n. 281.

[90] Ulp. D. 13, 6, 5, 10.

The same considerations applied where an object was given to a person for examination:

> "Si rem inspectori dedi, an similis sit ei cui commodata res est, quaeritur. et si quidem mea causa dedi, dum volo pretium exquirere, dolum mihi tantum praestabit: si sui, et custodiam."[91]

What if the contract is in the interest of both the lender and the borrower? Here the extreme options of either imposing custodia or merely dolus liability on the borrower are both equally unsatisfactory. Hence, we find Gaius suggesting the via media of culpa liability:

> ". . . si utriusque [gratia commodata sit res], veluti si communem amicum ad cenam invitaverimus tuque eius rei curam suscepisses et ego tibi argentum commodaverim, scriptum quidem apud quosdam invenio, quasi dolum tantum praestare debeas: sed videndum est, ne et culpa praestanda sit. . . ."[92]

Or, as Story put it:

> "When the bailment is reciprocally beneficial to both parties, the law requires ordinary diligence on the part of the bailee, and makes him responsible for ordinary neglect."[93]

As far as commodatum is concerned, this very differentiated way of looking at the borrower's position has not been preserved everywhere; according to the BGB, for instance, the normal principle of § 276 I 1 ("A debtor is responsible . . . for wilful conduct and negligence") applies.[94] Generally speaking, though, it is quite true that the determination of contractual liability on the basis of considerations of utility, that is, according to the parties' balance of interest in the particular type of contract, is so "rational, just, and convenient",[95] that it has not only left its mark on continental jurisprudence[96] but underlies even the common law to such an extent that Story saw the legal systems as being "in perfect conformity"[97] on this matter.

---

[91] Ulp. D. 13, 6, 10, 1.

[92] Gai. D. 13, 6, 18 pr.; on this text cf. Nörr, (1956) 73 *ZSS* 82 sqq.

[93] *Bailments*, § 23; cf. also § 238 and Pothier, *Traité du prêt à usage et du précaire*, nn. 50 sq.; Jones, *Bailments*, p. 72.

[94] Reasons: on the one hand custodia liability was not incorporated into the BGB. On the other hand, those cases where the loan is in the interest of the lender alone are too rare to warrant special consideration; furthermore, it is doubtful, under those circumstances, whether the parties really intend to contract a commodatum.

[95] Story, *Bailments*, § 23.

[96] Cf., for example, Heineccius, *Elementa Iuris Civilis*, Lib. III, Tit. XIV, § 788: "In contractibus, in quibus penes unum commodum, penes alterum incommodum est, ille ordinarie culpam et levissimam; hic non nisi latam praestat. Ubi par utriusque contrahentis commodum atque incommodum est, culpa etiam levis ab utroque praestanda est. Qui sua sponte se contractui obtulit, vel obligationem suscepit, in qua personae industria summa requiritur, quamvis solum incommodum sustineat, tamen ad culpam levissimam tenetur. Qui alteri rem ultro obtulit, ex qua ei soli commodum obveniat, non nisi latae culpae praestationem exigere potest"; Vinnius, *Institutiones*, Lib. III, Tit. XV, n. 12 (sub "commodatum"); Pothier, *Traité des obligations*, n. 142. Cf. further Michel, *Gratuité*, pp. 355 sqq.

[97] *Bailments*, § 18.

(e) The actio furti of the borrower

In Roman law, if the borrower was normally liable for custodia, this had a very interesting consequence in cases where the borrowed object was stolen. Here, the law provided (inter alia) the actio furti, a penal action for either twofold or fourfold the value of the stolen object.[98] This action was, of course, usually available to the owner.[99] In the case of commodatum, however, the owner did not really have to bear the risk of theft, since the borrower was always liable to him. Whether the latter, in looking after the object, had been negligent or not, whether he had made the theft possible or could have prevented it, this was one of the typical incidents for which he was liable in any event. The lender therefore being well protected, it was actually the borrower who had an interest in the safety of the thing (". . . cuius interest rem salvam esse").[100] This is why the classical jurists were prepared, as long as he was solvent, to allow him (and anybody else who was liable for custodia) to sue the thief.[101] Thus it was the borrower and not the lender/owner who could avail himself of the actio furti.

5. The actio commodati contraria

(a) Commodatum as imperfectly bilateral contract

We have thus far been dealing with the duties of the borrower. It has also already been mentioned that, if he did not duly restore the thing after the termination of the loan, the lender could bring the actio commodati. In turn, the borrower might, under certain circumstances, have an action against the lender: the actio commodati contraria. The existence of this contrarium iudicium was a characteristic difference between commodatum and both stipulatio and mutuum, which were unilaterally binding contracts. However, it would not be quite correct to place commodatum unqualifiedly into the opposite category of bilateral contracts. The decisive point is that it was not *necessarily* unilateral; a counterclaim *could* exist if (and only if) the borrower had incurred expenses or suffered damages. Whereas the actio commodati (directa) was an essential and indispensable element, intrinsically inherent in this type of legal relationship ("principalis actio", as Paulus puts it),[102] the counterclaim was only incidental; it was available to the borrower, depending on whether or not its specific prerequisites had been met in each individual case.[103] Thus we can call commodatum an

[98] For details cf. infra, pp. 932 sqq.
[99] Paul. D. 47, 2, 47; Paul. D. 47, 2, 67, 1; Pap. D. 47, 2, 81, 1.
[100] Gai. III, 203.
[101] Gai. III, 205 sq.; Mod. Coll. X, II, 6.
[102] D. 13, 6, 17, 1.
[103] In classical law, the contrarium iudicium could be brought irrespective of whether the lender had sued the borrower with the actio directa. Originally, the borrower's claims could probably be taken into consideration only by way of compensatio or retentio, later also by

imperfectly bilateral contract;[104] the writers of the ius commune spoke of a contractus bilateralis inaequalis.[105]

(b) Reimbursement of expenses

What were these specific prerequisites for the actio commodati contraria?[106] On the one hand, the borrower could claim reimbursement of expenses that he had incurred in connection with the borrowed object: the costs involved in retrieving a borrowed slave who had run away, or in curing his rather less adventurous companion who had fallen ill.[107] However, it was only for such extraordinary incidents that an action could be brought. The ordinary expenses of the preservation of the thing lent had to be borne by the borrower, as a matter of course.[108] This applied, for instance in the case of the loan of an animal or of a slave, to the cost of fodder or food respectively.[109] After all, it was his contractual duty to preserve and look after the thing properly, and this of necessity involved some expenditure. Only if something had happened that lay beyond the boundaries of his obligation of custodiam praestare could he ask the lender/owner for reimbursement of his impensae necessariae.

On account of such impensae, incidentally, the borrower also had a ius retentionis which enabled him effectively to bar the lender's claim until he had been reimbursed.[110] If the lender tried to frustrate this right of retention[111] by simply taking back his object without further ado, the borrower could bring an actio furti against him—a remedy that was otherwise not available to the borrower against the lender:

> "[E]rgo si ob aliquas impensas, quas in rem commodatam fecisti, retentionem eius habueris, etiam cum ipso domino, si eam subripiat, habebis furti actionem, quia eo casu quasi pignoris loco ea res fuit."[112]

---

way of a counterclaim stricto sensu, i.e. only when the actio directa had already been instituted by the lender. For details, see Giuseppe Provera, *Contributi alla teoria dei iudicia contraria* (1951), pp. 20 sqq.; Fritz Schwarz, "Die Konträrklagen", (1954) 71 *ZSS* 189 sqq.

[104] Kaser, *RPr* I, p. 528.

[105] Cf. e.g. Glück, vol. 4, pp. 285 sqq.

[106] For details, see Provera, loc. cit., passim and Schwarz, (1954) 71 *ZSS* 111 sqq.; Pothier, *Traité du prêt à usage et du précaire*, nn. 81 sqq.; Story, *Bailments*, §§ 273 sqq.

[107] Gai. D. 13, 6, 18, 2: "Possunt iustae causae intervenire, ex quibus cum eo qui commodasset agi deberet: veluti de impensis in valetudinem servi factis quaeve post fugam requirendi reducendique eius causa factae essent . . ."; Mod. Coll. X, II, 5.

[108] Gai. D. 13, 6, 18, 2: ". . . nam cibariorum impensae naturali scilicet ratione ad eum pertinent, qui utendum accepisset"; Mod. Coll. X, II, 5 in fine. Reason: qui habet commoda ferre debet onera; cf. infra, pp. 290 sq.

[109] Cf. also Pothier, *Traité du prêt à usage et du précaire*, n. 81, Story, *Bailments*, § 256, and, today, § 601 BGB.

[110] Schwarz, (1954) 71 *ZSS* 127; Alfons Bürge, *Retentio in römischen Sachen- und Obligationenrecht* (1979), pp. 176 sqq.

[111] On the ius retentionis in general, see Kaser, *RPr* I, pp. 521 sq.; Bürge, loc. cit., passim.

[112] Paul. D. 47, 2, 15, 2. On this text cf. Rosenthal, (1951) 68 *ZSS* 251 sq.; Schwarz, (1954) 71 *ZSS* 124 sq.

(c) Recovery of damages

On the other hand, the actio commodati contraria could be used to claim damages. Well known is the following example given by Gaius: "Item qui sciens vasa vitiosa commodavit, si ibi infusum vinum vel oleum corruptum effusumve est, condemnandus eo nomine est."[113] The vessels that had been lent proved to be defective, so that the wine or oil contained in them was spoilt or spilt. Another case in point is Paul. D. 13, 6, 17, 3; this text concerns the loan of decayed timber which was to be used for propping up a block of flats.[114] It is to be noted that the lender was liable only if he had known about the defects in the article lent ("sciens"). As it was the borrower and not the lender who was interested in and gained the advantage from the contract, it would have been unreasonable to subject the latter to strict and extensive liabilities. The standard of diligence required of the lender thus stood in a relationship of inverse reciprocity to that of the borrower: entirely in accordance with the principle of utility. The scientia requirement is stressed in other texts too, for example in Paul. D. 13, 6, 22. Here a slave had been handed over by way of loan and had subsequently stolen something from the borrower. Of course, the owner of the slave was under noxal liability—he could either pay what was due under the actio furti or surrender the slave.[115] But did the borrower in addition have a contractual action against the lender? Only if the latter had known that this particular slave had long fingers.

Later centuries tended to extend the lender's responsibility to gross negligence,[116] but apart from that his position remains unchanged in modern law. This has given rise to one particular problem. Where the lender has deliberately handed over a defective object and thus caused damage, the borrower will normally not only have a contractual but also a delictual action. The delictual action, however (based on the lex Aquilia) is not confined to cases of dolus but also lies against the negligent lender. Thus it is clear that to admit a delictual remedy in these cases would seriously undermine the lender's privileged position and make any restriction on his contractual liability more or less meaningless. Thus one could argue that the contractual degree of diligence expected in this situation should be applied to the delictual action too. But then: is it really acceptable to assume generally that what is not forbidden by contract is permitted under the law of delict?

[113] Gai. D. 13, 6, 18, 3.

[114] For a discussion of these and further texts, see Schwarz, (1954) 71 *ZSS* 129 sqq.; cf. also Provera, op. cit., note 103, pp. 103 sqq.

[115] Cf infra, pp. 916 sq., 1118.

[116] Cf. e.g. Vinnius, *Institutiones*, Lib. III, Tit. XV, 11 (sub "commodatum"); Pothier, *Traité du prêt à usage et du précaire*, nn. 80, 84; cf. also § 599 BGB ("The lender is responsible only for wilful conduct and gross negligence"). But see § 600: "If the lender *fraudulently* conceals a defect in title or in quality in the thing lent, he is bound to compensate the borrower for any damage arising therefrom." Cf. further the "melancholy case" (Erle CJ) of *Blakemore v. Bristol and Exeter Railway Co.* (1858) 8 El & Bl 1035 (obiter).

The law of delict sanctions general duties of behaviour which have to be observed, irrespective of whether a special (contractual) relationship exists in an individual case. Which of these two views the Roman lawyers took cannot be determined from the sources.[117] The authors of the ius commune were divided on this point.[118] Modern German lawyers tend to adopt the former approach and argue that the subjective requirements of § 823 I BGB must be modified by the standard set in § 599.[119]

Finally, it must be pointed out that the borrower could not only claim under the actio commodati contraria where the damage had been caused by the defective object of the loan. A case in point is Afr. D.13, 6, 21 pr.:

> "Rem mihi commodasti: eandem subripuisti: deinde cum commodati ageres nec a te scirem esse subreptam, iudex me condemnavit et solvi: postea comperi a te esse subreptam: quaesitum est, quae mihi tecum actio sit."

As we have seen, the actio furti was not available to the borrower. However, the lender was liable under the actio commodati contraria. ". . . adiuvari quippe nos, non decipi beneficio oportet," as Paulus put it;[120] when we lend we ought to confer a benefit and not to do a mischief, and this reasoning underlies all other cases in which the borrower was allowed to claim damages too.[121]

6. Loan for use today

Throughout the centuries, the law relating to commodatum has seen little change. Certain marginal adjustments have been made: according to the German code, for instance, the lender is as a rule responsible not only for wilful conduct but also for gross negligence; the borrower is liable for dolus and culpa only (custodia having been transformed into and superseded by culpa liability already in post-classical Roman law); and the handing over of the object is now regarded as involving transfer of (direct) possession to the borrower.[122] By and large, though, Paulus or Gaius would find their way through the modern law of commodatum with ease. This applies not only to the European continental systems and South African law, but even to the English common law.

---

[117] For a review of the relevant texts, see Norman S. Marsh, "The Liability of the Gratuitous Transferor: A Comparative Study", (1950) 66 *LQR* 51 sqq.

[118] Cf. e.g. Glück, vol. 10, pp. 310 sqq.; Vangerow, *Pandekten*, § 681, Anm. 3, n. II; Windscheid/Kipp, § 455, n. 12.

[119] Cf. e.g. BGH, 1974 *Neue Juristische Wochenschrift* 234 (235); Kollhosser, op. cit., note 76, § 599, n. 4. For a full analysis of this and similar problems arising from the concurrence of delictual and contractual liability, see Peter Schlechtriem, *Vertragsordnung und ausservertragliche Haftung* (1972), pp. 27 sqq. Cf. also infra, pp. 904 sqq.

[120] D. 13, 6, 17, 3.

[121] Especially in cases of an "importune repetere" of the object lent. Cf. e.g. Paul. D. 13, 6, 17, 3 (". . . si ad fulciendam insulam tigna commodasti, deinde protraxisti . . ."). For a discussion of this and further cases, see Schwarz, (1954) 71 *ZSS* 157 sqq.

[122] This is different in South African law, where the borrower is still regarded as detentor.

In medieval English law—which had "but a meagre stock of words that can be used to describe dealings with movable goods"[123]—a host of legal relationships were lumped together under the title of bailment.[124] This term is derived from the French *bailler*, "to deliver"; originally it even covered cases where the transferor (bailor) was parting with ownership. In more modern times, however, it has been restricted to the "delivery of goods on a condition, expressed or implied, that they shall be restored by the bailee to the bailor",[125] that is, to the temporary transfer of possession of a chattel which must ultimately be returned. Even in this limited form, therefore, it ranges from hire to mandate, from deposit to pledge, and it also includes gratuitous loans. To this day, bailment is a somewhat labyrinthine concept. It appears at various disjointed places in textbooks on personal property, torts and contracts. Bailment is often, or even generally, a contract, but it may also be independent of a contract. If it is a contract, how can the gratuitous bailment be reconciled with the doctrine of consideration? Various attempts to do so are puzzling and rather unconvincing.[126] Does bailment therefore have to be regarded as a relationship sui generis?[127] We cannot pursue these questions. To a certain extent, however, the law of bailment has been set, since the great and celebrated case of *Coggs v. Bernard* (decided in 1703),[128] "upon a much more rational footing".[129] In an elaborate judgment, Sir John Holt isolated and distinguished six sorts of bailment and determined the liability of the bailee according to his benefit derived from the individual type of transaction.[130] This analysis is squarely based on Roman law;[131] it is through *Coggs v. Bernard* (and the subsequent

[123] Pollock and Maitland, vol. II, p. 169.

[124] Cf. Pollock and Maitland, vol. II, pp. 169 sqq.

[125] Jones, *Bailments*, p. 1; cf. also Blackstone, vol. II, p. 452 ("a delivery of goods in trust, upon a contract expressed or implied, that the trust shall be faithfully executed on the part of the bailee").

[126] This is how Lord Holt (*Coggs v. Bernard* (1703) 2 Ld Raym 909 at 919) argued: "But secondly it is objected, that there is no consideration to ground this promise upon, and therefore the undertaking is but nudum pactum. But to this I answer, that the owner's trusting him with the goods is a sufficient consideration to oblige him to a careful management." But the borrower has not given his promise because the lender was parting with his goods; the delivery cannot be regarded as the "price" for the promise. Cf. Atiyah, *Rise and Fall*, pp. 177, 186 sq., who tries to expose the fallacy of reading the decision ahistorically in the light of modern doctrine.

[127] Cf. M.P. Furmston, in: Cheshire, Fifoot and Furmston, *Law of Contract* (11th ed. 1986), p. 83.

[128] (1703) 2 Ld Raym 909.

[129] Blackstone, vol. II, p. 453.

[130] (1703) 2 Ld Raym 909 at 912 sqq. On the influence of civilian jurisprudence on Sir John Holt, see Daniel R. Coquillette, *The Civilian Writers of Doctors' Commons* (London, 1988), pp. 271 sqq.

[131] And Bracton, who has in turn drawn from Roman law.

elegant and comprehensive treatises of Jones and Story,[132] building on this cornerstone) that (the Roman) commodatum, depositum and pignus entered into English law.

II. DEPOSITUM

1. The nature of depositum; depositum miserabile

Depositum was similar to commodatum in many ways. It was a contract re,[133] it was a gratuitous transaction and, like the commodatary, the depositary did not have the possessory interdicts, but was a mere detentor.[134] The most significant difference, however, was that the object was handed over not to be used but to be kept in safe custody.[135] If a depositary used what had been given to him, he committed furtum usus and was liable to the depositor under the penal actio furti.[136] It is clear, therefore, that the balance of benefit and interest in depositum was entirely different from that in commodatum: it was only the bailor and not the bailee who could normally have an interest in and derive an advantage from this type of transaction.[137] This was bound to find its reflection in the standard of diligence that could be expected from the bailee. It would not have been reasonable to impose custodia liability on an altruistic holder such as the depositary, who kept the object not for his own but for the depositor's benefit. In fact, his liability was restricted to dolus and that, of course, could easily be (and actually was) rationalized on the basis of utility considerations: ". . . nam quia nulla utilitas eius versatur apud quem deponitur, merito dolus praestatur solus."[138] A further consequence flowed from this: if the deposited object was stolen, the depositor had to bring the actio furti against the thief.[139] Unlike the commodatary, the depositary was not eligible to do so: seeing that he was not liable towards the owner for this incident, and in this sense did not have a specific interest in the

---

[132] Cf. further Winfield, *Province*, pp. 92 sqq. Story and especially Jones, however, do not find much favour with modern common-law writers such as Tyler and Palmer, *Crossley Vaines on Personal Property* (5th ed., 1973), pp. 70, 86.

[133] Gai. D. 44, 7, 1, 5. A mere pactum de deponendo (unlike today) was unenforceable.

[134] Flor. D. 16, 3, 17, 1.

[135] Ulp. D. 16, 3, 1 pr.: "Depositum est, quod custodiendum alicui datum est." Ulpian carries on to provide an etymological explanation: "dictum ex eo quod ponitur: praepositio enim 'de' auget positum . . ."; but cf. also Paul. Sent. II, XII, 2 ("depositum est quasi diu positum") and Giuseppe Gandolfi, *Il deposito nella problematica della giurisprudenza romana* (1971), pp. 107 sqq.

[136] Cf. Gai. III, 196; Inst. IV, 1, 6.

[137] Vinnius, *Institutiones*, Lib. III, Tit. XV (sub de deposito), 2: ". . . totum hoc negotium ex utilitate deponentis aestimetur"; 3: "In deposito nullum commodum est depositarii."

[138] Ulp. D. 13, 6, 5, 2; cf. also Ulp. D. 50, 17, 23 and Tafaro, *Regula*, pp. 242 sqq., 259 sqq.

[139] Gai. III, 207: "Sed is apud quem res deposita est custodiam non praestat, tantumque in eo obnoxius est, si quid ipse dolo malo fecerit. qua de causa si res ei subrepta fuerit, quia restituendae eius nomine depositi non tenetur nec ob id eius interest rem salvam esse, furti agere non potest, sed ea actio domino competit"; Mod. Coll. X, II, 6.

safety of the thing (custodia), the situation did not require a deviation from the normal rule, namely that it is up to the owner to sue for theft.

As in the case of commodatum, we find an actio directa (the actio depositi)[140] of which the bailor could avail himself if the bailee did not duly return the thing deposited,[141] and also a contrarium iudicium (the actio depositi contraria) which the bailee could bring for reimbursement of expenses and compensation for damages.[142] Again, of course, the latter action lay only where expenses had been incurred or damages caused; like commodatum, depositum was an imperfectly bilateral contract with the obligation of the depositary being the principal while that of the depositor was merely incidental. Unlike the lender in commodatum, the depositor must have been strictly liable to the depositary for damage caused by the object deposited; after all, it was he who benefited from the latter's kindness.[143]

Like the actio commodati, the (contractual) remedy of the depositor had its historical origin in delict;[144] even before the formula in factum

---

[140] Again, there was a praetorian action with a formula in factum concepta (". . . [rem] dolo malo N^i N^i A^o A^o redditam non esse", introduced in the days of the early Republic) to which a formula in ius concepta (". . . quidquid ob eam rem N^{um} N^{um} A^o A^o dare facere oportet ex fide bona") was later added. Cf. Gai. IV, 47 for the full formulae. For a discussion of both formulae cf. e.g. Gandolfi, op. cit., note 135, pp. 69 sqq.; on the characteristic features of the actio in factum, see, however, more recently, Robin Evans-Jones, "The penal characteristics of the 'actio depositi in factum'", (1986) 52 *SDHI* 105 sqq.

[141] The depositor could claim his object back at any time, even if he had originally deposited it for a specific time. Cf. e.g. Ulp. D. 16, 3, 1, 46: "Proinde et si sic deposuero, ut post mortem meam reddatur, potero et ego et heres meus agere depositi, *ego mutata voluntate*", and Glück, vol. 15, pp. 188 sqq. (Could the depositary hand back the deposit at any time and thus terminate the—for him often burdensome—contractual relationship? On this question, see Wieslaw Litewski, *Studien zur Verwahrung im römischen Recht* (1978), pp. 31 sqq.) If the depositary did not hand the thing back at the depositor's request, he normally acted in bad faith. Cf., however, Marcellus (Ulp. D. 16, 3, 1, 22), who rhetorically asks: ". . . quid enim si in provincia res sit vel in horreis, quorum aperiendorum condemnationis tempore non sit facultas?" Answer: "[N]on semper videri posse dolo facere eum, qui reposcenti non reddat." The actio in ius, of course, was available for the recovery of id quod interest (i.e. the actual damage suffered by the plaintiff). As far as the measure of damages in the actio in factum was concerned, cf. the discussion by Robin Evans-Jones, "The Measure of Damages in the actio depositi in factum", (1987) 55 *TR* 267 sqq. He argues that, in spite of the "quanti ea res erit" clause, condemnation was not confined to vera aestimatio rei but involved his id quod interest. This was advantageous for the plaintiff, where the action was brought because the deposit had not been returned at all, for the plaintiff could claim certain categories of consequential loss over and above the value of the object. Where the property was, however, returned in a deteriorated state (for this extension of the ambit of the actio, see e.g. Ulp. D. 16, 3, 1, 16: "Si res deposita deterior reddatur, quasi non reddita agi depositi potest: cum enim deterior redditur, potest dici dolo malo redditam non esse"), the plaintiff's loss was usually less than the full value of the object.

[142] Mod. D. 16, 3, 23; Schwarz, "Die Konträrklagen", (1954) 71 *ZSS* § 121; Story, *Bailments*, § 121; Windscheid/Kipp, § 378, 2.

[143] Cf. today § 694 BGB: "The depositor shall compensate the depositary for any damage caused by the nature of the thing deposited, unless at the time of the deposit he neither knew nor should have known of the dangerous nature of the thing . . ." (reversal of onus of proof!).

[144] According to the prevailing opinion, the (earlier) actio depositi in factum was a penal remedy, whereas the (later) actio in ius concepta performed a purely reipersecutory function;

concepta had been developed by the praetors, the XII Tables had granted a penal action for duplum in case of embezzlement.[145] Once, of course, the actio depositi had been introduced, it normally lay for simplum. One case always remained, though, where double the value of the object deposited was owed, and that was where the deposit had to be made suddenly and in a situation of emergency: tumultus, incendii, ruinae or naufragii causa.[146] Here the depositor did not have the time to approach a friend or to select a trustworthy person with whom to deposit the property and was more or less forced into this transaction. The Roman lawyers apparently regarded it as particularly perfidious if the depositary tried to take advantage of the depositor's predicament in such a situation. Even under normal circumstances, however, they looked at the depositary's breach of trust with such disgust[147] that he was taken to be famosus. Condemnation under the actio depositi, in other words, involved infamia,[148] that is, a diminution of the estimation of a person among his fellow citizens and also certain legal disabilities—for instance, concerning the right to hold public office.[149] The actio depositi was one of a number of actiones famosae based on contractual relationships to which the idea of honest behaviour was so fundamental that any violation was regarded as a particularly offensive breach of confidence. The institution of infamia (iuris) has lost its place in modern private law, but lives on as an ancillary penalty in criminal law.[150] The iudicium in duplum in case of the above-mentioned necessary deposit (which came to be called depositum miserabile) was also not received in France and Holland.[151] In Germany it survived until the 19th century,[152] but was

---

the history of depositum is therefore seen, essentially, as a development from delict to contract. This view has recently been challenged by Evans-Jones, (1986) 52 *SDHI* 105 sqq., tying in with the ideas developed by Geoffrey MacCormack, "Gift, Debt, Obligation and the Real Contracts", (1985) 31 *Labeo* 131 sqq.

[145] Tab. 8, 19; cf. Paul. Coll. X, VII, 11; von Lübtow, *Condictio*, pp. 91 sq.; Watson, *Evolution*, pp. 10 sqq.; MacCormack, (1985) 31 *Labeo* 145 sq.; Robin Evans-Jones, "The Action of the XII Tables 'ex causa depositi'", (1988) 34 *Labeo* 188 sqq.

[146] Ulp. D. 16, 3, 1, 1.

[147] Cf. e.g. Seneca, *De beneficiis*, Lib. IV, X, 1: "Depositum reddere, per se expetenda est." Cf. also Plinius, *Epistulae*, Lib. X, 97, 7, praising the Christians of his time in the following way: ". . . se sacramento non in scelus aliquod obstringere, sed ne furta, ne latrocinium, ne adulteria committerent, ne fidem fallerent, *ne depositum appellati abnegarent*."

[148] Gai. IV, 182; Iul. D. 3, 2, 1.

[149] On infamia in general, see Kaser, *RPr* I, pp. 274 sq.; idem, "Infamie und ignominia in den römischen Rechtsquellen", (1956) 73 *ZSS* 220 sqq.; Peter Garnsey, *Social Status and Legal Privilege in the Roman Empire* (1970), pp. 185 sqq.

[150] Cf. Savigny, *System*, vol. II, § 83; Windscheid/Kipp, § 56 and, today, for instance §§ 45 sqq. StGB.

[151] Cf. Pothier, *Traité du contrat de dépôt*, n. 76; Groenewegen, *De legibus abrogatis*, Digest. Lib. XVI, Tit. III, l. 1.

[152] Cf. Stryk, *Usus modernus pandectarum*, Lib. XVI, Tit. III, § 1; Windscheid/Kipp, § 378, 1 (in fine); §§ 43, 58 I 14 PrALR.

not taken over into the BGB.[153] Penal elements are alien to modern private law.

2. The liability of the depositary

(a) Dolus, culpa lata (and exceptions)

It has been said above that the depositary was liable only for dolus. This statement still needs some qualification. The formula in ius concepta with its "ex bona fide" clause was flexible enough to accommodate special contractual arrangements by the parties. Thus, depositor and depositary were free to agree to make the latter responsible for culpa or even custodia.[154] The liability of the depositary was increased *ex lege*, where the depositum was in his own interest. Such cases are rare, yet we find an example in the Digest:

> "Si quis nec causam nec propositum faenerandi habuerit et tu empturus praedia desideraveris mutuam pecuniam nec volueris creditae nomine antequam emisses suscipere atque ita creditor, quia necessitatem forte proficiscendi habebat, deposuerit apud te hanc eandem pecuniam, ut, si emisses, crediti nomine obligatus esses, hoc depositum periculo est eius qui suscepit."[155]

Here the only reason why the friend deposited his money before embarking on his voyage was to enable the depositary to pay the purchase price for a tract of land, when required to do so. Closely related was another situation.

> "[S]ed et si se quis deposito obtulit, idem Iulianus scribit periculo se depositi illigasse, ita tamen, ut non solum dolum, sed etiam culpam et custodiam praestet, non tamen casus fortuitos."[156]

Why the depositary was so keen to have the object for safekeeping we do not know; but the fact that he spontaneously and officiously urged the depositor to give it to him was enough to render him liable for custodia. But for such importunity on the part of the depositary, it has been argued, the depositor might well have chosen "a person of more approved vigilance".[157] This argument is not necessarily convincing, as the depositary's offer may just as well have been the result not of self-interest but "of strong affection, and a desire to oblige, and often a sense of duty, especially in cases of imminent peril or sudden

---

[153] The French code civil (artt. 1924, 1950) still grants a special privilege to depositaries in case of deposita miserabilia: oral proof by witnesses is admitted, whatever the value of the deposited objects; otherwise contracts involving a value of 5 000 Francs or more can be proved only by formal documents. On the depositum miserabile in general, see Voet, *Commentarius ad Pandectas*, Lib. XVI, Tit. III, XI; Pothier, *Traité du contrat de dépôt*, nn. 75 sq.; Glück, vol. 15, pp. 208 sqq; Story, *Bailments*, § 44; and, most recently, Wieslaw Litewski, "Studien zum sogenannten 'depositum necessarium'", (1977) 43 *SDHI* 188 sqq.

[154] Cf. Ulp. D. 16, 3, 1, 6; Ulp. D. 13, 6, 5, 2; C. 4, 34, 1 (Alex.): ". . . si non aliud specialiter convenit . . ."); Erich Sachers, "Die Verschuldenshaftung des Depositars", in: *Festschrift für Paul Koschaker*, vol. II (1939), pp. 100 sqq.

[155] Ulp. D. 12, 1, 4 pr. Cf. Pothier, *Traité du contrat de dépôt*, n. 32; Glück, pp. 179 sqq.; Jones, *Bailments*, p. 49.

[156] Ulp. D. 16, 3, 1, 35. Cf. further Glück, vol. 15, p. 177; Pothier, *Traité du contrat de dépôt*, n. 30.

[157] Jones, *Bailments*, p. 47; cf. also Domat, *Les loix civiles*, Lib. I, Tit. VII, Sec. III, VIII.

emergency".[158] Nevertheless, reminiscences of Iul. D. 16, 3, 1, 35 can still be found in both the French[159] and the Louisiana Civil Code[160]—not, however, in modern German law.

Then there was one case where the depositary was even liable for vis maior: if he used the object that had been deposited with him and thus committed furtum usus, he could not expect any sympathy and had to bear the consequences, no matter what happened.[161]

Most importantly, though, "quidquid ob eam rem N^{um} N^{um} A^{o} A^{o} dare facere oportet ex fide bona" was probably, already in classical times, taken to apply to cases where the depositary had not been guilty of intentional breach of contract, but where he had blatantly disregarded the most obvious and elementary standards of good and diligent behaviour; in other words, where his lack of care had been such as to be inconsistent with good faith and honest intention. The depositary's liability was thus extended to cases of culpa lata[162] (gross negligence), at first merely under the formula in ius concepta.[163] It was only in post-classical times, however, that this type of liability was conceptualized and generally placed on a par with dolus: "[M]agnam tamen neglegentiam placuit in doli crimine cadere",[164] as Justinian interpolated Gaius' discussion of the actio depositi, "dissoluta enim neglegentia prope dolum est",[165] or "lata culpa plane dolo comparabitur"[166] as we read at other places.[167] Thus, the rule in Justinian's time seems to have been: ". . . qui depositum accepit . . . dolum solum et latam culpam, si non aliud specialiter convenit,

[158] Story, *Bailments*, § 82.

[159] Artt. 1927, 1928.

[160] Artt. 2908, 2909.

[161] Cf. De Robertis, *Responsabilità contrattuale*, p. 396; Glück, vol. 15, p. 178. The same applied, of course, if the depositary had sold the object: "Si rem depositam vendidisti eamque postea redemisti in causam depositi, etiamsi sine dolo malo postea perierit, teneri te depositi, quia semel dolo fecisti, cum venderes" (Ulp. D. 16, 3, 1, 25). Again, the idea of versari in re illicita; cf. supra, p. 197.

[162] For a Roman definition, see Ulp. D. 50, 16, 213, 2 ("Lata culpa est nimia neglegentia, id est non intellegere quod omnes intellegunt").

[163] Kaser, *RPr* I, p. 535, n. 10; Buckland/Stein, p. 468. Dolus did not yet have a fixed, technical meaning (evil intention), but was merely the opposite of bona fides. Under the bonae fidei iudicia, the judge was instructed to condemn, if the defendant's behaviour had infringed the standards of good faith. Such a breach of good faith was called dolus malus. In the course of time, a more and more refined interpretation and application of the precepts of good faith and honest behaviour was bound to lead to an extension of the debtor's liability to cases of (as we would describe it) negligent behaviour. To a large extent, this development was, however, impeded by the fact that quite a few bonae fidei iudicia were actiones famosae. The Romans were highly sensitive in questions of honour and social reputation, and thus the sanction of infamia was not to be imposed too lightly.

[164] D. 44, 7, 1, 5.

[165] Ulp. D. 17, 1, 29 pr.

[166] Ulp. D. 11, 6, 1, 1.

[167] Cf. further De Robertis, *Responsabilità contrattuale*, pp. 58 sq.; Arangio-Ruiz, *Responsabilità contrattuale*, pp. 251 sqq.; Hoffmann, *Fahrlässigkeit*, pp. 4 sqq.; Geoffrey MacCormack, "Culpa", in: (1972) 38 *SDHI* 176 sqq.; Cannata, *Responsabilità contrattuale*, pp. 5 sq.

praestare debuit."[168] We still find this rule in some of the codifications of the 19th century.[169]

(b) Diligentia quam in suis

Usually, however, another standard of liability was advocated in the literature and laid down in the codes. § 690 BGB is an example: ". . . the depositary shall be responsible only for such care as he is accustomed to exercise in his own affairs."[170] Here, liability is not determined according to the abstract standard of the diligens paterfamilias, but according to a concrete, subjective criterion (hence, in non-Roman parlance, culpa in concreto): the diligence expected of the debtor is diligentia quam suis rebus adhibere solet. This type of liability (and with it the distinction between diligentia diligentis and diligentia quam in suis) was largely developed in post-classical Roman law, but it was not entirely without classical antecedents.[171] As far as depositum is concerned, we have to go back to a very interesting but much disputed text by Celsus:

> "Quod Nerva diceret latiorem culpam dolum esse, Proculo displicebat, mihi verissimum videtur. nam et si quis non ad eum modum quem hominum natura desiderat diligens est, nisi tamen ad suum modum curam in deposito praestat, fraude non caret: nec enim salva fide minorem is quam suis rebus diligentiam praestabit."[172]

We are dealing here with a controversy among the classical lawyers (more precisely, in fact, between members of one and the same—the Proculian—school). Liability of the depositary was originally restricted, as we have seen, to dolus. Nerva advocated extension to what he called culpa latior; we would say cases of gross negligence. This, according to Proculus, was going too far: where the depositary is a very careless person generally, one cannot regard it as breach of good faith (= dolus) if he also handles the depositor's property carelessly. Celsus, however, sided with Nerva and introduced what one might call the

---

[168] C. 4, 34, 1 (Alex.); but cf. also Paul. Coll. X, VII, 6. Cf. further De Robertis, *Responsabilità contrattuale*, pp. 373 sqq.; Maschi, *Contratti reali*, pp. 376 sqq.; Francesco Sitzia, "Sulla responsabilità del depositario in diritto bizantino", (1971) 13 *BIDR* 189 sqq.; Vinnius, *Institutiones*, Lib. III, Tit. XV (sub de deposito), 3 ("Qui autem dolum dicit, latam culpam non excludit"); Glück, vol. 15, pp. 171 sqq.; Arndts, *Pandekten*, § 285; Brinz, *Pandekten*, § 137, 2.

[169] Cf. e.g. §§ 1266 Sächs. BGB; for South African law, see Bester, in: Joubert (ed.), *The Law of South Africa*, vol. 8 (1979), n. 74.

[170] Cf. further, for example, § 11 I 14 PrALR; art. 1927 code civil; Herbert Hausmaninger, "Rechtsvergleichende Notizen zur diligentia quam in suis", in: *Festchrift für Hermann Baltl* (1978), pp. 283 sqq.

[171] Cf. Bernhard Kübler, "Die Haftung für Verschulden bei kontraktsähnlichen und deliktsähnlichen Schuldverhältnissen", (1918) 39 *ZSS* 179 sqq.; Arangio-Ruiz, *Responsabilità contrattuale*, pp. 257 sqq.; De Robertis, *Responsabilità contrattuale*, pp. 65 sqq.; Herbert Hausmaninger, "Diligentia quam in suis", in: *Festschrift für Max Kaser* (1976), pp. 265 sqq.

[172] D. 16, 3, 32. On this text, see especially Walter Selb, "Das Problem des relativen 'dolus' in D. 16, 3, 32", in: *Synteleia Vincenzo Arangio-Ruiz*, vol. II (1964), pp. 1173 sqq.; Hausmaninger, *Festschrift Kaser*, pp. 267 sqq., and the authors quoted in the previous note.

concept of relative dolus:[173] a careless person, too, acts in breach of good faith (= dolo malo), if he is more careless with regard to the depositor's property than with regard to his own.

Gaius—about one generation later—did not adopt this idea, but expressly excluded liability for culpa. For this he advanced an interesting reason: ". . . qui negligenti amico rem custodiendam committit," he said, "de se queri debet".[174] If you deposit your property with a friend, you have to take him as he is. If he is a careless person and duly loses your property, you must blame yourself for having trusted so improvident a person. You should have made your choice more prudently. Gaius used this argument to justify the depositary's dolus liability ("negligentiae vero nomine ideo non tenetur, quia . . ."). It is obvious, however, that the same thought can have an entirely different twist: taking the concept of culpa in abstracto as background and alternative (as it had come to be developed by the time of Justinian), it usually has the effect of restricting (rather than extending) the debtor's liability; and indeed, if we look into Justinian's Institutes, we find, for instance, the following reflections concerning the liability of one partner (socius) as against the others:

> ". . . praevaluit tamen, etiam culpae nomine teneri eum, culpa autem non ad exactissimam diligentiam dirigenda est: sufficit enim talem diligentiam in communibus rebus adhibere socium, qualem suis rebus adhibere solet. nam qui parum diligentem socium sibi adsumit, de se queri (hoc est sibi imputare) debet."[175]

This is Gaius' argument, revived under different auspices.

(c) The development of diligentia quam in suis

It is very difficult, if not impossible, to extricate the historical development of the distinction between negligence in abstracto (or diligentia diligentis, determined according to the standard of the diligens paterfamilias) and negligence in concreto (or diligentia quam in suis, determined from the point of view of the individual debtor) from thick layers of real or supposed interpolations and scholarly dispute surrounding the concept of culpa in general. It seems that one started evaluating the debtor's behaviour in relative terms, first of all, in situations where somebody in case of peril had saved his own property, but had left to its fate what had been entrusted to him. Under these circumstances he was made responsible, qua dolus, for not being able to restore his creditor's property.[176] Thus the idea gained ground that

[173] Hausmaninger, *Festschrift Kaser*, p. 268.

[174] D. 44, 7, 1, 5. Cf., in nearly the same terms, *Inst.* III, 14, 3 (which has, incidentally, in turn been adopted nearly verbatim by Bracton, as cited by Lord Holt in *Coggs v. Bernard* (1703) 2 Ld Raym 909 at 914).

[175] *Inst.* III, 25, 9. Cf. also Gai. D. 17, 2, 72, usually taken to be interpolated.

[176] Kaser, *RPr* II, 355; Franz Wieacker, "Haftungsformen des römischen Gesellschaftsrechts", (1934) 54 *ZSS* 73 sqq. The same idea, incidentally, prevailed in the old Germanic law: the debtor remained liable, if only the bailor's property and not his own as

the depositor could expect the person to whom he was about to entrust some objects to display the same degree of diligence with regard to them that he would display in any event, i.e. particularly with regard to his own property. In the course of time, this idea was isolated and conceptualized as a specific standard of liability. As such, it had two significant aspects: if the debtor did not display the same diligence that he was used to displaying with regard to his own property, this could hardly be regarded as consistent with the standards of decent and honest behaviour. He was therefore liable, no matter whether he had in actual fact acted fraudulently or whether his act or omission would, in abstracto, have been qualified as gross negligence. On the other hand, however—and, once culpa liability had become established in contractual relationships, more importantly—there was the fact that diligentia quam in suis might just as well entail a relaxation of liability: for if the debtor was not a diligent person generally, how could he be expected to rise to a standard of utmost care, as far as not his own but somebody else's property was concerned? After all, the creditor chose his debtor, and if he chose a frivolous spendthrift, he had to blame himself for any disappointments.

Justinian did, in certain instances, provide for this type of liability. Diligentia quam in suis applied, for instance, in cases of tutela, dos or communio.[177] Whether it applied to the contract of depositum also, at least perhaps in certain individual cases, is a matter of dispute.[178] There are many texts from which it is abundantly clear that the depositary was liable for dolus (and culpa lata) only.[179] But then, what about Cels. D. 16, 3, 32, which, after all, is also part of the Justinianic compilation? Was that merely an oversight? Or did Justinian only want to stress that not to comply with diligentia quam in suis should be regarded, in the case of depositum, as culpa lata or even dolus? Be that as it may, the idea of requiring the standard of diligentia quam in suis from the depositary has commended itself to a broad variety of authors of the ius commune[180] and also to modern legislators.[181]

---

well had been affected by (e.g.) a fire that had been raging at his place: cf. Planitz, *Grundzüge des Deutschen Privatrechts* (3rd ed., 1949), p. 162.

[177] Cf. Ulp. D. 27, 3, 1 pr., Paul. D. 23, 3, 17 pr., Paul. D. 20, 2, 25, 16. For details, see Hausmaninger, *Festschrift Kaser*, pp. 276 sqq.

[178] Cf., on the one hand, Kaser, *RPr* II, p. 355, on the other, De Robertis, *Responsabilità contrattuale*, pp. 386 sqq. Further Hausmaninger, *Festschrift Kaser*, p. 282; Hoffmann, *Fahrlässigkeit*, p. 8; MacCormack, (1972) 38 *SDHI* 176 sqq.

[179] Cf. e.g. *Inst.* III, 14, 3.

[180] Brunnemann, *Commentarius in Pandectas*, Lib. XVI, Tit. III, ad L. Quod Nerva. 32; Grotius, *Inleiding*, III, VII, 9; Domat, *Les loix civiles*, Lib. I, Tit. VII, Sec. III, III; Pothier, *Traité du contrat de dépôt*, n. 23; see, too, Story, *Bailments*, §§ 63 sqq., Hoffmann, *Fahrlässigkeit*, pp. 154 sqq.

[181] For details, see Hausmaninger, *Festschrift Baltl*, pp. 283 sqq., 286, 293 sqq. He also points out that the concept of diligentia quam in suis has filtered through into English law (via Lord Holt in *Coggs v. Bernard*, who refers, in this context, to Bracton) and has been employed, though only occasionally, by some American courts.

3. The gratuitous nature of depositum

Modern German law recognizes one further situation where an increased responsibility is imposed on the depositary: if a remuneration for the custody has been agreed upon, he is to be liable for dolus and culpa (in abstracto).[182] Depositum, then, is no longer regarded as necessarily gratuitous.[183] The Roman lawyers thought differently. Throughout the classical period, the element of gratuity was maintained as an essential characteristic of depositum. Justinian, too, subscribed to this view. Thus, we read:

> "Si vestimenta servanda balneatori data perierunt, si quidem nullam mercedem servandorum vestimentorum accepit, depositi eum teneri et dolum dumtaxat praestare debere puto: quod si accepit, ex conducto."[184]

This, incidentally, is one of quite a few texts relating directly or indirectly to the public baths (thermae),[185] and it provides an indication of their enormous importance in the daily life of the average Roman.[186]

> "The baths are one of the fairest creations of the Roman Empire", writes Carcopino;[187] "[they] in fact offered the Romans a microcosm of many of the things that make life attractive . . . [At the height of the Empire] the Roman people had contracted the habit of attending the baths daily and spending the greater part of their leisure there."[188]

For Rome, the Libellus de regionibus urbis Romae gave a total of 856 thermae; in a little provincial town of 15 000 inhabitants such as Timgad there were twelve.[189] The baths were usually run by a balneator, an independent contractor, to whom the owner had leased the bath. He exploited the baths on a commercial basis, but the entrance fee charged was very low.[190] At the time of Horace, it was a quadrans,

---

[182] Cf. § 688 as opposed to § 690 BGB.

[183] This is in accordance with old Germanic law: Planitz, op. cit., note 176, p. 162. The same situation prevails in South African law today: Bester, op. cit., note 169, n. 70; cf. also R.H. Christie, "What is a Contract of Depositum", 1981 *Zimbabwe LJ* 98 sq.

[184] Ulp. D. 16, 3, 1, 8.

[185] Cf. e.g. Alf. D. 19, 2, 30, 1; Scaev. D. 32, 35, 3.

[186] Ulpian mentions, among the criteria by which to establish a person's domicile, the place where he goes to the bath: D. 50, 1, 27, 1.

[187] *Daily Life*, pp. 277, 279, 280. Cf. also Ralph Jackson, *Doctors and Diseases in the Roman Empire* (1988), pp. 48 sqq.

[188] Not everybody overindulged to the extent of Emperor Commodus, who was said to have taken up to eight baths a day: *Scriptores Historiae Augustae*, Commodus, 11, 5. For a comprehensive account of Roman baths, their management, financing and staffing, terms and conditions for users (opening hours, the question of mixed bathing), amenities provided, maintenance (fuel- and water-supply), etc., see Olivia Robinson, "Baths: An Aspect of Roman Local Government Law", in: Sodalitas, *Scritti in onore di Antonio Guarino*, vol. III (1984), pp. 1065 sqq.

[189] Cf. Michel, *Gratuité*, p. 27. For further interesting details and anecdotes, see Carcopino, pp. 277 sqq.; Robinson, *Scritti Guarino*, vol. III, pp. 1065 sqq.

[190] Nevertheless, it seems to have been a profitable occupation. Juvenal (*Satura*, VII, 4 sqq.) warns young poets that without the patronage of the emperor, they might be forced by the threat of imminent starvation to take up some prosaic occupation, such as that of bathkeeping. In the later empire, the costs of running baths rose; fuel was the heaviest charge. The provision of firewood became one of the regular munera civilia (cf. also the

i.e. a quarter of an as.[191] Thus, the baths were accessible even to the poor. Nevertheless, it was a much appreciated and very popular act of liberality if a magistrate marked his term of office by undertaking to pay all entrance fees for a certain period of time,[192] or if a wealthy Roman in his will made his private bathing hall available to the general public for free.[193] This might have happened in the case discussed by Ulpianus; and where the entrance was free, it is more than likely that one did not have to pay for leaving one's clothes in the custody of the balneator or his changing-room assistant (the capsarius) either.[194] Under these circumstances, the contract could qualify as depositum; liability was confined to dolus (or dolus and culpa lata). If, on the other hand, a fee had been charged, the balneator's liability was increased to custodia (thus, the result is, mutatis mutandis, the same as in modern law), but not under the rules relating to depositum. We would be dealing with a different type of contract, in this case locatio conductio (operis). Whenever a remuneration had been promised, the contract, according to Roman law, could not be depositum.[195] This is confirmed by a variety of texts, for instance Ulp. D. 16, 3, 1, 9:

> "Si quis servum custodiendum coniecerit forte in pistrinum, si quidem merces intervenit custodiae, puto esse actionem adversus pistrinarium ex conducto: . . . si vero nihil aliud quam cibaria praestabat nec de operis quicquam convenit, depositi actio est."

Somebody had given his slave, probably in order to penalize him, into the custody of a baker (who would make him work in his mill).[196] As long as the master of the slave paid for his maintenance only (cibaria), the contract was one of deposit. As soon as he remunerated the miller, however, the contract fell into the category of locatio conductio.

4. "Deposit" of immovables?

If the BGB did not follow Roman law regarding the question of gratuitousness, it took a more traditional stand in another question also concerning the scope of application of depositum. According to Roman

legacy of wood to provide fuel for the baths in Ulp. D. 32, 55, 3), and the contractors were granted an additional income from the salt revenues. Cf. Robinson, *Scritti Guarino*, vol. III, pp. 1070 sqq.

[191] Horatius, *Saturae*, I, 3, 137. Entrance for children was free. According to the lex metalli Vipascensis, the entrance fee was $\frac{1}{2}$ as; and double the amount for women. An as was a bronze coin worth a quarter of a sesterce. An average family of three persons, in the second half of the 1st century A.D. could live on about 25 as per day. One as, according to Pompeian graffiti, bought one quart of local wine or a plate, 2 as a small fish. For further details, see Etienne, *Pompeji*, pp. 215 sqq.

[192] Cf. e.g. Alf. D. 19, 2, 30, 1.

[193] Cf. e.g. Scaev. D. 32, 35, 3.

[194] Cf. Michel, *Gratuité*, p. 57.

[195] This was the position in classical law and again under Justinian. In post-classical vulgar law, the distinctions between the various contracts had become blurred and lucrative deposita were recognized. Cf. Codex Euricianus 278 and Ulp. D. 13, 6, 5, 2; Ulp. D. 47, 5, 2, 23, both interpolated; see Levy, *Obligationenrecht*, pp. 173 sqq.

[196] Michel, *Gratuité*, p. 58.

law, this type of transaction was confined to movable property. "Depositum est, quod custodiendum alicui *datum* est . . ."; and the word "depositum" referred to "[id] quod ponitur".[197] In this very literal sense, land can hardly be said to be taken and put into somebody's custody. Based on lexical meaning and etymology, such an argument on its own, of course, carries only a limited degree of persuasiveness. It has therefore been suggested that the Roman lawyers did not recognize the "deposit" of immovables, because there was no need for it: if I ask a friend to look after and watch over my house while I am away, our relationship can be classified, according to the individual circumstances of the case, as precarium, commodatum or habitatio gratuita (if the friend is actually staying in the house); or else as a mandate (mandatum).[198] Be that as it may, the question was disputed in the ius commune,[199] and the opinion that immovable property can be "deposited" even found its way into some codifications[200] and into South African law.[201] Yet, the BGB has codified the pandectist doctrine when it says: "By a contract of deposit the depositary is bound to keep in his custody a movable delivered to him by the depositor."[202]

5. The depositum irregulare

(a) *The problem of the deposit of money*

"Praeterea et is, apud quem res aliqua deponitur, re obligatur et actione depositi, qui et ipse de ea re quam accepit restituenda tenetur":[203] just like the commodatary, but unlike the borrower under a contract of mutuum, the depositary had to restore the very same object(s) that had been entrusted to him. In this form, depositum can be found among the earliest institutions not only of Roman but of most of the ancient

[197] Ulp. D. 16, 3, 1 pr. In layman's language the word "commendare" was used (cf. e.g. Ulp. D. 50, 16, 186: "Commendare nihil aliud est quam deponere"). In post-classical times, this term totally superseded classical terminology: cf. Levy, *Obligationenrecht*, pp. 166 sqq. Justinian reintroduced the classical technical term. On the institution of commendatio in the Middle Ages and its Greek (and Roman) antecedents, see Paolo Frezza, "Commendatio nelle carte notarili dell'alto Medio Evo", (1969) 20 *Iura* 177 sqq.

[198] Michel, *Gratuité*, pp. 71 sq.; also "Motive", in: *Mugdan*, vol. II, p. 319; Glück, vol. 15, pp. 146 sqq.

[199] Cf. Voet, *Commentarius ad Pandectas*, Lib. XVI, Tit. III, III ("Deponi possunt res omnes, . . . sive mobiles sive immobiles; cum et immobilium custodia alteri tradi queat; et commendari, quae commendatio depositio est"); Van Leeuwen, *Censura Forensis*, Pars I, Lib. IV, Cap. VI, 3; on the other hand, Grotius, *Inleiding*, III, VII, 5; Glück, vol. 15, pp. 146 sqq. Cf. further Vinnius, *Institutiones*, Lib. III, Tit. XV (sub de deposito), 1; Pothier, *Traité du contrat de dépôt*, n. 3; Story, *Bailments*, § 51.

[200] §§ 90, 91 I 14 PrALR; § 960 ABGB.

[201] Bester, op. cit., note 169, n. 69.

[202] § 688 BGB and Windscheid/Kipp, § 377.

[203] *Inst.* III, 14, 3.

laws.[204] At all times, and particularly in less refined and rather insecure societies, people have felt the need to leave their valuables with a trustworthy friend in times of emergency, when marching out for war, and in similar situations.[205] Of course, they did not want to deposit only jewellery or valuable pieces of equipment and the like, but also fungible objects, especially money. This they could do and did by somehow individualizing the specific sum that was to be the object of the deposit: for instance, by depositing "viginti nummorum saccum"[206] or "pecuniam signatam".[207] Under these circumstances, as in all other cases of deposit, the depositor remained the owner;[208] the depositary committed theft if he used the money. However, in the case of money, the depositor does not normally have a special interest in getting back the very same coins. The specific characteristic of money is that it represents a certain value and hence one could argue that it is not really a corpus but a quantitas that has been deposited.[209] Relying not so much on the honesty and trustworthiness, but on the solvency of the depositary, the depositor is primarily interested in getting back eadem quantitas or "tantundem",[210] i.e. a sum of money of the same (nominal) value that he has given. The depositary would then be allowed to use the money; he would become owner, and as such he would naturally carry the risk of the money getting lost.[211] One might ask whether he should not possibly be required to pay some interest in return for being allowed to use the money.

(b) Depositum and mutuum

It is obvious, on the one hand, that such a transaction would go beyond the normal scope and framework of depositum: it would be a contractus "[qui] egreditur . . . depositi notissimos terminos".[212] However, there is a definite resemblance to mutuum. In both cases we are dealing with the handing over of a sum of money, involving both a transfer of ownership and an undertaking on the part of the recipient to return the same sum. Thus, one might be inclined to apply the rules pertaining to mutuum to this kind of deposit and to allow the "depositary" to avail himself of the condictio. The condictio being

---

[204] Cf., for example, §§ 120–126 Codex Hammurabi; Exodus 22, 9. For an interesting analysis of the ancient Mesopotamian law and practice, see Raymond Bogaert, *Les origines antiques de la banque de dépôt* (1966), pp. 41 sqq.

[205] Cf. e.g. the story related by Herodotus, *Historiae*, Lib. VI, Cap. 86.

[206] Paul. D. 47, 2, 21, 1.

[207] Afr. D. 46, 3, 39.

[208] As to the vindicatio nummorum, see Hannu Tapani Klami, *Mutua magis videtur quam deposita* (1969), pp. 174 sqq.; Max Kaser, "Das Geld im römischen Sachenrecht", (1961) 29 *TR* 173 sqq.

[209] Cf. e.g. Glück, vol. 15, p. 157.

[210] Pap. D. 16, 3, 25, 1.

[211] Cf. e.g. Paul. Coll. X, VII, 9.

[212] Pap. D. 16, 3, 24. Cf. also Paul. D. 16 3, 26, 1 (". . . eum contractum de quo quaeritur depositae pecuniae modum excedere").

stricti iuris, a practical disadvantage would then appear to be that the judge would not be empowered to award interest to the depositor (unless, of course, a special stipulation had been entered into).

On the other hand, there was one marked difference between the two transactions, relating, as it were, not so much to (legal) technicalities but to the fundamental balance of interest involved: a contract of mutuum was made in the interest of the borrower, whereas even in this irregular kind of deposit, it was primarily the depositor who was interested in entrusting his capital to another person. The advantage the depositary derived from the transaction was only incidental and did not motivate the contract. Hence, one could argue that if this type of transaction was to be accommodated within the contractual scheme of Roman law, it should have been squeezed into the niche of depositum. The actio depositi would have offered the flexibility (on account of its bona fide clause) to award interest in appropriate cases—for instance, where there had been an agreement between the parties to this effect.

(c) From condictio to actio depositi

What exactly the attitude of the Roman lawyers was to this question is not at all easy to make out. No clear picture emerges from the texts contained in the Digest: some of them contain contradictions,[213] and suspicions of interpolations abound.[214] This kind of irregular deposit has been called one of the most controversial institutions in the science of Roman law[215]—and it may well be asked whether one can, in fact, speak of an "institution", as this term suggests that it was more clearly defined than it actually seems to have been at any time in the development of Roman law.[216] Only a few things are reasonably clear. It was from the Hellenistic East that this type of transaction made its way into Roman business life.[217] There the παρακαταθήκη contract provided for the restoration of deposited things in genere[218] and was a convenient legal tool to accommodate the flourishing business of deposit banking.[219] Whatever banking business there was in the Roman Republic seems to have been mostly run by Greeks,[220] and the Greek

---

[213] Cf. e.g. Paul. D. 16, 3, 26, 1.

[214] For a very radical view, see Carlo Longo, "Appunti sul deposito irregolare", (1906) 18 *BIDR* 121 sqq.; Schulz, *CRL*, pp. 519 sqq.

[215] Wieslaw Litewski, "Le dépôt irrégulier", (1974) 21 *RIDA* 215.

[216] William M. Gordon, "Observations on 'depositum irregulare'", in: *Studi in onore di Arnaldo Biscardi*, vol. III (1982), pp. 363 sqq.

[217] Cf., for example, Paolo Frezza, Παρακαταθήκη, in: *Symbolae Raphaeli Taubenschlag*, vol. I (1956), pp. 139 sqq.; Hannu Tapani Klami, Depositum und Παρακαταθήκη, in: *Iuris Professio, Festgabe für Max Kaser* (1986), pp. 89 sqq. Cf. also, generally, Wieacker, *RR*, pp. 347 sqq.

[218] Arnold Ehrhardt, "Parakatatheke", (1958) 75 *ZSS* 32 sqq.; Dieter Simon, "Quasi-ΠΑΡΑΚΑΤΑΘΗΚΗ", (1965) 82 *ZSS* 39 sqq.

[219] Raymond Bogaert, *Banque et banquiers dans les cités grecques* (Leiden, 1968).

[220] Fritz Pringsheim, "Zum römischen Bankwesen", in: *Gesammelte Abhandlungen*, vol. II (1961), pp. 114 sqq.; Laum, *Bankwesen*, RE Suppl., vol. IV, pp. 68 sqq.

word "trapezitae" was used, at least occasionally, for the money dealers on the Forum Romanum.[221] Large-scale banking institutions, however, whose function it could have been to collect deposits in order to be able to finance investments, do not seem to have existed in Rome.[222] Hence, it appears not to have been perceived, either here, or in other spheres,[223] as an economic necessity to receive and incorporate into Roman law a transaction along the lines of the παρακαταθήκη. Conservative and possibly slightly supercilious as far as the value of legal institutions from the provinces was concerned,[224] the classical Roman lawyers were content, at first, to make available the standard remedy of condictio and thus to accommodate the new practice within the framework of the established rules of mutuum.[225] Justinian, on the other hand, was prepared to grant the actio depositi and to oblige the depositary, according to the requirements of bona fides, to compensate the depositor for the use that he was allowed to make of his money.[226] As to when and how this transition occurred, one reads many divergent accounts.[227] It is not unlikely, though, that the recognition of this special contract of deposit goes back to certain jurists of the late classical period.[228] The continental ius commune has retained this institution

---

[221] Cf. e.g. C. 12, 57, 12, 3 and Ludwig Mitteis, "Trapezitika", (1898) 19 *ZSS* 198 sqq. Τράπεζα was the word for the table on which the money was spread out. On the activities and the social status of the Roman nummularii and argentarii (and on the difference between these two professions), see the detailed analysis by Alfons Bürge, "Fiktion und Wirklichkeit: Soziale und rechtliche Strukturen des römischen Bankwesens", (1987) 104 *ZSS* 467 sqq., 476 sqq.; cf. also Frier, *Roman Jurists*, pp. 7 sqq. ("A gentleman did not willingly pursue banking as a profession").

[222] De Martino, *Wirtschaftsgeschichte*, pp. 174 sqq.; Bürge, (1987) 104 *ZSS* 465 sqq., 509 sqq. Unlike their Greek counterparts, the Roman temples did not fulfil the function of banking or credit institutions. Cf. e.g. Benjamin Bromberg, "Temple Banking in Rome", (1939–40) 10 *The Economic History Review* 128 sqq. For an instructive example of the business of an average "banker" in the 1st century A.D. (L. Caecilius Iucundus), see Étienne, *Pompeji*, pp. 172 sqq.; for further details Bürge, (1987) 104 *ZSS* 476 sqq.

[223] Many but not all the cases of depositum irregulare discussed in the Digest concern banking relationships; cf. Litewski, (1974) 21 *RIDA* 224, but also Gordon, *Studi Biscardi*, vol. III, pp. 364 sqq.

[224] Roger Vigneron, "Résistance du Droit romain aux influences hellénistiques: le cas du dépôt irrégulier", (1984) 31 *RIDA* 307 sqq.

[225] Ulp. D. 12, 1, 10; Ulp. D. 16, 3, 1, 34; Ulp. D. 12, 1, 9, 9; Paul. Coll. X, VII, 9; on these texts, see, most recently, Bürge, (1987) 104 *ZSS* 548 sqq.

[226] Especially where the parties had agreed on interest by way of a formless pactum (cf. Pap. D. 16, 3, 24 in fine; Paul. D. 16, 3, 26, 1), but also in other cases (cf. Scaev. D. 16, 3, 28: "respondi deberi ex bonae fidei iudicio usuras, sive percepit sive pecunia in re sua usus est.") Cf. further Klami, op. cit., note 208, pp. 118 sqq.; Litewski, (1975) 22 *RIDA* 304 sqq.; Gordon, *Studi Biscardi*, vol. III, pp. 369 sqq.; Honsell/Mayer-Maly/Selb, pp. 303 sq.; Bürge, (1987) 104 *ZSS* 536 sqq., 542 sqq. As to the law of Justinian in general, see Maschi, *Contratti reali*, pp. 390 sqq.

[227] The first modern (critical) monograph was that of Theodor Niemeyer, *Depositum irregulare* (1898). For an overview and critical discussion of the quite formidable amount of literature, see Klami, *Mutua magis videtur quam deposita* (1969); Gandolfi, op. cit., note 135, pp. 149 sqq.; Litewski, (1974) 21 *RIDA* 215 sqq. and (1975) 22 *RIDA* 279 sqq.

[228] Cf. e.g. Kaser, *RPr* I, p. 536; Vigneron, (1984) 32 *RIDA* 307 sqq.; Bürge, (1987) 104 *ZSS* 536 sqq., 552 sqq.; contra: Klami, *Festgabe Kaser*, pp. 89 sqq.

under the name of "depositum irregulare".[229] Usually, at least in more modern times, the rules of deposit are applied;[230] and, indeed, in most European languages money given to a bank is to this day called a deposit. The irregular deposit has found its way into the codifications, as for instance § 700 BGB,[231] and provides the legal basis for the modern current or giro account.[232]

6. Conventional sequestration

"Licet deponere tam plures quam unus possunt, attamen apud sequestrem non nisi plures deponere possunt",[233] we are informed by Florentinus: in any deposit there can be one or several depositors. But there was one special situation where the depositary necessarily kept the object for two (or more) parties: the depositum in sequestre.[234] In D. 50, 16, 110 we find the following definition: "'Sequester' dicitur, apud quem plures eandem rem, de qua controversia est deposuerunt."[235] Etymologically, a sequester is a person who has no interest, one who stands aside (secus) and hence is impartial.[236] His position differed from that of a normal depositary in one important respect:

---

229 Coined, apparently, by the commentator Jason de Mayno (1435–1519): cf. Niemeyer, op. cit., note 227, p. 110.

230 Cf., for example, Glück, vol. 15, pp. 139, 157 sqq.; Vangerow, *Pandekten*, § 630; Windscheid/Kipp, § 379. For a contrary view, see e.g. *Ex parte Smith* 1940 OPD 120 at 126 sq.

231 The fathers of the BGB, however, deviated from what they perceived to be the Roman law (and thus, in reality, returned to the position in classical Roman law) by treating the transaction as a loan: "If fungibles are deposited in such manner that the ownership is to pass to the depositary, and he is to be bound to return things of the same kind, quality and quantity, the provisions relating to loan for consumption apply. . . ." Cf. also §§ 83, 84 I 14 PrALR; differently, artt. 484, 445 OR. The code civil is silent on this point (adopting, probably, the opinion of Pothier, *Traité du contrat de dépôt*, n. 83, that in modern law there is no practical difference between the two views).

232 On the renaissance of deposit banking in the 12th century, see A.P. Usher, "The Origins of Banking: the Primitive Bank of Deposit, 1200–1600", (1932–34) 4 The *Economic History Review* 399 sqq.; on the relationship between medieval banking and banking practice in antiquity, see Raymond Bogaert, *Les origines antiques de la banque de dépôt* (1966), pp. 159 sqq. On the history of deposit banking in general, see Endemann, *Studien*, vol. I, pp. 423 sqq.

233 D. 16, 3, 17 pr.

234 For details, see Pothier, *Traité du contrat de dépôt*, nn. 90 sqq.; Vincenzo Arangio-Ruiz, "Studi sulla dottrina romana del sequestro", in: *Scritti di diritto romano*, vol. I (1974), pp. 59 sqq., 89 sqq.; Gerardo Broggini, "Introduction au sequester", in: *Mélanges Philippe Meylan*, vol. I (1963), pp. 43 sqq.; Litewski, *Studien*, op. cit., note 141, pp. 47 sqq. Cf. also Maschi, *Contratti reali*, pp. 408 sqq. (according to whom only Justinian regarded the conventional sequestration as a case of deposit. This view is based on excessive textual criticism).

235 Cf. also Paul. D. 16, 3, 6: "Proprie autem in sequestre est depositum, quod a pluribus in solidum certa condicione custodiendum reddendumque traditur."

236 Cf. Heumann/Seckel, p. 535; Windscheid/Kipp, § 380, n. 2. For the Romans, the word was derived from "sequi" (cf. e.g. Mod. D. 50, 16, 110 and Broggini, *Mélanges Meylan*, p. 54).

"Rei depositae proprietas apud deponentem manet: sed et possessio, nisi apud sequestrem deposita est: nam tum demum sequester possidet: id enim agitur ea depositione, ut neutrius possessioni id tempus procedat."[237]

It is not difficult to see the reason for this distinction. Where two parties had a dispute over a particular object, there was always the danger that, in the course of the dispute, one of the parties (the one in possession of the disputed object) might acquire ownership by usucapio. The period for usucaption was short in Roman law, and not even the commencement of legal proceedings had any influence on its running. Bona fides was required only at the time of obtaining possession—mala fides superveniens non nocet. Hence it was imperative that the object be given to a third party, not involved in the dispute, until the issue had been settled. It would, however, have frustrated the whole object of this exercise if this third party had not been considered as the possessor; otherwise the period of usucaption would still have run in favour of one of the parties. The sequester was bound to return the thing to the person in whose favour the dispute had been decided; the latter could avail himself of a special actio (depositi) sequestraria.[238]

Today, this type of conventional sequestration has largely sunk into oblivion; the German Code does not even mention it any more.[239] The period of usucaption is ten years; judicial enforcement of a claim averring title over the thing interrupts this period, and mala fides superveniens non nocet has (under the influence of canon law) long since been converted into its opposite.

III. PIGNUS

1. The nature of pignus

"Creditor quoque, qui pignus accepit, re tenetur: qui et ipse de ea ipsa re quam accepit restituenda tenetur."[240] The fourth of the real contracts was pignus and it entailed the handing over of a thing in order to secure a debt. Obviously the very same thing had to be restored by the creditor/pledgee to the pledgor once this underlying debt had been discharged (or otherwise extinguished). We can be fairly brief in our discussion; for the most important aspect of pignus was that it gave rise to a ius in rem, a (limited) real right in the property owned by the pledgor. Pignus was (and is) the paradigm of real security and as such it falls outside the ambit of our investigation.[241] In the present context

[237] Flor. D. 16, 3, 17, 1; Litewski, *Studien*, op. cit., note 141, pp. 71 sqq.

[238] Cf., for example, Ulp. D. 16, 3, 5, 1; Pomp. D. 16, 3, 12, 2; Litewski, *Studien*, op. cit., note 141, pp. 78 sqq.

[239] For judicial sequestrations (i.e. those made by order of a court in the course of judicial proceedings), see, however, § 938 ZPO.

[240] Gai. D. 44, 7, 1, 6.

[241] See, for instance, Heinrich Dernburg, *Das Pfandrecht nach den Grundsätzen des heutigen römischen Rechts*, 2 vols. (1860, 1864); Rabel, *Grundzüge*, pp. 157 sqq.; Rodger J. Goebel,

we are solely concerned with the obligatory side of pignus; for one of the requirements for pledging a thing was that pledgor and pledgee were in agreement about the creation of the pledge. A (formless) contract had to be concluded,[242] and where in actual fact possession of the pledged property was transferred to the creditor/pledgee, we have the real contract of pignus. This was invariably the case in early law. In classical law, however, it came to be recognized that a right of pledge could be created even though the pledged property remained with the pledgor.[243] It is clear that in these instances of (purely contractual) pledges without possession the *real right* pignus was no longer based on the *real contract* of pignus.

2. The actio pigneraticia

(a) *The formula in factum concepta*

Turning our attention back, therefore, to the pledge with possession, we must first of all consider the pledgor's position once the obligation which the pledge was designed to secure had fallen away. Of course, the pledgor had always been able to avail himself of the rei vindicatio.[244] This remedy could be used to claim the object back from any third party, not only from the pledgee. But it involved proof of ownership ex iure Quiritium—often a difficult stumbling block for the pledgor/owner. For the actio Publiciana, on the other hand, his "in bonis esse" was required.[245] Where these actions were unavailable, the plaintiff was probably able to resort to the condictio.[246] It was from this root that a more specialized contractual remedy came to be developed by the praetors, namely the actio pigneraticia. In the edict it was proposed under the title "De rebus creditis" and in close connection with condictio and actio commodati.[247] Like the actio commodati, it initially only had a formula in factum concepta, and has been reconstructed by Lenel as follows:

> "Si paret A^m A^m N^o N^o rem qua de agitur ob pecuniam debitam pignori dedisse eamqua pecuniam solutam esse eove nomine satisfactum esse aut per N^m N^m

"Reconstructing the Roman Law of Real Security", (1961–62) 36 *Tulane LR* 29 sqq.; Paolo Frezza, *Le garanzie delle obligazioni*, vol. II: *Le garanzie reali* (1963); Kaser, *RPr* I, p. 463 sqq.; idem, "Studien zum römischen Pfandrecht", (1976) 44 *TR* 233 sqq.

[242] On the conventio pignoris Max Kaser, "Besitzpfand und 'besitzloses' Pfand" (1979) 45 *SDHI* 29 sqq.

[243] For details, see Kaser, (1979) 45 *SDHI* 1 sqq.

[244] Cf. Kaser, (1976) 44 *TR* 262 sq.

[245] For details, see, most recently, Max Kaser, "Nochmals zu 'in bonis habere'", in: *Huldigingsbundel Paul van Warmelo* (1984), pp. 144 sqq.; Hans Ankum, Marjolijn van Gessel-de Roo, Eric Pool, "Die verschiedenen Bedeutungen des Ausdrucks in bonis alicuius esse/in bonis habere im klassischen römischen Recht", (1987) 104 *ZSS* 238 sqq. and (1988) 105 *ZSS* 334 sqq.

[246] Max Kaser, "Studien zum römischen Pfandrecht II", (1979) 47 *TR* 229, 234.

[247] Lenel, *EP*, pp. 231 sqq., 254 sqq.

stetisse, quo minus solveretur, eamque rem A° A° redditam non esse, quanti ea res erit, tantam pecuniam iudex N^m^ N^m^ A° A° codemnato, si non paret, absolvito."[248]

Three comments might be apposite. "Pignori dedisse", in this form of action, still reflects the idea that the pledge had to be handed over. Nevertheless, the actio pigneraticia was also available in cases of non-possessory pledges, where the creditor had subsequently managed to get hold of the object.[249] Furthermore, it is not stated in the intentio of the formula that the pledged object had to have belonged to the pledgor. The actio pigneraticia was therefore applicable even where the pledgor had encumbered someone else's property[250]—that is, in a situation where the real right of pledge did not come into existence.[251] Finally, still according to the intentio, the action could be brought not only where the underlying debt had been discharged or where the creditor had defaulted, but also where the latter had been (otherwise) "satisfied on that account". When or whether such "satisfaction" had taken place was decided solely from the creditor's own point of view. It did not matter whether he had in actual fact received what was owed to him, or at least an equivalent in value, as long as he regarded himself as satisfied:

"satisfactum autem accipimus, quemadmodum voluit creditor, licet non sit solutum: sive aliis pignoribus sibi caveri voluit, ut ab hoc recedat, sive fideiussoribus sive reo dato sive pretio aliquo vel nuda conventione, nascitur pigneraticia actio. et generaliter dicendum erit, quotiens recedere voluit creditor a pignore, videri ei satisfactum, si ut ipse voluit sibi cavit, licet in hoc deceptus sit."[252]

With this wide and subjectivized interpretation of the term "satisfactum" the Roman lawyers tried to cover all situations in which a need for retention of the security could no longer be taken to exist.

(b) The formula in ius concepta

The formula in factum concepta dates back to the times of the early Republic. As in the case of commodatum, the classical lawyers developed a more flexible alternative in the form of a formula in ius concepta with an "ex bona fide" clause as its essential characteristic. It started off with a demonstratio defining the facts of the case: "Quod A° A° N° N° mensam argenteam qua de agitur ob pecuniam debitam pignori dedit" and carried on in the normal way: ". . . quidquid ob eam rem N^m^ N^m^ A° A° dare facere oportet ex fide bona, eius iudex N^m^ N^m^

---

248 *EP*, p. 255.

249 Kaser, (1979) 45 *SDHI* 5 sq.

250 Ulp. D. 13, 7, 9, 4: "Is quoque, qui rem alienam pignori dedit, soluta pecunia potest pigneraticia experiri." Cf. further e.g. Ulp. D. 21, 2, 38; Paul. D. 13, 7, 16, 1; Marci. D. 13, 7, 32; C. 8, 15, 6 (Diocl.).

251 Schwarz, (1954) 71 *ZSS* 138 sqq.; F.B.J. Wubbe, *Res aliena pignori data* (1960), pp. 128 sq., 168 sqq.

252 Ulp. D. 13, 7, 9, 3. Cf. further Ulp. D. 13, 7, 11, 2; C. 8, 32, 1; and Kaser, (1979) 47 *TR* 201 sqq.

A° A° condemnato, si non paret, absolvito."[158] Besides allowing the judge to take into consideration whether the pledgee/creditor had complied with the requirements of good faith,[159] this formula was much better suited to deal with a specific problem arising after realization of the pledge. If the creditor did not obtain satisfaction and he thereupon sold the pledged property, the proceeds of this sale might easily exceed the sum of the debt owed to him. It would seem reasonable, under these circumstances, to allow the pledgor to claim superfluum,[160] but it is difficult to see how that could have been achieved under the formula in factum concepta. "Quanti ea res erit" refers to the pledged property, for the monetary value of which the judge could (or could not) condemn the defendant. The intentio incerta of the formula in ius concepta left the judge much more freedom; he could condemn in "whatever the defendant ought on that account to give to (or to do for) the plaintiff": be it the pledged property or its value, be it a superfluum after sale.

3. The consequences of non-redemption of the pledge

But was the creditor actually allowed to sell the pledge? In early Roman law the pledged property seems to have been forfeited if it was not redeemed in time (by way of payment of the underlying debt, for example).[161] In those days one did not yet distinguish between various types of real rights, and the position of the pledgee was conceived in terms of (part) ownership of the property.[162] Forfeiture merely meant that the pledgee became fully and solely entitled to the thing. Of course, under these circumstances he was perfectly free to sell it. Once, however, the pledgee's position had begun to be conceptualized as ius in re aliena, the situation was no longer that straightforward. Ownership vested in the pledgor and it did, of course, not pass to the pledgee simply by virtue of the fact that the underlying debt had not been discharged, or that the pledgee/creditor had not otherwise been satisfied. Thus, the somewhat strange and hybrid situation could arise that the pledgee was entitled to keep the pledge indefinitely without,

---

[158] Cf. Kaser, (1979) 47 *TR* 221. This formula was probably not contained in the edict. According to René Robaye, "Sanction judiciaire du contrat de gage en droit romain classique", (1987) 34 *RIDA* 309 sqq., the actio in ius concepta is of post-classical origin.

[159] For a discussion of cases in which the in factum formula did not lead to satisfactory results and a more flexible instrument was needed, cf. Kaser, (1979) 47 *TR* 216 sqq.

[160] C. 8, 27, 20 (Diocl.); cf. e.g. Ulrich von Lübtow, "Catos leges venditioni et locationi dictae", in: *Symbolae Raphaeli Taubenschlag*, vol. III (1957), pp. 329 sqq.

[161] Cf. A. Manigk, *RE*, 20, 1 (1941), col. 1248 sqq.; von Lübtow, *Symbolae Taubenschlag*, vol. III, pp. 314 sqq.; Kaser, (1976) 44 *TR* 244 sqq.; but see, for example, Frezza, *Garanzie*, vol. II, pp. 82 sqq.

[162] Kaser, (1976) 44 *TR* 254 sqq.; but see, for instance, György Diósdi, *Ownership in Ancient and Preclassical Roman Law* (1970), pp. 118 sqq.; Gerhard Schlichting, *Die Verfügungsbeschränkung des Verpfänders im klassischen römischen Recht* (1973), pp. 124 sqq.

however, being able to use it as a means of obtaining satisfaction.[258] In order to avoid this anomaly, the parties had to come to some arrangement regarding the consequences of non-redemption of the pledge as part of their conventio pignoris. Thus, for instance, they could agree on a conditional transfer of ownership on the basis of either sale[259] or datio in solutum.[260] If the debt remained undischarged, the pledgee was to be taken to have bought the pledge or to have received and accepted it in lieu of fulfilment.[261] Such clauses represent the contractual variant of the old forfeiture regime, and it is obvious that they are problematic and dangerous. If the pledge was valuable, the creditor would try to insist on their inclusion in the contract, and the debtor, hard pressed for money and overoptimistic as far as his ability to repay was concerned, was usually not in a position to resist these pressures. The Roman lawyers, therefore, tried in various ways to mitigate the effect of these forfeiture clauses, in order to protect the pledgor;[262] in post-classical times, such clauses fell foul of Constantine's prohibition of leges commissoriae[263] and were regarded as invalid.[264]

Alternatively, the conventio pignoris could contain a pactum de vendendo: the pledgee should be authorized to obtain satisfaction by selling the pledge.[265] From the time of the later Republic this was what the parties regularly agreed upon;[266] by the days of the Severan Emperors, the sale of pledges had become so common[267] that, even

---

[258] "Bewahrungspfand": Kaser, (1976) 44 *TR* 253 sq.; idem, *RPr* I, p. 461, n. 11. A creditor, incidentally, who used the pledged property without the permission of the pledgor, committed theft (Gai. D. 47, 2, 55 pr.). Frequently, however, the parties agreed that the creditor keep the proceeds of the pledged property in lieu of interest; this was known as ἀντίχρησις (Marci. D. 20, 1, 11, 1). For details, see Alfred Manigk, *Gläubigerbefriedigung durch Nutzung* (1910); Kaser, (1979) 45 *SDHI* 80 sqq.; Henryk Kupiszewski, "Antichrese und Nutzpfand in den Papyri", in: *Juris Professio, Festgabe für Max Kaser* (1986), pp. 133 sqq.; Honsell/Mayer-Maly/Selb, pp. 202 sqq.

[259] Cf. e.g. Tryph. D. 20, 5, 12 pr.; Pap. vat. 9; Marci. D. 20, 1, 16, 9.

[260] Cf. C. 8, 13, 13; C. 4, 51, 4 (both Diocl. et Max.).

[261] For details, see Frank Peters, "Der Erwerb des Pfandes durch den Pfandgläubiger im klassischen und im nachklassischen Recht", in: *Studien im römischen Recht* (1973), pp. 137 sqq.

[262] Cf. Ulp. D. 46, 3, 45 pr.; C. 18, 13, 1 (Sev. et Ant.); C. 8, 34, 1 (Alex.); cf. Peters, *Studien*, op. cit., note 261, pp. 145 sqq., 156 sqq.

[263] CT 3, 2, 1; cf. also C. 8, 34, 3.

[264] Peters, *Studien*, supra note 261 , pp. 161 sqq. However, the pledgee could obtain rescission of the clause only if he was prepared to pay off his debt. This considerably impaired the protective effect of Constantine's provision. Cf. Levy, *Obligationenrecht*, p. 192. As far as modern law is concerned, see 1229 BGB: "An agreement made before the existence of the right to sell, by which the ownership of the thing falls to the pledgee or is transferred to him, in case he does not, or does not in one time, receive satisfaction, is void."

[265] Alberto Burdese, *Lex commissoria e ius vendendi nella fiducia e nel pignus* (1949), pp. 131 sqq.; von Lübtow, *Symbolae Taubenschlag*, vol. III, pp. 321 sqq.; Frezza, *Garanzie*, vol. II, pp. 200 sqq.; Kaser, (1979) 47 *TR* 210 sqq. As far as the transfer of ownership is concerned, cf. Gai. II, 64; also Ulp. D. 13, 7, 4 and Ulp. D. 41, 1, 46.

[266] Apart from that, the pledgor (regularly?) appears to have undertaken not to alienate the object that had been given as a pledge. Cf. Marci. D. 20, 5, 7, 2 and, for details, Schlichting, op. cit., note 257, pp. 9 sqq., 27 sqq.; Kaser, (1976) 44 *TR* 233 sqq., 282 sqq.; Honsell/Mayer-Maly/Selb, p. 202.

[267] Cf. e.g. C. 4, 24, 4 ("pactum vulgare").

without any special agreement to that effect, the authority to sell was taken to be part of the contractual arrangement of the parties.[268] If the purchase price exceeded the amount of the secured debt, it was now the pledgor who was generally taken to be entitled to such a surplus.[269] The proceeds of the sale had taken the place of the pledge and afforded satisfaction to the extent that the pledgee deserved to be satisfied: up to the amount of the secured debt. Appreciation of the fact that the pledgee was not necessarily entitled to the full value of the pledge entailed another change of perspective: if necessary, the pledgee had to be forced to do what was now no longer only in his own but also in the pledgor's interest, and it could therefore no longer be left to his discretion to decide whether he wanted to sell the property or not. Our oldest testimony for this change of perspective is contained in D. 13, 7, 6 pr., where Atilicinus is reported to have advocated, albeit only "ex causa" and not as a general rule, that "cogendum creditorem esse ad vendendum . . .: quid enim si multo minus sit quod debeatur et hodie pluris venire possit pignus quam postea?"[270] Once the pledgee/creditor had obtained the purchase price, the debt was regarded as discharged. Complications could, however, arise, if the pledge had not belonged to the pledgor. Here, the pledgee was not able to transfer ownership to the purchaser and was therefore still exposed to liability for eviction. Under these circumstances, as Tryphoninus puts it, "in suspenso haberi liberationem".[271] In order to avoid this, the pledgee usually requested the pledgor to authorize him to sell the pledge subject to a pactum de non praestanda evictione:[272] the purchaser of the pledge was then asked to renounce his rights arising from the contract of sale in case of legal defects; this, of course, he did only against a reasonable reduction of the purchase price, which, in turn, reduced the pledgor's chances of receiving a substantial superfluum.

4. The liability of the pledgee

Once again, one can see here that the debtor's position was fairly weak. If possible, he would rather have tried to discharge his debt and to ask the pledgee to restore the pledge. To enable him to enforce this request

---

[268] Cf. Ulp. D. 13, 7, 4 and Pomp. D. 13, 7, 5, who both mention a pactum *ne veneat*. Cf. Kaser, (1979) 47 *TR* 213 sq.; von Lübtow, *Symbolae Taubenschlag*, vol. III, pp. 325 sqq.; Buckland/Stein, pp. 476 sq; Hausmaninger/Selb, p. 237; Honsell/Mayer-Maly/Selb, p. 199; Thomas, *TRL*, pp. 189 sq., 331; differently Burdese, op. cit., note 265, pp. 141 sqq.; Frezza, *Garanzie*, vol. II, pp. 200 sqq. The pledgee had to notify the debtor of his intention to sell the pledge (denuntiatio): C. 8, 27, 4 (Alex.). In post-classical times, three denuntiationes were required: Levy, pp. 187 sq. Justinian comprehensively regulated and reformed the procedure: cf. C. 8, 33, 3 for all details.

[269] Cf. Pap. D. 13, 7, 42; Marci. D. 20, 6, 8, 10; Pap. D. 20, 4, 17; C. 8, 27, 20 (Diocl.); Kaser, *Quanti ea res est* (1935), pp. 78 sqq.

[270] For details see Kaser, (1979) 47 *TR* 212 sq.

[271] D. 20, 5, 12, 1; Schwarz, (1954) 71 *ZSS* 147 sqq.

[272] Pap. D. 21, 2, 68 pr.; cf. also Paul. D. 20, 5, 10; Burdese, op. cit., note 265, pp. 173 sqq.; Frezza, *Garanzie*, vol. II, pp. 208 sqq.; Kaser, (1979) 47 *TR* 211 sq., 224 sq.

was, as we have seen, the main purpose of the actio pigneraticia. Of course, this remedy could not necessarily be brought only where the pledge was still in the pledgee's possession, but also where the latter could be held responsible for its loss or destruction. It is, however, very difficult to give a conclusive answer as to what was in actual fact expected of the pledgee in classical law, and how therefore the standard of liability was fixed.[273] Ulpian D. 50, 17, 23 rates the pledgee among those persons liable for dolus and culpa. This statement is confirmed by a variety of other fragments.[274] On the other hand, in Ulp. D. 13, 7, 13, 1 we read the following in connection with the actio pigneraticia:[275] "Venit autem in hac actione et dolus et culpa, ut in commodato: venit et custodia: vis maior non venit"; and seeing that Justinian tried to abolish the classical custodia liability, the words "venit et custodia" can hardly have been interpolated.[276] There are writers, however, who have even regarded the various allusions to culpa as interpolated; they consider the pledgee as having been liable for dolus only.[277] The most likely explanation for the confused state of our sources is that the question was controversial among the classical lawyers. An initial dolus liability was probably extended to cover cases of what we today would call negligence. After the formula in ius concepta with its bonae fidei clause had been introduced, some lawyers seem to have gone even further and advocated custodia liability, perhaps only for certain situations.[278] Seeing, however, that a pledge is normally agreed upon

[273] Cf. Arangio-Ruiz, *Responsabilità contrattuale*, pp. 138 sqq.; Luzzatto, op. cit., note 53, pp. 233 sqq.; Alvaro d'Ors, "Observaciones sobre el 'edictum de rebus creditis'", (1953) 19 *SDHI* 196 sqq.; Nörr, (1956) 73 *ZSS* 84 sqq.; Frezza, *Garanzie*, vol. II, pp. 241 sqq.; Kaser (1979) 46 *SDHI* 70 sqq.; idem, " 'Furtum pignoris' und 'furtum fiduciae' ", (1982) 99 *ZSS* 249 sqq.; Hans Ankum, "La responsabilità del creditore pignoratizio nel diritto romano classico", in: *Studi in onore di Arnaldo Biscardi*, vol. IV (1983), pp. 587 sqq.; Laura Rota, "Contrasti dottrinari e ipotesi di studio in tema di responsabilità del creditore pignoratizio", in: *Studi in onore di Arnaldo Biscardi*, vol. V (1984), pp. 329 sqq.; Robaye, (1987) 34 *RIDA* 311 sqq. On the closely related question of who could bring the actio furti (and thus receive duplum: the pledgee/creditor—on account of his custodia liability or for some other reason—or the pledgor as owner), cf. the recent contributions by Hans Ankum, "Furtum pignoris und furtum fiduciae im klassischen römischen Recht", (1979) 26 *RIDA* 127 sqq. (1980) 27 *RIDA* 95 sqq.; J.A.C. Thomas, "Furtum pignoris: a commentary on the commentaries", in: *Studi in onore di Cesare Sanfilippo*, vol. I (1982), pp. 585 sqq.; G.C.J.J. van den Bergh, "Custodiae and furtum pignoris", in: *Studi in onore di Cesare Sanfilippo*, vol. I (1982), pp. 601 sqq.; Kaser, (1982) 99 *ZSS* 249 sqq.; most recently cf. René Robaye, *L'obligation de garde. Essai sur la responsabilité contractuelle en droit romain*, (1988).

[274] Ulp. D. 13, 6, 5, 2; Paul. D. 13, 7, 30 (on this text Watson, *Obligations*, pp. 182 sqq.); Pap. D. 20, 1, 2: Ulp. D. 44, 4, 4, 8; Ulp. D. 47, 2, 14, 6.

[275] Differently Bertha Bergsma-van Krimpen, "Eine neue Interpretation von D. 13, 7, 13", (1979) 26 *RIDA* 163 sqq.

[276] Cf. also Ulp. D. 47, 2, 14, 16; C. 8, 13, 19 (Diocl.).

[277] Cf. Franz Haymann, "Textkritische Studien zum römischen Obligationenrecht", (1919) 40 *ZSS* 213 sqq.

[278] For custodia liability as the general rule in classical law, cf. especially Ankum, *Studi Biscardi*, vol. IV, pp. 587 sqq.; at least for late classical law now also Kaser, (1982) 99 *ZSS* 249 sqq.; cf. also Rota, *Studi Biscardi*, vol. V, pp. 329 sqq. Contra, most recently, Robaye, (1987) 34 *RIDA* 311 sqq., 321 sqq.

for the benefit of both parties ("quia pignus utriusque gratia datur, et debitoris, quo magis ei pecunia crederetur, et creditoris, quo magis ei in tuto sit creditum"),[279] the two extreme standards of dolus on the one and custodia on the other end of the spectrum do not really commend themselves as balanced solutions to the problem. Hence we find Justinian opting for culpa liability: ". . . placuit sufficere, quod ad eam rem custodiendam exactam diligentiam adhiberet."[280] Thus, to all intents and purposes he settled the question; throughout the ages,[281] the pledgee, in terms of the contract of pignus, has consistently been held responsible for culpa (levis).[282]

5. The actio pigneraticia contraria

We have thus far been dealing with the pledgor's (contractual) remedy against the pledgee. However, just like the commodatary and the depositary, the pledgee might have incurred expenses or suffered damages; hence the need for a iudicium contrarium. As far as expenses were concerned, we can obtain the necessary information from Pomp. D. 13, 7, 8 pr. (even though this text may well have dealt originally with fiducia):[283]

> "Si necessarias impensas fecerim in servum aut in fundum, quem pignoris causa acceperim, non tantum retentionem, sed etiam contrariam pigneraticiam actionem habebo: finge enim medicis, cum aegrotaret servus, dedisse me pecuniam et eum decessisse, item insulam fulsisse vel refecisse et postea deustam esse, nec habere quod possem retinere."

Originally, a ius retentionis seems to have been available to the pledgee: he did not have to return the pledge until he had been reimbursed for his necessary expenses. But what if there was nothing to retain any more? A slave had been pledged and had fallen sick. The medical bill was paid by the pledgee, but then the slave died. Here a ius retentionis did not help the pledgee as far as recovery of the medical expenses was concerned. Thus he was given the actio pigneraticia contraria.[284]

Damages, on the other hand, could always be claimed under the provisions of the actio de dolo.[285] But it was soon realized that this general remedy was too restricted and thus not able to provide satisfactory protection of the pledgee's reasonable expectations. It was felt especially that the pledgee could expect the pledged property to

---

[279] *Inst.* III, 14, 4; cf. also Ulp. D. 13, 6, 5, 2.

[280] *Inst.* III, 14, 4; De Robertis, *Responsabilità contrattuale*, pp. 345 sqq.

[281] Cf. e.g. Accursius, gl. Exactam ad. I. 3, 15, 4; Vinnius, *Institutiones*, Lib. III, Tit. XV, 4; Grotius, *Inleiding*, III, VIII, 4; Pothier, *Traité de l'hypothèke*, ch. IV (*Du nantissement*), III; Windscheid/Kipp, p. 382; Story, *Bailments*, p. 332.

[282] Paul. D. 13, 7, 14: "Ea igitur, quae diligens pater familias in suis rebus praestare solet, a creditore exiguntur."

[283] Justinian merged pignus and fiducia; it is therefore often difficult to decide with which of these two forms of security the classical authors in actual fact dealt.

[284] Cf. further C. 4, 24, 7, 1 (Gord.).

[285] Ulp. D. 13, 7, 36, 1.

belong to the pledgor and not to have been otherwise encumbered. The problems arising from res aliena pignori data vel alii obligata are discussed in a variety of texts; the picture that emerges is that the pledgor seems to have been strictly liable for these legal defects. In Paul. D. 13, 7, 16, 1 the position is summed up in the following words:

> "Contrariam pigneraticiam creditori actionem competere certum est. proinde si rem alienam vel alii pigneratam vel in publicum obligatam dedit, tenebitur, quamvis et stellionatus crimen committat. sed utrum ita demum, si scit, an et si ignoravit? et quantum ad crimen pertinet, excusat ignorantia: quantum ad contrarium iudicium, ignorantia eum non excusat, ut Marcellus libro sexto digestorum scribit. sed si sciens creditor accipiat vel alienum vel obligatum vel morbosum, contrarium ei non competit."[286]

This did not mean, however, that the pledgor would always be liable, regardless of fault, for damages caused to the pledgee. Ulpianus relates an incident where copper was given as a pledge instead of gold:

> "Si quis in pignore pro auro aes subiecisset creditori, qualiter teneatur, quaesitum est. in qua specie rectissime Sabinus scribit . . . si in dando aes subiecisset, turpitur fecisse. . . . sed et hic puto pigneraticiam iudicium locum habere, et ita Pomponius scribit."[287]

It is clear from the context that Sabinus had been dealing with a fraudulent manipulation on the part of the pledgor.[288] Pomponius seems to have granted the actio pigneraticia contraria under the same circumstances in which Sabinus originally used the actio de dolo.[289] In these "aes pro auro" cases,[290] the pledgor was liable for dolus in contrahendo.[291] Fraudulent behaviour on the part of the pledgor could, however, occur not only in the process of entering into the contract of pledge, but also when the pledge was returned.

> "Si quasi recepturus a debitore tuo comminus pecuniam reddidisti ei pignus isque per fenestram id misit excepturo eo, quem de industria ad id posuerit, Labeo ait furti te agere cum debitore posse et ad exhibendum: et, si agente te contraria pigneraticia excipiat debitor de pignore sibi reddito, replicabitur de dolo at fraude, per quam nec redditum, sed per fallaciam ablatum id intellegitur."[292]

The pledgee returns the pledge to his debtor in the expectation that the latter has come to repay the debt. Instead of doing that, the debtor takes the pledge and throws it out of the window. Outside he has posted an accomplice who has been instructed to catch the pledge. The pledgee, according to Pomponius, will succeed with his actio pigneraticia

---

[286] Cf. further Ulp. D. 13, 7, 9 pr.; Marci. D. 13, 7, 32; C. 8, 15, 6 (Diocl.); Schwarz, (1954) 71 *ZSS* 142 sqq.; Stein, *Fault*, pp. 128 sqq.; Kaser, (1979) 47 *TR* 223 sqq.

[287] Ulp. D. 13, 7, 36 pr.

[288] Schwarz, (1954) 71 *ZSS* 136; Stein, *Fault*, pp. 137 sq.

[289] The actio de dolo has probably been cut out by the compilers; Ulpian originally wrote this text in the course of a commentary on the actio de dolo (11 ad ed.).

[290] Cf. also Ulp. D. 13, 7, 1, 2.

[291] Cf. further Paul. D. 46, 1, 54.

[292] Pomp. D. 13, 7, 3. On this text Schwarz, (1954) 71 *ZSS* 160 sq. and especially Kaser, (1979) 47 *TR* 227 sq., vindicating it for classical law against a variety of interpolation hypotheses (e.g. Frezza, *Garanzie*, vol. I, p. 295; d'Ors, (1953) 19 *SDHI* 191).

contraria,[293] because even though the debtor might raise the exceptio de pignore sibi reddito (after all, the pledgee has returned the pledge to him), he will be able to counter this exceptio with a replicatio de dolo et fraude.

Instead of actively pursuing his claims against the pledgor by means of the contrarium iudicium, the pledgee could opt to wait and see: if he was sued under the actio pigneraticia, he could avail himself of his ius retentionis and refuse to hand back the pledge until his claims had been satisfied. The Emperor Gordian increased the strength of the pledgee's position by allowing him to retain the pledge even on account of any other claim that he might have against the debtor. On being sued for the return of the pledge, he could avail himself of the exceptio doli for this purpose.[294]

---

[293] Besides, the actio furti (possessionis) and the actio ad exhibendum are applicable.
[294] C. 8, 26, 1, 2; Enzo Nardi, *Studi sulla ritenzione in diritto romano*, vol. I (1947), pp. 203 sqq.; cf. also Story, *Bailments*, pp. 304 sq.

PART IV

CHAPTER 8

Emptio venditio I

I. THE BINDING NATURE OF CONSENSUAL SALE

1. Consensus

The development of the consensual contracts generally, and of the rules relating to the contract of sale in particular, is one of the most remarkable achievements of Roman jurisprudence. The Roman law of sale has provided us with the basic tools for our modern analysis of this economically most important of contracts, and it has invariably shaped our way of thinking about sale, irrespective of whether certain individual rules were preserved or rejected. Even where modern legislators have chosen not to follow the example of Roman law, the latter provides the background against which to evaluate such a decision and to appreciate its implications. Thus, the Roman law of sale has been emphatically described as "the most fruitful subject in Roman law for the English law-student";[1] and one could apply this statement with even greater justification to the English law student's Continental or South African counterpart.

The contract of sale (emptio venditio) was purely consensual. The sole basis for the respective obligations to deliver the goods and to pay the purchase price was the agreement between seller and purchaser. No form was needed, no witnesses had to be present, no rei interventio was required.

2. The question of arrha

(a) Arrha confirmatoria

Nor was the handing over of an arrha necessary in order to make the contract binding. Arrha is an object (in Rome, usually a ring[2] or a sum of money) given, upon entering into a contract, as an earnest.[3] The historical analysis of this institution is a favourite topic of discussion, especially amongst English romanists;[4] the disputes, however, rage mainly around the developments in the law of the Roman Republic and of Justinian, whereas the situation in classical law is relatively clear.

---

[1] De Zulueta, *Sale*, p. III.

[2] Cf. Ulp. D. 14, 3, 5, 15; Ulp. D. 19, 1, 11, 6; on the history of arrha, see Pringsheim, *Sale*, pp. 335 sqq.

[3] The German term "*Draufgabe*" is misleading in view of what is set out infra, note 8. The term "*Handgeld*" (Windscheid/Kipp, § 325) is more apposite.

[4] For a recent overview, see M. McAuley, "One Thousand Years of Arra", (1977) 25 *McGill LJ* 693 sqq.

> "Emptio venditio contrahitur cum de pretio convenerit, quamvis nondum pretium numeratum sit, ac ne arra quidem data fuerit. nam quod arrae nomine datur, argumentum est emptionis et venditionis contractae", says Gaius,[5] and in D. 18, 1, 35 pr. he expands: "Quod saepe arrae nomine pro emptione datur, non eo pertinet, quasi sine arra conventio nihil proficiat, set ut evidentius probari possit convenisse de pretio."[6]

Wherever such an earnest was given, it only provided some evidence that a contract of sale had been concluded. It did not have a constitutive effect or function, but merely played a confirmatory role (arrha confirmatoria).[7] Once the contractual obligations had been discharged, the ring could be claimed back. If a sum of money had been given as arrha, it was set off against the purchase price.[8]

(b) Greek arrha

D. 18, 1, 35 pr. makes it clear that the confirmation of a contract by means of an arrha was not a rare occurrence. The text also contains a pointed allusion to an alternative way of looking at arrha. This was the view prevailing in Greek law, which did not recognize consensual contracts and where the handing over of an earnest was therefore essential for creating (contractual) liability.[9] Here both parties were interested in the arrha for it was not only the buyer who was penalized by its forfeiture if he failed to pay the purchase price: it also served to secure the seller's obligation in that, if he defaulted, he not only had to return the buyer's arrha, but he also had to pay him alterum tantum, i.e. as much in addition. Arrha, in this form, "seems to have remained the real sanction of sale in the Greek East throughout the Hellenistic period"[10]; a mere agreement to buy or sell, unaccompanied by arrha, could be repudiated with impunity by either of the two parties. Roman practice was clearly influenced by this Hellenistic model, but to what extent Greek arrha was ever received into Roman law remains a matter of speculation.[11] In any case, it would have made sense only at a time when consensual contracts were not yet recognized as actionable; for once the aggrieved party was able to sue on the contract, there was no longer any real need to acknowledge a system of alternative sanctions. On the other hand, Plautus in his comedies refers to what can in

---

[5] Gai. III, 139.

[6] Gai. D. 18, 1, 35 pr.

[7] Cf., in this sense, also § 336 I BGB.

[8] Ulp. D. 19, 1, 11, 6; Knütel, *Contrarius consensus*, pp. 37 sqq. Cf. also § 337 I BGB: "The earnest shall, in case of doubt, be credited to the performance due from the giver, or when this cannot be done, shall be returned on performance of the contract."

[9] Cf. esp. Pringsheim, *Sale*, pp. 333 sqq.

[10] De Zulueta, *Sale*, pp. 22 sq.

[11] Cf. esp. Mario Talamanca, *L'arra della compravendita in diritto greco e in diritto romano* (1953), pp. 47 sqq.; Philippe Meylan, "Des arrhes de la vente dans Plaute", in: *Mélanges Henri Lévy-Bruhl* (1959), pp. 205 sqq.; Frezza, *Garanzie*, vol. I, pp. 299 sqq; Watson, *Obligations*, pp.46 sqq.; Geoffrey MacCormack, "A Note on Arra in Plautus", (1971) 6 *The Irish Jurist* 360 sqq.

substance only be the Hellenistic version of arrha.[12] These plays were written at a time when consensual contracts were probably already enforceable.[13] Did he therefore present Greek law to his audience? But would constant allusion to a foreign legal institution have succeeded in eliciting any response (let alone a comical one) from a crowd of spectators that has been characterized as "a noisy and unruly lot"?[14] Would it not, therefore, be more realistic to consider Plautus as "faithfully portraying an already romanized version of the Greek law"?[15] Alternatively, can one solve the problem by referring to the "social value" of arrha:

> "Even if it had no legal effects whatsoever, sellers would still want to extract substantial arra from the buyer. . . . In the mind of the man in the street, a consensual contract is that much more binding where arra has been given . . ."?[16]

Be that as it may, the practice of giving an arrha lived on, and even the impact of the Greek perception of this practice was only temporarily subdued.

(c) Post-classical arrha

With the decline of consensualism, arrha (re)gained its attraction. Justinian even received and incorporated Greek arrha into the Corpus Juris Civilis, but only in respect of sales effected in writing.[17] Reason:

> "[I]n his autem [emptionibus et venditionibus] quae scriptura conficiuntur non aliter perfectam esse emptionem et venditionem constituimus, nisi et instrumenta emptionis fuerint conscripta vel manu propria contrahentium, vel ab alio quidem scripta, a contrahente autem subscripta et, si per tabellionem fiunt, nisi et completiones acceperint et fuerint partibus absoluta. donec enim aliquid ex his deest, et paenitentiae locus est et potest emptor vel venditor sine poena recedere ab emptione."[18]

Whenever it was envisaged to reduce the agreement into writing, the document that was to be drawn up was regarded as the contract. Prior to its written formulation, no binding obligations existed; there was still room for reconsideration and either vendor or purchaser could withdraw from the contract with impunity. Hence the need for arrha. Its function was penal (arrha poenalis). On the other hand, however, Justinian also revived and preserved the classical (purely) consensual sale. For these contracts "quae sine scriptura consistunt", arrha still had

---

[12] Cf. *Curculio*, Act V, l. 612; *Pseudolus*, Act IV, Sc. VII, l. 1183, where the seller is given the choice of delivering the object sold or returning the arrha; further, for example *Rudens*, Act II, Sc. VI, l. 554 sq.; *Mostellaria*, Act V, Sc. II, l. 1099.

[13] For the date of origin of consensual sale (3rd century) cf. Fritz Pringsheim, "L'origine" des contrats consensuels", (1954) 32 *RH* 475 sqq.; Alan Watson, "The Origins of Consensual Sale: A Hyphothesis", (1964) 32 *TR* 253; Kaser, *RPr* I, p. 526.

[14] Duckworth, *The Nature of Roman Comedy* (1952), p. 82.

[15] McAuley, (1977) 23 *McGill LJ* 695.

[16] Watson, *Obligations*, pp. 49, 51.

[17] On the rise in the use of writing in post-classical sales law, cf. Wulf Eckart Voss, *Recht und Rhetorik in den Kaisergesetzen der Spätantike* (1982), pp. 195 sqq.

[18] *Inst.* III, 23 pr.

a merely evidentiary function.[19] Yet it is difficult to determine whether the distinction was really that straightforward. *Institutiones* III, 23 pr. in fine, contains a clause ("sive in scriptis sive sine scriptis venditio celebrata est") which cannot easily be reconciled with what is set out at the beginning of the text.

(d) Argumentum emptionis contractae or arrha poenitentialis?

C. 4, 21, 17, our other major source for the Justinianic arrha, is, if anything, even more difficult to understand. The interpretation of the sources has thus given rise to disputes which continue unabated.[20] As far as the position in the ius commune is concerned, the main point of controversy has always been the function of an arrha given after the sale had already come into existence: "Venditione perfecta, et arris datis, emptor, seu venditor recusat implere promissa, quaestio est quid iuris?"[21] Was the arrha merely argumentum emptionis et venditionis contractae (evidence that the contract had been concluded)?[22] If one of the parties subsequently withdrew from the contract and did not render performance as promised, the other would then have had a claim for damages on the contract in exactly the same way as if no arrha had been given.[23] Or are we dealing here with what came to be called arrha poenitentialis (*"Reugeld"*)? Both parties, it was often argued, had a right to withdraw from the contract; the purchaser, if he chose to exercise this right of withdrawal, forfeited what he had given as arrha, whereas the vendor, who no longer wanted to be bound by the contract, had to return double the amount of the arrha: "[H]oc in casu ad id, quod interest, actionem non esse dandam, sed arras datas omitti,

---

19 *Inst.* III, 23 pr.

20 Cf. e.g. Talamanca, op. cit., note 11, pp. 79 sqq.; Gérard Chalon-Secrétan, *Les arrhes de la vente sous Justinien* (1954); J.A.C. Thomas, "Arra in Sale in Justinian's Law", (1956) 24 *TR* 253 sqq.; idem, "Arra reagitata", (1956) *Butterworth's South African LR* 60 sqq.; idem, "A Postscript on Arra", (1959) 10 *Iura* 109 sqq.; Alan Watson, "Arra in the Law of Justinian", (1959) 6 *RIDA* 385 sqq.; T.H. Tylor, "Writing and Arra in Sale under the Corpus Juris", (1961) 77 *LQR* 77 sqq.; A.M. Honoré, "Arra as You Were", (1961) 77 *LQR* 172 sqq.; Mario Talamanca, "Osservazioni sull'arra nel diritto Giustinianeo", in: *Mélanges Philippe Meylan*, vol. I, pp. 325 sqq.; Joseph M. Thomson, "Arra in Sale In Justinian's Law", (1970) 5 *The Irish Jurist* 179 sqq.; M.L. Marasinghe, "Arra—Not in Dispute", (1973) 20 *RIDA* 349 sqq.; Henryk Kupiszewski, "Quelques remarques sur les vocabula ΑΝΤΙΧΡΗΣΙΣ, ΑΡΡΑ, ΠΑΡΑΦΝΡΗΑ dans le digeste", (1974) 18 *JJP* 235 sqq.

21 Fachinaeus, *Controversiae iuris*, Lib. II, Cap. XXVIII.

22 Cf. e.g. Pothier, *Traité du contrat du vente*, nn. 508 sq.

23 Except that the value forfeited might have counted towards damages. This was disputed, too. Cf., today, § 338 BGB: "If the performance due from the giver becomes impossible because of a circumstance for which he is responsible, or if the rescission of the contract is due to his fault, the holder of the earnest is entitled to retain it. If the holder of the earnest demands compensation for nonperformance, the earnest shall, in case of doubt, be credited, or if this cannot be done, it shall be returned upon payment of the compensation." The earnest, in this instance, represents a minimum amount of liquidated damages; the function of the earnest is that of a penalty clause.

aut duplum reddi oportere."[24] According to this view, arrha weakened rather than strengthened the contract. The fathers of the BGB favoured the former solution. Of course, the will of the parties is always of paramount importance, and it is therefore primarily up to them to determine the effects of arrha in detail.[25] However, in case of doubt, it is not to be regarded as arrha poenitentialis; it is deemed to be (merely) proof of the conclusion of the contract.[26]

3. The essentialia negotii

For a valid sale to come into existence, the parties had to agree on the object of the sale and the price. They could provide further details of their transaction: either of them could reserve the right to rescind the contract under certain circumstances, the purchaser could ask the vendor to guarantee certain qualities of the thing sold, the parties could specify the place of performance, etc. But these were merely accidentalia negotii, special arrangements of the parties, which did not determine the nature of the contract. As long as object and price had been agreed upon, the contract could be classified as sale; at least with regard to these essential elements, the contract had to be the work of the parties and an expression of their private autonomy. Exact determination of reciprocal rights and duties and of the effects and consequences of the transaction, on the other hand, was not necessarily the business of the parties; such regulations normally connected with or "naturally" flowing from any contract of sale (hence: "naturalia negotii") were (and still are) usually provided by the law.[27] We shall deal first with the essentialia and then with the naturalia negotii.

II. THE POSSIBLE OBJECTS OF A CONTRACT OF SALE

1. Demarcating the areas of emptio venditio and locatio conductio

Almost anything could be the object of a contract of sale,[28] whether corporeal or incorporeal: chattels (especially slaves) or land, claims against third parties or inheritances, servitudes, praedial or personal, etc. If, however, the benefit of the seller's services or the use of a thing

[24] Cf. e.g. Fachinaeus, loc. cit.; cf. also e.g. Perezius, *Praelectiones*, Lib. IV, Tit. XXXVIII, 20.

[25] For the modern version of arrha poenitentialis, cf. § 359 BGB.

[26] § 336 BGB.

[27] The distinction between essentialia, naturalia and accidentialia negotii was developed in the Middle Ages under the influence of Aristotelian logic. Cf. Helmut Coing, "A Typical Development in the Roman Law of Sales", in: *Gesammelte Aufsätze zu Rechtsgeschichte, Rechtsphilosophie und Zivilrecht*, vol. I (1982), pp. 73 sq.; idem, "Zum Einfluss der Philosophie des Aristoteles auf die Entwicklung des römischen Rechts", (1952) 69 *ZSS* 32 sq.

[28] Paul. D. 18, 1, 34, 1: "Omnium rerum, quas quis habere vel possidere vel persequi potest, venditio recte fit."

was the subject matter of the transaction, the contract was not sale but hire (locatio conductio). Wherever a legal system distinguishes between different types of contracts and wherever the naturalia negotii vary according to how a specific transaction is classified, intricate problems of where to draw the line arise. What, for instance, if I engage a goldsmith to make me a ring? Is it sale of the ring or hire of the goldsmith's services?

> "Item quaeritur, si cum aurifice mihi convenerit, ut is ex auro suo certi ponderis certaeque formae anulos mihi faceret, et acciperet verbi gratia denarios CC, utrum emptio et venditio an locatio et conductio contrahatur. Cassius ait materiae quidem emptionem venditionemque contrahi, operarum autem locationem et conductionem. sed plerisque placuit emptionem et venditionem contrahi. atqui, si meum aurum ei dedero, mercede pro opera constituta, convenit locationem conductionem contrahi."[29]

The question, as we see, was controversial. Cassius even argued that we are dealing here with a mixed type of transaction. Eventually the opinion came to prevail that the contract was one of sale, provided the vendor (maker) supplied the material.[30] The opposite was the case where the purchaser had given the goldsmith the gold; also in building contracts, for instance, where the "purchaser" had asked the "vendor" to build a house on his (the "purchaser's") ground.[31] These are subtle distinctions. In the latter two instances the hire of the services clearly dominates the transactions, whereas the transfer of ownership from the maker/builder to the customer, which might point in the direction of sale, is, at best, only incidental.[32] But to apply the rules of sale wherever the contractor is bound to produce the work from materials provided by himself (except in the "superficies-solo-cedit" situations), seems not always to be entirely satisfactory. Where the value of those materials, as compared with that of the work, is quite insignificant, it is hardly apposite to speak of a contract of sale.[33] Or take the case where the contractor produces a non-fungible object for a specific customer: it may well be argued that the rules relating to the contract for work are more suitable in this instance, particularly in view of the fact that it will be difficult for the customer to sell this object elsewhere.[34]

---

[29] Gai. III, 147.

[30] Cf. also Pomp. D. 18, 1, 20; Iav. D. 18, 1, 65.

[31] Pomp. D. 18, 1, 20 in fine; Paul. D. 19, 2, 22, 2.

[32] In the case of the building contract, ownership passed to the "purchaser" on account of accessio (superficies solo cedit) and not on account of delivery. Where the goldsmith made the ring from the "purchaser's" gold, we are dealing with a case of specificatio. According to the Sabinians, the "purchaser" continued to be the owner, whereas the Proculians saw the goldsmith as acquiring ownership. Only according to this latter opinion would the "seller" have had to (re)transfer ownership.

[33] De Zulueta, *Sale*, pp. 15 sq.

[34] Cf. "Protokolle"., in: *Mugdan*, vol. II, p. 919. § 651 BGB therefore reads as follows: "If the contractor binds himself to produce the work from material provided by him, he shall deliver the thing produced to the customer and convey ownership in the thing. The

Similar problems of demarcating the respective areas of emptio venditio and locatio conductio could arise in other cases, another famous example being the one discussed in Gaius III, 146:

> "Item, si gladiatores ea lege tibi tradiderim, ut in singulos qui integri exierint pro sudore denarii XX mihi darentur, in eos vero singulos qui occisi aut debilitati fuerint denarii mille, quaeritur utrum emptio et venditio an locatio et conductio contrahatur."

Somebody wants to organize a gladiatorial show. For each man who emerges unscathed, he agrees to pay 20 denarii in return for the slave's exertions ("his sweat"); for each gladiator who is killed or maimed, 1 000 denarii. Sale or hire? According to the prevailing opinion, it could be either, depending on what happened to each particular slave. Whomever the organizer of the games was able to return unscathed to the gladiators' masters (lanistae) was to be considered as having been hired: with respect to those killed or disabled, the contract was one of sale. Thus the nature of the transaction could be determined only once the outcome of the gladiatorial contest was known. Both sale and hire were dependent upon the fulfilment or non-fulfilment of a condition; until then the transaction was pending. This solution is hardly convenient, for it does not provide a remedy for the games-giver if the lanista fails to supply the gladiatorial games.[35]

2. Generic sales

(a) *The Roman rule and its origin*

The most interesting and, from a modern point of view, even startling exception to the range of possible objects of a contract of sale was provided by the fact that mere generic sales (or "sales by description") recognized in Roman law. Things which are normally counted, measured or weighed and are therefore usually defined by reference to their genus could, of course, be sold, but only if they were either specified ("these two amphorae of Tusculan country wine") or if a whole (specific) stock of such non-specific goods was sold ("all the wine in my cellar").[36] Even the sale of generic goods from an identified source, i.e. from a specified mass or stock, was possible ("ten amphorae of wine from my cellar").[37] But the sale of, say, "twenty amphorae of white wine", or of "a slave", that is, the pure generic emptio venditio,

---

provisions applicable to sale apply to such a contract; if a non-fungible thing is to be produced, the provisions relating to contract for work, with the exception of §§. . ., take the place of §§. . . ."

[35] De Zulueta, *Gaius* II, p. 174. Cf. also the detailed analysis of Gai. III, 146 by A.M. Prichard, in: *Studies in the Roman Law of Sale in memory of Francis de Zulueta* (1959), pp. 1 sqq.; Antonio Guarino, "Il leasing dei gladiatori", (1985) 13 *Index* 461 sqq.

[36] Cf. e.g. Gai. D. 18, 1, 35, 5.

[37] Gai. D. 18, 1, 35, 7; Paul. D. 18, 6, 5 (second part).

was unknown to Roman law.[38] This raises two questions: how could long-distance trading, especially among the big grain and wine merchants, be carried out without it? And secondly: what was the reason for this peculiarly restrictive state of affairs?

The answer to the latter question lies in the historical evolution of sale.[39] In all the ancient laws, sale was essentially a market transaction. It was concluded inter praesentes, and conclusion of the contract and execution of the mutual performances (i.e. the transfer of the object of the sale and payment of the purchase price) coincided. Thus, in early Roman law, sale was tantamount to an executed sale or cash sale. This is obvious regarding the formal act of mancipatio, in the course of which originally, in order to effect the sale, the price was weighed out and handed over in exchange for the acquisition of a res mancipi. But the informal sale, too, was first of all cash sale. In the course of time this strict and simple system of transfer against cash was gradually relaxed, first in that the purchase price could be credited, then also by allowing the delivery of the object sold to be separated from the conclusion of the sale. Thus, by the time of the later Roman Republic, the formless emptio venditio had become a fully executory contract.[40] It no longer contained all the elements necessary for the transfer of ownership of the object sold in itself; nor did it require payment of the purchase price for its validity. The contract merely gave rise to the obligations on the part of the vendor to perform whatever acts were necessary to transfer ownership, on the part of the purchaser to effect the payment. The contract of sale in this sense was conceived as a uniform transaction with an all-round range of application: it could be concluded as a cash or credit transaction, among Roman citizens and with peregrini, in respect of res mancipi and res nec mancipi. Mancipatio eventually degenerated into a mode of transfer of res mancipi; though retaining

[38] We find it in none of our sources. Cf. Emil Seckel, Ernst Levy, "Die Gefahrtragung beim Kauf im klassischen römischen Recht", (1927) 47 *ZSS* 122 sqq.; Buckland/McNair, p. 282; De Zulueta, *Sale*, p. 16; Arangio-Ruiz, *Compravendita*, pp. 122 sqq. Contra: Franz Haymann, "Haben die Römen den Gattungskauf gekannt?", (1928–29) 79 *JhJb* 95 sqq.; Honsell/Mayer-Maly/Selb, pp. 305 sqq.

[39] For what follows, see De Zulueta, *Sale*, pp. 2 sqq.; Arangio-Ruiz, *Compravendita*, pp. 4 sqq.; Kaser, *RPr* I, pp. 545 sq. Cf. also Joseph Georg Wolf, "Barkauf und Haftung", (1977) 45 *TR* 12 sq.

[40] "From the beginning of the second century B.C. the pulse of trade began to beat too fast for the leisurely methods which had suited the cautious Roman peasant well enough": De Zulueta, *Sale*, p. 5. Hypotheses on the origin of consensual sale and of the origins of the bonae fidei iudicia in general abound; see, for instance, Philippe Meylan, "Le rôle de la bona fides dans le passage de la vente au comptant à la vente consensuelle à Rome", in: *Aequitas und Bona Fides, Festgabe für August Simonius* (1955), p. 247 sqq.; Filippo Cancelli, *L'origine del contratto consensuale di compravendita nel diritto romano* (1963), passim; Franz Wieacker, "Zum Ursprung der bonae fidei iudicia", (1963) 80 *ZSS* 1 sqq. (cf. also idem, *RR* , pp. 441 sqq., 453 sq., 457 sq.); Alan Watson, "The Origins of Consensual Sale: A Hypothesis", (1964) 32 *TR* 245 sqq.; Luigi Labruna, "Plauto, Manilio, Catone: Premesse allo studio dell' 'emptio' consensuale", (1968) 14 *Labeo* 24 sqq.; Jolowicz/Nicholas, pp. 288 sqq.; Diósdi, pp. 44 sqq. The most recent contribution is Watson, *Evolution*, pp. 12 sqq.

many of its archaic features,[41] it no longer functioned in itself as (the) sale, but was regarded as a way of discharging the vendor's obligation arising from the underlying contract. It is an intriguing feature of the Roman law of sale, though, that the old cash sale ideas lingered on and that the fully developed, executory emptio venditio always retained certain features of the ancient executed type of transaction. One of these features was the fact that the sale of generic goods never came to be accommodated within the framework of emptio venditio by the Roman lawyers. As a matter of course, every sale in the olden days was the sale of one or a number of specific things; for in a system where the parties get together on the marketplace and exchange their performances on the spot, it is evident that the objects of the sale are those specific items which the vendor has actually brought along. A generic sale, under these circumstances, is a logical impossibility. The lawyers, however, retained what had once been a natural restriction, even at a time when it had become possible to envisage and conceptualize this type of transaction.

(b) Generic sale and sale of specific goods

Two factors may well have contributed towards this conservative attitude. On the one hand, the cash sale remained by far the most frequent type of sale and continued to dominate particularly the common transactions of everyday life. On the other hand (and this is, at the same time, the answer to the first of the above-mentioned questions), there does not seem to have been a great practical need for the purely generic emptio venditio. Big business (and whoever else might have been involved in such transactions) could (and actually did) avail itself of two stipulations in order to achieve the same practical result.[42] That was convenient enough and it also allowed the parties to stipulate, in the same breath, all the terms they deemed necessary in the individual circumstances. In any event, this procedure was hardly more cumbersome for the parties than adapting, by way of special pacta, the rules relating to the consensual emptio venditio to suit the envisaged generic sale. This would have been necessary, however, seeing that these rules were geared very much towards the (non-generic) sale of specific goods.[43] The latter observation, incidentally, is hardly less valid today than it was in Roman law. The generic sale has, of course, long since been recognized, but it has always been overshadowed by the sale of specific goods. Even modern legislators have given pride of place to

---

[41] The transferee still had to assert that he had *bought* the object ("Hunc ego hominem ex iure Quiritium meum esse aio isque mihi emptus esto hoc aere aeneaque libra"), which was as fictitious as the "price" paid, a copper coin which he handed over to the transferor after he had used it to knock at the scales which the libripens held.

[42] Seckel/Levy, (1927) 47 *ZSS* 137 sqq.; Buckland/McNair, pp. 282 sq.

[43] For instance, as far as liability for latent defects is concerned; cf. e.g. Seckel/Levy, (1927) 47 *ZSS* 136 sq. and, today, § 480 BGB, read together with § 243 BGB.

the sale of specific goods and have devoted careful and loving consideration to all the details and eventualities thereof. The sale of generic goods tends to be regarded traditionally as a deviation from the norm that can be dealt with by way of a mere appendix or some special provisions thrown in here and there. In modern life, however, it dominates to such an extent that it may well be asked whether the law should not also reverse its priorities.[44] In so far as this has not yet been achieved, we are still caught up in the thinking patterns of lost ages, where producer and consumer met, without any intermediaries, in a shop or marketplace, in order to effect their transactions. Ultimately, it is the cash sale of ancient Rome that still lurks in the background.

(c) The double function of the contract of sale

Another consideration may be added at this stage. Sale, as we have said, was an obligatory (or executory) act. It gave rise to certain obligations, which still had to be discharged, particularly the obligation to transfer the object sold. But at the same time the contract of sale itself contributed to the execution of this very obligation; it contained a "real" (as opposed to merely obligatory) element. This seemingly paradoxical situation can best be explained by a comparison with the position in modern German law. In § 433 I BGB we read that "by the contract of sale the seller of a thing is bound to deliver the thing to the purchaser and to transfer ownership of the thing". As far as this transfer of ownership is concerned, we have to refer to § 929 BGB. "For the transfer of ownership of a movable thing," this rule provides, "it is necessary that the owner of the thing deliver it to the acquirer and that both agree that the ownership be transferred." All in all, therefore, three acts are necessary to conclude and carry out the transaction. There is, first of all, the (purely obligatory) contract of sale. Then there is traditio, the act of physical transfer of the object sold. But over and above that, there is a further contract accompanying the delivery: transferor and transferee have to agree on the transfer of ownership. This second contract is conceptually detached from and unconnected to the contract of sale (the principle of separation); in German law, furthermore, its validity has to be determined in abstracto, i.e. independent of whether the underlying contract of sale is void or valid (or whether, indeed, such an underlying contract has even been concluded—the principle of abstraction).[45] It has been maintained that for the transfer of ownership in Roman law, apart from traditio, an

[44] Cf. e.g. Rabel, *Warenkauf*, vol. I, p. 65.

[45] Cf. e.g. Zweigert/Kötz, *Einführung in die Rechtsvergleichung* (1st ed.(!), 1971), vol. I, pp. 214 sqq.; Gerhard Kegel, "Verpflichtung und Verfügung", in: *Festschrift für F.A. Mann* (1977), pp. 57 sqq.; Reinhard Zimmermann, "Sittenwidrigkeit und Abstraktion", (1985) *Juristische Rundschau* 48 sqq. The principle of abstraction goes back to Friedrich Carl von Savigny; cf. his *Obligationenrecht*, vol. II, pp. 254 sqq. and Wilhelm Felgentraeger, *Friedrich Carl v. Savignys Einfluss auf die Übereignungslehre* (1927).

agreement of this kind, separate from the contract of sale, was required—but (unlike in German law) not an abstract one: a causa traditionis in the sense of an agreement on the legal purpose of transferring ownership, a special legal act determining why traditio is actually made: venditionis causa, donationis causa, mutui causa, etc.[46] Today, however, another view prevails.[47] It has been shown that transfer of ownership depended on two elements only: iusta causa traditionis and traditio. Gaius II 19, 20, for instance, states quite clearly:

> "Nam res nec mancipi ipsa traditione pleno iure alterius fiunt, si modo corporales sunt et ob id recipiunt traditionem. Itaque si tibi vestum vel aurum vel argentum tradidero sive ex venditionis causa sive ex donationis sive quavis alia ex causa, statim tua fit ea res. si modo ego eius dominus sim."

The contract of sale and traditio: no further acts were necessary. The contract of sale, then, had a double function: it was the obligatory act *and* iusta causa traditionis—iusta causa traditionis in the sense that it implicitly contained the will of the parties to transfer ownership on the basis of a contract of sale; and it was this common purpose that formed the basis of traditio and justified the transfer of ownership. If that was so, it becomes clear (and that is why we have made the point in the present context) that it was not merely their innate conservatism which prevented the Roman lawyers from recognizing generic sales. The very structure of the Roman emptio venditio did not lend itself to accommodating this type of transaction.[48] If the contract of sale served as iusta causa traditionis and thus contained everything that was necessary to transfer ownership except traditio, it could only refer to a specific thing; for, whilst it is perfectly possible to agree to sell goods described only by reference to their genus, ownership can logically be transferred with regard to only one or the other *specific* object.

3. The sale of non-existing objects

If the potential objects of a contract of sale were multifarious, a very basic requirement for its validity was that such object did in fact exist: "Nec emptio nec venditio sine re quae veneat potest intellegi."[49] Thus, if the slave who was to be the object of the sale had died before the contract was concluded, if a house had burnt down or a vessel had been smashed before it was sold, the contract was void. It was impossible for the vendor, under these circumstances, to fulfil what he had promised:

---

[46] Cf. e.g. Fritz Schulz, (1932) 52 *ZSS* 544 sqq.

[47] Max Kaser, "Zur 'iusta causa traditionis'", (1961) 64 *BIDR* 61 sqq.; Günther Jahr, "Zur iusta causa tradionis", (1963) 80 *ZSS* 141 sqq.; Uwe Wesel, "Zur dinglichen Wirkung der Rücktrittsvorbehalte des römischen Kaufs", (1968) 85 *ZSS* 100 sqq.; Robin Evans-Jones, Geoffrey MacCormack, "Iusta causa traditionis", in: *New Perspectives in the Roman Law of Property, Essays for Barry Nicholas* (1989), pp. 99 sqq.

[48] See, for this argument, Frank Peters, "Die Verschaffung des Eigentums durch den Verkäufer", (1979) 96 *ZSS* 189.

[49] Pomp. D. 18, 1, 8 pr.

he could not make delivery and provide undisturbed possession and enjoyment of something that had ceased to exist. "Impossibilium nulla obligatio est" was the fundamental principle governing these situations.[50] By the same token, a sale was not regarded as invalid merely because the vendor was not owner of what he sold: "Rem alienam distrahere quem posse nulla dubitatio est: nam emptio est et venditio."[51] However, as the text continues, ". . . res emptori auferri potest". On the consequences and implications of such an act of eviction, more anon.

4. The sale of res extra commercium or of a free man

(a) *Res publicae, res divini iuris and the liber homo*

Furthermore, there were certain categories of things, in which dealings were not factually (objectively) impossible, but prohibited by law. These were liberi homines—subjects rather than objects of rights—things in usu publico (such as public roads, fora, basilicae, stadia, theatra, cloacae or rivers)[52] and res divini iuris: res sacrae, dedicated to the gods above (such as temples or sacred groves), res religiosae, dedicated to the gods below (tombs, burial grounds, etc.) and res sanctae, places specifically under divine protection, such as the walls and gates of a city.[53] Res publicae and res divini iuris were taken to be extra commercium; they could not be the object of any commercial legal transaction between private individuals. Originally, therefore, any contract of sale involving either a free man or a res extra commercium was void.

(b) *The availability of the actio empti*

Soon, however, this solution was felt to be unsatisfactory in situations where the purchaser (but not the vendor) had been unaware of the true status of the thing. Cases of this nature were, of course, very unlikely to crop up with regard to res publicae and, to a lesser extent, res divini iuris:

---

[50] Cf. infra, pp. 687 sqq. On the sale of an object belonging to the purchaser (suae rei emptio) cf. Pomp. D. 18, 1, 16 pr. ("non valet"); Iul. D. 12, 6, 37; Ulp. D. 50, 17, 45 pr.; Antonio Carcaterra, "I negozi giuridici sulla cosa propria", (1940) 18 *Annali Bari* 1 sqq.; Giannetto Longo, "Negozi giuridici collegati e negozi su cosa propria", (1979) 45 *SDHI* 93 sqq.; Carmela Russo Ruggieri, "'Suae rei emptio consistere non potest'", in: *Sodalitas, Scritti in onore di Antonio Guarino*, vol. VI (1984), pp. 2813 sqq.; Arp, *Anfängliche Unmöglichkeit*, pp. 95 sq., 122.

[51] Ulp. D. 18, 1, 28; on this text, see David Daube, "Generalizations in D. 18, 1 de contrahenda emptione", in: *Studi in onore di Vincenzo Arangio-Ruiz*, vol. I, pp. 186 sqq.; cf. also Paul. D. 19, 1, 46.

[52] Cf. e.g. Kaser, *RPr* I, p. 381.

[53] Gai. II, 3 sqq.; Marci. D. 1, 8, 6, 2 sqq.; *Inst.* II, 1, 7 sqq.

> ". . . it is . . . difficult to credit that even the greenest provincial on his first visit to the mother city could honestly believe that he could take effective possession from another private individual of . . . the Temple of Venus . . . or the Via Sacra";[54]

they did, however, present a problem as far as the sale of a liber homo as a slave was concerned.[55] Of course it was not possible to transfer ownership in this instance; but that, as we shall see presently, was not the duty of the seller. The liber homo was an economic asset of which the purchaser could enjoy the habere licere and which was thus capable of being the object of a sale.[56] The sanction of invalidity was therefore already in classical Roman law restricted to those cases where the purchaser had been fully aware of the status of the "slave" at the time when the contract was concluded.[57] If, on the other hand, he had not known that what he had bought was not a slave but a free man, the contract was regarded as valid.[58] This implies that, once the truth had been discovered and the purchaser consequently lost possession of the man, he could bring the actio empti against his vendor in order to claim damages.[59] The position has been conveniently summed up by Licinius Rufinus:

> "Liberi hominis emptionem contrahi posse plerique existimaverunt, si modo inter ignorantes id fiat. quod idem placet etiam, si venditor sciat, emptor autem ignoret. quod si emptor sciens liberum esse emerit, nulla emptio contrahitur."[60]

The transaction was considered to be a valid sale "for the purpose of allowing the innocent purchaser an actio empti. Practicality—and the jurists were nothing if not practical—not legal technicality dictated this departure from nicety of principle."[61] Otherwise, the purchaser would have been able to avail himself only of an unjustified enrichment claim or of the actio doli—the former merely allowing him to recover the purchase price, the success of the latter being dependent on proof of the vendor's knowledge that the "slave" was free.

Whether the same pragmatic approach was adopted with regard to res divini iuris or whether the classical lawyers regarded the sale of res extra commercium as invalid even if the purchaser had entered the contract in good faith, is not entirely clear. It cannot have been easy, in these cases, for the purchaser to establish his ignorance. This might well be the reason why in texts such as D. 18, 1, 22 and 23 the nullity of the sale was proclaimed without any qualification and, as a consequence

---

[54] J.A.C. Thomas, "The Sale of Res Extra Commercium", (1976) 29 *Current Legal Problems* 139.

[55] Cf. Pap. D. 41, 3, 44 pr.: ". . . nam frequenter ignorantia liberos emimus"; Paul. D. 18, 1, 5: ". . . quia difficile dinosci potest liber homo a servo."

[56] Stein, *Fault*, p. 63.

[57] Cf. e.g. Paul. D. 18, 1, 34, 2.

[58] Cf. e.g. Pomp. D. 18, 1, 4.

[59] According to the rules relating to eviction; cf. infra, pp. 296 sqq.

[60] D. 18, 1, 70. Cf. also *Inst.* III, 23, 5.

[61] Thomas, (1976) 29 *Current Legal Problems* 141; cf. also Arangio-Ruiz, *Compravendita*, pp, 126 sqq.; Stein, *Fault*, pp. 62 sqq.; Medicus, *Id quod interest*, p. 163.

(only) the condictio was granted to recover the price. Nevertheless, where the purchaser had been "nesciens", invalidity probably implied only that the obligation could not in fact be discharged.[62] Ulpianus granted an actio in factum to the purchaser ("Si locus religiosus pro puro venisse dicetur, praetor in factum actionem in eum dat ei ad quem ea res pertinet"),[63] which paved the way for his pupil Modestinus finally to make the actio empti available in these cases too:

> "Qui nesciens loca sacra vel religiosa . . . pro privatis comparavit, licet emptio non teneat, ex empto tamen adversus venditorem experiatur ut consequatur quod interfuit eius ne deciperetur."[64]

Justinian consolidated the position and placed both cases (the sale of a res extra commercium and that of a free man) on a par.[65] But what could the purchaser recover with his actio empti? Modestinus says "quod interfuit eius ne deciperetur"; Justinian formulates "quod sua interest deceptum eum non esse". This sounds like what the modern lawyers would call the negative interest. And, indeed, these texts did provide the historical basis and dogmatic point of departure for that doctrine.[66] The aim of granting a claim for damages, so it was argued, is to put the injured party financially in whatever position he would have been in had the wrongdoer acted properly. Hence, in order to determine the quantum of damages, the fraudulent misrepresentation has to be eliminated in thought. If the vendor had not deceived the purchaser, the latter would not have entered into the contract. As a consequence, he can claim only his interest in the non-conclusion of the contract, not his (positive) interest in the validity of the contract. The hypothetical basis for assessing his damages should therefore be the position he would have been in had the contract not been concluded; not the position he would have been in if the contract had come into existence and been properly carried out.

The distinction between negative and positive interest has certainly proved to be a valuable one and plays a significant role in the modern

---

[62] Voci, *L'errore*, pp. 154 sqq., goes even further and argues that the sale was valid in classical Roman law.

[63] D. 11, 7, 8, 1. For a different interpretation of the text, see Stein, *Fault*, pp. 68 sqq.

[64] D. 18, 1, 62, 1. Cf. Stein, *Fault*, pp. 75 sqq.; Honsell, *Quod interest*, pp. 107 sq. Contra ("ex empto" interpolated) e.g. Arangio-Ruiz, *Compravendita*, pp. 132 sq.; Medicus, *Id quod interest*, pp. 164 sq.; Arp, *Anfängliche Unmöglichkeit*, pp. 104 sqq.

[65] *Inst.* III, 23, 5: "Loca sacra vel religiosa, item publica, veluti forum basilicam, frustra quis sciens emit, quas tamen si pro privatis vel profanis deceptus a venditore emerit, habebit actionem ex empto, quod non habere ei liceat, ut consequatur, quod sua interest deceptum eum non esse. idem iuris est, si hominem liberum pro servo emerit." Decipere indicates that the seller must be guilty of dolus, i.e. the action was granted only where the vendor was sciens, the purchaser ignorans. In decreeing the same as far as the sale of a liber homo was concerned, Justinian changed the law; according to classical law, in this instance, the purchaser could sue even where the seller had also been ignorans.

[66] Cf. Rudolf von Jhering, "Culpa in contrahendo, oder Schadensersatz bei nichtigen oder nicht zur Perfektion gelangten Verträgen", (1861) 4 *JhJb* 16 sqq.; Windscheid/Kipp, § 307, n. 5.

German law of damages.[67] But it does not represent Roman law. "Quod interest deceptum non esse" should not be taken as a conceptual deviation from the normal quod sua interest; it did not entail any restriction as far as the recoverable interest was concerned. The injured party could claim his (full) interest in not having been deceived. This interest, however, was probably assessed on the basis of what the purchaser would have had had the object of the sale in fact been what he had believed it to be, not only on the basis of what he would have done had he realized that the vendor was deceiving him.[68]

(c) Culpa in contrahendo

Ulp. D. 11, 7, 8, 1, Mod. D. 18, 1, 62, 1 and *Inst.* III, 23, 5, incidentally, did not only stand at the cradle of the concept of negative interest in the modern law of damages, but were also among the handful of texts which inspired Rudolf von Jhering to formulate his celebrated doctrine of culpa in contrahendo.[69] Contractual diligentia, he postulated, is owed not only where the contract has come into existence but also where it is still in statu nascendi. With the commencement of their negotiations, the parties are entering into a (quasi-)contractual relationship giving rise to rights and duties. Based on the reasonable expectations engendered by the precontractual contact, these rights and duties go beyond the compass of the law of delict and are to be determined in accordance with the contract which the parties intend to conclude. Infringement of the duties in contrahendo by one of the parties entitles the other to claim the damages that he has suffered in relying on the eventual conclusion/validity of the contract. The liability is contractual and it is based on culpa; compensation is limited to the negative interest. For a far-ranging theory of precontractual liability of this sort, the Roman texts naturally provide only tentative intimations. In fact, Jhering's "legal discovery"[70] was a product of the method of conceptual construction prevailing in the second half of the 19th century[71] rather than the result of an impartial exegesis of the historical Roman law.[72] We have seen, for instance, that in cases of sale of res

[67] Cf. e.g. § 122 I: "If a declaration of intention is . . . rescinded under §§ . . ., the declarant shall . . . compensate (the other) party . . . for the damage which the other . . . party sustained by relying upon the validity of the declaration, not, however, beyond the value of the interest which the other . . . party has in the validity of the declaration" (i.e. positive interest as the limit for the negative interest). Cf. also §§ 179 II, 307, 309 BGB and Lange, *Schadensersatz*, pp. 44 sqq.

[68] Cf. Honsell, *Quod interest*, pp. 87 sqq., 108 sq.; Kaser, *RPr* I, p. 549.

[69] In his article referred to supra, note 66.

[70] Hans Dölle, "Juristische Entdeckungen", in: *Verhandlungen des 42. Deutschen Juristentages*, vol. II (1959), pp. B1 sqq.

[71] For a detailed analysis, see Erich Schanze, "Culpa in contrahendo bei Jhering", (1978) 7 *Ius Commune* 326 sqq.

[72] On fault in the formation of contract in Roman law generally, see Karl Heldrich, *Das Verschulden beim Vertragsabschluss im klassischen römischen Recht und in der späteren Rechtsentwicklung* (1924); Stein, *Fault*, passim.

extra commercium the parties were liable only for dolus, not culpa in contrahendo. Here Jhering could draw attention to the Prussian code of 1794 as evidence for the fact that this result was no longer accepted as equitable. § 284 I 5 read:

> *"Was wegen des bei Erfüllung des Vertrages zu vertretenden Grades der Schuld Rechtens ist, gilt auch für den Fall, wenn einer der Contrahenten bei Abschliessung des Vertrages die ihm obliegenden Pflichten vernachlässigt hat."*[73]

Culpa in contrahendo has become a firmly established feature of the legal landscape of German private law, albeit praeter legem, i.e. as a growth of judge-made law.[74] It has even been (ab)used for a somewhat uncouth intrusion into the realm of delict; but this is a more domestic problem arising, largely, from an unfortunate stumbling block defacing the German law of delict.[75] Culpa in contrahendo falls squarely into the grey area between the law of contract and the law of delict, and there is much to be said for the proposition that it does not fit neatly into either of these, but rather forms an integral part of a third "track" of liability.[76] But however one might assess these systematic implications, the impact of Jhering's doctrine, both in Germany and abroad, shows the practical need for and legitimacy of (non-delictual) liability for culpa in contrahendo.[77]

5. Emptio rei speratae and emptio spei

(a) Emptio rei speratae

No valid sale without a thing to be sold: that was the rule. It sometimes happened, however, that objects were sold which had, as both parties knew, not yet come into existence, but were expected to do so in the foreseeable future; indeed, such transactions concerning res futurae

---

[73] "What is right with regard to the degree of fault for which (a debtor) is responsible when performing his contractual obligation, is also applicable if one of the contracting parties has neglected the duties incumbent on him in concluding the contract."

[74] Cf., for example, Hans Stoll, "Tatbestände und Funktionen der Haftung für culpa in contrahendo", in: *Festschrift für Ernst von Caemmerer* (1978), pp. 435 sqq.; Dieter Medicus, "Verschulden bei Vertragsverhandlungen", in: *Gutachten und Vorschläge zur Überarbeitung des Schuldrechts*, vol. I (1981), pp. 479 sqq.; Peter Gottwald, "Die Haftung für culpa in contrahendo", (1982) *Juristische Schulung* 877 sqq.

[75] This is § 831 BGB, dealing with vicarious liability. See infra, pp. 1125 sq.

[76] Cf., in particular, Claus-Wilhelm Canaris, *Die Vertrauenshaftung im deutschen Privatrecht* (1971); idem, "Schutzgesetze—Verkehrspflichten—Schutzpflichten", in: *(Zweite) Festschrift für Karl Larenz* (1983), pp. 27 sqq.

[77] Cf. e.g. § 45 of the Czech BGB (1950): "A party who has negligently or intentionally caused a legal transaction to be invalid, is bound to compensate for the damage suffered by the other party in relying on the validity of the contract"; artt. 1337 sq. codice civile. For comparative views on culpa in contrahendo, see Rudolf Nirk, "Rechtsvergleichendes zur Haftung für culpa in contrahendo", (1953) 18 *RabelsZ* 310 sqq.; Friedrich Kessler, Edith Fine, "Culpa in Contrahendo, Bargaining in Good Faith, and Freedom of Contract: A Comparative Study", (1964) 77 *Harvard LR* 401 sqq.; Friedrich Kessler, "Der Schutz des Vertrauens bei Vertragsverhandlungen in der neueren amerikanischen Rechtsprechung", in: *Festschrift für Ernst von Caemmerer* (1978), pp. 873 sqq.; Stoll, *Festschrift von Caemmerer*, pp. 435 sqq.

were very old and common in Rome. In Cato, *de agri cultura,*[78] we encounter the sale of olives on the tree, grapes on the vine, winter fodder which is still growing and the yield of a flock of sheep. The range of possible transactions was not confined, however, to situations where the object of the sale had not yet been harvested but was already growing. Next year's harvest from a specific field or the offspring of a certain number of dams (or of a slave) could be sold, even if the seed had not yet been sown, the mother-sheep or -slave not yet been inseminated.[79] Our main testimony dealing with the legal effects of such transactions is Pomp. D. 18, 1, 8 pr:

> "[E]t tamen fructus et partus futuri recte ementur, ut, cum editus esset partus, iam tunc, cum contractum esset negotium, venditio facta intellegatur: sed si id egerit venditor, ne nascatur aut fiant, ex empto agi posse."

The sale was taken to be subject to a condition.[80] Only if it eventually transpired that there was an object, did the contract of sale become effective (ex tunc, i.e. with retroactive effect). If the crop failed, the contract of sale failed too. As a consequence, it was only in the former case that the prospective purchaser had to pay the purchase price. The risk that the whole of his harvest might be destroyed by hail or inundation, or that his slave might turn out to be infertile was therefore still carried by the vendor. In order to provide for the possibility that the harvest be brought in, but prove to be disappointingly small, the purchase price was normally fixed proportionately to the actual yield (so and so much per bushel, per pound, etc.). If the vendor, subsequent to the conclusion of the contract, regretted the terms of the sale and therefore prevented fructus or partus (and with it the contract of sale) from coming into existence, the condition, in accordance with general principles,[81] was deemed to have been fulfilled, the contract deemed to have become effective. This type of transaction has come to be known as emptio rei speratae. The Roman lawyers themselves did not use a specific term to designate it and, indeed, the transaction had nothing abnormal about it. In particular, it did not constitute an exception to the rule that a valid sale required a thing to be sold.

(b) Emptio spei and its viability

However, the Roman lawyers were prepared to go even one step further. Could the parties not have intended to shift the risk of there

[78] CLV sqq., 146 sqq.

[79] For details of the development, see Volker Kurz, " 'Emptio rei speratae' 'pura' oder 'sub condicione'?", (1974) 20 *Labeo* 195 sqq.

[80] Arangio-Ruiz, *Compravendita*, pp. 118 sqq.; Masi, *Condizione*, pp. 63 sqq., 158 sqq., 224 sq.; Alfredo Calonge, "En torno al problema de la retroactividad de la condición en el derecho clásico", in: *Studi in onore di Edoardo Volterra*, vol. III (1969), pp. 158 sq.; Thomas, *TRL*, p. 282; unconvincing Kurz, (1974) 20 *Labeo* 194 sqq., 199 sqq., according to whom the emptio rei speratae was an unconditional sale.

[81] Cf. infra, pp. 730 sq.

being no crop onto the purchaser? One can easily imagine a situation where a farmer urgently needs money and, at the same time, wants to insure himself against the vagaries of the weather. The purchaser, on the other hand, might be prepared to speculate, and risk his money, in return for the chance of making a big profit.[82] Where, in fact, a lump sum was fixed at a fairly low level for the whole yield, it could be surmised that the parties intended their transaction to work this way. What we are dealing with, under these circumstances, is not a normal business transaction:[83] it contains a strong element of gambling. It is not surprising, therefore, that our sources concentrate on different examples when they discuss this type of contract: the purchase of a prospective haul of fish, of a catch of birds, or of the largesse which a triumphant princeps might have ordered to be thrown to the populace and which a particular person was able to pick up.[84] One might be tempted to ask whether such kinds of transactions are not too silly to deserve legal analysis. How often did it happen that a stroller along the shore came across some fishermen and decided to offer them his purse for the next haul?[85] And, assuming that a contract of sale did come into existence on these terms, would he not run the risk of having to pay the price, even though the fishermen subsequently neglected their duty to catch fish and merely spent two idle hours on a pleasure cruise around the bay?

But, firstly, as David Daube has pointed out, we should not only have in mind the casual stroller when assessing the viability of this type of contract.

> "[W]e must also think, say, of a firm of victuallers at Rome undertaking to pay certain fishermen at Pessinus a fixed sum for their catches of cod during the season."[86]

---

[82] Nicholas, *Introduction*, p. 173.

[83] But cf. Dennis Paling, "Emptio spei and emptio rei speratae", (1973) 8 *The Irish Jurist* 178 sqq.

[84] Cf. esp. Pomp. D. 18, 1, 8, 1.

[85] But cf. the famous case submitted to the Delphic oracle (Plutarch, *Vitae*, Solon, 4, 1 sqq.; cf. the discussion by Pothier, *Traité du contrat de vente*, n. 6; Herbert William Parke, D.E.W. Wormell, *The Delphic Oracle*, vol. I (1956), pp. 110 sqq.; David Daube, "Purchase of a Prospective Haul", in: *Studi in onore di Ugo Enrico Paoli* (1955), p. 203). Some Milesians bought from some fishermen the next haul of their net. It proved to include a golden tripod. Had the purchasers bought only such fish as might be caught or the haul, whatever it might contain? The Pythia awarded the tripod to neither of the parties but to the wisest man that could be found. It was sent to Thales of Miletos, the Ionian philosopher and natural scientist, who, however, declined to accept it and sent it to another philosopher, whom he considered wiser than himself. On the same argument the tripod passed through the hands of all the Seven Wise Men (tradition refers to Kleobulos of Lindos, Solon of Athens, Chilon of Sparta, Thales of Miletos, Pittakos of Mitylene, Bias of Priene and Periandros of Korinthos as the septem sapientes), until it was realized that no mortal was as wise as Apollo. Hence it was sent to the temple of Apollo at Delphi and dedicated to that god (that is, the master of the Delphic oracle, to whom the case had originally been submitted).

[86] "Certainty of Price", in: *Studies in the Roman Law of Sale in memory of Francis de Zulueta* (1959), p. 12. For another practical example, see the sale of a vindemia pendens, as related by Plinius, *Epistulae*, Lib. VIII, 2; cf. J.E. Spruit, "Schikanen anlässlich eines Traubenkaufs", in: *Satura Roberto Feenstra oblata* (1985), pp. 158 sqq.

And as to the second question, one has to remember that sale was a bonae fidei contract. The fishermen, under a contract of sale, had a duty to cast their net and to make a reasonable effort to procure a good haul.[87]

The third of the above-mentioned examples, too, is not as foolish as it sounds to us. True, the throwing of largesse is somewhat out of fashion today. In Rome, however, consuls, praetors or emperors liked to mark triumphs or other kinds of feasts with such an act of generosity: not only coins were thrown to the mob but also various kinds of food, tickets for grain, clothing, gold, silver, precious stones, pearls, paintings, slaves, and even animals.[88] What a skilled person could catch was certainly worth a considerable investment. Again, as concerns the temptation on the part of the seller to neglect his duties in the scramble for largesse, once he had secured his right to claim a purchase price, the fact that sale was bonae fidei implied that he could bring the action only if he himself had done his best. Furthermore, it has to be taken into consideration that for the purposes of analysing a specific problem, simple and more theoretical cases were sometimes used rather than the more complex situations which occurred in actual practice. Suppose the purchaser bought half of the largesse picked up by the vendor:[89] the latter would then have an economic incentive to catch "as catch can". The legal problem remains the same.

(c) ". . . quasi alea emitur"

As has already been indicated, the Roman lawyers accommodated this type of transaction within the framework of the contract of sale:

> "Aliquando tamen et sine re venditio intellegitur, veluti cum quasi alea emitur. quod fit, cum captum piscium vel avium vel missilium emitur: emptio enim contrahitur etiam si nihil inciderit, quia spei emptio est: at quod missilium nomine eo casu captum est si evictum fuerit, nulla eo nomine ex empto obligatio contrahitur, quia id actum intellegitur."[90]

This was emptio spei and, as opposed to the emptio rei speratae, it was not conditional but came into existence immediately. Whether,

[87] Cf. Cels. D. 19, 1, 12.

[88] Cf. Suetonius, *De vita Caesarum*, Nero, XI, 4, describing what was thrown to the streets at the occasion of one of Nero's entertainments. Another legal problem arising from the throwing of largesse (acquisition of ownership) is discussed in Gai. D. 41, 1, 9, 7 and *Inst.* II, 1, 46. For further discussion, see Daube, *Studi Paoli*, pp. 205 sqq.; Liebs, *RR*, pp. 165 sq.; Ferenc Benedek, "'Iactus missilium'", in: *Sodalitas, Scritti in onore di Antonio Guarino*, vol. V (1984), pp. 2108 sqq.

[89] Daube, *Studi Paoli*, p. 205.

[90] Pomp. D. 18, 1, 8, 1. The classicity of this text has been vindicated by Max Kaser, "Erbschaftskauf und Hoffnungskauf", (1971) 74 *BIDR* 47 sq.; cf. also already Daube, *Studi Paoli*, pp. 204 sqq. and J.A.C. Thomas, "Venditio hereditatis and emptio spei", (1959) 33 *Tulane LR* 541 sqq. Cf. also Ulp. D. 19, 1, 11, 18.

eventually, there was an object to be sold or not did not matter.[91] It is interesting to note that Pomponius acknowledged that this constituted, in fact, an exception to the rule "no sale without an object to be sold". At the same time, he gave an ingenious argument for allowing this exception. It is not necessarily the res futura which the purchaser buys; instead, if nothing comes up, it is the hope (spes) that something might have come up. Thus, one can look at the contract as if (not a res, but) a chance ("quasi alea"), which may or may not materialize, has been the object of the transaction.

A further interesting instance of an emptio spei can be found in Ulp. D. 18, 4, 11:

> "Nam hoc modo admittitur esse venditionem 'si qua sit hereditas, est tibi empta', et quasi spes hereditatis: ipsum enim incertum rei veneat, ut in retibus."

A hereditas could be the object of a contract of sale, but only if the person in respect of whose estate the transaction was effected had already died—contracts concerning the estate of living persons are (and were) unacceptable for reasons of public policy and morality.[92] If a person believed himself to be the heir and sold his inheritance, he was normally liable to the purchaser once it turned out that the inheritance had actually fallen to somebody else.[93] This was not so if it had specifically been provided "ut quidquid iuris haberet venditor emptor haberet".[94] The tacit guarantee was effectively excluded; the vendor was obliged to transfer the inheritance[95] if he became heir; otherwise his obligation fell away. It did, however, happen that the parties went one step further and agreed that the vendor was not only exempted from liability if he had not, in fact, become heir, but that he should be allowed to retain the purchase price too.[96] This is the situation referred to by Ulpianus, and this indeed resembles the purchase of the next haul of the net. It was an emptio spei.[97] Of course, the vendor remained liable for dolus.

---

[91] If the vendor failed to make a decent effort to procure the object, he was liable (under the actio empti) for damages, to be estimated according to the speculative value of the catch: cf. Cels. D. 19, 1, 12.

[92] Cf. e.g. Pap. D. 39, 5, 29, 2; Diocl. C. 8, 38, 4. The immorality of such transactions is based on the desire on the part of the acquirer to see his spes hereditatis materialize as soon as possible. See, too, Paul D. 18, 4, 7.

[93] Iav. D. 18, 4, 8; Paul. D. 18, 4, 9. This was the other group of texts, on which Jhering based his culpa in contrahendo theory; cf. supra, pp. 244 sq.

[94] Paul. D. 18, 4, 13.

[95] The normal mode of transfer was in iure cessio hereditatis; see Voci, *DER*, vol. I, pp. 98 sqq.; Kaser, *RPr* I, pp. 722 sq.

[96] One can think, for instance, of a Roman who hears that his uncle in Athens has died. He is sure that his uncle has instituted him as his heir. Being short of money, he sells his spes hereditatis. As the purchaser bears the risk of the vendor not having become heir, the purchase price will, however, not be very high. Cf. Kaser, (1971) 74 *BIDR* 55.

[97] Cf. Thomas, (1959) 33 *Tulane LR* 545 sqq. and especially Max Kaser, "Erbschaftskauf und Hoffnungskauf", (1971) 74 *BIDR* 50 sqq.

III. THE PURCHASE PRICE

1. Did the purchase price have to consist in money?

(a) *The Sabinian view*

The second essential element of any contract of sale was agreement about the price, and the first fundamental question that posed itself in this regard was whether the price necessarily had to consist in money. Or, to put the same question slightly differently: did the rules relating to sale apply to exchange transactions? This problem was the subject of one of the most famous school controversies in classical Roman law.[98] It must be borne in mind that the answer to it had an immediate and dramatic practical consequence: only if they could fly the flag of sale were consensual exchange deals at all actionable; otherwise they were bound to founder helplessly on the shallow sands of the Roman contractual system. This explains the persistent attempts of the Sabinians to broaden the only channel that was close enough to prevent this disaster: emptio venditio. Their proposition was based on an historical argument:

> "Origo emendi vendendique a permutationibus coepit. olim enim non ita erat nummus neque aliud merx, aliud pretium vocabatur, sed unusquisque secundum necessitatem temporum ac rerum utilibus inutilia permutabat, quando plerumque evenit, ut quod alteri superest alteri desit. sed quia non semper nec facile concurrebat, ut, cum tu haberes quod ego desiderarem, invicem haberem quod tu accipere velles, electa materia est, cuius publica ac perpetua aestimatio difficultatibus permutationum aequalitate quantitatis subveniret. eaque materia forma public percussa usum dominiumque non tam ex substantia praebet quam ex quantitate, nec ultra merx utrumque, sed alterum pretium vocatur."[99]

This is a most interesting lecture in economic history,[100] taking us back to the days of the early subsistence economy. Whatever was needed over and above what was produced on the own farm could be acquired only, before money was introduced, by way of exchange. The introduction of money finally solved the problem that the other party might not actually be interested in the goods offered in exchange; by virtue of the value that it represented, it came to be regarded as a generally acceptable counterperformance.[101] Thus sale was born, but it had its origin in exchange. It was in actual fact, in the Sabinian view, nothing more than a refined and specialized form of exchange. Or, the other way round: exchange is the most ancient form of sale.[102] If the latter was generally regarded as enforceable, then surely the mother transaction could not lack this most vital of attributes.

---

[98] Paul. D. 18, 1, 1, 1; Gai. III, 141. Cf. e.g. Arangio-Ruiz, *Compravendita*, pp. 134 sqq.; David Daube, "The Three Quotations from Homer in Digest 18, 1, 1, 1", (1949) 10 *Cambridge LJ* 213 sqq.

[99] Paul. D. 18, 1, 1, pr.

[100] For a discussion, see Herman van den Brink, *The Charme of Legal History*, 1974, pp. 79 sqq.; Alfons Bürge, "Geld- und Naturalwirtschaft im vorklassischen und klassischen römischen Recht", (1982) 99 *ZSS* 142 sqq.

[101] For details of the development, see Bürge, (1982) 99 *ZSS* 128 sqq.

[102] Gai. III, 141.

(b) *The Proculian view*

The Proculians were not impressed by this argument. They stressed the technical differences between the two types of transaction:

> ". . . nam ut aliud est vendere, aliud emere, alius emptor, alius venditor, sic aliud est pretium, aliud merx: quod in permutatione discerni non potest, uter emptor, uter venditor sit."[103]

And indeed, the praetor had to know to whom he had to grant the actio empti and to whom the actio venditi. A whole variety of substantive issues depended on who was vendor and who was purchaser.[104] The alternative, namely to regard both parties, at the same time, as vendor and purchaser, would not really have made sense either.[105] Caelius Sabinus tried to overcome this difficulty by suggesting that the rem venalem habens had to be regarded as seller.[106] However, quite apart from the practical difficulties of establishing who had in actual fact held out his thing for sale, such a distinction would have been unfair:[107] since both parties owe a thing (rather than money), it would not have been equitable to expect one of them (the "purchaser") to transfer ownership, the other only to provide habere licere. Ultimately, therefore, the Proculian view prevailed. Some sort of compromise was reached, though, in that the buyer was allowed to promise something in addition to money. As long as at least part of the price was in money, the Proculian objections were met and the actions on sale could be granted. No text deals specifically with the case where the counterperformance consisted in money and an object that was to be exchanged, but we find the actio venditi being granted in analogous situations: where, for instance, the purchaser, in addition to paying a certain price, had agreed to repair one of the vendor's houses[108] or to take a lease of one of the vendor's estates.[109] Transactions of this kind can, of course, lead to difficult questions of where to draw the line, for it would hardly be reasonable to apply the law of sale in all these cases no matter what the parties had actually intended, no matter, too, how insignificant the balance payable in money was compared to the rest of the counterperformance.

(c) *Sale and exchange*

The distinction between exchange and sale is less important today than it was under classical Roman law, for to us the one transaction is as

[103] Paul. D. 18, 1, 1, 1; cf. also Paul. D. 19, 4, 1 pr.

[104] For instance: the purchaser had to transfer ownership, the vendor only had to afford habere licere; the purchaser could avail himself of the actio empti if he was evicted. Cf. infra, pp. 296 sqq.

[105] "Absurdum videri": Gai. III, 141.

[106] Gai. III, 141 in fine.

[107] Seckel/Levy, (1927) 47 *ZSS* 133.

[108] Pomp. D. 19, 1, 6, 1.

[109] Iav. D. 18, 1, 79.

valid and enforceable as the other. It has, however, not entirely lost its practical significance, even in systems which boldly provide that the rules relating to sale "apply mutatis mutandis to exchange".[110] Such blanket provisions do not solve the problem, since, for instance, many of the rules implying an obligation to pay a purchase price cannot even be applied mutatis mutandis.[111] Today, the classification problem often arises with regard to the common trade-in agreements. If A buys a motor car from B for 10 000 rand, trading in his old car for 1 000 rand and paying the remainder in cash, the transaction is usually regarded as a contract of sale, the purchaser being allowed to provide a substitute for part of the purchase price.[112] The situation in German law has, however, been somewhat distorted owing to considerations of saving turnover tax. Thus the transaction has been split into a contract of sale and an agency agreement, the vendor (of the new car) undertaking to sell the purchaser's old car for him (i.e. not in his own name).[113]

2. Pretium verum

In conclusion then, the price generally had to consist in money. Furthermore, it had to be verum and certum but not necessarily iustum. The first of these requirements was fairly straightforward: "Cum in venditione quis pretium rei ponit donationis causa non exacturus, non videtur vendere."[114] The price had to be seriously meant; otherwise the transaction was merely a donation in disguise. That the price was very low did not in itself invalidate the sale, as long as the vendor seriously intended to demand it. Only if it was derisory ("nummo uno")[115] could it normally be assumed[116] that the parties did not actually have in mind the conclusion of a genuine contract of sale.

---

110 § 515 BGB. In other codifications, a distinction is recognized as far as remedies for eviction are concerned (under a contract of exchange a party that has been evicted may either claim damages or restitution of the thing delivered; cf. e.g. art. 238 OR); in the code civil the provisions relating to rescission for *lésion* do not apply to exchange: art. 1706. For further details and analysis, see T.B. Smith, "Exchange or Sale?", (1974) 48 *Tulane LR* 1031 sqq; A.D.M. Forte, "A Civilian Approach to the Contract of Exchange in Modern Scots Law", (1984) 101 *SALJ* 691 sqq; R.L. Purves, "Asset-Transfer Contracts", 1987 *Responsa meridiana* 237 sqq.

111 Cf. e.g. § 472 I BGB, which provides with regard to the actio quanti minoris (on which see infra, p. 318): "In case of reduction, the purchase price shall be reduced in the proportion which, at the time of the sale, the value of the thing in a condition free from defect would have borne to the actual value." For further criticism, see Theo Mayer-Maly, "Dogmengeschichtliches zu BGHZ 46, 338", in: *Festschrift für Karl Larenz* (1973), pp. 673 sqq.

112 The relation is different, for instance, if A and B swop their motorcars (A's car being worth 9 000 rand, B's 10 000 rand) and A has to throw in 1 000 rand as a makeweight. The crucial factor in determining the type of contract is the intention of the parties: cf. e.g. Voet, *Commentarius ad Pandectas*, Lib. XVIII, Tit. I, XXII; Kerr, *Sale and Lease*, pp. 23 sqq. See further Smith, (1974) 48 *Tulane LR* 1034 sqq; Forte, (1984) 101 *SALJ* 693 sqq.

113 For details, see H.P. Westermann, in: *Münchener Kommentar*, vol. III 1 (2nd ed., 1988), § 515, n. 4.

114 Ulp. D. 18, 1, 36. For a comprehensive discussion of this text, see David Daube, *Studi Arangio-Ruiz*, vol. I, pp. 192 sqq.

115 Cf. Ulp. D. 19, 2, 46 (dealing, however, with locatio conductio); Pothier, *Traité du contrat de vente*, n. 19.

116 But see Michel, *Gratuité*, pp. 244 sqq.

3. Pretium certum

(a) Borderline cases

The certainty requirement, on the other hand, led to a couple of very interesting borderline cases; for "certum pretium" was not taken to imply that the parties must necessarily name the actual figure. Thus we find the following statement by Ulpianus: "Huiusmodi emptio 'quanti tu eum emisti' . . . valet." Reason: ". . .magis enim ignoratur, quanti emptus sit, quam in rei veritate incertum est."[117] In this example the purchaser does not know the price. He seems to be very keen to have the object, whereas the vendor just has an interest not to sell at a loss. Perhaps he does not remember what he once had to pay for it when he himself bought the thing; hence, the parties do not specify a sum, but fix the price at "whatever sum the vendor has bought it for". Here the price is objectively certain, and this was sufficient for the validity of the sale. The fact that the parties did not know the actual amount, did not matter. In other words: the price had to be certum in the sense of at least being ascertainable. Whether the same holds true in the other example given in D. 18, 1, 7, 1 ("quantum pretii in arca habeo") is very doubtful.[118] First of all: do the parties really deserve protection for what can only be described as a gamble? What sober motive could induce a purchaser to promise whatever he happens to have in his safe as the purchase price? More importantly, though, there is, of course, the possibility that no money at all appears to be in the safe. In that case the sale cannot conceivably be valid. It is, one can say, a chance (alea) that the purchaser is substituting for a real price. Whilst, however, one might be able to buy or sell a chance ("emptio spei"), it can hardly have been regarded as possible to pay with a chance. After all, the price had to consist in money. There are thus, I think, strong reasons for regarding this second example as spurious.

We are back on safer ground with regard to the situation where a piece of land was sold for a certain figure, plus the possible profit made by a resale:

> "Si quis ita emerit: 'est mihi fundus emptus centum et quanto pluris eum vendidero', valet venditio . . .: habet enim certum pretium centum, augebitur autem pretium, si pluris emptor fundum vendiderit."[119]

This contract is valid, the price being centum and hence certum. The possible future payment is merely a subsidiary duty, also enforceable with the actio venditi, but not rendering the price uncertain. It has been suggested that transactions of this type are impractical: the vendor

---

117 D. 18, 1, 7, 1.

118 For a detailed analysis, see David Daube, "Certainty of Price", in: *Studies in the Roman Law of Sale in memory of Francis de Zulueta* (1959), pp. 9 sqq. Cf., however, also J.A.C. Thomas, "Marginalia on certum pretium", (1967) 35 *TR* 77 sqq., who comes to the conclusion that the two cases can "in fact stand perfectly well together".

119 Ulp. D. 18, 1, 7, 2; cf. also Ulp. D. 19, 1, 13, 24.

cannot hope to derive any advantage from a term such as this, since the purchaser has no incentive to make a profit.[120] But one has only to change the example slightly ("one hundred plus half of what I can (re)sell it for") in order to meet this objection.[121]

(b) Determination of the price at a later stage

The "certainty of price" requirement was primarily intended to help ensure that in its essential elements the bargain was the work of the parties. Secondly, however, the Roman lawyers seem to have wanted to ensure that the bargain was in actual fact struck; they tried to avoid recognizing a contract of sale where a breakdown of the transaction was still possible due to the fact that in the end a price might either be lacking or be unascertainable. Hence their reluctance to accept an arrangement by the parties "ut quanti Titius rem aestimaverit, tanti sit empta".[122] The possibility existed that Titius did not want to or could not fix a price. Opinions were divided in classical law,[123] for there may, of course, be good reasons why the parties do not want to determine the price themselves, but would rather leave that to an (impartial) third party. Justinian settled the dispute by construing the clause as a (suspensive) condition: if the third party names a price, the sale becomes effective; otherwise the transaction is void for lack of price.[124] This solution implied, however, that the sale did not already come into existence at the time of its conclusion. A different view was taken if the price had to be fixed, not by a third party, but by the purchaser. This was unacceptable in Roman law: "Illud constat imperfectum esse negotium, cum emere volenti sic venditor dicit: 'quanti velis, quanti aequum putaveris, quanti aestimaveris, habebis emptum'."[125] The problem here was not so much that the purchaser might in the end not fix a price at all—it was rather that the vendor would have had an interest in the failure of this disadvantageous arrangement. The main objection of the Roman lawyers was probably that the determination of an essentiale negotii had been left to one party and that thus the institutional check against the danger of gross and unreasonable contractual imbalance (namely negotiation about the price) had been removed. Other ways and means of seeing to it that the purchaser did

---

[120] Cf. e.g. Arangio-Ruiz, *Compravendita*, pp. 139 sq.

[121] Daube, *Studies De Zulueta*, p. 27. He continues: "As a matter of fact, one can think of situations, where even the term of 18, 1, 7, 2 . . . would be perfectly in order. I sell the farm next door to mine to a farmer though I have higher offers from building speculators. A clause obliging him to cede any profit by a resale will keep him out of temptation—to my advantage. Nor will it deprive him of his chief interest in the contract—which is to get and work the farm" (pp. 27 sq.).

[122] Gai. III, 140.

[123] Gai. III, 140.

[124] C. 4, 38, 15, 1; *Inst*. III, 23, 1.

[125] Gai. D. 18, 1, 35, 1. Cf. Arangio-Ruiz, *Compravendita*, p. 141; differently Daube, *Studies De Zulueta*, pp. 21 sqq.

not abuse his power were not available. More particularly, as we shall presently see, judicial control concerning fairness of price was not the policy of Roman law.

Modern legal systems tend to take a more liberal view with regard to the two last-mentioned problem areas. The German Code allows determination of the performance by a third party;[126] if the third party cannot or will not make the determination, or if he delays it, either his declaration is substituted by court decision[127] or the contract is void.[128] The determination of the price may, however, even be left to one of the contracting parties, be it that he has to decide "in an equitable manner" or even in his free discretion.[129] This represents a deviation from Roman law which is based on pandectist doctrine.[130] Finally, even an agreement to pay a fair and reasonable price is not regarded as too uncertain.[131] South African law is still more firmly wedded to Roman law,[132] even though Roman-Dutch practice may have been less cautious: attention has recently been drawn to a decision of the Hooge Raad of 1719, where the Court was actually prepared to determine the price boni viri arbitratu.[133]

4. Pretium iustum

(a) The Roman attitude

The price had to be meant seriously and it had to be certain. It was not a requirement for the validity of a contract of sale that the price be just or fair.[134] This is a reflection of the liberalistic (rather than paternalistic)

---

[126] § 317 I BGB.

[127] If the third party is to determine the performance in an equitable manner (which is to be presumed): § 319 I BGB.

[128] If the third party may make the decision at his discretion: § 319 II BGB. There can be no judicial substitution for or control of a discretionary declaration of this kind.

[129] § 315 I BGB. § 315 III provides: "If the determination is to be made in an equitable manner, the determination made is binding upon the other party only if it is equitable. If it is inequitable, the determination is made by court decision; the same applies if the determination is delayed."

[130] The pandectists tended to interpret "imperfectum" in Gai. D. 18, 1, 35, 1 not as invalid, but as (validly concluded but) not yet effective. On the pandectist doctrine with regard to determination of the purchase price by either one of the partners to the contract or a third party, see Windscheid/Kipp, § 386; Hans-Joachim Winter, *Die Bestimmung der Leistung durch den Vertragspartner oder Dritte (§§ 315 bis 319 BGB) unter besonderer Berücksichtigung der Rechtsprechung und Lehre des 19. Jahrhunderts* (unpublished Dr. iur. thesis, Frankfurt, 1979), passim.

[131] Cf. already Windscheid/Kipp, § 386, n. 5 d.

[132] For details, see Kerr, *Sale and Lease*, pp. 26 sqq. and e.g. *Adcorp Spares PE (Pty.) Ltd. v. Hydromulch (Pty.) Ltd.* 1972 (3) SA 663 (T) (with reference, i.a., to Vinnius, *Institutiones* 3, 24, 1, and Voet, 18, 1, 2).

[133] *Johannes van der Lip v. De Weduwe en boedelhoudster van Adolph Snellerwaart* (cf. Van Bynkershoek, *Observationes Tumultuariae*, n. 1558, but particularly the report in (1975) 92 *SALJ* 278 sq.); on this decision and its (possible) implications, see H.J. Erasmus, P. van Warmelo, D. Zeffertt, "Pretium certum and the Hooge Raad", (1975) 92 *SALJ* 268 sqq.

[134] On iustum pretium generally, see Theo Mayer-Maly, "Der gerechte Preis", in: *Festschrift für Heinrich Demelius* (1973), pp. 139 sqq.

spirit of Roman law,[135] as well as of the sovereign position and practically unfettered authority of the paterfamilias. Roman private law was the law of the free Roman citizen, who could not only be relied upon to look after his own interest, but whose duty it also was to protect the (economically, socially, intellectually or emotionally) weaker members of the community—notably women, children and slaves—in so far as they belonged to his household.[136] Determination of the price could thus be left to the parties; whatever they agreed upon could be taken to represent a fair price in the circumstances of the individual sale. Judicial reconsideration and interference would have been an improper infringement of the freedom of the parties to strike their own bargain and to assess the balance of performance and counterperformance according to their own economic needs and interests. This attitude is encapsulated in Paul. D. 19, 2, 22, 3:

> "Quemadmodum in emendo et vendendo naturaliter concessum est quod pluris sit minoris emere, quod minoris sit pluris vendere et ita invicem se circumscribere, ita in locationibus quoque et conductionibus iuris est."[137]

The parties were free to charge (much) more or (much) less than what others might consider to be a fair price. This, according to Paulus, is a matter of course and it applies not only to contracts of sale but to all bilateral contracts in which the performance of one of the parties is in money. "Invicem se circumscribere" is very difficult to translate: to "overreach" or "outwit" each other would perhaps come closest to what is meant. It would be inappropriate, though, to take this term as implying and thus condoning deceit.[138] That circumscribere cannot be equated with dolus is obvious if one takes into consideration that the contract of sale gives rise to iudicia bonae fidei.

(b) *Invicem se circumscribere*

Paul. D. 19, 2, 22, 3 does not contain a carte blanche for foul play, for neither actio empti nor actio venditi could be granted in case of fraudulent machinations. There was no licence for wangling and knavery. However, the Roman lawyers were realistic enough to see that the usages of trade and commerce do not always conform to particularly high standards of honesty: "Sed aliter leges, aliter

---

[135] See generally Schulz, *Principles*, pp. 140 sqq.

[136] Under the Principate, the Roman State looked after the basic needs of the poor by way of the cura annonae (public distribution of free grain) and cura carnis. Cf. e.g. Theodor Mommsen, *Staatsrecht*, vol. II, pp. 502 sqq.; Stephan Brassloff, *Sozialpolitische Motive in der römischen Rechtsentwicklung* (1933), pp. 167 sqq. The number of people on the corn dole was usually about 150 000 under Caesar and Augustus, 175 000 under Septimius Severus. In addition, the lex Iulia de annona was enacted in order to combat unfair practices in the sale and transportation of grain (on these, cf. Ulp. D. 47, 11, 6 pr.).

[137] Cf. further Ulp. D. 4, 4, 16, 4 ("Pomponius ait in pretio emptionis et venditionis naturaliter licere contrahentibus se circumvenire"); Hermog. D. 19, 2, 23.

[138] Cf., however, Ulrich von Lübtow, "De iustitia et iure", (1948) 66 *ZSS* 499 sqq.; Antonio Carcaterra, *Dolus bonus/dolus malus. Esegesi di D. 4, 3, 1, 2–3* (1970), pp. 143 sqq.

philosophi tollunt astutias",[139] or, more generally: "Non omne quod licet honestum est."[140] Some grain merchants sail from Alexandria to famine-stricken Rhodos, where grain has become a very precious commodity. May the merchant whose vessel arrives first sell his grain to the starving Rhodians without indicating that various other vessels are about to arrive within a short while? The answer of the philosopher might well be "No". He would tend to postulate a moral duty of disclosure.[141] The lawyer, on the other hand, will be reluctant to base his decision upon too moralizing an attitude. He will remember that the messenger god and intermediary Hermes (with whom its Roman counterpart Mercurius was largely identified) has always been taken to be the patron and protector of both merchants and thieves. Thus he will realize that a merchant is out to make a profit and that to be cunning and shrewd is part of business life.[142] It is, therefore, not according to abstract ethical ideals, but with a view to average business decency that his actions have to be evaluated. The behaviour of the fastest of the above-mentioned grain merchants, for instance, is clever exploitation of an advantageous situation, not deceitful machination.[143] Only the latter would have fallen foul of the bona fides requirement inherent in sale.[144] Anything short of dolus was invicem se circumscribere, and it was naturaliter concessum, not on account of the precepts of natural law (ius naturale) but in the sense of being in accordance with the nature of trade (natura contractus).[145] In a certain way, therefore, the Roman

---

[139] Cicero, *De officiis*, 3, XVII—68.

[140] Paul. D. 50, 17, 144. A similar attitude (and not as has often been alleged: cf. e.g. Leonhard Freund, *Lug und Trug unter den Germanen* (1863), passim, a higher moral standard) can be found in the old Germanic law. Here the words for "*tauschen*" (exchange) and "*täuschen*" (deceive) have the same etymological root; a horse-dealer was called rostiuschaere ("*Rosstäuscher*"). The basic principle was "*Jeder Kaufmann lobt seine Ware. Loben und bieten gehört zum Kauf*" (Every merchant praises his goods. Puffing and bidding are part of the game). Cf. Andreas Wacke, "Circumscribere, gerechter Preis und die Arten der List",(1977) 94 *ZSS* 202. As far as English law is concerned, see, for instance, *Smith v. Hughes* (1871) LR 6 QB 597 at 603: ". . . the question is not what a man of scrupulous morality or nice honour would do under such circumstances."

[141] Cicero, *De officiis*, 3, XXIII—57.

[142] Cf. e.g. Conradus Rittershusius, *Differentiarum iuris civilis et canonici seu Pontificii libri septem* (1638), Lib. III, Cap. X: ". . . illa industria et solertia et vigilantia in rebus propriis et suis commodis augendis . . . est homini naturalis et laudabilis potius quam vituperanda."

[143] For a similar, very interesting case cf. *Laidlaw v. Organ* 4 US (2 Wheat) 178 (1817) as discussed by Zweigert/Kötz, vol. II, p. 125. During the war of 1812–14 between England and the United States, and as a result of the British blockade, the tobacco prices in New Orleans had fallen drastically. One morning the plaintiff learnt that a treaty of peace had been signed in Ghent; he immediately proceeded to buy a great quantity of tobacco from the defendants, who were unaware of these developments. The tobacco price, as was to be expected, subsequently rose by some 50 %. Chief Justice Marshal upheld the contract. For England, see *Smith v. Hughes* (1871) LR 6 QB 597.

[144] Theo Mayer-Maly, "Privatautonomie und Vertragsethik im Digestenrecht", (1955) 6 *Iura* 128 sqq.; Wacke, (1977) 94 *ZSS* 184 sqq.

[145] Cf., for example, Glück, vol. 17, p. 19; Erich Genzmer, "Die antiken Grundlagen der Lehre vom gerechten Preis und der laesio enormis", in: *Deutsche Landesreferate zum II. Internationalen Kongress für Rechtsvergleichung im Haag* (1937), pp. 36 sq.

lawyers seem to have resigned themselves to the realities of life and business morals. The licentia they were prepared to grant to any party to a (prospective) contract of sale found its limitations only in the rejection of dolus, in the remedies available in case of latent defects and—above all—in the smartness and alertness of the other party.[146]

(c) *Private autonomy*

Ius vigilantibus scriptum: there was very little in the Roman law of contracts to limit this core feature of economic liberalism. The law merely provides the framework within which the individuals may operate;[147] it does not have protective functions. One notable exception was the legislation limiting interest rates on loans.[148] But no attempts were ever made in classical Roman law to interfere with the freedom of the parties to a contract of sale to fix their price. Yet, these situations are not at all dissimilar. In both instances, leaving technicalities aside,[149] it is an imbalance between performance and counterperformance with which the legal system is faced. It is on this basis that § 138 II BGB provides one and the same rule for all bilateral contracts: loans against interest, sale, hire, etc. According to this rule, not even an obvious disproportion between the performance and the pecuniary advantages granted in exchange for it is in itself sufficient reason to set aside the contract as invalid: in addition, there must have been exploitation of a distressed situation, inexperience, lack of judgemental ability, or grave weakness of will of the disadvantaged party.[150]

---

[146] Wacke, (1977) 94 *ZSS* 202 sqq., who also (pp. 198 sq.) draws attention to the fact that some haggling took place as a matter of course and commercial practice before a contract of sale was concluded. The parties usually took their time before they reached an agreement; on the weekly market days (dies nundinarum) no work was done on the farms. (The nundinae are apparently derived from the word for haggling.) The initial offer of the vendor could therefore not have created a reasonable expectation that the object was really worth this price. A philosopher such as Cicero looked down on the mercatores and found their occupation "sordid": "nihil enim proficiant, nisi admodum mentiantur" (*De officiis*, 1, XLII—150). As far as the bargaining process is concerned, cf. also C. 4, 44, 8 (Diocl.): ". . . quod videlicet si contractus emptionis atque venditionis cogitasses substantiam et quod emptor viliori comparandi, venditor cariori distrahendi votum gerentes ad hunc contractum accedant vixque post multas contentiones paulatim venditore de eo quod petierat detrahente, emptore autem huic quod obtulerat addente, ad certum consentiant pretium. . . ." For details about prices in Italy and the African provinces, see R. Duncan-Jones, *The Economy of the Roman Empire, Quantitative Studies* (1974), pp. 63 sqq.

[147] "The formal equality of Romans before the law became a shield behind which the mercantile economy of Rome could operate with greater confidence": Frier, *Roman Jurists*, p. 192.

[148] Cf. supra, pp. 166 sqq.

[149] Mutuum differed from sale in that it was a strictly unilaterally binding contract in Roman law. Interest could be promised only by way of a separate stipulation. Cf. supra, pp. 154 sq.

[150] For an analysis in English, see John P. Dawson, "Economic Duress, and the Fair Exchange in French and German Law", (1937) 12 *Tulane LR* 48 sqq.; idem, "Unconscionable Coercion: The German Version", (1976) 89 *Harvard LR* 1052 sqq. As far as English law is concerned, cf. e.g. *Lloyds Bank Ltd. v. Bundy* [1975] QB 326 (CA) at 337 (per Lord Denning MR).

§ 138 II was formulated in the second half of the 19th century.[151] It was a child of the then—once again—dominant ideas of economic liberalism:[152]

> "[E]very person who is not, from his peculiar condition or circumstances, under disability, is entitled to dispose of his property in such manner and upon such terms as he chooses; and whether his bargains are wise and discreet, or profitable or unprofitable, or otherwise, are considerations, not for courts of justice, but for the party himself to deliberate upon."[153]

5. Laesio enormis and equality in exchange

(a) C. 4, 44, 2

There were times, however, when an entirely different attitude prevailed. It found its legal expression in the doctrine of laesio enormis,[154] an awe-inspiring piece of legal architecture, built upon the frail foundations of two texts from Justinian's Code. The better known of these texts reads as follows:

> "Rem maioris pretii si tu vel pater tuus minoris pretii distraxit, humanum est, ut vel pretium te restituente emptoribus fundum venditum recipias auctoritate intercedente iudicis, vel, si emptor elegerit, quod deest iusto pretio recipies. minus autem pretium esse videtur, si nec dimidia pars veri pretii soluta sit."[155]

This rescript was ostensibly issued by Diocletian. It is not unlikely, however, that we are dealing with a Justinianic interpolation.[156] Even a

---

[151] On its history, see Zimmermann, *Moderationsrecht*, pp. 147 sqq.; Klaus Luig, "Vertragsfreiheit und Äquivalenzprinzip im gemeinen Recht und im BGB", in: *Festgabe für Helmut Coing* (1982), pp. 171 sqq.

[152] Cf. e.g. Franz Wieacker, *Das Sozialmodell der klassischen Privatrechtsgesetzbücher und die Entwicklung der modernen Gesellschaft* (1953).

[153] Joseph Story, *Commentaries on Equity Jurisprudence* (11th ed.), vol. I (1873), § 244. On the age of freedom of contract and its intellectual background, see, above all, Atiyah, *Rise and Fall*, pp. 219 sqq.

[154] The term was introduced by the glossators.

[155] C. 4, 44, 2. The other text is C. 4, 44, 8, a long and involved piece of legal draftsmanship ("Si voluntate tua fundum tuum filius tuus venumdedit, dolus ex calliditate atque insidiis emptoris argui debet vel metus mortis vel cruciatus corporis imminens detegi, ne habeatur rata venditio. hoc enim solum, quod paulo minori pretio fundum venumdatum significas, ad rescindendam emptionem invalidum est. quod videlicet si contractus emptionis atque venditionis cogitasses substantiam et quod emptor viliori comparandi, venditor cariori distrahendi votum gerentes ad hunc contractum accedant vixque post multas contentiones, paulatim venditore de eo quod petierat detrahente, emptore autem huic quod obtulerat addente, ad certum consentiant pretium, profecto perspiceres neque bonam fidem, quae emptionis atque venditionis conventionem tuetur, pati neque ullam rationem concedere rescindi propter hoc consensu finitum contractum vel statim vel post pretii quantitatis disceptationem: nisi minus dimidia iusti pretii, quod fuerat tempore venditionis, datum est, electione iam emptori praestita servanda").

[156] The question is much disputed. Arguing in favour of interpolation affecting the substance of the text cf., for example, René Dekkers, *La lésion énorme* (1937), pp. 16 sqq.; Genzmer, op. cit., note 145, pp. 55 sqq.; A.J.B. Sirks, "La *laesio enormis* en droit romain et byzantin", (1985) 53 *TR* 291 sqq.; Hannu Tapani Klami, "'Laesio enormis' in Roman Law", (1987) 33 *Labeo* 48 sqq.; cf. also idem, *Roman Law and Hardship* (1987), pp. 156 sqq.; contra e.g. Károly Visky, "Die Proportionalität von Wert und Preis in den römischen Rechtsquellen des III. Jahrhunderts", (1969) 16 *RIDA* 374 sqq., 385 sqq.; cf. now also idem, *Spuren*, pp. 24 sqq.; Karl Hackl, "Zu den Wurzeln der Anfechtung wegen laesio enormis",

superficial reading of the text raises suspicions. Thus, for instance, the object of the sale is referred to as "res" at the outset, as "fundus" later on. The first sentence has "iustum pretium", the second "verum pretium".[157] The vendor is at first "tu vel pater tuus" (the verb relating only to the third person), then only "tu". And the plurality of purchasers mentioned in the first part of the text (emptoribus) corresponds equally badly with the single emptor in the second part. But even if the text was indeed subjected to later alterations, it does not necessarily follow that the substance of this fragment is entirely spurious.[158] Yet, there are other arguments to confirm our suspicion. Up to the time of Justinian there is no sign that a remedy on the lines of that suggested in C. 4, 44, 2 was ever granted. The Codex Theodosianus, in particular, made no mention of such a remedy, even though there would have been occasion to do so had it already existed by that time.[159] Furthermore, it sounds unlikely that a conservative and classicist emperor such as Diocletian[160] should have been responsible for as uncouth an intrusion into a core principle of classical contract law as the remedy for laesio enormis represents.[161] Diocletian did indeed try to curb the freedom of the parties to determine the price of goods, but only by means of public-law regulations. His edictum de pretiis rerum venalium[162] was a sweeping attempt to relieve the lot of wage earners (mainly workmen, public officials and soldiers) suffering under the galloping inflation[163] by imposing maximum prices for a whole variety

(1981) 98 *ZSS* 147 sqq. Alan Watson, "The Hidden Origins of Enorm Lesion", (1981) 2 *Journal of Legal History* 186 sqq., finds that "it is simply logically impossible to provide [an answer]"; in the same vein, Klami ((1987) 33 *Labeo* 63; *Roman Law and Hardship*, p. 172) states: ". . . the riddle of laesio enormis cannot be solved, I suppose." For an analysis of the arguments pro and contra interpolation, see also Walter de Bondt, "Lesion in the Roman Law of Contracts", 1979 *Juridical Review* 45 sqq.

157 This point is emphasized by Klami, (1987) 33 *Labeo* 55 sqq.

158 Cf. e.g. Kaser, *RPr* II, p. 389.

159 CT 3, 1, 1 (a. 319); 3, 1, 4 (a. 383); 3, 1, 7 (a. 396). On the impact of these provisions on early medieval law, cf. Kenneth S. Cahn, "The Roman and Frankish Roots of the Just Price of Medieval Canon Law", (1969) 6 *Studies in Medieval and Renaissance History* 6 sqq., 43 sqq.

160 Typical for his approach to law, e.g. Coll. XV, III, 2: "Maximi enim criminis est retractare quae semel ab antiquis statuta et definita suum statum et cursum tenent ac possident."

161 Cf. e.g. C. 4, 44, 4 and C. 4, 44, 3, both also attributed to Diocletian; they are not in harmony with C. 4, 44, 2 and 8.

162 For details, see Hugo Blümner, "Der Maximaltarif des Diokletian vom Jahr 301, 1893", in: 72 *Preussische Jahrbücher* 453 sqq.; Graser, *The Edict of Diocletian on Maximum Prices* (1940); Siegfried Lauffer (ed.), *Diokletians Preisedikt* (1971); Marta Giacchero (ed.), *Edictum Diocletiani et Collegarum de pretiis rerum venalium* (1974).

163 In the second half of the 3rd century, the prices apparently rose by something like 800 %; in Egypt one unit of wheat seems to have cost 12–15 drachmai between A.D. 200 and 250, but 120 000 drachmai in about 300 B.C. For details, see Fritz Heichelheim, "Zur Währungskrise des römischen Imperiums im 3. Jahrhundert n. Chr.", (1933) 26 *Klio* 96 sqq.; Gunnar Mickwitz, *Geld und Wirtschaft im römischen Reich des vierten Jahrhunderts n. Chr.* (1932), pp. 45 sqq.; Jones, *The Roman Economy* (1974), pp. 187 sqq.; Jean-Pierre Callu, *La politique monétaire des empereurs romains de 238 à 311* (1969), pp. 196 sqq.; Michael H.

of goods and services.[164] It contained draconian sanctions (death penalty!)[165] but, remarkably enough, it did not declare invalid those contracts infringing the edict. Not even in order to enforce the cornerstone of his policy of price controls[166] did Diocletian tinker with what the parties had agreed upon.[167] Finally, C. 4, 44, 2 seems to fit in well with Justinian's concept of an absolutist welfare state. Christian teaching, as well as stoic moral philosophy, demanded an infusion of ethics and of humanitas into the law and it was in this spirit that the Emperor was supposed to render aid to the weak and poor and to relax the rigours of the law. The feeling for the importance of clarity and the educational value of firm and severe legal rules made way for the urge to show consideration and avoid harsh results in individual cases by allowing equitable exceptions.[168] C. 4, 44, 2 was designed to meet a special crisis. Justinian's ruthless taxation policy[169] tended to force peasant farmers to sell their smallholdings and it is obvious that this situation lent itself to exploitation by urban capitalists, keen to invest their wealth in assets of a more stable value than money. The farmers in their predicament had no bargaining power at all and were often forced to sell their property at far below its real value. It is in this situation that Justinian felt compelled to intervene and to make a remedy available to the seller.

Crawford, "Finance, Coinage and Money from the Severans to Constantine", in: *ANRW*, vol. II, 2 (1975), pp. 567 sq.; De Martino, *Wirtschaftsgeschichte*, pp. 391 sqq.; Klami, *Roman Law and Hardship* (1987), pp. 117 sqq., 130 sqq.

[164] For instance: 1 pound (= 327 g) of pork: 12 denarii, 1 pound of beef: 8 denarii, a chicken: 30 denarii, one fatted hen-pheasant: 200 denarii, half a litre of beer: 4 denarii, 20 cucumbers or 20 big edible snails: 4 denarii. A barber was allowed to take 2 denarii for a haircut, a primary teacher could charge 50 denarii per month and pupil, a teacher of grammar 200, of rhetoric 250 denarii.

[165] *Praefatio*, 18; cf. also Lactantius, *De mortibus persecutorum*, 7, §§ 6 sq.: "Idem cum variis iniquitatibus immensum faceret caritatem, legam pretiis rerum venalium statuere conatus est. Tunc ob exigua et vilia multus sanguis effusus, nec venale quicquam metu apparebat et caritas multo deterius exarsit, donec lex necessitate ipsa post multorum exitium solveretur."

[166] Which was, incidentally, not very successful and seems to have hardly outlived the Emperor who enacted it: cf. e.g. Ernst Schönbauer, "Untersuchungen über die Rechtsentwicklung in der Kaiserzeit", (1955–56) 9/10 *JJP* 53 sqq.

[167] De Bondt, 1979 *Juridical Review* 50, 52, 55 further argues that, whereas Diocletian's main aim (pursued by means of his edictum de pretiis rerum venalium and his reforms of the fiscal system) was to stabilize the value of the money and to combat inflation, the recognition of laesio enormis would have had the opposite effect.

[168] Cf. the clause "humanum est" in C. 4, 44, 2. On humanity in Roman Law, see Schulz, *Principles*, pp. 189 sqq.; Heinz Haffter, "Die römische Humanitas", in: Hans Oppermann (ed.), *Römische Wertbegriffe*, (1983), pp. 468 sqq.; Henryk Kupiszewski, "Humanitas et le droit romain", in: *Maior viginti quinque annis, Essays in commemoration of the sixth lustrum of the Institute for Legal History of the University of Utrecht* (ed. J.E. Spruit, 1979), pp. 85 sqq. Cf. also, more specifically, on humanitas and the regulation of labour relations, Johannes Michael Rainer, "Humanität und Arbeit im römischen Recht", (1988) 105 *ZSS* 745 sqq. For a very sceptical view of the "humanitas" displayed in C. 4, 44, 2, see De Bondt, 1979 *Juridical Review* 58 sq.

[169] Cf. e.g. A.H.M. Jones, *The Decline of the Ancient World* (1966), pp. 114, 154 sqq., 175 sqq.

(b) Extension of C. 4, 44, 2

It will have been noted that C. 4, 44, 2 is very far from establishing a clear and general rule. It deals with a specific situation and thus confines itself to granting relief to a particular applicant of the name of Aurelius Lupus. All one can say is that the emperor allows the vendor to rescind the contract if he has sold a tract of land for less than half its true value; the purchaser, however, is given the opportunity to avoid such a rescission by making up the true value. Yet, the underlying legal principle, namely that a contract can be so one-sided, the disproportion in the values exchanged so gross, that the law has to intervene and provide the disadvantaged party with a remedy: this principle, once it had been accepted in one individual situation, commended itself to be applied to a whole lot of further cases. Why should legal intervention be confined to combating exploitation of the peasantry (*"Bauernlegen"*)? If the purchaser is in such a predicament that the vendor is able to sell his object (why necessarily a piece of land?) for more than double its true value, does he not equally deserve the protection of the law? It is easy enough to imagine such situations, where it is the purchaser who is the disadvantaged party. The same problems can crop up with regard to other contracts, too: a house may have been let for a rental far in excess of anything that is fair and reasonable or that is normally asked for houses of that kind. Conversely, the lessor may have been forced to agree to a rent amounting to not even half of what he should normally be able to receive.

All these and a variety of other questions began to be asked in medieval jurisprudence; and as the principle expressed in C. 4, 44, 2 was generally accepted, it is clear in which way the answers were premised. A breathtaking expansion of the institute of laesio enormis took place, in the course of which all the arbitrary restrictions of the imperial constitution were thrown off:[170] relief came to be granted not only to the vendor but also[171] to the purchaser;[172] the scope of application of the rule was extended from the sale of land to that of houses and of movables[173] (this was supported by the general word "rem"); it was adopted from sale into all kinds of other contracts, including, for instance, letting and hiring, compromise, exchange and even donation.[174] There has, however, hardly ever been unanimity about how far one could go; most of these questions were hotly debated, the answers depending, largely, on how much the individual

[170] Cf. especially Dekkers, op. cit., note 156, pp. 66 sqq.; R.W.M. Dias, "Laesio Enormis, The Roman-Dutch Story", in: *Studies in the Roman Law of Sale in memory of Francis de Zulueta* (1959), pp. 46 sqq.; Wolfgang Georg Schulze, *Die laesio enormis in der deutschen Privatrechtsgeschichte* (unpublished Dr. iur. thesis, Münster, 1973).

[171] According to §§ 59, 69 I 11 PrALR, only to the purchaser.

[172] For a comprehensive discussion see Glück, vol. 17, pp. 27 sqq.

[173] Or only valuable movables: Voet, *Commentarius ad Pandectas*, Lib. VIII, Tit. V, XII.

[174] For details, see Glück, vol. 17, pp. 120 sqq.

authors were attracted by the idea of equality in exchange, and on how faithfully they tried to apply and interpret the sources of Roman law.

(c) Consequential problems

Still, however liberally one was prepared to dispense with the limitations of C. 4, 44, 2, the very fact that the remedy for laesio enormis originated in this text, led to some further consequential problems. Take, for example, the case where the purchaser is the disadvantaged party. How does one apply a remedy that has been designed for the reverse situation and therefore allows the seller to rescind the contract if he has obtained *less than half* of the true price?[175] Should one give the purchaser the same option if he has had to pay more than double?[176] Let us assume the "true value" of the object sold to be 100. The vendor would then enjoy the protection of the law if the purchase price was 49 or less, the purchaser only if it was 201 or more. Thus, on this construction, the purchaser seems to lose out, for from a purely arithmetical point of view the margin of what the law still expects him to tolerate before he can avail himself of a remedy is exactly double of what is laid down in the case of the vendor: the vendor can rescind if he has been overcharged by more than 50, whilst the purchaser must have been overcharged by more than 100. This is the reason why the glossators and commentators tended to reject the purely geometrical method (as they called it) of assessment if the purchaser had suffered laesio enormis and favoured an arithmetical calculation: the purchaser should be entitled to the remedy if he had had to pay more than the true value plus half, i.e., in our example, more than 150. On purely logical grounds, neither of these approaches can be faulted, and thus the dispute was never conclusively resolved.[177]

Laesio enormis has been compared to the hydra: each answer to any of the questions raised seemed to cause a host of new problems. "Vides quod capita habeat haec hydra?" exclaimed Christian Thomasius, exasperated by a string of more than thirty questions which he had just

[175] For a comprehensive discussion, see, again, Glück, vol. 17, pp. 35 sqq. He quotes (inter alia!) Azo, Accursius, Baldus, Bartolus, Gutierrez, Covarruvias, Gomezius, Augustin Barbosa, Jacobus Curtius, Johannes Voet, Gottlieb Gerhard Titius, Samuel von Cocceji and Darjes for the one opinion, Molinaeus, Cujacius, Duarenus, Donellus, Merenda, Perezius, Tulden, Böckelmann and Johann Ulrich von Cramer for the other. Cf. also the discussion by Cahn, (1969) 6 *Studies in Medieval and Renaissance History* 21 sqq.

[176] This was the prevailing opinion from about the 16th century onwards; cf. e.g. Molinaeus, "Tractatus contractuum et usurarum", in: *Opera omnia* (Parisiis, 1681), Quaest. XIV, n. 175; Grotius, *Inleiding*, III, LII, 2; Lauterbach, *Collegium theoretico-practicum*, Lib. XVIII, Tit. V, X; cf. further Dias, *Studies De Zulueta*, p. 52.

[177] For a discussion of further problems and limitations of the laesio enormis in the ius commune of the Roman-Dutch variant, see Dias, *Studies De Zulueta*, pp. 54 sqq.; for the ius commune generally, see Glück, vol. 17, pp. 79 sqq., 105 sqq.

formulated.[178] In the course of time, most of the features of laesio enormis came under attack. Dimidia pars veri pretii was not always perceived to be a sensible limit of laesio enormis and thus different (equally arbitrary) criteria were set: two-thirds for the region of Württemberg,[179] the charmingly extravagant figure of five-twelfths in the French code civil;[180] and canon law even made special provision for what was called laesio enormissima—where the lesion "longe dimidium justi pretii excedat".[181] A dispute arose as to whether it was justified to let the purchaser (if he so chose) make up the full value, or whether he should not only be required to pay up to whatever limit was set for laesio enormis, i.e. usually half the true price.[182] After all, if one-half or anything between one-half and the true value had been agreed upon, the vendor would not have been able to recover what was lacking of the true price. Why should he end up in a better position, where he had started off in a worse one?[183] Furthermore, the legal consequences of laesio enormis came to be questioned too. Why this odd alternativity of sanctions and why, of all people, let the *advantaged* party make the choice? Hence, we find the right of choice occasionally being granted to the disadvantaged party; more radically, though, the whole transaction was also sometimes considered invalid in case of laesio enormis.[184]

(d) The problem of establishing the iustum pretium

All these problems, however, are, in a certain sense of a merely technical nature. The real crux of laesio enormis lies elsewhere. However the limits might be fixed, and whatever the nature of its sanctions, the doctrine can work only if there is a true or just price for every article, against which one is able to assess what the parties have agreed upon. Economic liberalism denies the existence of such an objective yardstick. The value in a contract depends upon the judgement of the contracting parties themselves, not upon that of other people.

---

[178] *De aequitate cerebrina legis secundae C. De resc. vend.*, 2 § 13; for further details, see Klaus Luig, "Bemerkungen zum Problem des gerechten Preises bei Christian Thomasius", in: *Tradition and Entwicklung, Gedenkschrift für Johannes Riederer* (1981), pp. 167 sqq.

[179] Württembergische Landrechte of 1555 and 1610; cf. Schulze, op. cit., note 170, pp. 31 sqq.

[180] Article 1674, applicable only in favour of a seller of land. This restrictive tendency can be traced back to Cuiacius, Molinaeus, Domat and Pothier; for details, see Enrico Dell'Aquila, "L'adeguatezza tra i vantaggi nei contratti onerosi", (1979) 91 *Studi Senesi* 485 sqq. Article 1674 was inserted at the urging of Napoleon Bonaparte, who took a lively interest in the preparation of the code civil and left many marks on both the style and the substance of the code (which he is said to have considered his greatest achievement). Article 1674 is an exception to the general rule of art. 1118.

[181] Cf. e.g. Parladorius, *Res Quotidianae*, Lib. II, Cap. IV (pp. 246 sqq.).

[182] For details, see Glück, vol. 17, pp. 53 sqq.; Dias, *Studies De Zulueta*, pp. 55 sq.

[183] According to art. 1681, the purchaser may, if he chooses to pay rather than rescind, subtract 10 % from the iustum pretium.

[184] Cf. e.g. § 59 I 11, § 75 I 4 PrALR.

"The value of a thing . . . must be in its nature fluctuating, and will depend upon ten thousand different circumstances. One man, in the disposal of his property, may sell it for less than another would. He may sell it under a pressure of circumstances, which may induce him to part with it at a particular time. If courts of equity were to unravel all these transactions, they would throw every thing into confusion, and set afloat the contracts of mankind."[185]

Or, in the words of Thomas Hobbes: "The value of all things contracted for, is measured by the Appetite of the Contractors: and therefore the just value, is that which they be contented to give."[186] The astounding career of laesio enormis was possible only because the medieval scholastics, and later the natural lawyers, took an entirely different view of this matter and considered equality of exchange to be one of the basic principles of the law of contracts: ". . .carius vendere aut vilius emere rem quam valeat, est secundum se injustum et illicitum"[187] as St. Thomas Aquinas put it; "[i]n contractibus natura aequalitatem imperat, et ita quidem, ut ex inaequalitate jus oriatur minus habenti",[188] to quote the "father" of a natural law, that was no longer divinely inspired, but based on human reason. But how can such inaequalitas ever be established?[189] Admittedly, the price is determined by a subjective estimation. However, a price determined subjectively by all becomes objective to each. It would be sinful (or: contra ius naturale) to deviate from this common estimate in an individual transaction, for that would imply the exploitation of this particular purchaser (or vendor). Thus, the doctrine of equality in exchange was not based on the belief that each object has an intrinsic and immutable value, and that this value represents the iustum pretium.[190] Neither was the just price of goods linked to their cost of production.[191]

---

185 Story, op. cit., note 153, § 245.

186 Thomas Hobbes, *Leviathan*, Part I, chap. 15 (p. 208 of the ed. by C.B. Macpherson, 1968).

187 *Summa Theologiae*, Secunda secundae, Quaest. LXXVII, Art. I.

188 Grotius, *De jure belli ac pacis*, Lib. II, Cap. XII, 8.

189 For what follows, see Endemann, *Studien*, vol. II, pp. 6 sqq., 14, 30 sqq.; John T. Noonan, *The Scholastic Analysis of Usury* (1957); John W. Baldwin, *The Medieval Theories of the Just Price. Romanists, Canonists and Theologians in the Twelfth and Thirteenth Centuries* (1959); Winfried Trusen, *Spätmittelalterliche Jurisprudenz und Wirtschaftsethik, dargestellt an Wiener Gutachten des 13. Jahrhunderts* (1961), pp. 71 sqq.; idem, "Äquivalenzprinzip und gerechter Preis im Spätmittelalter", in: *Staat und Gesellschaft, Festgabe für Günther Küchenhoff* (1967), pp. 247 sqq.; Cahn, (1969) 6 *Studies in Medieval and Renaissance History* 3 sqq., 30 sqq.; Raymond de Roover, *La pensée économique des Scolastiques. Doctrines et méthodes* (1971); Wolter, *Ius canonicum in iure civili* pp. 113 sqq.; James Gordley, "Equality in Exchange", (1981) 69 *California LR* 1587 sqq.; Werner Goez, "Das Ringen um den 'gerechten Preis' in Spätmittelalter und Reformationszeit", in: *"Der Gerechte Preis", Beiträge zur Diskussion um das "pretium iustum"* (1982), pp. 21 sqq.

190 "Primum, in contractibus emptionum et venditionum, similibusque permutationibus, nequaquam attendi, nec constitui iustum pretium ex natura rei, sed hominum aestimatione, tametsi insana sit aestimatio: num si natura rei foret observanda, pluris esset aestimandus equus, quam gemma ob utilitatem equi": Covarruvias a Leyva, *Variae resolutiones*, vol. II, Lib. II, Cap. III, 4.

191 "Secundo hinc apparet in pretii iusti aestimatione non esse considerandum quanti res ipsa empta fuerit, nec quot labores pro eius adquisitione venditor fuerit perpessus, sed

Instead, it was identified with the market price set under competitive conditions.

> ". . . iustum cuiusque rei pretium non ex cuiuslibet affectione, aut sumptu constat, sed ex communi hominum aestimatione perpenditur: itaque tantum valet res, quantum absque fraude et iniuria communiter potest homini scienti eius conditionem. . . . Non ignoramus . . . pretia rerum, quae usquam posuimus, alia in aliis locis esse, et omnibus pene annis mutari."[192]

These ideas about equality of exchange go back to Aristotle (who had argued that neither party, as a matter of commutative justice, must be enriched at the expense of the other)[193] from where they were taken up and further developed by St. Thomas Aquinas. They profoundly influenced both the doctrine of canon law[194] and the earlier natural-law theorists: so much so that laesio enormis, which provided relief only in certain extreme cases, was regarded as entirely unsatisfactory.[195] Each deviation from the just price, so it was argued, constitutes a peccatum[196] and is sufficiently serious to grant an action in foro externo.[197] The writers of the ius commune, however, by and large adopted a more positivistic attitude; they continued to apply C. 4, 44,

---

tantum, habendam, esse rationem communis hominem aestimatione. Sic sane mercator, qui magnis expensis attulit merces e Flandria non poterit eas carius vendere, quam communi hominum aestimatione valeant in Hispania, alioqui restituere tenebitur quidquid ultra iustum pretium acceperit": Covarruvias a Leyva, loc. cit.

[192] Covarruvias a Leyva, loc. cit. Cf. also already Gai. D. 13, 4, 3 (". . . scimus quam varia pretia rerum per singulas civitates regionesque . . ."); Paul. D. 35, 2, 63, 2 ("Nonnullam tamen pretio varietatem loca temporaque adferunt: nec enim tantidem Romae et in Hispania oleum aestimabitur nec continuis sterilitatibus tantidem, quanti secundis fructibus, dum hic quoque non ex mentis temporum nec ex ea quae raro accidat caritate pretia constituantur"). On the individual factors to be taken into consideration in establishing the price of a thing, see, for the late Middle Ages e.g. Conrad Summenhard von Calw, as discussed by Trusen, *Festgabe G. Küchenhoff*, pp. 259 sqq., for the age of the law of reason Samuel Pufendorf, *De jure naturae et gentium*, Lib. V, Cap.I, § 1 (and the analysis by Herbert Niederländer, "Zum 'Pretium rei' bei den Vernunftrechtlern", in: *Gedächtnisschrift für Wolfgang Kunkel* (1984), pp. 283 sqq.

[193] *Nicomachean Ethics*, Book V, II, 6 sqq. (1130 b sqq.)

[194] Even though the Corpus Juris Canonici itself still faithfully reflects Roman law: "Tenet venditio, licet venditor sit deceptus ultra dimidiam iusti pretii; potest tamen venditor agere, ut restituatur res vel iustum pretium suppleatur, et, si alterum praecise petit, succumbit" (*Decretales Gregorii* IX., Lib. III, Tit. XVII, Cap. III).

[195] Cf., for example, the criticism by Pufendorf, *De jure naturae et gentium*, Lib. V, Cap. III, § 9, who argued that the rule works unfairly, in that a small deviation in the price of an expensive object can cause more harm than a large deviation in the price of a small item; yet the rule applied to the second case, but not the first.

[196] Cf., for example, Antonius Merenda (Alfred Pernice, *Labeo* , vol. I, p. 454, n. 2): "Concludamus ergo rationem naturalem non pati, ut contrahentes se invicem decipiant, et ideo peccare eos qui secus fecerint." The starting point is 1. Thessalonians 4, 6: "ne quis supergrediatur neque circumveniat in negotio fratrem suum" (vulgata-tr.); cf. also St. Matthew 6, 24. This did not mean that the Church condemned the economic activity of merchants and commercial enterprise per se; cf. supra, pp. 171, 173 sq.

[197] Cf. e.g. Covarruvias a Leyva, *Variae resolutiones*, vol. II, Lib. II, Cap. IV, 11: ". . . opinio verissima est, manifesta et urgenti admodum ratione quae dictat, naturali lege in contractibus commutativis a Republica et hominum moribus in utriusque utilitatem institutis, re ipsa exactam et summam aequalitatem requiri ex justitia commutativa partes ad partem . . . quo fit, deceptionem istam omnino esse contra virtutem justitiae commutativae, quae in aequalitate juxta proportionem consistit; si quis igitur ab ea virtute recesserit, id est,

2 and thus to require the contract price to deviate by more than half from the just price. The Aristotelian theory could, after all, be used to explain why the remedy was provided; and its limitations, as a matter of positive law, could be reconciled with the economic ethics of scholasticism by confining laesio ultra dimidium to the forum externum and dealing with the less severe cases of laesio in foro conscientiae,[198] by pointing to the flood of litigation that would ensue but for the clear limit set in C. 4, 44, 2 ("Permittit autem Jus utrimque deceptionem, quae non est ultra dimidium justi pretii, ad vitandas innumeras lites, quae sequerentur, si ex qualibet fraude daretur actio"),[199] or by adopting a sort of margin approach: the contract price is iustum if it has been fixed somewhere between the highest and the lowest value of the object sold.[200]

(e) The abolition of laesio enormis

Once, however, the belief in one's ability to assess equality in exchange had been shaken and once the idea of private autonomy had again started to gain ground and to supersede metaphysical, "natural", or paternalistic notions of contractual justice, the concept of laesio enormis was doomed. Inherently arbitrary and preposterous, full of pitfalls and anomalies, subversive and fatal, as it now appeared to disillusioned judges and academic writers,[201] suitable only to be the object of mockery and legal satire,[202] laesio enormis did not become part of the

---

a medio justitiae, vitium declinat, peccat et ad restitutionem tenetur"; Grotius, *De jure belli ac pacis*, Lib. II, Cap. XII, 12: "Hi vero qui legibus civilibus subjecti non sunt, id sequi debent quod aequuum esse ipsis ratio recta dictat: imo et illi qui legibus subjecti sunt, quoties de eo quod fas piumque est agitur, si modo leges non jus dant aut tollunt, sed juri duntaxat ob certas causas auxilium suum denegant."

[198] Cf. e.g. Molina, *De iustitia et iure*, Tract. II, Disp. 350, col. 404 sqq.

[199] Leonardus Lessius, *De justitia et jure ceterisque virtutibus cardinalibus libri quatuor* (Venetiis, 1734), Lib. 2, Cap. 21, Dubitatio IV (n. 20).

[200] Lauterbach, *Collegium theoretico-practicum*, Lib. XVIII, Tit. I, 53 sqq. St. Thomas Aquinas had already recognized that the iustum pretium cannot be exactly determined: ". . . et tenetur ille qui plus habet, recompensare ei qui damnificatus est, si sit notabile damnum. Quod ideo dico, quia justum pretium rerum non est punctualiter determinatum, sed magis in quadam aestimatione consistit; ita quod modica additio vel minutio non videtur tollere aequalitatem justitiae": *Summa Theologiae*, Secunda secundae, Quaest. LXXVII, Art I. He, and with him the other "realists", relied on the free (and unmanipulated) interplay of market forces to result in a iustum pretium. The "nominalists", on the other hand, argued for State intervention. Hence, the iustum pretium came to be fixed by public price regulations; cf. e.g. Gustaf Klemens Schmelzeisen, *Polizeiordnungen und Privatrecht* (1955), pp. 436 sq.

[201] These invectives have been taken from the judgment of Van den Heever JA in *Tjollo Ateljees (Eins.) Bpk. v. Small* 1949 (1) SA 856 (A) at 862 sqq. (esp. at 863 and 873) and Schulz, *CRL*, p. 528. For further harsh comments, see Ludwig Julius Friedrich Höpfner, *Naturrecht des einzelnen Menschen, der Gesellschaften und der Völker* (6th ed., Giessen, 1795), § 92; Adolph Dietrich Weber, *Systematische Entwickelung der Lehre von der natürlichen Verbindlichkeit und deren gerichtliche Wirkung* (4th ed., 1811) § 41.

[202] Cf. De Spinetto, *Apothecario de Venetia Politische Schnupf-Tobacs-Dose vor die Wächserne Nase der Justiz in sich fassend Juristische Streit-Fragen in Handel en Wandel von denen Kauf- und Mieth- oder Pacht- und anderen Contracten mit Satyrischer Feder entworfen und aus dem Italienischen ins Teutsche übersetzt (The Political Snuff-Box before the Waxen Nose of Justice)* (1739), prise 51 sqq.

BGB.[203] For the whole of the 19th century there are no reported cases in which an action arising from laesio enormis was successful.[204] In France[205] and Austria[206] the doctrine still exists, but it leads a very quiet, practically impotent, pensioner's life.[207] The South African courts, in turn, have seen no need to revivify the moribund.[208] The *Tjollo Ateljees* case struck the mortal blow,[209] but it was the legislator who finally ended its existence as far as Roman-Dutch law is concerned:[210] an interesting case of a formal abolition of a common-law rule.

(f) Equality in exchange today

However, as one knows, there is life after death. Modern codifications are generally disinclined to recognize inadequacy of price as an independent ground for relief. § 138 BGB is an example in point. According to its second subsection, it is not the disparity of values in itself that voids the contract; even a striking disproportion between performance and counterperformance is relevant only if it has been brought about by the exploitation of certain enumerated weaknesses on the part of the disadvantaged party.[211] The code, in other words, proceeds from the assumption that, as long as both parties are in a position to assess their circumstances properly and to draw the appropriate conclusions from such an assessment,[212] their contractual arrangements have to be given effect to. However, the courts have not always been happy to accept the results of such far-reaching party autonomy. On the one hand, they have begun to infer exploitation of one of the enumerated weaknesses, if the disproportion in the price is obvious and the contract therefore grossly unfair and inequitable.[213] The greater the disproportion, the more willing the courts have become

[203] For the arguments, see Franz Philipp von Kübel, "Recht der Schuldverhältnisse, Teil 2", in: Werner Schubert (ed.), *Vorentwürfe*, pp. 20 sq.

[204] The pandectists tended to regard laesio enormis as a somewhat anomalous exception to the normal principles of contract law, based merely on equity: cf. e.g. von Wächter, *Pandekten*, § 207, p. 472. For references to cases in which laesio enormis was discussed, see, for example, John P. Dawson, "Economic Duress and the Fair Exchange in French and German Law", (1937) 11 *Tulane LR* 368.

[205] Cf. supra, p. 264.

[206] § 934 ABGB.

[207] In France it has again been restricted to the sale of land; the Austrian provision used to be emasculated in practice by standardized renunciation clauses.

[208] Schreiner J, in *Botha v. Assad* 1945 TPD 1 at 9. For a full discussion of laesio enormis in South African law, see Wessels, *Contract*, vol. II, §§ 5071 sqq.

[209] *Tjollo Ateljees (Eins.) Bpk. v. Small* 1949 (1) SA 856 (A).

[210] S. 25 General Law Amendment Act 32/1952. Cf. further H.R. Hahlo, E. Kahn, "Good-Bye Laesio Enormis", (1952) *SALJ* 392 sqq.

[211] Cf. supra, p. 258.

[212] A "distressed situation" ("*Zwangslage*"), for instance, does not necessarily imply a threat to the economic existence of the disadvantaged party: see e.g. Theo Mayer-Maly, in: *Münchener Kommentar*, vol. I (2nd ed., 1984), § 138, n. 124.

[213] The question of lack of judgemental ability or willpower is investigated only with regard to the individual contract in question, no matter whether the disadvantaged party has shown these traits on other occasions; see e.g. Mayer-Maly, op. cit., note 212, § 138, n. 126.

to conclude that there is, for instance, inexperience or indiscretion.[214] On the other hand, § 138 BGB ("Legal transactions contra bonos mores are void") has been used to sidestep the restrictive requirements of § 138 II. A contract under which the one party obtains advantages in obvious disproportion to what he returns, is taken to be contra bonos mores, if the advantaged party displayed a reprehensible attitude, by either deliberately exploiting the weaker economic position of his opponent, or by grossly negligently failing to realize that the latter entered into the contract only because of his precarious situation.[215] This subjective component, however, has an almost fictitious character, as the courts are prepared to draw inferences from the objective circumstances of the contract (especially the disproportion in values) without requiring specific evidence as to whether the conduct in question was wilful or grossly negligent.[216] One court has even gone so far as to argue quite boldly that a particularly gross disproportion (as opposed to a merely obvious or striking one) is sufficient reason in itself to void the contract under § 138 I; and it has regarded a disproportion to be "particularly gross" if what has been promised exceeds the value of the performance by 100 %.[217] These and similar developments, both in Germany[218] and in other countries[219]—particularly the fact that the Austrian legislator in 1979 gave teeth to § 934 ABGB by disallowing renunciation of the remedy[220]—have led to a renaissance of laesio enormis. This renaissance is part of a rediscovery of equality in exchange.[221] The heyday of extreme individualism was short-lived and even before the BGB had come into existence the legislator started to take the first steps towards what is usually broadly referred to as consumer protection.[222] Today, the question is asked whether a

---

[214] John P. Dawson, "Unconscionable Coercion: The German Version", (1976) 89 *Harvard LR* 1061.

[215] Cf. e.g. BGHZ 80, 153 (160); for details, see Mayer-Maly, op. cit., note 212, § 138, nn. 98 sqq.; Helmut Koziol, "Sonderprivatrecht für Konsumentenkredite?", (1988) 188 *Archiv für die civilistische Praxis* 184 sqq.

[216] Cf. already RGZ 150, 1 (6).

[217] OLG Stuttgart, 1979 *Neue Juristische Wochenschrift* 2409 (dealing with a case of loan, where the annual interest was 31,08 %). Cf. also Karl Hackl, "Äquivalenzstörung und Sittenwidrigkeit", 1977 *Betriebsberater* 1412 sqq.

[218] Analysed critically by Theo Mayler-Maly, "Renaissance der laesio enormis?", in: *(Zweite) Festschrift für Karl Larenz* (1983), pp. 395 sqq.; cf. also Mayer-Maly, op. cit., note 212, § 138, nn. 104, 119.

[219] For a comparative analysis (France, Germany, United States) of modern remedies, cf. Gordley, (1981) 69 *California LR* 1625 sqq., 1645 sqq; for a crisp and lucid analysis of English law, see P.S. Atiyah, "Contract and Fair Exchange", (1985) 35 *University of Toronto LJ* 1 sqq.

[220] § 935 ABGB, amended version. Cf. the criticism by Mayer-Maly, *II. Festschrift Larenz*, pp. 398 sq., 408.

[0] Cf. e.g. Franz Bydlinkski, *Privatautonomie und objektive Grundlagen des verpflichtenden Rechtsgeschäfts* (1967), pp. 103 sqq., 151 sqq.; Gordley, (1981) 69 *California LR* 1587 sqq. Cf. also Wolfgang Blomeyer, "Der gerechte Preis im geltenden Recht", in: "*Der Gerechte Preis*", op. cit., note 189, pp. 39 sqq.

[222] Cf. e.g. Justus Wilhelm Hedemann, *Die Fortschritte des Zivilrechts im XIX. Jahrhundert*, vol. I (1910), pp. 3 sqq., 130 sqq.; Luig, *Festgabe Coing*, pp. 171 sqq.

piecemeal modification of the law of contract, in order to protect the socially and economically weaker party, is still a satisfactory way of tackling the problem, or whether one should not rather consolidate all these reforms and conceptualize a whole new body of consumer law. This is a wide field that cannot be explored in the present context.[223] Suffice it to say that this transition from freedom of contract to social responsibility can be seen, in a broader context, as a return to the ethical foundations of the earlier ius commune[224] (which, in turn, had superseded the individualism of classical Roman law). One may well be sceptical about the reintroduction of rigid and (necessarily) arbitrary limitations of the freedom of the parties to fix their price, on the model of the historical laesio enormis. C. 4, 44, 2 was a relatively crude attempt to strike a balance between invicem se circumscribere and equality in exchange.[225] Some degree of flexibility will have to be built into the modern remedies, in order to allow the judge to take into consideration the specific (objective and subjective) circumstances of the case.[226] But here, as everywhere, Jhering's "through Roman law beyond Roman law" has to be kept in mind. It is only by examining the continuity and transformation of Roman law within the history of the ius commune and by critically assessing our place within the rhythm of developments that we can make meaningful progress.

---

[223] For a general overview, see Ole Lando, "Unfair Contract Clauses and a European Uniform Commercial Code", in: Mauro Cappelletti, *New Perspectives for a Common Law of Europe* (1978), pp. 267 sqq. On the crisis of "classical" (liberal) contract doctrine today cf. also the literature quoted infra, p. 577, note 216.

[224] Franz Wieacker, "Das Sozialmodell der klassischen Privatrechtsgesetzbücher und die Entwicklung der modernen Gesellschaft", in: *Industriegesellschaft und Privatrechtsordnung* (1974), pp. 23 pp.

[225] Cf. also Gordley, (1981) 69 *California LR* 1644.

[226] This is the thrust of both Gordley's ((1981) 69 *California LR* 1637 sqq.) and Mayer-Maly's (*II. Festschrift Larenz*, pp. 395 sqq.; cf. also *Münchener Kommentar*, op. cit., note 212, § 138, nn. 98 sqq.) argument. On the other hand, the conflicting demands of equity and certainty of law have somehow to be balanced. Hence the repeated attempts by both courts and academic writers to suggest concrete figures to mark the borderline between what is still legal and what has to be regarded as illegal. Such attempts are understandable considering the trend to (over)extend § 138 BGB as (e.g.) an instrument of price-control. They are, however, in my view, irreconcilable with the nature of § 138 BGB as an outer limit of contractual freedom, and with the officium iudicis (cf. Zimmermann, *Moderationsrecht*, pp. 47 sqq., 83).

CHAPTER 9

Emptio venditio II

I. THE PASSING OF OWNERSHIP

1. The relationship between contract of sale and transfer of ownership

Thus far we have considered the basic requirements for a contract of sale to come into existence. We must now turn our attention to the main effects of such a contract. These were twofold. Firstly, certain obligations arose on the part of both the vendor and the purchaser (sale obviously being a bilaterally binding contract), and for the enforcement of these obligations the law provided two actions, the actiones empti and venditi. Secondly, upon perfection of the sale (that is, normally with its conclusion) the risk of accidental loss passed to the purchaser. One consequence, in particular, the contract of sale did not have: the passing of ownership. This required a separate act of conveyance: mancipatio in the case of res mancipi, traditio as far as res nec mancipi were concerned, alternatively for both categories of things in iure cessio.[1] All these acts aimed at publicity: real rights, potentially affecting everyone (they are enforceable against anyone who withholds the thing from the person entitled to it), were not to be acquired or transferred in private.

The Roman separation of obligatory act and conveyance is still maintained in many modern legal systems. In German and South African law conveyance of the property is not only separate from the underlying obligatory act, it is also to be evaluated entirely independently and on its own merits. It is thus abstract in the sense that ownership may pass, even though the contract of sale might be invalid or might not have come into existence at all. In Rome only mancipatio and in iure cessio were abstract. Traditio was causal in that, in order to transfer ownership, it had to be based on a iusta causa traditionis (as, for example, a valid contract of sale).[2] There are legal systems, however, which adopt an entirely different approach. They do not require a separate act of conveyance, but allow ownership to pass upon conclusion of the sale.[3] The French code civil provides a fine example.

---

[1] In iure cessio and mancipatio had fallen into disuse by the time of Justinian. According to the Digest, therefore, traditio is the only way of transferring ownership.

[2] Cf., for example, Kaser, *RPr* I, pp. 416 sqq.

[3] The doctrine that ownership passes by mere agreement of the parties goes back to the natural lawyers of the 17th and 18th centuries; cf. e.g. Hugo Grotius, *De jure belli ac pacis*, Lib. II, Cap. II, 1; Samuel Pufendorf, *De jure naturae et gentium*, Lib. IV, Cap. IX; Christian

Its art. 1583 reads:

> "Elle [sc.: the contract of sale] est parfaite entre les parties, et la propriété est acquise de droit à l'acheteur à l'égard du vendeur, dès qu'on est convenu de la chose et du prix, quoique la chose n'ait pas encore été livrée ni le prix payé."[4]

According to both the Roman and the French construction of sale, of course, the purchaser acquires a right to enforce the vendor's obligation to transfer the object sold; but, whereas this is a mere ius in personam in the one system, it is a ius in rem in the other. This difference has practical consequences in two situations.[5] If the vendor, after conclusion of the sale but before delivery, has fallen insolvent, the purchaser who is able to assert ownership and thus to remove his object from the bankrupt's estate, is in a much better position than his Roman counterpart, whose personal claim against the vendor competes with all the claims of other creditors. Again, the purchaser's position is more favourable under the French construction where the vendor first sold (but did not deliver) the object to him, and subsequently sold and delivered it to a third party, before either disappearing or becoming insolvent. He can then vindicate the object from the third party. According to Roman law, he would have only his fairly useless personal action against the vendor. Neither of the solutions, incidentally, can be said to be more just or equitable than the other. However one decides this conflict, one honest party (either the purchaser or the third party) will have to suffer for the act of a dishonest one. The Roman approach, however, seems to be more conducive to certainty of law and therefore more in line with the requirements of trade and commerce. Once delivery has been made, the position of the transferee is secure, at least in so far as he does not have to fear that previous purchasers might turn up and vindicate the thing from him.[6]

2. The payment of the purchase price

(a) *Inst. II, 1, 41*

Transfer of ownership in Roman law—and in the ius commune—was thus usually based on the two elements of iusta causa and traditio; or, to use the terminology of the German usus modernus, on titulus and modus.[7] Where such transfer resulted from a contract of sale, however, there was a further requirement. This is apparent from *Inst.* II, 1, 41:

Wolff, *Institutiones Juris Naturae et Gentium*, §§ 313 sqq.; and see William M. Gordon, *Studies in the Transfer of Property by traditio* (1970), pp. 172 sqq.

[4] As far as English law is concerned, cf. Buckland/McNair, pp. 291 sqq.

[5] Cf. e.g. Nicholas, *Introduction*, pp. 101 sqq.

[6] The transferee's position will be even safer where a legal system recognizes acquisition of ownership (from a non-owner) in good faith. This is the case in modern German law (§§ 932 sqq. BGB), but was different in Roman law (which did, however, offer some protection to the purchaser by way of establishing short periods for acquisitive prescription (usucapio)).

[7] Cf. only Coing, pp. 178 sqq.

> "Sed si quidem ex causa donationis aut dotis aut qualibet alia ex causa tradantur, sine dubio transferuntur: venditae vero et traditae non aliter emptori adquiruntur, quam si is venditori pretium solverit vel alio modo ei satisfecerit, veluti expromissore aut pignore dato. quod cavetur quidem etiam lege duodecim tabularum: tamen recte dicitur et iure gentium, id est iure naturali, id effici. sed si is qui vendidit fidem emptoris secutus fuerit, dicendum est statim rem emptoris fieri."

Ownership, according to the first sentence of this text, will pass only once the purchase price has been paid (or security been given). According to Justinian, this rule goes back to the XII Tables[8] and is based on natural law. But whatever its age, its venerability, or the breadth of its acceptance, the rule was rendered more or less nugatory in the very next sentence: for here it was said to be sufficient that the vendor "puts his trust in the buyer". It is, however, just in these cases, where the vendor has relied upon the purchaser's inclination and ability to pay the purchase price, that he would have needed the protection that the rule under discussion was obviously prepared to grant to him: namely that he should have been able, until the buyer had fulfilled his obligation, to assert his right of ownership and thus not lose out in case the purchaser became insolvent.

The rule contained in *Inst.* II, 1, 41 (which is in line with a Pomponius fragment of questionable authenticity)[9] has been consistently followed in the ius commune;[10] it is still applied in modern South African law.[11] In the course of this century, however, an intense discussion has arisen about its origin and development in Roman law.[12]

---

[8] Both Pringsheim and Schindler (cf. infra, notes 12, 13) maintain that the XII Tables cannot have contained a provision of this kind. But why should Justinian have invented (or grossly distorted) it? (Alfons Bürge, "Geld- und Naturalwirtschaft im vorklassischen und klassischen römischen Recht", (1982) 99 *ZSS* 149).

[9] Pomp. D. 18, 1, 19: "Quod vendidi non aliter fit accipientis, quam si aut pretium nobis solutum sit aut satis eo nomine factum vel etiam fidem habuerimus emptori sine ulla satisfactione."

[10] Cf., for example, Vinnius, *Institutiones*, Lib. II, Tit. I, 41; Voet, *Commentarius ad Pandectas*, Lib. VI, Tit. I, 14 sq.; Grotius, *Inleiding*, II, V, 14; Pothier, *Traité du contrat de vente*, § 323; Windscheid/Kipp, § 172, 7; *Daniels v. Cooper* (1880) 1 EDC 174 sqq.; for details, see Robert Feenstra, *Reclame en Revindicatie* (1949), pp. 98 sqq., 255 sqq.; idem, "Eigendomsovergang bij koop en terugvorderingsrecht van de onbetaalde verkoper: Romeins recht en Middeleeuws handelsrecht", (1987) 50 *THRHR* 134 sqq.; Coing, pp. 307 sq.; more particularly on the glossators and commentators, Klaus Luig, "Übergabe und Übereignung der verkauften Sache nach römischem und gemeinem Recht", in: *Satura Roberto Feenstra oblata* (1985), pp. 445 sqq. The rule has not been taken over into the BGB ("Motive", in: *Mugdan*, vol. III, p. 186).

[11] For details, see C.G. van der Merwe, *Sakereg* (1979), pp. 203 sq.; Kerr, *Sale and Lease*, pp. 112 sqq. According to Shippard J (*Daniels v. Cooper* (1880) 1 EDC 174), South African law in this regard is "at variance with every well-considered modern system of mercantile law throughout the world"; but cf. Art. 1191 BW and Feenstra, (1987) 50 *THRHR* 128.

[12] For a summary of the main views, see J.A.C. Thomas, "Institutes 2, 1, 41 and the Passage of Property on Sale" (1973) 90 *SALJ* 150 sqq.; cf. further Karl-Heinz Schindler, "Die Bedeutung der Kaufpreiszahlung im nachklassischen römischen Recht", in: *Festschrift für Konrad Duden* (1977), pp. 555 sqq.; Tony Honoré, "Sale and the Transfer of Ownership: the Compilers' Point of View", in: *Studies in Justinian's Institutes in Memory of J.A.C. Thomas* (1983), pp. 56 sqq.; Feenstra, (1987) 50 *THRHR* 127 sqq.

Fritz Pringsheim launched a sweeping attack on the classicity of the rule; he attributed it in its entirety to Justinian.[13] Some regard only the qualification to the rule (*Inst.* II, 1, 41, second sentence) as Justinianic.[14] Others relate the price requirement to the availability of the actio auctoritatis, by which the transferee in a mancipatio could sue the transferor upon eviction for double the purchase price.[15] Those who accept the classicity of our rule are divided as to whether it applied to traditio but not to mancipatio,[16] to mancipatio but not to traditio,[17] or to both forms of transfer of ownership.[18] Then there are those who are irritated by the fact that the rule is emasculated, for all practical purposes, by its qualification;[19] they have tried to save the former by assuming that an express grant of credit was necessary for the latter.[20]

Today one tends to believe that *Inst.* II, 1, 41 does in fact represent not only Justinianic but also classical Roman law.[21] This applies not only to the principle that transfer of ownership depended on payment of the purchase price but also to the qualification according to which fidem emptoris sequi was regarded as sufficient. Furthermore, it has been demonstrated by Robert Feenstra that this latter clause signifies *tacit* reliance on the faith of the buyer.[22]

(b) Pre-classical, classical and post-classical law

Any account of the development of the rule in pre-classical law must remain largely a matter of speculation. Personally, I would tend to

---

[13] *Der Kauf mit fremdem Geld* (1916), pp. 50 sqq.; but see also the same author in *The Greek Law of Sale*, pp. 179 sqq.; cf. further Schindler, *Festschrift Duden*, pp. 555 sqq.

[14] Cf. e.g. Ernst Schönbauer, "Zur Frage des Eigentumsüberganges beim Kauf", (1932) 52 *ZSS* 195 sqq.

[15] Cf. Arangio-Ruiz, *Compravendita*, pp. 276 sqq.; Buckland/Stein, p. 240; cf. also Thomas, (1973) 90 *SALJ* 158.

[16] Philippe Meylan, "Le paiement du prix et le transfert de la propriété de la chose vendue en droit romain classique", in: *Studi in onore de Pietro Bonfante*, vol. I (1930), pp. 441 sqq.; Watson, *Obligations*, pp. 62 sqq.

[17] Emilio Albertario, "Il momento del trasferimento della proprietà nella compravendita romana", in: *Studi di diritto romano*, vol. III (1936), 427 sqq.

[18] Max Kaser, (1966) 34 *TR* 412 sqq.; idem, "Stellvertretung und 'notwendige Entgeltlichkeit'", (1974) 91 *ZSS* 161 sq.

[19] Honoré, *Studies Thomas*, p. 58, has pointed out, though, that the result is not the same as it would be if ownership were to pass automatically with delivery. "For it is quite possible for the seller to make clear that he does not rely on the buyer's good faith alone, though he does not, at the moment of delivery, obtain payment or satisfaction, either. Thus, he may ask the buyer to provide security, e.g. to get a friend to guarantee payment of the price. The buyer may promise to do this, yet fail to carry out his promise. If, then, the seller parts with possession on the faith of such a promise, he does not . . . fidem emptoris sequi, but neither does he obtain payment or satisfaction." The same applies where the purchaser has promised to pay at once and then, after he has obtained possession of the thing, fails to honour his promise.

[20] Pothier, *Traité du contrat de vente*, n. 324; De Zulueta, *Sale*, pp. 37 sq.

[21] Cf. esp. Kaser, *RPr* I, p. 418; idem, *RPr* II, p. 284; Jörs/Kunkel/Wenger, pp. 129 sqq.; cf. also Honsell/Mayer-Maly/Selb, p. 162.

[22] Robert Feenstra, "Fidem emptoris sequi", in: *Studi in onore di Ugo Enrico Paoli* (1955), pp. 273 sqq. Approved by (e.g.) Watson, *Obligations*, pp. 62 sq.; Kaser, (1966) 34 *TR* 412; Thomas, (1973) 90 *SALJ* 151, 159.

relate it to the old Roman cash sale principle and to the gradual emergence of the fully executory consensual sale. In the olden days, when sale necessarily meant executed sale, it was a matter of course that payment of the purchase price and transfer of the object sold coincided. This reflected the fact that the one performance was made in exchange for the other. As time went on, the purchase price could be credited and it then no longer necessarily had to be paid at the time when the contract was concluded.[23] It was not unreasonable at all, under these circumstances, to limit the practical consequences of this relaxation of the cash sale principle and to make (or rather: continue to make) transfer of ownership dependent upon payment of the purchase price. This was the least one could do to maintain the balance of do ut des inherent in the sale. After all: why should the fact that the *purchaser* was granted indulgence put the *vendor* at a disadvantage? However, this rationale was bound to fade once sale had become a fully executory contract. If the parties agreed to a contract of sale, that was one thing. How and when they would carry out the obligations arising from this transaction was a different matter. Both the delivery of the thing and/or payment of the purchase price could be postponed and the special protection of the vendor was therefore no longer necessary in order to maintain the institutional balance of a sale transaction. Hence the indifference of the classical lawyers to our rule: they liberally extended exceptions that had long since been recognized[24] until they had largely neutralized the rule; they also sometimes seem to have simply ignored it.[25]

One may well ask why Justinian faithfully preserved the position in classical law for posterity rather than simply allow this process of oblivion to continue. The answer lies in the development of post-classical law: for under the influence of the Hellenistic legal systems,[26] with their principle of necessary remunerativeness, the idea of payment of the purchase price as a prerequisite for the transfer of ownership was not only not put to sleep—it was energetically revived.[27] The whole concept of the consensual and fully executory contract broke down and the sale was regarded as binding only once the

[23] Cf. supra, p. 237.

[24] The XII Tables already seem to have relaxed the principle by allowing a promise in the form of a stipulation (expromittere) as an acceptable substitute for the payment of the purchase price.

[25] Cf. e.g. Gai. II, 20: "Itaque, si tibi vestem vel aurum vel argentum tradidero, sive ex venditionis causa sive ex donationis sive quavis alia ex causa, statim tua fit ea res. . . ." Cf., further, C. 4, 49, 1 (Carac.); 3, 32, 12 (Diocl. et Max.).

[26] Cf. esp. Pringsheim, *Der Kauf mit fremdem Geld*, op. cit., note 13, pp. 1 sqq. and passim (e.g. 40 sqq., 163 sqq.); idem, *Sale*, e.g. pp. 190 sqq.

[27] Kaser, *RPr* II, pp. 278 sq.; Levy, *Vulgar Law*, pp. 131 sqq. (for the Roman-Germanic kingdoms cf. pp. 156 sqq.); but see Schindler, *Festschrift Duden*, pp. 560 sqq.; Wulf Eckart Voss, *Recht und Rhetorik in den Kaisergesetzen der Spätantike* (1982), pp. 190 sqq.

purchase price had been paid.[28] Payment of the purchase price made the purchaser owner of the object sold and gave him the right to demand its transfer. *Institutiones* II, 1, 41 does not, therefore, represent the final mark of a continuous development, but has to be seen as an attempt to reconcile generally accepted notions and practices of Justinian's time with the principles of classical Roman law. Hence the retention of the rule, combined however with the "fatal qualification".[29]

(c) Pactum reservati dominii

The vendor, then, who was prepared to grant the purchaser credit, but did not want to rely solely on the purchaser's solvency and honesty, was well advised to make special arrangements and let the purchaser have the object as a precarium tenens or as a conductor. This enabled the latter to use the object even before he had paid the purchase price, while at the same time securing the vendor's position. A traditio did not take place under these circumstances and the vendor therefore retained ownership (and in the case of locatio conductio even possession) of the object sold. "Cum venderem fundum, convenit, ut, donec pecunia omnis persolveretur, certa mercede emptor fundum conductum haberet":[30] such an agreement, which had the practical effect of what we would call a reservation of title (without, however, technically constituting it), and which the writers of the ius commune referred to as a pactum reservati dominii,[31] was construed by the Roman lawyers not as a single (sale) transaction but as a (cumulative) combination of sale (emptio venditio) and lease (locatio conductio). However, the contract of sale was the dominating feature, whereas the lease served a

---

[28] For details, see Pringsheim, *Der Kauf mit fremdem Geld*, op. cit., note 13, pp. 81 sqq. For a completely different view of post-classical law (the classical analysis of sale was preserved without major modifications; however, the private contract of sale came to be incorporated into a new social and economic framework (essentially: an authoritarian one) by means of regulations and enactments of a public legal character), cf. Voss, op. cit., note 27, pp. 81 sqq., 200 sqq.

[29] Watson, *Obligations*, p. 63. Tony Honoré has recently made an imaginative attempt to reconstruct by what stages Justinian's commissions came to form their view of the matter. According to him, they adopted three different views of the law (all set out somewhere within the Corpus Juris), each at a different stage of their deliberations. Cf. "Sale and the Transfer of Ownership: the Compilers' Point of View", in: *Studies in Justinian's Institutes in Memory of J.A.C. Thomas* (1983), pp. 56 sqq. Honoré's analysis provides the starting point for Luig's discussion of the medieval interpretations (and harmonizations) of the authoritative texts (*Satura Feenstra*, pp. 445 sqq.). But see also Feenstra, (1987) 50 *THRHR* 130 sqq.

[30] Iav. D. 19, 2, 21. The problem that arose in this case was that the full price had been paid before the time envisaged by the parties. On this text, see David Daube, "Tenancy of Purchaser (Digest 19, 2, 21)", (1948–50) 10 *Cambridge LJ* 77 sqq.; idem, "Si . . . tunc in D. 19, 2, 22 pr.", (1958) 5 *RIDA* 427 sqq.; J.A.C. Thomas, "Tenancy by Purchaser", (1959) 10 *Iura* 103 sqq.; Rolf Knütel, "Kauf und Pacht bei Abzahlungsgeschäften im römischen Recht", in: *Studien im römischen Recht* (1973), pp. 37 sqq.

[31] Cf. e.g. Glück, vol. 16, pp. 229 sqq.; Windscheid/ Kipp, § 172, n. 18. Cf. also Gottfried Schiemann, "Über die Funktion des pactum reservati dominii während der Rezeptionen des römischen Rechts in Italien und Mitteleuropa", (1976) 93 *ZSS* 161 sqq; Coing, p. 309.

subordinate function within this composite transaction and was adapted to fit into the framework set by the intention of the parties to effect a contract of sale. Hence, Paulus' generalizing statement "locator non obligatur, conductor obligatur".[32] The emptor/conductor is bound, under the actio locati,[33] to pay the rent. The actio conducti (of the emptor/conductor against the venditor/locator), on the other hand, is not applied, for it is overshadowed, and thus superseded, for all practical purposes by the actio empti.[34, 35]

II. THE DUTIES OF THE PARTIES

1. The duties of the purchaser

A contract of sale gave rise to two actions, the actio empti (of the purchaser against the vendor) and the actio venditi (which was available to the vendor against the purchaser). Both were iudicia bonae fidei with the following formula:

> "Quod A^s A^s de N° N° hominem Stichum emit (vendidit), quidquid ob eam rem N^m N^m A° A° dare facere oportet ex fide bona, eius iudex N^m N^m A° A° condemnato, si non paret, absolvito."[36]

Which were the respective duties of the parties, enforceable by means of these actions? The purchaser had to pay the purchase price, that is, to transfer the purchase money into the ownership of the vendor: "[E]mptor . . . nummos venditoris facere cogitur."[37] From the time of delivery of the object sold the vendor could charge interest on the purchase price ("item usurae pretii post diem traditionis [veniunt in hoc iudicium]");[38] furthermore, under certain circumstances he could claim

32 D. 19, 2, 20, 2.

33 According to Daube, (1958) 5 *RIDA* 430, 433, the actio venditi. He regards the text as interpolated.

34 For details, see Knütel, *Studien*, op. cit., note 30, pp. 35 sqq., 51 sqq. Cf. also infra, pp. 530 sqq.

35 Another possibility of securing the position of the vendor is intimated in Ulp. D. 43, 26, 20; on which see Anton Meinhart, "Dogmengeschichtliches und Dogmatisches zum Eigentumsvorbehalt", (1988) 105 *ZSS* 729 sqq.: the purchaser receives the object by way of traditio, but the parties agree that such traditio is not to have the effect of transferring ownership; instead, ownership is to pass only with payment of the purchase price. This agreement constitutes a pactum adiectum to the contract of sale (generally on the essence of pacta adiecta, cf. infra, pp. 509 sqq.) and also contains an understanding to the effect that the purchaser be, in the mean time, in the position of a precario tenens.

36 Cf. Lenel, *EP*, p. 299. On the interplay of the actiones empti and venditi, see J.A.C. Thomas, "Sale Actions and other Actions", (1979) 26 *RIDA* 417 sqq.

37 Ulp. D. 19, 1, 11, 2 in fine; cf. also Paul. D. 19, 4, 1 pr.

38 Ulp. D. 19, 1, 13, 20; reason: ". . . nam cum re emptor fruatur, aequissimum est eum usuras pretii pendere." Cf. also Pap. vat. 2 and cf. e.g. Giuliano Cervenca, *Contributo allo studio delle usurae c.d. legali vel diritto romano* (1969), pp. 13 sqq.; and, most recently, the comprehensive and thorough analysis by Rolf Knütel, "Zum Nutzungszins", (1988) 105 *ZSS* 514 sqq. The rule has been incorporated into the BGB (§ 452: "The purchaser is bound to pay interest on the purchase price from the date at which the emoluments of the purchased object accrue to him, unless the purchase price is payable at a fixed time"; the date at which the emoluments accrue to the purchaser is determined in § 446 (delivery, as far as movables

reimbursement of expenses,[39] the co-operation of the purchaser in implementing the contract,[40] etc.

2. The duties of the vendor

(a) *Uti frui habere possidereque licere*

The vendor, on the other hand, had to deliver the object sold. He was bound to transfer vacuam possessionem,[41] i.e. free and unimpeded possession, which the purchaser could enter into without being disturbed by either the vendor or a third party.[42] Moreover, he had to maintain the purchaser in undisturbed possession and enjoyment of the object; he had to afford him his habere licere or, as some sources put it more fully, his uti frui habere possidereque licere.[43] He was not bound, however, to make the purchaser owner.[44] In other words, what he owed was a facere;[45] he had to execute the legal act required for transferring ownership (mancipatio, in iure cessio or traditio, as the case may have been),[46] but was not responsible for the result—the transfer of ownership—itself. As a consequence of this, the actio empti could not be brought merely on account of the fact that the vendor had not made the purchaser owner of the object sold. As long as he retained his habere licere, the law did not give him any protection.

(b) *Transfer of ownership?*

For a modern lawyer this must sound both surprising and inequitable. We would regard a rule such as the one contained in § 433 I 1 ("By the contract of sale the seller of a thing is bound to deliver the thing to the purchaser and to transfer ownership of the thing") as appropriate and, indeed, self-evident. Was the Roman law "stiff and primitive" in this regard?[47] First of all, we have to remember what has been stated above[48] about the structure of the Roman emptio venditio: the contract of sale contained everything that was necessary to transfer ownership except traditio (or mancipatio). Once the object was handed over (or

---

are concerned)). It has occasionally been criticized as "anomalous" (cf. Franz Leonhard, *Besonderes Schuldrecht des BGB* (1931), pp. 90 sqq.), but has, more recently, most effectively been defended by Knütel, (1988) 105 *ZSS* 514 sqq., 538 sqq. For South African law cf. Kerr, *Sale and Lease*, pp. 145 sq.

[39] Cf., for example, Ulp. D. 19, 1, 13, 22; Stefan Weyand, "Kaufverständnis und Verkäuferhaftung im klassischen römischen Recht", (1983) 51 *TR* 249 sqq.

[40] Pomp. D. 19, 1, 9: "Si is, qui lapides ex fundo emerit, tollere eos nolit, ex vendito agi cum eo potest, ut eos tollat."

[41] Cf. e.g. Lab. D. 18, 1, 78, 1.

[42] Berger, *ED*, p. 757.

[43] Cf. e.g. Ulp. D. 45, 1, 38; *FIRA*, vol. III, nn. 88 sq.

[44] Cf. e.g. Paul. D. 19, 4, 1 pr.; Ulp. D. 18, 1, 25, 1; Arangio-Ruiz, *Compravendita*, pp. 149 sqq.

[45] Kaser, *RPr* I, p. 551.

[46] As far as mancipatio is concerned, cf. e.g. Gai. IV, 131 a.

[47] Schulz, *CRL*, p. 531.

[48] Cf. supra, pp. 239 sq.

mancipated), and provided the vendor himself had been owner, ownership passed:

> "Et in primis ipsam rem praestare venditorem oportet, id est tradere quae res, si quidem dominus fuit venditor, facit et emptorem dominum."[49]

Nothing else was necessary. But if that was so, there was neither room nor necessity for postulating a special duty to make the purchaser owner.[50] That would be the automatic consequence of traditio (or mancipatio), which, in turn, the vendor was bound to perform. One may be tempted to ask whether this did not bring an imbalance into the contract: the purchaser had to make the vendor owner of the purchase money,[51] whereas the vendor merely had to afford habere licere. This distinction does, however, quite correctly reflect the inherent difference between the object of the sale and the price. Money is available in random quantity, and the purchaser does not have to use specific coins to fulfil his obligation. Thus he can reasonably be expected to pay the price with coins of which he is able to make the vendor owner. The position is different as far as the object of the sale is concerned. The sale of generic goods was unknown in Roman law. It was always a specific thing that had been promised and that was owed, and this thing might in actual fact turn out to belong to a third party. Hence one would only expect the seller to do his best to transfer ownership; he could not be held bound to do what was sometimes impossible: that is actually to make the purchaser owner.[52]

(c) Practical implications

But did this not cause hardship for the purchaser? If he had known about the seller's lack of title, he did, of course, not deserve any protection. But what if it transpired after the contract of sale had been concluded that the object which had been transferred belonged to a third party? "Nemo plus iuris transferre potest quam ipse haberet" was the rule of Roman law, and acquisition of ownership in good faith on the part of the purchaser was therefore out of the question. That then left the purchaser in a somewhat awkward position:[53] as long as his habere licere had not been interfered with, he did not have an action against the vendor. Nor could he resell the object since he was now aware of his lack of title. But, on the one hand, this unsatisfactory state of affairs would normally not persist for a long time. The period for usucaption was short; after the lapse of one year the purchaser acquired

---

[49] Ulp. D. 19, 1, 11, 2.

[50] Frank Peters, "Die Verschaffung des Eigentums durch den Verkäufer", (1979) 96 *ZSS* 185 sq.; cf. also F.H. Lawson, "The Passing of Property and Risk in Sale—A Comparative Study", (1949) 65 *LQR* 364 sq.

[51] Cf. supra, p. 277.

[52] Peters, (1979) 96 *ZSS* 181 sq.

[53] Cf. e.g. Nicholas, *Introduction*, p. 181; Ernst Rabel, "Die Haftung des Verkäufers wegen Mangels im Rechte", vol. I (1902), p. 108.

ownership by prescription of any movable object he might have bought. The fact that he had subsequently learnt about the seller's lack of title did not matter: mala fides superveniens non nocet. Things were different, however, in the case of res furtivae. Yet, if the vendor had knowingly sold an object that had been stolen, the purchaser obviously had the actio empti to invoke:[54] not on account of the fact that the vendor had not made him owner, but because of the vendor's mala fides.

The real problem, therefore, arose only where the object had been stolen and the vendor had not known about that either. But here we are dealing with a situation that does not really allow for a smooth and easy solution: one of two honest parties is ultimately bound to lose out. That this should be the purchaser rather than the vendor may perhaps be justified on the ground that any claim for damages is ultimately based on the fact that a third party—rather than the purchaser—is owner of the object. Clarity in so far can only exist once the third party has been successful with his action against the purchaser. It seems to be at least expedient to resolve this matter before going into the question of damages.[55] Furthermore, the purchaser has undisturbed possession and enjoyment, after all. To allow him, at the same time, to claim damages (on account of the fact that he is not free to dispose of the object) would in turn have placed the vendor in an awkward position. It would hardly have been possible for him to assess the genuineness of the purchaser's intentions to resell or encumber the object of the sale.[56, 57]

(d) The liability of the vendor

The vendor, under the actio empti, was generally liable for dolus.[58] This is a natural consequence of the fact that the actio empti was a iudicium bonae fidei. Dolus being the opposite of bona fides, it did not necessarily follow that liability was restricted to what we would refer to as dolus in a technical sense, to deliberate and intentional breaches of

---

[54] Cf. especially Afr. D. 19, 1, 30, 1.

[55] Significantly enough, § 440 II BGB has adopted this eviction principle, even though the Code recognizes a duty of the vendor to make the purchaser owner; cf. infra, pp. 303 sq.

[56] Or the purchaser's intention to manumit the slave whom he had bought! Cf. Afr. D. 19, 1, 30, 1.

[57] Peters, (1979) 96 *ZSS* 197 sqq., who concludes that the Roman approach "unter den gegebenen Umständen als rechtspolitisch gut vertretbar gewertet werden [muss]" (under the circumstances, has to be evaluated as being easily defensible, from a policy point of view). Cf. also Rabel, op. cit., note 53, p. 111, who, despite his criticism of the approach of the Roman lawyers, admits: "Im übrigen dürfte es keine einzige bezeugtermassen in der Zeit der letzten Klassiker entschiedene Streitfrage des Gewährleistungsrechtes geben, deren Lösung dem heutigen Empfinden zuwiderliefe" (On the whole, there is probably no controversial question in the law relating to the vendor's liability which would, by the time of the late classical lawyers, not have found a solution conforming also to the modern sense of justice and fairness).

[58] Cf. supra, pp. 241 sqq. (dolus in contrahendo); cf. further e.g. Ulp. D. 18, 4, 2, 5.

contract. At least in some instances, the vendor was liable for culpa too.[59]

III. THE PASSING OF THE RISK

1. Periculum est emptoris

For the other important consequence of a contract of sale we must turn our attention to *Inst.* III, 23, 3:

> "Cum autem emptio et venditio contracta sit . . ., periculum rei venditae statim ad emptorem pertinet, tametsi adhuc ea res emptori tradita non sit."

The text continues to give some illustrations:

> "[I]taque si homo mortuus sit vel aliqua parte corporis laesus fuerit, aut aedes totae aut aliqua ex parti incendio consumptae fuerint, aut fundus vi fluminis totus vel aliqua ex parte ablatus sit, sive etiam inundatione aquae aut arboribus turbine deiectis longe minor aut deterior esse coeperit: emptoris damnum est, cui necesse est, licet rem non fuerit nactus, pretium solvere."

This is the famous risk rule, usually crisply expressed in the words "periculum est emptoris". Periculum refers to the chance or possibility that the object of the sale might be lost, destroyed or damaged.[60] This risk has to be borne as a matter of course by the vendor before the contract of sale is concluded. That it attaches to the purchaser, once ownership had been transferred to him, is equally obvious. In both instances we are dealing with a simple principle: "res perit domino" or "casum sentit dominus".

What we are concerned with in the present context is the period between conclusion of the contract of sale and the transfer of ownership. Here the problem arises whether the loss that has occurred affects the purchaser's obligation to pay the purchase price or not.[61] Does this obligation stand, i.e. does the purchaser have to pay, although he does not receive the goods, or receives them in a damaged state (this would be periculum emptoris)? Or is it the vendor who loses out in that he does no longer have the goods (or retains them in a deteriorated state) and will not be able to recover the purchase price (the full purchase price) either (periculum venditoris)? Piles of literature have been penned on this problem in general[62] and on the attitude of the

---

[59] Proc. D. 18, 1, 68 pr.; Pomp. D. 18, 4, 3; Ulp. D. 19, 1, 13, 16.

[60] For the meaning of periculum in legal texts generally, see Geoffrey MacCormack, "Periculum", (1979) 96 *ZSS* 129 sqq.; for the present context, see esp. Emil Seckel, Ernst Levy, "Die Gefahrtragung beim Kauf im klassischen römischen Recht", (1927) 47 *ZSS* 248 sqq.; Arangio-Ruiz, *Compravendita*, pp. 250 sqq.; Max Kaser, "Die actio furti des Verkäufers", (1979) 96 *ZSS* 111 sqq.

[61] *"Preisgefahr"* or *"Gegenleistungsgefahr"* as opposed to *"Sachgefahr"* (periculum rei). It is the former, too, that modern English and French law have in mind when they refer to "risk" or *"risque"*.

[62] For a comprehensive comparative investigation, see Günter Hager, *Die Gefahrtragung beim Kauf* (1982); for some elegant reflections based on the diversity of modern approaches, see Alan Watson, *Legal Transplants* (1974), pp. 82 sqq.

Roman lawyers towards it in particular.[63] As far as Roman law is concerned, it is essentially only one proposition that is above all doubt, and that is that Justinian opted for the first alternative: periculum emptoris. But whether that reflects the position in classical law is not at all easy to decide.

2. The position in classical law

True: there are statements in the Digest which accord fully with *Inst.* III, 23, 3. Paulus, for instance, is quoted as specifically stating ". . . perfecta emptione periculum ad emptorem respiciet".[64] But these statements have all been subjected to extensive textual criticism, and the result has been that some authors have been able to read the exact opposite, namely periculum est venditoris, into the sources.[65] Others have not gone that far. Meylan has tried to show that the Roman lawyers applied a very refined scheme and made their decision dependent upon whether a res mancipi or nec mancipi had been the object of the sale and, if it had been a res nec mancipi, whether it had been either lost or totally destroyed, or whether it had merely been damaged.[66] Rabel, on the other hand, came to the conclusion that the Roman lawyers decided without any principle at all and allocated the risk, according to the merits of each case, sometimes to the vendor, sometimes to the purchaser.[67] Today the opinion prevails that periculum est emptoris was the rule not only in Justinianic but also in classical law.[68] Methodically, one has abandoned the shifting sands of

---

[63] For a recent survey of the literature, see Wolfgang Ernst, *Das klassische römische Recht der Gefahrtragung beim Kauf: Periculum est emptoris*, (unpublished Dr. iur. thesis, Bonn, 1981) (for an abbreviated version, see idem, "Periculum est emptoris", (1982) 99 *ZSS* 216 sqq.).

[64] D. 18, 6, 8 pr.

[65] For example Franz Haymann, "Textkritische Studien zum römischen Obligationenrecht, Periculum est emptoris", (1920) 41 *ZSS* 44 sqq.; idem, "Zur Klassizität des periculum est emptoris", (1928) 48 *ZSS* 314 sqq.; Emilio Betti, "Zum Problem der Gefahrtragung bei zweiseitig verpflichtenden Verträgen", (1965) 82 *ZSS* 1 sqq. Cf. Jacobus Cuiacius, "Ad Africanum Tractatus VIII", Ad L. si fundus 33. loc. et cond., in: *Opera Omnia*, vol. I (Venetiis, 1768).

[66] Philippe Meylan, "Inst. III, 23, §§ 3 et 3a et l'unification du régime des risques dans le contrat de vente par Justinien", in: *Atti Verona*, vol. III (1951), pp. 387 sqq.; idem, "Paul. D. 21, 2, 11 pr. et la question des risques dans le contrat de vente", (1949) 3 *RIDA* 193 sqq.; idem, "Periculum est emptoris", in: *Festschrift für Theo Guhl* (1950), pp. 9 sqq.; idem, "Fr. Vat. 16 et la question des risques dans le contrat de vente", (1950) 1 *Iura* 253 sqq.

[67] Ernst Rabel, "Gefahrtragung beim Kauf", (1921) 42 *ZSS* 543 sqq. Cf. also Geoffrey MacCormack, "Alfenus Varus and the Law of Risk in Sale", (1985) 101 *LQR* 573 sqq., who argues that the law developed on a casuistic ad hoc basis. While, he says, the "trend" of the late classical law favoured perfection of the contract as the criterion for the passing of risk, Alfenus Varus favoured an approach under which the risk remained with the seller until traditio (cf. Paul. D. 18, 6, 13 and 15; but why did Paul—in whose days the law was periculum est emptoris—take the trouble to record Alfenus' decisions? I am not convinced by the explanations offered by MacCormack on p. 576).

[68] Emil Seckel, Ernst Levy, "Die Gefahrtragung beim Kauf im klassischen römischen Recht", (1927) 47 *ZSS* 117 sqq.; H.R. Hoetink, *Periculum est emptoris* (1928); De Zulueta, *Sale*, pp. 30 sqq.; Jörs/Kunkel/Wenger, pp. 228 sqq.; Schulz, *CRL*, pp. 532 sq.; Arangio-Ruiz, *Compravendita*, pp. 250 sqq.; Benöhr, *Synallagma*, pp. 86 sqq.; Kaser, *RPr* I,

far-reaching interpolation allegations and is therefore able to approach the classical texts from a more consolidated basis. Furthermore, one cannot help suspecting that at least some of the extreme opponents of the classicity of periculum est emptoris tended to approach the sources with preconceived ideas. Haymann, for instance, regarded this rule as a stain on the badge of honour of the Roman lawyers which he set out to efface.[69] This sounds like arguing on the pattern of what ought not to be, cannot be: ". . . *dass nicht sein kann, was nicht sein darf*."[70] It is true, however, that periculum est emptoris has often been regarded as a strange and anomalous peculiarity of Roman law. Pufendorf criticized it as being in conflict with "res perit domino".[71] This it is indeed, for the vendor, at the time when the goods are destroyed or damaged, has not yet transferred ownership and even retains possession. Would it therefore not be much more in accordance with natural justice to let the loss lie where it has struck, rather than to shift it to the purchaser who has, as yet, neither legal nor factual control over what had been sold? Periculum est emptoris continued to be applied in practice, but some of the attempts to provide a rational justification for this rule sound rather forced and awkward: "illustration[s] of the fertility of the Teutonic intellect when in search of a reason", as Williston[72] said of the theories of a man with the rather inauspicious name of Goose.[73]

3. The ambit of the rule

Before being able to evaluate these criticisms, we first have to define more exactly the ambit of the rule. The risk passed only once the sale was perfect, emptione perfecta. Hence: "Necessario sciendum est, quando perfecta sit emptio: tunc enim sciemus, cuius periculum sit."[74] Normally, perfection and conclusion of the sale coincided. "[E]t si id

pp. 552 sq.; Honsell/Mayer-Maly/Selb, pp. 309 sq.; Imre Molnár, "'Periculum emptoris' im römischen Recht der klassischen Periode", in: *Sodalitas, Scritti in onore di Antonio Guarino*, vol. V (1984), pp. 2227 sqq.; Frank Peters, "Periculum est emptoris", in: *Iuris Professio, Festgabe für Max Kaser* (1986), pp. 221 sqq.

[69] Haymann, (1920) 41 *ZSS* 48 sq. (*"[Unsere Aufgabe muss es sein, die] Linien des klassischen Rechts . . . in ihrer bewunderungswürdigen Einfachheit und Folgerichtigkeit wiederherzustellen und damit zugleich einen Fleck von dem wissenschaftlichen Ehrenschild jener grossen, unerreichbaren Meister endgültig auszutilgen"* (It has to be our task to reconstruct the outlines of classical law in their admirable simplicity and consistency and we must at the same time aim at wiping out, once and for all, a blot on the badge of honour of those great and unrivalled masters)).

[70] Christian Morgenstern, "Die unmögliche Tatsache", in: *Gesammelte Werke* (1967), pp. 262 sq.

[71] *De jure naturae et gentium*, Lib. V, Cap. V, 3. Cf. also Grotius, *De jure belli ac pacis*, Lib. II, Cap. XII, XV, 1.

[72] Samuel Williston, *The Law Governing Sales of Goods at Common Law and Under the Uniform Sales Act*, vol. II (1948), § 308. Cf. also the same author, "The Risk of Loss After an Executory Contract of Sale in the Civil Law", (1895–96) 9 *Harvard LR* 72 sqq.

[73] "Zur Lehre vom casus", (1868) 9 *JhJb* 197 sqq.

[74] Paul. D. 18, 6, 8 pr.

quod venierit appareat quid quale quantum sit, sit et pretium, et pure venit, perfecta est emptio."[75] As soon as there was agreement about the exact object of the sale and about the price, and the sale had been concluded unconditionally, the obligations came into existence; nothing remained to be done except to discharge them. Under these circumstances, emptio was perfecta. Matters were different where the sale was not pura but had been concluded subject to a suspensive condition. Here the effects of the contract were suspended, and the mutual obligations came into existence only once the condition had been fulfilled. Only then could the sale be said to be complete (perfecta). Condicione pendente, therefore, the risk remained with the seller.[76] The same applied where generic goods from an identified source were sold.[77] The contract was not complete until the objects of the sale had been identified, i.e. for instance, if "ten amphorae of wine from my cellar" had been sold, until the amphorae had been put aside for that transaction.[78] There were some further instances of such a postponement of the transfer of risk because the sale was not yet complete.[79] The most interesting one relates to an economically very important type of transaction, the sale of wine.[80]

4. Excursus: the sale of wine

Wine was either sold out of vats (dolia, hence vinum doliare) or bottled in amphorae (vinum amphoarium). Vinum doliare was usually new wine; while it was kept in doliis, it went through the fermentation process. These dolia were made from clay; they were pitched on the

[75] Paul. D. 18, 6, 8 pr.

[76] Perhaps only the risk of loss or total destruction, not of deterioration; cf. Pap. vat. 16; Paul. D. 18, 6, 8 pr. in fine. The question is controversial; see e.g. Seckel/Levy, (1927) 47 *ZSS* 154 sqq., 173 sqq.; Paul Krückmann, "Einige Randfragen zum periculum emptoris", (1939) 59 *ZSS* 18 sqq.; Arangio-Ruiz, *Compravendita*, pp. 260 sqq.; Ernst, op. cit., note 63, pp. 35 sqq. As to the question whether a sale subject to a dies incertus was regarded as perfect, see Alan Rodger, "Emptio perfecta Revisited: A Study of Digest 18, 6, 8, 1", (1982) 50 *TR* 337 sqq.

[77] Cf. supra, p. 236.

[78] Pap. vat. 16; Gai. D. 18, 1, 75, 7; Paul. D. 18, 6, 5; for details, see Seckel/Levy, (1927) 47 *ZSS* 189 sqq.; Ernst, op. cit., note 63, pp. 61 sqq.

[79] For details Seckel/Levy, (1927) 47 *ZSS* 214 sqq.

[80] On wine-growing, wine trade and wine-drinking in Rome, cf. generally A. Henderson, *The History of Ancient and Modern Wines* (1824); Joachim Marquardt/A. Mau, *Das Privatleben der Römer* (2nd ed., 1886), pp. 443 sqq.; Friedrich von Bassermann-Jordan, *Geschichte des Weinbaus* (2nd ed., 1923), vol. I, pp. 39 sqq., vol. II, pp. 1102 sq.; Charles Seltmann, *Wine in the Ancient World* (1957), pp. 129 sqq.; cf., too, Étienne, *Pompeji*, pp. 141 sqq.; Bruce W. Frier, "Roman Law and the Wine Trade: the Problem of 'Vinegar Sold As Wine'", (1983) 100 *ZSS* 257 sqq. Frier points out that, on one estimate, the residents of Rome drank more than one hundred million litres of wine per year. The distribution of so vast a quantity "required a sprawling network of merchants, called vinarii . . . Fortunes were made and lost quickly in the wine trade, and the ethical standards of the traders were reputedly none too high" (p. 258).

inside and could contain more than 1 000 ℓ.[81] They were usually sunk into the ground of the cella vinaria;[82] their openings were closed with clay lids. Older and better wine was poured into and kept in amphorae,[83] clay vessels with a volume of about 26 ℓ.[84] Unlike the dolia, amphorae had a narrow neck which could be corked up.[85] Such corks seem to have worked very well; we are told by Pliny, for instance, that under the Principate wine from the famous vintage of 121 B.C. (the so-called Opimianian wine) was still available.[86] The same cannot be said of the clay lids which were put on the dolia; here one could not always prevent the air from entering and hence there was a danger of the wine turning sour or musty. "Proprium autem inter liquores vino mucescere aut in acetum verti, extantque medicinae volumina."[87] Acor and mucor was a specific risk connected with the purchase of wine;[88] nevertheless, this risk normally passed to the purchaser with the conclusion of the sale, in accordance with emptione perfecta periculum est emptoris. There was, however, one way for the purchaser to avoid this consequence:

> "Si vinum venditum acuerit vel quid aliud vitii sustinuerit, emptoris erit damnum, quemadmodum si vinum esset effusum vel vasis contusis vel qua alia ex causa sed si venditor se periculo subiecit, in id tempus periculum sustinebit, quoad se subiecit."[89]

The purchaser could buy the wine subject to his approval and make perfection of the sale dependent upon degustatio.[90] This seems to have been very common for the sale of vinum doliare.[91] Cato recommended for the standard transaction a period of three days within which degustatio had to occur: ". . . in triduo proximo viri boni arbitratu degustato; si non ita fecerit, vinum pro degustato erit."[92] Perhaps the

---

[81] Cf. e.g. Hessel, *Die Weinveredelungsmethoden des Altertums verglichen mit denen der heutigen Zeit* (1856), pp. 54 sqq.; Mau, *RE*, vol. V (1903), col. 1283 sqq. One can get a good idea of the size of these dolia if one remembers that in Athens paupers (or a philosopher such as Diogenes) could live in them.

[82] Cf. e.g. Scaev. D. 32, 93, 4; Ulp. D. 33, 6, 3, 1.

[83] Cf. e.g. Proc. D. 33, 6, 15.

[84] Cf. e.g. Wernicke, *RE*, vol. I (1894), col. 1969 sqq.

[85] Bassermann-Jordan, op. cit., note 80, vol. II, pp. 716 sqq.; Marquardt/Mau, op. cit., note 80, p. 462.

[86] Plinius Secundus, *Historia naturalis*, Lib. XIV, 14, 94.

[87] Plinius, op. cit., note 86, Lib. XIV, 20, 131.

[88] For details, e.g. Frier, (1983) 100 *ZSS* 258 sq.

[89] Ulp. D. 18, 6, 1 pr.; Ulp. D. 18, 6, 1 and 18, 6, 4 provide a comprehensive treatment of the problems relating to the sale of wine. Cf. further Gai. D. 18, 6, 16; Pap. vat. 16; and the discussion by Seckel/Levy, (1927) 47 *ZSS* 204 sqq.; R. Yaron, "Sale of Wine", in: *Studies in the Roman Law of Sale in memory of Francis de Zulueta* (1959), pp. 71 sqq.; Wolf, *Error*, pp. 128 sqq.; Manfred Harder, "Weinkauf und Weinprobe im Römischen Recht", in: *Recht und Wirtschaft in Geschichte und Gegenwart, Festschrift für Johannes Bärmann* (1975), pp. 17 sqq.; Frier, (1983) 100 *ZSS* 278 sqq.; Molnár, *Scritti Guarino*, vol. V, pp. 2236 sqq.; Peters, *Festgabe Kaser*, pp. 225 sqq.

[90] If he found the wine to be musty or sour, he could rescind the contract; Paul. D. 18, 1, 34, 5: ". . . gustus enim ad hoc proficit, ut improbare liceat."

[91] Cf. Ulp. D. 18, 6, 4, 1: ". . . difficile autem est, ut quisquam sic emat, ut ne degustet."

[92] *De agri cultura*, CLVII, 148.

requirement of arbitratus boni viri was dropped in classical times, for, as Yaron points out, "one wishes to buy wine according to one's own judgement, and not according to that of some impartial vir bonus".[93] It has often been argued that an agreement regarding degustatio was read into any contract of sale concerning vinum doliare, so that the risk of acor and mucor was always on the vendor until such tasting had taken place. In the case of vinum amphorarium, however, the right of degustatio had to be specifically reserved.[94] This opinion hinges on the assumption that Ulpianus in D. 18, 6, 1 pr. originally referred to vinum amphorarium, and that only the compilers generalized this statement by way of interpolation. It seems preferable, however, to accept the text as it stands. Perhaps it referred to vinum doliare only, for an agreement concerning degustatio could in any event not have helped the purchaser very much in the case of vinum amphorarium.[95] He would have been confined to some sort of spot check. But whether the wine in one amphora had or had not turned sour or musty did not tell the purchaser much about the other amphorae; everything depended entirely on whether each individual amphora had been properly corked.[96]

Sometimes wine (or grain or oil, etc.)[97] was bought per aversionem,[98] or uno pretio:[99] a lump sum was agreed upon for a whole (unspecified) quantity (*"Kauf in Bausch und Bogen"*).[100] On these terms, the purchaser could buy, for instance, a large quantity of cheap, often adulterated wine, which he was then able to process in such a way that it could be used as a drink for his slaves.[101] Such transactions were, of course, not normally subject to degustatio and were perfecta the moment the contract had been concluded. Where, on the other hand, the price was determined by quantity (so and so much per unit), and where the exact sum therefore still had to be established adnumerando, admetiendo or adpendendo, the position—according to the prevailing Sabinian opinion—was different:

> "Sabinus et Cassius tunc perfici emptionem existimant, cum adnumerata admensa adpensave sint, quia venditio quasi sub hac condicione videtur fieri, ut in singulos

[93] *Studies de Zulueta*, p. 75; but see Alan Watson, (1960) 50 *JRS* 255; Frier, (1983) 100 *ZSS* 281 sq.: "improbare" (Paul. D. 18, 1, 34, 5) implies a judgment of fact; what matters is not whether the purchaser personally likes the wine, but whether, due to organic deterioration, the wine is no longer merchantable. On the arbitrium boni viri in general, see Voci, *Obbligazioni*, vol. I, 1, pp. 190 sqq.

[94] Cf. e.g. Seckel/Levy, (1927) 47 *ZSS* 204 sqq.; Kaser, *RPr* I, p. 553.

[95] Harder, *Festschrift Bärmann*, pp. 29 sq.

[96] Wolf, *Error*, p. 131, n. 73.

[97] C. 4, 48, 2, 2.

[98] Ulp. D. 18, 6, 4, 1; Mod. D. 18, 1, 62, 2.

[99] Gai. D. 18, 1, 35, 6.

[100] Usually in the case of vinum doliare, but this type of transaction was also possible with regard to vinum amphoarium: cf. C. 4, 48, 2, 1: "Cum autem universum, quod in horreis erat positum venisse sine mensura. . . ." Cf. e.g. Arangio-Ruiz, *Compravendita*, pp. 257 sqq.; the different types of sale of wine are listed by Frier, (1983) 100 *ZSS* 276 sq.

[101] Cf. Paul Thielscher, *Des Marcus Cato Belehrung über die Landwirtschaft* (1963), pp. 297 sq.

metretas aut in singulos modios quos quasve admensus eris, aut in singulas libras quas adpenderis, aut in singula corpora quae adnumeraveris."[102]

In other words, the risk passed only when the purchase price had been specified; prior to that, an essential element for a valid contract of sale was lacking.

5. The concept of periculum

There was another factor which even further limited the scope of application of the risk rule, namely a very narrow understanding of the central concept of periculum. Of course, it did not refer to any incidents caused by the vendor's negligence. These had to be borne by the vendor himself. But the lawyers went one important step further. In D. 18, 6, 3 we read:

"Custodiam autem venditor talem praestare debet, quam praestant hi quibus res commodata est, ut diligentiam praestet exactiorem, quam in suis rebus adhiberet."

After conclusion of the contract of sale, but before the object of sale has been handed over, the vendor is in the same position with regard to that object as a borrower. He is liable not only for negligence (be it according to the standard of the diligens paterfamilias or that of diligentia quam in suis) but for custodia.[103] Or, to state the same thing from a different angle: it was only the risk of loss by way of vis maior (periculum vis maioris) which passed, emptione perfecta, to the buyer. Only if the object sold had been lost, destroyed or damaged due to an event which nobody—neither buyer, nor seller, nor the most ideal custodian—could have prevented, did the purchaser have to pay the purchase price without receiving anything; in cases of casus minor, however, the vendor was responsible for damages due to non-performance. The two obligations could, of course, be set off against each other; the purchaser's compensation claim was then limited, for all practical intents and purposes, to the difference by which his interesse exceeded the (as yet unpaid) purchase price.[104]

---

[102] Gai. D. 18, 1, 35, 5. Cf. Seckel/Levy, (1927) 47 *ZSS* 179 sqq.; Arangio-Ruiz, *Compravendita*, pp. 271 sqq.; J.A.C. Thomas, "Marginalia on certum pretium", (1967) 35 *TR* 82 sqq.; Peters, *Festgabe Kaser*, pp. 226 sqq.

[103] Cf. also Paul. D. 19, 1, 36; Gai. D. 18, 6, 2, 1; Ulp. D. 18, 6, 4, 1 et al.; further Wolfgang Kunkel, "Diligentia", (1925) 45 *ZSS* 278 sqq.; Hoetink, op. cit., note 68, pp. 49 sqq.; Arangio-Ruiz, *Compravendita*, pp. 247 sqq.; Schulz, *CRL*, p. 533; Manlio Sargenti, "Problemi della responsabilità contrattuale", (1954) 20 *SDHI* 200 sqq.; Max Kaser, "Die actio furti des Verkäufers", (1979) 96 *ZSS* 105 sqq. The question is disputed. For a contrary view (custodia had to be specifically agreed upon), see Betti, *Istituzioni*, vol. II, 1, pp. 372 sq., 416 sqq.

[104] In case of theft, the vendor also had to "cede" to the purchaser his (reipersecutary and penal—as to this terminology cf. infra, pp. 918 sqq.) actions: condictio ex causa furtiva, actio furti and rei vindicatio; alternatively, if he had already brought one of these actions, he had to hand over what he had received (usually called "stellvertretendes commodum"). Cf. e.g. Ulp. D. 47, 2, 14 pr.: "Eum qui emit, si non tradita est ei res, furti actionem non habere, sed adhuc venditoris esse hanc actionem Celsus scripsit, mandare eum plane oportebit emptori furti actionem et condictionem et vindicationem, et si quid ex his actionibus fuerit

6. Afr. D. 19, 2, 33 et al.: evidence against periculum emptoris?

It is submitted that on this basis even those texts which have often been taken to provide evidence against periculum emptoris can be satisfactorily explained. Thus, for instance, Africanus seems to allocate the risk of expropriation (occurring after conclusion of the sale, but before transfer) to the vendor:

> ". . . nam et si vendideris mihi fundum isque priusquam vacuus traderetur publicatus fuerit, tenearis ex empto: quod hactenus verum erit, ut pretium restituas, non ut etiam id praestes, si quid pluris mea intersit eum vacuum mihi tradi."[105]

It is likely, however, that this decision was based on the fact that the vendor himself did not yet have vacua possessio when the expropriation (probably taken to be a case of vis maior) occurred. At that time, therefore, the contract of sale had not yet been "perfecta" and hence the risk had not passed to the purchaser.[106] Paul. D. 21, 2, 11 pr., too, deals with expropriation:

> "Lucius Titius praedia in Germania trans Renum emit et partem pretii intulit: cum in residuam quantitatem heres emptoris conveniretur, quaestionem rettulit dicens has possessiones ex praecepto principali partim distractas, partim veteranis in praemia adsignatas: quaero, an huius rei periculum ad venditorem pertinere possit. Paulus respondit futuros casus evictionis post contractam emptionem ad venditorem non pertinere et ideo secundum ea quae proponuntur pretium praediorum peti posse."

It is fairly obvious that the property was expropriated at a time when traditio had already taken place.[107] One might therefore be tempted to argue that, if (as Paulus decides) the purchaser has to pay (the remainder of) the purchase price in this case, he would—e contrario—not have been obliged to do so, had the expropriation occurred before traditio.[108] But Paulus does not even mention traditio, which leads one to believe that this factor cannot really have been relevant for his decision. Thus,

consecutus, id praestare eum emptori oportebit. . ."; also Gai. D. 18, 1, 35, 4; *Inst.* III, 23, 3 a. Reason: It would not have been in accordance with bona fides if the vendor were allowed to claim the purchase price and at the same time to retain what was still left of the object (albeit in the form of a substitute): cf. esp. Seckel/Levy, (1927) 47 *ZSS* 147 sq. The purchaser thus had a chance (under the rei vindicatio) to get the object restored to him once it had turned up again. Of course, if that happened (or if the purchaser successfully brought one of the other claims that had been ceded to him), he had to pay back (part of the) damages that he might have received from the vendor in the meantime. For details, see Manfred Harder, "Commodum eius esse debet, cuius periculum est", in: *Festschrift für Max Kaser* (1976), pp. 351 sqq.; Kaser, (1979) 96 *ZSS* 115 sqq.

[105] D. 19, 2, 33; cf. e.g. Haymann, (1928) 48 *ZSS* 406 sqq.

[106] Cf. e.g. Seckel/Levy, (1927) 47 *ZSS* 219 sqq.; Kaser, *RPr* I, p. 553. For a different interpretation, see Ernst, op. cit., note 63, pp. 8 sqq. For an overview of the discussion of this fragment in the literature of the ius commune, see Glück, vol. 17, pp. 135 sqq.

[107] Cf. e.g. Haymann, (1920) 41 *ZSS* 140; Seckel/Levy, (1927) 47 *ZSS* 231; Meylan, (1949) 3 *RIDA* 195, 207; Jörs/Kunkel/Wenger, p. 229, n. 11.

[108] Cf. Emilio Betti, "'Periculum'. Problema del rischio contrattuale in diritto romano classico e giustinianeo", in: *Studi in onore di Pietro de Francisci*, vol. I (1956), pp. 183 sq.

whether traditio had taken place or not, the purchaser was obliged to pay.[109]

Another type of action by the public authorities is at the heart of the following two fragments:

> "Lectos emptos aedilis, cum in via publica positi essent, concidit: si traditi essent emptori aut per eum stetisset quo minus traderentur, emptoris periculum esse placet. . . . Quod si neque traditi essent neque emptor in mora fuisset quo minus traderentur, venditoris periculum erit."[110]

The aedil had smashed to pieces some beds which had been sold and which were now standing in the street. Being responsible (inter alia) for the security of the Roman streets,[111] he could not tolerate unwieldy objects lying around and obstructing orderly traffic.[112] According to Paulus, the purchaser had to bear the loss if the beds had already been handed over to him (for then he had become their owner) or if he had been responsible for the fact that this transfer had not yet taken place (mora creditoris; thus, the parties might have agreed that the purchaser should come and collect the beds; when, however, he did not turn up at the right time, the vendor—usually hard pressed for space in his small shop or store-room—put them in the street). Otherwise, the risk was on the vendor. This can be reconciled with periculum est emptoris only if the aedil's action was not regarded as vis maior. A general proposition of this kind would be very doubtful; in the present context, however, such an evaluation seems reasonable and convincing.[113] Irrespective of whether the vendor actually knew what happened to the beds or not, irrespective of whether the aedil's intervention as such was one "cui resisti non potest": the incident had its origin within the vendor's sphere of influence. If he or his employees put the beds in the street, he increased the risk that something might happen to them. Such an action was not in accordance with his duty of custodiam praestare. He was thus responsible for the consequences on account of his custodia liability, and that seems to be the reason why Paulus does not allocate the risk to the purchaser.

---

[109] Seckel/Levy, (1927) 47 *ZSS* 231 sq.; Benöhr, *Synallagma*, p. 88. Cf. also Meylan, (1949) 3 *RIDA* 197 sqq., who, however, goes on to argue that in case of res nec mancipi (praedia in Germania trans Renum!) the risk passes with the due date of the purchase price (dies pretii solvendi). His theory, while providing an ingenious explanation for Paul. D. 21, 2, 11, is based on the mistaken assumption that transfer of ownership was, according to classical law, always dependent on payment of the purchase price. A curious explanation is offered by Voet, *Commentarius ad Pandectas*, Lib. XVIII, Tit. VI, 1.

[110] Paul. D. 18, 6, 13/15 pr.

[111] For details, see Mommsen, *Staatsrecht*, vol. II, 3, pp. 486 sqq.

[112] The Roman streets were very narrow; for a lively account, see Carcopino, pp. 57 sqq. In our case the aedil seems to have acted within his powers; argumentum e contrario from Iul. D. 18, 6, 14.

[113] Glück, vol. 17, pp. 143 sqq.; Seckel/Levy, (1927) 47 *ZSS* 244 sqq.; Kaser, *RPr* I, p. 533, n. 73; Theo Mayer-Maly, "Haftung aus Miete nach Staatsunrecht", (1957) 74 *ZSS* 364 sqq.; Benöhr, *Synallagma*, pp. 88 sq.; for a different interpretation, see, for instance, Krückmann, (1940) 60 *ZSS* 65 sqq.; MacCormack, (1985) 101 *ZSS* 573 sqq.

7. Evaluation of the Roman risk rule

Proper consideration of its application in practice may well make us differ from those who regard the risk rule as an inequitable anomaly. True, we are dealing with a deviation from res perit domino. Also, as a matter of history, the origin of the rule probably lies in the cash sale of the ancient Roman law.[114] Where every sale is executed immediately, both risk and ownership are bound to pass at one and the same time, namely when the contract is concluded. It was only with the rise of the fully executory contract that a divergence became possible. Whilst the transfer of the object (and with it the final act necessary for the transfer of ownership) could be postponed to a later date, one continued to think in terms of the cash sale pattern in some other respects, for instance with regard to the question of risk. But this does not mean that we are here dealing, as far as classical law is concerned, with an inappropriate atavism. Periculum est emptoris is a reasonable solution to the difficult problem of risk allocation,[115] corresponding entirely to the underlying economic interest structure. As between the parties, the object of the sale belongs (in an untechnical sense) to the purchaser.[116] It has become part of his economic sphere. Hence the duty, on the part of the purchaser, to reimburse the vendor for the expenses necessary for the maintenance of the thing whilst still in his possession;[117] hence the right of the purchaser to claim any accessions to or fruits of the thing which arose since completion (i.e. normally conclusion) of the sale.[118]

[114] Cf. e.g. Kaser, *RPr* I, p. 547; idem, (1979) 96 *ZSS* 114 sq.; Buckland/Stein, p. 487; Honsell/Mayer-Maly/Selb, p. 310; Watson, *Obligations*, p. 69. It was not imported only in the late classical period under the influence of Hellenistic law, as Haymann, (1930) 41 *ZSS* 172 sqq. and Betti, (1965) 82 *ZSS* 12 would have it.

[115] Schulz, *CRL*, p. 533 even calls it "an ideal solution". See, too, De Zulueta, *Sale*, p. 35; Nicholas, *Introduction*, p. 180; Ernst, op. cit., note 63, pp. 73 sqq.; Stefan Weyand, "Kaufverständnis und Verkäuferhaftung im klassischem römischen Recht", (1983) 51 *TR* 246 sqq.; Peters, *Festgabe Kaser*, pp. 221 sqq.; MacCormack, (1985) 101 *LQR* 574 (more "sophisticated").

[116] Cf. already Windscheid/Kipp, § 321, 3, as translated by Lawson, (1949) 46 *LQR* 361: "The reason for this exceptional provision is to be found in the fact that the declaration of intention to sell is a declaration of intention to alienate. That means that its content is not so much that the seller binds himself to surrender the thing sold, as rather that he actually surrenders it. In consequence of this characteristic of the declaration of intention to sell, the thing sold is treated by the law, so far as the relation of the seller to the buyer is concerned, as though it had already been severed from the seller's estate and passed into the buyer's." Cf. also § 390.

[117] Cf. supra, pp. 277 sq.

[118] Paul. D. 22, 1, 38, 7–8; Pomp. D. 19, 1, 3, 1; C. 4, 49, 13 and 16 (Diocl.); Ulp. D. 19, 1, 13, 13. For details, see Voet, *Commentarius ad Pandectas*, Lib. XVIII, Tit. VI, 9; Glück, vol. 17, pp. 189 sqq.; and esp. Weyand, (1983) 51 *TR* 229 sqq. Cf. also Paul. D. 18, 6, 7 pr.: "Id, quod post emptionem fundo accessit per alluvionem vel perit, ad emptoris commodum incommodumque pertinet: nam et si totus ager post emptionem flumine occupatus esset, periculum esset emptoris: sic igitur et commodum eius esse debet", and *Inst.* III, 23, 3 a, where the reason for this is crisply expressed in the rule "nam et commodum eius esse debet, cuius periculum est". This rule also appears among the regulae iuris antiqui in Paul. D. 50, 17, 10 ("Secundum naturam est commoda cuiusque rei eum sequi, quem sequentur incommoda"). For details, see G.C.J.J. van den Bergh, "Qui habet commoda fere debet

The purchaser may, furthermore, resell the thing; the vendor can't (unless he is prepared to commit a breach of contract). Thus it is the purchaser who benefits from a rise, but who also takes the risk of a fall in the market price.

The contract of sale embodies the will of the parties that the object of the sale shall belong to the purchaser, and we have seen[119] that in this regard it was more than a merely executory agreement. It contained the will to transfer ownership and it was only the act of traditio that was postponed for the time being. Ex fide bona, therefore, what the parties were aiming at was to be given effect to as soon and as far as possible. Under these circumstances, a regime of periculum est emptoris is not unnatural. It must be emphasized again that risk in this context referred only to events which did not originate in the vendor's sphere and which had nothing to do with the fact that the vendor still kept the object of the sale in his possession.

8. Reception and rejection of periculum est emptoris

If the reception and continued application of a Roman rule in later phases of legal history provides some indication of its soundness, the record of periculum est emptoris is not at all dismal.[120] True it is that both the writers and the legislators of the law of the Age of Reason were hostile to it.[121] So were the fathers of the BGB.[122] They did not see a rational justification for the rule and considered it to be in conflict with the nature and equity of the bilateral contract of sale. Hence, § 446 I 1 BGB provides: "On the delivery of the thing sold the risk of accidental destruction and accidental deterioration passes to the purchaser."[123] On the other hand, in art. 185 I OR we find a codified version of the Roman risk rule, and in the European ius commune it applied until the days of the pandectists.[124]

---

onera", in: *Flores legum H.J. Scheltema oblati* (1971), pp. 21 sqq.; Manfred Harder, "Commodum eius esse debet, cuius periculum est": in: *Festschrift für Max Kaser* (1976), pp. 362 sqq.

[119] Cf. supra, pp. 239 sq.

[120] The following comments refer only to the sale of individual things, not to emptio generis.

[121] Cf. supra, note 71 and §§ 95, 100 I 11; 364 I 5 PrALR; cf. also §§ 1064, 1048, 1051 ABGB. Critical of "periculum est emptoris" in his comparative evaluation, also Hager, op. cit., note 62, pp. 66 sqq.

[122] "Motive", in: *Mugdan*, vol. II, pp. 113 sq.

[123] § 446 I 2 BGB carries on to state that "after delivery the emoluments accrue to the purchaser, and he bears the burdens attached to the thing". This is in line with the maxim "secundum naturam est commoda cuiusque re eum sequi, quem sequentur incommoda" (Paul. D. 50, 17, 10).

[124] Cf. e.g. Vinnius, *Institutiones*, Lib. III, Tit. XXIV, 3; Voet, *Commentarius ad Pandectas*, Lib. XVIII, Tit. VI; Pothier, *Traité du contrat de vente*, n. 308; Grotius, *Inleiding*, III, XIV, 34; Glück, vol. 17, pp. 126 sqq.; Windscheid/Kipp, § 390; Vangerow, *Pandekten*, § 635; Bechmann, vol. II, pp. 99 sqq.; vol. III, 1, pp. 171 sqq.

In the South African variant of the ius commune it still applies today.[125] That is all the more remarkable, as periculum emptoris is no longer restricted to cases of vis maior, but refers to instances of accidental destruction or deterioration at large. Justinian, it will be remembered, abolished the concept of custodia liability, replacing it with culpa (in custodiendo).[126] In the present context this had the effect of a not inconsiderable extension of the risk rule. The French code civil retains "emptione perfecta periculum est emptoris" too; however, it makes not only the passing of the risk but also the transfer of ownership dependent upon the conclusion of the contract of sale.[127] Like the BGB, therefore, it tries to reconcile the passing of the risk with the overriding principle of res perit domino; but whereas the one code brings about this reconciliation on the level of the contract of sale, the other one detaches both transfer of ownership and passing of risk from the obligatory contract.

English law is very similar to French: the purchaser becomes owner with the conclusion of the contract of sale;[128] at the same time, the passing of the risk takes place.[129] As far as this latter consequence is concerned, the position is therefore not different to that in Roman law, and Lord Ellenborough, to mention but one example, might just as well have applied emptione perfecta periculum est emptoris when he said in the case of *Rugg v. Minett*:[130]

> ". . . and therefore according to the case of . . ., every thing having been done by the sellers, which lay upon them to perform, in order to put the goods in a deliverable state in the place from whence they were to be taken by the buyers, the goods remained there at the risk of the latter. But with respect to the other ten casks [sc.: of turpentine], as the filling them up according to the contract remained to be done by the sellers, the property did not pass to the buyers, and therefore they are not bound to pay for them."

---

[125] Cf. *Poppe, Schunhoff and Guttery v. Mosenthal & Co.* (1879) 9 Buch 91; *Taylor & Co. v. Mackie, Dunn & Co.* (1879) 9 Buch 166; for details, see De Wet en Yeats, pp. 308 sqq.; cf. also the acute analysis by M.A.K. Lambiris, (1984) 101 *SALJ* 656 sqq. For Scotland, see *Sloan's Dairies Ltd. v. Glasgow Corporation* 1977 SC 223 at 238 and A.D.M. Forte, "Must a Purchaser Buy Charred Remains?—An Analysis of the Passing of Risk on Civilian Principles", (1984) 19 *The Irish Jurist* 1 sqq. (who himself is critical of the rule: pp. 9 sqq.).

[126] Cf. supra, pp. 192 sq. and, in the present context, *Inst.* III, 23, 3 a, dealing with the sale of slaves, for which transaction special rules seem to have applied already in classical law; cf. Kaser, (1979) 96 *ZSS* 109 sqq.

[127] Artt. 1138, 1583 code civil.

[128] That was not always so; cf. Pollock and Maitland, vol. II, pp. 209 sq.: "That the ownership of the purchased goods did not pass to the buyer until they were delivered to him seems plain. We may gather from Bracton and Fleta that this was so even when the whole price had been paid. Unless there was some special agreement to the contrary, the risk remained with the party who was in possession of the goods." For the roots of the modern notion of sale as having the consequence of passing both title and risk, see Holdsworth, vol. III, pp. 354 sqq. "Res perit domino" seems to have been referred to for the first time by Blackburn J, in *Martineau v. Kitching* (1872) LR 7 QB 436 at 454. For a comparison between English and Roman law, see Buckland/McNair, pp. 289 sq.; Lawson, (1949) 65 *LQR* 352 sqq.

[129] Cf. ss. 20, 49 Sale of Goods Act 1979.

[130] (1809) 11 East 210 at 217.

CHAPTER 10

Emptio venditio III

I. LIABILITY FOR EVICTION

We have been looking at the basic requirements for a contract of sale and at its main effects. We shall now turn our attention to situations where the expectations engendered in one of the parties to the contract have been disappointed. For instance, the vendor's performance could become impossible (due to his fault or not) and either the vendor or the purchaser could be in default with their respective performances. These problems could emerge in all types of contracts and therefore we shall delay our discussion until we have dealt with all of them.[1] There are two situations, however, which specifically relate to contracts of sale: the vendor might fail to make the purchaser owner of the object sold; alternatively, that object might turn out to suffer from a latent defect. In any legal system, therefore, the question arises whether the law is prepared, under these circumstances, to protect the purchaser; whether, to use the terminology of modern English law, the contract of sale implies a warranty of title and of proper quality.

1. Warranty of peaceable possession

In Roman law, emptio venditio did not imply a warranty of title.[2] If the vendor was not the owner of what he sold, he was not able to transfer ownership to the purchaser: nemo plus iuris ad alium transferre potest, quam ipse haberet.[3] That, of course, did not mean that the contract of sale was invalid,[4] for it was not (objectively) impossible to perform what had been promised. The purchaser could sue the vendor if the object was not handed over to him, but he did not have a remedy merely on account of his lack of title. This followed from the fact that there was no obligation on the vendor to transfer ownership;[5] he merely had to grant the purchaser undisturbed possession. Being in possession, the latter was able to usucape and acquire ownership that way. However, the vendor was responsible not only for "vacuam possessionem *tradere*" but also for *sustaining* the continued enjoyment of the res.[6] There was therefore an implied warranty of peaceable

[1] Cf. infra, Chapter 25.

[2] For a comparative discussion, see Raphael Powell, "Eviction in Roman law and English Law", in: *Studies in the Roman Law of Sale in memory of Francis de Zulueta* (1959), pp. 78 sqq., 86 sqq.

[3] Ulp. D. 50, 17, 54.

[4] Ulp. D. 18, 1, 28.

[5] Cf. supra, pp. 278 sqq.

[6] Cf. supra, p. 278.

possession, for as soon as the true owner, by asserting his title, evicted the purchaser,[7] the latter could hold the vendor responsible. This liability for eviction,[8] as we find it in the law of Justinian and as it has become part and parcel of the ius commune, was the result of a long and interesting historical development, in the course of which several legal institutions, supplementing each other, eventually grew together.

2. Liability under the actio auctoritatis

First of all, there was auctoritas.[9] This was a guarantee implicit in sale by mancipatio, of which we find traces in tab. 6, 3 of the XII Tables.[10] If the position of the transferee was threatened because a third party brought the rei vindicatio against him, he could call on the transferor as his auctor to render procedural assistance. If the transferor refused to render such assistance or if the action was lost in spite of it, resulting in eviction, he was liable towards the transferee for double the purchase price. An actio auctoritatis must have been available for this purpose.[11]

---

[7] This is the main example that will be used for the purposes of the following discussion. The situation was the same, where the purchaser had become owner, but a third party could assert a real right against him: e.g. the holder of a non-possessory pledge (who could bring the actio Serviana) or a usufructuary (who could avail himself of the vindicatio ususfructus). What mattered was whether the purchaser had the habere licere or whether he was evicted (due to whatever real right of a third party); cf. e.g. Pomp. D. 21, 2, 34, 2; Paul. D. 21, 2, 35; Afr. D. 21, 2, 46 pr.; Cels. D. 21, 2, 62, 2; Windscheid/Kipp, § 391, 3.

[8] On evincere, evictio, see Heumann/Seckel, p. 177; Cuiacius, *Ad Africanum Tractatus VI*, Ad L. Non tamen 24 de eviction.: "Evincere igitur est legitimo certamine vincere, id est, cognitio judicis, et non vincere tantum, sed etiam rem abducere, et auferre. Plus enim est evincere quam vincere, quia est etiam rem abducere et auferre. Una litera auget significationem, ut in elugere, emereri, enavigare. . . ."

[9] The literature on this enigmatic concept of ancient Roman law is vast. Cf. e.g. Glück, vol. 20, pp. 179 sqq.; Ernst Eck, *Die Verpflichtung des Verkäufers zur Gewährung des Eigenthums nach römischem und gemeinem deutschen Recht* (1874), pp. 2 sqq.; Bechmann, vol. I, pp. 107 sqq.; Ernst Rabel, *Die Haftung des Verkäufers wegen Mangels im Rechte*, vol. I (1902), pp. 5 sqq.; Franz Haymann, *Die Haftung des Verkäufers für die Beschaffenheit der Kaufsache*, vol. I (1912), pp. 1 sqq.; Kaser, *Altrömisches ius*, pp. 135 sqq.; idem, *Eigentum und Besitz im älteren römischen Recht* (2nd ed., 1956), pp. 89 sqq., 109 sqq., 129 sqq.; Arangio-Ruiz, *Compravendita*, pp. 310 sqq.; Theo Mayer-Maly, "Studien zur Frühgeschichte der usucapio II", (1961) 78 *ZSS* 234 sqq.; Herman van den Brink, *Ius fasque* (1968), pp. 214 sqq.; Diósdi, *Ownership in Ancient and Preclassical Roman Law* (1970), pp. 75 sqq.; A.M. Prichard, "Auctoritas in Early Roman Law", (1974) 90 *LQR* 378 sqq.; Hans Ankum, "L'actio de auctoritate et la restitutio in integrum dans le droit romain classique", in: *Maior viginti quinque annis, Essays in commemoration of the sixth lustrum of the Institute for legal history of the University of Utrecht* (1979), pp. 1 sqq. For a modern overview over and summary of the discussion, see Jolowicz/Nicholas, pp. 146 sqq.; Kaser, *RPr* I, pp. 132 sqq.; Honsell/Mayer-Maly/Selb, pp.173 sqq.

[10] "Usus auctoritas fundi biennium, ceterarum rerum annos esto".

[11] The problem is that we have, at best, only indirect references to it, for Justinian deleted both mancipatio and the auctoritas liability flowing therefrom from the classical sources. It is not surprising, therefore, that it has even been argued that this liability never existed (cf. e.g. M. Sargenti, "Per una revisione della nozione dell'auctoritas come effetto della mancipatio", in: *Studi in onore di Emilio Betti*, vol. IV (1962), pp. 15 sqq.; Alfredo Calonge, *Evicción* (1968), pp. 15 sqq.); but see e.g. Rabel, Arangio-Ruiz, Kaser, Diósdi and Prichard, Ankum, all as above.

The origin of this liability seems to lie in delict.[12] The vendor had accepted the purchase price, even though he was not owner of the thing sold, and even though the acquirer was therefore in danger of losing out under the true owner's vindication. This was not unlike furtum nec manifestum, a non-manifest theft of the money; hence the sanction of duplum.[13] Of course, delictual liability required knowledge on the part of the vendor, but that could typically be presumed to exist[14] in the small and unsophisticated agrarian society of early Rome, where legal transactions were not the order of the day. Only when the cogency of this conclusion came to be less and less obvious, did one start to read a guarantee into the transaction itself; liability came to be seen as a consequence of the act of mancipatio rather than of a delict; duplum as a lump sum for damages rather than as a composition. Further-reaching guarantees could be undertaken by way of special dicta in mancipio or in venditione; if, for instance, a piece of land had been sold "ita ut optimus maximusque est", the vendor was responsible for the freedom of servitudes over it.[15]

3. Liability under a stipulatio duplae

Liability under the actio auctoritatis required mancipatio. It did not cover the sale of res nec mancipi; nor did it apply where res mancipi had been sold and were merely handed over by way of traditio (or transferred by way of in iure cessio). In these instances no right of recourse, implied in law, was at first available to the evicted purchaser. This situation was plainly unsatisfactory and thus the parties started to make specific contractual arrangements modelled on the pattern of auctoritas. It became standard practice for the purchaser (first of all, where res mancipi, then also where valuable res nec mancipi were sold) to require the vendor to promise double[16] the amount of the purchase price in case of eviction;[17] slave dealers were even forced by the aediles

---

[12] Cf. e.g. Rabel, op. cit., note 9, pp. 8 sqq.; Kaser, *Eigentum und Besitz*, op. cit., note 9, pp. 115 sqq.; idem, "Die römische Eviktionshaftung nach Weiterverkauf", in: *Sein und Werden im Recht, Festgabe für Ulrich von Lübtow* (1970), p. 488.

[13] Cf. infra, pp. 932 sqq.

[14] Cf. Max Kaser, "Typisierter 'dolus' im altrömischen Recht", (1962) 65 *BIDR* 79 sqq., 96 sq.

[15] Cels. D. 18, 1, 59; Ner. D. 21, 2, 48; Paul. D. 50, 16, 169; D. F. Mostert, "Uitwinning by die Koopkontrak in die Romeinse Reg", 1969 *Acta Juridica* 19 sqq.

[16] The parties were, of course, free to vary the sum; they could agree to simplum or to triplum, quadruplum, etc.: cf. e.g. Paul. D. 21, 2, 56 pr.; Glück, vol. 20, pp. 280 sqq.

[17] Cf. e.g. Varro, *De re rustica*, Lib. II, 10, 5; Gai. D. 21, 2, 6; Ulp. D. 21, 2, 37, 1; Rabel, op. cit., note 9, pp. 72 sqq.; Kaser, *Eigentum und Besitz*, op. cit., note 9, pp. 202 sqq.; Helmut Coing, "A Typical Development in the Roman law of Sale", in: *Gesammelte Aufsätze zu Rechtsgeschichte, Rechtsphilosophie und Zivilrecht*, vol. I (1982), pp. 64 sqq.; Arangio-Ruiz, *Compravendita*, pp. 341 sqq.; Watson, *Obligations*, pp. 83 sqq.; Pasquale Voci, "La responsibilità del debitore da 'stipulatio poenae'"; in: *Studi in onore di Edoardo Volterra*, vol. III (1971), pp. 339 sqq.; Mostert, 1969 *Acta Juridica* 67 sqq.; Knütel, *Stipulatio poenae*, pp. 37 sq. In the case of res mancipi, such a stipulation was necessary only where a mancipatio did not take place (e.g. where res mancipi were sold to peregrini), but the purchaser could also

curules to do so.[18] This was the stipulatio duplae, and its standard wording, as contained in the aedilitian edict, probably ran as follows:

> "Si quis eum hominem partemve quam ex eo evicerit, quo minus me eumve ad quem ea res pertinebit, habere recte liceat, qua de re lis tibi recte denuntiata erit, tam quanti is homo emptus est, tantam pecuniam duplam partemve eius duplam mihi dari spondesne?"[19]

The vendor was liable, if the purchaser lost his case under an actio in rem brought against him by a third party, provided he had called upon the vendor to assist him in defending the action. With regard to res nec mancipi of lesser value it was recommended to take a stipulatio habere licere.[20] The details are unclear: did it provide the purchaser with a claim for the recovery of the purchase price[21] or for damages?[22] And did it protect the purchaser against eviction by a third party (the true owner) or only against interference with his habere licere on the part of the vendor or his heirs?[23] Be that as it may, the protection of the purchaser still contained one grave weakness: the remedies against eviction where not inherent in sale, but required an additional act by the parties. If neither a mancipatio had occurred nor a special stipulation been made, a remedy was not available.

4. Liability under the actio empti

(a) "Emptorem duplam promitti a venditore oportet"

At this stage, however, the actio empti came to be activated by the classical jurists. It had, of course, always been available in cases of dolus: if the vendor knew that the object sold either did not belong to him or was encumbered with a real right, or if he had specifically guaranteed the freedom from legal defects, he was liable—even before eviction had taken place—for the purchaser's interest in the proper

take a stipulatio duplae from the seller where there was mancipatio ("satisdatio secundum mancipium"?; cf. Kaser, *RPr* I, p. 130; Mostert, 1969 *Acta Juridica* 24 sqq.) It could serve as a basis for suretyship in the form of either sponsio or fidepromissio.

[18] Ulp. D. 21, 2, 37, 1 in fine. If the vendor refused to give the guarantee within two months, the purchaser was granted the actio redhibitoria: Gai. D. 21, 1, 28.

[19] Kaser, *Festgabe von Lübtow*, pp. 484 sq.; cf. also Lenel, *EP*, p. 568.

[20] Varro, *De re rustica*, for example, Lib. II, 2, 6; Lib. II, 3, 5; Lib II, 4, 5; all relating to different kinds of pecus (". . . eam rem . . . recte mihi habere licere spondesne?").

[21] Rabel, op. cit., note 9, pp. 136 sqq.

[22] Max Kaser, "Das Ziel der actio empti nach Eviktion", (1934) 54 *ZSS* 176 sqq.

[23] In contrast to the stipulatio duplae, the stipulatio habere licere did not mention eviction as a requirement; hence the narrow interpretation (in accordance with "nemo alienum factum promittendo obligatur") by Ulpianus in D. 45, 1, 38 pr. Cf. esp. Max Kaser, "Neue Studien zum altrömischen Eigentum", (1951) 68 *ZSS* 152 sqq.; but see Ulp. D. 19, 1, 11, 18; Rabel, op. cit., note 9, pp. 30 sqq.; Watson, *Obligations*, pp. 85 sq.; Philippe Meylan, "La stipulation habere licere", (1970) 38 TR 67 sqq.; Arangio-Ruiz, *Compravendita*, pp. 332 sqq.; Mostert, 1969 *Acta Juridica* 60 sqq. The narrow interpretation only came to prevail once the actio empti had been made available to the purchaser to recover his interest; see D. 45, 1, 38 pr., the first sentence of which probably still represents the opinion of Sabinus.

implementation of this contract.[24] Now one went a step further. The actio empti was a iudicium bonae fidei. It was available to provide the purchaser with what was due to him ex fide bona. That in turn, however, was not only *tradere* vacuam possessionem but also the sustaining of continued enjoyment of the res. The accepted way of ensuring the latter was to make the stipulatio duplae. Where this had been neglected, the position of the purchaser was incompatible with good faith, and hence he could compel the vendor, by bringing the actio empti, to give that guarantee.[25] This does not seem to have applied to the sale of goods without much value[26] or to provincial land, where it was not usual, according to the consuetudo regionis, to enter into a stipulatio duplae;[27] nor could the purchaser pursue this avenue where it had been through mutual consent that a stipulatio duplae had not been entered into.[28] The position is summed up by Ulpianus:[29]

> "Emptori duplam promitti a venditore oportet, nisi aliud convenit: non tamen ut satisdetur . . . sed ut repromittatur. Quod autem diximus duplam promitti oportere, sic erit accipiendum, ut non ex omni re id accipiamus, sed de his rebus, quae pretiosiores essent, si margarita forte aut ornamenta pretiosa vel vestis Serica vel quid aliud non contemptibile veneat".

And then the special case of slaves: "[P]er edictum autem curulium etiam de servo cavere venditor iubetur." But what happened—apart from in this latter instance, dealt with in the aedilitian edict—if the vendor refused to give the stipulatio duplae? It was not possible in Roman law directly to compel the defendant to make a specific declaration. Paulus D. 21, 2, 2 supplies the answer: "Si dupla non promitteretur et eo nomine agetur, dupli condemnandus est reus."[30] The defendant was condemned immediately for the amount that would have been due under the stipulatio duplae. Such a threat was likely to induce the vendor rather to give the required guarantee, as he could then still hope that an eviction might not in fact occur. In certain instances, the purchaser was even allowed to sue for duplum at a time when he had already been evicted and when, therefore, events had gone beyond the stage where to compel the vendor to give a guarantee (in the

---

[24] Cf. e.g. Afr. D. 19, 1, 30, 1; Ulp. D. 19, 1, 1, 1; Ulp. D. 19, 1, 11, 15; Rabel, op. cit., note 9, pp. 93 sqq.; Antonius Louisius Olde Kalter, *Dicta et Promissa* (1963), pp. 69 sqq.

[25] Ulp. D. 21, 1, 31, 20: "Quia adsidua est duplae stipulatio, idcirco placuit etiam ex empto agi posse, si duplam venditor mancipii non caveat: ea enim, quae sunt moris et consuetudinis, in bonae fidei iudiciis debent venire." Cf. further Pomp. D. 45, 1, 5 pr.; Rabel, op. cit., note 9, pp. 75 sqq.; Kaser, (1934) 54 *ZSS* 182 sqq.; Arangio-Ruiz, *Compravendita*, pp. 346 sqq.; Mostert, 1969 *Acta Juridica* 109 sqq.; Honsell, *Quod interest*, pp. 20 sqq. Did that apply only to the stipulatio duplae or also to the stipulatio habere licere? Cf. Ner./Ulp. 19, 1, 11, 8, but (on this text) Kaser, (1934) 54 *ZSS* 185; Arangio-Ruiz, *Compravendita*, p. 347.

[26] Ulp. D. 21, 2, 37, 1.

[27] Gai. D. 21, 2, 6: "Si fundus venierit, ex consuetudine eius regionis in qua negotium gestum est pro evictione caveri oportet."

[28] Ulp. D. 21, 2, 37 pr.

[29] D. 21, 2, 37 pr.

[30] Cf. also Ner./Ulp. D. 19, 1, 11, 9.

form of a stipulatio duplae) would have made sense. In D. 21, 2, 37, 2 we find one case:

> "Si simplam pro dupla per errorem stipulatus sit emptor, re evicta consecuturum eum ex empto Neratius ait, quanto minus stipulatus sit, si modo omnia facit emptor, quae in stipulatione continentur: quod si non fecit, ex empto id tantum consecuturum, ut ei promittatur quod minus in stipulationem superiorem deductum est."

According to Ulpianus, it did not matter that the purchaser had, by way of mistake, asked the vendor to stipulate only simplum. As long as he had called on the vendor to help him defend the rei vindicatio, he was still entitled, even after he had been evicted, to bring the actio empti for duplum. Paul. Sent. II, XVII, 2 ("Si res simpliciter traditae evincantur, tanto venditor emptori condemnandus est, quanto si stipulatione pro evictione cavisset") presents a much more generalized statement to that effect; here the interposition of the guarantee is plainly fictitious. It is, however, uncertain how far this still represents the position in classical law.[31]

(b) Liability for the "positive interest"

Even then, however, there were still cases in which the purchaser eventually lost out.[32] If the res nec mancipi that had been sold was not "pretiosior" but only "contemptibilis" or if in the particular area of the Empire where a piece of land sold was situated, the conclusion of stipulationes duplae was not common, an action was not available, either for duplum or for simplum.[33] Furthermore, the defect in title might have caused damages to the purchaser without having led to a loss of possession: thus, the purchaser might have prevented eviction by acquiring the object from the third party (concursus causarum).[34] Finally, it was possible that the actual damages were in excess of duplum. In all these cases it was of practical significance that, from the time of Julian, the actio empti was generally made available in cases of eviction, irrespective of whether there had been dolus on the part of the vendor or not. Hence, for instance, the following statement by Iulianus: "Venditor hominis emptori praestare debet, quanti eius interest hominem venditoris fuisse."[35] We see that the action lay for

---

[31] Cf. particularly Levy, *Obligationenrecht*, pp. 213 sqq.; but see Honsell, *Quod interest*, pp. 23 sqq.

[32] Medicus, *Id quod interest*, p. 52; Honsell, *Quod interest*, pp. 25 sqq.

[33] Ulp. D. 21, 2, 37, 1; Gai. D. 21, 2, 6.

[34] Cf. Eck, op. cit., note 9, pp. 29 sqq.; Fritz Schulz, "Die Lehre vom Concursus Causarum im klassischen und justinianischen Recht", (1917) 38 *ZSS* 132 sqq.; Medicus, *Id quod interest*, pp. 100 sqq.

[35] D. 21, 2, 8; cf. further e.g. Iul./Ulp. D. 19, 1, 11, 18; Paul. D. 19, 1, 43; Iav. D. 21, 2, 60; Paul. D. 21, 2, 70; Kaser, (1934) 54 *ZSS* 163 sqq.; Arangio-Ruiz, *Compravendita*, pp. 349 sqq.; Medicus, *Id quod interest*, pp. 52 sqq.; Honsell, *Quod interest*, pp. 25 sqq.; Hans Ankum, "Das Ziel der 'actio empti' nach Eviktion", in: *Sodalitas, Scritti in onore di Antonio Guarino*, vol. VII (1984), pp. 3215 sqq.

"quanti (emptoris) interest hominem venditoris fuisse";[36] other texts describe what the purchaser could sue for as "quanti tua interest rem evictam non esse"[37] or "omne quod interest emptoris servum non evinci".[38] This is what modern parlance refers to as "positive interest".[39] What the judge had to estimate was the plaintiff's (purchaser's) interest in rem habere; he had to be placed, financially, in whatever position he would have been in had he not been evicted. As Donellus put it:

> ". . . id quod nostra interest persequitur haec actio, in quo non quid nobis absit, sed quid habere potuerimus, si res mansisset, aestimandum est."[40]

"Quid habere potuerimus" included not only the benefit of the use of the object (i.e. its—simple—value)[41] but also, for instance, everything that the purchaser would have acquired through the slave whom he had bought:

> ". . . quare sive partus ancillae sive hereditas, quam servus iussu emptoris adierit, evicta fuerit, agi ex empto potest: et sicut obligatus est venditor, ut praestet licere habere hominem quem vendidit, ita ea quoque quae per eum adquiri potuerunt praestare debet emptori, ut habeat."[42]

It was not very often that the purchaser resorted to the actio empti in order to claim quod interest; its exclusive scope of application was somewhat limited. Wherever the purchaser could use the actio empti in order to claim duplum or where, as was usual, a stipulatio duplae had in fact been concluded, he would rather pursue the latter opportunities.[43] For not only did he then not have to substantiate his positive interest, but he could claim, without further ado, a lump sum; this lump sum was also very likely to exceed his interest and would thus

[36] Not, however, in the cases of concursus causarum, where the actio empti only lay ad pretium reciperandum, i.e. for the return of the purchase price. The purchaser's habere licere was not infringed and therefore he could not claim quod interest rem habere licere. On the other hand, he had now paid the purchase price twice (where he had acquired the object from the true owner under a titulus onerosus—like sale) or he had paid a price, which, in the light of subsequent events, he need not have paid at all (acquisition from the true owner on account of a titulus lucrativus, e.g. he happened to become his heir). Cf. Honsell, *Quod interest*, p. 38 sqq. and the literature quoted above.

[37] C. 8, 44, 23 (Diocl.).

[38] Paul. D. 19, 1, 43. In Afr. D. 19, 1, 30, 1 we find "quanti mea intersit (rem) meam esse factam", but this refers to the (aggravated) liability under the actio empti for dolus; cf. Honsell, *Quod interest*, pp. 57 sq.

[39] For a comprehensive discussion, see Medicus, *Id quod interest*, pp. 53 sqq.; Honsell, *Quod interest*, pp. 30 sqq.

[40] "Comment. ad Tit. Dig. de Evictionib. et Duplae etc.", Cap. VII, 3, in: *Opera Omnia*, vol. X (Florentiae, 1847), col. 1401, discussed by Honsell, *Quod interest*, pp. 31 sq.

[41] The relevant value to be estimated was the value at the time of eviction; as a consequence any increase in value by way of improvements effected by the purchaser was taken into consideration. Cf. Paul./Afr. D. 19, 1, 43–45; on the difficult problems posed by this text, see Medicus, *Id quod interest*, pp. 80 sqq.; Honsell, *Quod interest*, pp. 50 sqq.; Knütel, *Stipulatio poenae*, pp. 338 sqq.

[42] Iul. D. 21, 2, 8. This is a typical case, where "quod interest" was for once likely to exceed dupla pecunia.

[43] The purchaser had a choice (elective concurrence of remedies): Knütel, *Stipulatio poenae*, pp. 335 sqq.

give him more than he could have got otherwise. After all, the purchase price is usually not a bad indicator of the value of the object sold and double the purchase price should normally have covered everything he could have hoped to gain from the transaction. Yet it was only with the general availability of the actio empti in case of eviction that a warranty of peaceable possession could be said to be inherent in this bonae fidei iudicium.[44]

5. The position under Justinian

Justinian preserved this achievement of classical jurisprudence for posterity essentially unchanged. Of course, mancipatio and auctoritas had become obsolete and had to be eradicated from the sources,[45] but otherwise he retained the Roman system of liability on eviction.[46] The purchaser could sue when he was—partially or totally—deprived of his habere licere, as a result of a real right vesting in a third party. His claim could arise from either a specific promise of guarantee given by the vendor (usually a stipulatio duplae) or the contract of sale itself. If he sued on the contract of sale (actio empti), he could claim his interest in rem habere. Alternatively, where he could have asked the vendor for a stipulatio duplae, he could also use the actio empti to claim what he would have got had such a promise been given (i.e. dupla pecunia).[47] Seeing that the actio empti covered his full interest (subject only to the general limitation imposed on the quantum of recoverable damages in C. 7, 47, 1),[48] a cogent reason for stipulationes duplae no longer

[44] If the purchaser was aware of the defect in title, he could not sue the vendor on account of eviction: cf. C. 8, 44, 27 and 30 (Diocl.). But see C. 6, 43, 3, 4 (Just.), where an action for the return of the purchase price is granted. This conflict between classical and Justinianic law has given rise to a dispute amongst the authors of the ius commune (Covarruvias, Donellus, Christinaeus, Fachinaeus, Carpzovius, Brunnemann, U. Huber and Van der Keessel on the one hand; Cujacius, Zoesius, Perezius, Groenewegen, Antonius Matthaeus III, Voet and Pothier on the other) that is fully canvassed in *Van der Westhuizen v. Yskor Werknemers se Onderlinge Bystandsversekering* 1960 (4) SA 803 (T) at 804H–812A. See Max Kaser, "Das römische Recht in Südafrika", (1964) 81 *ZSS* 23 sqq.; for modern German law: § 439 BGB. The parties were also able, in their contract of sale, to exclude liability for eviction (pactum de non praestanda evictione); cf. Ulp. D. 19, 1, 11, 18; Pothier, *Traité du contrat de vente*, nn. 182 sqq.; Glück, vol. 20, pp. 295 sqq.; Vangerow, *Pandekten*, § 610, n. 4; Calonge, op. cit., note 11, pp. 116 sqq. On partial eviction, see Ulp. D. 21, 2, 1; Paul. D. 21, 2, 36; Iul. D. 21, 2, 39, 2 (Voet, *Commentarius ad Pandectas*, Lib. XXI, Tit. II, XV sq.; Pothier, nn. 140 sqq.; Glück, vol. 20, pp. 332 sqq.). If the purchaser had not yet paid the purchase price, he could refuse to do so after litis contestatio had taken place with regard to the action by the third party brought against him (exceptio evictionis imminentis); cf. Pap. vat. 12, but see Pap. D. 18, 6, 19, 1; and Glück, vol. 20, pp. 370 sqq.; Benöhr, *Synallagma*, pp. 56 sqq. As far as the sale of claims (nomina) was concerned, see Cels./Ulp. D. 18, 4, 4 (". . . locupletem esse debitorem non debere praestare, debitorem autem esse praestare . . ."); Herm. D. 21, 2, 74, 3 (". . . dumtaxat ut sit, non ut exigi etiam aliquid possit . . . praestare cogitur"); Medicus, *Id quod interest*, pp. 167 sqq.

[45] Cf. e.g. Lenel, *EP*, pp. 542 sqq.

[46] Kaser, *RPr* II, pp. 391 sq.

[47] Cf. e.g. Levy, *Obligationenrecht*, pp. 216 sq.

[48] "Cum pro eo quod interest dubitationes antiquae in infinitum productae sunt, melius nobis visum est huiusmodi prolixitatem prout possibile est angustum coartare. Sancimus

existed. It was in order to accommodate the business practice of his time (which continued to use specific guarantee stipulations in the case of sale)[49] that Justinian refrained from further streamlining the protection of the purchaser against eviction.

6. The determination of quod interest

This was bound to happen, however, once the tradition of taking stipulationes (duplae) fell into disuse. Let us see, for instance, what Van Leeuwen says in this regard:

> "Quae stipulationes propterea paulatiin ab usu et moribus recesserunt, quibus emptori cui res evicta est, pretii, sumptuumque, damnorum, et interesse restitutio sufficere intellegitur."[50]

And Willem Schorer spells out the consequences: "Evictione locum habente non amplius duplum peti potest, sed tantum id quod interest; cessante moribus duplae stipulatione."[51] If stipulationes duplae had disappeared from the scene, because the claim for quod interest was regarded as satisfactory and sufficient under the circumstances, the raison d'être for the strange alternativity of how the purchaser could make use of the actio empti had fallen away. In Roman times it had been incompatible with good faith if the vendor refused to do what vendors normally did: to give a stipulatio duplae. Hence the purchaser was granted the actio empti to claim dupla pecunia. Now that the actio empti was available anyway, it would hardly have been in accordance with the precepts of good faith to read into the contract of sale what the parties would not normally have stipulated expressly and what the vendor would have been under no obligation to accept. The writers of the ius commune therefore generally restricted the scope of the actio

itaque in omnibus casibus, qui certam habent quantitatem vel naturam, veluti in venditionibus . . ., hoc quod interest dupli quantitatem minime excedere." It is unclear whether this arbitrary limitation of "dupli quantitas" refers to the ordinary value of the object sold or to the purchase price; cf. Medicus, *Id quod interest*, pp. 288 sqq.; Schindler, *Justinians Haltung zur Klassik*, pp. 259 sqq. Generally speaking, it does not seem to have been carried into effect in other parts of the compilation. In the context of eviction, however, we do find a hint in Afr. D. 19, 1, 44 (". . . et non ultra duplum periculum subire eum oportet"). Again, it is difficult to decide what the doubling referred to; also, there is a dispute as to whether this text was interpolated by Justinian (in order to bring the law into line with C. 7, 47, 1) or whether D. 19, 1, 44 expresses the opinion of at least one classical lawyer and perhaps even induced Justinian to formulate his generalized rule; cf. e.g. Honsell, *Quod interest*, pp. 54 sq.; Knütel, *Stipulatio poenae*, pp. 341 sqq. In any event, C. 7, 47 was usually applied to the "quod interest" claim during the time of the ius commune; cf. e.g. Cuiacius, *Ad Africanum Tractatus VIII*, Ad L. 44 de actio empt.; Windscheid/Kipp, § 391, 5.

[49] Levy, *Obligationenrecht*, pp. 216 sqq.; Kaser, *RPr* II, pp. 390 sq.

[50] *Censura Forensis*, Pars I, Lib. IV, Cap. XIX, 11; cf. further e.g. Groenewegen, *De legibus abrogatis*, Digest. Lib. XXI, Tit. I, l. 31 quod si nolit, Lib. XXI, Tit.II in initio; Voet, *Commentarius ad Pandectas*, Lib. XXI, Tit.II, XXVIII.

[51] *Aantekeningen*, III, XIV, 6 (in Hugo Grotius, *Inleiding*, Middelburg, 1767).

empti so as to exclude the claim for dupla pecunia.[52] The vendor was liable "ex natura ipsius contractus",[53] but only de eo quod interest, i.e. to the extent of the purchaser's interest in not being evicted. Opinions differed, however, on how this interest was to be determined. The most immediate consequence of the act of eviction was, of course, that the purchaser had lost the object sold to him. But did that mean that he could claim the value of this thing as at the time of eviction?[54] Or is the purchase price to be taken as a basis for evaluating the purchaser's loss? Does quod interest under these circumstances not rather have two objects: restitution of the price paid on the one hand; payment of all the purchaser has suffered over and above it on the other?[55] This dispute reflects the ambiguity of the Roman sources on the point. It survives in the continued controversy between modern Romanists[56] and still clouds the position in South African law.[57]

7. Roman-Dutch and modern German law

Of all modern systems, not surprisingly, South African law follows Roman law most closely.[58] It is squarely based on the Roman-Dutch branch of the ius commune[59] and the courts have, on that basis, usually

[52] As far as, specifically, Roman-Dutch law is concerned, see the detailed analysis by D.F. Mostert, "Uitwinning by die Koopkontrak in die Romeins-Hollandse Reg", 1967 *Acta Juridica* 49 sqq., 77 sqq. For the ius commune in general, see Coing, p. 452; Arndts, *Pandekten*, § 303, n. 8; Baron, *Pandekten*, § 288, II.

[53] Van Leeuwen, loc. cit.; Vinnius, *Selectae Juris Quaestiones* (Roterdami, 1685), Lib. II, Cap. VIII (". . . quae praestatio pars est obligationis empti et venditi") and many others.

[54] Cf. e.g. Donellus, *Commentarii de Jure Civili*, Cap. VII, 2, 3 (". . . Quibus verbis (sc. id quod interest) non pretium, ut dixi, continetur, sed quanti res valuit"); Domat, *Les loix civiles*, Tit. I, Sec. X, XII sqq.; Glück, vol. 20, p. 349; Baron, *Pandekten*, § 288, II; Windscheid/Kipp, § 391, 5.

[55] Molinaeus, *Tractatus de eo quod interest*, nn. 68 sqq.; Perezius, *Praelectiones*, Lib. VIII, Tit XLV, 11 (". . . re tamen evicta emptor consequitur rei pretium, et praeterea quanti interest rem evictam non esse"); Van Leeuwen, loc. cit. ("In qua causa, si succumbat, et rem ad alium pertinere compertum sit pretium restituere tenetur venditor cum usuris, et quod praeterea emptoris interest, rem evictam non fuisse"); Grotius, *Inleiding*, III, XIV, 6; Voet, *Commentarius ad Pandectas*, Lib. XXI, Tit. II, XXV; Pothier, *Traité du contrat de vente*, nn. 70, 119 sqq. and many others. In modern French law, the vendor is obliged to restore the price (apart from paying damages; art. 1630 code civil); such restitution is, however, not based upon an implied warranty, but upon the general principles of unjustified enrichment: the sale of a thing belonging to another person is void (art. 1599 code civil).

[56] According to Rabel (op. cit., note 9, pp. 145 sqq.) and Medicus (*Id quod interest*, pp. 49 sqq., 94 sqq.) the Roman lawyers took the price paid as the starting point for the id quod interest. Contra: Honsell, *Quod interest*, pp. 32 sqq.

[57] Cf. *Hendler Bros. Garage (Pty.) Ltd. v. Lambons Ltd.* 1967 (4) SA 115 (O) ("'n uitgewonne koper is slegs op skadevergoeding geregtig: die bedrag daarvan is die waarde van die verkoopte saak ten tye van die uitwinning") (according to De Wet en Yeats, p. 293, "'n bloemlesing van naïwiteite"); *Alpha Trust (Edms.) Bpk. v. Van der Watt* 1975 (3) SA 734 (A) at 748G (". . . as gevolg van die uitwinning (is respondent) geregtig om terugbetaling van die koopprys en vergoeding van sy skade met die actio empti van die verkoper te vorder") and see D.F. Mostert, "Uitwinning by die Koopkontrak in die Suid-Afrikaanse Reg", 1968 *Acta Juridica* 36 sqq.

[58] For a comprehensive analysis in historical perspective, see Mostert, 1968 *Acta Juridica* 5 sqq.

[59] For a detailed analysis, see Mostert, 1967 *Acta Juridica* 49 sqq.

done no more than to work out the details of the respective duties incumbent on the parties. Denuntiatio litis,[60] contrary to the practice in the olden days,[61] no longer has to be accompanied by a copy of the summons;[62] to give the vendor informal notice of the proceedings instituted by the third party is sufficient. On the other hand, such a notice to the auctor does not entitle the person threatened with eviction to rest on his laurels and throw all responsibility upon the vendor;[63] he has to put up a virilis defensio,[64] i.e. to conduct his case as a reasonable litigant.[65] South African law follows Roman and Roman-Dutch law even to the point that the vendor merely has to afford vacua possessio and is thus not under an obligation to make the purchaser owner of the object sold.[66] This idiosyncrasy of Roman law, faithfully preserved also in the European ius commune down to the time of the pandectists,[67] has been abandoned in the modern codes. They usually require the vendor, under the contract of sale, to transfer ownership.[68] That has

---

[60] For a general discussion, see Voet, *Commentarius ad Pandectas*, Lib. XXI, Tit. II, XX; Glück, vol. 20, pp. 388 sqq.

[61] Voet, *Commentarius ad Pandectas*, Lib. XXI, Tit. II, XX; Coing, p. 452.

[62] Cf. *Paarl Pretoria Gold Mining Co. v. Donovan & Wolff* 3 SAR 93 at 98, per Kotzé CJ (". . . it is clear that this was . . . only a local provision of the jus adjectivum or practice in the Netherlands . . . and forms no portion of the real substantive law, which is that by which alone we are bound, for we have our own rules and procedure in this country").

[63] *Lammers & Lammers v. Giovannoni* 1955 (3) SA 385 (A) at 397B (per Van den Heever JA).

[64] Voet, *Commentarius ad Pandectas*, Lib. XXI, Tit. II, XX; Mostert, 1967 *Acta Juridica* 102 sqq.

[65] *York & Co. (Pvt.) Ltd. v. Jones (1)* 1962 (1) SA 65 (SR) at 82 sqq.

[66] Cf. e.g. *Alpha Trust (Edms.) Bpk. v. Van der Watt* 1975 (3) SA 734 (A) at 743G. This applies at least in cases where the seller himself was not the owner. Otherwise, he seems to be obliged to transfer ownership; cf. Grotius, *Inleiding*, III, XV, 4: "Aen des verkoopers zijde bestaet de nakominge daer in, dat den verkooper, indien hy eigenaar is van het verkochte goed, schuldig is den kooper daer in te eigenen: 't welch gheschied door levering ende inleiding in het bezit . . ."; see also Kerr, *Sale and Lease*, pp. 110 sqq. This distinction seems to go back to the old Dutch (Germanic) concept of "waerhand": cf. Grotius, *Inleiding*, III, XIV, 6 and Mostert, 1967 *Acta Juridica* 85 sqq. It fits in with Roman law on the basis that, where an object has been sold by its owner, traditio is usually tantamount to transfer of ownership.

[67] Cf. e.g. Pothier, *Traité du contrat de vente*, nn. 41, 48; Glück vol. 20, p. 210; Windscheid/Kipp, § 389, 1; Coing, p. 451. A similar situation obtained in the English common law until well into the 19th century. As late as 1849 Baron Parke stated: ". . . the result of the older authorities is that there is by the law of England no warranty of title in the actual contract of sale, any more than there is of quality. The rule of caveat emptor applies to both" (*Morley v. Attenborough* (1849) 3 Exch 500 at 510; but see, only 15 years later, *Eichholz v. Bannister* (1864) 17 CB (NS) 708 at 723: ". . . in almost all the transactions of sale in common life, the seller by the very act of selling holds out to the buyer that he is the owner of the article he offers for sale" (per Erle CJ); cf. further Buckland/McNair, pp. 283 sq.; Powell, *Studies de Zulueta*, pp. 88 sqq.; Mostert, *Uitwinning by die Koopkontrak in die Suid-Afrikaanse reg* (unpublished LL.D. thesis, Pretoria, 1965), pp. 659 sqq.

[68] § 433 BGB has been quoted above (supra p. 278). § 434 adds: "The seller is bound to transfer to the purchaser the object sold free from rights enforceable by third parties against the purchaser." Ownership, in other words, must be transferred free from any real or personal rights which might affect the purchaser's habere licere (see § 434 read together with § 440 II BGB). This includes servitudes. The legislator thus rejected the approach of Roman law, according to which incumbrances on land by way of servitudes are so common, that the

not hindered them, however, from making the vendor's liability still dependent upon eviction:

> "If a movable[69] has been sold and delivered to the purchaser for the purpose of transferring ownership, the purchaser may not demand compensation for non-performance on account of the right of a third party involving the possession of the thing, unless he has delivered the thing to the third party in consideration of his right",[70]

as the German BGB puts it.[71] The underlying policy is that the purchaser must not be allowed to claim damages *and* still have the thing sold at his disposal; hence this deviation from the normal rules of breach of contract. It is no longer necessary for the purchaser to defend an action brought by the third party; he can claim compensation for non-performance, even where he has voluntarily surrendered the object to him who claimed to have a better title, provided only that such surrender is not in conflict with the requirements of good faith.[72]

---

purchaser cannot assume the vendor's land to be free from them unless he has been given a specific promise to that effect. This type of reasoning, however, still prevails today with regard to public burdens on land (§ 436 BGB: "The seller of a piece of land does not warrant the land to be free from public taxes and other public burdens which are not appropriate for entry in the Land Register"). In Roman-Dutch and modern South African law the question is whether the old Dutch (Germanic) rule, according to which the vendor is under a duty not only of *waeren* but also of *vrijen*, has survived the reception of Roman law; see Van der Keessel, *Praelectiones*, ad Gr. III, XV, 4, and the discussion by Mostert, 1967 *Acta Juridica* 87 sqq. Further, on the problem of how far the guarantee of the vendor extends to freedom from servitudes, see Donellus, *Commentarii de Jure Civili*, Cap. VI, 8 sqq.; Pothier, *Traité du contrat de vente*, nn. 200 sqq.; Vangerow, *Pandekten*, § 610, n. 2 (pp. 315 sqq.).

[69] In case of land (ownership of which is transferred not by agreement and delivery, but by agreement and registration in the Land Register) the general rule of § 440 I BGB applies ("If the seller does not fulfil the obligations imposed upon him by §§ 433 to 437, 439, the rights of the purchaser are determined according to the provisions of §§ 320 to 327").

[70] Or has returned it to the seller, or unless the thing has been destroyed (sc.: if such destruction has its origin in the defect in title).

[71] § 440 II. In evaluating this rule, it has to be taken into consideration that liability on account of eviction under the BGB does not have the same importance as in the ius commune, since the "nemo plus iuris" rule no longer applies: according to §§ 932 sqq. BGB the purchaser can acquire ownership in good faith from a non-owner. On the other hand, however, the periods for acquisitive prescription of ownership were much shorter in the ius commune than they are under the BGB. For similar considerations relating to the comparison between Roman and English law, see Powell, *Studies de Zulueta*, pp. 78 sqq. Cf. further already §§ 317 I 5, 135, 136, 143 I 11 PrALR (read together with § 1 I 11); §§ 922, 1053 ABGB; artt. 1625 sqq. code civil. For a comparative analysis (Roman Law, French law and Louisiana Civil Code), see Alexander E. Ralston, "Warranty of Title or Warranty of Peaceable Possession in Louisiana?", (1940–41) 15 *Tulane LR* 115 sqq.; John H. Baldwin, "Warranty Against Eviction in the Civil Law: Extent of the Vendee's Recovery", (1948–49) 23 *Tulane LR* 140 sqq.; Charles J. Boudreaux, "Warranty Against Eviction in the Civil Law: Limitations on the Extent of the Vendee's Recovery", (1948–49) 23 *Tulane LR* 154 sqq.; cf. also Coing, *Gesammelte Aufsätze*, vol. I, op. cit., note 17, pp. 65 sq.

[72] Cf. in this context § 442 BGB, according to which the purchaser has to prove the defect in title.

II. LIABILITY FOR LATENT DEFECTS

1. Introduction

(a) The remedies: Roman tradition and natural law

If the object that has been sold and handed over to the purchaser subsequently turns out to suffer from a defect which diminishes its value for its ordinary use or for the use provided for in the contract, the purchaser, according to modern German law, has a choice between two remedies: he may demand annulment of the sale (with the result that the parties are obliged to return their mutual performances) or he can ask for a reduction of the purchase price.[73] If a promised quality in the thing sold was absent at the time of the purchase, or if the seller has fraudulently concealed a defect, a third alternative is available to the purchaser: instead of cancellation or reduction, he may demand compensation for non-performance, i.e. his positive interest.[74] Except where the seller has fraudulently concealed the defect, all these claims prescribe within a very short time: within six months after delivery in the case of movables, within one year after transfer for land.[75]

These rules display quite a remarkable degree of traditionalism on the part of the fathers of the BGB; they have preserved all the essential elements of the Roman law relating to latent defects, as embodied in the Corpus Juris Civilis. Yet, the rules do not, I think, strike the unbiased reader as particularly simple or obvious solutions to the problem. They did, for instance, not commend themselves to those writers who wanted to get away from the idiosyncrasies of the ius positivum and who tried to create a system of law based on reason: the natural lawyers of the 17th and 18th centuries.[76] They proceeded from the basis of the objective equality of performances within a contract: "In contractibus natura aequalitatem imperat, et ita quidem ut ex inaequalitate jus oriatur minus habenti".[77] Whether this principle was based directly upon the precepts of social ethics or upon the presumptive wishes of the parties (". . . in emtione venditione is esse videtur animus contrahentibus, ut observetur aequalitas, nisi fortes rationes adsint in contrarium"),[78] latent defects in the object sold were for them *one* instance of inaequalitas which the law had to remedy. They did not present special problems and therefore did not need to be dealt with by way of a ius singulare. "Vitium rei", defines Christian Wolff,[79]

> "dicitur accidens, quod eidem inhaeret et rem usui suo minus aptam redidit. Cum res ementur propter eum, quam habere debent usum, consequenter nemo res vitiosas

---

[73] §§ 459, 462 BGB.
[74] § 463 BGB.
[75] § 477 BGB.
[76] For details, see Walter Jürgen Klempt, *Die Grundlagen der Sachmängelhaftung des Verkäufers im Vernunftrecht und Usus modernus* (1967), pp. 26 sqq.
[77] Grotius, *De jure belli ac pacis*, Lib. II, Cap. XII, 8.
[78] Christian Wolff, *Jus naturae*, Pars IV, Cap. IV, § 977.
[79] *Institutiones juris naturae et gentium*, § 618.

emere velle praesumatur; vitia rei, quae in oculos non incurrunt, vel aliunde nota sunt, emtori indicare tenetur venditor . . . Et quia vitium rei aestimabile quid est, quatenus scilicet rem per se ad aliquem usum aptam ineptam reddit; vitia pretium rei imminuunt, immo si quod vitium rem prorsus inutilem reddit, eam nullius pretii faciunt. . . . si res prorsus inutilis fuerit ob vitium latens, pretium emtori restituendum, si vero adhuc usum habere potest, aut alio modo damnum reparari, damnum saltem datum resarciendum. Haud difficulter patet, jura, quae tertius in re emta habet, vitiis annumeranda esse."

Defect in title and in quality are placed side by side.[80]

(b) The implied conditions of the Sale of Goods Act

The Romanistic system of remedies for latent defects did not commend itself to the English courts and legislators either. As in the case of the seller's duty to pass a good title, the courts had started to provide some measure of implied protection.[81] Today, however, the Sale of Goods Act imposes a series of graduated duties upon the seller. Where goods are sold by description, there is an implied condition that the goods correspond with their description.[82] Under certain circumstances there is the further implied condition that the goods are merchantable;[83] and, finally, in still more limited circumstances, the condition that the goods are fit for a particular purpose is implied in the contract of sale.[84] In case of a breach of one of these conditions, the purchaser may repudiate the contract of sale, reject the goods and claim damages, or he may claim damages only.[85] This intricate system of conditions, which frequently overlap in practice,[86] is certainly no less complicated than the corresponding rules of Roman law, but it is distinctly different. One thing, however, Roman law and the English common law originally had in common: both accepted a fairly harsh idea of caveat emptor,[87]

---

[80] Cf. also Pothier, *Pandectae Justinianae*, vol. VIII, Lib. XIX, Tit. 1, Art. V, XLVIII, XLIX: "Quum venditor praestare teneatur rem emptori habere licere, sequitur eum ex empto teneri praestare eas qualitates in re vendita abesse, per quas non liceat eam habere, aut per quas eam inutiliter haberet emptor . . . De caeteris autem vitiis quae non impediunt quominus rem habere liceat, venditor qui ea ignoravit et de his tacuit, nullatenus tenetur."

[81] Atiyah, *Rise and Fall*, pp. 464 sqq. For the historical development cf. Rheinstein, *Struktur*, pp. 42 sqq.; Samuel J. Stoljar, "Conditions, Warranties and Descriptions of Quality in Sale of Goods I", (1952) 15 *Modern LR* 432 sqq.

[82] S. 13 I, II.

[83] S. 14 II, 15 II.

[84] S. 14 III.

[85] Cf. ss. 11 III, 53.

[86] For details, see Patrick S. Atiyah, *The Sale of Goods* (7th ed., 1985).

[87] "[A] Latin proverb of late Anglican vintage": Walton H. Hamilton, "The Ancient Maxim Caveat Emptor", (1931) 40 *Yale LJ* 1186. Hamilton shows (pp. 1163 sqq.) how it won judicial acceptance with the rise of individualism and freedom of contract. "Not until the nineteenth century, did judges discover that caveat emptor sharpened wits, taught self-reliance, made a man—an economic man—out of the buyer, and served well its two masters, business and justice." Along the same lines Atiyah, *Rise and Fall*, pp. 178 sqq., 464 ("The doctrine of caveat emptor can be said to represent the apotheosis of nineteenth-century individualism"). The leading case had always been *Chandelor v. Lopus* (1603) Cro Jac 4, where a jeweller had sold a stone affirming it to be a Bezoar stone (i.e. a stone that is

before the attitude of the law gradually changed in favour of the purchaser. But, whereas this change came about at a relatively early stage in Rome, we still find English courts espousing the old idea in the beginning of the 19th century. If the object bought turned out to be defective, the purchaser could not normally avail himself of any remedy, because "it was [his] fault . . . that he did not insist on a [sc.: express] warranty".[88]

(c) Caveat emptor

Caveat emptor is the principle governing the sale of goods in all early legal systems. The old German law has several proverbial sayings to that effect: *"Augen auf, Kauf ist Kauf"*, *"Wer die Augen nicht auftut, der tue den Beutel auf"*, *"Wer närrisch kauft, muss weislich bezahlen"*, etc.[89] What all these maxims reflect is *"Kauf vor Augen"*, a situation in which the contract of sale is concluded and executed at one and the same time, in the presence of both parties. The purchaser has the object of the sale "before his eyes" and it can therefore be expected of him to examine it properly before he concludes the bargain.[90] After all: "ius vigilantibus scriptum"; as long as he can see what he buys and is able to satisfy himself of its quality, the Roman paterfamilias can be relied upon to look after his own interests and not, for instance, to pay the normal purchase price for a slave who is without one arm or leg.

It is a harsh but healthy attitude of the law to prevent the purchaser from trying to go back on the terms of the contract under these circumstances. For if an object turns out to be defective, it is in any event always very difficult to prove that such a defect existed already at the time when the contract was concluded or when the object was

---

found in the stomach or intestines of certain animals). It turned out that the stone was in fact not a Bezoar stone. Nevertheless, the purchaser lost his case because the vendor had only affirmed, not warranted it to be a Bezoar stone. In the Middle Ages, a very strict and detailed system of regulation of marketplaces and materials and methods of manufacture, and also the gild system compensated, to a certain extent, for the lack of common- law protection of the purchaser; cf. e.g. Hamilton, pp. 1141 sqq.; Gustav Klemens Schmelzeisen, *Polizeiordnungen und Privatrecht* (1955), pp. 423 sqq.

[88] *Parkinson v. Lee* (1802) 2 East 314; but cf. also still *Smith v. Hughes* (1871) LR 6 QB 597 at 604 sq. per Cockburn CJ: "Now, in this case, there was plainly no legal obligation in the plaintiff in the first instance to state whether the oats were new or old. He offered them for sale according to the sample, as he had a perfect right to do, and gave the buyer the fullest opportunity of inspecting the sample. . . . If, indeed, the buyer, instead of acting on his own opinion, had asked the question whether the oats were old or new, or had said anything which intimated his understanding that the seller was selling the oats as old oats, the case would have been wholly different . . . Here, however, nothing of the sort occurs. The buyer in no way refers to the seller, but acts entirely on his own judgement."

[89] Cf. Eduard Graf, Mathias Dietherr, *Deutsche Rechtssprichwörter* (2nd ed., 1869), pp. 259 sqq. The same applies in other countries; cf. the proverb "let their eye be their chapman" (cf. Hamilton, (1931) 40 *Yale LJ* 1164) or *"qui n'ouvre pas yeux doit ouvrir la bourse"*.

[90] "But when householders bought most of their commodities at local markets or fairs, when they were able to examine what they bought by look and feel, and haggle over the price, it may be that they 'would be more likely to feel ashamed of being outwitted than outraged at being swindled'" (Atiyah, *Rise and Fall*, pp. 179 sq.).

transferred. There is often a strong possibility that the deterioration in quality might have taken place subsequently; that is why modern German law lays down very short prescription periods, which begin to run, not when the purchaser has (or could have) detected the defect, but from the time of delivery (transfer). However, what may have been an acceptable (if somewhat crude) policy in the small rural community of old, which knew only the executed sale, did not tie in with the refined standards of good faith which governed the classical, executory contract. As in the case of liability for eviction, the protection of the purchaser developed gradually and from a variety of roots.

2. Early remedies

First of all, already in the ancient law we find the actio de modo agri.[91] Where land was mancipated and the vendor had stated by way of a lex mancipio dicta (a formal declaration made in the course of mancipatio) that it was of a particular size, he was liable for the proportionate amount of the price if the actual acreage turned out to be less than asserted. This liability was subject to litiscrescence,[92] i.e. if the vendor (defendant) disputed the claim and had to be sued, he was condemned to pay double the amount involved (infitiando lis crescit in duplum).[93] The actio de modo agri survived in classical law, albeit under new auspices,[94] but fell away together with mancipatio in Justinian's time.[95] Could the purchaser also make the vendor liable for dicta in mancipio, which did not relate to the size of land but to other characteristics, qualities or freedom from defects of res mancipi at large?[96] We do not know, for we have only a statement by Cicero[97] which may be read to imply that the phrase "uti lingua nuncupasset ita ius esto" in tab. 6, 1 of the XII Tables was applied to vitia in general. However, Cicero was no lawyer and his statements do at times display a certain lack of technical precision.

3. Liability for dolus and dicta in venditione

By the time of the late Republic the actio empti had become available where the vendor had acted in such a way that not to make him liable would have seemed in conflict with good faith. Two groups of cases fall into this category. Firstly, the vendor was responsible where he had

[91] Bechmann, vol. I, pp. 247 sqq.; Lenel, Quellenforschungen in den Edictcommentaren (1882) 3 *ZSS* 190 sqq.; Watson, *Obligations*, pp. 81 sqq.; Kaser, *RPr* I, pp. 133 sq.

[92] Cicero, *De officiis*, 3, XVI–65; Paul. Sent. I, XIX, 1.

[93] Kaser, *RZ*, pp. 99 sq.

[94] Levy, *Obligationenrecht*, pp. 229 sqq.

[95] Cf. e.g. Bechmann, vol. III, 2, pp. 218 sqq.

[96] Raymond Monier, *La garantie contre les vices cachés dans la vente romaine* (1930), pp. 6 sqq.; Arangio-Ruiz, *Compravendita*, pp. 353 sq.; Olde Kalter, op. cit., note 24, pp. 33 sqq.; Honsell, *Quod interest*, pp. 62 sqq.

[97] *De officiis*, 3, XVI–65.

fraudulently (dolo malo) failed to disclose a defect known to him.[98] The earliest case of which we know was decided by Marcus Porcius Cato. A man of the name of Titius Claudius Centumalus sold his house, which was situated on the mons Coelius, to Publius Calpurnius Lanarius. He did not mention that the augurs had ordered the demolition of this house, because its height obstructed their observation of the flight of birds.[99] About Cato's decision we hear: "[C]um in vendendo rem eam scisset et non pronuntiasset, emptori damnum praestari oportere."[100] A variety of further examples is contained in the Digest, for instance Paul. D. 19, 1, 4 pr.:[101] "Si servum mihi ignoranti, sciens furem vel noxium esse, vendideris, . . . teneris mihi ex empto, quanti mea intererit scisse. . . ." In order to sue the vendor, the purchaser did not have to wait until he lost the slave (by way of noxae deditio).

Secondly, the vendor was also liable under the actio empti, where he had specifically assured the purchaser, in the course of concluding the sale, that the object was free from certain (or all) defects or that it possessed certain qualities.[102] For an example of such liability arising from dicta in venditione we may turn to Pomp. D. 19, 1, 6, 4: "Si vas aliquod mihi vendideris et dixeris certam mensuram capere vel certum pondus habere, ex empto tecum agam, si minus praestes."[103] What necessitated a deviation from caveat emptor in this instance was not so much bad faith on the part of the vendor, but the fact that his dicta had engendered reasonable reliance in the person of the purchaser.

The actio empti, in all these cases, lay for quod actoris interest. One of the most explicit texts is Ulp. D. 19, 1, 13 pr.:[104]

> "Iulianus . . . ait . . . qui pecus morbosum aut tignum vitiosum vendidit . . . si . . . sciens reticuit et emptorem decepit, omnia detrimenta, quae ex ea emptione emptor traxerit, praestaturum ei: sive igitur aedes vitio tigni corruerunt, aedium aestimationem, sive pecora contagione morbosi pecoris perierunt, quod interfuit idone venisse erit praestandum."

Julian mentions two examples: the sale of defective timber and of animals suffering from a contagious disease. The vendor is liable not

---

[98] Monier, op. cit., note 96, pp. 177 sqq.; Paul van Warmelo, *Vrywaring teen gebreke by koop in Suid-Afrika* (1941), pp. 53 sqq; Stein, *Fault*, pp. 5 sqq.; Honsell, *Quod interest*, pp. 79 sqq. Cf. also David Daube, "Three Notes on Digest 18. 1, Conclusion of Sale", (1957) 73 *LQR* 379 sqq. (dealing with Gai. D. 18, 1, 35, 8 and fraudulent concealment of (the existence of) a neighbour, so that the estate sold appears larger than it is).

[99] This case lies on the borderline between defectiveness of the object sold and legal defects.

[100] Cicero, *De officiis*, 3, XVI—66.

[101] Cf. also, for instance, Viv./Ulp. D. 21, 1, 1, 10; Ulp. D. 21, 1, 38, 7 in fine.

[102] Monier, op. cit., note 96, pp. 134 sqq.; Olde Kalter, op. cit., note 24, pp. 54 sqq.; Stein, *Fault*, pp. 28 sqq. The use of specific words or forms was not required; this was different, for instance, in English law up to the 19th century following *Chandelor v. Lopus* (supra note 82).

[103] Cf. further e.g. Lab. D. 18, 1, 78, 3; Gai. D. 18, 6, 16 (relating to the sale of wine).

[104] Cf. further Pomp. D. 19, 1, 6, 4; Ulp. D. 19, 1, 13, 2; Marci. D. 18, 1, 45 and Medicus, *Id quod interest*, pp. 128, 299; Honsell, *Quod interest*, pp. 87 sqq.

only for the reduced value of the objects themselves but also for consequential loss: if the house that has been built with the bad timber collapses, or if the purchaser's cattle die owing to infection, compensation for these damages is within the compass of the actio empti.

4. Liability arising from specific promissa

If the purchaser wanted to make sure that the thing sold was either free from specific defects or that it had certain qualities, he could also ask the vendor for a stipulation to that effect.[105] Such promissa were usually combined with the stipulatio duplae against eviction;[106] unlike the latter, however, they did not lie for duplum, but covered the purchaser's interest in the truth of the affirmations. Again, quod interest (in this instance under the actio ex stipulatu) could go beyond compensation for the lesser value of the object sold.[107] There was a somewhat scholastic dispute as to whether such stipulations could in principle be regarded as valid:

> "Si ita quis stipulanti spondeat sanum esse, furem non esse, vispellionem non esse et cetera, inutilis stipulatio quibusdam videtur, quia si quis est in hac causa, impossibile est quod promittitur, si non est, frustra est. sed ego puto verius hanc stipulationem furem non esse, vispellionem[108] non esse, sanum esse utilem esse: hoc enim continere, quod interest horum quid esse vel horum quid non esse. . . ."[109]

A promise to the effect that the slave sold is healthy, it was argued, is useless: for either the slave is healthy, in which case the stipulation does not have any practical relevance; or he is not healthy—then the vendor has promised something which is objectively impossible. But this argument does not hold water. What the vendor promises is neither the absence of a defect nor the presence of a certain quality, but to pay damages if, contrary to his affirmation, the thing sold does have this defect or does lack the specific quality:

> ". . . hac stipulatione non agitur, ut factum infectum fiat, et quod est non sit, sed quanti interest, furem non esse praestari, vel quanti interest furtum non fieri, quod omnimodo utilem actionem efficiat."[110]

---

[105] Monier, op. cit., note 96, pp. 10 sqq.; Arangio-Ruiz, *Compravendita*, pp. 355 sqq.

[106] Cf. e.g. Varro, *De re rustica*, Lib. II, 2, 6; Lib. II, 3, 5; Lib. II, 4, 4; Lib. II, 10, 5.

[107] Honsell, *Quod interest*, pp. 63 sqq.; contra: Medicus, *Id quod interest*, pp. 110 sqq., 117.

[108] A vispellio was a person whose profession it was to carry corpses, not, as has frequently been assumed, a violator of graves. Why would a purchaser not wish to have a vispellio? They stood at the lowest end of the social hierarchy and were usually regarded as very shadowy figures. Meddling with sinister affairs, usually being found in bad company and making their money by burying the poor at night, they were turpes personae. For details, see Uwe Wesel, "Vispellio", (1963) 80 *ZSS* 392 sqq.

[109] Ulp. D. 21, 2, 31.

[110] Cuiacius, as quoted by Honsell, *Quod interest*, p. 66; Arangio-Ruiz, *Compravendita*, p. 357.

5. The aedilitian remedies

(a) The sale of slaves

The most interesting and—in the long run—influential inroad on the principle of caveat emptor originated in the jurisdiction of the aediles curules over market transactions.[111] Economically, one of the most important articles sold on the market were slaves. Slave-traders (mangones) were notoriously ill-reputed people, and thus one had to be particularly careful in one's dealings with them.[112] Warranties relating to the quality of slaves sold by way of stipulation seem to have been so common that the aediles curules felt called upon to regulate the matter comprehensively and to make certain remedies available in their edict.[113] The Digest still preserves the wording of this part of the aedilitian edict:

> "Qui mancipia vendunt certiores faciant emptores, quid morbi vitiive cuique sit, quis fugitivus errove sit noxave solutus non sit: eademque omnia, cum ea mancipia venibunt, palam recte pronuntianto,[114] quodsi mancipium adversus ea venisset, sive adversus quod dictum promissumve fuerit cum veniret, fuisset, quod eius praestari oportere dicetur: emptori omnibusque ad quos ea res pertinet iudicium dabimus, ut id mancipium redhibeatur. . . ."[115]

The individual slaves wore a board on which the vendor was required to inform potential purchasers of everything that could be classified as morbus or vitium.

(b) Morbus and vitium

What did these entail? First of all, only those diseases or physical defects that were not apparent. The aedilitian remedies applied only to latent defects.[116] After all, we are dealing with a market transaction and the purchaser had the opportunity to examine the slaves before he bought any of them. If he did not realize[117] that the slave was female instead of male, that his eyes had been knocked out or that he had a big and

[111] On the jurisdiction of the aediles generally, see Giambattista Impallomeni, *L'editto degli edili curuli* (1955), pp. 109 sqq.; Max Kaser, "Die Jurisdiktion der kurulischen Ädilen", in: *Mélanges Philippe Meylan*, vol. I (1963), pp. 173 sqq.

[112] Cf. e.g. Paul. D. 21, 1, 44, 1.

[113] Introduced in the early part of the 2nd century B.C., perhaps in the year 199; cf. A. de Senarclens, "La date de l'édit des Édiles de mancipiis vendundis", (1923) 4 *TR* 384 sqq.; idem, "Servus Recepticius", (1933) 12 *TR* 390 sqq.; Impallomeni, op. cit., note 111, pp. 90 sqq.; David Daube, *Forms of Roman Legislation*, pp. 91 sqq.

[114] On the use of imperatives in the aedilitian edict, see David Daube, *Forms of Roman Legislation* (1956), pp. 91 sqq.; Alan Watson, "The Imperatives of the Aedilitian Edict", (1971) 39 *TR* 73 sqq.

[115] Ulp. D. 21, 1, 1, 1.

[116] Ulp. D. 21, 1, 1, 6; Van Warmelo, op. cit., note 98, pp. 13 sqq.

[117] As to the relevant test, see Ulp. D. 21, 1, 14, 10: "Si nominatim morbus exceptus non sit, talis tamen morbus sit, qui omnibus potuit apparere . . ., eius nomine non teneri Caecilius ait, perinde ac si nominatim morbus exceptus fuisset: ad eos enim morbos vitiaque pertinere edictum aedilium probandum est, quae quis ignoravit vel ignorare potuit."

dangerous scar across his face,[118] he had, as Florentinus put it,[119] deceived himself and was precluded from taking recourse against the vendor. Secondly, it is obvious that not every defect could reasonably be expected to be displayed on the board. There is no standardized human being; everybody has some or other characteristics which may possibly be classified as a "defect". "Morbus" was usually defined as

> "habitu[s] cuiusque corporis contra naturam, qui usum eius ad id facit deteriorem, cuius causa natura nobis eius corporis sanitatem dedit".[120]

What mattered was whether the slave's fitness for use was impaired by the disease.[121] Therefore, the slave had to be suffering from a genuine, grave sickness—something which in a different context was referred to as morbus sonticus.[122] "Vitium", the other term mentioned in the edict, like morbus, referred only to physical defects;[123] how it related to morbus, was disputed. Sabinus insisted on the difference between both terms ("vitiumque a morbo multum differre"), but Ulpianus took them to constitute a hendiadys ("ego puto aediles tollendae dubitationis gratia bis κατὰ τοῦ αὑτοῦ idem dixisse, ne qua dubitatio superesset").[124] But whatever the relationship between morbus and vitium may have been, the more crucial distinction between what amounted to a physical defect or disease, of which the purchaser had to be notified, and what were seen as more minor matters which did not interfere with the use and services of the slave and with which the purchaser had to make do, was an apparently inexhaustible source of a somewhat weird casuistry.[125] Especially the first 15 fragments contained in the Digest titled "De aedilicio edicto et redhibitione et quanti minoris" preserve a wealth of examples.[126] Today they make curious and somewhat melancholic reading—and provide an idea of how eager many Romans

---

[118] Cf. Ulp. D. 21, 1, 14, 10: ". . . (ut puta caecus homo venibat, aut qui cicatricem evidentem et periculosam habebat vel in capite vel in alia parte [aperta?] corporis). . . ."

[119] D. 18, 1, 43, 1.

[120] Sab./Ulp. D. 21, 1, 1, 7; cf. also Aulus Gellius, *Noctes Atticae*, Lib. IV, II, 3.

[121] Ulp. D. 21, 1, 1, 8: "Proinde si quid tale fuerit vitii sive morbi, quod usum ministeriumque hominis impediat, id dabit redhibitioni locum. . . ."

[122] Ulp. D. 21, 1, 4, 5. Morbus sonticus excused the disregard of a summons (cf. tab. 2, 2 of the XII Tables and Aulus Gellius, *Noctes Atticae*, Lib. XX, I, 27). "Sonticus", etymologically, is an adjective from sum (in the sense of "definitely being", "overwhelmingly real"). The participle "sons" (the one who is) is used in the sense of guilty and lies at the root of the word for sin (both in English and German). On all this, see the analysis by David Daube, "Pecco Ergo Sum", (1985) 4 *RJ* 137 sqq.

[123] Ulp. D. 21, 1, 4, 3: "Et videmur hoc iure uti, ut vitii morbique appellatio non videatur pertinere nisi ad corpora."

[124] Sab./Ulp. D. 21, 1, 1, 7.

[125] "The jurists are perhaps not at their best in D. 21, 1": A. Rogerson, "Implied Warranty Against Latent Defects in Roman and English Law", in: *Studies in the Roman Law of Sale in memory of Francis de Zulueta* (1959), p. 121.

[126] But see also Aulus Gellius, *Noctes Atticae*, Lib. IV, II.

seem to have been to sell their old and sick slaves.[127] Thus, attention had to be drawn to the fact that the slave suffered from consumption[128] or podagra,[129] from a disease affecting lung, liver[130] or bladder,[131] from morbus comitialis (epileptic fits)[132] or any other chronic diseases.[133] The same applied if the slave was short-sighted,[134] blind during parts of the day[135] or dumb,[136] if he had a tumor or a nasal polypus,[137] if he had been castrated in a way that the organ required for the purposes of reproduction was totally absent,[138] or if he had been born with fingers that were joined together, so that he was prevented from properly using his hands.[139] A female slave was morbosa or vitiosa if due to a uterine disease she could give birth only to dead children,[140] if her vagina was so narrow that she could not become a woman,[141] or if she menstruated twice a month (or not at all, unless that was due to her age).[142] On the other hand, the purchaser could not complain if he subsequently found out that the slave suffered from slight feverishness, from an old quartan fever,[143] or from a light running of the eyes,[144] that in a spell of religious ecstasy he had made oracular pronouncements (as long as that did not occur habitually),[145] that he could only speak with difficulty,[146] stammered or lisped,[147] that he was knock-kneed or bow-legged,[148] that he had been born with a goiter, with protruding eyes,[149] or with more than the ordinary number of fingers or toes.[150] A left-handed slave was not diseased or defective,[151] nor was one who had bad breath or smelled like a goat,[152] who squinted[153] or who passed urine in bed (as long as this was due to sleep, wine or sluggishness in rising, not to a disease).[154] What if the slave had lost a tooth? He was not defective, since otherwise all babies (who have no teeth at all) would have had to be considered defective, too.[155]

---

[127] Cf. also Cato, *De agri cultura*, II; Honsell, "Von den ädilizischen Rechtsbehelfen zum modernen Sachmängelrecht", in: *Gedächtnisschrift für Wolfgang Kunkel* (1984), pp. 58 sq.

[128] Ulp. D. 21, 1, 1, 7. [129] Jav. D. 21, 1, 53.

[130] Ulp. D. 21, 1, 12, 4. [131] Ulp. D. 21, 1, 14, 4.

[132] Jav. D. 21, 1, 53. Epilepsy was referred to as morbus comitialis, because, if the fits occurred in a popular assembly (comitia), an immediate interruption and postponement of the gathering took place, since this was considered a bad omen. Cf. e.g. Berger, *ED*, p. 587.

[133] Ulp. D. 21, 1, 6 pr. [134] Ulp. D. 21, 1, 10, 3.

[135] Ulp. D. 21, 1, 10, 4 (". . . ubi homo neque matutino tempore videt neque vespertino").

[136] Ulp. D. 21, 1, 9. [137] Ulp. D. 21, 1, 12 pr. [138] Ulp. D. 21, 1, 7.

[139] Ulp. D. 21, 1, 14, 6. [140] Ulp. D. 21, 1, 14 pr. [141] Ulp. D. 21, 1, 14, 7.

[142] Paul. D. 21, 1, 15. [143] Ulp. D. 21, 1, 1, 8. [144] Ulp. D. 21, 1, 4, 6.

[145] Viv./Ulp. D. 21, 1, 1, 10. [146] Ulp. D. 21, 1, 9. [147] Ulp. D. 21, 1, 10, 5.

[148] Ulp. D. 21, 1, 10, 5. [149] Ulp. D. 21, 1, 12, 2. [150] Ulp. D. 21, 1, 10, 2.

[151] Ulp. D. 21, 1, 12, 3. [152] Ulp. D. 21, 1, 12, 4. [153] Ulp. D. 21, 1, 12, 4.

[154] Ulp. D. 21, 1, 14, 4. [155] Paul. D. 21, 1, 11.

(c) Defects of character

Defects of character, as has been indicated, were not covered by the term "vitium".[156] It would have been quite absurd to call every slave defective who was giddy, superstitious, irascible or insolent,[157] timid, avaricious[158] or melancholic,[159] given to gambling, drinking, lying or quarreling.[160] Hardly anybody could have been called healthy or normal under those circumstances. Yet, the lack of some of these vitia animi was so crucial to the purchasers that they usually asked the vendor for a specific assurance to that effect. The aediles curules therefore placed them on the same level as morbi and vitia and made the vendor declare a certain number of character defects, too: whether the slave was a runaway (fugitivus),[161] a person with the habit of roving about (erro),[162] or somebody who had perpetrated a capital crime,[163] who was prone to committing suicide[164] or who had fought wild beasts in the arena.[165] Besides these, there was one other flaw which had to be displayed on the board if the vendor wanted to avoid liability, even though it was neither a physical nor a character defect: whether the slave was still burdened with noxal liability (noxa non solutus).[166] If he had committed a delict, his master was liable: he could either pay the damages as if he had himself been guilty of the delict or he could

[156] Ulp. D. 21, 1, 4, 3: ". . . animi autem vitium ita demum praestabit venditor, si promisit, si minus, non"; Viv./Ulp. D. 21, 1, 1, 10. Brunnemann, *Commentarius*, Lib. XXI, 1, Ad L. Labeo, I, § 3, n. 8 gives this reason: ". . . quia animi vitia facilius poenis, aliisque modis in servis corrigi possunt."

[157] Viv./Ulp. D. 21, 1, 1, 9.

[158] Viv./Ulp. D. 21, 1, 1, 10.

[159] Paul. D. 21, 1, 2.

[160] Pomp./Ulp. D. 21, 1, 4, 2.

[161] For a massive amount of casuistry, see Ulp. D. 21, 1, 17.

[162] For a definition, see Ulp. D. 21, 1, 17, 14.

[163] Ulp. D. 21, 1, 1, 1; Ulp. D. 21, 1, 23, 2.

[164] Ulp. D. 21, 1, 1, 1; Ulp. D. 21, 1, 23, 3, with a very interesting reasoning: ". . . malus servus creditus est, qui aliquid facit, quo magis se rebus humanis extrahat, ut puta laqueum torsit sive medicamentum pro veneno bibit praecipitumve se ex alto miserit aliudve quid fecerit, quo facto speravit mortem perventuram, tamquam non nihil in alium ausurus, qui hoc adversus se ausus est." A breath-taking piece of early criminology; the person who had attempted suicide had demonstrated that he had no respect for life; he was a bad (and dangerous) person, because he was likely to try to do to another what he had attempted against himself. A modern variant of this idea can be found in §§ 211, 212 StGB (dealing with murder and wilful manslaughter), if Eberhard Schmidhäuser's argument ("Selbstmord und Beteiligung am Selbstmord in strafrechtlicher Sicht", in: *Festschrift für Hans Welzel* (1974), pp. 801 sqq.) is correct that both sections as far as their objective requirements are concerned, place the killing of another and suicide on the same level; their wording is: "Who kills a person . . .", not "Who kills another . . .". Schmidhäuser then carries on to argue that, since (attempted) suicide is an unlawful act (which is not punishable only due to an extra-legal exculpation ground), the aider and abettor has committed a crime and can consequently be punished. But see Albin Eser, in: Alfred Schönke, Horst Schröder, *Strafgesetzbuch* (23rd ed., 1988), Vorbem. §§ 211 sqq., nn. 33 sqq. for the prevailing opinion in German criminal law. On the fascinating topic of the evaluation of suicide in Roman law and society, see the study by Andreas Wacke, "Der Selbstmord im römischen Recht und in der Rechtsentwicklung", (1980) 97 *ZSS* 26 sqq.

[165] Ulp. D. 21, 1, 1, 1.

[166] Ulp. D. 21, 1, 1, 1; Ulp. D. 21, 1, 17, 17–19.

surrender the slave (noxae deditio). However, liability attached to the person who was master at the time when the noxal suit was brought: noxa caput sequitur.[167] Hence it was extremely important for the purchaser to know whether acquisition of the slave exposed him to possibly far-reaching delictual claims by third parties.[168]

(d) Dicta promissave

The parties were free to extend the scope of the vendor's warranty beyond these limits; an affirmation (be it by way of dictum in venditione, be it by way of formal promise) that the slave was free from further defects or that he possessed special qualities, which mattered to the purchaser in the individual case,[169] was sufficient.[170] The technical term for these formal or informal declarations was "dicta promissave".[171] They were binding and led to liability under the aedilitian edict.[172]

In practice, it was not always easy to draw a line between dicta and promissa on the one hand and the usual non-binding sales talk on the other. Each vendor is inclined to praise his goods[173] and as long as such praise remains either on a fairly general level or consists in the ostentatious exaggerations of notorious puffers, no sensible purchaser will take it all too seriously; the legal system consequently has no reason for making the vendor liable.

> "Ea quae commendandi causa in venditionibus dicuntur, si palam appareant, venditorem non obligant, veluti si dicat servum speciosum, domum bene aedificatam: at si dixerit hominem litteratum vel artificem, praestare debet: nam hoc ipso pluris vendit."[174]

That the slave is handsome, the horse well built are statements of a general, non-committal nature. Matters look different if the slave is said to be litteratus (which can mean either literate or learned) or a skilled artisan. Along the same lines Ulpianus distinguishes between "ea, quae

---

[167] Gai. IV, 77; Ulp. D. 47, 2, 41, 2; see infra, p. 917.

[168] The vendor also had to declare the nationality of the slave—certain nations seem to have had a very bad reputation concerning the quality of their people; Ulp. D. 21, 1, 31, 21: "Qui mancipia vendunt, nationem cuiusque in venditione pronuntiare debent: plerumque enim natio servi aut provocat aut deterret emptorem: idcirco interest nostra scire nationem . . .". Cf. Impallomeni, op. cit., note 111, pp. 63 sqq.

[169] For instance, that he was an excellent cook: Gai. D. 21, 1, 18, 1.

[170] Cf. Ulp., Gai. D. 21, 1, 17, 20—19, 4.

[171] As to the distinction between dicta and promissa, see Ulp. D. 21, 1, 19, 2. That distinction was not crucial; in fact, the two became increasingly amalgamated. Dictum possibly continued to refer to a (unilateral) declaration by the vendor; promissum implied a bilateral arrangement. See Max Kaser, "Unlautere Warenanpreisungen beim römischen Kauf", in: *Festschrift für Heinrich Demelius* (1973), pp. 128 sq.

[172] Except where the defect was patent. Where, for instance, a slave, whose eyes had been knocked out, was sold and the seller promised that he was "sanus", this stipulation was taken to mean that the slave did not suffer from physical defects apart from his blindness: cf. Flor. D. 18, 1, 43, 1.

[173] "To things of sale a seller's praise belongs": *Love's Labour's Lost*, Act IV, Scene III, line 237.

[174] Flor. D. 18, 1, 43 pr.

ad nudam laudem servi pertinent: veluti si dixerit frugi probum dicto audientem" and binding statements such as "aleatorem non esse, furem non esse, ad statuam numquam confugisse".[175]

Finally, the vendor was also liable under the edict if he had in any way acted fraudulently.[176]

(e) "Redhibendi iudicium"

Now let us examine the remedies that were provided by the edict. First of all, the purchaser was entitled to ask the vendor for an express warranty in the form of a stipulation that the slave was in fact free from all defects which should have been declared and which were not apparent.[177] Where that warranty was given, the purchaser had the standard remedy of the actio ex stipulatu to claim quod interest in case of breach of warranty. If the vendor refused to comply with this request, there was reason to suspect that something might be wrong with the slave. Hence the purchaser was given the right, within two months, to demand repayment of the price against the return of the slave:

> "Si venditor de his quae edicto aedilium continentur non caveat, pollicentur adversus eum redhibendi iudicium intra duos menses vel quanti emptoris intersit intra six menses."[178]

The point of this "redhibendi iudicium" was that a purchaser whose confidence in the regularity of the transaction had been shattered was allowed to withdraw from it even before a defect had become apparent.[179] After those two months that he was given to decide whether or not he wanted to have the slave, even without warranty, or not, he was still able, within a further four months, to claim quod interest—but only if his interesse had been infringed, i.e. if the slave had in fact turned out to be defective. This is what Gaius seems to state in the latter part of the fragment quoted above, and it may well have been that this claim was based on a fictitious actio ex stipulatu: the purchaser could sue the vendor for what he would have been able to sue him for had the warranty been given.[180] But whether and on what basis

---

[175] D. 21, 1, 19 pr. Cf. further Olde Kalter, op. cit., note 24, pp. 48 sqq.; Stein, *Fault*, pp. 29 sqq.; Kaser, *Festschrift Demelius*, pp. 127 sqq.

[176] Ulp. D. 21, 1, 1, 1 in fine: "[H]oc amplius si quis adversus ea sciens dolo malo vendidisse dicetur, iudicium dabimus." This clause is difficult to understand; see, for example, Monier, op. cit., note 96, pp. 56 sqq.; Impallomeni, op. cit., note 111, pp. 30 sqq.; A.M. Honoré, "The History of the Aedilitian Actions from Roman to Roman-Dutch Law", in: *Studies in the Roman Law of Sale in memory of Francis de Zulueta* (1959), pp. 136 sqq. It probably applied in cases such as Flor. D. 18, 1, 43, 2 and Ulp. D. 4, 3, 37; cf. Kaser, *Festschrift Demelius*, pp. 127 sqq., 136 sq.

[177] Ulp. D. 21, 2, 37, 1 in fine (". . . per edictum autem curulium etiam de servo cavere venditor iubetur") and Monier, op. cit., note 96, pp. 87 sqq.; Impallomeni, op. cit., note 111, pp. 44 sqq.

[178] Gai. D. 21, 1, 28. [179] Honsell, *Quod interest*, p. 69.

[180] i.e. the same principles as in the case of the stipulatio duplae: cf. supra pp. 295 sqq., 300; Honsell, *Quod interest*, pp. 68 sqq.

this claim was actually granted, remains a matter of speculation.[181] In the course of time, it was superseded in any event by what has generally become known as "the" aedilitian remedies, the actiones redhibitoria and quanti minoris.

(f) The actio redhibitoria

Only the first of these actiones was proposed in that part of the aedilitian edict that has come down to us in Ulp. D. 21, 1, 1, 1. If the slave turned out to have one of the defects referred to in the edict, without the vendor having declared it, if a quality that had been specifically warranted was absent or a defect whose absence had been promised was present (i.e. in case of breach of dicta promissave) or if the vendor had acted fraudulently, the purchaser could return the slave and receive back the purchase price.[182] This was the main content of the actio redhibitoria, but there were further implications.[183] Both vendor and purchaser had to be restored to the same position as if the sale had not been concluded ("Iulianus ait iudicium redhibitoriae actionis utrumque, id est venditorem et emptorem, quodammodo in integrum restituere debere").[184] Thus, for instance, the purchaser had to be indemnified if the slave had committed a theft or done some other damage to his property[185] and he had to be reimbursed for what he had expended in connection with the sale.[186] This did not apply to the cost of maintaining the slave, as he did not have to reimburse the vendor for the value of the slave's services either.[187] The vendor, on the other hand, was entitled to "quid ad emptorem pervenit vel culpa eius non pervenit"[188] as, for instance (the usual school-book example), an inheritance which the purchaser had acquired through the slave. Furthermore, the purchaser was liable for any deterioration of the slave due to his (the purchaser's) fault.[189] There was one very important practical restriction on the actio redhibitoria: it could only be brought

---

[181] Usually the text is regarded as interpolated, the claim for interesse being thought to have been added by a post-classical reviser; cf. e.g. Monier, op. cit., note 96, pp. 104 sqq.; Arangio-Ruiz, *Compravendita*, p. 389. For a different interpretation, see Medicus, *Id quod interest*, pp. 118 sqq.

[182] Technically, condemnation of the vendor was dependent upon restitution of the slave; there was no action that the vendor could bring to get the slave returned. Cf. Ulp. D. 21, 1, 29 pr. and Uwe Wesel, "Zur dinglichen Wirkung der Rücktrittsvorbehalte des römischen Kaufs", (1968) 85 *ZSS* 141 sqq.

[183] For details, see Bechmann, vol. III, 2, pp. 118 sqq.; Impallomeni, op. cit., note 111, pp. 137 sqq.; Georg Thielmann, "'Actio redhibitoria' und zufälliger Untergang der Kaufsache", in: *Studi in onore di Edoardo Volterra*, vol. II (1971), pp. 487 sqq.; Honsell, *Quod interest*, pp. 70 sqq.

[184] Ulp. D. 21, 1, 23, 7; cf. also Ulp. D. 21, 1, 21 pr.

[185] Ulp. D. 21, 1, 23, 8; Paul. D. 21, 1, 58 pr.

[186] Ulp. D. 21, 1, 27; Ulp. D. 21, 1, 29, 3.

[187] Aristo/Paul. D. 21, 1, 30, 1.

[188] Ulp. D. 21, 1, 23, 9.

[189] Or that of his people ("familia" and "procurator"): cf. Ulp. D. 21, 1, 1, 1,; Ulp. D. 21, 1, 25; Ulp. D. 21, 1, 31, 12.

within six months.[190] However, this period began to run only once the defect had become apparent and the purchaser was thus able to discover it[191] (no matter whether he had in actual fact discovered it or not), and it was what was called "useful" time ("sex menses utiles"), that is, those days during which the purchaser was unable to pursue his claim (because of disease, captivity, etc.) were not counted.[192]

(g) The actio quanti minoris; the sale "sub corona"

Alternatively, the purchaser could bring the actio quanti minoris. Even though this remedy is not mentioned in Ulp. D. 21, 1, 1, 1, there is no doubt that it was already available in early classical law.[193] It allowed the purchaser to claim from the vendor "quanto ob id vitium minoris [fu]erit,"[194] that is, an amount representing the difference between what the slave was actually worth and what he would have been worth had he been free from defects or possessed the promised qualities. In the end result, that led to a reimbursement of part of the purchase price.[195] The actio quanti minoris could be brought within a year of prima potestas experiundi (vitium).[196]

If the vendor did not want to be responsible at all for the quality of a particular slave (which happened particularly in the case of prisoners of war), he usually made him wear a hat or a wreath, thus selling him "sub corona".[197]

(h) The sale of iumenta

Along very much the same lines the aediles dealt with another typical market transaction that fell under their jurisdiction: the sale of certain livestock.

> "Aediles aiunt: 'Qui iumenta vendunt, palam recte dicunto, quid in quoque eorum morbi vitiique sit, utique optime ornata vendendi causa fuerint, ita emptoribus tradentur. si quid ita factum non erit, de ornamentis restituendis iumentisve ornamentorum nomine redhibendis in diebus sexaginta, morbi autem vitiive causa inemptis faciendis in six mensibus, vel quo minoris cum venirent fuerint, in anno iudicium dabimus. . . .'"[198]

---

[190] Ulp. D. 21, 1, 19, 6.
[191] Pap. D. 21, 1, 55.
[192] Windscheid/Kipp, § 104.
[193] Cf. Aulus Gellius, *Noctes Atticae*, Lib. IV, II, 5; and Fritz Pringsheim, "Das Alter der aedilizischen actio quanti minoris", (1952) 69 *ZSS* 234 sqq.; Arangio-Ruiz, *Compravendita*, pp. 381 sqq.; Impallomeni, op. cit., note 111, pp. 194 sqq.
[194] Aulus Gellius, loc. cit.; cf. also Ulp. D. 21, 1, 38 pr.
[195] For details, see Bechmann, vol. III, 2, pp. 160 sqq.; G.A. Mulligan, "Quanti Minoris Than What", (1953) 70 *SALJ* 132 sqq.; Medicus, *Id quod interest*, pp. 124 sq.; Honsell, *Quod interest*, pp. 74 sqq.
[196] Ulp. D. 21, 1, 38 pr. and cf. Pap. D. 21, 1, 55.
[197] Aulus Gellius, *Noctes Atticae*, Lib. VI, IV; as far as exclusion of liability is concerned, cf. also Ulp. D. 21, 1, 14, 9 and Impallomeni, op. cit., note 111, pp. 20 sqq.
[198] Ulp. D. 21, 1, 38 pr. See Monier, op. cit., note 96, pp. 46 sqq.; Arangio-Ruiz, *Compravendita*, pp. 380 sqq.; Impallomeni, op. cit., note 111, pp. 75 sqq.

Again, there was the actio redhibitoria, to be brought within six months, and the actio quanti minoris, available for a year. They applied in cases of physical defects or diseases, of which the purchaser had not been notified; also (even though that is not mentioned in the edict) in cases of dicta et promissa.[199] The term "iumenta" (beasts of burden) came to be seen as unduly restrictive; hence a special clause was added to the effect that the remedies were to apply to the sale of cattle in general (pecus).[200] The terms "morbus" and "vitium", again, had to be given concrete meaning in the application of individual cases. We are informed that not everything classed as a disease in slaves could be considered in the same light with regard to animals; castration was a case in point. A horse was taken as sound, even though it might have lost its powers of reproduction completely;[201] not so, for instance, if its tongue had been cut out.[202] Roman traders often seem to have tried to make their cattle look more attractive by splendidly caparisoning them, but then actually delivering them without all these ornamenta (harness, gear, etc.). The aediles did not condone such practices and required the vendor to hand over the cattle in whatever condition it had been offered for sale.[203] If a pair of cattle had been sold and only one turned out to be defective, the other one could also be returned.[204]

6. Extended liability under the actio empti

If we survey what has been said so far and try to sum up the law relating to latent defects at, say, the time of Salvius Iulianus, we must come to the conclusion that the picture was still somewhat patchy. The aedilitian remedies were restricted to the sale of slaves and cattle; furthermore, they applied to market transactions only. The seller of land was liable only if he had overstated its actual acreage. The actio empti covered all types of objects of sale, but was available only in cases of dolus. If the purchaser wished the vendor to be liable on a broader basis, he had to ask him for express warranties (by way of formless dicta in venditione or by formal promissa). Unless such warranties were given, the purchaser's protection was far from perfect. Caveat emptor still prevailed to a large extent.[205]

---

[199] Ulp. D. 21, 1, 38, 10 (referring only to the actio redhibitoria).

[200] Ulp. D. 21, 1, 38, 5.

[201] Ulp. D. 21, 1, 38, 7.

[202] Ofilius-Ulp. D. 21, 1, 8.

[203] Ulp. D. 21, 1, 38 pr.; Caelius/Ulp. D. 21, 1, 38, 11.

[204] Ulp. D. 21, 1, 38 pr.; for details, see Ulp. D. 21, 1, 38, 12 sqq.

[205] Of course, the purchaser could always insist on the inclusion of a pactum displicentiae into the contract. He could then call off the sale if he did not like the object he had bought, even though it might not be defective (cf. infra, pp. 739 sqq.). As far as the sale of slaves is concerned, a specific pactum redhibendi seems to have been in use: the sale was concluded "ita . . ., ut, nisi placuerit, intra praefinitum tempus redhibeatur" (Ulp. D. 21, 1, 31, 22). This clause served the same function as a pactum displicentiae but was modelled on the actio redhibitoria. Cf. Karlheinz Misera, "Der Kauf auf Probe", *ANRW*, vol. II, 14 (1982), pp. 531 sqq.

(a) Pomp. D. 19, 1, 6, 4 and other texts

Until about three decades ago it was the more or less generally accepted view that classical Roman law never advanced beyond that point. In the meantime, however, a different opinion has been gaining ground.

It is now widely recognized that we can see, in the course of classical jurisprudence, an energetic move towards a generalized liability for latent defects.[206] The vehicle for this development was the actio empti, its motor the "ex fide bona" clause inherent therein. Again (as in the case of liability for eviction) Iulianus seems to have played an important role, but he could take up and build upon the idea of a contemporary of Augustus, Marcus Antistius Labeo. The latter was commenting on a case involving the sale of a vessel,[207] to which we have already briefly referred.[208] According to the traditional opinion, the vendor was liable only for dolus, if that vessel did not turn out to be whole; unless, of course, he had given an express warranty to that effect:

> "[S]ed si vas mihi vendideris ita, ut adfirmares integrum, si id integrum non sit, etiam id, quod eo nomine perdiderim, praestabis mihi: si vero non id actum sit, ut integrum praestes, dolum malum dumtaxat preastare te debere".

Labeo, however, argued that specific dicta or promissa should not be necessary in order to ensure delivery of a vessel that is whole: ". . . et illum solum observandum, ut, nisi contrarium id actum sit, omnimodo integrum praestari debeat. . . ." In other words: the vendor does not have to give a specific warranty to the effect that the vessel is fit for use; on the contrary, if he does not want to be responsible for its defectiveness, he specifically has to exclude liability.[209] But what did the liability entail? This was spelt out by Iulianus:

> ". . . ait enim, qui pecus morbosum aut tignum vitiosum vendidit, si quidem ignorans fecit, id tantum ex empto actione praestaturum, quanto minoris essem empturus si id ita esse scissem."[210]

This seems to be the actio quanti minoris; and yet, as we can see from the second example (tignum vitiosum), we are not dealing with aedilitian liability but with the normal actio empti. That is confirmed by other texts. Marc. D. 18, 1, 45 deals with the sale of clothes which turned out to be renovated rather than new (". . . si vestimenta interpola quis pro novis emerit"). Iulianus opines "si quidem ignorabat venditor, ipsius rei nomine teneri". What this means is that, once again, the purchaser can achieve a reduction in the purchase price.[211] But this

---

206 Ulrich von Lübtow, "Zur Frage der Sachmängelhaftung im römischen Recht", in: *Studi in onore di Ugo Enrico Paoli* (1955), pp. 492 sqq.; Olde Kalter, op. cit., note 24, pp. 116 sqq.; Honsell, *Quod interest*, pp. 80 sqq.; Kaser, *RPr* I, p. 558.

207 Pomp. D. 19, 1, 6, 4.

208 Cf. supra, p. 309.

209 Cf. further Ulp. D. 19, 1, 11, 7: "Venditorem, etiamsi ignorans vendiderit, fugitivum non esse praestare emptori oportere Neratius ait."

210 Ulp. D. 19, 1, 13 pr.

211 For details, see Honsell, *Quod interest*, pp. 85 sqq.

was not the only result to which application of the actio empti could lead.

> "Si quis virginem se emere putasset, cum mulier venisset, et sciens errare eum venditor passus sit . . . ex empto competere actionem ad resolvendam emptionem. . . ."[212]

This looks like the actio redhibitoria in the guise of the actio empti; and a few lines above this text we find, indeed, the more generalized statement, attributed already to Labeo and Sabinus, that "[r]edhibitionem quoque contineri empti iudicio".[213]

(b) *Reception of the aedilitian principles into the ius civile*

What seems to have happened is that the principles laid down in the aedilitian edict were gradually received into the ius civile.[214] On the one hand, with the growing complexity of Roman economic life, there was less and less justification for the simple and straightforward caveat emptor. It became standard practice to add an express warranty to sale transactions, even outside the market place, and sooner or later this warranty was no longer perceived as a mere accidentale, but obtained the status of a naturale negotii. On the other hand, the aedilitian edict offered a reasonably satisfactory model set of rules, of which the lawyers could avail themselves in order to accommodate the need for an extended protection of the purchaser. These rules were well balanced, particularly in so far as they imposed an "objective" liability on the vendor (that is, he was liable irrespective of whether he was at fault or whether he had made special assertions), but they did not allow the purchaser to claim his full damages (quod interest); furthermore, their application was confined to certain, generally physical, defects. Thus, as far as the ius civile was concerned, a system of graduated liability could be built up by phasing in aedilitian principles where no liability had previously existed. Hence we find Iulianus stressing the difference between the vendor sciens and ignorans, the former being liable for "omnia detrimenta, quae ex ea emptione emptor traxerit", the latter only for quanti minoris.[215] All in all, then, warranty for latent defects was taken to be implicit in the contract of sale, even in cases where the seller had not known about the defects himself. This warranty, implied by law, was based on a generalization of the aedilitian remedies and was effected by means of a more refined interpretation of what was owed, in good faith, under the actio empti. The aedilitian rules were read into the "oportere ex fide bona" clause of the general action on sale and

---

[212] Ulp. D. 19, 1, 11, 5; Medicus, *Id quod interest*, pp. 146 sq.
[213] Ulp. D. 19, 1, 11, 3.
[214] Cf., particularly, Moritz Wlassak, *Zur Geschichte der negotiorum gestio* (1879), pp. 169 sqq.; Bechmann, vol. III, 2, pp. 174 sqq.
[215] Ulp. D. 19, 1, 13 pr.; cf. also Iul./Marci. D. 18, 1, 45.

there can be little doubt today that the texts, on which this statement is based, are substantially genuine.[216]

(c) The position under Justinian

Nothing much remained to be done by Justinian. With the actio empti a satisfactory remedy was available to cope with the problems arising from latent defects. The purchaser could use it to claim quod interest, to ask for redhibition or for quanti minoris. In view of this, one might have expected Justinian to abolish the aedilitian remedies, for they had become redundant. Since the office and jurisdiction of the aediles had been abolished,[217] the difference between the actiones redhibitoria and quanti minoris on the one hand and the actio empti on the other did not even have jurisdictional relevance and consequences any longer. In fact, however, they were not only retained as an appendage to the law of sale,[218] but their range of application was extended beyond slaves and cattle to cover the sale of all things "tam earum quae soli sint quam earum quae mobiles aut se moventes".[219] The continued existence of the aedilitian remedies is evidence of the traditionalism of both the East Roman school jurisprudence and Justinian.

7. Actio empti and aedilitian remedies in the ius commune

(a) "Miretur vero aliquis, cur Aediles introduxerunt actiones . . ."

From the time of the intellectual rediscovery of the Digest in Bologna down to the days of the pandectists, the unfortunate coexistence of two sets of remedies both dealing with latent defects in the thing sold has caused difficulties.[220] Of course, only the actio empti was available, if

[216] The classicality of the actio empti against the venditor ignorans has been recognized for centuries (cf. still Vangerow, *Pandekten*, vol. III, p. 302; Wlassak and Bechmann supra, note 214). In view of the texts referred to above, a contrary view can only be maintained on the basis of extensive interpolation assumptions: cf. Franz Haymann, *Die Haftung des Verkäufers für die Beschaffenheit der Kaufsache*, vol. I (1912), pp. 71 sqq.; Van Warmelo, op. cit., note 98, pp. 55 sqq.; Pringsheim (1952) 69 *ZSS* 293 sqq.; Impallomeni, op. cit., note 111, pp. 247 sqq.; Honoré, *Studies de Zulueta*, pp. 137 sqq. (but see pp. 143 sq.). Today, one tends to adopt a more conservative and cautious approach, as far as the corruption of classical texts is concerned; hence the renaissance of the pre-interpolationist view of the range of the actio empti.

[217] Mommsen, *Römisches Staatsrecht*, vol.II, 1, p. 522.

[218] Cf. Const. Omnem 4; Const. Tanta 5; Levy, *Obligationenrecht*, pp. 223 sq.; Monier, op. cit., note 96, pp. 186 sqq.

[219] Ulp. D. 21, 1, 1 pr. (interpolated); cf. further e.g. C. 4, 58, 4, 1 (dealing with the sale of "pestibilis fundus, id est pestibulas vel herbas letiferas habens"). Cf. e.g. Monier, op. cit., note 96, pp. 161 sqq.; Van Warmelo, op. cit., note 98, pp. 16 sqq.; Arangio-Ruiz, *Compravendita*, pp. 394 sqq.; Impallomeni, op. cit., not 111, pp. 265 sqq. The aedilitian remedies and the actio empti stood in a relationship of elective concurrence.

[220] For details of the historical development of the law relating to latent defects in things sold, cf. Van Warmelo, op. cit., note 98, pp. 58 sqq.; Honoré, *Studies de Zulueta*, pp. 132 sqq.; Norbert Burke, *Einschränkungen der ädilizischen Rechtsbehelfe beim Kauf von der Rezeption bis zur Gegenwart* (unpublished Dr. iur. thesis, Münster, 1967); Walter-Jürgen Klempt, *Die Grundlagen der Sachmängelhaftung des Verkäufers im Vernunftrecht und Usus modernus*

the purchaser wanted to claim damages and, as far as the requirements for this claim were concerned, the actio empti not only went beyond the aedilitian remedies, but also fell short of them. It went further, in that its range of application was not confined to what one could call aedilitian defects (namely those morbi and vitia covered by the edict),[221] but it was much narrower in that scientia on the part of the vendor was required.[222] However, regarding the objective liability for aedilitian defects, there was a very awkward overlap of remedies. Both the actio empti and the aedilitian remedies were available, either for quanti minoris or for redhibition.

In view of this, one could point out differences[223] and try to show that, for instance, quanti minoris actually meant one thing in the one context and something else in the other. This was the approach adopted by Accursius, the influential author of the authoritative *Glossa Ordinaria*:

> "No. hic differentiam", he wrote, "inter actionem quanto minoris, civilem et praetoriam. nam in civili agitur, quanto minoris esset empturus, si scisset, ut hic [sc.: D. 19, 1, 13 pr.]. Sed in praetoria quanto minoris valuit tempore contractus propter vitium: ut infra [D. 21, 1, 31, 5]."[224]

In other words: under the actio empti the purchaser could recover the difference between the contract price and what he personally would have paid had he known of the defect; the (aedilitian) actio quanti minoris[225] allowed him to recover the difference between the contract price and the (objective) market price for an object with that defect. Others also tried to distinguish the effects of the actio redhibitoria from the kind of redhibition (or resolutio venditionis) that could be obtained by bringing the actio empti.[226]

(b) Merging the remedies

Those, on the other hand, who did not see any difference between the praetorian and civilian way of dealing with redhibition or assessing

(1967). Cf. also the detailed commentary of Glück, vol. 20, pp. 3 sqq. and the presentation by Pothier, *Traité du contrat de vente*, nn. 203 sqq.

221 Cf. e.g. Wissenbach, *Exercitationes*, Disp. XLI, n. 9; Brunnemann, *Commentarius in Pandectas*, Lib. XXI, 1, Ad L. Labeo, I, § 3, n. 8; Glück, vol. 20, pp. 137 sq.

222 Cf. e.g. Bechmann, vol. III, 2, pp. 189 sqq.

223 Cf. e.g. Wissenbach, *Exercitationes*, Disp. XLI, n. 9: "Miretur vero aliquis, Cur Aediles introduxerint actiones, Redhibitoriam et Aestimatoriam, cum ex iisdem causis competant actiones Civiles. . . . Sed mirari desinat, Differentiae inter illas actiones Aedilitias et Civiles multae sunt."

224 Gl. Essem empturus ad D. 19, 1, 13 pr.; for details about the medieval discussions of the purchaser's actions for physical defects, see Van Warmelo, op. cit., note 98, pp. 58 sqq.; Hermann Dilcher, *Leistungsstörungen*, pp. 224 sqq.; Peter Stein, "Medieval Discussions of the Buyer's Actions for Physical Defects", in: *Studies in the Roman Law of Sale in memory of Francis de Zulueta*, 1959, pp. 102 sqq.

225 Also often referred to as actio aestimatoria.

226 e.g. Bechmann, vol. III, 2, pp. 189 sqq.

quanti minoris,[227] often attempted to obviate the problem by merging aedilitian remedies and actio empti, in so far as they overlapped. Digesta 21, 1 ("De aedilicio edicto et redhibitione et quanti minoris") was usually regarded as sedes materiae and the appropriate place to discuss the rules relating to latent defects. Whether, under these circumstances, the actio empti gradually faded away and finally disappeared from the scene[228] or whether—the other way around—the aedilitian remedies were fitted into the general framework of the actio empti and the corresponding duties arising from sale[229]—the practical result was the same: the whole complex was governed by a single set of rules (sometimes referred to as actio empti quanti minoris/actio empti redhibitoria). This was also the easiest way to cope with the one major difficulty arising in the practical application of the law; for however much the actions had become assimilated, there always remained one characteristic difference: the actiones redhibitoria and quanti minoris prescribed in six months and one year respectively, the actio empti was subject to the general prescription period of 30 years.[230] The greater the identity between the remedies, the more unsatisfactory this divergence. Few writers were prepared to acquiesce in the reasoning advanced, for instance, by Samuel Stryk—"Quid enim opus fuisset actionem empti ad materiam redhibitionis extendere, si iisdem cancellis cum aedilitia actione circumscribenda . . ."[231]—since the aediles had already created the actiones quanti minoris and redhibitoria, but had subjected them to a strict temporal limitation, what point would there have been in the introduction of the same remedies again, via the actio empti, if not to elevate them from the status of actiones temporales to that of actiones perpetuae? Yet, the practical result of such unrestricted concurrence of actions would have been a total erosion of the short prescription period laid down in the aedilitian edict, and such a result was usually regarded as absurd:

> "Nam si hic ex empto actio est, perpetuo quoque in eam rem dabitur. Est enim actio ex empto civilis, eoque etiam perpetua. Quod si est: erit inutile ex edicto aedilium intra six menses experiri, cum perpetua jure civili competat. Imo vero absurda sententia admodum efficietur, ut cum jure civili ex hac caussa actio competat perpetua: aediles, qui adiuvandi juris civilis, et aequitatis constituendae caussa edicta

[227] Cf. e.g. already Baldus de Ubaldis, *Consilia*, vol. V, CCCCXCIX ("emptor potest agere redhibitoria, vel certe quanto minoris . . . potest agi actione ex empto similiter").

[228] Cf. e.g. Ulrich Huber, *Praelectiones*, Lib. XXI, Tit. I, nn. 4 sq.; Justus Henning Boehmer, *Doctrina de actionibus* (Francofurti ad Moenum, 1738), Sect. II, Cap. VIII, § 77.

[229] Cf. e.g. Donellus, *Commentarii de Jure Civili*, Lib. XIII, Cap. II, III ("Earum praestationum, quae a venditore in re vendita citra aliam conventionem exiguntur, quatuor sunt capita. Primum, ut rem venditam tradat emptori . . . Tertium, ut dum emptor rem habebit, habeat incorruptam . . ."); for details Cap. III and "Commentaria ad titulum, de aediliticio edicto" (*Opera Omnia*, vol. X, col. 1327 sqq.); Lauterbach, *Collegium theoretico-practicum*, Lib. XXI, Tit. I, XXXIV.

[230] Based on C. 7, 39, 3, 1 (Honor. et Theodos.).

[231] *Usus modernus pandectarum*, Lib. XXI, Tit. I, § 52.

proponere debent, ac jus civili subsequi, intra sex tantum menses dent: idest, contrarium jus proponant."[232]

Even those who continued to maintain the availability of two sets of remedies on account of latent defects therefore usually subjected the actio empti to the short prescription periods as well, where this general remedy competed with those of the actiones aediliticiae.[233] Only the claim for damages was taken to prescribe within 30 years—the difficulty, however, being that quod interest could sometimes take the form of quanti minoris or redhibition![234]

(c) The scope of application of the actio redhibitoria

A further interesting dispute, which arose with the reception of Roman law in Europe, related more specifically to the availability of the actio redhibitoria. Some writers continued to maintain that, whenever an object sold suffered from an aedilitian defect, the purchaser was free to use either of the aedilitian remedies: "Est vero in electione emptoris, an velit redhibitoria, an vero quanti minoris agere."[235] Others (at times they represented the prevailing opinion) favoured a restriction of the purchaser's freedom of choice. Redhibition of the whole contract is a fairly drastic step, which the purchaser should not be allowed to take too lightly. Hence the purchaser should be able to use the actio redhibitoria only, if he would not have bought the object had he known about the defect. This, presumably, was only the case if the defect impeded proper use of the thing. On that basis, we often find the actio redhibitoria being granted only "[ob] tale vitium . . ., quod usum ministeriumque hominis plane impedit";[236] others based the availability of the actio redhibitoria more directly on the hypothetical will of the purchaser: ". . . si tale vitium in re vendita sit, propter quod actor eam rem empturus non fuerit."[237] Did that entail that the actio quanti minoris, in turn, was confined to those cases in which the actio redhibitoria could not be brought (i.e. "actio quanti minoris propter tale vitium datur, quod omnem usum non impedit, et sic emptor quidem emisset eam, verum non eodem, sed minori pretio"[238]), so that their fields of application were mutually exclusive? Or was the

[232] Donellus, "Commentaria ad titulum, de aedilitico edicto" (op. cit., note 229), Cap. V, n. 4; cf. further e.g. Heinrich Hahn, *Observata theoretico practica, Ad Matthaei Wesenbecii in L. libros Digestorum Commentarios* (Helmstadii, 1659), Pars II, Lib. XXI, Tit. I, Obs. n. 9; Lauterbach, *Collegium theoretico-practicum*, Lib. XXI, Tit. I, XXXIV.

[233] Glück, vol. 20, pp. 153 sqq.; Windscheid/Kipp, § 393, n. 1, 12.

[234] Windscheid/Kipp, § 393, n. 9.

[235] Struve, *Syntagma*, Exerc. XXVII, X; cf. further Pothier, *Traité du contrat de vente*, n. 233; Johann Paul Anselm Feuerbach (the great criminal lawyer), *Civilistische Versuche* (1803), Erster Theil, pp. 51 sqq.; Glück, vol. 20, p. 119.

[236] Stryk, *Usus modernus pandectarum*, Lib. XXI, Tit. I, § 11; cf. further e.g. Brunnemann, *Commentarius in Pandectas*, Lib. XXI, 1, Ad L. Labeo, I, § 3, 6.

[237] Ulrich Huber, *Praelectiones*, Lib. XXI, Tit. I, n. 6; cf. also Perezius, *Praelectiones*, Lib. IV, Tit. LVIII, n. 5; Voet, *Commentarius ad Pandectas*, Lib. XXI, Tit. I, IV.

[238] Cf. e.g. Stryk, *Usus modernus pandectarum*, Lib. XXI, Tit. I, § 11.

actio quanti minoris, as the less far-reaching of the two remedies, applicable in any event, whether the actio redhibitoria could be brought or not?[239] That was not entirely clear, either.

(d) Excursus: Special rules relating to the sale of cattle

It is interesting to note that, in the restriction of the actio redhibitoria, some influence of Germanic law manifested itself.[240] There the position of the purchaser was characterized, generally, by legal proverbs such as *"Augen auf, Kauf ist Kauf"*. Special rules existed only with regard to the sale of cattle (particularly horses), but even here the purchaser could cancel the sale only in case of certain grave defects (*"Hauptmängel"* or principal defects). The vendor's liability was objective, that is, independent of fault, but subject to very short periods of warranty. A remedy comparable with the actio quanti minoris was unknown.[241] These rules relating to the sale of cattle became so firmly entrenched in both the mores hodiernae and the local statutory laws that they largely withstood the reception of Roman law.[242] They are, for instance, still part and parcel of the German BGB which in that respect confirms Lord Simonds' dictum, that "the law . . . has grown up historically in separate compartments and . . . beasts have travelled in a compartment of their own".[243] The general rules relating to warranty against latent defects apply "to the sale of horses, asses, mules, hinnies, cattle, sheep and pigs only in so far as it is not otherwise provided by §§ 482 to 492".[244] According to § 482 I, the seller is responsible only for principal defects, and then only if they are discovered within specific periods of warranty. For details, § 482 II refers to an Imperial Ordinance.[245] This ordinance, enacted in March 1899, is still in force today and represents

---

239 Cf. e.g. Ulrich Huber, *Praelectiones*, Lib. XXI, Tit. I, n. 6.

240 Cf. particularly Feuerbach, loc. cit.

241 Cf. e.g. Otto Stobbe, Heinrich O. Lehmann, *Handbuch des Deutschen Privatrechts*, vol. III (3rd ed., 1898), § 232, pp. 304 sqq., 309 sqq; Georg Beseler, *System des gemeinen deutschen Privatrechts*, vol. I (4th ed., 1885), p. 507; Klempt, op. cit., note 76, pp. 50 sqq.

242 Cf. e.g. the compilation and analysis by von Kübel. By the end of the 19th century, the Germanic system of liability for principal defects held sway in most parts of Germany; the "Romanistic system" (i.e. no distinction as far as liability for latent defects in animals and other things is concerned) applied only in Mecklenburg, Braunschweig, Oldenburg, Schaumburg-Lippe, Lippe-Detmold, Sachsen-Weimar, Rudolstadt and in large parts of Schleswig-Holstein. In other parts of Europe, too, local rules relating to the sale of animals survived the reception of Roman law; cf., as far as French law is concerned, Van Warmelo, op. cit., note 98, p. 172 sqq. In Holland horses sold were warranted only "klaar van Sessen" (sound in six points, namely four legs and two eyes); cf. e.g. Van Leeuwen, *Censura Forensis*, Pars I, Lib. IV, Cap. XIX, n. 16 (". . . aliis vitiis, veluti si sit lunaticus, retrogradus aut pavidus, si transiungi nequeat, si sit calcitrosus . . . venditor moribus nostris non tenetur"; Voet, *Commentarius ad Pandectas*, Lib. XXI, Tit. I, XI; Van Warmelo, op. cit., note 98, pp. 85 sqq.

243 *Read v. J. Lyons & Co. Ltd.* [1947] AC 156 (HL) at 182.

244 § 481 BGB.

245 Its text is reproduced, for instance, in: *Mugdan*, vol. II, p. 1411; Putzo, in: *Palandt*, BGB (47th ed., 1988), sub § 482, in fine.

a somewhat anachronistic legal curiosity.[246] It gives a fairly detailed list of principal defects (ranging from red murrain in pigs to broken wind or staggers in horses) and provides for periods of warranty between three and 28 (usually: 14) days. It is obvious that, by not subjecting the sale of cattle to the general rules of the §§ 459 sqq.,[247] the fathers of the BGB favoured the interests of the cattle-selling, farming community; the general rules are much more sympathetic to the position of the purchaser. In an historical perspective, it is ironical to see that the aedilitian remedies did not (and do not, in their modern, codified version) apply to the sale of those very objects for which—apart from slaves—they were originally developed. The Germanic law, in turn, recognized special rules relating to the sale of cattle in order to tighten the vendor's liability; yet, once the aedilitian remedies had been received with regard to all other objects, they turned out to constitute a privilege for cattle-sellers.

(e) Modern German law

Leaving the special compartment reserved for animals (in reality: for farmers) aside, the German BGB attempted little more than to codify the current Roman common law on the topic of liability for latent defects.[248] The aedilitian remedies, which had originally applied only to slaves and cattle, dominated the scene, even though slavery had been abandoned and the sale of cattle was governed by special rules. As a consequence, the modern discussion still largely follows Roman thinking patterns. This does not have only beneficial effects. The question of when an object should be considered defective is often determined by reference to its fitness for use. This is in line with what Ulpianus sets out in D. 21, 1, 1, 8, but does not provide a useful criterion when it comes to (for instance) spurious paintings or imitated pearls.[249] Both types of objects are presumably fit for their ordinary "use" (i.e. to be hung up in the lounge or to be worn for a gala dinner); yet, provided they were sold as genuine, they should clearly be regarded as defective. The limitation of the claim for damages to cases where a promised quality in the thing sold is absent or where the vendor has fraudulently concealed a defect, has given rise to great difficulties, in so far as it is hard to reconcile and coordinate this

---

[246] One of the reasons why it was deemed necessary to lay down strict and detailed rules was the fear of making the outcome of judicial proceedings dependent upon the expert opinions of veterinary surgeons. Being generally speaking unenlightened and scientifically far behind the times, the latter were likely to confuse and misguide the court. For further about §§ 482 sqq. BGB and the Imperial Ordinance, see Fritz Ostler, "Kritik am Viehgewährschaftsrecht", 1956 *Juristenzeitung* 471 sqq.; Peters/Zimmermann, *Verjährungsfristen*, pp. 142 sqq.

[247] The best summary of all pros and cons can still be found in von Kübel's motivation of his draft, in: Werner Schubert (ed.), *Vorentwürfe, Schuldrecht 1* (1980), pp. 425 sqq.

[248] Cf. e.g. "Motive", in: *Mugdan*, vol.II, p. 123.

[249] Honsell, *Gedächtnisschrift Kunkel*, p. 62.

restrictive attitude with the general remedies of culpa in contrahendo and positive malperformance.[250] In both these latter instances, a claim for damages is granted, as a matter of course, even in cases of mere negligence.

The short prescription period, contained today in § 477 BGB, has proved to be a veritable minefield of problems. Not only is the period per se too short, it is also totally out of harmony with the general period of 30 years (!), applicable in cases of (for instance) culpa in contrahendo and positive malperformance. This has led to preposterous discrepancies in the solution of very closely related problems.[251] Finally, if we look at modern standard contract forms, we often find the statutory remedies of the purchaser being substituted by a right to demand removal of the defect.[252] This shows that the Romanistic fixation on redhibition, reduction of the purchase price and (under certain, limited circumstances) damages as the only possible remedies in cases of latent defects, is out of tune with the commercial consuetudines modernae.[253]

(f) The system of remedies in Roman-Dutch law

In an uncodified, namely their Roman-Dutch, version the aedilitian remedies still apply in modern South African law.[254] Not surprisingly, their coordination with the actio empti has in the course of time given rise to problems. Today the actio empti is usually taken to apply, if a vendor guarantees the absence of defects or promises the presence of certain qualities in the thing sold. If he then delivers a thing that is defective or lacks the promised qualities, he is guilty of a breach of contract and liable, in accordance with general principles, for

[250] For a discussion of this problem, see e.g. H.P. Westermann, in: *Münchener Kommentar*, vol. III, 1 (2nd ed., 1988), § 463, nn. 31 sqq. It does not arise in other modern European legal systems, where the purchaser is usually granted a contractual claim for damages (including consequential loss) if the vendor was at fault; sometimes, incidentally, not even fault is required: cf. Jürgen Basedow, *Die Reform des deutschen Kaufrechts* (1988), pp. 30 sqq., 73 sqq.

[251] For details, see Peters/Zimmermann, *Verjährungsfristen*, pp. 182, 202 sqq.

[252] This has, for instance, necessitated the regulations contained in § 11, n. 10 a–c of the *Gesetz zur Regelung des Rechts der Allgemeinen Geschäftsbedingungen* (AGBG; General Conditions of Business Act) of 1976. For details, see, for example, Hein Kötz, in: *Münchener Kommentar*, vol. I (2nd ed., 1984), § 11 ABGB, nn. 80 sqq; for a comparative analysis, see Basedow, op. cit., note 250, pp. 63 sqq.

[253] So, too, Honsell, *Gedächtnisschrift Kunkel*, p. 65. The BGB does not recognize a right to demand removal of the defect. Differently, for instance, § 932 ABGB. As far as the sale of fungibles is concerned, § 480 does, however, give the purchaser the right to demand, instead of cancellation or reduction, that in the place of the defective thing another one free from defects be delivered to him. During the 19th century, the question whether the aedilitian actions are applicable to generic sales or not was vehemently discussed; for details, see Burke, op. cit., note 220, pp. 86 sqq. (who also provides information about the attitude of modern legislators on this problem).

[254] Even to cattle (*Kock v. Du Plessis* 1923 OPD 113) and to the sale of incorporeals (cf. in this context Holmes JA, in *Phame (Pty.) Ltd. v. Paizes* 1973 (3) SA 397 (A) at 419H–420A: ". . . the aedilitian relief, recognized under the Roman-Dutch law, can, while retaining its basic principles, be adapted to apply to the modern circumstances . . .").

damages.[255] Again, the vendor is liable under the actio empti where he intentionally conceals from the purchaser the presence of certain defects known to him or where he makes statements relating to the quality of the thing, which he knows to be wrong and which induce the purchaser to enter into the contract.[256] Here we are dealing with fraudulent misrepresentation. Otherwise, that is, where the vendor sells a defective thing without, however, either giving an express or tacit guarantee or knowing about the defect, the purchaser can avail himself of only the actiones quanti minoris or redhibitoria. His choice is limited, in so far as the latter of these remedies applies only where he would not have bought the thing had he known about the defect, or where the defect is of such a nature, that it prevents the ordinary use of the thing.[257] The actio empti does not compete with the aedilitian remedies. That has been spelt out with regard to the actio redhibitoria by Watermeyer CJ, in the important case of *Hackett v. G. & G. Radio and Refrigerator Corporation*,[258] but it applies to the actio quanti minoris too. There is only one right of action[259] and Van Warmelo has characterized it in the following way:

> "Om te sê dat die actio empti die actiones aediliciae absorbeer, is dus ook 'n halwe waarheid. Dit is beter om te sê 'n nuwe aksie het ontstaan waarin die elemente van die actio empti en die actiones aediliciae verenig is."[260]

In *Hackett's* case the matter was raised because of the different prescription periods applicable to the aedilitian action, on the one hand, and the actio empti, on the other.[261] Today the discussion is largely academic, for the new Prescription Act subjects both kinds of "debts" to the general prescription period of three years.[262]

(g) Phame v. Paizes

More recently, attention has been focused on the precise ambit of liability for dicta et promissa. The point of controversy is whether the vendor is liable, under the aedilitian remedies, for what one could call innocent misrepresentation relating to the quality of the thing sold. The matter was decided in *Phame (Pty.) Ltd. v. Paizes*,[263] a *cause célèbre*, with J.C. de Wet, the grand old man of South African jurisprudence,[264] Hennie Erasmus (a well-known Latinist and law professor),[265] and

[255] Cf. e.g. *Minister van Landbou-Tegniese Dienste v. Scholtz* 1971 (3) SA 188 (A); De Wet en Yeats, pp. 300 sq.

[256] Cf. e.g. *Glaston House (Pty.) Ltd. v. Inag (Pty.) Ltd.* 1977 (2) SA 846 (A); De Wet en Yeats, pp. 301 sq.

[257] Cf. e.g. *Reed Bros. v. Bosch* 1914 TPD 578; Van Warmelo, op. cit., note 98, pp. 144 sqq.

[258] 1949 (3) SA 664 (A) at 684 and 685.

[259] So also De Wet en Yeats, pp. 303 sqq., but see Kerr, *Sale and Lease*, p. 54.

[260] Op. cit., note 98, p. 155.

[261] Act 18 (1943), s. 3.

[262] Act 68 (1969), s. 11(d).

[263] 1973 (3) SA 397 (A).

[264] 1973 (3) SA 397 (A) at 398 sqq.

[265] 1973 (3) SA 397 (A) at 403 sqq.

Holmes JA[266] (famous for bringing "colour and cogency . . . to the arid wastes" of the South African law reports)[267] as dramatis personae. After an extensive review of the old authorities (albeit in translation) and after consulting, inter alia, Paul van Warmelo's thorough monograph (which was specifically complimented as being "very learned"),[268] the court came to the conclusion that the aedilitian remedies are available not only if the res vendita suffered from a latent defect at the time of the sale but also if the seller made a dictum et promissum to the purchaser, on the strength of which the latter entered into the contract or agreed to the price in question and which later on turned out to be unfounded. Dicta et promissa are then defined as "material statement(s) made by the seller to the buyer during the negotiations, bearing on the quality of the res vendita and going beyond mere praise and commendation";[269] the decision carries on to carve out criteria for determining under which circumstances a statement by the vendor can be said to go beyond mere praise and commendation. These conclusions have been criticized by various authors,[270] but they do not appear to be in conflict with the Roman law in point.[271] Furthermore, they fit into a general trend in South African law towards imposing liability for non-fraudulent misrepresentation. Such liability can, since the famous *Trust Bank* case of 1979,[272] be based on delict. It remains to be seen how the aedilitian and delictual remedies will be able to co-exist.

8. Mortuus redhibetur

Before we conclude our reflections on latent defects, two marginalia should still be added. The one relates to the actio redhibitoria, the other to the claim for damages.

(a) *The problem of the impossibility of restoration*

As far as the aedilitian actio redhibitoria was concerned, we have seen that, where the purchaser chose to avail himself of this remedy, he had to restore the slave or animal to the vendor before the latter could be condemned to pay back the purchase price. Did this entail that the right to claim redhibition was excluded where the purchaser was no longer able to hand the (defective) object of the sale back, or to hand it back in the state in which he had received it, because it had in the meantime

---

[266] 1973 (3) SA 397 (A) at 407 sqq.
[267] J.J. Gauntlett, "The Sayings of Mr. Justice Holmes", (1974) 37 *THRHR* 169 sqq.
[268] 1973 (3) SA 397 (A) at 410E.
[269] 1973 (3) SA 397 (A) at 418A.
[270] S.W.J. van der Merwe, M.F.B. Reinecke, (1974) 37 *THRHR* 175 sqq.; De Wet en Yeats, pp. 306 sq.; Wouter de Vos," Onopsetlike wanvoorstelling by kontraksluiting", in: *J.C. Noster, 'n Feesbundel* (1979), pp. 63 sqq.
[271] Cf. supra, pp. 315 sq., 319.
[272] *Administrateur, Natal v. Trust Bank van Afrika Bpk.* 1979 (3) SA 824 (A); for details, cf. infra, pp. 674, 1042 sq.

been destroyed or damaged or had otherwise disappeared? The edict itself only gave an answer as to the consequences of a deterioration:

> "[S]i quid autem post venditionem traditionemque deterius emptoris opera familiae procuratorisve eius factum erit . . . ut ea omnia restituat."[273]

The actio redhibitoria can still be brought, but where the deterioration of the slave was caused by either the purchaser himself or by his people, the purchaser has to compensate the vendor for the decrease in value.[274] It is not entirely clear under which circumstances such compensation was due; the term "opera" is a fairly neutral one[275] and cannot, for instance, be equated with culpa or dolus. At the time the deterioration took place, the object belonged to the purchaser and thus it would hardly have been possible to think of applying fault criteria in the ordinary sense. Neither did opera necessarily imply specific actions on the part of the purchaser or his people; some influence on a psychological level was sufficient, "ut puta si imitatione conservorum apud emptorem talis factus est, aleator forte vel vinarius vel erro evasit".[276] Here, owing to the bad example of his new fellow-slaves, the homo venditus had deteriorated into a gambler, an alcoholic or a rover. The Roman lawyers probably made their decision dependent upon whether the deterioration would also have occurred had the slave continued to be with the vendor or whether it was due to his transfer to the purchaser.[277] In the latter instance, the purchaser had to compensate the vendor, no matter whether he had been at fault or not. This would seem to be in line with what the actio redhibitoria was generally taken to be designed for: namely to effect a restoration of both vendor and purchaser to the position they would have been in had the contract not been concluded.[278]

(b) The fiction of "mortuus redhibetur" and problems arising therefrom

It must come as a surprise, in view of this, that, according to a widely held opinion, the risk of accidental loss (as opposed to deterioration) always had to be borne by the vendor.[279] "Mortuus redhibetur" is the

---

[273] Ulp. D. 21, 1, 1, 11.

[274] Cf. today §§ 467, 351 BGB; Kerr, *Sale and Lease*, pp. 61 sqq.

[275] Cf. Rosalie Lederle, *Mortuus redhibetur, Die Rückabwicklung nach Wandlung im römischen Recht* (1983), pp. 23 sqq.

[276] Ulp. D. 21, 1, 25, 6.

[277] Ped./Ulp. D. 21, 1, 25, 4: "Pedius ait aequum fuisse id dumtaxat imputari emptori ex facto procuratoris et familiae, quod non fuit passurus servus nisi venisset: quod autem passurus erat etiam, si non venisset, in eo concedi emptori servi sui noxae deditionem et ex eo, inquit, quod procurator commisit, solum actionum praestandarum necessitatem ei iniungi." See Peter Mader, "Mortuus redhibetur?", (1984) 101 *ZSS* 225 sq.

[278] Cf. supra p. 317.

[279] Glück, vol. 20, p. 75; Ernst Eck, "Beitrag zur Lehre von den ädilizischen Klagen", in: *Juristische Abhandlungen, Festgabe für Georg Beseler* (1885), pp. 159 sqq.; Windscheid/Kipp, § 394, 2; Georg Thielmann, "Actio redhibitoria und zufälliger Untergang der Kaufsache", in: *Studi in onore di Edoardo Volterra*, vol. II (1971), pp. 487 sqq.; Lederle, op. cit., note 275, pp. 30 sqq.

famous tag extracted from the Roman sources;[280] or as §§ 467, 350 BGB put it:[281] the right to demand redhibition of the sale is not barred by the fact that the object which the purchaser received, has been destroyed. Taken as a general rule, however, designed to cover accidental loss at large,[282] the fiction of "mortuus redhibetur" is unsatisfactory.[283] The purchaser was owner of the object at the time it was destroyed. "Casum sentit dominus" is what one should naturally be inclined to say. Why make an exception to this rule and allow the purchaser to claim back the purchase price (even though he is not able to return the object), when the object was defective? The defect, from the purchaser's point of view, would then turn out to be a distinctly lucky coincidence.[284]

It has therefore been suggested that the fiction of mortuus redhibetur be restricted to those cases where the purchaser lost the slave due to the defect which gave rise to the actio redhibitoria.[285] This is, indeed, the solution adopted, mutatis mutandis, by the French and Italian codes,[286] and it would certainly be very attractive also to attribute it to classical Roman law.[287] It would fit in very well with the above-mentioned

[280] Cf. Paul. D. 21, 1, 47; Pomp. D. 21, 1, 48 pr.; Ulp. D. 21, 1, 31, 5 and 6; Ulp. D. 21, 1, 31, 24; Ulp. D. 21, 1, 38, 3. "Mortuus redhibetur" is a legal fiction, for the purchaser was (probably) not required to hand back the corpse of the slave. The situation has to be treated as if the purchaser was able to restore the (living) slave.

[281] The fathers of the BGB merely followed the ius commune (as it was then generally seen) and advanced no further argument for the adoption of the rule; cf. "Motive", in: *Mugdan*, vol. II, p. 156. Cf. also Wessels, *Contract*, § 4743, followed, for instance, in *Hall-Thermotank Natal (Pty.) Ltd. v. Hardman* 1968 (4) SA 818 (D) at 827F–H. For further discussion on the South African law, see *Mackeurtan's Sale of Goods in South Africa* (5th ed., 1984), pp. 149 sqq. For further comparative material on the topic, see Hermann Weitnauer, in: Hans Dölle, *Kommentar zum Einheitlichen Kaufrecht* (1976), Vorbem. Art. 78, pp. 499 sqq.

[282] As to where the purchaser had negligently caused the death of the slave, see Ulp. D. 21, 1, 31, 11.

[283] For further discussion, see Heinrich Honsell, "Gefahrtragung und Schadensersatz bei arglistiger Täuschung", (1970) *Monatsschrift für Deutsches Recht* 717 sqq.; Ernst von Caemmerer, "'Mortuus redhibetur', Bemerkungen zu den Urteilen BGHZ 53, 144 und 57, 137", in: *Festschrift für Karl Larenz* (1973), pp. 621 sqq.; Karl Larenz, *Lehrbuch des Schuldrechts*, vol. I (14th ed., 1987), pp. 406 sqq.

[284] For the various attempts to explain the principle of "mortuus redhibetur", see Lederle, op. cit., note 275, pp. 34 sqq.

[285] Heinrich Honsell (1970) *Monatsschrift für Deutsches Recht* 717 sqq.; idem, *Gedächtnisschrift Kunkel*, p. 61; Mader (1984) 101 *ZSS* 206 sqq.

[286] Art. 1647 code civil; art. 1492 III codice civile. Cf. also Pothier, *Traité du contrat de vente*, n. 221. A South African case in point is *Marks Ltd. v. Laughton* 1920 AD 12 at 21 (per Innes CJ).

[287] Arguably, this solution was in actual fact adopted by the Roman lawyers, where the slave had not died but had otherwise disappeared, as, for instance, where he had run away from the purchaser. This case is dealt with in Pomp./Ulp. D. 21, 1, 21, 3. According to Pomponius, the purchaser can still bring the actio redhibitoria (as long as he cannot be blamed for this behaviour of the slave—cf. e.g. Ulp. D. 21, 1, 23 pr. ". . . ut puta . . . saevitia emptoris fugitivum esse coeperit"). Instead of returning the slave, he had only to provide security (ensuring that he would continue searching for the slave and hand him back to the vendor once he had been found). It may be argued that the decision was based on the fact that the loss of the slave was caused by its defectiveness (sale of a servus fugitivus).

general idea, underlying function and application of the actio redhibitoria ("in integrum restituere debere"[288]):[289] if the slave would have died anyway (because he suffered from a physical defect), the loss would normally have fallen on the vendor; had the contract of sale not taken place, the vendor would have had neither the purchase price nor the slave. Consequently, if the actio redhibitoria aims at restoring this situation, the purchaser must be allowed to claim back the purchase price without having to hand back the slave. Otherwise, where the death of the slave had its origin in the sphere of the purchaser, or where it was purely accidental: had the contract of sale not taken place, the vendor would not have the purchase price but he would still be in possession of the slave (unless it can be assumed that the same accident would have struck the slave had he remained with the vendor).[290] The problem is, however, that we find no indication in the Roman sources for such a restrictive application of "mortuus redhibetur".[291] On the contrary, Ulp. D. 21, 1, 31, 11 appears to indicate that, unless the purchaser could be blamed for the death of the slave, the risk was on the vendor; for this text, by introducing a further fiction ("nam si culpa eius decessit, pro vivo habendus est"), makes the negligent purchaser liable to the vendor for the value of the slave.[292] But it may well be that post-classical compilers substituted subjective (fault) for the classical objective criteria of risk allocation. In other words: classical law may have applied the fiction of *mortuus redhibetur* in cases where the death would have occurred no matter whether the slave was with the purchaser or with the vendor (principal case: death caused by the defect, but also natural disaster hitting both estates). Consequence: the price can be reclaimed, even though the slave cannot be returned, i.e. the risk is on the vendor. The fiction of *pro vivo habendus est* applied to all other cases: the slave being actually dead, the situation nevertheless had to be looked at, as far as possible, as if he were still alive. Consequence: the purchaser had to return his value ("praestentur ea omnia, quae praestarentur, si viveret")[293] and would then receive the purchase price

However, Ulp. D. 21, 1, 21, 3, as it stands, raises a problem in that Pomponius makes his decision dependent upon scientia on the part of the vendor. But this is most probably an interpolation. On the fugitivus in fuga cf. Ulrich Manthe, "Zur Wandlung des servus fugitivus", (1976) 44 *TR* 133 sqq.; Lederle, op. cit., note 275, pp. 64 sqq.; Mader, (1984) 101 *ZSS* 221 sqq.

[288] Iul./Ulp. D. 21, 1, 23, 7 and supra, p. 317.

[289] This point is emphasized particularly by Mader, (1984) 101 *ZSS* 212 sqq.

[290] For instance, where an earthquake or a deluge had destroyed both the estates of the purchaser and of the vendor; cf. Thielmann, *Studi Volterra*, vol. II, pp. 507 sqq.

[291] But the sources are curiously terse, anyway, where they deal with "mortuus redhibetur"; they refer to the rule more or less in passing and are absolutely silent as to its rationale.

[292] Ulp. D. 21, 1, 31, 11 has been interpreted in various different ways. As in the text, most recently, Lederle, op. cit., note 275, pp. 41 sq.; Mader, (1984) 101 *ZSS* 227 sqq.

[293] Ulp. D. 21, 1, 31, 11.

(i.e. risk on purchaser/owner). But this is largely a matter of speculation.

9. Once again: "Si vas" (Pomp. D. 19, 1, 6, 4)

(a) The development of the "Pothier" rule

While discussing the availability of the actio empti in cases of latent defects, we came across a text by Pomponius, dealing with the sale of a defective vessel:

> "Si vas aliquod mihi vendideris . . . ita, ut adfirmares integrum, si id integrum non sit, etiam id, quod eo nomine perdiderim, praestabis mihi: si vero non id actum sit, ut integrum praestes, dolum malum dumtaxat praestare te debere. Labeo contra putat et illud solum observandum, ut, nisi in contrarium id actum sit, omnimodo integrum praestari debeat: et est verum."[294]

At first the traditional view is presented, according to which the seller was liable under the actio empti only in cases of dolus. In the end, however, Pomponius subscribes to Labeo's bold extension of the seller's liability. This text has played a very interesting role in the history of private law. Its interpretation always presented difficulties. Many have regarded the text as interpolated.[295] Others accept its genuineness, but are divided as to whether Labeo/Pomponius's statement is based on a tacit guarantee,[296] an implied term that the thing was not useless,[297] or on a liberal perception of the requirements of good faith inherent in sale.[298]

Similar disputes about the meaning and importance of D. 19, 1, 6, 4 have been raging since the Middle Ages. "Scis quantum glossatores et Doctores hic sudaverint, et frustra sursum deorsum sese jactaverint", as Molinaeus vividly puts it.[299] It was Molinaeus, however, who gave the whole discussion a new turn:

> "Cum enim vasculariam profiteatur, sive vasa cudat, sive at aliis facta vendat, et sic hanc artem vel negotiationem exercendo, si non semper expresse, saltem semper tacite ipso facto, et ex professo affirmat vasa ad usum, ad quem prostant, vaeneunt, vel elocantur, idonea, integra esse".[300]

By undertaking to produce or professionally to sell objects like the one sold, producer and merchant seller ipso facto and ex professo guarantee

---

[294] D. 19, 1, 6, 4; cf. supra, p. 320.
[295] Cf. e.g. Franz Haymann, *Die Haftung des Verkäufers für die Beschaffenheit der Kaufsache*, vol. I (1912), pp. 101 sqq.; Werner Flume, "Zum römischen Kaufrecht", (1934) 54 *ZSS* 330.
[296] Cf. e.g. Windscheid/Kipp, § 393, n. 2.
[297] Cf. e.g. Honoré, *Studies de Zulueta*, p. 144.
[298] Cf. e.g. Olde Kalter, op. cit., note 24, pp. 58 sqq.
[299] *Tractatus de eo quod interest*, § 49; for further details about these disputes, see § 19 (which has, however, been left out in Erasmus' edition and translation of the text (Johannesburg, n.d.)).
[300] § 49 (analysed by Honoré, *Studies de Zulueta*, pp. 147 sqq.).

the vessels to be fit for use.[301] Even if they were in ignorance, they are liable not only for quanti minoris, but for the purchaser's full interesse, consequential loss included.[302] Robert Joseph Pothier, as usual, put into elegant French what Molinaeus had already said in bad Latin.[303] If the vendor did not know about the defect of the article sold, he is not liable, normally, for consequential loss. But there is one exception: "*c'est le cas auquel le vendeur est on ouvrier, ou un marchand qui vend des ouvrages de son art, ou du commerce dont il fait profession.*"[304] Pothier explains this exception on the basis of the rule of imperitia culpae adnumeratur; the producer, in these instances, "*par la profession de son art*, spondet peritiam artis", and lack of professional skill is to be considered a form of culpa. The same applies to the merchant-seller: "*Par la profession publique, qu'il fait de son commerce,*" he guarantees that his articles are fit for use. This argument does not appear to be entirely convincing, for one can think of many instances where the vendor's lack of knowledge about the defect cannot really be attributed to imperitia. This may be one of the reasons why the producer-merchant seller's liability à la Pothier has not been received by either pandectist doctrine or by the BGB.[305] Nor did the Roman-Dutch authors adopt it; according to them a liability for consequential damages could attach only to the venditor sciens.[306] Voet alone recognized one exception, but only in the case of an artifex, not of a merchant-seller.[307] Nevertheless, the "Pothier rule" (as it has come to be called) has been received in modern South African law. "[L]iability for consequential damage caused by latent defect attaches to a merchant seller who was unaware of the defect", we read in the leading case of *Kroonstad Westelike Boere Ko-operatiewe Vereniging Bpk. v. Botha*,[308] "where he publicly professes to have attributes of skill and expert knowledge in relation to the kind of goods sold". Compared to what Pothier really says, however, this is a curiously amputated

[301] It follows that this rule does not apply to sales generally; not, for instance, "si quis paterfamilias non tanquam ejus professionis, sed tanquam haeres, vel alio casu dominus mobilium existentium in certa domo, in quibus quae vasa habentur, ea vendat. Cum enim nullam profiteatur horum industriam, sed incidenter, ut res indifferentes vendat, non tenetur de idoneitate, nisi quanto minoris" (§ 51).

[302] § 49. If, for instance, the liquid that was poured into the vessel, leaks out, the damage arising therefrom is a foreseeable consequence of the defectiveness of the vessel, a realization of the risk which the vendor has (tacitly) assumed (§§ 49, 50).

[303] Cf. Dumas, as quoted in Zweigert/Kötz/Weir, p. 73.

[304] Pothier, *Traité du contrat de vente*, n. 214; cf. also *Traité des obligations*, n. 163.

[305] As far as France is concerned, cf. e.g. Mazeaud/Mazeaud, *Leçons de Droit Civil*, vol. III, 2 (3rd ed., 1968), n. 988.

[306] Cf. e.g. H.D.J. Bodenstein, "A Few Aspects of the Actio emti and the Aedilitian Actions", (1914) 31 *SALJ* 20 sq.

[307] *Commentarius ad Pandectas*, Lib. XXI, Tit. I, 10; cf. further Van Warmelo, op. cit., note 98, pp. 91 sq. On what authority Voet bases this exception is not clear. The Roman texts he quotes, are not concerned with the position of an artifex; neither do the three writers to whom he refers (Mynsinger, Faber and Mevius) provide authority for his proposition.

[308] 1964 (3) SA 561 (A) at 571H. For criticism, see De Wet en Yeats, p. 303. The most recent decision in this line is *Gannet Manufacturing Co. (Pty.) Ltd. v. Postaflex (Pty.) Ltd.* 1981 (3) SA 216 (C) at 225F sqq.

version of the "Pothier rule". It seems to be based on an incorrect translation of the words: ". . . *ou un marchand qui vend des ouvrages . . . du commerce dont il fait profession*" by Solomon J, in *Erasmus v. Russell's Executor.*[309] There is obviously a significant difference between a merchant who is liable merely by virtue of selling "articles of commerce which it is his business to supply"[310] and one who must have publicly professed to have attributes of skill and expert knowledge.[311]

(b) The English Sale of Goods Act

It might not be inapposite in this context to refer also to English law.[312] § 14(1) of the Sale of Goods Act until 1973 contained the following provision:

> "Where the buyer, expressly or by implication, makes known to the seller the particular purpose for which the goods are required, so as to show that the buyer relies on the seller's skill or judgement, and the goods are of a description which it is in the course of the seller's business to supply, there is an implied condition that the goods shall be reasonably fit for such purpose",

and § 14(2) added specifically:

> "Where the goods are bought by description from a seller who deals in goods of that description, there is an implied condition that the goods shall be of merchantable quality."

There is every reason to believe that these rules were inspired by the "Pothier rule" and are thus ultimately based on Pomp. D. 19, 1, 6, 4 also. Sir Mackenzie Chalmers, the "father" of the Sale of Goods Act, had a very high regard for Pothier's *Traité du contrat de vente*: ". . . it is still", he wrote in 1894,[313] "the best reasoned treatise on the Law of Sale that has seen the light of day." This was very much in tune with the general sentiments prevailing in England at that time. When the English Courts and treatise writers, in the course of the 19th century, created the modern law of contract,[314] they were "engaged upon an enterprise which was new to the common law . . . but old to the civilian tradition".[315] It is hardly surprising, therefore, that they borrowed heavily from that civilian tradition, and Pothier's treatises,

---

[309] 1904 TS 365 at 374.

[310] These are the words of a correct translation by Jones J, in *Young's Provision Stores (Pty.) Ltd. v. Van Reyneveld* 1936 CPD 87 at 91 sq.

[311] For an example of a case which would be covered by this restricted version of the Pothier rule, see *Marais v. Commercial General Agency Ltd.* 1922 TPD 440. For a more detailed discussion of the implications, see Reinhard Zimmermann, "Der Einfluss Pothiers auf das römisch-holländische Recht in Südafrika", (1985) 102 *ZSS* (GA) 185 sqq.

[312] For a comprehensive comparative discussion, see Basedow, op. cit., note 250, pp. 15 sqq., 44 sqq.

[313] Reprinted, for instance, in *Chalmers' Sale of Goods Act, 1893* (17th ed., 1975), p. IX. Cf. further e.g. John B. Moyle, *The Contract of Sale in the Civil Law* (1892), p. 205.

[314] Cf. e.g. Atiyah, *Rise and Fall*, pp. 398 sqq., 681 sqq.

[315] A.W.B. Simpson, "Innovation in Nineteenth Century Contract Law", (1975) 91 *LQR* 254.

accessible to English lawyers in translated versions,[316] became one of the most influential sources.[317] As Best CJ once put it: "The authority of Pothier is as high as can be had next to the decision of a court of justice in this country."[318]

[316] A translation of the *Traité des obligations* by W.D. Evans appeared first in America (Philadelphia, 1802), four years later also in England (London, 1806). The *Traité du contrat de vente* was translated by L.S. Cushings in 1839, the *Traité du contrat de société* by O.D. Tudor in 1854.

[317] For further details, see Reinhard Zimmermann, "Synthesis in South African Private Law: Civil Law, Common Law and Usus Hodiernus Pandectarum", (1986) 103 *SALJ* 283 sq.; idem (1985) 102 *ZSS* (GA) 176 sqq.

[318] *Cox v. Troy* (1822) 5 B & Ald 474 at 480.

CHAPTER 11

Locatio conductio I

I. LOCATIO CONDUCTIO IN GENERAL

1. Locare and conducere

A lets his townhouse to B. He asks his employee C to maintain the garden of his country residence. Finally, he asks D to transport some columns from the one place to the other.—It does not strike the modern lawyer as particularly obvious that these three transactions should have more in common with each other than each of them with, say, a contract of sale. Indeed, according to modern German (or South African) law, we would be dealing with three different types of contract. B has been granted the use of a thing in return for money: A and B have concluded a (contract of) lease. C has promised to provide his services in return for money: he has entered into a contract of service (or employment). D has been assigned a specific task to be performed in return for money: we are dealing with a contract for work.

This scheme has been taken over from the pandectists.[1] They referred to locatio conductio rei (letting and hiring of things), locatio conductio operarum (letting and hiring of services) and locatio conductio operis (letting and hiring of work). The Roman lawyers, on the other hand, did not draw these distinctions. They did not think in terms of three different transactions, but accommodated all of them within the framework of one single contract called locatio conductio. The parallels with emptio venditio are obvious: we are dealing with a consensual contract[2] of a necessarily bilateral nature; the prestation of one of the parties has to consist in money; and the transaction is defined by what happens to the object of the contract seen from the point of view of first the one and then the other party (locare/conducere).[3]

---

[1] Cf., for example, Arndts, *Pandekten*, § 309; Dernburg, *Pandekten*, vol II, § 110; Thibaut, *System*, § 511. On the history of this trichotomy, see Félix Olivier-Martin, "Des divisions du louage en droit romain", (1936) 15 *RH* 463 sqq., who credits Voet (*Commentarius ad Pandectas*, Lib. XIX, Tit. II) with its invention. Most writers of the usus modernus pandectarum and of the natural-law school, however, drew a distinction only between locatio conductio rei and operae (the latter category comprising both contract of service and contract for work): Coing, pp. 456 sq. Cf. also art. 1708 code civil, art. 1568 codice civile, §§ 1090 sqq., 1151 ABGB, and Windscheid/Kipp, §§ 399, 401. On the question of classification, see too Jones, *Bailments*, pp. 85 sqq.; Story, *Bailments*, §§ 368 sqq.; F.B.J. Wubbe, "Opus selon la définition de Labéon", (1982) 50 *TR* 250.

[2] Gai. III, 135: "Consensu fiunt obligationes in emptionibus venditionibus, locationibus conductionibus, societatibus, mandatis."

[3] "We are accustomed, in the common law, to use words corresponding to those of the Roman law, almost in the same promiscuous manner. Thus letting (locatio) and hiring (conductio) are precise equivalents, used for the purpose of distinguishing the relative situation of different parties to the same contract": Story, *Bailments*, § 369.

"Locare" means to place, place out or place at the disposal, "conducere" to carry along, to take with one.[4] This, for the Romans, was the pivotal point, the core feature uniting the seemingly disparate contracts of lease, of service and for work under one and the same umbrella. The lessor places a thing at the lessee's disposal. The lessee may use it; he takes control of it and in this sense "carries it with himself". The employee places his services at the disposal of the employer, which the latter then "takes along", i.e. is in a position to make use of. And the customer (in the case of letting and hiring of work) places out a specific job, a piece of work to be done; the contractor takes over the object(s) with regard to which he has to perform that task.[5]

It becomes clear immediately that the Roman terminology must appear to be utterly confusing once one loses sight of these core concepts. For whilst in the contract of service (locatio conductio operarum) it is the locator who does the work (and the conductor who pays the remuneration), under a contract for work (locatio conductio operis) the conductor is bound to do the job, the locator to pay the money. Both the letting and hiring of things (locatio conductio rei) and of services often involve parties who are economically and socially unequal; but whereas in the first instance it is the conductor (lessee) who is typically in the weaker position, the same applies, in the second case, to the locator (employee). All in all, then, actiones locati are granted to a lessor, an employee and a customer, actiones conducti to the lessee, the employer and the contractor. The only key to understanding and determining this lies in the meaning of locare and conducere.

2. Three in one

If the modern trichotomy of contracts is alien to the Roman sources (neither Gaius nor D. 19, 2 separates the three basic forms of locatio conductio), this does not mean that the Romans applied the same rules to all varieties of this contract.[6] It would be quite wrong

---

[4] On etymology and meaning cf. e.g. Heinrich Degenkolb, *Platzrecht und Miete* (1867), pp. 133 sqq.; Kaufmann, *Altrömische Miete*, pp. 297 sq.; Ulrich von Lübtow, "Catos leges venditioni et locationi dictae", in: *Symbolae Raphaeli Taubenschlag dedicatae*, vol. III (1957), pp. 231 sqq. But see also e.g. Otto Karlowa, *Römische Rechtsgeschichte*, vol. II (1901), p. 638.

[5] The terms "locare" and "conducere" were not always employed in a strictly literal sense, but were sometimes used "metaphorically" (Schulz, *CRL*, p. 543). Thus, for instance, in a contract for work the conductor often does not "carry" anything "with him" (or away): take, for instance, the contractor who has undertaken to build a house on the property of the customer. The same applies to a lease of landed property (cf. Kaufmann, *Altrömische Miete*, pp. 237 sq.). On the terminology and the question of who could conclude a contract of locatio conductio, cf. Imre Molnár, "Subjekte der locatio conductio", in: *Studi in onore di Cesare Sanfilippo*, vol. II (1982), pp. 413 sqq.

[6] Cf., however, e.g. Arangio-Ruiz, *Istituzioni*, pp. 345 sq.; Ugo Brasiello, "L'unitarietà del concetto di locazione in diritto Romano", (1927) 2 *RISG* 529 sqq.; (1928) 3 *RISG* 1 sqq.;

to attribute any dogmatic significance to this essentially unitarian view.[7]

The Roman lawyers realized that not everything which came under the heading of locatio conductio could be treated alike, and, as usual, their approach to the individual cases brought before them was guided by pragmatic differentiation and careful analysis of typical conflicts of interest rather than by conceptual rigidity. While they themselves were quite uninterested in abstract categorization, their casuistry nevertheless provided the basis for the traditional civilian threefold classification.[8] This illustrates a fundamental dilemma with which the student of Roman law is often faced. It would be quite ahistorical to superimpose systematic distinctions over the Roman sources or to approach them with modern dogmatic categories in mind. On the other hand, the Roman sources usually provide the historical foundation, the casuistic basis for these classifying and structuring efforts of the later civilians; and in order to prevent the modern lawyer from drowning in the flood of Roman case law, some sort of systematic life jacket appears to be indispensable. This must be kept in mind, while we shall, in the following pages, deal with the three main types of locatio conductio separately.[9] In a way, of course, this procedure is un-Roman, because, as we have said, the Romans knew only the contract of locatio conductio. And yet, this unitarian concept was a matter of terminology and procedure rather than of practical impact and dogmatic consequences. This will become clearer if we remind ourselves of three things: that Roman law was actional law (and was thus developed under procedural auspices), that in this specific instance we are dealing with bonae fidei iudicia, and that the Roman lawyers were traditionalists rather than vigorous reformers.

3. Historical development

The early history of locatio conductio is obscured by the scarcity of sources.[10] It has been plausibly argued, however, that from early on the

---

Schulz, *CRL*, pp. 542 sq.; Luigi Amirante, "Ricerche in tema di locazione", (1959) 62 *BIDR* 9 sqq. Contra: A.D.E. Lewis, "The Trichotomy in Locatio Conductio", (1973) 8 *Irish Jurist* 164 sqq.

[7] Cf. e.g. Mayer-Maly, *Locatio conductio*, pp. 18 sqq.; idem, "Tipicità e unità della 'locatio conductio'", (1959) 5 *Labeo* 390 sqq.; Max Kaser, (1960) 11 *Iura* 229 sqq.; idem, *RPr* I, p. 563; more recently cf. e.g. Pinna Parpaglia, *Vitia ex ipsa re* (1983), pp. 181 sqq.

[8] ". . . far from constructing a bogus classification, the civilians were responsible for making explicit what, for the Roman jurists, was only implicit": Lewis, (1973) 8 *The Irish Jurist* 164.

[9] This is also how Kaser, *RPr* I, pp. 564 sqq. and Honsell/Mayer-Maly/Selb, §§ 118 sqq., deal with the matter. The alternative approach (discussion of locatio conductio in general; differentiation according to the various types of locatio conductio only in the context of individual problems) has been followed by Mayer-Maly in his book on locatio conductio.

[10] There are hardly any literary sources documenting the practice of letting and hiring before the 2nd century B.C. (i.e. before the time of the comedies of Plautus and Terentius). All available archaeological evidence has been carefully scrutinized by Kaufmann, *Altrömische Miete*, pp. 26 sqq. For the time of the XII Tables cf. Gai. IV, 28: "Lege autem introducta est pignoris capio veluti lege XII tabularum adversus eum, qui hostiam emisset nec pretium

letting and hiring of property, of services and of work must have occurred,[11] albeit possibly on a relatively small scale. Such transactions were at first not enforceable per se, but the contract verbis (stipulatio) was, of course, flexible enough to accommodate them just as any other arrangement. Some time during the course of the Republic, the praetor decided to enforce a purely consensual act and to grant a iudicium locati conducti.[12] Whether this first case involved a contract of lease, of services or for work, we do not know. The iudicium, in any event, contained a demonstratio which defined the facts on which the action rested, and the core feature of this definition consisted of the words "locavit" and "conduxit". Furthermore, the formula, which came to be incorporated into the edict, contained the ex bona fide clause. Take, for instance, what we today call locatio conductio rei:

> "Quod A^s A^s N^o N^o fundum quo de agitur locavit, quidquid ob eam rem N^m N^m A^o A^o dare facere oportet ex fide bona, eius iudex N^m N^m A^o A^o condemnato, si non paret, absolvito":

this was (probably), what the formula of the actio locati looked like;[13] and the conductor (lessee) could invoke the corresponding actio conducti:

> "Quod A^s A^s de N^o N^o fundum quo de agitur conduxerit, quidquid ob eam rem N^m N^m A^o A^o dare facere oportet ex fide bona, eius iudex N^m N^m A^o A^o condemnato, si non paret, absolvito."

A slight change in the demonstratio was all that was necessary to adapt the formula to suit a contract of services: "Quod A^s A^s N^o N^o se operasque suas locavit . . .", "Quod A^s A^s de N^o N^o operas eius conduxit . . .", and the actiones locati and conducti were applicable to this situation as well. Finally, the formula could be employed to suit a locatio conductio operis, too: "Quod A^s A^s N^o N^o (e.g.:) columnas transportandas locavit . . .", "Quod A^s A^s de N^o N^o columnas transportandas conduxit . . ." was how the parties would have defined the facts on which they based their action. A contract of locatio conductio was thus actionable, no matter whether it involved res, operae or opus; and in a legal system developed under procedural

---

redderet; item adversus eum, qui mercedem non redderet pro eo iumento, quod quis ideo locasset, ut inde pecuniam acceptam in dapem, id est in sacrificium, impenderet." A small farmer is unable to provide the prescribed sacrifices for the gods. He has to hire out his beasts of burden in order to raise the necessary money. If the hirer does not pay the remuneration, the farmer/lessor may resort to self-help, and distrain. Gaius' report relates to a time when locatio conductio was very much an extra-legal phenomenon. For further details, see Kaufmann, *Altrömische Miete*, pp. 35 sqq. On the early history of locatio conductio, see further Kaser, *RPr* I, pp. 564 sq.

[11] Kaufmann, *Altrömische Miete*, passim. Hardly anything is known about the (legal) shape and structure of these transactions.

[12] Cf. e.g. Kaufmann, *Altrömische Miete*, pp. 344 sqq. More particularly, contrary to the opinion of many, locatio conductio did not originate as contract re (cf. the discussion by Mayer-Maly, *Locatio conductio*, pp. 81 sqq.).

[13] Lenel, *EP*, pp. 229 sq. For detailed speculations on the structure of the formula, see Kaufmann, *Altrömische Miete*, pp. 349 sqq.

auspices ("ubi remedium, ibi ius") this is obviously of prime importance. Legal protection was available to lessors and lessees, to employers and employees, to customers and contractors; the carving out of the rules of substantive law was cura posterior and could be conveniently attended to within the wide range of bona fides. After all, the judge was instructed to decide what the defendant had to do or to give "ex bona fide", and that provided him with the necessary discretion to develop apposite distinctions and to make, for instance, the standard of liability dependent upon the individual type of locatio conductio which he happened to be dealing with. These distinctions, however, were never conceptualized or categorized, the reason being simply that it was not necessary to do so, from a procedural point of view. Thus, the Romans always contented themselves with locatio conductio as a residual category for all types of bilateral agreements except sale, where the prestation of one of the parties had to be in money.[14]

II. THE SOCIAL AND ECONOMIC FRAMEWORK OF LEASE

1. The quest for security of tenure

Lease, in modern law, is hardly less important than sale. More particularly, the lease of residential space is of great social and economic importance. Not everybody can afford to (or wants to) own his own home. But even if a person does not own it, his home is the centre of his social existence. He becomes attached to it and does not want to lose it. Thus, he has a special interest in security of tenure. If the landlord were totally free to terminate the lease at any time and for any reason, he would be able to cause a disproportionate amount of hardship to the tenant and his family. Furthermore, sometimes the market does not function properly. In Germany, for instance, the two world wars caused a dramatic housing shortage. By the end of the Second World

[14] Watson, *Evolution*, p. 16. Originally there seems to have been no distinction between selling and buying and letting and hiring. This would account for the promiscuous use of sale and hire terminology in early sources and is particularly plausible for the time before the introduction of money. Both "sale" and "letting and hiring" were, at that stage, exchange transactions: merchandise for merchandise in the one instance, merchandise for the letting of a thing or services in the others. The common denominator was that both parties delivered and received something. The fact that such transfer in the one case was intended only for a certain period was a more refined consideration which became important only gradually. As a consequence, sale was carved out as a transaction with a characteristic and homogeneous structure which was distinctly different from all the other types of bilateral agreement. A iudicium empti venditi, and with it a technical sale terminology, was developed. Thus, a distinction was drawn between sale and all the fairly disparate and heterogeneous exchange deals that remained of the old uniform category and which came to be referred to as locatio conductio. On all this, see especially Kaufmann, *Altrömische Miete*, pp. 303 sqq, also (pp. 309 sqq.) on Cato's (*De agri cultura* CLVIII, 149, 1) "pabulum hibernum venire" (pastoral lease or sale of the fodder growing on the pasture ground?).

War many houses had been destroyed or were uninhabitable; at the same time, millions of refugees and expellees from the East were in search of accommodation. Under such circumstances prospective tenants have an interest in the existing residential space being controlled and managed in an efficient manner; actual tenants who are already living in rented housing need protection against their landlords who might be tempted to exploit the situation and to demand exorbitant rents. Thus, in the course of time, a whole body of law was developed, amending, adapting and superseding the law of lease as it had once been laid down in the BGB.[15] Poorly drafted and scattered over several enactments,[16] this body of law rests on the cornerstones of notice protection and rent control. It introduces a great deal of ius cogens into the landlord–tenant relationship and seems to have a greater affinity to public law than to private law. The contract of lease, as it exists in modern German law, is no longer characterized so much by the private autonomy of the contracting parties; it has been converted into something of a publicly regulated, social owner-and-user relationship.[17] In Germany these changes partly reflect a balancing of interests determined by the "Constitution". For whilst the Basic Law of 1949[18] contains a guarantee both of private property[19] and of private autonomy,[20] it also acknowledges that property imposes duties and that its use must serve the public weal.[21] Property rights are limited in the social interest and freedom of contract must not become an instrument of domination, but has a social function too. On the other hand, the question may well be asked whether all these protective regulations are (still) necessary in order to achieve socially acceptable results.[22] Government aid for residential building over the past decades (far exceeding a hundred thousand million DM) and tax incentives have led to the completion of between 500 000 and 700 000 homes a year. Thus, today the supply of accommodation appears to be entirely satisfactory, both from a quantitative and a qualitative point of view: in

[15] For a detailed commentary cf. e.g. Volker Emmerich, Jürgen Sonnenschein, *Mietrecht* (2nd ed., 1984); Wolfgang Schmidt-Futterer, Hubert Blank, *Wohnraumschutzgesetze* (5th ed., 1984).

[16] For an attempt to remedy this state of affairs and to consolidate the law, see Jürgen Sonnenschein, *Die Bereinigung des Mietrechts im Bürgerlichen Gesetzbuch* (1985).

[17] Franz Wieacker, *Industriegesellschaft und Privatrechtsordnung* (1974), p. 27.

[18] The title "Basic law" is intended to convey the provisional nature of the (West) German "constitution". After 40 years of seperate development in the Federal Republic and the "German Democratic Republic" one can, however, hardly maintain any longer that the "Basic Law" is different in character (i.e. inferior) from a "proper" constitution. Cf., for example, Otto Kimminich, 1973 *Deutsche Verwaltungsblätter* 657 sqq. (659); Michael Kirn, 1974 *Zeitschrift für Rechtspolitik* 84 sqq. (86); Schmidt-Bleibtreu/Klein, *Kommentar zum Grundgesetz für die Bundesrepublik Deutschland* (6th ed., 1983), Einl. n. 45.

[19] Art. 14 I GG.

[20] Art. 2 I GG (as interpreted by the German Constitutional Supreme Court).

[21] Art. 14 II GG.

[22] Cf. particularly Heinrich Honsell, "Privatautonomie und Wohnungsmiete", (1986) 186 *Archiv für die civilistische Praxis* 115 sqq.

1984, 26,78 million homes were available for a total of 25,33 million households (as opposed to 9,4 million homes for 15,3 million households in 1950);[23] an average of more than 30 m^2 of living accommodation is available per person; only 13 % of the net income of a household, on average, has to be spent on rent. In view of this, some deregulation and a return to the laws of supply and demand would hardly appear to be unjustifiable. This would imply a return to the ius dispositivum of the BGB.[24] In any event, however, it is clear that the law no longer has to concern itself so much with the economic interest of the (essentially competitive) tenant but that security of tenure aims at protecting the tenant against the financial and (especially) the psychological consequences of a move of home.[25]

Other modern industrial societies, of course, have had to cope in similar ways with the "quest for security of tenure". But whereas the individually inclined French seem to be on the way back to the regulatory mechanisms of market forces,[26] the English legislator

> "gives a distinctly higher preference to the interest of tenants in remaining in their homes. . . . The middle class ideal of owning your own home and garden has in fact so infused English thinking that those who cannot afford to buy their homes are given the next best things; security for one, two or three lives."[27]

In comparison with its modern descendant, to which copious Acts of Parliament, voluminous court decisions and piles of literature have been devoted, the Roman lease may appear to be a fairly poor thing.[28] No particular concern for security of tenure is apparent from the pages of the Digest, none for substantive fairness of rent; hardly any protective legislative intervention is recorded, and only a comparatively modest amount of case law dealing with problems of lease can be found in D. 19, 2. Matters were left largely to the agreement of the parties.[29] The institution of giving notice was unknown. Rooms were either let for a certain time or, if no such limit had been set, the contract could entirely unceremoniously be terminated at any time by either party.

2. Living conditions in Rome

Does this mean that the letting and renting of accommodation was a rare and socially unimportant phenomenon in Rome that did not throw

---

[23] For these figures cf. Honsell, (1986) 186 *Archiv für die civilistische Praxis* 124 sqq.

[24] On a more general level, see Kurt H. Biedenkopf, "Die Wiederentdeckung des Privatrechts", in: *Europäisches Rechtsdenken in Geschichte und Gegenwart, Festschrift für Helmut Coing*, vol. II (1982), pp. 21 sqq.

[25] Tony Honoré, *The Quest for Security: Employees, Tenants, Wives* (1982), pp. 34 sqq.

[26] Honoré, op. cit., note 25, pp. 37 sqq. Today cf. Act 82—526, *Recueil Dalloz* 1982, 284 (22.6.1982).

[27] Honoré, op. cit., note 25, pp. 58 sq.

[28] Cf. Schulz, *CRL*, p. 544.

[29] "Roman jurisprudence displays, in urban leasehold as elsewhere, an emphasis on enforcement of the agreed-upon terms of contracts. Such emphasis can be defended as support for the security of the market-place": Frier, *Landlords and Tenants*, p. 186.

up problems? Quite the contrary is true. All too easily are we tempted, today, to visualize living conditions in Rome in terms of what we can glean from the excavation of leisurely country towns like Pompeii or Herculaneum. We think of wealthy Roman senators residing in private mansions of the type of a Villa dei Misteri or a Casa del Fauno.[30] In some instances we may be correct. But space in Rome was limited. It is estimated that the Imperial urbs did not extend beyond an area of eight square miles, yet had to accommodate about 1 200 000 inhabitants.[31] Owing to the lack of efficient transport systems, the suburban space could hardly be used for the housing of those who had to transact business in town. Only the wealthiest, under these circumstances, could afford to own their own home (domus). Most people had to live in insulae, imposing and often monumental blocks of flats which amazed the ancient world.[32] In the more luxurious of them, the ground floor was either let as a whole to one tenant or subdivided into comfortable multiple-room apartment units.[33] This ground-floor tenant, however, had to be prepared to pay a very substantial annual rent. Marcus Caelius Rufus, for instance, a contemporary and student of Cicero, is said to have paid 30 000 sesterces.[34] According to Carcopino, even "the humblest tenant [at that time] had to pay a rent of 2 000 sesterces a year".[35] And he did not get much comfort for that price, either: the insulae in which he lived were ill supplied with water, light and fireplaces. But for the ground floor, they lacked domestic

---

[30] On the Roman villa (architecture, conditions of living, daily routine of the owner of a villa, etc.), see Harald Mielsch, *Die römische Villa* (1987).

[31] For details Carcopino, pp. 20 sqq., 26 sqq. On the overcrowding of ancient towns, see in particular R. von Pöhlmann, *Die Übervölkerung der antiken Grossstädte* (1884). For quantitative studies on the size of cities and of city population in the Roman Empire, see Duncan-Jones, pp. 259 sqq.

[32] For this and what follows cf. Carcopino, pp. 33 sqq. According to the Regionaries, the city had 1 797 domus as opposed to 46 602 insulae. The most characteristic feature of these insulae was their height. "As early as the third century B.C. insulae of three storeys were so frequent that they had ceased to excite remarks." This can be gleaned from the anecdote (told by Livius, *Ab urbe condita*, Lib. XXI, LXII) of the (apparently) mad ox which "scaled the stairs of a riverside insula to fling itself into the void from the third storey amid the horrified cries of the onlookers" (Carcopino, pp. 35 sqq.): a bad omen indeed! Augustus imposed a limit of 20 m on the height of private houses.

[33] It is to these apartment units (as described in Ulp. D. 9, 3, 5, 2) that Frier, *Landlords and Tenants*, pp. 5 sqq. wishes to confine the use of the term "cenaculum" (as opposed to "diversoria" or "meritoria", the squalid tenement houses for the poor).

[34] Cicero, *Pro M. Caelio oratio*, VII—17.

[35] Carcopino, p. 56. Juvenal, *Satura*, III, 223 sqq., remarks that the annual rent for a miserable flat in town would have bought splendid estates in a medium-sized country town. The figure of 2 000 sesterces is probably exaggerated. Our legal and extra-legal texts deal with upper-class leases, not with "the hordes of depressed lower class tenants who constituted the vast majority of the Roman tenantry" (Frier, *Landlords and Tenants*, p. 39). The latter, according to Frier (p. 51), paid rent "on a short-term basis, perhaps most commonly daily". Payment at yearly intervals (as a rule: postnumerando!) in all probability applied only to upper-class tenants. English law seems to offer a parallel in so far as the law of lease has traditionally been reserved for relationships with some sort of permanence (as opposed to a mere licence).

drainage. They were usually dangerous to live in, overcrowded, squalid and noisy.

> "Almost everywhere, the higher you went in a building, the more breathless became the overcrowding, the more sordid the promiscuity. . . . Whatever the disposition of the ground floor, the upper storeys were gradually swamped by the mob: entire families were herded together in them; dust, rubbish, and filth accumulated; and . . . bugs ran riot."[36]

The insulae were normally exploited by a system of letting and subletting.[37] They were let to a principal lessee, who in turn sublet the cenacula (or meritoria) of the upper storeys and thus relieved the owner of all the troubles involved in the exploitation of his property. However, so

> "intolerable was the burden of rent that the sub-tenants of the first lessee almost invariably had to sub-let in their turn every room in their cenaculum which they could possibly spare".[38]

In other words: the free play of forces on the housing market can hardly be said to have produced socially acceptable conditions. If anything, there was a greater need to regulate the relationship between lessor and lessee in Rome than there is today. The extremes of wealth and poverty were much more marked; so was, of course, the inequality of

---

[36] Carcopino, loc. cit.

[37] For details Frier, *Landlords and Tenants*, pp. 29 sqq.; Guillaume Cardascia, "Sur une fonction de la sous-location en droit romain", in: *Studi in onore di Arnaldo Biscardi*, vol. II (1982), pp. 365 sqq. The same applied in the case of warehouses (horrea): the owner of a horreum usually let the whole warehouse to a principal tenant (the horrearius) who then in turn let out the storage space to the individual customers (cf. e.g. Andreas Wacke, "Rechtsfrage der römischen Lagerhausvermietung", (1980) 26 *Labeo* 304 sqq.; differently Claude Alzon, *Problèmes relatifs à la location des entrepôts en droit romain* (1965), according to whom the individual customer always contracted directly with the owner; the horrearius was merely a subordinate, something like a foreman of the staff of the horrea, acting in the employ of the owner. This view has however generally been rejected: cf. e.g. J.A.C. Thomas, "Return to 'Horrea' " (1966) 13 *RIDA* 357 sqq.).

It is obvious that the contract between owner and horrearius was locatio conductio rei. But what was the relationship between horrearius and his customers (the "depositors")? It cannot have been depositum wherever—as was usually the case—the horrearius received a merces. But was it locatio conductio operarum (Joachim Rosenthal, "Custodia und Aktivlegitimation zur Actio furti", (1951) 68 *ZSS* 231 sqq.) or locatio conductio operis (Felix Wubbe, "Zur Haftung des Horrearius", (1959) 76 *ZSS* 511 sqq.) or locatio conductio rei (prevailing opinion: cf. e.g. Thomas, (1966) 13 *RIDA* 362; Kaser, *RPr* I, p. 565; Wacke, (1980) 26 *Labeo* 309) or a combined locatio rei and operis faciendi (Alzon, pp. 201 sqq.)? The horrearius was an independent contractor who employed his own staff; thus he was probably not merely an employee of the "depositors" (thus: no locatio conductio operarum). In all our sources, the horrearius is referred to as locator, by customers as conductores. The relationship must therefore have been one of locatio conductio rei, despite the fact that the horrearius (unlike "normal" lessors) was liable for custodia (Paul. D. 19, 2, 55 pr.; Lab. D. 19, 2, 60, 6 and 9; C. 4, 65, 1 (Ant.); C. 4, 65, 4 (Alex.); Wubbe, (1959) 76 *ZSS* 508 sqq.; Carlo Augusto Cannata, "Su alcuni problemi relativi alla 'locatio horrei' nel diritto romano classico", (1964) 30 *SDHI* 244 sqq.; Alzon, pp. 41 sqq., and many others). The horrearius is providing a "safe-keeping place", i.e. he is *as locator* under an additional contractual duty of custodiam praestare. These (modern) disputes about the horrea contract are, incidentally, another confirmation of the fact that the Romans did not employ the scheme of three different types of locatio conductio (Thomas, (1966) 13 *RIDA* 362).

[38] Carcopino, loc. cit.

bargaining power as far as the scramble for urban accommodation was concerned.

3. Some typical problems

Apart from that, the tenant seems to have been surrounded by potential sources of disaster. A mere glance over the Digest reveals that his life cannot have been unexciting. Lofty as they were, the insulae were far too lightly built. Builders tried to economize. Thus it could happen that the piling up of earth against the wall of a house by a neighbour had disastrous effects: the earth was soaked by continual rain storms, and from the seepage of moisture the wall became wet and broke down.[39] The collapse of houses (ruina) is frequently mentioned, i.a. as one of the typical incidents falling outside the ambit of custodia liability.[40] Alfenus (D. 19, 2, 30 pr.) discusses the case of an owner of an insula who had leased it, for a sum of 30, to a principal tenant, who in turn sublet the various cenacula for a total of 40. Now the owner demolishes the building, allegedly in order to prevent its collapse. Can the principal tenant sue him for a refund of his rent (30) or also for what he has lost on account of the fact that he could not extract any profits from the subtenants? In D. 19, 2, 27, 1 we meet a tenant who decides to move out "timoris causa".[41] Does he have to pay the full amount of the rent agreed upon? Answer: not if there were grounds for his fears, even though a danger might in fact not have existed. What happens if a tenant has paid his rent for one year in advance and then, before the lapse of that year, the building collapses or burns down? He may reclaim the money for the remaining time,[42] not, interestingly, with a condictio,[43] but with the actio conducti.

Fires were, of course, the other great disaster which all inhabitants of an insula constantly dreaded.[44] Thus we find lessors insisting on the incorporation of special clauses into the contract: that the lessee may not bring easily inflammable substances (like hay) into his lodgings[45] or even that he may not have a fire ("ignem ne habeto").[46] In case of

---

[39] Iav. D. 19, 2, 57.

[40] Cf. e.g. supra, p. 192.

[41] On this text and the problem of iusta causa timoris in general, cf. Frier, *Landlords and Tenants*, pp. 94 sqq.

[42] Ulp. D. 19, 2, 19, 6.

[43] Reason: the payment had not been made per errorem.

[44] As to the justification of such fear, cf., for example, Ulp. D. 1, 15, 2 ("pluribus uno die incendiis exortis"). Cf. further e.g. Juvenal, *Satura*, III, 197 sqq. Aulus Gellius relates the story of a group of friends walking up the Cispian hill when they see a big urban insula on fire. "Magni reditus urbanorum praediorum", says one of them, "sed pericula sunt longe maxima. si quid autem possit remedii fore, ut ne tam adsidue domus Romae arderent, venum hercle dedissem res rusticas et urbicas emissem." It was mainly the risk of fire that made it more attractive for wealthy Romans to invest in farmland rather than in urban properties. For details, see Frier, *Landlords and Tenants*, pp. 21 sqq.

[45] Ulp. D. 19, 2, 11, 4.

[46] Ulp. D. 19, 2, 11, 1.

contravention, the lawyers were prepared to grant the actio locati to the lessor, irrespective of whether a third party had in actual fact set the hay on fire or whether—in the second example—the house had not burnt down on account of the lessee's fire but due to casus fortuitus.[47]

All these texts are suggestive in their implications. But they also show that the Roman lawyers dealt with the particulars of lease of residential space in very much the same manner as they dealt with any other problem brought before them. They appear to have been insensitive to the social dimensions of this type of contract,[48] and certainly they did not make any special effort to relieve the lot of tenants. Generally speaking, therefore, the Roman law of lease was landlord-friendly and it appears to have been entirely out of tune, at least by modern standards, with the social and economic problems of an ever-growing urban tenantry.

4. The Roman lawyers and the law of lease

The reason for this should not be sought in any social bias on the part of the lawyers. It is true that they may not have been fully aware of the acuteness of the problems. As respectable members of the class of clarissimi et amplissimi viri[49] they were unlikely to reside (or even to know anybody who resided) in the upper storeys of the insula of Felicula.[50] But that does not mean that they tailored the law to suit the needs of their fellow capitalists and to make the exploitation of slums a particularly profitable enterprise.[51] Nor, indeed, was the Roman law of lease totally detached from the social framework within which it was supposed to operate. By and large, the rules that were developed reflect a balancing of competing interests, based on the realities of the Roman rental market and, from a public policy perspective, apt to serve as a satisfactory instrument of social control.[52] The whole problem, however, lies in the fact that the jurists created the Roman lease law with only one segment of the market in mind: it was meant, primarily, to resolve the problems arising from upper-class housing. It was not designed to oppress or to relieve the lot of the poor: they simply did not feature.[53] Roman law was actional law and where there was no

---

[47] The idea of versari in re illicita; cf. supra, pp. 197, 209.

[48] Cf. generally Schulz, *Principles*, p. 24 (s. v. "Isolation").

[49] Cicero, *De oratore*, 1, XLV—45.

[50] An apartment block of extraordinary dimensions, that seems to have been famous throughout the ancient world (cf. Tertullius, *Adversus Valentinianos*, VII, 3). On the status and social background of the Roman jurists during the various periods of Roman law, see especially Fritz Schulz, *History of Roman Legal Science*, passim; Wolfgang Kunkel, *Herkunft und soziale Stellung der römischen Juristen* (2nd ed., 1967), passim.

[51] Cf. e.g. Schulz, *CRL*, p. 545.

[52] For all details, see Frier, *Landlords and Tenants*, pp. 21 sqq. ("The Social Institutions of the Roman Rental Market"), pp. 174 sqq. ("Recognition of Interests in Roman Lease Law"), pp. 196 sqq. ("Roman Jurisprudence as an Instrument of Social Control").

[53] This is the main thesis of Frier's book on the Roman law of urban leasehold, which is now authoritative.

litigation, no law could be developed. Thus, the procedural and social factors determining the incidence of litigiousness in Roman society in turn determined both the content and the structure of the private law. Lower-class tenants did not have the means to approach a jurisconsultus for his opinion and a whole variety of considerations effectively deterred them from making use of the judicial apparatus.[54] Usually the reward they might have been able to obtain by bringing a lawsuit did not warrant the amount of time, expense and trouble required. Moreover, members of the lower classes

> "were probably ignorant of the law, and they were also the victims of a social structure that was not only exaggeratedly pyramidal in its distribution of wealth and influence, but also bound by stark social conventions. . . . Simultaneously, however, their poverty effectively protected these same lower classes against private law suits by others. Much of Roman private law may therefore have remained confined for all practical purposes to the upper social tiers."[55]

Thus, our legal sources, like the literary, usually refer to the world of the Roman upper class. This is true even in the case of lease, for, as Bruce W. Frier has demonstrated, the inquilini of the jurists were not typically lower-class tenants.[56] Comfortable cenacula or whole apartment-house complexes were available for those who could afford them,[57] and we even know of members of the senatorial rank who were attracted by the advantages of renting.[58] The Roman lawyers contented themselves with finding solutions to the problems brought before them, and that, in this instance, led to the creation of what has been termed a "law of upper-class-leasehold".[59] Arguably, it is in any event only this sector of the rental market that can be adequately regulated by means of private law. Even today, as we have seen, the task of policing the market of urban housing in its entirety leads us into the area of administrative and legislative intervention and, more generally, into the field of public law.[60] The Roman lawyers worked within the

---

[54] For details, see Frier, *Landlords and Tenants*, pp. 48 sqq.

[55] Frier, *Landlords and Tenants*, pp. 50 sq. Cf., on a more general level, also David Daube, *Roman Law*, pp. 71 sqq. (". . . the sources, the legal ones in particular, concentrate on the haves; it is they who occupy the centre of the stage. . . . The have-nots are invisible: *die im Dunkeln sieht man nicht*").

[56] *Landlords and Tenants*, pp. 40 sqq.; cf. also p. 52: "The inquilini of slum tenements find no place in juristic decisions on leasehold, despite their numerical preponderance among urban tenants."

[57] The archaeological evidence in Ostia and Rome is discussed by Frier, *Landlords and Tenants*, pp. 3 sqq.

[58] Suetonius (*De vita Caesarum*, Tiberius, XXXV, 4), for instance, tells the story of a senator who was stripped of his rank by Tiberius, because he used to enter his urban leases only in the course of July, remaining, until then, on his country estates. In this way, he tried to take advantage of the sharp drop in (upper-class) rents which occurred annually after the 1st July, the day which traditionally marked the start of the rental year.

[59] Frier, *Landlords and Tenants*, p. 52.

[60] Cf. supra, p. 343. If in many Western legal systems this applies to the whole of the law of lease, modern South African law offers an even closer parallel to the situation in Roman law: the law of lease (locatio conductio rei) in its pure and proper sense applies, by and large,

framework of the existing social and procedural structures. Problems resulting from unequal bargaining power fell outside their sphere of competence and experience—as did social reform or social engineering in general. Hence the specific structure of the Roman law of lease: the characteristic lack of control over the formation and content of the contract and its focus on the allocation of (objectively existing) risks and on occurrences producing liabilities under the contract.

5. Legal rules and extra-legal restrictions

At this stage one further point should perhaps be mentioned which accounts, more generally, for the fact that there was so little law (comparatively speaking) relating to locatio conductio of whatever type. Roman law was originally based on status relationships; it concerned itself with the family unit rather than with the individual. There was a movement, as Sir Henry Maine has put it, from Status to Contract.[61] A characteristic feature of Roman law was that it tended to interfere with the internal aspects of these status relationships as little as possible; pietas, fides, reverentia and the mores maiorum were largely relied upon as entirely satisfactory regulatory mechanisms:

> "[T]he need of the Roman for liberty demands restraint in the matter of the creation and recognition of legal principles. He demands a wide space free of legal rules because of the number and power of extra-legal restrictions. The Romans were enmeshed in a web of such restrictions, the intricacy and strength of which can hardly be conceived by the isolated beings of modern times."[62]

Thus, for instance, contractual relationships between a paterfamilias and his sons in power or his slaves did not exist; and it is immediately obvious that where the need for skilled labour was largely satisfied by a slave economy, locatio conductio in its labour-law variant had to be of much less significance than it is today. Particularly important, in our context, is the patronatus, a comprehensive power-relationship (involving, for instance, the ius vitae necisque), mitigated only by pietas, fides and censorian supervision, which existed between the former master and his freedman, but which could also be created by way of deditio or applicatio. Thus, many peasants, artisans and workers were technically free, but in fact their situation was half-servile. They worked as clientes for their patrons, who in turn

---

only to upper-class housing. It is to this segment of the law and of society that books such as those by Kerr and Cooper (*The South African Law of Landlord and Tenant* (1973)) refer. A totally different body of (administrative) law governs the residential rights of urban blacks. Cf., for an overview, W.H.B. Dean, "The Legal Regime Governing Urban Africans in South Africa—An Administrative Law Perspective", (1984) *Acta Juridica* 105 sqq.

[61] *Ancient Law*, p. 100.

[62] Schulz, *Principles*, p. 21; cf. also Hans Kloesel, "Libertas", in: Hans Oppermann (ed.), *Römische Wertbegriffe* (1983), pp. 120 sqq.

provided them with accommodation, protection in case of need, etc.[63] Clientship created reciprocal duties, which were, however, based on fides rather than on law. Thus it involved a complex net of social relations, relations which would have been classified, in legal terminology, as contract of lease, contract of services and contract for work. Of course, there was no need for such distinctions yet. As a matter which fell outside the ambit of the law, everything remained jumbled up; and this may be one of the historical reasons for the hybrid nature of locatio conductio once clientship disintegrated and once the praetor started to "legalize" the relationship and to grant reciprocal actions.[64]

III. LOCATIO CONDUCTIO REI

1. The nature of lease

Locatio conductio rei, then, was a bilateral consensual contract which gave rise to two iudicia bonae fidei, the actiones locati and conducti. It involved the letting of a thing, either for use or for use and enjoyment of the fruits (res locata or fruenda locata).[65] Which of these two alternatives applied in an individual case depended on the nature of the thing and on the agreement between the parties. In any case, however, the arrangement was classified as locatio conductio (rei). Modern civilian legal systems have used this distinction to further refine the typology of contracts. They normally deal with the contract of hire or lease ("By a contract of lease the lessor is bound to give to the lessee the use of the leased thing . . ." (*Miete*)[66]) as opposed to what one could call, for want of a precise English terminus technicus, usufructuary lease ("By a contract of usufructuary lease the lessor is bound to give the lessee . . . the use of the object leased and the enjoyment of its fruits, insofar as they can be considered as proceeds under the rules of normal management" (*Pacht*)).[67]

2. The objects of lease

Both movables and immovables could be the object of locatio conductio rei;[68] thus, in our texts we find, for instance, the hire of

---

[63] Cf. e.g. Berger, *ED*, p. 391; Kaser, *RPr* I, pp. 118 sq. More specifically on client-coloni, cf. most recently P.W. de Neeve, *Colonus. Private Farm-Tenancy in Roman Italy During the Republic and the Early Principate* (1984), pp. 187 sqq.

[64] Kaser, *RPr* I, pp. 564 sq.; but see Kaufmann, *Altrömische Miete*, pp. 320 sqq.

[65] Cf. e.g. Afr. D. 19, 2, 35 pr.; Gai. D. 19, 2, 25. On what frui entailed (fructus percipere), see P.W. de Neeve, "Remissio Mercedis", (1983) 100 *ZSS* 303.

[66] § 535 BGB.

[67] § 581 I BGB. On the specific structure of the usufructuary lease *("Pacht")* in Roman law cf. recently Pinna Parpaglia, op. cit., note 7, p. 27 and passim; Wolfgang Ernst, "Das Nutzungsrisiko bei der Pacht in der Entwicklung seit Servius", (1988) 105 *ZSS* 589 sqq.

[68] Cf. in general Imre Molnár, "Object of locatio conductio", (1982) 85 *BIDR* 127 sqq. Recently, the thesis has been advanced that the object of locatio conductio (rei) was not a res

slaves[69] and animals,[70] of barns and stores (horrea),[71] as well as the lease of residential accommodation and of agricultural land, the latter usually in the form of "usufructuary lease", i.e. the lessee having both ius utendi and ius fruendi. The agricultural lease, of course, was often as problematic and potentially explosive from a social and an economic point of view as the letting and hiring of urban accommodation.

During the first two centuries A.D. a process of concentration of landed property took place.[72] "Latifundia perdidere Italiam" warned Plinius (Secundus),[73] whose own nephew, however, owned big estates scattered over the whole of Italy. Seneca, who seems to have owned a private fortune to the value of 300 million sesterces, became one of the greatest landowners of his time. Agricultural investment[74] yielded an annual return of around 5–6 % and was much more popular than investment in urban properties. Most of the landed aristocracy, however, preferred to reside in town and also found it inconvenient to run their estates, from a distance, by using slaves.[75] Strict discipline and control was necessary, and in addition, the owner had to carry the risk of crop failures and sluggish demand. Hence it became more and more common for the landed proprietors to leave the management and cultivation of their estates to free farmers and smallholders (coloni).[76] Their lot was generally a sorry one, for the economic conditions during the Imperial age were not favourable to the agricultural community.[77]

---

but an activity relating to this res: Pinna Parpaglia, *Vitia ex ipsa re* (1983), e.g. pp. 138, 145; cf. also Ernst, (1988) 105 *ZSS* 590 sq.; Frier, *Landlord and Tenant*, p. 215 ("To some extent . . . urban leasehold might better be thought of as the exchange of money for certain services from the landlord, and not just for a place (res)"); but see Theo Mayer-Maly, (1983) 34 *Iura* 155.

[69] Gai. III, 146; cf. supra, p. 236.

[70] Cf. e.g. Alf. D. 19, 2, 30, 2 and Sibylle von Bolla, *Untersuchungen zu Tiermiete und Viehpacht im Alterum* (1940).

[71] Lab. D. 19, 2, 60, 6; 9; Paul. D. 19, 2, 55 pr.; Alzon, loc. cit.; Cannata, (1964) 30 *SDHI* 235 sqq.; Thomas, (1966) 13 *RIDA* 353 sqq.; Wacke, (1980) 26 *Labeo* 299 sqq.

[72] Cf. e.g. Duncan-Jones, pp. 323 sqq.; De Martino, pp. 268 sqq.; most recently De Neeve, *Colonus*, pp. 217 sqq.

[73] *Historia naturalis*, Lib. XVIII, 6, 35.

[74] Duncan-Jones, pp. 33 sqq.; Moses I. Finley, *The Ancient Economy* (1975), pp. 95 sqq. On the size and cost of farms in the late Republic cf. also Frier, *Roman Jurists*, pp. 11 sq.

[75] Cf., for example, De Martino, pp. 314 sqq.

[76] "Colonus" is related to "colere"; the term indicates that the conductor was a farmer who was duty-bound to cultivate the land (as opposed to the "rather slangy word" (Frier, *Landlords and Tenants*, p. 59) "inquilinus" for the urban tenant). Originally, it did not necessarily refer to a small tenant; nor was it a terminus technicus for tenants of plots belonging to large estates. It was only in the period after Diocletian that what has become known as the "colonate" developed, the term "coloni" then referring to poor people of low social rank who were bound to their land and found themselves in a quasi-servile condition of dependency. On the term "colonus" and on the rise of what he prefers to call farm-tenancy in Italy in the course of the 1st century B.C., see De Neeve, *Colonus*, pp. 21, 31 sqq., 119 sqq. On the colonate of the later antiquity the literature abounds; cf. Kaser, *RPr* II, pp. 142 sqq.

[77] As to the crisis in Italian agriculture, see mainly M. Rostovtzeff, *The Social and Economic History of the Roman Empire* (2nd ed., 1957), e.g. 502 sqq. But see C.R. Whittaker, "Agri deserti", in M.I. Finley (ed.), *Studies in Roman Property* (1976), pp. 137 sqq.

Most tenants found it very difficult, if not impossible, to draw the kind of profit from the soil which they needed to be able to pay their rent and to maintain their family. Lamentations of poor coloni abound; very often they ran into debts vis-à-vis their lessors, which further increased their dependence and made them even more susceptible to exploitation. Their social and economic position gradually deteriorated,[78] so that it does not seem to have been a rare phenomenon to see coloni in their desperation run away in search of better soil or join a gang of brigands. Again, the law took very little account of these harsh realities of life.

Whether or not the lessor was owner of the object leased did not affect the validity of the contract of locatio conductio. Subletting was possible[79] and indeed widely practised.[80] Thus, it could happen that a person—be it by mistake or on purpose—hired a slave or rented a house which actually belonged to him. Such a conductio rei suae was, as a rule, invalid;[81] and if the lessee became owner of the res during the currency of the locatio conductio, the contract came to an end.[82] We find this principle suprisingly often affirmed in our sources and it may be inferred that locationes rei suae were by no means rare occurrences, particularly in post-classical times.[83] Also, unlike the emptio rei suae, the hiring of one's own thing was not a logical impossibility and the invalidity of the transaction was therefore less obvious. A number of exceptions existed and it appears, more particularly, that where the locator had a (real) right in the thing as against the owner, the latter was able to undertake a valid hiring of this thing.[84]

3. Merces locationis

(a) *Merces vera et certa*

The second essential element on which agreement had to be reached before a contract of locatio conductio could be said to have come into existence was the rent (merces locationis): ". . . nam ut emptio et venditio ita contrahitur, si de pretio convenerit, sic et locatio et conductio contrahi intellegitur, si de mercede convenerit."[85] If no

---

[78] For post-classical times, see Kaser, *RPr* II, pp. 401 sq.

[79] Cf. e.g. C. 4, 65, 6: "Nemo prohibetur rem quam conduxit fruendam alii locare, si nihil aliud convenit"; Molnár, *Studi Sanfilippo*, vol. II, pp. 420. Cf. today also § 1098 ABGB and art. 1573 codice civile. A different approach has been adopted by the PrALR (§ 309 I 21) and the BGB (§ 549 I, 1: "A lessee is not entitled, without the permission of the lessor, to transfer to a third party the use of the leased thing, particularly to sublet the thing").

[80] Cf., for example, Mayer-Maly, *Locatio conductio*, pp. 27 sqq; Cardascia, *Studi Biscardi*, vol. II, pp. 365 sqq. The right to sublease was presumed unless specifically excluded: cf. Frier, *Landlords and Tenants*, p. 62.

[81] Ulp. D. 50, 17, 45: "Neque pignus neque depositum neque precarium neque emptio neque locatio rei suae consistere potest"; Iul. D. 16, 3, 15.

[82] Ulp. D. 19, 2, 9, 6.

[83] Cf., in this context, the interesting hypothesis by Mayer-Maly, *Locatio conductio*, p. 118.

[84] For details, see J.A.C. Thomas, "Conductio rei suae", (1971) 2 *Index* 283 sqq.

[85] Gai. D. 19, 2, 2 pr.

remuneration for the letting had been agreed upon, the contract could be commodatum, depositum or mandatum, but it could not be locatio conductio. The merces locationis was subject to very much the same rules as pretium in sale.[86] It generally had to consist in money; and it had to be verum and certum, but not necessarily iustum. Only a few comments are necessary.

Obviously the locatio could not be made donationis causa[87] and thus, for instance, a conductio nummo uno was invalid.[88] There was no verum pretium. As to the "certainty of price" requirement, the same problem cases were discussed as in sale. What if I let my house for "quanti Titius aestimaverit" or what if no reward is fixed at the time of the conclusion of the contract, on the understanding that such agreement may be reached at a later stage? Gaius leaves these questions open,[89] but Justinian says "non proprie locatio et conductio contrahi intellegitur".[90] And as to the question of equality in exchange, we can refer to Paulus D. 19, 2, 22, 3, this notorious epitome of individualism in the domain of Roman private law:

> "Quemadmodum in emendo et vendendo naturaliter concessum est quod pluris sit minoris emere, quod minoris sit pluris vendere et ita invicem se circumscribere, ita in locationibus quoque et conductionibus iuris est."[91]

(b) Pecunia numerata?

Somewhat more complex is the situation with regard to the first of the above-mentioned requirements, namely that the merces had to consist in pecunia numerata. From early on,[92] there was at least one exception: in the case of agricultural tenancies it could be agreed that the locator should receive, in the place of a monetary reward, a specified proportion of the crops. This arrangement was called colonia partiaria[93] and, despite its affinity to societas, the contract was still locatio conductio (rei). Plinius recommended this type of transaction (albeit as a last resort) in view of the fact that the coloni were notoriously

---

[86] On the close relation between sale and hire cf. e.g. Gai. III, 142; Gai. D. 19, 1, 2 pr.; *Inst.* III, 24 pr.; Mayer-Maly, *Locatio conductio*, pp. 63 sqq.

[87] Paul. D. 19, 2, 20, 1.

[88] Ulp. D. 19, 2, 46.

[89] Gai. III, 143. On Cato, *De agri cultura*, XVII, 14, see Watson, *Obligations*, pp. 103 sqq.

[90] *Inst.* III, 24, 1. Justinian could afford to be strict on this point, since exclusion from the regime of locatio conductio no longer meant non-enforceability of the transaction. An actio praescriptis verbis was available.

[91] Cf. supra, p. 256.

[92] On negotia partiaria in Cato, *De agri cultura*, CXLV sq., 136 sq. see Watson, *Obligations*, pp. 104 sq.

[93] For details see Franz Kobler, *Der Teilbau im römischen und geltenden italienischen Recht* (1928); Mayer-Maly, *Locatio conductio*, pp. 135 sqq.; J.A.C. Thomas, "The Nature of Merces", 1958 *Acta Juridica* 197 sqq.; F.P. van den Heever, *The Partiarian Agricultural Lease in South African Law* (n.d). Specifically on the medieval concept of share-cropping, see E.J.H. Schrage, "Colonia partria, Zum Rechtsbegriff der Teilpacht aus der Sicht der Glossatoren", in: *Satura Roberto Feenstra oblata* (1985), pp. 393 sqq.

destitute and usually struggled to pay their rent.[94] Colonia partiaria, under these circumstances, was favourable for the lessor in that it gave him an income in kind where he might well have lost out otherwise. For the tenant it was advantageous in that he could share the risk of crop failure with the lessor: if the harvest was poor, the lessee's obligation towards the lessor was reduced proportionate.[95]

There is considerable dispute whether classical law recognized further exceptions to the pecunia numerata requirement. Two smallholders own one ox each. In order to pool their assets, they agree that each of them may in turn use both oxen for a period of ten days.[96] Locatio conductio? Two persons who do not get on with each other own a farm in common. They agree that each of them will in turn hire the other's share for a year at a time with the effect that they would be in a position, in alternate years, to use and draw the profits of the whole farm. After he has had the farm for one year, the one party sends his cattle onto the field, with the result that the prospects of the following year's crop are ruined. Can the other party avail himself of the actio conducti?[97] In the first example, the granting of an actio in factum was considered, in the second one (involving co-owners) the actio communi dividundo. Others seem to have argued that the actions arising from locatio conductio could be applied.[98] But ultimately, still in classical law,[99] the view came to prevail that locatio conductio required a merces in money.[100] This was Justinian's view too, and use-exchange transactions came to be accommodated as innominate contracts.

4. Leases for a fixed term

(a) Lustrum; ius repellendi and ius migrandi

Apart from these essentials of locatio conductio, the parties were, of course, entirely free to agree to any number of accidentalia negotii. Often, for example, they fixed a specific term during which the lessee was to have (and enjoy) the object of the lease; in the case of agricultural tenancies this was usually quinquennium (or: lustrum), a period of five

[94] *Epistulae*, Lib. IX, 37.
[95] Gai. D. 19, 2, 25, 6.
[96] Ulp. D. 19, 5, 17, 3; Inst. III, 24, 2.
[97] Ulp. D. 10, 3, 23.
[98] As can, for instance, be seen from "quaeritur" in Gai. III, 144. Cf. further Afr. D . 19, 2, 35, 1; on this text, see J.A.C. Thomas, "D. 19, 2, 35, 1", (1971) 74 *BIDR* 83 sqq.; Karlheinz Misera, "Der Nutzungstausch bei Nachbarn und Miteigentümern", (1977) 94 *ZSS* 273 sqq., 277 sqq.
[99] But probably only at a time when the availability of other remedies (esp. the actio in factum) for such use-exchange transactions was widely recognized.
[100] Cf. e.g. Mayer-Maly, *Locatio conductio*, pp. 129 sqq.; Thomas, 1958 *Acta Juridica* 191 sqq.; Watson, *Obligations*, pp. 101 sqq.; Misera, (1977) 94 *ZSS* 267 sqq. On Ulp. D. 19, 2, 19, 3, cf. Mayer-Maly, *Locatio conductio*, pp. 137 sq. and Károly Visky, "I contratti di locazione nella crisi economica del III secolo", in: *Studi in onore di Cesare Sanfilippo*, vol. I (1982), pp. 670 sqq.

years.[101] After the lapse of this period the contract came to an end and the lessee had to hand the object back. Only under certain circumstances was either of the parties allowed to dissolve the contractual relationship before that time: the lessor could expel the lessee if the latter did not pay the rent, if he neglected his duty to cultivate the land,[102] or grossly abused the former's property, if the object of the lease was in need of repair or if the lessor needed it for his own use;[103] the lessee could relinquish the object, if it had become unfit for use or if its continued use entailed a danger for him.[104] The lessor thus had a ius repellendi, the lessee a corresponding ius migrandi. Especially with regard to the latter, a rather restrictive tendency prevailed. This is not only in tune with the unfavourable treatment accorded to lessees generally, but also shows a specific desire to keep coloni on the soil and thus to ensure, in the public interest, that the land continued to be cultivated.[105] As far as public lands were concerned, there even seems to have been a practice of forcing lessees to stay on after expiry of the term of lease, if no other lessee could be found to look after the land. This device backfired, however, for fewer and fewer people were prepared, under these circumstances, to take public lands on lease in the first place. The penuria colonorum eventually forced the Emperor Hadrian to relent:

> "Valde inhumanus mos est iste. . . . facilius invenientur conductores, si scierint fore ut, si peracto lustro discedere voluerint, non teneantur."[106]

(b) Relocatio tacita

The desire to promote soil cultivation, incidentally, provides the policy background to another legal construction: "Qui ad certum tempus conducit, finito quoque tempore colonus est: intellegitur enim dominus, cum patitur colonum in fundo esse, ex integro locare."[107] This is what came to be called relocatio tacita: if the conductor remained on the land after the term of the lease had come to an end, the contract was deemed to have been renewed; its duration was extended.

---

[101] Cf. e.g. Paul. D. 19, 2, 24, 2–4; De Neeve, *Colonus*, p. 10; Visky, *Spuren*, pp. 205 sqq. For urban leasehold, cf. Frier, *Landlords and Tenants*, p. 37.

[102] Paul. D. 19, 2, 54, 1; on this text, see Giuseppe Giliberti, "La 'stipulatio poena', in D. 19, 2, 54, 1 (Paul. 5 Resp.)", (1983) 29 *Labeo* 44 sqq.

[103] C. 4, 65, 3 (Ant.); Mario Battaglini, "La risoluzione del contratto de locazione per necessità del locatore nel diritto Romano e comune", in: *Studi in onore di Emilio Betti*, vol. IV (1962), pp. 523 sqq.; Frier, *Landlords and Tenants*, pp. 92 sqq. This was not a numerus clausus of instances of justified expulsion. On cases where a third party was involved in the expulsion of a tenant, cf. Frier, pp. 79 sqq.

[104] Cf., for example, Gai. D. 19, 2, 25, 2 ("Si vicino aedificante obscurentur lumina cenaculi, teneri locatorem inquilino: certe quin liceat colono vel inquilino relinquere conductionem, nulla dubitatio est"); Alf. D. 19, 2, 27, 1 (". . . si quis timoris causa emigrasset . . ."); Ulp. D. 19, 2, 13, 7 ("Exercitu veniente migravit conductor . . ."): for details, see Frier, *Landlords and Tenants*, pp. 92 sqq.

[105] Mayer-Maly, *Locatio conductio*, pp. 216 sqq.

[106] Call. D. 49, 14, 3, 6.

[107] Ulp. D. 19, 2, 14.

It was the very same contract that continued to exist, and hence pignora (and other accessory rights) did not fall away either: "Qui impleto tempore conductionis remansit in conductione, non solum reconduxisse videbitur, sed etiam pignora videntur durare obligata."[108] Details about the length of time for which such (re-)locatio was deemed to have been concluded are not entirely clear[109] and were consequently controversial in later times.[110] The relocatio tacita as such, however, with tacit or implied consent as its dogmatic basis,[111] has survived the ages and can still be found in the modern German Civil Code.[112] § 568 BGB ("If, after the expiration of the term of the lease, the use of the thing is continued by the lessee, the lease is deemed to have been extended for an indeterminate time. . . .") has even gained in stature, for it applies not only where the lessee continues to use the thing after effluxion of the time for which the lease had originally been entered into but also where the lessor has terminated the lease by way of notice.[113] The relocatio tacita, in its modern form, has thus assumed a new function and plays a role (albeit a rather minor one) in the quest for security of tenure for housing tenants.

5. Leases for an indefinite period

We have so far been discussing the situation where the lease was for a fixed term. If, on the other hand, the parties did not agree on the duration of the lease and concluded their contract for an indefinite period, then either of the parties could unilaterally terminate the lease at any time. There was no security of tenure at all. Again, the termination of the contract happened in a relatively crude and unrefined manner: expellere or repellere in the case of the lessor, migrare, relinquere, deserere as far as the lessee was concerned.[114] The institution of giving notice was unknown to the Romans and so were specific periods of notice. Our modern rules relating to the giving of notice try to safeguard the reasonable interests of the debtor; historically, they derive from local customs which have varied from place to place and from

[108] Ulp. D. 19, 2, 13, 11; for details, see Frier, *Landlords and Tenants*, pp. 165 sqq.

[109] In cases of agricultural lease, the relocatio according to Ulp. D. 19, 2, 13, 11, was from year to year: the tenant allowing for the "planting of seeds, reaping etc., would need a year fully to derive benefit from the holding over" (Thomas, *TRL*, p. 295); this was different in the case of domestic premises or immovables. It is unclear, however, how far Ulp. D. 19, 2, 13, 11 can be accepted as being genuinely classical (cf. e.g. Mayer-Maly, *Locatio conductio*, pp. 220 sq.).

[110] Cf. e.g. Glück, vol. 17, pp. 278 sqq.; Vangerow, *Pandekten*, § 644.

[111] Ulp. D. 19, 2, 13, 11 (". . . hoc enim ipso, quo tacuerunt, consensisse videntur"; Kaser, *RPr* I, p. 229; *RPr* II, p. 88). In canon law (Liber Sextus, Lib. V, Tit. XII, De regulis iuris, XLIII) this became "qui tacet, consentire videtur").

[112] "Motive", in: *Mugdan*, vol. II, pp. 230 sqq.

[113] BGH, 1980 *Neue Juristische Wochenschrift* 1578.

[114] Kaser, *RPr* I, p. 568; Frier, *Landlords and Tenants*, pp. 70, 92.

time to time.[115] First of all, the debtor has to be left in no doubt whether the lease will come to an end (hence with regard to the lease of living accommodation, modern German law requires writing).[116] Secondly, the debtor must have some time to adjust himself to the new situation.[117] And thirdly, the law usually tries to ensure that the lessee be allowed sufficient time "to have some real benefit from the transaction".[118] This is the reason why, in the case of agricultural leases for an unspecified period, the lessee must be able to enjoy the property for at least one year (i.e. one farming cycle).[119]

6. Leases in perpetuity

Implicit in what has been said so far is, of course, the fact that lease (as opposed to sale) is concerned with a merely temporal transfer of the object.[120] Even if no definite period had been agreed upon, the contract was terminable by either of the parties at any time. Gaius mentions one exception,[121] which, however, related exclusively to agri vecticales belonging to a municipality. These were usually let in perpetuity,[122] i.e. upon the terms that, as long as the rent was paid, the land was not to be taken away from either the tenant or his heir. There seems to have been some debate about whether this was sale or hire: "sed magis placuit locationem conductionemque esse."[123] In post-classical times, long-term leases became more and more common as a device to attract competent managers to run the often uncultivated public estates.[124] Alongside the ordinary locatio conductio, emphyteusis (with regard to fundi patrimoniales, i.e. the private property of the emperor)[125] and a

---

[115] Cf. the statutes of the upper Italian city-states, for example the Statutes of Trient (1528): "Item statuimus et ordinamus, quod si aliquis locator velit aliquem conductorem expellere de domo . . ., debeat certiorare ipsum conductorem per mensem ante tempus locationis finitae" (cf. Klaus Genius, *Der Bestandsschutz des Mietverhältnisses in seiner historischen Entwicklung bis zu den Naturrechtskodifikationen* (1972), p. 74 sq.); Johannes à Sande, *Decisiones Frisicae* (Leovardiae, 1635), Lib. III, Tit. VI, Def. I (". . . consuetudine apud Frisios receptum est, ut dominus, qui vel ipse re locata uti frui, vel alteri eam locare aut alienare, vult colono aut inquilino ante Calendas Januarii denuntiet"; cf. further Genius, e.g. p. 144).

[116] § 564 a BGB.

[117] Hence the periods of notice, the length of which can be determined, for instance, according to whether the rent is measured by days, weeks or months; cf. § 565 BGB.

[118] *Mackay v. Naylor* 1917 TPD 533 at 538.

[119] Cf., for example, Grotius, *Inleiding*, III, XIX, 8; Van Leeuwen, *Censura Forensis*, Pars I, Lib. IV, Cap. XXII, 6; § 595 BGB; but see the more refined considerations by Pothier, *Traité du contrat de louage*, n. 28.

[120] Hence: "Non solet locatio dominium mutare": cf. Ulp. D. 19, 2, 39. For an exception (the so-called locatio conductio irregularis—a phenomenon similar to the depositum irregulare), see infra, p. 402, note 101.

[121] Gai. III, 145.

[122] Kaser, *RPr* I, p. 455.

[123] Gai. III, 145.

[124] Cf. Ludwig Mitteis, *Zur Geschichte der Erbpacht im Alterthum* (1901), pp. 33 sqq.; Levy, *Vulgar Law*, pp. 43 sqq.; Kaser, *RPr* II, pp. 308 sqq.

[125] For details, see Kaser, *RPr* II, pp. 151 sqq.

so-called ius perpetuum (relating to fundi rei privatae, i.e. State land)[125] came to be recognized; both institutions were covered by the vague and comprehensive concept of ownership in vulgar law.[126] As a consequence of this, the dividing lines between locatio conductio and ownership became blurred, a development which was stopped only by the Emperor Zeno, who recognized and accepted the ius emphyteuticarium as an institution sui generis, creating a ius in rem and being distinct from both locatio conductio and transfer of ownership subsequent to a contract of sale.[127] The European ius commune continued to provide special rules for long-term leases[128] and distinguished between locatio conductio simplex (or: ad modicum tempus) and locatio conductio ad longum tempus. Only the former was regarded as an obligatory contract of lease, to which the Roman rules relating to locatio conductio were applied. If the term for which the lease was entered into exceeded modicum tempus (usually ten years), the lessor was taken to have transferred dominium utile[129] to the lessee. The lessee's position was sometimes equated with that of an emphyteuta; more often, however, locatio conductio ad longum tempus was regarded as a separate institution (which did not preclude the application of some of the rules relating to emphyteusis). Others distinguished between locationes *in perpetuum* and emphyteusis.[130] Pothier mentions the *louage à longue temps*[131] but does not give any special rules. Modern German law no longer recognizes perpetual leases. If a lease is entered into for more than 30 years, either party may terminate the contract after 30 years by giving notice.[132] The emphyteusis has not survived codification. It continues to exist in South African law,[133] and with it the lease in perpetuity.[134]

---

[126] Levy, *Vulgar law*, pp. 45 sqq.

[127] C. 4, 66, 1; cf. *Inst.* III, 24, 3.

[128] For what follows, see Paolo Grossi, *Locatio ad longum tempus* (1963); Coing, pp. 369 sq. As to the glossators, cf., more recently, E.J.H. Schrage, "Emptio (Nondum) Tollit Locatum", 1978 *Acta Juridica* 6 sqq.

[129] On the distinction between dominium directum and dominium utile, cf. E. Meynial, "Notes sur la formation de la théorie du domaine divisé (domaine directe et domaine utile) du XIIe au XIVe siècle dans les romanistes—étude de dogmatique juridique", in: *Mélanges Fitting* (1908), vol. II, pp. 409 sqq.; Robert Feenstra, "Les origines du dominium utile chez les Glossateurs", in: Fata iuris romani (1974), pp. 215 sqq.; D.P. Visser, "The 'absoluteness' of ownership: the South African common law in perspective", 1986 *Acta Juridica* 39 sqq.

[130] Cf. e.g. Stryk, *Usus modernus pandectarum*, Lib. XIX, Tit. II, § 51.

[131] *Contrat de louage*, n. 27.

[132] § 567 BGB.

[133] C. G. van der Merwe, *Sakereg* (1979), pp. 420 sqq.

[134] Kerr, *Sale and Lease*, p. 183. Van Leeuwen, *Censura Forensis*, Pars I, Lib. IV, Cap. XXII, 4, says: "Caeterum quod a quibusdam alia dicatur quae ad certum tempus, alia quae in perpetuum initur, proprie ad locationem non pertinet, sed in alium contractum transit: Emphyteusin nimirum:. . . ."

7. The duties of the locator

If, as we have seen, locatio conductio involved the letting of a thing either for use, or for use and enjoyment of the fruits (fruenda locata), then obviously such frui licere was what the locator owed under the contract. He had to let the thing to the other party for the period agreed upon and he had to see to it that this thing was and remained fit for that other party's use and (possibly) enjoyment. Thus, for instance, he had to keep a house or stable that he had let in good repair.[135] Another example is discussed by Gaius:

> "Si vicino aedificante obscurentur lumina cenaculi, teneri locatorem inquilino: . . . de mercedibus . . . cum eo agatur, reputationis ratio habenda est. eadem intellegemus, si ostia fenestrasve nimium corruptas locator non restituat."[136]

Neither does the tenant have to dwell in darkness, nor does he have to suffer constant draught. If the locator sues for rent, a set-off will take place.

Apart from his main obligation of frui licere, the locator also had to comply with whatever the parties had agreed upon "in lege conductionis".[137] Locatio conductio was a consensual contract which gave rise to bonae fidei iudicia. Hence all ancillary agreements, with which the parties might have supplemented or adapted the content of locatio conductio to suit their individual case, became part and parcel of the contract[138] and were sanctioned by the actiones locati and conducti. They specified the contractual programme for this individual case and therefore had something like the force of law between these two parties: "contractus enim legem ex conventione accipiunt."[139] Often such special terms were not individually negotiated; instead, the parties adopted a standardized version, prepared and used by the locator. The lex conductionis (locationis)[140] under these circumstances fulfilled the function of what we today call standard contract terms.

8. The range of the lessor's liability

(a) Prevention of frui licere

Failure on the part of the locator to comply with his duties could, as we have seen, entitle the lessee to terminate the lease by simply moving out.[141] In addition, he was released (either partially or totally) from his obligation to pay the rent and, where he had already paid it, he could

[135] Ulp. D. 19, 2, 15, 1.
[136] Gai. D. 19, 2, 25, 2.
[137] Ulp. D. 19, 2, 15, 1.
[138] Cf. infra, pp. 509 sqq.
[139] Ulp. D. 16, 3, 1, 6.
[140] Cf. Mayer-Maly, *Locatio conductio*, pp. 106 sqq.; von Lübtow, *Symbolae Taubenschlag*, vol. III, pp. 239 sqq.; Frier, *Landlords and Tenants*, pp. 61 sqq.; De Neeve, *Colonus*, op. cit., note 101, pp. 5 sqq.; cf. also Kaser, *RPr* I, p. 229.
[141] Cf. supra, p. 356.

avail himself of the actio conducti to claim it (or part of it) back.[142] Finally, the actio conducti could be brought in order to claim damages. For such a claim to succeed it had to be shown, as a rule, that the lessee had been prevented from frui licere due to the lessor's fault.[143] Take the case of the owner of an insula who had leased it, for a sum of 30, to a principal tenant. The latter had in turn sublet the various cenacula for a total of 40. The owner then demolished the insula. Question: what can the principal tenant sue for? Alfenus draws a distinction:

> "si vitiatum aedificium necessario demolitus esset, pro portione, quanti dominus praediorum locasset, quod eius temporis habitatores habitare non potuissent, rationem duci et tanti litem aestimari: sin autem non fuisset necesse demoliri, sed quia melius aedificare vellet, id fecisset, quanti conductoris interesset, habitatores ne migrarent, tanti condemnari oportere."[144]

If the evacuation of the house was not due to the fault of the lessor, the lessee may claim back that part of the rent that he had paid for the time during which he could not use the house. If, on the other hand, the lessor had ordered the house to be demolished merely because he wanted to rebuild it in grand new style, he has to reimburse the (principal) tenant for his loss of profits (i.e. the amount of rent which the tenant had not been able to extract from his subtenants). In other words: the lessee may claim his positive interest.[145]

(b) Choosing unsuitable slaves

Digesta 19, 2, 30 pr. provides an example (one of several) where the damages arose due to the fact that the lessee was prevented from frui licere. But the loss could also be caused by the res locata itself. One merely has to think of the hire of slaves in this regard. The slave may be of an unpleasant or criminal disposition; he may start stealing the lessee's property or engage in other harmful activities. In these instances, however, classical lawyers preferred to apply the rules relating to noxal (i.e. delictual) liability.[146] The delict was not intrinsically linked to the contractual relationship; the lease had merely provided the occasion for committing it. But the situation was different where the slave turned out to be unsuitable for the very activity for which he had been hired. Two interesting texts discuss the contractual

---

[142] Cf. e.g. Alf. D. 19, 2, 27 pr.; Alf. D. 19, 2, 30 pr.; cf. also Gai. D. 19, 2, 25, 2 (supra, p. 360). Cf. further Bruce W. Frier, "Tenant Remedies for Unsuitable Conditions Arising after Entry", in: *Studies in Roman law in Memory of A. Arthur Schiller* (1986), pp. 65 sqq., 70 sqq.

[143] Max Kaser, (1957) 74 *ZSS* 157 sqq.; Imre Molnár, "Verantwortung und Gefahrtragung bei der locatio conductio zur Zeit des Prinzipats", in: ANRW, vol. II, 14 (1982), pp. 663 sqq. Cf. also Buckland/Stein, p. 500; Thomas, *TRL*, p. 294.

[144] Alf. D. 19, 2, 30 pr.

[145] Kaser, (1957) 74 *ZSS* 158; Honsell, *Quod interest*, pp. 119 sqq.; cf. further Afr. D. 19, 2, 33 (second part, from: ". . . nam et si colonus"); Afr. D. 19, 2, 35 pr.

[146] Paul. D. 19, 2, 45 pr., 1; Mayer-Maly, *Locatio conductio*, pp. 156 sqq. On noxal liability generally, see infra, pp. 916 sq., 1099 sq., 1118 sq.

liability of the lessor for an unfree muleteer who had caused, due to clumsiness in handling it, the death of the lessee's mule:

> "Servum meum mulionem conduxisti: neglegentia eius mulus tuus perit. si . . . eum locassem, non ultra me tibi praestaturum, quam dolum malum et culpam meam abesse: quod si sine definitione personae mulionem a me conduxisti et ego eum tibi dedissem, cuius neglegentia iumentum perierit, illam quoque culpam me tibi praestaturum aio, quod eum elegissem, qui eiusmodi damno te adficeret."[147]

What is the basis of the lessor's liability under the actio conducti? A distinction is drawn by Labeo as to whether a specific slave was hired for this purpose or whether the selection of the particular slave had been left to the locator. If, in the latter instance, the locator has chosen an unsuitable slave, he is liable on account of culpa in eligendo. For the former alternative, too, culpa seems to be the decisive criterion—culpa in contrahendo, as one could put it. In which respect the lessor has been negligent is, however, left to speculation. Perhaps his fault lies in not disclosing that the slave is too lazy, too weak or inexperienced to be a competent muleteer, but possibly he is blamed for the mere fact of having provided a slave who turns out to be incapable of properly handling a mule. In the latter case, the lessor's liability comes very close to a liability based on an implied guarantee that the object of the lease is fit for the purpose envisaged in the contract.

(c) Defect of title

Such a guarantee could, of course, be undertaken expressly by the lessor.[148] If the expectations raised by the lex conductionis were disappointed, the lessee could bring the actio conducti for his full interest. There were certain cases, however, apart from (possibly) the hire of muleteers, where the Roman lawyers took a guarantee to be implicit in the contract of lease. A variety of texts confirm that the problem of defect of title was handled in this way—just as, incidentally, in the case of emptio venditio.[149]

> "Si quis domum bona fide emptam vel fundum locaverit mihi isque sit evictus sine dolo malo culpaque eius, Pomponius ait nihilo minus eum teneri ex conducto ei qui conduxit, ut ei praestetur frui quod conduxit licere."[150]

---

[147] Lab. D. 19, 2, 60, 7. The other text is Ulp. D. 9, 2, 27, 34: "Si quis servum conductum ad mulum regendum commendaverit ei mulum ille ad pollicem suum eum alligaverit de loro et mulus eruperit sic, ut et pollicem avelleret servo et se praecipitaret, Mela scribit, si pro perito imperitus locatus sit, ex conducto agendum cum domino ob mulum ruptum vel debilitatum, sed si ictu aut terrore mulus turbatus sit, tum dominum eius, id est muli, et servi cum eo qui turbavit habiturum legis Aquiliae actionem. mihi autem videtur et eo casu, quo ex locato actio est, competere etiam Aquiliae." On these texts (and the question of their authenticity), cf. Mayer-Maly, *Locatio conductio*, pp. 159 sq.; Kaser, (1957) 74 *ZSS* 161 sqq.; Stein, *Fault*, pp. 105 sqq.; Molnár, *ANRW*, op. cit., note 143, pp. 622 sqq.

[148] Cf. Ulp. D. 19, 2, 15, 1 (". . . si quid in lege conductionis convenit").

[149] Cf. supra, pp. 293 sqq.

[150] Ulp. D. 19, 2, 9 pr. Cf. further Ulp. (Hans Kreller, (1948) 66 *ZSS* 76 sq.) D. 19, 2, 7; Tryph. D. 19, 2, 8; Ulp. D. 19, 2, 15, 8 and Kaser, (1957) 74 *ZSS* 166 sqq.; Medicus, *Id quod interest*, pp. 96 sqq.; Honsell, *Quod interest*, pp. 130 sqq.; Molnár, *ANRW*, op. cit., note 143,

If a third party asserted a real right in the object of the lease and evicted the lessee, the latter could take recourse against his lessor. It did not matter that the lessor had been in good faith himself and that not even negligence could be attributed to him. The lessee could reasonably expect not to have his frui licere disturbed by a third party with a better right to the object leased to him. Ulpianus (D. 19, 2, 7)[151] makes it clear that the lessee could recover his (positive) interest: he could claim the 60 that he had been prevented from extracting from his subtenant, not only the 50 that he himself owed to the lessor.[152] Here, as in some other instances too,[153] the lessor could, however, avert liability under the actio conducti by providing reasonable alternative accommodation: "plane si dominus non patitur et locator paratus sit aliam habitationem non minus commodam praestare, aequissimum esse ait absolvi locatorem."[154]

(d) *Publicatio*

Very similar (at least from the lessee's perspective) to these cases of eviction due to a defect in title on the part of the lessor were instances where the lessee was prevented from frui licere because of expropriation (publicatio).[155] The consequences of this form of State intervention on the lessor/lessee relationship are discussed in a most interesting, but very controversial text by Africanus.[156] Relating first of all the opinion of his teacher Iulianus, he writes:

> "Si fundus quem mihi locaveris publicatus sit, teneri te actione ex conducto, ut mihi frui liceat, quamvis per te non stet, quo minus id praestes."

It appears that Iulianus was prepared to grant a claim for the full (positive) interest even though, as he specifically states, the lessor could not in any way be blamed. This amounts to liability on the basis of an implied guarantee that the lessee will not be expropriated. But would exposure to such far-ranging liability not constitute an unprecedented

---

pp. 622 sqq. For a different opinion (liability only if the lessor knew about his defect in title), see Nicola Palazzolo, "Evizione della cosa locata e responsabilità del locatore", (1965) 48 *BIDR* 275 sqq. He leans particularly on Afr. D. 19, 2, 35 pr.

[151] "Si tibi alienam insulam locavero quinquaginta tuque eandam sexaginta Titio locaveris et Titius a domino prohibitus fuerit habitare, agentem te ex conducto sexaginta consequi debere placet, quia ipse Titio tenearis in sexaginta."

[152] Interestingly, the subtenants in their action against the sublessor could not claim quod interest, but only the prepaid rent. For an explanation, see Frier, *Landlords and Tenants*, pp. 79 sqq.

[153] Mayer-Maly, *Locatio conductio*, pp. 155 sq.

[154] Ulp. D. 19, 2, 9 pr. (not interpolated: see Kaser, (1957) 74 *ZSS* 168).

[155] Cf. e.g. Paul. D. 21, 2, 11 pr. ("futuros casus evictionis", relating to the expropriation of provincial land). On this text cf. supra, pp. 288 sq.

[156] D. 19, 2, 33. But see Hans Ankum, "Afr. Dig. 19, 2, 33, Haftung und Gefahr bei der publicatio eines verpachteten oder verkauften Grundstücks", (1980) 97 *ZSS* 165, according to whom "publicatio" in D. 19, 2, 33 refers to a sale of the fundus to a magistrate or imperial official in the public interest; formally, this was a voluntary sale, even though de facto the vendor was under some political pressure to sell.

hardship for the lessor?[157] And how can this be reconciled with what Africanus says a few lines later: ". . . et circa conductionem servandum puto, ut mercedem quam praestiterim restituas . . .: nec ultra actione ex conducto praestare cogeris"? This is Africanus himself speaking, and he makes it quite clear that the conductor should be able to reclaim only the rent that he might have paid and nothing more. For centuries, one has tried to interpret Julian's statement in this light,[158] but it is very difficult to see how "teneri te . . ., ut mihi frui liceat" can be understood to mean anything but a claim for the conductor's interest. Today it is no longer necessary to try at all costs to reconcile divergent views of Roman jurists for the sake of extracting easily applicable rules from the sources. Nor do we have to assume, more specifically, that Africanus only endorsed what his teacher Iulianus had pronounced. Classical Roman law developed in a casuistic fashion and, particularly where blanket clauses left a lot of leeway, controversies were bound to arise.[159] This seems to have been the case in the present instance, where a decision had to be taken whether, on the basis of the precepts of good faith, an actio conducti should be granted or not. Iulianus (whom we generally see vigorously using the ex bona fide clause inherent in the iudicia bonae fidei as a motor for law reform)[160] was evidently prepared to hold the lessor liable under the actio conducti.[161] In this particular case, however, his opinion does not seem to have prevailed; Africanus, about 20 years Iulianus' junior,[162] rejected it: cautiously and most politely, but none the less quite clearly.[163]

[157] Kaser, (1957) 74 *ZSS* 177. Contra: Andreas Wacke, "Dig. 19, 2, 33: Afrikans Verhältnis zu Julian und die Haftung für höhere Gewalt", in: *ANRW*, vol. II, 15, 1976, p. 481.

[158] Cf. e.g. Accursius, gl Ut mihi frui, ad D. 19, 2, 33; Donellus, *Commentari de Jure Civili*, Lib. XIII, Cap. VII, XVI; Glück, vol. 17, p. 370.

[159] On the nature of classical Roman law (and the consequences for the credibility of our sources) in this context, see especially Andreas Bertalan Schwarz, "Das strittige Recht der römischen Juristen", in: *Festschrift für Fritz Schulz*, vol. II (1951), pp. 201 sqq.; Max Kaser, *Zur Methode der römischen Rechtsfindung* (1962), pp. 74 sq.; idem, *RPr* I, pp. 181 sqq., 188 sqq.; Tomasz Giaro, "Über methodologische Werkmittel der Romanistik", (1988) 105 *ZSS* 180 sqq.

[160] Cf. supra, pp. 298 sq., 320.

[161] For an examplary exegesis of D. 19, 2, 33 in all its ramifications, see Wacke, *ANRW*, op. cit., note 157, pp. 455 sqq. He draws attention to the point (p. 481) that Iulianus did not hesitate to decide against the wealthy landed aristocracy (to which he himself probably belonged).

[162] A.M. Honoré, "Julian's Circle", (1964) 32 *TR* 17.

[163] Cf. especially Emil Seckel, Ernst Levy, "Die Gefahrtragung beim Kauf im klassischen römischen Recht", (1927) 47 *ZSS* 219 sqq.; Honsell, *Quod interest*, pp. 122 sqq.; Wacke, *ANRW*, op. cit., note 157, pp. 476 sqq.; Ankum, (1980) 97 *ZSS* 157 sqq. Contra especially Kaser, (1957) 74 *ZSS* 177 sqq.; Nicola Palazzolo, "Evizione della cosa locata e responsabilità del locatore", (1965) 68 *BIDR* 292 sqq. Modern German law would follow Africanus in the solution of this case: cf. Wacke, pp. 494 sq.

(e) Leaky vats and toxic plants

Another situation in which the locator's liability was arguably based on an implied guarantee brings us back to an old acquaintance, the fragment "Si vas".[164] It deals with emptio venditio, but says in the end: "[Q]uod et in locatis doliis praestandum Sabinum respondisse Minicius refert." This is confirmed by another celebrated text which deals more directly with the *hire* of (wine) jars:

> "Si quis dolia vitiosa ignarus locaverit, deinde vinum effluxerit, tenebitur in id quod interest nec ignorantia eius erit excusata: et ita Cassius[165] scripsit."[166]

It is not easy to understand this decision and to reconcile it with the general principles.[167] The difficulties are compounded by the fact that, in the very next sentence, Ulpianus seems to proceed from quite a different principle:

> "[A]liter atque si saltum pascuum locasti, in quo herba mala nascebatur: hic enim si pecora vel demortua sunt vel etiam deteriora facta, quod interest praestabitur, si scisti, si ignorasti, pensionem non petes et ita Servio Labeoni Sabino placuit."

In the one case, vats have been hired, but they were so damaged that the hirer's wine runs out. The lessor is liable, no matter whether he knew about the defect or not ("nec ignorantia eius erit excusata"). The position is different where a pasture that is leased out contains poisonous herbs. The lessee's cattle die. But he can claim damages only if the lessor had known about the evil weeds.[168] How can these statements be reconciled? Do we have to assume that the Roman lawyers decided casuistically and that the search for a general principle determining the liability of the lessor would be futile?[169] Did the Romans apply two (or possibly three) different types of liability: strict liability in the case of wine jars and related objects, liability only for dolus as far as pastures were concerned[170] (and possibly culpa liability for all other objects)? What would be the reason for such a differentiated system of liability? Or is it possible to reconcile the two statements with each other? Attempts to do just that have not been lacking. But does one have to (effectively) rewrite either the first part of D. 19, 2, 19, 1—in order to achieve such reconciliation on the basis of liability for

---

[164] Pomp. D. 19, 1, 6, 4. Cf. supra, pp. 309, 320, 334 sqq.

[165] Cassius was a student of Sabinus. Sabinus (whose opinion has been related by another of his students, Minicius) is quoted by Pomponius in D. 19, 1, 6, 4.

[166] Ulp. D. 19, 2, 19, 1.

[167] For a recent discussion, see Christoph Krampe, *Die Garantiehaftung des Vermieters für Sachmängel* (1980), pp. 21 sqq.

[168] However, in the case of ignorantia the lessor still loses his right to claim counterperformance (the merces locationis). On this aspect of the decision (and on its relation to Ulp. D. 19, 2, 15, 2, cf. the recent discussion by Ernst, (1988) 105 *ZSS* 554 sqq.

[169] Krampe, op. cit., note 167, p. 26.

[170] Prevailing opinion: see Stein, *Fault*, pp. 100 sqq.; Mayer-Maly, *Locatio conductio*, pp. 168 sqq.; Medicus, *Id quod interest*, p. 155.

dolus only[171]—or alternatively the second half of it (so that the lessor would always be strictly liable)?[172] It is very difficult, if not impossible, to reconstruct the true position in Roman law.

To my mind, the most convincing argument would run something like this.[173] The idea of different degrees of liability is bound to lead to problems. Why should the lessor of pasture always (i.e. even if he could have known that his field contained poisonous weeds) be liable only for dolus? And what is the justification for the strict liability of a lessor of vats for wine? Can one necessarily say that such a lessor implicitly promises to compensate for the loss of wine due to any leakage? And why does the text mention only these two extreme cases? Would all other objects have to be brought (together with the vats) under strict liability or (together with pasture) under dolus liability? These and other problems can be avoided only by postulating a common principle underlying both decisions. This common principle can neither be strict liability (for then the reference to scientia on the part of the lessor in the second example would be futile), nor dolus liability (for then the reference to ignorantia non excusata[174] in the first example would not make sense). It can therefore only be that type of liability which was normally applied to the lessor anyway, and that is culpa.[175] Or, to formulate in terms of D. 19, 2, 19, 1: the lessor is liable if he knows about the defect in the object of the lease, or if his ignorance cannot be excused. It is within this framework that the characteristics of the object of the lease become relevant. Where defective vats are let, the lessor's ignorance can normally not be excused and his negligence can therefore be presumed. It is a matter for speculation why that was so: possibly, because it was the lessor who chose the vats and because the lessee did not have any opportunity to acquaint himself with their fitness for holding wine.[176] Not so where a pasture is the object of the

[171] See Franz Haymann, *Die Haftung des Verkäufers für die Beschaffenheit der Kaufsache*, vol. I (1912), pp. 96 sqq.

[172] See Gerhard Beseler, "Et ideo-Declarare-Hic", (1931) 51 *ZSS* 70.

[173] Cf. Klaus Luig, "Zur Vorgeschichte der verschuldensunabhängigen Haftung des Vermieters für anfängliche Mängel nach § 538 BGB", in: *Festschrift für Heinz Hübner* (1984), pp. 129 sqq.

[174] Dismissed by many as interpolated (cf. e.g. Mayer-Maly, *Locatio conductio*, p. 169); but see, for instance, Voci, *L'errore*, p. 251.

[175] Luig, *Festschrift Hübner*, p. 132; cf. also Buckland/Stein, p. 500; Liebs, *RR*, p. 244.

[176] Cf., for example, Honsell, *Quod interest*, p. 134; also Ulrich von Lübtow, "Zur Frage der Sachmängelhaftung im römischen Recht", in: *Studi in onore di Ugo Enrico Paoli* (1955), pp. 490 sq. After all, the dolia were sunk into the ground. In the case of pasture, on the other hand, the lessee was in as good a position as the lessor to evaluate what was growing on it. It was not expected of the lessor to let his own cattle trial-graze on the pasture. According to Mayer-Maly (*Locatio conductio*, p. 170), the crucial difference lies in the fact that the effluxion of wine in the case of leaking vats is the typical kind of damage that is bound to happen, whereas the loss of cattle due to mala herba growing on the lessor's pasture is not so typically related to the defect. Others argue that a leaking vessel is not a receptacle, whilst a pasture with poisonous herbs is still a pasture (Thomas, *TRL*, p. 294; Kaser, (1957) 74 *ZSS* 166). Also, it has been pointed out that, in the case of vats, express guarantees were

lease: the lessor's ignorance about the toxic plants is much more easily excusable; as long as he had not known about their existence, no fault is normally attributable to him. He cannot normally be held responsible for not knowing that there happen to be poisonous weeds growing somewhere on his land. The standard of diligentia required of a lessor of vats was therefore different from what could reasonably be expected of a lessor of pasture; the one was required to know about certain defects (and if he didn't, this was bound, as a rule, to constitute culpa), the other one not.

(f) From Ulp. D. 19, 2, 19, 1 to § 538 BGB

Roman wine jars have left their mark on the history of private law. The subsequent fate of D. 19, 1, 6, 4 has already been briefly discussed.[177] Similarly interesting was the afterlife of D. 19, 2, 19, 1.[178] Throughout the various periods of European jurisprudence there were those who tried to see this fragment as an expression of the general principle of liability for fault: only for fault, but for every kind of it. This is very much in accordance with what has been suggested above. Accursius's Glossa ordinaria provides a good and early example. "Sed cur aliter?", he asks, apropos the words "in quo mala herba" in D. 19, 2, 19, 1. "Respon. quia in doliis ignorare non debuit. in pascuis vero iuste potuit ignorare. nam quae facilius sciri possunt, si ignoratur, gravius coercentur." In other words: ignorance in the case of vats is inexcusabilis, whilst in the case of pasture it is normally excusabilis. This was still the prevailing opinion centuries later, during the times of the usus modernus and of pandectism.[179] Voet—among others—tried to rationalize the decision with regard to the wine jars on the basis that the locator had himself manufactured them:

> "Praestetur denique reparatio damni totius, quod conductor ex rei conductae vitio passus est, sive sciverit locator vitium illud sive ignoraverit, quoties circa rem

originally given by the lessors. In the course of time, these accidentalia negotii became so common that they were ultimately turned into naturalia negotii (Karlowa, *Römische Rechtsgeschichte*, vol. II (1901), p. 640). According to Stein (*Fault*, p. 103) the vats were defined by mere description. "In such a case the lessor is liable for all loss caused by his failure to supply goods which answer to that description." (But it is very doubtful whether the Romans recognized the lease of unascertained goods; there appears to be no evidence for this proposition.) For a similar view, see Karl Heldrich, *Das Verschulden beim Vertragsabschluss* (1924), p. 21. Most recently, attention has been drawn to the economic background to D. 19, 2, 19, 1. Lessors of pasturage, frequently resident in Rome, could not be expected to know the toxic state of their plants, whereas the lessor of vats was easily able to determine whether the dolia were sound or not. Also, the lessors of pasturage (unlike the lessors of dolia) belonged typically to the upper class of society, and the jurists may not have regarded it as "socially practicable" to increase the scope of their liability: cf. Brigitte Clark, "Leaky Vats and Toxic Plants: Ulp. D. 19, 2, 19, 1 and the Liability of the Lessor", (1987) 50 *THRHR* 455.

177 Cf. supra, p. 365.

178 Cf. Luig, *Festschrift Hübner*, pp. 132 sqq.

179 Cf. e.g. Heineccius, *Elementa Iuris Civilis*, §§ 924, 929; Glück, vol. 17, pp. 361 sqq.; Arndts, *Pandekten*, § 311; Dernburg, *Pandekten*, vol. II, § 111, 2.

locatam artificium versatur, et locator artifex est; quippe qui tunc utique scire debuerat, quae suae artes erant. . . ."[180]

This interesting but, de lege lata, somewhat far-fetched argument (which Voet also tried to promote in the case of sale)[181] did not gain widespread acceptance.[182] Much more influential, in the long run, was a train of thought that can be traced back to Donellus. "Quaeritur igitur", we read with regard to the two cases discussed in D. 19, 2, 19, 1:[183]

> "cum utrobique sit ignorantia, cur, si pariter culpa est in locatore, non pariter is obligetur in id quod interest. . . . Scio dici posse, ignorantiam istam non pariter in his aestimari, propterea quod qui saltum locavit, potuerit juste ignorare in eo saltu malam herbam esse, cum non sit cujusvis noxias herba a bonis discernere. Qui autem vitiosa dolia locavit, potuerit vitium explorare et sine damno, aqua immissa. At ego de eo loquor, qui hoc ipsum explorans cognoscere primo non potuerit. Dicamus igitur hic quoque idem, quod modo in fundo evicto, quodque supra in vasis vitiosi venditione diximus, eum qui vasa vitiosa ignorans locavit, nihilominus teneri eo nomine in id quod interest, quia dolium locans hoc ipso quod dolium dixit, pro integro locavit, seu vi ipsa integrum dixit; quia non est dolium, nisi vas, nec vas, nisi instrumentum ad capiendum humorem paratum. Quidquid autem in emptione aut locatione emptor locatorve dixerunt, id praestare eos oportet."

By the word "vat" the lessor implicitly refers to a receptacle without leakage. If it does turn out to be leaky, the lessor is liable: not on account of negligence, but because of his implied guarantee. Donellus —in accordance with D. 19, 2, 19, 1—restricted his argument to dolia; but there is no reason why one should not also be able to ascribe to the term "saltus pascuus" the meaning "grazing ground without poisonous weeds". The argument proposed by Donellus thus lent itself to generalization which was bound to occur sooner or later. It did occur later rather than sooner, namely in Bernhard Windscheid's textbook of pandectist law. If the leased thing is affected by a defect which diminishes its fitness for use, we read in § 400, the lessor is liable to the lessee for his interest, if he has fraudulently concealed such defect or if he has either expressly or tacitly guaranteed its absence. The main basis for this assertion is D. 19, 2, 19, 1. It is indicative of Windscheid's influence on the first draft of the BGB that his suggestion to regulate the lessor's liability for defects in the thing accordingly was immediately accepted.[184] This is all the more remarkable since a preliminary draft

---

[180] *Commentarius ad Pandectas*, Lib. XIX, Tit. II, XIV.
[181] Cf. supra, p. 335.
[182] Pothier (*Traité du contrat de louage*, § 119), however, went even further. He argued that D. 19, 2, 19, 1 imposes liability not only on the manufacturer but also on the merchant, because his calling as such requires him to have knowledge of the goods in which he trades. This line of argument has been followed in the South African courts (*Hunter v. Cumnor Investments* 1952 (1) SA 735 (C) at 740H–742A. For details of the impact of D. 19, 2, 19, 1 with its "curious" distinction (*Alexander v. Armstrong* (1879) 9 Buch 233 at 237) on South African law, cf. Kerr, *Sale and Lease*, pp. 211 sqq.; Clark, (1987) 50 *THRHR* 456 sqq.
[183] *Commentarii de Jure Civili*, Lib. XIII, Cap. VII, XVI.
[184] For the reasons, see "Motive", in: *Mugdan*, vol. II, pp. 209 sq.

had made the lessor responsible only for fraudulent behaviour, and had not even accepted culpa liability.[185] Thus, the following rule was finally introduced into the BGB:

> "If a defect of the kind specified in § 537 exists at the time of entering into the contract . . . the lessee may demand compensation due to non-fulfillment."

There is no longer any mention of fault. The liability is based on an implied guarantee. Today, there is a great deal of debate whether this is a happy solution to the problem.[186] Within the German law of contract, the rule of § 538 BGB represents something of an anomaly;[187] its excessive strictness has repeatedly been criticized.[188] On the other hand, however, attention has been drawn to the social policy perspective of § 538 I;[189] it increases the protection of the lessee and can thus be seen as one of the few "drops of social oil"[190] within the machinery of the BGB.

9. The problem of risk

(a) Periculum locatoris

Over the preceding pages we have been discussing the locator's liability under the contract of locatio conductio (rei). Such liability, as we have seen, can be based either on fault or on a guarantee (be it express or implied), and the conductor can avail himself of the actio conducti to claim damages. A different, though closely related, question is whether the conductor has to pay the rent, even though he is not able to use (or use and enjoy) the object of the lease. The piece of land may have been swallowed by an earthquake. The (inevitable) invading army may have marauded the cornfields. Jackdaws and starlings may have swooped

---

[185] Cf. Horst Heinrich Jakobs, Werner Schubert, *Die Beratung des Bürgerlichen Gesetzbuchs, Recht der Schuldverhältnisse*, vol. II (1980), pp. 428 sqq.

[186] For a discussion of the problems involved and of the casuistry, see Krampe, op. cit., note 167, pp. 11 sqq. For an interesting parallel, see the landlord's implied warranty of liability for leased dwellings in American law, developed on the basis of the following dictum in *Jarvis v. First National Realty* 138 AppDC 369, 428 F 2d 1071 (DC Cir. 1970): ". . . in the case of the modern apartment dweller, the value of the lease is that it gives him a place to live. . . . When American city dwellers, both rich and poor, seek 'shelter' today, they seek a well known package of goods and services. . . . In order to reach results more in accord with legitimate expectations of the parties and standards of the community, courts have been gradually introducing more modern precepts of contract law in interpreting leases." The concept of implied warranty of habitability (representing one of these "more modern concepts") has been adopted by the *Restatement on Landlords and Tenants* in 1976. It is criticized by Frier, *Studies Schiller*, pp. 66 sqq., who argues that the Roman law of *urban lease* knew no warranty of this type and was thus more "socially adequate" than the modern American lease law.

[187] Heinrich Honsell, "Positive Vertragsverletzung", 1979 *Jura* 196.

[188] Cf. e.g. Walter Wilburg, *Die Elemente des Schadensrechts* (1941), p. 141.

[189] "Protokolle", in: *Mugdan*, vol. II, p. 814. Cf. Peter Schlechtriem, *Vertragsordnung und ausservertragliche Haftung* (1972), p. 337; Ingo Koller, *Die Risikozurechnung bei Vertragsstörungen in Austauschverhältnissen* (1979), pp. 118 sq. Cf. also Krampe, op. cit., note 167, pp. 38 sqq.

[190] Cf. Wieacker, *Privatrechtsgeschichte*, p. 470.

down, with disastrous consequences, upon the orchard. Neither of the parties can be blamed for any of these events. Yet, one of them will "feel" the loss: either the locator—who has let his property but may now lose out on the rent—or the conductor, who might have to pay the rent without having been afforded the benefit of frui licere. The former solution would be in accordance with "casum sentit dominus": after all, the locator is still owner of the object. In favour of the second alternative, it may be argued that a valid locatio conductio had been concluded and that the locator had done everything that could be expected of him; thus, the conductor should also have to carry out his part of the arrangement, i.e. to pay the rent. It is obvious that this is not a question of liability (for damages). We are dealing with the problem of risk. As in the case of sale,[191] "risk" in this context refers to the question whether counterperformance can still be demanded where the performance has become impossible. For an answer we must turn our attention to Ulp. D. 19, 2, 15, 2:

> "Si vis tempestatis calamitosae contigerit, an locator conductori aliquid praestare debeat, videamus. Servius omnem vim, cui resisti non potest, dominum colono praestare debere ait, ut puta fluminum graculorum sturnorum et si quid simile acciderit, aut si incursus hostium fiat."[192]

As a rule, the risk was on the lessor: periculum locatoris. The range of incidents for which the lessor had to carry the risk was defined as "vis, cui resisti non potest". Alfenus, in another text, refers to "vis extraria".[193] Both are tantamount to what, in another context,[194] we have termed vis maior.[195] Thus, not every incident for which neither of the parties could be blamed fell under periculum locatoris. Take, as far as agricultural leases are concerned, what one might describe as non-external vis ". . . si qua tamen vitia ex ipsa re oriantur, haec damno coloni esse, veluti si . . . raucis aut herbis segetes corruptae sint".[196] If the crops are destroyed by worms or weeds, we are dealing with a type of risk which is intrinsically related to the process of

---

[191] Cf. supra, p. 281.

[192] On this text cf. Kaser, "Periculum locatoris", (1957) 74 *ZSS* 169 sqq.; Theo Mayer-Maly, "Höhere Gewalt: Falltypen und Begriffsbildung", in: *Festschrift für Artur Steinwenter* (1958), pp. 60 sqq.; Giuseppe Provera, "Sul problema del rischio contrattuale nel diritto romano", in: *Studi in onore di Emilio Betti*, vol. III (1962), pp. 693 sqq.; Robin Seager, "Of 'vis' and Weeds: D. 19, 2, 19, 2 and 19, 2, 19, 1", (1965) 31 *SDHI* 330 sqq.; Claude Alzon, "Les risques dans la 'locatio conductio'", (1966) 12 *Labeo* 312 sqq.; Watson, *Obligations*, pp. 110 sqq.; Hans Ankum, "Remissio mercedis", (1972) 19 *RIDA* 223 sqq.; Chorus, *Handelen*, pp. 149 sqq.; Molnár, *ANRW*, op. cit., note 143, pp. 666 sqq.; P.W. de Neeve, "Remissio Mercedis", (1983) 100 *ZSS* 308 sqq.; Pinna Parpaglia, op. cit., note 7, pp. 4 sqq.; Ernst, (1988) 105 ZSS 541 sqq., 550 sqq.

[193] Alf. D. 19, 2, 30, 4.

[194] Cf. supra, p. 193.

[195] Cf. also Gai. D. 19, 2, 25, 6 ("Vis maior, quam Graeci θεοῦ βίαν appellant"); on this text, see, most recently, Theo Mayer-Maly, "Aequo animo ferre", in: *MNHMH Petropoulos*, vol. II (1984), pp. 108 sqq., and Ernst, (1988) 105 *ZSS* 545 sqq.

[196] Ulp. D. 19, 2, 15, 2.

cultivation[197] and therefore has to be borne by the person responsible for and entitled to such cultivation: the conductor.[198] More casuistry has been added by post-classical compilers to illustrate this distinction between the two parties' respective spheres of risk.[199] A variety of other texts deal with the lease of residential space[200] and attribute the risk of fire (incendium) as well as collapse (ruina) to the locator. Even if the conductor's frui licere is infringed due to aedificii vitia (forcing the locator to pull down the house or to carry out extensive repair works), the locator loses his right to claim the rent.[201]

(b) *Remissio mercedis*

Where a cornfield was destroyed terrae motu or where a house burnt down, frui became definitely and completely impossible. As a result, the conductor was entitled to a complete release from rent liability: periculum locatoris. Such remission then, as one can put it, was a matter of juristic law (formulary remissio). It has often been argued that the emperors went further and were prepared, under certain circumstances, to grant relief to the lessee in cases where his harvest had been exceptionally poor: remissio mercedis as a matter of imperial clemency.[202] Thus, we would be dealing with two different institutions: deductio ex mercede[203] where the conductor has lost the enjoyment as such, remissio mercedis where he retains enjoyment of the res locata without, however, being able to obtain the yield that was

[197] Views differ on what exactly vitia ex ipsa re refers to: faults which appear in the res (e.g. Watson, *Obligations*, p. 112), which result from the res (e.g. Molnár, *ANRW*, op. cit., note 143, p. 669), which arise in products or produce of the res (e.g. Seager, (1965) 31 *SDHI* 333), which could have been overcome by diligence and labour and are therefore ultimately due to negligence or imperitia on the part of the conductor (e.g. Parpaglia, op. cit., note 7, p. 32) or which occur "nell' ambito dell'attività agricola" (Francesco Sitzia, "Considerazioni in Tema di Periculum Locatoris e di Remissio Mercedis", in: *Studi in Memoria di Giuliana d'Amelio*, vol. I (1978), pp. 333 sqq.); cf. also Ernst, (1988) 105 *ZSS* 540 sqq., 554 sqq. (anything that prevents cultivation of the soil without constituting a blow of fate (*"schicksalhafte Einwirkung"* = vis maior).

[198] But see also Ulp. D. 19, 2, 19, 1 (". . . si saltum pascuum locasti, in quo herba mala nascebatur: . . . si ignorasti, pensionem non petes") and the analysis by Ernst, (1988) 105 *ZSS* 554 sqq.

[199] Ulp. D. 19, 2, 15, 2. According to Ernst, (1988) 105 *ZSS* 560 sqq., there was a significant shift in the post-classical analysis of risk-allocation; it was no longer based on the "fundamental content" of the contract of locatio conductio and the "basic concept" of vis maior (p. 559); the focus was now on the economic position of the lessee: could he reasonably be expected to pay the rent even though he had been unable to avert the incident that had prevented him from cultivating the land?

[200] Ulp. D. 19, 2, 19, 6; Alf. D. 19, 2, 30 pr., 1; Alf. D. 19, 2, 35 pr.; Alf. D. 19, 2, 27 pr.; Lab. D. 19, 2, 60 pr.

[201] This may appear to be surprising, because aedificii vitia could well be said to arise "ex ipsa re". But obviously the lawyers did not want to draw a distinction between ruina (which we find counted amongst the typical incidents of vis maior elsewhere, too) and those actions that were necessary to prevent ruina. Cf. Kaser, (1957) 74 *ZSS* 176.

[202] Mayer-Maly, *Locatio conductio*, pp. 140 sqq.; Kaser, (1957) 74 *ZSS* 173 sqq.; idem, *RPr* I, p. 567.

[203] Cf. e.g. Alf. D. 19, 2, 27 pr.

to be expected.[204] Alternatively, it has been suggested that complete destruction of the harvest was a question of risk, whereas remissio mercedis was applied in case of a partial destruction of the harvest.[205] Imperial remissio mercedis has traditionally been seen either as an instrument of social policy designed to help tenants in distress[206] or as the product of administrative policy aimed at counteracting the decline of Italian agriculture.[207] It has been shown, however, that the expressions, "deducere ex mercede" and "remittere mercedem", were not used with a strictly technical meaning in mind.[208] More particularly, remissio mercedis could refer to both a complete and a partial remission of rent.[209] Above all, it appears that imperial remissio mercedis did not go beyond the confines of the risk rule. Take, for instance, Ulp. D. 19, 2, 15, 5:

> "Cum quidam de fructuum exiguitate quereretur, non esse rationem eius habendam rescripto divi Antonini continetur. item alio rescripto ita continetur: 'Novam rem desideras, ut propter vetustatem vinearum remissio tibi detur.' "[210]

One may reasonably infer from this that exiguitas fructuum in itself was not a ground for remission of rent. Lack of care and insufficient cultivation are the most obvious causes of a bad crop, which must be attributed to the lessee. But even where we are dealing with the normal vagaries of agriculture, the tenant cannot claim relief: he could have acquainted himself with the quality of the soil, with the geographical situation of the farm and with the general weather patterns of that region.[211] Likewise (to come back to the example discussed in D. 19, 2, 15, 5) the lessee of a wine farm cannot base his claim for remissio mercedis on the age of the vines: as a competent farmer, he should have known that vines decline in productivity after they have reached a certain age.[212] Thus, even where we are dealing with exiguitas fructuum, remissio mercedis can be granted only if it was due to vis maior. Or, in risk-related terminology: a bad harvest caused by vis extraria is nothing other than an instance of impaired frui.[213] Imperial remissio mercedis, then, was not a separate institution; it was an

---

[204] Cf. especially Mayer-Maly, loc. cit.; also e.g. Watson, *Obligations*, p. 110.

[205] Alzon, (1966) 12 *Labeo* 315, Molnár, *ANRW*, op. cit., note 143, pp. 660 sqq., 674 sqq.

[206] Stephan Brassloff, *Sozialpolitische Motive in der römischen Rechtsentwicklung* (1933), pp. 87 sq.; Hans Ankum, "Remissio Mercedis", (1972) 19 *RIDA* 237.

[207] Mayer-Maly, *Locatio conductio*, p. 143; Kaser, (1957) 74 *ZSS* 174. Visky, *Studi Sanfilippo*, vol. I, pp. 679 sqq., 685 sq.

[208] Cf. e.g. Paul. D. 19, 2, 24, 5; Afr. D. 19, 2, 33 (both on remissio mercedis); Ulp. D. 19, 2, 19, 3 (deductio ex mercede). For details, see De Neeve, (1983) 100 *ZSS* 298 sqq.

[209] Ulp. D. 19, 2, 15, 7 and other literary and epigraphic sources: De Neeve, (1983) 100 *ZSS* 301.

[210] Cf. further Ulp. D. 19, 2, 15, 3; C. 4, 65, 8 (Alex.).

[211] Cf., in similar vein, J.A.C. Thomas, "Remissio Mercedis", in: *Studi in memoria di Guido Donátuti*, vol. III (1973), p. 1274.

[212] Molnár, *ANRW*, op. cit., note 143, p. 676; De Neeve, (1983) 100 ZSS 312; slightly differently Thomas, *Studi Donatuti*, vol. III, p. 1274.

[213] De Neeve, (1983) 100 *ZSS* 303.

instance of periculum locatoris.[214] It neither substantially improved the position of the tenants, nor seems to have been based on economic motives. Its advantages, as far as we can see, were mainly a matter of procedure; for to approach the Imperial chancellery was easier than to institute a formulary action.[215]

Bad harvests can be followed (or preceded) by abundant years. Where that was so, the lessor was entitled to refuse remissio mercedis or to recover what had been remitted. Such compensation seems to have been current practice and was discussed by Ulpianus in the following terms:

> "Papinianus . . . ait, si uno anno remissionem quis colono dederit ob sterilitatem,[216] deinde sequentibus annis contigit uberitas, nihil obesse domino remissionem, sed integram pensionem etiam eius anni quo remisit exigendam. . . . quid tamen, si novissimus erat annus sterilis, in quo ei remiserit? verius dicetur et si superiores uberes fuerunt et scit locator, non debere eum ad computationem vocari."[217]

The Roman rules relating remissio mercedis were applied throughout the history of the ius commune;[218] but it always remained doubtful whether they had to be regarded as natural emanations of the contractual risk regime (the lessor is bound to afford frui licere; this entails that the lessee has to be able to reap the fruits of the land (percipere fructus rei); if he is prevented, on account of vis maior, from doing so, he has not received what is due to him under the contract and does therefore not have to pay the rent either)[219] or as an extraordinary deviation from general principles, a special concession granted to the lessee by way of the ius "positivum" and based, ultimately, on equitable considerations.[220]

---

[214] Thomas, *Studi Donatuti*, vol. III, pp. 1271 sqq.; Sitzia, *Studi d'Amelio*, vol. I, pp. 331 sqq. (360 sq.); De Neeve, (1983) 100 *ZSS* 296 sqq.; cf. also Molnár, *ANRW*, op. cit., note 143, p. 661; Ernst, (1988) 105 *ZSS* 571 sq. (according to whom imperial remissio mercedis fitted in with the post-classical but not with the (early) classical risk regime (as espoused by Servius in Ulp. D. 19, 2, 15, 2)).

[215] De Neeve, (1983) 100 *ZSS* 332 sqq.; cf. also Ankum, (1972) 19 *RIDA* 222 sqq., 234 sq. For alternative explanations as to why imperial remissio was introduced, despite being, at least substantially, in accordance with the normal risk regime, see Giannetto Longo, "Osservazioni critiche sulla disciplina giustinianea della locatio-conductio", in: *Studi in onore di Biondo Biondi*, vol. II (1965), pp. 293 sqq.; Sitzia, *Studi d'Amelio*, vol. I, pp. 347 sq., 360 sq.

[216] On the significance of "sterilitas" cf. Ankum, (1972) 12 *RIDA* 229; Sitzia, *Studi d'Amelio*, vol. I, pp. 346 sqq.

[217] D. 19, 2, 15, 4. There is no reason to assume that this would have applied only to sterilitas or with regard to imperial remissio mercedis. Cf. Thomas, *Studi Donatuti*, vol. III, pp. 1274 sq.; De Neeve, (1983) 100 *ZSS* 321 sqq.; contra, for example, Molnár, *ANRW*, op. cit., note 143, p. 674; cf. also Ernst, (1988) 105 *ZSS* 569 sq.

[218] Cf. the analysis by Ernst, (1988) 105 *ZSS* 573 sqq.

[219] Cf., for example, Donellus, *Commentarii de Jure Civili*, Lib. XIII, Cap. VII, IX; Glück, vol. 17, pp. 454 sqq.

[220] The basic assumption, under these circumstances, being that the risk of enjoyment of the property is, naturally, with the lessee. Cf., for example, Grotius, *De jure belli ac pacis*, Lib. II, Cap. XII, XVIII.

The latter view dominated, when, at the turn of the 18th and 19th centuries, Prussia,[221] France and Austria codified their private law. The French and Austrian legislators saw a parallel to the equally exceptional rules of laesio enormis relating to contracts of sale and they thus determined that remissio mercedis was to be granted only if the actual yield was less than half of what could normally be expected.[222] To the fathers of the BGB, of course, the idea of an equitable interference with contractual terms in cases of changed circumstances did not appeal[223] and remissio mercedis thus shared the fate of laesio enormis[224] and of the clausula rebus sic slantibus:[225] it was not incorporated into the new code. The lessee was advised to insure himself against a typical disaster such as crop failure on account of hail; also, it was argued that he was always free to insert a clause into the individual contract reserving him the right of remissio mercedis. The liberalistic concept of the BGB collapsed, however, in the years of economic crisis following the First World War. As with both laesio enormis and clausula,[226] remissio mercedis experienced a remarkable renaissance. It was reintroduced by way of special legislation[227] and managed to establish itself so firmly that in 1985 it was able to crown its career by finally gaining entrance even into the BGB.[228]

10. The duties of the conductor

(a) Payment of rent, cultivation; the standard of care

The conductor, obviously, had to pay the rent. The due date was usually specified by the parties;[229] in case of doubt, payment postnumerando (i.e. after the lease, or a payment period that might

[221] §§ 500, 518, 561, 571 I 21.
[222] Artt. 1796 sq. code civil; § 1105 ABGB. Cf. also artt. 1635 sqq., 1648 codice civile.
[223] Cf. Ernst, (1988) 105 *ZSS* 583 sq.
[224] Cf. supra, pp. 267 sq.
[225] Cf. infra, p. 579, 681. The connection between remissio mercedis and clausula was seen, particularly clearly, by Leyser, *Meditationes ad Pandectas*, Spec. CCXVII, VI.
[226] Cf. supra, pp. 268 sqq. and infra, p. 582.
[227] Cf. the *Pachtschutzordnung* of 9.6.1920.
[228] § 593 BGB. The position under the Roman-Dutch common law in South Africa has been summed up by Solomon J in *Hansen, Schrader & Co. v. Kopelowitz* 1903 TS 707 (at 718 sq.) in the following words: "A lessee is entitled to remission of rent either wholly or in part where he has been prevented either entirely or to a considerable extent in making use of the property for the purposes for which it was let, by some vis maior or casus fortuitus, provided always that the loss of enjoyment of the property is the direct and immediate result of the vis maior or casus fortuitus, and is not merely indirectly or remotely connected therewith." However, these principles today only obtain in the Transvaal and Natal; in the other two provinces the legislator has curtailed the lessee's right to a remission of rent. For all details, see Kerr, *Sale and Lease*, pp. 222 sqq.
[229] Mayer-Maly, *Locatio conductio*, pp. 138 sqq.

have been set, had come to an end) seems to have been the rule.[230] Apart from that, the lex locationis frequently imposed further duties on the conductor, who, in turn, was obliged to comply with these terms.[231] Tenant–farmers, in particular, were required to cultivate the lessor's land in due season and also to keep farm buildings in good repair. A clause to that effect seems to have been so common, and it tied in so well with the official policy of preventing soil-exhaustion and deterioration into wasteland, that it came to be implied as a contractual duty, irrespective of whether it had been specified in the lex locationis or not.[232] Failure to cultivate entitled the lessor to bring the actio locati and to sue his tenant for damages.[233] The legal vehicle for the recognition of such a duty of cultivation was, of course, the "ex bona fide" clause contained in the formula of the actio locati: if the tenant farmer let the land lie fallow, he did not do what, in good faith, he ought to have done under a contract of (agricultural) lease.

With regard to other objects of lease, nothing so specific was required of the conductor. In general, one could expect him at least to take good care of the lessor's object and to see to it that its condition did not deteriorate during his tenure: "Item prospicere debet conductor, ne aliquo . . . corpus deterius faciat vel fieri patiatur."[234] If, in fact, the object did deteriorate and if such deterioration was due to the lessee's negligence, the lawyers were again prepared to grant the actio locati against him. For one of the earliest reported examples we may turn to Ulp. D. 19, 2, 13, 7:

> "Exercitu veniente migravit conductor, dein de hospitio milites fenestras et cetera sutstulerunt. . . . Labeo autem, si resistere potuit et non resistit, teneri ait, quae sententia vera est."[235]

---

[230] This conclusion has been (and is) usually drawn from the Roman sources (e.g. texts such as Paul. D. 19, 2, 24, 2); cf. e.g. Grotius, *Inleiding*, III, XIX, 11; Pothier, *Traité du contrat de louage*, n. 134; Windscheid/Kipp, § 400, n. 12; Frier, *Landlords and Tenants*, p. 37; *Ebrahim NO v. Hendricks* 1975 (2) SA 78 (C) at 81E.

[231] Cf., for example, Alf. D. 19, 2, 29 (duty not to fell, bark or burn the trees in a forest, nor to allow others to do so); Ulp. D. 19, 2, 11, 1 (prohibition on the use of fire); Ulp. D. 19, 2, 11, 4 (prohibition of storing hay in the villa urbana). For all details and for an analysis of how these clauses were interpreted by the Roman lawyers, see Bruce W. Frier, "Tenant's Liability for Damage to Landlord's Property in Classical Roman Law", (1978) 95 *ZSS* 243 sqq.

[232] Gai. D. 19, 2, 25, 3: "Conductor omnia secundum legem conductionis facere debet. et ante omnia colonus curare debet, ut opera rustica suo quoque tempore faciat, ne intempestiva cultura deteriorem fundum faceret. praeterea villarum curam agere debet, ut eas incorruptas habeat." On the basic duty to cultivate cf. Mayer-Maly, *Locatio conductio*, pp. 177, 180 sq.; Frier, (1978) 95 *ZSS* 240 sq.; De Neeve, *Colonus*, op. cit., note 101, p. 10; Ernst, (1988) 105 *ZSS* 554, 587 sqq.

[233] Cf. e.g. Paul. D. 19, 2, 24, 2. It also provided a justification for the tenant's expulsion; cf. supra, p. 356 and Mayer-Maly, *Locatio conductio*, p. 215.

[234] Ulp. D. 19, 2, 11, 2; cf. also Marci. D. 20, 2, 2.

[235] On this text Theo Mayer-Maly, "Haftung aus Miete nach Staatsunrecht", (1957) 74 *ZSS* 370 sqq.; Frier, (1978) 95 *ZSS* 235 sqq.

The tenant abandons the premises, because an army is approaching.[236] Thus, he is not in a position to prevent the soldiers from quartering in the abandoned dwelling and from damaging it. If he could have done so, had he not run away, he is liable to the locator. Thus, it is the possibility of resistance that gives rise to the liability for damages. The tenant in question did not act as an ordinary tenant should have acted in such a situation; his conduct, though not in itself harmful, enabled the soldiers to loot the premises and was characterized by an element of blameworthiness. It is on the basis of this and similar decisions that culpa was eventually recognized as the basis of the conductor's liability.[237] This fitted in well with the utility principle, since locatio conductio rei is an onerous contract, benefiting both the lessor and the lessee: ". . . sed ubi utriusque utilitas vertitur, ut in empto, ut in locato, ut in dote, ut in pignore, ut in societate, et dolus et culpa praestatur."[238] Again, one has to remember that the standard of conduct required of the tenant, and with it the concept of culpa, "was determined by the bona fides relationship between landlord and tenant, therefore by a socially conditioned standard of conduct". Thus, it was in principle an objective standard, "oriented to the deed, not to the doer".[239]

(b) Vicarious liability?

Problems could arise in cases where the lessor's property was not damaged by the tenant himself, but by one of the slaves (or other persons) who worked for him and whom he had brought onto the premises. Could the tenant be held liable, not only for his own fault,

[236] This must have been a (nominally) friendly army; the invasion by a hostile army was considered vis cui resisti non potest. Cf. Mayer-Maly, (1957) 74 *ZSS* 368 sqq.

[237] Frier (1978) 95 *ZSS* 234 sqq.; Tafaro, *Regula*, pp. 272 sqq. It has often been suggested that the conductor, under a contract of locatio conductio rei, apart from culpa, was liable, beyond culpa, for custodia: cf. Mayer-Maly, *Locatio conductio*, pp. 202 sqq.; Arangio-Ruiz, *Responsabilità*, pp. 130 sqq.; Wolfgang Hoffmann-Riem, "Die Custodia-Haftung des Sachmieters untersucht an Alf./Paul. D. 19, 2, 30, 2", (1969) 86 *ZSS* 394 sqq. This proposition is usually based on C. 4, 65, 28 (Diocl. et Max.) and Inst. III, 24, 5. But the former text deals with locatio conductio in general and is logically and systematically unconvincing (cf. e.g. Mayer-Maly, *Locatio conductio*, p. 214); and the diligentissimus paterfamilias of *Inst.* III, 24, 5 does not necessarily have to have been grafted on to a classical custodia liability, but may have been a rhetorical accentuation of the diligentia required of a careful debtor (cf. Kaser, *RPr* II, p. 354). Alfenus, in the above-mentioned timber case (D. 19, 2, 29), seems to refer to custodia (". . . an etiam ita silvam custodire". etc.). But, first of all, we are dealing here with a discussion of liability under a specific clause contained in the lex locationis, and secondly silvam custodire in this context expresses the content of the conductor's obligation rather than a standard of liability: Geoffrey MacCormack, "Custodia and Culpa", (1972) 89 *ZSS* 194 sq.

[238] Ulp. D. 13, 6, 5, 2 in fine.

[239] Frier, (1978) 95 *ZSS* 243. In modern private law negligence is also determined according to objective criteria. For details cf. e.g. Peter Hanau, in: *Münchener Kommentar*, vol. II (2nd ed., 1985), § 276, nn. 78 sqq. The reason is that private law is concerned with the protection of reasonable expectations and with a balancing of interests between two parties, rather than with an isolated adjudication of guilt.

but also for the fault of others? One of the key fragments, in the present context, relates to a drowsy furnace-tender:[240]

> "Si fornicarius servus coloni ad fornacem obdormisset et villa fuerit exusta, Neratius scribit ex locato conventum praestare debere, si neglegens in eligendis ministeriis fuit:. . . ."[241]

The slave fell asleep, and, as a consequence, the house burnt down. The master of the slave (i.e. the conductor) is liable ex locato, but only if he himself was negligent in choosing the slave. In other words: the conductor is not responsible for the fault of third parties, whose services he used, "to the same extent as for his own fault";[242] he is not subject to strict (= no fault) liability. For the actio locati to be successful, culpa must be attributable to him (and not only to the third party) in cases such as these too. Culpa remains the basis of the tenant's liability; it merely usually takes the form of culpa in eligendo.[243] The tenant is held responsible, because it was ultimately he who endangered the house by selecting an unsuitable slave to tend the furnace. Along very similar lines runs the argument in Ulp. D. 19, 2, 11 pr.:

> "Videamus, an et servorum culpam et quoscumque induxerit praestare conductor debeat? . . . mihi ita placet, ut culpam etiam eorum quos induxit praestet suo nomine, etsi nihil convenit, si tamen culpam in inducendis admittit, quod tales habuerit vel suos vel hospites: et ita Pomponius . . . probat."

Here it is not so convenient to refer to culpa in eligendo, because to bring both his family and his servants onto the estate is not really a matter of choice for the tenant. His fault seems rather to lie in the fact that he exposed the lessor's estate to people who were prone to cause damage, without properly supervising them.[244] Again, however, the tenant is held responsible for his own fault.[245]

11. The position of the lessee

(a) His protection against the lessor

We have thus far been discussing the requirements for a contract of lease, to which obligations on the parts of both the lessor and the lessee

---

[240] The example is not as outdated as it might seem. On Zimbabwean tobacco farms I have seen big barns in which the tobacco leaves are stored and dried. An open fire is kept burning in a furnace, and this furnace has to be watched by a servant (who still occasionally falls asleep).

[241] Ulp. D. 9, 2, 27, 9 (cf. also Coll. XII, VII, 7).

[242] In the words of § 278 BGB.

[243] Culpa in eligendo has often been regarded as spurious: cf. e.g. Wolfgang Kunkel, "Diligentia", (1925) 45 *ZSS* 329 sqq.; Manlio Sargenti, "Problemi della responsabilità contrattuale", (1954) 20 *SDHI* 210; von Lübtow, *Lex Aquilia*, p. 160. Contra: Mayer-Maly, *Locatio conductio*, p. 199; Geoffrey MacCormack, "Culpa in eligendo", (1971) 18 *RIDA* 539; Frier, (1978) 95 *ZSS* 256 sqq.; Rolf Knütel, "Die Haftung für Hilfspersonen im römischen Recht", (1983) 100 *ZSS* 399 sqq.

[244] Knütel, (1983) 100 *ZSS* 404.

[245] For further details about the vicarious liability of tenants and for a discussion of Proc./Ulp. D. 9, 2, 27, 11 and Coll. XII, VII, 9, see Frier, (1978) 95 *ZSS* 256 sqq. and Knütel, (1983) 100 *ZSS* 391 sqq.

it gave rise, and when and under which circumstances the contractual relationship came to an end. A final comment has to be made concerning the position of the lessee. From the point of view of a modern observer, it was stunningly weak. Not only did the conductor not acquire ownership or a limited real right, he did not even become possessor. He was a mere detentor. As a result of this, he did not have any protection through actiones in rem; nor could he avail himself of the possessory interdicts. Thus, the lessor could at any time expel his tenant, even where the parties had agreed upon a specific term of tenancy. Alternatively, he could evict the tenant by bringing the interdicta unde vi or uti possidetis. Of course, by doing so, the lessor committed a breach of contract and unless the expulsion was justified,[246] he became liable to the tenant under the actio conducti. But a mere actio in personam for damages must often have been cold comfort for somebody who had just lost his home.[247]

(b) Alienation of the leased property by the lessor

Most precarious, too, was the tenant's position if the lessor sold the leased property to a third party. Once ownership had been transferred, such a third party could evict the tenant, who again did not have any protection against the new owner/possessor. The latter did not even commit a breach of contract, since he did not become party to the contract of lease. Again, the only remedy the tenant could resort to, once he had been evicted, was the actio conducti against his lessor, i.e. the old owner/vendor. In order to achieve at least some indirect protection for the tenant, the lessor/vendor was required to include a special pactum in the contract of sale to the effect that the purchaser would allow the tenant to remain on the premises for the term of the lease:

> "Qui fundum fruendum vel habitationem alicui locavit, si aliqua ex causa fundum vel aedes vendat, curare debet, ut apud emptorem quoque eadem pactione et colono frui et inquilino habitare liceat: alioquin prohibitus is aget cum eo ex conducto."[248]

But this was not really a satisfactory solution to the problem. Of course, such a pactum did not give the tenant any direct claim or defence against the purchaser.[249] That would have been a direct contract

---

[246] Cf. supra, p. 356.

[247] It must be kept in mind, though, that this result was much less peculiar in Roman law than it would be in a modern legal system. For whatever remedy (real or personal) the lessee might have had—ultimately everything boiled down to condemnatio pecuniaria.

[248] Gai. D. 19, 2, 25, 1. Cf. also C. 4, 65, 9 (Alex.): "Emptori quidem fundi necesse non est stare colonum, cui prior dominus locavit, nisi ea lege emit. verum si probetur aliquo pacto consensisse, ut in eadem conductione maneat, quamvis sine scripto, bonae fidei iudicio ei quod placuit parere cogitur." On the reception (and the "productive misinterpretation") of this text by the glossators, cf. E.J.H. Schrage, "Emptio (Nondum) Tollit Locatum", 1978 *Acta Juridica* 3 sqq.

[249] Wesenberg, *Verträge zugunsten Dritter*, pp. 41 sqq.; Mayer-Maly, *Locatio conductio*, pp. 43 sqq.; Genius, op. cit., note 115, pp. 35 sqq.

in favour of a third party, which, as we know, was anathema to the Roman lawyers.[250] The pactum did, however, improve the position of the tenant in so far as the purchaser had to think twice before he resorted to expulsion: for, whilst the tenant still had only his actio conducti against the lessor/vendor, the latter was now able to take recourse against the purchaser and to sue him with the actio venditi for breach of his informal promise.

(c) Emptio tollit locatum

The authors of the European ius commune usually summed up the position which had been handed down to them from Roman law in the maxim "emptio tollit locatum": sale breaks hire. This is as crisp and poignant as it is inaccurate. First of all, it is not the contract of sale that has any detrimental effect on the relationship between the lessor/vendor and his tenant. It is only on account of the subsequent transfer of possession and of ownership that the lessor/vendor makes it impossible for himself to carry out his obligation under the contract of lease (namely to provide uti frui praestare licere), and that he exposes the tenant to the risk of being expelled by the purchaser.[251] And the second point: the contract of lease was, of course, not "broken" by either sale, transfer of ownership or any other transaction. It continued to exist and did, in fact, provide the tenant with his only remedy, the actio conducti against the lessor. Whatever transaction had taken place between the lessor and the third party did not affect the tenant's contractual position, but jeopardized his (continued) detention. Emptio tollit locatum therefore really means that the tenant was not in a position to counter the claims of any new owner of the property.

Harsh as it is, this rule, once again, cannot really be said to reflect a social bias on the part of the Roman lawyers. It was not designed as an instrument to oppress poor tenants. It was the logical consequence of certain basic and general concepts about real rights and personal rights and about their interplay and relationship. The actual cases cropping up in legal practice do not seem to have necessitated fundamental rethinking;[252] the fairly roundabout chain of contractual actions (tenant against lessor/vendor—lessor/vendor against purchaser) by and large

---

[250] Cf. supra, pp. 34 sqq.

[251] The position of the tenant, incidentally, was jeopardized not only on account of a transfer of ownership following a contract of sale; if, for instance, the lessor granted an ususfructus over the leased property to a third party, the same problem could arise. The tenant could not prevail against the claims of the usufructuary. For further details, see Mayer-Maly, *Locatio conductio*, pp. 46 sqq.; J.A.C. Thomas, "The Sitting Tenant", (1973) 41 *TR* 35 sqq.

[252] Mayer-Maly, *Locatio conductio*, pp. 45 sq.; Genius, op. cit., note 115, pp. 39 sqq.; Frier, *Landlords and Tenants*, pp. 64 sqq. (who discusses the "nuisance value" of expulsion).

appears to have worked well enough to provide a not inconsiderable deterrent against heedless expulsion.[253]

(d) D. 43, 16, 12 in fine

"Emptio tollit locatum" became part and parcel of the European Roman common law;[254] on the eve of codification it represented pandectist doctrine[255] and obtained in parts of Germany. By that time, however, strong tendencies against the retention of this rule had made themselves felt. They emanated from three entirely different quarters. Firstly, the Digest itself contained a rather curious inconsistency, which appeared to improve the position of the tenant. A small clause at the end of D. 43, 16, 12 strengthened the tenant's right of uti frui during the term of the lease,[256] in that it gave him the right to resist the purchaser, if the latter wanted to take possession, provided he (the tenant) did so on account of a iusta et probabilis causa. It appears plausible to accept the contract of lease as a iusta causa in this sense.[257] As soon as one did so, however, one had granted the tenant the right to prevent traditio of the property from the lessor/vendor to the purchaser and thus effectively to paralyse the purchaser's right of eviction—at least in all those cases where the purchaser's right to evict was dependent upon his position as owner and where the acquisition of such a position, in turn, depended, as it usually did, on traditio.[258]

Digesta 43, 16, 12 in fine is a post-classical addition and does not represent classical Roman law.[259] But in the days when the law of the Corpus Juris Civilis was still applicable and therefore had to be approached under systematic rather than historical auspices, the text provided—depending on the interpreter's point of view—either an awkward stumbling block or a welcome inroad into "sale breaks hire".

[253] Again, one must guard against evaluating Roman law, ahistorically, from a modern perspective. A claim for damages was not as "weak" as it might appear to us. First of all, all other claims ultimately gave the successful plaintiff not more than a sum of money either: omnis condemnatio pecuniaria. Secondly, the way in which damages were assessed in court, particularly the iusiurandum in litem (taken by the plaintiff!), put some pressure on the defendant rather to provide restitution in kind.

[254] But see Schrage, 1978 *Acta Juridica* 3 sqq. and now (more clearly) idem, "Zur mittelalterlichem Geschichte des Grundsatzes 'Kauf bricht nicht Miete' ", in: E.J.H. Schrage (ed.), *Das römische Recht im Mittelalter* (1987), pp. 283 sqq., where he demonstrates that the glossators and commentators interpreted C. 4, 65, 9 so restrictively and recognized so many exceptions that the main rule (emptio tollit locatum) did not have much practical significance.

[255] Cf. e.g. Windscheid/Kipp, § 400, n. 7.

[256] Cf. further Pap. D. 43, 16, 18 pr. and Mayer-Maly, *Locatio conductio*, pp. 53 sqq.; Genius, op. cit., note 115, pp. 30 sqq.

[257] Cf. e.g. Christian Friedrich Mühlenbruch, *Die Lehre von der Cession der Forderungsrechte* (3rd ed., 1836), p. 279; Rudolf von Jhering, *Der Besitzwille* (1889), p. 441. For a thorough discussion of this problem, see Karl Ziebarth, *Die Realexecution und die Obligation* (1866), passim, e.g. pp. 1 sqq., 163 sqq.

[258] Cf. e.g. Jhering, op. cit., note 257, pp. 448 sqq.

[259] Mayer-Maly, *Locatio conductio*, pp. 53 sqq.; Kaser, *RPr* II, p. 406; but see Thomas, (1973) 41 *TR* 37.

(e) *Huur gaat voor koop*

In a much more fundamental way, secondly, this principle came to be attacked during the eighteenth century by the natural lawyers. They proceeded from the basic proposition of a promise as being "aut via ad alienationem rei, aut alienatio particulae cujusdam nostrae libertatis".[260] Thus, the lessor, by concluding the contract of lease and thereby promising to let the tenant use and enjoy the property, had parted with and transferred a part of his own liberty (namely to use and enjoy the property himself) and he was therefore unable subsequently to confer this same particulum libertatis on another person, the purchaser. As a result, the lessee's right prevailed against any further transaction which the lessor might choose to effect and so the natural lawyers arrived at the exact opposite of sale breaks hire.[261] However, their view did not influence the contemporary practice of law.

The third source of opposition against emptio tollit locatum can best be located in 17th- and 18th-century Dutch law. Here, interestingly, the fronts were reversed in that the main thrust did not come from doctrinal jurisprudence but from local practice.

> "Dan by ons gheeft alle huur eenig eigen recht, als zijnde een bruick van korten tijd: 't welck daer uit blijckt, dat het verhuirde land ofte huis zijnde verkocht, den huirman evenwel sijn huir moet volghen."

These are the words of Hugo Grotius,[262] and we find similar statements in the works of all the other Roman-Dutch authors.[263] They tie in with the custom in other regions ("Moribus tamen Brabantiae, Flandriae, Hannoniae, aliarumque quarundam harum regionum contrarium ius est, ubi dictat lex municipalis potiorem esse conductionis quam emptionis causam"),[264] go back to medieval Germanic law[265] and were usually based, dogmatically, on the following consideration: "Moribus insuper . . . jus reale conductor adquirit, sic ut a successore singulari

---

[260] Hugo Grotius, *De jure belli ac pacis*, Lib. II, Cap. XI, IV; Christian Wolff, *Jus Naturae*, Pars III, Cap. IV, § 360 ("Qui alteri ad faciendum sese obligat perfecte, particulam quandam libertatis suae alienat"). Cf. further Diesselhorst, *Hugo Grotius*, pp. 34 sqq.; 50 sq.; Franz Wieacker, "Die vertragliche Obligation bei den Klassikern des Vernunftrechts", in: *Festschrift für Hans Welzel* (1974), pp. 11 sqq.

[261] For details, see Genius, op. cit., note 115, pp. 173 sqq.; cf. also Klaus Luig, "Der Einfluss des Naturrechts auf das positive Privatrecht im 18. Jahrhundert", (1979) 96 *ZSS* (GA) 44 sqq.

[262] *Inleiding*, II, XLIV, 9.

[263] For details, see J.C. de Wet, "Huur Gaat Voor Koop", (1944) 8 *THRHR* 166 sqq.; Genius, op. cit., note 115, pp. 138 sqq.; E.J.H. Schrage, "Sale Breaks Hire—Or Does It? Medieval Foundations of the Roman-Dutch Concept", (1986) 54 *TR* 294 sqq.

[264] Gudelinus, *Commentarii de iure novissimo*, Lib. III, Cap. VII, n 12. Cf. further, for instance, John Gilissen, " 'Huur gaat voor koop' in het oud-belgische Recht", (1939) 16 *TR* 281 sqq.

[265] For details Genius, op. cit., note 115, pp. 101 sqq.; Schrage, (1986) 54 *TR* 293 sq. The tenant had (although perhaps not always) *"Gewere"*, i.e. his position had the character of a real right, and he was granted legal protection against expulsion.

ante tempus expelli nequeat. . . ."[266] The position was summed up succinctly in the maxim "huur gaat voor koop". Where they dealt with Roman law, on the other hand, the Dutch jurists stressed the principle of emptio tollit locatum.[267]

It was under the influence of natural law that the great codifications at the turn of the 19th century departed in a more or less radical fashion from the Roman rule.[268] The South African courts apply "huur gaat voor koop",[269] and § 571 BGB states that

> "if the leased land is sold to a third party by the lessor after delivery to the lessee, the acquirer takes the place of the lessor in the rights and obligations arising from the lease during the existence of his ownership."

Thus, in most modern legal systems the tenant is well protected against the acquirer. It must be realized, though, that from a dogmatic point of view this presents something of an anomaly: for the tenant, on the basis of a conceptually purely obligatory contract of lease, acquires a quasi-real position, a "modified and exceptional" real right.[270]

12. Towards security of tenure

Naturally, the eventual abolition of emptio tollit locatum did not occur in isolation; even more basic is the tenant's protection against expulsion by his lessor. Over the centuries various ways were found to achieve at least some sort of protection. The locatio ad longum tempus[271] can be seen in this light, for it gave the tenant what he lacked with regard to locatio conductio simplex: possessory remedies, a real right and an actio in rem. Later on the actio spolii (that had made its way into the ius commune from the so-called Canon redintegranda of the Corpus Juris

---

[266] Paulus Voet, *Institutionum imperialium commentarius* (Ultrajecti, 1668), Lib. III, Tit. XXV, § 6, n. 4.

[267] Cf. e.g. Voet, *Commentarius ad Pandectas*, Lib. XIX, Tit. II, 17; Ulrich Huber, *Praelectiones*, Lib. III, Tit. XXV, 11 (". . . per venditionem (!) a locatore factam solvitur conductio"); Van Leeuwen, *Censura Forensis*, Pars I, Lib. IV, Cap. XXII, 19.

[268] §§ 3, 358 I 21 PrALR; art. 1743 code civil; §§ 1095, 1120 ABGB. For all details, see Genius, op. cit., note 115, pp. 193 sqq., 198 sqq., 204 sqq.

[269] De Wet, (1944) 8 *THRHR* 226 sqq.; De Wet en Yeats, pp. 330 sqq.; Kerr, *Sale and Lease*, pp. 277 sqq.

[270] *Cane v. Wynberg Municipality* (1893) 10 SC 118 at 120 (per De Villiers CJ). For Germany cf. RGZ 59, 326 (328): *"Mit der Übergabe der Mietsache entwächst das Recht des Mieters dem reinen Obligationenrechte. Es bestehen nicht mehr bloss zwischen den obligatorisch Verbundenen Rechte und Pflichten, sondern jedermann hat das durch den Besitz erkennbare Mietrecht zu achten"* (With the handing over of the leased object the lessee's right outgrows the pure law of obligations. There are no longer only rights and duties between the parties to the obligational relationship; everybody has to respect the lessee's right which is identifiable by virtue of his possession); Emmerich/Sonnenschein, op. cit., note 15, pp. 307 sqq. For a more radical and unequivocal approach, cf. the Prussian Code of 1794 which recognized the lessee's right as a ius in rem. For a detailed comparison and evaluation cf. Gerhard Otte, "Die dingliche Rechtsstellung des Mieters nach ALR und BGB", in: *Festschrift für Franz Wieacker* (1978), pp. 463 sqq.

[271] Cf. supra, p. 359.

Canonici)[272] was used to assist the tenant, even though he was only a detentor.[273] The whole topic of possession gave rise to one of the most complex and heated debates in 19th-century pandectist literature, but it was only the legislator who finally abolished the distinction between possessio and detentio. Since then, it has been beyond dispute that a tenant is possessor. The institution of notice, on the other hand, which was of Germanic origin and prevented the lessor from expelling his tenant without further ado, came to be received into the ius commune in the course of the later usus modernus pandectarum[274] and was firmly entrenched by the end of the 19th century. By that time, too, a clear distinction was drawn between contracts of lease for a specific period and those for an indefinite time.[275] In the latter instance, both parties were at liberty to give notice at any time, but had to observe customary periods of notice which varied from place to place.[276] If a specific time had been agreed upon, the contract normally came to an end with the lapse of that time. Under certain circumstances, however, both the lessor and the lessee had the right to terminate the contract prematurely. It was in this context that the Roman grounds for justified expulsion (mainly C. 4, 65, 3) and for justified abandonment[277] became relevant again.[278]

In the course of the present century, notice protection on the part of the tenant has been considerably increased. Today, according to the BGB, the lessor may terminate the lease of residential accommodation only if he can show a reasonable interest in such termination.[279] But even in the light of the legitimate interests of the lessor, the tenant can demand a continuation of the lease if hardship would otherwise ensue for himself or for his family.[280] Security of tenure reigns supreme.[281]

---

[272] For all details see, most recently, Duard G. Kleyn, *Die Mandament van spolie in die Suid-Afrikaanse Reg* (unpublished LLD thesis, Pretoria, 1986), pp. 73 sqq.

[273] Cf., for example, Leyser, *Meditationes ad Pandectas*, Spec. CCCCLI; Carl Georg Bruns, *Das Recht des Besitzes im Mittelalter und in der Gegenwart* (1848), pp. 393 sq.

[274] Cf. e.g. Justus Henning Boehmer, *Consultationes et Decisiones Iuris*, vol. II, Pars II (Halae Magdeburgicae, 1734), Resp. 1014, n. 6.

[275] Cf. e.g. Vangerow, *Pandekten*, § 643, n. 1.

[276] Cf. e.g. Windscheid/Kipp, § 402, 1.

[277] Cf. supra, pp. 355 sqq., 357 sq.

[278] Cf. e.g. Glück, vol. 17, pp. 373 sqq., 477 sqq.

[279] § 564 b BGB. The interpretation of this rule has recently been the subject of much controversy. Cf. BVerfG, 1989 *Neue Juristische Wochenschrift* 970 sqq., 972 sqq.; Johann Friedrich Henschel, "Eigentumsgewährleistung und Mieterschutz" 1989 *Neue Juristische Wochenschrift* 937 sqq.

[280] § 556 a BGB.

[281] The historical development of security of tenure of residential accommodation has been comprehensively analysed in the monographs of Genius op. cit., note 115 (from Roman law down to the times of usus modernus and the great natural-law codifications) and Udo Wolter, *Mietrechtlicher Bestandsschutz* (1986) (who takes the reader through from 1800 to the present-day law).

CHAPTER 12

Locatio conductio II

I. LOCATIO CONDUCTIO OPERARUM

1. Essential elements of Roman "labour law"

(a) *Locare conducere*

> "Simile est regnum coelorum homini patrifamilias, qui exiit primo mane conducere operarios in vineam suam. conventione autem facta cum operariis ex denario diurno, misit eos in vineam suam. Et egressus circa horam tertiam, vidit alios stantes in foro otiosos, et dixit illis: Ite et vos in vineam meam, et quod justum fuerit, dabo vobis. Illi autem abierunt. . . ."[1]

We all know the parable of the labourers in the vineyard. Quite apart from its theological significance, it gives us a vivid picture of how the labour market worked—in Rome as much as in Galilee. It was the place where people offered themselves into service. They were prepared to work for somebody else, and this involved, first of all, that they made themselves available for a change of place (locare,[2] as derived from locus). The employer/master, in turn, took them along or instructed them where to go, and his activity was described as conducere. We are dealing here with the second of the cardinal types of locatio conductio: the contract of service, or locatio conductio operarum, as it was termed by the lawyers of the ius commune. "Operae" are services,[3] services as such and without reference to a specific result to be achieved. Where such result was contemplated, one spoke of "opus".

(b) *Essentialia negotii; periculum conductoris*

By and large, locatio conductio operarum followed rules similar to locatio conductio rei. It was a consensual contract, and the parties had to agree on two essentialia negotii: the services to be rendered (operae) and the remuneration to be paid (merces).[4] The remuneration had to

---

[1] St. Matthew 20, 1–4.

[2] On se locare and operas suas locare cf. De Robertis, *I rapporti di lavoro nel diritto romano* (1946), pp. 18 sq., 25 sq., 52 sq.; J.A.C. Thomas, "Locatio and operae", (1961) 64 *BIDR* 234; Kaufmann, *Altrömische Miete*, p. 203. Could a slave let himself out? Cf. e.g. Lab. D. 19, 2, 60, 7; Pap. D. 33, 2, 2, and Thomas, (1961) 64 *BIDR* 232 sqq.; contra (on the basis that the texts are interpolated or untechnical) Mayer-Maly, "Römische Grundlagen des modernen Arbeitsrechts", 1967 *Recht der Arbeit* 285.

[3] For a detailed discussion, see Kaufmann, *Altrömische Miete*, pp. 182 sqq.; cf. also Mayer-Maly, 1967 *Recht der Arbeit* 282.

[4] On the history and etymology of merces and its derivatives, "mercennarius" (a person working for wages) and "Mercedonius" (an old, probably unofficial, name for the month of November(?), in the course of which the merces was due) see Kaufmann, *Altrömische Miete*, pp. 138 sqq.

consist in money and could not merely be a token amount.[5] The employer could avail himself of the actio conducti to enforce due performance of the services promised; if he did not pay the merces, he was liable to his employee under the actio locati. The contents of the contract and all details of the parties' obligations were determined by the agreement of the parties; failing that, by the standard of "dare facere oportere ex fide bona" as set out in the intentio of the actiones locati and conducti. Thus, questions of risk and liability, for instance, were settled on this basis in a very flexible and finely balanced manner. As far as risk is concerned, we find only one statement of a more general nature in the Digest: "Qui operas suas locavit, totius temporis mercedem accipere debet, si per eum non stetit, quo minus operas praestet."[6] "Periculum", in this context, again refers to the question whether counterperformance (in this instance: payment of the remuneration) still has to be made, even though rendering of the performance has become impossible. Digesta 19, 2, 38 pr. tells us that the employee did not, as a rule, lose his claim for the merces in this case; thus: periculum conductoris.[7] A very important exception, however, is expressed in the words "si per eum non stetit, quo minus operas praestet". Naturally, if it was due to the employee's fault that the services had not been rendered, he could not sue his employer for the wages. "Si per eum non stetit", however, takes things much further and goes beyond mere dolus and culpa. What mattered was whether the reason why the work had not been done had its origin within the *sphere* of the employee.[8] Which incidents were, in this sense, attributable to the employee and which were not, is very difficult to determine. This is due to the great

---

[5] On these requirements see, in general, Theo Mayer-Maly, "Dienstvertrag und Arbeitsvertrag", (1966) 1 *Zeitschrift für Arbeitsrecht und Sozialrecht* 2 sqq.

[6] Paul. D. 19, 2, 38 pr. See De Robertis, op. cit., note 2, pp. 148 sqq.; Mayer-Maly, *Locatio conductio*, pp. 181 sqq.; Max Kaser, "Periculum locatoris", (1957) 74 *ZSS* 194 sqq.; Giuseppe Provera, Sul problema del *rischio contrattuale nel* diritto romano", in: *Studi in* onore di Emilio Betti, vol. III (1962), pp. 693 sqq.; Claude Alzon, "Les risques dans la 'locatio conductio' ", (1966) 12 *Labeo* 319 sqq.; J.A.C. Thomas, "The Worker and His Wage", in: *Uit Het Recht, Rechtsgeleerde opstellen aangeboden aan mr. P. J. Verdam* (1971), pp. 201 sqq.; Imre Molnár, "Verantwortung und Gefahrtragung bei der locatio conductio zur Zeit des Prinzipats", *ANRW*, vol. II, 14 (1982), pp. 640 sqq.

[7] Differently Robert Röhle, "Das Problem der Gefahrtragung im Bereich des römischen Dienst- und Werkvertrages", (1968) 34 *SDHI* 184 sqq.

[8] The parallel with the "*Sphärentheorie*", which the modern German courts have developed to determine the allocations of risk (cf. supra p. 195) is obvious. The BGB itself, incidentally, had turned away (at least on a conceptual level) from the sphere-oriented way of risk allocation which dominated the earlier ius commune; it followed the generalized and will-oriented approach developed by the natural lawyers, as taken over by Savigny: in case of impossibility of performance, counter-performance also falls away on account of a "tacita conditio resolutiva" (Christian Wolff), i.e. the idea of the so-called conditional synallagma (cf. infra, p. 811). In the modern discussions about risk-allocation we see how even under the new normative roof of the BGB the old tradition of the ius commune still lives on (". . . *die gemeinrechtliche Erbschaft, die auch unter dem neuen normativen Dach des BGB fortwuchert*"). For an analysis of the historical development, see Joachim Rückert, "Vom casus zur Unmöglichkeit und vor den Sphäre zum Synallagma", (1984) 6 *ZNR* 50 sqq. (quotation on p. 52).

scarcity of sources dealing with locatio conductio operarum. We are not even sure how what must have been—and still is—one of the most relevant practical examples, sickness of the employee, was dealt with.[9] Death of the employer, on the other hand, certainly did not affect the employee's claim for wages.[10] The same must have applied to the usual cases of vis maior—earthquakes, invading armies and the like: the risk was on the employer. In actual practice, however, things often looked less favourable for the employee, for the parties frequently seem to have provided otherwise in their contract. One such clause has been preserved in the text of the Transylvanian wax tablets: ". . . [q]uod si fluor inpedierit, pro rata conputare debebit"[11]—if the mine was flooded, so that the mine worker was unable to work for part of the time for which the contract had been concluded, his claim for wages was reduced proportionately.

(c) Imperitia culpae adnumeratur

The employee obviously had to do what was required of him diligently. It is probable (though not certain),[12] that the employer was liable (only) for culpa and not for custodia. Such culpa could, however, appear in the interesting guise of imperitia: imperitia culpae adnumeratur.[13] The muleteer whose services were hired, provides an example:

> "Mulionum quoque, si per imperitiam impetum mularum retinere non potuerit, si eae alienum hominem obtriverint, vulgo dicitur culpae nomine teneri. idem dicitur et si propter infirmitatem sustinere mularum impetum non potuerit: nec videtur iniquum, si infirmitas culpae adnumeretur. . . ."[14]

Mules can be vicious and obstinate, and in order to be able to handle them, a considerable amount of skill and strength is required. If the muleteer lacks such skill or strength and consequently is unable to control the mules, he is liable, even though, considering his limited capabilities, it might be difficult to blame him either for his actions or for his failure to act at the time when the incident happened. His fault, however, consisted in offering to perform a service without being competent therefor; for the conductor may reasonably expect the

---

[9] Risk on employee (i.e. no claim for wages): Kaser, *RPr* I, p. 570; Benöhr, *Synallagma*, p. 107. Risk on employer (i.e. duty to pay wages): Mayer-Maly, *Locatio conductio*, p. 182; Provera, *Studi Betti*, vol. III, p. 712. The question was very controversial among the writers of the ius commune too; cf. e.g. Coing, p. 460 (today § 616 BGB).

[10] Ulp. D. 19, 2, 19, 9; 10. On these texts, See Nicola Palazzolo, "Le consueguenze della morte del Conductor operarum sul rapporto di lavoro", (1964) 30 *SDHI* 284 sqq., who argues that the question is not one of periculum but of "trasmissibilità ereditaria".

[11] *Corpus Inscriptionum Latinarum*, vol. III, 2, 948 X.

[12] For a discussion of this question, see Molnár, *ANRW*, op. cit., note 6, pp. 613 sqq.

[13] This rule can be found in Gai. D. 50, 17, 132.

[14] Gai. D. 9, 2, 8, 1; cf. also *Inst.* IV, 3, 8; both texts, however, deal with Aquilian liability. For an analysis, see Mayer-Maly, *Locatio conductio*, pp. 158 sq.; Molnár, *ANRW*, op. cit., note 6, pp. 611 sqq.; Okko Behrends, "Die Rechtsformen des römischen Handwerks", (1981) 22 *Abhandlungen der Akademie der Wissenschaften in Göttingen* 145 sqq.

locator to possess both peritia and firmitas for the specific service which the latter undertakes to render.[15]

2. The range of application of locatio conductio operarum

So much for Roman labour law, or perhaps rather: so little. Again we pose the question why this area of the law received so little attention from the Roman lawyers and why we do not find any attempt to mitigate the lack of equilibrium inherent in the relationship of employment. Particularly striking is the lack of any protection against socially unjustified dismissal of the employee.[16] As we have seen, the institution of giving notice to terminate the relationship was unknown in Roman law, and that meant that the contract of locatio conductio operarum came to an end either on the expiration of the time for which it had been entered into—this was what normally happened—or, if no time had been fixed, the contract could be terminated at any time by either of the parties.

(a) Status relationships

Again, however, we should not rashly attribute what seems to us to be a highly unsatisfactory state of affairs to a social bias or to sinister capitalistic machinations on the part of the Roman lawyers. For it is important to realize that locatio conductio operarum dealt with only a small segment of the Roman labour market. To a considerable extent,[17] the demand for both skilled and unskilled labour was met by slaves, and slaves, of course, did not enter into employment relationships. Their status was determined in terms of potestas and dominium, and it was not on a contractual basis that they worked for their masters. Where the master let out his slave to a third party, this constituted locatio conductio rei, not operarum.[18] If, therefore, the services rendered by slaves were excluded from the ambit of locatio conductio operarum, so were the operae which liberti owed towards their former masters (now patrons). These operae were usually rendered on the basis of a promise under oath[19] or of a stipulation; for the enforcement of such a promise, the ius civile provided a special action, the actio operarum.[20]

---

[15] Cf. today § 276 I 2 BGB: "A person who does not exercise ordinary care acts negligently." Negligence is determined according to an abstract objective criterion, not according to whether this particular debtor could have foreseen or prevented the damage.

[16] One of the main concerns of modern labour law; for a comparative analysis, see Tony Honoré, *The Quest for Security: Employees, Tenants, Wives* (1982), pp. 1 sqq.

[17] Cf., for example, Behrends, op. cit., note 14, pp. 182 sqq. But see also, as far as public works were concerned (such as large-scale imperial building programmes), P.A. Brunt, "Free Labour and Public Works at Rome", (1980) 70 *JRS* 81 sqq.

[18] Cf. e.g. Paul. D. 19, 2, 42; 43; 45, 1.

[19] Gai. III, 96.

[20] For details on the operae libertorum, cf. Kaser, *RPr* I, pp. 298 sqq.; Behrends, op. cit., note 14, pp. 184 sqq.; and now, in particular, the splendid work of Wolfgang Waldstein, *Operae Libertorum* (1986). He emphasizes that we are dealing here with a social phenomenon

(b) The artes liberales

Was locatio conductio operarum thus confined to service transactions between members of the upper classes? It would be wrong to draw such a conclusion. For not only at the lower, but also at the upper end of the social scale a whole range of services was largely excluded from this type of contract. We are dealing with the so-called artes liberales, activities which could be regarded as worthy of a free man[21]—such as those in which philosophers, advocates, architects, land surveyors or teachers and students involved in studia liberalia engaged.[22] These activities did not per se fall outside the scope of locatio conductio operarum; it was, however, regarded as inappropriate and unseemly among the higher echelons of Roman society to work for a wage.[23] Thus, "one" did not let one's (professional) services under a contract of locatio conductio.[24] A life of otium cum dignitate was the ideal of the Roman aristocracy:[25] otium, however, not implying a Mediterranean attitude of "dolce far niente", but providing the opportunity to concentrate one's efforts on the common weal. Only those who did not have to worry about their daily bread were able to seek self-fulfilment by devoting their lives to the service of the res publica.[26] A reflection of this attitude was the rather low estimation of labour, as it appears, for instance, from a famous passage of Cicero's de officiis:[27]

---

of great importance. On the actio operarum, cf. pp. 135 sqq., 345 sqq. and passim. Cf. also Johannes Michael Rainer, "Humanität und Arbeit im römischen Recht", (1988) 105 *ZSS* 745 sqq.

[21] Cf. e.g. Seneca, *Epistulae ad Lucilium*, Lib. XI, 88, 1, 2 and 20; referring, however, to "liberalia studia". There is an extensive literature dealing with the operae liberales (a term that does not appear in the legal sources; cf., however, Ulp. D. 50, 13, 1: ". . . liberalia autem studia . . ., quae Graeci ἐλευθέρια appellant"); cf., above all, Károly Visky, *Geistige Arbeit und die "artes liberales" in den Quellen des römischen Rechts* (1977), pp. 9 sqq.

[22] ". . . what might generally be described as 'the professions', with intellectual as distinct from skilled manual activity": Thomas, (1961) 64 *BIDR* 240 sq.

[23] Prevailing opinion; cf. e.g. Mayer-Maly, *Locatio conductio*, pp. 125 sqq.; Kaser, *RPr* I, p. 569; Thomas, *TRL*, p. 298; Watson, *Failures*, p. 78. For a different view, see, for instance, Heinrich Siber, "Operae liberales", (1939–40) 88 *JhJb* 161 sqq. (all types of operae liberales were typically rendered under a contract of locatio conductio) and Visky, op. cit., note 21, pp. 9 sqq. (operae liberales by law excluded from this contract). Others differentiate between the various professions (cf. e.g. Karl Heldrich, "Der Arzt im römischem Privatrecht", (1939–40) 88 *JhJb* 139 sqq.; Michel, *Gratuité*, pp. 198 sqq.), one of the main difficulties being that the term "artes liberales" lacked both precise definition and technical significance. Thus, a single coherent doctrine of the practice of "the" professions at Rome cannot be extracted from the sources (Thomas, (1961) 64 *BIDR* 241). For further standard literature on the topic, cf. Antoine Bernard, *La Rémunération des Professions Libérales en Droit Romain Classique* (1936); Jean Macqueron, *Le travail des hommes libres dans l'antiquité romaine* (1958).

[24] Cf. e.g. Ulp. D. 11, 6, 1 pr.: ". . . quia non crediderunt veteres inter talem personam locationem et conductionem esse . . ." (dealing with agri mensores).

[25] Cf. e.g. Cicero, *Pro P. Sextio oratio*, XLV—98; idem, *De oratore*, 1, I; Francesco M. de Robertis, *Lavoro e lavoratori nel mondo romano* (1963), pp. 21 sqq.

[26] Dieter Nörr, "Zur sozialen und rechtlichen Bewertung der freien Arbeit in Rom", (1965) 82 *ZSS* 76.

[27] 1, XLII—150 sq. On this text cf. e.g. De Robertis, op. cit., note 25, pp. 53 sqq.; Visky, op. cit., note 21, pp. 10 sqq.; Behrends, op. cit., note 14, pp. 149 sq.

"Inliberales autem et sordidi quaestus mercennariorum omnium quorum operae, non quorum artes emuntur: est enim in illis ipsa merces auctoramentum servitutis. . . . Opificesque omnes in sordida arte versantur: nec enim quicquam ingenuum habere potest officina, minimeque artes eae probandae quae ministrae sunt voluptatum: Cetarii, lanii, coqui, fartores, piscatores, ut ait Terentius; adde huc, si placet, unguentarios, saltatores totumque ludum talarium."

Sordidus: this is strong stuff. It should not induce us to paint too undifferentiated a picture.

(c) The value of "labour" in Roman society

First of all: we are dealing with upper-class attitudes. Among the Romans of less elevated station, middle-class artisans and traders, for instance, whose circumstances we know of through tombstones and inscriptions, a much more positive view about the value of labour prevailed.[28] Secondly, even among the upper classes it was not every type of work (operae, labor)[29] that was despised, not even every kind of manual labour. One merely has to think of the anecdotes about Republican statesmen being called away from their plough share[30] in order to realize that agriculture enjoyed a special status.[31] There can be little doubt that all activities connected with it were worthy of the sweat of even the most distinguished Romans. Thus, it was sometimes not so much the activity as such that was frowned upon, but rather whether the work was done for the working party himself or for a third person. To plough one's own field was in order, but to join the neighbour's workforce to harvest his olives was hardly suitable. But even that distinction must not be carried too far: it was one out of a variety of factors that influenced the social evaluation of labour.[32] To work for somebody else's benefit may be highly desirable, and genuinely altruistic behaviour was certainly never looked down upon by the Roman aristocracy. Thus, two further very important and closely connected factors determined the esteem in which a particular activity was held: whether it involved subjection to somebody else's will and whether or not the services were rendered gratuitously. A person who agreed to work for money somehow appeared to have sold himself.[33]

[28] On the necessity of differentiating between what he calls the ambiente volgare and the ambiente aulico, and on the social evaluation in both spheres, see De Robertis, op. cit., note 25, pp. 21 sqq. and passim.

[29] On the terminology, see De Robertis, op. cit., note 25, pp. 9 sqq.; cf. also Mayer-Maly, 1967 *Recht der Arbeit* 282.

[30] Cf. e.g. Valerius Maximus, Lib. IV, Cap. IV, §§ 4 sqq.; Plinius, *Historia naturalis*, XVIII sq.; Cicero, *Cato maior de senectute*, XVI.

[31] Cf. Cato, *De agri cultura, praefatio* (". . . pius stabilissimusque minimeque invidiosus") and Cicero, *De officiis* 1, XLII—151: "Omnium autem rerum ex quibus aliquid adquiritur, nihil est agricoltura melius, nihil uberius, nihil dulcius, nihil homine, nihil libero dignius." For details, see De Robertis, *Lavoro*, pp. 87 sqq.

[32] For an analysis of the various factors to be taken into consideration, see Nörr, (1965) 82 *ZSS* 73 sqq.

[33] Nörr, (1965) 82 *ZSS* 76.

Hence the exclusion of the activities of the upper classes from locatio conductio operarum. To engage in philosophy, mathematics, rhetoric or architecture was entirely respectable, as long as it served the purpose of edification, instruction or self-fulfilment. Apart from that, however, the Roman aristocracy felt honour-bound to make their skills available to assist others and operae liberales could therefore also be rendered to third parties. But this had to happen free of charge. The fiction had to be preserved that the work was done voluntarily, without legal obligation and as a matter of amicitia or public spirit. Take, for instance, the advocacy, a profession that carried high prestige.[34] Even though for many it was a professional activity, by means of which considerable sums of money were earned, it was not carried out on the basis of a contract of service. To be asked for help was an honour for the advocatus, and what he eventually received for his services was a ("voluntary") honorarium.[35] All this was ancestral or social convention, for a legal prohibition to enter into lucrative agreements does not seem to have existed for any of the more highly rated professional activities. Thus, for instance, physicians were obviously able to work for merces.[36] But then the activities of medici in general did not enjoy the same sort of prestige as the other "quaestus liberales";[37] medicine was usually practised by slaves or freedmen of Greek or Oriental origin;[38] ingenui seem to have remained an exception.[39]

---

[34] For details cf. Visky, op. cit., note 21, pp. 54 sqq. and, more generally, on the legal professions, their status and their members, Fritz Schulz, *Roman Legal Science* (1946), passim; Bruce W. Frier, *The Rise of the Roman Jurists* (1985), passim. Cf. also, in the present context, Thomas, (1961) 64 *BIDR* 245 sqq.; Michel, *Gratuité*, pp. 215 sqq.

[35] Cf. e.g. Ulp. D. 11, 6, 1 pr.: ". . . sed magis operam beneficii loco praeberi et id quod datur ei, ad remunerandum dari et inde honorarium appellari" (dealing, however, with agri mensores).

[36] Cf. e.g. Ulp. D. 9, 2, 7, 8; Gai. D. 9, 3, 7; Visky, pp. 73 sqq. Too extreme are Heldrich, (1939–40) 88 *JhJb* 141 sqq. (medici typically entered into a contract of locatio conductio) and Karl-Heinz Below, *Der Arzt im römischen Recht* (1953), pp. 57 (the medicus ingenuus—as opposed to servi and liberti—was excluded from entering into this type of contract).

[37] Cicero, *De officiis*, 1, XLII—150 sq. During the Republic, physicians were regarded as artisans (faber); cf. e.g. Plautus, *Aulularia*, Act III, Sc. II, l. 448 (on the notions of craft and craftsmen in Rome generally, see Behrends, op. cit., note 14, pp. 142 sqq.; cf. also Harald von Petrikovits, "Die Spezialisierung des römischen Handwerks", (1981) 122 *Abhandlungen der Akademie der Wissenschaften in Göttingen* 63 sqq.). For a long time (and in contrast to other Mediterranean nations) the Romans did not have any kind of scientific medicine at all. Cato is still reported to have treated all the members of his household himself. For his ideas about medicine cf. e.g. *De agri cultura*, CLXVIII, 160 ("Luxum si quod est, hac cantione sanum fiet"). According to Varro, *De re rustica*, Lib. I, 2, 27, gout could be cured by singing 27 times "Ego tui memini, medere meis pedibus, terra, pestem teneto, salus hic maneto in meis pedibus", whilst at the same time touching the soil and spitting out. But see Ulp. D. 50, 13, 1, 1 and 3 for a different assessment of the activity of doctors prevailing in classical times; cf. also Seneca, *De beneficiis*, Lib. VI, XIV, 3 sqq. and Watson, *Failures*, pp. 68 sqq.; Ralph Jackson, *Doctors and Diseases in the Roman Empire* (1988), pp. 56 sqq.

[38] Many of the most brilliant Roman doctors were of Greek origin: Asklepiades of Bythinia (who was friendly with Quintus Mucius Scaevola, Cicero, Marcus Antonius and other prominent Romans), his pupil, Themison of Laodikeia, and Galenos of Pergamon. Under their influence, the social evaluation of medicine and of those practising it seems to

(d) Common law (ius civile) and employment relationships

But wherever exactly the "upper" limit of locatio conductio operarum was drawn, it has become clear that this type of contract covered only a relatively small (middle) sector of the services available. If that was so, and if it is also kept in mind that the claims of middle-class wage-earners were not likely to come to the attention of the Roman jurists in great numbers,[40] the somewhat cursory treatment of this branch of law becomes much less surprising. Furthermore, there are other legal systems where the "common" law has not had a major formative influence on employment relationships either. In England, for instance, the courts traditionally paid no attention "to the reality of subordination which lurks behind the façade of contractual equality",[41] and as a result

> "the worker's obligation to obey the lawful commands given by management and the employer's obligation to remunerate the worker are [regarded as] contractual obligations freely incurred among equals. Pacta sunt servanda".[42]

The whole body of what we today know as labour law has been built up from different sources. One may well ask why this is so: are the courts simply not willing to lift the veil of equality, have they lacked the opportunity of doing so (because exploited workers have had no access to the courts or were deterred from litigating), or are we dealing with an inherent inability of (judge-made) case law to meet the expectations of society and to cope with the challenges presented by individual industrial relations?[43] Whatever the answer may be: one

have changed. The Emperors granted them immunitas and other privileges (Below, op. cit., note 36, pp. 22 sqq.). Antonius Musa (a libertus and another pupil of Asklepiades) became personal physician to Augustus and was able to cure a severe liver disease of the Emperor by way of hydrotherapy. He received the anulus aureus (entailing equestris dignitas), and a statue of him was made. For further details, see Manfred Just, "Der Honoraranspruch des medicus ingenuus', in: *Sodalitas, Scritti in onore di Antonio Guarino*, vol. VI (1984), pp. 3072 sqq.; generally on Roman physicians and their medicines cf. Jackson, op. cit., note 37, pp. 56 sqq. From C. 4, 43, 3 it is evident that even in Justinian's time medical practitioners could well be slaves. They were, incidentally, valued at three times the rate of slaves with no trade, and double the rate of skilled slaves (cf. Watson, *Failures*, pp. 67 sq.).

[39] Did medicine belong to the artes liberales, as opposed to the "quaestus illiberales", activities which could not be reconciled with upper-class status? Cf. e.g. Thomas, (1961) 64 *BIDR* 241 sqq. (yes); Visky, op. cit., note 21, pp. 73 sqq. (no); Just, *Scritti Guarino*, vol. VI, pp. 3057 sqq. (at first not, but later on yes). For a detailed analysis of the social status and legal position of medical practitioners cf. Bernard, op. cit., note 23, pp. 57 sqq.; Below, *Der Arzt im römischen Recht* (1953), passim; Visky, op. cit., note 21, pp. 73 sqq.; Watson, *Failures*, pp. 66 sqq.

[40] Cf. supra, pp. 348 sq. The same point has been emphasized with regard to English law; cf. Kahn-Freund's *Labour and the Law* (infra, note 41) p. 35; cf. also Otto Kahn-Freund, "Blackstone's Neglected Child: The Contract of Employment", (1977) 93 *LQR* 508 sqq., 521.

[41] Kahn-Freund's *Labour and the Law* (3rd ed., 1983, by Paul Davies, Marc Freedman (eds)), p. 36.

[42] Kahn-Freund's *Labour and the Law*, op. cit., note 41, p. 35.

[43] All these factors are discussed in Kahn-Freund's *Labour and the Law*, op. cit., note 41, pp. 29 sqq.

should in any event not blame the Roman lawyers for an exceptional and entirely unprecedented lack of social conscience.

(e) The contribution of Roman law

Finally, the great contributions the Roman lawyers have made even to this field of law must not be overlooked. Two major points, in my view, stand out. First of all, critical as we tend to be today of freedom of contract in labour relations, the move from status to contract, as it occurred during the Roman Republic,[44] represents a considerable advance in the management of human resources. Some of the more radical modern attempts to discredit contract as the basis for the relations between employers and workers, and to think in terms of incorporation and of what has been termed "*personenrechtliches Gemeinschaftsverhältnis*"[45] have soon become thoroughly discredited. And secondly: the nature of locatio conductio as a consensual contract giving rise to reciprocal rights and duties, the rules relating to merces and the refined way of determining liability and of allocating risks: these have remained essential elements of the contract of service ("*Dienstmiete*") of the continental ius commune. Much of it has been preserved in modern law.[46] And even though, for instance, it is often

---

[44] Not very much is known about the early history of service transactions. But it seems certain that, whereas locatio conductio presupposed at least formal equality of the parties, the legal institutions preceding it were based on a relationship of subordination; thus, the right of the paterfamilias to the services of his slaves and of his sons in power (and his right to transfer them into the service, i.e. the power, of another paterfamilias), the right of the patron to the services of his clientes and of the manumissor to those of his liberti were all based on relationships of power and status. For details, see Kaufmann, *Altrömische Miete*, e.g. pp. 44 sqq., 67 sqq., 118 sqq., but also the summary by Mayer-Maly, 1967 *Recht der Arbeit* 283. The contract of locatio conductio did not involve a change of the legal status on the part of the employee: Nörr, (1965) 82 *ZSS* 86 sqq. as against De Robertis, op. cit., note 25, pp. 143 sqq. More recently on the transition, as far as the activities of artisans are concerned, from status relationships to the liberalistic and individualistic contractual system, see Behrends, op. cit., note 14, pp. 193 sqq. Regarding the English common law, Kahn-Freund, (1977) 93 *LQR* 508 sqq. has argued that Blackstone's classification of the relationship of master and servant as essentially one of status impeded the development in England of a contractual approach to employment. Contra: John W. Cairns, "Blackstone, Kahn-Freund and the Contract of Employment", (1989) 105 *LQR* 300 sqq. One of the points at dispute between Kahn-Freund and Cairns is whether Blackstone's neglect of the contract of employment is a "specimen case to demonstrate the contrast between English legal thinking and the legal thinking of the continental nations of Western Europe". On Pothier's analysis (*Traité du contrat de louage*) cf. Kahn-Freund, (1977) 93 *LQR* 514 sqq. and Cairns, (1989) 105 *LQR* 302 sq. Other civilian authors did not deal with the master-and-servant relationship as part of the law of contract, but did so when they discussed various status relationships within the society at large. So did, incidentally, the Prussian General Land Law (§§ 1 sqq. II 5).

[45] On these developments, which occurred as part of the permeation of the law by national-socialistic thinking, see Bernd Rüthers, *Die unbegrenzte Auslegung. Zum Wandel der Privatrechtsordnung im Nationalsozialismus* (1968), pp. 379 sqq.

[46] Cf., for example, Mayer-Maly, 1967 *Recht der Arbeit* 281 sqq.; Reinhold Trinkner, Maria Wolfer, "Modernes Arbeitsrecht und seine Beziehung zum Zivilrecht und seiner Geschichte", 1986 *Betriebsberater* 4 sqq.; as far as the problem of risk allocation is concerned, cf. in particular Rückert, (1984) 6 *ZNR* 50 sqq. On the (earlier) ius commune, cf.,

claimed in Germany that labour law has become a distinctive and autonomous field of law, the §§ 611 sqq. BGB still remain of fundamental importance in individual labour relations. Apart from that, they govern all service contracts falling outside the area of labour law, particularly the services rendered by the so-called liberal professions: doctors, lawyers, chartered accountants, etc.[47]

II. LOCATIO CONDUCTIO OPERIS

1. Essential characteristics and range of application

We have seen that medici were able to work for merces.[48] In other words, they could render their services under a contract of locatio conductio. Such a contract was, however, not necessarily locatio conductio operarum. Indeed, in one of the texts referred to above,[49] the doctor was said to be liable ex locato: "Proculus ait, si medicus servum imperite secuerit, . . . ex locato . . . competere actionem."[50] Had he been employed under a contract of service, he would himself have been the locator. But since we are dealing with an operation, the services as such were not the object of the contract. What was owed was opus faciendum, a particular job to be done as a whole. This is the essential characteristic of locatio conductio operis.[51] One person undertakes to perform or execute a particular piece of work, and he promises to produce a certain specified result. This person is called the conductor (operis). The person commissioning the enterprise (the customer) is the

---

in this respect, Theo Mayer-Maly, "Elemente der Entwicklung des Arbeitsrecht", in: *La formazione storica*, vol. III, pp. 1320 sqq. He draws attention to the fact that the history of labour law does not commence with the Industrial Revolution, but that a scientific body of law dealing with labour relations already existed in the late Middle Ages.

[47] Cf. e.g. Gottfried Schiemann, "Der freie Dienstvertrag", 1983 *Juristische Schulung* 649 sqq. and also § 1163 ABGB. In so far as modern law deviates from the ius commune which, like Roman law, did not regard the services of members of the free (liberal) professions as being rendered under a contract of locatio conductio: cf. e.g. Glück, vol. 17, pp. 315 sqq.; D.J. Joubert, "Die kontraktuele verhouding tussen professionele man en kliënt", 1970 *Acta Juridica* 15 sqq.; Coing, pp. 458 sq.; cf. also Windscheid/Kipp, § 404 (emphasizing, however, that the legal regime is the same as if one were dealing with locatio conductio); § 895 I 11 PrALR; art. 1779 code civil. The situation in modern South African law is unclear (locatio conductio or mandatum?): cf. Joubert, 1970 *Acta Juridica* 22 sqq. (with very sensible suggestions). Generally on locatio conductio operarum in modern South African law, cf. James Fourie, *Die Dienskontrak in die Suid-Afrikaanse Arbeidsreg* (unpublished LLD thesis, Pretoria, 1977).

[48] Cf. supra, p. 390.

[49] At, p. 390, note 36.

[50] Ulp. D. 9, 2, 7, 8. Cf. e.g. Heldrich, (1939–40) 88 *JhJb* 150; Just, *Scritti Guarino*, vol. VI, p. 3061.

[51] Cf. e.g. Windscheid/Kipp, §§ 399, 401; Berger, *ED*, p. 567; Buckland/Stein, p. 505; Kaser, *RPr* I, p. 570; Thomas, (1961) 64 *BIDR* 236 sq.; F.B.J. Wubbe, "Opus selon la définition de Labéon" (1982) 50 *TR* 241 sqq.; for the historical development cf. particularly Kaufmann, *Altrömische Miete*, pp. 205 sqq.

locator: he places out the work to be done. "Locavi opus faciendum . . ."[52] or, as Paulus says:

> "Opere locato conducto: his verbis Labeo significari ait id opus, quod Graeci ἀποτέλεσμα vocant, non ἔργον, id est ea opere facto corpus aliquod perfectum."[53]

In what manner was this contract utilized? Very often there was a physical object to be worked upon or to be created: clothes to be cleaned or repaired,[54] cloth to be produced from wool,[55] jewels to be engraved,[56] a ring to be made,[57] a house to be built.[58] Sometimes the object did not undergo any physical change (for example: goods or passengers to be transported),[59] occasionally it was not a thing but a person (an apprentice to be taught)[60] and in other instances of locatio conductio operis there was no physical subject matter at all (games to be arranged or a trumpet signal to be given).[61] The decisive feature of all these transactions is that the customer was not interested in the services or the labour as such, but in the product or result of such labour. Indeed, he usually was not even interested in whether the conductor performed in person or whether he drew on the assistance of his employees. The conductor was responsible for producing the result; how he did this was (usually) up to him. Thus, the conductor was typically also not bound to obey orders or instructions as to the manner of carrying out the work.

2. Problems of classification

Obviously, where somebody employs a group of labourers to work, say, in his silver mine, we are dealing with a labour relationship (locatio conductio operarum); the jeweller, on the other hand, who engraves the initials of his customer on a bracelet, works under a contract of

[52] Iav. D. 19, 2, 51, 1.

[53] Paul. D. 50, 16, 5, 1. On this text, see Wubbe, (1982) 50 *TR* 241 sqq. He points out that opus does not refer to a material result (in the form of a physical object produced) but to an activity defined by and sustained up to an end (a τέλος).

[54] Cf. e.g. Gai. III, 205; Ulp. D. 19, 2, 9, 5.

[55] Ulp. D. 7, 8, 12, 6.

[56] Ulp. D. 19, 2, 13, 5.

[57] Gai. D. 19, 2, 2, 1; *Inst.* III, 24, 4.

[58] Alf. D. 19, 2, 30, 3; Lab. D. 19, 2, 60, 3; Iav. D. 19, 2, 59; Paul. D. 19, 2, 22, 2. Cf. Robert Röhle, "Das Problem der Gefahrtragung im Bereich des römischen Dienst- und Werkvertrages", (1968) 34 *SDHI* 206 sqq.; Susan D. Martin, *Building Contracts in Classical Roman Law*, (unpublished Ph.D. thesis, Michigan, 1982; not available to me). The codifications of the civil-law countries still regard building contracts as a normal instance of a contract for work (locatio conductio operis) and provide only very few special rules dealing with this subject matter. On the growth of self-made "law" in the building industry which has occurred since then, see Werner Lorenz, "Contracts for Work on Goods and Building Contracts", in: *International Encyclopedia of Comparative Law*, vol. VIII, 8, nn. 6 sqq. Modern commentators usually deal with building contracts as a distinctive category within the framework of locatio conductio operis.

[59] Ulp. D. 19, 2, 11, 3; Gai. D. 19, 2, 19, 7; Gai. D. 19, 2, 25, 7.

[60] Ulp. D. 19, 2, 13, 3; Kaser, *RPr* I, p. 569, n. 60, De Robertis, op. cit., note 2, pp. 197 sqq.

[61] Cf. Kaufmann, *Altrömische Miete*, p. 257.

locatio conductio operis (or, to use the terminology of English law, as an independent contractor). It is easy to establish the intention of the parties in these cases and to categorize their agreement accordingly. It is equally obvious, however, that there are a variety of marginal cases where it can be very difficult to decide on which side of the borderline between locatio conductio operis and operarum they fall.

These difficulties continue to persist in all those modern legal systems which have adopted the trichotomy of contracts grafted on to the Roman locatio conductio by the writers of the ius commune. Take, for example, the legal relationship between physician and patient. It is normally taken to be a contract of service by the modern German courts: the contract only obliges the physician to carry out, lege artis, an indicated medical treatment; it is not intended to make him liable for the success of such treatment.[62] But it is very doubtful whether the same applies if a physician accepts a patient for sterilization.[63] The Federal Supreme Court has gone further and even regarded it as a contract of service if a dentist promises to produce a dental prosthesis or to crown a tooth.[64] This appears to be wrong,[65] even if it is conceded that removal of the toothache cannot reasonably be taken to be the object of the contract. It is, indeed, not a therapeutic success that the dentist promises. Nevertheless, he undertakes to produce a more limited result (namely to prepare and fit onto the tooth a suitable crown), which in turn will (it is hoped) have the desired therapeutic consequences. Another notorious problem area in German law is the classification of the contract between an architect and his customer.[66]

One may ask, in view of the general recognition of "pacta sunt servanda",[67] why the classification of contracts still attracts so much of our attention. In German law it is mainly the fact that special (aedilitian-type) remedies have been introduced to deal with the problem of liability for defects under a contract for work.[68] They are

---

[62] Cf. e.g. Dieter Giesen, *Arzthaftungsrecht—Medical Malpractice Law* (1981), pp. 158, 283, who also refers to French law, where the position is the same as in German law: the *obligation médicale* is an *obligation de moyens*, not an *obligation de résultat*; Franz Bydlinski, "Verträge über ärztliche Leistungen, in: *Festschrift für Winfried Kralik* (1986), pp. 345 sqq.

[63] Cf. BGH, 1980 *Neue Juristische Wochenschrift* 1452 (1453) and LG Freiburg, 1977 *Neue Juristische Wochenschrift* 340.

[64] BGHZ 63, 306 sqq.

[65] Horst Heinrich Jakobs, "Die zahnärztliche Behandlung als Werkleistung", 1975 *Neue Juristische Wochenschrift* 1437 sqq.

[66] Cf. e.g. Horst Heinrich Jakobs, "Der Architektenvertrag im Verhältnis zum Dienst- und Werkvertragsrecht", in: *Beiträge zum Zivil- und Wirtschaftsrecht, Festschrift für Kurt Ballerstedt* (1975), pp. 355 sqq.

[67] Cf. infra, pp. 576 sqq.

[68] Neither Roman law nor the ius commune knew such special remedies. The conductor had to produce the work lege artis and according to the specifications laid down in the contract (cf. e.g. Pothier, *Traité du contrat de louage*, n. 419: he was under an obligation "*de faire bien l'ouvrage*"). If the work was defective, the customer could bring the actio locati: the conductor had not (properly) fulfilled his obligation. According to the BGB, the customer may, first of all, demand removal of the defect. In the second place, he may either cancel the

subject to very harsh prescription periods, however.[69] Claims based on malperformance under a contract of service, on the other hand, prescribe in 30 years. Such a vast discrepancy of prescription periods in closely related areas of law has proved to be a most unfortunate source of unsatisfactory distinctions and distortions.

In South Africa, the term "workman" in the Workmen's Compensation Act[70] has given rise to the most interesting and historically thorough judicial attempt at drawing a line between locatio conductio operis and operarum.[71] After reviewing Roman and classical Roman-Dutch law, Joubert JA rejected the supervision and control test of English law (that had been adopted in an earlier decision)[72] and stated that a right of supervision and control on the part of the employer is merely one out of several indicia (albeit an important one) in favour of a contract of service. The legal relationship between the parties as a whole has to be evaluated in order to establish the true object of the contract. In this context a variety of important legal characteristics are

---

contract or claim a reduction of the purchase price (i.e. bring the actiones redhibitoria or quanti minoris). If the defect was due to the fault of the conductor, damages may be claimed instead of cancellation or reduction (§§ 633 sqq. BGB). May the customer, instead of demanding removal of the defect, insist on the production of a new work? The BGB is silent on this point, the problem therefore controversial. It is obvious that the system of remedies as provided by the BGB has been inspired by the rules relating to the purchase of fungibles. This was not without precedent, for §§ 318 sqq. I 5 PrALR had already used the aedilitian remedies as a model for the contract of work. For a thorough comparative analysis concerning the obligation to execute the work free from defects and the remedies in case of breach of this obligation, cf. Lorenz, op. cit., note 58, nn. 50 sqq.; idem, "Rechtsvergleichendes zur Mängelhaftung des Werkunternehmers", in: *Festschrift für Ernst von Caemmerer* (1978), pp. 907 sqq. In fact, contracts of sale and for work are closely related. This is particularly obvious where the work is to be produced from material provided by the *contractor.* According to Roman law, this was a contract of sale (cf. supra, p. 235). The BGB deals with these cases under the heading of contract for the delivery of work. If a fungible thing is to be produced, the law of sale applies; in case of a non-fungible, most of the rules relating to the contract for work are applicable (§ 651 BGB). All in all, as Lorenz points out, the law of sale has in many respects provided the basis for the proper development of rules governing defects liability in contracts for work. As to the interaction, along very similar lines, between the law of sale and the law of contract for work in the English common law, cf. Lorenz, op. cit., note 58, nn. 86 sqq.: the rules relating to the seller's warranty against defects have been transferred to the contract for work.

[69] Six months; in the case of work on land, one year; in the case of work on buildings, five years. The prescription begins to run from the moment of acceptance of the work (§ 638 I BGB). Thus it can happen that the claims are prescribed before it was possible for the customer to discover the defect. For details, critical evaluation and, particularly, what we have termed "*systemsprengendende Kraft differenzierter Verjährungsfristen*" (distorting influence of diverging prescription periods), cf. Peters/Zimmermann, *Verjährungsfristen*, pp. 196 sqq.

[70] Act 30/1941.

[71] *Smit v. Workmen's Compensation Commissioner* 1979 (1) SA 51 (A).

[72] *Colonial Mutual Life Assurance Society Ltd. v. MacDonald* 1931 AD 412 at 434 sq. The court also rejected the "organisation test" (turning on the integration of the employee into the employer's business) as being of a "vague and nebulous nature"; cf. also the critical dictum by MacKenna J in the English case of *Ready Mixed Concrete (South East) Ltd. v. Minister of Pensions and National Insurance* [1968] 1 All ER 433 (QB) at 441H–444H.

listed in respect of which the two types of contract tend to differ.[73] They provide indicia as to the nature of the contract, and it is in this context that the problem of supervision and control, the employee's duty to obey lawful commands, orders or instructions, and his obligation to render his services in person feature prominently. The more independent, generally speaking, the position of the person rendering the services, the stronger the probability that we are dealing with locatio conductio operis. Very similar considerations prevail in German law.[74]

3. Range of liability of the conductor

With regard to the conductor's (the contractor's) liability we have the following interesting testimony by Gaius:

> "Qui columnam transportandam conduxit, si ea, dum tollitur aut portatur aut reponitur, fracta sit, ita id periculum praestat, si qua ipsius eorumque, quorum opera uteretur, culpa acciderit."[75]

We are dealing with the transportation of a column,[76] locatio conductio operis. Hence, "qui . . . conduxit". First of all, then, the conductor is liable for (his own) fault ("ipsius . . . culpa"). We see, secondly, that he was obviously allowed to use others in performing his obligation.[77] But how did this affect his liability: was he liable not only for his own fault but for theirs also? Or was his liability still dependent upon whether he himself had been at fault? This is the most interesting question addressed by our text.

(a) *Imperitia and custodia*

Before considering this problem, we should, however, first take note of the fact that the conductor's liability actually went beyond mere culpa in two important respects. On the one hand, he was taken to have guaranteed, by implication, that he possessed the skills necessary for the

---

[73] *Smit v. Workmen's Compensation Commissioner* 1979 (1) SA 51 (A) at 61 sqq., esp. 64A–68B.

[74] For a detailed discussion, see Gerald Weber, *Die Unterscheidung von Dienstvertrag und Werkvertrag* (unpublished Dr. iur. thesis, München, 1977).

[75] D. 19, 2, 25, 7. On this text cf., most recently, Rolf Knütel, "Die Haftung für Hilfspersonen im römischen Recht", (1983) 100 *ZSS* 419 sqq.

[76] Columns were very valuable and had to be handled with great care. In Rome whole columns rather than tambours were normally used and one can easily imagine that their transportation threw up problems and required special skills. For details cf. Vitruvius, *De architectura*, Lib. X, 2, § 11, and Knütel, (1983) 100 *ZSS* 420 sq.; also Story, *Bailments*, § 432.

[77] But see also Ulp. D. 45, 1, 38, 21; Ulp. D. 46, 3, 31. Cf. further Glück, vol. 17, p. 317; Mayer-Maly, *Locatio conductio*, pp. 27 sqq. In modern civil-law systems the conductor is, as a rule, permitted to employ servants; sub-contracting is deemed to have been authorized by the customer if the contract or the nature of the relationship so permits. For a comparative analysis, see Lorenz, op. cit., note 58, nn. 26 sqq. Artists, for instance, may often have to perform in person, even where that is not expressly stipulated (as it was in the case of Albrecht Dürer, who undertook to paint the middle section of the Heller altarpiece himself, "and no other human being than myself shall paint one stroke of it": Rudolf Huebner, *A History of Germanic Private Law* (1918), p. 555).

job that he had undertaken. After all, he had made himself contractually responsible for the finished product and had thus engendered a reasonable expectation in the person of his customer that he was competent to perform or execute such opus faciendum. If this was not in fact the case, he was liable for the resulting damages.[78] Again, this is liability based on imperitia and we find it wherever it could be said that the contractor "ut artifex . . . conduxit".[79] Jewellers and engravers provide an example ("si gemma includenda aut insculpenda data sit eaque fracta sit, si . . . imperitia facientis [factum sit, ex locato actio] erit"),[80] but so do those "[qui] vitulos pascendos vel sarciendum quid poliendumve condux[erunt]":[81] cattle-breeders, jobbing tailors and fullers.[82]

With regard to the objects, on the other hand, which the contractor received from his customer, there was a kind of guarantee too: for the contractor was liable for custodia. Gaius is very clear on this topic, at least as far as fullones and sarcinatores are concerned:

> "Item, si fullo polienda curandave aut sarcinator sarcienda vestimenta mercede certa acceperit eaque furto amiserit, ipse furti habet actionem, non dominus, quia domini nihil interest ea non periisse, cum iudicio locati a fullone aut sarcinatore suum consequi possit, si modo is fullo aut sarcinator rei praestandae sufficiat. . . ."[83]

It is the fuller or the tailor (i.e. the conductor) and not the locator/owner who can sue for theft if the clothes are stolen. The locator/owner does not need any protection in the form of an actio furti, for, irrespective of whether or not it was due to the conductor's negligence that the clothes were stolen, as long as the conductor was solvent, he was always able to recover his damages from him. Theft, of course, was a typical instance of what we have termed "vis minor", and it fell squarely within the conductor's duty of custodiam praestare.[84]

---

[78] For the inherent limitation of imperitia liability, Jones, *Bailments*, p. 99, gives the following example (borrowed from Muhammadan law): "A man who had a disorder in his eyes, called on a farrier for a remedy; and he applied to them a medicine commonly used for his patients: the man lost his sight, and brought an action for damages; but the judge said, 'No action lies, for, if the complainant had not himself been an ass, he would never have employed a farrier'." This example had already been discussed by Pufendorf, *De jure naturae et gentium*, Lib. V, Cap. V, 3, and was also taken up by Story, *Bailments*, § 435 (who referred to *Inst.* III, 15, 3 as a basis for the argument that liability ought not to be imposed in cases such as these).

[79] Cels./Ulp. D. 19, 2, 9, 5.

[80] Ulp. D. 19, 2, 13, 5; cf. also Ulp. D. 9, 2, 27, 29. On these texts cf. recently Peter Birks, "Other Man's Meat: Aquilian Liability for Proper User", (1981) 16 *The Irish Jurist* 163 sqq. (D. 9, 2, 27, 29) and 169 sqq. (D. 19, 2, 13, 5).

[81] Cels./Ulp. D. 19, 2, 9, 5.

[82] On imperitia cf. further Arangio-Ruiz, *Responsabilità*, pp. 188 sqq.; Cannata, *Colpa*, pp. 131 sqq., 241 sqq.; Behrends, op. cit., note 14, pp. 145 sqq. Pothier, *Traité du contrat de louage*, nn. 425 sq.; Coing, p. 460. Pothier, as usual, has had his impact on English law; in particular, courts and writers have drawn inspiration from the civil-law maxim "spondet peritiam artis—imperitia culpae adnumeratur": cf. *Harmer v. Cornelius* (1858) 5 CB (NS) 236 at 246 (per Willes J); cf. further Lorenz, op. cit., note 58, nn. 86 sqq. Cf. also Story, *Bailments*, §§ 428, 431.

[83] Gai. III, 205.

[84] Ulp. D. 47, 2, 12 pr.

This duty was imposed on the conductor, even though he received his merces primarily for performing the work, not for safeguarding the locator's clothes: "[N]am et fullo et sarcinator non pro custodia, sed pro arte mercedem accipiunt, et tamen custodiae nomine ex locato tenentur."[85]

It is likely that fullers and tailors are merely used as examples and that the custodia liability applied to other types of conductores also.[86] Yet, it is impossible to prove this suggestion, for other texts in the Digest also concentrate on those professions. Two fragments of Ulpianus (D. 47, 2, 12 pr. and D. 19, 2, 13, 6) may be quoted in this context, the latter of them, incidentally, making it clear that custodia liability did not only comprise theft. Here we read of mice gnawing the customer's clothes: "Si fullo vestimenta polienda acceperit eaque mures roserint, ex locato tenetur." Culpa on the part of the fuller seems to have been irrelevant and cannot simply be read into the text as a matter of course; for clothes were dried in via publica[87] and the conductor was therefore not always able to prevent damage. Nevertheless, this type of vis minor was attributed to his sphere of influence.[88]

(b) Gai. D. 19, 2, 25, 7 and the problem of vicarious liability

We are now better equipped to consider the problem of the liability of the conductor for the fault of his assistants, raised in D. 19, 2, 25, 7. ". . . ipsius eorumque, quorum opera uteretur, culpa . . ." is what this text says, and the crucial question is how to translate the particle, "que". "And", we would normally be inclined to think: the conductor is liable if he *and* his servants were at fault. But sometimes "que" can be used disjunctively, in the sense of "or".[89] In fact, Gaius himself occasionally used it this way, as we can see from D. 26, 8, 11. Our fragment concerning the transportation of the column, in my view, provides another example: the contractor is liable if the incident was due either to his own culpa *or* to that of his servants. In other words, D. 19, 2, 25, 7 presents an instance of vicarious liability stricto sensu,

[85] Gai. D. 4, 9, 5 pr.

[86] Cf. Ulp. D. 47, 2, 14, 17 (dealing with the liability of a nuntius) and Schulz, *CRL*, p. 547; Kaser, *RPr* I, p. 508; Molnár, *ANRW*, op. cit., note 6, pp. 599 sqq.; contra: Rosenthal, "Custodia und Aktivlegitimation zur Actio furti", (1951) 68 *ZSS* 239 sqq. Cf. further Arangio-Ruiz, *Responsabilità*, pp. 124 sqq.; De Robertis, op. cit., note 2, pp. 164 sqq.; also MacCormack, "Custodia and Culpa", (1972) 89 *ZSS* 159 sqq., 191 sqq. The horrearius was liable for custodia even though he was not conductor operis but locator rei (cf. supra p. 346, note 37). On the question of exemption from liability ("Locator horrei propositum habuit se aurum argentum margaritam non recipere suo periculo"), see Lab. D. 19, 2, 60, 6 and Andreas Wacke, "Rechtsfragen der römischen Lagerhausvermietung", (1980) 28 *Labeo* 312 sqq.

[87] D. 43, 10, 4; Arangio-Ruiz, *Responsabilità*, p. 127.

[88] Mayer-Maly, *Locatio conductio*, pp. 207 sq.

[89] Cf. e.g. Heumann/Seckel, p. 486.

i.e. of liability based (merely) on the fault of others.[90] Only this interpretation would seem to fit in with the conductor's custodia liability: for it would appear odd if he were held responsible for theft and for damage done by mice, but not for the fault of his own servants whom he used in performing his obligation. Their behaviour, after all, can hardly be qualified as vis maior. Thus, we are merely dealing with yet another example of a "lesser" accident which fell within the range of custodia liability. This is confirmed in the very next sentence, for our fragment continues, after the words "culpa acciderit": "culpa autem abest, si omnia facta sunt, quae diligentissimus quisque observaturus fuisset." Of course, the star-pupilish figure of the diligentissimus is suspect.[91] But even if we have to reckon with the possibility of an interpolation, there is nothing to suggest that the substance of this sentence does not represent good classical law. The conductor was under a very strict—in fact, under the strictest conceivable standard of liability short of an unmitigated no-fault liability, and Justinian merely tried to cast into subjective terminology what had originally been conceived of from a more objective point of view. Custodia thus provided—at least as far as locatio conductio operis was concerned—the basis for vicarious liability.[92]

In the course of time, Gai. D. 19, 2, 25, 7 became the central battlefield in the dispute surrounding the question of contractual liability for the acts of others. Those, of course, who were convinced that there could be no liability without fault ("It is not the occurrence of harm which obliges one to make compensation, but fault. This is as simple as the chemical fact that what burns is not the light but the oxygen in the air"),[93] took "que" in "eorumque" to mean "and" and quoted the Gaius fragment in support of their culpa theory.[94] Ultimately, however, the contrary opinion[95] prevailed and found its way into the BGB. In the formulation of § 278 (". . . and of persons whom he employs in performing his obligation") we are still able to recognize the phrase "quorum opera uteretur" of Gai. D. 19, 2, 25, 7. Thus, the code today imposes strict (contractual) liability for others,

[90] In this sense, in particular, Knütel, (1983) 100 *ZSS* 419 sqq. Contra (liability based on culpa) e.g. Mayer-Maly, *Locatio conductio*, pp. 28 sq.; MacCormack, "Culpa in eligendo", (1971) 18 *RIDA* 541 sq.

[91] Cf. supra, pp. 192 sq., 376. However, the superlative is not as objectionable here as in other texts, for in Gai. D. 19, 2, 25, 7 Gaius does not attempt to give a definition of culpa but merely says that there is no culpa if the utmost diligence is observed, (MacCormack, (1971) 18 *RIDA* 542). All interpolation hypotheses (many of them very far-reaching) relating to Gai. D. 19, 2, 25, 7 are listed by Knütel, (1983) 100 *ZSS* 419 sq. (n. 335), who himself accepts the text as genuine.

[92] Cf. further Ulp. D. 14, 3, 5, 10; Marcell./Ulp. D. 19, 2, 41 and the discussion by Knütel, (1983) 100 *ZSS* 407 sqq.

[93] Rudolf von Jhering, *Das Schuldmoment im römischen Privatrecht* (1867), p. 40 (as translated by Tony Weir, in Zweigert/Kötz/Weir, p. 295).

[94] Cf. e.g. Windscheid/Kipp, § 401.

[95] Cf. e.g. Dernburg, vol. II, § 38, n. 8.

the main policy reason being that a debtor who avails himself of the advantages of the distribution of labour creates additional risks for the creditor's property, for which, in turn, he must be responsible.[96] He must bear the consequences for performing his obligation in the way he does.

4. The problem of risk allocation

(a) *Periculum conductoris*

At the moment the contract is concluded, the promised work is not yet in existence; locatio conductio operis involves a process of production which usually takes some time. Thus, it may happen that the work is destroyed or damaged, or that it becomes incapable of performance before it has been completed. If this is due to some fortuitous event, the question of risk distribution arises. Does the contractor receive no remuneration for the time and effort that he has invested in the (unsuccessful) attempt to produce the work (periculum conductoris)? Or will the customer have to pay even though he does not receive the promised work (periculum locatoris)? It will be noted that we are dealing here again with price risk: what happens to the claim for the counterperformance agreed upon if the performance becomes impossible due to circumstances outside the control of either of the parties?[97] According to Labeo, the risk was on the contractor (conductor). "Si rivum, quem faciendum conduxeras et feceras, antequam eum probares, labes corrumpit, tuum periculum est."[98] Tu (the conductor) has undertaken to build a canal. The embankment collapses. Since the locator does not receive the work, the conductor will not receive his wages. Of course, there had to be a time when the risk would pass to the locator. One might have thought of the moment when the conductor had carried out his obligation to execute the work free from defects, or of the moment when the work was delivered to the locator.

In Roman law, the crucial event was adprobatio. "Antequam eum adprobares": it is a matter of course, and therefore not even mentioned, that after adprobatio the risk of accidental damage or destruction falls

---

[96] Cf. e.g. "Motive", in: *Mugdan*, vol. II, p. 16. For a detailed discussion of liability for persons employed in performing an obligation, see Karl Spiro, *Die Haftung für Erfüllungsgehilfen* (1984).

[97] Cf. particularly Kaser, (1957) 74 *ZSS* 186 sqq.; Emilio Betti, "Zum Problem der Gefahrtragung bei zweiseitig verplichtenden Verträgen", (1965) 82 *ZSS* 13 sqq.; Alzon, (1966) 12 *Labeo* 324 sqq.; Röhle, (1986) 34 *SDHI* 203 sqq.; Cannata, *Colpa*, pp. 219 sqq.; J.A.C. Thomas, "Reflections on Building Contracts", (1971) 18 *RIDA* 680 sqq.; Molnár, *ANRW*, op. cit., note 6, pp. 651 sqq.; Felix Wubbe, "Labeo zur Gefahrtragung im Bauvertrag", in: *L'homme dans son environment—Mensch und Umwelt, Festgabe der rechts-, wirtschafts-, und sozialwissenschaftlichem Fakultät der Universität Freiburg zum Schweizerischen Juristentag* (1980), pp. 131 sqq.; idem, (1982) 50 *TR* 247 sq. Generally on the passing of risk in contracts for work and on the different meanings of risk in this context, see Lorenz, op. cit., note 58, nn. 124.

[98] D. 19, 2, 62. Cf. also Lab. D. 14, 2, 10 pr.

on the customer (locator). But before adprobatio: (omne) periculum est conductoris.[99] A very similar approach, incidentally, was adopted in the famous English case of *Appleby v. Myers*; the conductor's action to recover payment for work done and materials supplied failed, because he was deemed to have entered into a contract "to complete the whole, and be paid when the whole is complete, and not till then".[100] And the BGB restates the Roman rule in § 644 I 1: "The contractor bears the risk up until acceptance of the work." But it is a harsh rule. To be sure: the workman, under a contract of locatio conductio operis, does not receive the merces for his services as such, but for the production of a certain specified work or result. This is a strong argument in favour of periculum conductoris. However, one should not lose sight of the fact that a contract of work does not only entail a straightforward exchange of a piece of work for money, but a whole production process too. The conductor has to put in time and effort, usually by working on a physical object provided by (and belonging to)[101] the other party. It is at least as much in the locator's interest as it is in his own that he undertakes to produce the work and one may therefore well ask why, under these circumstances, the whole of the production process should be at his risk.[102] Thus, a splitting of the risk suggests itself as an equitable alternative.

(b) Equitable distribution of the risks

This is exactly what we find being proposed in the later classical literature. Paulus, taking up Labeo's canal example, draws the

[99] But see Cannata, *Colpa*, pp. 216 sqq.; Wubbe, *Festgabe Schweizerischer Juristentag*, op. cit., note 97, pp. 131 sqq.

[100] (1867) LR 2 CP 651 at 660 (per Blackburn J).

[101] Occasionally the conductor became owner of what was handed over to him for the purposes of opus faciendum. Take Alf. D. 19, 2, 31, where grain was shot by several customers into one heap in Saufeius's vessel. Saufeius was to transport the grain. At the first port at which the ship called, one of the customers received back his share of the grain. In the course of the subsequent journey the vessel sank ("navis perierat": i.e. due to vis maior). The only thing that seems to be reasonably clear from Alf. D. 19, 2, 31 is that the contract was treated as one of locatio conductio operis. In later times, it became known as locatio conductio operis irregularis; for details, see Glück, vol. 17, pp. 424 sqq.; Windscheid/Kipp, § 401, n. 12; Nikolaus Benke, "Zum Eigentumserwerb des Unternehmers bei der 'locatio conductio irregularis'", (1987) 104 *ZSS* 156 sqq. (according to whom the distinction between locatio conductio regularis and irregularis was introduced by Lauterbach in his Collegium theoretico-practicum). Most of what has been written on this type of contract is based on speculation. One of the main problems with the Alfenus fragment is that it does not deal with the actio locati, but with an actio oneris aversi (of which, in turn, we do not know anything else). Cf. e.g. Mayer-Maly, *Locatio conductio*, pp. 34 sqq.; Francesco M. de Robertis, "D. 19, 2, 31 et il regime dei trasporti marittimi nell' ultima età repubblicana", (1965) 31 *SDHI* 92 sqq.; Watson, *Obligations*, pp. 106 sqq.; J.A.C. Thomas, "Trasporto marittimo, locazione ed 'actio oneris aversi' ", in: (1968) 1 *Antologia Giuridica Romanistica ed Antiquaria* 223 sqq.; Röhle, (1968) 34 *SDHI* 219 sq.; Kaser, *RPr* I, pp. 571 sq. and, most recently, Benke, (1987) 104 *ZSS* 156 sqq., 191 sqq.

[102] For a slightly different consideration cf. Glück, vol. 17, p. 439: the conductor can be required to provide only what the locator would have obtained had he done the work himself (or let it out to another conductor).

following distinction: "Immo si soli vitio id accidit, locatoris erit periculum, si operis vitio accidit, tuum erit detrimentum."[103] Vitium soli and vitium operis do not imply culpa but are to be taken as accidents, typically emanating from (and therefore attributable to) the risk sphere of the two parties concerned.[104] It is the locator who provides the place where the excavation work is to be done. If the soil turns out to be unsuitable for the building of a canal and makes the walls collapse, he has to carry the risk. On the other hand, it is the conductor who performs the work. Every accident related to the way in which the work is carried out is therefore attributable to him: if the walls collapse because the conductor falls ill and is therefore unable to get the work done according to schedule, he will not receive any remuneration for what he has done.

What D. 19, 2, 62 does not settle is the question of who, in post-Labeonic times, had to carry the risk for vis maior. Iav. D. 19, 2, 51, dealing with "vis naturalis veluti terrae motus", provides the answer: periculum *locatoris*.[105] This is in accordance with the allocation of risk under a contract of locatio conductio rei.[106]

The development[107] in Roman law from a very strict and dogmatic distribution of risks towards a more flexible one finds its parallels in other legal systems. In England the rule established in *Appleby v. Myers* seems to be widely regarded as unsatisfactory today.[108] In Germany the fathers of the BGB laid down a number of exceptions to the principle expressed in § 644 I 1 BGB: If the work, before its acceptance by the customer, is destroyed, or damaged, or becomes incapable of performance in consequence of a defect in the material provided by the customer, or in consequence of instructions given by him for its execution, the contractor may demand a part of the remuneration proportionate to the labour performed, and compensation for any outlay not included in the remuneration (§ 645 I 1). This rule is purportedly based on equitable considerations,[109] but finds its justification in the fact that the customer appears to be "closer" to the source of the risk. Another exception, eventually laid down in § 644 I 2 BGB, can be traced back to Iav. D. 19, 2, 37: the risk passes to the locator (customer) even before approval has taken place, if he ought to have approved the work. It has consistently been claimed that these

[103] D. 19, 2, 62.
[104] Cf. particularly Kaser, (1957) 74 *ZSS* 189 sq.
[105] Cf. further Afr. D. 19, 2, 33 ("quemadmodum . . ."); Iav. D. 19, 2, 37; Flor. D. 19, 2, 36. The arguments in favour of periculum locatoris are analysed succinctly by Wubbe, *Festgabe Schweizerischer Juristentag*, pp. 142 sqq.
[106] Cf. supra, pp. 369 sqq.
[107] According to Cannata and Wubbe (supra, note 97) there was no such development; the rules pertaining to risk of the time of Labeo were essentially the same as those in classical law.
[108] Lorenz, op. cit., note 58, n. 149.
[109] "Motive", in: *Mugdan*, vol. II, p. 280.

exceptions do not go far enough. Thus, the requirements of § 645 I 1 have been applied in a most liberal manner and the norm has been used, repeatedly, as the basis for an argumentum per analogiam.[110] Apart from that, a theory has attracted considerable support which favours the allocation of risk on the basis of typical spheres of risk:[111] a nice example of how ideas from the "Treasure House"[112] of the ius commune can prevail even against the odds of codificatory intervention.[113]

5. Adprobatio operis

We have been referring to adprobatio operis. In fact, in modern German law it is the key moment in most contracts for work.[114] Upon successful completion of adprobatio operis, the contractor's remuneration becomes due, any claims of the locator, based on defects in the work that were known to him, are excluded, with regard to all other defects the short prescription periods begin to run and, as we have seen, the price risk usually passes to the customer. But what does adprobatio operis entail? In the previous paragraph, we translated the German term "*Abnahme*" on one occasion as "acceptance" and on another as "approval". In fact, according to the prevailing opinion, it comprises both: it is regarded as a two-membered act consisting of (physical) acceptance and an acknowledgement by the locator that what is produced to him is what he had asked for.[115]

The discussion of adprobatio operis in Roman law seems to have been confined to building contracts.[116] In our sources we find two different forms of adprobatio.[117] Sometimes it is referred to as an act of the conductor: he has to demonstrate that the building has been constructed skilfully and according to the specifications of the contract:

[110] For details, see Hans Hermann Seiler, in: Erman, *Bürgerliches Gesetzbuch* (7th ed., 1981), vol. I, § 645, nn. 2 sqq.

[111] Walter Erman, "Der Sphärengedanke als Gesichtspunkt für die Verteilung der Preisgefahr beim Werkvertrag", 1965 *Juristenzeitung* 657 sqq.

[112] H.U. Kantorowicz, *Bractonian Problems* (1941), p. 126.

[113] On this subject, more generally, see Theo Mayer-Maly, "Die Wiederkehr von Rechtsfiguren", 1971 *Juristenzeitung* 1 sqq.

[114] Cf. § 640 I BGB ("The customer is bound to accept the work completed according to the contract, unless this is impossible by reason of the nature of the work"). On the significance of adprobatio operis in modern German law, cf. Horst Heinrich Jakobs, "Die Abnahme beim Werkvertrag", (1983) 183 *Archiv für die civilistische Praxis* 145 sqq.

[115] Cf. e.g. BGHZ 48, 257 (262); 50, 160 (162).

[116] Cf. e.g. Susan D. Martin, "A Reconsideration of probatio operis", (1986) 103 *ZSS* 321 sqq. She advances the interesting argument that probatio operis with regard to building contracts had a similar function to liability for imperitia in other types of locatio conductio operis. On probatio operis in Roman law cf. particularly Richard Samter, (1905) 26 *ZSS* 125 sqq.; Kaser, (1957) 74 *ZSS* 187 sq.; Thomas, (1971) 81 *RIDA* 679 sqq.; Cannata, *Colpa*, pp. 193 sqq.; and the study by Martin.

[117] Matthias Pietsch, *Die Abnahme im Werkvertragsrecht—Geschichtliche Entwicklung und geltendes Recht* (unpublished Dr. iur. thesis, Hamburg, 1976), pp. 37 sqq.

". . . ut bonitas [locatori] a conductore adprobaretur."[118] No declaration of approval is required. In other places, however, it is exactly this approval on the part of the locator that is emphasized; Paulus provides a detailed discussion:

> "Si in lege locationis comprehensum sit, ut arbitratu domini opus adprobetur, perinde habetur, ac si viri boni arbitrium comprehensum fuisset, idemque servatur, si alterius cuiuslibet arbitrium comprehensum sit: nam fides bona exigit, ut arbitrium tale praestetur, quale viro bono convenit. . . ."[119]

Whether he examines the structure himself or designates a knowledgeable third party to do so, probatio is incumbent upon the customer. The standard set for his approval is that of the arbitrium viri boni. From both D. 19, 2, 24 pr. and Lab. D. 19, 2, 60, 3 it appears that this second type of adprobatio obtained only where it had been agreed upon in lege conductionis. As a general rule, therefore, adprobatio was regarded as having taken place, if in the course of the conductor's demonstration of the work, the locator did not specifically disapprove of any of its features. This concept obviously avoids all difficulties arising from the possibility that the locator might delay or withhold a declaration of approval. It has therefore been suggested that the modern concept of "*Abnahme*" be re-evaluated in the light of the Roman sources.[120]

Where the construction work was let "per aversionem"[121] (i.e. as a whole and for a lump-sum price), probatio operis of the completed work was necessary to relieve the builder finally of whatever price risk he still had to carry. It also terminated his responsibility for defects in the work.[122] Problems could arise in cases where the work was let "in pedes mensurasve":[123] by units of measure, or where the price was quantified in singulos dies. The latter example is discussed by Iavolenus.[124] The payment plan fixed in the contract could have some bearing on the question of adprobatio operis. Especially where the progress of the work was determined by the orders and instructions of the locator, the day-by-day equivalent of probatio could be regarded as sufficient:

> "[S]i ita opus locasti, ut bonitas eius tibi a conductore adprobaretur, tametsi convenit, ut in singulas operas certa pecunia daretur, praestari tamen tibi a

---

[118] Iav. D. 19, 2, 51, 1; cf. also Lab. D. 19, 2, 62; Iav. D. 19, 2, 37.

[119] D. 19, 2, 24 pr.; cf. also Lab. D. 19, 2, 60, 3.

[120] Pietsch, op. cit., note 117, pp. 18 sq., 152 sqq., 220 sqq.; this suggestion has been followed e.g. by Seiler, op. cit., note 110, § 645, n. 6.

[121] Flor. D. 19, 2, 36.

[122] Cf. e.g. Cannata, *Colpa*, pp. 204, 207 sqq.; Thomas, (1971) 18 *RIDA* 688. The conductor continued to be liable only in the case of fraudulent behaviour: ". . . quibus consequens est, ut irrita sit adprobatio dolo conductoris facta, ut ex locato agi possit" (Paul. D. 19, 2, 24 pr. in fine).

[123] Flor. D. 19, 2, 36. Mayer-Maly, *Locatio conductio*, pp. 40 sq.; Kaser, (1957) 74 *ZSS* 187 sq.; Cannata, *Colpa*, pp. 209 sqq.; Röhle, (1968) 103 *ZSS* 327 sqq.; Thomas, (1971) 18 *RIDA* 677 sqq., 685 sq.; Martin, (1986) 103 *ZSS* 327 sqq.

[124] D. 19, 2, 51, 1. On this text, see, e.g. Cannata, *Colpa*, pp. 211 sqq.; Thomas, (1971) 18 *RIDA* 678 sq.; Molnár, *ANRW*, op. cit., note 6, pp. 655 sq.; Martin, (1986) 103 *ZSS* 330 sqq.

conductore debet, si id opus vitiosum factum est. . . . nisi si ideo in operas singulas merces constituta erit, ut arbitrio domini opus efficeretur: tum enim nihil conductor praestare domino de bonitate operis videtur."[125]

6. Lex Rhodia de iactu

"Opus" is a fairly abstract term, and hence locatio conductio operis, as we have seen, covered a wide variety of situations: building contracts, repair work, vocational training relationships and transportation, to mention a few. The fathers of the German Code, on the one hand, maintained this liberal definition of the scope of the contract for work;[126] on the other hand, however, they tried to lay down precise rules regulating the various details of this type of transaction. But since we are not dealing with a "type" of transaction in anything but a very abstract sense, problems were bound to arise.[127] Not all rules relating to an architect's contract are necessarily suitable for the carriage of passengers. The reason why these problems had not already cropped up in Roman law lies in the inherent flexibility of the iudicia locati and conducti: on the basis of the ex bona fide clause the Roman lawyers were able to make such adjustments as were necessary to suit the specific situation at hand. One example of how ingeniously this flexibility could be used is the incorporation of the so-called lex Rhodia de iactu into Roman jurisprudence.

(a) The reception of the lex Rhodia into Roman law

We are dealing with carriage by sea, an enterprise which had become increasingly important during the last two centuries of the Republic.[128] The trading of slaves depended on it, and it was vital for securing the Roman food supply (the annona),[129] more particularly the transportation of grain. Apart from that, luxury goods were brought to Rome from distant parts of the world: ivory from Africa, or even silk from China.[130] The two natural ports of Puteoli (Pozzuoli) and Ostia were soon no longer able to cope with the turnover of goods and thus an artificial Portus was built and connected, by means of a canal, with the Tiber.[131] Of course, persons also had to be transported by ship; indeed,

---

[125] Iav. D. 19, 2, 51, 1.

[126] § 631 II BGB.

[127] Cf. e.g. Seiler, op. cit., note 110, Vor § 631, n. 1.

[128] For details cf. Jean Rougé, *Recherches sur l'organisation du commerce maritime en méditerranée sous l'empire romain* (1966), pp. 459 sqq.; A.J.M. Meyer-Termeer, *Die Haftung der Schiffer im griechischen und römischen Recht* (1978), pp. 147 sqq.; De Martino, *Wirtschaftsgeschichte*, pp. 151 sqq.

[129] Cf. e.g. Meyer-Termeer, op. cit., note 128, pp. 148 sqq.; De Martino, *Wirtschaftsgeschichte*, pp. 366 sqq.

[130] De Martino, *Wirtschaftsgeschichte*, pp. 357 sq. On the trade with India and China cf. Albrecht Dihle, John Ferguson and Manfred G. Raschke, in: *ANRW*, vol. II, 9 (1978), pp. 546 sqq., 581 sqq., 604 sqq.; Lionel Casson, *Ancient Trade and Society* (1984), pp. 182 sqq.

[131] For details, cf. e.g. De Martino, *Wirtschaftsgeschichte*, pp. 365 sqq.; Russell Meiggs, *Roman Ostia* (2nd ed., 1973), pp. 149 sqq., 159.

certain ships were specifically designed for that purpose.[132] It has already been mentioned that any voyage by ship was a somewhat hazardous venture, particularly in the Mediterranean Sea.[133] It was (and still is) notorious for its storms, and shipwreck (naufragium) was no rare occurrence, even if one travelled in season (i.e. when the seas were not "closed").[134]

Sometimes, however, the ship's master (magister navis)[135] was able to save the vessel from foundering by throwing goods overboard and thus lightening the ship.[136] Of course, in a situation of distress there is no time carefully to pick and choose and thus the magister navis and his deck-hands grabbed and jettisoned what was nearest or what was heaviest. But must the unfortunate owner of these goods then carry the loss? That would most certainly not be equitable. After all, his property was sacrificed in order to save that of the others: he incurred a loss for the common benefit. Obviously then, if the benefit was common, so should be the loss. "Si commune periculum aliter depelli non possit, quam rem alienam perdendo; eam perdere licet, damnum vero commune esse debet":[137] this is how, long after the demise of the Roman Empire, the underlying principle of natural equity was formulated; or, on an even more general level: "Omnium contributione sarciatur, quod pro omnibus impensum est."[138] These words are taken, almost verbatim, from the Digest, where we find the following statement by the jurist Paulus: "Lege Rhodia cavetur, ut, si levandae navis gratia iactus mercium factus est, omnium contributione sarciatur quod pro omnibus datum est."[139] It is essentially what has become known in England as a general average,[140] and is referred to in Germany as "*(grosse) Haverei*".[141], [142] In antiquity the doctrine goes back to one of the seafaring nations par excellence, the Rhodians. Their sea law was a sort of common lex mercatoria maritima for the states

[132] Cf. e.g. Ulp. D. 14, 1, 1, 12.
[133] Cf. supra, p. 182.
[134] Cf. supra, p. 184, note 191.
[135] On the position and the duties of the magister navis cf. e.g. Ulp. D. 14, 1, 1, 1–5; on the management of a ship generally and on the role of dominus navis, exercitor, magister navis and gubernator, see Meyer-Termeer, op. cit., note 128, pp. 150 sqq.; Rougé, op. cit., note 128, pp. 213 sqq.; J.A.C. Thomas, "Juridical Aspects of Carriage by Sea and Warehousing in Roman Law", in: (1974) 32 *Recueils de la Société Jean Bodin pour l'Histoire Comparative des Institutions* 124 sq.
[136] For a well-known example of this practice cf. St. Paul's dangerous voyage towards Rome, as recounted in *Acta Apostolorum*, 27.
[137] Christian Wolff, *Jus Naturae*, Pars VI, Cap. IV, § 621.
[138] Leyser, *Meditationes ad Pandectas*, Sp. CLX.
[139] Paul. D. 14, 2, 1.
[140] Cf. e.g. Story, *Bailments*, § 583; Lowndes and Rudolf, *General Average and York Antwerp Rules* (10th ed., 1975).
[141] For details cf. §§ 700 sqq. HGB; Philipp Heck, *Das Recht der grossen Haverei* (1889).
[142] On the origin of the words *Haverei*/average cf. e.g. H. Kellenbenz, *HRG* vol. 2, col. 2 (from the Arabic word *awâr* (damaged cargo)) and Lowndes and Rudolf, op. cit., note 140, pp. 11 sq. (from the Italian *avere*, the having of property).

bordering on the Mediterranean Sea;[143] and part and parcel of these trade usages was the so-called lex Rhodia de iactu.[144] Based on the idea of a community of risk and emanating from the principle of aequitas,[145] late Republican jurisprudence received the lex Rhodia de iactu into Roman law:[146] not by way of legal surgery, but in a most natural or homeopathic manner. Carriage by sea was usually undertaken by way of locatio conductio operis.[147] This contract bound the magister navis to transport the customer's goods to the port of destination. He was not supposed to throw them overboard. This action (intentional, as it were!) amounted to a breach of contract, and he was therefore liable to his customer under the actio locati. If, however, it was inequitable to let the loss lie with the person whose goods had been sacrificed, it would have been equally inequitable to see the magister navis lose out. He was therefore able to proceed against the other customers whose goods had been saved; to this end he could avail himself of the actio conducti.[148] As, in the end, the loss was to be split equally between all participants of this communal enterprise, the actions were adjusted accordingly. The first locator could sue the magister navis for the value of his property that had been jettisoned, minus his own share of the loss; the magister navis, in turn, would sue the other locatores for their pro rata contribution. The Rhodian custom thus became an integral part of the contractual relationships existing between the parties to a contract of carriage by sea.[149]

Their conception of what was due, ex bona fide, between the parties gave the Roman lawyers ample scope to refine the application of the lex

[143] Cf. e.g. Rougé, op. cit., note 128, pp. 407 sqq. and, on a compilation of the 8th century A.D. and its influence in medieval law, Walter Ashburner, *The Rhodian Sea-Law,* 1909. Cf. also T.E. Dönges, *The Liability for Safe Carriage of Goods in Roman-Dutch Law* (1928), pp. 1 sqq.

[144] Hans Kreller, "Lex Rhodia. Untersuchungen zur Quellengeschichte des römischen Seerechtes", (1921) 85 *ZHR* 337 sqq.

[145] Paul. D. 14, 2, 2 pr. (". . . aequissimum enim est commune detrimentum fieri eorum, qui propter amissas res aliorum consecuti sunt, ut merces suas salvas haberent").

[146] Franz Wieacker, "Iactus in tributum nave salva venit (D. 14, 2, 4 pr.). Exegesen zur Lex Rhodia de iactu", in: *Studi in memoria di Emilio Albertario,* vol. I (1953), pp. 513 sqq.; Francesco M. de Robertis, "Lex Rhodia, Critica e anticritica su D. 14, 2, 9", in: *Studi in onore di Vincenzo Arangio-Ruiz,* vol. III (1953), pp. 155 sqq.; Thomas (1974) 32 *Recueils Jean Bodin* 152, 155.

[147] Depending on the object of transportation, it was locatio conductio rerum vehendarum or vectorum vehendorum. Alternatively, the contract could be locatio conductio rei (the hiring of space on the ship). In this case, a duty to carry out transportation was created only if the parties had added a special agreement to that effect. For details cf. Meyer-Termeer, op. cit., note 128, pp. 177 sqq.; J.A.C. Thomas, "Carriage by Sea", (1960) 7 *RIDA* 496 sq.; idem, (1974) 32 *Recueils Jean Bodin* 119 sqq.

[148] Or he could induce the other consignors to make their payment by withholding their goods; on this ius retentionis cf. Paul. D. 14, 2, 2 pr. According to Wieacker, *Studi Albertario,* vol. I, pp. 516 sq., this was the primary way of effecting the contribution: the ship's master availed himself of the ius retentionis ex iure tertiorum (i.e. the other consignors who have to receive their contribution from the cargo saved).

[149] Cf. Paul. D. 14, 2, 2 pr.; Wieacker, *Studi Albertario,* vol. I, p. 516; Kaser, *RPr* I, p. 572; Thomas, (1974) 32 *Recueils Jean Bodin* 152 sqq.; idem, *TRL,* p. 300.

Rhodia; one basic requirement for the duty of contribution being that the ship was saved from this specific danger.[150] The Digest title 14, 2 is full of interesting cases and distinctions. Thus, we read of a ship which encountered two storms on its voyage: from the first it emerged unscathed because the goods of one merchant had been thrown overboard, but in the second one it sank. The shipwreck, however, seems to have occurred in shallow waters, for paid divers managed to recover the cargo of some of the other merchants. Do they have to contribute to the first merchant's loss?[151] Do those locatores, whose goods added no weight to the ship ("velut gemmas margaritas") have to contribute like everyone else?[152] Or: the mast and the riggings of a ship were struck, adverso tempestate, by lightning. In Hippo, the ship was equipped with temporary riggings and was thus able to proceed to Ostia with the cargo safe and sound. Should the cargo-owners contribute towards the loss of the shipowners? (Interesting) answer: no, "hic enim sumptus instruendae magis navis, quam conservandarum mercium gratia factus est".[153]

(b) Subsequent history of the lex Rhodia

The history of the lex Rhodia de iactu can be told as one of gradual extension. Confined, originally, to iactus mercium, it was already in classical Roman law applied to cases where part of the cargo was used to ransom the ship from pirates (redemptio a piratis),[154] where the mast of the ship was cut down and cast off removendi communis periculi causa[155] or where a dinghy was lost, onto which part of the cargo had been transferred in order to lighten a ship that could otherwise not have entered a river or port.[156]

In the Middle Ages[157] the lex Rhodia began to be applied beyond the area of maritime law, because the basic underlying principle lent itself to generalization. Thus, Accursius emphazised: "Et not. quod si quid pro communi utilitate, vel alterius damni patior, quod mihi est restitutio facienda. . . ."[158] Fire and war were the principal disasters to

[150] On the nave salva requirement cf. Kreller, (1921) 85 *ZHR* 288 sqq.; Wieacker, *Studi Albertario*, vol. I, pp. 515 sqq. Today cf. §§ 700, 703 HGB (and Heck, op. cit., note 141, p. 600). Proof of causation (that iactus saved the ship) does not seem to have been required (cf., however, § 703 HBG and Wieacker, *Studi Albertario*, vol. I, pp. 530 sq.).

[151] Answer: yes; cf. Call. D. 14, 2, 4, 1. After all, the iactus has saved the remaining cargo; otherwise the ship would never have reached the point, where the water was shallow enough for the cargo to be saved by the divers; cf. Wieacker, *Studi Albertario*, vol. I, pp. 523 sqq., 531 sq.

[152] Paul. D. 14, 2, 2, 2.

[153] Iul. D. 14, 2, 6. Cf. today Rule XIV of the York Antwerp Rules (1974).

[154] Paul. D. 14, 2, 2, 3.

[155] Pap. D. 14, 2, 3; Herm. D. 14, 2, 5, 1.

[156] Call. D. 14, 2, 4 pr.; Wieacker, *Studi Albertario*, vol I, pp. 520 sqq.

[157] As to the following, see Gunter Wesener, "Von der Lex Rhodia de iactu zum § 1043 ABGB", in: *Festschrift für Johannes Bärmann* (1975), pp. 36 sqq.

[158] Gl. Aequissimum ad D. 14, 2, 2, pr.

which the idea of contribution was applied: "Igne orto in aliqua contrata, si domus alicuius destruitur a vicinis, ne ignis alterius extendatur, fieri potest iure", and "Milites, qui tempore propter defensionem vadunt ad bellum, si ibi perdunt equum, sibi per communem debet emendare."[159] As in the case of shipwreck, we are dealing with a common danger, in which the property of one party is used to save that of the others.

Another momentous innovation in the application of the lex Rhodia also goes back to Accursius. In his gloss "agere potest" ad D. 14, 2, 2 pr., he suggested that the person whose goods had been sacrificed should be able to proceed directly ("via recta") against the other persons deriving a benefit therefrom, for their pro rata contribution. Thus one would be able to avoid the somewhat cumbersome detour via the conductor. At the same time, the lex Rhodia moved into close proximity to another well-known institution, namely that of negotiorum gestio.[160] Various attempts were made, over the centuries, to locate and to categorize this direct claim properly; it was described as actio generalis, quae ex variis figuris causarum oritur,[161] as an actio in rem (based on consuetudo maritima)[162] and as a condictio ex lege (based on a quasi-contractual obligation).[163] But it was finally recognized that such a search for a procedural niche no longer really mattered; after all, one had moved away from the Roman concept of actional law, procedural formulae and "ubi remedium, ibi ius".[164] The natural lawyers, of course, seized upon the equitable principle of "omnium contributione sarciatur, quod pro omnibus impensum est" and were eager to entrench the lex Rhodia in its extended version.[165] Their discussions culminated in the incorporation of the following rule into the ABGB:

> "A person who has sacrificed his property in case of emergency in order to prevent greater damage to himself and others, shall be indemnified proportionally by those who have derived an advantage therefrom."[166]

In its typical fatherly tone, the second sentence of § 1043 ABGB kindly informs the reader that the particular application of the provision in regard to maritime risks is set forth in the maritime laws. This, then,

---

[159] This is how Baldus describes the relevant situations (*Commentaria*, Venetiis, 1586, ad D. 14, 2, 2). Cf. also e.g. Lauterbach, *Collegium theoretico-practicum*, Lib. XIV, Tit. II, XIV; Leyser, *Meditationes ad Pandectas*, Spec. CLX. Contra, for example, Voet, *Commentarius ad Pandectas*, Tit. XIV, Cap. II, XVIII; cf. also Glück, vol. 14, pp. 234 sqq.

[160] For a contrary view cf. e.g. Cuiacius, "Commentarii in Lib. XXXIV Pauli ad Edictum" (in: *Opera Omnia*, vol. v. (Mutinae, 1777), col. 518 sqq.).

[161] Modestinus Pistoris, *Consilia sive responsa*, vol. I, Cons. XVI, n. 19.

[162] Brunnemann, *Commentarius in Pandectas*, Lib. XIV, Tit. II, ad L. Si laborante 2 pr.

[163] Johann Schilter, *Praxis juris Romani, Exercitatio ad Pandectas XXVII*, §§ XXVI sq.

[164] Cf. Glück, vol. 14, pp. 232 sq.

[165] Cf. supra notes 138, 158, 159.

[166] § 1043, 1 ABGB. For the history of this provision cf. Wesener, *Festschrift Bärmann*, pp. 45 sqq. For a comparison with § 904 BGB (emergency) cf. Andreas Hatzung, *Dogmengeschichtliche Grundlagen und Entstehung des zivilrechtlichen Notstands* (1984), pp. 52 sqq.

is the lex Rhodia proper, but its range of application may well be somewhat limited in practice. Austria, after all, is not a naval power of the first order. However, all the great seafaring nations of modern times have adopted the same or very similar rules.[167] The lex Rhodia de iactu, as applied in Roman law, was taken over by the Italian city-states and became part of the medieval codifications of maritime law all over Europe, up to the Baltic Sea. It influenced artt. VIII and IX (dealing with the duty of contribution in cases of jettison at sea) of the Rôles d'Oléron[168] (which in turn were received, inter alia, in Flanders—under the name of Vonnisse van Damme—and Holland (Amsterdamsche Ordonantie)) and the town laws of Hamburg and Lübeck. These in turn provided the basis for the Sea Law of the Hanseatic League.[169] The Prussian General Land law dealt with what was by then called "*grosse Haverei*",[170] and so did the General German Commercial Code of 1861. From there these rules were taken over into the Commercial Code of 1897 which is still in force today. In England, the principle exemplified by the Rhodian law was also adopted: hardly surprising if one considers the complete monopoly of the civilians[171] over actions in

---

[167] Cf. H. Kellenbenz, "Haverei", in: *HRG*, vol. 2, col. 2 sqq.; Coing, pp. 554 sq.; Götz Landwehr, *Die Haverei in den mittelalterlichen deutschen Seerechtsquellen* (1985), passim. For an "intelligent and exhaustive" treatment of "one whose country was in its golden century the maritime leader of the world" (Percival Gane, *The Selective Voet*, vol. III (1956), p. 76), cf. Johannes Voet, *Commentarius ad Pandectas*, Lib. XIV, Tit. II (dealing e.g. with the community of property in food and drink which ought to exist among stranded castaways in order to protect them against the horrors of cannibalism).

[168] A collection of customary rules dealing, originally, with the transportion by sea of wine from the ports of Bordeaux and La Rochelle. The Rôles have played a central part in the formation of the sea law in north-western Europe. Cf. H. Kellenbenz, *HRG*, vol. 3, col. 1240 sqq.

[169] Götz Landwehr, "Die Hanseatischen Seerechte des 16. und 17. Jahrhunderts", in: *1667 års sjölag i ett 300-årigt perspektiv* (1984), pp. 75 sqq.; on "*grosse Haverei*" cf. pp. 103 sqq.

[170] §§ 1766 II 8; based on the Prussian Sea Law of 1727; cf. Götz Landwehr, "Das Preussische Seerecht vom Jahre 1727 im Rahmen der europäischen Rechtsentwicklung", (1986) 8 *ZNR* 132 sqq. For the first general definition of "*grosse Haverei*" cf. Quintijn Weijtsen, *Tractaet van 't Recht der Nederlantsche Avaryen* (1651), § 17: "Waer by men sonde mogen infereren, dat de schaden, die men gewillighlijk ende voluntairement doet aen 't Schip ofte Goeden, om meerder apparenter hinder te beschutten, souden moeten gerekent werden voor Avarye grosse." Vinnius, in his notes on Peckius, *In Titt. Dig. et Cod. ad rem nauticam pertinentes Commentarii* (1647), pp. 193, 206, writes: "Duae res concurrere debent, ut actio hujus contributionis nomine competat: 1. jactura rerum ex una parte, 2. conservatio rerum ex parte altra." On that basis he defines: "Avaria grossa vel grandis est, cum quaedam merces jaciuntur in mare levandae laborantis navis gratia, aut armamenta navis, malus, anchorae, rudentes, communis periculi removendi. causa dejiciuntur vel caeduntur voluntate navigantium, atque hoc damnum contributione omnium atque ipsius etiam nautae resarciatur." Dogmatically, the duty to contribute was by now usually based on "navalis societas" or a "societas et communio tacita". Cf. further e.g. Landwehr, (1986) 8 *ZNR* pp. 138 sqq.

[171] Cf. e.g. W. Senior, *Doctors' Commons and the Old Court of Admiralty* (1922); Brian P. Levack, *The Civil Lawyers in England 1603–1641* (1973); Daniel R. Coquillette, "Legal Ideology and Incorporation I: The English Civilian Writers, 1522–1607", (1981) 61 *Boston University LR* 1 sqq.

the High Court of Admiralty.[172] From here it came, inter alia, to the Cape of Good Hope,[173] and thus it is in the guise of the English doctrine of general average that the lex Rhodia applies in the South African usus modernus of Roman-Dutch law.

[172] For details, see *Potter's Historical Introduction to English Law* (4th ed., 1958), pp. 191 sqq.; Wiswall, *The Development of Admiralty Jurisdiction and Practice since 1800* (1970).

[173] On the Admiralty jurisdiction in South Africa and its history, see Gys Hofmeyr, 1982 *Acta Juridica* 30 sqq.

CHAPTER 13

Mandatum

1. The essential characteristics of mandatum

If a member of "the" professions, an advocatus, an agrimensor[1] or an architectus,[2] did not render his services under a contract of locatio conductio (be it operis or operarum), it did not mean that these activities took place in the purely social sphere without being sanctioned by the law at all. What was objectionable was to work for money, not to enter into a contractual relationship. If, for instance, an advocate[3] took care of somebody else's legal problems, he might consider it to be infra dignitatem to receive a salary. On the other hand, he could expect not to lose out. Thus, he ought to be able to claim damages and to be reimbursed for any expenses that he might have incurred on behalf of his client. The latter, in turn, would often rely on the advocate's undertaking to bring his case to court, to represent him in the trial or to make up a rhetorically convincing argument. Thus, where this sort of commitment was intended, the parties usually entered into a contract of mandatum.

Mandatum, like emptio venditio and locatio conductio, but unlike commodatum and depositum, was a consensual contract.[4] Like commodatum and depositum, but unlike the other consensual contracts, it was a necessarily gratuitous transaction: "Mandatum nisi gratuitum nullum est."[5] Where a reward was fixed, the contract was locatio conductio, not mandatum: "In summa sciendum est mandatum, nisi gratuitum sit, in aliam formam negotii cadere: nam mercede constituta incipit locatio et conductio esse."[6] In fact, the lack of any agreed upon counterperformance is emphasized so often as an essential characteristic of the contract of mandatum, that we may well doubt whether the actual practice was always in conformity with contractual theory.

A contract of mandatum gave rise, in any event, to the actio mandati (directa). This was a iudicium bonae fidei and lay for "quidquid ob eam

[1] On these cf. e.g. Ulp. D. 11, 6, 1 pr.; Antoine Bernard, *La Rémunération des Professions Libérales en Droit Romain Classique* (1936), pp. 103 sqq. and Karoly Visky, *Geistige Arbeit und die "artes liberales" in den Quellen des römischen Rechts* (1977), pp. 39 sqq.

[2] Visky, op. cit., note 1, pp. 95 sqq.

[3] Cf. supra, p. 390, note 34.

[4] Paul. D. 17, 1, 1 pr.: "Obligatio mandati consensu contrahentium consistit." Convenient consequence: "Ideo per nuntium quoque vel per epistulam mandatum suscipi potest." For details, see Watson, *Mandate*, pp. 61 sqq.

[5] Paul. D. 17, 1, 1, 4. Cf. further Gai. III, 162; Iav. D. 17, 1, 36, 1; Watson, *Mandate*, pp. 102 sqq.; Michel, *Gratuité*, pp. 185 sqq.

[6] *Inst.* III, 26, 13.

rem N^m N^m A^o A^o dare facere oportet ex fide bona".[7] Thus the mandator was able to enforce proper execution of what the mandatarius had undertaken to do;[8] apart from that, the mandatarius had to hand over to the mandator whatever he received on account of or in the execution of the mandate.[9] The mandatarius, on the other hand, could sue the mandator only if, in the course of carrying out the mandate, he had incurred expenses[10] or suffered damages.[11] To this end an actio mandati contraria, with a formula identical to that of the actio mandati directa,[12] was available to him. This did, however, make mandatum neither a (perfectly) bilateral[13] nor a reciprocal contract. The counterclaim was not bound to arise, but depended upon the circumstances of the case; and the mandatory did not agree to carry out the commission *in order* to obtain reimbursement of expenses or compensation for damages.

---

[7] Lenel, *EP*, pp. 295 sq. On the obligations of the mandatary cf. Vincenzo Arangio-Ruiz, *Il mandato in diritto romano* (1949), pp. 159 sqq.; Watson, *Mandate*, pp. 178 sqq.

[8] Particularly, the mandatarius was not allowed to exceed the terms of the mandate (fines mandati). If he did, he was liable to the mandator under the actio mandati, but was himself not able to sue the mandator for reimbursement of his expenses (actio mandati contraria). There was, however, a school dispute as to how far this principle should be carried. A commissions B to purchase a farm for not more than 100, but B buys it for 150. B is prepared to transfer the farm to A for 100; can he force A to accept it? No, according to the rigid approach of the Sabinians (Gai. III, 161); yes, according to the interpretatio benignior of the Proculians (favoured by Justinian and the writers in later centuries—cf. e.g. Glück, vol. 15, pp. 273 sqq.). Justinian relates the dispute in the following terms (III, 26, 8): "Is qui exsequitur mandatum non debet excedere fines mandati. ut ecce si quis usque ad centum aureos mandaverit tibi, ut fundum emeres . . ., [non] pluris emere debes . . .; alioquin non habebis cum eo mandati actionem: adeo quidem, ut Sabino et Cassio placuerit, etiam si usque ad centum aureos cum eo agere velis, inutiliter te acturum, diversae scholae auctores recte te usque ad centum aureos acturum existimant: quae sententia sane benignior est." There is much dispute, today, about what the prevailing view in classical law was and how certain other texts dealing with this problem (esp. Paul. D. 17, 1, 3–5; Gai. D. 17, 1, 41) ought to be understood; cf. Arangio-Ruiz, op. cit., note 7, pp. 168 sqq.; Fritz Pringsheim, "Noch einmal Gai. 3, 161 und Inst. Just. 3. 26. 8", (1955) 72 *ZSS* 54 sqq.; Watson, *Mandate*, pp. 185 sqq.; Paul van Warmelo, "Wanneer die Lashebber sy Opdrag te buite gaan", 1964 *Acta Juridica* 1 sqq.; F.B.J. Wubbe, "Benignus redivivus", in: *Symbolae iuridicae et historicae Martino David dedicatae*, vol. I (1968), pp. 246 sqq.

[9] Cf. e.g. Ulp. D. 17, 1, 10, 6; Ulp. D. 17, 1, 8, 3; Paul. D. 17, 1, 20 pr.

[10] Ulp. D. 17, 1, 12, 9; Pap. D. 17, 1, 56, 4; Gai. D. 17, 1, 27, 4; Cels. D. 17, 1, 50, 1; Watson, *Mandate*, pp. 154 sqq.; cf. also Bernardo Albanese, "'Judicium contrarium' e 'ignominia' nel mandato", (1970) 21 *Iura* 1 sqq. The test for the recoverability of expenses was not whether the mandator had actually benefited but whether the mandatarius had incurred them bona fide as a result of the mandate. Cf. today § 670 BGB (". . . which he may regard as necessary under the circumstances").

[11] Cf. infra, pp. 430 sq.

[12] Lenel, *EP*, pp. 295 sq.

[13] But see Guido Donatuti, "Contributi alla teoria del mandato in diritto romano, II. La volontà del mandante", in: *Studi di diritto romano*, vol. I (1976), pp. 351 sqq.; but see Arangio-Ruiz, op. cit., note 7, pp. 87 sqq.; cf. also Fritz Schwarz, "Die Konträrklagen", (1954) 71 *ZSS* 171 sqq., 218 sqq.; Kaser, *RPr* I, p. 579.

2. The gratuitousness of mandatum

(a) *Officium et amicitia*

"Mandatum . . . originem ex officio et amicitia trahit."[14] It was the extralegal social-value system of the Romans which accounted for the (relative) popularity of this type of contract. The (wealthy) Roman citizen, when called upon to take care of some matter for another person, felt honour-bound to carry out the task entrusted to his charge. He acted altruistically, in accordance with what could be expected of a man of his status and conforming to a code of ethics based on pietas, fides, reverentia and amicitia. He did not act for personal gain. Thus, he did not ask to be paid. Nothing, however, could prevent the mandator from showing his gratitude by way of a present.[15] If there was a moral duty on the iuris consultus to give an expert opinion to a friend who approached him, the latter was similarly obliged somehow to remunerate him for this service;[16] if it was a matter of honour for the mandatarius to act on behalf of the mandator, there was nothing wrong with the latter providing an honorarium in return for the services rendered: a visible sign of his estimation, with which he, in turn, honoured the mandatarius. This honorarium, as it came indeed to be called,[17] was a "remuneration" in the true sense of the word: a present given for a cause ("munus"), namely (in this instance) in return for a service.[18]

(b) *Payment of an honorarium*

So much emphasis on liberality and altruism sounds impressive but—considering the realities of daily life—also somewhat hypocritical. Take again the "free" professions such as the advocacy. By the time of classical law, an advocate expected to be remunerated for his services, and the giving of an honorarium had become generally accepted practice.[19] However, the contractual relationship was still regarded as a mandatum, with the consequence that such payment was not legally owed (and could not be enforced). The reason for this seems to have been that the advocacy and the pursuit of the other artes liberales was still not regarded as a "profession".[20] "One" did not have to work in order to earn one's living. Instead, one was able to devote one's time to

[14] Paul. D. 17, 1, 1, 4. Cf. also Cicero, *Pro Sexto Roscio Amerino oratio*, XXXVIII—111 sqq. and, generally, Schulz, *Principles*, pp. 223 sqq.

[15] "Gratiam vero referre, et gratuitam operam remunerare amicitiae non est contrarium, sed bene convenit" (Lauterbach, *Collegium theoretico-practicum*, Lib. XVII, Tit. I, XIV).

[16] For parallels in the case of loan transactions (mutuum was also, nominally, a gratuitous transaction!), cf. Alfons Bürge, "Vertrag und personale Abhängigkeiten im Rom der späten Republik und der frühen Kaiserzeit", (1980) 97 *ZSS* 122 sqq.

[17] Cf. e.g. Ulp. D. 11, 6, 1 pr.

[18] Cf. Michel, *Gratuité*, pp. 279 sq.

[19] Cf. e.g. Visky, op. cit., note 1, pp. 60 sqq.

[20] Michel, *Gratuité*, pp. 187 sq., 198 sqq.

serving the community by playing an active role in public life. The wealthy, well-connected Roman citizen of the time of the Republic tried to pass through the so-called cursus honorum,[21] until one day he became consul, proconsul, senator and elder statesman. These offices were not regarded as paid jobs, and the political independence of the office-bearers was always based, to some extent, on their material independence. Thus, it was one's leisure that one devoted to the public weal. The same applied in private affairs. If one took care of some matter for another person, one gave of one's free time. Any remuneration was therefore in the nature of a present, rather than a price for the time and trouble taken. That time did not have a price because it would in any event not have been invested profitably (in a material sense).[22]

(c) C. 4, 35, 1

If we have repeatedly referred to the impersonal "one", it was in order to indicate that to some degree (and increasingly so, with the withering away, in the course of time, of the old Roman value system) we are dealing with a pose. Many of the artes liberales had become profitable occupations, and many of those practising them made their living from the honoraria earned. Still, they preferred to be seen as generous and altruistic friends and counsellors. It was only in the course of the Principate that most of these social perceptions changed—changes which we finally find acknowledged and accommodated in late classical jurisprudence.

> "Adversus eum cuius negotia gesta sunt", we read in a rescript inscribed Severus and Antoninus,[23] "de pecunia quam de propriis opibus vel ab aliis mutuo acceptam erogasti, mandati actione pro sorte et usuris potes experiri. de salario quod promisit a praeside provinciae cognitio praebebitur."

The first sentence tells us nothing new. The mandatarius, in carrying out the mandate, has spent a sum of money. The actio mandati allows him to claim reimbursement of the capital and interest. But what about the "salary" that the mandator had promised? It cannot be sued for under the normal formulary procedure. However, the mandatarius is no longer without legal protection, for he will be able to proceed via the more modern and informal cognitio extra ordinem.

(d) Receipt of a salarium

By the time this rescript was drafted, receipt of a certain, predetermined sum of money in return for one's services no longer appeared to be in any way degrading. On the contrary: the term "salarium" carried

[21] Cf. e.g. Berger, *ED*, p. 422.
[22] Cf. Michel, *Gratuité*, p. 188.
[23] C. 4, 35, 1. According to Tony Honoré, *Emperors and Lawyers* (1981), pp. 97, 56 sqq., this rescript was drafted by Papinian, the then secretary a libellis.

distinctly aristocratic connotations and cannot, for instance, simply be equated with its modern English or French derivatives "salary" or "*salaire*".[24] The term "salarium" itself derives from "sal"[25] and can best be translated as salt-money. We only have to refer to St. Matthew 5, 13 ("Ye are the salt of the earth") in order to appreciate the high value set on salt in antiquity.[26] Its importance as an indispensable spice was often stressed; in Rome it also had a specific sacral significance, for it was an essential ingredient of the so-called mola salsa.[27]

But it was not only the term "salarium" as such that was free of low-class connotations. Since the time of Augustus, imperial functionaries of senatorial or equestrian rank outside Rome were in receipt of a fixed salarium; they had become "salaried" officials.[28] According to Cassius Dio,[29] a proconsul, for instance, received an annual sum of one million sesterces. These reforms constituted a significant break with the old idea of the important magistracies necessarily being gratuitous offices, and they did not leave the general social estimation of gratuity unaffected. If it was not demeaning for a former consul to administer one of the senatorial provinces for payment, how could it be socially objectionable for an advocate or a doctor to ask for a reward for their professional services? Thus, there was increasing pressure to make salaria that had been agreed upon for private services legally exactable too. This seems to have happened, first of all, in the case of procuratores.[30]

Originally, the procurator[31] omnium bonorum had been a freedman, sometimes even a slave, whom wealthy people used to have as a general manager of their property. Legal relationships between the patronus and his libertus, the dominus and his slave, did not exist. Nevertheless, both patronatus and patria potestas involved reciprocal (moral and social) duties, and thus the dominus negotii was expected either to allow his procurator enough free time to earn his own living, or he had to feed him. With the general dissolution of the extra-legal power relationships and with the corresponding rise of the procurator's social esteem, it became acceptable to base procuratio omnium bonorum on

---

24 Michel, *Gratuité*, p. 192.

25 Plinius Secundus, *Historia naturalis*, Lib. XXXI, 41, 89.

26 Cf. e.g. Walter Hatto Gross, in: *Kleiner Pauly*, vol. IV, col. 1528 sq.

27 Plinius Secundus, loc. cit. As to the meaning of "mola salsa", cf. e.g. Konrat Ziegler, in: *Kleiner Pauly*, vol. III, col. 1398; it was customary to strew a mixture of coarsely ground meal and salt over victims.

28 Cf. e.g. Mommsen, *Römisches Staatsrecht*, vol. I, pp. 300 sqq. This salarium succeeded the earlier vasarium, a lump sum which the Roman officials had received to cover the costs of outfit and equipment (derived from vasa, baggage); cf. Hans Gärtner, in: *Kleiner Pauly*, vol. V, col. 1141.

29 Cassius Dio, *Historia Romana*, LXXIX, 22, 5.

30 Arangio-Ruiz, op. cit., note 7, pp. 114 sqq.; Watson, *Mandate*, pp. 103 sqq.; Michel, *Gratuité*, pp. 192 sq.

31 Cf. the literature quoted supra, p. 53, note 138; on the relationship between mandatum and procuratio cf. also Watson, *Mandate*, pp. 36 sqq.

a mandate.[32] Of course, the procurator could not be expected to devote all his time to the administration of somebody else's property without any recompense. Thus, it became customary to give him, at regular intervals, instead of food, a sum of money: salarium in the place of (pars pro toto:) sal. By the time of Papinian, the claim for such a salarium had become legally enforceable.[33] The same applied to the salaria or honoraria of the members of the "liberal" professions.[34] Advocates, incidentally, seem to have been particularly greedy, as we can see from the repeated attempts of various emperors to fix maximum limits for their professional charges.[35]

All in all, then, by the end of the era of classical law, the lawyers had worked out a characteristically Roman solution. The old legal institutions remained unchanged; mandatum was still a gratuitous contract, and thus the actio mandati was not available to sue for either salarium or honorarium. At the same time, however, practical demands and new social perceptions were not simply ignored, for the mandatarius could resort to the cognitio extra ordinem procedure if the mandator refused to pay the recompense agreed upon. This is not contradicted by Ulp. D. 17, 1, 6 pr.: "Si remunerandi gratia honor intervenit, erit mandati actio." What this text says is not that, where an honorarium had been agreed upon, it could be sued for with the actio mandati.[36] Such an interpretation would be incompatible with all our other sources. Ulpianus rather seems to have stressed that the intervention of an ex gratia payment for the service rendered does not prevent the contractual relationship between the parties from being a mandate.[37]

(e) Mandatum nisi gratuitum nullum: the ius commune

Nevertheless, one cannot help remarking that the gratuitousness of mandatum was by now a matter of form rather than of substance. This must have become particularly obvious at a time when the distinction between formulary procedure and extraordinaria cognitio had

[32] Cf. e.g. Kaser, *RPr* II, pp. 100 sq. From the late Republic onwards, independent procurators of higher social standing made themselves available to look after the interests of their friends. They, too, acted under a mandate: Okko Behrends, "Die Prokuratur des klassischen römischen Zivilrechts", (1971) 88 *ZSS* 247 sqq.; Kaser, *RPr* II, p. 101.

[33] Cf., apart from C. 4, 35, 1, Pap. D. 17, 1, 7.

[34] Philosophers and "iuris professores", incidentally, remained excluded; the latter for the following reason: "est quidem res sanctissima civilis sapientia, sed quae pretio nummario non sit aestimanda nec dehonestanda" (Ulp. D. 50, 13, 1, 5; for an analysis, cf. Dieter Nörr, "Iurisperitus sacerdos", in: ΞENION, *Festschrift für Pan. J. Zepos*, vol. I (1973), pp. 555 sqq.

[35] Claudius fixed a maximum limit of 10 000 sesterces; cf. also e.g. C. 7, 72 of Diocletian's *edictum de pretiis rerum venalium* (Siegfried Lauffer (ed.), *Diokletians Preisedikt* (1971), p. 124); for further details about lawyers' fees cf. Ulp. D. 50, 13, 1, 9 sqq.; Paul. D. 19, 2, 38, 1; Michel, *Gratuité*, pp. 215 sqq.; Visky, op. cit., note 1, pp. 60 sqq. A pactum de quota litis was inadmissible: Ulp. D. 50, 13, 1, 12; Ulp. D. 17, 1, 6, 7; Pap. D. 17, 1, 7.

[36] Arangio-Ruiz, op. cit., note 7, pp. 117 sq., who consequently suspects interpolation.

[37] Cf. e.g. Glück, vol. 15, p. 286; Watson, *Mandate*, pp. 110 sqq.

vanished. Many authors of the ius commune still maintained the principle of "mandatum nisi gratuitum nullum est". On the other hand, they faithfully recorded that an actio extraordinaria was available for the recovery of salaria or honoraria that had been promised. But what was the practical relevance of hanging on to outdated procedural niceties? And if there was none, how could one still seriously maintain that mandatum was gratuitous?

Various solutions were suggested to resolve this problem. Thus, for example, a distinction was drawn between mandate and an innominate contract of the type of facio ut des,[38] depending on whether a remuneration for the professional services had been promised or not.[39] Others tried to distinguish between honorarium ("voluntaria operae gratis praestitae remuneratio")[40] and salarium ("[s]alarium . . . definimus, quod sit, iusta debitaque laboris sive operae sumptae sumendaeve, vel etiam officij in quacunque, re, ad referendam vicem compensatio, permutatio, remuneratio, adaequatio"):[41] only the former was compatible with the contract of mandatum.[42] Others, again,[43] focused on the nature of the service. If it was such that a value could not be attached to it—and that was usually the case with regard to the "liberal" professions—then whatever remuneration the mandator might have promised could not be regarded as the price of the service which the mandatory had agreed to perform: and whether such remuneration was called honorarium or salarium, it was thus compatible with the (essentially gratuitous) nature of mandatum. Pothier provides an example:[44]

> "I seek out a famous lawyer, in order to ask him to assume the defence of my case: he replies that he is willing to undertake it. I thank him for his reply, and I tell him that, to give him a slight indication of my gratitude,[45] I will present him with Meerman's Thesaurus, which does not figure in his library. He replies that he willingly accepts my present which I offer him with such good grace. Now, although I promise the lawyer Meerman's Thesaurus, the contract existing between us continues to be a contract of mandate, because what I promise to give him is not the price to be paid for the defence of my case which he has undertaken. The defence of my case which he undertakes, is something to which a specific value cannot be attached, and the mandate continues to be a contract of mandate. . . ."

A few lines later, however, it becomes obvious how tenuous this argument really is: for here the same author is prepared to admit that there are, none the less, certain services for which, even though they

[38] Cf. infra, pp. 534 sq. [39] Cf. e.g. Glück, vol. 15, pp. 285 sqq.

[40] Vinnius, *Institutiones*, Lib. III, Tit. XXVII, 13, n. 1.

[41] Iacobus Gothofredus, *Tractatus novus et practicus de salario* (Genevae, 1666), Cap. I, III.

[42] For details cf. D.J. Joubert, "Die kontraktuele verhouding tussen professionele man en kliënt", 1970 *Acta Juridica* 15 sqq.

[43] Cf. e.g. Pothier, *Traité du contrat de mandat*, n. 23; also Dernburg, *Pandekten*, vol. II, § 115 in fine.

[44] *Traité du contrat de mandat*, n. 23 (quoted from a translation by B.G. Rogers (ed.) (Lex Patria, 1979)).

[45] Pothier says: "*pour lui donner une faible marque de ma reconnaissance*".

belong to a liberal profession and in consequence fall under a contract of mandate rather than one of hire, those persons who have rendered them are allowed "en justice" to ask for the normal reward.[46]

Finally, therefore, there were those who abandoned all this camouflage[47] and recognized that mandatum was not necessarily gratuitous after all, and that the actio mandati (contraria) could be used to claim whatever remuneration had been promised. This view was based on a (mis-)interpretation of texts such as Ulp. D. 17, 1, 6 pr.,[48] on old Germanic customs[49] or simply on the changed perceptions and practices of modern business life.[50], [51] It was adopted, in the course of the 19th century, by a whole variety of drafts and codifications,[52] including the first draft of the BGB.[53] But in the end, as far as Germany is concerned, classical Roman law prevailed again. According to § 662 BGB, it is essential for a mandate that the mandatary binds himself *gratuitously* to take care of some matter for the mandator entrusted to him by the latter. The "quaestus liberales", however, were subjected to the regime of locatio conductio (operis or operarum, as the case might be):[54] against strong opposition from both the medical and legal professions.[55] Yet, in common parlance, the terms "Mandat" and "Honorar" live on, particularly with regard to services rendered by lawyers.[56]

3. The range of application of mandatum

(a) Factual and contractual activities of the mandatarius

All the other features of mandatum either follow from what has already been set out or from general principles. Mandatum, in a way, was a

---

[46] Pothier, *Traité du contrat de mandat*, n. 26.

[47] "Spitsvondighede", according to De Wet en Yeats, p. 341.

[48] Cf. e.g. Lauterbach, *Collegium theoretico-practicum*, Lib. XVII, Tit. I, XV; Stryk, *Usus modernus pandectarum*, Lib. XVII, Tit. I, § 18.

[49] Johann Gottlieb Heineccius, "Elementa Juris Germanici" (in: *Opera omnia* (Genevae, 1748)), Lib. II, § CCCLXXXII.

[50] Glück, vol. 15, p. 322; "Motive", in: *Mugdan*, vol. II, p. 295.

[51] Problem: was the honorarium then not really tantamount to merces? Why still maintain a distinction between operae liberales (contractual regime: mandatum) and other operae (locatio conductio)? A statement such as "[*Die operae liberales werden] nicht bezahlt, sondern honorirt*" (Dernburg, *Pandekten*, vol. II, § 115 in fine) sounds like a petitio principii. Further problem: could an honorarium be charged, if it had not been expressly promised at the time of conclusion of the contract, but where the mandatary was a person who did not normally render services of the kind in question gratuitously? Cf. (in the affirmative) Lauterbach, *Collegium theoretico-practicum*, Lib. XVII, Tit. I, XV; Stryk, *Usus modernus pandectarum*, Lib. XVII, Tit. I, § 18; Vinnius, *Institutiones*, Lib. III, Tit. XXVII, 13; Pothier, *Traité du contrat de mandat*, nn. 24, 26. Contra e.g. Glück, vol. 15, p. 291.

[52] References in "Motive", in: *Mugdan*, vol. II, p. 295.

[53] § 586 E I.

[54] Cf. supra, p. 393; but according to § 675 BGB, many of the rules relating to mandate are applicable, if the contract of service or for work has as its object the taking care of a matter. For details, see Hans-Joachim Musielak, "Entgeltliche Geschäftsbesorgung", in: *Gutachten und Vorschläge zur Überarbeitung des Schuldrechts*, vol. II (1981), pp. 1209 sqq.

[55] "Protokolle", in: *Mugdan*, vol. II, pp. 897 sq.

[56] As far as the "honoraria" of teachers are concerned, cf. § 196 I, n. 13.

counterpart to locatio conductio: depending on whether or not a reward had been fixed for the carrying out of the commission, the transaction fell either into the one or the other contractual niche.[57] Mandate therefore covered a wide range of situations. The mandator could request the mandatary to clean clothes,[58] to build a tomb[59] or to engage in any other (factual) activity. Usually, however, the mandatary was asked to enter into a contractual relationship with a third party: be it that the mandator wanted him to lend or borrow money,[60] to stand surety,[61] to buy or sell a farm or to let or hire a slave. This is what we call indirect representation: A could use B to conclude a contract for him with C. However, it was not A who became obliged and entitled to C (that would have been direct representation, which Roman law did not know)[62] but B, the "agent", himself. B was then bound under the mandate to hand over what he had acquired to A; A in turn had to indemnify B. Particularly the procurator acted in this manner as an indirect representative of his principal; as we have seen, in classical law his social status had become such that he was commissioned, as a rule, by way of a contract of mandate.

In later centuries, mandatum (extraiudiciale or iudiciale) became the contractual cornerstone of direct representation; for once this institution had come to be recognized,[63] and before Laband had isolated the granting of authority as something different (and abstract) from the internal contractual relationship between principal and agent,[64] the contract of mandate usually provided the basis for the agent's ability to act in the principal's name.[65]

(b) Illegal and immoral mandates; the mandatum tua tantum gratia

It hardly need be emphasized that illegal or immoral mandates were void;[66] thus one could not validly commission a person to sack a temple or to wound a slave.[67] Apart from that, as in any other contract, the object of the transaction had to be determined.[68] A mandatum incertum

[57] Cf. Gai. III, 162. However, where something was handed over for safekeeping without any reward being fixed, there was the more special contract of depositum: cf. Ulp. D. 16, 3, 1, 8. On this and other details relating to the object of mandatum, see Watson, *Mandate*, pp. 78 sqq.
[58] Gai. III, 162.
[59] Marc./Ulp. D. 17, 1, 12, 17.
[60] On the so-called "mandatum qualificatum", see supra, pp. 139 sqq.
[61] Cf. supra, p. 133.
[62] Cf. supra, pp. 45 sqq.
[63] Cf. supra, pp. 56 sqq.
[64] Supra, pp. 57 sq.
[65] Cf. e.g. Glück, vol. 15, pp. 323 sqq.; Coing, p. 463.
[66] Gai. III, 157; *Inst.* III, 26, 7; Voet, *Commentarius ad Pandectas*, Lib. XVII, Tit. I, VI; Glück, vol. 15, pp. 254 sqq.; Arangio-Ruiz, op. cit., note 7, pp. 105 sqq.; Watson, *Mandate*, pp. 88 sqq.
[67] Paul. D. 17, 1, 22, 6.
[68] Arangio-Ruiz, op. cit., note 7, pp. 109 sqq.; Watson, *Mandate*, pp. 92 sqq.

(e.g. to purchase for the principal any farm) was (probably) invalid,[69] although a certain discretion could be left to the mandatary, at least as far as incidental points were concerned.[70] However, there was one further, very interesting limit to the range of possible mandates: the mandatary could not bind himself to take care of his own affairs. Our sources consistently emphasize that a mandate cannot validly be concluded wholly in the interest of the mandatary. Such a mandatum tua tantum gratia, as it came to be called ("tua" as seen from the perspective of the mandator), was said to be "supervacuum". The reason is explained by Gaius[71] as follows: "[Q]uod . . . tu tua gratia facturus sis, id de tua sententia, non ex meo mandatu, facere debes"; and Justinian[72] added: "[C]uius generis mandatum magis consilium est quam mandatum et ob id non est obligatorium."[73] If I ask another person to invest his money by purchasing land or to grow tulips in his front garden, I am not giving him a commission but a piece of advice. What he does with his money or with his garden is entirely his own affair. He may consult me because I have special banking or gardening expertise. But whatever I advise him to do, I will ultimately have to leave it to him to decide, whether or not he follows that advice. Anything else would be an unacceptable interference with his natural prerogative to attend to his business according to his own discretion. "Qui mandat, vult, et urget, ut fiat quod mandatum est. Qui dat consilium, consultoris arbitrio rem permittit."[74] With regard to the own affairs of the "mandatarius", only the latter alternative is conceivable.[75]

(c) Types of mandate according to the interest involved

The discussion of the somewhat exceptional situation of the mandatum

---

[69] Cf. Cels. D. 17, 1, 48, 1 and 2; but see Watson, *Mandate*, pp. 96 sqq.
[70] Cf. e.g. Paul. D. 17, 1, 59, 6; Paul. D. 17, 1, 46.
[71] III, 156.
[72] III, 26, 6.
[73] Cf. further Gai. D. 17, 1, 2, 6.
[74] Vinnius, *Institutiones*, Lib. III, Tit. XXVII, 6, n. 1.
[75] On the question whether there can be a mandatum tua gratia which is not consilium, cf. e.g. Vangerow, *Pandekten*, § 659. Conversely, it is arguable that not every kind of advice or recommendation should be regarded as not binding. Cf., for example, Ulp. D. 17, 1, 16 for a mandatum (in the nature of a proposal) mea et tua gratia. Furthermore, it has often been argued that a mandatum tua tantum gratia is binding, and thus provides the mandatarius with a claim against the mandator, where he would not have acted as he did but for the mandate (arg. Ulp. D. 17, 1, 6, 5: "Plane si tibi mandavero quod tua intererat, nulla erit mandati actio, nisi mea quoque interfuit: aut, si non esses facturus, nisi ego mandassem, etsi mea non interfuit, tamen erit mandati actio"; itp., cf. e.g. Watson, *Mandate*, p. 120): Stryk, *Usus modernus pandectarum*, Lib. XVII, Tit. I, §§ 8 sqq.; Lauterbach, *Collegium theoretico-practicum*, Lib. XVII, Tit. I, XVI sq.; Voet, *Commentarius ad Pandectas*, Lib. XVII, Tit. I, IV; Glück, vol. 15, pp. 250 sqq. See also Windscheid/Kipp, § 412, n. 21, who, however, base the liability on a specific guarantee. Today, cf. § 676 BGB: "A person who gives advice or a recommendation to another is not bound to compensate him for any damage arising from following this advice or the recommendation, without prejudice to his responsibility resulting from a contract or delict."

tua tantum gratia gave rise to a slightly scholastic attempt positively to identify and categorize the circumstances under which a valid contract of mandatum could be concluded. Of course, it goes back to the law teacher, to Gaius. He drew a distinction between mandatum mea gratia, tua gratia and aliena gratia.[76] Later on, he refined this system by adding the possible combinations of mixed interest: "Mandatum inter nos contrahitur, sive mea tantum gratia tibi mandem sive aliena tantum sive mea et aliena sive mea et tua sive tua et aliena."[77] Thus (leaving out mandatum tua tantum gratia) we arrive at a fivefold subdivision. It is obvious that the mandate mea gratia (i.e. in the interest of the mandator) is the normal type and does not present any difficulties. Much more problematic is mandatum aliena gratia: a mandate in the interest (purely) of a third party. Justinian provides an example: "Aliena autem causa intervenit mandatum, veluti si tibi mandet, ut Titii negotia gereres, vel ut Titio fundum emeres, vel ut pro Titio sponderes."[78] A commissions B to take care of the affairs of C. Of course, this type of transaction cannot give rise to an action on the part of C; that would have been a (genuine) contract in favour of a third party. But even as far as the relationship between mandator and mandatary is concerned, it is difficult to see how B can incur an (enforceable) obligation: alteri stipulari nemo potest; and we know that this principle did not apply only to stipulations but also to all kinds of informal, consensual transactions.[79] A mandatum aliena tantum gratia is characterized, per definitionem, by a lack of an actionable interest in the person of the mandator. How, under these circumstances, can he bring the actio mandati against the mandatary? And yet, our sources treat the mandatum aliena tantum gratia as valid.[80] The solution to this apparent discrepancy seems to be implicit in the manner in which Ulpianus describes the situation in D. 17, 1, 8, 6: "Mandati actio tunc competit, cum coepit interesse eius qui mandavit: ceterum si nihil interest, cessat mandati actio." At the time when B promises A to take care of C's affairs, A does not have an (actionable) interest in the matter: otherwise we would be dealing not with mandatum aliena tantum, but with mea et aliena gratia. But such an interest may well arise subsequently. For once B has taken charge of C's affairs, A may be liable to C under an actio negotiorum gestorum (directa): by commissioning B in the way he did, A himself took care of a matter for another (C), without having received a mandate from him or being otherwise entitled to do so. This unsolicited meddling with his affairs[81] may be unwelcome to C. Even

---

[76] Gai. III, 155.

[77] Gai. D. 17, 1, 2 pr. (taken from his Res cottidianae). Cf. also *Inst.* III, 26 pr.

[78] *Inst.* III, 26, 3.

[79] Cf. supra, p. 35, note 6.

[80] Cf. e.g. Gai. D. 17, 1, 2, 2; Ulp. D. 17, 1, 6, 4.

[81] Watson, *Mandate*, p. 116. Cf. further the detailed analysis of Seiler, *Negotiorum gestio*, pp. 114 sqq., who confirms that it is the mandator, and not the mandatarius, whom the

if it is welcome, however, C may have suffered a loss, since he may well have relied on the action of the mandatary and thus abstained from taking care of the matter himself.[82] The actio mandati can therefore indeed only be brought by A against B, and the mandatum aliena tantum gratia can be regarded as valid only, if and when the former has an actionable interest: and that is entirely in harmony with what we have discussed above about the inherent limitation of alteri stipulari nemo potest.[83]

It is obvious that, if mandata mea and aliena gratia were valid, so were mandates based on a mixed interest:[84] for they were at least partially in the interest of the mandator and/or a third party, even though they might also be in the interest of the mandatarius. It may be remembered that in the form of a "mandatum qualificatum" the mandatum tua et aliena gratia provided a useful suretyship transaction. In Justinian's Institutes we find the typical example: "Tua et aliena, veluti si [quis] tibi mandet, ut Titio sub usuris crederes."[85] If Titius cannot repay, the mandatary may take recourse against the mandator. The latter is therefore effectively in the position of a surety.[86]

4. Mandatum morte solvitur

Mandatum was based on personal confidence, on fides and amicitia.[87] Any breach of trust on the part of the mandatarius was seen in a most serious light and condemnation under the actio mandati therefore involved infamia.[88] Furthermore, the mandate ended with the death of either of the parties: mandatum morte solvitur.[89], [90] Mandator and

---

classical lawyers regarded as negotiorum gestor in the case of mandata aliena tantum gratia. On the mandatum aliena gratia, see also Wieslaw Litewski, "Interesse des Auftraggebers, des Dritten und des Beauftragten", (1975) 78 *BIDR* 193 sqq. (227 sq.).

[82] For the traditional argument along these lines cf. e.g. Vinnius, *Institutiones*, Lib. III, Tit. XXVII, 3; Pothier, *Traité du contrat de mandat*, n. 17; Glück, vol. 15, p. 249. Contra Watson, *Mandate*, pp. 116 sqq., who does not, however, present an alternative solution.

[83] Cf. supra, pp. 35 sqq.

[84] For examples cf. Gai. D. 17, 1, 2, 3, 4 and 5; *Inst.* III, 26, 2, 4 and 5; for a discussion, see Litewski, (1975) 78 *BIDR* 193 sqq.

[85] *Inst.* III, 26, 5.

[86] For details cf. supra, pp. 139 sqq.

[87] Etymologically, "mandatum" is derived from "manus" and "dare" (cf. e.g. Voet, *Commentarius ad Pandectas*, Lib. XVII, Tit. I, I ("Mandatum dictum a datione manus . . . et manus fidei signum erat."); Vinnius, *Institutiones*, Lib. III, Tit. XXVII pr.). In Rome, one did not shake hands as profusely as one does in modern Germany, for instance. The gesture of offering one's right hand was a most intimate sign of friendship, and was reserved for grand and important occasions. Cf. Michel, *Gratuité*, pp. 170 sq.; W.H. Gross, "Salutatio", in: *Kleiner Pauly*, vol. IV, col. 1524 sq.

[88] Gai. IV, 182. Was the actio mandati contraria famosa too? Cf. Fritz Schwarz, "Die Konträrklagen", (1954) 71 *ZSS* 210 sqq.; Albanese, (1970) 21 *Iura* 1 sqq.

[89] Paul. D. 17, 1, 26 pr.; Gai. III, 160; Gai. D. 17, 1, 27, 3. For details, see Hamed A. Rabie, *L'acte juridique "post mortem" en droit romain* (1955), pp. 85 sqq.; Watson, *Mandate*, pp. 125 sqq.; Manfred Harder, "Zum transmortalen und postmortalen Auftrag nach römischem und geltendem Recht", in: *Sein und Werden im Recht, Festgabe für Ulrich von Lübtow* (1970), pp. 518 sqq. Today cf. § 673 BGB ("In case of doubt, a mandate is

mandatarius had placed their confidence in each other, not in each other's heirs. With the person of either of them, the essential basis of their contractual relationship falls away too. However, there were certain modifications to this rule. It applied "integro mandato" only, that is, before the mandate had been acted upon.[91] If the mandate was "under way",[92] i.e. if the mandatary had started to carry out the commission but had not yet completed it, it had to be carried out, irrespective of whether the mandator or the mandatarius had died over it. The practical effects of the principle of mandatum morte solvitur were also mitigated in instances where a mandatarius had executed the mandate in the belief that the mandator was still alive. Legal protection for such bona fide acts post finem mandati was accomplished by means of actiones utiles.[93]

A different, though closely related, question is whether the parties to a mandate could specifically arrange that it be carried out after the death of either of them. Justinian, while retaining the rule that a mandate was dissolved by death, allowed the conclusion of such mandata post mortem.[94] In this respect he deviated from the position adopted by the classical lawyers, who had disapproved of both mandata post mortem mandatarii and mandatoris as being in conflict with the personal nature of mandatum.[95] More particularly, the latter (example: "si, ut post mortem sibi monumentum fieret, quis mandavit")[96] would have run counter to the idea that the heirs of the mandator should be free to chose a person of *their* confidence; the mandatum post mortem mandatarii, on the other hand, is inutile[97] (in the sense of useless, impractical and

---

extinguished by the death of the mandatary") and § 672 BGB ("In case of doubt a mandate is not extinguished by the death of the mandator"). The latter rule was introduced in conscious deviation from the ius commune (Windscheid/Kipp, § 411, 2), § 186 I 13 PrALR, art. 2003 code civil and § 1022 ABGB; cf. "Motive", in: *Mugdan*, vol. II, p. 306; "Protokolle", in: *Mugdan* vol. II, pp. 954 sq. But see Harder, *Festgabe von Lübtow*, pp. 529 sqq. for a reinterpretation more in line with historical precedent.

[90] Similarly, the mandate came to an end if, re integra, the mandator revoked (revocare; cf. Gai. III, 159) or the mandatary renounced (renuntiare; cf. Paul. Sent. II, XV, 1) the contract. The second of these propositions is, however, questionable. For a discussion, see Glück, vol. 15, pp. 354 sqq.; Arangio-Ruiz, op. cit., note 7, pp. 134 sqq.; Watson, *Mandate*, pp. 70 sqq.; Philippe Meylan, "Révocation et renonciation du mandat en droit romain classique", in: *Studi in onore di Giuseppe Grosso*, vol. I (1968), pp. 463 sqq. Cf. today § 671 BGB.

[91] According to Harder, *Festgabe von Lübtow*, pp. 520 sqq., this restriction is of post-classical origin.

[92] Watson, *Mandate*, p. 130.

[93] Paul. D. 17, 1, 26 pr.; Gai. III, 160; *Inst.* III, 26, 10. Cf. today § 674 BGB: "If a mandate is extinguished other than by revocation, it is, nevertheless, deemed to continue in favour of the mandatary, until he knows or ought to know of its extinction."

[94] C. 8, 37, 11; C. 4, 11, 1.

[95] For details, see Arangio-Ruiz, op. cit., note 7, pp. 142 sqq.; J.C. van Oven, "Gaius, 3, 158: Mandatum post mortem mandantis", in: *Symbolae Raphaeli Taubenschlag*, vol. I (1956), pp. 529 sqq.; Watson, *Mandate*, pp. 133 sqq.; Harder, *Festgabe von Lübtow*, pp. 523 sqq.; Kaser, *RPr* I, p. 578; but see Cesare Sanfilippo, "Ancora un caso di 'mandatum post mortem'?", in: *Sodalitas, Scritti in onore di Antonio Guarino*, vol. V (1984), pp. 2047 sqq.

[96] Marc./Ulp. D. 17, 1, 12, 17.

[97] Gai. III, 158.

therefore invalid),[98] in that a mandator could not conceivably have a reasonable interest in commissioning, of all people, the heirs of a particular person: they are, after all, not even known yet!

5. The liability of the mandatarius

(a) *Dolus or dolus and culpa?*

Mandatum was a gratuitous transaction. This must have been an important feature in determining the standard of liability imposed upon the mandatary. Usually, as we have seen, the balance of interests within a contractual relationship and the standard of liability corresponded.[99] Thus, for instance, the depositarius, who did not receive any remuneration and who acted essentially altruistically, was normally liable only for dolus (and, to some extent, for culpa lata).[100] We might therefore expect the liability of the mandatarius to be restricted in a similar manner. And indeed, we possess a general statement by Modestinus (preserved outside the Corpus Juris Civilis) to this effect: "In mandati vero iudicium dolus, non etiam culpa deducitur."[101] Several texts in both the Digest and Code tie in with this. But then there is also a variety of fragments pointing in a different direction and declaring the mandatarius to be liable for culpa. Again, we even have a statement of a general nature, this time by Modestinus' teacher, Ulpian:

> "[D]olum et culpam mandatum, commodatum, venditum, pignori acceptum, locatum, item dotis datio, tutelae, negotia gesta [recipiunt]: in his quidem et diligentiam."[102]

How can we reconcile this apparent conflict of opinions? Interpolation hypotheses have provided a popular and convenient answer. As a result, for some time, the view prevailed that in classical law the mandatary was liable for dolus only. Later on, his liability came to be gradually extended, and references to culpa were interpolated into the classical texts in order to bring them into line with the more modern position.[103] Other authors have attributed the transition from dolus to culpa liability to late classical law.[104] More recently, an attempt has even been made to show that, already in high classical law, liability was for culpa.[105]

---

[98] Harder, *Festgabe von Lübtow*, p. 524.

[99] Cf. supra, pp. 198 sq.

[100] Cf. supra, pp. 209 sq.

[101] Coll. X, II, 3.

[102] Ulp. D. 50, 17, 23.

[103] Cf. e.g. Arangio-Ruiz, op. cit., note 7, pp. 188 sqq.; Schulz, *CRL*, p. 556; Jörs/Kunkel/Wenger, § 139, 2 a; William M. Gordon, "The Liability of the Mandatary", in: *Synteleia Vincenzo Arangio-Ruiz*, vol. I (1964), pp. 202 sqq.; Wieslaw Litewski, "La responsabilité du mandataire", (1983–84) 12 *Index* 106 sqq., 119 sqq.

[104] Cf. e.g. Buckland/Stein, p. 516; Hoffmann, *Fahrlässigkeit*, pp. 21 sqq.; cf. also, as far as Ulpian was concerned, Tafaro, *Regula*, pp. 276 sqq.

[105] Hannu Tapani Klami, *Teneor Mandati* (1976).

(b) Terminological problems

To me, there appears to be a certain element of truth in both the traditional and the two other points of view. For here, as elsewhere, Roman law was not static but developed in time; and this development is bound to have implied a broadening, not a restriction of liability. On the other hand, it is no longer permissible today summarily to suspect and brush aside all references to culpa in our classical sources relating to mandatum. Any analysis of the position in classical law must, however, take account of two further factors, which have been emphasized by Geoffrey MacCormack and Alan Watson respectively. The first of these relates to terminology.[106] Culpa, in classical Roman law, did not have a precise, rigidly defined meaning. It could cover a broad range of situations. More particularly, it could be used in (at least) two different ways: it provided (roughly) a Roman equivalent to the modern concept of negligence, i.e. the failure to exercise the care that a bonus paterfamilias would have exercised. But "culpa" could also refer to fault or blameworthiness in general, i.e. including dolus.[107] In the first sense, it was complementary to dolus, in the second it comprised it. If employed in the second sense, the term "culpa" could be used where the circumstances in fact disclosed a case of dolus. Thus, for instance, there is not necessarily an inconsistency between the proposition that the mandatary was liable for dolus but not for culpa and a decision in which a specific mandatary was held responsible on account of his "culpa".[108]

(c) Altruistic and not so altruistic mandatarii

The second point is this. Mandatum, as we have seen, covered a very wide and heterogeneous range of situations. There was the truly altruistic person who took care of his friend's affairs. There was the professional lawyer, doctor or surveyor. There was the procurator in receipt of a salarium. Was it really reasonable to treat all these mandatarii alike, as far as their liability was concerned? Also, we must remember that the mandatarius did not necessarily act solely in the interest of the mandator. Where the mandatum is either mea et tua or tua et aliena gratia, the mandatarius' activity can hardly be described as altruistic, even if he is not remunerated for his services. The contract is (also) in his interest, and thus the dolus liability might not seem adequate. Even in the case of depositum, the standard of liability

[106] Geoffrey MacCormack, "The Liability of the Mandatary", (1972) 18 *Labeo* 156 sqq.

[107] For a detailed analysis, see Geoffrey MacCormack, "Culpa", (1972) 38 *SDHI* 123 sqq.; cf. also idem, (1972) 18 *Labeo* 156 sqq.; Klami, op. cit., note 105, pp. 2 sqq.

[108] MacCormack, (1972) 18 *Labeo* 157. Contra: Litewski, (1983–84) 12 *Index* 107 and passim.

changed if, for once, the contract was not in the interest of the depositor, but of the depositarius.[109]

Whilst, therefore, liability for dolus seems to have been the historical starting point,[110] it is likely that by the time of classical law the question was approached in a very flexible manner.[111] After all, what the judge had to assess was "quidquid ob eam rem N^m N^m A^o A^o dare facere oportet ex bona fide"; and the yardstick of "bona fides" called for a comprehensive analysis of all factors determining the circumstances of each case.[112] Thus, on a more general level, it had to be considered that breach of contract in the case of mandatum was a matter of particular concern:

> "Mandati violatio violat duas res sanctissimas, amicitiam et fidem. Idcirco qui res mandatas non modo malitiosius, sed etiam negligentius gesserit, admittit summum deducus."[113]

On the other hand, condemnation involved infamia, a sanction not to be imposed too lightly. More specifically, however, the position of the parties had to be taken into consideration: whether the mandatum was in the interest of mandator, mandatarius and/or third party, and whether the services of the mandatarius were in fact, if not in law, remunerated.

(d) Mandatum: between suretyship and procuratio

If we want to gauge how all this worked out in practice,[114] we can take, at the one end of the scale, the liability of a person who stood surety at the request of the (main) debtor. According to Ulpian, he is liable, for instance, if, when sued for the amount owed, he fails to raise certain exceptions, even though he is aware of their availability.[115] The same applies if, having paid the debt, he omits to inform the debtor, who consequently pays again.[116] In both these instances, the fideiussor is probably not deliberately trying to prejudice the debtor; he simply does not bother to safeguard the position of the latter.[117] This type of behaviour does not accord with the precepts of good faith; in fact, it comes very close to dolus. It is, in the words of Ulpian, "dolo proximum";[118] or more fully: "dissoluta enim neglegentia prope dolum est."[119] Thus we can see that dolus was the normal standard of liability

---

[109] Cf. supra, pp. 208 sq.
[110] This is conceded even by Klami, op. cit., note 105, pp. 13 sqq.
[111] Watson, *Mandate*, pp. 198 sqq.
[112] Cf. e.g. Kaser, *RPr* I, pp. 509 sq.
[113] Donellus, *Commentarii de Jure Civili*, Lib. XIII, Cap. XI, XI (n. 5).
[114] For details of what follows, see Watson, *Mandate*, pp. 202 sqq.; MacCormack, (1972) 18 *Labeo* 158 sqq.
[115] Ulp. D. 17, 1, 29 pr.
[116] Ulp. D. 17, 1, 29, 3.
[117] MacCormack, (1972) 18 *Labeo* 159.
[118] D. 17, 1, 29, 3.
[119] D. 17, 1, 29 pr.

for this prototype of the altruistic mandatarius, but that there was a tendency to extend the scope of liability to cases of extreme recklessness which were not very far from dolus.[120]

At the other end of the scale we find the procurator. Here liability seems to have gone beyond what could conveniently be expressed in terms of dolus or dolo proximum: "A procuratore dolum et omnem culpam . . . praestandum esse iuris auctoritate manifeste declaratur."[121] All the remaining types of mandate fitted in somewhere between: depending upon the circumstances, liability appears to have been sometimes for dolus only,[122] sometimes for dolus and culpa lata[123] and in other instances for the full range of culpa.[124]

(e) Spondet diligentiam et industriam negotio gerendo parem

Arguably, then, Justinian's compilers interfered much less with the classical texts than has often been supposed; on the whole, they seem to have been happy to preserve the flexible interpretation of the classical Roman lawyers.[125] Such an attitude, of course, made it difficult in subsequent centuries to reconcile the texts on the basis of a unitary formula. Thus, there have always been attempts to show that liability was (or ought to have been) for dolus (and culpa lata).[126] By and large, however, when it came to the question of generalizing a standard of liability, Ulp. D. 50, 17, 23, the (not so) "ill-directed tirades of young Cicero"[127] and the fragments dealing with procuratio carried the day.[128] Even where mandatum was (or is) still regarded as gratuitous (as under the BGB), the scope of liability was usually widened to comprise culpa.[129, 130] This has often been justified, dogmatically, on the basis of an implied promise, on the part of the mandatarius, to exercise all the care and skill required by the business that he had undertaken to carry

---

[120] Further on the liability of the fideiussor, see Ulp. D. 17, 1, 8, 8.

[121] C. 4. 35, 13 (Diocl. et Max.). Cf. further C. 4, 35, 4 (Alex.); C. 4, 35, 9 (Diocl. et Max.); C. 4, 35, 11 (Diocl. et Max.); Ulp. D. 17, 1, 10, 1.

[122] Mod. Coll. X, II, 3; Paul. D. 17, 1, 26, 8.

[123] Ulp. D. 17, 1, 8, 10 (". . . si tibi mandavi, ut hominem emeres, tuque emisti, teneberis mihi, ut restituas. sed et si dolo emere neglexisti (forte enim pecunia accepta alii cessisti ut emeret) aut si lata culpa (forte si gratia ductus passus es alium emere) teneberis . . .").

[124] Ulp. D. 50, 17, 23; Paul. D. 17, 1, 22, 11; Paul. D. 17, 1, 26, 7.

[125] Watson, *Mandate*, pp. 198 sq.; Kaser, *RPr* II, p. 417.

[126] Cf., for example, the glossator Martinus (according to Hoffmann, *Fahrlässigkeit*, p. 44); Brunnemann, *Commentarius in Pandectas*, Lib. XVII, ad L. Idemque. 10. pr. et L. 12. pr, nn. 1, 2. Cf. further the discussion in Glück, vol. 15, pp. 262 sqq.

[127] Schulz, *CRL*, p. 556. He refers to *Pro Roscio Amerino oratio*, XXXVIII—111 sqq., on which, see Watson, *Mandate*, pp. 199 sqq.

[128] For the situation in modern South African law, cf. e.g. De Wet en Yeats, p. 341.

[129] But see art. 1992 II code civil (usually, however, ignored in the practice of the courts).

[130] Culpa levis or culpa levissima? A much-disputed question amongst the authors of the ius commune. During usus modernus and pandectism, the latter of these standards was usually advocated. For details, see Hoffmann, *Fahrlässigkeit*, pp. 44, 62, 95 sqq., 141 sqq., 212 sq.

out: "Spondet diligentiam et industriam negotio gerendo parem";[131] or, in the words of Donellus:

> "Quippe negotium aliquod gerendum suscipimus, quia geri quidquam sine industria et facultate gerendi non potest: ideo et hac ipsa industria ac facultate et profiteri et spondere intellegitur."[132]

6. The liability of the mandator

(a) Utility considerations

The fact that mandatum was gratuitous and that the mandatary usually acted in the interest of the mandator may also be expected to have played a role as far as the determination of liability in the reverse direction was concerned: could the mandatarius sue the mandator for any loss—not attributable to the fault of either of the parties—that he had suffered as a result of carrying out the mandate? Yes, is the answer given by Iulianus.[133] If A, at the request of B, purchases a slave, and this slave, before he can be transferred to B, steals some of A's property, A can recover his full damages from B under the actio mandati (contraria) ("damnum praestari debere"). Reason: ". . . multo tamen aequius esse nemini officium suum, quod eius, cum quo contraxerit, non etiam sui commodi causa susceperit, damnosum esse."[134] This is based on the well-known utility principle: the law should not allow a person to lose out on account of an obligation that he undertook in somebody else's interest. The loss must be shifted to where the benefit lies.[135]

(b) Casus a nullo praestantur

But the utility principle is not a hard-and-fast rule of law. It is based on considerations of equity. Furthermore, in the case of mandatum it is not always a realistic guideline for allocating risks and determining standards of liability: the mandatarius, as we have seen, did not necessarily act (solely) in the mandator's interest, and he might well receive a remuneration for his services. It is not surprising, therefore, that the question was controversial amongst the Roman jurists, and that in some of our texts we find a different assessment of the equities of the situation.

---

[131] Pothier, *Traité du contrat de mandat*, n. 46.

[132] *Commentarii de Jure Civili*, Lib. XIII, Cap. XI, XI; cf. further e.g. Windscheid/Kipp, § 410, n. 4; Hoffmann, *Fahrlässigkeit*, p. 141.

[133] As reported by Africanus in D. 47, 2, 62, 5.

[134] The last part of Afr. D. 47, 2, 62, 5 is interpolated; here the compilers attempted to reconcile the decision with the fault principle by means of a fiction. Cf. e.g. Dietrich Nörr, "Die Entwicklung des Utilitätsgedankens im römischem Haftungsrecht", (1956) 73 *ZSS* 95.

[135] Cf. also Grotius, *De jure belli ac pacis*, Lib. II, Cap. XII, § XIII: "ne quis . . . ex beneficio damnum sentiat."

"Exceptione, quae tibi prodesse debebat, usus iniuria iudicis damnatus es: nihil tibi praestabitur iure mandati, quia iniuriam, quae tibi facta est, penes te manere quam ad alium transferri aequius est."[136]

A stood surety for B. The creditor's claim may be countered by an exceptio, of which A, when sued by the creditor, in fact avails himself. The judge, however, nevertheless condemns A. According to Paulus, it is more equitable to let the loss lie where it has fallen than to shift it to the mandator. It is thus the mandatarius who carries the risk of the judge's mistake. If not in line with utility considerations, this decision is certainly in accordance with the principle of "casus a nullo praestantur".[137]

(c) The ius commune

Since the Middle Ages, jurists and (later) legislators have battled with this problem—and particularly with the confusing state of the sources—and have tried to apply and generalize either Julian's or Paul's view. Thus, for instance, during the 19th century the latter prevailed: the mandator was to be liable for dolus and culpa but not for casus.[138] This was in accordance with the general emphasis of the pandectists on fault. § 670 BGB appears to proceed from the same premise, for it grants the mandatary a claim only for *outlays* incurred in the course of carrying out the mandate, not for damages suffered.[139] This means that damages may be claimed only according to general principles, that is, if there was fault on the part of the debtor.

However, over the centuries many writers took the opposite view. "Nec hic § de curialitate debet servari" says, for instance, the gloss apropos Paul. D. 17, 1, 26, 6,[140] which is very similar to what, some centuries later, Groenewegen stated the Roman-Dutch law to be.[141] Voet, after pointing out that Roman law required fault on the part of the mandator and did not otherwise allow the mandatarius to recover

---

[136] Paul. D. 46, 1, 67. Sedes materiae has traditionally been taken to be Paul. D. 17, 1, 26, 6: "Non omnia quae impensurus non fuit mandatori imputabit, veluti quod spoliatus sit a latronibus aut naufragio res amiserit vel languore suo suorumque apprehensus quaedam erogaverit: nam haec magis casibus quam mandato imputari oportet." For a discussion, see Peter Stein, "Julian and liability for loss suffered in the execution of a contract in Roman law", 1956 *Butterworths South African LR* 67 sq.; Watson, *Mandate*, pp. 157 sqq.; Heinrich Honsell, "Die Risikohaftung des Geschäftsherrn", in: *De iustitia et iure, Festgabe für Ulrich von Lübtow* (1980), pp. 488 sqq.

[137] Ulp. D. 50, 17, 23 in fine.

[138] Cf. Hasse, *Culpa*, p. 403; Arndts, *Pandekten*, § 293; Baron, *Pandekten*, § 306 II 2; Dernburg, Pandekten, vol. II, § 116, 2 b; but cf. e.g. Donellus, *Commentarii de Jure Civili*, Lib. XIII, Cap. XII, XV; Glück, vol. 15, pp. 307 sqq.

[139] But see the comment in "Motive", in: *Mugdan*, vol. II, p. 302; "Protokolle", in: *Mugdan*, vol. II, pp. 951 sqq.

[140] Gl. Mandato ad D. 17, 1, 26, 6; contra e.g. Bartolus, *Commentaria*, ad lib. XVI Digest.: "Vult glossa dicere, quod iste § de aequitate non debet servari: quia aequitas rigori praefertur . . . quod non est verum hic: cum rigor iuris huius § sit scriptus, et ideo tenendus, licet duritiam contineat: non obstante aequitate, quia non est scripta."

[141] *Tractatus de legibus abrogatis*, Lib. XVII, Tit. I, l. 26, 6.

his loss, simply said: "Sed hodie mandatario ex aequitate hic quoque succurendum putant."[142] But did this mean that the mandator bore the full risk, including any kind of casus fortuitus? The most interesting and, in the long run, influential criterion for limiting the mandatarius' liability appears to have had its origin in the *Rationalia ad Pandectas* of Antonius Faber, where he grants the claim only for those damages which the mandatarius suffered ex causa mandati.[143] The natural lawyers elaborated this idea more fully and distinguished between loss sustained ex causa mandati or merely ex occasione mandati.

> "Idem quoque dicendum videtur", wrote Pufendorf,[144] "de damno in quo quis ex causa rei mandatae incidit: non tamen de illo, in quo tantum ex occasione eiusdem prolapsus est. adeoque illa dumtaxat damna erunt a mandante sarcienda, quae proprie ex ipsa negotio mandato profluxere: non autem, quae velut transversim intercurrerunt, dum negotium istud obitur."

This distinction found its way into the ABGB[145] and also, probably via Pothier,[146] into the code civil (although, strangely, the wrong way round).[147] We also find it in modern German law, where the narrow confines of § 670 BGB were soon left behind by courts and legal writers.[148] The principle of a liability (not based on fault) for risks arising from and connected with activities undertaken by another person in the debtor's interest, is widely acknowledged today.[149] "Ex occasione mandati" therefore refers to what one could call the general risks of life, which must, as usual, be borne by the gestor himself. He can therefore not claim damages for an accident which is not specifically related to the gestio, even though it may be causally linked to it.

---

[142] *Commentarius ad Pandectas*, Lib. XVII, Tit. I, XIII.

[143] Lib. XVII, Tit. I, 26, 6 (vol. IV, Genevae, 1626).

[144] *De jure naturae et gentium*, Lib. V, Cap. IV, § 4.

[145] § 1014 ABGB. Cf. also Windscheid/Kipp, § 410, 2.

[146] *Traité du contrat de mandat*, nn. 74 sq.

[147] Art. 2000 code civil provides for the recovery of damages which arose *à l'occasion de la gestion*. Perhaps, this is not based on a mistaken analysis of Pothier, but on Domat, *Les loix civiles*, Liv. I, Tit. XV, Sec. II, VI. Cf. also Coing, p. 463.

[148] Cf. e.g. Honsell, *Festgabe von Lübtow*, pp. 495 sqq.

[149] Claus-Wilhelm Canaris, "Risikohaftung bei schadensgeneigter Tätigkeit in fremdem Interesse", 1966 *Recht der Arbeit* 41 sqq.; Klaus Genius, "Risikohaftung des Geschäftsherrn", (1973) 173 *Archiv für die civilistische Praxis* 481 sqq.

CHAPTER 14

Negotiorum gestio

1. Negotiorum gestio and mandatum

(a) Similarities

Negotiorum gestio, in the German Civil Code, follows immediately upon mandate.[1] Both institutions, indeed, have much in common.[2] In both cases one person (the mandatarius/the gestor) manages somebody else's (the mandator's/principal's) affairs. As in mandate, the scope of matters which the gestor can take care of for the principal is very broad; they may be of a factual or of a legal nature.[3] As in mandate, the (negotiorum) gestor must, however, not have acted solely in his own interest. The negotium has to be alienum, or alterius; it may be alienum et suum, but it may not be suum tantum.[4] Like mandate, negotiorum gestio gives rise to an imperfectly bilateral relationship. There is, first of all, an actio directa, by means of which the principal may sue the gestor for damages in case of mismanagement and for the restoration of whatever the latter might have acquired in the course of executing the gestio.[5] The gestor, on the other hand, may avail himself of the actio negotiorum gestorum contraria, if and when he has incurred any expenses or suffered damages.[6] So close are the parallels between the mutual claims of gestor/principal and mandatarius/mandator that the BGB, in fact, refers the reader in its title dealing with negotiorum gestio to what has been laid down with regard to mandatum.[7] As a consequence, the same problems have to be solved in both areas, particularly those arising from the narrow formulation of § 670 BGB.

(b) Difference

The main difference between mandatum and negotiorum gestio is that

---

[1] Book II, Section VII, Title X: Mandate; Title XI: Negotiorum gestio.

[2] Cf. generally on the relationship between negotiorum gestio with contract and mandate S.J. Stoljar, "Negotiorum gestio", in: *International Encyclopedia of Comparative Law*, vol. X, 17 (1984), nn. 6 sqq.

[3] For Roman law cf. Seiler, *Negotiorum gestio*, pp. 10 sqq.; for modern German law: Hans Hermann Seiler, in: *Münchener Kommentar zum BGB*, vol. III, 2 (2nd ed., 1986), § 677, n. 2; for Roman-Dutch law: D.H. van Zyl, *Negotiorum gestio in South African Law* (1985) pp. 11 sqq.

[4] For Roman law cf. Seiler, *Negotiorum gestio*, pp. 16 sqq.; for modern German law: Seiler, in: *Münchener Kommentar*, op. cit., note 3, § 677, nn. 3 sqq.

[5] For Roman law, see Kaser, *RPr* I, pp. 589; for modern German law: Christian Wollschläger, *Die Geschäftsführung ohne Auftrag* (1976), pp. 262 sqq. and § 681 BGB; for Roman-Dutch and South African law: Van Zyl, *Negotiorum gestio*, pp. 49 sqq.; generally: Stoljar, op. cit., note 2, nn. 258 sqq.

[6] For Roman law: Kaser, *RPr* I, p. 590; for modern German law cf. § 683 BGB and Seiler, in: *Münchener Kommentar*, op. cit., note 3, § 683, nn. 1 sqq.; for Roman-Dutch and South African law: Van Zyl, *Negotiorum gestio*, pp. 67 sqq.; generally: Stoljar, op. cit., nn. 66 sqq.

[7] Cf. § 681 referring to §§ 666–668 and § 683 referring to § 670 BGB.

the one is a contract, the other an obligational relationship ex lege. The right–duty connection between gestor and principal, in other words, is not based on any kind of agreement but arises from the mere fact of the negotiorum (alterius) gestio.[8] As in the case of enrichment, we are dealing here with autonomous obligations which are neither contractual nor delictual, but fall somewhere in between these main categories.[9] Justinian therefore accommodated both of them in a special title dealing with obligationes quasi ex contractu;[10] *quasi* ex *contractu*, because even though they are not contractual, they derive from a lawful activity and give rise to claims which are more closely related to contract than delict. We have already seen that later centuries did not always look with much kindness on the quasi-contracts as a separate systematic entity, and that there was a tendency to amalgamate them with the contractual obligations.[11] Thus, one had to find (or construe) a consensual element, a consensus fictivus or praesumptus. In the case of negotiorum gestio the animus negotia aliena gerendi of the gestor (of which we find traces in the Roman sources) was emphasized as a special and indispensable requirement,[12] and likewise the actual or presumed will of the principal that the gestor should act for him. Thus, negotiorum gestio could conveniently be based on the corresponding intentions of the two parties. This (mis-)conception, incidentally, still

[8] May the dominus negotii, by way of ratification (ratihabitio), transform what was originally (or might have been) negotiorum gestio into a contract of mandatum? In post-classical and Justinianic times, it was evidently thought that he could. Cf., most clearly, Ulp. D. 46, 3, 12, 4 (". . . rati enim habitio mandato comparatur"); Ulp. D. 50, 17, 60: "Semper qui non prohibet pro se intervenire, mandare creditur. sed et si quis ratum habuerit quod gestum est, obstringitur mandati actione" (both texts itp.). Ratihabitio, in other words, provides the basis for a (fictitious) consent. In classical Roman law, however, ratihabitio was not of much significance. More particularly, for the granting of the actio negotiorum gestorum contraria it did not matter whether the principal had subsequently approved the transaction; what mattered was whether the gestio had been "utiliter". Ratihabitio could, however, limit the gestor's liability where negotium had been "male gestum" (Pomp./Scaev. D. 3, 5, 8); in certain other instances it could have the effect of bringing into existence a relationship of negotiorum gestio (esp.: collection of debts owing to the principal; C. 2, 18, 9: "Si pecuniam a debitore tuo Iulianus exegit eamque solutionem ratam habuisti, habes adversus eum negotiorum gestorum actionem" (Ant.)), but never of mandatum (for all details, see Seiler, *Negotiorum Gestio*, pp. 61 sqq.). Confusion in the sources, as usual, created confusion amongst the writers of the ius commune. Some related ratihabitio to mandatum, others to negotiorum gestio, and there were even those who abandoned the mutual exclusivity of both these institutions and maintained elective concurrence of the actions arising from mandatum and negotiorum gestio as a consequence of ratihabitio. Cf. Glück, vol. 5, pp. 333 sqq.; Van Zyl, *Negotiorum gestio*, pp. 20 sq.

[9] On *Negotiorum gestio* and quasi-contract generally, see Stoljar, op. cit., note 2, nn. 11 sqq.

[10] *Inst.* III, 27.

[11] Cf. supra, pp. 20 sq. The same tendency is already apparent in post-classical, Byzantine law. Thus, the establishment of a duty, on the part of the principal, to ratify the actions of the gestor is an attempt to assimilate negotiorum gestio and contract. Cf. also Ulp. D. 50, 17, 60 (first sentence).

[12] Cf., for example, Ruhstrat, "Beiträge zur Lehre von der Negotiorum Gestio", (1849) 32 *Archiv für die civilistische Praxis* 184 sqq.

lingers on in modern German doctrine, which tends to assign undue importance to these subjective elements.[13]

2. The value basis of negotiorum gestio

The institution of negotiorum gestio is a highly original creation of classical Roman[14] law which has been handed down to us, via Justinian[15] and the ius commune, without major changes. The BGB in particular follows Roman law very closely in this respect.[16] Unlike, for instance, the contracts of sale or loan, negotiorum gestio cannot be said to form a necessary part of every developed legal culture. According to Grotius,[17] it does not find a basis in natural law, and it is therefore not surprising that two of the main codifications of the age of the law of reason, the Prussian and the Austrian codes, contain a prohibition, in principle, of negotiorum alterius gestio.[18] English law, to mention another example, does not possess a doctrine of negotiorum gestio either—a highly characteristic trait, for it reflects the traditional individualism and the reserved mentality of the English people.[19] Management of another's affairs is regarded, first and foremost, as an undue curtailment of that other person's autonomy, and the unsolicited gestor is often somewhat contemptuously referred to as an officious meddler.[20] "Culpa est immiscere se rei ad se non pertinenti": this statement, attributed to Pomponius,[21] would neatly sum up such an attitude. For the Romans, however, it was only half the truth. Liberty was one of the basic principles inspiring the Roman jurists,[22] and thus their private law showed many essentially individualistic traits. But just as in the Roman conception of liberty certain limitations were inherent,[23] so individualism never reigned supreme.[24] Fides, amicitia,

---

[13] Cf. the discussion in Wollschläger, op. cit., note 5, pp. 44 sqq. Thus, for instance, the requirement that the gestor must have acted in accordance with the interest and the actual or presumptive wishes of the principal, which § 683 BGB lays down for the actio negotiorum gestorum contraria, has very often been promoted to a general requirement for negotiorum gestio. Critical (apart from Wollschläger) also, for example, Seiler, in: *Münchener Kommentar*, op. cit., note 3, § 677, n. 43.

[14] This is also emphasized, for instance, by Schulz, *CRL*, p. 624; Stoljar, op. cit., note 2, nn. 1 sqq., 24 sqq.

[15] Seiler, *Negotiorum gestio*, pp. 332 sqq.; Kaser, *RPr* II, pp. 417 sq.

[16] As to Roman-Dutch and South Africa law, cf. Van Zyl, *Negotiorum gestio*, p. 8 (". . .except to a very limited extent, the South African law of negotiorum gestio is the same as that recognized by the law of Justinian"). On negotiorum gestio in Louisiana, see J.M. Solis, "Management of the Affairs of Another", (1961–62) 36 *Tulane LR* 108 sqq.

[17] *De jure belli ac pacis*, Lib. II, Cap. X, 9.

[18] § 228 I 13 PrALR; § 1035 ABGB. French law, on the other hand, recognizes the negotiorum gestio; cf. artt. 1372 sqq. code civil and Stoljar, op. cit., note 2, nn. 31 sqq.

[19] Cf. e.g. John P. Dawson, *Unjust Enrichment* (1951), pp. 139 sqq.; Stoljar, op. cit., note 2, n. 17.

[20] John P. Dawson, "Negotiorum gestio: The Altruistic Intermeddler", (1961) 74 *Harvard LR* 817.

[21] D. 50, 17, 36. [22] Schulz, *Principles*, pp. 140 sqq. [23] Schulz, *Principles*, p. 140.

[24] Schulz, *Principles*, p. 238 even maintains that " 'Roman individualism' is nothing but a legend".

pietas, humanitas and officium have repeatedly been referred to: they created a value system and a specific kind of social ethics determining the behaviour of the (upper-class) Roman citizen.[25] Individualism was not his social ideal; on the contrary: he felt obliged to help his friends by lending them money, standing surety or simply giving advice. All this was part of the officium amici,[26] and it could matter little whether such help had been specifically solicited or not. For the Romans, these standards did not pertain to the lofty but non-committal heights of philosophical ideals; and their lawyers, practical and matter-of-fact, did what was necessary to provide favourable conditions for a behaviour along the accepted ethical lines and to protect the position of both parties. Mandatum can be seen in this light, but even more so negotiorum gestio.

> "It emanated from Roman humanitas. The underlying idea was that a man should help his fellow men in case of emergency. The Romans carried through this idea with their usual common sense without confusing morality and law. Nobody is legally bound to care for the affairs of another; but the law should favour and facilitate such altruistic action by granting the gestor the right to claim reimbursement of his expenses, which, of course, entails a liability of the gestor [himself]. The institution of negotiorum gestio was a happy invention, quite in the bold and original style of the republican jurisprudence."[27]

It is a prime example of the sober sense of realism with which the Roman lawyers were able to attune law and social ethics to each other and, more specifically, to balance the individualistic interest in not having one's own affairs interfered with and the interests of society in encouraging ethically desirable activities on behalf of others.

3. The history of negotiorum gestio in Roman law

Where, then, lie the roots of the Roman negotiorum gestio? Ulpian in his commentary ad edictum gives the following motivation for the edict de negotiis gestis:

> "Hoc edictum necessarium est, quoniam magna utilitas absentium versatur, ne indefensi rerum possessionem aut venditionem patiantur vel pignoris distractionem vel poenae committendae actionem, vel iniuria rem suam amittant."[28]

This laudatio edicti focuses on one specific type of situation: emergency actions in the interest of an absent friend, designed to avert some imminent danger to his property or to his reputation. It seems to have

---

[25] Cf. e.g. Schulz, *Principles*, pp. 189 sqq., 223 sqq.; Wieacker, *Vom römischen Recht*, pp. 14 sqq.; more specifically for negotiorum gestio: Theo Mayer-Maly, "Probleme der negotiorum gestio", (1969) 86 *ZSS* 420 sqq.

[26] Cf. supra, e.g. pp. 115, 119, 131.

[27] Schulz, *CRL*, p. 624.

[28] Ulp. D. 3, 5, 1.

been an old and important field of application for negotiorum gestio;[29] representation in litem features particularly prominently among the cases contained in the Digest, the gestor usually acting as defensor for the absent defendant.[30] Other groups of cases, too, tie in with the rationale given by Ulpianus: those, for instance, where the gestor discharges the principal's obligation,[31] or where he stands surety on his behalf.[32] But then we also see various gestores collecting debts,[33] purchasing farms or selling slaves for somebody else:[34] situations where it would hardly be appropriate to talk of an emergency and where, strictly speaking, a necessity to take care of the principal's affairs cannot normally have existed. Ulpianus D. 3, 5, 1 therefore does not seem to tell us the full story. And, indeed, it is widely accepted today that negotiorum gestio has two further roots: procuratio omnium rerum and cura furiosi.[35] It has been mentioned already that the procurator in pre-classical times did not act under a contract of mandatum. Nor was the curator in the position of a (private) mandatarius, since he was either called upon to act by law or appointed by the magistrate. The actio mandati, therefore, not being applicable to their case, both curator and procurator lacked a right of recourse, and could not be held accountable by their charges either. To cover these situations, two formulae became part of the praetorian edict, differing from each other as to who was plaintiff and defendant, but otherwise identical.[36] Their scope of application was defined by the broad and abstract requirement of negotium alterius gestio, and they contained the "ex bona fide" clause. Historically, however, these bonae fidei iudicia of civilian nature had been preceded by two praetorian claims with formulae in factum conceptae.[37] They seem to have been less broadly framed; in particular,

---

[29] Moritz Wlassak, *Zur Geschichte der negotiorum gestio* (1879), pp. 39 sqq.; Seiler, *Negotiorum gestio*, pp. 2 sq., 11 sq., 38 sq.; 47 sq.

[30] Iul. D. 5, 1, 74, 2; Pap. D. 3, 5, 30, 2; Pap. D. 3, 5, 30, 7; Paul. D. 3, 5, 40 et al. The gestor was thus avoiding missio in bona and, as its consequence, infamia.

[31] Iav./Lab. D. 3, 5, 42; Ulp. D. 3, 5, 5, 3; C. 2, 18, 12 (Alex.) et al.

[32] Cf. e.g. Afr. D. 3, 5, 45 pr. (in fine) and 1; Pap. D. 30, 5, 30 pr. and 31 pr.

[33] Cf. e.g. Iul. D. 46, 3, 34, 4; Paul. D. 3, 5, 22; Ulp. D. 3, 5, 5, 4.

[34] Cf. e.g. Proc./Pomp. D. 3, 5, 10; Afr. D. 3, 5, 45 pr.

[35] Seiler, *Negotiorum gestio*, e.g. pp. 314 sqq.; Kaser, *RPr* I, p. 587. On procuratio and negotiorum gestio specifically, see Watson, *Obligations*, pp. 193 sqq.; Seiler, *Negotiorum gestio*, pp. 104 sqq.

[36] Cf. Lenel, *EP*, p. 105.

[37] The early history of negotiorum gestio and, particularly, of the formulae is largely a matter of conjecture. Much of what is simply stated in the text has been disputed. Thus, for instance, according to Magdelain, *Consensualisme*, pp. 181 sqq., there was only the iudicium ex iure civili; the formulae in factum conceptae never existed. Hans Kreller, "Das Edikt de negotiis gestis in der Geschichte der Geschäftsbesorgung", in: *Festschrift Paul Koschaker*, vol. II (1939), p. 207 sqq. and Vicenzo Arangio-Ruiz, *Il mandato in diritto romano* (1949), pp. 29 sqq. maintain that the civilian iudicium was older than the praetorian one. Josef Partsch, *Studien zur negotiorum gestio* (1913), pp. 34 sqq. has argued that the iudicia based on negotiorum gestio were narrowly defined (negotia absentis; sine mandatu); in all other cases actiones utiles were granted. Against these and other hypotheses, see Seiler, *Negotiorum gestio*, pp. 316 sqq.

they probably required management of negotia absentis.[38] It is likely that these iudicia had been designed by the praetors to accommodate the above-mentioned cases of emergency assistance between friends, especially by way of defensio rei alterius (absentis) in litem.[39] We are not certain whether they continued to exist, side by side with the more modern bonae fidei iudicium; but if they did,[40] they cannot have been of much practical importance any longer and their requirements were probably assimilated with those of the bonae fidei actions.[41] The latter, in any event, dominated the scene.

4. The range of application of negotiorum gestio

"Quod A^s A^s negotia N^i N^i gessit": this demonstratio described the scope of negotiorum gestio in very abstract terms. It not only covered specific types of gestiones, but could accommodate a whole lot of entirely heterogeneous situations. That made negotiorum gestio a very useful tool to provide for restitution where this was deemed equitable, but it also gave it a somewhat un-concrete and un-descriptive character. Negotiorum gestio is (and has remained) "lawyer's law", a concept which does not really inspire the layman's imagination.[42] Of course, attempts have not been wanting to analyse negotiorum gestio, less abstractly, in terms of concrete phenomena of social life. Most influential, in modern times, has been Joseph Kohler's endeavour to turn the institution into a legal paradigm of human help.[43] Since then, German writers have been stressing the altruistic nature of negotiorum gestio and have based their discussion on cases characterized by the spontaneous benevolence of the gestor. They focus on the brave man hurrying to extinguish a fire in his absent neighbour's flat or on the philanthropist who takes home a crying child, and they rarely forget to mention the philatelist who buys a rare stamp for a friend in the belief that the latter has been wanting it for a long time.[44] But these are textbook examples, not the standard cases that come before the courts. Those, in turn, are largely characterized by an inextricable intertwining of the principal's and the gestor's own interest.[45] Thus, for instance, it often happens that the gestor is not only managing somebody else's affairs but also (and at the same time) discharging a duty imposed on

---

[38] Seiler, *Negotiorum gestio*, pp. 47 sqq.; 320 sq.

[39] Cf. Ulp. D. 3, 5, 3 pr. (containing, possibly, originally the word "absentis" in the place of "alterius").

[40] Owing to their conservatism?: Mayer-Maly, (1969) 86 *ZSS* 419.

[41] Seiler, *Negotiorum gestio*, pp. 48 sqq., 323 sqq.; Kaser, *RPr* I, p. 589.

[42] See, too, Seiler, *Negotiorum gestio*, pp. 3 sq.

[43] "Die Menschenhülfe im Privatrecht", (1887) 25 *JhJb* 42 sqq. Cf. also Ernst Rabel, "Ausbau oder Verwischung des Systems? Zwei praktische Fragen", (1919–20) 10 *RheinZ* 94 sqq.

[44] For these and further examples, see Wollschläger, op. cit., note 5, pp. 24 sq.

[45] For details Wollschläger, op. cit., note 5, pp. 28 sqq.

him;[46] and it is interesting to see the difficulties of a modern doctrine, based on the theory of human help, in dealing with these types of situations.[47] This shows that genuine altruism is both an unrealistic and an unhandy criterion to determine the scope of application of negotiorum gestio.[48] The Roman lawyers, for instance, were too practical to use it as such. For even though fides and the duties of friendship featured prominently within the value background of this institution,[49] neither altruism nor amicitia—nor even voluntariness of the gestor's activity ("sponte")—was required before an action could be granted. The actio negotiorum gestorum could be brought, according to Ulpian, against someone who "aliqua necessitate urguente vel necessitatis suspicione gessit".[50] This was the case, for example, where somebody had taken care of another person's affairs in the (mistaken) belief that he had been requested to do so.[51] Even the gestor who defends his absent friend in court can in fact be said to have acted not so much "sponte" but in compliance with his officium amicitiae. Furthermore, a certain type of amicitia, namely the amicitia paterna or pietas, could even have the opposite effect: for the actio negotiorum gestorum contraria was taken to be excluded, if the gestor had incurred expenses in the form of maintenance payments in favour of close relatives.[52]

All in all, one can therefore say that negotiorum gestio in classical law covered a wide variety of different situations. It began indeed where mandate ended.[53] But it was not only excluded by the contractual relationship of mandatum; it was subsidiary in a broader sense.[54]

---

[46] In modern German law, this is true even in many rescue cases, for according to § 323 c StGB, everybody is under a duty to render aid in an accident or common danger or emergency situation where aid is needed and may be expected under the circumstances.

[47] So called *"Auch-gestion"*: Seiler, in: *Münchener Kommentar*, op. cit., note 3, § 677, nn. 9, 15; Roland Wittmann, *Begriff und Funktionen der Geschäftsführung ohne Auftrag* (1981), pp. 10 sqq.; Werner Schubert, "Der Tatbestand der Geschäftsführung ohne Auftrag", (1978) 178 *Archiv für die civilistische Praxis* 425 sqq., 439 sqq.; Karl-Heinz Gursky, "Der Tatbestand der Geschäftsführung ohne Auftrag", (1985) 185 *Archiv für die civilistische Praxis* 13 sqq.

[48] For further criticism of the theory of human help cf. Wollschläger, op. cit., note 5, pp. 28 sqq., 38 sqq.; Stoljar, op. cit., note 2, nn. 19 sqq.; Seiler, in: *Münchener Kommentar*, op. cit., note 3, Vor § 677, n. 1; § 677, n. 12.

[49] Seiler, *Negotiorum gestio*, pp. 38 sqq.

[50] Ulp. D. 3, 5, 3, 10. For all details, see Seiler, *Negotiorum gestio*, pp. 40 sqq.

[51] Ulp. D. 3, 5, 5 pr.

[52] Cf. e.g. Paul. D. 3, 5, 33; for details see Ernst Rabel, "Negotium alienum und animus", in: *Studi in onore di Pietro Bonfante*, vol. IV (1930), pp. 296 sqq.; Seiler, *Negotiorum gestio*, pp. 42 sqq. The gestor, under these circumstances, was presumed not to have acted with the intention of recovering his expenses. On the animus recipiendi (as opposed to the animus donandi) as a requirement for the actio negotiorum gestorum contraria, see Glück, vol. 5, pp. 345 sqq., 383 sq.; Windscheid/Kipp, § 430, 2; Van Zyl, *Negotiorum gestio*, pp. 33, 37 sqq.; but see also Fritz Pringsheim, "Animus donandi", (1921) 42 *ZSS* 310 sqq. Today cf. § 685 BGB: "The manager does not have any claim if he did not have the intention to demand compensation from the principal. If parents or grandparents furnish maintenance to their descendants, or the latter to the former, it is to be presumed, in case of doubt, that there is no intention to demand compensation from the recipient."

[53] Stoljar, op. cit., note 2, nn. 6 sqq.

[54] Mayer-Maly, (1969) 86 *ZSS* 418.

Tutela, for instance, concerned the management of another's affairs and so did negotiorum gestorum pro tutore. Yet, the iudicia negotiorum gestorum were not applicable, for the Roman lawyers had developed special remedies to deal with these relationships.[55]

5. Requirements of the actio negotiorum gestorum

(a) "Taking care" of a "negotium" "for another"

We now have to turn our attention to further details relating to the actiones negotiorum gestorum directa and contraria. Basically, there had to be a gestio and a negotium which was being taken care of. The concept of negotium was understood in a most liberal sense and comprised factual and legal acts, but predominantly the latter. Most importantly, however, it had to be the principal's affair, negotium alterius. This meant, as we have already seen, that it could not be negotium suum of the gestor; a transaction in the nature of a negotium commune, however, did not exclude negotiorum gestio.[56] Was it necessary, apart from that, for the gestor to have acted with the intention of managing somebody else's affair? The question of how to determine when the gestor acted "for another" (these the words of the German Code)[57] is not even clear in modern law. Of the two most recent monographs on the topic the one proceeds from an objective,[58] the other one from a subjective point of view.[59] What matters, according to Wollschläger, is to whom the law attributes the benefits and expenses of this particular type of activity, into whose "sphere of attribution" they fall. Wittmann, on the other hand, insists on the gestor's intention as the relevant criterion.[60] Both these approaches have also been read into the Roman sources. Whereas Josef Partsch[61] argued that classical Roman law stuck to an objective concept of negotiorum gestio and that the Byzantine lawyers were the first to introduce the requirement of an animus negotia aliena gerendi on the part of the gestor, Salvatore Riccobono has tried to show that it was

[55] For a detailed discussion on tutela/protutela and negotiorum gestio, see Seiler, *Negotiorum gestio*, pp. 145 sqq., 208 sqq.

[56] Seiler, *Negotiorum gestio*, pp. 16 sqq.

[57] § 677 BGB.

[58] Wollschläger, op. cit., note 5, pp. 52 sqq.

[59] Wittmann, op. cit., note 47, pp. 18 sqq.

[60] This is the view that dominated during the centuries of the ius commune. Intention to act as a negotiorum gestor has been an essential requirement from the days of the glossators, via the Roman-Dutch authors down to modern South African law: Van Zyl, *Negotiorum gestio*, pp. 34 sqq.; cf. further Wittmann, op. cit., note 47, pp. 48 sqq. Many of the pandectists, however, do not mention the animus negotia aliena gerendi among the requirements of negotiorum gestio; cf. Glück, vol. 5, p. 345; Vangerow, *Pandekten*, § 664; Arndts, *Pandekten*, §§ 297 sq.; Dernburg, *Pandekten*, vol. II, § 122.

[61] *Aus nachgelassenen und kleineren verstreuten Schriften* (1931), pp. 88 sqq.

just the other way round: the gestor's intention was the basis of classical negotiorum gestio, and it was Justinian who abandoned it.[62]

(b) Animus negotia aliena gerendi?

The truth seems to lie somewhere in between these two options.[63] The animus negotia aliena gerendi does not appear to have been isolated and conceptualized as a specific requirement by the classical lawyers. That he took care, objectively, of a matter pertaining to another person and the gestor's knowledge of this fact: these two elements were often not conceptually separated. Nevertheless, an awareness that he was not (solely) managing his own affairs was usually present, albeit occasionally in a somewhat attenuated form. Thus, the liber homo bona fide serviens,[64] acting for his putative dominus, was both entitled and exposed to the actio negotiorum gestorum, even though he had been unaware of his position as a negotiorum gestor.[65] The same applied, for instance, where the gestor had erred about the person of the principal[66] or where he believed to be entitled to act on account of a mandate.[67] But in the Digest we also find at least one case where the subjective element was completely dispensed with:

> "Si rem, quam servus venditus subripuisset a me venditore, emptor vendiderit eaque in rerum natura esse desierit, de pretio negotiorum gestorum actio mihi danda sit. . . ."[68]

The purchaser (A) of a slave has sold, in good faith, an object, which the slave had stolen from the vendor (B). The object no longer exists; B therefore claims the price from A. According to Africanus, he can avail himself of the actio negotiorum gestorum. The fact that A believed he was transacting negotium suum does not matter, for objectively he managed another's affair. It is B's business to sell his (own) things. Their pecuniary value therefore is "assigned" (objectively) to B, the owner, not to the gestor, A. Thus it is perhaps not that wrong, after all, if a distinction is often drawn in modern law between negotia which are objectively somebody else's and those which are

[62] Salvatore Riccobono, *Scritti di diritto romano*, vol. II (1964), pp. 1 sqq., 73 sqq.

[63] Ernst Rabel, *Studi Bonfante*, vol. IV, pp. 279 sqq.; Seiler, *Negotiorum gestio*, pp. 22 sqq.; Kaser, *RPr* I, p. 588; idem, *RPr* II, p. 418; Wittmann, op. cit., note 47, pp. 39 sqq.; but see also Mayer-Maly, (1969) 86 *ZSS* 426 sqq; Honsell/Mayer-Maly/Selb, p. 349.

[64] "A free man who does not know his status as a free man and serves in good faith as another's slave": Berger, *ED*, p. 562.

[65] Lab./Paul. D. 3, 5, 18, 2; Ulp. D. 3, 5, 5, 7; Paul. D. 3, 5, 35; Seiler, *Negotiorum gestio*, pp. 95 sqq.

[66] Ulp. D. 3, 5, 5, 1.

[67] Ulp. D. 3, 5, 5 pr.

[68] Afr. D. 3, 5, 48. The correct interpretation of this text (interpolated?) is a controversial matter. Cf., most recently, Seiler, *Negotiorum gestio*, pp. 26 sq.; Mayer-Maly (1969) 86 *ZSS* 417; D.H. van Zyl, *Die Saakwaarnemingsaksie as Verrykingsaksie in die Suid-Afrikaanse Reg* (unpublished Dr. iur. thesis, Leiden, 1970), pp. 29 sqq.; Wollschläger, op. cit., note 5, pp. 43 sq.

objectively neutral and are "alterius" only on account of the intention of the gestor.[69]

(c) Utilitas gestionis

It has been emphasized already that neither the voluntariness of the action on the part of the gestor nor purely altruistic motive or amicitia nor absence of the principal was an essential or a fundamental condition for the actiones negotiorum gestorum to arise.[70] For the gestor's right of action against the principal (i.e. the so-called actio contraria) there was, however, one further requirement, which is referred to, in the sources, as utilitas gestionis: ". . . is enim negotiorum gestorum, inquit [Celsus], habet actionem, qui utiliter negotia gessit."[71] We have seen that the recognition of the institution of negotiorum gestio was one of the anti-individualistic traits of Roman law; it entailed a certain curtailment of the principal's autonomy. The utilitas requirement was the main safeguard designed to limit the extent of such curtailment. Some jurists took a very narrow view and were prepared to accept only necessary gestiones; Celsus/Ulpianus even define the useful in terms of what is necessary: ". . . non autem utiliter negotia gerit, qui rem non necessariam vel quae oneratura est patrem familias adgreditur."[72] Others, however, adopted a more liberal approach and were prepared to grant the claim on the basis of gestiones which had not been strictly necessary.[73] It was clear, however, that expenses incurred voluptatis causa (e.g. the ampla aedificia in Mod. D. 3, 5, 26 pr.) could not be recovered. Generally speaking, the Roman lawyers decided the question of utiliter gestum in a casuistic fashion, not according to abstract definitions.[74] That could not, of course, satisfy the more conceptually minded scholars of later centuries such as the pandectists, who engaged in a very scholarly and impractical, yet almost relentless debate on the topic. A monograph of 1878 provides an overview of the thirteen (!) most important doctrines.[75]

As in the case of mandatum, it did not matter whether the endeavours of the gestor were ultimately crowned with success: ". . . sufficit, si utiliter gessit, etsi effectum non habuit negotium." Example:

---

[69] Cf. e.g. Seiler, in: *Münchener Kommentar*, op. cit., note 3, § 677, nn. 3 sqq., 18.

[70] On voluntariness and amicitia, see Seiler, *Negotiorum gestio*, pp. 38 sqq. On absentia, see Seiler, *Negotiorum gestio*, pp. 47 sqq.; Van Zyl, *Negotiorum gestio*, pp. 28 sqq., but also Grotius, *Inleiding*, III, XXVII, 1; Stoljar, op. cit., note 2, nn. 71 sqq.

[71] Ulp. D. 3, 5, 9, 1; for details, see Seiler, *Negotiorum gestio*, pp. 51 sqq.

[72] Cels./Ulp. D. 3, 5, 9, 1. On necessitas and utilitas, see Mayer-Maly, (1969) 86 *ZSS* 423.

[73] Cf., for example, Pomp. D. 3, 5, 10. According to Seiler, *Negotiorum gestio*, pp. 54 sqq., this difference reflects the dual origin of negotiorum gestio in procuratorship/curatorship on the one hand and cases of emergency help on the other; cf. also pp. 109 sq.

[74] Similarly modern South African case law; cf. Van Zyl, *Negotiorum gestio*, pp. 42 sqq.

[75] August Sturm, *Das negotium utiliter gestum* (1878), pp. 104 sqq. Cf. also Windscheid/Kipp, § 430, 2 b; for the notion of utility in modern law, cf. Stoljar, op. cit., note 2, nn. 83 sqq.

"[E]t ideo si insulam fulsit vel servum aegrum curavit, etiamsi insula exusta est vel servus obiit, aget negotiorum gestorum."[76]

The wishes of the principal, incidentally, do not as a rule seem to have played a role in the assessment of the utilitas of the gestor's action.[77] Only in the most extreme case, namely that of negotiorum gestio prohibente domino, was the claim held to be excluded by some of the classical authors.[78, 79]

6. The actio negotiorum gestorum contraria

(a) *Its importance today*

The gestor's claims against the principal (as, for instance, laid down in §§ 683, 670 BGB) are today the very core of negotiorum gestio.[80] In Germany, between 70 and 80 per cent of all decided cases[81] deal with what the Romans only conceived of as the actio contraria. For them, the actio directa of the principal against the gestor was the main claim, and in our sources it occurs as often as the actio contraria. This change of emphasis may be due to the fact that our courts have to deal with different types of situations than the Roman lawyers: in the age of aeroplanes and telecommunications, cases of emergency help for an absent friend, particularly the unsolicited intervention as a defensor in legal proceedings, no longer feature prominently in the law reports. Even in classical Roman law, the procurator no longer acted as a negotiorum gestor, and the activities of the modern equivalent to the Roman curator (furiosi, prodigi or minoris) were governed by a set of special rules and not by negotiorum gestio either. But it highlights, more particularly, that the application of the modern actio contraria presents a variety of tricky problems.[82] The controversies surrounding the "utiliter gestum" requirement[83] are one example. Two further difficulties in the application of § 683 BGB are, in a manner of speaking, home-made. First of all, the narrow formulation of § 670 (to which

[76] Ulp. D. 3, 5, 9, 1. The same applies in modern law; cf. e.g. Seiler, in: *Münchener Kommentar*, op. cit., note 3, § 683, n. 16. For the ius commune, see Van Zyl, *Negotiorum gestio*, p. 42.

[77] Cf. Ulp. D. 17, 1, 50 pr. and Seiler, *Negotiorum gestio*, pp. 59 sqq.; Van Zyl, *Negotiorum gestio*, pp. 43 sq. Differently, for example, §§ 677, 683 BGB.

[78] But even this was controversial: cf. C. 2, 18, 24 (Just.); for all details, see Seiler, *Negotiorum gestio*, pp. 86 sqq. Cf. also Glück, vol. 5, pp. 338 sqq.

[79] Ratihabitio in classical Roman law was, of course, not a requirement for the actio negotiorum gestorum either; cf. supra, p. 434, note 8; in post-classical times, however, a duty on the part of the principal to ratify the actions of the gestor (if they were utiliter) seems to have been recognized: cf. Bas. Lib. XVII, Tit. I, IX (*Heimbach*, vol. II, p. 210)..

[80] Stoljar, op. cit., note 2, nn. 66 sqq.

[81] Wollschläger, op. cit., note 5, p. 32.

[82] Furthermore, the law of delict today largely satisfies the demand for a liability of the gestor for damages, and it is therefore often not necessary to resort to the actio negotiorum gestorum directa.

[83] For modern German law cf. e.g. Seiler, in: *Münchener Kommentar*, op. cit., note 3, § 683, nn. 3 sqq.

§ 683 refers) has given rise to the same controversy that we have already encountered in our discussion of mandate:[84] may the gestor claim only his "outlays" or can he also sue for damages incurred? The prevailing opinion, again, accepts the latter, partly on the basis of an "analogous" application of §§ 683, 670 BGB, and partly on the basis of a general liability for risks, which are related to activities in other peoples' interest.[85] One of the most interesting cases where such "outlays" (in reality: damages) were successfully claimed for concerns the self-sacrifice of a motorcar driver: in order to avoid an impending collision with (for instance) a small child who suddenly runs onto the street, he throws around his wheel and steers his car into a tree. This case raises several problems. Are we dealing with a (negotiorum) "gestio"? After all, the driver's reaction was probably purely in the nature of a reflex. Did he "take care of some matter" for the child? After all, had he not avoided the accident, he might well himself have been exposed to liability: not only (in case of negligence) in delict, but particularly under the strict liability of § 7 of the German Road Traffic Act. And finally: can he recover his damages? The Federal Supreme Court has allowed such a claim—not, however, for the full damages, but limited to "reasonable" compensation.[86]

(b) Remuneration of services rendered?

Secondly, it is unclear under the BGB whether the gestor may ask to be remunerated for the services rendered in the principal's interest. Take the following example:[87] a wine-grower is unable, for some or other reason, to look after his vineyard. His neighbour kindly intervenes and takes charge of the cultivation. Had he employed some workers to do the job (and provided he had acted in accordance with the interest and the actual or presumptive wishes of the principal), he would have been able to recover his expenses, especially the wages that he had had to pay. If, however, he does the work himself, he will, according to the BGB, not be able to recover compensation for his services as such: the gestor may demand reimbursement of his outlays "as a mandatary",[88] and the mandatary, as we know, acts gratuitously. Equitable? From the point of view of the Roman lawyers, perhaps. For them, it was in any event not the "done" thing to ask for the payment for services rendered. But that perception has changed: so much so that as early as

---

[84] Cf. supra, pp. 431 sq.

[85] Cf. e.g. Wollschläger, op. cit., note 5, pp. 286 sqq.; Wittmann, op. cit., note 47, pp. 81 sqq.; Seiler, in: *Münchener Kommentar*, § 683, nn. 18 sqq.; Stoljar, op. cit., note 2, n. 69.

[86] BGHZ 38, 270 sqq. For details and criticism, see Wollschläger, op. cit., note 5, pp. 305 sqq.; Rainer Frank, "Die Selbstaufopferung des Kraftfahrers im Strassenverkehr", 1982 *Juristenzeitung* 737 sqq.

[87] Franz von Kübel, in: Werner Schubert (ed.), *Die Vorentwürfe der Redaktoren zum BGB, Recht der Schuldverhältnisse* 2 (1980), pp. 978 sq.

[88] § 683 BGB.

the 19th century, the courts usually allowed the gestor to recover such remuneration.[89] The fathers of the BGB had no intention, in fact, of changing this and of reverting to classical Roman law in this regard. They did so inadvertently and due to a drafting mistake.[90] Mandatum, according to the first draft, was not gratuitous either;[91] and when this was subsequently changed, one forgot to consider the consequences that this change was bound to have for norms such as § 683, which simply refer the reader to the provisions on mandatum. The interpretatio moderna has in the meantime corrected this mistake and has returned, by and large, to the position of the later ius commune.[92]

7. The standard of liability of the gestor

(a) The position of the gestor

The most interesting aspect concerning the principal's right of action (i.e. the actio negotiorum gestorum contraria)[93] is the standard of liability of the gestor. As in the case of mandatum, the question has been disputed: among both modern Romanists[94] and the authors of the ius commune.[95] For a generalizing statement we may turn again to Ulp. D. 50, 17, 23: "[D]olum et culpam [recipiunt] mandatum, commodatum, venditum, pignori acceptum, locatum, item dotis datio, tutelae, negotia gesta."[96] But we must be careful not to take this as a hard-and-fast rule.[97] Nor must we—ahistorically—read any kind of modern conceptual rigidity into the text. Negotiorum gestio was based on a iudicium bonae fidei; the judge therefore had to determine in each individual case whether the debtor had complied with the precepts of good faith or not. The wording of the formula did not oblige him to evaluate the defendant's behaviour in terms of predetermined standards of liability; on the contrary, it left him a wide discretion to make his decision dependent upon all the circumstances of the case.

---

[89] Wollschläger, op. cit., note 5, pp. 313 sq.

[90] Hans Hermann Seiler, "Über die Vergütung von Dienstleistungen des Geschäftsführers ohne Auftrag", in: *Festschrift für Heinz Hübner* (1984), pp. 239 sqq.

[91] Cf. supra, p. 420, note 53.

[92] Wollschläger, op. cit., note 5, pp. 311 sqq.; Seiler, in: *Münchener Kommentar*, op. cit., note 3, § 683, nn. 24 sq.

[93] In general, see Stoljar, op. cit., note 2, nn. 258 sqq.

[94] Cf. e.g. Schulz, *CRL*, p. 621 (liability for omnis culpa); Franz Haymann, "Die Haftung des negotiorum gestor wegen Verschuldens im klassischen und iustinianischen Recht", in: *Atti del congresso internazionale di diritto romano*, vol. II (1935), pp. 451 sqq. (liability for dolus only); Arangio-Ruiz, *Responsabilità*, pp. 205 sqq. (liability at first only for dolus, but towards the end of the classical period also for culpa). Cf. further Erich Sachers, "Die Haftung des auftragslosen Geschäftsführers", (1938) 4 *SDHI* 309 sqq. and, especially, Hans Hermann Seiler, "Zur Haftung des auftraglosen Geschäftsführers im römischen Recht", in: *Studien im römischen Recht* (1973), pp. 195 sqq.

[95] Cf. e.g. Glück, vol. 5, pp. 351 sqq.

[96] Cf. also C. 2, 18, 20, 1 (Diocl. et. Max.).

[97] For what follows, see Seiler, op. cit., note 94, pp. 196 sq.

There are, however, two observations of a more general nature that may be made. The utility principle,[98] in many instances, would militate against a particularly strict type of liability. The gestor acts in the interests (at least: also) of the principal, and he usually does so gratuitously, if not out of pure altruism. This should count in his favour when it comes to the question of attribution of loss. On the other hand, however, the institution of negotiorum gestio has a strongly fiduciary flavour.[99] The law allows the gestor to interfere with the affairs of another person, and this other person must at least enjoy some protection against careless meddling. The law should not normally condone or encourage indifference towards the property of others.[100] In the end, therefore, the extent of the gestor's liability reflects the peculiar position of the institution of negotiorum gestio between amicitia and libertas. A limitation of liability may be used to encourage altruism, an extension of liability can serve to prevent undesirable intrusions into private autonomy.

(b) Pomp. D. 3, 5, 10 and Ulp. D. 3, 5, 3, 9

Thus, we are not surprised to find the Roman lawyers advocating, as a general guideline, an average level of responsibility, but deviating from it quite freely.[101] The two most interesting and, in the long run, influential texts are Pomp. D. 3, 5, 10 and Ulp. D. 3, 5, 3, 9. In the one instance, we read of a gestor who engages in a novel type of enterprise, which the absent principal himself was not accustomed to concern himself with. In this type of situation, the gestor is liable not only for dolus and culpa but also for casus (fortuitus). Ulpianus, on the other hand, discusses the case of the benevolent friend who prevents, "affectione coactus", the impending sale of the (absent) principal's property. Under these circumstances, only a minimum of liability is reasonable: ". . . aequissimum esse dolum dumtaxat [agentem] te praestare."[102] Pomponius, incidentally, was reporting an opinion of Proculus, Ulpianus drew upon Labeo. Both decisions thus go back to the days of early classical law. They formulated criteria for a graduated approach towards the gestor's liability that have found their way, through the various periods of Roman law[103] and the ius

[98] Cf. supra, pp. 198 sq.

[99] Also emphasized by Stoljar, op. cit., note 2, n. 26.

[100] The same considerations apply in the case of tutela; the tutor's liability therefore came to be extended, not restricted, by the classical lawyers. The actio tutelae was closely related to the actio negotiorum gestorum and was also based on bona fides. Cf. Kaser, *RPr* I, pp. 365 sq.

[101] For details, see Seiler, op. cit., note 94, pp. 197 sqq.

[102] Ulp. D. 3, 5, 3, 9.

[103] On the position in Justinianic law cf. De Robertis, *Responsabilità*, pp. 501 sqq.; but see, as to *Inst.* III, 27, 1 ("exactissima diligentia"), Seiler, op. cit., note 94, pp. 200 sq.

commune,[104] into a modern codification such as the BGB. § 680 BGB[105] generalizes the rationale underlying Ulp. D. 3, 5, 3, 9 when it states that, where the gestio has as its object the averting of an imminent danger which threatens the principal, the gestor's liability is limited to dolus and culpa lata. According to § 678 BGB,[106] on the other hand, the gestor is responsible even for casus fortuitus, if the taking care of this specific negotium is opposed to the actual or presumptive wishes of the principal and if the gestor should have recognized that. This is the modern version of Pomp. D. 3, 5, 10; the extrapolation of a more subjectively accentuated criterion ("novum negotium, quod non sit solitus absens facere" as a gestio the undertaking of which is typically against the wishes of the principal) is in line with a similar shift of emphasis concerning the utiliter requirement of the actio negotiorum gestorum contraria.[107] As a general rule, however, the gestor's standard of liability lies in between these two extremes: it comprises dolus and (all types of) culpa.[108]

8. Negotiorum gestio in modern law

(a) Evaluation of negotiorum gestio in German law

Over the centuries, the claims arising from negotiorum gestio have been called upon to deal with many totally different types of activity in another person's interest: payment of somebody else's debt, the supply of support for those in need of it, the preservation of property belonging to another, the rescue of life and limb.[109] Some of the traditional areas of application have been absorbed by more specialized remedies that have come to be developed;[110] on the other hand, new types of situations have had to be accommodated.[111] The institution of negotiorum gestio has been flexible enough to cope with such changes and has retained its importance as one of the tools ensuring a fair and

---

[104] Cf. e.g. Glück, vol. 5, pp. 365 sqq.; Pothier, "Traité du quasi-contrat negotiorum gestio" (appendix to *Traité du contrat de mandat*), nn. 208 sqq.; Windscheid/Kipp, § 430, 1. See also Van Zyl, *Negotiorum gestio*, pp. 60 sqq.

[105] Cf. also §§ 234, 237 I 13 PrALR, art. 420 II OR.

[106] Cf. also § 249 I 13 PrALR, § 1040 ABGB, art. 420 III OR.

[107] Cf. § 683 BGB and supra.

[108] The authors of the ius commune debated whether the gestor was liable for culpa levis or also culpa levissima: cf. the discussion and references in Glück, vol. 5, pp. 352 sqq., and Hoffmann, *Fahrlässigkeit*, pp. 44 sq., 63, 95 sq., 143 sqq., 213. The BGB does not draw this distinction; it differentiates only between culpa, culpa lata and diligentia quam in suis (cf. §§ 276 sq.).

[109] Cf. the general types of situation as listed by Stoljar, op. cit., note 2, nn. 92 sqq.; further Wollschläger, op. cit., note 5, pp. 76 sqq.; Johann Georg Helm, "Geschäftsführung ohne Auftrag", in: *Gutachten und Vorschläge zur Überarbeitung des Schuldrechts*, vol. III (1983), pp. 344 sqq.

[110] For instance, the problem of the right of recourse of a person who has paid somebody else's debt is often solved today by way of cessiones legis (assignment by operation of law) and similar devices; cf. e.g. Helm, op. cit., note 109, pp. 351 sqq.

[111] Cf., for example, the self-sacrifice of a motorcar driver, supra, p. 444.

reasonable allocation of risks. Not surprisingly, its retention in a revised German law of obligations has recently been advocated.[112]

(b) The individualistic approach of the common law

While both courts and legal writers in Germany are therefore happy to encourage useful activities in the interest of others, Anglo-American law continues to be concerned about officious interloping. Often quoted are the words of Bowen LJ in *Falcke v. Scottish Imperial Insurance Co.*:

> "The general principle is, beyond all question, that work and labour done or money expended by one man to preserve or benefit the property of another do not according to English law create any lien upon the property saved or benefited, nor, even if standing alone, create any obligation to repay the expenditure."[113]

And the *American Restatement of Restitution* states equally clearly: "A person who officiously confers a benefit upon another is not entitled to restitution therefor." Or, in the words of John P. Dawson, the great majority of common-law jurisdictions appear to "have done their best to discourage good Samaritans".[114] But the contrast between the "individualistic" common law and the humanitas-oriented civil law is (as usual) not really as dramatic as these general statements make it sound. True: the common law does not recognize a doctrine of negotiorum gestio. Nevertheless, in a variety of situations it has developed solutions completely comparable to those evolved by the civilian systems;[115] usually, incidentally, on the basis of a bit of civilian infusion.[116] Thus, for instance, it is generally accepted that a stranger who has buried a deceased may recover his reasonable expenses from the person primarily responsible for the burial.[117] This rule appears to be based on the Roman actio funeraria,[118] and it came to England via

---

[112] Helm, op. cit., note 109, pp. 385 sqq. [113] (1887) 34 ChD 234 (CA) at 248.

[114] "Rewards for the Rescue of Human Life?", in: *XXth Century Comparative and Conflicts Law, Legal Essays in Honor of Hessel E. Yntema* (1961) p. 142.

[115] Stoljar, op. cit., note 2, nn. 25, 59. Cf. further, Heilman, "The Rights of the Voluntary Agent Against His Principal in Roman Law and in Anglo-American Law", (1926) 4 *Tennessee LR* 34 sqq., 76 sqq.; Peter Birks, "Negotiorum gestio and the Common Law", (1971) 24 *Current Legal Problems* 110 sqq.; idem, "Restitution for Services", (1974) 27 *Current Legal Problems* 13 sqq.; Van Zyl, *Negotiorum gestio*, pp. 170 sqq. On the *American Restatement of Restitution* (where § 2, due to its prominent position, obscures the fact that in reality it contains a body of rules bearing a considerable resemblance to the civil law) cf. Stoljar, op. cit., note 2, nn. 60 sqq.

[116] This point has, most recently, been elaborated by Lee J.W. Aitken, "Negotiorum gestio and the Common Law: A Jurisdictional Approach", (1988) 11 *Sydney LR* 566 sqq.

[117] *Jenkins v. Tucker* (1788) 1 H Bl 90; *Ambrose v. Kerrison* (1851) 10 CB 776; Aitken, (1988) 11 *Sydney LR* 571 sqq.

[118] Closely related to negotiorum gestio; the praetor granted an action to a person who arranged a funeral at his own expense without being obliged to do so (Berger, *ED*, p. 343); for details cf. e.g. Ulp. D. 11, 7, 12, 2 sqq.; 11, 7, 14, 7 sqq.; Kaser, *RPr* II, p. 418; Stoljar, op. cit., note 2, n. 160. Why was this situation not absorbed by the institution of negotiorum gestio? There is a strong public interest in a prompt and proper disposal of the body (cf. Ulp. D. 11, 7, 12, 3 "ne insepulta corpora iacerent"); thus the claim lies even if the gestor has acted against the heir's wishes: cf. Ulp. D. 11, 7, 14, 13; Seiler, *Negotiorum gestio*, pp. 89 sq. In later

the jurisdiction of the medieval ecclesiastical courts.[119] From the Italian Law Merchant the Courts of Admiralty have adopted the principle that those who rescue persons or property from the perils of the sea should be rewarded.[120] Most importantly, however, there is the doctrine of "agency of necessity", according to which, in certain emergency situations, one person may render useful services to another without having been requested to do so, and receive compensation for those services.[121] This doctrine, too, is historically based on maritime usages, for it finds its origin in the power available to the master of a ship in an emergency to deal with the ship or her cargo outside the ordinary scope of his authority.[122] From there it has been extended to other cases where one party, by intervening on the other's behalf in an emergency, has gone beyond an existing authority. The agent, under these circumstances, is usually said to have had the *implied* authority of the dominus negotii to act as he has done.[123] But contract is not really a satisfactory basis for the doctrine of agency of necessity.[124] That becomes abundantly clear, for instance, in cases where necessaries are supplied to persons unable to provide for themselves and where the supplier has in fact been granted a restitutionary claim.[125] What we are dealing with is not a kind of "agency" but a nascent doctrine of necessitous intervention.[126]

(c) *Rescue cases*

Even in rescue cases, the Good Samaritan under the common law is not as unprotected as might appear at first blush. For if the act of rescue can be construed as the supply of necessaries, the rescuer falls under the

---

centuries, actio funeraria and negotiorum gestio merged; today, § 679 BGB takes care of the problem, when it states: "The fact that the management of the matter is opposed to the wishes of the principal is not taken into consideration if, without the management of the matter, a duty of the principal, the fulfilment of which is of public interest, . . . would not be fulfilled in due time."

119 Stoljar, op. cit., note 2, nn. 58, 161.

120 Holdsworth, vol. VIII, pp. 269 sqq.; for details of the modern law cf. Goff and Jones, *Restitution*, pp. 280 sqq. On maritime salvage in Roman-Dutch law, see Van Zyl, *Negotiorum gestio*, pp. 14, 74 sqq.

121 Stoljar, op. cit., note 2, n. 58. For details, see, for example, Goff and Jones, *Restitution*, pp. 264 sqq.; Aitken, (1988) 11 *Sydney LR* 585 sqq., 591 sqq.

122 Goff and Jones, *Restitution*, p. 264; for the historical background, see Holdsworth, vol. VIII, pp. 248 sqq.

123 Cf. e.g. Buckland/McNair, p. 336.

124 Cf., for example, the criticism by Goff and Jones, *Restitution*, p. 267; Stoljar, op. cit., note 2, n. 136.

125 *In re Rhodes* (1890) 44 ChD 94 (CA); for further details, see Stoljar, op. cit., note 2, nn. 134 sqq.

126 Goff and Jones, *Restitution*, pp. 278 sq.; cf. also Aitken, (1988) 11 *Sydney LR* 566 sqq., who points out that the historical connection between the—at first blush—rather heterogeneous instances in which English law permits the recovery of expenses of those who have intervened without prior solicitation in the affairs of others is jurisdictional: they were all connected with either the Court of Admiralty or with the ecclesiastical courts. These courts were controlled by civilian-oriented jurists who therefore had no hesitation to draw upon the doctrine of negotiorum gestio.

doctrine just mentioned. More importantly, however, the law of delict has been used to alleviate the rescuer's position. Here, too, the Anglo-American courts have moved away from the highly individualistic idea of rescue as constituting an infringement of a person's private autonomy to decide about his own fate; they are now quite prepared to grant a claim in damages if the rescuer is injured while trying to remove a danger caused, either intentionally or negligently, by the person to be rescued.

> "Danger invites rescue. The cry of distress is the summons to relief. The law does not ignore these reactions of the mind in tracing conduct to its consequences. It recognizes them as normal. It places their effects within the range of the natural and probable. The wrong that imperils life is a wrong also to his rescuer. The risk of rescue, if only it be not wanton, is born of the occasion. The emergency begets the man. The wrongdoer may not have foreseen the coming of a deliverer. He is accountable as if he had."[127]

These are the words of Cardozo and they show that neither the defence of volenti non fit iniuria nor the plea of novus actus interveniens is able any longer to defeat the rescuer's claim for the damages sustained. Civil-law jurisdictions such as Germany or South Africa grant relief to the rescuer by way of negotiorum gestio.[128] The actio negotiorum gestorum contraria, obviously, goes further than the claim in delict, in that it is applicable irrespective of whether the rescuee may be blamed for the danger in which he finds himself or whether this was due to vis maior. There is, however, at least one type of situation where negotiorum gestio does not always provide a satisfactory and suitable solution: the rescue of a person attempting to commit suicide. Where such an attempt is not just a cry for help, but is based on a serious desire to end one's own life,[129] the rescuer can hardly be said to have acted "in accordance with the . . . actual or presumptive wishes of the principal".[130] Here the civil law can in turn draw on the experiences gathered in the common law with rescue claims in delict.[131]

---

[127] *Wagner v. International Railway Co.* 232 NY 176, 133 NE 437 (1921) at 437 sq. Cf. further e.g. *Haynes v. Harwood* [1935] 1 KB 146 (CA).

[128] Cf. e.g. Wollschläger, op. cit., note 5, pp. 284 sqq.; Wittmann, op. cit., note 47, pp. 65 sqq.; A.K. Blommaert, "Negotiorum gestio and the life-rescuer", 1981 *TSAR* 123 sqq., 127 sqq. For a comparative analysis relating to rescue of life or limb cf. Stoljar, op. cit., note 2, nn. 242 sqq.

[129] The latter situation is a comparatively rare phenomenon in life, although it dominates in philosophical discussions about suicide (according to Camus, *Le Mythe de Sisyphe*, p. 15, the only question that really matters), and particularly in theatre, opera and literature. In reality, attempted suicides are the rule, and they cannot simply be regarded as failures to commit suicide. As a rule, it is a very ambivalent will that underlies the suicidal act. For further information, see Reinhard Zimmermann, "Self-Determination, Paternalism or Human Care?", 1979 *TSAR* 183 sqq. On suicide in Roman law, see Andreas Wacke, "Der Selbstmord im römischen Recht und in der Rechtsentwicklung", (1980) 97 *ZSS* 26 sqq.

[130] § 683 BGB.

[131] Reinhard Zimmermann, "Der Selbstmord als Gefährdungssachverhalt—Aufwendungs- oder Schadensersatz für den Retter?", 1979 *Zeitschrift für das gesamte Familienrecht* 103 sqq.

CHAPTER 15

Societas

I. ROMAN LAW

1. The nature of societas

The fourth of the consensual contracts was societas (partnership). Unlike sale or hire, it is not a transaction in which the parties' performances are reciprocal. A socius does not give or do anything *in order to* receive a counterperformance from his fellow socii. Societas is thus not based, primarily, on an antagonism of interests; its essence is the pooling of resources (money, property, expertise or labour, or a combination of them) for a *common purpose*. Socii, in the words of Daube, are not bent on getting the utmost out of each other; they are, in the first place, "friends", pursuing their common interests against third parties.[1]

2. Evolution of the contract of societas

(a) Erctum non citum

In *Institutiones* III, 154, Gaius refers to this type of consensual societas ("haec quidem societas de qua loquimur, id est quae nudo consensu contrahitur") as an institution iuris gentium, that is, not peculiar to Roman citizens. The implication appears to be that Roman law (at least at some stage of its development) knew a non-consensual societas which was not iuris gentium. In fact, one had always suspected as much. In February 1933, however, a parchment was discovered in an antiquarian bookshop in Cairo which confirmed this hypothesis.[2] It turned out to contain, inter alia, an entirely new fragment of Gaius' *Institutes*, which had not been preserved in the Veronese palimpsest[3] and which reads as follows:

> "Est autem aliud genus societatis proprium civium Romanorum. olim enim, mortuo patre familias, inter suos heredes quaedam erat legitima simul et naturalis societas, quae appellabatur ercto non cito, id est dominio non diviso. . . . Alii quoque, qui

[1] David Daube, "Societas as Consensual Contract", (1938) 6 *Cambridge LJ* 391. Cf. generally Jacques Heenen, "Business and Private Organisations", in: *International Encyclopedia of Comparative Law*, vol. XIII, 1, nn. 15 sqq.; Joseph Story, *Commentaries on the Law of Partnership* (5th ed., 1859), §§ 1 sqq., 15 sqq.

[2] Cf. e.g. Ernst Levy, "Neue Bruchstücke aus den Institutionen des Gaius", (1934) 54 *ZSS* 258 sqq.

[3] Why? Has this passage been omitted intentionally from the Veronese manuscript (which is from the late 5th century) because it dealt with an entirely outdated and obsolete institution, the discussion of which appeared to be unnecessary for elementary instruction purposes? Cf. e.g. Levy, (1934) 54 *ZSS* 270 sqq., but also Francis de Zulueta, "The New Fragments of Gaius (PSI. 1182)", (1934) 24 *JRS* 182.

volebant eandem habere societatem, poterant id consequi apud praetorem certa legis actione."[4]

This text draws our attention to an institution of pre-classical ("olim") law which must be seen as the earliest form and historical basis of partnership arrangements in Roman law. It refers to a specific aspect of the once all-important law of the family. On the death of the paterfamilias, the familia broke up into as many new familiae as there were sui heredes. However, in the old days, all these families remained united in a community of co-heirs (or, as Gaius puts it: brothers), a consortium which was called erctum non citum[5] and through which the old familia[6] continued to exist, in both its legal and its sacral substance. This consortium led to a complete community of property and was characterized by the fact that the individual co-heirs did not have a specific share in the inheritance: all rights vested in the community of co-heirs.

(b) Pre-classical consortium and classical societas

It was this type of consortium which parties who wished to pool their assets were then allowed to create artificially,[7] first by means of "certa legis actio", an ancient and formal type of procedure.[8] "[A]d exemplum fratrum societatem coierint", is how Gaius describes what these partners did:[9] they contracted a partnership on the model of the (natural) brothers of an undivided familia. In the course of time, however, the legis actio procedure proved to be too cumbrous, and eventually, therefore, the praetor granted an action on the basis of a purely consensual societas. The parties had pooled their property[10] in order to pursue a common purpose and good faith demanded that such an arrangement be honoured, no matter whether it was based on some outmoded formal act or not. It was still societas omnium bonorum, though, a partnership involving all the partners' assets of whatever source. Throughout classical and post-classical law it remained one of the basic types of partnership, and it retained certain characteristics of the old consortium.[11] It is, however, unlikely that this type of

[4] Cf. today Gai. III, 154 a, b. On this text, see particularly Franz Wieacker, *Societas, Hausgemeinschaft und Erwerbsgesellschaft* (1936), pp. 126 sqq.; Mario Bretone, " 'Consortium' e 'communio' ", (1960) 6 *Labeo* 168 sqq.

[5] On which see, for instance, Kaser, *RPr* I, pp. 99 sqq.; idem, "Neue Literatur zur 'societas' ", (1975) 41 *SDHI* 281 sqq.; Honsell/Mayer-Maly/Selb, p. 331; Voci, *DER*, vol. I, pp. 59 sqq.; Vincenzo Arangio-Ruiz, *La società in diritto romano* (1950), pp. 3 sqq.; Bretone, (1960) 6 *Labeo* 177 sqq., Herman van den Brink, *Ius Fasque* (1968), pp. 262 sqq.

[6] Kaser, *RPr* I, pp. 50 sqq.; Voci, *DER*, vol. I, pp. 23 sqq.

[7] Cf., above all, Wieacker, *Societas*, pp. 126 sqq.

[8] Comparable, probably, to an in iure cessio; Kaser, (1975) 41 *SDHI* 284 sq.

[9] Gai. III, 154 b.

[10] On how this was done cf. infra, pp. 465 sq.

[11] Wieacker, *Societas*, pp. 131 sqq., 153 sqq.; Kaser, *RPr* I, p. 573. Contra: Antonio Guarino, *Societas consensu contracta* (1972), pp. 13 sqq. According to him, the classical consensual societas has nothing to do, historically, with the pre-classical consortium. Only

transaction was widely practised in classical times.[12] Societas omnium bonorum finds its origin in family law and succession, not in mercantile practice. It may be suitable between close friends and relatives, or between farmers wishing to engage in a communal agricultural enterprise.[13] But already in the second century B.C. Rome was not the closely-knit agricultural community of old any longer. Trade and commerce flourished, and with it came an increasing desire to form profit-oriented business partnerships. Businessmen who wish jointly to run a bank,[14] to embark on the trading of slaves or on the building of roads do not normally want to pool all their (private) assets. They want to confine their association with each other to a specific type of business or sometimes even to one particular transaction. Societas omnium bonorum therefore being inconvenient for their purposes, the praetor (probably initially the praetor peregrinus) during the later Republic began to protect such informal unions created for the purpose of a joint commercial enterprise.[15] In the course of time the old civilian societas omnium bonorum and the more modern business partnership amalgamated and formed the basis for the classical consensual societas.[16] The contract of societas in classical law thus provided a general framework for all types of partnership arrangements, whether they be omnium bonorum, negotiationis alicuius or rei unius.[17] Apart

---

post-classical law created a societas omnium bonorum that fulfilled a function comparable to that of the old consortium. For a critical discussion of Guarino's views, see Kaser, (1975) 41 *SDHI* 278 sqq.; cf. also Kaser, *RPr* II, pp. 410. Originally, societas does not seem to have been able to be concluded sub condicione, for the question was disputed among the classical lawyers (C. 4, 36, 6 (Just.); Paul. D. 17, 2, 1 pr.; itp.). According to Wieacker, *Societas*, pp. 137 sq., this is one of the characteristics inherited by the consensual societas from the old consortium. The formal act which created the consortium of old entailed a change of status and could not therefore be conditional. Cf. also Arangio-Ruiz, op. cit., note 5, p. 121 sqq.; Kaser, *RPr* I, p. 573. But see now Kaser (1975) 41 *SDHI* 305; Guarino, *Societas*, p. 13. For yet another explanation cf. Watson, *Obligations*, pp. 130 sqq.

[12] Alan Watson, "Consensual societas between Romans and the Introduction of formulae", (1962) 9 *RIDA* 431 sqq.; cf. also idem, *Evolution*, p. 21.

[13] Cf. e.g. Wolfgang Kunkel, "Ein unbeachtetes Zeugnis über das römische consortium", in: (1954) 4 *Annales Faculté de Droit d'Istanbul* 56 sqq.; Watson, loc. cit.

[14] On argentarii socii cf., most recently, Alfons Bürge, "Fiktion und Wirklichkeit: Soziale und Strukturen des römischen Bankwesens", (1987) 104 *ZSS* 519 sqq.

[15] Cf. Arangio-Ruiz, op. cit., note 5, pp. 22 sqq.; Ulrich von Lübtow, "Catos leges venditioni et locationi dictae", in: *Symbolae Raphaeli Taubenschlag*, vol. III (1957), pp. 286 sqq.; Kaser, *RPr* I, pp. 573 sq.; Guarino, op. cit., note 11, passim.

[16] Wieacker, (1952) 69 *ZSS* 491 sqq. Previously (*Societas*, pp. 131 sqq.) Wieacker had emphasized exclusively the root of societas in consortium. For the opposite extreme (societas was since old a profit-oriented business organization—società di industria—and has no historical connection with the consortium at all), see Guarino, *Societas*. But cf. Kaser, (1975) 41 *SDHI* 278 sqq.

[17] Ulp. D. 17, 2, 5 pr.; cf. also Gai. III, 148; *Inst.* III, 25 pr. An example of alicuius negotiationis is to be found in Ulp. D. 17, 2, 52, 4 ("[q]uidam sagariam negotiationem coierunt") (for further details and examples—venalicii, argentarii, danistae, etc.—see Arangio-Ruiz, op. cit., note 5, pp. 141 sqq.; on societates argentariae cf. Manuel J. Garcia Garrido, "La sociedad de los banqueros ('Societas argentaria')", in: *Studi in onore di Arnaldo Biscardi*, vol. III (1982), pp. 377 sqq.); of unius rei is to be found in Ulp. D. 17, 2, 52, 13 ("Si

from these, there was a societas omnium bonorum quae ex quaestu veniunt which involved a pooling of all assets deriving from business activity (as opposed to, for instance, gifts or legacies). This seems to have become a popular type of societas for, according to Ulpian,[18] its conclusion was to be presumed in case of doubt, i.e. if the partners had simply entered into a societas without specifying which type it was to be.

3. Basic features of classical societas

The classical societas was based on the formless consent of the socii[19] which was apparent, usually, from their factual co-operation. Like the other consensual contracts, societas was therefore firmly rooted in the precepts of good faith. In addition, there were certain overtones of a distinctly fraternal nature, accountable, historically, to the old consortium as an imitated community of natural brothers.[20] Unlike emptio venditio, locatio conductio or mandatum, societas did not give rise to actiones directae and contrariae. The praetorian edict contained only one formula for the claims of socii against each other. This was the procedural reflection of the fact that the rights and duties of the members of a partnership towards each other are identical; they co-operate on the basis of a common purpose[21] rather than occupy

---

vicini semipedes inter se contulerunt, ut ibi craticium parietem inter se aedificarent ad onera utriusque sustinenda"), and see Wieacker, (1952) 69 *ZSS* 501. For the later Republic, see Watson, *Obligations*, pp. 134 sqq.

[18] D. 17, 2, 7. On this type of societas cf. also Paul and Ulpian in D. 17, 2, 8–13. Ferdinando Bona, "Contribute alla storia della 'societas universorum quae ex quaestu veniunt' in diritto romano", in: *Studi in onore di Giuseppe Grosso*, vol. I (1968), pp. 383 sqq., 395 sqq., argues that only Justinian made this the prototype of societas. But see e.g. Guarino, op. cit., note 11, pp. 26 sqq.

[19] Cf. Gai. III, 135, 154; cf. further, particularly, Daube, (1938) 6 *Cambridge LJ* 381 sqq.; Arangio-Ruiz, op. cit., note 5, pp. 63 sqq.; Watson, *Obligations*, pp. 128 sqq.; Kaser, (1975) 41 *SDHI* 299 sq.; but see also Wieacker, *Societas*, pp. 72 sqq. *Societas* could be a bilateral or even a plurilateral contract, depending on whether there were two or more socii; cf. e.g. Arangio-Ruiz, op. cit., note 5, pp. 70 sqq. According to Guarino, op. cit., note 11, pp. 38 sqq., 82 sqq. the consensual societas typically comprised only two socii, and it was essentially the structure of such a società "dualistica" which was reflected in classical law. For a critical discussion of this theory, see Kaser, (1975) 41 *SDHI* 321 sqq.

[20] Cf. e.g. Ulp. D. 17, 2, 63 pr.: "Verum est quod Sabino videtur, etiamsi non universorum bonorum socii sunt, sed unius rei, attamen in id quod facere possunt quodve dolo malo fecerint quo minus possint, condemnari oportere. hoc enim summam rationem habet, cum societas ius quodammodo fraternitatis in se habeat." This is the (later, i.e. since the 16th century) so-called beneficium competentiae: condemnation of the debtor only in id quod facere potest. Cf. further Ulp. D. 42, 1, 16; Wieacker, *Societas*, pp. 165 sq.; Watson, *Obligations*, p. 144; Wieslaw Litewski, "Das 'beneficium competentiae' im römischen Recht", in: *Studi in onore di Edoardo Volterra*, vol. IV (1971), pp. 546 sqq.; Joachim Gildemeister, *Das beneficium competentiae im klassischen römischen Recht* (1986), pp. 27 sqq. and passim. Cf. also Holdsworth, vol. VIII, p. 195.

[21] Of course, this common purpose was not to be illegal, immoral or impossible, otherwise the partnership was void; cf. Paul. D. 17, 2, 3, 3; Ulp. D. 17, 2, 57 and Thomas, *TRL*, p. 302, who draws attention to the interesting English case of *Everett v. Williams* of 1725; cf. (1893) 9 *LQR* 196 sqq. ("Truth is stranger than fiction. The story of a highwayman filing a Bill in Equity for an account against his partner . . . is correct after all").

distinct and separate roles (as a vendor and purchaser, letter and hirer, mandator and mandatarius) on the respective sides of their obligational relationship. The model form of the actio pro socio, of course, contained the ex bona fide clause and did not distinguish between the different types of societas.[22] Societas, furthermore, was not a corporate body, a legal person in its own right. It was a contract creating rights and duties merely between the socii themselves. Nobody could therefore act for "the societas". Nor could a socius represent his partners; if one partner bought something on behalf of all the socii, only he was entitled or obliged under such an emptio venditio, not the community of the partners as a whole.[23]

4. Termination of the societas

(a) Renuntiatio, mors socii, insolvency

These are the basic features of societas in classical Roman law, and most of the details set out on the following pages follow naturally from them. The operation of a partnership is usually designed to extend over some time, at least, as long as it is not merely unius rei; and because societas was based on the consent of the socii, it follows that their consensus had to be a continuing one. "Manet autem societas eo usque donec in eodem sensu perseverant [socii]."[24] The societas could exist only as long as the partners, in the pursuit of their common purpose, kept to their agreement. As a consequence, the partnership was dissolved if one of the partners renounced it.[25] It was not possible for him simply to withdraw and to leave the societas between the remaining partners intact.[26] His renuntiatio invariably terminated the contract as a whole, since it was now no longer carried by the original consensus.[27] If the remaining parties decided to carry on as partners,

---

[22] Cf. Lenel, *EP*, p. 297; Arangio-Ruiz, op. cit., note 5, p. 30; Kaser, (1975) 41 *SDHI* 290 sqq. ("Quod A^s A^s cum N° N° societatem omnium bonorum coiit, . . ."). Differently (without the words "omnium bonorum") Guarino, op. cit., note 11, p. 11.

[23] The classical societas was, in modern terminology, a mere undisclosed association ("*Innengesellschaft*"); it did not have any effects as far as third parties were concerned. For details, see, for example, Arangio-Ruiz, op. cit., note 5, pp. 78 sqq.

[24] Gai. III, 151. Cf. further *Inst.* III, 25, 4; Wieacker, *Societas*, pp. 285 sqq.

[25] Also, of course, if the partners mutually agreed to end their association (cf. Knütel, *Contrarius consensus*, pp. 124 sqq.), or if the period agreed for the continuance of the partnership expired.

[26] Of a different opinion is Guarino, op. cit., note 11, pp. 56 sqq., 90 sqq., according to whom only a societas comprising two socii was dissolved by renunciation. A "società pluralistica", on the other hand, continued to exist if only one partner decided to withdraw. Guarino draws the same distinction in cases of death, capitis deminutio and insolvency of one of the partners; cf. *Societas*, passim and idem, "Solutio societatis", (1968) 14 *Labeo* 139 sqq. Contra: Wieslaw Litewski, "Remarques sur la dissolution de la société en droit romain", (1972) 50 *RH* 70 sqq.; Kaser (1975) 41 *SDHI* 325 sqq.; cf. also J.A.C. Thomas, "Solutio societatis ex actione and dissensus sociorum", (1974) 48 *Tulane LR* 1103 sqq.

[27] Gai. III, 151; Mod. D. 17, 2, 4; *Inst.* III, 25, 4. For further details Paul. D. 17, 2, 65, 3–6; I.C. van Oven, " 'Societas in tempus coita' ", in: *Studi in onore di Vincenzo Arangio-Ruiz*, vol. II (1953), pp. 453 sqq.; Ferdinando Bona, *Studi sulla società consensuale in diritto romano*

this was held to be a new partnership.[28] Similarly, the death of one of the partners terminated the partnership: morte socii solvitur societas. Reason: "qui societatem contrahit certam personam sibi eligit."[29] We are reminded of the same rule and the same rationale in the case of mandatum:[30] both socius and mandator place their confidence in a particular person; if that person dies, the essential basis sustaining the contractual relationship falls away.[31] For the same reason the partners were not able to provide that the future heir of one of them should join the partnership.[32] The societas found its basis in the trust and faith existing between two or more specific individuals, and it was totally impossible to predict whether this type of relationship would extend to a party that was as yet unknown. Capitis deminutio being, civili ratione, equivalent to death, brought about the end of the partnership, too.[33] So did the insolvency of one of the partners.[34] Finally, and perhaps most interestingly, the bringing of the actio pro socio

(1973), pp. 117 sqq. The power to renounce at any time could not be excluded by way of agreement between the socii: Pomp./Ulp. D. 17, 2, 14; Paul. D. 17, 2, 17, 2; Wieslaw Litewski, "Les effets juridiques du pactum ne societate abeatur" (1978) 25 *RIDA* 279 sqq.

[28] Cf. Gai. III, 153; but see also Ulp. D. 17, 2, 58, 2; Arangio-Ruiz, op. cit., note 5, pp. 166 sqq.

[29] Gai. III, 152. Cf. further e.g. Paul. D. 17, 2, 65, 9 sq.; Arangio-Ruiz, op. cit., note 5, pp. 156 sqq. But see Watson, *Obligations*, pp. 131 sqq. "Qui societatem contrahit certam personam sibi elegit" is also the reason for the rule socii mei socius meus socius non est (Ulp. D. 17, 2, 20; Ulp. D. 50, 17, 47, 1). If, for instance, three socii run a taberna, and one of the socii accepts a fourth person as a socius in order to let him work in the shop, the latter does not become partner of the original societas. No. 1 and No. 4 form a subpartnership, of which Nos. 2 and 3, since they have not agreed to it, do not form part (Ulp. D. 17, 2, 19). Was No. 1 liable, towards Nos. 2 and 3, for the actions of No. 4? According to Ulp. D. 17, 2, 21, he has to sue No. 4 and then to bring what he receives by way of damages into the societas with Nos. 2 and 3. What if No. 4 (the sub-socius) is not able to pay damages? "Et puto", says Ulpian, "omnimodo eum teneri eius nomine, quem ipse solus admisit, quia difficile est negare culpa ipsius admissum." Does that mean that No. 1 is liable for culpa in eligendo? This is what the text has usually been understood to mean (cf. e.g. Etienne Laffely, *Responsabilité du "socius" et concours d'actions dans la société classique* (1979), pp. 36 sqq., 44 sq.). Consequently it has often been regarded as spurious. It is more likely, however, that Ulpian held No. 1 liable for breach of contract. He was not allowed, under the partnership agreement, to hand over the management of the taberna to a subpartner; the latter has therefore been able to cause the damages only as a consequence of No. 1's culpa. Cf., in this sense, Rolf Knütel, "Die Haftung für Hilfspersonen im römischen Recht", (1983) 100 *ZSS* 423 sqq.

[30] On the "coincidence" in this respect of the contract of partnership with that of mandate cf. Story, op. cit., note 1, § 270.

[31] Cf. also Story, op. cit., note 1, §§ 317 sq.; "[Partnership] is a mutual and reciprocal engagement of each partner with all the others, that the partnership shall be carried on with joint aid and coöperation of all; and, therefore, the survivors ought not to be held bound to continue the connection without a new consent, when the abilities, skill and character of the deceased partner either were, or at least might have been, a strong inducement to the original formation of the partnership"; Pothier, Traité du contrat de société, nn. 144 sqq.; Kaser, (1975) 41 *SDHI* 34.

[32] Ulp. D. 17, 2, 35; Pomp. D. 17, 2, 59 pr.

[33] Gai. III, 153; Arangio-Ruiz, op. cit., note 5, pp. 163 sqq.

[34] Gai. III, 154; Mod. D. 17, 2, 4, 1.

terminated the societas: ". . . si . . . actio interierit, distrahi videtur societas."[35]

(b) The bringing of an actio pro socio

Ultimately, of course, it was litis contestatio that extinguished the partnership obligations; but by initiating a lawsuit that necessarily entailed a general settlement of accounts,[36] a socius could be taken to have implicitly renounced the partnership: it was as clear a manifestation of his desire no longer to be associated with the other members of the societas as one might wish to get. An actio pro socio manente societate was thus excluded in classical law.[37] This reflects the "isolationist" and libertarian character of Roman jurisprudence.[38] Of course, societas gave rise to obligations between the socii. But the lawyers were loath to intervene in an existing and functioning unit. Thus, there were no legal rules determining the internal relationship among the partners, and the details of how they set about pursuing their common purpose were left entirely to their mutual good understanding.[39] It is the same attitude that prevailed, for instance, with regard to the regulation (or rather: non-regulation) of family affairs.[40] As long as the partnership functioned, the intervention of the law was neither necessary nor appropriate. If, on the other hand, there were problems that could no longer be resolved in an amicable manner, the co-operation between the partners had lost its gravitational centre: a type of trust, faith and loyalty that derived from and was reminiscent of the ancient fraternity. Litigation does not represent the pinnacle of good brotherly relations. The spirit of the partnership had broken down. It did not make sense, under these circumstances, to carry on with the empty shell.

5. Freedom of contract and its limitation

(a) The allocation of shares in profits and losses

The fact that societas was based on bona fides did, of course, not mean that the contents of the contract between the socii had to conform to any kind of objective standard of fairness or reasonableness. More particularly, the validity of a societas did not depend on an equivalence

---

[35] Ulp. D. 17, 2, 63, 10; cf. further Paul. D. 17, 2, 65 pr.; Ulp. D. 17, 2, 52, 14 and Thomas, (1974) 48 *Tulane LR* 1099 sqq.

[36] Cf. infra, p. 460.

[37] Cf. e.g. Wieacker, (1952) 69 *ZSS* 503 sq. But see Paul. D. 17, 2, 65, 15 (dealing, however, with societas vectigalium); Arangio-Ruiz, op. cit., note 5, pp. 176 sqq.; Kaser, (1975) 41 *SDHI* 329 sq.; contra: Thomas, (1974) 48 *Tulane LR* 1101 sqq.

[38] Cf. in general Schulz, *Principles*, pp. 19 sqq., 140 sqq.; more specifically on societas, see Schulz, *CRL*, p. 553; Franz Wieacker, "Das Gesellschaftsverhältnis des klassischen Rechts", (1952) 69 *ZSS* 315 sq.

[39] But cf. infra, p. 459.

[40] Cf. C. 8, 38, 2 (Alex.) ("Libera matrimonia esse antiquitus placuit"). For societas cf. Paul. D. 17, 2, 70: "Nulla societatis in aeternum coitio est."

of contribution and reward. "Quidquid ob eam rem N^m N^m A^o A^o dare facere oportet ex bona fide": that was determined, in the first place, according to what the parties had specifically agreed upon. For what can be more in accordance with good faith than to give effect to the arrangements of the parties concerned? A Roman paterfamilias may be relied upon to be the best guardian of his own interests. Naturally, if no specific agreement regarding profits and losses had been made, the presumption was that the parties would bear both in equal shares.[41] But if shares had been specified, the agreement had to be observed. Thus, for instance, the parties could arrange that one partner should receive two-thirds of the profits and bear one-third of any loss, while the other would bear two-thirds of any loss and get one-third of the profits.[42] It was even possible to allocate a share in the profits to a socius without making him share in the losses at all.[43]

True: in the days of the Republic, this matter had been very controversial. Quintus Mucius, for instance, had disapproved of these kinds of terms.[44] But his disapproval had not been based on the lack of equivalence between contribution and reward. Fairness was not an issue. Such arrangements had rather been regarded as "contra naturam societatis": as incompatible with the nature of partnership as such.[45] In this argument, we see again the old erctum non citum lurking behind the scenes of consensual societas.[46] This ancient type of consortium was formed by co-heirs. An heir, as Alan Watson has stressed,[47] is liable for the debts of the deceased, even if they exceed the assets. Co-heirs were liable in the same proportion as they inherited. They might have been instituted ex partes inaequales; but profit and loss, as far as each of the co-heirs was concerned, corresponded. Servius Sulpicius broke away from this traditional position.[48] He obviously did not regard such correspondence as essential for the modern, consensual type of partnership, and left the determination of shares, in both profits and losses, to the parties. If they gave one of them a better deal they might have good reason for doing so: ". . . saepe quorundam ita pretiosa est opera in societate, ut eos iustum sit meliore condicione in societatem admitti."[49] The services of one of the parties may be so valuable, in

41 Gai. III, 150; Ulp. D. 17, 2, 29 pr.
42 Cf. Gai. III, 149; cf. the example discussed in *Inst.* III, 25, 2.
43 Ulp. D. 17, 2, 29, 1.
44 Cf. the report of the controversy in Gai. III, 149; *Inst.* III, 25, 2.
45 Cf. the discussion by Horak, *Rationes decidendi*, pp. 158 sqq.
46 Alan Watson, "The Notion of Equivalence of Contractual Obligation and Classical Roman Partnership", (1981) 97 *LQR* 279 sqq.
47 *Evolution*, p. 21.
48 Gai. III, 149; *Inst.* III, 25, 2.
49 *Inst.* III, 25, 2.

comparison with the contributions of the others,[50] that such favourable treatment appears to be fully justified. Whether or not that is so must, however, be left to the discretion of the parties,[51] and it is not up to any third party to interfere with their evaluation of the matter.[52]

(b) The societas leonina

There was, however, one exception to this rule. A societas in which one partner shared only in the loss and not at all in the profit, was inadmissible.[53] It is in the fables of Phaedrus that we find the prototype of this so-called "societas leonina":

"Vacca et capella et patiens ovis iniuria
socii fuere cum leone in saltibus.
Hi cum cepissunt cervum vasti corporis,
sic est locutus partibus factis leo;
'Ego primam tollo; nominor quia rex meast;
secundam, quia sum socius, tribuetis mihi;
tum, quia plus valeo, me sequetur tertia;
malo adficietur siquis quartam tetigerit.'
Sic totam praedam sola improbitas abstulit."[54]

These are certainly powerful arguments on the part of the lion, but one must admit that from a more impartial point of view the distribution of the spoils is indeed "iniquissimum".[55] In fact, there is no distribution at all. Just as for a valid emptio venditio, there had to be at least some counterperformance in money (even though not necessarily a iustum pretium),[56] so in the case of a partnership contract each socius had to get at least some material benefit out of it (albeit not necessarily a fair share). For the Roman lawyers, this seems to have been inherent in the concept or nature of partnership.[57]

---

[50] On the problems raised by capital-service partnerships (in which one partner contributes money, the other services), see Ben Beinart, "Capital in Partnership", 1961 *Acta Juridica* 124 sqq.; Bona, op. cit., note 27, pp. 24 sqq.; Kaser, (1975) 41 *SDHI* 312 sqq.

[51] Arangio-Ruiz, *Società*, op. cit., pp. 101 sqq.; Watson, *Obligations*, pp. 138 sqq. Contra (such an arrangement was valid, not because it *could* be fair, but only when in fact it *was* fair) Watson, (1981) 97 *LQR* 283 sqq. The answer turns on the correct interpretation of the words "si modo" in Gai. III, 149 and on whether Ulp. D. 17, 2, 29, 1 is partly interpolated or not.

[52] On Paul. D. 17, 2, 30 cf. Glück, vol. 15, pp. 418 sqq.; Vangerow, *Pandekten*, vol. III, pp. 471 sq.; Arangio-Ruiz, op. cit., note 5, pp. 97 sqq.; Horak, *Rationes decidendi*, pp. 162 sqq.

[53] Ulp. D. 17, 2, 29, 2.

[54] *Fabulae Aesopiae*, I, 5. For details of its reception by Celsus, see Antonio Guarino, "La società col leone", (1972) 18 *Labeo* 72 sqq.

[55] Ulp. D. 17, 2, 29, 2.

[56] Cf. supra, pp. 252, 255 sqq.

[57] On societas leonina in modern law cf. Glück, vol 15, pp. 425 sq.; Pothier, *Traité du contrat de société*, n. 12; Story, op. cit., note 1, § 18; art. 1855 code civil; Christian Müller-Gugenberger, "Bemerkungen zur 'societas leonina': Fabel-haftes im Gesellschaftsrecht", in: *Gesetzgebungstheorie, Juristische Logik, Zivil- und Prozessrecht, Gedächtnisschrift für Jürgen Rödig* (1978), pp. 274 sqq.; J.J. Henning, H.J. Delport, "Partnership", in: Joubert (ed.), *The Law of South Africa*, vol. 19 (1983), n. 370 (n. 30); Peter Ulmer, in: *Münchener Kommentar*, vol. III 2 (2nd ed., 1986), § 705, n. 118; Heenen, op. cit., note 1, n. 22.

6. The actio pro socio

The actio pro socio, as we have seen, could be brought only after termination of the societas. Conversely, the institution of such an action involved dissolution of the societas. The actio pro socio entailed an allegation of breach of faith and it aimed at a condemnation which in turn entailed infamia.[58] It could reasonably be inferred that a person bringing to bear this type of heavy artillery no longer wished to be a socius.[59] The actio pro socio, therefore, did not aim at enforcing the obligations of the partners to make contributions to the (existing) societas;[60] it was concerned, solely, with a general settlement of accounts between the two (ex-)partners involved in the litigation.[61] "Quidquid ob eam rem N^m N^m A^o A^o dare facere oportet ex fide bona": this is, into what the judge was instructed to condemn the defendant. Thus, damages had to be taken into account which the plaintiff had suffered in the pursuit of the common purpose, or as a consequence of the defendant's fraudulent conduct.[62] Expenses which the plaintiff had incurred for the societas were included,[63] as were claims for his share in the profits[64] or for compensation for contributions to the societas which the defendant had failed to render.[65] On the other hand, however, the judge subtracted all the claims which the defendant might have, on account of the societas, against the plaintiff. In this way a kind of set-off was effected, and the defendant was condemned only into the balance.[66] This balance represented the final settlement of all claims of these two socii "ob eam rem" against each other.

In a very similar way, incidentally, the actions arising from mandatum and negotiorum gesto aimed at a general settlement of accounts; if the mandator sued the mandatarius for damages, the counterclaims of the latter were usually deducted, and he, too, was thus condemned into the balance only:

> "In bonae fidei autem iudiciis libera potestas permitti videtur iudici ex bono et aequo aestimandi quantum actori restitui debeat. in quo et illud continetur ut, habita ratione

[58] Gai. IV, 182; Arangio-Ruiz, op. cit., note 5, pp. 185 sq.; Watson, *Obligations*, pp. 144 sqq.

[59] Paul. D. 17, 2, 65 pr. makes it clear that the bringing of the action, in itself, imports renunciation of the societas.

[60] This obligation could, of course, be made indirectly enforceable by way of a stipulatio poenae: cf. e.g. Ulp. D. 17, 2, 41 sq.; Paul. D. 17, 2, 71 pr.; on the latter text cf. Apathy, *Animus novandi*, pp. 237 sqq.; Knütel, *Stipulatio poenae*, pp. 66 sqq.

[61] Cf., in particular, Wieacker, (1952) 69 *ZSS* 316 sqq. Contra: Guarino, (1968) 14 *Labeo* 158 sqq.; idem, *Società*, pp. 77 sqq., but see Kaser, (1975) 41 *SDHI* 329 sqq.

[62] Cf. infra, p. 462.

[63] Ulp. D. 17, 2, 52, 15; Paul. D. 17, 2, 67, 2.

[64] Paul. D. 17, 2, 65, 3.

[65] Ulp. D. 17, 2, 73; Paul. D. 17, 2, 74.

[66] Cf. e.g. Wieacker, (1952) 69 *ZSS* 326 sqq.

eius quod invicem actorem ex eadem causa praestare oporteret, in reliquum eum cum quo actum est condemnare."[67]

7. Liability between the partners

(a) The problem of contribution

A few words still have to be added about the circumstances under which (ex-)socii were liable to indemnify each other. On the one hand, as we have seen, there could be a claim if one of the partners, in the pursuit of the common purpose, had suffered a loss. Of course, this was not really a claim "for damages", for the aggrieved party did not blame his fellow socius for the loss. He merely asked him to contribute towards it by counting it as a disbursement on behalf of the partnership. But when could such a contribution be demanded?

> "Quidam sagariam negotiationem coierunt: alter ex his ad merces comparandas profectus in latrones incidit suamque pecuniam perdidit, servi eius vulnerati sunt resque proprias perdidit. dicit Iulianus damnum esse commune ideoque actione pro socio damni partem dimidiam adgnoscere debere tam pecuniae quam rerum ceterarum, quas secum non tulisset socius nisi ad merces communi nomine comparandas proficisceretur."[68]

In this example, the partners are dealing in clothing. On a journey to purchase new merchandise, one of them is attacked by robbers. He loses his money and the personal belongings that he carries with him; furthermore, the slaves accompanying him are wounded. If the travelling partner would not have taken these things with him but for the fact that he was on his way to purchase material for the common enterprise, the loss, according to Julian, must be shared. It is attributable to the partnership; hence the duty of the other partners to contribute. This view, however, was not undisputed amongst the Roman jurists. Labeo, for instance, rejected an actio pro socio on account of medical expenses incurred by one socius in a case where some slaves had been kept for sale by the partnership and one of the partners had been wounded in an attempt to prevent a slave from breaking out and escaping. Reason: ". . . non in societatem, quamvis propter societatem inpensum [est]."[69] That the expenses would not have been incurred but for the partnership is not sufficient; they must have been incurred (directly) for partnership purposes. This appears to be unduly harsh, even though it must be admitted that not all losses for which the partnership is a conditio sine qua non can sensibly be held to be recoverable.[70]

[67] Gai. IV, 61 (as restored in accordance with *Inst.* IV, 6, 30). Cf. further e.g. Kaser, *RPr* I, pp. 644 sq.
[68] Ulp. D. 17, 2, 52, 4. Cf. further Ulp. D. 17, 2, 52, 3 and Ulp. D. 17, 2, 58 pr. and 1.
[69] Lab./Pomp. D. 17, 2, 60, 1.
[70] Cf. the argumentum ad absurdum by Labeo (D. 17, 2, 60, 1): ". . . si propter societatem eum heredem quis instituere desisset aut legatum praetermisisset aut patrimonium suum neglegentius administrasset: . . ." The same, of course, applies to gains made

(b) *Dolus liability*

On the other hand, we have said that a partner could bring the actio pro socio for damages resulting from the defendant's fraudulent conduct. This is correct only for the early period, however. Socii were liable to each other for dolus, and up to the time of classical law for dolus only.[71] Thus, for instance, a socius who withdrew from the partnership inopportunely could be liable to his ex-partners. Renuntiatio, even on the part of only one partner, dissolved the societas. As a consequence, as Cassius put it, the renouncing partner released his colleagues from himself, but not himself from his colleagues (". . . eum qui renuntiaverit societati a se quidem liberare socios suos, se autem ab illis non liberare").[72] Thus, he could still be compelled to share profits,[73] and he had to compensate the others for any damages caused by the untimely dissolution of the societas:

> "Item si societatem ineamus ad aliquam rem emendam, deinde solus volueris eam emere ideoque renuntiaveris societati, ut solus emeres, teneberis quanti interest mea."[74]

(c) *Extension: culpa lata, diligentia quam in suis, culpa*

A liability between partners merely for fraud,[75] however, could not permanently satisfy the needs of a more and more sophisticated economy. Thus, in the course of classical law, we find a gradual extension of the scope of liability. To begin with, we have to remember that dolus was not a hard-and-fast terminus technicus, unproblematically relatable to our modern concepts of fraud or intention. Dolus (malus) must rather be seen, particularly in the context of the consensual contracts, as the reverse of bona fides. What mattered, according to the formula, was whether the defendant had complied with the precepts of good faith. That this was not the case if he had

merely "propter societatem"; cf. the example given by Bartolus, *Commentaria*, D. 17, 2, 61, § Socius 1: "Alio modo potest intelligi propter societatem, hoc est, quod societas fuit occasio remota. Verbi gratia: propter societatem habui necesse accedere ad curiam principis: et dum coram principe tractarem negotia, placui principi, ex quo donavit mihi castrum: certe hoc non facit contemplatione societatis, sed personae meae tantum: licet nunquam habuissem nec accessissem, nisi propter societatem." For further discussion, see Peter Stein, "Julian and Liability for Loss Suffered in the Execution of a Contract in Roman Law", 1956 *Butterworth's South African LJ* 64 sqq.; Giuseppe Gandolfi, "Damnum commune", in: *Studi in onore di Edoardo Volterra*, vol. III (1971), pp. 527 sqq.; Karlheinz Misera, "Zur Gefahrtragung bei der römischen societas", in: *Iuris Professio, Festgabe für Max Kaser* (1986), pp. 201 sqq.

[71] Cf. e.g. Franz Wieacker, "Haftungsformen des römischen Gesellschaftsrechts", (1934) 54 *ZSS* 35 sqq.; Arangio-Ruiz, op. cit., note 5, pp. 188 sqq.

[72] Cass./Paul. D. 17, 2, 65, 3. Prerequisite, however: ". . . quod utique observandum est, si dolo malo renuntiatio facta sit." Cf. further Paul. D. 17, 2, 65, 6; Bona, op. cit., note 27, pp. 79 sqq., but see Kaser, (1975) 41 *SDHI* 335 sq.

[73] Example: ". . . plane si quis in hoc renuntiaverit societati, ut obveniens aliquod lucrum solus habeat, veluti si mihi totorum bonorum socius, cum ab aliquo heres esset relictus, in hoc renuntiaverit societati, ut hereditatem solus lucri faciat, cogetur hoc lucrum communicare" (Gai. III, 151); cf. also Cass./Paul. D. 17, 2, 65, 3.

[74] Paul. D. 17, 2, 65, 4.

[75] For further texts cf. Paul. D. 2, 13, 9 pr.; Pomp. D. 17, 2, 59, 1; Ulp. D. 17, 2, 63 pr., 7.

knowingly and wilfully caused damage to his colleagues is fairly obvious. But even grossly negligent behaviour can hardly be regarded as reconcilable (in any event: not necessarily as reconcilable) with the standards to be expected of someone steeped in Roman bona fides. Thus the liability of a socius must have included, qua dolus (if not originally, then at least in classical law) cases which came to be classified, at a later stage, as culpa lata. An important step towards extending the liability of socii was taken when the idea underlying the fragment of D. 16, 3, 32 was transferred from tutela and/or depositum to the contract of societas. According to Celsus, it is to be regarded as a breach of good faith if a depositary is more diligent with regard to his own property than with regard to what has been deposited with him. Thus he has to be responsible not only for dolus but for diligentia quam in suis.

The same considerations, obviously, commend themselves in the case of partnership. Hence the following statement of Gaius:

> "Socius socio etiam culpae nomine tenetur . . . culpa autem non ad exactissimam diligentiam dirigenda est: sufficit etenim talem diligentiam communibus rebus adhibere, qualem suis rebus adhibere solet, quia qui parum diligentem sibi socium adquirit, de se queri debet."[76]

This is diligentia quam in suis. But, interestingly, Gaius no longer even argues why a socius should *also* be liable if he has not exercised the care that he is used to exercising in his own matters (sc.: and not only for dolus stricto sensu); his main concern appears to be the proper limitation of the socius' liability: he should be liable *only* for diligentia quam in suis (and not for culpa in abstracto). If somebody enters into a partnership with a careless person, he has to blame himself if his new partner does not rise above what may realistically be expected of him. This is a remarkable sign of proactive thinking,[77] for a further extension of the liability appears to have been in the air. Ulpianus, for instance, some 60 years later, seems to have been prepared to hold a partner liable, under the actio pro socio, where he had negligently damaged goods held in common by the partners (". . . quod si rei communi socius nocuit, magis admittit culpam quoque venire").[78] A liability not only for dolus but also for culpa in abstracto can easily be rationalized in terms of considerations of utility.[79] Societas, after all, falls under the negotia utriusque gratia: it has been entered into for the benefit of all the partners and not merely for that of either the plaintiff or defendant in

---

[76] Gai. D. 17, 2, 72; largely incorporated into *Inst.* III, 25, 9. Diligentia quam in suis in D. 17, 2, 72 is usually taken to be of post-classical origin; cf. e.g. Wieacker, (1934) 54 *ZSS* 67 sqq.; De Robertis, *Responsabilità*, pp. 549 sqq. But see Herbert Hausmaninger, "Diligentia quam in suis", in: *Festschrift für Max Kaser* (1976), pp. 271 sqq.; Laffely, op. cit., note 29, pp. 31 sq., 137; Liebs, *RR*, pp. 210 sq.

[77] See, too, Hausmaninger, *Festschrift Kaser*, pp. 275 sq.

[78] Ulp. D. 17, 2, 52, 2 in fine.

[79] See Wieacker, (1934) 54 *ZSS* 57 sqq.

the actio pro socio at issue. Hence the generalizing statement in Ulp. D. 13, 6, 5, 2 i.f.: ". . . sed ubi utriusque utilitas vertitur, ut in empto, ut in locato, ut in dote, ut in pignore, ut in societate, et dolus et culpa praestatur." It is impossible to determine whether this correctly reflects the position in (late) classical law or whether we are dealing with an interpolation of post-classical origin. But there was certainly a tendency towards a more generalized liability for culpa.[80]

(d) Custodia and imperitia

If the picture presented so far appears to be complex and multifaceted (and it must be emphasized that nearly everything—apart from the initial dolus liability—has been and still is the subject of scholarly dispute), we have yet to add a further dimension to the problem of a partner's standard of liability. For, under certain circumstances, a socius was liable even for custodia and imperitia.

> ". . . si in coeunda societate, inquit [Celsus], artem operamve pollicitus est alter, veluti cum pecus in commune pascendum aut agrum politori damus in commune quaerendis fructibus, nimirum ibi etiam custodia praestanda est: pretium enim operae artis est velamentum."[81]

It is true that this text, as it has come down to us, contains the word "culpa" in the place of "custodia". But this appears to be interpolated. Justinian, as we have seen,[82] generally attempted to dispose of the objective classical liability for custodia and substituted culpa for it. Apart from that, the "quod si" at the beginning of the next sentence ("quod si rei communi socius nocuit, magis admittit culpam quoque venire") would not make sense if both sentences had been dealing with liability for culpa.[83] The source of inspiration for this strict type of liability seems to have been the rules developed with regard to locatio conductio operis. For it can happen (as, indeed, it does in the examples mentioned in D. 17, 2, 52, 2) that the same opera which may be promised by way of locatio conductio became the object of a societas. The work, under these circumstances, is equivalent to a contribution of any other kind towards the common purpose.[84] Unlike under a

---

[80] Cf., apart from Ulp. D. 17, 2, 52, 2 and Ulp. D. 13, 6, 5, 2, Paul. D. 17, 2, 65, 9; Ulp. D. 50, 17, 23; Paul. Sent. II, XVI. These texts have all been suspected of interpolation; traditionally the liability of the socius for culpa has been regarded as being of post-classical origin. Cf. particularly Wieacker, (1934) 54 *ZSS* 52 sqq.; but, see more recently, Laffely, op. cit., note 29, pp. 22 sqq., 60 sqq., 137 sqq.; cf. also Hausmaninger, *Festschrift Kaser*, p. 275. For a further interesting case of liability for culpa (in eligendo?) (also, possibly, spurious), cf. supra, note 29.

[81] Ulp. D. 17, 2, 52, 2.

[82] Cf. supra, pp. 192 sq.

[83] Cf. further Ulp. D. 17, 2, 52, 3.

[84] The contribution of the partners to the societas could consist in money or other material assets, expertise or labour (or, of course, a combination of these); cf. e.g. Ulp. D. 17, 2, 5, 1; Pomp. D. 17, 2, 6; Proc. D. 17, 2, 80. "Pretium enim operae artis est velamentum" is a somewhat cryptic way of expressing this idea; cf. Arangio-Ruiz, op. cit., note 5, p. 192; Wieacker, (1934) 54 *ZSS* 48; Laffely, op. cit., note 29, p. 29.

contract of work, it is not done with a view to earning a merces. But societas and locatio conductio operis did not differ as to the nature of the work to be accomplished; and thus it is not unreasonable to expect of a socius in the role of a contractor what a contractor proper owes, too. The latter, as we have seen, was taken to have guaranteed that he was competent to perform the job that he had undertaken; and he was liable for custodia with regard to any objects handed over to him.[85] This applied, for instance, if a herd of animals was entrusted to a cattle-breeder or arable lands to a politor for the raising of crops; and if that was appropriate where the breeding or cultivation was a performance for which a remuneration had been promised, it was equally apposite where it constituted the contribution to a societas. It is, incidentally, highly significant that it is one and the same author, namely Celsus, whom we see discussing very similar examples in both D. 19, 2, 9, 5 and in D. 17, 2, 52, 3.[86]

8. Creation and partition of joint ownership

The bringing of the actio pro socio dissolved the societas. This was the end of the obligatory relationship between the partners. But what about the assets that were jointly owned by the partners? Apart, of course, from the societas omnium bonorum, the existence of such partnership property was not essential for a societas; a business partnership could be (and usually was) run without it.[87] But where the parties had decided to pool all or some of their property, they became co-owners, each of them having "totius corporis pro indiviso pro parte dominium",[88] and their relationship was subject to the rules relating to communio.[89] As a consequence, where the societas was terminated, the actio communi dividundo had to be brought in order to achieve a partition of the joint property:

> "Communi dividundo iudicium ideo necessarium fuit, quod pro socio actio magis ad personales invicem praestationes pertinet quam ad communium rerum divisionem. denique cessat communi dividundo iudicium, si res communis non sit."[90]

Thus, where societas and communio coincided, two actions were available, one for the settlement of the mutual claims of the partners against each other, the other aiming at the adjudicatio of all res communes. As, however, the actio communi dividundo also entailed

---

[85] Cf. supra, pp. 397 sqq.

[86] Cf. Wieacker, (1934) 54 *ZSS* 45 sqq.; Laffely, op. cit., note 29, pp. 46 sqq., 52 sqq.

[87] For details, see Wieacker, (1952) 69 *ZSS* 332 sqq. Conversely, of course, the mere existence of common property (res communes) did not entail societas, either: Ulp. D. 17, 2, 71; Pothier, *Traité du contrat de société*, n. 2; Story, op. cit., note 1, § 3.

[88] Cels./Ulp. D. 13, 6, 5, 15.

[89] For details, see Kaser, *RPr* I, pp. 590 sqq. Differently Guarino, op. cit., note 11, pp. 60 sqq. (according to whom societas could be combined with communio only by way of a special pactum adiectum); but see Kaser, (1975) 41 *SDHI* 293 sqq.

[90] Paul. D. 10, 3, 1.

settlement of the claims resulting from the former communio,[91] both actions could overlap. The procedural consequence is spelt out by Proculus: ". . . altera actione alteram tolli [ait]."[92]

Much less clear than how the partners achieved a division of their jointly owned property, incidentally, is the question of what they had to do to create it in the first place. One would expect one of the normal modes for transferring ownership to have been necessary, viz. traditio, mancipatio or in iure cessio. For the societas omnium bonorum we do, however, have some evidence for what is usually referred to as a transitus legalis:

> "In societate omnium bonorum omnes res quae coeuntium sunt continuo communicantur, quia, licet specialiter traditio non interveniat, tacita tamen creditur intervenire."[93]

This sounds as if the assets of the individual partners became common property automatically upon the formation of the partnership. But as cumbersome or even impossible as it would have been to require specific legal acts between all socii with regard to all their assets, it is hardly credible that it should have been possible, in classical law, to create co-ownership nudo consensu. The societas omnium bonorum finds its origin in the old consortium (ad exemplum fratrum suorum), which was constituted by way of "certa legis actio". It entailed, as a matter of course, community of property. It is not unlikely that this legis actio lived on, in a modernized version, as a collective (formal or merely factual?) act constituting joint ownership pro indiviso of the socii (omnium bonorum) in all their assets existing at the time of creation of the societas.[94]

II. JUSTINIAN, IUS COMMUNE AND MODERN DEVELOPMENTS

1. Liability between socii

Societas, as we have sketched it so far, was a typically Roman institution. It was based on good faith and fraternity, and it entailed a minimum of obligations.[95] The lawyers, as usual, were anxious not to impinge on the freedom of the individual. Essentially a creation of

---

[91] Cf. e.g. Kaser, *RPr* I, p. 591; idem, *RZ*, pp. 265 sq.

[92] Paul. D. 17, 2, 38, 1. Otherwise, of course, the two actions could be brought together. Cf. Ulp. D. 17, 2, 43 and Levy, *Konkurrenz*, vol. II, pp. 139 sqq.; Arangio-Ruiz, op. cit., note 5, pp. 195 sqq.; J.A.C. Thomas, "Concurrence of Actions with 'Actio Pro Socio' ", (1972) 7 *The Irish Jurist* 151 sqq.; Laffely, op. cit., note 29, pp. 89 sqq.

[93] Paul. D. 17, 2, 1, 1; Gai. D. 17, 2, 2.

[94] On this problem cf. Wieacker, *Societas*, pp. 138 sqq.; Arangio-Ruiz, op. cit., note 5, pp. 123 sqq.; Wieacker, (1952) 69 *ZSS* 498 sqq.; Paul van Warmelo, "Joint Ownership in Roman Law", (1957) 25 *TR* 150 sqq.; Pierre Cornioley, "De la 'communicatio rerum' dans la societas omnium bonorum"; in: *Sein und Werden im Recht, Festgabe für Ulrich von Lübtow* (1970), pp. 493 sqq.; Kaser, (1975) 41 *SDHI* 300 sqq.

[95] Wieacker, (1952) 69 *ZSS* 342; Schulz, *CRL*, p. 553; Kaser, *RPr* I, p. 576.

Republican jurisprudence, the consensual contract of societas survived the centuries and was preserved for posterity by Justinian. Even at this stage, it was still the only transaction allowing two or more parties to pool their assets for a common purpose.[96] Neither the classical lawyers nor Justinian had developed any new types of commercial associations. Nevertheless, the picture presented in the Corpus Juris Civilis is not without problems and even inner inconsistencies.[97] More particularly, there are those instances where the Digest reflects, rather disconnectedly, the different phases of development that a specific rule had undergone in classical law. The standard of the socius' liability is perhaps the best example.

Justinian himself seems to have been persuaded by the argument advanced by Gaius (". . . qui parum diligentem socium sibi adsumit, de se queri debet"); in his *Institutes*, he therefore declared diligentia quam in suis to be sufficient.[98] Ironically, in order to achieve a restriction of liability, he reverted to the very text (Gai. 2 rer. cott.) which had originally served as a bridge for the *extension* of liability from dolus to culpa (in abstracto). In the Digest, however, we find not only the diligentia quam in suis of D. 17, 2, 72 but other instances where liability is for culpa (in abstracto) or even only for dolus. This obviously created problems in later centuries.[99] Of the modern codes, § 211 I 17 PrALR, § 708 BGB[100] and art. 538 I OR have opted for diligentia quam in suis, art. 1850 code civil and § 1191 ABGB for culpa without any further qualification.

2. The societas and third parties

(a) Socii venaliciarii, actiones adiecticiae qualitatis and societates publicanorum

More importantly, though, Justinian's compilation contains certain nuances—disturbing for the purist but most welcome to more pragmatic modernizers of later ages—which are irreconcilable with the original concept of a partnership law concerned, nearly exclusively, with the relations of the partners inter se (and even that only for the purposes and in the context of winding up), not with those of "the"

[96] For an alternative way of organizing entrepreneurial activities (use of servi communes) cf. Andrea Di Porto, *Impresa collettiva e schiavo 'manager' in Roma antica (II sec. a.C.–II sec. d.C)*" (1984). According to Di Porto, certain deficiencies of the Roman societas (as, for instance, the instability of its structure) could thus be avoided. But see Alfons Bürge, (1988) 105 *ZSS* 856 sqq.

[97] On the law of partnership under Justinian, see Guarino, op. cit., note 11, pp. 41 sqq.; Kaser, *RPr* II, pp. 410 sqq.; idem, (1975) 41 *SDHI* 318 sqq.

[98] *Inst.* III, 25, 9; cf. further De Robertis, *Responsabilità*, pp. 545 sqq.

[99] Cf. Hoffmann, *Fahrlässigkeit*, pp. 100 sq., 146 sqq., 215 sq.; Glück, vol. 15, pp. 433 sqq.

[100] The diligentia quam in suis in § 708 BGB has repeatedly been criticized, and the courts have tried to limit its range of application in various ways. Cf., for example, BGHZ 46, 313 (317), relating to road-traffic situations; further Karsten Schmidt, "Gesellschaft bürgerlichen Rechts", in: *Gutachten und Vorschläge zur Überarbeitung des Schuldrechts*, vol. III (1983), pp. 525 sqq.

societas against third parties. We may mention here a special rule, attributed to Paul and relating to socii venaliciarii (firms of slave-dealers): where one of them had sold a slave, the aedilitian remedies could be brought not only against the vendor but also against other members of the firm, "ne cogeretur emptor cum multis litigare . . . nam id genus hominum ad lucrum potius vel turpiter faciendum pronius est".[101] Then there is the generalization of two of the actiones adiecticiae qualitatis in Pap. D. 17, 2, 82 and Lab. D. 17, 2, 84: socii are liable for each others' transactions "[si] in communem arcam pecuniae versae sunt", and if the societas had been formed at the request of one of the partners, he could be sued directly by third parties with whom his partners had contracted ("Quotiens iussu alicuius . . . societas coitur, directo cum illius persona agi posse. . .").[102] Furthermore, there was the interesting phenomenon of the societates publicanorum (or vectigalium), financial companies in which the farmers of public revenue organized themselves.[103] Despite their name, they were corporate entities of public law rather than private partnerships. Thus, at public auctions (where the various kinds of State revenue were let for lease) the "socii" could act collectively through their senior partner (manceps); death of one of the partners did not dissolve the firm; and it was even possible for outsiders to invest capital in the societas by purchasing share certificates which circulated on the financial markets. Of great significance also was the fact that the actio pro socio could be brought, between publicani, manente societate: a rule which Justinian extended, rather vaguely, to other societates as well: "Nonnumquam necessarium est et manente societate agi pro socio."[104]

(b) Societas and agency

These are some of the more atypical features of the Roman societas, as preserved in the Corpus Juris Civilis. How far some of them possibly reach back into classical law cannot and need not be decided; to the writers of the ius commune, whose interest in Roman law was not of a purely historical nature, they provided essential cornerstones for a

---

[101] D. 21, 1, 44, 1; cf. further Ulp. D. 14, 1, 4 pr. and 1, Ulp. D. 14, 1, 1, 25, relating to a partnership of exercitores; Paul. D. 2, 14, 9 pr.; Paul. D. 2, 14, 25 pr.; Paul. D. 2, 14, 27 pr. relating to socii argentarii. For details, see Feliciano Serrao, "Sulla rilevanza esterna del rapporto di società in diritto romano", in: *Studi in onore de Edoardo Volterra*, vol. V (1971), pp. 743 sqq.; Guarino, op. cit., note 11, pp. 104 sqq.; cf. also already Wieacker, (1952) 69 *ZSS* 496.

[102] On these fragments cf. e.g. Serrao, *Studi Volterra*, vol. V, pp. 744 sqq.; Claus, *Stellvertretung*, pp. 145 sqq., 354 sqq.; Kaser, *RPr* II, pp. 106 sq.

[103] Cf. e.g. Buckland/Stein, p. 513; Thomas, *TRL*, p. 472; P.W. Duff, *Personality in Roman Private Law* (1938), pp. 159 sqq.; J.A. Crook, *Law and Life in Rome* (1967), pp. 233 sqq.; for further details especially Ferdinand Kniep, *Societas publicanorum* (1896); Claude Nicolet, "Polybius VI, 17, 4 and the Composition of the societates publicanorum", (1971) 6 *The Irish Jurist* 163 sqq.; Maria Rosa Cimma, *Ricerche sulle società di publicani* (1981); for the social background cf. E. Badian, *Publicans and Sinners* (1972), passim.

[104] Paul. D. 17, 2, 65, 15.

re-interpretation of the classical partnership contract in the light of contemporary social and economic conditions. Societas was received throughout Europe as a convenient and flexible basis for all personal business associations;[105] but in the course of this reception it was changed, in turn, not inconsiderably.[106] Some of its more individualistic features were abandoned for the sake of a greater coherence of the association, and the management of the societas was facilitated in that it ceased to be a merely internal association.

Especially important in this respect was the development of the idea of agency.[107] Here one could draw, for instance, on the actio institoria. Once it was recognized, first of all, that the socii could authorize either each other or one or more of their number, by way of an express or implied mandate, to carry out transactions arising within the framework of the common purpose,[108] it was a relatively small step to regard anyone who had such an implied mandate to manage the partnership business as an institor.[109] As a consequence, he could make his fellow-socii liable under the actio institoriae, provided he had acted only "nomine communi"[110] and not in his own name. But were the other partners liable in solidum or only pro rata parte, qua socii sunt? The latter appears to have been the rule, but it was almost negated by the number and importance of the exceptions.[111] Thus, it was often argued that a creditor had a solidary action against all partners, where the partners had concluded the transaction "promiscue", where they had entrusted the management of the partnership to one of them, or to an outside factor, or where they had all undertaken the handling of the partnership, not, however, "communiter et pro indiviso", but "pro diviso, seu separatim, per partes aut regiones distributa administratione".[112] Sometimes local custom or a piece of legislation

---

[105] "The Roman Law is an inexhaustible treasure of various and valuable learning; and the principles applicable to the Law of Partnership are stated with uncommon clearness . . . A slight glance at them will at once show the true origin and basis of many of the general doctrines, incorporated into the modern jurisprudence of Continental Europe, as well as into that of the Common Law" (Story, op. cit., note 1, p. IX).

[106] For details, see Coing, pp. 464 sqq.

[107] On the development of agency in general cf. supra, pp. 54 sqq.; on agency of partners, see especially Peter Stein, "The Mutual Agency of Partners in the Civil Law", (1958–59) 33 *Tulane LR* 595 sqq., and Story, op. cit., note 1, § 1, §§ 101 sqq.

[108] This was done already by the glossators; cf. Stein, (1958–59) 53 *Tulane LR* 598.

[109] It seems to have been taken first by the commentators: Stein, (1958–59) 33 *Tulane LR* 599 sq.; cf. also Coing, pp. 466 sqq.

[110] "Titius et socii" was sufficient; the other socii did not have to be named; cf. e.g. Holdsworth, vol. VIII, p. 198; Coing, p. 468. Cf. further Story, op. cit., note 1, § 102. On the business name of a commercial partnership ("*Firma*") in modern law, see Heenen, op. cit., note 1, nn. 127 sqq.

[111] Coing, p. 468; cf. also Stein, (1958–59) 33 *Tulane LR* 600 sqq.; Henning/Delport, op. cit., note 57, n. 413.

[112] Voet, *Commentarius ad Pandectas*, Lib. XVII, Tit. II, XII. Example: one of the socii manages the business at Perugia, the other at Florence. It seems to have been possible to limit liability to the amount of capital which they had originally invested: cf. Coing, p. 468; also

provided differently; thus, for instance, the Dutch usus hodiernus inter mercatores limited the liability of partners pro rata parte "etiam tunc, cum plures socii unum ex suo numero vel extraneum velut institorem societati praefecerunt".[113] A French *Ordonnance* of 1673, on the other hand, imposed solidary liability on each partner for the debts of a commercial partnership.[114] Interestingly, both the Dutch custom and the French law were justified as favouring commerce.[115] Of course, merchants may be more easily inclined to embark on joint ventures if they know that their liability is limited; on the other hand, they may find it difficult to obtain credit, for potential creditors usually find a societas more attractive where all partners are liable jointly and severally.[116]

3. The actio pro socio

Another major change the law of partnership underwent under the ius commune related to the actio pro socio. Each partner was obliged to make some contribution to the societas: be it money, movable or immovable property, skill or labour.[117] Material contributions, for instance, usually had to be transferred, in the normal manner, into the common property of all partners; since the days of Justinian, endowment of the societas with a jointly owned partnership fund (arca communis)[118] had been the rule.[119] But what if one of the partners refused to give up his ownership in what was supposed to become a partnership asset? What if, contrary to the terms of the agreement, he did not provide the use, for the common benefit, of what he continued to own, or if he did not render his services? According to (classical) Roman law, any of the other partners could sue, under these circumstances, only if at the same time he accepted termination of the contractual relationship between the socii.[120] By the time of the usus

---

Henning/Delport, op. cit., note 57, n. 362 in fine. On the question whether the beneficium divisionis applied, cf. Stein, (1958–59) 33 *Tulane LR* 601.

[113] Voet, *Commentarius ad Pandectas*, Lib. XVII, Tit. II, XIII in fine.

[114] Cf. Pothier, *Traité du contrat de société*, n. 96.

[115] Grotius, *De jure belli ac pacis*, Lib. II, Cap. XI, 13; Pothier, *Traité du contrat de société*, n. 96.

[116] On the liability of members of a partnership to third parties, see Heenen, op. cit., note 1, nn. 91, 140 sqq. It is characteristic of a partnership (as opposed to other forms of business association) that all members are personally and without limit liable for partnership debts. On South African law, see Henning/Delport, op. cit., note 57, nn. 412 sqq.

[117] On the need for a contribution by each member in modern law, cf. Heenen, op. cit., note 1, nn. 23 sqq.

[118] Cf. e.g. Pap. D. 17, 2, 82 (classical, according to Kaser, *RPr* II, p. 410, n. 9).

[119] Kaser, *RPr* II, p. 410. In the terminology of the later ius commune, societas was normally (though nor necessarily) quoad sortem, not merely quoad usum; cf. e.g. Wieacker, (1952) 69 *ZSS* 302 sqq., and particularly Ben Beinart, "Capital in Partnership", 1961 *Acta Juridica* 122 sqq., 144 sqq. On partnership property cf. also Story, op. cit., note 1, §§ 88 sqq.

[120] The same applied, incidentally, according to the English common law; only in equity was a remedy granted under certain (narrow) circumstances. For the details, see Story, op. cit., note 1, §§ 216 sqq.

modernus pandectarum a different view prevailed, and one was generally prepared, on the basis of D. 17, 2, 65, 15, to entertain an actio pro socio manente societate.[121] This action had thus changed its nature: it no longer necessarily and exclusively aimed at a general settlement of accounts, but could be brought in order to obtain specific performance in terms of the partnership agreement, and to force the socii to honour their obligations to contribute to the partnership.

4. The "community of collective hand"

Many of the essentials of the societas of the ius commune live on in the so-called civil (or BGB-) partnership of modern German law,[122] most notably the fact that it finds its basis in a consensual, express or implied, obligatory contract which can accommodate the pursuit of any kind of lawful purpose by two or more (natural or juristic) persons.[123] There is, however, one most interesting and characteristic new element which was grafted on to this partnership contract in the course of the *traveaux préparatoires* of the German Civil Code. The partners of a personal business association form, as a rule, a community of collective hand (*Gesamthandsgemeinschaft*).[124] The contributions of the partners and the objects acquired for the partnership in the course of the management of the affairs of the partnership become the common property of the partners.[125] But this partnership property is not held in (fractionally shared) joint ownership.[126] It forms a separate group of assets distinct from the private estate of the partners,[127] and the rights attached to these assets can be exercised collectively only by the whole group of partners. An individual partner may not dispose of his share in the partnership property or in the individual objects belonging thereto; he is also not entitled to demand division.[128] The property regime

[121] Cf. e.g. Glück, vol. 15, pp. 445 sqq.; Pothier, *Traité du contrat de société*, n. 135.

[122] Like most modern civil-law jurisdictions, German law distinguishes between civil partnerships (§§ 705 sqq. BGB) and commercial partnerships (as regulated in §§ 105 sqq. of the Commercial Code (HGB)). The latter type must have as its object the carrying on of a commercial enterprise (as defined in §§ 1–3 HGB) of a kind or size which is that of a fully fledged merchant. For an overview cf. Heenen, op. cit., note 1, nn. 68 sqq., 96 sqq. On the history of the commercial companies cf., for example, H. Kellenbenz, *HRG*, vol. I, col. 1935 sqq.

[123] Cf. for instance, the analysis by Karsten Schmidt, op. cit., note 100, pp. 450 sqq.

[124] Cf. "Protokolle", in: *Mugdan*, vol. II, pp. 988 sqq., as opposed to "Motive", in: *Mugdan*, vol. II, p. 344; Windscheid/Kipp, § 405; for an overview cf. e.g. Heenen, op. cit., note 1, n. 8.

[125] § 718 I BGB.

[126] §§ 741 sqq. BGB.

[127] As a consequence, § 719 II BGB provides that a debtor may not set off a claim which he has against a single partner against a claim which belongs to the partnership property.

[128] § 719 I BGB. Furthermore, it is characteristic of the community of collective hand, that where a partner retires from the partnership (e.g. by giving notice, dying, or having bankruptcy proceedings instituted against him) and where the partnership continues among the other partners, the share of the retiring partner accrues to the remaining partners: cf. §§ 736, 738.

therefore gives the partnership the appearance, particularly in relation to third parties, of a self-sufficient body, as a legal entity in its own right. It has to be remembered, though, that the partnership does not possess independent legal personality (one of the characteristics of the Roman societas that has been maintained throughout the centuries), and that it is therefore not "the" partnership as such, but the individual partners (in their collectivity) who own the social property. The adoption of these principles into modern German law forms part of what Huebner enthusiastically celebrated as a "triumph great almost beyond expectation",[129] vouchsafed within the law of associations, for Germanic legal science.[130] We are dealing here with a form of group ownership that goes back to the communities of collective hand in medieval Germanic customary law,[131] which in turn find their origin in the family associations formed after the death of the housefather. It seems to have been a widespread practice that the sons, in order to maintain the unity of the family estate, continued to hold the inherited estate in a common household. These households (and similar forms of personal unions) did not exist as corporeal entities, independent of the individual members. That was evident, most notably, in the fact that they could engage in legal transactions only through the collective action of all associates or commoners. Originally, they had to clasp hands and then, as with collective hand ("cum communicatis manibus consimilique consensu", "unanimi consensu et manu composita"), perfect the juristic act.

Whether this type of property regime provides a particularly happy solution for the modern law of partnership may well be doubted; business organizations, run in the form of a civil company, appear to require for their effective management the status of fully fledged separate legal entities.[132] Not only have reform proposals been made along these lines,[133] but even de lege lata a variety of authors have attributed legal personality to the civil partnership.[134]

5. South African law of partnership

(a) Sources

The modern South African law of partnership, uncodified as it is, is still

---

[129] *A History of Germanic Private Law* (1918), p. 159.

[130] And propagated, in the course of the 19th century, most notably by Otto von Gierke; cf., for instance, *Das deutsche Genossenschaftsrecht*, vol. II (1873), pp. 923 sqq.

[131] For further reference cf. G. Buchda, *Geschichte und Kritik der deutschen Gesamthandlehre* (1936); idem, *HRG*, vol. I, col. 1587 sqq.; cf. also e.g. Huebner, op. cit., note 129, pp. 139 sqq.

[132] Karsten Schmidt, op. cit., note 100, pp. 471 sqq., 481 sqq.

[133] Karsten Schmidt, op. cit., note 100, pp. 491 sqq.

[134] Cf. e.g. Werner Flume, *Algemeiner Teil des Bürgerlichen Rechts*, vol. I, 1, *Die Personengesellschaft* (1977), pp. 54 sqq., 68 sqq. For a comparative analysis of the problem cf. Heenen, op. cit., note 1, nn. 6 sqq.; in France, for instance, civil and commercial partnerships are now legal entities by statute.

firmly rooted in the societas of the ius commune. Even where the courts have turned to English law, the position has not substantially been changed. Thus, for instance, partnership is said to be a contract uberrimae fidei.[135] This phrase, Latin, yet slightly illogical[136] and un-Roman, attempts to reflect what Ulpianus had referred to as "ius quodammodo fraternitatis", which is implicit in societas.[137] The notion of the implied authority of the socii to act for each other has been imported from English law[138] but finds, as we have seen, its correspondence in the ius commune. English literature has often been referred to (particularly: *Lindley on Partnership*), but more as a matter of persuasive authority and in view of the fundamental similarity between the English and the Roman-Dutch law of partnership.[139] This similarity is explicable partly because the medieval lex mercatoria was the historical basis of English commercial law (including commercial associations),[140] and partly on the basis that the jurisdiction of the Court of Chancery (due to the convenience of its procedure) extended to all matters which involved the taking of accounts, partnership being one of these.[141]

Much attention has been paid by the South African courts to Pothier, whose *Traité du contrat de société* was translated into Dutch by Johannes van der Linden, the last of the classical Roman-Dutch writers.[142] Thus,

---

[135] *Wegner v. Surgeson* 1910 TPD 571 at 579; *Purdon v. Muller* 1961 (2) SA 211 (A) at 230G.

[136] Cf. *Mutual and Federal Insurance Co. Ltd. v. Oudtshoorn Municipality* 1985 (1) SA 419 (A) at 433C–F (per Joubert JA), relating, however, to insurance contracts: ". . . Moreover, there is no magic in the expression uberrima fides. There are no degrees of good faith. It is entirely inconceivable that there could be a little, more or most [utmost] good faith. The distinction is between good faith or bad faith. There is no room for uberrima fides as a third category of faith in our law. . . . In my opinion uberrima fides is an alien, vague, useless expression without any particular meaning in law."

[137] D. 17, 2, 63 pr. It is a common characteristic of all modern personal business associations: cf. Heenen, op. cit., note 1, nn. 28 sqq.; on rights and liabilities flowing from the ius fraternitatis Heenen, op. cit., note 1, n. 111 sqq.

[138] Cf. e.g. *Braker & Co. v. Deiner* 1934 TPD 203 at 206 sqq.

[139] Cf. e.g. *Bester v. Van Niekerk* 1960 (2) SA 779 (A) at 784F–785A. For a detailed comparative investigation of the principles of Roman law, 17th and 18th century civil law and the old common law cf. Story, op. cit., note 1, passim; for a comparison between (classical) Roman law and (modern) English law cf. Buckland/McNair, pp. 300 sqq.; J.M. Barrett, Erwin Seago, *Partners and Partnerships in Law and Taxation*, vol. I (1956), pp. 7 sqq. ("The law of partnership is a noted exception to the common expression: The Roman law has not had an appreciable influence on the English Law"). In many respects, the English law reflects Roman ideas still more closely than modern Continental codes. Thus, for instance, Heenen (op. cit., note 1, n. 4) states that "[i]t is unquestionably in England and in the United States that the 'personal' character of the partnership has been taken the furthest: any change in the members or even the simple withdrawal of a member results in the dissolution of the partnership; if the business is continued, a new partnership is created." (This is different in Germany, Italy and France: Heenen, op. cit., note 1, n. 48.)

[140] Cf. e.g. Holdsworth, vol. VIII, pp. 194 sqq.

[141] Another factor bringing partnership cases under the jurisdiction of equity was the impossibility of actions at common law between partners and the firm, or between two firms having a common member; cf. Sir Frederick Pollock, *A Digest of the Law of Partnership* (11th ed., 1920), p. 24.

[142] *Verhandeling van het Recht omtrent Sociëteiten of Compagnieschappen en Andere Gemeenschappen* (1802). An English translation (*A Treatise on the Contract of Partnership*) by

the following formulation of the essentialia of a partnership contract is based on Pothier:

> "First, that each of the partners brings something into the partnership, or binds himself to bring something into it, whether it be money, or his labour or skill. The second essential is that the business should be carried on for the joint benefit of both parties. The third is that the object should be to make profit. Finally the contract between the parties should be a legitimate contract. . . . Where all these four essentials are present, in the absence of something showing that the contract between the parties is not an agreement of partnership, the court must come to the conclusion that it is a partnership."[143]

The first authoritative statement occurs in *Joubert v. Tarry & Co.*,[144] and it has been confirmed on a number of occasions.[145] It has, however, been pointed out that this definition is partly trivial[146] and partly inconclusive.[147] The authority of Pothier has also been invoked to justify continuation of the partnership for the benefit of a deceased partner's estate, where this was expressly provided in the partnership agreement.[148] Such pacta de stando in perpetua societate appear to have been common in the commercial practice of the usus modernus;[149] among the Roman-Dutch writers their validity was in dispute.[150]

(b) General features

Otherwise, the South African courts still recognize the general common-law principle that "a partnership is not a legal entity or persona separate from its members".[151] Occasionally, however, a

---

O.D. Tudor appeared in 1854. Van der Linden himself, incidentally, also wrote about the law of partnership in his *Regtsgeleerd Practicaal en Koopman's Handboek* (Boek IV, Afdeeling I, §§ XI sqq.), leaning heavily on Pothier's *Treatise*.

[143] Cf. Pothier, *Traité du contrat de société*, nn. 8 sqq.

[144] 1915 TPD 277.

[145] For example in *Bester v. Van Niekerk* 1960 (2) SA 779 (A) at 783H–784A; *Purdon v. Muller* 1961 (2) SA 211 (A) at 217H.

[146] *Delyannis v. Kapousousoglu* 1942 (2) PH A40 (W) (". . . illegality as a ground of invalidation seems to be part of the general law of contract; as such it does not seem to me to be convenient to include it in a category of the essentials of partnership").

[147] Criticism has in so far been levelled at the qualification ("Where all . . ."). F.P. van den Heever, *The Partiarian Agricultural Lease in South African Law* (n.d.), p. 23, for instance, writes: "The ruling is about as sound as the argument that because an ostrich is a two-legged, animate being it is, prima facie, and in the absence of proof of some non-essential disqualification, a man." Cf. further De Wet en Yeats, p. 384.

[148] *Torbet v. Executors of Attwell* (1879) 9 Buch 195 at 200 sq. (per de Villiers CJ).

[149] Coing, p. 469.

[150] Cf. e.g. Voet, *Commentarius ad Pandectas*, Lib. XVII, Tit. II, IV, as opposed to Van Bynkershoek, *Quaestiones Iuris Privati* (Lugduni Batavorum, 1744), Lib. III, Cap. X; Van der Linden, *Koopman's Handboek*, Boek IV, Afdeeling I, § XII; further: Story, op. cit., note 1, §§ 5, 196. Roman law had accepted only a contractual arrangement to the effect that the partnership should continue to exist between the remaining partners: Paul. D. 17, 2, 65, 9 (often, however, regarded as interpolated; cf. e.g. Arangio-Ruiz, op. cit., note 5, p. 159, but see Kaser, *RPr* II, p. 412; idem, (1975) 41 *SDHI* 323 sqq.); cf. also *Inst.* III, 25, 5.

[151] *Strydom v. Protea Eiendomsagente* 1979 (2) SA 206 (T) at 209C–D. Cf. also e.g. *Muller v. Pienaar* 1968 (3) SA 195 (A) at 202G–H.

"juristic ghost"[152] materializes, for the societas, even though not a legal person, may sue or be sued in its own name, and it is treated by the Insolvency Act (24/1936) as having a separate estate and as being in the position of any other debtor.[153] South African law accommodates all sorts of partnerships, universal and particular[154] (including unius rei).[155] Whether a universal partnership may be only universorum quae ex quaestu veniunt or also universorum bonorum is questionable.[156] Unlike in most modern civil-law jurisdictions, no distinction is drawn between civil and commercial partnerships.[157] The ordinary action with which one partner sues another is the actio pro socio.[158] It normally lies only after dissolution of the partnership, but may also be brought manente societate, most notably in order to enforce a partner's duty to contribute to the partnership.[159] The partnership may be quoad sortem or quoad usum, in other words, the establishment of a partnership fund is not essential for the constitution of a partnership, although it is very common.[160] The individual items contributed to such fund must be made the common property of all the partners.[161] At the termination of the partnership[162] the partnership assets therefore have to be divided or

[152] H.R. Hahlo, Ellison Kahn, *The Union of South Africa: The Development of its Laws and Constitution* (1960), p. 702.

[153] *Michalow v. Premier Milling Co. Ltd.* 1960 (2) SA 59 (W) at 63B–G; *Strydom v. Protea Eiendomsagente* 1979 (2) SA 206 (T) at 209F–210C. In *Potchefstroom Dairies and Industries Co. Ltd. v. Standard Fresh Milk Supply Co.* 1913 TPD 506 at 513, partnership has been referred to as a "quasi-persona".

[154] Cf. Henning/Delport, op. cit., note 57, n. 365; for the common law, see Story, op. cit., note 1, §§ 71 sqq., for the ius commune Glück, vol. 15, pp. 375 sqq.

[155] *Bester v. Van Niekerk* 1960 (2) SA 779 (A) at 783F–784A.

[156] *Annabhay v. Ramlall* 1960 (3) SA 802 (D) at 805A–F; Henning/Delport, op. cit., note 57, n. 366. The societas omnium bonorum has possibly fallen into disuse in Roman-Dutch law; according to Grotius, *Inleiding*, III, XXI, 3, it was even "van oude tijden in Holland . . . verboden geweest". But see Pothier, *Traité du contrat de société*, nn. 24 sqq. The French code civil forbade an absolute societas omnium bonorum except between husband and wife (art. 1837).

[157] This may be due to the influence of English law, where such a distinction does not obtain either. On the situation under the ius commune ("Il est manifeste que, pour nos anciens auteurs, la société de commerce n'est qu'une variété, à paine différenciée, de la société civile") cf. Levy-Bruhl, as quoted by Coing, p. 465. But cf. Pothier, *Traité du contrat de société*, n. 56.

[158] *Shingadia Brothers v. Shingadia* 1958 (1) SA 582 (FC) at 583H.

[159] Cf. e.g. *Munro v. Ekerold* 1949 (1) SA 584 (SWA) at 589; *Oosthuizen v. Swart* 1956 (2) SA 687 (SWA) at 690H–691A; *Shingadia's* case, at p. 583; Henning/Delport, op. cit., note 57, nn. 407 sqq.

[160] For details, see Henning/Delport, op. cit., note 57, n. 391; Beinart, 1961 *Acta Juridica* 118 sqq.

[161] For details, see Henning/Delport, op. cit., note 57, n. 395. According to Voet, *Commentarius ad Pandectas*, Lib. XVII, Tit. II, VI and *Oosthuizen v. Swart* 1956 (2) SA 687 (SWA) at 692A–E, movables which are in the possession of a partner at the date of entering into the partnership become ipso iure common to the partners, without genuine delivery. This is the transitus legalis of D. 17, 2, 1, 1 and 2, as understood by the jurists of the ius commune.

[162] On the various circumstances under which a partnership is dissolved (apart, of course, from the bringing of the actio pro socio substantially the same as in Roman law), cf. Henning/Delport, op. cit., note 57, n. 419. Cf. also Pothier, *Traité du contrat de société*,

distributed again.[163] Thus the question arises, whether such liquidation is to be effected in terms of the actio pro socio or of the actio communi dividundo. The Appellate Division of the Supreme Court had occasion to pronounce on it in a case involving the goodwill of a partnership practice of veterinary surgeons.[164] Joubert JA, in an interesting and most erudite judgment, conceded that, from a purely historical and technical point of view, the actiones pro socio and communi dividundo are separate and distinct legal remedies, each with their own characteristics. Nevertheless, he chose to follow the "logical and practical"[165] approach of Pothier (introduced by Van den Linden into Roman-Dutch law), according to whom the actio pro socio may be employed for the distribution or division of partnership assets in the same way and with the same result as the actio communi dividundo. As, in turn, the principles of the common law applicable to the actio communi dividundo have been extended in Roman-Dutch law by means of an utilis actio communi dividundo to res incorporales which are held in co-ownership,[166] the choice of remedy no longer matters. In the result, it was held that by virtue of either of the actions, the retiring partner was entitled to payment of his half-share of the goodwill of the partnership practice which the other partner continued to run.[167]

---

nn. 138 sqq.; Story, op. cit., note 1, §§ 265 sqq. (who concludes [§ 267]: "This general coincidence of opinion, in assigning the same causes for the dissolution of partnership, in so many countries, shows, that the doctrine has its true foundation in the general principles of natural justice and reason, rather than in the peculiar institutions of any particular age or nation"; cf. also § 281: "Pothier, Vinnius, and other learned jurists, have done little more than to state the [Roman] doctrine with a few appropriate illustrations." For a comparative survey of the modern law, see Heenen, op. cit., note 1, nn. 41 sqq.

[163] For a discussion of the problems arising, see Beinart, 1961 *Acta Juridica* 148 sqq.

[164] *Robson v. Theron* 1978 (1) SA 841 (A).

[165] *Robson's* case at 854E.

[166] At 857D.

[167] At 861G–862B. For a discussion of the problem of the goodwill in the context of the dissolution of a partnership, cf. also Story, op. cit., note 1, §§ 99 sq.

PART V

CHAPTER 16

Donatio

1. Introduction

(a) Promises of gifts and executed gifts

"Throughout the world it is regarded as normal for binding promises to be given for payment or some counterpart in kind. Gifts and gratuitous promises, on the other hand, are regarded as something abnormal and the law always treats them in a special way."[1]

Take the promise to confer a benefit on somebody else, for entirely altruistic reasons. Does the donor really want to be bound? If so, one would have to grant the promisee, even where he is the beneficiary, an action to enforce such a promise. But would it not be slightly odd, if not invidious, to offer legal protection to someone who has not sacrificed anything, and thus to see the donor caught by his own altruistic act? On the other hand, the donor's act may have created a basis for reasonable reliance on the part of the donee; this is particularly true where the donation has already been executed and where the donee may therefore well have made further dispositions over what he has in fact received. Hence the distinction that may be drawn between promises of gift and executed gifts; for while a legal system may be perfectly happy to accept the latter as valid, without further ado, it does not follow that the former must under all circumstances be binding too. In fact, as far as mere promises are concerned, legal systems usually require the donor to demonstrate his seriousness of purpose; they either insist on a special formality as evidence of the intention to be legally bound, or they go even further and lay down general indicia of seriousness[2] in order to distinguish promises which are legally significant and thus enforceable from those which are not.

(b) Reasons for policing the transfer of gratuitous benefits

But there are other problems that have to be considered. Genuinely altruistic behaviour is not really all that common, and the spiritually edifying notion of the "cheerful giver" (whom God loveth)[3] does not in general correctly reflect the realities of life. Gifts can be made for a whole variety of reasons. Many of them are perfectly acceptable per se, but raise questions as to whether the transaction can still properly be called a donation: a benefit may have been transferred as a remuneration for certain services rendered by the other party or as a reward for an act

[1] Zweigert/Kötz/Weir, p. 61.

[2] Konrad Zweigert, "Seriositätsindizien. Rechtsvergleichende Bemerkungen zur Scheidung verbindlicher Geschäfte von unverbindlichen" 1964 *Juristenzeitung* 349 sqq.

[3] 2. Corinthians 9, 7 ("ἱλαρὸν γὰρ δότην ἀγαπᾷ ὁ θεός").

of rescue, or the donor may have wished to induce the donee to act in a certain way or to produce a certain result. In this latter instance, the donor will often impose a charge on the gift (donatio sub modo), with the result that the transaction includes a strong element of exchange. But then there is also a whole variety of situations where the donor does not appear in a very respectable light at all: the gift may have been intended to bribe public officials, to "purchase" political influence (Germany has just been shaken by the "*Flick*" scandal, stirred up by the discovery of generous contributions by a large firm to political party funds), or to remove certain assets from an insolvent estate before the creditors are able to seize it. Donations are often made with tax advantages in mind, or in order to sidestep and evade statutory provisions affecting either the position of the donor or the validity of an exchange transaction. They can also be used to undermine the formal requirements relating to the making of a last will;[4] in particular, donations can lead to a substantial depletion of the donor's assets, which may in turn jeopardize the prospects of inheritance of the donor's next of kin.[5] Every legal system that accepts the notion of forced heirship[6] must therefore face the problem that gifts inter vivos may diminish the estate transmissible on death to such an extent that the compulsory portions of the necessary heirs may be eroded.

(c) Conceptual problems

There are thus many reasons for policing the transfer of gratuitous benefits. But any such policing requires first of all some conceptual clarity about what a donation is. Is it a contract or a unilateral promise? If a contract, is it a consensual or a real one? If not a contract, when and how does it become binding? Or does it not become binding at all? Is it merely a disposition, on account of which an unbargained-for transfer of assets takes place: the position of the donee being not dissimilar, under those circumstances, to that of an heir after the death of the testator? Is it, as Savigny[7] put it, not a specific type of transaction but "*ein allgemeiner Charakter . . ., welchen die allerverschiedensten Rechtsgeschäfte annehmen können*?"[8]

[4] Hence, for instance, provisions such as § 2301 I BGB: "The provisions relating to dispositions mortis causa apply to a promise of a gift made subject to the condition that the donee shall survive the donor." But see § 2301 II: "If the donor executes the gift by delivery of the object given, the provisions relating to gifts inter vivos apply." For details, see Hans-Joachim Musielak, in: *Münchener Kommentar*, vol. 6 (1982), § 2301, nn. 1 sqq.; on donatio mortis causa in Roman law, see Kaser, *RPr* I, pp. 763 sqq.; Yaron, *Gifts in Contemplation of Death in Jewish and Roman Law* (1960).

[5] This aspect has been emphasized, in particular, by John P. Dawson, *Gifts and Promises. Continental and American Law Compared* (1980).

[6] Cf. e.g. § 2303 BGB; art. 913 code civil and, on the origins of forced heirship, Dawson, op. cit., note 5, pp. 29 sqq.

[7] *System*, vol. IV, p. 3.

[8] A general character which the most divergent legal transactions may adopt.

What are the elements of a donation: a permanent diminution of the donor's capital resources, an increase in the resources of the recipient and, as the essential test for distinguishing gifts from other transactions, the intention of the donor to enrich the donee? Or does it suffice that the impoverishment involved be unrecompensed? The legal analysis of donation raises intricate problems[9] and, in dealing with them, modern civil-law legal systems have preserved many characteristic elements of their Roman heritage. Roman law itself, however, here as everywhere else, was not static, but went through various stages of development. As far as donations are concerned, we should look at three different periods: classical law, the Constantinian reform and the position at the time of Justinian.

2. The concept of donation in classical Roman law

(a) Donatio and the contractual scheme

For the classical lawyers, donation was a disposition for the benefit of somebody else, for which this other party was not expected to give any recompense.[10] Such a disposition could take many forms:[11] it could consist in the transfer of ownership, in the creation or extinction of a limited real right, or in the assumption of a debt; the donor could, by way of stipulation, incur an obligation towards the donee, "cede" a claim to him, discharge one or all of the donee's obligations towards a third party,[12] or release the donee from an obligation towards himself. All these, and similar, legal acts[13] constituted a donation if they were intended to confer a gratuitous benefit on the donee[14]—if, as several

---

[9] This is already evident from the wide range of opinions as to the appropriate systematical niche for the law of donations. Justinian dealt with it in the context of acquisition of ownership; Buckland/Stein still place it under the heading "The Law of Property; Iure civili Modes of Acquisition". Savigny's treatment of donation is part of his discussion of the principles relating to legal transactions in general. Others, too, have regarded the general part of the system of private law as the proper place to discuss donation (contra: Windscheid/Kipp, § 365, n. 18 (pp. 549 sqq.)). The Austrian ABGB places it between the general part of the law of obligations and the specific contracts, the BGB next to sale (i.e. as part of its section entitled "particular obligations"), the code civil alongside succession by will (both being gratuitous methods of acquisition).

[10] Gian Gualberto Archi, *La donazione* (1960), pp. 23 sqq.; Michel, *Gratuité*, pp. 290 sqq.; Kaser, *RPr* I, pp. 601 sq.

[11] Cf. e.g. Archi, op. cit., note 10, pp. 85 sqq.; Biondo Biondi, "Il concetto di donazione", in: *Scritti giuridici*, vol. III (1965), pp. 649 sqq.

[12] Cf. the example discussed by Schulz, *CRL*, pp. 566: A pays what D owes to C. A's payment is at one and the same time a solutio with regard to C and (provided there has been an agreement between A and D to that effect) donatio in respect of D.

[13] Or factual conduct: cf. e.g. Iul. D. 39, 5, 14 ("Qui alienum fundum donationis causa excolit . . ."); C. 3, 32, 2, 1 (". . . si non donandi animo aedificia alieno solo imposita sint"; Sev. et Ant.).

[14] Cf. Marc. D. 24, 1, 49; Iul. D. 12, 1, 20 (". . . non ea menta pecunia daretur . . ."); Iul. D. 39, 5, 1 pr.

texts put it, the donor acted animo donandi.[15] To determine the scope of the Roman concept of donatio is not at all easy. Theoretically, for instance, it would have been possible to include the unrecompensed transfer of a thing for use. But that situation was covered by commodatum; hence: "utendum dare non est donare"[16] or, to use a positive phrasing: "qui donat, sic dat, ne recipiat."[17] We do find occasional attempts by the Roman jurists to distinguish between donations and similar, related types of transactions.[18] What we look for in vain, however, is a crisp and clear-cut definition of donation. The reason for this seems to be that there was no specific necessity to develop one. Donations did not throw up many problems in practice. More particularly, they did not constitute a contract, and hence no need existed to develop and spell out specific requirements on the basis of which an action might be granted.[19] Of course, that did not mean that the Roman paterfamilias was not able to promise to make a gift. Neither did it entail that, where a gift had in actual fact been made, the benefit had to be retransferred because the whole transaction was a legal nullum.

(b) The executed gift

On the one hand stipulations were available for this, as for any other purpose. These all-round transactions were particularly well suited to accommodate the promise of a gift, for they were in any event unilateral by nature and gave rise to an action without being linked to any kind of counterperformance. Also, the oral formality attached to stipulatio constituted, in classical Roman law, the most appropriate of all possible indicia of seriousness.[20] Mere agreements or unilateral

---

[15] Cf., for example, Paul. D. 39, 5, 34 pr.; C. 5, 3, 1 (Sev. et Ant.). The origin of the concept of animus donandi is a controversial topic. All references to it were regarded as interpolated by Fritz Pringsheim, "Animus donandi", (1921) 42 *ZSS* 273 sqq. Biondo Biondi has gone to the opposite extreme and accepts animus donandi, wherever it occurs, as classical (op. cit., note 11, pp. 680 sqq.). For a balanced assessment, see Archi, op. cit., note 10, pp. 33 sqq., 49 sqq.; Kaser, *RPr* I, p. 160; for a full re-examination of the matter, see Sergio Broise, *Animus donandi* (1975) ("*in luogo di una rigida contrapposizione fra diritto classico e diritto giustinianeo, si potrebbe suppore una lenta e graduale trasformazione dei testi lungo tutto l'arco di tempo che va dalla fine della giurisprudenza classica alla codificazione di Giustiniano*" (pp. 48 sq.)).

[16] Vat. 269.

[17] Ulp. D. 43, 26, 1, 2.

[18] Cf. e.g. Ulp. D. 43, 26, 1, 2 and 3; for details, see Biondi, op. cit., note 11, pp. 674 sqq.; Klaus Slapnicar, *Gratis habitare, Unentgeltliches Wohnen nach römischem und geltendem Recht* (1981), pp. 70 sqq. According to Geoffrey MacCormack, "Gift, Debt, Obligation and the Real Contracts", (1985) 31 *Labeo* 137 sqq. gift is the earliest type of transaction in simple societies. According to him, loans, deposits and pledges (i.e. the real contracts) were only subsequently separated from the class of gifts. This would fit in with the fact that commodatum is much better defined than the broad concept of donatio.

[19] Hence, Schulz, *CRL*, p. 566 says that the classical donation can be defined only in a negative way. Since it did not give rise to obligations, there could, for instance, be no implied warranty of title or for latent defects: see Michel, *Gratuité*, pp. 294 sqq.

[20] Cf. supra, note 2.

promises, on the other hand, that were not reinforced by means of a stipulation, were unenforceable.[21] Donations, therefore, did not fit into the contractual scheme of classical law. But where a donation had in fact been executed, such disposition was legally recognized even where it was not based on a prior stipulation. The gift did not have to be retransferred, because the disposition was both effective and justified. In other words: donations, while not giving rise to contractual obligations, were taken to constitute an adequate basis for a transfer of assets that had already occurred.[22] To take the prototype of a donation, the unrecompensed transfer of ownership of a corporeal object: the fact that the transfer was intended to be a gift provided the iusta causa traditionis necessary to effect such transfer and to justify the resulting enrichment of the transferee. To a certain extent one can compare the Roman concept of donation to that of mutuum (or commodatum). In both cases the agreement of the parties (unless it was clothed in the form of a stipulation) did not give rise to an action. Only once the capital sum/object had been handed over did the transaction become legally effective. But, whereas in the case of mutuum the factual handing over brought about a contractual relationship on account of which the lender was able to bring the actio certae creditae pecuniae and thus to claim back an equivalent amount, the effects of a transfer donandi causa were more limited. An action to reclaim was of course, not needed, for what is given by way of donation is intended to vest permanently in the recipient. Hence (in contrast to commodatum or depositum) there was neither need nor basis for a contrarium iudicium either. All that was necessary was to secure the donee's position, and that was exactly what the causa donandi was designed to achieve.

The classical law of donation thus offers a fine example of the very economical way in which the Roman lawyers developed their law. They did not set about designing grand new schemes of contractual liability, but contented themselves, in truly pragmatic fashion, with providing those adjustments and refinements that were indispensable to make the existing system work. More specifically, individual types of contract were recognized only where there was a specific need to do so.[23]

(c) The prevailing attitude towards donations

If we look at the classical sources handed down to us, we find the Roman lawyers discussing the various incidents of a donation mainly in

---

[21] Exception: pollicitatio. Cf. infra, pp. 508 sqq. On pollicitatio cf. p. 496.

[22] This is the causa donandi which was based on the donor's intention to donate and on the corresponding will of the donee to receive the gift. Of course, it was particularly the former that was of vital importance for a donation and was therefore usually emphasized. But nobody had to accept somebody else's gifts against his will: "non potest liberalitas nolenti adquiri" (Ulp. D. 39, 5, 19, 2); cf. further Iav. D. 44, 7, 55 and Honsell/Mayer-Maly/Selb, p. 345.

[23] For a crisp and clear account of the development, see Watson, *Evolution*, pp. 6 sqq.

the context of two rules restricting this sort of transaction: the lex Cincia de donis et muneribus and the prohibition of donations between husband and wife. Both these restrictions as such, as well as the fact that they provided the focal point for analysing the essential elements of a gift, reveal something about the general attitude of the Romans towards the transfer of unrecompensed benefits. Practical and somewhat matter of fact, they tended to be unimpressed by the façade of unselfish liberalitas and generosity and looked with scepticism rather than with sympathetic feelings upon those who disregarded the precepts of commercial prudence to such an extent that they did not secure some consideration for their performance.[24] The bonus vir did not squander his assets but tried his best to preserve them for himself and his familia. Where he did not do so, the inference could be drawn that something might in fact be wrong.

3. The lex Cincia de muneribus

(a) Purpose and background of the enactment

The lex Cincia was a plebiscitum dating from 204 B.C.[25] It prohibited gifts[26] exceeding a certain value, the exact amount of which is unknown to us.[27] Only relatives down to the fifth degree, a number of in-laws and step-relatives, persons engaged to marry, slaves in the donor's power or former slaves released by him, and certain other personae exceptae[28] were allowed to receive larger donations. What was the purpose of this enactment? In 204 the second Punic war was drawing to a close. Agriculture and economy were devastated, and thus the lex Cincia, attempting to restrain conspicuous expenditure, may have been part of an austerity programme.[29] But it is difficult to see how one can

[24] Eberhard F. Bruck, *Über Römisches Recht im Rahmen der Kulturgeschichte* (1954), pp. 121 sqq. But see also Wolfgang Kunkel, (1955) 72 *ZSS* 478, who draws attention to the fact that munificentia and liberalitas were highly rated virtues amongst the aristocracy during the later Republic and Principate. But they were often rather ostentatiously displayed and became an object of political calculation.

[25] Livius, *Ab urbe condita*, Lib. XXXIV, IV, 9. Cf. generally vat. 250 sqq. and for the discussion of all details, Archi, op. cit., note 10, pp. 13 sqq., 145 sqq. and Franco Casavola, *Lex Cincia* (1960), passim. Cf. also, more recently, Amparo Gonzalez, "The Possible Motivation of the Lex Cincia de donis et muneribus", (1987) 34 *RIDA* 161 sqq.

[26] The lex Cincia applied not only to dona but also to munera. On the latter cf. Marci. D. 50, 16, 214: "Munus proprie est, quod necessarie obimus lege more imperiove eius, qui iubendi habet potestatem"; as to the former, cf. Pap. D. 50, 17, 82: "Donari videtur, quod nullo iure cogente conceditur." Ulpian (D. 50, 16, 194) explains the difference in the following way: "Inter donum et munus hoc interest, quod inter genus et speciem: nam genus esse donum Labeo a donando dictum, munus speciem: nam munus esse donum cum causa, ut puta natalicium [birthday present], nuptalicium [marriage present]."

[27] Advocates were not allowed to receive any gifts at all; cf. e.g. Tacitus, *Annales*, Lib. XI, 5, 3 (". . . ne quis ob causam orandam pecuniam donumve accipiat"); Casavola, op. cit., note 25, pp. 15 sqq.; Gonzalez, (1987) 34 *RIDA* 167 sqq. (who regards this part of the lex as the most important from a social and political point of view).

[28] Vat. 298–309.

[29] Cf. e.g. Casavola, op. cit., note 25, pp. 19 sqq.

either boost the economy or restrain luxurious living by prohibiting large gifts. Yet, in a more indirect way, the lex Cincia did possibly fit into the general policy pursued by a whole host of leges sumptuariae:[30] for what worried the legislator may well have been the fact that sumptuous gifts allowed those families which had been able, in the course of these turbulent times, to accumulate considerable wealth, to corrupt the electorate or recruit a large clientele and thus to "buy" political influence.

But there is an even more convincing alternative explanation for the lex Cincia.[31] It has this in common with the suggestion advanced above, that the possible abuse of an influential position raised doubts about the motives behind large-scale gifts. We have seen that "one" did not render services for an agreed-upon, enforceable reward.[32] The admired posture, as far as the upper echelons of society were concerned, was that of the generous friend and counsel.[33] Acceptance of payment was regarded as demeaning. Acceptance of a voluntary honorarium, on the other hand, was not; and one is perhaps not wrong in surmising that powerful and well-to-do members of the establishment knew ways and means to make the socially and economically less privileged recipients of their personal services, their help and advice and their patronal protection show their gratitude by offering "presents" of considerable value. The lex Cincia may well have been a move to curb extortionary abuses of this kind.

(b) The application of the lex Cincia

But whatever its background, the Roman lawyers (coming from the influential circles of society themselves) did not enforce its provisions with much vigour. The statute was "imperfecta". It did not contain a criminal sanction;[34] neither did it render (nor was it interpreted to render) donations in excess of the ceiling void. Its implementation was left to the praetor, and he was only prepared to grant an exceptio (legis Cinciae) which the donor could raise if he was sued for payment.[35] That limited the effect of the lex Cincia to situations where enforcement of an unperformed promise of a gift was sought; once the donation had been executed, it could no longer be attacked. Hence it was crucial to decide for each individual type of donation, when and under which

[30] Wieacker, *Vom römischen Recht*, pp. 62 sq. On the leges sumptuariae cf. further Nörr, *Rechtskritik*, pp. 73 sqq.

[31] Cf. especially Archi, op. cit., note 10, pp. 21 sq.; along similar lines cf. also Gonzalez, (1987) 34 *RIDA* 167 sqq.

[32] Cf. supra, pp. 388 sqq., 413, 415 sqq.

[33] Dawson, op. cit., note 5, p. 13.

[34] Exception: advocates accepting a gift (cf. supra, note 27) were liable, according to an enactment by Augustus, to pay a penalty of quadruplum: Cassius Dio, *Historia Romana*, LIV, 18, 2; Casavola, op. cit., note 25, pp. 16 sqq.

[35] Lenel, *EP*, p. 513; for details cf. Wolf, *Causa stipulationis*, pp. 136 sqq.; Behrends, *Fraus legis*, pp. 19 sqq.

circumstances the transaction was complete (perfecta). A considerable body of literature dealt with this question, and it came to be established, for instance, that release from a debt, granted animo donandi, became unassailable with acceptilatio.[36] Concerning the donation of a corporeal object, Paulus drew a distinction:

> "Sed in persona non excepti sola mancipatio vel promissio non perficit donationem. in rebus mobilibus etiamsi traditae sint, exigitur, ut et interdicto utrubi superior sit is cui donata est, sive mancipi mancipata sit sive nec mancipi tradita."[37]

Besides promissio or (where appropriate) mancipatio, the actual handing over of the object (traditio) was required for perfection; as far as movables were concerned, perfection also depended on whether the donor was still able to bring the interdictum utrubi against the donee. It has to be borne in mind, however, that perfectio donationis entailed only the exclusion of any remedies under the lex Cincia; more particularly, the praetor did not grant an in integrum restitutio. But the donor was still able to reclaim what he had given by way of the condictio indebiti:

> "Indebitum solutum accipimus non solum si omnino non debebatur sed et si per aliquam exceptionem peti non poterat, id est perpetuam exceptionem; quare hoc quoque repeti poterit, si quis perpetua exceptione tutus solverit."[38]

§ 813 I 1 BGB expresses the same principle in these words:

> "What was done with the object of fulfilling an obligation may be demanded back even if there was a defense to the claim whereby the enforcement of the claim was permanently barred."

Of course, such an unjustified enrichment claim was available only where the donor had performed without being aware that the donee's claim was barred peremptorily by the exceptio legis Cinciae.

In the course of the classical period, the lex Cincia came to be regarded as outmoded. First, the exceptio was reduced to a purely personal privilege that terminated with the donor's death ("morte Cincia removetur") and that could not be exercised by his heirs.[39] The donor himself, after all, had not changed his mind, and his perseverantia voluntatis[40] was to be respected. In post-classical times, the lex Cincia soon fell into disuse.[41]

4. The prohibition of donationes inter virum et uxorem

(a) Origin and purpose of the prohibition

The second of the above-mentioned restrictions of donations had a

[36] Cf. Ulp. D. 39, 5, 17.
[37] Paul. vat. 311.
[38] Ulp. vat. 266 (cf. also Ulp. D. 12, 6, 26, 3); Schwarz, *Condictio*, pp. 31 sqq.
[39] Pap. vat. 259; 266; 278; Heinrich Siber, "Confirmatio donationis", (1933) 53 *ZSS* 141 sqq.; Archi, op. cit., note 10, pp. 175 sqq.
[40] Cf. generally Jean Gaudemet, "Perseverantia voluntatis", in: *Mélanges Philippe Meylan*, vol. I (1963), pp. 139 sqq.
[41] Kaser, *RPr* II, p. 399.

much longer life; in South Africa it was not abolished until 1984, when the new Matrimonial Property Act[42] came into effect. Section 22 thereof provides that "no transaction . . . is void or voidable merely because it amounts to a donation between spouses". The somewhat "belated eradication of this anachronism"[43] was generally greeted with relief. Why had it ever been introduced?[44]

The first references to the prohibition of donations between spouses in legal writings that have come down to us date from the time of Augustus;[45] and, indeed, it fitted in with the Augustan marriage laws.[46] It will be recalled that Augustus was determined to stop the alarming decline of morality and family life that had set in, particularly amongst the upper classes. On the one hand, he therefore tried to promote marriage and the procreation of issue; on the other hand, he prohibited marriages between free-born citizens and certain women of evil reputation. One of the means of achieving these ends was the imposition of social and economic disadvantages, particularly in the form of severe restrictions on the capacity of those living in a prohibited marriage, or as a childless couple, to take under a will. The spouses must have tried to evade these restrictions by making donations inter vivos, and the prohibition of donations between spouses thus served a useful function in supporting the policies of the leges Iulia de maritandis ordinibus and Papia Poppaea. But it did not originate in this context.[47] "Moribus apud nos receptum est", said Massurius Sabinus;[48] the prohibition was based on the mores maiorum and probably goes back as far as the first half of the 2nd century B.C.[49] The explanation usually advanced is "ne mutuo amore invicem spoliarentur donationibus non temperantes, sed profusa erga se facilitate".[50] Love makes people do

---

[42] Act 88/1984.

[43] June Sinclair, *An Introduction to the Matrimonial Property Act 1984* (1984), p. 42.

[44] For a thorough analysis of the sources, cf. especially Karlheinz Misera, "Die Zeugnisse zum Grund des Schenkungsverbots unter Ehegatten", in: *Festschrift für Max Kaser* (1976), pp. 407 sqq.; cf. also Archi, op. cit., note 10, pp. 195 sqq. and Lothar Holzapfel, *Ehegattenschenkungen und Gläubigerschutz* (1979), pp. 69 sqq. Holzapfel (pp. 65 sqq.) draws attention to the protection of creditors resulting from (rather than providing the original rationale of) the prohibition.

[45] Treb./Lab. D. 24, 1, 64; Lab. D. 24, 1, 65 and 67; Alf. D. 24, 1, 35.

[46] Kaser, *RPr* I, p. 331; Misera, *Bereicherungsgedanke*, pp. 237 sqq.; cf. also Alan Watson, *The Law of Property in the Later Roman Republic* (1968), pp. 229 sqq.

[47] As has been argued, for instance, by Mario Lauria, "Il divieto delle donazioni fra coniugi", in: *Studi in memoria di Aldo Albertoni*, vol. II (1937), pp. 513 sqq.; Archi, op. cit., note 10, pp. 195 sqq.

[48] As quoted (probably) by Ulpianus in D. 24, 1, 1.

[49] Cf., in particular, Franz Wieacker, "Hausgenossenschaft und Erbeinsetzung", in: *Festschrift der Leipziger Juristenfakultät für Heinrich Siber*, vol. I (1941), pp. 45 sqq.; Misera, *Festschrift Kaser*, p. 420; both hint at a connection with the leges sumptuariae, esp. the lex Voconia (about 169 B.C., designed, inter alia, to restrain the luxury of women inheriting big patrimonies, cf. e.g. Kaser, *RPr* I, p. 684). The prohibition can, of course, have originated only in the context of free marriage (i.e. without conventio in manum).

[50] Ulp. D. 24, 1, 1.

many strange things. It may lead to a serious impairment of the lover's ability to behave rationally. More particularly, the spouses may be induced by marital affection to indulge in the most extravagant acts of liberality. As a result, amor alterius may despoil (usually) the husband of his fortune—and may thus lead to a rationally and economically unjustifiable shift of assets from one family to the other. That was, however, not desirable: the preservation of family fortunes was in general a priority of Roman policy.[51]

It was from this perspective that the prohibition of donations between spouses was usually applied.[52] Pomponius D. 24, 1, 31, 7 provides an interesting testimony for a teleological restriction of the rule:

> "Quod legaturus mihi aut hereditatis nomine relicturus es, potes rogatus a me uxori meae relinquere et non videtur ea esse donatio, quia nihil ex bonis meis deminuitur: in quo maxime maiores donanti succurrisse Proculus ait, ne amore alterius alter despoliaretur, non quasi malivolos, ne alter locupletior fieret."

A is about to grant a legacy to B, or even to institute him as his heir. B asks A to leave what was supposed to pass to him to his (B's) wife, and A complies with this request. Are we dealing here with a (prohibited) donatio inter virum et uxorem? The answer is no. The prohibition does not exist in order to prevent one of the spouses (the donee) from becoming richer. It wants to protect the family fortune of the donor from being squandered due to the follies of love. Where there is no impoverishment on the part of the donor, this rationale does not apply. This is the case, for instance, in our example where what the wife will one day acquire has never been part of her husband's assets.[53] The conception of a donation was thus restricted to transactions which had two effects at the same time: an increase in the patrimonium owned by one of the spouses[54] and a corresponding diminution of that of the other.[55] This antithesis of pauperior–locupletior was the cornerstone for the application of the prohibition of donations between spouses[56]

---

[51] Cf. e.g. Misera, *Festschrift Kaser*, pp. 419 sq.; Holzapfel, op. cit., note 44, pp. 76 sqq. This is also the reason why the prohibition did not apply only between the spouses themselves but between all the persons belonging to their two family units: cf. Ulp. D. 24, 1, 3, 2–8; Ulp. D. 24, 1, 32, 16–21.

[52] Hence, for instance, the rendering of gratuitous services to each other or the use or occupancy by one spouse of servants, lands or other assets belonging to the other were not prohibited; cf. infra, note 69.

[53] Cf. also Ulp. D. 24, 1, 5, 13; 14.

[54] For an example of a donation which was regarded as valid because the receiving spouse was left in the end with no net gain, see Ulp. D. 24, 1, 5, 8 (donatio sepulturae causa; discussed by Misera, *Bereicherungsgedanke*, pp. 15 sqq.).

[55] The donor could not recover more than the value by which he was impoverished. Cf., for example, Paul. D. 24, 1, 28, 3 (in fine): If a husband gives his wife 10 and she uses it to buy a slave worth 15, recovery could only be for 10. (On the other hand, if the wife bought a slave worth 5, she would be liable only for 5 (this being the sum by which she was ultimately enriched).)

[56] For a detailed analysis, see Misera, *Bereicherungsgedanke*, pp. 6 sqq.; Archi, op. cit., note 10, pp. 75 sqq.

and, in the course of time, it became one of the essential and characteristic features for donations in general.[57]

(b) Purity of marriage

During the classical period, the prohibition was frequently seen in a different light. ". . . ne cesset eis studium liberos potius educendi", says Paulus,[58] and he adds:

> "Sextus Caecilius et illam causam adiciebat, quia saepe futurum esset, ut discuterentur matrimonia, si non donaret is qui posset, atque ea ratione eventurum, ut venalicia essent matrimonia."

This is the moralizing tone and tendency that had gained ground in the regulation of family affairs with the great Augustan reform legislation; it also dominates the oratio Severi that has come down to us in D. 24, 1, 3 pr.:

> ". . . [m]aiores nostri inter virum et uxorem donationes prohibuerunt, amorem honestum solis animis aestimantes, famae etiam coniunctorum consulentes, ne concordia pretio conciliari viderentur neve melior in paupertatem incideret, deterior ditior fieret."

At the core of the argument there is the ideal image of the purity of marriage. The prohibition of donations between spouses serves to preserve it. For marriage must be based solely on "maritalis honor et affectio";[59] procreation and the education of children has to be its principal aim. But for the prohibition, the conclusion of marriages might be dependent on calculations of economic advantage, and marriages might in the end become venal; but for the prohibition, the spouses might well be out to get donations from each other and thus neglect their duty to bring up children. But for the prohibition, finally, divorces would be a frequent and undesirable consequence of the fact that one of the spouses proved to be less generous than expected.[60] Occasionally these moralizing views found their reflection in the application of the law; thus, for instance, the prohibition was not extended to cover donations to a concubine, "quia non erat affectione uxoris habita, sed magis concubinae".[61]

A further interesting reason for the prohibition of donationes inter vivum et uxorem, incidentally, was advanced by Plutarch.[62] In his view spouses should share all their wealth with each other. Donations between spouses would conflict with this ideal in so far as, by giving

---

[57] Emphasized by Dawson, op. cit., note 5, pp. 15 sqq. and passim.

[58] D. 24, 1, 2.

[59] Pap. D. 39, 5, 31 pr.; cf. Kaser, *RPr* I, p. 321.

[60] The divorce rate soared towards the end of the Republic, a fact which may have influenced the perception and application of the prohibition (Misera, *Festschrift Kaser*, p. 425). The prohibition did not, however, originate as a reaction to the divorce problem (as Wilens, *Over Schenkingen tusschen Echtgenooten in het Romeinsche Recht* (1934), pp. 9 sqq., 90 sqq. and others will have it).

[61] Ulp. D. 24, 1, 3, 1.

[62] *Quaestiones Romanae*, VII and VIII; Misera, *Festschrift Kaser*, pp. 415 sq.

each other some part of their patrimony as a gift, they would at the same time implicitly exclude each other from the remainder.

(c) The application of the prohibition

Unlike the lex Cincia, the prohibition of donations between spouses was vigorously enforced. Infringement entailed invalidity.[63] The donor of a corporeal object remained its owner and could therefore vindicate it.[64] However, the rule was subject to certain exceptions. Donations between spouses were valid where they were designed to provide maintenance or where the donor acted in compliance with a moral duty or with what was demanded by common decency.[65] These exceptions were not in conflict with whatever one considered to be the rationale of the prohibition. Furthermore, as in the case of the lex Cincia, the perseverantia voluntatis was respected; if the donor died without having revoked the donation, it became valid.[66] Donations mortis[67] or divortii causa[68] were valid too, for at the time when the transaction became effective, the marriage had, sadly, come to an end. Donations of this kind were normally intended to secure the wife's maintenance; even though they did lead to a transfer of assets between the families of the spouses as a consequence of the marriage, such transfer did not occur while the marriage lasted, and it did not endanger the moral foundations and ultimate goals of that institution, at least not to the same extent as normal donationes.

In actual practice, the prohibition never succeeded in suppressing donations between spouses.[69] This is reflected in the great number of

---

[63] For details, see Misera, *Bereicherungsverbot*, pp. 84 sqq.

[64] Ulp. D. 24, 1, 5, 18; Paul. D. 24, 1, 36 pr.; if the object had been consumed or destroyed, its value could be recovered, but only to the extent that the donee was still enriched. Cf. Misera, *Bereicherungsgedanke*, pp. 84 sqq.

[65] Cf. e.g. Ulp. D. 24, 1, 21 pr.; Pomp. D. 24, 1, 29, 1; Pomp. D. 24, 1, 31, 8.

[66] Ulp. D. 24, 1, 32 pr.–2; Pap. vat. 294, 2: C. 5, 16, 1 and 3 (both Ant.); Siber, (1933) 53 *ZSS* 103 sqq.; Archi, op. cit., note 10, pp. 219 sqq.

[67] Ulp. D. 24, 1, 9, 2; Gai. D. 24, 1, 10; Pap. D. 39, 6, 40.

[68] Ulp. D. 24, 1, 11, 11; Hermog. D. 24, 1, 60, 1. The divorce must be imminent: Paul. D. 24, 1, 12. "If . . . the gift is made vaguely in contemplation of a possible divorce . . . the donation is void" (*Van Schalkwyk v. Van Schalkwyk* 1947 (4) SA 86 (O) at 96–7).

[69] Misera, *Festschrift Kaser*, p. 433. The same author draws attention to the fact that, where a donation has in fact been made, the obligation to return or to make good the value is excluded where the recipient is no longer enriched. That shows that in actual practice the spouses were to a certain extent seen to be sharing in each other's assets. The same appears from the fact that where one spouse was permitted to use clothes or slaves, or to live in a house belonging to the other, this was not regarded as an infringement of the prohibition of donations between spouses. Cf. Pomp. D. 24, 1, 18: "Si vir uxoris aut uxor viri servis aut vestimentis usus vel usa fuerit vel in aedibus eius gratis habitaverit, valet donatio."

This text raises intricate problems. Does it imply that habitatio gratuita was, after all, regarded as donation (rather than commodatum; cf. supra, p. 191)? Slapnicar, op. cit., note 18, pp. 103 sqq., disputes that and translates "valet donatio" with: "it is to be treated as a donation" (rather than "the donation is valid"). He argues that while habitatio gratuita was commodatum, certain rules relating to donations were applied per analogiam (Pomp. D. 39, 5, 9 pr. as to the lex Cincia; Pomp. D. 24, 1, 18 as to the prohibition of donations between spouses). Thus he comes to the conclusion that even though the transaction was not

cases contained in D. 24, 1 as well as in some of the exceptions which the jurists obviously felt compelled to admit. In many instances the spouses tried to disguise their donations and concluded, for example, a contract of sale at a low price. Generally speaking, nothing could be said against donations in disguise as long as the price, albeit a very low one, was meant seriously.[70] The validity of a sale, after all, did not depend on a iustum pretium. Between spouses, however, such transactions could not be tolerated, for this would have led to an erosion of the prohibition of donations. Thus, "inter virum et uxorem donationis causa venditio facta pretio viliore nullius momenti est".[71] Could one avoid this harsh consequence (invalidity of the whole transaction) at least in cases where the husband/vendor had the intention to sell (animus vendendi)? Neratius proposed the following solution:

> "[ait] venditionem donationis causa inter virum et uxorem factam nullius esse momenti, si modo, cum animum maritus vendendi non haberet, idcirco venditionem commentus sit, ut donaret: enimvero si, cum animum vendendi haberet, ex pretio ei remisit, venditionem quidem valere, remissionem autem hactenus non valere, quatenus facta est locupletior: itaque si res quindecim venit quinque, nunc autem sit decem, quinque tantum praestanda sunt, quia in hoc locupletior videtur facta."[72]

His answer was partial invalidity, based on a fictitious splitting up of the transaction. On the one hand, there was a (valid) contract of sale (for the whole sum), on the other hand an agreement to grant a remission of part of the price owed, and this latter agreement was invalid in so far as it had enriched the wife. According to utile per inutile non vitiatur, the invalidity would be confined to whatever of the remissio mercedis constituted a donation in terms of the pauperior–locupletior rule. Consequence: the wife would have to pay the difference between what she had originally agreed to pay and the true value (at the time of litis contestatio, not at the time the contract had

---

donation, it was invalid. But his view is unconvincing (cf. e.g. Knütel, (1984) 184 *Archiv für die civilistische Praxis* 190). The prevailing opinion is that even though the transaction *was* a donation, it was *valid*. Cf. e.g. Karlheinz Misera, "Gebrauchsüberlassung und Schenkung unter Ehegatten", (1972) 3 *Index* 397 sqq. The solution seems to be that Pomponius is using the term "donatio" in D. 24, 1, 19 in a wide and untechnical sense. Here, as in so many other cases, one should not rashly assume that the Romans used and developed a fixed and technical terminology. In this particular instance, the Roman lawyers generally seem to have used a dual terminology: sometimes we find them referring to a particular transaction as a donation, and then stating that a particular rule did, nevertheless, not apply to it; on other occasions they (more narrowly) used the term "donatio" only to refer to those transactions that fitted into the framework of this particular rule. See Hugo Burckhard, *Zum Begriff der Schenkung* (1899), pp. 15 sqq.; Misera, *Bereicherungsgedanke*, pp. 161 sqq.

[70] Ulp. D. 18, 1, 38: "Si quis donationis causa minoris vendat, venditio valet. . . ." On verum pretium, see supra, p. 252.

[71] Ulp. D. 18, 1, 38 in fine. Cf. generally Karlheinz Misera, "Der Freundeskauf unter Ehegatten im römischen Recht", in: *Rechtswissenschaft und Gesetzgebung, Festschrift für Eduard Wahl* (1973), pp. 25 sqq.; Broise, op. cit., note 15, pp. 119 sqq.

[72] Ner./Ulp. D. 24, 1, 5, 5 (genuine; see Misera, *Bereicherungsgedanke*, pp. 120 sqq.; idem, *Festschrift Wahl*, pp. 34 sqq.)

been concluded) of the slave. Thus, if a slave that was worth 15 had been "sold" for 5, but had in the meantime decreased in value (to 10), the wife would have to pay another 5. This was an ingenious argument, but it did not prevail. Most Roman lawyers opted for the invalidity of the whole transaction.[73] The main reason for their rejection of Neratius' solution seems to have been that he effectively made the wife pay more than she had ever agreed to. Such imposition of an obligation would have been in conflict with the Roman notions of liberty and private autonomy.[74]

In post-classical times, the prohibition of donations between spouses became more and more unpopular.[75] In the West it gradually disappeared; in the East, however, it continued to exist. It was received in continental Europe and became part and parcel of the ius commune.[76] In some countries there were customs to the contrary, in others further exceptions came to be recognized.[77] In Germany it was abolished only by the BGB. In South Africa a refined set of rules, based on the writings of the ius commune and amplified by a whole variety of court decisions, still existed until recently.[78]

5. The law of donation under Constantine

(a) Promotion of acts of generosity

To recapitulate: classical law did not look at donations as a special type of transaction; it merely recognized them in so far as they could provide a causa for various types of disposition such as stipulationes, mancipationes, in iure cessiones or traditiones. A donation could also be the basis for the acquisition of ownership by way of usucapio or longi temporis praescriptio. It was Constantine who went one important step further towards the "emancipation" of donations. He was favourably disposed towards such acts of liberality[79] and himself

[73] Cf. Ulp. D. 18, 1, 38; Afr. D. 16, 1, 17 pr.; Pap. D. 24, 1, 52 pr.

[74] Hans Hermann Seiler, "Utile per inutile non vitiatur", in: *Festschrift für Max Kaser* (1976), p. 139; Zimmermann, *Moderationsrecht*, p. 129; differently, Misera, *Festschrift Wahl*, pp. 40 sqq., according to whom Neratius based his decision on the lack of a certum pretium.

[75] Kaser, *RPr* II, p. 172.

[76] Coing, p. 240; Windscheid/Kipp, § 509.

[77] Cf. e.g. Stryk, *Usus modernus pandectarum*, Lib. XXIV, Tit. I, § 6 with regard to "donationes . . . tempore nativitatis Christi" and "die natali donatio modica"; Huber, *Praelectiones*, Lib. XXIV, Tit. I, 4 ("Hinc etiam munera, quae sunt modicae praestationes esculentorum, potulentorum; vel strenae natalitiae aut novi anni, inter coniuges non prohibentur"). As far as remuneratory gifts are concerned, see, for instance, Brunnemann, *Commentarius in Pandectas*, Lib. XXIV, Tit. I, ad L. Quod autem 7, 3; Voet, *Commentarius ad Pandectas*, Lib. XXIV, Tit. I, X; Lib. XXXIX, Tit. V, XVII.

[78] For details, see H.R. Hahlo, *The South African Law of Husband and Wife* (4th ed., 1975), pp. 128 sqq. A variety of other modern legal systems have adopted the Roman prohibition of donations between spouses; see Holzapfel, op. cit., note 44, pp. 99 sqq. for an overview.

[79] On the rise of the term "liberalitas" in the imperial propaganda and on its meaning, cf. Armin U. Stylow, *Libertas und Liberalitas* (unpublished Dr. iur. thesis, München, 1972), pp. 58 sqq.

made large donations to, among many others, the poor and needy, to widows, soldiers and churches[80] (even though he did not go so far as to donate Rome and the entire Occident to Pope Sylvester).[81] His attitude was influenced by the teachings of Christianity,[82] which was gradually gaining ground and which promoted acts of generosity and charitableness. Furthermore, post-classical practice was obviously no longer able to master the complexities of classical law. By the time of the 4th century A.D., the law relating to donations appeared to be riddled with difficulties. Two problems were particularly apparent. On the one hand, the implementation of the lex Cincia involved subtle distinctions between donationes perfectae and those that had not yet been completed (inchoatae); and shrewd advocates were able to sow confusion and uncertainty by raising intricate arguments and trying to give out donationes perfectae as imperfectae and imperfect ones as perfect.[83] On the other hand, the classical donation did not represent a legal act sui generis, but was tied to a variety of other transactions, many of them formal ones. But these forms had by now been whittled

[80] Clémence Dupont, "Les donations dans les constitutions de Constantin", (1962) 9 *RIDA* 314 sqq.; as to the contemporary practice in general, see Dupont, pp. 308 sqq.

[81] The famous "Constantinian Donation" provided the formal legitimation for the establishment of the Papal State; the document was drawn up by Roman clergymen in the second half of the 8th century. Constantine allegedly made the donation when he moved his residence from Rome to what came to be known as Constantinople (Byzantium, today Istanbul). The Catholic Church regarded the document as so important that every new Emperor (of the Holy Roman Empire of German Nation) had to confirm it; whoever doubted its authenticity was regarded as a heretic. On all this, cf. Horst Fuhrmann, "Das frühmittelalterliche Papsttum und die konstantinische Schenkung", in: (1973) 20 *Settimane di studio del Centro Italiano di Studi sull' Alto Medioevo*; D. Waley, *The Papal State in the 13th century* (1961); P. Partner, *The Lands of St. Peter. The Papal State in the Middle Ages and the Early Renaissance* (1972).

[82] Constantine had been acquainted with the Christian religion from an early age. Amongst the servants of Diocletian's court (where he grew up) Christianity was widespread. Diocletian's wife and daughter inclined towards it, as did Constantine's own father, Constantius. Constantine was probably educated by Lactantius (one of the Fathers of the Church), who was a grammaticus (language instructor). One of Diocletian's co-emperors, Maximian, had a Christian wife (Eutropia); her daughter Theodora (also a Christian) became Constantius' wife (i.e. Constantine's step-mother; Constantine's mother was the famous concubine Helena). Their daughters (Constantine's step-sisters) received a Christian education. The decisive event regarding Constantine's attitude towards the Christian religion was, of course, the battle at the Milvian Bridge in Rome on 28 October 312 against the usurper Maxentius, and his famous vision preceding it. Constantine was baptized shortly before he died in 337. The new Christian ideas were bound to be reflected in Constantine's legislatorial activities. One of his (heathen) successors, Julianus Apostata, referred to him as "novator turbatorque priscarum legum" (Ammianus Marcellinus, *Res gestae*, Lib. XXI, 10, 8). Constantine's panegyrist Nazarius acknowledged the same, only from a different perspective: "Novae leges regendis moribus et frangendis vitiis constitutae. Veterum calumniosae ambages recisae captandae simplicitatis laqueos perdiderunt" (*Nazarii Panegyrius Const. Aug.*, XXXVIII). On Constantine as a Christian ruler cf. e.g. Ramsey MacMullen, *Constantine* (1987), pp. 101 sqq.; Avril Cameron, "Constantinus Christianus", (1983) 73 *JRS* 184 sqq.

[83] "Multas saepe natas ex donatione, causas cognavimus in quibus vel adumbrata pro expressis vel inchoata pro perfectis vel plurima pro omnibus controversiam faciant, cum agentium visa pro ingenio ac facultate dicendi aut perfecta deformarent aut inchoata perficerent": vat. 249, 1.

down considerably, and all the uncertainties surrounding particularly the requirements for a valid stipulatio or for the transfer of ownership by way of mancipatio, were bound to affect both the law and the practice of donations too.[84]

Constantine therefore set out to simplify and streamline the law.[85] He recognized donations as legal transactions in their own right, albeit in a peculiar way. For he did not conceive of donations as contracts in the classical sense: as legal acts which have the effect of bringing into existence one or several obligations. The mere informal promise to make a donation remained unenforceable. Donation was conceived by Constantine as a bilateral act that was immediately executed and that led to the instant transfer of ownership from the donor to the donee. Instead of being the causa of the transfer, it became one of its modes.[86] This was in line with the general development of post-classical law away from the classical distinction between obligatory act and transfer of ownership. The contract of sale, too, was now, once again, regarded as a transaction that had to be concluded and executed at one and the same time, and that was no longer merely an obligatory act providing the causal basis for the transfer of ownership by way (usually) of traditio; it involved the transfer of ownership itself.[87]

(b) Formalities

If donations, under Constantine, were thus put on a par with the contract of sale as far as their legal effects were concerned, they were at the same time singled out in that a special form was required for their conclusion. Every donation had to be recorded in a document that had to be drawn up in front of witnesses and that had to contain the name of the donor, the designation of the gift and proof of the donor's title.[88] Secondly, the gift had to be handed over "advocata vicinitate" (before witnesses drawn from the neighbourhood), and finally, official registration of the gift (insinuatio) had to be effected. Non-compliance entailed invalidity of the donation.[89] These formalities were designed to avoid invidious and complex legal proceedings by facilitating proof and by preventing non-authorized persons from liberally disposing of somebody else's property. They do not seem to have been intro-

---

[84] Dietrich V. Simon, *Konstantinisches Kaiserrecht* (1977), pp. 92 sqq.

[85] For details, see vat. 249 (date: A.D. 323); further Levy, *Vulgar Law*, pp. 138 sqq.; idem, *Obligationenrecht*, pp. 236 sqq.; Archi, op. cit., note 10, pp. 225 sqq.; Biondi, op. cit., note 11, pp. 707 sqq.; Kaser, *RPr* II, pp. 280 sqq., 394 sqq.; Simon, op. cit., note 84, pp. 84 sqq.

[86] Levy, *Vulgar Law*, p. 146.

[87] Levy, *Vulgar Law*, pp. 127 sqq.; idem, "Verkauf und Übereignung", (1963) 14 *Iura* 19 sqq.; William M. Gordon, *Studies in the Transfer of Property by Traditio* (1970), pp. 63 sqq.; Kaser, *RPr* II, pp. 276 sqq. Contra: Wulf Eckhart Voss, *Recht und Rhetorik in den Kaisergesetzen der Spätantike* (1982), pp. 131 sqq.

[88] On this latter requirement cf. Gothofredus, ad CT 8, 12, 1: "Ius eius, id est, ex qua causa, quo titulo dominii rem eam quam donat habeat, ne forte rem alienam donet" (Simon, op. cit., note 84, p. 108).

[89] Cf. also e.g. Codex Theodosianus 8, 12, 3.

duced for fiscal purposes,[90] for donations as such were not subject to taxation.

While being inspired by a desire to favour and promote acts of generosity, Constantine's enactment also shows the new authoritarian tendency to regiment the actions of the individual. It was no longer left to the parties to protect themselves against the risks and vagaries of legal dealings, and to the classical Roman lawyers forms such as those prescribed in vat. 249 would have seemed to be in irreconcilable conflict with the prevailing notion of liberty.

(c) *Donations and dispositions mortis causa*

But there was a further side to the law of donations as it developed in the post-classical period. Gifts inter vivos and testamentary dispositions, both from a functional and from a conceptual point of view, became more and more closely related.[91] Dispositions mortis causa, in West-Roman vulgar law, tended to be regarded as a particular species of donation,[92] and even in the East they were referred to as donationes in a very broad sense of that term.[93] Tertium comparationis, so to speak, was the donor's motive: normally either to provide for his family[94] or to display generosity towards the Church or the Church-run charitable institutions.[95] Redemption and salvation of the soul became a dominant concern for the growing number of Christians who pondered about the vanity of the world and the brevity of their lives, and soon it became an established custom[96] to devote part of one's

---

[90] As is usually believed; cf. e.g. Archi, op. cit., p. 236; Kaser, *RPr* II, p. 395. But see Simon, op. cit., note 84, pp. 116 sqq.

[91] For details, see Francisco Samper Polo, "La disposicion mortis causa en el derecho Romano vulgar", (1968) 38 *AHDE* 87 sqq.

[92] Codex Theodosianus 8, 17, 7.

[93] Pringsheim, "Liberalitas", in: *Studi in memoria di Emilio Albertario*, vol. I (1953), p. 667.

[94] Cf. e.g. Dupont, (1962) 9 *RIDA* 308 sqq.

[95] Generally called venerabiles domus. These include the xenodochia (locus venerabilis in quo peregrini suscipiuntur), ptochotrophia (in quo pauperes et infirmi homines pascuntur), nosotrophia (in quo aegroti homines curantur), orphanotrophia (in quo parentibus orbati pueri pascuntur); brephanotrophia (in quo infantes aluntur); gerontocomia (in quo pauperes et propter senectutem solam infirmi homines curantur). Cf. e.g. C. 1, 3, 45, 3 (for the definitions, see P.W. Duff, *Personality in Roman Private Law* (1938), p. 178). As to the establishment and administration of these so-called "piae causae", cf. Hans Rudolf Hagemann, *Die Stellung der Piae Causae nach justinianischem Rechte* (1953), pp. 42 sqq.; Kaser, *RPr* II, p. 158. The history of the law of foundations can be traced back to them: cf. Hans Liermann, *Handbuch des Stiftungsrechts* (1963), pp. 24 sqq. On the relief and welfare activities of the Church, based on Christian caritas, cf. generally Hagemann, pp. 5 sqq.; August Knecht, *System des Justinianischen Kirchenvermögensrechtes* (1905), pp. 43 sqq.; also Glück, vol. 39, pp. 448 sqq. Cf. further Eberhard F. Bruck, *Kirchenväter und soziales Erbrecht* (1956), pp. 31 sqq., 37 sqq.; Duff, pp. 189 sqq.; C.P. Joubert, *Die Stigting in die Romeins-Hollandse Reg en die Suid-Afrikaanse Reg* (1951), pp. 29 sqq.

[96] Cf. e.g. C. 1, 2, 25. The Greek Fathers of the Church had attempted to strike a compromise between the ideal of absolute poverty and the realities of a less perfect, secular (but none the less Christian) existence and postulated that part of the estate ought to be left to Christ (on behalf of the poor); for details, see Bruck, op. cit., note 95, pp. 1 sqq., 41 sqq., 55 sqq. Essential for these gifts pro animae redemptione was their voluntariness.

patrimony "ad pias causas".[97] The last will, of course, was a particularly suitable place to think of such gifts "pro animae remedio",[98] and the lawyers tried their best to encourage, uphold and privilege bequests "ad pias causas".[99] A substantial number of decisions have come down to us, and many of them apply to donationes inter vivos too.[100] Gifts can obviously be used to anticipate testamentary dispositions;[101] both types of transactions under these circumstances serve the same purpose. Both should therefore be approached from the same policy perspective.

6. Justinian and the law of donations

(a) *Donation as a binding contract*

Whether the Constantinian reform achieved its aim of simplifying and streamlining the law of donations is very doubtful. If old problems were solved, new practical difficulties[102] and dogmatic obscurities were thrown up. One need only look at the cumbrous, contorted and largely untechnical language of this piece of legislation[103] to appreciate that by the time of Justinian a need to clarify and restate the law relating to donations was evident again. Justinian,[104] to a certain extent, revived the classical conception. He drew a distinction, once again, between the obligatory contract and the acts necessary to carry out the obligations

---

Accordingly, Justinian did not fix a quota either (but see his advice in Nov. 7, 2, 1: "ἄριστον μέτρον ἡ τῶν δωρουμένων καθέστηκεν ἀμετρία ").

[97] On the meaning and interpretation of pia causa first in the East-Roman Empire, then (from the Middle Ages onwards) in continental Europe and in England (sub titulo "charitable purposes"), see Reinhard Zimmermann, "Cy-près", in: *Iuris Professio, Festgabe für Max Kaser* (1986), pp. 395 sqq.

[98] In the Middle Ages, the gift pro animae remedio was taken to be domina testamenti; the main function of the last will was to make provision for the salvation of the soul. Cf. generally Philippe Ariès, *Geschichte des Todes* (1980), p. 233 sqq., 242 sqq; Bruck, op. cit., note 95, pp. 257 sqq.; Liermann, op. cit., note 95, pp. 106 sqq.; Alfred Schultze, "Der Einfluss der Kirche auf die Entwicklung des germanischen Erbrechts", (1914) 35 *ZSS* (GA) 75 sqq., 98 sqq. In England, too, dispositions ad pias causas were part of every testament; cf. Pollock and Maitland, vol. II, pp. 337 sqq.; Joseph Willard, "Illustrations of the Origin of Cy Près", (1894) 8 *Harvard LR* 69 sqq.

[99] Cf. e.g. Andreas Tiraquelles, "De Privilegijs piae causae tractatus", in: *Opera Omnia*, vol. v. (Francofurti, 1574); Justus Henning Boehmer, *Ius Ecclesiasticum Protestantium* (3rd ed., Halae Magdeburgicae, 1732), III, XXVI, §§ 19 sqq.

[100] Kaser, *RPr* II, p. 467.

[101] Archi, op. cit., note 10, p. 255.

[102] Constantine himself found it advisable to admit certain exceptions from the new formal requirements he had devised (cf. Codex Theodosianus 8, 12, 5 (A.D. 332, concerning donationes inter liberos et parentes), Codex Theodosianus 3, 5, 3 (A.D. 330, concerning donationes ante nuptias)). To subject every occasional gift to public registration must have been entirely impracticable. Legal practice generally does not seem to have been much concerned about the official requirements: "It is striking to see how often the emperors took occasion to insist on Constantine's requirements." On all this, see Levy, *Vulgar Law*, pp. 140 sqq. As far as the traditio requirement is concerned, cf. Gordon, op. cit., note 87, pp. 68 sqq.

[103] Analysed in detail by Simon, op. cit., note 84, pp. 86 sqq.

[104] Levy, *Vulgar Law*, pp. 152 sq.; Archi, op. cit., note 10, pp. 272 sqq.; Kaser, *RPr* II, pp. 396 sqq.

that had arisen.[105] As far as the gift of a corporeal object was concerned, this meant that the donation provided a iusta causa for the transfer of ownership. Furthermore, the promise of a gift became binding and enforceable again. Such a promise, however, no longer had to be clothed in the form of a stipulation; a mere, informal agreement between the parties was sufficient.[106] Using the conceptual material of classical and post-classical law, Justinian had thus managed to create something new: donation as a binding contract[107] in its own right. As under Constantine, therefore, donation was conceived of as an independent type of transaction; but, as under classical law, the structure of this transaction was that of an executory contract.

There was one further element which Justinian took over from the Constantinian legislation: the requirement of public registration of the gift. Again, however, he introduced modifications. One of them followed from Justinian's changed perception of donation, for insinuatio could no longer be confined to executed gifts, but was extended to the newly enforceable informal executory contract of donation. The main trend evident in Justinian's legislation, however, was towards relaxation of this form of public control over gift transactions. Donations had to be registered only if the value of the gift exceeded 300,[108] later 500, solidi.[109] This was a very considerable sum: the solidus was a coin containing 4,55 grams of fine gold, and the quantity of gold that made up 500 solidi would have sold in June 1986 for 58 334 German Marks (to take a relatively stable currency).[110] Certain gifts were even exempted from registration, irrespective of the amount involved: those that had been made pro redemptione ab hostibus[111] or for the purpose of reconstructing houses that had burnt down or collapsed,[112] or gifts to the Emperor,[113] to mention some examples.

---

[105] Cf. generally Kaser, *RPr* II, pp. 282 sqq. As far as donations are concerned, cf. e.g. C. 8, 53, 35, 5 b (". . . non ex hoc inutilis sit donatio, quod res non traditae sunt, nec confirmetur ex traditione donatio") and *Inst.* II, 7, 2 (". . . et ad exemplum venditionis nostra constitutio eas etiam in se habere necessitatem traditionis voluit, ut, et si non tradantur, habeant plenissimum et perfectum robur et traditionis necessitas incumbat donatori").

[106] Cf. e.g. *Inst.* II, 7, 2: "[P]erficiuntur autem [donationes], cum donator suam voluntatem scriptis aut sine scriptis manifestaverit."

[107] Cf. e.g. C. 4, 21, 17 pr.; Pringsheim, (1921) 42 *ZSS* 275 sqq.

[108] C. 8, 53, 33 pr. (529 A.D.). [109] C. 8, 54, 36, 3 (531 A.D.); *Inst.* II, 7, 2.

[110] Certain provincial governors earned 300 solidi a year (of which 40–50 had to be passed on): Nov. 24–26.

[111] C. 8, 53, 36 pr. On redemptio ab hostibus in classical law, see Kaser, *RPr* I, p. 291; in post-classical times, see Knecht, pp. 105 sqq.; Ernst Levy, "Captivus redemptus", in: *Gesammelte Schriften*, vol. II (1963), pp. 40 sqq.; generally Adalbert Erler, *Der Loskauf Gefangener. Ein Rechtsproblem seit drei Jahrtausenden* (1978). Usually, one was dealing with the redemption of Christian prisoners who had fallen into heathen hands; in a wide sense of the term, the donor was thus promoting pia causa; hence the favourable treatment of the donation.

[112] C. 8, 53, 36, 2.

[113] Nov. 52, 2. As to gifts made by the Emperor, cf. C. 8, 53, 34, 1 a (and the case of Prince William of Orange, who promised to pay to "faeminae illustri" an annuity of 4 000 florins, as reported by Van Bynkershoek, *Observationes Tumultuariae*, nn. 260, 1870).

(b) *Enter the cheerful giver*

It is obvious that Justinian was very much inclined to favour acts of liberality and to promote generosity, and it is equally clear that this attitude found its basis in the teachings of Christianity. ". . . humanitas, per quam solam dei servatur imitatio"[114] was the general guideline for the application and reform of the law of donation. This is apparent, too, from the wide meaning given to the term "donation"[115] and from the fact that the motive for conferring the benefit became its dominant characteristic. The classical lawyers had referred to the animus donandi, but for them it was one of several attributes of a donation. In post-classical law the intention of the donor to donate had emerged as the essential feature establishing this type of transaction and distinguishing it from any other.[116] Justinian went yet one step further. Amending a statement by Iulianus, he inserted the following definition of donation into the Digest:

> "[D]at aliquis ea mente, ut statim velit accipientis fieri nec ullo casu ad se reverti, et propter nullam aliam causam facit, quam ut liberalitatem et munificentiam exerceat: haec proprie donatio appellatur."[117]

This text emphasizes the donor's noble spirit: he must have been moved by the desire to perform an unselfish act of liberality and must not have entered into the transaction for any egoistic motives. Here we see

---

[114] C. 5, 16, 27, 1.

[115] For details, see Kaser, *RPr* II, p. 398; Pringsheim, *Studi Albertario*, vol. I, pp. 667 sqq. Levy, *Obligationenrecht*, p. 240 refers to an "inflation" of the concept of donatio. The term "donation" was now also used to cover pollicitationes. Cf. e.g. Ulp. D. 39, 5, 19 pr. Both had been kept separate in classical law. A pollicitatio was the promise of a gift of money or of the performance of work (e.g. to build a monument) which a citizen made to his municipality, usually on the occasion of his candidacy for a municipal office or for a priesthood ("ob honorem"). Such a promise was binding and actionable in the cognitio extra ordinem, even though it was based on a unilateral, informal declaration. For details, see D. 50, 12 and Archi, op. cit., note 10, pp. 28 sqq.; Biondi, op. cit., note 11, pp. 677 sqq.; Pringsheim, *Studi Albertario*, vol. I, pp. 672 sqq.; cf. also T.B. Smith, "Pollicitatio—Promise and Offer", in: *Studies Critical and Comparative* (1962), pp. 168 sqq. Furthermore, "suffragium" had, in the course of the 4th century, come to be regarded as a variety of donation and was subjected to the formal requirements laid down in vat. 249 (Codex Theodosianus 2, 29, 2). Suffragium was the promise of a reward in order to obtain a public office; it provides a remarkable testimony to the corruption rampant during this period. If the donor obtained the office, he was bound to honour his promise. Nor could he claim back what he had given in advance. Cf. Levy, *Vulgar Law*, pp. 169 sq.; idem, *Obligationenrecht*, pp. 248 sq.; Claude Collot, "La pratique et l'institution du suffragium au Bas-Empire", (1965) 43 *RH* 185 sqq.

[116] Pringsheim, (1921) 42 *ZSS* 273 sqq. (but see supra, note 15); Bruck, op. cit., note 24, pp. 134 sqq.

[117] D. 39, 5, 1 pr. (generally held to be interpolated from "et propter" to "exercat"): Kaser, *RPr* II, p. 398.

Paulus' (the Apostle Paulus') cheerful giver,[118] after having penetrated the ethical and religious postulates of the Greek Fathers of the Church,[119] entering into the legal arena. There he was to set out on a long journey through much of the medieval and the modern law of donation;[120] for D. 39, 5, 1 pr. appeared at the outset of the title "De donationibus" and was too prominently placed to be able to be overlooked.

Pure altruism and unselfishness, of course, are much to be admired, but, regrettably, are rare in legal dealings. Human nature being what it is, "it is much more common for altruism to be somewhat impure",[121] and Justinian's infusion of contemporary Christian ethics into the law was to throw up problems; purity of motive is an unhandy criterion for legal distinctions. Justinian himself, incidentally, recognized one exception: a donation could be made animo remunerandi,[122] and it is due to Christian influence, once again, that even a naturalis obligatio came to be recognized to remunerate past services in this way.[123] Remunerative gifts[124] also received a special treatment in that they could not be revoked.[125]

(c) *Revocation of donations*

For "ordinary" gifts such a right of revocation had gradually been introduced on the ground of ingratitude. This was consistent with the general trend towards ethicizing the law of donations, and it would have been odd to scrutinize the donor's motives without also subjecting the donee's behaviour at least to certain moral minimum standards. First of all, the patron was given the right to revoke donations made to a freedman who turned out to be ungrateful.[126] In the course of time, this idea was extended to other donor/donee relationships,[127] until we find Justinian rounding the development off in the following way:

---

[118] Cf. supra, note 3.

[119] For a detailed analysis, see Bruck, op. cit., note 24, pp. 101 sqq. (first under the title "Ethics vs. Law: St. Paul, the Fathers of the Church, and the 'Cheerful Giver' in Roman Law", (1944) 2 *Traditio* 97 sqq.).

[120] Recounted by Bruck, op. cit., note 24, pp. 137 sqq. (first in (1946) 4 *Seminar* 45 sqq. sub titulo "The Ghost Story of the 'Cheerful Giver' in Medieval and Modern Civil Law").

[121] Dawson, op. cit., note 5, p. 86.

[122] Ulp. D. 15, 3, 10, 7.

[123] Ulp. D. 5, 3, 25, 11 (interpolated; Pierre Cornioley, *Naturalis obligatio* (1964), pp. 256 sq.).

[124] Cf. e.g. Levy, *Obligationenrecht*, p. 239; Ferdinando Bona, "Contributi alla storia della 'societas universorum quae ex quaestu veniunt' in diritto romano", in: *Studi in onore di Giuseppe Grosso*, vol. I (1968), pp. 418 sqq.; but see Michel, *Gratuité*, pp. 279 sqq., who concludes that for the Romans remuneratio and donation were two different things.

[125] Paul. D. 39, 5, 34, 1 (interpolated). This text deals with a rescue situation ("Si quis aliquem a latrumculis vel hostibus eripuit et aliquid pro eo ab ipso accipiat, haec donatio inrevocabilis est: non merces eximii laboris appellanda est, quod contemplatione salutes certo modo aestimari non placuit"). Cf., most recently, Broise, op. cit., note 15, pp. 89 sqq.

[126] C. 8, 55, 1 (A.D. 249).

[127] Vat. 248; Codex Theodosianus 8, 13, 1 and 2; Levy, *Obligationenrecht*, pp. 245 sqq.

> "Generaliter sancimus omnes donationes lege confectas firmas illibatasque manere, si non donationis acceptor ingratus circa donatorem inveniatur, ita ut iniurias atroces in eum effundat vel manus impias inferat vel iacturae molem ex insidiis suis ingerat, quae non levem sensum substantiae donatoris imponit vel vitae periculum aliquid ei intulerit vel quasdam conventiones sive in scriptis donationi impositas sive sine scriptis habitas, quas donationis acceptor spopondit, minime implere voluerit."[97]

This provision proceeded through the ius commune[98] into the modern codifications.[99] To see a woman cash in donations from her spouse and then commit adultery,[100] for example, is unlovely and hardly acceptable.

So is the idea of a donee bringing hunger and distress upon the donor and his family by insisting on fulfilment of the promise of a gift. § 519 BGB therefore entitles the donor to refuse such fulfilment if he is not in a position to honour his promise without endangering his own reasonable maintenance or the fulfilment of his obligations to furnish maintenance to others.[101] This equitable inroad on the effects of the promise to make a donation goes back, beyond Justinian, into the 2nd century A.D., when Antoninus Pius granted the donor the privilege to be condemned only in "id quod facere posset".[102] From the 16th century this became known as "beneficium competentiae". According to § 528 BGB, the donor may even demand the return of the gift on account of having been impoverished subsequent to its execution. This claim (which has no Roman precursor)[103] is, however, subject to certain limitations;[104] for the donor's distressed situation must be balanced against the interests of the donee, who may well have relied on the effectiveness of the transfer and made his disposition accordingly.[105]

7. Donation under the ius commune and in modern law

(a) The concept of donation; insinuatio actis

Of the various conceptions of donation which have been *en vogue* at one

---

[97] C. 8, 55, 10 pr.

[98] Cf. e.g. Voet, *Commentarius ad Pandectas*, Lib. XXXIX, Tit. II, XXII; Grotius, *Inleiding*, III, II, 17; Coing, p. 486; P.R. Owens, "Donation", in: Joubert (ed.), *The Law of South Africa*, vol. 8 (1979), n. 128.

[99] Artt. 953, 955 code civil; §§ 948 sq. ABGB; § 530 BGB.

[100] Cf. e.g. RG, 1910 *Juristische Wochenschrift* 148.

[101] Cf. also § 947 ABGB.

[102] Ulp. D. 23, 3, 33; Ulp. D. 39, 5, 12; Paul. D. 42, 1, 19, 1; for details, see Wieslaw Litewski, "Das 'beneficium competentiae' im römischen Recht", in: *Studi in onore di Edoardo Volterra*, vol. IV (1971), pp. 563 sqq.; Antonio Guarino, *La condanna nei limiti del possibile* (1975), pp. 44 sqq.; Joachim Gildemeister, *Das beneficium competentiae im klassischen römischen Recht* (1986), pp. 26 sq., 26 sqq.

[103] But see § 1123 I 11 PrALR.

[104] For details, see §§ 528, 529, 534 BGB.

[105] According to C. 8, 55, 8, a gift by a patron without filii to his freedman reverts to the patron if he subsequently has children. In the practice of the ius commune, this rule was often applied in an extended version: any gift could be revoked by the subsequent birth of children to the donor (cf. e.g. Voet, *Commentarius ad Pandectas*, Lib. XXXIX, Tit. V, XXVI); it was not, however, incorporated into the BGB. For details of the development, see William M. Gordon, "The Interpretation of C. 8, 55, 8", in: *Studi in onore di Edoardo Volterra*, vol. IV (1971), pp. 413 sqq.

or other time in the course of Roman legal history, it was, of course, Justinian's that made its way into the ius commune. Donation,[137] from the time that Roman law was received in medieval Europe, was an obligatory transaction, which, at the same time, provided a iusta causa for the transfer of ownership. This transfer could coincide with the conclusion of the contract, but it could also be effected subsequently. Donation, therefore, was not conceived of as a unilateral act; it was based on an agreement between donor and donee. Such an agreement did not have to be cast in a specific form; a mere ("naked") pactum was sufficient. However, there was one form of control over gift transactions which had been devised in post-classical Roman law and which has also been adopted in Europe: the requirement of insinuatio actis (curiae) for donations exceeding a certain, rather considerable sum.[138] Justinian had fixed the limit at 500 solidi, and there were constant disputes as to how this sum was to be "translated" into contemporary currency.

> "Tunc solidos non pro denobis florenis, ut quidam consulti responderunt . . . neque pro aureo anglico, een angelot, ut voluere Bodin[us] . . . neque pro auro hongarico, quamvis id vulgo receptum tradat Wesemb[eccius] . . . atque ita in senatu Frisiae judicatum referat Sande [accipiendus]."[139]

One wonders what could have prompted the Frisian Senate to adopt the Hungarian gold coin. In many places local statutes or customs prevailed.[140] For Savigny, 500 solidi were 2 000 gulden,[141] for Windscheid 500 ducats.[142] The Cape Supreme Court decided in 1886 that the pound sterling was the equivalent of the Roman aureus.[143] In

---

[137] Coing, pp. 485 sq. For a particularly detailed discussion, see Voet, *Commentarius ad Pandectas*, Lib. XXXIX, Tit. V.

[138] Grotius (*Inleiding*, III, II, 15) refrained from expressing an opinion on the matter. He saw the registration requirement as an attempt by the Romans to check excessive liberality ("om de overdadighe mildheid in te tomen") and proceeded to state, with a touch of dry humour: "I do not find anything to this effect in our own laws, perhaps because there is no excess of liberality in this country" ("waer van ich in onzes lands wetten niet en vinde, misschien omdat de mildheid hier niet te groot is geweest"). The background story on how Grotius tried to establish the law of Holland is told ("ut mihi pro certo relatum") by Van Leeuwen, *Censura Forensis*, Pars I, Lib. II, Cap. VIII, 7. But for Grotius, all authorities agreed that the registration rule was in force in Holland; cf. e.g. Voet, *Commentarius ad Pandectas*, Lib. XXXIX, Tit. V, 18, who states that there is no reason to abandon this requirement, since fictitious alienations in fraud of creditors are so commonly practised; Van der Keessel, *Praelectiones ad Grotium*, III, II, 15.

[139] Groenewegen, *De legibus abrogatis*, Cod. Lib. X, Tit. LXX, l. 5 quotiescumque.

[140] "Quotiescunque certa summa solidorum ab homine profertur, secundum consetudinem regionis intellegi atque taxari debent": Groenewegen, loc. cit.; Stryk, *Usus modernus pandectarum*, Lib. XXXIX, Tit. V, § 4.

[141] *System*, vol. IV, § 116 (p. 210).

[142] § 367, 2. Cf. also RGZ 1, 313 (4.666 2/3 Reichsmark).

[143] *Thorpe's Executors v. Thorpe's Tutor* (1886) 4 SC 488 at 490. Cf. further R.G. McKerron, "Registration of Gifts", (1935) 52 *SALJ* 17 sqq.; *Coronel's Curator v. Estate Coronel* 1941 AD 323 at 339 sqq.

post-colonial times this became 1 000 Rand[144] (which, in terms of contemporary monetary value does not bear the faintest resemblance to the ceiling set by Justinian).

(b) Restrictive policies in France

Whatever interests Constantine tried to protect by this form of control,[145] we have found that the general trend down to the time of Justinian was towards relaxation. It is highly intriguing to see how that trend has occasionally been reversed in more modern history. The central government in the France of the *ancien régime* tried to discourage and prevent transactions which had the effect of dissipating the wealth of the leading families.[146] Thus the requirement of registration was extended to gift transactions of every kind, large and small. The code civil essentially maintains these controls. Every gift inter vivos must be notarized, on pain of nullity[147]—and notarization in France is a cumbersome and costly business: donor as well as donee must appear before (usually) two notaries, the terms of the transaction must be reduced into writing, the document must be read aloud, signed by all present, and copied into a public record.

Conservation of the fortunes of the aristocracy (which had just been toppled) was, of course, not what concerned the fathers of the code civil. They saw gift transactions as being closely related to the law of succession:[148] and here the conviction had grown, since the late Middle Ages and throughout Europe, that the next of kin of every deceased person should be ensured a predetermined and substantial share in his estate.[149] This principle had become accepted by custom (in the form of a *légitime*) and was incorporated into the code civil.[150] As a result of this, the testator's freedom to dispose of his estate in his last will was limited. It is obvious that gifts inter vivos could seriously undermine this policy:

---

[144] See P.R. Owens, op. cit., note 129, n. 125. Today, s. 43 of the General Law Amendment Act (70/1968) applies; no longer are donations invalid merely through failure to register the donation. Executory contracts of donation, however, must now be reduced to writing and signed by the donor or by a person acting on a written authority granted by him in the presence of two witnesses. Failure to comply with these formalities appears to render the contract unenforceable, not void (i.e. subsequent performance is not recoverable).

[145] Cf. supra, pp. 492 sq. (note 90).

[146] For what follows, see Dawson, op. cit., note 5, pp. 29 sqq., 42 sqq.

[147] Art. 931 code civil. Cf. also artt. 932 sq., 1339 code civil.

[148] This is already apparent from the systematical position of donation next to the law of succession.

[149] For an overview, see Dawson, op. cit., note 5, pp. 29 sqq., 123 sqq.; cf. also Coing, pp. 610 sqq.

[150] Art. 913 code civil. The testator can dispose of $\frac{1}{2}$ of his estate only if one legitimate child survives him, of $\frac{1}{3}$ if two and of $\frac{1}{4}$ if three or more legitimate children survive. For further details, see artt. 914 sq. The BGB provides for a compulsory portion ("*Pflichtteil*"): "If a descendant of a testator is excluded by disposition mortis causa from succeeding, he may demand his compulsory portion from the heir. The compulsory portion amounts to one-half the statutory portion. The parents and spouse of the testator have the same rights if they have been excluded from succeeding by a disposition mortis causa" (§ 2303).

they could substantially diminish the estate transmissible on death and thus jeopardize the prospects of inheritance of the donor's closest relations. This open flank had to be covered;[151] hence the renewed endeavours of monitoring gift transactions.

However, the French code civil quite clearly overshot the mark. The courts soon started to map out two main routes of escape from notarization: they exempted the gift of a movable object by delivery from hand to hand (don manuel) from the sweeping provision of art. 931 code civil and they even went so far as to allow the parties to disguise their gift by dressing it up as an exchange transaction.[152]

The sad fate of the notarized gift in French law provides a good example of what can happen when a legislator tries to overreach himself. Even the unworldly, cheerful giver has reappeared in French jurisprudence to join the struggle;[153] for the main purpose of his resurrection has been to free his more mundane and calculating brother–donors from the fetters of notarization (and at the same time to strip them of the benefits of this and other protective mechanisms, especially the right of revocation). Wherever a transaction is tainted by selfish motives rather than inspired by unadulterated generosity, the courts have declared it to be onerous; they have thus been able to sustain and enforce informal gifts by holding that they are not gifts[154]—at least not for the purposes of art. 931 code civil.

(c) German law: form and definition of donation

The draftsmen of the German Code took a more balanced point of view as far as the question of authentication and identification of gift transactions was concerned. The requirement of public registration was abandoned and substituted by a comparatively uncomplicated form of notarization,[155] which was, furthermore, confined to promises of gift.[156] Any defect of form is "cured" by the performance of the

---

[151] Cf. § 2325 I BGB: "Where a testator has made a gift to a third party, a compulsory beneficiary may claim, as supplement to his compulsory portion, the amount by which the compulsory portion would be increased if the object given were added to the estate." However, a ten-year limit is imposed as far as this retrospective review of gifts is concerned (§ 2325 III BGB). According to the French code civil, donations can also be cancelled or scaled down retrospectively if the total of the descendant's gifts exceeded the disposable quota. Here not even a time limit exists. Cf. art. 922 code civil.

[152] For details, see Dawson, op. cit., note 5, pp. 70 sqq., 74 sqq.

[153] Marcel Planiol, Georges Ripert, *Traité pratique de droit civil francais* (2nd ed., 1957), vol. V, p. 325.

[154] Dawson, op. cit., note 5, p. 87.

[155] § 128 BGB: "If notarial authentication of a contract is prescribed by law, it is sufficient if first the offer and later the acceptance of the offer be authenticated by a notary."

[156] § 518 I BGB. The reasons given for the formality have been well summed up by Dawson, op. cit., note 5, p. 134: to ensure care and deliberation by promisors; the need for better evidence than the informal and ambiguous language often used in spontaneous expressions; the undesirability of allowing the strict requirements of form for testamentary gifts to be bypassed too easily; the need to prevent exploitation of the thoughtless and

promise.[157] As a result, the executed gift is valid, whether it be preceded by a formal promise of gift, an informal one or no promise at all. What are the essential elements constituting a gift? § 516 BGB provides the following definition:

> "A disposition whereby one person out of his property enriches another is a gift, if both parties agree that the disposition is to occur without recompense."

Certain time-honoured elements, on which this conception of gift is based, are immediately recognizable: we are dealing with a bilateral transaction which must have the characteristic double effect of impoverishing the donor and enriching the donee—the old pauperior–locupletior requirement that had once been carved out to check donations between husband and wife.[158] What is conspicuously absent from § 516 BGB is any reference to animus donandi. The intention of the donor to enrich was the cornerstone of Justinian's perception of a gift, and it remained the essential test for distinguishing gifts from other transactions, down to the days of the pandectists.[159] It was even incorporated into the first draft of the BGB. The great writers of the 19th century had stripped it of any unrealistic implication of magnanimity and unselfishness.[160] The donor, as Savigny had put it, may hope to gain, by way of his donation, some goodwill and affection which will in the long run bring him much greater advantages; he may make his gift out of mere vanity, in order to make others admire his wealth and generosity. In all these cases the transaction is a gift because the donor genuinely intends the other person's enrichment, albeit only in order to achieve certain ulterior purposes.[161]

---

good-natured and to protect their creditors and heirs. Cf. "Motive", in: *Mugdan*, vol. II, p. 162; Protokolle, in: *Mugdan*, vol. II, p. 743. Cf. also supra, pp. 85 sqq.

[157] § 518 II BGB.

[158] The same applies in French law. As to how this requirement and the ensuing restriction of the concept of donation fits in with the new purposes for policing gift transactions, see Dawson, op. cit., note 5, pp. 54 sqq., 142 sqq., 221 sqq. He emphasizes that, for instance, promises made without recompense to render a service or to permit the use of some piece of property are exempt from all restrictions because they are not regarded as promises of gift, but fall into separate contractual categories. In England, on the other hand, they will all be void for want of consideration. On locupletior–pauperior cf. further, for example, Savigny, *System*, vol. IV, §§ 145 sqq.; Archi, op. cit., note 10, pp. 75 sqq.

[159] Burckhard, op. cit., note 69, pp. 76 sqq.

[160] Cf. e.g. Savigny, *System*, vol. IV, § 153, pp. 86 sq.; Windscheid/Kipp, § 365; Dernburg, *Pandekten*, vol. II, § 106, 2.

[161] This, for Savigny, also settled the highly problematical question whether a remuneratory gift was a gift. For if the pursuit of selfish and egoistical purposes does not detract from the nature of the transaction as a gift, it would indeed be odd if the unselfish motive of gratitude for services rendered would. The qualification of remuneratory gifts has always been very controversial: Paul. D. 39, 5, 34, 1. Those who regarded donationes remuneratoriae as true donations and as such as being subject to all the positive rules governing donations (such as Savigny, *System*, vol. IV, § 153 or Windscheid/Kipp, § 368) tended to look at this text as an exception, which related specifically to rescue situations. Others regarded it as the expression of a general principle covering all instances of remuneratory gifts (cf. e.g. Mühlenbruch, *Doctrina pandectarum*, § 443). That led some writers to the conclusion that remuneratory gifts are not true donations at all, and,

(d) Absence of agreed-upon recompense

But however realistic the assessment of the donor's motives, and however penetrating the analysis of the Roman animus donandi requirement, the fact remained that it was an entirely subjective criterion; and to make legal distinctions depend on the purpose or intention of one of the parties is problematic, at least from the point of view of legal certainty. Also, if a donation is based on the consent of the

---

consequently, that none of the rules governing donations are applicable. Others tried to strike a compromise and contended that, while remuneratory donations had to be classified as donations, they were exempted at least from some of the rules applying to donations: the right to revoke the gift and possibly also the requirement of insinuation and the prohibition of donations between spouses. Most of the Roman-Dutch lawyers drew a distinction between donatio propria and impropria (or mera and non-mera or eygentlijke and oneygentlijke schenkinge). But whereas Voet put donationes remuneratoriae into the first category (*Commentarius ad Pandectas*, Lib. XXXIX, Tit. V, III), Huber (*Heedendaegse Rechtsgeleertheyt*, III. Boek, XIV. Kap.), Van Leeuwen (*Censura Forensis*, Pars I, Lib. IV, Cap. XII, 22) and others argued that they could not properly be called donations. This is, however, largely a merely terminological difference, for it did not follow for Voet that all the rules relating to donations had to be applied to remuneratory gifts. As a result, there was widespread agreement, for instance, that no registration was required. "The reason (for this) . . . is not far to seek. The formality of insinuatio was required in the interests of the donor and his heirs; it gave the donor time for reflection, thus putting him on guard against himself and at the same time protecting the interests of his heirs. Its object was to check impulsive liberality. . . . Where the donation is not a genuine donation and does not arise from sheer liberality, the donor having been influenced by some other inducing reason or reasons and, therefore, presumably having considered the matter and not having acted on a generous impulse of the moment, the safeguard of registration was not considered necessary" (*Avis v. Verseput* 1943 AD 331 at 365, per Tindall JA). Grotius based the exemption of remuneratory gifts from certain rules applying to donations on usage: "Doch is by ghebruick aenghenomen, dat schenckinge die uit verdienste gheschied niet en is onderworpen de wetten die tot nadeel van die schenckinghen iet bevelen" (*Inleiding*, III, II, 3). There was a difference of opinion, however, as to whether remuneratory donations were exempted from registration absolutely or only in so far as they did not exceed the value of the services received from the donee (in the latter sense, for instance, Voet, *Commentarius ad Pandectas*, Lib. XXXIX, Tit. V, XVII). But this limitation would have been totally impractical because it is hardly possible to draw up a comparison between the benefit received and the remuneration given (Savigny, *System*, vol. IV, § 153).

Modern South African law still draws the distinction between donatio mera and non mera; remuneratory and reciprocal donations fall into the second category and are not subject to the formalities and restrictions which apply to a donatio mera. Cf. for instance, *Brink, Executors of Van der Byl v. Meyer* (1832) 1 Menz. 552; *Fichardt Ltd. v. Faustmann* 1910 AD 168 and particularly the very thorough and interesting decision of *Avis v. Verseput* 1943 AD 331 sqq., esp. the judgments of Watermeyer ACJ (pp. 347 sqq.), Tindall JA (pp. 363 sqq.) and Fischer AJA (pp. 381 sqq.).

The German BGB makes one special concession for a certain group of remuneratory donations: "Gifts which are made in compliance with a moral duty or for the sake of common decency are not subject to recall or revocation" (§ 534). Apart from this, remuneratory donations do not enjoy a special status. In modern practice, difficulties of classification can crop up where employees receive an additional bonus, gratification, etc. from their employers. Remuneration or remuneratory donation? Interesting, too (even though very rarely the cause of litigation), the legal qualification of the tip (usually taken to be extra-remuneration for satisfactory fulfilment of contractual obligations on the part of the waiter, porter, etc., not donation; consequence: taxable as income. On the problems connected with the social institution of the tip, see Rudolf von Jhering, *Das Trinkgeld* (3rd ed., 1889)). On remuneratory donations in French law, see Dawson, op. cit., note 5, pp. 96 sqq.

parties and has to involve an enrichment of the donee, one may well ask whether anything was really gained by bringing in the intention of the donor as a separate requirement characterizing the enrichment: by postulating, in other words, that the purpose of enriching the donee must be to enrich the donee.[162] It was Otto Lenel, the distinguished Romanist, who did indeed ask this question and who argued that, in order to mark off gifts from other transactions, one should rather concentrate on a somewhat more objective characteristic of the former, namely the absence of any agreed recompense.[163] So convincing was this argument that it had an immediate impact on the *traveaux preparatoires* of the new Civil Code[164] and caused the second commission to change the draft BGB accordingly. The notion of the unrecompensed benefit has remained the most significant feature of donations ever since; it has proved to be a useful tool for confining the area within which the policing devices laid down in the §§ 516 sqq. BGB are to be applied. What matters is whether certain actions or abstentions on the part of the donee constitute a recompense for what the donor has given; whether, in other words, the "gift" is connected with a counterperformance. This has to be determined from the point of view of the parties to the contract. In so far the test is obviously not an objective one and can still throw up very difficult borderline questions.[165] But by relating the issue of compensation to the contractual agreement of the parties, one is effectively converting the whole enquiry into a question of interpretation of contract: a question which judges have to face wherever they are dealing with contractual relationships.

(e) English law: the doctrine of consideration

The idea of a recompense or, as one could also put it, a bargained-for exchange, must have a familiar ring to any common lawyer. For in order to define the scope of donation, the German Code is using here, under negative auspices, what has traditionally been, in a positive version, the essential test for the enforcement of promises in the English common law; the absence of any agreed-upon recompense characterizes

---

[162] Dawson, op. cit., note 5, p. 138.

[163] "Die Lehre von der Voraussetzung (im Hinblick auf den Entwurf eines bürgerlichen Gesetzbuches)", (1889) 74 *Archiv für die civilistische Praxis* 230 sqq.

[164] Cf. the account by Franz Haymann, *Die Schenkung unter einer Auflage* (1905), pp. 1 sqq.

[165] Cf., particularly, Werner Lorenz, "Entgeltliche und unentgeltliche Geschäfte", in: *Ius privatum gentium, Festschrift für Max Rheinstein*, vol. II (1969), pp. 547 sqq. One of the main problem areas is that of gifts with charge (donationes sub modo). Here it is often difficult to decide whether the parties intended to conclude a donation or an onerous contract. On donations sub modo, see Savigny, *System*, vol. IV, § 175; Windscheid/Kipp, § 369; Haymann, op. cit., note 164, pp. 22 sqq.; Schulz, *CRL*, pp. 568 sq.; Michel, *Gratuité*, pp. 265 sqq.; Coing, pp. 486 sq.; on modern law: Lorenz, *Festschrift Rheinstein*, vol. II, p. 561; Dawson, op. cit., note 5, pp. 103 sqq., 166 sqq.

donations in Germany, the presence of bargain consideration[166] provides the normal reason for enforcing a promise in England. The doctrine of consideration, as it has developed in English and American law,[167] is a most intricate and highly complex legal institution. Its application leads to many odd results.[168] The continental lawyer usually perceives it as one of the strange and idiosyncratic features which have the effect of turning the English common law into such an ungodly and impenetrable jumble. But even among Anglo-American lawyers it has evoked dismay, scorn and hostility.[169] The courts have tried to devise a variety of escape routes,[170] and legal writers have repeatedly pleaded for the total abolition of this doctrine.[171] This is

---

[166] For a classic "definition", see *Currie v. Misa* (1875) LR 10 Exch 153 at 162: "A valuable consideration, in the sense of the law, may consist either in some right, interest, profit, or benefit accruing to the one party, or some forbearance, detriment, loss, or responsibility, given, suffered, or undertaken by the other."

[167] For a recent summary of the position in modern law, see Treitel, *Contract*, pp. 52 sqq.; Basil S. Markesinis, "La notion de consideration dans la common law: vieux problèmes; nouvelles théories", (1983) 35 *Revue internationale de droit comparé* 735 sqq.; Clare Dalton, "An Essay in the Deconstruction of Contract Doctrine", (1985) 94 *Yale LJ* 1066 sqq.; cf. also infra, pp. 554 sqq.

[168] Cf. e.g. the famous case of *Stilk v. Myrich* (1809) 2 Camp 317.

[169] Cf. e.g. (Lord) Wright, "Ought the Doctrine of Consideration to be Abolished?", (1936) 49 *Harvard LR* 1225 sqq.; P.S. Atiyah, "Consideration: A Restatement", in: idem, *Essays on Contract* (1986), pp. 179 sqq.

[170] As an example of a successful one cf. the doctrine of promissory estoppel which has been developed in the United States (cf. e.g. *Restatement Contracts* 2d (1981), § 90: "A promise which the promisor should reasonably expect to induce action or forbearance on the part of the promisee or a third person and which does induce such action or forbearance is binding if injustice can be avoided only by enforcement of the promise. The remedy granted for breach may be limited as justice requires"; judicial adoption of this principle, which is designed to protect reliance, into German law has been urged by Zweigert, 1964 *Juristenzeitung* 354). For an unsuccessful attempt to break through the confines of the consideration doctrine, cf. Lord Mansfield's moral consideration theory ("Where a man is under a moral obligation, which no Court of law or equity can inforce, and promises, the honesty and rectitude of the thing is a consideration. . . . [T]he ties of conscience upon an upright mind are a sufficient consideration" (*Hawkes v. Saunders* (1782) 1 Cowp 289 at 290)); since every promise engenders a moral duty to perform, Lord Mansfield's theory would have led to a total collapse of the consideration doctrine. Not long after his death, it was rejected in *Eastwood v. Kenyon* (1840) 11 Ad & El 438, because, in the words of Lord Denman, it "might be attended with mischievous consequences to society; one of which would be the frequent preference of voluntary undertakings to claims for just debts. Suits would thereby be multiplied, and voluntary undertakings would also be multiplied, to the prejudice of real creditors. The temptations of executors would be much increased by the prevalence of such a doctrine, and the faithful discharge of their duty be rendered more difficult" (pp. 450 sq.). Some years before, Lord Mansfield (and his court) had, incidentally, launched an even more direct assault on the doctrine of consideration. In *Pillans v. Van Mierop* ((1765) 3 Burr 1663 sqq.) it was held that the enforceability of "naked promises" is not based on consideration; what matters is merely whether the undertaking "was entered into upon deliberation and reflection" (p. 1670). In this context, Wilmot J referred to civilian contractual doctrine and quotes Vinnius, Grotius and Pufendorf. Lord Mansfield argued that "the ancient notion about the want of consideration was for the sake of evidence only" (p. 1669). However, in 1778 the House of Lords confirmed the doctrine of consideration: "It is undoubtedly true that every man is by the law of nature bound to fulfil his engagements. It is equally true that the law of this country supplies no means nor affords any remedy to compel the performance of an agreement made without sufficient consideration. Such

obviously not the place to discuss the merits of these arguments. One point, however, may perhaps be borne in mind. The requirement of consideration (at least originally) is not really all that much of an insular curiosity. At the cradle of what appears to be such a striking and characteristic feature of the common law of contract there stood a midwife wrapped in Roman–Canon dressing: the medieval doctrine of causa.[172]

The word "consideration" originally indicated the reasons or motives for the giving of a promise. A promise without consideration was not binding;[173] being without reason or motive, it was somewhat silly[174] and could not have been seriously intended. In the course of time, it has been argued, the concept of consideration was "overloaded", it acquired

> "three superfluous functions, excluding as elements in any agreed exchange performances that are the subject of pre-existing duty, reinforcing offers, and promoting 'mutuality' ".[175]

Atiyah, too (albeit from a totally different perspective) emphasizes that consideration was "in search of a new role" in the course of the 19th century: "the doctrine . . . tended . . . to become fragmented into a number of subdoctrines concerned with specific [public policy]

---

agreement is nudum pactum ex quo non oritur actio; and whatsoever may be the sense of this maxim in the civil law, it is in the last-mentioned sense only that it is to be understood in our law" (per Lord Skynner). On *Pillans v. Van Mierop* cf. the analysis by Nikolaus Benke, "No inefficacy arises merely from a naked promise", (1987) 14 *Ius Commune* 1 sqq.; cf. also Peter Stein, "Continental Influences on English Legal Thought", in: *La formazione storica*, vol. III, p. 1117. *Ward v. Byham* [1956] 2 All ER 318 (CA) offers a good example of the doctrinal difficulties which the modern courts have to circumnavigate, in order to try to reach a reasonable result.

[171] Cf. e.g. A.G. Chloros, "The Doctrine of Consideration and the Reform of the Law of Contract", (1968) 17 *International and Comparative Law Quarterly* 137 sqq.

[172] On the origin of consideration cf., in particular, J.L. Barton, "The Early History of Consideration", (1969) 85 *LQR* 372 sqq.; Simpson, *History*, pp. 316 sqq., 375 sqq. The idea of causa, incidentally, reappeared in Lord Mansfield's moral consideration theory; cf. generally Holdsworth, vol. VIII, pp. 42 sqq. Lord Mansfield, the towering figure on the English legal scene in the second half of the 18th century, had attended lectures on Roman law at Oxford and was thus familiar with civil-law ideas. His Scottish background may have contributed too. For details cf. e.g. C.H.S. Fifoot, *Lord Mansfield* (1936); cf. also Daniel R. Coquillette, *The Civilian Writers of Doctors' Commons* (London, 1988), pp. 282 sqq.

[173] Cf., for example, St. Germain's famous dialogue *Doctor and Student* (1530), as quoted by Simpson, *History*, p. 322: ". . . But if his promise be so naked that there is no manner of consideration why it should be made, then I think him not bound to perform it." On St. Germain's work and his sources, see Simpson, pp. 376 sqq.

[174] In a similar vein Voet, *Commentarius ad Pandectas*, Lib. XXXIX, Tit. V, III: ". . . donatio sine ulla praecedente causa ad donandum impellente profusio magis ac prodigalitas, quam liberalitas est."

[175] Dawson, op. cit., note 5, pp. 220 sq.; for further details, see pp. 207 sqq. The point that "consideration . . . has given a spurious unity to legal problems that are substantially dissimilar" (Edwin W. Patterson, "An Apology for Consideration", (1958) 58 *Columbia LR* 938) has been made by many authors.

issues."[176] Perhaps one can say, therefore, that something has gone wrong with the doctrine of consideration[177] in the course of the last 200 years. That should not detract from the fact that consideration, as an indicium of seriousness,[178] performs a function for which analogous tools are employed in modern civil-law systems.[179] More particularly, in the present context, it excludes liability based upon informal promises of gift,[180] as did classical Roman and as does modern German law.

[176] *Rise and Fall*, p. 453. Atiyah relates the change of function and content of the doctrine of consideration to the profound changes in the conceptual structure of contractual liability, more particularly the rise of the executory contract during the "age of freedom of contract".

[177] Or, as Professor Atiyah would probably say, with the conceptual structure of contractual liability. For a critical analysis of Atiyah's views on consideration, see G.H. Treitel, "Consideration: A Critical Analysis of Professor Atiyah's Fundamental Restatement", (1976) 50 *Australian LJ* 439 sqq.

[178] Zweigert/Kötz/Weir, pp. 60 sqq., with a very valuable comparative review of the problem.

[179] On civil-law analogies to consideration in general, see Arthur T. von Mehren (1959) 72 *Harvard LR* 1009 sqq.; cf. also B.S. Markesinis, "Cause and Consideration: A Study in Parallel", (1978) 37 *CLJ* 53 sqq.

[180] Promises which have not been made against a consideration are actionable if they are "under seal" (i.e. contained in a sealed document).

CHAPTER 17

Pacta and Innominate Real Contracts

I. PACTA IN GENERAL

1. Nuda pactio obligationem non parit

". . . aut enim re contrahitur obligatio aut verbis aut litteris aut consensu."[1] This was the systematic subdivision upon which Gaius based his exposition of the law of contractual obligations. We have, by now, made our way through all the four categories mentioned. We have seen that an obligation could arise either on the basis of certain formal arrangements between the parties or by virtue of the real act of handing over an object. One of the most significant achievements of the Roman lawyers was, however, that they were prepared to grant an action even in cases where nothing more than a mere agreement had intervened. These were the consensual contracts. But their number was limited. Only if the (informal) arrangement between the parties could be classified as emptio venditio, locatio conductio, mandatum or societas was it enforceable. This was the numerus clausus of contracts concluded (nudo) consensu. Conversely, then, a mere pactum, that is, an agreement that did not fit into one of these categories, was not actionable: "nuda pactio obligationem non parit", as Ulpianus put this regula iuris.[2] This did not, however, mean that such a pactum—or pactio[3]—was entirely ineffective or invalid. ". . . sed parit exceptionem" is how Ulpian continues: in the course of the proceedings in iure, the defendant could ask, on the basis of a nudum pactum, for the insertion of an exceptio pacti into the formula. Most notably, an informal release from an obligation could become effective that way ("pactum de non petendo"), but also an agreement, according to which the creditor was not to claim performance for a certain period of time.[4]

---

[1] Gai. III, 89.

[2] D. 2, 14, 7, 4. Cf. further e.g. Ulp. D. 2, 14, 7, 5; Ulp. D. 19, 5, 15; Paul. Sent. II, XIV, 1; C. 2, 3, 10 (Alex.) and Schmidlin, *Rechtsregeln*, pp. 97 sqq. In later times this rule was usually referred to in a slightly different formulation: ex nudo pacto non oritur actio.

[3] On the terminology cf. André Magdelain, *Le consensualisme dans l'édit du préteur* (1958), pp. 5 sqq. Pactum/pactio is derived from pacisci/pacere and originally referred to redemption from liability, i.e. to the act by which the wrongdoer "bought off" the victim's right of vengeance: cf. e.g. 8, 2 of the XII Tables: "Si membrum rupsit, ni cum eo pacit, talio esto"; for details, see Kaser, *RPr* I, pp. 171 sqq. Ulpianus (D. 2, 14, 1, 1) draws attention to the fact that the word for peace has the same root: "Pactum autem a pactione dicitur (inde etiam pacis nomen appellatum est)."

[4] Cf. Gai. IV, 122: "Dilatoriae sunt exceptiones quae ad tempus valent, veluti illius pacti conventi, . . . ne intra quinquennium peteretur."

This is what the praetor referred to when he promised: "Pacta conventa . . . servabo."[5] With these words he did not intend to provide a positive sanction in the form of an action. For the protection of the debtor it was sufficient to make available a defence. On account of the pactum he could reasonably expect not to be sued at all, or not to be sued for some time. What he needed, therefore, was an exceptio in case the creditor instituted an action regardless of his promise.

2. Pacta ex continenti adiecta

There was, however, one group of cases where this kind of praetorian intervention was not even necessary, for the exceptio pacti (as well as, incidentally, the exceptio doli) was inherent in the bonae fidei iudicia.[6] If, therefore, for example, the actio venditi was brought against a purchaser or the actio locati against a lessee, the defendant did not have to insist on the insertion of the exceptio pacti into the formula if he wanted to bring the release or indulgence agreement to the attention of the judge. The latter was instructed to assess "quidquid ob eam rem N^m N^m A^o A^o dare facere oportet ex fide bona", and hence it was his duty to take such circumstances into consideration in any event: ". . . bonae fidei iudicio exceptiones pacti insunt."[7] But the oportere ex fide bona enabled the judge to go much further. "[B]ona fides exigit, ut quod convenit fiat":[8] if the parties had agreed on certain "adminicula [emptionis, locationis, etc.]"[9] and added a variety of provisions relating to, supporting and detailing the main contractus, what would have been more in tune with the precepts of good faith than to give effect to these agreements?[10] In the course of time, the term "pactum" came to be used in this context (i.e. in a very broad sense) too,[11] and the edictal clause of "pacta conventa . . . servabo" acquired a new dimension. As far as bonae fidei iudicia were concerned, all kinds of agreements had to be taken into account, whether they were favourable to the plaintiff or to the defendant.[12] It would have been inequitable merely to

[5] Ulp. D. 2, 14, 7, 7. Cf. e.g. Biondo Biondi, *Contratto e stipulatio* (1953), pp. 144 sqq.; Knütel, *Contrarius consensus*, pp. 63 sq. and, particularly, Gian Gualberto Archi, "Ait Praetor: 'Pacta conventa servabo' ", in: *De iustitia et iure, Festgabe für Ulrich von Lübtow* (1980), pp. 373 sqq. Differently Magdelain, *Consensualisme*, pp. 49 sqq., who reads into "[t]his rather high-sounding pronouncement" (Schulz, *CRL*, p. 470) the *"charte du consensualisme"*. Cf. further on this passage György Diósdi, "Pacta nuda servabo?", (1971) 74 *BIDR* 89 sqq.

[6] Cf. Paul. D. 18, 5, 3; Ulp. D. 2, 14, 7, 5 sq. and Rolf Knütel, "Die Inhärenz der exceptio pacti im bonae fidei iudicium", (1967) 84 *ZSS* 133 sqq.

[7] Paul. D. 18, 5, 3.

[8] Iav. D. 19, 2, 21; on this text, see, for example, J.A.C. Thomas, "Tenancy by Purchaser", (1959) 10 *Iura* 103 sqq.

[9] Pap. D. 18, 1, 72 pr.

[10] Ulp. D. 2, 14, 1 pr.; Ulp. D. 2, 14, 7, 5; Knütel, *Contrarius consensus*, pp. 64 sqq.

[11] Cf. e.g. Grosso, *Sistema*, pp. 187 sqq.

[12] The most prominent examples of pacta appended to contracts of sale were the in diem addictio, the lex commissoria and the pactum displicentiae. The former two gave the

give effect to pacta which defeated the designs of the specific plaintiff.

The iudicia bonae fidei provided the procedural framework within which so-called pacta adiecta became (indirectly) enforceable. The plaintiff could still not base an action on a "nudum" pactum, but if the agreement was ancillary to a contract of sale, lease or any other of the recognized contracts bonae fidei, it could determine the scope of application of the actiones empti, venditi, locati, conducti, etc. "[S]olemus enim dicere", in the words of Ulpian, "pacta conventa [and not only: exceptiones pacti!] inesse bonae fidei iudiciis."[13] However, a qualification is immediately added:

> "Sed hoc sic accipiendum est, ut si quidem ex continenti pacta subsecuta sunt, etiam ex parte actoris insint: si ex intervallo, non inerunt, nec valebunt, si agat, ne ex pacto actio nascatur."

A distinction is drawn between pacta ex continenti (entered into immediately, that is, at the time of conclusion of the contract) and pacta ex intervallo (which are added at a later stage). Only the former are part and parcel of the main transaction; subsequent modifications of the contract, on the other hand, retain their status as independent pacta and have to be dealt with separately, not within the ambit of the actio ex contractu. Pacta ex continenti "forma[n]t ipsam actionem",[14] pacta ex intervallo can be raised only by way of a defence.[15]

With regard to iudicia stricti iuris, pacta ex continenti adiecta could not, of course, have the same significance. They could provide the basis for an exceptio, but they were not enforceable within the framework of (for example) the condictio. This followed from the strict word formalism of old; the content of a stipulation was determined merely on the basis of what was contained in the formal declarations of the parties.[16] By the time of late classical law, however, a considerable relaxation had occurred and the emphasis was no longer exclusively placed on the (formal) verba. As far as possible, the actual will of the parties was taken into consideration;[17] and in the determination of the actual will, informal pacta could be of considerable importance. "[P]acta

---

vendor, the latter the purchaser the right to call off the sale under certain circumstances. For details cf. infra, pp. 735 sqq. Practically less important were the pactum de retroemendo (the vendor is granted the right to buy back the thing sold; cf. Proc. D. 19, 5, 12; C. 4, 54, 2 (Alex.); Glück, vol. 16, pp. 199 sqq.; Peters, *Rücktrittsvorbehalte*, pp. 277 sqq.; on the subsequent history, see Theo Mayer-Maly, "Beobachtungen und Gedanken zum Wiederkauf", in: *Festschrift für Franz Wieacker* (1978), pp. 424 sqq.) and the pactum protimiseos ("si ita fundum tibi vendidero, ut nulli alii eum quam mihi venderes"; cf. Paul. D. 19, 1, 21, 5; Hermog. D. 18, 1, 75; Glück, vol. 16, pp. 156 sqq.; Peters, *Rücktrittsvorbehalte*, pp. 282 sqq. On the historical development of the modern right of pre-emption (§§ 504 sqq. BGB) from this (and other) root(s), cf. Klaus Schurig, *Das Vorkaufsrecht im Privatrecht* (1975), pp. 36 sqq., 49 sqq.

[13] D. 2, 14, 7, 5. [14] Ulp. D. 2, 14, 7, 5.

[15] Cf. further e.g. Grosso, *Sistema*, pp. 179 sqq.; Biondi, op. cit., note 5, pp. 144 sqq.; Knütel, *Contrarius consensus*, pp. 67 sqq.

[16] Cf. supra, pp. 83 sq. and infra, pp. 622 sqq.

[17] Cf. e.g. Fritz Pringsheim, "Id quod actum est", (1961) 78 *ZSS* 54 sqq.

in continenti facta stipulationi inesse creduntur", we even read in Paul. D. 12, 1, 40,[18] a sweeping generalization which does, however, contain at least an element of truth. For, through the process of interpretation, informal pacta could indeed have some bearing on the content of the stipulation and, as a result, influence the range of the condictio.[19]

The special position of pacta in continenti adiecta, particularly as far as iudicia bonae fidei were concerned, was still compatible with the general rule of "ex nudo pacto non oritur actio". Yet there were also instances, where the emperors—or even the praetor—had been prepared to grant an action on the basis of an informal agreement that could not be classified as a consensual contract and that was also not ancillary to one. One traditionally refers to pacta vestita (as opposed to pacta nuda) and distinguishes between pacta praetoria (recognized by the praetor) and pacta legitima (upheld by the emperors).

II. PACTA PRAETORIA

There were two types of pacta praetoria: the constitutum debiti and the receptum.

1. Constitutum debiti

(a) The actio de pecunia constituta

A constitutum (derived from constituere = to fix, to appoint or to determine) is the informal[20] promise to pay an already existing debt, either one's own (constitutum debiti proprii) or that of another (constitutum debiti alieni), on a specific date.[21] "Qui pecuniam debitam constituit se soluturum esse, in eum iudicium dabo" is what the praetor promised,[22] and an actio de pecunia constituta was therefore made available to the creditor. In comparison with the condictio it had one great advantage for the creditor: the judge was instructed to assess "quanti ea res est"; he therefore had considerable latitude in determining the amount owed by the debtor. More particularly, not only could he condemn the latter into the sum of money or the monetary equivalent of what he had promised; he was able to take into consideration the creditor's interest in being paid timeously, i.e. to award damages for the delay in payment. If, for example, A had

[18] This text has usually been regarded as corrupt; cf. e.g. Riccobono/Kerr Wylie/Beinart, pp. 184 sqq.; but see e.g. Knütel, *Stipulatio poenae*, pp. 286 sq.

[19] For a detailed discussion and examples, see Rolf Knütel, "Stipulatio und pacta", in: *Festschrift für Max Kaser* (1976), pp. 201 sqq.

[20] Ulp. D. 13, 5, 14, 3.

[21] For what follows cf. Buckland/Stein, pp. 529 sq.; Schulz, *CRL*, pp. 560 sqq.; Magdelain, *Consensualisme*, pp. 126 sqq.; Jules Roussier, "Le constitut", in: (1958) 3 *Varia, Études de droit romain* 1 sqq.; Salvatore Tondo, "In tema di 'constitutem debiti'", (1958) 4 *Labeo* 208 sqq.; Frezza, *Garanzie*, vol. I, pp. 229 sqq.

[22] Cf. Lenel, *EP*, pp. 247 sqq.

promised by way of stipulation to pay ten aurei to B on 10 October, this was not a constitutum. The fixing of the date was part of the (original) contract, and constitutum presupposed an already existing obligation. If B defaulted, A could bring the condictio but was not able to recover his loss arising from the fact that performance had not been rendered in time.[23] If, however, it had become apparent, before 10 October, that B would not be able to pay in time, A and B could informally fix 1 November as the new due date. This was a constitutum debiti, and it was advantageous to B in that it granted him indulgence. A, in turn, could now claim his damages if B was still not able to meet the new deadline.

(b) Constitutum debiti alieni

Constitutum debiti was similar to novatio in that the parties were effecting a change to a rather significant detail of their original obligation; it did not, however, have the effect of a novation, since the action arising from the original obligation continued to exist[24] (but could be met with an exceptio as long as the new due date had not arrived). The fact that the original obligation was not extinguished was of particular significance for the constitutum debiti alieni. If A agreed that C was to pay B's debt by a certain date, B continued to be liable, but A had acquired a second debtor. We are dealing with a cumulative assumption of debt, and the transaction constituted, in effect, a form of suretyship, for which a stipulation was not required. Justinian assimilated it with fideiussio by making available to the third party the beneficia divisionis, excussionis and probably also cedendarum actionum.[25] Thus it is not surprising to see that in the practice of the ius commune there was no place for an institution that did not in effect differ from suretyship; the Roman-Dutch authors, for instance, regarded the constitutum debiti alieni as obsolete:

> "Sed postquam stipulationum solemnitas extra usum abierit, adeoque et ex nudis pactis obligationes oriri c[o]eperint, . . . hodie a fidejussione constitutum vix discerni potest. . . . Ideoque et huius actionis nomen foro cessit, praesertim cum moribus nostris in universum actionum nomina libellis exprimi non soleant."[26]

(c) Constitutum debiti proprii

The constitutum debiti proprii,[27] also, was too closely connected with the intricacies of the formulary procedure of classical law to be of great significance in later centuries. There were not many cases where the

---

[23] For details cf. infra, pp. 783 sqq., 790 sqq.
[24] Cf. Ulp. D. 13, 5, 18, 3.
[25] Cf. C. 4, 18, 3; Nov. 4, 1; Roussier, (1958) 3 *Varia* 142 sqq.; Frezza, *Garanzie*, vol. I, pp. 281 sqq.; Kaser, *RPr* II, p. 461.
[26] Groenewegen, *Tractatus de legibus abrogatis*, Cod. Lib. IV, Tit. XVIII, 2–3. Cf. further e.g. Voet, *Commentarius ad Pandectas*, Lib. XIII, Tit. V, XIV; Windscheid/Kipp, § 476; but see Glück, vol. 13, pp. 398 sqq.
[27] See the detailed exposition by Glück, vol. 13, pp. 373 sqq.

acquisition of a second claim could be of practical value to the creditor. After all, discharge of the one also let the other obligatio fall away.[28] Also, the constitutum could not be used to overcome defects in the first obligation, for its validity continued to depend upon the validity of the pre-existing obligation, which it was designed to confirm; there was no such thing as an abstract constitutum.[29]

One brief, but interesting, episode within the development towards a general law of contract, however, deserves mention in this context. In the Middle Ages, an obligatio naturalis was regarded as a sufficient basis for a constitutum. Since, as we shall presently see,[30] pacta nuda, according to the law of the Corpus Juris Civilis, engendered a naturalis obligatio, the constitutum could be used as a convenient means of rendering unenforceable consensual agreements (which did not fit into the category of either the contracts or the pacta praetoria or legitima) enforceable. In effect, therefore, one merely had to conclude a pactum nudum twice in order to elevate it to the status of a binding contract, or pactum vestitum. This curious institution was known as "pactum geminatum", and it was generally accepted by the legists (*"Legisten"*) of the later 15th century.[31] But with the increasing recognition being given to the principle of ex nudo pacto oritur actio, the practical importance of pacta geminata, and with it the historical significance of the medieval constitutum, was bound to fade away.[32]

2. Receptum arbitri

Receptum, the second of the so-called pacta praetoria, was the informal undertaking of a certain guarantee by either an arbitrator, a banker, or a carrier by sea, an innkeeper or a stablekeeper.

First of all, the receptum arbitri. We are dealing here with the undertaking by a person to act as arbitrator in a dispute between two or more parties. The Corpus Juris Civilis contains the following definition:

> "Recepisse autem arbitrium videtur, ut Pedius libro nono dicit, qui iudicis partes suscepit finemque se sua sententia controversiis impositurum pollicetur. quod si,

---

[28] Cf. e.g. Ulp. D. 13, 5, 18, 3.

[29] Cf. C. 4, 18, 2, 1 sq. On the constitutum in the law of Justinian cf. Gian Gualberto Archi, "Contributi alla critica del Corpus Juris", (1962) 65 *BIDR* 134 sqq.; Kaser, *RPr* II, pp. 383 sq.

[30] Cf. infra, note 147.

[31] Cf. Lothar Seuffert, *Zur Geschichte der obligatorischen Verträge* (1881), pp. 75 sqq.; Guido Astuti, "Pactum geminatum", in: *Studi in onore di Enrico Besta*, vol. I (1939), pp. 219 sqq.; Alfred Söllner, "Die causa im Kondiktionen- und Vertragsrecht des Mittelalters bei den Glossatoren, Kommentatoren und Kanonisten", (1960) 77 *ZSS* 262 sq.; Nanz, *Vertragsbegriff*, pp. 42 sqq.

[32] Once nuda pacta had become generally enforceable, there was little point in retaining constitutum as a special type of agreement. The BGB therefore no longer deals with it. For South African law cf. Percival Gane, *The Selective Voet*, vol. III (1956), p. 29 (translator's note); for the situation preceding codification in Germany, cf. Windscheid/Kipp, § 284.

inquit, hactenus intervenit, ut experiretur, an consilio suo vel auctoritate discuti litem paterentur, non videtur arbitrium recepisse."[33]

The arbitrator assumed the duty of settling a dispute submitted to him.[34] The receptum was based on and referred to an arbitration agreement (compromissum) between the parties. In modern parlance one could say that this compromissum constituted the offer to the third person to act as arbitrator. The latter had to accept the role of a judge, not that of a mere conciliator or adviser. The receptum did not, however, provide the parties involved in the dispute with an action against the arbitrator to honour his undertaking. They were able only to approach the praetor to apply the appropriate measures of coercion.[35] The receptum arbitri has survived the centuries.[36] Though it has not been incorporated into the BGB as one of the specific contracts, it is still generally recognized that the arbitrator can act only on the basis of a contractual relationship (sui generis) existing between himself and the parties to the dispute.[37] No action can be brought against him to carry out the arbitration and make his award.[38]

3. Receptum argentarii

The receptum argentarii was an informal[39] promise by means of which a banker guaranteed payment of his client's debt.[40] It was very similar to the constitutum debiti alieni, except that under the action arising from this receptum (the actio recepticia) the banker was liable even when the client's obligation was invalid. Like constitutum, the receptum argentarii originated, under Hellenistic influence, in Greek and Roman banking practice. Both transactions avoided the form of stipulatio. By the time of Justinian, the receptum argentarii had become obsolete; it was therefore fused with the constitutum debiti alieni.[41]

4. Receptum nautarum cauponum stabulariorum

(a) Actio de recepto; custodia liability

Finally, the receptum nautarum cauponum stabulariorum. It was

---

[33] Ulp. D. 4, 8, 13, 2. For details, see Magdelain, *Consensualisme*, pp. 156 sqq.; Ziegler, *Privates Schiedsgericht*, pp. 77 sqq.; Peter Stein, "Labeo's Reasoning on Arbitration", (1974) 91 *SALJ* 135 sqq.

[34] Cf. e.g. Paul. D. 4, 8, 19, 1.

[35] The edict provided: "Qui arbitrium pecunia compromissa receperit, eum sententiam dicere cogam"; cf. Ulp. D. 4, 8, 3, 2; Ulp. D. 4, 8, 3, 15; Lenel, *EP*, pp. 130 sq.; Ziegler, *Privates Schiedsgericht*, pp. 84 sqq.

[36] Cf. e.g. Glück, vol. 6, pp. 74 sqq., 87 sqq.; Windscheid/Kipp, § 417.

[37] Leo Rosenberg, Karl Heinz Schwab, *Zivilprozessrecht* (13th ed., 1981), p. 1113.

[38] Rosenberg/Schwab, op. cit., note 37, p. 1114.

[39] But see Alfons Bürge, "Fiktion und Wirklichkeit: Soziale und rechtliche Strukturen des römischen Bankwesens", (1987) 104 *ZSS* 527 sqq.: liability was undertaken by a formal act (i.e. the solemnity connected with the word "recipio").

[40] Lenel, *EP*, pp. 132 sqq., Berger, *ED*, p. 668; Magdelain, *Consensualisme*, pp. 152 sqq.; Frezza, *Garanzie*, vol. I, pp. 274 sqq.

[41] C. 4, 18, 2 pr.; *Inst.* IV, 6, 8; Kaser, *RPr* II, p. 383; Bürge, (1987) 104 *ZSS* 535 sq.

dogmatically the most interesting and historically the most significant of the pacta praetoria. We are dealing with an undertaking by a sea carrier, an innkeeper or a stablekeeper that their customers' goods would be safe while on the ship or on their premises. On the basis of this guarantee the praetor was prepared to grant an action, untechnically referred to as actio de recepto: "Nautae caupones stabularii quod cuiusque salvum fore receperint nisi restituent, in eos iudicium dabo."[42] Recipere res salvas fore is the extended version of the operative words: to undertake[43] that the goods will be safe. In case of damage, loss or destruction, the nauta, caupo or stabularius was liable, no matter whether he had been at fault or not. He was, in fact, acting like an insurer;[44] originally his guarantee was an absolute one and comprised all kinds of vis maior. Labeo, however, introduced an equitable inroad in favour of the nauta: he was to be relieved of liability if he had lost the goods "naufragio aut per vim piratarum".[45] Since the actio de recepto was stricti iuris, this adjustment had to be brought about by way of an exceptio. This was soon extended to other instances of vis maior and came to be applied to caupones and stabularii too.[46] According to classical Roman law, this type of receptum therefore gave rise to a form of liability which we have already repeatedly encountered: custodia. Gaius makes this quite clear when he states:

> "Nauta et caupo et stabularius mercedem accipiunt non pro custodia, sed nauta ut traiciat vectores, caupo ut viatores manere in caupona patiatur, stabularius ut permittat iumenta apud eum stabulari: et tamen custodiae nomine tenentur."[47]

As a consequence, for instance, it is not the customer who can bring the actio furti in case of theft, but the nauta/caupo/stabularius, "quia recipiendo periculum custodiae subit".[48]

(b) The reasons for the actio de recepto

What were the reasons that induced the praetor to grant the actio de recepto? At two places in the title 4, 9 we find Ulpian trying to answer

---

[42] Ulp. D. 4, 9, 1 pr.; cf. also Ulp. D. 4, 9, 3, 5 and Lenel, *EP*, p. 131. Were there originally separate edicts for nautae on the one hand and caupones and stabularii on the other? Cf. Francesco M. de Robertis, "Receptum nautarum. Studio sulla responsabilità dell' armatore in diritto romano, con riferimento alla disciplina particolare concernente il caupo e lo stabularius", (1953) 12 *Annali Bari* 125 sqq.; J.A.C. Thomas, "Carriage by Sea", (1960) 7 *RIDA* 489. On the origin of the edict, as far as nautae were concerned, in the Rhodian sea laws, see T.E. Dönges, *The Liability for Safe Carriage of Goods in Roman Dutch Law* (1928), pp. 8 sqq.

[43] On the meaning of "recipere" cf. e.g. A.J.M. Meyer-Termeer, *Die Haftung der Schiffer im griechischen und römischen Recht* (1978), pp. 201, 209; also e.g. Glück, vol. 6, p. 106.

[44] Otto Lenel, "Kritisches und Antikritisches", (1929) 49 *ZSS* 5.

[45] Lab./Ulp. D. 4, 9, 3, 1.

[46] Cf. Ulp. D. 4, 9, 3, 1 i.f.

[47] D. 4, 9, 5 pr. On this text cf., particularly, Robert Feenstra, "Deux textes de Gaius sur la responsabilité contractuelle: D. 19, 2, 40 et D. 4, 9, 5", in: *Droits de l'antiquité et sociologie juridique, Mélanges Henri Lévy-Bruhl* (1959), pp. 105 sqq. Cf. further Ulp. D. 4, 9, 1, 8 (". . . et puto omnium eum recipere custodiam, quae in navem illatae, sunt . . .").

[48] Ulp. D. 47, 5, 1, 4.

this question. First of all, he praises the edict ("[m]axima utilitas est huius edicti"),

> "quia necesse est plerumque eorum fidem sequi et res custodiae eorum committere. . . . nisi hoc esset statutum, materia daretur cum furibus adversus eos quos recipiunt coeundi, cum ne nunc quidem abstineant huiusmodi fraudibus";[49]

later on, he refers to Pomponius' somewhat tentative suggestion that the praetor might have liked to make it known to those engaged in these occupations that he was taking care to repress dishonesty.[50] Obviously, nautae, caupones and stabularii did not enjoy a very high reputation. One suspected them of conspiring with potential thieves against their customers, and even though there must have been differences in the moral and social standing of innkeepers and shipowners,[51] Pomponius lumped them all together, somewhat scornfully, as "hoc genus hominum". Common to these professions was the fact that they were in a position which lent itself to abuse. A customer who wanted his goods to be transported overseas, or who had to stay in an inn overnight, had to deliver his property (the goods or his baggage) into the custody of the persons in charge of either ship, inn or stable. He had to depend on their good faith and honesty, for better or for worse, since he had brought his property into a sphere which was under their control. In case of loss, destruction or damage it was often impossible for him to establish whether the incident was attributable to their fault, to the fault of their employees or to a mere accident. The least the praetor could do, under these circumstances, was to render binding informal guarantees which a nauta, caupo or stabularius might have given in order to attract potential customers to his business and to make them rely on his expertise and honesty.[52] The exceptio Labeoniana was what one would call, in modern parlance, a teleological restriction of the liability arising under the actio de recepto; for if the praetor wanted to protect customers against the possibility of collusion of the person in charge of the place with thieves, or against any other kind of dishonest behaviour, he merely had to make the latter carry periculum custodiae. Instances of vis maior cannot, by definition, be contrived or influenced by either of the parties concerned.

---

[49] D. 4, 9, 1, 1.

[50] D. 4, 9, 3, 1.

[51] A caupona was essentially a combination of hotel and pub; however, it often comprised a brothel too. Its reputation was so bad that it was regarded as degrading for a senator to lunch or dine in a caupona. The owner was called "caupo" (from which is derived the German word for merchant: *"Kauf"mann*). For details, see Tönnes Kleberg, *Hôtels, restaurants et cabarets dans l'antiquité Romaine* (1957), pp. 3, 37 sqq., 112 sqq.; cf. also Alfred Pernice, "Parerga", (1899) 20 *ZSS* 133 sqq. and the inscription mentioned by Honsell/Mayer-Maly/Selb, pp. 329 sqq. On nautae cf. De Robertis, (1953) 12 *Annali Bari* 17 sqq. (disputing that they were badly reputed).

[52] Was it not going too far to make nautae/caupones/ stabularii liable for custodia, i.e. also in cases where a fellow traveller (and not either they themselves or one of their employees) had committed the theft? Answer: no, "nam est in ipsorum arbitrio, ne quem recipiant" (Ulp. D. 4, 9, 1, 1).

(c) Actio de recepto and special delictual actions

If, therefore, the recipient of the customer's property was ultimately liable for custodia, the question arises whether the introduction of the actio de recepto had really been necessary. After all, the receptum did not stand on its own; it was an additional agreement, a guarantee that could be added to the underlying contract of carriage, lodging or stabling.[53] If we take by way of example the nauta,[54] we will remember that carriage by sea was normally undertaken on the basis of locatio conductio operis[55] and that the conductor under this type of contract was (probably) in any event liable for custodia.[56] Furthermore, two special, praetorian remedies were available in the event of the customer's goods being stolen or damaged on board, irrespective of whether the delict had been committed by the nauta himself, by one of his employees or by a fellow-traveller: the actiones furti and damni in factum adversus nautas.[57] The customer therefore appears to have been well protected even without receptum. Why, then, was the actio de recepto added to this armoury of legal processes? As far as the two delictual actions for theft and damage were concerned, the answer is still relatively easy. They were (probably) the older remedies and covered only two special types of situation. The actio de recepto, on the other hand, was based on the general provision of "res salvas fore"; it appears to be a more sophisticated creation, introduced, no doubt, "in the light of experience of particular provisions".[58] Furthermore, there was a difference in sanctions; the actiones furti and damni in factum adversus nautas lay for duplum, whereas redress under the actio de recepto was geared to compensation (simplum).

(d) Actio de recepto and actio locati

To disentangle the relationship between the actio de recepto and the actio locati is a much more difficult, if not impossible, task. The

[53] Cf. e.g. De Robertis, (1953) 12 *Annali Bari* 51 sqq. and passim; Meyer-Termeer, op. cit., note 43, pp. 185, 191. Contra: Manlio Sargenti, "Problemi della responsabilità contrattuale", (1954) 20 *SDHI* 150 sq.

[54] The term "nauta" in the context of the receptum refers to the exercitor navis; cf. Ulp. D. 4, 9, 1, 2: "Qui sunt igitur, qui teneantur, videndum est. ait praetor 'nautae'. nautam accipere debemus eum qui navem exercet: quamvis nautae appellantur omnes, qui navis navigandae causa in nave sint: sed de exercitore solummodo praetor sentit." Even where the magister navis concluded the receptum, it was the exercitor who was bound; his obligation arose "vel per se vel per navis magistrum" (Ulp. D. 4, 9, 1, 2 i.f.). On the position of exercitor navis, magister navis and others involved in the management of a ship, cf. Meyer-Termeer, op. cit., note 43, pp. 150 sqq.

[55] Cf. supra, p. 408.

[56] Cf. supra, pp. 398 sq.

[57] Paul. D. 4, 9, 6, 1 sqq.; Ulp. D. 47, 5, 1 sqq.; Sargenti, "Osservazioni sulla responsabilità dell' exercitor navis in diritto romano", in: *Studi in onore di Emilio Albertario*, vol. I (1953), pp. 555 sqq.; J.A.C. Thomas, "Juridical Aspects of Carriage by Sea and Warehousing in Roman Law", in: (1974) 32 *Recueils de la Société Jean Bodin pour l'Histoire Comparative des Institutions* 133 sqq.

[58] Thomas, (1974) 32 *Recueils Bodin* 136; cf. also Meyer-Termeer, op. cit., note 43, p. 194.

scarcity of sources and the prevailing uncertainty regarding the extent to which Justinian interfered with the classical texts inevitably brings a very strong element of speculation into the discussion. Even the very basic question as to which of the two remedies is the older is not beyond dispute. Van Oven, for instance, has argued that, historically, the strict receptum liability preceded the more modern and flexible regime of the consensual locatio conductio.[59] More often, however, a different development is held to have taken place. The contractual basis for carriage by sea was locatio conductio; it must have existed before the receptum guarantee as an accidentale negotii was recognized.[60] But what was its function? According to Fritz Schulz, for instance, the actio de recepto was created in order to subject the nauta to a liability that was stricter than that imposed under a contract of locatio conductio operis;[61] and indeed, we have seen that the receptum liability originally went beyond custodia and comprised all cases of vis maior. But whilst this consideration provides a plausible reason why the actio de recepto was introduced, it fails to explain why it continued to be used after the time of Labeo. Can this be attributed solely to the conservatism of the Roman lawyers?

De Robertis,[62] while sharing two of Schulz's basic assumptions (namely that the locatio conductio came first, and that all conductores operis were liable for custodia), ascribed exactly the opposite function to the actio de recepto; it was not introduced in order to stiffen, but rather as part of a policy to mitigate liability for sea carriage: the nauta was to be liable for custodia only if he had in fact entered into a receptum and thereby expressly assumed such a responsibility. According to Brecht,[63] the receptum was concerned only with the personal baggage brought on board by passengers. As long as we are dealing with locatio conductio rerum vehendarum, the nauta was liable for custodia, since the goods were the object of the transport. Locatio conductio vectorum vehendarum, on the other hand (i.e. the type of transaction that conspicuously dominates the Digest title 4, 9), focused exclusively on the person of the passenger. In this respect, custodia liability does not make sense. But if the carriage by sea of persons did not (and could not) entail custodia, the safety of the objects which the passenger brought with him and which were thus *incidentally* transported too, was not satisfactorily safeguarded. It was in order to attend to this specific problem—so Brecht argues—that the parties concluded the receptum and that the praetor granted an action.

[59] J.C. van Oven, "Actio de recepto et actio locati", (1956) 24 *TR* 137 sqq.; cf. also already Sargenti, *Studi Albertario*, vol. I, pp. 553 sqq.

[60] e.g. Meyer-Termeer, op. cit., note 43, pp. 185 sqq.

[61] *CRL*, p. 565.

[62] (1953) 12 *Annali Bari* 83 sqq.

[63] Christoph Heinrich Brecht, *Zur Haftung der Schiffer im antiken Recht* (1962), pp. 99 sqq.

Thomas,[64] too, tries to differentiate. He draws attention to the fact that locatio conductio operis was by no means the only form of carriage by sea. The contract could also be locatio conductio rei, i.e. the hiring of space on the ship.[65] In this latter instance, the nauta was the locator and could, as a matter of course, not be liable for custodia.[66] But even in case of locatio conductio operis, the nauta (here in the role of conductor) did not automatically incur this type of liability. For, according to Thomas, the job of the nauta "is the carrying of the cargo, the carrying as such: he should not do anything to the things given to him except transport them".[67] Thus, it was originally the receptum which gave the nauta responsibility—under a contract of locatio conductio operis—not merely to carry but to produce the carried cargo at the destination.

To show that the receptum was necessary in order to impose a type of liability that was not inherent in the contract of carriage by sea: this appears to be, indeed, the most convincing solution to our problem. We have seen above that fullers and tailors were liable for custodia, but that one cannot be certain whether these professions were merely referred to in our sources by way of example.[68] If, indeed, all other conductores under a contract of locatio conductio operis were liable only for culpa, then it must have been the function of the receptum to increase the nauta's responsibility to custodia.[69] But even if we assume that as a rule all conductores operis were contractually liable not only for culpa but also for custodia, this cannot have applied to the situation currently at issue. For it appears to have been generally established that the imposition of custodia liability was not appropriate where the risk of theft or damage was inherent in the contract and where, therefore, the debtor exposed what had been handed over to him to these perils with the consent of the other party.[70]

(e) From accidentale to naturale negotii

It is perhaps not surprising, under these circumstances, to see that even the Roman lawyers themselves were occasionally uncertain about the actual function of the actio de recepto. Pomponius was one of those who were rather puzzled: "[M]iratur igitur, cur honoraria actio sit

---

[64] J.A.C. Thomas, "Carriage by Sea", (1960) 7 *RIDA* 489 sqq.

[65] This was even the older type of transaction: Thomas, (1960) 7 *RIDA* 497; idem, (1974) 32 *Recueils Bodin* 138.

[66] Thus it was necessary for the praetor to introduce, by reason of the special circumstances of sea carriage, the actiones furti and damni in factum adversus nautas in order to subject the nauta–locator to a special liability which was not inherent in the contract of locatio conductio rei: Thomas, (1960) 7 *RIDA* 497; idem, (1974) 32 *Recueils Bodin* 137 sq.

[67] (1960) 7 *RIDA* 500, 501.

[68] Cf. supra, p. 399.

[69] This line of argument is taken, for instance, by Meyer-Termeer, op. cit., note 43, pp. 177 sqq., 185 sqq.

[70] Kaser, *RPr* I, pp. 508, 586.

inducta, cum sint civiles"[71] is what he asked. For him, of course, this was already a matter of legal history; at the time when he wrote his commentaries, the actio de recepto had already existed for about 300 years and it is very likely that in the course of these centuries the law had undergone considerable change. The conclusion of a receptum had become more and more a matter of course when goods were given to a nauta for transportation. The day must have come when it was simply read into a locatio conductio rerum vehendarum and when the onus was on the parties specifically to exclude the receptum liability if they so wished.[72] There was, in short, a tendency to associate the duty of carriage and the duty of restoring the cargo, to approximate (and ultimately: to merge) receptum and conductio liability, and to treat what had once been merely an accidentale negotii virtually as a naturale of the contract of carriage by sea.[73] When and exactly how this development occurred is unclear: and this uncertainty makes it even more difficult for us to disentangle locatio conductio and receptum today.

(f) The receptum in modern law

The praetor's edict on the liability of nautae, caupones and stabularii has become part of the European ius commune[74] and it is still in force in South Africa today.[75] Many of the modern civil codes, too, have adopted the strict receptum liability,[76] the BGB, however, only in the case of innkeepers.[77] It appears always to have been accepted that such a liability existed when a carrier by sea, an innkeeper or a stablekeeper had received the property of his customer under a contract of carriage, for lodging or for stabling, unless it had been specifically excluded by the parties.[78] But whether the liability was based on an implied contract

---

[71] Ulp. D. 4, 9, 3, 1.

[72] That was possible; cf. Ulp. D. 4, 9, 7 pr.

[73] Giuseppe Ignazio Luzzatto, *Caso fortuito e forza maggiore come limite alla responsabilitâ contrattuale* (1938), p. 170; Arangio-Ruiz, *Responsabilità*, pp. 103 sqq.; Van Oven, (1956) 24 *TR* 148 sqq.; Magdelain, *Consensualisme*, pp. 148 sqq.; Thomas, (1960) 7 *RIDA* 498 sq.; cf. also Kaser, *RPr* I, p. 585, but cf. also *RPr* II, p. 408 (n. 57). According to De Robertis, (1953) 12 *Annali Bari* 61 sqq. and Brecht, op. cit., note 63, pp. 112 sqq., these changes took place only in post-classical times. Against any such development, be it in classical or post-classical law, see however, E. Ude, "Das receptum nautarum, ein pactum praetorium", (1891) 12 *ZSS* 66 sqq. and Meyer-Termeer, op. cit., note 43, pp. 201 sqq.

[74] Cf. e.g. Story, *Bailments*, §§ 458 sq., 464 sqq., 488; for Roman-Dutch law cf. Dönges, op. cit., note 42, pp. 33 sqq.

[75] Cf. e.g. *Davis v. Lockstone* 1921 AD 153 sqq.; Chr. van der Horst, in: Joubert (ed.), *The Law of South Africa*, vol. 2 (1977), n. 166.

[76] Cf. e.g. artt. 1782 sqq., 1952 sqq. code civil (s.v. depositum necessarium).

[77] §§ 701 sqq. On the liability of carriers in Germany, cf. Windscheid/Kipp, § 384 i.f.; Johann Georg Helm, "Haftung für Schäden an Frachtgütern" (1966), passim; for a comparative analysis, see Jürgen Basedow, *Der Transportvertrag* (1987), pp. 392 sqq.

[78] Such exclusionary clauses have, on the basis of Ulp. D. 4, 9, 7 pr., always been regarded as permissible; cf., for example, Glück, vol. 6, p. 115; Voet, *Commentarius ad Pandectas*, Lib. IV, Tit. IX, XVII; Dönges, op. cit., note 42, pp. 100 sqq.; for modern South

to that effect or whether it arose, quasi ex contractu, ipso facto receptionis, was never beyond dispute.[79] This lack of dogmatic clarity persists in modern law.[80] It has often been noted that the reason given in the Digest for the edictum de nautis, cauponibus et stabulariis does not, under modern conditions, provide a very satisfactory justification for the imposition of this stringent type of liability. Carriers by sea, innkeepers and stablekeepers may, of course, still be individually unreliable; but it can hardly be maintained that in their collectivity, as members of the respective professions ("hoc genus hominum"),[81] they are particularly disreputable. After all, hotels without bawdyhouses are no longer that exceptional. Hence, the rule of cessante ratione legis cessat lex ipsa has been invoked by South African innkeepers,[82] and their German counterparts vigorously opposed the adoption of the rule that was to become § 701 BGB.[83] But in neither of these jurisdictions did the lobbyists prevail. There have always been good reasons for the receptum, quite apart from those advanced by Ulpianus, most notably those deriving from the fact that the customer and his property are exposed to dangers emanating from a sphere which only the other party is able to organize and control.[84]

(g) *Range of application*

Inevitably, under these circumstances, the question had to be asked why the receptum should be confined to nautae, caupones and stabularii; the policy considerations underlying this strict type of liability would seem to be applicable to a broader range of professional activities. Thus, over the centuries, we see indeed an extension of the provisions of the edict. This development had already started in classical Roman law: "De exercitoribus ratium, item lyntrariis nihil cavetur: sed idem constitui oportere Labeo scribit, et hoc iure utimur."[85] There appears to have been some discussion whether the edict should be applied only to exercitores navium engaged in transport over the open sea or also to river boatmen. Labeo advocated the

---

African law cf. Van der Horst, op. cit., note 75, n. 177. The same applied in Germany (to innkeepers) until 1966; but cf. now § 702 a BGB.

[79] Cf. e.g. Glück, vol. 6, pp. 112 sq.; Dönges, op. cit., note 42, pp. 27 sq.

[80] Liability of the innkeeper according to the §§ 701 sqq. BGB was first seen within the framework of the contract of lodging *("Beherbergungsvertrag")* concluded between the innkeeper and his customer; it was then viewed by some authors as being based on a separate contract of deposit. Today, the view prevails that we are dealing with a liability ex lege (quasi ex contractu?). For details cf. e.g. Peter Koch, "Zur Neuregelung der Gastwirtshaftung", 1966 *Versicherungsrecht* 707 sqq.; Uwe Hüffer, in: *Münchener Kommentar*, vol. III, 2 (2nd ed. 1986), § 701, nn. 3 sq.

[81] Pomp./Ulp. D. 4, 9, 3, 1.

[82] Cf. *Davis v. Lockstone* 1921 AD 153 at 159.

[83] "Motive", in: *Mugdan*, vol. II, p. 326.

[84] For details cf. e.g. Glück, vol. 6, pp. 110 sq.; Dönges, op. cit., note 42, pp. 21 sq.; "Motive", in: *Mugdan*, vol. II, pp. 326 sq.

[85] Ulp. D. 4, 9, 1, 4; cf. e.g. Glück, vol. 6, pp. 126 sq.; Dönges, op. cit., note 42, pp. 78 sq.; Meyer-Termeer, op. cit., note 43, pp. 188 sq.

extension to those in charge of rafts or barges, and his opinion has been followed. The next in line were carriers by land. At the time of the usus modernus pandectarum, we find some authors still maintaining the distinction between carriers by sea and by land. It would be unreasonable, so they argued, to subject the latter to the receptum liability also; they could do much less than a nauta to protect their customer's property, when they had to take their coaches over inconvenient roads and through dark and dangerous forests without any kind of convoy or protection.[86] In practice, however, carriers by land (*"Postmeister und Landkutscher"*) had generally come to be placed on a par with the nautae of the praetorian edict; predominantly this was approved in contemporary literature,[87] and has also been accepted in modern South African law.[88] The question has even been asked (though not yet decided) whether the edict should not also be extended to carriers by air.[89]

The South African courts have, however, balked at the idea of considering the owner of a parking garage as (the equivalent of) a stablekeeper. Schreiner JA had this to say on the matter:

> "The question whether the keeper of a parking garage comes under the term stabularius can, in my opinion, only be answered in the negative. The differences between a dead thing like a motor car, which, though in a sense self-propelled, requires human agency to set and keep it in motion, and a living creature like a horse, possessed of its own capacity to initiate movement and subject to the impulses and the needs that go with life, appear to me to be so obvious and so important as to make it highly artificial to treat them as legal equivalents. . . . It is not necessary to speculate on the question how far the analogy would have to be carried, and whether those who store bicycles, perambulators or roller-skates would also be subject to a stricter standard of obligation than those who store chairs and tables. For I am clear that . . . considerations of fairness . . . not only do not favour the proposed extension but militate strongly against it. The parking of motor vehicles in a modern city is a serious problem and it cannot be socially advantageous to increase the risks of those who in the course of their business contribute to the solution of the problem."[90]

One is left to wonder what the somewhat quixotic pronouncement on the similarities and dissimilarities between horses and motorcars was intended to prove.

---

[86] Cf. e.g. Ferdinand Christian Harpprecht and Wolfgang Adam Lauterbach, as quoted by Glück, vol. 6, p. 128 and discussed by Dönges, op. cit., note 42, pp. 73 sqq.

[87] Glück, vol. 6, pp. 126 sqq.; cf. further Story, *Bailments*, § 488; Dönges, op. cit., note 42, pp. 80 sqq.; on the codifications of the late 18th and 19th centuries (as, particularly, § 2459 II 8 PrALR and §§ 970, 1316 ABGB) cf. Ogorek, *Gefährdungshaftung*, pp. 83 sq. Contra, however, the pandectists; cf., for example, Vangerow, *Pandekten*, § 648; C.F. Müller, *Ueber die de recepto actio und deren analoge Ausdehnung auf die Postanstalten* (2nd ed., 1857); pp. 65 sqq.

[88] *Tregidga & Co. v. Sivewright* (1897) 14 SC 76 at 81 sq.; *CSAR v. Adlington & Co.* 1906 TS 964 at 970 sq. (but cf. also *Stocks & Stocks (Pty.) Ltd. v. T.J. Daly & Sons (Pty.) Ltd.* 1979 (3) SA 754 (A) at 761G–H).

[89] Van der Horst, op. cit., note 75, n. 170.

[90] *Essa v. Divaris* 1947 (1) SA 753 (A) at 775–6. Cf. also the judgment by Tindall JA, pp. 765 sq.

(h) The liability of common carriers

In his judgment, incidentally, Schreiner JA refers to the liability of the "common carrier"[91] (as opposed to a private carrier). This terminology has repeatedly been used by South African courts. It has been borrowed from English law, where carriers both by land and by sea have also traditionally been subjected to a particularly strict type of liability, as long as they are common carriers.[92] A common carrier has been defined as one who undertakes, for hire or reward, to transport the goods of those who choose to employ him from place to place.[93] Private carriers, who do not exercise the business of common carriers, are responsible only to the same degree as other bailees for hire. The reception of the term "common carrier" into Roman-Dutch law, however, is apt to create confusion;[94] not because under the ius commune both a professional and a private carrier would have been subject to the receptum-type liability, but because the extent of the common (professional) carrier's liability is different under the ius commune (and consequently under modern South African law) than under the English common law.[95] Joseph Story describes the historical development as follows:

> "By the common law, as understood in the reign of Henry the Eighth, a responsibility of the like extent and nature [s.c.: as under the civil law] seems to have existed in England; for it is said that at that time a common carrier was held chargeable in cases of a loss by robbery, only when he had travelled by roads dangerous for robbery, or had driven by night, or at any inconvenient hour. However this may be, it is certain that in the commercial reign of Elizabeth a different rule prevailed; and the doctrine has for a good length of time been firmly established, that a common carrier is responsible for all losses, except those occasioned by the act of God, or of the King's enemies."[96]

The common carrier is thus treated as an insurer against all but certain excepted perils, which are very narrowly circumscribed. What is the rationale?

> "And this is a politick establishment", said Lord Holt in *Coggs v. Bernard*, a decision already repeatedly referred to,[97] "contrived by the policy of the law, for the safety of

---

[91] *Essa v. Divaris* 1947 (1) SA 753 (A) at 775.

[92] Cf. e.g. Story, *Bailments*, §§ 488 sqq.

[93] Cf. the references in Story, *Bailments*, § 495. He adds: "To bring a person within the description of a common carrier, he must exercise it as a public employment; he must undertake to carry goods for persons generally; and he must hold himself out as ready to engage in the transportation of goods for hire as a business, not as a casual occupation pro hac vice". On the early history of the "common" callings in general, see Simpson, *History*, pp. 229 sqq.

[94] For a detailed comparison between the common carrier of English law and what is usually termed "public carrier" in South African law (a person who holds himself out to the public as undertaking the carriage of goods (or persons) as his profession; cf. *Prinsloo v. Venter* 1964 (3) SA 626 (O) at 627D–G), see Dönges, op cit., pp. 62 sqq.

[95] Cf. e.g. Dönges, op. cit., note 42, pp. 69 sqq.

[96] § 489. Cf. further the detailed exposition of the law relating to common carriers by Sir William Jones, *An Essay on the Law of Bailments* (1836), Appendix pp. 1–106.

[97] (1703) 2 Ld Raym 909 at 918.

> all persons, the necessity of whose affairs oblige them to trust these sorts of persons, that they may be safe in their ways of dealing; for else these carriers might have an opportunity of undoing all persons that had any dealings with them, by combining with thieves, etc. and yet doing it in such a clandestine manner, as would not be possible to be discovered. And this is the reason the law is founded upon in that point."[98]

It is obvious that these policy considerations are borrowed from Roman law;[99] interestingly, however, they are used to justify an even stricter liability than that comprised by the Roman custodia.[100]

(i) Range of liability under the ius commune

Among the authors of the ius commune, the scope of the public carrier's responsibility was in dispute.[101] This controversy arose from the fact that the glossators had attempted to translate the strict receptum liability into culpa terminology. They regarded liability for damages as a kind of punishment for a wrongful act and applied the principle of "nulla poena sine culpa".[102] Hence, they based the carrier's liability on "culpa levissima".[103] As a consequence, the carrier was not responsible,

---

[98] Cf. also Best CJ, in *Riley v. Horne* (1828) 5 Bing 217: "When goods are delivered to a carrier, they are usually no longer under the eye of the owner; he seldom follows, or sends any servants with them, to the place of their destination. If they should be lost or injured by the grossest negligence of the carrier or his servants, or stolen by them, or by thieves in collusion with them, the owner would be unable to prove either of these causes of loss. His witnesses must be the carrier's servants; and they, knowing that they could not be contradicted, would excuse their masters and themselves. To give due security to property, the law has added to that responsibility of a carrier which immediately arises out of his contract to carry for a reward, namely, that of taking all reasonable care of it, the responsibility of an insurer. From his liability as an insurer, the carrier is only to be relieved by two things, both so well known to all the country, when they happen, that no person would be so rash as to attempt to prove that they had happened when they had not, namely, the act of God, and the King's enemies" (p. 220).

[99] Cf. also *Lane v. Cotton* (1701) 12 Mod Rep 472: ". . . and the law will not expose him [sc. the carrier] to so great a temptation, but he must be honest at his peril. And this is the reason of the civil law in this case, which though I am loth to quote, yet inasmuch as the laws of all nations are doubtless raised out of the ruins of the civil law, . . . it must be owned that the principles of our law are borrowed from the civil law, therefore grounded upon the same reason in many things" (p. 482, per Holt CJ).

[100] One of the main differences is that under the common law the carrier is liable in case of robbery (unless committed by public enemies). In Roman (and Roman-Dutch) law this fell under the exception of vis maior (or damnum fatale). On the liability of innkeepers under the English common law, cf. Story, *Bailments*, nn. 469 sqq. He states at the outset of his discussion that the strict (though not as strict as the common carrier's!) liability of an innkeeper is usually said "to be founded on the custom of the realm. In point of fact, the origin of the latter may be clearly traced up to the Roman law, from which the common law, without any adequate acknowledgements, has from time to time borrowed many of the important principles which regulate the subjects of the contracts." One important difference, however, lies in the fact that the common carrier (unlike the Roman nauta) is under an obligation to contract.

[101] For what follows, cf. particularly W.J. Hosten, "Die Aanspreeklikheid van die depositarius en die vervoerder ingevolge die gemene reg", 1964 *Acta Juridica* 128 sqq.

[102] Lange, *Schadensersatz und Privatstrafe*, pp. 111 sqq.

[103] Cf. also Domenico Maffei, *Caso fortuito e responsabilità nell' étà dei glossatori* (1957), pp. 23 sqq.; Hoffmann, *Fahrlässigkeit*, pp. 35 sqq.

for instance, in cases of theft, provided no negligence was attributable to him. Even the slightest degree of negligence led to liability; on the other hand, however, if he could show that he had acted diligently, that was enough to relieve the carrier of his liability. "Casus fortuitus" was the term most often used to draw the line and it included vis maior as well as what we have referred to as "lesser accidents".[104] Many writers of the usus modernus pandectarum (including, more specifically, some Roman-Dutch authorities) still shared this view. A very clear statement to this effect is that of Vinnius, who refers to Ulp. D. 4, 9, 3, 1:

> "quo loco Jurisconsultus conferens actiones locati et depositi cum honoraria, quae ex edicto isto competit, utilitatem ejus, quae ex edicto est, hoc nomine maxime commendat: quod in locato conducto culpa, in deposito dolus duntaxat praestetur: edicto vero omnimodo, qui recepit, teneatur, etiamsi sine culpa ejus res periit aut damnum datum est, ita tamen, ut nec ille praestet casus fortuitos, seu quod damno fatali aut vi majore contigit. Igitur ex sententia Jurisconsulti is, qui recepit, praestat medium aliquid inter culpam et casum fortuitum, quod non praestat conductor: atqui hoc medium nihil aliud esse, fateri omnes debent, quam culpam levissimam."[105]

It is not surprising, in view of these authorities, that the South African courts have occasionally based the carrier's liability on culpa.[106] Today, however, a different view prevails:

> "The construction placed on this edict was that the bailees named were liable in every case of loss or damage occasioned by theft, injury or otherwise, although happening without any default on their part, unless it happened by superior force or by what was called 'fatal damage', as for instance by shipwreck, or by the act of pirates."[107]

As so often in a judgment by Lord De Villiers, this statement is squarely based on Voet.[108] It does, however, find support in the writings of a variety of other authors[109] and gives a fair reflection of the receptum (custodia) liability of classical Roman law.[110]

The passage quoted above from Vinnius' *Commentary on the Institutiones*, incidentally, also makes it clear, why the magna quaestio of modern historical research, namely that of the function of the actio de recepto in relation to the actio locati, did not unduly trouble the writers of the ius commune. Justinian had tried to redefine all instances of the classical contractual custodia liability in terms of culpa. Since the days of the glossators, it was therefore accepted that a conductor operis

---

[104] On the terminology cf. Dönges, op. cit., note 42, pp. 41 sqq.; Hosten, 1964 *Acta Juridica* 132 sq.; cf. also Windscheid/Kipp, §§ 384, n. 6.

[105] *Institutiones*, Lib. III, Tit. XXV, 5, 2.

[106] *Stephan Frazer & Co. v. Port Elizabeth Harbour Board* (1900) 17 SC 231 at 234; *Magaga v. Cole* (1908) 25 SC 434 at 436; *Postmaster-General v. Van Niekerk* 1918 CPD 378 at 382 sq.

[107] *Tregidga & Co. v. Sivewright* (1897) 14 SC 76 at 81, per Lord De Villiers CJ. Cf. further *Davis v. Lockstone* 1921 AD 153 at 158 sq., 164 sqq.; also *Essa v. Divaris* 1947 (1) SA 753 (A) at 764 sq.

[108] Cf. *Commentarius ad Pandectas*, Lib. IV, Tit. IX, II.

[109] Cf. e.g. Glück, vol. 6, p. 120.

[110] The same applies to the liability of the innkeeper in modern German law; cf. § 701 BGB.

was liable, as a rule, for culpa (levis); and liability of carriers under the praetorian edict was considerably stiffer in comparison, no matter whether it was conceived to be strict or construed as culpa levissima.

III. PACTA LEGITIMA: COMPROMISSUM AS EXAMPLE

1. Classical and post-classical compromissum

Informal agreements, which were not recognized by the praetor and which came to be regarded as binding and legally effective only in post-classical times, are usually referred to as pacta legitima.[111] The main cases falling into this category are dotis promissio, donatio and compromissum. By way of example,[112] we shall, at this stage, briefly consider the structure and history of the compromissum.[113] It owes its name[114] to the fact that two parties who wished to submit their dispute to arbitration formally promised each other to pay a penalty in case they did not abide by the arbitrator's decision. The mere agreement to submit to arbitration was not binding under classical law. But the parties could make their arrangement indirectly enforceable by means of two (non-genuine) stipulationes poenae. *Each* of the parties had to promise a penalty; a unilateral stipulatio poenae did not give rise to a valid compromissum.[115] This is an expression of the principle of reciprocity underpinning the arbitration proceedings.[116] In their compromissum, the parties had to appoint the arbiter (it was concluded "in aliquem arbitrum"), they had to confer upon him the full and unrestricted power to decide their dispute,[117] and they had to indicate which subject matter they wished to submit to him.[118] No appeal was possible against the arbiter's decision.[119]

---

[111] The term occurs in Ulp. D. 2, 14, 5 and Paul. D. 2, 14, 6 ("Legitima conventio est quae lege aliqua confirmatur. et ideo interdum ex pacto actio nascitur vel tollitur, quotiens lege vel senatus consulto adiuvatur.").

[112] On donatio cf. supra, pp. 477 sqq.

[113] It must immediately be stated that among modern scholars there is no unanimity on this topic. The views put forward in the following lines have been substantiated, in particular, by Ziegler, *Privates Schiedsgericht*, pp. 47 sqq., 180 sqq., 246 sqq.; cf. also Giorgio La Pira, " 'Compromissum' e 'litis contestatio' formulare", in: *Studi in onore di Salvatore Riccobono*, vol. II (1936), nn. 187 sqq. A different picture is presented, most notably, by Mario Talamanca, *Ricerche in tema di "compromissum"* (1958), passim; idem, "L'arbitrato romano dai 'veteres' a Giustiniano", (1974) 20 *Labeo* 86 sqq. He emphasizes (even for classical law) the informal arbitration agreement; the stipulationes poenae merely served to secure fulfilment of the obligations arising from it. In other words: he, more or less, regards as classical what is presented here as a postclassical conception.

[114] On the terminology ("compromittere", as used in the praetorian edict) cf. Ziegler, *Privates Schiedsgericht*, pp. 8 sqq.

[115] Ulp. D. 4, 8, 11, 4.

[116] Cf. further Ziegler, *Privates Schiedsgericht*, pp. 55 sq.

[117] Cf. e.g. Paul. D. 4, 8, 19 pr.; Ulp. D. 4, 8, 17, 3.

[118] A "compromissum plenum" ("quod . . . ad omnes controversias pertinet") was possible: Ulp. D. 4, 8, 21, 6.

[119] Cf. e.g. C. 2, 55, 1 (Ant.).

During the post-classical period we see a gradual shift of emphasis away from the formal penalty stipulations towards the underlying conventio, the arbitration agreement of the parties. This development is closely related to the general degeneration (or atrophy) of the classical stipulation as a formal, oral promise,[120] as well as to the rise (and eventual official recognition) of certain extraordinary forms of jurisdiction. Of these, the episcopalis audientia was the most important.[121] Based, originally, on St. Paul's request to the early Christians not to bring their disputes before a heathen judge ("Audet aliquis vestrum, habens negotium adversus alterum, iudicari apud iniquos, et non apud sanctos?")[122] the episcopalis audientia emerged when the bishops assumed the role of arbitrators in private disputes between clerics as well as between laymen. Provocatio ad episcopale iudicium was, of course, not based on a formal compromissum, since this, too, would have been enforceable only by the State courts. Once a concurring jurisdictional competence of the bishops had become recognized by the (by now) Christian State, a mutual assimilation between private and episcopal arbitration was bound to occur.

In the result, therefore, the compromissum sine poena began to be recognized in post-classical practice.[123] Oral formalities had, for all practical purposes, been abandoned, so that a compromissum (cum or sine poena) was nothing but a pactum in writing.[124] If the sententia arbitri was favourable to the defendant, he was granted an exceptio veluti pacti ex compromisso in order to prevent the plaintiff from further pursuing his claims against him.[125] Such a defence had not been available in classical law: "Ex compromisso placet exceptionem non nasci, sed poenae petitionem."[126] Strictly speaking, this principle of classical law was still respected; for it was not an exceptio pacti (based on the compromissum) that was granted to the defendant, but an exceptio veluti pacti arising from the sententia arbitri ex compromisso which the parties to the dispute had promised to comply with.

[120] Cf. supra, pp. 78 sqq.

[121] For details, see Walter Selb, "Episcopalis audientia von der Zeit Konstantins bis zur Nov. XXXV Valentinians III.", (1967) 84 *ZSS* 162 sqq.; Ziegler, *Privates Schiedsgericht*, pp. 167 sqq.; Giulio Vismara, "Ancora sulla 'episcopalis audientia'", (1987) 54 *SDHI* 53 sqq. Apart from episcopalis audientia, the special jurisdiction conceded by the Romans to the Jews was of some significance in the present context; cf. Ziegler, *Privates Schiedsgericht*, pp. 175 sq.; generally: Kaser, *RZ*, p. 527.

[122] 1. Corinthians 6, 1.

[123] Cf. C. 2, 55, 5 pr. (Just.).

[124] Cf. C. 2, 55, 4, 6 sq. (Just.). C. 2, 55, 4 pr. sqq. deal with a confirmation of this arbitration agreement by oath. But see Nov. 82, 11, 1 (repealing again the possibility of such confirmation).

[125] Cf. Ulp. D. 4, 8, 13, 1 (interpolated?: Talamanca, *Ricerche*, op. cit., note 113, pp. 125 sqq., but see Ziegler, *Privates Schiedsgericht*, pp. 51 sq., 183); C. 2, 55, 5 pr. (Just.).

[126] Ulp. D. 4, 8, 2; cf. further Ziegler, *Privates Schiedsgericht*, pp. 50 sq.

2. The compromissum of the ius commune

Justinian accepted and further consolidated these changes. Not only did he retain the protection for the victorious defendant;[127] he also made available an actio in factum to the plaintiff, in whose favour the arbitrator had pronounced.[128] On the other hand, however, as usual, Justinian tried to preserve and revive the institutions of classical law. He therefore encouraged the parties to take the matter into their own hands and to give teeth to their arbitration agreement by way of penalty clauses. Neither actio in factum nor exceptio veluti pacti applied to this standard type of compromissum and the penalty became a kind of forfeit-money, payment of which effectively released the parties from their obligation to stand by the sententia arbitri.[129] Nevertheless, the idea that the arbitration proceedings were based on an (independent) pactum, to which the penalties could (but did not necessarily have to) be added, was now firmly entrenched. In this form, the compromissum became part of the ius commune; and once the fetters of "ex nudo pacto non oritur actio" had been overcome,[130] there was nothing extraordinary in an informal arbitration agreement. "Constituitur arbiter compromisso partium, id est, conventione, qua contendentes arbitri sententiae se stituros promittunt, plerumque quidem poena apposita" is, for instance, the definition provided by Johannes Voet.[131]

3. Arbiter, arbitrator and amicabilis compositor

From the Middle Ages, however, another problem occupied the minds of the jurists. Secular as well as ecclesiastical arbitration practice had developed in a way that was not always in conformity with the sources of Roman Law. In particular, certain persons were now acceptable as arbitrators who had been disqualified under the provisions of the Corpus Juris Civilis.[132] Hence the attempts to distinguish between two types of arbitrator.[133] They found a textual

---

[127] Even in case of an entirely informal compromissum sine poena (". . . sub eo pacto in scriptis vel non in scriptis habito, ut eorum definitioni stetur"): C. 2, 55, 5 pr.

[128] C. 2, 55, 4, 4; C. 2, 55, 4, 6; C. 2, 55, 5 pr. sq. This actio in factum was based (dogmatically) on a recognition in writing of the sententia arbitri on the part of both parties (subscripto), i.e. on a special agreement post sententiam arbitri, not on the (informal) compromissum. However, a tacit recognition of the award was sufficient too ("si silentio eam roboraverint"); it was deemed to have taken place if the parties did not protest within a period of 10 days.

[129] Nov. 82, 11; Talamanca, *Ricerche*, op. cit., note 113, pp. 139 sqq.; Ziegler, *Privates Schiedsgericht*, pp. 239 sqq.

[130] Cf. infra, pp. 539 sqq.

[131] *Commentaruis ad Pandectas*, Lib. IV, Tit. VIII, III. For the modern South African common law, cf. Catherine Smith, in: Joubert (ed.), *The Law of South Africa*, vol. 1 (1976), n. 458.

[132] Cf. particularly C. 2, 55, 6 (women) and Ulp. D. 4, 8, 9, 2 (referring to the person who would otherwise have been judge in the same matter); Karl-Heinz Ziegler, "Arbiter, arbitrator und amicabilis compositor", (1967) 84 *ZSS* 376 sqq.

[133] Helmut Coing, "Zur Entwicklung des Schiedsvertrages im Jus Commune", in: *Festschrift für Heinz Hübner* (1984), pp. 35 sqq.

basis in a fragment taken from the epistulae of Proculus:

> "[A]rbitrorum enim genera sunt duo, unum eiusmodi, ut sive aequum sit sive iniquuum, parere debeamus [quod observatur, cum ex compromisso ad arbitrum itum est], alterum eiusmodi, ut ad boni viri arbitrium redigi debeat, etsi nominatim persona sit comprehensa, cuius arbitratu fiat."[134]

This text makes it clear, first of all, that in classical Roman law the arbiter (ex compromisso) was entirely free in his decision; he was not bound by any rules of substantive law.[135] Thus, his award was binding, even if it was unjust or inequitable. Apart from that, the parties could also leave the settlement of certain points to a third party who had to decide according to an objective standard, namely that of the arbitrium boni viri. This second type of "arbiter" was now (i.e. in medieval science) equated with the amicabilis compositor of Nov. 86, 2: a bishop, to whom the parties under certain circumstances had to refer their dispute and who acted as a kind of conciliator. This second type of "arbiter" also came to be termed "arbitrator", and in one of the most famous procedural treatises of the Middle Ages, Durantis' *Speculum iudiciale*, he is defined as follows:

> "Arbitrator vero est amicabilis compositor, nec sumitur super re litigiosa, vel ut cognoscat: sed ut pacificet, et quod certum est, dividat. . . . Nec tenetur iuris ordinem servare: nec statur eius sententiae, si sit iniqua: sed reducitur ad arbitrium boni viri."[136]

The regular arbiter, on the other hand, was now taken to perform the function of a judge: "Est enim arbiter, qui causam examinat in iudicii forma, sicut iudex."[137] He was chosen by the parties not merely in order to restore the peace between the parties or to determine, ex aequo et bono, points which the parties had left open in their agreement, but to decide a dispute ("Nam arbiter est, quem partes eligunt ad *cognoscendum* de quaestione, vel lite");[138] he was however bound to follow the rules of civil procedure ("Et debet iuris ordinem servare")[139] and had to apply the law ("Arbiter debet sequi iuris rigorem, et aequitatem scriptam").[140]

Many authors in later times maintained this distinction between arbiter and arbitrator, as, for example, Joost van Damhouder ("Een

---

[134] D. 17, 2, 76.

[135] Cf. further Paul. D. 4, 8, 19 pr. ("Qualem autem sententiam dicat arbiter, ad praetorem non pertinere Labeo ait, dummodo dicat, quod ipsi videtur"); Ulp. D. 4, 8, 27, 2; Ziegler, *Privates Schiedsgericht*, pp. 135 sqq.

[136] *Speculum iudiciale*, Pars I, Lib. I, Partic. I, Rubrica De Arbitro et Arbitratore, § 1, 3.

[137] Pillius, Tancredus, *Gratia, Libri de iudiciorum ordine* (ed.: F.C. Bergmann), 1842, p. 107 (n. 36). Cf. also already the Summa totius artis notariae Rolandini Rudolphini Bononiensis, as quoted by Ziegler, (1967) 84 *ZSS* 381.

[138] Durantis, *Speculum iudiciale*, loc. cit., § 1, 2.

[139] Durantis, *Speculum iudiciale*, § 1, 2. This was contrary to Roman law where, as far as the procedure was concerned, the arbiter was bound only by the terms of the compromissum: for details, see Ziegler, *Privates Schiedsgericht*, pp. 129 sqq.

[140] Baldus, as quoted in an appendix to the rubrica "De Arbitro et Arbitratore" of Durantis' *Speculum iudiciale*. This, too, was contrary to Roman law; cf. supra, note 134.

Arbiter procedeert gerechtelijck as een Rechter, Een arbitrateur procedeert vrundelijck")[141] or Johannes Voet ("Est vero arbiter, qui compromisso partium electus est, ut lites dirimat; diversus ab arbitratoribus, nomine quidem in jure nostro ignotis, re ipso notis; quippe qui absque ulla judicii forma ex aequo et bono lites componere suo consilio suaque auctoritate allaborant").[142] Others introduced, in effect, a new type of arbitrator, the "arbiter ex aequo et bono"; he not only had to conciliate but also had to make a decision, and yet he proceeded extra iudicium and decided ut bonus vir, i.e. without being bound by the ius.[143] This latter type of arbitrator lives on in modern German law, where the parties may in their arbitration agreement[144] authorize the *"Schiedsrichter"*[145] to decide in accordance with fairness and equity rather than to apply the substantive law.[146]

IV. COMBINED TRANSACTIONS: HIRE-PURCHASE IN ROMAN LAW

The picture presented so far was, of course, still somewhat patchy. Many (informal) agreements, which two or more parties might have wanted to enter into, were still "nudum"; since no action was available to enforce them, they were, in effect, not binding.[147] Thus, there were unsatisfactory gaps in the Roman contractual system, and it became crucially important to determine, for every slightly atypical arrangement, whether it could be squeezed into one of the existing contractual niches and, if so, into which one. Occasionally the Roman lawyers were, however, able to help by ingeniously combining two different sets of actions, a process of amalgamation through which a new kind of transaction could sometimes take shape. Hire-purchase agreements provide a good example.

It is by no means rare that a purchaser requires certain goods for his immediate use without, however, being able to pay the whole purchase

141 *Practycke in civile saecken* (Rotterdam 1649), Cap. CCIII.

142 *Commentarius ad Pandectas*, Lib. IV, Tit. VIII, II.

143 For details, see Coing, *Festschrift Hübner*, pp. 38 sqq., also on the meaning of ex aequo et bono under the ius commune.

144 *"Schiedsvertrag"*: §§ 1025 sqq. ZPO.

145 §§ 1026 sqq. ZPO.

146 As far as the procedure is concerned, the arbitrator must observe a number of special rules laid down by the ZPO, and certain general principles of (civil) procedure; otherwise he is free (within the terms of the arbitration agreement) to determine the award in his own discretion. Today, incidentally, the arbitration agreement normally has to be in writing (§ 1027 ZPO). On the historical development of arbitration in Germany, see Hermann Krause, *Die geschichtliche Entwicklung der Schiedsgerichtsbarkeit in Deutschland* (1930). The French code de procedure has taken over the *"amiable compositeur"* from the ius commune (art. 1019).

147 However, in the Corpus Juris Civilis nuda pacta are associated with aequitas naturalis (Ulp. D. 2, 14, 1 pr.); thus they could provide the basis for a naturalis obligatio (cf. e.g. Ulp. D. 46, 3, 5, 2; Pap. D. 46, 3, 95, 4; Guido Astuti, I *contratti obbligatori nella storia del diritto italiano*, vol. I (1952), pp. 176 sqq.).

price. Under these circumstances the vendor will often be prepared to give him credit, provided he retains some form of security. One of the most obvious ways of securing the vendor's claim is to make transfer of ownership of the res vendita dependent upon payment of the full purchase price.[148] Modern legal systems accommodate these needs and interests of the parties in the form of hire-purchase contracts[149] or instalment sales.[150]

In Rome, the parties were taken to have concluded two transactions: a contract of emptio venditio, combined with a locatio conductio (rei).[151] The Roman lawyers, however, did not deal with them in isolation, but adjusted the rights and duties of the parties in a most flexible and undogmatic manner. A generalizing statement about how the problems arising from the cumulative combination of sale and lease were tackled, is provided by Paulus:

> "Interdum locator non obligatur, conductor obligatur, veluti cum emptor fundum conducit, donec pretium ei solvat. . . . Item si pretio non soluto inempta res facta sit, tunc ex locato erit actio."[152]

A piece of property has been sold. Either the sale may have been unconditional (as presumably, for instance, in the example of the first sentence) or it may have been concluded subject to a lex commissoria (it is likely that this is the situation dealt with in the second sentence). The vendor has not yet transferred ownership, since the purchase price has not been paid. But he is prepared to allow the purchaser to live on the property in the meantime; he therefore leases it to him. This contract of lease is concluded "donec pretium emptor solvat": it is to fall away once the purchase price has been paid. According to Paulus, the vendor/lessor can avail himself of the actio locati. During the existence of the lease he can bring it in order to enforce payment of the

---

[148] On the pactum reservati dominii of the ius commune cf. e.g. Glück, vol. 16, pp. 229 sqq.; Windscheid/Kipp, § 172, 7; Gottfried Schiemann, "Über die Funktion des pactum reservati dominii während der Rezeptionen des römischen Rechts in Italien und Mitteleuropa", (1976) 93 *ZSS* 161 sqq. In South African law, considerable confusion exists about the legal effect of such pacts reserving ownership; this is due to the decision by Lord De Villiers CJ, in *Quirk's Trustees v. Assignees of Liddle & Co.* (1885) 3 SC 322. For a discussion, see M.A. Diemont, P.J. Aronstam, *The Law of Credit Agreements and Hire-Purchase in South Africa* (5th ed., 1982), pp. 13 sqq. On the reservation of title in Roman law cf., most recently, Anton Meinhart, "Dogmengeschichtliches und Dogmatisches zum Eigentumsvorbehalt", (1988) 105 *ZSS* 729 sqq.

[149] Cf., for South Africa, the provisions of the Hire-Purchase Act, 36/1942 and now the Credit Agreements Act, 75/1980. On the legal nature of this type of contract (sale or lease?), see Diemont/Aronstam, op. cit., note 148, pp. 20 sqq.

[150] Cf., for Germany, the *"Gesetz betreffend die Abzahlungsgeschäfte"* (Act relating to instalment-transactions) of 16 May 1894 (pre-BGB!); cf. e.g. Hans-Peter Benöhr, "Konsumentenschutz vor 80 Jahren", (1974) 138 *ZHR* 492 sqq.; Eike von Hippel, *Verbraucherschutz* (3rd ed. 1986), pp. 192 sqq.

[151] For details, see Rolf Knütel, "Kauf und Pacht bei Abzahlungsgeschäften im römischen Recht", in: *Studien im römischen Recht* (1973), pp. 33 sqq.

[152] Paul. D. 19, 2, 20, 2; idem, D. 19, 2, 22.

rent.[153] But he can also use this action to reclaim the property.[154] That is the case when the contract of sale has fallen away (due to the fact that the purchase price or the individual instalments have not been paid in time).[155] As a consequence, the lease must terminate too, since it was to exist only "donec pretium emptor solvat". That has now become impossible.

As long, however, as the purchaser/lessee paid the instalments of the purchase price, the vendor/lessor was not able to reclaim the land. Ulpianus D. 43, 26, 20 makes it clear that this was so, even where the purchaser was only precario tenens. It must have applied, a fortiori, where he was a lessee.[156] "Locator non obligatur, conductor obligatur": if the purchaser was bound under the contract of lease, he could, in turn, not bring the actio conducti against the vendor. The overriding intention of the parties was, after all, the conclusion of a sale. Questions of risk and liability therefore had to be decided according to the rules relating to emptio venditio, and the position of the purchaser was adequately protected by the actio empti. There was no room for an actio conducti: the sale, in so far, overshadowed all else.[157]

V. INNOMINATE REAL CONTRACTS

1. Permutatio and the rise of actiones praescriptis verbis

But, of course, not nearly all problems could be solved in this or a similar fashion. One need merely look at exchange agreements (permutatio). We have seen that the Sabinians were prepared to grant the actiones empti and venditi, but that in the end the Proculian view prevailed: without a purchase price in money there could be no sale.[158] Thus, permutatio remained within the "no man's land" of unenforceable pacta. Other informal arrangements which could not be brought under one of the existing contracts, or which combined certain elements of two or more of them, shared this fate. Under these circumstances it cannot always have been easy for the parties to determine whether their transaction was binding or not, and a rigid adherence by the Roman lawyers to a closed system of contracts and actions would have caused considerable hardship. A remedy therefore

---

[153] Contra: David Daube, (1958) 5 *RIDA* 430, 433; but see Knütel, op. cit., note 151, pp. 35 sqq.

[154] Paul. D. 19, 2, 20, 2 and 22, 1; cf. J.A.C. Thomas, "Tenancy by Purchaser", (1959) 10 *Iura* 107 sq.; Salvatore Tondo, " 'Pignus' e 'precarium' ", (1959) 5 *Labeo* 200 sqq.; Knütel, op. cit., note 151, pp. 41 sqq. For a different interpretation, see Daube, (1958) 5 *RIDA* 427 sqq.

[155] If there had been a lex commissoria, the sale could simply be called off by the vendor; if the sale was unconditional, it could be cancelled contrario consensu.

[156] Knütel, op. cit., note 151, pp. 47 sqq.

[157] Daube, (1958) 5 *RIDA* 431 sq.; Thomas, (1959) 10 *Iura* 108 sq.; Knütel, op. cit., note 151, pp. 51 sqq.

[158] Cf. supra, pp. 250 sqq.

came to be provided, at least in cases where one of the parties had visibly relied on the enforceability of the arrangement and had performed his side of it in the expectation that the counterperformance would also be forthcoming. A and B have agreed to swop their sedan chairs. Unless it had been couched in the form of two stipulations, this transaction was not enforceable. Once, however, A had handed over his sedan chair, the situation changed. True: if B did not reciprocate, A could always claim it back. In fact, this was one of the typical instances in which an unjustified enrichment claim was granted (viz. the condictio causa data causa non secuta).[159] But A had not given his sedan chair to B merely in order to get it back soon afterwards. He had honoured the arrangement made with B and could now reasonably expect B to do likewise. It is in this type of situation that the praetor intervened ("adiuvandi vel supplendi vel corrigendi iuris civilis gratia",[160] as usual) and granted an actio in factum to A.[161] It was an action "on the facts of the case", modelled as closely as possible on one of the existing contractual remedies. "Quod A^s A^s de N° N° [hominem Stichum] emit . . ." was the demonstratio of the formula for the actio empti.[162] Use of the technical term "emit" rendered redundant any further specification of what this transaction was about. Exchange was not sale, but it was similar to it. Hence one could conveniently use the actio empti as the basis for the claim and merely modify it by referring to the specific agreement which the parties had concluded. This was done by substituting the terms of this agreement (and in so far: the specific facts of the case) for the term "emit" in the demonstratio of the formula. Since the actio empti (and the other contractual actions used as models for the actiones in factum) were in ius concepta, one also referred to actiones in factum civiles.[163] Since the facts of the case (on the basis of which this action was granted) were spelt out at the outset of the formula (they were "prefaced"), the term "actio praescriptis verbis" also came to be used.[164] And since, apart from the demonstratio, the formula was identical to that of the actiones empti, venditi, locati or conducti, all these actiones in factum (civiles) or praescriptis verbis were bonae fidei iudicia.[165]

---

[159] Cf. infra, pp. 843 sqq . Apart from that, there was the actio doli (cf. e.g. Paul. D. 19, 5, 5, 3) which, however, also did not aim at enforcement of the agreement between the parties.

[160] Pap. D. 1, 1, 7, 1.

[161] Aristo/Iul./Ulp. D. 2, 14, 7, 2.

[162] Cf. supra, p. 277.

[163] Lab./Pap. D. 19, 5, 5, 1; Paul. D. 19, 5, 5, 2; Max Kaser, "Oportere und ius civile", (1966) 83 *ZSS* 37 sqq.

[164] D. 19, 5; C. 4, 64; Kaser, *RPr* II, pp. 419 sqq. Cf also James B. Thayer, "Actio Praescriptis verbis", (1944–45) 19 *Tulane LR* 62 sqq.; most recently, cf. Karlheinz Misera, "Julian-Afrikan D. 19, 5, 24. Ein Beitrag zu 'agere praescriptis verbis' ", in: *Sodalitas, Scritti in onore di Antonio Guarino*, vol. VI (1985), pp. 2591 sqq.

[165] Kaser, *RPr* I, p. 582.

2. Range of transactions

It can no longer be doubted today[166] that these remedies already began to be granted in classical law. They brought about, in actual practice, a considerable relaxation of the rigours of the classical scheme of contracts. On the other hand, the contributions of East-Roman school jurisprudence are considerable too, particularly in the field of systematic analysis. To try to disentangle details of the development is difficult, if not impossible. But the end result is clear: by the time of Justinian, a new class of contracts had come to be recognized.[167] These contracts were "innominate" in that the actions were not individualized by a specific name[168]—the demonstratio did not, as we have seen, merely refer to emptio or locatio, but to the specific terms of the arrangement; and they were "real", in that the right to claim counterperformance became enforceable only once performance had been rendered.[169,170] Hence the term "innominate real contracts". According to Paul (or rather: Tribonian) D. 19, 5, 5 pr., there were four types: ". . . aut enim do tibi ut des, aut do ut facias, aut facio ut des, aut facio ut facias."[171] This classification is of little systematic value, but it shows how broad the range of application was.[172] It covered all reciprocal consensual agreements apart from emptio venditio and

[166] As has been done for some time; cf. e.g. Pietro de Francisci, Συνάλλαγμα, vol. I (1913) and vol. II (1916), passim; Schulz, *CRL*, pp. 522 sqq.; but see e.g. Rabel, *Grundzüge*, pp. 116 sqq.; Buckland/ Stein, p. 522; Jörs/Kunkel/Wenger, pp. 243 sqq.; Biondi, op. cit., note 5, pp. 85 sqq., 101 sqq.; Kaser, *RPr* I, pp. 580 sqq.; Raimondo Santoro, "Il contratto nel pensiero di Labeone", (1983) 37 *Annali Palermo* 71 sqq.; Honsell/Mayer-Maly/Selb, pp. 340 sqq.

[167] On the question of how the innominate contracts fitted into Roman contractual theory, cf. Geoffrey MacCormack, "Contractual Theory and the Innominate Contracts", (1985) 51 *SDHI* 131 sqq.; but see Alberto Burdese, "Ancora in tema di contratti innominati", (1986) 52 *SDHI* 442 sqq.

[168] This notion already appears in Ulp. D. 2, 14, 1, 4; Ulp. D. 2, 14, 7, 1.

[169] Similar to the contracts re, there had to be "rei interventio", in the sense that something had to happen apart from the consent of the parties. Only here it was part performance, there performance (the real contracts were unilateral!), here a rendering of services or a transfer of an object, there only the latter.

[170] "In English legal terms, they were contracts made binding on executed consideration" (Thomas, *TRL*, p. 311).

[171] On the whole fragment D. 19, 5, 5, see Paul Collinet, "Le Fr. 5, Dig. 19, 5 De Praescr. Verbis et in F. Act.: Application de la Méthode critique de Décomposition des Textes", in: *Festschrift für Paul Koschaker*, vol. I (1939), pp. 70 sqq.; idem, *La genèse du digeste, du code et des institutions de Justinien* (1952), pp. 182 sqq. The fourfold subdivision (do, ut des; facio, ut facias; facio, ut des; do, ut facias) is, incidentally, referred to by Blackstone, *Commentaries*, vol. II, pp. 44 sq., not, however, in the context of innominate real contracts, but in order to discuss the concept of "valuable consideration"; cf. Nikolaus Benke, "No inefficacy arises merely from the naked promise", (1987) 14 *Ius Commune* 39 sqq.

[172] It is, however, not exhaustive; cf., for example, Kaser, *RPr* II, pp. 420 sq. Post-classical jurisprudence conceived of the actio praescriptis verbis as a (subsidiary) actio generalis. The innominate contracts "constitute the nearest approach that Roman law made to a generalized system of contract" (Thomas, *TRL*, p. 311). For a detailed analysis, see De Francisci, op. cit., note 166, vol. I, pp. 85 sqq.; cf. also Santoro, (1983) 37 *Annali Palermo* 95 sqq. and passim.

locatio conductio, no matter whether performance or counterperformance consisted in dare (aliquid) or facere (aliquid).

"Et si quidem pecuniam dem, ut rem accipiam, emptio et venditio est: sin autem rem do, ut rem accipiam, quia non placet permutationem rerum emptionem esse, dubium non est nasci civilem obligationem, in qua actione id veniet, non ut reddas quod acceperis, sed ut damneris mihi, quanti interest mea illud de quo convenit accipere."[173]

This is permutatio (exchange), and it was an innominate real contract of the type of do ut des. If one of the parties had performed and the other was unwilling to counterperform, an action was granted; and the aim of this action was not merely a restitutionary one, but it was designed to put the plaintiff in the position in which he would have been had the bargain been completed. "[D]edi tibi Stichum, ut Pamphilum manumittas" would be an example of do ut facias,[174] "si pacti sumus, . . . ut tu in meo, ego in tuo solo aedificem"[175] of facio ut facias. Many more could be added.[176] Particularly in close-knit agricultural communities it was probably not a rare occurrence for neighbouring farmers to "borrow" each other's oxen in order to plough their fields,[177] to work in each other's vineyards during the time of vintage (both cases of facio ut facias) or to remunerate certain services by payment in kind (facio ut des or do ut facias). No distinctions appear to have been drawn between these various "innominate" transactions; all were enforceable, under the same circumstances, by the same type of action.

3. Aestimatum

There was, however, one exception. One transaction which could otherwise have fallen under the actio praescriptis verbis too seems to have acquired such a degree of typicality already at an early stage that it was singled out by the praetor and "clothed" with a specific action. This was the actio de aestimato,[178] and it was proposed in the edict, according to Ulpianus

"tollendae dubitationis gratia: fuit enim magis dubitatum, cum res aestimata vendenda datur, utrum ex vendito sit actio propter aestimationem, an ex locato,

[173] Paul. D. 19, 5, 5, 1.

[174] Ulp. D. 2, 14, 7, 2.

[175] Paul. D. 19, 5, 5, 4.

[176] Cf. e.g. Afr. D. 19, 5, 24, dealing with a transaction of the type of do ut facias containing elements of mutuum and mandatum: Misera, *Scritti Guarino*, vol. VI, pp. 2591 sqq. For a recent discussion of further texts, see MacCormack, (1985) 51 *SDHI* 134 sqq.; cf. also the comprehensive analysis by De Francisci, op. cit., note 166, vol. I, pp. 105 sqq.

[177] Cf. supra, p. 355.

[178] Ulp. D. 19, 3, 1; De Francisci, op. cit., note 166, vol. I, pp. 85 sqq; W.W. Buckland, "Aestimatum", (1927) 43 *LQR* 74 sqq.; idem, "Aestimatum", (1932) 48 *LQR* 495 sqq.; Buckland/Stein, pp. 522 sqq.; Thayer, (1944–45) 19 *Tulane LR* 63 sqq.; Kudret Ayiter, "The Aestimatum Contract", in: J.E. Spruit (ed.), *Maior viginti quinque annis, Essays in commemoration of the sixth lustrum of the Institute for Legal History of the University of Utrecht* (1979), pp. 22 sqq.

quasi rem vendendam locasse videor, an ex conducto, quasi operas conduxissem, an mandati melius itaque visum est hanc actionem proponi".[179]

We are dealing here with a transaction called aestimatum. Goods are given to a person (usually a pedlar), and they are estimated (aestimare) at a fixed amount. Within a certain time, the recipient either has to pay the amount agreed upon or to return the goods. The real aim of this transaction was to give the pedlar some time within which to try to sell the goods. Whatever he received over and above the estimated sum was his. Aestimatum thus combined elements of emptio venditio, locatio conductio (operis), mandatum and even societas.[180] Hence the necessity to introduce a special action if some kind of recognition was to be given to this type of arrangement. The structure of the actio de aestimato resembled that of any other actio praescriptis verbis; in particular, it was based on good faith and became available only with the handing over of the goods to the person who was supposed to sell them.

There were other "innominate contracts" which by the time of Justinian had become so well established as to have their own names: permutatio has already been referred to repeatedly;[181] transactio and precarium may be added at this stage.[182] But none of them came to be individualized to the extent that a special action was created; actiones praescriptis verbis were available in all these cases.

4. Innominate contracts and the contractual scheme

All in all, it will have become clear that the advent of the innominate contracts entailed a fairly major inroad into, but not a complete abandonment of the rule ex nudo pacto non oritur actio.[183] A whole variety of consensual arrangements, of pacta in the broad sense of the word, had become legally recognized; but this recognition depended, first of all, on the fact that one of the parties had already fulfilled his side

[179] D. 19, 3, 1 pr.

[180] Cf., too, Ulp. D. 19, 5, 13 pr.

[181] Cf. e.g. the Digest title 19, 4 ("De rerum permutatione").

[182] Buckland/Stein, pp. 524 sqq.; Thomas, *TRL*, pp. 314 sq.; Kaser, *RPr* II, pp. 407, 445; more specifically on transactio, cf. Maria Emilia Peterlongo, *La transazione nel diritto romano* (1936); Aldo Schiavone, *Studi sulle logiche dei giuristi romani. "Nova negotia" e "transactio" da Labeone a Ulpiano* (1971), pp. 7 sqq., 163 sqq.; Friedrich Ebel, *Berichtung, transactio und Vergleich* (1978), pp. 50 sqq., who also deals specifically with the reception and post-reception development of transactio in the German ius commune; Károly Visky, "Les règles du droit romain relatives aux transactions judiciaires et extrajudiciaires à la fin de l'époque classique", (1983–84) 12 *Index* 87 sqq.; on the condictio ob transactionem, see Fritz Sturm, *Studi in onore di Cesare Sanfilippo*, vol. III (1983), pp. 627 sqq. On precarium cf. Pierpaolo Zamorani, *Precario habere* (1969); Max Kaser, "Zur Geschichte des precarium", (1972) 89 *ZSS* 94 sqq.

[183] With the general recognition of the enforceability of all kinds of pacts (also "naked" ones), the actio praescriptis verbis (and also the actio aestimatoria) became, of course, redundant ("inutilis et in desuetudinem abiit": Groenewegen, *Tractatus de legibus abrogatis*, Digest. Lib. XIX, Titt. III, V). On the treatment of innominate contracts by glossators and commentators, cf. Jean-Pierre Baud, "Contrats nommés et contrats innommés en droit savant", (1976) 19 *Studia Gratiana* 31 sqq.

of the arrangement; and secondly, this performance had to be intended to elicit a counterperformance. The innominate contracts, in other words, were modelled on the example of the contracts re[184] and they were confined to "synallagmatic" relationships.[185] Thirdly, their binding character was undermined, to some extent, by virtue of the fact that the condictio causa data causa non secuta remained available.[186] Having rendered performance, a party to an innominate contract could therefore choose whether to demand counterperformance or restoration. Thus, in effect, he had the right at any time to cancel the arrangement.

VI. TOWARDS A GENERAL LAW OF CONTRACT BASED ON CONSENT

1. Contract and pacta in the Corpus Juris Civilis

To sum up: What the glossators found when they started to work their way through the Digest was not a law of contract(s) based on any neat and rational system. On the one hand, there was the rule of "nuda pactio obligationem non parit". But, on the other hand, there was a whole variety of agreements which had in one way or another become legally recognized; having grown up historically, they now formed a somewhat haphazard lot. First, there were the contracts, i.e. those obligatory transactions which had a proper name (". . . transeunt in proprium nomen . . .").[187] Then there were the contractus innominati (or "anonyma synallagmata"); but some of them had actually acquired individual names (permutatio, aestimatum, transactio, precarium). Furthermore, consensual agreements were enforceable if they had been attached to one of the recognized contracts and had been concluded at one and the same time as the main contract (pacta in continenti adiecta). Then, again, there were two groups of agreements which were not classified as contracts but which were nevertheless enforceable: constitutum, receptum arbitri and receptum nautarum, cauponum, stabulariorum on the one hand, and those of which Paulus said: ". . .

---

[184] However, they were not merely an extension or generalization of the contracts re, for the notion of a quid pro quo was absent in the latter. On the relationship between contracts re and innominate real contracts, cf., most recently, MacCormack, (1985) 51 *SDHI* 131 sqq.

[185] The term "συνάλλαγμα" appears in Lab./Ulp. D. 50, 16, 19 and in Aristo/Ulp. D. 2, 14, 7, 2, but was not yet used as the terminus technicus that we know in modern law (hence the inverted commas); for details cf. Benöhr, *Synallagma*, passim; further: Constantin Despotopoulos, "La notion de synallagma chez Aristote", (1968) 13 *Archives de philosophie du droit* 115 sqq.; Schiavone, op. cit., note 182, pp. 37 sqq,.; Werner Macheiner, "Zu den Anfängen des Kontraktssystems", in: *Festgabe für Arnold Herdlitczka* (1972), pp. 172 sqq.; Santoro, (1983) 37 *Annali Palermo* 7 sqq., 35 sqq. (on D. 50, 16, 19) and 207 sqq., 277 sqq. (on D. 2, 14, 7, 2); Arnaldo Biscardi, "Quod Graeci synallagma vocant", (1983) 29 *Labeo* 127 sqq.; MacCormack, (1985) 51 *SDHI* 138 sqq.

[186] Cf. e.g. Paul. D. 19, 5, 5, 1.

[187] Ulp. D. 2, 14, 7, 1.

ex pacto actio nascitur . . ., quotiens lege vel senatus consulto adiuvatur"[188] on the other: donatio, compromissum, dotis promissio and some others.[189] Other informal arrangements which did not fall into these categories could be raised by way of defence; apart from that they could at least be regarded as obligationes naturales.

2. Pacta vestita and pacta nuda

How could all this be brought into a rational scheme? The glossators, first of all, tried to achieve some terminological clarity.[190] They proceeded from the definition given by Ulpianus ("Pactum . . . est pactio duorum pluriumve in idem placitum et consensus")[191] but specified that the parties had to have agreed "in idem dandum vel, faciendum".[192] Thus for them "pactum" was the general term comprising all agreements between two or more parties aimed at creating obligations.[193] Depending on whether these obligations were merely natural or whether they were enforceable, a distinction was drawn between pacta nuda and pacta vestita (literally: pacts which are clothed). As a result, the Roman contracts now fell into the group of pacta vestita: "Vestitur autem pactum sex modis: re, verbis, consensu, literis, contractus cohaerentia, rei interventu."[194] The first four garments were obviously taken from Gaius' classification of contracts,[195] the last two refer to the pacta adiecta[196] and the innominate real contracts. Accursius added the vestimentum legis auxilio ("Sed quando ex nudo pacto datur actio: potest dici vestitum legis auxilio"),[197] thus moving the pacta praetoria and legitima from the

[188] D. 2, 14, 6.

[189] Cf. e.g. Paul. D. 22, 1, 30; Scaev. D. 22, 2, 5, 1; C. 4, 32, 11 (all relating certain to exceptional cases of informal promises of interest; interpolated?). On these texts cf. Kaser, *RPr* I, p. 498, n. 37; *RPr* II, p. 371, n. 17; also (on the Scaevola text, dealing with fenus nauticum) Wieslaw Litewski, "Römisches Seedarlehen", (1973) 24 *Iura* 152 sqq., 165 sqq., and supra, p. 182, note 179 and p. 187.

[190] For details, see Hermann Dilcher, "Der Typenzwang im mittelalterlichen Vertragsrecht" (1960) 77 *ZSS* 273 sqq.

[191] D. 2, 14, 1, 1.

[192] Azo, *Summa Codicis*, Lib. II, Rubrica De Pactis, 1 ("Si enim ego et tu consentiamus: puta quod Socrates sit lapis, non est pactum").

[193] The commentators preferred "conventio" as the nomen generale; cf. Nanz, *Vertragsbegriff*, p. 45.

[194] Azo, *Summa Codicis*, Lib. II, Rubrica De Pactis, 15.

[195] The vestimentum "consensus" presented a specific difficulty: why did consensus give rise to an action only in the case of the consensual contracts and not also as far as pacta nuda were concerned (they are, after all, also based on consensus!)? Accursius (gl. Quinimo ad D. 2, 14, 7, 5) dismissed the problem in a rather playful manner: "Sed videtur quod nullum pactum sit nudum: cum quodlibet habeat in se consensum: unde vestiri consensu videtur . . . Respond. elegans, et tenuis vestis est consensus, quae non datur nisi certis contractibus enumeratis . . . qui cum sint favorabiles, et pingues, et calidi, levi veste vestiuntur."

[196] On these see specifically Pietro Vaccari, "Pactum vestitur contractus cohaerentia. La concezione dei patti aggiunti nella dottrina dei glossatori", in: *Scritti di storia del diritto privato* (1956), pp. 233 sqq.

[197] Gl. Legitima ad D. 2, 14, 6.

increasingly uncomfortable area of (irregular) pacta nuda[198] into the already rather densely populated haven of the pacta vestita. It was obvious from this system that pacta vestita were now very much the rule; the few remaining unenforceable pacta nuda appeared as something of an anomaly; and seeing that vestments were available so liberally, they were bound, sooner or later, to find a charitable champion who was prepared to save them too from the chill of death.[199]

As far as contractual *theory* is concerned, recognition of this process took its time. Too imposing was the authority of the Roman principle of "nuda pactio obligationem non parit". That the French humanists, for instance, should have been inclined to abandon it, was not to be expected.[200] But it continued to be asserted until well into the 17th century, though more and more sporadically. Simon van Leeuwen, for instance, leaves no doubt:

> "Quae nuda Conventio seu pactum nudum, licet revera et proprie pactum sit, et quam maxime serio et deliberato animo ineatur, eam tamen vim non habet, ut ex eo actio detur. Hinc vulgaris regula: Ex nudo pacto non datur actio."

And he adds: "Quod et in praxi est receptum."[201] But this is demonstrably wrong. Nearly all the other contemporary Roman-Dutch writers concede that, whatever the position in Roman law might have been, "moribus hodiernis" or "consuetudine nostra" nuda pacta were regarded as enforceable.[202] From about the 18th century onwards, this was no longer disputed.[203] "Ex nudo pacto oritur actio" was and

---

[198] ". . . nisi *mirabiliter* hoc in quibusdam casibus accidat, in quibus casibus nudum pactum parit actionem: ut in donatione": Azo, *Summa Codicis*, Lib. II, Rubrica De Pactis, 14.

[199] Azo's vivid description of the way in which pacta adiecta and innominate real contracts become clothed is quoted by Riccobono/Kerr Wylie/Beinart, p. 10; it fully exploits the garment metaphor: ". . . sed cum natum est ante et retro aspicit et oculis aperit an praecesserit vel sequi possit vel statim insit aliquis contractus cuius variis et grisiis pennis seu vestibus induatur; ut boream rabriemque procellae expellat; et suum suo domino in agendo auxilium praebeat."

[200] Cf. e.g. Franciscus Duarenus, Franciscus Connanus, Jacobus Cujacius and Hugo Donellus, as discussed by Seuffert, op. cit., note 31, pp. 108 sqq.; Nanz, *Vertragsbegriff*, pp. 65 sqq. But cf. also already Carolus Molinaeus, "Commentarius in Codicem", Lib. II, Tit. III, in: *Opera Omnia* (Parisiis, 1681), vol. III.

[201] *Censura Forensis*, Pars I, Lib. IV, Cap. II, n. 2.

[202] Cf. e.g. Voet, *Commentarius ad Pandectas*, Lib. II, Tit. XIV, IX; Groenewegen, *Tractatus de legibus abrogatis*, Cod. Lib. II, Tit. III, l. 10 legem; Vinnius, "Tractatus de pactis", in: idem, *Tractatus quatuor* (Lugduni 1748), Cap. VII, 6; cf. further Coenraad Visser, "The Principle pacta servanda sunt in Roman and Roman-Dutch Law, With Specific Reference to Contracts in Restraint of Trade", (1984) 101 *SALJ* 652 sqq.; Joubert, *Contract*, pp. 27 sqq. and, particularly, Nanz, *Vertragsbegriff*, pp. 95 sqq.

[203] Cf. e.g. Samuel Stryk, *Usus modernus pandectarum*, Lib. II, Tit. XIV, § 1; Glück, vol. 4, pp. 279 sqq.; Pothier, *Traité des obligations*, n. 3; Windscheid/Kipp, § 312; Seuffert, op. cit., note 31, pp. 130 sqq. The first and most influential writer of the usus modernus pandectarum to assert this principle was Matthaeus Wesenbecius (1531–86); cf. the quotation given in note 231 infra. Most of the writers of the 17th century referred to him. On Wesenbecius' significance for the development of a general law of contract, see Nanz, *Vertragsbegriff*, pp. 85 sqq.

remained the general rule, or, as it was also often expressed: "pacta sunt servanda"[204]—(all) pacts have to be honoured.[205]

3. The contribution of (commercial) practice

What were the decisive forces behind this change of attitude? First of all, in actual practice the rule of "nuda pactio obligationem non parit" began to be eroded virtually as soon as it had been resurrected from the pages of the Digest.[206] Already by the end of the Middle Ages, every informal agreement had, for all *practical* purposes, become legally binding.[207] The international lex Mercatoria was of considerable importance in this respect:

> ". . . in curia mercatorum, ubi de negotio potest decidi bona aequitate . . . non potest opponi ista exceptio, non intervenit stipulatio, sed pactum nudum fuit",

to quote the words of Bartolus;[208] the fact that the formalities of a stipulation had not been observed could not be raised against a pactum nudum. The consequence was spelt out clearly by Bartolus' pupil Baldus: "Ex pacto etiam nudo agunt mercatores, et numularii inter se. . . ."[209] In the states founded by the Crusaders *"outremer"* the maxim *"convenant vainc loi"* was applied;[210] it is based on a generalization of Ulp. D. 50, 17, 23 ("legem enim contractus dedit") and influenced, in turn (post-humanistic) contractual theory in France down to the code civil (*"Les conventions légalement formées tiennent lieu de loi à ceux qui les ont faites"*: art. 1134).[211] In the medieval French and Italian *"pratique coutumier"*, too, consensualism seems to have gained

[204] For the origin of this maxim cf. infra, pp. 543, 576.

[205] The most recent account of the historical development can be found in Klaus-Peter Nanz, *Die Entstehung des allgemeinen Vertragsbegriffs im 16. bis 18. Jahrhundert* (1985), pp. 5 sqq., 31 sqq. For a concise and modern survey cf. the discussion and the texts in Robert Feenstra, Margreet Ahsmann, *Contract. Aspecten van de begrippen contract en contractsvrijheid in historisch perspectief* (1980), pp. 1 sqq., 33 sqq. Cf. also A. Steinwenter, "Die Vertragstreue im bürgerlichen Recht", 1950 *Juristische Blätter* 173 sqq., 197 sqq.; Johannes Bärmann, "Pacta sunt servanda. Considérations sur l'histoire du contrat consensuel", (1961) 13 *RIDC* 18 sqq.; Coenraad Visser (1984) 101 *SALJ* 641 sqq.

[206] Yason de Mayno listed 16 exceptions, Andreas ab Exea, in a work on *Pacta* (1542), mentions no fewer than 67 exceptions (cf. Joubert, *Contract*, p. 27, n. 6). On the pactum geminatum—one of the most important enforceable pacta created during the Middle Ages—cf. supra, p. 513. Clearly, the problem of the unenforceability of pacta nuda was not an enormously important one.

[207] Hermann Dilcher, (1960) 77 *ZSS* 302.

[208] *Commentaria*, D. 17, 1, 48, 1, § Quintus Mucius.

[209] *Commentaria in Decretales*, I, Rubr. De pactis, Cap. I, n. 11; further Norbert Horn, *Aequitas in den Lehren des Baldus* (1968), pp. 90 sq., 189 sqq. This exception to the rigour of the Roman law was based on the "aequitas mercatoria" ("domus mercatorum debet esse domus veritatis et aequitatis": Angelus Aretinus; on the aequitas mercatoria in general, see Wilhelm Endemann, "Beiträge zur Kenntnis des Handelsrechts im Mittelalter", (1862) 5 *ZHR* 362 sqq.). Another transaction which developed in medieval commercial practice as a successor to the Roman stipulation was the bill of exchange: an abstract obligatio litteris. Cf. Endemann, *Studien*, vol. I, pp. 75 sqq.

[210] Cf. F. Spies, *De l'observation des simples conventions en droit canonique* (1928), pp. 150 sqq.

[211] Cf. also art. 1374 BW ("Alle wettiglijk gemaakte overeenkomsten strekken dengenen die dezelve hebben aangegaan tot wet") and Feenstra/Ahsmann, op. cit., note 205, pp. 5 sq.

ground;[212] the feudal nobility in particular felt (honour-)bound to observe informal "convenientia" or *"convenances"* (*"toutes convenances sont à tenir"*;[213] the terminology is derived from the Latin word "conventio", as used especially in Ulp. D. 2, 14, 1, 3).[214] Since the 17th century, the acceptance in practice of "ex nudo pacto oritur actio" has repeatedly been traced back to and justified as being in accordance with old Germanic customary law: "At inter Germanos, quibus sancta semper fides fuit, et verba dare ignotum aliud [sc.: quam inter Romanos] ab antiquo [fuit] servatum"[215] or:

> "Maer gelijck de Duitschen van alle oude tijden gheen deugd en hebben geacht boven de trouwe, zoo en is by de zelve . . . verstaen ende gebruickt, dat alle toezegginghen . . . door wat woorden het zoude mogen zijn . . . recht gaven om te eisschen."[216]

Both these texts allude to a famous passage in Tacitus' *Germania*, where the author muses on the stubborn determination with which the Germans honour gambling debts[217] and comments, somewhat unappreciatively: "ipsi fidem vocant." The old Germanic saying "one man one man, one word one word" has also often been referred to,[218] though entirely out of context.[219] Sources which could substantiate the argument are extremely scarce; a passage in the Stadrecht of Freiburg im Breisgau of 1520 (*"Wer bedechtlich zusagt, der sol es halten"*) is

[212] For details cf. Francesco Calasso, *La "convenientia"* (1932); Paul Ourliac, "La 'convenientia' ", in: *Études d'histoire du droit privé offertes à Pierre Petot* (1959), pp. 413 sqq.; Pierre-Clément Timbal, *Les obligations contractuelles dans le droit français des XIIIe et XIVe siècles d'après la jurisprudence du Parlement* (1973); cf. also Theo Mayer-Maly, "Der Konsens als Grundlage des Vertrages", in: *Festschrift für Erwin Seidl* (1975), pp. 121 sq.; Nanz, *Vertragsbegriff*, pp. 60 sqq.

[213] Cf. particularly the *Coutumes de Beauvaisis* (1283) of Philippe de Beaumanoir, Cap. 34, artt. 998 sqq.

[214] Antoine Loisel, *Institutes coutumières* (3rd ed., Paris, 1611), n. 342, expressed the situation in a metaphorical way: *"On lie les boeufs par les cornes et les hommes par les paroles, et autant vaut une simple promesse ou convenance, que les stipulations du droict Romain."* This is based on an addition to the Accursian gloss, which can be found in 16th- and 17th-century editions of that work (ad "iuris vinculum" in *Inst.* III, 13 pr.): "Verba ligant homines, taurorum cornua funes. Cornu bos capitur, voce ligatur homo", and gave rise to the French proverb: *"Comme les boeufs par les cornes on lie / Aussi les gens par leur mots font folie"* (for all this, see Feenstra/Ahsmann, op. cit., note 205, pp. 38, 43).

[215] Mevius, *Decisiones,* Pars V, Dec. CCCCVII.

[216] Hugo Grotius, *Inleiding*, III, I, 52.

[217] "Aleam, quod mirere, sobrii inter seria exercent, tanta lucrandi perdendive temeritate ut, cum omnia defecerunt, extremo ac novissimo iactu de libertate ac de corpore contendant. Victus voluntariam servitutem adit: quamvis iuvenior, quamvis robustior, adligari se ac venire patitur. Ea est in re prava pervicacia; ipsi fidem vocant. Servos condicionis huius per commercia tradunt, ut se quoque pudore victoriae exsolvant" (XXIV, 3 and 4).

[218] Cf. e.g. Glück, vol. 4, pp. 281 sqq.

[219] It meant originally that a man is bound, in court, by what he has said, even though he had meant to say something else; cf. Ekkehard Kaufmann, "Ein Mann—ein Wort", 1961 *Juristische Schulung* 120 sqq.

(possibly) the only evidence that the idea of consensuality was recognized in Germany prior to the reception of Roman law.[220]

4. The contribution of the canon lawyers

But be that as it may, the existence of "naked", non-enforceable pacta had for a long time been attacked on a more fundamental level by the canon lawyers. In the Middle Ages, contracts were usually confirmed by oath. This gave the Church the opportunity to assert its jurisdiction over disputes arising in these matters;[221] for a breach of contract, under these circumstances, necessarily involved laesio fidei—breach of a pledge of faith—and this amounted to the sin of perjury. However, before God there is no difference between an informal promise and one confirmed by oath, between a simple lie and perjury. Jesus Christ had even gone one step further; in the Gospel according to St. Matthew he is quoted in the following terms: "But I say unto you, Swear not at all. . . . But let your communication be, Yea, yea; Nay, nay: for whatsoever is more than these cometh of evil."[222] In a society where the oath played such a central role, this passage could not be taken to impose a blanket ban on iuramenta.[223] The least one could do, however, to bring the law into line with Christ's commandment was to insist that informal promissiones had to be kept in the same manner as an oath: "Promissio simplex obligat sicut et iuramentum. Nec inter haec Deus facit differentiam, cum uterque contraveniendo peccet mortaliter."[224] This was already reflected in the so-called canon Quicunque[225] of the Decretum Gratiani, the oldest compilation of canon law which was to form, eventually, the first part of the Corpus Juris Canonici. But it only dealt with (informal) unilateral promissiones. The locus classicus on the enforceability of consensual pacta was contained in the Decretals of Gregor IX, the Liber Extra of the Corpus Juris Canonici:

---

[220] Cf. W. Kunkel (ed.), *Quellen zur neueren Privatrechtsgeschichte Deutschlands*, vol. I, 1 (1936), p. 254. The *Stadtrecht* was drafted by Ulrich Zasius. On the passage quoted in the text and on Zasius' view on the matter in general, cf. Seuffert, op. cit., note 31, pp. 96 sqq.; Feenstra/Ahsmann, op. cit., note 205, p. 16; but also Theo Mayer-Maly, "Die Bedeutung des Konsenses in privatrechtsgeschichtlicher Sicht", in: G. Jakobs (ed.), *Rechtsgeltung und Konsens* (1976), pp. 101 sq. On forms of obligational transactions and on the question of contractual fidelity in the old German law prior to the reception of Roman law, see Rudolf Huebner, *A History of Germanic Private Law* (1918), pp. 490 sqq.; Nanz, *Vertragsbegriff*, pp. 24 sqq.

[221] Cf. e.g. Winfried Trusen, "Die gelehrte Gerichtsbarkeit der Kirche", in: *Handbuch der Quellen und Literatur der neueren europäischen Privatrechtsgeschichte* (1973), p. 486; Berman, *Law and Revolution*, p. 261.

[222] St. Matthew 5, 34 and 37. Cf. also Epistula Jacobi 5, 12.

[223] Mayer-Maly, *Rechtsgeltung und Konsens*, op. cit., note 220, p. 101.

[224] Albericus de Rosate, *Dictionarium iuris tam civilis quam canonici*, s.v. promissio. Cf. also St. Thomas Aquinas, *Summa theologiae*, Secunda Secundae, q. 110, art. 3, 5 ("mendacium est, si quis non impleat, quod promisit"), and Secunda Secundae, q. 88, art. 3.

[225] Secunda pars, Causa XII, Quaest. II, c. 66.

"Aut inita pacta suam obtineant firmitatem, aut conventus, si se non cohibuerit, ecclesiasticam sentiat disciplinam. Dixerunt universi: Pax servetur, pacta custodiantur."[226]

This text originally related to a dispute between two bishops about the boundaries of their dioceses which was decided at the first council of Carthage in the year A.D. 348 (hence: ex concilio Africano). In the Decretals of Gregor IX this same text was severed from its original context[227] and stated as a general rule. The intention of the compilers becomes abundantly clear when one looks at the heading under which the text appears (within the title "De pactis"); it is the famous adage "pacta quantumcunque nuda servanda sunt", formulated in pointed allusion to the legistic distinction between pacts which are "naked" and others which are "dressed", but also subtly reminiscent of the praetors' promise of "pacta conventa servabo". In the course of the 14th century it became the prevailing opinion among canonists that all informal contractual agreements were directly enforceable by means of a condictio ex canone[228] (so named in imitation of the Roman condictio ex lege), that is, not merely protected indirectly through the procedure of denuntiatio evangelica:[229] ex nudo pacto oritur actio.[230] But whether this rule of canon law could (or should) also be applied in foro civili remained disputed over the centuries.[231] On the one hand it could be argued that canon law had to be recurred to "ratione peccati"; for since the days of Bartolus and Baldus it had, generally speaking, been accepted that the law of the Church enjoyed precedence even in the secular sphere, where this was necessary in order to avert or prevent

[226] Lib. I, Tit. XXXV, Cap. I.

[227] Particularly, the fact was left out that the agreement between the two bishops had been in writing ("manuscriptiones nostrae tenentur et pittacia") and was therefore not an informal pactum.

[228] Johannes Teutonicus, gl. Promiserint ad. C. 12, q. 2, c. 66.

[229] An institute of canon law that was based on St. Matthew 18, 15–17: "Si peccaverit in te frater tuus, vade et corripe eum inter te et ipsum solum: si te audierit, lucratus eris fratris tuum: si te non audierit, adhibe tecum unum vel duos, ut in ore duorum vel trium testium stet omne verbum: quod si non audierit, dic ecclesiae: si autem ecclesiam non audierit, sit tibi sicut ethnicus et publicanus."

[230] For details of the development in canon law, cf. F. Spiess, *De l'observation des simples conventions en droit canonique* (1928); Jules Roussier, *Le fondement de l'obligation contractuelle dans le droit classique de l'Église* (1933); Hermann Dilcher, (1960) 77 *ZSS* 281 sqq.; Alfred Söllner, "Die causa im Kondiktionen- und Vertragsrecht des Mittelalters bei den Glossatoren, Kommentatoren und Kanonisten", (1960) 77 *ZSS* 240 sqq.; Nanz, *Vertragsbegriff*, pp. 46 sqq.

[231] Cf. e.g. Wesenbecius, *Commentarii in Pandectas*, Lib. II, Tit. XIV, 10 (p. 57): "Etsi vero longa est disputatio, an in reliquis Curiis, in quibus secundum ius civile pronunciatur, ius Pontificium obtinere debeat: tamen communis opinio est, et ita usus observat, ut indistincte ex pactis Nudis, serio et deliberate initis, etiam in foro Civili hodie detur actio". One of the first influential writers who unequivocally adopted the rule of canon law in iure civili was Carolus Molinaeus (cf. supra, note 200), who stated: "Sed hodie in praxi hae et omnes leges et theoriae de formulis stipulationum supervacuae sunt, qui etiam extra scripturam publicam vel privatam, sive confessione partis sive testibus aut alias legitime appareat de conventione serio pacta et conclusa in re licita nec prohibita nec inter prohibitos aut inhabilis, pro stipulatione habetur et oritur efficax actio iuxta notatum in c. 1, Extra de pactis, quod ita debet intelligi et restringi et ita in utroque foro seculari et ecclesiastico observatur".

sinful behaviour.[232] On the other hand, however, the sources contained in the Corpus Juris Canonici did not make it entirely clear whether an abrogation of the Roman law had been intended in this instance.[233] But it is indisputable, in any event, that recognition of the principle of ex nudo pacto oritur actio in the canon law contributed considerably to its general acceptance "usu".

5. The position of the natural lawyers; summary

As usually happened in cases where the tide of opinion over the centuries had been flowing increasingly strongly against a particular principle of Roman law, the final breakthrough on a doctrinal level was brought about by the natural lawyers. According to Grotius, the "father" of the modern conception of natural law, fides forms the basis of justice.[234] Hence, promises must be kept, whether they have been couched in a specific form or not. Even God would be acting against his nature were he not to keep his word.[235] From there it follows that all pacta must be binding. The supreme importance of this principle comes out well in Pufendorf's epochal work on the law of nature and of nations. "Si quae autem inter homines ineuntur pacta, illa sancte observanda esse, sociabilis natura hominum requirit", he writes, and concludes:

> "Igitur religiosissimum juris naturalis praeceptum, et quod universae humanae vitae decus, modum atque rationem temperat, habetur: Ut quilibet fidem datam servet, seu promissa atque pacta expleat."[236]

Thus, to the natural lawyers, contract was the essential tool for the regulation of human affairs, the cornerstone of all the institutions of the positive law[237] (including, incidentally, the State—the famous natural-law theory of the "contrat social").

All in all, then, the final establishment of a general law of contract based on consensus was the result of a long process, to which a whole

---

[232] Wolter, *Ius canonicum in iure civili*, pp. 43 sqq., 91 sqq.

[233] Wolter, *Ius canonicum in iure civili*, pp. 100 sqq.

[234] Cf. e.g. *De jure belli ac pacis*, Lib. II, Cap. XI, 1. On fides as basis of public international law, as conceived by Grotius, cf. Wolfgang Fikentscher, *De fide et perfidia. Der Treuegedanke in den "Staatsparallelen" des Hugo Grotius aus heutiger Sicht* (1979).

[235] *De jure belli ac pacis*, Lib. II, Cap. XI, 4. On the reception by Grotius of the Christian idea of the faithful God (cf., for example, 2. Timothy 2, 13), see Okko Behrends, "Treu und Glauben, Zu den christlichen Grundlagen der Willenstheorie im heutigen Vertragsrecht", in: L.L. Vallauri, G. Dilcher (eds.) *Christentum, Säkularisation und modernes Recht* (1981), vol. II, pp. 967 sqq.

[236] *De jure naturae et gentium*, Lib. III, Cap. IV, § 2. Cf. also Grotius, *De jure belli ac pacis*, Prolegomena, 15 sq.

[237] Characteristically, Grotius expounds his theory of contract as part of his discussion of the reasons for a just war; private persons, political entities and whole nations are all subject to the same rules. On the structure of Grotius' *De jure belli ac pacis*, cf. e.g. Wieacker, *Privatrechtsgeschichte*, pp. 290 sqq.; Hasso Hofmann, "Hugo Grotius", in: M. Stolleis (ed.), *Staatsdenker im 17. und 18. Jahrhundert*, pp. 65 sqq. On the central importance of contract within the system of natural law, cf. Franz Wieacker, "Die vertragliche Obligation bei den Klassikern des Vernunftrechts", in: *Festschrift für Hans Welzel* (1974), pp. 7 sqq.

variety of factors contributed. That contemporary writers realized the complexity of this process emerges very clearly from a passage of Augustin Leyser's *Meditationes ad Pandectas*, with which we may conclude this chapter:

> "Unde vero pacta nuda hodie vim obligandi accipiant, de ea non una Jurisconsultorum sententia est. Alii eam ex iure naturae derivant, atque rem hanc ad simplicitatem naturalem reductam dicerunt. Alii ad ius canonicum provocant. . . . Alii denique mores veteres Germanicos, quibus omnes pactiones validae sunt . . . mansisse perpetuum nec Iuris Romani receptione hac in parte interruptos fuisse perhibent. Sed parum interest, utrum subtilitatem Iuris Romani hac in parte iure naturali, an Germanico antiquo an canonico vinci dicas. Victa certe est et omnia pacta consensu perfecta vim eandem habent quam stipulationes."[238]

[238] Spec. XXXIX, V.

PART VI

CHAPTER 18
Formation of Contract

A contract is based on the consent of the parties thereto. The scope of such consent is not confined to a number of specifically recognized types of transactions. And the contract does not, as a rule, require compliance with any formalities for its validity. These are the three main elements characterizing our general law of contract, and it is obvious that the final and general recognition of the fact that every lawful agreement begets an action (ex nudo pacto oritur actio) was of momentous importance for the emergence of the modern concept of contract. Over the preceding pages we have tried to sketch the origin of this principle. We shall now have to consider certain of its implications.

I. THE ROMAN CONTRACT OF STIPULATION UNDER THE IUS COMMUNE

1. From contract verbis to contract litteris

There is one question that immediately springs to mind: but what about the stipulation? This contract verbis, it will be remembered, was the backbone of the contractual scheme of Roman law.[1] It was universally applicable; provided only the simple, oral formality was complied with, every lawful agreement could thus be made enforceable. Under these circumstances it commended itself as an institution which could have provided, par excellence, a foundation for a general law of contract. And indeed, the developments in post-classical law, as a result of which the stipulation was stripped of its formalism and adapted to the practice of the time,[2] may be regarded as a step in this direction. In a way, however, this trend was stopped by Justinian who, as we have seen,[3] attempted to reconcile the irreconcilable, namely the (classical) theory of an oral transaction and the (contemporary) practice of a written one. Thus, within the Corpus Juris Civilis we find (and, more importantly, the medieval lawyers found) two different historical layers of one and the same institution side by side; and at a time when little interest was displayed in the historicity of the Corpus Juris Civilis, this was bound to create a confusion which was decidedly unfavourable for

[1] Cf. supra, pp. 68 sqq., 89 sqq; see also, for example, Wolfgang Adam Lauterbach, *Collegium theoretico-practicum*, Lib. XLV, Tit. I, I (". . . apud Romanos fere omnia negotia in stipulationem deducebantur, propter eius firmitatem . . . Quasi nodus enim est omnium obligationum").

[2] Cf. supra, pp. 80 sqq.

[3] Cf. supra, pp. 81 sq.

the survival of the stipulation as a central element of the law of contract.[4] The glossators, true to the sources as they were, re-accentuated the requirements of the classical (oral) stipulatio, as they found them, particularly in title 45, 1 ("De verborum obligationibus") of the Digest. Thus, conclusion of the contract was seen to depend on the following five requirements: primo interrogatio, secundo responsio, tertio quod interrogatio precedat responsionem, quarto loco quod responsio fiat incontinenti post interrogationem, quinto quod responsio congrua id est intellegibilis. Of all this, however, one finds very little if account is taken of the way in which the stipulation lived on in medieval contractual practice. Here it was—along the lines of the post-classical Roman tradition—essentially a contract litteris, for the stipulation was usually incorporated into a (notarial) document.[5] All the requirements of the oral stipulation were projected into this instrument, whether they had in fact been complied with or not.[6] The bridge between theory and practice was established by a number of presumptions, but these presumptions operated only on the basis of specific words and clauses which had to be contained in the document (especially the verb "promittere" as opposed to, for example, "convenire").[7] Thus, it was a risky business to "stipulate" by way of "scriptura privata", and the proper drafting of the contract became more and more a matter for professional tabelliones.[8] The simple and uncomplicated stipulation, so familiar to every Roman citizen, had finally been turned into an arcanum of notarial practice.[9] As such it had lost its appeal as a practically viable and universally suitable cornerstone of contractual theory.

2. Ex nudo pacto oritur actio and the form of stipulation

As a consequence of these developments, a significant vacuum had now become apparent within the contractual scheme of Roman law as taken over by the medieval lawyers; for the convenient and universal availability of the stipulation was one of the main reasons why the Romans had been able to maintain the principle of "ex nudo pacto non oritur actio". It is obvious that this vacuum was bound to be filled by

[4] For details, see Romualdo Trifone, "La 'stipulatio' nelle dottrine dei glossatori", in: *Studi in onore di Enrico Besta*, vol. I (1939), pp. 171 sqq.; Nanz, *Vertragsbegriff*, pp. 36 sqq.

[5] Nanz, *Vertragsbegriff*, p. 38; cf. also Francisco Brandileone, "La 'stipulatio' nelle carte italiane del medio evo", in: *Mélanges Fitting*, vol. I (1907), pp. 101 sqq.

[6] Riccobono/Kerr Wylie/Beinart, pp. 7 sqq., 204 sqq.; Nanz, *Vertragsbegriff*, pp. 38 sq.

[7] Bartolus had tried to extend the presumption to this term too, but his opinion has not been followed; cf. C. Karsten, *Die Lehre vom Vertrage bei den italienischen Juristen des Mittelalters* (1882), pp. 187 sqq.

[8] The tabellio, in Rome, was a private, professional person who drew up written documents for private individuals (Berger, *ED*, p. 727). On the medieval notariate based on that tradition, cf. Armin Wolf, "Das öffentliche Notariat", in: *Handbuch der Quellen und Literatur der neueren europäischen Privatrechtsgeschichte*, vol. I (1973), pp. 505 sqq.; Winfried Trusen, "Zur Geschichte des mittelalterlichen Notariats", (1981) 98 *ZSS* 369 sqq.

[9] Wesenberg/Wesener, p. 47.

extending the range of enforceable pacta: a process that came to its logical end with the final abolition of the very notion of a pactum nudum. Thus it came about that the modern concept of contract descends, in direct line, from the consensual contracts, not from the stipulations of Roman law.[10] The medieval stipulation, with its strangely hybrid nature, became part of the glossatorial scheme of vestimenta, sub voce "verbis seu litteris", or "scriptura vel stipulatione".[11] But the advent of "ex nudo pacto oritur actio" heralded the end of its distinguished career. Some writers, of course, refused to acknowledge the inevitable and stood aghast at any intimation that the contract of stipulation had ceased to exist: "Neque audiendi sunt", they urged their readers, "qui stipulationes hodiernis moribus non amplius usitatas esse arbitrantur."[12] Predominantly, however, the writers of the usus modernus realized that there was no longer any room for a special type of contract "stipulation"; it does not make sense to accept every ("bare") pact as actionable, but to continue to cultivate certain solemnities (albeit not in reality but on the basis of certain more or less elaborate presumptions) which serve to clothe ("bare") pacta with actionability! Such formalities were now pointless; Hugo Grotius referred to "zodanige scherpzinnigheid", which, he noted with approval, had never been accepted "[by] de Duitschen".[13] But all was not lost. If the stipulation gradually sank into oblivion as a specific form of contract, this did not mean that the whole body of law built up around it by the Roman lawyers had become irrelevant too. In fact, the titles 45, 1 of the Digest and 8, (37) 38 of the Codex continued to be subjected to scholarly debate. For what had happened is described by Groenewegen as a fusion of the law of pacts and of stipulations ("Hodiernis moribus *confusa* sunt pactorum et stipulationum jura").[14] Others, as we have already seen, maintained that nuda pacta were as good as stipulations ("hodie . . . pro stipulatione habe[n]tur").[15] The consequence was spelt out, very clearly, by Johannes Voet: ". . . ea, quae de stipulationibus jure civili cauta inveniuntur, etiam ad hodierna pacta transferri debeant."[16] The rich casuistry, the principles and regulae developed by the Roman lawyers with regard to stipulations

[10] One important consequence of this was that contracts in general became subject to the regime of bona fides, which had governed the application and construction of consensual contracts in Roman law.

[11] Riccobono/Kerr Wylie/Beinart, p. 7.

[12] Voet, *Commentarius ad Pandectas*, Lib. XLV, Tit. I, I; other authors equally disinclined to part with such a venerable institution of Roman law are discussed by Nanz, *Vertragsbegriff*, pp. 123 sq. In particular, they admired the "firmitas" of the Roman stipulation.

[13] *Inleiding*, III, I, 52. In later centuries, a more positive attitude towards the stipulation prevailed once again. Savigny, for instance, stressed the advantages of this formal type of contract and regretted its abolition in contemporary practice: *Obligationenrecht*, vol. II, pp. 186 sqq; cf. also e.g. Puchta, *Pandekten*, § 250.

[14] *De legibus abrogatis*, Dig. Lib. XLV, Tit. I, l. 1.

[15] Cf. supra, p. 543, note 231 and p. 545.

[16] *Commentarius ad Pandectas*, Lib. XLV, Tit. I, I; his statement quoted above (note 12) has to be read in this light.

were thus preserved, and judiciously channelled, mutatis mutandis, into the mainstream of contractual theory and practice.

II. THE DOCTRINE OF CAUSA

1. Ex nudo pacto oritur actio and the notion of causa

The oral formality required for the classical Roman stipulatio had been a convenient way of establishing whether the parties seriously intended to be bound or not. The danger always exists that people will commit themselves rashly and without due consideration; but the question-and-answer ritual with, in particular, the use of a key verb, must have made it abundantly clear to any Roman citizen what he was letting himself in for. The rule of "ex nudo pacto *non* oritur actio", from this point of view, served to protect those who were inexperienced or careless in handling their affairs. This, in any event, was the opinion of the late medieval lawyers.[17] But how under these circumstances could one—particularly the canon lawyers!—justify giving up this rule? The answer to this question is simple: actionability was extended only to those pacta which were seriously intended.[18] Acceptance of the principle that every lawful agreement begets an action thus carried with it, as a corollary, the introduction of what Zweigert[19] has called an indicium of seriousness: a general requirement intended to distinguish serious promises from those which should not be regarded as binding. We have already come across this criterion; Grotius, for instance, referred to it when he said that all "toezegginghen die uit eenighe redelicke oorzaecken geschieden . . . recht gaven om te eisschen".[20] It is the idea that an agreement, in order to be enforceable, must be shown to be based on a (lawful) cause. This doctrine lives on in several modern legal systems, most notably in French law, where art. 1131 code civil provides that promissory contracts are valid only if they have a cause.[21] It found its origin in medieval law, which had in turn, as was so often the case, used a few Roman bricks in order to create a totally un-Roman doctrinal edifice.

2. Causa in Roman law

In the title 2, 14 of the Digest the term "causa" appears in two places, both times in connection with the innominate real contracts. In the one case, Ulpian quotes Aristo as stating that "et si in alium contractum res non transeat, subsit tamen causa, . . . esse obligationem": there is an obligation, even if the matter does not fall under any of the "nominate"

---

17 Cf. Lothar Seuffert, *Zur Geschichte der obligatorischen Verträge* (1881), pp. 68, 76 sq.
18 Hence, for instance, the recognition of pacta geminata; cf. supra, p. 513.
19 "Seriositätsindizien", 1964 *Juristenzeitung* 349 sqq.
20 *Inleiding*, III, I, 52.
21 Cf. also art. 1371 BW.

contracts (such as emptio venditio and locatio conductio), provided only that a "ground" exists. Some lines later, the same is said in a negative form: "Sed cum nulla subest causa, propter conventionem hic constat non posse constitui obligationem."[22] Causa, in this context, can easily be related to the characteristic element of an innominate real contract, namely the performance (be it a datio or a factum) of one of the parties concerned (which brings into existence the claim for counterperformance). This is, in any event, how the glossators understood the notion. "Id est datio vel factum, ex quo vestiatur contractus innominatus . . ." reads the gl. Causa ad D. 2, 14, 7, 4.[23]

Apart from that, causa appears in connection with the stipulation. Here it meant the underlying purpose of the promise which could, but did not have to be, mentioned in the stipulation. Depending on whether the stipulation had been framed causally or abstractly, lack of the causa stipulationis was either taken into consideration automatically or only if the promisee raised an exceptio (doli).[24] The latter was the case in Ulp. D. 44, 4, 2, 3 ("si quis sine causa ab aliquo fuerit stipulatus, deinde ex ea stipulatione experiatur, exceptio utique doli mali ei nocebit"): the parties had entered into a stipulation, but there had probably been a misunderstanding as to what the promise was all about; and since the stipulation had been abstractly drafted, this lack of causa could be raised only on the basis of an exceptio doli.[25] What this text did not do was to require specification of the causa as a requirement for the validity of stipulations in general. Yet, this is what the glossators read into it.[26] Their interpretation becomes understandable if one bears in mind the changes which had occurred since the days of classical Roman law. With the decline of the formulary procedure, the exceptio had lost its technical significance as an essentially procedural device and had thus acquired a new meaning as a term of substantive law.[27] As a consequence, the distinction between invalidity ipso iure and dismissal of the plaintiff's claim per exceptionem was blurred.[28] Moreover, as we have seen, by the days of the glossators the stipulation had in actual practice become a contract litteris. Stipulatio sine causa therefore, to

[22] In the comprehensive dissertation on innominate real contracts by Paulus (D. 19, 5, 5) causa is, however, neither mentioned as a word nor stated as a requirement.
[23] Cf. also gl. Causa ad D. 2, 14, 7, 2.
[24] Cf. supra, p. 93.
[25] Wolf, *Causa stipulationis*, pp. 12 sqq., 27 sqq.
[26] Cf. Alfred Söllner, "Die causa im Kondiktionen- und Vertragsrecht des Mittelalters bei den Glossatoren, Kommentatoren und Kanonisten", (1960) 77 *ZSS* 222 sqq.; J.L. Barton, "Causa promissionis again", (1966) 34 *TR* 41 sqq.; cf. also Berman, *Law and Revolution*, pp. 245 sqq. On post-classical Roman practice (stipulation increasingly became a causal transaction), see Kaser, *RPr* II, pp. 378 sqq.
[27] Riccobono/Kerr Wylie/Beinart, pp. 128 sqq.; Kaser, *RPr* II, pp. 69 sqq.; cf. also infra, p. 681.
[28] Thus, even in post-classical Roman law, whether a stipulation had been drafted abstractly or causally mattered only as far as the question of onus of proof was concerned. Cf. e.g. Riccobono/Kerr Wylie/Beinart, pp. 123 sqq.; Kaser, *RPr* II, p. 379.

them, essentially meant an instrument which testified to the conclusion of a stipulation without, however, mentioning the cause. If, according to D. 44, 4, 2, 3, the exceptio doli was available in such a case, this meant that the document (and with it: the stipulation) was rendered invalid. Or, to put the same idea positively: there had to be a causa for a valid stipulation, and this causa had to be expressly stated in the written document.

3. The scholastic doctrine of causation

These were two of the most important bricks available to the medieval lawyers.[29] The mortar was the scholastic doctrine of causation. Every effect, so the scholastics argued, is dependent upon its reason (causa), and causa is that without which a thing cannot exist: "Illud est proprie causa alicuius, sine quo esse non potest: omnis enim effectus dependet a sua causa."[30] According to St. Thomas Aquinas (and, ultimately, Aristotle), there are four kinds of causes: formalis, materialis, efficiens and finalis.[31] Obviously, it was attractive, particularly for the canon lawyers and the commentators, to apply this scheme to the law of contracts and thus to extend the concept of causa as they found it in the Corpus Juris Civilis. If everything is based on a cause, so must contracts be. Baldus appears to have been the first to draw the consequences.[32] Not only stipulations, all obligatory contracts are (must be) based on a specific causa. But whilst the former receive their causa from outside, the "nominate" contracts carry it within themselves:

> ". . . stipulatio est contractus aliunde tamen causandus, quod non est in aliis contractibus specificatis, ut in locatione, emptione et venditione etc., qui sunt causa sui ipsius."[33]

4. Causa as an extra piece of "garment"

The concept of causa, under these circumstances, could, of course, no longer be confined to datio vel factum or to a negotium antecedens (as had been the case when the glossators had discussed innominate real contracts and stipulations);[34] every causa extrinseca (that is, either

---

[29] Cf. further Riccobono/Kerr Wylie/Beinart, pp. 123 sqq.; Söllner, (1960) 77 *ZSS* 219 sqq.; on causa and synallagma cf., most recently, Raimondo Santoro, "Il contratto nel pensiero di Labeone", (1983) 37 *Annali Palermo* 221 sqq.

[30] St. Thomas Aquinas, *Summa theologiae*, Tertia Pars, q. 86, art. 6.

[31] *Summa theologiae*, e.g. Prima Secundae, q. 72, art. 3. Forma and materia were grouped together as causae intrinsicae as opposed to the causae extrinsicae, (i.e. the causae efficientes and finales). Cf. further e.g. Söllner, (1960) 77 *ZSS* 183 sqq.; Gerhard Otte, *Dialektik und Jurisprudenz* (1971), pp. 193 sqq.

[32] Söllner, (1960) 77 *ZSS* 236; cf. also Barton, (1966) 34 *TR* 59 sqq.

[33] Ad C. 4, 30, 13, n. 23.

[34] For details, see Söllner, (1960) 77 *ZSS* 219 sqq., 223. In the case of stipulations, the document had to refer to an existing legally enforceable obligation. This was the negotium antecedens, which the glossators referred to as the causa stipulationis; the sources most often quoted in this context were C. 4, 30, 13 and Paul. D. 22, 3, 25, 4. The situation was thus very similar to the well-known concept of a iusta causa traditionis. Paul. D. 41, 1, 31 pr.

finalis or efficiens) was sufficient. In particular, this entailed that even a causa impulsiva (that is, one which is "non cogens, sed persuadens", a reasonable motive as opposed to a pre-existing obligation)[35] could give rise to a binding obligation.[36] Inevitably, the next step was to transfer these ideas to pacta:

> "Ubi non est causa, ibi non est causatum, et ideo ex pacto nudo non insurgit actio, quia actio est quoddam causatum, ergo non potest sine causa oriri."[37]

Because there is no causa, a (bare) pact cannot beget an action. Conversely, therefore, if, and as long as, a (bare) pact is based on a causa, it may in fact be enforceable! The doctrine of causa could therefore be used as an ingenious way to bridge the rift that had developed between the legists and the canonists. The legists, as we have seen, distinguished between (enforceable) pacta vestita and (unenforceable) pacta nuda.[38] The canonists, on the other hand, were prepared to grant an action even on the basis of a pactum nudum. This was, however, justifiable only if the parties had seriously intended to enter into legal relations, and that in turn was ensured by generalizing the causa requirement.[39] If one therefore wanted to translate the situation under the canon law into the terminology developed by the glossators, one merely had to refer to causa as an extra piece of garment,[40] with which the canonists—charitable as could be expected—were prepared to save a poor and naked pactum from the chill of death. At least in theory and pro forma it was therefore possible to claim that the rule of ex nudo pacto non oritur actio still reigned supreme.

At the same time, however, a terminological ambiguity gained ground, which often made it very difficult to identify the position of individual authors; for the term "nudum pactum" came to be used not only where an informal agreement was not clothed by one of the traditional vestimenta but also in the sense of a pactum *nudum a causa*. Thus, for instance, Jason de Mayno still recognized the principle of ex nudo pacto non oritur actio (although he detailed no fewer than 16 limitationes), but confounded the doctrine of the vestimenta pactorum with the causa theory when he said: "[S]ed pactum nudum dicitur, cui non subest causa."[41] This is also the key to resolving the apparent contradiction in the works of Ulrich Zasius. If he still emphasized that

states: "Numquam nuda traditio transfert dominium, sed ita, si venditio aut aliqua iusta causa praecesserit, propter quam traditio sequeretur"; on which the gloss (gl. Iusta causa) remarks: ". . . idem in promissore per stipulationem. . . ."

[35] Baldus, ad C. 4, 30, 13, n. 22.

[36] Söllner, (1960) 77 *ZSS* 249; contra: Barton, (1966) 34 *TR* 60 sqq.

[37] Baldus, *Commentaria in Decretales*, I, De Pactis, n. 14.

[38] Supra, pp. 538 sq.

[39] Argument: if a causa was required even for the validity of a stipulation, the same had to apply, a fortiori, to pacta.

[40] Baldus, *Commentaria in Decretales*, I, De Pactis, nn. 4 sq. (causa as vestimentum); cf. also Norbert Horn, *Aequitas in den Lehren des Baldus* (1968), pp. 187 sqq.

[41] Commentaria, ad D. 2, 14, 7, 4, n. 1.

bare pacts were not actionable,[42] he meant pacta without a causa; and this is entirely in accordance with the famous rule of the *Freiburger Stadtrecht* (drafted by Zasius): "Wer bedechtlich zusagt, der sol es halten." For this is what causa meant: the pactum must have been made *"bedechtlich"* (deliberately) or, as others formulated it in Latin, serio et deliberate initum.[43]

5. The decline of causa

By the time of the usus modernus pandectarum, causa had played out its historically most important role: namely that of facilitating the transition from a closed shop of (enforceable) pacta vestita to the principle of modern law that every agreement begets an action.[44] That a contract, in order to be valid, must have been seriously intended by the parties is a matter of course. One does not really need causa as an independent requirement to call attention to this trivial point. Thus, amongst the German authors of the 17th and 18th centuries, both the term and the idea of a causa disappeared from the definition of contract, and the problem of whether the parties had indeed seriously and deliberately entered legal relations was shifted into the field of procedure and evidence.[45] In France and Italy a causa continued to be required as an element essential for the validity of contracts. *"Tout engagement doit avoir une cause honnête"* said Pothier,[46] and from here, as usual, the principle filtered through into the code civil. But it has been questioned, time and again, whether this "conceptual hippogriff"[47] serves a specific and indispensable function in the law of contract.[48] If it is correct that the term "causa" simply refers to the content of the contract as a whole,[49] it might just as well be jettisoned. For then there is no difference between, for instance, a statement to the effect that an unlawful contract is void and—this is what the code civil actually declares[50]—that a contract without lawful cause is void.

---

[42] Cf. Seuffert, op. cit., note 17, pp. 96 sqq.

[43] Cf. e.g. Wesenbecius, *Commentarii in Pandectas*, Lib. II, Tit. XIV, n. 10; Wissenbach, *Exercitationes*, Disp. IX, 35; Voet, *Commentarius ad Pandectas*, Lib. II, Tit. XIV, IX; Stryk, *Usus modernus pandectarum*, Lib. II, Tit. XIV, § 1.

[44] Cf. also John P. Dawson, *Gifts and Promises* (1980), p. 114 ("[cause] served as a catch-word in the long campaign, led by the canonists, to expand the range of enforceable promises. . . . In the gallery of ideas that have helped to liberate thought it therefore deserves a small corner located out in a distant wing").

[45] Coing, p. 403. Lord Mansfield (unsuccesfully) tried the same with regard to the doctrine of consideration: *Pillans v. Van Mierop* (1765) 3 Burr 1663 sqq.; cf. supra, p. 505, note 170.

[46] Pothier, *Traité des obligations*, n. 42.

[47] Zweigert/Kötz/Weir, p. 66.

[48] Cf. e.g. E. Lorenzen, "Causa and Consideration in Contracts", (1919) 28 *Yale LJ* 621 ("There is in reality no definable 'doctrine' of causa. The term 'causa' includes a variety of notions which may equally well be derived from the nature of the juristic act and from considerations of equity" (p. 646)) and, more recently, Dawson, op. cit., note 44, p. 114 (". . . in truth [causa] has no meaningful functions at all").

[49] Cf. Zweigert/Kötz/Weir, p. 67.

[50] Art. 1131 code civil.

6. Causa and consideration in English law

Finally, and perhaps most importantly, the requirement of causa became part and parcel of the English common law and survives, to this day, in the form of the doctrine of consideration.[51] It is, in fact, one of the central and most characteristic features of the English law of contract; and also one of its most problematic ones. The relationship with other core concepts of contractual liability (such as offer and acceptance) is strained and uneasy, to say the least, but so far consideration—like cause in France—has survived with extraordinary tenacity the attacks of all those critics who have questioned its utility.[52]

In a certain sense, the doctrine of consideration was little more than "the practical answer to an urgent problem".[53] In the course of the 16th century the English courts started to shake off the fetters of the medieval law of contract, a formulary system determined essentially by the catalogue of original writs in the Register (Registrum Brevium).[54] The rise of the action of assumpsit (around which the modern English law of contract has grown up) brought about an extension of liability.[55] Some sort of criterion was needed to define how far one was prepared to go. Consideration was brought in to ensure that the expansion of the law of contract remained under control; it was designed to delimit the actionability of informal promises by reference to the circumstances in which the promise in question was made.[56] The consideration for a promise originally meant the factors which the promisor considered when he promised, the circumstances which motivated his promising.[57] Christopher St. German, in his famous dialogue between a doctor of divinity and a student of the common law, put it thus:

> "[A]nd of . . . promyses made to a man vpon a certayne consyderacyon, yf the promyse be not agaynst the lawe. As yf A promyse to gyue B XX li. bycause he hathe made hym suche a house or hath lente hym suche a thynge or suche other lyke, I thynke hym bounde to kepe hys promyse. But yf hys promyse be so naked that there is no maner of consyderacyon why yt sholde be made, than I thynke hym not bounde to perfourme it. . . ."[58]

"In modern terms", as Professor Simpson comments,[59]

---

[51] Cf. supra, pp. 504 sqq.

[52] B.S. Markesinis, "Causa and Consideration: A Study in Parallel", (1978) 37 *Cambridge LJ* 53.

[53] C.H.S. Fifoot, *History and Sources of the Common Law. Tort and Contract* (1949), p. 399.

[54] On the Royal Writs and Writ Procedure cf. e.g. R.C. van Caenegem, *The Birth of the English Common Law* (1973), pp. 29 sqq.; for a comparison between the English writ and the Roman action, see Hans Peter, *Actio und Writ* (1957).

[55] For all details cf. Simpson, *A History of the Common Law of Contract. The Rise of the Action of Assumpsit* (1975), pp. 199 sqq.; cf. also infra, pp. 777 sqq.

[56] Simpson, *History*, pp. 316 sqq. (316, 321).

[57] Simpson, *History*, p. 321.

[58] *Second Dialogue*, Chapter 24, p. 229 (vol. 91 of the Publications of the Selden Society, 1974, eds. Plucknett and Barton).

[59] *History*, p. 322.

"one can see the plausibility of the theory—a promise which lacks any adequate motive cannot have been serious, and therefore ought not to be taken seriously."

All this by now sounds very familiar to us. The "naked" promise, the reasonable motive (causa impulsiva), the serious (and deliberate) intention of the parties: everything could have been stated in similar terms by many contemporary Continental lawyers. In fact, the very starting point of the whole dilemma, the Roman principle of "ex nudo pacto non oritur actio", had penetrated, almost three centuries before, and through the influence of Azo, into the common law of England.[60] This is apparent from a little couplet, quoted by Bracton in his great restatement of the laws and customs of England: "Re, verbis, scripto, consensu, traditione, iunctura vestes sumere pacta solent."[61] Now one could again refer to Roman–Canon doctrine; for there the causa requirement had been used to ease the way from ex nudo pacto non oritur actio to ex nudo pacto oritur actio, and had thus been instrumental in solving the very problem with which the common law, too, was faced. The prime agents of this process of assimilation were "Doctor and Student" and the Court of Chancery. St. German's dialogue, which contains a considerable amount of material derived from canon law, became a most popular and influential book;[62] the immediate sources of the theory of contract set forth in it have been identified as the *Summa Rosella* by the Franciscan Baptista de Salis[63] and the *Summa Angelica*, an encyclopedia compiled by another Franciscan, Angelus de Clavassio, doctor utriusque iuris of the University of Bologna.[64] And the Chancellors of the Court of Chancery, it must be remembered, down to the time of Henry VIII, were clergymen, usually

[60] On the concept of "nudum pactum" in England, see Nikolaus Benke, " 'No inefficacy arises merely from the naked promise'", (1987) 14 *Ius Commune* 1 sqq.

[61] *De Legibus et Consuetudinibus Angliae*, f. 16 b (p. 64); cf. also F.W. Maitland, *Bracton and Azo* (vol. 8 of the Publications of the Selden Society); Paul Vinogradoff, *Roman Law in Medieval Europe* (2nd ed., 1929), pp. 116. Even earlier than that, we find in the *Tractatus de legibus et consuetudinibus regni Angliae* (ascribed traditionally to Glanvill) the following enumeration of causae debendi: "Aut enim debetur quid ex causa mutui, aut ex venditionis causa aut ex commodato, aut ex locato, aut ex deposito, aut ex alia iusta debendi causa" (X, 3, p. 117). On the exact meaning and impact of this statement on the treatment of the law of obligations by Glanvill, on the Romanistic background thereto and on Glanvill's (Continental) sources, cf. the study of Horst Kaufmann, "'Causa debendi' und 'causa petendi' bei Glanvill sowie im römischen und kanonischen Recht seiner Zeit", (1961) 17 *Traditio* 107 sqq.

[62] Cf. e.g. Simpson, *History*, pp. 376 sq.

[63] It was "an encyclopedia with the material arranged under alphabetical headings"; first published under the title *Summa Casuum Utilissima*, it later became known as the *Summa Rosella*, "because it was a collection of the most elegant conclusions . . . which could be compared to a garland of sweet-smelling roses which Baptista had gathered together" (Simpson, *History*, p. 379).

[64] Cf. e.g. Paul Vinogradoff, "Reason and Conscience", (1908) 24 *LQR* 377 sqq.; Simpson, *History*, pp. 377 sqq.

well versed in canon law and Roman law; most of them were in fact law graduates of Oxford University.[65]

> ". . . [I]t is hardly conceivable, if [their] . . . careers . . . are borne in mind, that as judges in conscience they could avoid deriving ideas from the canon and civil law."[66]

7. Causa and consideration in South African law

(a) The reception of the consideration doctrine

Both cause and consideration are refined legal doctrines which have developed, from a common source, in their own individual way. Both of them perform the same function; they serve as a test of seriousness to distinguish between promissory transactions which are binding and those which are not.[67] Both of them, however, are highly problematic, and their utility within the modern law of contract has been repeatedly and severely queried. These problems are, of course, exacerbated if a legal system starts confounding the two doctrines. Such a legal system may well, as a result, land in "a nightmare of confusion".[68] This is what happened in the history of South African law.[69]

In the course of the 19th century the term "iusta causa" came to be translated as "consideration"; and the term "consideration", not unnaturally, was very soon equated with the English doctrine of valuable consideration.[70] In the first two decades of this century the question whether iusta causa, as understood by the classical Roman-Dutch lawyers, was or was not distinguishable from the consideration of English law, became the great cause célèbre of contractual theory, with the two most influential judges of their time as protagonists. J.G. Kotzé, Anthony Trollope's "boy judge",[71] the man who shaped the

[65] The law schools of both Oxford and Cambridge followed the continental pattern. The teaching of civil law at Oxford started with the Bologna-trained Italian, Magister Vacarius, in about the middle of the 12th century. Guilelmus de Drogheda (who died around 1245) was appointed "Regens in Legibus". For details, see H.G. Richardson, "The Oxford Law School under John", (1941) 57 *LQR* 319 sqq.

[66] Simpson, *History*, p. 400. Cf. further, especially William T. Barbour, *The History of Contract in Early English Equity* (1914), pp. 163 sqq. Generally on the influence of canon law on English law through the medium of the Court of Chancery, see, for example, Helmut Coing, "English Equity and the Denunciatio Evangelica of the Canon Law", (1955) 71 *LQR* 223 sqq.; John L. Barton, *Roman Law in England, Ius Romanum Medii Aevi, pars V, 13 a*, (1971), pp. 50 sqq.

[67] Zweigert/Kötz/Weir, pp. 60 sqq.; cf. also e.g. Markesinis, (1978) 37 *LQR* 55 (both doctrines "represent a kind of form—a check, one could say, on the unrestricted application of the philosophical doctrine of the autonomy of the will which is prepared to ascribe legally binding effects to the mere coincidence of the wills of the contracting parties").

[68] De Villiers AJA, in: *Conradie v. Rossouw* 1919 AD 279 at 323.

[69] On the situation in other mixed legal systems cf. Markesinis, (1978) 37 *Cambridge LJ* 53 sq. (n. 3).

[70] Cf. e.g. *Alexander v. Perry* (1874) 4 Buch 59 at 61; *Malan and Van der Merwe v. Secretan, Boon & Co.* 1880 Foord 94 at 95 sqq.; *Tradesmen's Benefit Society v. Du Preez* (1887) 5 SC 269 at 272 sqq. The history of the question is reviewed fully by De Villiers AJA, in *Conradie v. Rossouw* 1919 AD 279 at 299 sqq.

[71] *South Africa*, vol. II (1878), p. 121.

early history of the Transvaal Supreme Court, advocated the former position, while Lord De Villiers, who reigned as Chief Justice for 41 years—first of the Cape, then, since its inception, of the Union of South Africa[72]—took the rule of the "besoedelaar" or "pollutionist".[73] In *Rood v. Wallach*[74] and *Mtembu v. Webster*[75] this clash of judicial opinion came to a head. Five years after Lord De Villiers' death, the Appellate Division of the Supreme Court finally declined to endorse his view on the matter in the case of *Conradie v. Rossouw*.[76] "A good cause of action can be founded on a promise made seriously and deliberately and with the intention that a lawful obligation should be established": this is how the court defined the causa requirement,[77] and it rejected any idea of a reception of the English consideration doctrine.[78]

(b) Iusta causa and Grotius' notion of "redelicke oorzaecke"

It appears to be clear that Lord De Villiers was wrong in equating causa and consideration.[79] It is a far cry from Brother Baptista's garland of sweet-smelling roses to the refined and technical doctrine of consideration worked out over the centuries by the English courts. Continental causa and English consideration have developed in different directions, and the latter never formed part of the Roman-Dutch law of Holland. On the other hand, Kotzé[80] and his followers were probably not right either.

> "It may, indeed, be doubted whether the doctrine of causa really occupied the important place in the Roman-Dutch law which has been assigned to it in modern discussions",

says Lee,[81] and this is putting it mildly. Causa as an independent requirement for promissory transactions was on the way out in

---

[72] For a comprehensive yet eminently readable biography, see E.A. Walker, *Lord de Villiers and His Times* (1925).

[73] On this terminology and on the bellum iuridicum between the so-called purists, antiquarians, pollutionists and pragmatists raging over the nature and the true sources of South African private law cf. Reinhard Zimmermann, "Synthesis in South African Private law: Civil Law, Common Law and Usus Hodiernus Pandectarum", (1986) 103 *SALJ* 259 sqq.

[74] 1904 TS 187 sqq.

[75] (1904) 21 SC 323 sqq.

[76] 1919 AD 279 sqq. All three decisions are well worth reading.

[77] *Conradie v. Rossouw* 1919 AD 279 (headnote).

[78] At 288 sq. and 309 sqq.

[79] On other—English—lawyers who "have fallen into the error of treating causa and consideration as if they denote one and the same thing" (amongst them Blackstone, Sir Williams Evans (the translator of Pothier) and Sir Henry Maine), see John G. Kotzé, *Causa in the Roman and Roman-Dutch Law of Contract* (1922), pp. 8 sq. He also quotes Pollock, who glosses over Maine's slip with the following charming observation: "The use of the specially English term Consideration to represent the Roman causa is too dangerous a liberty to be allowed to any lesser man than Maine."

[80] Cf. particularly his monograph on "Causa" in the *Roman and Roman-Dutch Law of Contract* (1922), passim, e.g. pp. 26, 31, 56; also e.g. *Kennedy v. Steenkamp* 1936 CPD 113 at 117.

[81] *Introduction*, p. 224.

Germany, as it was in the Netherlands.[82] One of the main sources, always brought up in the debate, is Grotius' *Inleiding*. We have already referred to the famous passage where he makes mention of the "redelicke oorzaecken".[83] But the context in which this term appears is a rather peculiar one. In his *Inleiding* Grotius distinguishes between obligations arising from toezegging (promise) and from onevenheid (inequality).[84] A toezegging is either "uitdruckelick" (express) or "door wetduiding" (implied by law).[85] Express promise, in turn, is "door woorden, of schrift", i.e. verbis or litteris.[86] Grotius then explains that with regard to express verbal promises the subtleties of Roman law (he uses the word "scherpzinnigheid") no longer have to be complied with; "alle toezegginghen die uit eenighe redelicke oorzaecken geschieden" give rise to a right of action.[87] "Redelicke oorzaecke", so he continues,

> "werd verstaen zoo wanneer de toezegging ofte belofte geschied ter schenk, of dient tot eenige andere handelinge, 't zy zulcks geschied ten tijde vande handeling ofte daer nae."[88]

One cannot say that Grotius makes it entirely clear what he means. Thus, for instance, he may be taken to attribute significance to the concept of "redelicke oorzaecke" only in the case of express promises (though those of the modern, informal kind): auxiliary (incidental or accessory) transactions[89] and gifts.[90] More convincing, on balance, seems to be another interpretation. "Redelicke oorzaecke" is used in a very untechnical sense as the basis of every contractual agreement: it indicates that the law recognizes the agreement as reasonable, acceptable and thus enforceable. This is undoubtedly the case, for instance, as far as contracts of sale, hire, etc. are concerned: here, "de grond zelve van de handelinghe heeft een rechtelicke oorzaeck".[91] But the promise of a gift and auxiliary pacta, whether concluded in continenti *or ex intervallo* are reasonable bases for a contractual obligation too.[92] This appears to be the special import of III, I, 53.

---

[82] On Roman-Dutch authors, cf. Kotzé, op. cit., note 79, pp. 25 sqq.; Joubert, *Contract*, pp. 27 sqq.; J.C. Stassen, "Causa in die Kontraktereg", (1979) 42 *THRHR* 364 sqq.

[83] Cf. supra, p. 549, note 20.

[84] III, I, 9; III, I, 47. On onevenheid (comprising inter alia enrichment, delict and the real contracts), cf. III, I, 15 sqq.

[85] III, I, 49. On toezegging door wetduiding, cf. III, VI.

[86] III, I, 50. On schriftelicke toezegging, cf. III, V.

[87] III, I, 52.

[88] III, I, 53.

[89] Cf. the explanation of the meaning of toezegging welcke dient tot eenige andere handelinge in III, III, 1.

[90] Stassen, (1979) 42 *THRHR* 366 sq.

[91] *Inleiding*, III, XXX, 14.

[92] The question arises why Grotius singled out these two situations. The answer may be that all (or nearly all) other pacta were enforceable as a matter of course, i.e. normally as consensual contracts (toezegging door wetduiding; cf. III, VI (entitled: "Van overkoming in 't gemeen"). In III, I, 53 Grotius clarifies that even promises of gift and auxiliary (incidental or accessory) agreements were now actionable. In Roman law, both had been enforceable only if couched in the form of a stipulation (the latter also if they had been added by way of

But whatever the historically correct interpretation may be, in South African law Grotius' statement has contributed considerably to the prevailing confusion. More particularly, it has for a long time prevented courts and legal writers from recognizing that the requirement of iusta causa had in fact become redundant.[93] An agreement must be entered into with a serious intention to be bound, and it must not be tainted by illegality or immorality. If these conditions are present, an enforceable contract has come into existence.[94] Whether one lumps these two requirements together sub titulo "iusta causa" is a matter of terminology.[95] But under a regime of ex nudo pacto oritur actio, neither causa nor iusta causa are separate, additional requirements that have to be met before a contract can be said to have been validly concluded.[96]

III. CONSENSUS

1. Consent as the basis of contract in modern law

Having looked at two factors—form and causa—which are not essential to the modern concept of contract, we now have to turn our attention to the one which is: consensus. Consent forms the basis of the modern law of contract. But what exactly does that imply? It is obvious, first of all, that not every kind of consent can be relevant. A and B agree that Socrates is a stone,[97] or that Socrates is Socrates.[98] Clearly, their minds are ad idem, and thus there is consent. But it would be absurd to claim that this agreement can create a contract (or, for that matter, a pactum). Thus, consent between the parties has to

---

pactum adiectum *in continenti*). No matter whether these subtleties have been complied with or not, the mere pactum can be regarded (according to Grotius) as a redelicke oorzaecke = counts as a contract = gives rise to an action. Cf., apart from Stassen, (1979) 42 *THRHR* 366 sq., especially Kotzé, op. cit., note 79, pp. 28 sqq.; Lee, *Introduction*, pp. 431 sqq., and De Villiers AJA in *Conradie v. Rossouw* 1919 AD 279 at 314 sqq., all offering somewhat different interpretations. One basic difficulty in understanding the contractual theory of Grotius is that he nowhere clearly states whether (in his view) (1) all pacts are actionable and (2) all promises must be based on a iusta causa. Both propositions can merely be inferred. But by still discussing, in a separate chapter, the express verbal contract (i.e. the stipulation of Roman law, although in modern dress), he shows that he has not (or rather: not totally) thrown off the shackles of Roman law (Lee, *Introduction*, pp. 432 sq.)

[93] Cf., particularly, Kotzé, op. cit., note 79, pp. 25 sqq.

[94] Cf., particularly, Kotzé, op. cit., note 79, pp. 25 sqq.

[95] Cf., particularly, De Villiers AJA, in his erudite judgment in *Conradie v. Rossouw* 1919 AD 279 at 298 sqq.

[96] Cf. today, for example, Stassen, (1979) 42 *THRHR* 358 sq.; Joubert, *Contract*, pp. 32 sqq. Neither De Wet en Yeats nor Kerr, *The Principles of the Law of Contract* (3rd ed., 1982), in their textbooks deal with (iusta) causa as a special requirement for the validity of contracts. Cf. further Jansen JA, in *Saambou-Nasionale Bouvereniging v. Friedman* 1979 (3) SA 978 (A) at 990B–993C. A (iusta) causa, however, continues to be required for bills of exchange; cf. s. 25.1 of the (South African) Bills of Exchange Act 34/1964, and F.R. Malan, *Bills of Exchange, Cheques and Promissory Notes in South African Law* (1983), pp. 71 sqq.

[97] Cf. the example discussed by Azo, supra, p. 538, note 192.

[98] Petrus Placentinus, *Summa Codicis* (Moguntina, 1536), Lib. II, Tit. III.

relate to performance. This was already very clearly seen by the medieval lawyers; it is necessary

> "ut consentiant in idem, scilicet dandum faciendumve ex diversis motibus animorum, postmodum convenientes in quid unum faciendum vel dandum".[99]

But even where this is so and where, for instance, A wants to hand over his sedan chair to B, and B indeed wishes to receive it from A, the mere agreement as such, that is, the fact that both parties intend one and the same thing, cannot give rise to a binding obligation. This is because it is necessary that these intentions be communicated, in one way or another, between the parties. No specific formalities have to be complied with, but there has to be a declaration. The intention has to be expressed; whether verbally, or in writing or, for instance, by simply nodding one's head, does not matter. As a contract involves (at least) two parties, we have in fact two such declarations of intention. They are normally referred to as offer and acceptance.

This way of analysing the conclusion of contract reveals two specific problem areas which modern legal systems have to grapple with. On the one hand, an offer can sometimes not be accepted immediately. When a contract is concluded inter absentes, for instance by exchange of letters or through a messenger, the two declarations of intention have to be given in succession, and formation of the contract takes some time. The question then arises whether and to what extent the offeror is bound by the offer. What legal effects does the law attach to the offer as an individual declaration of intention, i.e. to the one element of an as yet incomplete transaction?[100] In Germany, the offeror is, as a rule, not able to withdraw his offer.[101] Other legal systems decide differently. The English common law, for instance, does not regard an offer as binding;[102] until it has been accepted by the offeree, it may be withdrawn at any time.[103]

---

[99] Placentinus, loc. cit. Cf., much later, also Wolfgang Adam Lauterbach, *Collegium theoretico-practicum*, Lib. II, Tit. XIV, IV.

[100] For a comparative discussion of this problem, see Zweigert/Kötz/Weir, pp. 27 sqq.; for a very comprehensive comparative investigation of all problems relating to offer and acceptance, see Rudolf B. Schlesinger, *Formation of Contracts, A Study in the Common Core of Legal Systems* (2 vols., 1968).

[101] § 145 BGB; for further details cf. §§ 146 sqq., particularly § 147 II: "An offer made to a person who is not present may be accepted only up to the moment when the offerer may expect to receive an answer under ordinary circumstances." Cf. also § 862 ABGB and Artur Nussbaum, "Comparative Aspects of the Anglo-American Offer-and-Acceptance Doctrine", (1936) 36 *Columbia LR* 920 sqq. ("Apparently it was only after the use of mail had become common in the 18th century that the traditional rule (sc. no binding effect to be attributed to an offer) was felt to be unsatisfactory" (p. 923)).

[102] The reason for this lies in the doctrine of consideration. No consideration is normally given for the offer, and hence the latter cannot bind the offeror. On South African law (where it is also accepted doctrine that an offer can be revoked, even though the doctrine of consideration has been rejected), cf. Ben Beinart, "Offers Stipulating a Period for Acceptance", 1964 *Acta Juridica* 200 sqq.; Joubert, *Contract*, pp. 36 sqq., 42.

[103] The practical effects of this rule are to a certain extent modified by the so-called mailbox theory (dating back to *Adams v. Lindsell* (1818) 1 B & Ald 681 sqq.): the contract is

On the other hand, it must be realized that both offer and acceptance are in turn composed of two essential elements, namely the intention of the party and his declaration. Hence the potential for a further conflict of interests: for will and declaration do not necessarily coincide. One (or even both) of the parties may have made a mistake in drawing up the declaration(s), or the opponent may have misunderstood it. It therefore has to be determined which of the two elements is to prevail. Does it matter, as far as both conclusion and interpretation of the contract are concerned, what the parties have intended or what they have in actual fact declared? Both views (normally dubbed will theory and declaration theory) are (and have been) advocated, though usually not without certain modifications.[104]

2. The Roman contribution

(a) Conceptual analysis in general

These are, in barest outline, some of the main features of modern contractual theory. It would be an entirely ahistorical enterprise to try to trace them back to Roman law. The modern general law of contract has essentially been developed by the natural lawyers, and our conceptual apparatus has thus been devised within the last three centuries.[105] But, of course, one did not start de novo; most of the individual parts that were needed for the new doctrinal building could conveniently be taken from the quarry of the Corpus Juris Civilis. All that was needed was a new scheme of putting things together: a coherent rational philosophy as a new basis and source of inspiration for systematic and conceptual clarity. The Roman lawyers did not think in terms of abstract propositions; they developed their law in casuistic fashion. Thus, as far as the voluntary transfer of assets was concerned, they did not look at phenomena such as "contract" or "legal act" as such; they paid attention to specific types of transactions carved out by experience rather than doctrinal thinking. In this manner, they devised transactions characterized by oral formalities, by rei interventio, by an entry into a ledger and by simple consent. The result was an abundant but imperfectly structured casuistry. And yet, their specific legal genius led the Roman lawyers to adjust their rules and precedents in such a

---

concluded (and thus the offer can no longer be revoked) when the offeree dispatches his acceptance (by, for instance, throwing it into the mailbox), not only when it reaches the offeror.

[104] Cf. infra, pp. 585 sqq., 621 sqq.

[105] Cf., in particular, Franz Wieacker, "Die vertragliche Obligation bei den Klassikern des Vernunftrechts", in: *Festschrift für Hans Welzel* (1974), pp. 8 sqq.; Theo Mayer-Maly, "Der Konsens als Grundlage des Vertrages", in: *Festschrift für Erwin Seidl* (1975), pp. 118 sqq.; idem, "Die Bedeutung des Konsenses in privatrechtsgeschichtlicher Sicht", in: G. Jakobs (ed.), *Rechtsgeltung und Konsens* (1976), pp. 96 sqq.; Flume, *AT*, pp. 1 sqq.; Martin Lipp, *Die Bedeutung des Naturrechts für die Ausbildung der Allgemeinen Lehren des deutschen Privatrechts* (1980), pp. 130 sqq.; Hans Hattenhauer, *Grundbegriffe des Bürgerlichen Rechts* (1982), pp. 58 sqq.; Nanz, *Vertragsbegriff*, pp. 135 sqq.

manner that the result was not unmanageable chaos. The germs of many of the modern general doctrines were slumbering in the sources.[106] Even most of the modern concepts were there, though they were rather diffuse and poorly defined; in addition, they had sometimes undergone considerable change in meaning before they were incorporated into the Corpus Juris Civilis.

(b) Contractus

Thus, first of all, there was the term "contractus". It is derived from the verb "contrahere" which, at least originally, meant "to contract" (in the sense of, for instance, "to contract a disease"). What one "contracted", in the legal context, was liability—any kind of liability, not only a "contractual" one.[107] The substantive contractus, too, was first of all used in the same wide and fairly untechnical sense. Characteristically, it was the law teacher, Gaius, with his systematic interests, who gave the term a narrower meaning and distinguished between obligationes ex delicto and ex contractu.[108] Since then contractus was used to identify those transactions that were enforceable according to the ius civile.[109] Later on, the innominate real "contracts" came to be included too.[110] No generally accepted definition of the term "contract" can be found in our sources.[111] There is only an "elegant" (in the opinion of Ulpianus) statement of Pedius to the effect that "nullum esse contractum, nullam obligationem, quae non habeat in se conventionem, sive re sive verbis fiat".[112]

(c) Pacta

The counterparts of the contractus were, on the one hand, the delicta and, on the other hand, the pacta. However, the term "pactum" was

[106] Cf. e.g. Gerhard Dulckeit, "Zur Lehre vom Rechtsgeschäft im klassischen römischen Recht", in: *Festschrift für Fritz Schulz*, vol. I (1951), pp. 148 sqq.; Kaser, *RPr* I, pp. 227 sqq.

[107] Cf. still e.g. Pap. D. 1, 3, 1 (delictum contrahere); Kaser, *RPr* I, p. 523; Biondi, *Contratto e stipulatio*, pp. 197 sqq.; Franz Wieacker (1967) 35 *TR* 130 sq.; Honsell/Mayer-Maly/Selb, p. 250. But cf. also Wunner, *Contractus*, pp. 10 sqq., 26 sqq.; Werner Macheiner, "Zu den Anfängen des Kontraktssystems", in: *Festsgabe für Arnold Herdlitczka* (1972), pp. 168 sqq.; Santoro, (1983) 37 *Annali Palermo* 31 sq.

[108] Gai. III, 88 sq.; Wieacker, (1967) 35 *TR* 132 sq.; Wunner, pp. 42 sqq. On the contract–delict dichotomy, see also supra, pp. 10 sqq.

[109] There is a vast literature on the Roman concept of contract; cf. e.g. Dulckeit, *Festschrift Schulz*, vol. I, pp. 152 sqq.; Kaser, *RPr* I, p. 523; Arnaldo Biscardi, "Some Critical Remarks on the Roman Concept of Obligations", (1977) 12 *The Irish Jurist* 371 sqq.; Santoro, (1983) 37 *Annali Palermo* 61 sqq. and passim (for the time of Labeo).

[110] Kaser, *RPr* II, pp. 362 sq.

[111] Labeo's attempt (Ulp. D. 50, 16, 19) to confine the term "contractus" to "ultro citroque obligationem, quod Graeci συνάλλαγμα vocant" is difficult to understand and possibly spurious. In any event, it has remained isolated and has never been followed up. Cf. e.g. Wunner, *Contactus*, pp. 33 sqq.; Benöhr, *Synallagma*, pp. 10 sqq.; Macheiner, *Festgabe Herdlitczka*, pp. 172 sqq.; but see the comprehensive analysis by Santoro, (1983) 37 *Annali Palermo* 7 sqq.

[112] Ulp. D. 2, 14, 1, 3.

ambiguous.[113] From early on, it referred to a transaction by means of which the person who had committed a delict "bought off" the injured parties' right of seizure. Apart from that, pactum could refer to what has come to be known as pactum de non petendo, an (informal) release agreement. Incidental agreements which could, if added to a contract with a iudicium bonae fidei, be indirectly enforceable, were also termed pacta (adiecta). Finally, and most importantly, pactum (or pactio) was the word used to denote all informal agreements which were not (independently) enforceable ("nuda pactio obligationem non parit"). But with the degeneration of the stipulation and the recognition of an increasing range of enforceable pacta, the distinction between contracts and pacta was, of course, greatly blurred and became more and more meaningless.[114]

(d) Conventio

Thirdly, then, there was the term "conventio". According to Ulpian this was a "verbum generale . . . ad omnia pertinens, de quibus negotii contrahendi transigendique causa consentiunt qui inter se agunt".[115] Conventio is derived from "convenire" = "to come together". In the same way as people are able to come together in one place, there can be a coming together of the minds, if two or more people agree on the same thing:

> "nam sicuti convenire dicuntur qui ex diversis locis in unum locum colliguntur et veniunt, ita et qui ex diversis animi motibus in unum consentiunt, id est in unam sententia decurrunt."[116]

But is conventio really the overarching generic term comprising both contractus and pacta? Or does it merely have a general significance in that it is an indispensable element contained in every pact or contract? The latter is what Pedius seems to imply (". . . nullum esse contractum, nullam obligationem, quae non habeat in se conventionem").[117] Conventio, in the context of this statement, appears more or less to be a synonym for consensus. In Ulp. D. 50, 12, 3 pr., too, both terms are used very much on the same level ("Pactum est duorum consensus atque conventio").

(e) Consensus

For consensus, in turn, the core concept of the modern law of contract, we do not find a definition or any attempt at a conceptual analysis in the Digest.[118] In Ulp. 2, 14, 1, 1 sq. we meet it as definiens, not as

113 Cf. supra, pp. 508 sqq.
114 Kaser, *RPr* II, pp. 362 sqq.
115 D. 2, 14, 1, 3.
116 Ulp. D. 2, 14, 1, 3.
117 Ulp. D. 2, 14, 1, 3.
118 Thus, the Romans did not concern themselves with questions relating to the actual formation of the contract as such. They looked at contract (and consensus) as a single,

definiendum: "Pactum autem a pactione dicitur . . . et est pactio duorum pluriumve in idem placitum et consensus." Did consensus refer to a subjective attitude of the parties to the contract (voluntas or animus) or rather to the (formal or informal) declarations made by them? Earlier this century attempts have not been wanting to eliminate every subjective notion from classical Roman law[119] and, in turn, to dispute the relevance of any objective criteria for post-classical contractual theory. But these are unacceptable doctrinal exaggerations.[120] True: there was a general tendency (prevalent in other developed legal systems too)[121] to "subjectivize" legal relations and to pay attention to the individual will rather than to strict and archetypal behaviour patterns, to move from form to formlessness, from a nearly exclusive emphasis on certainty of law to equity.[122] As far as the old liability transactions of pre-classical law were concerned, it did indeed matter only that the form had been complied with. The actual intention of the parties was irrelevant. Already in classical law, however, this situation had changed very considerably. No formal act was needed for the conclusion of consensual contracts; they were based merely on the consent of the parties, and they formed the nucleus around which the modern law of contract was to develop. Admittedly, consensus was not a well-analysed technical term but it did mean, first and foremost, what the English term "consent" is usually also taken to convey: a meeting of the minds, the concurrence of two or more wills, and hence something essentially subjective.[123] Of course, the only possible evidence of such intent is external facts, and thus, in order to be legally relevant, the agreement had to manifest itself somehow or other. Even the Byzantine lawyers could not entirely dispense with objective indications. But it is primarily the concurring wishes of the parties concerned that form the main element of contract. That this was so in classical Roman law appears most clearly from the approach adopted by the Roman lawyers towards the problem of error. The fact that a contract did not come into existence in cases where one of the parties

undivided unit and not at the individual declarationes voluntatis of the parties involved. Only after a general theory of contract had been developed by the natural lawyers and contract had come to be analysed in terms of offer and acceptance did, in particular, the question when a contract inter absentes can be taken to be concluded (e.g.: is it necessary that the offeror be notified of the acceptance of his offer?) come into the purview of scholarly debate. For a historical analysis, cf. Jörn Augner, *Vertragsschluss ohne Zugang der Annahmeerklärung: § 151 BGB in rechtshistorischer und rechtsvergleichender Sicht* (1985).

119 Cf. e.g. Silvio Perozzi, *Istituzioni di Diritto Romano* (2nd ed., 1928), vol. II, pp. 30 sqq.; Wieacker, *Societas*, pp. 80 sqq.

120 Very clear on this point is David Daube, "Societas as Consensual Contract", (1939) 7 *Cambridge LJ* 395 sqq.

121 Heinz Hübner, "Subjektivismus in der Entwicklung des Privatrechts", in: *Festschrift für Max Kaser* (1976), pp. 715 sqq., 720 sq.

122 Cf. supra, pp. 78 sqq., 82 sqq.

123 Cf. e.g. Daube, (1939) 7 *Cambridge LJ* 395 sqq.; Grosso, *Sistema*, pp. 53 sqq.

had erred with regard to certain essential aspects of it[124] amply demonstrates the significance attached to the will of the parties in the formation of a contract. In fact, classical law had already gone one important step further, for it is widely recognized today that consent was not only the basis of "consensual" contracts, but was also an essential element of all other contracts.[125] Pedius left no doubt about that when he stated that

> "nullum esse contractum, nullam obligationem, quae non habeat in se conventionem, sive re sive verbis fiat: nam et stipulatio quae verbis fit, nisi habeat consensum, nulla est".[126]

And, indeed, we have already seen in our discussion of stipulation and of mutuum how the "subjective" agreement of the parties increasingly came to be accepted as the cornerstone of and actual effective reason for all contractual obligations.[127] This development was already in full progress in classical law, but it was brought to a close by Byzantine jurisprudence. Their doctrine of volition, based on stoic moral philosophy and on the influence of Christian thinking,[128] led to what Kaser has called an "internalization"[129] of contractual obligations; every contract was taken to be based on and to derive its obligatory nature from a conventio (consensus), that is, a meeting of the minds. Rei interventio and verborum sollemnitas, where they were insisted upon, were merely additional, formal requirements. It is hardly necessary to mention that pacta, too, were based on consent in the sense discussed.[130]

3. Conventio, pactum and contractus under the ius commune

Since the time of the intellectual rediscovery of the Digest, a fairly sterile and pointless debate has been raging as to which term should be used as nomen generale for the law of contract. Conventio and pactum were the two obvious candidates. The French humanists, in particular, indulged in intricate and subtle deliberations which they sometimes

---

124 Cf. infra, pp. 587 sqq.

125 Fritz Raber, "Hoc animo dare", (1965) 33 *TR* 51 sqq.; Kaser, *RPr* II, pp. 365 sq.; Grosso, *Sistema*, pp. 53 sqq.; Thomas, *TRL*, pp. 225 sq.; Buckland/Stein, pp. 412 sqq.; Santoro, (1983) 37 *Annali Palermo* 184 sqq. (on "conventio re"); for the law of stipulations cf., most recently, Malte Dobbertin, *Zur Auslegung der Stipulation im klassischen Römischen Recht* (1987), pp. 51 sqq.

126 Ulp. D. 2, 14, 1, 3.

127 Cf. supra, pp. 156 sqq., 165, 510 sq.

128 Pietro De Francisci, ΣΥΝΑΛΛΑΓΜΑ, vol. II (1916), pp. 498 sqq.; Melchiorre Roberti, "L' influenza Cristiana nello svolgimento storico dei patti nudi", in: *Cristianesimo e diritto romano* (1935), pp. 87 sqq.; but cf. Biondi, *DRC*, vol. III, pp. 214 sqq.; Ugo Brasiello, "Sull' influenza del Cristianesimo in materia di elemento subbiettivo nei contratti", in: *Scritti di diritto romano in onore di Contardo Ferrini* (1946), pp. 505 sqq.

129 *"Verinnerlichung" der schuldrechtlichen Bindung*: *RPr* II, p. 366.

130 Ulp. D. 2, 14, 1, 1 sq.; Ulp. D. 50, 12, 3 pr.; Grosso, *Sistema*, pp. 171 sqq.; Magdelain, *Consensualisme*, pp. 5 sqq.

even spiced with personal invectives.[131] Ultimately in France, conventio came to be accepted as the main category.[132] Thus, the code civil states in its art. 1101:

> "*Le contrat est une convention par laquelle une ou plusieurs personnes s'obligent, envers une ou plusieurs autres, à donner, à faire ou à ne pas faire quelque chose.*"

The Dutch and German usus modernus finally settled for the term "pactum". Vinnius appears to have been one of the last authors to discuss the matter in detail.[133] When he wrote his *Tractatus de Pactis*, the crucial breakthrough towards recognition of the principle of "ex nudo pacto oritur actio" had been achieved. From a purely systematic point of view this meant that a distinction had to be drawn between pactum in a wider sense and the more specific term "pactum nudum". Pactum in the wider sense comprised both pacta nuda and contractus.

But did it still make sense to distinguish these two species of "pacta"? Both, after all, were based on consensus, and both were now enforceable. It slowly dawned upon contemporary authors that the whole basis for the Roman typology of contracts had fallen away.[134] Its raison d'être, after all, had been the fact that not all agreements beget an action. The usus modernus, however, by and large, lacked the boldness to draw the dogmatic consequences of this insight. A new vision of contractual liability was required. It was provided by the natural lawyers.

4. Domat and Pothier

In France, Jean Domat was the great initiator. In his main work, *"Les loix civiles dans leur ordre naturel"*, he developed his ideas with such an elegance and clarity that they became, via Pothier and the code civil, the basis of modern French contract law. Contract for Domat—as for most of the other natural lawyers—was of cardinal importance within human society:

> "*L'usage des conventions est une suite naturelle de l'ordre de la societé civile, et des liaisons que Dieu forme entre les hommes. Car comme il a rendu nécessaire pour tous leurs besoins, l'usage réciproque de leur industrie et de leur travail, et les différens commerces des choses; c'est principalement par les conventions qu'ils s'en accommodent.*"[135]

Pufendorf had put it similarly: contract is the vehicle for the exchange of goods which is necessary (and thus natural) in view of the innate

---

[131] Cf. e.g. Duarenus and Donellus, as discussed by Nanz, *Vertragsbegriff*, pp. 78 sqq. On the attitude of the glossators and commentators and of the authors of the usus modernus, cf. Nanz, *Vertragsbegriff*, pp. 44 sqq., 93 sq., 130 sqq.

[132] The general term for agreement in the medieval English common law was "covenant".

[133] *Tractatus de pactis*, Cap. I, 1 sqq. (A translation of this tractatus into Afrikaans by L.J. du Plessis has recently (1985) appeared.)

[134] Cf. e.g. Struve, *Syntagma*, Exercit. VI, Lib. II, Tit. XIV, 32; Stryk, *Usus modernus pandectarum*, Lib. II, Tit. XIV, §§ 4, 7; Voet, *Commentarius ad Pandectas*, Lib. II, Tit. XIV, IX;

[135] Liv. I, Introduction.

human imbecillitas.[136] The central significance attached to the law of contract led Domat to place it, very prominently, at the beginning of his new system of private law. *"Des Conventions en général"* is the first title of the first book of the Loix civiles, and at the outset the following definition is provided:

> *"Les conventions sont les engagements qui se forment par le consentement mutuel de deux ou plusieurs personnes qui se font entr'eux une loi d'exécuter ce qu'ils promettent."*[137]

The latter part of this phrase takes up a statement by Papinian (D. 50, 17, 23: "legem enim contractus dedit")[138] and is typical of Domat's attitude towards Roman law. He tried to avail himself of as much of the material contained in the Digest as possible, and regarded as his main task the elimination of those *"subtilitez"*, *"qui ne sont pas de notre usage"* and which had prevented the principles of Roman law from being entirely consonant with the precepts of the *"équité naturelle"*.[139] One of these subtleties which obviously had to be rejected was the Roman scheme of contracts; but, on the other hand, the Roman concept of consensus could be used as a constitutive element for a generalized law of contract. Hence: *"Les conventions s'accomplissent par le consentement mutuel donné et arrêté réciproquement."*[140] Domat did not analyse the concept of consensus any further. This was done only by Pothier, who distinguished offer and acceptance:

> *"Le contrat renferme le concours des volontés de deux personnes, dont l'une promet quelque chose à l'autre, et l'autre accepte la promesse qui lui est faite."*[141]

5. Grotius, Pufendorf and Wolff

In the other countries of central Europe consensus acquired an even greater importance, since here it had been able to emancipate itself entirely from causa as another requirement for the validity of contracts. On the other hand, however, the development took a peculiar detour. For the fundamental category in Grotius' system of natural law was neither contract (or conventio) nor consensus, but the (unilateral)

---

[136] *De jure naturae et gentium*, Lib. II, Cap. III, § 14; Lib. III, Cap. IV, § 1. For further details cf. Hans Welzel, *Die Naturrechtslehre Samuel Pufendorfs* (1958) (e.g. pp. 43 sqq.); Notker Hammerstein, "Samuel Pufendorf", in: M. Stolleis (ed.), *Staatsdenker im 17. und 18. Jahrhundert* (1977), pp. 174 sqq., 180 sqq.

[137] Liv. I, Introduction.

[138] Cf. also supra, p. 540.

[139] On Roman law as *"raison écrite"* and Domat's views in that regard cf. Jean Gaudemet, "Les tendances à l'unification du droit en France dans les derniers siècles de l'Ancien Régime (XVIe–XVIIIe)", in: *La formazione storica*, vol. I, pp. 179 sqq.; Klaus Luig, "Der Geltungsgrund des römischen Rechts im 18. Jahrhundert in Italien, Frankreich und Deutschland", in: *La formazione storica*, vol. II (1977), pp. 834 sqq. For much more hostile comment, see Christian Thomasius, *Institutiones Jurisprudentiae Divinae Italia* (1702), Lib. II, Cap. XI, 63 ("Hinc distinctiones . . . in nescio quas subspecies obscurissimas, quarum singulae infinitis litigiis inter Jurisconsultos dederunt occasionem ortae sunt"). On Thomasius' attitude towards the Roman law generally, see Wolfgang Ebner, *Kritik des römischen Rechts bei Christian Thomasius* (unpublished Dr. iur. thesis, Frankfurt, 1971).

[140] *Les loix civiles*, Liv. I, Tit. I, 8.

[141] *Traité des obligations*, n. 4.

promise.[142] This was a heritage of scholastic moral theology, where the binding nature of both the promissory oath and the simple promise had been emphasized; breach of faith displeases God and is a sinful deviation from the precepts of honesty and truthfulness.[143] Grotius blended this tradition with man's natural freedom to act or not to act in a specific manner. A binding promise thus has the effect of an "alienatio particulae cuiusdam nostrae libertatis";[144] and such an alienation can ultimately find its legitimation only in the fact that it has been willed by the alienor. On the other hand, however, Grotius also mentioned the requirements of a "signum volendi"[145]—the will to be bound has to find some external manifestation[146]—and of an "acceptatio" on the part of the promisee.[147,148] It was Pufendorf who installed the pactum (as opposed to the promissio) as the central category of the systematic endeavours of the natural lawyers,[149] and it was Christian Wolff who rounded off the development by introducing the modern term *"Vertrag"*.[150] Wolff also emphasized consensus as basis and reason for the contractual obligation and defined it as "volitio, ut fiat, vel non fiat, quod alter fieri vel non fieri vult".[151] Pufendorf, in so far as he was thinking along the lines mapped out by Grotius, had still required two "consents", one on the part of each of the parties to the contract: "Ut

---

[142] Cf. in particular Malte Diesselhorst, *Die Lehre des Hugo Grotius vom Versprechen* (1959); Nanz, *Vertragsbegriff*, pp. 139 sqq. Cf. also § 861 ABGB; for a general evaluation of the influences of the Roman ius commune and of natural law in the contract law of the ABGB, cf. Gunter Wesener, "Naturrechtliche und römisch-gemeinrechtliche Elemente im Vertragsrecht des ABGB", 1984 *ZNR* 113 sqq.

[143] For details of the tradition on which Grotius built (particularly Molina and Lessius), cf. Diesselhorst, *Hugo Grotius*, pp. 4 sqq., 10 sqq., 39 sqq.

[144] *De jure belli ac pacis*, Lib. II, Cap. XI, 4. Cf. also *Inleiding*, III, I, 1 and 12; see further Okko Behrends, "Treu und Glauben, Zu den christlichen Grundlagen der Willenstheorie im heutigen Vertragsrecht", in: L.L. Vallauri, G. Dilcher (eds.), *Christentum, Säkularisation und modernes Recht*, vol. II (1981), pp. 964 sqq.

[145] *De jure belli ac pacis*, Lib. II, Cap. XI, 3 and 4.

[146] Reason: ". . . nudis animis actibus efficientiam juris tribuere non fuerat congruum naturae humanae, quae nisi ex signis actus cognoscere non potest": *De jure belli ac pacis*, Lib. II, Cap. IV, 3.

[147] *De jure belli ac pacis*, Lib. II, Cap. XI, 14; cf. also *Inleiding*, III, I, 10: "Toezegging noemen wy een willighe daed eens mensches waer door hy aan een ander iet belooft, met meninghe dat den ander het zelve aennemen ende daer door op den belover eenig recht zal mogen verkrijgen." For details, see Diesselhorst, *Hugo Grotius*, pp. 106 sqq., 111 sqq.

[148] The question has recently been asked whether Grotius' view of contract as the sum of two unilaterally binding promises does not reflect the psychological realities much better than the "mystification" of a consensus: Eugen Bucher, "Für mehr Aktionendenken", (1986) 186 *Archiv für die civilistische Praxis* 21.

[149] *De jure naturae et gentium*, e.g. Lib. III, Cap. IV; cf. further Malte Diesselhorst, *Zum Vermögensrechtssystem Samuel Pufendorfs* (1976); Lipp, op. cit., note 105, pp. 141 sqq.; Nanz, *Vertragsbegriff*, pp. 149 sqq.

[150] *Grundsätze des Natur- und Völckerrechts* (Halle, 1754), § 438; Nanz, *Vertragsbegriff*, pp. 165 sqq. The term *"Vertrag"*, incidentally, is derived from *"sich vertragen"*, which means as much as to agree, to make peace, to be reconciled (with each other) and thus has connotations vaguely similar to the Latin "pactum".

[151] *Institutiones* § 27; cf. also Mayer-Maly, "Die Bedeutung des Konsenses", op. cit., note 105, pp. 98 sq.

promissio sit valida, requiri non solum consensum ejus, qui promittit, sed et ejus, cui promittitur."[152] Obviously, therefore, in terms of Pufendorf's analysis, the conclusion of a contract is dependent upon an act of volition on the part of both parties concerned. Apart from that, however, it is also necessary that these "actu[s] voluntatis . . . signis . . . manifestantur".[153] As a result, we have two declarationes voluntatis as essential elements for the formation of the contract. This analysis of contract in terms of two (coinciding) declarations of intention *("Willenserklärungen")*[154] was ultimately merged with Wolff's consensual theory of contract and became one of the legacies of natural law to the modern law of contract.[155,156]

6. Formation of contract in English law

(a) England and Continental legal science

This influence was not confined to the European continent. The history of the law of contract provides ample support for a thesis crisply stated by Edmund Burke in the words: "The Laws of all the nations of Europe are derived from the same sources."[157] It is in this spirit that William Strahan set about translating Domat's *Loix civiles* into English: it contains "all the Fundamental Maxims of Law and Equity, which must be the same in all countries".[158] It is in this spirit, too, that in 19th-century Britain treatises became the typical form of legal

---

[152] *De jure naturae et gentium*, Lib. III, Cap. VI, § 15.

[153] *De jure naturae et gentium*, Lib. III, Cap. VI, § 16.

[154] The doctrine of *"Willenserklärung"* (declaratio voluntatis) owes much to Wolfgang Adam Lauterbach; cf. his *Disputatio de voluntate*, as discussed by Mayer-Maly, "Die Bedeutung des Konsenses", op. cit., note 105, pp. 97 sq. and *Festschrift Seidl*, pp. 126 sq. Generally on the history of this concept, see Siegmund Schlossmann, "Willenserklärung und Rechtsgeschäft. Kritisches und Dogmengeschichtliches", in: *Festgabe der Kieler Juristen-Fakultät für Hänel* (1907), pp. 48 sqq.; Hermann Dilcher, "Die Willenserklärung nach dem preussischen ALR 'frei, ernstlich und zuverlässig' ", in: *Gedächtnisschrift für Hermann Conrad* (1979), pp. 85 sqq.

[155] Savigny dealt with the concept of contract and all questions relating to its formation within the general part of his system of private law (on the idea of a "general part" cf. supra, p. 31); he thus detached it from the law of obligations. Cf., for example, *System*, vol. III, pp. 7, 310, and Hammen, *Savigny*, pp. 95 sqq. This is also the approach adopted in the BGB which includes in book one its rules both on declarations of intention (*Willenserklärungen*; §§ 116 sqq. BGB), and on contracts (*Verträge*; §§ 145 sqq. BGB). Book two (containing the law of obligations) commences only with § 241. On the reasons cf. "Motive", in: *Mugdan*, vol. I, p. 422. The generic term, covering both *"Willenserklärung"* and *"Vertrag"* is that of *"Rechtsgeschäft"* (legal act); cf. the title of Book I, section III (§§ 104–185 BGB). On the history of this concept cf. Flume, *AT*, pp. 23 sqq., 28 sqq.; Hattenhauer, op. cit., note 105, pp. 58 sqq.

[156] In recent times, the concept of contractual liability based on consent has been questioned; cf., as far as England is concerned, Atiyah, *Rise and Fall*, passim, e.g. pp. 716 sqq.; for Germany cf. e.g. the discussion by Eugen Dietrich Graue, "Vertragsschluss durch Konsens?", in: G. Jakobs (ed.), *Rechtsgeltung und Konsens* (1975), pp. 105 sqq.

[157] Cf. Harold J. Berman, *Law and Revolution* (1983), p. 18.

[158] The translator's preface, p. X.

writing.[159] This is well illustrated by the first English monograph that can properly be called a legal treatise, Sir William Jones's essay on the *Law of Bailments* (1781). In the introduction to this work, Jones sets out his plan of work as follows:

> "I propose to begin with treating the subject analytically, and, having traced every part of it up to the first principles of natural reason, shall proceed historically, to show with what perfect harmony these principles are recognized and established by other nations, especially the Romans, as well as by our English Courts, when their decisions are properly understood and clearly distinguished. . . ."[160]

Significantly, it was a branch of the law of contract that was first subjected to this treatment; and in a sense, therefore, Jones's book heralded the era of innovation into which the English contract law was about to enter.[161] The stress on principles, as Atiyah has pointed out, was an important element in contemporary intellectual ideals.[162] Thus, in the law of contract the emphasis shifted from the traditional method of jumbling around individual precedents to a systematic exposition of general principles. Hence the need for books which dealt with the law of contract as a whole. These textbooks were written by scholars who were usually well versed in Roman law. They created the modern general law of contract,[163] and in doing this, they were

> "engaged upon an enterprise which was new to the common law . . . but old to the civilian tradition; they were trying to do what the civilians, the canonists and the natural lawyers had been doing for centuries".[164]

It is hardly surprising, therefore, that they borrowed heavily from that civilian tradition: from Roman law, from Domat, Grotius and Pufendorf, from Pothier and from Savigny. Domat's, Grotius' and Pufendorf's main works were all available in English translation by the end of the 18th century. Pothier's *Traité des obligations* was made accessible to English lawyers by W.D. Evans in 1806 and it soon became one of the most influential sources of modern English contract law. The high esteem in which Pothier's clear and eminently readable exposition of the law was held not only by academic writers but also by the English courts can perhaps best be gauged from the extravagant remark by Best J, in *Cox v. Troy*: "[T]he authority of Pothier . . . is as high as can be had, next to the decision of a Court of Justice in this

[159] Cf. especially A.W.B. Simpson, "The Rise and Fall of the Legal Treatise: Legal Principles and the Forms of Legal Literature", (1981) 48 *University of Chicago LR* 632 sqq.

[160] At p. 4.

[161] Cf. the analysis of A.W.B. Simpson, "Innovation in Nineteenth Century Contract Law", (1975) 91 *LQR* 247 sqq.

[162] *Rise and Fall*, p. 345. Cf. also at pp. 388 sqq., where the rise of formalism and, in conjunction with it, principle-orientation is discussed.

[163] Atiyah, *Rise and Fall*, pp. 398 sqq., 681 sqq.

[164] Simpson, (1975) 91 *LQR* 254.

country."[165] A translation of the first part of Savigny's *System des heutigen römischen Rechts* was published only in 1867[166] and came perhaps too late to exercise an equally profound influence on the development of English contract law. Sir Frederick Pollock (the first edition of whose treatise on the law of contract appeared eight years after Holloway's translation), in particular, however, relied heavily on Savigny.[167]

(b) The analysis of contract

If we look at the formation of contract, most modern textbooks analyse it in terms of offer and acceptance, an intention to create legal relations and the doctrine of consideration. All three requirements appear to be deeply engrained in the English common law. And yet, it is only the doctrine of consideration that has been an integral part of it for a considerable period of time; it evolved, as we have seen, in the 16th century,[168] and was closely related to the emergence of the action of assumpsit.

The analysis of contract as a legal transaction formed by offer and acceptance, was superimposed upon the doctrine of consideration in the course of the 19th century by treatise-writers such as Powell and Chitty, Pollock and Anson.[169] Essentially, they adopted the civilian doctrine as it had been developed by Grotius and Pufendorf, and as they had found it in Pothier. Judicial recognition came as early as 1818, in the famous case of *Adams v. Lindsell.*[170]

The third of the above-mentioned criteria serves to distinguish legal arrangements from extralegal, merely social ones. If—as was supposed—all contractual obligations are the product of the joint wills of the contracting parties, it does not follow—conversely—that every agreement must necessarily be legally enforceable. Whether or not an agreement should have any legal consequences must depend, in turn, on the intention of the parties.

> "If people make arrangements to go out for a walk or to read a book together, that is no agreement in a legal sense. Why not? Because their intention is not directed to

---

[165] (1822) 5 B & Ald 474 at 480. For further details concerning the reception of Pothier in England and (via England) South Africa, cf. Reinhard Zimmermann, "Der Einfluss Pothiers auf das römisch-holländische Recht in Südafrika", (1985) 102 *ZSS* (GA) 168 sqq., 176 sqq.

[166] *System of the Modern Roman Law*, translated by W. Holloway.

[167] "Considering the amount of coincidence (if not more than coincidence) between English and Roman law in the main principles of Contract, I have felt justified in making a pretty free use of the Roman law for purposes of illustration and analogy. . . . On points of Roman law (and to a considerable extent, indeed, on the principles it has in common with our own) I have consulted and generally followed Savigny's great work." (*Principles of Contract at Law and in Equity* (1st ed.), foreword).

[168] Cf. supra, pp. 554 sqq.

[169] Simpson, (1975) 91 *LQR* 258 sqq.; Atiyah, *Rise and Fall*, pp. 446 sqq.

[170] (1818) 1 B & Ald 681. Cf. also Stefan A. Riesenfeld, "The Impact of Roman Law on the Common Law Systems", (1985) 1 *Lesotho LJ* 269 sqq.

legal consequences, but merely to extralegal ones; no rights or duties are to be created."[171]

Hence the doctrine that a legally binding agreement must be accompanied by a joint intention of the parties to create legal relations.[172] Pollock took it over from Savigny,[173] but its civilian pedigree dates back, far beyond Pothier and Pufendorf, to the writings of the glossators.[174] In *Carlill v. Carbolic Smoke Ball Company*,[175] the new dogma received the stamp of judicial approval.

7. Contract and pollicitatio

(a) From promise to contract

Even more important, however, than the reception of these and other individual doctrines was the fact that in the course of the 19th-century contract emerged as the essential systematic cornerstone of the law of obligations. Contractual obligations, it was now argued, were those arising from voluntary acts of the will.[176] Everything that did not fall within the purview of contract was either tort or quasi-contract. Yet, traditionally, the common law had been primarily concerned with promissory liability[177] (as had indeed been continental canon law). It had grown up around the action of assumpsit,[178] a remedy for breach of promise.[179] Promise and breach of promise are essentially one-sided notions, and they were now replaced by an essentially two-sided conception.[180] As a consequence of this, unilateral acts, particularly the promise of a reward, were now bound to give rise to severe doctrinal headaches. Here we come, once again, across the ever-memorable smoke ball case.[181]

---

[171] Frederick Pollock, *Principles of Contract at Law and in Equity* (1876), p. 2.

[172] Simpson, (1975) 91 *LQR* 263 sqq.

[173] *System*, vol. III, § 140.

[174] Cf. supra, pp. 559 sq.

[175] [1893] 1 QB 256 (CA); on this aspect of the smoke ball case, see Simpson, (1985) 14 *Journal of Legal Studies* 375 sqq. Cf. further especially *Heilbut, Symons & Co. v. Buckleton* [1913] AC 30 (HL).

[176] Cf. e.g. Kindersley VC in *Haynes v. Haynes* (1861) 1 Dr & Sm 426 at 433: "When both parties will the same thing, and each communicates his will to the other, with a mutual agreement to carry it into effect, then an engagement or contract between the two is constituted"; Atiyah, *Rise and Fall*, pp. 405 sqq. (esp. p. 407).

[177] Cf. e.g. Simpson, (1975) 91 *LQR* 257 sqq.

[178] On the connection between canon law (laesio fidei) and the growth of assumpsit, see R.H. Helmholz, "Assumpsit and Fidei Laesio", (1975) 91 *LQR* 406 sqq. On the emergence and rise of the action of assumpsit generally, see A.W.B. Simpson, *History*, passim.

[179] Simpson, *History*, pp. 248 sqq.

[180] Simpson, (1975) 91 *LQR* 257.

[181] For a recreation "of the historical background and significance of this landmark in the history of contract law and its relationship to the seedy world of the late nineteenth-century vendors of patent medical appliances", cf. A.W.B. Simpson, "Quackery and Contract Law: The Case of the Carbolic Smoke Ball", (1985) 14 *Journal of Legal Studies* 345 sqq. The brief account that follows in the text is based on Simpson's analysis.

(b) The smoke ball case

A certain Frederick Augustus Roe had invented the carbolic smoke ball as a ". . . Device for Facilitating the Distribution, Inhalation and Application of Medicated and Other Powder". In the wake of the great influenza epidemic that swept through England in the winter of 1889–90, he began to market it as being able to "positively cure Influenza, Catarrh, Asthma, Bronchitis, Hay Fever, Neuralgia, Throat Deafness, Hoarseness, Loss of Voice, Whooping Cough, Croup, Coughs, Colds, and all other ailments caused by Taking Cold". A massive promotion campaign was launched, in the course of which an advertisement was placed in the *Pall Mall Gazette* of 13 November 1891, promising a reward of 100 Pounds Sterling to be paid by the Carbolic Smoke Ball Co.

> "to any person who contracts . . . Influenza, Colds, or any diseases caused by taking cold, after having used the ball 3 times daily for two weeks according to the printed directions supplied with each Ball".

Mrs. Carlill saw the advertisement, purchased a smoke ball and diligently snuffed and sneezed three times daily for two weeks. Despite all her exertions, she contracted influenza shortly afterwards. When she claimed the 100 Pounds Sterling promised, Roe refused to pay. Legal proceedings were instituted,[182] in the course of which a verdict was given in favour of Mrs. Carlill[183] and upheld on appeal.[184] The background story to this case, which has recently been unfolded, is full of interesting and amusing details. The crucial point, however, in our context, is that the court did not regard the promise of the reward as such as binding. It tried to fit the decision into the new doctrinal framework and declared that the reward could be claimed only on the basis of a "unilateral" contract. Like all contracts, it required the exchange of offer and acceptance. Consequently, the advertisement was taken to constitute an offer (ad incertas personas), which Mrs. Carlill had, in turn, accepted by performing the act specified therein. It can hardly be denied that this extension of the concept of acceptance (which need not be communicated to the offeror) is a somewhat strained construction.[185]

(c) "Auslobung" and pollicitatio

Yet, by attempting to reconcile these types of cases with (what had by then become) orthodox contractual theory, the English common law has been more rigid and dogmatic than some of the modern civilian

---

[182] The defence was led by H.H. Asquith, Q.C., who became Home Secretary shortly afterwards, and later Prime Minister (1908–1916).

[183] [1892] 2 QB 484; the trial was before Hawkins J ("assisted by his fox terrier Jack, which always sat on the bench with him": Simpson, (1985) 14 *Journal of Legal Studies* 362).

[184] [1893] 1 QB 256.

[185] Simpson, (1985) 14 *Journal of Legal Studies* 378.

jurisdictions themselves. In the German Civil Code, special provision is made for the promise of a reward.[186] It is known as *"Auslobung"*,[187] a unilateral act, which does not require acceptance. Whoever performs the condition of the reward is entitled to claim, whether he knew of the promise and acted with a view to the reward or not. Contrary to the prevailing opinion under the ius commune,[188] the BGB does therefore not regard *"Auslobung"* as a contract;[189] we are dealing here with one of those rare exceptions to the general principle of § 305, according to which for the creation of an obligation by legal transaction a contract between the parties is necessary.[190]

It is interesting to observe that the South African courts have not seen their way open to adopt a similar approach.[191] They have come to the same conclusion as the English courts and therefore had to dismiss—reluctantly[192]—the claim of a certain Mr. Bloom who had performed the act (for which a reward had been publicly announced) without, however, having had any knowledge of this offer of reward. Since under these circumstances he could not have intended to accept anything, no contract had come into existence; and as a result of this, no legal tie had been established between the parties.[193] This solution may be inconvenient and unsatisfactory but it cannot be described as wrong from a historical point of view; for a general institution of a promise of reward constituting a unilaterally binding legal act can be found in neither the Roman nor the classical Roman-Dutch sources.[194] Pollicitatio is probably the closest we get. But although this was indeed an informal, unilateral promise that was enforceable in the cognitio extra ordinem,[195] it was a far cry from a promise of reward à la §§ 657 sqq. BGB.[196] Firstly, the pollicitatio was made for the benefit of the promisor's municipality, that is, of a specific (public) body, whereas it is a characteristic feature of the promise of reward that a specific addressee does not in fact exist; it is a promise ad incertas personas. And secondly, the institution of pollicitatio was designed exclusively to serve the public interest; only as far as the promise of gifts or

[186] § 657 BGB.

[187] This term is of very recent origin (second half of the 19th century) and has not managed to establish itself in popular parlance; cf. Hans Hermann Seiler, in: *Münchener Kommentar*, vol. III, 2 (2nd ed., 1986), § 657, n. 1.

[188] "Contractual theory": cf. e.g. Vangerow, § 603, n. 2; Windscheid/Kipp, § 308.

[189] "Motive", in: *Mugdan*, vol. II, p. 290.

[190] Jost Wiechmann, *Der Ausschluss des Rechtsweges bei den öffentlichen Belohnungsversprechen* (1987), pp. 56 sqq.

[191] *Bloom v. The American Swiss Watch Company* 1915 AD 100.

[192] *Bloom's* case at 107 (per De Villiers AJA).

[193] *Bloom's* case at 103 (per Innes CJ).

[194] Karlheinz Dreiocker, *Zur Dogmengeschichte der Auslobung* (unpublished Dr. iur. thesis, Kiel, 1969), pp. 10 sqq., 65 sqq.

[195] Cf. supra, p. 496.

[196] In favour of a close historical connection, cf. Rudolf Düll, "Auslobung und Fund im antiken Recht", (1941) 61 *ZSS* 19 sqq. But see Dreiocker, op. cit., note 194, pp. 16 sqq.

performances of work "propter communem utilitatem" were concerned, was one prepared to deviate from general principles (that is, from the requirement of consensus). Promises of reward, on the other hand, are not thus confined; it is usually the promisor's private interest that dominates. All this is not to say that no private rewards were promised in Roman times. On the contrary: we find a variety of examples in Roman literature as well as, for instance, in inscriptions on walls and necklaces of slaves.[197] Characteristically, however, they were not treated as pollicitationes, but seem, by and large, to have remained extra-legal phenomena.[198]

(d) *Pollicitatio and contractual liability*

How does pollicitatio fit into the modern system of contractual liability, as designed, essentially, by the natural lawyers? Grotius, as we have seen, required acceptance in order that a promise may transfer a right.[199] Consequently, neither promissio nor pollicitatio was able to confer (iure naturali) a right upon another person to compel performance. Grotius' subtle distinction between promissio and pollicitatio[200] tended to be dropped by later writers,[201] but whether one identified the two or not, the result remained the same: "jus proprium alteri non dat".[202] This view, shared, as far as Roman-Dutch law is concerned, by Voet[203] and others, prevailed in most civilian systems down to the 19th century;[204] via Pufendorf and Pothier, it filtered through into the English common law. Pothier, as usual, stated the conceptual distinctions most clearly. A contract includes the concurrence of intention in two parties, one of whom promises something to the other, who on his part accepts such promise. A pollicitatio, on the other hand, is a promise not yet accepted by the person to whom it is made. *"[A]ux termes du pur droit naturel"*, it does not produce, without

---

[197] Cf. Dreiocker, op. cit., note 194, pp. 40 sqq. Cf., for example, Petronius, *Satiricon*, XCVII, 2: "Puer in balneo paulo ante aberravit, annorum circa XVI, crispus, mollis, formosus, nomine Giton. Si quis eum reddere aut commonstrare voluerit, accipiet nummos mille."

[198] Kaser, *RPr* I, p. 604.

[199] Cf. supra, p. 568, note 147.

[200] A promissio, according to Grotius, was designed, if accepted, to confer a ius upon another person; the person who uttered a pollicitatio, on the other hand, did not contemplate such a transfer of a right; cf. *De jure belli ac pacis*, Lib. II, Cap. XI, 3 sq. and Lib. II, Cap. XI, XIV. Pufendorf (*De iure naturae et gentium*, Lib. III, Cap. V, 6) describes pollicitatio as an "imperfecta promissio". Cf. also Geoffrey MacCormack, "A Note on Stair's Use of the Term Pollicitatio", 1976 *Juridical Review* 124.

[201] Cf., for example, Voet, *Commentarius ad Pandectas*, Lib. L, Tit. XII, I ("Pollicitatio est solius offerentis promissio").

[202] *De jure belli ac pacis*, Lib. II, Cap. XI, 3.

[203] *Commentarius ad Pandectas*, Lib. L, Tit. XII (listing, however, a considerable number of exceptions to the principle).

[204] T.B. Smith, "Pollicitatio—Promise and Offer", in: idem, *Studies Critical and Comparative* (1962), pp. 168 sqq.; cf. also Coing, p. 408.

such acceptance, what can properly be called an obligation.[205] This exposition (based; as it was on Ulp. D. 50, 12, 3)[206] became the basis of the English doctrine of offer and acceptance.[207] A pollicitation is "a promise made but not accepted";[208] but only an accepted promise can give rise to a (contractual) obligation.

The concept of pollicitatio as a unilateral but binding promise was revived in Germany only in the course of the 19th century. Somewhat surprisingly, the so-called *"Pollizitationstheorie"*[209] was, as we have seen, accepted by the drafters of the BGB.[210] In Scotland, the same view had already gained ground much earlier, since Viscount Stair in his *Institutions of the Law of Scotland* had refused to follow Grotius in this respect; in his view, an absolute promise which does not contemplate acceptance is enforceable as such.[211] Sir Percival Gane's suggestion that pollicitatio may yet figure prominently in South African law has thus far not been taken up. "It is curious", Gane wrote in 1957,[212]

> "that in a country in which promises to public concerns and civic bodies are not uncommon, and promises to religious bodies very common, more use has not been made of this title [sc. D. 50, 12 De pollicitationibus]."

It goes to show that the civilian doctrine of offer and acceptance in its inflexible English form still reigns supreme in this part of the world.

IV. PACTA SUNT SERVANDA

1. Pacta sunt servanda and classical contract doctrine

A final word on pacta sunt servanda. We have seen how the praetor's promise, as related by Ulpian in D. 2, 14, 7, 7, was turned into this general maxim by the canon lawyers.[213] Its import was, first of all, to assert the principle of consensualism: all pacts are binding, regardless of whether they are clothed or naked. However, once this principle had generally gained acceptance, the significance of "pacta sunt servanda" shifted slightly. The maxim was now taken to imply that contractual

---

205 *Traité des obligations*, n. 4.

206 "Pactum est duorum consensus atque conventio, pollicitatio vero offerentis solius promissum."

207 Simpson, (1975) 91 *LQR* 259.

208 John Austin, *Lectures on Jurisprudence*, vol. II (1885), p. 906.

209 Cf. e.g. Dernburg, *Pandekten*, vol. II, § 9; Arndts, *Pandekten*, § 241; Baron, *Pandekten*, § 211.

210 § 657 BGB.

211 *Institutions of the Law of Scotland* (4th ed.), vol. I (1826), Book I, Tit. X, IV; T. B. Smith, op. cit., note 204, pp. 168 sqq., 173 sqq.; cf. also D.I.C. Ashton Cross, "Bare Promise in Scots Law", (1957) 2 *Juridical Review* 138 sqq. There is considerable confusion as to the use of the terms "promissio" and "pollicitatio" by Stair; cf. Alan Rodger, "Molina, Stair and the Jus Quaesitum Tertio", 1969 *Juridical Review* 130 sqq.; MacCormack, 1976 *Juridical Review* 121 sqq.

212 Percival Gane, *The Selective Voet*, vol. VII (1957), Book L, Title 12, translator's note.

213 Cf. supra, p. 543.

promises must under all circumstances be honoured.[214] Thus, it became the hallowed basis of "classical" contract doctrine.

> "[I]f there is one thing which more than another public policy requires it is that men of full age and competent understanding shall have the utmost liberty of contracting, and that their contracts when entered into freely and voluntarily shall be held sacred and shall be enforced by Courts of justice. Therefore, you have this paramount public policy to consider—that you are not lightly to interfere with this freedom of contract."

This statement of Sir George Jessel MR[215] is representative of the attitude prevailing in the 19th century.[216] Everybody is free to decide whether he wants to enter into a contract or not *("Abschlussfreiheit")*, and it is up to the parties to determine the content of their transaction *("Inhaltsfreiheit")*.[217] Such content, of course, may not be illegal or immoral. But apart from that, there is no judicial interference. In particular, the validity of a contract does not depend on the (objective) adequacy of consideration. Equality in the values exchanged is immaterial. It is for the parties to make their bargain, not for the courts. The courts are merely concerned with the fairness of the bargaining *process*, the assumption being that the result of fair negotiations is likely to be substantially fair too. Hence, for instance, the defences of fraud, misrepresentation and duress. But once it has been established that the formation of the contract has not been affected by these kinds of cognitive weaknesses,[218] the parties are bound by their agreement. This was the principle in Roman law, where fides demanded that a man must keep his word.[219] Unilateral denunciation of a contract was therefore, in general, excluded. The canon lawyers, of course, eagerly reasserted the moral precept of faithfulness requiring that a promise must be honoured; and so did, under more secular auspices, the natural lawyers.

---

[214] Cf. e.g. Robert Feenstra/Margreet Ahsmann, *Contract* (1980), p. 21.
[215] *Printing and Numerical Registering Company v. Sampson* (1875) LR 19 Eq 462 at 465.
[216] Cf. e.g. Atiyah, *Rise and Fall*, pp. 398 sqq.; idem, "Contract and Fair Exchange", in: P.S. Atiyah, *Essays on Contract* (1986), pp. 329 sqq.; Arthur van Mehren, "A General View of Contract", in: *International Encyclopedia of Comparative Law*, vol. VII, 1 (1982), nn. 72 sqq.; Ludwig Raiser, "Vertragsfunktion und Vertragsfreiheit", in: *Hundert Jahre deutsches Rechtsleben, Festschrift zum 100jährigen Bestehen des Deutschen Juristentages*, vol. I (1960), pp. 101 sqq.; Franz Wieacker, *Industriegesellschaft und Privatrechtsordnung*, passim; Dieter Grimm, "Soziale, wirtschaftliche und politische Voraussetzungen der Vertragsfreiheit, Eine vergleichende Skizze", in: *La formazione storica*, vol. III, pp. 1221 sqq.; Günther Hönn, *Kompensation gestörter Vertragsparität* (1982), pp. 5 sqq., 18 sqq.; Ernst Kramer, in: *Münchener Kommentar*, vol. I (2nd ed., 1984), Vor § 145, nn. 2 sqq.
[217] Cf. e.g. Werner Scherrer, *Die geschichtliche Entwicklung des Prinzips der Vertragsfreiheit* (1948), pp. 31 sqq.
[218] Cf. Atiyah, *Essays on Contract*, op. cit., note 216, p. 330; or, in modern civilian parlance, defects of the will (cf. e.g. Honsell/Mayer-Maly/Selb, p. 119; Flume, *AT*, § 19).
[219] Cf. e.g. Schulz, *Principles*, pp. 223 sqq.

2. The right of unilateral withdrawal from a contract

But the principle of pacta sunt servanda was never carried through without exception.[220] Even in Roman law not every contract was binding absolutely and under all circumstances. A contract of locatio conductio rei, for instance, could unilaterally be terminated by the lessee if the lessor failed to comply with his duties.[221] Likewise, the lessor could expel the lessee in certain situations, for instance, if the latter did not pay his rent.[222] A contract of mandatum came to an end if the mandator revoked the contract, and probably also if the mandatarius renounced it.[223] A societas could be terminated at any time by any of the socii by simple renuntiatio.[224] And even a contract of sale could be unilaterally cancelled by the purchaser, albeit only when the requirements of the actio redhibitoria were met.[225] Later on the emperors gave the vendor a right to rescind a contract of sale if he had sold a tract of land for less than half its true value (laesio enormis).[226] As far as the innominate real contracts were concerned, we have seen that their binding character was undermined by virtue of the fact that the condictio causa data causa non secuta remained available.[227] In effect, therefore, once he had rendered performance himself, a party to an innominate real contract had the right at any time to cancel the arrangement. This jus poenitendi (as it came to be called)[228] featured prominently whenever in the centuries after the reception of Roman law in Europe the exact confines of the principle of pacta sunt servanda were discussed.[229] Down to the 19th century, there was support for its retention.[230] Other authors had realized, however, that the application of special rules for innominate real contracts did not make sense once the enforceability of all pacta (nuda) had become generally recognized;[231] and as far as both the nominate contracts of Roman law and the pacta in general were concerned, most civilian writers, true to the Roman tradition, continued to deny the parties a general right of

---

[220] For an overview cf., in particular, A. Steinwenter, "Die Vertragstreue im bürgerlichen Recht", 1950 *Juristische Blätter* 173 sqq.
[221] Cf. supra, p. 356.
[222] Cf. supra, p. 356.
[223] Cf. supra, p. 425, note 90.
[224] Cf. supra, p. 455.
[225] Cf. supra, pp. 317 sq., 318 sq.
[226] Cf. supra, pp. 259 sqq.
[227] Cf. supra, p. 537.
[228] Scherner, *Rücktrittsrecht*, pp. 23 sqq.; Coing, p. 404. On paenitentia in Roman law, cf. e.g. Berger, *ED*, p. 616.
[229] Cf. e.g. Scherner, *Rücktrittsrecht*, pp. 18 sqq.
[230] Scherner, *Rücktrittsrecht*, p. 27.
[231] Cf. e.g. Samuel Stryk, *Usus modernus pandectarum*, Lib. II, Tit. XIV, § 5; Augustin Leyser, *Meditationes ad Pandectas*, Spec. XXXIX, VII. Cf. further Coing, p. 404.

unilateral withdrawal.[232] Ultimately, however, an important exception was made in cases of what one could summarily term breach of contract. It is not based on Roman sources but was established, first of all, in canon law ("fidem frangenti fides frangitur"),[233] was taken up again by the natural lawyers,[234] and finally found its way into the BGB.[235] Today, further statutory rights of withdrawal from a contract have been granted in the interest of consumer protection.[236]

3. Clausula rebus sic stantibus

(a) Origin and development of the clausula

One of the most interesting, and potentially most dangerous, inroads into pacta sunt servanda has, however, been the so-called clausula rebus sic stantibus: a contract is binding only as long and as far as (literally:) matters remain the same as they were at the time of conclusion of the contract. It is obvious that such a proviso, if broadly interpreted, can be used to erode the binding nature of contractual promises very substantially; not surprisingly, therefore, the clausula doctrine fell into oblivion in the late 18th and the 19th centuries:[237] the heyday of "classical" contractual doctrine when freedom of contract, economic liberalism and certainty of law reigned supreme. The Roman lawyers had not known anything like it either. Moral philosophers were the first to draw attention to the change of circumstances and thus to sow the seed for the clausula rebus sic stantibus. "Omnia esse debent eadem, quae fuerunt, cum promitterem, ut promittentis fidem teneas . . .": this general proposition, which was to be quoted time and again, had originally been formulated by Seneca.[238] Equally influential was the example of the sword which does not have to be returned to a depositor who has become insane. It goes back to Cicero, *De officiis* ("Si gladium quis apud te sana mente deposuerit, repetat insaniens, reddere peccatum sit, officium non reddere"),[239] and was taken up by St. Augustine.[240]

---

[232] For details, cf. Scherner, *Rücktrittsrecht*, passim. A unilateral right of withdrawal from the contract was still rejected by the pandectists: for details, see Leser, *Rücktritt vom Vertrag*, pp. 2 sqq.

[233] Friedrich Merzbacher, "Die Regel 'Fidem frangenti fides frangitur' und ihre Anwendung", (1982) 99 *ZSS* (KA) 339 sqq; further, see Georges Boyer, *Recherches historiques sur la résolution des contrats* (1924), pp. 212 sqq., 235 sqq., 259 sqq.

[234] Scherner, *Rücktrittsrecht*, pp. 92 sqq.; Coing, p. 444.

[235] §§ 325 sq. BGB; for details cf. Leser, *Rücktritt vom Vertrag*, passim. For a comparative analysis cf. G.H. Treitel, "Remedies for Breach of Contract", in: *International Encyclopedia of Comparative Law*, vol. VII, 16 (1976), pp. 110 sqq. and Hans G. Leser, "Lösung vom Vertrag", in: *Recht und Rechtserkenntnis, Festschrift für Ernst Wolf* (1985), pp. 373 sqq.

[236] Cf. § 1 b AbzG (dealing with instalment sales) and § 1 HaustürWG (dealing with door-to-door sales).

[237] Cf. e.g. A.D. Weber, *Systematische Entwicklung der Lehre von der natürlichen Verbindlichkeit* (1784), § 90; for further details, see Leopold Pfaff, "Die Clausel: Rebus sic stantibus in der Doktrin und der österreichischen Gesetzgebung", in: *Festschrift für Joseph Unger* (1898), pp. 272 sqq.

[238] *De beneficiis*, Lib. IV, XXXV, 3. [239] 3, XXV—95.

[240] *Enarrationes in Psalmos*, V, 7.

St. Augustine's text, in turn, was incorporated into the *Decretum Gratiani* (c. Ne quis).[241] It was a gloss to this canon that became the real starting point for the medieval clausula doctrine—for it states quite categorically: ". . . semper subintellegitur haec conditio, si res in eodem statu manserit."[242] "Quod propter novum casum novum datur auxilium" was the reason provided for this assertion.[243] St. Thomas of Aquinas reaffirmed the same position from the point of view of moral theology; for, according to him, the breach of a promise is not a sin "si sint mutatae conditiones personarum et negotiorum".[244] Bartolus introduced the idea of an implied condition "rebus sic se habentibus" into the civil law—confined, however, to the specific legal act of renuntiatio.[245] Baldus extended it to cover all promissiones,[246] and by the end of the 15th century, its field of application was described in the broadest possible terms: in dispositione legum, in ultima voluntate, in contractibus, in privilegiis, in iuramento, in statutis iuratis,[247] or, quite simply, in omnibus actibus vel dispositionibus.[248] For the following three centuries, the doctrine was firmly entrenched; in the words of Augustin Leyser: "Omne pactum, omnis promissio, rebus sic stantibus, intelligenda est, ut Seneca lib. 4 de Beneficiis c. 35 rem clarius explicat."[249] Whether the contract has to be honoured or not depends on the hypothetical will of the parties; for the obligation falls away "si tanta incidat mutatio, ut non amplius pristina rerum facies supererit, atque promissor, si eam praevidisset, pacturus non fuisset". This explains what appears to be, at first blush, a strange coincidence: namely, that the clausula doctrine had been promoted most vigorously by those authors who had also been instrumental in establishing the very principle now qualified by the clausula: pacta sunt servanda. For at

[241] Secunda Pars, Causa XXII, Quaest. II, c. 14.

[242] Johannes Teutonicus, gl. Furens, ad C. 22, q. 2, c. 14. Cf. further Robert Feenstra, "Impossibilitas and Clausula rebus sic stantibus", in: *Daube Noster* (1974), pp. 81 sqq. The wording of the condition is taken from a text by Africanus (D. 46, 3, 38 pr: ". . . si in eodem statu maneat"), which does, however, not deal with the problem in question. The legal construction of the clausula remained that of an implied condition. A very similar construction, incidentally, appears in *Taylor v. Caldwell* (1863) 3 B & S 826, the decision which broke with the principle established in *Paradine v. Jane* (1647) Aleyn 26 and became one of the roots of the modern doctrine of frustration of contract (cf. infra, pp. 582, 817).

[243] Johannes Teutonicus, loc. cit.

[244] *Summa theologiae*, Secunda Secundae, q. 110, art. 3, ad quintum; the general rule is expressed in the following terms: "Si vero non faciat quod promisit, tunc videtur infideliter agere per hoc quod animum mutat."

[245] *Commentaria*, D. 12, 4, 8, § Quod Servius, 3.

[246] *Commentaria* (Venetiis, 1586), ad D. 12, 4, 8.

[247] Yason de Mayno, *Commentaria*, ad D. 12, 4, 8.

[248] Andreas Tiraquellus, as quoted by Pfaff, *Festschrift Unger*, p. 229.

[249] *Meditationes ad Pandectas*, Spec. XL, IV. For a detailed account of the historical development, cf. Pfaff, *Festschrift Unger*, pp. 225 sqq.; O. Fritze, "Clausula rebus sic stantibus", (1900) 17 *Archiv für Bürgerliches Recht* 29 sqq.; cf. also Margarethe Beck-Mannagetta, "Die clausula rebus sic stantibus und die Geschäftsgrundlage in der Dogmengeschichte", in: *La formazione storica*, vol. III, pp. 1263 sqq.

the bottom of both the principle that all pacts are actionable and of its limitation there lies the specific significance attributed by canon lawyers and moral theologians alike to the human will.[250]

(b) The clausula from the 17th century to today

The 17th century was a flowering time for the clausula doctrine (partly, perhaps, in response to the devastating wars of the time)[251] and it became part and parcel of the usus modernus as well as of the systematic endeavours of the natural lawyers.[252] It attained great prominence in the field of public international law,[253] but in the area of private law its star ultimately began to wane. Nineteenth-century legal science was predominantly hostile to it, and the clausula thus disappeared.[254] But the underlying idea had only temporarily lost its attraction. Thrown out by the door, as Windscheid put it,[255] it will always re-enter through the window. The will of a person usually relates to a certain given set of facts only; it has been formed on the basis of certain suppositions. If these turn out to be wrong, it is not always fair to hold that person by his word. On the other hand, however, the promisor's interest in having the contract set aside must be balanced against the interest of the community at large in certainty of the law. Some kind of criterion is therefore needed to attempt to achieve the balance. Windscheid's own *"Voraussetzungslehre"* (doctrine of tacit presupposition) was one such attempt,[256] but it did not commend itself to the drafters of the BGB.[257] The BGB does not, in fact, contain a general rule dealing with the problem of changed circumstances. The modern version of the clausula rebus sic stantibus therefore had to be developed

---

[250] Feenstra/Ahsmann, op. cit., note 214, p. 21.

[251] E.M. Meijers, "Essai historique sur la force majeure", in: *Études d'histoire du droit*, vol. IV (1966), p. 29.

[252] On Grotius' attitude cf. Feenstra, *Daube Noster*, pp. 84 sqq.; Beck-Mannagetta, in: *La formazione storica*, vol. III, pp. 1270 sqq.

[253] Cf. e.g. Pfaff, *Festschrift Unger*, pp. 282 sqq.; Erich Kaufmann, *Das Wesen des Völkerrechts und die clausula rebus sic stantibus* (1911).

[254] Cf. supra, note 237.

[255] "Die Voraussetzung", (1892) 78 *Archiv für die civilistische Praxis* 197.

[256] Windscheid defined the term "presupposition" in terms of an "undeveloped condition": one party wishes the effects of a transaction to be dependent on a certain state of affairs without, however, elevating such presupposition, by way of an express declaration, to the status of a term of the transaction. Such party may refuse to render performance, if his contractual opponent was in a position to gauge, from the circumstances of the transaction, that the presupposition in fact formed an element of his intention. Cf. esp. Bernhard Windscheid, *Die Lehre des römischen Rechts von der Voraussetzung* (1850); idem, in: Windscheid/Kipp, §§ 97 sqq. Contra e.g. Otto Lenel, "Nochmals die Lehre von der Voraussetzung", (1892) 79 *Archiv für die civilistische Praxis* 49 sqq.; cf. also Gerhard Kegel, "Empfielt es sich, den Einfluss grundlegender Veränderungen des Wirtschaftslebens auf Verträge gesetzlich zu regeln und in welchem Sinn?", in: *Verhandlungen des 40. Deutschen Juristentages* (1953), vol. I, pp. 143 sqq; for a recent analysis, cf. Ulrich Falk, *Ein Gelehrter wie Windscheid* (1989), pp. 193 sqq. The notion of "economic" impossibility (cf. e.g. RGZ 100, 129 (130)) may be mentioned as another attempt to cope with the problem of changed circumstances.

[257] "Protokolle", in: *Mugdan*, vol. II, p. 1174. On the clausula cf. "Motive", in: *Mugdan*, vol. II, pp. 109, 471.

extra legem by courts and legal writers; it is the doctrine of "*Wegfall der Geschäftsgrundlage*" (collapse of the underlying basis of the transaction), which was formulated, initially, in response to the problems posed by the consequences of the First World War on the performance of long-term contracts,[258] and which has become part and parcel of the modern German law of contract.[259] Its functional equivalent in English law is the doctrine of frustration of contract.[260]

[258] Paul Oertmann, *Die Geschäftsgrundlage, ein neuer Rechtsbegriff* (1921). On the judicial reception of this doctrine since the famous decision of RGZ 103, 328 sqq., see Bernd Rüthers, *Die unbegrenzte Auslegung* (1973), pp. 40 sqq.

[259] Cf., for example, Karl Larenz, *Geschäftsgrundlage und Vertragserfüllung* (3rd ed., 1963); Malte Diesselhorst, "Die Geschäftsgrundlage in der neueren Rechtsentwicklung", in: U. Immenga (ed.), *Rechtswissenschaft und Rechtsentwicklung* (1980), pp. 153 sqq.; Günther H. Roth, in: *Münchener Kommentar*, vol. II (2nd ed., 1985), § 242, nn. 465 sqq.; for a crisp account of the development cf. also Joachim Meinecke, "Frustration in the West German Law of Contract", (1978) 13 *The Irish Jurist* 83 sqq.

[260] Treitel, *The Law of Contract*, pp. 663 sqq.; on its history, see Kegel, op. cit., note 256, pp. 172 sqq.; for a comparison, cf. Stefan Schmiedlin, *Frustration of Contract und clausula rebus sic stantibus* (1985). The Louisiana Civil Code, interestingly, deals with the problem as being one of an error in motive, which can under certain circumstances constitute a ground for the voidability of contracts: "No error in motive can invalidate a contract, unless the other party was apprised that it was the principal cause of the agreement, or unless from the nature of the transaction it must be presumed that he knew it" (art. 1826). For details, see Timothy Hoff, "Error in the Formation of Contracts in Louisiana: A Comparative Analysis", (1978–79) 53 *Tulane LR* 358 sqq.

CHAPTER 19

Error

1. Error and contractual theory

(a) Cotton ex Peerless

Sometime in the 1860s two ships sailed from Bombay to Liverpool. Both were called *Peerless*. The one had left Bombay in October, the other in December. Meanwhile, back in England, 125 bales of cotton "to arrive ex Peerless from Bombay" had been sold. When the vendor tendered the cotton that had arrived with the December *Peerless*, the purchaser refused to accept it. He had meant and intended, so he alleged, to buy the cotton from the October *Peerless*.

We do not know what the (real) reason for the purchaser's reaction was. Possibly the price had fallen below the level of $17\frac{1}{2}$ pence per pound (which was the contract price) during the time between the arrival of the two ships. The court, in any event, gave judgment in his favour.[1] Again, we do not know the reasons, since none have been reported. Shortly after counsel for the defendant had risen, the court abruptly stopped him in his argument and announced its judgment. What had he said that so impressed the court? "That being so, there was no consensus ad idem, and therefore no binding contract."

Quite understandably, under these circumstances, the decision in *Raffles v. Wichelhaus* was taken to lend support to a subjective approach to the formation of contract. What matters is that the minds of the parties are ad idem; if that is not the case, there can be no contract. But there have also been different interpretations. Oliver Wendell Holmes, for instance, tried to "objectify" *Raffles v. Wichelhaus* and wrote:

> "It is commonly said that such a contract is void, because of mutual mistake as to the subject-matter, and because therefore the parties did not consent to the same thing. But this way of putting it seems to me misleading. The law has nothing to do with the actual state of the parties' minds. In contract, as elsewhere, it must go by externals, and judge parties by their conduct. . . . The true ground of the decision was not that each party meant a different thing from the other . . . but that each said a different thing. The plaintiff offered one thing, the defendant expressed his assent to another."[2]

These words remind us of what has been mentioned very briefly in the previous chapter.[3] A contract, in modern analysis, is made up of two

[1] *Raffles v. Wichelhaus* (1864) 2 H & C 906. On the rule developed on the basis of this decision cf., in particular, William F. Young, "Equivocation in the Making of Agreements", (1964) 64 *Columbia* LR 619 sqq.; for a critical evaluation, see also Grant Gilmore, *The Death of Contract* (1974), pp. 35 sqq.

[2] *The Common Law*, p. 309. "Even for Holmes this was an extraordinary tour de force", comments Gilmore (p. 41).

[3] Supra, pp. 567 sqq.

declarations of will, and each of these, as the term suggests, of two elements: verba and voluntas. As a rule, will and declaration will coincide. According to Holmes, this was the case in *Raffles v. Wichelhaus*: the vendor meant December *Peerless*, and though he only said *Peerless*, his declaration must also be interpreted as referring to the December *Peerless*. The purchaser, on the other hand, intended to buy his cotton from the October *Peerless*, and his declaration, too, has to be seen in the light of this intention. Thus, whether we emphasize will or declaration, the result is the same: in either case there is no correspondence, and hence a contract has not been concluded.

(b) Discrepancy between intention and declaration

Things begin to look quite different, though, if one of the parties has declared one thing but meant another. Suppose there had been but one *Peerless*, and Raffles (or Wichelhaus) had referred to it by mistake, meaning quite a different ship, with quite a different name, which he thought to be the *Peerless*. It is obvious that both declarations correspond. If this were the deciding factor, both parties would be bound, and the purchaser would have to accept the cotton from Bombay ex *Peerless*. It is equally obvious, however, that, as to their intentions, both parties are not in fact ad idem. Their minds have not met "in unam sententiam", and hence there is no consent. If this were crucial, a contract could not be said to have come into existence. Which of these two approaches—diametrically opposed as they appear to be—should a legal system adopt?

(c) Private autonomy and protection of expectations engendered

If freedom of contract and private autonomy were our guiding principles (and they are indeed entrenched, for instance, in the German constitution[4]), then everybody should be able to determine his legal relationships with other people according to his own free will. This will must, of course, be free of vices and thus, for instance, the contracting party must not be labouring under a mistake. A declaration affected by mistake—in terms of "classical" contract theory—is not likely to lead to a result that is substantially fair. Or, put differently (namely in the words of the Louisiana Civil Code): The basis of contract is consensus; and "consent being the concurrence of intention in two or more persons, with regard to a matter understood by all, reciprocally communicated, and resulting in each party from a free and deliberate exercise of the will, it follows that there is no consent, . . . where it has

[4] Art. 2 I GG; cf. e.g. Ludwig Raiser, "Vertragsfreiheit heute", 1958 *Juristenzeitung* 4 sqq.; Manfred Wolf, *Rechtsgeschäftliche Entscheidungsfreiheit und vertraglicher Interessenausgleich* (1970), pp. 21 sqq.

been procured by—Error; Fraud; Violence; Threats".[5] On the other hand, it has to be taken into account that freedom (and the exercise thereof) entails responsibility. The individual is free to determine whether he wants to enter into a contract or not. But once he decides to do so and communicates his intention to others, he engenders expectations, which the law has to protect too. This is the reason for the binding nature of a contract, from which, as we have seen,[6] the parties cannot be allowed (and are indeed not allowed) to withdraw at will. Hence, one could say that to be bound by one's declarations is the price to be paid for the freedom of will. As a result of this view, the risk of error would always have to be borne by the person making the declaration and not by the addressee.[7]

(d) *Will theory and declaration theory*

It is obvious that we are here again[8] dealing with a situation where neither of these two fundamentally irreconcilable approaches can sensibly be taken to any extreme. While it may be equitable to stress the individual will and to take into account any kind of mistake, certainty of law will be most detrimentally affected. Sole emphasis on the external manifestation of that intention, in turn, will be conducive to certainty of law, but is bound to lead to harsh and inequitable results. Every developed legal system will therefore have to find some balance between the two positions. If it proceeds from what is usually dubbed the "will theory", it must make some concession to the protection of the other party's reliance, and can therefore not give effect to every type of error. In the same way, the so-called "declaration theory" can serve only as a starting point and must be modified so as to accommodate the reasonable interests of the author of the declaration.

In modern South African case law both approaches have been vying for recognition.[9] On the one hand, it has been held that error excludes consensus and thus prevents the formation of a contract.[10] But not every kind of error has this effect. It must relate to one of the essential elements of the contract. Furthermore, the will theory is tempered by

---

[5] Art. 1819; cf. further Saúl Litvinoff, "'Error' in the Civil Law", in: Joseph Dainow (ed.), *Essays on the Civil Law of Obligations* (1969), pp. 222 sqq.

[6] Supra, pp. 577, 578.

[7] For a recent analysis of the "dynamic that operates in areas of doctrine caught between the commitment to objectivity, expressed as reliance on 'manifestation', and the commitment to subjectivity expressed as reliance on 'intent'" (p. 1065), cf. Clare Dalton, "An Essay in the Deconstruction of Contract Doctrine", (1985) 94 *Yale LJ* 1039 sqq.

[8] Cf., for example, supra, pp. 87 sqq.

[9] For a general discussion, see Konrad M. Kritzinger, "Approach to Contract: A Reconciliation", (100) 1983 *SALJ* 47 sqq.; De Wet en Yeats, pp. 7 sqq.; Joubert, *Contract*, pp. 79 sqq.

[10] Cf. e.g. *Robinson v. Randfontein Gold Mining Co., Ltd.* 1925 AD 173; *Trollip v. Jordaan* 1961 (1) SA 238 (A); *Ocean Cargo Line Ltd. v. F. R. Waring (Pty.) Ltd.* 1963 (4) SA 641 (A).

the doctrine of assent by estoppel[11] or, as many now prefer to say, of quasi-mutual assent:[12] a person who has deliberately or negligently[13] made a declaration which did not correctly reflect his true intention may be estopped from proving the truth and will thus be forced to proceed as if the misrepresentation had been true.[14] On the other hand, there are those who agree with Wessels CJ that "[t]he law does not concern itself with the working of the minds of the parties to a contract, but with the external manifestation of their minds".[15] This is an endorsement of the declaration theory, but it, in turn, is modified by the doctrine of iustus error: if a party to a contract has been labouring under a reasonable mistake, he may repudiate the contract (with the effect of in integrum restitutio). But when is a mistake reasonable? Usually it is said that it must relate to one of the vital elements of the agreement and that it must not have been due to inattention or negligence on the part of the mistaken party. But support can also be found for the proposition that an error is iustus when it has been

[11] The classic text in this regard is J.C. de Wet, *Estoppel by Representation in die Suid-Afrikaanse Reg* (1939).

[12] Cf. R.H. Christie, "The Doctrine of Quasi-Mutual Assent", 1976 *Acta Juridica* 149 sqq.

[13] But it is doubtful whether fault is always required: cf. the discussion by Tebbutt J, in *Sonday v. Surrey Estate Modern Meat Market (Pty.) Ltd.* 1983 (2) SA 521 (C); he himself answers the question in the negative. Another problem, which has not yet been authoritatively settled, is whether the party relying on estoppel must have acted to his prejudice (on which see e.g. *Peri-Urban Areas Health Board v. Breet* 1958 (3) SA 783 (T), which answers this question, too, essentially in the negative).

[14] The most recent authoritative statements by the Appellate Division are *Saambou-Nasionale Bouvereniging v. Friedman* 1979 (3) SA 978 (A); *Mondorp Eiendomsagentskap (Edms.) Bpk. v. Kemp en De Beer* 1979 (4) SA 74 (A) and *Spes Bona Bank Ltd. v. Portals Water Treatment South Africa (Pty.) Ltd.* 1983 (1) SA 978 (A). Historically, this modification of the "will theory" dates back to the famous leading English case of *Smith v. Hughes* (1871) LR 6 QB 597, which contains the following dictum by Blackburn J (at p. 607) : "If, whatever a man's real intention may be, he so conducts himself that a reasonable man would believe that he was assenting to the terms proposed by the other party, and that other party upon that belief enters into the contract with him, the man thus conducting himself would be equally bound as if he had intended to agree to the other party's terms." The dogmatic basis for this reception is unclear. Trollip J in *Connoch's (SA) Motor Co. Ltd. v. Sentraal Westelike Ko-operatiewe Maatskappy Bpk.* 1964 (2) SA 47 (T) at 49A–B described it thus: "The English doctrine of Estoppel by representation migrated to this country on the authority of a passport that it approximated the exceptio doli mali of Roman Law. However doubtful the validity of that passport might originally have been . . ., the doctrine has now become naturalized and domiciled here as part of our law." "The immigration authority who first stamped the doctrine's passport for entry into the Cape . . . appears to have been Lord de Villiers CJ": Tebbutt J, in *Sonday v. Surrey Estate Modern Meat Market* 1983 (2) SA 521 (C) at 525C.

[15] "Even, therefore, if from a philosophical standpoint the minds of the parties do not meet, yet, if by their acts their minds seem to have met, the law will, where fraud is not alleged, look to their acts and assume that their minds did meet and that they contracted in accordance with what the parties purport to accept as a record of their agreement. This is the only practical way in which courts of law can determine the terms of a contract": *South African Railways & Harbours v. National Bank of South Africa Ltd.* 1924 AD 704 at 716 sq. Cf. further e.g. *Collen v. Rietfontein Engineering Works* 1948 (1) SA 413 (A) at 431. For a nearly identical formulation of this proposition, see Holmes, *The Common Law*, p. 309 ("The law has nothing to do with the actual state of the parties' minds. In contract, as elsewhere, it must go by externals, and judge parties by their conduct").

induced by the wrongful misrepresentation of the other party. Others stress that the mistake must not have induced in that other party a reasonable belief that consensus has in fact been reached.[16] Closely related as they are, in actual practice all these approaches usually arrive at the same result as would have been achieved if the will theory and the doctrine of quasi-mutual assent had been applied.[17] Thus, South African law provides a good example of how two different theoretical perspectives are able to converge so as to lead to essentially the same solutions. Abstract theorizing in terms of will and declaration theory does not normally affect the direction of the law in action.

2. Basic types of error in Roman law

(a) Verba and voluntas

If we turn our attention to Roman law, the last thing we can expect to find is, of course, a neat and logical theoretical framework for the problem of error. Two things are clear, however.[18] In ancient Roman law it was only the declaration that counted. All legal acts were of a strictly formal nature, and whenever the prescribed form was complied with, mancipatio, stipulatio and whatever other legal acts existed were binding and effective. There was an irrebuttable presumption that the will of the parties was correctly and adequately reflected in, for instance, the verba of the old sponsio/stipulatio. Under these circumstances, there was, of course, no room for taking any kind of error into account. According to the law reflected in Justinian's compilation, on the other hand, certain types of mistake exclude consensus, the essential basis for the formation of contract. Ulpianus D. 18, 1, 9 pr. leaves no doubt about that:

---

[16] For these various meanings of iustus error cf. D.B. Hutchison/B.J. van Heerden, "Mistake in Contract, A Comedy of (Justus) Errors", (1987) 104 *SALJ* 522 sqq., who also draw attention to the anomaly that the iustus error doctrine is still applied in spite of the fact that the courts now generally appear to adhere to the (subjective) will theory, and no longer to the declaration theory. In fact, in recent years, there has been an unprecedented flood of decisions and case notes on the question of iustus error. Cf., most recently, *Horty Investments (Pty.) Ltd. v. Interior Acoustics (Pty.) Ltd.* 1984 (3) SA 537 (W); *Osman v. Standard Bank National Credit Corporation Ltd.* 1985 (2) SA 378 (C); *Du Toit v. Atkinson's Motors Bpk.* 1985 (2) SA 893 (A); *Spindrifter (Pty.) Ltd. v. Lester Donovan (Pty.) Ltd.* 1986 (1) SA 303 (A); *Nasionale Behuisingskommissie v. Greyling* 1986 (4) SA 917 (T); *Standard Credit Corporation Ltd. v. Naicker* 1987 (2) SA 49 (N); Carole Lewis, "Caveat Subscriptor and the Doctrine of Justus Error" (1987) 104 *SALJ* 317 sqq.; A.J. Kerr, "Uses and Misuses of the Term Iustus Error. Questions concerning Error in Corpore", (1987) 104 *SALJ* 377 sqq.; J.S. McLennan, "Justus Error, Snatching of Bargains, and Rectification", (1987) 104 *SALJ* 382 sqq.

[17] For a redefinition of iustus error in terms of quasi-mutual assent (an error is iustus when the other party, due to his unreasonable reliance, cannot uphold the contract on the basis of quasi-mutual assent), cf. M.F.B. Reinecke/Schalk van der Merwe, 1984 *TSAR* 290 sqq.; Hutchison/Van Heerden, (1987) 104 *SALJ* 522 sqq.

[18] Cf., for example, Voci, *L'errore* (1937); Gian Gualberto Archi, "Dal formalismo negoziale repubblicano al principio giustinianeo 'cum sit iustum voluntates contrahentium magis quam verborum conceptionem inspicere'", (1980) 46 *SDHI* 1 sqq.

> "In venditionibus et emptionibus consensum debere intercedere palam est: ceterum sive in ipsa emptione dissentient sive in pretio sive in quo alio, emptio imperfecta est. si igitur ego me fundum emere putarem Cornelianum, tu mihi te vendere Sempronianum putasti, quia in corpore dissensimus, emptio nulla est. idem est, si ego me Stichum, tu Pamphilum absentem vendere putasti: nam cum in corpore dissentiatur, apparet nullam esse emptionem."

For a valid contract (of sale) we need consensus. Such consent is lacking if the parties are not ad idem with regard (particularly) to the sale itself, or to the price, or to the object. For "not being ad idem" the term "dissensus" is used.

(b) Determination of the object of performance

Less clear, and consequently much disputed, is the position in classical Roman law. A variety of authors have argued that the reason why classical authors regarded certain types of error as operative was not the lack of consent, but rather the fact that the object of the performance was not sufficiently determined.[19] They claim that what Ulpian really said in D. 18, 1, 9 pr. ran something like this:

> "Si cum ego me fundum emere putarem Cornelianum, tu mihi te vendere Sempronianum putasti [the sale is invalid, because] nec emptio nec venditio sine re quae veneat potest intellegi."

A contract of sale requires the determination, by the parties, of two essential matters: object and price. In the example discussed by Ulpian, vendor and purchaser have two different tracts of land in mind. Thus there is no object to which the contract could refer; hence the invalidity of the transaction. This argument sounds plausible enough. But the path to this result is paved with interpolation hypotheses which are as far-reaching and radical as they are unacceptable. According to Joseph Georg Wolf, for instance, the whole of D. 18, 1, 9 pr., apart from the example concerning the sale of land, is spurious.[20] But the consensus-oriented argument in D. 18, 1, 9 pr. is supported by a variety of other texts.[21] In fact, we do not know of any classical discussion of mistake in the formation of contract unrelated to or detached from the consensus problem. Presumably, then (and this does indeed appear to

---

[19] Joseph Georg Wolf, *Error im römischen Vertragsrecht* (1961); Ugo Zilletti, *La dottrina dell' errore nella storia del diritto romano* (1961); Franz Wieacker, "Irrtum, Dissens oder gegenstandslose Leistungsbestimmung?", in: *Mélanges Philippe Meylan*, vol. I (1963), pp. 383 sqq.

[20] *Error*, pp. 23 sqq., 99 sq., 135 sq.

[21] For some more general statements cf. Iul./Ulp. D. 2, 1, 15 ("non consentiant qui errent"); Iul./Ulp. D. 5, 1, 2 pr. ("error . . . non habet consensum"); Pomp. D. 39, 3, 30 ("nulla enim voluntas errantis est"); Diocl. C. 1, 18, 8 ("cum errantis voluntas nulla sit"); Diocl. C. 1, 18, 9 ("cum nullus sit errantis consensus"). The identification theory is also in direct conflict with Iul. D. 18, 1, 41, 1, a text regarded as genuine even by Wolf (*Error*, pp. 160 sqq.): cf. e.g. Luigi Labruna, (1962) 8 *Labeo* 138.

be the prevailing opinion),[22] classical law did not differ much in this respect from what we find in the pages of the Digest. Of course, the object of a contract of sale had to be identified. But this identification took place in the agreement of the parties. It was one of the main features of the contractual consent. Without it, a contract could not be said to have been concluded. It is only under this perspective, i.e. from the point of view of the more general problem of impairment of consensus, that the determination of the object of performance, emphasized by Wolf and others, obtains a specific significance for the problem of mistake in contract.

(c) Ulp. D. 18, 1, 9 pr. and error in corpore

It must be obvious from what has been said so far that the consideration of error started with the consensual contracts. Not only were they based on the consent of the parties,[23] but the actions arising from them were also to be granted ex bona fide. This left the necessary room for the intention of the parties to be taken into account. Not surprisingly, then, the main dissertation on the problem of error contained in the Digest relates to the prototype of the consensual contracts, to emptio venditio. We have cited the first part of it already: it is the fragment D. 18, 1, 9 pr. Of central significance is the example relating to the Cornelian/Sempronian estate. The purchaser assumes that he is buying fundus Cornelianus, the vendor that he is selling fundus Sempronianus. These are the only facts provided by Ulpianus. He does not relate to us what the parties did in fact declare: a matter that would have been of the utmost interest to the modern analyst. Three different situations are conceivable:[24]

(1) The declarations of the parties were so vague and unclear that a specific fundus is not objectively identifiable—perhaps they referred only to a fundus in general, or they tried to individualize the tract of land by referring to certain features which were (unbeknown to them) common to both. This would be a dissensus (a hidden lack of agreement) in the narrow, modern sense of the word.[25]

[22] Theo Mayer-Maly, "Bemerkungen zum Aspekt der Konsensstörung in der klassischen Irrtumslehre", in: *Mélanges Philippe Meylan*, vol. I (1963), pp. 241 sqq.; Wunner, *Contractus*, pp. 134 sqq., 144 sqq., 193 sqq.; Kaser, *RPr* I, p. 237; Honsell/Mayer-Maly/Selb, p. 122.

[23] Gai. III, 135.

[24] Cf., in particular, Wunner, *Contractus*, pp. 145 sqq.

[25] Cf. e.g. § 155 BGB ("If the parties to a contract which they regard as concluded have in fact not agreed upon a point upon which agreement should have been arrived at . . ."). In the terminology of the English common law, we are dealing in this alternative with mutual mistake. For a comparative discussion cf. Dietrich Rothoeft, *System der Irrtumslehre* (1968), pp. 147 sqq. Earlier in this century, it was argued repeatedly that only a hidden lack of agreement (dissensus in the modern sense) vitiated the contract; texts such as D. 18, 1, 9 pr. were thus explained solely in terms of alternative (1), and it was argued that unilateral error did not affect the validity of the contract: cf., in particular, Werner Flume, "Irrtum und

(2) The declarations of the parties related to the fundus Cornelianus; however, the vendor wanted to sell a tract of land which was the fundus Sempronianus, but which he believed to be the fundus Cornelianus. This would be a unilateral mistake on the part of the vendor about the identity of the object of the transaction.
(3) The declarations of the parties related to fundus Sempronianus; however, the purchaser wanted to buy a tract of land which was fundus Cornelianus, but which he believed to be fundus Sempronianus: unilateral mistake regarding the identity of the object of sale, this time on the part of the purchaser.

For the Roman lawyers these distinctions did not matter. What mattered to Ulpianus was what he described as *putare* emere and *putare* vendere: the intentions of the parties. As long as they were not directed at the same thing, a contract could not come into being. This situation is referred to as dissensus. Dissent, in the terminology of Roman law, therefore embraced (unilateral) mistake, in this instance a mistake as to the identity of the thing which was the object of the contract. This type of mistake was material (or operative) in the sense that it excluded consensus.[26] It has come to be known as error in corpore.

(d) Error in pretio

Although it features particularly prominently in our sources, error in corpore was not the only material mistake. The identity of the object was but one of the essential elements of a contract of sale. There were other matters on which the parties had to be ad idem. The price was obviously one of them. Hence the statement by Ulpianus: "si in pretio dissentiant, emptio imperfecta est."[27] An error in pretio was thus also material. A case relating to locatio conductio deals with this problem: "Si decem tibi locem fundum, tu autem existimes quinque te conducere, nihil agitur."[28] This appears to be the rule; no consensus as to the rent has been reached, and thus there is no contract. Interestingly, however, the result is different in the following example: ". . . sed et si ego minoris me locare sensero, tu pluris te conducere, utique non pluris

Rechtsgeschäft im römischen Recht", in: *Festschrift für Fritz Schulz*, vol. I (1951), pp. 236 sqq. Contra (e.g.) Wieacker, *Mélanges Meylan*, pp. 389 sqq.; Wunner, *Contractus*, pp. 163 sqq.; Frier, (1983) 100 *ZSS* 262.

[26] This idea found its expression in the maxim "errantis voluntas nulla est" (e.g. Pomp. D. 39, 3, 20 and supra, p. 588). It does, of course, not mean that a person labouring under a mistake does not have a will at all, but only that his will is not his true will and thus a nullum. The idea that mistake excludes consensus can be traced back to Julian and appears to have been well established in high and late classical jurisprudence. Cf Arnold Ehrhardt, "Errantis voluntas nulla est", (1938) 58 *ZSS* 167 sqq.; idem, "Betrachtungen über die Lehre vom Error", (1952) 69 *ZSS* 402 sqq.; Wolf, *Error*, pp. 1 sqq.; Wunner, *Contractus*, pp. 195 sqq.

[27] Cf. D. 18, 1, 9 pr.

[28] Pomp. D. 19, 2, 52.

erit conductio, quam quanti ego putavi."[29] Here we are dealing with the rather uncommon situation where the lessor is content with much less than the lessee expects him to be: the lessor imagines the rent to be, say, five, whilst the lessee considers himself bound to pay ten. Pomponius does not regard this transaction as entirely invalid. There is a minimum consensus over five, since the lessee will obviously only be too happy to pay five rather than ten. "Minus in maiore inest":[30] his willingness to pay the higher sum can be taken to include acceptance of the lesser amount. Only as to the difference (between five and ten) is there a lack of consensus; but such partial lack of consensus does not affect the rest of the transaction.[31] From a very formalistic point of view, the same kind of reasoning could, of course, be applied to the other example too, where it had been the lessor who thought that he had contracted for ten, whilst the lessee was under the impression that he had promised only five. It is obvious, however, that here it would be against the interests of the lessor if one were to construe a consensus on the level of five. The fact that the Roman lawyers did not do so demonstrates again the flexible manner in which they handled a rule such as utile per inutile non vitiatur.[32]

(e) Error in negotio

Thirdly, there was the situation where the parties did not agree on the nature of their transaction. It is mentioned in D. 18, 1, 9 pr. (". . . sive in ipsa emptione dissentient") and is generally referred to as error in negotio. Ulpianus D. 12, 1, 18, 1 provides an example:

> "Si ego quasi deponens tibi dedero, tu quasi mutuam accipias, nec depositum nec mutuum est: idem est et si tu quasi mutuam pecuniam dederis, ego quasi commodatum ostendendi gratia accepi."[33]

In both these cases money has been handed over, but in neither are the parties ad idem as to the purpose of this act. One of them thinks that it is a deposit, the other takes it to be a loan for consumption; and in the second case the one party regards it as a loan for consumption whilst the other has a loan for use in mind. Neither of these contracts can come into existence under these circumstances. Again, incidentally, it is not clear (and therefore does not seem to matter)[34] whether we are dealing

---

[29] Pomp. D. 19, 2, 52. On this text cf. e.g. Wolf, *Error*, pp. 75 sqq.; Wunner, *Contractus*, pp. 199 sqq.; Wieacker, *Mélanges Meylan*, pp. 398 sq.; Hans Hermann Seiler, "Utile per inutile non vitiatur", in: *Festschrift für Max Kaser* (1976), pp. 129 sq.; Okko Behrends, "Institutionelles und prinzipielles Denken im römischen Privatrecht", (1978) 95 *ZSS* 209 sqq.

[30] Cf. supra, pp. 74 sq.

[31] Utile per inutile non vitiatur.

[32] Cf. supra, pp. 75 sqq.

[33] On this text and error in negotio in general, see Wolf, *Error*, pp. 86 sqq.; Wunner, *Contractus*, pp. 207 sqq.

[34] Contra: Flume, *Festschrift Schulz*, vol. I, p. 243; but see Wunner, loc. cit. For a different interpretation of this fragment (not based on lack of consensus), see Wolf, loc. cit.

with dissensus in the modern sense of the word or with a case involving error (in negotio).[35]

(f) Error in persona

Dissensus or mistake over the identity of the other contracting partner (error in persona) is not specifically referred to in our fragment D. 19, 1, 9 pr., but appears to have prevented the formation of a contract.

> "Si et me et Titium mutuam pecuniam rogaveris et ego meum debitorem tibi promittere iusserim, tu stipulatus sis, cum putares eum Titii debitorem esse, an mihi obligaris?"[36]

The person referred to as "tu" believes that he receives a loan from Titius, while in reality the money is paid out to him by order of "ego". Under these circumstances, "tu" is not under a contractual obligation towards "ego", for "nullum negotium mecum contraxisti". A little gloss, possibly only added at a later stage, specifies the reason: "[credita pecunia] nisi inter consentientes fieri non potest."

3. The problem of error in substantia

(a) Ulp. D. 18, 1, 9, 2

The most intriguing and disputed kind of mistake considered by the Roman lawyers is error in substantia. The core fragment stems, again, from Ulpian's commentary on Sabinus. It reads as follows:

> "Inde quaeritur, si in ipso corpore non erratur, sed in substantia error sit, ut puta si acetum pro vino veneat, aes pro auro vel plumbum pro argento vel quid aliud argento simile, an emptio et venditio sit. Marcellus scripsit . . . emptionem esse et venditionem, quia in corpus consensum est, etsi in materia sit erratum. ego in vino quidem consentio, quia eadem prope . . . οὐσία est, si modo vinum acuit: ceterum si vinum non acuit, sed ab initio acetum fuit, ut embamma, aliud pro alio venisse videtur. in ceteris autem nullam esse venditionem puto, quotiens in materia erratur."[37]

A variety of examples are presented: vinegar is sold as wine, bronze as gold, lead or some other metal resembling silver as silver. Clearly, we are not dealing with an error in corpore. The parties do not disagree as to the object of their contract of sale, for they both have the same specimen of liquid, the same lump of metal in mind. But the purchaser is seriously disadvantaged by the deal, for the liquid has turned out to be vinegar instead of wine, the metal is not gold, as he had thought, but it is bronze, etc. He has erred as to what the object of the sale really consisted of; his mistake relates to the substance of the thing. This is the crucial feature of the problem. Whether the vendor was labouring under the same mistake, we do not know. Ulpian seems to regard that

[35] For a modern definition of error in negotio cf. art. 1841 Louisiana Civil Code: "Error as to the nature of the contract will render it void. The nature of the contract is that which characterizes the obligation which it creates. . . ."

[36] Cels. D. 12, 1, 32; cf. Wunner, *Contractus*, pp. 210 sq.

[37] D. 18, 1, 9, 2.

as immaterial.[38] "Aliud pro alio venire" appears to indicate that the purchaser's error is not spontaneous, but has been induced by the seller.[39] But whether there was, to use the terminology of English law, fraudulent or innocent misrepresentation cannot be gauged from the text. The question, then, is: does this (unilateral or mutual) error in substantia prevent a valid contract of sale from coming into existence? Marcellus' answer is no; in his opinion this kind of mistake is not operative. But Ulpian disagrees. He assimilates error in substantia to error in corpore, for the deviation between declaration and intention is equally grave: what has in reality been sold (and to what therefore, from an objective point of view, the purchaser's declaration referred) is entirely different from the thing the purchaser had intended to buy. It is an aliud. Hence the result: nullam esse venditionem.

(b) Error relating to quality

The situation was quite different, however, if the purchaser's mistake did not relate to the substantia (sometimes also the terms "materia" or "qualitas" are used),[40] but merely to the quality of the object of sale: "Aliter atque si aurum quidem fuerit, deterius autem quam emptor existimaret: tunc enim emptio valet."[41] Here the object sold is gold, but the gold is of a lesser quality than the purchaser was entitled to expect. We are dealing with a latent defect, a type of situation for which, as we have seen,[42] a different set of rules applied. After all, by the time of classical Roman law, the days of an austere and categorical "caveat emptor" policy were gone and the purchaser was well protected. The sale of slaves and cattle was governed by the aedilitian remedies, whereas the purchaser of other goods was able to avail himself of the actio empti: for damages in case of dolus and breach of formless dicta in venditione or formal promissa, for quanti minoris or redhibition even against the honest vendor. The applicability of these remedies, of course, depended on the validity of the sale: without emptio venditio, no actio empti and no aedilitian remedies were available. It furthermore depended on the existence of a (latent) defect. Bronze, however, can

[38] Cf. Bruce W. Frier, "Roman Law and the Wine Trade: The Problem of 'Vinegar Sold As Wine'", (1983) 100 *ZSS* 268 sq.

[39] Stein, *Fault*, p. 44.

[40] On the question of terminology cf. Wolf, *Error*, pp. 121 sqq.; Pierre Cornioley, "Error in substantia, in materia, in qualitate", in: *Studi in onore di Giuseppe Grosso*, vol. II (1968), e.g. pp. 275 sqq., 293 sqq.; Robert Feenstra, "The Dutch Kantharos Case and the History of Error in Substantia", (1974) 48 *Tulane LR* 853 sqq.; Frier, (1983) 100 *ZSS* 267 sq. It is highly unlikely that each of these terms had a fixed and distinct technical meaning. Substantia was probably, at least in Ulpian's parlance, a wider concept that went beyond the mere question of "material". Qualitas (cf. e.g. Paul. D. 19, 1, 21, 2), incidentally, does not mean "goodness" in this context, but "characteristic" in the abstract; recognized already by Cuiacius ("dissensus in materia, qualitate et substantia eadem sunt"): *Comment. in Tit. I De contrah. empt.* Lib. XVIII Digest., ad L IX.

[41] Paul. D. 18, 1, 10.

[42] Cf. supra, pp. 311 sqq.

hardly be said to be defective gold, nor can lead be regarded as defective silver. Nevertheless, a purchaser can be disadvantaged even more if he receives lead rather than defective silver, and thus it would be highly anomalous if the law had been prepared to come to his rescue only in the second case and not also in the first. The doctrine of error in substantia provided the answer: it freed the purchaser from a contract which for him was fundamentally flawed.[43]

(c) Drawing the line: vinegar sold as wine

As a result of this, it became necessary to draw a line between cases where the object of the contract suffered from a defect and where it turned out to be of an entirely different substance. Obviously, this could involve some very fine distinctions. Apart from that, differences of opinion were bound to arise as to the proper solution of individual cases; after all, there was not even unanimity about whether error in substantia should be taken into consideration at all! Hence, it is very difficult to find a common denominator for the casuistry contained in the Digest title 18, 1.[44] Ulpian refers to the οὐσία, the "being", the

---

[43] I share the widely held opinion that the Roman lawyers considered error in substantia only from the point of view of the insufficiency of the prevailing system of remedies for breach of warranty (cf. e.g. Feenstra, (1974) 48 *Tulane LR* 854) and that the doctrine was developed—in typically casuistic fashion (Kaser, *RPr* I, p. 238; Schulz, *CRL*, p. 529)—to fill an unsatisfactory gap in the protection of the purchaser. Hence, only the mistake of a purchaser who paid too much was considered significant. The latter point has, most recently, also been emphasized by Frier. Frier, (1983) 100 *ZSS* 257 sqq., disagrees, however, with the general view on the historical development of the doctrine of error in substantia. According to him, it was devised in the early classical period as a primitive means of protecting the purchaser from unconscionable results of enforcing the sale. However, by the late classical period more refined ways of protecting the purchaser within sale had been developed, and consequently the error in substantia doctrine had become so hemmed in by limitations "as to be all but insignificant in practice" (p. 272). Many jurists (Marcellus!) therefore wished to abolish it altogether. But Ulpian "with his usual respect for tradition" was unwilling to follow their lead; he preserved "the doctrine even in its sharply truncated form" (p. 273). In fact, however, Frier is forced to admit that Ulpian began to broaden the doctrine once more (e.g. p. 284), thus paving the way for its survival (and even further extension) in the European ius commune. Frier's argument is most ingenious and contains a wealth of interesting observations. It is, however, ultimately unconvincing, because some of the premises are shaky. Thus, for instance, Frier argues (p. 275) that early classical jurists considered the sale to be void whenever vinegar was sold as wine. He deduces that from the words "ego in vino quidem consentio" in Ulp. D. 18, 1, 9, 2: for how, Frier asks rhetorically, could Ulpian "agree" with Marcellus, except to overrule a previous decision? But surely it can make sense to express one's agreement with a firmly established view, particularly if one wants to emphasize (as Ulpian does) that he agrees with it only in part.

[44] Cf. also, however, the notoriously difficult fragment of Paul. D. 19, 1, 21, 2, containing both a general statement and an example which appears to be in conflict with the approach adopted by the other Roman lawyers (and by Paul himself: D. 18, 1, 10): "Quamvis supra dicimus, cum in corpore consentiamus, de qualitate autem dissentiamus, emptionem esse, tamen venditor teneri debet . . .: veluti si mensas quasi citreas emat, quae non sunt." Does "qualitas" here, after all, mean "quality", not "characteristic" in the abstract? Has a controversy been dropped from the original text, so that it can be considered an inept summary by the compilers? Has a "non" been left out before "esse" ("emptionem non esse")? On this text see, most recently, Stein, *Fault*, pp. 46 sq.; Wolf, *Error*, pp. 157 sqq.; Honsell, *Quod interest*, pp. 99 sqq.; J.A.C. Thomas, "Error in persona and error in

nature or the essence of the object, and he illustrates this vaguely philosophical criterion[45] with the wine/vinegar example. Where something has been sold as wine that was in fact once wine but turned into vinegar in the meantime, the sale is valid. The wine has undergone acetic fermentation, an organic process which makes it unpalatable and destroys most of its commercial value; but the liquid is still virtually of one and the same continuous being.[46] The vinegar, in this instance, is wine turned sour (i.e. bad). The situation was different, where the vinegar sold as wine was (wine) vinegar from the start, and had been specifically prepared as such. Here, the object of the sale was neither wine nor wine turned sour, but an alternative substance. Despite the common origin of wine and vinegar in grape juice, the liquid in question never had the (original) "wineness" envisaged by the purchaser. His error does not relate to quality but to the substance, and thus invalidates the sale.

(d) Further borderline cases

Problems could arise in cases where the object of the sale contained at least some of the material of which it was supposed to consist in its entirety. We have seen that the contract is valid if the gold is merely of a lower quality than the purchaser expected. It is void if it is not gold but bronze. In D. 18, 1, 14 Ulpian discusses the sale of a bracelet said to be of gold but containing only "auri aliquid": the contract is valid. The same holds true, if it was gilded: "nam si inauratum aliquid sit, licet ego aureum putem, valet venditio." This statement is in direct conflict with an earlier opinion of Julian, concerning a silver-plated table which the parties believed to be of solid silver: "Mensam argento coopertam mihi ignoranti pro solida vendidisti imprudens: nulla est emptio pecuniaque eo nomine data condicetur."[47] Various attempts have been made to reconcile these texts.[48] It is more likely, however, that there was a difference of opinion between the two jurists. By insisting that the object must have consisted, in its entirety, of a

substantia", in: *La formazione storica*, vol. III, pp. 1219 sq., Marie Theres Fögen, "Citrusholz und Fussschemel", 1982 *RJ* 165 sqq.; Frier, (1983) 177 *ZSS* 286 sq. The example concerns the sale of a table which was supposed to have been made of the wood of citrus tuia, a cypress-like tree growing in North Africa, which was characterized by its beautiful grain. Rich Romans liked to buy expensive tables; in one case more than one million sesterces appear to have been paid for a mensa citrea, and Cicero once bought a table for half a million sesterces: Honsell, *Quod interest*, p. 101; cf. also Fögen, 1982 *RJ* 165, 170.

[45] On the Aristotelian background of the οὐσία clause, see Wolf, *Error*, pp. 139 sqq.; but cf. Frier (1983) 100 *ZSS* 284.

[46] On the problem of vinegar sold as wine, particularly on the jurist's evaluation of acetic fermentation, cf. the detailed analysis by Frier, (1983) 100 *ZSS* 257 sqq., 274 sqq.

[47] D. 18, 1, 41, 1.

[48] Cf. e.g. Wieacker, *Mélanges Meylan*, p. 396, who tries to distinguish the facts of the two cases; cf. also Stein, *Fault*, pp. 44 sqq.; Thomas, in: *La formazione storica*, vol. III, pp. 1212 sqq. But see Cornioley, *Studi Grosso*, vol. II, pp. 274 sq., 280 sqq.; Feenstra, (1974) 48 *Tulane LR* 853 sqq. For a comprehensive discussion of D. 18, 1, 41, 1, see Fritz Sturm, *Die rechtsgeschichtliche Exegese* (1972), pp. 62 sqq.

different material, Ulpian limited the scope of the error in substantia doctrine not inconsiderably.

Not in all cases, however, could the line be drawn so easily. ". . . si ego mulierem venderem, tu puerum emere existimasti, quia in sexu error est, nulla emptio, nulla venditio est."[49] A female slave was bought in the belief that she was a man. Here the purchaser's mistake obviously did not relate to the material of the object of sale: both male and female slaves are made of flesh and blood. Nevertheless, mistake as to the sex of a slave was regarded as "substantial". Men and women are essentially different; few persons of the female sex would presumably like to see themselves described as defective males. Where somebody had bargained for a boy and received a girl instead, this was a case of aliud pro alio venire. The situation was different where the object of the sale was not a virgin—as she was supposed to be—but had already been deflowered: "Quod si ego me virginem emere putarem, cum esset iam mulier, emptio valebit: in sexu enim non est erratum."[50] Here, indeed, the question was whether the purchaser could bring a remedy on account of a latent defect.

The definition drawn in D. 18, 1, 11, 1 thus demonstrates that the problem of error in substantia was not simply reduced to a question of material. At least, therefore, in the writings of Ulpian, and in spite of D. 18, 1, 14, we still find a fairly wide concept of substantia. This casts some doubt over the thesis recently advanced by Frier[51] that later classical jurists took a strongly negative stance towards error in substantia, and that its field of application was insignificant in practice.

4. Common mistake

We have already seen that it does not seem to have mattered whether only the purchaser mistook the object of the sale for something else, or whether his mistake was shared by the vendor. Frequently the latter will have been the case; both Ulp. D. 18, 1, 14 and Iul. D. 18, 1, 41, 1 do in actual fact provide examples of a common mistake. In these instances, the invalidity of the contract cannot have been based on a lack of consensus, for both parties were entirely ad idem. They had the same idea about the substance of the object. But it was a (common) misconception. Their consensus related to a different object: aliud pro alio venisse videtur. In their agreement the parties were supposed to identify the object of the transaction. In this they had failed. They had identified an object that did not in fact exist. In this sense the transaction was therefore frustrated, or incomplete, and hence no actions could arise therefrom.

---

[49] Ulp. D. 18, 1, 11, 1.
[50] Ulp. D. 18, 1, 11, 1.
[51] Cf. supra, note 43.

5. Error in motive and error in nomine

Errores in corpore, in persona, in negotio and in substantia were the most important forms of operative mistakes. If one of the parties was labouring under any of them, a valid contract (of sale) could not come into existence. In later centuries they were often described as mistakes relating to the content of the contract. Opposed to them are mistakes merely in the motive of the parties' declarations. These, at least as far as the law of contract is concerned, are generally irrelevant.[52] What has prompted a person to enter into a contract is entirely his own business. As long as the motive remains outside the content of the contract, it is of no concern to the contractual partner, and the consequences of any misconception in that regard must normally be borne by the declarant himself. The Roman lawyers did not conceptualize the problem in this way, but the Digest does not contain cases where the contract would have been regarded as invalid because of an error in motive.[53]

Another type of mistake, which was irrelevant, was the error in nomine:

> "Plane si in nomine dissentiamus, verum de corpore constet, nulla dubitatio est, quin valeat emptio et venditio: nihil enim facit error nominis, cum de corpore constat."[54]

Both parties have the same object (for instance a particular slave) in mind, but one of them errs as to its name. Such a mistake does not affect the content of the contract and hence does not exclude consensus. This is the reason, incidentally, why Ulpian in D. 18, 1, 9 pr. specifically refers to the fact that the slave in question was not present when the contract of sale was concluded ("[I]dem est, si ego me Stichum, tu Pamphilum *absentem* vendere putasti"): here we are dealing with an error in corpore, with the result "nullam esse emptionem". The two parties to the contract have two different slaves in mind. Had the slave been present, an error in corpore could hardly have occurred. We would have had a case of a mere error in nomine, and the contract would have been valid.

---

[52] For details, see Rothoeft, op. cit., note 25, pp. 80 sqq., 36 sqq., 283 sqq. The policy on which this distinction is based has been spelt out succinctly by Roscoe Pound, *Jurisprudence*, vol. IV (1959), p. 457: "The reason for denying relief where there is mistake only in the motive is the need of weighing against the individual interests of one who acts on mistaken motive the social interest in the security of transactions. The other party had nothing to do with the mistake and it does not inhere in the declaration of the will. But what is decisive is the economic reason, the security of transactions, which should be upheld in order to maintain the economic order, unless failure of an essential element of the transaction makes a strong case of impairment of the interest in individual free self-assertion. Motives are too shifting, too varying in degree of weight, too complex and too little susceptible of proof to be weighed against the security of transactions." Cf., further, Flume, *AT*, § 25, and Malte Diesselhorst, "Zum Irrtum bei Vertragsschluss", in: *Sympotica Franz Wieacker* (1970), pp. 186 sqq.

[53] The matter is different with regard to testamentary dispositions; cf. Hans Josef Wieling, *Testamentsauslegung im römischen Recht* (1972), pp. 208 sqq.; Honsell/Mayer-Maly/Selb, p. 124.

[54] Ulp. D. 18, 1, 9, 1.

6. Common error in nomine

Occasionally it occurs that the error in nomine is common to both parties. Take the famous case of RGZ 99, 147 sqq. revolving around the only Norwegian word every German law student is likely to know. Two parties had agreed to the sale of *"haakjöringsköd"* (shark meat), which they, however, took to mean whale meat. A case such as this would not have presented specific problems to the Roman lawyers, since there is consensus about whale meat. Whale meat, therefore, has become the object of the contract.

In modern German law it is more difficult to reach the same conclusion (the only sensible one); since emphasis is on the parties' declarations, the contract appears to relate to shark meat. The deviation from the declaration-oriented approach is normally justified by reference to the ostensibly time-honoured and venerable common-law maxim of falsa demonstratio non nocet.[55] It does indeed go back, via the ius commune, to classical Roman law, but there it served a different, and much more limited, function than is attributed to it today.[56] For one thing, it related only to testamentary dispositions; and for another it dealt specifically with a situation in which a person or an object had already been sufficiently identified within the will, but where the testator had added an additional (wrong, but superfluous) designation. "Demonstratio falsa est", as Gaius exemplifies,[57]

> "veluti si ita scriptum sit: 'servum Stichum, quem de Titio emi', 'fundum Tusculanum, qui mihi a Seio donatus est.' nam si constat, de quo homine, de quo fundo senserit testator, ad rem non pertinet, si is, quem emisse significavit, donatus esset, aut quem donatum sibi esse significaverat, emerit."

7. Will-orientation, mistake and the formal transactions

(a) Testaments

These last remarks have carried us into a field of law which presents problems similar to the law of contract, though in a distinctly different way: the law of testate succession. The testament of a person is supposed to convey and embody his or her last will, but it is a strictly formal declaration. Hence, again, the potential for a conflict between verba and voluntas, hence the problems of interpretation and of the effect of "cognitive weaknesses", of defects of the will on the validity of the testator's declaration. The stringency of the (external) formalism

---

55 Cf. e.g. Flume, *AT*, § 16, 2; for details, see Hans Josef Wieling, "Die Bedeutung der Regel 'falsa demonstratio non nocet' im Vertragsrecht", (1972) 172 *Archiv für die civilistische Praxis* 297 sqq.

56 Guido Donatuti, "Falsa demonstratio non nocet", in: *Studi di diritto romano*, vol. I (1976), pp. 247 sqq.; Giuseppe Grosso, "Sulla falsa demonstratio nelle disposizioni d'ultima volontà", in: *Studi in onore di Pietro Bonfante*, vol. II (1930), pp. 187 sqq.; Hans Josef Wieling, "Falsa demonstratio, condicio non scripta, condicio pro impleta im römischen Testament", (1970) 87 *ZSS* 197 sqq.

57 D. 35, 1, 17 pr.; cf. also Gai. D. 35, 1, 17, 1.

that dominates testate succession militates against a particularly liberal attitude to be adopted on these questions. On the other hand, however, account must always be taken of the fact that a contract creates a bond between two (or more) parties, whereas a will neither creates an obligation on the part of the testator nor involves the interests of any other party at all. The will is not addressed to anybody in particular, it does not confer any right (or even an expectation that could be of legal relevance), and it is freely revocable. Whilst, therefore, the law of contract has to balance the interests of both the declarant and the recipient of a contractual declaration, the law of testate succession can focus to a much greater extent on the interests of the former. Since a will cannot be taken to create a reasonable expectation, there is no need for the law to protect any such position. Hence the inclination of most legal systems to meet and carry through the (recognizable) intentions of the testator as far as possible.

(b) Stipulations

It is small wonder, under these circumstances, that testaments were the first formal transactions of Roman law in relation to which the more modern, will-oriented way of interpretation gained ground, and where defects of the will, and in particular error, were taken into consideration. Pre-classical jurisprudence already appears to have gone beyond the typical meaning of the testator's declaration in an attempt to give effect to his (real) intentions. For details, we must refer the reader to the literature on the Roman law of succession.[58] For our purposes, it is important to note the general trend of the development. For, once a more liberal attitude prevailed in relation to wills, the scene was set for a gradual relaxation of the strict word formalism in other transactions too, most notably with regard to the stipulatio. We have already stressed repeatedly that consensus, the subjective agreement, came to be increasingly accepted as cornerstone and actual effective reason for all contractual obligations.[59] Hence, for instance, the importance of informal pacta for the determination of the content of a stipulation;[60] and hence also a tendency to take account of deviations between verba and voluntas. ". . . nam et stipulatio quae verbis fit, nisi habeat consensum, nulla est":[61] in spite of formal correspondence between question and answer, a stipulation could be invalid if no actual agreement had been reached between the parties on one and the same object. This appears very clearly from Ven. D. 45, 1, 137, 1:

[58] Cf. e.g. Flume, *Festschrift Schulz*, vol. I, pp. 209 sqq.; Pasquale Voci, *Diritto ereditario romano* (2nd ed.), vol. II (1963), pp. 806 sqq.; Alan Watson, "Narrow, Rigid and Literal Interpretation in the Later Roman Republic", (1969) 37 *TR* 351 sqq.; Wieling, op. cit., note 53, passim; cf. also Kaser, *RPr* I, pp. 239 sq.; Honsell/Mayer-Maly/Selb, p. 123.

[59] Cf. e.g. supra, pp. 156 sqq., 165, 510 sq., 565.

[60] Cf. supra, pp. 510 sq.

[61] Ulp. D. 2, 14, 1, 3.

"Si hominem stipulatus sim et ego de alio sensero, tu de alio, nihil acti erit: nam stipulatio ex utriusque consensu perficitur."[62]

The stipulator had one slave in mind, the promisor another: no valid stipulation has been concluded. Or, as Justinian put it in the Institutes: the situation is the same as if no answer had been given to the question.[63] The above example can cover two situations:[64] question and answer may have referred to Stichus, but there is more than one slave of this name. The stipulator thought of the one Stichus and the promisor of the other. In modern terminology, this would be a case of dissensus. Alternatively, again, the stipulation may ostensibly have been about Stichus. The promisor, however, had a different slave in mind, whose name he believed to be Stichus but who was in actual fact called Pamphilus.[65] Here we are dealing with unilateral mistake.[66] In Rome, as has been pointed out already, this distinction did not matter[67] since in both cases there is dissensus in the broader sense (i.e. a lack of consensus).

As with the consensual contracts, not every form of error could, of course, be regarded as operative. A mere error in nomine, for instance, did not affect the validity of the transaction: "Si in nomine servi, quem stipularemur dari, erratum fuisset, cum de corpore constitisset, placet stipulationem valere."[68] Neither did, in the case of a stipulation, an error in substantia invalidate the contract: "Si id quod aurum putabam, cum aes esset, stipulatus de te fuero, teneberis mihi huius aeris nomine, quoniam in corpore consenserimus."[69] Only if the promisor had deceived the stipulator about the nature of the price of metal could the latter avail himself of an exceptio doli and thus escape condemnation.

8. Error and the protection of the promisee

(a) Modern approaches: English law and German law

Our overview of the Roman sources on the effect of error on the formation of contract may have left the modern reader slightly startled. The possibility of attacking the validity of a contract and thus escaping

---

[62] Cf. also Paul. D. 45, 1, 83, 1.

[63] "Si de alia re stipulator senserit, de alia promissor, perinde nulla contrahitur obligatio ac si ad interrogatum responsum non esset, veluti si hominem Stichum a te stipulatus quis fuerit, tu de Pamphilo senseris, quem Stichum vocari credideris": Inst. III, 19, 23.

[64] For a different view, see Flume, *Festschrift Schulz*, vol. I, pp. 245 sqq. (the text deals only with dissensus in the modern sense); Wolf, *Error*, pp. 61 sqq. (stipulation is invalid, because the object of the transaction has not been identified); cf. also Wieacker, *Mélanges Meylan*, pp. 400 sqq.; but see Wunner, *Contractus*, pp. 167 sqq.; Mayer-Maly, *Mélanges Meylan*, pp. 248 sq.; Fritz Raber, "Hoc animo dare", (1965) 33 *TR* 55 sqq.; Kaser, *RPr* I, p. 239.

[65] Cf. the example in *Inst.* III, 19, 23.

[66] Error in corpore, to be more specific.

[67] Cf. supra, pp. 589 sq.

[68] Ulp. D. 45, 1, 32.

[69] Paul. D. 45, 1, 22.

liability on the ground of error is a powerful legal weapon, and one expects the law to have granted some sort of protection to the reasonable reliance of the other party. Modern English law, for instance, attaches great significance to the position of the promisee. Despite their frequent use of will-related terminology[70] and, particularly, their obvious delight in the catch-phrase "consensus ad idem", as borrowed from Pothier, the English courts traditionally look at the *expression* of the will in order to determine whether (and with what content) a contract has been concluded. ". . . [F]or it is common learning that the intent of a man cannot be tried, for the Devil himself knows not the intent of a man", was the pragmatic insight of Brian CJ as far back as 1478,[71] and more recent writers have explained:

> "[T]he current phrase 'the intention of the parties governs the contract', is really only true to this extent; that it governs the contract where both parties are agreed what the intention was. Where there is a dispute as to the intention, the contract, or rather the contractual liability, is governed by the intention, as it is presumed from that sense which, under all the circumstances, the judge thinks ought fairly to be attached to the promise."[72]

This "objective test" approach is closely related to, if not derived from, estoppel by representation:[73] a party is bound by his declaration, because such declaration—whether or not it properly represents the declarant's true intention—is apt to engender reliance in the person of the addressee.[74] Of course, such reliance deserves protection only where it is reasonable. Thus, in particular, the promisor's mistake must not have been attributable to the promisee himself. Contrary to all Continental legal systems, English law has in fact made up a special category of the cases where the promisee has induced the promisor's

[70] Cf. e.g. Atiyah, *Rise and Fall*, pp. 407 sqq., quoting as an example Kindersley VC in *Haynes v. Haynes* (1861) 1 Dr & Sm 426 at 433: "When both parties will the same thing, and each communicates his will to the other, with a mutual agreement to carry it into effect, then an engagement or contract between the two is constituted."

[71] *Anon.* "(1478) YB 17 Edw IV, Pasch. f. 1, pl. 2", in: C.H.S. Fifoot, *History and Sources of the Common Law* (1949), pp. 252 sqq. (253).

[72] William Markby, *Elements of Law* (4th ed., 1889), n. 622. Cf. also e.g. Lord Wright, in *Norwich Union Fire Insurance Society Ltd. v. WH. M. Price Ltd.* [1934] AC 455 at 463: "[T]he test of intention in the formation of contracts . . . is objective; that is, intention is to be ascertained from what the parties said or did"; Furmston, in: Cheshire, Fifoot and Furmston, *Law of Contract* (11th ed., 1986), pp. 27 sq.: "Agreement, however, is not a mental state but an act and, as an act, is a matter of inference from conduct. The parties are to be judged, not by what is in their minds, but by what they have said or written or done. . . . The function of an English judge is not to seek and satisfy some elusive mental element. . . ." Further on the objective theory of contract and on the development from intent to responsibility, cf. Dalton, (1985) 94 *Yale LJ* 1039 sqq.; for Germany, cf. Gerhard Kegel, "Verwirkung, Vertrag und Vertrauen", in: *Festschrift für Klemens Pleyer* (1986), pp. 528 sqq.

[73] But see e.g. Treitel, *Contract*, p. 230.

[74] Cf. the leading case of *Smith v. Hughes* (1871) LR 6 QB 597 at 607: a party is bound, if, "whatever [his] real intention may be, he so conducts himself that a reasonable man would believe that he was assenting to the terms proposed by the other party, and that the party upon that belief enters into a contract with him". (Extreme) consequence: "It is even conceivable that a contract may be formed which is in accordance with the intention of neither party" (Williston, quoted by Dalton, (1985) 94 *Yale LJ* 1043).

mistake by some misrepresentation (innocent or otherwise).[75] Such misrepresentation renders the contract voidable at the option of the promisor.[76] Also, a mistake by one party may be operative (that is, have the effect of negativing consent) if it is known to the other party.[77] But apart from that, a mere unilateral mistake[78] does not normally affect the validity of the contract. English law thus provides a very far-reaching protection for the innocent promisee.[79] Arguably, it even overshoots the mark.[80] Modern German law, for instance, allows rescission of a contract on the basis of error much more readily,[81] but imposes a duty on the rescinding party to compensate the party, to whom the declaration of intention had been made, for the damage sustained in relying upon the validity of the contract.[82] This claim for compensation, incidentally, is not based on fault and cannot therefore be regarded as a (statutory) emanation of the culpa in contrahendo doctrine.[83] It finds its justification in the fact that the invalidity of the contract is attributable to the "sphere" of the maker of the declaration.[84]

(b) The position in Roman law

None of these devices was employed by the Roman lawyers. Neither was the promisor only relieved of his contractual obligation when the promisee did not deserve protection, nor was the latter granted a claim to recover his reliance interest. Nor, as a rule, did it matter whether the promisor could be blamed for his mistake; whether, in other words, the error was excusable or not.[85]

---

[75] For details, see Treitel, *Contract*, pp. 254 sqq.

[76] It is usually said that the representee may rescind the contract. On the various meanings of "rescission" cf. Treitel, *Contract*, pp. 283 sqq.

[77] Not every mistake has this effect: mistakes as to the person and as to the subject matter only if they are fundamental, mistakes as to the terms of the contract even though they may not have been fundamental. For details, see Treitel, pp. 224 sqq.

[78] As opposed to one which is common to both parties.

[79] In short, then, "Anglo-American law solves the problem of protecting the unerring party by giving relief only if there is no unerring party to the contract" (Timothy Hoff, "Error in the Formation of Contracts in Louisiana: A Comparative Analysis", (1978–79) 53 *Tulane LR* 374).

[80] So, too, Friedrich Kessler, Edith Fine, "Culpa in contrahendo, Bargaining in Good Faith, and Freedom of Contract: A Comparative Study", (1964) 77 *Harvard LR* 429; Diesselhorst, *Sympotica Wieacker*, pp. 206 sqq.

[81] § 119 I: "A person who, when making a declaration of intention, is in error as to its content, or did not intend to make a declaration of such content at all, may rescind the declaration if it may be assumed that he would not have made it with knowledge of the facts and with reasonable appreciation of the situation." § 119 II: "An error as to the content of the declaration is regarded in the same way as an error as to those characteristics of a person or a thing which are regarded in business as essential."

[82] § 122 BGB.

[83] Cf. infra, pp. 613 sq.

[84] Claus Wilhelm Canaris, *Die Vertrauenshaftung im deutschen Privatrecht* (1971), pp. 479 sqq., 532 sqq.

[85] Cf. e.g. Kaser, *RPr* I, p. 242.

About the reasons for this obvious lack of discrimination one can only speculate. First of all, it must, of course, be kept in mind that not every error excluded consent. The mistake had to relate to one of the essential elements of the contract. More particularly, the narrowness of the Roman doctrine of error in substantia has been described "as startling from a modern perspective".[86] Even mistakes regarding essential characteristics of the object of the contract, which could greatly disadvantage the purchaser, were ignored: by whom it had been made, what capacities or attributes it possessed, whether it was able to bear fruit, etc.[87] Thus, the ambit of operative errors in itself represented a kind of compromise between the interests of both parties concerned. Secondly, the potential for a deviation between intention and declaration was smaller in Roman law than it is today. Telegraphy, for instance, did not exist and the problems arising from the incorrect transmission of a telegram became a matter of concern only in the second half of the 19th century.[88] Furthermore, we have repeatedly stressed[89] that sale in early Roman law, being essentially a market transaction, was tantamount to cash sale. It was concluded inter praesentes, and the conclusion of the contract and the execution of the mutual performances necessarily coincided. It is obvious that errores in negotio, in pretio or in corpore are much less likely to occur (if not virtually impossible) where vendor and purchaser are present[90] and immediately exchange their mutual performances. By the time of the later Roman Republic, the formless emptio venditio had, of course, become a fully executory contract. But even then, and throughout the time of classical Roman law, sale to ultimate consumers in actual practice probably remained a transaction that was normally immediately executed. By and large, only merchants engaged in long-distance trading. They, in turn, appear to have formed reasonably close-knit

---

[86] Frier, (1983) 100 *ZSS* 274.

[87] Cf. today e.g. § 119 II BGB, covering every attribute or characteristic of the object of the contract relevant for the determination of its value (except the value itself).

[88] See, for example, the discussion by Rudolf von Jhering, "Culpa in contrahendo, Schadensersatz bei nichtigen oder nicht zur Perfektion gelangten Verträgen", (1861) 4 *JhJb* 106 sqq., stimulated by a decision of the District Court *("Landgericht")* of Cologne dating from 1856 and applying French law; for a report of this decision, dealing with the incorrect transmission of a telegraphic order (the recipient was instructed to buy rather than sell certain shares), see (1859) 19 *Zeitschrift für deutsches Recht und deutsche Rechtswissenschaft* 456 sqq. This case raised the question of the protection of the reasonable reliance of the recipient of the telegram. For contemporary pandectist doctrine it posed a major problem, since a contractual claim could not be construed in view of the fact that the contract was void; nor could a delictual claim be granted, since Aquilian liability for pure economic loss was generally rejected (cf. infra, pp. 1036 sqq.) Jhering's culpa in contrahendo doctrine and Bähr's declaration theory (cf. infra, note 188) were attempts to grapple with this difficulty. The *Landsgericht* of Cologne could resort to the famous general clause of delictual liability (art. 1382 code civil; on which, see infra, pp. 906, 1036) in order to achieve a satisfactory result.

[89] Cf. supra, pp. 237 sqq.

[90] In England, for instance, the question has been discussed whether an error in persona is possible inter praesentes; for details, see Treitel, *Contract*, pp. 225 sqq.

groups, developing and maintaining their own standards of trade.[91] Within an established market, as Frier argued recently,[92] merchants tend to look beyond the single transaction and to be motivated by the desire for repeat orders. They realize that it is to their own advantage to honour their undertakings without much wailing and lamenting. Both vendors and purchasers are usually keen to engender confidence and to build up a reputation for reliability. Under these circumstances, the possibility of attacking the validity of a contract on the ground of mistake was unlikely to lead to an unacceptable amount of confusion and commercial inconvenience.

Penultimately, it must be remembered that we are dealing here with a gradual development from a strictly objective, declaration-oriented approach towards a more flexible and individualistic one.[93] This development was in full swing during the time of classical Roman law. Even at the time of Ulpian, controversies still persisted.[94] Only slowly did the idea gain ground that a unilateral mistake can vitiate the contract. Thus, the picture presented over the previous pages is representative only of late classical jurisprudence. From this time onwards any appreciation for certainty of the law, for the inner discipline connected with form and formalism and for generally accepted social standards, faded away very quickly, anyway, and thus one could hardly expect post-classical jurisprudence to develop criteria which were suitable for checking the increasing emphasis on the intention of the parties.

9. Iuris ignorantia nocet, facti ignorantia non nocet

(a) *Error iuris nocet: the position in Roman law*

Finally, however, there was one kind of mistake which normally the Roman lawyers do not seem to have regarded as excusable, and that was the error iuris. "Regula est iuris quidem ignorantiam cuique nocere, facti vero ignorantiam non nocere", we read in Paul. D. 22, 6, 9 pr.[95] The same rule has come down to us in slightly different formulations: iuris ignorantia non prodest wrote Labeo,[96] iuris error nulli prodest, Paul in his commentary on the edict.[97] Error and

[91] Frier, (1983) 100 *ZSS* 293.

[92] (1983) 100 *ZSS* 289 sqq. (291).

[93] Cf. in general e.g. Heinz Hübner, "Subjektivismus in der Entwicklung des Privatrechts", in: *Festschrift für Max Kaser* (1976), pp. 715 sqq.

[94] Cf. Ulp. D. 18, 1, 9, 2.

[95] On this text cf. Schmidlin, *Rechtsregeln*, pp. 36 sqq.; Laurens C. Winkel, *Error iuris nocet—Rechtsdwaling als rechtsordeprobleem* (1982), pp. 149 sqq.

[96] Lab./Paul. D. 22, 6, 9, 3.

[97] Paul. D. 41, 4, 2, 15. On error iuris in Roman law generally (apart from the recent book by Winkel), cf. Voci, *L'errore*, pp. 211 sqq.; Paul van Warmelo, "Ignorantia iuris", (1954) 22 *TR* 1 sqq.; Zilletti, op. cit., note 19, pp. 254 sqq.; Theo Mayer-Maly, "Error iuris", in: *Ius Humanitatis, Festschrift für Alfred Verdross* (1980), pp. 147 sqq.; Henryk Kupiszewski, "Ignorantia iuris nocet", in: *Sodalitas, Scritti in onore di Antonio Guarino*, vol. III (1984), pp. 1357 sqq.

ignorantia are obviously used interchangeably.[98] Furthermore, the rule appears to be of considerable antiquity, for Labeo already advocated a restriction:

> "Sed iuris ignorantiam non prodesse Labeo ita accipiendum existimat, si iuris consulti copiam haberet vel sua prudentia instructus sit, ut, cui facile sit scire, ei detrimento sit iuris ignorantia. . . ."[99]

Originally it appears to have been taken for granted that a Roman citizen should know the law; after all, until the days of Cicero, schoolboys had to learn the text of the XII Tables by heart.[100] By that time, however, the ius civile, as contained in this venerable codification, had been overlaid with a number of individual enactments as well as by a whole body of law developed by the praetor. Labeo therefore confined the assumption to those who had legal advice readily available or who were themselves competent in law.[101] A layman could hardly be expected any longer to find his own way through either the ius honorarium or the lawyers' interpretation of the ius civile.[102] Neratius' argument in D. 22, 6, 2 therefore appears to be somewhat unrealistic: an error in iure (as opposed to ignorantia facti) is irrelevant, because the law can and should be definite (whereas the determination of factual circumstances may baffle even the homo prudentissimus).[103] Yet it is not too difficult to reconcile Neratius' reasoning with the restrictive tendency pursued by Labeo (and others): error iuris nocet applies not because the law is definite (or limited?; it is difficult to gauge the exact meaning of ius "finitum"),[104] but only if that is in fact the case. In other words: where the law is not (easily) determinable (for a layman), a mistake of law can possibly be regarded as excusable. It is in conformity

---

[98] Cf. also Mayer-Maly, *Festschrift Verdross*, p. 150.

[99] Lab./Paul. D. 22, 6, 9, 3; for details, see Winkel, op. cit., note 95, pp. 113 sqq.

[100] Cf. Alfred Pernice, *Labeo*, vol. II, 1 (2nd ed., 1895), p. 424.

[101] At the end of the fragment the comment, "quod raro accipiendum est", has been added (by Paul?; in post-classical times?), the intent of which is not entirely clear. Cf. Christian Friedrich Mühlenbruch, "Über iuris et facti ignorantia and deren Einfluss auf Rechtsverhältnisse", (1821) 2 *Archiv für die civilistische Praxis* 382 sqq.; but see Mayer-Maly, *Festschrift Verdross*, p. 151.

[102] "Late Republican sources paint a discouraging picture of indefiniteness and insecurity in the judicial system of Rome: the procedural forms of the Edict shifted constantly; rhetorical advocacy remained supreme in harsh adversary trials; broad social commitment to minimum standards of formal justice was still lacking; public ignorance of law was widespread . . .; and, at the margin of this pandemonium, a handful of jurists struggled to establish a place for their tenuous legal science": Frier, *Roman Jurists*, p. 183. All this changed as a result of the "revolution" of Roman jurisprudence during the late Republic (cf. infra, p. 627, note 33); this "revolution" brought about the emergence of the concept of "autonomous law" (Frier, pp. 188 sqq.) and entailed a strong movement towards legal security (on which, see Frier, pp. 188 sqq.).

[103] "In omni parte error in iure non eodem loco quo facti ignorantia haberi debebit, cum ius finitum et possit esse et debeat, facti interpretatio plerumque etiam prudentissimos fallat." Lauterbach, *Collegium theoretico-practicum*, Lib. XXII, Tit. VI, IV added that the interpretatio facti is a matter "ubi tamen ad minimum septem circumstantiae considerandae veniunt, scilicet, Causa, Persona, Locus, Tempus, Qualitas, Quantitas et Eventus".

[104] Cf. Vincenzo Scarano Ussani, *Valori e storia nella cultura giurudica fra Nerva e Adriano* (1979), pp. 5 sqq.; Winkel, op. cit., note 95, pp. 81 sqq.

with this kind of argument that a hard line on error iuris was usually taken with regard to specific, fairly recent acts of legislation[105]—as, for instance, decrees of the Senate such as the SC Silanianum,[106] the SC Macedonianum[107] or the SC Velleianum.[108] The constitutio Antoniniana led to a flurry of problem cases (and induced a policy of tightening-up),[109] for many of those who had been granted Roman citizenship lacked a detailed knowledge of the Roman laws.[110] But it was only in post-classical times that the emperors, concerned about the enforcement of the law, laid down a general duty to know the law: "Leges sacratissimae, quae constringunt omnium vitas, intellegi ab omnibus debent",[111] or, to quote the interpretatio to Codex Theodosianus 1, 1, 2: "Leges nescire nulli liceat, aut quae sunt statuta contemnere."[112] Certain groups of persons, however, were exempted from these stringent requirements: women, soldiers, minores XXV annis and rustici[113] (i.e. people stricken by rural simplicity).[114]

The maxim of error iuris nocet is based on the idea that one should know the law: "[non] stultis solere succurri, sed errantibus."[115] At least in classical Roman law, however, this was not considered to be a hard-and-fast rule. Its application depended to a certain extent on what could reasonably be expected of the people subject to the law.[116] The treatment of error iuris therefore demonstrates that the question (broadly speaking) of the reasonableness of the mistake did not necessarily remain entirely irrelevant. One may thus be justified in assuming that the other leg of Paul's regula in D. 22, 6, 9 pr. (facti ignorantiam non nocet) was also not always and necessarily applied without any regard to what could reasonably be expected.[117]

(b) Error vincibilis and invincibilis (ius commune)

In any event, the authors of the ius commune proceeded to restrict the relevance of ignorantia (or error) facti accordingly. By the time of the

[105] Mayer-Maly, *Festschrift Verdross*, pp. 161 sqq.
[106] Ulp. D. 29, 5, 3, 22.
[107] Ulp. D. 14, 6, 3 pr.; Pomp. D. 14, 6, 20; Ulp. D. 17, 1, 29, 1.
[108] C. 5, 6, 1 (Sev. et Ant.).
[109] Mayer-Maly, *Festschrift Verdross*, pp. 165 sq.; Winkel, op. cit., note 95, pp. 277 sq.
[110] On how imperial constitutions were published (and thus brought to the knowledge of those subject to them), cf. Fritz Schwind, *Zur Frage der Publikation im römischen Recht* (2nd ed., 1973), pp. 155 sqq.
[111] C. 1, 14, 9 (Val. et Marc.).
[112] Theo Mayer-Maly, "Einsicht und Erkundigungspflicht", (1976) 27 *Iura* 1 sqq.; Winkel, op. cit., note 95, pp. 275 sqq.
[113] They were allowed not to know the law (ius ignorare permissum est): cf. Paul. D. 22, 6, 9 pr.
[114] On rusticitas, e.g. C. 2, 2, 2 (Gord.) and Mayer-Maly, (1976) 27 *Iura* 2 sqq.; idem, "Rusticitas", in: *Studi in onore di Cesare Sanfilippo*, vol. I (1982), pp. 309 sqq.
[115] Paul. D. 22, 6, 9, 5 in fine.
[116] On the different restrictive strategies pursued, and criteria proposed by the Roman lawyers, see Winkel, pp. 79 sqq.
[117] Cf. also Kaser, *RPr* I, p. 242; Honsell/Mayer-Maly/Selb, p. 125.

usus modernus, the opinion had gained ground that a mistake relating to factual circumstances could be taken into account only if it was invincibilis[118] (or probabilis),[119] that is, if it could have been avoided by taking proper care. But what was to be regarded as proper care under these circumstances? By and large, it was held that gross negligence made the error inexcusable: "Error iustus est ille qui caret latissima et lata culpa."[120] The ignorance must not be based on negligentia crassa[121] or, as others put it, it must not be "supina et affectata".[122] Various attempts were made to refine these criteria. Thus, particularly, a distinction was drawn between ignorantia facti proprii and ignorantia facti alieni.[123] Of one's own personal sphere one could, as a rule, be expected to have a clear and detailed picture; exceptions were, however, made for very complicated affairs and propter memoriae imbecilitatem:[124] ". . . in iis quae antiqua sunt, aut valde intricata, facti proprii errorem tolerabilem esse ac excusare."[125] Matters falling outside one's own sphere one could, of course, not be required to know equally well. But even here an allegation of mistake could sometimes be of no avail, for instance, if the fact was known by all, or most, "in loco"[126] or "in ea civitate"[127] or if there had been a specific reason to make inquiries.

The distinction between own and other matters, incidentally, dates back to Pomponius, who had, however, introduced it in the context of mistakes relating to law.[128] This is quite typical of the specific relevance and influence of the Digest title 22, 6 on the development of the law of contract. An error iuris as such occurs but rarely when a contract is concluded.[129] Predominantly, the parties err about factual circum-

---

[118] Augustin Leyser, *Meditationes ad Pandectas*, Spec. CCLXXXIX, I and II; Glück, vol. 4, p. 164. The criterion of an error vincibilis appears to go back to Cuiacius (cf. Hübner, *Festschrift für Kaser*, p. 722), who had introduced it in respect of error iuris.

[119] Voet, *Commentarius ad Pandectas*, Lib. XXII, Tit. VI, VI.

[120] Blasius Altomarius, as quoted by Coing, p. 417. Cf. further Peter Haupt, *Die Entwicklung der Lehre vom Irrtum beim Rechtsgeschäft seit der Rezeption* (1941), pp. 17 sqq. For the Pandectists, see Windscheid/Kipp, § 79 a.

[121] Lauterbach, *Collegium theoretico-practicum*, Lib. XXII, Tit. VI, VIII.

[122] Voet, loc. cit. Cf. also Codex Maximilianeus Bavaricus civilis I, 1, 7.

[123] Lauterbach, *Collegium theoretico-practicum*, Lib. XXII, Tit. VI, V sqq.; Struve, *Syntagma*, Exerc. XXIX, Lib. 22, tit. 6, LIIX sqq.; Voet, loc. cit.

[124] Struve, *Syntagma*, Exerc. XXIX, Lib. 22, Tit. 6, LX.

[125] Voet, *Commentarius ad Pandectas*, Lib. XXII, Tit. VI, VII.

[126] Lauterbach, *Collegium theoretico-practicum*, Lib. XXII, Tit. VI, VIII.

[127] Voet, loc. cit.

[128] Pomp. D. 22, 6, 3.

[129] Both Haupt (infra note 130) and Coing (p. 418), incidentally, draw attention to the fact that the authors of the ius commune dealt with ignorantia iuris et facti in the form of a general doctrine (covering all areas of the law, including, particularly, criminal law). To what extent they specifically intended their propositions to be applied to the law of contract is occasionally unclear. In modern (German) criminal law the distinction between error iuris and error facti continues to be of great significance; cf. §§ 16 sqq. StGB and (e.g.) H.-J. Rudolphi, *Unrechtsbewusstsein, Verbotsirrtum und Vermeidbarkeit des Verbotsirrtums* (1969). In South African criminal law, the Appellate Division has recently set the cat among the

stances. But error iuris tended to be taken as the prototype of an error attributable to negligentia crassa and hence inexcusabilis. A generalization of this rationale provided the dogmatic basis for limiting the rule of ignorantia facti *non* nocet to cases of ignorantia invincibilis.[130]

(c) Error iuris (ius commune and modern law)

But what became of error iuris itself?[131] The glossators regarded a person who did not know the law as unworthy of legal protection.[132] The moral theologians were somewhat more lenient; a legal norm, they argued, can bind only those to whom it is known.[133] Nevertheless, the error iuris continued to be discriminated against; "error iuris regulariter non praesumitur, sed scientia" became a widely accepted rule of procedure, which lived on in France in the form of the famous adage "*nul n'est censé ignorer la loi*".[134] Some of the writers of the usus modernus questioned the distinction between ignorantia iuris and facti. Augustin Leyser abandoned it in favour of the more basic categories of error vincibilis and invincibilis.[135] Lauterbach advocated an exception from error iuris nocet "in juribus difficilioribus".[136] To 18th-century enlightened authoritarianism, on the other hand, "error iuris nocet" was bound to appeal. Condonation of ignorantia iuris militated against the educational and philosophical ideals of the time; and, in fact, the very idea of a codification, of a comprehensive and systematic reorganization of law (and society!) along the lines of natural reason, that became a hallmark of the age, aimed at making the law accessible, at instructing all subjects (and thus, indirectly, promoting their welfare) and at informing them about their rights, their duties and their position

pigeons in *S v. De Blom* 1977 (3) SA 513 (A) by suddenly reversing the principle of error iuris non excusat. The decision has remained controversial (cf. recently, for instance, *S v. Waglines (Pty.) Ltd.* 1986 (4) SA 1135 (N)).

[130] Haupt, op. cit., note 120, p. 20.

[131] For what follows cf. Theo Mayer-Maly, "Rechtsirrtum", in: *HRG*, vol. IV, col. 302 sqq.; as far as modern South African law is concerned, cf. Paul van Warmelo, "Regsdwaling", (1975) 38 *THRHR* 207 sqq.

[132] Cf. e.g. The Summula de iuris et facti ignorantia of Bulgarus ("Quia leges ab omnibus sciri debent et intelligi, qui ignarus iuris in aliquo labitur, indignus videtur auxilio"), printed on pp. 244 sqq. and commented upon on pp. 73 sqq. in Hermann Kantorowicz, *Studies in the Glossators of the Roman Law* (1938).

[133] Cf. still e.g. Grotius, *De jure belli ac pacis*, Lib. II, Cap. XX, XLIII: "Sicut ergo circa leges civiles eos excusamus qui legum notitiam aut intellectum non habuerunt, ita et circa naturae leges par est eos excusari quibus aut ratiocinationis imbecillitas aut prava educatio obstant. Nam ignorantia legis sicut inevitabilis si sit tollit peccatum."

[134] Cf. Hans Kiefner, "Die gegenwärtige Bedeutung der Maxime 'Nul n'est censé ignorer la loi'", in: E. v. Caemmerer, K. Zweigert (eds.), *Deutsche Landesreferate zum VII. Internationalen Kongress für Rechtsvergleichung in Uppsala* (1966), pp. 87 sqq. The Code Civil presupposes, but does not spell out, this maxim.

[135] *Meditationes ad Pandectas*, Spec. CCLXXXIX, I sqq.

[136] *Collegium theoretico-practicum*, Lib. XXII, Tit. VI, XIII.

within society.[137] Both the Prussian General Land Law and the Austrian ABGB therefore, not surprisingly, contain a rule to the effect that ignorance of a duly published law cannot be excused.[138] Many authors of the 19th century, again, adopted a more sceptical attitude towards the knowledge of the law one could expect of the general public,[139] and the BGB abandoned the distinction between error iuris and error facti altogether.[140] Today, the problem of ignorantia iuris is particularly topical[141] in view of the unprecedented flood of legislation emanating from our modern parliaments.[142]

10. The development of the modern error doctrine

(a) Usus modernus pandectarum

The sale of Stichus who was supposed to be Pamphilus, the problem of vinegar sold as wine, transactions concerning "golden" rings and "silver" tables, even the slave who is no longer a virgin but "iam mulier": the whole Roman repertory of cases was mulled over time and again by the authors of the ius commune. Together with these stock examples, all the solutions proposed and all the distinctions drawn by the Roman lawyers were faithfully preserved. Down to the end of the 18th century, the discussion of mistake in the formation of a contract did not receive any fundamentally new impulse, but dogmatized what was contained in the pages of the Digest.[143] A contract requires consensus, and "error excludit consensum".[144] Thus, a contract affected by error must be invalid.[145] This was the generally accepted starting point. But not every error could have this effect. This was an equally unquestioned proposition. It had to be fundamental in the sense

---

[137] For details, see, for instance, Franz Wieacker, "Aufstieg, Blüte und Krisis der Kodifikationsidee", in: *Festschrift für Gustav Boehmer* (1954), pp. 34 sqq.; Pio Caroni, "Kodifikation", in: *HRG* II, col. 907 sqq.

[138] § 12 Einleitung PrALR; § 2 ABGB.

[139] Cf. e.g. Savigny, *System*, vol. III, p. 336; Windscheid/Kipp, § 79 a.

[140] South African law appears to have moved in a similar direction; cf. Van Warmelo, (1975) 38 *THRHR* 207 sqq. According to the Louisiana Civil Code, errors of law usually have the same effect on contracts as errors of fact and invalidate a contract "where such error is its only or principal cause" (art. 1846): Hoff, (1978–79) 53 *Tulane LR* 370 sqq.

[141] Cf. e.g. Theo Mayer-Maly, "Rechtsirrtum und Rechtsunkenntnis als Probleme des Privatrechts", (1970) 170 *Archiv für die civilistische Praxis* 133 sqq.

[142] On this topic generally cf., for example, Theo Mayer-Maly, *Rechtskenntnis und Gesetzesflut* (1969); idem, "Gesetzesflut und Gesetzesqualität heute", in: *Festschrift zum 125jährigen Bestehen der Juristischen Gesellschaft zu Berlin* (1984), pp. 423 sqq.; Josef Isensee, "Mehr Recht durch weniger Gesetze", 1985 *Zeitschrift für Rechtspolitik* 139 sqq.; Dieter Strempel (ed.), *Mehr Recht durch weniger Gesetze* (1987), passim.

[143] For details cf. Peter Haupt, *Die Entwicklung der Lehre vom Irrtum beim Rechtsgeschäft seit der Rezeption* (1941), pp. 2 sqq.; cf. also the brief surveys by Coing, pp. 416 sqq., and Joubert, *Contract*, pp. 75 sq.

[144] Cf. e.g. Lauterbach, *Collegium theoretico-practicum*, Lib. XVIII, Tit. I, CV ("Error . . . voluntatem excludit, ac consensui est contrarius"); Voet, *Commentarius ad Pandectas*, Lib. XVIII, Tit. I, V ("Obest [consensui] error").

[145] No need existed to draw a distinction between dissensus in the narrow sense (mutual mistake) and (unilateral) mistake.

that it had to relate to the main content of the contract.[146] Thus, the parties must be ad idem as to each other's identity, as to the nature of their transaction and as to its subject matter (in the case of sale—still the standard example—object and price). Or, the other way round: consent is negatived by error in negotio, error in persona, error in corpore (plus error in substantia) and (where appropriate) error in pretio.[147] In these cases the rule of errantis voluntas nulla est was applied. An "error circa accessoria", on the other hand, was irrelevant. Likewise, a mistake about the quality, the value or the quantity of the object of the sale and (though this was very rarely expressly stated)[148] a mistake relating to the motive inducing a party to enter into the contract did not affect its validity.[149]

Certain features of the Roman doctrine of error were as vexing for the authors of the ius commune as they are for us. Error in substantia is the prime example. Much ingenuity was spent in an attempt to harmonize the sources and to draw the line between (irrelevant) mistakes as to the quality of the object of sale, and operative ones as to its substance or material.[150] Another dogmatic difficulty arose from the fact that an error in substantia was relevant in sale but did not matter as far as stipulations were concerned.[151] This discrepancy was often resolved by pointing out that in the latter case the recipient of the performance, who had been labouring under the mistake, would normally not be interested in the invalidity of the transaction. After all, he benefited from the stipulation (a unilaterally binding contract!), and

---

[146] ". . . circa id, quod (contrahentes) principaliter respiciunt": cf. e.g. Lauterbach, *Collegium theoretico-practicum*, Lib. XVIII, Tit. I, CV.

[147] Cf. e.g. Lauterbach, loc. cit., CVI sqq.; Voet, *Commentarius ad Pandectas*, Lib. XVIII, Tit. I, V; Glück, vol. 4, pp. 147 sqq. This is still the position in modern South African law: cf. e.g. Joubert, *Contract*, pp. 77 sqq.

[148] But see e.g. Pothier, *Traité des obligations*, n. 20.

[149] That does not mean that all these types of errors were necessarily entirely irrelevant. A motive, for instance, could have become part of the content of the contract. Under certain circumstances, the clausula rebus sic stantibus (cf. supra, pp. 579 sqq.) could be invoked (in Louisiana error in motive can invalidate the contract in these cases: cf. supra, p. 582, note 260). An error concerning the value of the object of sale could be taken into consideration under the rules relating to laesio enormis; the medieval authors in particular dealt with many error problems from this point of view (Feenstra, (1974) 48 *Tulane LR* 855). And as far as mistakes about the quality of the object of sale were concerned, the aedilitian remedies (as incorporated into the actio empti) provided the answer. The exact delimitation between the respective areas of application of the rules relating to mistake and the remedies for latent defects remains a matter of contention in modern German law; cf. e.g. Harm Peter Westermann, in: *Münchener Kommentar*, vol. III, 1 (2nd ed., 1988), § 459, nn. 73 sqq. Of course, the problem that the same fact may be looked upon as an error in substantia or as a latent defect appears in other civilian jurisdictions too. For Louisiana cf. Hoff, (1978–79) 55 *Tulane LR* 357.

[150] Cf. in particular Cuiacius, *Comment. in Tit. I. De contrah. empt. Lib. XVIII. Digest.*, Ad. L. IX, whose comments appear to have gained considerable influence (Haupt, op. cit., note 120, p. 11).

[151] Cf. supra, p. 600.

if he did not receive what he had believed he would receive, he should at least remain entitled to the object as it in fact existed.[152]

(b) Error in persona

Only occasionally did one leave the well-trodden ground and introduce new ideas or distinctions. Thus, some writers argued that only the party in error should be permitted to invoke the invalidity of the transaction:[153] a rule that had been introduced in someone's favour should not be allowed to be turned to his disadvantage.[154] Probably the most interesting dispute related to the error in persona. Some 18th-century authors recognized that the principle of error excludit consensum had been taken much too far in this regard.[155] Very often in everyday life the parties to a contract are not at all concerned about exactly whom they are contracting with, and their interests do not then require the transaction to be null and void in case of error in persona. On the contrary: invalidity would be inconvenient and undesirable.[156] Hence the attempts to limit the range of operative errores in persona to those cases where the identity of the other party had been essential for the conclusion of the contract: consideration of the person must form "an ingredient in the agreement", and anybody invoking error in persona must be able to show "that he would have been unwilling to enter into a contract in the same terms with anybody else". The two quotations are taken from a judgment by Carlisle AJ in *Gounder v. Saunders*, the first South African decision dealing with error in persona.[157] Pothier had been the great popularizer of this idea.[158] As so often, however, his views came to South Africa via a characteristic detour,[159] for the relevant passage in his *Traité des obligations* appears to have been cited with approval in every English case on error in persona since the latter half of the 19th century;[160] and for quite some time South African judges (those from Natal in particular!) liked to take their law from English sources, rather than to puzzle their heads over Dutch

[152] Cf. Bartolus, Cuiacius, Donellus, as quoted by Haupt, op. cit., note 120, pp. 22 sq.
[153] Cf. Haupt, op. cit., note 120, pp. 20 sq. (referring to Struve and Richelmann).
[154] Mod. D. 1, 3, 25.
[155] Haupt, op. cit., note 120, pp. 23 sqq.
[156] Cf., for instance, Treitel, *Contract*, p. 226, discussing the policy reasons why English courts have tried to restrict, as far as possible, the range of operative mistakes as to the identity of the other party.
[157] 1935 NPD 219 at 226.
[158] *Traité des obligations*, § 19; but cf. e.g. Barbeyrac in his annotations to Pufendorf, *Of the Law of Nature and Nations* (tr. B. Kennett, 4th ed., London 1729), Book III, Chap. VI, 7, n. 2.
[159] For details on the reception of this Pothier rule in South Africa, cf. Reinhard Zimmermann, "Der Einfluss Pothiers auf das römisch-holländische Recht in Südafrika", (1985) 102 *ZSS* (GA) 172 sqq.
[160] Cf. e.g. J.C. Smith, J.A.C. Thomas, "Pothier and the Three Dots", (1957) 20 *Modern LR* 38 sqq.; J.A.C. Thomas, "Error in persona and error in substantia", in: *La formazione storica*, vol. III, pp. 1203 sqq.

and Latin texts from old civilian writers.[161] The principle enunciated by Pothier (for which there is no authority in Roman law) has been repeatedly criticized; to Thibaut[162] and Savigny[163] (the great antagonists side by side!) it was irreconcilable with the will theory of contractual obligations, and so it still is for Professor De Wet of Stellenbosch.[164] English judges and writers, too, have occasionally expressed the wish to bury "this chief source of confusion" "once and for all".[165] Predominantly, however, the restriction of error in persona has been regarded as wholesome and practical, and thus it has prevailed not only in South Africa[166] and England,[167] but also on the European continent.[168]

(c) The contribution of the natural lawyers

The natural lawyers, of course, tried to put the whole doctrine of error on a new, more rational basis.[169] Thus, they rejected the Roman distinction between the various kinds of operative errors and quite a few of them not only redefined but also shifted the line dividing operative and inoperative errors not inconsiderably. Grotius, for instance, argued that every promise hinges on certain factual presumptions. If these turn out to be mistaken, the promise has lost its foundation and can no longer be enforced.

> ". . . si promissio fundata sit in praesumtione quadam facti quod non ita se habeat, naturaliter nullam ejus esse vim: quia omnino promissor non consensit in promissum, nisi sub quadam conditione, quae reipsa non exstitit":[170]

by way of a tacit condition, every motive that has induced a person to make a promise can therefore be read into his declaration. The whole

[161] For Natal cf. Hahlo/Kahn, *The Union of South Africa* (1960), pp. 64 sqq. and Peter Spiller, *A History of the District and Supreme Courts of Natal 1846–1910* (1986). On the process of reception of English law in South Africa generally, cf. Zimmermann, *RHR*, pp. 13 sqq.

[162] *System des Pandekten-Rechts* (6th ed.), vol. I 1823, § 146.

[163] *System*, vol. III, § 136.

[164] *Dwaling en Bedrog by die Kontraksluiting* (1943), pp. 11 sqq.; De Wet en Yeats, p. 22. Cf. also Joubert, *Contract*, pp. 77.

[165] A.L. Goodhart, "Mistake as to Identity in *Contract*", (1941) 57 *LQR* 235; cf. also *Lewis v. Averay* [1972] 1 QB 198 (CA) at 206F.

[166] Cf. e.g. *Bird v. Sumerville* 1961 (3) SA 194 (A) at 204G–H; *Landsbergen v. Van der Walt* 1972 (2) SA 667 (R) at 669C–G; Kerr, *Contract*, pp. 26 sqq.

[167] For details, see Treitel, *Contract*, pp. 224 sqq.; Thomas, in: *La formazione storica*, vol. III, pp. 1203 sqq.

[168] Cf. e.g. § 76 I 4 PrALR; art. 1110 code civil; art. 24, n. 2 OR; art. 1429, n. 3 codice civile; Glück, vol. 4, pp. 158 sq.; Wächter, *Pandekten*, vol. II, p. 371.

[169] For details, see Haupt, op. cit., note 120, pp. 25 sqq.; Klaus Luig, "Der Einfluss des Naturrechts auf das positive Privatrecht im 18. Jahrhundert", (1979) 96 *ZSS* (GA) 50 sqq.; idem, *Forschungsband von Zeiller* (cf. infra, note 174), pp. 157 sqq.; cf. also Coing, pp. 418 sq.

[170] *De jure belli ac pacis*, Lib. II, Cap. XI, VI. On Grotius' views on error cf. further Diesselhorst, *Hugo Grotius*, pp. 91 sqq.; cf. also Robert Feenstra, "L'influence de la scolastique espagnole sur Grotius en droit privé: quelques expériences dans les questions de fond et de forme, concernant notamment les doctrines de l'erreur et de l'enrichissement sans cause", in: *Fata Iuris Romani* (1974), pp. 338 sqq.

construction is obviously based on a fiction,[171] and it remained but an ephemeral episode.

The most important and lasting contribution of the natural lawyers in this area of the law, however, resulted from their analysis of contract as being based on two (coinciding) declarationes voluntatis, each of which, in turn, consists of two components: signum volendi and volitio, or declaration and intention.[172] Thus, it became possible to distinguish dissensus and (unilateral) error and to interpret error as a discrepancy or conflict between the two constituent elements of a declaratio voluntatis. Natural-law-inspired writers and legislators themselves, however, were not ad idem as to which of these two elements to emphasize. Some of them, placing the stress on commercial convenience and certainty, gave preference to the external manifestation of the will. Both the Bavarian Codex Maximilianeus[173] and the Austrian ABGB[174] were guided by the (supposedly old German) principle of "error noceat erranti"[175] and took account of any form of mistake by a party to a contract only under exceptional circumstances.[176] Grotius and his followers, as we have seen, were much less strict in their approach; in fact, they even extended the scope of operative mistakes beyond what had traditionally been recognized by the authorities of the ius commune. Significantly, however, they devised another way of protecting the interests of the recipient of the declaration: for, while recognizing that even fault on the part of the person in error did not alter the fact that the contract lacked consensus and could therefore not have come into existence, they provided the party to whom the declaration had been made with a claim to recover his damages.[177] This turned out to be a bold but, in the long run, influential innovation. Dogmatically, of course, it was difficult to see how it could be reconciled with established thinking patterns: a declaration made without intention is ineffective, and something that has no effect can hardly be the basis for a claim for damages. Culpa on its own, on the other hand, is not a suitable causa obligandi either.[178] Rudolf von Jhering's doctrine of culpa in contrahendo attempted to deal

---

[171] Cf. e.g. Diesselhorst, *Hugo Grotius*, pp. 97 sqq.

[172] Cf. supra, pp. 567 sqq.

[173] IV, 1, § 25.

[174] § 876. On the background and history of this section of the ABGB cf. Klaus Luig, "Franz von Zeiller und die Irrtumsregelung des ABGB", in: Selb/Hofmeister (eds.), *Forschungsband Franz von Zeiller* (1980), pp. 157 sqq.

[175] Cf. Haupt, op. cit., note 120, p. 36.

[176] According to the ABGB, if the mistake was induced by a misrepresentation by the other party or if the other party ought to have noticed the mistake.

[177] Grotius, *De jure belli ac pacis*, Lib. II, Cap. XI, VI; Pufendorf, *De jure naturae et gentium*, Lib. III, Cap. VI, § 6.

[178] In French law, the problem is obviated by the general clause of delictual liability (art. 1382), which, in turn, derives from the theories of natural law; cf. infra, pp. 906, 1036; also supra, note 88.

with these kinds of objections.[179] In the end, however, the fathers of the BGB went even further and resolved to grant a claim for the reliance interest, irrespective of whether the party in error had been at fault or not.[180]

(d) Error in Savigny's System and under the BGB

The most prominent voice against this new idea had, incidentally, been that of Savigny.[181] His exposition of the doctrine of error, as contained in volume three of the *System*, is usually regarded as a landmark par excellence for the interpretatio moderna of this topic;[182] Windscheid, for instance, did not hesitate to hail it as an "epoch-making" piece of legal writing.[183]

Savigny's importance in this area (as in many others) was not that of a great innovator. It lay in the manner in which he brought out and conceptualized the fundamental tenets underlying the sources of Roman law (as he understood them) and in which he tried to build up a coherent and logical doctrine on that basis. Thus, in this instance, his treatment provides the classic exposition of what has since become known as the "will theory".[184] Particularly important was the clear distinction that he drew between a mere error in motive (which does not affect the will of the contracting party but relates to the preliminary process of the formation of such a will) and an error in respect of the contents of the agreement. In the latter case there is no correspondence between will and declaration, and a declaration unsupported by a corresponding intention must be ineffective. More clearly than anybody else, Savigny spelt out the consequences of his basic premises: there can be no claim for damages, even if the party in error was at fault;[185] every error in persona relates to the content of the declaration and must therefore be taken into account;[186] and every transaction affected by an operative error must be regarded as null and void, irrespective of whether the party who had been labouring under the

[179] (1861) 4 *JhJb* 1 sqq. On Jhering's views, as expressed in this famous article, cf. recently Erich Schanze, "Culpa in Contrahendo bei Jhering", (1978) 7 *Ius Commune* 326 sqq.; Dieter Medicus, "Zur Entdeckungsgeschichte der culpa in contrahendo", in: *Iuris Professio, Festgabe für Max Kaser* (1986), pp. 169 sqq.

[180] § 122 BGB. Along different lines still, § 99 II E I. For a comparative analysis cf. Friedrich Kessler, Edith Fine, "Culpa in contrahendo, Bargaining in Good Faith, and Freedom of *Contract*: A Comparative Study", (1964) 77 *Harvard LR* 429 sqq. They note a trend in French law, too, to compensate the innocent party by awarding him reliance damages, and even a tendency in the common law to employ the idea of culpa in contrahendo as a weapon to soften the rigours of the "objective theory" of contracts.

[181] *System*, vol. III, § 138, n. (d).

[182] Cf. e.g. Wieacker, *Mélanges Meylan*, p. 385; Flume, *AT*, p. 445.

[183] Windscheid/Kipp, § 76, n.*

[184] *System*, vol. III, §§ 135 sqq. and Beylage VIII (pp. 326 sqq.). On Savigny's error doctrine cf. Haupt, op. cit., note 120, pp. 40 sqq.; Flume, *AT*, § 22, 2; Klaus Luig, "Savignys Irrtumslehre" (1979) 8 *Ius Commune* 36 sqq.; Hammen, *Savigny*, pp. 111 sqq.

[185] Cf. supra, note 88.

[186] Cf. supra, pp. 592, 612.

mistake wished this to be the case or not.[187] On all these points, Savigny took a stand against prevailing practice.

Ultimately, however, it was not doctrinal accuracy that won the day. For even though the "will theory" gained broad acceptance,[188] pragmatic modifications thereto continued to be made, particularly in the three areas mentioned above. The BGB does grant a claim for damages,[189] takes into consideration whether the mistake induced the declaration[190] and leaves any decision about the validity of the contract to the discretion of the party in error.[191] Thus, the transaction is not invalid ipso iure, but may be rescinded by way of an informal declaration to the other party.[192] Apart from that, the BGB no longer refers to the old categories of error in negotio, corpore, persona or pretio; they had become obsolete in the course of the later 19th century.[193] Ironically, only the error in substantia, that chief source of

[187] *System*, vol. III, § 138 (p. 294).

[188] Cf. e.g. Windscheid/Kipp, § 75; Ernst Zitelmann, *Irrtum und Rechtsgeschäft* (1879), passim; "Motive", in: *Mugdan*, vol. I, p. 457; De Wet en Yeats, pp. 7 sqq. A different view was taken by the adherents of the so-called "declaration theory", as developed since the 1870s: cf. e.g. Otto Bähr, "Ueber Irrungen im Contrahiren", (1875) 14 *JhJb* 393 sqq.; Rudolf Leonhard, *Der Irrtum als Ursache nichtiger Verträge* (2nd ed., 1907), pp. 14 sqq.

[189] § 122 BGB. The majority of pandectist writers had continued to protect the interests of the recipient of the declaration in a different manner: like the authors of the older ius commune, they regarded as operative only those mistakes for which the party labouring under them could not be blamed (error invincibilis). It was disputed whether every type of fault or only gross negligence was to be taken into account in this regard. Cf., for example, the discussion by Dernburg, *Pandekten*, vol. I, § 101, who refers to Savigny's solution as "mathematically" and abstractly correct, but as practically unsuitable (and as not being in accordance with the sources of Roman law); cf. further e.g. Windscheid/Kipp, § 76 in fine and, for modern South African law, Joubert, *Contract*, p. 83.

[190] Cf. § 119 I BGB (". . . may rescind the declaration if it may be assumed that he would not have made it with knowledge of the facts and with reasonable appreciation of the situation"); Ernst Kramer, in: *Münchener Kommentar*, vol. I (2nd ed., 1984), § 119, n. 129. On the earlier discussion about error in persona in this context, cf. supra, pp. 611 sq.

[191] This is in line with the principle of private autonomy: cf. Harder, (1973) 173 *Archiv für die civilistische Praxis* 225.

[192] §§ 119, 142 sqq. BGB. § 142 I BGB attributes ex-tunc effect to the declaration of rescission. Only a few of the pandectists had been prepared to follow Savigny and to regard the contract as null and void (cf. e.g. Wächter, *Pandekten*, vol. II, § 186, Beil. B). According to the majority view, only the party in error was allowed to invoke the invalidity of the transaction ("relative invalidity"); cf. e.g. Regelsberger, *Pandekten*, § 142, IV; Brinz, *Pandekten*, § 317, in fine. Towards the end of the century the term *"Anfechtbarkeit"* (rescindability) came into use and one started to require a declaration of rescission. It is interesting to note that this concept of *"Anfechtbarkeit"* can be traced back to Savigny too (who had, however, not applied it to error): *System*, vol. IV, pp. 536 sqq. For details, see Manfred Harder, "Die historische Entwicklung der Anfechtbarkeit von Willenserklärungen", (1973) 173 *Archiv für die civilistische Praxis* 209 sqq.; cf. also Hammen, *Savigny*, pp. 123 sqq. For modern South African law ("The way in which error is raised is . . . by the party who relies on it pleading it") cf. Joubert, *Contract*, pp. 83 sqq. According to Hoff, (1978–79) 53 *Tulane LR* 337, there has been a general tendency in both civil-law and common-law systems to expand the idea of voidability or relative nullity and to contract the scope of the notion of absolute nullity correspondingly.

[193] What mattered for adherents of the will theory was whether will and declaration coincided: without a corresponding will no (valid) declaration. Whether the deviation between will and declaration could be labelled error in persona, in objecto, etc. became more

doctrinal embarrassment, still shimmers through, albeit faintly. According to § 119 II BGB, a contract may be rescinded on the basis of an error as to those characteristics of a person or thing which are regarded in business as essential. It will be recognized immediately that this provision is much wider than the Roman notion of an error in substantia, particularly if the very liberal interpretation of the term "characteristics" by the German courts is kept in mind: it covers all legal or factual features of a thing that make up, contribute to or influence in the eyes of the general public its usefulness and value.[194] This includes, for instance, the age of a second-hand car and the existence of an expert opinion attesting to the genuineness of a work of art or the permissibility of building projects on a piece of property.[195] Rescission would also have been possible, according to German law, in that famous Dutch case[196] where some old metal cup, dug up in the course of dredging works, had been sold without knowledge of the fact that it was actually a hellenistic Kantharos of the 2nd century B.C. with Greek and Latin inscriptions (one of which concerned its owner, who may have been a Roman officer mentioned by Diodorus Siculus).

(e) Error in substantia

To most authors of the ius commune, such a wide-ranging recognition of a mistake, that related not really to the content of the contract, but rather to a quality of its object, would have been unthinkable. The somewhat exceptional category of error in substantia was usually taken to refer to cases where the material, in the sense of chemical substance, of the object of the contract had turned out to be different from the one contemplated by one or both of the contracting parties. Again, it was Savigny who pioneered a much more satisfactory approach. How odd that it should matter whether a sculpture by Benvenuto Cellini was plated with rather than made out of silver and not whether it was really attributable to that artist![197] Savigny therefore broadened the scope of error in substantia (a move for which, incidentally, he derived support

and more irrelevant. The fathers of the BGB did not want to put judiciary and legal science into the strait-jacket of these categories of the ius commune. A similar attitude was adopted when it came to the codification of the law of unjustified enrichment: cf. infra, pp. 887 sq. Other civilian codifications (as, for instance, the Swiss, Austrian and Italian ones) still use the categories of error in objecto, negotio and persona; for an overview cf. Diesselhorst, *Sympotica Wieacker*, pp. 181 sqq. The system of operative errors as recognized by the BGB (§ 119, cf. supra, note 81) is based on the analysis by Ernst Zitelmann as presented in his work on *Irrtum und Rechtsgeschäft* (1897). On the origin of § 119 BGB and on the theories of Zitelmann, cf., in particular, Rothoeft, op. cit., note 25, pp. 64 sqq., 92 sqq.; Werner Schubert, "Zu einer Edition unveröffentlichter Materialien zum BGB", (1975) 175 *Archiv für die civilistische Praxis* 430 sqq.; cf. also Hammen, *Savigny*, pp. 128 sqq.

[194] Cf. already RGZ 64, 266 (269); further e.g. BGHZ 34, 32 (41).

[195] For the (abundant) casuistry cf. e.g. Kramer, op. cit., note 190, § 119, nn. 108 sqq.

[196] Discussed by Feenstra, (1974) 48 *Tulane LR* 846 sqq. The Supreme Court of the Netherlands did not regard the contract as void or voidable.

[197] Savigny, *System*, vol. III, § 137, p. 280.

from the error in sexu discussed in D. 18, 1, 11, 1);[198] for he recognized that a contract may be void, if the mistake relates to a substantial *quality* of the object. Substantial qualities, however, are only those which, according to notions prevailing in everyday life, cause a thing to belong to a specific class of objects.[199] Thus, on the one hand, he did not stick to the rigid, outdated and unsatisfactory criterion of "materia", but was (in this instance) prepared to accommodate a more pragmatic approach.[200] Yet, on the other hand, he was keenly aware of the fact that recognition of every kind of mistake about (even essential) qualities was likely to undermine commercial certainty and be incompatible with the demands of business.[201] Hence the requirement that the thing must have turned out to be an aliud, must have belonged to a different commercial category of objects.

Savigny himself, incidentally, clearly recognized that error in substantia (however defined) was something of an anomaly in his doctrinal edifice; but respect for the sources of Roman law demanded not only its retention but also its rationalization as far as that was possible.[202] Even though Savigny's construction of error in substantia remained somewhat artificial,[203] it constituted an acceptable compromise solution and found its way into nearly all pandectist textbooks.[204] Only towards the end of the century was some opposition voiced. Ernst Zitelmann declared that every error relating to a quality of the object constituted an error in motive and as such was irrelevant.[205] The authors of the first draft of the BGB adopted this radical and rigidly dogmatic view.[206] But, as is so often the case, extreme views produce extreme reactions. The second commission wanted to be pragmatic, equitable and modern. Without much reflection,[207] it took a plunge into the dark and ventured to set out on what Leo Raape called a "mystery tour".[208] It is widely recognized today that in this instance the legislator has failed in his task to find plausible and determinable criteria by which to separate relevant from irrelevant forms of error.[209]

---

[198] Savigny, *System*, vol. III, § 137, p. 282. Zitelmann, *Irrtum und Rechtsgeschäft*, p. 574, on the other hand, criticized Savigny for distorting the sources.

[199] Savigny, *System*, vol. III, § 137, p. 283.

[200] Savigny, *System*, vol. III. § 137, p. 277.

[201] Savigny, loc. cit.

[202] Cf. also Haupt, op. cit., note 120, pp. 44 sqq.; Flume, *AT*, § 22, 2; Luig, (1979) 8 *Ius Commune* 54 sqq.; Hammen, *Savigny*, pp. 114 sqq.

[203] So Savigny himself (*System*, vol. III, § 138, p. 293).

[204] Cf. e.g. Windscheid/Kipp, § 76 a, e).

[205] *Irrtum und Rechtsgeschäft*, pp. 435 sqq., 549 sqq.; cf. also Flume, *AT*, § 22, 3.

[206] § 102 E I; "Motive", in: *Mugdan*, vol. I, p. 462.

[207] "Protokolle", in: *Mugdan*, vol. I, pp. 238 sq.; cf. the analysis by Flume, *AT*, § 24, 1.

[208] "'Fahrt ins Blaue, . . . eine Vorschrift aufs Geratewohl': Sachmängelhaftung und Irrtum beim Kauf", (1949) 150 *Archiv für die civilistische Praxis* 501.

[209] For a critical discussion of all modern views on § 119 II BGB, cf. Kramer, op. cit., note 190, § 119, nn. 10, 89 sqq.; cf. also Diesselhorst, *Sympotica Wieacker*, pp. 194 sqq.

(f) Developments in French and English law

In other European countries there have been similar tendencies to extend the scope of operative error beyond the mere terms of an agreement to parts of what one could call the contractual environment.[210] We have seen how far Grotius was prepared to go—his doctrine of implied supposition opened the door for mere motives to be taken into account.[211] Pufendorf modified and somewhat restricted this idea. He went back to the old distinction between essentialia and accidentalia negotii, but emphasized that the former also include "illae qualitates rei quas paciscens praecipue ob oculos habuit".[212] Via Jean Barbeyrac (who translated and annotated Pufendorf's main work), this formula gained entry into Pothier's influential Traité des obligations.[213] Pothier, of course, was not only the elegant stylist and a matchless popularizer; he was also a great amalgamator of legal ideas and various strands of tradition. Here we have an example, for it was Pothier who linked the view expressed by Pufendorf to the Roman error in substantia. *"L'erreur annule la convention"*, he wrote,[214] *"non seulement lorsqu'elle tombe sur la chose même, mais lorsqu 'elle tombe sur la qualité de la chose que les contractans ont eu principalement en vue, et qui fait la substance de cette chose."* And even though the French code civil refers only to the substance of the thing,[215] this clause is usually interpreted in the light of Pothier's statement on the matter.[216] Error in substantia has become a category subjectively determined, for it is taken to refer to the

---

[210] Cf. the analysis by F.H. Lawson, "Error in substantia", (1936) 52 *LQR* 79 sqq.

[211] Cf. supra, pp. 612 sq.

[212] This distinction was, however, not employed in the context of error by Pufendorf: cf. the analysis by G.E. Mulder, "De dwalingsleer van Samuel Pufendorf en zijn commentatoren", (1962) *Rechtsgeleerd Magazijn Themis* 111 sqq.; Feenstra, (1974) 48 *Tulane LR* 856 sq.

[213] Cf. Mulder and Feenstra, loc. cit.

[214] *Traité des obligations*, n. 18.

[215] Art. 1110 I code civil; cf. also art. 1358 I of the Civil Code of the Netherlands. But see artt. 1842 sqq. of the Louisiana Civil Code (1870) providing the following detailed regulation: "Error as to the thing, which is the subject of the contract, does not invalidate it, unless it bears on the substance or (!) some substantial quality of the thing" (art. 1842). "There is error as to the substance, when the object is of a totally different nature from that which is intended. Thus, if the object of the stipulation be supposed by one or both of the parties to be an ingot of silver, and it really is a mass of some other metal that resembles silver, there is an error bearing on the substance of the object" (art. 1843). "The error bears on the substantial quality of the object, when such quality is that which gives it its greatest value. A contract relative to a vase, supposed to be gold, is void, if it be only plated with that metal" (art. 1844). "Error as to the other qualities of the object of the contract, only invalidates it, when those qualities are such as were the principal cause of making the contract" (art. 1845). It is quite extraordinary to see how the code itself used to assume what would (for instance) in Germany be regarded as the role of a commentary. In 1984, these rules were replaced by the new art. 1950.

[216] For details, see Lawson, (1936) 52 *LQR* 81 sqq.; René David, "La doctrine de l'erreur dans Pothier et son interprétation dans la Common Law d'Angleterre", in: *Études de droit civil à la mémoire de Henri Capitant* (1939), pp. 145 sqq.; cf. also Watson, *Failures*, pp. 24 sq.

qualities which the parties had principally had in mind. Again, the dangers of this approach for commercial certainty are obvious.[217]

Even English judges have occasionally succumbed to the strange and luring spell of error in substantia. The English law relating to error is particularly complex and confusing,[218] and if Continental doctrine has been referred to as perplexa satis,[219] the English one is certainly perplexissima.[220] It has grown together from separate roots (common law and equity) and is based on certain characteristic premises that make any comparison with continental systems difficult.[221] The very fact, as Professor Lawson says very pointedly, that systems derived from Roman law accept a certain solution "is a reason why English law should not".[222] And yet, one comes across a statement such as the following:

> "And, as we apprehend, the principle of our law is the same as that of the civil law; and the difficulty in every case is to determine whether the mistake or misapprehension is as to the substance of the whole consideration, going, as it were, to the root of the matter, or only to some point, even though a material point, an error as to which does not affect the substance of the whole consideration."[223]

---

[217] Emphasized particularly by Lawson, loc. cit. Cf. also Hoff, (1978–79) 53 *Tulane LR* 353 ("very imprecise and uncontrollable device").

[218] For a brief overview from a comparative perspective cf. Zweigert/Kötz, pp. 108 sqq., 116 sqq.; T.B. Smith, "Error in the Scottish Law of *Contract*", (1955) 71 *LQR* 507 sqq.; Saúl Litvinoff, "'Error' in the Civil Law", in: Joseph Dainow (ed.), *Essays on the Civil Law of Obligations* (1969), pp. 222 sqq., 253 sqq.

[219] Grotius, *De jure belli ac pacis*, Lib. II, Cap. XI, VI.

[220] "The treatment of mistake is certainly one of the weakest aspects of (Anglo-American) contract law. The cases and 'rules' are contradictory and impossible to reconcile": Arthur I. Rosett, "Contract Performance: Promises, Conditions and the Obligation to Communicate", (1975) 22 *University of California at Los Angeles LR* 1095.

[221] Cf. e.g. Lawson, (1936) 52 *LQR* 105: "In fact, the instinct of English law is to isolate a contract as far as possible from its environment. This, though operating inequitably on occasion, gives greater certainty and makes parties more careful in settling the terms of their contract. Perhaps therefore the ultimate distinction is between a paternally minded equity and strict law." Any evaluation of the comparatively narrow ambit of the doctrine of error in English law must also (for instance) take account of the fact that it is interrelated with and supplementary to the doctrine of misrepresentation (which civilian legal systems do not know) and that Continental safeguards such as (for instance) culpa in contrahendo are not available in English law.

[222] (1936) 52 *LQR* 98. For a very thorough comparative analysis of German law and English law on the topic of mistake in general, see, however, Rothoeft, *System der Irrtumslehre* (1968), who demonstrates the functional equivalence of the solutions found in both legal systems. Cf. also Buckland/McNair, pp. 205 sqq.; Thomas, in: *La formazione storica*, vol. III, pp. 1203 sqq., 1208 sqq. and Timothy Hoff, "Error in the Formation of Contracts in Louisiana: A Comparative Analysis", (1978–79) 53 *Tulane LR* 329 sqq., who concludes that the doctrine of error in a modern civil code has a coherence within the legal system and a measure of predictability that the common law has yet to achieve (p. 379). Hoff refers in this context to Louisiana's paucity of case law. The Louisiana Civil Code enunciates a particularly thorough and detailed theory of contractual error (contained in 30 articles), which is largely based on Pothier and the French Code Civil.

[223] *Kennedy v. Panama, New Zealand and Australian Royal Mail Co. Ltd.* (1867) LR 2 QB 580 at 588 (per Blackburn J). For examples of the application of error in substantia in other common-law jurisdictions, cf. Hoff, (1978–79) 53 *Tulane LR* 355 sqq.

Blackburn J arrived at this conclusion after a lengthy review of Roman texts on error in substantia, and the whole passage has given rise to the inference that (common) mistake as to quality may under certain circumstances invalidate a contract in English law.[224] On the other hand, however, it is clear that a unilateral error in substantia does not in any way affect the contract.[225]

It need hardly be emphasized that the continental classification of error has in other respects, too, been regarded as useful at common law.[226] But, above all, the very idea that mistake can, under certain (albeit relatively narrow) circumstances, negative consensus,[227] has been received, via Domat, Pothier, Chitty, Colebrooke and the other treatise-writers from the civil law.[228] It has never fitted in very happily and has, in actual practice, been overlaid by estoppel ideas and the "objective test" approach.[229] But the fact remains that the English doctrine of mistake cannot be properly understood if one fails to realize that, essentially, it constituted a late importation into the common law, and one that was very closely related to the consensus doctrine of contract.[230]

[224] Treitel, *Contract*, pp. 215 sqq. (also discussing *Bell v. Lever Brothers, Ltd.* [1932] AC 161 (HL)).

[225] The leading case is *Smith v. Hughes* (1871) LR 6 QB 597.

[226] For America, cf. e.g. Roscoe Pound, *Jurisprudence*, vol. IV (1959), pp. 453 sqq. and, more recently, Timothy Hoff, (1978–79) 53 *Tulane LR* 348 sqq. For England, see e.g. Pollock, *Principles of Contract* (7th ed., 1902), pp. 461 sqq., referring to error in negotio, in persona, in substantia, in corpore and in pretio.

[227] Cf. Lord Atkin in *Bell v. Lever Brothers Ltd.* [1932] AC 161 (HL) at 217.

[228] A.W.B. Simpson, "Innovation in Nineteenth Century Contract Law", (1975) 91 *LQR* 265 sqq.; cf. also Peter Stein, "Continental Influences on English Legal Thought", in: *La formazione storica*, vol. III, pp. 1124 sq.

[229] Cf. supra, notes 14, 15.

[230] Simpson, (1975) 91 *LQR* 268 sq. According to Simpson, the common law had traditionally dealt with mistake by way of an implied condition: the agreement was taken to have included a condition to the effect that a certain state of affairs existed; if that proved to be a mistaken assumption "the contract was off not because the parties had failed to reach consensus, but because that was what they had in fact (tacitly) agreed upon." This is vaguely reminiscent of Grotius' construction of error (supra, pp. 612 sq.).

CHAPTER 20

Interpretation of Contracts

I. FRENCH FRANCS AND BELGIAN FRANCS (INTRODUCTION)

If a Frenchman and a Belgian meet in Hamburg, and the one sells his car to the other for 2 000 francs, the question arises as to what currency the parties have intended: 2 000 French or Belgian francs. Both parties have probably had their own currency in mind, and the reasonable and objective bystander may well be taken to have understood the mutual declarations accordingly. Thus, we would be dealing with a case of hidden lack of agreement (dissent): the one party intended and declared French francs, whilst the other party both meant and referred to Belgian francs. If the same transaction had taken place in Brussels, rather than in Hamburg, one would probably have to come to a different conclusion: in this case the declaration, not only of the Belgian, but also of the Frenchman, would have to be construed, from an objective point of view, as referring to Belgian francs. Thus, according at least to modern German law, a contract would have come into existence, since the declarations of both parties to the contract corresponded. However, due to the obvious deviation between intention and declaration, the Frenchman would be able to rescind the contract; but if he chooses to do so, he is under an obligation to compensate the other party for his reliance interest.

This very simple example shows how closely the questions of error and interpretation are intertwined. Whether the problem of error arises, and if so, in which way, often depends on how a contract or the declarations leading up to it are to be understood. And just as in the case of error the law can emphasize either the intention of the parties (their "consensus ad idem") or the external manifestation of their intention,[1] so it can adopt either a subjective or an objective approach in matters of interpretation.[2] Archaic legal systems are usually dominated by a very literal, word-oriented (i.e. objective) approach, and it is only with the increasing refinement of legal culture that subjective elements begin to be taken into consideration.[3] When a certain stage in this process is reached, however, progress ceases and decline begins.[4] Sole emphasis

---

[1] Cf. supra, pp. 584 sqq.

[2] Cf. e.g. Zweigert/Kötz, pp. 96 sqq.; Alexander Lüderitz, *Auslegung von Rechtsgeschäften* (1966), pp. 78 sqq.

[3] Cf. generally Heinz Hübner, "Subjektivismus in der Entwicklung des Privatrechts", in: *Festschrift für Max Kaser* (1976), pp. 715 sqq.

[4] Fritz Pringsheim, "Animus in Roman Law", (1933) 49 *LQR* 48.

on subjective criteria will seriously affect or even undermine the certainty of law and the security of commerce. Modern legal systems, therefore, usually attempt to establish a balance. The BGB, for instance, calls attention to both subjective and objective criteria. While § 133 BGB declares that, in interpreting a declaration of intention, the true intention shall be sought without regard to the literal meaning of the declaration, § 157 BGB instructs the judge to interpret contracts according to the requirements of good faith and in line with common usage.[5] Both of these rules find historical antecedents in the Digest: "In conventionibus contrahentium voluntatem potius quam verba spectari placuit",[6] says Papinian, whereas Paul asserts: "Cum in verbis nulla ambiguitas est, non debet admitti voluntatis quaestio."[7]

II. ROMAN LAW

1. From verba to voluntas

(a) Pre-classical Roman law

The two maxims just mentioned reflect the struggle between verba and voluntas that for a long time dominated any discussion about the interpretation of contracts in Roman law. Very generally speaking, it is indeed true to say that there has been a development from verba to voluntas, from a strictly objective to an excessively subjective approach. The most characteristic feature of archaic Roman jurisprudence is its tendency to endow every (sacral and) legal act with a definite form.[8] Specific rituals had to be meticulously performed, precisely set forms of words to be uttered with great punctiliousness.[9] The smallest mistake, a cough or a stutter, the use of a wrong term invalidated the whole act.[10] This actional formalism corresponded to a similarly strict formalism in the interpretation of those ancient legal acts. No regard was had to the intention of the parties; what mattered

---

[5] Both rules supplement each other: cf. e.g. Flume, *AT*, § 16, 3 a. For criticism of the apparent contradiction, see Zweigert/Kötz, pp. 101 sqq.; but see Staudinger/H. Dilcher, 1979, §§ 133, 157, nn. 7 sqq.

[6] Pap. D. 50, 16, 219. This maxim was almost literally taken over (via Pothier, *Traité des obligations*, n. 91) into art. 1156 code civil: *"On doit dans les conventions rechercher quelle a été la commune intention des parties contractantes, plutôt que se d'arrêter au sans littéral des termes."*

[7] Paul. D. 32, 25, 1. § 157 BGB takes up this view in so far as it postulates a strictly objective criterion. The reference to "good faith" has a double root in the Roman bona fides and in the (Germanic) concept of *"Treu und Glauben"* in the late Middle Ages (on the latter cf. Wolfgang Strätz, *Treu und Glauben*, vol. I (1974), pp. 47 sqq.). In England, this maxim (in a slightly different form: "Quoties in verbis nulla est ambiguitas, ibi nulla expositio contra verba expressa fienda est", cf. Blackstone, *Commentaries*, vol. II, p. 379) became the origin of the "plain meaning" rule and is thus to a large extent responsible for the expression-oriented approach of the English courts to contract interpretation.

[8] Schulz, *RLS*, pp. 24, referring to Jhering, *Geist*, vol. II, pp. 45 sqq., 470 sqq.

[9] For examples cf. Schulz, *RLS*, pp. 24 sqq.; Heinrich Honsell, "Das Gesetzesverständnis in der römischen Antike", in: *Europäisches Rechtsdenken in Geschichte und Gegenwart, Festschrift für Helmut Coing*, vol. I (1982), pp. 138 sqq.; cf. also Wieacker, *RR*, pp. 320 sq., 330 sqq.

[10] This is the "nimia subtilitas" to which Gaius (IV, 30) refers; cf. also Gai. IV, 11.

were the verba used by them. The more rigid the interpretation, the more care was, in turn, bestowed on the formulation of the formulae. The drafters had to try to eliminate every risk of ambiguity. This led to scrupulous attention to detail, to cumbrous enumerations and to the inclusion of standard clauses such as "quod ego sentio".[11] Anyone who failed to employ such devices ran the risk of having to face unwelcome and unexpected consequences: as was experienced, for instance, by those who had taken the vow to sacrifice "quaecumque proximo vere nata essent apud se animalia". Not only animals but their own children also were taken to be covered by these words.[12] The same interaction, incidentally, between techniques of interpretation and legal drafting is obvious in modern legal systems: flexibility in interpretation corresponds, on the whole, with a more mature approach to the drafting of legally relevant documents; and the clumsy, unabstract and casuistic manner in which it is usually deemed necessary to phrase legislation, wills and contracts in England (or South Africa) is a consequence and reflection of the strict and relatively formal canons of construction.[13]

---

[11] Examples in Schulz, *RLS*, p. 333. The anxious formalism and the excessive subtlety of the jurists were often caricatured; cf. e.g. Cicero, *Pro L. Licinio Murena oratio*, XII—26 sqq.; *Pro A. Caecina oratio*, XXIII—26; Nörr, *Rechtskritik*, pp. 84 sqq.; Frier, *Roman Jurists*, pp. 134 sq., 240 (". . . their [sc. the jurists'] supposed pretentiousness, pedantry, and conservatism are all often attacked, but in terms that imply more a lighthearted disdain for the 'lawyer class' than any deepseated animosity"); for a detailed analysis of rhetorical criticism of legal science in Cicero's *Pro Murena*, see Alfons Bürge, *Die Juristenkomik in Cicero's Rede Pro Murena—Übersetzung und Kommentar* (1974); Claude Cantegrit-Moatti, "Droit et politique dans le 'Pro Murena' de Cicéron", (1983) 61 *RH* 515 sqq.

[12] Festus, *De verborum significatione*, s.v. Ver sacrum, who continues: "[S]ed cum crudele videretur pueros ac puellas innocentes interficere, perductos in adultam aetatem velabant atque ita extra fines suos exigebant." On this incident, see Honsell, *Festschrift Coing*, vol. I, p. 139.

[13] For recent criticism of the style of English legislative drafting, see, for instance, the remarks by two distinguished Hamlyn lecturers: Tony Honoré, *The Quest For Security: Employees, Tenants, Wives* (1982), pp. 118 sqq. and P.S. Atiyah, *Pragmatism and Theory in English Law* (1987), p. 31 ("[M]ost legislation is not drafted in the form of a statement of true principle. . . . Much of it is drafted in the form of a set of specific rules, ad hoc solutions to particular problems. Nobody would read a modern English statute for its literary elegance as it was said that Flaubert used to read the French Code Civile. . . . Even when we do use legislation, an instrument well suited to the enactment of broad principles and generalisations, we find ourself so shackled by the traditional common law methodology, that we fail to use legislation in an effective and principled manner. . . . In particular, the detailed and crabbed style of legislative drafting means that it becomes almost impossible for the courts to draw principles from legislation, to treat legislation as a living graft on the common law, and to develop the law as an integral whole").

A considerable body of South African legislation is derived, either directly or indirectly, from English statutes, and so, too, is the South African style of legislative drafting. Statutes tend to be clumsily drafted, since the legislator anxiously tries to provide for every conceivable eventuality himself rather than to leave anything to the good sense of those interpreting the statute. Particularly odd, from a Continental perspective, are the long lists of (usually rather unhelpful) definitions with which many statutes commence (cf., for instance, Act 19/1893 where the term "banker" was defined as including "a body of persons . . . who carry on the business of banking"; on which, see *National Housing Commission v. Cape of Good Hope Savings Bank Society* 1963 (1) SA 230 (C) at 233). There is even an Interpretation Act (33/1957) which provides illuminating insights such as that "Christian name" means any name prefixed to the surname, whether received at Christian baptism or

(b) Post-classical jurisprudence

At the other end of the development of Roman legal science stood an exaggerated emphasis on subjective criteria.[14] It was closely related to the final disappearance of the old word formalism and to a general trend to judge all human behaviour according to moral, more particularly Christian standards.[15] The content and character of every contract were determined by the intention of the contracting parties, and this intention to attain a specific legal consequence was usually referred to as "animus". According to Fritz Pringsheim, whose research has fundamentally shaped our views on the post-classical animus doctrine,[16] the Byzantines were the first to attribute to the parties an intention directed towards procuring specific legal ends and to make the intention supreme, even where it was unexpressed and undemonstrable.[17] The Byzantine predilection to animus is obvious and unchallenged. Indisputably, it is the source of a considerable amount of interpolation of classical texts. But whether this theory was in fact "dangerous and alien to reality"[18] is somewhat more doubtful. One-sided and extreme as it may appear from a purely dogmatic point of view, it must be assessed against significant changes in the contemporary procedural background.[19]

Classical Roman law did not normally concern itself with problems of evidence; the taking of evidence and its evaluation could be left to the

not, that "month" means a calendar month, or that "law" means any law, proclamation, ordinance, Act of Parliament or other enactment having the force of law. This approach to legislation neither presupposes nor engenders a particularly liberal approach to the interpretation of statutes. And, indeed, statutory interpretation in South Africa, as in England, is traditionally governed by the so-called "golden rule": "The rule by which we are to be guided in construing acts of Parliament is to look at the precise words, and to construe them in their ordinary sense, unless it would lead to any absurdity or manifest injustice" (*Perry v. Skinner* (1837) 2 M & W 471 at 476); for all details, as far as South African law is concerned, cf. L.C. Steyn, *Die Uitleg van Wette* (5th ed., 1981); Lourens M. du Plessis, *The Interpretation of Statutes* (1986). The equivalent of the "golden rule" for contract interpretation is the "plain meaning rule" (cf. supra, note 7; for details, see Lüderitz, op. cit., note 2, pp. 65 sqq.) which applies to all those transactions that have been laid down in a document (no matter whether the formality is required by law or not). The plain meaning rule and the closely allied (procedural) "parol evidence rule" serve to protect reliance on the contractual declaration and are an expression of the objective (declaration-oriented) approach of the English courts to contract interpretation. According to the parol-evidence rule a written instrument may not be contradicted, added to or varied by oral evidence (cf. e.g. *Brown v. Selwin* (1734) Cases T. Talbot 240 at 242; Lüderitz, op. cit., note 2, pp. 111 sqq., 172 sqq.; Zweigert/Kötz, pp. 105 sqq.). South African law, again following English law, has traditionally adopted a rather rigid and formalistic approach to the interpretation of written contracts too; for details cf. E.L. Jansen, "Uitleg van Kontrakte en die bedoeling van die partye", 1981 *TSAR* 97 sqq.; Joubert, *Contract*, pp. 59 sqq.

[14] Kaser, *RPr* II, pp. 82 sqq.

[15] Cf. generally Kaser, *RPr* II, pp. 60 sqq.; Biondi, *DRC*, vol. II, pp. 1 sqq.

[16] Cf. particularly his article on "Animus in Roman Law", (1933) 49 *LQR* 43 sqq., 379 sqq.

[17] (1933) 49 *LQR* 48.

[18] Pringsheim, (1933) 49 *LQR* 48.

[19] Giuseppe Gandolfi, *Studi sull'interpretazione degli atti negoziali in diritto romano* (1966), pp. 243 sqq.; Franz Wieacker, (1966) 83 *ZSS* 437 sq., 444 sq.

discretion of the judge (normally not a professional lawyer), who decided the issue not on the basis of fixed rules of proof but on that of his personal authority.[20] This was different in the so-called bureaucratic, post-classical period of Roman jurisprudence.

> "The innate tendency of every bureaucracy to convert the development of the law into the monopoly of a central office, to codify the law and to assure and supervise its strict application and enforcement, produced a complete change in the structure of Roman legal science."[21]

Hence the tendency to tie the judge to specific rules of evidence and to emphasize the problem of proof.[22] "Nisi alia mens testatoris probetur",[23] "si voluntas testatoris . . . evidenter non ostenderetur":[24] these are the kinds of clauses which Justinian inserted into the classical texts. On the one hand, therefore, he instructed the judge to take account of the (real) intention of the parties; but at the same time he stressed the necessity that such an intention must be proved beyond reasonable doubt. In practice, such proof was normally bound to be based on the declaration of the party concerned.

(c) "Voluntas in primis spectanda est"

Nevertheless, Justinian's animus theory did, of course, greatly influence the authors of the ius commune and is responsible for the preponderance of subjective criteria in their writings. "[V]oluntas in primis spectanda est", as was stated crisply by the French humanist Alciatus.[25] The practically minded lawyers of the usus modernus were somewhat more cautious, though: "[I]ta verba minus curanda, si de mente constat . . . ne propter nimiam subtilitatem verborum, latitudo voluntatis contrahentium impediatur."[26] Here, again, we find the limitation inherent in the intention-oriented approach spelt out quite clearly: one must not prevent an equitable result by rigidly adhering to the external manifestation of the parties' intention, but the (unexpressed) will of the parties can prevail only if it is (objectively) determinable ("si de mente constat").

2. The position in classical Roman law

(a) Verba or voluntas?

But what about the centuries between the archaic period and Justinian? How much, in particular, does the Digest still reflect of the spirit of classical Roman jurisprudence when it comes to the interpretation of

[20] Kaser, *RZ*, pp. 276 sqq.
[21] Schulz, *RLS*, p. 263.
[22] For details, see Kaser, *RZ*, pp. 484 sqq.
[23] Scaev. D. 35, 2, 25, 1.
[24] Paul. D. 31, 85. Cf. further Wieacker, (1966) 83 *ZSS* 437.
[25] *De verborum significatione*, Lib. I, n. 2, in: Opera, Francofurti, vol. IV (1617), p. 755.
[26] Lauterbach, *Collegium theoretico-practicum*, Lib. XVIII, Tit. I, CXIX; cf. also Coing, pp. 410 sq.

contracts? During the 19th century, one was obviously inclined to see the whole question within the framework of the then prevailing notions of private autonomy and will theory. If every contract has its raison d'être in the will of the parties concerned,[27] then it is obvious that determination of the content of a contract requires ascertainment of the parties' true intention. Towards the end of the century, when the Corpus Juris Civilis ceased to be the basis of the living law in Germany and when one therefore started to look at it, once again, from a critical-historical point of view, rather than under purely dogmatic auspices, the pendulum swung radically to the other side. Long lists of interpolated words and phrases were drawn up, and the sources were purged of all subjective criteria determining both the content and the formation of a contract.[28] A (supposedly) classical Roman objectivity was opposed to Byzantine subjectivity. That contrast was encapsulated, as far as problems such as interpretation and error were concerned, in the antithesis of verba and voluntas.

(b) Flexibility

It is clear today that both these views on the matter are essentially ahistorical and that, indeed, the very framework within which the arguments were developed (namely the alternative of verba or voluntas) has for a long time obfuscated any unprejudiced appreciation of the sources.[29] Thus, what one has to guard against primarily is the temptation to put the past into the straitjacket of contemporary conceptions.[30] Classical Roman lawyers tended to look at legal transactions as a whole,[31] without isolating their individual components or dogmatizing the objective or subjective elements contained in them. The analysis of contract as being composed of two corresponding declarations of intention, both of which in turn are made up of an internal component (the intention—voluntas) and of an external one (the declaration—verba) is, as we have seen, of a much later date.[32] The Roman jurists did not think in terms of stereotyped categories; that obviously makes it difficult to generalize their solutions and to extract crisp and clear-cut formulae from our sources. Most remarkable and

---

[27] Cf. e.g. Savigny, *System*, vol. III, p. 258: "Intention per se is really the only important and effective thing, and only because it is an internal and invisible phenomenon do we need a sign by which we can recognize it" (cf. the translation by Weir in Zweigert/Kötz/Weir, p. 72).

[28] Cf. in particular Otto Gradenwitz, *Interpolationen in den Pandekten* (1887), pp. 170 sqq.; also e.g. Fritz Pringsheim, "Animus donandi", (1921) 42 *ZSS* 273 sqq.; Emilio Albertario, "La crisi del metodo interpolazionistico", in: *Studi in onore di Pietro Bonfante*, vol. I, pp. 611 sqq.

[29] Cf. Horak, *Rationes decidendi*, p. 194 *("quellenfremde Gelehrtenkonstruktion")*; Knütel, *Stipulatio und pacta, Festschrift für Max Kaser* (1976), pp. 202 sq.

[30] Cf. also the warning sounded, in a related context, by Robert Feenstra, "The Dutch *Kantharos* Case and the History of Error in Substantia", (1974) 48 *Tulane LR* 849 sq.

[31] Kaser, *RPr* I, p. 235.

[32] Supra, pp. 567 sqq.

characteristic, probably, is the flexibility with which questions of interpretation were approached and decided.

Already by the time of the later Republic, the narrowness and rigidity of the old literal approach to interpretation had been left behind.[33] To a considerable degree, this was a consequence of the relaxation of the "external" formalism of Roman law. Trade links with non-Romans facilitated (sub voce "ius gentium")[34] the introduction and increasing popularity of new, informal types of transactions: transactions which no longer found their effective cause in compliance with a specific formality, but in the consensus, or the conventio,[35] of the parties. Thus it was with the consensual contracts that the wider and more liberal manner of interpretation gained ground. Here one did not necessarily have to stick to the meaning that was typically associated with the words contained in formal declarations, but one could freely take into consideration—and was, on account of the "ex bona fide" clause even encouraged to do so—the individual circumstances of each case. As in the case of error, testaments were the first formal type of transactions where the more modern, flexible approach established itself,[36] and by the time of high classical law, it prevailed with regard to formal contracts too.[37] "Nullum esse contractum, nullam obligationem, quae non habeat in se conventionem": no matter whether a contract of sale, a mutuum[38] or a stipulation[39] had been concluded, the

---

[33] Cf. Alan Watson, "Narrow, Rigid and Literal Interpretation in the Later Roman Republic", (1969) 37 *TR* 351 sqq. This is a good example of the crucial importance of Republican jurisprudence for the development of Roman law. The decisive achievements of Roman law, according to the prevailing modern view, were already established by the end of the Republic. Wieacker, (1969) 2 *The Irish Jurist* 151 sq., writes: "First of all, I believe the development of an independent juristic technique made possible (perhaps for the first time in history) the solution of social conflicts according to a rational intellectual rule. In the second place there arose the great juristic abstractions, such as Person, Property, and Obligation, which all European legal systems have achieved only with the help of the Romans. Finally, it was already the Republic which had created the Praetor's ius honorarium, which supplemented the formalism of the old ius civile through a progressive legal ethic, i.e. through the ideas of bonum et aequum and bona fides, and through the struggle against dolus and the old rigidity of formalism. And all that was not only a mere promise of a great classical future, but had already been perfected in the finest technical detail."

In the same vein, see Frier, *Roman Jurists*, pp. 139 sqq.: "Around the middle of the second century B.C., Roman jurisprudence was profoundly transformed. [What emerged from this revolution was, first and foremost, the concept of] 'autonomous law'—a theory that not only became the guiding ethos of classical Roman law, but also is perhaps the single most important Roman contribution to the Western legal tradition" (pp. 156, 188 sqq.; on the doctrine of "autonomous law" cf. pp. 188 sqq.; 269 sqq.). For a comprehensive evaluation cf. now the authoritative study by Wieacker, *Römische Rechtsgeschichte*, pp. 519 sqq.

[34] On which, see Kaser, *RPr* I, pp. 202 sqq.; Honsell/Mayer-Maly/Selb, pp. 57 sqq.

[35] On these terms cf. supra, pp. 563 sqq.

[36] On the interpretation of wills cf. Voci, *DER*, vol. II, pp. 885 sqq.; Hans Josef Wieling, *Testamentsauslegung im römischen Recht* (1972), passim; Kaser, *RPr* I, pp. 241 sqq.; *RPr* II, pp. 84 sq.

[37] Cf. supra, pp. 599 sq.

[38] Supra, 156 sqq., 165.

[39] Supra, pp. 510 sq., 565

transaction was ultimately based on the consent of the individual parties concerned.

(c) The causa Curiana: the case before the court

The most prominent individual turning point within this development, incidentally, was the causa Curiana,[40] argued in 92 B.C. before the centumviral court.[41] It had all the ingredients of a sensational cause célèbre, for it involved a clash between Lucius Licinius Crassus, the leading orator of his time,[42] and Quintus Mucius Scaevola, Pontifex Maximus, Consul in 95 B.C., author of an influential treatise on the ius civile[43] and probably the most outstanding jurist of the late Republic. The case was of particular significance, since it concerned the interpretation of a testament, i.e. a strictly formal legal act. It must have occurred quite frequently that a paterfamilias instituted as his heir a son who had not as yet attained the age of puberty. When the testator died, the pupillus (if such he still was) would, of course, become sui iuris, but he would not be able to make a testament himself: for persons under the age of puberty lacked the ius testamenti faciendi.[44] Thus, the danger existed that the testator's property might ultimately pass ab intestato. Considering the specific importance attached by upper-class Roman citizens to testate succession (designation of an heir was regarded as the social duty of every bonus paterfamilias),[45] that was a result to be

[40] On the causa Curiana cf. Johannes Stroux, *Summum ius summa iniuria* (1926), pp. 29 sqq.; Gandolfi, op. cit., note 19, pp. 288 sqq.; Franz Wieacker, "The causa Curiana and Contemporary Roman Jurisprudence", (1967) 2 *The Irish Jurist* 151 sqq.; idem, "La 'causa Curiana' e gli orientamenti della giurisprudenza coeva", (1968) 1 *Antologia giuridica romanistica ed antiquaria* 111 sqq.; Wieling, *Testamentsauslegung*, op. cit., note 36, pp. 9 sqq., 60 sqq.; Alan Watson, *The Law of Succession in the Later Roman Republic* (1971), pp. 153 sqq., 94 sqq.; J.W. Tellegen, "Oratores, Iurisprudentes and the 'Causa Curiana' ", (1983) 30 *RIDA* 293 sqq.; Richard A. Bauman, *Lawyers in Roman Republican Politics* (1983), pp. 341 sqq.; Frier, *Roman Jurists*, pp. 135 sqq.

[41] On the jurisdiction of this court cf. Kaser, *RZ*, pp. 37 sqq.

[42] Was Crassus merely an orator, or also a recognized jurist? Cf. Bauman, op. cit., note 40, pp. 341 sqq.

[43] Cf. supra, pp. 24 sq. On the relationship between Crassus and Scaevola (they were of the same age and had held the quaestorship, aedileship, praetorship and consulship together), cf. Bauman, op. cit., note 40, pp. 341 sqq. He also discusses the question whether the causa Curiana had political overtones and whether it soured the relations between the two men.

[44] Gai. II, 113.

[45] On the "Roman Passion for Testacy" Maine, pp. 128 sq. ("No evil seems to have been considered a heavier visitation than the forfeiture of Testamentary privileges; no curse appears to have been bitterer than that which imprecated on an enemy that he might die without a Will"); Schulz, *Principles*, p. 156. But see David Daube, "The Preponderance of Intestacy at Rome", (1964–65) 39 *Tulane LR* 253 sqq. In support of the Roman dislike of intestacy, a famous remark by the elder Cato is usually referred to; according to Plutarch (*Vitae*, Cato maior, 9, 6), he had made three mistakes in his life, one of them being that he had remained without a will for an entire day. Daube, *Roman Law*, p. 73 finds it indefensible "to base on such an utterance by an eccentric one's estimate of the mores among, say, the tailors or carpenters or even the bankers of Rome. . . . The same Cato, let me remind you, remarked that he never made love to his wife except during a thunderstorm. Are we to

avoided. The paterfamilias was therefore allowed to appoint a substitute who was to become heir in case his son died as a pupillus. Such a clause, contained in the will of the paterfamilias, was known as a substitutio pupillaris, and it ran like this: "Titius filius meus mihi heres esto; si filius meus prius moriatur quam in suam tutelam venerit, tunc Seius heres mihi esto."[46] A substitutio pupillaris thus covered the situation where the heir died before attaining the age of puberty; whether this occurred after he had accepted the inheritance or before the paterfamilias himself had died was immaterial. It did not cover the situation where the son did not in fact die at all for the simple reason that he had never been born.

This, however, is exactly what had happened in the causa Curiana: a testator by the name of Marius Coponius had instituted as heir a son whom he had only hoped to have;[47] by way of a substitutio pupillaris, he had nominated a certain Curius as a substitute. But what Coponius had taken for granted did not materialize: for when he died, he neither had a son, nor was a postumus on its way. In such a case, a simple substitutio vulgaris would have helped. This was the appropriate device if the testator wanted to institute a third person as an alternative heir in the event of Titius (i.e. the person appointed in the first place) for some or other reason failing to inherit: be it because he refused to accept the inheritance, be it that he had predeceased the testator or that he had never been born. In order to be on the safe side, a testator who wanted to institute a future son was therefore well advised to combine a substitutio vulgaris (to cover the possibility that a son would not be born) and a substitutio pupillaris (to provide for the eventuality that by the time of the testator's death a son had been born but had died before having been in a position to make a will).[48] A substitutio vulgaris was, however, not contained—expressis verbis—in the will before the court in the causa Curiana. The question therefore arose whether it could not possibly be read into the substitutio pupillaris. Scaevola, the jurist, rejected such a proposition; and, in fact, on a strict and literal reading of the substitutio pupillaris he was undoubtedly correct.[49] The condition

generalize this too?" Contrary to Daube, the word ἀδιάθητος used by Plutarch can, incidentally, have the meaning "without a will". According to Daube, it means "without serious, planned work".

[46] On substitutio (pupillaris and vulgaris) Gai. II, 174 sqq.; D. 28, 6; *Inst.* II, 15 sq.; Schulz, *CRL*, pp. 260 sqq.; Voci, *DER*, vol. II, pp. 160 sqq.; Kaser, *RPr* I, pp. 688 sqq.

[47] On the institution of postumi, see Kaser, *RPr* I, pp. 684 sq. The postumus did not even have to have been conceived at the time the will was made: Ulp. D. 28, 2, 4.

[48] Cf., for example, Mod. D. 28, 6, 1, 1.

[49] Kaser, *RPr* I, p. 236, remarks that Scaevola's viewpoint was no mere formalism, but arose from the moral awareness of the educative force of compulsory form. For a sympathetic evaluation of the "legal" point of view, represented by Scaevola, cf. Wieacker, (1967) 2 *The Irish Jurist* 157 sqq. He also emphasizes that "[b]efore the great court of the centumviri the skilled jurist Scaevola, as advocate opposing the famous orator Crassus, was in an uncomfortable situation. As a rule, the old aristocratic jurist stood as an impartial adviser above the parties; Scaevola's cousin, the augur, looked down with amused contempt

under which Seius had been instituted as alternative heir had not been met.

(d) The causa Curiana: jurists and orators

But such a narrow construction no longer commended itself to the court. It was Crassus, the orator, who carried the day.[50] He placed the emphasis on the overriding intention of the testator, rather than on the wording of the will. The testator had evidently wanted his son to inherit, but had regarded Seius as his second choice. This is why he had instituted Seius to become heir after his son. The possibility that he might not have a son had evidently not occurred to him. It is quite obvious, however, that he would have preferred Seius to inherit his estate in this event too, rather than to die intestate. Undoubtedly, therefore, it was in accordance with the testator's (unexpressed and hypothetical) intention, and generally in his interests to construe the substitutio pupillaris as containing a substitutio vulgaris.[51]

The causa Curiana, no doubt, was only one milestone within a long development, and Crassus' victory did not mean that henceforth a will-oriented, subjective or individualizing approach had definitely superseded or replaced the old and rigid literal interpretation.[52] In fact,

on the juristic ignorance of the average court speaker. We do not know what duty of friendship . . . induced him to enter into the legal arena. In any case he tried, at least in the beginning, to accommodate himself to the rhetorical style. At length the jurist broke through. Therefore one has the impression that in his plea rhetorical and juristic arguments were not quite happily combined." Cicero, who of course favoured Crassus' point of view, pays tribute to Scaevola with a rather malicious compliment: he was "iuris peritorum eloquentissimus, eloquentium iuris peritissimus" (*De oratore*, 1, XXXIX—180; cf. also Brutus XLI—151: "videtur mihi in secunda arte [i.e. jurisprudence] primus esse maluisse quam in prima [rhetoric] secundus"). Watson, (1969) 37 *TR* 366 draws attention to the fact that Quintus Mucius Scaevola himself was prepared to take a wider view; he refers to Pomp. D. 35, 2, 33 concerning the rather queer case of a senator who wore women's dinner dresses; how was a legacy of "women's clothing" to be understood under those circumstances? On whether Watson's argument can be construed as an implied attack on Quintus Marcius' integrity (in that he "cut his coat according to his cloth"), see Bauman, op.cit., note 40, pp. 349 sqq. Wieacker's evaluation of the causa Curiana and of the role of the two main protagonists in the case are rejected by Tellegen, (1983) 30 *RIDA* 300 sqq. The latter asserts that the accepted distinction "between oratores and iurisprudentes is fundamentally wrong", and that the causa Curiana cannot be appreciated properly if one assumes that the members of these professions were "opposite extremes" (pp. 294 sq.); but see the detailed analysis of the (different) roles of orators and jurists by Frier, *Roman Jurists*, passim (e.g. pp. 127 sqq., 184 sqq.); cf. also Wieacker, *RR*, pp. 666 sqq.

[50] His speech was regarded as a masterpiece of forensic oratory; for details, see Wieacker (1967) 2 *The Irish Jurist* 160 sq.; Tellegen, (1983) 70 *RIDA* 297 sq., 307 sqq.

[51] In classical law, a pupillary substitution was in fact construed as containing a vulgar substitution and vice versa: cf. the constitutio by the Emperors Marcus Aurelius and Lucius Verus referred to in Mod. D. 28, 6, 4 pr. In our own time, § 2102 I BGB can mentioned: the appointment of a reversionary heir contains, in case of doubt, also the appointment of a substitutional heir.

[52] This was essentially the view of Stroux, op. cit., note 40, pp. 29 sqq.: the causa Curiana marked the victorious breakthrough of rhetoric and intention-oriented interpretation against the archaic formalism of the older lawyers. Contra e.g. Wieacker, (1967) 2 *The Irish Jurist* 155 sqq., 161 sqq., who in turn, however, appears to play down the importance of this

throughout classical Roman law we find cases where the verba prevailed against voluntas.[53] But it became an oft-quoted[54] precedent, a cause célèbre, where at a crucial juncture a free exegesis had triumphed over rigidity. For this is probably the most important feature of the causa Curiana: it demonstrates the flexibility that had been gained by the time of the late Republic. A case no longer necessarily had to be decided on the basis of the verba; other factors were taken into account and, where appropriate, they could even determine the result of the decision.

The causa Curiana is also characteristic of the influence of Hellenistic theories of forensic rhetoric on contemporary Roman jurisprudence.[55] Roman court orators adopted the Greek "status" doctrine,[56] particularly the antithesis of verba (scriptum) and voluntas (aequitas). Rhetoric, of course, was a theory of advocacy, and the orator had to adopt whichever view suited the interests of his clients.[57] Thus, he was not necessarily on the side of voluntas or aequitas; it could just as well be his duty to plead a case on the basis of a strictly literal interpretation.[58] The function of the Roman *jurist* was a different one.[59]

---

decision too much. For a rejection of Stroux's view cf. also Feliciano Serrao, *Classi, Partiti e Legge nella Repubblica Romana* (1974), pp. 142 sqq.; Bürge, op. cit., note 11, pp. 46 sqq.

[53] For the interpretation of wills cf. e.g. Wieling, *Testamentsauslegung*, op. cit., note 36, pp. 59 sqq., 107 sqq. and passim.; cf. also Felix Wubbe, "Der Wille des Erblassers bei Iav. D. 32, 100, 1", in: *Iuris Professio, Festgabe für Max Kaser* (1986), pp. 371 sqq.

[54] Cf. the references to Cicero and Quintilian in Schulz, *RLS*, p. 79, Gandolfi, op. cit., note 19, pp. 291 sqq. and Wieacker, (1967) 2 *The Irish Jurist* 157 sqq.

[55] Cf. generally Stroux, op. cit., note 40, passim (with too extreme and far-reaching conclusions); contra (equally extreme) e.g. Gerhard von Beseler, "Recuperationes iuris antiqui", (1938) 45 *BIDR* 169 sqq.; cf. also Schulz, *RLS*, pp. 76 sqq.; Behrends, *Fraus legis*, pp. 73 sqq.; for a more balanced evaluation, see Wunner, *Contractus*, pp. 182 sqq.; Kaser, *RPr* I, p. 236; Honsell, *Festschrift Coing*, vol. I, pp. 143 sq.; and, in particular, Franz Wieacker, "Über das Verhältnis der römischen Fachjurisprudenz zur griechisch-hellenistischen Theorie", (1969) 20 *Iura* 469 (on the whole, possibly still underrating the influence of rhetoric); Frier, *Roman Jurists*, pp. 95 sqq., 127 sqq. ("The Ciceronian court, with its shameless tattoo of loci communes, formed . . . an indispensable laboratory where Rome's fledgling legal scientists could create and test their abstract rules in relation both to specific cases and community values. . . . It seems reasonable to discover, within the intensely competitive arena of forensic discussion, many of the impulses towards breadth and equity which gave Roman private law its vitality as a living system and its vast influence as a dead one" (pp. 137 sq.); cf. also p. 267: "This indirect and selective flow of legal ideas from judicial oratory into law is perhaps . . . the real basis Roman law's growth into maturity"). Cf. now also the magisterial summary of the discussion by Wieacker, *RR*, pp. 662 sqq.

[56] For details cf. Uwe Wesel, *Rhetorische Statuslehre und Gesetzesauslegung der römischen Juristen* (1967), pp. 22 sqq.; Franz Horak, "Rhetorische Statuslehre und der moderne Aufbau des Verbrechensbegriffs", in: *Festgabe für Arnold Herdlitczka* (1972), pp. 121 sqq.; Richard A. Bauman, "The 'leges iudicorum publicorum' and their interpretation in the Republic, Principate and later Empire", *ANRW*, vol. II, 13 (1980), pp. 112 sqq.; Wieacker, *RR*, pp. 669 sqq.

[57] Schulz, *RLS*, pp. 76 sq.; cf. also Gandolfi, op. cit., note 19, pp. 257 sqq.; Wieacker, (1969) 20 *Iura* 475; Bürge, op. cit., note 11, pp. 58 sqq.

[58] On the "relativistic framework of rhetorical argument" see Frier, *Roman Jurists*, pp. 127 sqq. ("All that rhetoric offered was a loose framework of alternatives for interpretation"); Frier provides a brilliant and fascinating analysis of Cicero's speech pro Caecina which, according to him, reflects the crucial transformation that the Roman judicial system

He was concerned with questions of law, not with the selection and skilful presentation of an argument that could possibly strengthen the case of a particular client. "The question of law, namely which of the two interpretations, the literal or equitable, ought to prevail", states Schulz,[60] "was simply outside the province of rhetoric"; and he concludes that the Roman jurists cannot have found anything worth learning in rhetoric. But this view is much too negative. The elements of rhetoric were taught at school,[61] and every Roman jurist must therefore, from an early age, have been familiar with the relevant "status" and techniques of argument. The speeches of the orators in court merely reminded them of what they already knew themselves: namely, that, as for many other problems, more than one point of view can be adopted on the question of the interpretation of contracts, wills or statutes. The jurists were constantly made aware of the arguments for and against a literal interpretation, and it is hard to believe that this should not have affected them at all. Of course, they still had to decide which argument was to prevail. But the important progress that had been made lay in the fact that both rigid and wide, both objective and subjective interpretation could now prevail.[62]

(e) The "individualizing" approach

The causa Curiana has taken us into the field of the law of succession. So do most of the cases contained in the Digest which deal with problems of interpretation. They would all have to be considered for a more thorough appraisal of the approach of the classical Roman lawyers on this matter; for strict dogmatic borderlines between the interpretation of contracts, of testaments, and even of statutes did not exist.[63] Of course, the Roman lawyers were aware of the differences between the individual types of transactions: the conflict of interest between declarant and recipient of the declaration in the case of contract; strict observance of the prescribed formalities (but also: no reasonable reliance on the part of any addressee that needed to be protected!) in the case of wills. We do not find any express statement in the sources analysing or clarifying these policy issues, but they are reflected in the way the Roman lawyers dealt with the individual cases

underwent during the time of the late Republic (cf. e.g. pp. 252 sqq.; summary on p. 267). On "words vs. intent" within the context of pro Caecina, cf. pp. 128 sq.

[59] On the distinction (and antagonism!) between jurists and orators, cf. e.g. Schulz, *RLS*, pp. 53 sqq., 69 sqq., 108 sq.; Frier, *Roman Jurists*, pp. 130 sqq., 155 sqq.; Wieacker, *RR*, pp. 668 sqq. Contra: Tellegen, (1983) 30 *RIDA* 293 sqq.

[60] *RLS*, p. 76.

[61] Cicero, *De oratore*, 1, LVII—244; Schulz, *RLS*, p. 54; Wieacker, *RR*, p. 668. Cf. also the remarks by Tellegen, (1983) 30 *RIDA* 294 sq.

[62] For parallel developments with regard to the problem of interpretation of statutes, see Honsell, *Festschrift Coing*, vol. I, pp. 143 sq. Contra: Behrends, *Fraus legis*, pp. 33 sqq. and passim. Cf. also Wieacker, *RR*, pp. 670 sqq.

[63] So, too, Mayer-Maly, (1969) 37 *TR* 591.

brought before them. The dominant impression is the highly "individualizing" approach adopted throughout,[64] and as far as the construction of wills was concerned, that entailed specific significance of "mens testatoris" or "quid sensit testator".[65] In the case of contract, it was a slightly different criterion by which the process of interpretation was guided. "Id quod actum est" is the phrase that we find emphasized again and again. The felling of timber was sold for five years. Whose is the mast which might fall from the trees? "[P]rimum sequendum [est] quod appareret actum esse."[66] A piece of land had been sold, and the parties had provided that the water rights should go with it. Does that include the right of way to the water? "[R]espondit sibi videri id actum esse."[67] Some water pipes were supposed to pass into the property of the purchaser of an estate. What about the reservoir from which the water is drawn through the pipes? "[R]espondi apparere id actum esse, ut id quoque accederet, licet scriptura non continetur."[68] Or, to take the case of a stipulation: somebody had promised to give or to perform something "kalendis Ianuariis". Which date did he have in mind? "[S]i autem non addat quibus Ianuariis, facti quaestionem inducere . . . quid inter eos acti sit [utique enim hoc sequimur quod actum est]."[69]

(f) Id quod actum est

Id quod actum est[70] referred to the *common* intentions of the *individual* parties to a contract, as they became apparent from the specific context within which the negotiations had taken place and the declarations had been made. This "context" included the individual, personal circumstances of the contracting parties as well as those of their expectations that were based on other than purely internal motives. The literal meaning of the words used by the parties and other objective standards were relevant wherever they could help to determine id quod actum est; otherwise they were only fallen back upon where the individual circumstances remained in the dark ("si non appparet quid actum sit").[71] In this connection, certain standard arguments, based on general

---

[64] Betti, *Istituzioni*, vol. I, pp. 139 sqq. has tried to replace the clumsy and simplistic verba/voluntas doctrine by introducing a more refined distinction between typical (typifying) and individual (individualizing) interpretation (the former classical, the latter Justinianic). But it is not possible to draw a clear distinction between the two approaches; for terminological clarification, see Wieacker, (1966) 83 *ZSS* 438 sq.; Horak, *Rationes decidendi*, pp. 194 sqq.; cf. also Gandolfi, op. cit., note 19, pp. 83 sqq.

[65] For details cf. Voci, Wieling, Kaser, as quoted supra in n. 36.

[66] Lab. D. 18, 1, 80, 2.

[67] Paul. D. 18, 1, 40, 1.

[68] Lab. D. 18, 1, 78 pr.

[69] Ulp. D. 45, 1, 41.

[70] Of fundamental importance is Fritz Pringsheim, "Id quod actum est", (1961) 78 *ZSS* 1 sqq.; cf. further Wunner, *Contractus*, pp. 179 sqq.; Gandolfi, op. cit., note 19, pp. 116 sqq., 308 sqq.

[71] Cf. e.g. Ulp. D. 45, 1, 41.

experience or policy, could also be of assistance:[72] "commodissimum est id accipi, quo res de qua agitur magis valeat quam pereat";[73] "[i]n obscuris inspici solere, quod verisimilius est aut quod plerumque fieri solet"[74] or the well-known interpretation contra proferentem.[75] They were all of a fairly subordinate significance in Roman law; it was not until the time of the glossators that they began to be used as general maxims of interpretation.

All in all, I think that the position under classical Roman law can with some justification be described as an (unstable but) happy equilibrium.[76] Neither verba nor voluntas reigned supreme: the original archaic formalism in interpretation had been left behind, but it had not (yet) been replaced by an equally radical subjectivism. The advance of voluntas not only started in post-classical times; it in fact contributed to the refinement of classical law. The Byzantine animus theory was therefore neither novel nor intrinsically false: "The idea is an old and a great one; it is only its exaggeration that creates the novelty or the danger" and that turns what was once progress into decline.[77]

(g) Excursus: the animus novandi

Thus, not even every reference to animus is spurious. It was often only by isolating and dogmatizing it that Justinian interfered with the sources of classical law. Merely by way of example,[78] we may here refer to the problem of the animus novandi. Novation was defined by Ulpianus as "prioris debiti in aliam obligationem . . . transfusio atque translatio".[79] An existing obligation was extinguished and substituted by an new one. A novation was effected by way of a stipulation that was causally framed; it referred to what was owed under the previous obligation.[80] It was often used, for instance, in order to achieve a change in the person of the debtor or of the creditor. "Quod mihi Seius debet, mihi dari spondes?" "Spondeo":[81] on account of this stipulation the promisor replaced Seius as the debtor of "ego". Seius' obligation was terminated ipso iure. In order to have this "novatory" effect, the (new) stipulation basically had to comprise the same debt (idem

[72] Hans Erich Troje, "Ambiguitas contra stipulatorem", (1961) 27 *SDHI* 95.
[73] Ulp. D. 34, 5, 12; cf. also Ulp. D. 50, 17, 67.
[74] Paul. D. 50, 17, 114.
[75] Cf. infra, pp. 639 sqq.
[76] Pringsheim, (1933) 49 *LQR* 47.
[77] Pringsheim, (1933) 49 *LQR* 48.
[78] For an overview of the various acts for which animus became—at some time or other—an essential requirement, see Pringsheim, (1933) 49 *LQR* 49 sqq., 379 sqq.; Kaser, *RPr* II, pp. 87 sqq.
[79] D. 46, 2, 1 pr. Cf. also Gai. III, 176: "novatione . . . nova nascitur obligatio et prima tollitur, translata in posteriorem."
[80] Cf., most recently, Max Kaser, "Zu Novation und Delegation", in: *Satura Roberto Feenstra oblata* (1985), pp. 141 sqq.
[81] Cf. e.g. Ulp. D. 45, 1, 75, 6.

debitum), but it also had to contain a new element (aliquid novi).[82] In the above example, the change of creditor is the new element. Often this pair of objective criteria (idem debitum—aliquid novi) was both satisfactory and sufficient to determine when a particular stipulation had to be viewed as a novation. But sometimes it was not. In our discussion of suretyship stipulations we have seen that a sponsio could, according to Proculian practice, be concluded both ex intervallo and in the absence of the main debtor.[83] That entailed a change of the standard formula, which could now no longer refer to idem, but had to read, for instance, like this: "Quod Seius mihi debet, mihi dari spondes?" It was exactly the same as in the case of a novation. And yet, in the one instance (sponsio) the promisee was to become debtor alongside Seius, in the other (novatio) he was to replace him. It was in order to deal with these kinds of problems that the classical lawyers brought in a new, subjective requirement: they made the decision dependent upon the intention of the parties, and this was the origin of animus novandi.[84] In some of our sources even the very term appears to be of classical origin, although, as a rule, a formulation such as "hoc agere, ut (novetur)" was used.[85] Thus, for instance, Ulpian amplifies his definition of novation with the words: ". . . hoc est cum ex praecedenti causa ita nova constituatur, ut prior perematur."[86] As a result, therefore, the construction of a stipulation as a novation depended on a characteristic mixture of both objective and subjective criteria. It was only in post-classical times that animus novandi became the dominant feature in the dogmatic make-up of this institution and conclusively determined the novatory effect of a transaction.[87]

III. POST-RECEPTION DEVELOPMENTS

1. The older ius commune

Any more than a superficial or impressionistic assessment of the approach to the interpretation of contracts during the various phases of the ius commune would require a thorough analysis of the decisions of the courts: a task which has yet to be undertaken. Questions of

---

[82] Cf. e.g. Gai. III, 177; Ulp. D. 46, 2, 8, 5; Pomp. D. 45, 1, 18; David Daube, "Novation of Obligations Giving a Bonae Fidei Iudicium", (1948) 66 *ZSS* 91 sqq.; Robert Feenstra, "L'effet extinctif de la novation", (1961) 29 *TR* 400 sqq.; Franco Bonifacio, *La novazione nel diritto romano* (2nd ed., 1959), pp. 123 sqq.; Sturm, *Stipulatio Aquiliana*, pp. 200 sqq.

[83] Cf. supra, pp. 118 sq.

[84] For details, see Apathy, *Animus novandi*, passim, e.g. pp. 261 sqq.

[85] Apathy, *Animus novandi*, pp. 253 sqq. against earlier interpolationist views (e.g. Fritz Pringsheim, "Zur Geschichte des 'animus novandi'", in: *Studi in onore di Vincenzo Arangio-Ruiz*, vol. I (1952), pp. 509 sqq.).

[86] Ulp. D. 46, 2, 1 pr.

[87] Justinian ultimately required the parties expressly to declare their intention to novate; cf. C. 8, 41, 8 and *Inst.* III, 29, 3 sq. On the significance of animus novandi in Justinianic law, see Kaser, *RPr* II, pp. 450 sq.; Apathy, *Animus novandi*, pp. 266 sqq.

interpretation are (or can be) dependent upon so many different circumstances that it is particularly difficult to say whether the abstract formulations, the rules and guidelines found in contemporary literature do in fact reflect the actual jurisprudentia forensis, the law in action.[88] As far as the textbooks, the commentaries and the academic treatises are concerned, a subjective approach is prevalent throughout the centuries.[89] Papinian's statement to the effect that the will of the parties must be considered rather than the words[90] was quoted over and over again, and thus examination of the common intention of the parties was the primary objective of the interpreter.[91] "Quod actum est" was still an oft-quoted phrase, but it was now usually understood to refer to "id, de quo contrahentes senserunt".[92] The supremacy of subjective criteria was endorsed by humanists as well as by the writers of the usus modernus, and it found, of course, its culmination in the 19th century. For the pandectists, it became a natural consequence of private autonomy and of the "will theory" of contract. If contractual obligations are by definition self-imposed, it follows that the exclusive task of the courts is to discover what the parties have agreed upon and to give effect to this, their true intention.

2. True intention and justifiable reliance

Modern German law tends to follow a more objective, or normative, approach; the emphasis is not so much on what a party may have meant, but on how a reasonable man would have understood his declaration.[93] There is no room for an inquiry into the "true intention" of the parties if the justifiable reliance of the addressee deserves protection. A declaration of intention, as the emanation of an individual's autonomy, does not exist in a social vacuum; it gives rise to reasonable expectations on the part of others, which must not be disappointed. This reflects a significant shift from a theory of contract based on individualism to a perspective which accentuates the social

[88] Cf. also Coing, p. 411. On the nature of the ius commune in the 16th, 17th and 18th centuries, not as professorial law characterized by impractical abstractions, deductive reasoning and concept jurisprudence, but as judicial law, jurisprudentia forensis, developing through lawyers' interpretation and judicial opinions, cf. e.g. Gino Gorla, Luigi Moccia, "A 'Revisiting' of the Comparison between 'Continental Law' and 'English Law' (16th–19th century)", (1981) 2 *Journal of Legal History* 143 sqq. Protagonists of the law in action were judges and legal counsel, lawyers such as Molinaeus and Domat, Grotius and Bynkershoek, Huber and Sande, Carpzov and Mevius; the method of their decisions was largely casuistic; and a particularly important part of legal literature written or compiled during this time was forensic in character.

[89] Cf. supra, p. 625.

[90] D. 50, 16, 219.

[91] Cf. e.g. Pothier, *Traité des obligations*, n. 91.

[92] Donellus, "Ad. Tit. Dig. de Rebus dubii", Ad L. Ubi est 21., in: *Opera Omnia*, vol. XI (Lucae, 1767), col. 99.

[93] Cf. e.g. Flume, *AT*, pp. 51 sqq., 307 sqq.; Lüderitz, op. cit., note 2, pp. 278 sqq.; Wieacker, *Privatrechtsgeschichte*, p. 517.

consequences of human behaviour.[94] It is a change of perception which had been prepared and foreshadowed in the writings of the natural lawyers. They had laid, it will be recalled, the foundations for the modern concepts of contract and of a declaration of intention.[95] More particularly, they had emphasized that the will to be bound must find some external manifestation. Both voluntas and signum voluntatis are essential elements within the process of contract formation. Consequently, then, the interpretation of contracts cannot be determined by a purely subjective criterion either. Grotius firmly rejected Cicero's advice "[s]emper autem in fide quid senseris, non quid dixeris, cogitandum",[96] and expressed his own view in the following words:

> "Sed quia interni actus per se spectabiles non sunt, . . . ipsa dicante naturali ratione jus est ei cui quid promissum est promissorem cogere ad id quod recta interpretatio suggerit."[97]

But how is this recta interpretatio to be established? "Si nulla sit conjectura quae ducat alio, verba intelligenda sunt ex proprietate, non Grammatica quae est ex origine, sed populari ex usu."[96]

3. Rules of interpretation: in general

A second characteristic feature of the literature of the ius commune on the interpretation of contracts is the great variety of special rules and maxims that were collected and put forward, usually on the basis of some more or less isolated texts taken from the Digest.[98] Every clause in a contract must be interpreted in the light of all the other clauses, whether they precede or follow it ("Incivile est nisi tota lege perspecta una aliqua particula eius proposita iudicare vel respondere": Cels. D. 1, 3, 24);[99] ambiguous clauses must be construed in a sense which will give them some effect rather than render them inoperative ("Quotiens in stipulationibus ambigua oratio est, commodissimum est id accipi, quo res, qua de agitur in tuto sit": Ulp. D. 45, 1, 80);[100] of two possible constructions, the one which is most agreeable to the nature of the contract must be chosen ("Quotiens idem sermo duas sententias

---

[94] Bona fides and its Germanic counterpart *"Treu und Glauben"* have been instrumental in the shaping, first of the one, then of the other point of view; for details, see Okko Behrends, "Treu und Glauben. Zu den christlichen Grundlagen der Willenstheorie im heutigen Vertragsrecht", in: L.L. Vallauri, G. Dilcher (eds.), *Christentum, Säkularisation und modernes Recht*, vol. II (1981), pp. 957 sqq., 1001 sqq.

[95] Cf. supra, pp. 567 sqq.

[96] *De Officiis*, 1, XIII–40.

[97] Hugo Grotius, *De jure belli ac pacis*, Lib. II, Cap. XVI, 1; on Grotius' theory of interpretation, see Diesselhorst, *Hugo Grotius*, pp. 55 sqq.; cf. also Behrends, loc. cit., pp. 960 sqq. Cf. further Pufendorf, *De jure naturae et gentium*, Lib. V, Cap. XII, §§ 1 sqq.; Wolff, *Jus naturae*, Pars VI, Cap. III, §§ 459 sqq.

[98] Cf. e.g. the account in Wessels, *Contract*, vol. I, pp. 546 sqq., 552 sqq.

[99] Cf. e.g. Pothier, *Traité des obligations*, n. 96; art. 1161 code civil; also still Flume, *AT*, p. 309; A.G. Guest, *Anson's Law of Contract* (25th ed., 1979), p. 150.

[100] Pothier, *Traité des obligations*, n. 92; art. 1157 code civil; cf. also Flume, *AT*, p. 317; Anson, op. cit., note 99, pp. 149 sqq. ("Ut res magis valeat quam pereat").

exprimit, ea potissimum excipiatur, quae rei gerendae aptior est": Iul. D. 50, 17, 67);[101] the interpretation of ambiguous terms must be guided by the custom and trade usage of the country in which the contract has been concluded ("Semper in stipulationibus et in ceteris contractibus id sequimur . . . quod in regione in qua actum est frequentatur": Ulp. D. 50, 17, 34);[102] a contract is understood to contain the customary clauses, although they may not have been expressly inserted (". . . ea enim, quae sunt moris et consuetudinis, in bonae fidei iudiciis debent venire": Ulp. D. 21, 1, 31, 20);[103] however general the terms of a contract may be, they only apply to matters which were contemplated by the parties at the time of conclusion of the contract ("nam . . . iniquum est peremi pacto. id de quo cogitatum non docetur":[104] Ulp. D. 2, 15, 9, 3);[105] and so on. In an 18th-century German work, we find a hotchpotch of no fewer than 100 different rules of interpretation.[106] French authors—and their successors—were on the whole more successful in domesticating this casuistic jungle: Domat relates 15, Pothier 12 and Van der Linden merely 9 rules.[107] The first and most influential attempt to establish a hierarchy of criteria, incidentally, goes back to the glossator Johannes Bassianus: quod actum—ut magis valeat quam pereat—quod verisimilius—contra proferentem.[108] The scheme was later refined by Hugo Donellus, the main representative of the systematically oriented branch of the humanist school of jurisprudence. The importance attached to special canons of construction in the ius commune is probably a direct consequence of the narrowing down of "id quod actum est" to a purely subjective criterion; for if only the intention of the parties matters, then certain guidelines and criteria are needed to determine their presumed intention where the actual will cannot in fact be established. It is not surprising, therefore, that those who favoured a more objective approach to interpretation, more particularly the natural lawyers,[109] no longer held on to these canons of interpretation. The drafters of the BGB, too, abandoned them. The interpretation of contracts is dependent upon the individual circumstances of each case and must be undertaken "according to the requirements of good faith".[110] Within

[101] Pothier, *Traité des obligations*, n. 93; art. 1158 code civil; Flume, *AT*, p. 317.
[102] Pothier, *Traité des obligations*, n. 94; art. 1159 code civil.
[103] Pothier, *Traité des obligations*, n. 95; art. 1160 code civil.
[104] Cf. the note appended by Mommsen to his edition of this text: n. 10 in Mommsen/Krüger, D. 2, 15, 9, 3.
[105] Pothier, *Traité des obligations*, n. 98; art. 1163 code civil.
[106] Cf. Hans Erich Troje, "Ambiguitas contra stipulatorem", (1961) 27 *SDHI* 105.
[107] For a detailed synopsis, see Paul van Warmelo, "Die uitleg van kontrakte", (1960) 77 *SALJ* 69 sqq.
[108] Cf. Troje, (1961) 27 *SDHI* 99.
[109] Though not the codes inspired by natural law; cf. §§ 65 sqq. I 4 PrALR; artt. 1157 sqq. code civil and §§ 914 sqq. ABGB.
[110] § 157 BGB.

this framework courts of law need flexibility, and general and abstract rules are leading strings of rather doubtful value.[111]

4. Rules of interpretation: the contra proferentem rule

(a) *Interpretatio contra eum qui clarius loqui debuisset*

There is, however, one rule of construction which, though not incorporated into the BGB, has nevertheless experienced a surprising renaissance in modern German law. It appears last in the scheme devised by Johannes Bassianus and provides a good example of how isolated utterances of the Roman jurists were able to become the fons and origo of a general rule of law: the interpretatio contra proferentem.

"Cum quaeritur in stipulatione, quid acti sit, ambiguitas contra stipulatorem est":[112] this is how Celsus formulated the idea that in case of ambiguity the interpretation unfavourable to the stipulator has to be adopted. As will be remembered, it was the stipulator who formulated the question which, in turn, determined the content of the stipulation. Any ambiguity was therefore attributable to him, for he could just as well have made it clear what he wanted the other party to promise him.[113] The underlying idea is that of an "interpretatio contra eum qui clarius loqui debuisset".[114] It was applied not only to stipulations. "In contrahenda venditione ambiguum pactum contra venditorem interpretandum est":[115] as far as contracts of sale were concerned, the interpretatio was contra venditorem; and in case of locatio conductio, ambiguum pactum contra locatorem appears to have been the accepted guideline.[116] The reason is that the (ancillary) terms of a contract of sale (the leges venditionis) were drawn up by the vendor,[117] and those of a contract of lease (the leges locationis) by the locator.[118] Ambiguitas contra stipulatorem (emptorem, locatorem) appears in a variety of fragments in the Digest; most of them, however, are abstract statements, and examples of its practical application are conspicuously absent.[119] The only exception is Pomp. D. 18, 1, 33, where a provision

---

[111] Cf. "Motive", in: *Mugdan*, vol. I, pp. 436 sqq. and the evaluation of the rules contained in the code civil by Zweigert/Kötz, pp. 98 sqq. (trite, empty of content, rules of thumb, misleading).

[112] Cels. D. 34, 5, 26; cf. also Ulp. D. 45, 1, 38, 18.

[113] Cf. Cel. D. 45, 1, 99 pr.: ". . . ac fere secundum promissorem interpretamur, quia stipulatori liberum fuit verba late concipere"; cf. also Paul. D. 18, 1, 21 in fine; Pap. D. 2, 14, 39 in fine.

[114] Justus Henning Boehmer, *Dissertatio de interpretatione facienda contra eum qui clarius loqui debuisset* (Halae 1700); Christoph Krampe, *Die Unklarheitenregel* (1983), pp. 14 sq.

[115] Paul. D. 50, 17, 172; cf. further Paul. D. 18, 1, 21; Pap. D. 2, 14, 39 (referring to the "veteres").

[116] Pap. D. 2, 14, 39.

[117] Wolf, *Error*, p. 41.

[118] Mayer-Maly, *Locatio conductio*, pp. 106 sqq.

[119] For an analysis of the Roman sources, see Troje, (1961) 27 *SDHI* 115 sqq.; Gandolfi, op. cit., note 19, pp. 390 sqq.; Christoph Krampe, "Die ambiguitas-Regel: Interpretatio

in a sale determining that "flumina stillicidia uti nunc sunt, ut ita sint" was found to be ambiguous, because it was unclear to which flumina and stillicidia it referred. Pomponius gives the following opinion: "[P]rimum spectari oportet, quid acti sit: si non id appareat, tunc id accipitur quod venditori nocet: ambigua enim oratio est."[120] His answer shows that (at least by the time of classical law) the ambiguity rule was of a merely subsidiary nature: it was to be resorted to if determination of "id quod actum est" had not been possible. "Id quod actum est", however, as we have seen, was a very wide and flexible concept that could refer both to the individual will of the parties concerned and to the more objective and typical features of the contract. It allowed the jurists to read into the transaction what was either objectively or subjectively reasonable. Obviously, under these circumstances, little room was left for subsidiary rules such as ambiguitas contra stipulatorem (venditorem or locatorem).[121] For all practical purposes, they were on their way out.[122]

(b) The contra proferentem rule in medieval and in modern law

The revival of the ambiguity rule was due to medieval jurisprudence.[123] The glossators, first of all, established a general rule of interpretatio contra proferentem: for this is the common denominator of ambiguitas contra stipulatorem, venditorem and locatorem. Bartolus even took the generalization one step further. If the purchaser formulates the leges venditionis, they will usually reflect his interests. The contra proferentem policy is therefore regardful of the fact that "pactum appositum [fuit] gratia emptoris".[124] Hence the following reformulation of the rule: interpretatio fit contra proferentem seu contra eum, pro quo profertur.[125] More often than not, the person who benefits from the special clauses added to the contract is the creditor. Interpretatio contra

---

contra stipulatorem, venditorem, locatorem", (1983) 100 *ZSS* 185 sqq.; Heinrich Honsell, "Ambiguitas contra stipulatorem", in: *Iuris Professio, Festgabe für Max Kaser* (1986), pp. 75 sqq.

[120] On this text, see Troje, (1961) 27 *SDHI* 170 sqq.; Krampe, (1983) 100 *ZSS* 212 sqq.; Honsell, *Festgabe Kaser*, p. 81.

[121] Why do we find so many abstract formulations of the rule and so little case law in our sources? The most probable explanation is the one proposed by Honsell, *Festgabe Kaser*, pp. 76 sqq. Ambiguitas contra stipulatorem (attributed by Papinian to the "veteres": D. 2, 14, 39) goes far back in Roman legal history. Its origin appears to lie in sacral law. Every ambiguity had to be avoided ("in precibus nihil ambiguum esse debet") if one did not want to run the risk of being held bound, by the gods, to the (for them) more favourable interpretation of a promise. The same principle (which is intimately connected with the old word formalism) was applied to promises in private law, until (s.v. id quod actum est) the will of the parties concerned had become an essential element in the process of interpretation.

[122] Honsell, *Festgabe Kaser*, pp. 75 sqq.; cf. also Troje, (1961) 27 *SDHI* 115 sqq. Differently Gandolfi, op. cit., note 19, pp. 393 sqq.

[123] For what follows, see Troje, (1961) 27 *SDHI* 96 sqq.

[124] Bartolus, *Commentaria*, D. 2, 14, 39, § Veteribus, 2.

[125] Bartolus, *Commentaria*, D. 2, 14, 39 and D. 18, 1, 34 pr., § Si in emptione; Troje, (1961) 27 *SDHI* 100.

eum pro quo profertur is therefore often tantamount to interpretatio contra creditorem.[126] Here one can see how the ambiguity rule may be used in order to protect the position of the one who is perceived to be the weaker party to a contract. It is precisely this function that commended it to modern courts and writers who were desperately looking for devices to combat unfair standard contract terms. Standard contract terms are preformulated by one party and that party does not usually have the interests of his contractual partner at heart. The latter, particularly if he happens to be the ultimate consumer, lacks the economic power to insist on alterations, so as to achieve a fair balance of risk and interest. Individual negotiation is replaced by virtual imposition of a uniform and usually one-sided set of conditions, pushing aside the rules of the ius dispositivum.[127] It was soon discovered[128] that private autonomy no longer functions under these circumstances, for even according to "classical" contract theory only a fair bargaining process can be relied upon to produce a fair result. Thus the courts had to step in, but the code had poorly equipped them for this novel task.[129] It is not surprising, therefore, that they fell back upon the venerable contra proferentem rule,[130] particularly since that allowed them to achieve a reasonable solution without openly attacking the "idol" of freedom of contract.[131]

---

[126] "In dubio fit interpretatio contra creditorem": Bartolus, *Commentaria*, D. 45, 1, 38, 18. Cf. also Pothier, *Traité des obligations*, n. 97; art. 1162 code civil *("Dans le doute, la convention s'interprète contre celui qui a stipulé et en faveur de celui qui a contracté l'obligation")* and the criticism by Zweigert/Kötz/Weir, p. 73 (". . . is clearly based on the popular fallacy that the creditor is rich and the debtor is poor").

[127] Cf. e.g. Frank J in *Siegelman v. Cunard White Star Ltd* (1955) 221 F 2d 189 at 205–6 (as quoted by Sandrock, (1978) 26 *American Journal of Comparative Law* 552): "An ordinary contract has been called a sort of private statute, mutually made by the parties and governing their relations. But in a take-it-or-leave-it contract, absent actual freedom of contract, the parties do not 'legislate' by mutual agreement; the dominant party 'legislates' for both." For a general overview of the problems involved cf. Eike von Hippel, *Verbraucherschutz* (3rd ed., 1986), pp. 118 sqq.; Hein Kötz, "Welche gesetzgeberischen Massnahmen empfehlen sich zum Schutze der Endverbraucher gegenüber Allgemeinen Geschäftsbedingungen und Formularverträgen", in: *Verhandlungen des 50. Deutschen Juristentages* (1974), Gutachten A; Th. Bourgoignie (ed.), *Unfair Terms in Consumer Contracts* (1983); Hein Kötz, "Controlling Unfair Contract Terms: Options for Legislative Reform", (1986) 103 *SALJ* 405 sqq.

[128] Cf. in particular the by now classic work of Ludwig Raiser, *Das Recht der allgemeinen Geschäftsbedingungen* (1935).

[129] On the control of unfair standard contract terms by means of §§ 138, 242 and/or 315 BGB, cf. e.g. RGZ 62, 264 (266); RGZ 103, 82 (83 sq.); BGHZ 22, 90 (97 sqq.); BGHZ 38, 183 (186); BGHZ 41, 151 (155); BGHZ 54, 106 (109) and Wilhelm Weber, *Die Allgemeinen Geschäftsbedingungen, Eine rechtliche Gesamtdarstellung* (1967), pp. 364 sqq.

[130] Cf. e.g. RGZ 116, 274 (276); BGHZ 5, 111 (115); BGHZ 47, 207 (216); Raiser, op. cit., note 128, pp. 264 sqq.

[131] "[Judges] still had before them the idol 'freedom of contract'. They still knelt down and worshipped it, but they concealed under their cloaks a secret weapon. They used it to stab the idol in the back. This weapon was called the 'true construction of the contract' ": Lord Denning, in *George Mitchell (Chesterhall) Ltd. v. Finney Locky Seeds Ltd.* [1983] 1 All ER 108 (CA) at 113J.

But there are grave disadvantages in using rules of interpretation as a means of policing the substantive justice of standard contract terms.[132] More direct forms of intervention had to be devised, albeit extra or even contra legem. In 1977 the German Standard Terms Act[133] came into force and, even though it empowered the courts to strike down unfair standard contract terms,[134] the ambiguity rule was retained. § 5 ABGB represents its most modern statutory version:[135] "Uncertainty concerning the interpretation of standard contract terms shall be resolved against the proponent." Modern commentators usually stress that great restraint should be observed in the application of this rule.[136,137]

---

[132] Cf. e.g. Robert Fischer, (1963) 125 *ZHR* 205 sqq. and, more generally, Karl Llewellyn, (1938–39) 52 *Harvard LR* 703 (also referred to by Kötz, ((1986) 103 *SALJ* 407): "First, since they all rest on the admission that the clauses in question are permissible in purpose and content, they invite the draftsman to recur to the attack. Give him time, and he will make the grade. Second, since they do not face the issue, they fail to accumulate either experience or authority in the needed direction: that of making out for any given type of transaction what the *minimum decencies* are which a court will insist upon as essential to an enforceable bargain of a given type, or as being inherent in a bargain of that type. Third, since they purport to construe, and do not really construe, nor are intended to, but are instead tools of intentional and creative misconstruction, they seriously embarrass later efforts at true construction, later efforts to get at the true meaning of those wholly legitimate contracts and clauses which call for their meaning to be got at instead of avoided. The net effect is unnecessary confusion and unpredictability. . . . Covert tools are never reliable tools."

[133] *Gesetz zur Regelung des Rechts der Allgemeinen Geschäftsbedingungen* (ABGB). On this Act cf. e.g. Otto Sandrock, "The Standard Terms Act 1976 of West Germany", (1978) 26 *American Journal of Comparative Law* 551 sqq.; N. Reich/K.-W. Micklitz, *Consumer Legislation in the Federal Republic of Germany* (1981), pp. 269 sqq.; H.R. Hahlo, "Unfair Contract Terms in Civil Law Systems", (1981) 98 *SALJ* 70 sqq.

[134] §§ 9 sqq. ABGB.

[135] Others can be found in §§ 266 sq. I 5 PrALR; art. 1162 code civil (cf. also art. 1602 II, relating particularly to the contract of sale); § 915 ABGB. For details, see Troje, (1961) 27 *SDHI* 107 sqq.; Krampe, op. cit., note 114, pp. 15 sqq. The fathers of the BGB did not adopt the contra proferentem rule: "Motive", in: *Mugdan*, vol. I, pp. 437 sq. The contra proferentem rule has also made its way into the English common law; it is already documented in 15th-century case reports. By and large today, the rule still plays a greater role in England than on the Continent; it is used here as a formalized and schematic way of reliance protection. For details, see Lüderitz, op. cit., note 2, pp. 247 sqq.

[136] Cf. e.g. Ulmer/Brandner/Hensen, *ABG-Gesetz* (5th ed., 1987), § 5, nn. 1, 31. Admonitions of this kind run like a red thread through the history of the ambiguity rule. Many authors have stressed that it can be reverted to only as an ultima ratio and that it must not be allowed to subvert or replace a thorough examination of "id quod actum est". Cf. e.g. Antonius Faber (". . . non statim faciendam esse interpretationem contra venditorem aut locatorem, sed ita demum, si nihil sit quod melius dici possit . . .") and Donellus (". . . si ita quaeritur, ut nullis coniecturis possit constare, quidnam id sit, tum ambiguitas, quae tunc vere relinquitur, contra stipulatorem interpretanda est"), both in Troje, (1961) 27 *SDHI* 104 sq. Cf. also Raiser, op. cit., note 128, pp. 265, 270 and Krampe, op. cit., note 114, pp. 24 sqq.

[137] Already by the 15th century the contra proferentem rule had found its way into the English common law. It has come to be employed in situations where the content of the transaction is determined, on account of an imbalance of power, by one of the contracting parties. Standard contract terms provide a prominent example. For details, see Lüderitz, op. cit., note 2, pp. 247 sqq.; cf. also the comparative remarks by Krampe, op. cit., note 114, pp. 22 sq. Modern textbooks usually deal with the contra proferentem rule in connection with exemption clauses (cf. Treitel, *Contract*, pp. 171 sqq.). The subsidiary nature of the rule

IV. SPECIAL PROBLEM SITUATIONS

1. §§ 116, 117, 118, 122 BGB

Does it matter what the parties intended or what they declared? This is the central question around which the discussion of interpretation revolves. It also arises in three standard situations, which we must now still look at. In all three of them a contractual declaration has been made, but the declarant never wanted to be bound by it. Thus there is a conflict between that party's (real) intention and the signum voluntatis which has actually been set. In the first case, the contractual declaration was neither intended nor expected to be taken seriously. Secondly, there is the situation where the declarant indeed intended his declaration to be taken seriously, but made a mental reservation: in his own mind, he did not wish that declaration to become effective. And thirdly we are dealing with the problem that a contractual declaration, with the connivance of the partner to the contract, is made only in pretence. The BGB regards the lack of seriousness as a vitiating factor (§ 118), considers a reservatio mentalis to be irrelevant (§ 116)[138] and provides, in the case of simulation, that the sham transaction is void (§ 117 I).[139] If the latter served to disguise another bargain, the disguised transaction may be valid (§ 117 II).[140] These solutions may sound fairly obvious, but it should be appreciated that the treatment of the reservatio mentalis is highly problematic from the point of view of the will theory of contract, while from a more formalistic perspective the solution proposed in § 117 BGB may sound surprising and anomalous. Even in the case of a lack of seriousness, one may have second thoughts. For the other party may not have understood the declaration as expected and

is frequently emphasized ("the last straw moving the scale": cf. the references in Lüderitz, op. cit., note 2, p. 265). South African courts, too, do occasionally apply the contra proferentem rule (with regard to standard terms and other contractual clauses), but only as a last resort, when all attempts at ascertaining the common intention of the parties have failed. Cf. *Cairns (Pty.) Ltd. v. Playdon & Co. Ltd.* 1948 (3) SA 99 (A) at 123; Wessels, *Contract*, § 1956 ("[The rule] cuts the Gordian knot and arbitrarily determines against the stipulator"); Kerr, *Contract*, pp. 254 sq.; Joubert, *Contract*, pp. 63 sq. But cf. also the recent decision of *Lawrence v. Kondotel Inns (Pty) Ltd.* 1989 (1) SA 44 (D) 53 sq. There the contra proferentem rule was applied, without much ado, to an exemption clause which read: "All riders ride at their own risk: If any accident should occur, Kondotel . . . will not be held responsible." In the opinion of the court, this clause did not cover accidents arising from misconduct on the part of the animal (not convincing).

[138] However, the declaration of intention is void if made to a person who is aware of the mental reservation (§ 116, 2 BGB). This provision has been criticized as an unwarranted concession to the will theory of contract: Ernst Kramer, in: *Münchener Kommentar*, vol. I (2nd ed., 1984), § 116, n. 8; but cf. Flume, *AT*, § 20, 1.

[139] For details, see Karl Michaelis, "Scheingeschäft, verdecktes Geschäft und verkleidetes Geschäft im Gesetz und in der Rechtspraxis", in: *Festschrift für Franz Wieacker* (1978), pp. 444 sqq.

[140] This follows from the rule laid down in § 133 BGB according to which the true intention of the parties must be sought. The validity of the disguised transaction depends on whether the normal rules existing for such transactions have been complied with; thus, for instance, a transaction must be neither illegal nor immoral, and any formal requirements that may exist must have been met.

may therefore have relied on its effectiveness. Such reliance needs protection. Hence a specific claim for compensation is provided for in § 122 BGB.[141]

2. Lack of seriousness

As in the case of error,[142] this right to claim the negative interest does not have any precedent in Roman law. The basic proposition about the invalidity of the transaction, however, does. A stipulation made by way of a joke, for teaching or for demonstration purposes, was invalid. Interesting is the reason provided for this result:

> "Verborum quoque obligatio constat, si inter contrahentes id agatur: nec enim si per iocem puta vel demonstrandi intellectus causa ego tibi dixero 'spondes'? et tu responderis 'spondeo', nascetur obligatio."[143]

What matters is quod actum est, and part and parcel of quod actum est must obviously be the intention of the parties to enter into a legally relevant relationship with each other. As one can see from the examples used, the whole problem is of a somewhat academic nature.

3. Reservatio mentalis

(a) Roman law

The problem of a reservatio mentalis appears to have been of equally little practical importance in Roman law. To any practically minded lawyer it must be obvious that the secret (mental) reservation by one party to a contract not to be bound by his declared intention cannot affect the validity of the transaction.[144] Certainty of law and security of transactions would otherwise be undermined intolerably. Digesta 2, 15, 12 is about the only text in which a proposition of this kind has even been considered.[145] A person had made a composition that referred, quite generally, to everything that had been left to him by a specific testator. According to Celsus, he cannot afterwards claim that his intention had been directed towards the content of the first part of the will only.

(b) Pandectists and canon lawyers

One has to attribute extraordinary significance to the intention of the parties in order to find this result anomalous or questionable. Such a shift of perspective can be based on a desire to "ethicize" legal relations, but it can also be the consequence of doctrinal rigidity. Nineteenth-

---

[141] "Protokolle", in: *Mugdan*, vol. I, p. 712 and the remarks by Kramer, op. cit., note 138, § 118, n. 1.

[142] Cf. supra, pp. 613 sq.

[143] Paul. D. 44, 7, 3, 2. Cf. further Varro, *De Lingua Latina*, Lib. VI, 72 and Josef Partsch, "Die Lehre vom Scheingeschäft im römischen Rechte", (1921) 42 *ZSS* 248 sq. (dealing with a promise given by an actor "in tragoedia" on the stage).

[144] Most modern codifications therefore do not even deal with the problem.

[145] Cf. Albanese, *Atti negoziali*, pp. 162 sq.; Honsell/Mayer-Maly/Selb, p. 121.

century legal science provides an example of the latter alternative. The result was not in dispute: a reservatio mentalis must be irrelevant.[146] But how could this result be reconciled with the dominant will theory of contract? It is astonishing to see how this seemingly innocuous and rather impractical problem was able to acquire the awe-inspiring dimensions of a dogmatic "Cape Horn",[147] the dreaded rock on which any attempt to explain the legal world of contract from a purely intention-oriented point of view appeared to be bound to founder. As a consequence, the problem of the reservatio mentalis featured particularly prominently among the arguments of the opponents of the will theory.[148]

Many centuries earlier, canon law had even gone one important step further. In their aspiration to overcome the rigor iuris Romani, to refine and emphasize subjective elements in the law and to judge legal relations under the auspices of aequitas canonica, conscientia and honestas, canon lawyers had actually been prepared to take account of the (secret, but real) intention of a person not to be bound by a legal act which he had duly and consciously performed.[149] The first case known to us concerned a man who had not been able to seduce a girl, except by promising to marry her. He later on alleged that he had never intended to contract a marriage, and that it was for this reason that he had in fact made his declaration under a false name. Pope Innocent III, in a decretal addressed to the Bishop of Brixen,[150] decided in favour of the man.

In the tradition of the Catholic Church, this decision was taken to attribute operative effect to a reservatio mentalis. Throughout the centuries, marriages were "dissolved" on this basis[151] and, although the term "reservatio mentalis" is no longer used, contemporary Catholic marriage doctrine, as contained in the new Codex Juris Canonici, still places supreme importance on the "internus animi consensus" of the spouses. It is presumed to be in line with the "verb[a] vel sign[a] in celebrando matrimonio adhibit[a]",[152] but according to Can. 1101 II a marriage has not been validly contracted

---

[146] Cf. e.g. Savigny, *System*, vol. III, p. 258.

[147] Alfred Manigk, *Das rechtswirksame Verhalten* (1939), p. 142.

[148] On the role of the reservatio mentalis in the struggle between will theory and declaration theory cf. e.g. Otto Bähr, "Über Irrungen im Contrahiren", (1875) 14 *JhJb* 393 sqq.; Josef Kohler, "Studien über Mentalreservation und Simulation", (1878) 16 *JhJb* 91 sqq.; idem, (1878) 16 *JhJb* 325 sqq.; Bernhard Windscheid, "Wille und Willenserklärung", (1881) 63 *Archiv für die civilistische Praxis* 72 sqq.; Windscheid/Kipp, § 75; Rudolf Henle, *Vorstellungs- und Willenstheorie in der Lehre von der juristischen Willenserklärung* (1910), pp. 1 sqq.

[149] For what follows cf. Heinz Holzhauer, "Dogmatik und Rechtsgeschichte der Mentalreservation", in: *Festschrift für Rudolf Gmür* (1983), pp. 124 sqq.; idem, "Reservatio mentalis", in: *HRG*, vol. IV, col. 926 sqq.

[150] *Decretales Gregorii IX*, Lib. IV, Tit. I, Cap. XXVI.

[151] "Quid absurdius dici fingique potuisset, non video", comments the Protestant Justus Henning Boehmer, *Jus ecclesiasticum protestantium*, Lib. IV, Tit. I, § 142.

[152] Can. 1101 I Codex Juris Canonici (1983).

"si alterutra vel utraque pars positivo voluntatis actu excludat matrimonium ipsum vel matrimonii essentiale aliquod elementum, vel essentialem aliquam proprietatem".

The main difficulty, of course, lies in the proof of such a "positive act" of the will.[153] Lack of the (internal) intention to marry played a prominent role in the proceedings instituted by Henry VIII to get his marriage with Catherine of Aragon annulled,[154] and Napoleon Bonaparte (successfully) challenged the validity of his marriage to Josephine Beauharnais before the ecclesiastical courts on the basis of a reservatio mentalis.[155] Oaths, incidentally, were the other important legal act with regard to which the problem of a mental reservation became practically relevant.[156]

4. Simulatio

(a) Roman law

Simulatio brings us back from the lofty heights of State affairs to the dealings of more ordinary human beings: of purchasers and vendors of land, for instance, who wish to save taxes and notarial fees and hence record a lower purchase price in their notarial deed than the one they really intend to charge and pay. This is one of the standard examples for the application of § 117 BGB: the disguising contract (as recorded in the notarial deed) is void, because it was made only in pretence; the disguised transaction (sale of the land for the higher purchase price) is invalid too, since it lacks the statutory form.[157]

The Roman lawyers had to battle with very similar problems. Thus, for instance, contracts of sale sometimes appear to have been concluded

---

[153] Cf. Can. 1678–80 Codex Juris Canonici.

[154] Cf. e.g. Hans Thieme, "Die Ehescheidung Heinrichs VIII als europäischer Rechtsfall", in: *Syntagma Friburgense, Historische Studien für Hermann Aubin* (1956), pp. 257 sqq.

[155] For details, see e.g. Joseph Schnitzer, *Katholisches Eherecht* (1898), pp. 646 sqq. Napoleon and Josephine had contracted a civil marriage in 1796, but the Catholic marriage ceremony had taken place only on 1. 12. 1804, the eve of Napoleon's coronation as Emperor: Pope Pius VII had refused to crown a "concubine". Before the ecclesiastical court a variety of witnesses (inter alia Talleyrand) testified that Napoleon had not intended to enter into a marriage according to the rules of canon law. The civil marriage had already been dissolved beforehand, in accordance with art. 233 code civil. As is well known, Napoleon had taken a strong interest in the codification of French law, and left many marks upon the substance of the Code. The emphasis in the code civil on divorce "par consentement mutuel" is one example of this. Napoleon probably pressed for it, because he knew that his marriage to Josephine would remain childless (cf. Zweigert/Kötz, vol. I, p. 98). Dissolution of the marriage iure canonico had become necessary, because the (Habsburg) Emperor Franz I, whose daughter Marie Louise Napoleon now wished to marry for dynastic reasons, had insisted on it.

[156] For details, see Holzhauer, *Festschrift Gmür*, pp. 128 sqq. There are situations in which a person may feel (morally) obliged or may even be forced to conceal the truth and thus to commit what appears to be perjury. If, under these circumstances, he formulates his oath sufficiently ambiguously, he will not be liable (at least in foro conscientiae) for perjury, even though he intentionally deceives the (human) addressees of the oath. For to God "all hearts are open, all desires known, and from him no secrets are hid", and one will therefore be able to rely on the fact that he will realize the real (but hidden) intention behind the words.

[157] § 313 BGB.

without any intention on the part of the vendor to exact the purchase price. They were designed to disguise donations which the parties may have been unable to conclude: be it because of the provisions of the lex Cincia, or in view of the prohibition of donationes inter virum et uxorem. It is entirely in line with the flexibility with which the question of interpretation was approached in classical law that such simulated[158] transactions were, as a rule, not accepted at their face value: "Cum in venditione quis pretium rei ponit donationis causa non exacturus, non videtur vendere."[159] Originally, of course, transactions had been regarded as valid when and because all formalities had been complied with. The invalidity of the simulated transaction must have been unthinkable in the archaic days of Roman law. But this kind of rigorism had long been left behind.[160] With the rise of the consensual contracts, the will had become a key factor in the determination of id quod actum est, and the parties who merely pretend to conclude a sale do not, after all, really want to be bound by it. Their transaction could therefore not be accepted as a valid and effective sale; and where it had been used to disguise (for instance) a prohibited donation, the real intentions of the parties could, of course, not be given effect to either. In order to get around the prohibition of donations inter virum et uxorem, the spouses occasionally even seem to have taken the trouble to get divorced. The validity of the donation depended, according to Trebatius, on whether such a divorce was merely pretended or meant seriously: "Trebatius inter Terentiam et Maecenatem respondit, si verum divortium fuisset, ratam esse donationem, si simulatum, contra."[161] Invalid, too, were contracts of sale or lease where a price or rent of one coin had been agreed upon. This did not constitute pretium verum or merces vera. Sale or lease was merely simulated, in reality "et hoc donationis instar inducit".[162] The Digest contains a couple of generalizing statements: "Simulatae nuptiae nullius momenti sunt",[163] "[n]uda et imaginaria venditio pro non facta est",[164] "[c]ontractus imaginarii etiam in emptionibus iuris vinculum non optinent, cum fides facti simulatur non

[158] On the terms "simulare" und "simulatio" (derived from "similis") cf. Nadia Dumont-Kisliakoff, *La simulation en droit romain* (1970), pp. 15 sqq., 23 sqq.

[159] Ulp. D. 18, 1, 36; David Daube, "Generalisation in D. 18, 1, de contrahenda emptione", in: *Studi in onore di Vincenzo Arangio-Ruiz* vol. I, pp. 192 sqq.

[160] Contra, particularly, Partsch, (1921) 42 *ZSS* 227 sqq. who comes to the conclusion that simulated transactions were, as a rule, valid in classical Roman law. This view is based on unacceptable interpolation hypotheses. Giovanni Pugliese, *La simulazione nei negozi giuridici* (1938), argues that the Romans decided the question casuistically; neither were simulated transactions always valid, nor were they always invalid. A similar opinion is held by Kaser, *RPr* I, pp. 242 sq. For the view adopted here, cf. e.g. Honsell/Mayer-Maly/Selb, pp. 120 sqq.

[161] Iav. D. 24, 1, 64.

[162] Ulp. D. 19, 2, 46.

[163] Gai. D. 23, 2, 30. Marriages appear to have been simulated in order to avoid the disadvantages arising from the Augustan marriage laws for unmarried persons.

[164] Paul. D. 18, 1, 55.

intercedente veritate."[165] But it was the rubric chosen by Justinian for his Codex title 4, 22 which became the basis for all discussions about simulated transactions in the ius commune: the adage of "plus valere quod agitur quam quod simulate concipitur". Four out of the five rescripts contained in this title are attributed to Diocletian and Maximian, under whose reign a high point in the discrimination of simulated transactions appears to have been reached.[166] "Acta simulata . . . veritatis substantiam mutare non possunt",[167] they said, or: ". . . non quod scriptum, sed quod gestum est inspicitur."[168] As a consequence, all simulated acts were ineffective. Codex 4, 38, 9 makes it clear that the contract disguised by the simulated transaction may be valid: ". . . sed et donationis gratia praedii facta venditione si traditio sequitur, actione pretii nulla competente perficitur donatio." Obviously here an action on sale cannot be brought; but the donation (which was intended by the parties) is perfecta—and can therefore no longer be affected by the lex Cincia[169]—once traditio has taken place.

(b) Ius commune; simulatio and fraus legis

Fourteenth-century Italy again saw a proliferation of simulated transactions;[170] trade and commerce were flourishing, and simulation appears to have been a popular technique to get around cumbrous local statutes and inconvenient ecclesiastical decrees, particularly the vexed prohibition against usury. So, incidentally, was the conclusion of transactions in fraudem legis: transactions which, although complying with the words of a specific law, had nevertheless specifically been designed to defeat its purpose and were therefore contrary to the spirit of the law ("[f]raus enim legi fit, ubi quod fieri noluit, fieri autem non vetuit, id fit").[171] In actual practice it is often difficult to see whether a transaction has merely been simulated or is in fraudem legis, and it is hardly surprising that both doctrines have become intertwined and entangled in the course of the history of the ius commune. The term "simulation" was often used to cover all those situations where the parties had intended to circumvent a law.[172] The way for this development had been paved by the commentators who had developed the same criteria for both legal doctrines and had summed up their analysis in the sentence "tot modis committitur simulatio quot modis

---

[165] Mod. D. 44, 7, 54.

[166] For an overview cf. M.D. Blecher, "Simulated Transactions in the Later Civil Law", (1974) 91 *SALJ* 359 sqq.

[167] C. 4, 22, 2.

[168] C. 4, 22, 3.

[169] Cf. supra, pp. 483 sq.

[170] Blecher, (1974) 91 *SALJ* 365.

[171] Ulp. D. 1, 3, 30.

[172] Cf., in particular, Savigny, *System*, vol. I, pp. 324 sqq.; Jan Schröder, *Gesetzesauslegung und Gesetzesumgehung* (1985), pp. 15 sqq.

committitur fraus".[173] Nevertheless, at least in theory, they had still emphasized the crucial distinction between the two: in the case of simulation, a legal transaction is made only in pretence; the parties do not really intend the transaction which they appear to conclude. This transaction does not constitute a verus actus. Agere in fraudem, on the other hand, involves an actus verus,[174] albeit one that is iniustus. The parties do in fact want their act to be effective in order to achieve their aim of defeating the law.[175] Simulated transactions are mere "corpora sine spiritu, et cadavera sine anima",[176] acts in fraudem legis are "animated" by the intention of the parties.

Over the centuries, many refined distinctions were developed concerning simulatio.[177] The canon lawyers, for instance, moralized the issue and recognized that simulation may be a legitimate way of achieving a noble end;[178] after all, even the Lord himself had simulated a sinner: ". . . simulationem peccatricis carnis assumpserit, ut, condemnans in carne peccatum, nos in se faceret iustitiam Dei."[179] Reprehensible and to be rejected was a simulatio ex inhonesta causa. In practice, however, the law changed very little: id praevalere debet quod agitur, ei, quod simulatur, as Grotius put the basic principle in one of his opinions.[180] As a consequence, the simulated transaction was void. If the simulation had served to conceal another act,[181] it was usually acknowledged that the latter could be valid.[182]

In the course of the 19th century, the protection of third parties relying on the validity of the simulated transaction received attention. It was argued that the contract should not be treated as invalid with

---

[173] For details, see Helmut Coing, "Simulatio und Fraus in der Lehre des Bartolus und Baldus", in: *Festschrift für Paul Koschaker*, vol. III (1939), pp. 402 sqq.

[174] Coing, *Festschrift Koschaker*, vol. III, p. 412; cf. also Blecher, (1974) 91 *SALJ* 368; Otto Bähr, *Urteile des Reichsgerichts mit Besprechungen* (1883), pp. 59 sqq.

[175] For a similar view today cf. Kramer, op. cit., note 138, § 117, n. 10; Flume, *AT*, § 20, 2; but cf. Schröder, op. cit., note 172, pp. 42 sq.; Klaus Schurig, "Die Gesetzesumgehung im Privatrecht", in: *Festschrift für Murad Ferid* (1988), pp. 404 sqq.

[176] Lauterbach, *Collegium theoretico-practicum*, Lib. XVIII, Tit. I, CXVI.

[177] Very elaborate treatments of simulatio can be found in Bartholomaeus Cipolla, *De simulationibus* and Johannes Bertachinus, *Repertorium Juris*; cf. Partsch, (1921) 42 *ZSS* 234 and, particularly, Gunter Wesener, "Das Scheingeschäft in der spätmittelalterlichen Jurisprudenz, im Usus modernus und im Naturrecht", in: *Festschrift für Heinz Hübner* (1984), pp. 340 sqq.

[178] Blecher (1974) 91 *SALJ* 377 sqq.

[179] *Decretum Gratiani*, Secunda Pars, Causa XXII, Quaest. II, c. 21 (with further examples of simulation from the Old Testament). Blecher (p. 378) draws attention to the fact that we are dealing here with unilateral simulation, whereas the simulatio of the civil law is usually bilateral.

[180] "Hollandsche Consultatien en Advijsen", in: D.P. de Bruyn (ed.), *The Opinions of Grotius* (1894), pp. 553 sqq. For details of the development, see Wesener, *Festschrift Hübner*, pp. 338 sqq.

[181] In practice, this is nearly always the case; cf. e.g. Michaelis, *Festschrift Wieacker*, pp. 445 sqq.

[182] Cf. e.g. Lauterbach, *Collegium theoretico-practicum*, Lib. XVIII, Tit. I, CXVII. But see, for instance, the provision dealing with simulated transactions in the Codex Theresianus (Wesener, *Festschrift Hübner*, p. 353).

regard to them.[183] The BGB rejected this opinion,[184] but it ultimately found its way into § 916 II ABGB: evidence, again, of the relatively greater influence of the natural lawyers and their specific concern for a balance between subjective and objective elements in the concept of contract on the Austrian Code.[185, 186]

---

[183] Cf. the references in Windscheid/Kipp, § 75, n. 3.

[184] "Motive", in: *Mugdan*, vol. I, p. 459; "Protokolle", in: *Mugdan*, vol. I, pp. 711 sq. For modern attempts in German law to provide protection to third parties cf. e.g. Flume, *AT*, § 20, 2 c (the simulated transaction is, with regard to third parties, to be treated as reservatio mentalis!); but see Kramer, op. cit., note 138, § 117, nn. 17 sq.

[185] Cf. generally Klaus Luig, "Franz v. Zeiller und die Irrtumsregelung des ABGB", in: *Forschungsband Franz von Zeiller (1751–1828)* (1980), pp. 153 sqq. and, more specifically, Wesener, *Festschrift Hübner*, p. 355.

[186] South African courts refuse to enforce simulated transactions. They give effect to the true intention of the parties rather than to what they purport to have done. In *Zandberg v. Van Zyl* 1910 AD 302 at 309, Innes CJ said: "Not infrequently, . . . the parties to a transaction endeavour to conceal its real character. They call it by a name, or give it a shape, intended not to express but to disguise its true nature. And when a court is asked to decide any right under such agreement, it can only do so by giving effect to what the transaction really is; not what in form it purports to be." If the parties have decided to record their contract in writing, this principle even prevails over the parol evidence rule (which, if strictly applied, could lead to severe inequities in cases of simulated transactions); cf. Christie, *Contract*, pp. 162 sqq.

CHAPTER 21

Metus and Dolus

I. METUS

1. Historical background

During the last hundred years of its existence the Roman Republic was in constant turmoil. The clashes in the wake of the Gracchian reform legislation had set a pattern of political violence which was to lead, eventually, to the downfall of the old order. Violence was used to force legislation through an assembly and to influence the outcome of elections and of trials.[1] We read of tribunes, praetors[2] and candidates for the consulate being lynched, of a consul being stoned and his fasces broken, of riots at assemblies, attacks of the mob on the Senate and of politicians cutting their adversaries off in midspeech by blocking their mouths.[3] Since the days of the infamous Publius Clodius Pulcher[4] (himself murdered after a brawl on the via Appia), armed gangs, composed of slaves, freedmen and urban poor were employed to maraud the streets and to intimidate political opponents.[5] From time to time, a state of emergency had to be declared by passing the senatus consultum ultimum.[6] Even a man like Cicero,

> "who possessed by temperament and education refined sensibilities and a horror of internecine strife, encouraged violence, if it was undertaken by the boni in defence of the established order against the audaces and improbi who sought to disturb it. . . . The Romans of the Republic seem genuinely to have considered it an essential constituent of libertas that a man should be allowed to use force in his personal interest to secure what he believed to be his due. So, when a conflict could not be resolved constitutionally, it was not surprising that the frustrated party employed violence, and this in turn frequently could not be countered except by further partisan violence. This vicious circle continued until the military force which was finally summoned to break it moved the conflict to the higher plane of civil war".[7]

---

[1] For details, see A.W. Lintott, *Violence in Republican Rome* (1968), pp. 175 sqq., 208 sqq. On the annulment of laws passed by violence cf. pp. 132 sqq.

[2] Cf., for example, the episode involving the praetor Asellio who was assassinated by moneylenders: supra, pp. 167 sq.

[3] Cf., for example, the episode recounted in Plutarch, *Vitae*, Cato minor, 28, 1.

[4] On him cf. e.g. Hans Georg Gundel, in: *Kleiner Pauly*, vol. 1, col. 1227 sq.

[5] Lintott, op. cit., note 1, pp. 74 sqq.

[6] Details in Lintott, op. cit., note 1, pp. 149 sqq. Cf. further the observations by Frier, *Roman Jurists*, pp. 52, 270 sq.

[7] Lintott, op. cit., note 1, pp. 175, 204 sq. For a more detailed discussion of the morality of political violence, more particularly on Cicero's views ("misconceived and short-sighted"), cf. pp. 52 sqq.; but see also Frier, *Roman Jurists*, pp. 118 sqq. On Roman reliance on self-help cf. also Gunter Wesener, "Offensive Selbsthilfe im klassischen römischen Recht", in: *Festschrift Artur Steinwenter* (1958), pp. 100 sqq.; Theo Mayer-Maly, *RE*, vol. IX A 1, 1961, col. 315 sqq.; Alfons Bürge, "Vertrag und personale Abhängigkeiten im Rom der

In the provinces, people lived in constant fear of being extorted and exploited by corrupt governors and their agents. Being in a position of supreme authority, unchecked by a colleague or tribunus plebis, a provincial governor was often tempted to use his term of office to recover financially from the election campaigns fought at home, and to prepare his private purse for those that were yet to lead him to even higher office. The leges de rebus repetundis[8] (the mere volume of which is in itself an indication of the size of the problem) did little to ameliorate the situation: Rome was far away, and even if the worst came to the worst, a guilty governor could always slip away from Rome to the sanctuary of a provincial town.[9]

2. Coactus volui, tamen volui

Under these circumstances it is hardly surprising that people found themselves compelled, increasingly frequently, to give away movable and immovable property, to promise money, to waive claims, not to enter upon inheritances, etc. Whatever, therefore, the reaction of the public authorities on a constitutional level in these confused and turbulent times,[10] it was clear that the praetor had to step in to grant relief to those whose private transactions had been affected by fear or force. "Nihil consensui tam contrarium est . . . quam vis atque metus"[11]—nothing is as opposed to consent as force and fear: this is how Ulpian formulated, as far at least as bonae fidei transactions based on consensus were concerned, what was obviously equitable. But the ius civile did not provide a satisfactory solution to the problem. Coactus volui, tamen volui was the principle that we still find proclaimed by a late classical jurist such as Paulus:[12] even though I have formed my will under coercion, I have nevertheless formed a (legally relevant) will. There was no general rule declaring transactions concluded under the influence of duress or coercion invalid. On the

---

späten Republik und der frühen Kaiserzeit", (1980) 97 *ZSS* 107 sqq.; cf. also the case underlying Cicero's speech pro Caecina (on which see the detailed analysis by Frier, *Roman Jurists*, passim, e.g. pp. 24 sq.).

[8] Mommsen, *Römisches Strafrecht* (1899), pp. 705 sqq.; Berger, p. 675; D.V. Simon, in: *Kleiner Pauly*, vol 4, col. 1379 sq. The term "repetundae" indicates things or money given to an official under extortion as a bribe which could therefore be claimed back (repetere).

[9] This is what happened in the case of Verres, whose machinations Cicero exposed in a series of famous speeches. Verres withdrew to Massilia (Marseilles) where he lived most comfortably for the next 26 years off his proceeds and surrounded by the art treasures heaped up during the three years of his governorship in Sicily. He was killed in A.D. 43 after Antonius and Octavianus had seized power in Rome. Cf. e.g. M. Deissmann-Merten, in: *Kleiner Pauly*, col. 1207 sqq.

[10] It was entirely inadequate. On the control of violence by the executive, see Lintott, op. cit., note 1, pp. 89 sqq.; on legislation against violence, see Lintott, pp. 125 sqq.

[11] Ulp. D. 50, 17, 116 pr.

[12] "Si metu coactus adii hereditatem, puto me heredem effici, quia quamvis si liberum esset noluissem, tamen coactus volui": Paul. D. 4, 2, 21, 5; cf. also Cels. D. 23, 2, 22. On these texts, their possible philosophical background and their implications, see A.S. Hartkamp, *Der Zwang im Privatrecht* (1971), pp. 84 sqq., 124 sqq.

contrary: stipulations (and other formal transactions) were usually valid:

> ". . . si metu coactus . . . stipulanti Titio promisisti, quod non debueras promittere, palam est, iure civili te obligatum esse, et actio, qua intenditur dare te oportere, efficax est."[13]

3. "Quod metus causa gestum erit, ratum non habeo"

It was either in 79 or 78 B.C. that a praetor by the name of Octavius for the first time introduced a formula into the edict which appears to have been directed against "per vim aut metum auferre";[14] the actio Octaviana thus enabled the disadvantaged party to claim back what he had been compelled to hand over. This was the historic starting point for the legal protection against unconscionable coercion, as we find it laid down more fully in Hadrian's edictum perpetuum. "Quod metus causa gestum erit, ratum non habebo", were the generalizing words with which the relevant title was introduced.[15] What exactly did that entail? The key term "metus" was defined by Gaius in the following manner: "Metum autem non vani hominis, sed qui merito et in homine constantissimo cadat, ad hoc edictum pertinere dicemus."[16] This very restrictive concept of metus is a typical reflection of the Roman attitude towards "man's central virtue":[17] constantia. A Roman citizen could normally be held responsible for his actions and his declarations, and any attempt to get away from what he had done or said was instinctively frowned upon. The typical vir constans was not thrown off balance when faced with "timor quislibet";[18] if that made him rush into a contract then this was due, above all, to an embarrassing lack of resoluteness. Hence the requirement that the fear experienced must have been of such a magnitude that it would have had an impact even on a man of the most steadfast character, on the (model) vir constantissimus.[19] Fear of death,[20] imprisonment,[21] enslavement[22] or of

---

13 *Inst.* IV, 13, 1.

14 Hartkamp, op. cit., note 12, pp. 245 sqq.; Berthold Kupisch, *In integrum restitutio und vindicatio utilis bei Eigentumsübertragungen im klassischen römischen Recht* (1974), pp. 158 sqq.

15 Ulp. D. 4, 2, 1. Ulpian adds: "[O]lim ita edicebatur 'quod vi metusve causa': vis enim fiebat mentio propter necessitatem impositam contrariam voluntati: metus instantis vel futuri periculi causa mentis trepidatio. sed postea detracta est vis mentio ideo, quia quodcumque vi atroci fit, id metu quoque fieri videtur." On the relationship between vis and metus and the development sketched by Ulpian, cf. Udo Ebert, "Vi metusve causa", (1969) 86 *ZSS* 403 sqq.; Hartkamp, op. cit., note 12, pp. 1 sqq.; Kupisch, op. cit., note 14, pp. 192 sqq.

16 D. 4, 2, 6. Cf. also Ulp. D. 4, 2, 7 pr.: ". . . si quis meticulosus rem nullam frustra timuerit, per hoc edictum non restituitur, quoniam neque vi neque metus causa factum est."

17 Schulz, *Principles*, p. 224.

18 Cf. Ulp. D. 4, 2, 5.

19 He represents a Byzantine generalization of classic casuistry. For all details, see Hartkamp, op. cit., note 12, pp. 27 sqq.

20 Cf. e.g. Ulp. D. 4, 2, 3, 1.

21 Cf. e.g. Ulp. D. 4, 2, 7, 1.

22 Paul. D. 4, 2, 8, 1.

stuprum[23] fell into this category, not, for instance, fear of being exposed to legal proceedings[24] or to infamia.[25]

4. The meaning of metus causa

The exact meaning of the term "metus causa" as used in the praetor's edict ("quod metus causa gestum erit . . .") has given rise to scholarly dispute. Traditionally, the praetor was understood to disapprove of acts[26] which had been caused by fear;[27] but it has also been argued that the phrase refers to what has been done with the aim of causing fear.[28] More recently, a third interpretation has gained ground which regards—more widely—all acquisitions as being covered by the praetorian veto which have been made as a consequence of fear.[29] In other words: "metus causa" is not to be understood from the point of view of either the extortioner or the person who has been compelled to act, but from the position of whoever acquires something on the basis of duress: irrespective of whether he was himself responsible for the other party's predicament, whether he is merely exploiting it or whether he has acted in good faith. This latter opinion ties in best with the fact that the actio quod metus causa did not aim at penalizing extortionary behaviour (". . . haec actio . . . [non] personam vim facientis coerceat. . ."),[30] and that even bona fide third parties could therefore be liable.[31] If A has forced B to perform to C, who in turn sells the object to D, neither C nor D has acted "because of fear". Nevertheless, D's acquisition can be traced back to the fact that B once had to make a performance under compulsion; in this sense, it is (still) based on metus and can thus be regarded as something "quod metus causa factum est".[32]

5. The remedies

(a) *The actio quod metus causa*

This brings us to the remedies provided by the praetor in order to give teeth to his verdict of "ratum non habebo". The actio quod metus causa, without doubt, was the most potent and attractive weapon in the

[23] Paul. D. 4, 2, 8, 2.
[24] C. 2, 19, 10 (Diocl. et Max.).
[25] Ulp. D. 4, 2, 7 pr.
[26] Legal transactions and factual acts; for examples of the latter cf. Pomp./Ulp. D. 4, 2, 9, 2; Paul. D. 4, 2, 21, 2; Kupisch, op. cit., note 14, pp. 129 sqq.
[27] Cf. e.g. Fritz Schulz, "Die Lehre vom erzwungenen Rechtsgeschäft im antiken römischen Recht", (1922) 43 *ZSS* 220 and passim; Kaser, *RPr* I, p. 244; Hartkamp, op. cit., note 12, pp. 52 sqq.
[28] G.H. Maier, *Prätorische Bereicherungsklagen* (1932), pp. 96 sqq.
[29] Kupisch, op. cit., note 14, pp. 145 sqq.; Max Kaser, "Zur in integrum restitutio, besonders wegen metus und dolus", (1977) 94 *ZSS* 123 sq.
[30] Ulp. D. 4, 2, 9, 8.
[31] Cf. infra, p. 655.
[32] Cf. Ulp. D. 4, 2, 9, 8.

hands of a person who had acted under fear. It was characterized by a variety of interesting peculiarities. First of all, it was a penal action, for the defendant was liable for "quanti ea res erit, tantae pecuniae quadruplum":[33] fourfold the value which had been extorted.[34] Secondly, it was "in rem scripta",[35] that is, the defendant was not identified as the extortioner but only as the person who had acquired something on the basis of metus: "Si paret . . . N^{m} N^{m} fundum . . . [mancipio] accepisse. . . ."[36] This could be the person to whom the plaintiff had been forced to perform or also any other person into whose hands the object in question had ultimately come, for instance a bona fide purchaser.[37] Reason: ". . . in alterius praemium verti alienum metum non oportet."[38] Thirdly, the actio quod metus causa was an actio arbitraria; it contained, in between intentio and condemnatio, the clause "neque ea res [arbitrio iudicis] restituetur".[39] On the strength of it, the defendant was able to escape condemnation and payment of quadruplum by simply restoring the extorted objects. And finally, even if he refused such restoration, condemnation under the actio quod metus causa did not involve infamia.[40]

All of this presents a puzzling mixture of mildness and rigidity. On the one hand, one usually dealt with extortioners, or at least with persons who were not above suspicion. Hence the poena quadrupli, quadruplum being the highest multiple for which an action was available in Roman law.[41] On the other hand, however, the defendant could also be free from any blame. Hence the formula arbitraria and the exclusion of infamia. That extortioners would also benefit from these concessions was to be accepted nolens volens; volens probably rather than nolens in view of the extortionary practices of many influential Roman office-

---

[33] Lenel, *EP*, p. 112.

[34] After the lapse of one year, liability was confined to simplum: Ulp. D. 4, 2, 14, 1. Justinian broke down the amount of quadruplum into a (restitutionary) condemnation in simplum and a poena tripli. Cf. Ulp. D. 4, 2, 14, 10 sq. (itp.); Hartkamp, op. cit., note 12, pp. 285 sq. and, generally, Kaser, *RPr* II, p. 429.

[35] Cf. Ulp. D. 4, 2, 9, 8: "Cum autem haec actio in rem sit scripta nec personam vim facientis coerceat, sed adversus omnes restitui velit quod metus causa factum est . . ."; Ulp. D. 4, 2, 9, 1: "Animadvertendum autem, quod praetor in hoc edicto generaliter et in rem loquitur nec adicit a quo gestum." Very clear is Bartolus, *Commentaria*, ad D. 4, 2, 9, 8: "Haec actio est in rem scripta, ideo datur contra omnes, ad quos commodum pervenit ex metu."

[36] Kupisch, op. cit., note 14, pp. 176 sqq.; Kaser, (1977) 94 *ZSS* 126 sqq.

[37] That the actio quod metus causa could be brought against (bona fide) third parties who had acquired the extorted thing has been disputed in the past; cf. e.g. Schulz, (1922) 43 *ZSS* 240 sqq.; Ulrich von Lübtow, *Der Ediktstitel "Quod metus causa gestum erit"* (1932), pp. 168 sqq. But cf. Ulp. D. 4, 2, 14, 5; Ulp. 4, 2, 9, 8 (both not interpolated) and Hartkamp, op. cit., note 12, pp. 201 sqq.; Kaser, (1977) 94 *ZSS* 127 sqq. and particularly Kupisch, op. cit., note 14, pp. 199 sqq., who gives a detailed analysis of the historical development.

[38] Ulp. D. 4, 2, 14, 5 in fine.

[39] Cf. Ulp. D. 4, 2, 14, 4; *Inst.* IV, 6, 27; Lenel, *EP*, p. 112. On actiones arbitrariae in general, see Kaser, *RZ*, pp. 256 sqq.

[40] Cf. e.g. Hartkamp, op. cit., note 12, pp. 245, 274.

[41] *Inst.* IV, 6, 21.

bearers in the provinces, who were to be treated considerately for reasons of political expediency.[42]

(b) In integrum restitutio?

Orthodox doctrine has it that the person who had lost out on account of metus was also granted an in integrum restitutio. Actio quod metus causa and in integrum restitutio are thus seen as two distinct remedies, the one a purely penal one, the other of a restitutionary nature.[43] This picture does not, however, conform to our sources. In the Digest we find a far-reaching amalgamation of in integrum restitutio and actio quod metus causa which is attributed, traditionally, to Justinian.[44] The compilers, it is said, have modified the law by ruthlessly shortening and interpolating the classical texts; admittedly, therefore, "the short Digest title 4, 2 presents unusual difficulties".[45] These difficulties, however, find their origin in those strenuous attempts to bring the sources into harmony with certain preconceived ideas. They are not inherent in the sources themselves. For it has recently been demonstrated how things can be made to fall into place: the actio quod metus causa was the main remedy[46] which the praetor had made available *in order to effect* in integrum restitutio; we are not dealing with two separate remedies, but

---

[42] For speculations about the (political) background of the actio metus causa and its relationship with the leges de rebus repetundis, cf. in particular Hartkamp, op. cit., note 12, pp. 250 sqq.; Kupisch, op. cit., note 14, pp. 228 sqq.; Kaser, (1977) 94 *ZSS* 120 sqq.

[43] Cf. e.g. Lenel, *EP*, pp. 110 sqq.; Schulz, (1922) 43 *ZSS* 216 sqq.; idem, *CRL*, pp. 600 sqq.; von Lübtow, op. cit., note 37, pp. 81 sqq.; Ernst Levy, "Zur nachklassischen in integrum restitutio" (1951) 68 *ZSS* 361 sqq.; Hartkamp, op. cit., note 12, pp. 189 sqq.; Buckland/Stein, p. 593; Kaser, *RPr* I, p. 244; cf. also, most recently, Alvaro D'Ors, "El comentario de Ulpiano a los edictos del 'metus' ", (1981) 51 *AHDE* 287 sqq.; Hans Ankum, "Eine neue Interpretation von Ulpian Dig. 4, 2, 9, 5–6 über die Abhilfe gegen metus", in: *Festschrift für Heinz Hübner* (1984), pp. 3 sqq.

[44] Cf. e.g. Schulz, (1922) 43 *ZSS* 229 sqq.; von Lübtow, op. cit., note 37, pp. 218 sqq.; Levy, (1951) 68 *ZSS* 422 sq.; Hartkamp, op. cit., note 12, pp. 59 sqq., 285.

[45] Schulz, p. 604. Kaser, (1977) 94 *ZSS* 109 comments as follows: "Nur auf wenigen Gebieten des Juristenrechts erweckt . . . die neuzeitliche Interpolationen-Kritik durch Streichungen und Zusätze, zuweilen auch durch Umstellungen, so stark wie hier den Eindruck des Krampfhaften, die die angewandte Methode zu diskreditieren droht" (only rarely in modern contributions to the law of the Roman jurists does one find equally desperate and frantic efforts to spot interpolations and to amend the texts by way of deletions, additions and occasionally even by way of a rearrangement; efforts which threaten to discredit the method applied).

[46] Others, which could be used alternatively for the same purpose (namely that of restitutio in integrum) were the so-called rescissory (from "rescindere", "to pull down") actions modelled by the praetor according to the circumstances of each case and designed to set aside the effects of quod metus causa gestum erat. They were based on a fiction, for the judge was instructed to treat the matter as if the transaction had not taken place. Thus, for instance, where ownership had been transferred under duress, the plaintiff was granted an actio in rem on the model of the rei vindicatio. Cf. Ulp. D. 4, 2, 9, 4 and 6 and 7; for details, see Kupisch, op. cit., note 14, pp. 134 sqq.; Kaser, (1977) 94 *ZSS* 138 sqq. The plaintiff apparently had the choice between this rescissory action (which did not involve a poena quadrupli) and the actio quod metus causa.

the action was the means of attaining the aim of restoration.[47] This explains, for instance, why the actio quod metus causa was incorporated into the edictal title De in integrum restitutionibus and why the in integrum restitutio is often—also in other contexts—described as actio. The only major obstacle seems to lie in the fact that the actio quod metus causa lay for quadruplum and was an actio poenalis: not, it would appear, the appropriate attributes for a remedy supposed to serve the end of restoration. But we have already seen that the actio quod metus causa did not aim at penalizing the extortioner and that, furthermore, it was an actio arbitraria. Restoration was in fact its main objective, and the poena quadrupli was not (primarily) intended as a punishment for criminal behaviour but as an inducement for the debtor to return "quod metus causa accep[erat]".[48] Only on this basis was it possible, after all, to expose bona fide third parties to the actio quod metus causa: ". . . nec cuiquam iniquum videtur ex alieno facto alium in quadruplum condemnari, quia non statim quadrupli est actio, sed si res non restituatur."[49]

(c) Exceptio

In many cases, of course, it was not necessary for a person who had acted under the influence of fear to sound the charge by instituting an action. If, for instance, he had promised something by way of stipulation, he could just as well wait until the stipulator attempted to enforce the contract. He could then counter this action by asking for an exceptio to be inserted into the programme of litigation. This exceptio was known as the exceptio metus and it instructed the judge, quite simply, to inquire "si in ea re nihil metus causa factum est".[50] With the actio quod metus causa the exceptio metus shared the important characteristic that it was "in rem scripta" with the effect, "ut non inspiciamus, an is qui agit metus causa fecit aliquid, sed an omnino metus causa factum est in hac re a quocumque, non tantum ab eo qui agit".[51] The person of the extortioner was not identified in the formula of the exceptio, and thus it could be raised against any plaintiff, whether he himself had caused the fear or whether, for instance, he was a bona

---

[47] This is the main thesis of Kupisch's book on in integrum restitutio, op. cit., note 14, pp. 123 sqq. It was hailed as "revolutionary" by Kaser, (1977) 94 *ZSS* 110, 116.

[48] Kupisch, op. cit., note 14, pp. 145 sq., 228 sqq.; Kaser, (1977) 94 *ZSS* 115 sqq.; contra: Ankum, *Festschrift Hübner*, pp. 17 sq. This view appears to have prevailed among the authors of the ius commune too. Very clear on this point e.g. Voet, *Commentarius ad Pandectas*, Lib. IV, Tit. II, VII: ". . . Sed nec refert, an ipse metum faciens, an tertius bonae fidei possessor, justo etiam munitus titulo, conveniatur, quantum ad hanc quadrupli persecutionem: neque enim existimandum est, illum praestando quadruplum ex alieno admisso, seu illato per alium metu, poenam subire: nam cum haec actio arbitraria sit, et initio inspecto non nisi rei persecutionem comprehendat, . . . sic ut quadruplum non tamen metus illati quam contumaciae commissae coercitio dicenda sit."

[49] Ulp. D. 4, 2, 14, 3 in fine.

[50] Ulp. D. 44, 4, 4, 33.

[51] Ibid.

fide third party to whom the defendant had been coerced to make the promise.[52]

Naturally, it was not always easy to determine how actio and exceptio worked together in an individual case. Take the situation discussed in D. 4, 2, 14, 9.[53] A had, through force, procured a promise in the form of a stipulation from B. B had sued him with the actio metus causa, which meant that A had had the option of restoring B to the former position; such restitutio in integrum would, in this instance, have entailed a formal release. A had, however, refused to give it and had consequently been condemned to pay the poena quadrupli. He now sued B on the stipulation, which, though brought about by metus, was after all still in existence. Was B able, under these circumstances, to bar A's claim with the exceptio metus? Yes, according to Labeo, who thus allowed actio and exceptio to be cumulated. Not so, said Julian, who was therefore prepared to grant A a replicatio to counter B's exceptio. Without such replicatio B would in effect have been able to obtain both penalty and restitution: a result which had quite clearly not been envisaged by the praetor.[54]

Finally, there was a variety of situations where the defendant did not need to invoke praetorian help in order to escape the consequences of a transaction entered into metus causa. Most importantly, the exceptio metus was inherent in the bonae fidei iudicia;[55] it was part and parcel of the officium iudicis to refuse to entertain the plaintiff's claim under these circumstances. For all practical purposes that meant that the contract (of sale, lease etc.) was invalid.

6. The position under the ius commune

(a) *The relief for metus and its limits*

The Digest title 4, 2 provided the basis for all discussions about metus during the various ages of the ius commune; through the Roman-Dutch authorities it still exercises a dominant influence on modern South African law.[56] For centuries, texts such as D. 4, 2, 2–7 were accepted as defining the limits of relief for metus. It was emphasized that only fear of a severe evil ("metus maioris malitatis")[57] was a

[52] Example: A forces B to promise (by way of stipulation) to C. B is able to raise the exceptio metus against C's condictio. On the exceptio metus, see Hartkamp, op. cit., note 12, pp. 270 sqq.; Kupisch, op. cit., note 14, pp. 170 sqq.

[53] "Sed et si quis per vim stipulatus cum acceptum non faceret, fuerit in quadruplum condemnatus, ex stipulatu eum agentem adversus exceptionem replicatione adiuvari Iulianus putat, cum in quadruplo et simplum sit reus consecutus. Labeo autem etiam post quadrupli actionem nihilo minus exceptione summovendum eum, qui vim intulit, dicebat."

[54] Cf. also Schulz, *CRL*, p. 604.

[55] Kaser, *RPr* I, p. 245; Honsell/Mayer-Maly/Selb, p. 127. Cf. further the detailed analysis by Hartkamp, op. cit., note 12, pp. 84 sqq., 148 sqq.

[56] Cf. e.g. De Wet en Yeats, pp. 43 sqq.; Joubert, *Contract*, pp. 104 sqq.; Wessels, *Contract*, vol. I, nn. 1165 sqq.

[57] Ulp. D. 4, 2, 5.

sufficient cause of action, and the Roman case law on the topic was faithfully preserved. Instances of "maior malitas" came to be remembered by a little verse ("excusat carcer, status, mors, verbera, stuprum"),[58] and we find long discussions about metus infamiae, the main example of what continued to be considered "non satis gravis".[59] Metus reverentialis, fear due to the natural respect owed to persons in authority (such as parents or husbands), was identified by the Accursian gloss as a general ground for setting aside a contract,[60] but this extension of the concept of metus remained disputed.[61] "Ita expeditum illud", said Voet, "metum reverentialem huic restitutioni locum non facere";[62] but he recognized an exception where fathers or husbands could be proved to have gone beyond the bounds of respectful fear and to have instilled a "terror exheredationis", or something equally obnoxious, in their wives or children. Eventually, however, this kind of casuistry was abandoned in favour of a more generalized approach. For, as was pointed out by Lauterbach,[63] there could be vis in bonam partem and in malam partem, metus iustus and metus iniustus. Cutting, to a certain extent, across the established categories was therefore the more fundamental distinction whether the fear was inspired "contra bonos mores, adeoque injuste"[64] or not. This criterion, too, had been foreshadowed in the Digest; we find it mentioned both in Ulp. D. 4, 2, 3, 1 and in the famous regula iuris of D. 50, 17, 116. Pothier required that in order to provide the basis for a remedy, the fear had to be "injuste",[65] and this criterion has also been read into the French code civil.[66] Specific limits as to which form the pressure might take were no longer prescribed. In the same vein, the German BGB merely states that the transaction must have been induced "unlawfully" by duress.[67] This has brought about a considerable degree of flexibility and has enabled courts and legal writers to use the remedies provided in art. 1112 code civil and § 123 BGB in order to tackle the problem of economic duress[68]—a new and relatively subtle form of coercion which has come to the fore in the wake of the progress

[58] Cf. Lauterbach, *Collegium theoretico-practicum*, Lib. IV, Tit. II, XI.

[59] Voet, *Commentarius ad Pandectas*, Lib. IV, Tit. II, XII. Cf. also still art. 1114 code civil.

[60] This was based, mainly, on Ulp. D. 44, 5, 1, 5 and 6 concerning the relationship between freedman and patron.

[61] For a detailed discussion cf. J.E. Scholtens, "Undue Influence", 1960 *Acta Juridica* 276 sqq.

[62] *Commentarius ad Pandectas*, Lib. IV, Tit. II, XI.

[63] *Collegium theoretico-practicum*, Lib. IV, Tit. II, VI.

[64] Voet, *Commentarius ad Pandectas*, Lib. IV, Tit. II, X. For South African law cf. Joubert, *Contract*, p. 107.

[65] Pothier, *Traité des obligations*, n. 26.

[66] Nicholas, *FLC*, pp. 101 sq.

[67] § 123 BGB.

[68] John P. Dawson, "Economic Duress and the Fair Exchange in French and German Law", (1936–37) 11 *Tulane LR* 345 sqq.; cf. also, more recently, idem, "Unconscionable Coercion: The German Version", (1976) 89 *Harvard LR* 1041 sqq.

of economic individualism in the 19th century. Hand in hand with these developments went a relaxation of the standard for measuring the degree of pressure exercised on the contracting party.

By the time of Voet, the Roman vir constantissimus had been replaced by the more realistic homo constans,[69] and from there it was not far to the *"personne raisonnable"* of the code civil.[70] Apart from that, the standard was also individualized, for not everybody can be expected to display even an average degree of constantia or reasonableness. The judge was therefore usually asked to take into consideration the age, the sex and the condition of the person threatened.[71] The BGB ultimately abandoned any attempt to set up specific standards of hypothetical constancy in order to confirm the range of operative metus.

(b) Effect of metus on the contract

Whether contracts induced by metus were ipso iure void or merely voidable at the instance of the injured party remained disputed. The distinction between negotia bonae fidei and stricti iuris having become obsolete, it seemed appropriate to subject all contracts to one and the same regime.[72] Most authors of the later ius commune, when faced with this decision, seem to have been convinced by Paulus' "coactus volui" argument: ". . . consentire eum, qui metu conterritus quid fecit, ratio sana docet: eligit nempe ex duobus malis minimum."[73] Vis compulsiva (as the mere threat of violence had by now come to be called), after all, left the person exposed to it with a choice, albeit the hardly enviable one of embracing what he considered to be the lesser of two evils. This was different in the case of vis absoluta.[74] Where one party grabs the other's hand and makes him sign a document (not a very frequent incident outside of professorial textbooks) there is, of course, no freedom of choice: "Vis . . . absoluta . . . illius, qui eam patitur, excludit consensum."[75] The same kind of argument was bound

[69] *Commentarius ad Pandectas*, Lib. IV, Tit. II, XI.

[70] Art. 1112 code civil; cf. also Pothier, *Traité des obligations*, n. 25, who had specifically rejected the standard of the "most constant" man.

[71] Cf. e.g. Voet, *Commentarius ad Pandectas*, Lib. IV, Tit. II, XI; Pothier, *Traité des obligations*, n. 25; art. 1112 code civil (on the "unfortunate conflation of the objective Roman rule and the subjective approach preferred by Domat and Pothier", cf. Nicholas, *FLC*, p. 101). Contra e.g. Grotius, *De jure belli ac pacis*, Lib. II, Cap. XI, VII.

[72] But see the discussion in Glück, vol. 5, pp. 472 sqq.

[73] Voet, *Commentarius ad Pandectas*, Lib. IV, Tit. II, I; cf. further Joubert, *Contract*, p. 105; Wessels, *Contract*, vol. I, n. 1197. Often, however, certain exceptions were recognized, e.g. in case of a promise of dowry or of a datio libertatis (Voet, *Commentarius ad Pandectas*, Lib. IV, Tit. II, XV).

[74] The distinction between vis absoluta and vis compulsiva stems from the Middle Ages and has been developed by glossators and canonists; cf. Hartkamp, op. cit., note 12, pp. 3 sqq. The Romans did not deal with cases of vis absoluta.

[75] Voet, *Commentarius ad Pandectas*, Lib. IV, Tit. II, I; today cf. De Wet en Yeats, pp. 43 sq.

to appeal particularly to the will theorists of the 19th century: as long as two or more courses of action are open to the declarant, his declaration reflects a real will (and not only the semblance thereof).[76] This was the dominant view from Savigny[77] down to Windscheid/Kipp, and hence the BGB, too, leaves it to "whoever has been induced to make a declaration of intention . . . unlawfully by duress" to rescind the declaration.[78] Rescission here works in the same way as in the case of error, that is, ex tunc.[79] Pothier, too, refers to *"rescision"*,[80] and the code civil therefore does not regard contracts vitiated by violence as absolutely void either. The nullity is "relative", i.e. it may be invoked only by the victim of the threat.[81]

(c) Specific characteristics of the remedies for metus

According to both modern French and modern German law,[82] the contract may be rescinded (i.e. the nullity be invoked)—and consequently all performances made be reclaimed—even if the duress had been exercised not by the contractual partner but by a third party. The contractual partner need not even have known about the predicament of the victim of the threat. To this extent, it is still true to say that the remedy against duress is "in rem scripta".[83] Throughout the days of the ius commune, this characteristic of the Roman actio quod metus causa and of the exceptio metus had been faithfully retained;[84] modern South African writers have, however, questioned the wisdom of treating duress more strictly in this regard than the other vices of consent, particularly dolus (fraud).[85] In no modern legal system does the extortioner, or anybody else who happens to have received anything on account of metus, face a fourfold penalty any longer if he refuses to render restitution. This aspect of the actio quod metus causa was

[76] Cf. also, from a philosophical point of view, Thomas Hobbes in his *Leviathan*, as quoted by Atiyah, *Rise and Fall*, p. 43: "Feare and Liberty are consistent; as when man throweth his goods into the Sea for feare that the ship should sink, he doth it neverthelesse very willingly, and may refuse to doe it if he will: It is therefore the action, of one that was *free*; so a man sometimes pays his debt, only for *feare* of Imprisonment, which because no body hindered him from detaining was the action of a man at liberty." "Hobbes realizes, of course", Atiyah carries on, "that there must be certain exceptional cases where the civil law in a political society will . . . be disinclined to enforce a [promise extracted by duress]. But even in such case he appears to have some notion, peculiar though it may seem to us, that the promise is somehow prima facie binding, and it is only by the grace of the positive laws of the State that the promisor is freed from his promise."

[77] *System*, vol. III, pp. 102 sqq.

[78] § 123 BGB. [79] § 142 BGB.

[80] *Traité des obligations*, n. 26.

[81] Cf. Nicholas, *FLC*, pp. 74 sqq.

[82] But see § 875 ABGB; for a comparative analysis cf. Zweigert/Kötz, pp. 128 sq.

[83] Cf. "Motive", in: *Mugdan*, vol. I, pp. 465 sq.

[84] Cf. e.g. Voet, *Commentarius ad Pandectas*, Lib. IV, Tit. II, IV; Windscheid/Kipp, § 80, n. 5; Wessels, *Contract*, vol. I, n. 1202.

[85] De Wet en Yeats, pp. 45 sq.; Joubert, *Contract*, p. 110. Contra: H.R. Hahlo/Ellison Kahn, *The Union of South Africa* (1960), pp. 472 sq. Cf. also Savigny, *System*, vol. III, p. 117, who described metus as the worse and more dangerous form of disrupting law and order.

declared obsolete as far back as the 17th century: "Haec quadrupli poena nostris et Gallorum moribus exolevit. . . . In simplum actio . . . datur."[86] The intimidated party is entitled only to the simple value; the extortioner, moreover, is liable for full damages.[87] In modern German law this follows from the general principles of the law of restitution and of delict, and a specific (restitutionary or delictual) actio quod metus causa has therefore not been taken over by the code.

In the English common law, at least since the 19th century, duress used to be about as narrowly defined as metus in the earlier ius commune; a contract may be avoided, if there has been a threat of physical violence to, or unlawful constraint of, the person of one of the contracting parties.[88] More particularly, duress of goods and economic duress are traditionally not taken into consideration.[89] The narrow common-law definition induced the Courts of Equity to step in and grant relief in cases of "undue influence".[90]

In South Africa attempts have not been wanting to read the doctrine of "undue influence" into the Roman-Dutch authorities:[91] not particularly convincing[92] efforts (from a historical point of view) to justify or legitimize the contamination (as the "purists" would see it) of an essentially civilian jurisdiction by an English import.[93]

II. DOLUS

1. The remedies for dolus and metus compared

The three dots in our quotation of § 123 I BGB[94] stand for the words

---

[86] Groenewegen, Cod. Lib. II, Tit. XX, l. 4.

[87] Cf. e.g. Windscheid/Kipp, § 462.

[88] Cf. e.g. Treitel, *Contract*, p. 312. As under the ius commune, it is not clear whether a contract procured by duress is void or voidable. According to Atiyah, *Rise and Fall*, pp. 434 sqq., duress (and mistake) "were whittled away in the nineteenth century as defences to actions on executory contracts till virtually nothing was left of them". He sees the "severe limitations now imposed on the concept of duress [as] a natural corollary of the will theory". Cf. particularly his analysis of *Skeate v. Beale* (1841) 11 Ad & El 983.

[89] But see *Lloyds Bank Ltd. v. Bundy* [1975] QB 326 (CA) and Zweigert/Kötz, pp. 127 sq., as well as, more recently, *Pao On v. Lan Yin Long* [1980] AC 614 and Treitel, *Contract*, pp. 312 sqq.; Atiyah, *Pragmatism and Theory in English Law* (1987), pp. 15 sq. As to the exclusion of economic duress, Atiyah, *Rise and Fall*, p. 436, comments: ". . . the nineteenth-century rules were made in the context of a market-based law of contract. In the market economic pressures are commonplace, and a market-based law of contract cannot treat them as a vitiating ground."

[90] Treitel, *Contract*, pp. 314 sqq.

[91] Cf. e.g. *Mauerberger v. Mauerberger* 1948 (4) SA 902 (C) at 909–13; *Preller v. Jordaan* 1956 (1) SA 483 (A) at 492H–493B; Wessels, *Contract*, vol. I, nn. 1208 sqq.; Lee, *Introduction*, p. 231.

[92] Van den Heever JA in *Preller v. Jordaan* 1956 (1) SA 483 (A) at 499H sqq.; De Wet en Yeats, pp. 47 sqq.

[93] Generally on undue influence in South African law, see L.F. van Huysteen, *Onbehoorlike Beïnvloeding en Misbruik van Omstandighede in die Suid-Afrikaanse Verbintenisreg* (1980), pp. 108 sqq.; Joubert, *Contract*, pp. 111 sqq.; Ellison Kahn, "Undue Influence in the Formation of Contract", (1974) 91 *SALJ* 307 sqq.

[94] Cf. supra, p. 661.

"(by) fraud (or)" *("arglistige Täuschung")*. The BGB thus provides the same remedy in cases of metus and dolus: the affected party may rescind the contract. There is, however, one significant difference which becomes apparent if one reads § 123 II BGB:[95] rescission on account of dolus is not "in rem scripta", at least not to the same degree as the remedy for metus. As a rule, the remedy for dolus is available only if the other party to the contract has been guilty of the fraudulent behaviour. If the conclusion of the contract has been induced by fraud on the part of a third party, the contract may be rescinded only if the "second" party (i.e. the one affected by the rescission: the contractual partner or whoever else might have acquired a right under the contract) had known or should at least have known of the fraud.[96] The modern law thus still reflects the fact that the remedies against metus and dolus have grown up side by side, but not without characteristic differences. In classical Roman law no action could be granted on the basis of negotia bonae fidei affected by fraud (dolus): obviously a defrauder cannot successfully maintain that the other party "dare facere oportet ex fide bona". Like the exceptio metus, the exceptio doli was therefore inherent in the bonae fidei iudicia.[97] Other transactions, however, as in the case of metus, remained originally unaffected.[98] After all, the will to enter into the transaction was not lacking. Again, it was the praetor[99]

---

[95] "If a third party was guilty of the fraud, a declaration which was required to be made to another person may be rescinded only if the latter knew or should have known of the fraud. Insofar as a person other than the one to whom the declaration was required to be made has acquired a right directly through the declaration, the declaration may be rescinded as against him if he knew or should have known of the fraud."

[96] For the rationale and justification of this rule, cf. "Motive", in: *Mugdan*, vol. I, pp. 466 sq. On the problem of who may be regarded as third party in terms of this rule, cf. Flume, *AT*, § 29, 3; Ernst Kramer, in: *Münchener Kommentar*, vol. I (2nd ed., 1984), § 123, nn. 18 sq. French law permits rescission on account of dolus only if the other party to the contract has committed the fraud: *"Le dol ne peut entraîner la nullité que s'il émane du cocontractant"*: cf. Zweigert/Kötz, p. 126.

[97] Cf. e.g. Iul. D. 30, 84, 5: ". . . quia hoc iudicium fidei bonae est et continet in se doli mali exceptionem." On the classicity of this text (and others), cf. Rolf Knütel, "Die Inhärenz der exceptio pacti im fidei bonae iudicium", (1967) 84 *ZSS* 133 sqq.

[98] Cf., for example, the cause célèbre involving the banker Pythius from Syracuse who sold a seaside villa to the Roman knight Canius. In order to create the impression that this was the great fishing-ground in the area, he had hired a fishing fleet to cruise around in front of the villa. The story is told by Cicero, *De officiis*, 3, XIV—60; cf. further Theo Mayer-Maly, "Privatautonomie und Vertragsethik im Digestenrecht" (1955) 6 *Iura* 133 sqq.; von Lübtow, *Eranion Maridakis* (infra, note 99), pp. 184 sqq.; Max Kaser, "Unlautere Warenanpreisungen beim römischen Kauf", in: *Festschrift für Heinrich Demelius* (1973), pp. 133 sqq.; Ralf Michael Thilo, *Der Codex accepti et expensi im Römischen Recht* (1980), pp. 300 sqq; Geoffrey MacCormack, "Aliud simulatum, aliud actum", (1978) 104 *ZSS* 640 sq. The parties were, however, able to protect themselves by way of a specific undertaking in the form of a stipulation ("dolum malum abesse afuturumque esse", "ut a te dolus malus absit", etc.). For details on the clausula doli, see Helmut Coing, "Die clausula doli im klassischen Recht", in: *Festschrift für Fritz Schulz*, vol. I (1951), pp. 97 sqq.; Geoffrey MacCormack, "Juristic Use of the Term Dolus: Contract", (1983) 100 *ZSS* 522 sqq.; idem, "'Dolus' in Republican Law", (1985) 88 *BIDR* 17 sq.

[99] In this instance, it was Gaius Aquilius Gallus who either introduced or at least inspired the introduction of the relief (in about 66 B.C.). For details, see Ulrich von Lübtow, "Die

who had to intervene in order to grant equitable relief. Again, this relief could take the form either of an active or of a defensive remedy (the actio de dolo or the exceptio doli); again it has been controversial whether, apart from these two remedies, a separate in integrum restitutio was granted.[100] As in the case of metus, the most probable solution to this problem is that the actio de dolo was the normal procedural avenue for achieving the aim of restitution:[101] for, like the actio quod metus causa, the actio de dolo contained the clausula arbitraria.[102] Unlike the parallel remedy for duress, however, the actio de dolo was not "in rem scripta" but was available only against the perpetrator of the fraud.[103] Furthermore, it did not provide for a poena quadrupli: if the defrauder refused to render restitution, he was exposed merely to a condemnatio in simplum.[104] On the other hand, this condemnatio involved infamia.[105] Finally, the actio de dolo was subsidiary, that is, it could be brought only if no other remedy was available; for the words of the praetorian edict ran like this: "Quae dolo malo facta esse dicentur, *si de his rebus alia actio non erit* et iusta causa esse videbitur, iudicium dabo."[106] Again, one has the impression that one is dealing with a compromise solution; the praetor wanted to suppress objectionable behaviour but at the same time did not want to hit out too hard, since a variety of high-ranking Roman officials were bound to be affected.[107]

2. The concept of dolus

(a) Aliud simulare, aliud agere

How potent and effective these remedies were depended, of course, to a large extent on the interpretation of the words dolus malus. As far as the

Ursprungsgeschichte der exceptio doli und der actio de dolo malo", in: *Eranion Maridakis*, vol. I (1963), pp. 183 sqq.; Massimo Brutti, *La problematica del dolo processuale nell' esperienza romana* (1973), pp. 128 sqq. On C. Aquilius Gallus cf. Frier, *Roman Jurists*, pp. 140 sqq.; Wieacker, *RR*, pp. 600 sq.

[100] Cf. in particular Ernst Levy, "Zur nachklassischen in integrum restitutio", (1951) 68 *ZSS* 410 sqq.; Andreas Wacke, "Kannte das Edikt eine in integrum restitutio propter dolum?", (1971) 88 *ZSS* 105 sqq.

[101] Kupisch, op. cit., note 14, pp. 241 sqq.; cf. further Kaser, (1977) 94 *ZSS* 143 sqq.; Brutti, op. cit., note 99, pp. 352 sqq.; Arthur Hartkamp, "Die Drittwirkung der in integrum restitutio", in: *Daube Noster* (1974), pp. 133 sqq.

[102] Cf. Lenel, *EP*, p. 115.

[103] The same applied to the exceptio doli; cf. Ulp. D. 44, 4, 4, 33 (". . . exceptio doli personam complectitur eius, qui dolo fecit").

[104] Cf. Ulp. D. 4, 3, 17 pr.; Paul. D. 4, 3, 18 pr.

[105] Cf. e.g. Ulp. D. 4, 3, 1, 4; Ulp. D. 4, 3, 11, 1. Hence, for instance, ". . . quibusdam personis non dabitur, ut puta liberis vel libertis adversus parentes patronosve".

[106] Ulp. D. 4, 3, 1, 1. On the clause "si de his rebus alia actio non sit" cf. D. 4, 3, 1, 4 sqq.; Bernardo Albanese, "La sussidiarietà dell' actio de dolo", (1961) 28 *Annali Palermo* 173 sqq.; cf. also Alan Watson, "Actio de dolo and actiones in factum", (1961) 78 *ZSS* 392 sqq.; Klaus Slapnicar, "Über die Aktivlegitimation zur actio legis Aquiliae und actio de dolo im Dreipersonenverhältnis", in: *De iustitia et iure, Festgabe für Ulrich von Lübtow* (1980), pp. 233 sqq.

[107] Kaser, (1977) 94 *ZSS* 146.

actio de dolo was concerned, we find a gradual extension of its range of application. This becomes immediately apparent if we look at the two famous definitions of dolus malus contained in Ulp. D. 4, 3, 1, 2:

> "Dolum malum Servius quidem ita definiit machinationem quandam alterius decipiendi causa, cum aliud simulatur et aliud agitur. Labeo autem posse et sine simulatione id agi, ut quis circumveniatur: . . . itaque ipse sic definiit dolum malum esse omnem calliditatem fallaciam machinationem ad circumveniendum fallendum decipiendum alterum adhibitam."

And Ulpian added as his own commentary: "Labeoni, definitio vera est."[108] Originally, therefore, some simulation was required: a person was taken to have acted fraudulently if he had pretended one thing but actually intended another. This was the meaning attributed to dolus malus not only by Servius Sulpicius but also by Gaius Aquilius Gallus, the father of the actio de dolo: ". . . cum esset aliud simulatum, aliud actum."[109] Labeo/Ulpianus D. 4, 3, 9, 3 is a case that could have been decided along the lines of this definition.[110] Between A and B a dispute has arisen as to whom some oil belongs. B deposits the oil with C. C is supposed to sell the oil but to keep the proceeds until the dispute has finally been decided by a court of law. A subsequently refuses to join issue. As a result of this, B is unable to claim the money from C since the condition under which the deposit had been made has not yet been fulfilled: B has not been declared owner of the oil. In this situation B is given the actio de dolo against A. A has frustrated B's claim by first pretending to defend the action but then refusing to join issue. B has been misled by A's expressed intention which did not correspond to his (i.e. A's) real intention.[111]

(b) Lab. D. 4, 3, 1, 2

It was soon recognized, however, that the aliud simulare, aliud agere definition was too narrow in scope, since a person can intend to deceive another without misleading him by a pretence. Hence Labeo's attempt to provide a more comprehensive definition of dolus malus comprising every kind of cunning, trickery or contrivance practised in order to

---

[108] Ulp. D. 4, 3, 1, 2 in fine. For a detailed analysis of the definitions contained in D. 4, 3, 1, 2 and 3, cf. Antonio Carcaterra, *Dolus bonus/dolus malus. Esegesi di D. 4, 3, 1, 2–3* (1970).

[109] Cicero, *De officiis*, 3, XIV—60. For details cf. MacCormack, (1987) 104 *ZSS* 639 sqq.; on dolus in Republican law generally, see MacCormack, (1985) 88 *BIDR* 1 sqq.

[110] "Labeo libro trigensimo septimo posteriorum scribit, si oleum tuum quasi suum defendat Titius, et tu hoc oleum deposueris apud Seium, ut is hoc venderet et pretium servaret, donec inter vos deiudicetur cuius oleum esset, neque Titius velit iudicium accipere: quoniam neque mandati neque sequestraria Seium convenire potes nondum impleta condicione depositionis, de dolo adversus Titium agendum. sed Pomponius libro vicensimo septimo posse cum sequestre praescriptis verbis actione agi, vel si is solvendo non sit, cum Titio de dolo." Cf., on this and further examples, most recently Geoffrey MacCormack, "Dolus in the Law of the Early Classical Period (Labeo-Celsus)", (1986) 52 *SDHI* 237 sqq.

[111] However, the actio de dolo against A is granted only if C has fallen insolvent (i.e. as a last resort). In the first place, B is given an actio praescriptis verbis against C; any other solution would lead to the highly irregular result that C would be able to keep the oil.

cheat, trick or deceive another.[112] How the deceit was engineered was of no relevance. In terms of this definition, the actio de dolo could, for instance, be granted where the promisor of a slave had poisoned him before delivery, or where somebody who owed a piece of land under a stipulation, before delivering possession, had imposed a servitude on it or destroyed a building.[113] It was dolus, too, if, having to deliver a slave, the debtor knowingly gave a thief (who duly stole something from the recipient)[114] or if he deliberately gave a slave who did not belong to him (so that the recipient lost the slave through eviction),[115] or if somebody knowingly lent incorrect weights for the seller to weigh out goods to his customers.[116] But here, as elsewhere, the Roman lawyers were not fond of tying themselves down to abstract definitions: "Omnis definitio in iure civili periculosa est: parum est enim, ut non subverti posset."[117] If we survey the actual casuistry, we find a whole variety of decisions which can no longer have been squeezed even under the new definition.[118] In fact, Labeo's definition is hardly ever even referred to. Take, for instance, the example, discussed by Papinian, of an alternative obligation ("Stichum aut Pamphilum, utrum tu velis, dare spondes?"), where Stichus had been killed by the debtor and Pamphilus afterwards died too.[119] On account of the death of the first slave the promisor is not liable to the stipulator, since he is still able to specify Pamphilus as the slave he owes. Only with Pamphilus' demise has the stipulator lost out. Even though the latter event is not in any way attributable to the promisor (and even though, incidentally, it is also not specifically stated that he had intentionally murdered Stichus), Papinian is prepared to grant the actio de dolo against him. The mere fact that the promisor has (intentionally or negligently) reduced the stipulator's chances of receiving a (living) slave prevents the promisor from escaping liability. Or, to put it the other way round: refusal to pay

---

[112] Cf. e.g. Andreas Wacke, "Zum dolus-Begriff der actio de dolo", (1980) 27 *RIDA* 350 sqq. against Carcaterra, op. cit., note 108, pp. 40 sqq.

[113] Lab./Ulp. D. 4, 3, 7, 3. Cf. MacCormack, (1986) 52 *SDHI* 239 sq.

[114] Afr. D. 30, 110.

[115] Paul. D. 19, 5, 5, 2.

[116] Trebatius/Paul. D. 4, 3, 18, 3. Nota bene that the actio de dolo was granted in this instance even though the defendant had no intention of benefiting from the transaction.

[117] Iav. D. 50, 17, 202. Generally, on the role of definitions in Roman jurisprudence, see, most recently, Wieacker, *RR*, pp. 630 sqq.

[118] Cf. particularly Wacke, (1980) 27 *RIDA* 360 sqq.; MacCormack, (1986) 52 *SDHI* 242 sqq. and Glück, vol. 4, pp. 108 sqq.; Ludwig Mitteis, *Römisches Privatrecht bis auf die Zeit Diokletians*, vol. I, p. 320; also Kaser, *RPr* I, p. 628; Honsell/Mayer-Maly/Selb, pp. 371 sq. For a different view (extension of dolus concept only in post-classical times), cf. e.g. Fritz Litten, "Zum dolus-Begriff in der actio de dolo", *Festgabe für Karl Güterbock* (1910), pp. 257 sqq.

[119] Pap. D. 46, 3, 95, 1 (". . . Quod si promissoris fuerit electio, defuncto altero qui superest aeque peti poterit. enimvero si facto debitoris alter sit mortuus, cum debitoris esset electio . . ., si et alter servus postea sine culpa debitoris moriatur, nullo modo ex stipulatu agi poterit, cum illo in tempore, quo moriebatur, non commiserit stipulationem. sane quoniam impunita non debent esse admissa, doli actio non immerito desiderabitur . . .").

damages for the death of Pamphilus, under these circumstances, must appear as a violation of good faith.

(c) *Fidem placiti rumpere*

Codex 2, 20, 4[120] presents another interesting example. Two slaves belonging to different masters lived in a permanent marriage-like union (contubernium). The master of the servus, wanting to manumit his slave, tried to induce the master of the ancilla to release her also. To this end he offered to give the latter another slave in the place of the ancilla. After the ancilla had been released, the master of the servus refused to provide the substitute slave. We are dealing here with what was to become known as an innominate real contract (facio ut des).[121] An actio praescriptis verbis (in order to enforce counterperformance) does not (yet) seem to have been contemplated by the Emperors. In this case, the master of the ancilla could also not reverse his own transaction: "revocandae libertatis potestatem non habe[t]."[122] Under these circumstances, the actio de dolo is used to remedy the situation. The basis for its application is not fraudulent behaviour ("machinatio *ad* decipiendum alterum") in the narrow sense, but what is described by the Emperors as "fidem placiti rump[ere]": the mere fact that a person does not keep his word. Thus we see that the actio de dolo could conveniently be used to fill inequitable gaps within the Roman contractual system. In the same vein, Paul. D. 19, 5, 5, 3 had already stated: "Quod si faciam ut des et posteaquam feci, cessas dare, nulla erit civilis actio, et ideo de dolo dabitur."[123]

(d) *Bona fides and dolus*

In actual practice, therefore, the concept of dolus was similarly broadly interpreted in connection with the actio de dolo as it was with reference to the exceptio doli. For here it is generally recognized that the insertion of an exceptio doli into the procedural formula provided the judge with the same far-ranging discretion that he already had in bonae fidei iudicia, due to the ex bona fide clause contained in the intentio.[124] The exceptio was worded in the alternative: "si in ea re nihil dolo malo A^i A^i factum sit neque fiat",[125] and it was particularly the "neque fiat" clause that made it such a powerful instrument to bring about a just solution. "Factum est" referred to fraudulent behaviour before the institution of the action (against which the exceptio was now raised), particularly in the act of concluding the contract (dolus in

[120] Impp. Diocl. et Max.
[121] Cf. supra, pp. 534 sq.
[122] Generally e.g. Hartkamp, op. cit., note 12, pp. 137 sqq.
[123] D. 19, 5, 5, 3; cf. further Ulp. D. 11, 6, 5 pr. and Wacke, (1980) 27 *RIDA* 373 sqq.
[124] Kaser, *RPr* I, pp. 488 sq.; Honsell/Mayer-Maly/Selb, p. 372.
[125] Gai. IV, 119; on its origin, see von Lübtow, *Eranion Maridakis*, pp. 192 sqq.

contrahendo).[126] "Fiat", on the other hand, comprised all cases where the bringing of the action itself could be taken to constitute dolus. Thus, for instance, a person who claimed what he would have to return before long acted "dolo": "dolo facit, qui petit quod redditurus est."[127] But, as Geoffrey MacCormack has pointed out recently,[128] to pose the question in this form (does the bringing of the action itself constitute dolus?) invited an answer which located dolus not so much in personal misconduct, but rather in an inequity or injustice that would flow from the successful maintenance of the action. Thus, many cases came to be subsumed under the so-called exceptio doli generalis[129] where the actual misconduct of the plaintiff fell short of deceit or trickery in terms of the Labeonic definition. "Ideo autem hanc exceptionem praetor proposuit, ne cui dolus suus per occasionem iuris civilis contra naturalem aequitatem prosit":[130] the plaintiff was not supposed to turn a situation to his advantage against the precepts of natural equity. From here it is only a small step to the recognition of the fact that dolus was a kind of opposite number to bona fides.[131] Whenever the behaviour of the plaintiff did not conform to the overriding standard of good faith,[132] the exceptio doli could be granted; and it was ultimately the same criterion that determined whether or not the actio de dolo could be brought successfully. "Palam est autem hanc exceptionem ex eadem causa propositam, ex qua causa proposita est de dolo malo actio", said Ulpian,[133] who made it clear that actio and exceptio did not refer to different types of situation.

(e) Dolus and dolus malus

If, then, the crucial dividing line appears to have been drawn between bona fides on the one hand and dolus on the other, we must keep in mind two further points. Dolus, in classical Roman law, always retained an element of moral disapproval.[134] A person charged with dolus had not necessarily employed deceit and trickery, but had infringed one of the standard principles by which to conduct an honest

[126] The so-called exceptio doli praeteriti or specialis. On dolus in contrahendo cf. the monograph by Karl Heldrich, *Verschulden bei Vertragsabschluss* (1924), and Peter Stein, *Fault in the Formation of Contract* (1958).

[127] Paul. D. 44, 4, 8 pr.; also Paul. D. 50, 17, 173, 3.

[128] (1986) 52 *SDHI* 263 sq.

[129] Cass./Ulp. D. 44, 4, 4, 33; Brutti, op. cit., note 99, pp. 625 sqq. On the relationship between exceptio doli and exceptio pacti, see Brutti, op. cit., note 99, pp. 648 sqq.; Andreas Wacke, "Zur Lehre vom pactum tacitum und zur Aushilfsfunktion der exceptio doli", (1973) 90 *ZSS* 227 sqq.

[130] Paul. D. 44, 4, 1, 1.

[131] Cf. e.g. Paul. D. 17, 2, 3, 3 (referring to societas).

[132] As revealed, for instance, in Iav. D. 19, 2, 21: "[B]ona fides exigit, ut id quod convenit fiat."

[133] Ulp. D. 44, 4, 2 pr.; cf. also Ulp. D. 4, 3, 7, 8 and Wacke, (1980) 27 *RIDA* 371 sqq.

[134] Kaser, *RPr* II, p. 349; Wacke, (1980) 27 *RIDA* 384 sqq.; but cf. MacCormack, (1986) 56 *SDHI* 284 sq.

life: fidelity.[135] He had behaved in a manner in which a good Roman ought not to have behaved, and had thus departed from the premises and ethical precepts of the mores maiorum. After all, it must be remembered that the praetor spoke of "dolus malus", and even though the specific pejorative attribute was soon discarded, the term "dolus" was never taken to refer to what had once been designated dolus bonus.[136] Thus, for instance, fraud or trickery against an enemy or robber was not objectionable,[137] and even simulation (in the sense of Servius' old, more narrow definition) could be condoned where it had been resorted to in order to protect the simulating party's or somebody else's (legitimate) interests.[138] Another example is provided in Ulp. D. 4, 3, 7, 7:

> "Idem Labeo quaerit, si compeditum servum meum ut fugeret solveris, an de dolo actio danda sit? et ait Quintus apud eum notans: si non misericordia ductus fecisti, furti teneris: si misericordia, in factum actionem dari debere."

If A releases B's slave from his fetters with the result that the slave can run away, he has caused damage to B. However, he is not liable under the actio de dolo if he has acted out of compassion, that is, if his action has been prompted by a morally commendable impulse.[139]

(f) Dolus and sollertia

Even more important, practically, was a second factor limiting the range of application of the remedies against dolus. The standard of bona fides, as we have seen,[140] was determined in accordance with prevailing and average business decency, not from the refined but abstract point of view of moral philosophy. Thus, there was a broad grey area of "sollertia"[141] (cleverness, deftness, craftiness; MacCormack translates:[142] ingenuity) which fell short of constituting dolus (malus). In particular, invicem se circumscribere (or circumvenire) was not regarded as objectionable, but was expressly (and repeatedly) stated to be in accordance with the nature of trade and business.[143] Or, in the

---

[135] Generally Schulz, *Principles*, pp. 223 sqq.

[136] Ulp. D. 4, 3, 1, 3: "Non fuit autem contentus praetor dolum dicere, sed adiecit malum, quoniam veteres dolum etiam bonum dicebant et pro sollertia hoc nomen accipiebant. . . ." On dolus bonus cf. especially Carcaterra, op. cit., note 108, pp. 115 sqq.; Andreas Wacke, "Circumscribere, gerechter Preis und die Arten der List", (1977) 94 *ZSS* 221 sqq.

[137] Ulp. D. 4, 3, 1, 3 (". . . maxime si adversus hostem latronemve quis machinetur").

[138] Lab./Ulp. D. 4, 3, 1, 2; Wacke, (1977) 94 *ZSS* 227 sq.

[139] Cf. Wieslaw Litewski, "Dolus et misericordia dans le droit romain classique", (1972) 5 *Archivum Iuridicum Cracoviense* 91 sqq.

[140] Cf. supra, pp. 256 sqq.

[141] Ulp. D. 4, 3, 1, 3.

[142] Mommsen/Krüger/Watson, Ulp. D. 4, 3, 1, 3.

[143] Ulp. D. 4, 4, 16, 1; Paul. D. 19, 2, 22, 3; for details, see Mayer-Maly, (1955) 6 *Iura* 128 sqq.; Wacke, (1977) 94 *ZSS* 185 sqq.

words of the glossator Bulgarus: "[L]icet contrahentibus se invicem decipere, non tamen decere."[144]

3. Dolus causam dans and dolus incidens

(a) The medieval distinction

The most important and, in the long run, influential contribution of the medieval lawyers to the doctrine of dolus lay in the distinction they drew between dolus causam dans and dolus incidens (dolus qui incidit in contractum).[145] It was summed up by Azo in the following words:

> "De dolo malo dat causam contractui bonae fidei hoc est quia alias non erat contracturus nisi esset dolo inductus non tenet ipso iure contractus. Ubi autem deceptus erat alias contracturus . . . tenet venditio, sed purgatur dolus per actionem ex eo contractu."[146]

In both instances, the fraudulent behaviour must have caused the deception of the other party. That was inherent in Labeo's, and also in Servius', definition of dolus. But, whereas in the one case the innocent party[147] would not have contracted but for the fraud (so that the fraud could be said to have induced the fact that a contract had at all been concluded), dolus incidens merely concerned the terms of the contract, for instance the price: the innocent party would still have entered into the contract, but on different (i.e. better) terms. The glossators derived this distinction from an intricate and puzzling Digest fragment, attributed to Ulpian, which contained the phrase ". . . aut nullam esse venditionem, si in hoc ipso ut venderet [minor annis viginti quinque] circumscriptus est".[148] This was understood to indicate that, where the dolus had induced the vendor to sell, the contract of sale was ipso iure void. E contrario, then, the sale remained valid where the vendor had indeed intended to sell (in this instance:) the slave, but (again, in the example discussed in D. 4, 3, 7 pr.) without peculium. What the

---

[144] Cf. Carcaterra, op. cit., note 108, p. 164.

[145] For details of the development cf. Brutti, op. cit., note 99, pp. 11 sqq., 35 sqq.; cf. also Paul Wezel, *Dolus causam dans und dolus incidens* (unpublished Dr. iur. thesis, Tübingen, 1928), pp. 2 sqq.

[146] Azo, *Summa Codicis*, De dolo malo Rubrica.

[147] Where both parties have acted fraudulently, a kind of compensatio doli takes place; an application of the more general principle that an action cannot be brought by a person who has himself been guilty of behaviour tinged with turpitudo (nemo auditur turpitudinem suam allegans). Cf. Marc. D. 4, 3, 36 "Si duo dolo malo fecerint, invicem de dolo non agent"; further Ulp. D. 44, 4, 4, 13; Iul. D. 2, 10, 3, 3; Paul. D. 18, 1, 57, 3; Glück, vol. 4, pp. 120 sqq. Cf. also infra, pp. 865 sq.

[148] Ulp. D. 4, 3, 7 pr. For modern analyses of this text (which has often been regarded as being at least partly interpolated; cf. already Gerard Noodt, "De forma emendandi doli mali", in: *Opera omnia* (Lugduni Batavorum, 1724), Cap. XIV (pp. 377 sqq.), and many others, quoted by Glück, vol. 4, p. 115), cf. J.C. van Oven, "D. 4, 3, 7 pr. Contribution à l'histoire du dol dans les conventions", in: *Studi in onore di Emilio Albertario*, vol. I (1953), pp. 273 sqq.; Stein, *Fault*, pp. 88 sqq.; Albanese, (1961) 28 *Annali Palermo* 187 sqq.; Hartkamp, op. cit., note 12, pp. 140 sqq.; Brutti, op. cit., note 99, pp. 18 sqq.; Wacke, (1977) 94 *ZSS* 236 sqq.

distinction between dolus causam dans and dolus incidens[149] therefore sought to resolve, was the vexed question of the effects of dolus on a contract, more specifically: on a contract bonae fidei. Only dolus causam dans was taken to lead to its invalidity. If the dolus had merely been *incidental* to a contract of good faith, the transaction was not void, nor could the actio de dolo or the exceptio doli be resorted to: the appropriate bonae fidei iudicium itself (in the case of D. 4, 3, 7 pr.: the actio venditi) could be used to remedy the situation. Reason:

> ". . . contractibus bonae fidei semper ipso iure inest actio et exceptio doli; adeoque dolo probato, absolutio excipientis sequetur, aut agenti causa redintegrabitur."[150]

With regard to contracts stricti iuris, on the other hand, the actio de dolo or exceptio doli were available irrespective of whether the dolus had been causam dans or incidens.

(b) Usus modernus and pandectists

This scheme of dealing with the effects of dolus, based as it was on the bonae fidei/stricti iuris division of contracts, survived for a surprisingly long time: it was still faithfully preserved by Roman-Dutch lawyers[151] and authors of the German usus modernus.[152] Only slowly did one realize that it had been overtaken by the development of a general law of contract:

> "Voor het overige kunnen wy de verdeeling der contracten, in die van goede trouw en strict recht al mede zeer wel missen, nadien volgens onze gewoontens alle contracten van goede trouw geächt worden."[153]

In the end, therefore, the regime applicable to bonae fidei contracts was bound to prevail. Here, however, the notion that a contract affected by fraud could be void had increasingly come under attack.[154] A consent obtained by fraud is still a valid consent, it was now argued;[155] the declaration of the defrauded party does reflect a will that really

---

[149] Which, according to Wacke, (1977) 94 *ZSS* 236 sqq. (Honsell/Mayer-Maly/Selb, p. 128 concurring), indeed finds its root in classical Roman law.

[150] Voet, *Commentarius ad Pandectas*, Lib. IV, Tit. III, IV.

[151] Voet, *Commentarius ad Pandectas*, Lib. IV, Tit. III, III sqq.; Huber, *Heedendaagse Rechtsgeleertheyt*, IV. Boek, XXXIX. Kap. For other Roman-Dutch authors, see Wouter de Vos, "Skadevergoeding en terugtrede weens bedrog by kontraksluiting", 1964 *Acta Juridica* 28 sqq.

[152] Lauterbach, *Collegium theoretico-practicum*, Lib. IV, Tit. III, VI sqq.; Stryk, *Usus modernus pandectarum*, Lib. IV, Tit. III, § 5; Struve, *Syntagma*, Exerc. IIX, Lib. IV, Tit. III, XXVII sqq.

[153] Cornelis Willem Decker, n. 1 ad Simon van Leeuwen, *Het Roomsch Hollandsche Recht* (Amsteldam, 1783), IV. Boek, II. Deel, 1; cf. further e.g. Vinnius, *Institutiones*, Lib. IV, Tit. VI, 28; A.S. De Blécourt, H.F.W.D. Fischer, *Kort begrip van het oud-vaderlands burgerlijk recht* (7th ed., 1959), p. 275; Glück, vol. 4, p. 127.

[154] For a different view, see Noodt, op. cit., note 148, Cap. III sqq., who argued that all contracts bonae fidei affected by whatever kind of fraud were void. On Noodt's views cf. Brutti, op. cit., note 99, pp. 82 sqq.; G.C.J.J. van den Bergh, *The Life and Work of Gerard Noodt* (1647–1725), 1988, pp. 245 sqq.

[155] Cf. e.g. Pothier, *Traité des obligations*, n. 29.

existed.[156] Quite apart from that, ipso iure invalidity implies that it may be invoked not only by the victim of the fraud, but also, if it suits him, by the defrauder—a result which can hardly be reconciled with the idea that a defrauder should never be allowed to benefit from his own dolus.[157] Hence it came to be recognized that the effect of fraud could be, at most, to render the contract voidable at the instance of the defrauded party.

But when was the defrauded party able to rescind the contract? It was in the context of this question that the old distinction between dolus causam dans and dolus incidens received renewed attention.[158] For it was clear that the defrauded party was able (apart from raising the exceptio doli) to bring the normal (bonae fidei) action available to him under the contract, in order to claim restitution. Restitution could, however, mean two different things: if it was to be assumed that the defrauded party would have refrained from entering into the contract, had he known the truth (dolus causam dans), he could ask to have the contract set aside and claim any further damages that he might have suffered. If, on the other hand, it could be established that the person sought to be defrauded would nevertheless have concluded the contract, albeit (for instance) for a lower purchase price (dolus incidens), there was no basis for a rescission of the contract: in this case the claim had to be limited to the amount by which the sum paid (or promised) on account of the fraud exceeded the sum the innocent party would otherwise have been prepared to give.

(c) Modern law

Today, the distinction between dolus causam dans and dolus incidens survives in South African law[159] and (via Pothier)[160] in the French code civil,[161] but not in the German BGB. As in the case of metus, the drafters of the code civil employed the concept of relative nullity, where a contract is vitiated by fraud (dol):[162] it may be invoked only by

---

[156] Savigny, *System*, vol. III, pp. 112 sqq.; Windscheid/Kipp § 78.

[157] ". . . ne cui dolus suus per occasionem iuris civilis contra naturalem aequitatem prosit": Ulp. D. 44, 4, 1, 1. For further arguments cf. Vangerow, *Pandekten*, vol. III, pp. 274 sqq.

[158] Cf. e.g. Vangerow, *Pandekten*, vol. III, p. 275; Regelsberger, *Pandekten*, p. 537; Windscheid/Kipp, § 78.

[159] There is, however, some doubt as to its significance. More particularly, the question has not been authoritatively settled whether the remedy of rescission is available to the defrauded party even in cases of incidental fraud. For details, see *Gous v. De Kock, Combrinck v. De Kock* (1887) 5 SC 405; *Vlotman v. Landsberg* (1890) 7 SC 301; *Karroo and Eastern Board of Executors and Trust Co. v. Farr* 1921 AD 413; Lee, *Introduction*, pp. 226 sqq.; Wessels, *Contract*, vol. I, nn. 1097 sqq., 1126 sqq.; De Vos, 1964 *Acta Juridica* 33 sqq.; Van Rensburg, Lotz, van Rhijn, "Contract", in: Joubert (ed.), *The Law of South Africa*, vol. 5 (1978), n. 134.

[160] *Traité des obligations*, n. 31.

[161] Cf. also §§ 871 sq., 875 sq. ABGB.

[162] Art. 1117.

the party for whose protection the law has declared the transaction invalid. However, this applies only *"lorsque les manoeuvres pratiquées*[163] *par l'une des parties sont telles, qu'il est évident que, sans ces manoeuvres, l'autre partie n'aurait pas contracté"*.[164] Invalidity is thus confined to cases of dol principal (or *substantiel*), whereas in case of a mere dol incident (or *accidentel*) the defrauded party may claim damages only, usually in the form of a reduction of the price.[165] According to § 123 BGB, a contract may be rescinded no matter whether it has been affected by dolus causam dans or dolus incidens; it is only required that the declaration of intention has been "induced" by the fraudulent behaviour.[166] The fathers of the BGB did not, however,

---

163 The French code thus specifies the act by means of which the deceit must have been effected ("manoeuvres"). This is clearly reminiscent of the "machinationes" of the definitions provided by both Servius and Labeo and has also been adopted in the Italian (*"raggiri"*: art. 1439) and the Dutch (*"kunstgrepen"*: art. 1364) Code. Can this requirement be satisfied by mere silence *(dol par réticence)*? The French courts have displayed great flexibility and recognize today that dol can consist of the silence of one party concealing from the other a fact which, if he had known it, would have prevented him from contracting (Nicholas, *FLC*, pp. 98 sqq.). This has brought French law into line with modern German law, which does not require the deceit to have been effected by "manoeuvres"; failure to state a fact constitutes deceit if there was a duty to declare it, which in turn depends on the circumstances of the individual case. For details of this practically very important form of deceit according to German law, cf. Kramer, op. cit., note 98, § 123, nn. 13 sqq. English law follows a more conservative line (as did classical Roman law) and appears to be readier to hold a party drawing erroneous conclusions from the other party's silence to the contract. For a comparative analysis, see Zweigert/Kötz, pp. 124 sq.; for the two interesting and very similar cases of *Laidlaw v. Organ* and of the grain merchants sailing to the famine-stricken isle of Rhodes, cf. supra, p. 257. The English approach is summarized in *Smith v. Hughes* (as quoted above, p. 257, note 140 and p. 307, note 88.), the Roman in the sentence "aliud est celare, aliud tacere" (Cicero, *De officiis*, 3, XII—52).

164 Art. 1116; cf. also artt. 1439 sq. codice civile.

165 This distinction is criticized by Zweigert/Kötz, pp. 123 sq., but defended by Wacke, (1977) 94 *ZSS* 243 sqq.

166 Strictly speaking, § 123 BGB requires *"arglistige Täuschung"* (fraudulent misrepresentation). This is usually understood to mean intentional deceit (*absichtliche Täuschung*, as in art. 28 OR). In other words, a simple (unlawful) lie (Zweigert/Kötz, p. 123) is sufficient to render the contract voidable. For details cf. Ulrich von Lübtow, "Zur Anfechtung von Willenserklärungen wegen arglistiger Täuschung", in: *Festschrift für Horst Bartholomeyczik* (1973), pp. 249 sqq.; Kramer, op. cit., note 98, § 123, n. 6. In modern South African law, the remedy of rescission of the contract is available to the victim of a fraudulent misrepresentation—a fraudulent misrepresentation being an intentional misstatement of an existing, material fact which was intended to induce, and did in fact induce, the innocent party to enter into the contract: see, for example, Kerr, *Contract*, p. 267. This remedy, based squarely on dolus, is of Roman and Roman-Dutch provenance . However, the innocent party has also long been able to rescind the contract if the misrepresentation was "non-fraudulent", i.e. either negligent or innocent; see, for example, *Dickson & Co. v. Levy* 1894 (11) SC 33; *Parke v. Hamman*, 1907 TH 47; *Sampson v. Union & Rhodesia Wholesale (in liquidation)* 1929 AD 468 (480); *Harper v. Webster* 1956 (2) SA 495 (FC) at 501. This extension occurred under the influence of English law and, apparently, with no consideration of the issues involved. In this regard, see Joubert, *Contract*, pp. 92 sqq., 97 sq. It does not find a basis in Roman-Dutch law. For an extension of the *exceptio* doli to cases of dolus praesens (to cases, that is, where it was considered fraudulent to persist with a claim even though the claim itself may not have had its origin in any fraudulent behaviour), cf. Johannes van der Linden, *Supplementum commentarii ad pandectas* (J. Voet) (Utrecht, 1793), Lib. IV, Tit. III, I

want to deviate from the by then well-established doctrinal distinction. The Motive refer the reader to the rule relating to partial invalidity:[167] a transaction affected by fraud may be partly rescinded only if it is to be assumed that the defrauded party would have concluded it even if the rescindable part had been omitted.[168] The claim of the defrauded party for damages is usually based, today, on the law of delict.[169]

The fate of the exceptio doli was closely connected with that of the stipulatio. With the demise of the latter[170] it was bound to fall into oblivion too. The modern theory of contract, as has repeatedly been stressed, descends from the consensual contracts of Roman law,[171] and these were governed by the principle of bona fides. A specific procedural device in the form of an "exceptio" was thus no longer necessary in order to check the improper excercise of contractual rights; the judge had this discretion anyway.[172] The substantive content of the exceptio doli, in other words, had been absorbed into the requirement of bona fides; and if the term "exceptio doli" continued to be used, it was tantamount to a recourse to the principle of good faith inherent in

(referring to Ulp. D. 44, 4, 2, 5); *Karroo and Eastern Board of Executors and Trust Co. v. Farr* 1921 AD 413 at 415; cf. also Joubert, *Contract*, p. 97.

[167] "Motive", in: *Mugdan*, vol. I, p. 467; cf. also Wezel, op. cit. note 145, pp. 21 sqq.

[168] §§ 123, 142, 139 BGB; cf. further Wacke, (1977) 94 *ZSS* 244 sq.; Wezel, op. cit., note 145, pp. 28 sqq.

[169] In France § 1382 code civil is applicable; in Germany § 826 BGB and § 823 II BGB in connection with § 263 StGB (Kramer, op. cit., note 98, § 123, n. 30). In South Africa it has always been recognized that a delictual remedy (viz. the actio doli: cf., for instance, De Wet en Yeats, p. 38) is available to claim damages flowing from fraudulent misrepresentations; certain difficulties have been experienced with regard to the calculation of damages in cases of dolus incidens; cf. *Bill Harvey's Investment (Pty) Ltd. v. Oranjezicht Citrus Estates* 1958 (1) SA 479 (A); *Scheepers v. Handley* 1960 (3) SA 54 (A); *De Jager v. Grunder* 1964 (1) SA 446 (A); *Ranger v. Wykerd* 1977 (2) SA 976 (A); De Vos, *Acta Juridica* 26 sqq. But the magna quaestio in South African law today is whether damages may also be claimed in cases of negligent misrepresentation. The traditional view is that they cannot: see, in particular, *Hamman v. Moolman* 1968 (4) SA 340 (A); for criticism of this view as being illogical, indefensible in principle and alien to South African law, cf. the comprehensive references in Boberg, *Delict*, pp. 62 sq. However, in 1979 the Appellate Division took the momentous step of recognizing an action in delict for pure economic loss caused by a negligent misstatement (*Administrateur, Natal v. Trust Bank van Afrika, Bpk.* 1979 (3) SA 824 (A)—see infra, p. 1042). In the wake of this decision (which was confined to negligent statements outside the field of contract) there was renewed hope that the delictual remedy would also be extended into the contractual field. This hope was indeed fulfilled, only two years after the *Trust Bank* case, by the Cape Provincial Division of the Supreme Court in *Kern Trust (Edms.) Bpk. v. Hurter* 1981 (3) SA 607 (C). Here Friedman J held (at 616F–G) that ". . . [there is] no sound reason based either in principle or logic, why an action [for damages] for negligent misstatement inducing a contract, should [be denied]. . . . Such an action fits squarely in the confines of the lex Aquilia." The *Kern Trust* decision was enthusiastically welcomed by Dale Hutchison, (1981) 98 *SALJ* 486 sqq. In the meantime, the matter has been thrown into confusion, once again, by the recent decision of the Appellate Division of the Supreme Court in *Lillicrap, Wassenaar and Partners v. Pilkington Brothers (SA) (Pty.) Ltd.* 1985 (1) SA 475 (A) (see infra, p. 906), where a very restrictive attitude was adopted towards recognizing Aquilian liability "in a contractual setting" (at p. 500G).

[170] Cf. supra, pp. 546 sqq.

[171] Cf., for example, pp. 546 sq.

[172] Cf., for example, Regelsberger, *Pandekten*, p. 686; Windscheid/Kipp, § 47, n. 7.

the modern concept of contract. This is, essentially, still the position in modern German law, although the BGB itself would hardly lead the uninitiated reader to think so.[173] Its draftsmen had adopted a very cautious attitude;[174] nowhere did they expressly state that the exercise of contractual rights is subject to the principles of good faith. The standard of "good faith" appears only in a, seemingly, rather marginal provision (§ 242), where it relates specifically to the manner in which an obligation has to be performed.[175] Soon, however, the courts seized upon the rule and converted it into a general clause governing, and transforming, the whole of the German law of contract. It has provided a convenient starting point for countless new doctrines and for the modification, subversion or abrogation of old ones, in innumerable cases it has been resorted to in order to avoid harsh or inequitable results and it has often even been regarded as the magic wand[176] with which to eliminate any hardship in the world of private law. By 1961 the details of the application of this simple rule had reached such a degree of complexity that a standard commentary on the BGB devoted a whole volume of about 1 400 pages, predominantly in small print, to the compilation, classification and analysis of the rules and institutions derived from it.[177] Much criticism has, over the years, been levelled at the excessive proliferation of equitable inroads into established legal principles.[178] On the other hand, however, consensus has emerged over certain legitimate extensions of the principle enunciated in § 242 BGB; they have become so firmly established that they are seen today to form an indispensable part of the modern legal landscape.[179] One of those is the doctrine of the improper exercise of a right *("Lehre von der*

---

[173] Cf., for example, the discussion as to whether, even after the enactment of the BGB, the exceptio doli continued to exist, by Windscheid/Kipp, vol. I, pp. 214 sqq.

[174] "Protokolle", in: *Mugdan*, vol. I, pp. 796 sq.; for further examples of a similarly cautious attitude (firm and stable legal rules must not be replaced by equitable judicial discretion), cf. Fritz Rittner, "Ermessensfreiheit und Billigkeitsspielraum des Zivilrichters im deutschen Recht", in: *Ermessensfreiheit und Billigkeitsspielraum des Zivilrichters*, vol. 24 of *Arbeiten zur Rechtsvergleichung* (1964), pp. 32 sq.

[175] On which, see "Protokolle", in: *Mugdan*, vol. II, pp. 521 sqq. and Rudolf Henle, *Treu und Glauben im Rechtsverkehr* (1912), pp. 30 sq.

[176] *"Prätorische Zauberformel"*: Bruno Heusinger, *Rechtsfindung und Rechtsfortbildung im Spiegel richterlicher Erfahrung* (1975), pp. 109 sq.

[177] Wilhelm Weber, in: *Staudinger* (11th ed., 1961), § 242.

[178] For very strong, and early, criticism in this regard, cf. Henle, op. cit., note 175, pp. 3 sqq. (*"Diese Bestimmung mit ihrem redlichen Biedermannsgesicht ist zum Träger einer unheilvollen Seuche geworden, die am Mark unseres Rechtslebens vergiftend zehrt."* This provision has become, behind its mask of honesty, uprightness and trustworthiness, the source of a baneful pestilence, gnawing in a most sinister manner at the inner core of our legal culture). Cf. also the warnings by Justus Wilhelm Hedemann, *Die Flucht in die Generalklauseln, Eine Gefahr für Recht und Staat* (1933) (still a classic).

[179] Cf., in particular, the influential study by Franz Wieacker, *Zur rechtstheoretischen Präzisierung des § 242 BGB* (1956); today, for example, Günther H. Roth, in: *Münchener Kommentar*, vol. II (2nd ed., 1985), § 242, nn. 12 sqq., 52 sqq., 106 sqq. Generally on the problem of judge-made law in a codified system, from a constitutional point of view, cf. BVerfGE 34, 269 (286).

unzulässigen Rechtsausübung") in its various emanations.[180] It is this doctrine into which the "productive force of the exceptio doli"[181] has been channelled in modern German law.

A lively discussion whether the exceptio doli, as such, still exists in modern law has taken place in South Africa. Until recently, academic opinion was divided as to its existence and applicability. Some writers, including the influential Professor J.C. de Wet of Stellenbosch,[182] took a sharply negative attitude. Others were strongly in favour of it. A.J. Kerr called it "an outstanding example of equity at work".[183] The South African courts, too, failed for a long time to adopt a uniform approach; some judges expressed great scepticism as to the survival of the exceptio doli,[184] others merely assumed its existence,[185] while still others came out strongly and unambiguously in favour of it. In *Sonday v. Surrey Estate Modern Meat Market (Pty.) Ltd.*,[186] Tebbutt J went as far as to declare it to be

> "clear . . . that [the exceptio doli] has been accepted as part of our law, both by Provincial Divisions as well as the Appellate Division".

In the recent case of *Bank of Lisbon and South Africa Ltd. v. De Ornelas*,[187] the South African Appellate Division has, however, ultimately attempted to settle the matter. In an extraordinary judgment,[188] Joubert JA (speaking for the majority) embarked on a

---

[180] Roth, op. cit., note 179, § 242, nn. 224 sqq.

[181] Dernburg, *Pandekten*, vol. I, § 138, 4 in fine.

[182] *"Estoppel by Representation" in die Suid-Afrikaanse reg* (1939), pp. 83 sqq.

[183] Kerr, *Contract*, p. 137. For further comment, see, for example, P.J. Aronstam, "Unconscionable contracts: The South African solution?", (1979) 42 *THRHR* 21 sqq.; A.D. Botha, "Die exceptio doli generalis, rektifikasie en estoppel", (1980) 43 *THRHR* 255 sqq.; C.F.C. van der Walt, "Die huidige posisie in die Suid-Afrikaanse reg met betrekking tot onbillike kontraksbedinge", (1986) 103 *SALJ* 646 sqq.

[184] Cf. e.g. *Aris Enterprises (Finance) (Pty.) Ltd. v. Waterberg Koelkamers (Pty.) Ltd.* 1977 (2) SA 436 (T) at 437G–438C; *Novick v. Comair Holdings Ltd.* 1979 (2) SA 116 (W) at 156B–157B.

[185] *Paddock Motors (Pty.) Ltd. v. Igesund* 1976 (3) SA 16 (A) at 27H–28F; *Zuurbekom Ltd. v. Union Corporation Ltd.* 1947 (1) SA 514 (A) at 535–7.

[186] 1983 (2) SA 521 (C) at 530H.

[187] 1988 (3) SA 580 (A).

[188] To which (Judge) Alvin B. Rubin's remark, aimed at the American judiciary, would appear to apply: "Let me mention one other time-consuming task of judges that appears to me to be an obsessive preoccupation. It is our concern, particularly at the appellate level, with trying to write the kind of opinion that we think law school teachers will consider scholarly" ("Bureaucratization of the Federal Courts, The Tension Between Justice and Efficiency", (1979–80) 55 *Notre Dame Lawyer* 655). In the *Bank of Lisbon* case, Joubert JA took the opportunity to join the academic battlefield and to pass judgment, not only on the question of the existence of the exceptio doli in South African law, but also on the merit of the contributions of other academic writers. J.C. de Wet's doctoral thesis found favour in Joubert JA's eyes (". . . as De Wet correctly pointed out" (p. 598A)), but the unpublished (!) thesis of a relatively junior academic from Bloemfontein became the object of severe criticism ("These views of Botha are untenable and must be rejected . . ." (p. 604E); "They would seem to be pure speculation on his part" (p. 605C); "He also overlooked the fact that . . ." (p. 605C); all in all, more than 100 lines of the reported judgment are devoted to a

detailed analysis of Roman and Roman-Dutch sources on the basis of which he came to the conclusion that "the raison d'être of the exceptio doli generalis had disappeared in the law of contract at the end of the Middle Ages"[189] and that therefore

> "[a]ll things considered, the time has now arrived . . . once and for all, to bury the exceptio doli generalis as a superfluous, defunct anachronism. Requiescat in pace".[190]

It is, however, rather doubtful, whether the "productive force" of the exceptio doli can in fact be quelled that easily, particularly if one denies, as Joubert JA does,[191] that the underlying equitable principles were incorporated, under the aegis of bona fides, into classical Roman-Dutch and (consequently) modern South African law. The exceptio doli may well, therefore, haunt the courts and legal writers from its grave.[192]

---

discussion of Botha's views). For a comparative analysis of citation practices by appellate courts, see Hein Kötz, (1988) 52 *RabelsZ* 644 sqq. (where a fuller extract from Rubin's article appears on p. 657).

[189] 1988 (3) SA 580 (A) at 605D.

[190] At 607A–B.

[191] At 605B–F and 609I–610E; but see 599A–B read together with the statement on p. 596 H; cf. also Jansen JA, on p. 616 C.

[192] Cf. also Jansen JA in his dissenting opinion (at pp. 611 sqq.). He argues that the exceptio doli generalis still constitutes a substantive defence in modern South African law, based on the sense of justice of the community. Jansen's views are criticized, unusually severely, by Joubert JA ("His explanation . . . is, with respect, entirely unacceptable. It fails to take cognizance of the fact. . . . There is . . . not a scintilla of evidence . . . not supported by any authoritative Roman-Dutch legal sources. . . . He also, with respect, overlooks the fact . . ." (at 609G–610A)). For further comment on the *Bank of Lisbon* case, see Michael A. Lambiris, "The Exceptio Doli Generalis: An Obituary", (1988) 105 *SALJ* 644 sqq.

CHAPTER 22

Invalidity and Reasons for Invalidity

I. INVALIDITY

1. Terminological and conceptual problems

(a) The black cat which was not there

On 21 January 1942 in the Transvaal town of Germiston a certain Miss Van der Westhuizen married her lover, Mr Engelbrecht. Miss Van der Westhuizen was a minor and the marriage took place against the express prohibition of her parents; the marriage officer had been induced to believe that the bride was in fact of age. When Mr Van der Westhuizen sen. became aware of these facts, he promptly instituted an action against the couple (who had, in the meantime, broken off all relations with each other) to have the marriage declared null and void. Since a similar case had never been decided by a South African court, Mr Justice F.P. van den Heever took the opportunity to reflect on the meaning of the term "invalidity" in the old authorities.[1] Voet, he found, distinguished between juristic acts which are ipso iure null and void as opposed to those which require a declaration of nullity.[2] But then, virtually in the same breath, he recognized an almost universal practice, dictated by caution,[3] of obtaining judicial restitution, even with regard to juristic acts "quae vere nulla sunt". The words "ipso iure" (null and void) here, as in many other discussions on the topic, seem to be without any relevance; they are "thrown in for good measure and, apparently, for their sound".[4] After a lengthy historical exposition, Van den Heever J was driven to the conclusion that, in dealing with nullity ipso iure and seeking to attribute substantive significance to the distinction between the voidability and nullity of legal acts, the commentators of the ius commune "were like blind men looking in a dark room for a black cat which wasn't there".[5]

---

[1] *Van der Westhuizen v. Engelbrecht and Spouse and Engelbrecht v. Engelbrecht* 1942 OPD 191 at 195 sqq.

[2] *Commentarius ad Pandectas*, Lib. I, Tit. II, XVI.

[3] "Unde et quia nonnumquam ipso inter juris interpretes controversum est, an ipso jure quid nullum sit, an vero per judicem rescindendum, usu hodierno passim fere in tribunalibus obtinuit, ut et adversus ea, quae vere nulla sunt, majoris securitatis ergo, restitutio impetretur, eaque mediante rescindatur quod actum gestum contractumve fuit."

[4] *Van der Westhuizen v. Engelbrecht and Spouse & Engelbrecht v. Engelbrecht* 1942 OPD 191 at 196.

[5] At 199.

In fact, our discussion, in the previous two chapters, of the effects of mistake, duress and fraud on contracts, has already demonstrated[6] that Van den Heever's analysis is not far off the mark. Whether and under which circumstances a contract affected by these "vices of consent" was void, voidable, liable to be rescinded, relatively invalid, etc. has never been entirely clear. Additional difficulties arose from the fact that no generally accepted, uniform terminology was employed by the various authors of the ius commune;[7] what was referred to as "rescissio" by the one was termed *"résolution et nullité"* by another.[8] Only comparatively few of them stuck to clear-cut distinctions such as the ones proposed by Blasius Altimarius:[9] namely that there are contracts which are ipso facto nulli, others which have to be declared null and void by a court of law (such a declaration having ex tunc effect) and those which may be rescinded ex nunc.

(b) "Invalidity" according to the ius civile

The source of this confusion was, of course, the Roman law. There were two chief difficulties that systematically minded lawyers, who wanted to remain faithful to the sources, had to battle with. For, on the one hand, legal transactions could be "invalid", in classical Roman law, according to the ius civile. About 30 different terms survive in our sources to describe that result: nullum, nullius momenti, non esse, invalidum, nihil agere, inutile, inane, irritum, imperfectum, and vitiosum feature particularly prominently.[10] To bring them into any kind of systematic order would be an absolutely hopeless task. The Roman lawyers were mainly interested in whether an action was available in a given situation or not; they did not pay too much attention to a neat analysis of why an action could not be granted under certain circumstances and what further ramifications that entailed.[11] Thus, for instance, it was perfectly possible for them to declare the sale of a res religiosa to be invalid ("nullum esse emptionem")[12] and yet at the same time to make the actio empti available to the disappointed "purchaser" for "quod interfuit eius ne deciperetur".[13] Irritating for the modern lawyer is also the fact that no clear distinction was drawn

---

[6] Cf. supra, pp. 583 sqq., 651 sqq., 662 sqq.

[7] The same difficulty still persists today. Thus, for instance, the term "relative invalidity" (used by A.S. Hartkamp, *Der Zwang im Privatrecht* (1971), pp. 174 sqq.) has a different meaning in French law and in German law. In the former it refers to situations where only one of the parties may invoke the invalidity (cf. supra, pp. 661, 672), in the latter to cases where the transaction is to be treated as invalid only with regard to certain persons (cf. e.g. § 135 BGB and Hubert Beer, *Die relative Unwirksamkeit* (1975)).

[8] Cf. e.g. Coing, p. 414 (referring to Molina, Pothier and Perezius).

[9] *Tractatus de nullitatibus*, as quoted by Coing, p. 414.

[10] Santi di Paola, *Contributi ad una teoria della invalidità e della inefficacia in diritto romano* (1966), pp. 13 sqq, 72 sqq., 83 sqq., 93 sqq. and passim; Kaser, *RPr* I, p. 247.

[11] Kaser, *RPr* I, p. 246.

[12] Ulp. D. 18, 1, 22.

[13] Mod. D. 18, 1, 62, 1. For details cf. supra, p. 243.

between those cases where a valid contract had not come into existence (because of the lack of one of its requirements)[14] and where a transaction had in fact been concluded but was unenforceable "iure civili" because its content was, in some or other way, objectionable.[15] All that one may perhaps say by way of generalization is that the label "invalidity" usually implied that a transaction was denied its natural (or typical) consequences.[16] As a rule, this type of "civilian" invalidity could be invoked by anybody and at any time. But there were exceptions; the querela inofficiosi testamenti was probably the most important one. This was the complaint by a person, who would have been an intestate heir, but who was omitted or disinherited in the testator's will.[17] Even though such a will was contra officium pietatis and thus objectionable, it was valid until it had been declared null and void by the court with which the querela had been lodged. In this instance it was up to the aggrieved party, therefore, to decide whether to void the transaction or not. In this respect it resembles the modern concept of voidability (rescindability) of transactions.[18]

(c) Ius honorarium

Secondly, however, account must be taken of that other layer of legal rules of which classical Roman law was made up: the ius honorarium, developed by the praetors over the centuries and eventually revised and codified under Emperor Hadrian.[19] A variety of transactions, valid according to the civil law, were effectively invalidated by the praetor, in that he either refused to grant an action (denegatio actionis) or authorized the insertion of an exceptio into the procedural formula.[20] Alternatively, he ordered restitutio in integrum by granting remedies such as the actio quod metus causa, the actio de dolo or specific iudicia rescissoria.[21] This kind of reinstatement into the former legal position also effectively resulted in the annulment of a legal transaction, which was valid according to the ius civile. Again, the Roman lawyers were unconcerned about dogmatic niceties: was the transaction void or voidable and, if the latter, did the judicial or praetorian pronouncement have its rescissory effect ex tunc or merely ex nunc?[22]

(d) Classical and Justinianic law

To disentangle "civilian" and "praetorian" "invalidity" as such would

[14] Usually, however, the term "imperfectum" appears to have been used in this context.
[15] On this distinction, see, most recently, C.F.C. van der Walt, (1986) 103 *SALJ* 650.
[16] Kaser, *RPr* I, p. 247.
[17] Cf. generally Kaser, *RPr* I, pp. 709 sqq.; idem, *RPr* II, pp. 601 sq.
[18] Honsell/Mayer-Maly/Selb, p. 115.
[19] Cf. generally Max Kaser, "'Ius honorarium' und 'ius civile'", (1984) 101 *ZSS* 1 sqq.
[20] Kaser, *RPr* I, p. 248.
[21] Cf. supra, pp. 655 sqq., 662 sqq.
[22] Cf. Max Kaser, "Zur in integrum restitutio, besonders wegen metus und dolus", (1977) 94 *ZSS* 107 sq.

have been enough of a challenge for future generations of lawyers, to whom the contrast between ius civile and ius honorarium no longer mattered. Their task, however, was further complicated by the fact that terms such as "actio", "exceptio" and "in integrum restitutio" changed their meaning in post-classical times.[23] This was the inevitable consequence of the amalgamation of ius honorarium and ius civile and of the replacement of the formulary procedure of classical law by the imperial cognitio extra ordinem. Thus, for instance, the distinction between invalidity ipso iure and per exceptionem had lost any procedural significance and was consequently disregarded. Justinian, on the one hand (as usual), attempted to preserve the rules and concepts of classical substantive law; yet, on the other hand, he could not, of course, revive the procedural framework within which these rules had once been developed. This was bound to introduce an additional element of inconsistency into our sources. While, therefore, the term "exceptio" continued to be used, it had lost its characteristic classical contours. Justinian himself occasionally referred to invalidity where classical lawyers would have granted an exceptio, and as a result the difference between void and voidable was largely lost.[24]

(e) Pandectist doctrine

Only 19th-century pandectism eventually managed to establish some conceptual clarity.[25] Invalidity *("Ungültigkeit")* came to be accepted as the general, overall term, comprising (inter alia) ipso iure nullity *("Nichtigkeit")* and various forms of annulment of a legal act, either by a court of law or by the aggrieved party and, in the latter instance, either by raising an exceptio or by way of a declaration of rescission *("Anfechtung")*.[26] Within the BGB, the concept of rescission was linked to that of nullity, in that the effect of rescission was described in the following way: "If a legal transaction, which is liable to be rescinded, is rescinded, it is deemed to have been null and void from the outset"[27] (the ex tunc effect of the declaration of rescission). "Null and void" was interpreted, throughout the 19th century, in a quasi-naturalistic manner as absolutely and in every respect ineffective.[28] Today there is a

---

[23] Kaser, *RPr* II, pp. 65 sqq., 92 sq.

[24] Kaser, *RPr* II, p. 93.

[25] Cf. e.g. Windscheid/Kipp, § 82; cf. further Heinz Hübner, "Zum Abbau von Nichtigkeitsvorschriften", in: *Festschrift für Franz Wieacker* (1978), pp. 399 sqq. (also on the attempts by the natural lawyers to systematize the law in this regard on a rational basis). For the development of the principles of nullity in English law cf. Roberta Routledge, "The interaction of social and theoretical considerations in the development of the principle of nullity of contract in English law", in: *La formazione storica*, vol. III, pp. 1249 sqq.

[26] On rescission cf. supra, p. 615, note 192.

[27] § 142 I; but cf. still § 112 of the E I.

[28] Thus, for instance, it was deemed conceptually impossible to allow rescission of a transaction which was already null and void. This can, however, occasionally be desirable; for details cf. Theodor Kipp, "Über Doppelwirkungen im Recht, insbesondere über die Konkurrenz von Nichtigkeit und Anfechtbarkeit", in: *Festschrift für Ferdinand von Martitz*

tendency to try to regain a greater degree of flexibility and to escape the dogmatic and conceptual rigidity of the BGB.[29] Thus, for instance, it has been argued that under certain circumstances a transaction should not be regarded as absolutely void but only as relatively so: void against the one party but not against the other.[30] Even more notable has been the trend, in recent years, to restrict the invalidity of usurious transactions. Where a contract is contra bonos mores (and thus, according to § 138 BGB, "null and void") on account of an obvious disproportion between performance and counterperformance, courts have occasionally cut down the imbalance and upheld the contract in an acceptable, modified form.[31] This kind of judicial interference in, and reshaping of, contractual relationships occurs, to my mind, contra legem; nor is it necessitated by valid policy considerations.[32]

2. Convalescence; partial invalidity

Invalidity is normally a final verdict on the fate of a transaction. What is deficient in the beginning cannot become valid merely by the lapse of time.[33] There are, however, situations, where an—originally—invalid transaction is allowed to "convalesce". In modern law one can think of provisions, according to which a contract for the alienation of land, concluded without observance of the prescribed form, becomes valid if transfer and registration in the Land Register have taken place.[34] Likewise, the disposition of a non-owner over somebody else's property is invalid unless the owner has consented. The disposition becomes valid, however, if the owner (subsequently) ratifies it, or if the non-owner acquires the object.[35] This phenomenon of a "convalescence" occurs repeatedly in our Roman law sources. We have already come across a variety of examples. The rule of "morte Cincia removetur" falls into this category,[36] as does the idea that prohibited

---

(1911), pp. 211 sqq. In this article Kipp develops his famous theory of what he calls "double-effects" in the law. But cf. also Bernd Oellers, "Doppelwirkungen im Recht", (1969) 169 *Archiv für die civilistische Praxis* 67 sqq.

[29] Cf. generally Hübner, *Festschrift Wieacker*, pp. 399 sqq.; cf. also his comparative observations on p. 402.

[30] Ulrich Hübner, "Personale Relativierung der Unwirksamkeit von Rechtsgeschäften nach dem Schutzzweck der Norm", in: *Festschrift für Heinz Hübner* (1984), pp. 487 sqq.

[31] Cf. e.g. Theo Mayer-Maly, in: *Münchener Kommentar*, vol. I (2nd ed., 1984), § 138, nn. 134 sqq.

[32] For details, see Zimmermann, *Moderationsrecht*, passim; contra: Johannes Hager, *Gesetzes- und sittenkonforme Aufrechterhaltung von Rechtsgeschäften* (1983); Alfons Bürge, *Rechtsdogmatik und Wirtschaft* (1987); Manfred Lieb, in: *Münchener Kommentar*, vol. II, 3 (2nd ed., 1986), § 817, n. 17.

[33] Paul. D. 50, 17, 29: "Quod initio vitiosum est, non potest tractu temporis convalescere."

[34] § 313, 2 BGB.

[35] § 185 II BGB. For details, see Filippo Ranieri, *Alienatio convalescit* (1974), pp. 36 sqq., 51 sqq.

[36] Cf. supra, p. 484.

donations between spouses became valid with the death of the donor.[37] The exceptio senatus consulti Macedoniani, too, was removed (and the mutuum thus effectively validated) if the paterfamilias or the son (after he had ceased to be alieni iuris) ratified the loan.[38] Generally speaking, we are dealing here with situations where the obstacle to the validity of the transaction subsequently falls away.

Two further escape routes from the harshness connected with the complete and final invalidity of legal transactions were paved by the Roman lawyers. The one may be summed up in the maxim "utile per inutile non vitiatur":[39] if only part of a transaction was invalid, the rest of it, as a rule, remained unaffected. Attention has already been drawn to the very flexible manner in which this problem was approached.[40] "Utile per inutile non vitiatur" was adopted by the Swiss[41] and Austrian[42] codes, whereas the BGB has opted, in case of doubt, for the invalidity of the whole transaction.[43] Today, a tendency prevails to return to the Roman maxim.[44]

3. Conversion

(a) Traductio unius negotii in alterum (ius commune)

The other device is usually referred to as "conversion" (re-interpretation). The modern term goes back to a dissertatio iuridica inauguralis "de eo, quod iustum est, circa conversionem actuum negotiorumque iuridicorum iamiam peractorum" by the German scholar Christian Ferdinand Harpprecht, written in 1747.[45] In this inaugural dissertation he defined conversio as "traductio vel commutatio unius negotii in alterum pro obtinendo et salvando fine necessaria, actui et intentioni agentis conformis":[46] a transformation of one legal act into another, which is necessary in order to achieve and to save the aim of the transaction and which is in accordance with both the action and the intention of the acting party. This concept of "conversio" is based, interestingly, on the transsubstantiation doctrine of the Catholic Church, as laid down in the 4th Chapter of the *Decretum de Eucharistia* by the Council of Trent (1545–61):

> ". . . per consecrationem panis et vini conversionem fieri totius substantiae panis in substantiam corporis Christi Domini nostri, et totius substantiae vini in substantiam sanguinis eius. Quae conversio convenienter et proprie a sancta catholica Ecclesia transsubstantiatio est appellata."[47]

---

[37] Supra, p. 488. [38] Cf. supra, p. 180.
[39] Cf. Ulp. D. 45, 1, 1, 5. [40] Supra, pp. 75 sqq.
[41] Art. 20 II OR.
[42] § 878 ABGB.
[43] § 139 BGB.
[44] Cf. supra, p. 77.
[45] Cf. Christoph Krampe, *Die Konversion des Rechtsgeschäfts* (1980), pp. 28 sqq.
[46] At p. 8.
[47] For details, see Krampe, op. cit., note 45, pp. 36 sqq.

In the course of the 19th century the conversio actus iuridici became a generally accepted device for upholding invalid legal transactions in another form,[48] and was taken over into several of the modern codifications.[49] Thus, for instance, the BGB (§ 140) determines that if an invalid legal transaction satisfies the requirements of another legal transaction, the latter is effective, provided that it is covered by the hypothetical intention of the parties.[50] It is obvious that conversion and interpretation are very closely related to each other; in fact, it has been argued that we are not dealing here with distinct and separable legal techniques, but with a problem of (re-)interpretation (so that, ultimately, special rules such as § 140 BGB would be redundant when viewed against the general rules of interpretation).[51] Whether or not this view can be accepted as correct depends, of course, on how far one is prepared to take the notion of interpretation[52] and on how one perceives what actually takes place in the process of the "conversion" of a legal act: is there really a transformation (as Harpprecht would have it) from one thing into another, i.e. a judicial remodelling of the transaction, or does the judge, by uncovering a hidden side contained in it, uphold the act *as it is*, but from a different perspective?[53]

(b) Conversion in Roman law?

The Roman lawyers, as may be expected, did not bother with these subtle dogmatic distinctions. Nevertheless, they provided the casuistic basis for the modern doctrines. For, although they neither developed a specific set of rules nor knew the term "conversio", the problem was well known to them. The Digest contains a variety of situations, where ineffective legal acts are upheld by way of (as we would call it) conversion.[54] The best-known example is the one discussed in

---

[48] Krampe, op. cit., note 45, pp. 83 sqq.; Giuseppe Gandolfi, "La nozione pandettistica di 'conversione' al vaglio della giurisprudenza tedesca dell' ottocento", in: *Sodalitas, Scritti in onore di Antonio Guarino*, vol. VIII (1984), pp. 4053 sqq.

[49] Krampe, op. cit., note 45, pp. 123 sqq.; Giuseppe Gandolfi, "Il concetto moderno di 'conversione' e la sua genesi legislativa", in: *Studi in onore di Arnaldo Biscardi*, vol. II (1982), pp. 551 sqq.

[50] For details cf., e.g., Mayer-Maly, op. cit., note 31, § 140, nn. 1 sqq.; Hager, op. cit., note 32, pp. 115 sqq., 154 sqq.; Giuseppe Gandolfi, "Introduzione allo studio del concetto legislativo di 'conversione'", in: *Studi in onore di Cesare Sanfilippo*, vol. VI (1985), pp. 319 sqq.; idem, *La conversione dell' atto invalido, Il modello germanico* (1984), pp. 101 sqq., 145 sqq.

[51] Krampe, op. cit., note 45, pp. 286 sqq.

[52] Cf. e.g. Seiler, (1984) 184 *Archiv für die civilistische Praxis* 186 sq. In this respect the problem of what is usually referred to as "*ergänzende Vertragsauslegung*" is of particular relevance. May the courts fill gaps in the contractual arrangements on the basis of the hypothetical will of the parties (and thus do for the individuals "what they would have done for themselves, if their imagination had anticipated the march of nature": Jeremy Bentham, "A General View of a Complete Code of Laws", in: John Bowring (ed.) *Works* (1843), vol. III, p. 191) or do they have to stick to their real intention? Cf. generally Alexander Lüderitz, *Auslegung von Rechtsgeschäften* (1966), pp. 386 sqq., 392 sqq.; Flume, *AT*, pp. 321 sqq.

[53] Windscheid/Kipp, § 82, 5.

[54] Cf. generally Vincenzo Giuffré, *L'utilizzazione degli atti giuridici mediante 'conversione' in diritto romano* (1965), pp. 107 sqq.

D. 29, 1, 3.[55] Here a soldier had intended to make a will "communi iure", but he died before the document had been duly signed by the required number of witnesses. Under the general rules of the ius civile, a regular testamentum per aes et libram could not have come into existence under these circumstances. According to Ulpian, the testator's act is, however, valid as a soldier's will (testamentum militis), which was exempt from all formalities. But the desire to uphold invalid legal acts under different auspices was not confined to the law of testamentary dispositions.[56] In the field of contract we have, for instance, Ulp. D. 46, 4, 8 pr.: "An inutilis acceptilatio utile habeat pactum, quaeritur: et nisi in hoc quoque contra sensum est, habet pactum."[57] Acceptilatio was a transaction by which a debtor could be formally released from his obligations under a contract verbis.[58] It was actus contrarius to the stipulation of classical law[59] and subject to the same formal requirements. "Quod ego tibi promisi, habesne acceptum?"[60] was the question of the promisor, whereupon the stipulator had to answer "Habeo". If it did not comply with these formalities, the acceptilatio was invalid. The question arose, therefore, whether the transaction could not be seen as containing an informal pactum de non petendo, which would at least allow the debtor to defend himself against his creditor's claim by way of raising an exceptio pacti. Ulpian's answer is in the affirmative and this appears, indeed, to be a sensible solution, in view of what both parties had primarily intended. After all, by the time of classical law even formal acts such as stipulations (or acceptilationes) had to be founded on an agreement between the parties.[61] Thus, "inutilis acceptilatio utile habet pactum" was based, essentially, on a (re-) interpretation of the contract according to the principle of "id quod actum est";[62] hence the limitation contained in the "nisi in hoc" clause, hence also, particularly, the statement of Paulus in D. 2, 14, 27, 9: "Si acceptilatio inutilis fuit, tacita pactione id actum videtur, ne peteretur." Since a formal release had failed, the parties could be taken to have intended a pactum tacitum[63] (de non petendo).

---

[55] Giuffrè, op. cit., note 54, pp. 175 sqq.; Krampe, op. cit., note 45, pp. 64 sqq.

[56] Cf. Giuffrè, op. cit., note 54, pp. 207 sqq.

[57] On this text cf. in particular Christoph Krampe, "An inutilis acceptilatio utile habeat pactum, quaeritur—D. 46, 4, 8 pr. (Ulp. 48 Sab.)", (1985) 53 *TR* 3 sqq.

[58] Kaser, *RPr* I, p. 641; Honsell/Mayer-Maly/Selb, p. 265; Alan Watson, "The Form and Nature of 'acceptilatio' in Classical Roman Law", (1961) 8 *RIDA* 391 sqq.; cf. also infra, pp. 755, 756.

[59] Knütel, *Contrarius consensus*, p. 9; idem, "Zum Prinzip der formalen Korrespondenz im römischen Recht", (1971) 88 *ZSS* 87 sqq.; Detlef Liebs, "Contrarius actus, Zur Entstehung des römischen Erlassvertrags", in: *Sympotica Franz Wieacker* (1970), pp. 131 sqq.

[60] Gai. III, 169.

[61] Cf. supra, pp. 510 sq., 565, 627 sq.

[62] Krampe, (1985) 53 *TR* 16 sqq.

[63] For details, see Andreas Wacke, "Zur Lehre vom pactum tacitum und zur Aushilfsfunktion der exceptio doli", (1973) 90 *ZSS* 220 sqq., 254 sqq.

(c) Paul. D. 38, 1, 39 pr.

But there are other decisions where an invalid transaction was upheld without specific reference to id quod actum est and where it therefore remains a matter of speculation whether the Roman lawyers themselves viewed this kind of operation as a question of interpretation or of conversion in the modern sense. Paulus D. 38, 1, 39 pr. is a case in point.[64] According to the lex Aelia Sentia, patrons were not allowed to bind their freedmen to pay money rather than to render services;[65] such promises were regarded as an objectionable restriction of the freedman's liberty. The patron was, however, able to obtain a stipulation in the alternative ("certum operas aut in singulas HS quina milia dari?"),[66] for here the freedman could avoid payment of the promised sum by rendering the services. But what about a stipulation such as "si decem dierum operas non dederis, viginti nummos dare spondes?" We are dealing here with a non-genuine penalty clause: the freedman has promised the money, albeit only in case he does not provide ten days' work. The work as such has not been stipulated for; it is merely in condicione. Strictly speaking, therefore, the transaction is invalid. Effectively, however, the stipulatio poenae gave the libertus the same option as the alternative stipulation: provided he did the work, he did not have to pay. Hence the attempt to save the transaction, expressed in the following words:

> ". . . an vero operae dumtaxat promissae fingi debeant, ne patronus omnimodo excludatur? et hoc praetor quoque sentit operas dumtaxat promissas."[67]

All in all, it must be obvious that the Roman lawyers displayed considerable ingenuity in avoiding a verdict of complete and final invalidity and thereby helping the parties to achieve the ends they had intended to achieve with their transaction. Of course, these ends in themselves had to be legal, moral and attainable.

The last sentence leads us on to consider the reasons for the invalidity of a contract; it refers to the three most important and general ones: illegality, immorality and impossibility of performance.

II. INITIAL IMPOSSIBILITY

1. Impossibilium nulla obligatio est

"A contract, the performance of which is impossible, is void" states the BGB in its § 306, with characteristic precision and uncharacteristic

---

[64] On this text, see Knütel, *Stipulatio poenae*, pp. 76 sq.

[65] Ter. Cl. D. 40, 9, 32, 1; Iul. D. 38, 1, 25; Pierre Jaubert, "La Lex Aelia Sentia et la locatio conductio des operae liberti", (1965) 43 *RH* 5 sqq.

[66] Cf. Paul. D. 37, 14, 6, 1; Ter. Cl. D. 40, 9, 32, 2.

[67] Paul. D. 38, 1, 39 pr.

dash. Iuventius Celsus himself, well known for his succinct and trenchant style,[68] could hardly have faulted the German version of the famous principle that has come down to us under his name: "Impossibilium nulla obligatio est."[69] It thus appears to be a rule, not only of venerable antiquity, but also of obvious and even axiomatic validity. It is echoed in other modern legal systems[70] and corresponds to the maxim "ought implies can" of modern moral philosophy.[71] If we oblige somebody to do something, we presuppose in fact that he is able to do this act; anything else would be a kind of buffoonery ("lusisse tantum, et nihil egisse cense[m]ur" in the words of Pufendorf).[72] Impossibilium nulla obligatio est neatly encapsulates the idea that nobody can be obliged to perform what he cannot perform. But this is not identical to the assertion that a contract aimed at an impossible performance is bound to be void: at least in the eyes of the Roman lawyers, the one did not *necessarily* follow from the other. What, then, was the effect of impossibility of performance on the contractual relationship between two parties in Roman law?

2. The concept of impossibility

Before we answer this question, we must first of all attempt to define more precisely what is meant by "impossibility" in the present context. First of all, and most importantly, our discussion in this chapter refers only to initial (as opposed to supervening) impossibility. What matters is whether at the time of conclusion of the contract performance was impossible or not. Apart from that, "impossibilium nulla obligatio est" covered only cases in which performance was objectively impossible;[73] if somebody had promised what *he* could not, but another person could in fact perform, the obligatio was not "nulla": "Si ab eo stipulatus sim, qui efficere non possit, cum alio possibile sit, iure factam obligationem

[68] Cf. e.g. Franz Wieacker, "Amoenitates Iuventianae", (1962) 13 *Iura* 1 sqq.; Mario Bretone, "Note minime su Celsus filius", (1963) 9 *Labeo* 331 sqq.

[69] D. 50, 17, 185.

[70] Cf. e.g. *Peters, Flamman & Co. v. Kokstad Municipality* 1919 AD 427 at 434: "By the Civil Law a contract is void if at the time of its inception its performance is impossible: impossibilium nulla obligatio (D. 50, 17, 185)"; De Wet en Yeats, pp. 76 sqq.; Joubert, *Contract*, p. 124. The rule is used in an entirely different context in *Montsisi v. Minister of Police* 1984 (1) SA 619 (A) at 635A–638G (per Rabie CJ); cf. the discussion by Derek van der Merwe, "Regulae iuris and the axiomatization of the law in the sixteenth and seventeenth centuries", 1987 *TSAR* 300 sqq.

[71] Joachim Hruschka, "Zwei Axiome des Rechtsdenkens", in: *Aus dem Hamburger Rechtsleben, Festschrift für Walter Reimers* (1979), pp. 459 sqq.

[72] *De jure naturae et gentium*, Lib. III, Cap. VII, § 2; cf. Hruschka, *Festschrift Reimers*, p. 461.

[73] The same still applies to § 306 BGB; cf. § 275 II BGB e contrario. For South Africa cf. De Wet en Yeats, pp. 76 sq.; Joubert, *Contract*, pp. 124 sqq. As to the terminology ("subjective" and "objective" impossibility), cf. F. Mommsen, *Unmöglichkeit*, p. 5; Windscheid/Kipp, § 264, 1. Others (as, for instance, Savigny) had referred to absolute and relative impossibility.

Sabinus scribit."[74] Objective initial impossibility therefore comprised a large variety of situations: cases where the object of the contract cannot exist at all (the stipulation of a hippocentaurus),[75] where the object was no longer in rerum natura (the promise to deliver a slave who was already dead,[76] the sale of a house that had completely burnt down[77] or of an olive grove that had been devastated by a storm)[78] or where it was extra commercium (the sale of a res sacra or religiosa,[79] or of the campus Martius).[80] Transfer of ownership was also objectively impossible where the slave who had been stipulated for already belonged to the creditor[81] or turned out to be a homo liber.[82] If, on the other hand, what had been sold or promised did not belong to the vendor (or promisor) but to a third party, the obligation remained in any event unaffected: performance was not objectively impossible. In the case of a contract of sale, as we have seen, the vendor did not even have to transfer ownership, but merely vacua possessio; if he was evicted, the purchaser could bring the actio empti.[83] Finally, impossibilium nulla obligatio est could not be invoked where performance was merely difficult (as opposed to objectively impossible). The Roman lawyers drew a fine distinction between impedimentum naturale and facultas dandi: the latter, as they saw it, was a question of personal convenience or inconvenience, but did not affect the content of the promise. Hence the general rule that "causa difficultatis ad incommodum promissoris, non ad impedimentum stipulatoris pertinet".[84] Performance was therefore not (objectively) impossible if the debtor had no money and was unable to find a lender or if the slave whom he was supposed to hand over in Rome was in fact in Ephesos.[85] What if the slave who had been sold turned out to be in the hands of the enemy?

> ". . . Octavenus magis putabat valere emptionem et stipulationem, . . . potius enim difficultatem in praestando eo inesse, quam in natura, etiamsi officio iudicis sustinenda esset eius praestatio, donec praestari possit."[86]

---

[74] Ven. D. 45, 1, 137, 5; Dieter Medicus, "Zur Funktion der Leistungsunmöglichkeit im römischen Recht", (1969) 86 *ZSS* 83 sqq.

[75] Gai. III, 97 a; *Inst.* III, 19, 1.

[76] Gai. III, 97; *Inst.* III, 19, 1.

[77] Paul. D. 18, 1, 57 (with a detailed discussion about what happens when part of the house remains standing); Frank Peters, "Zur dogmatischen Einordnung der anfänglichen, objektiven Unmöglichkeit beim Kauf", in: *Festschrift für Max Kaser* (1976), pp. 289 sqq.; Arp, *Anfängliche Unmöglichkeit*, pp. 107 sqq.

[78] Pap. D. 18, 1, 58.

[79] Pomp., Paul., Cels./Pomp. D. 18, 1, 4–6 pr.; Mod. D. 18, 1, 62, 1; *Inst.* III, 23, 5.

[80] Cels./Pomp. D. 18, 1, 6 pr.

[81] Gai. D. 44, 7, 1, 10; Gai. III, 99; Ulp. D. 45, 1, 82 pr.; *Inst.* III, 19, 2 and 22.

[82] Gai. D. 44, 7, 1, 9; Gai. III, 97; Paul. D. 45, 1, 83, 5; Mod. D. 45, 1, 103; *Inst.* III, 19, 2.

[83] Cf. supra, pp. 293 sqq., 296 sqq.

[84] Ven. D. 45, 1, 137, 4.

[85] Cf. Ven. D. 45, 1, 137, 4.

[86] Pomp. D. 19, 1, 55. In place of "in natura" one probably has to read "quam eum non esse in rerum natura" (Mommsen). On the problem of slaves in hostium postestate and impossibility cf. further Paul. D. 46, 3, 98, 8 and Medicus, (1969) 86 *ZSS* 87 sqq.

On the borderline, too, was a stipulation, made in Rome "hodie Carthagine dare spondes?"[87] Ships could sail fast, but to cover the distance from Rome to Carthage within less than 24 hours was not only difficult, but impossible. Hence, as a rule, such a stipulation was said to depend on impossibilem causam. Likewise, Justinian regarded as impossible the promise by a person on his deathbed to build a house.[88]

3. Initial impossibility of stipulations

All the examples mentioned so far refer either to stipulation or to consensual sale. Impossibilium nulla obligatio est does not seem to have been discussed with regard to other contracts; as far as contractus re were concerned, such a discussion would, of course, have been a logical impossibility in any event, since they came into existence only with the handing over of the object. Dealing with the consequences of initial objective impossibility of contracts in Roman law, we must therefore distinguish between sale and stipulation. Only to the latter would a rule such as that contained in § 306 BGB have applied without qualification: "si id quod dari stipulamur tale sit, ut dari non possit, inutilis est stipulatio."[89]

The stipulation was invalid. No explanation is given for the result, and thus one is left to speculate. The stipulation was a contract stricti iuris, and the appropriate action was the condictio (certae rei). "Si paret N^{m} N^{m} A^{o} A^{o} hominem Stichum dare oportere, quanti ea rest est, tantam pecuniam iudex N^{m} N^{m} A^{o} A^{o} condemnato, si non paret, absolvito" was its formula. Condemnation, therefore, presupposed "that it appears that the plaintiff has to give the slave Stichus to the defendant". But how could this "appear" to be the case if the slave had ceased to exist at the time when the contract was concluded? To postulate a "dare oportere" under these circumstances was obviously not considered to be possible.[90] Apart from that, a second prerequisite for condemnation was that the defendant's (object of) performance was capable of being evaluated in monetary terms ("quanti ea res *est*, tantam pecuniam"). In most, if not in all, cases of initial objective impossibility, an object of which the value could sensibly be estimated, was, however, lacking; for what is the value of a hippocentaurus, of a

---

[87] Gai. D. 45, 1, 141, 4; Inst. III, 15, 5. Cf. also Ulp. D. 13, 4, 2, 6; Medicus, (1969) 86 *ZSS* 86 sq.; Arp, *Anfängliche Unmöglichkeit*, pp. 77 sq., 86.

[88] C. 8, 37, 15: "Si quis spoponderat insulam, cum moriebatur, aedificare stipulatori, impossibilis videbatur huiusmodi stipulatio."

[89] Gai. III, 97; see further Wollschläger, *Unmöglichkeitslehre*, pp. 8 sqq.; Arp, *Anfängliche Unmöglichkeit*, pp. 66 sqq. (according to whom nullity is the natural and logical consequence ("*sachlogisch richtige Rechtsfolge*", p. 88) of impossibility of performance of a unilateral promise such as a stipulation; but see also e.g. pp. 100 sq.)

[90] Cf. e.g. Franz Wieacker, "Leistungshandlung und Leistungserfolg im bürgerlichen Schuldrecht", in: *Festschrift für Hans Carl Nipperdey*, vol. I (1965), pp. 801 sq.; Wollschläger, *Unmöglichkeitslehre*, pp. 10 sq.; but see Arp, *Anfängliche Unmöglichkeit*, pp. 97 sqq.

res extra commercium or of the corpse of a slave whom the parties had intended to transfer alive?[91]

4. Initial impossibility and contracts of sale

Contracts of sale, on the other hand, gave rise to bonae fidei iudicia where such problems did not occur. The judge was neither asked to estimate "quanti ea res est" nor was he hemmed in by an awkward and narrow wording of the formula's intentio. He was invested with a broad discretion, for under the actiones empti and venditi he was instructed to condemn in "quidquid ob eam rem N^{m} N^{m} A^{o} A^{o} dare facere oportet ex fide bona".[92] As a result, the consequences of initial objective impossibility were determined with much greater flexibility than in the case of stipulations.[93] True: in many of our sources the sale is said to be invalid: ". . . si . . . corpus . . . in rerum natura ante venditionem esse desierit, nulla emptio est", said Paulus;[94] Nerva, Sabinus and Cassius are reported to have opined "nihil venisse" (and to have granted an unjustified enrichment claim to the purchaser if he had already paid the purchase price)[95] where the object of the sale had burnt down,[96] and Modestinus declared "emptio non teneat" in cases of a sale of sacred, religious or public land.[97] But we know by now that these pronouncements sound much more clear-cut and technical to us than they were intended by the Roman lawyers. Modestinus, in fact, in the very same sentence, goes on to grant the actio empti to the disappointed purchaser—despite the fact that the sale was "invalid". In other cases of objective initial impossibility, the actio empti was available too: "Si sterilis ancilla sit, cuius partus venit, . . . cum id emptor ignoraverit, ex empto tenetur venditor."[98] The sale of a liber homo as a slave was also valid provided that the purchaser did not know about the true status of the person involved.[99] Only where the object of the sale had been destroyed or had otherwise perished before the conclusion of the sale does the question of contractual liability never seem to have been discussed.[100] Thus, the only thing one can safely state in a more general

[91] For this line of argument, see Medicus, (1969) 86 *ZSS* 69 sqq. Contra: Arp, *Anfängliche Unmöglichkeit*, p. 100; he maintains that the stipulation was inutilis because of (and in so far as there was) a divergence between the content of the promise and the reality, on account of which the promise appeared to make no sense, to be absurd, and in this sense: to be impossible (pp. 86 sqq.; on the meaning of the term "impossibilis" cf. pp. 78 sqq.)

[92] Cf. supra, p. 277.

[93] Cf., in particular, Wollschläger, *Unmöglichkeitslehre*, pp. 11 sqq.; Peters, *Festschrift Kaser*, pp. 285 sqq.; Arp, *Anfängliche Unmöglichkeit*, pp. 101 sqq.

[94] D. 18, 1, 15 pr.

[95] We also find the condictio (indebiti) in Paul. D. 18, 4, 7.

[96] Paul. D. 18, 1, 57.

[97] D. 18, 1, 62, 1.

[98] Paul. D. 19, 1, 21 pr.

[99] Lic. Ruf. D. 18, 1, 70. For further details cf. supra, p. 242.

[100] For an attempt to rationalize and justify this differentiation, cf. Arp, *Anfängliche Unmöglichkeit*, pp. 106 sqq.: the sale of an object that did no longer exist was invalid because,

vein about the impact of initial objective impossibility on a contract of sale is that the (primary) obligation to transfer vacua possessio of the object did not exist: in that respect impossibilium was indeed nulla obligatio.[101] To say, however, that this always entailed invalidity of the whole transaction, is merely a modern and ahistorical *façon de parler*. The sale *was* invalid in so far as it did not have its normal or typical consequences: the vendor did not have to honour his primary obligation (because he could not), the purchaser did not owe the purchase price, and where he had paid it, he could claim it back by way of the condictio. This kind of "invalidity" did not, however, exclude the possibility that under certain circumstances a contractual action for the positive interest[102] could be brought against the vendor.

5. Impossibilium nulla obligatio est under the (earlier) ius commune

How, under these circumstances, could the development of the ius commune lead up to general statements such as the one pronounced by Solomon ACJ in *Peters, Flamman & Co. v. Kokstad Municipality*: "By the Civil Law a contract is void if at the time of its inception its performance is impossible"?[103] Glossators, commentators and writers up to the period of the usus modernus pandectarum[104] essentially stuck to the pattern which they found in the Roman sources: they differentiated between sale and stipulation. Only the latter type of transaction was invalid due to impossibilium nulla est obligatio. In actual practice the maxim was therefore ultimately bound to lose its field of application; with the acceptance of ex nudo pacto oritur actio, the stipulation was, after all, no longer of any significance as a special type of contract.[105] Savigny (one of the last authors who confined the Celsinian rule to stipulations) came to the conclusion, that contracts of sale and similar transactions were *valid*, except where the purchaser had known about the initial objective impossibility.[106] This view was based on sources such as Mod. D. 18, 1, 62, 1 and Lic. Ruf. D. 18, 1, 70, and meant that the vendor (even if he had been nesciens) was liable to pay "quod sua [i.e. the purchaser] interest deceptum non esse" (we would say: the positive interest). In this instance, however, Savigny did not prevail. Hugo Donellus had made the first attempt to elevate the crisp

due to the deviation between reality and the intentions of the parties, the transaction lacked any sense or purpose. Meaningful, however (despite impossibility of performance!), and therefore not invalid, the sale of a liber homo as a slave. This is hardly convincing.

[101] Cf. also Hausmaninger/Selb, pp. 286 sq. The argument of Peters, *Festschrift Kaser*, pp. 303 sqq., appears to be too radical.

[102] Cf. supra, pp. 241 sqq.

[103] 1919 AD 427 at 434.

[104] For details, see Wollschläger, *Unmöglichkeitslehre*, pp. 18 sqq., 23 sqq., 31 sqq.

[105] Cf. supra, pp. 546 sqq.

[106] *Obligationenrecht*, vol. II, p. 290; on Savigny's view cf., most recently, Arp, *Anfängliche Unmöglichkeit*, pp. 136 sqq.

and handy maxim contained in D. 50, 17, 185 to the status of a principle of universal applicability.[107] If the object of the transaction did not exist, every kind of contract, in his opinion had to be regarded as invalid; for, irrespective of whether a stipulation was involved or not, it would be absurd to allow one party to demand the impossible from the other. As far as the contract of sale was concerned, Donellus could refer to Paul. D. 18, 1, 57. Only in certain instances (cf. particularly Mod. D. 18, 1, 62, 1) did the contract have a limited form of validity. But these were narrowly confined exceptions to the general rule of "impossibilium nulla est obligatio".

6. The approach of the natural lawyers

Nevertheless, by accepting these exceptions, Donellus was still moving within the framework set out by the Roman sources. It was left to the natural lawyers to challenge traditional doctrine in a more fundamental way.[108] Discarding the subtleties of Roman law, they found an altogether new starting point for determining the effect of initial impossibility on contractual obligations in the idea that (in the words of Grotius:) "de verbintenisse is een gebruick van eens mensche vrije macht".[109] The content of a contractual obligation is attributable to the promisor only if it is based on the exercise of his free will. The promisor must have chosen to be bound, and as a rational being he can choose only what he is able to carry out. This train of thought goes back to medieval moral theology and, even beyond that, to the theory of attribution of human acts contained in Aristotle's *Nicomachean Ethics*.[110] St. Thomas Aquinas described this connection between electio and possibilitas particularly clearly ("Et ideo voluntas completa non est nisi de possibili, quod est bonum volenti. Sed voluntas incompleta est de impossibili: quae secundum quosdam velleitas dicitur, quia scilicet aliquis vellet illud, si esset possibile. Electio autem nominat actum voluntatis iam determinatum ad id quod est huic agendum. Ed ideo nullo modo est nisi possibilium")[111] and applied it to vow, oath and marriage promise. A vow (votum) is a promise made to God and it is obviously without any religious (and thus legal) significance if it involves an act that cannot possibly be carried out. An oath, too, is without much value (and thus invalid) "[s]i . . . est talis res quae in eius [i.e. the person taking the oath] potestate non fuit".[112] The

---

[107] The views of Donellus, as contained in his *Commentarii de Jure Civili*, are analysed by Wollschläger, *Unmöglichkeitslehre*, pp. 28 sqq.

[108] For what follows cf. Christian Wollschläger, "Die willenstheoretische Unmöglichkeitslehre im aristotelisch-thomistischen Naturrecht", in: *Sympotica Franz Wieacker* (1970), pp. 154 sqq.

[109] *Inleiding*, III, I, 19.

[110] For details, see Wollschläger, *Sympotica Wieacker*, pp. 156 sqq.

[111] *Summa Theologiae*, Prima Secundae, q. 13, art. 5, ad 1.

[112] *Summa Theologiae*, Secundae Secundae, q. 89, art. 7 (sub: respondeo).

impossibility is here conceived of as a vice of the will. The promise must have been made "voluntarie",[113] which entails, inter alia, that what has been promised must be subject to the free will of the promisor. What is (to him) impossible cannot, however, be subject to a person's will. Under this perspective, incidentally, "objective" and "subjective" impossibility appear to be on a par: attention is focused on the individual promisor and *his* ability to carry out what he has promised. A's vow cannot become acceptable due to the fact that B or C would be able to honour it. Impossibilitas and impotentia are therefore used synonymously and entail the same legal consequences. This is apparent particularly in the canon law of marriage, where impossibilitas coeundi (impotentia in the narrow, sexual sense), a classical example of merely subjective (initial) impossibility, was regarded as an impediment to a valid marriage. The phrase coined by St. Thomas Aquinas in this context ("nullus potest se obligare ad impossibile")[114] is more than vaguely reminiscent of Celsus' famous rule, but has, at the same time, acquired a new dimension: nobody can bind himself to do what is beyond his powers. Grotius generalized these ideas and Pufendorf further refined them.[115] Thus, already in Grotius' *Inleiding* (!) we read that, since contractual obligations

> "vereisschen voor eerst vrij oeffening des willes, . . . zoo en kan oock nae 't aengebooren recht niemand hem zelve verbinden tot zaken die alle menschen, ofte hem in 't byzonder, zijn onmoghelijck ofte ongeoorloft":[116]

by natural law man cannot bind himself to things which are impossible or not permitted for men generally or for him in particular. Reason: the free will of the promisor can be directed only towards an act or a performance which is within his (personal) potestas.

7. Pandectist doctrine

Based, as they were, on freedom of choice and of contract, these views could not fail to commend themselves to the pandectists. Man can will only what lies within the reach of his volition. The law of contract is based on the freedom of will. Ergo: a contract directed at something impossible must be invalid. What remained to be done was to test this result against the sources of Roman law (and then to claim that it was derived from them). For while Savigny and his followers (the so-called historical school of law) had once set out to return to the truth and purity of Roman law (as contained in the pages of the Corpus Juris

---

[113] Cf. e.g. *Summa Theologiae*, Secundae Secundae, q. 88, art. 1.

[114] *In quatuor libros Sententiarum* , Dist. 34, q. 1, art. 2, in: S. Thomae Aquinatis *Opera Omnia*, vol. I, Frommann, Holzboog, 1980 (ed. Robertus Busa), p. 604. Cf. also the regula iuris ("nemo potest ad impossibile obligari") in Pope Boniface's *Liber Sextus Decretalium*, Lib. V, Tit. XII, De regulis iuris, VI.

[115] On Pufendorf's views, see Wollschläger, *Sympotica Wieacker*, pp. 174 sqq.

[116] III, I, 19.

rather than in post-reception legal literature), it was nevertheless a somewhat idealized version of it which they had in mind; and in the course of the 19th century, the historical approach was overlaid and finally replaced by the exaggerated dogmatism of theorizing law professors, who attempted to bring the sources into some sort of systematical and conceptual shape, so as to fit in with their scientific calculus.

The man to do the job in this specific case was Friedrich Mommsen.[117] In D. 50, 17, 185 he found the necessary and authoritative confirmation of the fact that a contract is void if at the time of its inception performance is impossible. For Mommsen, this was a principle of universal validity. Irritating obstacles (in the form of texts such as D. 18, 1, 70, D. 18, 1, 62, 1 or *Inst.* III, 23, 5) were rather forcibly removed (for instance, by implying dolus, or 'culpa lata', on the part of the vendor).[118] On the other hand, Mommsen recognized that the problem had never been approached by the Roman lawyers from the point of view of the *individual* debtor's facultas dandi (or praestandi) and that application of "impossibilium nulla obligatio est" therefore had to be limited to cases of objective impossibility.[119] Mommsen's exposition satisfied the contemporary desire for neat and clear-cut principles. Within a short time, it gained wide-spread support[120] and duly received the highest possible accolade in the world of late 19th-century pandectism: it was adopted (and thus virtually canonized) by Bernhard Windscheid in his *Lehrbuch des Pandektenrechts*.[121] Its modern statutory version is § 306 BGB.

8. Recovery of damages

"A contract, the performance of which is impossible, is void"—"void" being, in modern parlance, an unambiguous terminus technicus,[122] it necessarily follows that the purchaser will not be able to avail himself of a contractual action (the actio empti) to claim what we would call his "positive" interest. Nevertheless, the vendor may under certain circumstances be obliged to compensate the purchaser for his (reliance) damages.[123] That was realized, first of all, by the natural lawyers, who merely applied the general principles of delictual liability to this situation. Fault, in their view, creates the obligation to make good any

[117] *Die Unmöglichkeit der Leistung in ihrem Einfluss auf obligatorische Verhältnisse* (1853), pp. 102 sqq.

[118] F. Mommsen, *Unmöglichkeit*, pp. 117 sqq.

[119] F. Mommsen, *Unmöglichkeit*, pp. 5 sq.; cf. further Dernburg, *Pandekten*, vol. II, § 16; Windscheid/Kipp, §§ 264, 315.

[120] But see Alois Brinz, (1857) 5 *Kritische Überschau der deutschen Gesetzgebung und Rechtswissenschaft* 281 sqq.

[121] §§ 264, 315.

[122] Cf. supra, p. 681.

[123] On the concepts of positive and negative interest cf. supra, pp. 243 sq., 298 sq.

damage caused,[124] and thus it is not surprising to find Pufendorf granting an action in case of negligence and dolus: if the vendor knew or could have known that he was unable to honour his obligation, he has to compensate the purchaser for "id quod interest ne ita sibi illuderetur".[125] Nineteenth-century legal science rejected the generalized form of delictual liability developed by the natural lawyers and returned to the established principles of Aquilian liability.[126] Both Savigny and Mommsen therefore confined the purchaser's claim to dolus.[127] Culpa as such could not be recognized as an independent causa obligationis, whereas in case of fraud the actio doli was available. It was Rudolf von Jhering, with his famous "discovery" of culpa in contrahendo,[128] who opened up a new perspective. He argued that the vendor could be liable for (as he termed it) the negative interest in case of pre-contractual negligence. According to Jhering, this form of liability was contractual in nature, and it is therefore amusing to see that he bolstered up his theory by referring to rules such as § 284 I 5 PrALR,[129] emanations of the natural-law theories of *delictual* liability. § 307 BGB ("If a person, in concluding a contract, the performance of which is impossible, knew or should have known about the impossibility, he is obliged to compensate for any damage which the other party has sustained by relying upon the validity of the contract . . .") has essentially codified Jhering's view,[130] despite the fact that Windscheid[131] had gone even further and postulated the same *strict* form of liability that was eventually adopted in the parallel situation of invalidity due to error.[132]

9. §§ 306 sq. BGB: evaluation

This ultimately leaves us with the question whether the solution adopted by the BGB is not only theoretically and conceptually but also practically satisfactory. That question is usually answered in the negative. Ever since Ernst Rabel launched his spirited attack on §§ 306 sq. BGB,[133] these rules have been regarded as unsound and unfortunate.[134] Neither logic nor policy compels a legal system to

[124] Cf. infra, pp. 1032, 1033 sq.
[125] *De jure naturae et gentium*, Lib. III, Cap. VII, § 2; cf. also § 1295 ABGB.
[126] Cf. infra, pp. 1036 sqq.
[127] Cf. Savigny, *System*, vol. III, pp. 293 sqq.; F. Mommsen, *Unmöglichkeit*, pp. 107 sqq.
[128] Cf. supra, pp. 244 sq.
[129] Cf. supra, p. 245.
[130] Cf. also De Wet en Yeats, p. 78; Joubert, *Contract*, p. 128 for South African law.
[131] Cf. Windscheid/Kipp, § 315, n. 7; but cf. "Motive", in: *Mugdan*, vol. II, p. 98; "Protokolle", in: *Mugdan*, vol. II, pp. 615 sqq.
[132] § 122 BGB; cf. supra, p. 602.
[133] *Unmöglichkeit der Leistung* (1907) and *Über Unmöglichkeit der Leistung und heutige Praxis* (1911), both today in Ernst Rabel, *Gesammelte Aufsätze*, vol. I (1965), pp. 1 sqq., 56 sqq.
[134] Cf. e.g. Zweigert/Kötz, pp. 204 sqq.; Alfred Söllner, in: *Münchener Kommentar* (2nd ed., 1985), § 306, n. 3; Ulrich Huber, Leistungsstörungen, in: *Gutachten und Vorschläge zur*

declare contracts, the performance of which is impossible, as void. It is obvious, of course, that the impossible performance as such cannot be rendered; but there is nothing inherently illogical in making a person pay damages for failure to do what he has undertaken to do. A claim for merely the negative interest (as provided for in § 307) is often insufficient. A contract of sale, for instance, induces in the purchaser a reasonable[135] reliance that he will in due course receive the promised object; if performance turns out to have been impossible from the outset, he can therefore expect to be put in the position he would have been in had the contract been properly carried out (as opposed to the position he would have been in had he not relied upon the validity of the contract). Textbooks and commentaries are therefore full of exhortations to apply § 306 BGB restrictively and to try to avoid the harshness inherent in the unequivocal verdict of invalidity wherever possible. Occasionally, for instance, the undertaking of a specific guarantee is read into the contract, with the effect that the risk of initial impossibility of performance is shifted to the person who has promised such performance. This was the solution adopted in an oft-quoted decision[136] of the Regional Appeal Court of Hamburg.[137] Here, 1 000 boxes of new potatoes from the Canary Islands "aboard S.S. *Thekla Bohlen* afloat" had been sold. As it turned out, however, only 106 boxes had been loaded. We are dealing here with a case of initial objective impossibility, since the specific goods that had been sold did not in fact exist.[138] Nevertheless, the court did not regard the sale as

---

Überarbeitung des Schuldrechts, vol. I (1981), pp. 813 sqq.; for a vigorous countercriticism, see Arp, *Anfängliche Unmöglichkeit*, pp. 35 sqq. and passim.

[135] Such *reasonable* reliance is lacking in cases where the content of the contract is patently absurd, as, for instance, where the inevitable hippocentaurus is sold. In these cases (which tend to crop up in textbooks rather than in court decisions) invalidity is the appropriate answer of a legal system (Rabel, *Gesammelte Aufsätze*, p. 47, who refers to an "*Obligationshindernis der höheren Dummheit*"). Along these lines, for instance, the Indian Contract Act declared an agreement to discover treasure by magic to be void (cf. Pollock, *Principles of Contract* (7th ed., 1902), p. 402). Also § 878, 1 ABGB ("What is downright impossible [geradezu unmöglich], cannot be the object of a valid contract") is usually interpreted as covering only these types of cases; this interpretation goes back to Ernst Rabel ("Zur Lehre von der Unmöglichkeit der Leistung nach Österreichischem Recht (1911)", in: *Gesammelte Aufsätze*, vol. I, pp. 79 sqq.), but is in conflict with what the legislator intended to express with this rule (Wollschläger, *Unmöglichkeitslehre*, pp. 100 sq.). "Normal" objective initial impossiblility (i.e., for instance, the object to be sold perished before conclusion of the contract) does not affect the validity of the transaction (arg. § 923 ABGB); thus, the positive interest may be claimed.

[136] Cf. e.g. Rabel, *Gesammelte Aufsätze*, vol. I, p. 68; Arp, *Anfängliche Unmöglichkeit*, pp. 43 sqq., 167 sqq.

[137] (1910) 65 *Seufferts Archiv*, n. 160.

[138] In the case of generic obligations there is always merely subjective impossibility if the debtor does not possess any goods of the kind to be supplied (as long as goods of this kind still exist); cf. e.g. § 279 BGB ("If a debt described by class is owed, and so long as delivery of this class of object is possible, the debtor is responsible for his inability to deliver, even though no fault may be imputed to him"). In the present case, however, the debt was not described by class (1 000 boxes of new potatoes from the Canary Islands), but the 1 000 boxes aboard the *Thekla Bohlen* were owed.

void, but awarded damages for non-performance to the disappointed purchaser. Reason:

> ". . . in the sale of a cargo described as 'afloat' merchants take the contractual declaration of the vendor to be a warranty or the undertaking of a guarantee that the cargo has been loaded on the named vessel."[139]

In the end, therefore, the real question seems to be which of the contracting parties should carry the risk of the possibility of performance; and this question can often be answered by a proper construction of the contract.[140] English courts, unhampered by an "impossibilium nulla obligatio est" dogma, have often been able to achieve satisfactory results by looking to what the parties might have contemplated.[141] Apart from that, it is often stated that a contract may be void if both parties believe that the contract is capable of being performed when this is not the case.[142] The operative feature here, however, is common mistake, not initial impossibility per se.

III. ILLEGALITY

1. The possible effects of illegality

(a) Subdivision of statutes according to their sanctio

Illegality is the second of the general grounds of invalidity referred to above. Broadly speaking, it can be described as a situation where either the conclusion or the content of a contract infringes a statutory prohibition. Illegality and (initial) impossibility have often been put on a par. Grotius' statement that by natural law man cannot bind himself to things which are impossible or unpermitted[143] may serve as an example. Like impossibility, illegality in Roman law did, however, not always and necessarily render contractual transactions void. Whether or not an illegal transaction was effective depended, in the first place, on the sanctio of the statutory prohibition (a formal clause appended to the lex, in which, amongst other matters, the consequences of any infringement were determined);[144] otherwise the question was resolved by way of interpretation. Three different types of statutes were distinguished in this context: leges imperfectae, leges minus quam

---

139 Trans. Weir, in Zweigert/Kötz/Weir, p. 161.

140 But cf. Arp, *Anfängliche Unmöglichkeit*, pp. 155 sqq. (who, however, also advocates a restriction of § 306 BGB).

141 Cf. Zweigert/Kötz, p. 228 and *Couturier v. Hastie* (1856) 5 HLC 673, the leading case in this field of the law, which turned upon the construction of the contract. On this case, see P.S. Atiyah,"*Couturier v. Hastie* and the Sale of Non-Existent Goods", (1957) 73 *LQR* 340 sqq. (but see now Atiyah, *Essays*, p. 250). For South African law cf. Christie, *Contract*, p. 82.

142 e.g. Treitel, *Contract*, p. 214.

143 Cf. supra, p. 693 (note 116).

144 Carlo Gioffredi, "La 'sanctio' della legge e la 'perfectio' della norma giuridica", (1946) 2 *Archivio penale* 166 sqq., 174 sqq.; Jochen Bleicken, *Lex publica* (1975), pp. 217 sqq.

perfectae and leges perfectae.[145] Only acts performed in violation of leges perfectae were void. Leges minus quam perfectae threatened the violator with a penalty, but did not invalidate the act itself. Infringement of a lex imperfecta led neither to a penalty nor to invalidity.

(b) Leges minus quam perfectae

It is particularly the existence of the latter category that tends to surprise the modern observer. Was it at all sensible to enact leges imperfectae? What hope could a legislator realistically have that his directions would be followed if, essentially, they merely constituted an appeal to the good will of the people?[146] In order to answer these questions, we must first of all take account of the fact that the oldest lex perfecta of which we can be certain dates from 169 B.C.[147] In the early days of Roman law the validity of a transaction seems to have been judged only from the point of view of the required form. If the formalities were not complied with, the transaction was invariably and irremediably void; where, on the other hand, they had been observed, it was unquestionably valid. That statutory prohibitions could interfere with, and indeed completely invalidate, formal private acts was inconceivable to the lawyers and law-makers of the earlier Republic; it was an idea that required a refined capacity of abstraction and analysis.[148] Thus, before approximately the middle of the second century, the Roman legislator was forced, if he wished to strengthen the efficacy of a statute, to sanction its violation by the imposition of a penalty. And, indeed, statutory prohibitions in the form of leges minus quam perfectae were the rule during this period. The lex Furia testamentaria (fixing the maximum amount of a legacy that a person was allowed to receive at one thousand asses)[149] is one example;[150] the various attempts to fight the taking of excessive interest by fixing certain "ceiling-rates"[151] provide us with another. In both instances a person who had obtained more money than he was allowed to was liable to pay fourfold the value of the surplus (poena quadrupli). The lex Laetoria for the protection of minores viginti

[145] Cf. UE 1, 1 sq. (with additions by Cuiacius); also Macrobius, *In somnium Scipionis*, Lib. II, 17, 3 and Chorus, *Handelen*, pp. 24 sqq.

[146] Generally on the question of how effective Republican legislation was, cf. Bleicken, op. cit, note 144, pp. 217 sqq.

[147] It was the lex Voconia; cf. Kaser, *Verbotsgesetze*, pp. 20, 50 sqq.; Hans Ankum, "Verbotsgesetze und Ius Publicum", (1980) 97 *ZSS* 291; for a different view (lex Poetelia Papiria, 326 B.C.), see Fritz Sturm, (1982) 99 *ZSS* 432.

[148] Giovanni Rotondi, *Leges publicae populi Romani* (1912), pp. 155 sqq.; Kaser, *Verbotsgesetze*, pp. 16 sqq.; cf. also Wieacker, *RR*, pp. 286 sq.

[149] Certain close relatives were excepted.

[150] UE 1, 2. On the content and function of the lex Furia cf. Gai. II, 225; Uwe Wesel, "Über den Zusammenhang der lex Furia, Voconia und Falcidia", (1964) 81 *ZSS* 310 sqq.; Alan Watson, *The Law of Succession in the Later Roman Republic* (1971), pp. 163 sqq.; Kaser, *Verbotsgesetze*, pp. 33 sqq.

[151] Cf. supra, pp. 166 sqq.

quinque annis was probably originally minus quam perfecta too:[152] an actio poenalis could be brought against the person who had taken unfair advantage of the minor, but the transaction itself, according to the ius civile, was not invalid.

(c) Leges imperfectae

Leges imperfectae, even in the old days, were resorted to only in exceptional circumstances. Invalidity of the transaction was out of the question; but sometimes special policy considerations prompted the legislator not to impose a penalty either. The lex Cincia de donis et muneribus provides the best example of this strange kind of compromise. It prohibited donations exceeding a certain amount and was designed to prevent rich and influential members of the establishment from extracting excessive and not always voluntary "gifts" from (amongst others) their clientes.[153] On the other hand, however, one did not want to embarrass the leading circles of society by exposing them to court proceedings and the concomitant publicity.[154] Quieta non movere was the precept of the legislator, which was carried through even when it came to determining the legal consequences of an act infringing the provisions of the lex.[155] A donation exceeding the limit was not invalid, and hence there could be no (enrichment) claim against the recipient of the gift. Where, however, the donor had so far merely promised to make the prohibited donation, he could not be sued by the promisee either; for the praetor, in his decision whether or not to grant an action, had to be guided by the fact that the promise had been made in violation of a statutory prohibition (albeit an "imperfect" one). A praetor who would have allowed an action under these circumstances would himself have been guilty of a violation of the legal order.[156] Denegatio actionis was the appropriate course for him to take.[157] Under the more modern formulary procedure the exceptio legis Cinciae became the standard way of bringing the illegality to judicial cognizance. Taking ius civile and ius honorarium together, transactions violating the lex Cincia therefore enjoyed only a limited kind of validity. This demonstrates that even leges imperfectae were not totally devoid of legal consequences. Whilst they did not lead to invalidity iure civili, mechanisms on another (the praetorian) level of the legal system[158] were available to

[152] Kaser, *Verbotsgesetze*, pp. 39 sqq.; idem, *RPr* I, pp. 276 sq.; Hans-Georg Knothe, *Die Geschäftsfähigkeit der Minderjährigen in geschichtlicher Entwicklung* (1983), pp. 53 sqq. (57)
[153] Cf. supra, p. 483.
[154] Kaser, *Verbotsgesetze*, p. 26.
[155] For details cf. supra, pp. 483 sq.
[156] Kaser, *Verbotsgesetze*, pp. 27 sq.; Behrends, *Fraus legis*, pp. 23 sq.
[157] The same applies, of course, to leges minus quam perfectae.
[158] Cf. generally Kaser, (1984) 101 *ZSS* 1 sqq.; more specifically with regard to illegal transactions, see Behrends, *Fraus legis*, pp. 21 sqq.; Walter Selb, "Gedanken zur römischen

prevent frustration of the legislator's policy. The granting of an exceptio, in particular, could lead to entirely satisfactory results. Thus, for instance, two famous senatus consulta, the s.c. Macedonianum and the s.c. Vellaeanum, were imperfecta:[159] loans or security transactions contravening their provisions were not invalid, and in neither case did the creditor have to pay a penalty.[160] By availing themselves of the exceptiones senatus consulti Macedoniani or Vellaeani, (former) sons in power and women did, however, effectively have the opportunity of invalidating the transaction.[161]

(d) Leges perfectae

The senatus consultum Macedonianum (enacted under Emperor Vespasian) was the last statutory prohibition of which we know that could be described as imperfectum. Since the time of the later Republic, leges perfectae had come to be accepted as a more modern and effective way of implementing the intentions of the legislator.[162] Very soon they gained the ascendancy and it became more or less a matter of course that contracts infringing newly enacted prohibitions were invalid. Old leges imperfectae and minus quam perfectae remained in existence, but new ones were not added to their number. The leges Falcidia, Fufia Caninia, Aelia Sentia and Iulia de adulteriis were among the more important leges perfectae dating from the days of the late Republic and the early Principate. Post-classical legislation displayed an increasing tendency to interfere with the freedom of the individual and to regulate his private sphere. All statutory prohibitions were now invested with the sanction of invalidity; and as a result of this, the distinction between the three traditional categories fell away. These were the words of the Emperor Theodosius:[163]

> "[N]ullum . . . pactum, nullam conventionem, nullum contractum inter eos videri volumus subsecutum, qui contrahunt lege contrahere prohibente. Quod ad omnes etiam legum interpretationes tam veteres quam novellas trahi generaliter imperamus, ut legis latori, quod fieri non vult, tantum prohibuisse sufficiat, cetera quasi expressa ex legis liceat voluntate colligere: hoc est ut ea quae lege fieri prohibentur, si fuerint facta, non solum inutilia, sed pro infectis etiam habeantur, licet legis lator fieri prohibuerit tantum nec specialiter dixerit inutile esse debere quod factum est";

"lex imperfecta" und zu modernen Normvorstellungen in der Rechtsgeschichte", in: *Festschrift für Heinz Hübner* (1984), pp. 253 sqq.

[159] Though not, of course, leges in the narrow, technical sense.

[160] Cf. supra, pp. 145, 177 and A. Arthur Schiller, "Senatus Consulta in the Principate", (1958–59) 33 *Tulane LR* 500 sq.

[161] Cf. e.g. Chorus, *Handelen*, pp. 35 sqq., who emphasizes that the difference between leges perfectae and imperfectae was of less practical consequence than might appear at first blush; further cf. Selb, *Festschrift Hübner*, pp. 253 sqq.

[162] For details, see Kaser, *Verbotsgesetze*, pp. 50 sqq., 62 sqq.

[163] *Nov. Theod.* 9 (dated 7th April 439); on this novella (the "Lex non dubium"), see Friedrich Endemann, *Über die civilrechtliche Wirkung der Verbotsgesetze nach gemeinem Rechte* (1887), pp. 24 sqq.; Chorus, *Handelen*, pp. 42 sqq.

whether or not they contained a special provision declaring the prohibited transaction invalid, all statutory prohibitions from now on had the status of a lex perfecta. Not even confirmation of the prohibited transaction by way of oath could change the situation.[164]

(e) The lex Non dubium and § 134 BGB

As part and parcel of the Corpus Juris,[165] Theodosius' regulation became the basis of the ius commune.[166] Throughout the centuries it has been emphasized that illegal transactions are invalid and without effect.[167] Only comparatively recently has there been a return to a greater degree of flexibility. Thus, § 134 BGB still provides that legal transactions which violate a statutory prohibition are void, but adds the rider: "unless a contrary intention appears from the statute."[168] What matters, therefore, is, once again, the sanctio (as the Romans would have called it) of the law itself; if it does not contain a special provision determining the consequences of its violation, the question has to be decided in accordance with the spirit and the purpose of the law, that is, by a proper construction of the statutory prohibition. There is a general presumption in favour of invalidity,[169] but this presumption is rebuttable. A contract of sale concluded in violation of the German Shop Closing Act,[170] for instance, is usually not regarded as invalid. The content of the transaction being entirely unobjectionable, invalidity of individual contracts can hardly be said to be a suitable means of enhancing the protection of sales personnel from working outside working hours.[171] It is even argued today that § 134 BGB does

---

[164] "Secundum praedictam itaque regulam, quam ubique servari factum lege prohibente censuimus, certum est nec stipulationem eiusmodi tenere . . . nec sacramentum admitti." This provision caused the medieval lawyers much headache, particularly in view of the fact that breach of a promissory oath entailed the sin of periurium. For details, see Chorus, *Handelen*, pp. 213 sqq.

[165] C. 1, 14, 5.

[166] For details, see Chorus, *Handelen*, pp. 177 sqq.; Endemann, op. cit., note 163, pp. 29 sqq., 41 sqq.; Coing, pp. 414 sq.

[167] According to Zweigert/Kötz, p. 73, in all systems of the world illegality is seen as a fact which invalidates contracts. For a comparative analysis of what makes a contract illegal, see Zweigert/Kötz, pp. 74 sqq.; for South Africa cf. Leon E. Trakman, "The Effect of Illegality in South African Law", (1977) 94 *SALJ* 327 sqq., 468 sqq. and Joubert, *Contract*, pp. 129 sqq.

[168] On the history and application of § 134 BGB cf. Hans Hermann Seiler, "Über verbotswidrige Rechtsgeschäfte (§ 134 BGB)", in: *Gedächtnisschrift für Wolfgang Martens* (1987), pp. 719 sqq. Article. 1131 code civil (relating to "*l'obligation . . . sur une cause illicite*"; cf. also art. 1133 defining what "*illicite*" means); § 879 ABGB and art. 20 I OR do not contain this kind of clause.

[169] Cf. e.g. Theo Mayer-Maly, in: *Münchener Kommentar*, vol. I (2nd ed., 1984), § 134, n. 1; contra: Flume, *AT*, § 17, 1.

[170] Gesetz über den Ladenschluss, 28. 11. 1956.

[171] Dieter Medicus, *Allgemeiner Teil des BGB* (2nd ed., 1985), nn. 648 sqq. Seiler, *Gedächtnisschrift Martens*, pp. 719 sqq. demonstrates that the courts have arrogated to themselves a far-ranging discretion to decide about the invalidity or otherwise of transactions violating statutory prohibitions. Their decisions are hardly predictable, and legal certainty is most detrimentally affected; cf. also already Endemann, op. cit., note 163,

not confine the judge to the alternative of all or nothing (i.e. contract either valid or invalid), but opens up the possibility of upholding the contract in a modified form.[172]

2. Transactions in fraudem legis

(a) *In fraudem legis agere*

Codex 1, 14, 5, Theodosius' Lex non dubium, had dealt with and, as far as the ius commune was concerned, conclusively settled, another problem connected with statutory prohibitions. "Non dubium est", the Emperor had asserted, "in legem committere eum qui verba legis amplexus contra legis nititur voluntatem: nec poenas insertas legibus evitabit, qui se contra iuris sententiam scaeva praerogativa verborum fraudulenter excusat."[173] The type of behaviour described in this paragraph was known as agere in fraudem legis: conclusion of a transaction which, whilst respecting the words of a specific statute, was designed[174] to thwart its purpose. The Digest contains the following elegant definition taken from a work of Paulus: "Contra legem facit, qui id facit quod lex prohibet, in fraudem vero, qui salvis verbis legis sententiam eius circumvenit";[175] and Ulpian put it equally succinctly when he stated that fraud in respect of the statute is practised when something is done which the statute does not wish anybody to do, yet which it has failed expressly to prohibit.[176] According to C. 1, 14, 5, such fraus legi facta was taken to be a violation of the statute and therefore led to invalidity.[177] This had not always been the case, though. Pre-classical jurisprudence was characterized, as we have

---

p. 125. More and more statutory prohibitions are issued by the modern legislator without any indication in their "sanctio" as to the fate of transactions infringing the prohibition. According to Seiler, invalidity should be restricted to cases where the illegality is grave and obvious, particularly where the core areas of criminal law are affected; § 134 BGB should not be (ab)used to transform ephemeral considerations of economic expediency into private law (p. 731). This would, in fact, entail a renaissance of the category of leges minus quam perfectae. For the development of English law in this regard, see Routledge, in: *La formazione storica*, vol. III, pp. 1254 sqq.

[172] Mayer-Maly, op. cit., note 31, § 134, n. 88; contra: Zimmermann, *Moderationsrecht*, pp. 113 sqq.

[173] C. 1, 14, 5 pr.

[174] On the importance of the subjective element (the intention to act against the spirit of the law—*Umgehungsabsicht*), see Giovanni Rotondi, *Gli atti in frodde alla legge nella dottrina romana e nella sua evoluzione posteriore* (1911), pp. 145 sqq.; Heinrich Honsell, "In fraudem legis agere", in: *Festschrift für Max Kaser* (1976), pp. 112, 124 sqq.; Behrends, *Fraus legis*, pp. 15 sq. On the meaning of the term "fraus" in "fraus legi facta", cf. also Ivo Pfaff, *Zur Lehre vom sogenannten in fraudem legis agere* (1892), pp. 62 sqq.; Rotondi, pp. 11 sqq.; Hugo Krüger/Max Kaser, Fraus, (1943) 63 *ZSS* 140 sqq.

[175] D. 1, 3, 29.

[176] D. 1, 3, 30: "Fraus enim legi fit, ubi quod fieri noluit, fieri autem non vetuit, id fit."

[177] On fraus legi facta in the history of the ius commune, see Pfaff, op. cit., note 174, pp. 20 sqq.; Rotondi, op. cit., note 174, pp. 160 sqq.; Helmut Coing, "Simulatio und fraus in der Lehre des Bartolus und Baldus", in: *Festschrift für Paul Koschaker*, vol. III (1939), pp. 402 sqq. For South Africa cf. *Dadoo Ltd. v. Krugersdorp Municipal Council* 1920 AD 530 at 543; Aquilius, "Immorality and Illegality in Contract", (1942) 59 *SALJ* 333 sqq.

repeatedly stressed,[178] by a strictly formalistic approach. Republican law-makers tried to provide, with cautious, unabstract and clumsy punctiliousness, for all kinds of eventualities:[179] where they wanted their law to apply to slaves or children of both sexes they had to be explicit ("servus serva"; "filius filia"), the lex Aquilia described the action of the wrongdoer in no less than three different verbs ("urere, frangere, rumpere"),[180] the prohibition against burying the dead with golden presents or ornaments (expressed in the words "neve aurum addito") would have covered gold fillings in the teeth, had a specific exception not been provided for.[181]

(b) *Republican jurisprudence*

The last example shows how closely legal drafting and techniques of interpretation are interrelated. To some degree both cause and consequence of this meticulous and formalistic attention to detail was a considerable rigidity in the interpretation of statutes: the literal meaning of the words used was the one and only decisive criterion. The average Republican lawyer was often criticized for his somewhat uninspiring narrowness; Cicero described him scathingly as "leguleius quidam cautus et acutus, praeco actionum, cantor formularum, auceps syllabarum".[182] Obviously, this kind of inflexibility lent itself to abuse and encouraged ingenious businessmen to find ways and means of achieving their ends without violating the letter of the law.[183] The number of devices used to get around the usury laws must have been legion: "Multisque plebis citis obviam itum fraudibus, quae, totiens repressae, miras per artes rursum oriebantur" comments Tacitus, half admiringly.[184] The leges Furia, Voconia and Falcidia,[185] the lex Cincia,[186] the leges sumptuariae:[187] no statute was impervious to

[178] Cf., e.g., supra, pp. 622 sq.

[179] For details, see Jhering, *Geist*, vol. II, 2, pp. 441 sqq.; Wieacker, *Vom römischen Recht*, pp. 45 sqq.; and, most recently, Heinrich Honsell, "Das Gesetzesverständnis in der römischen Antike", in: *Europäisches Rechtsdenken in Geschichte und Gegenwart, Festschrift für Helmut Coing*, vol. I (1982), pp. 129 sqq.

[180] Cf. infra, pp. 953, 983 sqq.

[181] Cf. Honsell, *Festschrift Coing*, p. 140.

[182] *De oratore* 1, LV—236; cf. further e.g. *Pro L. Murena oratio*, X—23 sqq. (the lawyer's arguments are "res parvae", "prope in singulis litteris atque interpunctionibus verborum occupatae"); *De officiis*, 1, X—33 ("nimis callida sed malitiosa iures interpretatio"); and see the literature quoted supra, p. 623, note 11.

[183] Jhering, *Geist*, vol. II, 2, pp. 467 sqq.; Pfaff, op. cit., note 174, pp. 7 sqq.; Honsell, *Festschrift Kaser*, pp. 115 sqq.

[184] *Annales*, Lib. VI, 16, 2; cf. further Pfaff, op. cit., note 174, pp. 149 sqq. In the Middle Ages, too, it was particularly the prohibition of usury which was circumvented time and again, and by way of a great variety of more or less subtle subterfuges; cf. supra, pp. 171 sq.

[185] All three of them imposing limits on the amounts of legacies. On fraus legis and the lex Voconia, see Pfaff, op. cit., note 174, pp. 114 sqq.

[186] On fraus legis and the lex Cincia, see Behrends, *Fraus legis*, pp. 19 sqq.

[187] Bleicken, op. cit., note 144, pp. 169 sqq.

attempts to circumvent it.[188] Even Marcus Porcius Cato (Censorius), that paragon of Republican uprightness, acted in fraudem legis when he conducted his maritime trade via a middleman by the name of Quinctius (one of his liberti),[189] since the lex Claudia de nave senatorum[190] had excluded Senators from this form of business activity. All these acts, although contrary to the spirit of the law, did not directly violate it and were therefore not affected by its sanctio. Only the legislator himself was able to address the problem by amending the statute that was circumvented.[191] Sometimes he tried to prevent such circumvention by including a general prohibition of fraus legi facta in the wording of the lex. In a similar vein the praetor promised:

> "Pacta conventa, quae neque dolo malo, neque adversus leges plebis scita senatus consulta decreta edicta principum, *neque quo fraus cui eorum fiat*, facta erunt, servabo."[192]

(c) *Scire leges non est verba earum tenere . . .*

All this changed only gradually during the late Republic and the Principate. Under the influence of Hellenistic philosophy and rhetoric a more liberal approach to interpretation gained ground—with regard to statutes as much as in relation to wills and contracts.[193] In the wake of the rhetorical antithesis between verba and voluntas, or scriptum and sententia, the intention of the statute, its purpose and its spirit became an acceptable criterion within the process of construction. One realized

---

[188] For details, see Pfaff, op. cit., note 174, pp. 104 sqq., 136 sqq.; Rotondi, op. cit., note 174, pp. 38 sqq.

[189] Plutarch, *Vitae*, Cato maior, 21, 5 sq.

[190] Berger, *ED*, p. 549.

[191] Cf. e.g. Gai. I, 46. This is, incidentally, still the attitude in England. A doctrine of evasion of the law has never been developed, not because English statutes are never evaded but because the common law is much less concerned with the law's authority than Continental legal systems. Statutes traditionally tend to be regarded as rather irritating encroachments on the common law, and they are strictly (literally) applied (and, therefore, have to be drafted with clumsy punctiliousness; cf. supra, p. 623). If there are any loopholes, it is up to the legislator and not to the courts to fill them. Cf. Ronald H. Graveson, "The Doctrine of Evasion of the Law of England and America", (1937) 19 *Journal of Comparative Legislation* 21 sqq. and the analysis by Klaus Schurig, "Die Gesetzesumgehung im Privatrecht", in: *Festschrift für Murad Ferid* (1988), pp. 392 sqq.

[192] Ulp. D. 2, 14, 7, 7. On fraus legis and the edictum de pactis cf., most recently, Behrends, *Fraus legis*, pp. 29 sqq.

[193] Cf. supra, pp. 625 sqq. For a totally different view of the development, see Behrends, *Fraus legis*, pp. 33 sqq., 39 sqq., 61 sqq. He argues that a more liberal, intention-oriented method of interpretation (advocated by the veteres of the 2nd century B.C.) was superseded, towards the end of the Republic, by a strictly literal, word-oriented approach (introduced by G. Aquilius Gallus and his pupil, Servius Sulpicius). Because of this narrower attitude towards statute interpretation, it became necessary to develop the doctrine of fraus legi facta to cover situations where not the wording but the intention of the statute had been violated. Behrends' thesis is based mainly on the somewhat shaky evidence of Cicero, *Pro A. Caecina oratio*, XVIII—78 sqq. and Cicero, *De oratore*. Contra Behrends, see Heinrich Honsell, (1985) 102 *ZSS* 573 sqq.; on the pro Caecina cf. Frier, *Roman Jurists*, passim, who provides quite a different interpretation from the one advanced by Behrends (cf. e.g. p. 151: "In sum, the argument at Caec. 79–85 is not serious").

that it was not possible (or even desirable)[194] for every detail to be specifically dealt with in leges or in any other form of legislation;[195] hence:

> ". . . cum in aliqua causa sententia eorum manifesta est, is qui iurisdictioni praeest ad similia procedere atque ita ius dicere debet."[196]

The new attitude was summed up particularly crisply by Celsus: "Scire leges non hoc est verba earum tenere, sed vim ac potestatem":[197] knowing laws (and, we may add, interpreting them) is not a matter of sticking to their words, but of grasping their force and tendency.[198] As a result of this purposive (or teleological)[199] approach, agere in fraudem legis came to be equated with agere contra legem: transactions which were contrary to the spirit of the law were just as much a violation of it as those that contravened its words. Thus, for instance, the senatus consultum Macedonianum was applied to a loan of corn or wine which the son in power was supposed to sell in order to be able to use the proceeds,[200] even though the words of the law merely referred to "mutua pecunia".[201] Likewise, the exceptio senatus consulti Vellaeani could be invoked if the parties had attempted to evade its provisions by way of a persona interposita: a man standing surety in the place and on behalf of the woman, who was prohibited by the senatus consultum from "pro aliis rea fieri".[202] The latter example, incidentally, shows us that the transaction in fraudem legis was not necessarily invalid. It was subject to the sanction of the statutory prohibition and was therefore treated in the same way as if the parties had agreed to what the law forbade directly and expressis verbis. Only when all statutory prohibitions had become leges perfectae[203] did agere in fraudem legis necessarily entail invalidity too. Today, again, it is the sanction of the law meant to be evaded that determines the fate of the transaction in fraudem legis ("*Umgehungsgeschäft*"); its applicability is widely regarded merely as a matter of the proper (purposive) construction of that law.[204]

---

[194] Cf. Pomp. D. 1, 3, 3: "Iura constitui oportet, ut dixit Theophrastus, in his, quae ἐπὶ τὸ πλεῖστον accidunt, non quae ἐκ παραλόγου"; Paul. D. 1, 3, 6.

[195] Iul. D. 1, 3, 12: "Non possunt omnes articuli singillatim aut legibus aut senatus consulti comprehendi. . . ."

[196] Iul. D. 1, 3, 12.

[197] D. 1, 3, 17.

[198] Trans. D.N. MacCormick, in: Mommsen/Krüger/Watson.

[199] Cf. supra, p. 148, note 214.

[200] Ulp. D. 14, 6, 7, 3.

[201] Ulp. D. 14, 6, 1 pr., for further details cf. supra, pp. 177, 181.

[202] Cf. Pomp. D. 16, 1, 32, 3; Ulp. D. 16, 1, 8, 4; Ulp. D. 16, 1, 8, 6; further Dieter Medicus, *Zur Geschichte des Senatus Consultum Velleianum* (1957), pp. 123 sqq. Acting through a persona interposita was a popular device, used in order to circumvent a statute; cf. e.g. Honsell, *Festschrift Kaser*, p. 124 and Proculus' categorical statement (D. 50, 8, 2, 1): "Quod quis suo nomine exercere prohibetur, id nec per subiecatam personam agere debet."

[203] Cf. supra, pp. 700 sq.

[204] Cf. e.g. Regelsberger, *Pandekten*, pp. 146 sq., 153; Vangerow, *Pandekten*, vol. I, § 24 (sub. 3 c); "Protokolle", in: *Mugdan*, vol. I, p. 725 (providing the motivation for the fact that the BGB (§ 134) does not contain a special rule dealing with the problem of fraus legi facta);

IV. IMMORALITY

1. Freedom of contract and extra-legal standards

In all modern legal systems the freedom of the parties to determine the content of their transaction is limited not only by statutory prohibitions but also by certain extra-legal standards.[205] If a contract is at variance with the sense of decency of all just and fair-thinking people,[206] if it carries a visible stamp of eccentricity[207] so as to scandalize the reasonable man, it cannot possibly be upheld. If it were upheld and if the courts were seen to assist the parties in its enforcement, the general esteem of the law would be detrimentally affected. All the great European codifications therefore contain a general clause declaring immoral contracts and/or those that offend against public policy null and void. These clauses go back, ultimately, to the suppression of transactions "contra bonos mores" by the Roman jurists and Emperors.

In primitive communities, religion, law and morals are usually inextricably interwoven.[208] The Ten Commandments, for instance, represent a motley collection of religious duties ("I am the Lord thy God: Thou shalt have none other Gods but me"), moral precepts ("Honour thy father and thy mother . . .") and legal rules ("Thou shalt not steal"). The disentanglement of these ideas belongs to the later and

---

Flume, *AT*, § 17, 5; Ernst Kramer, in: *Münchener Kommentar*, vol. I (2nd ed., 1984), § 117, n. 15; Behrends, *Fraus legis*, pp. 9 sqq., Schurig, *Festschrift Ferid*, pp. 375 sqq., 398 sqq.; and especially Arndt Teichmann, *Die Gesetzesumgehung* (1962), passim. Contra (a special doctrine of fraus legi facta outside the usual canons of interpretation is necessary) Mayer-Maly, op. cit., note 31, § 134, nn. 11 sqq.; cf. also, as far as Roman law is concerned, Honsell, *Festschrift Kaser*, pp. 122 sqq.; Behrends, Fraus legis, pp. 15 sq. and passim.

The more modern history has recently been analysed by Jan Schröder, *Gesetzesauslegung und Gesetzesumgehung* (1985), pp. 15 sqq. He demonstrates how closely, historically, the problem of fraus legi facta and the approach to the interpretation of statutes are interrelated. Until about the middle of the 19th century, a very restrictive view prevailed as to the question of statute interpretation; the judge was taken to be bound strictly to the words of the law (he was, in the words of Montesquieu, "*la bouche de la loi*"). As a result, recognition of a specific doctrine of fraus legis became necessary (unless one was still prepared to deal with the problem s.v. simulatio, cf. supra, pp. 648 sqq.). The change occurred in the course of the second half of the 19th century (Schröder, pp. 32 sqq.): recognition of the so-called "objective" theory of statutory interpretation made the doctrine of fraus legis redundant. The background for this change of approach is analysed in detail by Schröder, pp. 48 sqq.

For a modern comparative analysis, see Schurig, *Festschrift Ferid*, pp. 379 sqq. (Germany, Austria, Switzerland), pp. 387 sqq. (France) and pp. 392 sqq. (England—where, interestingly, the doctrine "is completely rejected, and life, none the less, goes on").

[205] For a comparative overview, see Zweigert/Kötz, pp. 72 sqq.; for South African law Joubert, *Contract*, pp. 132 sqq.

[206] This is the prevailing definition of the boni mores since the days of RGZ 48, 114 (124); 55, 367 (373); 79, 415 (418) (cf. also "Motive", in: *Mugdan*, vol. II, p. 406) in German law. For details see Helmut Haberstumpf, *Die Formel vom Anstandsgefühl aller billig und gerecht Denkenden in der Rechtsprechung des Bundesgerichtshofs* (1976); cf. also Mayer-Maly, op. cit., note 31, § 138, nn. 12 sq.

[207] Cf. John P. Dawson, "Unconscionable Coercion: The German Version", (1976) 89 *Harvard LR* 1063.

[208] Cf. e.g. Alfred Lord Denning, *The Changing Law* (1953), pp. 99 sqq.

more refined stages of mental progress. It is a sign of the specific legal genius of the Romans that they achieved this severance at a very early stage.[209] Supervision and enforcement of the public morals was entrusted to the censor[210] and thus separated from the civil (legal) jurisdiction, for which a different magistrate, the praetor, was responsible. By about the 1st century A.D., however, the specific censorial cura morum had lost its significance; from this time on the emperors felt responsible to see to it that the customary precepts of good and honest behaviour were respected and adhered to.

2. References to the boni mores in classical law

It is in line with these general observations that only in a few types of situation did the Roman lawyers have recourse to the standard of the boni mores.[211] One of these was the limitation of the freedom of legal transactions. But our sources do not take us back beyond the 2nd century A.D. Two texts by Gaius and by Julianus are our earliest testimonies to the consequences of an infringement of the boni mores by the contracting parties. "Illud constat", asserts Gaius,[212] "si quis de ea re mandet quae contra bonos mores est, non contrahi obligationem, veluti si tibi mandem ut Titio furtum aut iniuriam facias": no obligation is created if a morally objectionable mandate is given. Two examples are provided: the mandator charges the mandatarius with stealing something from Titius or with insulting him. We are dealing with a transaction involving a prohibited kind of behaviour. Theft and iniuria were strongly disapproved of: so much so that conviction entailed infamia.[213] But, of course, they were general forms of delict, not specific statutory prohibitions of the kind discussed above. Transactions referring to the commission (or omission) of such a delict or of criminal offences (such as homicidium, sacrilegium, stuprum, adulterium or lenocinium)[214] could therefore not be evaluated from the point of view of the lex perfecta/minus quam perfecta/imperfecta scheme, but had to be invalidated under different auspices: hence the reference to

---

[209] Schulz, *Principles*, pp. 19 sqq., who deals with this characteristic trait of Roman law under the heading "isolation"; cf. also, more recently, Joseph Plescia, "The Development of the Doctrine of Boni Mores in Roman Law", (1987) 34 *RIDA* 275 sqq..

[210] On his functions cf. e.g. Mommsen, *Staatsrecht*, vol. II, 1, pp. 331 sqq.; H. Hausmaninger, in: *Kleiner Pauly*, vol. I, col. 1107 sq.; Max Kaser, "Rechtswidrigkeit und Sittenwidrigkeit im klassischen römischen Recht", (1940) 60 *ZSS* 97 sqq.

[211] They are analysed by Theo Mayer-Maly, "Contra bonos mores", in: *Iuris Professio, Festgabe für Max Kaser* (1986), pp. 151 sqq.; cf. also by the same author, "The boni mores in historical perspective", (1987) 50 *THRHR* 60 sqq.; cf. also Plescia, (1987) 34 *RIDA* 275 sqq., 286 sqq.

[212] Gai. III, 157; cf. further Vincenzio Arangio-Ruiz, *Il mandato in diritto romano* (1949), pp. 105 sqq.; Watson, *Mandate*, p. 88.

[213] Cf. infra, pp. 933, 1062.

[214] The latter three (illicit intercourse with unmarried women of honourable social condition—stuprum—or with married women—adulterium—and pandering—lenocinium) were criminalized by the lex Iulia de adulteriis (18 B.C.); for details, see Mommsen, *Strafrecht*, pp. 688 sqq., 699 sqq.; cf. also Plescia, (1987) 34 *RIDA* 301 sqq.

the boni mores. Such transactions, although not specifically prohibited, were turpis and could therefore not be tolerated by the legal system.[215] This, of course, applied not only to mandates but to the other types of contract too. As far as stipulations were concerned, we find a clear statement to that effect in D. 45, 1, 26 and 27 pr.:

> "Generaliter novimus turpes stipulationes nullius esse momenti: veluti si quis homicidium vel sacrilegium se facturum promittat."[216]

A stipulation, quite openly obliging somebody to commit a murder, or to steal an object used for divine service: these must have been mere textbook examples. Of greater practical relevance was the type of situation dealt with by Iulianus:

> "Stipulatio hoc modo concepta: 'si heredem me non feceris, tantum dare spondes?' inutilis est, quia contra bonos mores est haec stipulatio."[217]

Ambulatoria est voluntas defuncti usque ad vitae supremum exitum:[218] up until the last moment of his life a testator has to be perfectly free to make up his mind as to his dispositions mortis causa, and every kind of commitment undertaken by the testator during his lifetime to dispose of his property in a specific way was therefore frowned upon. Hence the impropriety of the promise of a penalty for failing to institute a particular person as heir. The stipulation was invalid, and the unwritten standards of evaluation leading to this result were again summed up in the words "contra bonos mores".[219] It should be noted, incidentally, that the whole stipulation was regarded as invalid, not only its objectionable part. Strictly speaking, the infringement of the mos maiorum was confined to the condition ("si heredem me non feceris"); a promise of "tantum dare spondes" as such would have been quite in order. Utile per inutile non vitiatur? According to that rule, one could have been tempted to uphold the promise unconditionally. But we have already seen that the Roman lawyers did not subscribe to such a mechanical "blue pencil" approach.[220] The condition forms the basis upon which the remainder of the transaction depends. The promisor never contemplated paying, and the stipulator could never reasonably expect to receive, a sum of money straightaway. As a rule, it was therefore recognized that where a condition was invalid, the contingent part of the transaction fell away too. An exception was, however, made in cases of testamentary dispositions:

> ". . . legatum sub impossibili [and, we may add: turpi] condicione relictum . . . proinde deberi . . . ac si sine condicione relictum esset."[221]

---

215 For a detailed discussion, see Kaser, *Verbotsgesetze*, pp. 69 sqq.
216 Cf. also *Inst.* III, 19, 24.
217 D. 45, 1, 61.
218 Ulp. D. 34, 4, 4 in fine.
219 Cf. also C. 8, 38, 4 (Diocl.).
220 Supra, pp. 75 sqq.
221 Gai. III, 98; cf. Jens Peter Meincke, "Die Scheidungsklausel im Testament", in: *Festschrift für Max Kaser* (1976), pp. 451 sqq.; Kaser, *Verbotsgesetze*, pp. 103 sqq.

It was based on the favor testamenti.[222]

3. Conditions contra bonos mores and late classical jurisprudence

Quite a variety of texts deal with conditions that were denounced as being contra bonos mores. Paulus. D. 28, 7, 9 reflects the position in late classical law when he states quite generally:

> "Condiciones, quae contra bonos mores inseruntur, remittendae sunt, veluti 'si ab hostibus patrem suum non redemerit', 'si parentibus suis patronove alimenta non praestituit'."[223]

Both examples are concerned with an unacceptable lack of reverentia:[224] a legal system can hardly condone a condition not to redeem one's father from captivity or not to provide maintenance for patrons or parents. Other cases handed down to us in our sources refer to infringements of the freedom of (prospective) family relations ("si uxorem non duxeris", "si filius non susceperis"), to an incitement to commit atrocities ("si homicidium feceris") or to an objectionable disregard for decent and dignified behaviour ("si larvali habitu processeris").[225]

These texts have taken us to the late classical period, during which we see an increased interest in the legal relevance of the boni mores. Papinian in particular contributed substantially to the debate.[226] One of the texts ascribed to him is D. 28, 7, 15; it equates the immoral with the impossible (". . . nam quae facta . . . contra bonos mores fiunt, nec facere nos posse credendum est") and was to emerge as one of the focal points for the discussion of illegal and immoral conditions among the authors of the ius commune.[227] Thematically, a shift of emphasis in the suppression of immoral transactions is recognizable from the time of the Severan Emperors: pacta (rather than contracts) contra bonos mores became the centre of attention.[228] A whole string of statements, usually very generally phrased, has come down to us: "Pacta, quae contra leges constitutionesque vel contra bonos mores fiunt, nullam vim habere

---

[222] Cf. infra, pp. 720 sq.

[223] Paul. D. 28, 7, 9.

[224] On reverentia and boni mores cf. also Ulp. D. 44, 4, 4, 16.

[225] Paul. Sent. III, IV b, 2; on the latter example cf. Mayer-Maly, *Festgabe Kaser*, p. 165. On condiciones contra bonos mores contained in stipulations, see Kaser, *Verbotsgesetze*, pp. 88 sqq.

[226] Attention has been drawn to this point by Mayer-Maly, *Festgabe Kaser*, pp. 154, 160 sqq.; cf. also Mayer-Maly, (1987) 50 *THRHR* 71 sqq.

[227] Cf. Helmut Schmidt, *Die Lehre von der Sittenwidrigkeit der Rechtsgeschäfte in historischer Sicht* (1973), pp. 19, 21, 43, 60, 73, 104 sq. Cf. also still Wessels, *Contract*, §§ 459 sqq., who discusses illegal contracts under the heading "Contracts impossible by law"; Lee, *Introduction*, p. 232 ("Unlawful contracts are regarded by Roman law as civilly impossible").

[228] The most likely reason for this is that agreements contra bonos mores could probably frequently not be classified as one of the recognized types of contract: cf. Honsell, *Rückabwicklung*, pp. 77 sqq.

indubitati iuris est",[229] "Pacta vel conditiones contra leges vel decreta principum vel bonos mores nullius sunt momenti",[230] to mention two examples.[231] Characteristically, the boni mores appear in both of them as part and parcel of a catalogue of legal sources; by the end of the 3rd century A.D. they thus seem to have been perceived as a normative system equal to the ius.[232]

4. The effects of immorality

It is obvious that pacta contra bonos mores were invalid. The same applied to contracts with iudicia bonae fidei; what is against the boni mores cannot be claimed ex bona fide: "Generaliter observari convenit bonae fidei iudicium non recipere praestationem, quae contra bonos mores desideretur."[233] Stipulations, too, were ipso iure null and void, if the immorality was apparent from the wording of the formal promise. "Quod turpi ex causa promissum est, veluti si quis homicidium vel sacrilegium se facturum promittat, non valet",[234] provided, we must add, that the stipulation was causally drafted.[235] The situation was different where the stipulation was based on an immoral causa but had been framed abstractly, so that the content of the promise as such was not objectionable. Here the praetor had to come to the promisor's rescue, which he usually did by way of granting the exceptio doli. This is what happened, most probably, in a *cause célèbre* concerning the orator Gaius Visellius Varro, a cousin of Cicero.[236] Dangerously ill and expecting to die, Visellius had decided to leave a sum of 300 000 sesterces to his lover,[237] a woman by the name of Otacilia Laterensis. To effect this gift, he chose the form not of a will but of an (abstractly drafted) stipulation. "Trecenta milia sestertium te mihi dari oportere?" was what Otacilia was invited to ask, and Visellius replied with "Spondeo". That the sum was intended to be a donatio mortis causa in disguise and that it was based on a morally objectionable causa was not apparent from these words. When, to Otacilia's chagrin, Visellius recovered, she sued him for the money.

---

[229] C. 2, 3, 6 (Ant.).

[230] Consultatio veteris cuiusdam iurisconsulti, IV, 8.

[231] For a more extensive list, see Mayer-Maly, (1987) 50 *THRHR* 68.

[232] Mayer-Maly, (1987) 50 *THRHR* 70 sq.

[233] Pap. D. 22, 1, 5. On mandatum cf. supra, p. 421; as far as societas is concerned cf. e.g. Ulp. D. 17, 2, 53 and Vincenzo Arangio-Ruiz, *La società in diritto romano* (1960), pp. 116 sqq.; Antonio Guarino, *Societas consensu contracta* (1972), pp. 65 sqq.

[234] *Inst.* III, 19, 24; Kaser, *Verbotsgesetze*, pp. 76 sqq.

[235] For the difference between causally and abstractly drafted stipulations in general cf. supra, pp. 91 sq.

[236] Valerius Maximus, *Facta et dicta memorabilia*, Lib. XVIII, Cap. II, § 2. On this case, see Ulrich von Lübtow, "Die Ursprungsgeschichte der exceptio doli und der actio de dolo malo", in: *Eranion Maridakis*, vol. I (1963), pp. 196 sqq.; Watson, *Obligations*, pp. 32 sqq.; Massimo Brutti, *La problematica del dolo processuale nell'esperienza romana* (1973), pp. 219 sqq.; Kaser, *Verbotsgesetze*, pp. 80 sqq.; Geoffrey MacCormack, "'Dolus' in Republican Law", (1985) 88 *BIDR* 19 sqq.

[237] ". . . cum qua commercium libidinis habuerat. . . ."

Gaius Aquilius Gallus dismissed the claim, and as a "vir magnae auctoritatis et scientia iuris civilis excellens",[238] furthermore as father of the remedies concerning dolus[239] he could hardly have done so, had the programme of litigation not empowered him, by virtue of an exceptio doli, to go into the somewhat sordid background of the case.[240] It has even been suggested that this was the first time the new "neque fiat" clause was applied in practice.[241] Alternatively, it is perhaps not unthinkable that this was such a famous case (we hear that the principes civitatis were consulted in the matter) that it in turn inspired the introduction of either the exceptio doli or the "neque fiat" clause.[242] .

5. The content of the boni mores

Ultimately, then, the crucial question: what were the boni mores? No definition is contained in our sources. We have referred to Papinian's interest in attempting to grasp the importance of the boni mores for legal transactions, and it was he who probably came closest to revealing what the Roman lawyers meant when they used this general phrase. Contra bonos mores, he wrote, are acts which offend "pietatem existimationem verecundiam nostram".[243] The sense of duty and the natural affection towards gods, parents or near relatives, the respect or esteem enjoyed by a person in society and the innate sense of shame: these are the types of values which had from ancient times held together the community at large, and which in their entirety constituted the unquestioned and self-evident core of the boni mores.[244] A more detailed idea of what this entailed can be obtained only by an analysis of the casuistry contained in our sources.[245] Recourse to the boni mores was had, particularly frequently, where the moral integrity of family life in the widest sense was threatened: hence the invalidity of agreements pressurizing somebody (albeit indirectly) to enter into, not to enter into, to dissolve or not to dissolve a marriage,[246] hence also, for

---

238 Valerius Maximus, loc. cit.

239 Cicero, *De officiis*, 3, XIV–60; cf. also supra, pp. 663 sq. (note 99). Whether Aquilius was the father not only of the actio de dolo but also of the exceptio doli is not certain.

240 Cf. also the similar case, decided on the basis of an exceptio doli in Iul./Lab./Ulp. D. 44, 4, 4, 1; on which see, most recently, Geoffrey MacCormack, "Dolus in the Law of the Early Classical Period (Labeo-Celsus)", (1986) 52 *SDHI* 247 sq.

241 Von Lübtow, *Eranion Maridakis*, p. 201.

242 Cf. Kaser, *Verbotsgesetze*, pp. 85 sq.

243 Pap. D. 28, 7, 15.

244 Cf. e.g. Kaser, (1940) 60 *ZSS* 103; Mayer-Maly, *Festgabe Kaser*, p. 156; Plescia, (1987) 34 *RIDA* 275 sqq. The earliest references to the boni mores contained in authoritative texts can be found in three edicts on iniuria (Lenel, *EP*, pp. 400 sq.); they serve to delineate the still acceptable from the unacceptable behaviour. Already at this stage (i.e. before the time of Labeo) fairly precise ideas must have existed as to what the boni mores comprised. For details, see Mayer-Maly, *Festgabe Kaser*, pp. 157 sqq.; idem, (1987) 590 *THRHR* 64 sqq.

245 Cf., in particular, Kaser, (1940) 60 *ZSS* 120 sqq.; cf. also Plescia, (1987) 34 *RIDA* 286 sqq.

246 Kaser, (1940) 60 *ZSS* 121 sqq. On testamentary divorce clauses, see Meincke, *Festschrift Kaser*, pp. 437 sqq.

instance, the invalidity of stipulations de successione futura[247] or of arrangements in anticipation of somebody else's death.[248] But even outside this broadly defined area, the boni mores were occasionally invoked in order to limit the freedom of contract. Thus, for instance, the exclusion of liability for dolus was disapproved of as being contrary to the good morals,[249] and so was an undertaking between a plaintiff and his procedural representative that the latter was to be remunerated for his efforts by way of a share in the sum to be obtained through the defendant's condemnation.[250]

6. The boni mores and the ius commune

The writers of the ius commune largely contented themselves with referring to and commenting on the individual examples of transactions contra bonos mores contained in the Corpus Juris Civilis.[251] Occasionally, however, a different evaluation gained ground. Most notably perhaps, pacta successoria came to be recognized as being based on Germanic customary law: "Sic in Germania hodie per mores vulgatum est, ut non attenta amplius ea juris civilis veteri constitutione pacta successoria valeant."[252] Conditions in Rome were painted in a dark and sombre light in order to justify this deviation from the sources:

> "Summa nempe erat hac in parte Romanorum improbitas, ut illi, cui se successuros certa sciebant, non solum mortem optarent, sed et ferro, veneno aliisque artibus spem suam promoverent . . . Solebant securius alimenta aut medicamenta aegrotantibus denegare."[253]

Such insidious contrivances were, of course, entirely alien to the pure and honest German soul. Even pacta de hereditate tertii were no longer frowned upon as "odiosae . . . et plenae tristissimi et periculosi eventus".[254] On the other hand, new problem areas emerged, requiring moral value judgements. In the wake of the Reformation, for instance, heirs of legataries were frequently appointed under the condition of accepting the new or remaining faithful to the old religion. Predominantly, such clauses were regarded as unacceptable and therefore void:

---

247 C. 8, 38, 4 (Diocl. et Max.); cf. also Iul. D. 45, 1, 61.

248 Pactum de hereditate tertii: cf. Pap. D. 39, 5, 29, 2; C. 2, 3, 30 (Iust.).

249 Ulp. D. 16, 3, 1, 7; Tafaro, *Regula*, pp. 23 sqq., 44 sqq.

250 On redimere litem, see Pap. D. 17, 1, 7; C. 2, 12, 15 (Diocl.); Kaser, *RZ*, p. 162.

251 For details, see Schmidt, op. cit., note 227, passim.

252 Mevius, *Decisiones*, Pars III, Dec. CCLXX (5). For a detailed historical investigation cf. C.P. Joubert, "Pactum successorium", (1961) 24 *THRHR* 18 sqq., 106 sqq., 177 sqq.; (1962) 25 *THRHR* 46 sqq., 93 sqq.

253 Leyser, *Meditationes ad Pandectas*, Spec. XLIII, II.

254 These the words of C. 2, 3, 30, 2. On the recognition of such pacta by Schilter, Boehmer and others, cf. Schmidt, op. cit., note 227, pp. 54 sqq. But cf. also still Brunnemann, *Commentarius in Codicem*, Lib. II, Tit. III, L. de quaest. ult., 2 (". . . incivile [est], viventis hominis bona in sortem et divisionem vocare, et ita quasi ejus mortem voto ac spe praecipere") and Stryk, *Usus modernus pandectarum*, Lib. II, Tit. XIV, § 15, adding the somewhat sceptical comment: "Ego quantum praxin attinet, eam hodie a jure Romano diversam esse, asserere non ausim."

"[T]urpe est, et contra conscientiam agit, qui spe lucri mutat religionem, quam veram esse scit, et scire debet."[255]

Few authors, however, ventured beyond the mere casuistry. One of the first to adopt a more generalized approach was Hugo Donellus. "Quod attinet ad turpes conventiones, quae eaedem sunt contra bonos mores", he stated boldly,[256] "non dubitamus definire generaliter et sine exceptione, quod supra, omnes ipso iure non valere." Only the natural lawyers took a similar approach; thus we find Grotius, already in his *Inleiding*, setting out impossibility, illegality and immorality as three general grounds of invalidity in the law of obligations:

> "De verbintenissen zijn niet alleen nietig daer door belooft werd een unmoghelicke zaeck . . ., maer oock daer by iet belooft werd dat nae de burger-wet ende zeden oneerlick werd ghehouden."[257]

During the 18th and 19th centuries the general rule that all contracts (or even: all legal transactions) contra bonos mores are void established itself firmly. It impressed the fathers of the French code civil,[258] was taken over by the pandectists[259] and ultimately became part of the BGB.[260] Here it serves a crucial function as one of the few devices limiting the freedom of the parties to a contract to determine the contents of their transaction.

7. Reference to the boni mores in modern law

What types of contracts do we disapprove of today sub voce boni mores?[261] Many of the decisions of the Roman lawyers would still accord with modern attitudes. Pacta de quota litis, for instance, are still regarded as contra bonos mores in countries such as Germany[262] and

---

[255] Lauterbach, *Collegium theoretico-practicum*, Lib. XXVIII, Tit. VII, XI; cf. further Schmidt, op. cit., note 227, pp. 58 sqq.

[256] *Commentarii de jure civili*, Lib. XII, Cap. XXI, XVI.

[257] III, I, 42. The views of the natural lawyers are set out in detail by Schmidt, op. cit., note 227, pp. 65 sqq.; cf. also Wesenberg/Wesener, pp. 146 sq. For the natural lawyers, (natural) law and morals were most intimately related to each other.

[258] Cf. artt. 1108, 1133. According to the code civil, a contract is invalid if its "*cause*" is illicit. The cause is illicit when it is prohibited by the law, when it is "*contraire aux bonnes moeurs*" or contrary to the "*ordre public*". On these provisions, see Schmidt, op. cit., note 227, pp. 83 sqq.; Nicholas, *FLC*, pp. 122 sqq. "Public policy" features even more prominently in the English common law as a ground of invalidity; it is often taken to include the boni mores, cf. e.g. Treitel, *Contract*, pp. 334 sqq. But see, e.g., Sir Frederick Pollock, *Principles of Contract* (7th ed., 1902), pp. 273 sqq., who distinguishes immoral contracts from those against public policy. Cf. further Zweigert/Kötz, pp. 76 sqq.; for Germany, see Konstantin Simitis, *Gute Sitten und ordre public* (1960); Schmidt, op. cit., note 227, pp. 145 sqq.; for South Africa, see Aquilius, (1941) 58 *SALJ* 344 sqq.; Joubert, *Contract*, pp. 132 sq.

[259] Cf. e.g. Regelsberger, *Pandekten*, § 147 II; Windscheid/Kipp, §§ 81, 314; for all details, see Schmidt, op. cit., note 227, pp. 93 sqq.

[260] § 138 I BGB.

[261] Cf. in general Theo Mayer-Maly, "Die guten Sitten als Massstab des Rechts", 1986 *Juristische Schulung* 596 sqq.

[262] Cf. e.g. BGHZ 34, 64 (70); BGHZ 51, 290 (293).

South Africa[263] (but not in the United States);[264] a contingent fee, it is argued, would undermine the objectivity and integrity of an advocate/attorney, since it might lead him to confuse his own interest in a fair remuneration of his efforts with the interests of his client.[265] Agreements involving family relationships, too, are in many cases still regarded as morally offensive.[266] Artificial insemination, in vitro fertilization and the possibility of surrogate motherhood have, however, presented us with entirely new challenges to our established moral value judgements. Agreements between sperm donors and their doctors, or between the commissioning couple and the surrogate mother have to be evaluated against the standard of the boni mores,[267] which in turn, of course, has not remained unaffected by the dramatic advances of modern medical technology. But there are many other areas where the opinions on matters of good morals have changed in the course of time. Many transactions are upheld by modern courts which former generations would have avoided as being contrary to the moral values of the community (and vice versa): "The rule remains, but its application varies with the principles which for the time being guide public opinion."[268] Pacta successoria have already been mentioned in that regard; today we read in § 1941 BGB:

> "The deceased may by contract appoint an heir and create legacies and testamentary burdens (inheritance contract). Both the other contracting party or a third party may be appointed as heir (contractual heir) or legatee."

Those rules were unthinkable in Roman law (and would, incidentally, not be approved of by a present-day South African court either).[269] But the area where this shift of standards has occurred most patently is probably that of sexual morality and common decency. One cannot but think of the caustic comments by Stable J, in the Australian case of *Andrews v. Parker*:

> "What was apparently [once] regarded with pious horror . . . would, I observe, today hardly draw a raised eyebrow or a gentle 'tut-tut' . . . George Bernard Shaw's Eliza Doolittle . . . thought the suggestion that she have a bath in private with her

---

[263] Cf. e.g. Joubert, *Contract*, pp. 137 sq.

[264] For a comparative evaluation, see Zweigert/Kötz, pp. 78 sqq.

[265] RGZ 115, 141 (142 sq.); RGZ 142, 70 (73 sqq.).

[266] For an overview cf. Mayer-Maly, op. cit., note 31, § 138, nn. 48 sqq.; Joubert, *Contract*, pp. 134 sqq.

[267] Cf. Reinhard Zimmermann, "Die heterologe künstliche Insemination und das geltende Zivilrecht", 1981 *Zeitschrift für das gesamte Familienrecht* 932 sqq.; Dieter Giesen, "Recht und medizinischer Fortschritt", 1984 *Juristische Rundschau* 225, 227 (both on AID arrangements); Dagmar Coester-Waltjen, "Die künstliche Befruchtung beim Menschen—Zulässigkeit und zivilrechtliche Folgen", in: *Verhandlungen des 56. Deutschen Juristentages* (1986), vol. I, pp. B 79 sqq. (on surrogate motherhood agreements). For a thorough discussion of the validity of contracts concerning abortions, cf. Rolf Stürmer, "Das nicht abgetriebene Wunschkind", 1985 *Zeitschrift für das gesamte Familienrecht* 753 sqq.

[268] *Evanturel v. Evanturel* (1874–75) LR 6 PC 1 at 29; cf. also *Hurwitz v. Taylor* 1926 TPD 61 at 91 sq.; Mayer-Maly, op. cit., note 31, § 138, n. 17.

[269] In South Africa pacta successoria are still invalid. For a modern discussion of this rule, see Dale Hutchison, "Isolating the pactum successorium", (1983) 100 *SALJ* 221 sqq.

> clothes off was indecent. . . . One wonders what she would have thought and said to a suggestion that she wear in public one of today's miniscule and socially accepted bikinis, held miraculously in place apparently with the aid of providence, and, possibly, glue."[270]

In 1975, a German (county) court regarded a contract under which a hotel owner agreed to let a double room to an unmarried couple as morally offensive and therefore void.[271] Almost certainly, a similar case would be decided differently today.[272]

More important, however, than sex is economic power, at least as far as § 138 BGB is concerned. The boni mores have been invoked increasingly in order to tackle the problem of unfair contract terms arising from an inequality of the bargaining power of the contracting parties. As early as the second half of the 19th century (that is, still under the pandectist version of the ius commune) agreements in restraint of trade were subjected to close scrutiny, and, if necessary, declared null and void as being contra bonos mores.[273] In § 138 II (i.e. under the auspices of the boni mores) the German legislator has taken up the fight against usury:[274] not in a particularly dashing manner, and hence the modern attempts to sidestep the (subjective) requirements of this rule and to invalidate contracts under the general clause of § 138 I in cases of an exceptionally obvious disproportion between performance and counterperformance.[275] § 138 I BGB has been used to combat unfair standard-contract terms[276] and, even though the legislator has now intervened and attended to this specific problem area,[277] the general prohibition of contracts contra bonos mores continues to be a valuable tool in the hands of courts that are willing to protect the economically weaker party from exploitation.[278]

---

[270] [1973] Qd R 93 at 104; quoted by Zweigert/Kötz, p. 73.

[271] AG Emden, 1975 *Neue Juristische Wochenschrift* 1363 sq.

[272] Mayer-Maly, op. cit., note 31, § 138, n. 55.

[273] Zimmermann, *Moderationsrecht*, pp. 154 sqq. On agreements in restraint of trade in Roman law, see Andreas Wacke, "Wettbewerbsfreiheit und Konkurrenzverbotsklauseln im antiken und modernen Recht", (1982) 99 *ZSS* 188 sqq. For Roman-Dutch and South African law, see J.T. Schoombee, "Agreements in restraint of trade: The appellate division confirms new principles", (1985) 48 *THRHR* 127 sqq.; the leading modern case is *Magna Alloys and Research (SA) (Pty.) Ltd. v. Ellis* 1984 (4) SA 874 (A). On the approach of English courts (which has for a long time influenced South African decisions), cf. e.g. Treitel, *Contract*, pp. 345 sqq.

[274] Cf. supra, pp. 175 sqq., 268 sq.

[275] Cf. supra, p. 269.

[276] Cf. e.g. Ludwig Raiser, *Das Recht der Allgemeinen Geschäftsbedingungen* (1935), pp. 302 sqq.

[277] §§ 9, 10 and 11 AGBG

[278] Thus, for instance, agreements under which the owner of a restaurant is obliged to obtain his beer supply from a specific brewery for more than 20 years are usually regarded as being contra bonos mores by German courts. For details, see Zimmermann, *Moderationsrecht*, pp. 24 sqq. For an overview of further cases where § 138 BGB has been invoked in order to protect the freedom of trade and in order to curb the abuse of a superior bargaining position cf. Mayer-Maly, op. cit., note 31, § 138, nn. 64 sqq., 78 sqq.

CHAPTER 23

Condicio and Dies

I. INTRODUCTION

1. The dynamic nature of Western contract law

"Roman law", wrote one of the great masters of comparative law,[1]

> "is really very remarkable. Most early laws devote most of their attention to the static elements, especially problems of kinship and marriage and of crime; and they are composed mainly of prohibitions. But the element of tabu, which is so strong in them, is hardly visible in Roman law. Changes are regarded as normal, to be provided for by the appropriate legal instruments."

The most important of these instruments was contract, and it was largely the law of contract that gave the civilian legal tradition its peculiarly dynamic character.

> "Primitive and archaic law is a law of empirically known, psychologically sensed wrongs rather than theoretically conceived rights and duties. . . . These legal systems were therefore static and past oriented, since they dealt basically with wrongs and compensation, that is, the restitution as far as possible of a previously existing situation which had been wrongfully disturbed. Classical Roman and modern law, on the other hand, is future oriented and a law of movement concerned with the creation, transfer, and extinction of legal relations and prediction of this future movement."[2]

Yet, even contract law contains, of course, inherently "static" attributes. Once the parties have complied with whatever may be required for the conclusion of a contract, they are bound. "Pacta sunt servanda", as one was to say at a time when all consensual pacta had become enforceable and the formalities connected with the Roman all-round contract, the stipulation, had been jettisoned.[3] The law of contract thus provides the parties with a convenient tool to change their existing position; but it must also be concerned with the protection of reasonable expectations. A party to a contract may therefore, to his dismay, find himself bound, even though events have not taken the expected turn. Roman law, in principle, did not allow him to rescind the contract.[4] At the same time, however, it recognized special devices by means of which the parties could adapt their transaction, in advance, to certain developments which still lay somewhere in the future. Depending on whether they wanted to make the existence of

---

[1] F.H. Lawson, *A Common Lawyer Looks at the Civil Law* (1953), p. 101 (under the title: Roman Law a Law of Movement).

[2] J.C. Smith, "The Unique Nature of the Concepts of Western Law", in: J.C. Smith, David N. Weisstub, *The Western Idea of Law* (1983), p. 18; cf. also Lawson, op. cit., note 1, p. 100; Maine, *Ancient Law*, pp. 179 sqq.

[3] Cf. supra, p. 576.

[4] Cf. infra, p. 801.

the obligations, created by their contract, dependent upon a future certain event, or a future uncertain event, the parties could include a time clause or condition. These provisions introduced a greater degree of flexibility into the contract, without at the same time jeopardizing legal certainty: since they were part and parcel of the contract, both parties could adjust their expectations accordingly. Conditions, in particular, have always proved to be a most useful device, in Roman law even more so than in modern legal systems. Stipulations, it must be remembered, were unilaterally binding contracts; but by adding a condition, they could easily be adapted to serve the function of bilateral transactions such as hire, sale or permutatio.[5] Conditions could be employed in many different contexts and for a great variety of purposes; we have already referred to some of them in previous chapters.[6] The Roman lawyers devoted great attention to the problems arising from conditional transactions and the rich casuistry elaborating on them belongs to the showpieces of the Roman law of obligations. Modern legal systems, by and large, have not been able to add very much by way of doctrinal refinement.[7]

2. Conditions in general

A condition is a clause by means of which the effectiveness of a transaction is made dependent upon the occurrence or non-occurrence of a future and uncertain event. Depending on whether, upon the arrival (or non-arrival) of this event, the transaction is intended to take effect or to be terminated, we usually refer to either a suspensive or resolutive condition; today statutory definitions along this line are contained in § 158 BGB. The Roman lawyers, too, recognized this distinction, although their terminology does not reveal this very clearly. The phrase "sub condicionem (contrahere, legare, etc.)" was for them tantamount to effecting a transaction under a suspensive condition.[8] Known already in the law of the XII Tables,[9] suspensive conditions were, historically, the older variety and they always appear to have retained their status as conditions par excellence.[10] That a

[5] Cf., for example, supra, p. 91.

[6] Cf., in particular, the chapter on stipulatio poenae, pp. 95 sqq.

[7] Cf. infra, pp. 743 sqq.

[8] Cf., for example, Ulp. D. 18, 1, 3; Ulp. D. 18, 2, 2 pr.; Ulp. D. 18, 3, 1.

[9] Cf. UE 2, 4: "Sub hac condicione liber esse iussus: 'si decem milia heredi dederit', etsi ab herede abalienatus sit, emptori dando pecuniam ad libertatem perveniet; idque lex duodecim tabularum iubet." A slave could thus be manumitted in a testament upon the condition that he would pay a certain sum of money to the heir (as a compensation for the loss he suffered as a result of the manumission). The slave under these circumstances was known as "statuliber". The provision of the XII Tables dealt, more specifically, with the situation where the heir had sold the statuliber, and enabled him to satisfy the condition also by payment to his new master. Cf., for example, Ekkehard Kalchthaler, *Die historische Entwicklung des Satzes: "Die vom Gegner vereitelte Bedingung gilt als eingetreten" aus einer Interpretation zur Fiktio* (unpublished Dr. iur. thesis, Freiburg/Br., 1959), pp. 20 sqq.; Kaser, *RPr* I, p. 114.

[10] Buckland/Stein, p. 425: ". . . in fact the only real conditions."

transaction may first be effective and subsequently, upon the occurrence or non-occurrence of a specific event, relapse into a state of ineffectiveness, on the other hand, was a notion ill suited to the formalistic thinking patterns of pre-classical jurisprudence. Even in classical Roman law, obligations stricti iuris could not thus be limited in their effect.[11] The recognition of clauses of a resolutive character was therefore intimately linked to the rise of obligations, the actionability of which was determinable ex bona fide. Contracts of sale in particular were often subjected to what we would call resolutive conditions; but in many of these cases it was debatable whether the parties had not rather intended the clause to suspend the effects of their transaction. Difficult problems of interpretation were therefore bound to arise once the Roman lawyers had in effect, though not in name, begun to recognize two different types of condiciones. We shall deal first with suspensive and then with resolutive conditions before we return to the problem of where to draw the line between the two.

II. CONDICIO SUSPENSIVA

1. The nature of suspensive conditions

"[S]i Titius consul factus fuerit, quinque aureos dare spondes?":[12] this is a typical example of a suspensive condition, added, in this instance, to a stipulation.[13] The promisor had to give the ten aurei only once Titius had become consul. For the time being, he was not yet under any obligation to pay; whether, in fact, such an obligation would ever arise was quite uncertain; for, after all, Titius might never be elected consul. Essential for the conditional nature of the promise was thus the fact that its operation depended upon a future uncertain event. If the "si" clause related to a past event or to the present time, the characteristic state of pendency was lacking: for though the parties concerned might not yet be aware of it, it was immediately determinable from an objective point of view whether or not the promised sum had to be paid. "Si Titius consul fuit, [centum] dare spondes?"[14] and, "Si rex Parthorum vivit, centum mihi dari spondes?"[15] are promises falling into these two categories. If Titius had in fact been consul, or if the king of the

[11] Cf. infra, p. 733.
[12] *Inst.* III, 15, 4.
[13] Most of the examples discussed in the Digest (as well as on the following pages) concern either conditional dispositions contained in a will or conditional stipulations. Suspensive conditions could, however, be attached to all kinds of transactions (including, of course, consensual contracts), except those that were dubbed "actus legitimi" by Papinian. In D. 50, 17, 77 he says: "Actus legitimi, qui non recipiunt . . . condicionem, veluti emancipatio, acceptilatio, hereditatis aditio, servi optio, datio tutoris, in totum vitiantur per . . . condicionis adiectionem." In the place of "emancipatio" one possibly has to read "mancipatio". For further details, see Kaser, *RPr* I, p. 255.
[14] Cf. *Inst.* III, 15, 6.
[15] Pap. D. 12, 1, 37.

Parthians was still alive, the promise was instantly effective.[16] If, on the other hand, Titius had never held the coveted office, or if the foreign sovereign had already died, it could at once be said that the promise would never become effective, and the result was therefore "nihil valet stipulatio".[17] The "si" clauses did not, under these circumstances, constitute conditions.[18] If the event upon which the promise was made dependent did in fact lie in the future, but was not uncertain ("Decem aureos primis kalendis Martiis dare spondes"?),[19] there was a state of pendency, but we are dealing here with a time clause, not with a condition. Occasionally, incidentally, an obligation was not regarded as conditional, even though it was subject to an event both future and uncertain. This was the case where the clause in question had merely explicitly stated one of the requirements upon which the validity of the transaction depended anyway. The execution of a will in the following terms: "Titius heres esto. si Titius hereditatem meam adierit, Maevio decem dato" was one example.[20] It was a matter of course that Titius had to become heir before he could be obliged to pay the legacy of ten to Maevius. The "si" clause was thus "supervacua" and was treated pro non scripta; it was usually referred to as a (mere) condicio iuris—a "condition" imposed by law rather than by the testator.[21]

2. Impossible, illegal and immoral conditions

Conditions were, furthermore, subject to three rather self-evident restrictions: their realization had to be possible and they had to be untainted by illegality or immorality. "Si digito caelum attigero, [centum] dare spondes":[22] this was an (objectively) impossible condition ("condicio . . . cui natura impedimento est, quo minus existat"),[23] for no one can possibly touch the sky with his finger. As a result, the "si" clause was invalid ("impossibilium nulla est obligatio").[24] Did this partial invalidity affect the remainder of the transaction ("centum dare spondes")? Obviously it did, for the promisor can hardly be taken to have intended to be bound, without

---

16 ". . . si condicio vera sit, stipulatio tenet": Pap. D. 12, 1, 37.

17 *Inst.* III, 15, 6.

18 For the condicio in praesens vel praeteritum collata in modern law, cf. Flume, *AT*, § 38, 1 b; as far as English law is concerned, see Samuel J. Stoljar, "The Contractual Concept of Condition", (1953) 69 *LQR* 500 sqq.

19 *Inst.* III, 15, 2.

20 Pomp. D. 36, 2, 22, 1.

21 Iul. D. 35, 1, 21; Paul. D. 21, 1, 43, 10; cf. also Flume, *AT*, § 38, 1 c. On the closely related question of condiciones tacitae (inherent in the transaction itself), cf. Pap. D. 36, 2, 35, 1; Pap. D. 23, 3, 68; Pap D. 50, 17, 77; Max Kaser, "Condicio iuris und condicio tacita", in: *Symbolae Raphaeli Taubenschlag dedicatae*, vol. I (1956), pp. 427 sqq.; H.J. Légier, "Tacita condicio", (1966) 44 *RH* 5 sqq.; Wolf, *Causa stipulationis*, pp. 126 sq.

22 *Inst.* III, 19, 11; cf. also Gai. III, 98.

23 *Inst.* III, 19, 11.

24 Conversely, if the stipulation had been to the effect "Si ditio caelum non attigero, dare spondes?", it was valid and immediately enforceable (". . . pure facta obligatio intellegitur ideoque statim petere potest").

further ado, to pay a sum of one hundred. This obligation depended on something else being achieved first and if that event could not take place, the whole transaction had lost its basis. "[I]nutilis est stipulatio",[25] was therefore the appropriate answer and it appears to have been obvious to the Roman lawyers that a mechanical application of the "utile per inutile non vitiatur" rule[26] would not have made sense in these cases. Matters looked different, however, when it came to impossible conditions contained in testamentary dispositions. Take, for instance, the case where Lucius Titius was instituted heir "si . . . Fulvia filia mea vive[t]".[27] As it happened, the testator had never had a daughter named Fulvia. Here it could, as a rule, be assumed that the average, reasonable testator would rather have wanted his disposition in favour of Lucius Titius to stand without any strings attached to it than face the prospect of having his whole will set aside; the dreaded state of intestacy[28] would then have ensued. Thus, it was ultimately the general favor testamenti that induced the Roman lawyers to strike out merely the invalid part of the will, even where this invalid part was in the nature of a condition.[29]

The position was the same as far as illegal or immoral conditions were concerned. If they had been added to a will, they were simply struck out:

> "Condiciones contra edicta imperatorum aut contra leges aut quae legis vicem optinent scriptae vel quae contra bonos mores vel derisoriae sunt aut huiusmodi quas praetores improbaverunt pro non scriptis habentur."[30]

Thus, for instance, a person became heir even if he had been instituted under the condition that he divorce his spouse,[31] or that he throw the remains of the testator into the sea,[32] and irrespective of whether or not

[25] Gai. III, 98.
[26] On which see supra, pp. 75 sqq.
[27] Cf. Alf. D. 28, 5, 46.
[28] Cf. supra, p. 628, note 45.
[29] The question was, at first, the subject of a school dispute ("sed legatum sub impossibili condictione relictum nostri praeceptores proinde deberi putant ac si sine condicione relictum esset; diversae scholae auctores nihilo minus legatum inutile existimant quam stipulationem"). The opinion of the Sabinians prevailed: cf. Alf. D. 28, 5, 46; Ulp. D. 35, 1, 3; Pomp. D. 35, 1, 6, 1; *Inst.* II, 14, 10. For details, see Voci, *DER*, vol. II, pp. 609 sqq.; Hans Josef Wieling, "Falsa demonstratio, condicio pro non scripta, condicio pro impleta im römischen Recht", (1970) 87 *ZSS* 212 sqq.; Geoffrey MacCormack, "Impossible Conditions in Wills", (1974) 21 *RIDA* 263 sqq.; Gian Gualberto Archi, "Condizione nel negozio giuridico (diritto romano)", in: *Scritti di diritto romano*, vol. I (1981), pp. 253 sqq.
[30] Marci. D. 28, 7, 14; cf. further Pomp. D. 28, 7, 7; Pomp. D. 30, 54 pr.; Paul. D. 28, 7, 9; Voci, *DER*, vol. II, pp. 796 sqq.
[31] C. 6, 25, 5 (Val. at Gall.); on which see the analysis by Jens Peter Meincke, "Die Scheidungsklausel im Testament", in: *Festschrift für Max Kaser* (1976), pp. 437 sqq., 456 sqq. (containing a most instructive comparison with a decision by the German Federal Supreme Court of 1956).
[32] Modest. D. 28, 7, 27 pr. (". . . laudandus est magis quam accusandus heres, qui reliquias testatoris non in mare secundum ipsius voluntatem abiecit, sed memoria humanae condicionis sepulturae tradidit").

he had complied with these rather cranky demands of the testator. Stipulations as well as consensual contracts, on the other hand, were rendered invalid (in toto) on account of immoral or illegal conditions attached to them.

3. Casus perplexus

Occasionally a condition attached to a will was apt to lead to a puzzling logical stalemate when one tried to figure out its legal implications—as, for example, where a testator had provided "Stichus liber esto et, posteaquam liber erit, heres esto".[33] Stichus was to become free and once he was free, he was to become heir. Thus, according to the wording of the will, Stichus' institution as heir depended on his having been released from slavery. Such a release could, however, be effected only by someone who had succeeded the testator as his heir; and that, in terms of the will, could only be Stichus himself. The Roman jurists went to great lengths to save these kinds of dispositions.[34] In the present case, for instance, which appears to have been eagerly discussed,[35] Labeo, Neratius und Aristo cut the Gordian knot by arguing that "detracto verbo medio 'postea' simul ei et libertatem et hereditatem competere":[36] both freedom and the inheritance must be taken to be granted to him at one and the same time. Thus, Stichus can be regarded, for one logical second, alternatively as the heir, from whom he obtains his own liberty, and as the homo liber who may succeed the testator.[37] In other situations, however, one had to abandon all hope of finding a sensible solution to the conundrum and the disposition had to be declared invalid as a result of insurmountable perplexity. Marcianus D. 28, 7, 16 provides a somewhat silly but nevertheless rather instructive example: "Si Titius heres erit, Seius heres esto: si Seius heres erit, Titius heres esto"—the testator must have been either very confused or very malicious when he made Titius' institution as heir dependent upon that of Seius, and vice versa. "Iulianus inutilem esse institutionem scribit", we are, not surprisingly, informed, "cum condicio existere non possit."[38] Closely related is the case of the "preposterous" stipulation as discussed in *Inst.* III, 19, 14: "Item si quis ita stipulatus erat: si navis ex Asia venerit, hodie dare spondes? inutilis erat stipulatio, quia praepostere concepta est." In

---

[33] Ulp. D. 28, 5, 9, 14.

[34] Cf. further, as far as the conditional institution of an heir is concerned, Lab. D. 28, 7, 20, 1; Iul./Ulp. D. 28, 7, 4, 1; Lab. D. 28, 7, 20 pr. For a detailed analysis, see Ralph Backhaus, *Casus perplexus: die Lösung in sich widersprüchlicher Rechtsfälle durch die klassische römische Jurisprudenz* (1981), pp. 32 sqq.

[35] The same problem is raised in Marc. D. 28, 5, 52.

[36] Ulp. D. 28, 5, 9, 14.

[37] Franz Wieacker, "Die juristische Sekunde. Zur Legitimation der Konstruktionsjurisprudenz", in: *Existenz und Ordnung, Festschrift für Erik Wolf* (1962), p. 431; Backhaus, op. cit., note 34, pp. 41 sqq. (43).

[38] Marc. D. 28, 7, 16; cf. further Backhaus, op. cit., note 34, pp. 50 sqq.

terms of this odd provision performance is, on the one hand, due immediately ("hodie"); yet, on the other hand, the operation of the obligation is suspended until "the ship arrives from Asia". Performance, in other words, is supposed to be due before the obligation has come into existence.[39] This is logically impossible and the whole transaction must therefore be considered invalid. It has to be noted, however, that Justinian uses the past tense when relating this solution. The reason is that, as a result of an imperial ruling, stipulationes praeposterae had, in the meantime, become recognized as valid;[40] the incongruity had been resolved, rather arbitrarily, in favour of the suspension of the obligation.[41]

4. Condiciones casuales and potestativae

To return to our original example: "Si Titius consul factus fuerit" was a paradigm of what came to be referred to as a condicio casualis;[42] whether or not the promise became effective was dependent upon an event that was in principle outside the control of either of the parties. Satisfaction of the condition could, however, also depend on the stipulator's (i.e. the potential creditor's) will. A promise of the type "Si in Capitolium ascendero, quinque aureos dare spondes? Spondeo" was perfectly sound; the obligation to hand over the money was subject, in these cases, to a (suspensive) condicio "potestativa".[43] Not admissible, on the other hand, were conditions turning upon an event that was wholly in the control of the promisor.[44] A promise such as "Si in Capitolium ascenderis, quinque aureos dare spondes? Spondeo" was tantamount to "Si volueris, quinque aureos dare spondes? Spondeo"; it obviously lacked one of the essential ingredients of a legally recognizable promise, namely the will to be bound.

5. Positive and negative conditions

"Si Titius consul factus fuerit" and "Si in Capitolium ascendero" were positive conditions: something had to happen before the respective obligations could become effective. It was equally possible, however, to make the operation of an obligation dependent upon a particular event not happening. Of these negative conditions it was the negative

[39] Hence the term "preposterous", composed of the prepositions "prae" and "post". On *Inst.* III, 19, 14, see Antonio Masi, "Stipulatio praepostera", (1960) 63 *BIDR* 181 sqq.; Backhaus, op. cit., note 34, pp. 99 sqq.

[40] Cf. first the decision by the Emperor Leo, as reported in *Inst.* III, 19, 14 (dealing only with preposterous dowry stipulations), then, more generally, Justinian, in *Inst.* III, 19, 14 and C. 6, 23, 25.

[41] ". . . exactione videlicet post condicionem vel diem competente": C. 6, 23, 25.

[42] Cf. the classification in C. 6, 51, 1, 7.

[43] C. 6, 51, 1, 7. This text further mentions condiciones mixtae ("quarum eventus ex fortuna [et] ex honoratae personae voluntate . . . pendeat"; for example: marriage).

[44] Cf. Paul. D. 45, 1, 46, 3 ("Illam autem stipulationem 'si volueris, dari?' inutilem esse constat"); Ulp. D. 45, 1, 17; Ulp. D. 30, 43, 2; Ulp. D. 18, 1, 7 pr.

potestative condition that could throw up a special problem. "Si in Capitolium non ascenderit", "Si Stichum non manumiserit"[45]—conditions of this type would often be satisfied only with the death of the prospective creditor; for before his life's pilgrimage had finally been completed, one could rarely be certain that he might not perhaps one day still decide to saunter up Capitol hill. Yet, the moment of death was hardly the most apposite time to let him receive the reward for his abstention. It was the great Quintus Mucius Scaevola, the most famous representative of the "veteres" jurisprudence, who devised a way out of this predicament. A testator had bequeathed something to his wife under the condition that she would not remarry. Strictly speaking, the bequest would become effective only when she died without having contracted another marriage. Yet, Mucius reversed the position.[46] The widow, he opined, was to be given the legacy immediately, but she had to undertake to return it if she did, in fact, remarry. This undertaking took the form of a stipulation and came to be referred to as the cautio Muciana. It enabled the legatee to enjoy what had been left to her whilst she was still alive; at the same time considerable pressure was brought to bear upon her to comply with the condition set by the testator. Obviously this was a most satisfactory solution that commended itself to be extended; and the Roman jurists appear, indeed, to have availed themselves of the cautio Muciana wherever a negative potestative condition was included in a will,[47] even if the question of its satisfaction or otherwise might already become determinable during the lifetime of the (conditional) beneficiary.[48]

6. Condicio pendet

Conditions in the original, Roman sense of the word left the fate of the transactions to which they were appended in suspense and they thus created, for the time being, a state of uncertainty. Once the condition was satisfied (the technical expression normally used was "si exstiterit condicio"),[49] the transaction became fully effective; upon failure of the condition ("defectus condicionis")[50] the situation was the same as if the transaction had never been entered into. But what exactly was the legal position after conclusion of the (conditional) contract, but before the condition had either been satisfied or had failed? Did this legal relationship "in statu nascendi", as it were, have no legal significance at all?

---

[45] Cf. Ulp. D. 35, 1, 7 pr.

[46] Cf. Iul./Maec. D. 36, 1, 67, 1; Pap. D. 35, 1, 73.

[47] Cf. Ulp. D. 35, 1, 7 pr.; Gai. D. 35, 1, 18 (dealing with the institution of heirs). The question whether these are classical or post-classical generalizations is disputed; cf. Antonio Masi, "In tema di 'cautio Muciana'", (1962) 13 *Iura* 175 sqq.; Voci, *DER*, vol. II, pp. 606 sq.; Kaser, *RPr* I, p. 254; idem, *RPr* II, p. 97, n. 19.

[48] As, for example, in the case of "si Stichum non manumiserit" (Iav. D. 35, 1, 67). The condition could be satisfied if *Stichus* died before having been manumitted.

[49] Cf., for example, Paul. D. 18, 6, 8 pr.

[50] Cf., for example, Tryph. D. 28, 2, 28 pr.

And, secondly, what precisely did it mean when it is said that satisfaction of the condition made the transaction fully effective? Was that "effectiveness" of a retroactive nature or did it operate ex nunc? On neither of these two issues can a clear and straightforward answer be given.

(a) "Non est pro eo, quasi sit"

Turning to the first one, we find that the Romans sometimes used a slightly metaphorical expression to describe the situation. "Condicio pendet", they said[51] without, however, inferring specific legal consequences from this image of a state of "pendency". Generally speaking, the position was as Paulus summarized it: "Quod pendet, non est pro eo, quasi sit"[52]—what is pending is not (yet) in being, at least not as what it was intended to be. Thus, most importantly, a contract was not enforceable pendente condicione.[53] If performance had mistakenly been rendered, it was recoverable by means of a condictio indebiti;[54] for what was owed sub condicione was still indebitum. The situation could be different if the condition was bound at all events to be fulfilled: "Quod si ea condicione debetur, quae omnimodo exstatura est, solutum repeti non potest";[55] the reason either being that the Roman lawyers treated this "condition" as a dies[56] or that they regarded it as improper of the prospective debtor to claim what he subsequently had to hand over again in any event ("[d]olo facit, qui petit quod redditurus est").[57] A conditional contract of sale, as we have seen, was not "perfecta"[58] and did not therefore have the effect of transferring the risk to the purchaser. Nor did it provide a iusta causa, on account of which the purchaser could begin to usucapt the object delivered to him.[59] A person who had transferred ownership sub condicione remained, for the time being, owner of the object.[60] He was therefore free to transfer it to a third party or to incumber it, although these subsequent dispositions also remained in a state of pendency; they became fully effective only upon failure of the condition under which the first transaction was concluded.[61]

[51] Cf., for example, Iav. D. 12, 1, 36; Paul. D. 18, 6, 8 pr.; Iul. D. 28, 5, 38, 4 ("pendente condicione"); for a detailed analysis, see Carlo Gioffredi, "'Pendenza' e 'sospensione' dalle fonti romane alla dommatica odierna", (1956) 22 *SDHI* 113 sqq.

[52] D. 50, 17, 169, 1.

[53] Ulp. D. 50, 16, 54; Marci. D. 20, 1, 13, 5.

[54] Pomp. D. 12, 6, 16 pr.

[55] Ulp. D. 12, 6, 18.

[56] Cf. Daube, *Roman Law*, pp. 122 sq.; Alan Rodger, "Emptio perfecta Revisited: A Study of Digest 18, 6, 8, 1", (1982) 50 *TR* 344; cf. also Glück, vol. 13, p. 78.

[57] Paul. D. 44, 4, 8 pr.; Paul. D. 50, 17, 173, 3. Cf. also Liber Sextus, Lib. V, Tit. XII, De regulis iuris, LIX.

[58] Cf. supra, p. 284.

[59] Paul. D. 41, 4, 2, 2; Paul. D. 18, 6, 8 pr.

[60] UE 2, 2; Ulp. D. 24, 1, 11 pr.

[61] Cf. Gai. D. 30, 69, 1; Marci. D. 20, 1, 13, 1.

(b) *The spes debitum iri*

Yet, on the other hand, a conditional transaction did not constitute a legal "nothing". After all, the parties had already come to an arrangement, and some form of legal relationship had clearly been established. As far as conditional contracts were concerned, this legal relationship was described by Justinian as a "spes debitum iri",[62] an expectancy that the obligation(s) would become effective. This expectancy could, of course, not be equated to the obligation itself, but it was none the less a part of both parties' estates. As a consequence, it was both actively and passively transmissible on death: "eamque ipsam spem", in the words of Justinian, "transmittimus, si, priusquam condicio existat, mors nobis contigerit."[63] Furthermore, a novation as well as a formal release (acceptilatio) could be effected with regard to a conditional obligation[64] and it could also be secured by way of a pledge.[65] Transfer of ownership sub condicione, too, had certain preliminary effects. The freedom of the owner to dispose over the object was restricted in so far as he could no longer take any step that would conclusively have changed its status and thus have detrimentally affected the prospective acquirer's position: if the object of the transfer was a slave, he could no longer manumit him,[66] if it was a tract of land he could not dedicate a part of it as locus religiosus.[67] Again it was argued that neither the death of the transferor nor that of the transferee, pendente condicione, had any impact on the situation:[68] the respective heirs found themselves in exactly the same position as their deceased predecessors. Again, therefore, a rather secure expectancy[69] resulted from the conditional transaction.

---

[62] *Inst.* III, 15, 4; cf. also Ulp. D. 50, 16, 54.

[63] *Inst.* III, 15, 4; Paul. vat. 55; Iul. D. 36, 2, 19, 3; Paul. D. 18, 6, 8 pr.; but cf. also Ulp. D. 35, 1, 59 ("Intercidit legatum si ea persona decesserit, cui legatum est sub condicione"); Werner Flume, "Zur Vererblichkeit der suspensiv bedingten Obligation nach klassischem römischem Recht", (1936) 14 *TR* 19 sqq.; Masi, *Condizione*, pp. 19 sqq., 195 sqq.; Gottfried Schiemann, *Pendenz und Rückwirkung der Bedingung* (1973), pp. 8 sqq.; Kaser, *RPr* I, p. 256; Thomas, *TRL*, p. 236; contra (in classical Roman law the transaction lapsed when one of the parties died): F. Vassalli, "'Dies vel condicio'. Lineamenti della dottrina romana della condizione", in: *Studi giuridici*, vol. I (1960), pp. 268 sqq.; Salvatore Riccobono, "Formazione del domma della transmissibilità all' erede dei rapporti sotto condizione [fr. 23 D. XXIII, 4 Afr. VII qu. e V. F. 55]", in: *Studi in onore di Silvio Perozzi* (1923), pp. 351 sqq.; Buckland/Stein, pp. 424 sq.; cf. also Voci, *DER*, vol. I, pp. 291 sqq. (the question was controversial among classical jurists).

[64] Ulp. D. 46, 2, 14, 1; Pomp. D. 46, 3, 16; Pomp. D. 46, 4, 12; Pap. D. 50, 17, 77. These acts, of course, became effective only once the condition had been satisfied.

[65] Gai. D. 20, 4, 11, 1. The pledge, under these circumstances, was also sub condicione; cf. also Marci. D. 20, 1, 5 pr.; Afr. D. 20, 4, 9 pr.—2.

[66] Iav. D. 33, 5, 14; Gai. D. 40, 9, 29, 1.

[67] Pomp. D. 35, 1, 105; Paul. D. 11, 7, 34.

[68] Iul. D. 39, 5, 2, 5 ("Si pecuniam mihi Titius dederit absque ulla stipulatione, ea tamen condicione, ut tunc domum mea fieret, cum Seius consul factus esset: sive furente eo sive mortuo Seius consulatum adeptus fuerit, mea fiet"). The question was, however, controversial; cf. Ulp. D. 23, 3, 9, 1; Masi, *Condizione*, pp. 142 sqq.; Schiemann, op. cit., note 63, pp. 10 sqq.; Kaser, *RPr* I, p. 255.

[69] Schiemann, op. cit., note 63, p. 12.

7. The effect of satisfaction of the condition

(a) Operation ex nunc

Closely related to the question of how to determine the legal relationship between the parties during the state of pendency was the second of the above-mentioned issues; for if one were to accept that satisfaction of the condition generally had a retroactive effect, this could, at least to some extent, and with regard to certain problems, obviate the necessity of postulating preliminary effects pendente condicione.[70] Again, the attitude adopted by the Roman lawyers appears to have been rather equivocal[71] and the conflicting views expressed in our sources have given rise to lively controversies among modern scholars. Thus, on the one hand, we read: "Si rem meam sub condicione stipuler, utilis est stipulatio, si condicionis existentis tempore mea non sit"[72]—if I enter into a conditional stipulation that I be given my own property, the transaction is valid if the property has ceased to be mine at the time of satisfaction of the condition. Obviously, therefore, it is to this time, not to the moment when the contract was concluded, that we must look in order to determine its validity. The same view was adopted, with regard to a contract of sale, by Marcellus in D. 18, 1, 61: "Existimo posse me id quod meum est sub condicione emere, quia forte speratur meum esse desinere." There is still the prospect that the object of the sale, upon fulfilment of the condition, might no longer belong to the purchaser. If that should indeed turn out to be the case, the sale is valid.

(b) Retroactive effect

But then there is a variety of texts which appear to suggest that satisfaction of the condition had a retroactive effect. Some of them were quite generally phrased. ". . . in stipulationibus id tempus spectetur quo contrahimus", Paulus is reported to have opined[73] and this statement was even elevated by the compilers to the status of a regula iuris antiqui.[74] With regard to the contract of sale we have a passage, credited also to Paul, in which the position after satisfaction of the condition is described as "quasi iam contracta emptione in

---

[70] Cf., for example, the argument advanced by Vassalli, op. cit., note 63, pp. 268 sqq.: the positions of conditional debtor/creditor in classical law were intransmissible on death because retroactivity was unknown; cf. also Buckland/Stein, p. 424. Gai. D. 20, 4, 11, 1 also shows how closely the two issues were related.

[71] Thomas, *TRL*, p. 235.

[72] Pomp. D. 45, 1, 31; Masi, *Condizione*, pp. 98 sqq.

[73] D. 45, 1, 78 pr. (the decision to which this phrase was attached as an argument reads as follows: "Si filius familias sub condicione stipulatus emancipatus fuerit, deinde exstiterit condicio, patri actio competit").

[74] Paul. D. 50, 17, 144, 1.

praeteritum"[75]—as though the contract were related back to the time of the initial agreement. Other decisions deal with more specific issues. Here we may turn again to Gaius D. 20, 4, 11, 1, the case that dealt with a hypotheca aimed at securing a conditional stipulation.[76] A conditional debt, as we have seen, provided an adequate basis for a valid pledge;[77] but that pledge itself became operative only once the condition had been satisfied. If the same object had in the meantime been used once again as a security—this time, however, for an unconditional loan—the question arose as to which of the two creditors enjoyed preference. If the condition failed to materialize, there was, obviously, no problem. The first hypotheca having lapsed with the debt it was supposed to secure, the second creditor acquired the first rank. But if the condition was in fact satisfied, the second creditor remained second in line; for the matter, according to Gaius, had to be looked at as if the first stipulation had become effective at the time it was concluded: ". . . perinde habetur, ac si illo tempore, quo stipulatio interposita est, sine condicione facta esset." The first creditor thus enjoyed the rank he would have had in case of an unconditional transaction.

(c) *Modern interpretation*

Various attempts have been made to push the sources into some kind of doctrinal straitjacket. The Roman lawyers have, on the one hand, been taken to have made conditional transactions generally retroactive upon satisfaction of the condition.[78] Others have maintained that retroactivity was a Byzantine notion; in classical Roman law all conditions produced effects only from the moment of their satisfaction.[79] The truth, as usual, appears to lie somewhere in the middle. It is unlikely that there ever was a uniform rule one way or the other; neither was

---

[75] D. 18, 6, 8 pr. (the prime candidate, in the present context, of post-classical corruption of the classical law).

[76] "Videamus, an idem dicendum sit, si sub condicione stipulatione facta hypotheca data sit, qua pendente alius credidit pure et accepit eandem hypothecam, tunc deinde prioris stipulationis exsistat condicio, ut potior sit qui postea credidisset. sed vereor, num hic aliud sit dicendum: cum enim semel condicio exstitit, perinde habetur, ac si illo tempore, quo stipulatio interposita est, sine condicione facta esset. quod et melius est."

[77] Cf. supra, note 65.

[78] The general retroactivity doctrine has been developed by Bartolus, as Schiemann, op. cit., note 63, pp. 29 sqq. has pointed out. For a detailed analysis of its adoption and application during the various periods of the ius commune, see Schiemann, pp. 36 sqq. Among 19th-century pandectists it became one of the most widely discussed and controversial topics in the whole field of private law; cf., for example Fr. Eisele, "Das Dogma von der rückwirkenden Kraft der erfüllten Suspensiv-Bedingung", (1867) 50 *Archiv für die civilistische Praxis* 253 sqq.; Windscheid/Kipp, § 91. For a long time, the general retroactivity doctrine dominated the scene (cf., for example, Vangerow, *Pandekten*, § 95; Puchta, *Pandekten*, § 61). It was ultimately shattered by Windscheid.

[79] Cf., in particular, Vassalli, op. cit., note 63, pp. 273 sqq. (maintaining his view on the basis of rather sweeping interpolation allegations); cf. also Gian Gualberto Archi, "Il negozio sotto condizione sospensiva nella compilazione di Giustiniano", in: *Scritti di diritto romano*, vol. III (1981), pp. 2079 sqq.

retroactivity entirely alien to classical law,[80] nor did Justinian dramatically change the law.[81] The problem appears to have been approached in a characteristically pragmatic fashion;[82] more particularly, the approach adopted may well have differed according to the specific type of transaction (stricti iuris or bonae fidei) to which the condition was appended.[83] Also, it must always be kept in mind that a doctrine of binding precedent did not exist in classical Roman law. The jurists often differed as to how to deal with a specific problem, and in the present context, too, it is more than likely that the solution of individual cases remained controversial.[84]

8. Interpretation of conditions

(a) General considerations

We have been looking at the consequences of the satisfaction of conditions. But when were conditions satisfied? This depended entirely on how they were drafted and what they were intended to achieve; it was, in other words, a matter of interpretation. In many cases the issue was straightforward. Under a stipulation of the type "Si Capitolium ascenderis, quinque aureos dare spondes?" the five gold coins became exactable if the stipulator had walked up Capitol hill; where the stipulation said "Si intra biennium Capitolium non ascenderis, quinque aureos dare spondes?",[85] the same sum could be claimed if within the next two years the stipulator did not in fact embark on that ascent. But we have already come across examples where the matter was much more difficult to determine—as in the case of a negative potestative condition that did not set a time within which the stipulator had to act if he did not want to pay the money ("Si in Capitolium non ascenderis . . .").[86] Generally speaking, the classical Roman jurists adopted a flexible rather than a formalistic approach towards the interpretation of conditions.[87] Ambiguities in stipulations, as usual, tended to be resolved contra stipulatorem;[88] with regard to testamentary dispositions, the general favor testamenti prevailed[89] and in the case of conditional releases from slavery (whether by last will or on account of

[80] Cf., in general, Volker Kurz, *Vor- und Rückwirkungen im klassischen römischen Recht* (unpublished Dr. iur. thesis, Freiburg i. Br., 1971), pp. 5 sqq. and passim.
[81] Masi, *Condizione*, pp. 158 sqq.; Kaser, *RPr* II, p. 96.
[82] Thomas, *TRL*, p. 237.
[83] Cf. Masi, *Condizione*, pp. 109 sqq.; Alfredo Calonge, "En torno al problema de la retroactividad de la condición en el derecho clásico", in: *Studi in onore di Edoardo Volterra*, vol. III (1971), pp. 147 sqq., 158 sqq.; Kurz, op. cit., note 80, pp. 117 sqq.
[84] Kaser, *RPr* I, pp. 256 sq.
[85] Cf. the example discussed in Cels. D. 45, 1, 99, 1.
[86] Pap. D. 45, 1, 115, 1; for details, cf. supra, p. 723.
[87] As they did with regard to both dispositions mortis causa and inter viros in general; cf. supra, pp. 625 sqq.
[88] Cf. supra, pp. 639 sqq. and also, for example, p. 104.
[89] Cf., for example, Wieling, (1970) 87 *ZSS* 230 sqq.

a transaction inter vivos), the jurists were guided by the favor libertatis.[90]

(b) Interpretatio in favorem libertatis

Historically the most significant example of such an interpretatio in favorem libertatis concerned the statuliber. This was a slave manumitted in a testament upon the condition that he would pay a certain sum of money to the heir;[91] this money, obviously, he normally had to take from his peculium. Now, it could happen that at the time when the testator died the slave did not have the necessary sum available to effect his release, because, for instance, a third party had failed to repay a loan he had been given by the slave. In cases of this kind it was up to the heir to sue the borrower: he was the slave's new master and was thus, formally, in charge of the peculium. Of course, no legal duty was incumbent on him to collect the debt; but if he failed to do so, he effectively prevented the condition from materializing. This was not to be welcomed; for at one and the same time, he thus frustrated the expectation of the statuliber to attain his freedom and the testator's true intention—which had, typically, been to make over to his heir the value of the slave, rather than the slave as such. Under these circumstances, Servius[92] was prepared to read a tacit proviso into the condition that had been set by the testator:[93] the slave was to be released upon payment of a certain sum of money, or if the slave's failure to render such payment was attributable to the heir. Or, to put the same idea slightly differently: the condition was treated as if it had in fact been satisfied, if the heir had himself prevented it from materializing.[94] It was in this form that the rule came to be generalized. "[Q]uibus

---

[90] For details, see Masi, *Condizione*, pp. 227 sqq.

[91] For details, see Guido Donatuti, *Lo statulibero* (1940); Kaser, *RPr* I, p. 114.

[92] Cf. Ulp. D. 40, 7, 3, 2.

[93] Cf. also Watson, *Obligations*, pp. 1 sq. ("implied term"); Knütel, *Stipulatio poenae*, pp. 211 sq. Both authors deal with Ulp. D. 22, 2, 8, where Ulpian, once again, refers to Servius, this time for the proposition that a penalty cannot be claimed if the event upon which its forfeiture has been made dependent was brought about by the stipulator ("Servius ait pecuniae traiecticiae poenam peti non posse, si per creditorem stetisset, quo minus eam intra certum tempus praestitutum accipiat"). This is the historical origin of the rule embodied in § 162 II BGB: "If the fulfilment of a condition is brought about in bad faith by the party to whose advantage it would operate, the condition is deemed not to have been fulfilled." For South Africa, cf. Joubert, *Contract*, p. 177: "By parity of reasoning the same principle can be applied where the party who would be a creditor upon fulfilment actually ensures fulfilment of the condition contrary to the intention of the parties." As far as classical Roman law is concerned, cf. also Modest. D. 46, 1, 41 pr. (dealing with fideiussio indemnitatis; on which see supra, pp. 137, 140, 142), as interpreted by Rolf Knütel, "Zur Frage der sog. Diligenzpflichten des Gläubigers gegenüber dem Bürgen", in: *Festschrift für Werner Flume*, vol. I (1978), p. 568 sqq., 570.

[94] Cf. also UE 2, 5: "Si per heredem factum sit, quo minus statu liber condicioni pareat, proinde fit liber, atque si condicio expleta fuisset"; see further UE 2, 4, another decision in favorem libertatis, attributed by Ulpian to the XII Tables already. On the favor libertatis as motivation for the decisions concerning the statuliber, cf. also Kalchthaler, op. cit., note 9, pp. 53 sqq.

exemplis stipulationis quoque committi quidam recte putaverunt, cum per promissorem factum esset, quo minus stipulator condicioni pareret", as Julian reports.[95]

(c) Condition prevented from materializing

But what was recognized with regard to formal declarations (wills, first of all, then stipulations) was also, of course, applicable in the case of emptio venditio and other informal transactions. Here the equation of prevention with satisfaction—quite in line with the bonae fidei nature of these contracts—found an even broader field of operation. Take, for example, the case where a library is sold upon condition that the municipality sells to the purchaser the necessary ground to put it up.[96] This is what Justinian would have referred to as a condicio mixta: the municipality had to be prepared to make a site available but the purchaser had to do his bit too; unless, at least, he asked for a suitable site to be sold and transferred to him, there was no chance that the condition would materialize. The purchaser's cooperation towards the perfection of the sale was not, of course, enforceable; but if he failed to render it, the condition was treated as satisfied and the vendor was able, as a result, to bring the actio venditi. Why he had prevented the condition from materializing was relevant only in so far as his failure to act had to have been "attributable" to him; the standard expression used in this context was "si per emptorem steterit quo minus impleatur".[97] That implied neither an intention to defraud the other party nor plain dolus or even fault at large, in the sense of personal blame.[98] Provided only that the reason for the non-perfection of the sale fell within his sphere of responsibility, the purchaser's refusal to treat the contract as valid was seen, apparently, as an infringement of the precepts of good faith.[99]

How could all these cases (the one involving a will, the other a unilateral contract, the third a contract of sale) be reduced to one common denominator? What was objectionable, and had thus led the

---

[95] D. 35, 1, 24. By the time of Ulpian, the matter was no longer controversial: Ulp. D. 50, 17, 161 ("quibus exemplis stipulationes quoque committuntur . . ."). Cf. further David Daube, "Condition Prevented from Materializing", (1960) 28 *TR* 274 sqq.; Kalchthaler, op. cit., note 9, pp. 25 sqq.

[96] Ulp. D. 18, 1, 50. Cf. also Pomp. D. 18, 1, 8 pr. and Daube, (1960) 28 *TR* 281 sqq.; Kalchthaler, op. cit., note 9, pp. 59 sqq.

[97] Cf., for example, Ulp. D. 18, 1, 50; cf. also Serv./Ulp D. 22, 2, 8 (as far as stipulations were concerned). Other texts use the phrase "si per heredem (promisorem) factum sit": UE 2, 5; cf. also Iul. D. 35, 1, 24; Ulp. D. 50, 17, 161.

[98] Cf. supra, pp. 105 sq. and also Rolf Knütel, "Zur sogenannten Erfüllungs- und Nichterfüllungsfiktion bei der Bedingung", 1976 *Juristische Blätter* 616; idem, *Stipulatio poenae*, p. 197.

[99] Cf. also Karl Hackl, "Sulla finzione nel diritto privato", in: *Studi in onore di Arnaldo Biscardi*, vol. I (1982), p. 257. Whether or not, in an individual case, prevention could be equated with satisfaction, continued, however, to depend on the interpretation of the contract; hence, for example, the solution arrived at in Iul. D. 18, 1, 41 pr., where to treat condicio pro impleta (and consequently the contract of sale) as operative would obviously not have made sense: Daube, (1960) 28 *TR* 271 sqq.

jurists to apply the fiction, was the fact that satisfaction of the condition was prevented by a party who had an interest in its non-fulfilment; but for the satisfaction of the condition, the heir did not have to release the slave, and promisor as well as purchaser were under no obligation to pay. The general rule that eventually emerged was therefore formulated in the following terms:

> "In iure civili receptum est, quotiens per eum, cuius interest condicionem non impleri, fiat quo minus impleatur, perinde haberi, ac si impleta condicio fuisset."[100]

Or, as the fathers of the German BGB were to put it: if the fulfilment of a condition is prevented by the party to whose disadvantage it would operate, the condition is deemed to have been fulfilled.[101]

III. RESOLUTIVE CONDITIONS

1. The construction of resolutive conditions

> "If a legal transaction is entered into subject to a resolutive condition, the effect of the transaction lapses upon fulfilment of the condition; at this moment the former legal position is restored."

With these words the BGB[102] introduces the second type of condition recognized by most modern legal systems.[103] The Roman lawyers did not put it quite like that when they referred to an arrangement by the parties, according to which a contract was to be resolved upon the occurrence, or non-occurrence, of a future uncertain event. Only occasionally did they use formulations in which we can already detect a ring of the modern conceptual analysis. "[S]ub condicione resolvi emptio . . . videatur",[104] or "constat . . . resolvi emptionem sub condicione",[105] they said, thus indicating that a sale could be dissolved rather than contracted conditionally. But did they really mean to imply,

---

[100] Ulp. D. 50, 17, 161; cf. also Iul. D. 35, 1, 24; on which see Kalchthaler, op. cit., note 9, pp. 25 sqq.; Masi, *Condizione*, pp. 220 sqq. Another fiction, incidentally, that came to be recognized in post-classical, but possibly even in classical law, remained confined to the law of testamentary dispositions: a condition is held to be satisfied if the potential beneficiary was prevented from actual satisfaction due to circumstances which were outside his control (si per eum non stat, quominus impleatur); cf. UE 2, 6; Hermog. D. 35, 1, 94; Paul. D. 40, 7, 20, 3; Masi, *Condizione*, pp. 227 sqq.; Kaser, *RPr* I, p. 257; idem, *RPr* II, p. 97; for a modern comparative discussion, see A.B. Schwarz, "Bedingung", in: Franz Schlegelberger (ed.), *Rechtsvergleichendes Handwörterbuch für das Zivil- und Handelsrecht des In- und Auslandes*, vol. II (1929), pp. 415 sqq.

[101] However, the German legislator attempted to specify the manner in which fulfilment of the condition had to have been prevented and therefore added the words "in violation of the precepts of good faith" *("wider Treu und Glauben")*. He thus appears to have restricted the application of the "prevention equals satisfaction" rule. Yet this was not his intention; on the contrary, he devised this clause in order to emphasize the width of its range of operation; for a detailed analysis, see Knütel, 1976 *Juristische Blätter* 613 sqq., 616 sqq.

[102] § 158 II.

[103] For South African law, cf. Joubert, *Contract*, pp. 172 sq.; generally, see Schwarz, op. cit., note 100, pp. 395 sqq.

[104] Ulp. D. 18, 3, 1.

[105] Ulp. D. 18, 1, 3.

with these phrases, that the sale itself was subject to a (resolutive) condition?[106] Or did they not rather regard the sale as unconditional, yet accompanied by an informal pactum, according to which the contract was under certain circumstances to be dissolved?[107] It would then have been this dissolution pactum[108] which was subject to a condition, in the ordinary (Roman) sense of the word: it was supposed to become effective only upon the occurrence, or non-occurrence, of a future uncertain event. This is the kind of construction which Ulpian appears to have in mind in D. 18, 2, 2 pr., where he describes the situation in the following terms: ". . . pura emptio est, sed sub condicione resolvitur."[109] But we should be careful not to read all too subtle nuances into our sources and to use one or another specific turn of phrase as a basis for substantive distinctions.[110] Even if—as appears to me more likely—the Roman lawyers at least originally[111] tended to regard the resolutio venditionis as being sub condicione (suspensiva), they thereby recognized the possibility of subjecting a contract of sale to what in actual fact and for all practical purposes amounted to resolutive conditions.[112]

2. The admissibility of resolutive conditions

It is no mere accident that all the sources just referred to deal with emptio venditio. Sale was a bonae fidei contract, and it was the "ex bona fide" clause contained in the formulae of the actiones venditi and empti that enabled the Roman lawyers to take account of all informal arrangements between the parties when it came to determining whether either of the actions could be brought. If, therefore, the parties had arranged that their contract should be dissolved upon the occurrence, or non-occurrence, of an uncertain future event, what could have been more in accordance with good faith than to give effect to this

---

[106] Cf. Rudolf Henle, "Die rechtliche Natur der in diem addictio beim Kaufvertrage", in: *Festschrift für Paul Koschaker*, vol. II (1939), pp. 188 sqq.; Arangio-Ruiz, *Compravendita*, pp. 405, 407; Kaser, *RPr* I, p. 257; Honsell/Mayer-Maly/Selb, p. 92.

[107] Cf. Windscheid/Kipp, § 86, n. 6; Franz Wieacker, *Lex commissoria*, 1932, pp. 31 sqq. Generally on the construction of resolutive conditions and on the views adopted in 19th-century legal science, cf. also Markus Knellwolf, *Zur Konstruktion des Kaufs auf Probe* (1987), pp. 105 sqq.

[108] On which see, in general, Paul. D. 18, 5, 3 ("Emptio et venditio sicut consensu contrahitur, ita contrario consensu resolvitur, antequam fuerit res secuta"); Iul. D. 18, 5, 5, 1 ("Emptio nuda conventione dissolvitur, si res secuta non fuerit"); Knütel, *Contrarius consensus*, passim.

[109] Ulp. D. 18, 2, 2 pr.

[110] A point that has been emphasized by Peters, *Rücktrittsvorbehalte*, p. 94.

[111] Rabel, *Grundzüge*, pp. 175 sq.

[112] Contra: Werner Flume, "Die Aufhebungsabreden beim Kauf"—lex commissoria, in diem addictio und sogenanntes pactum displicentiae—und die Bedingung nach der Lehre der römischen Klassiker", in: *Festschrift für Max Kaser* (1976), pp. 309 sqq.; idem, "Der bedingte Rechtsakt nach den Vorstellungen der römischen Klassiker", (1975) 92 *ZSS* 68 sqq., 72 sq. He argues that, since the legal act itself (and not only the legal relationship created by it) was regarded as being sub condicione by the Roman lawyers, its subjection to a resolutive condition was conceptually impossible.

arrangement? The same considerations, of course, applied with regard to the other consensual contracts. They did not, however, apply to stipulations. Here the rigid formula of the condictio did not enable judges to pay attention to informal dissolution pacta, and a resolutive condition contained in the wording of the stipulation itself was, iure civili, simply ignored.[113] A stipulation for one hundred "nisi navis ex Asia venerit"[114] was therefore regarded as an absolute promise. Praetorian intervention, however, ensured that the clause at least had some effect; for if the stipulator sued for the promised sum after the ship had arrived from Asia, his claim could be barred by either the exceptio doli or the exceptio pacti.[115] Absolute legal rights and positions such as ownership, freedom or patria potestas could not be conferred or granted for some time only;[116] if they were subjected to a resolutive condition, the whole transaction was thus, apparently, invalid.[117] Actus legitimi,[118] too, could no more be resolved than brought about sub condicione.

3. The effects of resolutive conditions

What, then, were the effects of a resolutive condition where the parties were in fact able to append it to their contract? None for the time being; for the transaction was regarded as "pura",[119] which meant that it instantly became fully effective. Thus, for example, the parties had to render their performances, the contract provided a iusta causa traditionis as well as usucapionis, and a contract of sale was regarded as perfecta (with the result that the risk passed to the purchaser).[120] If the condition was satisfied, on the other hand, the contract was dissolved and restitution had to be effected: the purchaser could claim back the purchase price, the vendor the object of the sale. For this purpose the parties could avail themselves of the actiones empti and

[113] The reason is, presumably, that recognition of resolutive conditions in stipulations would have been in conflict with the non-recognition of suspensive conditions in formal releases (acceptilationes). Acceptilationes belonged to the actus legitimi of Pap. D. 50, 17, 77; cf. supra, note 13.

[114] Paul. D. 44, 7, 44, 2.

[115] Paul. D. 44, 7, 44, 2; Honsell/Mayer-Maly/Selb, p. 92.

[116] Cf. vat. 283 ("cum ad tempus [?; cf. infra, note 125] proprietas transferri nequiverit"); Paul. D. 40, 4, 33 ("Libertas ad tempus dari non potest"); Lab./Paul. D. 1, 7, 34 (". . . nec enim moribus nostris convenit filium temporalem habere"). As far as institutio heredis was concerned, the rule was semel heres, semper heres; cf. Gai. II, 184; Gai. D. 28, 5, 89.

[117] Honsell/Mayer-Maly/Selb, p. 92. A resolutive condition contained in a will—in violation of semel heres semper heres—was, however, regarded as pro non scripto (Kaser, *RPr* I, p. 688).

[118] Pap. D. 50, 17, 77.

[119] Cf. Ulp. D. 18, 2, 2 pr. On the technical term "purus" (unconditional, in the sense of not subject to a suspensive condition), see *Inst.* III, 15, 2 ("Omnis stipulatio aut pure aut in diem aut sub condicione fit. . . .") and, today still art. 1584 code civil ("*La vente peut être faite purement et simplement, ou sous une condition soit suspensive, soit résolutoire*"). In England, the term "absolute" is often used in contradistinction to "conditional".

[120] Iul./Ulp. D. 18, 2, 2, 1; for all details, see Peters, *Rücktrittsvorbehalte*, pp. 152 sqq.

venditi[121]—rather surprisingly so, in view of the fact that the contract of sale no longer existed.[122] Various attempts were made to explain this apparent dogmatical inconsistency; Papinian, for example, argued that, since the parties had initially contracted a sale, the dissolution of their relationship, too, had to follow the rules of sale.[123] This was not a particularly compelling proposition and thus we find Ulpian merely referring to an authoritative ruling on the matter: "[E]t quidem finita est emptio", he stressed, but then he added: "sed iam decisa quaestio est ex vendito actionem competere, ut rescriptis imperatoris Antonini et divi Severi declaratur."[124] Ownership in the object of the sale, incidentally, automatically reverted to the vendor on satisfaction of the resolutive condition. There is ample support in our sources for this proposition:[125] thus, for instance, we read that the purchaser could no longer avail himself of an action in rem after the event, upon which the resolution of the contract hinged, had occurred;[126] and if the purchaser had in the meantime pledged the object of the sale, the encumbrance fell away with the dissolution of the contract: "ex quo colligitur", writes Marcellus,[127] "quod emptor medio tempore dominus est: alioquin nec pignus teneret." But he was owner only "medio tempore", not after the condition had been satisfied. The vendor was therefore able to avail himself of the rei vindicatio to reclaim the object

[121] The relevant sources are analysed by Peters, *Rücktrittsvorbehalte*, pp. 262 sqq.

[122] The object of the sale was usually regarded as "inemptus": cf., for instance, Pomp. D. 18, 3, 2 and Uwe Wesel, "Zur dinglichen Wirkung der Rückttrittsvorbehalte des römischen Kaufs", (1968) 85 *ZSS* 163 sqq.

[123] Vat. 14 ("Lege venditionis inempto praedio facto fructus interea perceptos iudicio venditi restitui placuit, quoniam eo iure contractum in exordio videtur . . ."). Cf. further the somewhat strained explanation offered by Pomp. D. 18, 1, 6, 1.

[124] Ulp. D. 18, 3, 4 pr.

[125] Which is, nevertheless, rejected by a large body of opinion; cf. Wieacker, op. cit., note 107, pp. 45 sqq.; Ernst Levy, "Zu den Rücktrittsvorbehalten des römischen Kaufs", in: *Gesammelte Schriften*, vol. II (1963), pp. 117 sqq.; De Zulueta, *Sale*, p. 56; Arangio-Ruiz, *Compravendita*, pp. 420 sqq.; Flume, *Festschrift Kaser*, pp. 310 sqq., 320 sqq. The strongest argument in favour of these authors is vat. 283, which appears to declare, quite unequivocally, that ownership may not be transferred merely for some time (". . . cum ad tempus proprietas transferri nequiverit"). Attention has, however, been drawn to the fact that the manuscript of the Fragmenta Vaticana has "ad te" rather than "ad tempus". The text may therefore have referred to the individual case in question which involved a donation "ut post mortem eius qui accepit ad te rediret". Transfer of ownership on account of a donation may thus have been treated differently in this respect than a transfer based on sale. For a detailed analysis, see Peters, *Rücktrittsvorbehalte*, pp. 173 sqq.

In favour of an effect "in rem" of dissolution of a contract of sale are, apart from Peters, *Rücktrittsvorbehalte*, pp. 164 sqq., Wesel, (1968) 85 *ZSS* 94 sqq. and Kaser, *RPr* I, p. 562; cf. also Savigny, *System*, vol. III, p. 154; Vangerow, *Pandekten*, § 96; Windscheid/Kipp, § 90, n. 1. As far as the discussion among the authors of the ius commune is concerned, cf. Glück, vol. 16, pp. 263 sqq., 295 sqq.; Wesel, (1968) 85 *ZSS* 96 sqq.

[126] Ulp. D. 6, 1, 41 pr.

[127] Cf. Ulp. D. 18, 2, 4, 3; cf. also Marc./Ulp. D. 20, 6, 3.

of the sale; usually, however, he preferred to bring the more convenient actio venditi.[128]

IV. PROVISIONS FOR CALLING OFF A SALE

Most of our texts by far, concerning resolutive conditions, deal with three specific clauses, frequently appended, by way of pacta ex continenti adiecta,[129] to contracts of sale. These clauses were known as in diem addictio, lex commissoria and pactum displicentiae. Since they feature so prominently in our sources, it may not be inappropriate to pause for a moment and to look at how they operated.

1. In diem addictio

(a) Functions

"In diem addictio ita fit: 'ille fundus centum esto tibi emptus, nisi si quis intra kalendas Ianuarias proximas meliorem condicionem fecerit, quo res a domino abeat'."[130] This was the standard way[131] of phrasing an in diem addictio: let the land be sold to you, unless someone makes a better offer before the first of January next, on account of which the land departs from its owner. The clause was normally added to the contract at the instigation of the vendor;[132] it provided him with an opportunity to explore all the possibilities of how best to sell his piece of property, while at the same time protecting him against the consequences of unfavourable developments on the market—he was assured of at least the price he had agreed upon with the present purchaser. A sale sub in diem addictione could, furthermore, serve as a convenient means of raising credit. The vendor received the money that he needed, without suffering the disadvantages normally connected with somewhat hasty emergency sales: he still retained the chance of finally obtaining better value for his land. Occasionally, however, inclusion of the clause could also lie in the interest of a purchaser, who still entertained some doubts as to whether it was really so wise for him to buy the land; the in diem addictio gave him a suitable opportunity to get out of the transaction.

---

[128] On the advantages of the actio venditi (which allowed the vendor to claim compensation for damages, and profits), cf. Peters, *Rücktrittsvorbehalte*, pp. 202 sq., 263, 295.

[129] On which see, in general, supra, pp. 509 sqq.

[130] Paul. D. 18, 2, 1. On the phrase proposed in this fragment, see Wesel, (1968) 85 *ZSS* 138; J.A.C. Thomas, "Provisions for Calling Off a Sale", (1967) 35 *TR* 561 sqq.; Peters, *Rücktrittsvorbehalte*, pp. 8 sqq.

[131] According to Carlo Longo, "Sulla 'in diem addictio' e sulla 'lex commissoria' nella vendita", (1921) 31 *BIDR* 40 sqq., and others, the only one. Contra, however, the writers referred to in the previous note.

[132] For what follows, see Peters, *Rücktrittsvorbehalte*, p. 10.

(b) Construction

Was this particular type of pactum adiectum to be construed as a resolutive or rather as a suspensive condition?[133] Julian appears to have opined in favour of the former alternative,[134] Pomponius in favour of the latter.[135] Ulpian gave the typical lawyer's answer: it depends—

> "[q]uotiens fundus in diem addicitur, utrum pura emptio est, sed sub condicione resolvitur, an vero condicionalis sit magis emptio, quaestionis est. et mihi videtur verius interesse, quid actum sit."[136]

The decisive criterion was thus the intention of the parties. If they wanted performance and counterperformance to be rendered immediately, then what they had in mind was "pura emptio, quae sub condicione resolvitur"; if, on the other hand, they wished to defer the implementation of their transaction until either a better offer had been made or the time set for the receipt of a better offer had elapsed, the sale was obviously "condicionalis". What the matter usually boiled down to, in the end, was which of the two parties had been able to prevail with his ideas concerning how the contract was to operate: the purchaser, as a rule, being interested in a resolutive condition (since he would then immediately receive the object of the sale), the vendor normally favouring suspension of the contract (for as long as he was still in possession of the object he had a greater chance of finding third parties interested in acquiring it).

(c) Interpretation

But even apart from that, in diem addictiones offered the Roman jurists plenty of scope to display their interpretive skills.[137] Taking the typical intentions of reasonable Roman purchasers and vendors as their starting point, they worked out a refined and well-balanced set of principles. Generally speaking, they tended to favour the purchaser—quite in accordance with the notion that ambiguous terms should be interpreted to the disadvantage of the party that had (typically) introduced them into the transaction.[138] Any doubt, for instance, as to whether the condition had been satisfied was held against the vendor; if two slaves had been sold separately to two purchasers for ten apiece and someone

---

[133] Cf. Rudolf Henle, "Die rechtliche Natur der in diem addictio beim Kaufvertrage", in: *Festschrift für Paul Koschaker*, vol. II (1939), pp. 169 sqq.; Thomas, (1967) 35 *TR* 565 sqq.; Peters, *Rücktrittsvorbehalte*, pp. 98 sq., 100 sqq.

[134] Iul./Ulp. D. 18, 2, 2, 1; Iul./Paul. D. 41, 4, 2, 4.

[135] D. 18, 2, 4 pr.

[136] D. 18, 2, 2 pr. This text has often been regarded as interpolated; cf., for example, Longo, (1921) 31 *BIDR* 44 sq.; Arangio-Ruiz, *Compravendita*, pp. 408 sqq. Contra the authors referred to in note 133.

[137] For details, see Bechmann, *Kauf*, vol. II, pp. 502 sqq.; Glück, vol. 16, pp. 239 sqq.; Thomas, (1967) 35 *TR* 565 sqq.; Peters, *Rücktrittsvorbehalte*, pp. 26 sqq.; on the origin of the in diem addictio, see Thielmann, *Privatauktion*, pp. 17 sqq., 34 sqq.; Peters, *Rücktrittsvorbehalte*, pp. 21 sqq.

[138] On interpretatio contra stipulatorem, see supra, pp. 639 sqq.

offered thirty for the two, the sale was not dissolved as long as it remained uncertain for which of the slaves, if not for both, a better offer had been made.[139] Furthermore, the purchaser was normally allowed to solicit, and accept, only one better offer.[140] Whether or not in the end he accepted it, was left to his discretion; he was perfectly free to stand by the original contract.[141] If, however, he decided to take up the second offer, he had to inform the (first) purchaser, so as to give him a chance to improve his own bid;[142] and provided the first purchaser was prepared to match the second offer, the vendor could not call off the sale.[143] The crucial question, obviously, in many cases was, under which circumstances the second offer could be regarded as "melior condicio". An increased price, interestingly, was not necessarily required. Even without it, there was a better offer if easier or earlier payment was proposed; or if a more convenient place of payment was suggested. Moreover, the price could even be lower, provided the newcomer was prepared to waive certain onerous provisions contained in the (first) contract of sale.[144] Finally, an offer could also be deemed to be "better" if it was made by a more reliable person.[145] The position was summed up crisply by Pomponius: "Quidquid enim ad utilitatem venditoris pertinet, pro meliore condicione haberi debet."[146]

2. Lex commissoria

Just as in the case of an in diem addictio, a standard form appears to have been used by the parties when they wished to add what was usually referred to as a lex commissoria[147] to their sale: "si ad diem pecunia soluta non sit, ut fundus inemptus sit", they would tend to say or write.[148] What this clause was designed to achieve is rather obvious:

---

[139] Iul. D. 18, 2, 17 (". . . quod si incertum sit, ad utrius pretium addiderit, a priore emptione non videtur esse discessum").

[140] Sab./Ulp. D. 18, 2, 11 pr., as interpreted by Peters, *Rücktrittsvorbehalte*, pp. 41 sqq.; contra: Arangio-Ruiz, *Compravendita*, p. 402; Henle, *Festschrift Koschaker*, vol. II, p. 170. The parties were, however, able to provide differently (". . . sed Iulianus . . . scripsit interesse multum, quid inter contrahentes actum sit, nec impedire quicquam vel hoc agi, ut saepius fundus collocetur, dum vel prima vel secunda vel tertia adiectione res a venditore discedat").

[141] Sab./Ulp. D. 18, 2, 9. Again, there could be a special agreement to the contrary.

[142] Paul. D. 18, 2, 8.

[143] Paul. D. 18, 2, 7. There was thus an obvious functional similarity to an auction sale; the technical details of how the two institutions related to each other are disputed. Cf. Mario Talamanca, "Contributo allo studio delle vendite all'asta nel mondo classico", in: (1955) 6 *Atti della accademia nazionale dei lincei* 106 sq.; J.A.C. Thomas, "The Auction Sale in Roman Law", 1957 *Juridical Review* 42 sqq.; Thielmann, *Privatauktion*, pp. 17 sqq.; Peters, *Rücktrittsvorbehalte*, pp. 11 sqq.

[144] Ulp. D. 18, 2, 4, 6.

[145] Pomp./Ulp D. 18, 2, 4, 6.

[146] D. 18, 2, 5.

[147] From committere = to forfeit (cf. Heumann/Seckel, pp. 80 sq.); ownership of the object of the sale, as far as it had already been transferred, fell back (was forfeited) to the vendor.

[148] Pomp. D. 18, 3, 2. But other formulations were possible; cf., for example, Pomp. D. 18, 1, 6, 1 and Thomas, (1967) 35 *TR* 563 sqq.

the vendor was to be given the right to call off the sale if the purchase price had not been paid by a certain time.[149] But for the lex commissoria he could avail himself of the actio venditi against the purchaser only to claim the price or damages; a unilateral right of withdrawal on account of mora or any other form of breach of contract did not exist in Roman law.[150] Unlike an in diem addictio, a lex commissoria was thus solely in the vendor's interest and it was, as a rule, taken to have a resolutive rather than a suspensive effect;[151] after all, the lex commissoria aimed at inducing the purchaser to render payment timeously and the parties could thus normally be taken to have presupposed that the obligation to pay had in fact become effective. In order to make the whole arrangement workable, the jurists determined that the sale did not collapse, ipso iure, if by the due date the purchase price had not been paid; for that would, effectively, have allowed the purchaser to call off the sale if he no longer wanted to be bound by it. "Nam legem commissoriam . . . si volet venditor exercebit, non etiam invitus":[152] the vendor had the option of using the actio venditi either to claim the purchase price or to recover the object that he had given.[153] The reasonable interests of the purchaser were, however, safeguarded, in so far as the vendor had to make his election quickly and for good.[154] Whether, furthermore, the purchaser had to have defaulted in the technical sense of the word before the vendor could exercise his right under the lex commissoria is not quite clear.[155]

---

[149] Not unnaturally a lex commissoria was often agreed upon if the purchase price had to be paid in instalments; cf., for example, Pomp. D. 18, 1, 6, 1; Paul. D. 4, 4, 38 pr. (on the interpretation of the latter fragment, see Peters, *Rücktrittsvorbehalte*, pp. 77 sqq.; Detlef Liebs, "Der Sieg der schönen Rutiliana. Lex commissoria displicebat", in: *Festschrift für Max Kaser* (1976), pp. 373 sqq.; Berthold Kupisch, "Rutiliana pupilla—schön oder energisch? (Paul. D. 4, 4, 38 pr.)", (1977) 94 *ZSS* 247 sqq.). Not infrequently an arrha was given at the conclusion of the sale. It was forfeited to the vendor if the contract was called off; otherwise it was credited against the purchase price (cf. Peters, *Rücktrittsvorbehalte*, p. 61). On the relationship between the Roman sale sub lege commissoria and the arrha transaction of Greek provenance, see Wieacker, op. cit., note 107, pp. 79 sqq.; Levy, *Gesammelte Schriften*, vol. II, pp. 281 sqq.; Wesel, (1968) 85 *ZSS* 133 sqq.; Peters, *Rücktrittsvorbehalte*, pp. 60 sqq.

[150] Cf. supra, pp. 578 sq. and infra, p. 801.

[151] Ulp. D. 18, 3, 1: "Si fundus commissoria lege venierit, magis est, ut sub condicione resolvi emptio quam sub condicione contrahi videatur." Cf. further Sab./Paul. D. 41, 4, 2, 3; Pomp. D. 18, 3, 2; on which, see Wieacker, op. cit., note 107, pp. 19 sqq., 31 sqq., but also Peters, *Rücktrittsvorbehalte*, pp. 112 sqq., 115 sqq.

[152] Ulp. D. 18, 3, 3; cf. also Pomp. D. 18, 3, 2.

[153] Cf. also § 360 BGB, which still determines, for the same reason, that a forfeiture clause (i.e. a provision in the contract that the debtor shall forfeit his rights arising from the contract if he does not perform his obligation) grants the creditor a right to rescind the contract (*Mugdan*, vol. II, p. 158). § 360, obviously, looks at the notion of a "lex commissoria" from a more general point of view; the rule is not confined to contracts of sale. At the same time it has lost much of its practical significance as a result of the fact that the BGB recognizes a statutory right of rescission in case of mora debitoris; cf. infra, pp. 800, 802.

[154] Pap./Ulp. D. 18, 3, 4, 2.

[155] Was fault on the part of the purchaser required? And did the vendor have to make a special demand (interpellatio) before calling off the sale? Cf. Ulp. D. 18, 3, 4, 4; Lab. D. 19,

3. Pactum displicentiae

(a) Function

The subjection of a contract of sale to a pactum displicentiae, in turn, was solely in the interest of the purchaser. The clause was often phrased along the following lines: "ut si displicuisset [res] inempta [sit]",[156] and a provision of this kind clearly left the determination of whether or not the contract was to stand completely in the purchaser's discretion: if he did not like the object he had bought, he was able, without further ado, to terminate the sale.[157] As a rule, the parties specified a time within which the purchaser had to make up his mind;[158] what happened if they didn't cannot be said with any degree of certainty.[159] Occasionally, the right to invoke the pactum displicentiae was lost even before the period for approval had elapsed. Thus we read of the sale of three horses, which the purchaser was allowed to return within three days if he found them unsatisfactory. After having used the horses in a contest, and despite having won the first prize, he decided to return them. Under these circumstances, Ulpian allowed the vendor to claim the purchase price: "nam inter nos hoc actum", he argued,[160] "ut experimentum

---

1, 51, 1; Scaev. D. 18, 3, 6 pr. and the discussion by Heinrich Siber, "Interpellatio und Mora", (1908) 29 *ZSS* 101 sqq.; Wieacker, op. cit., note 107, pp. 35 sq.; Peters, *Rücktrittsvorbehalte*, pp. 71 sqq.

[156] Cf. Ulp. D. 18, 1, 3; Ulp. D. 43, 24, 11, 13; Paul. D. 41, 4, 2, 5; C. 4, 58, 4 (Diocl. et Max.). The formulation was less standardized than in the case of an in diem addictio and a lex commissoria. Significantly, the compilers did not devote a special title of the Digest to this type of pactum.

[157] No objective reasons for the decision (as, for instance, that the object was defective) had to be provided; cf. Peters, *Rücktrittsvorbehalte*, pp. 87, 93; Karlheinz Misera, Der Kauf auf Probe, *ANRW*, vol. II, 14 (1982), p. 561; Knellwolf, op. cit., note 107, pp. 16 sqq., 38 sqq. and passim. The pactum displicentiae thus constituted a potestative condition. In diem addictio and lex commissoria, on the other hand, were condiciones mixtae (i.e. potestative and casualis at one and the same time). Alternatively, it was, of course, quite possible that the vendor handed the object over to the purchaser "ad inspiciendum" (cf. Ulp. D. 19, 5, 17, 2) or "pretii explorandi gratia" (Pap. D. 19, 5, 1, 2), i.e. before a contract of sale had been concluded. The main problem, in these cases, was under which circumstances the inspector was liable if he lost the object. The answer was made to depend on utility considerations (cf. supra, pp. 198 sq.): for details, see Misera, pp. 526 sqq.

[158] Sab./Paul. D. 18, 5, 6; Paul. D. 41, 4, 2, 5; Mela/Ulp. D. 19, 5, 20, 1; Lab./Ulp. D. 19, 5, 20 pr. (triduum); *Inst.* III, 23, 4.

[159] Cf. the speculations by Peters, *Rücktrittsvorbehalte*, pp. 90 sq. If a slave was sold "ut, nisi placuerit, redhibeatur", the period of two months provided in the aedilitian edict for the actio redhibitoria "adversus eum [qui] de his quae edicto aedilium continentur non caveat" (Gai. D. 21, 1, 28; cf. further supra, pp. 296, 316) appears to have been applied per analogiam: ". . . si autem de tempore nihil convenerit, in factum actio intra sexaginta dies utiles accommodatur emptori ad redhibendum . . ." (Ulp. D. 21, 1, 31, 22). This pactum redhibendi relating to the sale of slaves served the same function, but was (probably) not identical to the pactum displicentiae relating to all other objects of sale. The former was closely related to the system of the aedilitian remedies and gave rise to an actio in factum ad redhibendum, not to the actiones empti or venditi; cf., apart from Ulp. D. 21, 1, 31, 22 sqq. also Pap. vat. 14 and the analysis by Misera, op. cit., note 157, pp. 531 sqq., 566 sqq. Contra (the two institutions were identical): Wieacker, op. cit., note 107, pp. 73 sq.; Levy, *Gesammelte Schriften*, vol. II, p. 277; Peters, *Rücktrittsvorbehalte*, pp. 84 sqq.

[160] D. 19, 5, 20 pr.

gratuitum acciperes, non ut etiam certares." Even though in this particular case a contract had probably not yet been concluded (which appears to be the reason why Ulpian granted an actio praescriptis verbis rather than the actio venditi),[161] the same considerations must have prevailed if the parties had entered into a sale on approval.

(b) Construction

How was the pactum displicentiae construed by the Roman jurists? According to Ulpian, the matter was determined in favour of a resolutive condition: "[C]onstat non esse sub condicione distractam, sed resolvi emptionem sub condicione", he stated unequivocally.[162] But this ruling referred only to clauses of the type "si displicuisset inemptus erit". Yet, occasionally, the parties seem to have settled on "si placuerit, erit tibi emptus"[163] and this formulation hinted rather strongly at a condicio suspensiva. The authors of Justinian's *Institutes*, in fact, understood it in this sense.[164] What mattered, therefore, was "quid actum sit":[165] how the parties, in each individual case, had intended their transaction to operate.[166] The different legal consequences resulting from the two courses available to the parties are illustrated in a text by Mela.[167] A number of mules were sold on approval. If the purchaser liked them, he had to pay the purchase price; if he did not, he owed a certain sum for every day he kept the animals. During the trial period the mules were taken away by a gang of robbers. What did the purchaser have to pay? If the pactum constituted a resolutive condition, the purchase price: emptione perfecta periculum est emptoris. If, on the other hand, the clause was of a suspensive

[161] Wieacker, op. cit., note 107, p. 74; Peters, *Rücktrittsvorbehalte*, pp. 88 sqq.; Flume, *Festschrift Kaser*, p. 325; Kaser, *RPr* I, p. 581; contra: Misera, op. cit., note 157, pp. 549 sqq. (sale under a resolutive condition); Thomas, (1967) 35 *TR* 570 sq.; Knellwolf, op. cit., note 107, pp. 92 sqq. (sale under a suspensive condition).

[162] D. 18, 1, 3.

[163] Cf. Mela/Ulp. D. 19, 5, 20, 1; *Inst.* III, 23, 4.

[164] *Inst.* III, 23, 4.

[165] Ulp. D. 18, 2, 2 pr.

[166] In the majority of cases, a pactum displicentiae was construed as a resolutive condition; for a detailed analysis of all our sources, see Misera, op. cit., note 157, pp. 539 sqq., 549 sqq., 556 sqq., 564 sq.; cf. also Knellwolf, op. cit., note 107, pp. 16 sqq. (suspensive condition), pp. 97 sqq. (resolutive condition). But see Peters, *Rücktrittsvorbehalte*, pp. 101 sqq., who argues that the classical Roman lawyers always regarded a pactum displicentiae as a resolutive condition.

[167] Ulp. D. 19, 5, 20, 1: "Item apud Melam quaeritur, si mulas tibi dedero ut experiaris et, si placuissent, emeres, si displicuissent, ut in dies singulos aliquid praestares, deinde mulae a grassatoribus fuerint ablatae intra dies experimenti, quid esset praestandum, utrum pretium et merces an merces tantum. et ait Mela interesse, utrum emptio iam erat contracta an futura, ut, si facta, pretium petatur, si futura, merces petatur: sed non exprimit de actionibus. puto autem, si quidem perfecta fuit emptio, competere ex vendito actionem, si vero nondum perfecta esset, actionem talem qualem adversus desultorem dari." (The latter remark refers to Lab./Ulp. D. 19, 5, 20 pr. in fine: actio praescriptis verbis.) On this text, see Peters, *Rücktrittsvorbehalte*, pp. 107 sqq.; Flume, *Festschrift Kaser*, p. 325; and, in particular, Misera, op. cit., note 157, pp. 543 sqq.

nature, the sale was nondum perfecta and the risk of loss or destruction on account of vis maior remained with the vendor. In this case he had to pay only the rent agreed upon.

V. DIES

1. Dies certus and dies incertus quando

A conditional obligation is subject to the occurrence, or non-occurrence, of an event both future and uncertain. If it is certain that the event will happen, we are not dealing with a condition but with a time clause (dies).[168] *When* it will happen may either be certain ("on the kalends of October") or uncertain ("on the death of Stichus"): as long as the futurity is certain to arise, we are still dealing with a dies. A clause of the type "on the kalends of October" is usually referred to as a dies certus; its opposite is the dies incertus quando. The latter could pose an interesting problem for the Roman lawyers. If it was not the death of Stichus, or of some other third party, but rather the demise of either of the contracting parties themselves that had been chosen as determinative dies, the obligation could become enforceable only by or against the heir of one of them—a result which would have been in conflict with the rule against contracts in favour, or to the detriment, of third parties. A stipulation of the type "post mortem meam dari spondes?" or "post mortem tuam dari spondes?" was therefore void.[169] "Pridie quam moriar [or: morieris] dari spondes?" was also frowned upon,[170] for the day before someone dies can be identified only once the death has actually occurred; in substance, therefore, the situation was again as if the stipulation had been in favour, or to the detriment, of the heir. Yet a promise of performance "cum moriar [or: morieris]" was valid, for it was construed to begin at the last moment of the stipulator's, or the promisor's, life.[171]

2. Dies ad quem

Not very much need be said about time clauses for, by and large, they followed the same rules as conditions. Thus, they also subdivided into two major categories: "[c]irca diem duplex inspectio est: nam vel ex die incipit obligatio aut confertur in diem."[172] The former of the two, known generally as dies a quo, corresponded to the suspensive

[168] Cf., in general, Ludwig Mitteis, *Römisches Privatrecht bis auf die Zeit Diokletians*, vol. I (1908), pp. 190 sqq.; Kaser, *RPr* I, p. 258; Thomas, *TRL*, pp. 233 sq.

[169] Gai. III, 100; for further discussion, see the references by Kaser, *RPr* I, p. 492, n. 34 and p. 543, n. 50.

[170] Gai. III, 100.

[171] Gai. III, 100; cf. also Thomas, *TRL*, p. 234, who draws attention to a similar reasoning in English law over tortious claims for loss of expectation of life: cf. *Morgan v. Scoulding* [1938] 1 KB 786.

[172] Paul. D. 44, 7, 44, 1.

condition, the latter (dies ad quem) found its counterpart in the resolutive condition. The range of application of a dies ad quem was subject to the same limitations as that of a resolutive condition. Only bonae fidei contracts could be entered into for a certain time;[173] with regard to stipulations, the dissolutive effect of the clause could at least be taken into account by way of an exceptio doli or pacti.[174] But absolute legal rights or positions could not be subjected to a time limit.[175]

3. Dies a quo

The dies a quo, like the suspensive condition, enjoyed a wider recognition. Only the actus legitimi did not admit of time clauses any more readily than of conditions.[176] The transfer of ownership, however, could be suspended for a certain period, and so could a contractual obligation, no matter whether bonae fidei or stricti iuris in character. Yet, with regard to contractual obligations, one significant difference existed between suspensive time clauses and conditions: a condition suspended the operation of the obligation,[177] a dies a quo merely postponed the due date.[178] In the latter case the obligation already existed from the moment of conclusion of the contract and, as a result, for instance, a debtor who mistakenly rendered performance before the dies had arrived could not claim restitution: "In diem debitor adeo debitor est, ut ante diem solutum repetere non possit."[179] Also, of course, a sale subject to a time clause was perfecta.

4. Navis ex Asia

Occasionally, incidentally, the distinction between condicio and dies could be blurred. Thus, there was the rather surprising concept of a condition which was bound to materialize; premature payment, as we have seen, was not recoverable and this "condition" was thus, as far as

---

[173] Cf. Ulp. D. 19, 2, 13, 11 (locatio conductio).
[174] Iul. D. 45, 1, 56, 4; Paul. D. 44, 7, 44, 1.
[175] Cf. supra, note 116.
[176] Pap. D. 50, 17, 77.
[177] Cf. supra, pp. 723 sqq.
[178] Cf., for example, Paul. D. 44, 7, 44, 1; Paul. D. 45, 1, 46 pr. (" 'Centesimis kalendis dari' utiliter stipulamur, quia praesens obligatio est, in diem autem dilata solutio").
[179] Paul. D. 12, 6, 10; Cels./Ulp. D. 12, 6, 17; cf. also the somewhat mysterious fragment Pomp. D. 12, 6, 16, 1: "Quod autem sub incerta die debetur, die existente non repetitur." Birks, in: Mommsen, Krüger, Watson, vol. I (1985), translates (or rather: interprets): "Where a debt falls due on an unfixed day, recovery is impossible since the day must come." But certainly the more natural translation would be ". . . recovery is impossible once the day has come". One would then have to conclude that before the day has come recovery was in fact possible: contrary to Paul. D. 12, 6, 10 and Cels./Ulp. D. 12, 6, 17. In order to resolve this difficulty, Cuiacius proposed the following emendation: ". . . die non existente non repetitur" (cf. the discussion in Glück, vol. 13, pp. 77 sq.). For a different explanation (the condictio was granted, originally, to a person prematurely paying a debt subject to dies *incertus*; Celsus was the first jurist to refuse it), cf. David Daube, "Zur Palingenesie einiger Klassikerfragmente", (1959) 76 *ZSS* 167 sqq.

the condictio indebiti is concerned, subjected to the same regime as a time clause.[180] Another particularly interesting example is related by Paulus in D. 18, 6, 8, 1. Here we read of the sale of a slave concluded in the following terms: "[E]st ille servus tibi emptus, sive navis ex Asia venerit sive non venerit." Is the contract immediately perfecta, so that the risk has passed to the purchaser? At first blush, one would probably not think so. Unquestionably, the sale is subject to two (suspensive) conditions and we know that even one of them would have been sufficient to prevent the passing of the risk. Yet, in this particular case the two conditions are contradictory: the slave is to be sold if the ship arrives and also if it does not arrive from Asia. In other words: the slave will, in any event, at some stage be sold, for it is absolutely certain that the voyage of the ship will come to an end—one way or the other. In substance, the two conditions therefore amount to a dies (incertus quando) and this is, probably,[181] the reason why Julian concludes "statim perfectam esse venditionem".

VI. USUS HODIERNUS

With codification, the voyages of "the ship from Asia" as well as the ascents of countless stipulators up Capitol hill have largely sunk into oblivion. Not so, however, the legal rules and institutions that they once served to illustrate. All legal systems based on Roman law still grant the parties to a contract the possibility, as it were, of extending their private autonomy into the future:[182] they may make the operation of their transaction dependent upon the occurrence, or non-occurrence, of a future, uncertain event.[183] In many countries, including, incidentally, England, such clauses are known by a word derived from the Latin "condicio".[184] Time clauses are also, of course, permissible;

---

[180] Cf. supra, p. 724.

[181] Cf. the arguments advanced by Alan Rodger, "Emptio perfecta Revisited: A Study of Digest 18, 6, 8, 1", (1982) 4 *TR* 337 sqq.

[182] Andreas von Tuhr, *Der Allgemeine Teil des Deutschen Bürgerlichen Rechts*, vol. II, 2 (1957), p. 271.

[183] Cf., for example, art. 1168 code civil: *"L'obligation est conditionelle lorsqu'on la fait dépendre d'un événement futur et incertain . . ."* (based on Pothier, *Traité des obligations*, n. 199). For a comprehensive comparative analysis of the law relating to conditions, see Schwarz, op. cit., note 100, pp. 391 sqq.; for South Africa, cf. D.P. de Villiers, "Die betekenis van die opskortende voorwaarde by 'n ooreenkoms", (1943) 7 *THRHR* 13 sqq., 154 sqq.; Joubert, *Contract*, pp. 169 sqq. On impossible, illegal and immoral conditions, see Schwarz, op. cit., note 100, pp. 406 sqq.; cf. also Denis A. Cooper, "Impossible Conditions in Roman and Modern Law: A Summary Review", (1941–42) 16 *Tulane LR* 433 sqq.; Flume, *AT*, § 38, 4 d.

[184] The term "condition" in English law is "a chameleon-like word which takes on its meaning, from its surroundings" (*Skips A/S Nordheim v. Syrian Petroleum Co. Ltd.* [1984] QB 599 at 618). Samuel J. Stoljar, "The Contractual Concept of Condition" (1953) 69 *LQR* 485 sqq. lists no fewer than twelve different legal meanings. The equivalent, roughly, of the Roman "condicio" is what is usually referred to as "contingent condition": specification of an event upon the occurrence, or non-occurrence, of which the obligations of both parties are contingent; cf., for example, Treitel, *Contract*, pp. 48 sqq. On "condition" in the sense

they focus on a future event that is not uncertain.[185] Conditions (as well as time clauses) subdivide into those with a suspensive and others with a resolutive effect.[186] The distinction between potestative, casual and mixed conditions is still maintained, whether merely by legal doctrine[187] or even by the code itself.[188,189] The pactum displicentiae has in modern German law become the sale on approval; the approval clause is to be construed, in case of doubt, as a suspensive condition.[190] The in diem addictio receives specific attention only in the Austrian Code: if the object of the sale has not yet been handed over to the (first) purchaser, it has to be construed as a suspensive condition, otherwise as a resolutive condition.[191] The lex commissoria has largely been replaced, in modern business practice,[192] by an arrangement according

---

of a contractual term, the breach of which gives the injured party the right to rescind the contract (as opposed to mere "warranties"), cf. Treitel, *Contract*, pp. 601 sqq. and infra, pp. 803 sq.; on "condition" in the sense of an implied term automatically discharging the parties in the case of frustration of contract cf. infra, p. 817. "The condition", in the words of Stoljar (p. 485), "is important because it vitally affects the law of performance and breach of contracts; and also because the whole development of this part of our contract law is inseparable from the history of conditions." For a general overview, from a comparative point of view, cf. also Schwarz, op. cit., note 100, pp. 392 sqq., 400 sqq. He points out that the notion of condition in England was first employed in the law of immovable property, from where it was taken over into the law of testamentary dispositions before it filtered through into the law of contract. But conditional bonds already played an important role in the medieval law of contract; cf. Simpson, *History*, pp. 90 sqq.

[185] Cf., for example, § 163 BGB; §§ 704 sqq. ABGB; artt. 1185 sqq. code civil.; Joubert, *Contract*, pp. 168 sq.

[186] § 158 BGB; § 696 ABGB; artt. 1168, 1181 ("*L'obligation contractée sous une condition suspensive* . . ."), 1183 ("*La condition résolutoire* . . .") code civil; *R v. Katz* 1959 (3) SA 408 (C); Joubert, *Contract*, p. 172; cf. also M.A.K. Lambiris, "The Incidence of Risk in Conditional Sales", (1984) 101 *SALJ* 656 sqq.

Similarly, contingent conditions in English law may be either precedent (i.e. the contract is not to be binding until the specified event occurs) or subsequent (i.e. a previously binding contract is to terminate on the occurrence of the specified event): Treitel, *Contract*, p. 48; Schwarz, op. cit., note 100, p. 396; but cf. also Stoljar, (1953) 69 *LQR* 506 sqq. Cf. also Blackstone, *Commentaries*, Book II, Ch. 10, II (dealing with Estates upon Condition): "These conditions are therefore either precedent, or subsequent. Precedent are such as must happen or be performed before the estate can vest or be enlarged; subsequent are such, by the failure or nonperformance of which an estate already vested may be defeated."

[187] Flume, *AT*, § 38, 2 c; Joubert, *Contract*, p. 172.

[188] Artt. 1169–1171 code civil.

[189] The definition of potestative condition has undergone a slight change in so far as it is no longer confined to cases where the occurrence, or non-occurrence, of the event is in the control of the stipulator (i.e. the conditional creditor); "*[l]a condition potestative est celle qui fait dépendre l'exécution de la convention d'un événement qu'il est au pouvoir de l'une ou de l'autre des parties contractantes de faire arriver ou d'empêcher*" (art. 1170 code civil). This change results from the abandonment of the unilateral Roman stipulation; under a bilateral contract both parties are in the role of debtor as well as creditor. Conditions turning upon an event wholly in the control of the promisor were, as we have seen, invalid in Roman law. More particularly, the Roman lawyers were averse to a promise of the type "Si volueris, . . . dare spondes?" (cf. Paul. D. 45, 1, 46, 3). The same aversion is reflected, in modern law, in the distinction between a potestative condition (valid) and condicio si voluero ("*Wollensbedingung*") (rendering the obligation ineffective); cf. Flume, *AT*, § 38, 2 d; H.P. Westermann, in: *Münchener Kommentar*, vol. I (2nd ed., 1984), § 158, n. 21. Substantially the same distinction is drawn in French law (*conditions potestatives ordinaires* as opposed to conditions purement

to which the vendor retains ownership of the res vendita until the purchaser has paid the purchase price. This modern variety of the pactum reservati dominii of the ius commune[193] is to be construed as envisaging a transfer of ownership sub condicione suspensiva.[194] Certain legal transactions are still what the Romans used to refer to as actus legitimi: they cannot be subjected to any condition. Marriage,[195] the admission of paternity of an illegitimate child[196] and the acceptance or disclaimer of an inheritance[197] are among the more important ones in German law.[198] In all these cases the public interest does not permit a state of pendency. This state of pendency is still the characteristic consequence of a condicio suspensiva.[199] Before the condition has been

---

potestatives); cf. also art. 1174 code civil, which is, however, unhappily drafted and appears to contradict art. 1170 code civil. In general cf. Schwarz, op. cit., note 100, pp. 398, 411 sq.

[190] § 495 I 2 BGB; cf. also § 1080 ABGB, art. 1588 code civil; *Florida Road Shopping Centre (Pty.) Ltd. v. Caine* 1968 (4) SA 587 (N) at 592 sq.; cf. also *Mackeurtan's Sale of Goods in South Africa* (5th ed., 1984), pp. 39 sqq. It is widely recognized that the sale on approval constitutes an exception to the rule (cf. supra, note 189) that a contract cannot be concluded under a condition of the type "si voluero". For a detailed analysis of 19th-century doctrinal disputes on the construction of the pactum displicentiae (usually without practical relevance), cf. Knellwolf, op. cit., note 107, passim.

[191] §§ 1083 sq. ABGB; cf. also Mackeurtan, op. cit., note 190, p. 44 ("It has no modern importance . . ."); "Protokolle", in: *Mugdan*, vol. II, p. 780.

[192] But see Mackeurtan, op. cit., note 190, pp. 230 sqq. on the lex commissoria in South African law, and § 360 BGB (supra, note 153) on its modern generalized German version. The history of the lex commissoria in Germany thus links up with the rules relating to the right of rescission of contract in two different ways: the lex commissoria is taken to grant a right to rescind the contract (with the result that restitution follows the rules of §§ 346 sqq. BGB); at the same time, the lex commissoria was the conceptual model for the recognition of a unilateral right of withdrawal from the contract in the second half of the 19th century (cf. infra, pp. 800 sqq.).

[193] On which see Gottfried Schiemann, "Über die Funktion des pactum reservati dominii während der Rezeptionen des römischen Rechts in Italien und Mitteleuropa", (1976) 93 *ZSS* 161 sqq., 184 sqq. (on its relationship with the lex commissoria), 191 sqq.; on another root of the modern "reservation of title" arrangements, see Anton Meinhart, "Dogmengeschichtliches und Dogmatisches zum Eigentumsvorbehalt", 1988 (105) *ZSS* 729 sqq.

[194] § 455 BGB; on which see, for example, Flume, *AT*, § 42; Gerhard Walter, *Kaufrecht* (1987), pp. 442 sqq.; for South Africa cf. the discussion by J.M. Otto, "Eiendomsvoorbehoud en opskortende voorwaardes by die koopkontrak", (1981) 44 *THRHR* 255 sqq., 396 sqq.; M.A. Diemont, P.J. Aronstam, *The Law of Credit-Agreements and Hire-Purchase in South Africa* (5th ed., 1982), pp. 12 sqq. It is obvious that the position of the vendor is secured in a more satisfactory manner by way of a retention of title than by way of a lex commissoria. A lex commissoria, after all, was to be construed rather ("magis") as a resolutive than a suspensive condition (Ulp. D. 18, 3, 1), with the result that the vendor was bound to transfer ownership. This would not have mattered that much had it been established that ownership would automatically have relapsed to him on the purchaser's failure to pay in time. It was, however, exactly the uncertainty regarding this point that bedevilled the application of the lex commissoria over the centuries; it resulted, essentially, from the antinomy between Ulp. D. 6, 1, 41 pr. and C. 4, 54, 3. Rather fine-spun, but practically unsatisfactory distinctions were already developed by the glossators in this respect (cf. Schiemann, (1976) 93 *ZSS* 184 sqq.). The Prussian General Land Law came down in favour of the purchaser (and his creditors): according to § 262 I 11, ownership does not fall back automatically but has to be retransferred. The lex commissoria was thus largely

satisfied the transaction does not yet have its characteristic consequences. The creditor cannot claim performance and has to render restitution if the debtor pays what he does not yet owe. At the same time, however, the creditor has an expectancy which the law recognizes and protects in various ways.[200] Most importantly, this expectancy is actively as well as passively transmissible upon death; and any disposition effected pendente condicione is invalid, on fulfilment of the condition, as far as it would frustrate or impair the conditional transaction. A condition can still be deemed to have been satisfied if its actual satisfaction has been prevented by the party to whose disadvantage it would have operated; likewise, a condition is deemed not to have been satisfied, if its satisfaction has been brought about by the party to whose advantage it would have operated.[201] And finally: a comparative analysis of modern legal systems still reveals the uncertainty that has, over the centuries, prevailed with regard to the effect of satisfaction.[202] According to the French code civil, for example, *"[l]a condition accomplie a un effet rétroactif au jour auquel l'engagement a été contracté"*.[203] § 158 I BGB, on the other hand, determines that the legal transaction becomes effective "upon satisfaction of the (suspensive) condition" ("ex nunc" effect).[204] But, as A.B.

emasculated as a viable means of securing the vendor against the purchaser's insolvency. For an analysis of the development in the 18th and 19th centuries, cf. Schiemann, op. cit., note 63, pp. 73 sqq., 82 sqq.

[195] § 13 II EheG.

[196] § 1600 b I BGB.

[197] § 1947 BGB.

[198] For details, see Flume, *AT*, § 38, 5; H.P. Westermann, op. cit., note 189, § 158, nn. 27 sqq.; cf. also the comparative analysis by Schwarz, op. cit., note 100, pp. 404 sqq.

[199] For details, see Flume, *AT*, § 39 (Germany); Joubert, *Contract*, pp. 173 sqq. (South Africa); Schwarz, op. cit., note 100, pp. 416 sqq. (comparative); Schiemann, op. cit., note 63, pp. 55 sqq. and passim.

[200] Cf., for example, Lauterbach, *Collegium theoretico-practicum*, Lib. II, Tit. XIV, LXXIX: "Ex quibus omnibus satis apparet, etiam pendente conditione aliquid subesse, quod conventionem quodammodo verificat et sustentat . . . ac obligationem nondum quidem natam, conceptam tamen esse, illamque tanquam in utero materno latere."

[201] § 162 BGB; Flume, *AT*, § 40, 1 (German law); Knütel, 1976 *Juristische Blätter* 613 sqq. (predominantly Austrian law); Joubert, *Contract*, pp. 175 sqq. (South African law); Schwarz, op. cit., note 100, pp. 414 sq. (comparative). Modern legal systems require in the case of both fictions that the party preventing or bringing about the satisfaction of the condition must either have acted against the precepts of good faith (§ 162 BGB) or must have been at fault ("designedly": Joubert, *Contract*, p. 176). For a critical evaluation, see Knütel, 1976 *Juristische Blätter* 615 sqq. Knütel maintains that the whole question whether or not a condition has to be treated as satisfied (or as not satisfied) remains a matter of interpretation (as it had, in fact, been in Roman law, supra, pp. 730 sq.); cf., further, especially, Flume, *AT*, § 40, 1. The same view appears to be taken, occasionally, in English law; cf. *Mackay v. Dick* (1881) 6 AC 251 (HL) and Schwarz, op. cit., note 100, pp. 414 sqq.; but cf. Treitel, *Contract*, pp. 49 sqq.

[202] For a detailed analysis, cf. Schiemann, op. cit., note 63, passim (esp. pp. 29 sqq., 36 sqq., 82 sqq.)

[203] Art. 1179 code civil; based on Pothier, *Traité des obligations*, n. 220.

[204] Cf. already Windscheid/Kipp, § 91.

Schwarz has pointed out,[205] the practical differences between the two regimes are not at all significant: neither is retroactivity carried to all its logical consequences, nor does it, as a rule, entail results which could not also be achieved on an alternative doctrinal basis.

[205] Op. cit., note 100, pp. 419 sqq. As Schiemann, op. cit., note 63, passim, has shown, it corresponds to this observation that the approach adopted by the authors of the ius commune towards explaining the "preliminary" effects of the legal transaction pendente condicione continually oscillated between the two poles of postulating an expectancy and espousing the retroactivity doctrine.

CHAPTER 24

Termination of Obligations

We have thus far been discussing the content and creation of contractual obligations. We shall now have to turn our attention to questions relating to their performance. Just as man is destined to die, so a contract is intended to be terminated. It does not exist for its own sake. Every contractual promise gives rise to the expectation, on the part of the promisee, that it will be honoured. If the promisor does what he has promised, he is free, and the obligation falls away. If, on the other hand, he either does not perform properly or does not perform at all, the question arises what form of relief the legal system is prepared to offer to the disappointed promisee: may he enforce (specific) performance of the contract, is he able to claim damages or can he possibly even rescind the contract? We shall first deal with the situation where the life of a contractual obligation ends according to plan: by way of performance. We shall then have to consider other ways of terminating an existing obligation. Finally, the pathological cases have to be dealt with: the various forms of breach of contract and the remedies available to the aggrieved party.

I. SOLUTIO

1. Praestatio eius quod debetur

" '[S]olvere' dicimus eum, qui fecit quod facere promisit":[1] we say that someone who does what he has promised "performs". Or, in the words of Voet: "Solutio . . . est naturalis praestatio ejus quod debetur."[2] Every obligation imposes on the debtor a duty to give, to do or to perform (dare facere praestare oportere).[3] When such performance is effected, the raison d'être of the obligation has materialized. At the same time, the obligatory relation between the parties has come to its natural end. "Tollitur autem obligatio praecipue solutione eius quod debeatur" says Gaius;[4] "an obligation is extinguished if the performance owed is made to the creditor", reads the German BGB.[5] The debtor is released immediately and ipso iure; he does not have to avail himself of an exceptio when sued after having rendered performance.[6] Details as to where, how and when performance had to be rendered

---

[1] Ulp. D. 50, 16, 176; cf. also Pomp. D. 46, 3, 54.
[2] *Commentarius ad Pandectas*, Lib. XLVI, Tit. III, I.
[3] Cf. supra, pp. 6 sq.
[4] III, 168.
[5] § 362 I.
[6] Kaser, *RPr* I, p. 636; Honsell/Mayer-Maly/Selb, p. 263.

could, in the first place, be determined by the contracting parties themselves; alternatively, the law provided certain rules dealing with the specific modalities of performance. Most of these rules had their origin in the equitable discretion accorded to the judge in the iudicia bonae fidei; based on and derived from the precepts of good faith as they were, they survived the centuries and commended themselves even to modern legislators. As in Roman law, these rules do, however, only have the status of what we call "ius dispositivum", i.e. the parties are entitled to make their own arrangements which may be better suited to their individual circumstances.

Obviously, the object of performance[7] had to correspond with what was contemplated in the contract. Thus, performance could consist in the payment of a certain sum of money, in the handing over of an object, in the rendering of services or in the execution of some other (legal or factual) act. If a res mancipi was owed, mancipatio or in iure cessio had to be performed, with regard to the delivery of other objects the formless traditio was sufficient. In the case of dare obligations (for instance: the promise to deliver a certain slave),[8] the debtor was not released if a possibility existed that the creditor might be evicted.[9] Similarly, if a homo had been stipulated for and a statuliber (that is, a person who was to become free upon fulfilment of a certain condition) was delivered, the condictio[10] could still be brought by the creditor for a "proper" slave.[11] Only when the condition failed was the debtor's obligation extinguished. The position was different as far as contracts of sale were concerned. Here the vendor merely owed "vacuam possessionem tradere", not transfer of ownership.[12] The purchaser was not entitled to expect more than an undisturbed position of habere licere; as long as he had provided that, the seller had discharged his obligation and the actio empti could not be brought against him.[13] Obviously, too, the creditor did not have to accept part-performance unless either a specific law[14] or the contract obliged him to do so.[15] If a debtor owed a specific sum of money and tendered payment in instalments only, the creditor was able to reject the first instalment without incurring the consequences of mora creditoris.

---

[7] For details, see Siro Solazzi, *L'estinzione dell' obbligazione nel diritto romano* (2nd ed., 1935), pp. 81 sqq.

[8] Cf., for example, infra, pp. 783 sqq.

[9] Cf. Pomp. D. 46, 3, 20.

[10] Cf., for example, supra, pp. 89 sq.

[11] Afr. D. 46, 3, 38, 3: "Qui hominem promisit si statuliberum solvat, magis puto non esse expectandam condicionem: sed et creditorem agere posse et illi condictionem competere. quod si interim condicio defecerit, liberatur."

[12] Cf. supra, p. 278.

[13] On the liability for eviction, see supra, pp. 293 sqq.

[14] Cf. supra, pp. 119, 131 sq.

[15] Cf. e.g. Iul. D. 12, 1, 21; Ulp. D. 19, 1, 13, 8; Windscheid/Kipp, § 342, 2; § 266 BGB; Joubert, *Contract*, pp. 278 sq.

2. Unum debitum ex pluribus causis

Occasionally a debtor may be bound to render similar performances by virtue of several obligations to one and the same creditor; he may, for instance, owe money on account of a contract of sale, as a result of having received a loan and under the law of unjustified enrichment. If the debtor pays an amount which is insufficient to satisfy all these debts, the question arises against which of them this payment is to be credited. It has always been generally acknowledged that it is, in the first place, the debtor who may specify the debt(s) that he wishes to be discharged.[16] Failing such specification on the part of the debtor, the creditor could, according to Roman law, determine the matter. He was, however, bound to make the choice in accordance with what the interest of the debtor demanded: "aequissimum enim visum est creditorem ita agere rem debitoris, ut suam ageret."[17] If both parties remained silent, a debt due was to be taken to be discharged before a debt not yet due,[18] among several debts due the one most burdensome for the debtor,[19] among several equally burdensome debts the oldest;[20] failing all these criteria, all debts were regarded as having been satisfied proportionately.[21] By and large, these rules have found their way into the BGB, except that here the creditor is not given a say in the matter.[22] But since most of the subsidiary rules are based on the presumed will of a reasonable debtor,[23] by which the creditor, too, had to be guided in his decision, the difference between Roman and modern law is not significant.[24]

3. Time and place of performance

The time at which performance could be demanded by the creditor (i.e. the due date) had to be determined in accordance with the special circumstances of the case, particularly with the nature of the transaction. If somebody promised in Rome to hand over a slave in Carthage, such a debt could hardly be taken to fall due before the

[16] Ulp. D. 46, 3, 1: "Quotiens quis debitor ex pluribus causis unum debitum solvit, est in arbitrio solventis dicere, quod potius debitum voluerit solutum, et quod dixerit, id erit solutum"; Paul. D. 46, 3, 101, 1; Windscheid/Kipp, § 343; § 366 I BGB; Joubert, *Contract*, p. 283.

[17] Ulp. D. 46, 3, 1.

[18] Ulp. D. 46, 3, 1.

[19] Ulp. D. 46, 3, 5 pr.; for further details, see Pap. D. 46, 3, 97.

[20] Ulp. D. 46, 3, 5 pr.

[21] Paul. D. 46, 3, 8. For a discussion cf. Fritz Schulz, *Einführung in das Studium der Digesten* (1916), pp. 109 sqq.; Heinrich Siber, "Beiträge zur Interpolationenforschung", (1925) 45 *ZSS* 174 sqq.

[22] "Motive", in: *Mugdan*, vol. II, p. 48.

[23] Helmut Heinrichs, in: *Münchener Kommentar*, vol. II (2nd. ed., 1985), § 366, n. 12. Contrary to Roman law, however, according to § 366 II BGB, among several debts due the one which affords the creditor the least security is first discharged; among several equally secure debts the one most burdensome to the debtor, etc. The Roman rules of allocation were thus slightly more favourable to the debtor.

[24] For Roman-Dutch law cf. Joubert, *Contract*, pp. 283 sqq.

promisor had been able to make his way across the sea to northern Africa.[25] Failing any such indications to the contrary, the creditor could demand performance at once.[26] If, on the other hand, a specific due date had been set by the parties, the creditor could—of course—not claim performance before the time stated. But was the debtor free to discharge his obligation even before the due date? Several texts in our sources indicate that he was;[27] according to the BGB, this is to be presumed in case of doubt.[28]

The place of performance, too (if it had not been fixed by the parties), was to be deduced from the circumstances of the case. Thus, for instance, a freedman had to render his services at the place where his patron resided.[29] If no such inference could be drawn, fungibles had to be delivered at the place where the creditor could sue for them,[30] and that was usually the domicile of the debtor.[31] Specific things, on the other hand, had to be delivered where they were at the time of conclusion of the contract.[32] Generally speaking, one can thus say that it was incumbent on the creditor to go and collect the performance due to him ("*Holschuld*" or "haalskuld" in modern parlance), not on the debtor to effect his performance at the creditor's place ("*Bringschuld*" or "bringskuld").[33]

---

[25] Paul. D. 45, 1, 73 pr. (". . . tacite tempus complecti videtur, quo perveniri Carthaginem potest"); cf. also Pomp. D. 45, 1, 14 (relating to domum aedificari).

[26] Pomp. D. 50, 17, 14: "In omnibus obligationibus, in quibus dies non ponitur, praesenti die debitur." Cf. also § 271 I BGB.

[27] Cels. D. 46, 3, 70; Ulp. D. 45, 1, 38, 16; Ulp. D. 45, 1, 41, 1; Ulp D. 50, 17, 17. The decision depends on the determination of the question in whose interest the time clause has been inserted into the contract; cf. e.g. Windscheid/Kipp, § 273; Joubert, *Contract*, pp. 282 sq.

[28] § 271 II BGB.

[29] Iav. D. 38, 1, 21, who adds, however, that the freedman came to the patronus' place at the expense of the latter ("sumptu scilicet et vectura patroni").

[30] Lic. Ruf. D. 5, 1, 38 (". . . quod pondere aut numero aut mensura continetur, ibi dari debet ubi petitur"); Ulp. D. 30, 47, 1.

[31] Kaser, *RZ*, p. 183. The general rule is actor sequitur forum rei; cf. C. 3, 19, 3; C. 3, 13, 2; vat. 325, 326. A similar situation obtained in the old Germanic law: cf. G.W. Wetzell, *System des ordentlichen Civilprozesses* (1878), p. 485. "Actor sequitur forum rei" became the rule in the German Code of Civil Procedure (§§ 12 sq. *Civilprozessordnung* of 1877), but since the parties were free to determine the question of jurisdiction by way of agreement (§ 38 *Civilprozessordnung*), it lost much of its significance (cf. e.g. Richard Schmidt, *Lehrbuch des deutschen Zivilprozessrechts* (1906), pp. 252, 274). This trend has, however, in the meantime been decisively reversed by the legislator (cf. the new §§ 38 sqq. ZPO, introduced in 1974, drastically curtailing the possibility of jurisdiction agreements). The rule of "actor sequitur forum rei" is generally seen today to be based on considerations of justice rather than mere convenience (BGHZ 41, 151 (154) and, for instance, Max Vollkommer, 1973 *Neue Juristische Wochenschrift* 1592). Generally on "actor sequitur forum rei", see Andreas Wacke, 1980 *Juristische Arbeitsblätter* 654 sqq.

[32] Lic. Ruf. D. 5, 1, 38 (". . . ibi dari debet ubi est"); Ulp. D. 30, 47, 1.

[33] On the terminology cf. e.g. Joachim Gernhuber, *Die Erfüllung und ihre Surrogate* (1983), pp. 15 sqq. For all details on the place of performance in Roman law cf. Solazzi, op. cit., note 7, pp. 106 sqq.; Francesco Amarelli, *Locus solutionis* (1984); on the later history, Roman-Dutch and South African law, see D.J. Joubert, "Die Locus Solutionis", 1971 *Acta*

4. Performance rendered by third parties/to third parties

In many cases (particularly when he is owed a sum of money) the creditor will be concerned only about receiving performance, not necessarily about receiving it from his debtor. Hence the provision in the BGB (§ 267) that third parties are entitled to make performance on behalf of the debtor even without the approval of the latter. In the same vein, Gaius states: "Solvendo quisque pro alio licet invito et ignorante liberat eum."[34] Neither in Roman nor in modern law,[35] however, does this rule apply without exception. Whenever the nature of the performance is determined by special qualities of the debtor—his skill, knowledge or experience—performance has to be made in person. If the creditor has asked a specific entrepreneur to build a ship or a house for him, he is entitled to expect performance in person and cannot be obliged to accept the work of another manufacturer: "[i]nter artifices longa differentia est et ingenii et naturae et doctrinae et institutionis."[36]

If it often does not matter who renders performance, it is, as a rule, important that it is made to the creditor and not to any third party. The creditor has, however, always been able to authorize another to receive performance.[37] The procurator,[38] particularly, was often in such a position. Alternatively, performance to a third party could terminate the obligation if the creditor was prepared (subsequently) to ratify it.[39] Occasionally, even an ostensible authority was sufficient. Iulianus gives the following example:

> "Si Titium omnibus negotiis meis praeposuero, deinde vetuero eum ignorantibus debitoribus administrare negotia mea, debitores ei solvendo liberabuntur: nam is, qui omnibus negotiis suis aliquem proponit, intellegitur etiam debitoribus mandare, ut procuratori solvant."[40]

At the time of performance Titius' authority to manage the creditor's affairs had been withdrawn. This was not known to the debtors, who still relied on the appointment of Titius as the creditor's procurator. Such reliance deserves protection, and thus the debtors' performance to Titius was taken to have discharged their obligations. Very similar considerations prevail in the modern law of agency.[41] Finally, a debtor was able to discharge his obligation by performing towards a solutionis

---

Juridica 105 sqq.; for a comprehensive comparative analysis of modern law cf. Haimo Schack, *Der Erfüllungsort im deutschen, ausländischen und internationalen Privat- und Zivilprozessrecht* (1985).

[34] Gai. D. 3, 5, 38; cf. also Gai. D. 46, 3, 53.

[35] For English law cf. Treitel, *Contract*, pp. 572 sqq.

[36] Ulp. D. 46, 3, 31. Cf. further Solazzi, op. cit., note 7, pp. 39 sqq.; Windscheid/Kipp, § 342, 4; § 267 BGB; Joubert, *Contract*, p. 275.

[37] Ulp. D. 46, 3, 12 pr.; Marci. D. 46, 3, 48. Cf. also Solazzi, op. cit., note 7, pp. 54 sqq.; Windscheid/Kipp, § 342, 5; § 362 II, read together with § 185 BGB; Joubert, *Contract*, p. 276.

[38] Cf. supra, pp. 53, 417.

[39] Ulp. D. 46, 3, 12, 4 ("rati enim habitio mandato comparatur").

[40] D. 46, 3, 34, 3; cf. also Gai. III, 160.

[41] §§ 167, 170 BGB.

causa adiectus:[42] this was a third party (for instance, a bank) specifically incorporated into the wording of a stipulation as an alternative recipient of the promisor's performance ("mihi aut Titio dari spondes?").[43] Of course, he could not sue for performance, for then we would have been dealing with a stipulatio alteri.[44] Once the debtor had been given the choice of performing either to the stipulator himself or to a solutionis causa adiectus, the creditor could no longer unilaterally withdraw that choice.[45]

5. Datio in solutum

It has been stated above that the debtor was obliged to perform what he owed under the contract. If he gave something else in lieu of what he owed, the obligation was not discharged. The creditor was, however, free to accept the substitute performance. If he decided to do so, such datio in solutum had the same effect as the ordinary solutio: it released the debtor from his obligation.[46] Problems could arise if, for instance, a debtor owing money gave a movable object in solutum. Acceptance of that object by the creditor terminated the obligation. But what if the creditor was subsequently evicted due to the fact that a third party turned out to have a better title? According to Marcianus, he was able to fall back upon the original obligation: "Si quis aliam rem pro alia volenti solverit et evicta fuerit res, manet pristina obligatio."[47] In other words, the (original) obligation fell away only if the alternative performance led to full and final satisfaction of the creditor. There are, however, texts in the Corpus Juris, according to which even an ultimately unsuccessful attempt to satisfy the creditor appears to have had the effect of terminating the original obligation, for in the event of an eviction the creditor was not allowed to sue on the original debt but was granted an actio empti utilis.

> "Si praedium tibi pro soluto datum aliis creditoribus fuerat obligatum, causa pignoris mutata non est. igitur si hoc iure fuerit evictum, utilis tibi actio contra debitorem competit. nam eiusmodi contractus vicem venditionis obtinet."[48]

The datio in solutum is seen here as a kind of sale, for the creditor is treated as if he had purchased the object given to him in lieu of payment

---

[42] Cf. generally Solazzi, op. cit., note 7, pp. 64 sqq.; D.J. Joubert, "Solutionis causa adjectus", (1979) 42 *THRHR* 1 sqq; cf. supra, pp. 38 sq.

[43] Cf. e.g. Paul. D. 46, 3, 10; Ulp. D. 46, 3, 12, 3.

[44] Cf. supra, pp. 34 sqq., 39.

[45] Ulp. D. 46, 3, 12, 3; Gai. D. 46, 3, 106; but see Pothier, *Traité des obligations*, n. 525; *Cassim v. Latha* 1930 TPD 659 sqq.; *Mahomed v. Lockhat Bros. Co. Ltd.* 1944 AD 230 at 237 sq.; cf. Joubert, (1979) 42 *THRHR* 6 sqq.

[46] There was a school dispute as to whether the debtor was released ipso iure or could only bar the creditor's claim under the original action by means of an exceptio doli: the Sabinians took the former view, the Proculians the latter; cf. Gai. III, 168. The Sabinian view eventually gained the upper hand: Kaser, *RPr* II, p. 442. Cf. also today § 364 I BGB.

[47] D. 46, 3, 46 pr.; the same opinion is expressed by Paulus in D. 46, 3, 98 pr.

[48] C. 8, 44, 4 (Ant.). Cf. also Ulp. D. 13, 7, 24 pr.

of the original debt. Codex 8, 44, 4 and a variety of other texts expressing similar ideas[49] are probably interpolated,[50] for it was Justinian who tried to bring datio in solutum into line with the contract of emptio venditio.[51] Nevertheless, in the history of the ius commune they have exerted great influence.[52] This is apparent, for instance, from the rule adopted in the BGB:

> "If a thing, a claim against a third party, or any other right is given in lieu of fulfilment, the debtor shall grant warranty in the same manner as a seller, against a defect in title and against a defect in the thing."[53]

It is very doubtful, however, whether this construction correctly reflects the intentions of the parties, for the average creditor can hardly be taken to have given up his claim in return for a performance which might still be taken away from him.[54]

II. RELEASE

1. Solutio per aes et libram and acceptilatio as actus contrarii

The Latin word for performance/fulfilment of an obligation was "solutio", acceptance in lieu of fulfilment (or substituted performance) was referred to as datio in solutum. This may appear to be a strange terminology, because literally speaking, the verb "solvere" means to unbind, to untie (somebody). This word and all its derivations possess a distinctly archaic flavour. They take us back to the days when an obligatio was not merely a vinculum iuris but a physical bond, through which a pledge-like power of seizure was established over the body of the person liable for a wrong.[55] In the case of what came to be called "contract", one person subjected himself to this power of seizure by means of a formal transaction. Naturally, however, there had to be some way of bringing to an end this uncomfortable sojourn in the "creditor's" dungeons. Neither of the two parties concerned normally had any interest in bringing matters to a head: to a sale of the "debtor"

---

[49] Cf., apart from Ulp. D. 13, 7, 24 pr., Paul. D. 41, 3, 4, 17; Ulp. D. 42, 4, 15; and Ulp. D. 44, 4, 4, 31.

[50] Cf., most recently, Manfred Harder, *Die Leistung an Erfüllungs statt* (1976), pp. 93 sqq.; for a different opinion, see e.g. Generoso Melillo, *In solutum dare* (1970), pp. 91 sqq., 111 sqq.; cf. also Kaser, *RPr* I, p. 638; *RPr* II, pp. 442 sq.; Honsell/Mayer-Maly/Selb, p. 264 (controversy amongst the classical jurists; but cf. Harder, pp. 97 sq.). For a discussion of the attempts, from the time of the glossators down to the pandectists, to harmonize the divergent sources cf. Harder, pp. 69 sqq. On Roman-Dutch and South African law, see D.J. Joubert, "Datio in Solutum", (1977) 10 *De Jure* 29 sqq.

[51] For his reasons cf. Ernst Rabel, "Nachgeformte Rechtsgeschäfte", (1907) 28 *ZSS* 312 sqq.; Harder, op. cit., note 50, pp. 103 sq.

[52] Frequently the creditor was given a choice whether to use the original action or the actio empti; cf. e.g. Glück, vol. 21, p. 197; Windscheid/Kipp, p. 420.

[53] § 365 II.

[54] For further detailed criticism of § 365 II BGB cf. Harder, op. cit., note 50, pp. 106 sqq.; cf. also Gernhuber, op. cit., note 33, pp. 180 sqq.

[55] Cf. supra, pp. 2 sq.

trans Tiberim or perhaps even to his being cut into pieces.[56] If we look, for instance, at nexum as one of the oldest liability transactions,[57] we see that the "debtor" was supposed to redeem himself by repaying, within a certain time, a specific sum that had been lent to him. It was only where he failed to do so that the question of his liability—that is, of the creditor's power of seizure—became relevant. But (informal) payment as such, although in a substantial sense it satisfied the "creditor", did not release the person liable from his bondage. The obligation had been created by a strictly formal act, and thus it could be "solved" only by another formal act, which, as a rule, had to correspond to the former. Thus, where the person liable had assumed his obligation by way of nexum (a solemn act per aes et libram), he could disentangle himself only by performing another act involving copper, scales and witnesses: the solutio per aes et libram (or nexi liberatio).[58] With the rise of the contract verbis (stipulation in particular), acceptilatio was developed as an oral form of dissolving oral obligations. Solutio per aes et libram and acceptilatio were thus devised as symmetrical actus contrarii to the transactions they were intended to discharge; they provide a good illustration of the ancient idea (featuring particularly prominently in the religious and magical spheres)[59] that what has once been done cannot be undone but by a corresponding act[60]—and since all (legally) relevant acts in ancient times were formal, the actus contrarius necessarily had to be formal too.

2. The rise of informal solutio

All this changed in the course of the Republic, and by the time of the 3rd century[61] the performance as such (i.e. an informal solutio) was generally regarded as sufficient for the termination of the obligation. Legal thinking had emancipated itself from the fetters of formalism, magic and religion, and one had come to realize that there was no point in preserving an obligation which had in actual fact been fulfilled. After all, the creditor had received what was due to him and it would have been entirely improper of him to invoke the debtor's liability. More particularly, the recognition of the informal, consensual transactions gave considerable impetus to this development; they had, of course,

---

[56] Cf. supra, pp. 3 sq. (note 13).

[57] Cf. supra, pp. 4 sq.

[58] Characteristically, solutio per aes et libram even in classical law still retained the formula "me a te solvo liberoque": Gai. III, 174. Cf. further Kaser, *Altrömisches ius*, pp. 240 sqq.; Detlef Liebs, "Contrarius actus", in: *Sympotica Franz Wieacker* (1970), pp. 128 sqq.; Rolf Knütel, "Zum Prinzip der formalen Korrespondenz im römischen Recht", (1971) 88 *ZSS* 73 sqq.

[59] See Liebs, *Sympotica Wieacker*, pp. 116 sqq. for details.

[60] On the principle of formal correspondence in Roman law, see generally Schmidlin, *Rechtsregeln*, pp. 74 sqq.; Liebs, *Sympotica Wieacker*, pp. 111 sqq.; Knütel, (1971) 88 *ZSS* 67 sqq.

[61] Kaser, *RPr* I, p. 634.

never required a formal solutio in order to be discharged, and thus provided a model that could be conveniently adopted for other legal acts too.[62] In the end, therefore, nearly all that survived of the old regime was the word "solutio", but it was used in the sense of "to perform", "to fulfil" or "to satisfy" (an obligation). At least in one respect, however,[63] the archaic origins lived on even in classical substantive law: for if it was accepted that any third party could make performance on behalf of the debtor (and thus discharge his obligation),[64] then the historical reason for this rule lies in the fact that the person liable was literally obligated, in the sense of being put into fetters, and had to rely, in any event, on the intervention of a friend or family member for his liberation.[65]

3. Formal release by way of solutio per aes et libram and acceptilatio

This evolution of solutio as an informal way of terminating obligations did not, incidentally, render solutio per aes et libram and acceptilatio entirely redundant: for it was only when they were accompanied by payment of whatever was owed that the formal acts no longer fulfilled any essential function. Both of them could, however, conveniently be used where the creditor wished to release his debtor from his obligation *without* receiving the performance that was due to him. Solutio per aes et libram could, under these circumstances, be executed nummo uno, i.e. on a purely imaginary or fictitious basis, and in the case of acceptilatio the formal question and answer ("Quod ego tibi promisi, habesne acceptum?" "Habeo") settled the issue, no matter whether performance had in actual fact been made or not. Both institutions thus continued to be used: not in connection with solutio, but as a means of terminating obligations by way of release. Solutio per aes et libram was applicable where the obligation was based either on a transaction per aes et libram, on a judgment or on a legatum per damnationem;[66] acceptilatio had to be used as far as contracts verbis were concerned: "consentaneum enim visum est verbis factam obligationem posse aliis verbis dissolvi."[67] If something was due on some other ground, it first had to be recast (by way of novation) into the form of a stipulation before release by acceptilatio could be effected.[68] It therefore involved but a minimum of inconvenience to make acceptilatio universally applicable.

---

62 Cf. Kaser, *RPr* I, p. 634.
63 For another example, see infra , p. 841, note 51.
64 Cf. supra, p. 752.
65 Kaser, *RPr* I, p. 172.
66 Gai. III, 173 sqq.
67 Gai. III, 170. On acceptilatio cf. supra, pp. 685, 755.
68 Gai. III, 170 ("sed id quod ex alia causa debeatur potest in stipulationem deduci et per acceptilationem dissolvi").

4. Excursus: the stipulatio Aquiliana

One of the most interesting illustrations of this combination of novatio and acceptilatio occurred in the case of the so-called stipulatio Aquiliana. Its formula had been composed by the Republican jurist Gaius Aquilius Gallus and read like this:

> "[Q]uidquid te mihi ex quacumque causa dare facere oportet, oportebit . . . quarumque rerum mihi tecum actio . . . petitio . . . persecutio est erit . . . tantam pecuniam mihi dari spondes?"[69]

It covered all debts, present and future, due and not yet owing, arising ex iure civili and under praetorian law, of the particular promisor against the stipulator and replaced them by a single comprehensive stipulation. Instead of many individual sums under various different kinds of obligations, only the grand total was now owed in terms of a contract verbis. This debt was then discharged by way of acceptilatio: "Quidquid tibi hodierno die per Aquilianam stipulationem spopondi, id omne habesne acceptum?" "Habeo acceptum." Ulpian describes what happened in the following words: "Aquiliana stipulatio omnimodo omnes praecedentes obligationes novat et peremit ipsaque peremitur per acceptilationem."[70] What the parties achieved through this double transaction was a kind of general settlement. They had to go through, discuss and evaluate all claims of the stipulator against the promisor, as well as those counterclaims of the promisor against the stipulator that could be used for set-off purposes. If there turned out to be a balance in favour of the stipulator, the money was either paid back immediately, in which case the acceptilatio constituted a formal, general and comprehensive receipt, or the balance could again be credited to the promisor, usually by way of a further stipulation. This had to occur after conclusion of the acceptilatio, since otherwise the latter would automatically have covered—and thus discharged—the former. In both cases the acceptilatio had the effect of protecting the promisor against any further claims on the part of the stipulator that had their origin in a legal relationship predating the stipulatio Aquiliana. In other words, the promisor owed the stipulator either nothing at all (and could always refer to the acceptilatio in that regard) or only one single and specific sum that had to be spelt out and promised in a subsequent transaction.

5. Informal release

Acceptilatio was a fairly convenient and universally applicable form of release. It did, however, require the conclusion of a stipulation. With the rise of the informal, consensual transactions, a growing demand for an informal type of release was bound, sooner or later, to make itself

---

[69] Cf. *Inst.* III, 29, 2; Flor. D. 46, 4, 18, 1. For all details, see Sturm, *Stipulatio Aquiliana*, pp. 51 sqq.; cf. also Max Kaser, "Stipulatio Aquiliana", (1973) 90 *ZSS* 346 sqq.

[70] D. 2, 15, 4.

felt. Already the praetorian edict contained the clause "pacta conventa . . . . servabo",[71] and we have seen[72] that this referred to pacta de non petendo, on the basis of which the debtor could raise the exceptio pacti conventi against the action of the creditor.[73] Moreover, in bonae fidei iudicia this exceptio was inherent[74] and the judge therefore had to take cognizance of an informal release immediately and ex officio. But the pactum de non petendo referred only to an individual claim, not to the legal relationship, the contract, in its entirety. In classical Roman law it was, however, recognized that even the latter could be resolved informally: as long as no performance had yet been effected (that is, "re integra"), the parties could bring any consensual contract to an end by mere agreement.[75] This agreement was sometimes referred to as contrarius consensus, for instance in the following text by Paulus: "Emptio et vendito sicut consensu contrahitur, ita contrario consensu resolvitur, antequam fuerit res secuta."[76] It is not difficult to see how happily this fitted the general "contrarius actus" scheme according to which the acts creating and resolving an obligation were seen as symmetrical counterparts:

> "Nihil tam naturale est quam eo genere quidque dissolvere, quo colligatum est. ideo verborum obligatio verbis tollitur: nudi consensus obligatio contrario consensu dissolvitur";[77]

and also: "cum re contraxerimus, re solvi debet."[78]

III. OTHER FORMS OF "SOLUTIO IMPROPRIA"

"Solutio propria", "in praecisa forma et specie obligationis"[79] (to use the terminology of the European ius commune) has always been, and still is, the most important way of terminating obligations. Datio in solutum and release have been mentioned as two forms of what was usually referred to as "solutio impropria". But there was a whole variety of further situations which entailed the extinction of an existing obligation. Novatio was one of them: the old obligatio was translated into a new one (always a stipulation), with the effect that the former fell

---

[71] Ulp. D. 2, 14, 7, 7.

[72] Supra, pp. 508 sq.

[73] Gai. IV, 119 ("si inter A^m A^m et N^m N^m non convenit, ne ea pecunia peteretur"); cf. also Gai. IV, 122 ("si inter A^m A^m et N^m N^m non convenit, ne ea pecunia intra quinquennium peteretur": the granting of indulgence, as opposed to a total release).

[74] Cf. supra, pp. 509 sq.

[75] Iul. D. 18, 5, 5, 1; Pap. D. 18, 1, 72 pr.; Ulp. D. 2, 14, 7, 6; *Inst.* III, 29, 4; Knütel, *Contrarius consensus*, pp. 23 sqq. (dealing with the requirement of res integra), 102 sqq., 120 sqq., 137 sqq.

[76] D. 18, 5, 3. On the application of this principle to other consensual transactions, see Knütel, *Contrarius consensus*, pp. 120 sqq.

[77] Ulp. D. 50, 17, 35.

[78] Pomp. D. 46, 3, 80; on this text, see Knütel, *Contrarius consensus*, pp. 10 sqq.

[79] Coing, p. 431.

away ipso iure.[80] Litis contestatio had a similar effect, at least as far as iudicia legitima were concerned: the original obligation was dissolved by operation of the law (ipso iure), and the defendant became bound to respect any condemnation that might ensue (condemnari oportere).[81] As a result, the plaintiff was prevented from enforcing the old (now extinct) obligation a second time. Confusio brought about the end of an obligation, and so did concursus causarum. Confusio refers to the situation where the position of debtor and creditor with regard to one and the same obligation merge in one person;[82] this can occur, for instance, if the debtor becomes the creditor's heir or if—conversely—the creditor succeeds his debtor. After all, it is essential for an obligation that it establishes a legal relationship between (at least) two different parties.[83] Concursus causarum was the concurrence of two or more titles of acquisition concerning one specific thing in one and the same person.[84] If somebody was entitled to receive delivery of a particular sedan chair by virtue of both a stipulatio and a contract of sale, one of the obligations had to fall away, for the creditor could, after all, receive delivery only once. If he had acquired the sedan-chair by traditio under the stipulation, he could not afterwards bring the actio empti for the same object; in this particular instance, that already followed from the more specific rule of "suae rei emptio non valet".[85] This brings us into the vicinity of another reason why an obligation could fall away: supervening impossibility in general had that effect, provided the debtor could not be held responsible therefor. Impossibilium nulla obligatio: if performance was initially impossible, an obligation could not come into existence;[86] impossibility occurring after conclusion of the contract made it fall away again.[87] And as we find the former of these principles codified in § 306 BGB, so § 275 BGB still formulates the basic proposition concerning supervening impossibility in the following words:

---

[80] "Novatio est prioris debiti in aliam obligationem . . . transfusio atque translatio": Ulp. D. 46, 2, 1 pr.; cf. also Gai. III, 176 and supra, pp. 60, 634 sq.

[81] "[E]t hoc est quod apud veteres scriptum est: ante litem contestatam dare debitorem oportere, post litem contestatam condemnari oportere, post iudicatum facere oportere": Gai. III, 180 (following immediately on the discussion of novatio). On condemnari oportere, see Günther Jahr, *Litis contestatio* (1960), pp. 70 sqq., 146 sqq.; Kaser, *RZ*, pp. 227 sq.

[82] Pomp. D. 46, 3, 107; Mod. D. 46, 3, 75; Frezza, *Garanzie*, vol. I, pp. 144 sqq.; Solazzi, op. cit., note 7, pp. 277 sqq.

[83] On confusio in the ius commune: Windscheid/Kipp, § 352; in South African law: Joubert, *Contract*, pp. 285 sq.; in modern German law: Gernhuber, op. cit., note 33, pp. 384 sqq.

[84] Fritz Schulz, "Die Lehre vom Concursus Causarum im klassischen und justinianischen Recht", (1917) 38 *ZSS* 114 sqq.; Kaser, *RPr* I, pp. 643 sq.

[85] Pomp. D. 18, 1, 16; cf. supra, p. 241. An exception was made, however, where one of the concurring titles of acquisition was a causa lucrativa; cf. e.g. Iul. D. 30, 84, 5 and Honsell, *Quod interest*, pp. 38 sqq. On concursus causarum lucrativarum, see *Inst.* II, 20, 6; Iul. D. 30, 82 pr. and 1 and Michel, *Gratuité*, pp. 404 sqq.

[86] Cf., for example, supra, pp. 687 sqq.

[87] Cf. e.g. Dieter Medicus, "Zur Funktion der Leistungsunmöglichkeit im römischen Recht", (1969) 86 *ZSS* 67 sqq.; Windscheid/Kipp, § 264.

"The debtor is relieved from his obligation to perform if the performance becomes impossible because of a circumstance, for which he is not responsible and which occurs after the creation of the obligation."

IV. COMPENSATIO

1. Set-off in modern law

Much less straightforward, both in modern and in Roman law, are the rules relating to compensatio or set-off—from a purely dogmatic point of view probably the most interesting manner of terminating an obligation. Strictly speaking, set-off even affects two obligations at the same time, though one of them in many cases only partly. If A owes 200 sesterces to B and B owes 100 to A, both parties face each other in the role of debtor as well as that of creditor. If the legal system were to look at each of these claims in isolation, an unnecessarily circuitous and uneconomical procedure would ensue: A would have to give 200 to B merely to receive part of the amount back in full satisfaction of his own claim. If neither A nor B is willing to render performance, both of them would ultimately have to sue each other: two separate court cases between the same parties would be the result. It is not difficult to realize that matters can be considerably streamlined by looking at the obligational relationships between A and B as a whole. It is only by a balance of 100 sesterces that their mutual claims against each other differ, and it is only this balance that has to be transferred between them. As a result of a set-off, only B retains part of his original claim and only he can therefore institute an action against A. The other part of his claim as well as A's counterclaim can be taken to be satisfied: for where two parties have to pay 100 to each other, the legal system can just as well allow them to maintain the status quo.

Indisputably, therefore, set-off is a convenient way of satisfying mutual debts. The magna quaestio, however, is how it becomes effective. Modern legal systems deriving from Roman law essentially fall into two groups in this regard. § 388 BGB represents a good example of the one, when it states that "[t]he set-off is made by declaration to the other party".[88] This rule is based on a tradition dating back to the glossator Azo.[89] Both French[90] and Austrian law,[91] on the other hand, do not require any such declaration. As soon (and as far) as two debts capable of being set off against each other confront each

[88] Cf. also art. 124 OR.

[89] "[S]ed ego puto ea[m] ipso iure tunc demum fieri cum a partibus est opposita . . .": *Summa Codicis*, Lib. IV, De compensationibus rubrica (p. 140, left column); for details, see Heinrich Dernburg, *Geschichte und Theorie der Kompensation* (2nd ed., 1868), pp. 284 sq.

[90] Art. 1290 code civil.

[91] § 1438 ABGB.

other, both of them are extinguished ipso iure;[92] no account is taken of the will of the two parties concerned. Again, this conception of a set-off can be traced back to the glossators.[93] Down to the days of the pandectists both theories have vied for recognition,[94] and thus it is small wonder that in an essentially ius commune-based jurisdiction such as the South African one the law is still unsettled in this regard.[95] In some cases it has been held that set-off operates ipso iure;[96] in others a declaration by one of the parties has been required.[97] Support for both views can be found in the writings of the Roman-Dutch authorities.[98] The reason for this age-old dispute essentially lies in Justinian's somewhat half-hearted attempts to consolidate the rules of classical Roman jurisprudence.[99]

2. The procedural framework for set-off in Roman law

(a) *Iudicia bonae fidei*

One of the most characteristic features of set-off in Roman law was its distinctly procedural flavour.[100] Whether, and if so, in which manner and under which circumstances a set-off could be effected depended entirely on the nature of the formula applicable in a given situation. Thus, first of all, there were the iudicia bonae fidei. If a purchaser brought the actio empti, a locator the actio locati, etc., the judge was always instructed to assess "quidquid ob eam rem N^m N^m A^o A^o dare

[92] On the term "ipso iure" in this context cf. Pothier, *Traité des obligations*, § 635: "*Cette interpretation est conforme à l'explication que tous les lexicographes donnent à ces termes, ipso iure. Ipso iure fieri dicitur, dit Brisson, quod ipsa legis potestate et auctoritate, absque magistratus auxilio et sine exceptionis ope fit . . . Verba ipso iure, dit Spigelius, intellegitur sine facto hominis. Ipso jure consistere dicitur, dit Pratejus, quod ex sola legum potestate et auctoritate, sine magistratus opera consistit.*"

[93] Cf. Dernburg, op. cit., note 89, pp. 283 sq., who refers in particular to the glossator Martinus.

[94] Cf. e.g. Dernburg, op. cit., note 89, pp. 281 sqq.; Fridolin Eisele, *Die Compensation nach römischem und gemeinem Recht* (1876), pp. 211 sqq.

[95] Joubert, *Contract*, pp. 288 sqq.

[96] Cf. e.g. *Toucker v. Stinnes (SA) Ltd.* 1934 CPD 184; *Clark v. Van Rensburg* 1964 (4) SA 153 (O); *Great North Farms (Edms.) Bpk. v. Ras* 1972 (4) SA 7 (T). Cf. also B.v.D. van Niekerk, "Some Thoughts on the Problem of Set-off", (1968) 85 *SALJ* 31 sqq.

[97] *Hardy & Mostert v. Harsant* 1913 TPD 433; *Harris v. Tancred* 1960 (1) SA 839 (C) at 843F–G; De Wet en Yeats, pp. 253 sq. The declaration has retroactive effect; cf. also § 389 BGB: "The set-off has the effect that the claims, insofar as they cover each other, are deemed to have expired at the moment at which, being suitable for set-off, they have first confronted each other."

[98] Cf. e.g. Voet, *Commentarius ad Pandectas*, Lib. XVI, Tit. II, II and Grotius, *Inleiding*, III, XL, 7 on the one hand, Van Leeuwen, *Rooms-Hollands-Regt*, IV. Bouk, XL. Deel, 2 on the other. Cf. further J.H. Loots, P. van Warmelo, "Compensatio", (1956) 19 *THRHR* 179 sqq.

[99] On the great and mysterious "riddle" set by the Roman sources for modern private law, cf. Lippmann, "Zur Lehre von der Kompensation nach dem Entwurfe des bürgerlichen Gezetsbuches", (1893) 32 *JhJb* 157 sqq.; cf. also Wladyslaw Rozwadowski, "Studi sulla compensazione nel diritto romano", (1978) 81 *BIDR* 76 sq. ("*. . . uno dei più grande misteri nella storia dello sviluppo delle obbligazioni romane*").

[100] Both Gaius and Justinian deal with compensatio as part of their discussion of the law of actions: Gai. IV, 61 sqq.; *Inst.* IV, 6, 30.

facere oportet ex fide bona". This entailed a complete discretion to take into account any counterclaim arising from the same transaction, and to condemn the defendant only in the difference.[101] It did not matter whether money or another kind of performance was owed, for, due to the principle of omnis condemnatio pecuniaria, judicial assessment of a specific sum of money was required even in the latter case. The one sum could then conveniently be subtracted from the other. Unlike in modern law,[102] set-off did therefore not require that the parties owed each other acts of performance of the same kind and nature. But apart from that, the Roman compensatio ex bona fide was more narrowly circumscribed than its modern counterpart: the counterclaim had to arise ex eadem causa;[103] and whether set-off was effected at all was in the court's discretion. If, for instance, ascertainment of the counterclaim was likely to delay the proceedings unduly, the judge usually refused to take account of it. The defendant was then free to institute a separate action.[104]

(b) Actiones stricti iuris

Secondly, the actiones stricti iuris. Their formulae did not contain such a convenient opening for the judge to consider the possibility of a set-off ex officio. Unless the parties came to a specific agreement (which could be informal)[105] to set their claims off against each other, they had to sue each other separately. If, however, during the proceedings in iure (that is, before the praetor) it turned out that the defendant had a counterclaim which was both due and entailed performance of the same kind as the one expected of himself, the praetor could ask the plaintiff to reduce his claim accordingly and to limit his request for condemnation to the difference between claim and counterclaim. If the plaintiff was unwilling to do that, the praetor could refuse to grant an action (denegatio actionis). This he would, however, only contemplate either if the counterclaim was undisputed or if the defendant was able immediately to prove its existence and the amount involved: for under these circumstances the plaintiff's insistence on condemnation into the full amount of his claim could hardly be regarded as fair and proper. If, on the other hand, the praetor regarded the defendant's demand for a set-off as inappropriate, he refused to accept any such possibility (compensationem denegare)[106] and pro-

[101] "In bonae fidei autem iudiciis libera potestas permitti videtur iudici ex bono et aequo aestimandi quantum actori restitui debeat. in quo et illud continetur ut, habita ratione eius quod invicem actorem ex eadem causa praestare oporteret, in reliquum eum cum quo actum est condemnare": Gai. IV, 61.

[102] Windscheid/Kipp, § 350, 4; § 387 BGB; Joubert, *Contract*, p. 290.

[103] Gai. IV, 61.

[104] Kaser, *RPr* I, p. 645.

[105] Kaser, *RPr* I, p. 646.

[106] Gai. D. 16, 2, 8.

ceeded to grant the action, as requested, to the plaintiff.

But what happened if the praetor was not sure about the substance of the defendant's counterclaim? It was, of course, not up to him to hear and evaluate the evidence and to pronounce upon the merits of the case; that was the task of the iudex in the second stage of the formulary proceedings. But the iudex could investigate these matters only if he was expressly instructed by the praetor to do so, and such instruction had to be part and parcel of the procedural formula granted to the plaintiff. The obvious solution, therefore, was the insertion of an exceptio into the formula. This is indeed what appears to have happened, for Justinian reports that the Emperor Marcus Aurelius had made the exceptio doli available for that purpose: ". . . sed et in strictis iudiciis ex rescripto divi Marci opposita doli mali exceptione compensatio inducebatur."[107] But this is where the problems really start. It is unlikely that this passage, and with it the attribution of a set-off, ope exceptionis, to (late) classical law, are entirely spurious,[108] though it is much less clear whether Marcus Aurelius really introduced a new idea or did not rather sanction an existing practice.[109] If, however, the whole scheme originated in classical jurisprudence, it is very difficult to make out how it operated within the rather stringent framework of the formulary procedure. Two particularly awkward questions had to be addressed. On the one hand, a plaintiff who disputed the existence of the counterclaim in the course of the proceedings in iure could not necessarily be taken to have acted in contravention of good faith and average business decency. If the defendant was able to substantiate his claim only apud iudicem, the requirements of the exceptio doli cannot usually have been satisfied, and thus any possibility of a set-off was bound to fail. On the other hand, there was the difficulty that, depending on whether the plaintiff had acted dolo malo or not, the defendant could be condemned only into the full amount claimed by the plaintiff or had to be absolved completely. "Si in ea re nihil dolo malo A^i A^i factum sit vel fiat" was what the exceptio instructed the judge to investigate,[110] and "iudex N^m N^m A^o A^o condemnato, si non paret, absolvito" were the two alternatives offered to him in the condemnatio. This strict all-or-nothing approach obviously entailed a grave risk for the plaintiff, for if he refused to accept the suggestion of the judge to reduce his claim by the amount of the defendant's counterclaim and if, as a result, he obtained only a formula containing the exceptio doli, he had to face the very real prospect of losing his claim altogether rather than having it cut in size.

[107] *Inst.* IV, 6, 30.

[108] Kaser, *RPr* I, p. 646. Contra: Thielmann, *Privatauktion*, pp. 151 sq.

[109] Cf. e.g. Waclaw Osuchowski, "Quelques remarques sur la 'deductio bonorum emptoris' et l'interpretation de D. 16.2.2", in: *Studi in onore di Edoardo Volterra*, vol. II (1971), p. 476; Rozwadowski, (1978) 81 *BIDR* 77 sqq., 98 sqq., 115 sqq.; Honsell/Mayer-Maly/Selb, p. 275.

[110] Gai. IV, 119.

What solutions (if any) the Roman jurists found to obviate these problems, we do not know. Only speculations are possible. Thus, it has, for instance, been suggested[111] that the "neque fiat" clause of the exceptio doli (in any event a powerful tool to advance the cause of equity and fairness)[112] may have been taken to refer not only to cases where the bringing of the action could be regarded as an infringement of the precepts of good faith, but also to those where something in the behaviour of the plaintiff, after litis contestatio right up to the time of judgment, constituted dolus. If this was in fact the case, one could have argued as follows. In view of the exceptio doli, it was the judge's duty to establish whether the defendant had a counterclaim which could be used for set-off purposes. If he had satisfied himself that such a claim existed, he would have to ask the plaintiff to accept the balance between claim and counterclaim in full settlement of the defendant's debt. Normally the plaintiff could be expected to accede to this request. If he did, the defendant was asked to pay the balance; and once payment had taken place, the judge could absolve the defendant. This was a somewhat roundabout procedure, but in the end a set-off was effected. If, on the other hand, the plaintiff insisted on payment of the whole sum due to him (despite the fact that the existence of an offsettable counterclaim had in the meantime been established), he could now with some justification be said to have overstepped the line dividing bona fides and dolus (malus), and it was neither strange nor inequitable if the judge proceeded to absolve the defendant under these circumstances (with the result that the plaintiff lost his entire claim).

(c) Special kinds of set-off: argentarius and bonorum emptor

There was, thirdly, however, one actio stricti iuris where an automatic set-off was already built into the formula. A banker (argentarius) who sued his customer was granted a formula with the following intentio: "Si paret N^{m} N^{m} A^{o} A^{o} HS X milia dare oportere amplius quam A^{s} A^{s} N^{o} N^{o} debet. . . ."[113] It required the banker to establish his customer's counterclaims and to reduce his own claim accordingly, for his action was limited to the balance due to him ("amplius quam").[114] The range of counterclaims that had to be taken into account was not limited to those arising ex eadem causa; it was sufficient that things of the same kind and nature were the object of both claim and

[111] Kaser, *RPr* I, p. 646; for different suggestions and further discussion, see Paul van Warmelo, "Le rescrit de Marc-Aurèle à propos de la compensation", in: *Mélanges Henri Lévy-Bruhl* (1959), pp. 335 sqq.; Siro Solazzi, *La compensazione nel diritto romano* (2nd ed., 1950), pp. 97 sqq.; Rozwadowski (1978) 81 *BIDR* 77 sqq.

[112] Cf. supra, pp. 667 sq.

[113] Gai. IV, 64; Lenel, *EP*, p. 256; cf. further e.g. Solazzi, op. cit., note 111, pp. 31 sqq.; Thielmann, *Privatauktion*, pp. 159 sqq.

[114] Set-off thus operated "ipso iure" in this instance; cf. Honsell/Mayer-Maly/Selb, p. 273.

counterclaim[115]—usually, of course, we are dealing here with money. In drawing up the balance, the banker had to be extremely careful, for if it turned out, apud iudicem, that he had claimed too much (albeit only a farthing),[116] he lost his entire claim: ". . . si facta compensatione plus nummo uno intendat argentarius, causa cadat et ob id rem perdat."[117] Such was the harsh consequence of pluris petitio:[118] the judge could condemn only into exactly the sum that the plaintiff had asked for; alternatively, he had to absolve the defendant. After all, a defendant who in actual fact owed 99 could not be said to owe the sum of 100, which a plaintiff might have claimed erroneously.

Finally, there was a special kind of set-off operating with regard to debts due to an insolvent estate. Whenever a bonorum emptor (that is, the purchaser of the property of an insolvent debtor) instituted an action, he had to do so "cum deductione": he had to deduct from his claim whatever he himself owed to the defendant by virtue of having become the insolvent person's successor.[119] In IV, 65-68 Gaius compares agere cum compensatione of the argentarius with agere cum deductione of the bonorum emptor, and notes three main differences: it was not in the intentio but only in the condemnatio of the formula that account was taken of deductio (which meant that the bonorum possessor was not faced with the dire consequences of pluris petitio); deductio did not operate only where performances of the same kind and nature were the object of both claim and counterclaim, but allowed a set-off even of "quod non est eiusdem generis";[120] and it also operated with regard to counterclaims that had not yet fallen due.

3. Towards a generalized form of set-off

(a) Assimilation

All in all, therefore, one cannot say that the Roman lawyers developed a uniform, logical and systematic approach to the problem of set-off; what we are faced with appears—at least from a modern perspective—as a rather confused hotchpotch of different principles and criteria, dictated by procedural niceties. In the one case, set-off operated ope exceptionis, in the other essentially ipso iure (though not quite).[121] Sometimes claim and counterclaim had to relate to performances of the

---

[115] Gai. IV, 66.

[116] De Zulueta's translation of nummus unus in Gai. IV, 68.

[117] Gai. IV, 68.

[118] On pluris petitio cf. Gai. IV, 53 sqq.; Guiseppe Provera, *La pluris petitio nel processo romano*, vol. I (1958); Kaser, *RZ*, pp. 246 sqq.; Guiseppina Sacconi, *La "pluris petitio" nel processo formulare* (1977); for the later history cf. Wolfgang Wiegand, *Plus petitio* (1974).

[119] Gai. IV, 65; cf. further e.g. Solazzi, op. cit., note 111, pp. 65 sqq.; Thielmann, *Privatauktion*, pp. 168 sqq.; Osuchowski, *Studi Volterra*, vol. II, pp. 461 sqq.; for details of the procedure, see Kaser, *RZ*, pp. 310 sqq.

[120] Gai. IV, 66.

[121] Discretion of the judge! (Cf. supra, p. 762.)

same kind, but in other instances this was not essential for setting off the one against the other. Here the counterclaim had to be due, there even debts falling due in future were brought into account. In one situation set-off operated only where claim and counterclaim had arisen ex eadem causa; in another, it did not matter in which transaction the counterclaim found its origin. Justinian therefore faced a formidable task when he set out to streamline and rationalize this area of the law.[122] The characteristic peculiarities of the classical formulary procedure had, of course, fallen away by his time, and thus there had been a trend, already for some time, towards assimilation and generalization.[123] Post-classical procedure was no longer divided into two different stages (proceedings in iure and apud iudicem). The actiones had lost their specific procedural significance, and the differences between stricti iuris and bonae fidei iudicia had largely been levelled out.[124] Particularly important in the present context was the change of attitude towards excessive claims. The strict all-or-nothing approach had not survived the demise of the formulary procedure, and thus pluris petitio no longer entailed dismissal (and consequent loss) of the entire claim. A plaintiff who had not taken account of the defendant's offsettable counterclaims could now be awarded the difference between claim and counterclaim.[125] This paved the way for the generalized form of set-off as introduced (or in any event recognized) by Justinian: ". . . nostra constitutio eas compensationes quae iure aperto nituntur, latius introduxit, ut actiones ipso iure minuant", as the emperor himself described his intervention.[126] In other words: it is the judge (and no longer the plaintiff) who determines the *amount* into which the defendant has to be condemned, and that amount, in the case of set-off, is the balance between claim and counterclaim. To a large extent, therefore, the regime governing the iudicia bonae fidei appears to have won the upper hand; thus, for instance, according to "nostra constitutio" (C. 4, 31, 14) a counterclaim could be taken into account only for the purposes of set-off "si causa . . . liquida sit et non multis ambagibus innodata". The same is meant when *Inst.* IV, 6, 30 refers to set-offs "quae iure aperto nituntur". Justinian merely formalized one of the main criteria that had guided the classical judge in the exercise of his discretion. But there were also important differences. A set-off was admissible even where claim and counterclaim originated in dispari

---

[122] Using "compensatio" as a terminus technicus; for all details, see Solazzi, op. cit., note 111, pp. 191 sqq.

[123] Cf. e.g. Levy, *Obligationenrecht*, pp. 145 sqq.; Solazzi, op. cit., note 111, pp. 111 sqq., 142 sqq.

[124] Cf. e.g. Kaser, *RPr* II, pp. 333 sqq.

[125] The plaintiff, as a consequence of the pluris petitio, merely incurred the penalty of a threefold reimbursement of his opponent's expenses ("in triplum restituat damnum, quod ipsius culpa adversario contigit"): C. 3, 10, 2 (Iust.); cf. also *Inst.* IV, 6, 24 and Francesco Sitzia, "Su una costituzione di Giustiniano in tema sportulae", (1972) 75 *BIDR* 221 sqq.

[126] *Inst.* IV, 6, 30.

causa; late classical jurisprudence already appears to have abandoned the ex eadem causa requirement which had originally restricted the set-off when it came to bonae fidei iudicia.[127] On the other hand, however, the performances owed under claim and counterclaim now had to be of the same nature:[128] this was a consequence of the fact that the principle of omnis condemnatio pecuniaria had been abandoned in post-classical procedure[129] and that thus not every claim ultimately led to a condemnation to pay a certain sum of money.[130]

(b) *Set-off in the Corpus Juris Civilis*

How did Justinian's compensation work? ". . . ut actiones ipso iure minuant" say the *Institutes*,[131] and in the Codex, too, it is emphasized that "[c]ompensationes ex omnibus actionibus ipso iure fieri".[132] The implication appears to be that both claims were regarded as being satisfied without any intervention of either of the parties being necessary. That is, however, in strange contrast to the language used in other places ("compensationis obici", "opponi compensationem")[133] and also to the fact that the ipso iure effect of compensatio has not been stressed more strongly (by way of interpolations) in the Digest.[134] Looking at the Corpus Juris as a whole, it is not difficult to see how a division of opinion could arise among the medieval lawyers about how best to harmonize the sources dealing with the operation (ope exceptionis or ipso iure?) of compensatio.

V. EXTINCTIVE PRESCRIPTION

Some modern legal systems recognize a further, practically very dangerous, threat to the life of obligations: the lapse of time. South African law provides a good example. According to § 10 I of the Prescription Act 68/1969, debts are extinguished (as a rule) three

---

[127] Kaser, *RPr* I, pp. 646 sq.

[128] Cf. e.g. Loots/Van Warmelo, (1956) 19 *THRHR* 181.

[129] For details, see Kaser, *RZ*, pp. 498 sq.

[130] Modern German law requires that the performances are of the same kind and nature and that the claim of the person declaring the set-off is due; claim and counterclaim need not have arisen ex eadem causa. Cf. § 387 BGB; also Windscheid/Kipp, § 350, 3 and 4, and (for South Africa) Joubert, *Contract*, pp. 290 sq. On the requirement of liquidity of the counterclaim cf. Windscheid/Kipp, § 350, 5; "Motive", in: *Mugdan*, vol. II, p. 58. According to § 393 BGB, set-off is not permissible against a claim arising from a wilful delict. This is a generalization of a rule contained in C. 4, 31, 14, 2; cf. "Motive", in: *Mugdan*, vol. II, p. 62.

[131] IV, 6, 30.

[132] C. 4, 31, 14; cf. also C. 4, 31, 4 (Alex.); Paul. D. 16, 2, 4; Paul. D. 16, 2, 21 (all interpolated).

[133] C. 4, 31, 14, 1; cf. further Solazzi, op. cit., note 111, pp. 166 sqq.; Loots/Van Warmelo, (1956) 19 *THRHR* 178.

[134] Cf. Rozwadowski, (1978) 81 *BIDR* 77 sqq., 98 sqq.

years[135] after they have become due.[136] In certain cases prescription may be interrupted[137] or its completion may be delayed,[138] but under normal circumstances a creditor may be expected to pursue (and, if necessary, enforce) his claims within a reasonable period. The reason lies, as Windscheid/Kipp[139] somewhat romantically describe it, in the obfuscating power of time: as the years pass by, it becomes more and more difficult for the debtor to defend himself.[140] He may no longer be able to remember and to prove those circumstances which thwart the plaintiff's claim. More particularly, he can hardly be required to keep all his receipts indefinitely; yet, without them it may be impossible for him to establish that he has already satisfied the claim. Prescription[141] thus provides the debtor with a convenient all-round protection against the claims of a creditor who has shown little interest in pursuing them. Of course, prescription is somewhat of a double-edged sword, for it affects unfounded as well as justified claims. But that is a price most modern legal systems are prepared to pay: long dormant claims, as a rule, "have more cruelty than justice in them".[142] Not all modern legal

---

[135] Exceptions: 30 years for debts secured by mortgage bond, judgment debts and some others, 15 years for certain debts owing to the State and six years for debts arising from a bill of exchange or other negotiable instrument. For details, see § 11 of the Prescription Act.

[136] In Scotland, too, prescription has the effect of extinguishing the obligation. The (regular) prescription period is, however, 5 years (§ 6 of the Prescription and Limitation (Scotland) Act 1973). For details, see David M. Walker, *The Law of Prescription and Limitation of Actions in Scotland* (3rd ed., 1981).

[137] The effect of an interruption of prescription is essentially that the prescription begins to run afresh on the termination of the interruption; the time that has elapsed before the interruption is not taken into consideration. Cf. also § 217 BGB. Example: acknowledgement of liability by the debtor.

[138] In other words, prescription is suspended for some time. The period of prescription is lengthened by the period during which the prescription is suspended. Cf. also § 205 BGB. Example: the creditor is a minor, or the debt is subject to a dispute submitted to arbitration.

[139] § 105: "*Die Zeit ist eine Macht, der sich kein menschliches Gemüt entziehen kann; . . . [sie] heiligt nicht bloss, sie verdunkelt auch.*" According to Savigny, *System*, vol. V, p. 272, prescription is one of the most important and beneficial ("*wohlthätigsten*") legal institutions.

[140] On the purposes and functions of prescription, see Karl Spiro, *Die Begrenzung privater Rechte durch Verjährungs-, Verwirkungs- und Fatalfristen*, vol. I (1975), §§ 3 sqq.

[141] We are, of course, dealing here only with what is often also referred to as "extinctive" (or negative) prescription (as opposed to "acquisitive" (or positive) prescription, e.g. usucaption). Following the tradition of the (older) ius commune (for the 19th century, cf. Savigny, *System*, vol. IV, pp. 309 sqq.), the South African Prescription Act 68/1969 still deals with both kinds of prescription. So does the Scottish Prescription and Limitation Act 1973. Cf. generally Karl August Dominik Unterholzner, Theodor Schirmer, *Ausführliche Entwickelung der gesammten Verjährungslehre aus den gemeinen in Deutschland geltenden Rechten* (2nd ed., 1858); Windscheid/Kipp, § 105; J.C. de Wet (the "father" of the South African Act) "Verjaring", in: *Opuscula Miscellanea* (1980), pp. 77 sqq.; Walker, op. cit., note 136. Modern legal systems generally do not require good faith on the part of the debtor; extinctive prescription, in other words, is based merely on the lapse of time, not on whether or not the debtor knew that he was obliged to pay. The opposite view had been adopted by the canon lawyers; cf. also still § 569 I 9 PrALR and Windscheid/Kipp, § 111. The canon lawyers, in so far, had merely extended to extinctive prescription what had always been recognized with regard to acquisitive prescription (usucapio).

[142] *R.B. Policies at Lloyd's v. Butler* [1950] 1 KB 76 at 82, quoting Best CJ in *A'Court v. Cross (a)* (1825) 3 Bing 329 at 332. German courts often tend to relax the rules of prescription in

systems, however, regard a debt which has prescribed as extinct. According to § 222 I BGB, for instance,[143] the debtor is entitled to refuse performance after the period of prescription has expired. The obligation thus continues to exist but the person bound by it is granted a peremptory defence. Yet the difference between these two constructions of prescription is largely of a technical nature. Even in South African law, prescription has to be raised in court by the defendant; the court cannot of its own motion take notice of the fact that the debt has fallen away.[144] Also payment in satisfaction of a claim which has prescribed is—rather irregularly—not regarded as indebitum solutum and may therefore not be claimed back.[145] Hence in practice, both under the South African system of a "strong" prescription and under the "weak" approach adopted by the BGB, it is up to the debtor either to render performance or to invoke the rules of prescription; if he decides to do the latter, the creditor has lost any possibility of enforcing his claim.

Much more important is the difference in the actual periods of prescription. According to § 195 BGB, the regular period of prescription is 30 years.[146] As so often, this provision of the German Code only restates a rule of the European ius commune. It ultimately derives from the praescriptio longi temporis, introduced by the Emperor Theodosius II in A.D. 424 for all actiones perpetuae, i.e. for claims which had hitherto not been subject to any temporal

---

order to alleviate the hardship undoubtedly connected with the fact that the creditor may lose a well-founded claim (and is therefore, in a sense, expropriated). Much less attention tends to be focused on the many cases in which strict application of the prescription rules prevents unjustified claims from being (successfully) pursued. For a comparative overview of modern legislation dealing with extinctive prescription cf. Peters/Zimmermann, *Verjährungsfristen*, pp. 267 sqq.; cf. also the stimulating analysis by M.M. Loubser, "Towards a Theory of Extinctive Prescription", (1988) 105 *SALJ* 34 sqq.

[143] A model for what is usually referred to as the "weak" form of prescription. Cf. also art. 142 OR.

[144] § 17 I Prescription Act; cf. also art. 2938 codice civile, read together with art. 2934 I.

[145] § 10 III Prescription Act; in the same sense § 222 II BGB and art. 2940 codice civile.

[146] Exceptions: certain claims (exactly specified in 17 numbers) arising—broadly speaking—from transactions of daily life (2 years; § 196 BGB), claims to arrears of interest, of rents, annuities, salaries, etc. (4 years; § 197 BGB); the actiones quanti minoris and redhibitoria in their modern version (6 months and 1 year; § 477 BGB); warranty claims in the case of the sale of livestock (6 weeks; § 490 BGB); certain claims for compensation arising from a contract of lease (6 months; § 558 BGB); warranty claims arising from a contract for work (6 months, 1 year, 5 years; § 638 BGB); claims arising from delict (3 years; § 852 BGB); and many more both in other parts of the BGB and (particularly) outside the BGB: for all the details, see Peters/Zimmermann, *Verjährungsfristen*, pp. 106 sqq., 148 sqq. So numerous are the exceptions that one may well doubt whether the 30 years of § 195 BGB can still be said to be the "regular" period of prescription. But despite a certain tendency of the courts to restrict the field of application of § 195 even further, this rule still covers a variety of practically very important claims; cf. Peters/Zimmermann, *Verjährungsfristen*, pp. 189 sqq. More progressive than the German is the Swiss codification, according to which the regular prescription period is 10 years: art. 127 OR and cf. Spiro, op. cit., note 140, §§ 331 sq.; the same applies in Italy (art. 2946 codice civile).

limitation.[147] Whatever its merits in the (also not-so-tranquil) circumstances of the 5th century, a prescription period of 30 years is totally unsuitable for times in which history appears to have "accelerated" in an entirely unprecedented manner; it is so long that it completely frustrates the aims sought to be achieved with periods of prescription.[148] A radical readjustment (which would at the same time obviate the countless problems arising from the number and diversity of exceptios from the "regular" period)[149] is urgently required.[150]

VI. EXCURSUS: THE PROBLEM OF SPECIFIC PERFORMANCE

1. Condemnation or absolution

We have repeatedly referred, in this chapter as well as in previous ones, to obligations being "enforceable" and to the creditor having to "pursue" his claim against his debtor. What exactly did this entail? It was a significant (and lasting) advance of legal culture that a creditor, already in pre-classical times, could no longer take the law into his own hands and resort to self-help.[151] Instead, he had to go to court in order to establish his claim in accordance with the rules of civil procedure. Under the formulary system of classical law he first had to ask the

[147] C. 7, 39, 3, 1. Classical Roman law did not know a general law of prescription; most actions could be brought at any time. Exceptions existed with regard to praetorian penal actions (cf. Gai. IV, 110; Paul. D. 44, 7, 35 pr.; Kaser, *RPr* I, p. 613) and the actiones redhibitoria and quanti minoris (cf. supra, pp. 317 sq.). The lack of prescription accentuated the importance of institutions such as the stipulatio Aquiliana. On the development of longi temporis praescriptio in Roman (provincial) law (first of all as a form of acquisitive prescription), see Dieter Nörr, *Die Entstehung der longi temporis praescriptio* (1969); on its post-classical (Theodosius II) extension to all actiones perpetuae (in the form of extinctive prescription), see Mario Amelotti, *La prescrizione delle azioni in diritto romano* (1958), pp. 211 sqq. For an overview cf. also Kaser, *RPr* I, pp. 424 sq.; *RPr* II, pp. 71 sq.; Peters/Zimmermann, *Verjährungsfristen*, pp. 112 sq.

[148] Of the other extreme (prescription period so short that creditor is unreasonably prejudiced in the pursuit of his claim) § 638 BGB provides a good example: the claim of the customer for removal of a defect in the work and his claims for cancellation, reduction, or compensation on account of the defect are barred by prescription in six months, unless the contractor has fraudulently concealed the defect. Since prescription begins to run from the acceptance of the work, the claims may be prescribed before the defect has become apparent. For details, see Peters/Zimmermann, *Verjährungsfristen*, pp. 187 sqq., 206 sqq., 226 sqq. The same problem arises with regard to § 477 (covering the law of sale).

[149] Cf. e.g. Peters/Zimmermann, *Verjährungsfristen*, pp. 196 sqq.

[150] For a set of concrete proposals, see Peters/Zimmermann, *Verjährungsfristen*, pp. 285 sqq., 315 sqq.; for a discussion, see Helmut Heinrichs, "Reform des Verjährungsrechts?", 1982 *Neue Juristische Wochenschrift* 2021 sqq.; cf. also the comments by the Minister of Justice, Hans A. Engelhard, "Zu den Aufgaben einer Kommission für die Überarbeitung des Schuldrechts", 1984 *Neue Juristische Wochenschrift* 1201 sqq., 1205 sq.; Loubser, (1988) 105 *SALJ* 34 sqq., 52 sq.

[151] For the historical development cf. Kaser, *RZ*, pp. 19 sqq.; idem, *RPr* I, p. 222. There were, however, some exceptional cases where self-help remained admissible, as is evident, especially, from the interdicta uti possidetis, utrubi and unde vi. For details, see Kaser, loc. cit.

praetor to grant him an action; the formula of this action contained the programme of litigation, i.e. the sum total of all matters which the iudex had to investigate in the second stage of the proceedings and which thus determined his decision. As far as that decision was concerned, there were only two alternatives: condemnation or absolution. All formulae ended with the stereotype order (to the judge) ". . . condemnato, si non paret, absolvito".[152] In the latter case the plaintiff lost his claim completely.[153] But what did he ultimately get if the defendant was condemned? Where a specific sum of money (certa pecunia) was owed, it was, of course, this sum of money which became the object of the condemnation: "Si paret N^{m} N^{m} A^{o} A^{o} sestertium decem milia dare oportere, iudex N^{m} N^{m} A^{o} A^{o} sestertium decem milia condemnato, si non paret, absolvito."[154] Where a specific object was owed (certum dare obligation), the judge had to assess the pecuniary value of that object:

> "Si paret N^{m} N^{m} A^{o} A^{o} tritici Africi optimi modios centum dare oportere, quanti ea res est, tantam pecuniam iudex N^{m} N^{m} A^{o} A^{o} condemnato, si non paret, absolvito."[155]

Then there was a variety of situations where the relevant clause read "quanti ea res erit, tantam pecuniam . . ."[156] or "quanti ea res fuit, tantam pecuniam . . .":[157] here, again, the judge was required to assess the pecuniary value of the object in dispute: either at the time when judgment was rendered or at a certain moment in the past (namely the instant when the delict was committed). Many practically very important claims were based on a formula which contained the clause "quidquid N^{m} N^{m} A^{o} A^{o} dare facere oportet" in their intentio: the bonae fidei iudicia belonged to this category, and so did actiones stricti iuris where an incertum was owed. "Quidquid" being taken to imply a conversion into a sum of money, the judge was once again instructed "tantam pecuniam . . . N^{m} N^{m} A^{o} A^{o} condemnato, si non paret, absolvito". The same applied in those cases where the action lay for "quantum iudici bonum et aequum videbitur".[158]

2. Omnis condemnatio pecuniaria

The situation was thus relatively simple and straightforward: whatever performance the defendant owed, he was invariably condemned into a

---

[152] Cf. Gai. IV, 43.

[153] More precisely, of course, he lost his (original) claim already at the time of litis contestatio: the dare or facere oportere was turned into a condemnari oportere.

[154] Cf. supra, p. 36.

[155] Cf. supra, p. 36.

[156] As in the actiones in rem; cf. e.g. Gai. IV, 51.

[157] As in the case of the actio furti; cf. infra, p. 932.

[158] As in the case of the actio iniuriarum: cf. infra, p. 1062.

specific sum of money.[159] "Omnis condemnatio pecuniaria" was the general rule which dominated the formulary procedure[160] and indirectly also exercised a significant influence on the rules of substantive Roman law (ubi remedium, ibi ius!).[161] With the demise of the formulary procedure, however, the necessity of a condemnatio pecuniaria was bound to wane. Cognitio, which developed under the Principate as a procedure extra ordinem,[162] but soon became exclusive in post-classical times,[163] was characterized by its lack of formality and by the prominent role attributed to the imperial jurisdictional official. He was the master of the trial from beginning to end, and the search for equitable solutions to the problems submitted to him was largely left to his discretion. This entailed that the judicial officer was no longer bound either to absolve or to condemn the defendant into the equivalent in money of what had been claimed. Judgment could be for less than the plaintiff had originally asked for,[164] and it could also be for other kinds of performances than payment of money.[165] The trend towards judicial decrees of specific performance was reinforced by the inflationary tendencies and the general decline of the economy during the 3rd and 4th centuries.[166] Where performance in specie was possible, it could, as a rule, be enforced by the creditor. Thus the defendant could, for instance, be condemned to transfer a specific object, to conclude a contract or to provide security. Execution of the judgment, too, became entirely State-controlled and aimed at providing the plaintiff with whatever performance was due to him under the judgment rendered in his favour.[167]

3. Condemnatio pecuniaria and specific performance under Justinian

Justinian, the great champion and restorer of classical Roman private law, did not resuscitate the structure and principles of the formulae procedure. In that regard he usually accepted and consolidated the policy of his predecessors.[168] Thus it is obvious that he did not revert to

[159] Gai. IV, 48: "Omnium autem formularum quae condemnationem habent ad pecuniariam aestimationem condemnatio concepta est"; Gai. IV, 51: "Iudex, si condemnet, certam pecuniam condemnare debet."

[160] For details, see Kaser, *RZ*, pp. 286 sqq.; Kelly, *Roman Litigation*, pp. 69 sqq.; Angela Romano, "Condanna 'in ipsam rem' e condanna pecuniaria nella storia del processo romano", (1982) 28 *Labeo* 131 sqq.

[161] Cf. e.g. supra, pp. 35 sq.

[162] Kaser, *RZ*, pp. 339 sqq.

[163] For all details, see Kaser, *RZ*, pp. 410 sqq.

[164] Kaser, *RZ*, pp. 383 sq., 475 sq.

[165] Kaser, *RZ*, pp. 392, 498 sq.; Károly Visky, "Quelques remarques sur la thèse ipsam rem condemnare et ses rapports économiques", (1972) 19 *RIDA* 474 sqq.

[166] Kaser, *RPr* II, p. 343; Visky, (1972) 19 *RIDA* 489 sqq.

[167] For details, see Kaser, *RZ*, pp. 511 sqq.

[168] Although, of course, the separation of the (classical) rules of substantive law from their procedural framework was bound to lead to awkward incongruities.

the principle of *omnis* condemnatio pecuniaria. *Institutiones IV*, 6, 32 ("Curare autem debet iudex, ut omnimodo, quantum possibile ei sit, certae pecuniae vel rei sententiam ferat, etiam si de incerta quantitate apud eum actum est") may even lead us to believe that the creditor was in principle entitled to demand that a contractual obligation be performed in specie.[169] A phrase contained in Ulp. D. 6, 1, 68 has been taken to point in the same direction. Here we find a statement (attributed to Ulpian, but inserted into the text by the interpolators) to the effect that having been ordered by the judge to hand over a thing, a party could be dispossessed "manu militari" at the judge's direction, provided the party still had the object in question. This assertion is then generalized in the following way:

> "[H]aec sententia generalis est et ad omnia, sive interdicta sive actiones in rem sive in personam sunt, ex quibus arbitratu iudicis quid restituitur, locum habet."[170]

Strictly speaking, however, this passage deals only with claims directed at a restitutio. Read in conjunction with a variety of other texts scattered throughout the Corpus Juris, it rather leads one to the conclusion that the principle of specific performance was restricted to dare (and reddere) obligations.[171] Both where a praestare and a facere was owed, Justinian may well be seen to have retained (or reverted to) the principle of the condemnatio pecuniaria. How else can one interpret the fact that he incorporated the following statement of Ulpian referring to the actio empti (that is, the practically most important praestare obligation) into the Digest: "Si res vendita non tradatur, in id quod interest agitur, hoc est quod rem habere interest emptoris"?[172] And as far as those cases were concerned where the debtor was bound to do something (facere), we have a very clear and generally worded testimony in D. 42, 1, 13, 1: ". . . quia non facit quod promisit, in pecuniam numeratam condemnatur, sicut evenit in omnibus faciendi obligationibus."[173] All in all, the Corpus Juris provides a somewhat patchy picture and leaves it open to considerable doubt how far the principle of specific performance had in actual practice been substituted for that of omnis condemnatio pecuniaria.

4. The distinctions of the ius commune

Not surprisingly, therefore, this topic became the subject of an intense and controversial discussion among the medieval lawyers. Since the

---

169 Kaser, *RPr* II, pp. 343 sq.

170 Cf. also C. 7, 4, 17 (Just.).

171 Cf. Hermann Dilcher, "Geldkondemnation und Sachkondemnation in der mittelalterlichen Rechtstheorie", (1961) 78 *ZSS* 278 sqq.; but cf. recently also J.J. du Plessis, "Spesifieke nakoming: 'n Regshistoriese herwaardering", (1988) 51 *THRHR* 349 sqq., 353 sqq.

172 Ulp. D. 19, 1, 1 pr. This is, however, in conflict with *Inst.* II, 7, 2 (dealing with donation, but referring also to the contract of sale).

173 But there were exceptions; cf. D. 3, 3, 35, 3 and D. 4, 8, 3.

days of the glossators, the threefold subdivision of the possible contents of an obligation as contained, for instance, in D. 44, 7, 3 pr. ("Obligationum substantia . . . in eo consistit . . . ut alium nobis obstringat ad dandum aliquid vel faciendum vel praestandum"),[174] provided the generally accepted starting point for this debate.[175] But even within these categories, further subtle distinctions were drawn in order to provide some sort of systematic framework for the rich casuistry of the Corpus Juris.[176] Thus, by the end of the Middle Ages, cases where the creditor could insist on specific performance were recognised within all three groups of obligations; but they stood side by side with other instances where the debtor could be forced only to pay the equivalent in money. Generally speaking, though, there was a continuing trend towards condemnation in specie: "praecise tenetur" is what was said about the debtor in these cases. Most of the dare obligations fell into this category,[177] and so, according to the majority view[178] and because it so closely resembled a dare obligation, did the actio empti. Other tradere obligations (as far as they were discussed at all) were usually subjected to the regime of condemnatio pecuniaria. With respect to facere obligations, Azo, Accursius and many other glossators, by giving the creditor the choice,[179] in fact recognized the possibility of a condemnation in specie. The commentators were at first reluctant to accept this. "Nemo potest praecise cogi ad factum" was the view they tended to adopt, but in the course of time more and more exceptions came to be identified.[180] Petrus de Bellapertica (Pierre de Belleperche) accepted condemnation in specie in the case of a scriptor; Jacobus de Ravanis (Jacques de Revigny), wherever services (operae) were owed; Johannes Faber, whenever the debtor was insolvent; Bartholomaeus Salicetus (and others), in cases where the obligation had been confirmed by oath; and Yason de Mayno, in a sweeping statement, "quando est tale pactum, quod faciliter et de levi potest expediri".

5. Roman-Dutch law; modern German law

The controversy continued among the humanists as well as among the authors of the usus modernus pandectarum.[181] The rule of "nemo

[174] Derived from Gai. IV, 2.

[175] In the place of praestare, one soon started to refer, more specifically, to tradere.

[176] For a detailed discussion, see H. Dilcher, (1961) 78 *ZSS* 283 sqq.

[177] But not those arising from innominate real contracts; cf. e.g. Bartolus, *Commentaria*, D. 19, 5, 5, 1, § Etsi quidem, 4.

[178] The dispute arose among the quattuor doctores. Martinus argued in favour of specific performance; his view was adopted by Pillius, Roffredus, Accursius, Ravanis, Bellapertica, Cinus, Bartolus, Baldus, Paulus de Castro and Jason de Mayno. Contra (". . . non tenetur emptor precise ad rem tradendam") Bulgarus and, following him, Rogerius, Placentinus, Johannes Bassianus and Azo. Cf. H. Dilcher, (1961) 78 *ZSS* 287 sqq.; H.F.W.D. Fischer, *De geschiedenis van de reële executie bij koop* (1934), pp. 123 sqq.

[179] Cf. e.g. Accursius, gl. In aliis autem casibus ad C. 7, 47.

[180] For all this cf. H. Dilcher, (1961) 78 *ZSS* 293 sqq., 298 sq., 301 sq.

[181] Coing, pp. 432 sqq.

potest praecise cogi ad factum" dominated the discussions relating to obligationes ad faciendum. It appears to have been widely accepted that a debtor cannot be forced to do something and that he is therefore able to discharge his obligation by paying damages (id quod interest). Ludovicus de Molina even referred to a communis opinio (of which he himself, however, disapproved).[182] Via Pothier[183] this doctrine found its way into art. 1142 code civil, which states: "*Toute obligation de faire ou de ne pas faire se résout en dommages et intérêts en cas d'inexécution de la part du débiteur.*"[184] The actio empti,[185] on the other hand, was likened by a majority of writers to the dare obligations; strictly speaking, to be sure, the vendor merely owed vacuam possessionem tradere, but this handing over was intended to transfer ownership and hence to constitute a datio in the technical sense of the word.[186] As a result, it was widely recognized that the purchaser could insist on specific performance, as long as the vendor was still able to transfer the object: "non enim solvendo interesse liberari potuit, qui rei tradendae facultatem habuit." This is how the Hooge Raad van Holland, Zeeland en West-Vriesland put it very crisply.[187]

Roman-Dutch law generally took a remarkably progressive attitude.[188] Few authors were prepared to follow Grotius when he stated that although by natural law a person who has promised to do something is bound to do it in case it admits of being done, he may, nevertheless, "nae 't burger-recht" effect his release by paying id quod interest.[189] Only Voet took a similarly antiquarian line and regarded specific performance as both impossible and undesirable in cases of obligationes ad faciendum.[190] Contrary to Grotius[191] (but like Donellus before him),[192] he viewed the vendor's duty under a contract of sale in

---

[182] Molina, *De iustitia et iure*, Tract. II, Disp. 562.

[183] *Traité des obligations*, n. 157.

[184] "The underlying idea is that, man being a free and responsible being, he should not be coerced by the state into behaving in a particular way. This is a most praiseworthy idea but it is far too vague, and its formulation in art. 1142 Code civil . . . is much too sweeping": Zweigert/Kötz/Weir, p. 145.

[185] For a comprehensive discussion of the historical development of specific performance with regard to the contract of sale, cf. Fischer, op. cit., note 178, passim, e.g. pp. 181 sqq.

[186] Cf. e.g. Gai. IV, 4.

[187] Reported by Cornelius Neostadius, "Decisiones supremi senatus Hollandiae, Zelandiae et Frisiae", in: idem, *Decisiones* (Hagae Comitis, 1667), Decis. L. Cf. also Pothier, *Traité du contrat de vente*, n. 68 and art. 1610 code civil. This ties in with the general principle laid down in art. 1184 II code civil, according to which a creditor who has not received what he was promised may require his debtor to perform the agreement in so far as that is still possible. For further details of the application of this rule in French practice (and particularly on the specific coercive technique of "*astreinte*"), see Zweigert/Kötz, pp. 186 sqq.

[188] Cf. Wessels, *History*, pp. 612 sqq.; Philip Gross, "Specific Performance of Contracts in South Africa", (1934) 51 *SALJ* 348 sqq.; Du Plessis, (1988) 51 *THRHR* 357 sqq.

[189] *Inleiding*, III, III, 41.

[190] *Commentarius ad Pandectas*, Lib. XLV, Tit. I, VIII.

[191] *Inleiding*, III, XV, 6.

[192] Cf. Fischer, op. cit., note 178, pp. 184 sq.

the same light.[193] By and large, however, Groenewegen's comment appears to be representative:

> "Hodie in omnibus faciendi obligationibus praecise ad factum cogi potest neque solvendo interesse liberatur promisor, qui faciendi facultatem habet."[194]

If a creditor was thus given the right to claim specific performance (not only of obligationes ad dandum but also) with regard to facere obligations, then the same was bound to apply to the tradere obligations (such as the actio empti) which fell somewhere in between the two. "Senatus condemnatum civili custodia sistendum (quod gyselinge houden dicimus) pronunciavit, quoad rem tradidisset":[195] this gives an impression of how a decree of specific performance was enforced.

In Germany, the last vestiges of omnis condemnatio pecuniaria were ultimately overcome in the course of the 19th century; for the pandectists, this principle was merely a kind of historical reminiscence which they discarded without much ado.[196] In modern German law, it is a matter of course that the parties to a contract are entitled to demand performance of their respective obligations in specie. "The effect of an obligation", says § 241 at the outset of Book II of the BGB, "is that the creditor is entitled to claim performance from the debtor." The implication is: specific performance.[197]

6. Specific performance in English law

(a) *The concept of contract*

It is most interesting to see that the same battle between specific performance and release from an obligation by payment of damages has been raging in the English common law. Unlike in Germany, it has not, however, ended in an out-and-out-victory for the former remedy, but in a rather uneasy truce between the two. The English common law does not traditionally conceive of contract as engendering enforceable duties to perform what has been promised.[198] A promisor is merely seen to assume the risk of a certain event either happening or not happening, no matter whether he promises to deliver a bale of cotton or whether the promise is that it shall rain tomorrow.[199] The only universal consequence of a legally binding promise is

---

[193] *Commentarius ad Pandectas*, Lib. XIX, Tit. I, XIV; cf. in this context Ben Beinart, "Roman Law in South African Practice", (1952) 69 *SALJ* 158.

[194] *De legibus abrogatis*, Digest. Lib. XLII, Tit. I, l. 13. Si quis ab alio.

[195] Cf. Neostadius, loc. cit.

[196] Cf. Arndts, *Pandekten*, § 219; Wächter, *Pandekten*, § 167.

[197] For further discussion, see John P. Dawson, "Specific Performance in France and Germany", (1959) 57 *Michigan LR* 495 sqq.; Zweigert/Kötz, pp. 181 sqq.

[198] Cf. generally Rheinstein, *Struktur*, pp. 122 sqq.

[199] Cf. the examples discussed by Holmes, *The Common Law*, pp. 298 sqq.

"that the law makes the promisor pay damages if the promised event does not come to pass. In every case it leaves him free from interference until the time for fulfilment has gone by, and therefore free to break his contract if he chooses".[200]

The reason for this (from a civilian perspective) rather peculiar attitude lies in the historical origin of modern English contract law in the action of assumpsit.[201] Assumpsit, in turn, grew out of tresspass—that is (in modern parlance), a delictual remedy[202] by means of which the plaintiff was allowed to claim compensation in money for a wrong that had been done to him.[203] In every writ of tresspass the defendant's harmful behaviour had to be described. In many cases it was quite obvious that such behaviour constituted a wrong, and in the course of time a number of standard forms were developed to cover these situations. Sometimes, however, additional explanations had to be provided by the plaintiff in order to establish the wrongfulness of the defendant's act: more particularly, he had to allege that the defendant had been under a duty to do or not to do what he had done or failed to do. This allegation was set out in a kind of demonstratio, a specific part of the formula introduced by the word "cum"; and since this "cum" clause contained all the relevant details particular to the case in question, such an action was referred to as a "special" writ of tresspass or as an action "on the case".

(b) *The rise of assumpsit*

Amongst these early actions on the case there was a group in which the duty of the defendant (and hence his liability in case of failure to comply with it) was based upon a prior (informal) transaction which he had entered into with the plaintiff. Thus, for example, we read of suits against a surgeon who treated a finger of his patient so incautiously that a great part of it was lost;[204] of a ferryman who killed a mare, entrusted

---

[200] Holmes, *The Common Law*, p. 301.

[201] For what follows, see A.W.B. Simpson, *History*, pp. 199 sqq.

[202] In a very similar fashion, of course, contract had grown out of delict in Roman law: cf. supra, pp. 4 sqq. And if its delictual origin is the historical reason why a contractual remedy for specific performance is (normally) not available according to the English common law, the same is true of the Roman rule of omnis condemnatio pecuniaria. A person who was "liable" because he had committed a wrong, was originally exposed to the injured party's power of seizure. But he could redeem himself by payment of a (monetary) composition. The State, of course, favoured this kind of release from liability which avoided crude forms of corporeal execution. Thus it had to make sure that the person liable (and his friends and relations) knew exactly how much money had to be paid in order to prevent manus iniectio from being granted. Thus, in every case where somebody was liable, a specific sum of money had to be determined in order to facilitate release from liability. This stage of the development was petrified in the rule of omnis condemnatio pecuniaria. Cf. e.g. Kaser, *RZ*, p. 287.

[203] For details, see S.F.C. Milsom, "Tresspass from Henry III to Edward III", (1958) 74 *LQR* 195 sqq., 407 sqq., 561 sqq.

[204] Cf. A.K.R. Kiralfy, *The Action on the Case* (1951), pp. 224 sq.

to him, as a result of overloading his boat;[205] or of a farrier who lamed a horse which he was shoeing.[206] In the course of the 14th century, the word "assumpsit" came to be commonly used in these kinds of actions: the defendant had undertaken to cure the finger, to transport the mare or to shoe the horse and could thus be seen to have assumed responsibility if something were to go wrong due to his lack of skill.[207] For more than a century, the development of assumpsit was checked by the "nonfeasance doctrine":[208] an action on the case based upon an assumpsit could not succeed if the defendant had merely failed to comply with what he had agreed to do; he had to have done something wrong (a misfeasance). It was only at the beginning of the 16th century[209] that assumpsit was made available also in cases of a pure nonfeasance. As a result of this, it had become a general action for the breach of informal agreements and thus effectively superseded the ancient contractual action of covenant: under covenant, the plaintiff had also been able to claim damages for breach of an agreement, but only if he was able to produce a sealed instrument ("make profert a specialty") to witness the latter.[210] This change of legal doctrine may well have been motivated by the activities of the Chancellors who had established a wide-ranging jurisdiction over contracts in cases where no remedy was provided by the common law.[211] Parole agreements were one such situation, and by abandoning the nonfeasance doctrine, the "ordinary" courts merely accepted for the common law what reason and conscience had obliged the Chancellors to recognize in equity. This entailed a (from the point of view of the common-law courts, welcome) shift in jurisdiction, for the extension of assumpsit largely removed the necessity for plaintiffs who wanted to enforce parole agreements to turn to equity.

The celebrated decision in *Slade's* case[212] was a further important milestone in the advance of assumpsit, for here it was settled that assumpsit could be used to force a person to pay a debt, i.e. a definite

[205] The case of the Humber Ferryman (*Buckton v. Townsend* 1348); for the text, see Simpson, *History*, pp. 623 sq.; for a discussion, see A.K.R. Kiralfy, "The Humber Ferryman and the Action on the Case", (1951–53) 11 *Cambridge LJ* 421 sqq.; Simpson, *History*, pp. 210 sqq.

[206] Cf. Kiralfy, op. cit., note 204, p. 142.

[207] On the exact meaning of the term "assumpsit", cf. Simpson, *History*, pp. 215 sqq.

[208] On which, see Simpson, *History*, pp. 222 sqq.

[209] With *Orwell v. Mortoft* (1505); cf. A.K.R. Kiralfy, *A Source Book of English Law* (1957), pp. 150 sqq.; for a comprehensive discussion, see Simpson, *History*, pp. 248 sqq.

[210] On covenant, see Simpson, *History*, pp. 9 sqq. He draws attention to the fact that originally specific relief could be granted under covenant.

[211] W.T. Barbour, "The History of Contract in Early English Equity", in: *Oxford Studies in Social and Legal History*, vol. IV (1914), pp. 66 sqq.; Simpson, *History*, pp. 275 sqq.

[212] *Slade's* case (1602) 4 Co Rep 91 a; for a discussion, see Kiralfy, op. cit., note 204, pp. 164 sqq.; A.W.B. Simpson, "The Place of Slade's Case in the History of Contract", (1958) 74 *LQR* 381 sqq. (but cf. idem, *History*, p. 305); H.K. Lücke, "Slade's Case and the Origin of the Common Counts", (1965) 81 *LQR* 422 sqq., 539 sqq.; (1966) 82 *LQR* 81 sqq.; J.H. Baker, "New Light on Slade's Case", (1971) 29 *Cambridge LJ* 51 sqq., 213 sqq.

sum of money owed. Again, this development heralded the demise of an older remedy. The action of debt "sur contract" had once been designed to cover exactly this type of situation, but it involved the outdated and unsatisfactory trial by wager of law (compurgation).[213] Based on the more rational procedure of trial by jury, assumpsit appealed to plaintiffs as well as judges; with *Slade's* case, debt sur contract was bound to sink into oblivion, and assumpsit firmly established itself as the regular common-law contractual action. As a matter of course, assumpsit lay for damages only, and thus the common law effectively gave the promisor an option to perform his contract or to compensate the promisee for non-performance.

(c) Common-law remedy and equitable relief

It soon became apparent, though, that the availability merely of a remedy for breach of contract rather than for the actual performance thereof could not always be regarded, from the point of view of the creditor, as adequate and equitable. Of course there are many cases in which specific relief is simply not possible. In other instances substantial practical difficulties can arise: one may think, for instance, of promises to paint a picture, to build a house or to sing in an opera.[214] And even in cases where the enforcement of specific performance would not create any difficulty,[215] the award of damages may often be regarded as perfectly adequate. Thus it can be argued, for instance, that in a market economy money ought to enable the disappointed purchaser of chattels to arrange a substitute transaction.[216] Things appear different, however, when it comes to items which are considered to be unique.[217] For the medieval English lawyers the "unique" item par excellence was land. If a vendor refused to transfer the piece of property which he had sold, the purchaser could hardly be

---

[213] On the action of debt sur contract, see Simpson, *History*, pp. 53 sqq.; on trial by wager of law, idem, pp. 136 sqq. The defendant had to find 11 compurgators who were prepared to swear an oath with their hands upon the Bible that he owed nothing, and then to kiss the Bible. If this procedure had been performed successfully, the defendant was said to have made his law "twelvehanded" (for he himself had to go through the same ceremony) and won the action.

[214] The main difficulty in these and similar cases lies in the fact that specific relief requires the cooperation of the (defaulting) promisor: cf. e.g. E.A. Farnsworth, "Legal Remedies for Breach of Contract", (1970) 70 *Columbia LR* 1150. How, under these circumstances, can a judgment for specific performance be enforced? For the answer in German law cf. §§ 883 sqq. ZPO and Zweigert/Kötz, pp. 183 sqq.; for French Law (with its characteristic institution of "*astreinte*"), see Zweigert/Kötz, pp. 187 sqq.

[215] As, for instance, with regard to an obligation to pay a sum of money.

[216] Farnsworth, (1970) 70 *Columbia LR* 1154, quoting a book by C.A. Huston on the enforcement of decrees in equity: "The law, concerning itself more and more with merchandise bought or sold for money, with things having a definite and calculable exchange value, came to conceive that the money compensation . . . was an entirely adequate remedy in the common case."

[217] On the traditional distinction between unique and non-unique goods, see Anthony F. Kronman, "Specific Performance", (1978) 45 *University of Chicago LR* 351 sqq.

expected to accept with equanimity a sum of money and look for a similar estate elsewhere. He wanted the vendor to honour his promise in a more specific manner. Under these circumstances, it was again to the equitable jurisdiction of the Chancellors that disappointed plaintiffs turned; for even if equity was no longer concerned with the enforceability of promises that would have been unenforceable at common law, it could, of course, still be invoked where the common-law remedy turned out to be deficient. The Chancellors, in turn, merely had to draw upon the canon law that they had studied (usually at Oxford) in order to find the appropriate answer to the problem.

The medieval canonists had been the first to break away decisively from omnis condemnatio pecuniaria; even for obligationes ad faciendum they had advocated the possibility of a condemnatio in specie.[218] A promise must be kept, for "mendacium est, si quis non impleat, quod promisit".[219] A decree of specific performance was thus ultimately designed to make the defendant act in accordance with good conscience and to coerce him to honour his promise, for the avoidance of sin. This is exactly what suited the Chancellors,[220] who could (as clerics) not be attracted at all by the common-law notion that promises may be broken and paid for rather than be kept. Not surprisingly, therefore, they were quite prepared to grant specific relief within their sphere of jurisdiction. These decrees in equity took the form of a personal command to the defendant to do or not to do something, and as a consequence it was said that equity acted in personam, that is, against the person of the defendant, whilst the common law acted in rem, i.e. against his property.[221] But when did the common-law remedy have to be applied for and when could equitable relief be obtained? The long jurisdictional struggle was ultimately settled by means of an "adequacy" test: specific performance was available only where the award of damages was inadequate. Payment of damages remained the rule, specific performance the exception. Moreover, specific relief was not granted as a matter of right; the equitable remedy was not only extraordinary but also discretionary; for since the Chancellor acted according to conscience, he could withhold relief where considerations of fairness or morality induced him to do so.[222]

(d) The position today

Today, only one Supreme Court of Judicature exists, and all its branches are empowered to apply the rules developed "at law" and "in

[218] H. Dilcher, (1961) 78 *ZSS* 302 sqq.
[219] Cf. supra, p. 542, note 224.
[220] Cf. also Simpson, *History*, pp. 595 sq.
[221] Farnsworth, (1970) 70 *Columbia LR* 1152 sq.
[222] Farnsworth, (1970) 70 *Columbia LR* 1154 sqq.

equity". Nevertheless, the idea still prevails that specific performance is an exceptional remedy.[223] It will not be granted where damages can adequately compensate the plaintiff, particularly in cases where a satisfactory substitute for what had been contracted for is readily available. Apart from that, contracts involving the rendering of personal services,[224] the erection of a building, or the performance of continuous contractual duties[225] are not specifically enforceable.[226, 227] Furthermore, a decree of specific performance continues to be at the discretion of the judge: "Equity will only grant specific performance if, under all the circumstances, it is just and equitable to do so."[228] This discretion has, however, largely come to be governed by fixed rules and principles. Thus, for instance,[229] specific performance can be refused if it would cause severe hardship to the defendant, if the contract has been obtained by unfair means or is unconscionable, if the conduct of the plaintiff himself has not been beyond reproach, or if the same remedy would not have been available to the defendant had the plaintiff been in breach of the contract (mutuality of remedy). Although there is a growing realization among Anglo-American authors "that many of the arguments for restricting specific performance are no longer wholly convincing",[230] and even though the courts, too, have in recent years been inclined to expand the scope of the remedy, the attitude adopted towards enforcement of the actual performance of a contract remains one of the fundamental differences between continental legal systems and the common law.[231]

7. Specific performance in South African law

Both traditions have to some extent been amalgamated in modern South African law. Its historical starting point, as we have seen, was a marked trend in favour of specific performance amongst the authoritative Roman-Dutch writers. Thus it was stated by Kotzé CJ that

---

[223] For details cf. Treitel, *Contract*, pp. 785 sqq.; cf. also Zweigert/Kötz, pp. 192 sqq.

[224] For the underlying reasons, see Zweigert/Kötz, p. 196.

[225] *Ryan v. Mutual Tontine Westminster Chambers Association* [1893] 1 Ch 116.

[226] Reason: the execution of a judgment for specific performance would involve great inconvenience. Hence also the exclusion of specific performance with regard to contracts that are "vague".

[227] On the other hand, specific performance is normally granted with regard to contracts involving the sale of land (also in favour of the vendor, even though his claim is only for money); where a satisfactory substitute cannot be obtained (sale of "unique" goods); where it would be difficult to assess or recover damages; where the damages would be purely nominal.

[228] *Stickney v. Keeble* [1915] AC 386 at 419.

[229] Treitel, *Contract* , pp. 788 sqq.

[230] Treitel, *Contract*, p. 785; cf. also Dawson, (1959) 57 *Michigan LR* 532; Alan Schwartz, "The Case for Specific Performance", (1979) 89 *Yale LJ* 271 sqq.; but see William Bishop, "The Choice of Remedy for Breach of Contract", (1985) 14 *Journal of Legal Studies* 299 sqq.

[231] For a comparative evaluation, see Zweigert/Kötz, pp. 197 sqq.

> "[b]y the well-established practice of South Africa, agreeing with the Roman-Dutch law, suits for specific performance are matters of daily occurrence".[232]

Nevertheless, in the course of the 19th century, rules and criteria of the English common law crept in "insidiously and, as it were, almost by accident",[233] so much so that the grounds for refusing specific performance listed by some academic writers in the early part of the 20th century were virtually the same as those applied by English courts.[234] In *Haynes v. King Williamstown Municipality*,[235] for many years the leading case, it was held that the court has a discretion to refuse specific performance, and that such refusal would be appropriate,

> "(a) where damages would adequately compensate the plaintiff; (b) where it would be difficult for the court to enforce its decree; (c) where the thing claimed can readily be bought anywhere; (d) where specific performance entails the rendering of services of a personal nature . . .; (e) where it would operate unreasonably harshly on the defendant, or where the agreement giving rise to the claim is unreasonable, or where the decree would produce injustice or would be inequitable under all the circumstances".[236]

Only in the 1980s have the courts begun to reassess these principles and to shed the limitations of specific performance derived from English practice.[237] In *Benson v. SA Mutual Life Assurance Society*[238] the Appellate Division firmly and authoritatively set its face against the continuation of a reception process which disregarded the fundamental difference in principle between Roman-Dutch and English law. The right of every plaintiff to claim specific performance has, once again, become "the cornerstone"[239] of South African law. It is the primary and regular remedy. To this extent, therefore, the civilian principle has prevailed. Unlike their modern continental counterparts, however, the courts do retain a discretion to refuse specific performance. This discretion obviously has its roots in English Equity: but it is no longer subject to any rules save that it be judiciously excercised in order to prevent injustice.[240] In particular, therefore, South African law has freed itself from the restrictive categories developed by the English courts.[241]

---

[232] *Cohen v. Shires, McHattie and King* (1882) 1 SAR 41 at 45.

[233] Sir John Wessels, "The Future of Roman Dutch Law in South Africa", (1920) 37 *SALJ* 272.

[234] Wessels, *Contract*, §§ 3113 sqq.; Gross, (1934) 51 *SALJ* 364 sqq.

[235] 1951 (2) SA 371 (A).

[236] At 378H–379A.

[237] Cf. e.g. *Isep Structural Engineering and Plating (Pty.) Ltd. v. Inland Exploration Co. (Pty.) Ltd.* 1981 (4) SA 1 (A); cf. also De Wet en Yeats, pp. 190 sq.

[238] 1986 (1) SA 776 (A).

[239] At 782J.

[240] At 782J–783F.

[241] For a more detailed discussion of the approach of the South African courts, cf. Joubert, *Contract*, pp. 224 sqq.; Andrew Beck, "The coming of age of specific performance", 1987 *Cilsa* 195 sqq., 204 sqq. As a consequence, for instance, the mere fact that a contract involves personal services does not automatically bar a decree of specific performance; cf. e.g. *National Union of Textile Workers v. Stag Packings (Pty.) Ltd.* 1982 (4) SA 151 (T) at 158A–C.

CHAPTER 25

Breach of Contract

I. BREACH OF CONTRACT IN GENERAL

1. Introduction

Every contractual promise engenders expectations in the person of the promisee. These expectations can be disappointed in various ways: the promisor may fail entirely to perform, he may offer performance belatedly or at the wrong place, or his performance may turn out to be unsatisfactory: In all these cases the promisor has not complied with the duties imposed upon him by the contract. In the terminology of the English common law, a breach of contract has occurred. The French code civil refers to non-performance ("*inexécution*").[1] The German BGB, however, does not appear to know such a unitary concept. It deals with only two specific forms of breach of contract (or: reasons for non-performance)—supervening impossibility and delay of performance—and provides separate sets of rules for both of them.[2] These rules are of a general nature in so far as they apply to all contracts. The same is true of the doctrine of "positive malperformance", which is not embodied in the code, but had to be developed, extra legem, by courts and legal writers.[3] Special rules dealing with liability for defective performance are set out in some of the titles of the BGB dealing with specific contracts.[4] This fragmented and unnecessarily intricate way of dealing with the problem of breach of contract has been severely criticized and is widely regarded today as one of the more unfortunate features of the German Code.[5] It is based on pandectist doctrine, and, through it, ultimately on the sources contained in the Corpus Juris Civilis. This leads us back to the approach adopted by the Roman lawyers which, in turn, depended on the type of action applicable in an individual case.

2. Certam rem dare obligations

(a) *Supervening impossibility*

We shall start our discussion by looking at the actiones stricti iuris entailing certam rem dare obligations. A has promised, by way of stipulation, to deliver the slave, Pamphilus, to B on 10 October. After

[1] Cf. art. 1147 code civil, also art. 1184; Zweigert/Kötz, pp. 213 sqq.

[2] § 280 sqq., 325 sq. BGB.

[3] Cf. infra, pp. 812 sq.

[4] §§ 459 sqq. (sale), §§ 537 sqq. (lease), §§ 633 sqq. (contract for work).

[5] Cf. e.g. Ulrich Huber, "Leistungsstörungen", in: *Gutachten und Vorschläge zur Überarbeitung des Schuldrechts*, vol. I (1981), pp. 756 sqq.; Zweigert/Kötz, pp. 232 sqq.

this promise has been made, but before the time for delivery arrives, Pamphilus dies. Thus on 10 October A is unable to satisfy B's claim. If B were to sue A, the judge would have to absolve the latter. From the point of view of substantive law, this result may be justified in terms of the rule that "ought" implies "can": if A cannot perform, he can be under no obligation to do so. Impossibilium nulla est obligatio: in case of *initial* impossibility of performance an obligation cannot come into existence,[6] impossibility occurring *after* conclusion of the contract makes it fall away again. Hence the statement by Pomponius: "Verborum obligatio . . . naturaliter resolvitur . . . cum res in stipulationem deducta sine culpa promissoris in rebus humanis esse desiit."[7] Under procedural auspices, the matter was determined by the wording of the formula. On account of a stipulation concerning delivery of a specific thing B could ask to be granted the condictio (certae rei).[8] The programme of litigation was therefore settled in the following terms: "Si paret N^m N^m A^o A^o Pamphilum servum dare oportere, quanti ea res est, tantam pecuniam iudex N^m N^m A^o A^o condemnato, si non paret absolvito." First of all, therefore, the judge had to determine whether "it appeared" that A had to hand over the slave Pamphilus to B. The answer was clearly in the negative; for how can a person be obliged to hand over what does not exist?[9] Both obligation and iudicium had lost their object. And, secondly: condemnation involved assessment of the pecuniary value of the object in question at the time of litis contestatio ("quanti ea res *est*").[10] At the relevant moment Pamphilus was dead, his value zero. As a result, A could not be condemned in any sum of money, and B's claim was therefore bound to fail.[11]

(b) *Perpetuatio obligationis*

Clear-cut and straightforward as it may seem, this result is clearly unsatisfactory if Pamphilus' death had been attributable to A: for it would be strange to see a debtor terminate his obligation by negligently or perhaps intentionally removing the object[12] that he was supposed to hand over. It was in order to address this problem that the Roman lawyers resorted to a simple and pragmatic device: they introduced a fiction.[13] If the impossibility was due, in some way or other, to the

---

[6] Cf. supra, pp. 687 sqq.
[7] D. 46, 3, 107.
[8] Cf. supra, pp. 36, 90.
[9] Cf. supra, p. 687.
[10] Kaser, *RZ*, p. 242.
[11] Cf. Dieter Medicus, "Zur Funktion der Leistungsunmöglichkeit im römischen Recht", (1969) 86 *ZSS* 75 sqq.; Max Kaser, "Perpetuari obligationem", (1980) 46 *SDHI* 127 sq.
[12] Cf. e.g. Pomp. D. 45, 1, 23 (". . . si . . . occidisti eum").
[13] A fiction often helped them to achieve a satisfactory solution to a problem by making it possible to apply an already existing (set of) rule(s) that would otherwise not have covered

behaviour of the debtor, the object of the performance was deemed to be still in existence: "Cum facto promissoris res in stipulatum deducta intercidit, perinde agi ex stipulatu potest, ac si ea res extaret: ideoque promissor aestimatione eius punitur."[14] If the situation is to be treated as if Pamphilus were still alive, it is in fact possible to say that A "appears to have to give the slave to B". Also, the judge can condemn A into "quanti ea res est, tantam pecuniam", that is, the (presumptive) market value of Pamphilus at the time of litis contestatio. As a result, therefore, the obligation continues to exist; it is, as the Roman lawyers put it, "perpetuated".[15] It was the perpetuatio obligationis, which enabled the creditor to claim the slave (and thus to obtain its pecuniary value), even though performance was no longer possible: "Effectus huius constitutionis[16] ille est, ut adhuc homo peti possit."[17]

It should be noted that impossibility, in the present context, means objective impossibility. If the debtor was not able to perform, whereas another, third party was (subjective impossibility), no fiction was necessary to hold the debtor liable. "Si paret . . . Pamphilum servum dare oportere" was not untrue, for Pamphilus could in fact be transferred (though not by this particular debtor). Also, since he was still alive at the time of litis contestatio, the "quanti ea res est, tantam pecuniam" clause presented no difficulty. Just as subjective initial impossibility did not prevent the obligation from coming into being,[18] so mere subjective supervening impossibility had no effect on its continued existence;[19] whoever promised something which was and remained objectively possible to perform was seen to guarantee his ability to render such performance.

(c) *Culpa*

Perpetuatio obligationis required that the (objective) impossibility was attributable to the debtor; or, in the parlance of the Roman lawyers: the debtor was liable "si per eum stetit, quo minus daret."[20] But when was

---

this situation; for another example cf. supra, p. 135. As far as the development of the English common law is concerned, cf. e.g. Simpson, *History*, pp. 301 sq.

[14] Paul. Sent. V, VII, 4; cf. also Ulp. D. 45, 1, 82, 1 (". . . perinde ac si homo viveret").

[15] Cf. particularly Paul. D. 45, 1, 91, 3–6. On this treatise ("*Schultraktat*") Theo Mayer-Maly, "Perpetuatio obligationis: D. 45, 1, 91", (1956) 7 *Iura* 6 sqq. On perpetuatio obligationis, cf. further Horst Heinrich Jakobs, *Unmöglichkeit und Nichterfüllung* (1969), pp. 173 sqq. and Maria Bianchi Fossati Vanzetti, *Perpetuatio obligationis* (1979), passim, who argue however that it was an institution applicable to all types of contractual obligations ("*l'unica e generale soluzione romana del problema [dell' inadempimento]*"); contra: Kaser, (1980) 46 *SDHI* 130 sqq.

[16] This refers to Paul. D. 45, 1, 91, 3, where the device of perpetuatio obligationis is ascribed to a constitutio veterum. On the history of perpetuatio obligationis, see Kaser, (1980) 46 *SDHI* 129 sq.

[17] Paul. D. 45, 1, 91, 6.

[18] Cf. supra, pp. 293, 687 sq.

[19] Kaser, *RPr* I, p. 514.

[20] Cf. e.g. Pomp. D. 45, 1, 23.

an event "attributable" to the debtor? The answer is provided by Paulus, according to whom "quotiens culpa intervenit debitoris, perpetuari obligationem".[21] "Culpa", in this context, is not just the Roman equivalent of our modern concept of negligence; nor does it merely indicate that the debtor must have caused the impossibility. The term "culpa"[22] contained an element of disapproval, in that the debtor's behaviour had fallen short of what was expected of him according to the precepts of both ius and mos. At the same time, however, it was not the notion of individual blame that lay at the heart of the investigation, but the typicality of the debtor's behaviour. What mattered was whether the debtor had acted in a manner that was typical for a person to whom "fault" could be attributed. This was the case, particularly, where he had brought about by his own act (factum) the destruction of the object, which he knew or ought to have known he was bound to deliver.[23] Thus, for instance, a promisor who killed the slave he owed continued to be bound: ". . . si quidem occidat eum promissor, expeditum est."[24] The direct act of killing warranted the label "culpa": the debtor could be seen to have been at "fault" when he put himself in a position in which performance of the obligation was no longer possible.[25] Factum implied culpa and was therefore often substituted for it. This did, however, not mean that culpa relevant to liability under a stipulation could not consist in an omission. It was only much less obvious and could not be accepted except after careful examination and under special circumstances. In D. 45, 1, 91 pr. Paulus considers the position of a promisor who omitted to provide medical treatment for a sick slave that he was bound to deliver. Eventually the slave died.

> "[C]ulpa, quod ad stipulatorem attinet, in faciendo accipienda sit, non in non faciendo . . . quia qui dari promisit, ad dandum, non faciendum tenetur."[26]

This is a slightly formalistic argument: the promisor is required merely to convey the slave (dare), not to perform any other activity (facere); hence there can be no liability for a non-facere such as failure to provide medical treatment. But the solution appears to have been controversial,

---

[21] D. 45, 1, 91, 3.

[22] Cf. particularly Cannata, *Colpa*, pp. 90 sqq.; Geoffrey MacCormack, "Culpa", (1972) 38 *SDHI* 123 sqq; Kaser, (1980) 46 *SDHI* 93 sqq.

[23] Cannata, *Colpa*, pp. 90 sqq.; Geoffrey MacCormack, "Factum debitoris and culpa debitoris", (1973) 41 *TR* 59 sqq.

[24] Paul D. 45, 1, 91 pr.

[25] Cf. MacCormack, (1973) 41 *TR* 68, who lists the following possibilities: "The promisor, aware of the promise, may deliberately kill the slave in order to prevent his acquisition by the promisee; or temporarily unmindful of the promisee he might kill him in a fit of anger. Or he might bring about the death of the slave through some careless act. In all these cases it can be held that the promisor has been at fault. The essence of fault lies in the fact that the promisor ought to be aware of the promise and therefore not behave in a way that will make it impossible for him to convey the slave to the promisee."

[26] Paul D. 45, 1, 91 pr.

and even Paulus cannot be seen as having ruled out in principle liability for behaviour other than a factum.[27]

(d) *Mora debitoris*

"Quotiens culpa intervenit debitoris, perpetuari obligationem": this statement applied to cases where the promisor's "fault" related to the event which made his performance (objectively) impossible. But it was also applicable in another situation. Even if the promisor had not himself brought about his inability to convey what he had promised: that is, even if the object in question perished accidentally, he was still held liable if he had delayed performance beyond the due date (mora debitoris). Mora debitoris, too, was based on culpa[28] and therefore justified perpetuation of the promisor's obligation; for in a certain, albeit somewhat indirect sense, the supervening impossibility was still attributable to the debtor's behaviour. Since it entailed an extension of the debtor's liability, the requirements for mora debitoris had to be specified, and it thus became the second type of "breach of contract" giving rise to liability for "quanti ea res est".

(e) *Deterioration of the object promised*

Performance, of course, need not be completely impossible; the debtor may still be able to transfer the object promised, but the object may have deteriorated in the meantime. If such deterioration was attributable to the promisor, performance no longer terminated his liability: ". . . qui hominem dari promisit et vulneratum a se offert, non liberatur."[29] Again, the promisor's obligation was "perpetuated" fictitiously, for the "rem dare oportere" of the intentio was deemed not to have been satisfied, although the (defective) object had in fact been handed over. As a result, performance could still be demanded: ". . . adhuc tamen ipsa res petenda est."[30] When it came to the assessment of "quanti ea res est", the judge was, however, probably required to take into account the value of what the stipulator had received;[31] thus, in the end, he obtained judgment for the difference in value between the object as it actually was and as it should have been.

3. Other types of obligations stricti iuris

We have so far only been looking at "certam rem dare" obligations and the actions applicable to them. Wherever a specific sum of money or the

---

[27] MacCormack, (1973) 41 *TR* 64; Kaser, (1980) 46 *SDHI* 95.

[28] Cf. infra, pp. 791 sqq.

[29] Iul. D. 46, 3, 33, 1; cf. further e.g. Iul. D. 30, 84, 4 and Erich Genzmer, "Der subjektive Tatbestand des Schuldnerverzugs im klassischen römischen Recht", (1924) 44 *ZSS* 103 sqq.; Manlio Sargenti, "Problemi della responsabilità contrattuale" (1954) 20 *SDHI* 194 sqq.; Kaser, (1980) 46 *SDHI* 103 sq. For the time before Julian, cf. Lab./Ulp. D. 4, 3, 7, 3. Labeo operates with the actio de dolo.

[30] Ulp. D. 46, 3, 27; cf. also Scaev. D. 45, 1, 131, 1.

[31] Kaser, (1980) 46 *SDHI* 138.

supply of unascertained goods was owed under an obligation stricti iuris (actio certae creditae pecuniae, "condictio triticaria"), no fictitious perpetuation was required to keep alive the debtor's obligation. Even when the debtor himself had run out of money, it was still not untrue to maintain "si paret N^m N^m A^o A^o sestertium decem milia dare oportere". Owing to the availability of money in general, performance could not become objectively impossible; the debtor always remained liable to pay.[32] The actio depositi in factum concepta presents an example of another type of claim—what the debtor owed was certam rem reddere:

> "Si paret A^m A^m apud N^m N^m mensam argenteam deposuisse eamque dolo malo N^i N^i A^o A^o redditam non esse, quanti ea res erit, tantam pecuniam. . . ."[33]

Condemnation of the depositary depended on non-performance of his obligation to return the silver table. Why the depositor did not receive his table back was immaterial, save that it had to be owing to the depositary's dolus malus; thus, for instance, it did not matter whether the table had been destroyed (objective impossibility) or sold to a third party (subjective impossibility) or whether the depositary merely did not wish to hand it back. Neither did one have to employ the device of perpetuatio obligationis, nor was it in fact necessary to distinguish between different forms of breach of contract.[34] More particularly, objective impossibility did not have the same key significance that it had in the case of "certam rem dare" obligations. Problems could arise only in cases where the object of the deposit had deteriorated; for here, according to the formula, the depositary could not be condemned even when the deterioration had been attributable to his dolus malus; for the condition on which condemnation depended ("eamque . . . redditam non esse") had not materialized. The difficulty was resolved essentially in the same way as in the case of certam dare obligations:

> "Si reddita quidem sit res [deposita], sed deterior reddita, non videbitur reddita, quae deterior facta redditur, nisi quid interest praestetur: proprie enim dicitur res non redditur, quae deterior redditur."[35]

Something which is returned in a worse condition is deemed not to have been returned at all.

4. Actions with a formula incerta

Finally, there were the claims with a formula incerta. They were all characterized by the clause "quidquid ob eam rem N^m N^m A^o A^o dare facere oportet, eius iudex N^m N^m A^o A^o condemna . . .", the "quidquid ob eam rem" in turn referring to a set of facts related in the

[32] As far as obligations to deliver fungible things are concerned, cf. Cannata, *Colpa*, pp. 58 sqq.
[33] Gai. IV, 47.
[34] Cf. also Medicus, (1969) 86 *ZSS* 98 sq.
[35] Ulp. D. 13, 6, 3, 1; cf. also Ulp. D. 16, 3, 1, 16.

preceding demonstratio. The actio ex stipulatio (incerti) fell into this category ("Quod A^s A^s d^e N^o N^o incertum stipulatus est . . ."[36]); so did the actio depositi in ius concepta ("Quod A^s A^s apud N^m N^m mensam argenteam deposuit, qua de re agitur . . ."[37]) as well as all actions arising from any of the consensual contracts. In these latter instances the intentio was extended by the words "ex fide bona". "Quidquid ob eam rem . . . dare facere oportet" remained "true", even if the object deposited or sold had been destroyed. "In obligatione" was not merely the duty to give or return a specific (existing) object, but "to give or to do" whatever the debtor/defendant ought to give or do on account of (for instance) the deposit or the sale. This could obviously be, in appropriate cases, the payment of id quod interest (damages). Again, therefore, no perpetuatio obligationis was required in order to arrive at liability for non-performance; and again, the crucial factor for determining condemnation or absolution was the standard of liability for which the debtor was responsible (dolus and, possibly, culpa lata in case of a depositum,[38] custodia when the object of a sale had been destroyed "emptione perfecta" but before delivery);[39] a specific categorization of the reasons for non-performance was not required. The debtor was thus liable whenever he had not performed at all or had not performed properly, provided only that such failure was attributable to him according to the rules of the specific contract.

Particularly interesting, in the present context, are the bonae fidei iudicia, where the judge was asked to establish "quidquid . . . N^m N^m A^o A^o dare facere oportet *ex fide bona*": with regard both to the estimation of the object of performance and to the establishment of the ambit of the debtor's liability the judge enjoyed a far-reaching discretion. The debtor had to adjust his behaviour in accordance with the precepts of good faith, and was thus subject to a whole range of duties of care. Infringement of these duties led to a claim for damages. Thus, a mandatarius was liable who had reported falsely that a person was solvent to whom the mandator was about to make a loan.[40] The actio pro socio was available if one of the partners had fraudulently or negligently failed to make a good bargain.[41] A shoemaker was liable under the actio locati, if he had struck the neck of his apprentice with a shoe last so forcefully that the poor boy's eye popped out.[42] Many more cases could be quoted.[43] Under certain circumstances, the

[36] Gai. IV, 136.
[37] Gai. IV, 47.
[38] Cf. supra, pp. 208 sqq.
[39] Cf. supra, p. 287.
[40] Ulp. D. 17, 1, 42.
[41] Cf. Ulp. D. 17, 2, 52, 11.
[42] Ulp. D. 19, 2, 13, 4; cf. also Ulp. D. 9, 2, 5, 3.
[43] Cf. e.g. Friedhelm Harting, Die "*positiven Vertragsverletzungen" in der neueren deutschen Privatrechtsgeschichte* (unpublished Dr. iur. thesis, Hamburg, 1967), pp. 22 sqq.

plaintiff was even able to recover consequential damages; the leaky vats and toxic plants of Pomp. D. 19, 1, 6, 4 and Ulp. D. 19, 2, 19, 1[44] immediately spring to mind in this regard.[45]

II. MORA DEBITORIS

1. Consequences of mora debitoris in Roman law

All in all it has become apparent that the way in which the Roman lawyers dealt with breach of contract depended on the type of procedural remedy applicable in the individual case. There was only one form of breach of contract on the part of the debtor that received special attention and became institutionalized across the board, and that was mora debitoris. We have already seen that failure by the debtor to discharge a "certam rem dare" obligation within the time allotted to him had the effect of increasing his liability: he became responsible for any incident that made performance impossible, no matter whether it was due to his fault or whether it had occurred accidentally.[46] But this rule was not confined to certam rem dare obligations. Whatever the debtor owed, mora (debitoris) placed the risk of any accidental destruction of the object of performance on his shoulders. This appears to have been the case even if the loss was not in any way causally related to the delay of performance. Thus, for instance, a debtor in mora was liable if the piece of property that he had promised was destroyed by virtue of a landslide.[47] The fact that the landslide would have hit the estate, even if it had been transferred in time, does not seem to have mattered.[48] With regard to claims for an incertum, particularly the iudicia bonae fidei, mora debitoris had further consequences: the creditor could claim the fruits which the object of performance yielded

[44] Cf. supra, pp. 365 sqq.

[45] Cf. further, for example, Ulp. D. 19, 1, 13 pr.; Ulp. D. 19, 1, 13, 1 and 2.; Lab. D. 19, 2, 60, 7; Ulp. D. 9, 2, 27, 34; Paul. D. 19, 1, 21, 3; for details see Medicus, *Id quod interest*, passim.

[46] For details, see Kaser, (1980) 46 *SDHI* 139 sqq; Schulz, *Einführung* , pp. 106 sqq.

[47] Ulp. D. 30, 47, 6: "Item si fundus chasmate perierit, Labeo ait utique aestimationem non deberi: quod ita verum est, si non post moram factam id evenerit: potuit enim eum acceptum legatarius vendere."

[48] But the rationalization of this result (the creditor could/might have sold the estate before its destruction; cf. the sentence commencing with "potuit") is probably spurious; cf. Schulz, *Einführung*, p. 108, but see also Kaser, (1980) 46 *SDHI* 143 sq.; Andreas Wacke, "Gefahrerhöhung als Besitzerverschulden", in: *Festschrift für Heinz Hübner* (1984), pp. 681 sqq. Gai. D. 16, 3, 14 is often quoted in support of the proposition that with regard to incertum claims the position was different: debtor released if object would have been destroyed in any event, i.e. also in cases of timeous performance; cf., for example, Kaser, *RPr* I, p. 516; Honsell/Mayer-Maly/Selb, pp. 246 sq. This text does, however, not deal with mora debitoris; cf. Bianchi Fossati Vanzetti, op. cit., note 15, pp. 49 sq.; Max Kaser, "Grenzfragen der Aktivlegitimation zur actio furti", in: *De iustitia et iure, Festgabe für Ulrich von Lübtow* (1980), pp. 301 sq.

during the delay.[49] Where money was owed, the debtor became liable for interest.[50] Apart from that, he had to compensate the creditor for any damage arising from the default.[51]

2. Requirements of mora debitoris in Roman law

(a) In general

What, then, were the requirements for mora debitoris? First of all, of course, there had to be a debt which was both actionable[52] and due.[53] Secondly, the debtor had to have failed to make performance at the proper time. But whether (thirdly) such failure to perform had to have been due to his fault and whether (fourthly) the debtor had to receive a special warning (interpellatio) from the creditor before he could be considered in mora, is much more doubtful. For both of these additional requirements there appears to be some textual support, and thus, for instance, we find them entrenched in the German Civil Code, albeit in a somewhat attenuated form: it is the debtor who has to prove that he was *not* at fault in failing to render performance;[54] an interpellatio, on the other hand, is dispensable if a specific time on the calendar had been fixed for performance.[55] Modern Romanistic doctrine has come up with different suggestions. Thus, it has been held that mora debitoris in classical Roman law required fault but not a special warning.[56] Others have come to exactly the opposite conclusion: mora debitoris was not based on fault but, as a rule, on an interpellation issued by the creditor.[57] Those who require fault are again not ad idem as to whether culpa at large was sufficient or whether the debtor, in failing to perform, had to have acted dolo malo.[58]

(b) Mora ex persona

The truth appears to lie somewhere in the middle; for neither did the Roman lawyers think in terms of the clear-cut modern concepts of

---

[49] Pap. vat. 15; Paul. D. 22, 1, 38, 8; Ulp. D. 17, 1, 10, 2 and 3 and 8 and 9; Ulp. D. 3, 5, 7, 1; Paul. D. 17, 2, 38, 1; Paul. Sent. II, XII, 7; III, VIII, 4.

[50] Marci. D. 22, 1, 32, 2; Afr. D. 46, 6, 10; Paul. D. 19, 2, 54 pr.

[51] Honsell/Mayer-Maly/Selb, p. 247; Honsell, *Quod interest*, pp. 16 sqq., 167 sqq.

[52] Scaev. D. 45, 1, 127.

[53] Paul. D. 45, 1, 49, 3: "Si promissor hominis ante diem, in quem promiserat, interpellatus sit et servus decesserit, non videtur per eum stetisse."

[54] This appears from the way in which § 285 BGB has been drafted: "The debtor is not in default so long as the performance does not take place because of a circumstance for which he is not responsible."

[55] § 284 II BGB.

[56] Heinrich Siber, Interpellatio und Mora, (1908) 29 *ZSS* 47 sqq.; cf. also Kaser, *RPr* I, p. 515.

[57] Agostino Elefante, " 'Interpellatio' e 'mora' ", (1960) 6 *Labeo* 30 sqq.; Horst Heinrich Jakobs, "Culpa und interpellatio bei der mora debitoris nach klassischem Recht", (1974) 42 *TR* 23 sqq.; Honsell/Mayer-Maly/Selb, p. 245.

[58] Cf., in particular, Genzmer, (1924) 44 *ZSS* 86 sqq.

dolus and culpa, nor were they interested in isolating and delimitating subjective (culpa) and objective (interpellatio) elements of liability. The best starting point to understanding their way of thinking appears to be the constitutio veterum: "[Q]uotiens culpa intervenit debitoris, perpetuari obligationem."[59] Culpa (in the sense described above) was thus essential for perpetuatio obligationis in both cases covered by the fiction. In other words: the debtor's "fault" either had to relate to the supervening impossibility itself or to the delay of performance in the course of which such impossibility occurred (albeit accidentally). Essentially, therefore, mora debitoris depended on culpa. Marcianus expresses the same idea only slightly differently when he says: "Mora fieri intellegitur non ex re, sed ex persona, id est, si interpellatus oportuno loco non solverit."[60] The question of mora debitoris was not determined merely by the external criterion ("ex re") of whether performance had in fact been made or not. The judge's enquiry had to focus on the person of the debtor ("ex persona"), i.e. on whether or not he knew that the due date had arrived.[61] If, indeed, he knew and still did not perform (without good reason),[62] the term "dolus malus" could be appropriately used to label his behaviour.[63]

(c) The role of interpellatio

But how could one ensure that the debtor knew about the proper time for performance? The most expedient way to do so was to give a special warning. Such an interpellatio was designed to let the debtor know that he was about to do what the jurists normally referred to as "moram facere".[64] It was such a convenient device for making the debtor incur the consequences of mora debitoris that the terms "interpellatum" and "in mora" were repeatedly used as synonyms. Thus, we read in Pomp. D. 45, 1, 23 that the promisor of a certain slave was liable only, after the death of that slave, "si per [promissorem] steterit, quo minus . . . eum mihi dares: quod ita fit, si aut interpellatus non dedisti aut occidisti eum". In D. 22, 1, 32 pr., too, the concept of mora "in persona" is described without further ado as a situation where the debtor does not perform at the proper place, even though he has been warned ("interpellatus"). Indeed, mora and interpellatio were seen to be so intimately linked with each other that a special reference to the requirement of culpa was often regarded as dispensable;[65] for if the

---

59 Paul. D. 45, 1, 91, 3.

60 D. 22, 1, 32 pr.

61 Cf., for example, Kaser, (1980) 46 *SDHI* 111 sq.

62 Cf., for example, Ulp. D. 22, 1, 23 pr. ("si rei publicae causa abesse subito coactus sit", "si . . . in vinculis hostiumve potestate esse coeperit"); Ulp. D. 22, 3, 19, 1; Ulp. D. 38, 1, 15 pr.; for further details, see Kaser, (1980) 46 *SDHI* 116 sqq.

63 Cf. e.g. Iul. D. 50, 17, 63.

64 Cf. e.g. Marci D. 22, 1, 32 pr.; Kaser, (1980) 46 *SDHI* 106.

65 Hence the fact that culpa is often not mentioned in our sources as a special requirement for mora.

debtor had received a warning, non-performance could be attributed, as a rule, to his "fault".[66] On the other hand, however, interpellatio was not a strict requirement for mora; it was an important indication, but not an essential prerequisite for establishing the debtor's "fault". What was required was a careful investigation into all the facets of each individual case: ". . . an mora facta intellegatur, neque constitutione ulla neque iuris auctorum quaestione decidi posse, cum sit magis facti quam iuris."[67] Objective and subjective criteria were inextricably interwoven, and the Roman lawyers were not inclined to work out fixed and rigid rules. In particular, it was left to the judge's discretion to decide whether in an individual case an interpellatio was (or would have been) necessary in order to make the debtor aware of the fact that he was about to default. No interpellatio was required where one person had deprived another of an object by a delictual act. If A had stolen something from B, he knew (or was supposed to know) that he was bound to restore it to the latter; in fact, he should not even have created a situation in which such a duty of restoration could arise. All the consequences of mora debitoris (particularly the strict liability) were thus immediately attributable to the debtor: "semper enim moram fur facere videtur."[68]

3. Requirements of mora debitoris (ius commune)

(a) *The role of culpa*

Throughout the various periods of the ius commune, mora debitoris was usually allotted a dogmatic compartment of its own. "Mora est solutionis faciendae . . . frustratoria dilatio"[69] is a definition representative not only of 17th-century jurisprudence. Struve has "solutionis debito tempore praestandae . . . injusta seu frustratoria dilatio",[70] Mühlenbruch "injustam restitutionis solutionisve . . . faciendae . . . cessationem".[71] Particularly important is the reference to fault. Mora is

---

[66] Cf. e.g. Pomp. D. 12, 1, 5: "[S]ed cum quaeratur, an per te factum sit, animadverti debebit . . . si aliqua iusta causa sit, propter quam intellegere deberes te dare oportere." The term "iusta causa" must be taken to refer to an interpellatio; cf., particularly, Kaser, (1980) 46 *SDHI* 106 sqq.

[67] Marci. D. 22, 1, 32 pr. in fine.

[68] Ulp. D. 13, 1, 8, 1; cf. further Pap. D. 13, 1, 17; Tryph. D. 13, 1, 20; Kaser, (1980) 46 *SDHI* 115 sq. The rule of "fur semper in mora" became part of the ius commune; cf. e.g. Voet, *Commentarius ad Pandectas*, Lib. XXII, Tit. I, XXVII; Windscheid/Kipp, § 278, 2. The BGB did not specifically adopt the rule (cf. "Motive", in *Mugdan*, vol. II, p. 33), without, however, wanting to reject it. § 848 BGB does not deal with the question of whether an interpellatio is dispensable or not, but merely states that a person who is bound to return a thing of which he has deprived another by delict, is responsible for accidental impossibility of returning it. On the background and significance of this rule in modern law, cf. Jens Peter Meincke, "Kann § 848 BGB gestrichen werden?", 1980 *Juristenzeitung* 677 sq.; Wacke, *Festschrift Hübner*, pp. 683 sqq.

[69] Voet, *Comamentarius ad Pandectas*, Lib. XXII, Tit. I, XXIV.

[70] *Syntagma*, Exerc. XXVII, Lib. XXII, Tit. I, LXV.

[71] *Doctrina Pandectarum*, § 355.

culpable delay of performance.[72] However, such culpa usually appears to have been presumed to exist if all the other requirements of mora were met; for most writers were not so much concerned with the details of fault as such and with its (positive) establishment as with the enumeration and discussion of (exceptional) circumstances, which excluded fault: "Evenit tamen aliquando, ut mora excusationem mereatur; in quantum non omne, quod differendi causa fit, morae adnumerandum est."[73] Thus there was no mora if the debtor did not know about his obligation (which he might, for instance, have inherited), if he could not ascertain the amount he had to pay, or if he was prevented from performing timeously due to his absence "rei publicae causa", due to the fact that the creditor was a minor for whom no tutor had been appointed, or because it was difficult to find out who the creditor was.[74]

(b) Impossibility and difficultas praestationis

Impossibilitas superveniens was sometimes regarded as a specific causa excusandi,[75] but only if it was owing to a casus fortuitus. Under these circumstances, it tied in with the general maxim of "casus a nullo praestantur".[76] Since impossibility on account of casus, however, had the effect of releasing the debtor from his obligation,[77] it did not have to be specifically stressed that the debtor was excused from not rendering performance. Much more interesting was the question whether a mere difficultas praestationis could be equated to impossibility. The answer given by the civilians, by and large, was in the negative: even where performance had become difficult, it still had to be rendered; in other words: the debtor's obligation was not terminated.[78] A concession was, however, made in that difficultas came to be accepted as a valid excusatio morae. The medieval canon lawyers generally tended to regard the debtor as the weaker party, requiring the assistance of the law; and more particularly, they were concerned about protecting him from the consequences of mora (which they regarded as

---

[72] Cf. e.g. *West Rand Estates Ltd. v. New Zealand Insurance Co. Ltd.* 1926 AD 173; Ernst Heymann, *Das Verschulden beim Erfüllungsverzug* (1913), pp. 88 sqq., 108 sqq. and passim; I. van Zijl Steyn, *Mora Debitoris volgens die Hedendaagse Romeins-Hollandse Reg* (1929), pp. 43 sqq.; Wouter de Vos, "Mora Debitoris and Rescission", (1970) 87 *SALJ* 307.

[73] Voet, *Commentarius ad Pandectas*, Lib. XXII, Tit. I, XXIX.

[74] For details cf. e.g. Dilcher, *Leistungsstörungen*, pp. 40 sqq.; Van Zijl Steyn, op. cit., note 72, pp. 43 sqq.

[75] Wollschläger, *Unmöglichkeitslehre*, pp. 46 sqq.; Van Zijl Steyn, op. cit., note 72, pp. 45 sqq.; cf. still Wessels, *Contract*, § 2862 ("Impossibility of performance is, of course, also an excuse").

[76] Ulp. D. 50, 17, 23 in fine; cf. further Dilcher, *Leistungsstörungen*, pp. 90 sqq.; Glück, vol. IV, pp. 368 sqq.; Wollschläger, *Unmöglichkeitslehre*, pp. 45 sq.

[77] Cf. e.g. supra, pp. 759, 784.

[78] But cf. e.g. Zasius ("magna difficultas impossibilitati aequiparatur"), as quoted by Wollschläger, *Unmöglichkeitslehre*, p. 48.

a delict), unless his behaviour was ethically unacceptable.[79] It was (probably) under their influence that the commentators formulated the doctrine of "difficultas non tollit obligationem, sed excusat a mora".[80] Some writers wanted to restrict this rule to obligations involving specific objects, but the extension of "difficultas excusat a mora" to obligations concerning generic things, particularly money debts, dominated the scene, even after the end of the Middle Ages.[81] Poverty (insolvency), as long as it was not attributable to his fault, thus protected the debtor from the consequences of mora debitoris.[82] Modern law is less favourable to the debtor: the mere difficulty of rendering performance, especially the lack of money on the part of the debtor, is not considered a valid excuse.[83]

(c) *Interpellatio and mora ex persona*

The general principle that delay leads to the inference of fault has, however, survived. Thus, even according to the BGB, it is not the creditor who has to prove the debtor's fault but the debtor on whom it is incumbent to show that he was not to blame for the delay.[84] Such inference of fault is, however justifiable only on account of the fact that the law, as a rule, still requires a special warning before a debtor can be seen to be in mora.[85] This, obviously, is the Roman interpellatio. Since the days of the glossators,[86] it was one of the standard prerequisites for what was first termed "mora regularis" and later, with reference to Marci. D. 22, 1, 32, "mora in persona". "Mora ex persona fit", defines, for instance, Johannes Voet, "si interpellatus opportuno loco et tempore non solverit".[87] One informal, extrajudicial interpellatio appears to have been very widely regarded as sufficient,[88] although Wissenbach clearly goes too far when he refers to a "communis Doctorum opinio".[89] According to Perezius,[90] the question was

---

[79] Cf. e.g. Endemann, *Studien*, vol. II, pp. 258 sq.; Heymann, op. cit., note 71, pp. 102 ff.; E.M. Meijers, "Essai historique sur la force majeure", in: *Études d'Histoire du Droit*, vol. IV (1966), p. 48 sqq. According to canonist doctrine, it was the *creditor* who had to prove that the delay of performance on the part of the debtor was inexcusabilis.

[80] For details, see Dilcher, *Leistungsstörungen*, pp. 43 sq.; cf. also Robert Feenstra, "Impossibilitas and Clausula rebus sic stantibus", in: *Daube Noster* (1974), p. 80; Coing, p. 436.

[81] Heymann, op. cit., note 72, pp. 105 sqq.; Feenstra, *Daube Noster*, p. 80; Coing, p. 436.

[82] Cf. still Windscheid/Kipp, § 277, 4 in fine.

[83] Joubert, *Contract*, p. 206; Alfred Walchshöfer, in: *Münchener Kommentar*, vol. II (2nd ed., 1985), § 285, n. 4; Volker Emmerich in: *Münchener Kommentar*, op. cit., § 275, n. 53.

[84] § 285 BGB; for South Africa cf. Joubert, *Contract*, p. 205.

[85] § 284 I BGB; for South Africa cf. Van Zijl Steyn, op. cit., note 72, pp. 52 sqq.; Joubert, *Contract*, pp. 202 sqq.

[86] Heymann, op. cit., note 72, pp. 88 sqq.; Dilcher, *Leistungsstörungen*, pp. 44 sqq., 51.

[87] *Commentarius ad Pandectas*, Lib. XXII, Tit. I, XXV.

[88] Cf., for example, Voet, *Commentarius ad Pandectas*, Lib. XXII, Tit. I, XXV; Van Zijl Steyn, op. cit., note 72, p. 54.

[89] *Exercitationes*, Disp. XLII, Lib. XXII, 15.

[90] *Praelectiones in Codicem*, Lib. IV, Tit. XXXII, 27.

controversial and, in fact, there were authors who required more than one warning.[91] But, as Perezius put it: ". . . rectius illi sentiunt, qui unicam legitime factam sufficere arbitrantur, cum qui certior factus est, non debet amplius certiorari."[92] Others were not so much concerned with the number of interpellationes, and (implicitly) with the consistency of the creditor's behaviour,[93] but with the form and manner in which the demand was made. Thus, in France the debtor was traditionally ("*suivant nos usages*")[94] seen to be in mora only if he had received "*une interpellation judiciaire*". Even under the code civil, "*mise en demeuere*" still requires "*une sommation*", a formal notice demanding performance and served through a *huissier.*[95] Some writers, though, saw the requirement of a summons as limited to contracts stricti iuris:

> "Quod autem dicunt interpellationem extrajudicialem sufficere, id referendum est ad eum, qui debitor est ex contractu bonae fidei, non ad eum, qui ex stricti Juris contractu tenetur, nam ut hic periculum morae sustineat, necesse est ut iudicialiter interpellatus sit."[96]

The reason was essentially a procedural one: in bonae fidei iudicia the judge had a very wide discretion and could thus condemn the defendant to pay damages or interest where this seemed reasonable (that is, even after the latter had merely received an informal demand). Iudicia stricti iuris did not give the judge that much leeway; he could only condemn in what was "nominatim . . . petit[um]".[97] Hence, if "interesse, usurae et similia"[98] were to be claimed on account of mora debitoris, they had to be included in the "petitio iudicialis".

(d) Interpellatio and litis contestatio

This difference in the requirements for mora debitoris was, of course, bound to fall away once the distinction between iudicia bonae fidei and stricti iuris had become obsolete and all contracts were seen to be governed by the precepts of bona fides.[99] Nevertheless, in a strange and

---

91 Cf. Van Zijl Steyn, op. cit., note 72, p. 57.

92 *Praelectiones in Codicem*, Lib. IV, Tit. XXXII, 27.

93 Cf. the qualifying remark by Voet, *Commentarius ad Pandectas*, Lib. XXII, Tit. I, XXV: ". . . si modo ei interpellans inhaeserit." Perezius, loc. cit., writes: "Itaque instantia post interpellationem perseverare debet; sed non est repetenda interpellatio, seu admonitio coram testibus nuncupata."

94 Pothier, *Traité des obligations*, n. 144.

95 Art. 1139 code civil, but the code adds: "*ou [un] autre acte équivalent*"; on this clause, see, for example, Nicholas, *FLC*, p. 232. In contrast to modern German law, incidentally, *mise en demeure* is an essential prerequisite for every claim for damages in case of breach of contract, no matter whether for delay or non-performance: art. 1146 code civil; cf. further Zweigert/Kötz, pp. 213 sqq., 217.

96 Perezius, *Praelectiones in Codicem*, Lib. IV, Tit. XXXII, 28; based on Iul. D. 12, 1, 22 (". . . per iudicem petitum est").

97 Perezius, loc. cit.

98 Perezius, loc. cit.

99 Cf. supra, pp. 547 sqq.

rather confusing way the older view lingered on, at least amongst the Roman-Dutch authors. For even though it was usually recognized that an informal, extrajudicial demand was sufficient to put the debtor in mora, many authors held that *interest* could be claimed only from the time of litis contestatio. Voet provides a good example. His statement in Lib. XXII, Tit. I, XXV of the *Commentarius ad Pandectas* on the general requirements of mora ex persona appears to be quite unequivocal: ". . . induci potest [sc.: mora] per unam interpellationem legitime factam, sive judicialem sive extrajudicialem." But this did not mean that all the consequences of mora debitoris came into effect immediately. If we look to section XI of the same title of book XXII, we find the following assertion:

> "Nostris vero moribus . . . regulariter ex sola mora extrajudiciali usurae nec in bonae fidei nec in stricti iuris negotiis adjudicandae sunt; post litem vero contestatam utrobique omnino. . . ."[100]

Thus, for mora interest to be awarded, an interpellatio extrajudicialis was not sufficient, and in that respect the regime originally applicable only to contracts stricti iuris appears to have gained the upper hand. Proceeding, inter alia, from Voet XXII, I, XI, South African courts have come to the (erroneous) conclusion that according to (classical) Roman-Dutch law "litis contestatio constituted that due demand from the date of which mora existed".[101] It was only in the 1926 case of *West Rand Estates Ltd. v. New Zealand Insurance Co. Ltd.* that Solomon JA clearly stated that neither a demand in the form of a summons nor litis contestatio was required for either mora as such or any of its consequences. "[M]ora begins from the date of receipt of the letter of demand",[102] he pronounced, thereby in turn implying incorrectly that the interpellatio had to be in writing. Today, however, it is recognized that no specific form has to be observed.[103] Even an oral warning is sufficient. The position is thus the same as in modern German law.

(e) Mora ex re

Where we have mora regularis, there must be mora irregularis; and if mora ex persona was equated to the former, its obvious "irregular" counterpart was the mora ex re of Marci. D. 22, 1, 32 pr:

> "Mora ex re est, quae fit sine interpellatione, adeoque lege introducitur sine facto hominis, seu quando res ipsam moram in se continet, unde a Paulo mora in re appellatur":[104]

mora arises from or is inherent in the circumstances of the case and thus the law does not insist on a specific intervention on the part of the

[100] Cf. further Van Zijl Steyn, op. cit., note 72, p. 55.
[101] *Victoria Falls & Transvaal Power Co. Ltd. v. Consolidated Langlaagte Mines Ltd.* 1915 AD 1 at 31.
[102] 1926 AD 173 at 183.
[103] Joubert, *Contract*, p. 203; De Wet en Yeats, p. 145.
[104] Voet, *Commentarius ad Pandectas*, Lib. XXII, Tit. I, XXVI.

creditor in the form of a demand or warning. Mora ex persona was seen to be based on an interpellatio, mora ex re covered a number of situations where one could do without it. By far the most important of them concerned the debtor who had to render performance certo tempore. Where the contract specifically determined a date for performance, the debtor did not need to be reminded; any delay was attributable to his fault in the same way as if he had received a warning: ". . . ea quae promisit ipse in memoria suo servare, non ab aliis sibi manifestari poscere [debet]."[105] Essentially it was the "certus dies" as expressed in the contract which was seen to make its own demand; hence "dies interpellat pro homine".[106] This maxim was based on a constitution of Justinian that had declared a special warning (the interpellatio of classical law, now termed "admonitio") to be dispensable "si quis certo tempore facturum se aliquid vel daturum se stipuletur".[107] The glossators generalized the idea inherent in this piece of legislation,[108] and thus "dies interpellat pro homine" emerged as a widely recognized principle of the ius commune.[109] Over the centuries, it became so firmly engrained in the practice of (particularly) the Dutch and German courts that not even the controversies among 19th-century pandectist writers[110] about the true position in Roman law were able to endanger its continued application.[111] Dies interpellat pro homine has become part and parcel of South African law[112] and § 284 II BGB presents its modern codified version. Only French jurisprudence has remained unsympathetic to the glossatorial emphasis on the lex "Magnam" and has rather taken its inspiration from texts such as D. 50, 17, 88. "Nulla intellegitur mora fieri, ubi nulla petitio est" said Scaevola, and he intended this to mean that a debtor could be guilty of mora only with regard to an actionable claim. He was, however, understood to consider a summons (petitio judicialis) as a prerequisite for mora; hence the emphasis on a "*sommation (ou autre acte équivalent*)" which we still find in the code civil.[113] It is essential for the *mise en demeure* even where the contract has specified a time for performance.[114] Only where the nature of the obligation is such that it *can* only be

---

[105] C. 8, 37, 12 (Just.).

[106] Arrival of the due day takes the place of the creditor in demanding performance: Nicholas, *FLC*, p. 234.

[107] C. 8, 37, 12. The motive that prompted Justinian to act was to remove "magnam legum veterum obscuritatem, quae protrahendarum litium maximam occasionem usque adhuc praebebat".

[108] Cf. Rogerius ("dies habetur pro interpellatione"); Accursius (". . . quia in mora est die interpellante pro homine"): Dilcher, *Leistungsstörungen*, p. 48.

[109] W. Ogris, *HRG*, vol. I, col. 740 sq.; Van Zijl Steyn, op. cit., note 72, pp. 64 sqq.

[110] For details, see Windscheid/Kipp, § 278, 1.

[111] Cf. e.g. "Motive", in: *Mugdan*, vol. II, pp. 31 sq.

[112] Cf. Joubert, *Contract*, p. 202; De Wet en Yeats, p. 143.

[113] Cf. supra, p. 796.

[114] Cf. e.g. Nicholas, *FLC*, pp. 233 sq. (who comments: "This rule is widely deplored, but well-settled"); but see also Zweigert/Kötz, p. 217.

performed within a certain time may damages be claimed without formally putting the debtor in delay.[115]

4. Consequences of mora debitoris (ius commune)

What were (and what are) the effects of mora debitoris? The medieval lawyers were presented with a specific problem by the Roman rule that interest could be charged in bonae fidei contracts. For how could this be reconciled with the canonical usura prohibition?[116] Interest on account of mora, ran the argument usually presented to resolve the difficulty, was not to be regarded as genuine (illicit) usura, but as a (lawful) way of compensating the creditor for his damages: "hic usuras ut interesse peti" (Accursius) or ". . . pro interesse petatur" (Gofredus de Trano), and such a claim was not dishonest, "quia tale lucrum ex mutuo non speratur" (Cinus da Pistoia).[117] Mora thus became one of the most important titles for awarding interest. The statutory or customary rates differed from town to town, from region to region. In the medieval upper Italian city states up to 20 % or even 30 % could be charged:[118] in later centuries 5 % came to be widely accepted.[119] "Moribus tamen hodiernis etiam in stricti juris judiciis ex mora usurae debentur quincunces", says Lauterbach,[120] and he makes it clear that a distinction was no longer drawn between contracts bonae fidei and stricti juris. In modern German law every money debt bears interest during default at 4 %.[121] Apart from that, as in the Roman law relating to incertum obligations, the creditor can claim compensation for damages[122] and delivery of or restitution for emoluments.[123] Furthermore, mora still has the effect of increasing the debtor's liability; he is responsible not only for negligence but also for impossibility of performance arising accidentally during the default.[124]

For centuries it has been controversial whether the debtor is to be held liable even if the damage would also have arisen in the case of

[115] Art. 1146 code civil.

[116] Supra, pp. 170 sqq.

[117] Cf. the references in Dilcher, *Leistungsstörungen*, pp. 151, 156, 155. Cinus alludes to the famous precept of "mutuum date nihil inde sperantes" of St. Luke, 6, 35. Cf. also Heymann, op. cit., note 72, pp. 75 sqq.

[118] Dilcher, *Leistungsstörungen*, pp. 152, 155.

[119] Cf. still Windscheid/Kipp, § 280, 1.

[120] *Collegium theoretico-practicum*, Lib. XXII, Tit. I, XVIII; cf. also e.g. Voet, *Commentarius ad Pandectas*, Lib. XXII, Tit. I, XI.

[121] § 288 BGB.

[122] § 286 BGB. The BGB draws a distinction between damages arising from the default (§ 286 I) and damages for non-performance (§ 286 II). This is a consequence of the fact that—unlike in Roman law—condemnation is in the first place in forma specifica. Thus, the creditor normally has the right to demand specific performance and—in case of mora—damages arising from the default. Damages for non-performance (including damages arising from the default) can according to § 286 II BGB, be claimed if, owing to the debtor's default, specific performance is no longer of any interest to the creditor. Cf. also § 326 BGB for synallagmatic obligations.

[123] § 292 BGB.

[124] § 287,2 BGB; Wacke, *Festschrift Hübner*, pp. 681 sqq.

timeous performance.[125] The BGB has settled this moot point in favour of the debtor.[126] South African writers still refer to perpetuatio obligationis where they deal with the extension of the debtor's liability as a consequence of mora debitoris.[127] So did many of the writers of the ius commune.[128] Already by the time of Justinian, however, the debtor's obligation no longer had to be fictitiously perpetuated in order to preserve it as a basis of his liability. For even certum dare obligations were now adjudged according to the requirements of "aequitas", that is, as freely as the contracts bonae fidei under classical Roman law.[129] In particular, liability was no longer strictly circumscribed by a procedural formula of the type: "Si paret . . . dare oportere, quanti ea res est, tantam pecuniam . . ."—with the result that the obligation automatically fell away when the object of the performance was destroyed. As in the case of bonae fidei transactions, the debtor could be liable for id quod interest if he had not complied with his contractual duties. The same, of course, applies today.

III. RESCISSION AS A REMEDY FOR BREACH OF CONTRACT

1. The "iron" rule of Roman law and the notion of an implied lex commissoria

> "If, in the case of a synallagmatic contract, one party is in default in performing, the other party may give him a reasonable period within which to perform and warn him of his intention to refuse to accept the performance after the expiration of the period. After the expiration of the period he is entitled to demand compensation for non-performance, or to withdraw from the contract, if the performance has not been made in due time. . . . If, in consequence of the default, the performance of the contract is of no use to the other party, such other party has the rights specified above without giving any notice"—

thus § 326 BGB.[130] Particularly interesting, from an historical point of view, is the right of the creditor to rescind the contract in case of mora debitoris. This is contrary to "an iron rule of Roman law" which the

---

[125] Cf. Dilcher, *Leistungsstörungen*, pp. 108 sqq.; Fachinaeus, *Controversiae iuris*, Lib. VIII, Cap. C and CI; Van Zijl Steyn, op. cit., note 72, pp. 90 sqq.; Windscheid/Kipp, § 280, 2.

[126] § 287 BGB in fine. The solution of the BGB is, however, less favourable to the debtor than, for instance, the one adopted in § 965 ABGB. The difference revolves around the question raised in Ulp. D. 30, 47, 6 in fine: if the creditor had received the object of the performance in time, would he have sold it and thus avoided its destruction? According to the ABGB, the *creditor* has to prove that he would indeed have sold it, according to the BGB, it is the debtor on whom it is incumbent to prove that the creditor would have kept it.

[127] Van Zijl Steyn, op. cit., note 72, pp. 90 sqq.; De Wet en Yeats, p. 148; Joubert, *Contract*, p. 206.

[128] Cf. e.g. Struve, *Syntagma*, Exerc. XXVII, Lib. XXII, Tit. I, LXX; Voet, *Commentarius ad Pandectas*, Lib. XXII, Tit. I, XXVIII.

[129] Kaser, *RPr* II, pp. 333 sq., 357.

[130] Cf. also § 286 II BGB.

classical lawyers "unflinchingly observed";[131] and although we have already seen that the rule was not quite as "iron" as Schulz leads us to believe,[132] it is certainly true that a *general* right of rescission in case of breach of contract was never recognized in Roman law.[133] Despite several attempts to reverse the principle (especially by the canon

[131] Schulz, *CRL*, p. 532.

[132] Supra, p. 578.

[133] However, if one of the parties to a reciprocal contract did not perform, the other party could refuse to counterperform ("functional synallagma": cf. Benöhr, *Synallagma*, p. 1). Such mutual interdependence of the two obligations had to be brought about, originally, by way of a special clause appended to the contract (cf. e.g. Lab. D. 18, 1, 78, 2 (". . . ea lege emerat, ut soluta pecunia traderetur ei possessio"); cf. further Benöhr, *Synallagma*, pp. 20 sqq.); in classical law, however, the judge was taken to be empowered, by virtue of the "ex bona fide" clause contained in the formulae of the actiones empti, vendiditi, locati and conducti, to take account of the fact whether the plaintiff had himself performed his obligation. If he had not done so up to the time when judgment was given, the defendant had to be absolved. In other words: the exceptio non adimpleti contractus (as this right of the defendant to retain his own performance came to be called from about the 15th century onwards) was inherent in the Roman bonae fidei iudicia. Cf. Ulp. D. 19, 1, 13, 8; Scaev. D. 18, 4, 22; Marcell./Ulp. D. 21, 1, 31, 8; Benöhr, *Synallagma*, pp. 27 sq.; Alfons Bürge, *Retentio im römischen Sachen- und Obligationenrecht* (1979), pp. 186 sqq. The same applied in cases of contractus bilaterales inaequales, if the plaintiff brought the actio directa without having discharged his obligations arising under the actio contraria; cf. Pomp. D. 13, 7, 8 pr. and 1; Paul. D. 47, 2, 15, 2; Iul. D. 47, 2, 60 and, for a detailed analysis, Bürge, *Retentionsrecht*, pp. 163 sqq. The idea underlying the Roman sources was generalized by the commentators ("Ex contracto ultro citroque obligatorio non potest effectualiter agi nisi ab eo qui totum contractum ex parte sua impleverit": Bartolus, *Commentaria*, ad D. 19, 1, 13, 8; apart from the individual instances of Roman law, this rule was often based on the general principle of fidem frangenti fides frangitur of the medieval canon law; on which see, in the present context, Friedrich Merzbacher, "Die Regel 'Fidem frangenti fides frangitur' und ihre Anwendung", (1982) 68 *ZSS* (KA) 347 sqq.) and the "exceptio non adimpleti contractus" remained part and parcel of the ius commune down to the days of the pandectists (cf. e.g. Glück, vol. 17, pp. 225 sqq.; Windscheid/Kipp, § 321, 1; for a historical analysis, see Scherner, *Rücktrittsrecht*, pp. 53 sqq.; cf. also Jansen JA in *BK Tooling (Edms.) Bpk. v. Scope Precision Engineering (Edms.) Bpk.* 1979 (1) SA 391 (A) 416 sqq.) and was incorporated into the BGB ("Whoever is bound by a mutual contract may refuse to perform his part until the other party has performed his part, unless the former party is bound to perform his part first" (§ 320 I 1 BGB; cf. also § 271 I 5 PrALR)). No provision corresponding to § 320 BGB exists in the French code civil, but courts and legal writers have applied the law as if it did (for details, see Nicholas, *FLC*, pp. 207 sqq.; cf. also Jansen JA in the *BK Tooling* case at p. 417A–D). The application of the exceptio non adimpleti contractus in modern South African law has led to considerable difficulties and confusion in cases where the plaintiff has been guilty of malperformance. May the defendant refuse to render counterperformance even though he is in possession of, and possibly even uses, the plaintiff's defective performance? In a famous trilogy of cases (*Hauman v. Nortje* 1914 AD 293; *Breslin v. Hichens* 1914 AD 312; *Van Rensburg v. Straughan* 1914 AD 317) it was established that the absolute nature of the exceptio non adimpleti contractus indeed precluded any contractual claim by the malperforming plaintiff; yet, in order to avoid inequitable results, an enrichment action for "quantum meruit" was granted (calculated by deducting the cost of remedying the defective performance from the contract price). This approach (based, probably, on a misunderstanding—De Vos, *Verrykingsaanspreeklikheid*, pp. 275 sqq.; De Wet en Yeats, pp. 181—of Voet, *Commentarius ad Pandectas*, Lib. XIX, Tit. II, XL) has been subjected to severe criticism (cf. De Vos and De Wet en Yeats, loc. cit.; J.C. de Wet, "Die sogenaamde

lawyers and, later, by the adherents of the school of natural law),[134] it was retained—at least as far as the theory of the Roman ius commune was concerned—down to the days of the pandectists.[135] It had taken a long time to establish the principle that even formless, merely consensual pacta are binding, and there appears to have been a natural reluctance to jeopardize the grand new idea of pacta sunt servanda by recognizing a general unilateral right of withdrawal from contract.[136] In the case of mora a narrowly circumscribed exception had come to be recognized in 19th-century legal science,[137] but the fundamental break with traditional doctrine was effected only by the fathers of the BGB.[138] Conceptually, it was the lex commissoria that stood at the cradle of this development.[139] Thus we find Windscheid arguing that the right of withdrawal in case of mora debitoris could, under certain circumstances, be taken to have been (tacitly) agreed upon;[140] and even the BGB still refers to its provisions dealing with rights of rescission ex contractu[141] when it deals with statutory rights of rescission in case of non-performance.[142] Furthermore, since a lex commissoria had a resolutive effect, rescission of the contract was seen to remove the basis for a claim for damages. This explains the strict alternativity between damages for non-performance and rescission according to §§ 325 sq. BGB.[143]

'exceptio non adimpleti contractus' in die praktyk van vandag", (1945) 9 *THRHR* 239 sqq.); in the *BK Tooling* case (1979 (1) SA 391 (A)) the Appellate Division ultimately took the opportunity to re-examine the matter. Use of the plaintiff's defective performance, it was now argued by Jansen JA, creates a discretion for the court to determine whether the defendant may raise the exceptio (and thus bar the plaintiff's claim for remuneration). In cases where the exceptio may not be raised, the plaintiff may bring his contractual action, albeit only for a reduced remuneration. For details, see Christie, *Contract*, pp. 419 sqq.; Joubert, *Contract*, pp. 232 sqq.; Zimmermann, *RHR*, pp. 116 sq.; cf. now also *Thomas Construction (Pty.) Ltd. v. Grafton Furniture Manufacturers (Pty.) Ltd.* 1986 (4) SA 510 (N); for the solution in German law of cases of this nature, cf. Emmerich, op. cit., note 83, § 320, nn. 11, 37 sqq.

[134] Cf. supra, p. 579.

[135] Cf. e.g. Windscheid/Kipp, § 321, 2.

[136] Leser, *Rücktritt vom Vertrag*, p. 4.

[137] Cf. Windscheid/Kipp, § 280, n. 1; on the developments in 19th- century commercial law, see Karl Scherner, *Rücktrittsrecht*, pp. 157 sqq.

[138] For a detailed discussion, see Leser, *Rücktritt vom Vertrag*, pp. 26 sqq.

[139] Leser, *Rücktritt vom Vertrag*, pp. 16 sqq.

[140] Windscheid/Kipp, § 280, n. 1.

[141] §§ 346 sqq. For a concise overview of the remedy of rescission in German law (under which circumstances is it available?; what are its characteristic features?), see Brice Dickson, "The Law of Restitution in the Federal Republic of Germany: A Comparison with English Law", (1987) 36 *International and Comparative Law Quarterly* 762 sqq.

[142] § 327.

[143] "Motive", in: *Mugdan*, vol. II, p. 116. The position is different in, for instance, French (art. 1184 II code civil), English and South African law. The alternativity of remedies in the BGB has often been criticized; cf. e.g. Leser, *Rücktritt vom Vertrag*, pp. 138 sqq.; Huber, op. cit., note 5, pp. 713 sqq., 763.

2. The notion of an implied condition (natural law)

The natural lawyers adopted a slightly different point of departure. They argued that the obligations of the two parties to a mutual contract were dependent, in the sense of being conditional, upon each other. If one of them did not perform, the other did not have to make performance either and he thus gained the right to abstain from the contract:

> "[n]am unius ejusdemque contractus capita singula alia aliis inesse videntur per modum conditionis, quasi expressum esset, haec ita faciam si et alter faciat quae promisit."[144]

This idea found its most mature expression in art. 1184 code civil: a resolutive condition is always implied in synallagmatic contracts to provide for the case where one of the parties does not fulfil his undertaking. However, the contract is not resolved by operation of law in this case, but at the choice of the party with regard to whom the undertaking has not been performed. This provision, inspired by Domat and Pothier,[145] tied in nicely with the practice which the French courts had been following anyway;[146] already since the days of Molinaeus one had felt to be both entitled and compelled "*de se déporter, dans les tribunaux, de la rigeur de ces principes*" (that is, the Roman rejection of a general right of rescission).[147]

3. Condition and warranty in English law

The idea of a condition as basis and justification for a right of rescission has not been confined to continental jurisprudence; in England it has been described as the "key to the modern theory of breach of contract".[148] We have seen that traditionally the claim for damages for breach of contract is the central contractual remedy according to the English common law.[149] Every contractual term, express or implied, is in law a "warranty", and breach of a warranty entitles the innocent party to claim damages. If, however, the term which has been broken is not only a warranty but also a "condition", the innocent party has the option of withdrawing from the contract: he can refuse to render performance or reclaim whatever has already been transferred.[150]

---

[144] Grotius, *De jure belli ac pacis*, Lib. III, Cap. XIX, 14; cf. further Scherner, *Rücktrittsrecht*, pp. 92 sqq.

[145] Georges Boyer, *Recherches historiques sur la résolution des contrats* (1924), pp. 381 sqq.

[146] For details, see Boyer, op. cit., note 145, pp. 329 sqq., 343 sqq., 350 sqq. Cf. also Coing, pp. 443 sq.

[147] Pothier, *Traité du contrat de vente*, n. 476.

[148] Samuel J. Stoljar, "The Contractual Concept of Condition", (1953) 69 *LQR* 485.

[149] Cf. supra, pp. 776 sqq.

[150] On the development and specific meaning of the notion of a condition in this context, see Rheinstein, *Struktur*, pp. 192 sqq. As on the Continent, rescission was a relatively late addition to the remedial processes available to the aggrieved party. It became established only in the late 18th century. Of cardinal importance were two decisions of Lord Mansfield in *Kingston v. Preston*, reported sub *Jones v. Barkley* (1781) 2 Dougl 684 at 690 sq., and *Boone v. Eyre* (1779) 1 H Bl 273.

The term "condition" has been defined as

> "[a] stipulation [which] goes to the root of the matter, so that a failure to perform it would render the performance of the rest of the contract . . . a thing different in substance from what [had been] stipulated for";[151]

failure of performance must have "substantially" deprived the other party of what he had bargained for. Today the formal categories of warranty and condition have largely been abandoned in favour of the distinction between the essential and non-essential terms of a contract.[152] This means, in the case of mora debitoris, that the creditor may, of course, claim damages in any event; in addition, he is entitled to rescind the contract, if the time within which performance must be made is "essential" to the contract. The right of rescission thus requires, in the phraseology of English law, that "time is of the essence of the contract".[153] Whether the parties intended time to be of the essence, is determined by the judge according to the individual circumstances of each case; the fact that a specific time for performance has been expressly fixed in the contract is no longer[154] regarded as conclusive.[155] If time does not appear to be "of the essence", the creditor is still able to elevate it to that status by giving the debtor a notice of rescission and allowing him a further reasonable time for performance.

4. Condition, lex commissoria and rescission in South African law

Both the notion of "time is of the essence" and that of the notice of rescission have, incidentally, percolated into South African law. Despite an old Dutch custom in favour of a right of rescission in case of delay of performance,[156] the Roman-Dutch writers (unlike their French counterparts) stuck to the principle of Roman law. Thus, for instance, as far as the law of sale is concerned, Voet states quite unambiguously that

> ". . . ob pretium non solutum non recte venditor contendit ad emptionis dissolutionem, reique jam per traditionem translatae restitutionem; sed magis ad

[151] *Bettini v. Gye* (1876) 1 QB 183 at 188.

[152] Cf. e.g. *Hongkong Fir Shipping Co. Ltd. v. Kawasaki Kisen Kaisha Ltd.* [1962] 2 QB 26 ("There are . . . many contractual undertakings of a more complex character which cannot be categorized as being 'conditions' or 'warranties' ": p. 70, per Diplock LJ); Treitel, *Contract*, pp. 585 sqq.; Zweigert/Kötz, pp. 223 sqq.

[153] For details cf. e.g. Treitel, *Contract*, pp. 631 sqq.

[154] Since s. 27(7) of the Judicature Act (1873), which caused the rules developed by Equity to prevail over those applicable "at law".

[155] According to *United Scientific Holdings Ltd. v. Burnley Borough Council* [1977] 2 WLR 806 (HL) at 826F, time, in modern English law, is prima facie not of the essence of the contract.

[156] Heinrich Mitteis, *Rechtsfolgen des Leistungsverzugs beim Kaufvertrag nach niederländischen Quellen des Mittelalters* (1913), pp. 176 sqq.

implementum ejus experiendum est. . . .; nisi ab initio id nominatim convenerit, ut ab emptione ob moram in ea implenda factam recedere liceat".[157]

When, therefore, the South African courts started looking for a basis upon which to grant disappointed creditors the right to rescind the contract, the traditional sources of Roman-Dutch law did not provide much inspiration. Not that great efforts were made to analyse these sources; for those were the days of the "pollutionists",[158] who did not hesitate to draw on English law whenever that appeared to be convenient. The theoretical foundations of such reception were usually somewhat fragile: a scanty remark to the effect that the "general rule of English law and . . . of Roman-Dutch Jurisprudence" have always been the same[159] could do the trick. It was blatantly wrong in the present case; but by the time the "purists" exposed such mistaken assumptions, the English doctrine had often firmly taken root. All one could do, under those circumstances, was to sort out the doctrinal confusion that almost invariably arose as a consequence of such a development and to integrate the new institution as harmoniously as possible into the framework of the Roman-Dutch ius commune. Obviously, recognition of a right of rescission on account of mora debitoris as such was a welcome event; but its English paraphernalia threw many established doctrines into disarray. More particularly, the requirements for the new right of rescission were frequently confused with the basic requirements for mora debitoris and the relationship between the concept of "time is of the essence of the contract" and the rule of "dies interpellat pro homine" became as obscure as that between interpellatio and a notice of rescission.[160] A particularly extravagant approach was adopted in a line of cases starting with the decision in *Federal Tobacco Works v. Barron & Co.*:[161] failure to deliver within a reasonable time can lead to a right of rescission even though *(a)* no specific date was fixed in the contract (i.e.: there is no mora ex re),

---

[157] *Commentarius ad Pandectas*, Lib. XIX, Cap. I, XXI; cf. further Van Zijl Steyn, op. cit., note 72, pp. 95 sqq.; De Wet en Yeats, p. 148.

[158] On the South African bellum iuridicum—concerning the proper sources of the common law—between pollutionists, purists, antiquarians and pragmatists, see Reinhard Zimmermann, "Synthesis in South African Private Law: Civil Law, Common Law and Usus Hodiernus Pandectarum", (1986) 103 *SALJ* 259 sqq.

[159] Cf., in the present context, *Mitchell v. Howard Farrar & Co.* (1886) 5 EDC 131 at 140 (per Barry JP). Generally cf. Reinhard Zimmermann, "Die Rechtsprechung des Supreme Court of the Cape of Good Hope am Ende der sechziger Jahre des 19. Jahrhunderts", in: *Huldigingsbundel Paul von Warmelo* (1984), pp. 286 sqq. In other cases relating to the right of rescission on account of mora Pothier has been referred to; cf. *Radue v. Kirsch* 1920 OPD 181 at 186; *Lewis & Co. v. Malkin* 1926 TPD 665 at 670.

[160] Cf., for example, *Wehr v. Botha* 1965 (3) SA 46 (A) at 59 sqq.; *Stapleford Estates (Pty.) Ltd. v. Wright* 1968 (1) SA 1 (E) at 3F ("Where time is not of the essence, a party may clearly make it so by placing the other party in mora").

[161] 1904 TS 483; cf. further *Benoni Produce & Coal Co. Ltd. v. Gundelfinger* 1918 TPD 453; *Graf & Co. v. Bassa* (1925) 46 NLR 2, and other decisions; cf. also *Broderick Properties Ltd. v. Rood* 1962 (4) SA 447 (T) (on which, see De Vos, (1970) 87 *SALJ* 314 sqq.; A.J. Kerr, (1978) 95 *SALJ* 143 sqq.).

(b) no interpellatio occurred (i.e.: there is no mora ex persona) and *(c)* no notice of rescission was given to the debtor (i.e. time was, strictly speaking, not made "of the essence" of the contract). For a long time, mora debitoris could thus be described as "een van die verwaarloosde onderdele van [die Suid-Afrikaanse] reg",[162] characterized, as a result, by "endless controversy"[163] and "complete . . . confusion".[164] Today it is widely recognized[165] that a right of rescission can arise only where the debtor is guilty of mora. Where no time for performance has been specified, an interpellatio is therefore required. In addition, the contract must either contain a lex commissoria or time must be made "of the essence" by way of a notice of rescission.[166] The lex commissoria does not have to be expressly agreed upon. Where a specific time has been fixed by the parties and where this time, in their view, is essential for the performance of the contract (as is, for instance, usually the case in commercial transactions), it may be read into the transaction.[167] A notice of rescission is required whenever there is neither an express nor an implied lex commissoria; that is, irrespective of whether we are dealing with mora ex re or mora ex persona. In the case of mora ex persona it may be combined with the interpellatio, but conceptually the two declarations have to be kept apart.[168, 169]

IV. IMPOSSIBILITY OF PERFORMANCE AND BREACH OF CONTRACT

1. Breach of contract in Roman law

What about the other forms of breach of contract? We have seen that, according to the formulary procedure of classical law, the answer

[162] Van Zijl Steyn, op. cit., note 72, p. 1.

[163] J.R. Harker, "The Nature and Scope of Rescission as a Remedy for Breach of Contract in American and South African Law", 1980 *Acta Juridica* 75.

[164] De Vos, (1970) 87 *SALJ* 312 sq.

[165] As to what follows, see W. de Vos, (1970) 87 *SALJ* 304 sqq.; idem, "Aspekte van mora debitoris", (1978) 41 *THRHR* 252 sqq.; De Wet en Yeats, pp. 148 sqq.; Harker, 1980 *Acta Juridica* 72 sqq.; also Van Zijl Steyn, op. cit., note 72, pp. 103 sqq. As far as judicial pronouncements are concerned, the decisions in *Nel v. Cloete* 1972 (2) SA 150 (A) at 159 sqq. and *Greenfield Manufacturers (Temba) (Pty.) Ltd. v. Royton Electrical Engineering (Pty.) Ltd.* 1976 (2) SA 565 (A) at 568 sqq. are of particular interest.

[166] The term "notice of rescission" is somewhat misleading, since its effect is not (yet) the rescission of the contract; it merely creates the right for the creditor to rescind once the period set for performance has elapsed; cf. De Vos, (1970) 87 *SALJ* 310; Harker, 1980 *Acta Juridica* 77.

[167] These are the cases where, in English law, time is presumed to be "of the essence" even though no notice of rescission has been given.

[168] Cf. *Nel v. Cloete* 1972 (2) SA 150 (A) at 162D–164D; *Ponisammy v. Versailles Estates (Pty.) Ltd.* 1973 (1) SA 372 (A) at 387H–389D; W. de Vos, (1978) 41 *THRHR* 258 sq.

[169] For details of the nature of rescission (*résolution, Rücktritt*) as a remedy for breach of contract in modern law (how does it work? what are its effects?), cf. Treitel, "Remedies for Breach of Contract", in: *International Encyclopedia of Comparative Law*, vol. VII, 16, nn. 143 sqq.; Hans G. Leser, *Der Rücktritt vom Vertrag* (1975); idem, "Lösung vom Vertrag", in: *Recht und Rechtserkenntnis, Festschrift für Ernst Wolf* (1985), pp. 373 sqq.; Harker, 1980 *Acta Juridica* 61 sqq.

depended on the type of action available to the creditor. The device of a perpetuatio obligationis was necessary in order to establish the liability, under the condictio, of a promisor who was responsible for the fact that the object of performance could no longer be transferred. But for the perpetuatio obligationis, the debtor of a certum dare obligation would have been released whenever performance became impossible. The position was different in the case of obligations for an incertum. Here the judge had to determine "quidquid dare facere oportet (ex fide bona)", which means that the debtor could be condemned in id quod interest irrespective of whether the object of performance still existed, provided only that the failure to perform (properly) was attributable to him according to whatever standard of liability appeared reasonable ("oportet ex fide bona") under the circumstances. In other words: a promisor automatically became free if the object of the stipulation was destroyed; as a result of the perpetuatio obligationis, however, he was liable for the value of that object, if he had culpably destroyed it. The vendor under a contract of emptio venditio, on the other hand, was liable for id quod interest, if he had made transfer of the object of the sale impossible or if he was guilty of any other form of breach of contract. Where he was not to blame for not performing (properly), however, it could hardly be said that he "ought to do or to give ex bona fide", and the actio empti was therefore unsuccessful.[170] If the liability of the stipulator (for the value of the object) was (dogmatically) a somewhat artificial exception to the rule, the liability of the vendor flowed naturally from the basic principles governing bonae fidei iudicia.

2. Breach of contract under the ius commune

By the time of Justinian the procedural basis for these kinds of distinctions had fallen away; the formulary system had long since been abandoned and in its place the post-classical cognitio procedure reigned supreme. All claims were now adjudged from the point of view of aequitas,[171] and thus, irrespective of whether a specific object or what the classical lawyers had termed an "incertum" was owed, irrespective also of the way in which the debtor had failed to comply with his contractual duties, he could now ultimately be condemned to id quod interest.[172] It was therefore essentially the regime applicable to bonae fidei iudicia that survived. The perpetuatio obligationis had lost its function, but was, nevertheless, still incorporated into the Corpus

[170] In the result, therefore, the vendor became free. Could he still demand payment of the purchase price or was the purchaser released from his obligation too? Or, in other words: who had to carry the risk of accidental destruction of the merx? The answer is provided by the rule "periculum est emptoris": cf. supra, pp. 281 sqq.

[171] Cf. supra, p. 548, note 10.

[172] Cf. e.g. Kaser, *RPr* II, p. 357.

Juris Civilis[173] and it has, not surprisingly, puzzled subsequent generations of lawyers.[174] By and large, however, Justinian's codification had settled the problem of liability for breach of contract and from the days of the glossators down to the first half of the 19th century the basic principles remained unchallenged. More particularly, apart from mora debitoris, no specific types of breach of contract were singled out and dealt with separately. The debtor was liable for id quod interest (or, in the terminology coined by the glossators, the "interesse"),[175] and supervening impossibility due to the destruction of the object of performance no longer automatically terminated his liability. Non-performance on account of supervening impossibility therefore created no further problems than any other kind of breach of contract. What mattered was simply whether the debtor had complied with his contractual obligations and, if not, whether his failure to perform (properly) was attributable to his fault;[176] hence the emphasis throughout the various periods of the ius commune on the subjective requirements for liability for breach of contract and the attempts to analyse, refine and systematize the various degrees of culpa (in the broad sense of the word).[177] For a typical formulation of the prevailing doctrine, we may refer to the Codex Maximilianeus Bavaricus Civilis (1756), where it is crisply stated that "dolum, culpam vel casum in conventione praest[are]" means as much as to be liable for the loss arising through the contract due to the malice or negligence of one of the contracting parties or due to some unforeseen accident.[178] Specific objective requirements for liability are not mentioned, and not even mora debitoris is specifically singled out. Following the pattern of the ius commune, too, is the French code civil. Its art. 1147 refers to *"inexécution"*, a broad concept which covers all forms of breach of contract (that is, those cases where one of the parties *"ne satisfera point*

---

[173] Cf. the sources discussed supra, pp. 784 sq., 792.

[174] Take, for example, the situation in South African law. According to W.A. Ramsden, *Supervening Impossibility of Performance in the South African Law of Contract* (1985), pp. 55 sqq., perpetuatio obligationis obtains in case of impossibility (due to the fault of the debtor) and mora debitoris. De Wet en Yeats refer to perpetuatio obligationis only with regard to mora (p. 148); cf. also Van Zijl Steyn, op. cit., note 72, pp. 90 sqq. Others do not refer to perpetuatio obligationis at all.

[175] Dilcher, *Leistungsstörungen*, pp. 120 sqq.; cf. further Hermann Lange, *Schadensersatz und Privatstrafe*, pp. 13 sqq., 100 sqq.

[176] During the time of the usus modernus, liability for damages arising as a consequence of deficient performance (*"positive Vertragsverletzung"*; cf. infra, pp. 812 sq.) tended to be based on the lex Aquilia rather than on contractual principles: cf. Harting, op. cit., note 43, pp. 65 sqq.; Kaufmann, *Lex Aquilia*, pp. 46 sqq., 110 sqq.; Coing, p. 442 and infra, p. 1024.

[177] Dilcher, *Leistungsstörungen*, pp. 17 sqq.; Hoffmann, *Fahrlässigkeit* , pp. 35 sqq.

[178] IV 1 § 20. Praestatio casus refers to the case of a casus quem culpa praecessit, i.e. liability for casus where there has been either culpa praecedens or mora praecedens. Cf. generally Dilcher, *Leistungsstörungen*, pp. 109 sqq.; Stephan Kuttner, *Kanonistische Schuldlehre von Gratian bis auf die Dekretalen Gregors IX* (1935), pp. 185 sqq. The culpa praecedens doctrine is clearly related to the concept of versari in re illicita.

à son engagement").[179] The debtor is liable wherever such non-performance is not due to vis maior or casus fortuitus.[180]

3. The notion of impossibility under the ius commune

What has been said so far does not, of course, mean that the notion of impossibility of performance was unknown or entirely irrelevant. First of all there was, as we have seen, the problem of initial impossibility of performance (impossibilium nulla est obligatio).[181] Secondly, the trend towards specific performance must be kept in mind. Wherever the creditor (contrary to the classical Roman omnis condemnatio pecuniaria) was given the right to enforce performance in forma specifica,[182] an exception had to be recognized for cases where such performance had become impossible. If the object that was to be transferred had been destroyed, the creditor could, as a matter of course, claim compensation only in money.[183] And thirdly: where the object of performance had been accidentally destroyed and where the resulting impossibility was therefore not attributable to the debtor, the latter was seen to be released from his obligation. "Debitor speciei liberatur casuali interitu rei" became the general principle of the ius commune:[184] an extension to bonae fidei contracts (especially to the contract of sale) of D. 46, 3, 107, a statement by Pomponius relating to verborum obligationes.[185] Nevertheless, however, neither the interitus rei nor the concept of impossibility featured as a general systematic category in the law relating to breach of contract. If the object of performance was accidentally destroyed, the debtor's obligation fell away. If the debtor was responsible for the destruction, he was liable for breach of contract; but he was liable in the same way and according to the same principles as wherever else he had failed to comply with his contractual duties. Culpa (with its various grades) and casus remained the central categories for the determination of the debtor's liability, not the specific type of breach of contract the debtor had committed.

4. Friedrich Mommsen's impossibility doctrine

Non-German readers will be wondering why this point needs emphasizing. The reason is that in the course of the 19th century the

---

179 Art. 1184 code civil. Art. 1147, however, also mentions *"retard"* (mora debitoris) as a special form of breach of contract. Cf. further e.g. Zweigert/Kötz, pp. 213 sqq.; Nicholas, *FLC*, pp. 193 sqq.

180 Artt. 1147 sq.

181 Cf. supra, pp. 687 sqq.

182 Cf. supra, pp. 772 sqq.

183 Wollschläger, *Unmöglichkeitslehre*, pp. 41 sq. As he points out, the crucial question for the authors of the ius commune was a different one: may a vendor (such as the debtor under an obligatio faciendi—nemo potest praecise cogi ad factum!; cf. supra, pp. 774 sq.) discharge his obligation by paying the interest, i.e. is he able to force the creditor to accept a monetary compensation in the place of specific performance, even where the latter is still possible?

184 Dilcher, *Leistungsstörungen*, pp. 185 sqq., Wollschläger, *Unmöglichkeitslehre*, pp. 42 sq.

185 Cf. supra, note 7.

whole perspective changed considerably. This was due, essentially, to a book by Friedrich Mommsen,[186] brother of the famous historian and Nobel prize winner, Theodor. He[187] superimposed a concept of "impossibility of performance" on the sources, which covered all cases in which the debtor was unable to perform: non impleat quia non potest (as opposed to quia non vult).[188] Impossibility became a very broad conceptual abstraction, a common systematic denominator for a whole range of situations. Thus, Mommsen distinguished, inter alia, between initial and supervening, natural and legal, absolute and relative, objective and subjective, permanent and temporary, complete and partial, apparent and "real" impossibility.[189] The legal consequences in a given situation depended, in the first place, on its appropriate niche within this typology of "impossibilities". It was one of the consequences of this new approach that the category of "supervening impossibility" became the essential dogmatic cornerstone of the law relating to breach of contract.

Mommsen's book is characterized by that abstract and excessive conceptualism which is so typical of pandectist writing. It forced the sources into a scheme which was alien to the Roman lawyers and which, today, fails to appeal to legal historians and modern lawyers alike. It would probably have been largely forgotten, had it not managed to impress the most influential of the pandectists, Bernhard Windscheid[190] and, through him, the fathers of the BGB.[191] If we look into the German codification, we find the following rules:

5. Supervening impossibility in modern German law

(1) If performance becomes impossible owing to circumstances for which the debtor is not responsible, his obligation falls away.[192] This rule has taken the place of the old tenet of "debitor speciei liberatur casuali interitu rei"[193]. It is formulated more broadly than the latter,[194] since it refers not only to obligationes ad dandum but also to obligationes ad faciendum. Obligationes ad faciendum, as will be

---

[186] *Die Unmöglichkeit der Leistung in ihrem Einfluss auf obligatorische Verhältnisse* (1853).

[187] On the roots of his ideas in the tradition of both the ius commune and (particularly) the law of the Age of Reason, see Wollschläger, *Unmöglichkeitslehre*, pp. 75 sqq., 118 sqq. On the Prussian General Land Law, which for the first time attributed central importance to the concept of impossibility within the law relating to breach of contract, see Wollschläger, pp. 106 sqq.

[188] For this alternative cf. Lauterbach, as discussed by Wollschläger, *Unmöglichkeitslehre*, pp. 72 sq.

[189] Cf. the categories listed and discussed by Wollschläger, *Unmöglichkeitslehre*, pp. 125 sqq.

[190] Windscheid/Kipp, §§ 264, 315, 360.

[191] Wollschläger, *Unmöglichkeitslehre*, pp. 167 sqq.

[192] § 275 BGB.

[193] Cf. supra, p. 809.

[194] And art. 1302 code civil.

remembered, were in any case not enforceable in forma specifica under the ius commune[195] ("nemo potest praecise cogi ad factum").

(2) There is an exception in cases where the debtor is obliged to pay money or to deliver fungible things: the debtor is responsible for his inability to deliver, even though no fault is attributable to him.[196] This reflects the old maxim "genus perire non potest" of the ius commune.[197]

(3) If the performance due by one party under a reciprocal contract becomes impossible because of circumstances for which neither he nor the other party is responsible, he loses his right to demand counterperformance.[198] This gives expression to what has been termed the "conditional synallagma":[199] obligation and counterobligation share the same fate; if one of them falls away, so does the other. Both obligations are interdependent and they should therefore not be looked at in isolation—the consequence of the fact that the one party has promised to perform *in order* to receive the counterperformance ("do ut des").[200] § 323 BGB contains the general risk rule developed during the age of the law of reason and embodied, for the first time, in §§ 364 I 5 of the Prussian General Land Law.[201] It is in conflict with the older ius commune, which tended to place the risk of casus in some of the most important bilateral contracts on the creditor;[202] thus, it is the purchaser who has to pay the purchase price, even though he does not receive the merx, and the customer who is bound to pay the remuneration agreed upon, although the promised work has been destroyed. This was, of course, the result of the Roman periculum emptoris, locatoris, etc.[203]

(4) Where the performance becomes impossible because of a circumstance for which the debtor is responsible, the creditor may demand compensation for non-performance;[204] alternatively, if the impossibility relates to a synallagmatic obligation, he may withdraw from the contract.[205] The right of withdrawal from the contract is

---

[195] And under the code civil: art. 1142. Cf. further Harting, op. cit., note 43, p. 92.

[196] § 279 BGB.

[197] Glück, vol. IV, pp. 386 sqq.; Dilcher, *Leistungsstörungen*, pp. 277 sqq.; Wollschläger, *Unmöglichkeitslehre*, p. 43.

[198] § 323 BGB.

[199] Benöhr, *Synallagma*, p. 1.

[200] On the exceptio non adimpleti contractus (§ 320 BGB) (another expression of the mutual interdependence of obligations arising under a reciprocal contract) cf. supra, pp. 801 sq.

[201] The historical development is traced by Wollschläger, *Unmöglichkeitslehre*, pp. 64 sqq., 106 sqq., 142 sq. and Joachim Rückert, "Vom casus zur Unmöglichkeit und von der Sphäre zum Synallagma", (1984) 6 *ZNR* 40 sqq. Rückert emphasizes that both under the Prussian Land Law and under the BGB the crisp and plucky general rule is subject to many exceptions for specific contracts.

[202] Dilcher, *Leistungsstörungen*, pp. 191 sqq.; Wollschläger, *Unmöglichkeitslehre*, pp. 50 sq.; Scherner, *Rücktrittsrecht*, pp. 37 sqq.; Rückert, (1984) 6 *ZNR* 40 sqq.

[203] Cf. supra, pp. 281 sqq., 370 sq., 403.

[204] §§ 280, 325 BGB.

[205] § 325 BGB.

essentially the same as in the case of mora debitoris.[206] The emphasis on (supervening) impossibility is the influence of Mommsen/Windscheid. Particularly odd, or even eccentric, appears to be the fact that supervening impossibility and mora debitoris[207] are the only two forms of breach of contract recognized by the BGB. Furthermore, a debtor is not only bound to perform at all and to perform at the right time; there are further obligations arising from the contract with which he can be expected to comply. Most importantly, his performance must not be deficient. Thus, the vendor of poisonous horsefodder should be liable for damages if the purchaser's horses die as a result of being exposed to such an unsuitable diet.[208] So should the vendor of defective fuel which damages the engines in the purchaser's vehicles.[209] Liability should also arise, for instance, where the damage was caused as a result of inadequate information or incorrect instructions supplied by the vendor of some piece of equipment.[210] As early as 1902 (two years after the BGB had come into effect) Hermann Staub[211] discovered that for these and similar cases the BGB contained a "giant gap". Concentrating solely on delay of performance and impossibility, the legislator had, apparently, forgotten to deal with what Staub termed *"positive Vertragsverletzungen"* (positive breach of contract; "positiewe wanprestasie" in the terminology of De Wet en Yeats).[212] The courts immediately set about filling this gap and today *"positive Vertragsverletzung"* is generally recognized as a judge-made institution extra legem.[213] As with the other forms of breach of contract, it entitles the creditor to claim damages or (under certain circumstances)[214] to rescind the contract. As a matter of fact, however, the BGB did not contain the blatant defect that Staub claimed to have "discovered".[215] In Mommsen's impossibility doctrine, cases of malperformance featured in the guise of partial impossibility as to the quality of the object of performance.[216] If the vendor delivers horsefodder that is poisonous, he

---

[206] Cf. supra, p. 802; for a comparative overview cf. Jürgen Basedow, *Die Reform des deutschen Kaufrechts* (1988), pp. 36 sqq.

[207] §§ 286, 326 BGB.

[208] RGZ 66, 289 sqq.

[209] BGH, 1968 *Neue Jurisitsche Wochenschrift* 2238.

[210] Cf. e.g. BGHZ 47, 312 (315 sq.).

[211] "Die positiven Vertragsverletzungen und ihre Rechtsfolgen", in: *Festschrift für den 26. Deutschen Juristentag* (1902), pp. 29 sqq.

[212] At pp. 161 sqq.

[213] BGHZ 11, 80 (83 sqq.) and, for all details, Emmerich, op. cit., note 83, Vor § 275, nn. 95 sqq.

[214] Emmerich, op. cit., note 83, Vor § 275, nn. 135 sqq.

[215] On "legal discoveries" in this context, see Hans Dölle, "Juristische Entdeckungen", in: *Verhandlungen des 42. Deutschen Juristentags*, vol. II (1959), pp. B 1 sqq., B 15 sq.

[216] Mommsen, *Unmöglichkeit*, pp. 193 sqq.; cf. also Jury Himmelschein, "Erfüllungszwang und Lehre von den positiven Vertragsverletzungen", (1932) 135 *Archiv für die civilistische Praxis* 255 sqq., 297 sqq.; Wollschläger, *Unmöglichkeitslehre*, pp. 132 sqq. On

has only partially complied with his contractual duties: he has made delivery, but what he has delivered is not suitable for use. The type of performance he was bound to render (delivery of horsefodder at the right time and of the right quality) has thus become impossible. The development of the doctrine of "*positive Vertragsverletzung*" therefore merely demonstrates a lack of sympathy and understanding for Mommsen's abstract conceptualism that still underlies the provisions of the BGB relating to breach of contract. Apart from that, however, it provides an example of the scope of judicial law-making, even under a codified system.

(5) Finally, it must be kept in mind that for some contracts the BGB provides a number of special rules and remedies dealing with the problem of defective performance. They take precedence over the general rules relating to breach of contract (lex specialis derogat legi generali). Particularly important are the rights of a customer under a contract for work and of a purchaser to demand annulment of the contract or reduction of the remuneration/purchase price.[217] These remedies are obviously either based on or inspired by the aedilitian remedies of Roman law.

6. Breach of contract in German law

The German way of dealing with the problem of breach of contract, particularly the attempt to categorize the various forms of breach of contract, has not attracted much favourable comment.[218] It is widely regarded today as one of the most unfortunate features of the German law of obligations. Breach of contract and ("extinctive") prescription have been earmarked as the two areas where fundamental reforms are necessary.[219] It is not surprising that the draft proposals, commissioned by the Minister of Justice, abandon the distinction between impossibility, default and delay of performance and adopt, instead, a unitary

positive malperformance under the ius commune, see Harting, op. cit., note 43, pp. 55 sqq., 65 sqq., 75 sqq. (natural law); cf. also infra, p. 1024 (liability under the lex Aquilia rather than the contract).

[217] §§ 459, 462, 634 BGB. Under certain circumstances (if a promised quality in the thing sold is absent at the time of the purchase, if the vendor has fraudulently concealed a defect or if the defect in the work is caused by circumstances for which the contractor is responsible) the purchaser/customer may demand compensation for non-fulfilment in the place of cancellation or reduction: §§ 463, 635 BGB.

[218] Cf., for example, Ernst Rabel, "Unmöglichkeit der Leistung", in: *Aus römischem und bürgerlichem Recht, Festschrift für Ernst I. Bekker*, (1907), pp. 171 sqq.; Heinrich Stoll, *Die Lehre von den Leistungsstörungen* (1936), pp. 1 sqq.; Wieacker, *Privatrechtsgeschichte*, p. 519; Zweigert/Kötz, pp. 232 sqq.; Huber, op. cit., note 5, pp. 756 sqq.; Basedow, op. cit., note 206, pp. 35 sqq.; but see also Horst Heinrich Jakobs, *Gesetzgebung im Leistungsstörungsrecht* (1985), who embarks on a defence of the system underlying the rules of the BGB and does not regard any reform legislation as necessary. For a criticism of Jakobs' point of view, see, however, Dieter Medicus, "Gesetzgebung und Jurisprudenz im Recht der Leistungsstörungen", (1986) 186 *Archiv für die civilistische Praxis* 268 sqq.

[219] Hans A. Engelhard (Minister of Justice), "Zu den Aufgaben einer Kommission für die Überarbeitung des Schuldrechts", 1984 *Neue Juristische Wochenschrift* 1201 sqq.

concept of breach of contract.[220] Mommsen's scheme, as endorsed by the BGB, strangely resembles the regime applied in Roman law to certum dare obligations. It is still the old idea of a perpetuatio obligationis in case of mora debitoris and of culpable supervening impossibility that lurks behind the scenes.[221] In a way, therefore, German legal science is, once again, about to take the step from a scheme determined by a somewhat outdated conceptual rigour to a pattern of thinking moulded upon, and more suitable to, the traditions of the bonae fidei iudicia.

7. Breach of contract in English law

In modern discussions de lege ferenda it is, in this instance, the English common law that has for some time set the trend.[222] Here we find a reasonably streamlined set of rules dealing with all forms of breach of contract, including liability for defects in contracts of sale or contracts for work.[223] Whenever one of the parties fails to perform his contractual duties, the other party has a claim for damages for breach of contract. If the failure of performance is substantial, the innocent party may, in addition, rescind the contract. Contrary to the tradition of the ius commune, the debtor's liability does not depend on fault.[224] The reason is, of course, that the common law regards all contractual promises as guarantees:[225]

> "[W]hen [a] party by his own contract creates a duty or charge upon himself, he is bound to make it good, . . . notwithstanding any accident by inevitable necessity";[226]

---

[220] Huber, op. cit., note 5, pp. 671 sqq., 699 sqq.

[221] Rabel, *Festschrift Bekker*, pp. 185, 201 sq.; Harting, op. cit., note 43, pp. 128 sqq., 139 sqq.; cf. also Wollschläger, *Unmöglichkeitslehre*, pp. 146 sq.

[222] Particularly in the discussion leading up to the Uniform Law for International Sales of Goods as adopted in 1964 by the Hague Conference for the Unification of the Law of Sales, and to the United Nations Convention on Contracts for the International Sale of Goods adopted in 1980 at a conference in Vienna; on these two important milestones towards legal unification cf. e.g. Hans Dölle (ed.), *Kommentar zum Einheitlichen Kaufrecht* (1976); John O. Honnold, *Uniform Law of International Sales under the 1980 United Nations Convention* (1982); on the *travaux préparatoires* to the Uniform Law for International Sales of Goods, cf., for example, the articles by Ernst Rabel as collected in: *Gesammelte Aufsätze*, vol. III (1967), pp. 381 sqq.; for a comparative evaluation of the United Nations Convention, see J. Barrigan Marcantonio, "Unifying the Law of Impossibility", (1984) 8 *Hastings International and Comparative LR* 41 sqq.

[223] For an overview cf. Zweigert/Kötz, pp. 221 sqq.; cf. also their evaluation, pp. 232 sqq.

[224] But cf. Basedow, op. cit., note 206, pp. 38 sqq., who points out that in actual practice the differences between English law and continental law have to a large extent been levelled out. Essential for the debtor's liability even on the Continent is (judicial) determination of his range of duties under the contract (i.e. an objective criterion). Breach of such contractual duty, as a rule, implies fault. Thus it is up to the debtor to establish (and prove) that he was *not* at fault; cf. e.g. § 282 BGB.

[225] Cf. supra, pp. 776, 803.

[226] *Paradine v. Jane* (1647) Aleyn 26 (dealing with a landlord's action to recover rent; the tenant was not excused from payment, even though he had been evicted from the land by a royalist army under the command of Prince Rupert). On this leading case and its reception, cf. e.g. Grant Gilmore, *The Death of Contract* (1974), pp. 44 sqq.

if he had not wanted to be bound under those circumstances, he should have specifically excluded his liability. This does not mean, however, that without an express exemption clause the debtor's liability is unlimited. Determination of its scope is a matter of the proper interpretation of the contract. Or, according to art. 74 of the Uniform Law for International Sales of Goods: the debtor continues to be bound unless he is able to prove that the non-performance is attributable to circumstances which, according to the common intentions at the time of conclusion of the contract, he did not have to take into account, to avoid or to overcome. Thus, in the leading case of *Taylor v. Caldwell*,[227] a contract concerning the hire of a music hall for the presentation of a series of concerts was held to contain an "implied condition" that

> "the parties shall be excused in case . . . performance becomes impossible from the perishing of the thing [i.e. the music-hall] without default of the contractor".

The German lawyer would refer to supervening impossibility.[228] The

---

[227] (1863) 3 B & S 826; on the development cf., apart from the standard English literature, L.W. Murcott, "Oormag in die Engelse en in die Suid-Afrikaanse Reg", (1942) 6 *THRHR* 169 sqq.

[228] The lessor would be released from his obligation according to § 275 I BGB, the lessee according to § 323 I BGB. This is one of many examples which demonstrate that despite the widely divergent theoretical starting points, the actual problems are often solved in very much the same way; cf. e.g. Zweigert/Kötz, pp. 229 sqq., and also Marcantonio, (1984) 8 *Hastings International and Comparative LR* 41 sqq. Better than by anything else, Zweigert/Kötz's contention is confirmed, incidentally, by the development of modern South African law. The systematic exposition of breach of contract in modern textbooks is so diverse that one can hardly believe that these books are dealing with one and the same legal system. Christie, *The Law of Contract in South Africa* (1981), deals with mora and breach, Kerr, *The Principles of the Law of Contract* (3rd ed., 1982), subdivides his chapter on breach of contract into repudiation, anticipatory breach, ordinary breach and major and minor breach. Van Rensburg/Lotz/Van Rhijn, in: Joubert (ed.), *The Law of South Africa*, vol. 5 (1978), nn. 199 have negative malperformance (mora creditoris and debitoris), positive malperformance and anticipatory breach (repudiation and prevention of performance). De Wet en Yeats, as in many other cases, adopt more modern German (pandectist) thinking patterns and distinguish between mora debitoris, impossibility (onmoontlikmaking van die prestasie) and positiewe wanprestasie. However, they add repudiation (repudiëring) as a fourth category. The discussion by Joubert, *Contract*, is along the same lines. The South African courts have not been unduly worried about the theoretical differences. Typical of their approach is the leading case on impossibility, *Peters, Flamman and Co. v. Kokstad Municipality* 1919 AD 427. In this case Solomon ACJ recognizes that for the old authorities it is clear that if a person is prevented from performing his contract by vis maior or casus fortuitus, he is discharged from liability. Joseph Averanius (*Interpretationes Iuris*) is quoted for this proposition. The judge then remarks that "unfortunately" the rules of the civil law appear to have been ignored in several South African cases and that the courts have been guided entirely by the decisions of the English courts. More particularly, the rule of *Paradine v. Jane* has been invoked (cf. e.g. *Hay v. The Divisional Council of King William's Town* 1 EDC 97 at 102). It is not consistent with the principles of the civil law. Even in English law, it has been considerably modified by later decisions. Solomon ACJ then proceeds to quote from *Horlock v. Beal* [1916] 1 AC 486 (HL) at 525, and *F.A. Tamplin Steamship Co. Ltd. v. Anglo-Mexican Petroleum Products Co. Ltd.* [1916] 2 AC 397 (HL) at 422 and comes to the conclusion: "It will be seen, therefore, that although the English law looks at the subject from a different point of view from ours, in the result the difference is not very great. And indeed, if this case had been tried in an English Court of Justice, I am disposed to think that the defendants would have been held to have been discharged from their obligations under the contract" (p. 437). Cf. further *Hersman v. Shapiro & Co.* 1926 TPD 367 at 371 sqq.;

somewhat fictitious nature of the construction chosen in *Taylor v. Caldwell* becomes apparent when one reads what Blackburn J says at the outset of his opinion—namely, that "[t]he parties when framing [their] agreement evidently had not present to their minds the possibility of such a disaster".[229] Only a few lines later, however, we see him express his confidence that "[the] implication tends to further the great object of making the legal construction such as to fulfil the intention of those who entered into the contract".[230] The inconsistency is obvious.[231] But somehow or other the desired legal result had to be connected to the intention of the parties and the most convenient, and fashionable, device that could be used in order to achieve that was the implied condition.

The basic inspiration came from Roman law, though, ironically, as in the case of the parallel rule of § 323 BGB, from the obligationes stricti iuris. For in Blackburn J's opinion we meet an old acquaintance. It is Pomp. D. 45, 1, 23 to which the judge refers for the proposition that a debtor corporis certi is freed from his obligation when there is no longer a corpus certum.[232] As so often,[233] incidentally, Pothier's *Traité*

Murcott, (1942) 6 *THRHR* 169 sqq., 190 sqq. (very solid) and W.A. Ramsden, *Supervening Impossibility of Performance in the South African Law of Contract* (1985) (the only monograph on the topic).

Repudiation (as a form of breach of contract in anticipando; in German: "*Erfüllungsverweigerung*") has been taken over from English law (leading case: *Hochster v. De la Tour* (1853) 2 El & Bl 678) and is today generally accepted as a special type of breach of contract (even by Roman-Dutch "purists" such as De Wet en Yeats); cf. e.g. P.M. Nienaber, "Enkele beskouinge oor kontrakbreuk in anticipando", (1963) 26 *THRHR* 19 sqq.; idem, *Anticipatory Repudiation in English and South African Law of Contract*, pp. 111 sqq.: "Roman-Dutch law did not know a form of breach of contract corresponding to the English breach by anticipatory repudiation. In South Africa the doctrine was superimposed on the forms of breach known to Roman-Dutch law. The courts acted on the English principle, apparently without realizing that an entirely new doctrine, unknown to Roman-Dutch law, thereby came to form part and parcel of South African law . . . and if even a twinge of doubt was experienced this was finally laid to rest in *Dennill v. Atkins & Co.* 1905 TS 282. . . . English authorities were quoted in abundance and so it hardly occasions surprise that not only the principle, but the underlying reasons for the principle as expressed in the leading English cases, were adopted." This passage was quoted with approval by Holmes JA in *Crest Enterprises (Pty.) Ltd. v. Rycklof Beleggings (Edms.) Bpk.* 1972 (2) SA 863 (A) at 869D–E; for final confirmation of the recognition of the doctrine cf. also *Novick v. Benjamin* 1972 (2) SA 842 (A) at 853H–858F. For recent trends, see *Tuckers Land and Development Corporation (Pty.) Ltd. v. Hovis* 1980 (1) SA 645 (A) at 650G–653A and David Carey Miller, (1980) 97 *SALJ* 531 sqq. In German law, the rules of positive malperformance are usually applied; cf. Emmerich, op. cit., note 83, Vor § 275, nn. 120 sqq.; but cf. also e.g. Klaus Friedrich, "Der Vertragsbruch", (1978) 178 *Archiv für die civilistische Praxis* 488, arguing for a separate institution. On historical and comparative aspects of the doctrine of anticipatory breach, cf. Francis Dawson, "Metaphors and Anticipatory Breach of Contract", (1981) 40 *CLJ* 83 sqq.; James C. Gulotta jr., "Anticipatory Breach—A Comparative Analysis", (1975–76) 50 *Tulane LR* 927 sqq.

[229] At 833.

[230] At 834.

[231] "It is hard to see how much further inconsistency is possible": A.W.B. Simpson, "Innovation in Nineteenth Century Contract Law", (1975) 91 *LQR* 271.

[232] At 834.

[233] Cf. e.g. supra, pp. 336 sq., pp. 611 sq.

des obligations[234] provided the vital link for the transfer of the civilian doctrine into the fabric of the common law. *Taylor v. Caldwell* may be regarded as one of the roots of the modern English doctrine of frustration of contract, for the underlying idea of an "implied condition" soon came to be fused with that of a "frustration of adventure", as developed in a line of cases dealing with charterparties and their construction.[235] By implying a condition that no event would occur that would defeat the object of the contract, the courts created an effective tool to bring about a just and fair solution, not only in cases of factual or legal impossibility but also where the foundation of the contract is affected by a supervening change of circumstances;[236] it is thus the functional equivalent to the continental clausula rebus sic stantibus.[237] "Viewed historically", writes Simpson,[238] "[the doctrine of frustration] represents a curiously complex blend of common and civil law development, linked, inevitably, to the central doctrine of consensus by fiction." It was King Edward VII's indisposition on the day of his projected coronation that gave rise to a particularly interesting and famous set of cases.[239]

V. MORA CREDITORIS

1. Mora creditoris, mora debitoris and breach of contract

When we were discussing mora, reference was made to the definition contained in Voet's *Commentarius ad Pandectas*: "Mora est solutionis faciendae . . . frustratoria dilatio."[240] It provided a convenient starting point for our examination of mora debitoris. We must now turn our attention to what, at that stage, we left out and merely represented by three dots: the words "vel accipiendae". If the debtor can upset the smooth exchange of performances, so can the creditor: the one by delaying his performance, the other by delaying acceptance of the performance offered by his debtor. Again, Voet's statement is typical of the view taken by the authors of the ius commune: they saw mora

[234] N. 660: *"L'extinction de la chose due éteint la dette."*

[235] *Freeman v. Taylor* (1831) 8 Bing 124; *Jackson v. Union Marine Insurance Co. Ltd. ("Spirit of Dawn")* (1874) LR 10 CP 125.

[236] Cf. e.g. Zweigert/Kötz, pp. 252 sqq.; Simpson, (1975) 91 *LQR* 271 sqq.

[237] Cf. supra, pp. 579 sqq.

[238] (1975) 91 *LQR* 273.

[239] C.f. e.g. *Krell v. Henry* [1903] 2 KB 740 (CA), dealing with the situation that the owner of a house en route of the coronation procession had let it to the defendant for the day. The procession was cancelled. It was held that the defendant was entitled to refuse to pay the rent under these circumstances. For a discussion of the coronation cases, see e.g. R.G. McElroy, Glanville Williams, "The Coronation Cases", (1940–41) 4 *Modern LR* 241 sqq.; (1941–42) 5 *Modern LR* 1 sqq.

[240] Cf. supra, p. 793 (note 69).

creditoris as a counterpart, or twin image, of mora debitoris.[241] Obviously, mora creditoris is practically much less important ("[moram] frequentius quidem debitor committit, rarius creditor"), but it does not, in essence, differ from mora debitoris. Both are, after all, two different types of mora and both are therefore based on fault (culpa). But where there is fault, there must also be the breach of a duty, for fault can be attributable only to someone who has done what he should not have done or who has failed to do what he should have done; hence the general assumption that the creditor is *obliged* to receive performance and that mora on his part constitutes a culpable breach of this obligation. "Mora est delictum culpabile in debito solvendo, vel credito recipiendo commissum"; or "Mora est culpa praetermittendi officii in solvendo, recipiendove debito, quae alteri damnosa est".[242] As a result of this construction, the debtor had a claim for damages against the defaulting creditor.[243]

In a way, therefore, the position under the ius commune did not differ much from that under the English common law, where mora creditoris is unknown as a specific legal institution.[244] The creditor is liable, in the same way as the debtor, for breach of contract; the debtor's remedies depend (as do those of the creditor) on whether the breach of contract is "substantial", "goes to the root of the contract" or is "material".[245] It is interesting (but no longer surprising) to see that the creditor's liability is based, dogmatically, on the (judicial) implication of an appropriate term into the contract. According to Anson/Guest,[246] the courts "are most ready to imply a condition that each party undertakes to do all that is necessary to secure performance of the contract"; and it is the infringement of this duty to co-operate that constitutes the creditor's breach of contract.

2. Mora creditoris in modern German law

The concept of mora creditoris underlying the provisions of the BGB is quite a different one. Unlike the creditor in a case of mora debitoris, the debtor in the event of mora creditoris does not have a right to sue for damages. The reason is that mora creditoris under the BGB is not based on fault but merely on the fact that the creditor does not accept

---

[241] Cf. e.g. Glück, vol. 4, pp. 401 sqq.; Carl Otto von Madai, *Die Lehre von der Mora, Dargestellt nach Grundsätzen des Römischen Rechts* (1837), pp. 227 sqq.; A.B. de Villiers, *Mora creditoris as vorm van kontrakbreuk* (unpublished LLD thesis, Stellenbosch, 1953), pp. 78 sqq., 186 sqq.

[242] Salicetus, *Tractatus de mora* and Hotomannus, *Tractatus de mora*, both quoted by von Madai, op. cit., note 241, p. 5.

[243] This is still the position in South African law; cf. De Wet en Yeats, pp. 163 sqq., 174 sq.; Joubert, *Contract*, pp. 214 sqq., 220 sq.

[244] For a comparative investigation, see Uwe Hüffer, *Leistungsstörungen durch Gläubigerhandeln* (1976), pp. 134 sqq.

[245] Cf. supra, pp. 803 sq.

[246] 23rd ed., 1969, p. 491.

performance offered to him in the proper manner.[247] Fault as a requirement for mora creditoris, in turn, had lost its basis when it came to be recognized in the second half of the 19th century that the creditor is not *obliged* to receive performance but merely *entitled* to do so. The debtor, in other words, does not have a claim against the creditor to make him accept performance, even where it has been duly tendered. The institution of mora debitoris is merely designed to relieve in certain respects the position of a debtor who has done whatever one could reasonably expect him to do.[248] This doctrine, again, goes back to Friedrich Mommsen;[249] it was emphatically reasserted by Josef Kohler[250] and impressed the fathers of the BGB.[251] Of course, both Mommsen and the (earlier) authors of the ius commune claimed that their views were derived from, or at least reconcilable with, the sources of Roman law. Contemporary Romanist doctrine tends to side with Mommsen and to attribute the modern, objective construction of mora creditoris to the Roman lawyers.[252] However, not all our sources do confirm such a general pattern; not even the solution adopted by the BGB, incidentally, is as straightforward as a reading of §§ 293 sqq. might suggest. With regard to one of the most important transactions, the contract of sale, the code deviates from the general principle: the purchaser is not bound only to pay the purchase price but also to take delivery of the object of the sale.[253] Delay in accepting a res vendita is, therefore, first and foremost mora *debitoris*!

3. Requirements of mora creditoris in Roman law

Mora creditoris in Roman law appears to have had two requirements. On the one hand, performance had to be offered to the creditor at the right time, in the right place and in the proper manner. What that entailed depended on the circumstances of the individual case. As a general rule one can say that the debtor had to do whatever he was able to do without the co-operation of the creditor. Thus, where, according to the contract, performance had to be rendered at the creditor's premises, the debtor had to bring the goods, or the money, or whatever he owed, to that place and to offer it there. If, however, the creditor was required to collect the object of performance from the debtor's premises, a verbal offer was sufficient.[254] Even that appears to have been dispensable, where a specific time had been fixed when the

[247] § 293 BGB.

[248] §§ 298 sqq.

[249] *Die Lehre von der Mora nebst Beiträgen zur Lehre von der culpa* (1855), pp. 133 sqq.

[250] "Annahme und Annahmeverzug", (1879) 17 *JhJb* 261 sqq.

[251] "Motive", in: *Mugdan*, vol. II, pp. 37 sqq.; cf. also Hüffer, op. cit., note 244, pp. 14 sqq.

[252] Cf. Kaser, *RPr* I, pp. 517 sq.; Honsell/Mayer-Maly/Selb, pp. 247 sq.; Hausmaninger/Selb, p. 370; but see also Buckland/Stein, p. 551; Thomas, *TRL*, pp. 254 sq.

[253] § 433 II BGB.

[254] Pomp. D. 19, 1, 3, 4.

creditor was supposed to come around to collect whatever was due to him.[255] On the other hand, the failure of the debtor's attempt to render performance had to be attributable to the creditor. "Si per creditorem steterit quo minus accipiat" was the phrase used in this context by the Roman lawyers.[256] This, as we have seen repeatedly,[257] was a very broad and general expression, which did not in itself disclose *under which circumstances* a certain event was to be attributed to the creditor's sphere of risk. Marcellus[258] refers to a "iusta causa" which might entitle the creditor to refuse payment from his debtor. But only a hitch in the performance itself could constitute such a iusta causa: the fact that it was not tendered at the right time, at the right place or in the right manner. That he had fallen sick or was prevented from receiving performance by force or by bad weather was no excuse, as we know from Ulp. D. 13, 5, 18 pr.: ". . . proinde si valetudine impeditus aut vi aut tempestate petitor non venit, ipsi nocere Pomponius scribit." Thus it is widely accepted today that a creditor in Roman law—unlike a debtor—could be in mora, irrespective of whether he had been at fault or not.[259]

4. Consequences of mora creditoris in Roman law

(a) Alleviation of liability

What were the consequences of mora creditoris? First of all, and most importantly, the debtor was not released from his obligation. But since he had done what he was expected to do and since the fact that he had not been able to discharge his obligation was attributable to the creditor, he no longer had to carry the risk of accidental destruction. Moreover, just as his liability was augmented in a case of mora debitoris, it was relaxed as a consequence of mora creditoris: whatever he might have been responsible for previously, he was now liable only for dolus.[260] Thus, where he owed a specific thing and where this thing perished due to anything but his own dolus, he became free.[261] If fungibles or money were owed, the solution was slightly different; for even if (for instance) the specific slave that had been offered to the creditor subsequently died, the debtor was, strictly speaking, still both bound and able to deliver another one. The jurists helped by granting an exceptio doli:

> "Si cui homo legatus fuisset et per legatarium stetisset, quo minus Stichum, cum heres tradere volebat, acciperet, mortuo Sticho exceptio doli mali heredi proderit."[262]

[255] Paul. D. 18, 6, 5.
[256] Afr. D. 17, 1, 37; Cels. D. 19, 1, 38, 1; Ulp. D. 46, 3, 9, 1.
[257] Cf. supra, pp. 105 sq., 385, 730, 785 sqq.
[258] D. 46, 3, 72 pr.
[259] Cf. supra, note 252.
[260] Pomp. D. 18, 6, 18; Paul. D. 18, 6, 5; Pomp. D. 24, 3, 9.
[261] Sab./Iav. D. 45, 1, 105; Marc. D. 46, 3, 72 pr.
[262] Iul. D. 30, 84, 3; cf. also Marc. D. 46, 3, 72 pr.

(b) *Obsignatio and depositio*

Moreover, a debtor who had unsuccessfully tendered a sum of money was able to seal and thus deposit it at a public place.[263] The specific advantages of an offer followed by obsignatio and depositio were, firstly, that the accrual of interest was suspended ("ex eo die ratio non habebitur usurarum")[264] and, secondly, that it relieved the debtor of the risk of not being able to prove—if the money disappeared—that these specific coins had in fact been earmarked to discharge his debt and that their disappearance was not due to his dolus malus. Since the time of Diocletian, obsignatio and depositio had the effect of releasing the debtor from his obligation.[265] The authors of the ius commune, incidentally, received this institution,[266] a fact which probably goes some way towards explaining their lack of interest in mora creditoris. Strictly speaking, however, down to the days of codification, a debtor was able to place his creditor in mora by offering performance ("oblatio"), but he could effect complete release by following up oblatio by obsignatio and depositio. This is, for instance, the position as reflected in Pothier's *Traité des obligations*.[267] Oddly enough, and for no obvious reason, the code civil abandoned the institution of mora creditoris completely and merely provided a number of rules for what it refers to as "*consignation*".[268] In contrast to modern German law (and also, for instance, South African law)[269] the mere offer of performance does not have any consequences; the debtor must go through the whole cumbersome procedure of *consignation* if he wants to safeguard his position. What was once devised as a means of protecting the interests of the debtor has thus been strangely turned into an entirely unnecessary burden.[270]

(c) *Recovery of expenses and damages*

The alleviation of his liability with regard to the object owed and the possibility, as far as money was concerned, of depositing it in a public place: that did not always help the debtor. He could reasonably expect to be protected, too, where he had incurred—or was likely to

---

[263] Pap. D. 22, 1, 7; C. 4, 32, 19 pr. (Diocl.); Kaser, *RPr* I, pp. 639 sq.; R. Vigneron, *Offerre aut deponere. De l'origine de la procédure des offres réelles suivies de consignation* (1979), pp. 19 sqq., 51 sqq.

[264] Pap. D. 22, 1, 7.

[265] C. 8, 42, 9: "Obsignatione totius debitae pecuniae sollemniter facta liberationem contingere manifestum est. . . ."

[266] De Villiers, op. cit., note 241, pp. 353 sqq., 360 sqq.; Windscheid/Kipp, § 347; today §§ 372 sqq. BGB; De Wet en Yeats, pp. 171 sq.; *Odendaal v. Du Plessis* 1918 AD 470. Obsignatio and depositio were (and still are) no longer confined to money but may also be effected with regard to certain other movables.

[267] Cf. nn. 144, 283, 574.

[268] Artt. 1257 sqq. code civil; for a comparative discussion cf. Hüffer, op. cit., note 244, pp. 61 sqq.

[269] De Wet en Yeats, pp. 163 sqq.; Joubert, *Contract*, pp. 214 sqq.

[270] Cf. Vigneron, op. cit., note 263, pp. 13 sqq., 199 sqq.

incur—expenses for looking after and maintaining the object that he had been unable to transfer. Occasionally, the debtor was allowed to abandon the object in order to avoid such expenses. Thus, particularly, a vendor of wine was entitled to pour away the merchandise if the purchaser had failed to take delivery in time (normally 1 October);[271] after all, he needed the casks for his new harvest. "Licet autem venditori . . . effundere vinum", says Ulpian,[272] but he also tries to encourage the vendor to adopt, whenever possible, a less ruthless procedure:

> "[S]i tamen, cum posset effundere, non effundit, laudandus est potius: eapropter mercedem quoque doliorum potest exigere, sed ita demum, si interfuit eius inania esse vasa in quibus vinum fuit . . . vel si necesse habuit alia conducere dolia."

In other words if he chose to keep the wine, the vendor was able to claim the damages he had suffered as a result either of not being able to let his dolia or of having to hire somebody else's dolia in order to accommodate his new wine. This claim for damages[273] was also available to him in all those cases where he did not have the option of abandoning the object sold. This was the case, for instance, where the object concerned was a slave:

> "Si per emptorem steterit, quo minus ei mancipium traderetur, pro cibariis per arbitrium indemnitatem posse servari Sextus Aelius, Drusus dixerunt, quorum et mihi iustissima videtur esse sententia."[274]

The slave has to be fed during the time of the purchaser/creditor's mora and, according to Sextus Aelius, Livius Drusus and Celsus, the vendor could recover the respective expenses. This claim is based on the bona fides inherent in the contract of sale.[275] The purchaser's behaviour must thus have constituted a breach of good faith: it could not have been based on a good cause and must, at least typically, have constituted dolus. It appears to be likely, therefore, that the debtor's claim for damages on account of mora creditoris was based on fault and that, at least in this context, the "si per creditorem steterit" has to be interpreted in a narrower sense than for the other consequences of mora creditoris.[276]

---

[271] Cato, *De re rustica*, Cap. CXLVIII ("Locus vinis ad K. Octobres primas dabitur, Si ante non deportaverit, dominus vino quid volet faciet").

[272] D. 18, 6, 1, 3; for a different interpretation, see Otto Gradenwitz, "Das Ausgiessen des Weins und L. 1 § 3 de periculo et commodo", (1929) 37 *BIDR* 53 sqq.; contra: Wolf, *Error*, pp. 130 sq.Roman-Dutch customs did not tolerate such waste; see Groenewegen, *De Legibus Abrogatis*, ad Digest. Lib. XVIII, Tit. VI, l.1 § 3 licet; Voet, *Commentarius ad Pandectas*, Lib. XVIII, Tit. VI, IV.

[273] Cf. in particular Peter Apathy, "Mora accipiendi und Schadensersatz", (1984) 101 *ZSS* 190 sqq. According to the prevailing opinion, the debtor had only a ius retentionis which he was able to assert by way of an exceptio doli; cf. Kaser, *RPr* I, p. 518; Alfons Bürge, *Retentio im römischen Sachen- und Obligationenrecht* (1979), pp. 190 sq. For modern South African law, cf. supra, note 243.

[274] Cels. D. 19, 1, 38, 1.

[275] Cf. e.g. Okko Behrends, *Fraus legis*, p. 92; Apathy, (1984) 101 *ZSS* 195.

[276] Apathy, (1984) 101 *ZSS* 193 sqq.

(d) Purgatio morae

This way of looking at things would, incidentally, also bring the requirements for mora creditoris and mora debitoris into better harmony. That both institutions are sometimes hardly distinguishable is apparent from Pomp. D. 19, 1, 9: "Si is, qui lapides ex fundo emerit, tollere eos nolit, ex vendito agi cum eo potest, ut eos tollat." Stones have been sold, but the purchaser fails to remove them from the vendor's estate. Pomponius does not specify whether we are dealing with a case of mora creditoris or mora debitoris (the purchaser having infringed an ancillary duty imposed upon him by the contract).[277] Whatever the case may be, he is prepared to grant the actio venditi (for the vendor's interest in the removal of the stones). It is thus not inconceivable that the differentiation did not matter to the Roman lawyers, at least as far as the claim for damages arising from contracts of sale was concerned. As under § 433 II BGB, the purchaser was seen to be obliged to take delivery of the object sold, and if he culpably infringed that duty, he was exposed to a claim for damages.

But whatever the exact delimitation between mora debitoris and mora creditoris, it is obvious that both could not exist at the same time with regard to one and the same performance. If A had promised to deliver a slave by 10 October, he fell in mora debitoris unless he had offered performance by the end of that day. If in fact he had made such an offer, it was the creditor who was in mora. What happened if the debtor attempted to perform on 20 October? Provided that his belated "oblatio" met all the other contractual requirements (i.e. proper manner, proper place), it had the effect of bringing the consequences of mora debitoris to an end; it resulted in what was called purgatio (or: emendatio) morae. This idea goes back to Celsus "adulescens", who is reported to have stated "eum, qui moram fecit in solvendo Sticho quem promiserat, posse emendare eam moram postea offerendo".[278] Such purgatio morae occurred even if the creditor did not accept performance, because then, again, it was he who fell in mora (creditoris). Or, to put it the other way round: mora creditoris terminated mora debitoris. The reverse, incidentally, is also true: mora debitoris terminated mora creditoris. For the creditor, too, had the opportunity of "purging" his delay by subsequently being prepared to accept performance.[279] Any further delay was then attributable to the debtor and entailed the consequences of mora debitoris.

---

277 In the latter sense e.g. Friedrich Mommsen, *Mora*, op. cit., note 249, pp. 134 sq.; Kaser, *RPr* I, p. 551.

278 Paul. D. 45, 1, 91, 3; cf. further e.g. Paul. D. 45, 1, 73, 2; Magdelain, "Note sur la 'Purgatio Morae' ", in: *Droits de l'Antiquité et Sociologie Juridique, Mélanges Henri Lévy-Bruhl* (1959), pp. 199 sqq.; Sturm, *Stipulatio Aquiliana*, pp. 78 sqq.; Knütel, *Stipulatio poenae*, pp. 185 sqq.

279 Pomp. D. 18, 6, 18.

VI. QUOD INTEREST, DAMAGES AND BREACH OF CONTRACT

1. Restoration, damages and *"Differenztheorie"*

Before concluding this chapter, we still have to say something about what a plaintiff could claim in case of breach of contract—more particularly, about the crucial concepts of "quod interest" or, as the modern lawyer would put it, of "damages". The loose equation of "quod interest" and "damages" must, however, not lead us to the conclusion that both are in fact the same. The focal point of the modern German law of damages is a uniform and comprehensive concept of damages,[280] as embodied in the famous *"Differenztheorie"*.[281] In terms of this "theory", the recoverable loss is defined as the difference between the plaintiff's position as in fact it is and as it would have been but for the interference of the damaging event. Since, as a rule, only material damages are recoverable, this involves a comparison of the actual value of the plaintiff's assets after the damaging event with their hypothetical value, established on the assumption that this event had not occurred. Does that mean that compensation consists in payment of a sum of money and that therefore a claim for breach of contract necessarily leads to a condemnatio pecuniaria? Not according to the BGB and some of the other codes of central Europe:[282] in the first place the defendant owes (and has to be condemned in) restoration and only in the second instance a sum of money. Thus we read in § 249, 1 BGB:

> "A person obliged to make compensation shall *restore* the situation which would have existed if the circumstances rendering him liable to make compensation had not occurred."[283]

---

[280] For a comprehensive comparative analysis, see Treitel, op. cit., note 169, nn. 40 sqq.

[281] Cf. Lange, *Schadensersatz*, pp. 17 sqq. For England cf. e.g. *Livingstone v. The Rawyards Coal Co.* (1880) 5 AC 25 at 39; for South Africa: *Union Government v. Warneke* 1911 AD 657 at 665.

[282] Cf. e.g. § 1323 ABGB; § 79 I 6 PrALR.

[283] The idea that, in the first place, restoration (in kind) is owed did not originate in Roman law, but in the teachings of the Church. Of crucial importance was a passage in a letter of St. Augustine to a bishop by the name of Macedonius (cf. *Decretum Gratiani*, Secunda Pars, Causa XIV, Quaestio VI, c. 1.), according to which restoration is a necessary part of and prerequisite for true penitence: "non remittetur peccatum, nisi restituatur ablatum." St. Thomas Aquinas further developed this idea and created the dogmatical foundations of the theological doctrine of restitution ("restitutio est actus commutativae justitiae"); in Pope Boniface VIII's Liber Sextus it received final, legislative sanction ("peccatum non dimittitur, nisi restituatur ablatum": Regula iuris IV). Via the late Spanish scholastic writers and their followers (most notably the Jesuit Leonardus Lessius in Leuven) the doctrine influenced Grotius ("Culpam obligare ad restitutionem damni": *De jure belli ac pacis*, Lib. II, Cap. XVII, I) and, through him, the subsequent natural lawyers. To them, the obligation to make restitution (where possible) appeared to be the obvious consequence of a breach of the natural duty of alterum non laedere: why should the aggrieved party be obliged to accept a compensation in money, if something had been taken away from him or damaged that he had particularly treasured (Joachim Georg Darjes). Courts and writers under the usus modernus and during the early 19th century remained sceptical, and the final breakthrough came only with the acceptance of the restitution doctrine by Friedrich

And § 251 I BGB adds:

> "Insofar as restitution is impossible or is insufficient to compensate the creditor, the person liable shall compensate him in money."[284]

2. Omnis condemnatio pecuniaria

Roman procedure, on the other hand, as we have stressed repeatedly, was dominated by the principle of omnis condemnatio pecuniaria.[285] Every judgment had to be for a definite sum of money, and that implied, for instance, that restoration in kind was not enforceable. Nor, more importantly, was specific performance.[286] Furthermore, as has been set out previously, the disadvantaged party was not able to rescind the contract.[287] A claim for the payment of "damages" was therefore not just one out of the several remedies available to the parties to a contract; condemnatio pecuniaria was the only form of legal redress obtainable to them. The concept of "damages" as a *specific kind of remedy* was alien to the Roman lawyers; for every single action the question had to be asked in what sum of money the defendant had to be condemned.

This was determined, to a certain extent, by the procedural formula. With regard to actiones stricti iuris containing an intentio certa, the judge was usually asked to determine "quanti ea res est" and to condemn the defendant accordingly.[288] "Si paret N^{m} N^{m} A^{o} A^{o} Pamphilum servum dare oportere" is a typical intentio certa, and the judge could only condemn the defendant in the value of the slave Pamphilus or absolve. Thus, at least originally, the yardstick for the determination of the sum for which judgment had to be given was an entirely objective one.[289] Whether or not the individual plaintiff had suffered a loss that went beyond the value of the object owed was (at least originally) not important.[290]

Mommsen, *Zur Lehre von dem Interesse* (1855), pp. 12 sqq., Windscheid/Kipp, § 257 and other pandectists; cf. further "Motive", in: *Mugdan*, vol. II, p. 11, but also Heinrich von Degenkolb, "Der spezifische Inhalt des Schadensersatzes", (1890) 76 *Archiv für die civilistische Praxis* 1 sqq. For all this, see the thorough historical study by Udo Wolter, *Das Prinzip der Naturalrestitution in § 249 BGB* (1985). In Roman law, some formulae (most notably the rei vindicatio) contained a clausula arbitraria ("neque ea res restituetur"). Whilst the defendant was thus free to absolve himself by restoring the object of the dispute, condemnation ultimately had to be for a sum of money (for details Kaser, *RZ*, pp. 256 sqq.).

[284] Relief in money is, however, also available under the conditions laid down in §§ 249,2, 250 and 251 II BGB. In actual practice, relief in money is the rule, restoration in kind the exception.

[285] Cf. e.g. supra, pp. 35 sq., 771 sq.

[286] Cf. supra, pp. 770 sqq.

[287] Cf. supra, pp. 578 sq., 801 sq.

[288] Cf. supra, pp. 95 sq., 771, 784.

[289] Cf. e.g. Ulp. D. 2, 7, 5, 1 ("quod in veritate est"); Ulp. D. 27, 3, 1, 20 ("rei tantum aestimationem").

[290] Already in classical law cautious attempts were made to take into account the concrete loss of the disadvantaged party, particularly as far as actions for certam rem reddere (cf. supra, p. 788), for restituere (cf., for example, supra, p. 665, note 39, p. 664, note 101, p. 825, note 283 in fine) and those that required estimation of quanti ea

The situation was different in the case of incertum obligations, particularly the bonae fidei iudicia, where the judge had to condemn in "quidquid ob eam N^m N^m A^o A^o dare facere oportet (ex fide bona)". Here all the individual circumstances of the case had to be taken into account and what the judge was, essentially, instructed to do was to estimate what sum of money it would be equitable for the defendant to give to the plaintiff.[291] That did, of course, not necessarily coincide with the (objective) value of the object of performance. It could comprise a whole variety of further items; for naturally it was equitable to compensate the plaintiff, as far as possible, for any loss that he had suffered as a result of the defendant's behaviour. This, then, is where both the problem and the notion of "damages" appeared on the scene, but the Roman lawyers were far from conceptualizing this notion or from tying it to rigid definitions.

3. Id quod interest

They usually referred to "id quod interest" that had to be awarded to the plaintiff. "Quod interest" did not denote a specific method of assessment; in particular, it did not encapsulate a Roman form of "*Differenztheorie*". Quod actoris interest refers to the plaintiff's "interest" (in the modern sense of the word): he has to get what he was interested in, what concerned him, what was of consequence to him; for, interestingly, the expression is not derived from interesse (= to be in between) but from the phrase "quod (mea, tua, nostra etc.) in re est" (what is in it for me, you, us, etc.).[292] Generally speaking, quod interest was the more modern and flexible counterconcept to the somewhat crude and limiting idea of awarding "quanti ea res est", and it signified a shift from an objective, standardized point of view to a more sophisticated and equitable approach, characterized by individualizing and, on the whole, subjective[293] criteria. What quod interest entailed could differ from action to action and from case to case and every generalization would be dangerous. The classical lawyers did little to develop and systematize this area of the law. Assessment of quod interest was largely left to the individual iudex, about whose activity, in turn, we hardly possess any sources.[294] All we can do, therefore, is to list a variety of items that were capable of being included sub titulo quod interest.

Obviously, in case of non-performance, the value of the object owed provided the most convenient starting point for the assessment: this

---

res *erit* (supra, p. 771) were concerned: Kaser, *RPr* I, pp. 499 sq.; Medicus, *Id quod interest*, pp. 245 sqq., 260 sqq., 266 sqq.; cf. further on this development Sebastiano Tafaro, *La interpretatio ai verba 'quanti ea res est' nella giurisprudenza romana* (1980).

[291] Cf. *Inst.* IV, 6, 30: "In bonae fidei autem iudiciis libera potestas permitti videtur iudici ex bono et aequo aestimandi, quantum actori restitui debeat."

[292] Honsell, *Quod interest*, pp. 30 sqq., 63 sq.; Kaser, *RPr* I, p. 500; Honsell/Mayer-Maly/Selb, p. 224.

[293] Honsell, *Quod interest*, p. 172; but see Medicus, *Id quod interest*, pp. 326 sq.

[294] Medicus, *Id quod interest*, p. 337; on the scarcity of sources dealing with individual items of "damages", cf. further Honsell/Mayer-Maly/Selb, p. 227.

value, after all, was according to the contractual "programme" supposed to have been transferred to the plaintiff. Apart from that, the plaintiff's loss of profits could be included. Paulus (". . . quantum mea interfuit, id est quantum mihi abest quantumque lucrari potui")[295] confirms that in abstracto, and Neratius provides a good example when he writes:

> "Et non solum quod ipse per eum adquisii praestare debeo, sed et id, quod emptor iam tunc sibi tradito servo adquisiturus fuisset."[296]

A vendor who owes a slave falls in mora. He has to hand over to the purchaser whatever he acquires, in the course of his mora, through the slave. But if the purchaser would have acquired more, had the slave been handed over in time, the vendor is even liable for this extra amount. This form of loss has since the Middle Ages come to be referred to as "lucrum cessans", as opposed to "damnum emergens", the damage to the existing assets of the plaintiff.[297] Under certain circumstances, consequential loss could be recovered, particularly where defective objects had been sold or leased. The discussions surrounding leaky vats, toxic plants and the delivery of infectious cattle spring to mind.[298] Where the creditor had incurred a penalty or forfeited a pledge as a result of his debtor's mora, he was able to assert this loss too.[299] The same applied if it turned out that the creditor himself had now become liable to a third party.[300] Where a purchaser had a specific interest in an object that exceeded its (objective) market value, he could claim on the basis of the former: what mattered was quod *actoris* interest. This is confirmed by Ulp. D. 19, 1, 1 pr.:

> "Si res vendita non tradatur, in id quod interest agitur, hoc est quod rem habere interest emptoris: hoc autem interdum pretium egreditur, si pluris interest, quam res valet vel empta est."[301]

---

[295] D. 46, 8, 13 pr.

[296] D. 19, 1, 31, 1; Honsell, *Quod interest*, pp. 18 sq.

[297] For further details on the recoverability of lucrum cessans in Roman law, see C. 7, 47, 2 ("Et hoc non solum in damno, sed etiam in lucro nostra amplectitur constitutio, quia et ex eo veteres quod interest statuerunt"); Honsell, *Quod interest*, pp. 16 sqq. In later centuries, recovery of lucrum cessans was often refused (except as far as merchants were concerned) on the basis of Paul. D. 19, 1, 21, 3 (according to Honsell, *Quod interest*, pp. 7 sqq. a special case, not capable of generalization). The canonists in particular emphasized the distinction between damnum emergens and lucrum cessans, since recovery of the latter tended to come into conflict with the usury doctrine of the Church. For all details on lucrum cessans during the history of the ius commune, cf. Endemann, *Studien*, vol. II, pp. 276 sqq.; Lange, *Schadensersatz und Privatstrafe*, pp. 32 sqq.; Wieling, *Interesse und Privatstrafe*, pp. 109 sqq. In the modern law of damages, the compensation also has to include lost profits; the distinction between damnum emergens and lucrum cessans is without practical significance: cf. e.g. art. 1149 Code Civil, § 252 BGB.

[298] Cf. Ulp. D. 19, 2, 19, 1; Pomp. D. 19, 1, 6, 4; Iul./Ulp. D. 19, 1, 13 pr. and 1, and the discussion supra, pp. 309 sq., 365 sqq.

[299] Ulp. D. 13, 4, 2, 8; Honsell, *Quod interest*, pp. 169 sqq.

[300] Kaser, *RPr* I, p. 501.

[301] Honsell, *Quod interest*, pp. 15 sq.; also Berthold Kupisch, "Id quod interest bei Nichterfüllung und Verzug des Verkäufers", (1975) 43 *TR* 18 sq.; for an example, taken from the law of delict, cf. Paul. D. 9, 2, 22, 1. Special rules may have applied for the sale of fungible goods with a constantly varying market price (such as oil, wine or grain): Honsell,

4. The lex Sancimus (C. 7, 47, 1)

By the time of Justinian, the formulae had disappeared and the distinction between the estimation, in some cases, of quanti ea res est and, in others, of quod interest no longer needed to be perpetuated. Thus, the individualized way of assessing the specific plaintiff's loss was extended to the actiones stricti iuris; wherever the judge ordered compensation in money (rather than specific performance),[302] the defendant was condemned in id quod interest.[303] Yet Justinian was not altogether pleased with the intricacies of the case law surrounding this key concept. He complained about the possibility that "quod re vera inducitur damnum . . . ex quibusdam machinationibus et immodicis perversionibus in circuitus inextricabiles redigatur".[304] Thus he may have cut down on classical distinctions and controversies. More importantly, however, he resurrected the ancient policy of clumsy generalizations, by introducing an arbitrary and purely mechanical limit to the extent of the defendant's liability for damages. "In omnibus casibus", he ruled,

> "qui certam habent quantitatem vel naturam . . . hoc quod interest dupli quantitatem minime excedere: in aliis autem casibus, qui incerti esse videntur, iudices . . . requirere, ut, quod re vera inducitur damnum, hoc reddatur."[305]

Generations of lawyers have been mystified by the terms of this poorly drafted enactment. What was the difference between "cases which have a certain quantity or nature" and "other cases which appear to be uncertain"? What was to be regarded as the simplum on which the calculation of quantitas dupli had to be based? These were the two main questions that agitated the minds of countless writers down to the 19th century;[306] for C. 7, 47, 1 remained part and parcel of the ius commune, and the continued validity of the limit of quantitas dupli was accepted, at least as far as contractual claims for damages were concerned, by the

---

Quod interest, pp. 1 sqq.; but see Medicus, *Id quod interest*, pp. 30 sqq.; Kupisch, (1975) 43 *TR* 1 sqq. An immaterial interest could not normally be recovered; cf. e.g. Kaser, *RPr* I, p. 491; but see also Pap. D. 17, 1, 54 pr. and Honsell, *Quod interest*, pp. 153 sqq.; Fritz Raber, "Zum 'pretium affectionis'", in: *Festgabe für Arnold Herdlitczka* (1972), pp. 197 sqq. For the ius commune, see Lange, *Schadensersatz und Privatstrafe*, pp. 46 sqq.; Wieling, *Interesse und Privatstrafe*, pp. 123 sqq.; for modern law cf. § 253 BGB; Lange, *Schadensersatz*, pp. 34 sqq.; Treitel, op. cit., note 169, nn. 110 sqq. On the question "an commodum . . . compensari cum damno . . . debeat" we find an isolated decision by the Emperor Marc Aurel ("abstine commodo si damnum petis"): Ulp. D. 17, 2, 23, 1; further Honsell, *Quod interest*, pp. 163 sqq. On compensatio lucri cum damno under the ius commune, see Lange, *Schadensersatz und Privatstrafe*, pp. 65 sqq.; Wieling, *Interesse und Privatstrafe*, pp. 215 sqq.; on its modern German equivalent of "*Vorteilsausgleichung*", see Lange, *Schadensersatz*, pp. 298 sqq.; Treitel, op. cit., note 169, n. 105.

[302] Cf. supra, pp. 772 sqq.

[303] Medicus, *Id quod interest*, pp. 338 sqq.; Kaser, *RPr* II, pp. 344 sqq.

[304] C. 7, 47, 1.

[305] C. 7, 47, 1, on which, see Medicus, *Id quod interest*, pp. 288 sqq.; Schindler, *Justinians Haltung zur Klassik*, pp. 259 sqq.; H.J. Erasmus, " 'n Regshistoriese Beskouing van Codex 7, 47", (1968) 31 *THRHR* 213 sqq.

[306] Cf. Lange, *Schadensersatz und Privatstrafe*, pp. 56 sqq.; Wieling, *Interesse und Privatstrafe*, pp. 89 sqq.; Mommsen, *Interesse*, op. cit., note 283, pp. 235 sqq.

Roman-Dutch authorities[307] as much as under the German usus modernus[308] and pandectist doctrine.[309]

5. Foreseeability and contemplation test

(a) *Molinaeus, Pothier and the code civil*

A very interesting and, in the long run, influential twist was given to the discussion about C. 7, 47, 1 in French literature. It appears to have been Molinaeus who for the first time tried to rationalize the statutory limitation of duplum in terms of foreseeability.[310] "Ut enim ratio decidendi totius legis est odium immensitatis", he wrote,[311]

> ". . . ita particularis ratio limitationis in casibus certis est, *quia verisimiliter non fuit praevisum*, nec cogitatum de suscipiendo maiori damno, vel periculo ultra rem principalem, quam sit res ipsa principalis. Haec autem ratio quandoque; etiam in casibus incertis quadantenus reperitur".

For both casus certi and incerti it is equitable to limit the amount of damages recoverable to those that could be foreseen at the time when the contract was entered into: this is the rationale which underlies and finds expression in both parts of Justinian's enactment (casus certus and casus incertus).[312] Pothier generalized this idea and detached it from the specific provisions contained in C. 7, 47, 1. According to him, these provisions were part of French law, not because but only as far as they were based on *"la raison et l'équité naturelle"*.[313] Thus he formulated the following test for the limitation of (contractual) damages:

> *". . . le débiteur n'est tenu que des dommages et intérêts qu'on a pu prévoir, lors du contrat, que le créancier pourrait souffrir de l'inexécution de l'obligation."*[314]

Reason: the debtor cannot be considered as having subjected himself to any risks that lie beyond the limits of foreseeability.[315]

---

307 Groenewegen, *Tractatus de legibus abrogatis*, Cod. Lib. VII, Tit. XLVII; Voet, *Commentarius ad Pandectas*, Lib. XLV, Tit. I, X. The rule has been abrogated by disuse in South Africa: Erasmus, (1968) 31 *THRHR* 237 sqq.; De Wet en Yeats, p. 207.

308 Cf. e.g. Struve, *Syntagma*, Exerc. XLIV, Lib. XLII, Tit. I, V.

309 Windscheid/Kipp, § 258, 1; cf. further Wieling, *Interesse und Privatstrafe*, pp. 106 sqq.

310 Generally on foreseeability as a device in order to limit damages, cf. Treitel, op. cit., note 169, nn. 77 sqq.

311 *Tractatus de eo quod interest* (Venetiis, 1574), n. 60. "No treatise on damages has perhaps had a more profound influence on the development of the law of damages than the Tractatus de eo quod interest of Molinaeus": H.J. Erasmus, "Aspects of the History of the South African Law of Damages", (1975) 38 *THRHR* 116 sq. For a recent translation of Molinaeus' treatise into Afrikaans ("Verhandeling oor skadevergoeding") cf. H.J. Erasmus (ed.) (Lex Patria, Johannesburg, 1973).

312 Thus he argues that obviously "hanc legem aequissimam esse, et optimis rationibus fundatam, non otiosam, nec incongruam" (n. 58).

313 *Traité des obligations*, n. 164.

314 *Traité des obligations*, n. 160.

315 *Traité des obligations*, n. 160; "de schuldenaar wordt geächt zig alleenlijk aan deezen onderworpen te hebben" (Van der Linden, *Verhandeling van Contracten en andere Verbintenissen* (Leyden, 1804)).

(b) *Hadley v. Baxendale*

Pothier's views, as usual, were avidly received by the 19th-century English courts and formed the basis, in this instance, of the contemplation doctrine, as formulated in the celebrated decision of *Hadley v. Baxendale*: in cases of breach of contract such damages (apart from the "general damages") can be claimed

> "as may reasonably be supposed to have been in the contemplation of both parties, at the time they made the contract, as a probable result of the breach of it."[316]

This test still dominates the discussion in England[317] and it has also been taken over into South African law.[318] As early as 1908 Kotzé JP referred to the contemplation theory, as enunciated in *Hadley v. Baxendale*, as "the clear rule of our law",[319] and in the *Victoria Falls* case of 1915 the Appellate Division confirmed that it would be inequitable to make one of the parties to a contract responsible for "special consequences", "which could not have been in his contemplation when he entered into the contract".[320] Via Ernst Rabel[321] and Ernst von Caemmerer,[322] and in the form of the doctrine of the attribution of risks in accordance with the protective ambit of the contract,[323] the contemplation test has even found its way into German textbooks and commentaries.

6. Interesse circa rem and extra rem

Codex 7, 47, 1 was historically one of the first deliberate attempts to grapple with the problem of limiting liability for damages. Another most influential distinction aiming in the same directon was drawn on the basis of an isolated reference by Paulus (?) to the interest (of a purchaser) *relating to the object (of the sale) itself*:

---

[316] (1854) 9 Exch 341 at 354; on the socio-historical importance of this decision, see Richard Danzig, (1975) 4 *Journal of Legal Studies* 249 sqq. (also in (1977) 6 *Ius Commune* 234 sqq.); cf. also Janet T. Lauda, "*Hadley v. Baxendale* and the Expansion of the Middleman Economy", (1987) 16 *Journal of Legal Studies* 455 sqq.

[317] Cf. e.g. *Koufos v. Czarnikow Ltd.* [1969] 1 AC 350 (HL) at 421 sq.; *McGregor on Damages* (13th ed., 1972), nn. 180 sqq.

[318] For details, see Erasmus, (1975) 38 *THRHR* 362 sqq.; Reinhard Zimmermann, "Der Einfluss Pothiers auf das römisch-holländische Recht in Südafrika" (1985) 102 *ZSS* (GA) 178 sqq.

[319] *Emslie v. African Merchants Ltd.* 1908 EDC 82 at 91.

[320] *Victoria Falls & Transvaal Power Co. Ltd. v. Consolidated Langlaagte Mines Ltd.* 1915 AD 1 at 22. But see subsequently *Lavery & Co. Ltd. v. Jungheinrich* 1931 AD 156 at 162 sqq., 176, where the contemplation test has (possibly) been superseded by a "convention principle": the expectations of the parties may only be taken into account, if they have become "virtually . . . a term of the contract". Cf. further *Shatz Investments (Pty.) Ltd. v. Kalovyrnas* 1976 (2) SA 545 (A) at 551B–554F (obiter); Kerr, *Contract*, pp. 454 sqq. For a very critical evaluation of Pothier's theory, see De Wet en Yeats, p. 205 ("gekunsteld, teoreties onsuiwer en prakties onbruikbaar"); but cf. e.g. Wieling, *Interesse und Privatstrafe*, p. 53.

[321] *Warenkauf*, vol. I, pp. 491 sqq.

[322] "Das Problem des Kausalzusammenhangs im Privatrecht", in: *Gesammelte Schriften*, vol. I (1968), pp. 395 sqq.

[323] *Lehre von der Zurechnung nach dem Schutzzweck des Vertrages* or, more generally, *der haftungsbegründenden Norm*: cf. e.g. Lange, *Schadensersatz*, pp. 76 sqq.

"Cum per venditorem steterit, quo minus rem tradat, omnis utilitas emptoris in aestimationem venit, quae modo circa ipsam rem consistit."[324]

He then gives two examples to illustrate the type of interest that goes beyond this limit:

". . . neque enim si potuit ex vino puta negotiari et lucrum facere, id aestimandum est, non magis si triticum emerit et ob eam rem, quod non sit traditum, familia eius fame laboraverit: nam pretium tritici, non servorum fame necatorum consequitur"—

the disappointed purchaser of wine cannot claim his loss of profits, a vendor who failed to deliver grain cannot be held responsible for the damage that arose as a result of the fact that his slaves did not have anything to eat. Whether the limitation of the recoverable interest to the utilitas circa ipsam rem represents classical Roman law[325] or whether the text has in its essential parts been corrupted by Tribonian,[326] cannot be determined with any degree of certainty. Historically, in any event, it provided the starting point for the distinction between the interesse circa rem and extra rem that was introduced by the glossators[327] and has, in one or other form, dominated the discussion for centuries.[328] According to Accursius, for instance, only the direct loss (interesse circa rem) could be claimed in the case of what he termed a "non factum" (for example: failure to effect delivery); when it came to a malefactum, however (for example: delivery of a defective object), the vendor was liable for the full interesse extra rem (that is, consequential loss). This was an attempt to reconcile D. 19, 1, 21, 3 with Ulp. D. 19, 1, 13 pr.: here we find the vendor of a piece of cattle infected with a contagious disease being held liable not only for quanti minoris emptor empturus esset but for "omnia detrimenta, quae ex ea emptione emptor traxerit"—and that means for the damage the purchaser suffered on account of the fact that his other animals caught the infection and consequently died.

Of course, it is possible to distinguish these two cases on the basis that in the one a deficient merx was delivered, whereas in the other no delivery took place at all, and then to argue "peius est male tradere quam omnino non tradere".[329] But there is another feature of Ulpian's text which is equally suitable as a starting point for dogmatic distinctions. The vendor of the cattle knew about the infection: "sciens retinuit et emptorem decepit". Paulus D. 19, 1, 21, 3, on the other hand, merely states "[c]um per venditorem steterit, quo minus rem tradat". Thus, it became increasingly popular to award interesse extra

---

[324] D. 19, 1, 21, 3.

[325] Arangio-Ruiz, *Compravendita*, pp. 232 sqq.; Medicus, *Id quod interest*, pp. 35 sqq., 321 sq.; Kupisch, (1975) 43 *TR* 16 sqq.; cf. also Honsell, *Quod interest*, pp. 7 sqq. (special case, not capable of generalization).

[326] Franz Heymann, "Haftung für unmittelbaren und mittelbaren Schaden beim Kauf", in: *Studi in onore di Pietro Bonfante*, vol. II (1930), pp. 450 sqq.

[327] Lange, *Schadensersatz und Privatstrafe*, pp. 19 sqq.; also Erasmus, (1975) 38 *THRHR* 115 sq.

[328] Wieling, *Interesse und Privatstrafe*, pp. 26 sqq., 41 sqq.

[329] Gl. Non servorum ad D. 19, 1, 21, 3.

rem only in cases of fraud.[330] Pothier was one of the authors who adopted this line of argument and combined it with his contemplation theory. In general, he said, the parties are deemed to have contemplated the damages which the creditor might suffer with respect to the thing which is the object of the contract (damni propter rem ipsam).[331] When, however, it is the fraud of the debtor that gives rise to the claim for damages, liability extends to all damages in respect of any other property (*dommages extrinsèques*), irrespective of whether the debtor could be presumed to have subjected himself to them or not; *"car celui, qui commet un dol, s'oblige, velit, nolit, à la réparation de tout le tort que ce dol causera"*.[332] This is (of course) also the view of the French code civil.[333]

In Roman-Dutch jurisprudence and the German usus modernus the twofold division of interesse (circa rem or intrinsecum and extra rem or extrinsecum) lost much of its significance. The terminology became imprecise and was muddled up with other criteria. Some equated damnum extrinsecum with damnum remotum,[334] others interesse extra rem and lucrum cessans.[335, 336] South African courts have sometimes even used the terms "extrinsic damages" and "intrinsic damages" in

[330] Cf. e.g. Ulrich Huber, *Praelectiones*, Pars II, Lib. XIII, Tit. III, n. 11; cf. further §§ 285 sqq. I 5 PrALR, § 1324 ABGB; Rudolf von Jhering, "Das Schuldmoment im römischen Privatrecht", in: *Vermischte Schriften juristischen Inhalts* (1879), pp. 215 sqq., all differentiating the extent to which damages may be recovered according to the degree of the wrongdoer's fault. According to Glück, vol. 4, p. 447, lucrum cessans may be claimed only in case of dolus (or culpa lata). In modern German law, full damages are recoverable in case of (any kind of) fault. There have, however, been tendencies to move away from this harsh all-or-nothing view; for a comparative overview, see Hans Stoll, "Die Reduktionsklausel im Schadensrecht aus rechtsvergleichender Sicht", (1970) 34 *RabelsZ* 481 sqq.

[331] *Traité des obligations*, n. 161. Example: If the vendor does not deliver the horse that he has sold, the purchaser may claim the sum he needed to spend in order to buy another horse; "[b]ut if this purchaser was a canon, who for want of having the horse that I had engaged to deliver to him, and not having been enabled to get another, was prevented from arriving at the place of his benefice in time to be entitled to his revenue; I should not be liable for the loss which he sustained thereby, although it was occasioned by the non-performance of my obligation." (trans. W.D. Evans).

[332] *Traité des obligations*, n. 166.

[333] Artt. 1150 sq. Even in case of "dol", however, recovery of damages is limited to those that are direct ("*une suite immediate et directe de l'inexécution de la convention*"): art. 1151; Pothier, *Traité des obligations*, n. 167. This is not based, as Rabel thought (*Warenkauf*, p. 477), on the circa rem/extra rem distinction, but serves to exclude those damages that have no "necessary relation" to the vendor's dol (Nicholas, *FLC*, p. 224); cf. the example discussed by Pothier, n. 167; further Wieling, *Interesse und Privatstrafe*, pp. 52 sqq.

[334] Struve, *Syntagma*, Exerc. XLIV, Lib. XLII, Tit. I, V.

[335] Glück, vol. 4, p. 447; Andreas Gail, cf. Erasmus, (1975) 38 *THRHR* 116; Wieling, *Interesse und Privatstrafe*, p. 117; cf. also Endemann, *Studien*, vol. II, p. 292.

[336] A new line of argument was developed by Contius (Professor at Bourges during the 16th century) and Donellus, who stressed the need for a causal link between the damaging act and the loss suffered. Only the loss for which the act was a conditio sine qua non is recoverable (and thus constitutes the interesse circa rem): cf. Wieling, *Interesse und Privatstrafe*, pp. 45 sqq.; Erasmus, (1975) 38 *THRHR* 116; also Glück, vol. 4, pp. 443 sqq. On causation (in Germany: "adequate" causation) as a device to limit liability, cf. Rabel, *Warenkauf*, pp. 486 sqq.; Treitel, op. cit., note 169, nn. 91 sqq.; Wieling, *Interesse und Privatstrafe*, pp. 228 sqq.

order to refer to the (English) distinction between special and general damages.[337]

7. "Mare amplissimum, in quo pauci sine periculo navigarunt"

All in all, the rules and principles governing (and limiting) the recovery of (contractual) damages degenerated into one of the largest and most complex legal minefields of the ius commune.[338] Petrus Rebuffus' well-known "Arbor super interesse"[339] gives some idea of the efforts that were made to accommodate the Roman sources within a comprehensive conceptual framework: on it we find no less than 48 subdivisions of the interesse. Such subdivisions were ultimately rendered superfluous with the advent, in the 19th century, of the *"Differenztheorie"*.[340] Based on a misinterpretation of the Roman concept of "quod interest" ("what is in between"), it nevertheless had an immediate and lasting impact, for it satisfied the pandectists' desire for a clear conceptual formula, which appeared to reduce the problem to a simple mathematical operation without involving any value judgements.[341] The man who so ingeniously read into the sources what suited contemporary legal science? It was Friedrich Mommsen, once again.[342]

---

[337] *Lavery & Co. Ltd. v. Jungheinrich* 1931 AD 156 at 174 sq.; *Whitfield v. Phillips* 1957 (3) SA 318 (A) at 329D–E; *Shatz Investments (Pty.) Ltd. v. Kalovyrnas* 1976 (2) SA 545 (A) at 550F–551A. On "general" and "special" damages in English law, see MacGregor, op. cit., note 317, nn. 16 sqq.; in South African law Erasmus/Gauntlett, in: Joubert (ed.), *The Law of South Africa*, vol. 7 (1979), n. 11.

[338] Coing, p. 438. Scaccia exclaimed "haec materia est profundissima et longissima, et est obscura sicut alia, quae sit in corpore juris, et amplectitur mare amplissimum, in quo pauci sine periculo navigarunt et propter ejus subjectam materiam turbatur totus mundus" (cf. Endemann, *Studien*, vol. II, p. 244); Anton Fumeus likened anybody venturing into this field of law to Daedalus: "Qui de eo quod interest, pro iure civili scripserunt, mihi videntur optimo iure Dedali nominandi, struxerunt enim multis ambagibus inextricabiles vias, vel potius pervias" (cf. Wieling, *Interesse und Privatstrafe*, p. 4; cf. further the quotations on p. 2).

[339] Reproduced in Lange, *Schadensersatz und Privatstrafe*, p. 30. The most important of these—apart from the distinction of interesse circa rem and extra rem—was the threefold subdivision into interesse commune (market value of the res (concerned), interesse conventum (its agreed price) and interesse singulare (based on the affectio of the particular plaintiff); it was derived from Paul. D. 9, 2, 33 pr. and Paul. D. 35, 2, 63 pr. For details, see Lange, *Schadensersatz und Privatstrafe*, pp. 22 sqq.; cf. also Wieling, *Interesse und Privatstrafe*, pp. 67 sqq.; Erasmus, (1975) 38 *THRHR* 14 sq. It was rejected earlier by Jacobus de Ravanis, later by Molinaeus (*Tractatus de eo quod interest*, n. 12) and others, and it subsequently disappeared.

[340] Cf. supra, p. 824.

[341] For a criticism of the *Differenztheorie* cf. e.g. Heinrich Honsell, "Herkunft und Kritik des Interessebegriffs im Schadensersatzrecht", 1973 *Juristische Schulung* 69 sqq.; Wolfgang Grunsky, in: *Münchener Kommentar*, vol, II (2nd ed., 1985), Vor § 249, n. 7.

[342] *Interesse*, op. cit., note 283, pp. 3 sqq.; the French humanist, Franciscus Hotomannus, had, however, already defined the concept of interest in very similar terms some centuries earlier; cf. Wieling, *Interesse und Privatstrafe*, p. 18 sq.

PART VII

CHAPTER 26

Unjustified Enrichment

I. CONDICTIO

1. Indebitum solutum

A sells his horse to B. Some weeks later, he duly delivers the animal to the purchaser. When he sues him for the purchase price, the contract of sale turns out to have been invalid.

Obviously, under these circumstances, A must be able to recover the horse from B: for it would be blatantly unfair if B were allowed to keep what he has acquired without having to render counterperformance. A's claim can, however, be based neither on delict nor on contract; B, by accepting delivery of the animal, did not act unlawfully, and A, by making delivery, intended to *discharge* his own contractual obligation, not to *create* one on the part of B (to return the horse).[1] Occasionally, A will still be able to institute the rei vindicatio. In modern French law, for example, it is the contract of sale that transfers ownership;[2] if the sale is invalid, ownership remains with the vendor, and B merely acquires possession. Very often, however, the vendor can no longer avail himself of an actio in rem. In modern German law, the transfer of ownership constitutes a separate transaction (separate, that is, from the underlying contract of sale),[3] which, moreover, has to be evaluated "abstractly": invalidity of the contract of sale does not, as a rule, affect the transfer of ownership.[4] In Roman law, too, A would have lost his real right: horses were res mancipi, and transfer of (quiritary) ownership therefore required either mancipatio or in iure cessio. Both acts were abstract and remained valid irrespective of the fate of the obligatory transaction they were supposed to discharge.[5]

A special remedy is thus required, a remedy in personam and based on the fact that the purchaser has received what subsequently turned out to be "indebitum": a performance that was never owed to him and that he therefore has no right to keep. This remedy was instituted by the Roman lawyers and it is usually referred to as condictio indebiti. Over the centuries, it has become one of the cornerstones of our

[1] Cf. the argument advanced in Gai. III, 91 and Gai. D. 44, 7, 5, 3.

[2] Art. 1583 code civil.

[3] § 929 BGB.

[4] Cf. § 829 of the First Draft (E I) of the BGB; Andreas Wacke, in: *Münchener Kommentar*, vol. IV (2nd ed., 1986), § 873, n. 20; Gerhard Kegel, "Verpflichtung und Verfügung", in: *Festschrift für F.A. Mann* (1977), pp. 57 sqq.; Reinhard Zimmermann, "Sittenwidrigkeit und Abstraktion", 1984 *Juristische Rundschau* 48 sqq.

[5] Kaser, *RPr* I, pp. 413 sqq.

modern law of unjustified enrichment. Whence the term, "condictio", to designate the claim?

2. "Si paret . . . dare oportere"

It must appear somewhat ironic that the origin of our law of unjustified enrichment (which is often regarded as a rather irregular branch of the law, providing for a more or less discretionary remedy in cases of inequitable hardship)[6] should lie in the actiones stricti iuris of Roman law. One can even trace the name "condictio" back to the time when the formulary procedure was not yet known, but when the parties to the proceedings before the magistrate (in iure) had to make their assertions in prescribed and precisely set forms of words. A trial could be founded upon five different legis actiones, one of which was the so-called legis actio per condictionem.[7] Its name is derived from "condicere", which means as much as "to give notice" ("Condicere autem denuntiare est prisca lingua").[8] If, at the first appearance by the parties, the defendant denied the plaintiff's assertions that he owed him a sum of money, or a specific thing, the plaintiff "gave him notice" to appear again before the magistrate after 30 days.[9] This period gave the parties an opportunity to settle their dispute; only if they failed do so was a judge appointed so that the proceedings could begin in earnest apud iudicem.

The most important characteristic, for our present purposes, of the legis actio per condictionem[10] was its abstract nature. The substantive basis of the claim, its causa debendi, was never mentioned; what was referred to was the mere fact that a particular sum of money or a specific object was owing (the "dare oportere").[11] When the formulary process with written formulae slowly superseded the legis actiones, it followed their model in many respects; after all, the Roman lawyers were always loath to disrupt the even flow of legal development more

---

[6] Cf., for example, "Protokolle", in: *Mugdan*, vol. II, pp. 1182 sqq. (where restitution is said to rest solely on grounds of equity); BGHZ 36, 232 (235) ("*Die Bereicherungsansprüche gehören dem Billigkeitsrecht an und stehen daher in besonderen Masse unter den Grundsätzen von Treu und Glauben*"—The unjustified enrichment claims are based upon equity and hence they are governed, specifically, by the principle of good faith). Otto von Gierke is reputed to have said that in viewing the law of unjustified enrichment one stood "at the threshold of the most holy" (cf. John P. Dawson, "Erasable Enrichment in German Law", (1981) 61 *Boston University LR* 276). Contra: Walter Wilburg, *Die Lehre von der ungerechtfertigten Bereicherung nach österreichischem und deutschem Recht* (1934), pp. 18 sqq.; Zweigert/Kötz, p. 294 and many others. Cf. also Birks, *Restitution*, pp. 9 sqq., 22 sqq.

[7] For details, see Kaser, *RZ*, pp. 80 sqq.

[8] Gai. IV, 18; cf. also Okko Behrends, *Der Zwölftafelprozess* (1974), pp. 97 sqq.

[9] Gai. IV, 17 b.

[10] Introduced by the lex Silia as far as certa pecunia, and by the lex Calpurnia, as far as omnis certa res was concerned: Gai. IV, 19. On the lex Silia, cf., most recently, Carlo Augusto Cannata, "Das faktische Vertragsverhältnis oder die ewige Wiederkunft des Gleichen", (1987) 53 *SDHI* 299 sqq.

[11] Cf. Gai. IV, 17 b.

than was absolutely necessary.[12] Thus, in particular, the intentio of the more modern successor of the legis actio per condictionem was also framed abstractly: "Si paret N^m N^m A^o A^o tritici Africi optimi modios centum dare oportere."[13]

Although the giving of notice had by now disappeared,[14] the new remedy retained the name "condictio": condictio certae pecuniae or condictio certae rei, as the case might be. It was the prototype of an actio stricti iuris in classical Roman law: the judge merely had the choice to condemn in "decem milia" ("quanti ea res est tanta pecunia"), or to absolve. But since the standard formula did not refer to the causa debendi, the condictio turned out to be applicable to a broad variety of situations. Thus, at a comparatively early stage,[15] it became the remedy by means of which promises in the form of stipulations for a certum were enforceable;[16] for if B has promised A to pay ten thousand sesterces, it is indeed appropriate to say that B "ought to give" ten thousand sesterces to A. Also attributable to the "veteres" (i.e. the Republican jurists)[17] is its application, in a delictual context, as condictio ex causa furtiva;[18] for again, if a certain object had been stolen, it was perfectly apposite for its owner to allege that the thief must give it back to him. Somewhat later (though still before the year 76 B.C.)[19] it was extended to the new informal loan-transaction mutuum[20] and, closely related to it, to obligationes litteris.[21] And ultimately, certain instances of unjustified retention

[12] See generally Schulz, *Principles*, pp. 83 sqq.

[13] Cf. Lenel, *EP*, p. 240.

[14] In all formulary claims, the plaintiff now had to notify the defendant, informally and extrajudicially, of the nature of the action to be brought against the latter ("editio actionis"): cf. Kaser, RZ, pp. 162 sqq.; Berger, *ED*, p. 450.

[15] For speculation as to the historical development, cf. Schwarz, *Condictio*, pp. 281 sqq.; von Lübtow, *Condictio*, pp. 59 sqq., 85 sqq., 115 sqq.; Kaser, *RPr* I, p. 593; Fritz Sturm, "La condictio ob transactionem", in: *Studi in onore di Cesare Sanfilippo*, vol. III (1983), pp. 631 sqq.; Detlef Liebs, "The History of the Roman Condictio up to Justinian", in: *The Legal Mind, Essays for Tony Honoré* (1986), pp. 165 sqq.

[16] Cf. supra, pp. 89 sq.

[17] Cf. Tryphon. D. 13, 1, 20.

[18] Cf. infra, pp. 941 sq.

[19] When Cicero appeared for the wealthy actor Roscius against whom a condictio had been brought. Cicero, *Pro Roscio comoedo*, 5, 14 refers to three different bases for a condictio: pecuniae datio, expensilatio and stipulatio. For a discussion, cf. e.g. Schwarz, *Condictio*, pp. 281 sqq.

[20] Cf. supra, p. 153. According to Kaser, *RPr* I, p. 593, the condictio based on mutuum may have been an offshoot of the condictio ex causa furtiva. Before being considered to be a contract, mutuum was possibly merely regarded as a factual act of handing over something; the refusal to pay back was taken to constitute an act of fraudulent appropriation. After mutuum came to be considered as a (real) contract, where ownership was to be transferred to the borrower, the condictio basically became a contractual action. The condictio ex causa furtiva survived as the only application of a condictio which could be brought by the owner. Contra: Liebs, *Essays Honoré*, pp. 165 sqq.; cf. also already idem, *Klagenkonkurrenz*, pp. 98 sqq.

[21] The entry ("expensum ferre"; hence expensilatio) by the creditor into his codex accepti et expensi, which gave rise to the obligatio litteris, was based on a fictitious loan; cf. supra, pp. 32 sq. (note 178).

were regarded as sufficiently similar to these types of situations as also to be remedied by means of the condictio. This heralded the birth of the condictio as an unjustified enrichment action. Gaius emphasized its structural similarity with mutuum: "Is quoque qui non debitum accepit ab eo qui per errorem solvit, re obligatur", he wrote[22] and proceeded to argue that the condictio with the pleading "si paret eum dare oportere" lay against such a person, precisely as if he had received the payment by way of a loan. This argument could, indeed, not be faulted at a time when obligationes re were taken to be based exclusively on rei interventio (or datio). By the time of Gaius, however, the consensual leg of mutuum was already far enough developed[23] that the crucial distinction between condictiones based on mutuum and those based on unjustified retention had become obvious. To quote Gaius once again:

> "[S]ed haec species obligationis [i.e., the one arising from indebitum solutum] non videtur ex contractu consistere, quia is qui solvendi animo dat magis distrahere vult negotium quam contrahere."[24]

3. Indebitum solutum and unjustified enrichment

If unjustified enrichment was *not* founded on contract, the question was bound to arise as to how it could be positively classified. In his Institutes Gaius appears to shirk the problem, but in another work of his, the so-called *Res cottidianae*, we find an answer of a sort: together with a variety of other obligations that did not appear to fit into the neat "summa divisio" of contract and delict,[25] he placed it in a third class of "obligationes . . . ex variis causarum figuris".[26] Justinian, in his Institutes, devoted a special title to "obligation(es) quasi ex contractu", in which he included the case of "is cui quis per errorem non debitum solvit".[27] This settled the matter, as far as the ius commune was concerned: liability arising from unjustified enrichment was consistently classified as quasi-contractual.[28] Even some of our modern

[22] Gai. III, 91.
[23] Cf. supra, pp. 156 sqq.
[24] Gai. III, 91.
[25] On which see supra, pp. 10 sqq.
[26] Gai. D. 44, 7, 5, 3, read in conjunction with Gai. D. 44, 7, 1 pr.
[27] *Inst.* III, 27, 6.
[28] By Lord Mansfield (in *Moses v. Macferlan* [1760] 2 Burr 1005) the systematizing conclusion that certain restitutionary remedies should be described as arising quasi ex contractu was introduced into English law (cf. Peter Birks, "English and Roman Learning in Moses v. Macferlan", (1984) 37 *Current Legal Problems* 5 sqq.). It was the source of the "implied contract heresy" (Birks, *Restitution*, pp. 29 sqq. (83)), which became firmly engrained in the English common law via Blackstone's *Commentaries* (Book III, Chapter 9). For an analysis of the civilian tradition from which Lord Mansfield and Blackstone borrowed, cf. Peter Birks, Grant McLeod, "The Implied Contract Theory of Quasi-Contract: Civilian Opinion Current in the Century Before Blackstone", (1986) 6 *Oxford Journal of Legal Studies* 46 sqq. French authors tended to regard payment of an indebitum as "promutuum"; cf. Pothier, *Traité du contrat du prêt de consomption*, nn. 132 sqq. ("*Du quasi-contrat appelé promutuum*"); Coing, p. 495.

codes—among them, most notably, the French code civil,[29]—still perpetuate this tradition.

We have so far referred to indebitum solutum (condictio indebiti) and unjustified enrichment interchangeably. This is justifiable only as long as we confine our attention to Gaius' and Justinian's *Institutes*, for both of them do, indeed, deal only with this one form of enrichment liability. But this was merely a kind of pars pro toto treatment, suitable at best for an introductory textbook. The briefest glance into either Code or Digest will show us that the Roman lawyers recognized a variety of other "condictiones". Yet, so influential was the "institutional" abridgement, that writers and legislators of later centuries have sometimes exclusively focused their attention on the condictio indebiti. Again, the French code civil provides the most prominent example:

> "*Celui qui reçoit par erreur ou sciemment ce qui ne lui est pas dû s'oblige à le restituer à celui de qui il l'a indûment reçu*",

it states in art. 1376, thereby adopting, as it generally tended to, the views propounded by Robert Joseph Pothier.[30]

II. THE CONDICTIONES IN ROMAN LAW

1. The typology of condictiones: classical or post-classical?

What were the other "condictiones"? The Digest contains separate titles for the condictio causa data causa non secuta (D. 12, 4), the condictio ob turpem vel iniustam causam (D. 12, 5), the condictio sine causa (D. 12, 7) and the condictio furtiva (D. 13, 1);[31] the condictio indebiti is dealt with in D. 12, 6, the longest and most substantial title of them all.[32] To what extent these categories of enrichment liability were shaped by the classical Roman lawyers, by post-classical jurisprudence or by Tribonian, is not entirely clear. It is obvious that the classical jurists already attempted to carve out certain typical situations in which they were prepared to grant the condictio. Yet, for them the condictio was still a uniform procedural institution, without specifically

[29] Artt. 1376 sqq. code civil (sub titulo: "Des quasi-contrats").

[30] For details of the development, cf. Walter Lang, *Der allgemeine Bereicherungsanspruch im französischen Recht vor und nach dem code civil* (unpublished Dr. iur. thesis, Frankfurt, 1975), pp. 40 sqq., 48 sqq., 61 sq.

[31] There was a further title (D. 13, 2), devoted to a condictio ex lege. It consisted of a single fragment, which said that if a new obligation were to be introduced and no provision made as to what kind of action one were to use, then "ex lege agendum est". The Codex contains a brief title (C. 4, 9) devoted to "de condictione ex lege et sine causa vel iniusta causa". On the condictio ex lege cf. Glück, vol. 13, pp. 237 sqq.; Theo Mayer-Maly, "Das Gesetz als Entstehungsgrund von Obligationen", (1965) 12 *RIDA* 444 sqq.; Kaser, *RPr* II, p. 424; Liebs, *Essays Honoré*, p. 182.

[32] The Code presents the condictiones in the following order: De condictione indebiti (C. 4, 5), de condictione ob causam datorum (C. 4, 6), de condictione ob turpem causam (C. 4, 7), de condictione furtiva (C. 4, 8) and de condictione ex lege et sine causa vel iniusta causa (C. 4, 9). For a comparison, in historical perspective, of the two systems presented in the Digest and the Code, see Liebs, *Essays Honoré*, pp. 167 sqq.

differentiated requirements. Thus it would be wrong to insist on the classicity of the condictiones indebiti, ex causa furtiva, etc. as such—that is, as separate legal institutions. Classical law, strictly speaking, did not recognize specific types of condictiones, but applied *the* condictio to a number of situations in which it was thought to be unfair to leave the plaintiff without redress. It was only in post-classical times, when the formulae fell away and the classical concept of an "actional law" ultimately broke down, that the term "condictio" in its original procedural sense was no longer meaningful. In vulgar law, it disappeared completely,[33] and when Justinian revived it in his usual classicist spirit, its meaning had shifted: "condictio" had come to be a term of substantive law, and it was used to designate all those non-contractual and non-delictual claims, which the classical lawyers had been prepared to enforce by means of a condictio (in the old sense of the word). These claims were taken over, further developed, refined and systematized[34] by the East-Roman school of jurists, and it is in this form that they were ultimately received into the Corpus Juris Civilis. All in all, they constitute "one of [the] most distinctive and important achievements [of Roman jurisprudence]",[35] which has had a lasting impact on modern civilian systems.

We shall now deal with each of these "condictiones" (in the Justinianic sense) in turn.

2. Condictio ex causa furtiva

At a comparatively early stage, the condictio was applied in cases of theft; we shall return to the condictio (ex causa) furtiva, as it came to be dubbed, when we deal with furtum.[36] In the present context, three observations appear to be apposite. Firstly, for the purposes of this specific claim, the "dare oportere" of the intentio of the condictio was not (yet) taken to imply a transfer of ownership. The thief was liable, even though the act of stealing as such did not deprive the original owner of his ownership and the thief could therefore be obliged only to retransfer possession. Secondly, it should be noted that theft (furtum) in Roman law was a very wide concept: much wider, for example, than the modern German crime by that name. Accordingly, the scope of the condictio ex causa furtiva was rather extensive and covered, inter alia,

---

[33] Ernst Levy, "West-östliches Vulgarrecht und Justinian", (1959) 76 *ZSS* 11 sq.

[34] ". . . not only cautiously but also not without subtlety", as Liebs, *Essays Honoré*, p. 183, remarks. But cf. also Berthold Kupisch, *Ungerechtfertigte Bereicherung: geschichtliche Entwicklungen* (1987), pp. 21 sqq. For a completely different evaluation, cf. Schulz, *CRL*, p. 611 (". . . the compilers have completely ruined the classical law. . . . [The Byzantine] law is one of the worst parts of Justinian's law; it has confused and irritated generations of lawyers and exercised an evil influence on continental codifications down to our times").

[35] Thomas, *TRL*, p. 326.

[36] Cf. infra, pp. 941 sq.

furtum usus and embezzlement.[37] But (and this is the third point) it went even further than that. The condictio was granted even in cases that could no longer be classified as theft. Take, for instance, the following decision by Sabinus, approved by Celsus and reported by Ulpian:

> "Sed et ei, qui vi aliquem de fundo deiecit, posse fundum condici Sabinus scribit, et ita et Celsus, sed ita, si dominus sit qui deiectus condicat: ceterum si non sit, possessionem eum condicere Celsus ait."[38]

Only movable property could be the object of theft.[39] Nevertheless, the condictio was granted, in the present case, to a person who had been evicted from his land; that person did not even have to be the owner, for Celsus allowed him to bring the condictio in respect of his mere possession.[40] Cases of that nature may well have been referred to as condictio "ex iniusta causa",[41] to which Sabinus' generalizing statement was applicable that anything "quod ex iniusta causa apud aliquem sit, posse condici".[42] But the condictio was made available even against a person who had acquired something through (as a modern German lawyer would put it)[43] an innocent encroachment on somebody else's property or through the force of nature.[44] If, for instance, a ward transferred a sum of money as a loan without his tutor's authority, he remained the owner of that money[45] until the recipient had inseparably mixed it with his own. It was only as a result of this intermixture (referred to as "consumptio nummorum")[46] that the ward lost ownership (and, with it, the rei vindicatio). "Consumpta pecunia condictionem habet", said Julian;[47] the condictio (sine causa) compensated the ward for the loss of his real right. Or take the case reported by Africanus in D. 19, 1, 30 pr. in fine. A slave was sold, but before he was delivered he stole something from the vendor. After delivery, the purchaser in good faith consumed the goods, because he believed them

[37] Cf. infra, pp. 923 sq.
[38] D. 13, 3, 2.
[39] But cf. also p. 929 (note 56).
[40] This type of situation came to be known as condictio possessionis; cf. also Lab./Cass./Ulp. D. 47, 2, 25, 1 and Gai. II, 79 in fine (". . . condici tamen furibus et quibusdam aliis possessoribus possunt"); Liebs, *Essays Honoré*, p. 170; Wolfram Pika, *Ex causa furtiva condicere im klassischen römischen Recht* (1988), pp. 73 sqq.
[41] As Liebs, *Essays Honoré*, p. 170 suggests.
[42] Ulp. D. 12, 5, 6. For a detailed analysis of this fragment, cf. Raimondo Santoro, "Studi sulla condictio", (1971) 32 *Annali Palermo* 189 sqq., 219 sqq. Cf. also Schwarz, *Condictio*, pp. 276 sq.; Honsell/Mayer-Maly/Selb, p. 353; contra, however, most recently, Pika, op. cit., note 40, p. 25 and many others before him.
[43] Cf. infra, p. 890.
[44] Emphasized particularly by Savigny, *System*, vol. V, pp. 523 sqq.
[45] Cf. Gai. II, 82.
[46] For details, see Andreas Wacke, "Die Zahlung mit fremdem Geld", (1976) 79 *BIDR* 49 sqq., 89 sqq., 124 sqq.; Sven Erik Wunner, "Rechtsfolgen der Konsumtion fremder Sachen", in: *Gedächtnisschrift für Wolfang Kunkel* (1984), pp. 584 sqq.
[47] D. 12, 1, 19, 1. Cf. Schwarz, *Condictio*, pp. 240 sqq.; Max Kaser, "Das Geld im römischen Sachenrecht", (1961) 29 *TR* 208 sqq.; Kupisch, op. cit., note 34, p. 10; but cf. also Wunner, *Gedächtnisschrift Kunkel*, pp. 589 sqq., 602 sq. Cf. further Iav. D. 12, 1, 18, 1.

to have been part of the slave's peculium. Result: "condictio eo nomine [venditori] adversus [emptorem] competet, quasi res mea ad te sine causa pervenerit." Or, to come to the case involving unjustified enrichment by force of nature: the condictio could also be instituted, according to Ulpian, in respect of "ea, quae vi fluminum importata sunt".[48]

3. Enrichment by transfer

All the other special enrichment claims are characterized by the fact that the plaintiff tries to reclaim what he has transferred to the defendant. Broadly speaking, the condictio is granted if the purpose which this transfer was intended to attain has either been frustrated or is, for some or other reason, frowned upon by the community. In this specific function, the condictiones tied in with and supplemented the Roman contractual system.[49] Thus, the main situations to be considered were the following.

(a) Transfer solvendi causa

The transfer between plaintiff and defendant has taken place solvendi causa; in particular, the plaintiff may have intended to discharge an obligation created either by stipulation or by a contract of sale. That this obligation did not in fact exist, was not, as a rule, of any consequence as far as the transfer of ownership from plaintiff to defendant was concerned. Mancipatio and in iure cessio were "abstract", anyway; and traditio, though "causal",[50] did not depend on the validity of the underlying stipulatio or emptio venditio. In other words: the fact that performance was rendered solutionis causa was in itself sufficient as a iusta causa traditionis.[51] An exception existed only in so far as the *vendor's* performance was not regarded as solutio.[52] As a result, therefore, a promisor who transferred ownership in either money or any other object, or a purchaser who paid the purchase price, lost their ownership on account of such a transfer, even if the stipulation or contract of sale were invalid.[53] Thus, the rei vindicatio was of no avail, and a remedy was required to enable the promisor or

[48] D. 12, 1, 4, 2. This case is interpreted differently by Kaser, *RPr* I, p. 595 (n. 23) and Liebs, *Essays Honoré*, p. 171; cf. also Santoro, (1971) 32 *Annali Palermo* 197 sqq.

[49] This point has also recently been emphasized by Kupisch, op. cit., note 34, pp. 4 sqq., 9 sqq.

[50] Kaser, *RPr* I, pp. 416 sqq.

[51] The reason for this lies in the historical origin of solutio as a specific transaction designed to release the debtor from his personal liability (supra, pp. 754 sqq.). Cf. generally Rabel, *Grundzüge*, p. 68; Max Kaser, "Zur 'iusta causa traditionis'", (1961) 64 *BIDR* 69 sqq.; cf. also Kupisch, op. cit., note 34, pp. 17 sqq.; Liebs, *Essays Honoré*, p. 177. But see now Robin Evans-Jones, Geoffrey MacCormack, "Iusta causa traditionis", in *New Perspectives in the Roman Law of Property, Essays for Barry Nicholas* (1989), pp. 102 sqq.

[52] Kaser, (1961) 64 *BIDR* 77 sqq., 83. This exception was probably another relict of the old notion of sale as a transaction that was immediately executed (cf. supra, pp. 237 sq.).

[53] Kaser, (1961) 29 *TR* 218 sqq.

purchaser to claim retransfer of ownership. This remedy was the condictio indebiti. The vendor, on the other hand, who handed over the object of the sale, retained his ownership if the contract of sale turned out to be defective. Since he could use the rei vindicatio, he did not have to be protected by means of a condictio.

(b) Executed transactions

Where a contract of sale was concluded and executed at one and the same time (executed sale), the transfer could not be said to have been made solvendi causa: there was no pre-existing obligation which the performance was supposed to discharge. Thus, it was the causa emptionis, or causa venditionis, itself upon which the effect of the traditio depended; and, as a result, ownership did not pass if the contract of sale was in any way defective. Again, no condictio was required.[54] The same applied where a transfer was made donationis causa or by way of datio dotis.[55]

(c) Transfer credendi causa

If a sum of money was handed over credendi causa (that is, as a loan for consumption), ownership remained with the lender if the contract of mutuum turned out to be invalid.[56] Only consumptio nummorum on the part of the recipient could change the situation:[57] the rei vindicatio was then replaced by a condictio; not, however, by one of those based on a transfer.[58]

(d) Datio ob rem

Not rarely did it happen that someone made a performance in order to elicit some form of counterperformance on the part of the recipient. Unless the recipient became bound to render such a counterperformance (that is, unless a contract had come into existence), the transferor required some form of protection, in case his expectations were disappointed. Being unable to enforce the counterperformance, he had to be able to reclaim his own performance and was therefore duly granted a condictio. Since his transfer was usually referred to as datio ob rem (transfer for a purpose envisaged),[59] this particular form of

---

[54] We do not know what the position was if an (invalid) sale was immediately executed by way of mancipatio or in iure cessio. Since these two forms of transfer of ownership were abstract, ownership must have passed, and a condictio (sine causa?; cf. Kupisch, op. cit., note 34, pp. 10 sq.) may have been available to the vendor. As Justinian eradicated mancipatio and in iure cessio, no sources have come down to us.

[55] Kaser, (1961) 64 *BIDR* 83 sqq.; Kupisch, op. cit., note 34, p. 20.

[56] Kaser, (1961) 64 *BIDR* 84.

[57] For details, see Wacke, (1976) 79 *BIDR* 49 sqq.

[58] Cf. supra, p. 840.

[59] The datio ob rem is contrasted by Paulus and Pomponius to datio ob causam: cf. Paul. D. 12, 5, 1 pr. ("Omne quod datur aut ob rem datur aut ob causam"); Pomp. D. 12, 6, 52 ("Damus aut ob causam aut ob rem . . . ob rem vero datur, ut aliquid sequatur"); cf. also

condictio was called condictio ob rem. Rather confusingly, it also came to be referred to as condictio ob rem dati, ob causam datorum and causa data causa non secuta.[60] It was the last name[61] which Justinian decided to use in the Digest.

4. Condictio causa data causa non secuta

The condictio causa data causa non secuta[62] derived its special significance from the fact that not every agreement was enforceable in Roman law. There was, as we have seen, a numerus clausus of contracts, among them only four consensual contracts. Thus, for example, if someone paid another a sum of money in order to make him emancipate a son, manumit a slave, or abandon a lawsuit,[63] he had no means of enforcing the counterperformance that he had envisaged. None of these transactions could be classified as a sale, or hire, or partnership, or mandate; nor, of course, did the handing over of the money bring any of the four recognized real contracts into existence. Or take the case of an exchange transaction. If A gave B his sedan chair in order to obtain B's golden bracelet, his expectation might well be disappointed, for B was under no obligation to deliver the bracelet.[64] Yet, if he failed to counterperform, B had no right to retain A's performance; after all, the sedan chair had been given to him ob rem, not as a present. "[O]b rem vero datur, ut aliquid sequatur" explained Pomponius and concluded "quo non sequente repetitio competit."[65] If, on the other hand, the desired state of affairs had in fact come about (the other party had delivered the bracelet, emancipated the son, manumitted the slave, etc.), this right to reclaim the performance fell away: "Si ob rem . . . data sit pecunia, . . . causa secuta repetitio cessat."[66] Both

---

Paul. D. 12, 6, 65 pr. For an analysis, see Schwarz, *Condictio*, pp. 117 sqq.; Honsell, *Rückabwicklung*, pp. 73 sqq.; François Chaudet, *Condictio causa data causa non secuta* (unpublished *doctorat en droit* thesis, Lausanne, 1973), pp.89 sqq.On datio ob transactionem (mentioned, for instance, in Paul. D. 12, 6, 65 pr., 1) and condictio ob transactionem, cf. Schwarz, *Condictio*, pp. 159 sqq., 257 sqq.; Sturm, *Studi Sanfilippo*, vol. III, pp. 629 sqq.

[60] Reason: some late classical authors used the term "causa" in place of "res"; cf., e.g. Ulp. D. 12, 4, 1 pr.; Ulp. D. 12, 6, 23, 3; and the analysis by Liebs, *Essays Honoré*, p. 173.

[61] On which cf. Schwarz, *Condictio*, pp. 132 sqq.

[62] Literally: the action of debt arising where things have been given on a basis, which basis has failed to sustain itself; more freely: debt for non-materialization (tr. Birks, (1983) 36 *Current Legal Problems* 156).

[63] These are the examples mentioned by Ulpian, D. 12, 4, 1 pr. For a detailed list of cases of application of the condictio causa data causa non secuta, cf. Chaudet, op. cit., note 59, pp. 47 sqq.; cf. also Detlef Liebs, "Bereicherungsanspruch wegen Misserfolgs und Wegfall der Geschäftsgrundlage", 1978 *Juristenzeitung* 698 sq.

[64] For details cf. supra, pp. 250 sqq.

[65] D. 12, 6, 52. For a detailed analysis of the requirements (datio, ob causam, causa non secuta), cf. Glück, vol. 13, pp. 10 sqq.; Chaudet, op. cit., note 59, pp. 49 sqq.; cf. also De Vos, *Verrykingsaanspreeklikheid*, pp. 10 sqq.

[66] Ulp. D. 12, 4, 1 pr. Does this mean that, before the moment of causa secuta, the (first) performance could be reclaimed at any time and for any reason (in particular, because of a mere change of mind)? No, according to the traditional opinion: cf. Schwarz, *Condictio* pp. 266 sqq. Contra: Honsell, *Rückabwicklung*, p. 74; Liebs, *Essays Honoré*, pp. 172 sq.; cf. also the discussion by Chaudet, op. cit., note 59, pp. 66 sqq.

rules were retained, even when actiones in factum (or praescriptis verbis) began to be granted to the party who had made the first performance, a development from which eventually Justinian's system of innominate real contracts emerged.[67] Once he had handed over his sedan chair to B, A could now enforce counterperformance. But he retained the option of claiming back his own performance; for as long as B had not delivered the bracelet, it was still true to say that the state of affairs envisaged by A had not yet come about ("causa non secuta"). Effectively, therefore, the condictio causa data causa non secuta gave A a right of withdrawal from the contract.[68] B had it in his hands, however, to terminate this state of pendency and to commit A to the contract, for the rule remained: causa secuta repetitio cessat. Nevertheless, the continued existence of the condictio[69] was bound to undermine the binding character of innominate real contracts; and the remedy was thus destined to play an important role when, in later centuries, the exact confines of the principle of pacta sunt servanda were sought to be established.[70]

5. Condictio ob turpem (vel iniustam) causam

(a) *Turpitudo accipientis dumtaxat*

We have been proceeding from the tacit assumption that what the plaintiff sought to recover had been handed over for an honest purpose

[67] For details, cf. supra, pp. 532 sqq.

[68] If the condictio was brought on account of the fact that the person who had first performed had changed his mind, one often spoke of condictio ex paenitentia rather than condictio causa data non secuta (cf. e.g. Bartolus, *Commentaria*, ad D. 12, 4, 5 (Si pecuniam): "In contractibus innominatis, si ex una parte impletur, ex alia non: propter casum cessat condictio ob causam, quasi causa non sequuta: sed habet locum ex poenitentia"); on the condictio ex paenitentia (which was just a subspecies of the condictio causa data causa non secuta), cf. Ulp. D. 12, 4, 3, 2 and 3; 12, 4, 5 pr. sqq. (particularly 12, 4, 5 pr., involving the case of "si pecuniam ideo acceperis, ut Capuam eas"); Glück, vol. 13, pp. 20 sqq.; Scherner, *Rücktrittsrecht*, pp. 23 sqq.; Chaudet, op. cit., note 59, pp. 66 sqq.; Kaser, *RPr* II, p. 423; De Vos, *Verrykingsaanspreeklikheid*, p. 10. Dogmatically, the ius poenitendi can be explained on account of the fact that the person who had first performed had not yet himself received the counterperformance. He could, therefore, not be sued by means of an actio praescriptis verbis (and was thus not bound to the innominate real contract), for that action was available only against the recipient of the first performance.

[69] Originally the condictio causa data causa non secuta was confined to cases where the first performance consisted in a datio ob rem (cases, that is, that were to become innominate real contracts of the type of either do ut des or do ut facias); cf. Schwarz, *Condictio*, pp. 137 sqq. By the time of Justinian (if not already in classical law) an extension had taken place and the requirement of dare ob rem (as opposed to facere ob rem) had lost its technical significance. Thus, the condictio causa data causa non secuta could be instituted to reclaim any (first) performance under any form of innominate real contract. Cf. Chaudet, op. cit., note 59, pp. 51 sqq. On the recoverability of operae in general, see Ulp. D. 12, 6, 26, 12; von Lübtow, *Condictio*, pp. 51 sqq.; Werner Flume, "Der Wegfall der Bereicherung in der Entwicklung vom römischen zum geltenden Recht", in: *Festschrift für Hans Niedermeyer* (1953), pp. 111 sqq.; D.J. Joubert, "'n factum as Grondslag van 'n Verrykingsaksie", (1975) 8 *De Jure* 166 sqq.; Wolfgang Waldstein, "Zur Frage der condictio bei irrtümlicher Leistung nichtgeschuldeter operae", in: *Iuris Professio, Festgabe für Max Kaser* (1986), pp. 319 sqq.

[70] Cf. supra, pp. 578 sq.

(datio ob rem honestam). If the performance had been such that its acceptance offended the traditional standards of honest and moral behaviour (datio ob turpem causam), the condictio ob turpem causam was applicable. It lay, for instance,[71] against a person who had accepted money in order not to commit a crime (". . . dedi tibi ne sacrilegium facias, ne furtum, ne hominem occides")[72] or in order to do what he was obliged to do in any event (". . . si tibi dedero, ut rem mihi reddas depositam apud te").[73] The payment of a ransom to a kidnapper would be another case in point. Extortionary practices of this kind could, of course, not be condoned, and thus the transfer of the money could hardly be sanctioned by the legal system.[74] As long as, in spite of the payment, the desired result did not ensue (the crime was nevertheless committed, the deposit still not given back, the hostage not released) it would not even have been necessary to introduce a new type of enrichment action; the condictio causa data causa non secuta would have done the job. The point about the condictio ob turpem causam was that it could also be used if the purpose for which the money had been given *had* in fact been accomplished (causa data causa secuta, so to speak).[75] For even if the recipient did abstain from killing (to mention just the one example), this could by no means earn him the right to keep the money that he had extorted. Generally speaking, as one can see from the scarcity of case law reported in the Corpus Juris, the ambit of this particular enrichment claim was rather restricted. It was a subcategory of the condictio causa data causa non secuta, in that it also required a datio ob rem; yet, its success did not depend on the further requirement of "causa non secuta", but merely on the infringement of the boni mores on the part of the recipient. Justinian also allowed the recovery of dationes ob iniustam (as opposed to turpem) causam;[76] he did not, however, thereby substantially widen the scope of application of the remedy.[77]

---

[71] On Iul. D. 12, 5, 5, see David Daube, "Turpitude in Digest 12. 5. 5", in: *Studies in Roman law in Memory of A. Arthur Schiller* (1986), pp. 33 sqq.

[72] Ulp. D. 12, 5, 2, pr.

[73] Ulp. D. 12, 5, 2, 1.

[74] Ownership of the money obviously passed despite the causa being turpis; cf. Kaser, (1961) 29 *TR* 220; idem, (1961) 64 *BIDR* 85; Kupisch, op. cit., note 34, pp. 13 sqq.; Liebs, *Essays Honoré*, pp. 174 sqq.

[75] Paul. D. 12, 5, 1, 2: "Quod si turpis causa accipientis fuerit, etiamsi res secuta sit, repeti potest"; Iul. D. 12, 5, 5; Paul. D. 12, 5, 9 pr. For all details, see Schwarz, *Condictio*, pp. 169 sqq.; Honsell, *Rückabwicklung*, pp. 80 sqq.; De Vos, *Verrykingsaanspreeklikheid*, pp. 20 sqq.; Liebs, *Essays Honoré*, pp. 174 sqq.

[76] Cf. the heading of the Digest title 12, 5. He thus included the general statement by Ulpian about enrichment ex iniusta causa (D. 12, 5, 6; on which see supra) in this title.

[77] Ulp. D. 12, 5, 6 is the only text relating to the condictio ob iniustam causam. No case law has come down to us. It is probable that this condictio was tagged on to the condictio ob turpem causam as a result of Theodosius' Lex non dubium, which had turned every

(b) *Turpitudo utriusque*

The range of cases in which a plaintiff could successfully bring the condictio ob turpem causam was further reduced by virtue of the famous "in pari turpitudine" rule. Where both the giver and the recipient had been guilty of morally reprehensible behaviour, there was no reason for the law to intervene. For though the recipient might not deserve what had been handed over to him, the giver does not deserve to be protected either. Under these circumstances, it is preferable to leave things as they are, rather than to assist one villain in his claim against the other; for in order to succeed, a plaintiff must always be able to demonstrate a *better* right than the defendant.[78] This perception found its expression in the rule that where both parties are tainted by the evil, the position of the possessor is to be regarded as the stronger one: ". . . si et dantis et accipientis turpis causa [est], possessorem potiorem esse";[79] or, as it was usually expressed in later centuries: in pari turpitudine·melior est causa possidentis. It was applied in a variety of cases involving crime and grave infringements of the moral code;[80] mere illegality of the transfer that could not at the same time be qualified as "turpis", was not sufficient. Thus, for example, recovery was excluded where someone had given money ob stuprum (for illicit sexual intercourse)[81] or, according to some older authors, where a person had paid a prostitute.[82] The same applied where a thief had paid another in order to avoid being given away by him ("si dederit fur, ne proderetur")[83] or where someone bribed a judge in order to pervert the course of justice ("si pecunia detur, ut male iudicetur").[84] If, on the other hand, judgment had to be given in favour of the person who had

statutory prohibition into a lex perfecta (cf. supra, pp. 700 sq.); infringement entailed invalidity. "Ex iniusta causa apud aliquem esse" was thus taken to mean that the recipient of a datio ob rem had acted in breach of a statutory prohibition. The classical Roman lawyers, on the other hand, characterized notable breaches of statutory provisions (irrespective of whether they were perfect, less than perfect or imperfect) as turpis and would thus have granted the condictio ob turpem causam. Cf. Kaser, *Verbotsgesetze*, pp. 69 sqq.; Liebs, *Essays Honoré*, pp. 174 sqq. The question of whether we are dealing in D. 12, 5 with one or two kinds of (enrichment) actions is discussed by Glück, vol. 13, pp. 50 sqq.; De Vos, *Verrykingsaanspreeklikheid*, pp. 20 sqq.

[78] Cf. also Honsell, *Rückabwicklung*, pp. 88 sq. and the following passage from Faber's *Rationalia in Pandectas*, quoted by Honsell (n. 2): "Et tamen alterutrum evenire necesse est, ut vel is, qui turpiter accepit, retineat, aut qui turpiter dedit, condicat . . . minus tamen iniquum est, retentionem dari ei, qui accepit turpiter, quia iniquius et difficilius est dari actionem, quam retentionem: actio enim non datur, nisi iure, retentio autem plerumque occasione magis, quam iure."

[79] Paul. D. 12, 5, 8; cf. also Ulp. D. 3, 6, 5, 1; Pap. D. 12, 7, 5; C. 4, 7, 2 (Ant.).

[80] Hans Hermann Seiler, "§ 817 S. 2 BGB und das römische Recht", in: *Festschrift für Wilhelm Felgentraeger* (1969), pp. 381 sqq.; cf. also Honsell, *Rückabwicklung*, p. 86.

[81] Ulp. D. 12, 5, 4 pr. On the crime of stuprum generally, see Mommsen, *Strafrecht*, pp. 691 sqq., 694 sqq.

[82] Ulp. D. 12, 5, 4, 3: "Sed quod meretrici datur, repeti non potest, ut Labeo et Marcellus scribunt. . . ."

[83] Ulp. D. 12, 5, 4, 1.

[84] Paul. D. 12, 5, 3.

paid the bribe anyway ("si dedi, ut secundum me in bona causa iudex pronuntiaret"),[85] the solution was less clear. Traditionally, the condictio seems to have been granted in this case, presumably because the giver was regarded as less blameworthy than the judge, who accepted the money for doing what it was, in any event, his duty to do. An imperial constitution was required to decide that the giver, too, had committed an offence that was serious enough to warrant exclusion of the condictio (". . . sed hic quoque crimen contrahit (iudicem enim corrumpere videtur) et non ita pridem imperator noster constituit litem enim perdere").[86] Particularly interesting about the former of these two views is the fact that the jurists do not seem to have hesitated to evaluate and compare the degree of turpitude of both parties involved in the transaction and to decide in favour of the party who was less to blame.[87] A similarly flexible approach to the in pari turpitudine rule appears to have prevailed in other cases. Thus, we hear of a woman who intended to marry her uncle and therefore gave him money as a dowry. The marriage (which eventually did not occur) would have had to be classified as incestuous; and since incest was regarded as a case of stuprum, the dowry had been given, strictly speaking, ob rem turpem. Nevertheless, Papinian allowed the woman to reclaim her money, for her behaviour was rather less obnoxious than that of most other persons who paid ob stuprum (". . . non enim stupri, sed matrimonii gratia datam esse").[88]

(c) *Turpitudo solius dantis*

The evil may taint the recipient alone ("turpitudo accipientis dumtaxat"; consequence: condictio ob turpem causam) or it may affect both the giver and the recipient ("turpitudo utriusque"; consequence (normally): no enrichment action). But, of course, it could also be only the giver who had infringed the boni mores ("turpitudo solius dantis").[89] Such was the case, according to a strong body of opinion, where money was given to a prostitute. Traditionally, the condictio had been excluded on account of turpitudo utriusque;[90] now ("nova ratione") it was held that only the giver was tainted. Reason: the recipient could only be blamed for *being* a prostitute; but being one, it was hardly fair to label the receipt of the money as turpis.[91]

---

[85] Ulp. D. 12, 5, 2, 2.
[86] Ulp. D. 12, 5, 2, 2.
[87] Seiler, *Festschrift Felgentraeger*, p. 386; De Vos, *Verrykingsaanspreeklikheid*, p. 23.
[88] Pap. D. 12, 7, 5 pr.; and the interpretation given by Seiler, *Festschrift Felgentraeger*, pp. 386 sqq.
[89] Cf. the enumeration of the various possibilities in Paul. D. 12, 5, 1 pr. On turpitudo solius dantis in general, see Honsell, *Rückabwicklung*, pp. 90 sqq.
[90] Ulp. D. 12, 5, 4, 3: cf. supra, p. 846, note 82.
[91] ". . . illam enim turpiter facere, quod sit meretrix, non turpiter accipere, cum sit meretrix": a rather sophistic reasoning. Seiler (*Festschrift Felgentraeger*, pp. 383 sq.) draws attention to the fact that prostitutes registered with the aediles did not fall under the

6. Condictio indebiti

(a) *Indebitum solutum*

Though probably not the oldest of the Roman unjustified enrichment claims,[92] the condictio indebiti became undoubtedly their most important species. We have already briefly sketched the function of this remedy; it served to retransfer indebitum solutum. A performance rendered with the object of fulfilling an obligation constituted indebitum solutum, if the obligation did not in fact exist. The transfer of Pamphilus was indebitum solutum if the debtor thought he owed either Pamphilus or Stichus, whereas, however, he actually owed Stichus.[93] Where a person was under an alternative obligation (he owed either Stichus or ten), he could reclaim Stichus if he had delivered him without realizing that he could have paid the sum of ten instead.[94] Furthermore, the condictio indebiti could also be brought if performance had been made in discharge of a debt which was valid at civil law but defeasible, ex iure praetorio, by an exceptio perpetua.[95] A conditional debt remained indebitum, as long as the condition was not satisfied, and whatever had been given to discharge it could, therefore, also be reclaimed.[96] An obligatio naturalis, on the other hand, excluded the condictio indebiti; for though he could not have forced the other party to render performance, the creditor had nevertheless received what was owing to him.[97] All this is perfectly straightforward.[98] Much more obscure are the particulars of the second main requirement of the

---

provisions of the lex Iulia de adulteriis and were liable (since the time of Caligula) to pay tax. Thus it may have appeared to be inappropriate to label as "turpis" the acceptance of remuneration for an activity which was not only officially tolerated, but from which the State derived an income; cf. also Glück, vol. 13, p. 53 and Honsell, *Rückabwicklung*, p. 92. On the position of a meretrix in general, see also Max Kaser, "Rechtswidrigkeit und Sittenwidrigkeit im klassischen römischen Recht", (1940) 60 *ZSS* 135; Joseph Plescia, "The Development of the Doctrine of Boni Mores in Roman Law", (1987) 34 *RIDA* 304 sqq. The authors of the ius commune appear to have entertained a lively discussion on when exactly a person may be classified as meretrix. Thus, for example, an 18th-century compendium gave the following definition: "Meretrix est, quae passim et palam omnibus patet, et cujus turpitudo est publice venalis, sicut in lupanari vel in alio loco, sive cum quaestu sive sine quaestu, pudori suo non parcens, palam se prostituat"; the author then asks how many men a woman must have had in order to qualify as meretrix and reports the view adopted by the glossators: "Glossa requirit, ut plures quam 23.000 admiserit"; on which, in turn, Count von Kreittmayr, the father of the Codex Juris Bavarici Criminalis (1751), remarked that, under those circumstances, no person in the world could be regarded as a harlot any longer. For all this, see (1983) 2 *RJ* 302.

[92] Liebs, *Essays Honoré*, pp. 168, 177.

[93] Pomp. D. 12, 6, 19, 3.

[94] Iul. D. 12, 6, 32, 3.

[95] Ulp. D. 12, 6, 26, 3: "Indebitum autem solutum accipimus non solum si omnino non debeatur, sed et si per aliquam exceptionem perpetuam peti non poterat: quare hoc quoque repeti poterit, nisi sciens se tutum exceptione solvit."

[96] Pomp. D. 12, 6, 16 pr.

[97] Afr. D. 12, 6, 38, 1; Ner. D. 12, 6, 41; Tryphon. D. 12, 6, 64.

[98] For further casuistry on "indebitum solutum", see Glück, vol. 13, pp. 76 sqq.; Buckland/Stein, pp. 541 sq.; Schwarz, *Condictio*, pp. 21 sqq.

condictio indebiti: the plaintiff had to have made his performance in the mistaken belief that it was owing.[99]

(b) Solutio per errorem

Questions surrounding this "error" requirement have been the subject of lively debates throughout the history of the ius commune;[100] in fact, one can justly claim that we are dealing here with the single most disputed area of the Roman law of unjustified enrichment.[101] Some of the more extreme interpolationists have even denied that error on the part of the person rendering performance was at all required in classical Roman law;[102] even if he knew that what he gave was an indebitum, they claimed, he could demand its retransfer. Today one is inclined to reject these somewhat ruthless attempts to purge the classical sources—here as in many other contexts—of all subjective elements. Yet, on the other hand, it is also obvious that to some extent the compilers have indeed tampered with the sources that they found; they did not, however, succeed in eradicating all traces of the classical regime. A variety of texts within the Corpus Juris Civilis therefore seem to be in irreconcilable conflict with each other;[103] and every analysis based upon such unreliable sources must thus of necessity contain some element of speculation. As a result of the research undertaken over the last three or four decades,[104] the following picture, in broad outline, appears to have emerged.

In classical Roman law error on the part of the plaintiff was an essential element of the condictio indebiti. This is confirmed by too many sources to be disputed or explained away. We have already repeatedly referred to the famous passage in Gaius' *Institutes* in which the condictio indebiti is introduced in the following terms: "Is quoque

[99] The defendant, incidentally, also had to have acted under the influence of error, for a person who accepted a performance, although he knew that it was not owing to him, committed theft: Scaev. D. 13, 1, 18; Ulp. D. 47, 2, 43 pr. and 1; cf. H.F. Jolowicz, *Digest XLVII. 2, De Furtis* (1940), pp. XXV sqq.

[100] Cf. the detailed analysis by D.P. Visser, *Die rol van dwaling by die condictio indebiti* (unpublished Dr. iur. thesis, Leiden, 1985), pp. 66 sqq.

[101] For an even more dramatic comment ("one of the most notorious controversies in the field of Roman private law") cf. August Herrmann, "Beiträge zur Lehre vom Irrthum, Erster Beitrag", (1847) 3 (Neue Folge) *Zeitschrift für Civilrecht und Prozess* 87.

[102] Cf., in particular, Siro Solazzi, "L'errore nella 'condictio indebiti' ", in: *Scritti di diritto romano*, vol. IV (1963), pp. 99 sqq.; idem, "Ancora dell'errore nella 'condictio indebiti' ", in: *Scritti*, vol. IV (1963), pp. 405 sqq.; idem, "Le 'condictiones' e l'errore", in: *Scritti*, vol. V (1972), pp. 1 sqq.

[103] Cf., for example, C. 4, 5, 5 compared with C. 1, 18, 10 (both by Diocl. et Max., the one text from A.D. 293, the other from A.D. 294.).

[104] Cf. Schwarz, *Condictio*, pp. 17 sqq., 65 sqq.; Sven Erik Wunner, "Der Begriff causa und der Tatbestand der condictio indebiti", (1970) 9 *Romanitas* 463 sqq.; Harald Koch, *Bereicherung und Irrtum* (1973), pp. 105 sqq.; Laurens C. Winkel, *Error iuris nocet—Rechtsdwaling als rechtsordeprobleem* (1982), pp. 189 sqq.; H. Gaspart-Jones, "La 'condictio indebiti' et l'erreur dans le droit de Justinien", in: *Hommage à René Dekkers* (1982), pp. 93 sqq.; Visser, op. cit., note 100, pp. 22 sqq.; idem, "Die grondslag van die condictio indebiti", (1988) 51 *THRHR* 492 sqq.; De Vos, *Verrykingsaanspreeklikheid*, pp. 24 sqq.

qui non debitum accepit ab eo qui per errorem solvit, re obligatur."[105] At the very outset of the Digest title 12, 6 this is confirmed by a fragment taken from Ulpian's commentary on the edict: "Et quidem si quis indebitum ignorans solvit, per hanc actionem condicere potest: sed si sciens se non debere solvit, cessat repetitio."[106] Yet it would probably not be quite correct to say that error was a (positive) requirement of the condictio indebiti, the implication being that the plaintiff had to prove it. It appears more likely that the plaintiff merely had to establish the fact of having rendered a performance, which constituted an indebitum solutum. The presence of an error could, under these circumstances, be presumed. It was up to the defendant to rebut this presumption, and this he did by demonstrating that the plaintiff had been aware of the non-existence of the debt.[107] Thus, it was not so much the plaintiff's error which made the condictio indebiti applicable; it was rather his knowledge, at the time of rendering performance, which barred the claim.[108] This onus of proof was one of the two essential points with regard to which Justinian changed the law.

> ". . . eum, qui dicit indebitas solvisse", he determined,[109] "compelli ad probationes, quod per dolum accipientis vel aliquam iustam ignorantiae causam indebitum ab eo solutum, et nisi hoc ostenderit, nullam eum repetitionem habere."

Thus, he elevated error to a core requirement of the plaintiff's claim: it was the plaintiff who had to show that his performance had been based on "some just case of ignorance". But, on the other hand, he also made it clear that he was not prepared to take account of every kind of error. In fact, even the classical lawyers may well already have started to pay attention to issues of reasonableness in this regard.[110] This idea was bound to appeal to the compilers, for it suited their desire to "ethicize" the law. But what they still required was some kind of criterion to determine under which circumstances a mistake could be regarded as unreasonable. They found it in the error iuris/error facti dichotomy, which had already been recognized by the classical lawyers[111] in one specific situation and which was now generally brought to bear on whether or not to grant the plaintiff his condictio indebiti. Ignorantia

[105] Gai. III, 91.

[106] D. 12, 6, 1, 1; cf. also Ulp. D. 12, 6, 26, 3.

[107] Cf., in particular, Schwarz, *Condictio*, pp. 96 sqq. An exception appears to have existed in the case of fideicommissa; cf. infra, note 111.

[108] Schulz, *CRL*, p. 616.

[109] Paul. D. 22, 3, 25 pr. (interpolated; cf. Schwarz, *Condictio*, pp. 107 sqq.).

[110] Cf. supra, pp. 604 sqq., 606.

[111] Cf., for example, C. 4, 5, 7 (Diocl. et Max.); C. 6, 50, 9 (Gord.); Paul. D. 22, 6, 9, 5. All these texts deal with a fideicommissum indebitum per errorem solutum; the heir had not realized that he could subtract the quarta Pegasiana. Fideicommissa were linked particularly intimately to good faith, trust and honour. The moral duty of the heir to comply with the wishes of the testator ("fidem praestare") was thus taken to prevail over his interest to assert his error iuris. For details, see Fritz Schwarz, "Die Funktion des Irrtums bei Erfüllung gänzlich oder teilweise nicht geschuldeter Fideikommisse", (1951) 68 *ZSS* 266 sqq.; cf. also Winkel, op. cit., note 104, pp. 192 sqq.; Visser, op. cit., note 100, pp. 41 sqq.

iuris nocet, facti vero ignorantia non nocet was the general rule,[112] and it was based on the assumption that an error of fact was typically excusable, whereas an error of law was not.[113] Thus, we now come across statements like the one contained in C. 1, 18, 10:

> "Cum quis ius ignorans indebitam pecuniam persolverit, cessat repetitio. per ignorantiam enim facti tantum repetitionem indebiti soluti competere tibi notum est."[114]

But some adjustments continued to be made at both ends of the spectrum. At least for certain groups of persons even an error iuris was regarded as excusable, and likewise even an error facti could sometimes be taken to be inexcusable.[115]

What was the function of the error requirement, as far as the condictio indebiti was concerned? A man who gave something in the knowledge that he was not bound to do so did not deserve to be protected if he decided to reclaim this object, after all. He appeared more like someone who had executed a donation;[116] and a donation, as we know,[117] could not be reclaimed either. In both instances, it was rather the recipient who could reasonably ask to be protected, for both solvens and donor had engendered in him the expectation that he might keep what he was given. On balance, this interest had to prevail against that of the other party to still be able to change his mind. Or, to put it slightly differently: in the absence of a good reason to grant a claim, the policy of the law was always quieta non movere.[118] Justinian's distinction between error iuris and error facti, of course, added another facet to the ratio legis: the general public was required to know the law, and exclusion of the condictio indebiti in case of error iuris was regarded as a suitable way of sanctioning this duty.

7. Miscellaneous cases

(a) Pomponius' enrichment principle

The carving out of specific claims, each with their own requirements,

---

[112] Paul. D. 22, 6, 9 pr.; cf. supra, pp. 604 sq.

[113] Interestingly, the English common law, since the beginning of the 19th century, adopted a very similar approach; a plaintiff may not reclaim money that he has paid under a mistake of law: cf. *Bilbie v. Lumley* (1802) 2 East 469. The reason given by Lord Ellenborough was that "[e]very man must be taken to be cognizant of the law; otherwise there is no saying to what extent the excuse of ignorance might not be carried" (p. 472).

[114] Cf. further the analysis by Schwarz, *Condictio*, pp. 105 sqq.; Visser, op. cit., note 100, pp. 45 sqq.

[115] Visser, op. cit., note 100, pp. 52 sqq. But see also Gaspart-Jones, *Hommage Dekkers*, pp. 93 sqq., who disputes that any rule existed, at least in Justinian's time; whether or not the condictio indebiti was to be granted was determined according to what appeared to be equitable in the circumstances of the individual case.

[116] Cf. Paul. D. 50, 17, 53 ("Cuius per errorem dati repetitio est, eius consulto dati donatio est"); Paul. D. 46, 2, 12 ("Si quis delegaverit debitorem, qui doli mali exceptione tueri se posse sciebat, similis videbitur ei qui donat, quoniam remittere exceptionem videtur"); Schwarz, *Condictio*, pp. 111 sqq.; Visser, op. cit., note 100, pp. 56 sqq.

[117] Cf. supra, pp. 480 sq.

[118] Cf. already supra, p. 846 (in pari turpitudine).

is clearly conducive to legal certainty; at the same time, however, there is always a good chance of new cases cropping up which also deserve to be remedied but which do not fit into one of the existing niches. The question then arises whether, and if so how, to adapt the system in order to accommodate such novel situations. This question naturally presented itself to the Roman lawyers as far as unjustified enrichment claims were concerned; and what they obviously had to do was to try to find a common denominator for all the existing condictiones. What was the general principle that had justified the granting of specific enrichment actions and that could now be used to expand, but at the same time suitably contain, the range of claims?

Originally, of course, the condictio had been the fertile (procedural) mother of the (substantive) claims.[119] But, for one thing, it had become barren with the demise of the formulary procedure; and, for another the "dare oportere" had, of course, been much too abstract to play any useful role in giving shape and substance to the individual unjustified enrichment claims. Another similarly resourceful mother of legal rules and institutions was natural equity. That nobody should enrich himself at the expense of another, was an important precept based on it: "Nam hoc natura aequum est neminem cum alterius detrimento fieri locupletiorem", in Pomponius' well-known words.[120] Justinian regarded this statement as so important that he included it, in a slightly modified version, among the diversae regulae iuris antiqui with which he rounded off his compilation.[121] But, of course, it had never been a legal rule of immediate applicability. The Roman economy could hardly have flourished as it did if every enrichment at the expense of another had been frowned upon: all businessmen, after all, tend to make their profits at the expense of their competitors. The general equitable principle needed to be transformed into more specific legal rules. This is in fact what happened after the time of the Republic, and in a whole variety of fields do we find Pomponius' principle at work behind the scenes.[122]

One of these fields was the condictio, as far as it was used as an enrichment action. Thus we see, for instance, Papinian claiming that "[h]aec condictio ex bono et aequo introducta, quod alterius apud alterum sine causa deprehenditur, revocare consuevit".[123] Which type of enrichment condictio he had in mind when he referred to "haec

[119] John P. Dawson, *Unjust Enrichment* (1951), p. 42 elegantly describes the condictio as "the Roman general assumpsit" (on which, see supra, pp. 777 sqq. and infra, pp. 892 sqq.).

[120] D. 12, 6, 14. On the origin and background of this principle (stoic moral philosophy) and its reception into the legal system, see Christian Wollschläger, "Das stoische Bereicherungsverbot in der römischen Rechtswissenschaft", in: *Römisches Recht in der europäischen Tradition, Symposion für Franz Wieacker* (1985), pp. 41 sqq.

[121] D. 50, 17, 206: "Iure naturae aequum est neminem cum alterius detrimento et iniuria fieri locupletiorem."

[122] For all details, see Wollschläger, *Symposion Wieacker*, pp. 61 sqq.

[123] D. 12, 6, 66.

condictio", we do not know; it may have been the condictio indebiti (after all, the fragment was placed by Justinian in the title 12, 6) or the condictio ex causa furtiva. What is significant about the text is the historical link, of which it bears witness, between the precepts of fairness and equity and the use of the condictio as a claim to recover whatever of one's property happened to be, without good cause, in the hands of another. The condictio causa data causa non secuta is likewise said to be grounded on the idea of what is just and fair;[124] and in a variety of other places naturalis aequitas,[125] natura[126] and ius gentium[127] are referred to in the context of enrichment condictiones. All these texts have been subjected to radical criticism: how could the classical Roman lawyers, one argued, be taken to have conceived of such an intimate connection between the various emanations of the condictio (an actio stricti iuris!) on the one hand and natural law and equity on the other! We must be dealing here with one of those typically Byzantine attempts to replace the clear rules of classical Roman law by a somewhat amorphous equity jurisprudence.[128] Yet it is not at all difficult to reconcile the one with the other. The condictio was, of course, an actio stricti iuris and once the praetor was prepared to grant the action, the judge had no discretion. Under which circumstances the plaintiff's duty of "dare oportere" could, however, be accepted, was a matter of interpretation, and in this regard the aequitas naturalis could indeed be of great significance. Thus it helped to shape the various enrichment condictiones; but at the same time it always remained available in a residuary function and never completely lost its creative potential. Occasionally, individual decisions continued to be based directly on what appeared to be right and fair. Celsus D. 12, 1, 32[129] is probably the most prominent case in point. We are dealing here with the situation where A orders his debtor B to promise a loan to C.[130] C, however,

[124] Paul. D. 12, 6, 65, 4: "Quod ob rem datur, ex bono et aequo habet repetitionem: veluti si dem tibi, ut aliquid facias, nec feceris."

[125] Ulp. D. 12, 4, 3, 7 (". . . sed ipse Celsus naturali aequitate motus putat repeti posse").

[126] Paul. D. 12, 6, 15 pr. ("Indebiti soluti condictio naturalis est . . ."); Tryphon. D. 12, 6, 64 (". . . ita debiti vel non debiti ratio in condictione naturaliter intellegenda est").

[127] Cels. D. 12, 6, 47 (". . . quoniam indebitam iure gentium pecuniam solvit"); Marci. D. 25, 2, 25 (". . . nam iure gentium condici puto posse res ab his, qui non ex iusta causa possident").

[128] Cf., for example, Fritz Pringsheim, "Bonum et aequum", (1932) 52 *ZSS* 138 sqq.; Cesare Sanfilippo, *Condictio indebiti* (1943), pp. 56 sqq.; Schwarz, *Condictio*, pp. 304 sqq. Contra, especially, Santoro, (1971) 32 *Annali Palermo* 216 sqq.; Wollschläger, *Symposion Wieacker*, pp. 82 sqq.; cf. also Kupisch, op. cit., note 34, pp. 25 sq.

[129] "Si et me et Titium mutuam pecuniam rogaveris et ego meum debitorem tibi promittere iusserim, tu stipulatus sis, cum putares eum Titii debitorem esse, an mihi obligaris? subsisto, si quidem nullum negotium mecum contraxisti: sed propius est, ut obligari te existimem, non quia pecuniam tibi credidi (hoc enim nisi inter consentientes fieri non potest): sed quia pecunia mea quae ad te pervenit, eam mihi a te reddi bonum et aequum est." On this text, see Schwarz, *Condictio*, pp. 245 sqq.; Santoro, (1971) 32 *Annali Palermo* 273 sqq.

[130] A delegatio nominis, or debiti; on which cf. Kaser, *RPr* I, pp. 651 sq.

believes B to be the debtor of Titius, not of A. As a result of C's error in persona, a contract between A and C has not come into existence.[131] Nevertheless, C is under an obligation to return to A what he has received from him. Since A is deemed to have given the money that he was owed by B, to C,[132] a mutuum would have come into existence between A and C but for C's mistake about the identity of his contractual partner. The situation is thus that C is deemed to have received the money from A: but as the intended loan transaction did not come into being, he appears to be enriched, sine causa, at the expense of A. A must therefore clearly be granted a claim; since, however, the transfer constituted neither an indebitum solutum nor a datio ob rem, neither condictio indebiti nor condictio causa data causa non secuta is applicable to effectuate the retransfer. Celsus, under these circumstances, merely refers to "[quod] bonum et aequum est" as the basis for A's claim.

(b) Retinere sine causa

Bonum et aequum, naturalis aequitas, ius gentium: these were, of course, rather unspecific guidelines to determine unjustified enrichment problems. It is hardly surprising, therefore, that the Roman lawyers attempted to identify criteria on a somewhat lower level of abstraction, but still transcending the specific requirements of the individual condictiones. Some of them, for example, experimented with the concept of negotium contractum; a condictio, they claimed, could be instituted only if the datio had been based on a cooperation between giver and recipient, supported by the intention of both of them to enter into a transaction. But although this criterion was occasionally used in order to exclude restitution,[133] it could hardly hope to gain widespread support as a common denominator embracing all varieties of (enrichment) condictiones:[134] the condictio ex causa furtiva, for example, obviously did not require a negotium contractum. Much more promising was the notion advanced by, among others, Papinian, when he reflected on the origins of "[h]aec condictio":[135] the notion that something is found "apud alterum sine causa". Sine causa did not, of course, signify a lack of the causal basis required for the transfer of ownership. If, for example, a sedan chair was handed over in fulfilment of an invalid stipulatory promise, ownership passed to the recipient, for

---

[131] Cf. supra, p. 592.

[132] "Qui debitorem suum delegat, pecuniam dare intellegitur, quanta ei debetur": Iul. D. 46, 1, 18.

[133] Iul. D. 12, 6, 33: "Si in area tua aedificassem et tu aedes possideres, condictio locum non habebit, quia nullum negotium inter nos contraheretur: nam is, qui non debitam pecuniam solverit, hoc ipso aliquid negotii gerit: cum autem aedificium in area sua ab alio positum dominus occupat, nullum negotium contrahit." On this text, cf. Schwarz, *Condictio*, pp. 192 sq.

[134] But cf. Kaser, *RPr* I, pp. 594 sq.

[135] D. 12, 6, 66: cf. supra, p. 852 (note 123).

the traditio found sufficient "causal" support in the causa solvendi. Yet, since the underlying obligatory act was invalid, the recipient had acquired ownership "sine causa": his enrichment was not justified in the sense that he did not deserve to retain the object of the transfer. It was this absence of a causa retinendi, resulting either from the failure of the purpose of the performance (condictio indebiti, condictio causa data causa non secuta) or from an unjustified interference (condictio ex causa furtiva) that provided the key to the non-contractual condictiones.[136]

(c) Condictio ob causam finitam and condictio liberationis

But if the "sine causa" requirement lay at the root of all the recognized enrichment condictiones, it could also be used as a convenient touchstone of liability when it came to the discussion of novel types of situations. Thus we find, indeed, a variety of texts expanding the existing system of condictiones on the basis merely that the defendant appeared to have acquired something sine causa. Take, for example, the case discussed by Ulpian and reported in D. 12, 7, 2.[137] The owner of a laundry receives clothes from a client. When he loses the clothes, his client brings the actio locati and obtains reimbursement of the value of the clothes. Later the client finds the clothes. It is obvious that the launderer should be allowed to reclaim what he had to pay under the actio locati. Yet that payment, at the time when it was made, was not indebitum solutum. The launderer owed the money and his client did not acquire it sine causa. It was only subsequently that his causa retinendi fell away: "etenim vestimentis inventis quasi sine causa datum videtur." Hence the (rather tentative) conclusion: "quasi sine causa datum . . . putamus condici posse". Cases of this kind were even allotted a special terminological compartment of their own: they came to be referred to as condictiones ob causam finitam. One of the first references to the new species of condictio[138] is contained in a text on sale.[139] A purchaser of wine had given an arrha; later, however, the parties agreed to rescind their contract. As a result, the arrha obviously had to be given back, but, again, the condictio indebiti was of no avail. Julian therefore granted the condictio sine causa: "certe etiam condici poterit, quia iam sine causa apud venditorem est anulus." Ulpian

---

[136] There is a vast literature dealing with the concept of causa (retinendi) in terms of the enrichment condictiones (as opposed to the causa required for the transfer by traditio), particularly as far as the condictio indebiti is concerned. Cf., for example, Sanfilippo, op. cit., note 128, pp. 52 sqq.; Schwarz, *Condictio*, pp. 191 sqq., 212 sqq.; August Simonius, "Zur Frage einer einheitlichen 'causa condictionis' ", in: *Festschrift für Hans Lewald* (1953), pp. 161 sqq.; Wunner, (1970) 9 *Romanitas* 459 sqq.; Kaser, *RPr* I, pp. 595 sq.; Visser, op. cit., note 100, pp. 1 sqq.; idem (1988) 51 *THRHR* 492 sqq.; Kupisch, op. cit., note 34, pp. 16 sq. Cf. also J.E. Scholtens, "Condictio indebiti and condictio sine causa", (1957) 74 *SALJ* 261 sqq.

[137] On which see David Hughes, "D. 12. 7. 2", 1976 *Juridical Review* 156 sqq.

[138] On the historical development, cf. Liebs, *Essays Honoré*, pp. 178 sq.

[139] Iul./Ulp. D. 19, 1, 11, 6.

concurred and specified "quasi ob causam datus sit [sc.: anulus] et causa finita sit".[140]

Another important example of a condictio sine causa was the so-called condictio liberationis. If someone had undertaken, by way of an abstract stipulation, to pay a certain sum of money or to deliver a specific object, the promise was valid irrespective of whether the underlying reason (causa) for which it had been given was flawed or not.[141] If it was, the stipulator had received the promise sine causa. Despite the fact that this was neither a case of indebitum solutum nor of causa data causa non secuta, he had to render restitution. A specific procedural avenue was even made available for this purpose, because what the promisor asked for was neither certa res nor certa pecunia but "ut promissione liberetur", or simply "liberatio" (i.e. an incertum). Unless, therefore, the stipulator released him by means of acceptilatio, the promisor could institute a condictio incerti (sine causa) against him.[142]

(d) Condictio sine causa

Justinian accommodated these two special types of situations in a separate Digest title: D. 12, 7, De condictione sine causa. "Est et haec species condictionis, si quis sine causa promiserit . . .", it starts[143] and picks up the same theme (the condictio liberationis) at a later stage.[144] The condictio ob causam finitam is referred to in the second fragment.[145] Another case (Pap. D. 12, 7, 5)[146] is possibly included because of the uncertainty whether to subsume it under the condictio ob rem or ob turpem vel iniustam causam. All this creates the impression that D. 12, 7 was meant to serve as a residuary category, comprising whatever did not fit in neatly with any of the other condictiones. When they referred to it in this particular function, the writers of the ius commune usually spoke of the condictio sine causa specialis.[147] But there is another side to D. 12, 7, too. The introductory

[140] D. 19, 1, 11, 6.

[141] Cf. supra, pp. 91 sq., 550.

[142] Cf., for example, Iul. D. 12, 7, 3 ("Qui sine causa obligantur, incerti condictione consequi possunt ut liberentur . . ."); Iul. D. 39, 5, 2, 3 and 4; Ulp. D. 44, 4, 7 pr. and 1; Pomp./Paul. D. 19, 1, 5, 1; Wolf, *Causa stipulationis*, pp. 152 sqq.; Kaser, *RPr* I, pp. 598 sq.; Kupisch, op. cit., note 34, pp. 3 sq., 11 sq. Apart from suing for liberatio, the promisor could also defend himself against the stipulator's claim by means of the exceptio doli.

[143] Ulp. D. 12, 7, 1 pr.

[144] Iul. D. 12, 7, 3.

[145] Ulp. D. 12, 7, 2; cf. also Ulp. D. 12, 7, 1, 2.

[146] On which see Glück, vol. 13, pp. 189 sq.

[147] A third group of cases usually classified and discussed sub titulo condictio sine causa specialis were those that fell somewhere in between the condictiones by transfer and the condictio ex causa furtiva. Cf., for example, Iul. D. 12, 1, 19, 1, as discussed supra, p. 840. This group of cases is included in Ulpian's comprehensive phrase "[c]onstat id demum posse condici alicui, quod . . . non ex iusta causa ad eum pervenit" (cf. also Liebs, *Essays Honoré*,

fragment already assures the reader that "this kind of condictio" (the condictio sine causa, one is bound to infer) also lies "si solverit quis indebitum".[148] "[S]i ob causam promisit, causa tamen secuta non est" is then given as a further example of where it has to be said "*condictionem* locum habere".[149] A condictio, the condictio, the condictio sine causa? If these (and some other) texts[150] have to be taken to relate to the condictio sine causa, we must be dealing here with a remedy of very wide applicability; a remedy, in fact, that could be brought whenever any of the other, more specialized, condictiones could be instituted too. As such, it not only covered a hotchpotch of special cases but also swallowed up, as a kind of condictio (sine causa) generalis,[151] all the standard situations of enrichment liability qua condictio. The whole of the title D. 12, 7 oscillates uneasily between the two poles of a condictio sine causa specialis and generalis. It was, however, only in its former function that the condictio sine causa trod new ground. As condictio generalis it did not extend the range of enrichment liability; its main significance, in this respect, was to pinpoint the common basis of all enrichment condictiones.

III. THE SUBSEQUENT FATE OF THE CONDICTIONES

Just like the Roman contractual system, the whole range of condictiones supplementing it was received into the ius commune; and although the creation of a generalized law of contract was bound to jeopardize the basis on which they had once been devised, the Roman condictiones proved extraordinarily long-lived and made their way into many modern legal systems. To this day, they form the foundation of the South African law of unjustified enrichment and even make a somewhat quaint appearance in the German BGB. They are all still unmistakably Roman, but both their function and range of application have changed considerably. This is particularly obvious in the case of the condictio causa data causa non secuta.

1. Condictio causa data causa non secuta

(a) *Ius poenitentiae*

Originally, the condictio causa data causa non secuta was an integral part of the Roman law of restitution. It correlated to the datio ob rem,

p. 180). Generally on the condictio sine causa specialis, see Glück, vol. 13, pp. 183 sqq., 187 sqq.; De Vos, *Verrykingsaanspreeklikheid*, pp. 29 sqq.

[148] Ulp. D. 12, 7, 1 pr.

[149] Ulp. D. 12, 7, 1, 1.

[150] Cf., for example, Afr. D. 12, 7, 4.

[151] On which see, in particular, Wolf, *Causa stipulationis*, pp. 33 sqq., 40 sqq.

which, in turn, derived its specific significance from the fact that the range of consensual contracts was strictly limited. Wherever two parties could not, nudo consensu, create contractual obligations, the position of the party performing first deserved protection. Since he could not enforce counterperformance, he had to be able, at least, to claim his own performance back.

This right to ask for restitution, causa non secuta, already lost its absolutely essential character with the rise of the actiones praescriptis verbis:[152] for as soon as the recipient of the first performance could be sued to counterperform, the giver appeared to be sufficiently protected. In a way, therefore, recognition of the innominate real contracts stole the thunder of the condictio causa data causa non secuta; no longer indispensable, it remained available merely as an alternative remedy that provided whoever performed first with what effectively constituted a right of withdrawal from the contract. This right of withdrawal was peculiar to the innominate real contracts; an anomaly, incidentally, that was still enhanced by virtue of the fact that it could even be exercised on account of a simple change of mind.[153] Medieval lawyers tended to distinguish these two issues. A person may withdraw from an innominate real contract, they said, either ex capite causae non secutae or ex capite poenitentiae.[154] The ius poenitendi could be exercised until such time as the recipient of the first performance had counterperformed: "Cum enim is, qui dedit, non sit obligatus alteri", it was argued for several centuries,[155] "a conventione recedere et mutare voluntatem potest", irrespective of whether or not the other party was prepared to honour his obligation and had perhaps even already incurred expenses on this account.[156] A person who had given ob rem thus enjoyed a free discretion whether to institute a contractual claim or the condictio:

> ". . . in contractibus innominatis . . . in arbitrio est dantis, an actione praescriptis verbis ad contractum implendum, an vero . . . ad datum repetendum agere velit."[157]

(b) Condictio ratione cessationis causae

In strange contrast to these extremely liberal provisions, the condictio ratione cessationis causae (or: ex defectu causae)[158] was much more narrowly confined. Justinian had regarded it as inequitable that the

---

[152] Cf. supra, pp. 532 sqq.

[153] Cf. supra, p. 844.

[154] Cf. Scherner, *Rücktrittsrecht*, pp. 23 sqq.; Wollschläger, *Unmöglichkeitslehre*, pp. 61 sqq.

[155] The quotation is taken from Struve, *Syntagma*, Exerc. XVIII, Lib. XII, Tit. IV, XV.

[156] He could, however, demand indemnification for these expenses: cf. Struve, *Syntagma*, Exerc. XVIII, Lib. XII, Tit. IV, XV; Scherner, *Rücktrittsrecht*, pp. 23 sq.

[157] Lauterbach, *Collegium theoretico-practicum*, Lib. XII, Tit. IV, Tab. ad IX.

[158] On the interpretation of "causa" in terms of the condictio causa data causa non secuta by the medieval lawyers (causa finalis), see Alfred Söllner, "Die causa im Kondiktionen- und Vertragsrecht des Mittelalters bei den Glossatoren, Kommentatoren und Kanonisten", (1960) 77 *ZSS* 195 sq., 203 sqq.

recipient of the first performance should be exposed to a condictio, even where he was prevented from counterperforming as a result of fortuitous circumstances.

> "Pecuniam a te datam", he ruled,[159] "licet causa pro qua data est, non culpa accipientis, sed fortuito casu secuta non est, minime repeti posse certum est."

Having thus, in principle, introduced the criterion of fault into the sources dealing with the condictio causa data causa non secuta, he proceeded to qualify its range of application by retaining texts such as C. 4, 6, 5 where the condictio was granted, in spite of the fact that the recipient could not be blamed for being unable to do what was expected of him. C. 4, 6, 5, however, concerns a case of what we would today refer to as initial impossibility—a soldier had received money in order to act as procurator, an activity which he was not permitted to undertake.[160] Even more importantly, Justinian also omitted to bring the relevant Digest title in line with the new regime. Generations of interpreters have thus been perplexed by the obvious discrepancy between the generally worded statement in C. 4, 6, 10 and Celsus' decision concerning a case where one party gave another money in order to receive the slave Stichus:[161]

> ". . . nulla hic alia obligatio est quam ob rem dati re non secuta . . . et ideo, si mortuus est Stichus, repetere possum quod ideo tibi dedi, ut mihi Stichum dares."

There is no reference in this text to the possibility that the death of Stichus may have been attributable to the fault of the recipient of that sum of money.

(c) *Periculum debitoris and conditional synallagma*

For the writers of the ius commune all these sources were, of course, equally authoritative and a most refined and intricate set of distinctions was therefore developed to bring about some form of reconciliation.[162] In particular, one started to differentiate between various kinds of impossibility (initial or supervening, iure or facto, culpa or casu)[163] and thus, incidentally, to lay the foundations for the modern, general

---

[159] C. 4, 6, 10 (Diocl.; interpolated: cf. Schwarz, *Condictio*, p. 147).

[160] "Si militem ad negotium tuum procuratorem fecisti, cum hoc legibus interdictum sit, ac propter hoc pecuniam ei numerasti, quidquid ob causam datum est, causa non secuta restitui tibi competens iudex curae habebit."

[161] D. 12, 4, 16 ("Dedi tibi pecuniam, ut mihi Stichum dares . . ."). This arrangement was classified as datio ob rem, not as a contract of sale; cf. Emil Seckel, Ernst Levy, "Die Gefahrtragung beim Kauf im klassischen römischen Recht", (1927) 47 *ZSS* 131 sqq.; Arangio-Ruiz, *Compravendita*, pp. 150 sqq.; J.A.C. Thomas, "Celsus: Sale and the Passage of Property", in: *Studies in the Roman Law of Sale in memory of Francis de Zulueta* (1959), pp. 160 sqq.; D.E.C. Yale, "Celsus: Sale and Conditional Gift", in: *Studies De Zulueta*, pp. 171 sqq.

[162] Cf., for example, Struve, *Syntagma*, Exerc. XVIII, Lib. XII, Tit. IV, VI sqq.; the schematic exposition by Lauterbach, *Collegium theoretico-practicum*, Lib. XII, Tit. IV, Tab. ad IX; Glück, vol. 13, pp. 30 sqq. and the discussion by Wollschläger, *Unmöglichkeitslehre*, pp. 56 sqq.; cf. also Coing, p. 496.

[163] Cf., today, still § 815 BGB; infra, note 175.

impossibility doctrine.[164] But the leniency displayed, by and large, towards a debtor who could not be blamed for not performing, must have been largely a matter of theory; for how a restricted right of restitution ratione cessationis causae could be made to coexist in a meaningful manner with a virtually unrestricted condictio ob poenitentiam dantis remained obscure. It was the French humanist Donellus who saw this unsatisfactory discrepancy and who attempted therefore to elevate the rule of D. 12, 4, 16, once again, to the status of a general principle. Even if the recipient was prevented from performing on account of casus fortuitous, he argued,[165] he was liable, under the condictio causa data causa non secuta, for restoration. Donellus thus removed the necessity for strictly separating the condictiones ex defectu causae and propter poenitentiam. At the same time, he established the foundation of the general risk rule, contained today in § 323 BGB:[166] for if the recipient of the performance (i.e. the debtor of the counterperformance) remained exposed to the condictio causa data causa non secuta, irrespective of whether or not he could be blamed for not counterperforming, the risk of casus was in effect placed on his—the debtor's—shoulder. This regime of periculum debitoris gives expression to what is usually termed "conditional synallagma":[167] the one party gives (or does) only in order to receive what the other party has agreed to give (or do) in return. Originating, historically, in the discussions surrounding the interplay between innominate real contract and condictio causa data causa non secuta, the principle of periculum debitoris eventually came to be extended to bilateral contracts in general: (supervening) impossibility of performance entails the loss of the right to claim, or to retain, the counterperformance agreed upon.

(d) "Hodie [haec] condictio rara est"

Having thus displayed a remarkable capacity for initiating new doctrinal developments, the innominate real contracts were, however, ultimately doomed to wither away.[168] It was, of course, the ascendancy of the notion that every ("naked") pact begets an action (ex nudo pacto oritur actio)[169] that sealed their fate: if the consensus of the parties already creates a contract, it no longer makes sense to maintain that in certain situations a person is bound only when he receives performance. With the innominate real contracts the so-called ius poenitendi, or condictio ex poenitentia, was also bound to fall away. In Germany this remained disputed for some time ("Gravis inde controversia resultat; an supposita simplici illa pactorum validitate, poenitentiae adhuc locus sit

[164] On which see supra, pp. 687 sq., 809 sqq.
[165] *Commentarii de jure civili*, Lib. XIV, Cap. XXI, V. sqq.
[166] Wollschläger, *Unmöglichkeitslehre*, pp. 64 sqq.
[167] Cf. supra, p. 811.
[168] Cf., as far as the parallel problem of the real contracts is concerned, supra, pp. 164 sq.
[169] Cf. supra, pp. 537 sqq.

in contractibus innominatis?"),[170] but the Roman-Dutch authorities were practically unanimous as early as the 17th century:

". . . cum jure canonico et moribus nostris nuda pacta eandem, quam stipulationes, vim habeant, . . . ideo hodie ex quolibet contractu innominato efficax actio oritur, quae etiam re integra poenitentiam excludit, nisi aliud actum appareat."[171]

Furthermore, the condictio causa data causa non secuta in the narrower sense (ratione cessationis causae) had lost its main field of application. "Hodie [haec] condictio rara est", acknowledged Stryk,[172] and it is easy enough to see why that was so. If someone performs in order to receive a counterperformance, the parties will usually have concluded a contract. The first performance can then not be classified as a datio ob rem but occurs solvendi causa. If, on the other hand, the parties have not reached a contractual agreement, the reason for this will often lie in the fact that the purpose of the performance was not communicated to the recipient: in which case we are not dealing with a datio ob rem but merely with a unilateral motive that is irrelevant in law.[173] Thus it is only in a very small range of situations that the condictio causa data causa non secuta remains applicable:[174, 175] situations, essentially, in which the parties have come to some kind of arrangement that does not have the quality of an obligatory contract. One may think here of cases in which the parties cannot, or do not wish to, bind the recipient of the first performance: as, for example, where a person receives something in order to marry the giver[176] or to institute him as his heir, to adopt a child or to donate blood (in all these cases a contractual obligation on the part of the recipient would be frowned upon), where the

[170] Stryk, *Usus modernus pandectarum*, Lib. II, Tit. XIV, § 5; but cf. also idem, Lib. XII, Tit. IV, § 3; Glück, vol. 13, p. 48.

[171] Groenewegen, *De legibus abrogatis*, Digest. Lib. XII, Tit. IV, l. 5 si pecuniam; Voet, *Commentarius ad Pandectas*, Lib. XII, Tit. IV, VI.

[172] *Usus modernus pandectarum*, Lib. XII, Tit. IV, § 3.

[173] Cf. Schwarz, *Condictio*, pp. 117 sqq.

[174] The question as to which cases exactly (if any!) are still covered by the condictio causa data causa non secuta is highly controversial: one of the many major battlefields of legal dispute in the law of unjustified enrichment. Cf., as far as modern German law is concerned, Alfred Söllner, "Der Bereicherungsanspruch wegen Nichteintritt des mit der Leistung bezweckten Erfolges (§ 812 Abs. 1 S. 2, 2. Halbsatz BGB)", (1963) 163 *Archiv für die civilistische Praxis* 20 sqq.; Honsell, *Rückabwicklung*, pp. 75 sqq.; Liebs, 1978 *Juristenzeitung* 697 sqq.; Dieter Reuter, Michael Martinek, *Ungerechtfertigte Bereicherung* (1983), pp. 146 sqq.; Manfred Lieb, in: *Münchener Kommentar*, vol. III, 2 (2nd. ed., 1986), § 812, nn. 158 sqq.; Martin Weber, "Bereicherungsansprüche wegen enttäuschter Erwartung?", 1989 *Juristenzeitung* 25 sqq. For Roman-Dutch and South African law, cf. Wessels, *Contract*, nn. 3721 sqq.; De Vos, *Verrykingsaanspreeklikheid*, pp. 62 sqq., 154 sqq.; the position in Swiss law (art. 62, 2 OR) is analysed by Chaudet, op. cit., note 59, pp. 15 sqq. and passim (who comes to the conclusion that the condictio causa data causa non secuta is a relic of the past that has no place in modern law; for a similar verdict, cf. already Ernst von Caemmerer, "Bereicherung und unerlaubte Handlung", in: *Gesammelte Schriften*, vol. I (1968), pp. 222 sq.).

[175] The right to demand restitution is barred, however, if the attainment of the intended result was impossible from the beginning, and the person performing knew this: § 815 BGB.

[176] Cf. already C. 5, 3, 2 (Alex.); as to the recoverability of a dowry given for a marriage which subsequently does not take place, cf. D. 12, 4, 6 sqq. and many other texts (cf. Chaudet, op. cit., note 59, p. 47, n. 10).

performance is supposed to induce the other party to accompany the giver on a trip abroad[177] or to play a game of chess with him (such arrangements are usually not intended to leave the purely social level). Payment of part of a purchase price in the expectation that a contract of sale is going to be concluded may also be regarded as a datio ob rem;[178] if the contract does not subsequently come into existence, the condictio causa data causa non secuta is also still available.[179]

2. Condictio ob turpem vel iniustam causam

The decline of the condictio causa data causa non secuta was bound to be followed by that of the condictio ob turpem vel iniustam causam:[180] after all, it was also based on a datio ob rem, although one ob inhonestam causam. Again, therefore, all cases in which the parties intended to conclude a contract fall outside the scope of this condictio; such a contract almost invariably being void for illegality or immorality, the question arises here whether the first performance (rendered either solvendi or obligandi causa) may be reclaimed by means of the condictio indebiti or the condictio sine causa. But even where a datio ob rem has in fact taken place, it is doubtful whether the condictio ob turpem vel iniustam causam retains an independent and essential function. Every datio ob rem is based on an agreement between the parties that the recipient may, under certain circumstances, keep what has been handed over to him. If the purpose of the performance is such that its recipient is tainted by turpitude, this agreement underpinning the datio can hardly ever be regarded as valid. Yet, if the agreement is invalid, a claim for restitution lies on that account, rather than because one would have to recognize a specific exception to the principles governing the condictio causa data causa non secuta.

---

177 Cf. already C. 4, 6, 7 (Diocl. et Max.).

178 Cf. already Ulp. D. 19, 1, 11, 6.

179 On donationes sub modo (which could, according to Roman law, be reclaimed by means of the condictio causa data causa non secuta if the beneficiary did not fulfil the donor's wish), cf. Kaser, *RPr* I, p. 259; Liebs, 1978 *Juristenzeitung* 699; Stryk, *Usus modernus pandectarum*, Lib. XII, Tit. IV, § 8; Wessels, *Contract*, n. 3734; Windscheid/Kipp, § 368; as far as modern German law is concerned, see the statutory provisions of §§ 525 sqq. BGB (§ 527: "If the execution of the burden remains unperformed the donor may, under the conditions specified for the right of rescission in the case of mutual contracts, demand return of the gift under the provisions relating to the return of unjust enrichment to the extent that the gift ought to have been applied to the execution of the burden").

180 On the meaning of "turpis" and "iniusta" in this context, and on the question whether we are dealing with a single condictio or with two different ones, see Glück, vol. 13, pp. 50 sqq.; De Vos, *Verrykingsaanspreeklikheid*, pp. 66 sq. (Roman-Dutch law); pp. 160 sqq. (modern South African law); *Jajbhay v. Cassim* 1939 AD 537 at 547 sq. Today, in any event, we are faced with one condictio, covering both illegality and immorality: cf. § 817, 1 (on its legislative history, see Honsell, *Rückabwicklung*, pp. 98 sqq.); Leon E. Trakman, "The Effect of Illegality in South African Law", (1977) 94 *SALJ* 332.

3. In pari turpitudine causa est melior possidentis

(a) *Extension of the rule in modern German law*

But does it matter whether the exclusive field of application of the condictio ob turpem vel iniustam causam has indeed been narrowed down to zero?[181] Is there any point in determining whether the plaintiff may avail himself of this or any of the other condictiones? The whole discussion would, indeed, be rather academic were it not for the problem of the in pari turpitudine rule. The dilemma, at least in modern German law, is this: if the in pari turpitudine rule (as adopted by § 817, 2 BGB) were to be strictly confined to the condictio ob turpem vel iniustam causam (as laid down today in § 817, 1 BGB), it would be rendered practically meaningless. The modern statutory version of the condictio indebiti (§ 812 I 1 BGB) would in any event be applicable and could be used to sidestep the bar to the condictio ob turpem vel iniustam causam. The obvious way to avoid such a result (which would patently frustrate the intentions of the legislator)[182] is to extend the in pari turpitudine rule to all condictiones based on a transfer. This is indeed what the German courts have done.[183] But once one makes the rule so broadly applicable, one is immediately faced with a host of consequential problems. For one thing, cases of turpitudo solius dantis have to be covered:[184] it would be utterly unreasonable if only a recipient who had acted immorally himself were allowed to keep the performance, whereas the condictio would not be barred against a blameless receiver. As a result, the in pari turpitudine rule becomes applicable in cases of usurious loan transactions. But is it really palatable that the recipient of the capital may now retain the money without paying any interest at all? The initial exploitation would then eventually have turned out to be a rather arbitrary stroke of good luck.[185] For another thing, account must be taken of the fact that a sordid plaintiff may sometimes bring the rei vindicatio rather than an unjustified enrichment action. Should this claim not also be barred? In other words, why should a borrower who has charged exorbitant interest rates not be allowed to reclaim his capital, whereas a lessor who has charged an exorbitant rental should be able to have his property restored immediately? A lessee's interest in retaining his accommoda-

---

[181] As has been claimed, correctly, it is submitted, by Honsell, *Rückabwicklung*, pp. 10 sqq.; others contend that a need for the condictio ob turpem vel iniustam causam still exists, but that its range of application is very small. For a discussion, see Reuter/Martinek, op. cit., note 174, pp. 175 sqq.; Lieb, op. cit., note 174, § 817, nn. 4 sqq.

[182] "*Gesetzesvereitlung*": Philipp Heck, "Die Ausdehnung des § 817, S. 2, auf alle Bereicherungsansprüche", (1925) 124 *Archiv für die civilistische Praxis* 24.

[183] RGZ 151, 70 (72); RGZ 161, 52 (55); BGHZ 44, 1 (6); BGHZ 50, 90 (91); approved and followed by the prevailing opinion in the literature: cf., for example, Reuter/Martinek, op. cit., note 174, pp. 201 sq.

[184] Cf., for example, RGZ 161, 52 (55); Reuter/Martinek, op. cit., note 174, p. 202. This is, however, against the express wording of § 817, 2 BGB ("*gleichfalls*").

[185] Cf. supra, pp. 176 sq.

tion deserves at least as much protection as that of a borrower in not losing the capital.[186]

(b) "Sinister" and "disastrous" results

Then there is the problem[187] that the in pari turpitudine rule may be at variance with the basic proposition that immoral and illegal transactions are void. If both parties have carried out their respective obligations, exclusion of the right to bring enrichment actions leads to a perpetuation of the status quo: of a position, that is, of which the legal system expressly disapproves. The sanction of invalidity thus loses its practical effect. If, on the other hand, only one party has performed, application of the in pari turpitudine rule exposes him to a strange kind of double sanction: he may neither demand counterperformance nor is he allowed to claim back his own performance.[188] The eccentricity of those results is furthermore compounded by the fact that the in pari turpitudine rule is no longer confined to cases involving crimes and other grave infringements of the moral code: it applies to immoral and illegal transactions at large. Yet it can hardly be maintained that the original (or any other) rationale of the rule[189] covers situations in which the parties have committed a relatively minor infringement of one of the many modern, morally indifferent, statutory prohibitions.[190] Cut off from its historical moorings (that is, the condictio ob rem), the in pari turpitudine rule is lurching through the modern German law of unjustified enrichment without direction and has become one of the most dreaded perils in the sea of legal doctrine.[191] It has been described

[186] The courts have, however, refused to apply the in pari turpitudine rule to the rei vindicatio: RG, 1923 *Leipziger Zeitschrift für Deutsches Recht* 565 (566 sq.); OGHZ 4, 57 (65); BGHZ 39, 87 (91). Contra: Lieb, op. cit., note 174, § 817, nn. 20, 25; Zimmermann, *Moderationsrecht*, pp. 159 sqq. and many others.

[187] Cf. especially Honsell, *Rückabwicklung*, pp. 1 sqq.

[188] Cf. also Stratford CJ in *Jajbhay v. Cassim* 1939 AD 537 at 543 sq.: "It may be said that contracts of that nature are more discouraged by leaving the bereft plaintiff unhelped and the doubly delinquent defendant in possession of his ill-gotten gains. I cannot agree with this view, which I think would not so much discourage such transactions but would tend to promote a more reprehensible form of trickery by scoundrels without such honour as even thieves are sometimes supposed to possess, and public policy should properly take into account the doing of simple justice between man and man."

[189] Cf. supra, p. 846. For a modern discussion of the ratio legis, cf. Honsell, *Rückabwicklung*, pp. 58 sqq.; Reuter/Martinek, op. cit., note 174, pp. 203 sqq.; cf. also Trakman, (1977) 94 *SALJ* 330 sq.; Zweigert/Kötz, pp. 309 sq.

[190] Cf., in particular, Seiler, *Festschrift Felgentraeger*, pp. 389 sqq.; Andreas Wacke, "Vorzüge und Nachteile des deutschen Bereicherungsrechts", in: *Beiträge zum deutschen und israelischen Privatrecht* (1977), p. 146; Zweigert/Kötz, p. 309. The same point is emphasized, for South African law, by De Vos, *Verrykingsaanspreeklikheid*, p. 162; as far as French law is concerned, see Zweigert/Kötz, pp. 314 sqq.

[191] For an overview of the problems arising from the application of § 817, 2 BGB and of the various suggestions that have been made to deal with them, see Honsell, *Rückabwicklung*, pp. 1 sqq., 32 sqq. (who himself (pp. 136 sqq.) proposes drastically to restrict the range of application of the rule); contra: Zimmermann, *Moderationsrecht*, pp. 164 sqq.; Barbara

as ill-boding and sinister,[192] and the German Federal Supreme Court, in a startling pronouncement, has even contended that it intentionally disregards the precepts of justice.[193]

(c) The approach adopted by the South African courts

Much more in tune with the spirit in which the in pari turpitudine rule was once devised by the Roman lawyers is the attitude adopted in modern South African law.[194] Although they, too, no longer draw a distinction between immorality and lesser forms of illegality, the South African courts approach the matter in a much more flexible manner than their German counterparts.

> "[T]he rule expressed in the maxim in pari delicto potior conditio defendentis is not one that can or ought to be applied in all cases; . . . it is subject to exceptions which in each case must be found to exist only by regard to the principle of public policy",

said Stratford CJ, in the seminal decision of *Jajbhay v. Cassim*,[195] and Watermeyer JA, after a review of Roman and Roman-Dutch authorities,[196] came to the same conclusion:

Dauner, "Der Kondiktionsausschluss gem. § 817 S. 2", 1980 *Juristenzeitung* 495 sqq.; Reuter/Martinek, op. cit., note 174, pp. 199 sqq.; König, *Bereicherung*, pp. 130 sqq.; Lieb, op. cit., note 174, § 817, nn. 9 sqq.

[192] Walter Wilburg, *Entwicklung eines beweglichen Systems im bürgerlichen Recht* (1950), p. 11.

[193] BGHZ 8, 348 (373).

[194] For a discussion, see Trakman, (1977) 94 *SALJ* 468 sqq.; De Vos, *Verrykingsaanspreeklikheid*, pp. 160 sqq.

[195] 1939 AD 537 at 544.

[196] At 547 sqq. On Roman-Dutch law cf. also De Vos, *Verrykingsaanspreeklikheid*, p. 68. Generally speaking, the in pari turpitudine rule does not appear to have been of much practical relevance in the ius commune. Most writers contented themselves with mentioning the rule and referring to the examples discussed by the Roman lawyers (particularly the meretrix case: Ulp. D. 12, 5, 4, 3). Glück, vol. 13, p. 59 mentions, in addition, the case of a person who appears to have persuaded a great number of farmers (in Franconia) to give him money and to accept, in return, a sealed box in which they would find, after some time and due to the machinations of an earth goblin, a multiple of the original sum. After they had discovered the fraud, the farmers claimed their money back, but they lost their case on account of the in pari turpitudine rule. Cf. also Windscheid/Kipp, § 428, n. 11, who mention the rule only in a relatively obscure place. Occasionally it was argued that the recipient should not be allowed to keep his ill-gotten gains, but that the treasury should be able to take them from him; cf., for example, Stryk, *Usus modernus pandectarum*, Lib. XII, Tit. V, § 3; Glück, vol. 13, p. 60; §§ 172 sq. I 16 PrALR; cf. also Zweigert/Kötz, p. 310.

Since the days of the commentators, the in pari turpitudine rule was often regarded as one of the most important expressions of the general principle of "nemo auditur suam turpitudinem allegans": nobody will be heard (in court) if he has to plead his own turpitude; or, in the words of Lord Mansfield (*Holman v. Johnson* (1775) 1 Cowp 341): "No Court will lend its aid to a man who founds his cause of action upon an immoral or an illegal act." This maxim, developed by the glossators (cf. Fritz Sturm, "Aperçu sur l'origine du brocard Nemo auditur propiam turpitudinem allegans", (1970–71) 30 *Mémoires de la Société pour l'histoire du droit et des institutions des anciens pays bourguignons, comtois et romands* 289 sqq.; Robert Feenstra, "Nemo auditur suam turpitudinem allegans", in: *Brocardica in honorem G.C.J.J. van den Bergh* (1987), pp. 31 sqq.) and not by the canonists (as P. Savey-Casard, *Le refus d'action pour cause d'indignité, Etude sur la maxime Nemo auditur propiam turpitudinem allegans* (unpublished thesis, Lyon, 1930), passim, would have it) had nothing to do, originally, with the law of unjustified enrichment. It was devised in view of certain texts

> "The principle underlying the [in pari turpitudine] rule is that the Courts will discourage illegal transactions, but the exceptions show that where it is necessary to prevent injustice or to promote public policy, it will not rigidly enforce the general rule."[197]

The fact that the plaintiff has been guilty of dishonourable conduct does not, therefore, constitute an absolute bar to an enrichment action. It is the balance of equities between the parties that the courts have to consider[198] and in this context they take account of, inter alia, the relative degree of turpitude displayed by plaintiff and defendant and the extent to which the contract has been executed.[199]

4. Condictio indebiti

(a) *Function and range of application*

If the condictiones causa data causa non secuta and ob turpem vel iniustam causam dwindled in importance, the condictio indebiti went from strength to strength. One important development favouring its prospects was the gradual recognition of the principle of ex nudo pacto oritur actio. If every agreement gave rise to a binding contract, performance was made, more often than not, solvendi causa: in order to discharge an already existing obligation; and where such an obligation subsequently turned out not to have existed after all,

---

dealing with acts in fraudem creditoris and with the position of the mala fide possessor. For Roman antecedents of the maxim, cf. Ulp. D. 50, 17, 134, 1 ("Nemo ex suo delicto meliorem suam condicionem facere potest") and Ulp. D. 50, 17, 161. On "nemo auditur turpitudinem suam allegans" in the usus modernus, see the disputatio "De allegatione propriae turpitudinis", in: Samuel Stryk, *Opera*, vol. XI (Florentiae, 1840), Disputat. XVII; for a modern comparative analysis, see Hubert Niederländer, "Nemo turpitudinem suam allegans auditur—Ein rechtsvergleichender Versuch", in: *Ius et Lex, Festgabe für Max Gutzwiller* (1959), pp. 621 sqq.

[197] *Jajbhay v. Cassim* 1939 AD 537 at 550.

[198] Stratford CJ in *Jajbhay v. Cassim* 1939 AD 537 at 544 refers to "public policy" and "simple justice between man and man". Sharply critical are De Wet en Yeats, p. 83, who speak of " 'n grenslose moeras van onsekerheid". In favour of a great degree of flexibility also, as far as German law is concerned, is König, *Bereicherung*, pp. 126 sqq.; de lege ferenda idem, in: *Gutachten und Vorschläge zur Überarbeitung des Schuldrechts*, vol. II (1981), pp. 1531 sqq.

[199] For a comparative analysis of the application of the in pari turpitudine rule (as laid down, for instance, in § 1174 ABGB, art. 66 OR and art. 2035 codice civile and as recognized in France by the courts) cf. Honsell, *Rückabwicklung*, pp. 109 sqq.; cf. also Zweigert/Kötz, pp. 308 sqq. and the remarks by Seiler, *Festschrift Felgentraeger*, pp. 390 sq. and König, *Bereicherung*, pp. 146 sqq. Nowhere does it appear to be applied as broadly and inflexibly as in Germany. More specifically regarding English law, into which the in pari turpitudine rule was received by Lord Mansfield (cf. *Smith v. Bromley* (1760) 2 Dougl 696 ("If the act is in itself immoral, or a violation of the general laws of public policy, there the party paying shall not have this action; for where both parties are equally criminal against such general laws, the rule is potior est conditio defendentis"; the source of inspiration may either have been directly the Digest or the writings of Grotius, Pufendorf or Pothier)), see J.K. Grodecki, "In pari delicto potior est conditio defendentis", (1955) 71 *LQR* 254 sqq.; Muthard Hackbarth, *In pari turpitudine melior est conditio possidentis* (unpublished Dr. iur. thesis, Hamburg, 1967); Goff and Jones, *Restitution*, pp. 324 sqq. In modern Dutch law the rule has not been received at all (cf. Honsell, *Rückabwicklung*, pp. 130 sqq.; Feenstra, *Brocardica Van den Bergh*, p. 31).

restitution had to occur in terms of the condictio indebiti. Its fortunes were further boosted by the recognition of the principle of abstraction. The transfer of ownership, so Savigny taught,[200] is based on an agreement between the owner and the acquirer that ownership be transferred. This agreement constitutes a legal transaction that is completely separate from, and independent of, the underlying obligatory act (the contract of sale, exchange, donation etc.). More particularly, its validity remains unaffected in principle by any vice from which this underlying act might suffer. It is obvious that that doctrine was bound to broaden the field of application of the law of unjustified enrichment at the expense of the rei vindicatio; for if transfer of ownership no longer required a valid "causa", the transferor was usually destined to lose his title and could merely argue that this change of title was unjustified and had to be reversed. Thus, in the words of the great pandectist Heinrich Dernburg,[201] it is by means of an enrichment action that the law attempts to heal the wounds that it itself inflicts (by virtue of the abstract transfer of ownership). Again, we are dealing in

---

[200] *System*, vol. III, pp. 312 sq., 321; *Obligationenrecht*, vol. II, pp. 256 sq. For a detailed analysis, cf. Wilhelm Felgentraeger, *Friedrich Carl v. Savignys Einfluss auf die Übereignungslehre* (1927); Hammen, *Savigny*, pp. 146 sqq., 152 sqq. Traditionally, transfer of ownership had been seen to depend on what the jurists of the German usus modernus referred to as titulus (= causa) and modus (= the different forms of traditio). One of the main problems for them was to reconcile the *causal* transfer of ownership, as it appeared from texts such as Paul. D. 41, 1, 31 pr. ("Numquam nuda traditio transfert dominium, sed ita, si venditio aut aliqua iusta causa praecesserit, propter quam traditio sequeretur"), with the existence of the title D. 12, 6 on the condictio indebiti; for the condictio indebiti obviously presupposed a transfer of ownership in spite of the lack of causa. This dilemma was generally resolved by postulating that a causa putativa (or erronea) was sufficient to transfer ownership. Characteristically, the gloss remarked: "[V]era vel putativa alioquin si dicas ex putativa non transferri dominium, totus titulus de condictione indebiti repugnaret: qui titulus habet locum quando transfertur dominium alicuius rei ex putativa causa" (gl. Iusta causa ad D. 41, 1, 31 pr.; cf. also Kupisch, op. cit., note 34, pp. 32 sq.). The causa putativa doctrine (on which, see, for example, Coing, p. 304) was clearly a make-shift one and meant, in effect, that only lip service was paid to the causal system; after all, the parties failed to produce an effective causal transaction. But whatever they might have intended the causa to be, implicit in their arrangement was also the will to effect a transfer of ownership. This was the nucleus of the abstract contract that eventually replaced the "titulus"; cf. already Donellus, *Commentarii de Jure Civili*, Lib. IV, Cap. XVI, IX and Pothier, *Traité de la propriété*, n. 230 read together with *Traité du prêt de consomption*, n. 178 (*"Celui, qui paie à quelqu'un, par erreur, une chose qu'il croit lui devoir a la volonté de lui en transférer le domaine par la tradition qu'il lui en fait; celui, à qui elle est payée, a pareillement la volonté d'en acquérir le domaine: ce concours de leurs volontés suffit, avec la tradition, pour la translation de la propriété"*); cf. also the discussion by Filippo Ranieri, "Brevi note sull'origine della nozione di negozio reale ed astratto", (1970) 38 *TR* 315 sqq.; Kupisch, op. cit., note 34, pp. 33 sqq. Savigny's magisterial exposition of the doctrine marked its breakthrough as far as German legal science was concerned; cf. Filippo Ranieri, "Die Lehre der abstrakten Übereignung in der deutschen Zivilrechtswissenschaft des 19. Jahrhunderts", in: H. Coing, W. Wilhelm (eds.), *Wissenschaft und Kodifikation des Privatrechts im 19. Jahrhundert* (1977), pp. 90 sqq.; Hammen, *Savigny*, pp. 156 sqq.

The principle of abstraction is still of fundamental importance in the modern German law of property (cf. the literature referred to supra, p. 834, note 4; see further Zweigert/Kötz, *Einführung in die Rechtsvergleichung* (1st ed. (!)), vol. I (1971), pp. 213 sqq.); it is also recognized in South Africa (cf. C.G. van der Merwe, *Sakereg* (1979), pp. 204 sqq.).

[201] *Bürgerliches Recht*, vol. II, 2 (3rd ed., 1906), pp. 677 sq.

most of these cases with an unsuccessful attempt to effect the discharge of an obligation (a transfer solvendi causa), and the appropriate medication is therefore the condictio indebiti.

(b) The error requirement: sententia Papiniani

The requirements of the condictio indebiti have not changed much over the centuries. The plaintiff had to have rendered a performance in order to discharge an obligation which did not in fact exist (indebitum solutum).[202] Furthermore, he had to have acted in the mistaken belief that he was bound to make that performance. Error thus remained an essential prerequisite for this type of claim. All details as to what exactly that implied were, however, endlessly disputed. The main controversy raged over the problem of how to deal with error iuris. "Cum quis ius ignorans indebitam pecuniam persolverit, cessat repetitio":[203] the emperors Diocletian and Maximian could hardly have given a clearer expression to their view that a mere error iuris excluded the condictio. Yet, on the other hand, the Digest contains a statement by Papinian to the effect that, while a mistake of law does not benefit those who wish to acquire, it does not prejudice those who sue for what is theirs.[204] The plaintiff under a condictio indebiti clearly claimed back what should have remained his; he did not intend to make a gain, but attempted to prevent a permanent (unjustified) diminution of his assets. Consequently, an error iuris should not be taken to prejudice his chances of success. The authors of the ius commune were thus faced with a dilemma. Having to apply the Corpus Juris Civilis as it stood, it would have been of little concern for them to know that the one text represented Justinianic law, whereas the other one reflected the view held by the classical jurists. They had somehow to harmonize the sources. In century after century ever more refined distinctions were drawn.[205] Majority support, broadly speaking, oscillated between two different points of view.

> "Veteres omnes fere . . . ita rem hanc explicant, ut concludant, hanc Constitutionem [scil. C. 1, 18, 10] accipiendam non esse de omni indebito soluto iuris ignorantiam, sed de indebito civiliter, debito autem naturaliter."[206]

---

[202] For a detailed discussion, see Glück, vol. 13, pp. 73 sqq., 76 sqq.; as far as modern law is concerned, see §§ 813 and 814 in fine BGB and Reuter/Martinek, op. cit., note 174, pp. 129 sqq. On the notions of "causa" and performance "sine causa" in the context of the condictio indebiti, see Visser, (1988) 51 *THRHR* 498 sqq., 502 sqq.

[203] C. 1, 18, 10.

[204] D. 22, 6, 7: "Iuris ignorantia non prodest adquirere volentibus, suum vero petentibus non nocet." On this text, see Winkel, op. cit., note 104, pp. 109 sqq.; on its relevance for the right to bring the condictio indebiti, see pp. 200 sqq.

[205] For a detailed analysis, cf. Visser, op. cit., note 100, pp. 66 sqq.; for brief overviews, cf. Koch, op. cit., note 104, pp. 116 sqq.; Coing, p. 494.

[206] Fachinaeus, *Controversiae iuris*, Lib. VIII, Cap. CVI.

This was the basic tenet of the one opinion.[207] The principle of error iuris nocet was to be confined to cases where the plaintiff had honoured an obligatio naturalis; if he had wrongly assumed that his performance was not only naturaliter but also civiliter debitum, he could not demand its retransfer. If, however, he had given what he owed neither civiliter nor naturaliter, he could bring the condictio indebiti irrespective of whether his mistake had been one of fact or law:

> "Caeterum, si nec civiliter nec naturaliter sit debitor, et solverit, repetere id potest, ne damnum sentiat omissionis pecuniae suae contra sententiam Papiniani."[208]

(c) *Error iuris nocet, error facti non nocet*

Proponents of the other major line of argument[209] embraced the principle of C 1, 18, 10, and with it the division between error facti and error iuris, much less equivocally. Error iuris nocet, whilst error facti non nocet, they claimed. Of Pap. D. 22, 6, 7 they made rather short shrift. "Iuris ignorantia . . . . suum . . . . petentibus non nocet" were the words used by Papinian; but since a person proceeding under a condictio indebiti had lost his ownership and was not reclaiming what belonged to him but merely what was owed to him, this passage did not actually apply to the present type of situation:

> ". . . non enim hic de rei suae petitione questio est, eum secundum ante dicta is, qui solvit, dominus esse desierit, ac condictione indebiti non *suum* repetat, sed sibi debitum ex quasi contractu."[210]

By the time of the usus modernus pandectarum both points of view still found support, though the balance was shifting increasingly towards the latter.[211]

(d) *Ignorantia vincibilis and invincibilis*

At the same time, however, a third solution began to be aired. "Ego certe neminem adhuc vidi, qui pugnantes in hac juris parte invicem

---

[207] It was essentially developed by the glossators and dominated during the Middle Ages: cf. Visser, op. cit., note 100, pp. 66 sqq., 92 sqq., 113 sqq.

[208] Fachinaeus, *Controversiae iuris*, Lib. VIII, Cap. CVI.

[209] In particular, the ultramontani and the humanists. For details, see Visser, op. cit., note 100, pp. 110 sqq., 122 sqq.

[210] Voet, *Commentarius ad Pandectas*, Lib. XII, Tit. VI, VII.

[211] In favour of the strict distinction between error iuris and error facti were, for example, Benedict Carpzov, *Jurisprudentia forensis Romano-Saxonica, Francofurti ad Moenum* (1650), Pars III, Const. XV, Definit. XLII; Lauterbach, *Collegium theoretico-practicum*, Lib. XII, Tit. VI, XVIII; cf. further the discussion by Fachinaeus, *Controversiae*, Lib. VIII, Cap. CVI; Glück, vol. 13, pp., 135 sqq. As far as Dutch legal science was concerned, cf., in favour of the error iuris/error facti dichotomy, Perezius, *Praelectiones*, Lib. IV, Tit. V, 14; Voet, *Commentarius ad Pandectas*, Lib. XII, Tit. VI, VI sq.; contra: Vinnius, *Institutiones*, Lib. III, Tit. XXVIII, 6, n. 3; Huber, *Praelectiones*, Pars I, Lib. III, Tit. XXVIII, 7; cf. also Grotius, *Inleiding*, III, XXX, 9. For further analysis, see Visser, op. cit., note 100, pp. 152 sqq.

South African courts have adopted the view that error iuris, generally speaking, excludes the condictio indebiti; cf. *Rooth v. S* (1888) 2 SAR 259 (per Kotzé CJ; the decision contains an extensive investigation of the ius commune) and the analyses by De Vos, *Verrykingsaanspreeklikheid*, pp. 182 sqq.; Visser, op. cit., note 100, pp. 235 sqq.

leges satis conciliarit", declared Augustin Leyser,[212] taking stock of 500 years of doctrinal dispute. "Quae quum ita sint", he concluded, "alium fontem, ex quo decisio dubiorum circa doctrinam de ignorantia et errore emergentium hauriatur investigari oportebit." The source of inspiration that he had in mind was "recta ratio", and it induced him to cut the Gordian knot by distinguishing between ignorantia vincibilis (surmountable and hence unreasonable or inexcusable)[213] and invincibilis. Excusability of the mistake as a general criterion to determine whether or not to grant the condictio indebiti quickly gained ascendancy among the 19th-century pandectists, though not, of course, merely on the basis of "sound reason". General statements such as those contained in C. 1, 18, 10 or D. 22, 6, 7, it was now argued,[214] could not be seen as absolute and rigid legal rules; they provided no more than guidelines that had to be interpreted in the light of a whole range of qualifications which could emerge from the decisions of specific cases.[215] The consequence was not a complete rejection of the error iuris/error facti dichotomy, but merely its relegation to a secondary place. For even if excusability (or reasonableness) now appeared to commend itself as the principal criterion that was bound, to a certain extent, to cut across all the established distinctions, it could still be maintained that errores facti, as a rule, were excusable, whereas errores iuris, by and large, were not. Yet, legal certainty was seriously jeopardized. An error of law could, after all, sometimes be regarded as reasonable, an error of fact as unreasonable; certain presumptions were sometimes applied and at other times rejected in this regard, and the whole issue eventually got entangled in an inordinate amount of casuistry.[216] When the BGB was drafted, its compilers were therefore determined to reform the law. Error iuris and error facti were placed on a par and the excusability criterion abolished. Moreover, error was dropped as a specific requirement of the condictio indebiti; instead, the onus was now placed on the defendant to show that the plaintiff had known, at the time of rendering performance, about the absence of an

---

[212] *Meditationes ad Pandectas*, Spec. CCLXXXIX, I and II.

[213] "Illam [sc.: ignorantiam vincibilem] vocamus, quam quis, adhibita attentione et diligentia debita, discutere potuisset; hanc [sc.: ignorantiam invicibilem], quae admota licet omni cura, quam vitae communis ratio et personarum conditio fert, dispelli nequivisset" (Leyser, loc. cit.).

[214] Cf., in particular, Vangerow, *Pandekten*, § 625, Anm. 1; cf. also § 83, Anm. 1, V; further: Windscheid/Kipp, § 426, 3; Dernburg, *Pandekten*, vol. II, § 141, 3; also already Savigny, *System*, vol. III, pp. 447 sqq. (on Pap. D. 22, 6, 7, cf. pp. 346 sqq.); and see the analyses by Koch, op. cit., note 104, pp. 119 sqq.; Visser, op. cit., note 100, pp. 190 sqq.

[215] Likewise, the common-law rule that excludes recovery of money paid under a mistake of law (cf. supra, note 113) has, in the course of time, been considerably watered down. Cf. Goff and Jones, *Restitution*, pp. 90 sqq. (claiming that "[f]ew subjects are more confused"); Birks, *Restitution*, pp. 164 sqq.; and, for a comparative analysis, Zweigert/ Kötz, pp. 299 sqq.

[216] König, *Bereicherung*, pp. 33, 40 sq.

obligation.[217] Without realizing it, the legislator had thus come close to the position that had once prevailed in classical Roman law.

5. Condictio sine causa

(a) Condictio sine causa specialis

The condictio sine causa remained ianus-faced and enigmatic.[218] Johannes Voet described its two functions in the following terms:

> "Et vel generalis est vel specialis: generalis, quae cum aliis condictionibus concurrere potest, veluti condictio indebiti, causa data, causa non secuta, ob turpem injustamve causam, aliisque similibus: cum utique his omnibus in casibus res merito dici possit sine causa penes possidentem esse . . .; [s]pecialis sine causa condictio est, quae tunc locum habet, cum aliis actionibus locus non est."[219]

This subdivision into a general and a special condictio sine causa represented the prevailing doctrine of the ius commune.[220] Its "special" variety was the rag-picker among the condictiones: it served to gather all instances of an unjustified retention that did not fit into one of the established categories of enrichment liability. There was no other common denominator for this hotchpotch of cases than the fact that one person had somehow or other (that is, by transfer or otherwise) acquired something which he now appeared to retain without cause. "[S]i causa, quae initio erat, postea casu aliquo desiit esse"[221] was one such case; initially there was a causa for the transfer, but it subsequently fell away. This particular species of a condictio sine causa was occasionally even elevated to the status of a specific, "nominate" enrichment claim in its own right.[222] Apart from that we find, for example, the cases of the ring that had been given as an arrha and was still kept, "precio ac re solutis", by the vendor, or of the promissory note "quod soluto debito penes creditorem sine causa manet".[223] Of particular importance, at least in the light of modern discussions, were those situations where the acquisition had not come about by way of transfer but, for example, "vi fluminum",[224] or as a result of specificatio or consumptio.[225] Among two of the leading luminaries of

---

[217] § 814 BGB. For an analysis of the problems arising in modern law and a comparative evaluation of § 814 BGB, cf. Zweigert/Kötz, pp. 299 sqq.; König, *Bereicherung*, pp. 39 sqq., 73 sqq.

[218] For an overview, cf. Rolf Schmitt, *Die Subsidiarität der Bereicherungsansprüche* (1969), pp. 67 sqq. On the medieval condictio sine causa generalis, cf. the detailed analysis by Söllner, (1960) 77 *ZSS* 190 sqq., 202 sqq.

[219] *Commentarius ad Pandectas*, Lib. XII, Tit. VII, I.

[220] On Roman-Dutch law, cf. the analysis by De Vos, *Verrykingsaanspreeklikheid*, pp. 71 sqq.

[221] Samuel Cocceji, *Jus civile controversum, Francofurti et Lipsiae* (1740), Lib. XII, Tit. VII.

[222] The condictio ob causam finitam; cf., for instance, § 1435 ABGB.

[223] Cocceji, loc. cit. (based on Ulp. D. 19, 1, 11, 6 and C. 4, 9, 2).

[224] Ulp. D. 12, 1, 4, 2.

[225] Cf., for example, Vangerow, *Pandekten*, § 628, II and III; Dernburg, vol. II, § 143; Windscheid/Kipp, § 422; "Motive", in: *Mugdan*, vol. II, pp. 475 sqq.

19th-century legal science there was a lively dispute about whether a bona fide possessor was liable, on the basis of the Roman sources, under a condictio sine causa if he consumed or sold somebody else's object (and thus encroached upon his ownership).[226]

(b) *Condictio sine causa generalis*

The condictio sine causa generalis, on the other hand, was available whenever any of the other enrichment condictiones could also be brought: it "concurred" with them.[227] As such, in a way, it was a rather meaningless institution and was consequently dropped by quite a few of the writers of the ius commune.[228] Yet Lauterbach (who, in turn, emphasized the condictio sine causa generalis at the expense of its more special sidekick) noted an important point when he wrote: "Nam causa honesta non secuta, aut turpis, vel injusta, aut erronea, quoad hanc actionem, habetur pro nulla."[229] "Sine causa" may thus be seen as a common denominator for the whole range of Roman enrichment condictiones,[230] and as such it presented itself as a suitable starting point for streamlining the law of unjustified enrichment. Rather than eliminate the condictio sine causa generalis as redundant, one could abandon the system of the "nominate" condictiones, haphazard as it now (with the recognition, at long last, of ex nudo pacto oritur actio) appeared to be. This is exactly what Friedrich Carl von Savigny proposed to do. Examining the multitude of Roman condictiones on a "historical" basis—from the condictio ex mutuo, which was, to him, the paradigm, via all those other cases where the enrichment had come about as a result of a "datio", down to the instances (often previously overlooked!) of an enrichment arising from the defendant's own act or from accidental circumstances[231]—he came to the conclusion that the true basis of all of them consists in claiming something back which has come from the plaintiff's property. Their common feature, he proclaimed, was the enlargement of the assets of one party by way of diminution of the assets of another, leading to a state of unjustified

[226] Bernhard Windscheid, "Zwei Fragen aus der Lehre von der Verpflichtung wegen ungerechtfertigter Bereicherung", in: *Gesammelte Reden und Abhandlungen"* (1904), pp. 301 sqq.; contra: Rudolf von Jhering, "Ist der ehemalige gutgläubige Besitzer einer fremden Sache verpflichtet, nach deren Untergang dem Eigenthümer derselben den gelösten Kaufpreis herauszugeben?" (1878) 16 *JhJb* 230 sqq.; cf. also Windscheid/Kipp, § 422; König, *Bereicherung*, pp. 157 sqq.

[227] Cf., for example, gl. Est et haec species ad D. 12, 7, 1: "Ipsa tamen generalissima est. nam concurrit fere cum omnibus aliis. . . ."

[228] Cf., for example, Stryk, *Usus modernus pandectarum*, Lib. XII, Tit. VII; Glück, vol. 13, pp. 183 sqq.; Reinhard, "Zur Lehre von der condictio sine causa", (1846) 29 *Archiv für die civilistische Praxis* 233 sqq.

[229] *Collegium theoretico-practicum*, Lib. XII, Tit. VII, V.

[230] Cf. also, as far as the condictio indebiti is concerned, Visser, (1988) 51 *THRHR* 498 sqq.

[231] *System*, vol. V, pp. 503 sqq. Savigny's theory is analysed by Jan Wilhelm, *Rechtsverletzung und Vermögensentscheidung als Grundlagen und Grenzen des Anspruchs aus ungerechtfertigter Bereicherung* (1973), pp. 19 sqq.; cf. also Hammen, *Savigny*, pp. 187 sqq.

"habere"; unjustified, because a legal basis (a causa) for this shift of assets had either not existed in the first place or had subsequently fallen away.[232] In the case of the condictiones indebiti and ob causam finitam, for example, this causa was obviously the underlying obligatory act. Savigny's lucid exposition marked the birth of the famous German general enrichment action. It gained widespread recognition in 19th-century legal doctrine[233] and was, most importantly, eventually also received into the BGB.

IV. ENRICHMENT LIABILITY OUTSIDE THE CONDICTIONES

1. Aequitas naturalis and the lex Si et me et Titium

It was, however, not only through their analysis of the various condictiones that the lawyers of the ius commune worked towards the modern generalized law of unjustified enrichment. A "seductive idea"[234] such as the prohibition of unjust enrichment was bound to shape the solution of a whole range of problems other than those eventually compiled in titles 12, 4-7 of the Digest or the equivalent subsections of the Code. The evidence for this was scattered throughout the Corpus Juris and no part of it missed the enquiring eyes of legal geologists[235] who started digging in the Middle Ages. One of the first, and most notable, finds in this huge quarry was, of course, the general equitable principle enunciated by Pomponius: ". . . hoc natura aequum est neminem cum alterius detrimento fieri locupletiorem." The mere fact that it had been elevated by the compilers to the status of a regula iuris antiqui, and as such had been included in the final Digest title[236] indicated to the medieval lawyers that its influence extended far beyond the condictiones. They realized that it did not contain a non-committal theoretical statement on natural law or equity, but that it constituted, instead, a formative force behind a variety of rules and institutions of the positive law.[237] On the other hand, however, they were too faithful to the sources to convert it into a rule of positive jurisprudence in its own right and thus to start exploiting its conceivably rather explosive potential. Primarily, therefore, they saw their task in listing both emanations and limitations of the principle as far as they could find them in the Corpus Juris.[238] This very process,

---

232 *System*, vol. V, p. 525.

233 For an analysis, cf. Wilhelm, op. cit., note 231, pp. 38 sqq.; Hammen, *Savigny*, pp. 198 sqq.

234 Dawson, op. cit., note 119, p. 61.

235 Cf. the metaphor by Dawson, op. cit., note 119, p. 63.

236 Pomp. D. 50, 17, 206.

237 Cf. Helmut Coing, "Zur Lehre von der ungerechtfertigten Bereicherung bei Accursius", (1963) 80 *ZSS* 396 sqq.

238 Coing, (1963) 80 *ZSS* 396 sqq.

however, brought to light apparent contradictions and discrepancies, which had to be resolved; and it was usually in the unravelling of these puzzling details that recourse was had to aequitas naturalis, aequitas generalis, and the like.[239] A particularly important part was played, in this context, by the so-called lex Si et me et Titium,[240] a text in which Celsus himself appeared to have derived the right to (re-)claim directly from the precepts of good faith and equity. D. 12, 1, 32 concerns what may be referred to as third-party enrichment, the most notoriously difficult of all enrichment constellations:[241] C (in terms of our discussion above)[242] has been enriched on account of the fact that B has transferred to him, sine causa, what he (B) owed to A. Obviously, this precedent could not be used for too ambitious generalizations, for there was always the negotium requirement of the lex Si in area[243] that had to be kept in mind.[244] Yet, some extension was permissible and thus the medieval lawyers were prepared to consider favourably the position of a person who had lent some money to a pauper. The pauper, before falling insolvent, had used the money to buy food for his sons, who, in turn, subsequently inherited their mother's estate. The remedy against the insolvent father being without any value, the lender was allowed to proceed "contra ipsos filios habentes forte res maternas, ex aequitate huius legis [sc.: D. 12, 1, 32]".[245] This solution might, at first glance, appear to be in conflict with D. 12, 6, 49 (the lex His solis),[246] where Modestinus made it clear that the condictio was available only against those to whom payment had been made and not against those who had benefited from such payment. The necessary reconciliation was achieved on the basis that the lex His solis was taken to pertain only to those cases where the recipient of the performance had not become insolvent.[247]

[239] The productive role played by the glossators in the advancement of the unjust enrichment principle has recently been emphasized by E.J.H. Schrage, "Qui in fundo alieno aedificavit. Die actio negotiorum gestorum utilis als Vorstufe einer allgemeinen Bereicherungsklage", lecture presented at the congress of the SIHDA in Salzburg (September 1988).

[240] Cels. D. 12, 1, 32, on which, see supra, pp. 853 sq.

[241] On third-party enrichment in Roman law in general, see A.M. Honoré, "Third Party Enrichment", 1960 *Acta Juridica* 236 sqq.

[242] Supra, pp. 853 sq.

[243] Iul. D. 12, 6, 33, on which see supra, p. 854 (note 133).

[244] Dawson, op. cit., note 119, p. 67 refers to the "problem that haunted the doctors".

[245] Yason de Mayno, ad D. 12, 1, 32 (Robert Feenstra, "De betekenis van De Groot en Huber voor de ontwikkeling van een algemene actie uit ongerechtvaardigde verrijking", in: *Uit het recht, Rechtsgeleerde opstellen aangeboden aan mr. P.J. Verdam* (1971), p. 141); cf. also Dawson, op. cit, note 119, pp. 75 sq.

[246] "His solis pecunia condicitur, quibus quoquo modo soluta est, non quibus proficit."

[247] Robert Feenstra, "Die ungerechtfertigte Bereicherung in dogmengeschichtlicher Sicht", in: (1972) 29 *Ankara Üniversitesi Hukuk Fakültesi Dergisi* 226 sq.

2. The actio negotiorum gestorum (contraria) as enrichment action

(a) *Mala fide administration of another's affairs*

The most exciting and, in the long run, significant advances towards a more generalized enrichment liability were made in two closely related areas. The one was negotiorum gestio.[248] Like the condictio indebiti, the unauthorized management of somebody else's affairs was classified as a quasi-contractual obligation.[249] We have seen that, under certain circumstances, the principal was granted a claim against the gestor (the so-called actio negotiorum gestorum directa) and the gestor, in turn, an actio contraria against the principal.[250] It was this actio negotiorum gestorum contraria that was occasionally used as an enrichment action. Two fragments from the Digest are of particular importance. Digesta 3, 5, 5, 5 is one of them.

> "Sed et si quis negotia mea gessit non mei contemplatione, sed sui lucri causa, Labeo scripsit suum eum potius quam meum negotium gessisse . . .: sed nihilo minus, immo magis et is tenebitur negotiorum gestorum actione. ipse tamen si circa res meas aliquid impenderit, non in id quod ei abest, quia improbe ad negotia mea accessit, sed in quod ego locupletior factus sum habet contra me actionem."[251]

We are dealing with the mala fide administration of the affairs of another; despite the fact that the gestor has transacted his own business rather than that of the principal—in fact, even more so than if he had—he can be held liable under the actio negotiorum gestorum directa. But can he, on his part, demand reimbursement for his expenses from the principal? Intuitively, one may perhaps be inclined to answer in the negative: after all, he meddled with the affairs of another, not for that other person's sake, but for his own profit. Yet, at the same time it must also be acknowledged that it would hardly be equitable if the principal were allowed to keep what he had gained as a result of the gestor's expenses. Hence the compromise solution, perhaps already advocated by the classical Roman lawyers:[252] the gestor may claim his expenses only in so far as the principal has been enriched thereby. Liability under the actio negotiorum gestio contraria was thus limited to "quanto locupletior factus est". This phrase did not, incidentally, refer to the defendant's actual enrichment at the time of litis contestatio (that is, to the amount by which he was still enriched when he was

[248] For what follows, see the detailed analysis by D.H. van Zyl, *Die saakwaarnemingsaksie as verrykingsaksie in die Suid-Afrikaanse reg* (unpublished Dr. iur. thesis, Leiden, 1970), pp. 38 sqq. For a summary in English cf. also, by the same author, *Negotiorum gestio in South African Law* (1985), pp. 84 sqq.

[249] Cf. *Inst.* III, 27, 1.

[250] For details, see supra, pp. 433 sqq., 443 sqq.

[251] On this text, see Ernst Rabel, "Negotium alienum and animus", in: *Studi in onore di Pietro Bonfante*, vol. IV (1930), pp. 279 sqq.; Seiler, *Negotiorum gestio*, pp. 29 sq.; Van Zyl, *Saakwaarnemingsaksie*, op. cit., note 248, pp. 22 sqq.; Kaser *RPr* I, p. 588, n. 20.

[252] Kaser, op. cit.

sued) but to what he had originally received.[253] The position of a malae fidei gestor was obviously not very different from that of a malae fidei possessor who made improvements on somebody else's land. This brought the principle enunciated in D. 12, 6, 33, the famous lex Si in area, into the discussion, and suddenly the medieval interpreters were faced with a serious inconsistency: for according to the lex Si in area not even the bona fide possessor could institute an action on account of the fact that he had improved somebody else's property. It was the glossator Martinus who seized the opportunity to unhinge the troublesome and inconvenient lex Si in area. Boldly he pronounced "quod malae fidei possessor, etiam si suo nomine expensas fecit, habeat non solum retentionem . . . sed etiam actionem",[254] and referred to Pomponius' famous unjust enrichment principle for support. Many of his contemporaries refused to follow suit;[255] they regarded his well-known bias in favour of equity[256] as somewhat exaggerated. Yet, slowly but surely, his interpretation gained ground. Grotius[257] and Voet[258] were among its most prominent advocates in Holland, Cuiacius, Molinaeus and Pothier in France.[259] Pothier considered the action to be based "*sur la seule raison de l'équité naturelle, qui ne permet pas de s'enricher et de profiter aux dépens d'autrui*".[260] Molinaeus, as usual, had expressed the same idea before him, though less elegantly and not in the vernacular.[261] Even in Germany, where legal writers remained, on the whole, more cautious, the actio negotiorum gestorum utilis of the malae fidei possessor appears to have been widely accepted in practice.[262, 263]

---

[253] Hubert Niederländer, *Die Bereicherungshaftung im klassischen römischen Recht* (1953), pp. 141, 145 sqq.; Kaser, *RPr* I, p. 600.

[254] Cf. gl. Actionem ad D. 3, 5, 5, 5.

[255] For details of the development, see Van Zyl, *Saakwaarnemingsaksie*, op. cit., note 248, pp. 42 sqq., 51 sq., 57 sq., 64 sqq., 77 sqq., 85 sq., 91 sqq.; cf. also *Festschrift Verdam*, pp. 138, 150.

[256] Cf. Hermann Kantorowicz, *Studies in the Glossators of the Roman Law* (1938), pp. 86 sqq.

[257] *Inleiding*, III, I, 15.

[258] *Commentarius ad Pandectas*, Lib. V, Tit. III, XXIII.

[259] For all details, see Van Zyl, *Saakwaarnemingsaksie*, op. cit., note 248, pp. 62 sqq.

[260] *Traité du contrat de mandat (appendice)*, n. 193.

[261] Carolus Molinaeus, "Commentarius in priores Titulos antiqui Consuetudinis Parisiensis", Tit. I (De fiefs), Gloss V, n. 103 ("Patet enim in ratione in qua se fundat ille text. nempe in illa sola aequitate naturali, ne quis aliena jactura locupletetur"), in: *Opera omnia* (Parisiis, 1681), vol. I, p. 88.

[262] Cf., for example, Glück, vol. 8, pp. 309 sq.; further Van Zyl, *Saakwaarnemingsaksie*, op. cit., note 248, pp. 77 sqq., 85 sq.

[263] By way of analogy of this extension of the actio negotiorum gestorum and, again, on the basis of equity an utilis actio negotiorum gestorum was also, occasionally, granted to the gestor who had managed the principal's affairs contrary to his express wishes. Again, it was the glossator Martinus who initiated this extension. For all details, see Van Zyl, *Saakwaarnemingsaksie*, op. cit., note 248, pp. 48 sqq., 55, 61 sqq., 71 sqq., 81 sq., 88, 96 sq.

(b) *Afr. D. 3, 5, 48*

The second text of major importance was Afr. D. 3, 5, 48. A slave is sold and takes with him an object that he has stolen from the vendor. The purchaser in good faith sells that object to a third party where it is destroyed. The original owner/vendor can thus no longer make use of his rei vindicatio. Under these circumstances Africanus is prepared to grant the actio negotiorum gestorum to him against the purchaser, in respect of the price received by the latter.[264] This is a rather atypical case of a negotiorum gestio, for the gestor has managed somebody else's affairs in the mistaken belief that they are his own.[265] Hence the generalizing statement, in the middle of the text, according to which the actio (directa) is applicable "si negotium, quod tuum esse existimares, cum esset meum, gessisses". But where there is a relationship of negotiorum gestio, the gestor must also be able to avail himself of the actio contraria against the principal. This is confirmed in the last part of our fragment: the gestor is allowed to sue the principal for whatever the latter has acquired through the gestio.[266] It is likely that the negotiorum gestio in D. 3, 5, 48 was merely used as a device to establish what essentially constituted mutual enrichment actions.[267] This is, in any event, how the text was understood by the writers of the ius commune, and they were able, in support of their interpretation to draw attention to Afr. D. 12, 1, 23—a text in which Julian advocated a condictio "quasi ex re tua locupletior factus sim"; again, the defendant (ego) had sold, in good faith, an object belonging to the plaintiff (tu), the object was subsequently destroyed and the question arose whether "tu" could sue "ego" for the purchase price.[268] Over the centuries, the designation of the remedy for and against the bonae fidei gestor vacillated somewhat uneasily between actio negotiorum gestorum utilis, condictio certi (generalis) and condictio sine causa; but whatever the name, it was always retained as a specific source of enrichment liability.[269] Usually it was regarded as another emanation of the precepts of natural equity, as spelt out, for example, in D. 50, 17, 206, and some writers therefore even spoke of an actio in factum (or utilis) ex aequitate. Again, there was an inclination to extend its scope. Often, for instance,

---

[264] "Si rem, quam servus venditus subripuisset a me venditore, emptor vendiderit eaque in rerum natura esse desierit, de pretio negotiorum gestorum actio mihi danda sit. . . ."

[265] Cf. supra, pp. 441 sq.

[266] ". . . sicut ex contrario in me tibi daretur (actio), si, cum hereditatem quae ad me pertinet tuam putares, res tuas proprias legatas solvisses, quandoque de ea solutione liberarer."

[267] Cf., in particular, Theo Mayer-Maly, "Probleme der negotiorum gestio", (1969) 86 *ZSS* 427.

[268] "Si eum servum, qui tibi legatus sit, quasi mihi legatum possederim et vendiderim, mortuo eo posse te mihi pretium condicere Iulianus ait, quasi ex re tua locupletior factus sim."

[269] For all details, see Van Zyl, *Saakwaarnemingsaksie*, op. cit., note 248, pp. 45 sqq., 58 sqq., 68 sqq., 79 sqq., 86 sqq., 94 sqq.; cf. also, as far as medieval jurisprudence is concerned, Dawson, op. cit., note 119, pp. 70 sqq.

the remedy arising from D. 3, 5, 48 was granted to a bonae fidei possessor and could thus be used as another instrument to dislodge the unpopular rule of D. 12, 6, 33 (lex Si in area). The latter was now bound to appear in an even less favourable light; constituting one of those Roman subtleties arising "de mero iure, et rigore juris civilis vel positivi",[270] it was bound, eventually, to give way to the more equitable dispensation: "Mais l'équité," in the words of Pothier,[271]

> "qui ne permet pas qu'on s'enrichisse aux dépens d'autrui, m'accorde, en ce cas, contre la subtilité du droit, une action contre vous, pour répéter de vous les frais de ma gestion, jusqua'à concurrance de ce que vous en avez profité."

3. The actio de in rem verso

(a) The Roman actio de in rem verso

The other Roman institution that stimulated the advance towards a broadly based enrichment liability in an even more effective manner was the actio de in rem verso. In Rome, it had been one of the "actiones adiecticiae qualitatis" that served, to some extent, as a substitute for the lack of (direct) agency.[272] A person in power, it will be remembered, could not normally bind his paterfamilias if he transacted business on his behalf; nor could he himself be sued. Yet, under certain circumstances, the praetor allowed the third party to proceed against the paterfamilias; and one of these situations was referred to in the words "si quid in rem N^{i} N^{i} inde versum est":[273] the person in power had to have used what he had acquired under the contract in order to enrich the property of the paterfamilias.[274] The liability of the paterfamilias was confined to the value of his enrichment at the time when judgment was given.[275] These were fairly humble beginnings, and one might have expected the actio de in rem verso to wither away when, in the course of European legal history, slavery was abolished, agency recognized, the contractual capacity of children over the age of majority accepted and the Roman patria potestas replaced by less authoritarian principles of household organization. That the remedy turned out to be destined for vicissitudes, to which in its innocent specificity it hardly appeared to be born, is certainly one of the more

[270] Molinaeus, op. cit., note 261, n. 105.
[271] *Traité du contrat de mandat (appendice)*, n. 189.
[272] Cf. supra, pp. 52 sq.
[273] Those were the terms of the formula: Lenel, *EP*, p. 282. On the Roman actio de in rem verso cf. Niederländer, op. cit., note 253, pp. 37 sqq.; Axel Brandi, *Bereicherung aus fremdem Vertrag. Der Verzicht des BGB auf die Versionsklage* (unpublished Dr. iur. thesis, Münster, 1966), pp. 3 sqq.; and, most recently, Geoffrey MacCormack, "The Early History of the 'actio de in rem verso' (Alfenus to Labeo)", in: *Studi in onore di Arnaldo Biscardi*, vol. II (1982), pp. 319 sqq.; idem, "The Later History of the 'actio de in rem verso' (Proculus-Ulpian)", (1982) 48 *SDHI* 318 sqq.
[274] Dawson, op. cit., note 119, p. 85 translates "de in rem verso" as "concerning what has been converted to [the master's] account".
[275] Cf. Niederländer, op. cit., note 253, pp. 37 sqq.

extravagant episodes within the history of the European ius commune.[276] One single text contained in the Code proved to be the catalyst. It read:[277]

> "Alioquin si cum libero rem agente eius, cuius precibus meministi, contractum habuisti et eius personam elegisti, pervides contra dominum nullam te habuisse actionem, nisi vel in rem eius pecunia processit vel hunc contractum ratum habuit."

A has given a loan to B who, however, acted on behalf of C. Normally, A would be confined to an action against B, the person whom, after all, he chose to contract with. Yet, two exceptions are recognized in the final clause of our text: A may proceed against C (the "dominus"), if the money has been converted to his account or if he has ratified the contract. We are, of course, concerned here with the first alternative. It is the actio de in rem verso; but the significant, or even startling, feature lies in the fact that it is granted although B was neither slave nor son in power. He is expressly described as a liber (homo). It is almost certain that the "nisi vel" clause is interpolated and represents Justinianic law rather than the views of Diocletian and Maximian.[278] But, whether Roman or Byzantine: here there was an authoritative statement to the effect that a remedy could be available against third parties who derived a benefit from a transaction to which they were strangers. It is a plain case of third-party enrichment.[279]

(b) Actio utilis de in rem verso

The writers of the ius commune usually referred to this remedy as an actio utilis de in rem verso.[280] They saw it as yet another emanation of the equitable principle that nobody should be allowed to enrich himself at the expense of another. The traditional core example remained the one where C had been enriched as a result of a contract between A and B, and it was this contract which was seen by many as the basis of the action against the third party.[281] Others focused on the versio in rem

[276] Dawson, op. cit., note 119, p. 85 speaks of "one of the most extraordinary accidents of history".
[277] C. 4, 26, 7, 3 (Diocl. et Max.).
[278] Kaser, *RPr* I, p. 607, n. 17; idem, *RPr* II, p. 107, n. 53; Honsell/Mayer-Maly/Selb, p. 379.
[279] Cf., in particular, the discussion by Honoré, 1960 *Acta Juridica* 237 sqq. De Vos, *Verrykingsaanspreeklikheid*, pp. 44 sqq. regards the decision as fundamentally unsound and contrary to elementary legal principles.
[280] For what follows, see the comprehensive study by Berthold Kupisch, *Die Versionsklage* (1965), passim; cf. also Brandi, op. cit., note 273, pp. 24 sqq.; and, for briefer overviews, cf. Dawson, op. cit., note 119, pp. 85 sqq.; Feenstra, (1972) 29 *Ankara Üniversitesi Hukuk Fakültesi Dergisi*, pp. 298 sqq.; Coing, pp. 498 sqq.; Kupisch, op. cit., note 34, pp. 37 sqq. More specifically on the glossators, cf. Schrage, loc. cit., note 239; on Roman-Dutch law, see Honoré, 1960 *Acta Juridica* 243 sqq. and De Vos, *Verrykingsaanspreeklikheid*, pp. 86 sqq.
[281] Cf., for example, Struve, *Syntagma*, Exerc. XXI; Lib. XV, Tit. III, LXXII: "Fundamentum hujus actionis est ille contractus, qui cum filiofam. aut servo est initus, ex quo utilitas domino patrive obvenit, adeoque hic isto perinde obligatur et convenitur, ac si cum ipso potius contractum esset."

itself, on the gain received by C.[282] For them the actio de in rem verso was a quasi-contractual action[283] that could be likened to negotiorum gestio. This parallel[284] was the more obvious, since both institutions followed the same rules. "In rem autem versum intellegitur, quod utiliter vel necessario impensum:"[285] only necessary or useful expenses could be taken to have been converted to the third party's account. This definition, in turn, could be deduced from a statement in the Digest, according to which

> "totiens de in rem verso esse actionem, quibus casibus procurator mandati vel qui negotia gessit negotiorum gestorum haberet actionem quotiensque aliquid consumpsit servus, ut aut meliorem rem dominus habuerit aut non deteriorem".[286]

B, in concluding the contract with A, had to have acted as C's negotiorum gestor;[287] and A could sue only C in those cases in which B could have availed himself of the actio negotiorum gestorum (contraria). So close was the relationship between actio utilis de in rem verso and actio negotiorum gestorum, in fact, that the borderlines were often blurred and an actio negotiorum gestorum was granted in place of an actio utilis de in rem verso.[288] Others, however, maintained the distinction:

> "in hoc tamen ab illa differt, quod actio negotiorum gestorum detur illi, qui ipse pecuniam in absentis negotia vertit . . .: actio autem de in rem verso datur illi, qui ipse pecuniam in alterius utilitatem non impendit, sed filio vel servo [aut libero, we have to add], credidit, ut ille in rem patris vel domini verteret."[289]

A's remedy, in other words, was not an actio negotiorum gestorum because he had not managed C's affairs himself.

(c) C. 4, 26, 7, 3 and third-party enrichment

In the course of time, however, C. 4, 26, 7, 3 was taken as authority for even further-reaching propositions. Some of the commentators had already established a link between this text and D. 12, 1, 32, the enigmatic lex Si et me et Titium, which also dealt with third-party enrichment. The common basis, claimed Baldus, was "equitas generalis que quocunque casu representata parit actionem generalem,

---

[282] Cf. Lauterbach, *Collegium theoretico-practicum*, Lib. XIV, Tit. I, II (". . . propter Utilitatem Praetor concedit actionem de in Rem verso"); Stryk, *Usus modernus pandectarum*, Lib. XV, Tit. III, § 2; Kupisch, *Versionsklage*, p. 24.

[283] Cf. already Ulp. D. 15, 3, 1 pr. (". . . quasi cum ipsis potius contractum videatur"). But this phrase did not refer to a quasi-contractual obligation in the technical sense.

[284] ". . . idem fere fundamentum habet [actio de in rem verso], quod actio negotiorum gestorum": Stryk, *Usus modernus pandectarum*, Lib. XV, Tit. III, § 1.

[285] Struve, *Syntagma*, Exerc. XX, Lib. XV, Tit. I, LXXIII.

[286] Ulp. D. 15, 3, 3, 2.

[287] Or, according to D. 15, 3, 3, 2, as mandatarius; in this regard, the actio de in rem verso had, however, become redundant in the meantime: Kupisch, *Versionsklage*, pp. 33 sqq.

[288] Cf., in this light, the analysis by Van Zyl, *Negotiorum gestio*, pp. 113 sqq.; cf. further the sources referred to by Schrage, loc. cit. (note 239), Kupisch, *Versionsklage*, p. 28 and Brandi, op. cit., note 273, pp. 31 sqq.

[289] Stryk, *Usus modernus pandectarum*, Lib. XV, Tit. III, § 4.

scilicet certi condictionem. quod est notandum".[290] This put the actio utilis de in rem verso into close proximity with the condictiones; and although most writers tried to keep the remedies apart, the obvious parallels between C. 4, 26, 7, 3 and D. 12, 1, 32 continued to confound the issues. Some three hundred years after Baldus, Ulrich Huber used D. 12, 1, 32 apropos his discussion of the actio de in rem verso to support his general proposition that

> "ex aequitate contra Alium dandam in subsidium actionem, quia quod de meo ad te pervenit, hoc a te mihi reddi, bonum et aequum est".[291]

Augustin Leyser, in turn, referred to the actio de in rem verso when he discussed D. 12, 1, 32. "It is impossible to describe the extent", he wrote,[292]

> "to which the expositors have busied themselves with this text, the resources and the treasures of wisdom and equity they extract from it, the numbers of lawsuits and disputations they occasion in explaining and applying it. . . . We ourselves are not endowed with the light of genius that can detect all the mysteries that lie hidden in this text. . . . The expositors, however, have no need to carve out a special territory around this text, for they already have the expanded (utilis) actio de in rem verso which most exactly coincides with the condiction of this text."

The actio utilis de in rem verso was thus applicable, according to Leyser, whenever somebody had been enriched ex alieno contractu, irrespective of whether the contractual partner (B) or the plaintiff (A) had acted as negotiorum gestor for the defendant (C) or not.

(d) Versio in rem and two-party relationships

Of even greater significance was another development that occurred in the course of the 18th century.[293] Hitherto the actio utilis de in rem verso had always been confined to what we have referred to as third-party enrichment. But the more the general attention was directed at the versio in rem itself (rather than the contractus aliorum) as the real basis of this remedy, the less emphasis was placed on the position of the middleman (B). Was it at all necessary to confine the actio de in rem verso to cases where a negotiorum gestor had converted the money (or whatever else he might have received from A) to C's account? Increasingly this question was answered in the negative. After all, it was quite imaginable that C might have been enriched, sine causa and at A's expense, through an act of A himself. In fact, the Roman sources themselves knew some such cases, and by making the actio de in rem verso applicable in two-party relationships, one was finally able

---

[290] *In quartum et quintum Codicis libr. praelectiones* (Lugduni, 1561), ad C. 4, 26, 7 n. 5 in fine: cf. also Dawson, op. cit., note 119, pp. 86 sq., 171.

[291] *Praelectiones*, Pars II, Lib. XV, Tit. III, 2. On Huber's enrichment theory in general, see Feenstra, *Festschrift Verdam*, pp. 145 sqq. and De Vos, *Verrykingsaanspreeklikheid*, pp. 88 sqq.

[292] *Meditationes ad Pandectas*, Spec. CXXX, VIII, as translated by Dawson, op. cit., note 119, p. 172.

[293] Kupisch, *Versionsklage*, pp. 38 sqq.; Coing, pp. 500 sq.

to assign a convenient systematic niche to them. The prime example concerned the liability of a pupillus infantia maior under a contract that he had concluded sine auctoritate tutoris. Of course, he could not be held contractually responsible; yet, on the other hand, there was no reason to allow him to keep any enrichment arising as a result of such a transaction. The Emperor Antoninus Pius therefore determined that an action was to be granted against the minor "in quantum locupletior fact[us] est".[294] That meant, as one saw it now, that the creditor could sue if he was able to prove a versio in rem:

> "Contractus . . . cum pupillo initus tam diu erit nullus, usque dum creditor versionem in rem, sive hunc exinde factum esse locupletiorem, probaverit";[295]

and the actio de in rem verso could thus be seen to lie "adversus eum quoque . . ., qui ex negotio se ipsum obligare nequit".[296] This could be not only a pupillus infantia maior but also aliae personae "defectu quodam laborantes", "foeminae . . . in illis locis ubi curatore opus habe(n)t ad contrahendum", and, particularly interesting, "persona(e) morales jure minorennium gaudentes" (as, for example, "civitates, ecclesiae et collegia omnia, quae ad instar minorum alieno auxilio reguntur, et hinc suos curatores vel administratores habent").[297] Thus there was a strong tendency to broaden the scope of the actio de in rem verso to such an extent that it approached something like a general enrichment action: it could be used wherever someone had made a gain, directly or indirectly, at somebody else's expense.[298] Not everybody was prepared, however, to follow Augustin Leyser, who even saw in it, under certain circumstances, a remedy in rem. Whenever something has been expended "in conservationem aut meliorationem rei alienae" in such a manner that the benefit was not to pertain to a specific person, "sed cum re ipsa in quosvis alios transeat, tunc actio de in rem verso realis", he claimed and referred, by way of example, to the case of a brewer who saved his village from being marauded by a hostile army by handing over to the soldiers his entire supply of beer (to the value of over 2 000 Thaler). According to Leyser, the brewer may institute an actio de in rem verso against the owner of every house in that village,

[294] Ulp. D. 26, 8, 1 pr.; Ulp. D. 26, 8, 5 pr. On these texts and the rescript of the emperor cf. von Lübtow, *Condictio*, pp. 47 sqq.; Niederländer, op. cit., note 253, pp. 111 sqq.; Luigi Labruna, *Rescriptum Divi Pii* (1962), passim; Van Zyl, *Saakwaarnemingsaksie*, op. cit., note 248, pp. 12 sqq.; J.A.C. Thomas, "Naturalis obligatio pupilli", in: *Sein und Werden im Recht, Festgabe für Ulrich von Lübtow* (1970), pp 457 sqq., 470 sqq.

[295] Stryk, *Usus modernus pandectarum*, Lib. XII, Tit. I, § 17; and he adds: "hoc enim casu cum aequitati naturali consentaneum sit, neminem cum alterius damno fieri locupletiorem." More specifically on the situation where the other party manages the affairs of the minor (negotiorum gestio), cf. the analysis, stretching over all the periods of the ius commune, by Van Zyl, *Saakwaarnemingsaksie*, op. cit., note 248, pp. 40 sqq., 51, 56 sq., 63 sq., 76 sq., 84 sq., 90 sq.

[296] Io. August Hellfeld, *Iurisprudentia forensis secundum pandectarum ordinem* (3rd ed., Jenae, n.d.), § 918.

[297] Cf. Stryk, *Usus modernus pandectarum*, Lib. XII, Tit. I, §§ 23 sqq.

[298] Cf. also Coing, p. 501.

irrespective of whether or not it has changed hands in the meantime.[299]

(e) The actio de in rem verso in the natural-law codifications

This was the situation when, in the second half of the 18th century, Austria and Prussia set the wheels in motion to codify their private law. The actio de in rem verso in its extended version was firmly entrenched in the usus modernus pandectarum and appeared to conform fully with, if not even to derive from, the precepts of natural equity. Neither of the two legislators therefore hesitated to retain it.

> "He, from whose property something has been converted to somebody else's benefit, is entitled either to claim the same back or to demand to be compensated for its value",

determined § 262 I 13 of the Prussian General Land Law,[300] and the Austrian General Civil Code put it very similarly (§ 1041), but it added that the versio in rem alterius had to have come about otherwise than by way of "management of affairs".[301] In both codes these claims were systematically closely related to, but nevertheless quite separate from, negotiorum gestio. At the same time, they were very broadly phrased. Thus they presented themselves as suitable devices to remedy perceived shortcomings of the law of unjustified enrichment. In Austria, § 1041 ABGB, became, in the course of time, the sedes materiae for all enrichment claims arising not from transfer,[302] and Prussian legal science used § 262 I 13 to smuggle the general condictio sine causa (that had, of late, become fashionable among contemporary pandectists) into the local code.[303]

But the true culmination of the astonishing career of the actio de in rem verso occurred in France.[304] On the whole, French legal science had never been very favourably disposed towards this claim.[305] In cases of third-party enrichment the actio negotiorum gestorum contraria utilis was usually resorted to, rather than the actio utilis de in rem verso,[306] and thus there was no basis for applying the latter remedy to two-party relationships either. Pothier gave much scope to the

---

[299] *Meditationes ad Pandectas*, Spec. CLXVII, I. Contra: Glück, vol. 14, pp. 421 sq.

[300] On the background, the meaning and the subsequent interpretation of this section, cf. Kupisch, *Versionsklage*, pp. 57 sqq.; cf. also Brandi, op. cit., note 273, pp. 35 sqq.

[301] For all details, see Kupisch, *Versionsklage*, pp. 92 sqq.

[302] Cf. Rummel, in: Peter Rummel (ed.), *Kommentar zum ABGB*, vol. I (1983), § 1041 (pp. 1320 sqq.).

[303] Kupisch, *Versionsklage*, pp. 70 sqq.

[304] For Italy cf. Giuseppe Bruno, *L'actio de in rem verso* (1900), who demonstrates that the actio de in rem verso continued to be used, until the end of the 19th century, as a general enrichment claim, even though it had not been adopted by the codice civile of 1865.

[305] Generally on the history of the law relating to unjust enrichment in France, cf. Lang, op. cit., note 30, pp. 34 sqq., 40 sqq.; cf. also Dawson, op. cit., note 119, pp. 92 sqq.; Coing, p. 493.

[306] Cf., for example, Cuiacius, Lib. III, Tit. XXVI Codicis, Ad L. VII, in: *Opera*, vol. IX (Mutinae, 1781), col. 288; further, see Kupisch, *Versionsklage*, p. 122.

institution of negotiorum gestio,[307] but for the rest he concentrated on the condictio indebiti.[308] His view, as usual, shaped the provisions of the code civil,[309] and, as a result, both the condictio sine causa and the general actio de in rem verso remained outside its purview. A German professor writing a textbook on French private law[310] did, however, manage to find some scattered provisions[311] which appeared to be based on the concept of a versio in rem and which could be reduced to the common denominator of Pomponius' unjust enrichment principle. His views commended themselves to two influential French authors[312] and, through them, ultimately to the Court of Cassation, which, in the famous *arrêt Boudier* of 1892 recognized the actio de in rem verso as a general enrichment action "*dérivant du principe d'équité qui défend de s'enrichir au détriment d'autrui*".[313] It soon became apparent that this formulation was too wide and that not every enrichment which has accrued at someone else's expense may be recoverable. The enrichment, it came to be accepted, must have occurred "*sans cause légitime*", or, in the terminology of the ius commune, sine causa.[314] The modern French version of the actio de in rem verso has thus become synonymous with *enrichissement sans cause* —a development, incidentally, which has heralded the destruction of the very basis from which it had once set out on its triumphal march through European legal history. For if an action lies only where the defendant has been enriched sine causa, it cannot normally apply in cases of third-party enrichment such as the one discussed in C. 4, 26, 7, 3; the middleman's negotiorum gestio, after all, provides a *cause légitime* for what the third party has acquired.[315]

---

[307] *Appendice* to the *Traité du contrat de mandat*, nn. 167 sqq.

[308] *Traité du contrat du prêt de consomption*, nn. 140 sqq. (these sections have recently been translated by W.J. Hosten, C. van Soelen, P. Ellis, *Treatise on the quasi-contract called promutuum and on the condictio indebiti* (Pretoria, 1987)).

[309] Cf. artt. 1371 sqq. ("*Des quasi-contrats*") dealing merely with "*gestion d'affaires*" and "*paiement de l'indu*". For details cf. Zweigert/Kötz, pp. 273 sqq.; Lang, op. cit., note 30, pp. 55 sqq.; cf. also Barry Nicholas, "Unjustified Enrichment in the Civil Law and Louisiana Law", (1961–62) 36 *Tulane LR* 619 sqq.; on "quasi-contractual" liability in French law, cf. also Carlo Augusto Cannata, "Das faktische Vertragsverhältnis oder die ewige Wiederkunft des Gleichen", (1987) 53 *SDHI* 310 sqq.

[310] Karl Salomo Zachariä von Lingenthal, *Handbuch des Französischen Civilrechts* (1808), vol. II, §§ 399 sqq.

[311] Cf., for example, artt. 1241, 1312, 1926 code civil. The operative phrase is "*tourner au profit*". Cf. further Lang, op. cit., note 30, pp. 62 sqq.

[312] C. Aubry, C. Rau, *Cours de droit civil français d'après la méthode de Zachariae* (4th ed.), vol. VI (1873), pp. 246 sq.

[313] 15. 6. 1892, *Recueil Dalloz* 1892 (*Première partie*), p. 596.

[314] For details, see Zweigert/Kötz, pp. 276 sqq.; Dawson, op. cit., note 119, pp. 100 sqq., Nicholas, (1961–62) 36 *Tulane LR* 622 sqq.; Detlef König, *Der Bereicherungsanspruch gegen den Drittempfänger einer Vertragsleistung nach französischem Recht* (1967). The actio de in rem verso can be resorted to only if no other remedy is available to the plaintiff ("*subsidiarité de l'action de in rem verso*").

[315] Cf. Kupisch, *Ungerechtfertigte Bereicherung*, op. cit., note 34, p. 43; cf. also, for Austrian law, p. 41.

4. The general enrichment action that was

(a) Grotius and Huber

Obviously, then, in the 19th century a general enrichment claim was "in the air" throughout central Europe. But neither the French Court of Cassation nor Savigny was the first to devise and recognize it. It was Hugo Grotius, who had, in the first half of the 17th century, already drawn together all the different threads and woven them into a single, crisp and comprehensive formula. He saw the different condictiones[316] and the medieval action against the person whose hunger had been stilled at somebody else's expense;[317] he noticed that the actio negotiorum gestorum contraria was used, occasionally, as an enrichment claim;[318] he examined, time and again, the famous lex Si et me et Titium[319] and he read the restitution doctrine of the late medieval Spanish scholastics.[320] Above all, however, he was inspired by the precepts of natural justice and equity. "De rebus non extantibus hoc humano generi placuit", he finally concluded,[321] "ut si tu ex re mea factus es locupletior, me rem non habente, in tantum tenearis, in quantum es factus locupletior."[322]

But was this perhaps to be understood merely as a rule of natural law, rather than one of positive jurisprudence? In his *Inleiding tot de Hollandsche Rechtsgeleertheyd* Grotius took the opportunity to answer this question. Obligations, he stated, have their source either in contract or in inequality ("toezegging [ofte] onevenheid").[323] Obligations arising from inequality are subdivided again into those where the inequality is caused by another person, on the one hand (delict); and where it actually benefits another, or would benefit him, if something were withheld, on the other (". . . onevenheid . . . die een ander datelick batet, ofte door onthoudinge baten zoude").[324] Inequality

---

[316] *Inleiding*, III, XXX, 4 sqq.

[317] *De jure belli ac pacis*, Lib. II, Cap. X, II (". . . ut qui pecuniam patri credidit ad alendum filium, si pater solvendo non sit, in ipsum filium bona materna habentem actionem habeat").

[318] Marginal note in Grotius' own copy of the *Inleiding*; cf. Feenstra, *Festschrift Verdam*, p. 138.

[319] Cf., for example, *Inleiding*, III, XXX, 18 and a letter to his brother, Willem, written in March 1616 (as quoted and discussed by Feenstra, *Festschrift Verdam*, pp. 143 sq.).

[320] Robert Feenstra, "L'influence de la scolastique espagnole sur Grotius en droit privé: quelques expériences dans des questions de fond et de forme, concernant notamment les doctrines de l'erreur et de l'enrichissement sans cause", in: *Fata iuris Romani* (1974), pp. 338 sqq.

[321] *De jure belli ac pacis*, Lib. II, Cap. X, II. On the systematic division between obligations arising "e rebus extantibus" and "e rebus non extantibus" (both subdivisions of obligations "ex dominio") cf. Feenstra, *Festschrift Verdam*, p. 140; idem, *Fata iuris Romani*, pp. 354 sqq. For an analysis of what constituted, in Grotius' view, the basis of the obligation to render restitution cf. Birks/McLeod, (1986) 6 *Oxford Journal of Legal Studies* 59 sqq.

[322] Reason: "quia quatenus ex meo lucratus es, plus habes, cum ego minus habeam: introducta autem sunt dominia ad servandam aequalitatem in eo scilicet, ut quisque suum haberet."

[323] III, I, 9.

[324] III, I, 14.

which benefits or might benefit another, Grotius then declared, binds the person who received the benefit to make compensation, without regard to the way in which he came to acquire it.[325] After these general, introductory remarks he turned to a detailed discussion of the individual obligations, and when he came to those arising from enrichment ("baet-trecking"), he opened the discussion, again, on a very general level: "Verbintenisse door baet-trecking ontstaet, wanneer iemand zonder voorige recht-gunnige baet treckt, ofte zoude komen te trecken, uit eens anders goed."[326] He then went through the individual condictiones until he wound up by acknowledging a claim for the "weder-eissching van alle 't gunt andersins zonder gheven, betalen ofte belooven, aen iemand is gekomen uit eens anders goed buiten rechtelicke oorzake".[327] It is clear from the context that this is not merely the Roman condictio sine causa (specialis) but enrichment sine causa at somebody else's expense as a general source of obligation.[328] Ulrich Huber referred to Grotius, when he, too, espoused the idea of a general enrichment action[329] and, perhaps most importantly, the Hooge Raad van Holland en Zeeland also was quite prepared to grant actiones ex aequitate arising from "baettrekking".[330]

(b) South African law

Strangely enough, the modern South African courts have not followed suit. "[T]he rule against enrichment is not one of general application—if it were, all commerce would be stultified": this terse pronouncement of Van den Heever J[331] represents, to this day, the prevailing judicial attitude.[332] As a result, a principle "vibrant with life and struggling for

---

[325] III, I, 15.

[326] III, XXX, 1 ("Obligation from enrichment arises when someone without legal title derives or may derive advantage from another person's property"; transl. by Lee).

[327] III, XXX, 18 (". . . repetition of anything which in any other way, without gift, payment, or promise, has come to a man from another man's property apart from any lawful cause"; transl. by Lee).

[328] Feenstra, *Festschrift Verdam*, pp. 137 sqq. Contra: De Vos, *Verrykingsaanspreeklikheid*, pp. 71 sqq.

[329] *Praelectiones*, Pars II, Lib. XV, Tit. III, 2; for details, see Feenstra, *Festschrift Verdam*, pp. 145 sqq.; cf. also Birks/McLeod, (1986) 6 *Oxford Journal of Legal Studies* 72 sqq.

[330] For details, see J.E. Scholtens, "The General Enrichment Action That Was", (1966) 83 *SALJ* 395 sqq.; De Vos, *Verrykingsaanspreeklikheid*, pp. 110 sqq.

[331] *Muller v. Grobbelaar* 1946 OPD 272 at 278; cf. also *Pucjlowski v. Johnston's Executor* 1946 WLD 1 at 3 sq.: "Save, as a rather nebulous generalization, there was not in Roman law and there is now in Roman-Dutch law no rule which lays down categorically that no person shall be enriched at the expense of another, without legal cause. The alleged rule is a generalization, not borne out by legal phenomena." But see also *Pretorius v. Van Zyl* 1927 OPD 226 at 229.

[332] The *cause célèbre*, in which the restrictive attitude has been confirmed (though, possibly, not for all time; cf. the indication by Botha JA on pp. 139 sq. that the time may come when South African law will be ripe to accept and integrate a general enrichment action), is *Nortje v. Pool* 1966 (3) SA 96 (A). For criticism of this decision, see Scholtens, (1966) 83 *SALJ* 391 sqq.; J.C. van der Walt, (1966) 29 *THRHR* 374 sqq.; De Vos, *Verrykingsaanspreeklikheid*, pp. 311 sqq.

growth [has been] locked . . . in tight compartments, a prisoner of the past".[333] An odd assortment of individual enrichment actions (to wit, the condictiones indebiti, causa data causa non secuta, ob turpem vel iniustam causam and sine causa, the actiones negotiorum gestorum, the action against persons with limited capacity to act and the one arising from accessio or processing[334]—though not, apparently, the actio de in rem verso[335]) is still at hand to clank the ancient chains. Only here and there have some of the remedies been modernized, rather coyly, by means of what is usually referred to as "ad hoc extensions".[336] The law relating to unjustified enrichment has, as a result, become one of the most awkward and perplexing dungeons within the edifice of South African private law.

V. ENRICHMENT REMEDIES IN MODERN LAW

1. German law

(a) *The general enrichment action of the BGB*

German legal science, in turn, has taken its lead from Savigny[337] and so the general enrichment claim came to be incorporated, eventually, into the BGB. The 24th title of the 7th section of the book on obligations thus starts off with the general rule that a person who, through an act performed by another, or in any other way, acquires something at the expense of that other person[338] without any legal ground, is bound to make restitution. Neither this rule nor the title on unjustified enrichment as a whole can be regarded as a legislative masterpiece.[339] The story of their genesis is rather unfortunate, in that the decision to

---

[333] Weeramantry J, in *Da Costa v. Bank of Ceylon* (1970) 72 New Law Reports (Ceylon) 457 at 544 sq. The learned judge strongly criticized the decision in *Nortje's* case (pp. 539 sqq.) and came, as far as Ceylon is concerned, to the opposite conclusion.

[334] Cf. the discussion by De Vos, *Verrykingsaanspreeklikheid*, pp. 153 sqq.

[335] De Vos, *Verrykingsaanspreeklikheid*, pp. 86 sqq. maintains that the actio (utilis) de in rem verso was not recognized by the Roman-Dutch authors and that it is, consequently, also out of use in modern South African law. But see Honoré, 1960 *Acta Juridica* 243 sqq., 246 sqq.

[336] As to which *Nortje v. Pool* 1966 (3) SA 96 (A) at 139H provides the helpful comment that they are admissible "[onder] bepaalde omstandighede". For details cf. De Vos, *Verrykingsaanspreeklikheid*, pp. 244 sqq. and passim; see also Zimmermann, *RHR*, pp. 135 sqq.

[337] Cf. supra, pp. 872 sq.

[338] The wide term "at the plaintiff's expense" was chosen instead of the narrower "out of the plaintiff's property", which, in turn, can be found in the Swiss Code. The enrichment action may be brought regardless of whether the plaintiff has suffered any provable loss. Cf. "Protokolle", in: *Mugdan*, vol. II, p. 1171; but see also Wilhelm, op. cit., note 231, pp. 45 sq., 53 sq., 55 sq.

[339] But see Dawson, op. cit., note 119, pp. 91 sq.: "The end result was the Code of 1900, which contains the most carefully considered solutions to be found in any modern legislative system."

adopt the general action was taken at a comparatively late stage.[340] Thorough discussions were devoted only to the condictio indebiti, and many of the rules contained in §§ 813 sqq. BGB were tailored to suit that particular enrichment claim. When the general action was introduced, the consequences of this sweeping change for the remaining sections of that title were not considered.[341] Furthermore, the old condictiones were not entirely abandoned. §§ 812 I and 817 I BGB specifically mention enrichment claims ob causam finitam, causa data causa non secuta and ob turpem vel iniustam causam,[342] but their function and practical value have remained unclear. The highly sophisticated and perplexing disputes surrounding the application of the "in pari turpitudine" rule, as laid down in § 817, 2 BGB, provide perhaps the most striking example of the practical difficulties that have arisen in this regard.[343]

But what has become of the general enrichment action of the BGB over the last nine decades?[344] After the code entered into effect on 1 January 1900, the practical application of § 812 BGB proved to be difficult. "At the expense", "without legal ground": how were these requirements to be interpreted? Several attempts were made to find appropriate guidelines to carve out and establish basic principles upon which all unjustified enrichment claims are to be based.[345] None of these theories have, however, managed to gain acceptance. What remained was a somewhat unfortunate picture of the courts pragmatically trying to muddle their way through, and of a legal literature unable to give them much help and guidance. Generally acceptable formulae covering all enrichment claims remained on a similar level of abstraction as Pomponius' famous natural-law maxim.

---

[340] In the second commission; cf. "Protokolle", in: *Mugdan*, vol. II, pp. 1169 sqq. as opposed to §§ 737 sqq. of the first draft (on which, see "Motive", in: *Mugdan*, vol. II, pp. 463 sqq.). On the influence of Bernhard Windscheid (who had retained the Roman condictiones as specific expressions of his *Voraussetzungs-* (presupposition) doctrine; cf. Windscheid/Kipp, §§ 421 sqq.) on the first draft, as far as the law of unjustified enrichment is concerned, cf. Werner Schubert, "Windscheid und das Bereicherungsrecht des 1. Entwurfs des BGB", (1975) 92 *ZSS* 186 sqq.

[341] Especially not concerning the question of the extent of the enrichment claim (§ 818 BGB); cf. Axel Flessner, *Wegfall der Bereicherung* (1970), pp. 26 sqq. referring to Andreas von Tuhr, Walter Wilburg and Werner Flume as the most influential critics.

[342] The distinction between condictio indebiti and condictio sine causa is not reflected in the wording of § 812 I 1 BGB. On the distinction, and the respective spheres of application, of the condictiones indebiti and sine causa, cf. Reuter/Martinek, op. cit., note 174, pp. 126 sqq. The issue is without any practical relevance.

[343] Cf. supra, pp. 863 sqq.

[344] For a crisp and lucid exposition of the modern German law of unjustified enrichment in English, see Brice Dickson, "The Law of Restitution in the Federal Republic of Germany: A comparison with English Law", (1987) 36 *International and Comparative Law Quarterly* 771 sqq.; cf. also Dawson, op. cit., note 119, pp. 119 sqq.; Zweigert/Kötz/Weir, pp. 210 sqq., 232 sqq.

[345] Erich Jung, *Die Bereicherungsansprüche und der Mangel des rechtlichen Grundes* (1902); Robert Krawielicki, *Grundlagen des Bereicherungsanspruchs* (1936); Fritz Schulz, "System der Rechte auf den Eingriffserwerb", (1909) 105 *Archiv für die civilistische Praxis* 1 sqq.

(b) The Wilburg/von Caemmerer typology

It was Walter Wilburg who in 1934[346] acknowledged for the first time that a uniform answer as to when an enrichment is unjustified cannot be given. For whereas it is quite possible to state positively when an enrichment is justified—to wit, when the defendant is entitled, under a contract or by law, to keep the enrichment that he has acquired—the converse does not, apparently, apply. It cannot be maintained that a person who increases his property at the expense of another, without a specific contractual or legal causa, is bound to return the enrichment to this other person.[347] Such a proposition would not take into account, for instance, that the enrichment may be due to the display of particular skills in (lawful) competition. Somebody builds a dam and the neighbours, who have refused to participate in the expenses, also benefit from its construction.[348] This benefit accrues to them without specific contractual or legal reason; and yet they are not unjustifiedly enriched. Wilburg, and 20 years later especially von Caemmerer, therefore distinguished different types of enrichment claims. Admittedly, the fathers of the BGB had undertaken to incorporate a general enrichment action into their codification. However, in drafting § 812 BGB they had emphasized the enrichment by transfer as one of the traditional core examples. Wilburg and von Caemmerer now argued that this accentuation was not only historically but also dogmatically justified. If one wishes to arrive at workable criteria as to when an enrichment is unjustified, one has to separate the claim arising from enrichment by transfer from the claims based on enrichment "in any other manner". The enrichment-by-transfer claim (*"Leistungskondiktion"*) concerns the recovery of performances which have gone awry for some reason or other. Central to determining when and between which parties this type of claim may be granted is the concept of performance (*"Leistung"*).[349] If someone renders performance to another person, he does so with a specific purpose in mind (solvendi causa, obligandi causa, donandi causa); and if this purpose is not achieved, or turns out to have been frustrated, the performance may be said to have been made without legal ground. Thus, the legal requirement of "at the expense" as a further criterion for enrichment

---

346 *Die Lehre von der ungerechtfertigten Bereicherung nach österreichischem und deutschem Recht* (1934).

347 Ernst von Caemmerer, "Grundprobleme des Bereicherungsrechts", in: *Gesammelte Schriften*, vol. I (1968), pp. 374 sq.

348 Von Caemmerer, loc. cit.

349 Cf., for example, Hans-Wilhelm Kötter, "Zur Rechtsnatur der Leistungskondiktion", (1954) 153 *Archiv für die civilistische Praxis* 193 sqq.; Hermann Weitnauer, "Die Leistung", in: *Festschrift für Ernst von Caemmerer* (1978), pp. 255 sqq.; Reuter/Martinek, op. cit., note 174, pp. 80 sqq.; for criticism, see Berthold Kupisch, *Gesetzespositivismus im Bereicherungsrecht* (1978); Lieb, op. cit., note 174, § 812, nn. 23 sqq.

liability becomes superfluous in this context.[350] It is crucial, however, for determining when an enrichment-in-any-other-way claim, particularly one based on an encroachment (*"Eingriffskondiktion"*),[351] may be granted: for there is no specific causa in these cases, in terms of which one could establish whether an enrichment is unjustified or not.[352] The relevant test question rather has to be who was entitled to the right, with regard to which there was the interference. Thus, for example, it is the purpose of the right of ownership to afford the owner the uti, frui, habere. If anybody else derives a benefit by using or consuming this object, he has been enriched at the owner's expense, and, provided there is no specific justification for him to retain the benefit,[353] he has to render restitution.

The typological differentiation proposed by Wilburg and von Caemmerer turned out to be so convincing that, over the years, it has become very widely accepted.[354] Most textbooks and commentaries follow this theoretical framework, and since the Federal Supreme

---

[350] The courts have, for some time, taken "at the expense" to mean that the person instituting the enrichment claim must have suffered a loss and that, furthermore, this loss and the enrichment of the other party must be directly related to each other (for a discussion cf. Ernst von Caemmerer, "Bereicherungsansprüche und Drittbeziehungen", in: *Gesammelte Schriften*, vol. I (1968), pp. 321 sqq.). This proposition is not acceptable, however: the law of unjustified enrichment is not concerned with the compensation of losses.

[351] The condictio based on an encroachment by the defendant is the most important enrichment-in-any-other-way claim within the typology proposed by von Caemmerer. The two others derive from the fulfilment of somebody else's debt (*"Rückgriffskondiktion"*) and from unauthorized expenditure on someone else's property (*"Verwendungskondiktion"*); cf. von Caemmerer, *Gesammelte Schriften*, vol. I, pp. 378 sqq.; idem, "Bereicherung und unerlaubte Handlung", in: Gesammelte Schriften, vol. I, pp. 228 sqq. But in this regard there is still considerable discord among German writers. Thus, for example, Lieb, op. cit., note 174, § 812, nn. 182 sqq. favours a greater diversification of the enrichment-in-any-other-way claims. Reuter/Martinek, op. cit., note 174, pp. 56 sqq., 232 sqq., 371 sqq. postulate a distinction between encroachment and "absorption" actions (*"Abschöpfungskondiktionen"*).

[352] Nor, incidentally, can the unlawfulness of the encroachment be regarded as the decisive element: cf. Lieb, op. cit., note 174, § 812, nn. 199 sqq.; but cf. Schulz, (1909) 105 *Archiv für die civilistische Praxis* 1 sqq.; Horst Heinrich Jakobs, *Eingriffserwerb und Vermögensverschiebung in der Lehre von der ungerechtfertigten Bereicherung* (1964), pp. 54 sqq. If a businessman overtakes somebody else in contravention of the traffic laws in order not to miss a business appointment, he makes a profit by unlawful means, but is nevertheless not enriched at the expense of the person whom he overtook.

[353] As, for instance, where the owner has allowed the other party to use or consume his object.

[354] Cf., for example, Reuter/Martinek, op. cit., note 174, pp. 32 sqq. Detlef König, commissioned by the German Minister of Justice, has recently recommended recodification along these lines: "Ungerechtfertigte Bereicherung", in: *Gutachten und Vorschläge zur Überarbeitung des Schuldrechts*, vol. II (1981), pp. 1515 sqq. However, he also recommends inclusion of a general clause to accommodate miscellaneous cases. The positioning of the general clause (at the end of the draft provisions) corresponds to that of the condictio sine causa (§ 748 E I) within the system proposed by the first commission charged with the drafting of the BGB. For comment and criticism of the reform draft, see Manfred Lieb, "Das Bereicherungsrecht de lege ferenda", 1982 *Neue Juristische Wochenschrift* 2034 sqq.; Reuter/Martinek, op. cit., note 174, pp. 67 sqq.

Court has also applied it in a great number of precedents,[355] the matter can for all practical purposes be regarded as settled. The rule expressed in § 812 BGB is usually taken to have two largely independent sides to it: the one, roughly speaking, quasi-contractual; the other quasi-delictual in nature; and it is very widely interpreted to read:

> "A person who acquires something without any legal ground (1) through an act performed by another or (2) at the expense of another in any other manner, is bound to render restitution."

Recognition of a general enrichment action has therefore been only a transitional phenomenon, but it has provided the basis for a rational reorganization of the rules and precedents in this area of the law.[356]

2. English law

(a) The basic options for the legal system

Unjustified enrichment is not a contextual category: it does not deal with one particular aspect of life, but tends to crop up in a broad variety of widely divergent circumstances.[357] An error made in the course of discharging a contract of sale may give rise to an unjustified enrichment claim, but so can the break-up of a "de facto" marriage or the unauthorized use of someone else's photograph in a TV commercial. Unjustified enrichment may occur as a result of the mistaken payment of money, but it may also derive from the rendering of services, from the acknowledgement of the non-existence of a debt, or from the unlawful appropriation of someone else's property. As soon as a legal system is therefore prepared to transcend the basic contract/tort dichotomy, it is faced with the following dilemma. It may either develop a motley assortment of rules and remedies, clustering around individual types of factual situations and tending to develop their own language and technicalities.[358] As a result, the law is in danger of becoming unnecessarily complex, diffuse, and even unintelligible. Or it may attempt to devise a unitary basis of enrichment liability, but then the general formula resulting from these efforts is bound to remain on

---

[355] Cf., for example, BGHZ 40, 272 sqq.; BGHZ 68, 276 (277); BGHZ 72, 246 (248 sq.); BGHZ 82, 28 (30); cf. further Otto Mühl, "Wandlungen im Bereicherungsrecht und die Rechtsprechung des Bundesgerichtshofs", in: *De iustitia et iure, Festgabe für Ulrich von Lübtow* (1980), pp. 547 sqq.

[356] More recently, attempts to establish a uniform formula for all enrichment claims have been revived, but they have, so far, not had any influence on the courts; cf. especially Christian-Michael Kaehler, *Bereicherungsausgleich und Vindikation. Allgemeine Prinzipien der Restitution* (1972); Kupisch, op. cit., note 349, pp. 19 sqq.; Wilhelm, op. cit., note 231, pp. 62 sqq., 173 sqq. The view that the new doctrine has stood the test of time is substantiated by Johannes Köndgen, "Wandlungen im Bereicherungsrecht", in: *Dogmatik und Methode, Josef Esser zum 65. Geburtstag* (1975), pp. 55 sqq. and Andreas Wacke, "Vorzüge und Nachteile des deutschen Bereicherungsrechts", in: *Beiträge zum deutschen und israelischen Privatrecht* (1977), pp. 131 sqq.

[357] Cf. also Zweigert/Kötz/Weir, p. 208: "The layman can make nothing of the expression, and can hardly be blamed for it."

[358] Cf. Birks, *Restitution*, p. 20.

such an abstract level that it does not, in itself, lead to greater legal certainty either. Some form of typological fragmentation must therefore occur, certain structural refinements and conceptual tools have to be developed and a stable pattern of analysis be agreed upon, an indispensable harness preventing Pomponius' "natural justice" from running wild. Modern German law has, obviously, been following the latter of these two courses. Scores of legal writers are sternly marching on, with the heavy tread of German scholarship, through the enrichment forest:[359] meticulously mapping the great trunk road 812, conscientiously exploring complex side-paths and penetrating with the most unrelenting scrupulousness the remotest corners of the dreaded third-party enrichment jungle.[360] So elaborate are the discussions that one may well ask whether the matter has not been taken too far and whether the results of all the theoretical efforts are really worth the trouble.[361]

(b) *Rearing the backward child*

English law, on the other hand, traditionally presents an entirely different picture.[362] Bedevilled by historical accident and legalistic fiction,[363] the law of restitution[364] has remained something of a

[359] Cf., for example, the literature list provided by Lieb, op. cit., note 174, § 812, at the beginning.

[360] On third-party enrichment in German law cf., in particular, the influential study by Claus-Wilhelm Canaris, "Der Bereicherungsausgleich im Dreipersonenverhältnis", in: *Festschrift für Karl Larenz* (1973), pp. 799 sqq.; cf. further the overviews by Reuter/Martinek, op. cit., note 174, pp. 387–515; Lieb, op. cit., note 174, § 812, nn. 30–135 and König, *Bereicherung*, pp. 177 sqq. For a comparative analysis, see John P. Dawson, "Indirect Enrichment", in: *Ius Privatum Gentium, Festschrift für Max Rheinstein*, vol. II (1969), pp. 789 sqq.; König, *Bereicherung*, pp. 219 sqq. Of fundamental importance in this respect is the refusal, on the part of the legislator, to recognize the actio de in rem verso ("Motive", in: *Mugdan*, vol. II, pp. 871 sqq.; on the application of that remedy in 19th-century German law—it was essentially confined, again, to third-party enrichment cases such as the one discussed in C. 4, 26, 7, 3—see Rudolf von Jhering, "Mitwirkung für fremde Rechtsgeschäfte", (1857) 1 *JhJb* 330 sqq.; Windscheid/Kipp, § 483; Kupisch, *Versionsklage*, pp. 114 sqq.; Brandi, op. cit., note 273, pp. 47 sqq., 55 sqq.; Reuter/Martinek, op. cit., note 174, pp. 18 sqq.; König, *Bereicherung*, pp. 182 sqq., 203 sqq.). The underlying policy in not allowing the plaintiff to sue the third party is hinted at already in the genuine part of C. 4, 26, 7, 3 (". . . eius personam elegisti"): the plaintiff has chosen the middleman as his contractual partner and has thus relied on the willingness and ability of the latter to honour his obligation. He must seek his reward where he has placed his trust and cannot now decide to turn against a third party who has acquired the benefit through the middleman. This policy is generally regarded as sound today: cf., for example, Zweigert/Kötz, pp. 294 sqq.; cf. also (de lege ferenda) König, op. cit., note 354, pp. 1577 sqq.

[361] Karl Larenz, *Lehrbuch des Schuldrechts, Besonderer Teil* (11th ed., 1977), preface and p. 466; König, *Bereicherung*, p. 225 (from a comparative perspective). It has been pointed out repeatedly that the practical solutions to individual cases are not normally in dispute; cf. König, op. cit., note 354, p. 1520.

[362] Zweigert/Kötz, p. 297: ". . . one appears to be entering another world."

[363] For a brief summary of the development, cf. Dickson, (1987) 36 *International and Comparative Law Quarterly* 753: "Just as the law of contract developed out of the action in 'assumpsit', so, in turn, the law of quasi-contract developed out of the form of action known as 'indebitatus assumpsit'. Common heads of recovery under that action ('counts') were

backward child of the legal family.[365] An amorphous and somewhat muddled multitude of restitutionary remedies at law and in equity have come to be recognized over the centuries and are still entrenched in modern English law.[366] "My Lords", as Lord Diplock stated emphatically in 1978,[367]

> "there is no general doctrine of unjust enrichment recognised in English law. What it does is to provide specific remedies in particular cases of what might be classified as unjust enrichment in a legal system that is based upon the civil law."

It is, essentially, the fear of an indeterminate liability that motivates judicial pronouncements such as this. But there have also been courageous attempts to shake off the fetters of the past, to extricate the

---

'money had and received', 'money paid', 'quantum meruit', and 'quantum valebant'. Each of these counts had its own set of rules for determining whether recovery was allowable, and unless the plaintiff brought his or her action within one of them the action was bound to fail, except in the rare instance where a court of equity could step in to do justice according to the particular circumstances of the case. A regrettable by-product of the employment of indebitatus assumpsit to remedy restitutionary claims was the importation of the 'implied contract' notion, whereby a claim could succeed only if the defendant could be said to have impliedly promised to grant it. This idea of a fictional contract impeded the development of the English law of restitution from the middle of the eighteenth century to the middle of the twentieth. It prevented plaintiffs from recovering against defendants when the contract between them was ultra vires, it barred actions against defendants who were too young or mentally imbalanced, and it restricted damages recoverable from a tortfeasor. Indeed, it could be said that the whole subject of quasi-contract, and of its modern manifestation, restitution, has suffered from its identification with the term 'contract' in much the same way as the subject of constructive trusts has been badly handicapped by its identification with the concept 'trust'."

For a detailed analysis of the development of implied assumpsit, see Simpson, *History*, pp. 489 sqq. On unjust enrichment and the concept of quasi-contract in English law, cf. Dawson, op. cit., note 119, pp. 9 sqq.; Goff and Jones, *Restitution*, pp. 5 sqq. and, most recently, Birks, *Restitution*, pp. 22, 29 sqq.; cf. also Birks/McLeod, (1986) 6 *Oxford Journal of Legal Studies* 46 sqq. Birks draws attention to the fact that "quasi ex contractu", as used in the fourfold Justinianic subdivision of obligations, means "as though upon a contract" (i.e., in reality there is none). The anglicized version "quasi-contract", on the other hand, has never lost the overtones of "sort of contract". This is why unjustified enrichment has been driven into the category of contract and is usually dealt with as a somewhat anomalous appendage to the law of contract. The traditional position is epitomized by Lord Haldane's statement in *Sinclair v. Brougham* [1914] AC 398 (HL) at 415: "[B]roadly speaking, so far as proceedings in personam are concerned, the common law of England really recognizes (unlike the Roman law) only actions of two classes, those founded on contract and those founded on tort. When it speaks of actions arising quasi ex contractu it refers merely to a class of action in theory based on a contract which is imputed to the defendant by a fiction of law. The fiction can only be set up with effect if such a contract would be valid if it really existed." Birks, *Restitution* (p. 22): "When the law behaves like this you know it is in trouble, its intellect is either genuinely defeated or deliberately indulging in some benevolent dishonesty."

[364] On the relationship between restitution and unjust enrichment, see Birks, *Restitution*, pp. 16 sqq. ("Restitution and unjust enrichment identify exactly the same area of law. The one term simply quadrates with the other"). Is there a historical link with the restitution doctrine of the Spanish scholastics of the late Middle Ages (possibly via Grotius and Viscount Stair)? Cf. the suggestion by Coing, p. 191; cf. also supra, note 320.

[365] Birks, *Restitution*, pp. 2 sq., taking up a remark by H.W.R Wade, *Administrative Law* (1st ed., 1961), preface.

[366] For a comprehensive discussion, see Goff and Jones, *Restitution*, pp. 69 sqq.

[367] *Orakpo v. Manson Investments Ltd.* [1978] AC 95 (HL) at 104.

unjust enrichment principle from its "quasi-contractual" niche and to break through to a general enrichment action. Such attempts date back to Lord Mansfield's famous ruling in *Moses v. Macferlan*, according to which "the defendant, upon the circumstances of the case, is obliged by the ties of natural justice and equity" to render restitution.[368] More recently, Sir Robert Goff and Gareth Jones, in their leading textbook on the law of restitution, have expressed the view that the law "is now sufficiently mature for the courts to recognize a generalized right to restitution".[369] The "predominant principle", under which the restitutionary remedies have to be brought home, consists in their opinion of three elements: "firstly, that the defendant has been enriched by the receipt of *a benefit*; secondly, that he has been so enriched *at the plaintiff's expense*; and thirdly, that it would be *unjust* to allow him to retain the benefit."[370] Lord Denning must be mentioned as a further prominent protagonist of the unjustified enrichment doctrine in the judicial sphere,[371] and so must be, among the academic writers, Professor Birks of Oxford.[372] Generally speaking, the opinion appears to be gaining ground these days that the recognition of generalized principles of enrichment liability does not necessarily lead to anarchy, but is in fact the only way of sorting out the present mess.[373] Yet, there are also

[368] (1760) 2 Burr 1005 (KB). For a most stimulating analysis of Lord Mansfield's use of his Roman learning in this case, see Peter Birks, "English and Roman Learning in *Moses v. Macferlan*", (1984) 37 *Current Legal Problems* 1 sqq. Generally speaking, the equitable principle enunciated in *Moses v. Macferlan* has not been well received; cf., for example, *Holt v. Markham* [1923] 1 KB 504 at 513 ("well-meaning sloppiness of thought"); H.G. Hanbury, "The Recovery of Money", (1924) 40 *LQR* 35 ("Lord Mansfield definitely crossed the all too narrow bridge which leads from the sound soil of implied contract to the shifting quicksands of natural equity"); cf. further Dawson, op. cit., note 119, pp. 15 sqq.

[369] *The Law of Restitution* (2nd ed., 1978), pp. 13, 24.

[370] Goff and Jones, *Restitution*, pp. 13 sq. Birks, *Restitution*, pp. 7, 16 sqq., 20 sq. and passim proposes a very similar pattern of analysis: the defendant must have been enriched, he must have been enriched at the expense of the plaintiff, the enrichment must have been unjust and there must be no other consideration that might bar the claim.

[371] Cf., for example, *Hussey v. Palmer* [1972] 3 All ER 744 (CA); *Eves v. Eves* [1975] 3 All ER 768 (CA), both decisions relating to the problem of "constructive trust".

[372] Cf., in particular, his splendid *Introduction to the Law of Restitution* (1985). The purpose of his book, as he himself describes it, is to find "the simplest structure on which the material in Goff and Jones can hang" (p. 3).

[373] For further indicia of this "wider movement by which Anglo-American common law has set about rectifying the error of having overlooked the subject for most of the century in which textbooks have re-shaped the law", see Birks, *Restitution*, p. 5; Michael Martinek, "Der Weg des Common Law zur allgemeinen Bereicherungsklage—Ein später Sieg des Pomponius?", (1983) 47 *RabelsZ* 294 sqq., 305 sqq. Contra, most recently, Steve Hedley, "Contract, Tort and Restitution; or, On cutting the legal system down to size", (1988) 8 *Journal of Legal Studies* 137 sqq.; cf. also Atiyah, *Rise and Fall*, pp. 764 sqq. arguing that, while ideas of unjust enrichment permeate many aspects of the law, it would be wrong to extricate a separate body of law under that name; for a reply cf. Peter Birks, "Restitution and the Freedom of Contract", (1983) 36 *Current Legal Problems* 141 sqq.; on which, in turn, see P.S. Atiyah, *Essays on Contract* (1986), pp. 48 sqq. In Scotland restitution has been recognized as an established and independent source of obligations since the 17th century. For an analysis of the historical development, see Peter Birks, "Restitution: A View of the Scots Law", (1985) 38 *Current Legal Problems* 57 sqq.

indications that it is not a general enrichment action which will mark the end of all endeavours to rationalize this branch of the law. In the United States, the law of restitution has evolved very much along the lines mapped out by Lord Mansfield. The first important milestone was the recognition of the unjust enrichment principle in the *Restatement of the Law of Restitution* (1937). This principle has over the years been developed into a general, law-generating rule.[374] But, at the same time, we find, starting with the *Restatement*, a disintegration of this general action into a new typology of enrichment claims.[375] The task of reorganizing a diffuse and variegated mass of casuistry, under the auspices of a general rule, has also been tackled by some English authors. Goff and Jones, for example, have suggested a distinction between cases "where the plaintiff himself conferred the benefit on the defendant" and "where the defendant has acquired the benefit through his own wrongful act"[376]—a classification which is more than vaguely reminiscent of the German pair of *"Leistungskondiktion"* and *"Eingriffskondiktion"*. It may well turn out to be the starting point, if not for a convergence, then at least for a rational and meaningful comparison between the Anglo-American common law and one of the major civilian jurisdictions.[377]

VI. THE MEASURE OF ENRICHMENT LIABILITY

1. The "weakness" of enrichment claims in German law

We have so far been looking at the requirements for liability deriving from unjustified enrichment. We must now still add a few words about the extent, or measure, of this liability. If we turn our attention, first of all, to modern German law, we find § 812 I 1 BGB merely providing that the recipient has to make restitution of whatever he has acquired without legal ground at somebody else's expense. Obviously, if restitution in kind is impossible on account of the nature of what the recipient has acquired, he is bound to make good the value.[378] But then there is a highly significant restriction placed upon all unjustified enrichment claims: the obligation to make restitution in kind, or to

---

[374] Cf. Dawson, op. cit., note 119, pp. 3 sqq., 111 sqq.

[375] Cf., in particular, George Palmer, *The Law of Restitution* (1978), vol. I, pp. 40 sqq.; vol. II, pp. 358 sqq. ("benefits conferred pursuant to an actual or supposed contract", "benefits actively acquired by the defendant through his own wrong", "unsolicited benefits").

[376] *Restitution*, pp. 43 sqq. Birks, *Restitution*, pp. 99 sqq. distinguishes between restitution for wrongs and restitution for unjust enrichment by subtraction. The latter category is subdivided according to three different factors rendering an enrichment unjust, namely non-voluntary transfer (in the sense of a transfer that, under the circumstances, the plaintiff did not want to happen), free acceptance (i.e. what is recognized in equity under the name "acquiescence") and other miscellaneous cases.

[377] Martinek, (1983) 47 *RabelsZ* 318 sqq., 330 sqq.; König, op. cit., note 354, p. 1521.

[378] § 818 II BGB.

restore the value, is excluded in so far as the recipient has ceased to be enriched.[379] Thus it is the enrichment creditor who is made to bear the risk of all events which adversely affect the economic benefit accruing to the recipient: the destruction or confiscation of the object concerned as well as, for example, the unfavourable consequences of imprudent investment decisions on the part of the recipient.[380] This is the characteristic "weakness" of unjustified enrichment claims in German law:[381] the defendant is liable only for his actual "enrichment" at the time of litispendence—of the amount, that is, by which all the advantages accruing to him from the event on which the enrichment action is based outweigh the associated or consequential disadvantages. Other modern legal systems tend to be less well disposed towards the recipient/defendant.[382] What induced the German legislator to make enrichment claims so unattractive?

2. Instances of "weak" enrichment liability in Rome

Roman law knew this restricted version of enrichment liability only in certain rather exceptional situations.[383] One of them has already been referred to briefly: the case of the pupillus who had concluded a contract without the authority of his tutor. According to a rescript of the Emperor Antoninus Pius, he could be held liable "in quantum locupletior fact[us] est";[384] and when the question arose which point in time was relevant in order to establish the extent of his enrichment, the answer was given that the moment of litis contestatio had to be referred to:

> "In pupillo, cui sine tutoris auctoritate solutum est, si quaeratur, quo tempore sit locupletior, tempus quo agitur inspicitur."[385]

The same applied when spouses reclaimed what they had given to each other in contravention of the prohibition of donationes inter virum et uxorem.[386]

---

[379] § 818 III BGB. But see §§ 818 IV, 819: from the time of litispendence or from the moment the recipient knows about the absence of a legal ground he is liable "under the general provisions" (§§ 292, 987 sqq. BGB); for further details, see Dawson, "Erasable Enrichment in German Law", (1981) 61 *Boston University LR* 277 sq., 303 sqq.

[380] For an analysis of § 818 III and of the casuistry that has developed in this regard, see Dawson, (1981) 61 *Boston University LR* 271 sqq.; Reuter/Martinek, op. cit., note 174, pp. 576 sqq.; Lieb, op. cit., note 174, § 818, nn. 1 sqq.

[381] Cf., for example, Flessner, op. cit., note 341, p. 2.

[382] For a comparative analysis, cf. Flessner, op. cit., note 341, pp. 37 sqq.; cf. also König, *Bereicherung*, pp. 51 sqq., 73 sqq.; Zweigert/Kötz, pp. 316 sqq.; as far as American law is concerned, cf. John P. Dawson, "Restitution without Enrichment", (1981) 61 *Boston University LR* 563 sqq.

[383] Cf. supra, p. 882.

[384] Ulp. D. 26, 8, 1 pr.; Ulp. D. 26, 8, 5 pr.

[385] Marci. D. 46, 3, 47 pr. For all details, see Hubert Niederländer, *Die Bereicherungshaftung im klassischen römischen Recht* (1953), pp. 11 sqq., 56 sqq., 89 sqq.; Werner Flume, "Der Wegfall der Bereicherung in der Entwicklung vom römischen zum geltenden Recht", in: *Festschrift für Hans Niedermeyer*, 1953, pp. 124 sqq.

[386] On which see supra, p. 486.

"[N]am ius constitutum ad eas donationes pertinet, ex quibus et locupletior mulier et pauperior maritus in suis rebus fit"[387]—

this is how the range of transactions covered by the prohibition was usually described and the element of "locupletior" (enrichment) obviously played a crucial role.[388] But it was also relevant in determining what the impoverished party was allowed to claim back. Again, therefore, the question was asked "[q]uod autem spectetur tempus, an locupletior [est facta]" and, again, it was held, in response, "verum est litis contestatae tempus spectari oportere".[389]

3. Liability of the defendant under the condictio

Normally, however, quite a different regime applied. The condictio was an actio stricti iuris and its formula did not, therefore, allow for any flexibility. The defendant, provided it could be established that he "appeared to have to give", was condemned in either the sum or the value of the object(s) that he had received. If 10 000 had been transferred to him by mistake, he owed 10 000 sesterces; if he had received a specific object, he was liable for "quanti ea res est, tantam pecuniam". As far as money was concerned, this was where the matter ended. The possibility that he might have spent or lost it, or that for any other reason he might be unable to return the very same coins that he had received, did not matter: "Quod indebitum per errorem solvitur, aut ipsum aut tantundem repetitur."[390] The recipient was in the same position as a borrower under a contract of mutuum[391]—he did not have to return the same objects but objects of the same kind and to the same value. That he was no longer "enriched" and was therefore unable to pay even "tantundem" was of no consequence for the existence of his obligation either: after all, payment of 10 000 sesterces always remained objectively possible. The same considerations applied with regard to objects "quae pondere numero mensura consistunt";[392] the liability of the defendant always remained unimpaired, for the very reason that the objects "in obligatione" were merely reckoned by weight, number or measure.[393] Matters looked different, though, where the defendant had received a specific, individual object (species). If this object was destroyed, he was normally automatically released from his obligation: it had become (objectively) impossible to give the

---

[387] Ter. Cl. D. 24, 1, 25.

[388] For all details, see Karlheinz Misera, *Der Bereicherungsgedanke bei der Schenkung unter Ehegatten* (1974), pp. 6 sqq.

[389] Ulp. D. 24, 1, 7 pr.; Niederländer, op. cit., note 253, pp. 11 sqq., 56 sqq., 67 sqq.; Flume, *Festschrift Niedermeyer*, pp. 116 sqq.; Misera, op. cit., note 388, pp. 91 sqq., 189 sqq. For a detailed analysis of the reasons that may have induced the Roman lawyers thus to restrict the plaintiff's claim, see Misera, op. cit., note 388, pp. 216 sqq., 248 sqq.

[390] Pomp. D. 12, 6, 7.

[391] Gai. III, 91; *Inst.* III, 14, 1.

[392] Paul. D. 12, 1, 2, 1; Gai. III, 90.

[393] Cf., for example, Marci. D. 19, 5, 25; Flume, *Festschrift Niedermeyer*, p. 130.

object he was bound to give and "impossibilium nulla est obligatio".[394] Yet under certain circumstances the obligation was deemed to be perpetuated: the defendant either had to have been in mora or the impossibility to perform must have come about as a result of his "fault".[395] No fictitious perpetuatio obligationis was necessary—because the obligation remained unaffected—if the enrichment debtor had sold the object that he had received. It was still (objectively) possible to render restitution, and thus he could be condemned, without further ado, to pay the value. Only if the object that the defendant had sold in good faith was subsequently destroyed, did the perpetuatio obligationis construction have, once again, to be resorted to. As a rule, however, it did not provide the plaintiff with a cause of action either, since the destruction was not normally attributable to the defendant/vendor's fault. The result was therefore that the latter was released from his enrichment obligation.

4. Condictio pretii

Yet, if that would have been the end of the matter, he would have been left with a comfortable—and quite undeserved—gain: he was no longer exposed to a condictio and could at the same time keep the purchase price he had received from the third party, where the object had ultimately perished. It was in order to address this inequity that Julian allowed the plaintiff to institute an action for that purchase price; it had, after all, merely replaced the original object of the plaintiff's condictio in the defendant's property.

> "Si eum servum, qui tibi legatus sit, quasi mihi legatum possederim et vendiderim, mortuo eo posse te mihi pretium condicere Iulianus ait, quasi ex re tua locupletior factus sim":[396]

the new claim was still referred to as condictio and it was obviously based on the idea of a surrogation. If this solution commended itself in cases where the object sold had been destroyed, it was also, arguably, appropriate if the object still existed. Whether the one or the other was the case, was, from the point of view of the relationship between plaintiff and defendant, entirely accidental. Why then should the practical result be different? Or, to put it slightly differently: why should the condictio pretii be a suitable device only to establish, and not also to limit, the defendant's liability? Whether the object in question

[394] Cf. supra, pp. 687 sqq.

[395] Paul. D. 45, 1, 91, 3: ". . . quotiens culpa intervenit debitoris, perpetuari obligationem." For further details, see supra, pp. 786 sq., 791 sq. An enrichment debtor cannot, however, normally have been held responsible for the event preventing him from honouring his obligation in just the same way as a promisor; for it can hardly be expected of him to be aware of his obligation to make restitution (and thus to adjust his behaviour accordingly) to the same extent as this can be expected of a person who has promised, say, to convey a slave. If he was actually aware of the fact that he received indebitum, he committed theft (cf. supra, note 99).

[396] Afr. D. 12, 1, 23.

was ultimately destroyed or not: in *both* cases the defendant no longer had the object in his property, but had, instead, received the price; and hence it was the price for which he should be liable, rather than either for the (full) value of the object or, alternatively, for nothing. This is how the Roman lawyers may have argued, for in a famous and much-debated fragment Ulpian, indeed, appears to have confined the plaintiff's claim to the purchase price (which is specifically stated to have been rather small), although the slave that the defendant had originally received is not reported to have died:

> ". . . et interdum licet aliud praestemus, inquit, aliud condicimus: ut puta . . . hominem indebitum [dedi], et hunc sine fraude modico distraxisti, nempe hoc solum refundere debes, quod ex pretio habes."[397]

"Quod ex pretio habes" here does not mean "what you have left from the price"[398] but "what you have received as price",[399] and Ulp. D. 12, 6, 26, 12 can therefore not be taken to have determined the content of enrichment condictiones, on a gliding scale, according to the enrichment still extant at the time of litis contestatio.[400]

5. The regime of the ius commune: all or nothing

Until the time of Justinian the general rule was all or nothing. Predominantly this meant "all": the plaintiff was able to claim the full value of what the defendant had received. The alternative of "nothing" applied only in cases of interitus speciei not attributable to the fault of the defendant. The condictio pretii constituted the only exception from this simple scheme: if the defendant, in good faith, sold the object that he had received, the purchase price took the place of that object as far as the plaintiff's condictio was concerned. Considerably less indulgence was thus afforded to the defendant by the Roman lawyers than by the BGB, and the lawyers of the ius commune by and large accepted this position for a long time.[401] More particularly, the distinction between condictiones aimed at the recovery of a species or a quantitas remained firmly entrenched and in the latter case the debtor continued to be held liable, in conformity with D. 12, 6, 7, for tantundem: "Sed quando quantitas solvitur: tunc indistincte dicitur quis locupletior in eo quod recipit. Quantitas enim perire non potest."[402] Usually the parallel with mutuum was drawn, and Cuiacius and many subsequent French

---

[397] Ulp. D. 12, 6, 26, 12.

[398] As Peter Birks (Mommsen, Krüger, Watson, *The Digest of Justinian*, vol. I (1985)) translates.

[399] Flume, *Festschrift Niedermeyer*, p. 105.

[400] Cf., in particular, Flume, *Festschrift Niedermeyer*, pp. 104 sqq.; cf. also: Niederländer, op. cit., note 253, pp. 4 sqq.; Malte Diesselhorst, *Die Natur der Sache als aussergesetzliche Rechtsquelle, verfolgt an der Rechtsprechung zur Saldotheorie* (1968), pp. 36 sqq. Contra: Heinrich Siber, "Retentio propter res donatas", in: *Studi in onore di Salvatore Riccobono*, vol. III (1936), pp. 252, 257; von Lübtow, *Condictio*, pp. 20 sqq. and others.

[401] Flume, *Festschrift Niedermeyer*, pp. 140 sqq.

[402] Bartolus, *Commentaria*, ad D. 12, 6, 7 (Quod indebitum).

authors even referred to a quasi-contract of "promutuum" in these cases.[403] Lauterbach, in the 17th century, summarized the then prevailing opinion in the following terms:

> "Si quantitas indebiti soluta, tantundem in eodem genere [petitur] . . . Si vero species soluta, repetitur illa ipsa . . . Si vero res in specie restitui non potest, bonae fidei possessor, qui nullam moram admisit, non tenetur, nisi in quantum locupletior factus est [i.e. the price that he has actually received] . . . Malae fidei vero possessor, aut qui moram admisit, verum pretium restituit [i.e. the actual value of the object in question]."[404]

6. The change of opinion in the 19th century

The turnabout came only in the 19th century,[405] and in the wake of a variety of tendencies to facilitate enrichment actions. The error requirement of the condictio indebiti was relaxed, Savigny's generalized condictio sine causa gained recognition and the naturalis aequitas was emphasized (possibly still under the influence of the enthusiasm displayed by the natural lawyers for Pomponius' famous declaration) as the true basis on which the law of unjustified enrichment rested. The further one was prepared, however, to take the principle against unjust enrichment, the more anxious one became to protect the reasonable reliance of those who had disposed of what they had received; and such protection appeared to be required, irrespective of whether a species, fungibles or money was involved. If the plaintiff's claim was subject to the precepts of what was fair and equitable, it followed not only that every unjust benefit must be recoverable, but also that the defendant may be held liable only as far as a benefit had in fact accrued to him.[406] "Neminem cum alterius detrimento fieri locupletiorem": the defendant was not to be enriched at the plaintiff's expense; but where he had lost or spent the money, or given away the fungibles, he could hardly be seen to be "enriched". Thus it came to be regarded not only as manifestly equitable, but as inherent in the very nature of "enrichment" liability, that a duty to make restitution existed only in so far as the recipient was (still) enriched.[407] The most influential legal writers of the

---

[403] Cf. supra, p. 837, note 28.

[404] *Collegium theoretico-practicum*, Lib. XII, Tit. VI, XXIX.

[405] Flume, *Festschrift Niedermeyer*, pp. 145 sqq. (who, however, at p. 144, draws attention to the fact that Duarenus had already abandoned the distinction between species and quantitas as the object of the enrichment claim and merely stated "eum a quo condicitur indebitum, eatenus damnari, quaternus sit factus locupletior"); Diesselhorst, op. cit., note 400, pp. 42 sqq.; Flessner, op. cit., note 341, pp. 5 sqq.; König, *Bereicherung*, pp. 52 sqq. The provisions of the Prussian General Land Law are still in tune with the traditional opinion; cf., in particular, § 193 I 16 PrALR.

[406] Or, as it is often put, "innocent" receivers of unjustified gain must not be allowed to incur any loss as a result of the enrichment claim; they must not be required to "reach into their own pockets".

[407] Cf. Dawson, (1981) 61 *Boston University LR* 271 sqq., who draws attention to a statement of the imperial Supreme Court (RGZ 118, 185 (187)) according to which the "principle of enrichment that is highest of all is that the duty of the enriched person to surrender . . . must in no event lead to a reduction of his estate by more than the amount of

19th century adopted this view[408] and so it could not fail to impress the draftsmen of the BGB.[409] Modern comparative research, as well as historical investigation, demonstrates, however, that there is nothing axiomatic or intrinsically self-evident about the rule expressed in § 818 III BGB.[410]

---

the enrichment". This principle, Dawson comments, is enforced "with an unrelieved rigor and disregard of consequences that would be hard to find elsewhere in modern German law" (p. 272).

[408] Glück, vol. 13, pp. 152 sqq.; Vangerow, *Pandekten*, § 625, Anm. 3; Windscheid/Kipp, § 424, 1.

[409] "Protokolle", in: *Mugdan*, vol. II, pp. 1181 sqq.

[410] Cf., in particular, the trenchant criticism by Dawson, (1981) 61 *Boston University LR* 271 sqq., 306 sq. who, after pointing out that the surviving net gain as the measure of enrichment "had emanated not from some 'most holy' sanctum of the legal order [cf., for instance, the remark by Otto von Gierke, quoted supra, p. 835, note 6] but from the private studios of Pandectist authors", proceeds to argue that the pandectist authors and their followers gave a basic misdirection to the German law of restitution. Their aim "was the promotion of virtue by giving honesty, based on ignorance, both reward and protection". Thus they concentrated attention and concern "on the 'innocent' recipients of unjustified gain". Their view, however, is fundamentally flawed and one-sided for "it took no account of the other side in what has for centuries been conceived as a two-sided relation—enrichment acquired at the expense of *another*. . . . An encompassing principle of exoneration that ensures against any loss all those who do not know that the gain they derived and acquired at another's expense will have to be restored, therefore seems (to an unsympathetic observer from abroad) to show a basic though well-meaning confusion of thought" (pp. 302, 306, 314).

PART VIII

CHAPTER 27

Delict in General

1. Delict and crime

When a person injures another by an act of reckless driving, he is accountable both to the victim of the wrong and to the community at large. To the former he has to render compensation for the resulting damage, whereas the State, as representative of the community, will institute proceedings with the aim of punishing the offender. One and the same act can therefore constitute a wrong both against a private and against the public interest: it can be a delict as well as a crime. It is the law of delict which protects the interests of the injured individual and which determines whether and under which circumstances redress may be claimed; criminal law, on the other hand, subjects the wrongdoer to a sanction[1] in order to prevent a repetition of the wrongful act and to deter others from committing it.[2] Of course, there are many delicts that do not at the same time constitute crimes: negligent damage to somebody else's corporeal assets is an example. Public interest does not appear to call for a criminal sanction in these cases. Occasionally, social policy requires the abrogation of a criminal penalty. This has happened in South Africa with regard to adultery.[3] Yet, though no longer criminal, the act can still constitute a delict and give rise to a claim for damages.[4] Conversely, not every crime is a delict either. High treason and (in South Africa) blasphemy are crimes but they do not affect the interests of private individuals.[5]

2. Delict and contract

(a) Death of contract, death of delict?

Both criminal law and the law of delict deal with unlawful conduct; but

[1] ". . . malum passionis quod infligitur propter malum actionis": Grotius, *De jure belli ac pacis*, Lib. II, Cap. XX, I; generally, see Eberhard Schmidhäuser, *Vom Sinn der Strafe* (2nd ed., 1971), pp. 34 sqq.

[2] Generally, on the distinction between criminal law and the law of delict, see Pierre Catala, John Anthony Weir, "Delict and Torts: A Study in Parallel", (1963) 37 *Tulane LR* 582 sqq.; André Tunc, "Introduction", in: *International Encyclopedia of Comparative Law*, vol. XI, 1 (1983), nn. 49 sqq.; more specifically for England (crime and tort), see Percy H. Winfield, *The Province of the Law of Tort* (1971), pp. 190 sqq.; cf. also Van den Heever, *Aquilian Damages*, pp. 1 sqq.

[3] *Green v. Fitzgerald, Fitzgerald v. Green* 1914 AD 88 sqq.

[4] Cf., for example, Pauw, *Persoonlikheidskrenking*, pp. 190 sqq.; J. Neethling, *Persoonlikheidsreg* (2nd ed., 1985), pp. 203 sqq. For Germany, see Andreas Wacke, in: *Münchener Kommentar*, vol. V, 1 (2nd ed., 1989), § 1353, nn. 39 sqq.

[5] Crimes that result in harm to individuals do, however, normally constitute a delict. For a more detailed analysis, see Jean Limpens, Robert M. Kruithof, Anne Meinertzhagen-Limpens, "Liability for One's Own Act", in: *International Encyclopedia of Comparative Law*, vol. XI, 2 (1983), nn. 151 sqq.

whereas crime may be said to be a public wrong, a delict is a civil wrong. Yet breach of contract, in a broad sense, may also be dubbed a civil wrong. Within the province of private law, the necessity of drawing a second distinction thus presents itself. Ever since the days of Gaius,[6] civilian tradition has conceived of contract and delict as two separate branches of the law of obligations, and in the English common law, too, a very similar conceptual classification (contract and tort) has become firmly entrenched.[7] It has already been mentioned repeatedly that the distinction between delict (or tort) and contract is a most delicate one and that the borderline has in many respects become blurred.[8] What is regarded as contractual liability in one country may be added to the province of delict in another, and vice versa, and certain cases even appear to defy all attempts at classification:[9] being in the nature of hermaphrodites,[10] they lead an unsettled existence within the no man's land somewhere between the traditional and established categories. Moreover, we have seen[11] that the whole basis of the classification has been challenged by the death-of-contract theorists: contract, they claim, is in the process of being reabsorbed into the mainstream of the law of tort (whence it originally sprang).

It is not without irony, though, that contract is said to have rejoined tort just at the time when tort itself "has been subjected to the most intense theoretical and practical attacks in its long history".[12] The explosion of civil liability, of traffic accidents and medical malpractice law has drawn attention to the "creaking joint[s] of our arthritic tort system".[13]

"The toll on life, limb, and property exacted by today's industrial operations, methods of transport, and many another activity benignly associated with the

---

[6] Gai. III, 88; cf. supra, pp. 10 sqq.

[7] Cf. generally Tunc, op. cit., note 2, nn. 32 sqq.

[8] Supra, pp. 11 sqq. Cf. also G.H.L. Fridman, "The Interaction of Tort and Contract" (1977) 93 *LQR* 422 (who recommends a fusion of the two categories) and J.C. Smith, "Economic Loss and the Common Law Marriage of Contracts and Torts", (1984) 18 *University of British Columbia LR* 95 sqq. (who records the union of contract and tort, but warns that it may be premature to celebrate the nuptials).

[9] Even comparative lawyers have their difficulties. Thus, Basil Markesinis, "An Expanding Tort Law—The Price of a Rigid Contract Law", (1987) 103 *LQR* 354, after an analysis of how German courts deal with economic loss cases, criticizes English courts for expanding the law of torts rather than the law of contract. Christian von Bar, "Deliktsrecht", in: *Gutachten und Vorschläge zur Überarbeitung des Schuldrechts*, vol. II (1981), pp. 1685 sqq., 1771 sqq., on the other hand, after having examined the modern trends in French and English law, advocates de lege ferenda an expansion of the German law of delict at the expense of the contractual constructions employed de lege lata. On the nature of the liability arising from culpa in contrahendo (cf. supra, pp. 11 sq., 244 sq.) cf., most recently, Dieter Medicus, "Die culpa in contrahendo zwischen Vertrag und Delikt", in: *Festschrift für Max Keller* (1989), pp. 205 sqq.

[10] Robert Stevens, "*Hedley Byrne v. Heller*: Judicial Creativity and Doctrinal Possibility" (1964) 27 *Modern LR* 161.

[11] Supra, pp. 12 sq.

[12] Jeffrey O'Connell, "The Interlocking Death and Rebirth of Contract and Tort", (1976-77) 75 *Michigan LR* 662.

[13] John G. Fleming, (1982) 30 *American Journal of Comparative Law* 704.

> 'modern way of life' ", writes Fleming,[14] "has reached proportions so staggering that the economic cost of accidents represents a constant and mounting drain on the community's human and material resources, calculable as a significant fraction of the gross national product. The principal, nay paramount, task of the law of torts is to play an important regulatory role in the adjustment of these losses and the eventual allocation of their cost."

Does that imply the death of tort? Probably not, but it does entail an ever-increasing shift from the classical model of individual loss-bearing towards a collectivization of losses, a gradual absorption of tort law, or at least large parts of it, into the modern social security system.[15] Yet, despite these somewhat sombre prospects, both contract and delict have, to date, displayed a remarkable longevity; and whether jurisprudentially justifiable and practically satisfactory or not, the distinction does, as a matter of fact, continue to exist in modern legal systems. Contract law ratifies and enforces the joint ventures of two or more parties beyond the boundaries of the existing status quo;[16] it seeks to protect specific expectations engendered by a binding promise. Tort law, on the other hand, attempts to coordinate the freedom of the individuals by deliminating and protecting their respective spheres against intrusions by each other; it is concerned with the degree of care owed even between strangers, and liability thus arises solely from the unlawful act committed by the wrongdoer, quite irrespective of whether any prior relationship existed between the parties concerned.

(b) Exclusivity or alternativity of remedies?

Given, then, the existence of two different bodies of rules and of two different types of remedy, the danger of a considerable overlap is obvious. Thus, if a complete stranger in a particular situation enjoys protection under the law of delict, should not—at least!—the same protection be accorded to contractual partners? Would it not be absurd to maintain that the general duty not to destroy other people's property does not also apply to the person who has leased the piece of property in question from its owner? Or take the case of products liability: the consumer's claim for damages resulting from the defective product may be based on the contract with his vendor, but it may also be, against the manufacturer, of a delictual character. Does that mean that, if vendor and manufacturer are one and the same person, two actions are available against him? Ultimately one may even ask whether every breach of contract that results in damage does not also constitute a delict.[17]

The answer to these questions is not of a purely academic nature. Whether damages are claimed in contract or in delict can have a whole

---

[14] John G. Fleming, *An Introduction to the law of Torts* (1977), p. 1.
[15] Cf., for example, John G. Fleming, "Is There a Future for Tort?", (1975) 58 *Australian LJ* 131 sqq.; Zweigert/Kötz, pp. 433 sqq.; Tunc, op. cit., note 2, nn. 21 sqq.
[16] Charles Fried, *Contract as Promise* (1981), pp. 2 sq.
[17] Cf. W.B.C. Palton, "Tort or Contract", (1966) 82 *LQR* 346 sqq.

variety of implications. The details differ from country to country.[18] In Germany, for example, delictual claims are subject to a three-year period of prescription,[19] whereas contractual claims often prescribe only after 30 years.[20] A plaintiff in delict has to prove fault, in contract the onus of proof is reversed.[21] The place of jurisdiction differs[22] and so does, occasionally, the degree of fault required for both actions.[23] In delict immaterial interest is, under certain circumstances, recoverable,[24] whereas contractual claims are strictly confined to material loss.[25] A further rather odd, but most important, distinction exists when it comes to liability for the fault of third parties: the defendant in a delictual action can exonerate himself by showing that no culpa in eligendo, custodiendo or inspiciendo was attributable to him.[26] Contract, on the other hand, entails strict liability of the debtor for the fault of those employed in performing his obligation.[27]

In spite of these differences, German law allows, in principle, a choice of remedies:[28] if a set of facts gives rise to a claim in delict and in contract, the plaintiff may proceed on either basis.[29] But this approach is practicable only where, as indeed in Germany, the scope of delict is defined in such a manner that it cannot be used to turn the flank of contract. The German law of delict does not protect a person's property at large, and thus it is mainly via the law of contract that pure economic (or patrimonial) loss[30] which has been negligently caused may be recovered.[31] As a result, a sufficiently large range of cases is left

---

[18] For details, see Tony Weir, "Complex Liabilities", in: *International Encyclopedia of Comparative Law*, vol. XI, 12 (1983), nn. 10 sqq. For a recent comparative discussion on the question of concurrence or alternativity of remedies in medical malpractice claims, see Dieter Giesen, *International Medical Malpractice Law* (1988), pp. 33 sqq.

[19] § 852 BGB.

[20] § 195 BGB; for details, see Peters/Zimmermann, *Verjährungsfristen*, pp. 218 sqq.

[21] § 282 BGB.

[22] §§ 29, 32 ZPO.

[23] Cf., for example, §§ 599 (loan for use), 690 (deposit), as opposed to § 823 I BGB.

[24] § 847 BGB; cf. infra, pp. 1027, 1092 sqq.

[25] § 253 BGB.

[26] § 831 BGB.

[27] § 278 BGB.

[28] For details, see Peter Schlechtriem, *Vertragsordnung und ausservertragliche Haftung* (1972), pp. 289 sqq.

[29] Both claims can, however, not be treated as completely independent. On the interaction between the two notionally independent claims, see Weir, op. cit., note 18, n. 61. Cf. also the example discussed supra, pp. 202 sq.

[30] That is loss, which does not flow from (usually: physical) damage to a specific right or interest of the plaintiff (such as life, body, health, freedom or a specific asset within his property).

[31] The patrimony as such is not listed among the rights or interests enumerated in § 823 I, the core provision of the German law of delict (cf. infra, p. 1036). Pure economic loss may be recovered under § 823 II, provided that some statute—usually of a criminal nature—has been violated which aims at the protection of the injured party's patrimony, and—most importantly—under § 826 BGB (which is, however, limited to intentional activities which

to the exclusive regulation of the law of contract to prevent the existing differences between contractual and delictual remedies from being rendered meaningless.

The situation is entirely different under the French code civil.[32] Here we find the famous general clause of delictual liability,[33] according to which "every act whatever of man which causes damage to another obliges him by whose fault the damage occurred to repair it".[34] It is so wide that the admission of an elective concurrence of liability would lead to every culpable breach of contract being actionable in delict too. As a result, French doctrine has to protect the rules relating to contractual liability by means of the principle of "*non-cumul des responsabilités*". Where a contractual bond exists between two parties, the law of contract must be given preference as the lex specialis; and even though all the elements of a cause of action in delict may be present, the availability of a contractual remedy is taken automatically to preclude any recourse to it.

In this context it is interesting to note a recent shift of approach by the South African courts. For while contractual and delictual liability have traditionally never been regarded as exclusive of each other,[35] the *Lillicrap* decision has introduced an important qualification to the principle.[36] Significantly, it follows closely on the heels of the extension of Aquilian (i.e. delictual) liability to cases involving purely economic loss,[37] and it may be inferred from *Lillicrap* that a concurrence of delictual and contractual liability is no longer permissible where the harm does not flow from physical damage to the person or to a specific piece of property of the plaintiff, but where it is of a purely economic nature.[38] English law, incidentally, which also does not exclude pure economic loss, a limine, from the confines of the law of torts,[39] appears to adopt an intermediate position too.[40]

---

must, in addition, be contra bonos mores). For an overview of the German provisions, cf. B.S. Markesinis, *A Comparative Introduction to the German Law of Tort* (1986), pp. 24 sqq., 509 sqq., 513 sqq.

[32] Cf. Schlechtriem, op. cit., note 28, pp. 63 sqq.; Weir, op. cit., note 18, nn. 52 sqq.

[33] Art. 1382: "*Tout fait quelconque de l'homme, qui cause à autrui un dommage, oblige celui par la faute duquel il est arrivé, a le réparer.*"

[34] Tr. Weir, in Zweigert/Kötz/Weir, p. 283.

[35] *Van Wyk v. Lewis* 1924 AD 438 sqq.

[36] *Lillicrap, Wassenaar and Partners v. Pilkington Brothers (SA) (Pty.) Ltd.* 1985 (1) SA 475 (A); cf. p. 500G, where Grosskopf AJA states that "the Aquilian action does not fit comfortably in a contractual setting like the present".

[37] See infra, pp. 1042 sq.

[38] P.Q.R. Boberg, "Back to *Winterbottom v. Wright*?—Not Quite!", (1985) 102 *SALJ* 213 sqq.; Dale Hutchison and D.P. Visser, "Lillicrap Revisited: Further Thoughts on Pure Economic Loss and Concurrence of Actions", (1985) 102 *SALJ* 587 sqq., 590 sqq.

[39] Cf. infra, pp. 1038 sqq.

[40] "It is a familiar position in our law that the same wrongful act may be made the subject of an action either in contract or in tort at the election of the claimant, and, although the course chosen may produce certain incidental consequences which would not have followed had the other course been adopted, it is a mistake to regard the two kinds of liability as

3. Delict and tort

We have, so far, been referring rather indiscriminately to the notions of delict and tort. "Delict" (derived from "delinquere"—hence also the word "delinquent") is the civilian term generally used to designate a civil (as opposed to criminal) wrong. Its common-law counterpart is "tort" which, in turn, has its etymological root in the Latin term "tortus", meaning "crooked" or "twisted".[41] Delict and tort are functional equivalents, since both of them refer to certain wrongful acts which the law is prepared to redress, either with a decree for restitution in kind[42] or with an award of damages. But the approach adopted towards defining the scope and essence of such wrongful acts is entirely dissimilar.[43] The continental law of delict presents the picture of a coherent body of rules based on general principles and abstract concepts; and though the inordinate amount of case law that can be found in any modern commentary on the topic[44] considerably mars the neatness of this picture, the crisp provisions of the modern codes,[45] still essentially shaping our ideas about delictual liability, are the result of a long and characteristic process of generalization, systematization and abstraction.[46] Of prime importance, in this context, are the notions of causation, unlawfulness, fault and damages: they constitute the four essential features of the modern, actionable delict. Tort, by comparison,

> "is a bag of nuts and bolts. History can say how they came there, but science is pressed to rationalize their presence. It follows from the impossibility of discovering a highest common factor of contentual quiddity that the common law should be said to know not tort but torts".[47]

"Tort" does not constitute a coherent body of law, definable in general and abstract terms, but is no more than the sum total of a variety of individual torts that have developed, under the writ system, in characteristically casuistic and haphazard fashion. Each of these specific torts is still regarded as an independent cause of liability, each has its own constituent elements, and each protects a special interest from being interfered with.[48] That does not mean, however, that the English

---

themselves necessarily exclusive of each other": *Lister v. Romford Ice and Cold Storage Co.* [1957] AC 555 (HL) at 587 (per Lord Radcliffe). Cf. Weir, op. cit., note 18, nn. 67 sq. For criticism see Fridman, (1966) 82 *LQR* 428 sqq.

41 Winfield, op. cit., note 2, pp. 8 sqq.; Tunc, op. cit., note 2, n. 5.

42 Supra, pp. 824 sq.

43 For a comparison, see Buckland/McNair, pp. 338 sqq.; Catala/Weir, (1963) 37 *Tulane LR* 573 sqq.; B.S. Markesinis, "The Not So Dissimilar Tort and Delict", (1977) 93 *LQR* 78 sqq.

44 Cf., for example, Karl Schäfer, in: *Staudinger* (12th ed.), §§ 823–832 (1986), § 823, nn. 1-625 (334 pages).

45 For an overview cf. Limpens/Kruithof/Meinertzhagen-Limpens, op. cit., note 5, nn. 5 sqq.

46 For details, see infra, pp. 1031 sqq.

47 Catala/Weir, (1963) 37 *Tulane LR* 580.

48 Zweigert/Kötz, p. 343.

law of torts has become entirely petrified. For even though the courts do not approach the cases brought before them from the point of view of general requirements of tortious liability, but rather try to fit them into one of the existing pigeon-holes, they have never been reluctant to expand the scope of protection by adding yet another of these pigeon-holes:

> "[T]ortious liability is constantly expanding and there is ample evidence that a plaintiff's claim is not necessarily prejudiced because he is unable to find a specific label for the wrong of which he complains. New and innominate torts have been constantly emerging in the long course of our history and the courts have shown no inclination at any stage to disclaim their creative functions, if considerations of policy pointed to the need of recognizing a new cause of action."[49]

4. The development of the law of torts

(a) Trespass and the rise of "case"

The "fertile mother of actions"[50] in English legal history was trespass.[51] It emerged in the course of the 13th century as a remedy for a class of very obvious and dangerous wrongs: wrongs that had been committed with force and arms and that constituted a breach of the king's peace ("vi et armis, et contra pacem Domini Regis"). This grave allegation was necessary, originally, to justify the intervention of the royal courts; for the great bulk of trespasses at that time was dealt with by the local courts. It was only towards the end of the 14th century that the royal courts openly started to exercise jurisdiction over trespass actions in which the king could not be said to have a special interest. One of the first cases appears to have been the "*Farrier's* Case",[52] concerning a smith's liability for laming a horse that he was, rather unskilfully, shoeing: obviously, the smith's action could hardly be said to endanger the king's peace. Thus, a category of writs gradually came to be established that was characterized by the absence of the contra pacem clause: the special writ of trespass as opposed to the common writs that contained the allegation of a breach of peace. More important, from the point of view of substantive law, was another feature common to the cases where proceedings were initiated by a special writ: the wrong

---

[49] Fleming, *Torts*, p. 5. Cf. also *Ashby v. White* (1703) 2 Ld Raym 938 (per Holt CJ); *Chapman v. Pickersgill* (1762) 2 Wils 145 ("This action is for a tort: torts are infinitely various, not limited or confined, for there is nothing in nature but may be an instrument of mischief": p. 146). For a more modern case in point, see *Rookes v. Barnard* [1964] AC 1129 (HL) (establishing the tort of intimidation).

[50] *Pollock and Maitland*, vol. II, p. 525.

[51] Derived from the Latin "transgressio" (Pollock and Maitland, vol. II, pp. 511 sq.). For what follows see S.F.C. Milsom, "Trespass from Henry III. to Edward III.", (1958) 74 *LQR* 195 sqq., 407 sqq., 561 sqq.; idem, *Historical Foundations of the Common Law* (1969), pp. 244 sqq. Cf. also Theodore F.T. Plucknett, *A Concise History of the Common Law* (5th ed., 1956), pp. 455 sqq.; C.H.S. Fifoot, *History and Sources of the Common Law* (1949), pp. 44 sqq.

[52] Cf. Fifoot, op. cit., note 51, pp. 81 sq. (A.D. 1373); on which, see Milsom, *Historical Foundations*, op. cit., note 51, pp. 249 sqq.

allegedly committed by the defendant was less obvious and some explanation was needed to substantiate the plaintiff's claim. In a common writ, the plaintiff had to describe only what the defendant had either done or failed to do. But in the case of the farrier, for instance, the mere allegation that the smith had driven his nails into the quick of the horse's hoof and thereby caused the plaintiff damage was hardly sufficient to establish the wrongfulness of his behaviour. In addition, the plaintiff had to set out why the smith should have been under a duty to shoe the plaintiff's horse. Thus, a special clause introduced by the word "cum" (whereas) had to be included in the writ[53]—the Roman lawyers would probably have called it a demonstratio. This clause contained the special facts of the case on which the success of the action depended, and hence the expressions "super casum", "*sur son cas*" or "on the case" were used to describe the new kind of writ. This was the origin of the distinction between (general) trespass and "case", a distinction that became firmly entrenched on account of certain procedural consequences attaching to the contra pacem clause in (general) trespass: breach of the king's peace was a most serious matter and had therefore always carried arrest and outlawry.[54]

(b) The distinction between trespass and "case"

Trespass and case remained the principal writs which the common law offered against wrongful misconduct, but in the course of time standard

---

[53] Milsom, (1958) 74 *LQR* 407 sqq.; Simpson, *History*, pp. 200 sqq.

[54] Milsom, *Historical Foundations*, op. cit., note 51, p. 263. It is significant to note that the defendant, if convicted, was liable to a fine and imprisonment (abolished only in 1694) since every trespass constituted a punishable offence; originally, no clear-cut division existed between crime and civil injury. Trespass, the action which exercised dominance over the growing law of torts, was "quasi-criminal" in character (Winfield, op. cit., note 2, p. 10). It aimed "at a punitive and exemplary result", and throughout the time of the Year Books, men were "punished" for their trespasses (Pollock and Maitland, vol. II, p. 573). The transition from what we would call "criminal" to "civil" justice is described by Pollock and Maitland (vol. II, p. 522) in the following words: "[U]nder Edward I a favorite device of our legislators is that of giving double or treble damages to 'the party grieved'. They have little faith in 'communal accusation' or in any procedure that expects either royal officials or people in general to be active in bringing malefactors to justice. More was to be hoped from the man who had suffered. He would move if they made it worth his while. And so in a characteristically English fashion punishment was to be inflicted in the course of civil actions: it took the form of manifold reparation, of penal and exemplary damages." Further on the history of the distinction between tort and crime, see Winfield, op. cit., note 2, pp. 8 sqq.; Buckland/MacNair, pp. 344 sqq.

While, generally speaking, the common law of torts (like its civilian counterpart, the law of delict) has moved from punishment to compensation, it has (unlike the civil law) never entirely abandoned the penal element. Some traces of the old link between tort and crime have survived to the present day, in particular the notion of exemplary ("punitive") damages to punish contumelious and outrageous wrongdoing (cf. *Rookes v. Barnard* [1964] AC 1192; Fleming, *Torts*, pp. 1 sq.; Winfield and Jolowicz, pp. 616 sqq.). The old common-law rule that tort claims survive neither the death of the wrongdoer nor that of the victim (also due to the historical connection of trespass with criminal law, usually expressed in the adage "actio personalis moritur cum persona") was abrogated by statute in 1934 (Fleming, *Torts*, pp. 638 sqq.; Winfield and Jolowicz, pp. 657 sqq.).

forms were evolved to cover the most common types of both of them. Thus, a whole variety of specific torts came to be recognized, among them assault, battery and false imprisonment as special forms of trespass to the person, trespass to land and trespass to chattels, libel and slander, nuisance, deceit, conversion and conspiracy. The appropriate actions were in the nature of trespass, if they involved a forcible and direct injury; they constituted a subspecies of case, where the defendant's conduct had either not been forcible or not been direct. Assumpsit, it will be remembered, was a typical example of case,[55] and so were malicious prosecution, slander or deceit. The choice of the appropriate remedy could depend on rather delicate distinctions as the oft-quoted remark by Blackstone demonstrates:

> "[I]f I throw a log of timber into the highway, (which is an unlawful act), and another man tumbles over it, and is hurt, an action on the case only lies, it being a consequential damage; but if in throwing it I hit another man, he may bring trespass, because it is an immediate wrong."[56]

What was the practical relevance of the division between case and trespass and of all the "finespun and cabalistic"[57] learning connected with it? Trespass, as a direct forcible injury, was prima facie wrongful, and thus it was up to the defendant to rebut the presumption by invoking a specific excuse or justification. Moreover, trespass was actionable per se, and thus the plaintiff succeeded without proof of actual damage. Case, on the other hand, covered situations where the plaintiff's act was not so obviously "wrong" and where, therefore, the form of conduct as such and the (eventual) infliction of an injury (in other words: the issue of causation) could hardly be taken to provide a satisfactory basis for an action. Further criteria had to be resorted to: the plaintiff had to have suffered damages and, even more importantly, proof of either wrongful intent or negligence on the part of the defendant was required.

(c) The rise of the tort of "negligence"

Case could thus be brought for inadvertent injuries and it became common, in the course of the 19th century, to refer to actions upon the case for negligence, to actions for negligence or, simply, to actionable negligence. At first, these expressions clearly referred to the old action of trespass on the case, justified, in certain types of situations, by an allegation of negligence. Gradually, however, their meaning began to shift, and "negligence" was no longer merely conceived of as one of the ways of committing one of the established torts, but rather as a separate basis of tort liability in its own right. This shift

> "broadly coincided with the Industrial Revolution and was undoubtedly stimulated by the advent of machinery, urbanization and the faster traffic along turnpike and

[55] Cf. supra, pp. 777 sqq.
[56] *Scott v. Shepherd* (1773) 2 Black W 892 at 894 sq.
[57] Fleming, *Torts*, p. 17.

railway. Untold new sources of risk and losses made their appearance and confronted the law with problems it was unable to solve by recourse to its inherited, archaic tort remedies. At this crucial stage of social and economic reorientation, the courts responded to the call for a new pattern of loss adjustment by fastening on the concept of negligence".[58]

It was the famous case of *Donoghue v. Stevenson*[59] in which the new tort of negligence came to be recognized unequivocally by the House of Lords: "The law", as Lord Atkin put it in his speech,[60]

> ". . . appears to be that in order to support an action for damages for negligence the complainant has to show that he has been injured by the breach of a duty owed to him in the circumstances by the defendant to take reasonable care to avoid such injury."

Negligence—with duty, breach and damage as its three essential requirements—is the closest the English common law has come to a generalized form of tortious liability. Today it "overwhelmingly" occupies the attention both of courts and academic writers and has become "a unifying force of vast potential".[61]

(d) *The ghosts of the past*

It has even been able to transform the basis of the liability for trespass. Trespass, it has been emphasized, was the remedy for forcible and direct injuries—for situations, that is, in which the defendant could typically be taken to have acted with unlawful intent: if one person rams a knife into another, he will not normally be able to claim that he did not intend to inflict an injury. Yet, proof of such intention (or, for that matter: of negligence) was not required. Liability for trespass was thus traditionally strict.[62] As such, it was bound to be regarded as an intolerable atavism by 19th-century legal science. The principle of "no liability without fault", reflecting the needs and aspirations of contemporary individualism, was quickly raised to the status of an axiomatic truth.[63] Fault therefore became an essential ingredient of trespass; but since this happened at the very time when negligence emerged as a separate basis of tort liability, the range of trespass came to be limited, largely, to cases of intentional harm. For a long time it has been maintained, however, that if the plaintiff could show a direct

---

[58] Fleming, *Torts*, pp. 93; cf. also Tunc, op. cit., note 2, nn. 71 sqq.

[59] [1932] AC 562 (HL); on which see R.F.V. Heuston, "Donoghue v. Stevenson in Retrospect", (1957) 12 *Modern LR* 1 sqq.; idem, "*Donoghue v. Stevenson*: A Fresh Appraisal", (1971) 24 *Current Legal Problems* 37 sqq.; J.C. Smith, *Liability in Negligence* (1984), pp. 15 sqq.

[60] [1932] AC 562 (HL) at 579.

[61] Fleming, *Torts*, p. 94. But cf. also Smith, op. cit., note 59, pp. 15 sqq. and passim, who argues that the law of negligence cannot be reduced to a single principle of liability.

[62] Cf., for example, *Leame v. Bray* (1803) 3 East 593 at 600; but see also Percy H. Winfield, "The Myth of Absolute Liability", (1926) 42 *LQR* 37 sqq.; S.F.C. Milsom, "Trespass from Henry III to Edward III, Part III: More Special Writs and Conclusions", (1958) 74 *LQR* 578 sqq.

[63] Cf. Fleming, *Torts*, pp. 18, 93 sqq.; Tunc, op. cit., note 2, nn. 71 sqq.; cf. also infra, pp. 1034 sq., 1129 sq.

injury caused by the act of the defendant, he was able to proceed in trespass rather than negligence—the advantage for him of this cause of action being that the defendant could escape liability only by proving inevitable accident.[64] This was established in *Stanley v. Powell*[65] and meant, in effect, that while liability for trespass to the person had ceased to be strict, there was still a decisive difference in the onus of proof between the two torts of trespass and negligence. Only in 1959 was it held that the burden of proving negligence in actions for unintentional trespass to the person rests upon the plaintiff, just as it does in actions for negligence.[66] Yet, one further distinction appeared at first to persist, and it was brought up in the 1965 case of *Letang v. Cooper*.[67] Here the injured plaintiff[68] had waited for more than three years before finally deciding to sue, and it was obvious that by that time her claim in negligence was statute barred. Could she, under these circumstances, still fall back on an alternative claim in trespass? This depended on the interpretation given to the phrase, "actions for damages for negligence", as used in the Limitation (of Actions) Act. According to Diplock LJ, a cause of action today means no more than a factual situation which entitles one person to obtain a remedy from another in the courts, and an action founded upon a failure to exercise reasonable care must therefore be regarded as an action for negligence, notwithstanding the fact that it can also be called an action for trespass to the person.[69] Lord Denning MR took matters to their logical conclusion when he indicated that he

> "would go this one step further: when the injury is not inflicted intentionally, but negligently, I would say that the only cause of action is negligence and not trespass".[70]

This episode is characteristic of the gradual process of adjustment following the abolition of the forms of action by the Judicature Act in 1873. It took a long time to discard most of the doctrinal vestiges of the now obsolete procedural heritage,[71] but, as Lord Atkin gallantly

---

[64] For what follows, see Winfield and Jolowicz, pp. 116 sqq.

[65] [1891] 1 QB 86 (cf. infra, p. 1006, note 50).

[66] *Fowler v. Lanning* [1959] 1 QB 426. The same view had already been adopted earlier in the so-called highway cases (plaintiff injured by accident on highway): *Holmes v. Mather* (1875) LR 10 Exch 261.

[67] [1965] 1 QB 232.

[68] She had been sunbathing on a lawn outside a hotel when defendant had driven his car over her legs.

[69] [1965] 1 QB 232 at 242 sqq. But see still Elwes J, in *Letang v. Cooper* [1964] 2 QB 53.

[70] [1965] 1 QB 232 at 240.

[71] Fleming, *Torts*, p. 17. Cf. also John W. Salmond, "Observations on Trover and Conversion", (1905) 21 *LQR* 43: "Forms of action are dead, but their ghosts still haunt the precincts of the law. In their life they were powers of evil, and even in death they have not wholly ceased from troubling"; Winfield and Jolowicz, p. 43: "Maitland's famous phrase, 'The forms of action we have buried, but they still rule us from their graves', has been

pronounced, "[w]hen [the] ghosts of the past stand in the path of justice clanking their medieval chains the proper course for the judge is to pass through them undeterred".[72] Thus, it is no longer necessary today to canvass the procedural niceties of trespass and case. "Remedies", in the words of Denning J,[73] "now depend upon the substance of the right, not on whether they can be fitted into a particular framework". But how a common lawyer thinks about the "substance of a right" is still determined, as far as redress for the wrongful inflictional harm is concerned, by the traditional types of tortious liability that once developed in the procedural cast-iron moulds.[74]

5. Roman law and English law

If we now turn our attention to Roman law, we shall see that in certain significant respects it bore a greater resemblance to the English law of torts than to its modern civilian descendant. Delict is one of those areas which Pringsheim could have referred to when he analysed the "inner relationship" between English and Roman law,[75] and it substantiates the claim that there is

> "more affinity between the Roman jurist and the common lawyer than . . . between the Roman jurist and his modern civilian successor".[76]

Like trespass, the Roman notion of delict had a strongly criminal flavour; and even though the compensatory function came increasingly to the fore, in the course of Roman legal history the penal element was never entirely abandoned. As a result, the distinction between crime and delict was much less clear-cut than it is today. More importantly, however, the Roman law of delicts, like the English law of torts, displayed a wholly casuistic character. It was based on a variety of nominate delicts but could, ad hoc, conveniently be expanded by praetorian intervention. This intervention took the form of new formulae, sometimes issued in close analogy to the established ones, in other cases drafted independently. Designed to accommodate, and thus to turn upon, a specific combination of facts, the new remedies may be regarded as the Roman equivalent of the English writs "upon the case".[77] Unlike the modern civilians, but very similar to the English common lawyers, the Roman jurists avoided generalizations and abstract definitions. Proceeding from case to case, they were "more

---

repeated often enough to become a cliché. One does not venture to polish any aphorism of Maitland's, but we shall see that in some respects it may be questioned whether the forms of action have not been buried alive."

[72] *United Australia Ltd. v. Barclays Bank Ltd.* [1941] AC 1 (HL) at 29.

[73] *Nelson v. Larholt* [1948] 1 KB 339 at 343.

[74] Cf. also the remarks by Markesinis, (1977) 93 *LQR* 85 sqq.

[75] Fritz Pringsheim, "The Inner Relationship between English and Roman law", (1935) 5 *Cambridge LJ* 347 sqq.

[76] Buckland/MacNair, p. XIV.

[77] Cf., in particular, the actiones in factum by means of which the lex Aquilia was extended: infra, pp. 977 sqq., 986 sq., 993 sqq.

anxious to establish a good working set of rules . . . than to set up anything like a logical system".[78] Their efforts did not culminate in a streamlined law of *delict* but remained a somewhat haphazard assemblage of individual *delicts*. Yet, the ingenuity with which they penetrated the problems of a vast mass of casuistry and with which they devised suitable rules and criteria paved the way for the modern endeavours to conceptualize, generalize and systematize the law of delictual liability.

6. The origins of delict in Roman law

The law of delict originated in private vengeance.[79] A person who was wronged by another acquired a pledge-like power of seizure over the wrongdoer's body. It gave him the right, at first, to kill the wrongdoer; later, to inflict no more than the same form of harm that he had suffered (lex talionis). In addition, the victim's power of seizure came to be tied to formal, State-controlled legal proceedings (manus iniectio). Then the right of vengeance was made redeemable: the victim of the wrong was encouraged, and later required, to abstain from avenging himself by accepting a composition paid either by the wrongdoer himself or by his relatives. This composition consisted first in cattle (pecus), later in a sum of money (pecunia); in the beginning freely negotiable, the amount to be paid was ultimately fixed by the State. Thus, for each specific wrong "atonement tariffs" came to be established and they were known as "poenae". Early, and prominent, examples are contained in the XII Tables ("Manu fustive si os fregit libero CCC, si servo CL poenam subito" (8, 3); "Si iniuria alteri faxsit, XXV poenae sunto" (8, 4)), but this enactment also still contains rules representing earlier stages in the development of delictual liability ("Si membrum rupsit, ni cum eo pacit, talio esto" (8, 2)).[80] In tab. 8, 3 and 4 the poena consisted in an arbitrary amount that was fixed across the board. Usually, though, and particularly with regard to property-related offences, the estimated value of the particular piece of property concerned was taken as a point of reference, the amount of the poena thus being either the estimated value itself[81] or a multiple thereof:[82] the double, treble, or even quadruple value. Occasionally, the determination of the sum into which the defendant was to be condemned was left to the discretion of the judge; thus, the formula of the actio iniuriarum merely referred to "quantam pecuniam recuperatoribus bonum aequum videbitur".[83] By the time of classical Roman law this system of (private) poenae had become firmly established and they were no longer regarded as a means

---

[78] Buckland/McNair, p. XIV; cf. also Markesinis, (1977) 93 *LQR* 83 sqq.
[79] For what follows see supra, pp. 1 sqq.
[80] On tab. VIII, 2-4, see infra, pp. 1050 sq.
[81] Cf., for example, infra, pp. 961 sq.
[82] Cf., for example, infra, pp. 932 sqq.
[83] Cf. infra, p. 1062.

to avert the victim's revenge, but as a form of penalty that was enforced by way of civil proceedings. The actions available for this purpose were known as actiones poenales. Some were based on the ius civile—among them, most notably, the actio furti in case of theft and the actio legis Aquiliae for damnum iniuria datum. The actio iniuriarum, covering the somewhat enigmatic delict of "iniuria",[84] had a civilian origin too. Other remedies[85] owed their existence to the activities of the praetors and were thus rooted in the ius honorarium. Their formulae were in factum conceptae, which means that the judge was empowered to condemn or absolve on the basis merely of an initial statement of what had in fact happened ("nominato eo quod factum est").[86] These praetorian actions reflected the far-reaching changes on a social, political and economic level that occurred in the course of the later Republic, and they were introduced, as usual, "adiuvandi vel supplendi vel corrigendi iuris civilis gratia":[87] in order to adjust the law to new societal demands and challenges. The actiones quod metus causa and the actio de dolo are usually mentioned in this context; introduced in the first half of the 1st century B.C., they were designed to cope with the increasing violence and lawlessness that foreshadowed the fall of the Republic. Yet they do not appear to have had a penal function but were merely designed to serve the ends of restoration.[88] But the actio vi bonorum raptorum, dealing, essentially, with robbery (rapina)[89] was an example of a praetorian actio poenalis and so were the actio de deiectis vel effusis, the actio de posito vel suspenso,[90] the actio de sepulchro violato and many others.[91]

7. Characteristics of the Roman actiones poenales

(a) *Passive intransmissibility*

All penal remedies, whether in ius or in factum concepta, were subject to three characteristic rules, which still reflected their origin in private vengeance and atonement. First of all, no actio poenalis survived the wrongdoer's death:[92] against his heirs, after all, there had been no right of vengeance, for the victim's erstwhile power of seizure had extended

[84] Infra, pp. 1050 sqq.
[85] Not all of them actiones poenales.
[86] Gai. IV, 46.
[87] Pap. D. 1, 1, 7, 1.
[88] See supra, pp. 654 sqq., 664.
[89] Gai. III, 209 and see the discussion in D. 47, 8; further: Udo Ebert, *Die Geschichte des Edikts de hominibus armatis coactisve* (1968); Marco Balzarini, *Ricerche in tema di danno violento e rapina nel diritto romano* (1969); Letizia Vacca, *Ricerche in tema di 'actio vi bonorum raptorum'* (1972); Kaser, *RPr* I, pp. 626 sqq. The actio vi bonorum raptorum had (at least also) a penal character (cf. infra, p. 920).
[90] Cf. supra, pp. 16 sqq.
[91] For an overview, see Kaser, *RPr* I, pp. 628 sqq.
[92] Cf., for example, Gai. IV, 112 ("certissima iuris regula"); *Inst.* IV, 12, 1; Pasquale Voci, *DER*, vol. I, pp. 51 sqq., 302 sqq.

only to the body of the wrongdoer himself. Actiones poenales were thus, to use the technical term, "passively intransmissible" on death. They were, however, as a rule,[93] not also actively intransmissible. Whilst, therefore, they could still be brought by the victim's (i.e. the creditor's) heir, they never lay against the heir of the wrongdoer (i.e. the debtor). Once, of course, litis contestatio had taken place, the wrongdoer's death was no longer of any consequence ("Sciendum est ex omnibus causis lites contestatas et in heredem . . . transire"),[94] for under the rules of Roman civil procedure a plaintiff was entitled to receive what was due to him tempore litis contestatae.

In the second place, joint perpetrators of the wrong were, in principle, liable cumulatively and the injured party could thus receive the full composition several times over.[95] This sounds odd to us, for it means that the victim turned out, in the end, to be the better off, the more persons had participated in the infliction of the injury. But the explanation is simply that each individual person's act resulted in an obligation to expiate the wrong; and no such expiation could be taken to have occurred in relation to someone who had not paid the full statutory sum in question. No distinction was drawn between mere aiding and abetting on the one hand and joint perpetration of the wrong on the other: any form of participation entitled the victim to sue for the whole amount.

(b) Noxal liability

And thirdly: where the wrongful act had been committed by a person in power (filius- or filiafamilias and slave),[96] the actio poenalis lay as a noxal action against his or her paterfamilias. Liability was thus in the alternative: the paterfamilias could either defend the action and, ultimately, render payment as if he had himself committed the offence, or he could simply surrender the actual offender to the injured person.[97] Surrender tended to be regarded in classical law as a means of avoiding the (primary) obligation to pay the composition;[98] but this was an inversion of the original principle.[99] When, in the olden days, the victim wanted to wreak his vengeance upon a person in power, the paterfamilias' potestas posed a serious obstacle: any attempt to avenge the wrong would normally have interfered with it. Hence the request to surrender the wrongdoer. Later on, the State favoured abstention

---

[93] But see infra, p. 1061.
[94] Call. D. 44, 7, 59.
[95] For details, see Levy, *Konkurrenz*, vol. I, pp. 476 sqq.; Liebs, *Klagenkonkurrenz*, pp. 125 sqq., 181 sqq., 265 sq.; Kaser, *RPr* II, p. 429.
[96] In post-classical times only slaves; see *Inst.* IV, 8.
[97] Gai. IV, 75; *Inst.* IV, 8 pr. The surrender took the form of mancipatio in the case of slaves, alternatively, of in iure cessio. For further details as to the basis and origin of noxal liability, and to the details of its application, see the literature referred to infra, p. 1118, note 177.
[98] Gai. D. 9, 4, 1.
[99] Thomas, *Institutes*, p. 305.

from vengeance and fixed specific penalties. But, of course, an obligation to pay such penalties could be imposed neither on slaves nor on sons or daughters in power. It was their paterfamilias to whom all property belonged and who was thus the only possible addressee for a claim to pay the fine. Yet, since he himself had not committed the wrong, it was regarded as inappropriate to expose him to liability without, at least, retaining for him the option of surrender. "Summa autem ratione permissum est noxae deditione defungi: namque erat iniquum, nequitiam eorum ultra ipsorum corpora dominis damnosam esse":[100] this is how Justinian rationalized the legal position. If the poena was particularly high, the paterfamilias could escape liability by giving up the wrongdoer; if, on the other hand, he had an overriding interest in keeping the latter, he could justly be taken to have attracted the liability to pay the penalty upon himself. Although, therefore, the defendant in a noxal action was always the paterfamilias, it was still the slave who was regarded as the wrongdoer. Liability was thus seen, as the Romans put it, to "follow his (i.e. the slave's) head": noxa caput sequitur.[101] If the slave or child in power was transferred into somebody else's patria potestas, the noxal action followed suit. The person to be proceeded against was thus (oddly, perhaps, in our view) whoever just happened to have the wrongdoer in his power at that particular moment, not his master at the time when the wrong had been committed; hence, for instance, the concern of Roman purchasers, reflected in the provisions of the aedilitian edict, that slaves be free from noxal liability.[102] If the person in power attained his freedom before action was taken, he became liable himself and the (former) master's noxal liability fell away.

8. Private criminal law and public criminal law

A delict was a private wrong and yet the actio poenalis served to penalize the wrongdoer. It is obvious, therefore, that the private actio poenalis discharged what we would consider to be the proper function of a criminal prosecution. On the other hand, however, Roman lawyers also recognized a number of crimes; in fact, the modern distinction between crime and delict goes back to the Roman notions of crimen and delictum. But the boundary between the two was not drawn along the same lines as it is today.[103]

The term "crimen" was used to designate offences prosecuted in the public interest and punishable by a public penalty upon accusation and

[100] *Inst.* IV, 8, 2; cf. also already Gai. IV, 75.

[101] Gai. IV, 77; Ulp. D. 47, 2, 41, 2; *Inst.* IV, 8, 5.

[102] Cf. supra, pp. 314 sq.

[103] Cf., for example, Buckland/McNair, p. 344: "[T]he law of delict [is allied] with that of crime rather than with that of other civil obligations, so much so that Mommsen in his *Strafrecht*, somewhat to the confusion of his readers, hardly distinguishes between delict and crime except in matters of procedure."

subsequent condemnation in a special court and according to a strict and largely State-controlled procedure, differing considerably from the one that governed civil trials.[104] The list of such offences was very small at first; it comprised only a number of acts that were regarded as affecting the community at large particularly severely: treason (perduellio) and certain sacral wrongs, later also murder and crimes involving violence. The lesser forms of criminality were covered by what Kunkel/Kelly refer to as "private criminal law":[105] punishment was to be inflicted in the course of civil actions. Just as in the early English common law,[106] the State thus relied on the initiative of the aggrieved party to get the wheels of justice rolling. In Rome this policy was maintained even when, in the course of the later Republic, and under the early Principate, the number of crimes was increased drastically, the system of criminal tribunals rigorously reformed, and the efficiency of the administration of criminal justice generally improved; for, by that time, the private penal actions were already firmly entrenched and remained in force throughout the entire classical period. Even in the genuinely criminal proceedings, however, the system of privately instituted prosecution was the rule: apart from the aggrieved party,[107] even the quivis ex populo could initiate the trial and thus assume the role of (private) prosecutor. Of course, the average Roman citizen did not usually do so out of a genuine desire to promote the public interest—the criminal statutes tended to promise considerable rewards for victorious prosecutors.

9. The nature of the remedies available

(a) *Actiones poenales and reipersecutoriae*

The availability of actiones poenales was an important and characteristic feature of the Roman law of delict. But the desire of the injured party to obtain redress for the loss that he had suffered was also catered for. "Agimus autem interdum ut rem tantum consequamur, interdum ut poenam tantum, alias ut rem et poenam", as we are informed by Gaius,[108] and Justinian amplifies:

---

[104] For all details, see Theodor Mommsen, *Römisches Strafrecht* (1899); Wolfgang Kunkel, *Untersuchungen zur Entwicklung des römischen Kriminalverfahrens in vorsullanischer Zeit* (1962); A.H.M. Jones, *The Criminal Courts of the Roman Republic and Principate* (1972); cf. also Jolowicz/Nicholas, pp. 305 sqq., 401 sqq.; Liebs, *Klagenkonkurrenz*, pp. 266 sqq.; Artur Völkl, *Die Verfolgung der Körperverletzung im frühen Römischen Recht* (1984), pp. 217 sqq.

[105] *An Introduction to Roman Legal and Constitutional History* (2nd ed., 1973), pp. 29, 64.

[106] Cf. the quotation by Pollock and Maitland, supra, note 54, which is also referred to by Fritz Schulz, *CRL*, p. 573, in this context. Generally on delict and crime in ancient law, see Maine, *Ancient Law*, pp. 216 sqq.

[107] Who could, in certain instances, be compensated for his loss from the (public) penalty.

[108] Gai. IV, 6.

"Sequens illa divisio est, quod quaedam actiones rei persequendae gratia comparatae sunt, quaedam poenae persequendae, quaedam mixtae sunt."[109]

There was thus a threefold subdivision: actions were either purely penal in nature, or purely "reipersecutory", or both penal and reipersecutory at one and the same time. An actio ad poenam tantum persequendam (or simply: an actio poenalis) served merely to penalize the wrongdoer. Actiones ad rem persequendam (literally: actions to recover a (or the) thing) had a completely different function: they aimed exclusively at compensation. "[I]llae autem rei persecutionem continent", as Paulus put it,[110] "quibus persequimur quod ex patrimonio nobis abest." Since, as we know,[111] restitution in kind could never be sued for in classical Roman law, condemnation always led to the award of a specific sum of money. Determination of the sum depended, of course, on the formula of each particular action, but by and large it was designed to cover the plaintiff's (typical) loss. In any event, there was no penal element involved in the assessment. A typical reipersecutory action was, for instance, the rei vindicatio. It could be brought against a thief (as against any other non-owner) who was still in possession of the stolen object and it lay for "quanti ea res erit, tantam pecuniam . . .".

Contractual actions were of a purely reipersecutory nature too.[112] If someone damaged a sedan chair that he had hired, he was liable under the actio locati, and here the iudex was invested with a very wide discretion to assess the lessor's actual damages. ". . . quidquid ob eam rem . . . dare facere oportet et bona fide, eius . . ." read the crucial passage of the formula: it focused exclusively on the injury to the plaintiff, without including—as the English lawyer would put it—a punitive award. Apart from such more general remedies, which could be used in a delictual context, the Roman lawyers sometimes also made purely reipersecutory actions available to deal with a specific wrong: the condictio ex causa furtiva in the case of theft was one of the most prominent examples.[113]

(b) Actiones mixtae

Thirdly, then, there was a group of actions which was taken to serve both a penal and a reipersecutory function at one and the same time: actiones quibus rem et poenam persequimur or, in Justinian's terminology,[114] actiones mixtae. The sum to be awarded was a penalty,

[109] *Inst.* IV, 6, 16.
[110] D. 44, 7, 35 pr.
[111] Cf. supra, pp. 770 sqq.
[112] Emphasized by Gaius IV, 7; *Inst.* IV, 6, 17.
[113] Infra, pp. 941 sqq.
[114] Did the classical lawyers use the term "actio mixta"? Cf. Detlef Liebs, "Gemischte Begriffe im römischen Recht", (1970) 1 *Index* 143 sqq.; but see also Kaser, *RPr* II, p. 343 and

but it was understood also to compensate the plaintiff for his harm. If that sum happened to be a multiple of the value of the object in question, it normally far exceeded the plaintiff's actual loss; and to this excess a compensatory function could, of course, hardly be attributed. Not unnaturally, therefore, the opinion came to prevail[115] that the whole award had to be split into a reipersecutory simplum and the (purely penal) amount by which the award exceeded the simple value. Justinian's exposition of the action for robbery provides a good example: "Vi autem bonorum raptorum actio mixta est, quia in quadruplo rei persecutio continetur, poena autem tripli est."[116] According to the original praetorian provision, the defendant was liable to pay quadruplum,[117] and in classical law there had never been any doubt that one was dealing with *poena* quadrupli (although there had been some doubt as to whether the action was purely penal or also reipersecutory in character).[118] Justinian came down in favour of an actio mixta, but for him this entailed that only the triplum exceeding the simple value could be regarded as a penalty. The action was thus partly (purely) penal and partly (purely) reipersecutory, with the result that only in the penal part (i.e., as far as triplum was concerned) did the remedy retain the typical characteristics of a penal action.[119]

(c) *Concurrence of actions*

The classification of the remedies according to the aim pursued by them was of particular importance when several actions were available on account of one specific delict. "Bis de eadem re agere non licet" was the general procedural rule determining all questions of concurrence:[120] litis contestatio prevented the plaintiff from bringing any other action in the same matter. This meant, in the present context, that the wrongdoer could not be punished twice; likewise, of course, the victim of the wrong was not to receive his compensation more than once. No plaintiff could thus avail himself of two (private) penal actions[121] with regard to one and the same delict; nor could he use two reipersecutory

Hans Ankum, "Gaius, Theophilus and Tribonian and the Actiones Mixtae", in: *Studies in Justinian's Institutes in memory of J.A.C. Thomas* (1983), pp. 4 sqq.

115 According to Hans Ankum, "Actions by which we claim a thing (res) and a penalty (poena) in classical Roman law", (1982) 24 *BIDR* 28 sqq., already in classical law. Traditionally it is held that the splitting up of the award is of post-classical origin; cf., for example, Kaser, *RPr* II, p. 429.

116 *Inst.* IV, 6, 19.

117 Cf. Paul. D. 47, 8, 1.

118 Gai. IV, 8 ("secundum quorundam opinione"); Gai. IV, 112; Ulp. D. 47, 8, 2, 27; Ankum, (1982) 24 *BIDR* 18 sq., 30 sq.

119 Generally on actiones mixtae, see Liebs, *Klagenkonkurrenz*, pp. 53 sqq. and the two articles by Ankum, *Studies Thomas*, pp. 4 sqq. and (1982) 24 *BIDR* 15 sqq.

120 Levy, *Konkurrenz*, vol. I, pp. 76 sqq.; Kaser, *RZ*, pp. 229 sqq.

121 On the concurrence of private penal actions and criminal proceedings cf. Liebs, *Klagenkonkurrenz*, pp. 266 sqq.

remedies. Once he had sued the wrongdoer, all subsequent actions pursuing the same aim were barred. On the other hand, however, no obstacle existed which could have prevented the plaintiff from cumulating a penal and a reipersecutory remedy. The imposition of a penalty and compensation for the harm suffered were not eadem res, and thus the one action did not "consume" the other. It followed logically that actiones mixtae could be cumulated neither with an actio poenalis nor with an actio ad rem tantum persequendam: an actio mixta covered (and thus consumed) both aspects peculiar to the Roman law of delicts and left no room for any other remedy.[122]

10. Plan of treatment

It is in conformity with our initial programme[123] if we confine ourselves to these somewhat sketchy general remarks. Just as the Roman lawyers did not develop a general law of contract, so they were not interested in carving out a set of rules and principles governing delictual liability at large. They had a law of delicts rather than of delict. We, too, should therefore rather look at the specific private wrongs on which they focused their attention. Since, however, we cannot provide a comprehensive survey, we have to confine our attention to the three most important delicts originating in the ius civile: furtum, damnum iniuria datum and iniuria. One of them, damnum iniuria datum, as regulated by the lex Aquilia, was to become the nucleus of the modern generalized law of delict. Historically older, however, were furtum and iniuria; both were already recognized by the time of the XII Tables as two specific types of delict. Following the traditional order of the ius commune,[124] we shall commence our discussion with furtum.

---

[122] For all details, see Levy, *Konkurrenz*, vol. I and II; Liebs, *Klagenkonkurrenz*, passim; cf. also Kaser, *RZ*, pp. 232 sqq.

[123] Supra, p. 32.

[124] "Inter Delicta Privata primo loco ponitur Furtum, quia ejus correctio est antiquissima": Lauterbach, *Collegium theoretico-practicum*, Lib. XLVII, Tit. II, II.

CHAPTER 28

Furtum

I. THE ROMAN CONCEPT OF FURTUM

1. The definition of D. 47, 2, 1, 3

The translation usually given for furtum is theft. Theft is recognized as a criminal offence all over the world, be it on the basis of the common law,[1] be it on a statutory basis[2] or as part and parcel of a comprehensive penal code.[3] But its scope differs considerably from that of its Roman ancestor, the "private delict" furtum. In modern German criminal law, for example, theft is just one of a whole variety of neatly compartmentalized property-related offences.[4] It consists in the taking away of a movable thing belonging to someone else, with the intent of unlawfully appropriating it to one's own use, and it has to be carefully distinguished from embezzlement,[5] fraud[6] and the reception of stolen property.[7]

The traditional civilian concept of furtum was much broader. "Furtum crimen omnium generalissimum", wrote a famous 16th-century treatise writer,[8] and he added: ". . . ubique gentium tam est familiare ut vix ullum . . . reperiatur aut frequentius aut notius."[9] He then proceeded to cite what must have been the most celebrated definition in the entire law of liability for wrongful acts. Taken from

---

[1] As in South Africa; cf. J.R.L. Milton, *South African Criminal Law and Procedure*, vol. II (2nd ed., 1982), pp. 595 sqq.; De Wet en Swanepoel, *Strafreg* (4th ed., 1985), pp. 296 sqq.

[2] As in England; cf. today the Theft Act of 1968. In terms of its s. 1(1) "a person is guilty of theft if he dishonestly appropriates property belonging to another with the intention of permanently depriving the other of it". The traditional English term for theft is larceny (from latrocinium).

[3] As in Germany: § 242 StGB.

[4] Cf. also De Wet en Swanepoel, op. cit., note 1, pp. 302 sqq. For a discussion of theft and all related offences in modern English law, cf. J.C. Smith, *The Law of Theft* (5th ed., 1984); for South Africa, cf. Milton, op. cit., note 1, p. 602.

[5] § 246 StGB ("Anybody who unlawfully appropriates to his own use a movable thing not belonging to him, which is in his possession or custody . . .").

[6] § 263 StGB ("Anybody who, for the purpose of unlawfully enriching himself or a third person, causes pecuniary damage to another by procuring or interposing an error through deception or distortion or suppression of true facts . . .").

[7] § 259 StGB ("Anybody who for gain purchases, or otherwise acquires for himself or for a third party property that has been acquired by means of a punishable act, or who disposes of or participates in the disposal of such property . . .").

[8] Van Damhouder, *Praxis rerum criminalium*, Cap. CX, 1; cf. also Benedict Carpzov, *Practica nova rerum criminalium Imperialis Saxonica* (Lipsiae, 1739), Pars II, Quaest. LXXVII, 1.

[9] Cf. also James Fitzjames Stephen, *A History of the Criminal Law of England*, vol. III (1883), p. 129 (referring to the laws of the early English kings): "Theft . . . seems to have been the crime of crimes."

D. 47, 2, 1, 3, it was repeated by countless generations of lawyers[10] and determined the scope of application of the wrong called "furtum" until well into the 18th century: "Furtum est contractatio rei fraudulosa[11] lucri faciendi gratia vel ipsius rei vel etiam usus eius possessionisve"—theft is the dishonest handling of a thing in order to make gain either out of the thing itself or else out of the use or possession thereof. This definition is attributed to the late classical jurist Paulus; and though it may ultimately have been put together only by post-classical compilers,[12] there is no reason to suspect that it did not correctly reflect the range of theftuous conduct at around the turn of the 2nd to the 3rd century A.D. Of course, it embraced every form of asportation that would be covered by the modern German notion of theft. It did, however, go beyond the latter in at least four important respects.

2. D. 47, 2, 1, 3 and the modern German concept compared

First of all, mere furtum usus constituted theft. Thus, for instance, the depositary was liable if he decided to use the thing deposited with him,[13] and so was a borrower who took the lender's horse further than he was meant to take it.[14] Likewise, a fuller or tailor who received clothes for cleaning or repair: ". . . si forte his utatur, ex contrectatione eorum furtum fecisse videtur, quia non in eam causam ab eo videntur accepta."[15] Secondly, the Roman notion of theft covered furtum possessionis. The main example was that discussed by Gaius: "Aliquando etiam suae rei quisque furtum committit, veluti si debitor rem quam creditori pignori dedit subtraxerit"[16]—if someone has pledged a piece of property to his creditor, and subsequently taken it away from him, he has committed theft; for although the object that he

[10] Also in England. Cf. the version given by Bracton, *De Legibus et Consuetudinibus Angliae* f. 150 b ("[Fu]rtum est secundum leges contrectatio rei alienae fraudulenta cum animo furandi, invito illo cuius res illa fuerit"; on. p. 425 in the edition by S.E. Thorne, vol. II (1968)) containing the essential elements of D. 47, 2, 1, 3. For a discussion of Bracton's definition, cf. Stephen, op. cit., note 9, pp. 130 sqq.; cf. also Holdsworth, vol. III, pp. 360 sqq.

[11] The significance of this element is illustrated by Lauterbach, *Collegium theoretico-practicum*, Lib. XLVII, Tit. II, XXIX with the following nice example: "Hinc Israëlitae e captivitate egressi furtum non commiserunt, quia res Aegyptiis, supremo rerum Domino authore, subtraxerunt." It appears to have been much discussed; cf. also Carpzov, op. cit., note 8, Pars II, Quaest. LXXVII, 2, who argues that "qui rem mandato et auctorate Dei tanquam supremi justissimique judicis accipit, fur dici vix poterit".

[12] The text is regarded as interpolated by, among others, H.F. Jolowicz, *Digest XLVII, 2 De Furtis* (1940), pp. 1 sq.; Schulz, *CRL*, pp. 580 sq.; Alan Watson, "The Definition of furtum and the Trichotomy", (1960) 28 *TR* 197 sqq.; Kaser, *RPr* I, p. 615. Contra: J.A.C. Thomas, "Animus furandi", (1968) 19 *Iura* 31 sq.

[13] Gai. III, 196.

[14] Gai. III, 196; Paul. D. 47, 2, 40; cf. also Honsell/Mayer-Maly/Selb, p. 301, n. 13; as to the historical development, see Wieacker, *RR*, p. 578.

[15] Paul. D. 47, 2, 83 pr.

[16] Gai. III, 200.

took belonged to him,[17] he has still deprived the pledgee/creditor of its possession. In the third place, theft comprised what we have just referred to as embezzlement. "Eum creditorem, qui post solutam pecuniam pignus non reddat, teneri furti Mela ait, si celandi animo retineat", writes Ulpianus and approves "quod verum esse arbitror."[18] The pledgee/creditor who holds on to the pledge after the debt has already been paid, merely keeps what is in his possession anyway. Yet, provided he has acted with a view to concealing the object in question from the debtor, the latter is able to institute the actio furti.[19] Finally, certain instances of fraud were taken to constitute furtum. Thus, for example, a false creditor ("hoc est is, qui se simulat creditorem")[20] was regarded as a thief if he accepted payment tendered by the debtor—"furtum fit", in the more generalizing words of Scaevola, "cum quis indebitos nummos sciens acceperit".[21] All these cases fit Paul's definition: there was a physical contact between thief and stolen property that could be described as contrectatio,[22] and the thief acted with the intention of making an unlawful gain.

3. D. 47, 2, 1, 3 and the Roman case law

(a) *Of mule drivers, peacocks, weights and spread-out togas*

Yet, the Digest also reports a number of decisions that appear to

[17] In which case the rule "rei . . . nostrae furtum facere non possumus" normally applied (Paul. Sent. II, XXXI, 21). A res nullius could not be stolen either; cf., for example, Sab./Cass./Ulp. D. 47, 2, 43, 5 and Raphael Powell, "Furtum by a Finder", (1958–59) 33 *Tulane LR* 509 sqq. (containing also a comparison with English law). A fugitive slave was considered as having stolen himself: cf. Afr. D. 47, 2, 61; C. 6, 1, 1; C. 6, 2, 10 (both Diocl.) and Fritz Pringsheim, "Servus fugitivus sui furtum facit", in: *Festschrift für Fritz Schulz*, vol. I (1951), pp. 279 sqq.

[18] D. 47, 2, 52, 7.

[19] The same must have applied if somebody refused to restore a deposit. On the other hand, however, mere denial of the receipt of a deposit did not as such constitute theft: cf. Paul. D. 47, 2, 1, 2; Cels. D. 47, 2, 68 pr. ("Infitiando depositum nemo facit furtum"); this is in line with the principle of "sola cogitatio furti faciendi non facit furem" (Paul. D. 47, 2, 1, 1); for an analysis of the subtle differences, cf. J.A.C. Thomas, "Infitiando depositum nemo facit furtum", in: *Studi in onore de Edoardo Volterra*, vol. II (1971), 759 sqq.

[20] Ulp. D. 47, 2, 43 pr.

[21] D. 13, 1, 18. On furtum and false pretences generally, see Jolowicz, op. cit., note 12, pp. XXV sqq. More specifically on the position of a falsus procurator, see Dieter Medicus, "Zur Leistungsannahme durch den 'falsus procurator' ", in: *Synteleia Vincenzo Arangio-Ruiz*, vol. I (1964), pp. 214 sqq.; J.A.C. Thomas, "A Note on 'falsus procurator' ", in: *Studi in honore di Giuseppe Grosso*, vol. II (1968), pp. 409 sqq.

[22] This was, of course, a fifth essential difference between the modern and the Roman concept of theft. Whatever may have been the exact meaning of "contrectatio" (the term is usually translated as "handling", "touching", or "some sort of physical meddling"; cf., however, also David Pugsley, "Contrectatio", (1980) 15 *The Irish Jurist* 341: "Contrectatio is a nasty word. . . . It means touching, handling, fondling, pawing, interfering with"; according to MacCormack, 1977 *Acta Juridica* 146 sq., these derogatory overtones made the term suitable for use "in a legal context where the idea to be conveyed is not just 'touching' but 'illicit touching' "), it did in any event not require the actual asportation of the object (nor its "apprehension", which § 242 StGB is generally understood to require, in a somewhat free interpretation of the term "*Wegnahme*" = "carrying away"). Thus, for example, the defacing of documents could constitute theft in Roman law: cf. Paul./Ulp./Iul. D. 9, 2, 40–42; Ulp./Paul. D. 47, 2, 27–32 and J.A.C. Thomas, "Furtum of Documents", (1968) 15 *RIDA* 429 sqq.; idem, "Furtum of documents II", (1969) 20 *Iura* 301 sqq.

overstep these boundaries (liberal though they were) and to assume a conception of theft so wide as to include almost any species of dishonesty.[23] The "veteres", according to Paul, held a person responsible for theft who caused the loss of someone else's mules by fraudulently summoning him to court (so that, one has to gather, he was forced to leave the animals unguarded).[24] The text ("Eum, qui mulionem dolo malo in ius vocasset, si interea mulae perissent, furti teneri veteres responderunt") mentions neither whether the mules were in fact stolen[25] nor whether the "thief" intended them to be stolen; also, it does not disclose whether the summons was issued lucri faciendi gratia nor does it appear to be relevant whether or not the physical element of contrectatio was present.[26] The veteres also seem to have been prepared to grant the actio furti against a person who chased, and thus caused the loss of, somebody else's tame peacock.[27] Again, the mere fact that the owner was deprived of his peacock by an act of the defendant (which can hardly have involved a particularly manifest element of "handling") seems to have been a sufficient cause of action. In the opinion of Mela (cited by Ulpian), a vendor could bring the actio furti against the person from whom the purchaser had borrowed weights which were heavier than they were meant to be ("Maiora quis pondera tibi commodavit, cum emeres ad pondus: furti eum venditori teneri Mela scribit");[28] whether the purchaser knew of the manipulation and could therefore be taken to have acted in concert with the borrower did not matter. Sabinus was prepared to grant the actio furti against a man who spread out his toga in order to conceal a servus fugitivus from his master's eyes.[29] At a push, one may construe this as a contrectatio, but there is certainly no reference to an intention to steal on the part of the toga wearer.

(b) The nature of Roman definitions

Several strategies have been developed to deal with the apparent discrepancy between these texts and Paul's definition. Occasionally, for example, it has been suggested that one or the other of these rather

[23] Jolowicz, op. cit., note 12, p. XX.
[24] Paul. D. 47, 2, 67, 2.
[25] W.W. Buckland, "Contrectatio", (1941) 57 *LQR* 470, and many others, assume that the animals strayed.
[26] Cf. Paul Huvelin, *Études sur le furtum dans le très ancien droit romain* (1915), pp. 380 sq.; Bernardo Albanese, "La nozione del furtum fino a Nerazio", (1953) 23 *Annali Palermo* 44 sq.
[27] Cf. D. 47, 2, 37. The original version of the decision is reflected in the words "Si pavonem meum mansuetum, cum de domo mea effugisset, persecutus sis, quoad is perit, agere tecum furti potero". Pomponius qualified it by adding ". . . ita potero, si aliquis eum habere coeperit". Cf. Huvelin, op. cit., note 26, p. 619; Albanese, (1953) 23 *Annali Palermo* 51 sq.; J.A.C. Thomas, "Contrectatio, complicity and furtum", (1962) 13 *Iura* 82 sqq.
[28] Ulp. D. 47, 2, 52, 22.
[29] Aulus Gellius, *Noctes Atticae*, Lib. XI, XVIII, 14.

extravagant decisions must be spurious.[30] More often, however, it is Paul's definition that has attracted criticism: both the animus lucri faciendi (or animus furandi)[31] and the requirement of contrectatio[32] have been held to have been incorporated by the compilers. Then there are those who have attempted to bring about a reconciliation by interpreting these two requirements loosely enough to cover even the apparent exceptions. Thus, lucrum has been interpreted as not necessarily connoting gain in any economic sense,[33] and the element of contrectatio has been held to have been satisfied even where there was no direct physical contact (as, for instance, in the case of the peacock).[34] Others, again, have read into the texts what they intended to get out of them. Jolowicz, among others, interpreted the word "perire" in the case of the peacock as " 'get lost' with the implication of theft",[35] Buckland believed the "veteres" in the case of the mule driver to have decided

> "that if I meddle with the thing [sc.: the mule] willfully so as to deprive you of an economic interest in the thing, that is a contrectatio fraudulosa",[36]

and Watson presumes that both the person who summoned the mule driver to court and he who chased the peacock were held liable as accomplices: since it was their deliberate wrongdoing that permitted the theft to occur, the main offender's animus furandi is imputed to them and his contrectatio makes them liable.[37] More plausible, however, is yet another explanation. Roman definitions cannot, as a rule, be taken as a definitive statement of all the necessary and sufficient conditions for specific legal consequences to arise; they are often more in the nature of "a useful guideline or a convenient summary of the main characteristics" of a particular concept.[38] Thus not even Paul, who (probably) devised at least the substance of the definition of

---

[30] Cf., for example, Schulz, *CRL*, p. 572 (referring to Mela/Ulp. D. 47, 2, 52, 22).

[31] Paul Huvelin, "L'animus lucri faciendi dans la théorie romaine du vol", (1918) 42 *NRH* 73 sqq.; Emilio Albertario, "Animus furandi", in: *Studi di diritto romano*, vol. III (1936), pp. 211 sqq. But see Jolowicz, op. cit., note 12, pp. LV sqq.; Thomas, (1968) 19 *Iura* 1 sqq.; David Pugsley, "Animus furandi", in: *Scritti in onore di Antonio Guarino*, vol. V (1984), pp. 2419 sqq.

[32] Cf., for example, David Pugsley (1980) 15 *The Irish Jurist* 341 sqq. But see Alan Watson, "Contrectatio as an Essential of Furtum", (1961) 77 *LQR* 526 sqq.; J.A.C. Thomas (1962) 13 *Iura* 70 sqq.; Geoffrey MacCormack, "Definitions: Furtum and Contrectatio", 1977 *Acta Juridica* 129 sqq.

[33] Thomas, (1968) 19 *Iura* 28 sqq.; idem, *TRL*, p. 353; J.P. verLoren van Themaat, *Diefstal en, in verband daarmee, bedrog in die Romeins-Hollandse Reg* (1949), pp. 23 sqq., 125 sqq.

[34] Thomas, (1962) 13 *Iura* 85; idem, *TRL*, p. 354 (Contrectatio "is best conceived as some positive physical interference with, not necessarily entailing actual touching of, the thing stolen").

[35] Op. cit., note 12, p. 48.

[36] (1941) 57 *LQR* 470 sq.

[37] (1961) 77 *LQR* 526 sqq. and "Contrectatio again", (1962) 28 *SDHI* 331 sqq. Contra: Thomas, (1962) 13 *Iura* 70 sqq. (pointing out that this would mean that one person can be liable as an accomplice, even though he was not working in concert with the actual thief). As far as the case involving the toga is concerned, cf. also Jolowicz, op. cit., note 12, p. XXIV.

[38] MacCormack, 1977 *Acta Juridica* 129 sqq. (quotation from p. 130).

furtum, can be taken to have had in mind a dogmatic strait-jacket fitting every type of theft. Much less can one expect the earlier jurists of classical Roman law to have adhered to it particularly strictly. The individual elements of which the definition was composed were fairly broad and lent themselves to differing interpretations;[39] we may therefore assume that many borderline cases were controversial, and quite possibly the proper scope of furtum was at one time even the subject of a school dispute between Proculians and Sabinians.[40]

(c) *Furtum in ancient law*

Most importantly, however, one must not forget that Roman law was never static. Between the enactment of the XII Tables and the end of the classical period of Roman jurisprudence lies a period of some 750 years, and it would be highly anomalous if the notion of furtum should not have undergone considerable changes in the course of it. Many details of the development are shrouded in speculation but its broad outlines are reasonably clearly discernible.[41] When with the codification of the XII Tables furtum emerged into the dawning of early legal history, it was already a specific type of civil wrong; and though we do not as yet find any definition, we may safely assume that it was rather narrowly confined to cases involving the asportation of a movable object that was in someone else's possession or detention.[42] That this must have constituted the original core notion of furtum is revealed particularly clearly by its etymology; for "fur" and "furtum" are derivatives of "ferre" (to take, to carry away).[43] It is implicit, too, in Gaius' statement of what constituted theft in his own time, that is, around the middle of the 2nd century A.D. "Furtum autem fit non solum cum quid intercipiendi causa rem alienam amovet", he states at

[39] Thus, for instance, the terms "dolus malus", "animus furandi", "animus celandi", "animus lucri faciendi" and others are used to denote the mental element of furtum. On the factual element of contrectatio, see MacCormack, 1977 *Acta Juridica* 144: ". . . [an] extraordinarily wide range of meaning . . . attaches to contrectatio. It is never defined in the texts and an attempt to express its essence produces some such statement as: contrectatio denotes a physical connection or contact between the property stolen and the thief. The point is both that the range of circumstances which might be held to constitute a physical connection is infinite, and that the opportunity for disagreement is immense." De Wet en Swanepoel, op. cit., note 1, pp. 301, 311 regard contrectatio as a term without any specific meaning. On contrectatio, cf. further (apart from the literature already referred to) VerLoren van Themaat, op. cit., note 33, pp. 8 sqq. and Carel Rainier Snyman, *Die animus lucri faciendi en die toe-eieningsbegrip by diefstal: 'n regsvergelykende studie*, (unpublished LLD thesis, Bloemfontein, 1972), pp. 14 sqq.; on lucri faciendi gratia, see Snyman, pp. 33 sqq.

[40] Peter Stein, "School Attitudes in the Law of Delicts", in: *Studi in onore di Arnaldo Biscardi*, vol. II (1982), pp. 281 sqq.

[41] Cf., for example, Albanese, (1953) 23 *Annali Palermo* 43 sqq.; Jolowicz, op. cit., note 12, pp. XX sqq.; Thomas, (1962) 13 *Iura* 86 sqq.; Kaser, *RPr* I, pp. 614 sq.

[42] Contra: Peter Birks, (1973) 8 *The Irish Jurist* 349 sqq.

[43] Cf. Paul. D. 47, 2, 1 pr. (also drawing attention to the equivalent Greek expressions). For details, see Hubert Niederländer, "Die Entwicklung des furtum und seine etymologischen Ableitungen", (1950) 67 *ZSS* 253 sqq.

the outset,[44] thereby suggesting that it was at some time thus confined.

(d) Developments in Republican and classical Roman law

In the course of the Republic, the notion of furtum came to be extended considerably. Furtum and damnum iniuria datum were, after all, the two principal offences against property, and the scope of damnum iniuria datum was fairly rigidly determined by the provisions of the lex Aquilia.[45] Thus it was to the as yet undefined notion of furtum that one tended to turn when a property-related offence occurred that deserved to be punished, without however, strictly speaking, fitting the requirements of either of these delicts. By the end of the Republic furtum had attained an indeterminate and almost boundless scope. It had been made to cover almost any situation in which a person, through someone else's deliberate act, suffered patrimonial loss other than by physical damage to the object in question.[46] All the rather extraordinary cases discussed above: the peacock and the toga cases, as well as the ones concerning the mule driver and the false weights are characteristic of this period; neither was a particular type of "handling" required, nor need the offender have acted for the purpose of gain. In the meantime, however, the praetors had explored and opened up other avenues of granting protection against wrongful harm. The range of application of the lex Aquilia was considerably extended by means of actiones in factum,[47] the actio de dolo,[48] the actio servi corrupti and a variety of other remedies[49] had been introduced, and the criminal justice system, too, had been improved appreciably. As a result of these developments a tendency to reappraise, retrench and reformulate[50] the notion of furtum gained ground: for since the actio furti no longer served a kind of catch-all function, the need arose to reintroduce precision and coherence by carving out characteristic features distinguishing the old from the more recent remedies. Here, as elsewhere, the great "Proculian" Labeo appears to have been the harbinger of the new approach. Distancing himself from the "cruel and severe"[51] judgments given by the veteres, he no longer regarded the intention, on

[44] Gai. III, 195.

[45] Cf. infra, pp. 975 sqq. On the borderline between furtum and the lex Aquilia were cases involving the defacing of documents. Cf., for example, Ulp. D. 9, 2, 41, 1 ("Interdum evenire Pomponius eleganter ait, ut quis tabulas delendo furti non teneatur, sed tantum damni iniuriae, ut puta si non animo furti faciendi, sed tantum damni dandi delevit: nam furti non tenebitur; cum facto enim etiam animum furis furtum exigit") and Ulp. D. 47, 2, 27, 3 ("Sed si quis non amovit huiusmodi instrumenta, sed interleverit, non tantum furti actio locum habet, verum etiam legis Aquiliae: nam rupisse videtur qui corrupit"). Cf. further supra, note 22 and, in particular, Thomas, (1968) 15 *RIDA* 440 sqq.

[46] Thomas, (1962) 13 *Iura* 87.

[47] Infra, pp. 977 sqq., 986 sq., 993 sqq.

[48] Supra, pp. 664 sqq.

[49] For an overview, see Kaser, *RPr* I, pp. 625 sqq.

[50] Thomas, (1962) 13 *Iura* 87 sq.

[51] Cf. Aulus Gellius, *Noctes Atticae*, Lib. VI, XV, 1.

the part of the thief, to deprive another of his property as sufficient to constitute theft, but rather emphasized appropriation of the stolen property as a distinctive element of theft.[52] He also drew attention to the (spurious) etymology of furtum suggested by Varro: "Furtum a furvo, id est nigro dictum Labeo ait", as Paul reports—a derivation insinuating an act done "clam et obscuro . . . et plerumque nocte".[53] Sabinus, the head of the opposing school, was prepared to follow the veteres as far as the subjective side of theft was concerned. Deriving the word "furtum" from "fraus" (fraud),[54] he inclined towards a wider basic concept of theft than Labeo.[55] He even suggested that immovable property might be stolen.[56] On the other hand, however, he introduced the notion of adtrectatio into the discussion[57] as a convenient means of covering cases where a person unlawfully kept what was already in his possession,[58] as well as situations where he committed furtum through an act of asportation.[59] If Labeo thus stressed, and refined, the subjective side of theft, Sabinus called attention to a factual feature, characteristic, at least, of a variety of paradigm cases. Both aspects ultimately came to be combined, and thus we find contrectatio[60] and animus lucri faciendi emerging, in Paul's definition, as the two distinctive elements normally to be found in cases of theft.[61] The

[52] Stein, *Studi Biscardi*, vol. II, pp. 283 sqq.

[53] Paul. D. 47, 2, 1 pr. For a detailed discussion, see Niederländer, (1950) 67 *ZSS* 186 sqq. The English adjective "furtive" retains the meaning suggested by Labeo.

[54] Paul. D. 47, 2, 1 pr.; for a discussion, see Niederländer, (1950) 67 *ZSS* 239 sqq.

[55] Cf. Stein, *Studi Biscardi*, vol. II, pp. 286 sq.

[56] Cf. Aulus Gellius, *Noctes Atticae*, Lib. XI, XVIII, 13; Kaser, *RPr* I, p. 157.

[57] Cf. the definition of theft provided by Aulus Gellius, *Noctes Atticae*, Lib. XI, XVIII, 20 ("Verba sunt Sabini . . .: Qui alienam rem adtrectavit, cum id se invito domino facere iudicare deberet, furti tenetur").

[58] And where the use of the older terms such as "amovere", "subripere" or "tollere" would therefore have been inappropriate and misleading.

[59] The development is analysed in detail by MacCormack, 1977 *Acta Juridica* 131 sqq.

[60] The definition of theft in terms of "contrectatio" gave rise to the following problem that was much discussed among the Roman lawyers ("Volgaris est quaestio": Ulp. (not Paul.) D. 47, 2, 21 pr.): if only a part of a heap or collection is taken, does that entail theft of the whole? The question was of great practical importance, since under the actio furti the thief was liable for twofold or fourfold the value of the object stolen. As long as actual asportation was the key element of theft, the answer cannot have been uncertain, but in later Republican and classical law it was arguable that the removal of part constituted contrectatio of the whole. Digest 47, 2, 21 preserves a "rather garbled discussion . . . of a medley of cases" relating to heaps of corn, barrels of wine and beams too heavy for removal by one person (MacCormack, 1977 *Acta Juridica* 134). It is impossible to reconstruct the position in classical law with any degree of certainty. The writers of the ius commune tended to be as perplexed (cf. Antonius Matthaeus, *De Criminibus* (Amstelodami, 1661), Lib. XLVII, Dig. Tit. I, Cap. I, 3: "De qua quaestione Ulpianus and Paulus . . . ita perplexe disserunt, ut exclamare cum Poëta possis: Quo teneam vultus mutantem Protea modo?") as some modern authors (cf. Pugsley, (1980) 15 *The Irish Jurist* 350 sq.: "absurd", "ridiculous"). For a discussion, see Albanese, (1953) 23 *Annali Palermo* 139 sqq.; Jolowicz, op. cit., note 12, pp. 29 sqq.; J.A.C. Thomas, "Digest 47. 2. 21", in: *Synteleia Vincenzo Arangio-Ruiz*, vol. II (1964), pp. 607 sqq.; MacCormack, 1977 *Acta Juridica* 134 sqq.

[61] Neither contrectatio alone (without the appropriate mental attitude) nor the mere theftuous intent (unaccompanied by a physical element) constituted theft. For the first

borderline between the actio furti and the actio de dolo always remained somewhat blurred, though: on the one hand there were, of course, certain core situations for which the actio de dolo was clearly the proper remedy; yet, on the other hand, it was granted only "si alia actio non sit".[62] Whenever the fraud therefore led to a situation that was characterized by contrectatio as well as by an intention to make a profit, the actio furti continued to be granted.[63]

4. Complicity in theft

As a consequence of this retrenchment of the notion of furtum a further, very important distinction came to be drawn which, in turn, prevented the range of liability from being confined too narrowly. "Interdum furti tenetur", explains Gaius,[64]

> "qui ipse furtum non fecerit, qualis est cuius ope consilio furtum factum est. in quo numero est qui nummos tibi excussit ut eos alius subriperet . . . aut oves aut boves tuas fugavit ut alius eas exciperet."

This is the locus classicus on complicity in theft: a person may be liable under the actio furti, even though he has not himself perpetrated the delict, but merely either rendered physical assistance ("ops") or mentally participated in the theft by way of instigation or advice ("consilium").[65] Gaius provides two stock examples to illustrate this proposition: A knocks some coins out of B's hand so that C can run away with them; D stampedes E's sheep or cattle to enable F to catch them. There is no question that C and F can be charged with theft. But A and D are also liable, even though they did not "handle" (in the sense of contrectare) any of the coins or cattle. This distinction between main perpetrator and accomplice had, of course, been entirely unnecessary at a time when the notion of furtum was so vague and imprecise as to cover almost every form of dishonesty. There is in fact evidence that the veteres went so far as to hold A liable for theft, quite irrespective of the eventual fate of the coins: neither did they require him to have acted in concert with C nor did they regard it as necessary that there was such a third party as C who benefited from A's act; the coins could merely have rolled into the sea or into a sewer.[66] Likewise, the man who waved the red banner in order to stampede somebody else's cattle: as long as he intended the cattle to stampede, it did not matter whether they were taken by a third party, fell over a cliff and died or merely ran away and

---

proposition, see Paul. D. 47, 2, 22 pr. ("Si quid fur fregerit aut ruperit, quod non etiam furandi causa contrectaverit, eius nomine cum eo furti agere non potest"), for the second, Paul. D. 47, 2, 1, 1 ("Sola cogitatio furti faciendi non facit furem").

[62] Supra, p. 664.

[63] Supra, pp. 923 sq.

[64] Gai. III, 202.

[65] On the distinction between ops and consilium, cf. Ulp. D. 47, 2, 50, 3.

[66] Ulp. D. 9, 2, 27, 21, as interpreted by Geoffrey MacCormack, "Ope consilio furtum factum", (1983) 51 *TR* 271 sqq., 275 sq.; and cf. Albanese, (1953) 23 *Annali Palermo* 162 sqq.

disappeared.[67] With the recognition of contrectatio as a characteristic element of theft neither the striker nor the banner waver could, however, any longer be regarded as thieves. Where their actions had resulted in the loss of the coins or in the death or disappearance of the cattle, Aquilian protection had become available;[68] where, on the other hand, they had participated in somebody else's theft they were held liable as accomplices.[69] The requirement of contrectatio thus provided both the substantive cause and the touchstone[70] for the distinction between principal offender and accomplice. Dogmatically, it was based on an ingenious reinterpretation of the clause "ope consilio Numerii Negidii furtum factum" contained, from of old, in the formula of the actio furti non manifesti.[71] Originally it was taken as a compendious phrase embracing the physical and mental requirements of theft: it had to be committed "by act *and* design" of Numeriis Negidius.[72] It may have been Labeo who for the first time advocated a disjunctive interpretation and understood the words "ope consilio" in the sense of "by (Numerius Negidius') help *or* advice".[73] This interpretation must rapidly have established itself as authoritative, for we find it in a variety of texts dating from either the end of the 1st or the beginning of the 2nd century A.D.[74] "[S]icut nemo furtum facit sine dolo malo, ita nec consilium vel opem ferre sine dolo malo posse", remarks Pedius,[75] thus clearly distinguishing between the person who commits the theft (furtum facere) and those who merely assist, whether it be consilio or ope. It is likely that even the formula was slightly changed[76] to accommodate the new, and differentiated, way of looking at liability for theft: "Si paret Aulo Agerio a Numerio Negidio opeve consilio Numerii Negidii furtum factum esse paterae aurae . . .";[77] for if ope consilio entailed liability (merely) for complicity in theft, a special clause had to be inserted to cover liability for theft proper.

---

[67] Cf. Ulp. D. 47, 2, 50, 4; Gai. III, 202; Albanese, (1953) 23 *Annali Palermo* 54 sq.; MacCormack, (1983) 51 *TR* 274 sqq.

[68] Cf. infra, pp. 976 sq., 986 sq.

[69] For another interesting case of complicity, see Ulp. D. 47, 2, 52, 21: A wants to invest money by lending it to a person of good credit. He asks B for advice, who recommends C. C is indeed a man of substance. When it comes to handing over the money, however, B presents someone else (a penniless D, rather than the respectable C) under the name of C. B and D subsequently share the money. D has committed theft, B is liable "quasi ope . . . consilioque furtum factum sit". In this case, too, the veteres would not have hesitated to regard both B and D as actual thieves: cf. Paul. (ad Plautium) D. 47, 2, 67, 4.

[70] MacCormack, (1983) 51 *TR* 283.

[71] Huvelin, op. cit., note 26, pp. 385 sqq.; Jolowicz, op. cit., note 12, pp. LXV sqq.; Albanese, (1951) 23 *Annali Palermo* 164 sqq.

[72] Cf., for example, Stein, *Studi Biscardi*, vol. II, p. 285.

[73] The crucial text is Lab./Paul. D. 50, 16, 53, 2, on which see, most recently, Stein, *Studi Biscardi*, vol. II, pp. 285 sq., but also MacCormack, (1983) 51 *TR* 276 sqq.

[74] Iav. D. 47, 2, 91, 1; Pedius/Paul. D. 25, 2, 21, 1; Pedius/Ulp. D. 47, 2, 50, 2; Cels./Ulp. D. 47, 2, 50, 1; analysed, most recently, by MacCormack, (1983) 51 *TR* 282 sqq.

[75] Ulp. D. 47, 2, 50, 2.

[76] MacCormack, (1983) 51 *TR* 293.

[77] Cf. Gai. IV, 37; Lenel, *EP*, p. 328; Kaser, *RPr* I, p. 616.

II. THE ACTIONS ARISING FROM THEFT

1. Actio furti nec manifesti

(a) *"Quanti es res fuit, duplum"*

What we have just quoted was the intentio of the formula of the actio furti nec manifesti: if it appears that a golden cup has been stolen from the plaintiff by the defendant or with the aid or through the incitement of the defendant. . . . Depending on whether or not the matter did in fact so appear, the judge was instructed either to absolve the defendant or to condemn him to the plaintiff into "quanti ea res fuit, cum furtum factum est, tantae pecuniae duplum". The thief was liable for double, and what had to be doubled was, generally speaking, not the plaintiff's interest in the object not being stolen (his "damages", as we would put it), but the value of the stolen object at the time of the commission of the delict.[78] If, however, its value subsequently increased, assessment of the sum of condemnation had to be based on that higher value: the reason being that the object in question could be considered as stolen, not only at the moment of the first contrectatio, but at the time of the rise in value too (". . . quia et tunc furtum eius factum esse verius est").[79] Theft, in other words, was construed as an ongoing wrong ("*Dauerdelikt*").

Assessment of "quanti ea res fuit, duplum" could cause problems where a document that had been drawn up to evidence a claim or payment was stolen. Should one base the claim merely on the value of the material of which the document consisted and thus consider the matter merely in terms of the disappearance of a tablet or a piece of paper? This would, in many cases, hardly have been satisfactory: after all, the document was designed to represent the sum that had been specified therein. Very widely, therefore, the full value of the sum in question came to be accepted as the measure of the value of the document removed: "Qui tabulas cautionesve subripuit, in adscriptam summam furti actione tenebitur."[80] But this approach led to a logical dilemma. For if it was possible to prove adscripta summa to the judge in the theft proceedings, the loss of the document had not really deprived the plaintiff of anything more than a tablet or a piece of paper: he would still be able to pursue his claim against the defendant, even without the use of the document. If, on the other hand, the document was of essential importance for establishing that claim, the plaintiff was not really able to prove adscripta summa (and that is: the sum specified in the document on which assessment of the poena furti was to be

[78] Ulp. D. 47, 2, 50 pr.: "In furti actione non quod interest . . . duplabitur, sed rei verum pretium"; cf. also Ulp. D. 50, 16, 193.
[79] Ulp. D. 47, 2, 50 pr.
[80] Paul. D. 47, 2, 83, 3; cf. also D. 47, 2, 27 pr. sqq.

based) in the theft proceedings either.[81] How the Roman lawyers ultimately resolved this difficulty is not entirely clear.[82] Generally speaking, they appear to have been concerned with evaluating the plaintiff's interest in the document ("quanti ea res fuit" in the sense of "what the matter was worth for him"),[83] which in turn depended on its real probative value. Post-classical jurisprudence seems to have reverted to the choice of simply doubling the adscripta summa (wherever it could be established).[84] Although in these and certain other cases[85] the notion of interesse was brought into the discussion, the actio furti (nec manifesti) always remained a purely penal remedy:[86] the duplum was not designed to compensate the victim for his loss; it served merely to penalize the thief. Condemnation entailed infamia.[87] The person to be sued, as is apparent from the formula, could either be the thief himself or an accomplice.

(b) The right to sue: ex iure dominii and custodia liability

But who could bring the actio furti? Very often, of course, this question was not difficult to answer either: if A steals clothes belonging to B, the right of action must obviously vest in B: "iure dominii defertur furti actio."[88] This solution did, however, not always commend itself as appropriate. Take the case where B has given his clothes to a tailor to be mended, and it is the tailor (C) who loses them by theft. In this situation it is ultimately C who loses out, not B, the owner. For as long as C has been promised a remuneration for the job, a contract of locatio conductio operis exists between him and his customer. On account of this contract he is liable for custodia.[89] Custodia, as we have emphasized repeatedly,[90] included liability for loss resulting from theft, quite irrespective of whether the debtor himself could be blamed for the incident or not. B's position was therefore well protected, because,

---

[81] Cf. the argument reported by Paulus in D. 47, 2, 32 pr.: ". . . si iudici, apud quem furti agatur, possit probari, quantum debitum fuerit, possit etiam apud eum iudicem eadem probare, apud quem pecuniam petat: si vero in furti iudicio probare non potest, ne illud quidem posse ostendi, quanti eius interest." Hence the conclusion of "quidam": "tabularum dumtaxat existimationem faciendam in furti actione." Paul's own answer to the problem (". . . potest post furtum factum tabulas nanctus esse actor, ut ex eo probet quanti sua interfuerit, si tabulas nanctus non esset") has been described, appositely, as "partial and rather desperate": Thomas, (1968) 15 *RIDA* 436.

[82] For a discussion, see Medicus, *Id quod interest*, pp. 233 sqq.; Franz Wieacker, "Furtum tabularum", in: *Synteleia Vincenzo Arangio-Ruiz*, vol. I (1964), pp. 562 sqq.; Thomas, (1968) 15 *RIDA* 432 sqq.

[83] Possibly under the influence of the developing conception of interesse in the lex Aquilia (cf. infra, pp. 969 sqq.): Thomas, (1968) 15 *RIDA* 437 sqq.

[84] Paul. Sent. II, XXXI, 32.

[85] Cf. Medicus, *Id quod interest*, p. 232.

[86] Cf. still *Inst.* IV, 1, 19.

[87] Iul. D. 3, 2, 1; Paul. Sent. II, XXXI, 15.

[88] Pap. D. 47, 2, 81, 1.

[89] Cf. supra, pp. 397 sqq.

[90] Cf. for example, supra, pp. 192 sqq.

unless C could plead vis maior (which, however, he was unable to do in case of theft), he could obtain redress on the basis of his actio locati. Under these circumstances it was hardly equitable to grant him the actio furti too. It was C who was the ultimate victim of A's wrongful behaviour and who thus deserved to claim the penalty. This was generally recognized in Roman law: "[S]i . . . sarcinator sarcienda vestimenta mercede certa acceperit eaque furto amiserit, ipse furti habet actionem, non dominus", as Gaius crisply put it.[91] He rationalized this result in terms of an old rule according to which the actio furti could only be given to the person who had an interest in the safety of the thing that had been stolen: "Cuius interfuit non subripi, is actionem furti habet."[92] This was usually the owner, but if the owner could proceed against someone who was liable to him under a contract involving custodia, that other party took his place. Not only could the contractor in a locatio conductio operis relationship be in such a position, but also a lessee (locatio conductio rei),[93] a borrower (commodatum)[94] and a pledgee (pignus).[95] A depositary, on the other hand, was normally liable only for dolus (and culpa lata);[96] he did not therefore have a specific responsibility for (and interest in) the safety of the thing. If the deposit was stolen from him, his position remained unaffected: he neither could be sued by the depositor nor could he, in turn, sue the thief for duplum.[97] The matter was different only if the

[91] Gai. III, 205.

[92] Ulp. (possibly Sab.) D. 47, 2, 10; the rule is also referred to in Quintus Mucius Scaevola/Pomp. D. 47, 2, 77, 1. Gaius has "[cuius] interesit rem non perire" and "[cuius] interest rem salvam esse".

[93] Iul. D. 47, 2, 59; Gai. D. 19, 2, 6. For further details concerning both locatio conductio operis and rei, see Fritz Schulz, "Die Aktivlegitimation zur actio furti im klassischen römischen Recht", (1911) 22 *ZSS* 59 sqq.

[94] Gai. III, 206; Mod. Coll. X, II, 6; cf. also C. 6, 2, 22, 1; Schulz, (1911) 32 *ZSS* 37 sqq.

[95] Gai. III, 204 ("Unde constat creditorem de pignore subrepto furti agere posse"); Paul. D. 47, 2, 15 pr.; Paul. D. 47, 2, 88; Hans Ankum, "'Furtum pignoris' und 'furtum fiduciae (II)", (1980) 27 *RIDA* 95 sqq.; Max Kaser, " 'Furtum pignoris' und 'furtum fiduciae' ", (1982) 99 *ZSS* 249 sqq.; cf. also Schulz, (1911) 32 *ZSS* 43 sqq. But the question has been (and still is) controversial; for contrary views and interpretations, cf. J.A.C. Thomas, "Furtum pignoris: a commentary on the commentaries", in: *Studi in onore di Cesare Sanfilippo*, vol. I (1982), pp. 585 sqq.; G.C.J.J. van den Bergh, "Custodia and furtum pignoris", in: *Studi in onore di Cesare Sanfilippo*, vol. I (1982), pp. 601 sqq.; cf. also still Max Kaser, "Besitzpfand und besitzloses Pfand", (1979) 45 *SDHI* 63 sqq. The answer depends on whether one accepts (1) that the pledgee was liable for custodia and (2) that his entitlement to the actio furti rested on this custodia liability rather than on his security interest. It is interesting to note that Gaius discusses the position of the pledgee (without reference to custodia) *before* he deals with fullo, sarcinator and commodatary (where he specifically links entitlement to the actio furti and custodia). It may therefore well be that in earlier classical law the pledgee's security interest (based on his real right in the object pledged to him) was regarded as the relevant criterion; the actio furti would then have been granted to the pledgee only up to double the value of the claim that was secured by the pledge but to the pledgor/owner for (double) the amount by which the value of the pledge exceeded the claim; cf. also Ulp. D. 47, 2, 12, 2; Ulp. D. 47, 2, 14, 5–7 and Kaser, (1982) 99 *ZSS* 255 sqq.

[96] Supra, pp. 208 sqq.

[97] Gai. III, 207.

depositary had specifically agreed to be liable for custodia.[98]

(c) *The right to sue: emptio venditio and miscellaneous other cases*

What about the vendor who had sold, but not yet delivered, the merx? Ownership had not yet passed, but the risk was already, emptione perfecta, on the purchaser. Yet the practical impact of the risk rule was limited by virtue of the fact that the vendor was under a custodia liability: if the merx was stolen before delivery, the purchaser could bring the actio empti and claim damages for non-performance.[99] We are not surprised, therefore, to find the actio furti being granted to the vendor rather than the purchaser: "Eum qui emit, si non tradita est ei res, furti actionem non habere, sed adhuc venditoris esse hanc actionem Celsus scripsit."[100] Yet, the actual reason for this proposition was not the vendor's liability for custodia. Of overriding importance was the fact that the vendor was still owner of the object sold[101]—for, after all, we are dealing here with the rather exceptional, in fact unique, situation that an *owner* was liable for custodia to a non-owner. That the vendor could thus avail himself of the actio furti iure dominii was not of purely academic interest. Conductor, commodatary and pledgee were granted the actio furti only as long as they were able to honour their obligation towards the owner; as soon as they fell insolvent, the right to bring the actio furti reverted to the latter, "quia hoc casu ipsius interest rem salvam esse".[102] The vendor, on the other hand, on account of being owner, retained the actio furti irrespective of whether he was still solvent or not. The purchaser merely had an obligatory claim to have the object handed over, and such a claim could not prevail against the vendor's ownership when it came to determining "cuius interest rem salvam fore". This principle, incidentally (obligatory claim not a sufficient basis to sue for theft), was of general application; a person, for example, to whom a thing was due under a stipulation did not have the actio furti either.[103]

Yet, ownership and custodia liability were not the only bases for entitlement to bring the actio furti. A somewhat haphazard group of cases existed, where the Roman lawyers were prepared to recognize a legally relevant interest[104] in the possession, the use and enjoyment or

[98] Cf. Ulp. D. 47, 8, 2, 22 sq. and Kaser, (1979) 45 *SDHI* 72.

[99] For details cf. supra, p. 287.

[100] Ulp. D. 47, 2, 14 pr.

[101] Cf. Pap. D. 47, 2, 81 pr. ("Si vendidero neque tradidero servum et is sine culpa mea subripiatur, magis est, ut mihi furti competat actio: et mea videtur interesse, *quia dominium apud me fuit*"); for all details, see Max Kaser, "Die actio furti des Verkäufers", (1979) 96 *ZSS* 118 sqq.

[102] Gai. III, 205; cf. also Ulp. D. 47, 2, 12 pr. (who provides the following reason: "nam qui non habet quod perdat, eius periculo nihil est").

[103] Paul. D. 47, 2, 13.

[104] Such interest was in any event only recognized if it arose "ex honesta causa": Pomp. D. 47, 2, 77, 1 (dealing with the situation where a thing was stolen from a thief; the first thief

retention of a thing: the position of the usufructuary, for example, enjoyed such recognition, and so did that of a bonae fidei possessor or of a person entitled to a ius retentionis.[105] In all these cases the actio furti was, however, split; the owner of the stolen object was still entitled to bring the actio furti for any amount exceeding the usufructuary's, possessor's etc. interest.

2. Actio furti manifesti

(a) *The discrimination of the manifest thief*

Where there was an actio furti nec manifesti there must, of course, have been an actio furti manifesti. It lay for poena quadrupli: for fourfold the value of the object stolen.[106] Throughout its entire history, Roman law distinguished between furtum nec manifestum and furtum manifestum and dealt with the latter much more severely than with the former.[107] This must appear to be rather odd, for there was no difference in guilt between the two forms of theft;[108] nor could it have been maintained that the one was the more vicious or dangerous form of wrongful behaviour.[109] The only distinctive feature of furtum manifestum was that the thief was caught in flagrante delicto, that is, in the act of stealing;[110] and furtum nec manifestum, in turn, could only be defined negatively, and rather trivially, as every form of theft that was not manifest.[111] But that was hardly a rational basis for such a drastic

---

may not bring the actio furti against the second one "ideo quod domino interfuit, non prioris furis, ut id quod subreptum et salvum esset").

[105] Ulp. D. 47, 2, 46, 1–6; Iav. D. 47, 2, 75; Ulp. D. 47, 2, 52, 10; Iul./Paul. D. 47, 2, 54, 4; Kaser, (1979) 96 *ZSS* 103 sq.; idem, "Grenzfragen der Aktivlegitimation zur actio furti", in: *De iustitia et iure, Festgabe für Ulrich von Lübtow* (1980), pp. 291 sqq.

[106] On the significance of quadruplum cf. Vincenzo Arangio-Ruiz, "La répression du vol flagrant et du non flagrant dans l'ancien droit romain", in: *Scritti di diritto romano*, vol. II (1974), pp. 371 sqq. (unconvincing); contra, for example, Honsell/Mayer-Maly/Selb, p. 359. For a general discussion, cf. Kelly, *Roman Litigation*, pp. 153 sqq.

[107] For Justinianic law, cf. *Inst.* IV, 1, 3 sqq.

[108] This point is also emphasized by Jolowicz, op. cit., note 12, pp. LXVIII and others.

[109] Some writers of the ius commune even took the view that non-manifest theft was the more serious offence: cf. infra, note 185. Others who defended the traditional distinction (which was still preserved in artt. 157 sq. of the Constitutio Criminalis Carolina) drew attention to the fact that the apprehension of the thief was very disgraceful ("quia deprehensio tanta turpitudo") and gave rise to clamour and commotion ("quia clamorem, tumultum . . . excitavit"): cf. Heinrich Janssen, *Der Diebstahl in seiner Entwicklung von der Carolina bis zum Ausgang des 18. Jahrhunderts*, (unpublished Dr. iur. thesis, Göttingen, 1969), pp. 69 sq. (with the quotations from a commentary on the Carolina by Johann Paul Kress from 1721). For a more frivolous comment, cf. Plucknett, *History*, p. 447: "No reasons seem to be evident for the rule [sc.: that the manifest thief fared much worse than the one whose guilt was only established after a lapse of time] . . ., but some savages are said to adopt it as a special condemnation for those who are not merely thieves, but incompetent thieves."

[110] On concept and etymology of furtum manifestum, see Fernand de Visscher, "Le 'fur manifestus' ", (1922) 46 *RH* 442 sqq. (unconvincing); contra: Ernst Rabel, (1932) 52 *ZSS* 473 sqq.; cf. also the discussion by Jolowicz, op. cit., note 12, pp. LXVIII.

[111] Cf. Gai. III, 185 ("nam quod manifestum non est, id nec manifestum est"); Gai. D. 47, 2, 8 ("Nec manifestum furtum quid sit, apparet: nam quod manifestum non est, hoc scilicet nec manifestum est"). Cf. also MacCormack, (1983) 51 *TR* 271.

differentiation of the penalties. What both the classical lawyers and Justinian faithfully preserved[112] was a rather rough-and-ready distinction characteristic of the early Roman jurisprudence (as, perhaps, of any early legal system)[113] and based on unrefined perceptions of what was just and fair. "In early law there is all the difference between obvious guilt and guilt which has to be proved" writes Jolowicz,[114] thus pinpointing the one essential factor that explains the comparatively heavier penalty imposed on manifest thieves: a conspicuous apprehension about indirect (or circumstantial) evidence and a marked reluctance to accept it as tantamount to what was self-evident and, seemingly, indisputable.[115] The other point has been emphasized by Sir Henry Maine, when he said:

> "The ancient lawgiver doubtless considered that the injured proprietor, if left to himself, would inflict a very different punishment when his blood was hot from that with which he would be satisfied when the Thief was detected after a considerable interval; and to this calculation the legal scale of penalties was adjusted."[116]

The manifest thief deserved to be treated more harshly on account of the fresh and acute resentment he had aroused in the victim: another one[117] of those traits of the developed law of delict that were clearly reminiscent of its origin in private vengeance. At the time of the XII Tables the manifest thief did not even receive the benefit of a proper trial. After having been caught, he merely had to be brought before the magistrate; there a liber homo was first scourged and then assigned for life to the party from whom he had stolen.[118] Such a magisterial addictio[119] was all that was required before the victim of the theft could wreak his vengeance. A slave, after having been similarly beaten, was hurled down from the Tarpeian rock.[120] In two cases it was even lawful to kill a fur manifestus out of hand: if he was caught at night ("Si nox furtum faxsit")[121] or if he defended himself with a weapon ("Luci . . .

[112] ". . . discreditable example of Roman conservatism": De Zulueta, *Gaius II*, p. 199; cf. also Thomas, *Institutes*, p. 264.

[113] For Germanic law cf. Heinrich Brunner/Claudius Freiherr von Schwerin, *Deutsche Rechtsgeschichte*, vol. II (1928), pp. 626 sqq.; for the old English common law, cf. Pollock and Maitland, vol. II, pp. 495 sqq.; cf. also Stephen, op. cit., note 9, p. 132, who draws attention to the fact that the division of thefts into manifest and non-manifest theft by Bracton was taken directly from Roman law.

[114] Op. cit., note 12, p. LXIX.

[115] Cf. also Pollock and Maitland, vol. II, p. 495 (". . . we doubt whether we can wholly acquit our forefathers of the [il-]logical idea that half-proven guilt is proven half-guilt").

[116] *Ancient Law*, p. 223.

[117] Cf. supra, pp. 915 sqq.

[118] Cf. Gai. III, 189.

[119] On which see, most recently, Walter Selb, "Vom geschichtlichen Wandel der Aufgabe des 'iudex' in der 'legis actio'", in: *Gedächtnisschrift für Wolfgang Kunkel* (1984), pp. 423, 443; Max Kaser, "Unmittelbare Vollstreckbarkeit und Bürgenregress", (1983) 100 *ZSS* 94. For a parallel in the old English common law (summary mode of dealing with "hand-having" thieves), see Pollock and Maitland, vol. II, pp. 160 sq.

[120] Aulus Gellius, *Noctes Atticae*, Lib. XI, XVIII, 8.

[121] Tab. 8, 12.

si se telo defendit").[122] But here the law had to ensure, at least, that it did not indirectly sanction secret murder. Therefore the victim of the theft was required to make public the lawfulness of his killing by shouting aloud (endoplarare) and thus alarming whoever might be near.[123] Thus it was originally only the fur nec manifestus who had to be sued and whose guilt had to be made incontestable according to the ordinary rules of civil procedure; the actio furti nec manifesti for double the value of the thing stolen was in fact already recognized by the XII Tables.[124] Sometime within the next three hundred years[125] the praetors, appalled by the "asperitas poenae"[126] for manifest theft, introduced an actio furti manifesti along very similar lines.[127] Their intervention heralded the end of the archaic forms of self-redress in theft—though not the end of the discrimination against the manifest thief.

(b) The concept of furtum manifestum

With one important exception, the concept of what constituted furtum manifestum had remained unchanged. It covered all those situations where the thief was caught in flagrante delicto and where his guilt was therefore evident. But what exactly did that mean?[128] Did the thief have to be apprehended in the very act of stealing ("dum fit")? Or did it suffice if he was caught in the place where he had committed the delict ("eo loco . . . ubi fit")? In that case, the actio furti manifesti would still

---

[122] Tab. 8, 13. Cf. generally the sources and literature in Kaser, *RPr* I, p. 158 (n. 34); Wieacker, *RR*, p. 244 (n. 38); also Jolowicz, op. cit., note 12, pp. LXXIV sq.

[123] Cf. Gai. D. 9, 2, 4, 1 ("cum clamore testific[are]"). On the parallel in Germanic law ("*Gerüfte*"), see Wieacker, *Festschrift für Leopold Wenger*, vol. I (1944), pp. 129 sq.; for England, cf. Pollock and Maitland, vol. II, pp. 160 sq.

[124] Gai. III, 190; cf. tab. 8, 16, as reconstructed on the basis of Festus, *De verborum significatione*, sub "nec" (but see Reuven Yaron, "Si adorat furto", (1966) 34 *TR* 510 sqq.). The duplum is perhaps explainable, originally, as a form of taliation: the defendant must be placed in the same position, financially, as he had placed the plaintiff. Cf. Kelly, *Roman Litigation*, pp. 154 sqq.; Detlef Liebs, "Damnum, damnare und damnas", (1968) 85 *ZSS* 191 sq.

[125] Cf. Schulz, *CRL*, p. 582; Watson, *Obligations*, pp. 231 sq.; as far as slaves were concerned, cf. still Pomp. D. 12, 4, 15.

[126] Gai. III, 189.

[127] The following were the main differences between the actio furti nec manifesti and the actio furti manifesti: the former had a formula in ius concepta (thus, it applied only to Roman citizens; to peregrini it had to be extended by way of fiction: cf. Gai. IV, 37 and De Zulueta, *Gaius II*, p. 257), it lay for double the value and could be brought against the main perpetrator as well as his accomplices (on account of the "opeve consiliove" clause). The actio furti manifesti had a formula in factum concepta (since it was a praetorian creation), lay for fourfold the value and could only be brought against the thief himself, not against any of his accomplices (the formula did not contain the "opeve consiliove" clause; reason: "[i]s, qui opem furtum facienti fert, numquam manifestus est: itaque accidit, ut is quidem, qui opem tulit, furti nec manifesti, is autem, qui deprehensus est, ob eandem rem manifesti teneatur").

[128] For what follows, see Gai. III, 184; Ulp. and Paul. D. 47, 2, 3–7; *Inst.* IV, 1, 3; De Visscher, (1922) 46 *RH* 493 sqq.; Rabel, (1932) 52 *ZSS* 475 sqq.; Jolowicz, op. cit., note 12, pp. LXXIII sq.

have been available if a theft of olives committed in an olive grove, or of grapes committed in a vineyard, was detected as long as the thief had not yet left the olive grove or vineyard. Or could one possibly extend the notion of furtum manifestum to all those situations where the thief had not yet carried the stolen object to its intended hiding place ("donec perferret eo quo perferre fur destinasset")? Or did it even embrace cases where the thief was seen, at any time, with the particular object in his hands ("quandoque eam rem fur tenens visus fuerit")? All four approaches were advocated in classical Roman law, as Gaius informs us. He himself regarded either of the first two opinions as tenable, but reported that the second was favoured by most.[129] Justinian ultimately adopted the third solution,[130] as had Julian and Ulpian before him.[131] This dispute, in a slightly modified form, still lives on in modern German criminal law when it comes to drawing the line between attempted and completed theft. The "theories" of contrectatio, apprehensio, ablatio and illatio are mentioned by the textbook writers in this context: the choice thus being between the moment when the object in question is handled, apprehended, carried away or brought into safety.[132]

(c) The quaestio lance et licio

The one exception concerned an ancient institution which even Gaius could no longer understand. Under the law of the XII Tables a person was considered to be fur manifestus if the stolen goods were found on his premises in the course of a formal, highly ritualistic search.[133] This was the famous quaestio lance et licio: to be performed (but for the licium) in stark nakedness and with a dish (lanx) in both hands.[134] Streams of ink have flowed in ever-repeated attempts to explain these rather mysterious particulars. Gaius[135] opened the roundabout of speculation by suggesting that the licium was some sort of apron, designed to cover the privy parts of the searcher. He also mentions two possible reasons why the searcher had to carry a dish (or perhaps rather

[129] Gai. III, 184. For interesting case law, see Ulp. D. 47, 2, 7, 1–3.

[130] *Inst.* IV, 1, 3.

[131] Iul./Ulp. D. 47, 2, 3, 2. Gaius' objection to this solution (". . . magnam recipit dubitationem utrum unius dici an etiam plurium dierum spatio id terminandum sit") was answered by accepting the limitation suggested by Paul ("'Quo destinaverit quis auferre' sic accipiendum est 'quo destinaverit eo die manere eum eo furto' ").

[132] Cf., for example, Reinhart Maurach, Friedrich-Christian Schroeder, *Strafrecht, Besonderer Teil*, Part I (6th ed., 1977), § 34 III B I. The moment of apprehensio is generally regarded as relevant today (that is, a contrectatio that amounts to an assumption of control and gives the thief the opportunity to remove the object). I doubt whether this correctly reflects the meaning of the notion of "*Wegnahme*" (taking away), as used in § 242 StGB.

[133] Gai. III, 192; Aulus Gellius, *Noctes Atticae*, Lib. XI, XVIII, 9.

[134] For similar ritualistic searches in other early legal systems, cf. Claudius Freiherr von Schwerin, *Die Formen der Haussuchung in indogermanischen Rechten* (1924).

[135] III, 193.

a platter) with him: either it was to engage his hands and so to prevent him from palming anything off, or else he may have required it as a receptacle for whatever he found. But these theories are almost certainly too rationalistic, and Gaius himself refused to accept them.[136] Over the centuries, many other views have been propounded,[137] but no certainty has, as yet, been reached. Theodor Mommsen, writing in 1898, refused even to detail all the old and new "pieces of folly" ("*Thorheiten*")[138] advanced in this context. Yet the most plausible view appears to be that all the three characteristic elements of the quaestio—nakedness as well as lanx and licium—were required for an expiatory offering to the household gods;[139] for, after all, the search constituted a grave breach of the peace of the house, a sacrilege (nefas) that had to be expiated somehow. The lanx may then have been an offering-cup, the licium a kind of sacral fillet. The nakedness may have been symbolic for the plaintiff's purity; at the same time, it clearly demonstrated that he entered the house unarmed and with nothing in his pocket that he could later pretend to find. The whole procedure became obsolete sometime during the 2nd century B.C.,[140] and by the middle of the 2nd century A.D. it could already be dismissed, rather curtly, as ridiculous.[141] Yet, even in classical Roman law, a thief whose guilt was established through an informal search of his premises—in front of witnesses—was dealt with more severely than a mere fur nec manifestus, although he was no longer branded a fur manifestus either. An actio furti concepti for three times the value of the object stolen was available against him.[142] If a suspect refused to have his premises searched, he was liable to be charged fourfold (actio furti prohibiti).[143]

3. Other remedies available in case of theft

The penal actio furti, in its various manifestations, was not the only remedy available to the victim of a theft. The owner of the stolen object could obviously bring the rei vindicatio for its recovery. According to its formula, the defendant was asked, in the first place, to return the

---

[136] ". . . neutrum eorum procedit, si id quod quaeratur eius magnitudinis aut naturae sit, ut neque subici neque ibi imponi possit."

[137] For an overview, cf., for example, Egon Weiss, "Lance et licio", (1922) 43 *ZSS* 455 sqq.; Franz Horak, *RE*, vol. XXIV, col. 788 sqq.; Wieacker, *RR*, p. 245.

[138] *Römisches Strafrecht*, p. 748.

[139] For a detailed analysis, cf. Joseph Georg Wolf, "Lanx und licium. Das Ritual der Haussuchung im altrömischen Recht", in: *Sympotica Franz Wieacker* (1970), pp. 59 sqq.

[140] Cf. Watson, *Obligations*, pp. 232 sq.

[141] Gai. III, 193 ("quae res ridicula est").

[142] Gai. III, 186, 191; Aulus Gellius, *Noctes Atticae*, Lib. XI, XVIII, 11. Cf. David Daube, "Some Comparative Law—Furtum conceptum", (1937) 15 *TR* 48 sqq.; Jolowicz, op. cit., note 12, pp. LXXV sqq.; De Zulueta, *Gaius II*, pp. 201 sqq.; Jolowicz/Nicholas, pp. 168 sq. Of course, it could happen that the object had not in fact been stolen by the occupier of the premises but had been placed there by someone else. If that was the case, the latter was liable to the occupier under an actio furti oblati: Gai. III, 187, 191.

[143] Gai. III, 188, 192. By the time of Justinian not only the actio furti prohibiti but also the actiones furti concepti and oblati were obsolete: *Inst.* IV, 1, 4.

object;[144] if he refused to do so, he was condemned to pay "quanti ea res erit, tantam pecuniam". Clearly, therefore, the rei vindicatio was a reipersecutory remedy.[145] The same was true of the contractual claim, of which the plaintiff was sometimes able to avail himself against the thief.[146] If the depositary used the object deposited with him, he committed furtum.[147] At the same time, however, his behaviour constituted breach of contract, and thus the actio depositi could be brought against him. If the borrower took the lender's horse further than he was meant to take it, he was liable under the actio commodati. In other cases, again, the actio locati was available: as, for example, when a fuller used the clothes that he was meant to clean.[148] Even on account of these more general avenues for obtaining redress, the victim of a wrong was therefore well protected. But there was yet another action in his armoury of remedies, tailored more specifically to the case of theft: the condictio ex causa furtiva. Just like the rei vindicatio, it was at the disposal of the owner of the object stolen,[149] and thus it differed in one important respect from all the other condictiones. "Si paret N^{m} N^{m} A^{o} A^{o} . . . dare oportere" (the intentio of the condictio) was normally taken to refer to situations where the defendant had (without good reason) acquired ownership and was now obliged to retransfer it to the plaintiff.[150] The thief, however, as a result of his theftuous behaviour, had not, of course, acquired ownership. Gaius recognized the anomaly of the situation and attributed the rather peculiar use to which the condictio was put to the hatred of thieves. "[P]lane odio furum", he said,[151]

> "quo magis pluribus actionibus teneantur, receptum est ut, extra poenam dupli aut quadrupli, rei recipiendae nomine fures etiam hac actione teneantur: si paret eos dare oportere, quamvis sit etiam adversus eos haec actio qua rem nostram esse petimus."

Whether or not this speculation as to why the condictio was thus extended is soundly based,[152] it is clear that the condictio ex causa

[144] ". . . neque ea res arbitrio tuo restituetur": the clausula arbitraria.

[145] Like all other actiones in rem: *Inst.* IV, 6, 17.

[146] Gai. IV, 7.

[147] Supra, note 13.

[148] Cf. supra, note 15. Generally on the relationship between contractual liability and redress for furtum in locatio conductio, and on their interplay, see J.A.C. Thomas, "Furtum and locatio conductio", (1976) 11 *The Irish Jurist* 170 sqq.

[149] Ulp. D. 13, 1, 1 ("In furtiva re soli domino condictio competit"). For further details, see Wolfram Pika, *Ex causa furtiva condicere im klassischen römischen Recht* (1988), pp. 35 sqq.

[150] Cf., for example, supra, pp. 6, 835.

[151] IV, 4.

[152] For a discussion, see Pika, op. cit., note 149, pp. 20 sqq. It is likely that the condictio was extended to cases of furtum at a time when "dare oportere" had not yet acquired the technical meaning of "to have to transfer ownership". Cf. further Pernice, *Labeo*, vol. III, p. 233; Schwarz, *Condictio*, p. 278; Roy Stone, "Gaius noster and 'Res nostra' ", (1966) 83 *ZSS* 357 sqq.; Kaser, *RPr* I, p. 618; but cf. also Liebs, *Klagenkonkurrenz*, pp. 96 sq.

furtiva was generally recognized in classical law.[153] Unlike the actio furti, but just as the rei vindicatio, it was reipersecutory in character ("Poenam tantum persequimur . . . actione furti . . .; nam ipsius rei et vindicatio et condictio nobis competit").[154] It was available in cases of manifest and non-manifest theft,[155] provided, of course, the thief had dispossessed the owner[156] and the latter had not, in the meantime, regained possession of the object stolen.[157] Under a condictio ex causa furtiva a thief was liable even if he had lost what he had stolen or if it had been accidentally destroyed. This was already recognized by the veteres, as Tryphoninus reports:

> "Licet fur paratus fuerit excipere condictionem et per me steterit, dum in rebus humanis res fuerat, condicere eam, postea autem perempta est, tamen durare condictionem veteres voluerunt, quia videtur, qui prima invito domino rem contrectaverit, semper in restituenda ea, quam nec debuit auferre, moram facere."[158]

A thief was always considered to be in default ("fur semper in mora"), and all the consequences of mora debitoris were thus applicable to him without interpellatio.[159] Herein lay the main advantage of the condictio in comparison with the rei vindicatio; for the rei vindicatio, being a remedy in rem, was bound to fail wherever the defendant no longer had the object of the dispute.[160]

4. Concurrence of actions

Determination of the concurrence of all the various actions available in case of theft was reasonably straightforward. Any of the actiones poenales could be brought together with any of the reipersecutory remedies. Thus, the actio furti could be cumulated with either the rei vindicatio or the condictio ex causa furtiva or a contractual action.[161] As a result, the plaintiff had the chance to obtain, in cases of furtum nec

---

[153] Possibly not under that name, though: Schwarz, *Condictio*, p. 53; Pika, op. cit., note 149, pp. 21 sq.

[154] Gai. IV, 8; cf. also Iul./Ulp. D. 11, 3, 11, 2 (". . . quamvis enim condictione hominem, poenam autem furti actione consecutus sit"); Ulp. D. 13, 1, 7, 1; Pika, op. cit., note 149, pp. 28 sqq.

[155] Ulp. D. 13, 1, 10 pr.

[156] Pomp./Ulp. D. 47, 2, 21, 10: "Quamvis autem earum quoque rerum, quas quis non abstulit, furti teneatur, attamen condici ei non potest, idcirco quia condici ea res, quae ablata est, potest: et ita Pomponius scribit."

[157] Ulp. D. 13, 1, 10 pr.

[158] D. 13, 1, 20.

[159] Liebs, *Klagenkonkurrenz*, pp. 136 sqq.; Pika, op. cit., note 149, pp. 30 sqq.

[160] Apart from that, the plaintiff did not (as under the rei vindicatio) have the notoriously difficult task of proving his quiritary ownership. A third point was that, as a result of "fur semper in mora", the defendant was condemned into the highest value that the object had had since the commission of the theft (i.e. the plaintiff was indemnified for lucrum cessans): Ulp. D. 13, 1, 8, 1; Paul. D. 13, 1, 13; Tryph. D. 25, 2, 29. For condemnation under the rei vindicatio the time of litis contestatio was relevant. On the advantages of the condictio ex causa furtiva, cf. generally Glück, vol. 13, pp. 212 sqq.; Pieter Pauw, "Historical Notes on the Nature of the condictio furtiva", (1976) 93 *SALJ* 396.

[161] Gai. D. 47, 2, 55, 3; Ulp. D. 13, 1, 7 pr. and 1; Levy, *Konkurrenz*, vol. I, pp. 416 sqq., 428 sq.; Liebs, *Klagenkonkurrenz*, pp. 91 sqq.; Pika, op. cit., note 149, p. 108.

manifestum, three times—and, in the event of furtum manifestum, even five times—the value of the object stolen. Rei vindicatio, condictio ex causa furtiva and (if available) a contractual claim, on the other hand, stood in a relationship of elective concurrence towards each other; once either of these remedies had been brought, the plaintiff's legitimate interest in receiving compensation had been satisfied and another lawsuit ad rem persequandam was thus out of the question.[162] Finally, it need hardly be emphasized that the penal actions could not be cumulated either.[163]

III. FURTUM IN THE IUS COMMUNE

1. The demise of the actio furti

Very little of the Roman law relating to furtum has made its way into our modern legal systems.[164] Theft is today a crime, and its history is part and parcel of the history of criminal law. Even in classical Roman law the availability of private penal remedies was already a matter more of theoretical than of any practical significance, for thieves, as Thomas[165] aptly remarks, are not generally well endowed with this world's goods; and to expect them to pay two-, three- or fourfold the value of the object stolen (apart from the simple value or quod interest on account of one of the actiones ad rem persequendum) must often

---

[162] For the technical details, see Pomp. D. 47, 2, 9, 1; Levy, *Konkurrenz*, vol. II, pp. 90 sqq.; Pika, op. cit., note 149, pp. 109 sqq.

[163] If a wife, in view of an imminent divorce, had stolen something from her husband, a special actio rerum amotarum (here the edict used the term "amovere" as opposed to merely "contrectare") was made available by the praetors to the husband (in classical law wives enjoyed the same protection against thefts by their husbands). It was a purely reipersecutory remedy and appears to have been introduced because theft was regarded as conceptually impossible between husband and wife (". . . quibusdam existimantibus ne quidem furtum eam [i.e.: the wife] facere, ut Nerva Cassio, quia societas vitae quodammodo dominam eam faceret": Paul. D. 25, 2, 1). The actio rerum amotarum thus replaced both the actio furti and the condictio ex causa furtiva. Later, however, it was argued that theft was in fact possible in this situation, but that the matrimonial reverence owed by the spouses to each other prevented them from suing each other with the actio furti, a remedy which was penal and entailed infamia (". . . aliis, ut Sabino et Proculo, furto quidem eam facere . . ., sed furti non esse actionem constituto iure . . . nam in honorem matrimonii turpis actio adversus uxorem negatur": Paul. D. 25, 2, 1 and Gai. D. 25, 2, 2). This does not, however, explain why the condictio ex causa furtiva should have been excluded between husband and wife; in fact, it may well have become available as an alternative remedy (perhaps only through Justinian's intervention) to recover the stolen property. Whether or not the condictio ex causa furtiva may be brought by spouses against each other has always remained disputed (cf., for example, Glück, vol. 28, pp. 48 sq. on the one hand, Windscheid/Kipp, § 454, n. 24 on the other). Those who answered the question in the affirmative usually argued that the actio rerum amotarum had been abrogated by disuse, since it did not give the spouse anything over and above what he could obtain by the condictio (Windscheid/Kipp, loc. cit.). For all details on the development and scope of application of the Roman actio rerum amotarum, see Andreas Wacke, *Actio rerum amotarum* (1963), passim; Liebs, *Klagenkonkurrenz*, pp. 146 sqq.; Kaser *RPr* I, pp. 618 sq.; idem, *RPr* II, p. 436.

[164] For an example, cf. supra, p. 939 (with note 132).

[165] *TRL*, p. 360.

have been rather illusory.[166] With the rise of the cognitio extraordinaria[167] the emphasis, as far as the suppression of theft was concerned, shifted decisively in favour of criminal proceedings.[168] In a way, therefore, the concluding fragment 93 is historically the most significant of all the texts collected in title D. 47, 2, De furtis; over all our discussions about private remedies and their various incidents we must not forget, warns Ulpian, that by now "furti plerumque criminaliter agi et eum qui agit in crimen subscribere".[169] According to Julian (who wrote nearly a century earlier), the institution of criminal proceedings even had the effect of precluding the injured party from bringing the actio furti and thus exposing the thief to the danger of being penalized more than once.[170] Justinian preserved the private penal actions,[171] and since they featured so prominently in both his Digest and the *Institutes*, they were bound to become part of the Roman–canon ius commune that was received in Germany.[172] But neither Justinian nor any of the post-reception jurists, mapping out and analysing the Roman law of furtum,[173] could halt the ascendancy of criminal penalties for theft. By the end of the Middle Ages, the suppression of crime and imposition of punishment had become essential functions of the State authorities,[174] and in the famous Constitutio Criminalis Carolina of 1532 theft was therefore no longer regarded as a private wrong but as a public crime. Duplum and quadruplum were still preserved as penalties (though only for two

---

[166] Cf. also Kelly, *Roman Litigation*, pp. 162 sq. (". . . the classical actio furti . . . must have been in practice a fairly useless remedy").

[167] Cf., for example, Mommsen, *Strafrecht*, pp. 260 sqq., 346 sqq. and passim; A.H.M. Jones, *The Criminal Courts of the Roman Republic and Principate* (1972), pp. 107 sqq.; Jolowicz/Nicholas, pp. 401 sqq. Some thefts were public offences already under Republican law—for example, plagium (kidnapping: D. 48, 15; Mommsen, *Strafrecht*, pp. 780 sqq.; Berger, *ED*, p. 632) and abigeatus (cattle-rustling; D. 47, 14; Mommsen, *Strafrecht*, pp. 775 sq.)—many others were added under the Principate (on furtum balnearium, theft committed in a bath-house, see D. 47, 17; on the crimen expilatae hereditatis, D. 47, 19; Mommsen, *Strafrecht*, pp. 777 sqq.; Berger, *ED*, p. 418); generally cf. Mommsen, *Strafrecht*, pp. 733 sqq., 760 sqq.; cf. also Jolowicz, op. cit., note 12, pp. XII sqq.

[168] For a similar process in the history of the early common law, cf. Pollock and Maitland, vol. II, pp. 157 sqq., 494 sq.

[169] Genuine, according to Kaser, *RPr* I, p. 617; idem, *RPr* II, p. 435.

[170] D. 47, 2, 57, 1 (suspected by Jolowicz, op. cit., note 12, pp. 86 sq. and others).

[171] He even emphasized that it was open to the victim of a theft to resort to civil rather than criminal proceedings: cf. D. 47, 2, 93 in fine (interpolated: Kaser, *RPr* I, p. 435).

[172] They were not received in France: cf. Auguste Dumas, *Histoire des obligations dans l'ancien droit français* (1972), pp. 33 sq.; Coing, pp. 506 sq.

[173] Cf. VerLoren van Themaat, op. cit., note 33, pp. 38 sqq.; Snyman, op. cit., note 39, pp. 45 sqq.

[174] Cf., for example, Gudelinus, *Commentarii de iure novissimo* , Lib. III, Cap. XIII, n. 18 (". . . fisco solo poenas ob vindictam publicam iudicio criminali persequente"). On the factors militating against dealing with crime by way of delicta privata in general, cf. Coing, pp. 504 sqq. On the history (and eventual decline) of the poena dupli generally, see Karl Otto Scherner, "Der doppelte Fahrpreis oder der Geist des deutschen Privatrechts", in: *Wege europäischer Rechtsgeschichte, Karl Kroeschell zum 60. Geburtstag* (1987), pp. 361 sqq., 367 sqq.

different forms of petty theft),[175] but it was no longer the private actio furti by means of which they were enforceable. Whether the latter remedy was still available as an alternative way of proceeding against the thief remained in dispute for some time. Lauterbach and Stryk were among the last influential writers who advocated the survival of the Roman actio furti, the one, however, conceding that it was "hodie in quibusdam locis abrogata, in aliis infrequens",[176] the other suggesting ("Illud interim juris hodierni esse puto") that the duplum was no longer "mera poena" but had to be taken as embracing "ipsam rei restitutionem".[177] Among the "quidam loci" in which the remedy was abrogated were, most notably, Belgium[178] and Holland.[179] In the course of the 18th century this view gained ground in Germany too,[180] and it was widely accepted even by the 19th-century pandectists.[181] If the actio furti was retained by the one or other textbook writer, it was in a purely reipersecutory function and in order to compensate for certain (alleged) weaknesses inherent in the other private remedies.[182]

2. The history of the modern concept of theft

Apart from endorsing duplum and quadruplum as two suitable forms of penalty, the Constitutio Criminalis Carolina dealt with theft in the tradition of Germanic law. The severity of the punishment must be mentioned in this context,[183] as well as the distinction between petty theft and furtum magnum,[184] and (possibly) also the further distinction

---

[175] Artt. 157, 158. In the case of art 157 the thief was, however, liable to be incarcerated if he could not pay the duplum (in accordance with the maxim "qui non habet in aere, luat in corpore"; cf. Ulp. D. 48, 19, 1, 3 in fine); according to art. 158, condemnation in quadruplum was applicable only if the thief was a respectable person and provided one could expect him to improve his ways (otherwise the penalties were pillory, whipping and banishment). Neither the duplum nor the quadruplum appears to have been applied in practice: cf. H. Holzhauer, *HRG*, vol. III, col. 1996.

[176] Lauterbach, *Collegium theoretico-practicum*, Lib. XLVII, Tit. I, XLVII.

[177] Stryk, *Usus modernus pandectarum*, Lib. XLVII, Tit. I, § 1.

[178] Cf. Gudelinus, op. cit., note 174, Lib. III, Cap. XIII: ". . . omnes actiones apud nos reipersecutorias esse dicendum est earumque omnium conceptionem esse in simplum."

[179] As far as Holland was concerned, cf. Groenewegen, *De legibus abrogatis*, Inst. Lib. IV, Tit. I, § 5 poena; Voet, *Commentarius ad Pandectas*, Lib. XLVII, Tit. II, XV.

[180] At the same time, the distinction between manifest and non-manifest theft became obsolete.

[181] Wächter, *Pandekten*, § 214; Windscheid/Kipp, § 453, 2.

[182] Dernburg, vol. II, § 130 in fine; cf. also Arndts, *Pandekten*, § 323 in fine.

[183] Originally, every act of theft carried capital punishment. According to art. 160 CCC (dealing with furtum magnum) the judge was no longer obliged to impose the death penalty. For details cf. Janssen, op. cit., note 109, pp. 91 sqq. For England cf. Stephen, op. cit., note 9, p. 129; Pollock and Maitland, vol. II, pp. 495 sqq.

[184] Cf. artt. 157 sq. as opposed to art. 160 CCC. For a definition, cf., for example, Lauterbach, *Collegium theoretico-practicum*, Lib. XLVII, Tit. II, XII ("Ab Objecti quantitate in Magnum, secundum Const. Car. quod 5 solidos vel aureos eorumve aestimationem continet, vel excedit; et Parvum, quod est infra illam summam"); for a discussion of the distinction and its historical foundations, see Janssen, op. cit., note 109, pp. 68 sqq., 82 sqq. For England, where "both an old English and an old Frankish tradition may have conspired

between "secret" and "public" (manifest and non-manifest)[185] theft. Most interesting, however, from a purely dogmatic point of view was the fact that "theft" (though undefined) was much more narrowly conceived than the Roman furtum; in particular, it did not cover cases of embezzlement.[186] Again, this was in line with the Germanic concept of the crime, which had always emphasized the element of the actual removal of an object from another person's custody.[187] It is somewhat surprising to see how slowly legal doctrine followed suit.[188] Even after the Carolina had firmly entrenched the notion of theft as a crime, the writers of the ius commune—private-law oriented as they were—continued to base their discussion on Paulus' definition and on the case law of the Digest and thus to equate, or rather confuse, the Roman delict of furtum with the Germanic crime of theft.[189] Only in the early

to draw the line between 'grand' and 'petty larceny' at twelve pence", see Pollock and Maitland, vol. II, pp. 495 sqq.; Holdsworth, vol. III, pp. 366 sq.

[185] This distinction related only to petty theft and it determined whether the thief had to pay duplum or quadruplum: see artt. 157 sq. CCC. Whether it derived (via the Italian jurisprudence) from Roman law or from Germanic roots is disputed: cf. Janssen, op. cit., note 109, pp. 68 sq. It appears that already by the beginning of the 17th century the distinction was no longer observed in practice. Some authors even claimed that manifest theft deserved to be punished more mildly, not more severely, than non-manifest theft; among these authors were Carpzov, who argued (on the basis of the theory of ablatio; on which cf. supra, p. 939) that manifest theft was tantamount merely to attempted theft, and Johann Paul Kress, who drew attention to the fact that the manifest thief did not usually cause any damage, since he was able to return the object stolen: cf. Janssen, op. cit., note 109, pp. 71 sq.

[186] Cf. art. 170 CCC e contrario.

[187] Cf. R. Lieberwirth, "Diebstahl", in: *HRG*, vol. I, 1971, col. 730 sq.; Snyman, op. cit., note 39, pp. 55 sqq. This view of theft prevailed throughout the history of the English common law: "There can . . . be little doubt that the 'taking and carrying away', upon which our later law insists, had been from the first the very core of the English idea of theft. 'He stole, took and carried away': this is the charge made against the thief." Even Bracton's definition of the crime in terms of contrectatio (cf. supra, p. 923, note 10) did not change that, for the notion of contrectatio was "narrowed down to the case where there has been an actual physical change of possession effected by the act of the thief without the consent of the person entitled to the goods" (Holdsworth, vol. III, p. 361); cf. further Stephen, op. cit., note 9, pp. 134 sqq. In the same vein, the Larceny Act of 1916 still provided that "a person steals who, without the consent of the owner, fraudulently and without a claim of right made in good faith, takes and carries away anything capable of being stolen with intent, at the time of such taking, permanently to deprive the owner thereof". The expression "carries away", it was further specified, "includes any removal of anything from the place which it occupies, but in the case of a thing attached only if it has been completely detached". This definition of theft obviously did not include embezzlement, which, in turn, was made a separate crime in 1799 (with regard to servants or clerks; later extended to other persons too). For details, see Stephen, op. cit., note 9, pp. 152 sqq.; Plucknett, *History*, pp. 449 sqq. and s. 17 of the Larceny Act of 1916. The Theft Act of 1968, however, has redefined theft so as to include (inter alia) embezzlement; it no longer requires an act of asportation but refers, instead, to the dishonest appropriation of property belonging to another. For details, see Smith, op. cit., note 4, nn. 17 sqq.

[188] Friedrich Schaffstein, *Studien zur Entwicklung der Deliktstatbestände im Gemeinen Deutschen Strafrecht* (1984), p. 35.

[189] For a discussion, see Janssen, op. cit., note 109, pp. 4 sqq.

17th century[190] did it dawn upon them that the wide Roman definition might not provide an entirely satisfactory framework for the stiff sanctions of contemporary criminal law. Decapitation is hardly the appropriate penalty for a man who takes a borrowed horse beyond the town where he was meant to take it![191]

The decisive step, as far as German jurisprudence was concerned, was taken by the Saxonian professor and practitioner, Benedict Carpzov.[192] Though still proceeding from the Pauline notion of contrectatio, he advocated a distinction between two different types of "handling". The poena ordinaria furti was to be confined to cases involving contrectatio vera, and contrectatio vera, in turn, was characterized by an *ablatio* rei alienae. Where, on the other hand, one was merely dealing with a contrectatio ficta (that is, a translatio ad alium usum contra voluntatem domini), a milder form of punishment was called for. This doctrine soon gained widespread acceptance and provided the starting point for the development of a differentiated system of more precisely defined forms of criminal behaviour that took place over the next 250 years. Theft was eventually defined along the lines of the Germanic crime[193] and so became entirely detached from the Roman notion of furtum. Within the area thus vacated, crimes such as embezzlement, fraud and receiving stolen property established themselves.[194] Furtum usus and furtum possessionis as such[195] were eventually taken not to require any criminal sanction at all; they were regarded as a breach of (private) trust rather than an infringement of the public order.

3. The condictio ex causa furtiva

With the demise of the actio furti private law was left with the task of protecting the interest "ad rem persequendam" of the injured individual by granting either restoration or compensation. The rei vindicatio and (where appropriate) contractual actions remained, of course, available for that purpose. But these were remedies of a general nature, the availability of which did not depend on whether or not a

[190] That is, at the very time when public law (of which criminal law is a prominent part; cf. Ulp. D. 2, 1, 3) emerged as a scientific discipline in its own right—a process which has recently been analysed by Michael Stolleis, *Geschichte des öffentlichen Rechts in Deutschland*, vol. I (1988).

[191] Cf. the observation by Vinnius, *Institutiones*, Lib. IV, Tit. I, 6, based on the example discussed in Paul. D. 47, 2, 40.

[192] *Practica nova*, op. cit., note 8, Pars II, Quaest. LXXXV, 1; for a discussion of Carpzov's doctrine (and also of his fellow Saxonian Matthias Berlich's work, on which it was based), see Janssen, op. cit., note 109, pp. 8 sqq., 13 sqq.

[193] For details of the development, see Janssen, op. cit., note 109, pp. 17 sqq., 26 sqq., 42 sqq.; cf. also Lieberwirth, op. cit., note 187, col. 733 sqq.

[194] Cf. supra, p. 922; for the development in England (where the narrow, Germanic concept of theft had always been adhered to), see Stephen, op. cit., note 9, pp. 145 sqq.; Plucknett, *History*, pp. 446 sqq.

[195] That is, where they did not at the same time fulfil the requirements of any of the other crimes (as, for example, fraud).

delict of theft (however defined) had been committed. The concept of furtum therefore retained its significance only with regard to the condictio ex causa furtiva; and the ambit of this remedy continued, indeed, to be described in terms of Paulus' definition right until the end of the 19th century.[196] But the whole discussion had become a typical example of pandectist textbook jurisprudence. Hovering forever uneasily somewhere between the fields of delict and unjustified enrichment,[197] the condictio ex causa furtiva was about to be swallowed by both the usus modernus legis Aquiliae and the generalized enrichment action. In the opinion of the fathers of the BGB, at any rate, it had lost its practical significance and was therefore denied entry into the code.[198] As a result, theft has ceased to be a specific institution of private law, and all questions as to its proper scope of application have become a matter of purely academic interest. A person whose property is unlawfully interfered with enjoys comprehensive protection, both under § 823 I BGB[199] (compensation for any damage arising) and under § 812 I 1[200] (restoration of unjustified enrichment arising as a result of interference).

IV. SOUTH AFRICAN DEVELOPMENTS

1. The concept of theft in criminal law

South African law, as usual, still maintains a somewhat closer link with the tradition of the ius commune. On the one hand, theft is still a common-law crime. It is based on the Roman-Dutch notion of furtum, which is, in turn, essentially still that of Paul. D. 47, 2, 1, 3.[201] Over the last 150 years, however, the old, pre-1968 English law[202] has exercised considerable influence[203] and eroded some of the civilian

[196] Glück, vol. 13, pp. 229 sqq.; Wächter, *Pandekten*, § 214; Windscheid/Kipp, § 452.

[197] On the nature of the condictio ex causa furtiva, cf. Pika, op. cit., note 149, pp. 102 sqq.; Glück, vol. 13, pp. 230 sqq.; Pauw, (1976) 93 *SALJ* 396 sqq.; Windscheid/Kipp, §§ 425, 453, 1; Baron, *Pandekten*, § 311, II.

[198] "Motive", in: *Mugdan*, vol. II, p. 475.

[199] Infra, p. 1036; cf. also Hugo Grotius, *Inleiding*, III, XXXVII, drawing together damage to property and theft under the heading of "misdaed tegens goed" (on which see *Smit v. Saipem* 1974 (4) SA 918 (A) at 929 sq.).

[200] Cf. supra, pp. 889 sq.

[201] For a detailed analysis of Roman-Dutch law, cf. VerLoren van Themaat, op. cit., note 33, pp. 61 sqq.; cf. also Snyman, op. cit., note 39, pp. 61 sqq. The main respect in which the Roman-Dutch crime of theft appears to have differed from the Roman delict of furtum was that depositaries, borrowers, pledgees, etc., exceeding their contractual rights in respect of the thing, were not liable "moribus nostris" to criminal prosecution; reason: "quasi minores sint tales a pudore recessus, quam ut infamiae et corporali subjacerent coercitioni" (Voet, *Commentarius ad Pandectas*, Lib. XLVII, Tit. II, XV); cf. also Groenewegen, *De legibus abrogatis*, Inst. Lib. IV, Tit. I, § 7 placuit; Vinnius, *Institutiones*, Lib. IV, Tit. I, 6; but see also the analysis by VerLoren van Themaat, op. cit., note 33, pp. 132 sqq.

[202] Cf. supra, note 187.

[203] An important catalyst in this reception process was the Native Territories' Penal Code of 1886 (applicable in Transkei). Its definition of theft (copied from Sir James Fitzjames

foundations.[204] Among the "tattered remnants"[205] is, most prominently, the factual element of contrectatio. It vaguely insinuates some kind of "dealing" with the property; but what precisely it entails is entirely unclear—as unclear, in fact, as it was even in Roman law.[206] Is a mere touching of the thing sufficient?[207] Or does contrectatio imply an assumption of control on the part of the thief?[208] Does the victim of the theft have to be deprived of his control?[209] Must there be an actual physical handling or does an act which is "tantamount to a physical dealing with the property by the thief or at his instance and in his presence"[210] suffice for conviction under a charge of theft?[211] Occasionally, it has even been suggested that "the taking and removal of the stolen property" is necessary.[212] "Few parts of criminal law", says Milton,[213] "present as much difficulty as contrectatio", and the

---

Stephen's draft Criminal Code) was substantially adopted by the most prominent South African textbook (Gardiner and Lansdowne, p. 1082) when it first appeared in 1919. In the same year, the definition was adopted by Kotzé JP in *R v. Siboya* 1919 EDL 41 at 43 sq. Kotzé JP (one of the most influential judges in the late 19th and early 20th centuries) seems to have had a particular predilection "om ons gemene reg oor diefstal in die [Transkeian Penal Code] te soek" (De Wet en Swanepoel, op. cit., note 1, p. 311; cf. also pp. 313 sq.). For another prominent example of this tendency, cf. *R v. Carelse and Kay* 1920 CPD 471 at 474 (per Kotzé JP), where s. 180 of the Native Territories' Penal Code is referred to as authority for the proposition that theft requires actual asportation.

[204] For a concise summary of where South African courts have followed and where they have refused to follow English law, cf. Milton, op. cit., note 1, pp. 601 sqq. According to J.C. de Wet (De Wet en Swanepoel, op. cit., note 1, p. 307), this partial reception of English law has turned theft into " 'n byna onhanteerbare regsfiguur". "So seer is dit die geval", he continues, "dat daar vandag op hierdie terrein omtrent geen reël is waaroor daar duidelikheid en eenstemmigheid bestaan nie."

[205] Percival Gane, *The Selective Voet*, vol. VII (1957), p. 150.

[206] Cf., in this context, the remarks by MacCormack, quoted supra, note 39.

[207] Cf. *R v. Tarusika* 1959 (1) R & N 51 (SR) at 51–2, where contrectatio is defined as a mere "touching or handling [of] the thing with a view to its asportation". Contra ("[a] mere touching of the thing is not enough") Milton, op. cit., note 1, p. 607 ; cf. also VerLoren van Themaat, op. cit., note 33, p. 71 (". . . uit ons hofbeslissings blyk dat blote aanraak nie voldoende is nie maar hanteer vereis word").

[208] Milton, op. cit., note 1, pp. 607 sq.

[209] De Wet en Swanepoel, op. cit., note 1, pp. 308 sqq.; contra: Milton, op. cit., note 1, p. 608.

[210] *R v. Makonie* 1942 OPD 164 at 165.

[211] According to *R v. Strydom* 1952 (2) SA 397 (T) at 399H–400A, in the case of theft of money the manipulation of cheques or a book entry may constitute a contrectatio even without the actual physical handling of any individual coins; but "[w]hen it comes to theft of an individual object such as a beast . . . the rule still seems to be that there must be an actual physical dealing with the thing concerned or some conduct which is akin to physical handling. As an example of the latter type may be mentioned the case where a bird or animal the property of another is enticed into an enclosure and captured and appropriated". Contra: Milton, op. cit., note 1, p. 607.

[212] Cf. *R v. Nerera* 1939 SR 297 at 299; *R v. Carelse and Kay* 1920 CPD 471 at 474 (both under the influence of English law; cf. s. 1 of the Larceny Act of 1916). Contra: *Moodley v. R* (1914) 35 NLR 514 at 519; *R v. Mlooi* 1925 AD 131 at 152; Milton, op. cit., note 1, pp. 606 sq.; Snyman, op. cit., note 39, p. 209. English law itself has now abandoned this criterion.

[213] Op. cit., note 1, p. 603. Cf. also the detailed discussion (33 pages) by VerLoren van Themaat, op. cit., note 33, pp. 66 sqq. (whose work also contains a valuable analysis of

retention of this rather ambiguous and indistinct notion of the Roman law of delict and its transformation into a key element of the modern crime of theft was not, probably, a very happy idea. The equally unspecific subjective requirement of lucri faciendi gratia is the most notable victim of the partial anglicization of the South African law of theft.[214] It has been replaced by the intention to deprive the owner of the full benefits of his ownership.[215] As a result, mere furtum usus no longer constitutes theft. This was generally accepted[216] until 1948 when the Orange Free State Provincial Division attempted to turn back the clock, at least as far as cases of unauthorized borrowing were concerned.[217] The court acknowledged that even (at least some of) the Roman-Dutch authors, motivated by a desire to circumscribe the range of application of the harsh post-medieval penalties for theft,[218] regarded furtum usus as not punishable. But they had confined their remarks to the standard examples discussed in the Digest: cases of furtum usus characterized by the fact that the fur exceeded certain rights in respect of a thing that had previously been conveyed to him. A person therefore still committed theft, so it was argued, if he *took away* somebody else's property with the intention of using it for a certain period before eventually restoring it. This proposition was, however, rejected by the Appellate Division in *R v. Sibiya*,[219] the decision that authoritatively settled the common law in favour of the "intention to deprive permanently" test: in the words of Schreiner ACJ,[220]

> "[T]he law requires for the crime of theft . . . that the taker should have intended to terminate the owner's enjoyment of his rights or, in other words, to deprive him of the whole benefit of his ownership."

If furtum usus falls outside the scope of the modern South African law of theft, its definition is nevertheless still wide enough to cover

---

contrectatio in Roman law: pp. 8 sqq.). De Wet (De Wet en Swanepoel, op. cit., note 1, p. 311) argues that already in Roman law contrectatio was " 'n uitgediende uitdrukking sonder 'n spesifieke betekenis".

[214] *R v. Siboya* 1919 EDL 41 at 43 sq.; Milton, op. cit., note 1, pp. 621 sqq.; Snyman, op. cit., note 39, pp. 222 sqq.; but see VerLoren van Themaat, op. cit., note 33, pp. 125 sqq. English law itself has toyed for some time with the idea of including lucri faciendi gratia into the definition of theft (cf. Blackstone, *Commentaries*, Book IV, chapter XVII, I and the discussion by Snyman, op. cit., note 39, pp. 167 sqq.); it was rejected only in the case of *R v. Cabbage* (1815) Russ & Ry 292.

[215] Cf. the analysis by Milton, op. cit., note 1, pp. 616 sqq.; Snyman, op. cit., note 39, pp. 235 sqq.; but see also De Wet en Swanepoel, op. cit., note 1, pp. 312 sqq., who argue that the essential requirement is "die bedoeling van die dader om hom die goed toe te eien".

[216] Cf., for example, *R v. Fortuin* (1883) 1 Buch AC 290 (theft of the use of an ox is not a crime).

[217] *R v. Mtaung* 1948 (4) SA 120 (O).

[218] Cf. supra, p. 945 (with note 183).

[219] 1955 (4) SA 247 (A).

[220] *R v. Sibiya* 1955 (4) SA 247 (A) at 257C. The decision contains a very interesting dissenting opinion by Van den Heever JA (at pp. 257E sqq.).

cases of embezzlement[221] as well as of furtum possessionis.[222] In that respect, again, it is the traditional Roman and Roman-Dutch approach that has prevailed.

2. The condictio ex causa furtiva

On the other hand—and that takes us back to the field of private law—the condictio ex causa furtiva also still lives on in modern South African law.[223] This would not be surprising if it were regarded as a special unjustified enrichment claim; the South African courts, after all, do not recognize a general enrichment action.[224] Very widely, however, this specific condictio is held to be a delictual remedy,[225] and thus one wonders what its practical significance might be: for the lex Aquilia, in its modern South African version, protects the injured party as comprehensively as its modern German statutory counterpart.[226] Textbooks on delict thus hardly ever mention the condictio ex causa furtiva, but here and there, though very rarely, it still becomes the subject of a court decision. A recent case in point is *Clifford v. Farinha*.[227] The plaintiff had leased a BMW motorcar, which was subsequently, without his consent, taken and used by the defendant. When the defendant parked and left the car for a short while, it was stolen by a third party. What attracted the court to resort to the condictio ex causa furtiva was the rule of fur semper in mora. The defendant had secured the windows of the car and locked its doors. No fault was thus attributable to her as far as the loss of the car through (the second) theft was concerned, and the actio legis Aquiliae therefore appeared to be unavailable.[228] But since she had herself committed an

---

[221] Cf. *The State v. Nellmapius* 2 SAR 121 at 126 ("But this distinction [sc.: between theft and embezzlement] does not exist in the Roman-Dutch law. . . . Just as one may by our law commit theft by means of false pretences, so likewise may he commit theft by means of embezzlement"); De Wet en Swanepoel, op. cit., note 1, p. 317.

[222] Milton, op. cit., note 1, pp. 629 sq. ("[An owner] commits theft where he effects a contrectatio of his own property when someone else has a special property or interest in it of which the owner intends permanently to deprive him").

[223] The various actiones furti were already obsolete in Roman-Dutch law: cf. supra, note 179.

[224] Cf. supra, pp. 886 sq.

[225] *Minister van Verdediging v. Van Wyk* 1976 (1) SA 397 (T) at 400C–H; De Vos, *Verrykingsaanspreeklikheid*, p. 213; Pauw, (1976) 93 *SALJ* 399 sq.

[226] Cf. supra, p. 948.

[227] 1988 (4) SA 315 (W). The last cases before *Clifford v. Farinha* were that of *Minister van Verdediging v. Van Wyk* (supra, note 225) and *John Bell & Co. Ltd. v. Esselen* 1954 (1) SA 147 (A).

[228] *Clifford v. Farinha* 1988 (4) SA 315 (W) at 320D–E: "The difficulty experienced by the plaintiff in establishing Aquilian liability, on the facts of the present case is that the defendant's intentional acts . . . were not intended to cause the loss of the vehicle, while the act which proximately caused the loss of the vehicle—namely the theft by a third party—was not attributable to any fault on the part of the defendant." But quaere. The question is not so much whether the defendant was liable for the second theft but whether—under Aquilian principles—she was liable for her own act of furtum. If so, she was liable to pay damages, covering the plaintiff's interest in the car. The fact that this claim would normally (i.e. without the interference by the second thief) have been settled by way of restitution of the car is quite irrelevant. Cf., as far as German law is concerned (to which

act of furtum, she carried the risk of accidental loss or damage.[229] It is interesting to note that the defendant's conduct did not constitute theft in terms of South African criminal law, for it is a typical example of mere furtum usus. If that did not prevent the court from granting the condictio, we must be dealing here with the very last preserve in which the Roman notion of furtum survives in an unadulterated form.[230]

Cilliers AJ refers (at p. 321) when dealing with the principle of fur semper in mora), § 251 I BGB and Jens Peter Meincke, 1980 *Juristenzeitung* 677 sqq.

[229] *Minister van Verdediging v. Van Wyk* 1976 (1) SA 397 (T) turned on the same point. In that case the defendant had unlawfully taken the plaintiff's car and driven it to a dance. He parked the truck at a parking lot, where it caught fire and burnt out. The court applied the condictio ex causa furtiva because it allowed the plaintiff to recover the highest value of the stolen thing since the commission of the theft. Again, I think, the plaintiff could also have received the same amount (value of the truck before it burnt out) under Aquilian principles.

[230] *Clifford v. Farinha* 1988 (4) SA 315 (W) at 322G (". . . there is nothing to indicate that the Roman-Dutch writers . . ., in dealing with civil actions based on theft in its various manifestations, considered a civil claim to be dependent on the particular manifestation of theft also being a crime").

CHAPTER 29

Lex Aquilia I

I. ORIGIN AND CONTENT OF THE LEX AQUILIA

1. The essential data provided in the Digest

The lex Aquilia was undoubtedly the most important statutory enactment on Roman private law subsequent to the XII Tables. It was passed by an assembly of the plebs after it had been proposed by a tribune by the name of Aquilius (". . . lex Aquilia plebiscitum est, cum eam Aquilius tribunus plebis a plebe rogaverit"[1]). It repealed and superseded all earlier laws that had dealt with unlawful damage (to property)—XII Tables and others alike ("[l]ex Aquilia omnibus legibus, quae ante se de damno iniuria locutae sunt, derogavit, sive duodecim tabulis, sive alia quae fuit"[2]). The lex Aquilia was not particularly long or complex;[3] it contained three "chapters" (we would rather say sections or paragraphs), the second of which was no longer in use in classical Roman law ("[h]uius legis secundum quidem capitulum in desuetudinem abiit").[4] The first and the third chapters are preserved verbatim; they were quoted by Gaius in his commentary on the edictum provinciale (first chapter) and by Ulpian in his commentary on the Edict (third chapter), and these quotations have been incorporated into the Corpus Juris Civilis. Drafted no longer in the clumsy monumental style of the XII Tables nor, as yet, displaying the hairsplitting pedantry of the later Republican legislation,[5] they read as follows:

> "[Si quis] servum servamve alienum alienamve quadrupedem vel pecudem iniuria occiderit, quanti id in eo anno plurimi fuit, tantum aes dare domino damnas esto";[6]
>
> "Ceterarum rerum praeter hominem et pecudem occisos si quis alteri damnum faxit, quod usserit fregerit ruperit iniuria, quanti ea res erit in diebus triginta proximis, tantum aes domino dare damnas esto."[7]

---

[1] Ulp. D. 9, 2, 1, 1.

[2] Ulp. D. 9, 2, 1 pr. On the effect of this clausula derogatoria and on the provisions preceding the lex Aquilia, see Pernice, *Sachbeschädigungen*, pp. 21 sqq.; Van den Heever, *Aquilian Damages*, pp. 15 sqq. ("Oh how I wish that Ulpian had given us an inkling of these prior laws": Franciscus Balduinus); Kaser, *Altrömisches ius*, pp. 132 sqq.; Fritz Pringsheim, "The origin of the lex Aquilia", in: *Gesammelte Abhandlungen*, vol. II (1961), pp. 410 sqq.; J.M. Kelly, "The Meaning of the Lex Aquilia", (1964) 80 *LQR* 81 sqq.; von Lübtow, *Lex Aquilia*, pp. 22 sqq.; Lawson/Markesinis, pp. 2 sq.

[3] But see J.A. Crook, "Lex Aquilia", (1984) 72 *Athenaeum* 75 sq.

[4] Ulp. D. 9, 2, 27, 4.

[5] Nörr, *Causa mortis*, p. 128.

[6] Gai. D. 9, 2, 2 pr.

[7] Ulp. D. 9, 2, 27, 5.

2. The problem of the second chapter

This is practically all the information about the origin and content of the lex Aquilia with which we are provided by the Digest. A whole variety of questions remain open. Perhaps the most obvious one concerns the content of the second chapter. Generations of lawyers have engaged in speculations and conjectures. Johannes Voet, for instance, regarded it as probable that the second chapter dealt with the corruption of the morals of a slave ("de moribus servi corruptis"); the lex Aquilia was thus put together, he argued, "methodo quadam non inconcinna":

> "sic ut primum quidem caput de toto servo perempto, secundum de parte ejus nobiliore, puta animo corrupto, tertium autem de parte minus nobili, corpore scilicet laeso."[8]

As it turned out, this view was wide off the mark,[9] for the discovery (by Niebuhr) of the text of Gaius' *Institutes* in 1816[10] finally terminated all speculation. "Capite secundo," we read in Gai. III, 215, "adversus stipulatorem qui pecuniam in fraudem stipulatoris acceptam fecerit, quanti ea res est, tanti actio constituitur." An adstipulator was a person whom a stipulator asked to act as a kind of trustee and to recover what he (the stipulator) was owed by the promisor.[11] The adstipulator therefore took a promise of "idem" from the (first) stipulator's debtor. He was thus in a position to dispose over the claim and could, in particular, release the debtor from his obligation (by way of acceptilatio). Where he did so "in fraudem stipulatoris", he was liable under chapter two of the lex Aquilia to make good the loss.[12] Since the adstipulator normally acted at the request of the principal stipulator, the actio mandati was, of course, available too; and it was in fact the advent of this more convenient remedy that made the older action fall into obsolescence.[13]

---

[8] *Commentarius ad Pandectas*, Lib. IX, Tit. II, V.

[9] Ben Beinart, "Roman Law in South African Practice", (1952) 69 *SALJ* 157; for a collection of further conjectures (Cuiacius, Bynkershoek and many others) cf. Johannes van der Linden in his notes on Voet, *Commentarius ad Pandectas*, printed (in translation) in Percival Gane, *The Selective Voet*, vol. II (1955), p. 550; Glück, vol. 10, pp. 359 sqq.

[10] The manuscript was found in a Veronese library; it is a palimpsest: some works of St. Jerome had been written over the Gaius text.

[11] Siro Solazzi, *L'estinzione dell' obbligazione nel diritto romano* (2nd ed., 1935), pp. 72 sqq.; Frezza, *Garanzie*, vol. I, pp. 5 sqq.; Gaetano Scherillo, "L'adstipulator", (1963) 10 *RIDA* 241 sqq.; Kaser, *RPr* I, p. 660; Honsell/Mayer-Maly/Selb, p. 285. An adstipulatio was primarily applied when the stipulator wanted to make sure that payment would be made after his death; a direct stipulation post mortem was invalid: Gai. III, 117; Berger, *ED*, p. 352.

[12] For details cf. Lévy-Bruhl, "La deuxième chapitre de la loi Aquilia", (1958) 5 *RIDA* 507 sqq.; Giuseppe Grosso, "La distinzione fra 'res corporales' e 'res incorporales' e il secondo capo della 'lex Aquilia' ", in: *Synteleia Vincenzo Arangio-Ruiz*, vol. II (1964), pp. 791 sqq.; C. St. Tomulescu, "Les trois chapitres de la lex Aquilia", (1970) 21 *Iura* 191 sqq.; Bernhard Schebitz, *Berechnung als Ersatzes nach der lex Aquilia* (unpublished Dr. iur. thesis, Berlin, 1987), pp. 147 sqq.

[13] Gai. III, 216.

3. Dating the lex Aquilia

No palimpsest has as yet (like a deus ex machina) yielded a solution to the other disputes and uncertainties enveloping the early history of the lex Aquilia. To start with, unanimity does not even exist among modern scholars as to the date of its enactment; and any attempt to establish its policy background, the specific reason why or the occasion when the lex Aquilia was proposed, leads us inevitably even further into the field of speculation. A fairly strong body of opinion favours either the year 287 or 286 B.C. as the date of origin.[14] This view is based mainly on a passage in Theophilus' paraphrase of Justinian's *Institutes*,[15] where the lex Aquilia is connected with the so-called third secession of the plebs (to the mons Ianiculus); it is thus indirectly connected, too, with the passing of the lex Hortensia, which provided that plebiscites should have full binding force for the whole Roman people, plebs and patricians alike (". . . qua cautum est ut plebiscita universum populum tenerent").[16] The lex Aquilia may thus have been one of the very first plebiscita enacted as a consequence of the lex Hortensia. On the other hand, however, it must be taken into consideration that Theophilus wrote more than 800 years after the (alleged) event and that, furthermore, he mentions the origin of the lex quite incidentally, when dealing with the absence of the word "plurimi" from the third chapter of the lex.[17] Being a busy Dean of the Constantinople law faculty,[18] he may neither have had the time nor the interest to research thoroughly a historical detail that was hardly relevant for the purpose of his exposition.[19] He probably merely took over what he found in some source or other, which we, in turn, are no longer able to check. Whether or not he went even further (as Honoré suspects)[20] and blended various scraps of information, by a free association of ideas,

---

[14] Cf. e.g. Van den Heever, *Aquilian Damages*, p. 7; Ben Beinart, "Once More on the Origin of the lex Aquilia", 1956 *Butterworth's South African LR* 70; Theodor Joseph Gerke, "Geschichtliche Entwicklung der Bemessung der Ansprüche aus der 'Lex Aquilia' ", (1957) 23 *SDHI* 61; Watson, *Obligations*, p. 234; Thomas, *TRL*, p. 363; Kaser, *RPr* I, p. 161; Paul van Warmelo, "A propos de la loi Aquilia", (1980) 27 *RIDA* 333; Richard A. Bauman, *Lawyers in Republican Roman Politics* (1983), pp. 83 sqq.; Honsell/Mayer-Maly/Selb, p. 364; Hans Ankum, "Quanti ea res erit in diebus XXX proximis dans le troisième chapitre de la lex Aquilia: un fantasme florentin", in: *Religion, société et politique, Mélanges en hommage à Jacques Ellul* (1983), p. 171.

[15] Paraphrasis institutionum, Lib. IV, Tit. III, § 15.

[16] Gai. I, 3; plebiscita were thus practically equated to leges.

[17] This point is emphasized by W.M. Gordon, "Dating the lex Aquilia", 1976 *Acta Juridica* 316.

[18] Cf. A.M. Honoré, "The Background to Justinian's Codification", (1974) 48 *Tulane LR* 873. On Theophilus, who was also a member of the commission charged by Justinian with the drafting of the Institutes, cf. C. 1, 17, 2, 9 (". . . virum illustrem magistrum iurisque peritum in hac splendidissima civitate laudabiliter optimam legum gubernationem extendentem").

[19] A.M. Honoré, "Linguistic and Social Context of the Lex Aquilia", (1972) 7 *The Irish Jurist* 145 sq.

[20] (1972) 7 *The Irish Jurist* 145 sq.

into what appeared to him a plausible story:[21] his account can certainly not be regarded as incontestable authority for placing an exact date on the lex Aquilia. Nor, incidentally, does it provide a dependable basis for establishing the context within which the lex Aquilia originated. Beinart's view that the lex was introduced as a result of the disturbances preceding or accompanying the (third) secessio plebis[22] has therefore not found much support.[23]

Equally little support has, however, been attracted by Tony Honoré for his all too radical departure from the chronological framework suggested by the Byzantine sources. In his view,[24] the lex Aquilia was part of a legislative programme to ensure the preservation of property rights. Its main point was to substitute for the fixed penalties of the earlier law a more flexible and equitable assessment of the damages suffered by the victim of the wrong. Fixed penalties were acceptable as long as the value of the currency was stable. It was the second Punic war that brought about the first serious inflation and within a short period the weight of the "as"[25] was substantially reduced.[26] In this situation, according to Honoré, the lex Aquilia was necessary to protect the propertied classes against the effects of inflation. As a result, he suggests a date between about 209 and 195 B.C.[27] But this kind of argument provides at best plausibility, not proof.[28] Considering the economic context at the turn of the century, it is unlikely that the Romans still operated with fixed penalties; thus, one may perhaps deduce that the lex Aquilia could in any event hardly have been introduced at a later date. Nothing, however, compels one to believe that the Romans could not have found the transition from a fixed penalty to some kind of assessment of the actual damages convenient, or perhaps even necessary, at an earlier period.

---

[21] Gordon, 1976 *Acta Juridica* 315 sq. comments (sarcastically?): "It is, of course, well known that deans of faculties are accustomed to putting together scraps of information and blending them into what they hope will be a plausible story. . . ."

[22] 1956 *Butterworth's South African LR* 70 sqq.; he argues that the main purpose of the statute was to protect plebeian property owners and to enable them to exact reparations for the losses which they had suffered at the hands of the patricians.

[23] Cf. von Lübtow, *Lex Aquilia*, p. 16; Jolowicz/Nicholas, p. 275; Nörr, *Causa mortis*, pp. 126 sq.; but see, in support of Beinart, Bauman, op. cit., note 14, p. 83.

[24] (1972) 7 *The Irish Jurist* 145 sqq.

[25] On which see, for example, H. Chantraine, in: *Kleiner Pauly*, vol. I, col. 632 sqq.

[26] Cf., for example, Plinius, *Historia naturalis*, Lib. XXXIII, XIII (42 sqq.).

[27] (1972) 7 *The Irish Jurist* 149 sq. Cf. also Schebitz, op. cit., note 12, pp. 36 sqq. who, for different reasons than Honoré, argues in favour of a date around 210 B.C. For an overview of other opinions differing from the majority view, cf. Arnaldo Biscardi, "Sulla data della 'lex Aquilia' ", in: *Scritti in memoria di Antonio Giuffrè*, vol. I (1967), pp. 77 sqq.

[28] Cf. e.g. Nörr, *Causa mortis*, p. 128; against Honoré, see also Alan Watson, "Personal Injuries in the XII Tables", (1975) 43 *TR* 217; Georg Thielmann, " 'Actio utilis' und 'actio in factum'—Zu den Klagen im Umfeld der lex Aquilia", in: *Studi in onore di Arnaldo Biscardi*, vol. II (1982), p. 297; Schebitz, op. cit., note 12, pp. 31 sqq.

Most probably, the lex Aquilia was younger than the lex Hortensia;[29] by the middle of the 2nd century, on the other hand, it must already have been in force for quite a considerable period, for it would otherwise be surprising to find Marcus Iunius Brutus advocating, without further ado, an extensive application of one of the terms used in the third chapter.[30] Within the framework set by these dates, stylistic and linguistic arguments point to the first rather than the second half of the 3rd century.[31] This coincides roughly with the period suggested by the Byzantine sources;[32] and while certain details may over the centuries have got muddled, or may perhaps even have been conjured up,[33] it is unlikely that Theophilus should either have tried to mislead his readers or should himself have been completely misled by his sources as to—roughly—the period when the lex Aquilia was enacted. After all, at least up to the time of Ulpian, the history of this enactment appears to have been known:[34] hardly surprising if one considers its significance.

4. The composition of the lex Aquilia

The next of our open questions concerns the strange way in which the lex Aquilia was composed. The first chapter dealt with the wrongful killing of (male or female) slaves and of grazing animals (literally: four-footed beasts of the class of cattle), the third chapter provided a remedy for all other wrongful damage to property,[35] inflicted by burning, breaking or tearing. The second chapter, in turn, was concerned with a rather special situation, namely release of the debtor by an adstipulator in fraudem creditoris. It is obvious that chapters one and three belong together, and that chapter two is something of a corpus alienum in this context. True: all three chapters are, in a way, united by virtue of the fact that one person has caused another

---

[29] It may, however, have been validly enacted even before 286 (the year of the lex Hortensia) as a plebiscite, provided it was endorsed by the Senate; cf. Biscardi, *Scritti Giuffré*, p. 81; Honoré, (1972) 7 *The Irish Jurist* 146; Theo Mayer-Maly, (1974) 126 *Göttingische Gelehrte Anzeigen* 132; Nörr, *Causa mortis*, p. 128.

[30] Cf. Ulp. D. 9, 2, 27, 22 ("Si mulier pugno vel equa ictu a te percussa eiecerit, Brutus ait Aquilia teneri quasi rupto").

[31] Cf. e.g. Biscardi, *Studi Giuffré*, pp. 83 sqq.; von Lübtow, *Lex Aquilia*, pp. 16 sq.; Mayer-Maly, (1974) 226 *Göttingische Gelehrte Anzeigen* 132; G. Cardascia, "La Portée Primitive de la Loi Aquilia", in: *Daube Noster* (1974), pp. 53 sqq.; Kaser, *RPr* I, p. 161; Thomas, *TRL*, p. 363; Nörr, *Causa mortis*, pp. 124 sqq.; Honsell/Mayer-Maly/Selb, p. 364.

[32] Theophilus' statement is confirmed by the scholiast to Basilica 60, 3, 1. Bauman, op. cit., note 14, p. 83 thinks that the accounts of Theophilus and of the scholiast are based on different sources (which would be an argument in favour of their credibility). According to Nörr, *Causa mortis*, p. 127, the scholiast does in fact not link the lex Aquilia with the secessio plebis. Generally on the reliability of the two Byzantine statements on the lex Aquilia, see Gordon, 1976 *Acta Juridica* 315 sqq.

[33] Kaser, for instance, thinks that the connection between lex Aquilia and lex Hortensia is spurious (*RPr* I, p. 161); but cf. Honsell/Mayer-Maly/Selb, p. 364.

[34] Emphasized by Bauman, op. cit., note 14, p. 83.

[35] Cf. the summary given by Gai. III, 217.

damage—damage to a specific piece of property in the first and third instances, (pure) pecuniary loss in the second one. Gaius specifically tries to demonstrate this common thread running through the provisions of the lex Aquilia ("Qua et ipsa [sc.: secunda] parte legis damni nomine actionem introduci manifestum est.").[36] But this kind of rationalization does not take us very far.[37] It still remains to be explained why chapters one and three are separated in such a peculiar fashion; a rational legislator would hardly have structured the lex Aquilia in that manner.

The idea thus suggests itself that the provisions of the lex Aquilia were not drafted at one and the same time.[38] Ulpian, as we have seen,[39] refers to certain provisions of the XII Tables, as well as to "some other statute",[40] as having been replaced by the lex Aquilia. Since the XII Tables far from covered all the ground (regarding damage to res se moventes, we know only of a fine prescribed for the os fractum of a slave[41]), it is not at all unlikely that such a "lex alia", preceding the enactment of the lex Aquilia, did in fact exist and that it dealt with the most important case of damage to two (in an agrarian society) particularly vital pieces of movable property, namely the killing of slaves or grazing quadrupeds. This statute may have established fixed rates of compensation and was either published together with[42] or at a later date followed by[43] an enactment dealing with adstipulatio.[44] These were the predecessors of chapters one and two of the lex Aquilia which, in turn, set out to reform the rules on killing and also added a general clause dealing with damage to property "praeter hominem et pecudem occisos".[45] Chapter two could not yet be abandonded, since the actio mandati still had to be developed to provide a satisfactory solution to the problem of adstipulatio. Thus, the new provision was simply added as chapter three to the two old ones. This was practically much more

[36] Gai. III, 216.

[37] Cf. David Daube, "On the Use of the Term Damnum", in: *Studi in onore di Siro Solazzi* (1948), p. 155 ("Gaius' explanation is no explanation. It fails from whatever angle we look at it. It is one of the many rationalisations of historical difficulties undertaken by the Roman jurists").

[38] Cf., particularly, David Daube, "On the Third Chapter of the Lex Aquilia", (1936) 52 *LQR* 267 sq.; idem, *Studi Solazzi*, pp. 154 sqq.; Pringsheim, *Gesammelte Abhandlungen*, vol. II, pp. 410 sqq.

[39] Supra, note 2.

[40] Ulp. D. 9, 2, 1 pr. (". . . sive alia [lex] quae fuit").

[41] Tabula 8, 3; for all details cf. Artur Völkl, *Die Verfolgung der Körperverletzung im frühen Römischen Recht* (1984), pp. 144 sqq.

[42] Daube, (1936) 52 *LQR* 267 sq.

[43] Pringsheim, *Gesammelte Abhandlungen*, vol. II, p. 414.

[44] According to David Pugsley, "Si quis alteri damnum faxit", 1977 *Acta Juridica* 299, the three chapters were originally three different leges.

[45] According to Pringsheim, *Gesammelte Abhandlungen*, vol. II, pp. 410 sqq., chapter 3 had its predecessors, too. In fact, he detects five historical layers which succeeded each other in a logically and historically understandable manner. Pringsheim's analysis is based on the account provided by Gaius III, 210 sqq.

convenient (though not entirely satisfactory from a systematic point of view) than altering the whole structure of the existing statute.[46]

5. The text of the lex Aquilia

This leads us to the question of how far the text of the lex Aquilia, handed down to us by Gaius and Ulpian, is genuine. There may well have been certain linguistic modernizations:[47] the old-fashioned "erus" in chapter one was replaced by the word "dominus"[48] and "quadrupedemve pecudem" was probably changed into "quadrupedem vel pecudem";[49] on the other hand, archaisms such as "damnas" or "faxit" (in place of "fecerit") were retained. Such changes, of course, left the substance of the text unaffected. A prime candidate for a much more substantial interference[50] with the classical text is the phrase at the outset of chapter three: "Ceterarum rerum praeter hominem et pecudem occisos." Quite a few modern authors delete these words when they reproduce the text of chapter three;[51] according to a widespread view, the introductory "ceterarum rerum" is to be attributed either to Justinian's compilers or to Ulpian or perhaps even to alterations effected by Republican jurisprudence;[52] "praeter . . . occisos" is often regarded as an explanatory gloss that was also added only at a later stage.[53] According to Kaser, the whole passage is "presumably a retrospective summary of a number of specific provisions".[54] It is very unlikely, however, that Republican jurists would have tampered with the text of the lex Aquilia to such an extent. Republican leges and plebiscita were usually posted in such a way that

[46] Cf. Daube, (1936) 52 *LQR* 268, who argues that it requires a much more developed technique to amalgamate new and old rules than only to add the new ones to the old. He also suggests that it may have had some influence that, for a long time, statutes were written on stone; making an appendix was then easier than fitting in an interpolation. Cf., however, the reservations by Cardascia, *Daube Noster*, pp. 67 sq. and Schebitz, op. cit., note 12, pp. 9 sqq.

[47] But see Crook, (1984) 72 *Athenaeum* 76 (". . . all too likely that what was quoted as the lex Aquilia in the days of Gaius and Ulpian was a heavily modernized text into which a sprinkling of obvious archaisms had been reintroduced for verisimilitude").

[48] Cf. Ulp. D. 9, 2, 11, 6 ("Legis autem Aquiliae actio ero competit, hoc erat domino"); cf. also Gai. III, 154 a; Pernice, *Sachbeschädigungen*, pp. 14 sq.; von Lübtow, *Lex Aquilia*, p. 19; also, generally, Wittmann, *Körperverletzung*, pp. 44 sq.

[49] Cf. e.g. von Lübtow, *Lex Aquilia*, p. 19; Crook, (1984) 72 *Athenaeum* 70.

[50] A comprehensive reconstruction of both chapters one and three in general has been proposed by Pugsley, 1977 *Acta Juridica* 295, 302. His views have not, however, gained acceptance.

[51] Cf. e.g. Kelly, (1964) 80 *LQR* 78; von Lübtow, *Lex Aquilia*, p. 21; Wittmann, *Körperverletzung*, p. 40; Crook, (1984) 72 *Athenaeum* 77; Hausmaninger, *Lex Aquilia*, p. 7.

[52] Cf. e.g. Otto Lenel, (1922) 43 *ZSS* 577; De Zulueta, *Gaius II*, p. 210 ("It is as certain as such a thing can be that Ceterarum—occisos is a gloss"); Pringsheim, *Gesammelte Abhandlungen*, vol. II, p. 416; von Lübtow, *Lex Aquilia*, p. 21; Wittmann, *Körperverletzung*, pp. 39 sqq.; Schebitz, op. cit., note 12, pp. 114 sqq.

[53] Pernice, *Sachbeschädigungen*, p. 14; Lenel, (1922) 43 *ZSS* 575; H.F. Jolowicz, "The Original Scope of the Lex Aquilia and the Question of Damages", (1922) 38 *LQR* 221; von Lübtow, *Lex Aquilia*, p. 21.

[54] *RPr* I, p. 161 (trans. Honoré, (1972) 7 *The Irish Jurist* 138); cf. also the interpretation by Cardascia, *Daube Noster*, pp. 60 sq.

anybody was able to read them;[55] the term "figere" (to affix) was sometimes used, metaphorically, to say that a law had been enacted. Later on the authentic version was kept in an archives, either in the aerarium Saturni or in the temple of Ceres on the forum Romanum;[56] and although the Roman system of collecting, filing and recording legal enactments was defective,[57] a reliable text was nevertheless fairly easily accessible. The lex Aquilia was of considerable importance, and it was regularly commented upon from the time of M. Iunius Brutus[58] and Quintus Mucius Scaevola.[59] Neither is it imaginable under these circumstances that substantial alterations crept in as a result of simple carelessness, nor that the text was falsified;[60] the Roman jurists were, of course, aware of the distinction between the actual content of an enactment and the supplementing and interpretative activities of magistrates and jurisprudence.[61] Naturally, this applies to Ulpian too. He would hardly have purported to give a direct quotation (". . . ait eadem lex Aquilia") and then proceeded to throw in explanatory glosses. If there was an interference with the text, it must therefore be attributed to the (Justinianic) compilers. There are, however, no convincing reasons to suspect the introductory "ceterarum rerum"; neither the generalizing phrase as such nor the "genitive of respect"[62] is objectionable.[63] "Praeter hominem et pecudem occisos", on the other hand, appears to be faulty Latin.[64] Apart from that, it is strange that the drafters of the lex Aquilia should have used the words "homo" and "pecus" in order to refer to what they had previously specified as "servus" and "quadrupes pecus".[65] Tony Honoré[66] has drawn attention to the fact that the terms "homo" and "pecus" are used in the very next fragment from Ulpian's commentary on the Edict;[67] the commissioner in charge of excerpting this part of Ulpian's work probably lifted them from fr. 27, 6 and used them to construct his little gloss. This gloss, in

---

[55] For all details, see Fritz Schwind, *Zur Frage der Publikation im römischen Recht* (2nd ed., 1973), pp. 26 sqq.

[56] Dieter Nörr, "Texte zur lex Aquilia", in: *Iuris Professio, Festgabe für Max Kaser* (1986), p. 215; cf. also Honoré, (1972) 7 *The Irish Jurist* 139 sq.

[57] Honoré, loc. cit.

[58] Cf. Ulp. D. 9, 2, 27, 22.

[59] Cf. Paul. D. 9, 2, 31.

[60] Honoré, (1972) 7 *The Irish Jurist* 140.

[61] This point is emphasized by Nörr, *Causa mortis*, p. 125.

[62] "*Forensischer Genitiv*": Nörr, *Festgabe Kaser*, p. 216.

[63] Cf. Honoré, (1972) 7 *The Irish Jurist* 140 (who argues that the term "res" was used in an abstract sense before 120 B.C.) and Nörr, Festgabe Kaser, pp. 215 sq., who shows that the words "ceterarum rerum" were used (in a generalizing sense: as far as other matters are concerned) by the Roman legislator; further, see Pugsley, 1977 *Acta Juridica* 302.

[64] It should have been "praeter hominem et pecudem occisum". But see Crook, (1984) 72 *Athenaeum* 73.

[65] This discrepancy of terminology may, however, also be explicable on the basis that chapter three was drafted at another (later) time than chapter one.

[66] (1972) 7 *The Irish Jurist* 141.

[67] Ulp. D. 9, 2, 27, 6 ("Si quis igitur non occiderit hominem vel pecudem . . .").

turn, was thought to be necessary in order to give an authentic interpretation of "ceterarum rerum"; for without explanation "ceterarum rerum" can either be taken to mean "as regards things other than slaves and grazing animals" or "as to matters other than killing a slave or grazing animal".[68] Only in the second alternative was the mere wounding of slaves or grazing animals covered by the (third chapter of the) lex Aquilia.

II. THE ASSESSMENT OF THE SUM OF CONDEMNATION

1. Chapter one

We have already seen that the most important change brought about by the lex Aquilia was the transition from a system of fixed penalties to a more flexible assessment of the damages suffered by the victim of the wrong. This assessment, however, appears to have been (at least from a modern point of view) rather odd. The judge was not instructed to determine (for instance:) "quod actoris interest", but "quanti id in eo anno plurimi fuit" (chapter one) and "quanti ea res erit in diebus triginta proximis" (chapter three). Where a slave or grazing animal had been killed (first chapter), the wrongdoer thus had to pay the owner the highest value which that object had had during the "previous year". Previous to what? That was problematic (and consequently controversial) in cases where the slave or animal had first been (mortally) wounded and only died at a later date. According to Julian, the year had to be calculated from the time the wound had been inflicted, Celsus regarded the time of death as relevant.[69] But what was the sense of throwing the calculation back into the past? Did those who drafted the lex Aquilia want to make up for the fact that, prices being unsteady, "the owner of the slave might not have sold him just at the time when the wrong was committed?"[70] More likely is another explanation.[71] If a slave was killed, the death sometimes occurred as a result of a wound

[68] Honoré, (1972) 7 *The Irish Jurist* 140 sq. Nörr, *Festgabe Kaser*, p. 216, incidentally, regards even this part of the text as (substantially) genuine; so do Pugsley, 1977 *Acta Iuridica* 302 sq. and Schebitz, op. cit., note 12, pp. 114 sqq.

[69] Ulp. D. 9, 2, 21, 1; cf. Pringsheim, *Gesammelte Abhandlungen*, vol. II, p. 416.

[70] Daube, (1936) 52 *LQR* 259; cf. also von Lübtow, *Lex Aquilia*, p. 120; but see Pringsheim, *Gesammelte Abhandlungen*, vol. I, pp. 416 sq. Cardascia, *Daube Noster*, pp. 63 sq. draws attention to the fact that even in an economy where prices are stable (as in Rome during the first half of the 3rd century B.C.) the value of slaves and grazing animals (that is, of the most important work tools in an agrarian society) must have been subject to seasonal fluctuations. Hence the time period of one year, to take into account the fact that the delict might have happened during the bad season, and to allow the plaintiff to make good his true loss. Cf. also F.P. van den Heever, *Aquilian Damages*, p. 9; but see Pugsley, 1977 *Acta Juridica* 298 sq.; Pieter Pauw, "Once Again on the Origin of the Lex Aquilia", (1978) 95 *SALJ* 188.

[71] Kaser, *RPr* I; p. 161; Honsell/Mayer-Maly/Selb, pp. 365 sq.; Hausmaninger, *Lex Aquilia*, p. 28; cf. also Lawson/Markesinis, p. 5; Schebitz, op. cit., note 12, pp. 63 sqq.

that he had received some time before. At the time of his death, he would thus have considerably decreased in value and it would have been inequitable to allow the owner merely to recover the value of an ailing slave with a mortal wound in his body. Even if the slave was stabbed and died immediately, it was at least arguable that for a second or so before his death he was mortally wounded and thus, at the time of death, without much value. But quite apart from such hairsplitting, the owner may often have found it difficult to prove how much a slave was worth at a specific point in time. It was in order to facilitate this proof and to cut off the kind of arguments mentioned, that the plaintiff was simply allowed to claim the highest value during the previous year: a somewhat rough-and-ready[72] but nevertheless fairly effective method of avoiding difficulties. Sometimes the owner of the slave (or grazing animal) thus received something over and above the compensation of his actual loss;[73] this could occur, for instance, where the slave had already decreased in value due to a previous, unrelated injury. If a valuable painter had his thumb cut off,[74] it was, in a way, quite fortunate for the owner, if he was subsequently killed within a year after that injury had occurred; for under chapter one of the lex Aquilia the owner received "quanti fuit priusquam artem cum pollice amisisset":[75] not the value of a thumbless invalid, but that of a highly skilled painter.[76]

2. Chapter three

(a) *Chapters one and three compared*

The manner in which the compensation was determined in chapter one was thus reasonably straightforward. More particularly, since one was dealing with the complete destruction of an object, reference to its real value made good sense. We can hardly expect to find a refined assessment of the concrete "quod actoris interest" in these early days, and restoration of the value of the slave (or animal) provided the plaintiff with what he was at least typically "interested" in. A good deal more mysterious is the position under chapter three. "Quanti ea res erit in diebus triginta proximis": this clause differs in three important respects from the one contained in chapter one, but appears to correspond with it regarding the very issue in which one would least expect such correspondence. First of all, the period here is not one year, but merely 30 days. Secondly, this period is not retrospective but prospective: it is the 30 days *after* the infliction of the wound that

[72] Lawson/Markesinis, p. 5.

[73] Gai. III, 214 (". . . quo fit ut quis plus interdum consequatur quam ei damnum datum est").

[74] Iul./Ulp. D. 9, 2, 23, 3.

[75] Iul./Ulp. D. 9, 2, 23, 3.

[76] For another example, see Ulp. D. 9, 2, 23, 5.

matter, not the month preceding this event. Thirdly, the word "plurimi" is missing in the third chapter of the lex Aquilia. And fourthly (and perhaps most surprisingly): the principle of the real value seems to determine assessment of the compensation here, too ("quanti *ea res* erit"); irrespective, therefore, of whether a slave was killed (chapter one) or whether he had merely been bumped into or scratched, the owner could claim his full value. Damage worth threepence, slave worth 300 pounds: the wrongdoer had to pay 300 pounds.[77]

(b) "Erit" or "fuit" ("fuerit")?

Of these four propositions—the one more mystifying than the other—only the first has remained uncontested; nobody has as yet disputed that the third chapter did in fact specify a period of 30 days. The tradition of discarding the word "erit", on the other hand, goes back to Gaius and Ulpianus. Gaius explains "[h]oc tamen capite non quanti in eo anno, sed quanti in diebus XXX proximis ea res fuerit, damnatur is qui damnum dederit",[78] and Ulpian (D. 9, 2, 29, 8) has "fuit" in place of "erit" (or "fuerit"). Both of them appear to read the time backwards rather than forwards. Gregor Haloander, one of the most famous philologists of the late Middle Ages, followed suit. In his edition of the Digest he replaced the "erit" of the Florentina by "fuit".[79] Many modern authors approve of this emendation;[80] they usually regard "erit" as a scribal error[81] and are thus able to explain the retrospective period in the same way as the "annus" of chapter one. Having thus (possibly) resolved one problem, the proponents of this view are, however, immediately faced with another: "quanti ea res fuit in diebus triginta proximis" does not make much sense if any moment of the last month might come into question. In other words: we would expect a reference to the highest value, as indeed it was contained in chapter one. Again, Sabinus already saw the problem and resolved it by way of interpretation: "proinde habendum ac si etiam hac parte plurimi verbum adiectum esset."[82] Gaius in fact attempted to provide a rationalization: the legislator had thought it sufficient to have used the

[77] Daube, *Roman Law*, p. 67; cf. also Van den Heever, *Aquilian Damages*, p. 12.
[78] III, 218; cf. also *Inst.* IV, 3, 14.
[79] Cf. n. 17 on p. 158 of the Mommsen/Krüger edition.
[80] Pernice, *Sachbeschädigungen*, pp. 14 sq.; Lenel, (1922) 43 *ZSS* 575; Max Kaser, *Quanti ea res est* (1935) pp. 168 sq. (but cf. today *RPr* I, p. 161); Schulz, *CRL*, p. 588; Gerke, (1957) 23 *SDHI* 78 sqq.; Pringsheim, *Gesammelte Abhandlungen*, vol. II, pp. 416 sq.; Medicus, *Id quod interest*, p. 239; Geoffrey MacCormack, "On the Third Chapter of the Lex Aquilia", (1970) 5 *The Irish Jurist* 169 sq.; Tomulescu, (1970) 21 *Iura* 195 sq.; von Lübtow, *Lex Aquilia*, p. 21; Pugsley, 1977 *Acta Juridica* 305; Van Warmelo, (1980) 27 *RIDA* 347; Ankum, *Mélanges Ellul*, pp. 171 sqq.; Behrends, 1985 *Juristische Schulung* 880.
[81] Cf., in particular, Ankum, *Mélanges Ellul*, pp. 180 sq.
[82] Gai. III, 218; cf. also Ulp. D. 9, 2, 29, 8.

word "plurimi" in the first chapter[83] (sc.: and did not deem it necessary to repeat it in the third).

(c) *The meaning of "ea res"*

As far as the fourth of the above-mentioned propositions is concerned, modern writers are split down the middle. The traditional, prevailing view has been indeed that the principle of the real value applied to the third as it did to the first chapter.[84] It is relatively easy to point out the absurdities to which this approach is apt to lead and David Daube has done so with nearly irresistible panache. "There is no child", he writes,

> "that does not at some time or other scratch a letter or two, or even four, on the wall of a house. At Rome, on the basis of the prevalent view, the father would have to pay for the entire estate—not just the house, but the grounds as well. . . . That in a society governed by this kind of regulation nobody will be rich or poor for long is evident . . . Nothing mattered when all material life became a joke through the third chapter of this statute, which equated damaging with destruction."[85]

And he concludes:

> "[N]o economy could go on for a fortnight with the regulation ascribed to the Romans by the orthodox school; maybe it would not be viable for one day."[86]

Daube therefore suggests that one should read the phrase "quanti ea res erit" (not "fuit"!) in the sense of "the sum this affair will come to".[87] Res does not refer to the object that has been damaged, and what the judge has to assess is therefore not the full value of that object but the actual damage suffered by the plaintiff (i.e., in particular, the mere difference between the full value and the reduced value after interference).[88] But why does one have to wait for 30 days? Because, answers Daube, the plaintiff has to be given some time to see how the injury develops.[89] Immediately after its infliction the plaintiff may still be in the dark: he does not know whether his slave will recover or remain disabled, whether the cost of hospitalization will be high or low, and so on. On the other hand, a certain time limit was indispensable, lest the wrongdoer be responsible for every indisposition

---

[83] Gai. III, 218; cf. also *Inst.* IV, 3, 15 ("nam plebem Romanam, quae Aquilio tribuno rogante hanc legem tulit, contentam fuisse, quod prima parte eo verbo usa est").

[84] Lenel, (1922) 43 *ZSS* 577; Kaser, *Quanti ea res est*, p. 169; Schulz, *CRL*, p. 590; Gerke, (1957) 23 *SDHI* 79 sq.; Medicus, *Id quod interest*, p. 238; MacCormack, (1970) 5 *The Irish Jurist* 170; Van Warmelo, (1980) 27 *RIDA* 347.

[85] *Roman Law*, pp. 67, 68. It is great fun to read this whole *tour de force*.

[86] *Roman Law*, p. 71.

[87] Cf. (1936) 52 *LQR* 257.

[88] Daube's interpretation has been followed, at least essentially, by Watson, *Obligations*, pp. 234 sq.; Wittmann, *Körperverletzung*, pp. 40 sqq.; Cardascia, *Daube Noster*, pp. 53 sqq.; Kaser, *RPr* I, p. 161; Thielmann, *Studi Biscardi*, vol. II, pp. 299 sq.; Honsell/Mayer-Maly/Selb, p. 366; Hausmaninger, *Lex Aquilia*, p. 29; Schebitz, op. cit., note 12, pp. 165 sqq. All these authors reject the view that the full value could be claimed. But while some think (with Daube) that the plaintiff could recover his full interesse, others confine his claim to the diminution in value of the damaged object. Cf. also Pauw, (1978) 95 *SALJ* 189 sqq. (who argues that the question was approached in a flexible manner).

[89] (1936) 52 *LQR* 256.

which henceforth befell the injured person. A period of 30 days presents a reasonable compromise.

(d) The original scope of chapter three

There is, however, one obvious difficulty implicit in this explanation. The 30 days rule makes sense only in the case of damage to res se moventes: slaves, grazing quadrupeds and other animals. Where an inanimate object is damaged, the extent of the loss is clear immediately, and there is hardly any point in waiting another 30 days to see what happens. Daube is thus forced to postulate that the third chapter of the lex Aquilia applied originally only to the wounding of slaves and animals; damage to inanimate objects, far less momentous according to Daube, was only included by way of interpretatio in the second half of the 1st century B.C.[90]

Here we are entering another arena of scholarly dispute, namely the discussion about the original scope of chapter three. It hardly comes as a surprise to see that some authors even maintain that exactly the opposite development took place: at the time the lex was passed, the third chapter dealt only with the destruction of inanimate objects and it was subsequent juristic interpretation of the lex that brought in partial damage (to inanimate objects as well as to res se moventes). The protagonist of this view is Jolowicz,[91] and the main point of his theory is that it makes intelligible the "quanti ea res fuit" in its traditional interpretation: if the lex Aquilia originally envisaged only the destruction of property there was, of course, nothing odd about sticking to the principle of awarding the full value in chapters one as well as three. But is it really plausible to assume that damage to slaves or cattle (short of complete destruction—that is, killing) would not have been dealt with at all by the lex Aquilia? After all, even the XII Tables had already contained a rule concerning os fractum of a slave![92] Daube's theory, of course, provokes a similar objection, for it is hardly imaginable that Roman law could have been able to dispense with a comprehensive remedy for injury to chattels until the second half of the 1st century B.C. Another major weakness of both Jolowicz's and Daube's views lies in their assumption that considerable changes must have taken place between the date of the lex Aquilia and the end of the republican period: changes of which we find no traces in our sources; changes, furthermore, which even the lawyers of the classical age no longer remembered. Thus Daube admits that the original meaning of the third chapter was "utterly forgotten" already at the time of

[90] (1936) 52 *LQR* 255 sqq.; cf. also Schulz, *CRL*, p. 588; von Lübtow, *Lex Aquilia*, pp. 109 sq.; Cardascia, *Daube Noster*, pp. 53 sqq.; Alan Watson, "Personal Injuries in the XII Tables", (1975) 43 *TR* 214 sqq.; Schebitz, op. cit., note 12, pp. 116 sqq.

[91] H.F. Jolowicz, "The Original Scope of the lex Aquilia and the Question of Damages", (1922) 38 *LQR* 220 sqq.; cf. also Van Warmelo, (1980) 27 *RIDA* 340 sqq.

[92] Cf. supra, p. 958 (note 41).

Sabinus:[93] not a very plausible suggestion in view of the great practical importance of this provision, which must have been constantly before the courts.[94] Ultimately everything that is said or written about the original scope of chapter three is based on speculation, and some of the indirect evidence advanced can be used in such a manner that it fits both views. Thus both Jolowicz and Daube try to draw support from the words which describe the type of damnum relevant for chapter three: urere, frangere, rumpere. Jolowicz interprets them as expressing damage of a total kind. An object that has been burnt, smashed or broken must be damaged to such an extent that it is virtually useless.[95] Daube, on the other hand, regards the three words as particularly appropriate to describe three different kinds of wounding. The terms "frangere" and "rumpere" were in fact taken over from the XII Tables ("os fractum", "membrum ruptum"), where they had also not referred to inanimate objects but only to injury to living beings.[96]

(e) "Is anything . . . exempt from doubt?"

It may have become apparent by now that the third chapter of the lex Aquilia is like an equation with too many variables. Whatever view one embraces, it appears to be impossible to adduce the type of evidence that would exclude any possibility of alternative solutions.[97] Much of the evidence that we have can be explained one way or the other. Take the controversy about "erit" or "fuit" ("fuerit"). Of course, "erit" can be explained as a copyist's slip. This kind of slip can happen, and thus the explanation is not, per se, implausible. In a way, however, textual emendations always smack of an emergency solution and may therefore not appear to be entirely satisfactory. But even this challenge can be countered. If, at the time when Ulpian wrote, damages under the third chapter were assessed on the basis of the loss suffered, "quanti ea res erit" can be taken to mean "how much the affair will come to (when the items of loss have been added up)".[98] If one accepts this interpretation

---

[93] (1936) 52 *LQR* 264 sq.

[94] Daube himself, in another context, points to the "enormous prestige of the lex Aquilia in the first few centuries of its existence" (*Studi Solazzi*, p. 149). But see Nörr, "Zur Interdependenz von Prozessrecht und materiellem Recht am Beispiel der lex Aquilia", (1987) 6 *RJ* 101, 112 (the lex Aquilia was of little practical relevance).

[95] (1922) 38 *LQR* 220 sqq.

[96] (1936) 52 *LQR* 255, 260. Burning does not appear in the XII Tables, but Daube draws attention to the fact that in biblical law burning, breaking and crushing are used to describe three different types of wounding. On "urere frangere rumpere", in this context, cf. further MacCormack, (1970) 5 *The Irish Jurist* 171 sqq.; Watson, (1975) 43 *TR* 215 sqq.; Artur Völkl, "Quanti ea res erit in diebus triginta proximis. Zum dritten Kapitel der lex Aquilia", (1977) 24 *RIDA* 465 sqq.; Van Warmelo, (1980) 27 *RIDA* 339 sq.; on membrum ruptum and os fractum in the XII Tables, cf. Peter Birks, "The Early History of Iniuria", (1969) 37 *TR* 179 sqq.; Völkl, op. cit., note 41, pp. 40 sqq., 144 sqq.

[97] "The proper verdict is non liquet": De Zulueta, *Gaius II*, p. 212; "Is anything . . . exempt from doubt?": Crook, (1984) 72 *Athenaeum* 75.

[98] This argument has been advanced by MacCormack, (1970) 5 *The Irish Jurist* 170.

(not, however, a particularly convincing one), even the assumption of a scribal error is unnecessary. Those, on the other hand, who wish to take "erit" in D. 9, 2, 27, 5 at its face value and who are thus prepared to throw the calculation forward,[99] have to face the objection that Ulpian at another place uses "fuit", whereas Gaius has "fuerit".[100] Of course it would hardly be acceptable to postulate two scribal mistakes. But it may be argued that the law had changed over the centuries:[101] while the lex Aquilia originally had "erit", it was applied in classical times as if it had "fuit". As we have seen, there are certain problems with this kind of scenario.[102] Again, however, an alternative explanation for the use of "fuit" or "fuerit" is at hand.[103] The lex Aquilia itself determined the matter from the moment of the injury: the plaintiff was to receive compensation for such consequences as would appear within the next 30 days after the infliction of the wound (hence the use of "erit"). The relevant formula of the lex Aquilia, however, which had to be applied when the plaintiff brought his suit, approached the matter, not unnaturally, from the point of view of the iudex. After all, the iudex had to be instructed to assess the damage which the plaintiff "had" suffered; at the time when he became concerned with the matter, the 30-day period lay in the past (although it was still the one *following* the injury). The formula of the actio legis Aquiliae, as proposed in the Edict, therefore used the past tense; and it is this phrasing that was taken up by Ulpian in D. 9, 2, 29, 8 and Gaius in III, 218 of his *Institutes*.

All in all, I think, firstly, that in case of doubt the texts should be taken as they stand and, secondly, that D. 9, 2, 27, 5, the text where Ulpian purports to give the actual wording of the lex, should be the cardinal point of our investigation into chapter three.[104] It follows, therefore, that "erit" should be taken to be authentic and that the time rule has to be read forwards. If, furthermore, one accepts "ceterarum

[99] J. A. Iliffe, " 'Thirty days hath *Lex Aquilia*' ", (1958) 5 *RIDA* 493 sqq.; Watson, *Obligations*, pp. 234 sq.; Wittmann, *Körperverletzung*, pp. 40 sqq.; John M. Kelly, "Further Reflections on the '*Lex Aquilia*' ", in: *Studi in onore di Edoardo Volterra*, vol. I (1971), pp. 239 sqq.; Thomas, *TRL*, p. 364; Völkl, (1977) 24 *RIDA* 478; Thielmann, *Studi Biscardi*, vol. II, pp. 299 sq.; Crook, (1984) 72 *Athenaeum* 74; Hausmaninger, *Lex Aquilia*, p. 29; Schebitz, op. cit., note 12, pp. 116 sqq.—Nörr, *Festgabe Kaser*, p. 217 contemplates retrospectivity in spite of "erit"; Cardascia, *Daube Noster*, pp. 72 sq. argues the other way round—that one can maintain prospectivity despite reading "fuit".

[100] Cf. supra, p. 963.

[101] Cf. e.g. Daube, (1936) 52 *LQR* 261; cf. also, most recently, Schebitz, op. cit., note 12, pp. 114 sqq.

[102] Cf. supra, pp. 959 sq., 965 sq. (note 94).

[103] It has been advanced by Wittmann, *Körperverletzung*, pp. 40 sqq.; approved by Honsell/Mayer-Maly/Selb, p. 366; Schebitz, op. cit., note 12, pp. 123 sq.; rejected by Ankum, *Mélanges Ellul*, p. 178. For exactly the opposite view cf. Van Warmelo, (1980) 27 *RIDA* 347.

[104] Cf. also Daube, *Studi Solazzi*, p. 146 (lectio difficilior); Cardascia, *Daube Noster*, p. 59.

rerum" as genuine,[105] it is not unreasonable to attribute the same abstract, or generalizing, meaning to the word "res" in "quanti ea res erit" as in "ceterarum rerum": if in the one case we may translate "matters other than the foregoing", we can just as well read the other clause in the sense of "as much as this affair will be". In other words: the wrongdoer did not have to pay the full value (nor, probably, as yet, the full financial loss, in the sense of quod interest, of the victim) but merely the diminution in value of the object damaged. Acceptance of the "ceterarum rerum" clause also implies that the third chapter did not originally have only a limited scope of application: from the time of its enactment it comprised injury to slaves and grazing animals *and* damage (partial damage as well as complete destruction) to all other objects.[106] Thus it applied to all forms of damage to property, with the exception of the killing of slaves and grazing quadrupeds. As a result of this, we can no longer maintain Daube's rationalization of the significance of the "quanti ea res erit in diebus triginta proximis" clause: with regard to inanimate objects it would not have been necessary to wait for 30 days in order to assess the damage. But an alternative explanation is available. The period of 30 days may well have been taken over from the XII Tables;[107] for in the olden days the condemned debtor had been granted exactly this period of time to pay or render restitution and thus to avert the harsh consequences of manus iniectio.[108] This kind of regime made perfect sense under the lex Aquilia too:[109] before the judge could be asked to assess the damages, a period of 30 days had to elapse; within this time-span a wound might have healed, the debtor might have paid a sum that satisfied the other party, he might have

---

[105] Cf. supra, p. 960.

[106] Cf. e.g. Völkl, (1977) 24 *RIDA* 465 sqq.; also MacCormack, (1970) 5 *The Irish Jurist* 171 sqq. MacCormack agrees that the third chapter covered all types of objects, but he reads the "quanti ea res" clause backwards (fuit). In order to avoid the absurdities pointed out above, he is thus forced to argue that "urere frangere rumpere" originally expressed types of physical damage, which constituted a serious injury to a slave, animal or other object. Thus, it makes good sense to say that the owner received the highest value within the previous year (along similar lines, see Van den Heever, *Aquilian Damages*, pp. 11 sqq.; Beinart, 1956 *Butterworth's South African LR* 77; Iliffe, (1958) 5 *RIDA* 502 sqq.; Detlef Liebs, "Damnum, damnare, damnas", (1968) 85 *ZSS* 197). But it is implausible that no protection should have existed against less serious (but more frequent!) forms of damage.

[107] Cf. Kelly, *Studi Volterra*, vol. I, pp. 240 sq.; Völkl, (1977) 24 *RIDA* 477 sqq.

[108] Cf. generally Kaser, *RZ*, p. 97.

[109] Why did the first chapter not provide for a similar 30-day period? Cf. the suggestions and arguments advanced by Kelly and Völkl, loc. cit. Perhaps the policy reasons in favour of retrospectivity (cf. supra, pp. 961 sq.) prevailed as far as chapter one was concerned; with regard to chapter three, on the other hand, retrospectivity à la chapter one was out of the question, if one accepts that chapter three gave the plaintiff a claim only for the diminution in value, not for the full value of the object damaged. "What is the 'highest value' in the last thirty days of a crack in a wine-jar?" (Kelly, *Studi Volterra*, vol. I, p. 237).

repaired the sedan chair that he had damaged or he might have given his creditor a new one.[110]

III. THE NATURE OF THE ACTIO LEGIS AQUILIAE

1. The reipersecutory character of the remedy

(a) Chapter one

What was the nature of the actio legis Aquiliae de damno iniuria dato?

---

[110] The weak point in the scenario sketched above appears to lie, at first blush, in Gai. III, 218 and Ulp. D. 9, 2, 29, 8, and here not so much in the use of the words "fuit" and "fuerit" (on these cf. supra, p. 967), but in the suggestion to read "plurimi" into the text of the third chapter. Does that mean that the classical jurists reckoned backwards (as is usually taken for granted)? If that was so, we face the problem of a change of "interpretation" from "erit" to "fuit" sometime between 286 B.C. and classical law. This is indeed a serious obstacle, since such an "interpretation" against the words of the lex is neither very likely per se (cf. supra, pp. 960, 965 sq. (note 94)), nor would it have made much sense, since it would have involved a retrogression from a more refined to a more "primitive" way of assessing the damage (but see Völkl, (1977) 24 *RIDA* 479 sqq. for an interesting attempt to resolve these problems—which, incidentally, are in any event less serious than those faced by adherents of the "scribal error" viewpoint; for a detailed list of problems arising if one reads "fuit" or "fuerit" into the original text of the lex Aquilia, cf. Cardascia, *Daube Noster*, pp. 54 sqq). Yet, it is by no means necessary to assume that the classical jurists calculated the 30-day period backwards (cf. also Wittmann, *Körperverletzung*, p. 41). They may in fact have retained "erit" without, however, understanding any longer why such a period had originally been inserted into chapter three: (legal) history was not the strong point of the Roman jurists. This would be particularly likely if the 30-day period was reminiscent of, or tied up with, procedural niceties from the days of the XII Tables and the legis actiones, which were long since obsolete by Sabinus' time. (If the lex Aquilia dates from the first half of the third century, litigation resulting from it would, at first, have been by legis actio.) Since nobody understood (or approved of) the rationale of the 30-day rule, one simply applied it, under different auspices, as if it contained the word "plurimi" (under the influence of the first chapter, with which chapter three had by now been combined for about 300 years). The practical effect of this change of perspective was that the plaintiff was to receive quanti ea res est, to be assessed at that time within a 30-day period after the injury, when it was the highest. Thus, if a slave had been injured and the wound had nearly healed within the month following the injury, the diminution in value of the slave had to be assessed at the time of the injury, not at the time when the slave had nearly reached his full value again; if, on the other hand, the slave became progressively more ill (that is, less valuable), the end of the 30-day period had to be chosen for the assessment of the diminution in value. It is, therefore, submitted that the classical lawyers attributed exactly the kind of rationale to the 30-day rule in chapter three that, according to Daube, was assigned to it by those who had drafted that part of the lex Aquilia. Of course, this rationale—and with it the 30-day rule—applied only to res se moventes, not to the (more frequent) cases of damage to inanimate objects. This may be one of the reasons why the classical lawyers appear to have been so surprisingly uninterested in it—we do not find any case law concerning the 30-day rule in the Digest. There is, however, one important text which indirectly alludes to the 30-day rule and which appears to me to confirm the view advanced above. In D. 9, 2, 24 Paulus deals with the case where somebody has confessed to having injured a slave; but then it turns out that the slave is not injured at all. Paulus poses two (rhetorical) questions: ". . . aestimationem cuius vulneris faciemus? vel ad quod tempus recurramus?" The text (genuine; cf. Watson, *Obligations*, p. 235; also Völkl, (1977) 24 *RIDA* 483) implies that the classical lawyers regarded aestimatio vulneris as relevant for the award of the sum into which the wrongdoer had to be condemned. The second question refers to a time which has to be taken into account for the purposes of aestimatio vulneris. One can draw the inference that the 30-day rule was still applied. If that was so, it can, however, hardly have been reckoned backwards. For how can one assess a wound (within) 30 days before it has been inflicted?

We have seen that delictual remedies could either be penal in character or reipersecutory, or both penal and reipersecutory at one and the same time.[111] The actio legis Aquiliae belonged to the latter category: "[r]em vero et poenam persequimur . . . ex h[aec] caus[a]", as we are informed by Gaius.[112] It was the most interesting example[113] of an actio mixta.[114] On the one hand, it therefore aimed at compensating the injured party for his loss; hence the emphasis, in chapter one, on the value of the slave or grazing animal that had been killed. Restoration of that value was perhaps a somewhat rough, but nevertheless normally not entirely unsatisfactory method of providing the plaintiff with compensation. In the course of time, however,[115] more refined considerations came to prevail. And whilst over the centuries aestimatio corporis always remained the basis for assessing the sum in which the defendant had to be condemned, certain further items came to be included, if that was required in an individual case. If, for instance, a slave who had been instituted heir was killed, the award of merely the value of the slave would not have compensated the plaintiff for his actual loss. For had his slave still been alive, he could have ordered him to accept the inheritance: with the result that it would have vested in himself. Of this chance he was deprived as a result of the slave's death and thus Neratius allowed the value of the inheritance to be included in the sum which the defendant had to pay under chapter one.[116] Gaius took the same view: ". . . non enim tantum ipsius

---

[111] Cf. supra, pp. 918 sqq.
[112] IV, 9.
[113] "Prototype": Kaser, op. cit., note 84, p. 167.
[114] *Inst.* IV, 6, 19. In favour of a dual nature of the lex Aquilia even in classical law (whether under the name of actio mixta or not; cf. supra, pp. 919 sq. (note 114)) cf. e.g. Ernst Levy, *Privatstrafe und Schadensersatz im klassischen römischen Recht* (1915), pp. 135 sqq.; Kaser, *RPr* I, p. 621; Honsell/Mayer-Maly/Selb, p. 365. Contra: Schulz, *CRL*, p. 589; von Lübtow, *Lex Aquilia*, pp. 36 sqq., who attribute a purely penal character to the actio legis Aquiliae. They regard many of the texts contained in the Digest as interpolated and do not even believe Gaius (". . . has been added by a man who had in mind Gai. 4, 171": Schulz, p. 589); but cf. Mayer-Maly (1974) 226 *Göttingische Gelehrte Anzeigen* 133. More recently, Hans Ankum, "Actions by which we claim a thing (res) and a penalty (poena) in classical Roman law", (1982) 24 *BIDR* 31 sqq. has also argued that the actio legis Aquiliae was purely penal. While rejecting von Lübtow's opinion as "[t]otally inacceptable" (p. 17), he argues that Gaius made a mistake (p. 19). Generally, one tends to believe that at least the penal element (if not also the compensatory one) was characteristic of the lex Aquilia from early on. For a different view (the original lex Aquilia did not have a penal character at all), cf. Cardascia, *Daube Noster*, p. 63.

Since the actio legis Aquiliae was an actio mixta, it could not be cumulated with other reipersecutory actions; cf. Levy, *Konkurrenz*, vol. II, pp. 1 sqq.; Kaser, *RPr* I, p. 621; Hausmaninger, *Lex Aquilia*, pp. 35 sqq.; contra: von Lübtow, *Lex Aquilia*, pp. 69 sqq.
[115] But see Geoffrey MacCormack, "Aquilian Studies", (1975) 41 *SDHI* 67 sqq., who regards it as misleading to picture the development of the law as a progression from objective (market) value to subjective interest. In his opinion, it cannot be assumed that the jurists, even at the time of the enactment of the lex Aquilia, applied inflexibly some particular standard for the assessment of compensation.
[116] Cf. Ulp. D. 9, 2, 23 pr.

pretium aestimatur, sed et hereditatis amissae quantitas."[117] Similar considerations prevailed if one member of a troupe of actors or musicians was killed, or a horse that formed part of a chariot team: not only did the dead person (or animal) as such have to be taken into account, but also the amount by which the others had decreased in value.[118] These were the kinds of examples that induced Gaius to state, in a more general vein, "si servo occiso plus dominus capiat damni quam pretium servi sit, id quoque aestimatur";[119] Paulus referred to "other heads of damage necessarily connected"[120] (sc.: with the damaging event—"causae corpori cohaerentes").[121] Thus there was a gradual relaxation of the rather inflexible measure of "damages" set by chapter one: a relaxation brought about by way of interpretation[122] and based upon a more and more individualizing approach. By the end of the classical period assessment of "quanti id . . . fuit" was no longer confined to the value of the object itself plus certain typical forms of consequential loss, but aimed at quod actoris interest: account had to be taken of whatever damages the individual plaintiff in each specific case had suffered as a result of the damaging event.[123] "[H]oc iure utimur, ut eius quod interest fiat aestimatio"—this statement of Ulpian marks the end of the development.[124] The practical consequences of this new formula can be gauged from the example discussed in D. 9, 2, 23, 4 (also a fragment taken from Ulpian's commentary of the Edict):[125] a

[117] III, 212. For further discussion of the problems arising from the killing of slaves instituted as heirs, cf. Ulp. D. 9, 2, 15, 1 in fine; Marci. D. 9, 2, 16; Ulp. D. 9, 2, 23, 1 and 2; Gerke, (1957) 23 *SDHI* 66 sqq.; Alan Rodger, "Damages for the Loss of an Inheritance", in: *Daube Noster* (1974), pp. 289 sqq.; MacCormack, (1975) 41 *SDHI* 71 sqq.; Schebitz, op. cit., note 12, pp. 290 sqq.

[118] Paul. D. 9, 2, 22, 1 ("non solum . . . perempti corporis aestimatio facienda est, sed et eius ratio haberi debet, quo cetera corpora depretiata sunt"); Gai. III, 212 ("non solum occisi fit aestimatio, sed eo amplius id quoque computatur, quod ceteri qui supersunt depretiati sunt"); for a recent analysis, see Schebitz, op. cit., note 12, pp. 273 sqq.

[119] III, 212.

[120] Trans. C.F. Kolbert, in: *Justinian, The Digest of Roman Law, Theft, Rapine, Damage and Insult* (1979), p. 80.

[121] Paul. D. 9, 2, 22, 1.

[122] "Illud non ex verbis legis, sed ex interpretatione placuit . . .": *Inst.* IV, 3, 10.

[123] Cf. e.g. Kaser, *RPr* I, p. 621; MacCormack, (1975) 41 *SDHI* 69 sqq.; Lawson/Markesinis, pp. 35 sq.; Hans Ankum, "L'actio de pauperie et l'actio legis Aquiliae dans le droit romain classique", in: *Studi in onore di Cesare Sanfilippo*, vol. II (1982), pp. 47 sqq.; Honsell/Mayer-Maly/Selb, pp. 367 sq.; Hausmaninger, *Lex Aquilia*, pp. 28 sqq. Contra: von Lübtow, *Lex Aquilia*, pp. 121 sqq.; cf. also Gerke, (1957) 23 *SDHI* 66 sqq., 82 sqq.; Medicus, *Id quod interest*, pp. 238 sqq.; Schebitz, op. cit., note 12, pp. 268 sqq., 355 sqq.

[124] D. 9, 2, 21, 2; regarded as interpolated by von Lübtow, *Lex Aquilia*, p. 122; Gerke, (1957) 23 *SDHI* 82 sqq.; Schebitz, op. cit., note 12, pp. 361 sqq.; but see e.g. Ankum, *Studi Sanfilippo*, vol. II, p. 51. Cf. also Ulp. D. 9, 2, 23, 6.

[125] Ulpian, however, refers to Labeo. Ankum, *Studi Sanfilippo*, vol. II, p. 50 therefore attributes the transition from the (objective) aestimatio corporis to the plaintiff's id quod interest to Labeo. Others refer to Julian (Kaser) or late classical jurisprudence (Hausmaninger); cf. also supra, note 115 above. Ulp. D. 9, 2, 23, 4 has (of course) also often been regarded as suspect; cf. Gerke, (1957) 23 *SDHI* 93 sqq.; but see Medicus, *Id quod interest*, pp. 241 sq.; MacCormack, (1975) 41 *SDHI* 69 sq.; Ankum, *Studi Sanfilippo*, vol. II, pp. 49 sq.

slave had committed serious acts of embezzlement in the plaintiff's business; he was killed before the plaintiff had been able to extract from him—by means of torture (quaestio)—the names of his accomplices and thus to clear up all the details of this crime. What the plaintiff could claim from the person who killed the slaves is described as "quanti mea intererat fraudes . . . per eum commissas detegi": his interest in detecting the acts committed by the slave (and his accomplices).

(b) Chapter three

The same development from a standardized way of evaluating merely the diminution in value of the damaged object to a refined evaluation of the individual plaintiff's damages took place with regard to the "quanti ea res erit" clause in chapter three.[126] Generally speaking, the plaintiff received compensation for what the jurists of the ius commune dubbed damnum emergens and lucrum cessans.[127] Like aestimatio corporis in the first chapter, so was aestimatio vulneris in the third chapter (in the case of injury to animate objects; otherwise: estimation of the damage to the object itself) the starting point for any assessment of the sum to be awarded.[128] But apart from that, medical expenses could, for instance, be recovered if a slave was injured; and that was so even in cases where the value of the slave had not been diminished by the injury he had received.[129] Problems could arise as far as lucrum cessans was concerned. Where someone had destroyed the nets of a fisherman, he was liable for the value of the nets but not for the value of the fish which the fisherman was unable to catch on account of the damage: "incertum fuerit, an caperentur."[130] The mere chance that some fish might have been caught is too vague and unspecific to deserve legal protection qua damages.[131] The same argument probably prompted Marcellus to refuse to entertain the claim (based on the third chapter of the lex Aquilia) of a prospective heir against the person who had destroyed the will under which he had been instituted.[132] Ulpian, however, dissented; in his view the position was the same as when a debt certificate

[126] According to Daube, (1936) 52 *LRQ*, 258 sqq., cf. also *Studi Solazzi*, pp. 146 sqq., the principle of interesse was first established in the third chapter of the lex Aquilia (it was inherent in the "quanti ea res erit" clause), which, according to him, at first applied only to the wounding of res se moventes. When it was extended to cover inanimate objects, the method of calculation applicable under chapter one (estimation of the market value) filtered through to chapter three, at least as far as cases of complete destruction were concerned. But this is unconvincing; cf. e.g. Medicus, *Id quod interest*, p. 239; Völkl, (1977) 24 *RIDA* 483 sq.

[127] Cf. supra, p. 827. There was no compensation for immaterial damages (mental pain and suffering); cf. Paul. D. 9, 2, 33 pr.: "Si servum meum occidisti, non affectiones aestimandas esse puto, veluti si filium tuum naturalem quis occiderit. . . ."

[128] Cf. Paul. D. 9, 2, 24.

[129] Ulp. D. 9, 2, 27, 17 in fine.

[130] Lab./Proc./Ulp. D. 9, 2, 29, 3.

[131] "Too speculative": Lawson/Markesinis, p. 35.

[132] Cf. Ulp. D. 9, 2, 41 pr.

("chirographum") had been destroyed. In both instances, according to Ulpian, the judge had to assess "quod interest".[133]

2. The penal character of the remedy

The penal aspect of the lex Aquilia, on the other hand, was slightly less straightforward. True: the actio legis Aquiliae displayed the characteristics of a typical actio poenalis. It was passively intransmissible and could therefore not be brought against the wrongdoer's heirs: ". . . in heredem . . . haec actio non dabitur, cum sit poenalis."[134] When several persons had been involved in the act of killing a slave, each of them was liable under chapter one, unless it could be established which of them had dealt the mortal blow.[135] The plaintiff could cumulate his actions and the fact that one of the co-delinquents paid the full amount did not release the others from their liability: "nam ex lege Aquilia, quod alius praestitit, alium non relevat, cum sit poena."[136] Furthermore, when the delict described in chapters one or three had been committed by a son in power or a slave, the paterfamilias was liable under an actio noxalis: he either had to pay the sum that was due as a result of the delict himself, or he had to surrender the delinquent.[137] But despite all this: was it really appropriate to state that the wrongdoer was punished by the actio legis Aquiliae ("[i]n hac . . . actione . . . dolus et culpa *punitur*")?[138] After all, unlike in the case of furtum,[139] the wrongdoer did not have to pay duplum or quadruplum, but merely the simple value of (as far as chapter one was concerned) the slave or grazing animal.

---

[133] D. 9, 2, 41 pr. For a detailed, and recent, discussion of what could be claimed under chapter three, cf. Schebitz, op. cit., note 12, pp. 165 sqq. He deals with D. 9, 2, 41 pr. and other cases involving the destruction of instruments (pp. 218 sqq.); in his opinion, all these texts are largely spurious.

[134] Ulp. D. 9, 2, 23, 8; cf. also Gai. IV, 112; further: Tobias Johannes Scott, *Die Geskiedenis van die Oorerflikheid van Aksies op grond van Onregmatige Daad in die Suid-Afrikaanse Reg* (unpublished Dr. iur. thesis, Leiden, 1976), pp. 19 sqq.

[135] Ulp. D. 9, 2, 11, 2; Iul./Ulp. D. 9, 2, 51, 1.

[136] Ulp. D. 9, 2, 11, 2; cf. further Levy, *Konkurrenz*, vol. I, pp. 484 sqq.; von Lübtow, *Lex Aquilia*, pp. 57 sqq.; Liebs, *Klagenkonkurrenz*, p. 181.

[137] The lex Aquilia is reported to have contained special rules about the paterfamilias's noxal liability: cf. Gai. IV, 76; Cels./Ulp. D. 9, 4, 2, 1. The paterfamilias seems to have been liable under the actio directa, "si servus sciente domino occidit"; reason: "ipse enim videtur dominus occidisse" (Ulp. D. 9, 4, 2 pr.). Knowledge by the paterfamilias, however, was not easily to be assumed: "Scientiam hic pro patientia accipimus, ut qui prohibere potuit teneatur, si non fecerit" (Paul. D. 9, 2, 45 pr.). Of course, the paterfamilias was also liable under the actio directa if the slave or son in power had acted under his orders. The same principle applied if a free man acting under orders committed an Aquilian delict: "actio legis Aquiliae cum eo est qui iussit, si modo ius imperandi habuit" (Iav. D. 9, 2, 37 pr.). For a detailed discussion, see von Lübtow, *Lex Aquilia*, pp. 41 sqq.; Hans-Peter Benöhr, "Zur Haftung für Sklavendelikte", (1980) 97 *ZSS* 273 sqq.; cf. also Hausmaninger, *Lex Aquilia*, p. 35.

[138] Paul. D. 9, 2, 30, 3; cf. also Gai. III, 202 (". . . etiam culpa puniatur").

[139] Cf. supra, pp. 932 sqq., 936 sqq.

Gaius therefore pointed to the provision that the sums under chapters one and three had to be doubled if the defendant denied liability.[140] "Infitiando lis crescit in duplum" is a rule that dates back to the days of the legis actio per manus iniectionem.[141] Manus iniectio could be granted only if the defendant's liability had already been established, for instance by a previous trial. The creditor was now allowed to exercise his power of seizure over the debtor. However, a third party (referred to as vindex) was still able to intervene and to dispute the creditor's right of seizure. Another trial between vindex and creditor ensued. But since the vindex had disputed what had already previously been placed beyond doubt and what was therefore manifest, he was made to pay duplum if defeated in the second trial. Litiscrescence was thus a penalty imposed for litigating under circumstances where litigation appeared to be unwarranted. Similar considerations must have prompted the drafters of the lex Aquilia to include a provision on the doubling of damages contra infitiantem.[142] As a result thereof, only the defendant who confessed in iure was liable for simplum; if the suit was defended, the wrongdoer had to be condemned in duplum.[143] The lex Aquilia dealt with matters that were very obviously wrong and a person who was charged with an offence under this statute and who denied liability must have been regarded with some scepticism.[144] All this reveals, however, that what was penalized by doubling the amount of damages was the defendant's reluctance to confess, not the Aquilian delict as such. If Gaius' somewhat unfortunate intimation in IV, 9 were to be accepted as correct, the actio legis Aquiliae in simplum could not have been penal: which is, however, manifestly wrong.[145]

This was seen by Justinian's compilers, who therefore drew attention, in addition to litiscrescence, to the "quanti id in eo anno plurimi fuit" clause of chapter one.[146] Usually under this provision the plaintiff merely received a compensation for his loss; as a result of

---

[140] Gai. IV, 9.

[141] For what follows, cf. Kaser, *RZ*, pp. 94 sqq.

[142] In what form was the doubling of the damages expressed in the statute? Cf. the synopsis of the discussion by Crook, (1984) 72 *Athenaeum* 75 sq.

[143] Kaser, *Altrömisches ius*, pp. 132 sqq.; idem, *RZ*, p. 95; idem, *RPr* I, p. 162; cf. also J. Paoli, *Lis infitiando crescit in duplum* (1933), pp. 95 sqq.; von Lübtow, *Lex Aquilia*, pp. 26 sqq.; Lawson/Markesinis, pp. 12 sqq. Cf., most recently, the interesting speculations by Nörr, (1987) 6 *RJ* 113. He thinks the actio legis Aquiliae in duplum may have been available only if the wrongdoer denied that he had committed the delict, not if he merely disputed that he had acted iniuria.

[144] According to Nörr, (1987) 6 *RJ* 113, the jurists in Rome were typically concerned only with cases where the question whether a particular person had committed the delict could not easily be disputed.

[145] That litiscrescence could not have been what gave the actio legis Aquilia its penal nature is also emphasized by De Zulueta, *Gaius II*, p. 230; von Lübtow, *Lex Aquilia*, pp. 37 sq.; Cardascia, *Daube Noster*, p. 70; Lawson/Markesinis, p. 5; Hausmaninger, *Lex Aquilia*, pp. 34 sq.; but see e.g. Wittmann, *Körperverletzung*, p. 41 and others.

[146] *Inst.* IV, 3, 9 ("qua ratione creditum est poenalem esse huius legis actionem"); *Inst.* IV, 6, 19.

the necessity to assess the highest value within the last year before the injury, it could, however, sometimes[147] happen that the award went far beyond this limit. It was this surplus that could no longer be reconciled with the reipersecutory nature of the lex Aquilia and that therefore contributed the penal element inherent in this action. But what a strange kind of penalty we are dealing with![148] It can have affected only a very small number of delinquents and these, in turn, were hit in an entirely arbitrary manner. Whether two, or four, or perhaps ten times more than the actual value of the dead slave or animal had to be paid did not depend on the extent of the wrongdoer's blameworthiness, or similar criteria, but on completely unrelated considerations. A penalty implying such absurdities is in fact so odd that we can hardly attribute it even to a legislator of the 3rd century B.C.[149] It was, as we have seen, for entirely different reasons that the calculation was thrown into the past,[150] and Justinian's explanation looks like a not particularly successful attempt to rationalize the ambiguity that undoubtedly existed between an action that was penal in its legal characteristics, but compensatory in its normal result.[151] The real answer appears to be, quite simply, that poena did not necessarily imply that something was recoverable in excess of compensation.[152] One and the same sum could have a dual function: it could be poena in the guise of compensation.

IV. THE STATUTORY DEFINITION OF THE DELICT: HARMFUL RESULT

We have now sketched the framework within which to appreciate how the Roman jurists applied and interpreted the individual requirements for condemnation in terms of the lex Aquilia. It is obvious that, in order to be liable, the defendant had to have brought about some kind of harmful result: an object must have been damaged and the damage must have arisen as the result of some conduct of the wrongdoer. Both the result and the wrongdoer's action were described in the first chapter with the words "servum servamve alienum alienamve quadrupedem vel pecudem . . . occidere", while the third chapter referred to "damnum facere", specified by the terms "urere frangere rumpere". But in neither case were these merely objective, or factual, requirements sufficient. If it was to rate as an Aquilian delict, occidere, urere

[147] "Aliquando" (*Inst.* IV, 3, 9); "interdum" (*Inst.* IV, 6, 19); but see Ankum, (1982) 24 *BIDR* 31 ("in many cases").

[148] Cf., particularly, Cardascia, *Daube Noster*, pp. 57 sqq. ("*une véritable loterie avec un petit nombre de numéros perdants*"); also already, Pernice, *Sachbeschädigungen*, p. 121.

[149] Cardascia, *Daube Noster*, p. 63 therefore thinks that the actio legis Aquiliae was originally not an actio poenalis. But cf. e.g. Mayer-Maly, (1974) 226 *Göttingische Gelehrte Anzeigen* 133.

[150] Supra, pp. 961 sq.

[151] Cf. the formulation by De Zulueta, *Gaius II*, p. 210.

[152] But see Ankum, (1982) 24 *BIDR* 31 ("the excess is a penalty").

frangere rumpere (or, more generally: damnum facere) had to be evaluated in a specific manner: it had to be labelled "iniuria". Under both chapters, iniuria was thus the essential term that gave the injury inflicted its distinctly delictual flavour.

1. Quadrupedes pecudes

As far as, first of all, the potential objects of the delict under chapter one were concerned, the terms "servus" and "servam" presented little difficulty. But which animals could be classified as "quadrupedes pecudes"? Gaius regarded as essential that they were kept in herds and gave as examples sheep, goats, horses, mules and asses.[153] The qualification of pigs was doubtful,[154] but since the time of Labeo they were also taken to fall under chapter one. Dogs were not included, and neither were (a fortiori) wild animals such as bears, lions or panthers. Elephants and camels were on the borderline: "natura eorum fera est", but on the other hand they served as draught animals.[155] This was sufficient to bring them within the scope of chapter one.[156]

2. Occidere and mortis causam praebere

The real interpretive crux, however, was the term "occidere". Whether or not a slave or grazing animal was dead, could, of course, normally be established reasonably easily; but the specific problem lay in investigating whether the defendant's act, that had caused the death, could be dubbed "occidere". If someone holds up a red flag and thereby chases somebody else's oxen into a narrow confine so that they perish by falling over a cliff,[157] it is obvious that the person with the flag in his hand caused the death of the animals and that, provided he has acted "iniuria", he should be liable for the resulting damage to the owner. But whether the act of flag-waving can be referred to as "killing" is quite a different matter. Or take the case where someone scares a horse, on which somebody else's slave is riding. The horse, as a result, throws off its rider, who falls into a river and drowns.[158] Again, whoever is prepared to take words seriously can hardly say that the act of scaring a horse constitutes an act of killing. We are therefore faced with a situation where we have an act by the defendant (the waving of the flag, the scaring of a horse), the kind of delictual result envisaged by chapter one of the lex Aquilia (oxen and slave are dead) and also a causal connection between act and result (oxen and slave have died because

---

[153] D. 9, 2, 2, 2; cf. also *Inst.* IV, 3, 1.

[154] For the reason, see Wesel, *Statuslehre*, pp. 50 sq. Unlike the other typical grazing animals, pigs are kept for no other purpose than to provide meat. On pigs and the lex Aquilia, see also Glück, vol. 10, pp. 354 sq.

[155] Gai. D. 9, 2, 2, 2.

[156] Wounding of quadrupedes pecudes and wounding and killing of all other animals was covered by chapter three; cf. Gai. III, 217; *Inst.* IV, 3, 13.

[157] Cf. the cases in Ulp. D. 47, 2, 50, 4 together with Gai. D. 47, 2, 51; Nerat. D. 9, 2, 53.

[158] Ofilius/Ulp. D. 9, 2, 9, 3.

defendant waved the flag or scared the horse). But the lex Aquilia does, strictly speaking, not make the defendant liable for having caused the death of the animal (for "mortis causam praebere" or "praestare"), but describes the wrongful behaviour with the term "occidere". "Occidere" and "mortis causam praebere" cannot simply be equated; there is a subtle difference between the two and the Roman lawyers were very conscious of it when they determined the scope of chapter one. Celsus formulated the basic proposition with characteristic boldness:

> ". . . multum interesse dicit, occiderit an mortis causam praestiterit, ut qui mortis causam praestitit, non Aquilia, sed in factum actione teneatur."[159]

We see, incidentally, that a defendant who had merely caused death, but not killed, did not escape liability: an analogous action modelled on the lex Aquilia was available which is described by Celsus in D. 9, 2, 7, 6 as an actio in factum. The development of these actiones in factum obviously occurred as a kind of compensation for the narrow, or literal, interpretation of occidere.

The Roman lawyers thus appear to have been faced with the necessity of broadening an originally fairly restricted form of liability. The position is exactly the opposite today. Like chapter one of the lex Aquilia, § 823 I BGB does not read "a person who . . . causes the death of another" but "a person who injures . . . the life of another". Unlike the Roman jurists, the courts and legal writers in Germany are, however, not particularly sensitive to this distinction. If a delinquent who finds himself trapped by a police squad runs away, and one of the policemen chasing him falls to his death,[160] the delinquent is usually taken to have "injured the policeman's life", although, strictly speaking, he has merely caused his death.[161] As a result of such a wide, and undifferentiated, interpretation of the objective requirements for liability, German lawyers have traditionally been engaged in lively debates about how to *limit* liability in a reasonable manner. After all, even the manufacturer of a knife or motorcar may be said to have caused the death of whoever may later be killed with the knife or run over by the car;[162] and since it is not at all improbable that these

---

[159] Cels./Ulp. D. 9, 2, 7, 6. For a detailed analysis and the historical development of the phrase "causam mortis praestare", see Dieter Nörr, *Causa mortis*; for a summary in English of the main points, see Dieter Nörr, "Causam mortis praebere", in: *The Legal Mind, Essays for Tony Honoré* (1986), pp. 203 sqq. Nörr's views have been favourably received by, inter alia, Willvonseder, (1988) 105 *ZSS* 737 sqq.; Mayer-Maly, (1986) 37 *Iura* 148 sqq. and MacCormack, (1988) 56 *TR* 209 sqq.; for very critical comments, see Watson, *Failures*, p. 83.

[160] Cf. e.g. BGH, 1971 *Neue Juristische Wochenschrift* 1980 (1981); BGH, 1971 *Neue Juristische Wochenschrift* 1982 (1983) (though not dealing with injury to life but to bodily integrity); Wolfgang Grunsky, in: *Münchener Kommentar*, vol. II (2nd ed., 1985), Vor § 249, nn. 61 sqq.

[161] For further discussion, see Reinhard Zimmermann, "Herausforderungsformel und Haftung für fremde Willensbetätigungen nach § 823 I BGB", 1980 *Juristenzeitung* 10 sqq.

[162] Cf. e.g. the discussion by Ernst von Caemmerer, "Wandlungen des Deliktrechts", in: *Gesammelte Schriften*, vol. I (1968), pp. 478 sqq.

consequences may ensue from the use of dangerous instruments such as knives and cars, one could even attribute negligence to the manufacturer. Yet it is obvious that he should not be liable under § 823 I BGB, the modern equivalent of the Roman lex Aquilia.

3. The meaning of "occidere"

"Occidere", for the Roman lawyers, was different from (and entailed another legal sanction than) "causam mortis praebere". But what exactly did the term positively imply? Etymologically, it was thought to derive from "caedere" and "caedes", that is, from words connoting direct slaying.[163] Hence the following definition was suggested by Iulianus: ". . . lege Aquilia is demum teneri visus est, qui adhibita vi et quasi manu causam mortis praebuisset";[164] the death must have been brought about by force, and as the direct result of the defendant's physical action. Ulpian is perhaps slightly more precise when he states that the word "killing" implies either the use of a sword or similar weapon or a direct and violent application of the wrongdoer's body or any part of it against the victim (as, for instance, strangling, kicking or butting).[165] But Roman definitions cannot always be taken at face value. What Julian and Ulpian are providing is the core meaning of the word;[166] but not every element of their definition was absolutely indispensable. More particularly, the Roman lawyers did not always require the use of force. Thus, Labeo was prepared to grant the actio legis Aquiliae against a midwife who administered a poisonous drug to one of her clients, provided only she administered the drug with her own hands. "[S]i quidem suis manibus supposuit":[167] nothing in the text suggests that the midwife must have forced the potion down the other woman's throat. Ulpian placed this point beyond all doubt when he commented: "[s]i . . . per vim vel suasum medicamentum . . . infundit . . ., lege Aquilia teneri."[168] The position was the same where someone killed another by injecting a lethal substance into his arm or

[163] Iul. D. 9, 2, 51 pr.; von Lübtow, *Lex Aquilia*, p. 138. Cf. also Lab./Ulp. D. 29, 5, 1, 17 concerning the senatus consultum Silanianum ("Occisorum appellatione eos contineri Labeo scribit, qui per vim aut caedem sunt interfecti . . .").

[164] Iul. D. 9, 2, 51 pr. Likewise, tresspass has traditionally been defined as the tort of inflicting direct and forcible injury; the formal allegation of the writ of trespass was that the defendant had acted "vi et armis et contra pacem Domini Regis". It was on the strength of this allegation (whether true or not) that the jurisdiction of the king's courts (as opposed to the local courts) was established. Cf. F.W. Maitland, *The Forms of Action at Common Law* (1965), pp. 48 sqq.

[165] D. 9, 2, 7, 1: "Occisum autem accipere debemus, sive gladio sive etiam fuste vel alio telo vel manibus (si forte strangulavit eum) vel calce petiit vel capite [lapide? cf. Wesel, *Statuslehre*, p. 83] vel qualiter qualiter."

[166] Cf., in particular, N.H. Andrews, " 'Occidere' and the lex Aquilia", (1987) 46 *Cambridge LJ* 315 sqq.

[167] Lab./Ulp. D. 9, 2, 9 pr. On this text cf. Nörr, *Causa mortis*, pp. 166 sqq.

[168] Cf. Ulp. D. 9, 2, 9, 1.

by rubbing him with a poisonous potion.[169] Again, it was irrelevant whether the patient was forced or merely persuaded to undergo this kind of treatment. What mattered was whether the murderer had with his own hands given the injection or rubbed in the potion. The mere act of handing the drug or potion over to the patient, with the request to apply it to himself, was not regarded as sufficient. It did not constitute "occidere". Since, however, it involved "mortis causam praestare", an actio in factum was available.[170] "Si quis corpore suo damnum dederit": this is how Gaius described the essential criterion for the range of application of the actio legis Aquiliae.[171] The death must have been brought about by the wrongdoer "with his own body", it must have been the direct consequence of a physical action of his.[172] Thus,[173] the lex Aquilia was applicable when someone had killed a slave by dashing him against a rock,[174] by dropping a heavy load upon him[175] or by piercing him with a javelin.[176] A decretal actio in factum,[177] on the other hand, had to be resorted to against a person who held a slave so that a third party could murder him;[178] who persuaded a slave to go down a dangerous well where he was killed;[179] who gave a madman a sword, which the latter promptly used to commit suicide[180] or who caused the slave's death by pushing a third party into him.[181] The cases involving the red flag[182] and the scared horse[183] also fall into this category, and so do, very importantly, those cases where the death ultimately had occurred as the result of an omission. "Si quis hominem fame necaverit, in factum actione teneri Neratius ait":[184] this was apparently a much discussed example. It is obvious that if someone caused another person to starve to death, the "corpore suo"

---

[169] Cf. Ulp. D. 9, 2, 9, 1.
[170] Cf. Lab./Ulp. D. 9, 2, 9 pr.; cf. also Cels./Ulp. D, 9, 2, 7, 6.
[171] III, 219; cf. also *Inst.* IV, 3, 16.
[172] The same applies to the tort of trespass: the wrong must have been committed by "direct means". For details cf., for example, Winfield and Jolowicz, pp. 42 sqq., 53 sqq.; Fleming, *Torts*, pp. 15 sqq., 23 sqq.; cf. also Maitland, op. cit., note 164, p. 50 (". . . it was to the last necessary that there should be some wrongful application of physical force to the defendant's lands or goods or person—but . . . a wrongful touch to his person or chattels was held to be force enough and an adequate breach of the king's peace").
[173] For very useful schemes of cases falling under chapter one and being remedied by actiones in factum, cf. Andrews, (1987) 46 *Cambridge LJ* 316 sqq.
[174] Cels./Ulp. D. 9, 2, 7, 7.
[175] Ulp. D. 9, 2, 7, 2.
[176] Ulp. D. 9, 2, 9, 4; cf. also Alf. D. 9, 2, 52, 2 ("aeque si quis . . .").
[177] Sometimes (cf. e.g. Gai. III, 219) also referred to as actiones utiles.
[178] Ulp. D. 9, 2, 11, 1.
[179] Cf. Gai. III, 219.
[180] Cels./Ulp. D. 9, 2, 7, 6.
[181] Proc./Ulp. D. 9, 2, 7, 3 ("Proinde si quis alterius impulsu damnum dederit, Proculus scribit neque eum qui impulit teneri, quia non occidit, neque eum qui impulsus est, quia damnum iniuria non dedit").
[182] Supra, p. 976, note 157.
[183] Supra, p. 976, note 158.
[184] Ulp. D. 9, 2, 9, 2.

requirement inherent in the term "occidere" was not complied with.[185]

Of course, it cannot always have been easy to draw the line, and many cases must have been controversial.[186] Celsus, for instance, was prepared to grant an actio legis Aquiliae where someone drowned as a result of having been thrown off a bridge.[187] Unlike the person who had scared the horse, the wrongdoer had in this case used direct bodily violence against his victim: he had thrown him into the water. Arguably, however, he had thereby furnished only a cause of death—for ultimately it was the force of the current that had killed the man. Hence we find Gaius arguing in favour of a mere action on the case.[188] Another interesting case is discussed by Proculus. Someone irritates a dog in order to make him bite and kill somebody else's slave. Proculus appears to regard the dog as a kind of weapon (such as a javelin thrown at another) and therefore considers the actio legis Aquiliae to be applicable.[189] Julian disagrees; in his opinion, the owner of the slave had to use an actio in factum, unless the dog had in fact been "held" by the defendant (in his hands? on a lead?)[190]

---

[185] Cf. further Gai. III, 219; Ulp. D. 9, 2, 29, 7; Lab./Ulp. D. 47, 8, 2, 20; von Lübtow, *Lex Aquilia*, pp. 148 sq. Ulp. D. 19, 5, 14, 1 deals with a case where a slave freezes to death because his clothes have been taken away. In both instances we are, however, not dealing with a "mere" omission; here, too, the death occurred as an indirect result of a previous action of the defendant: he had locked the slave in (so that he starved); he had taken away his clothes (so that he was exposed to the chill of a winter night).

[186] Similar problems arose with regard to the tort of trespass. For an instructive example cf. *Scott v. Shepherd* (1773) 2 Black W 892: A throws a lighted squib into a crowd, where it falls upon B. B, in alarm, throws it away and it falls upon C, who does the same as B. The squib ends its journey by falling upon D, exploding and putting out his eye. The whole incident took place on a fair day, close to Guy Fawkes Night. Three of the judges regarded this as trespass by A to D; Blackstone J dissented and held an action on the case to be necessary. To read the judgment is indeed to "step back into the age of Julian and Ulpian and to be surprised by the anachronism that the Roman discussion is conducted in the prose of Boswell" (Andrews, (1987) 46 *Cambridge LJ* 321). For an in-depth analysis, cf. M.J. Prichard, *Scott v. Shepherd (1773) and the Emergence of the Tort of Negligence* (1976).

[187] Cf. Ulp. D. 9, 2, 7, 7. It did not matter "sive ipso ictu perierit aut continuo submersus est aut lassatus vi fluminus victus perierit".

[188] III, 219: ". . . item si quis alienum servum de ponte aut ripa in flumen proiecit"; cf. von Lübtow, *Lex Aquilia*, pp. 145 sq. But some editors read "sed si" in place of "item si"; Gaius would then have to be taken to have shared Celsus's opinion (as did, incidentally, Justinian: Inst. IV, 3, 16).

[189] Ulp. D. 9, 2, 11, 5; not interpolated: cf. MacCormack, (1975) 41 *SDHI* 14 sqq. against von Lübtow, *Lex Aquilia*, p. 152 and others.

[190] Cf. Ulp. D. 9, 2, 11, 5. Or was it the slave who was held so that the dog could bite him? The text does not make that clear: "Item cum eo, qui canem irritaverat et effecerat, ut aliquem morderet, quamvis eum non tenuit, Proculus respondit Aquiliae actionem esse: sed Julianus eum demum Aquilia teneri ait, qui tenuit et effecit ut aliquem morderet: ceterum si non tenuit, in factum agendum." Cf. e.g. von Lübtow, *Lex Aquilia*, p. 152 ("tenere" refers to the slave); Geoffrey MacCormack, "Juristic Interpretation of the lex Aquilia", in: *Studi in onore di Cesare Sanfilippo*, vol. I (1982), p. 277 ("tenere" refers to the dog); cf. further Jean Macqueron, "Les dommages causés par des chiens dans la jurisprudence Romaine", in: *Flores legum H. J. Scheltema oblati* (1971), pp. 147 sqq.

4. Actio directa and actio in factum

It is obvious from our classical sources that the term "occidere" never came to be interpreted more liberally. It remained limited to cases of direct causation of death. Even Justinian continued this tradition by referring, in his *Institutes*, to the test devised by Gaius.[191] What was it that prompted the Roman lawyers to retain such a conservative, or restrictive, attitude, even though, as they themselves acknowledged, the meaning of "occidere" in lay usage had become much wider? "Occidisse dicitur vulgo quidem, qui mortis causam quolibet modo praebuit", said Iulianus, but he proceeded to restate the narrow Aquilian usage.[192] In fact, the beginnings of the broader meaning of the term "occidere" in common parlance can even be traced back to the beginning of the 2nd century B.C.[193] For the lawyers, however, there was no necessity to follow suit and to change the by that time well-established, legal usage.[194] At least in classical law, entirely satisfactory alternative remedies were available: decretal actiones in factum which appear to have provided adequate protection in cases of indirect causation. But the possibility of extending the lex Aquilia by means of granting, where appropriate, an actio in factum, can hardly have existed all along. The first decision of which we know is attributed to Ofilius. He gave an actio in factum in the case involving the slave who was killed because the horse on which he was riding had been scared.[195] He does not give a reason for his ruling, but provides a precedent: the situation is the same as when a slave is lured by one man into an ambush and then killed by another.[196] The implication of this kind of argument is clear: the actio in factum in cases of indirect killing must already have existed before Ofilius' days. But it cannot go back further than (at the earliest) the latter part of the 2nd century B.C., for decretal actiones in factum (modelled on one of the actions proposed in

---

[191] "Ceterum placuit ita demum ex hac lege actionem esse, si quis praecipue corpore suo damnum dederit": *Inst.* IV, 3, 16. Only by adding the word "praecipue", did Justinian acknowledge a somewhat more liberal usage that may have gained ground in post-classical times; cf. e.g. von Lübtow, *Lex Aquilia*, p. 213.

[192] D. 9, 2, 51 pr.

[193] Cf. Nörr, *Causa mortis*, pp. 7 sq., who draws attention to a passage in Plautus' play *Pseudolus* where the author achieves a comical effect by opposing "occidere gladio" and "occidere fame".

[194] "Occidere" was also interpreted strictly in another statutory context: Lab./Ulp. D. 29, 5, 1, 17; cf. Peter Stein, "School Attitudes in the Law of Delicts", in: *Studi in onore di Arnaldo Biscardi*, vol. II (1982), pp. 287 sq.; Nörr, *Causa mortis*, pp. 166 sq.

[195] Ofilius/Ulp. D. 9, 2, 9, 3. For an analysis, see Schipani, *Lex Aquilia*, pp. 165 sqq.; MacCormack, (1975) 41 *SDHI* 17 sq.; Stein, *Studi Biscardi*, vol. II, pp. 289 sq. and, particularly, Nörr, *Causa mortis*, pp. 139 sqq.

[196] ". . . quemadmodum si servus meus ab alio in insidias deductus, ab alio esset occisus." On the use of the word "quemadmodum" and arguments by analogy in the texts on the lex Aquilia, see MacCormack, *Studi Sanfilippo*, vol. I, pp. 255 sqq.

the edict) are inextricably linked with the formulary procedure.[197] From the date of the enactment of the lex Aquilia until the time when the praetorian edict allowed the formulation of actiones in factum, an unsatisfactory lack of legal protection appears therefore to have existed in all cases of mortis causam praebere, which did not fall under the narrow, Aquilian concept of "occidere". How could such a situation ever have been tolerated by the Roman lawyers?

In order to avoid this dilemma, it has occasionally been suggested that the interpretation of "occidere" was, in fact, much wider in the days of the Republic; either gradually[198] or at some or other specific point,[199] the meaning of the word was restricted. But neither is this kind of development from a more liberal to a narrower interpretation generally very plausible, nor, more importantly, can our sources be brought in line with it.[200] In a legal context, the term "occidere" always appears to have had a very narrow core meaning, which, in all likelihood, even antedates the lex Aquilia.[201] When the word appeared in this statute, the Roman lawyers remained faithful to the traditional interpretation. In actual practice, situations of an indirect killing of a slave or grazing animal were probably rare and did not usually come to the attention of the courts.[202] The jurists in those early days may well have been content to provide a remedy for what was obviously and manifestly wrong and may not have felt the need for a specific action covering all cases of mortis causam praebere. Apart from that, we must remember that, when the lex Aquilia was enacted, the procedure per legis actiones still reigned supreme. Dieter Nörr has recently advanced the attractive suggestion that, whatever need may still have existed to remedy at least certain instances of indirect killing, could possibly have been met by the use of fictions.[203] Gaius, in a famous passage,[204] states that an action for the cutting down of "vines" could succeed only if the plaintiff used the word "trees"; seeing that the XII Tables spoke of cutting down trees in general, vines had to be fictitiously represented as trees. It is not impossible that the same kind of fictitious reasoning was

---

[197] Cf. generally Max Kaser, " 'Ius honorarium' and 'ius civile' ", (1984) 101 *ZSS* 48 sqq., 65 sqq.; also Nörr, *Causa mortis*, pp. 146 sqq.; Wieacker, *RR*, pp. 470 sqq.

[198] Watson, *Obligations*, pp. 241 sqq.; cf. also Stein, *Studi Biscardi*, vol. II, p. 288.

[199] Behrends, *Fraus legis*, pp. 33 sqq.

[200] The discussion turns mainly on Alf. D. 9, 2, 52, 2 (a case involving two heavily laden carts proceeding up the Capitoline hill. The first cart rolled back and crashed into the second one, which, in turn, knocked down a slave. The text does not make it clear whether the slave was killed or merely wounded; whether, in other words, the decision concerned a case of "occidere" or of "rumpere"). On D. 9, 2, 52, 2 cf. Watson, *Obligations*, p. 242; Schipani, *Lex Aquilia*, pp. 179 sqq.; MacCormack, (1975) 41 *SDHI* 13 sqq.; idem, *Studi Sanfilippo*, vol. I, pp. 257 sq.; Nörr, *Causa mortis*, pp. 142 sqq.; Andrews, (1987) 46 *Cambridge LJ* 323.

[201] Cf. Nörr, *Causa mortis*, pp. 6 sq.; Andrews, (1987) 46 *Cambridge LJ* 322 sq.

[202] Nörr, *Causa mortis*, pp. 126, 136 sq. He draws attention to the fact that many of the examples concerning the actio in factum have the air of the schoolroom.

[203] *Causa mortis*, pp. 126, 137 sq., 149; cf. also idem, (1987) 6 *RJ* 105 sqq.

[204] IV, 11.

employed in cases of indirect killing. When, however, the legis actio system was replaced by the formulary procedure, jurists were no longer able, for the purposes of bringing a lawsuit, to use the word "occidere" when they actually merely meant "mortis causam praestare". The scope of a remedy was determined, from now on, by the process of interpretation, and that excluded all instances of indirect killing from the ambit of the lex Aquilia. It was in this situation that actiones in factum began to be used to fill the gap. As Geoffrey MacCormack has pointed out,[205] these developments provide a fascinating illustration of Sir Henry Maine's famous remark[206] on the secretion of the substantive law in the interstices of procedure.

5. Urere frangere rumpere—corrumpere

In view of Gaius' (and Justinian's) generalizing remark that an action under the lex Aquilia could only be granted "si quis corpore suo damnum dederit",[207] we may expect that the words in the third chapter corresponding to "occidere" in the first (namely: urere frangere rumpere) were similarly restrictively interpreted. This was in fact the case. Singeing a slave by throwing a lighted torch into his face was, of course, unquestionably "urere",[208] and so was setting fire to an orchard or a country house.[209] In all these cases, the damage was the direct result of a physical action of the wrongdoer. Again, this concept of "corpore suo damnum dare" excluded liability for omissions. If a stoker-slave charged with watching the fire fell asleep and thus did not prevent the house from burning down, the actio legis Aquiliae did not apply—"nam qui custodit, nihil fecit."[210,211] The term "frangere" covered cases where a craftsman broke a chalice meant for diatretion[212] that had

[205] (1988) 56 *TR* 210.

[206] *Early Law and Custom* (1861), p. 389.

[207] Gai. III, 219; Inst. IV, 3, 16.

[208] Ulp. D. 9, 2, 27, 6.

[209] Ulp. D. 9, 2, 27, 7. A person who sets fire to a house is also liable to the neighbour to whose house the fire spreads: Ulp. D. 9, 2, 27, 8 ("Si quis insulam voluerit meam exurere et ignis etiam ad vicini insulam pervenerit, Aquilia tenebitur etiam vicino"). But this was a borderline case; cf. the dispute concerning a rather similar case (fire on a stubble-field spreads to the neighbour's praedium) in Coll. XII, VII, 4–7; for a discussion, see MacCormack, *Studi Sanfilippo*, vol. I, pp. 275 sq. Further on "urere" (with a discussion of the interesting case of Ulp. D. 9, 2, 27, 10—oven against party wall), cf. Peter Birks, "Cooking the Meat: Aquilian Liability for Hearths and Ovens", (1985) 20 *The Irish Jurist* 352 sqq., 365 sqq.

[210] Nerat./Ulp. D. 9, 2, 27, 9; for a discussion, see Ben Beinart, "Culpa in omittendo", (1949) 12 *THRHR* 145 sqq.; von Lübtow, *Lex Aquilia*, pp. 159 sqq; Kemp J. Kemp, *Delictual Liability for Omissions* (unpublished LLD thesis, Port Elizabeth, 1978), pp. 91 sqq.

[211] Further on urere, cf. Schipani, *Lex Aquilia*, pp. 334 sqq.

[212] "Within the category of cut glass the diatreta or the so-called 'cage-cups' (*Netzgläser*) are the ultimate marvel in the sphere of artistic glass. . . . These marvels of craftsmanship were probably cut from a thick walled vessel. But to the present day it remains a mystery how this work could be carried out, for the infinite patience, fanatical concentration and calm deliberation required to produce such a work of art seem to go beyond the realm of possibility. There was such a danger of seeing the whole work ruined by a break in an unguarded moment . . . A possible explanation of the mystery might be that the

been handed over to him[213] or where somebody staved in the doors of a house or smashed the house itself.[214] "Rumpere", in turn, appears originally to have meant something like "to break", "to smash" or "to rend asunder", and it was primarily used, from the days of the XII Tables, to describe situations where a severe bodily injury was directly inflicted on a slave or animal.[215] This traditional core meaning is still reflected in the definition provided by Ulpianus:

> "Rupisse eum utique accipiemus, qui vulneravit, vel virgis vel loris vel pugnis cecidit, vel telo vel quo alio, ut scinderet alicui corpus, vel tumorem fecerit."[216]

Problems could arise in cases where a direct injury was inflicted and damage caused, but where the object of the injury itself nevertheless remained whole. Prototype was the situation where someone caused a miscarriage by striking a pregnant mare or woman. Iunius Brutus was prepared cautiously to extend the scope of "rumpere" (and thus: of the third chapter of the lex Aquilia): "Si mulier pugno vel equa ictu a te percussa eiecerit, Brutus ait Aquilia teneri quasi rupto."[217] In a way, of course, the body of the mare (or woman) had indeed been "broken" when the foal (or child) was ejected prematurely. Celsus, however, took matters much beyond the concept of a "quasi rumpere". He boldly equated rumpere with corrumpere ("ruptum enim intellegitur, quod quoquo modo corruptum est"),[218] which meant as much as to "spoil", "to make something worse", "to deteriorate". As a result, every form of physical deterioration was now covered by the lex

undercutting was performed entirely under water. For if glass is fully immersed in water, the even distribution of pressure on all sides prevents chipping and cracking": F. Neuberg, *Ancient Glass*, as translated by M. Bullock and A. Jaffa, and quoted by Peter Birks, "Other Men's Meat: Aquilian Liability for Proper User", (1981) 16 *The Irish Jurist* 168. The process of diatretion is thus the drilling and piercing which makes the net of glass and separates it from the inner cup and which turns the pre-diatreton (a beaker clad in an outer layer of differently coloured glass) into a calix diatretra (cf. Birks, loc. cit.); cf. further Okko Behrends, "Die Rechtsformen des römischen Handwerks", in: (1981) 22 *Abhandlungen der Akademie der Wissenschaften in Göttingen* 146.

213 Ulp. D. 9, 2, 27, 29; cf. Birks, (1981) 16 *The Irish Jurist* 163 sqq. (suggesting a fairly far-reaching reconstruction of the text).

214 Ulp. D. 9, 2, 27, 31.

215 For details, see Wittmann, *Körperverletzung*, pp. 3 sqq.; Völkl, op. cit., note 41, pp. 40 sqq.

216 D. 9, 2, 27, 17.

217 Ulp. D. 9, 2, 27, 22. Cf. also Pomp. D. 9, 2, 39 pr.: "Quintus Mucius scribit: equa cum in alieno pasceretur, in cogendo quod praegnas erat eiecit: quaerebatur, dominus eius possetne cum eo qui coegisset lege Aquilia agere, quia equam in iciendo ruperat. si percussisset aut consulto vehementius egisset, visum est agere posse." On these texts, see Schipani, *Lex Aquilia*, pp. 133 sqq.; von Lübtow, *Lex Aquilia*, pp. 112 sq., 167 sq.; MacCormack, (1975) 41 *SDHI* 3 sq.; Herbert Hausmaninger, "Zur Gesetzesinterpretation des Celsus", in: *Studi in onore di Giuseppe Grosso*, vol. V, pp. 265 sq.; Behrends, 1985 *Juristische Schulung* 878 sqq.; Nörr, *Causa mortis*, pp. 130 sqq. For an interesting alternative explanation of the phrase "quasi occidere", see Nörr, (1987) 6 *RJ* 106 sq.

218 This is how Gaius (III, 217) describes the new approach.

Aquilia,[219] and thus an action could be brought, for instance, if wine was adulterated or poured away,[220] if clothes were torn or stained,[221] if millet or grain was thrown into a river,[222] if a document was rendered illegible,[223] if a ship was scuttled[224] or damaged in a collision,[225] if a mule broke down because it had been overloaded[226] or if unripe grapes were cut down from their vine.[227]

Celsus' view appears to have been readily received by the majority of Roman jurists. Of course, it was bound to render the other two verbs contained in chapter three, "urere" and "frangere", somewhat redundant. Celsus himself did not deny that,[228] but, as he himself explained: ". . . non esse novum, ut lex specialiter quibusdam enumeratis generale subiciat verbum, quo specialia complectatur."[229] Furthermore, the surprisingly liberal approach with regard to the word "rumpere" in chapter three may be said to correspond rather badly with the strict interpretation of "occidere" in chapter one. But the significance of reading "corrumpere" into chapter three was to make irrelevant any enquiry into the type of physical result that had occurred.[230] This was a problem that could not arise in chapter one, where the physical result was always death. Only as far as the question of indirect causation was concerned were the jurists faced with a similar problem under both chapters, and in this regard the same narrow approach was as consistently maintained under chapter three as under chapter one. Again, however, actiones in factum were available where the defendant had not injured the object corpore suo. This was the case, for instance, where a cooper who had been hired to mend a vat, punctured it so that the wine contained in it ran out.[231] The wine had been "corrupted", but the link between the cooper's physical action and the damage was not direct enough.

---

[219] Gai. III, 217; cf. also *Inst.* IV, 3, 13. Ulpian (D. 9, 2, 27, 13) attributed this extension to "fere omnes veteres"; but cf. Hausmaninger, *Studi Grosso*, vol. V, p. 265; MacCormack, (1975) 41 *SDHI* 4 sq.

[220] Ulp. D. 9, 2, 27, 15.

[221] Ulp. D. 9, 2, 27, 18 ("quasi ruperit").

[222] Ulp. D. 9, 2, 27, 19.

[223] Ulp. D. 47, 2, 27, 3; Iul. D. 9, 2, 42.

[224] Ulp. D. 9, 2, 27, 24.

[225] Proc./Ulp. D. 9, 2, 29, 2 (". . . parvi refert navem immittendo aut serraculum ad navem ducendo an tua manu damnum dederis"); Schipani, *Lex Aquilia*, pp. 341 sqq.

[226] Ulp. D. 9, 2, 27, 23.

[227] Ulp. D. 9, 2, 27, 25. If ripe grapes were cut down and then taken away this was not damnum iniuria datum but could be furtum or contempt iniuria (in the sense of the actio iniuriarum). For a discussion of Ulp. D. 9, 2, 27, 25, see Birks, (1981) 16 *The Irish Jurist* 153 sqq.

[228] ". . . non negat fractum et ustum contineri corrupti appellatione": Ulp. D. 9, 2, 27, 16.

[229] Ulp. D. 9, 2, 27, 16.

[230] Andrews, (1987) 46 *Cambridge LJ* 325 sq.

[231] Ulp. D. 9, 2, 27, 35.

6. The limits of the notion of "corrumpere"

Even within the wide notion of "corrumpere", however, certain additional limitations were inherent. First, it required that the object involved had to have *deteriorated*. The actio legis Aquiliae could therefore not be brought against a person who castrated somebody else's slave and thereby rendered him more valuable.[232] Secondly, there was no corrumpere unless the object in question was changed in some way.[233] Thus, the sowing of tares or wild oats into somebody else's crops gave rise only to an actio in factum:

> ". . . nam alia quaedam species damni est ipsum quid corrumpere et mutare, ut lex Aquilia locum habeat, alia nulla ipsius mutatione applicare aliud, cuius molesta separatio sit."[234]

But this seems to have been a borderline case, for Ulpian came down (though somewhat haltingly)[235] in favour of the actio legis Aquiliae in the rather similar situation that grain had been mixed up with sand.[236] Closely related was (thirdly) a whole group of situations where the owner was deprived of a specific item of his property but where this piece of property was neither destroyed nor damaged (nor, incidentally, appropriated by the offender to his own use).[237] Two friends take a stroll along the banks of the Tiber; one of them, while admiring the other's ring, inadvertently drops it into the river.[238] A person knocks some coins out of somebody else's hand, so that they roll into the sea

[232] Viv./Ulp. D. 9, 2, 27, 28 ("Et si puerum quis castraverit et pretiosiorem fecerit, Vivianus scribit cessare Aquiliam, sed iniuriarum erit agendum . . ."); cf. also Ulp. D. 9, 2, 27, 17. The fact that no Aquilian action could be brought in these cases may, alternatively, have been due to the absence of damnum. The third chapter started off with the words "si quis alteri damnum faxit", before it proceeded to specify "quod usserit fregerit ruperit". It is, however, not clear how damnum must be understood. Does it refer to the actual damage done to the object concerned (cf. e.g. Liebs, (1968) 85 *ZSS* 197; MacCormack, (1970) 5 *The Irish Jurist* 172)? Then it would scarcely have any independent significance, but would merely be a summarizing reference to whatever has happened to the object by means of urere frangere rumpere (or rather: corrumpere). Or does it refer to the loss caused to the owner of the object (cf. e.g. Daube, *Studi Solazzi*, pp. 98 sqq.; von Lübtow, *Lex Aquilia*, pp. 132 sqq.; Hausmaninger, *Lex Aquilia*, p. 31), so that urere frangere rumpere was relevant in terms of chapter three only *if* it resulted in such loss? Only in the latter case could one say that, even though an object had been subjected to a rumpere iniuria, liability could still be negatived by a further factor, namely the absence of damnum. Cf., on D. 9, 2, 27, 28 in this context, von Lübtow, *Lex Aquilia*, pp. 132 sqq.; Birks, (1981) 16 *The Irish Jurist* 160 sqq. As far as the term "damnum" is concerned, cf., above all, Daube, *Studi Solazzi*, pp. 93 sqq.; Liebs, (1968) 85 *ZSS* 173 sqq.

[233] MacCormack, (1975) 41 *SDHI* 6.

[234] Cels./Ulp. D. 9, 2, 27, 14; Geoffrey MacCormack, "Celsus quaerit: D. 9, 2, 27, 14", (1973) 20 *RIDA* 341 sqq.

[235] He advocated an action on the rather contorted basis of quasi *cor*rumpere.

[236] Ulp. D. 9, 2, 27, 20 ("Item si quis frumento harenam vel aliud quid immiscuit, ut difficilis separatio sit, . . ."). On the divergence between D. 9, 2, 27, 14 and D. 9, 2, 27, 20 cf. Hausmaninger, *Studi Grosso*, vol. V, p. 268.

[237] On these cases, cf. von Lübtow, *Lex Aquilia*, pp. 180 sqq.; J.L. Barton, "The Lex Aquilia and Decretal Actions", in: *Daube Noster* (1974), pp. 15 sqq.; MacCormack, (1975) 41 *SDHI* 30 sqq.

[238] Alf. D. 19, 5, 23.

or down a drain.[239] A boar that has been trapped in A's boar trap is released by B and thus regains its natural liberty.[240] Or take another variation of the pannum rubrum case: somebody waves a red flag, but this time the startled cattle do not fall over a precipice but merely stampede, and are not seen again.[241] In all these cases, an actio furti does not lie.[242] Nor can the ring, the coins, the boar or the cattle be said to be "corrupted". Yet, the owner has undoubtedly incurred a loss, but it is damnum sine laesione corporis. It is for this reason that the plaintiff can resort only to an actio in factum, not to the actio legis Aquiliae. Only Sabinus appears to have been prepared to extend the scope of chapter three by equating irretrievable loss with physical destruction[243]—a view, however, that did not find much support.[244]

Finally there was the issue of "other men's meat":[245] cases where one person inflicted loss upon another by putting some item of his wealth precisely to its proper use: eating other people's food, drinking their wine, using their incense, or trampling their grapes to make wine. "Si quis alienum vinum vel frumentum consumpserit, non videtur damnum iniuria dare ideoque utilis danda est actio", says Paul,[246] and in these instances it can scarcely have been the lack of laesio corporis that made him reject the possibility of Aquilian liability: the food is chewed up and swallowed, the grapes burst under the offender's feet, etc. It is not clear, however, whether destruction in the course of proper user was nevertheless taken not to constitute "corruption" in terms of chapter three,[247] or whether, as Birks has suggested,[248] the issue turned around the "iniuria" requirement: (cor-)ruptiones, which are in harmony with the natural order of things do not amount to (cor-)rumpere iniuria.

---

[239] Sab./Ulp. D. 9, 2, 27, 21.

[240] Proc. D. 41, 1, 55.

[241] Cf. Ulp. D. 47, 2, 50, 4.

[242] In D. 47, 2, 50, 4, the flag-waver is held liable under the actio furti if he acted "furti faciendi causa". But where the waving of the flag is merely a silly practical joke ("lusus perniciosus") there is no theft. In some instances, the actio de dolo was available. On the relationship between actio de dolo and actiones in factum, see Alan Watson, "Actio de dolo and actiones in factum", (1961) 78 *ZSS* 392 sqq.

[243] Cf. Ulp. D. 9, 2, 27, 21 (often regarded as interpolated; cf. e.g. von Lübtow, *Lex Aquilia*, p. 181; but cf. MacCormack, (1975) 41 *SDHI* 31 sq.). To make things even more puzzling, Ulpian attributes to Sabinus also the opinion that an actio in factum was applicable (D. 9, 2, 27, 21 in fine). Did Sabinus possibly express different opinions on the question in different works (Barton, *Daube Noster*, p. 19)?

[244] "The suggestion that a direct Aquilian action may lie in the circumstances can only be described as pretty startling": Barton, *Daube Noster*, p. 19.

[245] Birks, (1981) 16 *The Irish Jurist* 141.

[246] D. 9, 2, 30, 2.

[247] Cf. e.g. von Lübtow, *Lex Aquilia*, pp. 185 sq.

[248] (1981) 16 *The Irish Jurist* 141 sqq.; cf. also the sequel in (1985) 20 *The Irish Jurist* 352 sqq. (under the title "Cooking the meat: Aquilian Liability for Hearths and Ovens" and concerning Ulp. D. 9, 2, 27, 10 and Coll. XII, VII, 8 (oven against party wall)—a case "of particular obscurity" (MacCormack, (1975) 41 *SDHI* 30); for further discussion of these texts, cf. von Lübtow, *Lex Aquilia*, pp. 162 sqq.; MacCormack, (1975) 41 *SDHI* 36 sqq.; Nörr, *Causa mortis*, pp. 171 sq.).

V. SOME ADDITIONAL REFLECTIONS

1. Causation in the Roman law of delict

Before proceeding to the other requirements of delictual liability under the lex Aquilia, two issues arising from the foregoing discussion still have to be considered. Delict has to do with human behaviour and with a harmful result. Both must be connected in a specific manner: the harmful result must have been caused by the defendant's conduct. The question thus arises whether the Roman lawyers developed or applied a specific doctrine of causation. And secondly: the range of application of the actio legis Aquiliae was, as we have seen, (surprisingly) limited. In particular, it did not cover cases where death or injury had only been brought about indirectly. However, even in these situations the plaintiff did not remain without protection: actiones in factum were available so as to extend the range of liability for civil wrongs in a suitable manner. What were the distinctive features of these remedies "on the case" and, in particular, what was their relationship to the actio legis Aquiliae?

(a) "Factual" and "legal" causation

The first of these two questions can be answered with a straightforward "no". The analysis of delict in terms of objective and subjective requirements, of factual and normative elements and, more generally, of abstract conceptual thinking, is thoroughly un-Roman. The issue of causation provides a good example. That a defendant cannot be held liable unless his conduct has in fact "caused" the injury is one of the few more or less universally accepted propositions of the modern law of delict. But what does that imply? When can the relevant causal connection between conduct and injury be said to be established? Hosts of theories have been developed to address the "never ending and insoluble problems" arising from these questions; theories which have, in view of their "ugly and barely intelligible jargon",[249] not seldom even contributed to the "uncertainties and confusions which continue to surround the legal use of causal language".[250] Thus, one often encounters a very basic distinction between factual causation and legal causation.[251] Factual causation is usually defined in terms of the sine qua

[249] *Overseas Tankships (U.K.) Ltd. v. Morts Dock & Engineering Co. Ltd. (The Wagon Mound)* [1961] AC 388 (HL) at 423, 419.

[250] H.L.A. Hart, A.M. Honoré, *Causation in the Law* (2nd ed., 1985), p. 1 (the standard work in the field).

[251] Cf. e.g. Boberg, *Delict*, pp. 380 sqq. (an exceptionally lucid account of Aquilian liability in the South African usus hodiernus); cf. also Hart and Honoré, op. cit., note 250, p. 110 ("bifurcation of causal questions"); Dieter Giesen, *International Medical Malpractice Law* (1988), pp. 163 sqq.

non ("but for") test.[252] To apply it, one has to ask whether, but for the defendant's (wrongful) conduct, the harmful result would have occurred. If it would, that conduct has not caused the harmful result; it cannot be counted among its necessary conditions.[253] Whether or not the sine qua non test (which, after all, involves a process of elimination in thought)[254] can really be said to reduce causation to a pure question of fact and merely to reflect scientific notions of physical sequence, the main problem is that it casts the net of liability far too widely. It has been pointed out above that the phrase "to injure somebody else's life", as used in § 823 I BGB, is taken to mean "to cause (that person's) death";[255] and "causing death", in turn, is usually interpreted in terms of the sine qua non test: "to furnish a condition without which the death would not have occurred." Hence the daunting prospect that a motorcar manufacturer might be liable for any accident in which his cars are subsequently involved (had he not produced the car, nobody could have been killed by it) or that a parent may be held responsible for the crimes committed by his children (if one eliminates in thought the acts of conception, the specific crimes in question would not have been perpetrated).

This is where a second unquestioned premise of the modern law of delict comes in: the defendant cannot be liable merely because his conduct has "in fact" caused the harmful result. Some means must be found of limiting his liability.[256] Fault is not sufficient for this purpose, for it would hardly be acceptable either, from the point of view of social policy, to establish liability wherever harm has been culpably caused. Such a regime would stifle, for instance, all forms of lawful competition. What is required, is "a policy-based mechanism for eliminating from the causal net these factual consequences for which it would be unreasonable or undesirable to impose liability".[257] Should one[258] therefore limit the actor's liability to those consequences that were

---

[252] Cf. e.g. Hart and Honoré, op. cit., note 250, pp. 108 sqq.; A.M. Honoré, "Causation and Remoteness of Damage", in: *International Encyclopedia of Comparative Law*, vol. XI, 7, nn. 106 sqq.; Fleming, *Torts*, pp. 173 sqq.; for South Africa cf. e.g. *Minister of Police v. Skosana* 1977 (1) SA 31 (A) at 33 sqq.

[253] On the use of the term "condition" and on the (German) "*Äquivalenztheorie*", cf. Hart and Honoré, op. cit., note 250, pp. 431 sqq.

[254] And therefore, in a way, presupposes what it sets out to prove, on the basis of a priori conclusions derived from experience. For criticism of the sine qua non test, cf., for example, the discussions by Honoré, op. cit., note 252, nn. 108 sqq and Boberg, *Delict*, pp. 383 sqq.; cf. also e.g. Jürgen Rödig, *Die Denkform der Alternative in der Jurisprudenz* (1969), pp. 115 sqq.

[255] Supra, p. 977.

[256] Boberg, *Delict*, p. 380.

[257] Boberg, *Delict*, p. 387; cf. also Fleming, *Torts*, pp. 173, 181 sqq.; Hart and Honoré, op. cit., note 250, passim, e.g. pp. 88 sqq.

[258] For an overview of the different theories that have been developed, cf. Boberg, *Delict*, pp. 439 sqq.; Honoré, op. cit., note 252, nn. 67 sqq.; Fleming, *Torts*, pp. 181 sqq.; Lange, *Schadensersatz*, pp. 51 sqq.

reasonably foreseeable at the time of acting?[259] Or perhaps rather to those that flowed directly from his conduct, without the operation of a novus actus interveniens (irrespective of whether the specific result in question was reasonably foreseeable)?[260] Or should one require the causal bond between conduct and harmful result to be "adequate" in the sense that, according to common experience, the result can be regarded as a normal or natural consequence of the conduct?[261] Does one have to focus on the purpose of the rule violated and eliminate all those consequences that are not covered by its protective scope?[262] Or would it be more appropriate in this context to activate the requirements of wrongfulness and fault and to ask not (as has traditionally been done) whether the defendant's conduct was wrongful and culpable in abstracto, but whether it was wrongful and culpable in relation to the harm complained of?[263] Does one have to establish (and limit) two causal connections: namely that between the defendant's conduct and the harmful result (existence of liability) as opposed to that between the harmful result (for instance: the injury to bodily integrity or life) and the resulting damages (extent of liability)?[264] These are a few of the criteria suggested and some of the issues canvassed in modern legal literature. Two things are obvious: since we are dealing with questions of legal policy[265] rather than with logic or scientific notions, the idea of a specific province of legal causation (as opposed to factual causation) seems to be unsound and misleading. And secondly: causal questions cannot sensibly be discussed in isolation. They frequently interrelate with wrongfulness and fault as well as with broader policy considerations.[266] To try to isolate an explicit doctrine of causation

[259] The leading case embracing the foreseeability test is *The Wagon Mound* (supra, note 249). For a detailed analysis (and a proposed restatement) of the foreseeability test, see J.C. Smith, *Liability in Negligence* (1984), pp. 91 sqq., 131 sqq.

[260] Leading case (dethroned by *The Wagon Mound*) *In re Polemis (In re an arbitration between Polemis and Furness, Withy & Co. Ltd.)*, [1921] 3 KB 560 (CA), but cf. Bacon's maxim "in jure non remota causa sed proxima spectatur" which is analysed by Joseph H. Beale, "The Proximate Consequences of an Act", (1919–20) 33 *Harvard LR* 633 sqq.

[261] On the so-called adequate cause theory cf., for example, Lange, *Schadensersatz*, pp. 57 sqq.; Hart and Honoré, op. cit., note 250, pp. 465 sqq.

[262] Prevailing view in modern German law; cf., in particular, Ernst von Caemmerer, "Das Problem des Kausalzusammenhangs im Privatrecht", in: *Gesammelte Schriften*, vol. I (1968), pp. 395 sqq.; Lange, *Schadensersatz*, pp. 76 sqq.

[263] This approach is strongly urged by Boberg, *Delict*, pp. 274 sqq., 380 sqq. On the difference between the abstract and the relative concept of negligence, cf. the clear analysis by W.H.B. Dean, "Culpability or Remoteness", (1974) 91 *SALJ* 47 sqq.

[264] "Haftungsbegründende Kausalität" as opposed to "haftungsausfüllende Kausalität"; cf. e.g. Hart and Honoré, op. cit., note 250, p. 85; Lange, *Schadensersatz*, pp. 54 sq.; Zimmermann, 1980 *Juristenzeitung* 16.

[265] Cf. e.g. Andrews J in *Palsgraf v. Long Island Railroad Co.* (1928) 248 NY 339 at 352, 162 NE 99 at 103: ". . . because of convenience, of public policy, or a rough sense of justice, the law arbitrarily declines to trace a series of events beyond a certain point. This is not logic. It is practical politics."

[266] This point is made particularly clearly with regard to Roman law by MacCormack, *Studi Sanfilippo*, vol. I, p. 283.

from the Roman sources would therefore be a doubly inappropriate endeavour.

(b) *The Roman approach*

Of course, the Roman lawyers did not grant an action, if there was no "causal" connection between harmful result and the defendant's conduct. But this was more a matter of common sense than of conceptualizing and applying logical or philosophic notions.[267] There is no evidence for the use by the jurists of a specific theory of causation. Even the phrase "causam mortis praestare" was used as a term of common parlance rather than as a vehicle for the reception of Greek philosophical discussions on causation;[268] and the idea of a conditio sine qua non, though known and used as an argument to establish or to reject liability in other contexts,[269] hardly ever surfaces in our texts dealing with the lex Aquilia. These texts always take for granted that the defendant's conduct did cause the injury. What remained to be discussed was merely whether the specific manner in which the injury had been brought about justified the application of the lex Aquilia or merely of an actio in factum.[270] The answer to this enquiry, in turn, did not depend on considerations of causation either. The narrow scope of chapters one and three was not attributable to the fact that the Romans of the 3rd century B.C. should have been unable to conceive of the idea of indirect causality;[271] it was merely determined by the (linguistic) meaning of the operative verbs.[272] "Occidere, urere, frangere, rumpere" all implied, as a matter of course, that death or injury had to have been "caused" by the defendant, but so did "causam mortis praestare". Yet the specific terms had once been chosen in order to describe as clearly and forcibly as possible an action that was manifestly and palpably wrong; and it was this traditional core meaning which was perpetuated by way of a restrictive interpretation. The decision whether a particular act was a direct or indirect cause of damage therefore did not depend "on an abstract exercise in causation. It (was)

---

[267] Károly Visky, "Die Frage der Kausalität aufgrund des D. 9, 2 (ad legem Aquiliam)", (1979) 26 *RIDA* 475 sqq., 501; MacCormack, *Studi Sanfilippo*, vol. I, pp. 263 sqq.; cf. also e.g. Lord Dunedin in *Leyland Shipping Co. Ltd. v. Norwich Union Fire Insurance Society* [1918] AC 350 (HL) at 362 (". . . question . . . to be determined by common-sense principles").

[268] Cf. the comprehensive analysis of this phrase in philosophical, rhetorical and legal literature by Nörr, *Causa mortis*, passim.

[269] For a detailed analysis, see Reinhard Willvonseder, *Die Verwendung der Denkfigur der "conditio sine qua non" bei den römischen Juristen* (1984), pp. 32 sqq.

[270] Willvonseder, op. cit., note 269, pp. 12 sqq., 194.

[271] Dieter Nörr, *Essays Honoré*, p. 205 writes: "If that were right we would have to conclude that the Romans, a warlike people, did not properly understand what they were doing when they killed enemies or criminals by starvation." The argument is developed in greater detail in *Causa mortis*, pp. 2, 122 sq.

[272] Particularly clear on this point is Andrews, (1987) *Cambridge LJ* 315 sqq., 328.

firmly anchored in the interpretation of . . . one of the . . . operative words of the lex Aquilia."[273]

(c) Concurrent causation

What did this approach imply with regard to notorious problem areas such as concurrent causation?[274] Take the case of a slave who is mortally wounded by A. Before he dies, however, he receives another wound from B which immediately kills him. Application of the conditio sine qua non test poses a problem. If we put the test question: "Would the slave have died but for A's conduct?", the answer is clearly "Yes". The same applies if we ask: "Would the death have occurred if B had not intervened?" Neither A nor B, therefore, seems to have caused the death: hardly an acceptable result. It could be avoided by accepting a sine qua non relation, if the harmful result would not have occurred in this specific manner and at this specific moment without the interference of A (or B). But would one then not have to hold a surgeon liable who has "caused" his patient's death in the course of an unskilful operation, even though the patient would not have survived a skilful operation either?[275]

The Roman lawyers were not hemmed in by this or any other dogma and decided the case according to their understanding of the word "occidere". "Celsus scribit", reports Ulpian,[276]

> "si alius mortifero vulnere percusserit, alius postea exanimaverit, priorem quidem non teneri quasi occiderit, sed quasi vulneraverit, quia ex alio vulnere periit, posteriorem teneri, quia occidit. quod et Marcello videtur et est probabilis."

Undoubtedly, according to Celsus, Marcellus and Ulpian, B has committed "occidere". A, on the other hand, has not directly brought about the slave's death. B's action intervened and (as a modern lawyer might say)[277] "broke" "the chain of causation". A's conduct can therefore not be labelled "occidere"; liability can arise only under chapter three of the lex Aquilia. But this solution was not undisputed. Julian took the view that both B *and* A were liable under chapter one:

---

[273] MacCormack, *Studi Sanfilippo*, vol. I, p. 282.

[274] See, generally, Honoré, op. cit., note 252, nn. 130 sqq.; Hart and Honoré, op. cit., note 250, pp. 205 sqq.; Ernst von Caemmerer, "Das Problem der überholenden Kausalität im Schadensersatzrecht", in: *Gesammelte Schriften*, vol. I (1968), pp. 411 sqq.; Lange, *Schadensersatz*, pp. 110 sqq.

[275] Honoré, op. cit., note 252, n. 111. This is only one of the conundra raised by the sine qua non test. For exceptions and alleged exceptions to the conditio sine qua non rule, see Honoré, op. cit., note 252, nn. 119 sqq.

[276] D. 9, 2, 11, 3.

[277] Cf. e.g. Honoré, op. cit., note 252, n. 130 read in conjunction with nn. 77 sqq. Cf., in this context, *Weld-Blundell v. Stephens* [1920] AC 956 (HL) at 986: "Perhaps one may be forgiven for saying that B snaps the chain of causation; that he is no mere conduit pipe through which consequences flow from A to C, no mere moving part in a transmission gear set in motion by A; that, in a word, he insulates A from C"; on which, see A.L. Goodhart, "The Third Man or Novus Actor Interveniens" (1951) 4 *Current Legal Problems* 190: "My only comment is that four metaphors do not constitute one argument."

> "rursus Aquilia lege teneri existimati sunt non solum qui ita vulnerassent, ut confestim vita privarent, sed etiam hi, quorum ex vulnere certum esset aliquem vita excessurum."[278]

It is the action of inflicting a fatal wound as such that must be termed "occidere"; as long as death is certain to result from it, it does not matter whether it occurs immediately or only after a while.[279] This conception of occidere, incidentally, was also the reason why Julian calculated the period determined in the "quanti id in eo anno plurimi fuerit" clause from the moment the slave received the mortal injury.[280] At this stage he had already committed occidere. Celsus, in line with the argument advanced in D. 9, 2, 11, 3, regarded the moment of death as crucial.[281]

2. The actio legis Aquiliae and analogous remedies

(a) Actio directa and actiones in factum

We may now turn to our second question. The actio legis Aquiliae was proposed in the edict, the actiones in factum were not. It was therefore not on account of a specific promise, contained in his "annual statute",[282] that the praetor was prepared to grant an action, but he decided on the allegations in each particular case and on the basis of his general imperium whether that would be the equitable and appropriate thing for him to do. How exactly the formulae of these actiones in factum were drafted, we do not know; but we can safely assume that they were very closely modelled on the ones applicable to the actio legis Aquiliae (directa). If we take the second of the cases mentioned by Ofilius as an example,[283] the intentio may have read "Si paret N^m N^m servum A^i A^i in insidias deduxisse causamve mortis praebuisse . . .".[284] The essential facts of the case, as alleged by the plaintiff, had to be specifically stated; of course, they could not be summed up by the term "occidere", for the whole point of applying for an actio in factum was to escape the narrow interpretive confines of this term. The actiones in

---

[278] Iul. D. 9, 2, 51 pr.

[279] But see also Ulp. D. 9, 2, 15, 1, where Iulianus is purported to have adopted the same view as Celsus. This contradiction has given rise to a host of speculations. The three texts D. 9, 2, 11, 3, D. 9, 2, 15, 1 and D. 9, 2, 51 and the problem of the "overtaking cause" have frequently been discussed; cf., in particular, Karl-Heinz Schindler, "Ein Streit zwischen Julian und Celsus", (1957) 74 *ZSS* 201 sqq.; David Pugsley, "Causation and Confessions in the lex Aquilia", (1970) 38 *TR* 163 sqq.; von Lübtow, *Lex Aquilia*, pp. 59 sqq.; MacCormack, (1975) 41 *SDHI* 26 sqq.; Visky, (1979) 26 *RIDA* 486 sqq.; Hans Ankum, "Das Problem der 'überholenden Kausalität' bei der Anwendung der lex Aquilia im klassischen römischen Recht", in: *De iustitia et iure, Festgabe für Ulrich von Lübtow* (1980), pp. 325 sqq.; Lawson/Markesinis, pp. 30 sqq.; Willvonseder, op. cit., note 269, pp. 144 sqq.; Nörr, *Causa mortis*, pp. 181 sqq.; Hausmaninger, *Lex Aquilia*, pp. 17 sq.

[280] Cf. Ulp. D. 9, 2, 21, 1; supra, p. 961, note 69.

[281] Cf. Ulp. D. 9, 2, 21, 1; supra, p. 961, note 69.

[282] Frier, *Roman Jurists*, p. 44.

[283] Supra, p. 981, note 196.

[284] Nörr, *Causa mortis*, p. 158.

factum were possibly slightly more streamlined than the actio directa in that certain features of the latter, which had come to be regarded as rather odd or as outdated, were not grafted onto the former. Thus, the praetorian actions for indirect damage may not have entailed litiscrescence (they could, in other words, be granted only as an actio in simplum),[285] they may have simply been for "quanti ea res erit" (rather than requiring calculations running forwards or backwards) and they may have lost certain of the penal attributes of the actio legis Aquiliae.[286] Generally speaking, however, the plaintiff was no worse off if he could proceed "only" under an actio in factum rather than under the actio directa; more particularly, at least in classical law, he was not exposed to the vagaries of an entirely discretionary decision on the part of the praetor, for actiones in factum appear to have been granted as a matter of course. They served to extend the protective ambit of the lex Aquilia by way of analogy:[287] the only difference to the modern argumentum per analogiam being that we would approach the issue from the point of view of substantive law whereas Roman law was actional law: it was, first and foremost, not the analogous rule as such that had to be carved out, but the analogous remedy that had to be provided (ubi remedium ibi ius).

(b) Actiones utiles

Furthermore, there were a variety of situations where neither the actio directa nor an actio in factum but an actio utilis was granted. Some of the cases of indirect causation fall into this category,[288] and so do certain instances where Aquilian-type protection was accorded to non-owners.[289] Under the lex Aquilia, it was only the dominus (erus) who could sue,[290] but, at least by the time of classical law,

[285] Barton, *Daube Noster*, pp. 21 sqq. (who argues that this explains the "hostility" and "viciously restrictive [attitude]" of the classical lawyers towards the actio directa; they wished to force plaintiffs to use praetorian actions in the greatest possible number of cases, because they could thus avoid the inequitable doubling of damages); Nörr, *Causa mortis*, pp. 149 sqq.; idem, (1987) 6 *RJ* 111 sqq. (on the basis of a most ingenious reconstruction of the "drama" in front of the praetor, when the correct type of action had to be chosen).

[286] Thielmann, *Studi Biscardi*, vol. II, pp. 314 sqq.

[287] Cf. e.g. Walter Selb, "Formulare Analogien in 'actiones utiles' und 'actiones in factum' am Beispiel Julians", in: *Studi in onore di Arnaldo Biscardi*, vol. III (1982), pp. 315 sqq.

[288] Cf. e.g. Ulp. D. 47, 8, 2, 20; Gai. D. 47, 2, 51; Ulp. D. 9, 2, 27, 9; Paul. D. 9, 2, 30, 2.

[289] For an overview cf. von Lübtow, *Lex Aquilia*, pp. 169 sqq.; Kaser, *RPr* I, p. 622; Hausmaninger, *Lex Aquilia*, pp. 33 sq. Cf. also J.M. Thomson, Who Could Sue on the lex Aquilia? (1975) 91 *LQR* 207 sqq. He argues that the actio *directa* was granted to persons who were not strictly dominus. Only towards the end of the Republic and in the course of a general move towards an interpretative restriction of the lex Aquilia (cf., in another context, supra, p. 982, notes 198, 199) was the actio directa confined to owners and did the praetor therefore have to devise analogous claims for non-owners.

[290] Cf. supra, note 48.

usufructuaries[291] and pledgees[292] were counted among those who could bring an actio utilis. Even the commodatary may, according to the opinion of Marcellus, have been able to avail himself of this remedy: for Marcellus that must have followed from his contention that the commodatary's custodia liability covered instances of damnum iniuria datum.[293] Yet there are also cases where a non-owner was granted, rather oddly, an actio in factum: a tenant (provided he gave an undertaking that the lessor/owner would not himself institute an action),[294] a bonae fidei possessor (when the object in question had been destroyed by the owner)[295] and occasionally even the pledgee[296] (who could resort, in other cases, to the actio utilis).[297] What was the difference between these two types of actions, and why did one sometimes turn to the one and sometimes to the other? Originally, actiones in factum and actiones utiles appear to have been two separate techniques by means of which the praetors were able to supplement, to correct and to adapt the ius civile.[298] As far as the lex Aquilia is concerned, the actio in factum was competent where the factual circumstances of a specific case did not fit in with the statutory verbs (occidere, urere frangere rumpere); an actio utilis, on the other hand, was the apposite remedy to extend the right to sue to persons other than the owner.[299] With the final codification of the praetorian edict by Iulianus sometime around A.D. 130, the creative and innovatory activity of the praetors was practically stopped and the ius honorarium lost its flexibility. At the same time, the responsibility for the administration of justice shifted to the imperial courts and chancellery; closely connected

[291] Ulp. D. 7, 1, 17, 3; ("Si quis servum occiderit, utilem actionem exemplo Aquiliae fructuario dandam numquam dubitavi"); Ulp. D. 9, 2, 11, 10; but see the discussion by John Iliffe, "The Usufructuary as Plaintiff under the lex Aquilia according to the Classical Jurists", (1965) 12 *RIDA* 325 sqq.

[292] But only "propter inopiam debitoris vel quod litem amisit" and limited "ad modum debiti": Paul. D. 9, 2, 30, 1. Normally, the actio legis Aquiliae was available to the pledgor/debtor, and it would have been inequitable to give an action against the wrongdoer both to the pledgor and to the pledgee. For details cf. Joseph Georg Wolf, "D. 20, 1, 27 Marc. 5 dig. Zur Aktivlegitimation des Pfandgläubigers für die actio legis Aquiliae", (1959) 76 *ZSS* 520 sqq.

[293] Cf. Ulp. D. 19, 2, 41; contra: Iul./Ulp. D. 9, 2, 11, 9 (based on Iul. D. 13, 6, 19: "Ad eos, qui . . . utendum [aliquid] accipiunt, damnum iniuria ab alio datum non pertinere procul dubio est").

[294] Cels./Ulp. D. 9, 2, 27, 14; for details: MacCormack, (1973) 20 *RIDA* 341 sqq.

[295] Ulp. D. 9, 2, 17; for details: Pernice, *Sachbeschädigungen*, pp. 190 sqq.; Felix Wubbe, "Der gutgläubige Besitzer, Mensch oder Begriff?", (1963) 80 *ZSS* 193 sqq.

[296] Ulp. D. 9, 2, 17.

[297] Supra n. 292.

[298] Cf. Pap. D. 1, 1, 7, 1 ("Ius praetorium est, quod praetores introduxerunt adiuvandi vel supplendi vel corrigendi iuris civilis gratia propter utilitatem publicam"); Marci. D. 1, 1, 8 ("Nam et ipsum ius honorarium viva vox est iuris civilis").

[299] Cf., in particular, Walter Selb, "Actiones in factum und Formeltechnik", in: *Festschrift für Heinrich Demelius* (1973), pp. 230 sqq.; idem, *Studi Biscardi*, vol. III, pp. 312 sqq.; idem, "Formulare Analogien in actiones utiles und actiones in factum vor Julian", in: *Studi in onore di Cesare Sanfilippo*, vol. V (1984), pp. 729 sqq.; Max Kaser, " 'Ius honorarium' und 'ius civile' ", (1984) 101 *ZSS* 95 sqq.

with those developments was the rise of the new cognitio procedure ("extra ordinem"). As a result, the intricacies of the conceptiones formularum were of less and less practical relevance and no longer interested the jurists very much.

> "Nec refert directa quis an utili actione agat vel conveniatur, quia in extraordinariis iudiciis, ubi conceptio formularum non observatur, haec suptilitas supervacua est, maxime cum utraque actio eiusdem potestatis est eundemque habet effectum",

says Paul;[300] and if even the distinction between "actio directa" and "analogous claim" was regarded as a cumbersome and rather unnecessary subtlety, how much less appreciation can one expect for the outmoded difference between different types of analogous claims! Gaius, in fact, already made the first attempt to simplify matters: he used the term "actio utilis" whenever a claim was granted on the model of the actio legis Aquiliae directa.[301] Most of the other lawyers, however, continued to use the traditional terms. But since all that mattered to them was that both the actiones utiles and actiones in factum had the effect of extending the range of application of the lex Aquilia, they employed both phrases, entirely promiscuously, whenever they referred to an action other than the actio directa[302]—hence the enormous terminological confusion in our sources.

(c) *Justinian's rationalization*

Justinian, in turn, even added to this confusion. In his Digest he perpetuated the terminology as employed by the classical jurists. Obviously it was not inappropriate, under those circumstances, to attempt to provide some kind of rational explanation in his statutory textbook. He probably adopted the one currently in use at the East-Roman faculties of law[303] and thus arrived at the famous three-membered classification in *Inst.* IV, 3, 16:[304] actio legis Aquiliae directa in cases of damnum corpore corpori datum, actio utilis where the damage corpori had not been brought about corpore,[305] actio in factum "si non corpore damnum fuerit datum neque corpus laesum

---

[300] D. 3, 5, 46, 1.

[301] III, 219.

[302] Selb, *Festschrift Demelius*, pp. 223 sqq.; idem, *Studi Biscardi*, vol. III, pp. 328.; but cf. also Hasse, *Culpa*, pp. 36 sq.; Pernice, *Sachbeschädigungen*, pp. 145, 157 sqq.; Schulz, *CRL*, p. 591; Kaser, *RPr* I, p. 621; idem, (1984) 101 *ZSS* 101; Thielmann, *Studi Biscardi*, vol. II, pp. 303 sqq.; Paul van Warmelo, "Les actions autour de la loi Aquilie", in: *Studi in onore di Arnaldo Biscardi*, vol. III (1982), pp. 351 sqq.; Honsell/Mayer-Maly/Selb, p. 367; Gunter Wesener, "Utiles actiones in factum", in: *Studi in onore di Emilio Betti*, vol. IV (1962), pp. 503 sqq.

[303] Van Warmelo, *Studi Biscardi*, vol. III, p. 360.

[304] On which see, for example, von Lübtow, *Lex Aquilia*, pp. 209 sqq.; Paul van Warmelo, "The Institutes of Justinian as Students' Manual", in: *Studies in Justinian's Institutes in memory of J.A.C. Thomas* (1983), pp. 175 sqq.

[305] That is, the cases where an object was damaged, but not as a direct consequence of a physical action of the wrongdoer.

fuerit, sed alio modo damnum alicui contigit."[306] This scheme, of course, had little to do with the historical truth;[307] nor did it really correspond with the sources contained in the Digest.[308] Still, it was not without elegance; and since, in any event, the whole question was devoid of any practical relevance, it survived the centuries essentially unchallenged. Down to the days of the pandectists, Justinian's threefold classification was faithfully preserved,[309] but it was noted that for all practical purposes there was no difference between the various types of actions.[310]

---

[306] That is, cases where the owner was deprived of the use of his object which, in turn, was, however, neither damaged nor stolen; cf. the examples supra, pp. 986 sq.

[307] Thomas, *Institutes*, pp. 274 sq. writes with mild irony: ". . . the imperial assertion in respect of the niceties of a system of procedure several centuries out of use may be received with scepticism."

[308] Cf. already Pernice, *Sachbeschädigungen*, pp. 144 sqq. Von Lübtow, *Lex Aquilia*, pp. 135 sqq., 180 sqq., 202 sqq., cf. also idem, (1984) 30 *Labeo* 317 sqq. has, however, argued that *Inst.* IV, 3, 16 reflects the position in classical law.

[309] Cf., for example, Glück, vol. 10, pp. 334 sq.

[310] Windscheid/Kipp, § 455, n. 3.

CHAPTER 30

Lex Aquilia II

I. THE STATUTORY DEFINITION OF THE DELICT: INIURIA

1. Damnum iniuria datum

(a) The notion of "non iure facere"

"Occidere" and "urere frangere rumpere" were relatively straightforward, predominantly factual and descriptive requirements of the Aquilian delict. Matters were more intricate when it came to the notion of iniuria,[1] as contained in chapters one and three. Only "damnum facere" of a specific kind could be labelled as a private wrong and it was the complex concept of "iniuria" that gave the action of the defendant its distinctly delictual flavour. A stabs to death B's slave who is lying in ambush to rob him.[2] C pulls down his neighbour's house to keep a fire off his own.[3] The aedil D smashes some beds that have been left lying around in via publica so as to endanger the traffic.[4] E enters a slave of his for a public boxing and wrestling contest (pancratium) in the course of which the latter is killed by his opponent F.[5] There can be no doubt that in all of these cases we are dealing with damage that has been directly inflicted: with "occidere" (A and F) or "corrumpere" (C and D) in the most literal and manifest sense of the words. And yet, it would scarcely be appropriate to award damages to B, to the neighbour, to the owner of the beds or to E. Why not? Because, as we would put it, in none of these instances had the damage been wrongfully inflicted.[6] For the Romans, this was the first, and possibly the most obvious, implication of "iniuria": "Iniuria ex eo dicta est, quod non iure fiat: omne enim, quod non iure fit, iniuria fieri dicitur."[7]

---

[1] "[O]ne of the most impressive achievements of the Roman legal mind": Lawson/Markesinis, p. 19.

[2] Cf. Gai. D. 9, 2, 4 pr.

[3] Cf. Cels./Ulp. D. 9, 2, 49, 1.

[4] Cf. Ulp. D. 18, 6, 13.

[5] Cf. Ulp. D. 9, 2, 7, 4.

[6] For the modern concept of wrongfulness, cf. e.g. Jean Limpens/Robert M. Kruithof/Anne Meinertzhagen-Limpens, "Liability for One's Own Act", in: *International Encyclopedia of Comparative Law*, vol. XI, 2 (1983), nn. 28 sqq.; Erwin Deutsch, *Haftungsrecht*, vol. I (1976), pp. 190 sqq.; Boberg, *Delict*, pp. 30 sqq. In French legal science, no clear distinction is drawn between unlawfulness and fault; both are taken to be implicit in the concept of faute, as contained in art. 1382 code civil; cf. e.g. Zweigert/Kötz, pp. 356 sqq.

[7] Ulp. D. 47, 10, 1 pr.; cf. also Ulp. D. 9, 2, 5, 1 ("Iniuriam autem hic accipere nos oportet . . . quod non iure factum est, hoc est contra ius . . ."); Paul. Coll. II, V, 1 ("Generaliter dicitur iniuria omne, quod non iure fit"); Inst. IV, 4 pr.; for a discussion cf.

Normally, one did not have to worry very much about this element of wrongfulness, for, as a rule, it was inherent in the very acts of killing and of injuring. Anybody who committed "occidere" or "urere frangere rumpere" could prima facie be said to have acted wrongfully.[8] But there were certain exceptional situations, where the equation occidere/urere frangere rumpere = occidere/urere frangere rumpere iniuria did not work out; situations where, as the modern lawyer would say, the injury, although it had been inflicted both directly and intentionally, was justified.[9]

(b) Self-defence

Self-defence was the first of these grounds of justification. "Vim vi repellere licere Cassius scribit idque ius natura comparatur":[10] natural reason permits a person to defend himself, even if he has to resort to violence. Of course, there were certain limits to the right of self-defence. It was admissible only against an unlawful attack. Thus, if A was assaulted by B and threw a stone to defend himself, he was still liable if the stone did not hit B, but the innocent passer-by C;[11] C had not launched the attack against A, and any infringement of his bodily integrity was therefore unlawful. Furthermore, the attack had to be

---

Pernice, *Sachbeschädigungen*, pp. 26 sqq., 34 sqq.; Schipani, *Lex Aquilia*, pp. 51 sqq., 296 sqq.; Peter Birks, "The Early History of iniuria", (1969) 37 *TR* 163 sqq.; von Lübtow, *Lex Aquilia*, pp. 83 sqq., 94 sqq.

[8] A similar argument is usually adopted as far as the interpretation of § 823 I BGB is concerned and hence the distinction, even in the interpretatio moderna of the German statutory version of Aquilian liability, between direct injuries on the one hand, and those brought about indirectly and liability for omissions on the other. Here the wrongfulness of the defendant's behaviour has to be positively established (did he owe a duty of care to the plaintiff and did he act in breach of this duty? The enquiry is thus very similar to the one conducted in English law in order to establish "negligence" (cf., for example, infra, p. 1039, note 264); it involves the balancing of conflicting interests and is thus ultimately a matter of public policy; cf. e.g. Fleming, *Torts*, pp. 125 sqq.; Boberg, *Delict*, pp. 33 sqq.); there the element of wrongfulness is taken to be automatically satisfied and is removed only if a specific legally recognized defence can be invoked. Cf. Ernst von Caemmerer, "Wandlungen des Deliktrechts", in: *Gesammelte Schriften*, vol. I (1968), pp. 478 sqq.; Hans Stoll, "Unrechtstypen bei Verletzung absoluter Rechte", (1963) 162 *Archiv für die civilistische Praxis* 205 sqq. For a similar distinction in South African law, cf. Boberg, *Delict*, pp. 32 sq.; cf. also J.C. Smith, *Liability in Negligence* (1984), pp. 26, 29 sqq. and passim.

[9] Cf., in particular, Pernice, *Sachbeschädigungen*, pp. 34 sqq.; Ben Beinart, "The relationship of iniuria and culpa in the lex Aquilia", in: *Studi in onore di Vincenzo Arangio-Ruiz*, vol. I (1953), pp. 282 sqq.; Lawson/Markesinis, pp. 19 sqq.; Hausmaninger, *Lex Aquilia*, pp. 20 sqq.

[10] Ulp. D. 43, 16, 1, 27; cf. also Gai. D. 9, 2, 4 pr. (". . . nam adversus periculum naturalis ratio permittit se defendere"); Paul. D. 9, 2, 45, 4 ("vim enim vi defendere omnes leges omniaque iura permittunt"); Alfred Pernice, *Labeo*, vol. II, 1 (2nd ed., 1895), pp. 73 sqq.; Paul van Warmelo, "Noodweer", 1967 *Acta Juridica* 10 sqq; Giannetto Longo, "Sulla legittima difesa e sullo stato di necessità in diritto romano", in: *Sein und Werden im Recht, Festgabe für Ulrich von Lübtow* (1970), pp. 321 sqq.; Hausmaninger, *Lex Aquilia*, pp. 20 sq.; Andreas Wacke, "Defence and necessity in Aquilian liability", (1987) 20 *De Jure* 83 sqq. On the philosophical justification of defence in terms of the ius naturale and the ius gentium, cf. Stephan Kuttner, *Kanonistische Schuldlehre von Gratian bis auf die Dekretalen Gregors IX* (1935), pp. 334 sqq.

[11] Paul. D. 9, 2, 45, 4.

imminent. Use of force against a person who has already completed his attack cannot be justified, since it constitutes an act of revenge, rather than self-defence: "illum . . . solum qui vim infert ferire conceditur, et hoc, si tuendi dumtaxat, non etiam ulciscendi causa factum sit."[12] And finally, even if the attack was both unlawful and imminent, the prospective victim was not allowed to resort to unreasonable and excessive means in order to try to ward it off.[13] Of course, if one's life was threatened, one was allowed to kill the attacker.[14] But if an imminent theft could have been prevented by arresting the thief, it was not permissible quite simply to stab him to death.[15] If somebody was hit with a whip and, in the resulting brawl, poked out one of the attacker's eyes, he had not acted iniuria;[16] but if a shopkeeper, whose lantern was taken away, pursued the thief, got hold of him, tried to snatch back his lantern and, in the course of doing so, put out the thief's eye with a spiked whip[17] which he was carrying, he was accountable for the injury inflicted.[18,19]

(c) Necessity

If we turn our attention to the second of the above-mentioned

[12] Paul. D. 9, 2, 45, 4; cf. also *Cockroft v. Smith* (1705) 11 Mod Rep 43.

[13] Cf. also Limpens/Kruithof/Meinertzhagen-Limpens, op. cit., note 6, n. 168 ("The force used in defence must be proportionate to the attack"); Fleming, *Torts*, p. 77 ("The force used must not exceed what reasonably appears to be necessary to beat off the attack"), § 227 II BGB.

[14] Ulp. D. 9, 2, 5 pr. ("Sed et si quemcumque alium ferro se petentem quis occiderit, non videbitur iniuria occidisse").

[15] Ulp. D. 9, 2, 5 pr. (". . . sin autem cum posset adprehendere, maluit occidere, magis est ut iniuria fecisse videatur"); cf. also *Cook v. Beal* 1 Ld Raym 176 at 177.

[16] Alf. D. 9, 2, 52, 1.

[17] Or sword-cane: flagellum, in quo dolor inerat.

[18] Alf. D. 9, 2, 52, 1. The taker of the lantern was, incidentally, not treated as a thief in this text; the incident, from which the scuffle developed, was probably nothing but a "drunken prank": cf. Geoffrey MacCormack, "Aquilian Studies", (1975) 41 *SDHI* 46 sq. For a full interpretation of Alf. D. 9, 2, 52, 1 from the point of view of defence, see Wacke, (1987) 20 *De Jure* 88 sqq.

[19] The Roman sources thus contained all the essential elements still constituting the justification of self-defence in modern law; cf. Limpens/Kruithof/Meinertzhagen-Limpens, op. cit., note 6, nn. 167 sqq.; Fleming, *Torts*, pp. 76 sq.; § 227 BGB. For details of the historical development cf. Hans Schmitt-Lermann, *Die Lehre von der Notwehr in der Wissenschaft des gemeinen Strafrechts* (1930), pp. 12 sqq.; Kuttner, op. cit., note 10, pp. 334 sqq.; cf. also Van Warmelo, 1967 *Acta Juridica* 10 sqq., 15 sqq. (Roman-Dutch law); Wacke, (1987) 20 *De Jure* 86 sq. Bartolus and Baldus labelled the three requirements restricting the right of defence "circa causam" (the causa of the act must be defence not revenge), "circa tempus" (attack must be imminent) and "circa modum" (the requirement of paritas armorum). Christian doctrine had some difficulty in reconciling the right of self-defence with Christ's admonition in his Sermon on the Mount: "But I say unto you that ye resist not evil: but whosoever shall smite thee on thy right cheek turn to him the other also" (St. Matthew 5, 39). A whole variety of arguments were advanced in the course of time: Christ did not intend to abrogate the ius naturale (implication: natural law and the teachings of the Bible have equal ranking!); a person who allowed himself to be killed without offering resistance was like a person who committed suicide, and suicide is a tresspass against God (cf. Andreas Wacke, "Der Selbstmord im römischen Recht und in der Rechtsentwicklung", (1980) 97 *ZSS* 32 sqq.).

examples, we encounter a different kind of justification. If C pulls down his neighbour's house in order to save his own, he does not act in self-defence. After all, no unlawful attack is emanating from that neighbour or his house. Nevertheless, C's action may be justified on the basis of, as a modern lawyer would say, (inevitable) necessity.[20] The defence of necessity involves "more obviously than any (other) a hard choice between competing values and a sacrifice of one to the other":[21] without having himself committed any wrong, the neighbour is made to suffer the destruction of his property. Obviously, this can be expected of him only under very special circumstances. Just how special was disputed amongst the Roman lawyers.[22] According to Servius,[23] C's interference with his neighbour's property must have been (objectively) necessary in order to avert a present danger from his own house: only if the fire did in fact reach the neighbour's piece of land was C not taken to have acted unlawfully. Celsus drew the line slightly differently. He did not make the decision dependent on an ex post facto evaluation of the situation, but looked at it from the perspective of the person whose house was threatened by the fire: he was allowed to pull down his neighbour's house, irrespective of whether the fire eventually reached that plot or not—provided only he had been moved by a reasonable fear ("iusto enim metu ductus").[24] Ulpian appears to have approved of this more liberal view when he said "nec enim iniuria hoc fecit, qui se tueri voluit, cum alias non posset".[25] But however this particular issue was settled, nobody appears to have found anything wrong with the fact that the interest protected (the security of C's house) can hardly be said to have outweighed, in principle, the interest of the neighbour not to have his property interfered with. This is rather surprising. Modern legal systems tend to require that the object saved must be considerably more valuable than the one sacrificed;[26] and while

[20] For details, see Limpens/Kruithof/Meinertzhagen-Limpens, op. cit., note 6, nn. 170 sqq.; Fleming, *Torts*, pp. 86 sqq.; §§ 228, 904 BGB.

[21] Fleming, *Torts*, p. 86.

[22] For details, see Pernice, *Labeo*, op. cit., note 10, pp. 66 sqq.; Longo, *Festgabe von Lübtow*, pp. 331 sqq.; Geoffrey MacCormack, "Aquilian Studies", (1975) 41 *SDHI* 53 sqq.; Lawson/Markesinis, pp. 20 sqq.; Hausmaninger, *Lex Aquilia*, pp. 21 sq.; Wacke, (1987) 20 *De Jure* 97 sqq.

[23] Ulp. D. 43, 24, 7, 4; on this text, see Schipani, *Lex Aquilia*, pp. 153 sqq.

[24] Ulp. D. 9, 2, 49, 1 (also emphasizing, however, that the person pulling down his neighbour's house acted iniuria, "nisi magna vi cogente fuerit factum"). On D. 9, 2, 49, 1, see Schipani, *Lex Aquilia*, pp. 310 sqq. Cf. also *Cope v. Sharpe* [1912] 1 KB 496 (CA), where the defence of necessity was successful, even though the fire was eventually extinguished before it reached the defendant's property; at the moment, however, at which the defendant acted, there appeared to be real and imminent danger.

[25] Ulp. D. 47, 9, 3, 7 in fine; for a discussion of the whole text, see Schipani, *Lex Aquilia*, pp. 206 sqq. Ulpian's view was regarded as authoritative on the matter by the authors of the ius commune: cf. Andreas von Tuhr, "Der Nothstand im Civilrecht" (1888), p. 62.

[26] Cf. e.g. § 228 BGB (harm must not be disproportionate to the danger), § 904 BGB (imminent harm must be out of all proportion to the harm inflicted); for France and the French legal family cf. Limpens/Kruithof/Meinertzhagen-Limpens, op. cit., note 6, nn. 173

one may therefore destroy one's neighbours' flowerbeds in an attempt to save one's own house, it is much less obvious that a person should be allowed to sacrifice someone else's house in order to save his own.

It would, however, be rash to generalize the solution adopted by the Roman lawyers in the fire cases. Their lack of concern for the neighbour's property may have been based on the fact that his house was (or at least: appeared to be) doomed by the fire anyway. Under those circumstances, C, in a way, did not save his own house by causing his neighbour any damage; he merely anticipated, as far as the neighbour's house was concerned, what was about to happen to it in any event.[27] At the same time—and that may well have been a second factor militating against imposing liability on the trespasser—C not only saved his own house, but in most cases must have made a significant contribution towards preventing the fire from spreading to other parts of the town. Fires, it will be remembered,[28] were a constant source of apprehension; considering the cramped living conditions in large parts of urban Rome, one was all too often unable to contain them.[29] Once a fire was raging, any private initiative to try to stop it must have been welcome and deserved to be encouraged; and while C may merely have had the safety of his own house in his mind, he usually acted at the same time as a "public champion".[30]

In other cases of emergency the Roman lawyers never seem to have carried the trespasser's exemption from liability that far; there are no other decisions which would have allowed him to infringe upon an interest equal to or even more valuable than the one saved.[31] We merely

sqq. (things sacrificed must be less valuable than the things saved (France); the damage caused must be less serious in kind and quantity than the one the defendant tried to avoid (Argentina)). Only in the common-law countries does there appear to be no specific requirement of this kind; but even here, the measures which are taken must be "reasonable" (cf. Winfield and Jolowicz, p. 723, cf. also p. 725 (more latitude in the protection of the actor's person than of his property)). German law (§ 904, 2 BGB) as well as some other legal systems, whilst maintaining that the infringement of the third party's interest is justified, nevertheless grant a claim for compensation on equitable grounds to that third party; cf. e.g. Limpens/Kruithof/Meinertzhagen-Limpens, op. cit., note 6, nn. 179 sqq.; Fleming, *Torts*, pp. 88 sq.; Winfield and Jolowicz, pp. 723 sqq.

[27] Cf., along very similar lines, Reinhard Willvonseder, *Die Verwendung der Denkfigur der "condicio sine qua non" bei den römischen Juristen* (1984), pp. 157 sqq.; Lawson/Markesinis, p. 21.

[28] Cf. supra, pp. 347 sq.

[29] "The terrible frequency of devastating conflagrations is one of the most remarkable things in the history of Ancient Rome, and hardly less extraordinary is the apparent inadequacy of counteracting measures": P.K. Baillie Reynolds, *The Vigiles of Imperial Rome* (1926), p. 13. Only Augustus established the vigiles, who acted as police force as well as a fire brigade; for details, see W. Krenkel, in: *Kleiner Pauly*, vol. V, col. 1270 and the work by Baillie Reynolds.

[30] Cf. Fleming, *Torts*, p. 86; cf. also *King's Prerogative in Salpetre* (1607) 12 Co Rep 12 (dealing with the case of a person who blew up a house to prevent the fire spreading to the whole town).

[31] Ulp. D. 19, 5, 14 pr. discusses a case where in a situation of maritime distress someone threw somebody else's merchandise overboard in order to save his own. But here, again, the

read of sailors who cut the anchor ropes of another vessel into which their ship was blown, or of fishermen who slashed some fishing nets in which their boat got caught.[32] Provided that vessel and boat could not be extricated in any other way and provided, too, that the emergency was not attributable to any fault on the part of the sailors or the fishermen, no liability under the lex Aquilia ensued. Any modern lawyer would probably come to the same conclusion.[33]

(d) *Actions of a magistrate*

Thirdly, then, the aedil D. Since he was responsible, inter alia, for the safety on the roads, he could take the steps that were necessary to secure safe traffic. If that involved the smashing of some beds, he could not be held liable under the lex Aquilia. The same principle applied to other magistrates who had to cause damage in the exercise of their official functions: "Is, qui iure publico utitur, non videtur iniuriae faciendae causa hoc facere: iuris enim executio non habet iniuriam."[34] Of course, the magistrate could be liable under the lex Aquilia, or an actio in factum, if he exceeded the confines of his authority or acted improperly. Thus, if he returned worn and spoilt what he had seized by way of security, the actio directa could be brought against him;[35] the actio in factum was applicable if the objects seized were cattle and if the animals died in his custody as a result of not being fed.[36]

(e) *Consent*

Finally, concerning the boxing and wrestling contest between E's slave and F in the course of which the slave was mortally wounded, the answer of the jurists was also: lex Aquilia cessat.[37] After all, the slave's owner had consented to the bout. Pancratium was a dangerous sport, where nearly every manoeuvre of hands, feet and body was permitted:

"trespasser" also acted for the benefit of everybody else on board. Cf. also *Mouse's* case, (1609) 12 Co Rep 63. On Quint. Muc./Pomp. D. 9, 2, 39, cf. Okko Behrends, 1985 *Juristische Schulung* 878 sqq.; Hausmaninger, *Lex Aquilia*, p. 23; Wacke, (1987) 20 *De Jure* 92 sqq.

[32] Lab./Proc./Ulp. D. 9, 2, 29, 3; Wacke, (1987) 20 *De Jure* 94 sqq.; cf. also RGZ 5, 160; 88, 211.

[33] For the historical development of the modern doctrine of necessity in private law, cf. Andreas Hatzung, *Dogmengeschichtliche Grundlagen und Entstehung des zivilrechtlichen Notstands* (1984), pp. 56 sqq. (usus modernus), 63 sqq. (natural law), 69 sqq. (pandectism), 90 sqq. (codifications of the age of reason), 134 sqq. (origin of the §§ 228, 904 BGB).

[34] Ulp. D. 47, 10, 13, 1. For examples cf. Ulp. D. 9, 2, 29, 7 (where the magistrate was compelled "quid . . . adversus resistentem violentius [facere]"); Ulp. D. 43, 24, 7, 4 ("incendii arcendi causa vicini aedes intercid[ere]"). Cf. generally Hausmaninger, *Lex Aquilia*, pp. 23 sq.; for modern law Limpens/Kruithof/Meinertzhagen-Limpens, op. cit., note 6, nn. 181 sqq.; Boberg, *Delict*, pp. 771 sqq.

[35] Ulp. D. 9, 2, 29, 7.

[36] Ulp. D. 9, 2, 29, 7.

[37] Ulp. D. 9, 2, 7, 4. On this text cf. Pernice, *Labeo*, op. cit., note 10, pp. 82 sqq.; Schipani, *Lex Aquilia*, pp. 319 sqq.; Wittmann, *Körperverletzung*, pp. 95 sqq.; Andreas Wacke, "Accidents in sport and games in Roman and modern German law", (1979) 42 *THRHR* 282 sq.

a kick in the stomach, all kinds of neck-holds (including strangling), breaking one's opponent's arm or fingers, and the like.[38] And although biting and gouging were forbidden, there was an obvious risk that one of the fighters might not survive this somewhat rough engagement. If a slave was entered for it, his owner could be taken to have waived, to a certain extent, the Aquilian protection that his property normally enjoyed. As long as he kept within the rules of the game,[39] the slave's opponent no longer had to observe the general precept of "alterum non laedere" and could inflict all kinds of injuries. Since the owner had given his consent, these injuries were not "iniuria datum" and did, therefore, not give rise to a claim for damages.[40]

2. The relationship between iniuria and culpa

(a) The new interpretation: damnum culpa datum

We have been trying to isolate a variety of situations where the act of causing death or damage could not be said to have been "non iure factum"; where the defendant had not acted "without right" or, in modern parlance, wrongfully. But this was only one aspect (for us possibly the more obvious one) of the complex notion of iniuria. For the Roman lawyers, Aquilian liability was based on fault (culpa in the broadest sense of the word), and it was the term "iniuria" that provided the obvious point of departure for this remarkable interpretive refinement of the requirements of the lex Aquilia. Only if the defendant could be "blamed" for death or damage were the Roman lawyers of the classical (and even of the Republican) period prepared to attach the label "iniuria" to his act and to make him thus accountable for the damage caused. "[I]d est si culpa quis occiderit" was the phrase that Ulpian appended to his explanation of iniuria,[41] and Gaius stated boldly: "Iniuria autem occidere intellegitur, cuius dolo aut culpa id acciderit."[42] Damnum iniuria datum was taken to imply damnum culpa datum.[43]

---

[38] F.A. Wright, in: *The Oxford Classical Dictionary* (2nd ed., 1970), p. 775; H.A. Harris, *Greek Athletes and Athletics* (1964), pp. 105 sqq.; O.W. Reinmuth, in: *Kleiner Pauly*, vol. IV, col. 460; Wacke, (1979) 42 *THRHR* 282 sq.; Ingomar Weiler, *Der Sport bei den Völkern der Alten Welt* (2nd ed., 1988), pp. 183 sqq.

[39] Such as there were; according to Wright, loc. cit., they were strictly enforced by umpires, who closely watched the combatants.

[40] On consent in modern law cf. Limpens/Kruithof/Meinertzhagen-Limpens, op. cit., note 6, nn. 184 sqq.; Fleming, *Torts*, pp. 72 sqq.; Deutsch, op. cit., note 6, pp. 226 sqq.; Boberg, *Delict*, pp. 724 sqq. The problem of consent is particularly topical in medical malpractice cases: cf. the comprehensive discussion by Dieter Giesen, *International Medical Malpractice Law* (1988), pp. 252 sqq.

[41] D. 9, 2, 5, 1.

[42] III, 211.

[43] Ulp. D. 47, 10, 1 pr.; Ulp. D. 47, 6, 1, 2; Ulp. D. 47, 10, 15, 46; Paul. D. 44, 7, 34 pr.

(b) "Occidere", "urere frangere rumpere" iniuria

How precisely one arrived at this kind of interpretation is a matter of speculation.[44] It is likely, though, that originally (both before and at the time of the enactment of the lex Aquilia) "occidere" and "urere frangere rumpere" were used to describe certain acts that could typically only be committed intentionally. If a slave is stabbed to death or if a lighted torch is thrust into his face, this is not only prima facie wrongful, but can normally only have been done dolo. In a way, therefore, one can say that this ancient type of liability was strict, or absolute: the wrongdoer was liable irrespective of whether or not he, in this specific case, had been at fault. But the (objective) requirements of the delict were such that it was rather unlikely that he had caused the death or damage without intention. Inclusion of the term "iniuria" in chapters one and three of the lex Aquilia was an acknowledgement of the fact that certain exceptional situations existed where the defendant ought to escape liability (though he had committed "occidere" or "urere frangere rumpere"). If the slave had attacked the defendant, the latter did not act non iure when he singed or stabbed him. It was still quite natural that his action had been wilful, but he was now allowed to assert that he had acted in pursuance of a right which justified infliction of the damnum (the wrongfulness aspect of iniuria).

(c) From (typical) dolus to fault at large

But then cases may have arisen where the injury had still been caused directly and where the defendant could not be said to have acted "iure", but where it was nevertheless deemed unreasonable to impose liability. Somebody burns stubble on his fields; it is a quiet day, and he watches the fire most diligently. A sudden and entirely unforeseeable gust of wind makes the fire flare up and spread to the neighbour's field.[45] Or take the example of a ship ramming another vessel coming towards it, not as a result of a steering mistake, but because it was thrown about by a tempest in such a manner that it could no longer be controlled.[46] These kinds of cases must have come up for consideration increasingly frequently, once the requirement of the use of force in chapter one was no longer taken very seriously,[47] the "urere frangere rumpere" of chapter three had been replaced by the much less descriptive term "corrumpere"[48] and Aquilian-type liability was generally extended by actiones in factum. And even if the requirement of "corpore damnum datum" was retained, as far as the actio legis Aquiliae (directa) was

[44] On the relationship between iniuria and culpa and on the historical development, cf. Beinart, *Studi Arangio-Ruiz*, vol. I, pp. 279 sqq.; von Lübtow, *Lex Aquilia*, pp. 83 sqq.; Lawson/Markesinis, pp. 19 sqq., 22 sqq.; Honsell/Mayer-Maly/Selb, pp. 229 sqq.

[45] Cf. the situation in Paul. D. 9, 2, 30, 3.

[46] Cf. Alf./Ulp. D. 9, 2, 29, 4.

[47] Cf. supra, pp. 978 sq.

[48] Cf. supra, pp. 984 sq.

concerned, it can hardly be denied that there is some element of indirectness in the situations mentioned. The stubble case was in fact much disputed; Celsus was in favour of granting an actio in factum rather than the actio legis Aquiliae.[49] In any event, we are dealing here with borderline cases, where it was no longer possible to infer from the factual situation that the damage must—typically—have been caused intentionally. Thus, not unlike the courts in England many centuries later, the Roman lawyers may have recognized a defence of (inevitable) accident.[50] It was new in that it did not fit in with the "non iure" interpretation of iniuria; but it was perfectly possible to maintain that wherever death or damage constituted casus, the defendant had not acted iniuria. All that was involved was a reinterpretation, or perhaps rather an interpretative extension, of the concept of iniuria. The next step was, obviously, to formulate positively what had so far been recognized by way of exception: if the defendant was *not* liable for casus, that meant as much as that he *was* liable for fault.[51] His fault could, of course, but did not necessarily have to, take the form of dolus.

(d) Wrongfulness and fault

As a result of these developments, one had overcome the archaic form of strict liability and had adopted a flexible and ethically more satisfactory approach that turned on the inquiry of whether or not the defendant had in fact behaved as he should have behaved. This more refined criterion must soon have superseded or swallowed the older concept of iniuria:[52] damnum iniuria datum was replaced, for all practical purposes, by damnum culpa datum. And, indeed, as long as the notion of culpa was not converted into the equivalent of our modern idea of negligence,[53] it was perfectly possible to make it cover the same ground as the earlier "iniuria" concept. If the aedil (by smashing the beds) had done what the law permitted him to do, how could one say that he had been at fault? Or if the sailors cut the anchor

---

[49] Cels. Coll. XII, VII, 5.

[50] Lawson/Markesinis, pp. 19 sq. In England, this has become the generally accepted view since the end of the 19th century (!), as a result of the decision of *Stanley v. Powell* [1891] 1 QB 86 (per Denman J; the defendant, while firing at a pheasant, had shot the plaintiff (who was employed to carry cartridges) with a pellet which ricochetted from a tree at a considerable angle. Since the injury was held to have been accidental, the action for tresspass was unsuccessful).

[51] For the development in England cf. *Salmond and Heuston on the Law of Torts* (18th ed., 1981), p. 128: "In so far as *Stanley v. Powell* decided that inevitable accident was a good defence to an action of tresspass it probably cannot now be questioned. But in recent years a series of decisions . . . have extended *Stanley v. Powell* so far as to hold that a plaintiff in an action of tresspass for injuries to the person must always prove intention or negligence on the part of the defendant."

[52] Beinart, *Studi Arangio-Ruiz*, vol. I, pp. 284 sqq.; Lawson/Markesinis, p. 25. Contra: MacCormack, (1975) 41 *SDHI* 56 (according to whom iniuria was probably understood by the jurists, from the time of the enactment of the lex, as expressing the requirement of fault).

[53] That that was not the case in classical law has been emphasized by Geoffrey MacCormack, "Aquilian Culpa", in: *Daube Noster* (1974), pp. 201 sqq.

ropes of the ship into which their own vessel had been blown: how could one refer to this act as damnum *culpa* datum? After all, they had done what they were allowed to do under the circumstances.[54] Culpa, in other words, became the all-embracing criterion upon which the liability of whoever had committed "occidere" or "corrumpere" depended.[55] Iniuria, in the sense of "non iure", was submerged, and thus we find the Roman jurists thinking mainly in terms of dolus and culpa, even in what we would regard as the proper province of wrongfulness.[56] The modern systematic distinction between wrongfulness and fault as two separate elements of delictual liability is alien to our classical sources. Its foundations were laid by Justinian. In his *Institutes* he states that "iniuria occidere" means "nullo iure occidere" and he illustrates the meaning of "non iure" with the example of self-defence.[57] He then turns to the concept of culpa, without referring to the term "iniuria" or to problems of wrongfulness any longer.[58] But by his time the notion of culpa had acquired the more specialized and technical meaning of "negligence"[59] (did the defendant exercise the care of a bonus paterfamilias?—hardly a meaningful test question to determine issues of wrongfulness).

3. Aquilian culpa in classical Roman law

As with regard to the operative verbs in chapters one and three, we find a whole range of interesting cases dealing with the culpa requirement and specifying it for individual situations.[60] A pruner lops off the branch of a tree, which falls and kills a passer-by. The pruner is liable, if he had done the job over a public thoroughfare and had failed to shout a warning.[61] A farmer is liable for the damage to his neighbour's crops if he burns stubble on a windy day and is therefore unable to control the fire.[62] A person who is throwing a javelin by way of sport, but outside a proper sports field, is held responsible under the lex Aquilia if he hits and kills a slave who happens to be passing by.[63] A barber is accountable for the death of his customer, if, having set up his business in close proximity to a playing ground, his hand is hit by a ball, the razor thereby jerked against the customer's throat and the throat, in

[54] Cf. Beinart, *Studi Arangio-Ruiz*, vol. I, p. 286.
[55] Like the concept of "faute" in art. 1382 code civil; cf. supra, note 6.
[56] Beinart, *Studi Arangio-Ruiz*, vol. I, p. 285; Kaser, *RPr* I, p. 505.
[57] *Inst.* IV, 3, 2.
[58] *Inst.* IV, 3, 3 sqq.
[59] Cf. Schipani, *Lex Aquilia*, pp. 439 sqq.; Kaser, *RPr* II, p. 438.
[60] Analysed in great detail by Schipani, *Lex Aquilia*, pp. 133 sqq.; MacCormack, *Daube Noster*, pp. 203 sqq.; idem, (1975) 41 *SDHI* 43 sqq.; cf. also von Lübtow, *Lex Aquilia*, pp. 98 sqq.
[61] Paul. D. 9, 2, 31.
[62] Paul. D. 9, 2, 30, 3.
[63] Ulp. D. 9, 2, 9, 4. On javelins and javelin throwing in the Ancient World, see Harris, op. cit., note 38, pp. 92 sqq.; idem, *Athletics in Ancient Greece* (1976), pp. 196 sqq.

turn, cut rather than shaved.[64] In all these cases careful attempts are made to draw the line: no fault is attributable to the pruner if he either shouted a warning or threw the branch down on to private land and in a place where there was no path; to the farmer if he selected a still day and took all reasonable precautions to prevent the fire from spreading; to the javelin-thrower if he exercised in a campus iaculatorius; or to the barber if he did not shave at a place "ubi ex consuetudine ludebatur vel ubi transitus frequens erat". It is apparent from these and other texts that the Roman lawyers approached the question of culpa in a casuistic manner. They did not try to subsume the facts of the individual case under a standardized test or formula.[65] More particularly, they did not ask in each case whether the defendant ought to have foreseen the damage.[66] Foreseeability or carelessness could be important issues[67] but they did not necessarily and conclusively determine the question of liability. The crucial issue was whether, more generally, the defendant had been at fault; whether, in other words, he had behaved as he should not have behaved;[68] and that, in turn, depended on an evaluation of all the circumstances of the case and tended to be determined from an objective point of view.[69] Only in some respects does a certain degree

---

[64] Mela/Proc./Ulp. D. 9, 2, 11 pr.

[65] Cf. also Pernice, *Sachbeschädigungen*, p. 51; von Lübtow, *Lex Aquilia*, pp. 87, 105.

[66] MacCormack, *Daube Noster*, pp. 202, 204.

[67] As, for instance, they were in Paul. D. 9, 2, 31.

[68] MacCormack, *Daube Noster*, p. 202. Neither furiosus nor infans can be made liable under the lex Aquilia; reason: "quae enim in eo culpa sit, cum suae mentis non sit" (Pegasus/Ulp. D. 9, 2, 5, 2). On the delictual liability of an impubes infantia maior, see Lab./Ulp. D. 9, 2, 5, 2; Lab./Iul./Ulp. D. 47, 2, 23; Bernard Perrin, "Le caractère subjectif de l'iniuria Aquilienne à l'époque classique", in: *Studi in onore di Pietro de Francisci*, vol. IV (1956), pp. 271 sqq.; MacCormack, *Daube Noster*, pp. 218 sq.; Schipani, *Lex Aquilia*, pp. 219 sqq., 270 sqq.; Hausmaninger, *Lex Aquilia*, p. 26.

[69] Cf. von Lübtow, *Lex Aquilia*, pp. 83 sqq.; Schipani, *Lex Aquilia*, passim, e.g. pp. 131 sqq., 192 sqq.; MacCormack, *Daube Noster*, pp. 201 sqq.; Honsell/Mayer-Maly/Selb, p. 366; Hausmaninger, *Lex Aquilia*, p. 25. That culpa was seen in an objective light is also apparent, for instance, from the one (apparently) more generalizing statement on culpa that we possess: ". . . culpam autem esse, quod cum a diligente provideri poterit, non erit provisum" (Paul. D. 9, 2, 31; attributed by Paul to Quintus Mucius). This phrase has often been regarded as spurious (cf. e.g. Arangio-Ruiz, *Responsabilità*, pp. 234 sqq.; von Lübtow, *Lex Aquilia*, pp. 99 sq.), but see, for example, Schipani, *Lex Aquilia*, pp. 141 sqq., 371 sqq. It should, however, not be seen as providing a general definition of culpa (in terms of foreseeability); the remark was probably related by Quintus Mucius more directly to the circumstances of the case than appears from D. 9, 2, 31: MacCormack, *Daube Noster*, pp. 203 sqq. For a different evaluation, cf. Okko Behrends, "Die Rechtsformen der römischen Handwerks", (1981) 22 *Abhandlungen der Akademie der Wissenschaften in Göttingen* 145. It should also be noted that the problem of fault was not considered in isolation. The Roman lawyers did not go through a list of specific requirements, defined and categorized as neatly as in a modern textbook, when they tried to establish whether a particular plaintiff was liable under the lex Aquilia. Just as fault and unlawfulness were not neatly separated, so the issue of fault was frequently merged with causal questions: a higher degree of fault could, for instance, "compensate" for a certain lack of directness in the infliction of the injury. The point has been emphasized and illustrated by Geoffrey MacCormack, "Juristic Interpretation of the Lex Aquilia", in: *Studi in onore di Cesare Sanfilippo*, vol. I (1982), pp. 270 sqq. The bonus (or diligens) paterfamilias as a general model of the standard by which the issue of

of generality appear to have been achieved. Thus the notion of imperitia culpae adnumeratur was applied to Aquilian liability as it was to liability arising under a contract of locatio conductio operis or operarum.[70] Nobody who had undertaken a particular job could escape liability by claiming that he did not possess the necessary skill to carry out that job. If a doctor operated unskilfully[71] or if he caused damage by making the wrong use of a drug,[72] he was liable under the lex Aquilia as well as ex locato. The same applied if a muleteer was so inexperienced that he was unable to control his mules and to stop them from running over somebody's slave.[73] Imperitia liability, incidentally, provides a good example of the objective approach adopted by the Roman lawyers.[74] Doctor and muleteer were not judged in relation to *their* experience or according to whether *they* could have foreseen the harm; what mattered was whether they possessed the skills that could reasonably be expected of a man of their profession.

---

culpa, or negligence, is determined (and as such, i.e. as a *general* standard, of Justinianic vintage; cf. Kaser, *RPr* II, pp. 350 sqq.) lives on in modern South African law. Representing "an embodiment of all the qualities which we require of a good citizen" (Van der Walt, *Delict*, § 39), he displays neither "the foresight of a Hebrew prophet" in anticipating harm nor "the agility of an acrobat" in avoiding it (*Broom v. Administrator, Natal* 1966 (3) SA 505 (D) at 516G–H. Or, as Holmes JA put it (*S v. Burger* 1975 (4) SA 877 (A) at 879D–E): "One does not expect of a diligens paterfamilias any extremes such as Solomonic wisdom, prophetic foresight, chameleonic caution, headlong haste, nervous timidity, or the trained reflexes of a racing driver. In short, a diligens paterfamilias treads life's pathway with moderation and prudent common sense." His English counterpart is the famous reasonable man, an "excellent but odious character" (A.P. Herbert, *Uncommon Law* (1982), p. 4 (Is there a reasonable woman?)) who is "free both from over-apprehension and from over-confidence" (*Glasgow Corporation v. Muir* [1943] AC 448 (HL) at 457). He is variously described as "the man in the street", "the man in the Clapham omnibus" or "the man who takes the magazines at home, and in the evening pushes the lawn mower in his shirt sleeves" (*Hall v. Brooklands Auto Racing Club* [1933] 1 KB 205 (CA) at 224; for details, see Fleming, *Torts*, pp. 97 sqq.; André Tunc, "Introduction", in: *International Encyclopedia of Comparative Law*, vol. XI, 1 (1983), nn. 133 sqq.; cf. also Holmes, *The Common Law*, p. 108: "[The law] does not attempt to see men as God sees them").

[70] Cf. supra, pp. 386 sq., 397 sq.

[71] Proc./Ulp. D. 9, 2, 7, 8.

[72] Gai. D. 9, 2, 8 pr.

[73] Gai. D. 9, 2, 8, 1. The position was the same if the muleteer did not possess the (physical) strength required to hold back the mules. Cf. further Ulp. D. 9, 2, 27, 29, where a diatretarius is held liable if he breaks a calix meant for diatreting because of a lack of skill; on this text cf. Peter Birks, "Other Men's Meat: Aquilian Liability for Proper User", (1981) 16 *The Irish Jurist* 163 sqq., but also von Lübtow, *Lex Aquilia*, pp. 100 sqq. On imperitia culpae adnumeratur and Aquilian liability in general, see Schipani, *Lex Aquilia*, pp. 246 sqq. (D. 9, 2, 8, 1), 324 sqq. (D. 9, 2, 7, 8); von Lübtow, *Lex Aquilia*, pp. 103 sqq.; MacCormack, *Daube Noster*, pp. 210 sqq.; T.J. Scott, "Die reël imperitia culpae adnumeratur as grondslag vir die nalatigheidstoets vir deskundiges in die deliktereg", in: *Petere Fontes*, L.C. Steyn—*Gedenkbundel* (n.d.), pp. 124 sqq. (especially on Roman law: pp. 130 sqq.); Van der Walt, *Delict*, § 41; cf. also Behrends, op. cit., note 69, pp. 144 sqq. The position is the same in the English common law. " 'Imperitia culpae adnumeratur' says the Digest. 'Spondet peritiam artis', says Story on Bailments": Buckland/McNair, pp. 259 sq. "Those who undertake work calling for special skill must not only exercise reasonable care but measure up to the standard of proficiency that can be expected from persons of such profession" (Fleming, *Torts*, p. 104); cf. also Scott, op. cit., pp. 140 sqq.

[74] But see Lawson/Markesinis, p. 28.

4. "Contributory negligence" in Roman law

(a) The Roman all-or-nothing approach

If fault was the relevant criterion to determine whether a person who had committed occidere or corrumpere was liable under the lex Aquilia, the modern lawyer will be inclined to imagine that considerations of fault determined also the extent to which that person could be held responsible. Not rarely does it happen that some fault of the victim has contributed to the injury, and it would appear to be unreasonable completely to overlook this contributory factor when it comes to the assessment of damages. In particular, one might be disposed to compare the relative contributions of tortfeasor and victim and to reduce the extent of the compensation accordingly. Most modern legal systems do, in fact, know rules about contributory negligence and recognize the possibility of an apportionment of damages.[75] Not so the Roman lawyers.[76] If somebody suffered harm through his own fault, he was denied recovery, unless the tortfeasor had acted intentionally (in which case he could recover his full damages[77]). This strict principle of all-or-nothing was predetermined by the procedural formula. The judge only had the alternative to condemn in the full amount or to absolve the defendant—tertium non datur. Translated into the terms of substantive law, this meant that the judge had to determine whether the act of the defendant satisfied all the requirements of the lex Aquilia or not. If he came to the conclusion that there had been damnum *culpa* datum, he had to condemn, otherwise to absolve. The Roman lawyers thus approached the question of "contributory negligence" under a very specific perspective. They did not ask (as we do): was there fault on both sides?; they merely enquired whether the injury was due to the fault of *either* the tortfeasor *or* the victim. A pruner who dropped a branch on a public road without having shouted a warning was liable if the branch killed a slave who happened to be passing by. According to Quintus Mucius, he was even liable if the incident occurred on the putator's private ground, also, of course, if he had shouted out too late. But if the branch was dropped on a private ground, and there was no path underneath the tree (so that it was entirely unlikely that people would be passing by), he could not be

[75] For a comparative survey, cf. A.M. Honoré, "Causation and Remoteness of Damage", in: *International Encyclopedia of Comparative Law*, vol. XI, 7 (1983), nn. 144 sqq.; additionally (for South African law) Boberg, *Delict*, pp. 652 sq.

[76] Cf., for example, Pernice, *Labeo*, op. cit., note 10, pp. 97 sqq.; Buckland/McNair, pp. 370 sqq.; Medicus, *Id quod interest*, pp. 322 sqq.; Buckland/Stein, p. 587; Peter Aumann, *Das mitwirkende Verschulden in der neueren juristischen Dogmengeschichte*, (unpublished Dr. iur. thesis, Hamburg, 1964), pp. 4 sqq.; Klaus Luig, "Überwiegendes Mitverschulden", (1968) 2 *Ius Commune* 192 sqq.; von Lübtow, *Lex Aquilia*, pp. 106 sqq.; Christian Wollschläger, "Das eigene Verschulden des Verletzten im römischen Recht", (1976) 93 *ZSS* 115 sqq.; Lawson/Markesinis, pp. 33 sq.; Hausmaninger, *Lex Aquilia*, pp. 26 sqq.

[77] Cf. Ulp. 9, 2, 9, 4 in fine; Paul. D. 9, 2, 31 ("quod si nullam iter erit, dolum dumtaxat praestare debet, ne immittat in eum, quem viderit transeuntem").

held responsible.[78] If a slave was hit under these circumstances, it was due to his own fault, not to that of the pruner. A very similar solution was arrived at in the case of the hunter who dug pits to catch deer:[79] if the pits were on a private ground and if an adequate warning had been put up, any injury sustained by third parties was not attributable to the hunter. If, on the other hand, he had dug the pits on public ground, or on a private ground but without any warning, he was liable to the full extent.

(b) Of javelin-throwers and itinerant barbers

The two cases that have featured most prominently in subsequent discussions about "contributory negligence", were that of the javelin-thrower[80] and that of the barber putting his shaving-chair next to a playing ground.[81] In the former instance the Aquilian action was held to lie "si per lusum iaculantibus servus fuerit occisus"; but there was no liability if the javelin was thrown in a field set aside for that purpose. Reason: "quia non debuit [sc.: servus] per campum iaculatorium iter intempestive facere." If a slave crosses a sports field while people are busy practising javelin-throwing and if he is pierced by a javelin as a result thereof, it is entirely his own fault. It is, in any event, not the javelin-thrower who can be blamed for the incident.[82]

More complex was the barber case. It was much discussed in Roman law,[83] and at least three different solutions were proposed. None of the lawyers dealing with the case advocated an apportionment of damages, however. Mela isolated the relevant criterion: "in quocumque eorum culpa sit, eum lege Aquilia teneri." That could either be the person who had hit the ball (after all, he had hit it "vehementius")[84] or the barber (he had set up his chair "ubi ex consuetudine ludebatur vel ubi transitus frequens erat"). Proculus argued in favour of the latter alternative. But the argument that it was dangerous to shave in the immediate vicinity of a playing ground could just as well be turned against the customer. He was by no means forced to have his beard shaved in such a

[78] Paul. D. 9, 2, 31.

[79] Paul. D. 9, 2, 28.

[80] Ulp. D. 9, 2, 9, 4 (cf. supra, note 63).

[81] Mela/Proc./Ulp. D. 9, 2, 11 pr. (cf. supra, note 64).

[82] Cf. further Wollschläger, (1976) 93 *ZSS* 128 sqq., who draws attention to a Greek parallel (or rather: model) for the case of the javelin-thrower.

[83] "[A] stock . . . case in classical jurisprudence": MacCormack, *Daube Noster*, p. 215.

[84] But, on the other hand, he could hardly be thought to have caused the damage directly (damnum *corpori* datum). Did Mela, therefore, only contemplate an actio in factum? What kind of game were the players busy playing? Wacke, (1979) 42 *THRHR* 277 thinks it was a game similar to hockey (where the ball was hit); according to Wollschläger, (1976) 93 *ZSS* 132, the ball had been thrown by hand; the text merely says "pila percussa". On Roman ball games generally, see H.A. Harris, *Sport in Greece and Rome* (1972), pp. 75 sqq.; Weiler, op. cit., note 38, pp. 265 sqq.

precarious place. The barber might have chosen a more suitable spot[85] to offer his services, but, in the last resort, it was the slave who had himself to blame for having availed himself of such an offer. This argument was advanced with the words "si in loco periculoso sellam habenti tonsori se quis commiserit, ipsum de se queri debere",[86] and Ulpian regarded it as absolutely tenable ("nec illud male dicetur").

(c) *Balancing of fault, preponderant negligence or assumption of risk?*

Did this involve a balancing of fault which was seen to exist on the part of both the barber and his "victim"? This is quite possible; and since nothing at all is said about the gravity of the respective faults, one may come to the conclusion that, in the opinion of the Roman lawyers—or at any rate of some of them—any form of contributory negligence cost the victim/plaintiff his remedy.[87] Alternatively, one might argue that implicit in the view reported by Ulpian was the assumption that the victim's fault was much graver; compared with that of the barber, it made the latter pale into insignificance. The Roman rule may then have been that *preponderant* negligence on the part of the victim excluded the plaintiff's liability.[88] Or did the Roman lawyers solve these cases by applying a theory of causation?[89] It was the barber's customer who had had the last opportunity of avoiding the "accident" by exercising reasonable care, and it is for that reason that he ought to be liable. His intervention, in a way, "broke" the chain of causation linking barber's fault and injury. The Roman approach would then have been very similar to that adopted by the English common law.[90]

---

[85] People of lower rank were shaved by itinerant barbers in the open air; for the wealthier Romans, elegant barbershops were available; for details, see e.g. Carcopino, pp. 175 sqq.

[86] Genuine? No, says von Lübtow, *Lex Aquilia*, p. 107 ("*naive Glosse*"). Contra: Theo Mayer-Maly, "De se queri debere, officia erga se und Verschulden gegen sich selbst", in: *Festschrift für Max Kaser* (1976), p. 248.

[87] The idea of compensatio culpae; cf. infra, pp. 1030, 1047.

[88] Cf., in particular, Luig, (1968) 2 *Ius Commune* pp. 193 sqq. Wacke, (1979) 42 *THRHR* 276 explains the decision in D. 9, 2, 9, 4 (javelin-thrower) on this basis.

[89] Cf. Buckland/McNair, pp. 370 sqq., but also Pernice, *Sachbeschädigungen*, p. 60. Contra, in particular, MacCormack, *Studi Sanfilippo*, vol. I, pp. 277 sqq. ("In a sense one can say that the jurists reduced the question of causation to one of fault").

[90] Originally, the common law treated contributory negligence as a complete defence: it not only impaired but completely barred recovery except against an intentional wrongdoer. "[I]f there is blame causing the accident on both sides, however small the blame may be on one side, the loss lies where it falls" was the principle, as formulated by Lord Blackburn, in *Cayzer, Irvine & Co. v. Carron Co.* [1884] 9 AC 873 (HL) at 881. It was justified on the basis that, in a practical sense, the plaintiff was the author of his own wrong (*Butterfield v. Forrester* (1809) 11 East 60 at 61) and therefore the only effective cause of his injury (Fleming, *Torts*, p. 243, who criticizes this argument as being "a hollow pretence" and "hypocritical"). Subsequently, this harsh rule was mitigated by the "proximate cause", or "last opportunity", test. As a result of it, the entire blame was now thrown on whoever had had the last opportunity of avoiding the harm. "Not surprisingly", writes Fleming, p. 244, "the result [which was still all or nothing] was again explained in the abracadabra of causation,"

But D. 9, 2, 11 pr. in fine can also be explained in an entirely different manner.[91] By availing himself of the services of this specific barber, the customer voluntarily exposed himself to the risk that the shaving process might be rather awkwardly disrupted or interfered with, and it is this aspect of the assumption of a risk[92] which made it appear unreasonable to grant a claim for damages to the plaintiff. Neither barber nor customer had therefore been "at fault"; both engaged in a somewhat risky kind of activity and therefore had to bear the consequences.[93] Since this explanation accords much better with our other sources (which do not evidence any recognition of the notion of a concurrence of faults—that is, of "contributory" negligence in the true sense of the word[94]), it is the one to be preferred.

---

possibly still under the influence of the canonical distinction between causa proxima and causa remota (Luig, (1968) 2 *Ius Commune* 223). On the "last opportunity" rule in South African law, cf. Boberg, *Delict*, pp. 653 sqq.

[91] Wollschläger, (1976) 93 *ZSS* 131 sqq.

[92] Cf. also Mayer-Maly, (1974) 226 *Göttingische Gelehrte Anzeigen* 130; Hausmaninger, *Lex Aquilia*, p. 27. The idea of an exclusion of delictual liability on the grounds of an assumption of risk ("*Handeln auf eigene Gefahr*") has also been advanced with regard to Alf. D. 9, 2, 52, 4 ("Cum pila complures luderent, quidam ex his servulum, cum pila percipere conaretur, impulit, servus cecidit et crus fregit: quaerebatur, an dominus servuli lege Aquilia cum eo, cuius impulsu ceciderat, agere potest"): von Lübtow, *Lex Aquilia*, pp. 108 sq.; Wacke, (1979) 42 *THRHR* 278 sq. Alfenus, however, rather appears to have stressed the fact that there was no fault involved ("respondi non posse, cum casu magis quam culpa videretur factum"). But, of course, all disputes about whether the exclusion of liability in a specific situation depended on "wrongfulness" or "fault" are, as far as Roman law is concerned, of a somewhat academic nature. That the Roman lawyers took account of the special circumstances obtaining in combative sport is apparent from Ulp. D. 9, 2, 7, 4 (a case dealing with wrestling, boxing and pancratium): "cessat [lex] Aquilia, quia gloriae causa et virtutis, non iniuriae gratia videtur damnum datum." Generally on liability for accidents in sport and games in Roman law, see Wacke, (1979) 42 *THRHR* 273—specifically on Ulp. D. 9, 2, 7, 4 cf. pp. 281 sqq.

In modern law, the opinion tends to prevail that the crucial issue is one of wrongfulness, not of fault: as long as the rules of the game are not infringed, participants in any form of contact sport do not act unlawfully if they injure each other. The appropriate dogmatic tool to achieve this result is, however, in dispute: consent (volenti non fit iniuria), assumption of risk, application of special standards of behaviour (i.e. modification of the usual "alterum non laedere" precept for contact sport)? For details, see Reinhard Zimmermann, "Verletzungserfolg, Spielregeln und allgemeines Sportrisiko", 1980 *Versicherungsrecht* 497 sqq. These special considerations are, however, justifiable for injuries inflicted only while the game (or fight) is in progress. For the time before (knocking up) and after (final whistle has been blown, towel has been thrown in) the normal rules apply, and any injury is (prima facie) unlawful. For Roman law cf., along similar lines, Ulp. D. 9, 2, 7, 4 (". . . plane si cedentem vulneraverit, erit Aquiliae locus").

[93] On the meaning of "de se queri debet" in this context, see Wollschläger, (1976) 93 *ZSS* 132 sqq.; generally, cf. Mayer-Maly, *Festschrift Kaser*, pp. 236 sqq.

[94] Aumann, op. cit., note 76, pp. 6 sq., 18; Wollschläger, (1976) 93 *ZSS* 115 sqq.; cf. also Schipani, *Lex Aquilia*, pp. 420 sqq.; contra, for example, Medicus, *Id quod interest*, pp. 322 sqq.; Luig, (1968) 2 *Ius Commune* 192 sqq.; Honsell/Mayer-Maly/Selb, p. 232.

II. THE PROTECTION OF A FREEMAN'S BODILY INTEGRITY

1. Damage to property

We have been dealing in the previous pages with a range of issues in respect of which the original scope of the lex Aquilia came to be gradually extended. "Urere frangere rumpere" was superseded by the all-embracing term "corrumpere";[95] remedies were granted in cases of indirect causation[96] and even in situations where the substance of the object concerned was not at all affected;[97] fault in the broadest sense of the word became a sufficient basis for liability;[98] the injured party could recover his full quod interest;[99] and the role of plaintiff was no longer confined to the owner of the object killed or damaged.[100] All this had been achieved by Republican and classical jurisprudence. But by the end of classical law one further, very significant development had taken place. Essentially, the lex Aquilia was intended to deal with damage to property: slaves, grazing animals, res se moventes other than grazing animals, and inanimate objects.[101] Damage to freemen was not covered by its provisions: "Liber homo . . . enim [Aquiliae] non habet [actionem], quoniam dominus membrorum suorum nemo videtur."[102] If a slave lost his limb, his owner's property was damaged; but if the same thing happened to a freeman, nobody's property had been interfered with: the limb can hardly be said to "belong" to the person whose body it makes up. In the case of the lex Aquilia it was the erus (dominus) who was entitled to sue;[103] and even if Aquilian protection was extended to certain non-owners,[104] the fact remained that the lex drew a distinction between the object damaged and the person who could bring the action. But was this not a strange result? Generous protection was provided with regard to damage to property—but when it came to personal injuries we find only a somewhat patchy assortment of remedies: the actio iniuriarum dealt with situations that were typically characterized by the presence of dolus,[105] and the

[95] Supra, pp. 984 sq.
[96] Supra, pp. 978 sqq.
[97] Supra, pp. 986 sq.
[98] Supra, pp. 1005 sqq.; cf. also Ulp. D. 9, 2, 44 pr. ("In lege Aquilia et levissima culpa venit").
[99] Supra, pp. 969 sqq., 973 sq.
[100] Supra, pp. 994 sqq.
[101] Supra, pp. 965 sqq., 976, 983 sqq.
[102] Ulp. D. 9, 2, 13 pr. (a text, incidentally, which is frequently referred to in discussions concerning the question who owns the body of a deceased person; this, in turn, is relevant when a request is made to dissect that body or to use it for transplant purposes. Cf. e.g. 1979 *Neue Juristische Wochenschrift* 570).
[103] Cf. supra, p. 959, note 48.
[104] Supra, p. 995.
[105] Cf. infra, pp. 1059 sqq.

actiones de effusis vel deiectis, de pauperie and de feris pertained to very special situations.[106]

2. Liberum corpus nullam recipit aestimationem

Nevertheless, for the Romans this result was much less disturbing than it appears to us. For what did the judge have to assess under chapters one and three of the lex Aquilia? Originally only either the full value of the object killed (chapter one) or the diminution in value that had occurred as a result of the injury (chapter three); and even at a time when the full interest had become recoverable, aestimatio corporis or aestimatio vulneris remained the starting point and cornerstone for its assessment.[107] Under both chapters one and three, therefore, a specific pecuniary value had to be assigned to the object in question. Exactly this, however, was impossible as far as the body of a freeman was concerned. "[L]iberum corpus nullam recipit aestimationem"[108] was the principle of Roman law: the value of a freeman's body cannot be expressed in pecuniary terms.

3. Injury to sons in power

But once one was prepared to go beyond the mere aestimatio corporis or vulneris in the case of slaves, there was no reason not to contemplate some form of compensation when, say, a filius familias was injured. It can hardly have been comprehensible to a Roman paterfamilias why he should be able to recover medical expenses as well as loss of earnings when a slave of his was injured, but not when it came to his son in power. The jurists did not find that comprehensible either, and thus they started granting actiones legis Aquiliae utiles, where filii familias had been injured.[109] Our main source[110] is Iul./Ulp. D. 9, 2, 5, 3, the famous case of the shoemaker's apprentice:

[106] For details, see Wittmann, *Körperverletzung*, pp. 62 sqq.; cf. also Lawson/Markesinis, p. 11.

[107] For details cf. supra, pp. 970, 972.

[108] Gai. D. 9, 3, 7; cf. also Gai. D. 9, 1, 3; Ulp. D. 9, 3, 1, 5; Wittmann, *Körperverletzung*, pp. 66 sqq.; N.J.J. Olivier, *Die aksie weens die nalatige veroorsaking van pyn en lyding* (unpublished Dr. iur. thesis, Leiden, 1978), pp. 21 sqq.

[109] All texts inferring that an actio utilis was granted in cases of damage to freemen have often been regarded as interpolated; cf., most recently, von Lübtow, *Lex Aquilia*, pp. 116 sqq. Cf. also Schulz, *CRL*, p. 591 ("It is . . . hardly credible that an actio utilis was ever granted in classical times when a free person had suffered injury") and many others.

[110] But cf. also Ulp. D. 9, 2, 7, 4 (the wrestling, boxing and pancration case); our only source dealing with the applicability of the lex Aquilia where a freeman had been killed. It is very widely held, however, that the actio legis Aquiliae utilis was not available in classical Roman law in the case of death of freemen; cf. e.g. Thomas, *TRL*, p. 368; but cf. Robert Feenstra, "Die Glossatoren und die actio legis Aquiliae utilis bei Tötung eines freien Menschen", in: Eltjo J.H. Schrage, *Das römische Recht im Mittelalter* (1987), pp. 205 sqq.; Bernhard Schebitz, *Berechnung des Ersatzes nach der lex Aquilia* (unpublished Dr. iur. thesis, Berlin, 1987), p. 100. As far as Byzantine law is concerned, see Stephan Brassloff, "Zur Lehre von den Rechtsfolgen der schuldhaften Tötung einer Person im byzantinischen Recht", (1911) 25 *Zeitschrift für vergleichende Rechtswissenschaft* 378 sqq.

> "[S]utor . . . puero discenti ingenuo filio familias, parum bene facienti quod demonstraverit, forma calcei cervicem percusserit, ut oculus puero perfunderetur."[111]

The shoemaker obviously became impatient because his apprentice (a freeborn youngster) did not grasp what he was being taught. He thus resorted to a somewhat rough and ready teaching tool: a last, with which he struck at the neck of the boy. As a result of this, something rather unforeseen and unfortunate happened: the boy's eye was knocked out.[112] According to Julian, the actio iniuriarum did not lie "quia non faciendae iniuriae causa percusserit, sed monendi et docendi causa"; and whether the actio locati could be brought was rather doubtful.[113] There was, however, no doubt in Julian's mind that Aquilian protection was available to the paterfamilias;[114] and as far as the content of the claim was concerned, he referred to "quod minus ex operis filii sui propter vitiatum oculum sit habiturus, et impendia, quae pro curatione fecerit."[115]

4. The liber homo bona fide serviens

The actio legis Aquiliae utilis was granted in a second type of situation by the classical lawyers: where a freeman had been injured, who did not know about his status and served in good faith as someone else's slave (liber homo bona fide serviens). Ulpian must have referred to him when he said: "Liber homo suo nomine utilem Aquiliae habet actionem."[116] Extension of Aquilian protection to the injury of sons in power could still be explained on the basis that the position of the paterfamilias was not altogether dissimilar to that of the erus (dominus)

---

[111] The same incident is discussed in Iul./Ulp. D. 19, 2, 13, 4 and on a parchment discovered in Egypt: cf. (1957) 14 *Papiri della Società Italiana*, n. 1449; Vincenzo Arangio-Ruiz, "Frammenti di Ulpiano, libro 32 ad edictum, in una pergamena di provenienza egiziana", (1957) 153 *Archivio Giuridico Filippo Serafini* 140 sqq.; idem, "Di nuovo sul frammento di Ulpiano in PSI. 1449 R.", (1960) 2 *BIDR* 281 sqq.

[112] How was this possible? Can a stroke at the neck make an eye pop out? This is, indeed, what Arangio-Ruiz, (1960) 2 *BIDR* 292 (and before him Cuiacius and other humanists) maintained. Or did the stroke at the neck push the apprentice's head against an awl which he held in his hand at that particular moment (cf. Schulz, *Einführung*, p. 56; Mayer-Maly, *Locatio conductio*, p. 187; Wittmann, *Körperverletzung*, p. 84). More recently, it has been argued that due to the specific shape of a Roman shoe-last, eye and neck may well have been hit with one and the same stroke: cf. Max Schubert, "Der Schlag des Schusters", (1975) 92 *ZSS* 267 sqq.

[113] The question depended on how severely an instructor was allowed to punish his apprentices. Julian says: ". . . levis dumtaxat castigatio concessa est docenti." For a discussion, see Mayer-Maly, *Locatio conductio*, pp. 186 sqq; Friedhelm Harting, *Die "positiven Vertragsverletzungen" in der neueren deutschen Privatrechtsgeschichte* (unpublished Dr. iur. thesis, Hamburg, 1967), pp. 29 sqq.

[114] "Sed lege Aquilia posse agi non dubito." The text is, however, corrupt, in so far as neither Julian nor Ulpian can have granted the actio directa (cf. Wittmann, *Körperverletzung*, p. 89); but cf. also Schebitz, op. cit., note 110, p. 91.

[115] Iul./Ulp. D. 9, 2, 7 pr.

[116] D. 9, 2, 13 pr.; Jörs/Kunkel/Wenger, p. 257; Wittmann, *Körperverletzung*, pp. 76 sqq.; Kaser, *RPr* I, p. 622; Olivier, op. cit., note 108, pp. 28 sqq.; Schebitz, op. cit., note 110, pp. 82 sqq.

as contemplated by the lex Aquilia. In the case of Ulp. D. 9, 2, 13 pr. we are, however, for the first time dealing with a situation where the injured person was allowed to bring the action himself ("suo nomine"). This was another significant advance, justified, probably, on the ground that, since this person had so far been treated as a slave, it would have been inequitable to withhold the specific protection accorded to a slave from him.[117] Of course, the liber homo bona fide serviens was not able to claim what his dominus would have been able to claim had he been his slave, particularly not his diminution in value; this was prevented by the principle of "liberum corpus nullam recepit aestimationem". Again, however, the action could be brought to recover medical expenses and the loss of earnings that resulted from his injury.

Was this breakthrough further exploited by the Roman lawyers, in that they made the actio utilis available in other cases of injuries to persons sui iuris? The Digest contains a certain number of texts where any reference to the status of the injured person is lacking: the cases concerning the theft of the shopkeeper's lantern,[118] the dog who is made to bite "aliquem"[119] and the fatal fall from the bridge[120] belong to this category. But it may well have been taken for granted that the injured person was a slave, and any argument based merely on an occasional generalizing "quidam" or "aliquis", is far too tenuous. D. 9, 2, 13 pr., as it stands, would of course provide a much more solid basis, but it is virtually certain that the text was generalized by the compilers.[121] They, rather than the classical lawyers, appear to have been responsible for taking the final step and extending the ambit of Aquilian protection to damage to freemen in general.[122]

III. THE USUS MODERNUS LEGIS AQUILIAE

1. Introduction

"Tituli praesentis usus amplissimus est, cum omnium damnorum reparatio ex hoc petatur, si modo ulla alterius culpa doceri possit": this is how Samuel Stryk[123] introduced his discussion of the usus modernus legis Aquiliae. Even in Roman law, the lex Aquilia had been extended, adapted and modernized in so many ways that a jurist from the time of

[117] Wittmann, *Körperverletzung*, p. 104.

[118] Alf. D. 9, 2, 52, 1; cf. supra, p. 1000.

[119] Proc./Ulp. D. 9, 2, 11, 5; cf. supra, p. 980 (notes 189, 190).

[120] Cels./Ulp. D. 9, 2, 7, 7; cf. supra, p. 980 (note 187).

[121] Cf. the authors mentioned supra, note 116.

[122] Cf. e.g. Wieacker, (1975) 92 *ZSS* 357; Kaser, *RPr* II, p. 438; Schebitz, op. cit., note 110, pp. 79 sqq.; but cf. Brassloff, (1911) 25 *Zeitschrift für vergleichende Rechtswissenschaft*, pp. 378 sqq.; Wittmann, *Körperverletzung*, pp. 98 sqq.; undecided is Hausmaninger, *Lex Aquilia*, p. 32.

[123] *Usus modernus pandectarum*, Lib. IX, Tit. II, § 1.

its enactment would hardly have recognized the late classical (or Justinianic[124]) delict of damnum culpa datum as specifically Aquilian; and any legal advice based merely on the wording of the lex would have been hopelessly inadequate. This process of extension, adaptation and modernization was carried on by courts and writers of the ius commune: almost imperceptibly at first, and with small and hesitating steps, but leading, eventually, to the far-ranging popular ("usus amplissimus")[125] and comprehensive remedy described by Stryk. This transformation was, first and foremost, the work of legal practice.[126] Very little of it can be gauged from the writings of glossators and commentators[127] (nor, of course, from authors of the subsequent humanist school). Even many of the writers of the (Dutch and German) usus modernus were reluctant to deviate from Roman law. But by their time the transformation of the actio legis Aquiliae was so firmly entrenched in practice that further doctrinal resistance must have appeared rather futile. One by one the changes came to be accepted, or at least acknowledged: rather haltingly and not always very consistently, but in the end the "mores hodiernae" triumphed all along the line. And just as the Aquilian delict of the Corpus Juris Civilis was a far cry from the one contemplated by those who had, in the 3rd century B.C., set out to draft the lex Aquilia, so it had become manifest, by the end of the 17th century, that the modern law in action no longer reflected the Aquilian delict of the Corpus Juris. The famous enlightenment lawyer, Christian Thomasius, even argued that "actio nostra, qua utimur, ab actione legis Aquiliae magis differat, quam avis a quadrupede", and he thus decided to put an end to the kind of mummery that was going on. "Larva legis Aquiliae detracta actioni de damno dato"[128] was the programmatic title of his polemical treatise: the Aquilian mask torn away from the action concerning damage done. What was the basis of his argument?

---

[124] On the lex Aquilia in post-classical law and under Justinian, cf. the clear and instructive exposition in *Inst.* IV, 3; Giovanni Rotondi, "Teorie postclassiche sull' 'actio legis Aquiliae' ", in: *Scritti giuridici*, vol. II (1922), pp. 411 sqq.; idem, "Dalla 'lex Aquilia' all'art 1151 Cod. Civ., in: *Scritti*, op. cit., pp. 468 sqq.; Levy, *Obligationenrecht*, pp. 335 sqq.; Schipani, *Lex Aquilia*, pp. 387 sqq., 439 sqq.; Kaser, *RPr* II, pp. 437 sqq.

[125] Cf. also Molinaeus, *Commentarius in Codicem*, Lib. II, Tit. XXXV (*Opera omnia*, vol. III (Parisiis, 1681), p. 625): ". . . in omnibus iudiciis nulla actio (est) frequentior illa."

[126] For a comprehensive analysis of the usus modernus of the actio legis Aquiliae, cf. Kaufmann, *Lex Aquilia*, passim; cf. also Rotondi, *Scritti*, vol. II, pp. 501 sqq.; Coing, pp. 509 sqq.; Thomas Kiefer, *Die Aquilische Haftung im "Allgemeinen Landrecht für die Preussischen Staaten" von 1794* (1989), pp. 58 sqq.; as far as France is concerned, cf. Coing, pp. 506 sq.

[127] Cf., in particular, Rudolf König, *Das allgemeine Schadensersatzrecht im Mittelalter im Anschluss an die lex Aquilia* (unpublished Dr. iur. thesis, Frankfurt, 1954), passim; most recently, cf. Kiefer, op. cit., note 126, pp. 29 sqq.; cf. also Charles Fried, "The Lex Aquilia as a Source of Law For Bartolus and Baldus", (1960) 4 *American Journal of Legal History* 142 sqq.; Harvey Chalmers, "The Concurrence of Criminal and Civil Actions in Medieval Law", (1973) 39 *SDHI* 385 sqq.

[128] It appeared in 1703; I have used the edition Halae Magdeburgicae, 1750. The quotation ("actio nostra . . .") is taken from § I of this treatise.

2. The assessment clauses and litiscrescence

One of the peculiar features of the Roman lex Aquilia that never appears to have been received in Europe was the retrospective (or prospective) assessment of the value of the object killed or damaged, as required by the "quanti in eo anno plurimi fuit" and "quanti ea res erit in diebus triginta proximis" clauses of chapters one and three respectively.[129] While legal writers tried to puzzle out the reasons for these strange provisions,[130] the courts simply assessed the plaintiff's interest "secundum statum praesentem in quo (res) fuit tempore damni dati".[131] Johann Sichard and Johannes Brunnemann still opposed this deviation from the Roman sources,[132] but a mere generation later it was more or less universally accepted. Stryk, Brunnemann's son-in-law, reported ". . . quod usum fori attinet, communiter . . . approbata est [haec] sententia", and he justified it on the basis that in that respect the old Germanic customary law had not been superseded by the Roman rule "recepto jure romano, pristinae Germanorum consuetudines non penitus sublatae".[133]

The rule of lis infitiando crescit in duplum[134] proved somewhat more long-lived. Although it was tied up with certain niceties of Roman civil procedure, it had still become part of the ius commune as a convenient means of preventing parties to a lawsuit from lying: ". . . jus civile in judicia hoc casu reducendum est, quo coercerentur eo melius publica illa in judicio prolata mendacia", as the matter was put by Stryk.[135] But by his time the tide had turned in practice[136] and Stryk himself acknowledged that "usu fori hoc duplum cessare plerique censent". In the course of the 18th century, this opinion came to prevail in legal literature, too.[137]

3. The penal nature of the remedy

As a result of the odd assessment clauses, it could happen that the award in Roman times went far beyond the plaintiff's interest. It was this surplus which in Justinian's view contributed the penal element inherent in the actio legis Aquiliae.[138] Apart from that, only

---

[129] Cf. supra, pp. 961 sqq.

[130] Cf., for example, König, op. cit., note 127, p. 38.

[131] Cf. Kaufmann, *Lex Aquilia*, pp. 85 sq.; the quotation is taken from Stryk, *Usus modernus pandectarum*, Lib. IX, Tit. II, § 2.

[132] Cf. Kaufmann, *Lex Aquilia*, p. 86.

[133] *Usus modernus pandectarum*, Lib. IX, Tit. II, §§ 2 sq.; cf. also Struve, *Syntagma*, Exerc. XIV, Lib. IX, Tit. II, XXV; Lauterbach, *Collegium theoretico-practicum*, Lib. IX, Tit. II, XXIV.

[134] Cf. supra, p. 974.

[135] *Usus modernus pandectarum*, Lib. IX, Tit. II, § 20.

[136] Kaufmann, *Lex Aquilia*, p. 88.

[137] Glück, vol. 10, p. 385. For the 19th century, cf. Windscheid/Kipp, §§ 263, 455, 5 in fine.

[138] *Inst.* IV, 3, 9; cf. supra, pp. 974 sq.

litiscrescence could possibly (if somewhat vaguely) be taken to constitute a non-compensatory component of the remedy, justifying its classification as actio mixta.[139] Once it had lost these two features, the Aquilian action was bound to change its character. This was widely recognized by the authors of the (later) usus modernus. "Actio legis Aquiliae hodie non poenalis est, sed rei persecutoria" was the principle enunciated by Groenewegen,[140] and it was approved of even by some of those who continued to apply infitiando lis crescit in duplum:[141] ". . . per accidens fit mixta [sc.: non sua natura]", as was explained by Lauterbach.

4. Cumulative liability

As in a game of dominoes, this change of character entailed further consequences. Where several persons had caused the damage, the injured party was able, in Roman law, to claim the full amount from all of them.[142] This form of cumulative liability was squarely based upon the penal nature of the lex Aquilia. Once it had become a purely reipersecutory remedy, however, cumulation could no longer be rationalized.[143] "Nam quae ab Ulpiano subjicitur ratio . . . hodie falsa est",[144] and the consequence was: liability of the several delinquents in solidum, but if one of them paid, all the others were released from their obligation (". . . quia actio tendit tantum ad reparationem damni, hoc ab uno ex illis refuso, liberantur reliqui, cum nihil amplius intersit"[145]).

5. Passive intransmissibility

(a) *Canonist doctrine*

Another domino was bound to fall sooner or later: the Roman rule that the Aquilian action was passively intransmissible.[146] Unless legal proceedings against the wrongdoer had already reached the stage of litis contestatio (in which case the wrongdoer's death no longer affected the

---

[139] Gai. IV, 9; cf. supra, p. 970.

[140] *De legibus abrogatis*, Inst., Lib. IV, Tit. III, § 15. For further details on the development, see Tobias Johannes Scott, *Die Geskiedenis van die Oorerflikheid van Aksies op grond van Onregmatige Daad in die Suid-Afrikaanse Reg* (unpublished Dr. iur. thesis, Leiden, 1976), pp. 48 sqq., 154 sqq.

[141] Cf. e.g. Stryk, *Usus modernus pandectarum*, Lib. IX, Tit. II, §§ 4, 21; Lauterbach, *Collegium theoretico-practicum*, Lib. IX, Tit. II, XXIV.

[142] Cf. supra, pp. 916, 973.

[143] The medieval lawyers (who still regarded the actio legis Aquiliae as both reipersecutoria and poenalis) had confined the cumulation to the amount by which the award exceeded the plaintiff's interesse, i.e. the duplum (in the case of litiscrescence) or any surplus on account of the assessment clauses: cf. König, op. cit., note 127, pp. 46 sq.; Lange, *Schadensersatz und Privatstrafe*, pp. 135 sq., 138.

[144] Stryk, *Usus modernus pandectarum*, Lib. IX, Tit. II, § 21.

[145] Stryk, loc. cit.; cf. also Glück, vol. 10, pp. 385 sqq.; Kaufmann, *Lex Aquilia*, pp. 91 sqq.

[146] Supra, p. 973.

enforceability of the claim[147]), the heir was liable only for any enrichment derived from the delict (id quod pervenit[148]). It took a surprisingly long time to topple this dogma, for until well into the 17th century even legal practice tended to steer a much more conservative course as in the case of cumulative liability.[149] But in the end it was the aequitas canonica that came to prevail, not only in foro conscientiae, but also in iure civili. The canonists had always recognized the passive transmissibility of delictual claims:

> "[S]ecundum canones tenetur haeres ex delicto defuncti, etiam si cum ipso lis non fuerit contestata . . . et quamvis ex delicto nihil pervenerit ad [eundem]."[150]

The reason for this was rather interesting. Commission of a delict, of course, constituted a sin.[151] Remission from this sin, according to canonist doctrine, required restitution ("peccatum non dimittitur, nisi restituatur ablatum").[152] The deceased wrongdoer was, unfortunately, no longer able to effect such restitution, and thus it was incumbent (at least in conscientia) on his heirs to save his soul from a prolonged sojourn in purgatory:

> "Quia vero ecclesia Romana non tantum in hac vita, sed etiam post mortem peccata dimitti credit, ceu doctrina de purgatorio et de offertorio pro defunctis praesupponit, inde etiam ex hoc principio constituerunt pontifices, heredes in genere ob damnum a defuncto per delictum datum obstringi in conscientia ad id restituendum, quod absque hoc medio in altera vita peccatum dimitti non possit."[153]

This result was even brought into line with Roman doctrine. The deceased would normally have received absolution before his death. Absolution required a confession of sins on the part of the dying person, and this confession could be construed as containing a tacit guarantee to redress all wrongs. The wrongdoer's obligation had thus been converted into a contractual one and contractual obligations were passively transmissible.

(b) *Forum civile*

For a long time such arguments did not really commend themselves to the civil lawyers; a certain reluctance seems to have prevailed to accept the canonist intruder, where the rule of Roman law was not obviously

---

147 Cf. Gai. D. 50, 17, 139 pr.; Paul. D. 50, 17, 164; Call. D. 44, 7, 59.

148 Cf. Scott, op cit., note 140, pp. 21 sqq.

149 Kaufmann, *Lex Aquilia*, pp. 95 sqq.

150 Henricus de Segusio (Hostiensis), *In Decretalium Commentaria*, Lib. V, De raptoribus, incendiariis, et violatoribus ecclesiarum (Tit. XVII), Cap. V, 1 and Lib. III, De sepulturis (Tit. XXVIII), Cap. XIV, 10. For a detailed analysis, cf. T.J. Scott, "Passive Transmissibility of Delictual Actions in Old Canon Law", 1978 *Acta Juridica* 15 sqq.

151 Hence the jurisdiction of the Church ("ratione peccati"); cf. Wieacker, *Privatrechtsgeschichte*, p. 76. On the criterion of ratione peccati, cf. also Wolter, *Ius canonicum in iure civili*, pp. 43 sqq., 91 sqq., 161 sqq., 193 sqq.

152 Cf. supra, p. 824, note 283.

153 Boehmer, *Ius ecclesiasticum protestantium*, Lib. V, Tit. XVII, § CXXXII; cf. also Scott, 1978 *Acta Juridica* 18.

morally intolerable.[154] Once one had realized that the real reason for the intransmissibility of the actio legis Aquiliae (its penal character) had fallen away, however, it was only natural to turn to canon law for guidance. Vinnius rather cautiously asserted "quod cum jure Canonico primum cautum esset . . . propter aequitatem etiam in foro civili receptum videtur",[155] but Thomasius put it more bluntly when he asked:

> "Quid ergo de moribus hodiernis hoc respectu dicendum? Respondendum, cum actio hodierna de damno dato sit actio fundata in aequitate Canonica et Jure Gentium: ideo actio hodierna dabitur contra heredes."[156]

This in fact remained the rule.[157]

6. Purely patrimonial loss

(a) Roman law and Inst. IV, 3, 16 i.f.

Other changes were even more significant, though unrelated to the (reipersecutory or penal) nature of the claim de damno dato. As far as the possible objects of Aquilian protection were concerned, Stryk's rather comprehensive formulation ("omnium damnorum reparatio ex hoc petatur") suggests that all limits had come to be abandoned. This was indeed the case. For, firstly, the lex Aquilia had been extended, rather surreptitiously, to cover purely patrimonial loss as such. No specific precedent for this development was available in the Roman sources. Wherever a Roman lawyer (including Justinian's compilers) had been prepared to grant the actio legis Aquiliae, or an actio in factum, the defendant's conduct had to have related to a specific corporeal asset in the plaintiff's property. Corruption of a res was not necessarily required;[158] but even where the lawyers awarded damages sine laesione corporis, these damages were still the result of the plaintiff's having been deprived of a particular item of his property, not purely patrimonial loss as such. This appears quite clearly, for instance, from the example provided by Justinian: a person, moved by pity, releases somebody else's slave from his bonds and the slave runs away.[159] Obviously, the plaintiff could recover patrimonial loss, but it

---

154 Kaufmann, *Lex Aquilia*, pp. 95 sqq.

155 *Institutiones*, Lib. IV, Tit. XII, 1, n. 8.

156 Op. cit., note 128, § LVIII; cf. further Brunnemann, *Commentarius in Pandectas*, Lib. IX, Tit. II, Ad L. Inde Neratius 23, n. 12 sq.; Stryk, *Usus modernus pandectarum*, Lib. IX, Tit. II, § 5; Voet, *Commentarius ad Pandectas*, Lib. IX, Tit. II, XII; Grotius, *Inleiding*, III, XXXII, 10; Glück, vol. 10, pp. 387 sq.; Scott, op. cit., note 73, pp. 127 sqq., 164 sqq.

157 To what extent was the heir liable: merely iuxta facultates hereditatis (liability restricted to the amount of the inheritance) or ultra facultates hereditatis (the heir had to satisfy the claim from his own assets, if necessary)? For a discussion, see Scott, 1978 *Acta Juridica* 15 sqq.

158 Cf. supra, pp. 986 sq.

159 *Inst.* IV, 3, 16; cf. also Paul. D. 9, 2, 33, 1. On these texts, and on the position in post-classical Roman law, cf. Rotondi, *Scritti*, vol. II, op. cit., note 124, pp. 440 sqq., 479;

was the patrimonial loss that resulted from the loss of the slave. When he tried to describe this kind of case in an abstract formula, however, Justinian used a very broad and rather equivocal phrase.

> "[S]ed si non corpore damnum fuerit datum neque corpus laesum fuerit, sed alio modo damnum alicui contigit . . . placuit eum qui obnoxius fuerit in factum actione teneri",

he said,[160] and this passage, if taken out of context, could indeed be taken to imply that any form of damnum was recoverable, irrespective of whether a specific res had in any way been affected or interfered with.

(b) Damnum datum, sed non in corpus

This wide interpretation gained ground in the Middle Ages; in Wilhelm Durantis' influential *Speculum iudiciale* we find the following instructive example:

> "Quid si propter faeces quas proiecisti in viam ante domum meam, condemnatus sum in decem secundum statutum loci Dic, quod agere possum contra te ad illa decem: quia qui occasionem damni [dat damnum dedisse videtur]."[161]

B throws rubbish in front of A's door, and A is subsequently fined by the public authorities for contravening some kind of statute dealing with waste removal. A is allowed to recover this fine from B on account of the fact that B's act occasioned A's loss. It does not appear to have struck Durantis as particularly problematic that A merely suffered purely patrimonial loss; the lex Aquilia is applied without any apparent realization of the momentous implications of this step. Courts and writers of the usus modernus perpetuated this interpretation of *Inst.* IV, 3, 16, they, too, in the belief that they were merely following in the footsteps of the Roman lawyers.[162] Of course, it was not the original actio legis Aquiliae itself that covered cases of this nature, it was a praetorian extension of it, an actio in factum, or, as it was sometimes put rather clumsily, an "actio subsidiaria in factum Praetoria ad exemplum actionis legis Aquiliae".[163] But since it was generally recognized that no practical difference existed between actio directa, actio utilis and actio in factum ("inter haec nihil interesse"[164]), this was an entirely irrelevant matter merely of nomenclature; relevant alone was the fact that Aquilian protection had become available in cases of

---

König, op. cit., note 127, pp. 6 sq., 54; F.H. Lawson, "The Duty of Care in Negligence: A Comparative Study", (1947–48) 22 *Tulane LR* 115 sq.; but see Kaufmann, *Lex Aquilia*, pp. 12 sqq.

[160] *Inst.* IV, 3, 16 in fine.

[161] *Speculum iudiciale*, Lib. IV, Partic. IV, De Iniuriis et damno dato, § 2 sequitur, 14; cf. further König, op. cit., note 127, pp. 22 sqq.

[162] For all details, see Kaufmann, *Lex Aquilia*, pp. 46 sqq., 62 sqq.

[163] Cf. Kaufmann, *Lex Aquilia*, p. 53.

[164] Cf., for example, Brunnemann, *Commentarius in Pandectas*, Lib. IX, Tit. II, Ad L. Item Mela, 11, n. 14; Stryk, *Usus modernus pandectarum*, Lib. IX, Tit. II, §§ 6 sq.; Glück, vol. 10, pp. 339 sq.; Rotondi, *Scritti*, vol. II, op. cit., note 124, pp. 524 sq.

purely patrimonial loss. "Fundamentum et causa hujus actionis est damnum injuria datum, . . . quo *patrimonium seu res aliena* dolo, aut culpa diminuitur" was a 17th-century definition of the Aquilian delict[165] which sums up contemporary opinion on the matter. Cases of purely patrimonial loss could arise, for instance, from the bad advice or the unsatisfactory conduct of a case on the part of an advocate, as is apparent from the discussion by Lauterbach: ". . . Praetor ex aequitate contra illum dat actionem subsidiariam in factum; e.g. si Advocatus per imperitiam parti damnum dederit"; and he adds: "quod etiam procedit in aliis casibus, ubi quis damnum dedit sua culpa; sed non in corpus."[166]

It was as a consequence of this extension of delictual liability that the lex Aquilia came to make deep inroads into the province of contractual liability. More particularly, it covered all the cases for which we are accustomed today to use the rather artificial term of "positive malperformance".[167] Purely patrimonial loss, according to the German BGB, can be recovered within a contractual relationship only and by way of a contractual claim for damages. This would apply, for instance, in the case of the incompetent advocate:[168] he could be held responsible by his client only on the basis of a breach of contract.[169] The jurists of the usus modernus do not seem to have known or respected such boundaries. Irrespective of whether or not contractual relationships existed between the parties concerned, the actio legis Aquiliae was applied in all cases of damnum culpa datum.[170] It was thus clearly on its way to becoming *the* general comprehensive remedy available for the recovery of damages.[171]

7. The protection of a freeman's life and bodily integrity

Secondly, and no less importantly, since the days of the glossators[172] the lex Aquilia was taken to cover cases of physical injury inflicted upon freemen. This view could be based on D. 9, 2, 13 pr. and remained uncontroversial. The *killing* of a liber homo was a more difficult matter. Sedes materiae for the glossators was D. 9, 2, 7, 4, the fragment "Si

---

[165] Struve, *Syntagma*, Exerc. XIV, Lib. IX, Tit. II, XX; cf. also Lauterbach, *Collegium theoretico-practicum*, Lib. IX, Tit. II, VII ("Ut damnum sit datum pecuniarium, scilicet, quo alterius diminuitur patrimonium").

[166] *Collegium theoretico-practicum*, Lib. IX, Tit. II, XV; for Roman-Dutch law cf., for example, Van Bynkershoek, *Observationes tumultuariae*, n. 1195; Pieter Pauw, "Aanspreeklikheid vir 'suiwer vermoënskade' in die Suid-Afrikaanse reg", (1975) 8 *De Jure* 26 sqq.; J.C. van der Walt, "Nalatige wanvoorstelling en suiwer vermoënskade: die appèlhof spreek 'n duidelike woord", 1979 *TSAR* 145 sqq.; *Administrateur, Natal v. Trust Bank van Afrika Bpk.* 1979 (3) SA 824 (A) at 830 sq.

[167] Cf. supra, pp. 783, 812 sq.

[168] Supra, note 166.

[169] Or, possibly, of culpa in contrahendo.

[170] Cf. Kaufmann, *Lex Aquilia*, pp. 110 sqq.; Harting, op. cit., note 113, pp. 65 sqq.

[171] See, too, Kaufmann, *Lex Aquilia*, pp. 117 sq.; Rotondi, *Scritti*, vol. II, op. cit., note 124, pp. 523 sqq.

[172] König, op. cit., note 127, p. 33.

quis in colluctatione".[173] "Sic ergo tenebitur lege Aquilia qui occidit liberum hominem", opined Azo,[174] and with him the majority of contemporary writers.[175] Bulgarus took the opposite view based, mainly, on the principle of "liberum corpus non recipit aestimationem".[176] It was Azo's view that prevailed in the long run. As far as the usus modernus was concerned, legal practice, as usual, took the lead; in the course of the 17th century the mores hodiernae also filtered through into legal literature.[177] But if injury to life led to Aquilian liability, it could hardly be the victim of the crime himself to whom the action was granted.[178] His heirs or relatives might, of course, have incurred expenses for hospitalization, medical care, etc. Some writers confined the availability of the lex Aquilia to these kinds of items. Hence, for instance, Lauterbach's remark that no action could be brought against an occisor "[qui] liberum hominem statim examinaverit".[179] What about the funeral expenses? There is no legal action available, said Stryk; if the wrongdoer reimburses those who have incurred them, he acts "magis in solatium haeredum pauperum, quam ex juris necessitate".[180] But at the same time he indicated that the reimbursement was perhaps not *merely* a voluntary gesture of consolation but that it was rendered as a matter of custom(ary law?).[181] The most important issue was, however, whether the wife and children of the deceased were able to claim compensation for the loss of support resulting from the death of the family's breadwinner (". . . id quod illorum interest, ob difficiliorem vitae sustentationem, quae operis defuncti potuit sublevari"[182]). It was this claim for which the glossators had laid the foundations[183] and which had become a widely accepted addition to the Aquilian repertory by the end of the 17th century. "Nec dubium", asserted Voet[184] in 1698, "quin ex usu hodierno latius illa

---

[173] Cf. supra, p. 1003, note 37; p. 1015, note 110.

[174] *Summa Codicis*, Lib. III, De lege Aquilia (p. 89, left column).

[175] For a penetrating interpretation of glossatorial writings on the matter, see Feenstra, in: Schrage, op. cit., note 110, pp. 207 sqq.

[176] Cf. Feenstra, in: Schrage, op. cit., note 110, pp. 211 sqq.

[177] For details, see Kaufmann, *Lex Aquilia*, pp. 34 sqq., 43 sqq.

[178] See, however, the remark "sed certe heres liberi hominis non agit lege Aquilia" by Azo, loc. cit., as interpreted by König, op. cit., note 127, p. 34. Contra: Feenstra, in: Schrage, op. cit., note 110, pp. 217 sqq.

[179] *Collegium theoretico-practicum*, Lib. IX, Tit. II, VIII; cf. also Stryk, *Usus modernus pandectarum*, Lib. IX, Tit. II, § 9.

[180] *Usus modernus pandectarum*, Lib. IX, Tit. II, § 9.

[181] Cf. also Grotius, *Inleiding*, III, XXXIII, 2; *Lockhat's Estate v. North British & Mercantile Insurance Co. Ltd.* 1959 (3) SA 295 (A) at 304; Dernburg, *Pandekten*, vol. II, § 132, 2; § 844 I BGB.

[182] Lauterbach, *Collegium theoretico-practicum*, Lib. IX, Tit. II, VIII.

[183] Feenstra, in: Schrage, op. cit., note 110, pp. 205 sqq.; cf. also Durantis, *Speculum iudiciale*, as quoted by König, op. cit., note 127, p. 40.

[184] *Commentarius ad Pandectas*, Lib. IX, Tit. II, XI. Cf. also Struve, Syntagma, Exerc. XIV, Lib. IX, Tit. II, XXII; Grotius, *Inleiding*, III, XXXIII, 2; Glück, vol. 10, pp. 341 sq; for the 19th century, see Dernburg, *Pandekten*, vol. II, § 132, 2; Windscheid/Kipp, § 455, 5

agendi potestas extensa sit", and he added some advice as to the assessment of the quod interest of the deceased's dependants:

> ". . . in quantum ob hominem liberum culpa occisum uxori et liberis actio datur in id, quod religioni judicantis aequum videbitur, habita ratione victus, quem occisus uxori liberisque suis aut aliis propinquis ex operis potuisset ac solitus esset subministrare."[185]

8. Compensation for pain, suffering and disfigurement

This brings us to the content of the Aquilian claim. The most interesting changes that occurred in this regard related to the infliction of bodily harm upon freemen. That medical expenses and loss of income could be claimed[186] was never doubted. But could the injured person ask to be compensated for pain, suffering and disfigurement? The answer of the Roman lawyers had been in the negative; at least as far as disfigurement was concerned, Gaius (D. 9, 3, 7) had left no doubt about that.[187] On the other hand, however, the idea of providing victims of violence with fixed amounts of money to comfort them was firmly rooted in Germanic (or perhaps rather: local) customary law.[188] People were thus used to the fact that their immaterial interest was taken into account when it came to the award of damages. Hence the continuous pressure by plaintiffs and counsel to abandon the rule of Roman law, a pressure to which 17th- and 18th-century courts eventually succumbed.[189] Academic writers tended for a long time to lash out at the uneducated practitioners ("Unde errare indoctos rabulas forenses . . ."[190]) and to take an uncompromisingly conservative attitude:

(who draw attention to the fact that the claim, recognized in practice, is "certainly not" justifiable theoretically); today § 844 II BGB.

[185] For which period did one have to assume that the relatives lost the opera of the dead person? Bartolus and Baldus argued (on the authority of Pap. D. 7, 1, 56 in fine) that the assessment had to be based on the presumption that the deceased would have become 100 years old. Durantis said "usque ad tempus quo verisimile est eum occisum vivere potuisse" (Kaufmann, *Lex Aquilia*, p. 20), but also referred (like Azo and Roffredus before him) to D. 35, 2, 68 pr. (the so-called lex Hereditatum computationi, providing a table for the computation of the value of a legatum concerning alimenta (problem: does it infringe the lex Falcidia?)); cf. the detailed analysis by Feenstra, in: Schrage, op. cit., note 110, pp. 223 sqq. As far as Roman-Dutch and South African law are concerned, cf. Groenewegen, *De legibus abrogatis*, Digest. Lib. XXXV, Tit. II, 1. 68; J.E. Scholtens, "Damages for Death", (1959) 76 *SALJ* 373 sqq.

[186] Supra, p. 1015.

[187] Cf. supra, p. 1015.

[188] Cf. Robert Feenstra, "Theories sur la responsabilité civile en cas d'homicide et en cas de lésion corporelle avant Grotius", in: idem, *Fata iuris romani* (1974), pp. 327 sqq.; Wieling, *Interesse und Privatstrafe*, pp. 136 sqq.; Olivier, op. cit., note 108, pp. 37 sqq., 120 sqq., 155 sqq.

[189] Kaufmann, *Lex Aquilia*, pp. 30 sqq.; Manfred Herrmann, *Der Schutz der Persönlichkeit in der Rechtslehre des 16. bis 19. Jahrhunderts* (1968), pp. 64 sqq.; Olivier, op. cit., note 108, pp. 121 sqq., 152 sqq., 160 sqq.

[190] Stryk, *Usus modernus pandectarum*, Lib. IX, Tit. II, § 10.

"Si liber homo laesus est, agitur tantum ad operas amissas,[191] et expensas in curationem factas, deformitatis vero et dolorum nulla habetur ratio."[192]

In the end, however, they had to resign themselves, velit nolit, to the practical realities:

". . . et cicatricis et doloris atque deformitatis aestimatio moribus praestanda veniat, si per laesum laesamve petita sit."[193]

It may be noted that injury to women paved the way for this development, at least as far as compensation for disfigurement was concerned.[194] For whereas men do not have to care very much about their appearance (only to them should Gai. D. 9, 3, 7 therefore be taken to apply![195]), beauty is a matter of vital importance to women: it facilitates their prospects of marriage and, as a result, of financial security.

9. Culpa

(a) In general

About the only requirement of Aquilian liability that remained essentially unchanged was culpa (in the sense of fault). It could take the form of intention (dolus) or negligence (culpa in the narrow sense, as it was conceptualized in the Justinianic sources[196]). The wrongdoer was

---

[191] Or, more precisely: ad operas, "quibus caruit aut cariturus est" (Gai. D. 9, 3, 7). On the operarum aestimatio see, again, Feenstra, in: Schrage, op. cit., note 110, pp. 223 sqq.

[192] Lauterbach, *Collegium theoretico-practicum*, Lib. IX, Tit. II, XXIV.

[193] Voet, *Commentarius ad Pandectas*, Lib. IX, Tit. II, XI. Cf. also Vinnius, *Institutiones*, Lib. IV, Tit. III, 13, n. 2; and, in particular, Grotius, *Inleiding*, III, XXXIV, 2 ("De smert ende ontciering van 't lichaem, hoewel eighentlick niet en zijn vergoedelick, werden op geld geschat, soo wanneer sulcks versocht word"); Glück, vol. 10, pp. 388 sqq.; as far as pecunia doloris is concerned, cf. also Stryk, *Usus modernus pandectarum*, Lib. IX, Tit. II, § 10 (on the basis of an analogy to art. 20 of the Constitutio Criminalis Carolina). For a discussion cf. Robert Feenstra, "Over de oorsprong van twee omstreden paragrafen uit de Inleidinge van Hugo de Groot (III, 33, 2 en III, 34, 2)", 1958 *Acta Juridica* 27 sqq.; idem, *Fata iuris romani*, pp. 323 sqq.; Wieling, *Interesse und Privatstrafe*, pp. 133 sqq.; Pieter Pauw, "Aspects of the origin of the action for pain, suffering and disfigurement", 1977 *TSAR* 244 sqq.; Olivier, op. cit., note 108, pp. 135 sqq., 162 sqq.; Boberg, *Delict*, pp. 516 sqq.; *Hoffa v. SA Mutual Fire & General Insurance Co. Ltd.* 1965 (2) SA 944 (C) at 950 sqq.; *Government of the Republic of South Africa v. Ngubane* 1972 (2) SA 601 (A) at 606A–611A. Feenstra, loc. cit., has drawn attention to the fact that this development was inspired not only by local customs but (particularly in the person of Hugo Grotius) by concepts of the law of nature, as formulated by 16th-century Spanish writers on the basis of medieval canonist doctrine (particularly the doctrine of restitution); cf. also Olivier, op. cit., note 108, pp. 83 sqq., 91 sqq., 135 sqq.

For the position in the 19th century, see Windscheid/Kipp, § 455, 7; Wieling, *Interesse und Privatstrafe*, pp. 147 sq.; today cf. § 847 BGB. On the recoverability of *dommage moral* in French law, see Geneviève Viney, in: Jacques Ghestin, *Traité de droit civil, Les obligations, La responsabilité: effets* (1988), nn. 142 sqq.; Pauw, *Persoonlikheidskrenking*, pp. 139 sqq.

[194] Cf. still Dernburg, *Pandekten*, vol. II, § 132, 1.

[195] Cf. Jacobus de Ravanis, as quoted by Pauw, 1977 *TSAR* 244.

[196] For a historical analysis, cf. Bert Krikke, "Rechtshistorische en dogmatische problemen rond het culpa-begrip", in: *Strafrecht in perspectief* (1980), pp. 201 sqq.

liable for all possible degrees of culpa, including culpa levissima.[197] Imperitia was still equated to culpa.[198] Wrongfulness remained an essential prerequisite for delictual liability, but was terminologically not distinguished from fault.[199] A general theory of causation was never

[197] Cf., for example, Voet, *Commentarius ad Pandectas*, Lib. IX, Tit. II, XIII; Rotondi, *Scritti*, vol. II, op. cit., note 124, pp. 513 sq.; Kaufmann, *Lex Aquilia*, pp. 74 sqq.; for the 19th century cf. Ogorek, *Gefährdungshaftung*, pp. 37 sqq. It was frequently argued, though, that liability for culpa levissima was excluded if the damage had been done within a contractual relationship which, in turn, did not impose such a strict degree of diligence on the parties; in other words, the special, contractual standard of diligence could modify what was generally (under the law of delict) expected of a person. Example: ". . . si depositarius in rebus suis negligens ex levissima culpa damnum dederit in re deposita, ad illud resarciendum, cum locum non habeat depositi actio, multo minus haec poenalis" (Lauterbach, *Collegium theoretico-practicum*, Lib. IX, Tit. II, IX—not taking into account, though, that the Aquilian action was no longer penal, but purely reipersecutory, as he himself acknowledged in other places, cf. e.g. loc. cit. XXIV); reason: "alias frustranea esset omnis de culpa juris dispositio." Cf. also Stryk, *Usus modernus pandectarum*, Lib. IX, Tit. II, § 14; Glück, vol. 10, pp. 310 sqq. The same case is still decided in exactly the same way according to modern German law. A depositarius is liable for diligentia quam in suis (§§ 690, 277 BGB), whereas liability in delict is for negligence in general (§§ 823 I, 276 I BGB). If an object that has been deposited is damaged or destroyed, the requirements for both a contractual and a delictual claim for damages are usually satisfied, but the standard of diligence envisaged in §§ 690, 277 BGB is applied to the delictual claim also; otherwise the intentions of the legislator, as expressed in § 690 BGB, would be frustrated. Cf., for example, Uwe Hüffer, in: *Münchener Kommentar*, vol. II, 2 (2nd ed., 1986), § 690, n. 7; generally on the problems arising from the concurrence of liabilities, see Peter Schlechtriem, *Vertragsordnung und ausservertragliche Haftung* (1972), passim; Fleming, *Torts*, pp. 168 sqq.; Tony Weir, "Complex Liabilities", in: *International Encyclopedia of Comparative Law*, vol. XI, 12 (1983), nn. 10 sqq.; for South Africa cf. *Lillicrap, Wassenaar and Partners v. Pilkington Brothers (SA) (Pty.) Ltd.* 1985 (1) SA 475 (A) at 500F–501H; Dale Hutchison, D.P. Visser, (1985) 102 *SALJ* 590 sqq.; Boberg, *Delict*, pp. 3 sqq. Cf. also supra, pp. 904 sqq.

[198] In discussions concerning imperitia, liability for medical malpractice played a particularly prominent role. What the lawyers of the usus modernus had to say about the medical profession, in this context, was not particularly flattering. For Stryk, the medical profession was full of sycophants (". . . nulla ars plures habeat Sicophantes quam medicina, et plerumque hic barbitonsores et pharmacopolae officii sui limites excedant . . ."; he then proceeds to report a case of "pillularum imperite adhibitarum contra chirurgum"); Lauterbach regretfully reported that negligent doctors were only rarely brought before a court of law and that they were therefore the only people who might kill with impunity ("Raro . . . culpa Medici in judicium vocatur. Unde: Errata Medicorum terra occultat, benefacta autem Sol illustrat. Et Plinius: Soli Medico hominem occidere impune est"); and Groenewegen came to the conclusion: "Imperitia hodie non solet imputari medicis . . . Medicorum imperitia terra tegit, ideoque in judicium non vocatur, aut alioqui fere excusatur" (*De legibus abrogatis*, Inst., Lib. IV, Tit. III, § 7); cf. also Vinnius, *Institutiones*, Lib. IV, Tit. III, 8, n. 2. On the history of medical malpractice law in England, cf. the remarks by Giesen, op. cit., note 40, pp. 4 sqq. Generally on imperitia culpae adnumeratur in Roman-Dutch law, cf. Scott, *Gedenkbundel Steyn*, pp. 134 sqq.

[199] Cf. , for example, Struve, *Syntagma*, Exerc. XIV, Lib. IX, Tit. II, XXI ("Quod si nec dolus nec culpa intervenit, non intelligitur damnum injuria datum . . ."); Voet, *Commentarius ad Pandectas*, Lib. XLVII, Tit. I, I; Glück, vol. 10, pp. 319 sqq; Kaufmann, *Lex Aquilia*, pp. 73 sqq. As far as damages caused by an act which is "licit and permitted by law" (a traditional ball game) are concerned, cf. the interesting decision of the Rota Fiorentina of 1780, discussed by Gino Gorla, (1975) 49 *Tulane LR* 346 sqq. The decision, inter alia, refers to D. 9, 2, 11 pr. (the barber case). The case of the barber also features prominently (art. 146) in the Constitutio Criminalis Carolina of 1532, the codification that heralded a new era in the science of criminal law.

developed or applied.[200] The difference between causam mortis dare and occidere continued to be discussed, although it had lost any significance.[201] What mattered was whether the wrongdoer had provided occasionem damni, but that enquiry was often linked to the broader problem of fault.[202]

(b) *Culpa in omittendo*

Discussion of the knotty question of liability for omissions was also conducted, from the time of the glossators,[203] in terms of the culpa requirement. The approach to be adopted was controversial. For, on the one hand, there was a fragment, attributed to Ulpian (but dealing with the (possibly) rather special situation of a usufructuary who neglects to plough the land, to plant new vines or to repair an aqueduct[204]), that appeared to reject any possibility of liability for mere omissions; and on the basis of this text even Voet asserted that the lex Aquilia did not cover cases of culpa in omittendo.[205] On the other hand, however, there was the doctor who abandoned the treatment of his patient and of the stoker who took a nap by his furnace: both of them had been liable in Roman law.[206] Thus it was generally recognized that Aquilian protection existed where the damage had been "committendo et omittendo simul datum"[207] or, in the words of Lauterbach, "si quis circa factum praeteritum culpam committat in omittendo".[208] But some authors went further and accepted liability for omissions, wherever more than mere culpa levissima was attributable to the

[200] But cf. the somewhat unfortunate attempts of (for example) Lauterbach to apply the scholastic causa doctrine: *Collegium theoretico-practicum*, Lib. IX, Tit. II, I–III, XI. For further details, see Kaufmann *Lex Aquilia*, pp. 64 sqq.

[201] Cf. e.g. Stryk, *Usus modernus pandectarum*, Lib. IX, Tit. II, § 7 ("Quale ergo hic subest interesse? scil. nullum aliud, quam ut constet, an actione directa, l. aquil. an in factum agendum. Verum inter haec nihil interesse, jam dictum est").

[202] Cf. e.g. Lauterbach, *Collegium theoretico-practicum*, Lib. IX, Tit. II, II and III: "Causa sive factum, ex quo oritur, est damnum facientis injuria . . . Causa efficiens remota est Lex; . . . [p]roxima est malitia, infirmitas, ignorantia, negligentia vel imperitia hominis. . . ."

[203] König, op. cit., note 127, pp. 31 sq.

[204] D. 7, 1, 13, 2 (". . . nam qui agrum non proscindit, qui vites non subserit, item aquarum ductus conrumpi patitur, lege Aquilia non tenetur"); on this text cf. Pernice, *Sachbeschädigungen*, pp. 166 sqq.; Van den Heever, *Aquilian Damages*, pp. 41 sqq; Ben Beinart, "Culpa in omittendo", (1949) 12 *THRHR* 152 sqq.; von Lübtow, *Lex Aquilia*, p. 97; Alan Watson, "D. 7. 1. 13. 2 (Ulp. 18 ad Sab.): the lex Aquilia and decretal actions", (1966) 17 *Iura* 174 sqq.; Kemp J. Kemp, *Delictual Liability for Omissions* (unpublished LLD thesis, Port Elizabeth, 1978), pp. 75 sqq.

[205] *Commentarius ad Pandectas*, Lib. IX, Tit. II, III.

[206] Cf. Ulp. D. 9, 2, 27, 9; Gai. D. 9, 2, 8 pr.; see also the discussion by Van den Heever, *Aquilian Damages*, pp. 37 sqq.; Kemp, op. cit., note 204, pp. 62 sqq., 88 sqq.

[207] Voet, *Commentarius ad Pandectas*, Lib. IX, Tit. II, III; Glück, vol. 10, pp 319 sq.; *Halliwell v. Johannesburg Municipal Council* 1912 AD 659 at 670 sq.; Kemp, op. cit., note 204, pp. 137 sqq.

[208] *Collegium theoretico-practicum*, Lib. IX, Tit. II, X.

wrongdoer;[209] others were even prepared to drop any distinction between faults of commission and omission: "Sufficit autem, culpa levissima damnum illatum esse, . . . sive committendo, sive omittendo."[210]

(c) *Concurrence of fault*

Of central importance for the discussion of contributory negligence were the cases of the javelin-thrower and the barber;[211] both were now interpreted in the light of the Justinianic regula iuris "[q]uod quis ex culpa sua damnum sentit, non intellegitur damnum sentire"[212]—which in turn was taken to imply that fault on the part of the victim of a wrong had the effect of excluding any claim for compensation against the wrongdoer (unless, of course, the latter had acted dolo). While, therefore, the Roman all-or-nothing approach[213] was retained, the problem was now conceived in terms of a concurrence of fault:

> "Cum itaque moraliter nemo damnum sentire videatur, qui sua culpa damnum sentit, . . . sequitur inde, quod, si patientis quoque culpa concurrat, hoc delictum non videatur commissum."[214]

The fault of the plaintiff/victim was, in a way, "set off" against that of the defendant/wrongdoer, with the result that "culpa culpam abolet".[215] Hence the expression of compensatio culpae or culpa compensation[216] that came to be used to label the uncompromising approach to the problem of contributory negligence. Whether every contributory fault on the part of the victim—even culpa levissima—was originally taken to deprive him of his remedy is not quite clear. In the later usus modernus, at any rate, the issue appears to have been decided on the basis of a preponderance of fault:[217] only if he had displayed the same or a greater degree of negligence than the wrongdoer did the victim lose his claim. Where, on the other hand, his negligence was less significant, when compared with that of the wrongdoer, his claim for damages remained completely unaffected.

---

[209] Stryk, *Usus modernus pandectarum*, Lib. IX, Tit. II, § 14.

[210] Struve, *Syntagma*, Exerc. XIV, Lib. IX, Tit. II, XX; cf. also Grotius, *Inleiding*, III, XXXII, 3, 4, 12, 14.

[211] Cf. supra, pp. 1011 sq.

[212] Pomp. D. 50, 17, 203, on which see Medicus, *Id quod interest*, pp. 323 sq.; Aumann, op. cit., note 76, pp. 30 sq.; Lange, *Schadensersatz und Privatstrafe*, pp. 71 sq.

[213] Supra, pp. 1010 sqq.

[214] Lauterbach, *Collegium theoretico-practicum*, Lib. IX, Tit. II, VII; cf. also XI.

[215] Gl. Tenebitur ad D. 9, 2, 9, 4.

[216] An unsuitable name, according to Buckland/McNair, p. 371; cf. also Lawson/Markesinis, pp. 33 sq.

[217] Luig, (1969) 2 *Ius Commune* 206 sqq.; cf. further Kaufmann, *Lex Aquilia*, pp. 77 sqq.; Aumann, op. cit., note 76, pp. 50 sqq.; Wieling, *Interesse und Privatstrafe*, pp. 222 sqq.

IV. TOWARDS THE MODERN, GENERALIZED LAW OF DELICT

1. Legal theory and mores hodiernae

All in all, I think, one can understand, perhaps even sympathize with, Thomasius' emphatic rejection of any link between the Roman lex Aquilia and the modern delict de damno dato. Historically he was wrong, but under purely dogmatic auspices he certainly had a point. Though the enactment from the 3rd century B.C. was still (in the terminology of Lauterbach) causa efficiens remota ex quo oritur actio,[218] many new strands had been woven into it.[219] The usus modernus of the Aquilian delict had absorbed Germanic customary law, some elements from canon law and medieval moral theology, but above all it had been shaped by the efforts of generations of judges and counsel: practical lawyers who made the lex Aquilia suit the needs of their time. It was thus part and parcel of a vigorous, yet flexible, jurisprudentia forensis. But the time was clearly ripe for a new theoretical framework. Contemporary tractatus, discursus, collegii and commentarii were still full of dogmatic ballast: distinctions between actiones in factum, utiles and directae, between occidere and causam mortis praebere, or between the computation of the interesse in chapter one and that prescribed in chapter three, litiscrescence and the problem of the penal nature or otherwise of the action, the requirement of corruptio rei and the principle of liberum corpus nullam recipit aestimationem—all this was more or less respectfully dragged along, but became increasingly overshadowed by the "mores hodiernae". Reference to the latter was all too often merely added, fairly abruptly, at the end of the respective section of the treatise. Legal theory had failed to provide a suitable doctrinal edifice to accommodate the law in action. This task was finally undertaken by the natural lawyers, and it was in fact the vitality of their ideas that inspired Thomasius to "pull down the Aquilian mask".[220]

---

[218] *Collegium theoretico-practicum*, Lib. IX, Tit. II, III and II.

[219] Cf., once again, in particular Feenstra, *Fata iuris romani*, pp. 323 sqq.; also Thomasius, op. cit., note 128, § LI and passim.

[220] He tried to show not only that the actio hodierna was entirely different from the actio legis Aquiliae, but also that it corresponded to the precepts juris naturae vel gentium. Characteristic is the following passage: "Cum . . . conveni[at] hac parte Canonicum jus cum aequitate naturali & moribus Gentium, sane in tantum se commendavit hac parte Jus Canonicum Germanis ut duritiam morum proprium ad aequitatem Juris Canonici reducerunt: Quo facto plane non fuerunt apti, ut introducto, integro seculo post Jus Canonicum, Jure Justinianeo in Academias Germaniae, relicta hac parte Juris Canonici aequitate, recipere potuerint irregularem illam et omni ratione destitutam duritiam legis Aquiliae" (§ LI).

On Thomasius' views on the relationship between ius civile and ius canonicum in general, see Wolter, *Ius canonicum in iure civili*, pp. 161 sqq.; on his natural-law theory, cf. Hinrich Rüping, *Die Naturrechtslehre des Christian Thomasius und ihre Fortbildung in der Thomasius-Schule* (1968).

2. The "natural" law of delict

The new foundations had been laid about 80 years before the publication of the "Larva", by Hugo Grotius. An obligation, he said, can arise from three sources: pactio, maleficium, and lex. Maleficium was his word for delict and he defined it in terms which have become famous:

> "Maleficium hic appellamus culpam omnem, sive in faciendo, sive in non faciendo, pugnantem cum eo quod aut homines communiter, aut pro ratione certae qualitatis facere debent. Ex tali culpa obligatio naturaliter oritur, si damnum datum est, nempe ut id resarciatur."[221]

This was the principal and fundamental proposition of the "natural" law of delict; if someone causes damage because he culpably does what he ought not to do, he is obliged to make it good.[222] Samuel Pufendorf elaborated the moral foundations of this principle. Innate in man is what he calls socialitas: he has to live, and get on, with his fellow human beings.[223] The most important precept flowing from man's social nature is this: "(I.) Ut ne quis alterum laedat, utque (II.) si quod damnum alteri dederit, id reparet."[224] (I.), incidentally, is the second of Ulpian's three fundamental iuris praecepta: "honeste vivere, alterum non laedere, suum cuique tribuere."[225] It is based, ultimately, on the golden rule of moral philosophy: "Do as you would be done by"—a point, perhaps most clearly emphasized by Christian Thomasius:

---

[221] *De jure belli ac pacis*, Lib. II, Cap. XVII, I. Cf. also *Inleiding*, III, XXXII, 7, 9, 12 (referring to "het aengheboren recht" (natural law).

[222] For a discussion, see Hans-Peter Benöhr, "Ausservertragliche Schadensersatzpflicht ohne Verschulden? Die Argumente der Naturrechtslehren und -kodifikationen", (1976) 93 *ZSS* 209 sqq.; Kiefer, op. cit., note 126, pp. 78 sqq.

[223] Characteristic is the following passage from his *De jure naturae et gentium*: "Ex hisce positis facile est fundamentum legis naturalis invenire. Scilicet manifesto apparet, hominem esse animal sui conservandi studiosissimum, per se egenum, sine sui similium auxilio servari ineptum, ad mutua commoda promovenda maxime idoneum, idem tamen saepe malitiosum, petulans, et facile irritabile, ac ad noxam inferendam promtum, ac validum. Ejusmodi animali, ut salvum sit, bonisque fruatur, quae in ipsius conditionem hic cadunt, necessarium est, ut sit sociabile, id est, ut conjungi cum sui similibus velit, et adversus illos ita se gerat, ut ne isti ansam accipiant eum laedendi, sed potius rationem habeant ejusdem commoda servandi, aut promovendi" (Lib. II, Cap. III, XV).

[224] *De jure naturae et gentium*, Lib. III, Cap. I, I; cf. further Benöhr, (1976) 93 *ZSS* 213 sqq.; Kiefer, op. cit., note 126, pp. 83 sqq. "Ut ne quis alterum laedat" (alterum non laedere) is the more basic of the two statements; (II.) has to be added, though, because, as Thomasius (op. cit., note 128, § II) explains "[f]rustraneum hoc esset praeceptum, si post laesionem non tenerer laeso ad satisfactionem").

[225] D. 1, 1, 10, 1 (on which, see Malte Diesselhorst, "Die Gerechtigkeitsdefinition Ulpians in D. 1, 1, 10 pr. und die Praecepta iuris nach D. 1, 1, 10, 1 sowie ihre Rezeption bei Leibnitz und Kant", in: *Römisches Recht in der europäischen Tradition, Symposion Franz Wieacker* (1985), pp. 185 sqq.; Gottfried Schiemann, "Das allgemeine Schädigungsverbot: 'alterum non laedere' ", 1989 *Juristische Schulung* 345 sqq.). On the precept of alterum non laedere, cf., most recently, Hans Hattenhauer, *Grundbegriffe des Bürgerlichen Rechts* (1982), pp. 103 sq.; Diesselhorst, op. cit., pp. 196 sqq.; Klaus Luig, "Digesten und Dogmatik", (1986) 5 *RJ* 307 sqq.; Eduard Picker, "Vertragliche und deliktische Schadenshaftung", 1987 *Juristenzeitung* 1048 sqq.; Schiemann, 1989 *Juristische Schulung* 345 sqq.

"Damnum alteri a nobis datum, esse resarciendum, . . . cordibus hominum inscriptum est . . . Postulat id communis tranquillitas, postulat aequalitas humani generis. Nemo sibi vult damnum dari, non itaque det aliis. Quilibet vult sibi damnum ab aliis datum resarciri; resarciat aliis."[226]

3. Fault as the basis of delictual liability

(a) Thomasius

But why should the obligation to make good the damage arise only in case of fault? This is by no means as self-evident (or "natural") as Grotius' magisterial assertion makes it sound. If the basic precept is "alterum non laedere", *strict* liability based merely on the fact that one person caused the other damage may well be seen to be the more appropriate consequence. This was, in fact, the point of view adopted by Thomasius. "Aequum non solum, sed et justum est, ut damnum casu datum resarciam", he postulated[227] and proceeded to give the following example. While visiting a friend, my attention is drawn to a very valuable crystal glass of his. Admiringly I turn the glass around in my hands, when suddenly something entirely unforeseen happens, which frightens both me and my friend out of our wits. As a result I drop the glass, which breaks into pieces. Who has to carry the loss? I do, according to Thomasius, for without my interference (however innocent it was) the glass would still be whole:

"Sufficit, quod factum meum dominus adversus me allegare possit. Nam si vitrum non sumsissem in manus, non etiam id fuisset fractum. Quam innocens igitur sit curiositas mea, mea tamen est, non domini vitri."[228]

Looked at merely from the point of view of the injured party, this argument is certainly not unconvincing. In a way, the person dropping the glass is indeed "closer" to the loss.[229]

(b) Grotius, Pufendorf and others

Grotius, Pufendorf and most of the other natural lawyers, however, took a different perspective. Focusing their attention on the injuring (rather than the injured) party, they emphasized the duty aspect of the

---

[226] Op. cit., note 128, § II.

[227] Op. cit., note 128, § IV; "[a]equum est, quia pium et humanum est, aliis, quibus etiam non a nobis damnum datum est, ex abundantia nostra succurrere et in solatium rerum amissarum quaedam donare; quanto magis iis, qui facto nostro damnum passi sunt: Justum est, quia tranquillitas humani generis id postulat." On the notions of aequalitas and tranquillitas, in this context, cf. Benöhr, (1976) 93 *ZSS* 220 sqq.

[228] Op. cit., note 128, § IV. Cf. further § VII, but also § V.

[229] Blackburn J, in the famous case of *Rylands v. Fletcher* [1861–73] All ER 1 at 11 appears to have had something similar in mind, for his way of arguing implies that he regarded no-fault liability as the primary principle of delictual liability, negligence as an exception (cf. also A.W.B. Simpson, "Legal Liability for Bursting Reservoirs: The Historical Context of *Rylands v. Fletcher*", (1984) 13 *Journal of Legal Studies* 213 sqq.). In the course of the 19th century, English courts vacillated on the question of whether to deduce negligence based liability or no-fault liability from the maxim of "sic utere tuo ut alieno non laedas"; cf. infra, p. 1137, note 317.

matter.[230] A person can be held liable only if he has done what he ought not to have done, or if he has not done what he ought to have done. The damage, in Pufendorf's terminology, must have been "imputable" to the person who had caused the damage. Such imputation,[231] in turn, required a free and moral action; and that implied, inter alia, that the acting party had to be able to foresee the consequences and to recognize the wrongfulness of what he was doing (or failing to do).[232] Liability for damages required an avoidable deviation from the path of lawful behaviour—"defectus rectitudinis actionis . . . vincibilis", in the words of Christian Wolff[233]—and was thus based on fault. Purely accidental loss, on the other hand, had to be carried by whoever had been hit by it—entirely in accordance with the maxim "casus a nullo praestantur".[234] It was the latter view that commended itself to the draftsmen of the codifications, in which the age of the law of reason culminated, and thus we find fault (*faute, Verschulden*) as the cornerstone of delictual liability in the two famous general clauses of § 1295 ABGB and art. 1382 code civil.[235]

(c) *Nineteenth-century legal science*

In the course of the 19th century, the principle that liability is based on fault acquired the status of an unquestionable, axiomatic truth. For even though Grotius (and the other natural lawyers) had not referred to Roman law,[236] the fault principle commended itself to the pandectists for a whole variety of reasons.[237] It tied in with the basic precepts of Kant's moral philosophy[238] (as adopted by Savigny,[239] the founder of

[230] Benöhr, (1976) 93 *ZSS* 226 sq.

[231] On this notion cf. from an analytical point of view, Joachim Hruschka, "Imputation", in: Albin Eser, George P. Fletcher, *Rechtfertigung und Entschuldigung*, vol. I (1987), pp. 121 sqq.

[232] On Pufendorf's concepts of an actio moralis, of imputatio and imputativitas, cf. e.g. *De jure naturae et gentium*, Lib. I, Cap. V; W. Hardwig, *Die Zurechnung* (1957), pp. 35 sqq.; Joachim Hruschka, "Ordentliche und ausserordentliche Zurechnung bei Pufendorf", (1984) 76 *ZStrW* 661 sqq.

[233] *Philosophia practica universalis*, Pars I (Francofurti et Lipsiae, 1738), § 692 ("Defectus rectitudinis actionis dicitur vincibilis, si eum evitare potuisses, modo voluisses"); § 696 ("Defectus rectitudinis actionis vincibilis dicitur in genere culpa"); § 701 ("Defectus actionis a rectitudine quoad voluntatem et voluntatum dicitur Dolus"); § 717 ("Culpa in specie dicitur defectus rectitudinis actionis quoad intellectum vincibilis").

[234] Cf. Ulp. D. 50, 17, 23 in fine.

[235] On the fault principle in the natural law codifications, see Benöhr, (1976) 93 *ZSS* 228 sq. (Codex Maximilianeus), pp. 229 sqq. (Prussian General Land Law), 233 sqq. (ABGB), 242 sqq. (code civil). On the most direct sources of art. 1382 code civil, cf. infra, note 248.

[236] Grotius had used certain passages from Aristotle's *Nicomachaean Ethics* as the starting point for his views on delict: cf. *De jure belli ac pacis*, Lib. III, Tit. XI, II sqq.

[237] Analysed in detail by Hans-Peter Benöhr, "Die Entscheidung des BGB für das Verschuldensprinzip", (1978) 46 *TR* 1 sqq.

[238] Cf. e.g. Josef Esser, *Grundlagen und Entwicklung der Gefährdungshaftung* (2nd ed., 1969), pp. 50 sqq.; Roscoe Pound, "The Role of the Will in Law", (1954) 68 *Harvard LR* 1 sqq. (8, 17); Ogorek, *Gefährdungshaftung*, pp. 23 sq.

[239] Cf. e.g. *System*, vol. V, pp. 1 sqq.; *Obligationenrecht*, vol. II, p. 295.

the historical school of jurisprudence), it fitted the prevailing economic liberalism[240] and served the interests of expanding industry and of the rising middle class:[241] it was seen to provide adequate protection without unduly restricting the freedom of the individual will or hampering entrepreneurial activities.[242] Apart from that, it did not prove too difficult to reconcile it with the Roman sources: Aquilian liability had been based on culpa anyway, and instances of a stricter form of liability could, somehow or other, also be made to fit the picture that was painted of a triumphal march of the fault principle through Roman law.[243] The idea that there can be no liability without fault was seen to be both the product and the symbol of a high stage of cultural development. Thus, of course, it underlies the provisions on the law of delict of that apotheosis of 19th-century legal thinking, the BGB. "The fault-principle", its draftsmen argued,[244]

> "is of central importance for the delineation of the spheres of rights within which the citizens can develop their individuality. In determining whether or how to act, one should have to take account of the legal interests of others only if the requisite forethought suggests that they may be affected. If after careful reflection an act seems to present no danger to others, one should be free to do it, and if it nevertheless causes harm to someone else's legal rights, that person must put up with it just as if it were an accident."

Strict liability had thus been (almost) entirely removed from the province of the "proper" law of delict; and since the dogmatic category of the "quasi-delicts" had become obsolete in the course of time, isolated instances of no-fault liability were thought of as anomalous and exceptional[245] and remained for a long time outside the mainstream of private-law legal theory. We still have to battle today with the consequences of this ahistorical dogmatism.[246]

4. Purely patrimonial loss

(a) *The natural lawyers*

Apart from their insistence on fault, the most characteristic feature of natural law theories concerning delictual liability was their readiness to

---

[240] Cf. e.g. Hein Kötz, "Haftung für besondere Gefahr", (1970) 170 *Archiv für die civilistische Praxis* 2 sqq.

[241] Fleming, *Torts*, pp. 93 sqq., 302 sqq. ("'No liability without fault' became the banner of an individualistic society set on commercial exploitation and self-help").

[242] Benöhr, (1978) 46 *TR* 10 sqq.

[243] Cf., in particular, Rudolf von Jhering, *Das Schuldmoment im römischen Privatrecht* (1867).

[244] "Protokolle", in: *Mugdan*, vol. II, p. 1074; I have, in general, followed the translation by Weir, in Zweigert/Kötz/Weir, p. 311.

[245] "[V]estigial anomalies of an uncivilised past when individual freedom was less esteemed than in the new era of middle class democracy": Fleming, *Torts*, p. 302; for Roman law, cf. Jhering, op. cit., note 243, pp. 41 sq.

[246] Cf. infra, pp. 1132 sqq.

provide compensation for purely patrimonial loss.[247] Both § 1295 ABGB and art. 1382 code civil[248] reflect this way of thinking and neither of these norms therefore requires that the plaintiff's pecuniary loss must have flowed from damage to his person or property.[249]

(b) Germany (19th century)

Unlike in the case of fault, the pandectists did not follow suit, however. Nineteenth-century legal science predominantly advocated a return to the more limited scope of Aquilian liability in Roman law,[250] and it was this view which found expression in § 823 I BGB.[251] A certain number of specific rights and interests are listed, and it is only by violating one of them that a person may become liable in delict. The list[252] contains life, body, health, freedom, property and "any other right"; but there is unanimity that, whatever may be smuggled into § 823 I under cover of the "other right" clause,[253] it does in any event not refer to the

[247] Cf. e.g. Hans Jentsch, *Die Entwicklung von den Einzeltatbeständen des Deliktrechts zur Generalnorm und die Berechtigung einer solchen* (unpublished Dr. iur. thesis, Leipzig, 1939), pp. 5 sqq.; Friedhelm Keppmann, *Die neuere Entwicklung der objektiven Tatbestände der §§ 823, 826 BGB* (unpublished Dr. iur. thesis, Münster, 1959), pp. 18 sqq.

[248] The way to the famous general clause of art. 1382 led via Jean Domat, *Les loix civiles*, Lib. II, Tit. VIII, Sect. IV, 1; cf. the analysis by Yosiyuki Noda, "Jean Domat et le Code civil français" (1956) 3 *Comparative Law Review (Japan Institute of Comparative Law)* 1 sqq.; cf. also Pothier, *Traité des obligations*, nn. 116, 123. Art. 1382 code civil has been received by the Dutch legislator: art. 1401 BW. There is one interesting difference, however: the Dutch Code has "elke onregtmatige daad" as opposed to the "*tout fait quelconque*" of art. 1382 code civil (for details of the development cf. Robert Feenstra, *Vergelding en vergoeding* (1982), pp. 3 sqq.). French legal science has, however, read the requirement of wrongfulness into the notion of "*faute*": cf. supra, p. 998, note 6.

[249] Cf. also §§ 1, 8, 10 I 6 PrALR, on which see Kiefer, op. cit., note 126, passim. He draws attention to the continuity between the doctrines of the usus modernus and the provisions of the Prussian General Land Law on the law of delictual liability. The natural-law theories merely provided the philosophical framework.

[250] Cf., for example, Dernburg, *Pandekten*, vol. II, §§ 131, 135; Hasse, *Culpa*, pp. 26 sq.; Vangerow, *Pandekten*, § 681; Windscheid/Kipp, §§ 451, 455; RGZ 9, 158 sqq. (163 sqq.); for a discussion, see Keppmann, op. cit., note 247, pp. 52 sqq. Legal practice did not always follow suit; cf. August Hefke, "Das Wesen des damnum iniuria datum", (1886) 14 *Archiv für praktische Rechtswissenschaft* 212 sq. Under the influence of pandectist doctrine the provisions of the PrALR (cf. supra, note 249) were also restrictively interpreted and brought into line, as far as possible, with the scope of Aquilian liability in Roman law. Cf. Kiefer, op. cit., note 126, pp. 165 sqq., 189 sqq., 224 sqq.

[251] The first draft had still opted for a general clause: cf. §§ 704 sq. E I. On the discussions in the course of the *traveaux préparatoires*, cf. Keppmann, op. cit., note 247, pp. 97 sqq.; Michael Fraenkel, *Tatbestand und Zurechnung bei § 823 Abs. 1 BGB* (1979), pp. 97 sqq.; Kiefer, op. cit., note 126, pp. 270 sqq. In the end, the general clause was rejected by the second commission by a bare majority of ten to eight votes.

[252] Which, incidentally, can also be traced back to Grotius (cf. his *Inleiding*, III, XXXIII (Van misdaed tegen 't leven), III, XXXIV (Van misdaed tegen 't lichaem), III, XXXV (Van hoon), III, XXXVI (Van misdaed tegens goed)) and beyond him, ultimately, to Donellus (cf. infra, p. 1086, notes 270 and 274); Feenstra, op. cit., note 248, pp. 13 sq.

[253] Delictual protection of family relationships, of the right to an established and operative business, and of the general right to one's personality, to mention the three most notable examples. For an overview, cf. B.S. Markesinis, *A Comparative Introduction to the German Law of Tort* (1986), pp. 34 sqq. (with reproduction, in translated form, of some of the most important cases: pp. 173 sqq.); Zweigert/Kötz, pp. 340 sqq. The "or any other right" clause

injured party's patrimony as such. Thus, to mention three notorious problem cases, there is no liability in delict for negligent statements,[254] for the negligent interruption of an electricity supply[255] or for negligence, on the part of a notary, in the execution of a will.[256] The German approach is based on the fear of liability "in an indeterminate amount for an indeterminate time to an indeterminate class":[257] the assumption being that refusal in principle to recover pure economic loss is the only effective means of preventing an appalling variety of claims by hosts of people which would stifle commercial activities and make ordinary life intolerable.[258] "Just think", exclaimed Rudolf von Jhering,[259]

> "what it would lead to if everyone could be sued in tort for gross negligence [!] as well as fraud! Anything and everything—an unwitting utterance, carrying a tale, making a false report, giving bad advice . . . answering a traveller's question about the way or the time or whatever—all this, if grossly negligent, would make one liable for the harm even if one was in perfect good faith; if the actio de dolo were so

---

was, in fact, intended to refer only to absolute rights similar to ownership (as, for example, patents, copyrights, trade marks, or the right to one's image).

[254] Unless, of course, there is a contract between the two parties concerned (in which case recovery for pure economic loss presents no problem), or unless the negligent statement leads to physical damage (for an instructive example, see *Bristow v. Lycett* 1971 (4) SA 223 (RAD), where the defendant's assurances relating to an elephant had turned out to be unduly sanguine).

[255] In these cases, § 823 I BGB leads to strange distinctions. If the interruption of the electricity supply merely brings to a halt the machines in a factory, the owner of the factory has no claim for the resulting loss of production (pure economic loss; but was there perhaps an infringement of the plaintiff's right to an established and operative business? No, say the courts: the interference was not "direct"; cf. e.g. BGHZ 66, 388 sqq.); but if it causes the incubators in a poultry farm to cool off with the result that all the eggs are spoilt, the plaintiff may recover his loss (s.v. injury to property; cf. BGHZ 41, 123 sqq.). For a discussion of the cable cases cf. e.g. Günter Hager, "Haftung bei Störung der Energiezufuhr", 1979 *Juristenzeitung* 53 sqq.; Alfons Bürge, "Die Kabelbruchfälle", 1981 *Juristische Blätter* 57 sqq.; Markesinis, op. cit., note 253, pp. 112 sqq., 125 sqq. The leading English cable case is *Spartan Steel & Alloys Ltd. v. Martin & Co. (Contractors) Ltd.* [1973] 1 QB 27 (CA); for a comparative analysis, see Gerold Herrmann, *Zum Nachteil des Vermögens* (1978), pp. 23 sqq.; for South African law, see *Coronation Brick (Pty.) Ltd. v. Strachan Construction Co. (Pty.) Ltd.* 1982 (4) SA 371 (D) (and the discussion in Boberg, *Delict*, pp. 144 sqq.).

[256] With the result that the will is invalid and the property of the deceased passes to the intestate heirs. In England, a negligent solicitor has been held liable to the disappointed beneficiary in a case of this kind: *Ross v. Caunters* [1980] Ch 297. For an analysis of the situation in German law, see Reinhard Zimmermann, "Lachende Doppelerben?—Erbfolge und Schadensersatz bei Anwaltsverschulden", 1980 *Zeitschrift für das gesamte Familienrecht* 99 sqq.; as far as common-law jurisdictions are concerned, cf. Owen Rogers, "The Action of the Disappointed Beneficiary", (1986) 103 *SALJ* 583 sqq.; cf. also Werner Lorenz, "Some thoughts about contract and tort", in: *Essays in Memory of Professor F.H. Lawson* (1986), pp. 86 sqq.

[257] Cardozo CJ, in *Ultramares Corporation v. Touche* (1931) 255 NY 170, 174 NE 441 at 444.

[258] Cf. *Weller & Co. v. Foot and Mouth Disease Research Institute* [1966] 1 QB 569 at 585; generally cf., for example, Herrmann, op. cit., note 255, pp. 1 sqq., 15 sqq. (a book written in an unusually brisk and lively style); cf. also the analysis by W. Bishop, "Economic Loss in Tort", (1982) 2 *Oxford Journal of Legal Studies* 1 sqq.

[259] "Culpa in contrahendo oder Schadensersatz bei nichtigen oder nicht zur Perfektion gelangten Verträgen", (1861) 4 *JhJb* 12 sq., as translated by Weir, in Zweigert/Kötz/Weir, p. 266.

extended, it would become the veritable scourge of social and commercial intercourse, conversation would be gravely inhibited, and the most innocent language would become a snare!"[260]

(c) England

In other jurisdictions the distinction between (physical) damage to a specific corporeal asset and economic loss has, however, come in for trenchant criticism. "I can find neither logic nor common sense in this", said Lord Devlin in the leading English case on negligent statements,[261] and he therefore felt

> "bound to say, my Lords, that I think this to be nonsense. It is not the kind of nonsense that can arise even in the best system of law out of the need to draw nice distinctions between borderline cases. It arises, if it is the law, simply out of a refusal to make sense. The line is not drawn on any intelligible principle."

Cases of pure economic loss are thus no longer excluded, a limine, from the ambit of the English tort of negligence, but they are seen to require special treatment on policy grounds. Whether or not a duty of care was owed to the injured party in a particular situation and whether or not there was a breach of such duty of care:[262] these questions are determined with more circumspection than in cases of loss arising from physical injury. In recent years, a tendency appeared to gain ground to draw the line much more liberally in favour of the injured party than in the period immediately following Hedley Byrne and Heller.[263] Thus, a prima facie duty was said to arise if a relationship of proximity or neighbourhood exists between the parties, "such that, in the reasonable contemplation of the [alleged wrongdoer], carelessness on his part may

[260] Cf. also, as far as negligent statements are concerned, the famous dictum by Lord Pearce: "Negligence in word creates problems different from those of negligence in act. Words are more volatile than deeds. They travel fast and far afield. They are used without being expended and take effect in combination with innumerable facts and other words. . . . If the mere hearing or reading of words were held to create proximity, there might be no limit to the persons to whom the speaker or writer could be liable. Damage by negligent acts to persons and property on the other hand is more visible and obvious; its limits are more easily defined" (*Hedley Byrne & Co. Ltd. v. Heller & Partners Ltd.* [1964] AC 465 (HL) at 534).

[261] *Hedley Byrne & Co. Ltd. v. Heller & Partners Ltd.* [1964] AC 465 (HL); cf. P.S. Atiyah, "Negligence and Economic Loss", (1967) 83 *LQR* 248 sqq.; Smith, op. cit., note 8, pp. 49 sqq., 163 sqq. The distinction between economic loss and physical damage is defended by Bruce Feldthusen, *Economic Negligence* (1984), pp. 8 sqq.; cf. further, as far as the United States is concerned, the recent analyses by Robert L. Rabin, "Tort Recovery for Negligently Inflicted Economic Loss: A Reassessment", (1985) 37 *Stanford LR* 1513 sqq. and, more specifically on California, Justin Sweet, *Deliktshaftung für reinen Vermögensschaden, Festschrift für Max Keller* (1989), pp. 129 sqq.

[262] Duty, breach and damage are the three essential requirements in English law for the tort of negligence; cf. e.g. Lord Atkin in the famous case of *Donoghue v. Stevenson* [1932] AC 562 (HL) at 579; Fleming, *Torts*, pp. 94 sqq. On the concept of duty of care, cf. the detailed (and critical) analysis by Smith, op. cit., note 8, pp. 1 sqq.

[263] When "the horns of 'judicial valour' . . . were hastily withdrawn into their judicial shell" (Boberg, *Delict*, p. 92): cf., in particular, *Mutual Life and Citizens' Assurance Co. Ltd. v. Clive Raleigh Evatt* [1971] AC 793 (PC) and the comment by Fleming, *Torts*, p. 609.

be likely to cause damage to [the other party]".[264] It is then up to the injured party to point to some consideration which might reduce or negative this duty. This implies a remarkable shift of emphasis of judicial favour from the defendant to the plaintiff:[265] recovery for pure economic loss is no longer refused, unless there is a good reason to

[264] *Anns v. Merton London Borough Council* [1978] AC 728 (HL) at 751 sq. (per Lord Wilberforce). The famous "neighbour test", reaffirmed by Lord Wilberforce in the *Anns'* case, for determining whether a duty of care exists, has been formulated by Lord Atkin in *Donoghue v. Stevenson* [1932] AC 562 (HL) at 580 ("one of the most oft-quoted dicta in the law of tort": Boberg, *Delict*, p. 53; cf. also Smith, op. cit., note 8, p. 20: "Seldom in the history of the common law has a single statement of a single judge in a single case had such a profound effect on the development of the law"): "The liability for negligence . . . is no doubt based upon a general public sentiment of moral wrongdoing for which the offender must pay. But acts or omissions which any moral code would censure cannot in a practical world be treated so as to give a right to every person injured by them to demand relief. In this way rules of law arise which limit the range of complainants and the extent of their remedy. The rule that you are to love your neighbour becomes in law, you must not injure your neighbour; and the lawyer's question, Who is my neighbour? receives a restricted reply. You must take reasonable care to avoid acts or omissions which you can reasonably foresee would be likely to injure your neighbour. Who, then, in law is my neighbour? The answer seems to be—persons who are so closely and directly affected by my act that I ought reasonably to have them in contemplation as being so affected when I am directing my mind to the acts or omissions which are called in question."

Lord Atkin's famous dictum has been hailed, rather extravagantly, as "a seed of an oak tree, a source of inspiration, a beacon of hope, a fountain of sparkling wisdom, a skyrocket in the midnight sky" ((Mr. Justice) A.M. Linden, "The Good Neighbour on Trial: A Fountain of Sparkling Wisdom", (1983) 17 *University of British Columbia LR* 67). For a somewhat more critical analysis, see Smith, op. cit., note 8, pp. 15 sqq. He refers to a "judicial platitude" which "is now a liability to the law of negligence" and should be "laid gracefully to rest in the tombs of the law reports alongside the myriad of other cases which are no longer relevant in the last two decades of the 20th century." On the impact of *Anns'* decision, see Smith, op. cit., note 8, pp. 38 sqq.

[265] Cf., in this context, also *Junior Books Ltd. v. The Veitchi Co. Ltd.* [1983] 1 AC 520 (HL) and the conclusions drawn by J.C. Smith, "Economic Loss and the Common Law Marriage of Contracts and Torts", (1984) 18 *University of British Columbia LR* 95 sqq.; but cf. also Peter Cane, "Economic Loss in Tort: Is the Pendulum out of Control?", (1989) 52 *Modern LR* 201 sqq. ("constructively" overruled?; p. 203). For further comments, from a comparative perspective, see Werner Lorenz, "Verkehrspflichten zum Schutze fremden Vermögens?" and Peter Schlechtriem, "Deliktshaftung des Subunternehmers gegenüber dem Bauherrn wegen Minderwert seines Werks—Eine neue Entscheidung des House of Lords", in: *25 Jahre Karlsruher Forum* (1983), pp. 48 sqq., 64 sqq.; B.S. Markesinis, "An Expanding Tort Law—The Price of a Rigid Contract Law", (1987) 103 *LQR* 357 sqq., 376 sqq., 385 sqq.; Lorenz, *Essays Lawson*, pp. 95 sqq.

allow it; rather it appears to be allowed unless special (secondary) policy considerations can be adduced to refuse it.[266]

(d) Germany (20th century)

This is exactly the approach that has recently been advocated, in the tradition of natural-law ideas, for the German law of delict. The fundamental precept, says Picker,[267] is alterum non laedere. It applies, in principle, to physical damage as much as to pure economic loss. Secondary policy considerations do, however, require a limitation of liability, for unlimited liability would lead to socially unacceptable consequences. Hence the decision of the legislator to list a number of specific rights and interests, one of which must have been infringed by the tortfeasor. But this decision must not be taken to imply that pure economic loss, per se, is unworthy of protection. It is merely intended to limit the number of potential creditors. What matters, according to the BGB, is that the range of those who may possibly be entitled to claim damages must be determinable abstractly and ex ante. Provided

[266] In the meantime, however, "a strong reaction against this tendency has . . . prompted a return to the traditional caution against generalized principles, if not a repudiation of the idea that a new start, untrammelled by past experiences, was now in order": Fleming, *Torts*, p. 162, referring, inter alia, to *Governor of the Peabody Donation Fund v. Sir Lindsay Parkinson & Co. Ltd.* [1985] AC 210 (HL) and *Candlewood Navigation Corporation Ltd. v. Mitsui O.S.K. Lines Ltd. (The Mineral Transporter)* [1986] AC 1 (PC). Later cases also show a tendency to return to the earlier view. In *Leigh & Sillavan Ltd. v. Aliakmon Shipping Co. Ltd.* [1986] 2 All ER 145 (HL), the fear of "opening the floodgates so as to expose a person guilty of want of care to unlimited liability to an indefinite number of . . . persons" (at 154G) prompted the court to dismiss the action (on the *Aliakmon* case, see Markesinis, (1987) 103 *LQR* 387 sqq. (". . . an opinion that at times displays an inadequate consideration for the repercussions of the decision, opts for a solution that is clearly utopic, and unforgivably misses the opportunity to bring some order into the prevailing chaos")). The same tendency is revealed in the trilogy of 1987 cases, viz. *Smith v. Littlewood Organisation Ltd.* [1987] 1 AC 241 (HL) (where Lord Goff opined that too general a notion of reasonable foresight or proximity could not "accommodate all the untidy complexities of life" (at 736A)), *Curran v. Northern Ireland Co-ownership Housing Association Ltd.* [1987] 2 All ER 13 (HL) (where their Lordships felt themselves "entitled to be wary of effecting any extension of the principle appplied in *Anns v. Merton London Borough*" (at 18D)) and *Yuen Kun-yeu v. Attorney General of Hong Kong* [1987] 2 All ER 705 (PC); cf. now also *D & F Estates Ltd. v. Church Commissioners for England* [1988] 3 WLR 368 (HL); on which see J.N. Duncan Wallace, (1989) 105 *LQR* 46 sqq.; Cane, (1989) 52 *Modern LR* 200 sqq. In view of these constantly changing judicial sentiments, one can certainly subscribe to the statement that "the English law on the recoverability of mere economic loss is today possibly in greater confusion than ever before" (Dale Hutchison, "Negligent Statements: Why the Reluctance to Impose Liability? ", (1978) 95 *SALJ* 519); cf. also Smith, op. cit., note 8, p. 49 ("The one thing which is clear about the topic of economic loss is that the principles regarding recovery are obscure") and the concluding remark by Cane, (1989) 52 *Modern LR* 214: "Given this conceptual morass, it seems unlikely that the law of tort liability for economic loss is yet in its final form. The pendulum is swinging wildly and is yet to find a regular rhythm."

[267] 1987 *Juristenzeitung* 1041 sqq., 1047 sqq.

a suitable mechanism can be found to secure this objective, even in cases of pure economic loss, nothing prevents us from reverting to the basic rule of alterum non laedere.

Traditionally, though, German lawyers have tended to adopt a different approach. Many of them, too, are dissatisfied with the way the line has been drawn in § 823 I BGB. Since, however, they still accept exclusion of delictual liability for pure economic loss as the (natural) principle, they have to try to identify certain criteria *increasing* the range and intensity of the duties owed by the defendant to the plaintiff in specific types of situations and thus, by way of exception, justifying the imposition of liability. The protection of reasonable reliance engendered by the plaintiff,[268] his specific professional qualifications,[269] or some kind of "social contact"[270] between the parties have been proposed as such criteria.[271] Apart from that, certain rather strained contractual constructions have been used—particularly by the courts—in order to overcome the all too narrow limitations of delictual liability.[272] But whatever the approach adopted, the tendency

[268] Cf. Claus-Wilhelm Canaris, "Schutzgesetze—Verkehrspflichten—Schutzpflichten", in: *(Zweite) Festschrift für Karl Larenz* (1983), pp. 27 sqq.

[269] Cf. Klaus J. Hopt, "Nichtvertragliche Haftung ausserhalb von Schadens- und Bereicherungshaftung", (1983) 183 *Archiv für die civilistische Praxis* 608 sqq.

[270] Cf. Hans Dölle, "Aussergesetzliche Schuldpflichten", (1943) 103 *ZStW* 67 sqq., 72 sqq.

[271] For further attempts to provide a theoretical justification for an expansion of liability in the no man's land between contract and delict, cf. Hans Stoll, "Vertrauensschutz bei einseitigen Leistungsversprechen", in: *Festschrift für Werner Flume*, vol. I (1978), pp. 741 sqq.; Johannes Köndgen, *Selbstbindung ohne Vertrag* (1981); Christian von Bar, *Verkehrspflichten* (1980), pp. 204 sqq.

[272] As far as negligent misstatement cases are concerned, cf., for example, the analysis by Werner Lorenz, "Das Problem der Haftung für primäre Vermögensschäden bei der Erteilung einer unrichtigen Auskunft", in: *Festschrift für Karl Larenz* (1973), pp. 575 sqq.; Siegbert Lammel, "Zur Auskunftshaftung", (1979) 179 *Archiv für die civilistische Praxis* 337 sqq. Lawson/Markesinis, p. 85 sum up as follows: "The extension of the law of contract thus seems to be attempted whenever the maker of the statement occupies some 'responsible position' and/or stands to make a gain from his statement, provided always that he knows that some other person, usually though not necessarily clearly identified, is going to rely on it and (if it is wrong) suffer loss. In practice, more often than not, this is done in the sort of circumstances that would lead the common law to discover a 'special relationship'. But in German law, if such a 'special relationship' is discovered, it will lead to the creation of a *contract* between the maker and the ultimate receiver of the statement, rather than give rise to a duty to take care which, if breached, will be actionable in tort." Alternatively, the courts tend to water down the requirements of § 826 BGB (plaintiff must have acted intentionally and his behaviour must constitute an infringement of the boni mores) in order to be able to impose liability (cf. the references in Lorenz and Lammel, loc. cit.). That the giving of erroneous advice does not, by itself, lead to liability, is specifically stated in § 676 BGB (cf. supra, p. 422). In the disappointed beneficiary cases (supra, p. 1037, note 256), the German Supreme Court has employed the construction of a contract with protective ambit in favour of third parties (BGH, 1965 *Neue Juristische Wochenschrift* 1955 (1956 sq.)); on this method of extending contractual protection in general, cf., for example, Peter Gottwald, in: *Münchener Kommentar*, vol. II (2nd ed., 1985), § 328, nn. 60 sqq. Generally on the German approach to economic loss cases, cf. also Lorenz, *Essays Lawson*, pp. 86 sqq., and the (rather sympathetic) comparative analysis by Markesinis, (1987) 103 *LQR* 356 sqq. A similarly well-stocked armoury of theories and constructions designed to undermine the economic loss rule is available in Swiss law: cf. Peter Gauch, "Deliktshaftung für reinen Vermögensschaden", in: *Festschrift für Max Keller* (1989), pp. 121 sqq.

is clear: even in German law, pure economic loss has, within certain, hitherto rather ill-defined limits, become recoverable once again.

(e) *Austria and South Africa*

The same tendency, of course, prevails in other jurisdictions. Austria and South Africa are interesting cases in point. That Austrian lawyers should be struggling with the problem of extending rather than restricting delictual liability, is slightly odd: their starting point is, after all, a codified version, par excellence, of natural-law theories on liability for delict.[273] Perpetual peering, first at German pandectism, and, since 1900, at the BGB, appears to have had the effect of converting § 1295 ABGB into a kind of condensed version of §§ 823 I, 823 II BGB.[274]

South African law, too, has for some time succumbed to the temptation of abandoning the more liberal principles inherent in its historical heritage in favour of the more restrictive views propounded in a foreign legal system. The distinction between physical damage and pure economic loss as a method of limiting delictual liability appears to have crept in under the influence of English law.[275] The "Hedley Byrne of South African law",[276] in which recoverability of pure economic loss under Aquilian principles was ultimately authoritatively re-established, dates from only 1979.[277] Courts and legal writers are now engaged in

---

[273] § 1295 ABGB.

[274] In 1916 the legislator even added (totally unnecessarily, one should have thought) a second subsection to § 1295 ABGB which corresponds to § 826 BGB. For a critical evaluation of the assimilation between German and Austrian law of delict, cf. Rudolf Reischauer, in: Peter Rummel (ed.), *Kommentar zum ABGB*, vol. II (1984), § 1294, n. 16; for a different view, see Friedrich Harrer, in: Michael Schwimann (ed.), *Praxiskommentar zum ABGB*, vol. V (1987), § 1295, nn. 1 sqq. Very much the same development, interestingly, appears to have occurred in Swiss law (with regard to the general clause of art. 41 I OR); cf. Gauch, *Festschrift Keller*, p. 136. The French general clause (art. 1382 code civil), on the other hand, has not been narrowed down, by way of interpretation, in a similar manner. French courts have thus arrived at results, which, as Harrer points out, are hardly imaginable under Austrian law (cf. e.g. the action of a soccer club against a person who carelessly killed one of their (professional) players. The club was allowed to claim damages for having to pay a high transfer fee to obtain the services of a substitute player: Zweigert/Kötz, p. 361). For a comparative discussion, cf. Lawson/Markesinis, pp. 80 sqq.

[275] Van der Walt, *Delict*, n. 24.

[276] Boberg, *Delict*, p. 103.

[277] *Administrateur, Natal v. Trust Bank van Afrika Bpk.* 1979 (3) SA 824 (A) at 829 sqq. Rumpff CJ specifically referred to Roman-Dutch law in this context. He also drew attention to the fact that, for a long time, an unsatisfactory situation of uncertainty prevailed in South African law. Taking up a metaphor by Learned Hand J ("Nor is it desirable for a lower court to embrace the exhilarating opportunity of anticipating a doctrine which may be in the womb of time, but whose birth is distant"), he continued: "The birthpangs of such a right of action have endured so long that the time has arrived, perhaps even with a Cesarian section, that this child should be brought into the world. It should immediately be added that it can be foretold that the child will be a problem child" (p. 831, as rendered into English on p. 825). *Administrateur, Natal v. Trust Bank van Afrika Bpk.* in fact vindicates the liberal view of Watermeyer J in *Perlman v. Zoutendyk* 1934 CPD 151, who stated, inter alia, that "Roman-Dutch law approaches a new problem in the continental rather than the English

exploring the implications of this move[278] and finding ways and means of containing this kind of liability within socially acceptable limits.[279] Once again, therefore, the crucial issue has become one of confining, rather than expanding, delictual protection.[280]

5. Liability for omissions

(a) *The priest, the Levite and the Good Samaritan*

The same is true if we look at the issue of liability for omissions. The Roman lawyers, as will be remembered, did not put occidere or corrumpere per commissionem and per omissionem on a par: there are no abstract statements, nor is there any case law to the effect that Aquilian liability could ensue from "mere" omissions. An action was granted, however, in certain cases where the omission was connected with some prior conduct of the alleged wrongdoer;[281] where, as Voet was later to put it, the damage had been "committendo et omittendo simul datum".[282] If a person had exposed somebody else's objects to the

way, because in general all damage caused unjustifiably [injuria] is actionable, whether caused intentionally [dolus] or by negligence [culpa]". *Perlman v. Zoutendyk*, in its time, was on the one hand hailed as "a classic example of the method of Roman-Dutch law" (T.W. Price, "Aquilian Liability for Negligent Statements", (1950) 67 *SALJ* 414), but on the other hand denounced as "the leading heresy in the law of delict" (R.G. McKerron, (1973) 90 *SALJ* 1; McKerron's view, in turn, has been referred to as "one of the most stupid statements that has yet appeared in South African legal literature": J.C. van der Walt, 1979 *TSAR* 151). *Perlman v. Zoutendyk* concerned liability for negligent statements, and so did *Herschel v. Mrupe* 1954 (3) SA 464 (A), a decision that adopted a much more conservative line (though how conservative exactly, it is difficult, if not impossible, to state because of the diversity of views expressed by the five judges concerned—"[q]uot judices, tot sententiae" commented G.A. Mulligan, (1954) 71 *SALJ* 321; "only one Judge . . . correctly enunciates the proper rules of law . . . but applies them wrongly to the facts" said T.W. Price, 1955 *Butterworth's South African LR* 154, and Dale Hutchison, 1975 *Responsa Meridiana* 134 declared the whole decision to be obiter). Nevertheless, *Herschel v. Mrupe* set the tone for more than 20 years, until the advent of the *Trust Bank* decision. For an analysis of the most important cases of the pre- and post-*Trust Bank* period as well as the views expressed in the South African legal literature, cf. Boberg, *Delict*, pp. 58 sqq., 103 sqq.

[278] For instance, as far as negligent misrepresentation inducing a contract is concerned. Traditionally, the courts have denied delictual liability in these cases (cf. *Hamman v. Moolman* 1968 (4) SA 340 (A) at 348A–349H; under the influence of English law); but see now *Esso Petroleum Co. Ltd. v. Mardon* [1976] 1 QB 801 (CA) (for English law), *Kern Trust (Edms.) Bpk. v. Hurter* 1981 (3) SA 607 (C); Hutchison, (1981) 98 *SALJ* 486 sqq. and Boberg, *Delict*, pp. 62 sq. (for South African law).

[279] The courts often refer to the "duty of care" concept as the appropriate dogmatic tool (cf. e.g. *Shell & BP South African Petroleum Refineries (Pty.) Ltd. v. Osborne Panama SA* 1980 (3) SA 653 (D) at 659A–660A; *Franschhoekse Wynkelder (Ko-operatief) Bpk. v. South African Railways & Harbours* 1981 (3) SA 36 (C) at 40A–41F), legal writers tend to find the key to the problem in the requirement of wrongfulness (cf. e.g. Pauw, (1975) 8 *De Jure* 31; Hutchison, (1978) 95 *SALJ* 519; Van der Walt, *Delict*, n. 24).On the nature of wrongfulness and on its relationship to the duty-of-care concept, cf. Boberg, *Delict*, pp. 30 sqq.; for a comparative analysis of "duty of care in negligence", see Lawson, (1947–48) 22 *Tulane LR* 111 sqq.

[280] Cf. also Coetzee J, in *Suid-Afrikaanse Bantoetrust v. Ross en Jacobsz* 1977 (3) SA 184 (T) at 187.

[281] Cf. supra, p. 980, note 185.

[282] Supra, p. 1029.

risk of being destroyed or damaged, he had to take appropriate steps to contain and avert the danger; but a duty to act (to help or to rescue) in general did not exist. Nobody was to be compelled, in order to avoid liability, to meddle with the affairs of his neighbours, to the neglect of his own,[283] and it is obvious that this attitude was motivated by the characteristic reluctance of the Roman lawyers to interfere (or to encourage any interference) with the freedom of the individual.[284] The same disinclination to extend the reach of legal obligation has traditionally been displayed by English courts and legal writers where, too, it

> "drew sustenance from the . . . philosophy of individualism, which was content to condone the indifference of the Priest and the Levite and to dismiss the solicitude of the Samaritan as an aspiration merely of private morality".[285]

In continental Europe this very restrictive attitude commended itself, of course, to the pandectists; they focused their attention on D. 7, 1, 13, 2[286] and argued that liability for omissions was, in principle, excluded.[287] Again, therefore, they attempted to turn back the wheel of history, for the natural lawyers had, for all practical purposes, abandoned the distinction between commission and omission and had subjected delictual liability for both forms of human behaviour to the same requirements. Thus, Grotius refers to "culpam omnem, sive in faciendo, sive in non faciendo" and proceeds to state that, according to the law of nature, an obligation arises "ex tali culpa".[288] In the same vein (and like a legal textbook) the ABGB declares that damage can arise from an unlawful act or omission; provided only the wrongdoer has been at fault, the injured party may claim damages.[289] Some of the later writers of the usus modernus, too, as we have seen,[290] had adopted

[283] Cf. Van den Heever, *Aquilian Damages*, pp. 37 sqq.

[284] Cf., in general, Schulz, *Principles*, pp. 140 sqq.

[285] Fleming, *Torts*, p. 134; cf. also the discussion by Kemp, op. cit., note 204, pp. 403 sqq. For a (sympathetic) analysis of the arguments in favour of a general rule "no liability for mere omissions", cf. further Kemp J. Kemp, "The duty to rescue—compulsion or laissez faire?", (1985) 18 *CILSA* 166 sqq.; and see the analysis by Smith, op. cit., note 8, pp. 29 sqq. ("The grounds of liability for nonfeasance are different from the grounds of liability for action"). A critical evaluation is offered by Ernest J. Weinrib, "The Case for a Duty to Rescue", (1980–81) 90 *Yale LJ* 247 sqq.; Robert Justin Lipkin, "Beyond Good Samaritans and Moral Monsters: An Individualistic Justification of the General Duty to Rescue", (1983) 31 *University of California at Los Angeles LR* 252 sqq.; B.S. Markesinis, "Negligence, Nuisance and Affirmative Duties of Action", (1989) 105 *LQR* 104 sqq. (suggesting that the latest decision by the House of Lords on the matter, *Smith v. Littlewood Ltd.* [1987] 1 AC 241, may herald a change of (judicial) attitude).

[286] Cf. supra, p. 1029, note 204.

[287] Representative: Windscheid/Kipp, § 455, 2.

[288] Supra, p. 1032.

[289] §§ 1294, 1295 ABGB.

[290] Supra, p. 1030.

this view: culpa was the decisive criterion; the kind of conduct displayed was irrelevant.

(b) Modern approach

Unlike in the case of pure economic loss, the pandectist reaction was fairly short-lived and thus even the BGB no longer discriminates between liability for commission and for omission. This does, of course, not entail the imposition of random duties to help the needy, to rescue the imperilled or to warn the incautious. Not every moral duty has a legal counterpart, and thus it is still true to say that a legal duty not to cause harm is much more readily accepted than a legal duty to prevent it.[291] But whether or not such a duty exists is determined in a flexible manner and not according to blunt and categorical distinctions. Just as not every (potentially) harmful activity leads to liability, so the mere failure to act does not per se exempt from liability. Common sense and public policy can demand dispensation from liability in cases of commission just as they can call for the imposition of liability in cases of omission. A balancing of conflicting interests is required, and the result of this process of balancing determines whether a particular form of human behaviour may be labelled wrongful or not.[292] The central issue is therefore, once again, not one of conduct but of the appropriate adjustment of a general requirement of delictual liability: wrongfulness, in terms of modern conceptual thinking.[293] The same view, incidentally, prevails today in South African law,[294] after the courts have finally managed to extricate themselves[295] from the fetters of a very narrow prior conduct doctrine.[296]

But when is an omission wrongful?[297] Are certain standardized

[291] Boberg, *Delict*, p. 211; cf. also Kemp, (1985) 18 *CILSA* 163 sqq. (who adopts a very restrictive attitude and argues against a delictual duty to rescue); Smith, op. cit., note 8, pp. 29 sqq.

[292] Cf. already supra, p. 999, note 8 and Boberg, *Delict*, pp. 30 sqq.

[293] Culpa, according to the writers of the usus modernus and the natural lawyers. The modern distinction between unlawfulness and fault appears to go back to Jhering (op. cit., note 243, pp. 4 sqq.).

[294] For all details, see Boberg, *Delict*, pp. 210 sqq.

[295] *Minister van Polisie v. Ewels* 1975 (3) SA 590 (A); but cf. also the earlier cases, *Regal v. African Superslate (Pty.) Ltd.* 1963 (1) SA 102 (A) at 109E, 117B–C, and 121D–F and *Peri-Urban Areas Health Board v. Munarin* 1965 (3) SA 367 (A) at 373E.

[296] *Halliwell v. Johannesburg Municipal Council* 1912 AD 659; *Cape Town Municipality v. Paine*, 1923 AD 207 at 217; reaffirmed in (and perhaps best illustrated by) a whole string of "municipality cases" (a local authority is not liable for damage arising as a result of its omission to repair a road within its jurisdiction, unless, by previously building the road, it had introduced a new source of danger which would not otherwise have existed; for details and references, see Boberg, *Delict*, pp. 221 sq.)

[297] For a comparative analysis, cf. Limpens/Kruithof/Meinertzhagen-Limpens, op. cit., note 6, nn. 76 sqq.; Lawson/Markesinis, pp. 71 sqq. As far as English law is concerned, see Fleming, *Torts*, pp. 133 sqq. More specifically on liability in negligence for an omission by medical practitioners, see Giesen, op. cit., note 40, pp. 144 sqq., 157 sqq.

criteria available with reference to which the crucial policy decision may be made?[298] Or may one (must one) refer to specific stereotyped categories of liability in order to determine where to draw the line between the conflicting ideals of *laissez-faire* and social responsibility? South African courts have invoked the legal convictions of the community as the ultimate criterion,[299] but apart from indicating that the community's mere moral indignation is irrelevant, this statement does not take us any further. *All* decisions on the matter of wrongfulness should, after all, reflect the prevailing ideas of what is fair and reasonable under the circumstances. According to Boberg, the previously established categories of liability should be regarded as "crystallised applications of the objective reasonableness criterion".[300] They thus provide, at least in certain areas, some kind of guideline for the proper exercise of the judicial discretion.

(c) "Verkehrssicherungspflichten"

German courts, in turn, have over the past six decades developed a comprehensive network of duty situations which are based neither on statute, nor on contract, nor on prior conduct. Of cardinal importance in this context is the concept of "*Verkehrssicherungspflichten*":[301] anybody who either establishes, or is in charge of, a source of potential danger for the rights or interests (as enumerated in § 823 I BGB) of other people is obliged to take appropriate precautions to prevent the risk from materializing.[302] If he negligently fails to do so, he is liable in delict. Thus, for instance, the owner of a shop has to ensure that no vegetable leaves are lying on the floor,[303] municipalities in charge of public roads must ensure safe traffic and are thus obliged, inter alia,[304]

---

[298] As in the case of direct infliction of an injury where the action is taken to be wrongful unless the requirements of a specific legally recognized defence are satisfied; cf. supra, p. 999, note 8 and Boberg, *Delict*, p. 32 (". . . it is settled law that all harm to person or property caused by a positive act is prima facie wrongful"); Smith, op. cit., note 8, p. 26 (". . . the prima facie duty doctrine has application only to risks of physical harm arising out of action").

[299] *Minister van Polisie v. Ewels* 1975 (3) SA 590 (A) at 597B.

[300] *Delict*, p. 214.

[301] Declared untranslatable by Lawson/Markesinis, p. 78.

[302] For a comprehensive analysis, see Christian von Bar, *Verkehrspflichten* (1980), pp. 83 sqq. and passim. For the historical development (starting with RGZ 52, 373 sqq.; RGZ 54, 53 sqq.), cf. von Bar, pp. 1 sqq., 15 sqq.

[303] BGHZ 66, 51 sqq. (though transposing the whole problem, rather oddly, into the law of contract).

[304] For all details, see Hans-Joachim Mertens, in: *Münchener Kommentar*, vol. III, 2 (2nd ed., 1986), § 823, nn. 223 sqq.

to carry out the necessary repair works, to remove ice and snow from busy crossings, to examine (and, if necessary, chop down) potentially dangerous trees, or to place and maintain the appropriate signposts and robots, the organizers of a big soccer match or of a rock concert have to ensure the safety not only of the players and spectators but also of the property of those living in the immediate vicinity of the match or concert venue,[305] and an innkeeper has to see to it that billiard players do not injure other guests.[306] Under cover of the term "*Verkehrssicherungspflichten*" a vast province of case law has established itself within the German law of delict, defined and contained not by legal rules but by the dictates of social policy as perceived by the judiciary; and as in South Africa, the notion of wrongfulness has thus become a "cloak of respectability"[307] for the process of judicial law-making.

6. Contributory negligence

(a) *Developments in continental Europe*

Finally, a word about contributory negligence. Here, too, we have a situation where the conservative attitude of 19th-century legal science ultimately did not prevail against a more equitable dispensation advocated by 18th-century natural lawyers. Mommsen, Windscheid and most of the other pandectists embraced the so-called principle of "culpa-compensation". Digesta 50, 17, 203[308] was their dogmatic starting point:[309] everybody has to carry the consequences of his own fault. As a result of this "most natural"[310] precept, the victim of a wrong was bound to lose his claim for damages if he could have avoided the injury through the exercise of proper care. This entailed the old, though somewhat rough-and-ready, notion of "all or nothing". Nineteenth-century legal practice was dominated by it, too.[311] Thus, for instance, the courts dismissed the claim of a traveller against an innkeeper for the loss of his suitcase, because he had handed over the suitcase to one of the innkeeper's servants without specifically drawing attention to its valuable content;[312] or the action of a horseman who crashed into a coach while charging down a road at night.[313] Towards

[305] Mertens, op. cit., note 304, nn. 215 sqq.
[306] RGZ 85, 185 (186).
[307] Boberg, *Delict*, p. 146.
[308] Cf. supra, p. 1030 (note 212).
[309] Cf. Friedrich Mommsen, *Zur Lehre von dem Interesse* (1855), p. 158; Windscheid/Kipp, § 258, 2; cf. further Werner Rother, *Haftungsbeschränkung im Schadensrecht* (1965), pp. 30 sqq.; Aumann, op. cit., note 76, pp. 80 sqq.
[310] Mommsen, op. cit., note 309, p. 157.
[311] See Rother, op. cit., note 309, pp. 35 sqq.; Aumann, op. cit., note 76, pp. 168 sqq.
[312] RGZ 1, 83 sqq.
[313] RG, in: (1889) 44 *SeuffA.*, n. 86. Both the owner of the coach and the horseman had infringed several police regulations.

the end of the 19th century, the courts tended to balk at the idea that even the slightest negligence on the part of the plaintiff should have such drastic consequences. They therefore decided the matter on a preponderance of fault (the old culpa maior doctrine),[314] but still according to the hallowed "all or nothing". The BGB, however, went the decisive step further. It codified a solution that completely broke with romanistic doctrine and that had first been expounded by Christian Wolff. Dealing with the position of a depositor who had negligently chosen a careless depositee (who, in turn, had duly lost the object deposited with him), Wolff had advocated an apportionment of damages according to the relative degree of fault:

> "Si deponens rem custodiendam committit homini negligenti, quem negligentem esse novit, vel nosse poterat, et res deposita negligentia depositarii vel perit, vel deterioratur; damnum inter deponentem et depositarium dividendum in ratione culpae utriusque."[315]

Though Wolff acknowledged that his idea, appealing in theory, might be difficult to realize in practice,[316] it was adopted by the Austrian[317] and Swiss[318] legislators as well as by French legal science.[319] The BGB ultimately followed suit and provided as follows:

> "If any fault of the injured party has contributed to the occurrence of the damage, the duty to compensate and the extent of the compensation to be made depend upon the circumstances, especially upon the extent to which the injury was caused predominantly by the one or the other party."[320]

(b) *South African law*

In South Africa contributory negligence ceased to be a complete defence only with the introduction of the Apportionment of Damages Act in 1956.[321] Unlike in modern German law, the damages awarded are to be reduced, not in proportion to the causal contribution of the parties, but to the degree of fault displayed by them.[322] Does that mean that the determination of the degree of the plaintiff's fault (say 70 %) will automatically determine the degree of the defendant's fault (30 %)?[323] Or does one first have to assess the degree of both parties'

---

[314] Aumann, op. cit., note 76, pp. 170 sqq.; Luig (1969) 2 *Ius Commune* 234.
[315] Christian Wolff, *Jus naturae*, Pars IV, Cap. III, § 591. Cf. further Pars II, Cap. II, §§ 628 sqq. and Aumann, op. cit., note 76, pp. 42 sqq.
[316] *Jus Naturae*, Pars II, Cap. III, § 632.
[317] § 1304 ABGB.
[318] Art. 51 II OR (1881); Art. 44 I OR (1911).
[319] Lawson/Markesinis, pp. 132 sqq.; Aumann, op. cit., note 76, pp. 132 sqq.
[320] § 254 I; on the legislative history cf. Aumann, op. cit., note 76, pp. 140 sqq., 175 sqq.
[321] Act 34/1956.
[322] Fault, however, also plays an important (though secondary) role in German law in determining the amount of the reduction; cf., for example, Wolfgang Grunsky, in: *Münchener Kommentar*, vol. II (2nd ed., 1985), § 254, nn. 61 sqq.
[323] *South British Insurance Co. Ltd. v. Smit* 1962 (3) SA 826 (A) at 835H.

faults separately (by asking how far each of them deviated from the norm of the diligens paterfamilias—which may be 90 % in the one and 60 % in the other case; or 20 % as opposed to 40 %) before proceeding to compare the results?[324] This is only one of a whole variety of practical problems[325] raised by this rather clumsily drafted enactment.[326] Nevertheless, the new dispensation is generally regarded as much more satisfactory than the old uncompromising common-law approach—which was based, incidentally, not on Roman and Roman-Dutch authority but on a wholesale reception of the English law of contributory negligence[327] (including the notorious "last opportunity" rule as a device to mitigate the harshness of the "all or nothing"). "The law relating to the subject of contributory negligence which is applied by our courts", said Watermeyer CJ,[328] when it was too late,

> "has been taken over from English law and it is seldom that any Roman-Dutch authority is referred to. In fact there is plenty of authority in Roman law . . . and also in Roman-Dutch law. . . . It may be that if Roman-Dutch authorities had been more fully referred to in earlier South African cases our law of contributory negligence might have developed on different lines from the English law."

Without that source of inspiration, however, South African law became completely entrapped by the "abracadabra"[329] of the causal approach to contributory negligence.[330] Ultimately, therefore, only the legislator was able to save the day.[331]

---

[324] *Jones v. Santam Bpk.* 1965 (2) SA 542 (A) at 555A–555D.

[325] For a discussion, see Boberg, *Delict*, pp. 655 sqq., 663 sqq.

[326] Cf. Holmes J in *Taylor v. South African Railways & Harbours* 1958 (1) SA 139 (D) at 142A–B: "This brings me to the Apportionment of Damages Act of 1956. The law in England was adjusted in this regard in 1945. Its counterpart in South Africa was long in reaching our statute books. 'No matter', one thought with Voltaire, 'perfection walks slowly—she requires the hand of time'. And so it is a little disappointing to find that after all the lawgiver, with two and possibly three languages at its disposal, has not expressed itself in words so simple and clear that he who runs may read."

[327] On which cf. supra, pp. 1012 sq. (note 90).

[328] *Pierce v. Hau Mon* 1944 AD 175 at 195.

[329] Fleming, *Torts*, p. 244.

[330] For a vivid description of the way South African law ultimately found itself in a Cloud-cuckoo-land, cf. Boberg, *Delict*, pp. 653 sq.

[331] The relevant section of the South African Apportionment of Damages Act is very closely modelled on the English Law Reform (Contributory Negligence) Act which had already in 1945 transformed the English law relating to contributory negligence. For a discussion of the English law, cf. Fleming, *Torts*, pp. 242 sqq.; for a comparative discussion, cf. A.M. Honoré, "Causation and Remoteness of Damages", in: *International Encyclopedia of Comparative Law*, vol XI, 7 (1983), nn. 145 sqq.; Lawson/Markesinis, pp. 131 sqq.; Aumann, op. cit., note 76, pp. 199 sqq.

CHAPTER 31

Actio iniuriarum

I. THE EARLY HISTORY OF INIURIA

1. Iniuria in the XII Tables

Iniuria was a complex and intriguing concept. As one of the requirements for Aquilian liability it was taken to embrace the notions of wrongfulness and fault.[1] Apart from that, however, it had a further, more specialized meaning. "Iniuria ex eo dicta est", explains Ulpian,[2]

> "quod non iure fiat: omne enim, quod non iure fit, iniuria fieri dicitur. hoc generaliter. specialiter autem iniuria dicitur contumelia."

In this latter sense, iniuria was a delict in its own right, and thus it was not the actio legis Aquiliae but an actio iniuriarum that provided protection for the injured party.

The historical origin of the actio iniuriarum appears to lie in tab. 8, 4 of the XII Tables, the text of which was either "Si iniuria alteri faxsit, XXV poenae sunto" (this is the version handed down to us by Aulus Gellius)[3] or, as many modern editors will have it, "Si iniuriam [alteri?] faxsit, . . .".[4] Depending on whether one chooses to follow Gellius[5] or the modern emendation, the XII Tables thus contained a delict of "iniuria alteri facere" (in the sense of "to act in a wrongful manner with regard to somebody else") or of "iniuria".[6] But, whatever the answer to this problem, it is obvious that tab. 8, 4 must be read in conjunction with the two provisions that preceded it. These were tab. 8, 2 ("Si membrum rupsit, ni cum eo pacit, talio esto") and tab. 8, 3 ("Manu fustive si os fregit libero, CCC, si servo, CL poenam subito"). Membrum ruptum was probably[7] the mutilation of a limb, a

---

[1] Supra, pp. 998 sqq., 1004 sqq.

[2] Ulp. D. 47, 10, 1 pr.

[3] *Noctes Atticae*, Lib. XX, I, 12 (according to the manuscripts); cf. also Paul. Coll. II, V, 5 (according to a manuscript from Vercelli).

[4] Cf. e.g. S. Riccobono (ed.), *Fontes Iuris Romani Antejustiniani*, Pars Prima (Leges) (1968), p. 54. Cf. also Dietrich V. Simon, "Begriff und Tatbestand der 'Iniuria' im altrömischen Recht", (1965) 82 *ZSS* 132 sqq.; Kaser, *RPr* I, p. 156; Arrigo Manfredini, *Contributi allo studio dell "iniuria" in età repubblicana* (1977), pp. 15 sqq.

[5] As do Peter Birks, "The Early History of Iniuria", (1969) 37 *TR* 188 sq. and Artur Völkl, *Die Verfolgung der Körperverletzung im frühen Römischen Recht* (1984), pp. 169 sqq.

[6] Peter Birks, (1969) 37 *TR* 163 sqq., has argued, however, that tab. 8, 4 had nothing to do with the later delict of iniuria; it did not constitute a separate and independent delict, but was an integral part of the provision for os frangere of tab. 8, 3. According to Manfredini, op. cit., note 4, tab. 8, 4 (and also tab. 8, 5) did not form part of the XII Tables but has to be regarded as a rule of interpretation, worked out in the course of the 4th century by priests. Against both Birks and Manfredini, see Völkl, op. cit., note 5, pp. 18 sqq.

[7] The exact meaning of membrum ruptum is much disputed. Cf. Santi di Paola, "La genesi storica del delitto di 'iniuria' ", (1947) 1 *Annali Catania* 268 sqq.; Ulrich von Lübtow,

particularly severe infringement of the victim's bodily integrity. Tab. 8, 3 dealt with the mere breaking of a bone, committed by a blow with hand or stick[8] and iniuria (or iniuria alteri facere), in turn, must have covered physical assaults of an even less serious nature: a slap in the face, a blow or a kick, a box on the ear or a stroke with a stick (that did not have either of the consequences contemplated in tab. 8, 2 or 8, 3).[9] This gradation was clearly reflected by the penalties imposed in each of these three instances. In the case of membrum ruptum, the old and somewhat crude lex talionis still prevailed;[10] the victim of the wrong was not obliged to accept a composition offered by the wrongdoer (or his relatives) but could avenge the wrong by doing to the wrongdoer what he had done to him. For os fractum and iniuria, on the other hand, the principle of retaliation had already been abandoned, and the delinquent was allowed to expiate the wrong by paying a specific sum of money. This sum varied according to whether (in the case of os fractum) the injured person was a free man or a slave;[11] for injuria the penalty was 25 asses.

"Zum römischen Injurienrecht", (1969) 15 *Labeo* 131 sqq.; Wittmann, *Körperverletzung*, pp. 3 sqq.; Kaser, *RPr* I, p. 156; Honsell/Mayer-Maly/Selb, p. 368; Elemér Pólay, "Iniuria-Tatbestände im archaischen Zeitalter des antiken Rom", (1984) 101 *ZSS* 152 sqq. (all in the sense mentioned in the text).

For different views cf. Paul Huvelin, "La notion de l''iniuria' dans le très ancien droit Romain", in: *Mélanges Ch. Appleton* (1903), pp. 377 sqq. (membrum rumpere included only amputations); Ch. Appleton, "Notre enseignement du droit romain", in: *Mélanges de droit romain dédiés à Georges Cornil*, vol. I (1926), pp. 51 sqq.; Giovanni Pugliese, *Studi sull' "iniuria" I* (1941), pp. 29 sqq.; Simon, (1965) 82 *ZSS* 163 sqq.; Birks, (1969) 37 *TR* 179 sqq.; Manfredini, op. cit., note 4, p. 54; Völkl, op. cit., note 5, pp. 42 sqq. (all kinds of bodily harm). In favour of a wide interpretation of the term "membrum" (more general than "limb"), cf. Birks, (1969) 37 *TR* 183 sqq.; Alan Watson, "Personal Injuries in the XII Tables", (1975) 43 *TR* 218; Völkl, op. cit., note 5, pp. 47 sq.

[8] On tab. 8, 3, see, most recently, Völkl, op. cit., note 5, pp. 144 sqq. He argues that this provision was designed to exempt the wrongdoer from the harsh consequences of tab. 8, 2, because a person who hit another man manu fustive did not normally intend to break a bone. Traditionally, the justification for the special rule contained in tab. 8, 3 is seen in the fact that os fractum was a less serious injury, when compared with the membrum ruptum of tab. 8, 2; whether the wrongdoer acted intentionally or merely negligently is widely held to be irrelevant.

[9] Cf., most recently, Völkl, op. cit., note 5, pp. 184 sqq. and Pólay, (1984) 101 *ZSS* 160 sqq. For an ingenious explanation why the word "iniuria" was used to denote physical assaults in the nature of an insult, see David Daube, "Societas as a Consensual Contract"(!) (1938) 6 *Cambridge LJ* 401 sqq. and idem, "Matthew v. 38 f." (1944) 45 *Journal of Theological Studies* 182 sq. ("Were membrum ruptum and os fractum not also instances of iniuria in [a wide untechnical] sense? They were, and no doubt the Romans knew it. But it was only in cases like a slap in the face that unlawfulness alone, so to speak, constituted the offence . . . [and was] not concealed behind any more concrete facts like a broken limb or a torn out eye. . . . Consequently it was cases like a slap in the face, cases of wrong pure and simple, that received the technical appellation of iniuria, 'unlawfulness proper' ").

[10] On which cf. supra, pp. 2 sq., 914.

[11] It is interesting to note that slaves were still equated to free persons and not yet (as in the lex Aquilia) seen as things.

2. The rise of the actio iniuriarum

A sum of 25 asses may have been a lot of money around 450 B.C.,[12] but in the course of the following three centuries the value of the as depreciated so considerably[13] that the statutory penalty became derisory. Who could be so poor, asked Aulus Gellius,[14] that 25 asses would discourage him from indulging in the pleasure of injuring another person? And he related[15] the story of a man called Lucius Veratius, who amused himself by slapping the faces of people he happened to meet. He was followed by a slave whose task it was to hand over 25 asses to the puzzled victims. This incident precipitated a reform of the law.[16] Around the turn of the third to the second century B.C. the praetors introduced an edictum de iniuriis aestumandis,[17] according to which courts of recuperatores were instructed to determine a sum that appeared to them to be equitable under the circumstances (". . . quantum ob eam rem bonum et aequum recuperatoribus videbitur").[18] The edictum de iniuriis aestumandis involved a modernization of both penalty and procedure. A reform of the substantive law soon ensued. Taken merely as an infringement of bodily integrity, the iniuria of the XII Tables was of a rather trifling nature. An important (if not even the main) element inherent in the delict was the humiliation suffered by its victim. The law could thus be seen to provide protection against insults, and it was only natural that the specific manner in which the insult had to be inflicted receded increasingly into the background. In the course of the later Roman Republic the requirement of a physical assault was dropped and protection thus extended to non-physical aspects of the personality.[19, 20] Again, it was by way of praetorian intervention that

---

[12] Cf., for example, von Lübtow, (1969) 15 *Labeo* 139 (25 pounds of copper).

[13] For details, see Peter Birks, "Lucius Veratius and the Lex Aebutia", in: *Daube Noster* (1974), pp. 44 sq.

[14] *Noctes Atticae*, Lib. XX, I, 12.

[15] *Noctes Atticae*, Lib. XX, I, 13 (on the authority of Labeo). On this story, cf. von Lübtow, (1969) 15 *Labeo* 133 sq.; Alan Watson, "The Development of the Praetor's Edict", (1970) 60 *JRS* 112 sq.; Birks, *Daube Noster*, pp. 39 sqq.; Manfredini, op. cit., note 4, pp. 79 sqq.

[16] But see Birks, *Daube Noster*, pp. 40 sqq.

[17] On which see Aulus Gellius, *Noctes Atticae*, Lib. XX, I, 13; von Lübtow, (1969) 15 *Labeo* 139 sqq.; Wittmann, *Körperverletzung*, pp. 25 sqq.; Völkl, op. cit., note 5, pp. 208 sqq.

[18] Cf. the reconstruction by Völkl, op. cit., note 5, p. 214; Walter Selb, "Die Formel der Injurienklage", 1978 *Acta Juridica* 36.

[19] But the actio iniuriarum continued to be granted also in cases of physical harm. For all details, see Wittmann, *Körperverletzung*, pp. 34 sqq., 47 sqq. He argues that in classical Roman law (since the time of Labeo) minor bodily injuries constituting contumelia gave rise to an action only if the wrongdoer had acted intentionally (as in all other cases of contumelia iniuria; cf. infra, pp. 1059 sqq.). With regard to bodily harm going beyond mere contumelia, the actio iniuriarum could, however, still be instituted even in cases of negligence. But the evidence is very scanty (see, however, Lab./Ulp. D. 47, 10, 15 pr., as interpreted by Wittmann, *Körperverletzung*, pp. 48 sqq.), since the compilers (apparently) regarded protection under the lex Aquilia (which had been developed in the meantime; cf. supra, pp. 1015 sqq.) as sufficient and therefore limited the actio iniuriarum generally to cases of dolus.

this change occurred. Four specific edictal promises were introduced, dealing with convicium, adtemptata pudicitia, infamandi causa quid facere and servum alienum verberare. It was primarily the claims arising from these edicts that came to be referred to in classical Roman law by the nomen collectivum actio iniuriarum. Ulpian/Labeo, in a somewhat cryptic passage, allude to a further edict dealing generally with iniuria and making the special edictal promises practically redundant: "Hoc edictum [sc.: ne quid infamandi causa fiat] supervacuum esse Labeo ait, quippe cum ex generali iniuriarum agere possumus."[21] But whether such an edictum generale ever existed is very doubtful.[22] Even if one accepts the text as genuine, it probably merely referred to the actio de iniuriis aestumandis, which may have been considered by the classical Roman lawyers as providing a general basis for the actio iniuriarum.[23] But whatever the true position in this matter, the four special edicts were in the forefront of the lawyers' interest and provided the essential substance with which the rather abstract notion of iniuria came to be fleshed out.[24] We shall therefore briefly have to examine each of them.

II. CLASSICAL FOUNDATIONS OF THE ACTIO INIURIARUM

1. The different forms of iniuria

(a) *Convicium*

Convicium was probably the oldest of the four, having already had a

---

[20] Was this development inspired by Greek law (cf., for example, Fritz Pringsheim, "Bonum et aequum", (1932) 52 *ZSS* 86 sqq.; von Lübtow, (1969) 15 *Labeo* 140 sq.; Honsell/Mayer-Maly/Selb, p. 369)? Contra ("The law of iniuria is genuinely Roman law") Schulz, *CRL*, p. 598; Pugliese, op. cit., note 7, pp. 39 sqq.; Wittmann, *Körperverletzung*, pp. 36 sq.

[21] Ulp. D. 47, 10, 15, 26.

[22] Cf. Pugliese, op. cit., note 7, pp. 81 sqq., 96 sqq.; Simon, (1965) 82 *ZSS* 178 sq.; Elemér Polay, " 'Iniuria dicitur omne, quod non iure fit' ", (1985) 27 *BIDR* 76.

[23] Roland Wittmann, "Die Entwicklungslinien der klassischen Injurienklage", (1974) 91 *ZSS* 299 sqq.; cf. also Jolowicz/Nicholas, pp. 272 sq.; Thomas, *TRL*, p. 369.

[24] Too extreme, however, is the proposition by Raber, *Injurienansprüche*, pp. 6 sq.
Contumely iniuria was, of course, a private wrong. In 81 B.C. (that is, at a time of great domestic upheaval) certain violent forms of it (pulsare, verberare and vi domum introire: Ulp. D. 47, 10, 5 pr.) became the object of criminal proceedings, when Cornelius Sulla introduced the lex Cornelia de iniuriis. The actio iniuriarum ex lege Cornelia, though criminal in nature (it aimed at punishing those who endangered the public order), had to be instituted by the injured party. For details, see Pugliese, op. cit., note 7, pp. 117 sqq.; von Lübtow, (1969) 15 *Labeo* 157 sqq.; Okko Behrends, *Die römische Geschworenenverfassung* (1970), pp. 115 sqq.; Manfredini, op. cit., note 4, pp. 217 sqq.; Artur Völkl, "Zum Verfahren der 'actio legis Corneliae de iniuriis' ", in: *Sodalitas, Scritti in onore di Antonio Guarino*, vol. II (1984), pp. 561 sqq. On the concurrence of actions, cf. Paul. D. 47, 10, 6; *Inst.* IV, 4, 10.

forerunner in the XII Tables.[25] Ulpian quotes the praetor in the following terms:

> "[Q]ui adversus bonos mores convicium cui fecisse cuiusve opera factum esse dicetur, quo adversus bonos mores convicium fieret: in eum iudicium dabo";[26]

and he refers to Labeo for the proposition that "convicium iniuriam esse".[27] We are dealing here with a kind of stylized defamation, with roots both in the realm of magic and in traditional forms of people's justice.[28] A number of people were called together and assembled at somebody's house in order to raise an insulting and abusive clamour. Not every kind of verbal abuse was thus convicium. It had to be bawled aloud ("id solum, quod cum vociferatione dictum est"),[29] and it had to be voiced within a crowd of people (". . . quod in coetu dictum est").[30] In order to constitute a delict, the clamour had to be raised against a specific person (the word "cui", according to Ulpian, was not added by the praetor without reason, "nam si incertae personae convicium fiat, nulla executio est"),[31] but it was not necessary that the addressee be present while he was thus insulted ("Convicium non tantum praesenti, verum absenti quoque fieri posse Labeo scribit").[32] Finally, an action could be brought only if the convicium had been at variance with the moral standards of the community concerned ("adversus bonos mores huius civitatis")[33] and was apt to bring the person exposed to it into disrepute or contempt ("quae . . . [sc.: vociferationem] ad infamiam vel invidiam alicuius spectaret").[34]

(b) De adtemptata pudicitia

The edict de adtemptata pudicitia[35] was designed to protect the moral reputation of honest women and of young Romans who still wore the

---

[25] On "malum carmen incantare" (magical incantations) and "occentare" as a form of public defamation (both contained in tab. 8, 1), see Franz Beckmann, *Zauberei und Recht in Roms Frühzeit* (unpublished Dr. iur. thesis, Münster, 1923); Eduard Fraenkel (1925) 1 *Gnomon* 185 sqq.; Max Kaser, "Infamia und ignominia in den römischen Rechtsquellen", (1956) 73 *ZSS* 222; Liebs, *RR*, p. 217; but see also Arrigo Manfredini, *La diffamazione verbale nel diritto romano*, vol. I (1979), pp. 24 sqq.

[26] D. 47, 10, 15, 2.

[27] Ulp. D. 47, 10, 15, 3. Cf. also Ulp. D. 47, 10, 1, 1.

[28] Cf. the literature cited supra, note 25; Birks, (1969) 37 *TR* 206 sq.; Honsell/Mayer-Maly/Selb, p. 369; cf. also Manfredini, op. cit., note 25, pp. 49 sqq., maintaining that convicium originated as a political delict (unconvincing); and see Polay, (1985) 27 *BIDR* 76. On the etymology of convicium, cf. Ulp. D. 47, 10, 15, 4 ("Convicium autem dicitur vel a concitatione vel a conventu, hoc est a collatione vocum. cum enim in unum complures voces conferuntur, convicium appellatur quasi convocium"); Raber, *Injurienansprüche*, pp. 23 sq.; Wittmann, (1974) 91 *ZSS* 308 sq.

[29] Ulp. D. 47, 10, 15, 11.

[30] Ulp. D. 47, 10, 15, 12. Could an individual person commit the offence of convicium (provided he acted in the presence of a crowd of people)? Cf. Ulp. D. 47, 10, 15, 4 and Ulp. D. 47, 10, 15, 11 and 12; Raber, *Injurienansprüche*, pp. 27 sqq.

[31] D. 47, 10, 15, 9. [32] Ulp. D. 47, 10, 15, 7.

[33] Ulp. D. 47, 10, 15, 6. [34] Ulp. D. 47, 10, 15, 5.

[35] On its wording, see Lenel, *EP*, p. 400; for a general discussion, see, in particular, Raber, *Injurienansprüche*, pp. 39 sqq.; Wittmann, (1974) 91 *ZSS* 314 sqq.

toga praetexta.[36] It covered three closely related situations: "Tenetur hoc edicto non tantum qui comitem abduxit, verum etiam si quis eorum quem appellavisset adsectatusve est."[37] Abducere comitem was the removal, or abduction, of the companion, without whom a lady could not in all propriety appear in public. Adsectari literally means to follow somebody about, appellare to accost a person. Both types of conduct, however, gave rise to an actio iniuriarum only if they infringed the boni mores[38] (whereas comitem abducere appears to have been regarded as immoral—and thus unlawful—per se).[39] Thus, for instance, to follow a boy or woman could be a merry prank or even constitute an honourable service.[40] What was damaging to the reputation, and thus objectionable, was a constant and silent pursuit ("adsidua[41] enim frequentia quasi praebet nonnullam infamiam"[42]); it permitted the inference that one could take one's liberties with that particular person. Appellare, in turn, was confined by virtue of the contra bonos mores requirement to the kind of accosting that constituted an attempt upon a person's chastity: "Appellare est blanda oratione alterius pudicitiam adtemptare."[43]

But just as a clamour raised against infamous persons did not amount to iniuria,[44] so not every woman could complain if exposed to indecent proposals. For a certain group of women this was in fact part of their business; and it is thus obvious that prostitutes did not possess the chastity that could have been infringed by an appellare, even in the narrow, technical sense.[45] But how could a potential customer see whether he was dealing with a decent woman or a lady of the night? Usually the dress she wore gave him some indication. A prostitute was not allowed to walk around matronali habitu (wearing the clothes of a respectable materfamilias, more particularly the long stola);[46] instead she was normally dressed in a short tunica and preferred colourful and often quite transparent silk designs.[47] In time, however, these differences of garment became blurred. Thus it could happen that a man accosted a respectable woman who was dressed non matronali habitu, but meretricia veste. Did he commit an offence? Yes, according

[36] On which see, for instance, Berger, *ED*, p. 738.
[37] Ulp. D. 47, 10, 15, 19.
[38] Ulp. D. 47, 10, 15, 23.
[39] Cf. Raber, *Injurienansprüche*, pp. 54 sq.
[40] Cf. Ulp. D. 47, 10, 15, 23.
[41] Mommsen/Krüger, D. 47, 10, 15, 22, n. 5.
[42] Ulp. D. 47, 10, 15, 22.
[43] Ulp. D. 47, 10, 15, 20.
[44] Raber, *Injurienansprüche*, p. 26.
[45] Raber, *Injurienansprüche*, p. 50.
[46] For details, see Ulp. D. 34, 2, 23, 2.
[47] Raber, *Injurienansprüche*, p. 47.

to Ulpian, but only a very minor one.[48] Slightly more serious was an insult to a virgo, dressed as a slave,[49] for even the pudicitia of a slave enjoyed the protection of the law, though not quite to the same extent as that of a freeborn woman.[50] "[S]i igitur non matronali habitu femina fuerit et quis eam appellavit vel ei comitem abduxit, iniuriarum tenetur"[51] is the summarizing comment by Ulpian, which does, however, not appear to tie in particularly well with the line of argument developed in the two examples concerning ancillaris and meretricia vestis.[52] The text (our most interesting and important source dealing with de adtemptata pudicitia) has therefore often been declared spurious[53] and various attempts have been made to provide an amended version. Thus, for instance, the word "non" has been added between "iniuriarum" and "tenetur";[54] alternatively, "matronali habitu" has been read in place of "non matronali habitu".[55] Cornelis van Bynkershoek[56] argued that the sentence may originally have been meant as a question, which Ulpian, in turn, might quite possibly have answered in the negative. More recently, it has been suggested that some lines contained in the original text may have been dropped by mistake.[57] None of these hypotheses can be proved and the question regarding the exact circumstances under which the actio iniuriarum could be brought against a person who had accosted a woman not wearing matronly clothes must therefore ultimately remain open.

(c) Ne quid infamandi causa fiat

The most general of the edictal provisions dealing with iniuria was couched in the following terms: "[N]e quid infamandi causa fiat. si quis adversus ea fecerit, prout quaeque res erit, animadvertam."[58] Any act which was apt to bring another person into disrepute gave rise to an actio iniuriarum.[59] As we have seen repeatedly, the Romans tended to

---

[48] Ulp. D. 47, 10, 15, 15 (". . . multo minus [peccare videtur], si meretricia veste feminae, non matrum familiarum vestitae fuissent"). Wittmann, (1974) 91 *ZSS* 317 translates "minus" as "not" rather than "less" and therefore concludes that the edict did not apply in this case.

[49] Ulp. D. 47, 10, 15, 15; but see Wittmann, (1974) 91 *ZSS* 316 sq.

[50] Ulp. D. 47, 10, 9, 4; Raber, *Injurienansprüche*, pp. 50 sq.

[51] Ulp. D. 47, 10, 15, 15.

[52] But see Wittmann, (1974) 91 *ZSS* 318 sqq.

[53] Cf., for example, Schulz, *CRL*, p. 597.

[54] Cf. the humanist Heinrich Brenkmann (Hans Peters, "Brenkmanns Papiere zu Göttingen", (1911) 32 *ZSS* 375).

[55] Cornelis van Bynkershoek, *Observationes Juris Romani* (Lugduni Batavorum, 1710), Lib. IV, Cap. XXV.

[56] Loc. cit.

[57] Raber, *Injurienansprüche*, pp. 51 sq. Contra: Wittmann, (1974) 91 *ZSS* 319 sq.

[58] Ulp. D. 47, 10, 15, 25.

[59] But see David Daube: "'Ne quid infamandi causa fiat.' The Roman Law of Defamation", in: *Atti del congresso internazionale di diritto romano e di storia del diritto* (Verona), vol. III (1951), pp. 418 sqq. ("[T]he edict contemplated nothing but infamare in the full

be remarkably sensitive when it came to questions of honour and reputation, and the range of behaviour falling under the edict ne quid infamandi causa fiat was therefore rather wide. Thus, for instance, the malicious use of mourning dress or filthy clothes, allowing one's beard to grow unkempt or one's hair to hang down in an untidy manner could constitute the edictal offence.[60] These were all signs of mourning, displayed not only when a close relative had died or a great public calamity had happened[61] but also by a person who was formally charged with a crime.[62] In the latter case close relatives were allowed also to express their sympathy by way of vestis mutatio; but if other people joined in, their behaviour was taken to constitute an insult to the prosecutor.[63] Mourning attire was also inappropriately used by a person who followed around, "sordidatus", the man whom he suspected to be his father's murderer.[64] Carmen conscribere vel proponere vel cantare aliquod quod pudorem laedat[65] were further acts that could give rise to an actio iniuriarum: the composition, publication or recitation of a song that hurt another's honour. A person who, in a petition presented to the emperor, attacked the reputation of another, committed an offence,[66] and so did a person who pretended to be able to influence the outcome of a lawsuit by bribing the judge concerned with the matter.[67] Interference with somebody else's property could affect that person's reputation too.[68] Thus, the actio iniuriarum was available to a debtor whose goods had been wrongfully taken into possession by his creditor:[69] the inference obviously being that the former was not prepared to honour his obligations and could only be got at by way of self-help. Injurious also was the public announcement of the sale of a pledge which a person pretended to have received from another;[70] again, the impression was created that this other person had commitments which could be honoured only by selling a pledge that he had—ostensibly—given.

---

sense, 'to make a man incur infamy', i.e. infamy before the censor or praetor"). Contra: Max Kaser, (1956) 73 *ZSS* 224; Raber, *Injurienansprüche*, pp. 68 sqq.

[60] Ulp. D. 47, 10, 15, 27 (". . . ut puta ad invidiam alicuius veste lugubri utitur aut squalida, aut si barbam demittat, vel capillos submittat").

[61] Cf., for example, Suetonius, *De vita Caesarum*, Divus Iulius, LXVII, 2 (". . . audita clade Tituriana barbam capillumque summiserit [sc.: Caesar] nec ante dempserit quam vindicasset"); Divus Augustus, XXIII, 2 (". . . per continuos menses barba capilloque summisso caput interdum foribus illideret").

[62] Cf. Raber, *Injurienansprüche*, pp. 57 sq.

[63] Wittmann, (1974) 91 *ZSS* 323 (referring to Ven. D. 47, 10, 39).

[64] Cf. the case reported by Seneca, *Controversiae*, Lib. X, I (30), on which see Daube, *Atti Verona*, vol. III, pp. 433 sqq.; Raber, *Injurienansprüche*, pp. 58 sq.; Wittmann, (1974) 91 *ZSS* 330 sqq.; Peter Birks, "Infamandi causa facta in disguise", 1976 *Acta Juridica* 83 sqq.

[65] Ulp. D. 47, 10, 15, 27; Manfredini, op. cit., note 25, pp. 196 sqq.

[66] Ulp. D. 47, 10, 15, 29.

[67] Ulp. D. 47, 10, 15, 30; Daube, *Atti Verona*, vol. III, pp. 423 sq.; Raber, *Injurienansprüche*, pp. 64 sq.

[68] For details, see Raber, *Injurienansprüche*, pp. 65 sqq.

[69] Ulp. D. 47, 10, 15, 31.

[70] Ulp. D. 47, 10, 15, 32; Daube, *Atti Verona*, vol. III, pp. 426 sq.

(d) Servum alienum verberare

Finally, there was the edict dealing with the beating or torturing of another person's slave:

> "Praetor ait: Qui servum alienum adversus bonos mores verberavisse deve eo iniussu domini quaestionem habuisse dicetur, in eum iudicium dabo. item si quid aliud factum esse dicetur, causa cognita iudicium dabo."[71]

Of course, it was not so much the insult to the slave that mattered as that inflicted on his master: ". . . spectat enim ad nos iniuria, quae in his fit, qui . . . potestati nostrae . . . subiecti sint."[72] Beating[73] somebody else's slave was thus a typical example of what came to be referred to as an indirect iniuria.[74] Again, however, not every verberatio fell under the provisions of the edict: there had to be an infringement of the boni mores. This requirement for liability was not satisfied, for instance, if the blows had merely been inflicted corrigendi aut emendandi causa;[75] hence, incidentally, Julian's statement that the shoemaker who had knocked out his apprentice's eye[76] was not liable under the actio iniuriarum.[77]

(e) Residual cases

However liberally one was prepared to interpret the provisions of the special edicts, certain cases were bound to crop up which, though not being covered by any of them, still required to be remedied by means of an actio iniuriarum.[78] Entering another man's house without his

---

[71] Ulp. D. 47, 10, 15, 34. For details, see Raber, *Injurienansprüche*, pp. 77 sqq.; Wittmann, (1974) 91 *ZSS* 339 sqq.

[72] Ulp. D. 47, 10, 1, 3. Could a slave also be personally insulted? No, according to Gai. III, 222 ("Servo autem ipsi quidem nulla iniuria intellegitur fieri . . ."); but cf. Ulp. D. 47, 10, 15, 35 ("ipsi servo facta iniuria").

[73] As to the exact meaning of "verberare" cf. Ulp. D. 47, 10, 5, 1 (". . . verberare est eum dolore caedere, pulsare sine dolore"); Ulp. D. 47, 10, 15, 40 (" 'Verberasse' dicitur abusive et qui pugnis ceciderit").

[74] "Iniuria . . . per alias personas" (Ulp. D. 47, 10, 1, 3). Insulting a married woman was another instance of an indirect iniuria (". . . spectat enim ad nos iniuria, quae in his fit, qui . . . affectui (nostrae) subiecti sint" : Ulp. D. 47, 10, 1, 3). It gained great importance within the very honour-conscious upper echelons of 19th-century society—cf., as a typical example, the plot of Theodor Fontane's little masterpiece *Cécile*. For a judicial pronouncement on the matter, see *Jacobs v. Macdonald* 1909 TS 442 at 443 (per Innes CJ). A rather peculiar case of an "indirect" iniuria is dealt with by Paul. D. 47, 10, 26: someone makes a mockery of another person's slave by taking him, "anim[o] iniuriae faciendae", into a popina ("cook-shop": J.A.C. Thomas, in Mommsen/Krüger/Watson) or by playing dice with him; the slave is here used in order to insult his master. On this text, see Raber, *Injurienansprüche*, pp. 139 sqq. and Marek Kurylowicz, "Paul. D. 47.10.26 und die Tatbestände der römischen 'iniuria' ", (1987) 38 *Labeo* 298 sqq.

[75] Ulp. D. 47, 10, 15, 38.

[76] Cf. supra, p. 1016.

[77] Iul./Ulp. D. 9, 2, 5, 3.

[78] For details, see Ernst Landsberg, *Iniuria und Beleidigung* (1886), pp. 42 sqq.; Wittmann, (1974) 91 *ZSS* 346 sqq. and also David McQuoid-Mason, *The Law of Privacy in South Africa* (1978), pp. 23 sqq., who attempts to subsume a variety of iniuriae under the heads of "intrusions" (as where somebody enters someone else's home; see immediately below in the text), "publication of private facts" (for instance: the premature disclosure of the contents of

permission was one such case; if it happened vi, the lex Cornelia de iniuriis was applicable, but if the intruder had not used force, the actio iniuriarum was granted.[79] Preventing a person from using his own property could constitute another example, as where the owner of a house situated lower down created smoke in order to fumigate his neighbour's dwellings higher up.[80] Dogmatically, the action was probably based on what the classical Roman lawyers referred to as the "edictum generale";[81] in actual fact, however, it marks an advance (a rather cautious one) beyond the confines of the edict.

2. The essential elements of iniuria

(a) Contumelia; contra bonos mores

What were the common elements justifying the grouping together of the special edicts, and their eventual absorption into a so-called "edictum generale", under the common denominator of iniuria? In the first place, of course, the disregarding of another person's personality was common to all the situations examined above: iniuria in the sense of contumelia.[82] Secondly, the offender's act constituted an infringement of the boni mores.[83] This was either expressly stated in the specific edict or implicit in the description of the offence.

(b) The problem of the animus iniuriandi

Thirdly, it has often been maintained that animus iniuriandi, the

another person's will, as discussed in Ulp. D. 9, 2, 41 pr.) and "putting a person in a false light" (for example: falsely proclaiming a freeman to be one's slave; cf. Ulp. D. 47, 10, 11, 9; Gai. D. 47, 10, 12; Daube, *Atti Verona*, vol. III, pp. 428 sq.) and thus to relate them to the modern concept of invasion of privacy, as developed in the United States.

[79] Paul. D. 47, 2, 21, 7; cf. also Raber, *Injurienansprüche*, pp. 152 sqq.

[80] Iav. D. 47, 10, 44 ("Si inferiorum dominus aedium superioris vicini fumigandi causa fumum faceret, aut si superior vicinus in inferiores aedes quid aut proiecerit aut infunderit, negat *Labeo* iniuriarum agi posse: quod falsum puto, si tamen iniriae faciendae causa immittitur"). Cf. further Ulp. D. 47, 10, 24 ("Si quis proprium servum distrahere prohibetur a quolibet, iniuriarum experiri potest"); Ulp. D. 47, 10, 13, 7 (someone is prevented from fishing in the sea or from lowering his nets); and, on these two cases, Raber, *Injurienansprüche*, pp. 161 sqq.; on D. 47, 10, 13, 7 cf. also Daube, *Atti Verona*, vol. III, pp. 430 sqq.; Iul. D. 19, 1, 25 (a seller of grapes prevents the purchaser, after delivery, from treading the grapes or from taking away the unfermented wine), on which see J.E. Spruit, "Schikanen anlässlich eines Traubenkaufs", in: *Satura Roberto Feenstra oblata* (1985), pp. 157 sqq.

[81] Lab./Ulp. D. 47, 10, 15, 26; cf. supra, p. 1053.

[82] Ulp. D. 47, 10, 1 pr. Cf. also Paul. Coll. II, V, 1 and 3; *Inst.* IV, 4 pr. ("Generaliter iniuria dicitur omne quod non iure fit: specialiter alias contumelia, quae a contemnendo dicta est, quam Graeci ὕβριν appellant"); von Lübtow, (1969) 15 *Labeo* 162 sqq.; Wittmann, (1974) 91 *ZSS* 290 sqq.; Buckland/Stein, p. 590 (". . . in the law as we know it, the wrong consisted in outrage or insult or wanton interference with rights, any act, in short, which shewed contempt of the personality of the victim or was such as to lower him in the estimation of others").

[83] Paul. Coll. II, V, 2: "Commune omnibus iniuriis est, quod semper adversus bonos mores fit . . ."; Raber, *Injurienansprüche*, pp. 5 sq.; Wittmann, (1974) 91 *ZSS* 303 sqq.; Theo Mayer-Maly, "Contra bonos mores", in: *Iuris Professio, Festgabe für Max Kaser* (1986), pp. 157 sqq.

intention to insult, was an essential requirement for the actio iniuriarum in all its emanations.[84] But this is an inadmissible and ahistorical generalization. Only some of our texts can possibly be taken to lend support to such a view; but even they are usually not unambiguous. Nor can one be certain whether they have not been interpolated by Justinian's compilers who, as we know, generally favoured subjective criteria to determine legal consequences. Thus, in particular, there is Ulpian's statement that "iniuria ex affectu facientis consistat" (consequence: madmen and persons under the age of puberty—"impube[re]s, qui doli capa[ces] non [sunt]"—cannot be liable under the actio iniuriarum),[85] but this text is taken from Ulpian's commentary on the lex Cornelia de iniuriis, not on iniuria in terms of the praetorian edict;[86] and even apart from that, it does not state clearly what exactly was meant by the term "affectus". Considering the context within which the phrase appears, it is not necessarily synonymous with animus iniuriandi but may simply have been used to indicate that the offender had to have been able to form a legally relevant will;[87] since unless a person is able to distinguish between good and evil, the results of his actions are not attributable to him in law. Reference has also often been made to a variety of texts adverting to the offender's animus iniuriae faciendae. We may think, once again, of the shoemaker's case where liability under the actio iniuriarum is excluded "quia non faciendae iniuriae causa percusserit, sed monendi et docendi causa".[88] Had he chastised iniuriae faciendae causa, one could be inclined to conclude, he would have been held responsible. But it would be wrong to isolate a purely subjective criterion and to assume that its presence was essential to establishing liability. The reason why the boy was beaten was relevant within the wider enquiry of whether the shoemaker's action could be labelled "contra bonos mores"; and it was this rather more objective criterion that ultimately mattered, as is stated specifically, for cases of this kind, by Ulp. D. 47, 10, 15, 38:

> "Adicitur 'adversus bonos mores', ut non omnis omnino qui verberavit, sed qui adversus bonos mores verberaverit, teneatur: ceterum si quis corrigendi animo aut si quis emendandi, non tenetur."

A purely subjective mental element was thus, to put it cautiously, not indispensable for purposes of liability, and it is quite in accordance with its rather limited function that many texts do not even mention it.[89]

[84] Cf., for example, Melius de Villiers, "The Roman Law of Defamation", (1918) 34 *LQR* 412 sqq. and infra, notes 228, 229.
[85] Ulp. D. 47, 10, 3, 1; interpolated according to Giannetto Longo, "La complicità nel diritto penale romano", (1958) 61 *BIDR* 120; Max Kaser, "Gaius und die Klassiker", (1953) 70 *ZSS* 174; but see Raber, *Injurienansprüche*, pp. 108 sqq.
[86] Cf. the inscription (Ulpian 56 ad ed.) and Lenel, *EP*, p. 397.
[87] Pauw, *Persoonlikheidskrenking*, p. 18.
[88] Ulp. D. 9, 2, 5, 3.
[89] Cf., for instance, Ulp. D. 47, 10, 15, 23.

Proof that he lacked the intention to insult did not (in any event not necessarily) exclude the wrongdoer's liability. Objective and subjective ingredients were inextricably interwoven within the concept of iniuria, and the relative weight attached to each depended, furthermore, on the type of injury in question. This makes it impossible to generalize. The most one can probably say[90] is that here, as in many other instances, the Roman lawyers did not think in terms of specific, isolated requirements for liability that had to be satisfied, but tended to look at the typicality of a situation. Thus it is obvious from the examples contained in the Digest that the delict of iniuria only covered situations where dolus on the part of the offender could typically be presumed to have been present. "Conduct", in the words of Ranchod,[91] "which was classified as iniuria usually did not occur without some form of dolus"; and while it would therefore be quite in order to refer to dolus as a characteristic ingredient of the different forms of contumelia iniuria, it would at the same time be wrong to assert that liability under the actio iniuriarum was strictly and necessarily confined to persons who could be shown to have acted with the intention to insult.

(c) Characteristics of the actio iniuriarum

Fourthly, the actio iniuriarum, on whatever basis it was granted, was of a purely penal nature.[92] Like all other actiones poenales, it was therefore passively intransmissible.[93] Unlike the others, however, it was also actively intransmissible,[94] that is, it could not be brought by the heirs of the deceased victim of the insult. The actio iniuriarum was thus a strictly personal remedy; it was only the injured party himself who deserved to receive compensation for the disregarding of his personality.[95] Although this compensation was of a financial nature, the claim was not held to be part of the injured party's property: "Iniuriarum actio in bonis nostris non computatur, antequam litem contestemur."[96] Modern legal systems still retain this principle; thus, according to § 847 I 2 BGB, the claim for compensation in money for

[90] Cf., in particular, the detailed analysis by Raber, *Injurienansprüche*, pp. 107 sqq.; further Bhadra Ranchod, *Foundations of the South African Law of Defamation* (unpublished Dr. iur. thesis, Leiden, 1972), pp. 12 sqq.; Pauw, *Persoonlikheidskrenking*, pp. 17 sqq.; N.J.J. Olivier, *Die aksie weens die nalatige veroorsaking van pyn en lyding* (unpublished Dr. iur. thesis, Leiden, 1978), pp. 12 sqq.

[91] Op. cit., note 90, p. 15.

[92] Gai. IV, 112.

[93] Gai. IV, 112.

[94] Gai. IV, 112. For details, see Tobias Johannes Scott, *Die Geskiedenis van die Oorerflikheid van Aksies op grond van Onregmatige Daad in die Suid-Afrikaanse Reg* (unpublished Dr. iur. thesis, Leiden, 1976), pp. 13 sqq.; 31 sqq.

[95] Furthermore, the actio iniuriarum had to be brought within a year (while the resentment was still (reasonably) fresh): cf. C. 9, 35, 5; Kaser, *RPr* I, p. 625; but cf. Pugliese, op. cit., note 7, pp. 109 sqq.

[96] Ulp. D. 47, 10, 28.

immaterial damages[97] does not pass to the heirs, unless it has been acknowledged by way of contract or an action has been instituted.[98]

Finally, condemnation under the actio iniuriarum was for "quantam pecuniam . . . bonum aequum videbitur"[99] and involved infamia.[100]

III. THE USUS MODERNUS OF THE ACTIO INIURIARUM

1. "Mine honour is my life . . ."

All in all, I think one can agree with Fritz Schulz:[101] the actio iniuriarum afforded a strong and efficient protection against injuries to immaterial interests, and in particular against insulting behaviour of any kind. Reflecting, as it did, the high value attributed to the respect or esteem which a person enjoys within society,[102] it was bound to appeal to medieval lawyers: glossators, ultramontani and commentators alike.[103] They lived within a society that prized good name, dignity and honour even more highly and imbued it with the spirit of the feudal codes of chivalry. For the source of the chivalrous idea "is pride aspiring to beauty, and formalized pride

---

[97] Which is, however, unlike in Roman law, confined to two specific cases: injury to the body or health and deprivation of liberty. In particular, it does not apply to situations where honour or reputation are impaired: cf. infra, p. 1092.

[98] This provision is widely criticized, however, and its abolition has been recommended de lege ferenda: cf. Hans-Joachim Mertens, in: *Münchener Kommentar*, vol. III, 2 (2nd ed., 1986), §§ 52 sqq.; Gerhard Hohloch, in: *Gutachten und Vorschläge zur Überarbeitung des Schuldrechts*, vol. I (1981), pp. 442 sq. For South African law, see Scott, op. cit., note 94, pp. 190 sq. Here the old English adage of "actio personalis moritur cum persona" has occasionally been referred to, quite wrongly, as Scott, (1976) 39 *THRHR* 288 sqq. shows.

[99] Cf. Lenel, *EP*, pp. 397 sqq.; Selb, 1978 *Acta Juridica* 29 sqq. As to the criteria applied, cf. *Inst.* IV, 4, 7. Details of the procedure are described by Gaius III, 224: "[P]ermittitur enim nobis a praetore ipsis iniuriam aestimare, et iudex vel tanti condemnat quanti nos aestimaverimus, vel minoris, prout illi visum fuerit"; cf. also Paul. Coll. II, VI, 1. The matter was different, though, in cases which were referred to as iniuria atrox. Here it was not the plaintiff who made his own assessment of the injury (which the iudex could then reduce, at his discretion); it was the praetor who determined the appropriate amount (which the iudex in turn did not venture to reduce (cf. Gai. III, 224, second half)). The category of iniuria atrox was also used to determine when a libertus could sue his patronus (to whom he owed reverentia, pietas and obsequium; cf., for example, Ulp. D. 37, 15, 9) for contumelia: cf. Ulp. D. 2, 4, 10, 12; Ulp. D. 47, 10, 7, 2 and 3. For a classification of iniuriae atroces (ex facto, ex persona, ex loco), see Gai. III, 225; Ulp. D. 47, 10, 7, 8. For a general discussion, see Raber, *Injurienansprüche*, pp. 91 sqq. Occasionally it has been maintained (wrongly) that all injuries below the level of atrox were eliminated from the scope of the actio iniuriarum: cf. Manfred Herrmann, *Der Schutz der Persönlichkeit in der Rechtslehre des 16.–18. Jahrhunderts* (1968), pp. 12 sq.

[100] Gai. IV, 182.

[101] *CRL*, p. 599.

[102] The technical term was "existimatio": cf. Call. D. 50, 13, 5, 1: "Existimatio est dignitatis inlaesae status, legisbus ac moribus comprobatus, qui ex delicto nostra auctoritate legum aut minuitur aut consumitur."

[103] For an analysis cf. Robert Mainzer, *Die ästimatorische Injurienklage in der geschichtlichen Entwicklung* (1908), pp. 61 sqq.; Ranchod, op. cit., note 90, pp. 32 sqq.; cf. also Herrmann, op. cit., note 99, pp. 17 sqq.

gives rise to a conception of honour, which is the pole of noble life".[104] "The purest treasure mortal times afford/", says Shakespeare,[105] "is spotless reputation; that away/Men are but gilded loam or painted clay./A jewel in a ten-times-barr'd-up chest/Is a bold spirit in a loyal breast./Mine honour is my life; both grown in one;/Take honour from me, and my life is done."

Given the violent tenor of life in the Middle Ages, and the extreme excitability of medieval man,[106] it is not surprising that honour and revenge were closely tied up with each other; in fact, the duel as a ritualized form of obtaining satisfaction for outraged honour survived, within certain segments of society, until well into our century.[107] But revenge is a crude form of private self-help that can hardly be tolerated within any developed community. It is one of the principal functions of public authorities to see to it that disputes are settled in a peaceable manner.[108] This can occur only if a satisfactory set of legal remedies is available; and just as, therefore, the actio legis Aquiliae came to be received for the recovery of damnum iniuria datum, so the actio iniuriarum (aestimatoria, as it was usually called) was adopted from the Romans in order to provide protection against interference with man's

[104] Johan Huizinga, *The Waning of the Middle Ages* (trans. F. Hopman, Penguin reprint, 1982), p. 67; cf. also p. 68, where he points out that "[t]he thirst for honour and glory proper to the men of the Renaissance is essentially the same as the chivalrous ambition of earlier times".

[105] *Richard II*, Act I, sc. i, l. 177 sqq. (also quoted by Jonathan Burchell, *The Law of Defamation in South Africa* (1985), p. 18 and Leon J, in *Payne v. Republican Press (Pty.) Ltd.* 1980 (2) PH J44 (D) at 111).

[106] Cf. the magnificent first chapter of Huizinga's famous book (op. cit., note 104, pp. 9 sqq.).

[107] Cf. generally K. Demeter, *Duell*, in: *HRG*, vol. I, col. 789 sq. More specifically on the medieval trial by combat, on the chivalrous tradition of jousting and on the "duel of honour" of the late Middle Ages, see V.G. Kiernan, *The Duel in European History* (1988), pp. 31 sqq. They were the direct ancestors of the modern duel which emerged in Italy amidst the chronic warfare of the 16th century. From there it spread to France and all other parts of Europe (including England which, in turn, exported it to her colonies); for details, see Kiernan, pp. 46 sqq., 68 sqq. In the late 19th and early 20th centuries the historical origin of duelling became the subject of lively controversies among supporters and opponents of this social institution; the one side argued that it was historically and psychologically intimately linked to a specifically Germanic concept of honour, the other claimed that it was entirely alien to the German character and constituted a fateful and objectionable import from the frivolous Mediterranean countries (cf., in particular, the spirited comments by the historian Georg von Below, *Das Duell und der germanische Ehrbegriff* (1896); for a balanced evaluation of these disputes, see Johannes Slawig, *Der Kampf gegen das Duellwesen im 19. und 20. Jahrhundert in Deutschland unter besonderer Berücksichtigung Preussens* (unpublished Dr. phil. thesis, Münster, 1986), pp. 7 sqq.). For a discussion of the complex and ambivalent relationship between the social institution of duelling and the formal legal system, cf. Slawig, pp. 49 sqq. and, in particular, Warren F. Schwartz, Keith Baxter, David Ryan, "The Duel: Can These Gentlemen Be Acting Efficiently?", (1984) 13 *Journal of Legal Studies* 320 sqq. Schwartz, Baxter and Ryan base their observations on 19th-century American duelling conventions.

[108] Hence the anti-duelling laws, the first of which were already enacted in the latter part of the 16th century. Among the German principalities, Saxony appears to have led the way. For details, see Slawig, op. cit., note 107, pp. 49 sqq.; Kiernan, op. cit., note 107, pp. 185 sqq., 191 sqq.

(non-material) interest in his dignity and honour.[109] The penal nature of the actio iniuriarum tied in well with the traditions of Germanic customary law,[110] but its inherent flexibility rendered it superior to the system of fixed penalties prevailing in the latter. Thus, it was the more convenient aestimatio of the penalty that was taken over from the Roman sources, but, in its wake, the substantive concept of iniuria followed suit.[111]

2. The definition of iniuria

Down to the days of the Dutch and German usus modernus we therefore find iniuria, in terms of the actio iniuriarum, defined in the special sense of contumelia: "Hoc loco et in specie denotat [sc.: iniuria] contumeliam a contemnendo", wrote Lauterbach[112] and he added the following German equivalents: "*Eine Schmach, Verleümdung, Ehrenrührige, verkleinerliche Wort und Werck.*" Some authors tried to be more specific; thus, for instance, Voet described iniuria as a wrongful act committed in contempt of a free man by another who thereby with evil intention impairs either his person, his dignity or his reputation (". . . delictum in contemptum hominis liberi admissum, quo ejus corpus, vel dignitas, vel fama laeditur dolo malo").[113] Availing themselves of a distinction dating back to Labeo,[114] most writers stated that iniuria may be committed by acts or words ("aut re aut verbis"). Iniuria litteris ("quae fit verbis contumeliosis in scripturam redactis")[115] was either added as a third category[116] or subsumed under either iniuria

---

[109] If one and the same act constituted contumely iniuria and satisfied the requirements of the lex Aquilia, and if therefore both immaterial and patrimonial loss was caused, the actio iniuriarum and the actio legis Aquiliae could be cumulated: cf. Voet, *Commentarius ad Pandectas*, Lib. XLVII, Tit. X, XVIII.

[110] Ekkehard Kaufmann, "Das spätmittelalterliche deutsche Schadensersatzrecht und die Rezeption der 'actio iniuriarum aestimatoria' ", (1961) 78 *ZSS* (GA) 93 sqq.

[111] Kaufmann, (1961) 78 *ZSS* (GA) 97 sqq.; cf. also Mainzer, op. cit., note 103, pp. 47 sqq.

[112] *Collegium theoretico-practicum*, Lib. XLVII, Tit. X, I. For further definitions of the concept of iniuria, see Karlheinz Bartels, *Die Dogmatik der Ehrverletzung in der Wissenschaft des gemeinen Rechts bis zum Ausgang des 18. Jahrhunderts* (unpublished Dr. iur. thesis, Göttingen, 1959), pp. 72 sqq.; Herrmann, op. cit., note 99, p. 51.

[113] *Commentarius ad Pandectas*, Lib. XLVII, Tit. X, I (trans by Melius de Villiers, *The Roman and Roman-Dutch Law of Injuries* (1899), p. 17). The triad of corpus, dignitas and fama is taken from Ulp. D. 47, 10, 1, 2. As in Roman law, the iniuria could be either "vel immediate per semetipsum, nulla alia persona interveniente" or "vel mediate per consequentiam" (Lauterbach, *Collegium theoretico-practicum*, Lib. XLVII, Tit. X, X; for details cf. Bartels, op. cit., note 112, pp. 150 sqq.). According to Stryk, *Usus modernus pandectarum*, Lib. XLVII, Tit. X, § 9, a man could be (indirectly) insulted by an insult inflicted upon his wife, but not vice versa ("Ita quoque uxori injuria illata marito illata esse censetur, . . . sed non vice versa"). Reason: "defendi uxores a vires, non viros ab uxoribus aequum est." On iniuria per consequentias in modern South African law, see J. Neethling, *Persoonlikheidsreg* (2nd ed., 1985), pp. 70 sqq.

[114] Lab./Ulp. D. 47, 10, 1, 1.

[115] Lauterbach, *Collegium theoretico-practicum*, Lib. XLVII, Tit. X, II.

[116] Cf., for example, Azo, *Summa Codicis*, Lib. IX, De iniuriis (p. 338, right column).

realis or (more often) iniuria verbalis.[117] A specific form of iniuria litteris, the libellus famosus, was often[118] treated as a separate kind of delict.[119] Voet, suggesting a somewhat fanciful[120] analogy between obligations arising from iniuria and those arising from contract, added a fourth class of iniuriae quae consensu inferuntur.[121] Others simply appended a general, salvatory clause (iniuria committitur facto, vel verbo, vel scriptura, "vel aliis multis modis").[122] Many of the examples provided in 13th- to 17th-century literature for each of these two, or three, or four modes of committing iniuria were still the ones[123] discussed in title 10 of Digest 47: convicium facere and barbam dimittere as much as, for instance, comitem abducere or matronam honestam adsectari.[124]

3. Of hunchbacks, cuckolds, clergymen and flouncy skirts

More interesting, however, are the instances of injurious behaviour taken from contemporary practice rather than from Roman law. They are a valuable source of information about the mores of the time. Thus, it could be injurious to taunt a person with his natural impediment by calling him a cripple, or a hunchback, to refer to someone, ironically, as a "bonus patiens vir" (and thus suggesting that he was a cuckold), to state emphatically "*ego saltem* scortator non sum" (and thus insinuate that a particular other person *is* a fornicator), to use obscene language, particularly in the presence of a virgo, to address a clergyman "*du Pfaff*", or to use the familiar "*du*" when talking German to persona honorabilis.[125] These are all cases of verbal injuries. Pulling faces, putting out one's tongue at another or kissing a woman against her will are examples of iniuriae reales.[126] Iniuria litteris (in the form of the

[117] Cf. Vinnius, *Institutiones*, Lib. IV, Tit. IV, 1.

[118] But see, for instance, Voet, *Commentarius ad Pandectas*, Lib. XLVII, Tit. X, X.

[119] Cf. Lauterbach, *Collegium theoretico-practicum*, Lib. XLVII, Tit. X, LXVI sqq. (emphasizing, however, that famosus libellus "ab aliis injuriis nec Causa Efficiente, nec Subjecto differt"). Perezius, *Praelectiones*, Lib. IX, Tit. XXXVI, appears to regard famosus libellus and iniuria literis as synonymous ("Gravioris injuriae species est, quae scripto fit").

[120] De Villiers, op. cit., note 113, p. 77.

[121] *Commentarius ad Pandectas*, Lib. XLVII, Tit. X, XI ("Consulto denique injuriam quis facit, si alteri injuriam fieri mandet, aut generaliter procuret, ut alteri contumelia inferatur"). Joost van Damhouder, *Praxis rerum criminalium*, Cap. CXXXV also had four classes, but they were verbis, facto, scriptis and gestibus.

[122] Angelus Aretinus, as quoted by Ranchod, op. cit., note 90, p. 32. On injuriae, quae in non faciendo consistunt (for instance: debitos alicui honoris titulos non tribuere, dominum aliquem non nominare), see Leyser, *Meditationes ad Pandectas*, Spec. DXLIX.

[123] Cf., in particular, Leyser, *Meditationes ad Pandectas*, Spec. DXLVIII.

[124] For a detailed exposition cf., for instance, Voet, *Commentarius ad Pandectas*, Lib. XLVII, Tit. X, VII sqq. and De Villiers, op. cit., note 113, pp. 73 sqq.; Landsberg, op. cit., note 78, pp. 69 sqq.; cf. also Bartels, op. cit., note 112, pp. 128 sqq.

[125] All these examples from Lauterbach, *Collegium theoretico-practicum*, Lib. XLVII, Tit. X, XVI, and Voet, *Commentarius ad Pandectas*, Lib. XLVII, Tit. X, VIII. Cf. further the casuistry compiled by Bartels, op. cit., note 112, pp. 93 sqq.

[126] Lauterbach, *Collegium theoretico-practicum*, Lib. XLVII, Tit. X, XVII; Stryk, *Usus modernus pandectarum*, Lib. XLVII, Tit. X, § 7; cf. also the examples provided by Bartels, op.

delict famosus libellus) covered "quamlibet scripturam infamantem, epigramma, carmen malum, satyram, picturam, historiam, comoediam".[127] Eagerly discussed were questions of pre-eminence and precedence;[128] for to refuse someone his rightful place at table, in a procession or at any other ceremonious occasion could constitute a grave insult within a hierarchically structured society, intensely concerned with rank, form and ritual.[129] A particularly interesting debate raged around the problem of insults inflicted by the clergy in the pursuit of their duties. Many a drastic invective seems to have emanated, in true Lutheran fashion, from protestant pulpits—and provides us with some inkling of the tight moral control exercised by the Church in those days. Thus, for instance, we hear of a superintendent in Saxony who was engaged in a strenuous fight against the fashion of wearing flouncy skirts.[130] Having referred in one of his Sunday sermons to women wearing such "vainglorious" garments as brutes and whores, he did not hesitate on subsequent occasions to identify individual ladies sitting in his congregation. Pointing his finger at them, he exclaimed that they were conceited women with the head of a devil, doomed to suffer the fires of hell, and he refused to administer the Holy Communion to them. The women concerned and their husbands thereupon sued the superintendent, and the law faculty of the University of Halle, to which the matter was referred, opined in their favour. While it was acknowledged that the clergy had a duty to admonish and impel their congregations to adopt a virtuous course of life, there were still certain limits to how far they could go in publicly upbraiding individual members. Thus they were, in a way, privileged, but not exempt from being sued for contumely iniuria.[131] This reflects the prevailing trend in the contemporary literature:

> "[N]ec excipiuntur Clerici et Ecclesiae Ministri, si scil. non ex pietatis zelo, nec observatis gradibus admonitionis; sed privato affectu pro concione, vel alibi in certam personam injuriose invehunt, vel eandem depingant, ut omnes intelligant, quis notetur."[132]

---

cit., note 112, pp. 108 sqq. Generally on iniuriae reales, see A. Ranjit B. Amerasinghe, "The law relating to Iniuriae reales", 1967 *Acta Juridica* 159 sqq.; more specifically on ignominious gestures ("sannae"): Leyser, *Meditationes ad Pandectas*, Spec. DXLV.

[127] Lauterbach, *Collegium theoretico-practicum*, Lib. XLVII, Tit. X, LXVI.

[128] Cf. Coing, pp. 513 sq.; Leyser, *Meditationes ad Pandectas*, Spec. DXLVI, XII (dealing with "alterum, cui dignior locus debetur, antegredi").

[129] Cf., for the Middle Ages, Joachim Bumke, *Höfische Kultur* (1986), for example pp. 248 sqq. (seating order), 276 sqq. (court ceremonies); on the hierarchical conception of society, see Huizinga, op. cit., note 104, pp. 54 sqq.; Bumke, pp. 43 sqq.

[130] Stryk, *Usus modernus pandectarum*, Lib. XLVII, Tit. X, § 3.

[131] Cf. also De Villiers, op. cit., note 113, pp. 98, 201.

[132] Lauterbach, *Collegium theoretico-practicum*, Lib. XLVII, Tit. X, VI. Cf. also, for instance, Leyser, *Meditationes ad Pandectas*, Spec. DXLVIII, VIII.

4. Animus iniuriandi

(a) Presumption of animus iniuriandi

"Zelus pietatis", "privatus affectus": these are subjective criteria, taking us into the field of what was usually referred to as animus iniuriandi. "Injuriae fundamentum est animus injuriandi":[133] the intention to inflict contumely iniuria (that is: to impair the person, dignity or reputation of another) was the gist and hallmark of the actio iniuriarum.[134] This pronounced emphasis on a purely mental element had been introduced into the sources—here as elsewhere—by Justinian's compilers ("nam maleficia voluntas et propositum delinquentis distinguit")[135] and was therefore bound to become part of the heritage of the ius commune. Highly commendable under ethical auspices, animus iniuriandi as the decisive criterion for establishing iniuria is, however, unwieldy in practice: for it is often difficult, if not impossible, for the injured plaintiff to prove the specific intention behind the alleged wrongdoer's behaviour. From the time of the gloss, lawyers were therefore intent on alleviating the plaintiff's predicament and established a presumption that prima facie defamatory acts were committed with an intention to defame.[136] Thus it was incumbent upon the defendant to show that animus iniuriandi had been absent from his mind:

> "Sin tales fuerint prolati sermones qui per se et propria significatione contumeliam inferunt, injuriandi animus adfuisse creditur, eique, qui illa protulit, probatio incumbit, injuriae faciandae consilium defuisse."[137]

Certain situations were, however, always recognized where such a presumption did not operate. Persons in a position of authority ("magistratus"), for instance, were not presumed to have acted animo

---

[133] Lauterbach, *Collegium theoretico-practicum*, Lib. XLVII, Tit. X, XIX.

[134] "Quicquid enim fit animo et intentione iniuriandi aliumque aut commovendi, aut laedendi" (Van Damhouder, *Praxis Rerum Criminalium*, Cap. CXXXV); ". . . met een oogmerk om te beledigen, tot schending van iemands eer" (Joannes van der Linden, *Regtsgeleerd, practicaal en Koopman's handboek* (Amsteldam, 1806), I. Boek, XVI Afd., § IV). For detailed analyses, see Ranchod, op. cit., note 90, pp. 34 sqq., 75 sqq.; Pauw, *Persoonlikheidskrenking*, pp. 37 sqq., 77 sqq.; cf. also Bartels, op. cit., note 112, pp. 75 sqq.

[135] Paul. D. 47, 2, 54 pr.; Ranchod, op. cit., note 90, pp. 21 sqq. For a good summary cf. Jolowicz, as quoted by Ranchod, p. 21; "The compilers had no doubt a predilection for animus, particularly in the sense that when there was doubt as to the existence of a legal relationship they tended to seek the criterion in the intention of the party or parties concerned to bring about the particular relationship as it was known to the law, whereas the classical jurists had been content to decide the matter by applying objective legal rules to the facts, including of course the intention of the parties."

[136] Bartels, op. cit., note 112, pp. 81 sqq., 84 sqq.; Ranchod, op. cit., note 90, pp. 36 sqq.; Pauw, *Persoonlikheidskrenking*, pp. 48 sqq.

[137] Voet, *Commentarius ad Pandectas*, Lib. XLVII, Tit. X, XX; cf. also Lauterbach, *Collegium theoretico-practicum*, Lib. XLVII, Tit. X, XIX: "Quod cum directe per testes aut instrumenta fieri nequeat, proin conjecturae et praesumptiones quoque admittuntur; puta ex verbis et factis sua natura vel loci consuetudine injuriosis."

iniuriandi.[138] This was usually justified with reference to D. 47, 10, 13, 1: "Is, qui iure publico utitur, non videtur iniuriae faciendae causa hoc facere: iuris enim executio non habet iniuriam." Thus it was up to the plaintiff to establish abuse of authority on the part of the public official. Similar considerations prevailed in the case of teachers and other persons standing in loco parentis, who administered a (reasonable) chastisement to their charges. Nor could a person who had been consulted in his professional capacity be presumed to have acted with the intention to insult: a doctor (mistakenly) advising his patient that he suffered from leprosy[139] or an astrologer calling his client a thief.[140, 141] Again, the behaviour of clergymen posed a problem: what, for instance, if they embraced a woman and gave her a kiss? Not everybody, after all, is fond of such intimate contact with his pastor.[142] Yet, according to many, the clergyman was presumed to have acted benedicendi causa; others credited him with a (perhaps somewhat exaggerated) charitable zeal (". . . quod clericus, si deoscultetur mulierem, facere id praesumatur zelo charitatis").[143] Some authors, however, were opposed to any kind of preferential treatment accorded to the clergy; "a tali charitate libera nos Domine", they exclaimed and proceeded to grant the actio iniuriarum.[144]

(b) Rebuttal of the presumption

If, then, apart from such exceptional cases, a presumption operated in favour of the plaintiff "puta ex verbis et factis sua natura vel loci consuetudine injuriosis",[145] what could the defendant do in order to rebut it? He could show, for instance, that he had acted merely in jest.[146] Mistake, too, could be a valid defence, though not, apparently, error in persona.[147] Violent anger was sometimes taken to negative the defendant's animus iniuriandi, and thus he was not liable under the

[138] Cf. Ranchod, op. cit., note 90, pp. 39 sq.; De Villiers, op. cit., note 113, pp. 199 sqq.
[139] Voet, *Commentarius ad Pandectas*, Lib. XLVII, Tit. X, XX.
[140] This case was the prototype: Ulp. D. 47, 10, 15, 13.
[141] On the position of advocates using injurious language in their professional capacity, see the detailed analysis by Leyser, *Meditationes ad Pandectas*, Spec. DXLVII. Advocates do not appear to have enjoyed the best of reputations ("Vulgata est et quotidiana querela de improbitate et imperitia advocatorum"); cf. also Stryk (infra, note 289), § 5 (most advocates earn their money through squalid trials—particularly those involving the actio iniuriarum).
[142] Cf. the case discussed by Stryk, *Usus modernus pandectarum*, Lib XLVII, Tit. X, § 7 (". . . si [clericus] foeminae invitae obtrudat osculum").
[143] Cf. the authorities referred to by Stryk, loc. cit.
[144] Stryk, loc. cit.
[145] Lauterbach, *Collegium theoretico-practicum*, Lib. XLVII, Tit. X, XIX.
[146] Bartels, op. cit., note 112, pp. 163 sq.; Ranchod, op. cit., note 90, pp. 41 sq.; Pauw, *Persoonlikheidskrenking*, p. 57; De Villiers, op. cit., note 113, p. 195.
[147] Pauw, *Persoonlikheidskrenking*, pp. 52 sqq.; for a very detailed discussion, see Leyser, *Meditationes ad Pandectas*, Spec. DL.

actio iniuriarum for "quod calore iracundiae vel fit vel dicitur"[148] unless he had persisted in these acts or statements after having had time to cool down. A blow inflicted in a sportive combat was not regarded as iniuria nor (interestingly) a swearword uttered by a chess-player against his opponent.[149] Furthermore, a person could escape liability for an insult inflicted on another if he could show that he had merely retaliated (retorsio).[150] While it was argued by some that, given the nature of human beings, one could hardly expect them to control themselves when provoked by the other person's defamatory statement,[151] others maintained that the retorsion had not so much been made animo iniuriandi as rather honoris tuendi gratia.[152] Truth could also constitute a valid defence against an actio iniuriarum, but the exact scope of the defence was much disputed.[153] The prevailing view seems to have been that defamatory statements entailed liability, even if they were true. Only if exposure of the matter concerned was in the public interest, was the actio iniuriarum excluded[154]—for here it could be presumed that amor iustitiae,[155] and not the desire to insult the other, had induced the defendant to make his allegation. Thus, for instance, the statement that someone is a leper constituted iniuria if that other person had already been identified as such by the authorities in charge of public health. If, on the other hand, his exposure led to his identification and subsequent removal from the community, the same statement did not give rise to an actio iniuriarum.[156]

Not infrequently, insulting remarks appear to have been accompanied by a protestation to the effect that no offence was intended:

---

[148] Voet, *Commentarius ad Pandectas*, Lib. XLVII, Tit. X, I in fine; cf. also Ranchod, op. cit., note 90, pp. 44 sqq., 81 sq.; De Villiers, op. cit., note 113, pp. 33 sq.

[149] Reason: ". . . sicut fieri consuevit in ludis talibus": Azo, *Commentarius ad singulas leges Codicis* (Parisiis, 1577), Lib IX, Tit. XXXV, L. 5.

[150] Ranchod, op. cit., note 90, pp. 48 sq., 82 sq.; De Villiers, op. cit., note 113, pp. 215 sqq. Cf. also the comprehensive analysis by Ernst Beling, *Die geschichtliche Entwickelung der Retorsion und Kompensation von Beleidigungen und Körperverletzungen* (1894), pp. 1 sqq., 24 sqq., 67 sqq., 120 sqq., 153 sqq.

[151] Ulrich Huber, *Heedendaegse Rechtsgeleertheyt*, II Deel, III Boek, VIII Kap., 10.

[152] Lauterbach, *Collegium theoretico-practicum*, Lib. XLVII, Tit. X, LVII. He maintains that retorsio is illicit in foro conscientiae (reason: "revera nihil aliud est quam privata vindicta") as well as in foro externo de Jure Civili: "Quamvis autem haec ita sese habeant, Moribus tamen nostris hoc remedium in toto fere Imperio est permissum, ita, ut retorsio in foro soli non sit punibilis" (LX). For a defence of retorsio ("Retorsione injuriarum meliores sunt et utiliores actionibus injuriarum"), see Leyser, *Meditationes ad Pandectas*, Spec. DXLII, IX.

[153] For a discussion, see Leyser, *Meditationes ad Pandectas*, Spec. DLI, introducing his discussion with the words: "Utraque regula: Veritas convitii excusat; et veritas convitii non excusat; vera est"; Bartels, op. cit., note 112, pp. 171 sqq., 181 sqq.; Ranchod, op. cit., note 90, pp. 49 sqq., 84 sqq.; cf. also Pauw, *Persoonlikheidskrenking*, pp. 54 sqq.; De Villiers, op. cit., note 113, pp. 103 sqq. The main authority on the matter was Paul. D. 47, 10, 18 pr.: "Eum, qui nocentem infamavit non esse bonum aequum ob eam rem condemnari: peccata enim nocentium nota esse et oportere et expedire."

[154] Cf., for example, Voet, *Commentarius ad Pandectas*, Lib. XLVII, Tit. X, IX.

[155] Lauterbach, *Collegium theoretico-practicum*, Lib. XLVII, Tit. X, XXI.

[156] Cf. the example discussed already by Pierre de Belleperche and Faber (Ranchod, op. cit., note 90, p. 51).

someone called another a thief, a robber or a forger "salvo honore" (without prejudice to his character); or he added the clause "absit dicto contumelia".[157] Such a protestation did not rebut the presumption that the speaker had acted animo iniuriandi: "[n]am si actus sit potentior protestatione, haec nihil operatur."[158] Nor, incidentally, could a person who merely repeated a slanderous comment escape liability under the actio iniuriarum by giving the name of the person from whom he had heard it; "nam injurias ab alio auditas proferens famam non minus laedit".[159] Many writers referred in this context to the old German maxim "*Wehrmann haben hilft nicht*" (it is of no use to have a warrantor).[160]

5. Remedies

(a) Actio iniuriarum aestimatoria

If we turn our attention to the remedies available to the victim of the insult, we find in the first place the so-called actio iniuriarum aestimatoria. Though it may ultimately have originated in Germanic customary law,[161] the essential attributes of the Roman actio iniuriarum had been grafted onto it; it was, as Lauterbach put it, "nihil aliud . . . quam actio praetoria, personalis, poenalis, civilis, famosa, annalis".[162] Most importantly, therefore, it could not be brought by the heir of the victim[163] (nor, of course, against the heir of the wrongdoer); condemnation still involved infamia[164] (though not if the insult had been only slight or moderate[165]); and it prescribed within a

[157] Cf. Lauterbach, *Collegium theoretico-practicum*, Lib XLVII, Tit. X, XX.

[158] Lauterbach, loc. cit. Cf. also Stryk, *Usus modernus pandectarum*, Lib. XLVII, Tit. X, § 6: "[p]rotestatio facto contraria est." On this legal proverb in general, see Arndt Teichmann, "Die protestatio facto contraria", in: *Festschrift für Karl Michaelis* (1972), pp. 294 sqq.; Helmut Köhler, "Kritik der Regel 'protestatio facto contraria non valet'", 1981 *Juristenzeitung* 464 sqq.

[159] Lauterbach, *Collegium theoretico-practicum*, Lib. XLVII, Tit. X, XXII.

[160] Cf., for example, Stryk, *Usus modernus pandectarum*, Lib. XLVII, Tit. X, § 14; cf. also the discussion by De Villiers, op. cit., note 113, pp. 111 sqq.; Bartels, op. cit., note 112, pp. 188 sqq.

[161] As Robert Feenstra (quoted by Ranchod, op. cit., note 90, pp. 66 sq.) believes.

[162] *Collegium theoretico-practicum*, Lib. XLVII, Tit. X, XXVI.

[163] For details, see Scott, op. cit., note 94, pp. 125 sq., 161 sqq.

[164] "Infamia enim vitae amissioni aequalis est, et oculorum privatione major habetur"(!): Lauterbach, *Collegium theoretico-practicum*, Lib. XLVII, Tit. X, XXXII.

[165] ". . . si modica vel levis injuria illata sit." Reason: "Praetor minima non curat, et propter rem minimam non detur actio famosa": Lauterbach, loc. cit. Generally on the distinction between iniuria atrox on the one hand and iniuria modica and levis on the other during the time of the usus modernus, see Herrmann, op. cit., note 99, pp. 59 sqq.; De Villiers, op. cit., note 113, pp. 153 sqq.; cf. also the case discussed by L. Roeleveld, 1981 *Acta Juridica* 157 sqq. South African criminal law still requires "seriousness" of the offence with regard to both the crimen iniuriae and the crime of defamation: J.R.L. Milton, *South African Criminal Law and Procedure*, vol. II (2nd ed., 1982), pp. 528 sqq., 561 sqq.; Burchell, op. cit., note 105, pp. 325 sqq., but see, most recently, John van den Berg, "Is gravity really an element of crimen iniuria and criminal defamation in our law?", (1988) 51 *THRHR* 54 sqq.

year.[166] As in Roman law, the plaintiff was required to assess the amount at which he estimated the injury, but the judge was able to reduce the sum according to what he considered bonum et aequum.[167] The formula used by the plaintiff for that purpose, however, had a characteristically medieval–customary ring to it:[168] "*Wolte lieber 1 000 Thaler verlihren alss selbige* [sc.: iniuria] *ungeandet lassen*",[169] he would declare—I would rather lose a sum of 1 000 than suffer such iniuria. Whether the sum in which the defendant was ultimately condemned went to himself or to the poor was apparently up to the plaintiff to decide.[170]

(b) Criminal proceedings

Then there was, of course, the possibility of laying a criminal charge against the wrongdoer. Whether criminal and civil proceedings could be cumulated was disputed. Carpzov[171] and Voet[172] were prepared to allow cumulation, but a substantial number of authors argued against it; both actions, the latter argued, were "mere poenalis", and the wrongdoer should not be punished twice on account of one and the same crime.[173]

---

[166] Prescription effectively terminated the possibility of bringing the actio iniuriarum ("Tollitur praescriptione": Lauterbach, *Collegium theoretico-practicum*, Lib. XLVII, Tit. X, XXXVII; "[C]essat . . . injuriarum persecutio": Voet, *Commentarius ad Pandectas*, Lib. XLVII, Tit. X, XIX). Dissimulatio was another, very interesting way of putting an end to the right to sue. It dates back to Roman law (Ulp. D. 47, 10, 11, 1: "Iniuriarum actio ex bono et aequo est et dissimulatione aboletur. si quis enim iniuriam dereliquerit, hoc est statim passus ad animum suum non revocaverit, postea ex paenitentia remissam iniuriam non poterit recolere"; if someone at first ignores the affront, he cannot later change his mind and seek to recover) and was much discussed by the writers of the ius commune (often sub voce tacita remissio). On account of which circumstances could it be inferred that someone had not taken the insult to heart and therefore waived the matter? "[E]x. gr. cum injuriante pristina familiaritate sponte utendo, amice salutando, osculo amplectando, conversando"; likewise the drinking out of one cup (which the Germans of old considered to be the most effectual token of friendship: Grotius, *Inleiding*, III, XXXV, 3). Merely keeping up the normal proprieties ("ut communis salutatio in publico, propinatio in convivio") did not imply a remissio tacita. Nor, incidentally, did the act of going to confession to the pastor by whom one had been insulted, "quia hic tantum consideratur ut Vicarius Dei, et principaliter agitur inter Deum et peccatorem" (all quotations from Lauterbach, *Collegium theoretico-practicum*, Lib. XLVII, Tit. X, XXXVI). Cf. also Ranchod, op. cit., note 90, pp. 55 sq. 89; De Villiers, op. cit., note 113, pp. 187 sqq.

[167] For details cf., for example, Voet, *Commentarius ad Pandectas*, Lib. XLVII, Tit. X, XIII; Stryk, *Usus modernus pandectarum*, Lib. XLVII, Tit. X, §§ 17 sqq. (distinguishing between Saxony and other territories).

[168] Kaufmann, (1961) 78 *ZSS* (GA) 98 sq.

[169] Lauterbach, *Collegium theoretico-practicum*, Lib. XLVII, Tit. X, XXX.

[170] Voet, *Commentarius ad Pandectas*, Lib. XLVII, Tit. X, XVII.

[171] Cf., for example, *Verhandeling der lyfstraffelyke misdaaden* (trans. van Hogendorp) (Amsterdam, 1772), 87. Hoofstuk, XV sqq.

[172] *Commentarius ad Pandectas*, Lib. XLVII, Tit. X, XXIV; cf. also De Villiers, op. cit., note 113, pp. 248 sqq.

[173] Cf., for example, Stryk, *Usus modernus pandectarum*, Lib. XLVII, Tit. X, § 21; Lauterbach, *Collegium theoretico-practicum*, Lib. XLVII, Tit. X, LV.

(c) Amende honorable

But the latest, and most interesting, addition to the arsenal of remedies was what came to be referred to (particularly in Roman-Dutch law) as amende honorable.[174] Essentially, it constituted an amalgam of three originally distinct institutions. First of all, there was the declaratio honoris: a formal declaration, on the part of the offender, that he had made his allegation in heat and without any intention to defame the other. It had its roots in Germanic customary law.[175] Furthermore, there was the notion of recantatio, revocatio or palinodia: the retraction of the defamatory words as being untrue. It had the effect of repairing the injured person's honour and derived from medieval canon law.[176] The Church, of course, had jurisdiction over defamation matters ratione peccati, and one of the fundamental prerequisites for the remission of sins in general was restitution: "peccatum non dimittitur, nisi restituatur ablatum."[177] It was the famous Dominican scholar Albertus Magnus who applied this principle to the sin of defamation, since he argued that restitution of fama was possible:

> "[I]d quod possidetur, invitissime amittitur: fama autem carius possidetur, quam aurum et argentum, ergo invitissime amittitur; ergo videtur quod maxime debet restitui."[178]

Based, ultimately, on fundamental precepts of iustitia distributiva,[179] the idea of a remedy concerned with restitutio laesae famae commended itself to secular courts and writers and was generally recognized as being moribus recepta.[180]

Finally, we encounter the concept of a deprecatio Christiana: an acknowledgement by the person who had committed the iniuria that he had done wrong, combined with a prayer that he may be forgiven. It is obvious that this institution, too, had its origin in the teachings of the Christian Church. As God forgives us, so we are bound to forgive

---

[174] An "extraordinarium remedium", in the terminology of Lauterbach. The challenge to a duel was another "extraordinary" remedy recognized at least by some ("Aliud extraordinarium remedium re vincendae injuriae quidam ponunt in provocatione ad duellum ex proverb. *Auf eine Lüge gehört eine Maultasche oder Dolch*"). Lauterbach's comment (*Collegium theoretico-practicum*, Lib. XLVII, Tit. X, LXV): "Verum abominandum hoc et omni jure prohibitum esse nemo Christianorum inficias ibis, cum provocantes gravissime peccent in Deum Magistratum, cui ultionis munus demandandum est, et proximum, cujus corpori et animae struere conantur, et dum putativam temporalem ignominiam evitare satagunt, periculum aeternae infamiae atque exitii incurrunt, sive vincant, sive vincantur."

[175] For details, see C. von Wallenrodt, "Die Injurienklage auf Abbitte, Widerruf und Ehrenerklärung in ihrer Entstehung, Fortbildung und ihrem Verfall", (1864) 3 *Zeitschrift für Rechtsgeschichte* 243 sqq.

[176] For details, see Wallenrodt, (1864) 3 *Zeitschrift für Rechtsgeschichte* 255 sqq.; Udo Wolter, *Das Prinzip der Naturalrestitution in § 249 BGB* (1985), pp. 72 sq. Interesting historical examples of recantationes are provided by Leyser, *Meditationes ad Pandectas*, Spec. DXLIII, I.

[177] Cf. supra, pp. 824 sq., note 283.

[178] Cf. Wallenrodt, (1864) 3 *Zeitschrift für Rechtsgeschichte* 261.

[179] Cf. supra, p. 824, note 283.

[180] For a detailed list of the ways in which reparatio iniuriarum could be effected, see Van Damhouder, *Praxis rerum criminalium*, Cap. CXXXVI, 11.

those who trespass against us; but the trespasser, in turn, must repent before a true reconciliation can take place:

> "Si quis rixam faciat de clericis aut ministris Dei, hebdomadam dierum poeniteat . . . et petat veniam a Deo et proximo suo plena confessione et humilitate, et sic potest Deo reconciliare et proximo suo."[181]

Of these three constituent elements of the amende honorable, the actio ad palinodiam emerged as the dominant ingredient in the course of the late ius commune.[182] How exactly it related to the other two was unclear. According to Stryk,[183] the declaratio honoris was applicable "quando dubium est, an verba sit injuriosa, et contumeliosa, nec in proferente animus injuriandi liquido apparet", the deprecatio Christiana, by and large, in cases of slighter injuries ("quando alter alteri aliquid imputavit quod crimen magnum non importat, aut si eo modo fit improperatio, ut adsit quaedam injuriantis excusatio, vel levior honoris laesio, vel etiam, si injuriae quidem leves non sunt, injurians tamen et injuriatus ejusdem est conditionis, status atque dignitatis"), and the palinodia "quando injuria illata admodum atrox, quae famam honesti viri gravissime violat".

(d) The relation between amende honorable and amende profitable

Controversial, too, was the question whether amende honorable and actio iniuriarum aestimatoria (or, as it was often called, amende profitable) could be cumulated. Since it was obvious that the amende profitable was mere poenalis,[184] the answer depended, in the first place, on the proper qualification of the amende honorable. If it was mere reipersecutoria, the two remedies could be cumulated, but if it also had a penal character, a regime of elective concurrence was bound to be the consequence. In view of the fact that palinodia originally aimed at reparation of the injured party's honour, it is not surprising that the first alternative was favoured by many; particularly in Holland the custom appears to have prevailed to institute an action for honourable and profitable amends at one and the same time.[185] But the second alternative also found its champions. Thus it was argued that the main

---

[181] *Poenitentiale Viviani*, as quoted by Wallenrodt, (1864) 3 *Zeitschrift für Rechtsgeschichte* 265.

[182] Cf., for example, the discussion by Lauterbach, *Collegium theoretico-practicum*, Lib. XLVII, Tit. X, XLVII sqq.

[183] *Usus modernus pandectarum*, Lib. XLVII, Tit. X, § 30; cf. also Wolter, op. cit., note 176, p. 73. Leyser, *Meditationes ad Pandectas*, Spec. DXLIII, I states that there are no rules specifying which remedy is available when, "sed ex arbitrio judicis pendet".

[184] Cf. supra, p. 1070 (note 162).

[185] Voet, *Commentarius ad Pandectas*, Lib. LXVII, Tit. X, XVII; cf. also Ranchod, op. cit., note 90, p. 66; De Villiers, op. cit., note 113, p. 179.

function of insisting on recantation was to hurt one's opponent[186]—an opinion that found some support in the fact that the circumstances under which the latter was made to repent were often of a somewhat humiliating nature: he had to fall on his knees, appear bare-footed, slap himself on his mouth, or even suffer the sombre presence of a hangman.[187]

IV. DEFAMATION IN ENGLISH LAW

1. Technicalities beyond belief

It may be apparent by now that the history of the delict of iniuria is a rather complex matter—according to one modern commentator, one of the most complex in the history of private law.[188] In South Africa, the issue has been further confounded by a partial, though in some respects only temporary, reception of English law, that occurred in a particularly prominent province within the broad field of iniuria—the law of defamation, which aims, specifically at the protection of a person's reputation or good name.[189] The English law of defamation, in turn, can hardly be credited with the virtues of clarity and simplicity either. It is, in fact, an exceptionally messy branch of the common law, full of curious niceties, of artificial and irrational distinctions, and of "technicalities beyond belief".[190] Thus, for instance, a person defamed in a letter which only one other person (the addressee) ever reads may claim damages without proof of loss of any kind; yet, if someone is insulted in front of a huge audience (though "merely" orally), he can bring an action only if either a serious crime or a contagious disease has been imputed to him, or if he can prove that he has suffered pecuniary damages.[191] This is due to the fact that English law draws a fundamental distinction between libel and slander as two different forms of defamation.

2. Libel and slander

Libel, essentially, is defamation litteris, the English equivalent of the civilian libellus famosus: any publication of defamatory matter in permanent form. Slander (deriving etymologically from the word

---

[186] Cf. Wallenrodt, (1864) 3 *Zeitschrift für Rechtsgeschichte* 297; cf. also the discussion by Stryk, *Usus modernus pandectarum*, Lib. XLVII, Tit. X, § 28; Van Damhouder, *Praxis rerum criminalium*, Cap. CXXXVI, 11, who, when referring to reparatio iniuriarum, remarks "qua iniuriantes puniendos esse diximus".

[187] Wallenrodt, (1864) 3 *Zeitschrift für Rechtsgeschichte* 296; De Villiers, op. cit., note 113, p. 178.

[188] R. Lieberwirth, in: *HRG*, vol. I, col. 358.

[189] Cf., for instance, *Martens v. Short* (1919) 40 NLR 193 at 194: "There is no branch of the law so uncertain, and therefore so unscientific, as that of defamation" (per Tatham J).

[190] Cf. the chapter title in Lord Denning, *What Next in the Law* (1982), p. 179.

[191] Zweigert/Kötz, p. 454.

"scandalum")[192] is a form of iniuria re aut verbis: an attack on somebody else's reputation that is communicated by word of mouth or in some other transitory form—such as insulting noises or derisory gestures.[193] The common-law delict of slander originated in the early 16th century, and it evolved around an action "on the case". Averment of damages was therefore essential.[194] Thus, it was not actionable to call an unmarried woman a whore if she was not engaged in trade or could not show loss of a marriage.[195] The tort of libel was younger.[196] With the invention of printing, the production of libelli famosi had taken on a new dimension and was considered to entail dangers for the King's Peace.[197] Thus, the notorious Star

---

[192] A.K.R. Kiralfy, *The Action on the Case* (1951), p. 118.

[193] The distinction between libel and slander ("the result, less of conscious policy than of a series of historical accidents": John G. Fleming, *Torts*, p. 517; cf. also J.M. Kaye, "Libel and Slander—Two Torts or One?", (1975) 91 *LQR* 539: "Lassitude, not policy or reason, brought the distinction between libel and slander to its finished state") is generally severely criticized; cf., for instance, Fleming, *Torts*, p. 517 (". . . absurd in theory and very often mischievous in its practical operation"); *Gatley on Libel and Slander* (8th ed., 1981), nn. 141, 145. For satirical comments cf. the fictitious case reports of *Chicken v. Ham* and *Temper v. Hume and Haddock*, in: A.P. Herbert, *Uncommon Law* (1969), pp. 71 sqq.; idem, *Codd's Last Case and Other Misleading Cases* (1952), pp. 125 sqq.

[194] Holdsworth, *History*, vol. VIII, pp. 363, 367; *Potter's Historical Introduction to English Law* (4th ed., 1958), p. 436. On the relation between damage and action on the case, cf. also Simpson, *History*, pp. 580 sqq. One type of slander was, however, held to be actionable without proof of damage: the imputation of a crime triable at common-law ("slander per se"). This was the first inroad the common law courts were able to break into the comprehensive jurisdiction of the ecclesiastical courts (ratione peccati) over defamation matters. In all other cases, it was the averment of (temporal) damages that became the decisive factor in justifying a temporal remedy and that therefore allowed the common-law courts to assert their jurisdiction against their ecclesiastical rivals. The first case appears to have been *Davis v. Gardiner* (1593) 4 Co Rep 16 b (the imputation being that a woman had a bastard child; as a result of this scandalous (slanderous) statement, the woman suffered special damage in the form of loss of marriage; Plucknett, *History*, p. 494).

[195] Cf. Potter, op. cit., note 194, p. 435.

[196] Generally on the history of libel and slander, cf. the magisterial work of Holdsworth, *History*, vol. VIII, pp. 333 sqq.; cf. also V.V. Veeder, "The History of the Law of Defamation", in: *Select Essays in Anglo-American Legal History*, vol. III (1909), pp. 446 sqq.; C.H.S. *Fifoot, History and Sources of the Common Law* (1949), pp. 126 sqq.; Plucknett, *History*, pp. 483 sqq.; Potter op. cit., note 194, pp. 429 sqq.; Kaye, (1975) 81 *LQR* 524 sqq. On the history of libel, cf. also Denning, op. cit., note 190, pp. 163 sqq. The influence of the civilian delict of iniuria on the development of the English law of defamation and the historical interaction between civil law and common law have, to date, received hardly any attention; cf., however, Heinz Hübner, "Defamation, Privacy", in: Helmut Coing, Knut Wolfgang Nörr, *Englische und kontinentale Rechtsgeschichte: ein Forschungsprojekt* (1985), pp. 72 sqq. The most obvious point of contact is the canon law which has, through the jurisdiction of the ecclesiastical courts, greatly influenced the development in England. As late as 1497 Fineux CJ declared defamation to be "entirely a spiritual offence" (cf. Potter, op. cit., note 194, p. 431).

[197] Cf., for instance, William Blackstone, *Commentaries*, Book IV, Ch. XI, 13: ". . . [they] are malicious defamations of any person, and especially a magistrate, made public by either printing, writing, signs or pictures, in order to provoke him to wrath, or expose him to public hatred, contempt and ridicule. The direct tendency of these libels is the breach of the public peace, by stirring up the objects of them to revenge, and perhaps to bloodshed. . . . [B]lasphemous, immoral, treasonable, schismatical, seditious, or scandalous libels are punished by the English law, some with a greater, others with a less degree of severity."

Chamber[198] assumed (an essentially criminal) jurisdiction over the matter and imposed penalties such as fines, pillory, branding or loss of ears. The Long Parliament abolished the Star Chamber in 1641, but the notion that libel constituted a grave offence tending "to the breaking of the peace and great mischief"[199] lingered on. When the common-law courts therefore developed the doctrine of civil libel, they considered it to be in the nature of trespass (rather than case), and consequently not to require the averment of damages.[200] This was established in the 1670 case of *King v. Lake*, where Sir Matthew Hale allowed the plaintiff to sue on account of certain insulting allegations which, if spoken, would not have been actionable without proof of damage; "yet here", Hale CB continued, "they were being writ and published, which contains more malice than if they had been spoken".[201]

3. Common elements

On the other hand, however, libel and slander have much in common.[202] In both cases, a defamatory imputation is required—that is, an imputation which may tend "to lower the plaintiff in the estimation of right-thinking members of society generally"[203] or "to expose him to hatred, contempt or ridicule".[204] Furthermore, the element of publication is essential for both forms of defamation: the defamatory matter must have been communicated to somebody other than the person who is the subject of the defamatory imputation.[205] Thus it is obvious that the interest protected is only man's estimation in the eyes of others—his reputation—and not his dignity or self-esteem. If this constitutes a significant deviation from civilian contumely iniuria,[206] another feature common to libel and slander is even more

---

[198] The Court of the Star Chamber was a conciliar court, namely the Privy Council sitting in the Star Chamber (*camera stellata*, so called from the gilded stars on the roof); on its jurisdiction in general, see Holdsworth, *History*, vol. V, pp. 155 sqq.

[199] Lord Coke, as quoted by Denning, op. cit., note 190, p. 163.

[200] Holdsworth, *History*, vol. VIII, pp. 363 sq.

[201] A.K.R. Kiralfy, *A Source Book of English Law* (1957), p. 163. For a different interpretation of this case, see Kaye, (1975) 91 LQR 531 sqq. In any event, the matter was finally settled in *Thorley v. Lord Kerry*, in: Fifoot, op. cit., note 196, pp. 149 sqq.

[202] As appears already from the way in which the discussion of the law of defamation is arranged in books such as Fleming, *Torts*, pp. 500 sqq., 518; *Winfield and Jolowicz on Tort* (12th ed., 1984), pp. 293 sqq. or *Gatley on Libel and Slander*, note 193.

[203] *Sim v. Stretch* (1936) 52 TLR 669 at 671 (per Lord Atkin).

[204] *Parmiter v. Coupland* (1840) 6 M & W 105 at 108 (per Parke B).

[205] For all details, see Gatley, op. cit., note 193, nn. 221 sqq.

[206] Cf., for instance, F.G. Gardiner, "Is Publication Essential to an Action for Defamation", (1897) 14 *Cape LJ* 184 sqq; T.W. Price, "Animus Injuriandi in Defamation", (1949) 66 *SALJ* 6; *Die Spoorbond v. South African Railways, Van Heerden v. South African Railways* 1946 AD 999 at 1010; *African Life Assurance Society Ltd. v. Robinson & Co. Ltd. and Central News Agency Ltd.* 1938 NPD 277 at 295 sqq.; cf. also Voet, *Commentarius ad Pandectas*, Lib. XLVII, Tit. X, I ("vel dignitas") and De Villiers, op. cit., note 113, pp. 90, 132; Grotius, *Inleiding*, III, XXXV, 2 (". . . in 't heimelick ofte in 't openbaer"). The reason for this difference between common law and civil law lies in the fact that in England the emphasis is on reputation (which can be impaired only by publication of defamatory matter),

startling from a continental point of view. It relates to the subjective side of the notion of defamation—or perhaps rather the lack of it.

Sir Matthew Hale's words in *King v. Lake* appear to suggest that the defamatory statement should have occurred with malice in order to be actionable. In fact it seems to have been necessary for the plaintiff to allege that the defendant had acted "falsely and maliciously". But this clause increasingly degenerated into a mere form of pleading, devoid of any substantive import.[207] Eventually it was laid down that actual malice was unnecessary to support an action in defamation.[208] It does not even matter whether the defendant intended to injure the plaintiff's reputation:

> "A person charged with libel cannot defend himself by showing that he intended in his own breast not to defame, or that he intended not to defame the plaintiff, if in fact he did both."[209]

This statement is taken from the most famous (or perhaps most infamous) case in the law of libel, the landmark at which, according to Lord Denning,[210] the law took a wrong turning.

4. "Animus iniuriandi" and Artemus Jones

The Paris correspondent of the *Sunday Chronicle* had written an article in which he commented on the miraculous change of behaviour of the average English holiday-maker when going abroad. Mention was made of a certain Artemus Jones whom, "by his goings on", one would never have expected to be a churchwarden at Peckham:

> "No one, indeed, would assume that Jones in the atmosphere of London would take on so austere a job. . . . Here, in the atmosphere of Dieppe, on the French side of the Channel, he is the life and soul of a gay little band that haunts the Casino and turns night into day, besides betraying a most unholy delight in the society of female butterflies."

Of course, the correspondent had used Artemus Jones as a purely fictitious character and he had no intention of referring to a specific person of that name. A real Artemus Jones happened to exist, however. He spent his life as a barrister on the North Wales Circuit—"rarely going to London and never to Peckham".[211] But since he could show that his acquaintances had identified him with the hero of the article, he was allowed to claim no less than £1 750 in damages.

Thus, under the English common law, a person may well be liable for defamation, even if no blame attaches to him. He can escape liability

---

whereas in Roman law it was on outraged feelings (cf. also Buckland/McNair, p. 380). Not convincing, in this respect, is Burchell, op. cit., note 105, pp. 71 sq.

[207] Cf., for instance, Potter, op. cit., note 194, p. 437.

[208] *Bromage v. Prosser* (1825), in: Fifoot, op. cit., note 196, pp. 151 sqq.; Holdsworth, *History*, vol. VIII, pp. 374 sq.

[209] *E. Hulton & Co. v. Jones* [1910] AC 20 at 23 (per Lord Loreburn).

[210] Op. cit., note 190, p. 173.

[211] Denning, op. cit., note 190, p. 173.

only by proving that his allegation was true,[212] that it constituted a fair comment in the public interest[213] or that it was justified on account of either an "absolute" or "relative" privilege. Absolute privilege completely exempts from liability for defamation, but it covers only a very limited range of situations. The main examples are things said in court or parliament.[214] The scope of qualified privilege is much more extensive; it includes, for instance, statements made in the discharge of a public or private duty or on a subject-matter in which the defendant has a legitimate interest.[215] A qualified privilege is lost, however, upon proof that the defendant has abused the situation; and it is in this context that the requirement of malice becomes relevant. For while it may be in the public interest that a person should be allowed, under certain circumstances, to speak freely and to state openly whatever he knows or believes about another, the law still requires him to act honestly and without improper motive.[216] Qualified privilege thus covers a variety of situations where a statement is both defamatory and in fact untrue but has been made in good faith.

V. SOUTH AFRICAN USUS MODERNUS OF THE ACTIO INIURIARUM

1. The battle about animus iniuriandi

The English tort of defamation is thus, in many respects, distinctly different from the civilian delict of iniuria.[217] Yet there is also at least one very obvious structural similarity. In both systems, a (prima facie) defamatory imputation (no matter whether verbis or litteris) may give rise to a cause of action unless the person who has made the imputation is able to invoke one of a certain number of "defences" or "privileges". This basic similarity enabled South African courts and writers to graft many of the English rules of defamation onto the Roman-Dutch actio iniuriam that had originally been transplanted to the Cape.[218] The development followed the general pattern of South African legal history: in the course of the 19th century an ever-increasing tendency to find one's law in an English textbook or in English case reports rather than "to wade through a sea of Latin or to puzzle [one's] head over old

[212] On the defence of truth, see Gatley, op. cit., note 193, nn. 351 sqq.
[213] For all details, see Gatley, op. cit., note 193, nn. 691 sqq.
[214] Generally on absolute privilege, cf. Gatley, op. cit., note 193, nn. 381 sqq.
[215] For a detailed analysis, see Gatley, op. cit., note 193, nn. 441 sqq.
[216] The same applies in the case of "fair comment"; the plea is defeated if the plaintiff can show that the còmment was actuated by malice.
[217] For an overview, cf. Price, (1949) 66 *SALJ* 4 sqq; idem, "The Basis of the South African Law of Defamation", 1960 *Acta Juridica* 254 sqq.; Ranchod, op. cit., note 90, pp. 133 sqq.
[218] Cf., for example, Ranchod, op. cit., note 90, pp. 135 sqq. On the interaction of English and Roman-Dutch law in Ceylon, see Lalith W. Athulathmudali, "The Law of Defamation in Ceylon", (1964) 13 *International and Comparative Law Quarterly* 1368 sqq.

Dutch writers and black letter consultations",[219] then, from about the 1920s onwards, a strong backlash culminating in judicial attempts to return the oak tree of the specifically South African usus modernus to the Roman-Dutch acorn whence it sprang,[220] until ultimately some form of pragmatic compromise was reached and the hybrid nature of contemporary South African common law accepted.

In the case of defamation it was particularly the requirement of animus iniuriandi that became one of the major battlefields of the famous bellum iuridicum raging between the so-called pollutionists on the one side and the purists and antiquarians on the other.[221] Without animus iniuriandi no iniuria: this was the Roman-Dutch principle adopted at the Cape and taken for granted in leading decisions such as *Mackay v. Philip*.[222] Gradually, though, English terminology crept into the decisions of the courts and, most notably, the term "malice" began to be used by Lord De Villiers[223] and others in place of animus iniuriandi.[224] Sooner or later, the "contagion"[225] was bound to spread, the new terminological germ bound to infect the thinking on substantive law. Thus it was held, in a variety of decisions, that the defendant in a defamation suit is confined to pleading certain set defences. The mere absence of any intention to insult was no longer of avail to him.[226] Animus iniuriandi thus having been reduced to a hollow fiction,[227] it had ceased to be an essential element of defamation. Only in 1960 was it reinstated in its former splendour. The decisive turning point was *Maisel v. Van Naeren*, where De Villiers AJ reaffirmed that

> "[i]n Roman-Dutch law defamation is a species of injuria, and a claim for general damages for defamation is merely an instance of amende profitable being claimed under the actio injuriarum. Inasmuch as dolus, or animus injuriandi as it is called in relation to injuriae, is an essential for liability under the actio injuriarum, it is likewise an essential for liability for defamation".[228]

---

[219] Sir John Wessels, "The Future of Roman-Dutch Law in South Africa", (1920) 37 *SALJ* 276.

[220] Cf. the eleganter dictum by Holmes J, in: *Ex parte Winnaar* 1959 (1) SA 837 (N) 839 ("The original sources of the Roman-Dutch law are important; but exclusive preoccupation with them is like trying to return an oak tree to its acorn"); cf. also P.Q.R. Boberg, "Oak Tree or Acorn?—Conflicting Approaches to Our Law of Delict", (1966) 83 *SALJ* 150 sqq.

[221] Cf. supra, p. 557, note 73; p. 805.

[222] (1830) 1 Menz 455.

[223] Chief Justice of the Cape of Good Hope (and later of the Union of South Africa) from 1877 to 1914. The standard biography is Eric A. Walker, *Lord de Villiers and His Times* (1925).

[224] Cf., inter alia, *Botha v. Brink* (1878) 8 Buch 118 at 123, 128 and 130.

[225] Price, (1949) 66 *SALJ* 17.

[226] *Jooste v. Claassens* 1916 TPD 723 at 732; *Laloe Janoe v. Bronkhorst* 1918 TPD 165 at 168; *Tothill v. Foster* 1925 TPD 857 at 862 sq.; *Kleinhans v. Usmar* 1929 AD 121 at 126.

[227] McKerron, "Fact and Fiction in the Law of Defamation", (1931) 48 *SALJ* 154 (172).

[228] 1960 (4) SA 836 (C) at 840C–D.

This view has been repeatedly endorsed by the Appellate Division of the Supreme Court,[229] and as a result, the defendant is, once again, free today to rebut the presumption of animus injuriandi in whatever way he chooses. Of course, he can avail himself of any of the "stereotyped defences", but they have lost their status of exclusiveness.[230]

2. Compromise solutions

As far as the theoretical basis of the delict of iniuria is concerned, the pendulum has therefore swung between the two extremes: from dolus to strict liability and back again to dolus. Would it not have been sensible to arrest it somewhere in the middle and base liability (as under the Aquilian action) on negligence? This suggestion has indeed been made repeatedly,[231] but it has so far failed to gain decisive judicial support.[232] The courts, in turn, have in the meantime settled for a different kind of compromise solution: while generally emphasizing the requirement of animus iniuriandi, they have made a very significant exception in the case of defamatory reports by the newspapers, by radio and by television. The dictates of public policy, according to Rumpff CJ,[233] require the protection of the ordinary citizen against the powerful media with their potential for injuring his reputation in a situation where it may be difficult to pinpoint animus iniuriandi; and in order to provide this protection the principle of strict liability has therefore, at least partially, been retained.

3. A hybrid law of defamation

But strict liability of the press is not the only strand from the English common law that remains woven into the fabric of the modern South African law of defamation. What has emerged, over the years, is a truly hybrid system that has emancipated itself from its Roman-Dutch and English roots and has, instead, acquired a distinctive flavour of its own. Essentially, it is still the civilian actio iniuriarum that forms the basis of the law of defamation, and the gist of it[234] is, as a rule, the animus iniuriandi. Courts and legal writers have for some time toyed with the

[229] See especially *Jordaan v. Van Biljon* 1962 (1) SA 286 (A); *Craig v. Voortrekkerpers Bpk.* 1963 (1) SA 149 (A); *Nydoo v. Vengtas* 1965 (1) SA 1 (A).

[230] For an analysis and critical evaluation of the position today, see Burchell, op. cit., note 105, pp. 149 sqq.

[231] *Hassen v. Post Newspapers (Pty.) Ltd.* 1965 (3) SA 562 (W); *Suttonmere (Pty.) Ltd. v. Hills* 1982 (2) SA 74 (N) at 79A–B; P.J. Visser, "Nalatige krenking van die reg op fama", (1982) 45 *THRHR* 168 sqq; Burchell, op. cit., note 105, p. 168.

[232] Cf., in particular, *Suid-Afrikaanse Uitsaaikorporasie v. O'Malley* 1977 (3) SA 394 (A) at 407A–D.

[233] *Suid-Afrikaanse Uitsaaikorporasie v. O'Malley*, 1977 (3) SA 394 (A) at 404 sq. (obiter); *Pakendorf v. De Flamingh* 1982 (3) SA 146 (A) at 156C. For further discussion, see Burchell, op. cit., note 105, pp. 181 sqq.

[234] Cf. the phrase used by Schreiner JA in *Basner v. Trigger* 1946 AD 83 at 94.

idea of a distinction, in principle, between libel and slander,[235] but their view has failed to make an impact. Truth alone is not a defence in South African law; as in Roman-Dutch law, the additional requirement of the public benefit must be satisfied.[236] On the other hand, however, English case law and writers continue to be cited by the South African courts.[237] The test for determining what constitutes defamatory matter[238] and the defence of fair comment[239] are English in origin, and so is the element of "publication" required for the modern South African version of iniuria.[240] Many details relating to the stereotyped or crystallized defences have been taken over from English law,[241] together with the term "privilege" or "privileged occasion"[242] and the distinction between an absolute and a qualified (or provisional) privilege.[243] The further systematic division into defences rebutting the inference of unlawfulness (justification grounds) and those relating to the element of fault (that is: excluding the presence of animus iniuriandi)[244] is, however, of civilian (though not specifically Roman-Dutch)[245] provenance.

4. The concept of iniuria

Yet ultimately, and perhaps most importantly, it is still the civilian concept of iniuria that determines the scope and range of application of the actio iniuriarum. Protection of a person's reputation has always been a particularly important objective of that remedy.[246] But neither in

---

[235] Cf., for instance, Manfred Nathan, *The South African Law of Torts*, 1921, pp. 98 sqq. On the distinction between verbal and literal injuries by Voet, see De Villiers, op. cit., note 113, pp. 105 sqq.

[236] For the details, see Chittharanjan Felix Amerasinghe, *Defamation and other aspects of the actio iniuriarum in Roman-Dutch Law* (1968), pp. 82 sqq.; Burchell, op. cit., note 105, pp. 206 sqq.

[237] Cf., for instance, Ben Beinart, "The English Legal Contribution in South Africa: The Interaction of Civil and Common Law", 1981 *Acta Juridica* 58.

[238] See Amerasinghe, op. cit., note 236, pp. 9 sqq., 19 sqq.; Burchell, op. cit., note 105, pp. 95 sqq.

[239] Cf. *Crawford v. Albu* 1917 AD 102 at 113 sq.; *Marais v. Richard* 1981 (1) SA 1157 (A) at 1166E–F; for details, see Amerasinghe, op. cit., note 236, pp. 144 sqq.; Burchell, op. cit., note 105, pp. 219 sqq.

[240] Amerasinghe, op. cit., note 236, pp. 55 sqq.; Burchell, op. cit., note 105, pp. 67 sqq.

[241] For example: the notion of malice as a means to defeat the defence of privilege; cf. *Basner v. Trigger* 1946 AD 83 at 94 sq.; *May v. Udwin* 1981 (1) SA 1 (A) at 14H sqq.; Burchell, op. cit., note 105, pp. 249 sq.

[242] Cf., for example, *Maisel v. Van Naeren* 1960 (4) SA 836 (C) at 841B.

[243] For details, see Amerasinghe, op. cit., note 236, pp. 93 sqq.; P.R. MacMillan, "Animus iniuriandi and privilege", (1975) 92 *SALJ* 144 sqq.; Burchell, op. cit., note 105, pp. 237 sqq.

[244] Cf., for example, Burchell, op. cit., note 105, p. 205; as far as judicial privilege is concerned, cf. the detailed analysis of Roman and Roman-Dutch authorities by Joubert JA in *May v. Udwin* 1981 (1) SA 1 (A).

[245] The Roman-Dutch writers did not yet draw a clear-cut distinction between unlawfulness and fault; cf., for example, supra, p. 1028, note 199.

[246] For Roman law cf., for example, Neethling, op. cit., note 113, pp. 51 sqq., who attempts to analyse the provisions of the praetorian edict in terms of the individual interest protected.

Roman law nor in the tradition of the ius commune down to the days of the Roman-Dutch authorities[247] was contumelia iniuria synonymous with defamation. Fama, it will be remembered,[248] was only one of the objects of legal protection mentioned by Johannes Voet; corpus and dignitas were also included. Other authors referred to pudicitia, honor or existimatio;[249] and while it is difficult to unravel the precise meaning in which the individual terms were used,[250] it is obvious that the delict of iniuria did not necessarily imply a lowering of the individual's esteem in the eyes of others. It covered a whole variety of situations of which the common denominator was an intentional disregard for another person's personality.[251] Unlike the English common law which is still essentially confined to the traditional number of specific torts,[252] South African law thus had at its disposal an instrument that could be adjusted suitably to cope with the problem of the ever-increasing potential for intrusions upon a person's sphere of privacy. "Of the desirability—indeed of the necessity—of (affording) some . . . protection", wrote Warren and Brandeis in a famous article,[253]

> "there can . . . be no doubt. The press is overstepping in every direction the obvious bounds of propriety and decency. Gossip is no longer a resource of the idle and the vicious, but has become a trade, which is pursued with industry as well as effrontery. . . . The intensity and complexity of life, attending upon advancing civilization, have rendered necessary some retreat from the world, and man, under the refining influence of culture, has become more sensitive to publicity, so that solitude and privacy have become more essential to the individual; but modern

---

[247] In the later German usus modernus there appears to have been a tendency to restrict the scope of protection of the actio iniuriarum; for details, see Mainzer, op. cit., note 103, pp. 81 sqq.; Bartels, op. cit., note 112, pp. 52 sqq.; Herrmann, op. cit., note 99, pp. 51 sqq.

[248] Cf. supra, p. 1064, note 113.

[249] Cf., for instance, the analyses by Bartels, op. cit., note 112, pp. 52 sqq.; Herrmann, op. cit., note 99, pp. 51 sqq. and Neethling, op. cit., note 113, pp. 58 sqq.

[250] The most enigmatic of them is "dignitas". According to De Villiers, op. cit., note 113, p. 24, it meant "that valued and serene condition in [a person's] social or individual life which is violated when he is, either publicly or privately, subjected by another to abusive and degrading treatment, or when he is exposed to ill-will, ridicule, disesteem or contempt". De Villiers appends a footnote in which he declares that the word "dignity" must be understood in a wide sense. "Injuries against dignity evidently comprise all those injuries which are not aggressions upon either the person or the reputation." Cf. also Neethling, op. cit., note 113, p. 58.

[251] As had been the position in Roman law; cf. supra, p. 1059 (note 82).

[252] Traditionally, therefore, intrusions into a person's privacy have to be squeezed into one of the established torts, particularly defamation. For an overview, see Zweigert/Kötz, pp. 459 sqq.; but see now David J. Seipp, "English Judicial Recognition of a Right to Privacy", (1982) 3 *Oxford Journal of Legal Studies* 325 sqq. A similar approach appears to have been on its way in South African law; attention was focused very largely on defamation which was usually dealt with as a specific wrong in its own right. Iniuria at large remained, for a long time, in its shade and constituted a somewhat awkward collection of individual cases that did not fit into any of the normal "pigeon-holes". Cf. still, for example, the discussion by R.G. McKerron, *The Law of Delict* (6th ed., 1965), pp. 51 sqq., 160 sqq.

[253] "The Right to Privacy", (1890) 4 *Harvard LR* 193; according to a book entitled *Landmarks of Law* (referred to by Zweigert/Kötz, p. 457), "certainly the most influential law review article ever written".

enterprise and invention have, through invasions upon his privacy, subjected him to mental pain and distress, far greater than could be inflicted by mere bodily harm."

Modern advertising methods contain similar dangers for the interests of private individuals, and so do, for example, computerized information networks or modern technological devices allowing the tapping of private telephone conversations. In America these arguments have ultimately prompted the courts to recognize a general "right of privacy".[254] For South Africa, on the other hand, the solution lay in the recognition of specific rights of personality on the basis, and within the confines, of the concept of iniuria. Innes CJ gave the decisive hint when he defined iniuria, as early as 1908, as

> "a wrongful act designedly done in contempt of another, which infringes his dignity, his person or his reputation. If we look at the essentials of injuria we find . . . that they are three. The act complained of must be wrongful; it must be intentional; and it must violate one or other of those real rights, those rights in rem, related to personality, which every free man is entitled to enjoy."[255]

It took another 45 years, however, before the implications of this approach were fully grasped and the first systematic exposition of the doctrine of the rights of personality was undertaken.[256]

5. Corpus, dignitas and fama

Subsequently a whole variety of personality rights were identified and they are more and more frequently seen today as forming a distinctive group of subjective rights.[257] The starting point is still Voet's[258] well-known triad of legal interests protected by the delict of iniuria:

---

[254] For an overview, cf. Zweigert/Kötz, pp. 457 sqq. or McQuoid-Mason, op. cit., note 78, pp. 35 sqq.

[255] *R v. Umfaan* 1908 TS 62 at 66; Cf. also *Whittaker v. Roos and Bateman*; *Morant v. Roos and Bateman* 1912 AD 92 at 122.

[256] W.A. Joubert, *Grondslae van die Persoonlikheidsreg* (1953), pp. 115 sqq. and passim. Joubert's views have been inspired by Carl Gareis (cf. e.g. "Das juristische Wesen der Autorrechte" (1877) 35 *Archiv für Theorie und Praxis des Allgemeinen Deutschen Handels- und Wechselrechts* 185 sqq.), Otto von Gierke (*Deutsches Privatrecht*, vol. I (1895), pp. 702 sqq.) and Josef Kohler (cf. e.g. "Das Autorrecht", (1880) 18 *JhJb* 129 sqq., 329 sqq.). On their contributions to the idea of a general right of personality, see (apart from Joubert) Robert Scheyhing, "Zur Geschichte des Persönlichkeitsrechts im 19. Jahrhundert", (1959–60) 158 *Archiv für die civilistische Praxis* 521 sqq.; Diethelm Klippel, "Historische Wurzeln und Funktionen von Immaterialgüter- und Persönlichkeitsrechten im 19. Jahrhundert", 1982 *ZNR* 132 sqq., 144 sqq.; Eberhard Klingenberg, "Vom persönlichen Recht zum Persönlichkeitsrecht", (1979) 96 *ZSS* (GA) 203 sqq.; Dieter Leuze, *Die Entwicklung des Persönlichkeitsrechts im 19. Jahrhundert* (1962), pp. 93 sqq., 103 sqq., 111 sqq.; Neethling, op. cit., note 113, pp. 5 sqq.; Helmut Coing, "Die Entwicklung der Persönlichkeitsrechte im 19. Jahrhundert", in: *Festschrift für Werner Maihofer* (1988), pp. 78 sqq. On the protection of personality rights in 19th-century German legal practice, cf. Karl Irmscher, *Der privatrechtliche Schultz der Persönlichkeit in der Praxis des gemeinen und der partikularen Rechte des 19. Jahrhunderts* (unpublished Dr. iur. thesis, Frankfurt/Main, 1953), passim.

[257] Cf., in particular, Neethling, op. cit., note 113, pp. 1 sqq. and passim; *Universiteit van Pretoria v. Tommie Meyer Films (Edms.) Bpk.* 1977 (4) SA 376 (T) at 381D sqq. As far as crimen iniuriae is concerned, see De Wet en Swanepoel, *Strafreg* (4th ed., 1985), pp. 250 sqq.

[258] Ultimately Ulpian's: D. 47, 10, 1, 2.

corpus, dignitas and fama.[259] Fama leads us straight into the law of defamation. As far as the right to corpus is concerned, South African courts and legal writers usually distinguish between infringement of a person's physical (or bodily) integrity and interference with his personal liberty.[260] Determination of the meaning of the term "dignitas" has proved to be more difficult. Yet it is widely accepted today that it should not be strictly limited to dignity or honour, but should rather be seen as a general clause, or nomen collectivum, comprising all rights of personality not yet specifically identified and delimited in the sources of the (Roman-Dutch) common law: everything, that is, except the rights to corpus and fama.[261] It is within this broad framework that the protection of dignity and honour finds its place; so do the protection of a person's right to his feelings of piety or chastity, of his right of identity and, most importantly, his right to privacy.[262] Infringement of the right to privacy, in particular, has been recognized by South African courts on various occasions as a "dignitary wrong" in the broad sense of the word.[263] As in *all* other cases of iniuria, the action lies for sentimental damages,[264] but animus iniuriandi

---

[259] South African criminal law, too, still avails itself of this distinction. The various forms of assault are concerned with bodily integrity, crimen iniuriae serves to protect dignitas, and the crime of defamation takes care of fama.

[260] For all details, see Neethling, op. cit., note 113, pp. 83 sqq.

[261] The leading case is *O'Keeffe v. Argus Printing and Publishing Co. Ltd.* 1954 (3) SA 244 (C) at 247G (referring to De Villiers, op. cit., note 113, p. 24; cf. supra, note 250); cf. further Amerasinghe, 1967 *Acta Juridica* 192 sqq.; McQuoid-Mason, op. cit., note 78, pp. 124 sqq.; Neethling, op. cit., note 113, pp. 63 sqq. Contra: *Walker v. Van Wezel* 1940 WLD 66 at 70. From the point of view of criminal law (crimen iniuriae), see Milton, op. cit., note 165, pp. 535 sqq.; De Wet en Swanepoel, op. cit., note 257, pp. 245 sqq.

[262] For all details, see Neethling, op. cit., note 113, pp. 36 sqq., 83 sqq. On the right of privacy, see McQuoid-Mason, op. cit., note 78, pp. 86 sqq., 100 sqq. and passim.

[263] *O'Keeffe v. Argus Printing and Publishing Co. Ltd.* 1954 (3) SA 244 (C) at 249D–E ("The unauthorised publication of a person's photograph and name for advertising purposes is . . . capable of constituting an aggression of that person's dignitas"); *S v. A* 1971 (2) SA 293 (T) at 297 ("I have no doubt that the right to privacy is included in the concept of dignitas, and that there is no dearth of authority for this proposition"); *S v. I* 1976 (1) SA 781 (RAD) at 784 ("Looking through (complainant's) window was clearly an invasion of her privacy. Put another way her dignitas was injured by the invasion of her privacy").

[264] What is the position of a plaintiff who has suffered patrimonial loss too? Generally speaking, the actio iniuriarum lies for sentimental damages, the actio legis Aquiliae for patrimonial loss. A plaintiff wishing to recover for both forms of harm must, therefore, bring (and prove the requirements of) two different claims, which can, however, be combined in a single action. This is unproblematic in cases where the patrimonial loss flows from physical injury (cases of assault): it can be recovered under Aquilian principles (i.e. in cases of dolus and culpa). If the same injury also constituted contumelia iniuria (in the form of infringement of the plaintiff's right to corpus), sentimental loss can be claimed, provided the defendant had acted animo iniuriandi. Defamation presents a more difficult problem, since the wrong is of a non-physical nature. Again, however, if animus iniuriandi can be established, both kinds of damages may be recovered (whether on the basis of an actio legis Aquiliae and an actio iniuriarum "rolled into one"—pure economic loss, after all, has, once again, become recoverable under the actio legis Aquiliae (cf. supra, pp. 1042 sq.)—or merely of the actio iniuriarum—which would thus, by way of exception, also cover patrimonial loss (possibly only if it is not "too remote")—is not quite clear). A defamation action based on negligence can, in any event, be brought only for patrimonial loss and must satisfy the

(as in *most* other cases of iniuria)[265] has remained the key requirement for liability.

VI. THE FATE OF THE ACTIO INIURIARUM IN GERMANY

1. Usus modernus and natural law

All in all, therefore, the actio iniuriarum, though considerably modified, is alive and well in South Africa and still forms one of the two pillars of delictual liability at large. The same cannot be said of Germany, where the development took quite a different course. During the days of the usus modernus pandectarum, the action for iniuria enjoyed great popularity and tended to be brought as frequently and indiscriminately as in Holland.[266] ". . . qua frequentius fere hodie delictum est nullum"[267] is the phrase with which Lauterbach introduces his discussion of iniuria. The rulers of the various kingdoms and principalities traditionally tended to be favourably disposed towards the poena iniuriarum. Specific statutes were issued dealing with the matter;[268] after all, the imposition of a penalty (no matter whether by way of actio civilis or persecutio criminalis) was a rather more salutary alternative to duelling as a way of reacting to insults.[269] The natural

---

requirements of the actio legis Aquiliae. For details, see Boberg, *Delict*, pp. 19 sq.; Neethling, op. cit., note 113, pp. 75 sqq.; also already De Villiers, op. cit., note 113, pp. 182 sqq.; specifically on defamation: Burchell, op. cit., note 105, pp. 305 sq.; specifically on intrusions into the right of privacy: McQuoid-Mason, op. cit., note 78, pp. 252 sqq. There is one further point that must be remembered with regard to physical injury. We have said that the plaintiff may recover patrimonial loss under Aquilian principles (in cases of dolus and negligence) and sentimental loss on account of the actio iniuriarum (only in cases of dolus). Yet, even if the defendant acted negligently, there is an action available to the plaintiff for pain and suffering. The historical origin of this action has been briefly discussed in a previous chapter (pp. 1026 sq.). It is widely thought today that we are dealing here with an actio sui generis (cf., in particular, *Hoffa v. S.A. Mutual Fire & General Insurance Co. Ltd.* 1965 (2) SA 944 (C)). Yet there are also those who regard the remedy for pain and suffering as an exceptional form of Aquilian liability (exceptional, because it violates its patrimonial-loss principle) or of an extension of the actio iniuriarum (into the field of negligence). For a comprehensive discussion, see Olivier, op. cit., note 90, pp. 233 sqq.; Boberg, *Delict*, pp. 516 sqq. For a codified version of the action for pain and suffering, cf. § 847 BGB.

[265] For the exceptions (all under the influence of English law), see Neethling, op. cit., note 113, pp. 116 sq. (false imprisonment), p. 185 (wrongful execution against property) and supra, p. 1080 (liability of mass media for defamation).

[266] Cf. Lee, *Introduction*, p. 334.

[267] *Collegium theoretico-practicum*, Lib. XLVII, Tit. X, I.

[268] Cf., for instance, the edicta contra duella in Brandenburg and Saxonia, as quoted by Stryk, *Usus modernus pandectarum*, Lib. XLVII, Tit. X, §§ 23 sq.

[269] Generally on anti-duelling legislation (starting in the late 16th century) and on the motives inspiring it, cf. Slawig, op. cit., note 107, pp. 49 sqq; on the attitudes of the churches cf. pp. 92 sqq. Slawig proceeds to give a detailed account of the fight against duelling in Germany (more particularly: Prussia) during the 19th and 20th centuries. For an analysis of the opposition to duelling on a European level during the Age of Enlightenment and in the 19th century, see Kiernan, op. cit., note 107, pp. 165 sqq., 185 sqq. As far as England is concerned, cf. Blackstone, *Commentaries*, Book IV, Ch. 14, III (quoted by

lawyers, if anything, even extended the protection of honour, dignity and fama; abandoning the notion of a separate action with its own specific requirements, they dealt with the problem of contumely iniuria as an integral part of their general law of delict.[270] Fault, said Grotius,[271] creates the obligation to make good the damage that has been inflicted. Damage, in turn, means that someone has less than belongs to him.[272] But what belongs to man? On the one hand, what he is entitled to "accedente facto humano", as for instance, by means of ownership, contract or law. On the other hand, and more importantly, however, he is also entitled to that which accrues to him from the law of nature alone;[273] and by nature not only man's life, body, limbs and the acts of his will are his own, but also his reputation and honour.[274] In essence,

Kiernan, p. 165): "Express malice . . . takes in the case of deliberate duelling, where both parties meet avowedly with an intent to murder: thinking it their duty as gentlemen, and claiming it as their right . . . and therefore the law has justly fixed the crime and punishment of murder on them, and on their seconds also."

On the Continent, too, punishment could be hefty; for an account of a particularly spectacular incident, in which a duellist was ultimately decapitated, cf. Adolph Kohut, *Das Buch berühmter Duelle* (1888), pp. 57 sqq. Yet the self-defined elite that embraced the social convention of duelling as a means of defending their honour failed, for a long time, to respect anti-duelling laws and refused to resort to the alternative of instituting a defamation action. Duelling remained "a feature of the 'noble' life. . . . One point was its being normally illegal, especially for civilians. The duellist put himself above the law, and demonstrated that his self-respect, or, what came to the same thing, his respect for his class, mattered more to him than any external fact. . . . In what he deemed questions of honour the gentleman stood outside any social contract binding on the common man; he belonged to a superior social order which made its own rules" (Kiernan, op. cit., note 107, p. 153). Indicative of the 19th-century attitude towards duelling is also a statement made by Albrecht von Roon, Prussian Minister of War, during a parliamentary debate: "*Die persönliche Ehre des Mannes ist sein Eigenstes, und es giebt keine Macht der Erde, auch nicht die höchste, welche darüber Richter sein kann*" (The personal honour of a gentleman is his most cherished attribute, and there is no power in the world, not even the Supreme one, which could set itself up to judge about it); cf. Slawig, op. cit., note 107, p. 170. While duelling declined in 19th-century Britain, it remained an influencial social institution in Germany until the First World War. For details of the development, see Kiernan, op. cit., note 107, pp. 204 sqq. (Britain), pp. 271 sqq. (the "Old Monarchies"). Generally on the relationship of duelling and the legal system, see Schwartz/Baxter/Ryan, (1984) 13 *Journal of Legal Studies* 325 sqq.; Slawig, op. cit., note 107, pp. 49 sqq.

[270] Cf., however, Donellus, who is the true father of this line of thought. He used the three famous precepts of Ulp. D. 1, 1, 10, 1 ("honeste vivere, alterum non laedere, suum cuique tribuere") as a starting point and argued: "Alterum non laedere est non laedere alterius personam aut vitam ejus petendo aut violando incolumitatem, libertatem, existimationem" (*Commentarii*, Lib. II, Cap. I, X). For a general discussion of Donellus' views, see Herrmann, op. cit., note 99, pp. 19 sqq. "Alterum non laedere" as the foundation of the law of delict was later also emphasized by Pufendorf (supra, p. 1032); for him, too, the protection of fama, honor and other constituent elements of the personality (conceived by him, as previously by Donellus and Grotius, as "personality rights") was an integral part of it. On Pufendorf's views, see Herrmann, op. cit., note 99, pp. 37 sqq.

[271] *De jure belli ac pacis*, Lib. II, Cap. XVII, I; cf. supra, p. 1032 (note 221).

[272] "Damnum forte a demendo dictum . . . cum quis minus habet suo."

[273] ". . . sive illud suum ipsi competit ex mera natura. . . ."

[274] Cf. also *Inleiding*, II, I, 42 and, already, Donellus, *Commentarii*, Lib. II, Cap. I, XI: "Siquidem jus cujusque, id est quod jure cujusque est, non est tantum in rebus externis, sed et in persona cujusque. Quod genus vita, incolumitas, fama, libertas" (cf. also supra, note 270).

that meant liability for defamation based on negligence.[275] But how can reputation and honour be damaged and how can such damage be repaired? Grotius answered that damage may be inflicted by blows, insults, abuse, calumny, ridicule and other similar means.[276] Damni reparatio is made "culpae confessione, exhibitione honoris, testimonio innocentiae et quae his similia sunt" (this is the amende honorable), and also, if the injured party so wishes, by payment of a sum of money, "quia pecunia communis est rerum utilium mensura"[277] (the so-called amende profitable). Clearly to be distinguished from this obligation to make good the damage is the further obligation to suffer punishment; the latter is purely a matter of criminal law, for, as Grotius explains elsewhere, "het recht om te straffen komt toe de overheden".[278] The later natural lawyers (especially Pufendorf, Thomasius and Wolff) elaborated on the idea of natural rights, innate to man and based on his natural freedom. More particularly, they advocated everyone's right to develop his own personality freely and without undue interference by others.[279] Part and parcel of these all-embracing "personality rights" were the rights of honour, dignity and reputation.

2. De iniquitate et iniustitia actionum iniuriarum

But these somewhat lofty speculations[280] had little impact on the

[275] For further details, as far as the positive (Roman-Dutch) law was concerned, cf. *Inleiding*, III, XXXV (Van hoon) and III, XXXVI (Van lasteringh). On the difference between hoon (translated by Lee as "injury") and lasteringh ("defamation"), cf. Ranchod, op. cit., note 90, p. 68.

[276] *De jure belli ac pacis*, Lib. II, Cap. XVII, XXII.

[277] *De jure belli ac pacis*, Lib. II, Cap. XVII, XXII. In this regard Grotius follows Domingo de Soto (". . . cum pecunia pretium sit omnium rerum, illa aestimatur et honor et fama"). This view was, however, not uncontested; thus, Leonardus Lessius in his work De iustitia et iure stated: "Pecunia secundum communem usum hominum non est mensura nisi rerum venalium, quas homines solent pecunia commutare; fama autem aeque natura sua neque gentium consuetudine pecunia solet aestimari." Cf. Ranchod, op. cit., note 90, pp. 67 sq.

[278] *Inleiding*, III, XXXII, 7.

[279] Both the concepts of subjective rights as such and of the protection of the personality in terms of (a system of) subjective (personality) rights find their origin in the *Commentarii de Jure Civili* of Donellus. On Donellus' revolutionary ideas, on their reception by the natural lawyers and on the specific contributions of Althusius, Grotius, Pufendorf, Thomasius and Wolff to the development of a comprehensive protection of personality rights, cf. Herrmann, op. cit., note 99, pp. 19 sqq. 29 sqq.; Scheyhing, (1959–60) 158 *Archiv für die civilistische Praxis* 508 sqq.; Leuze, op. cit., note 256, pp. 12 sqq.; H.J. Becker, "Persönlichkeitsrecht", in: *HRG*, vol. II, col. 1626 sqq.; Klingenberg, (1979) 96 *ZSS* (GA) 195. Cf. also the programmatic statement of § 83 Einl. PrALR. Nineteenth-century legal science was predominantly hostile to the idea of a right of personality: cf., in particular, Savigny, *System*, vol. I, pp. 335 sqq. and, for a discussion, Scheyhing, (1959–60) 158 *Archiv für die civilistische Praxis* 503 sqq.; Leuze, op. cit., note 256, pp. 46 sqq. Towards the end of the century, however, we find a revival of the idea in the writings of Gareis, Gierke and Kohler: cf. supra, note 256.

[280] Epitomized in the work of Christian Wolff, who recognized, apart from the right of honour and reputation (for details, see *Institutiones* §§ 142 sqq.), innate human rights (inter alia!) to the use of one's organs, to food, drink and medication, to sensual enjoyment and to

practice of the law (particularly during the Restoration period). At any rate, they were unable to bolster the fortunes of the actio iniuriarum; for in the course of the 18th century legal opinion had started to swing decisively against both the actio aestimatoria and delictual protection of fama and honour[281] in general.[282] One of the first influential voices was that of Justus Henning Boehmer, who published a dissertation in 1714 entitled, programmatically, *De iniquitate et injustitia actionum injuriarum*. "Puto", he thundered,[283]

> "actione injuriarum indoli Christianismi, legibus, divinis, regulis philosophiae, peaeceptis prudentiae, rectae rationi, ipsis philosophorum ethnicorum sententiis, praxi primitivae ecclesiae, et denique toti sacrae scripturae adversari, omniaque argumenta, quae pro illis excusandis adduci solent, esse petita ex pseudopatientia et funesta persuasione vulgi."

It was, of course, no mere coincidence that this attack was launched by a great ecclesiastical lawyer, for it is indeed difficult to reconcile the image of the average plaintiff in a defamation suit with the Christian virtues of tolerantia and patientia; resist not evil, directs the Bible, and a smite on the cheek (no matter how much it hurts one's pride) should therefore elicit neither a counterattack[284] nor any desire to humiliate or penalize the wrongdoer.

3. The shift from private law to criminal law

Given man's sinful nature, however, the precepts of the Sermon on the Mount alone do not, unfortunately, appear to guarantee the proper functioning of human society; and thus, if public peace is to be maintained, the delict of iniuria cannot remain entirely without sanction: ". . . reipublicae interest, ut hi, qui injuriis alios adficiunt, non puniantur solum, sed et graviter puniantur."[285] But whether this penalty should be private or public in character was quite a different matter. The actio iniuriarum was the only (civil) actio mere poenalis

---

the pursuit of happiness (*Jus naturae*, Pars I, Cap. II, § 376 ("jus . . . utendi organis suis"), § 383 ("jus . . . ad eas res, quae cibo ac potui inserviunt seu corpus alere possunt"), § 416 ("[j]us ad medicamenta"), § 410 ("jus . . . fruendi voluptate transitoria, si fuerit innocua"), § 284 ("jus ad ea, quae ad felicitatem consequendam, conservandam et augendam requiruntur"). This is not the kind of doctrine likely to appeal to either legal practice or a legislator.

[281] The main (if not exclusive) function of the delict of iniuria at the time of the late usus modernus. The contraction of the actio iniuriarum was partly offset by the extension of Aquilian protection, which occurred at about the same time. As has been discussed above, the actio legis Aquiliae became available to claim compensation for pain, suffering and disfigurement (but only in cases of infliction of bodily harm, not as far as other forms of iniuriae were concerned).

[282] For what follows, see Mainzer, op. cit., note 103, pp. 90 sqq.

[283] The quotation is taken from Leyser, *Meditationes ad Pandectas*, Spec. DXLII, I.

[284] Cf. supra, p. 1069 (retorsio), pp. 1063, 1085 (duel).

[285] Leyser, *Meditationes ad Pandectas*, Spec. DXLII, VII. Leyser's work contains a very interesting and fair ("[e]xsequitur haec . . . eleganter et docte, ut semper solet") discussion of Boehmer's view and a comprehensive attempt to justify the existence of the actio iniuriarum.

that had been received from Roman law; and within a law of delict increasingly directed towards the compensation for loss sustained,[286] it was bound to remain something of a corpus alienum. "[In iniuriis] non minus quam in furto atque aliis criminibus vitiositas actus ab effectu discernenda est", as Grotius[287] had put it: just as in theft and other crimes, the criminality of the act must be distinguished from its effect (that is, the damage caused). To deal with the "vitiositas", the criminal side of the matter, was perceived to be the proper concern of the State; and thus, the imposition of a poena iniuriandi drifted away from private law into the province of criminal law.[288] But once the actio iniuriarum aestimatoria had been deprived of its main function, the question was bound to arise whether any action at all, on the level of private law, was still apposite as far as the wrong of iniuria was concerned. It was answered with a straightforward "no" by an influential author such as Samuel Stryk. All too often, he claimed,[289] people tried to enrich themselves by suing upon the slightest occasion on account of an alleged iniuria; and he expressed his surprise at the fact that the actio iniuriarum was not yet counted as a modus adquirendi. Christian Thomasius, of course, who did not even want to accept the actio legis Aquiliae,[290] was another prominent opponent of the Roman delict of iniuria. Others, while admitting that the actio iniuriarum was "ex parte actoris non prudenter nec generose nec christiane", still regarded it as "juste tamen":[291] a somewhat lacklustre defence.

In the course of the 19th century more and more of the German states abolished the remedy by way of legislation,[292] and as far as the Reich was concerned, the penal code of 1872 sounded its death knell. Some 19th-century legal writers tried to stem the tide and claim at least a residual field of application for a remedy in private law,[293] but conventional wisdom was that the delict of iniuria had in its entirety been removed from the scene by the provisions of the penal code.[294] What were the reasons for this radical departure from tradition?

---

[286] Cf., for example, supra, pp. 1019 sq. and infra, p. 1111.

[287] *De jure belli ac pacis*, Lib. II, Cap. XVII, XXII. Cf. also *Inleiding*, III, XXXII, 7.

[288] Cf. e.g. Bartels, op. cit., note 112, pp. 46 sqq.; also Irmscher, op. cit., note 256, pp. 123 sqq.

[289] Eines christlichen Jurisconsulti Bedencken von Injurienprocessen, in: *Supplementum dissertationum et operum*, vol. XIII (Florentiae, 1840), pp. 1022 sqq. (§ 7)—a beautifully written piece that is still well worth reading today.

[290] Cf. supra, pp. 1018, 1031.

[291] Cf. Mainzer, op. cit., note 103, p. 91.

[292] Mainzer, op. cit., note 103, pp. 96 sqq.

[293] Cf. Rudolf von Jhering, "Rechtsschutz gegen injuriöse Rechtsverletzungen", in: *Gesammelte Aufsätze*, vol. III (1886), pp. 233 sqq.; Landsberg, op. cit., note 78, pp. 83 sqq.; Dernburg, *Pandekten*, § 137 in fine, and others; for a discussion, see Mainzer, op. cit., note 103, pp. 14 sqq.; Ekkehard Kaufmann, "Dogmatische und rechtspolitische Grundlagen des § 253 BGB", (1963) 162 *Archiv für die civilistische Praxis* 425 sqq.

[294] Windscheid/Kipp, § 472; Mainzer, op. cit., note 103, pp. 101 sqq.

4. Criticism of the actio ad palinodiam

As far as the amende honorable was concerned, there were, as we have seen,[295] quite often penal elements involved which were no longer regarded as appropriate in a private-law remedy. Quite apart from that, there was also the awkward problem of enforcement. If the offender was not prepared to recant, to furnish the required declaratio honoris, or to pray for forgiveness, he had to go to gaol or to a penitentiary until he gave in. Occasionally, a hangman was asked to act in his place (and presence).[296] But what value could a declaration thus enforced have for the victim of the insult? Not even he, let alone anybody else, could seriously believe, under these circumstances, that the offender regretted the incident and regarded the plaintiff as a man of honour, after all. If anything, it was only a rather shallow kind of satisfaction that a plaintiff could obtain by instituting the actio ad palinodiam. Most importantly, perhaps, it was now argued[297] that this remedy did not even serve a useful restitutionary purpose. The honour of a person as such, his dignitas, so the argument ran, can never be affected by an insult. Thus, the actio ad palinodiam cannot "restore" anything to a person that has not been taken away from him in the first place. What can, however, be impaired by the iniuria is the esteem in which that person is held by others (his reputation, or fama). Yet, even in this regard the action is unnecessary, for a person's injured reputation is already restored when the offender is punished.[298]

5. The decline of the actio iniuriarum aestimatoria

To a certain extent, the latter argument applied to the actio iniuriarum aestimatoria too. Since it had lost its penal function, it could serve only to compensate the victim for any damage sustained as a result of the iniuria. On account of an attack against his honour, no damage could, however, have been caused, for his honour was in no way detrimentally affected. Only if his reputation was impaired was there any possibility of damages. As far as pecuniary damages were concerned, special provision was made in the penal code,[299] and the

[295] Supra, p. 1074.

[296] For details cf., for example, Lauterbach, *Collegium theoretico-practicum*, Lib. XLVII, Tit. X, LIII; Leyser, *Meditationes ad Pandectas*, Spec. DXLIII, IV.

[297] For details, see Kaufmann, (1963) 162 *Archiv für die civilistische Praxis* 430 sqq. (with regard to the Prussian General Land Law).

[298] In South African law, the Roman-Dutch amende honorable has fallen into desuetude: cf. *Lumley v. Owen*, as quoted by De Villiers, op. cit., note 113, p. 178 ("an archaism"); *Hare v. White* (1865) 1 Roscoe 246 at 247; Burchell, op. cit., note 105, pp. 315 sq. For a more favourable opinion on the amende honorable cf. recently *Kritzinger v. Perskorporasie van Suid-Afrika (Edms.) Bpk.* 1981 (2) SA 373 (O). Burchell (p. 316) reports that the actio ad palinodiam has been received, and still lives on, in the Code of Zulu Law (Natal).

[299] § 188 StGB, on which cf., for instance, Baron, *Pandekten*, § 321, 3; Freiesleben, in: *von Olshausen's Kommentar zum Strafgesetzbuch* (11th ed., 1927), § 188. The rule was abolished in 1974.

BGB, too, was to allow for their recovery.[300] Usually, however, the damages are of a non-material, or sentimental, nature; and the main function of a sustained actio iniuriarum would thus have been to afford the plaintiff some compensation in the form of a solatium in order to assuage his injured feelings. But then one would have had to express the value of these feelings in financial terms; and it was exactly this kind of trade-off that repelled the contemporary sense of decency. Freiherr von Kreittmayer, the famous "father" of the Bavarian Civil Code of 1756, gave the argument a slightly nationalistic slant: assessment of a person's *point d'Honneur*, he maintained,[301] was completely alien to German tradition and mentality; hence the low esteem in which the actio aestimatoria was held among decent and reputable people. The Romans may have regarded the person convicted under an actio iniuriarum as infamous;[302] yet in Germany it was rather the person bringing such a "squalid" action who exposed himself to ridicule and disrepute. The same ideas still prevailed when the BGB was drafted.[303] Immaterial interest, in the opinion of the German gentleman, cannot be weighed up against money. Honour and good reputation are of an inestimable value, and whoever is prepared to "trade them in" against a sum of money can hardly be a man of honour who deserves to be respected anyway.[304] The BGB therefore does not include honour and reputation

[300] § 823 II BGB imposes an obligation to make amends upon anyone who violates a statutory provision intended for the protection of others. Among these "protective norms", are the provisions of the penal code dealing with insult and defamation (§§ 185 sqq. StGB). Cf. also § 824 BGB.

[301] Cf. Mainzer, op. cit., note 103, p. 93. On the concept of honour in the late 18th and in the 19th centuries, see also Slawig, op. cit., note 107, pp. 14 sqq.; Kiernan, op. cit., note 107, pp. 152 sqq., 223 sqq. (on the views presented by Walter Scott and later British writers).

[302] Supra, p. 1062 (note 100).

[303] Cf. "Protokolle", in: *Mugdan*, vol. II, p. 1119; "Kommissionsbericht", in: *Mugdan*, vol. II, p. 1297; also, for example, G. Hartmann, "Der Civilgesetzentwurf, das Aequitätsprincip und die Richterstellung", (1888) 73 *Archiv für die civilistische Praxis* 364: "It runs counter to the most profound German sensibilities to assess the most sacred emotions in terms of base mammon and to compensate every culpable interference with those feelings by means of a money payment" (trans.: Handford, (1978) 27 *Comparative and International Law Quarterly* 855).

[304] It was the same "psychology of honour" that kept alive the institution of duelling as an alternative social mechanism to settle disputes relating to a point of honour: cf. the analysis by Kiernan, op. cit., note 107, pp. 152 sqq.; cf. also pp. 116 sqq. (detailing the "grudges and grievances" that could give rise to a duel). Duelling was not confined to officers or to the nobility ("Barons from head to toe, in every drop of blood the fruit of sixty-four equal marriages, and in every glance a challenge!": as Friedrich Engels saw it; cf. Kiernan, p. 271) but had spread to the top echelons of the bourgeoisie. It had become an upper-class phenomenon; doctors, lawyers, statesmen and newspaper editors were among the highly represented groups. Involvement in duels or challenges included, among many others, Napoleon, La Fontaine, Voltaire, Heinrich Heine, Otto von Bismarck, and at least five men who were destined to become British prime ministers: Lord Bath, Lord Shelborne, William Pitt, George Canning, the Duke of Wellington and Sir Robert Peel (who was twice in the role of challenger). Alexander Pushkin and the German socialist Ferdinand Lassalle were killed in duels. For details, see Schwartz/Baxter/Ryan, (1984) 13 *Journal of Legal Studies* 325; Kiernan, op. cit., note 107, pp. 6 sqq., 216, 277 sqq. and passim; cf. also Kohut, op. cit., note 269, pp. 69 sqq. In Germany, a country that was "succumbing to atavistic

within the list of rights or interests enumerated in § 823 I BGB;[305] furthermore, it specifically provides that compensation for non-pecuniary loss may be claimed only in the case of injury to body or health, or in the case of deprivation of liberty.[306] Over and above that, § 253 BGB contains an express prohibition against awarding non-pecuniary damages in any cases other than those specified by law.[307]

6. The renaissance of the actio iniuriarum

These very rigorous provisions have, however, not stood the test of time. Thrown out by the front door, the actio iniuriarum has managed to sneak in through the back window—in the guise and under the cover of the general right of personality.[308] It was under the impact of the totalitarianism of the Nazi regime that the Bonn "constitution"[309] of 1949 entrenched the respect for human dignity and the right to personal freedom, very prominently, in its first two articles. Soon the argument began to gain ground that these constitutional provisions were of fundamental importance not only in the field of public law; and

---

'neo-feudalism' and strident militarism", the duelling conventions retained their hold until the First World War; ". . . so long disunited and timidly subservient to princelings and prelates, [the German nation was] well fitted for a double life of reality and fantasy" (Kiernan, op. cit., note 107, pp. 271, 272). The prevailing views among the upper classes are encapsulated in the remark by Minister von Roon (cf. supra, p. 1086, note 269). Highly significant, too, the case of Reinhold von Thadden (who refused to accept a challenge and was, as a result, subjected to severe social and professional discrimination) and of the three Counts Schmising-Kerssenbrock (who were dismissed from the army as a result of having rejected, for religious reasons, the institution of duelling); they are related and analysed by Slawig, op. cit., note 107, pp. 175 sqq., 188 sqq. Slawig (p. 76) also draws attention to the fact that the persons involved in duelling tended to receive milder forms of punishment in 19th-century Prussia and Germany than under 18th century anti-duelling laws. Why was the opposition to duelling so much more successful in Britain (for details, see Kiernan, op. cit., note 107, pp. 204 sqq.) than in Germany? Kiernan's suggestion (p. 131) that "the availability of pecuniary satisfaction must be one reason for the early demise of the duel in England" is hardly satisfactory; for in Germany a pecuniary alternative (in the form of the private poena iniuriarum) could, after all, easily have been available, too.

[305] Supra, p. 1036. The first draft (which was based on a general clause (supra, p. 1036, note 251)) had, however, specifically included a reference to the protection of honour: § 704 II E I.

[306] § 847 I BGB. On the history and background of this provision, see Olivier, op. cit., note 90, pp. 173 sqq., 179 sqq.

[307] § 253 BGB; on which see, particularly, Kaufmann, (1963) 162 *Archiv für die civilistische Praxis* 421 sqq. For a comparative discussion and evaluation, and for proposals de lege ferenda, see Gerhard Hohloch, "Allgemeines Schadensrecht", in: *Gutachten und Vorschläge zur Überarbeitung des Schuldrechts*, vol. I (1981), pp. 426 sqq.; cf. also Lange, *Schadensersatz*, pp. 256 sqq.

[308] Generally on the general right of personality in German law, see Peter Schwerdtner, in: *Münchener Kommentar*, vol. I (2nd ed., 1984), § 12, nn. 163 sqq.; Ernst von Caemmerer, "Der privatrechtliche Persönlichkeitsschutz nach deutschem Recht", in: *Festschrift für Fritz von Hippel* (1967), pp. 27 sqq.; Hans-Erich Brandner, "Das allgemeine Persönlichheitsrecht in der Entwicklung der Rechtsprechung", 1983 *Juristenzeitung* 689 sqq.; in English: Zweigert/Kötz/Weir, pp. 342 sqq.; B.S. Markesinis, *A Comparative Introduction to the German Law of Tort* (1986), pp. 37 sqq., 191 sqq., 542 sq., and P.R. Handford, "Moral Damage in Germany", (1978) 27 *International and Comparative Law Quarterly* 849 sqq.

[309] Cf. supra, p. 343, note 18.

since their spirit was to pervade every branch of the legal system, they should also be given material effect on the level of the private law. More particularly, delictual protection of the personality was deemed to be desirable and necessary. It was introduced in 1954 by the Federal Supreme Court via the "or other right" clause[310] contained in § 823 I BGB[311] and has, since then, been reaffirmed on numerous occasions. Invasions of the right of personality[312] are thus subject to the general rules of delictual liability; they give rise to a claim for damages, provided the requirements of wrongfulness and fault are satisfied. Negligence, as with all the other rights and interests of § 823 I BGB, suffices. Yet, a further step had to be taken by the courts. According to §§ 823 I, 847, 253 BGB, the aggrieved plaintiff is confined to a claim for the pecuniary loss that he has suffered. Typically, however, merely non-pecuniary loss flows from an invasion of the general personality right. Thus, for instance, the brewery-owner whose picture was taken at a show-jumping competition, to be subsequently used—without his permission—in an advert for a sexual stimulant, could show no loss of income. Nor did the professor of international and ecclesiastical law suffer any financial harm who, through a curious chain of circumstances, was referred to in a popular scientific article as an authority on ginseng roots and their erotic properties. Nevertheless, the Federal Supreme Court in both cases awarded compensation (or perhaps rather satisfaction) for the plaintiff's pain and suffering (usually referred to as "solatium").[313] The elimination of damages for immaterial loss from the protection of personality would in the opinion of the court have meant that injury to the dignity and honour of a human being would have remained without satisfactory sanction by the civil law and such a state of affairs could no longer be considered as being in conformity with the fundamental value system established by the Basic Law. In the wake of these two decisions it has become standard practice[314] for the courts to award a financial compensation for non-pecuniary harm in all cases where the intrusion into the plaintiff's personality right is grave and objectively serious.[315] It is hard to imagine a line of decisions more

---

[310] Cf. supra, p. 1036 (note 253).

[311] BGHZ 13, 334 sqq. Ironically, this breakthrough decision concerned a letter written on behalf of a former Nazi minister of economic affairs, who felt insulted by a newspaper article dealing with his activities in pre- and post-war Germany. For a translation of the main parts of the judgment, see Markesinis, op. cit., note 308, pp. 191 sqq. For further cases, cf., for example, BGHZ 39, 124 sqq. (a television announcer was described in a newspaper article as a "milked out nanny-goat" who really belonged in a "second-class honky-tonk" on the Reeperbahn) and BGH, 1965 *Neue Juristische Wochenschrift* 685 sq. (fictitious interview with Princess Soraya about her life with the Shah of Persia).

[312] Which does not only protect a person's honour and reputation but his privacy at large.

[313] BGHZ 26, 349 sqq.; BGHZ 35, 363 sqq. (both cases, in translation, in Markesinis, op. cit., note 308, pp. 195 sqq.)

[314] For all details, see Schwerdtner, op. cit., note 308, nn. 291 sqq.

[315] Iniuria atrox rediviva!

blatantly contra legem than this.[316] Yet it demonstrates that even a codification as monumental as the BGB is not completely detached from the ebb and flow of legal development. The radical renunciation of the delict of iniuria has remained a mere episode, for in essence the judges are today, once again, required to award "quantam pecuniam bonum aequum videbitur"[317] to the plaintiff to assuage his injured feelings.[318]

---

[316] Are German courts allowed (and if so, under which circumstances) to decide contra legem? After all, they are bound by the law: cf. art. 20 III GG. Art. 97 I GG makes it clear that this subjection of the judge to the law is inextricably linked with, and has to be regarded as a necessary prerequisite for, judicial independence. I have tried to deal with the intricate implications of judge-made law within a codified system in general, and with the constitutional parameters set by the German Basic Law in *Moderationsrecht*, pp. 97 sqq., 177 sqq. Cf. also Jörn Ipsen, *Richterrecht und Verfassung* (1975); Otto Rudolf Kissel, "Grenzen der rechtsprechenden Gewalt", 1982 *Neue Juristische Wochenschrift* 1777 sqq.; Eduard Picker, "Richterrecht oder Rechtsdogmatik—Alternativen der Rechtsgewinnung", 1988 *Juristenzeitung* 1 sqq., 62 sqq.; Fritz Ossenbühl, "Gesetz und Recht—Die Rechtsquellen im demokratischen Rechtstaat", in: *Josef Isensee, Paul* Kirchhof (eds.), *Handbuch des Staatsrechts*, vol. III (1988), § 61, nn. 35 sqq. The Federal Constitutional Court has, however, condoned the judicial derogation of § 253 BGB: BVerfGE 34, 269 sqq. ("Soraya"). Contra: Wolfgang Grunsky, in: *Münchener Kommentar*, vol. II (2nd ed., 1985), § 253, n. 6.

[317] For the factors to be taken into consideration, see Schwerdtner, op. cit., note 308, nn. 294 sqq. For South Africa cf. Burchell, op. cit., note 105, pp. 289 sqq. English law has had considerable influence in this regard. In the main, it is accepted that the award of damages should compensate the plaintiff for his sentimental loss. Whether, in addition, punitive or exemplary damages may be awarded is very controversial. But in any event, as has been pointed out repeatedly, it is difficult, if not impossible, to separate the punitive and the compensatory elements in sentimental damages: cf., for instance, *S.A. Associated Newspaper Ltd. v. Samuels* 1980 (1) SA 24 (A) at 48E–H; also (for England) *Cassell & Co. Ltd. v. Broome* [1972] AC 1027 (HL) at 1072 ("the whole process of assessing damages where they are 'at large' is essentially a matter of impression and not addition", per Lord Hailsham). For a comprehensive comparative analysis of the elements of compensation and satisfaction in the modern remedies for sentimental loss (pain and suffering), see Petrus Johannes Visser, *Kompensasie en genoegdoening volgens die aksie weens pyn en leed* (unpublished LLD thesis, Pretoria, 1980); cf. now also idem, "Genoegdoening in die deliktereg", (1988) 51 *THRHR* 468 sqq.

[318] French courts and legal writers have always been able to grant adequate protection to personality interests on the basis of the general clause of art. 1382 code civil ("Every act whatever of man which causes damage to another obliges him by whose fault the damage occurred to repair it"). Neither are honour, reputation, privacy or any other personality rights excluded from the scope of this provision nor does the code draw a distinction between pecuniary damages and sentimental loss (*dommage moral*). For a comparative analysis, see Zweigert/Kötz, pp. 448 sqq.; Léontin-Jean Constantinesco, "Die Persönlichkeitsrechte und ihr Schutz im französischen Recht", (1960–61) 159 *Archiv für die civilistische Praxis* 320 sqq.

CHAPTER 32

Strict Liability

I. LIABILITY FOR DAMAGE DONE BY ANIMALS

1. A special compartment

"[T]he law of torts has grown up historically in separate compartments and . . . beasts have travelled in a compartment of their own." This statement by Lord Simonds[1] applies to civilian legal systems no less than it does to the English common law. It reflects a common appreciation of the fact that animals are a rather anomalous type of chattel. They kick and butt and gore;[2] they lie around in inappropriate places for people to stumble over them and they stray onto busy highways or railway lines where they collide with hapless cyclists[3] or cause trains to be derailed;[4] they attack human beings, as well as each other, they cause damage to movable and immovable property, they roam around, and they pick up and transmit all sorts of infectious diseases.[5] Dogs, "for ages the companion[s] and hunting agent[s] of man",[6] chase, kill and eat the neighbour's chickens,[7] they bite innocent postmen as well as unlawful intruders; they throw over little children in clumsy attempts to hug them; and they leave behind excrement on which people can slip. They also impregnate good-looking bitches and thus deprive them of their chances of winning for their owners handsome sums in beauty competitions.[8]

Animals, obviously, constitute a constant source of danger. Yet, the law cannot simply aim at preventing people from keeping them, for

---

[1] *Read v. J. Lyons & Co. Ltd.* [1947] AC 156 (HL) at 185.

[2] Cf. Servius/Ulp. D. 9, 1, 1, 4. Generally on the theme of "the goring ox" ("a popular one in the legal thought of the civilizations of the ancient Near East"), see J.J. Finkelstein, *The Ox That Gored* (1981), pp. 5 sqq. On the biblical laws concerning goring oxen, cf. also, apart from Finkelstein, Bernard S. Jackson, *Essays in Jewish and Comparative Legal Thought* (1975), pp. 108 sqq.

[3] Cf. *Searle v. Wallbank* [1947] AC 341, where it was held that an occupier of land adjoining a highway owes no duty of care to maintain fencing or otherwise prevent his animals from escaping onto the highway; a rule which has been described, with judicial moderation, as "difficult, archaic and ill-adapted to urban communities" (*Gomberg v. Smith* [1963] 1 QB 25 at 31) and, in the bolder spirit of academic analysis, as "an outrageous subsidy shamelessly exacted by the farming lobby at the expense of public safety" (John G. Fleming, *An Introduction to the Law of Torts* (1967), p. 170); cf. today § 8 of the Animals Act 1971 and Fleming, *Torts*, pp. 337 sq.; see also *Ellis v. Johnstone* [1963] 2 QB 8; OLG Celle, 1980 *Versicherungsrecht* 430 sq. (dealing with a dead animal lying on a road).

[4] *Cooper v. Railway Executive* [1953] 1 All ER 477.

[5] Cf. RGZ 80, 237 (239 sq.).

[6] *Boyce v. Robertson* 1912 TPD 381 at 383.

[7] *Maree v. Diedericks* 1962 (1) SA 231 (T) at 237C ("baldadige slagting").

[8] Cf. BGHZ 67, 129 sqq. (concerning loss of earnings that would have resulted from the sale of purebred puppies).

animals can also serve a whole variety of useful, even necessary functions. They provide milk and wool and meat, they can be used for transportation, sporting and entertainment purposes; dogs can assist the police as well as rescue workers and they can be indispensable to the blind. Animals are things, not persons, and they can be owned like cupboards, cars or toilet paper. But the person in charge of them has to be responsible for the mischief that they cause. This liability, generally speaking, must be rather strict, for a person should not be allowed to derive the benefit from keeping animals, without at the same time being required to carry the concomitant risks. On the other hand, however, there must also be limits to the keeper's liability. Where a cat is picked up and used as a projectile,[9] the person hit by it has, in a way, been injured by an animal; yet, his injury can hardly be said to constitute a realization of the specific risks attached to keeping animals. A cat has no greater propensity to be thrown about at other people than, say, a book or a tennis ball. This is a rather obvious example, but it illustrates that the law is faced with the necessity of carving out criteria to demarcate the keeper's sphere of risk. It may also be advisable to draw distinctions between different types of situations or animals. The farmer who depends for his livelihood on breeding sheep may have to be treated differently from the city dweller who keeps a horse to ride for pleasure.[10] Some people keep dogs to guard their homes, others have pet racoons[11] or snakes. Lions, generally speaking, are more dangerous than rabbits;[12] but where, for instance, does the elephant fit in? After all, there is "the world of difference between the wild elephant in the jungle" and a docile circus elephant which may be as harmless "[as] a cow".[13]

2. The actio de pauperie in Roman law

(a) The meaning of pauperies

The roots of liability for damage done by animals in countries of the civil-law tradition lie in the Roman actio de pauperie. The XII Tables are already said to have provided a remedy "[s]i quadrupes pauperiem fecisse dicetur".[14] The term "pauperies" derives from "pauper"; it

[9] Cf. the example used by Karl Larenz, *Lehrbuch des Schuldrechts*, vol. II (12th ed., 1981), p. 707; cf. also the case decided in OLG Braunschweig, 1983 *Versicherungsrecht* 347 sq.

[10] Cf. the distinction made in § 833 BGB.

[11] *Andrew v. Kilgour* (1910) 13 WLR 608 (Canada).

[12] Cf., for example, the Report of the New South Wales Law Reform Commission 1970, in: W.L. Morison, C.S. Phegan, C. Sappiden, *Cases on Torts* (6th ed., 1985), pp. 909 sqq.

[13] *Behrens v. Bertram Mills Circus Ltd.* [1957] 2 QB 1 at 14; and see the comment in the Report of the New South Wales Law Reform Commission (supra, note 12), p. 910.

[14] Ulp. D. 9, 1, 1 pr.; *Inst.* IV, 9 pr. On the decemviral remedy, see, most recently, Bernard S. Jackson, "Liability for Animals in Roman Law: An Historical Sketch", (1978) 37 *Cambridge LJ* 122 sqq.

meant, at least in later, non-legal sources, "poverty".[15] Why the XII Tables used it in the present context (rather than the seemingly more appropriate word "damnum")[16] has remained something of a mystery. Was it intended to indicate damage on account of which the injured party became poorer?[17] But it should then also have applied to other harmful events, such as those that were ultimately regulated by the lex Aquilia. Or was its original sense something like "the state of producing little or of being unproductive"?[18] The XII Tables would then have referred to incidents in which four-footed animals "caused the state of being unproductive"; which, in turn, would suggest that originally only injuries to the instruments of production, in the first place slaves and pecudes, were covered.[19] But whatever its meaning may have been around 450 B.C., Ulpian understood it, some 650 years later, to stand for damage done without any legal wrong on the part of the doer: "[P]auperies est damnum sine iniuria facientis datum."[20] This definition has two important implications. First of all, the "doer" in terms of the actio de pauperie was obviously the animal itself. But, secondly, the animal did not commit a legal wrong when it inflicted damage by kicking, goring, biting, or in any other manner. Ulpian, in fact, specifically elaborated on this point: an animal, he said, is quite incapable of committing a legal wrong, because it is devoid of reasoning (". . . nec enim potest animal iniuria fecisse, quod sensu caret").[21]

This argument, self-evident perhaps to us,[22] is rather remarkable in view of the fact that during various periods in European legal history a different attitude prevailed.[23] In ancient Greece, for instance, animals tended to be personified and were rewarded, as well as punished, like

---

[15] Lewis and Short, *A Latin Dictionary* (1979; 1966 impression), p. 1318.

[16] Which was used in the lex Aquilia; cf. Ulp. D. 9, 2, 27, 5 and supra, pp. 953, 986.

[17] Kaser, *Altrömisches ius*, pp. 224 sqq.; cf. also Detlef Liebs, "Damnum, damnare und damnas", (1968) 85 *ZSS* 195 sq.

[18] Alan Watson, "The Original Meaning of Pauperies", (1970) 17 *RIDA* 361 sqq. Watson, pp. 363 sqq., also refutes Kerr Wylie's view, according to which the XII Tables did not in fact use the term "pauperies" (J. Kerr Wylie, "'Actio de pauperie' Dig. Lib. IX, Tit. I", in: *Studi in onore di Salvatore Riccobono*, vol. IV (1936), pp. 465, 482).

[19] Watson, (1970) 17 *RIDA* 362; cf. also Jackson, (1978) 37 *Cambridge LJ* 123 sq. This would put the beginnings of the actio de pauperie in line with the lex Aquilia where, too, slaves and grazing animals were the principal objects of legal protection.

[20] D. 9, 1, 1, 3.

[21] D. 9, 1, 1, 3.

[22] ". . . [f]or a dog cannot reason like a human being, and there is something bizarre in seeking the mens rea [guilty mind] of a pony": *Salmond and Heuston on the Law of Torts* (18th ed., 1981), p. 318.

[23] Cf. generally, Karl von Amira, "Thierstrafen und Thierprocesse", in: (1891) 12 *Mittheilungen des Instituts für oesterreichische Geschichtsforschung* 545 sqq., 574 sqq., 587 sqq.; Wolfgang Sellert, "Das Tier in der abendländischen Rechtsauffassung", in: *Studium generale. Vorträge zum Thema Tier und Mensch* (1984), pp. 66 sqq.; cf. also (for Anglo-Saxon and English law) Glanville Williams, *Liability for Animals* (1939), pp. 7 sqq., 265 sqq.

human beings.[24] In post-classical Rome they were taken to be subject to the rules of natural law,[25] and when an ox gored, such unruly behaviour could be regarded as a culpable breach of the good conduct owed by him to all human beings.[26] In the Middle Ages, a specifically Christian perception of the world and its relationship to God, blended curiously with some superstitious elements, moulded the approach adopted towards animals.[27] Not everybody, of course, went as far as St. Francis of Assisi, who even gave them the benefit of his sermons. Generally speaking, however, one appears to have looked upon animals as creatures of God in which, as in human beings, the good and evil forces could reveal themselves.[28] The evil, however, had to be rooted out, no matter where it appeared. Hence the necessity to punish wicked animals: cockerels that had violated the natural order of things by laying eggs, hens that crowed like cockerels, dogs or sows that killed or injured children, and so on. From about the 13th century onwards until well into the 18th century,[29] in some places even until the beginning of the 19th century, animals could be prosecuted, tried[30] and condemned—be it to be burnt at the stake, to be hung by their neck,[31] to be exiled to Siberia, or to suffer corporal punishment.[32] Yet, it was not

[24] Thus, for instance, Plutarch relates the case of a dog who was awarded a lifelong pension since he had chased a criminal from Athens almost to Corinth. For details, see Rudolf Düll, "Archaische Sachprozesse und Losverfahren", (1941) 61 *ZSS* 1 sqq.; idem, "Zum Anthropomorphismus im antiken Recht", (1944) 64 *ZSS* 346 sqq.; but cf. also Finkelstein, op. cit., note 2, pp. 58 sqq. A streak of anthropomorphism is also clearly perceptible in the attitude adopted by contemporary lovers of animals towards their pets. The German philosopher, Arthur Schopenhauer, incidentally, did not regard the intellect, but rather the will to live, as the essential characteristic of every creature. Since, however, in that respect there is no difference between animals and human beings (cf. E. Grisebach (ed.) *Die Welt als Wille und Vorstellung*, vol. II (2nd ed.), pp. 235 sqq.), animals were, to him, not merely legal objects but had to be respected as the subjects of (moral) rights. Schopenhauer thus became the intellectual ancestor of the modern "ethical" approach towards animal protection (animals have to be protected for their own sake). The contrary view (human beings owe no duties towards animals since animals lack reason) was adopted by Kant and the other Enlightenment philosophers. They consequently argued in favour of animal protection, only in so far as it benefits man (the anthropocentric view of animal protection): cf. Sellert, op. cit., note 23, pp. 80 sqq.

[25] Cf. infra, p. 1114.

[26] Cf. still *Cowell v. Friedman & Co.* (1888) 5 HCG 22 at 44: "[B]ut when an ox gores, the act may be regarded as a breach of the good behaviour which is its second nature."

[27] For all details, see von Amira, (1891) 12 *Mittheilungen des Instituts für oesterreichische Geschichtsforschung* 545 sqq. Williams, op. cit., note 23, p. 266 refers to a "curious recrudescence of earlier notions".

[28] Sellert, op. cit., note 23, pp. 73 sqq.

[29] As far as legal literature is concerned, the practice of killing animals that killed a human being was still defended by an author like Stryk, *Usus modernus pandectarum*, Lib. IX, Tit. I, § 20.

[30] On the nature of that trial cf., however, von Amira, loc. cit. and Finkelstein, op. cit., note 2, pp. 64 sqq.

[31] Cf. the vivid description of a case in the 16th-century Netherlands by C.G. van der Merwe, "Diere voor die Gereg", Mei 1972 *Codicillus* 35.

[32] Cf. also Finkelstein, op. cit., note 2, pp. 7 sqq., 48 sqq., 64 sqq., who emphasizes that "[t]he notion that trials and punishments of irrational creatures and of inanimate things are

so much the animal itself that had to be punished as the obnoxious demon that manifested itself in the sinister deed.[33] For the very same reason, incidentally, one had to burn witches: the fire was supposed to exterminate the evil.[34]

(b) The principle of noxality

Rather similar ideas may originally have prevailed in ancient Rome.[35] Our evidence is too scanty to determine whether or not animals causing damage were at some stage taken to be possessed by a demoniacal spirit. Alternatively, the Romans may have proceeded from a rather similar kind of anthropomorphism to that of the Greeks.[36] But, for whatever reason, it was generally the animal that was seen to have committed the delict. The victim of the injury was thus allowed to wreak his vengeance upon the body of the animal—in the very same way as if the wrongdoer had been a human being.[37] If the animal was owned by someone, there was, however, a specific problem—the same problem that we have encountered when considering injuries done by slaves and children in power:[38] by simply killing the animal, the victim would have violated the owner's rights. Hence it was the delinquent's surrender that he could request. This surrender was known as "noxae deditio" and it remained a characteristic feature of the liability for damage caused by animals throughout the history of Roman law[39]

a valid legal procedure occurs *uniquely* in Western society"; it was unknown to any society, past or present, which falls outside "the Western cosmological tradition" (pp. 64, 5).

[33] Cf. Hans Fehr, "Gottesurteil und Folter. Eine Studie zur Dämonologie des Mittelalters und der neuen Zeit", in: *Festgabe für Rudolf Stammler* (1926), pp. 231 sqq., 252. But cf. also Finkelstein, op. cit., note 2, pp. 64 sqq., according to whom the animal had to be executed, because the very act of killing a human being ". . . had rendered it an object of public horror. This horror is engendered by the implications of such a killing: the animal was seen as a living rebuttal of the divinely ordained hierarchy of creation; by an action that itself could not be judged on a moral standard the ox turned into an instrument that undermined the moral foundations of the universe" (p. 70). In the phenomenon of real animal trials in early Christian Europe, Finkelstein argues, "a uniquely biblical conception of sovereignity" manifested itself; cf. pp. 25 sqq.

[34] Sellert, op. cit., note 23, pp. 74 sq.

[35] Kaser, *RPr* I, p. 165.

[36] Cf. Düll, (1941) 61 *ZSS* 1 sqq.; but see Franz Haymann, "Textkritische Studien zum römischen Obligationenrecht", (1921) 42 *ZSS* 367 sqq. On the question of a historical connection between Greek law and the Roman actio de pauperie, cf. also Jackson, (1978) 37 *Cambridge LJ* 122 sq.

[37] On the origin of delict in private vengeance, cf. supra, pp. 2 sq., 914. For parallels between the Roman and the Anglo-Saxon development, see Williams, op. cit., note 23, pp. 265 sqq. (272); cf. also p. 7 sqq.

[38] Supra, pp. 916 sq.

[39] Cf., in particular, Otto Lenel, "Die Formula der actiones noxales", (1927) 47 *ZSS* 2 sqq.; Cornelius Gerhardus van der Merwe, *Skuldlose aanspreeklikheid vir skade veroorsaak deur diere* (unpublished LLD thesis, Pretoria, 1970), pp. 5 sqq., 12 sqq.; Kaser, *RPr* I, pp. 165, 633. Contra: Kerr Wylie, *Studi Riccobono*, vol. IV, pp. 461 sqq.; Ubaldo Robbe, "L'actio de pauperie", (1932) 7 *RISG* 359 sqq. On the differences between the actiones legis Aquiliae and de pauperie noxalis, see Hans Ankum, "L'actio de pauperie et l'actio legis Aquiliae dans le droit romain classique", in: *Studi in onore di Cesare Sanfilippo*, vol. II (1982), pp. 14 sq.

(and, indeed, much of the ius commune). "Noxia autem est ipsum delictum", as Ulpian emphasized;[40] and as a result, the actio de pauperie had the usual characteristics of a noxal action: it was the owner of the animal at the time of litis contestatio (not at the time when it had done the damage) who was liable ("noxa caput sequitur");[41] and if the animal died before litis contestatio, the right to bring the actio de pauperie fell away.[42] This was the more archaic side of the Roman regime of liability for damage caused by animals. But in the very notion of a noxal liability there also lay the key to a more rational and matter-of-fact approach to the issue.[43] For it was obviously not the animal against whom the victim had to institute proceedings, but its owner; and though the aim of these proceedings was, initially, to seize the animal and to avenge the injury, the notion of private vengeance as the basis of the law of delict gradually faded away.[44] A claim for damages was regarded as a more appropriate remedy and obviously, again, it was the owner of the animal who was the target of this claim. As a result, in both classical and post-classical Roman law, the victim was given a choice: he could sue either for damages or for the surrender of the animal (". . . aut noxam sarcire aut in noxam dedere").[45] The new view gained the ascendancy to such an extent that surrender was increasingly regarded as a means of avoiding the primary obligation of noxam sarcire.[46] But in any event it was firmly established that, one way or another, liability attached to the owner of the animal. The animal had caused the damage, but it was no longer thought to have committed a delict. The owner, of course, had not committed a delict either, but he was liable merely for being in charge of a potential source of risk for others. Fault on his part was required no more than "blameworthy" conduct on the part of the animal.[47]

---

[40] Ulp. D. 9, 1, 1, 1; on this text, see Van der Merwe, op. cit., note 39, pp. 15 sq.

[41] Ulp. D. 9, 1, 1, 12; and see, in general, supra, p. 917.

[42] Ulp. D. 9, 1, 1, 13. If the animal that had caused the damage was killed by a third party after the victim had instituted proceedings against the owner of the animal, the owner's liability under the actio de pauperie had to be taken into account when it came to determining the sum that had to be awarded to the owner in his lawsuit against the third party under the lex Aquilia; cf. Iav. D. 9, 2, 37, 1; Ulp. D. 9, 1, 1, 16; and, for a detailed analysis, Ankum, *Studi Sanfilippo*, vol. II, pp. 13 sqq.

[43] On the approach adopted by the Romans towards animals along these lines, see Haymann (1921) 42 *ZSS* 368 sqq.; Slavomir Condanari-Michler, "Vis extrinsecus admota. Ein Beitrag zum Einfluss der griechischen Philosophie auf Roms Juristen", in: *Festschrift für Leopold Wenger*, vol. I (1944), pp. 236 sqq.; Sellert, op. cit., note 23, p. 71.

[44] Cf. supra, pp. 3, 914 sq.

[45] Ulp. D. 9, 1, 1, 11; cf. also Ulp. D. 9, 1, 1 pr. On the formula, see Lenel, *EP*, p. 195.

[46] Gai. D. 9, 4, 1.

[47] Cf., for example, Condanari-Michler, *Festschrift Wenger*, vol. I, pp. 237 sqq.; Buckland/Stein, p. 603; Van der Merwe, op. cit., note 39, pp. 2 sq.; Kaser, *RPr* I, p. 633; Sellert, op. cit., note 23, p. 72. But cf. Paul. D. 9, 1, 2, 1, where a distinction is drawn that is most easily explainable on the basis that in the one case the owner was at fault and in the other he was not: "Si quis aliquem evitans, magistratum forte, in taberna proxima se immisisset ibique a cane feroce laesus esset, non posse agi canis nomine quidam putant: at si

(c) *Range of application*

After these more general remarks about the nature of the actio de pauperie we may now turn to the details of its application. The remedy was available in cases of bodily harm to children in power and to free persons,[48] as well as damage to property. In the latter instance it was, of course, as a rule the owner who could sue; but where a non-owner, as a result of being liable for custodia, had a specific interest in the integrity of the object, he, rather than the owner, could bring the action.[49] The damage had to be done, according to the provision of the XII Tables, by a quadrupes. Implicit in this term was probably a limitation that was to appear more clearly from the text of the lex Aquilia:[50] it was intended to cover four-footed beasts of the class of cattle (". . . quadrupedemve pecudem"). By the time that Ulpian wrote his commentary on the Edict, this restriction had been dropped, however: "Quae actio ad omnes quadrupedes pertinet", he remarked.[51] The classical lawyers were, in fact, even prepared to grant an actio utilis "et si non quadrupes, sed aliud animal pauperiem fecit":[52] if the damage had been caused by two-footed animals like chicken, geese or ducks. But was the actio de pauperie only applicable to domesticated animals

solutus fuisset, contra." But the somewhat abrupt second alternative ("at si . . .") may well constitute a shortened and distorted version of the classical original. Unconvincing are the explanations by Haymann, (1921) 42 *ZSS* 362 sq. and Kerr Wylie, *Studi Riccobono*, vol. IV, pp. 508 sq. On D. 9, 1, 2, 1 cf. also Jean Macqueron, "Les dommages causés par des chiens dans la jurisprudence Romaine", in: *Flores legum H.J. Scheltema oblati* (1971), pp. 137 sqq. As far as the discussion of D. 9, 1, 2, 1 by the authors of the ius commune is concerned, cf. C.G. van der Merwe, op. cit., note 39, p. 101.

[48] Gai. D. 9, 1, 3 ("Ex hac lege iam non dubitatur etiam liberarum personarum nomine agi posse . . ."). From this text it can be deduced that in earlier times the matter was in doubt; originally probably, as in the case of the lex Aquilia, only injury to slaves (and grazing animals) could be recovered. Cf. Kerr Wylie, *Studi Riccobono*, vol. IV, pp. 465, 510; Van der Merwe, op. cit., note 39, pp. 115 sqq.; Watson, (1970) 17 *RIDA* 365 sq.; Jackson, (1978) 37 *Cambridge LJ* 124 sq.

[49] Paul. D. 9, 1, 2 pr. (mentioning as an example the fullo).

[50] Cf. supra, pp. 953, 959, 976.

[51] D. 9, 1, 1, 2. This development appears to have occurred partly by interpretation, partly by statute. The statute in question was the so-called lex Pesolania, which is referred to in Paul. Sent. I, XV, 1 (". . . etiam lege Pesolania de cane cavetur"); cf. Macqueron, *Festschrift Scheltema*, pp. 136 sq.; contra: Jackson, (1978) 37 *Cambridge LJ* 129 sq. (who argues that Cuiacius' conjecture that the term derives from a comparative reference to the lex Solonia (Solon's law), which was later misunderstood or erroneously copied, is still persuasive). Cf. also Voet, *Commentarius ad Pandectas*, Lib. IX, Tit. I, VI (lex Colonia); on which see Gane, *The Selective Voet*, vol. II, (1955), p. 541; cf. also Glück, vol. 10, pp. 279 sq.). Determination of the legal regime applicable to dogs, incidentally, always appears to have presented certain difficulties. On the one hand, dogs "have been domesticated for ages: I am not quite sure, but I believe we find dogs associated with Neolithic man" (*Boyce v. Robertson* 1912 TPD 381 at 383). Yet, on the other hand, they display a "certain propensity towards ferocity" and are, therefore, "in some respects ferae naturae" (*Boyce v. Robertson* 1912 TPD 381 at 384). Cf., apart from the lex Pesolania and the article by Macqueron (dealing specifically with damage done by dogs), Williams, op. cit., note 23, pp. 137 sqq., 343 sqq., 354 sqq.; ss. 3 and 9 of the English Animals Act 1971 and P.M. North, *The Modern Law of Animals* (1972), pp. 184 sqq.

[52] Paul. D. 9, 1, 4.

or also to those which are wild by nature? This question may have been disputed among the classical Roman lawyers (it certainly is among contemporary Romanists),[53] but there can, I think, be little doubt that Ulpian reflected the prevailing view when he wrote: "In bestiis autem propter naturalem feritatem haec actio locum non habet."[54]

(d) The "contra naturam" test

By far the most interesting texts on the actio de pauperie are those which discuss the type of conduct on account of which the animal had to have caused the damage. As has been mentioned, the owner's liability, though strict, must still be kept within certain reasonable limits; and the Roman lawyers appear to have attempted, originally, to bring about the necessary delimitation by requiring a spontaneous action on the part of the animal. "[C]um commota feritate nocuit quadrupes"[55] the remedy could be brought, but not if some external cause was ultimately responsible for the damage. Thus, the actio de pauperie was not applicable, for instance, if a horse kicked someone because it was pricked or hit or wounded;[56] if one bull was provoked by another into doing damage;[57] or if a mule upset its load onto someone because it was overloaded, because it tripped as a result of the unevenness of the road or because the mule-driver had been negligent.[58] Yet there were certain situations where the owner was held responsible even though the behaviour of his animal could hardly be said to have been spontaneous. Thus we read of a mule that kicked out and broke a groom's leg after the groom had brought along a horse that had started to sniff at the mule. "[C]onsulebatur", reports Alfenus, "possetne cum domino mulae agi, quod ea pauperiem fecisset. respondi

[53] Fritz Litten, "Beiträge zur Lehre von der Schadenszurechnung nach römischem und bürgerlichem Rechte", (1907) 49 *JhJb* 425 sqq.; Haymann, (1921) 42 *ZSS* 373 sqq.; Barry Nicholas, "Liability for Animals in Roman Law", 1958 *Acta Juridica* 187 sq.; Kerr Wylie, Studi Riccobono, vol. IV, p. 477; Thomas, *TRL*, p. 383; Jackson, (1978) 37 *Cambridge LJ* 135 sq.; but cf. Robbe, (1932) 7 *RISG* 348 sqq.; D.I.C. Ashton-Cross, "Liability in Roman Law for Damage Caused by Animals", (1953) 11 *Cambridge LJ* 395 sqq.; idem, "Liability for Animals in Roman Law", 1959 *Cambridge LJ* 189 sqq.; Van der Merwe, op. cit., note 39, pp. 59 sqq.

[54] Ulp. D. 9, 1, 1, 10. Cf. also *Inst.* IV, 9 pr.

[55] Servius/Ulp. D. 9, 1, 1, 4; Van der Merwe, op. cit., note 39, pp. 69 sqq.

[56] Ulp. D. 9, 1, 1, 7.

[57] Quintus Mucius/Ulp. D. 9, 1, 1, 11.

[58] Ulp. D. 9, 1, 1, 4. Cf. also the case involving the two loaded carts pulling up the Capitoline hill (Alf. D. 9, 2, 52, 2; on which cf. supra p. 982, note 200; cf. further Kerr Wylie, *Studi Riccobono*, vol. IV, pp. 511 sqq.). If the first cart had rolled back (crashed into the second one and, as a result, knocked down a slave), because the mules had shied at something, the actio de pauperie could be brought against their owner ("sed si mulae, quia aliquid reformidassent et muliones timore permoti, ne opprimerentur, plostrum reliquissent . . . eum domino mularum [actionem] esse"). But the action did not lie if the drivers had been at fault (if, for example, they had tried to lift the back of the first cart in order to make it easier for the mules to pull it up the hill, but had then suddenly, "sua sponte", let go), or if the mules just could not take the weight, or if in trying to do so, they had slipped and fallen and the (first) cart had then started to roll down the hill.

posse."[59] The same answer was given in the case of a horse that kicked someone who was stroking or patting it.[60] The spontaneity doctrine was obviously thought to overshoot the mark: it confined the owner's liability too narrowly. Another, more refined criterion was thus required to draw the line more aptly. It was ultimately formulated by Ulpian in the following terms: "Et generaliter haec actio locum habet, quotiens contra naturam fera mota pauperiem dedit":[61] the general rule is that the action lies whenever an animal is moved against its nature to commit pauperies. "Contra naturam" was a conveniently flexible concept and allowed the Roman jurists to delimit the respective risk spheres of the owner of the animal, the victim of the injury and any third party that might have been involved, in a pragmatic fashion.[62] It was not designed to focus on the general disposition of the individual animal that had caused the damage, for Servius/Ulp. D. 9, 1, 1, 4 specifically state that the owner is liable even if a horse given to kicking actually kicks and thus inflicts an injury, or if an ox that is prone to goring gores someone; in cases, that is, where the damaging form of behaviour can hardly be regarded as uncharacteristic of the individual animal concerned. Nor, on the other hand, did "contra naturam" refer to the "nature" of the whole species of animals to which the one that had caused the damage belonged (contra naturam sui generis).[63] Kicking, after all, is not an unnatural form of behaviour in horses, goring is not unnatural in oxen:[64] and yet, it is clear from our sources that the owner was liable. "Contra naturam" must rather have been used in classical Roman law as a common denominator for forms of behaviour that were uncharacteristic of a domesticated animal. Domesticated animals could be expected to be tame and peaceful, and thus a horse was not supposed to kick, nor was an ox supposed to gore. If they did, it was either because their innate, original wildness[65] broke through what had become their second nature—and it was this risk which the owner had to bear—or they had acted secundum naturam: the horse had kicked because it had been hit, the ox had gored because it had been provoked, the mule had slipped because of the unevenness

[59] Alf. D. 9, 1, 5.
[60] Ulp. D. 9, 1, 1, 7 in fine.
[61] Ulp. D. 9, 1, 1, 7.
[62] Cf., in particular, Van der Merwe, op. cit., note 39, pp. 72 sqq. Many authors take the contra naturam requirement to be of post-classical origin; cf. Haymann, (1921) 42 ZSS 373 sqq.; Robbe, (1932) 7 *RISG* 343 sqq.; Kerr Wylie, *Studi Riccobono*, vol. IV, pp. 461 sqq.; Nicholas, 1958 *Acta Juridica* 187 sqq. But see, apart from Van der Merwe, Kaser, *RPr* I, p. 634; idem, *RPr* II, p. 433.
[63] This is how Colin Kolbert (Mommsen/Krüger/Watson, vol. I (1985) wrongly translates the phrase. Cf. also, for example, Windscheid/Kipp, § 457, 3 and other pandectists; Ashton-Cross, (1953) 11 *Cambridge LJ* 400.
[64] But, for example, goring would be a behaviour contra naturam sui generis for horses, kicking contra naturam sui generis for oxen; cf. Fr. Eisele, "Civilistische Kleinigkeiten", (1886) 24 *JhJb* 482.
[65] Cf. Servius/Ulp. D. 9, 1, 1, 4 ("cum commota feritate nocuit quadrupes").

of the road. Such reactions could scarcely be seen as inconsistent with the peaceful nature of domesticated animals and the owner was thus relieved of liability.[66]

3. The edictum de feris in Roman law

(a) *Wild animals in Rome*

But what about wild animals? Large numbers of lions and bears, of cheetahs and elephants, of tigers and rhinoceroses, of crocodiles and hippopotamuses[67] were needed for circuses and training schools.[68] Ever more sensational venationes[69] were put up for the amusement of the populace. As early as 169 B.C. did the aediles curules P. Cornelius Scipio Nasica and P. Lentulus display, amongst others, 63 "African beasts"[70] and 40 bears at a show in the Circus Maximus.[71] No less a personage than Quintus Mucius Scaevola (pontifex) is credited by Pliny with having arranged the first fight "of a number of lions together"

---

[66] The case of the dog biting a man who, when fleeing from a magistrate, rushes into a taberna also fits in here (Paul. D. 9, 1, 2, 1, first alternative: ". . . non posse agi canis nomine quidam putant"; cf. supra, note 47). Cf. also Proc./Ulp. D. 9, 2, 11, 5 (someone irritates a dog and thus causes it to bite another person); Ofilius/Ulp. D. 9, 2, 9, 3 (someone scares a horse which, as a result, throws its rider into the river).

If it was due to the fault of a third party that the animal had inflicted the injury (as in the two last-mentioned cases) the injured person could bring an actio legis Aquiliae in factum against that third party. Cf. also Ulp. D. 9, 1, 1, 5, where it is held that a person who takes a dog out on a lead will be liable if the dog breaks loose "asperitate sua" and does some harm to someone else, provided it could have been better restrained or it should never have been taken to that particular place. According to Ulpian, this action excludes the victim's right to bring the actio de pauperie against the owner of the dog. This can, however, hardly have been a general rule; cf. also Glück, vol. 10, p. 274; Haymann, (1921) 42 *ZSS* 386 sq.; but see Van der Merwe, op. cit., note 39, pp. 96 sq.

[67] On the types of animals used in the Roman games cf. George Jennison, *Animals for Show and Pleasure in Ancient Rome* (1937), pp. 42 sqq.

[68] On the "training of man-eaters", see Jennison, op. cit., note 67, pp. 194 sq. The schools were for the training of the bestiarii (who had to fight the animals) as well as of the beasts themselves (to turn them, where that was still necessary, into eager and ferocious fighters).

[69] These were the animal contests or hunts with which the day in the circus usually started. "They finished before midday, the afternoons were always devoted to the far more important gladiatorial combats—the amusement of the cultured classes" (Jennison, op. cit., note 67, p. 176). Carcopino, pp. 260 sq., summarizes as follows: "There were some relatively innocent [animal shows] to break the monotony of the massacre: . . . teams of panthers obediently drawing chariots; lions releasing from their jaws a live hare they had caught; tigers coming to lick the hand of the tamer who had just been lashing them; elephants gravely kneeling before the imperial box or tracing Latin phrases in the sand with their trunks. There were terrible spectacles, in which ferocious beasts fought duels to the death: bear against buffalo, buffalo against elephant, elephant against rhinoceros. There were disgusting ones in which the men, from the safe shelter of iron bars or from the height of the imperial box—like Commodus later—let fly their arrows at animals roaring with baffled rage, and flooded the arena with the blood of butchery. . . ." For a description of the venationes given at the dedication of the Colosseum, see the *Liber Spectaculorum* of Martialis.

[70] The term "Africanae bestiae", or simply, "Africanae", was normally used to refer to leopards and other large cats. They did not necessarily come from Africa but could also have been imported from the East. Cf. Jennison, op. cit., note 67, pp. 45 sq.

[71] Livius, *Ab urbe condita*, XLIV, XVIII, 8.

during his aedilship.[72] In 58 B.C. 150 large spotted cats (predominantly leopards) were let loose together in the arena.[73] Augustus records that 3 500 Africanae bestiae were killed in his 26 venationes;[74] and during the games with which Titus inaugurated the Colosseum in 80 A.D., 5 000 beasts were killed in one single day.[75] These animals had to be imported from all parts of the Empire,[76] displayed for sale, shoved from their travelling dens into stockyards[77] or cages and transported through the Roman streets before, ultimately, ending up in the carnage of the amphitheatres. There was an obvious risk that they, in turn, might find an opportunity to cause a bloodbath. The famous sculptor Praxiteles, for example, very nearly became one of their victims; while working at the docks in Ostia on the figure of a lion which had just arrived from overseas, he was attacked by a leopard that had managed to escape from another cage nearby.[78] But then there were also people who earned their money as snake charmers[79] or who displayed tame lions in a cage.[80] Rich Romans fancied exotic animals as household pets[81] or they kept big game in special hunting parks close to their country villae.[82] Nero even had a multitude of all kinds of "pecudes et ferae" in his famous domus aurea at Rome.[83] Again, the presence of these animals—whether tame or otherwise—in a densely populated city must have been somewhat more hazardous than the rural co-existence of man with sheep or mules or horses; and if it was thought necessary to make the owner strictly liable for injuries inflicted by a cow, the rules of the lex Aquilia can hardly have been regarded as having provided sufficient protection against the dangers emanating from ferocious panthers.

---

[72] Plinius, *Historia naturalis*, Lib. VIII, XX (53).

[73] Plinius, *Historia naturalis*, Lib. VIII, XXIV (64). These games were given by an aedil by the name of M. Scaurus and also included, as a special highlight, the first hippopotamus brought to Rome; it was exhibited with five crocodiles.

[74] Cf. Jennison, op. cit., note 67, pp. 63 sq.

[75] Suetonius, *De vita Caesarum*, Titus, VII, in fine. For further details on the animal shows under the Empire, see Jennison, op. cit., note 67, pp. 60 sqq., 83 sqq.

[76] Some came from as far afield as Scotland (ursus Caledonicus); cf. Jackson, (1978) 37 *Cambridge LJ* 134.

[77] Described by Jennison, op. cit., note 67, pp. 174 sqq.

[78] Plinius, *Historia naturalis*, Lib. XXXVI, IV (4) (40).

[79] Cf. Paul. D. 47, 11, 11: "In circulatores, qui serpentes circumferunt et proponunt, si cui ob eorum metum damnum datum est, pro modo admissi actio dabitur"; cf. Ashton-Cross, (1953) 11 *Cambridge LJ* 400.

[80] Epictetus, *Dissertationes ab Arriani digestae*, Lib. IV, I, 25.

[81] For details, see Jennison, op. cit., note 67, pp. 126 sqq. "The Emperor Caracalla . . . kept a number of lions which he took with him on his journeys, and one of them, called Scimetar, ate and slept in the same room with him . . . [The Emperor] Elagabalus . . ., a fantastic, effeminate, and vicious youth, is represented in the *Historia Augusta* as having a taste for . . . employing (his animals) in childish amusements and very disagreeable practical jokes" (pp. 132, 90). He used to let lions, leopards and bears (who had been deprived of their teeth and claws) loose on his guests, at table or in their beds.

[82] For details, see Jennison, op. cit., note 67, pp. 133 sqq.

[83] Suetonius, *De vita Caesarum*, Nero, XXXI.

(b) The intervention of the praetor

In this instance it was, however, not the ius civile that took up the issue. The safety of the public roads was a matter for which the curules aediles were responsible—the same magistrates that were also charged with the cura ludorum.[84] They must soon have perceived that none of the existing remedies could adequately cope with the problems presented by transporting and marketing the animals that were required for the games and thus they issued an "edictum de feris". Very little, unfortunately, is known about this edict, not even its date of promulgation. Originally, it probably referred to dogs and boars;[85] both were not, at that stage, covered by the actio de pauperie.[86] Foreign animals began to be used for the games only around the beginning of the 2nd century B.C.[87] The range of application of the aedilitian edict was then gradually extended; by the time of classical Roman law it appears to have included wolves, bears, "panthers"[88] and lions.[89] A person who had brought these kinds of wild beasts into the vicinity of a public road, or who kept them there, was liable for any damage that they did.[90] It did not matter whether they were tied up or allowed to run around,[91] nor whether they escaped or merely mauled a passer-by.[92] The person in charge of the animal—who did not have to be its owner[93]—was liable, irrespective of whether he could have prevented the incident or not. The basis of his liability was thus not fault but the mere fact that by having a dangerous animal "qua vulgo iter fiet", he had created a risk to others. For the death of a freeman the edict provided a penalty of 200 solidi,[94] in cases of non-fatal injuries to freemen the judge was instructed to award "quanti bonum aequum

[84] On the double responsibility of the aediles, in this context, see Alan Watson, *Law Making in the Later Roman Republic* (1974), p. 86.

[85] Cf. the analysis by Jackson, (1978) 37 *Cambridge LJ* 128 sqq.

[86] Dogs probably had to be brought under the actio de pauperie by way of a special statute (cf. supra, note 51); they remained excluded from the ambit of the first chapter of the lex Aquilia (Gai. D. 9, 2, 2, 2). The same text reveals the interpretive difficulties that were experienced with regard to pigs. It is likely that for the same reason pigs (and that means also boars) were not originally taken to be included among the quadrupedes in terms of the actio de pauperie.

[87] Jennison, op. cit., note 67, pp. 44 sq. One of the first foreign animals seen in a Roman circus was possibly the ostrich from Africa.

[88] On the meaning of the term "panthera", see Jennison, op. cit., note 67, pp. 183 sqq.

[89] Ulp. D. 21, 1, 40; cf. also *Inst.* IV, 9, 1 (leaving out the wolf and panther); Paul. D. 21, 1, 41 ("aliudve quod noceret animal"). According to Ashton-Cross, (1953) 11 *Cambridge LJ*, application of this edict was even extended to domestic animals. Contra: Nicholas, 1958 *Acta Juridica* 186 sq.; Van der Merwe, op. cit., note 39, p. 142.

[90] "[A]iunt aediles: 'ne quis canem, verrem vel minorem aprum, lupum, ursum, pantheram, leonem, . . . qua vulgo iter fiet, ita habuisse velit, ut cuiquam nocere damnumve dare possit" (Ulp. D. 21, 1, 40 and 42; Lenel, *EP*, p. 566).

[91] Cf. Paul. D. 21, 1, 41 (". . . sive soluta sint, sive alligata, ut contineri vinculis . . .").

[92] Nicholas, 1958 *Acta Juridica* 186; Van der Merwe, op. cit., note 39, p. 143.

[93] Nicholas, 1958 *Acta Juridica* 185; Van der Merwe, op. cit., note 39, p. 143; but cf. Ashton-Cross, (1953) 11 *Cambridge LJ* 395 sqq.

[94] But cf. Lenel, *EP*, p. 566.

. . . videbitur", and in cases of damage to property "duplum" was recoverable.[95] None of these consequences could be averted by way of noxal surrender. Provocation of the animal by the victim of the injury did perhaps exclude liability.[96] According to *Inst.* IV, 9, 1 the actio de pauperie and the aedilitian action could be brought concurrently; but this can have applied only in the case of dogs and, possibly, boars.[97]

4. The actio de pastu in Roman law

Even less than about the edictum de feris is known about a third remedy that was available for damage caused by animals. It dealt with a specific form of damage—depasturization of another person's land—and is known as the actio de pastu. It must have been of considerable importance at a time when Rome was still a predominantly agrarian society and in fact it is said to have been part and parcel already of the decemviral remedies.[98] Whether only deliberate depasturization was actionable (in the sense that the defendant had to have driven his animals onto the plaintiff's land)[99] or whether we are dealing with another instance of strict liability, based on the principles of noxality[100] is a matter of uncertainty. Of our three sources which allude to the actio de pastu one appears to support the former,[101] and two the latter proposition.[102] The most explicit of the three is Pauli Sententiae I, XV, 1 ("Si quadrupes pauperiem fecerit damnumve dederit quidve depasta sit, in dominum actio datur, ut aut damni aestimationem subeat aut quadrupedem dedat . . ."); and although there are certain indications that Paulus' original text may have suffered somewhat at the hands of the post-classical compilers of the Sententiae, the reasons to suspect the clause "quidve depasta sit" cannot really be regarded as conclusive. But even if, as appears likely, the owner of the cattle was under a strict noxal liability, the practical importance of the actio de pastu dwindled considerably when liability under Aquilian principles came to be extended, by means of actiones in factum and

[95] Ulp. D. 21, 1, 42; Inst. IV, 9, 1. For further details on the edictum de feris, cf. Van der Merwe, op. cit., note 39, pp. 142 sqq.; Jackson, (1978) 37 *Cambridge LJ* 132 sqq.

[96] Cf. Paul. Sent. I, XV, 3.

[97] Cf. also Van der Merwe, op. cit., note 39, p. 145.

[98] Ulp. D. 19, 5, 14, 3.

[99] Kerr Wylie, *Studi Riccobono*, vol. IV, p. 475; A. Fliniaux, "Une vieille action du droit romain. L' 'actio de pastu'", in: *Mélanges de droit romain dédiés à Georges Cornil*, vol. I, pp. 252 sqq., 280 sqq.; cf. also Jackson, (1978) 37 *Cambridge LJ* 137, who suggests that culpa may have been sufficient.

[100] Cf. C.G. van der Merwe, "Die actio de pastu", (1973) 36 *THRHR* 107 sqq.; Kaser, *RPr* I, pp. 162 (n. 67), 633 (n. 29); cf. also *Van Zyl v. Van Biljon* 1987 (2) SA 372 (O) at 401.

[101] Ulp. D. 19, 5, 14, 3: "Si glans ex arbore tua in meum fundum cadat eamque ego immisso pecore depascam: Aristo scribit non sibi occurrere legitimam actionem, qua experiri possim: nam neque ex lege duodecim tabularum de pastu pecoris (quia non in tuo pascitur) neque de pauperie neque de damni iniuriae agi posse: in factum itaque erit agendum."

[102] Paul. Sent. I, XV, 1; C. 3, 35, 6.

actiones utiles, to cases of indirect causation of damage.[103] Diocletian and Maximian specifically encouraged plaintiffs to use the actio legis Aquiliae in cases of depasturization when they decreed: "De his, quae per iniuriam depasta contendis, ex sententia legis Aquiliae agere minime prohiberis";[104] and as long as fault could be established on the part of the defendant, this was indeed the more convenient remedy for the plaintiff.[105] It may, however, also be concluded, e contrario, from C. 3, 35, 6, that where the land was not "depasta per iniuriam" the actio de pastu was thought to remain available.[106]

5. The actio de pastu in South African law

All three remedies have come to be incorporated into the ius commune. Via the old Roman-Dutch authorities they were transplanted to the Cape of Good Hope, from where they spread to the other European settlements in Southern Africa. There they have survived to this day. The range of application of the actio de pastu has, generally speaking, been defined rather liberally.[107] It is applicable wherever damage has been done by grazing and it does not matter whether grass, crops, shrubs or trees have been affected.[108] The defendant is liable even if his animals devour crops that have been reaped;[109] and if, in the course of satisfying their appetite, the animals have trampled down the plaintiff's crops, the resulting damage is also recoverable by means of the actio de pastu.[110] Not only four-footed animals but also birds are covered by the remedy, as long, of course, as they can cause damage by grazing. Whether their owner is strictly liable, or only if he intentionally drove his animals onto the plaintiff's land, is still disputed; the Rhodesian Court of Appeal has adopted the latter view,[111] but the (only) authority

[103] Cf. supra, for example, pp. 903 sq.

[104] C. 3, 35, 6.

[105] The defendant did, for example, not have the option of noxal surrender; in case of denial the amount of condemnation "crescit in duplum" (cf. supra, p. 974).

[106] For further discussion, see Fliniaux, *Mélanges Cornil*, vol. I, pp. 247 sqq.; Van der Merwe, op. cit., note 39, pp. 121 sqq.; idem, (1973) 36 *THRHR* 105 sqq.; Jackson, (1978) 37 *Cambridge LJ* 127 sq., 136 sqq.

[107] For details, see Van der Merwe, op. cit., note 39, pp. 130 sqq., 135 sqq.; idem, (1973) 36 *THRHR* 105 sqq., 110 sqq.; *Van Zyl v. Van Biljon* 1987 (2) SA 372 (O) at 381 sqq. (a decision running over 40 pages and comprehensively covering all available historical sources, contemporary literature and South African precedents; cf. also the case note by J. Neethling, (1988) 51 *THRHR* 547 sqq.). In the 19th century the actio de pastu was in danger of being ousted by the (English) common-law remedy of "cattle trespass": *De Blanche v. Zietsman* (1880) 1 NLR 185; *Westhuyzen v. Lotter* (1898) 19 NLR 162; cf. also *Thomson v. Schietekat* (1893) 10 SC 46.

[108] *Thomson v. Schietekat* (1893) 10 SC 46; *Van Zyl v. Kotze* 1961 (4) SA 214 (T).

[109] Voet, *Commentarius ad Pandectas*, Lib. IX, Tit. I, II; *Crous v. Jaffe Bros.* 1921 OPD 2; cf. also Struve, *Syntagma*, Exerc. XIV, Lib. IX, Tit. I, III (". . . ut si columbae in alterius granariis frumentum absumserint").

[110] *Vermaak v. Du Plessis* 1974 (4) SA 353 (O).

[111] *Heron v. Skinner* 1971 (1) SA 399 (RAD).

referred to, Voet's *Commentarius ad Pandectas*,[112] does not actually support it. On the contrary: ever since the French humanist Cuiacius attempted to reconstruct the Sententiae Pauli, the actio de pastu has predominantly been held not to require proof of fault.[113]

An alternative remedy that originated in Germanic customary law has, incidentally, been recognized by the Roman-Dutch writers, and is still applicable today in the Republic of South Africa on the basis of provincial ordinances: rather than institute the actio de pastu to claim damages, the plaintiff may impound the animals trespassing on his land and keep them until their owner has paid both the pound fees and compensation for the damage caused.[114]

6. The edictum de feris in South African law

The edictum de feris has apparently only once been applied by a South African court[115]—a dog had been taken onto a public road and had bitten to death an ostrich that was lawfully feeding on the commonage adjoining that road—but it has been mentioned in a number of other decisions.[116] According to Wessels JA,[117] "canis", in terms of the edict, refers only to a vicious dog, not to "a lady's lap dog". On the authority

---

[112] Lib. IX, Tit. I, I.

[113] Cf., for example, Struve, *Syntagma*, Exerc. XIV, Lib. IX, Tit. I, III; cf. also *Van Zyl v. Kotze* 1961 (4) SA 214 (T); *Constant v. Louw* 1951 (4) SA 143 (C) at 148B; *Vermaak v. Du Plessis* 1974 (4) SA 353 (O); *Van Zyl v. Van Biljon* 1987 (2) SA 372 (O) at 381 sqq. The main point to be decided in the latter case was whether or not vis maior constitutes a defence against the actio de pastu. The court held that it does, provided "the animal [was] directly motivated to act by vis maior". If, on the other hand, the vis maior merely made available to the animals an access to the other person's land (in casu defendant's cattle had gained access to plaintiff's maize field due to the fact that the boundary fence had been struck down by lightning), "and the animals then made use of that access from their own volition to graze on the damaged land, the damage would have been caused by their own independent conduct . . . and the owner of the animals would be strictly liable for the damage done". It is hardly convincing, however, to derive this distinction (as M.T. Steyn J does) from "the decisive effect of the principle of causality" (all quotations from the translation of the headnote on pp. 373 sq.).

[114] The "licentia pignorandi" derives from Germanic customary law; for details, cf. Leyser, *Meditationes ad Pandectas*, Spec. CXI; Stryk, *Usus modernus pandectarum*, Lib. IX, Tit. I, §§ 15 sqq.; Glück, vol. 10, pp. 302 sqq.; Van der Merwe, (1973) 76 *THRHR* 112 sqq. The custom was recognized in Anglo-Saxon law, too, and has become part of the English common law ("distress damage feasant", defined by Williams, op. cit., note 23, p. XLVII, as "a process of self-help whereby chattels that are doing damage to or (perhaps) encumbering land or depasturing chattels may be taken and retained by way of security until compensation is paid". On its history (". . . for many centuries . . . a history of attenuation—almost of decay") and all details of its application, see Williams, op. cit., note 23, pp. 7 sqq.; cf. also Fleming, *Torts*, pp. 80 sq. A person who distrains animals has to impound them as soon as reasonably possible (see Williams, pp. 90 sqq.).

[115] *Le Roux v. Fick* (1879) 9 Buch 29 (cf. *O'Callaghan v. Chaplin* 1927 AD 310 at 325 and 367).

[116] *Cowell v. Friedman & Co.* (1888) 5 HCG 22 at 38; *Chandler v. The Middelburg Municipality* 1924 TPD 450 at 465 and 467; *O'Callaghan v. Chaplin* 1927 AD 310 (passim); *Bristow v. Lycett* 1971 (4) SA 223 (RAD) at 229.

[117] *O'Callaghan v. Chaplin* 1927 AD 310 at 371.

of Brunnemann[118] wild animals other than those specifically mentioned in the Edict have been held to be included—as, for example, snakes and crocodiles.[119] Occasionally, a departure from the requirement that the animal must have been kept in the vicinity of a public road has been suggested,[120] but in *O'Callaghan v. Chaplin*—where a dog had caused the damage in a private house—the edictum de feris was not in fact applied.[121] Liability is still, predominantly, regarded to be strict.[122]

7. The actio de pauperie in South African law

(a) *The nature of the remedy*

Last, but not least, of course, there is the actio de pauperie. It is this remedy, more than any other, that has shaped the modern civilian approach to liability for damage caused by animals.[123] But while in continental Europe, it has come to be incorporated into the modern codes of private law over the last two hundred years,[124] it still subsists as part and parcel of the Roman-Dutch branch of the ius commune in South Africa.[125] In the course of time, however, certain changes have

[118] *Commentarius in Pandectas*, Lib. XXI, Tit. I, ad L. Hi enim. 40.

[119] *O'Callaghan v. Chaplin* 1927 AD 310 at 346.

[120] Van Damhouder, *Praxis rerum criminalium*, Cap. CXLII, 9; cf. also *O'Callaghan v. Chaplin* 1927 AD 310 at 342 (per Kotzé JA).

[121] 1927 AD 310 at 330 (per Innes CJ).

[122] *Le Roux v. Fick* (1879) 9 Buch 29 at 41; *O'Callaghan v. Chaplin* 1927 AD 310 at 377 (per Wessels JA). But see also *Robertson v. Boyce* 1912 AD 367 at 382; *O'Callaghan v. Chaplin* 1927 AD 310 at 314 (per Innes CJ). For further details of the application of the edictum de feris in South African law, see Van der Merwe, op. cit., note 39, pp. 153 sqq.; but cf. also N.J. van der Merwe/P.J.J. Olivier, *Die onregmatige daad in die Suid-Afrikaanse reg* (5th ed., 1985), p. 495.

[123] In Germany the edictum de feris was abrogated by § 367, n. 11 StGB (Windscheid/Kipp, § 457, 3); cf. also already Glück, vol. 10, p. 272 (arguing that it had been replaced by art. 136 Constitutio Criminalis Carolina). The continued existence of the actio de pastu was in dispute (Windscheid/Kipp, loc. cit.; Rudolf Bienenfeld, *Die Haftungen ohne Verschulden* (1933), p. 45); it was not taken over into the BGB (cf. "Motive", in: *Mugdan*, vol. II, p. 452).

[124] Cf. art. 1385 code civil (on which see Watson, *Failures*, pp. 4 sqq., 17 sq.), § 1320 ABGB, art. 356 OR, § 833 BGB.

[125] In some of the earlier South African decisions liability of the owner was based on the English scienter doctrine (on which see infra, p. 1136 sq.); cf., in particular, *Botha v. Raubenheimer* 1918 EDL 200 (". . . however vicious a stallion may be by common knowledge, as there was no evidence to show that it is in the habit of kicking mares or is likely to do so, and as it was not shown that the defendant had knowledge of such vicious propensity on the part of his stallion, absolution from the instance should have been granted"); cf. further the cases referred to in *Beatty v. Donelly* (1876) 6 Buch 51. Contra: *Storey v. Stanner* (1882) 1 HCG 40 at 41; *Cowell v. Friedman & Co.* (1888) 5 HCG 22 at 50; *O'Callaghan v. Chaplin* 1927 AD 310 at 378. For some time, however, the notion has lingered on that the owner had to have been at fault: *Spires v. Scheepers* 3 EDC 173 at 176; *Parker v. Reed* (1904) 21 SC 496; *Sephton v. Benson* 1911 CPD 502; *Chandler v. The Middelburg Municipality* 1924 TPD 450; cf. also still *O'Callaghan v. Chaplin* 1927 AD 310 at 375 sqq. (per Wessels JA). Contra: *O'Callaghan v. Chaplin* 1927 AD 310 (with a very comprehensive discussion of the question by Innes CJ at pp. 313 sqq., and Kotzé JA at pp. 334 sqq.). This decision has authoritively settled the matter in favour of strict liability. Two very recent judicial utterances on the matter are *Van Zyl v. Van Biljon* 1987 (2) SA 372 (O) at 375 sqq. and *Lawrence v. Kondotel Inns (Pty.) Ltd.*

occurred. Most importantly, perhaps, the compensatory function of the actio de pauperie was increasingly stressed by the authors of the ius commune.[126] In the first place, the plaintiff had to be compensated for the damage caused by the defendant's animal; in fact, it was often pointed out that this was what he had to ask for when he brought the action.[127] The handing over of the animal was merely regarded as a way in which the defendant, if he so chose, was able to discharge his obligation. Clearly, the noxal surrender was a rather atavistic notion; as odd, in fact, as the concomitant rule that the action had to be brought against the owner tempore litis contestatae ("noxa caput sequitur"!).

For centuries, jurists were at pains to provide a rational explanation for the principle of noxality. One argument, for instance, that was frequently advanced, proceeded from the fact that it is the owner who derives the benefit from having the animal among his assets; it is only reasonable, under these circumstances, that he must also carry all the burdens associated with this piece of property.[128] But why was he then liable only for the consequences of the animal's conduct contra naturam and not also for the damages caused secundum naturam? Others, therefore, rather emphasized the principle of "alterum non laedere": every person had to be responsible for all the damage that either he, or one of the assets under his control, inflicted upon others.[129] But this, too, was a somewhat awkward explanation. For why should the owner of an animal be strictly liable if his liability depended otherwise on fault (lex Aquilia!)?[130] Yet it was the notion of strict liability that provided the most popular justification for the option of noxal surrender: in view of the fact that the owner was free of any blame,[131] it would have been

1989 (1) SA 44 (D) at 50 sqq.

In Scottish legal history, too, pauperian liability and the scienter principle have vied for recognition; today, the position in Scottish law appears to correspond to that in modern English law (i.e.: liability for damage done by "harmless" animals based on foreknowledge—scienter); cf. D.L. Carey-Miller, "The Scottish Institutional Writers on Animal Liability; Civilian or Scienter?", 1974 *Juridical Review* 5 sqq.; Bernard S. Jackson, "Liability for Animals in Scottish Legal Literature: From the Auld Lawes to the Sixteenth Century", (1975) 10 *The Irish Jurist* 334 sqq.; idem, "Liability for Animals in Scottish Legal Literature: From Stair to the Modern Law", 1977 *Juridical Review* 139 sqq.

[126] Cf. the discussion by Van der Merwe, op. cit., note 39, pp. 31 sq.

[127] Glück, vol. 10, p. 292; cf. also *O'Callaghan v. Chaplin* 1927 AD 310 at 352.

[128] Cf., for example, Gabriel Vasques, as quoted by Struve, *Syntagma*, Exerc. XIV, Lib. IX, Tit. I, VIII; Stryk, *Usus modernus pandectarum*, Lib. IX, Tit. I, § 4 (". . . ut qui commodum ex bestia captat, etiam incommodum ex reparatione damni sustineat") (quoted by De Villiers JA, in *O'Callaghan v. Chaplin* 1927 AD 310 at 334).

[129] Cf. Van der Merwe, op. cit., note 39, p. 33; Glück, vol. 10, p. 289.

[130] For a justification of ownership (rather than fault) as the basis of the actio de pauperie, see *O'Callaghan v. Chaplin* 1927 AD 310 at 313 sqq., 320 sqq., 334 sqq., 365 and 370 sqq.; Van der Merwe, op. cit., note 39, pp. 51 sqq.

[131] If the owner had been at fault, he was liable under Aquilian principles.

unreasonable to extend his liability beyond the intrinsic value of the animal.[132]

All this, at least to us, sounds rather unconvincing and it is surprising that the principle of noxality survived, in Germany, until the eve of codification.[133] In actual practice, however, things often looked quite different. Saxonian law, for instance, did not recognize the option of a noxal surrender,[134] and in other parts of Europe, too, the question was debated whether it had not been rendered obsolete. This view was, indeed, adopted by a whole variety of Frisian and Flemish authors,[135] but not in Holland: ". . . mane[t] in reliquis apud nos intacta romani juris definitio [. . .], etiam quantum ad ipsam noxae dandi licentiam, et subsequentem inde liberationem", as Voet specifically stressed.[136] The South African courts, though (in theory) applying "romeins-hollandse reg",[137] have not perpetuated this tradition. As a means of escaping "just liability for damage done by one's animals acting contra naturam", noxae deditio is regarded "as the remnant of an archaic practice wholly at variance with and unsuited to the notions of justice prevailing in modern times. Its observance was not in keeping with the legal philosophy of the past century and of our own day. The surrender of a harmful, and it may be worthless, animal is no compensation to an injured person".[138] With noxae deditio, the doctrine of noxa caput sequitur, with all its consequences, was also bound to go.[139] The only person liable is the original owner, "and he [is] liable for compensation pure and simple".[140]

---

[132] Cf., for example, Struve, *Syntagma*, Exerc. XIV, Lib. IX, Tit. I, VIII; Van der Merwe, op. cit., note 39, p. 33; cf. also Glück, vol. 10, p. 290.

[133] Windscheid/Kipp, § 457, 3; Bienenfeld, op. cit., note 123, p. 45.

[134] On Saxonian law (based on II, 40 Sachsenspiegel), see Wesenbeck, *Commentarius*, Lib. IX, Tit. I, 6; Stryk, *Usus modernus pandectarum*, Lib. IX, Tit. I, §§ 6 sqq. Nor did art. 136 of the Constitutio Criminalis Carolina recognize the possibility of noxal surrender.

[135] Cf., for example, Sande, *Decisiones Frisicae*, Lib. II, Tit. VII, V; Ulrich Huber, *Eunomia Romana sive Censura Censurae Juris Justinianaei* (Franequerae, 1700), Lib. IV, Ulp. Lib. XVIII ad Edict.; cf. further Van der Merwe, op. cit., note 39, pp. 36 sq.; *O'Callaghan v. Chaplin* 1927 AD 310 at 342 sqq.; see also Wesenbeck, *Commentarius*, loc. cit.; Vinnius, *Institutiones*, Lib. IV, Tit. IX, 1, n. 1.

[136] *Commentarius ad Pandectas*, Lib. IX, Tit. I, VIII; cf. further Grotius, *Inleiding*, III, XXXVIII, 10; Groenewegen, *De legibus abrogatis*, Inst. Lib. IV, Tit. IX, Princ., 5. But see Grotius, *Inleiding*, III, XXXVIII, 13 recognizing an exception in cases where a dog has killed somebody's swans or other birds ("Den eigenaar van een hond die iemands zwaenen ofte andere vogelen heeft dood ghebeten, is ghehouden zulcks te beteren, zonder te moghen volstaen met overgewing van de hond").

[137] Zimmermann, *RHR*, pp. 4 sqq.

[138] *O'Callaghan v. Chaplin* 1927 AD 310 at 360; cf. also *Le Roux v. Fick* (1879) 9 Buch 29 at 40 ("I am afraid a suitor would scarcely think that, moribus hujus seculi, a judge was acting in accordance with the highest principles of equity in deciding that a Kafir dog was all the compensation he could obtain for the loss of a valuable breeding bird that had been bitten to death by that dog").

[139] *O'Callaghan v. Chaplin* 1927 AD 310 at 322.

[140] Ibid.

(b) Range of animals

A second point on which there has been some development is the range of animals covered by the pauperian remedy. It has always been generally agreed that the actio directa was applicable in the case of quadrupedes, while an actio utilis had to be granted if a two-footed animal had caused the damage;[141] but this distinction was not of practical significance. A large number of writers, however, understood Paulus D. 9, 1, 4 ("Haec actio utilis competit et si . . . aliud animal pauperiem fecit") as referring also to *wild* animals (no matter whether two- of four-footed). "Quando autem Dominus illas bestias habet in domo et custodia sua quodammodo domesticorum animalium, aequum est, ut teneatur perinde ac aliorum nomine", it was argued:[142] if a person preferred to keep a crocodile rather than a lap dog, this could hardly be regarded as a good reason to relax his liability.[143] In modern South African practice the question has not yet been settled conclusively. On the one hand there are judicial dicta in favour of the view that the damage must have been caused by a domestic animal;[144] yet, on the other hand, the action has been granted where bees or meerkats have displayed their innate viciousness.[145]

(c) Contra ius naturale

This brings us to a third important aspect. The question of whether or not liability under the actio de pauperie extends to wild animals is obviously closely related to the way in which the "contra naturam" test is taken to operate; for if one requires that an animal must have acted in "breach of the good behaviour that is its second nature"[146] in order to make its owner liable, one can hardly apply the actio de pauperie to animals still persisting in a state of natural ferocity. This is why Struve, amongst others, argued:

---

[141] Cf., for example, Glück, vol. 10, pp. 292 sq.

[142] Lauterbach, *Collegium theoretico-practicum*, Lib. IX, Tit. I, IX sq. Cf. further Voet, *Commentarius ad Pandectas*, Lib. IX, Tit. I, IV; Van Leeuwen, *Censura Forensis*, Pars I, Lib. V, Cap. XXXI, 3.

[143] But cf. Glück, vol. 10, pp. 271 sq.: a person who does not take specific care when encountering a wild animal can only blame himself if he is attacked. A person approaching a domestic animal, on the other hand, can normally expect not to be attacked by it.

Occasionally, the question was discussed whether the actio de pauperie utilis could also be granted if a lunatic had caused the damage. After all, the furiosus could, arguably, be regarded as an "animal . . . quod sensu caret" (Ulp. D. 9, 1, 1, 3); and in D. 9, 2, 5, 2 Ulpian himself makes a comparative reference to the case of "si quadrupes damnum dederit" when discussing the situation of "si furiosus damnum dederit". For further discussion, see Stryk, *Usus modernus pandectarum*, Lib. IX, Tit. I, §§ 1 sq.; Glück, vol. 10, pp. 294 sqq.

[144] *O'Callaghan v. Chaplin* 1927 AD 310 at 337 and 370; *South African Railways & Harbours v. Edwards* 1930 AD 3 at 9 sq.

[145] *Goosen v. Reeders* 1926 TPD 436 at 439 (where bees are classified as "animals of vicious propensities"); *Klem v. Boshoff* 1931 CPD 188. Cf. also *Beatty v. Donelly* (1876) 6 Buch 51 at 52 (concerning monkeys).

[146] *Cowell v. Friedman & Co.* (1888) 5 HCG 12 at 44.

> "Ad feras autem, licet in custodia retineantur, non recte applicatur utilis actio de pauperie: quia et verba et mens atque ratio legis, quod se. animal contra indolem suam et consuetudinem noceat, cessat."[147]

Interpretation of the "contra naturam" requirement, unfortunately, turned out to be a highly volatile affair. Even by the time of Justinian it was no longer used in the sense in which it had once been devised. The conduct of animals as well as human beings was thought by the Byzantines to be governed by certain rules of natural law. As "companion and hunting agent of man",[148] a dog has to respect his master's property and person; and a cow is supposed to provide meat and milk, but not to fight with human beings. If they failed to comply with these standards, they acted "contra ius naturale", and their misbehaviour made the owner liable.[149]

(d) Contra naturam sui generis

The glossators further obscured the issue by introducing an amendment, which became almost universally accepted. Accursius, in his glossa "Contra naturam" ad Inst. IV, 9, provides the following definition:

> "id est, consuetudinem generis illius animalis: licet sit sua consuetudo ut calcitret . . . [n]am maior pars equorum non pessundat: et maior pars bo[v]um cornu non petit: quia equi, et boves dicuntur mansueti."

The "contra naturam" test had thus been turned into a "contra naturam sui generis" test.[150] It was obviously intended to accommodate cases such as the ones discussed in Servius/Ulp. D. 9, 1, 1, 4 and thus to make it clear that, even if the individual animal was in the habit of acting rather viciously, the damage could still be taken to have been inflicted "contra naturam" if the class of animal to which it happened to belong, was not supposed to behave in such a way. In other words, horses in general act contra naturam if they kick, and hence the owner of a horse that has caused damage by kicking, is liable, even if this specific horse is notorious for kicking. But the choice of phrase ("contra naturam sui generis") was rather unfortunate in that it conveyed the idea that certain forms of behaviour are characteristic of specific classes of animals—the implication being that the owner would be liable only

---

147 *Syntagma*, Exerc. XIV, Lib. IX, Tit. I, IX. It is also the main reason why in modern South African law application of the actio de pauperie is, as a rule, restricted to domestic animals: Van der Merwe, op. cit., note 39, p. 65. Other authors, who were in fact prepared to apply pauperian principles to damage done by wild animals tended to do this on the basis of an actio utilis; the contra naturam requirement, however, according to them, was confined to the actio de pauperie directa. Cf., for example, Lauterbach, *Collegium theoretico-practicum*, Lib. IX, Tit. I, VII, X.

148 *Boyce v. Robertson* 1912 TPD 381 at 383.

149 Haymann, (1921) 42 *ZSS* 366; Kerr Wylie, *Studi Riccobono*, vol. IV, pp. 464, 477; Nicholas, 1958 *Acta Juridica* 187; Van der Merwe, op. cit., note 39, pp. 81 sq.

150 Cf. further F. Litten, "Über das 'contra naturam "sui generis"'", (1905) 28 *ZSS* 494 sqq.; idem, (1907) 49 *JhJb* 422 sqq.

if (to pursue the example) his horse had behaved in a way contrary to the nature of the class of horses. This inference, however, was very rarely, if ever, drawn;[151] for it would largely have eroded the substance of the actio de pauperie. Kicking, after all, is a form of behaviour that can hardly be regarded as "unnatural" for horses in general. Most of the writers of the ius commune understood "contra naturam sui generis" in the sense of contrary to the "nature" of the animal as a domesticated being. This is apparent from their general definitions ("Contra naturam nocere dicuntur animalia, quotiens mansueta feritatem assumunt")[152] as well as from the examples provided to illustrate the notion of an act "secundum naturam": a dog satisfying his hunger by eating bread or meat, cattle feasting on grass, a horse kicking out while in pain, a mule stumbling because of its too heavy load.[153] But there was obviously a lot of room for manoeuvre. Accursius,[154] for instance, argued that a dog that had been tied up, did not expose its owner to an actio de pauperie when it bit a passer-by: dogs that are not allowed to run around, are usually more ferocious and can therefore not be taken to act contra naturam sui generis if they attack a human being. Johannes Faber, to mention another example, contended that on account of special ferocity and mischievousness even an act that had to be classified, normally, as secundum naturam could acquire contra naturam dimensions.[155] The same criterion has been employed by Jansen J in the case of *Maree v. Diedericks*.[156]

(e) The "reasonable cow" test

Modern South African courts, as is apparent from this example, still apply the "contra naturam (sui generis)" test in order to determine whether the owner of an animal that has caused damage, is liable or not.[157] But the case law that has emerged over the years clearly reveals its chameleonic nature. Occasionally, the courts have adopted what one

---

[151] Van der Merwe, (1979) 42 *THRHR* 17.

[152] Voet, *Commentarius ad Pandectas*, Lib. IX, Tit. I, IV.

[153] For details, see Van der Merwe, op. cit., note 39, pp. 84 sqq.

[154] Gl. Putant ad D. 9, 1, 2.

[155] *In quatuor Institutionum Libros Commentaria* (Venetiis, 1582), Rub. Si quadrupes pauperiem fecisse dicatur (ad Inst. IV, 9), 3. The example discussed is the following: ". . . si habebam pratum clausum, cuius clausuram bos tuus, vel taurus rupit per lasciviam, vel ferocitate, et herbam, vel bladum depastus est. hoc casu non esset deneganda haec actio de pauperie." Absente lascivia and ferocitate, however, the actio de pauperie did not lie: "Quid ergo si animalia tua . . . depasta fuerunt glandem meam, vel prata, vel blada mea, quaeritur an agere possim . . .? glossa dicit, quod potest agi actione de pauperie. . . . Sed hoc non videtur verum . . . quia haec actio non datur, nisi quando animal delinquit contra naturam sui generis."

[156] 1962 (1) SA 231 (T) at 237: "As die landdros se bevinding dat die twee honde gesamentlik al die hoenders doodgebyt het, korrek is, dan was beide honde nie besig om op 'n natuurlike wyse honger te stil nie—hulle was besig met 'n baldadige slagting wat as contra naturam aangemerk moet word."

[157] For a detailed analysis, see Van der Merwe, op. cit., note 39, pp. 89 sqq., 91 sqq.; cf. also idem, (1979) 42 *THRHR* 17 sqq.

could call a subjective approach: the animal must have been moved by its innate wildness, viciousness or perverseness to inflict the injury.[158] An over-friendly, large dog that hugs a visitor can thus, for instance, not be taken to conduct himself contra naturam sui generis. Other decisions proceed from a more objective perspective. There the view has been adopted that, in order to be contra naturam sui generis, the action of the animal in question must have been in conflict with what may be expected of a well-behaved animal of its kind.[159] What this boils down to, effectively, is the judicial creation of the "reasonable cow" or the "reasonable duck" as a criterion to determine the owner's liability. The absurdity inherent in this form of anthropomorphism hardly needs to be elaborated upon.[160]

8. Liability for damage done by animals in modern German law

The European legislators of the late 18th and of the 19th centuries must have realized that the "contra naturam sui generis" test was not a particularly happy conceptual concoction,[161] for they all abandoned it. In addition, they also tended to jettison both the option of noxal surrender and the principle of noxa caput sequitur.[162] As a result of these changes, the owner's liability was considerably extended and the question was therefore bound to arise whether it was still justifiable to dispense with what was otherwise a regular prerequisite for any claim for damages: the element of fault.

Some codes persisted in holding the owner strictly liable,[163] others introduced the fault requirement.[164] The fathers of the BGB vacillated for a long time.[165] Eventually, the dice fell in favour of a comprehensively formulated § 833, that was based on the notion of strict liability:

---

[158] *Le Roux v. Fick* (1879) 9 Buch 29 at 33; *Cowell v. Friedman & Co.* (1888) 5 HCG 22 at 40; *Boyce v. Robertson* 1912 TPD 381 at 384; *Solomon v. De Waal* 1972 (1) SA 575 (A) at 582E.

[159] *O'Callaghan v. Chaplin* 1927 AD 310 at 314; *South African Railways & Harbours v. Edwards* 1930 AD 3 at 6, 10 and 12; *Solomon v. De Waal* 1972 (1) SA 575 (A) at 582E; *Lawrence v. Kondotel Inns (Pty.) Ltd.* 1989 (1) SA 44 (D) at 51 sq.

[160] On the defences available against the actio de pauperie (vis maior, culpable conduct on the part of the injured or of a third party, provocation by another animal, unlawful presence of the injured person at the place of injury) cf. Van der Merwe, op. cit., note 39, pp. 100 sqq., 105 sqq.

[161] So, too, as far as South Africa is concerned, Van der Merwe, (1979) 42 *THRHR* 26.

[162] Cf. the discussion in "Motive", in: *Mugdan*, vol. II, p. 452.

[163] Cf., in particular, art. 1385 code civil; and see §§ 1560 sq. Saxonian Civil Code (which, however, retained the alternative of noxae deditio).

[164] Cf., in particular, § 1320 ABGB, art. 65 OR (both operating, however, with a reversal of the burden of proof: it is up to the keeper of the animal to show that he exercised the necessary care in supervising the animal); § 73 I 6 PrALR, but see also §§ 70–72 (detailing instances of strict liability).

[165] Cf. § 734 E I (read with "Motive", in: *Mugdan*, vol. II, pp. 452 sqq.: liability based on fault); § 756 E II (read with "Protokolle", in: *Mugdan*, vol. II, pp. 1123 sqq.: reversal of onus of proof of fault, as far as domestic animals are concerned; strict liability with regard to all other animals); § 817 Reichstagsvorlage (read with "Bericht der XII. Kommission des Reichstages", in: *Mugdan*, vol. II, pp. 1301, 1403 sqq.).

> "If a person is killed, or the body or health of a person is injured, or a thing is damaged, by an animal, the person who keeps the animal is bound to compensate the injured party."

Nevertheless, the agricultural lobby in the German Reichstag was to have the last word. In 1908 an amendment was accepted, according to which the duty to make compensation does not arise if the damage was caused by a domestic animal, which is kept for professional purposes (as opposed to merely constituting a luxury), provided its keeper either exercised the necessary care in supervising that animal or the damage would have occurred notwithstanding the exercise of such care.[166] Foresters, officers, the police, the owners of horse-cabs and, in particular, farmers[167] are thus allowed to exculpate themselves.

But even the liability of people who keep "luxury animals" has come to be restricted. In this case it was tradition, not partisan interest that prevailed, and it did not require legislative intervention, but worked through judicial interpretation. For a long time the courts have held that, in order to make its keeper liable, the animal must have acted in a spontaneous, arbitrary or capricious manner, unguided by any reasonable purpose or intention.[168] More recently, the Federal Supreme Court has slightly changed the relevant criterion.[169] Animals, it is now argued, can never be credited with acts of free volition: they do not, in this sense, act "arbitrarily", but their whole behaviour is guided rather by their instincts, whether inborn or acquired. The specific risk associated with the keeping of animals lies in the utter unpredictability of their conduct. Only if the damage is a realization of this risk may its keeper be held liable. Excluded, in particular, are the cases where the animal merely makes a reflex movement (a dog that has been narcotized, bites the doctor on the operating table)[170] or where its actions are entirely determined by a human being (a horse, led by the bridle, treads on a person's heels).[171] Whether the natural unpredictability of an animal is a particularly appropriate criterion by which to determine the respective risk spheres of the keeper and its victim, remains disputed.[172] Apart from that, the courts are often called upon to decide whether the keeper's liability may be reduced, or even excluded, because of contributory negligence or voluntary assumption

---

[166] § 833, 2 BGB.

[167] For details as to who may avail himself of the benefit of exculpation and as to which animals may be classified as domestic, see Hans-Joachim Mertens, in: *Münchener Kommentar*, vol. III, 2 (2nd ed., 1986), § 833, nn. 28 sqq.

[168] RGZ 141, 406 (407) ("*von keinem vernünftigen Wollen geleitete[s] willkürliche[s] Verhalten*"); BGH, 1971 *Neue Juristische Wochenschrift* 509.

[169] BGHZ 67, 129 sqq. (dealing with the case of a roaming dog covering the plaintiff's purebred chow bitch).

[170] OLG München, 1976 *Versicherungsrecht* 334.

[171] OLG Schleswig, 1983 *Versicherungsrecht* 470.

[172] For a critical evaluation cf. Mertens, op. cit., note 167, § 833, nn. 13 sqq.; Erwin Deutsch, "Die Haftung des Tierhalters", 1987 *Juristische Schulung* 675 sq.

of risk on the part of the injured person (A is injured by B's horse which he has hired for a ride;[173] C, in spite of several warning signs, parks his car on D's private property and is bitten by D's dogs[174]).[175] Among contemporary legal writers it is, furthermore, disputed whether the principles laid down in § 833 BGB may be extended to micro-organisms that have been cultivated or preserved in a laboratory.[176]

II. VICARIOUS LIABILITY

1. The principle of noxality

(a) *Roman law*

If the BGB came down in favour of strict liability in the case of damage done by animals, it opted for a different regime with regard to another historically rather closely related problem. When slaves or children in power had committed a delict, it was, in classical Roman law, their paterfamilias whom the victim had to sue.[177] This was another instance of no-fault liability, mitigated, again, by the fact that it was effectively limited by the intrinsic value of the delinquent: the paterfamilias, rather than pay the damages, could surrender the slave or child. The paterfamilias, in other words, was "vicariously" liable for the wrongful acts or persons in his power, but his liability was of a "noxal" character. One might therefore have expected a similar development to have occurred as in the case of the South African usus modernus of the actio de pauperie: noxae deditio and the rule of noxa caput sequitur falling into disuse and leaving behind a strict liability on the part of the master to render compensation.[178]

(b) *"[N]oxalium actionum nullus est usus"*

This is, however, not what actually happened. As far as delicts by children in power were concerned, the principle of noxality had already

[173] Cf., for example, OLG Düsseldorf, 1976 *Neue Juristische Wochenschrift* 2137; Kammergericht, 1986 *Versicherungsrecht* 820; but see BGH, 1986 *Versicherungsrecht* 1206.

[174] OLG Frankfurt, 1983 *Versicherungsrecht* 1040.

[175] Cf. further Rolf Knütel, "Tierhalterhaftung gegenüber dem Vertragspartner?", 1978 *Neue Juristische Wochenschrift* 297 sqq. (dealing with the liability of the keeper of the animal towards his contractual partner); Elke Herrmann, "Die Einschränkung der Tierhalterhaftung nach § 833 S. 1 BGB in der modernen Judikatur und Literatur", 1980 *Juristische Rundschau* 489 sqq.; Deutsch, 1987 *Juristische Schulung* 676 sqq.

[176] Erwin Deutsch, "Gefährdungshaftung für laborgezüchtete Mikroorganismen", 1976 *Neue Juristische Wochenschrift* 1137 sqq.; Mertens, op. cit., note 167, § 833, n. 10. But cf. also Bienenfeld, op. cit., note 123, p. 210.

[177] For details, see Kaser, *RPr* I, pp. 161 sqq., 630 sqq.; von Lübtow, *Lex Aquilia*, pp. 41 sqq.; Gian Luigi Falchi, *Ricerche sulla legittimazione passiva delle azioni nossali* (1976); Hans-Peter Benöhr, "Zur Haftung für Sklavendelikte", (1980) 97 *ZSS* 273 sqq.; Hans Ankum, (1981) 32 *Iura* 233 sqq.; Honsell/Mayer-Maly/Selb, pp. 381 sqq. Cf. also Lawson/Markesinis, pp. 160 sqq. and supra, pp. 916 sq.

[178] Cf., as far as the development in France is concerned, Watson, *Failures*, pp. 6 sq.

been abandoned in post-classical Roman law,[179] and even Justinian, for once, did not revert to the classical position. What man, he asked rhetorically, would contemplate giving up his son, and especially his daughter, in surrender to the victim of the wrong?[180] "[E]t ideo placuit, in servos tantummodo noxales actiones esse proponendas", he concluded; filiifamilias could now be proceeded against directly.[181] By the time of the usus modernus, however, noxal liability had also fallen into disuse with regard to slaves, the reason simply being that the institution of slavery had largely been relinquished:[182] "Nostris Moribus, quoniam tales servos non habemus, noxalium actionum nullus est usus."[183] Did this mean that a master was no longer vicariously liable for wrongful acts committed by his servants? Many writers evidently thought so. "[S]ervi nostri s[u]nt liberi homines", they argued, "et hinc ipsi ex suis delictis, non autem domini illorum conveniendi."[184] The master could be held liable, under general principles, if he himself had been at fault, particularly if he had failed to show due care in the selection of his staff (". . . si in eligendis famulis culpam commiserit dominus, hos negotiis suis adhibendo, quos scivit vel scire potuit, perditi ingenii homines esse").[185] Others, however, were prepared to go further. "Door der dienaers misdaed en werden de meesters ende vrouwen in 't ghemeen niet verbonden, dan zoo veel de onbetaelde huir mag bedragen", we read in Grotius' *Inleiding*:[186] the master was "vicariously" liable, but only up to the amount of unpaid wages. This kind of wage liability appears to have had its origin in

[179] Kaser, *RPr* II, p. 430.

[180] *Inst.* IV, 8, 7: ". . . quis enim patitur filium suum et maxime filiam in noxam alii dare, ut paene per corpus pater magis quam filius periclitetur, cum in filiabus etiam pudicitiae favor hoc bene excludit?"

[181] On the decline (or "humanization") of patria potestas in post-classical Roman law in general, see Kaser, *RPr* II, pp. 202 sqq.; cf. also (humanity) Schulz, *Principles*, pp. 189 sqq., 198 sqq.

[182] Cf. Groenewegen, *De legibus abrogatis*, Inst. Lib. I, Tit. VIII, 3: ". . . servitus paulatim ab usu recessit, ejusque nomen hodie apud nos exolevit" (he also points out, however, that "servos habere Christianis nefas non [est], si modo herili in servos potestate non abutantur, sed eos secundum Christianam levitatem mansuetudinem tractent . . ."). Cf. also Coing, pp. 205 sq.

[183] Lauterbach, *Collegium theoretico-practicum*, Lib. IX, Tit. IV, IX. But cf. also, in the present context, Stryk, *Usus modernus pandectarum*, Lib. IX, Tit. IV, § 2: "Cum tamen huc usque post Budam in Ungaria occupatam frequentissima fuerint turcarum mancipia servitiis christianorum adhibita, nullus dubito, si aliquis horum delictum privatum commisisset, actioni noxali adhuc locum fore, ut hujus mancipi dominus, vel damnum resarciat, vel turcam noxae dedat, nam nec hic ultra corpus ipsorum nequitia dominis damnosa esse debet."

[184] Stryk, *Usus modernus pandectarum*, Lib. IX, Tit. IV, § 2.

[185] Stryk, *Usus modernus pandectarum*, Lib. IX, Tit. IV, § 5; cf. also, particularly clearly, Leyser, *Meditationes ad Pandectas*, Spec. CXIII, I; Glück, vol. 10, pp. 417 sq.

[186] III, XXXVIII, 8.

Saxonian law[187] and became widely accepted in 17th- and 18th-century Roman-Dutch jurisprudence.[188] By a variety of authors it was confined, however, to instances where the servant had acted beyond the scope of his employment. For delicts committed within the scope of his employment, so these authors argued, the master was liable for full compensation. The locus classicus on the matter is Voet, *Commentarius ad Pandectas*, Lib. IX, Tit. IV, X:

> "Ac primo quidem admonendi sumus, dominos ac patres in solidum teneri ex delictis famulorum ac filiorum . . . quoties illi deliquerunt in officio aut ministerio, cui a patre dominove fuerunt praepositi."

This was not based on the *Sachsenspiegel* or any other Germanic source, but, ostensibly, on a rule of Roman law.

2. Liability for others in Roman law (apart from noxal liability)

(a) *Within a contractual context*

The Roman lawyers had, indeed, dealt with a whole variety of instances of liability for others even apart from those situations where the principle of noxality applied; but they did not develop any general and clear-cut rules in this regard. Thus, in particular, there were all those cases where a third party (no matter whether slave or freeman) was employed in performing a *contractual* obligation.[189] Normally, the debtor could be held responsible only for his own fault and not (merely) for that of other persons. But in the present context his fault could take the form of culpa in eligendo.[190] Thus, for example, we read of the stoker–slave of a colonus who dropped asleep at the furnace. As a result of his drowsiness the locator's house burnt down. According to Neratius, the colonus was liable ex locato "si neglegens in eligendis ministriis fuit".[191] Occasionally, however, the level of what was expected of the debtor was pitched rather high—so high, in fact, that one came very close to no-fault liability. Julian, for instance, required a messenger whom a debtor employed to send back borrowed silver to

---

[187] Cf. II, 32 *Sachsenspiegel*; Stryk, Usus modernus pandectarum, Lib. IX, Tit. IV, § 4. On the liability of the master in early German law in general cf. T.B. Barlow, *The South African Law of Vicarious Liability in Delict and a Comparison of the Principles of Other Legal Systems* (1939), pp. 25 sqq.

[188] Cf., for instance, Voet, *Commentarius ad Pandectas*, Lib. IX, Tit. IV, X; Groenewegen, *De legibus abrogatis*, Digest. Lib. XV, Tit. I, 1; Van Leeuwen, *Censura Forensis*, Pars I, Lib. II, Cap. XII, 3.

[189] For a detailed analysis, see now the authoritative study by Rolf Knütel, "Die Haftung für Hilfspersonen im römischen Recht", (1983) 100 *ZSS* 340 sqq.

[190] On which, in general, cf. Geoffrey MacCormack, (1971) 18 *RIDA* 525 sqq.

[191] Ulp. D. 9, 2, 27, 9; cf. also Ulp. Coll. XII, VII, 7. On this text, see Bruce W. Frier, "Tenant's Liability for Damage to Landlord's Property", (1978) 95 *ZSS* 256 sqq.; Knütel, (1983) 100 *ZSS* 399 sqq. The culpa in eligendo has in the past often been regarded as spurious; cf. Wolfgang Kunkel, "Diligentia", (1925) 45 *ZSS* 329 sqq.

be of such a character that nobody should have been able to divine that he could possibly be led astray by crooks.[192] Ulpian and Pomponius even held a conductor liable for damage caused by guests or members of his household, merely on account of his having admitted "such persons" onto his property:

> ". . . placet, ut culpam etiam eorum quos induxit praestet suo nomine, etsi nihil convenit, si tamen culpam in inducendis admittit, quod tales habuerit vel suos vel hospites."[193]

(b) *Custodia*

Then there were the cases where the debtor was responsible for custodia;[194] and custodia, as a matter of course, covered theft by servants of the debtor and, at least according to Marcellus and Ulpian, also damnum iniuria ab alio datum.[195] Closely related was the strict liability of nautae, caupones and stabularii based on "receptum",[196] where, too, it did not matter whether the destruction, loss or damage of the customer's property had come about as a result of the sea carrier's, innkeeper's or stablekeeper's own fault, of the fault of their employees or of some other incident that could not be regarded as vis maior. Most significantly, perhaps, there was the famous fragment "Qui columnam transportandam",[197] where a conductor operis was held responsible for his own fault as well as for that of his employees. Again, we are dealing here with vicarious liability stricto sensu, albeit in a contractual context.

(c) *Delictual and quasi-delictual remedies*

If we turn our attention to delictual and quasi-delictual remedies, we find a similarly casuistic approach. In late classical jurisprudence an actio legis Aquiliae in factum was occasionally granted against a person whose servants had damaged someone else's property. According to general principles of Aquilian liability, the master had to have been at fault (usually, again, in the form of culpa in eligendo). This appears to be confirmed by Proc./Ulp. D. 9, 2, 27, 11, where it is stated: ". . . si

[192] Iul. D. 13, 6, 20: "Argentum commodatum si tam idoneo servo meo tradidissem ad te perferendum, ut non debuerit quis aestimare futurum, ut a quibusdam malis hominibus deciperetur, tuum, non meum detrimentum erit, si id mali homines intercepissent." Cf. MacCormack, (1971) 18 *RIDA* 531 sq.; Knütel, (1983) 100 *ZSS* 381 sqq.

[193] D. 19, 2, 11 pr.; cf. Mayer-Maly, *Locatio conductio*, pp. 200 sq.; MacCormack, (1971) 18 *RIDA* 540 sq.; Frier, (1978) 95 *ZSS* 258 sqq.; Knütel, (1983) 100 *ZSS* 401 sqq.

[194] Cf., in general, Fritz Schulz, "Die Haftung für das Verschulden der Angestellten im klassischen römischen Recht", (1911) 38 *GrünhZ* 9 sqq.

[195] D. 19, 2, 41; cf. Knütel, (1983) 100 *ZSS* 411 sqq. Generally on custodia cf. supra, pp. 193 sqq. The prevailing opinion, according to which custodia was an objective (strict) liability, has repeatedly been challenged, most recently by René Robaye, *L' obligation de garde. Essai sur la responsablité contractuelle en droit romain* (1988).

[196] Cf. supra, pp. 514 sqq.; also Schulz, (1911) 38 *GrünhZ* 41 sqq.

[197] Gai. D. 19, 2, 25, 7; on which see supra, pp. 399 sqq.

noxios servos habuit, damni eum iniuria teneri, cur tales habuit."[198] The phrase is not, however, unambiguous. The master is held responsible for the resulting damage—resulting, in this case, from the fact that his servants had burnt down a house he had hired—"by reason of having such slaves"; and it is easy to see how this formulation may be taken to establish a fiction or presumption of culpa as the basis of the master's liability, rather than to require actual proof of fault. A strict vicarious liability, in turn, was imposed by the edict in the case of the actio de deiectis vel effusis:[199] the habitator[200] was held responsible, for reasons of public policy, if something was thrown out or poured down from his house and it did not matter whether he himself, a member of his household, a free servant or anybody else who happened to be in the house had actually done the throwing out or pouring down.[201] "[C]ulpa enim penes eum [sc.: qui inhabitat] est", Ulpian added in order to justify the habitator's—as opposed to the owner's—liability: without thereby, however, introducing a requirement of personal fault.[202] But, obviously, this sentence was bound to lend itself to misinterpretation; Justinian himself must have seen it as an expression of the fault-based nature of quasi-delictual liability—if he did not insert it for this very purpose.[203] Similarly ambiguous was the position concerning furtum vel damnum in navi aut caupone aut stabulo.[204] Again, sea carriers, innkeepers and stablekeepers were strictly liable if their customer's property was damaged or stolen by one of their employees. Again, however, this liability was rationalized (by the compilers?) in terms of a fault presumption: ". . . cum enim . . . aliquatenus culpae reus est, quod opera malorum hominum uteretur, ideo quasi ex maleficio teneri videtur."[205] The reus is not blamed for actual negligence in the selection of his staff, but for the mere fact that he availed himself of the services of mali homines.[206]

[198] Substantially genuine; cf. MacCormack, (1971) 18 *RIDA* 536 sqq.; Knütel, (1983) 100 *ZSS* 392 sqq., 396 sqq. But see also Frier, (1978) 95 *ZSS* 261 sq. and also Ulp. Coll. XII, VII, 9.

[199] Cf. supra, pp. 16 sq.

[200] Ulp. D. 9, 3, 1, 4.

[201] The praetor merely said "Unde in eum locum, quo vulgo iter fiet vel in quo consistetur, deiectum vel effusum quid erit . . .": Ulp. D. 9, 3, 1 pr.; and see Paul. D. 9, 3, 6, 2: "Habitator suam suorumque culpam praestare debet."

[202] MacCormack, (1971) 18 *RIDA* 547 sq. "The justification made by the jurists is related to the fact that the habitator not the dominus is the person made liable. The habitator is liable because he is the person in charge of the household and is therefore in a position to take the measures necessary to . . . organiz[e] his household in such a way as to prevent things being thrown or poured out"; Kaser, *RPr* II, p. 428.

[203] Cf., for example, Wittmann, *Körperverletzung*, p. 64.

[204] Supra, pp. 16 sq.

[205] Gai. D. 44, 7, 5, 6.

[206] Cf. further the liability of publicani for the acts of slaves which they had used in order to collect taxes: Ulp. D. 39, 4, 1, 6; Gai. D. 39, 4, 2; Ulp. D. 39, 4, 3 pr.; MacCormack, (1971) 18 *RIDA* 551; Barlow, op. cit., note 187, pp. 21 sq.

3. Vicarious liability in South African law

Looking back at Voet's bold assertion of vicarious liability for wrongful acts by employees within the scope of their employment, we can now appreciate that here, as so often, a general principle was arrived at by a process of generalization and abstraction on the basis of the massive casuistry contained in the Roman sources. The focal point for the formulation of the new doctrine, in this instance, was the idea of selection: ". . . cum his [sc.: patre dominove] imputandum sit, quod negligentium aut malignorum operas ministerio certo aut officio addixerint", in the words, again, of Voet.[207] The servant's delict was attributable to the master on account of the fact that he had chosen him to do the job at hand. By and large, the principle of strict vicarious liability managed to establish itself in Roman-Dutch law,[208] but there were also those who drew attention to and criticized the false generalization of the Roman sources upon which it was based.[209]

South African courts, when they were first confronted with the issue, did not delve deeply into the sources, whether those of Roman law or of Roman-Dutch law.[210] They tended to accept what fitted in with the corresponding English doctrine, which was much more familiar to them. The wage liability for acts beyond the scope of employment was hardly ever mentioned[211] and passed into complete oblivion. At the same time the master's liability in full for acts within the scope of employment was unhesitatingly accepted, sources of the ius commune merely being used, selectively, to support Anglo-American authorities. "The law on the subject is thus broadly stated by *Story on Agency* . . .", reads a highly characteristic passage by De Villiers CJ, in the 1874 decision of *Gifford v. Table Bay Dock and Breakwater Management Commission*,[212]

> "[t]he principal is liable to third persons for the torts, negligences, and other malfeasances or misfeasances and omissions of his servant or agent in the course of his employment, although the principal did not authorize or justify or participate in, or indeed know of such misconduct, or even if he forbade the acts or disproved of them. 'In all such cases', he adds, 'the rule applies respondeat superior; and it is founded upon public policy and convenience; for in no other way could there be any safety to third persons in their dealings either directly or indirectly with him through

---

[207] *Commentarius ad Pandectas*, Lib. IX, Tit. IV, X.

[208] Barlow, op. cit., note 187, pp. 73 sqq.

[209] Van der Keessel, *Praelectiones iuris hodierni*, ad Gr. 3, 1, 34 (vol. IV, p. 25); cf. also Van der Linden in his notes on Voet, *Commentarius ad Pandectas*, in: Gane, *The Selective Voet*, vol. II, p. 607; for further details, see Barlow, op. cit., note 187, pp. 61 sqq.

[210] For an analysis, cf. Barlow, op. cit., note 187, pp. 84 sqq. ("A study of the cases on the subject before the hearing of *Mkize v. Martens* in May 1914, indicates that the courts have failed to make any deep study of a very complex question, yet in *Mkize v. Martens*, the Appellate Division regarded the matter as definitely settled by precedent, and held that there was no need to go into the old authorities": p. 91). The decision of *Mkize v. Martens* is reported in 1914 AD 382.

[211] But cf. *Estate Van der Byl v. Swanepoel* 1927 AD 141 at 153 sq. (per Kotzé JA).

[212] (1874) 4 Buch 96 at 114.

the instrumentality of agents . . .'. Story then proceeds to point out . . . that similar principles are recognized, though not with the same distinctness, by the Roman law (see also Pothier on Obligations, nn. 121 and 453). The passage from the Digest, which has already been quoted, clearly supports the same view."

This passage, incidentally, is the famous fragment Qui columnam.[213] The particle "que" in "eorumque" must have been understood disjunctively by the Chief Justice. Despite occasional criticism,[214] South African courts have continued to rely on English precedents, particularly when they were called upon to determine the concept of a servant and to define the scope of the employment.[215] The doctrine of common employment, according to which a servant may not sue his master for the negligence of a fellow-servant, has, however, been rejected, after a thorough examination of Roman-Dutch, English, American, Scottish and modern continental authorities, by Kotzé CJ,[216] Lord De Villiers' great counterpart in the Transvaal.

4. The position in modern French and German law

In the rather lengthy quotation from *Gifford's* case reference was made to D. 19, 2, 25, 7 and to a passage in Pothier's *Traité des obligations.*[217] Both had by that time exercised a significant influence on liability for others in continental European law, though in completely different directions. Pothier, of course, became the intellectual father of the strict vicarious liability of art. 1384 code civil, which states concisely that one is responsible, not only for the injury which one causes by one's own action, but also for that which is caused "*par le fait des personnes dont on doit répondre*".[218] Digesta 19, 2, 25, 7 (the "que" interpreted conjunc-

---

[213] Ulp. D. 19, 2, 25, 7.

[214] Cf. Van den Heever, *Aquilian Damages*, pp. IV sqq. ("[I]n a highly industrialised country [such as England] . . . it may be expedient that the employer's responsibility for damage caused by his workmen or machinery should be co-extensive with these artificial extensions of his own activities and personality. . . . [But] in a young and undeveloped country such as South Africa was at the time, application of the principle of unlimited liability was calculated to stifle initiative and entrench monopoly"). Paul Boberg comments: "This is no doubt very true, but it can have no application today, when we pride ourselves on being the most highly developed and industrialized state in Africa. Certainly we are now as industrialized as was nineteenth-century England. The adoption of this doctrine has thus enabled our law to move with the times and to reflect the social requirements of the age in which we live": "Oak Tree or Acorn? Conflicting Approaches to Our Law of Delict", (1966) 83 *SALJ* 170.

[215] For details, see Barlow, op. cit., note 187, pp. 95 sqq., 120 sqq.

[216] *Lewis v. Salisbury Gold Mining Co.* (1894) 1 OR 1 sqq. ("the best [judgment] ever delivered in this country on the question of vicarious liability": Barlow, op. cit., note 187, p. 907).

[217] *Traité des obligations*, nn. 121, 456.

[218] On the origin of this provision (Domat and Pothier), cf., most recently, Watson, *Failures*, pp. 6 sq., 15 sqq.; on its application cf. Zweigert/Kötz, pp. 380 sqq.; Lawson/Markesinis, pp. 167 sqq. The (strict) vicarious liability of the employer is based, traditionally, on the principle of "Ex qua persona quis lucrum capit, eius factum praestare

tively), on the other hand, was one of the key sources upon which 19th-century German legal writers relied in order to reject the notion that one person could be held strictly responsible for the acts of others.[219] "No liability without fault" was one of the great axioms of pandectist doctrine,[220] and the Roman texts tended to be read in such a way as to conform thereto. By the time the BGB was drafted the idea of vicarious liability had gained some ground,[221] but ultimately it managed to establish itself only in the contractual context. According to § 278 BGB, a debtor is responsible for the fault of those whom he employs in performing his obligation, to the same extent as for his own fault.[222] But when it came to the law of delict, the forces of tradition largely had their way: strongly supported—for obvious reasons—by lobbyists representing the interests of trade, industry and agriculture.[223] Nationalistic sentiments, strangely, also played their role. The principle enunciated in art. 1384 code civil was regarded as entirely alien to traditional "German" notions of justice and fairness.[224] The rather extensive way in which the French courts applied their regime of vicarious liability did not inspire the German observers with much confidence either.[225] A master, horribile dictu, had even been ordered to pay damages because his servant had sounded a trumpet at night and thus disrupted the neighbours' tranquillity! In the end, liability for the unlawful acts of employees under the BGB was thus made to hinge on culpa in eligendo vel custodiendo vel inspiciendo; the less traditionally minded proponents of the French system merely managed to achieve a reversal of the onus of proof.[226] Despite this concession, § 831 BGB has

---

debet" (Ulp. D. 50, 17, 149); cf. Knütel (1983) 100 *ZSS* 441 sqq. On the justification of vicarious liability in English law cf. P.S. Atiyah, *Vicarious Liability in the Law of Torts* (1967), pp. 15 sqq., 22 sqq.

[219] Cf., for example, Windscheid/Kipp, § 401, n. 5.

[220] Cf. supra, pp. 1034 sq.

[221] For details of the development cf. Hans Hermann Seiler, "Die deliktische Gehilfenhaftung in historischer Sicht", 1967 *Juristenzeitung* 525 sqq.; Günther Niethammer, *Entwicklung der Haftung für Gehilfenhandeln unter besonderer Berücksichtigung der dogmengeschichtlichen Grundlagen der deliktischen Gehilfenhaftung in der neueren Privatrechtsgeschichte thesis* (unpublished Dr. iur. thesis, München, 1973), pp. 7 sqq., 78 sqq.; Ogorek, *Gefährdungshaftung*, pp. 68 sqq. Cf. also "Motive", in: *Mugdan*, vol. II, p. 16 ("one of the most disputed questions of modern German common law").

[222] This was justified (and thus reconciled with the general culpa principle) on the basis that a person concluding a contract undertakes that, whatever he has promised, shall be carried out diligently, no matter by whom; thus, if he chooses to employ another person in performing his obligation, he is liable for that person's fault. Cf. Enneccerus, *Verhandlungen des 17. deutschen Juristentages*, vol. II (1885), pp. 102 sqq., and also "Motive", in: *Mugdan*, vol. II, p. 16.

[223] Seiler, 1967 *Juristenzeitung* 527 sqq.

[224] "Protokolle", in: *Mugdan*, vol. II, p. 1094.

[225] Seiler, 1967 *Juristenzeitung* 528.

[226] § 831 BGB thus reads: "A person who employs another to do any work, is bound to compensate for any damage which the other unlawfully causes to a third party in the performance of this work. The duty to compensate does not arise if the employer has exercised the necessary care in the selection of the employee, and, where he has to supply

turned out to be a major source of embarrassment. Countless ways have been developed by both courts and legal writers to bypass this unsound rule:[227] the rather extravagant encroachment of contractual remedies on the law of delict, for instance, a characteristic feature of the modern German law of obligations, is based largely on the desire to make available, for the benefit of the injured party, the stricter rule of § 278 BGB.[228]

III. QUASI-DELICTUAL LIABILITY

1. The fate of the Roman quasi-delicts

Noxal liability did not depend on fault; a Roman paterfamilias was liable for damage caused by children and slaves in his power, as well as by (domesticated) animals belonging to him, but his liability was effectively limited by virtue of the option of noxae deditio that was available to him. Other instances of strict liability in classical Roman law, as we have seen, were thrown together sub titulo "obligationes quasi ex delicto":[229] the action against a judge qui litem suam fecit and the actiones de deiectis vel effusis, de posito vel suspenso and de damno aut furto in navi aut caupone aut stabulo. But although all four remedies were incorporated into the ius commune, none of them can be said to have prospered. By the time of the usus modernus pandectarum, the strict liability of the iudex qui litem suam fecit had largely fallen into disuse; ". . . moribus hujus aevi non tenetur judex qui per imperitiam male judicavit", as Groenewegen reports.[230] He paints a somewhat sombre picture of the

apparatus or equipment or to supervise the work, has also exercised ordinary care as regards such supply or supervision, or if the damage would have arisen notwithstanding the exercise of such care."

[227] For an overview, from a comparative point of view, cf. Zweigert/Kötz, pp. 374 sqq.; B.S. Markesinis, *A Comparative Introduction to the German Law of Tort* (1986), pp. 349 sqq. (for the most important cases—in translation see—pp. 391 sqq.).

[228] Cf. also the observation in Zweigert/Kötz/Weir, p. 299: "The English jurist Pollock stated that the strict liability of a master for the torts of his servants, such as exists at Common Law, was justified by the consideration that if it did not exist a 'huge expansion of implied, i.e. fictitious contracts, to no great advantage of either law or conscience, would ensue'; the development of German law has vindicated this prediction to the hilt"; cf. also the speculation by Sir Frederick Pollock in (1916) 32 *LQR* 227 ("Denial of the 'superior's' responsibility in tort would surely have led to a luxuriant and perplexed growth of contracts implied in law, for which the substance of justice would have been no better from any point of view, and the science of law much the worse").

[229] Cf. supra, pp. 16 sqq. For a list of further instances of liability without fault, see Bienenfeld, op. cit., note 123, pp. 13 sqq., 45 sqq.

[230] *De legibus abrogatis*, Inst. Lib. IV, Tit. V, Princ.; cf. also, for example, Vinnius, *Institutiones*, Lib. IV, Tit. V, pr., 2 sq.; Lauterbach, *Collegium theoretico-practicum*, Lib. L, Tit. XIII, III. Writers in earlier centuries tended to be puzzled as to why a medical doctor, who operated badly or gave his patient the wrong medicine, was liable under the lex Aquilia ("Imperitia quoque culpae adnumeratur, veluti si medicus ideo servum tuum occiderit, quod eum male secuerit aut perperam ei medicamentum dederit": *Inst.* IV, III, 7) whereas a judge was held responsible, for his lack of skill, merely quasi ex delicto. Donellus, *Commentarii*, Lib. XV, Cap. XLIII, XIII, proposed to resolve the discrepancy by classifying the liability

competence of judicial officers of his time: ". . . manifestum esse videtur, quod imperitissimi quoque Iudicandi munus ambiant", he stated, the implication being that it would have been both unfeasible and inappropriate to hold them liable for giving wrong decisions merely because they did not know the law. Most importantly, however, disadvantaged litigants were no longer taken to require this specific form of protection, for they could seek redress by lodging an appeal against the incorrect decision: ". . . iniquitati sententiae occurrendum est remedio appellationis."[231] The actio de posito vel suspenso, too, was obsolete by the end of the 18th century. It had never served to compensate an injured party for his damages but had merely imposed a penalty on persons endangering safe traffic.[232] With the rise of the modern territorial states and their administrative organs, the maintenance of public safety became increasingly a concern of the State authorities and the remedy in private law was thus effectively superseded by recourse to the police, who could be asked to take appropriate steps to avert the danger:

> ". . . hoc casu nulla actio hodie instituatur, sed potius ab eo, cui cura aedium et platearum forique publici commissa est, simpliciter mandatum inhibitoriale impetretur."[233]

---

of the iudex qui litem suam fecit as (genuinely) delictual, Franciscus Hotomanus, *Commentarius in quatuor liberos Institutionum* (Lugduni, 1588), Lib. IV, Tit. III, III, the other way round, by treating the imperitia liability of the medicus as another instance of an obligatio quasi ex delicto. For further details, see Hochstein, *Obligationes*, pp. 38 sqq., 64 sqq.

[231] Vinnius, *Institutiones*, Lib. IV, Tit. V, pr., 1, and many others. The possibility of an appellatio had already led Bartolus as well as the humanists to suggest qualifications and restrictions of the liability of the iudex qui litem suam fecit; cf. Hochstein, *Obligationes*, pp. 44 sqq., 67 sqq.; as far as the usus modernus is concerned, cf. pp. 80 sqq.; cf. also Coing, p. 517. The iudex always remained liable for dolus; cf., today, § 839 II BGB (and the exception contained in § 839 III BGB), on which see "Motive", in: *Mugdan*, vol. II, pp. 460 sq.

The parallel to the liability of medici, incidentally, continued to be stressed (despite the fact that no "appeal" was available as an alternative remedy against a botched-up operation); cf., for example, Lauterbach, *Collegium theoretico-practicum*, Lib. L, Tit. XIII, III: "Hodie, sicut nec Medicorum errata, ita nec Judicantium imperitiam in jus vocari . . ."; lack of skill in doctors was scarcely ever brought to court and hence the somewhat cynical saying that for them it is permitted to kill with impunity. Cf. supra, p. 1028, note 198 and also Watson, *Failures*, pp. 65 sq.

[232] Ulp. D. 9, 3, 5, 6; Ulp. D. 9, 3, 5, 11. Cf. also *Bowden v. Rudman* 1964 (4) SA 686 (N) at 691E–F: ". . . it is clear that the object was to prevent harm being done by anything that might fall, and that the law did not wait till the harm was done but provided punishment if the harm were possible."

[233] Justus Henning Boehmer, *Doctrina de actionibus* (Halae Magdeburgicae, 1789), Sect. II, Cap. XI, § XVIII; Glück, vol. 10, pp. 411 sq.; cf. also Windscheid/Kipp, § 457, n. 4. The actio de posito vel suspenso was, however, carried forward into Roman-Dutch law—cf. Grotius, *Inleiding*, III, XXXVIII, 5 sqq.; Voet, *Commentarius ad Pandectas*, Lib. IX, Tit. III, VI—and has even been discussed (though not applied) in the South African case of *Bowden v. Rudman* 1964 (4) SA 686 (N) at 690E sqq. In this case Caney J argued that the action had lost its penal character and was available only to recover damages for injury actually done (i.e. where the things lodged or hung had fallen down). But what, under these circumstances, is its relationship to the actio de deiectis vel effusis? Cf. Voet, loc. cit., on the

The actio de damno aut furto adversus nautas, caupones, stabularios was obliterated, for all practical purposes, when it lost the specific sting attached to it: recovery of *double* the value of the thing stolen or damage done.[234] Once it had become available for no more than simplum,[235] it did not give the customer anything which he could not obtain by means of the receptum liability of nauta, stabularius or caupo. In certain respects, in fact, it was more advantageous for him to proceed under the receptum rather than the quasi-delictual remedy.[236]

A slightly more valiant struggle for survival was put up by the actio de deiectis vel effusis; in some half-forgotten corner of both Austrian[237] and South African law,[238] indeed, it still exists today.[239] In Germany it passed relatively unmolested through usus modernus[240] and pandectism[241] and even made its way into the first draft of the BGB.[242] In the end, however, the legislator decided to jettison the remedy.[243] A special edict dealing with injuries caused by pouring down from or throwing out of houses may have been appropriate under the conditions prevailing in ancient Rome; but in 19th-century Germany police regulations and the provisions of the penal code could be relied upon to prevent people from emptying the contents of their chamber-pots over the heads of unsuspecting passers-by.

2. Delictual and quasi-delictual liability

If, therefore, the four quasi-delicts have left hardly any traces in modern legal science, the systematic niche carved out for them in Justinian's *Institutes*, too, was ultimately bound to wither away. Throughout the

one hand, *Bowden v. Rudman* 1964 (4) SA 686 (N) at 692D–E ("The situation is analogous to that of the thing thrown out or poured out upon a passer-by") on the other. In *Bowden v. Rudman*, incidentally, the actio de posito vel suspenso was held not to be applicable to the case of a gate opened outwards across the pavement. In the headnote (p. 686) this action is confused with the actio de effusis vel deiectis.

[234] Ulp. D. 4, 9, 7, 1; Ulp. D. 47, 5, 1, 2.

[235] Groenewegen, *De legibus abrogatis*, Digest. Lib. IV, Tit. IX, l. ult. § 1; Voet, *Commentarius ad Pandectas*, Lib. IV, Tit. IX, X.

[236] Thus, for example, the actio quasi ex delicto was limited to theft or damage caused by employees. Liability under the receptum was much wider; it also covered, for example, theft committed or damage caused by other guests or passengers; cf. Ulp. D. 4, 9, 1, 8; Gai. D. 4, 9, 2; Pomp./Ulp. D. 4, 9, 3 pr. For further details, see Glück, vol. 6, pp. 140 sqq.; T.E. Dönges, *The Liability for Safe Carriage of Goods in Roman-Dutch Law* (1928), pp. 24 sqq.

[237] § 1318 ABGB. On the survival of the actio de deiectis vel effusis in a generalized form (art. 1384 code civil, last alternative) cf. infra, p. 1142.

[238] Gane, *The Selective Voet*, vol. II, p. 595 (who remarks with classic understatement that the Digest title 9, 3 "cannot be said to have been of leading importance in South African law"); N.J. van der Merwe, P.J.J. Olivier, *Die onregmatige daad in die Suid-Afrikaanse reg* (5th ed., 1985), p. 496.

[239] It does, of course, no longer lie for duplum (as it did in Roman law: Inst. IV, 5, 1).

[240] Stryk, *Usus modernus pandectarum*, Lib. IX, Tit. III, §§ 1 sqq.; Glück, vol. 10, pp. 409 sqq.

[241] Windscheid/Kipp, § 457, 1; Bienenfeld, op. cit., note 123, pp. 45 sq.

[242] §§ 729 sqq. E I; cf. "Motive", in: *Mugdan*, vol. II, pp. 448 sq. and the discussion by Joseph Unger, "Die actio de dejectis et effusis im deutschen Entwurfe", (1891) 30 *JhJb* 226 sqq.

[243] "Protokolle", in: *Mugdan*, vol. II, p. 1123.

centuries scholars hypothesized inconclusively about the distinctive characteristic of quasi-delicts, as opposed to delicts.[244] Some authors, rather vaguely, suggested "culpa aliqua" as the basis of quasi-delictual liability,[245] others referred to wrongs by construction of law where "waerelick geen misdaed en is"[246] or of "factum omne ex quo qui convenitur, . . . quod sit maleficio finitum"[247] or "quod maleficio est proximum".[248] Some jurists of the usus modernus tried to argue that liability, in the one case, is based on the fault of the defendant himself, in the other on culpa imputativa.[249] Others argued that only the intentional infliction of harm gives rise to delictual liability, whereas obligationes quasi ex delicto are characterized by negligence ("culpa propria").[250] Occasionally, the category of the quasi-delicts was also regarded as a kind of legal ragpicker which could be used conveniently to accommodate all instances of non-/quasi-contractual liability, that did not fall under either the lex Aquilia or the actio iniuriarum. Thus, in particular, liability under the actio de pauperie was often said to be of a quasi-delictual nature.[251] But whatever new turn the discussion took, it became increasingly apparent that its practical significance was rather limited. Liability, as a rule, was based on fault, and as long as this remained the fundamental precept (as it did, particularly prominently, in the 19th century),[252] it mattered little whether an action was classified as delictual or quasi-delictual.[253] Isolated instances of no-fault liability, insofar as they still existed,[254] tended to be regarded as rather

---

[244] For a detailed discussion, see Hochstein, *Obligationes*, pp. 35 sqq., 48 sqq., 71 sqq., 94 sqq., 129 sqq.; cf. also Coing, pp. 395 sq.

[245] Ulrich Zasius, as quoted and analysed by Hochstein, *Obligationes*, pp. 50 sqq., cf. also pp. 73 sq.

[246] Grotius, *Inleiding*, III, XXXVIII, 1.

[247] Donellus, *Commentarii*, Lib. XV, Cap. XLIII, V.

[248] Vinnius, *Institutiones*, Lib. IV, Tit. V.

[249] Cf. supra, p. 19, note 107.

[250] Cf. supra, p. 19, note 108; Lauterbach, *Collegium theoretico-practicum*, Lib. XLVII, Tit. I, VIII; Coing, p. 395. But what was the position of the actio legis Aquiliae in this scheme of things? According to Lauterbach, loc. cit., it had to be classified as an obligatio ex delicto (vero) despite the fact that it was available in cases of dolus and culpa.

[251] Cf. Grotius, *Inleiding*, III, XXXVIII, 10; Van Leeuwen, *Censura Forensis*, Pars I, Lib. V, Cap. XXXI, 2; for a detailed analysis cf. Hochstein, *Obligationes*, pp. 86 sqq.; cf. also Van der Merwe, op. cit., note 39, pp. 27 sq.

[252] Cf. supra, pp. 1034 sq.

[253] Cf. supra, p. 20.

[254] Or were not brought in line with the principle of "no liability without fault" too; cf., for example, as far as the actio de pauperie is concerned, Van der Linden in his annotations on Voet, as translated by Gane, *The Selective Voet*, vol. II (1955), pp. 533 sq.; *Parker v. Reed* (1904) 21 SC 496 at 501 sq.; *O'Callaghan v. Chaplin* 1927 AD 310 at 375 sqq. (per Wessels JA); cf. also Van der Merwe, op. cit., note 39, pp. 29 sqq.; on the actio de deiectis vel effusis cf., for example, Voet, *Commentarius ad Pandectas*, Lib. IX, Tit. III, I (". . . cum culpa ipsius non in dejectione consistat, sed in eo poties, quod aut malignos, aut negligentes intra domus suae vel coenaculi septa receperit, quos jure suo repellere poterat, quorumque ideo culpam tenetur praestare"). Cf. further Justus Wilhelm Hedemann, *Die Fortschritte des*

anomalous and antiquated elements of the Roman heritage, as ius singulare based on "positive"[255] rulings of the praetor rather than on any principles with wider implications.[256] By the time the BGB was drafted the dogmatic category of "quasi-delict" was regarded as defunct and useless; it did not, therefore, commend itself for reception into the new code. Nor did any of the traditional instances of no-fault liability, except one: the actio de pauperie. Even this rather peripheral remedy, however, was cut down in scope, for the notion of strict liability was preserved only with regard to damage done by so-called "luxury animals".[257] But apart from that, the principle of no liability without fault reigned supreme and the law of delict in the BGB, in that respect, neatly reflects the prevailing doctrine of 19th-century German legal science.[258]

IV. NEW INSTANCES OF NO-FAULT LIABILITY

1. Legislation in the 19th century

Yet, while the leading luminaries of the pandectist school of thought were engaged in their study of Ulpian and Papinian,[259] the world around them changed dramatically. The Industrial Revolution led to an unprecedented "acceleration of history" and brought with it untold new sources of risk and losses.[260] From the 1830s monstrous machines called railway engines[261] steamed through the German territories,

---

Zivilrechts im XIX. Jahrhundert vol. I (1910), pp. 86 sq.; Bienenfeld, op. cit., note 123, pp. 100 sqq.; Hans-Peter Benöhr, "Zur ausservertraglichen Haftung im gemeinen Recht", in: *Festschrift für Max Kaser* (1976), p. 705.

[255] "Motive", in: *Mugdan*, vol. II, pp. 449; cf. also p. 453.

[256] See Bienenfeld, op. cit., note 123, pp. 23 sqq.; Ogorek, *Gefährdungshaftung*, pp. 48 sqq. and, as a particularly blatant example, the cursory reference to obligationes ex variis causarum figuris by Savigny, *Obligationenrecht*, vol. II, pp. 330 sq.

[257] § 833, 1 BGB.

[258] Cf. supra, pp. 1034 sq.

[259] Cf. the criticism by Lorenz von Stein, *Zur Eisenbahnrechts-Bildung* (1872), p. 15.

[260] For some modern figures, see André Tunc, "Introduction", in: *International Encyclopedia of Comparative Law*, vol. XI, 1 (1983), nn. 1, 72 ("The accident age"). According to him, in the United States alone 115 000 persons die every year as a result of accidents, more than 11 million suffer temporary disablement, and more than 5 million others suffer some kind of injury. During the Second World War, the toll of industrial accidents was nearly as heavy as the toll of war itself in countries such as the United Kingdom and the United States. For more facts and figures, see P.S. Atiyah, *Accidents, Compensation and the Law* (3rd ed., 1980), pp. 18 sqq.; on motor accidents, see also André Tunc, "Traffic Accident Compensation: Law and Proposals", in: *International Encyclopedia of Comparative Law* vol. XI, 14 (1983), n. 1.

[261] For a notorious definition of a railway enterprise (in no fewer than 111 words, all crammed into a single sentence) cf. RGZ 1, 247 (252). On the eve of the opening of the first Prussian railway line a pastor in Berlin implored his congregation to keep away, for the sake of their eternal salvation, from these "infernal dragons". On the hostility and opposition which railways and motorcars at first aroused in England, see J.R. Spencer, "Motor-Cars and the Rule in Rylands v. Fletcher: A Chapter of Accidents in the History of Law and Motoring", (1983) 42 *Cambridge LJ* 69 sqq. Some (from a modern perspective) rather amusing highlights of the campaign against the use of these dangerous machines: in 1932 the

pulling carriages for the transportation of goods and persons but, occasionally, also wreaking death and destruction around them.[262] The advent of machinery and urbanization facilitated the production processes; but at the same time these developments brought with them a vastly increased potential for danger. Workmen became involved in hazardous mining ventures or had to handle menacing blast furnaces and combustion engines; and an explosion in a factory, or a burst of sparks from an engine in a densely populated area could obviously have disastrous consequences. In many cases of this kind it is difficult, if not impossible, to prove negligence on the part of the person in charge of the installation and hence it became manifest, at least to more practically minded lawyers, that new patterns of loss adjustment had to be devised. As early as 1838 (a mere three years after the first railway line on any German territory[263] and a mere four days (!) after the first one operating in Prussia[264] had been opened) a rather revolutionary step was taken by the Prussian legislature: it introduced a special statute imposing strict liability on railways for all harm to persons or property occurring "through carriage on the railway"; the defendant could exonerate himself only by showing that the harm had been caused through the fault of the victim or by an external and unavoidable event.[265] This pioneering piece of legislation triggered off similar statutes in other German states,[266] and when in 1871 the Empire was founded, the imperial parliament followed suit almost immediately. The "imperial law of liability"[267]—which, albeit under another name

---

proprietor of the Stockton and Darlington Railway was prosecuted for the crime of public nuisance because the locomotives scared horses; when the first traction engines appeared on the roads, Parliament reacted by requiring a man with a red flag to walk in front (Locomotive Act of 1865); and cars at first were occasionally pelted with stones; enraged farmers even fired shotguns at them.

[262] For an account of some 19th-century railway accidents, see Gustav Lehmann, *Körperverletzungen und Tödtungen auf deutschen Eisenbahnen* (1869).

[263] 7th December 1835 (from Nürnberg to Fürth).

[264] 30th October 1838 (from Berlin to Potsdam; the length of this railway line was a mere 3,5 miles).

[265] § 25 Gesetz über die Eisenbahn-Unternehmungen, 3rd November 1838. It has recently been discovered that the "father" of this piece of legislation (and that is, of the modern form of strict liability) was none other than Friedrich Carl von Savigny, (in his capacity as member of the council of state in Prussia): cf. the documents presented by Theodor Baums, "Die Einführung der Gefährdungshaftung durch F.C. von Savigny", (1987) 104 *ZSS* (GA) 277 sqq. Thus, in spite of the fact that he made short shrift with the obligationes ex variis causarum figuris in his *Obligationenrecht* (cf. supra, note 256), it would be wrong to argue that Savigny was insensitive or indifferent towards the challenges of the industrial age. In his *Obligationenrecht* he intended to develop general concepts and principles (cf. vol. II, p. 4); and for this specific purpose the individual instances of quasi-delictual liability did not appear to him to be of any significance.

[266] On the development of the railway law in the 19th century, see Justus Wilhelm Hedemann, *Die Fortschritte des Zivilrechts im XIX. Jahrhundert*, vol. I (1910), pp. 88 sqq.; Ogorek, *Gefährdungshaftung*, pp. 61 sqq.; Michael R. Will, *Quellen erhöhter Gefahr* (1980), pp. 2 sqq.; cf. also Bienenfeld, op. cit., note 123, pp. 460 sqq.

[267] Reichs-Haftpflichtgesetz, 7th June 1871; on the origin of which, see Ogorek, *Gefährdungshaftung*, pp. 98 sqq.

and in a substantially expanded form, is still in force today—provided for strict liability for harm to persons[268] arising "through the operation" of a railway.[269] The same statute made factory-owners liable for the fault of senior employees.[270] Mention must also be made, in this context, of Bismarck's famous system of workmen's compensation for industrial accidents; it, too, constituted a rather radical deviation from the principle of letting losses lie where they had fallen, unless they were attributable to somebody else's fault;[271] in this case, however, a social insurance scheme, rather than strict liability on the part of the factory-owner, provided the solution.[272]

2. Strict liability in disguise

Ironically, therefore, in the very moment of its triumph, the shadows of decline began to fall upon the fault principle; fostered by the economic liberalism of the 19th century, it was unsuited to the emerging paternalistic spirit of the 20th.[273] But the new forms of strict liability tended to be regarded, just as the old ones, as anomalous instances of a ius singulare; they were locked into special statutes and thus remained isolated from the mainstream of private-law legal theory. When it was suggested that the railway liability of the imperial law of liability be received into the BGB, this was rather curtly rejected;[274] one obviously balked at the idea of recognizing a two-track system of liability law. This uncompromising attitude was to have two rather unfortunate consequences. Having been denied an official passport for entry into the BGB, the notion of strict liability began to infiltrate the traditional core areas of delictual liability in disguise. The degree of care expected of the defendant in a delictual action has on occasion been pitched at such a high level as to amount almost to no-fault liability.[275] "In general", Zweigert/Kötz/Weir have summed up the situation,[276]

---

[268] Strict liability for damage to property was introduced only in 1940 by means of the *Sachschädenhaftpflichtgesetz*.

[269] § 1 *Reichs-Haftpflichtgesetz*; cf. today § 1 *Haftpflichtgesetz*.

[270] § 2 *Reichs-Haftpflichtgesetz*; cf. today § 3 *Haftpflichtgesetz*.

[271] Cf. the famous phrase, coined by Holmes, *The Common Law*, p. 50: "[S]ound policy lets losses lie where they fall, except where a special reason can be shown for interference."

[272] On the development cf. Hedemann, op. cit., note 266, pp. 90 sqq.; Ogorek, *Gefährdungshaftung*, pp. 113 sqq. For Switzerland cf. the recent study by Herbert Bracher, "Die Entwicklung der Fabrikhaftpflicht in der Schweiz und ihre Ablösung durch Kranken- und Unfallversicherung", (1986) 8 *ZNR* 157 sqq.

[273] M.A. Millner, *Negligence in Modern Law* (1967), pp. 234 sq.; cf. also Benöhr, *Festschrift Kaser*, pp. 694 sqq.

[274] "Bericht der XII. Kommission des Reichstages", in: *Mugdan*, vol. II, p. 1300. Cf. also Gottlieb Planck, as quoted by Tunc, op. cit., note 260, vol. XI, 1, n. 83: "It is not the task of a Civil Code to intervene here."

[275] For examples, see Josef Esser, "Die Zweispurigkeit unseres Haftpflichtrechts", 1953 *Juristenzeitung* 129 sqq.; Will, op. cit., note 266, pp. 41 sqq.

[276] At p. 312.

> "whenever it seems necessary in order to achieve a socially acceptable distribution of the accident risks peculiar to modern life, the courts tend to insist on precautions which it is virtually impossible to satisfy, and they can do this because, judging a case ex post facto, they can always discover some precaution or other which, had the defendant adopted it in time, would have prevented the occurrence of the harm."

In other cases, the courts have alleviated the injured party's burden of proof by accepting prima facie evidence: if the plaintiff is unable to adduce direct evidence establishing negligence on the part of the defendant, he may still succeed if he proves other facts justifying the conclusion that the defendant failed to exercise the necessary care. This is of particular importance in medical malpractice suits. When sponges, tubes or scalpel blades are found, after an operation, in the body of the patient,[277] or when a physician mistakes the organ on which or, even worse, the patient on whom he is supposed to operate,[278] the doctor may be taken to have been at fault, unless he is able to demonstrate the reasonable possibility of an alternative explanation of the incident.[279] Occasionally the courts have even reversed the onus of proof. In German law this has happened, most notably, in cases involving products liability.[280]

3. 20th-century ad hoc legislation

If these and similar instances of a stricter-than-normal liability have grown up rather surreptitiously, and have tended to undermine the borderline between fault- and risk-based liability,[281] ad hoc legislation has until recently been regarded as the only proper and legitimate means of accommodating the need for an expansion of no-fault liability

---

[277] For pertinent case law (comparative) cf. Dieter Giesen, *International Medical Malpractice Law* (1988), pp. 139 sq.

[278] Cf. Giesen, op. cit., note 277, pp. 142 sqq., 519.

[279] As far as German law is concerned, cf. Dieter Giesen, *Wandlungen des Arzthaftungsrechts* (2nd ed., 1983), pp. 90 sqq.

[280] BGHZ 51, 91 sqq.—the famous "fowl pest" case. The plaintiff, who ran a chicken farm, had her chickens inoculated against fowl pest by a veterinary surgeon who used vaccine produced by the defendants. A few days later fowl pest broke out, as a result of which more than 4 000 chickens died. For a translation of this landmark decision into English, cf. Markesinis, op. cit., note 227, pp. 245 sqq. On products liability in German Law in general, see Ernst von Cämmerer, "Products Liability", in: *Ius privatum gentium, Festschrift für Max Rheinstein,* vol. II (1969), pp. 659 sqq.; Zweigert/Kötz, pp. 431 sqq.; Markesinis, op. cit., note 227, pp. 50 sqq.; Mertens, op. cit., note 167, § 823, nn. 279 sqq.

The law relating to products liability is about to be unified, on the basis of a regime of strict liability, within the European community: cf. the *Richtlinie des Rates vom 25.7.1985 zur Angleichung der Rechts- und Verwaltungsvorschriften der Mitgliedsstaaten über die Haftung für fehlerhafte Produkte* (85/374/EWG); for Germany cf., most recently, Hans Claudius Taschner, 1988 *Neue Juristische Wochenschrift* 1432 sqq.; further (comparative) Dieter Giesen, "Produkthaftung im Umbruch", 1989 *Juristenzeitung* 517 sqq.

[281] Cf. also Lawson/Markesinis, p. 144 (". . . the confusion of the two concepts is not only intellectually untidy; it has other disadvantages as well. . . ."). But cf. Hans G. Leser, "Zu den Instrumenten des Rechtsgüterschutzes im Delikts- und Gefährdungshaftungsrecht", (1983) 183 *Archiv für die civilistische Praxis* 601 (no-fault liability represents the bottom line on a sliding scale of liability law); cf. also Heinz Hübner, "Noch einmal: Gefährdungshaftung und Verantwortung", in: *Festschrift für Wolfram Müller-Freienfels* (1986), pp. 329 sqq.

stricto sensu. A string of special statutes have thus been enacted over the years, dealing with road traffic,[282] air transport,[283] electricity and gas supply,[284] atomic energy,[285] water pollution[286] and pharmaceutical products.[287], [288] As a result of this casuistic approach, as well as of the traditional reluctance of German courts to extend the scope of application of these statutes analogically,[289] one is faced today with a whole variety of rather haphazard distinctions. Thus, for instance, it does not make much sense that a person who injures himself in the course of boarding a boat should be worse off (his claim being based on fault) than someone who falls while stepping aboard a train (strict liability of the railway). Nor is there any good reason why the liability of a contractor should depend on whether he uses a field railway or a bulldozer for some excavation works.[290] A confusingly patchy picture also emerges if one looks at the way in which the strict liability is limited in each individual case.[291] The custodian[292] of a motor vehicle is not liable if the accident was caused by an unavoidable event, attributable neither to a defect in the construction of the vehicle nor to the failure of any of its functional parts.[293] The liability of the railway, on the other hand, is excluded only in cases of vis maior ("*höhere Gewalt*"),[294] while for the custodian of an aeroplane not even vis maior constitutes a good defence. Passengers in a motor vehicle cannot hold the custodian liable under the provisions of the Road Traffic Act, unless they were being carried by way of business or for reward;[295] nor does the custodian's strict liability cover injuries sustained by persons who have been engaged in the operation of the vehicle (as, for example,

---

282 § 7 *Kraftfahrzeuggesetz*, 3 May 1909 (today: *Strassenverkehrsgesetz*—Road Traffic Act).

283 § 19 (today: § 33) *Luftverkehrsgesetz*—Air Traffic Act—1 August 1922.

284 § 1 a *Reichs-Haftpflichtgesetz* (today: § 2 *Haftpflichtgesetz*).

285 *Atomgesetz*—Atomic Energy Act—23 December 1959; cf. today §§ 25 sqq. *Atomgesetz*, as promulgated on 15 July 1985.

286 § 22 *Wasserhaushaltsgesetz*—Water Maintenance Act—27 July 1957.

287 § 84 *Arzneimittelgesetz*—Pharmaceutical Products Act—24 August 1976.

288 For an overview of the development, cf. Will, op. cit., note 266, pp. 2 sqq., 20 sqq., 27 sqq.; Zweigert/Kötz, pp. 399 sqq.

289 Will, op. cit., note 266, pp. 70 sqq. Cf., for example, RGZ 78, 171 sqq., a case involving one of Count Zeppelin's famous airships. The court refused to extend the provisions of the Imperial Law of Liability and the Road Traffic Act to cover this case even though the operation of an airship involves, at least, the same degree of risk than that of motorcars or railways.

290 For these and further examples, cf. Hein Kötz, "Gefährdungshaftung", in: *Gutachten und Vorschläge zur Überarbeitung des Schuldrechts*, vol. II (1981), pp. 1786 sq.

291 For details, see, again, Kötz, op. cit., note 290, pp. 1803 sq., 1825 sqq.

292 On the concept of "*Halter*" (custodian; normally, but not necessarily, the owner of the car), cf. Adalbert Kunschert, in: Geigel, *Der Haftpflichtprozess* (19th ed., 1986), pp. 599 sqq.

293 § 7 II *Strassenverkehrsgesetz*.

294 § 1 II *Haftpflichtgesetz*. On the concept of vis maior, see Adolf Exner, "Der Begriff der höheren Gewalt (vis major), im römischen und heutigen Verkehrsrecht", (1883) 10 *GrünhZ* 497 sqq.; Adamkiewiecz, "Die 'höhere Gewalt' im Bürgerlichen Gesetzbuch", (1915) 59 *Beiträge zur Erläuterung des Deutschen Rechts* 577 sqq.; Ulrike Städtler, *Schadensersatz im Falle höherer Gewalt* (1986), pp. 13 sqq.

295 § 8 a, 1 *Strassenverkehrsgesetz*.

agents employed to tow away or repair the car).[296] Neither the liability of the railway nor that imposed by the Air Traffic Law knows similar limitations. Very often (as with regard to rail, road and air traffic) specific limits are fixed for the amount of damages recoverable,[297] but then there are also statutes (as, in particular, the Water Maintenance Act) which do not contain any upper limit. All in all, it is obvious that the present mosaic of special provisions is not the result of any principled choice, but of the determination of both courts and legislature to meddle as little as possible with the familiar system of a fault-based liability. Only comparatively recently has one begun to formulate generalized principles and to attempt to integrate a unified concept of strict liability into the German delictual system.[298]

V. STRICT LIABILITY IN ENGLISH LAW

1. Vicarious liability

If, in conclusion, one looks at the development of the notion of strict liability in English law, one is immediately struck by the fact that in many essential respects it took a very similar course to that in German or South African law.[299] Thus, in particular, it is traditionally unorganized and fragmentary in application.[300] Certain specific instances of strict liability have emerged over the centuries, among them,

---

[296] § 8 *Strassenverkehrsgesetz*.

[297] §§ 9 sq. *Haftpflichtgesetz*, § 12 *Strassenverkehrsgesetz*, § 37 *Luftverkehrsgesetz*.

[298] Cf., in particular, Will, op. cit., note 266, pp. 243 sqq.; Kötz, op. cit., note 290, pp. 1779 sqq.; but see also Hübner, *Festschrift Müller-Freienfels*, pp. 331 sqq.

[299] Regarding modern South African law, see J.C. van der Walt, "Strict Liability in the South African Law of Delict", (1968) 1 *Cilsa* 49 sqq.; idem, "Risiko-aanspreeklikheid: Erkenning in die regspraak", 1984 *TSAR* 211 sqq.; Van der Merwe/Olivier, op. cit., note 238, pp. 485 sqq. On the old common-law (=ius commune) forms of strict liability still in use today (actio de pauperie, actio de pastu, edictum de feris, actiones de deiectis vel effusis and positi vel suspensi) cf. supra, pp. 1108 sqq., 1127 sq. Modern legislation was sparked off by the criticism of the status quo expressed in *Union Government v. Sykes* 1913 AD 156 (". . . my sympathies are entirely with the plaintiff. The South African Railways are administered by the Government, in the public interest, and it seems to me only fair that private persons whose farms are injured by sparks from engines should be compensated at the public expense. That, however, is a matter for the Legislature to deal with" (p. 185, per Solomon JA). Thereupon § 70 Railways Act 22/1916 introduced a reversal of the onus of proof in favour of the injured party. After dissatisfaction had been expressed in *Ross v. S.A. Railways* (1938 OPD 128, per Krause J), the legislator finally made the railways strictly liable for fire damage; cf., today, s. 65 South African Transport Services Act 65/1981. For other individual instances of strict liability, cf. s. 26 Electricity Act 41/1987 (presumption of negligence), s. 11 II Aviation Act 74/1962 and s. 41 Nuclear Energy Act 92/1982. There is, however, no strict liability for road traffic accidents. The rule of *Rylands v. Fletcher*, incidentally (on which see infra pp. 1138 sqq), has not become part of South African law; cf. T.W. Price, "Is the rule in *Rylands v. Fletcher* part of Roman-Dutch law?", (1953) 70 *SALJ* 381 sqq., 395 sqq.; but cf. also *Eastern Telegraph Co. v. Cape Town Tramways* 1902 AC 382 at 393 sq. Today the question of whether a more broadly based principle of risk liability should be recognized receives increasing attention. The matter has even been considered by the Law (Reform) Commission.

[300] Fleming, *Torts*, p. 304; cf. also Atiyah, op. cit., note 260, pp. 157 sqq.

most notably, vicarious liability.[301] The foundations of the doctrine that an employer is strictly liable for the tort of his servants were laid by Lord Holt in the late 17th and 18th centuries[302] and it is not unlikely that the Roman quasi-delicts, more particularly the praetorian liability of the nauta,[303] the actio de deiectis vel effusis[304] and the idea of selection, as expressed in the Justinianic sources,[305] had some influence in this regard. Unlike in Germany, but as in South Africa (strict) vicarious liability has become a feature of the modern law of torts in England, its application depending essentially on two requirements: that there is a relationship of master and servant between defendant and tortfeasor and that the latter caused the harm in the course of his employment.[306]

2. Liability for damage done by animals

Then there was the problem of liability for damage done by animals. As in early Roman law, it was originally the animal that was regarded as the culprit; the victim of the injury could therefore not proceed against its keeper, but had to take out his revenge on the animal itself.[307] Later, however, the idea gained ground that the keeper could be held responsible if he could in any way be blamed for what had happened. This was the origin of the "scienter"[308] doctrine: the plaintiff had to charge the defendant with knowingly keeping an animal of vicious propensities.[309] If the animal was ferae naturae, such knowledge came

---

[301] ". . . one of the most firmly established legal principles throughout the common law world": P.S. Atiyah, op. cit., note 218, p. 12.

[302] Cf. *Boson v. Sandford* 2 Salkeld 440; *Turberville v. Stampe* 1 Ld Raym 264; *Anonymous* 1 Ld Raym 739, and others; for details of the development cf. Barlow, op. cit., note 187, pp. 36 sqq.; Holdsworth, vol. VIII, pp. 472 sqq.; John H. Wigmore, "Responsibility for Tortious Acts: Its History" (1893–94) 7 *Harvard LR* 315 sqq., 383 sqq.; Oliver Wendell Holmes, "The History of Agency", in: *Select Essays in Anglo-American Legal History*, vol. III (1909), pp. 387 sqq.

[303] Which came into England via the courts of Admiralty and as part of the lex Mercatoria; cf. Holdsworth, vol. VIII, pp. 250 sqq. The first case in which the modern doctrine of vicarious liability made its appearance in a common-law court (*Boson v. Sandford;* cf. supra, note 302) involved an action by a shipper of goods against the captain of the ship.

[304] Holdsworth, vol. VIII, p. 476.

[305] Cf. Barlow, op. cit., note 187, p. 44.

[306] For details, see P.S. Atiyah, op. cit., note 218, pp. 31 sqq., 171 sqq.; Fleming, *Torts*, pp. 339 sqq.; cf. also Zweigert/Kötz, pp. 383 sqq. On the doctrine of common employment ("[t]he most nefarious judicial ploy for reducing the charges on industry"; employers are relieved of vicarious liability if the injury was caused by the negligence of a fellow servant), cf. Fleming, *Torts*, p. 491; Atiyah, op. cit., note 218, p. 415.

[307] But the owner was allowed to buy off the right of vengeance. Unlike in Roman law, he had to pay the value of the animal and not the amount of damages suffered by the injured person. Generally on the historical development of liability for damage done by animals in English law, cf. Holmes, *Common Law*, pp. 17 sqq.; Williams, op. cit., note 23, pp. 7 sqq., 265 sqq. For Scotland cf. Carey-Miller, 1974 *Juridical Review* 1 sqq.

[308] From "scienter retinuit" in the old form of the writ: see Williams, op. cit., note 23, pp. 273 sqq., for details, see pp. 278 sqq.

[309] ". . . the courts were not prepared to hold that all the acts of animals involved their owners; there had to be some culpability in the owner himself, and of this culpability

to be irrebuttably presumed,[310] and thus the keepers of bears, zebras, elephants, chimpanzees and dingoes (but not of camels)[311] were held liable, irrespective of whether or not they had been negligent; there is nothing unlawful in keeping a pet chimpanzee, but if one does so, one bears the risk of any damage it may do. When the animal was of a harmless species, however,[312] the plaintiff had to show that on at least one previous occasion it had, to the defendant's knowledge, displayed an inclination to do the specific kind of harm complained about.[313] In a way, therefore, even the keeper of an animal mansuetae naturae was thus subjected to strict liability, for, provided scienter could be proved, it did not matter whether or not he had in fact been able to prevent the damage.[314] Apart from that the English common law also recognized an equivalent to the Roman actio de pastu: if animals falling within the class of "cattle" (including oxen, donkeys, pigs, fowls, ducks and geese, but excluding cats and dogs)[315] escaped and trespassed on another's land, their owner was held strictly liable (cattle trespass).[316] This rule was based on the principle of "sic utere tuo ut neminem laedas": "[E]very one", as Lord Holt put it,[317]

---

knowledge of the animal's past mischief was a rough practical test." On the history of the scienter principle, see Williams, op. cit., note 23, pp. 273 sqq. (the quotation is taken from p. 282).

[310] Williams, op. cit., note 23, pp. 292 sqq. Cf. today s. 2 I of the Animals Act 1971 (strict liability in respect of any damage caused by an animal which belongs to a dangerous species); for details, see North, op. cit., note 51, pp. 21 sqq.

[311] Fleming, *Torts*, p. 332. On the meaning of "dangerous species" in terms of the new Act, see North, op. cit., note 51, pp. 34 sqq.

[312] But under which circumstances can an animal be said to be of a "harmless species"? Traditionally, the relevant test for classifying a species was whether the animals belonging to it were "harmless to mankind"; whether or not it was in their nature to cause damage to property did not matter. For details cf. Williams, op. cit., note 23, pp. 286 sqq. The rigid division of all animals into dangerous and harmless species has often been criticized; "[s]uch a division", as the New South Wales Law Reform Commission (cf. supra, p. 1096, note 12, quoted here according to North, op. cit., note 51, p. 4) commented, "is not to be found in nature. The different species of animals in fact present different degrees of danger to mankind and within each species the danger presented is not constant but varies according to age, sex, time of the year and many other matters; and individual animals within the one species differ". In spite of these criticisms, the Animals Act 1971 still classes animals by species (cf. ss. 2, 6 II), although the line is now drawn differently. For details, cf. North, op. cit., note 51, pp. 34 sq., 48 sqq.

[313] As to details of the proof of scienter, see Williams, op. cit., note 23, pp. 299 sqq.; cf. also North, op. cit., note 51, pp. 48 sqq. According to Salmond/Heuston, op. cit., note 22, p. 317, it was uncertain, at common law, whether the animal's vicious tendency had to have been contrary to the nature of animals of that class; contra naturam sui generis!

[314] Cf. today s. 2 II Animals Act 1971.

[315] North, op. cit., note 51, p. 92; for further details, see Williams, op. cit., note 23, pp. 136 sqq.

[316] For a detailed historical analysis, see Williams, op. cit., note 23, pp. 127 sqq. Today s. 4 of the Animals Act 1971 applies (referring to "livestock"); on which, see North, op. cit., note 51, pp. 91 sqq.

[317] *Tenant v. Goldwin* 2 Ld Raym 1089 at 1092. The maxim "sic utere tuo ut neminem laedas", incidentally, was referred to in a variety of different contexts. In 19th-century decisions it was sometimes used to establish strict liability (cf. *Rylands v. Fletcher* [1861–73] All ER 1 at 8), while at other times it was, interestingly, taken to entail liability for fault (cf. *Vaughan v. Menlove* (1873) 3 Bing (NC) 468 at 476).

"must so use his own, as not to do damage to another [a]nd . . . every man is [therefore] bound so to look to his cattle, as to keep them out of his neighbour's ground, that so he may receive no damage."

Finally, there were certain scattered miscellaneous instances of no-fault-liability, as particularly in cases of escaping fires;[318] there was also the dictum of Lord Holt (that was to play a role in *Rylands v. Fletcher*) concerning the flow of filth from a house or office so as to damnify another.[319]

3. *Rylands v. Fletcher*

This was the position when, in the 19th century, negligence as an independent basis of liability appeared upon the scene.[320] Its advent was stimulated by, and in turn contributed to the growing belief that liability must be based on fault; a belief that became as firmly entrenched in England as it was in contemporary continental science.[321] Again, however, we see the interesting phenomenon that at the moment of triumph a shadow began to fall over the principle of "no liability without fault", for from what were then generally regarded as "vestigial anomalies of an uncivilized past"[322] (namely strict liability on account of cattle trespass or of the flow of filth from house or office)[323] there arose a principle that could well have become the germ of a generalized risk-based liability. Characteristically, of course, the bold step[324] was taken not by the legislator but by a court of law. "We think", pronounced Blackburn J, in the famous case of *Rylands v. Fletcher*,[325]

"that the true rule of law is that the person who, for his own purposes, brings on his lands, and collects and keeps there anything likely to do mischief if it escapes, must

[318] For a historical analysis, see A.I. Ogus, "Vagaries in Liability For the Escape of Fire", (1969) 27 *Cambridge LJ* 104 sqq.
[319] *Tenant v. Goldwin* 2 Ld Raym 1089 at 1092; cf. also *Turberville v. Stampe* 1 Ld Raym 264 ("if my servant throws dirt into the highway, I am indictable").
[320] Cf. supra, pp. 910 sq.
[321] Cf. supra, pp. 1034 sq.; but cf. also Sir Frederick Pollock, (1923) 39 *LQR* 167; on which, in turn, see P.S. Atiyah, *Pragmatism and Theory in English Law* (1987), p. 179.
[322] Fleming, *Torts*, p. 300.
[323] On the antecedents of *Rylands v. Fletcher*, cf. also *Benning v. Wong* (1969) 122 CLR 249 at 294 sqq. (High Court of Australia; per Windeyer J).
[324] It was, as is often the case, not regarded by the judges concerned as either very bold or novel; cf. for example, Lord Cairns in [1861–73] All ER 1 at 12 sq.: "The principles on which this case must be determined appear to me to be extremely simple"; "[t]hese simple principles". Cf. also the rather vivid description of what happened by John H. Wigmore, "Responsibility for Tortious Acts: Its History—III", (1894) 7 *Harvard LR* 454 ("Briefly, [those scattered classes of cases] wandered about, unhoused and unshepherded, except for a casual attention, in the pathless fields of jurisprudence, until they were met, some thirty years ago, by the master-mind of Mr. Justice Blackburn, who guided them to the safe fold where they have since rested." But then he goes on to describe the principle enunciated by Mr. Justice Blackburn as "epochal in its consequences").
[325] [1861–73] All ER 1 at 7. On its historical context cf. the study by A.W.B. Simpson, "Legal Liability for Bursting Reservoirs: The Historical Context of *Rylands v. Fletcher*", (1984) 13 *Journal of Legal Studies* 209 sqq.

> keep it in at his peril, and, if he does not do so, he is prima facie answerable for all the damage which is the natural consequence of its escape."

In *Rylands v. Fletcher* itself, this pronouncement applied to water escaping from a reservoir on the land of the defendants,[326] breaking into a disused shaft of an abandoned mine and flooding the plaintiff's adjoining mine through communicating passages. Soon the rule was extended from water to fire[327] and electricity,[328] gas[329] and explosives,[330] chemical fumes,[331] flag-poles,[332] poisonous trees[333] and even (intangible) vibrations.[334] But in the long run it has not been allowed to display its potential "as a catalyst for a broader and more systematic pattern of loss distribution pertaining to accidents caused by dangerous operations".[335] From its inception, it was hedged in by the rather awkward requirement that the storage of the object on the defendant's property must have constituted a "non-natural user" of the land.[336] An even more effective brake was applied to the rule of *Rylands v. Fletcher*, however, when in 1947 the House of Lords came down in favour of a rather restrictive interpretation of the "escape"-requirement: it is not sufficient that the dangerous substance has escaped from the control of the defendant—it must in fact have left his land.[337] This move not only introduced artificial and haphazard distinctions into the law[338] but reduced the rule to a rather peripheral existence as another one of the exceptional and anomalous instances of

---

[326] According to Simpson, (1984) 13 *Journal of Legal Studies* 216 sqq., the decision in *Rylands v. Fletcher* has to be seen in the context of two contemporary, major dam disasters; "the case was about bursting reservoirs and about what, if anything, the law ought to do about them. . . .[I]t is not improbable that the [. . .] unique features [of dams or reservoirs] . . . received special examination at common law [in *Rylands v. Fletcher*]" (p. 216). Ironically, as Simpson points out on pp. 251 sqq., *Rylands v. Fletcher* had hardly any impact on this specific problem area, for it did not apply to public water reservoirs (that is, the vast majority of large reservoirs).

[327] *Jones v. The Festinog Railway Company* (1868) LR 3 QB 733.

[328] *National Telephone Co. v. Baker* [1893] 2 Ch 186.

[329] *Batcheller v. Tunbridge Wells Gas Co.* (1901) 84 LT 765.

[330] *Miles v. Forest Rock Granite Co.* (1918) 35 TLR 500.

[331] *West v. Bristol Tramways Company* [1908] 2 KB 14.

[332] *Shiffman v. The Grand Priory in the British Realm of the Venerable Order of the Hospital of St. John* [1936] 1 All ER 557.

[333] *Crowhurst v. The Burial Board of the Parish of Amersham* (1878) 4 Ex D 5.

[334] *Hoare and Company v. McAlpine* [1923] 1 Ch 167. Cf. further, for example, *Attorney-General v. Corke* [1933] Ch 89, where the owner of a disused brickfield had allowed gypsies to camp on his land and was held liable to his neighbours for harm caused by their unhygienic habits.

[335] Fleming, *Torts*, p. 309.

[336] Cf. *Rylands v. Fletcher* [1861–73] All ER 1 at 12 sq., per Lord Cairns (otherwise confirming the principle enunciated by Blackburn J); but cf. also already Blackburn J [1861–73] All ER 1 at 7.

[337] *Read v. J. Lyons & Co. Ltd.* [1947] AC 156 (HL).

[338] Take, for example, the case of *Read v. J. Lyons & Co. Ltd.* ([1947] AC (HL) 156), itself, where the plaintiff was injured by an explosion occurring in the defendant's ammunition factory in which she was working. Why should it make a difference whether she was injured within the confines of the factory or after she had just left its gates (Zweigert/Kötz, p. 421)?

no-fault liability.[339] As in Germany, fault has thus retained its prominent position in the theory of loss adjustment;[340] and attempts have not been wanting either, to rationalize the isolated instances of strict liability in terms of a generalized fault requirement.[341]

4. The quest for strict liability in modern law

Yet, on the other hand, the ascendancy of fault has not been able to stifle all progress. Again, the quest for a more broadly based responsibility for the creation of an abnormal risk has manifested itself in three different ways. On the one hand the courts have occasionally stretched the standard of care expected of the defendant to such an extent that it is hardly distinguishable from strict liability. Thus, for example, in *Daly v. Liverpool Corporation*[342] a pedestrian who had been knocked down by a bus succeeded in a claim based on negligence although Stable J specifically stated that in his judgment "there was no sort of culpable negligence on the part of the driver". But, the learned judge continued, a motorcar has today become "a lethal weapon" and the standard of care and skill which the law requires in the driver "is very high indeed". It is in fact a standard "which it is impossible to reconcile with the discharge of the duties of drivers of public vehicles".[343] In other cases, the courts have alleviated or even reversed the burden of proof by means of the doctrine of res ipsa loquitur.[344]

---

[339] For a general evaluation of the rule of *Rylands v. Fletcher* in modern English law, cf. Windeyer J, in *Benning v. Wong* (1969) 122 CLR 249 at 296 sqq.; Will, op. cit., note 266, pp. 122 sqq.; Simpson, (1984) 13 *Journal of Legal Studies* 214 sqq.; Zweigert/Kötz, pp. 418 sqq.; Fleming, *Torts*, pp. 308 sqq. Cf. also Spencer, (1983) 42 *Cambridge LJ* 65 sqq. He argues that, in some ways, the decision that the use of a motor-vehicle on the highway involves fault rather than strict liability (*Wing v. L.G.C.O.* [1909] 2 KB 652), "is the most significant event in the history of the law of tort this century".

[340] More particularly, there is no strict liability for motorcar accidents; this is severely criticized, for instance, by Lord Denning, *What Next in the Law* (1982), p. 128; cf. also Spencer, (1983) 42 *Cambridge LJ* 80 sqq. On the problems raised by traffic accidents in general and on the ways in which different modern legal systems have responded (or failed to respond) to them, see Tunc, op. cit., note 260, vol. XI, 14, nn. 1 sqq.

[341] For examples, see Fleming, *Torts*, p. 302; as far as Scots law is concerned, cf. Geoffrey MacCormack, "Culpa in the Scots Law of Reparation", 1974 *Juridical Review* 13 sqq., 18.

[342] [1939] 2 All ER 142.

[343] Cf. also, as far as motorcar accidents are concerned, Spencer, (1983) 42 *Cambridge LJ* 80 ("Consequently, in cases where the plaintiff excited their compassion, the courts began to twist the law of negligence to make a defendant liable for negligence when he was really not negligent at all, to make his insurers pay"); cf. further the (comparative) observations by Lawson/Markesinis, pp. 142 sqq. They quote, inter alia, from an American study according to which even a "good driver commits on average more than nine errors of four different natures in five minutes of driving". This type of inevitable error, Lawson and Markesinis conclude, "makes the moral and educational value of a fault-based system meaningless in so far as it makes people responsible for 'faults' for which they cannot be reproached". See also Tunc, op. cit., note 260, vol. XI, 1, nn. 72, 144 sqq. and, as far as Louisiana is concerned, the green snake case, as discussed by Vernon V. Palmer, "In Quest of a Strict Liability under the Code", (1982) 56 *Tulane LR* 1317 sqq.

[344] "Ever since that barrel of flour rolled out of that English warehouse window and fell upon the usual hapless pedestrian, giving rise to Baron Pollock's remarks during argument

And finally, there have also been instances where Parliament has openly introduced new forms of strict liability; this has happened in the Civil Aviation Act of 1949, the Nuclear Installations Act of 1965, the Gas Act also of 1965 and the Vaccine Damage Payments Act of 1979. Proposals to add to this list have been flourishing in recent years,[345] but, as in Germany the question has also repeatedly been debated whether the extension of the notion of strict liability by piecemeal legislation still provides a satisfactory solution to the modern problems of loss distribution.[346]

VI. ORIGIN AND APPLICATION OF ART. 1384 CODE CIVIL

What a more generalized approach can look like, may be gleaned, inter alia,[347] from the development of French jurisprudence in the course of the last century. A fairly insignificant-looking clause in art. 1384 code civil ("One is responsible not only for the injury which one causes by one's own action, but also for that which is caused by the action of persons for whom one is responsible, or of things which one has under one's guard") has been used by courts and legal writers to build a second track of delictual liability alongside the famous general clause of art. 1382 code civil.[348] A landmark within this development was the *arrêt Jand'heur*, a decision handed down by the *Cour de cassation* in plenary session.[349] Here it was held that the custodian of a thing is liable, irrespective of fault, provided, however, the damage did not arise from an external and irresistible event, that is, vis maior. Whether

of *Byrne v. Boadle* (1863) 2 H & C 722 . . ., that Latin phrase—'res ipsa loquitur'—has been beguiling, bewitching and bewildering the Anglo-American bench and bar": Stuart M. Speiser, *Res ipsa loquitur* (1972) (a two-volume work of more than 1 000 pages), vol. I, p. III. Cf. also, most recently, in a special context and from a comparative point of view, Giesen, op. cit., note 277, pp. 511 sqq., 515 sqq.

[345] Fleming, *Torts*, p. 307.

[346] Cf., for example, J.A. Jolowicz, "Liability for Accidents", (1968) 26 *Cambridge LJ* 50 sqq.; the report of the "Pearson Commission" on Civil Liability and Compensation for Personal Injury (1978), Cmnd. 7054; J.A. Jolowicz, "Compensation for Personal Injury and Fault", in: D.V. Allen, C.J. Bourn, J.H. Holyoak, *Accident Compensation after Pearson* (1979), pp. 33 sqq.; Atiyah, op. cit., note 260, pp. 323 sqq., 443 sqq.; idem, "No Fault Compensation: A Question That Will Not Go Away", (1980) 54 *Tulane LR* 271 sqq.

[347] A comparative analysis of other legal systems that have left the numerus clausus model behind can be found in Will, op. cit., note 266, pp. 150 sqq.; a general theory of the inner nature of strict liability based on the experiences of common law and civil law has recently been presented by Vernon Palmer, (1988) 62 *Tulane LR* 1303 sqq. For an even more radical departure from the fault principle, cf. the accident compensation scheme operating in New Zealand; for a comparative discussion of which, see, for example, D.B. Hutchison, "Accident Compensation: New Zealand Shows the Way", (1985) 48 *THRHR* 24 sqq.; Giesen, op. cit., note 277, pp. 529 sqq., 532 sqq.; John G. Fleming, Jan Hellner, Eike von Hippel, *Haftungsersetzung durch Versicherungsschutz* (1980), pp. 11 sqq., 51 sqq.

[348] On which cf. supra, pp. 906, 1034, 1036.

[349] *Court de Cassation*, Ch. réun., 13.2.1930, *Recueil Dalloz* (1930), Première Partie, pp. 57 sqq.

or not the thing in question is intrinsically dangerous or not, is irrelevant. Razor-blades, hatpins, toy balloons and tennis balls have been held to constitute things in terms of art. 1384 code civil, as have all kinds of machinery, motorcars, trains, ships, bicycles and elevators, gas, electricity, water, chemicals and X-rays.[350] As a result of the remarkably extensive interpretation given to this provision of the code, it has largely been unnecessary for the legislator to intervene and introduce strict liability by way of special statutes.[351]

The modern French doctrine on liability for things under one's guard has been compared to a skyscraper constructed on the head of a pin.[352] Yet, in reality, this pinhead was perhaps not quite as insignificant as it used to appear—and still appears—to many;[353] for the custodian's liability, as it found its way into art. 1384 code civil, probably descends from a passage in Domat's *Loix Civiles*,[354] which was designed to link, and at the same to generalize, the principles underlying the contemporary French version of the pauperian remedy, on the one hand, and the actiones de effusis vel deiectis and de posito vel suspenso on the other.[355]

[350] For an analysis of the development cf. Ulrich M. Hübner, *Die Haftung des Gardien im französischen Zivilrecht* (1972); Will, op. cit., note 266, pp. 131 sqq.; Lawson/Markesinis, pp. 146 sqq.; Zweigert/Kötz, pp. 407 sqq.; André Tunc, "'It is not wise to take the Civil Codes too seriously'. Traffic accident compensation in France", in: *Essays in Memory of Professor F.H. Lawson* (1986), pp. 71 sqq. On custodial liability in Louisiana (based on art. 2317 Louisiana Civil Code), see Palmer, (1988) 62 *Tulane LR* 1334 sqq.

[351] According to Tunc, *Essays Lawson*, p. 72, art. 1384 is "by far the most frequently applied of all the Civil Code provisions".

[352] Jean Boulanger, "Notations sur le pouvoir créateur de la jurisprudence civile", (1961) 59 *Revue trimestrielle de droit civil* 431.

[353] Cf., for example Tunc, *Essays Lawson*, p. 72: "This sentence . . . was a transition, a mere *élégance de style*. It did not express any rule of law; it was not meant to be applied and had no place in a code." This was, in fact, the view that prevailed in 19th-century French legal science. So obscure was the true origin of the final clause of art. 1384 I code civil (and so irresistible—in France as well—the ascendancy of the fault principle!) that reference to liability for things under one's guard was denied any independent significance; in the course of the 19th century the clause was taken to refer merely to the liabilities imposed by artt. 1385 and 1386 on the guardians of an animal and the owner of a building. Only towards the end of the century did one begin to realize the true potential of the rule as a catalyst for a broadly based risk liability.

[354] Liv. II, Tit. VIII, Sect. II; cf. also Yosiyuki Noda, "Jean Domat et le Code civil français", (1956) 3 *Comparative Law Review (Japan Institute of Comparative Law)* 31 sq.

[355] Cf. also the analysis by Watson, *Failures*, pp. 4. sq., 14 sq., 27, who, however, suggests an even more direct link between the actiones de deiectis vel effusis and de posito vel suspenso, and art. 1384 code civil.

Index of Main Sources

1. ROMAN LEGAL SOURCES

(a) Justinianic

Institutiones

Page

2. ANCIENT NON-LEGAL SOURCES

Wherever available, the edition of the *Collection des Universités de France* has been used and referred to.

3. CORPUS JURIS CANONICI

Decretum Gratiani

Decretales Gregorii IX

Liber Sextus

Constitutiones Clementis V

4. CONTINENTAL CODIFICATIONS

(a) Constitutio Criminalis Carolina

(b) Preussisches Allgemeines Landrecht (Prussian General Land Law)

(c) Code civil (French civil code)

(e) Bürgerliches Gesetzbuch (Civil Code, Germany)

Generally, the edition by Ian S. Forrester, Simon L. Goren and Hans-Michael Ilgen, *The German Civil Code* (1975), has been used as a starting point wherever I have translated a section of the German Code, or parts of it, into English.

5. *TABLE OF CASES*

(a) United Kingdom, United States and Commonwealth

(b) South Africa

(c) Germany

Subject Index

A

D

E

F

M

T

U